Peterson's College Money Handbook

2008

PETERSON'S
A nelnet COMPANY

PETERSON'S

A nelnet COMPANY

About Peterson's, a Nelnet company

Peterson's (www.petersons.com) is a leading provider of education information and advice, with books and online resources focusing on education search, test preparation, and financial aid. Its Web site offers searchable databases and interactive tools for contacting educational institutions, online practice tests and instruction, and planning tools for securing financial aid. Peterson's serves 110 million education consumers annually.

For more information, contact Peterson's, 2000 Lenox Drive, Lawrenceville, NJ 08648; 800-338-3282; or find us on the World Wide Web at www.petersons.com/about.

Previous editions published as *Peterson's College Money Handbook* © 1983, 1984, 1985, 1986, 1987, 1988, 1989, 1990, 1991, 1996, 1997, 1998, 1999, 2000, 2001 2002, 2003, 2004, 2005, 2006 and as *Paying Less for College* © 1992, 1993, 1994, 1995

Editor: Linda Seghers; Production Editor: Mark D. Snider; Copy Editor: Sally Ross; Research Project Manager: Dan Margolin; Research Associate: James Feichthaler; Programmer: Phyllis Johnson; Manufacturing Manager: Ray Golaszewski; Composition Manager: Linda M. Williams

ISSN 1089-831X
ISBN-13: 978-0-7689-2489-3
ISBN-10: 0-7689-2489-8

Printed in the United States of America

10 9 8 7 6 5 4 3 2 1 09 08 07

Twenty-fifth Edition

Other Recommended Titles

Peterson's Scholarships, Grants & Prizes
Peterson's Sports Scholarships & College Athletic Programs

Contents

A Note from the Peterson's Editors

The news media seem to constantly remind us that a college education is expensive. It certainly appears to be beyond the means of many Americans. The sticker price for four years at state-supported colleges can be more than $45,000, and private colleges and universities can cost more than $150,000. And these numbers continue to rise.

But there is good news. The system operates to provide the needed money so that most families and students are able to afford a college education while making only a reasonable financial sacrifice. However, because the college financial aid system is complex, finding the money is often easier said than done. That is why the process demands study, planning, calculation, flexibility, filling out forms, and meeting deadlines. Fortunately, for most people it can produce positive results. There are many ways to manage college costs and many channels through which you can receive help. Be sure to take full advantage of the opportunities that have been opened up to students and their families by the many organizations, foundations, and businesses that have organized to help you with the burden of college expenses.

For nearly forty years, Peterson's has given students and parents the most comprehensive, up-to-date information on how to get their fair share of the financial aid pie.

Peterson's College Money Handbook 2008 is both a quick reference and a comprehensive resource that puts valuable information about college costs and financial aid opportunities at your fingertips.

- **The ABCs of Paying for College** provides insight into federal financial aid programs that are available, offers an overview of the financial aid landscape, walks you through the process of filing for aid, and provides proven tips on how to successfully navigate the financial aid process to obtain the federal, state, and institutional aid you deserve.
- The **Quick-Reference Chart** offers a snapshot comparison of the financial aid programs available at more than 2,000 four-year institutions across the country.
- The **Profiles of College Financial Aid Programs** provide unbiased financial aid data for each of the more than 2,000 four-year institutions listed.
- The **Appendix** lists the state scholarship and grant programs offered by all fifty states and the District of Columbia.
- The six **Indexes** included in the back of the book allow you to search for specific award programs based on a variety of criteria, including merit-based awards, athletic grants, ROTC programs, and much more.

Peterson's publishes a full line of resources to help guide you and your family through the financial aid and college admission process. Peterson's publications can be found at your local bookstore, library, and high school guidance office, and you can access us online at www.petersons.com.

We welcome any comments or suggestions you may have about this publication and invite you to complete our online survey at www.petersons.com/booksurvey. Or you can fill out the survey at the back of this book, tear it out, and mail it to us at:

Publishing Department
Peterson's, a Nelnet company
2000 Lenox Drive
Lawrenceville, NJ 08648

Your feedback will help us make your educational dreams possible.

The editors at Peterson's wish you the best of luck during the financial aid process!

The ABCs of Paying for College

A Guide to Financing Your Child's College Education

Don Betterton

Given the lifelong benefit of a college degree (college graduates are projected to earn in a lifetime $1 million more than those with only a high school diploma), higher education is a worthwhile investment. However, it is also an expensive one made even harder to manage by cost increases that have outpaced both inflation and gains in family income. This reality of higher education economics means that parental concern about how to pay for a child's college education is a dilemma that shows no sign of getting easier.

Because of the high cost involved (even the most inexpensive four-year education at a public institution costs about $10,000 a year), good information about college budgets and strategies for reducing the "sticker price" is essential. You have made a good start by taking the time to read *Peterson's College Money Handbook*. In the pages that follow, you will find valuable information about the four main sources of aid—federal, state, institutional, and private. Before you learn about the various programs, however, it will be helpful if you have an overview of how the college financial aid system operates and what long-range financing strategies are available.

Financial Aid

Financial aid refers to money that is awarded to a student, usually in a "package" that consists of gift aid (commonly called a scholarship or grant), a student loan, and a campus job.

College Costs

The starting point for organizing a plan to pay for your child's college education is to make a good estimate of the yearly cost of attendance. You can use the **College Cost Worksheet** on the next page to do this.

To estimate your college costs for 2008–09, refer to the tuition and fees and room and board figures shown in the **College Costs At-a-Glance** chart on page 39. If your child will commute from your home, use $2500 instead of the college's room and board charges and $900 for transportation. We have used $800 for books and $1300 for personal expenses. Finally, estimate the cost of two round trips if your home is more than a few hundred miles from the college. Add the items to calculate the total budget. You should now have a reasonably good estimate of college costs for 2008–09. (To determine the costs for later years, adding 5 percent per year will probably give you a fairly accurate estimate.)

Do You Qualify for Need-Based Aid?

The next step is to evaluate whether or not you are likely to qualify for financial aid based on need. This step is critical, since more than 90 percent of the yearly total of $128 billion in student aid is awarded only after a determination is made that the family lacks sufficient financial resources to pay the full cost of college on its own. To judge your chance of receiving need-based aid, it is necessary to estimate an Expected Family Contribution (EFC) according to a government formula known as the Federal Methodology (FM). You can do so by referring to the **Approximate Expected Family Contribution Chart** for 2008–09 on page 4.

Applying for Need-Based Aid

Because the federal government provides about 67 percent of all aid awarded, the application and need evaluation process is controlled by Congress and the U.S. Department of Education. The application is the Free Application for Federal Student Aid, or FAFSA. In addition, nearly every state that offers student assistance uses the federal government's system to award its own aid. Furthermore, in addition to arranging for the payment of federal and state aid, many colleges use the FAFSA to award their own funds to eligible students. (Note: In addition to the FAFSA, some colleges also ask the family to complete the CSS/PROFILE® application.)

The FAFSA is your "passport" to receiving your share of the billions of dollars awarded annually in need-based aid. Even if you're uncertain as to whether or not you qualify for need-based aid, everyone who might need assistance in financing an education should pick up

College Cost Worksheet

	College 1	College 2	College 3	Commuter College
Tuition and Fees	______	______	______	______
Room and Board	______	______	______	$2,500
Books	$ 800	$ 800	$ 800	$ 750
Personal Expenses	$1,300	$1,300	$1,300	$1,300
Travel	______	______	______	$ 900
Total Budget	______	______	______	______

a FAFSA from the high school guidance office after mid-November 2007. This form will ask for 2007 financial data, and it should be filed after January 1, 2008, in time to meet the earliest college or state scholarship deadline. Within two to four weeks after you submit the form, you will receive a summary of the FAFSA information, called the Student Aid Report, or SAR. The SAR will give you the EFC and also allow you to make corrections to the data you submitted.

You can also apply for federal student aid via the Internet using FAFSA on the Web. FAFSA on the Web can be accessed at www.fafsa.ed.gov. Both the student and at least one parent should apply for a federal PIN number at www.pin.ed.gov. The PIN number serves as your electronic signature when applying for aid on the Web. (Note: Many colleges provide the option to apply for early decision or early action admission. If you apply for this before January 1, 2008, which is prior to when the FAFSA can be used, follow the college's instructions. Many colleges use either PROFILE or their own application form for early admission candidates.)

How Need Is Calculated and Aid Is Awarded

	College X	College Y
Total Cost of Attendance	$10,000	$ 24,000
−Expected Family Contribution	− 5,500	− 5,500
= Financial Need	$ 4,500	$ 18,500
− Grant Aid Awarded	− 675	−14,575
− Campus Job (Work-Study) Awarded	− 1,400	− 1,300
− Student Loan Awarded	− 2,425	− 2,625
= Unmet Need	0	0

Note: Sometimes an institution is unable to meet all need. The amount of unmet need is called "the gap."

Awarding Aid

About the same time you receive the SAR, the colleges you list will receive your FAFSA information so they can calculate a financial aid award in a package that typically includes aid from at least one of the major sources—federal, state, college, or private. In addition, the award will probably consist of a combination of a scholarship or a grant, a loan, and a campus job. These last two pieces—loan and job—are called self-help aid because they require effort on your part (that is, the aid must be either earned through work or paid back later). Scholarships or grants are outright gifts that have no such obligation.

It is important that you understand each part of the package. You'll want to know, for example, how much is gift aid, the interest rate and repayment terms of the student loan, and how many hours per week the campus job requires. There should be an enclosure with the award letter that answers these questions. If not, make a list of your questions and call or visit the financial aid office.

Once you understand the terms of each item in the award letter, you should turn your attention to the "bottom line"—how much you will have to pay at each college where your child was accepted. In addition to understanding the aid award, this means having a good estimate of the college budget so you can accurately calculate how much you and your child will have to contribute. (Often, an aid package does not cover the entire need.) Colleges follow different practices in how much detail they include in their award notifications. Many colleges provide full information—types and amounts of aid, yearly costs, and the EFC divided into the parent and student shares. If these important items are missing or incomplete, you can do the work on your own. (See the Comparing Financial Aid Awards and Family Contribution Worksheet on this page.) For example, if only the college's

Approximate Expected Family Contribution Chart

	Income Before Taxes								
Assets	**$20,000**	**30,000**	**40,000**	**50,000**	**60,000**	**70,000**	**80,000**	**90,000**	**100,000**
$20,000									
Family Size 3	$ 0	160	1,800	3,500	5,800	9,100	12,600	14,100	17,400
4	0	0	850	2,500	4,400	7,100	10,600	12,000	15,300
5	0	0	0	1,600	3,300	5,500	8,600	10,100	13,400
6	0	0	0	600	2,200	4,100	6,600	7,900	11,200
$30,000									
Family Size 3	$ 0	160	1,800	3,500	5,800	9,100	12,600	14,100	17,400
4	0	0	850	2,500	4,400	7,100	10,600	12,000	15,300
5	0	0	0	1,600	3,300	5,500	8,600	10,100	13,400
6	0	0	0	600	2,200	4,100	6,600	7,900	11,200
$40,000									
Family Size 3	$ 0	160	1,800	3,500	5,800	9,100	12,600	14,100	17,400
4	0	0	850	2,500	4,400	7,100	10,600	12,000	15,300
5	0	0	0	1,600	3,300	5,500	8,600	10,100	13,400
6	0	0	0	600	2,200	4,100	6,600	7,900	11,200
$50,000									
Family Size 3	$ 0	340	2,000	3,800	6,200	9,500	13,000	14,500	17,800
4	0	0	1,100	2,700	4,700	7,400	11,000	12,400	15,700
5	0	0	0	1,800	3,500	5,800	9,000	10,400	13,750
6	0	0	0	800	2,400	4,300	6,900	8,300	11,600
$60,000									
Family Size 3	$ 0	600	2,300	4,100	6,600	10,000	13,600	15,000	18,300
4	0	0	1,300	3,000	5,000	8,000	11,500	13,000	16,300
5	0	0	400	2,050	3,800	6,200	9,600	11,000	14,300
6	0	0	0	1,000	2,700	4,600	7,400	8,800	12,150
$80,000									
Family Size 3	$ 0	1,130	2,800	4,800	7,600	11,200	14,700	16,150	19,500
4	0	170	1,800	3,600	5,900	9,100	9,600	14,100	17,400
5	0	0	900	2,600	4,500	7,200	10,700	12,100	15,450
6	0	0	0	1,600	3,200	5,400	8,500	10,000	13,300
$100,000									
Family Size 3	$ 0	1,660	3,400	5,600	8,800	12,300	15,900	17,300	20,600
4	0	700	2,400	4,200	6,800	10,250	13,800	15,200	18,500
5	0	0	1,400	3,100	5,300	8,300	11,800	13,300	16,600
6	0	0	400	2,100	3,900	6,300	9,700	11,100	14,400
$120,000									
Family Size 3	$ 0	2,190	4,000	6,500	9,900	13,400	17,000	18,400	21,700
4	0	1,220	3,000	4,900	7,800	11,400	14,900	16,350	19,650
5	0	310	2,000	3,700	6,100	9,500	13,000	14,400	17,700
6	0	0	1,000	2,600	4,600	7,300	10,800	12,200	15,550
$140,000									
Family Size 3	$ 0	2,700	4,700	7,500	11,000	13,400	18,100	19,500	22,850
4	0	1,750	3,500	5,700	9,000	12,500	16,000	17,750	20,800
5	0	850	2,500	4,400	7,100	10,500	14,100	15,500	18,850
6	0	0	1,500	3,200	5,300	8,400	11,900	13,350	16,650

This chart makes the following assumptions:

- $20,000 income files 1040A or 1040EZ, all other incomes file regular 1040
- Age of older parent is 45+
- No parental untaxed income reported
- Estimated federal income tax for incomes $20,000 to $80,000 is 10 percent
- Estimated federal income tax for incomes $90,000 to $100,000 is 15 percent
- One student in college, two parent family
- No student income or assets reported

Comparing Financial Aid Awards and Family Contribution Worksheet

	College 1	College 2	College 3
Cost of Attendance	________	________	________
Aid Awarded	________	________	________
Grant/Scholarship	________	________	________
Loan	________	________	________
Job	________	________	________
Total Aid	________	________	________
Expected Family Contribution	________	________	________
Student Contribution	________	________	________
Parent Contribution	________	________	________

direct charges for tuition, room, and board are shown on the award letter, make your own estimate of indirect costs like books, personal expenses, and travel. Then subtract the total aid awarded from the yearly cost to get the EFC. A portion of that amount may be your child's contribution (20 percent of student assets and 50 percent of student earnings over $3000) and the remainder is the parental share. If you can afford this amount at your child's first-choice college, the financial aid system has worked well for you, and your child's college enrollment plans can go forward.

But if you think your EFC is too high, you should contact the college's financial aid office and ask whether additional aid is available. Many colleges, private high-cost colleges in particular, are enrollment-oriented—they are willing to work with families to help make attendance at their institutions possible. Most colleges also allow applicants to appeal their financial aid awards, the budget used for you, or any of the elements used to determine the family contribution, especially if there are extenuating circumstances or if the information has changed since the application was submitted. Some colleges may also reconsider an award based on a "competitive appeal," the submission of a more favorable award letter from another college.

If your appeal is unsuccessful and there is still a gap between the expected family contribution and what you feel you can pay from income and savings, you are left with two choices. One option is for your child to attend a college where paying your share of the bill will not be a problem. (This assumes that an affordable option was included on your child's original list of colleges, a wise admission application strategy.) The second is to look into alternate methods of financing. At this stage, parental loans and tuition payment plans are the best financing options. A parental loan can bring the yearly cost down to a manageable level by spreading payments over a number of years. This is the type of financing that families use when purchasing a home or automobile. A tuition payment plan is essentially a short-term loan and allows you to pay the costs over ten to twelve months. It is an option for families who have the resources available but need help with managing their cash flow. See the "Financing Your Child's College Education" section for more information.

Non-Need-Based Aid

Regardless of whether you might qualify for a need-based award, it is always worthwhile to look into merit, or non-need, scholarships from sources such as foundations, agencies, religious groups, and service organizations. For a family that isn't eligible for need-based aid, merit scholarships are the only form of gift aid available. If you later qualify for a need-based award, a merit scholarship can be quite helpful in providing additional resources if the aid does not fully cover the costs. Even if the college meets 100 percent of need, a merit scholarship can benefit you by reducing the self-help (loan and job) portion of an award.

In searching for merit-based scholarships, keep in mind that there are relatively few awards (compared to those that are need-based), and most of them are highly competitive. Use the following checklist when investigating merit scholarships.

- Take advantage of any scholarships for which your child is automatically eligible based on parents' employer benefits, military service, association or church membership, other affiliations, or student or parent attributes (ethnic background, nationality, etc.). Company or union tuition remissions are the most common examples of these awards.
- Look for other awards for which your child might be eligible based on the characteristics and affiliations indicated above but where there is a selection process and an application is required. Free computerized searches are available on the Internet. (You should not pay a fee for a scholarship search.) Peterson's free scholarship search can be accessed by logging on to www.petersons.com/finaid. Scholarship directories, such as *Peterson's Scholarships, Grants & Prizes*, which details more than 5,000 scholarship programs, are useful resources and

What Is CSS/PROFILE®?

There are many complexities in the financial aid process: knowing which aid is merit-based and which aid is need-based; understanding the difference between grants, loans, and work-study; and determining whether funds are from federal, state, institutional, or private sources.

In addition, the aid application process itself can be confusing. It can involve more than the Free Application for Federal Student Aid (FAFSA) and the Federal Methodology (FM). Many colleges feel that the federal aid system (FAFSA and FM) does not collect or evaluate information thoroughly enough for them to award their own institutional funds. These colleges have made an arrangement with the College Scholarship Service, a branch of the College Board, to establish a separate application system.

The application is called the CSS/PROFILE®, and the need-analysis formula is referred to as the Institutional Methodology (IM). If you apply for financial aid at one of the colleges that uses PROFILE, the admission material will state that PROFILE is required in addition to the FAFSA. You should read the information carefully and file PROFILE to meet the earliest college deadline. Before you can receive PROFILE, however, you must register, either by phone or through the Web (http://profileonline.collegeboard.com/index.jsp), providing enough basic information so the PROFILE package can be designed specifically for you. The FAFSA is free, but there is a charge for PROFILE. As with the FAFSA, PROFILE can be submitted via the Internet.

In addition to the requirement by certain colleges that you submit both the FAFSA and PROFILE (when used, PROFILE is always in addition to the FAFSA; it does not replace it), you should understand that each system has its own method for analyzing a family's ability to pay for college. The main differences between PROFILE's Institutional Methodology and the FAFSA's Federal Methodology are:

- PROFILE includes equity in the family home as an asset; the FAFSA doesn't.
- PROFILE takes a broader look at assets not included on the FAFSA.
- PROFILE expects a minimum student contribution, usually in the form of summer earnings; the FAFSA has no such minimum.
- PROFILE may collect information on the noncustodial parent; the FAFSA does not.
- PROFILE allows for more professional judgment than the FAFSA. Medical expenses, private secondary school costs, and a variety of special circumstances are considered under PROFILE, subject to the discretion of the aid counselor on campus.
- PROFILE includes information on assets not reported on the FAFSA, including life insurance, annuities, retirement plans, etc.

To summarize: PROFILE's Institutional Methodology tends to be both more complete in its data collection and more rigorous in its analysis than the FAFSA's Federal Methodology. When IM results are compared to FM results for thousands of applicants, IM will usually come up with a somewhat higher expected parental contribution than FM.

can be found in bookstores, high school guidance offices, or public libraries.

- See if your state has a merit scholarship program.
- Look into national scholarship competitions. High school guidance counselors usually know about these scholarships. Examples of these awards are the National Merit Scholarship, the Coca-Cola Scholarship, Aid Association for Lutherans, Gates Millennium Scholars, Intel Science Talent Search, and the U.S. Senate Youth Program.

Creditworthiness

If you will be borrowing to pay for your child's college education, making sure you qualify for a loan is critical. For the most part, that means your credit record must be free of default or delinquency. You can check your credit history with one or more of the following three major credit bureaus and clean up any adverse information that appears. The numbers below will offer specific information on what you need to provide to obtain a report. All of the credit bureaus accept credit report requests over their Web sites. You will usually be asked to provide your full name, phone number, social security number, birth date, and addresses for the last five years. You are entitled to a free report from each bureau.

Equifax
P.O. Box 740241
Atlanta, GA 30374
800-685-5000
http://www.equifax.com

Trans Union[SM]
P.O. Box 2000
Chester, PA 19022
800-888-4213
http://www.tuc.com

Experian National Consumer Assistance Center
475 Anton Boulevard
Costa Mesa, CA 92626
888-397-3742
800-972-0322 (TTY/TDD)
http://www.experian.com

- ROTC (Reserve Officers' Training Corps) scholarships are offered by the Army, Navy, Air Force, and Marine Corps. A full ROTC scholarship covers tuition, fees, textbook costs and, in some cases, a stipend. Acceptance of an ROTC scholarship entails a commitment to take military science courses and to serve for a specific number of years as an officer in the sponsoring branch of the service. Competition is heavy, and preference may be given to students in certain fields of study, such as engineering, languages, science, and health professions. Application procedures vary by service. Contact an armed services recruiter or high school guidance counselor for further information.
- Investigate community scholarships. High school guidance counselors usually have a list of these awards, and announcements are published in local newspapers. Most common are awards given by service organizations like the American Legion, Rotary International, and the local women's club.

If your child is strong academically (for example, a National Merit® Commended Student or better) or is very talented in fields such as athletics or performing/creative arts, you may want to consider colleges that offer their own merit awards to gifted students they wish to enroll. Refer to the *Non-Need Scholarships for Undergraduates* index.

In addition to merit scholarships, there are loan and job opportunities for students who do not qualify for need-based aid. Federal loan programs include the unsubsidized federal Stafford and Direct Loans. See the "Federal Financial Aid Programs" article for more information. Some of the organizations that sponsor scholarships—for example, the Air Force Aid Society—also provide loans.

Note

A point of clarification about whether to put college savings in your name or your child's: If you are certain that your child will not be a candidate for need-based aid, there may be a tax advantage to accumulating money in his or her name. However, when it comes to maximizing aid eligibility, it is important to understand that student assets are assessed at a 20 percent rate and parental assets at about 5 percent. Therefore, if your college savings are in your child's name, it may be wise to reestablish title to these funds before applying for financial aid. You should contact your financial planner or accountant before making any modifications to your asset structure.

Work opportunities during the academic year are another type of assistance that is not restricted to aid recipients. Many colleges will, after assigning jobs to students on aid, open campus positions to all students looking for work. In addition, there are usually off-campus employment opportunities available to everyone.

Financing Your Child's College Education

In this section, "financing" means putting together resources to pay the balance due the college over and above payments from the primary sources of aid—grants, scholarships, student loans, and jobs. Financing strategies are important because the high cost of a college education today often requires a family, whether or not it receives aid, to think about stretching its college payment beyond the four-year period of enrollment. For high-cost colleges, it is not unreasonable to think about a 10-4-10 plan: ten years of saving; four years of paying college bills out of current income, savings, and borrowing; and ten years to repay a parental loan.

Savings

Although saving for college is always a good idea, many families are unclear about its advantages. Some families do not save because after normal living expenses have been covered, they do not have much money to set aside. An affordable but regular savings plan through a payroll deduction is usually the answer to the problem of spending your entire paycheck every month.

The second reason why saving for college is not a high priority is the belief that the financial aid system penalizes a family by lowering aid eligibility. The Federal Methodology of need determination is very kind to savers. In fact, savings are ignored completely for most families that earn less than $50,000. Savings in the form of home equity, retirement plans, and most annuities are excluded from the calculation. And even when savings are counted, a maximum of 5 percent of the total is expected each year. In other words, if a family has $40,000 in savings after an asset protection allowance is considered, the contribution is no greater than $2000. Given the impact of compound interest it is easy to see that a long-term savings plan can make paying for college much easier.

A sensible savings plan is important because of the financial advantage of saving compared to borrowing. The amount of money students borrow for college is now greater than the amount they receive in grants and scholarships. With loans becoming so widespread, savings should be carefully considered as an alternative to borrowing. Your incentive for saving is that a dollar saved is a dollar not borrowed.

Borrowing

Once you've calculated your "bottom-line" parental contribution and determined that the amount is not affordable out of your current income and assets, the most likely alternative is borrowing. First determine if you are eligible for a larger subsidized federal Stafford or Direct Loan. Because no interest is due while your child attends college, these are the most favorable loans. If this is not possible, look into the unsubsidized Stafford or Direct Loan, which is not based on need but the interest accrues each year. The freshman year limit (either subsidized or unsubsidized) is $3500.

After you have taken out the maximum amount of student loans, the next step is to look into parental loans. The federal government's parent loan program is called PLUS and is the standard against which other loans should be judged. A local bank that participates in the PLUS program can give you a schedule of monthly repayments per $1000 borrowed. Use this repayment figure to compare other parental loans available from commercial lenders (including home equity loans), state programs, or colleges themselves. Choose the one that offers the best terms after all up-front costs, tax advantages, and the amount of monthly payments are considered. Be sure to check with your financial aid office before making a final decision. Often, the financial aid office will have reviewed the various programs that are available and can help direct you to the best choice.

Make Financial Aid Work for You

This overview is intended to provide you with a road map to help you think about financing strategies and navigate through the complexities of the financial aid process. Much of the information you will need to help you determine your plan to pay for your child's education can be found within the pages of this guide. First use the **Approximate Expected Family Contribution Chart** in conjunction with the **College Cost Worksheet** to estimate need eligibility. Complete the FAFSA (and PROFILE, if required). At the same time, look into merit scholarships. Once your child is accepted at a school, use the **Comparing Financial Aid Awards and Family Contribution Worksheet** to figure out your parental obligation. If you can't afford the payment, present your arguments to the institution's financial aid office before checking out the terms of PLUS and other parental loan options. And finally, if there are younger children at home, think about starting a college savings fund to get a head start on their future education costs.

If you are like millions of families that benefit from financial aid, it is likely that your child's college plans can go forward without undue worry about the costs involved. The key is to understand the financial aid system and to follow the best path for your family. The result of good information and good planning should be that you will receive your fair share of the billions of dollars available each year and that the cost of college will not prevent your child from attending.

Don Betterton is a former Director of Undergraduate Financial Aid at Princeton University.

Middle-Income Families: Making the Financial Aid Process Work

Richard Woodland

The U.S. Department of Education's National Center for Education Statistics has researched how middle-income families finance a college education. Their 2001 report, *Middle Income Undergraduates: Where They Enroll and How They Pay for Their Education*, states that although 31 percent of middle-income families have the entire cost of college covered by financial aid, there is widespread angst among these families that, while they earn too much to qualify for grant assistance, they are financially unable to pay the spiraling cost of higher education.

First, we have to agree on what constitutes a "middle-income" family. For the purposes of the federal study, middle-income families are defined as those families with incomes between $35,000 and $70,000. The good news is that 52 percent of these families received grants, while the balance received loans. Other sources of aid, including work-study, also helped close the gap.

So how do these families do it? Is there a magic key that opens the door to significant amounts of grants and scholarships?

The report shows some interesting trends. One way middle-income families make college more affordable is by choosing a less expensive school. In fact, in the report, 29 percent of middle-income students chose to enroll in low- to moderate-cost schools, with a total cost of less than $8500 per year, including community colleges and lower-priced state colleges and universities. But almost half of these middle-income families chose higher-priced schools, with costs between $8500 and $16,000. The remaining 23 percent enrolled at the highest-priced schools, with costs above $16,000. Clearly cost is a factor, but middle-income families are not limiting their choices based on cost alone.

The report shows that families pay these higher costs through a combination of family assets, current income, and long-term borrowing. This is often referred to as the "past-present-future" model of financing. In fact, just by looking at the Expected Family Contributions, it is clear that there is a significant gap in what families need and what the financial aid process can provide. Families are closing this gap by making the necessary financial sacrifices to pay the current price of higher-cost schools, especially if they think their child is academically strong. The report concludes that parents are more likely to pay for a higher-priced education if their child scores above 2000 on the SAT.

Where to Start

The best place for middle-income families to start is their high school guidance office. Here they can find valuable information on financial aid and leads on local scholarships. Most guidance counselors report that there are far fewer applicants for these locally based scholarships than one would expect. So read the information they send home, and be sure to follow up during the application process. A few of those $500 to $1000 scholarships can really add up.

Then, be sure to attend a financial aid awareness program. If your school does not offer one, contact your local college financial aid office and see when and where one is available. These programs offer a lot of inside information on how the financial aid process works.

Next, be sure to file the correct applications for aid. Remember, each school can have a different set of requirements. For example, many higher-cost private colleges require the CSS/PROFILE® application, which should be filed in September or October of the senior year. Other schools may have their own institutional aid applications. All schools require the Free Application for Federal Student Aid (FAFSA). Watch the deadlines! It is important that you meet the school's published application deadline. Generally, schools are not very flexible about this, so be sure to double-check the due date of your application.

Finally, become a smart educational consumer. Peterson's has a wide range of resources available to help you understand the process. Be sure to check your local library, bookstore, and of course, the

Internet. Two great Web sites to check out are www.petersons.com and www.finaid.org.

Closing the Gap

Once your child is accepted, you will receive an award notice outlining the aid you are eligible to receive. If you feel the offer is not sufficient, or if you have some unique financial problems, call the college or university's financial aid office to see if you can have your case reviewed. The financial aid office is the best source for putting the pieces together to help you finance your college education.

The financial aid office will help you determine what the "net price" is. This is the actual out-of-pocket cost that you will need to cover. Through a combination of student and parent loans, along with other forms of financial aid and family resources, most families are able to meet these expenses.

Furthermore, many students help close the gap by working throughout their college career. While this works for many students, research shows that too many hours spent away from studies can negatively affect academic success. Most experts feel that working 10 to 15 hours a week is optimal.

An overlooked source of aid is the recent tax credits given to middle-income families. Rather than extending eligibility for traditional sources of grant assistance to middle-income families, the federal tax system has built in a number of significant tax benefits for middle-income families, including the Hope Scholarship and Lifetime Learning Tax Credit. While it may take seven or eight months before you see the tax credit, most families in this income group can count on this benefit, usually between $1500 and $2000 per student. This is real money in your pocket and you do not need to itemize your deductions to qualify for this tax credit. Another option for upper-middle-income families not qualifying for the Hope/Lifetime tax credit is a tuition and fee deduction of up to $4000 from their taxable income.

A tool to help you get a handle on the ever-rising costs of college is to assume you can pay a third of "net charges" from savings, another third from available (nonretirement) assets, and the rest from parent borrowing. If any one of these is not available, shift that amount to one of the other resources. But if it looks like you will be financing most or all of the costs from future income (borrowing), it may be wise to consider a lower-cost college.

Millions of middle-income families send their children to colleges and universities every year. Only 8 percent attend the lowest-priced schools. By using the concept of past-present-future financing, institutional assistance, federal and state aid, meaningful targeted tax relief, and student earnings, you can afford even the highest-priced schools.

Alternative Financing Options

For many families, traditional financial aid programs come up short in meeting the tuition bill each semester. Rather than exhausting their savings, many families are turning to private or alternative loans to help defray the cost. The world of private/alternative educational loans can be confusing. There are varying interest rates, loan fees, up-front costs, and capitalization dates. There is no single place to go and search for the best deal. But the private/alternative loan financing market is today's fastest-growing source of financial aid. Organizations such as Sallie Mae offer a number of money-saving options in alternative loan financing. Consult the micro-site content center at www.petersons.com/finaid for more information on the types of financing plans available.

The most common source of alternative funding is the federal Parent Loans for Undergraduate Students (PLUS). These are federally insured loans that offer creditworthy borrowers significant funding at reasonable interest rates. To qualify, you need to pass a credit check. It is a good idea to check your credit report annually. This can be done for free at FreeCreditReport.com. Contact the college financial aid office; some schools are in the Direct Loan program and will process the application from the financial aid office. Other schools will recommend a bank or other financial institution where you can begin the PLUS process. In general, you can borrow the full cost of tuition less any other aid received. This can run into the thousands of dollars.

Remember, though, that PLUS is not always the best deal. Many states have alternative loan programs that offer far better terms than PLUS. For example, New Jersey and Pennsylvania offer programs backed by state bond issues that generally are more attractive than the federal PLUS. Check with your state Higher Education Office or with a school in your area for more information. In most cases, these loans are portable, meaning they can be used at any school across the country. By doing some research you can save hundreds of dollars in interest charges.

Many schools have arranged special financing plans with private lenders. When you are working with the financial aid office to put your total aid package together, be sure to check for any special programs that may be available. There are many lenders available to help families finance higher education. You can trust the financial aid counselors. They do this work every day and can point you in the right direction.

Richard Woodland is Director of Student Services and Financial Aid at The Curtis Institute of Music.

Common Questions Answered

Q ***Are a student's chances of being admitted to a college reduced if the student applies for financial aid?***

A Generally no. Nearly all colleges have a policy of "need-blind" admissions, which means that a student's financial need is not taken into account in the admission decision. There are a few selective colleges, however, that do consider ability to pay before deciding whether or not to admit a student. Some colleges will mention this in their literature; others may not. The best advice is to apply for financial aid if the student needs assistance to attend college.

Q ***Are parents penalized for saving money for college?***

A No. As a matter of fact, families that have made a concerted effort to save money for college are in a much better position than those that have not. For example, a student from a family that has saved money may not have to borrow as much. Furthermore, the "taxing rate" on savings is quite low—only about 5 percent of the parents' assets are assessed and neither the home equity nor retirement savings are included. For example, a single 40-year-old parent who saved $40,000 for college expenses will have about $1900 counted as part of the parental contribution. Two parents, if the older one is 40 years old (a parent's age factors into the formula-tion), would have about $300 counted. (Note: The "taxing rate" for student assets is much higher—20 percent—compared to 5 percent for parents.)

Q ***How does the financial aid system work in cases of divorce or separation? How are stepparents treated?***

A In cases of divorce or separation, the financial aid application(s) should be completed by the parent with whom the student lived for the longest period of time in the past twelve months (custodial parent). If the custodial parent has remarried, the stepparent is considered a family member and must complete the application along with the biological parent. If your family has any special circumstances, you should discuss these directly with the financial aid office. (Note: Colleges that award their own aid may ask the noncustodial biological parent to complete a separate aid application and a contribution will be calculated.)

Q ***When are students considered independent of parental support in applying for financial aid?***

A The student must be at least 24 years of age in order to be considered independent. If younger than 24, the student must be married, be a graduate or professional student, have legal dependents other than a spouse, be an orphan or ward of the court, or be a veteran of the armed forces or on active military duty. However, in very unusual situations, students who can clearly document estrangement from their parents can appeal to the financial aid office for additional consideration.

Q ***What can a family do if a job loss occurs?***

A Financial aid eligibility is based on the previous year's income. So the family's 2006 income would be reported to determine eligibility for the 2007–08 academic year. In that way, the family's income can be verified with an income tax return. But the previous year's income may not accurately reflect the current financial situation, particularly if a parent lost a job or retired. In these instances, the projected income for the coming year can be used instead. Families should discuss the situation directly with the financial aid office and be prepared to provide appropriate documentation.

Q ***When my daughter first went to college, we applied for financial aid and were denied because our Expected Family Contribution was too high. Now, my son is a high school senior, and we will soon have two in college. Will we get the same results?***

A The results will definitely be different. Both your son and your daughter should apply. As we described earlier, need-based financial aid is based on your Expected Family Contribution, or EFC. When you have two children in college, this amount is divided in half for each child.

Q ***I've heard about the "middle-income squeeze" in regard to financial aid. What is it?***

A The so-called "middle-income squeeze" is the idea that low-income families qualify for aid, high-income families have adequate resources to pay for education, and those in the middle are not eligible for aid but do not have the ability to pay full college costs. There is no provision in the Federal Methodology that treats middle-income students differently than others (such as an income cutoff for eligibility). The Expected Family Contribution rises proportionately as income and assets increase. If a middle-income family does not qualify for aid, it is because the need analysis formula yields a contribution that exceeds college costs. But keep in mind that if a $65,000-income family does not qualify for grant aid at a public university with a $16,000 cost, the same family will likely be eligible for aid at a private college with a cost of $25,000 or more. Also, there are loan programs available to parents and students that are not based on need. Middle-income families should realize, however, that many of the grant programs funded by federal and state governments are directed at lower-income families. It is therefore likely that a larger share of an aid package for a middle-income student will consist of loans rather than grants.

Q ***Given our financial condition, my daughter will be receiving financial aid. We will help out as much as we can, and, in fact, we ourselves will be borrowing. But I am concerned that she will have to take on a lot of loans in order to go to the college of her choice. Does she have any options?***

A She does. If offered a loan, she can decline all or part of it. One option is for her to ask in the financial aid office to have some of the loan changed to a work-study job. If this is not possible, she can find her own part-time work. Often there is an employment office on campus that can help her locate a job. In most cases, the more she works, the less she has to borrow. It is important to remember that the educational loans offered to students have very attractive terms and conditions, with flexible repayment options. Students should look upon these loans as a long-term investment that will reap significant rewards.

Q ***Is it possible to change your financial aid package?***

A Yes. Most colleges have an appeal process. A request to change a need-based loan to a work-study job is usually approved if funds are available. A request to consider special financial circumstances may also be granted. At most colleges, a request for more grant money is rarely approved unless it is based on a change in the information reported. Applicants should speak with the financial aid office if they have concerns about their financial package. Some colleges may even respond to a competitive appeal, that is, a request to match another college's offer.

Q ***My son was awarded a federal Stafford Loan as part of his financial aid package. His award letter also indicated that we could take out a PLUS Loan. How do we go about choosing our lender? Do we go to our local bank?***

A Read the material that came with the financial aid award letter. It is likely that the college has a "preferred lender" list for Stafford and PLUS Loans. However, you can borrow from any bank that participates in the federal loan programs.

Q ***The cost of attending college seems to be going up so much faster than the Consumer Price Index. Why is that, and how can I plan for my child's four years?***

A The cost of higher education cannot be compared to the Consumer Price Index (CPI). The CPI does not take into account most of the costs faced by colleges. For example, the dollars that universities spend on grants and scholarships have risen rapidly. Many universities have increased enrollment of students from less affluent families, further increasing the need for institutional financial aid. Colleges are expected to be on the cutting edge of technology, not only in research but also in the classroom and in the library. Many colleges have deferred needed maintenance and repairs that can now no longer be put off. In addition, there is market pressure to provide many expensive lifestyle amenities that were not expected ten years ago. In general, you can expect that college costs will rise at least 2 to 3 percent faster than inflation.

Q ***I'm struggling with the idea that all students should apply to the college of their choice, regardless of cost, because financial aid will level the playing field. I feel I will be penalized because I have saved for college. My son has been required to save half of his allowance since age six for his college education. Will that count against him when he applies for financial aid? It's difficult to explain to him that his college choices may be limited because of the responsible choices and sacrifices we have made as a family. What can we do to make the most of our situation?***

A In general, it is always better to have planned ahead for college by saving. Families that have put away sufficient funds to pay for college will quickly realize that they have made the burden easier for themselves and their children. In today's college financing world, schools assume that paying for the cost of attendance is a 10-year commitment. So by saving when your child is young, you reap significant advantages from compound interest on the assets and reduce the need to borrow as much while in school. This should reduce the number of years after college that you will be burdened with student and parent loans. We advise families to spend the student's assets first, since the financial aid formulas count these more heavily than parental assets. Then, after the first year, you can explain to the college how you spent these assets, and why you might now need assistance. When looking at parental information, the income of the family is by far the most important component. Contrary to popular belief, parental assets play a minor role in the calculation of need. With this strategy, you have done the right thing, and in the long run, it should prove to be a wise financial plan.

Picking the right college also involves other factors. Students should select the colleges they are going to apply to in two ways. First and most important is to look at colleges that meet your son's academic and lifestyle interests. Most experts will tell him to pick a few "reach" schools (i.e., schools where he is not sure he has the grades and scores required) and at least one or two academically "safe" schools. He should also select one or two financially "safe" schools that you are sure you can afford with either moderate or little financial aid. Most students do not get into all of their first-choice schools, and not everyone can afford the schools they are admitted to. By working closely with the guidance office in high school and the admissions and financial aid offices at the college, you can maximize your options.

Q ***My son was awarded a $2500 scholarship. This can be split and used for two years. When filling out the FAFSA, do we have to claim the full amount, or just the $1250 he plans to use the first year?***

A Congratulations to your son on the scholarship. Nowhere on the FAFSA should you report this scholarship. It is not considered income or an asset. However, once you choose a school to attend, you must notify the financial aid office for its advice on how to take the funds. But remember, do NOT report it on the FAFSA.

Q ***I will be receiving a scholarship from my local high school. How will this scholarship be treated in my financial aid award?***

A Federal student aid regulations specify that all forms of aid must be included within the defined level of need. This means that additional aid, such as outside scholarships, must be combined with any need-based aid you receive; it may not be kept separate and used to reduce your family's contribution. If the college has not filled 100 percent of your need, it will usually allow outside scholarships to close the gap. Once your total need has been met, the college must reduce other aid and replace it with the outside award. Most colleges will allow you to use some, if not all, of an outside scholarship to replace self-help aid (loans and Federal Work-Study) rather than grant aid.

Q ***I know we're supposed to apply for financial aid as soon as possible after January 1. What if I don't have my W-2s yet and my tax return isn't done?***

A The first financial aid application deadlines usually fall in early February. Most colleges use either March 1 or March 15 as their "priority filing date." Chances are you'll have your W-2 forms by then, but you won't have a completed tax return. If that is the case, complete the financial aid application using your best estimates. Then, when you receive the Student Aid Report (SAR), you can use your tax return to make corrections. Just be sure to check with each college for its deadline.

Q ***Is there enough aid available to make it worthwhile for me to consider colleges that are more expensive than I can afford?***

A Definitely. More than $100 billion in aid is awarded to undergraduates every year. With more than half of all enrolled students qualifying for some type of assistance, this totals more than $5500 per student. You should view financial aid as a large, national system of tuition discounts, some given according to a student's ability and talent, others based on what a student's family can afford to pay. If you qualify for need-based financial aid, you will essentially pay only your calculated family contribution, regardless of the cost of the college. You will not pay the "sticker price" (the cost of attendance listed in the college catalog) but a lower rate that is reduced by the amount of aid you receive. No college should be ruled out until after financial aid is considered. In addition, when deciding which college to attend, consider that the short-term cost of a college education is only one criterion. If the college meets your educational needs and you are convinced it can launch you on an exciting career, a significant up-front investment may turn out to be a bargain over the long run.

Q ***If I don't qualify for need-based aid, what options are available?***

A You should try to put together your own aid package to help reduce your parents' share. There are three sources to look into. First, search for merit scholarships. Second, seek employment, during both the summer and the academic year. The student employment office should be able to help you find a campus job. Third, look into borrowing. Even if you don't qualify for the need-based loan programs, the unsubsidized federal Stafford and Direct Loans are available to all students. The terms and conditions are the same as the subsidized loan programs except that interest accrues while you are in college.

After you have contributed what you can through scholarships, employment, and loans, your parents will be faced with their share of the college bill. Many colleges have monthly payment plans that allow families to spread their payments over the academic year. If these monthly payments turn out to be more than your parents can afford, they can take out a parent loan. By borrowing from the college itself, from a commercial agency or lender, or through PLUS, your parents can extend their college payments over a ten-year period or longer. Borrowing reduces the monthly obligation to its lowest level, but the total amount paid will be the highest due to principal and interest payments. Before making a decision on where to borrow parental loan funds, be sure to first check with the financial aid office to determine what is the best source of alternative funds.

Federal Financial Aid Programs

There are a number of sources of financial aid available to students: federal and state governments, private agencies, and the colleges themselves. In addition, as discussed earlier, there are three different forms of aid: grants, earnings, and loans.

The federal government is the single largest source of financial aid for students. For the 2005–06 academic year, the U.S. Department of Education's student financial aid programs made an estimated $94 billion available in loans, grants, and other aid to nearly 10 million students, while 11 million families benefited from various education tax cuts and deductions. At the present time, there are four federal grant programs—Federal Pell Grant, Federal Supplemental Educational Opportunity Grant (FSEOG), Academic Competitiveness Grant (ACG), and National Smart Grant (SMART). There are three federal loan programs: Federal Perkins Loan, Direct Loan, and Stafford Loan. The federal government also has a job program, Federal Work-Study (FWS), which helps colleges provide employment for students. In addition to the student aid programs, there are also tuition tax credits and deductions. They are the HOPE Scholarship for freshmen and sophomores, the Lifetime Learning Tax Credit for undergraduate students after their second year, and the Tuition and Fees Tax Deduction.

The majority of federal higher education loans are made either in the Direct Loan program or the Stafford Loan program. The difference between these loans is the lending source, but, for the borrower, the terms and conditions are essentially the same. Both Direct and Stafford programs make available two kinds of loans: loans to students and PLUS loans to parents and graduate or professional students. These loans are either subsidized or unsubsidized. Subsidized loans are made on the basis of demonstrated student need, and the interest is paid by the government during the time the student is in school. For the unsubsidized (non-need-based) loans and PLUS Loans, interest begins to accrue as funds are disbursed.

To qualify for the Federal Pell Grant, ACG, SMART, FSEOG, Federal Work-Study, and Federal Perkins Loan pro-

Table Used to Estimate Federal Pell Grants for 2007–2008

Adjusted Gross Income	Family Assets							
	$50,000	$55,000	$60,000	$65,000	$70,000	$75,000	$80,000	$85,000
$ 5,000	$ 4,310	$ 4,310	$ 4,310	$ 4,310	$ 4,310	$ 4,310	$ 4,310	$ 4,310
$10,000	4,310	4,310	4,310	4,310	4,310	4,310	4,310	4,310
$15,000	4,310	4,310	4,310	4,310	4,310	4,310	4,310	4,310
$20,000	4,310	4,310	4,310	4,310	4,310	4,310	4,000	4,000
$25,000	3,980	3,980	3,780	3,680	3,180	2,980	2,780	2,580
$30,000	3,380	3,200	3,180	3,000	2,980	2,780	2,580	2,300
$35,000	2,300	2,180	2,000	1,980	1,980	1,880	1,780	1,680

Note: Based on family of four, one child enrolled in college, oldest parent age 41+.
This chart should only be used as an estimate since the formula to determine EFC takes into account a number of variables.

grams and the subsidized Stafford Loan, you must demonstrate financial need.

Pell Grant

The Federal Pell Grant is the largest grant program; more than 6 million students receive Pell Grants annually. This grant is intended to be the starting point of assistance for lower-income families. Eligibility for a Federal Pell Grant is based on the Expected Family Contribution. The amount you receive will depend on your EFC and the cost of education at the college you will attend. The highest award depends on how much funding the program receives from the government. The maximum for 2007–08 is $4310.

To give you some idea of your possible eligibility for a Pell Grant, the table in this section may be helpful. The amounts shown are based on a family of four, with one student in college, no emergency expenses, no contribution from student income or assets, and college costs of at least $4050 per year. Pell Grants range from $400 to $4310.

Federal Supplemental Educational Opportunity Grant (FSEOG)

As its name implies, Federal Supplemental Educational Opportunity Grants provide additional need-based federal grant money to supplement the Federal Pell Grant. Each participating college is given funds to award to especially needy students. The maximum award is $4000 per year, but the amount you receive depends on the college's awarding policy, the availability of FSEOG funds, the total cost of education, and the amount of other aid awarded.

Academic Competitiveness Grants

U.S. citizens who are Pell Grant–eligible and who attended a "rigorous" high school program, as defined by the U.S. Secretary of Education, can receive up to $750 in their first year and $1300 in their second year if they have a minimum 3.0 GPA. More information about this program is available from your child's high school or college financial aid office.

National Smart Grants

Third- and fourth-year undergraduates who are Pell Grant–eligible and major in math, science, technology, or certain foreign languages and have a minimum 3.0 in their major can qualify for a grant of up to $4000. More information about this program is available from your high school or college financial aid office.

Federal Work-Study (FWS)

This program provides jobs for students who demonstrate need. Salaries are paid by funds from the federal government as well as the college. You work on an hourly basis on or off campus and must be paid at least the federal minimum wage. You may earn only up to the amount awarded in the financial aid package.

Federal Perkins Loan

This is a low-interest (5 percent) loan for students with exceptional financial need. Federal Perkins Loans are made through the college's financial aid office with the college as the lender. You can borrow a maximum of $4000 per year for up to five years of undergraduate study. Borrowers may take up to ten years to repay the loan, beginning nine months after they graduate, leave school, or drop below half-time status. No interest accrues while they are in school, and, under certain conditions (e.g., they teach in low-income areas, work in law enforcement, are full-time nurses or medical technicians, serve as Peace Corps or VISTA volunteers, etc.), some or all of the loan can be cancelled. In addition, payments can be deferred under certain conditions such as unemployment.

Federal Stafford and Direct Loans

Stafford and Direct Loans generally have the same interest rates, loan maximums, deferments, and cancellation benefits. A Stafford Loan may be borrowed from a commercial lender, such as a bank or a credit union. A Direct Loan is borrowed directly from the U.S. Department of Education through the college's financial aid office.

The Direct and Stafford Loan programs carry a fixed 6.8 percent interest rate. If a student qualifies for a need-based subsidized Stafford or Direct Loan, the interest is paid by the federal government while he is enrolled in college. There is also the unsubsidized loan that is not based on need.

The maximum amount dependent students may borrow in any one year is $3500 for freshmen, $4500 for sophomores, and $5500 for juniors and seniors, with a maximum of $23,000 for the total undergraduate program. The maximum amount independent students can borrow is $7500 for freshmen (of which no more than $3500 can be subsidized), $8500 for sophomores (of which no more than $4500 can be subsidized), and $10,500 for juniors and seniors (of which no more than $5500 can be subsidized). Borrowers may be charged a small origination fee (usually less than 3 percent), which is deducted

Federal Financial Aid Programs

Name of Program	Type of Program	Maximum Award Per Year
Federal Pell Grant	need-based grant	$4310
Federal Supplemental Educational Opportunity Grant (FSEOG)	need-based grant	$4000
Academic Competitiveness Grant (ACG)	need/merit	$750 (freshman) $1300 (sophomore)
National Smart Grant (SMART)	need/merit/program	Up to $4000 (third- and fourth-year undergraduate)
Federal Work-Study	need-based part-time job	no maximum
Federal Perkins Loan	need-based loan	$4000
Subsidized Stafford/Direct Loan	need-based student loan	$3500 (first year)
Unsubsidized Stafford/Direct Loan	non-need-based student loan	$3500 (first year, dependent student)

from the loan proceeds. Some lenders offer reduced or no-fee loans.

To apply for a Stafford Loan, you must first complete the FAFSA to determine eligibility for a subsidized loan and then complete a separate loan application that is submitted to a lender. The financial aid office can help in selecting a lender, but students are free to select any lender they choose. The lender will send a master promissory for completion. The proceeds of the loan, less the origination fee, will be sent to the college to be either credited to your account or released to you directly. Direct Loans are processed by the financial aid office as part of your overall financial aid package.

Once the repayment period starts, borrowers of both subsidized and unsubsidized Stafford or Direct Loans have to pay a combination of interest and principal monthly for up to a ten-year period. There are a number of repayment options as well as opportunities to consolidate federal loans. There are also provisions for extended repayments, deferments, and repayment forbearance, if needed.

Federal PLUS Loans

PLUS Loans are for parents of dependent students to help families with the cost of education. There is no needs test to qualify. The loan has a fixed interest rate of 8.5 percent for Stafford Loans and 7.9 percent for Direct Loans (subject to change). There is no yearly limit; you can borrow up to the cost of your child's education, less other financial aid received. Repayment begins sixty days after the funds are disbursed. A small origination fee (usually about 3 percent or less) may be subtracted from the proceeds. Parent borrowers must generally have a good credit record to qualify. PLUS may be processed under either the Direct or Stafford Loan system, depending on the type of loan program for which the college has contracted.

Tuition Tax Credits

Tuition tax credits allow families to reduce their tax bill by the out-of-pocket college tuition expense. Unlike a tax deduction, which is modified according to your tax bracket, a tax credit is a dollar-for-dollar reduction in taxes paid.

There are two programs: the HOPE Scholarship and the Lifetime Learning Tax Credit. As is true of many federal programs, there are numerous rules and restrictions that apply. You should check with your tax preparer or financial adviser for information about your own particular situation.

HOPE Scholarship

The HOPE Scholarship offsets some of the expense for the first two years of college or vocational school. Students or the parents of dependent students can claim an annual income tax credit of up to $1650—100 percent of the first $1100 of tuition and required fees and 50 percent of the second $1100. Grants, scholarships, and other tax-free educational assistance must be deducted from the total tuition and fee payments.

This credit can be claimed for students who are in their first two years of college and who are enrolled on at least a half-time basis in a degree or certificate program for any portion of the year. This credit phases out for joint filers who have an income between $90,000 and $110,000 and for single filers who have between $45,000 and $55,000 of income. Parents may claim credits for more than one qualifying student. (The income figures are subject to change.)

Lifetime Learning Tax Credit

The Lifetime Learning Tax Credit is the counterpart of the HOPE Scholarship; it is for college juniors, seniors, graduate students, and part-time students pursuing lifelong learning to improve or upgrade their job skills. The qualifying taxpayer can claim an annual tax credit of up to $2000—20 percent of the first $10,000 of tuition. The credit is available for net tuition and fees, less grant aid. The total credit available is limited to $2000 per year per taxpayer (or joint-filing couple), and is phased out at the same income levels as the HOPE Scholarship. (The income figures are subject to change each year.)

Tuition and Fees Tax Deduction

The Tuition and Fees Tax Deduction could reduce taxable income by as much as $4000. This deduction is taken as an adjustment to income, which means you can claim this deduction even if you do not itemize deductions on Schedule A of Form 1040. This deduction may benefit taxpayers who do not qualify for either the Hope or Lifetime Learning Tax Credits.

Up to $4000 may be deducted for tuition and fees required for enrollment or attendance at an eligible postsecondary institution. Personal living and family expenses, including room and board, insurance, medical, and transportation, are not deductible expenses.

The exact amount of the Tuition and Fees Tax Deduction depends on the amount of qualified tuition and related expenses paid for one's self, spouse, or dependents, and your Adjusted Gross Income. Consult the IRS or your tax preparer for more information.

Student Loan Interest Tax Deducation

If you made student loan interest payments in 2007, you may be able to reduce your taxable income by up to $2500 if the current tax law for 2006 is extended by the federal government. You should check with your lender and your tax preparer or the IRS for additional information.

AmeriCorps

AmeriCorps is a national umbrella group of service programs for students. Participants work in a public or private nonprofit agency and provide service to the community in one of four priority areas: education, human services, the environment, and public safety. In exchange, they earn a stipend (for living expenses) of between $7400 and $14,800 a year, health insurance coverage, and $4725 per year for up to two years to apply toward college expenses. Many student-loan lenders will postpone the repayment of student loans during service in AmeriCorps, and AmeriCorps will pay the interest that is accrued on qualified student loans for members who complete the service program. Participants can work before, during, or after college and can use the funds to either pay current educational expenses or repay federal student loans. For more information, visit www.americorps.org.

Analyzing Financial Aid Award Letters

Richard Woodland

You have just received the financial aid award letters. Now what? This is the time to do a detailed analysis of each college's offer to help you pay for your child's education. Remember, accepting financial aid is a family matter. More often than not, parents need to borrow money to send their dependent children to college. You need to clearly understand the types of aid you and your child are being offered. How much is "free" money in the form of grants and/or scholarships that does not have to be repaid? If your financial aid award package includes loans, what are the terms and conditions for these loans? A good tool to have with you is the federal government's most recent issue of *The Student Guide,* available from the school's financial aid office or at http://studentaid.ed.gov/students/publications/student_guide/index.html. This publication is very helpful in explaining the federal grant and loan programs that are usually a part of the aid package.

Let's take a minute to explain what is meant by "financial aid award package." A college will offer an aid applicant a combination of aid types, "packaged" in the form of grants and scholarships, loans, and a work-study job, based on the information provided on the FAFSA and/or another application. Many schools use a priority filing date, which guarantees that all applications received by this date will be considered for the full range of institutional aid programs available. Late applicants (by even one day!) often are only awarded the basic aid programs from state and federal sources. *It is important to apply on time.*

Evaluate Each Letter

As each award letter comes in, read it through carefully. The following are some critical points to consider:

- **Does the Cost of Attendance (COA) include all projected costs?** Each award letter should state the school's academic year COA. Tuition, fees, room, board, books, transportation, and personal expenses are what normally make up the COA. Does the award letter itemize all these components? Or does it omit some? This is crucial because this is what you will need to budget for. If you need additional information, be sure to contact the financial aid office. They will be glad to provide you with information or answer any questions you may have about their costs.
- **What is your Expected Family Contribution (EFC)?** Is the school's—not just the federal government's—EFC listed on the award letter? Some schools may require a higher EFC than you expected. Be aware that the EFC may increase or decrease each year depending on the information you provide on the renewal FAFSA or other financial aid application.
- **Is there unmet need?** Does the aid package cover the difference between the COA and the EFC? Not every school can cover your full need. If the aid package does not cover your full need, does the information with the award letter provide you with alternative loan options? If not, contact the financial aid office for more information.
- **Is the scholarship renewable for four years?** If your child is awarded a scholarship based on scholastic achievement or talent, you need to ask these questions: Is there a minimum grade point average he has to maintain? Can he switch majors but keep the scholarship? Does he need to participate in an "honors college" program to maintain the scholarship? If he needs to change to part-time status, will the award amount be pro-rated, or does he need to maintain full-time status? If it is an athletic or "special talent" scholarship, will he continue to receive the award if for some reason he cannot continue with the specific program? Renewal of scholarship funds is often the biggest misunderstanding between families and colleges. Be sure you clearly understand the terms and conditions of all grants and scholarships.
- **What will the college do to your child's award if she receives outside, noninstitutional scholarships?** Will the award be used to cover unmet need or reduce her student loans? Will the college reduce her institutional grants or scholarships? Or will they reduce her work-study award? (This is a good time to compare each school's policy on this matter.) Remember, your overall aid cannot total more than the COA, and many programs cannot exceed your financial need.

- **What are the interest rates of the loans that are offered?** Did another school offer you more than one loan and why? *Do not* sign the award letter until you understand your loan obligations. Again, *The Student Guide* can be very helpful with this part of the analysis.
- **Is the school likely to cover the same expenses every year?** In particular, ask if grant or scholarship funds are normally reduced or increased after the freshman year, even if family income and EFC remain the same. Some colleges will *increase* the self-help (loan, job) percentage every year but not necessarily the free money.
- **If work-study was awarded, how many hours a week will your child be expected to work?** If you feel working that many hours will have a negative impact on your child's academic performance, you may want to request that the awarded job funds be changed to a loan. You must ask immediately because funds are limited. Many schools are flexible with these funds early in the process.
- **What happens if (or more likely, when) tuition increases?** Check with the financial aid office to find out what its policy is for renewing an aid package. If, for example, tuition increases by 5 percent each of the next three years and your EFC remains the same, what will happen to your scholarships, grants, and loans?

You can always appeal your award letter if you feel that your needs are not being met, if your family situation has changed, or if you have received a better award from a competitive school. You have the right to ask for a reconsideration of your award. (Do not use the word *negotiate*.) When asking for reconsideration, be sure to provide the aid officer with all relevant information.

Compare Letters

After you have received and reviewed all the award letters from the schools your child is considering, the next step is to compare them and determine which schools are offering the best aid packages. Following are three sample award letters and a sample spreadsheet that shows you how to analyze and compare each school's awards.

Note: These award letters are simply for discussion purposes. They should not be considered to be representative award letters with an EFC of $9550.

UNIVERSITY A
FINANCIAL AID AWARD LETTER
2007–2008

Date: 4/21/07
ID#: 000000009

Dear Courtney Applicant,

We are pleased to inform you that you are eligible to receive the financial assistance indicated in the area labeled "Your Financial Aid." We estimated your budget based on the following assumptions:

In-state resident and living on campus.

	FALL	**SPRING**	**TOTAL**
Tuition and Fees	$3,849	$3,849	$ 7,698
Room & Board	3,769	3,770	7,539
Books	420	420	840
Transportation	973	974	1,947
Personal Expenses	369	369	738
Estimated Cost of Attendance	**$9,380**	**$9,382**	**$18,762**

Your Financial Aid

	FALL	**SPRING**	**TOTAL**
Federal Pell Grant	$1,950	$1,950	$ 3,900
Federal Direct Subsidized Loan	1,750	1,750	3,500
State Grant	432	432	864
Total Financial Aid	**$4,132**	**$4,132**	**$ 8,264**
Unmet Need	**$5,248**	**$5,250**	**$10,498**

What to Do Next:

- Verify that accurate assumptions have been used to determine your awards.
- Carefully review and follow the instructions on the Data Changes Form.
- To reduce or decline all or part of your loans, you must complete and return the Data Changes Form.
- We will assume you fully accept the awards above unless you submit changes to us immediately.
- Return corrections and required documents promptly.
- Retain this letter for your records.

UNIVERSITY B
FINANCIAL AID AWARD LETTER
2007–2008

Date: 4/21/07
ID#: 000000009

Dear Courtney Applicant,

We are pleased to inform you that you are eligible to receive the financial assistance indicated in the area labeled "Your Financial Aid." We estimated your budget based on the following assumptions:

Nonresident and living on campus.

	FALL	SPRING	TOTAL
Tuition and Fees	$ 9,085	$ 9,085	$18,170
Room & Board	2,835	2,835	5,670
Books	410	410	820
Transportation	875	875	1,750
Personal Expenses	378	377	755
Estimated Cost of Attendance	**$13,583**	**$13,582**	**$27,165**

Your Financial Aid

	FALL	SPRING	TOTAL
Federal Pell Grant	$ 1,950	$ 1,950	$ 3,900
Federal SEOG Grant	225	225	450
Academic Excellence Scholarship	500	500	1,000
Federal Work-Study Program	1,250	1,250	2,500
Federal Perkins Loan	1,250	1,250	2,500
Subsidized Stafford Loan	1,750	1,750	3,500
University Student Loan	2,000	2,000	4,000
Total Financial Aid	**$ 8,925**	**$ 8,925**	**$17,850**
Unmet Need	**$ 4,658**	**$ 4,657**	**$ 9,315**

What to Do Next:

- Verify that accurate assumptions have been used to determine your awards.
- Carefully review and follow the instructions on the Data Changes Form.
- To reduce or decline all or part of your loans, you must complete and return the Data Changes Form.
- We will assume you fully accept the awards above unless you submit changes to us immediately.
- Return corrections and required documents promptly.
- Retain this letter for your records.

UNIVERSITY C
FINANCIAL AID AWARD LETTER
2007–2008

Date: 4/21/07
ID#: 000000009

Dear Courtney Applicant,

We are pleased to inform you that you are eligible to receive the financial assistance indicated in the area labeled "Your Financial Aid." We estimated your budget based on the following assumptions:

Living on campus.

	FALL	**SPRING**	**TOTAL**
Tuition and Fees	$14,955	$14,955	$29,910
Room & Board	4,194	4,193	8,387
Books	450	450	900
Transportation	350	350	700
Personal Expenses	1,295	1,293	2,588
Estimated Cost of Attendance	**$21,244**	**$21,241**	**$42,485**

Your Financial Aid

	FALL	**SPRING**	**TOTAL**
Institutional Grant	$10,805	$10,805	$21,610
Federal Pell Grant	1,950	1,950	3,900
Federal SEOG Grant	2,000	2,000	4,000
Federal Work-Study Program	1,713	1,712	3,425
Total Financial Aid	**$16,468**	**$16,467**	**$32,935**
Unmet Need	**$ 4,776**	**$ 4,774**	**$ 9,550**

What to Do Next:

- Verify that accurate assumptions have been used to determine your awards.
- Carefully review and follow the instructions on the Data Changes Form.
- To reduce or decline all or part of your loans, you must complete and return the Data Changes Form.
- We will assume you fully accept the awards above unless you submit changes to us immediately.
- Return corrections and required documents promptly.
- Retain this letter for your records.

Comparison Grid

	University A (State University)	University B (Nonresident State University)	University C (Private College)
Cost of Attendance	**$18,762**	**$27,165**	**$42,485**
Tuition and Fees	7,698	18,170	29,910
Room and Board	7,539	5,670	8,367
Books	840	820	900
Transportation	1,947	1,750	700
Personal Expenses	738	755	2,558
Grants and Scholarships	**4,764**	**5,350**	**29,510**
Loans	**3,500**	**6,000**	**0**
Work-Study	**0**	**2,500**	**3,425**
Expected Family Contribution	**9,550**	**9,550**	**9,550**
Balance	**$ 948**	**$ 165**	**$ 0**

Some things to notice:

- At all schools, the Federal Pell grant remains the same.
- Even though University C (a private college) has the highest "sticker price," the net cost is less than the state schools.
- University B is a state university, but you are classified as an out-of-state resident (or nonresident). Many students in this situation find that the higher out-of-state costs combined with lower grant aid make this a costly decision.
- All schools assume that you will be residing in on-campus housing. But if you choose to commute to University A, you would save a substantial amount because you would not have the $7539 room and board cost.

Once you have entered all the information into a spreadsheet of your own and come up with the balances, here are some things to consider for each school:

- **How much is the balance?** Ideally, your balance should be $0, but look to see which school has the lowest balance amount.
- **What part of the aid package comes in the form of grants and scholarships?** It is important to note this because these awards (gift aid) do not have to be paid back.
- **Look at the loans.** Usually, the best financial deal contains more money in scholarships and less in loan dollars. Based on expected freshman-year borrowing, determine the debt burden at each school once your child graduates. You have to multiply the amount of your loan by four or five years, depending on how long it will take for your child to graduate. And remember that the loan amounts will probably increase each year. You also should take into consideration that you will have to borrow even more as the COA increases each year. To determine the best loan deal, consider:
  - —What are the terms of the loans?
  - —What are interest rates?
  - —Do you pay the yearly interest rate during enrollment or is the interest subsidized or paid by the government?
  - —Is any money due during enrollment or is it deferred until after graduation? Figuring out how much you will owe at each school at graduation will give you a clear picture of what your financial situation will be *after* graduation.

However, unless cost is your only concern, you shouldn't simply choose the school offering the lowest loan amounts. Many other factors need to be considered, such as academic and social environment. And you should never reject a school based solely on insufficient financial aid. Consult with an aid administrator to discuss possible alternatives.

Finally, if the college that costs the most is still the one your child wants to attend, there are a number of ways to find money to cover the gap between the aid package and your actual cost, including paying more than the EFC figure, increasing student borrowing, working more hours, and taking out a PLUS loan.

Richard Woodland is Director of Student Services and Financial Aid at The Curtis Institute of Music.

Online Filing of FAFSA and CSS/PROFILE® Applications

Richard Woodland

Over the past few years, there have been major advancements in the way students apply both for admission to college and for financial aid. The two primary financial aid applications, the Free Application for Federal Student Aid (FAFSA) and the CSS/PROFILE® application from the College Scholarship Service now offer direct, online applications. FAFSA on the Web and PROFILE are available in both English and Spanish.

Why File Online?

There are two reasons why it is a good idea to file online. First, the online environment prevents you from making many mistakes. For example, if there is a question that is required of all applicants, you cannot inadvertently skip it. If the application software thinks your answer may not be accurate, it will prompt you to check it before proceeding. The financial aid process can be complicated, and applying online greatly reduces the chance for error. The second reason is turnaround time. The online applications are processed in a matter of days, not weeks. Since time is an important factor when applying for financial aid, it is prudent to have your application processed as quickly as possible.

Some Common Concerns About Online Filing

Both the FASFA and PROFILE online applications have become much more user-friendly. You do not have to be a computer expert to use these programs. Both applications allow you to save your completed data and return later if you are interrupted or need to gather additional information. Both systems use secure encryption technology to protect your privacy. FASFA information is shared with other federal agencies as required as part of the application process, online or paper. FAFSA information is also sent to your state of legal residence for state aid purposes and to any college or program your child lists on the application. The information on the application is highly personal, and every precaution is taken to safeguard your privacy.

Now, let's discuss some specific issues related to each application.

The FAFSA

The FAFSA is the universal application for all federal financial aid programs. It is the primary application used for most state and college financial aid programs. Before using the FAFSA online application, you need to secure an electronic signature, or Personal Identification Number (PIN). This is similar to the access codes used at ATM machines, online banking, etc. It is easy to obtain a PIN number. Simply go to www.pin.ed.gov and apply online. You will receive a reply via e-mail in about 48 hours. If your child is under 24 years of age, he or she and one parent will need a PIN number. If there is more than one child in college, a parent only needs one PIN number. However, each college applicant will need to have his or her own PIN.

The FASFA online application is not presented in the same format as the paper FAFSA. Although all of the questions are exactly the same, the order of some of the items on the online application has been rearranged to make it easier to complete and allow for some built-in skip-logic. You can easily obtain a copy of the electronic FAFSA by logging on to www.fafsa.ed.gov. Just click on "FAFSA on the Web Worksheet." Completing this first will make the online entry that much easier. There are a number of other worksheets available that can also make the process easier. You should print them out and decide which are applicable to your situation. Everyone should review Worksheets A, B, and C. If you have not completed your federal tax return, the "Income Estimator" worksheets are easy to use and can reduce much of the guesswork.

After completing the online FASFA, be sure to print a copy of the pages at the end of the process so that you have a copy of your answers and the confirmation number. Although lost applications are extremely rare, having this information will give you peace of mind. You can go online as often as you wish to check the status of your application.

The CSS/PROFILE®

The CSS/PROFILE® is a more comprehensive financial aid application that is used primarily at private, higher-cost colleges and universities to award nonfederal student aid funds. Many private scholarship programs also use the PROFILE. A complete list of colleges and programs that use the PROFILE can be found at https://profileonline.collegeboard.com/index.jsp.

The PROFILE application has a $5 registration fee and an additional $18 for each school or program you select to receive your information. You must have a credit card, debit card, or checking account to use this service.

> *Note:* A limited number of fee waivers are available for families with incomes below the poverty line. See your high school guidance officer for more information on the fee waiver program.

Complete information on the online PROFILE application is available at www.collegeboard.com/profile. Although the customized PROFILE application is processed in about one week, you should allow for enough processing time (usually 2 to 3 weeks) to meet the earliest deadline established by the school or program.

What Happens Next?

Both the FAFSA and CSS/PROFILE® processors want more applicants to use the online environment. Not only is the process easier for them, but it is faster and more accurate. Once you decide to apply online, the processors will only respond to you electronically. You will not receive any paper acknowledgments—all confirmations will be sent via e-mail. When it is time to reapply for aid in subsequent years (usually quite easy as most of the data are carried over from the previous application), all reminders will be sent to the e-mail address that is on file, so it is important to report any changes in your e-mail address.

It is easy to update the FAFSA following your initial application. For example, if you used estimated income information and now you have your federal tax return completed, you can simply return to www.fafsa.ed.gov and change your income figures. But be sure to go through the entire process and print out the updated confirmation page. In general, the PROFILE is a one-time application, filed well before tax season. Any updates are usually done directly through the schools.

Both processors offer helpful information, both in print and online. Check with your high school guidance office or local college financial aid office for additional assistance. If you need to call the FAFSA processor, the phone number is 800-4-FED-AID (toll-free). You can contact PROFILE customer service via e-mail at help@cssprofile.org or by phone at 305-829-9793.

Richard Woodland is Director of Student Services and Financial Aid at The Curtis Institute of Music.

Searching for Scholarships Online

Today's students need all the help they can get when looking for ways to pay for their college education. Skyrocketing tuition costs, state budget cuts, and diminished personal savings have combined to make financing a college education perhaps the number one concern for parents. College sticker shock is driving many families away from college. No wonder. The "purchasing power" of all aid programs from federal, state, and institutional sources has declined over the past two decades. State education budgets have been slashed. In 2006–07, tuition and fees increased 5.9 percent at four-year public institutions and 6.3 percent at four-year private colleges. And it's not only lower-income families who are affected. Some fear they make *too much* money to qualify for financial aid. Regardless of their situation, most families struggle to make sense of the college financial aid process and to decide which aid package is the right one for them.

Despite the confusion, students and parents can and should continue to research as many sources as they can to find the money they need. The Internet can be a great source of information. There are many worthwhile sites that are ready to help you search and apply for your fair share of awards, including Peterson's comprehensive financial aid site at www.petersons.com/finaid.

Peterson's "Pay For School"

Peterson's "Pay for School" financial aid Web site at www.petersons.com/finaid provides families with a wealth of information on college funding for every step of their college admission process.

Expert Advice

By logging on to www.petersons.com/finaid you gain access to comprehensive articles that describe the ins and outs of federal and state funding; tips for filing the FAFSA and the CSS/PROFILE®; step-by-step advice on what you should be doing junior and senior year of high school; and an audio clip of an interview with a real live financial aid expert. Links to state programs and agencies help you connect directly to those resources. The **Advice Center** lets you access articles on specific topics, such as advice on 529 Plans, loans and payment plans, scholarship scams, the military, and international students. There is also a section called "Financial Aid This Month," which contains the latest-breaking news on government programs and other college funding topics.

Scholarship Search

Peterson's free **Scholarship Search** connects you to more than 1.6 million scholarships, grants, and prizes totaling nearly $7 billion and lets you do an individualized search for awards that match your financial and educational needs. In just three easy steps you can

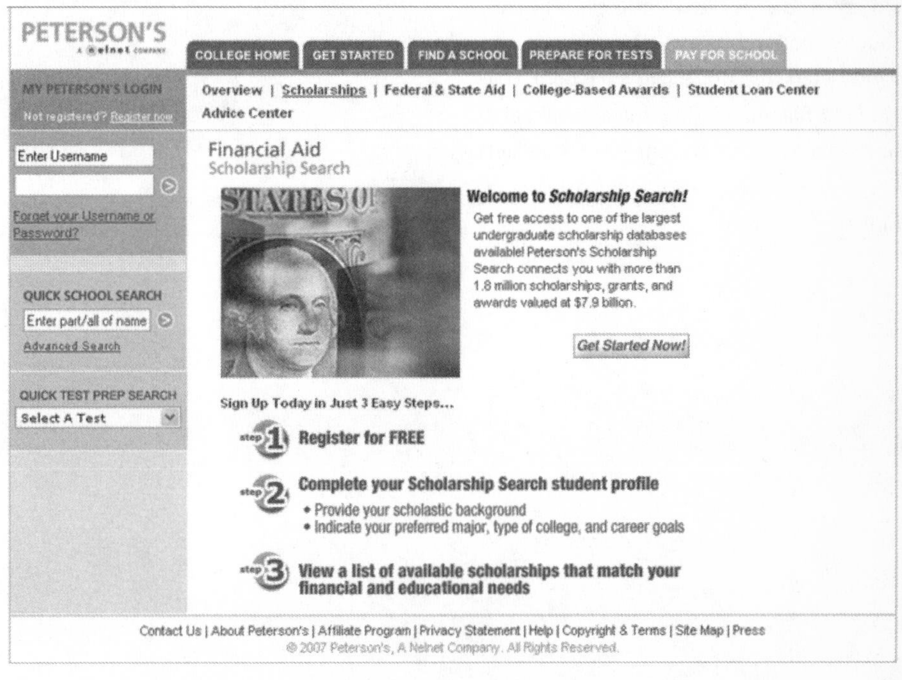

register; complete a customized profile indicating your scholastic and personal background, intended major, work experience, and a host of other criteria; and access a list of scholarships that match your needs. Each scholarship is described in detail, including eligibility and application requirements and contact information with links to its e-mail address and Web site. Finding money for college couldn't be easier!

Interactive Tools

When it's time to get to the nuts and bolts of your college financial planning, Peterson's has the tools to help. You can access a calculator to find your Estimated Family Contribution (EFC) as well as a **College Financial Planning Calculator** that lets you figure out your own personal savings plan. After you have received award letters from the colleges you've applied to, you can use the **Award Analyzer,** which helps you compare award letters to determine which school is prepared to give you the most aid. You simply enter the information from each award letter you received, press the Calculate button, and you discover which school has offered you the best package.

Searching and applying for financial aid is a complicated process. The resources and tools available to you on www.petersons.com/finaid can help you get your fair share of the financial aid pie. So, what are you waiting for? Log on! Free money for college may be just a mouse click away.

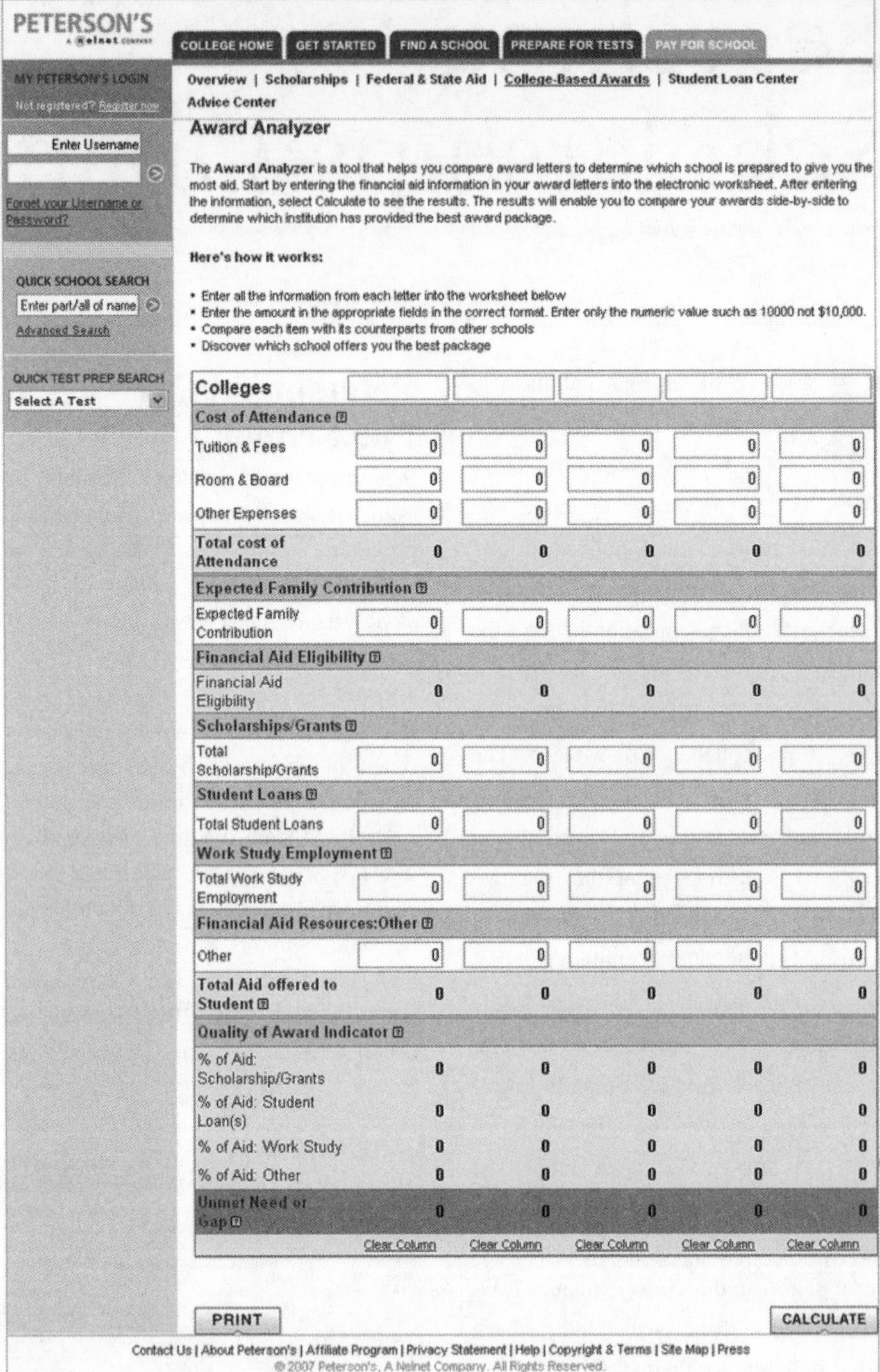

PETERSON'S

COLLEGE HOME | GET STARTED | FIND A SCHOOL | PREPARE FOR TESTS | PAY FOR SCHOOL

MY PETERSON'S LOGIN

Not registered? Register now

Enter Username

Forgot your Username or Password?

QUICK SCHOOL SEARCH

Enter part/all of name

Advanced Search

QUICK TEST PREP SEARCH

Select A Test

Overview | Scholarships | Federal & State Aid | College-Based Awards | Student Loan Center

Advice Center

Award Analyzer

The **Award Analyzer** is a tool that helps you compare award letters to determine which school is prepared to give you the most aid. Start by entering the financial aid information in your award letters into the electronic worksheet. After entering the information, select Calculate to see the results. The results will enable you to compare your awards side-by-side to determine which institution has provided the best award package.

Here's how it works:

- Enter all the information from each letter into the worksheet below
- Enter the amount in the appropriate fields in the correct format. Enter only the numeric value such as 10000 not $10,000.
- Compare each item with its counterparts from other schools
- Discover which school offers you the best package

Colleges					
Cost of Attendance					
Tuition & Fees	0	0	0	0	0
Room & Board	0	0	0	0	0
Other Expenses	0	0	0	0	0
Total cost of Attendance	0	0	0	0	0
Expected Family Contribution					
Expected Family Contribution	0	0	0	0	0
Financial Aid Eligibility					
Financial Aid Eligibility	0	0	0	0	0
Scholarships/Grants					
Total Scholarship/Grants	0	0	0	0	0
Student Loans					
Total Student Loans	0	0	0	0	0
Work Study Employment					
Total Work Study Employment	0	0	0	0	0
Financial Aid Resources:Other					
Other	0	0	0	0	0
Total Aid offered to Student	0	0	0	0	0
Quality of Award Indicator					
% of Aid: Scholarship/Grants	0	0	0	0	0
% of Aid: Student Loan(s)	0	0	0	0	0
% of Aid: Work Study	0	0	0	0	0
% of Aid: Other	0	0	0	0	0
Unmet Need or Gap	0	0	0	0	0
	Clear Column	Clear Column	Clear Column	Clear Column	Clear Column

PRINT | CALCULATE

Contact Us | About Peterson's | Affiliate Program | Privacy Statement | Help | Copyright & Terms | Site Map | Press

© 2007 Peterson's, A Nelnet Company. All Rights Reserved.

How to Use This Guide

Quick-Reference Chart

The amount of aid available at colleges can vary greatly. "College Costs At-a-Glance" lists the percent of freshmen who applied for and received need-based gift aid and the percent of those whose need was fully met. Also listed are the average freshman financial aid package, the average cost after aid, and the average indebtedness upon graduation.

Profiles of College Financial Aid Programs

After the federal government, colleges provide the largest amount of financial aid to students. In addition, they control most of the money channeled to students from the federal government. The amount and makeup of your financial aid package will depend on the institution's particular circumstances and its decisions concerning your application. The main section of this book shows you the pattern and extent of each college's current awards. The profiles present detailed factual and statistical data for each school in a uniform format to enable easy, quick references and comparisons. Items that could not be collected in time for publication are designated as *N/A*. Items for which the specific figures could not be gathered in time are given as *available.* Colleges that supplied no data are listed by name and address only so that you do not overlook them in your search for colleges.

There is much anecdotal evidence that students and their families fail to apply for financial aid under the misconception that student aid goes only to poor families. Financial need in the context of college expenses is not the same as being needy in the broad social context. Middle-class families typically qualify for need-based financial aid; at expensive schools, even upper-middle-income families can qualify for need-based financial aid. Peterson's encourages you to apply for financial aid whether or not you think that you will qualify.

To help you understand the definition and significance of each item, the following outline of the profile format explains what is covered in each section. The term college or colleges is frequently used below to refer to any institution of higher education, regardless of its official definition.

The College

The name of the college is the official name as it appears on the institution's charter. The city and state listed are the official location of the school. The subhead line shows tuition and required fees, as they were charged to the majority of full-time undergraduate students in the 2006–07 academic year. Any exceptions to the 2006–07 academic year are so noted. For a public institution, the tuition and fees shown are for state residents, and this is noted. If a college's annual expenses are expressed as a comprehensive fee (including full-time tuition, mandatory fees, and college room and board), this is noted, as are any unusual definitions, such as tuition only. The average undergraduate aid package is the average total package of grant, loan, and work-study aid that was awarded to meet the officially defined financial need of full-time undergraduates enrolled in fall 2006 (or fall 2005) who applied for financial aid, were determined to have need, and then actually received financial aid. This information appears in more detail in each profile.

About the Institution

This paragraph gives the reader a brief introduction to a college. It contains the following elements:

Institutional Control

Private institutions are designated as *independent* (nonprofit), *independent/religious* (sponsored by or affiliated with a religious group or having a nondenominational or interdenominational religious orientation), or *proprietary* (profit-making). Public institutions are designated by their primary source of support, such as *federal*, *state*, *commonwealth* (Puerto Rico), *territory* (U.S. territories), *county, district* (an administrative unit of public education, often having boundaries different from those of units of local government), *state- and locally-supported* ("locally" refers to county, district, or city), *state-supported* (funded by the state), or *state-related* (funded primarily by the state but administered autonomously).

Type of Student Body

The categories are *men* (100 percent of student body), *coed-primarily men, women* (100 percent of student body), *coed-primarily women*, and *coed.* A few schools are designated as *undergraduate: women only, graduate: coed* or *undergraduate: men only, graduate: coed.*

Degrees Awarded

Associate, bachelor's (baccalaureate), *master's, doctoral* (doctorate), and *first pro-*

fessional (in such fields as law and medicine). There are no institutions in this book that award the associate degree only. Many award the bachelor's as their highest degree. Your student will need to discuss this with you and his or her guidance counselor to decide whether a college that concentrates on undergraduate education or an institution with professional schools and research activities better meets his or her needs.

Number of Undergraduate Majors

This shows the number of academic fields in which the institution offers associate and/or bachelor's degrees. The purpose of this is to give you an indication of the range of subjects available.

Enrollment

These figures are based on the actual number of full-time and part-time students enrolled in degree programs as of fall 2006. In most instances, they are designated as *total enrollment* (for the specific college or university) and *freshmen*. If the institution is a university and its total enrollment figure includes graduate students, a separate figure for *undergraduates* may be provided. If the profiled institution is a subunit of a university, the figures may be designated *total university enrollment* for the entire university and *total unit enrollment* for the specific subunit.

Methodology Used for Determining Need

Private colleges usually have larger financial aid programs, but public colleges usually have lower sticker prices, especially for in-state or local students. At a public college, your financial need will be less, and you will receive a smaller financial aid package. The note on whether a college uses federal (FAFSA) or institutional methodology (usually PROFILE) will let you know whether you will have to complete one or two kinds of financial aid application forms. Federal Methodology is the needs-analysis formula used by the U.S. Department of Education to determine the Expected Family Contribution (EFC), which, when subtracted from the cost of attendance at an institution, determines the financial need of a student. There is no relative advantage or disadvantage to using one methodology over the other.

Undergraduate Expenses

If provided by the institution, the one-time application fee is listed. Costs are given for the 2007–08 academic year or for the 2006–07 academic year if 2007–08 figures were not yet available. Annual expenses may be expressed as a comprehensive fee (including full-time tuition, mandatory fees, and college room and board) or may be given as separate figures for full-time tuition, fees, room and board, or room only. For public institutions where tuition differs according to state residence, separate figures are given for area or state residents and for nonresidents. Part-time tuition is expressed in terms of a per-unit rate (per credit, per semester hour, etc.), as specified by the institution.

The tuition structure at some institutions is complex. Freshmen and sophomores may be charged a different rate from that charged juniors and seniors, a professional or vocational division may have a different fee structure from the liberal arts division of the same institution, or part-time tuition may be prorated on a sliding scale according to the number of credit hours taken. Tuition and fees may vary according to academic program, campus/location, class time (day, evening, weekend), course/credit load, course level, degree level, reciprocity agreements, and student level. If tuition and fees differ for international students, the rate charged is listed.

Room and board charges are reported as an average for one academic year and may vary according to board plan selected, campus/location, gender, type of housing facility, or student level. If no college-owned or -operated housing facilities are offered, the phrase *college housing not available* will appear.

If a college offers a *guaranteed tuition* plan, it promises that the tuition rate of an entering student will not increase for the entire term of enrollment, from entrance to graduation. Other payment plans might include *tuition prepayment*, which allows an entering student to lock in the current tuition rate for the entire term of enrollment by paying the full amount in advance rather than year by year, and *installment* and *deferred payment* plans, which allow students to delay the payment of the full tuition.

Guaranteed tuition and tuition prepayment help you to plan the total cost of your child's education and can save you from the financial distress sometimes caused by tuition hikes. Colleges that offer such plans may also help you to arrange financing, which in the long run can cost less than the total of four years of increasing tuition rates. Deferred payment or installment payments may better fit your personal financial situation, especially if you do not qualify for financial aid and, due to other financial commitments, find that obtaining the entire amount due is burdensome. Carefully investigate these plans, however, to see what premium you may pay at the end to allow you to defer immediate payment.

Freshman Financial Aid

Usually, these are actual figures for the 2005–06 term, beginning in fall 2005; figures may also be estimated for the 2006–07 term. The particular term for which these data apply is indicated. The figures are for degree-seeking full-time freshman students. The first figure is the number of freshmen who applied for any kind of financial aid. The next figure is the percentage of those freshmen financial aid applicants who were determined to have financial need—that is, through the formal needs-assessment process, had a calculated expected family contribution that was less than the total college cost. The next figure is the percentage of this group of eligible freshmen who received any financial aid. The next figure is the percentage of this preceding group of eligible aid recipients whose need was fully met by financial aid. The *Average percent of need met* is the average percentage of financial need met for freshmen who received any need-based aid. The *Average financial aid package* is the average dollar amount awarded (need-based or non-need-based) to freshmen who applied for aid, were deemed eligible, and received any aid; awards used to reduce the expected family contribution are excluded from this average. The final line in most profiles is the percentage of freshmen who had no financial need but who received non-need-based aid other than athletic scholarships or special-group tuition benefits.

What do these data mean to you? If financial aid is important in your comparison of colleges, the relative percentage of students who received any aid, whose need was fully met, and the average percentage of need met have the most weight. These figures reflect the relative abundance of student aid available to the average eligible applicant. The average dollar amount of the aid package has real meaning, but only in relation to the college's expense; you will be especially interested in the difference between this figure and the costs figure, which is what the average student (in any given statistical group, there actually may be no average individual) will have to pay. Of course, if the financial aid package is largely loans rather than grants, you will have to pay this amount eventually. Relative differences in the figures of the number of students who apply for aid and who are deemed eligible can hinge on any number of factors: the relative sticker price of the college, the relative level of wealth of the students' families, the proportion of only children in college and students with siblings in college (families with two or more children in college are more likely to apply for aid and be considered eligible), or the relative sophistication in financial aid matters (or quality of college counseling they may have received) of the students and their families. While these may be interesting, they will not mean too much to most students and families. If you are among the unlucky (or, perhaps, lucky) families who do not qualify for need-based financial aid, the final sentence of this paragraph in the profile will be of interest because it reveals the relative policies that the college has in distributing merit-based aid to students who cannot demonstrate need.

Undergraduate Financial Aid

This is the parallel paragraph to the Freshman Financial Aid paragraph (see above). The same definitions apply, except that the group being considered is degree-seeking full-time undergraduate students (including freshmen).

There are cases of students who chose a particular college because they received a really generous financial aid package in their freshman year and then had to scramble to pay the tuition bill in their later years. If a financial aid package is a key factor in your child's decision to attend a particular college, you want to be certain that the package offered to all undergraduates is not too far from that offered to freshmen. The key figures are those for the percentage of students who received any aid, the percentage of financial aid recipients whose need was fully met, the average percentage of need met, and the dollar figure of the average financial aid package. Generally, colleges assume that after the freshman year, students develop study habits and time-management skills that will allow them to take on part-time and summer employment without hurting their academic performance. So, the proportion of self-help aid (work-study and student loans) in the financial aid package tends to increase after the freshman year. This pattern, which is true of most colleges, can be verified below, in the freshman-undergraduate figures in the paragraph on Gift Aid (Need-Based).

Gift Aid (Need-Based)

Total amount is the total dollar figure in 2006–07 (estimated) or 2005–06 (actual) of need-based scholarships and grant (gift) aid awarded to degree-seeking full-time and part-time students that was used to meet financial need. The percentages of this aid from federal, state, institutional (college or university), and external (e.g., foundations, civic organizations, etc.) sources are shown. *Receiving aid* shows the percentages (and number, in parentheses) of freshmen and of all undergraduates who applied for aid, were considered eligible, and received any need-based gift aid. *Scholarships, grants, and awards* cites major categories of need-based gift aid provided by the college; these include Federal Pell Grants, Federal Supplemental Educational Opportunity Grants (FSEOG), state scholarships, private scholarships, college/university gift aid from institutional funds, United Negro College Fund aid, Federal Nursing Scholarships, and others.

Scholarships and grants are gifts awarded to students that do not need to be repaid. These are preferable to loans, which have to be repaid, or work-study wages, which may take time away from studies and personal pursuits. The total amount of need-based gift aid has to be placed into the context of the total number of undergraduate students (shown above, in the About the Institution paragraph) and the relative expense of the institution. Filing the FAFSA automatically puts you in line to receive any available federal grants for which you may qualify. However, if the college that your child is considering has a higher than usual proportion of gift aid coming from state, institutional, or external sources, be sure to check with the financial aid office to find out what these sources may be and how to apply for them. For almost all colleges, the percentage of freshmen receiving need-based gift aid will be higher than the percentage of all undergraduates receiving need-based gift aid. However, if your family is dependent on need-based gift aid and the particular college your child is considering shows a sharper drop from the freshman to undergraduate years than other colleges of a similar type, you might want to think about how this change will affect your ability to pay for later years at this college.

Gift Aid (Non-Need-Based)

Total amount is the total dollar figure in 2006–07 (estimated) or 2005–06 (actual) of non-need-based scholarships and grant (gift) aid awarded to degree-seeking full-time and part-time students. Non-need-based aid that was used to meet financial need is not included in this total. The percentages of this aid from federal, state, institutional (college or university), and external (e.g., National Merit Scholarships, civic, religious, fraternal organizations, etc.) sources are shown. *Receiving aid* shows the percentages (and number, in parentheses) of freshmen and of all undergraduates who did not receive need-based aid but who received non-need-based gift aid. *Average award* is the average dollar amount of awards to the students in this immediately preceding group. *Scholarships, grants, and awards by category* cites the major categories in which non-need-based awards are available and the number of awards made in that category (in parentheses, the total dollar value of these awards). The categories listed are *Academic Interests/Achievement*, *Creative Arts/Performance*, *Special Achievements/Activities*, and *Special Characteristics*. *Tuition waivers* indicate special categories of students (minority students, children of alumni, college employees or children of employees, adult students, and senior citizens) who may qualify for a full or partial waiver of tuition. *ROTC* indicates Army, Naval, and Air Force ROTC programs that are offered on campus; a program offered by arrangement on another campus is indicated by the word *cooperative*.

This section covers college-administered scholarships awarded to undergraduates on the basis of merit or personal attributes without regard to need. If you do not qualify for financial aid but nevertheless lack the resources to pay for college, non-need-based awards will be of special interest to you. Some personal characteristics are completely beyond an individual's control, and talents and achievements take a number of years to develop or attain. However, certain criteria for these awards, such as religious involvement, community service, and special academic interests can be attained in a relatively brief period of time. ROTC programs offer such benefits as tuition, the cost of textbooks, and living allowances. In return, you must fulfill a service obligation after graduating from college. Because they can be a significant help in paying for college, these programs have become quite competitive. Certain subject areas, such as nursing, health care, or the technical fields, are in stronger demand than others. Among the obligations to consider about ROTC are that you must spend a regular portion of your available time in military training programs and that ROTC entails a multiyear commitment after your graduation to serve as an officer in the armed services branch sponsoring the program.

Loans

The figures here represent loans that are part of the financial aid award package. These are typically offered at rates lower than can be found in the normal loan marketplace. *Student loans* represents the total dollar amount of loans from all sources to full-time and part-time degree-seeking undergraduates or their parents. The percentage of these loans that goes to meet financial need and the percentage that goes to pay the non-need portion (the expected family contribution) are indicated. The percentage of a past graduating class who borrowed through any loan program (except parent loans) while enrolled at the college is shown, as is the average dollar figure per-borrower of cumulative undergraduate indebtedness (this does not include loans from other institutions). *Parent loans* shows the total amount borrowed through parent loan programs as well as the percentages that were applied to the need-based and non-need-based portions of financial need. *Programs* indicates the major loan programs available to undergraduates. These include Direct and Stafford Loans (subsidized and unsubsidized and PLUS), Perkins Loans, Federal Nursing Loans, state loans, college/university loans, and other types.

Loans are forms of aid that must be repaid with interest. Most people will borrow money to pay college costs. The loans available through financial aid programs are offered at very favorable interest rates. Student loans are preferable to parent loans because the payoff is deferred. In comparing colleges, the dollar amount of total indebtedness of the last class is a factor to be considered. Typically, this amount would increase proportionate to the tuition. However, if it does not, this could mean that the college provides relatively generous grant or work-study aid rather than loans in its financial aid package.

Work-Study

The total dollar amounts, number, and average dollar amount of *Federal work-study* (FWS) jobs appear first. The total dollar figure of *State or other work-study/employment*, if available, is shown, as is the percentage of those dollars that go to meet financial need. The number of part-time jobs available on campus to undergraduates, other than work-study, is shown last.

FWS is a federally funded program that enables students with demonstrated need to earn money by working on or off campus, usually in a nonprofit organization. FWS jobs are a special category of jobs that are open to students only through the financial aid office. Other kinds of part-time jobs are routinely available at most colleges and may vary widely. In comparing colleges, you may find characteristic differences in how the "self-help" amounts (loans and work-study) are apportioned.

Athletic Awards

The total dollar amount of athletic scholarships given by the college to undergraduate students, including percentages that are need-based and non-need-based, is indicated.

If your child is a serious student-athlete candidate, this may provide a broad context, but actual awards will depend upon her specific talents and the college's athletic needs at the particular time. If she is a good athlete but not of starter caliber in a marquee sport, she might be able to secure a partial scholarship, depending on talent and the college's needs. In this case, the number of students receiving athletic awards in relation to the number of total undergraduates may be important.

Applying for Financial Aid

Required financial aid forms include the FAFSA (Free Application for Federal Student Aid), the institution's own form, CSS/PROFILE®, a state aid form, a noncustodial (divorced/separated) parent's statement, a business/farm supplement, and others. The college's financial aid application deadline is noted as the *Financial aid deadline* and is shown in one of three ways: as a specific date if it is an absolute deadline; noted as *continuous*, which means processing goes on without a deadline or until all available aid has been awarded; or as a date with the note *(priority)*, meaning that you are encouraged to apply before that date in order to have the best chance of obtaining aid. *Notification date* is listed as either a specific date or *continuous*. The date by which your child must reply to the college with her decision to accept or decline its financial aid package is listed as either a specific date or as a number of weeks from the date of notification.

Be prepared to check early with the colleges your child is interested in as to exactly which forms will be required from you. All colleges require the FAFSA for students applying for federal aid. In most cases, colleges have a limited amount of funds set aside to use as financial aid. It is possible that the first eligible students will get a larger share of what is available.

Contact

The name, title, address, telephone and fax numbers, and e-mail address of the person to contact for further information (student financial aid contact, chief financial aid officer, or office of financial aid) are given at the end of the profile. You should feel free to write or call for any materials you need or if you have questions.

Appendix

This section lists more than 400 state-specific grants and loans. Eligibility requirements, award amounts, and contact information are given for all programs.

Indexes

Six indexes in the back of the book allow you to search for particular award programs based on the following criteria:

Non-Need Scholarships for Undergraduates

This index lists the colleges that report that they offer scholarships based on academic interests, abilities, achievements, or personal characteristics other than financial need. Specific categories appear in alphabetical order under the following broad groups:

- Academic Interests/Achievements
- Creative Arts/Performance
- Special Achievements/Activities
- Special Characteristics

See the index for specific categories in each group.

Athletic Grants for Undergraduates

This index lists the colleges that report offering scholarships on the basis of athletic abilities.

Co-op Programs

This index lists colleges that report offering cooperative education programs. These are formal arrangements with off-campus employers that are designed to allow students to combine study and work, often in a position related to the student's field of study. Salaries typically are set at regular marketplace levels, and academic credit is often given.

ROTC Programs

This index lists colleges that offer Reserve Officers' Training Corps programs. The index is arranged by the branch of service that sponsors the program.

Tuition Waivers

This index lists colleges that report offering full or partial tuition waivers for certain categories of students. A majority of colleges offer tuition waivers to employees or children of employees. Because this benefit is so common and the affected employees usually are aware of it, no separate index of schools offering this option is provided. However, this information is included in the individual college profiles.

Tuition Payment Alternatives

This index lists colleges that report offering tuition payment alternatives. These payment alternatives include deferred payment plans, guaranteed tuition plans, installment payment plans, and prepayment plans.

Data Collection Procedures

The data contained in the college chart, profiles, and indexes were collected in fall and winter 2006 and spring 2007 through *Peterson's Annual Survey of Undergraduate Financial Aid* and *Peterson's Annual Survey of Undergraduate Institutions*. Questionnaires were sent to the more than 2,000 institutions of higher education that are accredited in the U.S. and U.S. territories and offer full four- or five-year baccalaureate degrees via full-time on-campus programs of study. Officials at the colleges—usually financial aid or admission officers but sometimes registrars or institutional research staff members—completed and returned the forms. Peterson's has every reason to believe that the data presented in this book are accurate. However, students should always confirm costs and other facts with a specific school at the time of application, since colleges can and do change policies and fees whenever necessary.

The state aid data presented in *Peterson's College Money Handbook* was submitted by state officials (usually the director of the state scholarship commission) to Peterson's in spring 2007. Because regulations for any government-sponsored program may be changed at any time, you should request written descriptive materials from the office administering a program in which you are interested.

Criteria for Inclusion in This Book

Peterson's College Money Handbook 2008 covers accredited baccalaureate-degree-granting institutions in the United States and U.S. territories. Institutions have full accreditation or candidate-for-accreditation (preaccreditation) status granted by an institutional or specialized accrediting body recognized by the U.S. Department of Education or Council for Higher Education Accreditation. Recognized institutional accrediting bodies, which consider each institution as a whole, are the six regional associations of schools and colleges (Middle States, New England, North Central, Northwest, Southern, and Western), each of which is responsible for a specified portion of the United States and its territories; the Association for Biblical Higher Education (ABHE); the Accrediting Council for Independent Colleges and Schools (ACICS); the Accrediting Commission of Career Schools and Colleges of Technology (ACCSCT); the Distance Education and Training Council (DETC); the American Academy for Liberal Education; the Council on Occupational Education; and the Transnational Association of Christian Colleges and Schools (TRACS). Program registration by the New York State Board of Regents is considered to be the equivalent of institutional accreditation, since the Board requires that all programs offered by an institution meet its standards before recognition is granted. There are recognized specialized accrediting bodies in more than forty different fields, each of which is authorized to accredit specific programs in its particular field. This can serve as the equivalent of institutional accreditation for specialized institutions that offer programs in one field only (schools of art, music, optometry, theology, etc.).

Quick-Reference Chart

College Costs At-a-Glance

Michael Steidel

To help shed some light on the typical patterns of financial aid offered by colleges, we have prepared the following chart. This chart can help you to better understand financial aid practices in general, form realistic expectations about the amounts of aid that might be provided by specific colleges or universities, and prepare for meaningful discussions with the financial aid officers at colleges you are considering. The data appearing in the chart have been supplied by the schools themselves and are also shown in the individual college profiles.

Tuition and fees are based on the total of full-time tuition and mandatory fees for the 2007–08 academic year or for the 2006–07 academic year if 2007–08 figures are not available. More information about these costs, as well as the costs of room and board and the year for which they are current, can be found in the individual college profiles. For institutions that have two or more tuition rates for different categories of students or types of programs, the lowest rate is used in figuring the cost.

The colleges are listed alphabetically by state. An "NR" in any individual column indicates that the applicable data element was "Not Reported."

The chart is divided into eight columns of information for each college:

1. Institutional Control
Whether the school is independent (ind.), including independent, independent–religious, and proprietary, or public, including federal, state, commonwealth, territory, county, district, city, state, local, and state-related.

2. Tuition and Fees
Based on the total of full-time tuition and mandatory fees. An asterisk indicates that the school includes room and board in their mandatory fees.

3. Room and Board
If a school has room and board costs that vary according to the type of accommodation and meal plan, either the lowest figures are represented or the figures are for the most common room arrangement and a full meal plan. If a school has only housing arrangements, a dagger appears to the right of the number. An "NA" will appear in this column if no college-owned or -operated housing facilities are offered.

4. Percent of Eligible Freshmen Receiving Need-Based Gift Awards
Calculated by dividing the number of freshman students determined to have need who received need-based gift aid by the number of full-time freshmen.

5. Percent of Freshmen Whose Need Was Fully Met
Calculated by dividing the number of freshman students whose financial need was fully met by the number of freshmen with need.

6. Average Financial Aid Package for Freshmen
The average dollar amount from all sources, including *gift aid* (scholarships and grants) and *self-help* (jobs and loans), awarded to aided freshmen. Note that this aid package may exceed tuition and fees if the average aid package included coverage of room and board expenses.

7. Average Net Cost After Aid
Average aid package subtracted from published costs (tuition, fees, room, and board) to produce what the average student will have to pay.

8. Average Indebtedness Upon Graduation
Average per-student indebtedness of graduating seniors.

Because personal situations vary widely, it is very important to note that an individual's aid package can be quite different from the averages. Moreover, the data shown for each school can fluctuate widely from year to year, depending on the number of applicants, the amount of need to be met, and the financial resources and policies of the college. Our intent in presenting this chart is to provide you with useful facts and figures that can serve as general guidelines in your pursuit of financial aid. We caution you to use the data only as a jumping-off point for further investigation and analysis, not as a means to rank or select colleges.

After you have narrowed down the colleges in which you are interested based on academic and personal criteria, we recommend that you carefully study this chart. From it, you can develop a list of questions for financial aid officers at the colleges you are seriously considering attending. Here are just a few questions you might want to ask:

- What are the specific types and sources of aid provided to freshmen at this school?
- What factors does this college consider in determining whether a

financial aid applicant is qualified for its need-based aid programs?

- How does the college determine the combination of types of aid that make up an individual's package?
- How are non-need-based awards treated: as a part of the aid package or as a part of the parental/family contribution?
- Does this school "guarantee" financial aid and, if so, how is its policy implemented? Guaranteed aid means that, by policy, 100 percent of need is met for all students judged to have need. Implementation determines *how* need is met and varies widely from school to school. For example, grade point average may determine the apportioning of scholarship, loan, and work-study aid. Rules for freshmen may be different from those for upperclass students.
- To what degree is the admission process "need-blind"? Need-blind means that admission decisions are made without regard to the student's need for financial aid.
- What are the norms and practices for upperclass students? Our chart presents information on *freshman* financial aid only; however, the financial aid office should be able and willing to provide you with comparable figures for upperclass students. A college might offer a wonderful package for the freshman year, then leave you mostly on your own to fund the remaining three years. Or the school may provide a higher proportion of scholarship money for freshmen, then rebalance its aid packages to contain more self-help aid (loans and work-study) in upperclass years. There is an assumption that, all other factors being equal, students who have settled into the pattern of college time management can handle more work-study hours than freshmen. Grade point average, tuition increases, changes in parental financial circumstances, and other factors may also affect the redistribution.

Michael Steidel is Director of Admission at Carnegie Mellon University.

College Costs At-a-Glance

College Costs At-a-Glance	Institutional Control ind.=independent; pub.=public	Tuition and Fees	Room and Board	Percent of Eligible Freshmen Receiving Need-Based Gift Awards	Percent of Freshmen Whose Need Was Fully Met	Average Financial Aid Package for Freshmen	Average Net Cost After Aid	Average Indebtedness Upon Graduation
Alabama								
Alabama Agricultural and Mechanical University	pub.	$ 3900	$4770	96%	1%	$ 3680	$ 4990	$17,125
Alabama State University	pub.	$ 4008	$3400	83%	15%	$ 7212	$ 196	$26,903
Auburn University	pub.	$ 5496	$7564	71%	14%	$ 7061	$ 5999	$21,256
Auburn University Montgomery	pub.	$ 5020	$3050	72%	97%	$ 4507	$ 3563	$15,000
Birmingham-Southern College	ind.	$24,300	$8062	72%	35%	$23,562	$ 8800	NR
Faulkner University	ind.	$11,565	$5400	71%	12%	$ 5800	$11,165	$18,900
Jacksonville State University	pub.	$ 5070	$3764	40%	60%	$ 6675	$ 2159	$17,125
Judson College	ind.	$10,710	$6564	98%	7%	$11,256	$ 6018	$15,917
Samford University	ind.	$16,000	$6060	94%	27%	$12,642	$ 9418	$18,501
Southeastern Bible College	ind.	$ 9070	$2000†	100%	NR	$ 5125	$ 5945	$20,000
South University	ind.	$15,800	NA	77%	NR	$ 5146	$10,654	$ 9600
Spring Hill College	ind.	$22,000	$8120	100%	72%	$21,532	$ 8588	$12,864
Troy University	pub.	$ 4104	$5491	64%	NR	$ 3002	$ 6593	NR
Tuskegee University	ind.	$14,615	$6783	85%	70%	$13,824	$ 7574	$30,000
The University of Alabama	pub.	$ 5278	$5380	50%	19%	$ 7518	$ 3140	$18,653
The University of Alabama at Birmingham	pub.	$ 4792	$7111	59%	15%	$14,145	—	$17,650
The University of Alabama in Huntsville	pub.	$ 4848	$5110	87%	19%	$ 5941	$ 4017	$20,273
University of North Alabama	pub.	$ 4651	$4372	65%	26%	$ 3565	$ 5458	NR
The University of West Alabama	pub.	$ 4326	$3438	NR	74%	$ 6145	$ 1619	$16,043
Alaska								
University of Alaska Fairbanks	pub.	$ 4308	$6030	72%	29%	$ 7973	$ 2365	$24,656
University of Alaska Southeast	pub.	$ 4396	$5790	60%	19%	$ 6134	$ 4052	$19,979
Arizona								
Arizona State University	pub.	$ 4688	$6900	92%	23%	$ 8503	$ 3085	$15,894
Arizona State University at the Polytechnic Campus	pub.	$ 4448	$5100	94%	17%	$10,513	—	NR
The Art Institute of Phoenix	ind.	$18,576	$6028†	NR	NR	NR	NR	NR
Collins College: A School of Design and Technology	ind.	$24,250	$4600†	72%	3%	$10,000	$18,850	$18,000
Embry-Riddle Aeronautical University	ind.	$26,130	$7214	100%	NR	$13,951	$19,393	$49,037
Northern Arizona University	pub.	$ 4546	$6260	62%	20%	$ 7537	$ 3269	$17,563
The University of Arizona	pub.	$ 4766	$7850	95%	18%	$ 7443	$ 5173	$17,392
University of Phoenix Online Campus	ind.	$14,180	NA	67%	NR	$ 2200	$11,980	NR
University of Phoenix–Phoenix Campus	ind.	$ 9630	NA	55%	NR	$ 2763	$ 6867	NR
University of Phoenix–Southern Arizona Campus	ind.	$ 9990	NA	66%	NR	$ 3335	$ 6655	NR
Arkansas								
Arkansas State University	pub.	$ 5710	$4440	93%	21%	$ 8100	$ 2050	$18,500
Arkansas Tech University	pub.	$ 4880	$4422	81%	29%	$ 3832	$ 5470	$18,155
Harding University	ind.	$11,650	$5442	94%	31%	$ 9911	$ 7181	$28,717
Hendrix College	ind.	$22,916	$6738	100%	44%	$18,394	$11,260	$16,360
John Brown University	ind.	$16,158	$5956	91%	16%	$10,413	$11,701	$19,262
Lyon College	ind.	$15,960	$6644	100%	44%	$13,452	$ 9152	$15,495
Ouachita Baptist University	ind.	$17,950	$5400	98%	43%	$14,767	$ 8583	$13,504
Southern Arkansas University–Magnolia	pub.	$ 4650	$3970	67%	82%	$ 1532	$ 7088	$14,423

NA = not applicable; NR = not reported; * = includes room and board; † = room only; — = not available.

College Costs At-a-Glance

	Institutional Control ind.=independent; pub.=public	Tuition and Fees	Room and Board	Percent of Eligible Freshmen Receiving Need-Based Gift Awards	Percent of Freshmen Whose Need Was Fully Met	Average Financial Aid Package for Freshmen	Average Net Cost After Aid	Average Indebtedness Upon Graduation
Arkansas—*continued*								
University of Arkansas	pub.	$ 5808	$ 6522	61%	21%	$ 7805	$ 4525	$18,170
University of Arkansas at Monticello	pub.	$ 4150	$ 3440	NR	NR	NR	NR	NR
University of Arkansas at Pine Bluff	pub.	$ 4454	$ 5940	74%	44%	$ 7569	$ 2825	NR
University of Phoenix–Little Rock Campus	ind.	$ 9750	NA	76%	NR	$ 2649	$ 7101	NR
University of the Ozarks	ind.	$14,950	$ 5260	100%	19%	$12,963	$ 7247	$18,292
Williams Baptist College	ind.	$10,370	$ 4700	67%	NR	$ 9321	$ 5749	$14,739
California								
Academy of Art University	ind.	$14,680	$12,600	53%	1%	$ 4685	$22,595	$32,000
Alliant International University	ind.	$14,770	NR	80%	20%	$16,250	—	$17,125
Art Center College of Design	ind.	$27,910	NA	70%	NR	$12,836	$15,074	$70,000
Azusa Pacific University	ind.	$23,750	$ 7328	97%	15%	$19,684	$11,394	$18,777
California Baptist University	ind.	$18,900	$ 6810	97%	22%	$ 9860	$15,850	$21,700
California College of the Arts	ind.	$27,914	$ 8615	100%	9%	$18,881	$17,648	$33,188
California Institute of Technology	ind.	$32,835	$ 9540	100%	100%	$25,212	$17,163	$ 5156
California Institute of the Arts	ind.	$31,855	$ 8000	96%	1%	$26,334	$13,521	$30,051
California Polytechnic State University, San Luis Obispo	pub.	$ 4350	$ 8453	73%	8%	$ 6058	$ 6745	$14,032
California State University, Chico	pub.	$ 3412	$ 8314	65%	24%	$ 8099	$ 3627	NR
California State University, Dominguez Hills	pub.	$ 3051	$ 8690	98%	5%	$ 7488	$ 4253	$15,232
California State University, East Bay	pub.	$ 2916	$ 8939	91%	19%	$ 8400	$ 3455	$12,627
California State University, Fresno	pub.	$ 3039	$ 6880	84%	24%	$ 6817	$ 3102	$14,648
California State University, Fullerton	pub.	$ 3030	$ 4408†	87%	8%	$ 6358	$ 1080	$14,508
California State University, Los Angeles	pub.	$ 3080	$ 7866	100%	15%	$ 7927	$ 3019	NR
California State University, Northridge	pub.	$ 3042	$ 9328	90%	NR	$ 7645	$ 4725	$14,027
California State University, Sacramento	pub.	$ 3284	$ 7966	81%	1%	$ 8096	$ 3154	$10,868
California State University, San Bernardino	pub.	$ 3398	$ 5886	89%	8%	$ 6927	$ 2357	$17,946
California State University, Stanislaus	pub.	$ 3043	$ 7178	87%	4%	$ 8537	$ 1684	$ 8500
Chapman University	ind.	$30,748	$10,500	100%	100%	$22,931	$18,317	$22,277
Claremont McKenna College	ind.	$34,850	$10,740	99%	100%	$29,432	$16,158	$10,518
Cogswell Polytechnical College	ind.	$14,984	$ 3000†	100%	NR	NR	NR	$46,689
Concordia University	ind.	$21,130	$ 7060	97%	17%	$22,802	$ 5388	$19,733
Dominican University of California	ind.	$30,780	$12,000	99%	10%	$20,825	$21,955	$49,337
Fresno Pacific University	ind.	$20,790	$ 5990	98%	15%	$17,037	$ 9743	$15,588
Harvey Mudd College	ind.	$34,670	$11,412	94%	100%	$30,439	$15,643	$18,288
Holy Names University	ind.	$22,710	$ 8000	100%	15%	$18,950	$11,760	$10,500
La Sierra University	ind.	$21,846	$ 6330	100%	12%	$14,520	$13,656	$28,876
The Master's College and Seminary	ind.	$20,770	$ 6900	98%	16%	$14,368	$13,302	$15,383
Menlo College	ind.	$26,220	$ 9800	99%	5%	$21,120	$14,900	$26,243
Mills College	ind.	$33,024	$10,240	NR	NR	$26,407	$16,857	$19,206
Mount St. Mary's College	ind.	$24,150	$ 8747	NR	NR	NR	NR	NR
National University	ind.	$ 9132	NA	44%	NR	$ 7033	$ 2099	$32,312
Occidental College	ind.	$35,333	$ 9500	98%	100%	$26,747	$18,086	$20,640
Otis College of Art and Design	ind.	$28,346	NR	100%	1%	$18,367	$ 9979	$44,706

NA = not applicable; NR = not reported; * = includes room and board; † = room only; — = not available.

College Costs At-a-Glance

	Institutional Control ind.=independent; pub.=public	Tuition and Fees	Room and Board	Percent of Eligible Freshmen Receiving Need-Based Gift Awards	Percent of Freshmen Whose Need Was Fully Met	Average Financial Aid Package for Freshmen	Average Net Cost After Aid	Average Indebtedness Upon Graduation
California—*continued*								
Pacific Oaks College	ind.	$19,140	NA	NR	NR	NR	NR	NR
Pacific Union College	ind.	$20,265	$ 5652	100%	27%	$11,652	$14,265	$17,000
Pepperdine University	ind.	$32,740	$ 9500	95%	52%	$30,500	$11,740	$31,848
Pitzer College	ind.	$34,038	$ 9670	98%	100%	$30,194	$13,514	$20,701
Point Loma Nazarene University	ind.	$23,730	$ 7470	97%	23%	$14,630	$16,570	NR
Pomona College	ind.	$31,865	$11,291	100%	100%	$32,250	$10,906	$11,250
Saint Mary's College of California	ind.	$29,050	$10,566	88%	6%	$20,431	$19,185	$23,402
San Diego Christian College	ind.	$18,886	$ 7540	71%	70%	$12,705	$13,721	$16,000
San Diego State University	pub.	$ 3160	$10,093	67%	17%	$ 5800	$ 7453	$14,700
San Francisco Art Institute	ind.	$27,235	$ 7200†	100%	9%	$24,054	$10,381	NR
San Francisco State University	pub.	$ 3166	$ 9544	71%	8%	$ 7532	$ 5178	$15,288
San Jose State University	pub.	$13,466	$ 9096	78%	2%	$ 9797	$12,765	$18,521
Santa Clara University	ind.	$30,900	$10,380	82%	74%	$18,545	$22,735	$17,527
Scripps College	ind.	$33,700	$10,100	100%	100%	$29,145	$14,655	$12,071
Shasta Bible College	ind.	$ 7580	$ 1650†	100%	27%	$ 5544	$ 3686	NR
Simpson University	ind.	$18,600	$ 6400	100%	23%	$ 9912	$15,088	$17,940
Sonoma State University	pub.	$ 3648	NR	66%	26%	$ 9960	—	$ 8210
Southern California Institute of Architecture	ind.	$10,696	NA	21%	NR	$ 8867	$ 1829	$33,000
Stanford University	ind.	$32,994	$10,367	99%	77%	$30,088	$13,273	$15,758
Thomas Aquinas College	ind.	$20,400	$ 6600	86%	100%	$14,700	$12,300	$14,000
University of California, Berkeley	pub.	$ 6654	$13,074	97%	66%	$17,250	$ 2478	$14,751
University of California, Davis	pub.	$ 7593	$11,354	95%	16%	$12,281	$ 6666	$12,701
University of California, Irvine	pub.	$ 6141	$ 9815	89%	47%	$13,006	$ 2950	$13,587
University of California, Los Angeles	pub.	$ 7143	$11,141	95%	32%	$15,446	$ 2838	$15,996
University of California, Riverside	pub.	$ 6591	$10,200	89%	56%	$15,335	$ 1456	$14,965
University of California, San Diego	pub.	$ 6685	$ 9657	91%	21%	$13,701	$ 2641	$15,170
University of California, Santa Barbara	pub.	$ 7277	$11,178	88%	46%	$14,055	$ 4400	NR
University of California, Santa Cruz	pub.	$ 7962	$11,805	86%	49%	$14,955	$ 4812	$14,381
University of Judaism	ind.	$20,300	$10,778	50%	100%	$19,860	$11,218	$17,000
University of La Verne	ind.	$25,590	$ 9750	102%	7%	$18,223	$17,117	$28,856
University of Phoenix–Bay Area Campus	ind.	$13,390	NA	43%	NR	$ 2109	$11,281	NR
University of Phoenix–Sacramento Valley Campus	ind.	$12,900	NA	57%	NR	$ 2138	$10,762	NR
University of Phoenix–San Diego Campus	ind.	$12,450	NA	55%	NR	$ 2830	$ 9620	NR
University of Phoenix–Southern California Campus	ind.	$13,710	NA	62%	NR	$ 2486	$11,224	NR
University of Redlands	ind.	$28,776	$ 9360	99%	49%	$27,366	$10,770	$15,125
University of San Diego	ind.	$32,564	$10,960	82%	9%	$19,667	$23,857	$28,842
University of San Francisco	ind.	$31,180	$10,730	84%	12%	$23,143	$18,767	$28,000
University of Southern California	ind.	$33,892	$10,144	86%	96%	$29,256	$14,780	$27,420
University of the Pacific	ind.	$27,350	$ 8700	98%	30%	$23,192	$12,858	NR
Vanguard University of Southern California	ind.	$21,564	$ 3568†	81%	11%	$20,573	$ 4559	$16,979
Westmont College	ind.	$29,470	$ 9232	98%	11%	$20,388	$18,314	$16,801
Whittier College	ind.	$28,206	$ 8542	90%	31%	$22,027	$14,721	$27,335
Woodbury University	ind.	$23,572	$ 8104	100%	5%	$17,485	$14,191	$27,115

NA = not applicable; NR = not reported; * = includes room and board; † = room only; — = not available.

College Costs At-a-Glance	Institutional Control ind.=independent; pub.=public	Tuition and Fees	Room and Board	Percent of Eligible Freshmen Receiving Need-Based Gift Awards	Percent of Freshmen Whose Need Was Fully Met	Average Financial Aid Package for Freshmen	Average Net Cost After Aid	Average Indebtedness Upon Graduation
Colorado								
Adams State College	pub.	$ 2925	$ 6160	80%	6%	$ 6213	$ 2872	$17,605
The Colorado College	ind.	$32,124	$ 8052	93%	56%	$28,705	$11,471	NR
Colorado School of Mines	pub.	$ 9010	$ 6880	88%	81%	$14,800	$ 1090	$18,700
Colorado State University	pub.	$ 4717	$ 6602	74%	38%	$ 7381	$ 3938	$16,887
Colorado State University-Pueblo	pub.	$ 4190	$ 5810	86%	11%	$ 7264	$ 2736	$ 30
Fort Lewis College	pub.	$ 5973	$ 6468	57%	18%	$ 6164	$ 6277	NR
Johnson & Wales University	ind.	$21,462	$ 8550	76%	3%	$14,382	$15,630	$14,798
Mesa State College	pub.	$ 3840	$ 7214	66%	15%	$ 6576	$ 4478	$18,353
Metropolitan State College of Denver	pub.	$ 3431	NA	78%	1%	$ 4922	—	$23,678
Naropa University	ind.	$19,426	$ 6894	76%	NR	$18,795	$ 7525	NR
Nazarene Bible College	ind.	$ 8400	NA	100%	NR	NR	NR	$19,908
Regis University	ind.	$26,900	$ 8830	100%	47%	$17,806	$17,924	NR
University of Colorado at Boulder	pub.	$ 5643	$ 8300	56%	80%	$ 8458	$ 5485	$17,141
University of Colorado at Colorado Springs	pub.	$ 6537	$ 7662	78%	12%	$ 5756	$ 8443	$12,438
University of Denver	ind.	$30,372	$ 9228	98%	15%	$21,878	$17,722	$27,008
University of Northern Colorado	pub.	$ 3950	$ 6832	47%	44%	$ 8383	$ 2399	NR
University of Phoenix–Denver Campus	ind.	$ 9750	NA	41%	NR	$ 2757	$ 6993	NR
University of Phoenix–Southern Colorado Campus	ind.	$ 9750	NA	54%	NR	$ 3121	$ 6629	NR
Western State College of Colorado	pub.	$ 3349	$ 6976	50%	15%	$ 6625	$ 3700	$16,000
Connecticut								
Central Connecticut State University	pub.	$ 6734	$ 8348	74%	12%	$ 5943	$ 9139	$10,500
Connecticut College	ind.	*$44,240	NR	92%	100%	$27,578	$16,662	$22,160
Fairfield University	ind.	$31,955	$ 9980	88%	29%	$22,654	$19,281	$28,751
Quinnipiac University	ind.	$28,720	$11,200	99%	14%	$15,201	$24,719	$31,070
Sacred Heart University	ind.	$25,400	$10,320	99%	32%	$16,090	$19,630	$21,166
Southern Connecticut State University	pub.	$ 6591	$ 8432	66%	37%	$ 6930	$ 8093	$15,197
Trinity College	ind.	$35,130	$ 8970	96%	100%	$27,916	$16,184	$18,122
University of Bridgeport	ind.	$21,710	$ 9600	91%	8%	$20,453	$10,857	NR
University of Connecticut	pub.	$ 8842	$ 8850	80%	19%	$10,740	$ 6952	$20,030
University of Hartford	ind.	$26,996	$10,418	72%	27%	$16,153	$21,261	$25,553
University of New Haven	ind.	$24,645	$10,130	98%	13%	$16,402	$18,373	$35,118
Wesleyan University	ind.	$35,144	$ 9540	94%	100%	$29,476	$15,208	$23,375
Western Connecticut State University	pub.	$ 6731	$ 7784	91%	33%	$ 6917	$ 7598	$ 6005
Yale University	ind.	$33,030	$10,020	98%	100%	$32,260	$10,790	$13,344
Delaware								
University of Delaware	pub.	$ 7740	$ 7366	74%	56%	$ 9706	$ 5400	$17,200
Wesley College	ind.	$17,579	$ 7800	94%	NR	$15,250	$10,129	$19,500
District of Columbia								
American University	ind.	$29,673	$11,570	76%	49%	$24,350	$16,893	$19,766
The Catholic University of America	ind.	$28,990	$10,808	99%	55%	$19,157	$20,641	NR
Corcoran College of Art and Design	ind.	$24,489	$10,795	81%	NR	$ 5794	$29,490	$31,541
Georgetown University	ind.	$35,568	$12,146	98%	100%	$27,330	$20,384	$24,816

NA = not applicable; NR = not reported; * = includes room and board; † = room only; — = not available.

College Costs At-a-Glance

	Institutional Control ind.=independent; pub.=public	Tuition and Fees	Room and Board	Percent of Eligible Freshmen Receiving Need-Based Gift Awards	Percent of Freshmen Whose Need Was Fully Met	Average Financial Aid Package for Freshmen	Average Net Cost After Aid	Average Indebtedness Upon Graduation
District of Columbia—*continued*								
The George Washington University	ind.	$39,240	$11,520	97%	65%	$34,139	$16,621	$29,304
Florida								
The Baptist College of Florida	ind.	$ 7550	$ 3736	96%	4%	$ 5287	$ 5999	$ 670
Bethune-Cookman College	ind.	$11,792	$ 7206	79%	29%	$14,605	$ 4393	$32,500
Clearwater Christian College	ind.	$12,500	$ 5330	57%	4%	$ 8052	$ 9778	$16,800
Eckerd College	ind.	$27,618	$ 7868	100%	27%	$19,716	$15,770	$ 9448
Embry-Riddle Aeronautical University	ind.	$26,496	$ 9150	100%	NR	$13,913	$21,733	$52,495
Embry-Riddle Aeronautical University Worldwide	ind.	$ 4584	NR	78%	NR	$ 5294	—	$24,494
Flagler College	ind.	$11,200	$ 6800	40%	8%	$11,858	$ 6142	$15,535
Florida Atlantic University	pub.	$ 3327	$ 8280	91%	20%	$ 7750	$ 3857	NR
Florida College	ind.	$11,380	$ 5460	39%	15%	$ 3961	$12,879	$ 7574
Florida Gulf Coast University	pub.	$ 3730	$ 7740	62%	11%	$ 6099	$ 5371	$11,332
Florida Institute of Technology	ind.	$27,540	$ 7400	100%	32%	$22,383	$12,557	$25,768
Florida Metropolitan University–Pinellas Campus	ind.	$15,120	NA	100%	NR	$ 6625	$ 8495	$45,000
Florida Southern College	ind.	$21,190	$ 7500	95%	42%	$18,403	$10,287	$16,072
Florida State University	pub.	$ 3307	$ 7078	56%	72%	$ 8483	$ 1902	$13,290
International College	ind.	$13,130	NA	76%	6%	$ 6925	$ 6205	$18,400
Jacksonville University	ind.	$21,200	$ 6780	66%	20%	$17,510	$10,470	$21,483
Johnson & Wales University	ind.	$21,460	$ 9600	93%	1%	$16,741	$14,319	$18,633
New College of Florida	pub.	$ 3850	$ 7080	100%	72%	$11,662	—	$15,334
Northwood University, Florida Campus	ind.	$16,455	$ 7767	80%	23%	$13,772	$10,450	$21,654
Nova Southeastern University	ind.	$18,650	$ 6012	88%	6%	$15,322	$ 9340	$31,368
Palm Beach Atlantic University	ind.	$18,740	$ 6780	55%	48%	$ 2540	$22,980	$24,393
Ringling College of Art and Design	ind.	$23,125	$ 9999	85%	3%	$ 8366	$24,758	$71,865
Rollins College	ind.	$30,860	$ 9626	97%	32%	$30,213	$10,273	$21,540
Saint Leo University	ind.	$16,420	$ 8102	100%	34%	$14,430	$10,092	$15,300
St. Thomas University	ind.	$18,750	$ 5910	80%	40%	NR	NR	$12,000
Southeastern University	ind.	$13,480	$ 6430	98%	12%	$ 6953	$12,957	$21,569
Stetson University	ind.	$28,780	$ 7968	99%	39%	$23,644	$13,104	$22,000
University of Central Florida	pub.	$ 3492	$ 8000	40%	21%	$ 5374	$ 6118	$12,876
University of Florida	pub.	$ 3206	$ 6590	61%	30%	$10,511	—	$15,045
University of Miami	ind.	$33,070	$ 9606	97%	36%	$24,674	$18,002	$24,673
University of North Florida	pub.	$ 3353	$ 6268	71%	39%	$ 1271	$ 8350	$16,707
University of Phoenix–Central Florida Campus	ind.	$10,058	NA	57%	NR	$ 2776	$ 7282	NR
University of Phoenix–Fort Lauderdale Campus	ind.	$10,058	NA	64%	NR	$ 2761	$ 7297	NR
University of Phoenix–West Florida Campus	ind.	$10,058	NA	67%	NR	$ 2736	$ 7322	NR
University of South Florida	pub.	$ 3490	$ 7180	51%	16%	$ 8603	$ 2067	$17,995
The University of Tampa	ind.	$19,628	$ 7254	95%	26%	$15,050	$11,832	$23,099
University of West Florida	pub.	$ 3311	$ 6600	NR	NR	NR	NR	NR
Webber International University	ind.	$15,900	$ 4990	100%	35%	$16,104	$ 4786	$23,642
Georgia								
Agnes Scott College	ind.	$27,387	$ 9350	99%	79%	$25,543	$11,194	$20,772

NA = not applicable; NR = not reported; * = includes room and board; † = room only; — = not available.

College Costs At-a-Glance

	Institutional Control ind.=independent; pub.=public	Tuition and Fees	Room and Board	Percent of Eligible Freshmen Receiving Need-Based Gift Awards	Percent of Freshmen Whose Need Was Fully Met	Average Financial Aid Package for Freshmen	Average Net Cost After Aid	Average Indebtedness Upon Graduation
Georgia—*continued*								
Armstrong Atlantic State University	pub.	$ 3074	$ 6000†	48%	85%	$ 5818	$ 3256	$11,000
Augusta State University	pub.	$ 3066	$ 4920†	69%	NR	$11,232	—	$ 3191
Berry College	ind.	$18,950	$ 7164	100%	27%	$14,621	$11,493	$13,882
Brenau University	ind.	$17,700	$ 8950	100%	39%	$16,585	$10,065	$16,426
Clark Atlanta University	ind.	$16,100	$ 7014	68%	47%	$14,103	$ 9011	$17,751
Columbus State University	pub.	$ 3188	$ 6284	81%	86%	$ 3524	$ 5948	NR
Dalton State College	pub.	$ 1742	NA	55%	9%	$ 1526	$ 216	$ 4049
Emory University	ind.	$34,336	$11,020	96%	100%	$27,760	$17,596	$24,272
Georgia College & State University	pub.	$ 4424	$ 7116	34%	3%	$ 5253	$ 6287	$15,128
Georgia Institute of Technology	pub.	$ 4926	$ 7094	57%	53%	$ 9901	$ 2119	$14,895
Georgia Southern University	pub.	$ 4082	$ 6860	95%	23%	$ 6377	$ 4565	$18,146
Georgia Southwestern State University	pub.	$ 3162	$ 4956	64%	15%	$ 6169	$ 1949	$15,346
Kennesaw State University	pub.	$ 3266	$ 4620†	41%	15%	$ 7975	—	$15,346
LaGrange College	ind.	$18,575	$ 7598	100%	33%	$13,841	$12,332	$19,596
Life University	ind.	$ 5823	$12,000	62%	10%	$ 5800	$12,023	$30,000
Macon State College	pub.	$ 1792	NA	80%	10%	$ 5334	—	NR
Medical College of Georgia	pub.	$ 4288	$ 2556†	NR	NR	NR	NR	$10,365
Mercer University	ind.	$25,256	$ 7710	100%	61%	$26,194	$ 6772	$22,529
North Georgia College & State University	pub.	$ 3452	$ 4780	NR	NR	NR	NR	$ 9852
Oglethorpe University	ind.	$23,510	$ 8000	100%	15%	$21,503	$10,007	$17,024
Piedmont College	ind.	$16,500	$ 6000	69%	40%	$15,249	$ 7251	$15,537
Reinhardt College	ind.	$14,970	$ 6018	76%	72%	$ 2421	$18,567	NR
Savannah College of Art and Design	ind.	$24,890	$10,015	24%	42%	$ 9500	$25,405	$28,000
Shorter College	ind.	$14,300	$ 6600	100%	22%	$11,495	$ 9405	$16,193
Southern Polytechnic State University	pub.	$ 3348	$ 5610	50%	35%	$ 2207	$ 6751	$28,364
Spelman College	ind.	$17,005	$ 8750	75%	1%	$10,500	$15,255	$23,500
Toccoa Falls College	ind.	$13,825	$ 5050	100%	13%	$ 9336	$ 9539	$17,273
University of Georgia	pub.	$ 4964	$ 6848	96%	38%	$ 7854	$ 3958	$13,478
University of Phoenix–Atlanta Campus	ind.	$11,558	NA	63%	NR	$ 2712	$ 8846	NR
University of Phoenix–Columbus Georgia Campus	ind.	$10,500	NA	78%	NR	$ 2720	$ 7780	NR
University of West Georgia	pub.	$ 3460	$ 5162	89%	18%	$ 6612	$ 2010	$14,781
Valdosta State University	pub.	$ 3490	$ 5680	93%	19%	$ 7332	$ 1838	$16,220
Wesleyan College	ind.	$15,200	$ 7600	100%	27%	$11,641	$11,159	$20,988
Hawaii								
Brigham Young University–Hawaii	ind.	$ 3040	$ 5170	91%	55%	$ 4200	$ 4010	$12,418
Hawai'i Pacific University	ind.	$13,080	$10,560	44%	18%	$11,390	$12,250	$17,125
University of Hawaii at Hilo	pub.	$ 3148	$ 6292	66%	9%	$ 5283	$ 4157	$11,206
University of Hawaii at Manoa	pub.	$ 5390	$ 7185	85%	32%	$ 7177	$ 5398	$11,748
University of Phoenix–Hawaii Campus	ind.	$11,700	NA	74%	NR	$ 2796	$ 8904	NR
Idaho								
Albertson College of Idaho	ind.	$17,680	$ 6325	56%	29%	$15,783	$ 8222	$26,461
Boise State University	pub.	$ 4154	$ 5778	90%	15%	$ 7554	$ 2378	$20,004

NA = not applicable; NR = not reported; * = includes room and board; † = room only; — = not available.

College Costs At-a-Glance

	Institutional Control ind.=independent; pub.=public	Tuition and Fees	Room and Board	Percent of Eligible Freshmen Receiving Need-Based Gift Awards	Percent of Freshmen Whose Need Was Fully Met	Average Financial Aid Package for Freshmen	Average Net Cost After Aid	Average Indebtedness Upon Graduation
Idaho—*continued*								
Idaho State University	pub.	$ 4190	$ 4950	60%	11%	$ 4067	$ 5073	$20,253
Lewis-Clark State College	pub.	$ 3897	$ 4670	66%	8%	$ 3659	$ 4908	NR
Northwest Nazarene University	ind.	$19,970	$ 5300	85%	17%	$12,801	$12,469	$25,301
University of Idaho	pub.	$ 4200	$ 5696	57%	29%	$ 8572	$ 1324	$20,002
University of Phoenix–Idaho Campus	ind.	$10,200	NA	57%	NR	$ 2118	$ 8082	NR
Illinois								
Augustana College	ind.	$24,924	$ 6807	35%	29%	$17,950	$13,781	$17,100
Aurora University	ind.	$16,850	$ 7034	71%	28%	$18,138	$ 5746	$18,517
Benedictine University	ind.	$20,310	$ 6700	58%	38%	$13,630	$13,380	NR
Blessing-Rieman College of Nursing	ind.	$17,300	$ 6550	NR	NR	NR	NR	$11,000
Bradley University	ind.	$20,060	$ 6750	99%	51%	$13,984	$12,826	$15,079
Columbia College Chicago	ind.	$16,788	$ 9765	NR	NR	NR	NR	NR
Concordia University	ind.	$21,320	$ 6992	90%	38%	$13,800	$14,512	$15,426
DePaul University	ind.	$22,575	$10,392	76%	14%	$16,928	$16,039	$21,061
Dominican University	ind.	$21,250	$ 6620	100%	14%	$16,458	$11,412	$16,137
Eastern Illinois University	pub.	$ 7069	$ 6660	45%	76%	$11,249	$ 2480	$16,890
Elmhurst College	ind.	$24,660	$ 7164	92%	27%	$17,669	$14,155	$17,244
Eureka College	ind.	$14,180	$ 6220	100%	34%	$12,570	$ 7830	$14,727
Greenville College	ind.	$17,932	$ 6136	100%	15%	$15,099	$ 8969	$19,820
Illinois College	ind.	$17,100	$ 6730	73%	61%	$13,253	$10,577	$17,733
Illinois Institute of Technology	ind.	$24,113	$ 8049	99%	21%	$22,239	$ 9923	$20,155
Illinois State University	pub.	$ 8040	$ 6148	62%	44%	$ 8714	$ 5474	$17,015
Illinois Wesleyan University	ind.	$30,750	$ 7030	100%	53%	$20,928	$16,852	$21,794
Judson College	ind.	$20,420	$ 7200	93%	2%	$12,149	$15,471	$21,960
Knox College	ind.	$27,900	$ 5925	100%	32%	$22,948	$10,877	$22,860
Lake Forest College	ind.	$29,164	$ 6960	100%	100%	$21,963	$14,161	$19,976
Lexington College	ind.	$17,810	NA	100%	4%	$13,850	$ 3960	$25,000
Lincoln Christian College	ind.	$11,100	$ 4580	NR	NR	$ 7500	$ 8180	$16,379
Loyola University Chicago	ind.	$27,966	$ 9930	97%	8%	$21,722	$16,174	$25,470
MacMurray College	ind.	$16,730	$ 6166	100%	23%	$12,291	$10,605	$22,487
McKendree College	ind.	$18,900	$ 7380	100%	44%	$17,910	$ 8370	$18,956
North Central College	ind.	$23,115	$ 7440	100%	29%	$18,433	$12,122	$21,078
Northeastern Illinois University	pub.	$ 6261	NA	95%	3%	$ 6599	—	$12,569
Northern Illinois University	pub.	$ 7125	$ 6848	59%	22%	$ 8830	$ 5143	$19,764
Northwestern University	ind.	$33,559	$10,266	100%	100%	$26,676	$17,149	$18,860
Olivet Nazarene University	ind.	$17,590	$ 6400	99%	31%	$12,610	$11,380	$20,062
Principia College	ind.	$21,450	$ 7896	88%	66%	$19,672	$ 9674	$12,740
Robert Morris College	ind.	$16,800	NR	98%	4%	$10,187	$ 6613	$18,479
Saint Anthony College of Nursing	ind.	$17,336	NA	NR	NR	NR	NR	$21,000
Saint Francis Medical Center College of Nursing	ind.	$13,720	$ 1880†	NR	NR	NR	NR	NR
Saint Xavier University	ind.	$19,860	$ 7414	100%	21%	$18,973	$ 8301	$18,730
Shimer College	ind.	$21,000	$ 8049	88%	12%	$10,736	$18,313	NR

NA = not applicable; NR = not reported; * = includes room and board; † = room only; — = not available.

College Costs At-a-Glance

	Institutional Control ind.=independent; pub.=public	Tuition and Fees	Room and Board	Percent of Eligible Freshmen Receiving Need-Based Gift Awards	Percent of Freshmen Whose Need Was Fully Met	Average Financial Aid Package for Freshmen	Average Net Cost After Aid	Average Indebtedness Upon Graduation
Illinois—*continued*								
Southern Illinois University Carbondale	pub.	$ 8071	$6666	76%	87%	$10,608	$ 4129	$15,748
Southern Illinois University Edwardsville	pub.	$ 7118	$6500	73%	35%	$ 8945	$ 4673	$17,491
Trinity College of Nursing and Health Sciences	ind.	$ 8562	NA	33%	NR	NR	NR	$ 5000
Trinity International University	ind.	$20,106	$6550	95%	19%	$19,509	$ 7147	$17,794
University of Illinois at Chicago	pub.	$ 9742	$7446	74%	67%	$10,892	$ 6296	$15,897
University of Illinois at Springfield	pub.	$ 7244	$7495	49%	52%	$ 7923	$ 6816	$12,696
University of Illinois at Urbana–Champaign	pub.	$11,130	$8196	62%	51%	$ 9733	$ 9593	$15,413
University of Phoenix–Chicago Campus	ind.	$11,190	NA	69%	NR	$ 2404	$ 8786	NR
University of St. Francis	ind.	$19,540	$7280	78%	85%	$17,703	$ 9117	$18,547
VanderCook College of Music	ind.	$17,890	$8050	NR	NR	NR	NR	NR
Western Illinois University	pub.	$ 7411	$6446	71%	39%	$ 6972	$ 6885	$16,400
Wheaton College	ind.	$22,450	$7040	85%	38%	$19,359	$10,131	$19,343
Indiana								
Anderson University	ind.	$19,990	$6460	100%	45%	$13,818	$12,632	$25,777
Ball State University	pub.	$ 6810	$6898	71%	30%	$ 7426	$ 6282	$17,418
Bethel College	ind.	$17,450	$5380	79%	5%	$14,632	$ 8198	$16,337
Butler University	ind.	$25,414	$8530	94%	24%	$20,264	$13,680	NR
Calumet College of Saint Joseph	ind.	$10,650	NA	82%	NR	NR	NR	$22,800
DePauw University	ind.	$27,780	$7800	76%	70%	$25,384	$10,196	$15,635
Franklin College	ind.	$20,325	$5970	100%	19%	$16,994	$ 9301	$32,778
Goshen College	ind.	$21,300	$7000	100%	34%	$16,599	$11,701	$18,680
Grace College	ind.	$17,350	$6360	100%	37%	$15,011	$ 8699	$18,017
Hanover College	ind.	$22,700	$6800	99%	49%	$16,949	$12,551	$18,181
Huntington University	ind.	$19,430	$6730	98%	17%	$14,555	$11,605	$23,005
Indiana State University	pub.	$ 6436	$6294	59%	16%	$ 6329	$ 6401	$22,724
Indiana University Bloomington	pub.	$ 7460	$6352	82%	26%	$ 7369	$ 6443	$19,756
Indiana University East	pub.	$ 5040	NA	92%	10%	$ 5559	—	$25,402
Indiana University Kokomo	pub.	$ 5072	NA	83%	13%	$ 4465	$ 607	$19,667
Indiana University Northwest	pub.	$ 5142	NA	75%	9%	$ 6046	—	$20,622
Indiana University–Purdue University Indianapolis	pub.	$ 6524	$4834	82%	8%	$ 6378	$ 4980	$22,542
Indiana University South Bend	pub.	$ 5232	NA	81%	9%	$ 4808	$ 424	$19,139
Indiana University Southeast	pub.	$ 5118	NA	79%	13%	$ 4487	$ 631	$16,676
Manchester College	ind.	$21,700	$7450	100%	35%	$20,858	$ 8292	$19,929
Marian College	ind.	$20,800	$7100	61%	51%	$17,749	$10,151	$14,815
Martin University	ind.	$12,170	NA	88%	38%	$ 7346	$ 4824	$27,193
Purdue University	pub.	$ 7096	$7546	36%	33%	$12,578	$ 2064	$20,102
Purdue University Calumet	pub.	$ 5467	$4150†	69%	NR	$ 4968	$ 4649	$15,833
Rose-Hulman Institute of Technology	ind.	$28,995	$7869	100%	7%	$25,411	$11,453	$29,491
Saint Joseph's College	ind.	$20,960	$6720	99%	36%	$17,773	$ 9907	$22,603
Saint Mary-of-the-Woods College	ind.	$20,180	$7380	NR	NR	NR	NR	$20,180
Saint Mary's College	ind.	$26,872	$8678	79%	47%	$19,709	$15,841	$35,143
Taylor University	ind.	$22,028	$5867	94%	23%	$15,135	$12,760	$17,712

NA = not applicable; NR = not reported; * = includes room and board; † = room only; — = not available.

College Costs At-a-Glance

	Institutional Control ind.=independent; pub.=public	Tuition and Fees	Room and Board	Percent of Eligible Freshmen Receiving Need-Based Gift Awards	Percent of Freshmen Whose Need Was Fully Met	Average Financial Aid Package for Freshmen	Average Net Cost After Aid	Average Indebtedness Upon Graduation
Indiana—*continued*								
Taylor University Fort Wayne	ind.	$19,056	$5180	99%	19%	$16,174	$ 8062	$20,780
Tri-State University	ind.	$21,210	$6240	100%	98%	$17,990	$ 9460	$15,780
University of Evansville	ind.	$22,980	$7120	98%	32%	$22,031	$ 8069	$20,368
University of Notre Dame	ind.	$35,187	$9290	96%	99%	$28,331	$16,146	$26,285
University of Phoenix–Indianapolis Campus	ind.	$10,320	NA	82%	NR	$ 2925	$ 7395	NR
University of Saint Francis	ind.	$18,478	$5834	100%	29%	$13,139	$11,173	$21,352
University of Southern Indiana	pub.	$ 4520	$6492	71%	13%	$ 7728	$ 3284	$15,623
Valparaiso University	ind.	$24,000	$6640	99%	29%	$19,817	$10,823	$25,524
Wabash College	ind.	$24,792	$7064	98%	100%	$22,581	$ 9275	$18,137
Iowa								
Allen College	ind.	$13,472	$5712	80%	12%	$15,034	$ 4150	$20,811
Ashford University	ind.	$15,340	$5800	NR	NR	NR	NR	$20,468
Buena Vista University	ind.	$22,556	$6296	99%	24%	$23,280	$ 5572	$29,578
Central College	ind.	$21,222	$7224	100%	20%	$18,228	$10,218	$23,490
Clarke College	ind.	$20,297	$6574	100%	25%	$18,578	$ 8293	$22,268
Coe College	ind.	$26,390	$6600	100%	34%	$22,197	$10,793	$26,625
Cornell College	ind.	$24,800	$6660	100%	77%	$22,080	$ 9380	$24,622
Dordt College	ind.	$18,660	$5160	100%	18%	$16,682	$ 7138	$19,157
Drake University	ind.	$22,682	$6500	99%	31%	$18,860	$10,322	$26,482
Graceland University	ind.	$17,900	$6000	99%	37%	$18,449	$ 5451	$26,892
Grand View College	ind.	$16,940	$5596	99%	14%	$11,811	$10,725	NR
Grinnell College	ind.	$29,030	$7700	97%	100%	$26,136	$10,594	$17,975
Iowa Wesleyan College	ind.	$18,870	$5880	100%	54%	$16,253	$ 8497	$20,794
Loras College	ind.	$22,053	$6305	84%	33%	$16,791	$11,567	$28,800
Luther College	ind.	$26,380	$4290	99%	41%	$22,101	$ 8569	$18,271
Maharishi University of Management	ind.	$24,430	$6000	100%	25%	$23,963	$ 6467	$26,800
Morningside College	ind.	$19,902	$6227	80%	64%	$16,962	$ 9167	$26,816
Mount Mercy College	ind.	$18,930	$5970	100%	47%	$16,355	$ 8545	$27,083
Northwestern College	ind.	$18,296	$5210	100%	35%	$14,480	$ 9026	$23,143
Palmer College of Chiropractic	ind.	$ 6416	NA	57%	81%	$ 6498	—	$10,895
Simpson College	ind.	$23,596	$6655	100%	22%	$20,105	$10,146	$24,644
The University of Iowa	pub.	$ 6293	NR	64%	99%	$ 7226	—	$20,234
University of Northern Iowa	pub.	$ 6112	$5740	69%	19%	$ 6283	$ 5569	$21,561
Wartburg College	ind.	$22,410	$6715	100%	36%	$17,853	$11,272	$22,122
William Penn University	ind.	$16,880	$5042	100%	31%	$17,782	$ 4140	$22,169
Kansas								
Baker University	ind.	$17,580	$5850	99%	28%	$15,911	$ 7519	$25,844
Benedictine College	ind.	$16,710	$6208	99%	46%	$12,379	$10,539	$22,333
Bethany College	ind.	$17,110	$5500	86%	34%	$17,434	$ 5176	$16,958
Bethel College	ind.	$16,700	$6100	77%	34%	$17,228	$ 5572	$18,722
Emporia State University	pub.	$ 3586	$5170	68%	26%	$ 4880	$ 3876	$16,005
MidAmerica Nazarene University	ind.	$15,968	$5830	99%	2%	$10,620	$11,178	$19,222

NA = not applicable; NR = not reported; * = includes room and board; † = room only; — = not available.

College Costs At-a-Glance	Institutional Control ind.=independent; pub.=public	Tuition and Fees	Room and Board	Percent of Eligible Freshmen Receiving Need-Based Gift Awards	Percent of Freshmen Whose Need Was Fully Met	Average Financial Aid Package for Freshmen	Average Net Cost After Aid	Average Indebtedness Upon Graduation
Kansas—*continued*								
Newman University	ind.	$17,308	$5372	70%	20%	$10,739	$11,941	$20,504
Pittsburg State University	pub.	$ 3790	$4844	85%	14%	$ 6431	$ 2203	$11,502
Tabor College	ind.	$16,734	$5900	86%	25%	$16,198	$ 6436	$20,181
University of Kansas	pub.	$ 6153	$5747	69%	91%	$ 6281	$ 5619	$18,869
University of Phoenix–Wichita Campus	ind.	$10,770	NR	87%	NR	$ 2476	$ 8294	NR
Wichita State University	pub.	$ 4481	$5276	46%	17%	$ 4775	$ 4982	$21,368
Kentucky								
Alice Lloyd College	ind.	$ 1200	$3900	100%	40%	$ 9143	—	$ 3495
Asbury College	ind.	$21,286	$5152	99%	33%	$15,680	$10,758	$24,739
Bellarmine University	ind.	$24,150	$6880	100%	29%	$19,416	$11,614	$15,295
Berea College	ind.	$ 775	$5230	100%	8%	$28,683	—	$ 7638
Campbellsville University	ind.	$17,260	$6230	100%	27%	$13,932	$ 9558	$17,083
Centre College	ind.	*$33,000	NR	100%	39%	$21,263	$11,737	$16,760
Clear Creek Baptist Bible College	ind.	$ 5262	$3310	100%	NR	$ 4969	$ 3603	NR
Eastern Kentucky University	pub.	$ 5192	$5392	79%	13%	$ 7545	$ 3039	$14,257
Georgetown College	ind.	$22,360	$6380	100%	48%	$19,525	$ 9215	$17,326
Kentucky Christian University	ind.	$12,630	$4624	86%	11%	$10,633	$ 6621	$19,200
Kentucky State University	pub.	$ 5378	$6272	NR	NR	NR	NR	NR
Kentucky Wesleyan College	ind.	$13,600	$5750	100%	19%	$12,462	$ 6888	$15,428
Lindsey Wilson College	ind.	$15,806	$6540	100%	26%	$12,636	$ 9710	$14,712
Morehead State University	pub.	$ 4870	$5208	64%	35%	$ 7517	$ 2561	$18,167
Murray State University	pub.	$ 5418	$5670	75%	94%	$ 4595	$ 6493	$15,010
Pikeville College	ind.	$12,750	$5000	100%	62%	$13,656	$ 4094	$11,973
Thomas More College	ind.	$21,220	$6250	94%	100%	$17,950	$ 9520	$22,165
Transylvania University	ind.	$22,300	$7130	99%	33%	$18,044	$11,386	$17,616
Union College	ind.	$15,650	$5000	100%	26%	$13,326	$ 7324	$22,434
University of Kentucky	pub.	$ 7096	$7970	51%	45%	$ 7252	$ 7814	$17,692
University of Louisville	pub.	$ 6252	$5096	95%	21%	$ 9110	$ 2238	$10,906
University of the Cumberlands	ind.	$13,658	$6626	100%	70%	$16,137	$ 4147	$19,497
Louisiana								
Centenary College of Louisiana	ind.	$18,900	$6780	100%	31%	$17,119	$ 8561	$17,300
Grambling State University	pub.	$ 3606	$4718	85%	5%	$ 5950	$ 2374	$30,000
Louisiana State University and Agricultural and Mechanical College	pub.	$ 4449	$6498	96%	18%	$ 7644	$ 3303	$16,354
Louisiana Tech University	pub.	$ 4502	$4365	94%	24%	$ 5520	$ 3347	$17,142
Loyola University New Orleans	ind.	$26,508	$9150	84%	37%	$23,346	$12,312	NR
Nicholls State University	pub.	$ 3470	$4038	88%	67%	$ 5235	$ 2273	$14,095
Northwestern State University of Louisiana	pub.	$ 3553	$4686	69%	34%	$ 4308	$ 3931	$18,812
Southeastern Louisiana University	pub.	$ 3423	$5750	77%	NR	$ 3886	$ 5287	$19,006
Southern University and Agricultural and Mechanical College	pub.	$ 3666	$5030	65%	12%	$ 8455	$ 241	$23,000
Tulane University	ind.	$34,896	$8397	98%	52%	$25,580	$17,713	$21,202
University of Louisiana at Lafayette	pub.	$ 3382	$3770	92%	13%	$ 4876	$ 2276	NR
University of New Orleans	pub.	$ 3810	$4734	74%	17%	$ 5031	$ 3513	$22,350

NA = not applicable; NR = not reported; * = includes room and board; † = room only; — = not available.

College Costs At-a-Glance

	Institutional Control ind.=independent; pub.=public	Tuition and Fees	Room and Board	Percent of Eligible Freshmen Receiving Need-Based Gift Awards	Percent of Freshmen Whose Need Was Fully Met	Average Financial Aid Package for Freshmen	Average Net Cost After Aid	Average Indebtedness Upon Graduation
Louisiana—*continued*								
University of Phoenix–Louisiana Campus	ind.	$ 9090	NA	85%	NR	$ 3011	$ 6079	NR
Maine								
Bates College	ind.	*$44,350	NR	98%	97%	$27,545	$16,805	$13,636
Bowdoin College	ind.	$34,640	$ 9310	99%	100%	$29,899	$14,051	$16,160
Colby College	ind.	*$44,080	NR	97%	100%	$30,042	$14,038	$17,542
Husson College	ind.	$11,770	$ 6240	96%	8%	$10,374	$ 7636	$19,380
Maine College of Art	ind.	$26,060	$ 9270	100%	3%	$13,152	$22,178	$33,350
Maine Maritime Academy	pub.	$ 8195	$ 7050	87%	12%	$ 6911	$ 8334	$26,508
New England School of Communications	ind.	$10,270	$ 6500	54%	23%	$ 2300	$14,470	$20,000
Saint Joseph's College of Maine	ind.	$21,760	$ 9030	100%	33%	$17,642	$13,148	$34,488
Thomas College	ind.	$17,730	$ 7430	100%	15%	$16,850	$ 8310	$21,025
Unity College	ind.	$19,630	NR	100%	35%	$14,904	$ 4726	NR
University of Maine	pub.	$ 7464	$ 7125	83%	34%	$11,269	$ 3320	$21,795
University of Maine at Farmington	pub.	$ 6408	$ 6312	89%	10%	$ 8880	$ 3840	$16,555
University of Maine at Presque Isle	pub.	$ 5380	$ 5658	90%	41%	$ 6790	$ 4248	$11,181
University of New England	ind.	$23,790	$ 9255	100%	50%	$22,497	$10,548	$39,014
University of Southern Maine	pub.	$ 6326	$ 7444	85%	14%	$ 8224	$ 5546	$22,000
Maryland								
Bowie State University	pub.	$ 5730	$ 5992	78%	10%	$ 6396	$ 5326	NR
Coppin State University	pub.	$ 4910	$ 6511	80%	12%	$ 7704	$ 3717	$17,843
Frostburg State University	pub.	$ 6550	$ 6746	84%	27%	$ 7494	$ 5802	$11,423
Goucher College	ind.	$29,325	$ 8925	95%	23%	$19,796	$18,454	$17,097
Hood College	ind.	$23,655	$ 8135	99%	42%	$21,864	$ 9926	$21,112
The Johns Hopkins University	ind.	$33,900	$10,622	91%	100%	$31,612	$12,910	$16,932
Loyola College in Maryland	ind.	$31,715	$ 9578	93%	93%	$21,900	$19,393	$16,073
McDaniel College	ind.	$27,280	$ 5900	98%	30%	$21,013	$12,167	$22,753
Mount St. Mary's University	ind.	$25,890	$ 9130	100%	26%	$15,682	$19,338	$20,703
Peabody Conservatory of Music of The Johns Hopkins University	ind.	$29,990	$ 9500	78%	4%	$11,012	$28,478	$19,196
St. John's College	ind.	$34,506	$ 8270	92%	70%	$27,149	$15,627	NR
St. Mary's College of Maryland	pub.	$11,989	$ 8855	38%	NR	$ 7500	$13,344	$17,125
Salisbury University	pub.	$ 6412	$ 7058	81%	22%	$ 6519	$ 6951	$18,330
Sojourner-Douglass College	ind.	$ 6748	NA	92%	NR	$ 2831	$ 3917	NR
Towson University	pub.	$ 7164	$ 7506	67%	20%	$ 7320	$ 7350	$12,472
University of Baltimore	pub.	$ 6069	NA	NR	NR	NR	NR	$18,050
University of Maryland, Baltimore County	pub.	$ 8622	$ 8381	85%	34%	$10,204	$ 6799	$19,910
University of Maryland, College Park	pub.	$ 7906	$ 8422	74%	28%	$12,078	$ 4250	$17,731
University of Maryland University College	pub.	$ 5520	NA	65%	NR	$ 3909	$ 1611	NR
University of Phoenix–Maryland Campus	ind.	$11,820	NA	57%	NR	$ 2362	$ 9458	NR
Villa Julie College	ind.	$16,770	$ 9188	98%	31%	$14,046	$11,912	$15,580
Washington College	ind.	$30,200	$ 6450	97%	70%	$15,528	$21,122	$19,800
Massachusetts								
American International College	ind.	$20,990	$ 9270	99%	17%	$15,462	$14,798	$23,522

NA = not applicable; NR = not reported; * = includes room and board; † = room only; — = not available.

College Costs At-a-Glance

	Institutional Control ind.=independent; pub.=public	Tuition and Fees	Room and Board	Percent of Eligible Freshmen Receiving Need-Based Gift Awards	Percent of Freshmen Whose Need Was Fully Met	Average Financial Aid Package for Freshmen	Average Net Cost After Aid	Average Indebtedness Upon Graduation
Massachusetts—*continued*								
Amherst College	ind.	$34,916	$ 9080	100%	100%	$33,882	$10,114	$11,626
Anna Maria College	ind.	$23,234	$ 8410	97%	23%	$16,855	$14,789	$23,513
Assumption College	ind.	$26,060	$ 5775	98%	20%	$16,233	$15,602	$21,304
Atlantic Union College	ind.	$16,080	$ 4800	98%	19%	$ 9609	$11,271	$20,023
Babson College	ind.	$34,112	$11,670	92%	84%	$26,179	$19,603	$33,458
Becker College	ind.	$21,460	$ 8500	99%	9%	$ 9879	$20,081	$32,121
Bentley College	ind.	$30,044	$10,530	84%	31%	$23,941	$16,633	$24,393
Berklee College of Music	ind.	$29,331	$12,550	30%	NR	$19,220	$22,661	NR
Boston College	ind.	$33,506	$11,438	87%	100%	$25,075	$19,869	$19,137
The Boston Conservatory	ind.	$27,835	$14,320	29%	5%	$15,580	$26,575	$15,000
Boston University	ind.	$33,792	$10,480	87%	55%	$27,009	$17,263	$21,196
Brandeis University	ind.	$34,035	$ 9463	96%	40%	$24,964	$18,534	$19,892
Bridgewater State College	pub.	$ 5866	$ 6852	80%	NR	$ 6067	$ 6651	$16,634
Clark University	ind.	$31,465	$ 5900	100%	67%	$24,072	$13,293	$19,125
College of the Holy Cross	ind.	$33,313	$ 9580	82%	100%	$23,745	$19,148	$18,090
Curry College	ind.	$24,300	$ 9640	94%	5%	$15,231	$18,709	$27,145
Emerson College	ind.	$25,894	$10,870	82%	96%	$13,502	$23,262	$25,108
Emmanuel College	ind.	$24,200	$10,400	87%	36%	$17,636	$16,964	$18,637
Endicott College	ind.	$21,374	$10,254	76%	11%	$12,557	$19,071	$27,725
Fitchburg State College	pub.	$ 5542	$ 6486	84%	94%	$ 6167	$ 5861	$13,228
Framingham State College	pub.	$ 5449	$ 6699	81%	57%	$ 6424	$ 5724	$15,328
Gordon College	ind.	$24,278	$ 6640	98%	20%	$13,799	$17,119	$11,193
Hampshire College	ind.	$34,605	$ 9030	100%	80%	$28,725	$14,910	$22,830
Harvard University	ind.	$33,709	$ 9946	99%	100%	$35,036	$ 8619	$ 9717
Hellenic College	ind.	$16,515	$10,370	100%	NR	$ 9700	$17,185	$ 7300
Lasell College	ind.	$20,900	$ 9200	99%	9%	$15,100	$15,000	$20,800
Lesley University	ind.	$25,850	$12,100	97%	7%	$20,175	$17,775	$15,000
Massachusetts College of Art	pub.	$ 7200	$11,090	53%	NR	$ 6696	$11,594	NR
Massachusetts College of Liberal Arts	pub.	$ 6326	$ 6542	71%	38%	$ 7131	$ 5737	$18,628
Massachusetts College of Pharmacy and Health Sciences	ind.	$21,880	$11,300	90%	8%	$13,333	$19,847	$54,495
Massachusetts Institute of Technology	ind.	$33,600	$ 9950	97%	100%	$30,466	$13,084	$17,956
Massachusetts Maritime Academy	pub.	$ 5466	$ 6935	45%	51%	$ 5925	$ 6476	$12,972
Merrimack College	ind.	$27,070	$10,705	100%	84%	$17,500	$20,275	$17,125
Montserrat College of Art	ind.	$21,355	$ 5500†	100%	NR	$10,457	$16,398	NR
Mount Holyoke College	ind.	$34,266	$10,040	99%	100%	$30,145	$14,161	$23,900
Mount Ida College	ind.	$21,330	$10,635	99%	9%	$11,513	$20,452	NR
Nichols College	ind.	$23,900	$ 8800	99%	26%	$16,272	$16,428	$27,483
Northeastern University	ind.	$30,309	$10,970	97%	17%	$17,553	$23,726	NR
Regis College	ind.	$23,680	$10,580	90%	16%	$22,545	$11,715	$23,472
School of the Museum of Fine Arts, Boston	ind.	$26,244	$11,380†	99%	NR	$14,981	$22,643	$23,898
Simmons College	ind.	$26,705	$10,710	82%	6%	$14,638	$22,777	$26,300
Smith College	ind.	$32,558	$10,880	100%	100%	$32,307	$11,131	$19,760
Stonehill College	ind.	$26,345	$11,040	96%	38%	$19,839	$17,546	$21,595

NA = not applicable; NR = not reported; * = includes room and board; † = room only; — = not available.

College Costs At-a-Glance	Institutional Control ind.=independent; pub.=public	Tuition and Fees	Room and Board	Percent of Eligible Freshmen Receiving Need-Based Gift Awards	Percent of Freshmen Whose Need Was Fully Met	Average Financial Aid Package for Freshmen	Average Net Cost After Aid	Average Indebtedness Upon Graduation
Massachusetts—*continued*								
Suffolk University	ind.	$22,690	$12,756	89%	13%	$13,387	$22,059	NR
Tufts University	ind.	$34,730	$ 9770	90%	100%	$26,302	$18,198	$14,200
University of Massachusetts Amherst	pub.	$ 9595	$ 6989	81%	16%	$10,220	$ 6364	$14,094
University of Massachusetts Boston	pub.	$ 8546	NA	91%	52%	$ 9777	—	$18,755
University of Massachusetts Dartmouth	pub.	$ 8309	$ 8162	74%	56%	$11,010	$ 5461	$16,214
University of Massachusetts Lowell	pub.	$ 8444	$ 6365	92%	67%	$ 8300	$ 6509	$14,833
University of Phoenix–Boston Campus	ind.	$13,050	NA	61%	NR	$ 1857	$11,193	NR
University of Phoenix–Central Massachusetts Campus	ind.	$13,050	NA	43%	NR	$ 1798	$11,252	NR
Wellesley College	ind.	$33,072	$10,216	95%	100%	$29,793	$15,289	$10,206
Wentworth Institute of Technology	ind.	$19,300	$ 9300	29%	4%	$ 8443	$20,157	$20,928
Western New England College	ind.	$37,658	$ 9998	100%	14%	$16,485	$31,171	NR
Westfield State College	pub.	$ 5657	$ 6470	71%	16%	$ 6097	$ 6030	NR
Wheaton College	ind.	$34,610	$ 8150	95%	50%	$25,556	$17,204	$23,880
Wheelock College	ind.	$24,890	$ 9910	84%	3%	$15,101	$19,699	$18,231
Williams College	ind.	$33,700	$ 8950	100%	100%	$33,948	$ 8702	$ 9943
Worcester Polytechnic Institute	ind.	$33,318	$ 9950	99%	38%	$21,654	$21,614	$34,409
Michigan								
Adrian College	ind.	$19,900	$ 6780	100%	85%	$17,672	$ 9008	$20,849
Albion College	ind.	$26,122	$ 7406	100%	43%	$21,044	$12,484	$22,504
Alma College	ind.	$22,380	$ 7774	100%	32%	$19,787	$10,367	$23,470
Andrews University	ind.	$19,528	$ 6750	66%	39%	$20,043	$ 6235	$25,083
Calvin College	ind.	$20,470	$ 7040	100%	27%	$15,400	$12,110	$21,600
Central Michigan University	pub.	$ 6753	$ 6824	90%	81%	$10,016	$ 3561	$17,365
Cleary University	ind.	$14,160	NA	79%	6%	$11,255	$ 2905	NR
College for Creative Studies	ind.	$26,375	$ 3900†	NR	NR	NR	NR	$36,848
Concordia University	ind.	$19,060	$ 7350	100%	26%	$16,979	$ 9431	$28,280
Eastern Michigan University	pub.	$ 6935	$ 6610	66%	4%	$ 6949	$ 6596	$22,757
Ferris State University	pub.	$ 7342	$ 7220	58%	11%	$ 7000	$ 7562	$15,000
Grace Bible College	ind.	$11,290	$ 6570	100%	6%	$ 6864	$10,996	$13,640
Grand Valley State University	pub.	$ 6588	$ 6600	98%	100%	$ 8416	$ 4772	$18,003
Hillsdale College	ind.	$18,260	$ 7030	100%	34%	$13,750	$11,540	$16,000
Hope College	ind.	$22,570	$ 6982	84%	28%	$18,879	$10,673	$23,324
Kalamazoo College	ind.	$27,054	$ 6915	100%	76%	$22,830	$11,139	$25,000
Kettering University	ind.	$24,908	$ 5690	93%	12%	$15,433	$15,165	$47,487
Kuyper College	ind.	$12,725	$ 5700	100%	18%	$ 8557	$ 9868	$12,900
Lake Superior State University	pub.	$ 6698	$ 6836	43%	54%	$ 8436	$ 5098	$19,825
Lawrence Technological University	ind.	$19,443	$ 7266	95%	26%	$14,255	$12,454	$29,224
Michigan State University	pub.	$ 8843	$ 6044	55%	41%	$ 9798	$ 5089	$22,147
Michigan Technological University	pub.	$ 8910	$ 6840	99%	33%	$10,177	$ 5573	$13,807
Northern Michigan University	pub.	$ 6141	$ 6874	62%	22%	$ 6674	$ 6341	$15,799
Northwood University	ind.	$16,455	$ 7194	86%	29%	$14,665	$ 8984	$23,445
Olivet College	ind.	$17,594	$ 6060	100%	11%	$12,733	$10,921	$23,258

NA = not applicable; NR = not reported; * = includes room and board; † = room only; — = not available.

College Costs At-a-Glance	Institutional Control ind.=independent; pub.=public	Tuition and Fees	Room and Board	Percent of Eligible Freshmen Receiving Need-Based Gift Awards	Percent of Freshmen Whose Need Was Fully Met	Average Financial Aid Package for Freshmen	Average Net Cost After Aid	Average Indebtedness Upon Graduation
Michigan—*continued*								
Spring Arbor University	ind.	$17,386	$6070	97%	57%	$17,088	$ 6368	$13,230
University of Detroit Mercy	ind.	$23,970	$7622	91%	33%	$26,028	$ 5564	NR
University of Michigan	pub.	$ 9798	$7838	54%	90%	$ 9317	$ 8319	$23,533
University of Michigan–Dearborn	pub.	$ 7392	NA	65%	12%	$ 3825	$ 3567	$22,908
University of Michigan–Flint	pub.	$ 6902	NA	60%	23%	$ 6369	$ 533	$19,315
University of Phoenix–Metro Detroit Campus	ind.	$11,700	NA	70%	NR	$ 2632	$ 9068	NR
University of Phoenix–West Michigan Campus	ind.	$11,400	NA	87%	NR	$ 2558	$ 8842	NR
Walsh College of Accountancy and Business Administration	ind.	$ 9526	NA	NR	NR	NR	NR	$10,472
Wayne State University	pub.	$ 6812	$6575	72%	7%	$ 6233	$ 7154	$19,329
Minnesota								
Augsburg College	ind.	$23,422	$6604	96%	28%	$12,862	$17,164	$25,750
Bemidji State University	pub.	$ 6690	$5860	72%	20%	$ 6954	$ 5596	$18,850
Bethany Lutheran College	ind.	$17,760	$5278	100%	27%	$12,114	$10,924	$23,115
Bethel University	ind.	$24,510	$7380	100%	19%	$17,120	$14,770	$28,085
Carleton College	ind.	$34,272	$8592	100%	100%	$28,714	$14,150	$19,429
College of Saint Benedict	ind.	$24,924	$6898	95%	58%	$20,417	$11,405	$24,764
College of St. Catherine	ind.	$22,880	$6432	81%	1%	$25,793	$ 3519	$27,519
The College of St. Scholastica	ind.	$23,574	$6514	80%	16%	$18,298	$11,790	$31,549
College of Visual Arts	ind.	$21,684	NA	100%	3%	$ 8787	$12,897	NR
Concordia College	ind.	$20,980	$5090	100%	27%	$16,409	$ 9661	$27,896
Concordia University, St. Paul	ind.	$23,496	$6776	100%	12%	$16,861	$13,411	$27,710
Crown College	ind.	$18,588	$6922	63%	10%	$12,432	$13,078	$30,444
Gustavus Adolphus College	ind.	$28,515	$4275	100%	NR	$19,800	$12,990	$21,300
Macalester College	ind.	$33,694	$8220	100%	100%	$24,854	$17,060	$14,889
Martin Luther College	ind.	$ 9850	$3825	100%	18%	$ 8790	$ 4885	$15,315
Minnesota State University Mankato	pub.	$ 5840	$5099	64%	39%	$ 6719	$ 4220	$20,826
Northwestern College	ind.	$20,990	$6750	100%	9%	$14,142	$13,598	$22,650
St. Cloud State University	pub.	$ 5718	$5194	77%	75%	$10,698	$ 214	$21,869
Saint John's University	ind.	$24,924	$6496	99%	46%	$20,993	$10,427	$25,407
Saint Mary's University of Minnesota	ind.	$22,398	$6130	100%	60%	$15,830	$12,698	$28,500
St. Olaf College	ind.	$30,600	$7900	100%	100%	$22,416	$16,084	$23,993
Southwest Minnesota State University	pub.	$ 6240	$5360	70%	24%	$ 7647	$ 3953	$16,438
University of Minnesota, Crookston	pub.	$ 9065	$5750	93%	47%	$11,764	$ 3051	NR
University of Minnesota, Duluth	pub.	$ 9439	$5722	81%	56%	$ 7122	$ 8039	$20,205
University of Minnesota, Morris	pub.	$ 9112	$6260	90%	44%	$12,676	$ 2696	$15,490
University of Minnesota, Twin Cities Campus	pub.	$ 9173	$6996	77%	57%	$12,148	$ 4021	NR
University of St. Thomas	ind.	$24,808	$6882	99%	32%	$17,014	$14,676	$31,065
Winona State University	pub.	$ 7100	$6300	45%	10%	$ 4893	$ 8507	$20,889
Mississippi								
Alcorn State University	pub.	$ 4156	$4616	76%	45%	$ 6610	$ 2162	$10,000
Belhaven College	ind.	$15,580	$6000	86%	25%	$10,562	$11,018	$18,126
Blue Mountain College	ind.	$ 7490	$3766	81%	41%	$ 7589	$ 3667	$11,500

NA = not applicable; NR = not reported; * = includes room and board; † = room only; — = not available.

College Costs At-a-Glance

College Costs At-a-Glance	Institutional Control ind.=independent; pub.=public	Tuition and Fees	Room and Board	Percent of Eligible Freshmen Receiving Need-Based Gift Awards	Percent of Freshmen Whose Need Was Fully Met	Average Financial Aid Package for Freshmen	Average Net Cost After Aid	Average Indebtedness Upon Graduation
Mississippi—*continued*								
Jackson State University	pub.	$ 4224	$ 5212	NR	NR	NR	NR	NR
Millsaps College	ind.	$23,352	$ 8368	100%	41%	$18,462	$13,258	$21,495
Mississippi State University	pub.	$ 4596	$ 6331	95%	22%	$ 7106	$ 3821	$19,780
University of Southern Mississippi	pub.	$ 4714	$ 5070	94%	38%	$ 9192	$ 592	$17,429
Wesley College	ind.	$ 8040	$ 3640	67%	NR	$ 3090	$ 8590	$ 6750
William Carey College	ind.	$ 8715	$ 3615	NR	NR	NR	NR	$17,000
Missouri								
Avila University	ind.	$18,850	$ 5750	98%	27%	$10,776	$13,824	$16,398
Baptist Bible College	ind.	$13,460	$ 5500	NR	NR	NR	NR	NR
Central Methodist University	ind.	$17,160	$ 5720	100%	4%	$12,359	$10,521	$22,904
Columbia College	ind.	$12,414	$ 5164	89%	24%	$ 9448	$ 8130	$12,707
Conception Seminary College	ind.	$13,024	$ 7230	29%	86%	$19,188	$ 1066	$16,375
Culver-Stockton College	ind.	$16,600	$ 6850	100%	15%	$12,960	$10,490	$17,695
Drury University	ind.	$15,512	$ 5790	95%	84%	$ 7428	$13,874	$17,885
Evangel University	ind.	$14,300	$ 5120	91%	8%	$ 7940	$11,480	$22,105
Hannibal-LaGrange College	ind.	$12,608	$ 4930	54%	NR	NR	NR	$16,689
Kansas City Art Institute	ind.	$25,680	$ 7874	100%	13%	$15,912	$17,642	$30,000
Lincoln University	pub.	$ 5123	$ 3990	65%	16%	$ 6000	$ 3113	$20,974
Lindenwood University	ind.	$12,700	$ 6200	NR	NR	NR	NR	NR
Maryville University of Saint Louis	ind.	$18,120	$ 7720	100%	13%	$13,980	$11,860	$23,560
Messenger College	ind.	$ 5860	$ 3900	71%	NR	$ 5600	$ 4160	$19,342
Missouri Baptist University	ind.	$14,810	$ 5990	NR	NR	NR	NR	$18,358
Missouri State University	pub.	$ 5738	$ 5358	79%	24%	$ 5921	$ 5175	$16,003
Missouri Valley College	ind.	$15,450	$ 5850	100%	36%	$12,150	$ 9150	$14,200
Rockhurst University	ind.	$22,990	$ 6200	60%	27%	$20,426	$ 8764	$17,525
St. Louis College of Pharmacy	ind.	$19,750	$ 7823	100%	20%	$11,023	$16,550	$80,000
Saint Louis University	ind.	$26,648	$ 8230	96%	15%	$19,061	$15,817	$34,539
Southeast Missouri State University	pub.	$ 5505	$ 5647	84%	21%	$ 6132	$ 5020	$17,198
Southwest Baptist University	ind.	$14,100	$ 4200	38%	29%	$10,869	$ 7431	$18,380
Stephens College	ind.	$20,500	$ 7975	66%	14%	$16,787	$11,688	$18,810
Truman State University	pub.	$ 6342	$ 5570	51%	65%	$ 6682	$ 5230	$16,656
University of Central Missouri	pub.	$ 5835	$ 5109	52%	27%	$ 6006	$ 4938	$ 9576
University of Missouri–Columbia	pub.	$ 7308	$ 6977	90%	21%	$12,611	$ 1674	$18,983
University of Missouri–Kansas City	pub.	$ 7592	$ 6823	73%	59%	$11,419	$ 2996	$18,227
University of Missouri–St. Louis	pub.	$ 7968	$ 7178	78%	24%	$11,022	$ 4124	$18,143
University of Phoenix–Kansas City Campus	ind.	$11,064	NA	59%	NR	$ 2473	$ 8591	NR
University of Phoenix–St. Louis Campus	ind.	$11,910	NA	80%	NR	$ 2451	$ 9459	NR
University of Phoenix–Springfield Campus	ind.	$ 9750	NA	77%	NR	$ 2881	$ 6869	NR
Washington University in St. Louis	ind.	$35,524	$11,252	99%	100%	$27,621	$19,155	NR
Webster University	ind.	$18,240	$ 7403	85%	NR	$18,807	$ 6836	$22,690
Westminster College	ind.	$15,030	$ 6140	99%	63%	$14,117	$ 7053	$16,477
William Jewell College	ind.	$21,400	$ 5840	100%	NR	$16,761	$10,479	$18,093

NA = not applicable; NR = not reported; * = includes room and board; † = room only; — = not available.

College Costs At-a-Glance

	Institutional Control ind.=independent; pub.=public	Tuition and Fees	Room and Board	Percent of Eligible Freshmen Receiving Need-Based Gift Awards	Percent of Freshmen Whose Need Was Fully Met	Average Financial Aid Package for Freshmen	Average Net Cost After Aid	Average Indebtedness Upon Graduation
Missouri—*continued*								
William Woods University	ind.	$15,570	$6100	100%	30%	$12,541	$ 9129	$13,865
Montana								
Carroll College	ind.	$18,410	$6350	89%	18%	$14,916	$ 9844	$25,659
Montana State University	pub.	$ 5673	$6450	75%	12%	$ 6808	$ 5315	$18,081
Montana State University–Billings	pub.	$ 5055	$4310	86%	19%	$ 7208	$ 2157	$15,461
Montana Tech of The University of Montana	pub.	$ 5605	$5594	71%	50%	$ 5000	$ 6199	$20,000
University of Great Falls	ind.	$16,350	$5800	69%	1%	$10,701	$11,449	$26,450
The University of Montana	pub.	$ 4977	$5860	67%	15%	$ 6740	$ 4097	$15,185
Nebraska								
College of Saint Mary	ind.	$20,055	$6252	96%	20%	$15,001	$11,306	$18,047
Concordia University	ind.	$19,790	$5070	99%	23%	$14,810	$10,050	$18,923
Creighton University	ind.	$25,126	$7842	100%	44%	$23,087	$ 9881	$27,427
Dana College	ind.	$18,650	$5390	46%	29%	$16,516	$ 7524	$17,029
Doane College	ind.	$19,150	$5410	98%	77%	$18,590	$ 5970	$13,647
Grace University	ind.	$13,970	$5350	100%	18%	$10,631	$ 8689	$17,823
Hastings College	ind.	$18,302	$5148	100%	32%	$12,216	$11,234	$17,634
Nebraska Methodist College	ind.	$13,230	$2384†	94%	56%	$ 7001	$ 8613	$24,901
Nebraska Wesleyan University	ind.	$19,302	$5165	99%	25%	$14,117	$10,350	$18,944
Union College	ind.	$15,230	$4218	NR	NR	$11,989	$ 7459	$23,379
University of Nebraska at Kearney	pub.	$ 4765	$5686	72%	31%	$ 7162	$ 3289	$16,175
University of Nebraska at Omaha	pub.	$ 5118	$6630	61%	NR	NR	NR	$18,800
University of Nebraska Medical Center	pub.	$ 4830	NA	NR	NR	NR	NR	$26,226
Wayne State College	pub.	$ 4013	$4470	66%	25%	$ 3882	$ 4601	NR
Nevada								
University of Nevada, Las Vegas	pub.	$ 4166	$8857	40%	50%	$ 5801	$ 7222	$17,394
University of Phoenix–Nevada Campus	ind.	$10,200	NA	54%	NR	$ 2530	$ 7670	NR
New Hampshire								
Chester College of New England	ind.	$15,930	$7850	30%	NR	$ 6692	$17,088	$32,915
Daniel Webster College	ind.	$24,385	$8750	78%	NR	$16,187	$16,948	$45,000
Dartmouth College	ind.	$33,297	$9840	97%	100%	$33,208	$ 9929	$21,561
Franklin Pierce University	ind.	$25,300	$8200	99%	11%	$15,089	$18,411	$28,036
Keene State College	pub.	$ 7822	$7026	64%	20%	$ 7331	$ 7517	$20,992
Rivier College	ind.	$21,695	$7942	98%	25%	$15,011	$14,626	$25,959
Southern New Hampshire University	ind.	$23,346	$8970	97%	5%	$15,320	$16,996	NR
Thomas More College of Liberal Arts	ind.	$11,150	$8000	100%	83%	$ 9842	$ 9308	$21,417
University of New Hampshire	pub.	$10,401	$7584	67%	28%	$15,617	$ 2368	$23,928
University of New Hampshire at Manchester	pub.	$ 7788	NA	29%	7%	$ 5864	$ 1924	$17,562
New Jersey								
Bloomfield College	ind.	$16,400	$8100	96%	57%	$15,269	$ 9231	$18,404
Centenary College	ind.	$22,415	$8400	96%	20%	$16,206	$14,609	$20,571
The College of New Jersey	pub.	$10,553	$8843	34%	32%	$ 9805	$ 9591	$19,459
College of Saint Elizabeth	ind.	$21,150	$9424	75%	14%	$18,092	$12,482	NR

NA = not applicable; NR = not reported; * = includes room and board; † = room only; — = not available.

College Costs At-a-Glance

	Institutional Control ind.=independent; pub.=public	Tuition and Fees	Room and Board	Percent of Eligible Freshmen Receiving Need-Based Gift Awards	Percent of Freshmen Whose Need Was Fully Met	Average Financial Aid Package for Freshmen	Average Net Cost After Aid	Average Indebtedness Upon Graduation
New Jersey—*continued*								
Drew University	ind.	$33,068	$ 9000	100%	26%	$23,523	$18,545	$18,275
Felician College	ind.	$19,950	$ 7432	65%	13%	$14,340	$13,042	$19,500
Kean University	pub.	$ 8036	$ 8880	99%	9%	$ 7154	$ 9762	$20,037
Monmouth University	ind.	$21,868	$ 8472	34%	23%	$12,409	$17,931	$53,092
Montclair State University	pub.	$ 8404	$ 8988	45%	39%	$ 5982	$11,410	NR
New Jersey City University	pub.	$ 7536	$ 7880	76%	10%	$ 7496	$ 7920	$26,344
Princeton University	ind.	$33,000	$10,980	100%	100%	$29,443	$14,537	$ 4965
Ramapo College of New Jersey	pub.	$ 9496	$ 9924	47%	17%	$10,943	$ 8477	$15,937
The Richard Stockton College of New Jersey	pub.	$ 9058	$ 8446	50%	49%	$11,840	$ 5664	NR
Rider University	ind.	$24,790	$ 9280	96%	20%	$17,925	$16,145	$28,636
Rowan University	pub.	$ 9330	$ 8742	65%	35%	$ 6584	$11,488	$16,253
Rutgers, The State University of New Jersey, Camden	pub.	$ 9758	$ 8596	69%	50%	$11,846	$ 6508	$18,645
Rutgers, The State University of New Jersey, Newark	pub.	$ 9534	$ 9535	78%	31%	$11,960	$ 7109	$17,143
Rutgers, The State University of New Jersey, New Brunswick	pub.	$ 9958	$ 9312	60%	40%	$12,573	$ 6697	$16,283
Stevens Institute of Technology	ind.	$33,115	$10,000	80%	27%	$25,792	$17,323	$14,113
William Paterson University of New Jersey	pub.	$ 9422	$ 9380	59%	52%	$12,477	$ 6325	$18,386
New Mexico								
College of Santa Fe	ind.	$26,072	$ 7585	87%	20%	$18,101	$15,556	$17,540
College of the Southwest	ind.	$10,500	$ 5400	76%	45%	$11,144	$ 4756	$17,420
New Mexico State University	pub.	$ 4230	$ 5576	91%	13%	$ 6405	$ 3401	NR
St. John's College	ind.	$36,596	$ 8684	90%	95%	$24,205	$21,075	$28,770
University of Phoenix–New Mexico Campus	ind.	$ 9750	NA	81%	NR	$ 3440	$ 6310	NR
New York								
Adelphi University	ind.	$20,900	$ 9500	85%	1%	$14,500	$15,900	$23,246
Alfred University	ind.	$23,162	$10,384	99%	16%	$20,541	$13,005	$23,292
Bard College	ind.	$34,080	$ 9850	96%	58%	$25,008	$18,922	$18,345
Barnard College	ind.	$33,078	$11,392	96%	100%	$31,377	$13,093	$19,400
Bernard M. Baruch College of the City University of New York	pub.	$ 4320	NA	83%	26%	$ 5406	—	$11,700
Canisius College	ind.	$24,937	$ 9480	100%	37%	$22,199	$12,218	$24,386
Cazenovia College	ind.	$21,490	$ 8940	NR	NR	NR	NR	$28,814
City College of the City University of New York	pub.	$ 4359	$ 9135†	90%	75%	$ 7547	$ 5947	$16,080
Clarkson University	ind.	$27,090	$ 9648	64%	NR	$22,513	$14,225	$27,927
Colgate University	ind.	$35,030	$ 8530	100%	100%	$33,221	$10,339	$16,093
The College of New Rochelle	ind.	$21,910	$ 8200	97%	4%	$23,468	$ 6642	$26,486
The College of Saint Rose	ind.	$19,258	$ 8116	94%	5%	$ 7858	$19,516	$24,732
College of Staten Island of the City University of New York	pub.	$ 4328	NA	98%	9%	$ 5790	—	NR
Columbia University, School of General Studies	ind.	$33,906	$ 8913	NR	NR	NR	NR	NR
Cooper Union for the Advancement of Science and Art	ind.	$ 1550	$13,500	100%	75%	$27,500	—	$ 3478
Cornell University	ind.	$32,981	$10,776	95%	100%	$28,929	$14,828	$18,938
The Culinary Institute of America	ind.	$21,280	$ 7170	NR	NR	NR	NR	$18,000
Daemen College	ind.	$17,690	$ 8190	92%	27%	$15,506	$10,374	$13,323
Dominican College	ind.	$18,610	$ 8980	98%	12%	$12,675	$14,915	$23,091

NA = not applicable; NR = not reported; * = includes room and board; † = room only; — = not available.

College Costs At-a-Glance

	Institutional Control ind.=independent; pub.=public	Tuition and Fees	Room and Board	Percent of Eligible Freshmen Receiving Need-Based Gift Awards	Percent of Freshmen Whose Need Was Fully Met	Average Financial Aid Package for Freshmen	Average Net Cost After Aid	Average Indebtedness Upon Graduation
New York—*continued*								
Dowling College	ind.	$18,430	$ 8988	100%	4%	$12,734	$14,684	$22,735
D'Youville College	ind.	$17,000	$ 8300	100%	30%	$13,639	$11,661	$26,897
Elmira College	ind.	$30,050	$ 9100	100%	15%	$24,400	$14,750	$29,058
Eugene Lang College The New School for Liberal Arts	ind.	$29,210	$11,750	95%	9%	$25,068	$15,892	$21,293
Fashion Institute of Technology	pub.	$ 4770	$11,213	74%	17%	$ 7947	$ 8036	$12,869
Five Towns College	ind.	$17,085	$16,800	90%	56%	$ 5350	$28,535	$18,000
Hamilton College	ind.	$34,980	$ 8910	99%	100%	$30,355	$13,535	$19,371
Hilbert College	ind.	$15,700	$ 5900	97%	23%	$10,917	$10,683	$22,282
Hobart and William Smith Colleges	ind.	$34,688	$ 8828	100%	81%	$25,182	$18,334	$25,913
Hofstra University	ind.	$24,830	$ 9800	87%	10%	$15,404	$19,226	$31,196
Houghton College	ind.	$20,400	$ 6680	100%	13%	$13,883	$13,197	$24,125
Iona College	ind.	$23,218	$ 9998	76%	20%	$15,293	$17,923	$19,457
Ithaca College	ind.	$26,832	$10,314	88%	52%	$22,875	$14,271	NR
Keuka College	ind.	$19,120	$ 8210	100%	29%	$18,135	$ 9195	$18,645
Laboratory Institute of Merchandising	ind.	$17,700	$13,000	57%	NR	$ 5260	$25,440	$17,662
Lehman College of the City University of New York	pub.	$ 4290	NA	92%	2%	$ 3524	$ 766	$10,500
Le Moyne College	ind.	$22,580	$ 8620	100%	37%	$18,423	$12,777	$18,360
Manhattan College	ind.	$21,550	$ 9325	96%	23%	$16,225	$14,650	$35,130
Manhattanville College	ind.	$30,776	$12,240	85%	15%	$25,039	$17,977	$23,253
Mannes College The New School for Music	ind.	$28,210	$11,750	50%	12%	$11,396	$28,564	$18,025
Marist College	ind.	$22,576	$ 9790	100%	21%	$14,291	$18,075	$28,450
Marymount Manhattan College	ind.	$19,638	$12,090	94%	8%	NR	NR	$17,125
Medaille College	ind.	$15,780	$ 8024	95%	10%	$13,500	$10,304	$23,000
Medgar Evers College of the City University of New York	pub.	$ 4230	NA	96%	NR	NR	NR	NR
Molloy College	ind.	$17,310	NA	96%	22%	$11,788	$ 5522	$23,000
Monroe College (Bronx)	ind.	$10,200	$10,120	81%	31%	$ 9905	$10,415	$ 6240
Mount Saint Mary College	ind.	$18,290	$ 9040	92%	10%	$11,817	$15,513	$20,000
Nazareth College of Rochester	ind.	$21,640	$ 9080	100%	14%	$16,446	$14,274	$26,795
The New School for Jazz and Contemporary Music	ind.	$28,210	$11,750	23%	13%	$ 9918	$30,042	$28,106
New York Institute of Technology	ind.	$20,358	$11,452	68%	NR	$12,061	$19,749	$17,125
New York School of Interior Design	ind.	$20,750	NA	NR	NR	NR	NR	$30,000
New York University	ind.	$33,420	$11,780	92%	NR	$20,643	$24,557	$34,417
Niagara University	ind.	$21,240	$ 8850	99%	49%	$17,508	$12,582	$21,594
Nyack College	ind.	$15,400	$ 7600	99%	20%	$13,872	$ 9128	$19,351
Parsons The New School for Design	ind.	$30,930	$11,750	96%	18%	$10,471	$32,209	$42,784
Paul Smith's College of Arts and Sciences	ind.	$19,500	$ 7800	99%	16%	$14,752	$12,548	$ 6625
Polytechnic University, Brooklyn Campus	ind.	$29,789	$ 8500	81%	69%	$23,011	$15,278	$25,012
Purchase College, State University of New York	pub.	$ 5709	$ 9078	83%	11%	$ 7357	$ 7430	$16,058
Rensselaer Polytechnic Institute	ind.	$33,496	$ 9915	100%	50%	$27,220	$16,191	$27,235
Roberts Wesleyan College	ind.	$21,656	$ 7774	100%	25%	$17,964	$11,466	NR
Rochester Institute of Technology	ind.	$25,011	$ 8748	95%	83%	$17,600	$16,159	NR
Russell Sage College	ind.	$24,670	$ 8520	57%	2%	NR	NR	$26,000
Sage College of Albany	ind.	$17,670	$ 8520	62%	NR	NR	NR	$18,000

NA = not applicable; NR = not reported; * = includes room and board; † = room only; — = not available.

College Costs At-a-Glance	Institutional Control ind.=independent; pub.=public	Tuition and Fees	Room and Board	Percent of Eligible Freshmen Receiving Need-Based Gift Awards	Percent of Freshmen Whose Need Was Fully Met	Average Financial Aid Package for Freshmen	Average Net Cost After Aid	Average Indebtedness Upon Graduation
New York—*continued*								
St. Bonaventure University	ind.	$22,515	$ 7760	100%	34%	$18,581	$11,694	$16,900
St. Francis College	ind.	$14,020	NR	67%	15%	$ 9100	$ 4920	NR
St. John Fisher College	ind.	$20,710	$ 8880	100%	11%	$17,458	$12,132	$31,206
St. Joseph's College, New York	ind.	$12,946	NR	100%	70%	$11,500	$ 1446	$17,978
St. Joseph's College, Suffolk Campus	ind.	$13,610	NA	100%	68%	$ 7433	$ 6177	$17,806
St. Lawrence University	ind.	$33,910	$ 8630	99%	60%	$33,307	$ 9233	$28,611
Sarah Lawrence College	ind.	$36,088	$12,152	93%	90%	$26,119	$22,121	$45,300
School of Visual Arts	ind.	$22,080	$12,300	62%	1%	$11,366	$23,014	$30,600
Skidmore College	ind.	$34,694	$ 9556	100%	84%	$26,224	$18,026	$16,078
State University of New York at Binghamton	pub.	$ 5910	$ 8588	88%	89%	$11,224	$ 3274	$15,167
State University of New York at Fredonia	pub.	$ 5482	$ 8120	91%	24%	$ 7750	$ 5852	$22,303
State University of New York at New Paltz	pub.	$ 5340	$ 7630	87%	18%	$ 2040	$10,930	$ 1900
State University of New York at Oswego	pub.	$ 5322	$ 8940	94%	38%	$ 7132	$ 7130	$21,467
State University of New York at Plattsburgh	pub.	$ 5337	$ 7728	96%	28%	$ 8628	$ 4437	$17,596
State University of New York College at Geneseo	pub.	$ 5560	$ 7788	80%	73%	$ 9055	$ 4293	$17,000
State University of New York College at Old Westbury	pub.	$ 5076	$ 8083	NR	NR	$ 6880	$ 6279	$15,533
State University of New York College at Oneonta	pub.	$ 5412	$ 7696	88%	17%	$ 8828	$ 4280	$12,100
State University of New York College at Potsdam	pub.	$ 5357	$ 8220	95%	85%	$12,479	$ 1098	$17,495
State University of New York College of Agriculture and Technology at Cobleskill	pub.	$ 5650	$ 8630	70%	12%	$ 6923	$ 7357	$22,463
State University of New York College of Environmental Science and Forestry	pub.	$ 5069	$10,600	77%	100%	$11,150	$ 4519	$19,000
State University of New York Downstate Medical Center	pub.	$ 4745	$12,260	NR	NR	NR	NR	NR
State University of New York Institute of Technology	pub.	$ 5317	$ 7600	93%	28%	$ 8354	$ 4563	$16,318
Stony Brook University, State University of New York	pub.	$ 5631	$ 8394	96%	8%	$ 8012	$ 6013	$14,816
Syracuse University	ind.	$29,965	$10,420	90%	65%	$23,100	$17,285	$23,500
Union College	ind.	*$44,043	NR	100%	100%	$26,636	$17,407	$22,602
University at Albany, State University of New York	pub.	$ 5939	$ 8605	94%	26%	$ 8763	$ 5781	$11,856
University at Buffalo, the State University of New York	pub.	$ 6128	$ 8108	92%	19%	$ 5581	$ 8655	$19,062
University of Rochester	ind.	$35,190	$10,640	99%	100%	$27,987	$17,843	$27,497
Utica College	ind.	$23,440	$ 9510	100%	9%	$19,483	$13,467	$25,565
Vassar College	ind.	$36,030	$ 8130	100%	100%	$27,803	$16,357	$19,313
Vaughn College of Aeronautics and Technology	ind.	$14,280	$10,000	100%	12%	$ 5600	$18,680	$17,125
Wagner College	ind.	$27,400	$ 8400	97%	22%	$14,960	$20,840	NR
Webb Institute	ind.	$ 0	$ 9000	17%	33%	$ 2626	$ 6374	$11,612
Wells College	ind.	$16,680	$ 7500	100%	25%	$17,747	$ 6433	$20,923
York College of the City University of New York	pub.	$ 4180	NA	99%	NR	$ 3313	$ 867	NR
North Carolina								
Appalachian State University	pub.	$ 4187	$ 5760	86%	21%	$ 5314	$ 4633	$14,838
Barton College	ind.	$17,654	$ 6264	72%	15%	$16,697	$ 7221	$22,809
Belmont Abbey College	ind.	$17,302	$ 9430	98%	26%	$13,461	$13,271	$16,608
Bennett College For Women	ind.	$14,150	$ 6258	84%	5%	$ 8449	$11,959	$15,531
Brevard College	ind.	$17,220	$ 6150	100%	25%	$16,330	$ 7040	$19,293

NA = not applicable; NR = not reported; * = includes room and board; † = room only; — = not available.

College Costs At-a-Glance	Institutional Control ind.=independent; pub.=public	Tuition and Fees	Room and Board	Percent of Eligible Freshmen Receiving Need-Based Gift Awards	Percent of Freshmen Whose Need Was Fully Met	Average Financial Aid Package for Freshmen	Average Net Cost After Aid	Average Indebtedness Upon Graduation
North Carolina—*continued*								
Cabarrus College of Health Sciences	ind.	$ 7700	NA	NR	NR	NR	NR	NR
Campbell University	ind.	$18,598	$6160	72%	100%	$25,545	—	$21,703
Catawba College	ind.	$19,690	$6570	57%	34%	$18,096	$ 8164	$18,133
Chowan University	ind.	$16,040	$6800	98%	11%	$12,525	$10,315	$23,370
Davidson College	ind.	$30,194	$8590	96%	100%	$19,379	$19,405	$26,130
Duke University	ind.	$33,963	$9152	97%	100%	$28,996	$14,119	$23,499
East Carolina University	pub.	$ 4003	$6940	67%	97%	$ 7978	$ 2965	$19,614
Elon University	ind.	$20,441	$6850	85%	NR	$11,903	$15,388	$21,991
Gardner-Webb University	ind.	$17,590	$5740	75%	25%	$14,568	$ 8762	NR
Guilford College	ind.	$23,020	$6690	100%	27%	$17,950	$11,760	$22,130
Heritage Bible College	ind.	$ 4200	$2400	82%	NR	$ 4250	$ 2350	$14,554
Johnson & Wales University	ind.	$21,462	$8550	92%	1%	$15,217	$14,795	NR
Johnson C. Smith University	ind.	$15,004	$5840	90%	5%	$ 7625	$13,219	$25,000
Meredith College	ind.	$21,200	$5940	100%	21%	$14,731	$12,409	$18,962
Methodist University	ind.	$20,080	$7550	96%	45%	$18,377	$ 9253	$26,640
Montreat College	ind.	$16,182	$5258	100%	NR	$14,051	$ 7389	$17,682
Mount Olive College	ind.	$13,126	$5300	99%	22%	$ 7843	$10,583	$ 9786
North Carolina Agricultural and Technical State University	pub.	$ 3872	$6686	78%	4%	$ 5720	$ 4838	$20,052
North Carolina School of the Arts	pub.	$ 4891	$6139	92%	8%	$ 9884	$ 1146	$20,574
North Carolina State University	pub.	$ 5117	$7373	97%	38%	$ 8588	$ 3902	$14,719
Peace College	ind.	$21,140	$7230	100%	12%	$14,649	$13,721	NR
Pfeiffer University	ind.	$16,450	$6650	100%	22%	$12,245	$10,855	$17,350
Roanoke Bible College	ind.	$ 9915	$5720	100%	4%	$ 4827	$10,808	$19,486
St. Andrews Presbyterian College	ind.	$17,162	$7540	100%	27%	$12,778	$11,924	$18,951
Shaw University	ind.	$10,020	$6410	99%	9%	$ 8846	$ 7584	$15,982
The University of North Carolina at Asheville	pub.	$ 3882	$5880	96%	32%	$ 6464	$ 3298	$14,211
The University of North Carolina at Chapel Hill	pub.	$ 5033	$6846	99%	95%	$10,103	$ 1776	NR
The University of North Carolina at Charlotte	pub.	$ 3895	$5790	86%	25%	$ 7190	$ 2495	$17,730
The University of North Carolina at Greensboro	pub.	$ 4029	$6051	47%	24%	$ 7480	$ 2600	$19,146
The University of North Carolina at Pembroke	pub.	$ 5262	$5517	90%	12%	$ 6557	$ 4222	$16,296
The University of North Carolina Wilmington	pub.	$ 4160	$6722	80%	67%	$ 5411	$ 5471	$15,620
University of Phoenix–Charlotte Campus	ind.	$10,770	NA	71%	NR	$ 2744	$ 8026	NR
University of Phoenix–Raleigh Campus	ind.	$10,770	NA	82%	NR	$ 2801	$ 7969	NR
Wake Forest University	ind.	$34,330	$9500	88%	44%	$24,308	$19,522	$20,655
Warren Wilson College	ind.	$21,084	$6700	88%	17%	$14,683	$13,101	$15,713
Western Carolina University	pub.	$ 4609	$5210	99%	34%	$ 6623	$ 3196	$17,964
Wingate University	ind.	$17,650	$6750	94%	27%	$15,348	$ 9052	$ 2424
Winston-Salem State University	pub.	$ 3109	$5476	96%	1%	$ 3782	$ 4803	$10,200
North Dakota								
Dickinson State University	pub.	$ 5295	$3882	69%	20%	$ 4910	$ 4267	NR
Jamestown College	ind.	$11,235	$4620	100%	26%	$ 7744	$ 8111	$21,879
Mayville State University	pub.	$ 5257	$3884	75%	40%	$ 4039	$ 5102	$15,758

NA = not applicable; NR = not reported; * = includes room and board; † = room only; — = not available.

College Costs At-a-Glance

	Institutional Control ind.=independent; pub.=public	Tuition and Fees	Room and Board	Percent of Eligible Freshmen Receiving Need-Based Gift Awards	Percent of Freshmen Whose Need Was Fully Met	Average Financial Aid Package for Freshmen	Average Net Cost After Aid	Average Indebtedness Upon Graduation
North Dakota—*continued*								
Medcenter One College of Nursing	ind.	$10,017	NA	NR	NR	NR	NR	$24,471
Minot State University	pub.	$ 4492	$5294	81%	33%	$ 4019	$ 5767	$16,354
North Dakota State University	pub.	$ 5722	$5477	61%	40%	$ 4106	$ 7093	$23,197
University of North Dakota	pub.	$ 5792	$5085	57%	27%	$ 6316	$ 4561	NR
Valley City State University	pub.	$ 5307	$3716	85%	43%	$ 5525	$ 3498	$15,544
Ohio								
Antioch College	ind.	$28,550	$7354	79%	18%	$26,620	$ 9284	$17,112
Antioch University McGregor	ind.	$13,137	NA	NR	NR	NR	NR	$20,625
Ashland University	ind.	$22,990	$8374	100%	NR	NR	NR	$18,250
Baldwin-Wallace College	ind.	$21,236	$6974	100%	61%	$18,198	$10,012	$17,849
Bluffton University	ind.	$20,570	$7082	100%	63%	$19,980	$ 7672	$22,183
Bowling Green State University	pub.	$ 9060	$6684	76%	20%	$10,288	$ 5456	$22,929
Capital University	ind.	$25,100	$6552	64%	25%	$18,372	$13,280	$25,171
Case Western Reserve University	ind.	$31,738	$9280	100%	85%	$32,096	$ 8922	$28,081
Cedarville University	ind.	$19,800	$5010	42%	50%	$15,654	$ 9156	$21,746
Central State University	pub.	$ 5294	$7402	75%	NR	NR	NR	NR
Cleveland Institute of Music	ind.	$29,034	$9334	100%	23%	$18,481	$19,887	$23,657
Cleveland State University	pub.	$ 7920	$7800	87%	10%	$ 7508	$ 8212	NR
College of Mount St. Joseph	ind.	$20,050	$6300	98%	63%	$16,596	$ 9754	$13,400
The College of Wooster	ind.	$30,060	$7520	100%	92%	$25,922	$11,658	$23,527
Columbus College of Art & Design	ind.	$21,346	$6600	100%	21%	$14,550	$13,396	$31,288
Defiance College	ind.	$19,740	$6170	51%	NR	$14,053	$11,857	$17,359
Denison University	ind.	$30,660	$8560	100%	64%	$25,983	$13,237	$15,263
Heidelberg College	ind.	$18,618	$7902	100%	18%	$16,443	$10,077	$30,979
Kent State University	pub.	$ 8430	$6880	79%	14%	$ 7972	$ 7338	$22,230
Kenyon College	ind.	$36,050	$5900	96%	59%	$26,300	$15,650	$20,627
Laura and Alvin Siegal College of Judaic Studies	ind.	$15,775	NA	100%	NR	$ 1000	$14,775	NR
Lourdes College	ind.	$13,200	NA	70%	NR	$ 9530	$ 3670	NR
Malone College	ind.	$17,790	$6400	100%	15%	$13,770	$10,420	$20,505
Miami University	pub.	$10,502	$8140	37%	36%	$17,660	$ 982	$22,255
Mount Union College	ind.	$20,970	$6350	100%	21%	$15,665	$11,655	$18,627
Mount Vernon Nazarene University	ind.	$18,064	$5286	99%	16%	$13,706	$ 9644	$21,719
Oberlin College	ind.	$34,426	$8720	86%	100%	$22,919	$20,227	$16,922
Ohio Northern University	ind.	$28,260	$7080	70%	38%	$23,865	$11,475	$38,203
The Ohio State University	pub.	$ 8559	$6720	89%	30%	$10,391	$ 4888	$18,130
Ohio University	pub.	$ 8847	$7839	41%	14%	$ 5985	$10,701	$19,194
Ohio University–Zanesville	pub.	$ 4596	NA	72%	17%	$ 5862	—	$19,194
Ohio Wesleyan University	ind.	$30,290	$7790	100%	30%	$21,893	$16,187	$22,619
Tiffin University	ind.	$15,870	$6775	51%	17%	$16,949	$ 5696	$19,624
The University of Akron	pub.	$ 8382	$7640	51%	6%	$ 5866	$10,156	$16,105
University of Cincinnati	pub.	$ 9399	$9246	48%	6%	$ 7618	$11,027	$16,794
University of Dayton	ind.	$23,970	$7190	96%	47%	$13,091	$18,069	$20,731

NA = not applicable; NR = not reported; * = includes room and board; † = room only; — = not available.

College Costs At-a-Glance

	Institutional Control ind.=independent; pub.=public	Tuition and Fees	Room and Board	Percent of Eligible Freshmen Receiving Need-Based Gift Awards	Percent of Freshmen Whose Need Was Fully Met	Average Financial Aid Package for Freshmen	Average Net Cost After Aid	Average Indebtedness Upon Graduation
Ohio—*continued*								
The University of Findlay	ind.	$22,796	$7792	100%	20%	$17,213	$13,375	$19,000
University of Phoenix–Cincinnati Campus	ind.	$11,910	NA	61%	NR	$ 1987	$ 9923	NR
University of Phoenix–Cleveland Campus	ind.	$11,910	NA	70%	NR	$ 2732	$ 9178	NR
University of Phoenix–Columbus Ohio Campus	ind.	$10,080	NA	64%	NR	$ 1934	$ 8146	NR
The University of Toledo	pub.	$ 7927	$7894	83%	10%	$ 6364	$ 9457	$21,531
Urbana University	ind.	$16,254	$6612	93%	30%	$13,224	$ 9642	$21,125
Walsh University	ind.	$18,900	$7430	93%	60%	$13,625	$12,705	$18,775
Wittenberg University	ind.	$31,400	$7870	100%	38%	$22,839	$16,431	$24,298
Xavier University	ind.	$23,880	$8640	98%	27%	$15,823	$16,697	$21,753
Youngstown State University	pub.	$ 6697	$6490	NR	NR	NR	NR	NR
Oklahoma								
East Central University	pub.	$ 3496	$3190	68%	35%	$ 4466	$ 2220	$12,196
Northeastern State University	pub.	$ 3489	$3600	71%	66%	$ 5854	$ 1235	$18,981
Northwestern Oklahoma State University	pub.	$ 3450	$3310	87%	52%	$ 4786	$ 1974	$11,478
Oklahoma Baptist University	ind.	$14,666	$4330	94%	44%	$12,627	$ 6369	$16,614
Oklahoma Panhandle State University	pub.	$ 3521	$3200	NR	NR	NR	NR	NR
Oklahoma State University	pub.	$ 4996	$6015	73%	18%	$ 9112	$ 1899	NR
Oral Roberts University	ind.	$17,400	$7350	99%	50%	$18,541	$ 6209	$32,978
St. Gregory's University	ind.	$13,772	$5636	52%	17%	$10,686	$ 8722	$10,160
Southeastern Oklahoma State University	pub.	$ 3574	$5348	61%	38%	$ 1086	$ 7836	$ 6430
Southern Nazarene University	ind.	$15,024	$5378	NR	NR	NR	NR	NR
Southwestern Christian University	ind.	$ 4585	$2400	89%	53%	$ 7925	—	$17,000
University of Central Oklahoma	pub.	$ 3539	$4763	95%	10%	$ 5121	$ 3181	$16,211
University of Oklahoma	pub.	$ 5110	$6863	24%	50%	$ 9234	$ 2739	$19,206
University of Phoenix–Oklahoma City Campus	ind.	$ 9750	NA	82%	NR	$ 2731	$ 7019	NR
University of Phoenix–Tulsa Campus	ind.	$ 9750	NA	82%	NR	$ 2778	$ 6972	NR
University of Science and Arts of Oklahoma	pub.	$ 3720	$4360	96%	14%	$ 6694	$ 1386	$13,129
University of Tulsa	ind.	$21,770	$7404	41%	48%	$22,431	$ 6743	$12,411
Oregon								
The Art Institute of Portland	ind.	$18,630	$8250	44%	1%	$ 4759	$22,121	$39,434
Cascade College	ind.	$12,800	$6120	20%	NR	$12,213	$ 6707	$24,988
Corban College	ind.	$19,294	$7070	100%	10%	$11,964	$14,400	$28,021
Eugene Bible College	ind.	$ 8720	$4805	35%	NR	$ 8811	$ 4714	$10,550
George Fox University	ind.	$23,790	$7600	92%	16%	$16,623	$14,767	$17,903
Lewis & Clark College	ind.	$29,772	$8048	92%	49%	$26,051	$11,769	$19,489
Linfield College	ind.	$24,174	$7080	94%	44%	$18,758	$12,496	$25,447
Northwest Christian College	ind.	$19,890	$6424	100%	20%	$15,379	$10,935	$14,415
Oregon College of Art & Craft	ind.	$17,900	$3600†	67%	17%	$11,743	$ 9757	$32,000
Oregon Health & Science University	pub.	$11,540	NA	NR	NR	NR	NR	NR
Oregon State University	pub.	$ 5643	$7344	79%	28%	$ 9095	$ 3892	$19,550
Pacific Northwest College of Art	ind.	$18,208	$6300	79%	7%	$11,185	$13,323	$22,155
Pacific University	ind.	$26,670	$7170	97%	39%	$18,266	$15,574	$25,581

NA = not applicable; NR = not reported; * = includes room and board; † = room only; — = not available.

College Costs At-a-Glance	Institutional Control ind.=independent; pub.=public	Tuition and Fees	Room and Board	Percent of Eligible Freshmen Receiving Need-Based Gift Awards	Percent of Freshmen Whose Need Was Fully Met	Average Financial Aid Package for Freshmen	Average Net Cost After Aid	Average Indebtedness Upon Graduation
Oregon—*continued*								
Portland State University	pub.	$ 5600	$ 8940	61%	11%	$ 6323	$ 8217	$17,629
Reed College	ind.	$34,530	$ 9000	93%	96%	$28,205	$15,325	$17,175
Southern Oregon University	pub.	$ 4986	$ 6468	87%	17%	$ 7606	$ 3848	$22,851
University of Oregon	pub.	$ 5838	$ 7827	46%	20%	$ 6938	$ 6727	$18,813
University of Phoenix–Oregon Campus	ind.	$10,770	NA	58%	NR	$ 2512	$ 8258	NR
University of Portland	ind.	$26,390	$ 7850	100%	25%	$20,356	$13,884	$22,253
Warner Pacific College	ind.	$22,408	$ 5740	87%	16%	$13,887	$14,261	$24,717
Western Oregon University	pub.	$ 4683	$ 7030	80%	21%	$ 6317	$ 5396	$19,337
Willamette University	ind.	$30,018	$ 7250	98%	25%	$26,019	$11,249	$25,240
Pennsylvania								
Albright College	ind.	$27,420	$ 8158	100%	16%	$ 965	$34,613	$30,992
Allegheny College	ind.	$30,000	$ 7500	100%	40%	$23,500	$14,000	NR
Alvernia College	ind.	$20,422	$ 8193	100%	36%	$13,986	$14,629	$ 6985
Arcadia University	ind.	$25,990	$ 9660	99%	28%	$21,330	$14,320	$32,875
Bloomsburg University of Pennsylvania	pub.	$ 6412	$ 5616	49%	90%	$ 9461	$ 2567	$17,234
Bryn Mawr College	ind.	$33,010	$10,550	100%	100%	$26,815	$16,745	$18,787
Bucknell University	ind.	$38,134	$ 8052	100%	100%	$24,500	$21,686	$17,500
Cabrini College	ind.	$25,950	$ 9900	76%	16%	$18,023	$17,827	$17,515
California University of Pennsylvania	pub.	$ 6586	$ 8144	67%	5%	$ 7735	$ 6995	$21,860
Carnegie Mellon University	ind.	$34,578	$ 9280	96%	36%	$21,613	$22,245	$26,500
Cedar Crest College	ind.	$25,340	$ 8624	100%	13%	$18,901	$15,063	$28,730
Central Pennsylvania College	ind.	$12,165	$ 5925	NR	NR	NR	NR	NR
Chatham University	ind.	$24,808	$ 7586	100%	NR	$21,400	$10,994	$22,895
Chestnut Hill College	ind.	$22,750	$ 7950	90%	1%	$17,121	$13,579	$29,000
Clarion University of Pennsylvania	pub.	$ 6616	$ 5546	80%	14%	$ 6629	$ 5533	$18,628
College Misericordia	ind.	$20,860	$ 8640	99%	16%	$14,324	$15,176	$22,437
Delaware Valley College	ind.	$23,110	$ 8965	100%	21%	$15,663	$16,412	$17,482
DeSales University	ind.	$22,000	$ 8250	82%	54%	$15,566	$14,684	$13,977
Dickinson College	ind.	$35,784	$ 8980	94%	88%	$26,916	$17,848	$19,413
Drexel University	ind.	$33,650	$11,010	39%	14%	$15,921	$28,739	$25,347
Duquesne University	ind.	$22,665	$ 8296	100%	60%	$15,268	$15,693	$27,080
Elizabethtown College	ind.	$29,000	$ 7600	100%	27%	$17,642	$18,958	NR
Franklin & Marshall College	ind.	$34,450	$ 8540	93%	100%	$28,961	$14,029	$23,043
Gannon University	ind.	$19,996	$ 7880	98%	35%	$16,413	$11,463	$20,423
Geneva College	ind.	$19,430	$ 7200	100%	23%	$15,277	$11,353	$26,034
Gettysburg College	ind.	$34,050	$ 8260	100%	100%	$24,487	$17,823	$21,810
Grove City College	ind.	$10,962	$ 5766	100%	14%	$ 5187	$11,541	$22,532
Gwynedd-Mercy College	ind.	$21,000	$ 8600	100%	15%	$12,895	$16,705	$18,877
Haverford College	ind.	$33,710	$10,390	92%	100%	$28,531	$15,569	$15,875
Indiana University of Pennsylvania	pub.	$ 6390	$ 5162	76%	20%	$ 8137	$ 3415	$21,716
Juniata College	ind.	$28,920	$ 8040	93%	23%	$22,124	$14,836	$23,405
King's College	ind.	$22,280	$ 8590	70%	18%	$15,246	$15,624	$25,391

NA = not applicable; NR = not reported; * = includes room and board; † = room only; — = not available.

College Costs At-a-Glance

	Institutional Control ind.=independent; pub.=public	Tuition and Fees	Room and Board	Percent of Eligible Freshmen Receiving Need-Based Gift Awards	Percent of Freshmen Whose Need Was Fully Met	Average Financial Aid Package for Freshmen	Average Net Cost After Aid	Average Indebtedness Upon Graduation
Pennsylvania—*continued*								
Kutztown University of Pennsylvania	pub.	$ 6619	$ 6208	69%	50%	$ 5905	$ 6922	$15,559
Lancaster Bible College	ind.	$13,800	$ 5980	96%	10%	$10,582	$ 9198	$19,229
La Roche College	ind.	$18,220	$ 7564	65%	NR	$14,598	$11,186	$18,000
Lebanon Valley College	ind.	$26,385	$ 7115	99%	35%	$18,510	$14,990	$28,051
Lehigh University	ind.	$33,770	$ 8920	91%	52%	$26,697	$15,993	$25,603
Lincoln University	pub.	$ 7892	$ 7142	76%	35%	$ 7550	$ 7484	$28,858
Lock Haven University of Pennsylvania	pub.	$ 6445	$ 6060	78%	19%	$ 9852	$ 2653	$21,340
Lycoming College	ind.	$25,605	$ 6826	100%	12%	$19,798	$12,633	$23,343
Mansfield University of Pennsylvania	pub.	$ 6676	$ 5934	50%	4%	$ 5303	$ 7307	$19,262
Marywood University	ind.	$24,090	$10,410	100%	17%	$17,301	$17,199	$34,364
Mercyhurst College	ind.	$20,364	$ 7458	100%	79%	$16,288	$11,534	$21,000
Messiah College	ind.	$23,290	$ 7060	88%	26%	$12,349	$18,001	$27,322
Millersville University of Pennsylvania	pub.	$ 6398	$ 6566	79%	19%	$ 6744	$ 6220	$17,885
Moore College of Art & Design	ind.	$26,154	$ 9906	99%	2%	$14,091	$21,969	$36,778
Moravian College	ind.	$26,775	$ 7760	100%	18%	$18,668	$15,867	NR
Mount Aloysius College	ind.	$15,350	$ 6470	100%	NR	$10,845	$10,975	$23,458
Neumann College	ind.	$18,632	$ 8418	92%	65%	$17,000	$10,050	$20,000
Peirce College	ind.	$13,240	NA	5%	95%	$ 4611	$ 8629	$15,662
Penn State Abington	pub.	$10,520	NA	83%	5%	$10,118	$ 402	$23,500
Penn State Altoona	pub.	$10,958	$ 6850	69%	6%	$12,860	$ 4948	$23,500
Penn State Berks	pub.	$10,958	$ 7490	64%	6%	$11,482	$ 6966	$23,500
Penn State Erie, The Behrend College	pub.	$10,958	$ 6850	68%	10%	$13,641	$ 4167	$23,500
Penn State Harrisburg	pub.	$10,948	$ 8430	68%	7%	$14,019	$ 5359	$23,500
Penn State University Park	pub.	$12,164	$ 6850	54%	10%	$14,778	$ 4236	$23,500
Pennsylvania College of Technology	pub.	$10,620	$ 7300	NR	NR	NR	NR	NR
Philadelphia Biblical University	ind.	$15,875	$ 6550	99%	25%	$13,605	$ 8820	NR
Philadelphia University	ind.	$23,818	$ 8212	100%	12%	$17,838	$14,192	$27,991
Robert Morris University	ind.	$16,290	$ 8410	97%	31%	$14,295	$10,405	NR
Rosemont College	ind.	$22,835	$ 9200	100%	13%	$16,135	$15,900	$23,091
Saint Francis University	ind.	$22,224	$ 7640	100%	22%	$16,603	$13,261	$15,600
Saint Joseph's University	ind.	$29,095	$10,170	76%	23%	$12,854	$26,411	$16,120
Saint Vincent College	ind.	$23,000	$ 7242	100%	21%	$19,109	$11,133	NR
Seton Hill University	ind.	$23,380	$ 7230	100%	20%	$18,632	$11,978	$24,657
Shippensburg University of Pennsylvania	pub.	$ 6549	$ 5962	73%	12%	$ 5775	$ 6736	$18,505
Slippery Rock University of Pennsylvania	pub.	$ 6363	$ 4998	69%	44%	$ 7136	$ 4225	$21,025
Swarthmore College	ind.	$33,232	$10,300	100%	100%	$30,596	$12,936	$13,404
Temple University	pub.	$10,180	$ 8230	100%	34%	$13,836	$ 4574	$27,355
Thiel College	ind.	$18,720	$ 7574	100%	35%	$12,924	$13,370	$21,427
Thomas Jefferson University	ind.	$22,884	$ 3021†	67%	4%	NR	NR	$25,975
University of Pennsylvania	ind.	$34,156	$ 9804	92%	100%	$27,948	$16,012	$20,927
University of Phoenix–Philadelphia Campus	ind.	$13,050	NA	65%	NR	$ 2307	$10,743	NR
University of Phoenix–Pittsburgh Campus	ind.	$13,050	NA	66%	NR	$ 2171	$10,879	NR
University of Pittsburgh	pub.	$12,138	$ 7800	80%	42%	$ 9309	$10,629	NR

NA = not applicable; NR = not reported; * = includes room and board; † = room only; — = not available.

College Costs At-a-Glance

	Institutional Control ind.=independent; pub.=public	Tuition and Fees	Room and Board	Percent of Eligible Freshmen Receiving Need-Based Gift Awards	Percent of Freshmen Whose Need Was Fully Met	Average Financial Aid Package for Freshmen	Average Net Cost After Aid	Average Indebtedness Upon Graduation
Pennsylvania—*continued*								
University of Pittsburgh at Bradford	pub.	$10,894	$ 6650	73%	18%	$11,400	$ 6144	$27,684
University of Pittsburgh at Greensburg	pub.	$11,612	$ 6680	82%	57%	$ 8176	$10,116	$15,260
University of Pittsburgh at Johnstown	pub.	$10,876	$ 6200	84%	10%	$ 8638	$ 8438	$23,609
University of the Sciences in Philadelphia	ind.	$25,392	$ 9936	96%	59%	$16,087	$19,241	$36,145
Ursinus College	ind.	$33,350	$ 7600	100%	75%	$22,364	$18,586	$26,997
Valley Forge Christian College	ind.	$12,600	$ 6742	95%	8%	$ 7373	$11,969	$24,253
Villanova University	ind.	$31,135	$ 9560	91%	23%	$22,149	$18,546	$28,549
Washington & Jefferson College	ind.	$28,080	$ 7602	87%	19%	$19,380	$16,302	$20,000
Waynesburg College	ind.	$15,780	$ 6370	100%	22%	$12,743	$ 9407	$20,000
Westminster College	ind.	$24,325	$ 7070	98%	26%	$21,108	$10,287	$23,592
Widener University	ind.	$26,750	$ 9640	88%	21%	$21,998	$14,392	$29,514
Wilkes University	ind.	$22,990	$ 9860	100%	12%	$17,746	$15,104	$27,729
Wilson College	ind.	$21,830	$ 7916	100%	24%	$15,863	$13,883	$26,224
York College of Pennsylvania	ind.	$11,160	$ 6950	73%	29%	$ 8611	$ 9499	$20,639
Puerto Rico								
Pontifical Catholic University of Puerto Rico	ind.	$ 5098	$ 3565	98%	3%	$ 6930	$ 1733	$ 3500
University of Phoenix–Puerto Rico Campus	ind.	$ 5880	NA	80%	NR	$ 3272	$ 2608	NR
Rhode Island								
Bryant University	ind.	$27,639	$10,715	84%	16%	$16,731	$21,623	$29,128
Johnson & Wales University	ind.	$21,462	$ 7650	91%	2%	$14,058	$15,054	$17,704
Providence College	ind.	$27,345	$ 9765	93%	21%	$18,901	$18,209	NR
Roger Williams University	ind.	$25,759	$10,943	70%	53%	$15,111	$21,591	$28,147
Salve Regina University	ind.	$25,175	$ 9800	96%	11%	$18,616	$16,359	$24,631
University of Rhode Island	pub.	$ 7724	$ 8466	100%	86%	$13,735	$ 2455	$16,200
South Carolina								
Anderson University	ind.	$17,850	$ 7000	99%	30%	$16,985	$ 7865	$15,125
The Citadel, The Military College of South Carolina	pub.	$ 8168	$ 5090	70%	7%	$ 8364	$ 4894	$16,127
Claflin University	ind.	$11,764	$ 6322	95%	11%	$10,930	$ 7156	$19,993
Clemson University	pub.	$ 9868	$ 5874	38%	34%	$11,217	$ 4525	NR
Coastal Carolina University	pub.	$ 7500	$ 6690	37%	14%	$ 6479	$ 7711	$24,250
College of Charleston	pub.	$ 7234	$ 7596	73%	36%	$10,035	$ 4795	$16,761
Columbia College	ind.	$20,302	$ 6022	98%	71%	$21,723	$ 4601	$25,333
Columbia International University	ind.	$14,400	$ 5712	100%	8%	$10,874	$ 9238	$21,678
Converse College	ind.	$22,234	$ 6848	100%	38%	$19,681	$ 9401	$20,861
Erskine College	ind.	$20,275	$ 6951	95%	49%	$19,100	$ 8126	$16,940
Francis Marion University	pub.	$ 7038	$ 5860	71%	NR	NR	NR	$20,640
Furman University	ind.	$28,840	$ 7552	100%	36%	$24,282	$12,110	$24,538
Limestone College	ind.	$15,900	$ 6200	99%	19%	$10,738	$11,362	$16,761
Newberry College	ind.	$20,891	$ 6890	100%	32%	$13,857	$13,924	$13,477
North Greenville University	ind.	$11,180	NR	NR	NR	NR	NR	NR
Southern Methodist College	ind.	$ 5800	$ 4400	100%	NR	$ 2025	$ 8175	$12,600
Southern Wesleyan University	ind.	$16,150	$ 5800	100%	37%	$13,314	$ 8636	$18,072

NA = not applicable; NR = not reported; * = includes room and board; † = room only; — = not available.

College Costs At-a-Glance

	Institutional Control ind.=independent; pub.=public	Tuition and Fees	Room and Board	Percent of Eligible Freshmen Receiving Need-Based Gift Awards	Percent of Freshmen Whose Need Was Fully Met	Average Financial Aid Package for Freshmen	Average Net Cost After Aid	Average Indebtedness Upon Graduation
South Carolina—*continued*								
University of South Carolina	pub.	$ 7808	$6520	42%	32%	$ 9448	$ 4880	$19,360
University of South Carolina Upstate	pub.	$ 7314	$5240	59%	19%	$ 8424	$ 4130	$19,359
Winthrop University	pub.	$ 9500	$5570	96%	22%	$ 9737	$ 5333	NR
Wofford College	ind.	$26,110	$7260	100%	54%	$21,456	$11,914	$10,242
South Dakota								
Augustana College	ind.	$19,986	$5664	100%	17%	$17,137	$ 8513	$26,006
Black Hills State University	pub.	$ 5335	$3988	NR	NR	NR	NR	$19,266
Dakota State University	pub.	$ 5699	$3927	48%	16%	$ 5754	$ 3872	$23,250
Dakota Wesleyan University	ind.	$17,500	$5400	100%	20%	$12,787	$10,113	$24,000
Mount Marty College	ind.	$16,582	$4958	99%	17%	$14,336	$ 7204	$26,304
Northern State University	pub.	$ 4962	$4102	89%	100%	$ 6627	$ 2437	$21,123
Presentation College	ind.	$12,300	$4775	72%	18%	$ 7357	$ 9718	$21,152
South Dakota State University	pub.	$ 5052	$5029	52%	71%	$ 6364	$ 3717	$20,682
The University of South Dakota	pub.	$ 5380	$4964	43%	82%	$ 4200	$ 6144	$20,163
Tennessee								
American Baptist College of American Baptist Theological Seminary	ind.	$ 4172	$1600†	100%	NR	$ 2025	$ 3747	NR
Austin Peay State University	pub.	$ 4837	$5190	51%	NR	$ 6551	$ 3476	NR
Belmont University	ind.	$19,780	$9529	57%	32%	$10,031	$19,278	$10,200
Bryan College	ind.	$16,320	$4540	70%	44%	$14,284	$ 6576	$12,588
Carson-Newman College	ind.	$16,060	$5200	99%	33%	$14,645	$ 6615	$10,870
Christian Brothers University	ind.	$20,080	$5650	51%	32%	$18,951	$ 6779	$26,539
Cumberland University	ind.	$15,510	$5313	49%	18%	$11,755	$ 9068	$21,562
East Tennessee State University	pub.	$ 4637	$5024	87%	33%	$ 7402	$ 2259	$19,707
Freed-Hardeman University	ind.	$13,192	$6560	99%	29%	$11,541	$ 8211	$30,584
Free Will Baptist Bible College	ind.	$11,166	$4708	NR	NR	NR	NR	$14,509
Johnson Bible College	ind.	$ 6830	$4490	99%	NR	$ 5047	$ 6273	$11,425
King College	ind.	$19,262	$6508	100%	33%	$16,372	$ 9398	$18,635
Lambuth University	ind.	$17,400	$7160	96%	36%	$18,465	$ 6095	$19,008
Lee University	ind.	$10,258	$5024	9%	26%	$ 8591	$ 6691	$27,308
LeMoyne-Owen College	ind.	$10,318	$4568	95%	4%	$ 7197	$ 7689	$13,354
Lipscomb University	ind.	$15,566	$6730	40%	28%	$12,485	$ 9811	$25,589
Maryville College	ind.	$23,800	$7400	100%	34%	$23,787	$ 7413	$18,473
Memphis College of Art	ind.	$20,660	$5760†	65%	29%	$ 6625	$19,795	$34,360
Middle Tennessee State University	pub.	$ 4670	$5626	52%	57%	$ 7800	$ 2496	$21,301
Milligan College	ind.	$18,320	$5030	33%	50%	$14,551	$ 8799	$18,500
Rhodes College	ind.	$29,112	$7180	100%	55%	$25,656	$10,636	$23,710
Sewanee: The University of the South	ind.	$30,660	$8780	100%	77%	$24,809	$14,631	$16,866
Southern Adventist University	ind.	$15,596	$4734	59%	50%	$16,414	$ 3916	$10,935
Tennessee State University	pub.	$ 4564	$5000	66%	47%	$ 6485	$ 3079	$21,644
Tennessee Technological University	pub.	$ 4590	$5964	54%	30%	$ 8466	$ 2088	$15,195
Tennessee Wesleyan College	ind.	$15,550	$5700	100%	23%	$12,076	$ 9174	$16,490
Trevecca Nazarene University	ind.	$14,774	$6470	96%	26%	$10,502	$10,742	$16,072

NA = not applicable; NR = not reported; * = includes room and board; † = room only; — = not available.

College Costs At-a-Glance

	Institutional Control ind.=independent; pub.=public	Tuition and Fees	Room and Board	Percent of Eligible Freshmen Receiving Need-Based Gift Awards	Percent of Freshmen Whose Need Was Fully Met	Average Financial Aid Package for Freshmen	Average Net Cost After Aid	Average Indebtedness Upon Graduation
Tennessee—*continued*								
Tusculum College	ind.	$16,215	$ 6500	72%	4%	$10,336	$12,379	$20,928
Union University	ind.	$17,900	NR	72%	NR	$16,748	$ 1152	$21,088
University of Phoenix–Nashville Campus	ind.	$10,470	NR	68%	NR	$ 2406	$ 8064	NR
The University of Tennessee	pub.	$ 5864	$ 6358	95%	35%	$ 8910	$ 3312	$18,254
The University of Tennessee at Martin	pub.	$ 4665	$ 4410	63%	44%	$ 9368	—	$22,854
Vanderbilt University	ind.	$33,440	$10,890	91%	96%	$34,594	$ 9736	$19,429
Watkins College of Art and Design	ind.	$12,720	$ 5600†	58%	5%	$ 4778	$13,542	$18,000
Texas								
Abilene Christian University	ind.	$17,410	$ 6350	100%	23%	$11,546	$12,214	$27,980
Arlington Baptist College	ind.	$ 6090	$ 4100	NR	91%	$ 8062	$ 2128	$ 8100
Austin College	ind.	$24,945	$ 8234	99%	100%	$24,107	$ 9072	NR
Austin Graduate School of Theology	ind.	$ 6150	NA	NR	NR	NR	NR	$11,625
Baylor University	ind.	$24,490	$ 7526	97%	19%	$15,591	$16,425	NR
The College of Saint Thomas More	ind.	$12,000	$ 3690†	33%	83%	$ 8600	$ 7090	$ 9250
Concordia University at Austin	ind.	$18,910	$ 7300	88%	27%	$14,034	$12,176	$20,202
Dallas Baptist University	ind.	$13,650	$ 4959	71%	53%	$11,553	$ 7056	$19,679
Dallas Christian College	ind.	$ 8850	$ 5500	NR	NR	$ 5700	$ 8650	$15,000
East Texas Baptist University	ind.	$13,700	$ 4190	100%	29%	$11,566	$ 6324	$18,551
Hardin-Simmons University	ind.	$16,946	$ 4950	77%	15%	$12,172	$ 9724	$24,837
Houston Baptist University	ind.	$17,716	$ 4995	97%	18%	$13,128	$ 9583	$17,256
Lamar University	pub.	$ 4080	$ 5888	NR	17%	$ 1391	$ 8577	$ 7408
LeTourneau University	ind.	$16,920	$ 6570	100%	15%	$11,611	$11,879	NR
Lubbock Christian University	ind.	$14,290	$ 4750	100%	15%	$11,506	$ 7534	$22,814
McMurry University	ind.	$16,300	$ 6425	96%	17%	$19,763	$ 2962	$22,446
Midwestern State University	pub.	$ 4716	$ 5220	84%	18%	$ 6190	$ 3746	$17,882
Northwood University, Texas Campus	ind.	$16,455	$ 6888	78%	19%	$15,449	$ 7894	$16,206
Rice University	ind.	$28,900	$10,250	100%	100%	$23,754	$15,396	$15,873
St. Edward's University	ind.	$20,400	$ 7460	95%	36%	$16,278	$11,582	$25,832
Sam Houston State University	pub.	$ 4896	$ 5880	54%	3%	$ 5658	$ 5118	$16,948
Southern Methodist University	ind.	$30,880	$10,825	78%	46%	$25,764	$15,941	$17,424
Southwestern University	ind.	$25,740	$ 8710	99%	58%	$22,249	$12,201	$22,652
Stephen F. Austin State University	pub.	$ 5232	$ 6544	84%	20%	$ 4361	$ 7415	$19,177
Tarleton State University	pub.	$ 4626	$ 5802	48%	59%	$ 7874	$ 2554	$16,776
Texas A&M University	pub.	$ 6966	$ 7660	92%	66%	$11,418	$ 3208	$16,027
Texas A&M University at Galveston	pub.	$ 4743	$ 4870	54%	24%	$11,057	—	$15,793
Texas A&M University–Commerce	pub.	$ 5242	$ 5740	100%	28%	$ 7292	$ 3690	$19,032
Texas A&M University–Corpus Christi	pub.	$ 5148	NR	86%	11%	$ 6974	—	$18,625
Texas A&M University–Texarkana	pub.	$ 2644	NA	NR	NR	NR	NR	NR
Texas Christian University	ind.	$23,020	$ 7520	90%	48%	$14,337	$16,203	$23,220
Texas Lutheran University	ind.	$18,840	$ 5600	91%	26%	$14,256	$10,184	$26,707
Texas Southern University	pub.	$ 4998	$ 6402	85%	29%	$14,065	—	$25,310
Texas State University-San Marcos	pub.	$ 5652	$ 5878	69%	14%	$10,209	$ 1321	$16,420

NA = not applicable; NR = not reported; * = includes room and board; † = room only; — = not available.

College Costs At-a-Glance

	Institutional Control ind.=independent; pub.=public	Tuition and Fees	Room and Board	Percent of Eligible Freshmen Receiving Need-Based Gift Awards	Percent of Freshmen Whose Need Was Fully Met	Average Financial Aid Package for Freshmen	Average Net Cost After Aid	Average Indebtedness Upon Graduation
Texas—*continued*								
Texas Tech University	pub.	$ 6459	$ 7288	46%	6%	$ 5812	$ 7935	$21,355
Texas Woman's University	pub.	$ 5832	$ 5846	66%	68%	$ 9712	$ 1966	$19,409
University of Dallas	ind.	$23,267	$ 7615	100%	31%	$18,840	$12,042	$24,737
University of Houston–Victoria	pub.	$ 4680	NA	NR	NR	NR	NR	NR
University of Mary Hardin-Baylor	ind.	$15,660	$ 5728	88%	24%	$10,113	$11,275	$15,819
University of Phoenix–Dallas Campus	ind.	$11,190	NA	66%	NR	$ 2509	$ 8681	NR
University of Phoenix–Houston Campus	ind.	$11,190	NA	60%	NR	$ 2872	$ 8318	NR
University of St. Thomas	ind.	$17,868	$ 6700	99%	16%	$13,452	$11,116	$19,668
The University of Texas at Arlington	pub.	$ 6400	$ 5553	69%	16%	$ 7898	$ 4055	$16,780
The University of Texas at Austin	pub.	$ 7630	$ 8176	98%	89%	$ 9800	$ 6006	$16,800
The University of Texas at Brownsville	pub.	$ 3657	$ 2300†	94%	NR	$ 2915	$ 3042	NR
The University of Texas at Dallas	pub.	$ 7570	$ 6540	69%	68%	$12,179	$ 1931	$16,895
The University of Texas at El Paso	pub.	$ 5262	$ 4185†	90%	19%	$ 8691	$ 756	$ 6538
The University of Texas at San Antonio	pub.	$ 6699	$ 8169	79%	22%	$ 6644	$ 8224	$16,888
The University of Texas at Tyler	pub.	$ 4476	NR	84%	16%	$ 6442	—	$11,286
The University of Texas Medical Branch	pub.	$ 4302	$ 3060†	NR	NR	NR	NR	$25,083
The University of Texas–Pan American	pub.	$ 4165	$ 5095	95%	6%	$ 7324	$ 1936	$12,630
The University of Texas Southwestern Medical Center at Dallas	pub.	$ 4105	NA	NR	NR	NR	NR	$36,000
University of the Incarnate Word	ind.	$19,060	$ 6994	100%	62%	$14,050	$12,004	$31,681
Wayland Baptist University	ind.	$10,800	$ 3584	99%	16%	$ 9195	$ 5189	$23,896
Utah								
Brigham Young University	ind.	$ 7680	$ 6460	53%	NR	$ 2331	$11,809	$13,714
Southern Utah University	pub.	$ 4068	$ 4154	100%	12%	$ 4710	$ 3512	$ 9223
University of Phoenix–Utah Campus	ind.	$10,200	NA	61%	NR	$ 2597	$ 7603	NR
University of Utah	pub.	$ 4663	$ 5828	75%	16%	$ 7506	$ 2985	$12,806
Utah State University	pub.	$ 3949	$ 4400	52%	25%	$ 5680	$ 2669	$11,040
Westminster College	ind.	$21,030	$ 6140	100%	85%	$15,920	$11,250	$16,450
Vermont								
Bennington College	ind.	$36,800	$ 9380	95%	5%	$24,825	$21,355	$25,463
Burlington College	ind.	$15,760	$ 4500†	50%	NR	$ 7816	$12,444	$40,153
Champlain College	ind.	$22,550	$10,910	63%	NR	$ 6658	$26,802	NR
College of St. Joseph	ind.	$14,900	$ 7150	100%	9%	$13,043	$ 9007	$28,522
Goddard College	ind.	$11,442	NA	56%	NR	$ 4672	$ 6770	$23,054
Green Mountain College	ind.	$23,329	$ 8426	100%	22%	$18,730	$13,025	$28,026
Lyndon State College	pub.	$ 6828	$ 6942	68%	17%	$ 8843	$ 4927	NR
Marlboro College	ind.	$30,680	$ 8860	100%	NR	NR	NR	$18,404
Middlebury College	ind.	*$44,330	NR	100%	100%	$29,286	$15,044	$12,322
Saint Michael's College	ind.	$28,515	$ 6990	99%	14%	$24,067	$11,438	$22,264
Southern Vermont College	ind.	$15,100	$ 7350	94%	10%	$14,074	$ 8376	$20,244
Sterling College	ind.	$17,780	$ 6520	100%	20%	$17,547	$ 6753	$15,880
University of Vermont	pub.	$11,324	$ 7642	89%	24%	$16,068	$ 2898	$23,328
Vermont Technical College	pub.	$ 8704	$ 6942	79%	21%	$ 9238	$ 6408	$25,456

NA = not applicable; NR = not reported; * = includes room and board; † = room only; — = not available.

College Costs At-a-Glance

	Institutional Control ind.=independent; pub.=public	Tuition and Fees	Room and Board	Percent of Eligible Freshmen Receiving Need-Based Gift Awards	Percent of Freshmen Whose Need Was Fully Met	Average Financial Aid Package for Freshmen	Average Net Cost After Aid	Average Indebtedness Upon Graduation
Vermont—*continued*								
Woodbury College	ind.	$15,900	NA	100%	14%	$ 8580	$ 7320	$21,879
Virgin Islands								
University of the Virgin Islands	pub.	$ 3726	$ 7550	94%	3%	$ 4145	$ 7131	$ 8782
Virginia								
Averett University	ind.	$20,512	$ 7100	98%	20%	$12,837	$14,775	$29,813
Bridgewater College	ind.	$21,490	$ 9310	100%	31%	$18,869	$11,931	$24,601
Christendom College	ind.	$16,740	$ 6066	98%	100%	$13,500	$ 9306	$16,180
Christopher Newport University	pub.	$ 9106	$ 8100	73%	24%	$ 5930	$11,276	$16,534
The College of William and Mary	pub.	$ 8490	$ 6932	74%	44%	$12,312	$ 3110	$14,524
Emory & Henry College	ind.	$20,860	$ 7360	99%	30%	$19,173	$ 9047	$13,312
George Mason University	pub.	$ 6408	$ 6750	75%	14%	$ 8397	$ 4761	$15,791
Hampden-Sydney College	ind.	$27,732	$ 8671	100%	37%	$18,564	$17,839	$16,244
Hampton University	ind.	$14,818	$ 6746	46%	83%	$ 2893	$18,671	$ 3645
Hollins University	ind.	$24,325	$ 8650	100%	25%	$18,826	$14,149	$16,853
James Madison University	pub.	$ 6290	$ 6756	50%	93%	$ 6693	$ 6353	$11,932
Jefferson College of Health Sciences	ind.	$13,860	$ 3600†	100%	7%	$ 9999	$ 7461	$20,780
Longwood University	pub.	$ 7589	$ 6058	95%	27%	$ 8094	$ 5553	NR
Lynchburg College	ind.	$25,265	$ 7000	100%	30%	$18,519	$13,746	$18,517
Mary Baldwin College	ind.	$21,450	$ 6100	96%	62%	$23,300	$ 4250	$23,598
Marymount University	ind.	$19,199	$ 8212	85%	17%	$15,233	$12,178	$24,661
Radford University	pub.	$ 5746	$ 6218	64%	32%	$ 7407	$ 4557	$14,729
Randolph College	ind.	$24,410	$ 8800	100%	46%	$23,152	$10,058	$26,650
Randolph-Macon College	ind.	$25,345	$ 7695	100%	25%	$19,042	$13,998	$15,130
Roanoke College	ind.	$24,653	$ 8152	80%	23%	$21,013	$11,792	$21,807
Shenandoah University	ind.	$21,240	$ 7650	52%	19%	$15,063	$13,827	$19,518
Southern Virginia University	ind.	$16,500	$ 4900	98%	18%	$ 8395	$13,005	$15,444
Sweet Briar College	ind.	$25,015	$10,040	NR	NR	$16,143	$18,912	$ 5496
University of Phoenix–Richmond Campus	ind.	$11,820	NR	61%	NR	$ 1890	$ 9930	NR
University of Richmond	ind.	$37,610	$ 7200	99%	95%	$31,115	$13,695	$17,165
University of Virginia	pub.	$ 7845	$ 6909	86%	100%	$15,553	—	$12,726
Virginia Commonwealth University	pub.	$ 4227	$ 7473	80%	4%	$ 7285	$ 4415	$20,737
Virginia Intermont College	ind.	$17,845	$ 6095	14%	10%	$11,514	$12,426	$20,051
Virginia Military Institute	pub.	$ 7609	$ 5930	85%	35%	$12,749	$ 790	$11,754
Virginia Polytechnic Institute and State University	pub.	$ 6973	$ 4700	76%	14%	$ 8786	$ 2887	$19,807
Virginia State University	pub.	$ 5440	$ 6884	75%	30%	$ 8452	$ 3872	$28,250
Virginia Wesleyan College	ind.	$23,136	$ 6850	40%	3%	$17,594	$12,392	$18,604
Washington and Lee University	ind.	$31,875	$ 8920	89%	93%	$28,588	$12,207	$21,846
Washington								
Antioch University Seattle	ind.	$15,105	NA	NR	NR	NR	NR	$15,999
Bastyr University	ind.	$16,365	$ 3650†	NR	NR	NR	NR	$30,000
Central Washington University	pub.	$ 5238	$ 7140	73%	28%	$ 7238	$ 5140	$14,591
Gonzaga University	ind.	$25,012	$ 7220	100%	27%	$18,076	$14,156	$23,416

NA = not applicable; NR = not reported; * = includes room and board; † = room only; — = not available.

College Costs At-a-Glance

	Institutional Control ind.=independent; pub.=public	Tuition and Fees	Room and Board	Percent of Eligible Freshmen Receiving Need-Based Gift Awards	Percent of Freshmen Whose Need Was Fully Met	Average Financial Aid Package for Freshmen	Average Net Cost After Aid	Average Indebtedness Upon Graduation
Washington—*continued*								
Northwest University	ind.	$19,762	$6578	100%	24%	$13,577	$12,763	$20,133
Pacific Lutheran University	ind.	$23,450	$7140	76%	43%	$22,190	$ 8400	$22,101
Saint Martin's University	ind.	$20,965	$6400	100%	47%	$19,549	$ 7816	$27,846
Seattle Pacific University	ind.	$23,391	$7818	98%	15%	$19,043	$12,166	$22,709
Seattle University	ind.	$24,615	$7503	54%	11%	$23,000	$ 9118	$18,329
University of Phoenix–Spokane Campus	ind.	$10,260	NA	68%	NR	$ 2144	$ 8116	NR
University of Phoenix–Washington Campus	ind.	$11,190	NA	54%	NR	$ 2506	$ 8684	NR
University of Puget Sound	ind.	$30,060	$7670	98%	31%	$23,409	$14,321	$26,762
University of Washington	pub.	$ 5988	$6561	63%	66%	$11,000	$ 1549	$15,900
Walla Walla College	ind.	$21,014	$4710	83%	23%	$16,300	$ 9424	$32,283
Washington State University	pub.	$ 6447	$6890	53%	27%	$ 8297	$ 5040	NR
Western Washington University	pub.	$ 5002	$6785	82%	31%	$ 8879	$ 2908	$14,887
Whitman College	ind.	$30,806	$7840	100%	84%	$22,000	$16,646	$16,300
Whitworth University	ind.	$25,692	$7294	98%	22%	$16,975	$16,011	$18,478
West Virginia								
Alderson-Broaddus College	ind.	$19,090	$6160	100%	24%	$17,817	$ 7433	$26,459
Bethany College	ind.	$18,205	$7770	NR	NR	NR	NR	$18,500
Bluefield State College	pub.	$ 3648	NA	100%	58%	$ 5800	—	$17,500
Concord University	pub.	$ 4084	$6070	72%	37%	$ 7384	$ 2770	$12,989
Davis & Elkins College	ind.	$17,730	$6300	64%	27%	$13,003	$11,027	$23,973
Glenville State College	pub.	$ 4042	$5370	75%	17%	$ 7903	$ 1509	$17,057
Marshall University	pub.	$ 4150	$6492	66%	35%	$ 7158	$ 3484	$16,639
Mountain State University	ind.	$ 7800	$5636	84%	3%	$ 4844	$ 8592	$29,045
Ohio Valley University	ind.	$14,262	$5860	41%	NR	$ 9500	$10,622	$15,000
Salem International University	ind.	$12,660	$5360	71%	58%	$11,535	$ 6485	$15,794
Shepherd University	pub.	$ 4348	$6456	47%	NR	$ 7677	$ 3127	$17,357
University of Charleston	ind.	$21,000	$7600	45%	39%	$17,500	$11,100	$24,310
West Liberty State College	pub.	$ 3996	$5734	NR	NR	NR	NR	$13,800
West Virginia University	pub.	$ 4476	$6630	57%	45%	$ 4911	$ 6195	$20,100
West Virginia Wesleyan College	ind.	$20,980	$6160	100%	32%	$20,750	$ 6390	$19,090
Wheeling Jesuit University	ind.	$23,490	$7230	81%	40%	$21,339	$ 9381	$23,218
Wisconsin								
Alverno College	ind.	$17,296	$6106	NR	NR	NR	NR	NR
Bellin College of Nursing	ind.	$15,839	NA	NR	NR	NR	NR	$23,702
Beloit College	ind.	$28,350	$6162	98%	100%	$22,425	$12,087	$22,424
Carroll College	ind.	$20,830	$6350	100%	50%	$15,067	$12,113	$19,267
Carthage College	ind.	$23,650	$6800	100%	25%	$15,031	$15,419	NR
Concordia University Wisconsin	ind.	$18,140	$6860	95%	33%	$19,205	$ 5795	$21,030
Edgewood College	ind.	$19,080	$6535	99%	21%	$13,363	$12,252	$24,727
Lakeland College	ind.	$17,595	$6145	99%	22%	$13,183	$10,557	NR
Lawrence University	ind.	$29,598	$6882	100%	79%	$23,800	$12,680	$22,626
Maranatha Baptist Bible College	ind.	$ 9030	$5150	60%	4%	$ 6084	$ 8096	$13,689

NA = not applicable; NR = not reported; * = includes room and board; † = room only; — = not available.

College Costs At-a-Glance

	Institutional Control ind.=independent; pub.=public	Tuition and Fees	Room and Board	Percent of Eligible Freshmen Receiving Need-Based Gift Awards	Percent of Freshmen Whose Need Was Fully Met	Average Financial Aid Package for Freshmen	Average Net Cost After Aid	Average Indebtedness Upon Graduation
Wisconsin—*continued*								
Marian College of Fond du Lac	ind.	$17,625	$5200	100%	32%	$18,191	$ 4634	$21,500
Marquette University	ind.	$25,074	$8120	89%	37%	$18,761	$14,433	$25,753
Milwaukee School of Engineering	ind.	$25,980	$6501	100%	15%	$16,759	$15,722	$34,862
Mount Mary College	ind.	$19,204	$6195	100%	8%	$13,647	$11,752	$18,125
Northland College	ind.	$21,901	$6160	98%	18%	$17,050	$11,011	$20,911
Ripon College	ind.	$22,437	$6060	100%	48%	$19,019	$ 9478	$19,468
St. Norbert College	ind.	$23,497	$6319	97%	38%	$17,598	$12,218	$24,808
Silver Lake College	ind.	$18,288	$4650†	100%	27%	$14,873	$ 8065	$19,116
University of Phoenix–Wisconsin Campus	ind.	$11,010	NA	73%	NR	$ 2650	$ 8360	NR
University of Wisconsin–Green Bay	pub.	$ 5716	$4700	64%	37%	$ 7559	$ 2857	$17,000
University of Wisconsin–La Crosse	pub.	$ 5555	$4970	43%	17%	$ 4692	$ 5833	$16,793
University of Wisconsin–Madison	pub.	$ 6726	$6920	74%	33%	$11,469	$ 2177	$20,282
University of Wisconsin–Milwaukee	pub.	$ 7392	$5314	37%	25%	$ 5275	$ 7431	$16,683
University of Wisconsin–Parkside	pub.	$ 5386	$5277	54%	15%	$ 5273	$ 5390	NR
University of Wisconsin–Stevens Point	pub.	$ 5459	$4542	49%	68%	$ 5462	$ 4539	$17,025
University of Wisconsin–Stout	pub.	$ 6963	$4884	42%	49%	$ 7402	$ 4445	$21,665
University of Wisconsin–Superior	pub.	$ 5567	$4576	45%	30%	$ 5303	$ 4840	$20,114
University of Wisconsin–Whitewater	pub.	$ 6407	$4190	40%	44%	$ 5691	$ 4906	$17,712
Wisconsin Lutheran College	ind.	$19,564	$6910	100%	21%	$14,213	$12,261	$14,028
Wyoming								
University of Wyoming	pub.	$ 3554	$7274	46%	15%	$ 6702	$ 4126	$16,855

NA = not applicable; NR = not reported; * = includes room and board; † = room only; — = not available.

Profiles of College Financial Aid Programs

ABILENE CHRISTIAN UNIVERSITY

Abilene, TX

Tuition & fees: $17,410 **Average undergraduate aid package: $11,431**

ABOUT THE INSTITUTION Independent religious, coed. Awards: associate, bachelor's, master's, doctoral, and first professional degrees and post-bachelor's and post-master's certificates. 78 undergraduate majors. Total enrollment: 4,777. Undergraduates: 4,145. Freshmen: 964. Federal methodology is used as a basis for awarding need-based institutional aid.

UNDERGRADUATE EXPENSES for 2007–08 ***Application fee:*** $25. ***Comprehensive fee:*** $23,760 includes full-time tuition ($16,710), mandatory fees ($700), and room and board ($6350). ***College room only:*** $2950. ***Part-time tuition:*** $557 per semester hour. ***Part-time fees:*** $33.50 per semester hour; $10 per term.

FRESHMAN FINANCIAL AID (Fall 2006, est.) 914 applied for aid; of those 64% were deemed to have need. 100% of freshmen with need received aid; of those 23% had need fully met. ***Average percent of need met:*** 68% (excluding resources awarded to replace EFC). ***Average financial aid package:*** $11,546 (excluding resources awarded to replace EFC). 31% of all full-time freshmen had no need and received non-need-based gift aid.

UNDERGRADUATE FINANCIAL AID (Fall 2006, est.) 3,797 applied for aid; of those 61% were deemed to have need. 100% of undergraduates with need received aid; of those 23% had need fully met. ***Average percent of need met:*** 68% (excluding resources awarded to replace EFC). ***Average financial aid package:*** $11,431 (excluding resources awarded to replace EFC). 28% of all full-time undergraduates had no need and received non-need-based gift aid.

GIFT AID (NEED-BASED) ***Total amount:*** $18,016,268 (18% federal, 23% state, 53% institutional, 6% external sources). ***Receiving aid:*** Freshmen: 61% (587); All full-time undergraduates: 57% (2,240). ***Average award:*** Freshmen: $9604; Undergraduates: $8260. ***Scholarships, grants, and awards:*** Federal Pell, FSEOG, state, private, college/university gift aid from institutional funds, United Negro College Fund.

GIFT AID (NON-NEED-BASED) ***Total amount:*** $7,032,664 (1% federal, 1% state, 84% institutional, 14% external sources). ***Receiving aid:*** Freshmen: 60% (576); Undergraduates: 50% (1,981). ***Average award:*** Freshmen: $6117; Undergraduates: $6007. ***Scholarships, grants, and awards by category:*** *Academic Interests/Achievement:* agriculture, biological sciences, business, communication, education, English, foreign languages, general academic interests/achievements, mathematics, physical sciences, religion/biblical studies, social sciences. *Creative Arts/Performance:* art/fine arts, debating, journalism/publications, music, theater/drama. *Special Achievements/Activities:* cheerleading/drum major, leadership. *Special Characteristics:* 873 awards ($2,762,377 total): children of faculty/staff, ethnic background, first-generation college students, local/state students, members of minority groups, out-of-state students, previous college experience, relatives of clergy, religious affiliation.

LOANS ***Student loans:*** $21,983,521 (36% need-based, 64% non-need-based). 70% of past graduating class borrowed through all loan programs. *Average indebtedness per student:* $27,980. ***Average need-based loan:*** Freshmen: $2648; Undergraduates: $4047. ***Parent loans:*** $5,413,402 (100% non-need-based). ***Programs:*** FFEL (Subsidized and Unsubsidized Stafford, PLUS), Perkins, state, college/university.

WORK-STUDY ***Federal work-study:*** Total amount: $400,774; 440 jobs averaging $1454. ***State or other work-study/employment:*** Total amount: $1,536,882 (3% need-based, 97% non-need-based). Part-time jobs available.

ATHLETIC AWARDS Total amount: $2,497,862 (47% need-based, 53% non-need-based).

APPLYING FOR FINANCIAL AID ***Required financial aid forms:*** FAFSA, institution's own form. ***Financial aid deadline (priority):*** 3/1. ***Notification date:*** Continuous beginning 4/1. Students must reply within 3 weeks of notification.

CONTACT Michael Lewis, Director of Student Financial Services, Abilene Christian University, ACU Box 29007, Abilene, TX 79699-9007, 325-674-2643 or toll-free 800-460-6228. *E-mail:* moll06g@acu.edu.

ACADEMY OF ART UNIVERSITY

San Francisco, CA

Tuition & fees: $14,680 **Average undergraduate aid package: $5875**

ABOUT THE INSTITUTION Proprietary, coed. Awards: associate, bachelor's, and master's degrees. 26 undergraduate majors. Total enrollment: 9,483. Undergraduates: 7,438. Freshmen: 984. Federal methodology is used as a basis for awarding need-based institutional aid.

UNDERGRADUATE EXPENSES for 2007–08 ***Application fee:*** $100. ***Comprehensive fee:*** $27,280 includes full-time tuition ($14,400), mandatory fees ($280), and room and board ($12,600). ***Part-time tuition:*** $600 per credit.

FRESHMAN FINANCIAL AID (Fall 2005) 383 applied for aid; of those 84% were deemed to have need. 98% of freshmen with need received aid; of those 1% had need fully met. ***Average percent of need met:*** 23% (excluding resources awarded to replace EFC). ***Average financial aid package:*** $4685 (excluding resources awarded to replace EFC).

UNDERGRADUATE FINANCIAL AID (Fall 2005) 2,365 applied for aid; of those 88% were deemed to have need. 98% of undergraduates with need received aid; of those 2% had need fully met. ***Average percent of need met:*** 29% (excluding resources awarded to replace EFC). ***Average financial aid package:*** $5875 (excluding resources awarded to replace EFC).

GIFT AID (NEED-BASED) ***Total amount:*** $7,174,840 (76% federal, 24% state). ***Receiving aid:*** Freshmen: 24% (166); All full-time undergraduates: 24% (1,152). ***Average award:*** Freshmen: $4238; Undergraduates: $4510. ***Scholarships, grants, and awards:*** Federal Pell, FSEOG, state, private.

GIFT AID (NON-NEED-BASED) ***Total amount:*** $388,163 (100% institutional). ***Receiving aid:*** Freshmen: 4% (30); Undergraduates: 2% (87).

LOANS ***Student loans:*** $36,843,561 (51% need-based, 49% non-need-based). 55% of past graduating class borrowed through all loan programs. *Average indebtedness per student:* $32,000. ***Average need-based loan:*** Freshmen: $2250; Undergraduates: $3556. ***Parent loans:*** $18,184,419 (100% non-need-based). ***Programs:*** Federal Direct (Subsidized and Unsubsidized Stafford, PLUS), alternative loans.

WORK-STUDY ***Federal work-study:*** Total amount: $198,780; 57 jobs averaging $3487.

APPLYING FOR FINANCIAL AID ***Required financial aid forms:*** FAFSA, institution's own form. ***Financial aid deadline (priority):*** 3/2. ***Notification date:*** Continuous beginning 3/1. Students must reply within 3 weeks of notification.

CONTACT Mr. Joe Vollaro, Executive Vice President of Financial Aid and Compliance, Academy of Art University, 79 New Montgomery Street, San Francisco, CA 94105-3410, 415-618-6528 or toll-free 800-544-ARTS. *Fax:* 415-618-6273. *E-mail:* jvollaro@academyart.edu.

ADAMS STATE COLLEGE

Alamosa, CO

Tuition & fees (CO res): $2925 **Average undergraduate aid package: $6865**

ABOUT THE INSTITUTION State-supported, coed. Awards: associate, bachelor's, and master's degrees. 31 undergraduate majors. Total enrollment: 4,899. Undergraduates: 2,308. Freshmen: 513. Federal methodology is used as a basis for awarding need-based institutional aid.

UNDERGRADUATE EXPENSES for 2006–07 ***Application fee:*** $20. ***Tuition, state resident:*** full-time $2030; part-time $92 per credit hour. ***Tuition, nonresident:*** full-time $8456; part-time $384 per credit hour. ***Required fees:*** full-time $895; $33 per credit hour. Full-time tuition and fees vary according to course load and student level. Part-time tuition and fees vary according to course load. ***College room and board:*** $6160; ***Room only:*** $3290. Room and board charges vary according to board plan and housing facility. The Colorado College Opportunity Fund stipend has been applied to instate tuition. ***Payment plans:*** Installment, deferred payment.

FRESHMAN FINANCIAL AID (Fall 2005) 435 applied for aid; of those 76% were deemed to have need. 95% of freshmen with need received aid; of those 6% had need fully met. ***Average percent of need met:*** 53% (excluding resources awarded to replace EFC). ***Average financial aid package:*** $6213 (excluding resources awarded to replace EFC). 8% of all full-time freshmen had no need and received non-need-based gift aid.

UNDERGRADUATE FINANCIAL AID (Fall 2005) 1,586 applied for aid; of those 81% were deemed to have need. 97% of undergraduates with need received aid; of those 5% had need fully met. ***Average percent of need met:*** 54% (excluding resources awarded to replace EFC). ***Average financial aid package:*** $6865 (excluding resources awarded to replace EFC). 12% of all full-time undergraduates had no need and received non-need-based gift aid.

GIFT AID (NEED-BASED) ***Total amount:*** $4,432,270 (72% federal, 27% state, 1% external sources). ***Receiving aid:*** Freshmen: 49% (251); All full-time undergraduates: 57% (1,005). ***Average award:*** Freshmen: $4005; Undergraduates: $3943. ***Scholarships, grants, and awards:*** Federal Pell, FSEOG, state, private, college/university gift aid from institutional funds.

GIFT AID (NON-NEED-BASED) ***Total amount:*** $971,835 (7% state, 55% institutional, 38% external sources). ***Receiving aid:*** Freshmen: 31% (157); Undergraduates: 29% (512). ***Average award:*** Freshmen: $1483; Undergraduates: $1756. ***Scholarships, grants, and awards by category:*** *Academic Interests/Achievement:* business, education, English, foreign languages, physical sciences. *Creative Arts/Performance:* art/fine arts, music, theater/drama. ***Tuition waivers:*** Full or partial for employees or children of employees, senior citizens.

LOANS ***Student loans:*** $6,767,520 (56% need-based, 44% non-need-based). 71% of past graduating class borrowed through all loan programs. *Average indebtedness per student:* $17,605. ***Average need-based loan:*** Freshmen: $2390; Undergraduates: $3262. ***Parent loans:*** $610,714 (100% non-need-based). ***Programs:*** FFEL (Subsidized and Unsubsidized Stafford, PLUS), Perkins, alternative loans.

WORK-STUDY ***Federal work-study:*** Total amount: $354,923; jobs available. ***State or other work-study/employment:*** Total amount: $928,710 (54% need-based, 46% non-need-based). Part-time jobs available.

ATHLETIC AWARDS Total amount: $660,999 (100% non-need-based).

APPLYING FOR FINANCIAL AID ***Required financial aid form:*** FAFSA. ***Financial aid deadline:*** Continuous. ***Notification date:*** Continuous.

CONTACT Phil Schroeder, Student Financial Aid Director, Adams State College, 208 Edgemont Boulevard, Alamosa, CO 81102, 719-587-7306 or toll-free 800-824-6494. *Fax:* 719-587-7366.

ADELPHI UNIVERSITY

Garden City, NY

Tuition & fees: $20,900 **Average undergraduate aid package: $14,500**

ABOUT THE INSTITUTION Independent, coed. Awards: associate, bachelor's, master's, and doctoral degrees and post-bachelor's and post-master's certificates. 41 undergraduate majors. Total enrollment: 8,053. Undergraduates: 4,930. Freshmen: 839. Federal methodology is used as a basis for awarding need-based institutional aid.

UNDERGRADUATE EXPENSES for 2006–07 ***Application fee:*** $35. ***Comprehensive fee:*** $30,400 includes full-time tuition ($19,800), mandatory fees ($1100), and room and board ($9500). ***College room only:*** $6350. Full-time tuition and fees vary according to course level, location, and program. Room and board charges vary according to board plan and housing facility. ***Part-time tuition:*** $640 per credit. ***Part-time fees:*** $550 per year. Part-time tuition and fees vary according to course level, location, and program. ***Payment plans:*** Installment, deferred payment.

FRESHMAN FINANCIAL AID (Fall 2005) 648 applied for aid; of those 79% were deemed to have need. 100% of freshmen with need received aid; of those 1% had need fully met. ***Average percent of need met:*** 28% (excluding resources awarded to replace EFC). ***Average financial aid package:*** $14,500 (excluding resources awarded to replace EFC). 4% of all full-time freshmen had no need and received non-need-based gift aid.

UNDERGRADUATE FINANCIAL AID (Fall 2005) 3,034 applied for aid; of those 85% were deemed to have need. 100% of undergraduates with need received aid; of those 1% had need fully met. ***Average percent of need met:*** 30% (excluding resources awarded to replace EFC). ***Average financial aid package:*** $14,500 (excluding resources awarded to replace EFC). 17% of all full-time undergraduates had no need and received non-need-based gift aid.

GIFT AID (NEED-BASED) ***Total amount:*** $20,967,486 (16% federal, 24% state, 60% institutional). ***Receiving aid:*** Freshmen: 58% (436); All full-time undergraduates: 59% (2,318). ***Average award:*** Freshmen: $5440; Undergraduates: $5245. ***Scholarships, grants, and awards:*** Federal Pell, FSEOG, state, private, college/university gift aid from institutional funds, United Negro College Fund, endowed-donor scholarships.

GIFT AID (NON-NEED-BASED) ***Total amount:*** $7,207,827 (81% institutional, 19% external sources). ***Receiving aid:*** Freshmen: 39% (293); Undergraduates: 40% (1,594). ***Average award:*** Freshmen: $8574; Undergraduates: $7726. ***Scholarships, grants, and awards by category:*** *Academic Interests/Achievement:* 1,938 awards ($14,167,294 total): communication, foreign languages, general academic interests/achievements. *Creative Arts/Performance:* 311 awards ($2,484,402 total): art/fine arts, dance, music, performing arts, theater/drama. *Special Achievements/Activities:* 224 awards ($172,250 total): community service, general special achievements/activities, memberships. *Special Characteristics:* 222 awards ($972,388 total): children and siblings of alumni, children of faculty/staff. ***Tuition waivers:*** Full or partial for employees or children of employees. ***ROTC:*** Army cooperative, Air Force cooperative.

LOANS ***Student loans:*** $27,874,063 (70% need-based, 30% non-need-based). 84% of past graduating class borrowed through all loan programs. *Average indebtedness per student:* $23,246. ***Average need-based loan:*** Freshmen: $3510; Undergraduates: $4242. ***Parent loans:*** $31,528,903 (76% need-based, 24% non-need-based). ***Programs:*** FFEL (Subsidized and Unsubsidized Stafford, PLUS), Perkins, Federal Nursing, alternative loans.

WORK-STUDY ***Federal work-study:*** Total amount: $1,730,433; 1,138 jobs averaging $1672. ***State or other work-study/employment:*** Total amount: $1,769,997 (100% non-need-based). 661 part-time jobs averaging $2103.

ATHLETIC AWARDS Total amount: $1,813,102 (61% need-based, 39% non-need-based).

APPLYING FOR FINANCIAL AID ***Required financial aid forms:*** FAFSA, state aid form. ***Financial aid deadline (priority):*** 3/1. ***Notification date:*** Continuous beginning 3/1.

CONTACT Ms. Sheryl Mihopulos, Director of Student Financial Services, Adelphi University, 1 South Avenue, PO Box 701, Garden City, NY 11530, 516-877-3365 or toll-free 800-ADELPHI. *Fax:* 516-877-3380.

ADRIAN COLLEGE

Adrian, MI

ABOUT THE INSTITUTION Independent religious, coed. Awards: associate and bachelor's degrees. 45 undergraduate majors. Total enrollment: 1,051. Undergraduates: 1,051. Freshmen: 364.

GIFT AID (NEED-BASED) ***Scholarships, grants, and awards:*** Federal Pell, FSEOG, state, private, college/university gift aid from institutional funds.

GIFT AID (NON-NEED-BASED) ***Scholarships, grants, and awards by category:*** *Academic Interests/Achievement:* business, general academic interests/achievements. *Creative Arts/Performance:* art/fine arts, music, theater/drama. *Special Achievements/Activities:* religious involvement. *Special Characteristics:* children and siblings of alumni, children of faculty/staff, children of union members/company employees, international students, religious affiliation.

LOANS ***Programs:*** FFEL (Subsidized and Unsubsidized Stafford, PLUS), Perkins.

WORK-STUDY ***Federal work-study:*** Total amount: $183,211; 102 jobs averaging $1800. ***State or other work-study/employment:*** Total amount: $723,466 (98% need-based, 2% non-need-based). 414 part-time jobs averaging $1747.

APPLYING FOR FINANCIAL AID ***Required financial aid form:*** FAFSA.

CONTACT Mr. Michael Hague, Associate Vice President for Student Financial Services, Adrian College, 110 South Madison Street, Adrian, MI 49221-2575, 517-265-5161 Ext. 4523 or toll-free 800-877-2246. *E-mail:* mhague@adrian.edu.

AGNES SCOTT COLLEGE

Decatur, GA

Tuition & fees: $27,387 **Average undergraduate aid package: $24,823**

ABOUT THE INSTITUTION Independent religious, undergraduate: women only; graduate: coed. Awards: bachelor's and master's degrees and post-bachelor's certificates. 27 undergraduate majors. Total enrollment: 902. Undergraduates: 886. Freshmen: 221. Both federal and institutional methodology are used as a basis for awarding need-based institutional aid.

UNDERGRADUATE EXPENSES for 2007–08 ***Application fee:*** $35. ***Comprehensive fee:*** $36,737 includes full-time tuition ($26,600), mandatory fees ($787), and room and board ($9350).

FRESHMAN FINANCIAL AID (Fall 2006, est.) 199 applied for aid; of those 82% were deemed to have need. 100% of freshmen with need received aid; of those 79% had need fully met. ***Average percent of need met:*** 94% (excluding resources awarded to replace EFC). ***Average financial aid package:*** $25,543 (excluding resources awarded to replace EFC). 26% of all full-time freshmen had no need and received non-need-based gift aid.

UNDERGRADUATE FINANCIAL AID (Fall 2006, est.) 628 applied for aid; of those 86% were deemed to have need. 100% of undergraduates with need received aid; of those 56% had need fully met. ***Average percent of need met:*** 94% (excluding resources awarded to replace EFC). ***Average financial aid***

package: $24,823 (excluding resources awarded to replace EFC). 31% of all full-time undergraduates had no need and received non-need-based gift aid.

GIFT AID (NEED-BASED) ***Total amount:*** $9,856,263 (9% federal, 6% state, 84% institutional, 1% external sources). ***Receiving aid:*** Freshmen: 74% (163); All full-time undergraduates: 66% (534). ***Average award:*** Freshmen: $18,670; Undergraduates: $18,385. ***Scholarships, grants, and awards:*** Federal Pell, FSEOG, state, private, college/university gift aid from institutional funds.

GIFT AID (NON-NEED-BASED) ***Total amount:*** $4,155,408 (13% state, 83% institutional, 4% external sources). ***Receiving aid:*** Freshmen: 36% (80); Undergraduates: 25% (202). ***Average award:*** Freshmen: $13,831; Undergraduates: $12,801. ***Scholarships, grants, and awards by category:*** *Academic Interests/Achievement:* general academic interests/achievements. *Creative Arts/Performance:* music. *Special Achievements/Activities:* community service, leadership. *Special Characteristics:* adult students, children of educators, children of faculty/staff, international students, local/state students, religious affiliation. ***ROTC:*** Army cooperative, Air Force cooperative.

LOANS ***Student loans:*** $2,973,972 (60% need-based, 40% non-need-based). 66% of past graduating class borrowed through all loan programs. *Average indebtedness per student:* $20,772. ***Average need-based loan:*** Freshmen: $2472; Undergraduates: $3852. ***Parent loans:*** $2,000,793 (9% need-based, 91% non-need-based). ***Programs:*** FFEL (Subsidized and Unsubsidized Stafford, PLUS), college/university.

WORK-STUDY ***Federal work-study:*** Total amount: $726,947; 370 jobs averaging $1965. ***State or other work-study/employment:*** Total amount: $267,000 (4% need-based, 96% non-need-based). 140 part-time jobs averaging $1907.

APPLYING FOR FINANCIAL AID ***Required financial aid forms:*** FAFSA, previous year's tax returns. ***Financial aid deadline:*** 5/1 (priority: 2/15). ***Notification date:*** Continuous beginning 3/1. Students must reply by 5/1 or within 2 weeks of notification.

CONTACT Diane Clark, Director of Financial Aid, Agnes Scott College, 141 East College Avenue, Decatur, GA 30030-3797, 404-471-6395 or toll-free 800-868-8602. *Fax:* 404-471-6159. *E-mail:* finaid@agnesscott.edu.

ALABAMA AGRICULTURAL AND MECHANICAL UNIVERSITY

Huntsville, AL

ABOUT THE INSTITUTION State-supported, coed. Awards: bachelor's, master's, and doctoral degrees. 36 undergraduate majors. Total enrollment: 6,076. Undergraduates: 4,978. Freshmen: 1,137.

GIFT AID (NEED-BASED) ***Scholarships, grants, and awards:*** Federal Pell, FSEOG, state, private, college/university gift aid from institutional funds, United Negro College Fund.

GIFT AID (NON-NEED-BASED) ***Scholarships, grants, and awards by category:*** *Academic Interests/Achievement:* general academic interests/achievements. *Creative Arts/Performance:* music, theater/drama. *Special Characteristics:* children of faculty/staff, parents of current students.

LOANS ***Programs:*** Federal Direct (Subsidized and Unsubsidized Stafford, PLUS), FFEL (Subsidized and Unsubsidized Stafford, PLUS), Perkins, state.

WORK-STUDY ***Federal work-study:*** Total amount: $478,174; jobs available. ***State or other work-study/employment:*** Part-time jobs available.

APPLYING FOR FINANCIAL AID ***Required financial aid forms:*** FAFSA, institution's own form.

CONTACT Dr. Carlos Clark, Financial Aid Officer, Alabama Agricultural and Mechanical University, 4900 Meridian Street, Normal, AL 35762, 256-851-5400 or toll-free 800-553-0816. *Fax:* 256-851-5407.

ALABAMA STATE UNIVERSITY

Montgomery, AL

Tuition & fees (AL res): $4008 Average undergraduate aid package: $7108

ABOUT THE INSTITUTION State-supported, coed. Awards: associate, bachelor's, master's, and doctoral degrees and post-master's certificates. 49 undergraduate majors. Total enrollment: 5,565. Undergraduates: 4,584. Freshmen: 1,343. Federal methodology is used as a basis for awarding need-based institutional aid.

UNDERGRADUATE EXPENSES for 2007–08 ***Tuition, state resident:*** full-time $4008; part-time $167 per credit hour. ***Tuition, nonresident:*** full-time $8016; part-time $334 per credit hour. ***College room and board:*** $3400; ***Room only:*** $1980.

FRESHMAN FINANCIAL AID (Fall 2006, est.) 1316 applied for aid; of those 92% were deemed to have need. 97% of freshmen with need received aid; of those 15% had need fully met. ***Average percent of need met:*** 72% (excluding resources awarded to replace EFC). ***Average financial aid package:*** $7212 (excluding resources awarded to replace EFC). 3% of all full-time freshmen had no need and received non-need-based gift aid.

UNDERGRADUATE FINANCIAL AID (Fall 2006, est.) 4,060 applied for aid; of those 92% were deemed to have need. 93% of undergraduates with need received aid; of those 16% had need fully met. ***Average percent of need met:*** 69% (excluding resources awarded to replace EFC). ***Average financial aid package:*** $7108 (excluding resources awarded to replace EFC). 2% of all full-time undergraduates had no need and received non-need-based gift aid.

GIFT AID (NEED-BASED) ***Total amount:*** $15,115,942 (79% federal, 3% state, 12% institutional, 6% external sources). ***Receiving aid:*** Freshmen: 73% (977); All full-time undergraduates: 63% (2,906). ***Average award:*** Freshmen: $3823; Undergraduates: $3759. ***Scholarships, grants, and awards:*** Federal Pell, FSEOG, state, private, college/university gift aid from institutional funds, United Negro College Fund.

GIFT AID (NON-NEED-BASED) ***Total amount:*** $440,220 (5% federal, 33% state, 43% institutional, 19% external sources). ***Receiving aid:*** Freshmen: 30% (408); Undergraduates: 20% (933). ***Average award:*** Freshmen: $5635; Undergraduates: $5102. ***Scholarships, grants, and awards by category:*** *Academic Interests/Achievement:* 618 awards ($2,356,419 total): biological sciences, business, education, general academic interests/achievements, health fields, mathematics. *Creative Arts/Performance:* 248 awards ($417,704 total): art/fine arts, music, performing arts, theater/drama. *Special Achievements/Activities:* 40 awards ($101,212 total): cheerleading/drum major, general special achievements/activities, leadership. *Special Characteristics:* 648 awards ($1,172,949 total): children of union members/company employees, ethnic background, general special characteristics, handicapped students, local/state students, members of minority groups, out-of-state students, religious affiliation, veterans, veterans' children. ***ROTC:*** Army cooperative, Air Force.

LOANS ***Student loans:*** $22,836,252 (90% need-based, 10% non-need-based). 90% of past graduating class borrowed through all loan programs. *Average indebtedness per student:* $26,903. ***Average need-based loan:*** Freshmen: $2784; Undergraduates: $3440. ***Parent loans:*** $1,376,802 (54% need-based, 46% non-need-based). ***Programs:*** FFEL (Subsidized and Unsubsidized Stafford, PLUS), Perkins, state.

WORK-STUDY ***Federal work-study:*** Total amount: $1,823,170; 593 jobs averaging $2532. ***State or other work-study/employment:*** Total amount: $154,360 (100% non-need-based). 65 part-time jobs averaging $1631.

ATHLETIC AWARDS Total amount: $986,090 (88% need-based, 12% non-need-based).

APPLYING FOR FINANCIAL AID ***Required financial aid form:*** FAFSA. ***Financial aid deadline (priority):*** 4/1. ***Notification date:*** Continuous beginning 5/15. Students must reply within 2 weeks of notification.

CONTACT Mrs. Dorenda A. Adams, Director of Financial Aid, Alabama State University, PO Box 271, Montgomery, AL 36101-0271, 334-229-4323 or toll-free 800-253-5037. *Fax:* 334-299-4924. *E-mail:* dadams@alasu.edu.

ALASKA BIBLE COLLEGE

Glennallen, AK

ABOUT THE INSTITUTION Independent nondenominational, coed. Awards: associate and bachelor's degrees. 1 undergraduate major. Total enrollment: 38. Undergraduates: 38. Freshmen: 6.

GIFT AID (NEED-BASED) ***Scholarships, grants, and awards:*** private, college/university gift aid from institutional funds.

GIFT AID (NON-NEED-BASED) ***Scholarships, grants, and awards by category:*** *Academic Interests/Achievement:* general academic interests/achievements, religion/biblical studies. *Creative Arts/Performance:* music. *Special Achievements/Activities:* religious involvement. *Special Characteristics:* children of faculty/staff, local/state students, religious affiliation, spouses of current students.

LOANS ***Programs:*** state.

APPLYING FOR FINANCIAL AID ***Required financial aid form:*** institution's own form.

CONTACT Kevin Newman, Financial Aid Officer, Alaska Bible College, PO Box 289, Glennallen, AK 99588-0289, 907-822-3201 Ext. 253 or toll-free 800-478-7884. *Fax:* 907-822-5027. *E-mail:* knewman@akbible.edu.

ALASKA PACIFIC UNIVERSITY

Anchorage, AK

ABOUT THE INSTITUTION Independent, coed. Awards: associate, bachelor's, and master's degrees. 12 undergraduate majors. Total enrollment: 733. Undergraduates: 510. Freshmen: 58.

GIFT AID (NEED-BASED) ***Scholarships, grants, and awards:*** Federal Pell, FSEOG, state, private, college/university gift aid from institutional funds, Bureau of Indian Affairs Grants.

GIFT AID (NON-NEED-BASED) ***Scholarships, grants, and awards by category:*** *Academic Interests/Achievement:* biological sciences, business, education, general academic interests/achievements, humanities, physical sciences, social sciences. *Special Achievements/Activities:* community service, general special achievements/activities, leadership, religious involvement. *Special Characteristics:* children and siblings of alumni, children of faculty/staff, ethnic background, general special characteristics, international students, local/state students, members of minority groups, out-of-state students, religious affiliation.

LOANS ***Programs:*** FFEL (Subsidized and Unsubsidized Stafford, PLUS), state.

APPLYING FOR FINANCIAL AID ***Required financial aid form:*** FAFSA.

CONTACT Peter Miller, Director of Financial Aid, Alaska Pacific University, 4101 University Drive, Grant Hall, Room 115, Anchorage, AK 99508-4672, 907-564-8341 or toll-free 800-252-7528. *Fax:* 907-564-8372. *E-mail:* sfs@alaskapacific.edu.

ALBANY COLLEGE OF PHARMACY OF UNION UNIVERSITY

Albany, NY

CONTACT Tiffany M. Gutierrez, Director of Financial Aid, Albany College of Pharmacy of Union University, 106 New Scotland Avenue, Albany, NY 12208-3425, 518-445-7256 or toll-free 888-203-8010. *Fax:* 518-445-7322. *E-mail:* gutierrt@mail.acp.edu.

ALBANY STATE UNIVERSITY

Albany, GA

CONTACT Ms. Kathleen J. Caldwell, Director of Financial Aid, Albany State University, 504 College Drive, Albany, GA 31705-2717, 912-430-4650 or toll-free 800-822-RAMS (in-state). *Fax:* 912-430-3936. *E-mail:* finaid@asurams.edu.

ALBERTSON COLLEGE OF IDAHO

Caldwell, ID

Tuition & fees: $17,680 **Average undergraduate aid package: $14,850**

ABOUT THE INSTITUTION Independent, coed. Awards: bachelor's and master's degrees. 26 undergraduate majors. Total enrollment: 822. Undergraduates: 793. Freshmen: 211. Federal methodology is used as a basis for awarding need-based institutional aid.

UNDERGRADUATE EXPENSES for 2007–08 ***Application fee:*** $50. ***Comprehensive fee:*** $24,005 includes full-time tuition ($17,000), mandatory fees ($680), and room and board ($6325). ***College room only:*** $2850.

FRESHMAN FINANCIAL AID (Fall 2006, est.) 131 applied for aid; of those 100% were deemed to have need. 100% of freshmen with need received aid; of those 29% had need fully met. ***Average percent of need met:*** 95% (excluding resources awarded to replace EFC). ***Average financial aid package:*** $15,783 (excluding resources awarded to replace EFC). 38% of all full-time freshmen had no need and received non-need-based gift aid.

UNDERGRADUATE FINANCIAL AID (Fall 2006, est.) 430 applied for aid; of those 100% were deemed to have need. 100% of undergraduates with need received aid; of those 17% had need fully met. ***Average percent of need met:*** 90% (excluding resources awarded to replace EFC). ***Average financial aid package:*** $14,850 (excluding resources awarded to replace EFC). 33% of all full-time undergraduates had no need and received non-need-based gift aid.

GIFT AID (NEED-BASED) ***Total amount:*** $1,312,879 (63% federal, 2% state, 26% institutional, 9% external sources). ***Receiving aid:*** Freshmen: 35% (74); All full-time undergraduates: 36% (283). ***Average award:*** Freshmen: $4519; Undergraduates: $4423. ***Scholarships, grants, and awards:*** Federal Pell, FSEOG, state, private, college/university gift aid from institutional funds.

GIFT AID (NON-NEED-BASED) ***Total amount:*** $4,727,226 (4% state, 89% institutional, 7% external sources). ***Receiving aid:*** Freshmen: 59% (124); Undergraduates: 53% (416). ***Average award:*** Freshmen: $9340; Undergraduates: $8271. ***Scholarships, grants, and awards by category:*** *Academic Interests/Achievement:* $3,321,666 total. *Creative Arts/Performance:* $281,686 total. *Special Achievements/Activities:* $1500 total. *Special Characteristics:* $764,601 total. ***ROTC:*** Army cooperative.

LOANS ***Student loans:*** $2,483,476 (64% need-based, 36% non-need-based). 76% of past graduating class borrowed through all loan programs. *Average indebtedness per student:* $26,461. ***Average need-based loan:*** Freshmen: $2736; Undergraduates: $4627. ***Parent loans:*** $622,610 (100% non-need-based). ***Programs:*** FFEL (Subsidized and Unsubsidized Stafford, PLUS), Perkins.

WORK-STUDY ***Federal work-study:*** Total amount: $137,290. ***State or other work-study/employment:*** Total amount: $44,300 (37% need-based, 63% non-need-based).

ATHLETIC AWARDS Total amount: $910,577 (100% non-need-based).

APPLYING FOR FINANCIAL AID ***Required financial aid forms:*** FAFSA, institution's own form. ***Financial aid deadline (priority):*** 2/15. ***Notification date:*** Continuous beginning 3/1. Students must reply within 3 weeks of notification.

CONTACT Merna Davis, Data Coordinator, Albertson College of Idaho, 2112 Cleveland Boulevard, Caldwell, ID 83605-4432, 208-459-5380 or toll-free 800-244-3246. *Fax:* 208-459-5844. *E-mail:* mdavis@albertson.edu.

ALBERTUS MAGNUS COLLEGE

New Haven, CT

ABOUT THE INSTITUTION Independent Roman Catholic, coed. Awards: associate, bachelor's, and master's degrees. 56 undergraduate majors. Total enrollment: 2,186. Undergraduates: 1,769. Freshmen: 176.

GIFT AID (NEED-BASED) ***Scholarships, grants, and awards:*** Federal Pell, FSEOG, state, college/university gift aid from institutional funds.

GIFT AID (NON-NEED-BASED) ***Scholarships, grants, and awards by category:*** *Academic Interests/Achievement:* biological sciences, business, communication, computer science, education, English, foreign languages, general academic interests/achievements, humanities, international studies, mathematics, physical sciences, premedicine, religion/biblical studies, social sciences. *Creative Arts/Performance:* art/fine arts, performing arts, theater/drama. *Special Achievements/Activities:* community service, leadership. *Special Characteristics:* religious affiliation.

LOANS ***Programs:*** FFEL (Subsidized and Unsubsidized Stafford, PLUS), Perkins.

APPLYING FOR FINANCIAL AID ***Required financial aid forms:*** FAFSA, institution's own form.

CONTACT Andrew Foster, Director of Financial Aid, Albertus Magnus College, 700 Prospect Street, New Haven, CT 06511-1189, 203-773-8508 or toll-free 800-578-9160. *Fax:* 203-773-8972. *E-mail:* financial_aid@albertus.edu.

ALBION COLLEGE

Albion, MI

Tuition & fees: $26,122 **Average undergraduate aid package: $20,965**

ABOUT THE INSTITUTION Independent Methodist, coed. Awards: bachelor's degrees. 37 undergraduate majors. Total enrollment: 1,941. Undergraduates: 1,941. Freshmen: 480. Federal methodology is used as a basis for awarding need-based institutional aid.

UNDERGRADUATE EXPENSES for 2006–07 ***Application fee:*** $20. ***Comprehensive fee:*** $33,528 includes full-time tuition ($25,668), mandatory fees ($454), and room and board ($7406). ***College room only:*** $3622. Room and board charges vary according to housing facility. ***Part-time tuition:*** $1090 per semester hour. ***Payment plans:*** Tuition prepayment, installment, deferred payment.

FRESHMAN FINANCIAL AID (Fall 2006, est.) 366 applied for aid; of those 75% were deemed to have need. 100% of freshmen with need received aid; of those 43% had need fully met. ***Average percent of need met:*** 91% (excluding

resources awarded to replace EFC). ***Average financial aid package:*** $21,044 (excluding resources awarded to replace EFC). 40% of all full-time freshmen had no need and received non-need-based gift aid.

UNDERGRADUATE FINANCIAL AID (Fall 2006, est.) 1,346 applied for aid; of those 85% were deemed to have need. 100% of undergraduates with need received aid; of those 48% had need fully met. ***Average percent of need met:*** 92% (excluding resources awarded to replace EFC). ***Average financial aid package:*** $20,965 (excluding resources awarded to replace EFC). 38% of all full-time undergraduates had no need and received non-need-based gift aid.

GIFT AID (NEED-BASED) ***Total amount:*** $19,723,858 (5% federal, 12% state, 81% institutional, 2% external sources). ***Receiving aid:*** Freshmen: 58% (276); All full-time undergraduates: 60% (1,144). ***Average award:*** Freshmen: $17,700; Undergraduates: $16,498. ***Scholarships, grants, and awards:*** Federal Pell, FSEOG, state, private, college/university gift aid from institutional funds.

GIFT AID (NON-NEED-BASED) ***Total amount:*** $9,154,508 (5% state, 94% institutional, 1% external sources). ***Receiving aid:*** Freshmen: 54% (257); Undergraduates: 56% (1,071). ***Average award:*** Freshmen: $12,226; Undergraduates: $11,824. ***Scholarships, grants, and awards by category:*** *Academic Interests/Achievement:* 1,693 awards ($19,319,920 total): business, communication, education, general academic interests/achievements, mathematics, premedicine. *Creative Arts/Performance:* 170 awards ($207,200 total): art/fine arts, music, performing arts, theater/drama. *Special Characteristics:* 291 awards ($436,326 total): children and siblings of alumni, relatives of clergy. ***Tuition waivers:*** Full or partial for children of alumni, employees or children of employees.

LOANS ***Student loans:*** $9,336,153 (44% need-based, 56% non-need-based). 65% of past graduating class borrowed through all loan programs. *Average indebtedness per student:* $22,504. ***Average need-based loan:*** Freshmen: $3174; Undergraduates: $4644. ***Parent loans:*** $2,468,013 (100% non-need-based). ***Programs:*** FFEL (Subsidized and Unsubsidized Stafford, PLUS), Perkins, state.

WORK-STUDY ***Federal work-study:*** Total amount: $848,421; 640 jobs averaging $1326.

APPLYING FOR FINANCIAL AID ***Required financial aid form:*** FAFSA. ***Financial aid deadline (priority):*** 3/1. ***Notification date:*** Continuous beginning 3/15.

CONTACT Doug Kellar, Associate Vice President for Enrollment, Albion College, Kellogg Center Box 4670, Albion, MI 49224-1831, 517-629-0440 or toll-free 800-858-6770. *Fax:* 517-629-0581. *E-mail:* dkellar@albion.edu.

ALBRIGHT COLLEGE

Reading, PA

Tuition & fees: $27,420 **Average undergraduate aid package: $18,291**

ABOUT THE INSTITUTION Independent religious, coed. Awards: bachelor's and master's degrees. 45 undergraduate majors. Total enrollment: 2,222. Undergraduates: 2,150. Freshmen: 458. Federal methodology is used as a basis for awarding need-based institutional aid.

UNDERGRADUATE EXPENSES for 2006–07 ***Application fee:*** $25. ***Comprehensive fee:*** $35,578 includes full-time tuition ($26,620), mandatory fees ($800), and room and board ($8158). ***College room only:*** $4644. Full-time tuition and fees vary according to program. Room and board charges vary according to board plan and housing facility. ***Part-time tuition:*** $3328 per course. Part-time tuition and fees vary according to class time. ***Payment plan:*** Installment.

FRESHMAN FINANCIAL AID (Fall 2005) 397 applied for aid; of those 91% were deemed to have need. 99% of freshmen with need received aid; of those 16% had need fully met. ***Average financial aid package:*** $965 (excluding resources awarded to replace EFC).

UNDERGRADUATE FINANCIAL AID (Fall 2005) 710 applied for aid; of those 67% were deemed to have need. 96% of undergraduates with need received aid; of those 53% had need fully met. ***Average financial aid package:*** $18,291 (excluding resources awarded to replace EFC).

GIFT AID (NON-NEED-BASED) ***Total amount:*** $3,424,908 (1% state, 79% institutional, 20% external sources). ***Receiving aid:*** Freshmen: 39; Undergraduates: 160. ***Average award:*** Freshmen: $13,863; Undergraduates: $12,601. ***Scholarships, grants, and awards by category:*** *Academic Interests/Achievement:* 5 awards ($4000 total). *Creative Arts/Performance:* 117 awards ($160,000 total): journalism/publications. *Special Achievements/Activities:* 505 awards ($624,937 total): hobbies/interests, religious involvement. *Special Characteristics:* 233 awards ($596,500 total). ***Tuition waivers:*** Full or partial for children of alumni, employees or children of employees, senior citizens.

LOANS ***Student loans:*** $12,622,935 (69% need-based, 31% non-need-based). 2% of past graduating class borrowed through all loan programs. *Average indebtedness per student:* $30,992. ***Average need-based loan:*** Freshmen: $4122; Undergraduates: $4367. ***Parent loans:*** $4,421,163 (33% need-based, 67% non-need-based).

WORK-STUDY ***Federal work-study:*** Total amount: $717,388; 548 jobs averaging $1308. ***State or other work-study/employment:*** Total amount: $574,832 (5% need-based, 95% non-need-based). 394 part-time jobs averaging $1391.

CONTACT Mary Ellen Duffy, Director of Financial Aid, Albright College, PO Box 15234, Reading, PA 19612-5234, 610-921-7515 or toll-free 800-252-1856. *Fax:* 610-921-7729. *E-mail:* mduffy@alb.edu.

ALCORN STATE UNIVERSITY

Alcorn State, MS

Tuition & fees (MS res): $4156 **Average undergraduate aid package: $9552**

ABOUT THE INSTITUTION State-supported, coed. Awards: associate, bachelor's, and master's degrees and post-master's certificates. 37 undergraduate majors. Total enrollment: 3,584. Undergraduates: 3,015. Freshmen: 489. Federal methodology is used as a basis for awarding need-based institutional aid.

UNDERGRADUATE EXPENSES for 2006–07 ***Tuition, state resident:*** full-time $4156; part-time $173 per hour. ***Tuition, nonresident:*** full-time $9332; part-time $389 per hour. ***College room and board:*** $4616; ***Room only:*** $2330.

FRESHMAN FINANCIAL AID (Fall 2006, est.) 486 applied for aid; of those 98% were deemed to have need. 100% of freshmen with need received aid; of those 45% had need fully met. ***Average percent of need met:*** 45% (excluding resources awarded to replace EFC). ***Average financial aid package:*** $6610 (excluding resources awarded to replace EFC). 14% of all full-time freshmen had no need and received non-need-based gift aid.

UNDERGRADUATE FINANCIAL AID (Fall 2006, est.) 2,710 applied for aid; of those 86% were deemed to have need. 100% of undergraduates with need received aid; of those 56% had need fully met. ***Average percent of need met:*** 56% (excluding resources awarded to replace EFC). ***Average financial aid package:*** $9552 (excluding resources awarded to replace EFC). 9% of all full-time undergraduates had no need and received non-need-based gift aid.

GIFT AID (NEED-BASED) ***Total amount:*** $7,470,904 (100% federal). ***Receiving aid:*** Freshmen: 74% (362); All full-time undergraduates: 86% (2,337). ***Average award:*** Freshmen: $4074; Undergraduates: $4240. ***Scholarships, grants, and awards:*** Federal Pell, FSEOG, state, private, college/university gift aid from institutional funds.

GIFT AID (NON-NEED-BASED) ***Total amount:*** $2,386,777 (23% state, 77% institutional). ***Receiving aid:*** Freshmen: 31% (153); Undergraduates: 23% (634). ***Average award:*** Freshmen: $9118; Undergraduates: $10,023. ***Scholarships, grants, and awards by category:*** *Academic Interests/Achievement:* 352 awards ($1,437,625 total): general academic interests/achievements. *Creative Arts/Performance:* 208 awards ($1,033,169 total): music. *Special Characteristics:* 477 awards ($484,169 total): children of faculty/staff, local/state students, members of minority groups. ***Tuition waivers:*** Full or partial for employees or children of employees. ***ROTC:*** Army.

LOANS ***Student loans:*** $16,394,399 (62% need-based, 38% non-need-based). 67% of past graduating class borrowed through all loan programs. *Average indebtedness per student:* $10,000. ***Average need-based loan:*** Freshmen: $2536; Undergraduates: $3742. ***Parent loans:*** $1,161,039 (100% non-need-based). ***Programs:*** Federal Direct (Subsidized and Unsubsidized Stafford, PLUS).

WORK-STUDY ***Federal work-study:*** Total amount: $336,337; 244 jobs averaging $2060.

ATHLETIC AWARDS Total amount: $2,041,500 (100% non-need-based).

APPLYING FOR FINANCIAL AID ***Required financial aid forms:*** FAFSA, institution's own form. ***Financial aid deadline (priority):*** 4/1. ***Notification date:*** Continuous. Students must reply within 4 weeks of notification.

CONTACT Juanita M. Russell, Director of Financial Aid, Alcorn State University, 1000 ASU Drive #28, Alcorn State, MS 39096-7500, 601-877-6190 or toll-free 800-222-6790. *Fax:* 601-877-6110. *E-mail:* juanita@lorman.alcorn.edu.

ALDERSON-BROADDUS COLLEGE

Philippi, WV

Tuition & fees: $19,090 **Average undergraduate aid package: $18,186**

ABOUT THE INSTITUTION Independent religious, coed. Awards: associate, bachelor's, and master's degrees. 43 undergraduate majors. Total enrollment: 747. Undergraduates: 623. Freshmen: 140. Federal methodology is used as a basis for awarding need-based institutional aid.

UNDERGRADUATE EXPENSES for 2006–07 ***Application fee:*** $10. ***Comprehensive fee:*** $25,250 includes full-time tuition ($18,890), mandatory fees ($200), and room and board ($6160). ***College room only:*** $3000. Full-time tuition and fees vary according to degree level. Room and board charges vary according to housing facility. ***Part-time tuition:*** $630 per credit hour. ***Part-time fees:*** $50 per term. Part-time tuition and fees vary according to degree level. ***Payment plan:*** Installment.

FRESHMAN FINANCIAL AID (Fall 2005) 122 applied for aid; of those 91% were deemed to have need. 100% of freshmen with need received aid; of those 24% had need fully met. ***Average percent of need met:*** 84% (excluding resources awarded to replace EFC). ***Average financial aid package:*** $17,817 (excluding resources awarded to replace EFC). 6% of all full-time freshmen had no need and received non-need-based gift aid.

UNDERGRADUATE FINANCIAL AID (Fall 2005) 562 applied for aid; of those 92% were deemed to have need. 100% of undergraduates with need received aid; of those 28% had need fully met. ***Average percent of need met:*** 86% (excluding resources awarded to replace EFC). ***Average financial aid package:*** $18,186 (excluding resources awarded to replace EFC). 6% of all full-time undergraduates had no need and received non-need-based gift aid.

GIFT AID (NEED-BASED) ***Total amount:*** $5,516,841 (19% federal, 14% state, 61% institutional, 6% external sources). ***Receiving aid:*** Freshmen: 90% (111); All full-time undergraduates: 87% (501). ***Average award:*** Freshmen: $12,921; Undergraduates: $13,418. ***Scholarships, grants, and awards:*** Federal Pell, FSEOG, state, private, college/university gift aid from institutional funds, Federal Nursing, National Health Service Corp., Scholarship for Disadvantaged Students.

GIFT AID (NON-NEED-BASED) ***Total amount:*** $370,966 (8% state, 80% institutional, 12% external sources). ***Receiving aid:*** Freshmen: 13% (16); Undergraduates: 11% (63). ***Average award:*** Freshmen: $6321; Undergraduates: $6220. ***Scholarships, grants, and awards by category:*** *Academic Interests/Achievement:* 508 awards ($2,513,147 total): biological sciences, business, communication, computer science, education, general academic interests/achievements, health fields, humanities, mathematics, physical sciences, premedicine, religion/biblical studies, social sciences. *Creative Arts/Performance:* 84 awards ($431,930 total): art/fine arts, creative writing, debating, journalism/publications, music, performing arts, theater/drama. *Special Achievements/Activities:* general special achievements/activities, leadership. *Special Characteristics:* 31 awards ($380,252 total): children of faculty/staff, ethnic background, general special characteristics, international students, religious affiliation. ***Tuition waivers:*** Full or partial for employees or children of employees.

LOANS ***Student loans:*** $4,160,781 (68% need-based, 32% non-need-based). 80% of past graduating class borrowed through all loan programs. *Average indebtedness per student:* $26,459. ***Average need-based loan:*** Freshmen: $3621; Undergraduates: $4865. ***Parent loans:*** $542,526 (85% need-based, 15% non-need-based). ***Programs:*** FFEL (Subsidized and Unsubsidized Stafford, PLUS), Perkins, Federal Nursing.

WORK-STUDY ***Federal work-study:*** Total amount: $251,800; 195 jobs averaging $1400. ***State or other work-study/employment:*** Total amount: $232,631 (100% non-need-based). 132 part-time jobs averaging $1400.

ATHLETIC AWARDS Total amount: $882,450 (75% need-based, 25% non-need-based).

APPLYING FOR FINANCIAL AID ***Required financial aid form:*** FAFSA. ***Financial aid deadline (priority):*** 3/1. ***Notification date:*** Continuous beginning 2/15. Students must reply within 2 weeks of notification.

CONTACT Brian Weingart, Director of Financial Aid, Alderson-Broaddus College, College Hill Road, Philippi, WV 26416, 304-457-6354 or toll-free 800-263-1549. *Fax:* 304-457-6239.

ALFRED UNIVERSITY

Alfred, NY

Tuition & fees: $23,162 **Average undergraduate aid package: $19,697**

ABOUT THE INSTITUTION Independent, coed. Awards: bachelor's, master's, and doctoral degrees and post-master's certificates. 41 undergraduate majors. Total enrollment: 2,310. Undergraduates: 1,991. Freshmen: 489. Both federal and institutional methodology are used as a basis for awarding need-based institutional aid.

UNDERGRADUATE EXPENSES for 2007–08 ***Application fee:*** $40. ***Comprehensive fee:*** $33,546 includes full-time tuition ($22,312), mandatory fees ($850), and room and board ($10,384). ***College room only:*** $5384. ***Part-time tuition:*** $724 per credit hour. ***Part-time fees:*** $70 per term.

FRESHMAN FINANCIAL AID (Fall 2006, est.) 428 applied for aid; of those 85% were deemed to have need. 100% of freshmen with need received aid; of those 16% had need fully met. ***Average percent of need met:*** 89% (excluding resources awarded to replace EFC). ***Average financial aid package:*** $20,541 (excluding resources awarded to replace EFC). 8% of all full-time freshmen had no need and received non-need-based gift aid.

UNDERGRADUATE FINANCIAL AID (Fall 2006, est.) 1,611 applied for aid; of those 88% were deemed to have need. 100% of undergraduates with need received aid; of those 20% had need fully met. ***Average percent of need met:*** 86% (excluding resources awarded to replace EFC). ***Average financial aid package:*** $19,697 (excluding resources awarded to replace EFC). 9% of all full-time undergraduates had no need and received non-need-based gift aid.

GIFT AID (NEED-BASED) ***Total amount:*** $20,863,235 (11% federal, 11% state, 78% institutional). ***Receiving aid:*** Freshmen: 74% (362); All full-time undergraduates: 75% (1,392). ***Average award:*** Freshmen: $15,390; Undergraduates: $14,194. ***Scholarships, grants, and awards:*** Federal Pell, FSEOG, state, private, college/university gift aid from institutional funds.

GIFT AID (NON-NEED-BASED) ***Total amount:*** $2,321,743 (4% federal, 2% state, 79% institutional, 15% external sources). ***Receiving aid:*** Freshmen: 44% (215); Undergraduates: 40% (736). ***Average award:*** Freshmen: $7862; Undergraduates: $8794. ***Scholarships, grants, and awards by category:*** *Academic Interests/Achievement:* biological sciences, business, communication, education, engineering/technologies, English, foreign languages, general academic interests/achievements, humanities, international studies, mathematics, military science, physical sciences, premedicine, social sciences. *Creative Arts/Performance:* art/fine arts, general creative arts/performance, performing arts. *Special Achievements/Activities:* leadership. *Special Characteristics:* children of educators, children of faculty/staff, international students. ***ROTC:*** Army cooperative.

LOANS ***Student loans:*** $5,708,929 (8% need-based, 92% non-need-based). 83% of past graduating class borrowed through all loan programs. *Average indebtedness per student:* $23,292. ***Average need-based loan:*** Freshmen: $4243; Undergraduates: $5118. ***Parent loans:*** $3,094,956 (100% non-need-based). ***Programs:*** FFEL (Subsidized and Unsubsidized Stafford, PLUS), Perkins, college/university, alternative loans.

WORK-STUDY ***Federal work-study:*** Total amount: $459,726; jobs available.

APPLYING FOR FINANCIAL AID ***Required financial aid forms:*** FAFSA, institution's own form, state aid form, noncustodial (divorced/separated) parent's statement, business/farm supplement. ***Financial aid deadline:*** 3/15. ***Notification date:*** Continuous beginning 2/15. Students must reply by 5/1 or within 2 weeks of notification.

CONTACT Mr. Earl Pierce, Director of Financial Aid, Alfred University, Alumni Hall, One Saxon Drive, Alfred, NY 14802-1205, 607-871-2159 or toll-free 800-541-9229. *Fax:* 607-871-2252. *E-mail:* pierce@alfred.edu.

ALICE LLOYD COLLEGE

Pippa Passes, KY

ABOUT THE INSTITUTION Independent, coed. Awards: bachelor's degrees. 14 undergraduate majors. Total enrollment: 613. Undergraduates: 613. Freshmen: 193.

GIFT AID (NEED-BASED) ***Scholarships, grants, and awards:*** Federal Pell, FSEOG, state, private, college/university gift aid from institutional funds.

GIFT AID (NON-NEED-BASED) ***Scholarships, grants, and awards by category:*** *Special Achievements/Activities:* general special achievements/activities. *Special Characteristics:* members of minority groups.

LOANS ***Programs:*** FFEL (Subsidized and Unsubsidized Stafford, PLUS), college/university, Bagby Loans (for freshmen).

WORK-STUDY ***Federal work-study:*** Total amount: $710,000; 402 jobs averaging $1600. ***State or other work-study/employment:*** Total amount: $400,000 (100% non-need-based). 241 part-time jobs averaging $1591.

APPLYING FOR FINANCIAL AID ***Required financial aid form:*** FAFSA.

CONTACT Ms. Nancy M. Melton, Director of Financial Aid, Alice Lloyd College, 100 Purpose Road, Pippa Passes, KY 41844, 606-368-6059. *E-mail:* nancymelton@alc.edu.

ALLEGHENY COLLEGE
Meadville, PA

Tuition & fees: $30,000 **Average undergraduate aid package: $22,400**

ABOUT THE INSTITUTION Independent, coed. Awards: bachelor's degrees. 47 undergraduate majors. Total enrollment: 2,095. Undergraduates: 2,095. Freshmen: 573. Federal methodology is used as a basis for awarding need-based institutional aid.

UNDERGRADUATE EXPENSES for 2007–08 ***Application fee:*** $35. ***Comprehensive fee:*** $37,500 includes full-time tuition ($29,680), mandatory fees ($320), and room and board ($7500). ***College room only:*** $3900. ***Part-time tuition:*** $1237 per credit hour. ***Part-time fees:*** $160 per term.

FRESHMAN FINANCIAL AID (Fall 2006, est.) 494 applied for aid; of those 81% were deemed to have need. 100% of freshmen with need received aid; of those 40% had need fully met. ***Average percent of need met:*** 92% (excluding resources awarded to replace EFC). ***Average financial aid package:*** $23,500 (excluding resources awarded to replace EFC). 27% of all full-time freshmen had no need and received non-need-based gift aid.

UNDERGRADUATE FINANCIAL AID (Fall 2006, est.) 1,605 applied for aid; of those 86% were deemed to have need. 100% of undergraduates with need received aid; of those 38% had need fully met. ***Average percent of need met:*** 91% (excluding resources awarded to replace EFC). ***Average financial aid package:*** $22,400 (excluding resources awarded to replace EFC). 29% of all full-time undergraduates had no need and received non-need-based gift aid.

GIFT AID (NEED-BASED) ***Total amount:*** $21,542,751 (7% federal, 11% state, 78% institutional, 4% external sources). ***Receiving aid:*** Freshmen: 70% (401); All full-time undergraduates: 67% (1,376). ***Average award:*** Freshmen: $17,450; Undergraduates: $16,050. ***Scholarships, grants, and awards:*** Federal Pell, FSEOG, state, private, college/university gift aid from institutional funds, Federal Academic Competitiveness Grant, National Smart Grant, Veterans Educational Benefits.

GIFT AID (NON-NEED-BASED) ***Total amount:*** $7,908,420 (95% institutional, 5% external sources). ***Receiving aid:*** Freshmen: 11% (64); Undergraduates: 10% (212). ***Average award:*** Freshmen: $10,500; Undergraduates: $10,900. ***Scholarships, grants, and awards by category:*** *Academic Interests/Achievement:* 1,668 awards ($19,109,233 total): general academic interests/achievements. *Special Characteristics:* 66 awards ($1,264,446 total): adult students, children of educators, children of faculty/staff, international students.

LOANS ***Student loans:*** $11,351,456 (48% need-based, 52% non-need-based). ***Average need-based loan:*** Freshmen: $4675; Undergraduates: $4850. ***Parent loans:*** $3,859,904 (100% non-need-based). ***Programs:*** FFEL (Subsidized and Unsubsidized Stafford, PLUS), Perkins, private loans from commercial lenders.

WORK-STUDY ***Federal work-study:*** Total amount: $1,740,565; 1,092 jobs averaging $1600. ***State or other work-study/employment:*** Total amount: $699,810 (100% non-need-based). 400 part-time jobs averaging $1750.

APPLYING FOR FINANCIAL AID ***Required financial aid form:*** FAFSA. ***Financial aid deadline (priority):*** 2/15. ***Notification date:*** Continuous beginning 3/1. Students must reply by 5/1 or within 4 weeks of notification.

CONTACT Ms. Sheryle Proper, Director of Financial Aid, Allegheny College, 520 North Main Street, Meadville, PA 16335, 800-835-7780 or toll-free 800-521-5293. *Fax:* 814-337-0431. *E-mail:* fao@allegheny.edu.

ALLEGHENY WESLEYAN COLLEGE
Salem, OH

CONTACT Financial Aid Office, Allegheny Wesleyan College, 2161 Woodsdale Road, Salem, OH 44460, 330-337-6403 or toll-free 800-292-3153.

ALLEN COLLEGE
Waterloo, IA

Tuition & fees: $13,472 **Average undergraduate aid package: $14,428**

ABOUT THE INSTITUTION Independent, coed, primarily women. Awards: associate, bachelor's, and master's degrees (liberal arts and general education courses offered at either University of North Iowa or Wartburg College). 2 undergraduate majors. Total enrollment: 426. Undergraduates: 359. Freshmen: 31. Federal methodology is used as a basis for awarding need-based institutional aid.

UNDERGRADUATE EXPENSES for 2006–07 ***Application fee:*** $50. ***Comprehensive fee:*** $19,184 includes full-time tuition ($11,958), mandatory fees ($1514), and room and board ($5712). ***College room only:*** $2666. ***Part-time tuition:*** $415 per credit hour. ***Part-time fees:*** $37 per credit hour; $170 per term.

FRESHMAN FINANCIAL AID (Fall 2005) 35 applied for aid; of those 71% were deemed to have need. 100% of freshmen with need received aid; of those 12% had need fully met. ***Average percent of need met:*** 75% (excluding resources awarded to replace EFC). ***Average financial aid package:*** $15,034 (excluding resources awarded to replace EFC).

UNDERGRADUATE FINANCIAL AID (Fall 2005) 289 applied for aid; of those 81% were deemed to have need. 100% of undergraduates with need received aid; of those 10% had need fully met. ***Average percent of need met:*** 80% (excluding resources awarded to replace EFC). ***Average financial aid package:*** $14,428 (excluding resources awarded to replace EFC).

GIFT AID (NEED-BASED) ***Total amount:*** $1,271,733 (27% federal, 60% state, 7% institutional, 6% external sources). ***Receiving aid:*** Freshmen: 51% (20); All full-time undergraduates: 54% (177). ***Average award:*** Freshmen: $4515; Undergraduates: $5988. ***Scholarships, grants, and awards:*** Federal Pell, FSEOG, state, private, college/university gift aid from institutional funds, Federal Nursing, Federal Scholarships for Disadvantaged Students.

GIFT AID (NON-NEED-BASED) ***Total amount:*** $17,910 (54% institutional, 46% external sources). ***Scholarships, grants, and awards by category:*** *Academic Interests/Achievement:* 20 awards ($12,101 total): health fields. *Special Achievements/Activities:* community service, general special achievements/activities, leadership. *Special Characteristics:* local/state students, members of minority groups, out-of-state students. ***ROTC:*** Army cooperative.

LOANS ***Student loans:*** $2,838,029 (70% need-based, 30% non-need-based). 100% of past graduating class borrowed through all loan programs. *Average indebtedness per student:* $20,811. ***Average need-based loan:*** Freshmen: $2344; Undergraduates: $3982. ***Parent loans:*** $398,139 (9% need-based, 91% non-need-based). ***Programs:*** Federal Direct (Subsidized and Unsubsidized Stafford, PLUS), Perkins, Federal Nursing, state, college/university.

WORK-STUDY ***Federal work-study:*** Total amount: $15,353; 18 jobs averaging $2000. ***State or other work-study/employment:*** Part-time jobs available.

APPLYING FOR FINANCIAL AID ***Required financial aid forms:*** FAFSA, institution's own form. ***Financial aid deadline:*** Continuous. ***Notification date:*** Continuous beginning 4/1.

CONTACT Kathie S. Walters, Financial Aid Director, Allen College, Barrett Forum, 1825 Logan Avenue, Waterloo, IA 50703, 319-226-2003. *Fax:* 319-226-2051. *E-mail:* walterks@ihs.org.

ALLEN UNIVERSITY
Columbia, SC

CONTACT Ms. Donna Foster, Director of Financial Aid, Allen University, 1530 Harden Street, Columbia, SC 29204-1085, 803-376-5736 or toll-free 877-625-5368 (in-state). *E-mail:* donnaf@allenuniversity.edu.

ALLIANT INTERNATIONAL UNIVERSITY
San Diego, CA

Tuition & fees: $14,770 **Average undergraduate aid package: $16,250**

ABOUT THE INSTITUTION Independent, coed. Awards: bachelor's, master's, and doctoral degrees and post-bachelor's certificates. 10 undergraduate majors. Total enrollment: 3,521. Undergraduates: 178. Federal methodology is used as a basis for awarding need-based institutional aid.

UNDERGRADUATE EXPENSES for 2007–08 ***Application fee:*** $45. ***Tuition:*** full-time $14,400; part-time $530 per unit.

FRESHMAN FINANCIAL AID (Fall 2006, est.) 20 applied for aid; of those 100% were deemed to have need. 100% of freshmen with need received aid; of those 20% had need fully met. ***Average percent of need met:*** 80% (excluding resources awarded to replace EFC). ***Average financial aid package:*** $16,250 (excluding resources awarded to replace EFC). 20% of all full-time freshmen had no need and received non-need-based gift aid.

UNDERGRADUATE FINANCIAL AID (Fall 2006, est.) 142 applied for aid; of those 100% were deemed to have need. 100% of undergraduates with need received aid; of those 26% had need fully met. ***Average percent of need met:*** 80% (excluding resources awarded to replace EFC). ***Average financial aid***

package: $16,250 (excluding resources awarded to replace EFC). 24% of all full-time undergraduates had no need and received non-need-based gift aid.

GIFT AID (NEED-BASED) ***Total amount:*** $586,637 (74% federal, 26% state). ***Receiving aid:*** Freshmen: 80% (16); All full-time undergraduates: 55% (82). ***Average award:*** Freshmen: $6000; Undergraduates: $6000. ***Scholarships, grants, and awards:*** Federal Pell, FSEOG, state, private, college/university gift aid from institutional funds.

GIFT AID (NON-NEED-BASED) ***Total amount:*** $264,106 (92% institutional, 8% external sources). ***Receiving aid:*** Freshmen: 100% (20); Undergraduates: 96% (142). ***Average award:*** Freshmen: $1400; Undergraduates: $1400. ***Scholarships, grants, and awards by category:*** *Academic Interests/Achievement:* business, communication, computer science, education, English, foreign languages, general academic interests/achievements, humanities, international studies, social sciences. *Special Achievements/Activities:* community service, general special achievements/activities, leadership. *Special Characteristics:* children and siblings of alumni, children of current students, children of faculty/staff, ethnic background, international students, local/state students, members of minority groups, veterans. ***ROTC:*** Army cooperative.

LOANS ***Student loans:*** $911,120 (40% need-based, 60% non-need-based). 67% of past graduating class borrowed through all loan programs. *Average indebtedness per student:* $17,125. ***Average need-based loan:*** Freshmen: $2625; Undergraduates: $3500. ***Parent loans:*** $86,782 (100% non-need-based). ***Programs:*** FFEL (Subsidized and Unsubsidized Stafford, PLUS), Perkins, alternative loans.

WORK-STUDY ***Federal work-study:*** Total amount: $68,324; 20 jobs averaging $4250. ***State or other work-study/employment:*** Total amount: $47,783 (100% need-based). 18 part-time jobs averaging $4207.

ATHLETIC AWARDS Total amount: $328,879 (100% non-need-based).

APPLYING FOR FINANCIAL AID ***Required financial aid form:*** FAFSA. ***Financial aid deadline (priority):*** 3/2. ***Notification date:*** Continuous beginning 3/15. Students must reply within 3 weeks of notification.

CONTACT Deborah Spindler, Director of Financial Aid, Alliant International University, 10455 Pomerado Road, San Diego, CA 92131-1799, 858-635-4559 Ext. 4700 or toll-free 866-825-5426. *Fax:* 858-635-4848.

ALMA COLLEGE

Alma, MI

Tuition & fees: $22,380 **Average undergraduate aid package: $19,393**

ABOUT THE INSTITUTION Independent Presbyterian, coed. Awards: bachelor's degrees. 69 undergraduate majors. Total enrollment: 1,215. Undergraduates: 1,215. Freshmen: 313. Federal methodology is used as a basis for awarding need-based institutional aid.

UNDERGRADUATE EXPENSES for 2006–07 ***Application fee:*** $25. ***One-time required fee:*** $300. ***Comprehensive fee:*** $30,154 includes full-time tuition ($22,170), mandatory fees ($210), and room and board ($7774). ***College room only:*** $3830. Room and board charges vary according to board plan and housing facility. ***Part-time tuition:*** $860 per credit. Part-time tuition and fees vary according to course load. ***Payment plans:*** Installment, deferred payment.

FRESHMAN FINANCIAL AID (Fall 2006, est.) 313 applied for aid; of those 78% were deemed to have need. 100% of freshmen with need received aid; of those 32% had need fully met. ***Average percent of need met:*** 85% (excluding resources awarded to replace EFC). ***Average financial aid package:*** $19,787 (excluding resources awarded to replace EFC). 22% of all full-time freshmen had no need and received non-need-based gift aid.

UNDERGRADUATE FINANCIAL AID (Fall 2006, est.) 1,177 applied for aid; of those 77% were deemed to have need. 100% of undergraduates with need received aid; of those 29% had need fully met. ***Average percent of need met:*** 84% (excluding resources awarded to replace EFC). ***Average financial aid package:*** $19,393 (excluding resources awarded to replace EFC). 21% of all full-time undergraduates had no need and received non-need-based gift aid.

GIFT AID (NEED-BASED) ***Total amount:*** $12,961,453 (8% federal, 16% state, 74% institutional, 2% external sources). ***Receiving aid:*** Freshmen: 78% (244); All full-time undergraduates: 77% (904). ***Average award:*** Freshmen: $16,163; Undergraduates: $14,725. ***Scholarships, grants, and awards:*** Federal Pell, FSEOG, state, private, college/university gift aid from institutional funds.

GIFT AID (NON-NEED-BASED) ***Total amount:*** $2,928,554 (8% state, 88% institutional, 4% external sources). ***Receiving aid:*** Freshmen: 14% (43); Undergraduates: 9% (107). ***Average award:*** Freshmen: $15,244; Undergraduates: $13,726. ***Scholarships, grants, and awards by category:*** *Academic Interests/Achievement:* 859 awards ($5,995,941 total): general academic interests/achievements. *Creative Arts/Performance:* 330 awards ($619,310 total): art/fine arts, dance, music, theater/drama. *Special Characteristics:* 254 awards ($1,149,137 total): children and siblings of alumni, children of faculty/staff, previous college experience. ***Tuition waivers:*** Full or partial for employees or children of employees. ***ROTC:*** Army cooperative.

LOANS ***Student loans:*** $6,827,252 (67% need-based, 33% non-need-based). 95% of past graduating class borrowed through all loan programs. *Average indebtedness per student:* $23,470. ***Average need-based loan:*** Freshmen: $4659; Undergraduates: $5637. ***Parent loans:*** $3,126,419 (27% need-based, 73% non-need-based). ***Programs:*** FFEL (Subsidized and Unsubsidized Stafford, PLUS), Perkins, state, college/university, alternative loans.

WORK-STUDY ***Federal work-study:*** Total amount: $174,000; 140 jobs averaging $950. ***State or other work-study/employment:*** Total amount: $21,000 (100% need-based). 30 part-time jobs averaging $700.

APPLYING FOR FINANCIAL AID ***Required financial aid form:*** FAFSA. ***Financial aid deadline (priority):*** 3/1. ***Notification date:*** Continuous beginning 3/1. Students must reply within 3 weeks of notification.

CONTACT Mr. Christopher A. Brown, Director of Student Financial Assistance, Alma College, 614 West Superior Street, Alma, MI 48801-1599, 989-463-7347 or toll-free 800-321-ALMA. *Fax:* 989-463-7993. *E-mail:* cabrown@alma.edu.

ALVERNIA COLLEGE

Reading, PA

ABOUT THE INSTITUTION Independent Roman Catholic, coed. Awards: associate, bachelor's, and master's degrees and post-bachelor's and post-master's certificates. 40 undergraduate majors. Total enrollment: 2,735. Undergraduates: 1,996. Freshmen: 277.

GIFT AID (NEED-BASED) ***Scholarships, grants, and awards:*** Federal Pell, FSEOG, state, private, college/university gift aid from institutional funds.

GIFT AID (NON-NEED-BASED) ***Scholarships, grants, and awards by category:*** *Academic Interests/Achievement:* general academic interests/achievements. *Special Achievements/Activities:* community service, junior miss, leadership, religious involvement. *Special Characteristics:* children and siblings of alumni, children of faculty/staff, international students, local/state students, out-of-state students, previous college experience, religious affiliation, siblings of current students.

LOANS ***Programs:*** FFEL (Subsidized and Unsubsidized Stafford, PLUS), Perkins, college/university, Health Professions Loans.

WORK-STUDY ***Federal work-study:*** Total amount: $682,044; 620 jobs averaging $1950. ***State or other work-study/employment:*** Total amount: $89,780 (5% need-based, 95% non-need-based). Part-time jobs available.

APPLYING FOR FINANCIAL AID ***Required financial aid forms:*** FAFSA, state aid form, noncustodial (divorced/separated) parent's statement.

CONTACT Lora Myers, Director of Financial Aid, Alvernia College, 400 St. Bernardine Street, Reading, PA 19607-1799, 610-796-8200 Ext. 1473 or toll-free 888-ALVERNIA (in-state). *Fax:* 610-796-8336. *E-mail:* bra.myers@alvernia.edu.

ALVERNO COLLEGE

Milwaukee, WI

Tuition & fees: $17,296 **Average undergraduate aid package: N/A**

ABOUT THE INSTITUTION Independent Roman Catholic, undergraduate: women only; graduate: coed. Awards: associate, bachelor's, and master's degrees and post-bachelor's certificates (also offers weekend program with significant enrollment not reflected in profile). 42 undergraduate majors. Total enrollment: 2,480. Undergraduates: 2,245. Freshmen: 283. Federal methodology is used as a basis for awarding need-based institutional aid.

UNDERGRADUATE EXPENSES for 2007–08 ***Application fee:*** $20. ***Comprehensive fee:*** $23,402 includes full-time tuition ($16,896), mandatory fees ($400), and room and board ($6106). ***Part-time tuition:*** $704 per credit. ***Part-time fees:*** $200 per term.

GIFT AID (NEED-BASED) ***Total amount:*** $11,807,532 (27% federal, 23% state, 50% institutional). ***Scholarships, grants, and awards:*** Federal Pell, FSEOG, state, private, college/university gift aid from institutional funds, transfer student scholarships.

GIFT AID (NON-NEED-BASED) ***Total amount:*** $265,986 (27% institutional, 73% external sources). ***Scholarships, grants, and awards by category:*** *Academic Interests/Achievement:* general academic interests/achievements. *Creative Arts/Performance:* art/fine arts, music. *Special Achievements/Activities:* community service. *Special Characteristics:* general special characteristics, previous college experience. ***ROTC:*** Army cooperative, Air Force cooperative.

LOANS ***Student loans:*** $13,729,695 (48% need-based, 52% non-need-based). ***Parent loans:*** $776,320 (100% non-need-based). ***Programs:*** FFEL (Subsidized and Unsubsidized Stafford, PLUS), Perkins, Federal Nursing, state.

WORK-STUDY ***Federal work-study:*** Total amount: $254,953; 185 jobs averaging $1445.

APPLYING FOR FINANCIAL AID ***Required financial aid forms:*** FAFSA, institution's own form. ***Financial aid deadline (priority):*** 3/15. ***Notification date:*** Continuous beginning 3/15. Students must reply within 2 weeks of notification.

CONTACT Dan Goyette, Director of Financial Aid, Alverno College, 3400 South 43rd Street, PO Box 343922, Milwaukee, WI 53234-3922, 414-382-6046 or toll-free 800-933-3401. *Fax:* 414-382-6354. *E-mail:* dan.goyette@alverno.edu.

AMERICAN ACADEMY OF ART
Chicago, IL

CONTACT Ms. Ione Fitzgerald, Director of Financial Aid, American Academy of Art, 332 South Michigan Avenue, Suite 300, Chicago, IL 60604, 312-461-0600. *Fax:* 312-294-9570.

AMERICAN BAPTIST COLLEGE OF AMERICAN BAPTIST THEOLOGICAL SEMINARY
Nashville, TN

ABOUT THE INSTITUTION Independent Baptist, coed. Awards: associate and bachelor's degrees. 2 undergraduate majors. Total enrollment: 186. Undergraduates: 186. Freshmen: 54.

GIFT AID (NEED-BASED) ***Scholarships, grants, and awards:*** Federal Pell, FSEOG, state.

GIFT AID (NON-NEED-BASED) ***Scholarships, grants, and awards by category:*** *Special Characteristics:* religious affiliation.

WORK-STUDY ***Federal work-study:*** Total amount: $7391; 2 jobs averaging $3695.

APPLYING FOR FINANCIAL AID ***Required financial aid form:*** FAFSA.

CONTACT Marcella Lockhart, Executive Assistant for Administrator, American Baptist College of American Baptist Theological Seminary, 1800 Baptist World Center Drive, Nashville, TN 37207, 615-256-1463 Ext. 2227. *Fax:* 615-226-7855. *E-mail:* mlockhart@abcnash.edu.

AMERICAN INDIAN COLLEGE OF THE ASSEMBLIES OF GOD, INC.
Phoenix, AZ

CONTACT Office of Student Financial Aid, American Indian College of the Assemblies of God, Inc., 10020 North Fifteenth Avenue, Phoenix, AZ 85021-2199, 800-933-3828.

AMERICAN INTERCONTINENTAL UNIVERSITY
Los Angeles, CA

CONTACT Mr. Joe Johnson, Director of Financial Aid, American InterContinental University, 12655 West Jefferson Boulevard, Los Angeles, CA 90066, 310-302-2000 Ext. 2447 or toll-free 800-333-2652 (out-of-state). *Fax:* 310-302-2002.

AMERICAN INTERCONTINENTAL UNIVERSITY
Weston, FL

CONTACT Financial Aid Office, American InterContinental University, 2250 North Commerce Parkway, Suite 100, Weston, FL 33326, 954-446-6100 or toll-free 866-248-4723 (out-of-state).

AMERICAN INTERCONTINENTAL UNIVERSITY
Atlanta, GA

CONTACT Sherry Rizzi, Financial Aid Director, American InterContinental University, 3330 Peachtree Road NE, Atlanta, GA 30326, 404-965-5796 or toll-free 888-999-4248 (out-of-state). *Fax:* 404-965-5704.

AMERICAN INTERCONTINENTAL UNIVERSITY
Atlanta, GA

CONTACT Financial Aid Office, American InterContinental University, 6600 Peachtree-Dunwoody Road, 500 Embassy Row, Atlanta, GA 30328, 404-965-6500 or toll-free 800-255-6839.

AMERICAN INTERCONTINENTAL UNIVERSITY
Houston, TX

CONTACT Financial Aid Office, American InterContinental University, 9999 Richmond Avenue, Houston, TX 77042, 832-242-5788.

AMERICAN INTERCONTINENTAL UNIVERSITY ONLINE
Hoffman Estates, IL

CONTACT Financial Aid Office, American InterContinental University Online, 5550 Prairie Stone Parkway, Suite 400, Hoffman Estates, IL 60192, 847-851-5000 or toll-free 877-701-3800.

AMERICAN INTERNATIONAL COLLEGE
Springfield, MA

Tuition & fees: $20,990 **Average undergraduate aid package: $13,854**

ABOUT THE INSTITUTION Independent, coed. Awards: associate, bachelor's, master's, and doctoral degrees and post-bachelor's and post-master's certificates. 45 undergraduate majors. Total enrollment: 1,815. Undergraduates: 1,398. Freshmen: 331. Federal methodology is used as a basis for awarding need-based institutional aid.

UNDERGRADUATE EXPENSES for 2006–07 ***Application fee:*** $20. ***Comprehensive fee:*** $30,260 includes full-time tuition ($20,990) and room and board ($9270). ***Part-time tuition:*** $470 per credit.

FRESHMAN FINANCIAL AID (Fall 2005) 314 applied for aid; of those 89% were deemed to have need. 100% of freshmen with need received aid; of those 17% had need fully met. ***Average percent of need met:*** 73% (excluding resources awarded to replace EFC). ***Average financial aid package:*** $15,462 (excluding resources awarded to replace EFC). 18% of all full-time freshmen had no need and received non-need-based gift aid.

UNDERGRADUATE FINANCIAL AID (Fall 2005) 1,130 applied for aid; of those 91% were deemed to have need. 97% of undergraduates with need received aid; of those 18% had need fully met. ***Average percent of need met:*** 67% (excluding resources awarded to replace EFC). ***Average financial aid package:*** $13,854 (excluding resources awarded to replace EFC). 13% of all full-time undergraduates had no need and received non-need-based gift aid.

GIFT AID (NEED-BASED) ***Total amount:*** $9,669,441 (19% federal, 6% state, 74% institutional, 1% external sources). ***Receiving aid:*** Freshmen: 81% (275); All full-time undergraduates: 81% (982). ***Average award:*** Freshmen: $12,501; Undergraduates: $10,505. ***Scholarships, grants, and awards:*** Federal Pell, FSEOG, state, private, college/university gift aid from institutional funds.

GIFT AID (NON-NEED-BASED) ***Total amount:*** $1,300,550 (2% federal, 1% state, 94% institutional, 3% external sources). ***Receiving aid:*** Freshmen: 9% (32); Undergraduates: 10% (123). ***Average award:*** Freshmen: $12,485; Undergraduates: $11,734. ***Scholarships, grants, and awards by category:*** *Academic Interests/Achievement:* 749 awards ($4,046,435 total): general academic interests/achievements. *Special Achievements/Activities:* 10 awards ($66,000 total): general special achievements/activities. ***ROTC:*** Army cooperative, Air Force cooperative.

LOANS ***Student loans:*** $10,651,969 (74% need-based, 26% non-need-based). 96% of past graduating class borrowed through all loan programs. *Average indebtedness per student:* $23,522. ***Average need-based loan:*** Freshmen: $2984; Undergraduates: $3640. ***Parent loans:*** $1,808,479 (36% need-based, 64% non-need-based). ***Programs:*** FFEL (Subsidized and Unsubsidized Stafford, PLUS), Perkins, state, college/university, alternative loans.

WORK-STUDY ***Federal work-study:*** Total amount: $302,532; 220 jobs averaging $2400.

ATHLETIC AWARDS Total amount: $2,322,448 (62% need-based, 38% non-need-based).

APPLYING FOR FINANCIAL AID ***Required financial aid form:*** FAFSA. ***Financial aid deadline (priority):*** 5/1. ***Notification date:*** Continuous beginning 3/15. Students must reply within 4 weeks of notification.

CONTACT Mr. Douglas E. Fish, Director of Financial Services, American International College, 1000 State Street, Springfield, MA 01109-3189, 413-205-3259. *Fax:* 413-205-3912. *E-mail:* douglas.fish@aic.edu.

AMERICAN SENTINEL UNIVERSITY

Englewood, CO

CONTACT Financial Aid Office, American Sentinel University, 385 Inverness Parkway, Englewood, CO 80112.

AMERICAN UNIVERSITY

Washington, DC

ABOUT THE INSTITUTION Independent Methodist, coed. Awards: associate, bachelor's, master's, doctoral, and first professional degrees and post-bachelor's certificates. 53 undergraduate majors. Total enrollment: 11,279. Undergraduates: 5,921. Freshmen: 1,223.

GIFT AID (NEED-BASED) ***Scholarships, grants, and awards:*** Federal Pell, FSEOG, state, private, college/university gift aid from institutional funds.

GIFT AID (NON-NEED-BASED) ***Scholarships, grants, and awards by category:*** *Academic Interests/Achievement:* general academic interests/achievements. *Creative Arts/Performance:* general creative arts/performance. *Special Achievements/Activities:* general special achievements/activities, leadership, memberships. *Special Characteristics:* adult students, children and siblings of alumni, children of faculty/staff, ethnic background, first-generation college students, local/state students, members of minority groups, previous college experience, relatives of clergy, spouses of current students.

LOANS ***Programs:*** Federal Direct (Subsidized and Unsubsidized Stafford, PLUS), FFEL (PLUS), Perkins, college/university.

WORK-STUDY ***Federal work-study:*** Total amount: $4,080,467; 2,169 jobs averaging $2016.

APPLYING FOR FINANCIAL AID ***Required financial aid forms:*** FAFSA, institution's own form.

CONTACT Brian Lee Sang, Office of Enrollment, American University, 4400 Massachusetts Avenue, NW, Washington, DC 20016-8001, 202-885-6100. *Fax:* 202-885-1025. *E-mail:* financialaid@american.edu.

AMERICAN UNIVERSITY OF PUERTO RICO

Bayamón, PR

CONTACT Mr. Yahaira Melendez, Financial Aid Director, American University of Puerto Rico, PO Box 2037, Bayamón, PR 00960-2037, 787-620-2040 Ext. 2031. *Fax:* 787-785-7377. *E-mail:* melendezy@aupr.edu.

AMHERST COLLEGE

Amherst, MA

Tuition & fees: $34,916 **Average undergraduate aid package: $32,041**

ABOUT THE INSTITUTION Independent, coed. Awards: bachelor's degrees. 36 undergraduate majors. Total enrollment: 1,648. Undergraduates: 1,648. Freshmen: 433. Institutional methodology is used as a basis for awarding need-based institutional aid.

UNDERGRADUATE EXPENSES for 2006–07 ***Application fee:*** $55. ***Comprehensive fee:*** $43,996 includes full-time tuition ($34,280), mandatory fees ($636), and room and board ($9080). ***College room only:*** $4870. ***Payment plans:*** Installment, deferred payment.

FRESHMAN FINANCIAL AID (Fall 2006, est.) 275 applied for aid; of those 82% were deemed to have need. 100% of freshmen with need received aid; of those 100% had need fully met. ***Average percent of need met:*** 100% (excluding resources awarded to replace EFC). ***Average financial aid package:*** $33,882 (excluding resources awarded to replace EFC).

UNDERGRADUATE FINANCIAL AID (Fall 2006, est.) 908 applied for aid; of those 85% were deemed to have need. 100% of undergraduates with need received aid; of those 100% had need fully met. ***Average percent of need met:*** 100% (excluding resources awarded to replace EFC). ***Average financial aid package:*** $32,041 (excluding resources awarded to replace EFC).

GIFT AID (NEED-BASED) ***Total amount:*** $25,284,962 (4% federal, 93% institutional, 3% external sources). ***Receiving aid:*** Freshmen: 52% (225); All full-time undergraduates: 46% (768). ***Average award:*** Freshmen: $33,274; Undergraduates: $31,393. ***Scholarships, grants, and awards:*** Federal Pell, FSEOG, state, private, college/university gift aid from institutional funds, United Negro College Fund.

GIFT AID (NON-NEED-BASED) ***Total amount:*** $1,039,942 (6% federal, 94% external sources).

LOANS ***Student loans:*** $2,342,546 (61% need-based, 39% non-need-based). 43% of past graduating class borrowed through all loan programs. *Average indebtedness per student:* $11,626. ***Average need-based loan:*** Freshmen: $1287; Undergraduates: $1833. ***Parent loans:*** $2,732,464 (100% non-need-based). ***Programs:*** Federal Direct (Subsidized and Unsubsidized Stafford, PLUS), Perkins, college/university.

WORK-STUDY ***Federal work-study:*** Total amount: $818,029; 520 jobs averaging $1573. ***State or other work-study/employment:*** Total amount: $253,542 (100% need-based). 157 part-time jobs averaging $1615.

APPLYING FOR FINANCIAL AID ***Required financial aid forms:*** FAFSA, CSS Financial Aid PROFILE, noncustodial (divorced/separated) parent's statement, income tax form(s), W-2 forms. ***Financial aid deadline (priority):*** 2/15. ***Notification date:*** 4/1. Students must reply by 5/1.

CONTACT Joe Paul Case, Dean/Director of Financial Aid, Amherst College, B-5 Converse Hall, PO Box 5000, Amherst, MA 01002-5000, 413-542-2296. *Fax:* 413-542-2628. *E-mail:* finaid@amherst.edu.

ANDERSON UNIVERSITY

Anderson, IN

Tuition & fees: $19,990 **Average undergraduate aid package: $16,181**

ABOUT THE INSTITUTION Independent religious, coed. Awards: associate, bachelor's, master's, doctoral, and first professional degrees. 58 undergraduate majors. Total enrollment: 2,730. Undergraduates: 2,199. Freshmen: 457. Federal methodology is used as a basis for awarding need-based institutional aid.

UNDERGRADUATE EXPENSES for 2006–07 ***Application fee:*** $25. ***Comprehensive fee:*** $26,450 includes full-time tuition ($19,990) and room and board ($6460). ***College room only:*** $3940. ***Part-time tuition:*** $850 per semester hour.

FRESHMAN FINANCIAL AID (Fall 2006, est.) 376 applied for aid; of those 90% were deemed to have need. 100% of freshmen with need received aid; of those 45% had need fully met. ***Average percent of need met:*** 88% (excluding resources awarded to replace EFC). ***Average financial aid package:*** $13,818 (excluding resources awarded to replace EFC). 18% of all full-time freshmen had no need and received non-need-based gift aid.

UNDERGRADUATE FINANCIAL AID (Fall 2006, est.) 1,642 applied for aid; of those 90% were deemed to have need. 100% of undergraduates with need received aid; of those 45% had need fully met. ***Average percent of need met:*** 76% (excluding resources awarded to replace EFC). ***Average financial aid package:*** $16,181 (excluding resources awarded to replace EFC). 23% of all full-time undergraduates had no need and received non-need-based gift aid.

GIFT AID (NEED-BASED) ***Total amount:*** $16,539,069 (11% federal, 19% state, 63% institutional, 7% external sources). ***Receiving aid:*** Freshmen: 82% (338); All full-time undergraduates: 77% (1,470). ***Average award:*** Freshmen: $10,901; Undergraduates: $11,960. ***Scholarships, grants, and awards:*** Federal Pell, FSEOG, state, private, college/university gift aid from institutional funds.

GIFT AID (NON-NEED-BASED) ***Total amount:*** $3,803,264 (85% institutional, 15% external sources). ***Receiving aid:*** Freshmen: 11% (46); Undergraduates:

10% (181). ***Average award:*** Freshmen: $8821; Undergraduates: $8792. ***Scholarships, grants, and awards by category:*** *Academic Interests/Achievement:* 1,824 awards ($8,380,000 total): general academic interests/achievements. *Creative Arts/Performance:* 60 awards ($70,000 total): art/fine arts, music. *Special Achievements/Activities:* 30 awards ($74,000 total): leadership. *Special Characteristics:* 373 awards ($2,200,000 total): adult students, children of faculty/staff, international students, relatives of clergy.

LOANS ***Student loans:*** $12,730,772 (89% need-based, 11% non-need-based). 95% of past graduating class borrowed through all loan programs. *Average indebtedness per student:* $25,777. ***Average need-based loan:*** Freshmen: $3127; Undergraduates: $4586. ***Parent loans:*** $3,664,822 (78% need-based, 22% non-need-based). ***Programs:*** FFEL (Subsidized and Unsubsidized Stafford, PLUS), Perkins.

WORK-STUDY ***Federal work-study:*** Total amount: $500,000; 1,480 jobs averaging $2160. ***State or other work-study/employment:*** Part-time jobs available.

APPLYING FOR FINANCIAL AID ***Required financial aid form:*** FAFSA. ***Financial aid deadline (priority):*** 3/1. ***Notification date:*** Continuous beginning 3/1.

CONTACT Mr. Kenneth Nieman, Director of Student Financial Services, Anderson University, 1100 East Fifth Street, Anderson, IN 46012-3495, 765-641-4180 or toll-free 800-421-3014 (in-state), 800-428-6414 (out-of-state). *Fax:* 765-641-3831. *E-mail:* kfnieman@anderson.edu.

ANDERSON UNIVERSITY

Anderson, SC

Tuition & fees: $17,850 **Average undergraduate aid package: $15,834**

ABOUT THE INSTITUTION Independent Baptist, coed. Awards: bachelor's and master's degrees. 46 undergraduate majors. Total enrollment: 1,706. Undergraduates: 1,682. Freshmen: 399. Federal methodology is used as a basis for awarding need-based institutional aid.

UNDERGRADUATE EXPENSES for 2007–08 ***Application fee:*** $25. ***Comprehensive fee:*** $24,850 includes full-time tuition ($16,600), mandatory fees ($1250), and room and board ($7000). ***College room only:*** $3450. ***Part-time tuition:*** $425 per credit hour.

FRESHMAN FINANCIAL AID (Fall 2005) 362 applied for aid; of those 89% were deemed to have need. 100% of freshmen with need received aid; of those 30% had need fully met. ***Average percent of need met:*** 64% (excluding resources awarded to replace EFC). ***Average financial aid package:*** $16,985 (excluding resources awarded to replace EFC). 10% of all full-time freshmen had no need and received non-need-based gift aid.

UNDERGRADUATE FINANCIAL AID (Fall 2005) 1,228 applied for aid; of those 90% were deemed to have need. 99% of undergraduates with need received aid; of those 29% had need fully met. ***Average percent of need met:*** 66% (excluding resources awarded to replace EFC). ***Average financial aid package:*** $15,834 (excluding resources awarded to replace EFC). 8% of all full-time undergraduates had no need and received non-need-based gift aid.

GIFT AID (NEED-BASED) ***Total amount:*** $8,423,467 (17% federal, 22% state, 61% institutional). ***Receiving aid:*** Freshmen: 87% (319); All full-time undergraduates: 83% (1,056). ***Average award:*** Freshmen: $8098; Undergraduates: $7160. ***Scholarships, grants, and awards:*** Federal Pell, FSEOG, state, college/university gift aid from institutional funds.

GIFT AID (NON-NEED-BASED) ***Total amount:*** $3,090,365 (100% state). ***Receiving aid:*** Freshmen: 78% (288); Undergraduates: 56% (719). ***Average award:*** Freshmen: $5772; Undergraduates: $5652. ***ROTC:*** Army cooperative, Air Force cooperative.

LOANS ***Student loans:*** $3,382,574 (89% need-based, 11% non-need-based). 76% of past graduating class borrowed through all loan programs. *Average indebtedness per student:* $15,125. ***Average need-based loan:*** Freshmen: $3608; Undergraduates: $4596. ***Parent loans:*** $3,284,030 (100% need-based). ***Programs:*** FFEL (Subsidized and Unsubsidized Stafford, PLUS), Perkins.

WORK-STUDY ***Federal work-study:*** Total amount: $234,672; 127 jobs averaging $1662. ***State or other work-study/employment:*** Part-time jobs available.

ATHLETIC AWARDS Total amount: $888,509 (100% non-need-based).

APPLYING FOR FINANCIAL AID ***Required financial aid form:*** FAFSA. ***Financial aid deadline:*** 7/30 (priority: 3/1). ***Notification date:*** Continuous beginning 3/15. Students must reply within 2 weeks of notification.

CONTACT Becky Pressley, Director of Financial Aid, Anderson University, 316 Boulevard, Anderson, SC 29621-4035, 864-231-2070 or toll-free 800-542-3594. *Fax:* 864-231-2008. *E-mail:* bpressley@andersonuniversity.edu.

ANDREWS UNIVERSITY

Berrien Springs, MI

Tuition & fees: $19,528 **Average undergraduate aid package: $21,664**

ABOUT THE INSTITUTION Independent Seventh-day Adventist, coed. Awards: associate, bachelor's, master's, doctoral, and first professional degrees and post-master's certificates. 82 undergraduate majors. Total enrollment: 3,195. Undergraduates: 1,733. Freshmen: 290. Federal methodology is used as a basis for awarding need-based institutional aid.

UNDERGRADUATE EXPENSES for 2007–08 ***Application fee:*** $32. ***Comprehensive fee:*** $26,278 includes full-time tuition ($18,968), mandatory fees ($560), and room and board ($6750). ***College room only:*** $3250. ***Part-time tuition:*** $767 per credit hour.

FRESHMAN FINANCIAL AID (Fall 2006, est.) 285 applied for aid; of those 64% were deemed to have need. 100% of freshmen with need received aid; of those 39% had need fully met. ***Average percent of need met:*** 94% (excluding resources awarded to replace EFC). ***Average financial aid package:*** $20,043 (excluding resources awarded to replace EFC). 36% of all full-time freshmen had no need and received non-need-based gift aid.

UNDERGRADUATE FINANCIAL AID (Fall 2006, est.) 1,544 applied for aid; of those 64% were deemed to have need. 100% of undergraduates with need received aid; of those 42% had need fully met. ***Average percent of need met:*** 93% (excluding resources awarded to replace EFC). ***Average financial aid package:*** $21,664 (excluding resources awarded to replace EFC). 36% of all full-time undergraduates had no need and received non-need-based gift aid.

GIFT AID (NEED-BASED) ***Total amount:*** $5,076,075 (40% federal, 6% state, 54% institutional). ***Receiving aid:*** Freshmen: 42% (120); All full-time undergraduates: 44% (691). ***Average award:*** Freshmen: $5267; Undergraduates: $3486. ***Scholarships, grants, and awards:*** Federal Pell, FSEOG, state, private, college/university gift aid from institutional funds.

GIFT AID (NON-NEED-BASED) ***Total amount:*** $8,954,606 (3% state, 71% institutional, 26% external sources). ***Receiving aid:*** Freshmen: 64% (181); Undergraduates: 59% (922). ***Average award:*** Freshmen: $8173; Undergraduates: $6036. ***Scholarships, grants, and awards by category:*** *Academic Interests/Achievement:* 1,561 awards ($5,866,385 total): general academic interests/achievements. *Creative Arts/Performance:* 62 awards ($49,394 total): music. *Special Achievements/Activities:* 184 awards ($197,305 total): leadership, religious involvement. *Special Characteristics:* 172 awards ($2,019,569 total): children of faculty/staff, general special characteristics, international students.

LOANS ***Student loans:*** $15,529,417 (24% need-based, 76% non-need-based). 68% of past graduating class borrowed through all loan programs. *Average indebtedness per student:* $25,083. ***Average need-based loan:*** Freshmen: $5443; Undergraduates: $4660. ***Parent loans:*** $11,786,243 (100% non-need-based). ***Programs:*** Federal Direct (Subsidized and Unsubsidized Stafford, PLUS), Perkins.

WORK-STUDY ***Federal work-study:*** Total amount: $662,438. ***State or other work-study/employment:*** Total amount: $290,592 (100% need-based).

APPLYING FOR FINANCIAL AID ***Required financial aid forms:*** FAFSA, institution's own form. ***Financial aid deadline:*** Continuous.

CONTACT Cynthia Schulz, Assistant Director of Student Financial Services, Andrews University, Student Financial Services-Administration Building, Berrien Springs, MI 49104, 800-253-2874. *Fax:* 269-471-3228. *E-mail:* sfs@andrews.edu.

ANGELO STATE UNIVERSITY

San Angelo, TX

CONTACT Ms. Lyn Wheeler, Director of Financial Aid, Angelo State University, ASU Station #11015, San Angelo, TX 76909-1015, 325-942-2246 or toll-free 800-946-8627 (in-state). *Fax:* 325-942-2082. *E-mail:* lyn.wheeler@angelo.edu.

ANNA MARIA COLLEGE

Paxton, MA

ABOUT THE INSTITUTION Independent Roman Catholic, coed. Awards: associate, bachelor's, and master's degrees and post-bachelor's and post-master's certificates. 28 undergraduate majors. Total enrollment: 1,200. Undergraduates: 809. Freshmen: 182.

GIFT AID (NEED-BASED) ***Scholarships, grants, and awards:*** Federal Pell, FSEOG, state, private, college/university gift aid from institutional funds, United Negro College Fund, Federal Nursing.

GIFT AID (NON-NEED-BASED) ***Scholarships, grants, and awards by category:*** *Academic Interests/Achievement:* general academic interests/achievements. *Creative Arts/Performance:* music. *Special Achievements/Activities:* religious involvement. *Special Characteristics:* children and siblings of alumni, children of faculty/staff, children with a deceased or disabled parent, general special characteristics, local/state students, previous college experience, siblings of current students.

LOANS ***Programs:*** FFEL (Subsidized and Unsubsidized Stafford, PLUS), Perkins, state, college/university.

WORK-STUDY ***Federal work-study:*** Total amount: $90,500; 82 jobs averaging $1103.

APPLYING FOR FINANCIAL AID ***Required financial aid form:*** FAFSA.

CONTACT Nicole Brennan, Director of Financial Aid and Admission, Anna Maria College, 50 Sunset Lane, Paxton, MA 01612-1198, 508-849-3367 or toll-free 800-344-4586 Ext. 360. *Fax:* 508-849-3362. *E-mail:* nbrennan@annamaria.edu.

ANTIOCH COLLEGE

Yellow Springs, OH

Tuition & fees: $28,550 **Average undergraduate aid package: $30,640**

ABOUT THE INSTITUTION Independent, coed. Awards: bachelor's degrees. 56 undergraduate majors. Total enrollment: 341. Undergraduates: 330. Freshmen: 98. Both federal and institutional methodology are used as a basis for awarding need-based institutional aid.

UNDERGRADUATE EXPENSES for 2007–08 ***Comprehensive fee:*** $35,904 includes full-time tuition ($27,800), mandatory fees ($750), and room and board ($7354). ***College room only:*** $3597. ***Part-time tuition:*** $458 per credit hour.

FRESHMAN FINANCIAL AID (Fall 2006, est.) 94 applied for aid; of those 90% were deemed to have need. 100% of freshmen with need received aid; of those 18% had need fully met. ***Average percent of need met:*** 93% (excluding resources awarded to replace EFC). ***Average financial aid package:*** $26,620 (excluding resources awarded to replace EFC). 14% of all full-time freshmen had no need and received non-need-based gift aid.

UNDERGRADUATE FINANCIAL AID (Fall 2006, est.) 279 applied for aid; of those 91% were deemed to have need. 100% of undergraduates with need received aid; of those 47% had need fully met. ***Average percent of need met:*** 94% (excluding resources awarded to replace EFC). ***Average financial aid package:*** $30,640 (excluding resources awarded to replace EFC). 17% of all full-time undergraduates had no need and received non-need-based gift aid.

GIFT AID (NEED-BASED) ***Total amount:*** $2,635,998 (39% federal, 4% state, 57% institutional). ***Receiving aid:*** Freshmen: 61% (67); All full-time undergraduates: 72% (238). ***Average award:*** Freshmen: $21,950; Undergraduates: $11,076. ***Scholarships, grants, and awards:*** Federal Pell, FSEOG, state, private, college/university gift aid from institutional funds, United Negro College Fund.

GIFT AID (NON-NEED-BASED) ***Total amount:*** $2,780,544 (4% state, 90% institutional, 6% external sources). ***Receiving aid:*** Freshmen: 77% (85); Undergraduates: 77% (254). ***Average award:*** Freshmen: $13,700; Undergraduates: $23,327. ***Scholarships, grants, and awards by category:*** *Academic Interests/Achievement:* 23 awards ($156,214 total): biological sciences, education, general academic interests/achievements, humanities, international studies, mathematics, physical sciences, social sciences. *Special Characteristics:* 150 awards ($367,875 total): local/state students.

LOANS ***Student loans:*** $1,250,468 (67% need-based, 33% non-need-based). 85% of past graduating class borrowed through all loan programs. *Average indebtedness per student:* $17,112. ***Average need-based loan:*** Freshmen: $2487; Undergraduates: $3656. ***Parent loans:*** $1,497,286 (100% non-need-based). ***Programs:*** FFEL (Subsidized and Unsubsidized Stafford, PLUS), Perkins.

WORK-STUDY ***Federal work-study:*** Total amount: $813,494; 263 jobs averaging $2500. ***State or other work-study/employment:*** Total amount: $302,000 (100% non-need-based). Part-time jobs available (averaging $1000).

APPLYING FOR FINANCIAL AID ***Required financial aid forms:*** FAFSA, institution's own form. ***Financial aid deadline (priority):*** 3/1. ***Notification date:*** Continuous beginning 3/15. Students must reply within 4 weeks of notification.

CONTACT Jennifer Rhyner, Associate Director of Admissions and Financial Aid, Antioch College, 795 Livermore Street, Yellow Springs, OH 45387, 937-769-1120 or toll-free 800-543-9436. *Fax:* 937-769-1133. *E-mail:* jrhyner@antioch-college.edu.

ANTIOCH UNIVERSITY MCGREGOR

Yellow Springs, OH

Tuition & fees: $13,137 **Average undergraduate aid package: $6000**

ABOUT THE INSTITUTION Independent, coed. Awards: bachelor's and master's degrees and post-master's certificates. 6 undergraduate majors. Total enrollment: 679. Undergraduates: 160. Federal methodology is used as a basis for awarding need-based institutional aid.

UNDERGRADUATE EXPENSES for 2006–07 ***Application fee:*** $45. ***Tuition:*** full-time $12,912; part-time $269 per credit hour. ***Required fees:*** full-time $225; $75 per term part-time.

UNDERGRADUATE FINANCIAL AID (Fall 2006, est.) 41 applied for aid; of those 98% were deemed to have need. 100% of undergraduates with need received aid. ***Average percent of need met:*** 22% (excluding resources awarded to replace EFC). ***Average financial aid package:*** $6000 (excluding resources awarded to replace EFC).

GIFT AID (NEED-BASED) ***Total amount:*** $90,299 (72% federal, 28% state). ***Receiving aid:*** All full-time undergraduates: 63% (27). ***Average award:*** Undergraduates: $745. ***Scholarships, grants, and awards:*** Federal Pell, FSEOG, state.

GIFT AID (NON-NEED-BASED) ***Total amount:*** $13,800 (100% state).

LOANS ***Student loans:*** $375,401 (55% need-based, 45% non-need-based). 92% of past graduating class borrowed through all loan programs. *Average indebtedness per student:* $20,625. ***Average need-based loan:*** Undergraduates: $4000. ***Programs:*** FFEL (Subsidized and Unsubsidized Stafford, PLUS), Perkins.

WORK-STUDY Federal work-study jobs available.

APPLYING FOR FINANCIAL AID ***Required financial aid forms:*** FAFSA, institution's own form. ***Financial aid deadline:*** Continuous.

CONTACT Kathy John, Director of Financial Aid, Antioch University McGregor, 800 Livermore Street, Yellow Springs, OH 45387, 937-769-1840 or toll-free 937-769-1818. *Fax:* 937-769-1804. *E-mail:* kjohn@mcgregor.edu.

ANTIOCH UNIVERSITY SANTA BARBARA

Santa Barbara, CA

CONTACT Cecilia Schneider, Financial Aid Director, Antioch University Santa Barbara, 801 Garden Street, Santa Barbara, CA 93101-1580, 805-962-8179 Ext. 108. *Fax:* 805-962-4786.

ANTIOCH UNIVERSITY SEATTLE

Seattle, WA

Tuition & fees: $15,105 **Average undergraduate aid package: $6681**

ABOUT THE INSTITUTION Independent, coed. Awards: bachelor's, master's, and doctoral degrees. 1 undergraduate major. Total enrollment: 950. Undergraduates: 209. Federal methodology is used as a basis for awarding need-based institutional aid.

UNDERGRADUATE EXPENSES for 2006–07 ***Application fee:*** $50. ***Tuition:*** full-time $14,940; part-time $415 per credit. ***Required fees:*** full-time $165; $35 per quarter hour. ***Payment plan:*** Installment.

UNDERGRADUATE FINANCIAL AID (Fall 2005) 300 applied for aid; of those 83% were deemed to have need. 100% of undergraduates with need received aid; of those 60% had need fully met. ***Average percent of need met:*** 75% (excluding resources awarded to replace EFC). ***Average financial aid package:*** $6681 (excluding resources awarded to replace EFC).

GIFT AID (NEED-BASED) ***Total amount:*** $1,022,379 (27% federal, 29% state, 11% institutional, 33% external sources). ***Receiving aid:*** All full-time undergraduates: 43% (150). ***Average award:*** Undergraduates: $4000. ***Scholarships, grants, and awards:*** Federal Pell, FSEOG, state, private, college/university gift aid from institutional funds, United Negro College Fund.

GIFT AID (NON-NEED-BASED) ***Receiving aid:*** Undergraduates: 4% (15). ***Tuition waivers:*** Full or partial for employees or children of employees.

LOANS ***Student loans:*** $1,706,553 (53% need-based, 47% non-need-based). 85% of past graduating class borrowed through all loan programs. *Average indebtedness per student:* $15,999. ***Average need-based loan:*** Undergraduates: $5500. ***Parent loans:*** $8125 (100% non-need-based). ***Programs:*** FFEL (Subsidized and Unsubsidized Stafford, PLUS), Perkins.

WORK-STUDY ***Federal work-study:*** Total amount: $105,000; 18 jobs averaging $6000. ***State or other work-study/employment:*** Total amount: $10,000 (100% need-based). 2 part-time jobs averaging $5000.

APPLYING FOR FINANCIAL AID ***Required financial aid form:*** FAFSA. ***Financial aid deadline (priority):*** 4/15. ***Notification date:*** Continuous beginning 3/15. Students must reply within 2 weeks of notification.

CONTACT Katy Gilroy, Director of Financial Aid, Antioch University Seattle, 2326 Sixth Avenue, Seattle, WA 98121-1814, 206-268-4004. *Fax:* 206-268-4242. *E-mail:* kgilroy@antiochseattle.edu.

APEX SCHOOL OF THEOLOGY

Durham, NC

CONTACT Financial Aid Office, Apex School of Theology, 5104 Revere Road, Durham, NC 27713, 919-572-1625.

APPALACHIAN BIBLE COLLEGE

Bradley, WV

CONTACT Mrs. Shirley Carfrey, Director of Financial Aid, Appalachian Bible College, PO Box ABC, Sandbranch Road, Bradley, WV 25818, 304-877-6428 Ext. 3244 or toll-free 800-678-9ABC Ext. 3213. *Fax:* 304-877-5082. *E-mail:* scarfrey@abc.edu.

APPALACHIAN STATE UNIVERSITY

Boone, NC

Tuition & fees (NC res): $4187 **Average undergraduate aid package: $5844**

ABOUT THE INSTITUTION State-supported, coed. Awards: bachelor's, master's, and doctoral degrees and post-master's certificates. 84 undergraduate majors. Total enrollment: 15,117. Undergraduates: 13,447. Freshmen: 2,716. Federal methodology is used as a basis for awarding need-based institutional aid.

UNDERGRADUATE EXPENSES for 2006–07 ***Application fee:*** $45. ***Tuition, state resident:*** full-time $2221; part-time $75 per credit hour. ***Tuition, nonresident:*** full-time $11,963; part-time $404 per credit hour. ***Required fees:*** full-time $1966; $9 per credit hour. Part-time tuition and fees vary according to course load. ***College room and board:*** $5760; ***Room only:*** $3100. Room and board charges vary according to board plan and housing facility. ***Payment plans:*** Installment, deferred payment.

FRESHMAN FINANCIAL AID (Fall 2006, est.) 1788 applied for aid; of those 51% were deemed to have need. 96% of freshmen with need received aid; of those 21% had need fully met. ***Average percent of need met:*** 72% (excluding resources awarded to replace EFC). ***Average financial aid package:*** $5314 (excluding resources awarded to replace EFC). 11% of all full-time freshmen had no need and received non-need-based gift aid.

UNDERGRADUATE FINANCIAL AID (Fall 2006, est.) 7,977 applied for aid; of those 59% were deemed to have need. 94% of undergraduates with need received aid; of those 24% had need fully met. ***Average percent of need met:*** 76% (excluding resources awarded to replace EFC). ***Average financial aid package:*** $5844 (excluding resources awarded to replace EFC). 6% of all full-time undergraduates had no need and received non-need-based gift aid.

GIFT AID (NEED-BASED) ***Total amount:*** $16,388,413 (40% federal, 37% state, 16% institutional, 7% external sources). ***Receiving aid:*** Freshmen: 27% (744); All full-time undergraduates: 30% (3,702). ***Average award:*** Freshmen: $5040; Undergraduates: $4711. ***Scholarships, grants, and awards:*** Federal Pell, FSEOG, state, private, college/university gift aid from institutional funds.

GIFT AID (NON-NEED-BASED) ***Total amount:*** $5,198,613 (17% federal, 42% state, 21% institutional, 20% external sources). ***Receiving aid:*** Freshmen: 11% (310); Undergraduates: 7% (875). ***Average award:*** Freshmen: $2346; Undergraduates: $3016. ***Scholarships, grants, and awards by category:*** *Academic Interests/Achievement:* 3,490 awards ($3,564,490 total): general academic interests/achievements. *Creative Arts/Performance:* general creative arts/performance. *Special Achievements/Activities:* general special achievements/activities. *Special Characteristics:* 182 awards ($1,701,683 total): first-generation college students, general special characteristics, handicapped students, members of minority groups, out-of-state students, veterans, veterans' children. ***Tuition waivers:*** Full or partial for employees or children of employees. ***ROTC:*** Army.

LOANS ***Student loans:*** $26,385,977 (70% need-based, 30% non-need-based). 49% of past graduating class borrowed through all loan programs. *Average indebtedness per student:* $14,838. ***Average need-based loan:*** Freshmen: $2489; Undergraduates: $3381. ***Parent loans:*** $16,874,410 (49% need-based, 51% non-need-based). ***Programs:*** FFEL (Subsidized and Unsubsidized Stafford, PLUS), Perkins, college/university.

WORK-STUDY ***Federal work-study:*** Total amount: $560,361; 340 jobs averaging $1648. ***State or other work-study/employment:*** Total amount: $921,244 (100% non-need-based). 2,859 part-time jobs averaging $1236.

ATHLETIC AWARDS Total amount: $2,280,782 (34% need-based, 66% non-need-based).

APPLYING FOR FINANCIAL AID ***Required financial aid form:*** FAFSA. ***Financial aid deadline (priority):*** 3/15. ***Notification date:*** Continuous beginning 4/1. Students must reply within 3 weeks of notification.

CONTACT Kay Stroud, Associate Director of Student Financial Aid, Appalachian State University, Office of Student Financial Aid, ASU Box 32059, Boone, NC 28608-2059, 828-262-8687. *Fax:* 828-262-2585. *E-mail:* stroudkn@appstate.edu.

AQUINAS COLLEGE

Grand Rapids, MI

CONTACT David J. Steffee, Director Financial Aid, Aquinas College, 1607 Robinson Road, Grand Rapids, MI 49506-1799, 616-459-8281 Ext. 5127 or toll-free 800-678-9593. *Fax:* 616-732-4547. *E-mail:* steffdav@aquinas.edu.

AQUINAS COLLEGE

Nashville, TN

CONTACT Zelena O'Sullivan, Director of Financial Aid, Aquinas College, 4210 Harding Road, Nashville, TN 37205-2005, 615-297-7545 Ext. 431 or toll-free 800-649-9956. *Fax:* 615-279-3891. *E-mail:* osullivanz@aquinas-tn.edu.

ARCADIA UNIVERSITY

Glenside, PA

Tuition & fees: $25,990 **Average undergraduate aid package: $19,540**

ABOUT THE INSTITUTION Independent religious, coed. Awards: bachelor's, master's, and doctoral degrees. 52 undergraduate majors. Total enrollment: 3,595. Undergraduates: 2,119. Freshmen: 574. Federal methodology is used as a basis for awarding need-based institutional aid.

UNDERGRADUATE EXPENSES for 2006–07 ***Application fee:*** $30. ***Comprehensive fee:*** $35,650 includes full-time tuition ($25,650), mandatory fees ($340), and room and board ($9660). ***College room only:*** $6680. Full-time tuition and fees vary according to course load, degree level, and program. Room and board charges vary according to board plan. ***Part-time tuition:*** $442 per credit. ***Payment plans:*** Installment, deferred payment.

FRESHMAN FINANCIAL AID (Fall 2006, est.) 540 applied for aid; of those 93% were deemed to have need. 100% of freshmen with need received aid; of those 28% had need fully met. ***Average percent of need met:*** 81% (excluding resources awarded to replace EFC). ***Average financial aid package:*** $21,330 (excluding resources awarded to replace EFC). 10% of all full-time freshmen had no need and received non-need-based gift aid.

UNDERGRADUATE FINANCIAL AID (Fall 2006, est.) 1,759 applied for aid; of those 97% were deemed to have need. 98% of undergraduates with need received aid; of those 31% had need fully met. ***Average percent of need met:*** 74% (excluding resources awarded to replace EFC). ***Average financial aid package:*** $19,540 (excluding resources awarded to replace EFC). 9% of all full-time undergraduates had no need and received non-need-based gift aid.

GIFT AID (NEED-BASED) ***Total amount:*** $22,266,052 (8% federal, 10% state, 78% institutional, 4% external sources). ***Receiving aid:*** Freshmen: 86% (492); All full-time undergraduates: 88% (1,659). ***Average award:*** Freshmen: $16,443; Undergraduates: $16,562. ***Scholarships, grants, and awards:*** Federal Pell, FSEOG, state, private, college/university gift aid from institutional funds.

GIFT AID (NON-NEED-BASED) ***Total amount:*** $4,694,168 (90% institutional, 10% external sources). ***Receiving aid:*** Freshmen: 83% (476); Undergraduates:

82% (1,540). ***Average award:*** Freshmen: $10,744; Undergraduates: $9315. ***Scholarships, grants, and awards by category:*** *Academic Interests/Achievement:* 1,215 awards ($12,473,520 total): general academic interests/achievements. *Creative Arts/Performance:* 83 awards ($214,000 total): applied art and design, art/fine arts, theater/drama. *Special Achievements/Activities:* 712 awards ($2,187,645 total): community service, general special achievements/activities, leadership, memberships. *Special Characteristics:* 34 awards ($83,723 total): children and siblings of alumni, relatives of clergy, religious affiliation. ***Tuition waivers:*** Full or partial for employees or children of employees.

LOANS ***Student loans:*** $15,726,760 (67% need-based, 33% non-need-based). 79% of past graduating class borrowed through all loan programs. *Average indebtedness per student:* $32,875. ***Average need-based loan:*** Freshmen: $4455; Undergraduates: $5365. ***Parent loans:*** $3,808,381 (40% need-based, 60% non-need-based). ***Programs:*** FFEL (Subsidized and Unsubsidized Stafford, PLUS), Perkins, college/university.

WORK-STUDY ***Federal work-study:*** Total amount: $1,190,487; 872 jobs averaging $1287. ***State or other work-study/employment:*** Total amount: $306,345 (14% need-based, 86% non-need-based). 245 part-time jobs averaging $1196.

APPLYING FOR FINANCIAL AID ***Required financial aid forms:*** FAFSA, institution's own form. ***Financial aid deadline (priority):*** 3/1. ***Notification date:*** Continuous. Students must reply by 5/1.

CONTACT Holly Kirkpatrick, Director of Financial Aid, Arcadia University, 450 South Easton Road, Glenside, PA 19038, 215-572-4475 or toll-free 877-ARCADIA. *Fax:* 215-572-4049. *E-mail:* kirkpath@arcadia.edu.

ARGOSY UNIVERSITY, ATLANTA

Atlanta, GA

CONTACT Ashley Manker, Financial Aid Office, Argosy University, Atlanta, One Lakeside Commons, Building One, 990 Hammond Drive, 11th Floor, Atlanta, GA 30328, 770-671-1200 Ext. 1036 or toll-free 888-671-4777. *Fax:* 770-407-1110. *E-mail:* amanker@argosyu.edu.

ARGOSY UNIVERSITY, CHICAGO

Chicago, IL

CONTACT Ardie Elgersma, Financial Aid Office, Argosy University, Chicago, Two First National Plaza, 20 South Clark Street, Third Floor, Chicago, IL 60603, 312-201-0200 Ext. 3909 or toll-free 800-626-4123 (in-state). *Fax:* 312-201-1907. *E-mail:* aelgersma@argosyu.edu.

ARGOSY UNIVERSITY, DALLAS

Dallas, TX

CONTACT Beth Kirkman, Financial Aid Office, Argosy University, Dallas, One North Park, Suite 315, 8950 North Central Expressway, Dallas, TX 75231, 214-459-2204 or toll-free 866-954-9900. *Fax:* 214-696-3900. *E-mail:* bkirkman@argosyu.edu.

ARGOSY UNIVERSITY, DENVER

Denver, CO

CONTACT Financial Aid Office, Argosy University, Denver, 1200 Lincoln Street, Denver, CO 80203, 303-248-2700 or toll-free 866-431-5981.

ARGOSY UNIVERSITY, HAWAI'I

Honolulu, HI

CONTACT Mary Vee Cheung, Financial Aid Office, Argosy University, Hawai'i, 400 Pacific Tower, 1001 Bishop Street, Honolulu, HI 96813, 808-536-5555 Ext. 204 or toll-free 888-323-2777 (in-state). *Fax:* 808-536-5505. *E-mail:* mvee@argosyu.edu.

ARGOSY UNIVERSITY, INLAND EMPIRE

San Bernardino, CA

CONTACT Financial Aid Office, Argosy University, Inland Empire, 636 East Brier Drive, Suite 235, San Bernardino, CA 92408, 909-915-3800 or toll-free 866-217-9075.

ARGOSY UNIVERSITY, NASHVILLE

Franklin, TN

CONTACT Financial Aid Office, Argosy University, Nashville, 341 Cool Springs Boulevard, Suite 210, Franklin, TN 37067-7226, 615-369-0616.

ARGOSY UNIVERSITY, ORANGE COUNTY

Santa Ana, CA

CONTACT Thomas Cameron, Financial Aid Officer, Argosy University, Orange County, 3745 West Chapman Avenue, Suite 100, Orange, CA 92868, 714-450-4826 or toll-free 800-716-9598. *Fax:* 714-450-0776. *E-mail:* tcameron@argosyu.edu.

ARGOSY UNIVERSITY, PHOENIX

Phoenix, AZ

CONTACT Amy Vincent, Financial Aid Office, Argosy University, Phoenix, 2301 West Dunlap, Suite 211, Phoenix, AZ 85021, 602-216-2600 or toll-free 866-216-2777. *Fax:* 602-216-2601. *E-mail:* avincent@argosyu.edu.

ARGOSY UNIVERSITY, SAN DIEGO

San Diego, CA

CONTACT Financial Aid Office, Argosy University, San Diego, 7650 Mission Valley Road, San Diego, CA 92108, toll-free 866-505-0333.

ARGOSY UNIVERSITY, SAN FRANCISCO BAY AREA

Point Richmond, CA

CONTACT Adrian Ramos, Financial Aid Office, Argosy University, San Francisco Bay Area, 999 Canal Boulevard, Point Richmond, CA 94804, 510-215-0277 Ext. 217 or toll-free 866-215-2777 Ext. 205 (in-state), 866-215-2777 (out-of-state). *Fax:* 510-215-0299. *E-mail:* aramos@argosyu.edu.

ARGOSY UNIVERSITY, SARASOTA

Sarasota, FL

CONTACT Deborah Kerris, Financial Aid Office, Argosy University, Sarasota, 5250 17th Street, Sarasota, FL 34235, 800-331-5995 Ext. 244 or toll-free 800-331-5995. *Fax:* 941-371-8910. *E-mail:* dkerris@argosyu.edu.

ARGOSY UNIVERSITY, SCHAUMBURG

Schaumburg, IL

CONTACT Virginia Carlin, Financial Aid Office, Argosy University, Schaumburg, One Continental Towers, 1701 Golf Road, Suite 101, Rolling Meadows, IL 60008, 847-290-7400 or toll-free 866-290-2777. *Fax:* 847-290-8432. *E-mail:* vcarlin@argosyu.edu.

ARGOSY UNIVERSITY, SEATTLE

Seattle, WA

CONTACT Eun-Ju Lee, Assistant Director of Student Services, Argosy University, Seattle, 1019 Eighth Avenue North, Seattle, WA 98109, 206-283-4500 Ext. 235 or toll-free 866-283-2777 (out-of-state). *Fax:* 206-283-5777. *E-mail:* elee@argosyu.edu.

ARGOSY UNIVERSITY, TAMPA

Tampa, FL

CONTACT Donna Page, Financial Aid Office, Argosy University, Tampa, 4401 North Hines Avenue, Tampa, FL 33614, 813-393-5290 or toll-free 800-850-6488 Ext. 5260 (in-state), 800-850-6488 (out-of-state). *Fax:* 813-874-1989. *E-mail:* dpage@edmc.edu.

ARGOSY UNIVERSITY, TWIN CITIES

Eagan, MN

CONTACT Office of Student Finance, Argosy University, Twin Cities, 1515 Central Parkway, Eagan, MN 55121-1756, 651-846-3384 or toll-free 888-844-2004. *Fax:* 651-994-0170. *E-mail:* financialaidautc@argosyu.edu.

ARGOSY UNIVERSITY, WASHINGTON D.C.

Arlington, VA

CONTACT Financial Aid Office, Argosy University, Washington D.C., 1550 Wilson Boulevard, Suite 600, Arlington, VA 22209, 703-526-5800 or toll-free 866-703-2777 Ext. 5833.

ARIZONA STATE UNIVERSITY

Tempe, AZ

Tuition & fees (AZ res): $4688 Average undergraduate aid package: $8649

ABOUT THE INSTITUTION State-supported, coed. Awards: bachelor's, master's, doctoral, and first professional degrees and post-bachelor's and post-master's certificates. 86 undergraduate majors. Total enrollment: 51,234. Undergraduates: 41,815. Freshmen: 7,894. Federal methodology is used as a basis for awarding need-based institutional aid.

UNDERGRADUATE EXPENSES for 2006–07 ***Application fee:*** $25; $50 for nonresidents. ***Tuition, state resident:*** full-time $4591; part-time $240 per credit. ***Tuition, nonresident:*** full-time $15,750; part-time $656 per credit. Full-time tuition and fees vary according to location and program. Part-time tuition and fees vary according to location and program. ***College room and board:*** $6900; ***Room only:*** $4200. Room and board charges vary according to board plan, housing facility, and location. ***Payment plan:*** Installment.

FRESHMAN FINANCIAL AID (Fall 2005) 3966 applied for aid; of those 72% were deemed to have need. 100% of freshmen with need received aid; of those 23% had need fully met. ***Average percent of need met:*** 65% (excluding resources awarded to replace EFC). ***Average financial aid package:*** $8503 (excluding resources awarded to replace EFC). 24% of all full-time freshmen had no need and received non-need-based gift aid.

UNDERGRADUATE FINANCIAL AID (Fall 2005) 17,003 applied for aid; of those 77% were deemed to have need. 100% of undergraduates with need received aid; of those 19% had need fully met. ***Average percent of need met:*** 64% (excluding resources awarded to replace EFC). ***Average financial aid package:*** $8649 (excluding resources awarded to replace EFC). 14% of all full-time undergraduates had no need and received non-need-based gift aid.

GIFT AID (NEED-BASED) ***Total amount:*** $69,470,222 (40% federal, 1% state, 49% institutional, 10% external sources). ***Receiving aid:*** Freshmen: 35% (2,609); All full-time undergraduates: 34% (11,173). ***Average award:*** Freshmen: $8745; Undergraduates: $5652. ***Scholarships, grants, and awards:*** Federal Pell, FSEOG, state, private, college/university gift aid from institutional funds, Federal Nursing.

GIFT AID (NON-NEED-BASED) ***Total amount:*** $38,556,256 (1% federal, 1% state, 81% institutional, 17% external sources). ***Receiving aid:*** Freshmen: 6% (412); Undergraduates: 3% (937). ***Average award:*** Freshmen: $6317; Undergraduates: $8031. ***Scholarships, grants, and awards by category:*** *Academic Interests/Achievement:* architecture, area/ethnic studies, biological sciences, business, communication, computer science, education, engineering/technologies, English, foreign languages, general academic interests/achievements, health fields, home economics, humanities, mathematics, military science, physical sciences, premedicine, social sciences. *Creative Arts/Performance:* applied art and design, art/fine arts, cinema/film/broadcasting, creative writing, dance, debating, general creative arts/performance, journalism/publications, music, performing arts, theater/drama. *Special Achievements/Activities:* general special achievements/activities. ***Tuition waivers:*** Full or partial for employees or children of employees. ***ROTC:*** Army, Air Force.

LOANS ***Student loans:*** $95,926,737 (72% need-based, 28% non-need-based). 45% of past graduating class borrowed through all loan programs. *Average indebtedness per student:* $15,894. ***Average need-based loan:*** Freshmen: $2486; Undergraduates: $4123. ***Parent loans:*** $31,241,330 (29% need-based, 71% non-need-based). ***Programs:*** Federal Direct (Subsidized and Unsubsidized Stafford, PLUS), FFEL (PLUS), Perkins.

WORK-STUDY ***Federal work-study:*** Total amount: $1,096,940; 605 jobs averaging $1813. ***State or other work-study/employment:*** Total amount: $13,025,165 (21% need-based, 79% non-need-based). 4,554 part-time jobs averaging $2860.

ATHLETIC AWARDS Total amount: $5,826,001 (25% need-based, 75% non-need-based).

APPLYING FOR FINANCIAL AID ***Required financial aid form:*** FAFSA. ***Financial aid deadline (priority):*** 3/1.

CONTACT Craig Fennell, Director of Student Financial Assistance, Arizona State University, Box 870412, Tempe, AZ 85287-0412, 480-965-3355. *Fax:* 480-965-9484. *E-mail:* financialaid@asu.edu.

ARIZONA STATE UNIVERSITY AT THE DOWNTOWN PHOENIX CAMPUS

Phoenix, AZ

CONTACT Financial Aid Office, Arizona State University at the Downtown Phoenix Campus, 411 N. Central Avenue, Phoenix, AZ 85004, 602-496-4636.

ARIZONA STATE UNIVERSITY AT THE POLYTECHNIC CAMPUS

Mesa, AZ

Tuition & fees (AZ res): $4448 Average undergraduate aid package: $8439

ABOUT THE INSTITUTION State-supported, coed. Awards: bachelor's and master's degrees. 25 undergraduate majors. Total enrollment: 6,545. Undergraduates: 5,589. Freshmen: 236. Federal methodology is used as a basis for awarding need-based institutional aid.

UNDERGRADUATE EXPENSES for 2006–07 ***Application fee:*** $50. ***Tuition, state resident:*** full-time $4400; part-time $229 per credit hour. ***Tuition, nonresident:*** full-time $15,750; part-time $656 per credit hour. Full-time tuition and fees vary according to degree level, location, and program. Part-time tuition and fees vary according to course load, degree level, location, and program. ***College room and board:*** $5100; ***Room only:*** $3200. Room and board charges vary according to board plan, housing facility, location, and student level. ***Payment plan:*** Installment.

FRESHMAN FINANCIAL AID (Fall 2005) 34 applied for aid; of those 53% were deemed to have need. 100% of freshmen with need received aid; of those 17% had need fully met. ***Average percent of need met:*** 70% (excluding resources awarded to replace EFC). ***Average financial aid package:*** $10,513 (excluding resources awarded to replace EFC). 37% of all full-time freshmen had no need and received non-need-based gift aid.

UNDERGRADUATE FINANCIAL AID (Fall 2005) 796 applied for aid; of those 73% were deemed to have need. 100% of undergraduates with need received aid; of those 14% had need fully met. ***Average percent of need met:*** 60% (excluding resources awarded to replace EFC). ***Average financial aid package:*** $8439 (excluding resources awarded to replace EFC). 6% of all full-time undergraduates had no need and received non-need-based gift aid.

GIFT AID (NEED-BASED) ***Total amount:*** $4,408,571 (46% federal, 44% institutional, 10% external sources). ***Receiving aid:*** Freshmen: 45% (17); All full-time undergraduates: 41% (499). ***Average award:*** Freshmen: $9456; Undergraduates: $4823. ***Scholarships, grants, and awards:*** Federal Pell, FSEOG, state, private, college/university gift aid from institutional funds.

GIFT AID (NON-NEED-BASED) ***Total amount:*** $932,222 (72% institutional, 28% external sources). ***Receiving aid:*** Freshmen: 3% (1); Undergraduates: 1% (11). ***Average award:*** Freshmen: $7280; Undergraduates: $4327. ***Scholarships, grants, and awards by category:*** *Academic Interests/Achievement:* general academic interests/achievements. *Creative Arts/Performance:* general creative arts/performance. *Special Achievements/Activities:* general special achievements/activities. *Special Characteristics:* general special characteristics. ***Tuition waivers:*** Full or partial for employees or children of employees. ***ROTC:*** Army cooperative, Air Force cooperative.

LOANS ***Student loans:*** $9,244,806 (76% need-based, 24% non-need-based). ***Average need-based loan:*** Freshmen: $2600; Undergraduates: $4677. ***Parent loans:*** $2,033,639 (36% need-based, 64% non-need-based). ***Programs:*** Federal Direct (Subsidized and Unsubsidized Stafford, PLUS), FFEL (PLUS), Perkins.

WORK-STUDY ***Federal work-study:*** Total amount: $69,703; 37 jobs averaging $1833. ***State or other work-study/employment:*** Total amount: $641,413 (22% need-based, 78% non-need-based). 207 part-time jobs averaging $3098.

ATHLETIC AWARDS Total amount: $22,498 (100% non-need-based).

APPLYING FOR FINANCIAL AID ***Required financial aid form:*** FAFSA. ***Financial aid deadline (priority):*** 3/1. ***Notification date:*** Continuous beginning 4/15. Students must reply within 4 weeks of notification.

CONTACT Heather Klotz, Financial Aid Counselor, Arizona State University at the Polytechnic Campus, 7001 East Williams Field Road, Building 370, Mesa, AZ 85212, 480-727-1042. *Fax:* 480-727-1008. *E-mail:* heather.klotz@asu.edu.

ARIZONA STATE UNIVERSITY EAST

Mesa, AZ

See Arizona State University at the Polytechnic Campus.

ARIZONA STATE UNIVERSITY WEST

Phoenix, AZ

ABOUT THE INSTITUTION State-supported, coed. Awards: bachelor's and master's degrees and post-bachelor's certificates. 23 undergraduate majors. Total enrollment: 8,211. Undergraduates: 6,941. Freshmen: 539.

GIFT AID (NEED-BASED) ***Scholarships, grants, and awards:*** Federal Pell, FSEOG, state, private, college/university gift aid from institutional funds.

GIFT AID (NON-NEED-BASED) ***Scholarships, grants, and awards by category:*** *Academic Interests/Achievement:* general academic interests/achievements.

LOANS ***Programs:*** Federal Direct (Subsidized and Unsubsidized Stafford), FFEL (PLUS), Perkins, college/university.

APPLYING FOR FINANCIAL AID ***Required financial aid form:*** FAFSA.

CONTACT Leah Samudio, Financial Aid Manager, Arizona State University West, 4701 West Thunderbird Road, PO Box 37100, Phoenix, AZ 85069-7100, 602-543-8178. *E-mail:* leah.samudio@asu.edu.

ARKANSAS BAPTIST COLLEGE

Little Rock, AR

CONTACT Director of Financial Aid, Arkansas Baptist College, 1600 Bishop Street, Little Rock, AR 72202-6067, 501-374-7856.

ARKANSAS STATE UNIVERSITY

Jonesboro, AR

Tuition & fees (AR res): $5710   Average undergraduate aid package: $9200

ABOUT THE INSTITUTION State-supported, coed. Awards: associate, bachelor's, master's, and doctoral degrees and post-bachelor's and post-master's certificates (specialist). 80 undergraduate majors. Total enrollment: 10,727. Undergraduates: 9,340. Freshmen: 1,727. Both federal and institutional methodology are used as a basis for awarding need-based institutional aid.

UNDERGRADUATE EXPENSES for 2006–07 ***Application fee:*** $15. ***Tuition, state resident:*** full-time $4470; part-time $149 per credit hour. ***Tuition, nonresident:*** full-time $11,520; part-time $384 per credit hour. ***Required fees:*** full-time $1240; $39 per credit hour or $25 per term part-time. Full-time tuition and fees vary according to course load, location, and program. Part-time tuition and fees vary according to course load, location, and program. ***College room and board:*** $4440. Room and board charges vary according to board plan and housing facility. ***Payment plan:*** Installment.

FRESHMAN FINANCIAL AID (Fall 2006, est.) 1522 applied for aid; of those 96% were deemed to have need. 100% of freshmen with need received aid; of those 21% had need fully met. ***Average percent of need met:*** 67% (excluding resources awarded to replace EFC). ***Average financial aid package:*** $8100 (excluding resources awarded to replace EFC). 17% of all full-time freshmen had no need and received non-need-based gift aid.

UNDERGRADUATE FINANCIAL AID (Fall 2006, est.) 6,085 applied for aid; of those 95% were deemed to have need. 100% of undergraduates with need received aid; of those 27% had need fully met. ***Average percent of need met:*** 55% (excluding resources awarded to replace EFC). ***Average financial aid package:*** $9200 (excluding resources awarded to replace EFC). 10% of all full-time undergraduates had no need and received non-need-based gift aid.

GIFT AID (NEED-BASED) ***Total amount:*** $27,926,090 (51% federal, 12% state, 29% institutional, 8% external sources). ***Receiving aid:*** Freshmen: 82% (1,358); All full-time undergraduates: 66% (4,852). ***Average award:*** Freshmen: $6000; Undergraduates: $5400. ***Scholarships, grants, and awards:*** Federal Pell, FSEOG, state, private, college/university gift aid from institutional funds.

GIFT AID (NON-NEED-BASED) ***Receiving aid:*** Freshmen: 31% (510); Undergraduates: 37% (2,750). ***Average award:*** Freshmen: $3500; Undergraduates: $3500. ***Scholarships, grants, and awards by category:*** *Academic Interests/Achievement:* 3,000 awards ($8,200,000 total): agriculture, biological sciences, business, communication, computer science, education, engineering/technologies, English, general academic interests/achievements, health fields, humanities, library science, mathematics, military science, physical sciences, premedicine, social sciences. *Creative Arts/Performance:* 340 awards ($720,000 total): art/fine arts, cinema/film/broadcasting, debating, journalism/publications, music, performing arts, theater/drama. *Special Achievements/Activities:* 300 awards ($350,000 total): cheerleading/drum major, community service, general special achievements/activities. *Special Characteristics:* 150 awards ($380,000 total): adult students, children and siblings of alumni, children of faculty/staff, ethnic background, first-generation college students, general special characteristics, handicapped students, local/state students, members of minority groups, out-of-state students, veterans, veterans' children. ***Tuition waivers:*** Full or partial for children of alumni, employees or children of employees, senior citizens. ***ROTC:*** Army.

LOANS ***Student loans:*** $32,875,227 (68% need-based, 32% non-need-based). 68% of past graduating class borrowed through all loan programs. *Average indebtedness per student:* $18,500. ***Average need-based loan:*** Freshmen: $3000; Undergraduates: $4100. ***Programs:*** FFEL (Subsidized and Unsubsidized Stafford, PLUS), Perkins.

WORK-STUDY ***Federal work-study:*** Total amount: $818,020; 300 jobs averaging $3200. ***State or other work-study/employment:*** Total amount: $1,980,000 (100% non-need-based). Part-time jobs available.

ATHLETIC AWARDS Total amount: $2,355,860 (39% need-based, 61% non-need-based).

APPLYING FOR FINANCIAL AID ***Required financial aid forms:*** FAFSA, institution's own form. ***Financial aid deadline:*** 7/1 (priority: 2/15). ***Notification date:*** Continuous beginning 6/1. Students must reply within 2 weeks of notification.

CONTACT Mr. Gregory Thornburg, Director of Financial Aid/Dean of Enrollment Services, Arkansas State University, PO Box 1620, State University, AR 72467, 870-972-2310 or toll-free 800-382-3030 (in-state). *Fax:* 870-972-2794. *E-mail:* gthorn@astate.edu.

ARKANSAS TECH UNIVERSITY

Russellville, AR

Tuition & fees (AR res): $4880   Average undergraduate aid package: $4960

ABOUT THE INSTITUTION State-supported, coed. Awards: associate, bachelor's, and master's degrees (Educational Specialist's). 53 undergraduate majors. Total enrollment: 7,038. Undergraduates: 6,435. Freshmen: 1,515. Federal methodology is used as a basis for awarding need-based institutional aid.

UNDERGRADUATE EXPENSES for 2006–07 ***Tuition, state resident:*** full-time $4470; part-time $149 per credit hour. ***Tuition, nonresident:*** full-time $8940; part-time $298 per credit hour. ***Required fees:*** full-time $410; $4 per credit hour or $145 per term part-time. Full-time tuition and fees vary according to course load and location. Part-time tuition and fees vary according to course load and location. ***College room and board:*** $4422; ***Room only:*** $2412. Room and board charges vary according to board plan and housing facility. ***Payment plans:*** Installment, deferred payment.

FRESHMAN FINANCIAL AID (Fall 2005) 1066 applied for aid; of those 83% were deemed to have need. 99% of freshmen with need received aid; of those 29% had need fully met. ***Average percent of need met:*** 39% (excluding resources awarded to replace EFC). ***Average financial aid package:*** $3832 (excluding resources awarded to replace EFC). 26% of all full-time freshmen had no need and received non-need-based gift aid.

UNDERGRADUATE FINANCIAL AID (Fall 2005) 3,784 applied for aid; of those 86% were deemed to have need. 99% of undergraduates with need received aid; of those 24% had need fully met. ***Average percent of need met:*** 43% (excluding resources awarded to replace EFC). ***Average financial aid package:*** $4960 (excluding resources awarded to replace EFC). 20% of all full-time undergraduates had no need and received non-need-based gift aid.

GIFT AID (NEED-BASED) ***Total amount:*** $9,354,249 (78% federal, 22% state). ***Receiving aid:*** Freshmen: 48% (706); All full-time undergraduates: 47% (2,451). ***Average award:*** Freshmen: $2682; Undergraduates: $2547. ***Scholarships, grants, and awards:*** Federal Pell, FSEOG, state, private, college/university gift aid from institutional funds.

GIFT AID (NON-NEED-BASED) ***Total amount:*** $10,731,109 (1% federal, 7% state, 83% institutional, 9% external sources). ***Receiving aid:*** Freshmen: 33% (483); Undergraduates: 22% (1,158). ***Average award:*** Freshmen: $5732; Undergraduates: $5884. ***Scholarships, grants, and awards by category:*** *Academic Interests/Achievement:* 1,888 awards ($7,832,592 total): agriculture, engineering/technologies, general academic interests/achievements, international studies. *Creative Arts/Performance:* 293 awards ($589,313 total): creative writing, general creative arts/performance, music, theater/drama. *Special Achievements/Activities:* 60 awards ($39,289 total): leadership. *Special Characteristics:* 139 awards ($330,265 total): adult students, children of faculty/staff, ethnic background, international students, out-of-state students, previous college experience, public servants. ***Tuition waivers:*** Full or partial for employees or children of employees, senior citizens. ***ROTC:*** Army cooperative.

LOANS ***Student loans:*** $18,312,175 (52% need-based, 48% non-need-based). 58% of past graduating class borrowed through all loan programs. *Average indebtedness per student:* $18,155. ***Average need-based loan:*** Freshmen: $1111; Undergraduates: $2299. ***Parent loans:*** $1,256,363 (100% non-need-based). ***Programs:*** FFEL (Subsidized and Unsubsidized Stafford, PLUS), Perkins.

WORK-STUDY ***Federal work-study:*** Total amount: $247,194; 250 jobs averaging $1109. ***State or other work-study/employment:*** Total amount: $620,263 (100% non-need-based). 435 part-time jobs averaging $1077.

ATHLETIC AWARDS Total amount: $741,955 (100% non-need-based).

APPLYING FOR FINANCIAL AID ***Required financial aid form:*** FAFSA. ***Financial aid deadline (priority):*** 4/15. ***Notification date:*** Continuous beginning 5/1. Students must reply within 2 weeks of notification.

CONTACT Niki Harrison, Financial Aid Officer, Arkansas Tech University, Bryan Student Services Building, Room 117, Russellville, AR 72801-2222, 479-968-0399 or toll-free 800-582-6953. *Fax:* 479-964-0857. *E-mail:* niki.harrison@atu.edu.

ARLINGTON BAPTIST COLLEGE

Arlington, TX

Tuition & fees: $6090 **Average undergraduate aid package: $7690**

ABOUT THE INSTITUTION Independent Baptist, coed. Awards: bachelor's degrees. 10 undergraduate majors. Total enrollment: 153. Undergraduates: 153. Freshmen: 27. Federal methodology is used as a basis for awarding need-based institutional aid.

UNDERGRADUATE EXPENSES for 2007–08 ***Application fee:*** $15. ***Comprehensive fee:*** $10,190 includes full-time tuition ($5550), mandatory fees ($540), and room and board ($4100). ***Part-time tuition:*** $185 per hour.

FRESHMAN FINANCIAL AID (Fall 2005) 32 applied for aid; of those 69% were deemed to have need. 100% of freshmen with need received aid; of those 91% had need fully met. ***Average financial aid package:*** $8062 (excluding resources awarded to replace EFC).

UNDERGRADUATE FINANCIAL AID (Fall 2005) 145 applied for aid; of those 89% were deemed to have need. 100% of undergraduates with need received aid; of those 83% had need fully met. ***Average financial aid package:*** $7690 (excluding resources awarded to replace EFC).

GIFT AID (NEED-BASED) ***Total amount:*** $380,696 (51% federal, 49% institutional). ***Scholarships, grants, and awards:*** Federal Pell, private, college/university gift aid from institutional funds.

GIFT AID (NON-NEED-BASED) ***Scholarships, grants, and awards by category:*** *Special Characteristics:* children of faculty/staff, spouses of current students.

LOANS ***Student loans:*** $611,395 (100% need-based). 70% of past graduating class borrowed through all loan programs. *Average indebtedness per student:* $8100. ***Programs:*** FFEL (Subsidized and Unsubsidized Stafford, PLUS).

WORK-STUDY Federal work-study jobs available.

APPLYING FOR FINANCIAL AID ***Required financial aid form:*** FAFSA. ***Financial aid deadline (priority):*** 8/1. ***Notification date:*** Continuous beginning 9/1.

CONTACT Mr. David B. Clogston Jr., Business Manager, Arlington Baptist College, 3001 West Division Street, Arlington, TX 76012-3425, 817-461-8741 Ext. 110. *Fax:* 817-274-1138.

ARMSTRONG ATLANTIC STATE UNIVERSITY

Savannah, GA

Tuition & fees (GA res): $3074 **Average undergraduate aid package: $6848**

ABOUT THE INSTITUTION State-supported, coed. Awards: associate, bachelor's, and master's degrees. 34 undergraduate majors. Total enrollment: 6,728. Undergraduates: 6,086. Freshmen: 855. Federal methodology is used as a basis for awarding need-based institutional aid.

UNDERGRADUATE EXPENSES for 2007–08 ***Application fee:*** $20. ***Tuition, state resident:*** full-time $2560; part-time $107 per credit hour. ***Tuition, nonresident:*** full-time $10,242; part-time $427 per credit hour. ***Required fees:*** full-time $514; $257 per term part-time. ***College room and board:*** ***Room only:*** $6000.

FRESHMAN FINANCIAL AID (Fall 2005) 595 applied for aid; of those 62% were deemed to have need. 100% of freshmen with need received aid; of those 85% had need fully met. ***Average percent of need met:*** 85% (excluding resources awarded to replace EFC). ***Average financial aid package:*** $5818 (excluding resources awarded to replace EFC). 33% of all full-time freshmen had no need and received non-need-based gift aid.

UNDERGRADUATE FINANCIAL AID (Fall 2005) 4,362 applied for aid; of those 64% were deemed to have need. 100% of undergraduates with need received aid; of those 59% had need fully met. ***Average percent of need met:*** 85% (excluding resources awarded to replace EFC). ***Average financial aid package:*** $6848 (excluding resources awarded to replace EFC). 12% of all full-time undergraduates had no need and received non-need-based gift aid.

GIFT AID (NEED-BASED) ***Total amount:*** $4,986,678 (99% federal, 1% external sources). ***Receiving aid:*** Freshmen: 25% (178); All full-time undergraduates: 33% (1,701). ***Average award:*** Freshmen: $2706; Undergraduates: $2796. ***Scholarships, grants, and awards:*** Federal Pell, FSEOG, state, private, college/university gift aid from institutional funds, Federal Nursing.

GIFT AID (NON-NEED-BASED) ***Total amount:*** $5,257,888 (92% state, 2% institutional, 6% external sources). ***Receiving aid:*** Freshmen: 40% (278); Undergraduates: 16% (829). ***Average award:*** Freshmen: $2989; Undergraduates: $2779. ***Scholarships, grants, and awards by category:*** *Academic Interests/Achievement:* 479 awards ($537,127 total): biological sciences, computer science, education, engineering/technologies, English, foreign languages, general academic interests/achievements, health fields, humanities, international studies, mathematics, military science, physical sciences. *Creative Arts/Performance:* 77 awards ($48,300 total): art/fine arts, music. *Special Achievements/Activities:* 2 awards ($450 total): community service. *Special Characteristics:* 34 awards ($70,285 total): ethnic background, international students, religious affiliation. ***ROTC:*** Army, Naval cooperative.

LOANS ***Student loans:*** $17,454,171 (61% need-based, 39% non-need-based). 55% of past graduating class borrowed through all loan programs. *Average indebtedness per student:* $11,000. ***Average need-based loan:*** Freshmen: $2368; Undergraduates: $3418. ***Parent loans:*** $582,964 (100% non-need-based). ***Programs:*** FFEL (Subsidized and Unsubsidized Stafford, PLUS), college/university, alternative loans.

WORK-STUDY ***Federal work-study:*** Total amount: $349,362; 109 jobs averaging $3500. ***State or other work-study/employment:*** Part-time jobs available.

ATHLETIC AWARDS Total amount: $627,168 (100% non-need-based).

APPLYING FOR FINANCIAL AID ***Required financial aid form:*** FAFSA. ***Financial aid deadline (priority):*** 3/15. ***Notification date:*** Continuous beginning 4/1. Students must reply within 2 weeks of notification.

CONTACT Lee Ann Kirkland, Director of Financial Aid, Armstrong Atlantic State University, 11935 Abercorn Street, Savannah, GA 31419-1997, 912-921-5990 or toll-free 800-633-2349. *Fax:* 912-921-7357. *E-mail:* finaid@mail.armstrong.edu.

ART ACADEMY OF CINCINNATI

Cincinnati, OH

CONTACT Ms. Karen Geiger, Director of Financial Aid, Art Academy of Cincinnati, 1125 Saint Gregory Street, Cincinnati, OH 45202-1700, 513-562-8773 or toll-free 800-323-5692 (in-state). *Fax:* 513-562-8778. *E-mail:* financialaid@artacademy.edu.

ART CENTER COLLEGE OF DESIGN

Pasadena, CA

ABOUT THE INSTITUTION Independent, coed. Awards: bachelor's and master's degrees. 19 undergraduate majors. Total enrollment: 1,631. Undergraduates: 1,485. Freshmen: 55.

GIFT AID (NEED-BASED) ***Scholarships, grants, and awards:*** Federal Pell, FSEOG, state, private, college/university gift aid from institutional funds.

GIFT AID (NON-NEED-BASED) ***Scholarships, grants, and awards by category:*** *Creative Arts/Performance:* art/fine arts.

LOANS ***Programs:*** FFEL (Subsidized and Unsubsidized Stafford, PLUS), college/university, alternative loans.

WORK-STUDY ***Federal work-study:*** Total amount: $300,000; 150 jobs averaging $2000.

APPLYING FOR FINANCIAL AID ***Required financial aid form:*** FAFSA.

CONTACT Clema McKenzie, Director of Financial Aid, Art Center College of Design, 1700 Lida Street, Pasadena, CA 91103-1999, 626-396-2215. *Fax:* 626-683-8684.

THE ART CENTER DESIGN COLLEGE

Tucson, AZ

CONTACT Ms. Margarita Carey, Education Finance Director, The Art Center Design College, 2525 North Country Club Road, Tucson, AZ 85716-2505, 520-325-0123 or toll-free 800-825-8753. *Fax:* 520-325-5535.

THE ART INSTITUTE OF ATLANTA

Atlanta, GA

CONTACT Rena Marroquin, Financial Aid Office, The Art Institute of Atlanta, 6600 Peachtree Dunwoody Road, 100 Embassy Road, Atlanta, GA 30326, 770-394-8300 or toll-free 800-275-4242.

THE ART INSTITUTE OF BOSTON AT LESLEY UNIVERSITY

Boston, MA

CONTACT Financial Aid Officer, The Art Institute of Boston at Lesley University, 700 Beacon Street, Boston, MA 02215-2598, 617-349-8714 or toll-free 800-773-0494 (in-state). *Fax:* 617-437-1226.

THE ART INSTITUTE OF CALIFORNIA–INLAND EMPIRE

San Bernardino, CA

CONTACT Financial Aid Office, The Art Institute of California–Inland Empire, 630 East Brier Drive, San Bernardino, CA 92408, 909-915-2100 or toll-free 800-353-0812 (out-of-state).

THE ART INSTITUTE OF CALIFORNIA–LOS ANGELES

Santa Monica, CA

CONTACT Financial Aid Office, The Art Institute of California–Los Angeles, 2900 31st Street, Santa Monica, CA 90405-3035, 310-752-4700 or toll-free 888-646-4610.

THE ART INSTITUTE OF CALIFORNIA–ORANGE COUNTY

Santa Ana, CA

CONTACT Financial Aid Office, The Art Institute of California–Orange County, 3601 West Sunflower Avenue, Santa Ana, CA 92704-9888, 714-830-0200 or toll-free 888-549-3055.

THE ART INSTITUTE OF CALIFORNIA–SAN DIEGO

San Diego, CA

CONTACT Monica McCormick, Financial Aid Administrator, The Art Institute of California–San Diego, 10025 Mesa Rim Road, San Diego, CA 92121, 619-546-0602 or toll-free 800-591-2422 Ext. 3117 (in-state).

THE ART INSTITUTE OF CALIFORNIA–SAN FRANCISCO

San Francisco, CA

CONTACT Director of Student Financial Services, The Art Institute of California–San Francisco, 1170 Market Street, San Francisco, CA 94102-4908, 415-865-0198 or toll-free 888-493-3261. *Fax:* 415-863-5831.

THE ART INSTITUTE OF CHARLESTON

Charleston, SC

CONTACT Financial Aid Office, The Art Institute of Charleston, The Carroll Building, 24 North Market Street, Charleston, SC 29401, 843-727-3500 or toll-free 866-211-0107.

THE ART INSTITUTE OF COLORADO

Denver, CO

CONTACT Shannon May, Director of Student Financial Services, The Art Institute of Colorado, 1200 Lincoln Street, Denver, CO 80203-2903, 303-837-0825 Ext. 4747 or toll-free 800-275-2420. *Fax:* 303-860-8520. *E-mail:* mays@aii.edu.

THE ART INSTITUTE OF DALLAS

Dallas, TX

ABOUT THE INSTITUTION Proprietary, coed. Awards: associate and bachelor's degrees. 10 undergraduate majors. Total enrollment: 1,354. Undergraduates: 1,354. Freshmen: 326.

GIFT AID (NEED-BASED) ***Scholarships, grants, and awards:*** Federal Pell, FSEOG, private, college/university gift aid from institutional funds.

LOANS ***Programs:*** FFEL (Subsidized and Unsubsidized Stafford, PLUS), Perkins.

APPLYING FOR FINANCIAL AID ***Required financial aid forms:*** FAFSA, institution's own form.

CONTACT Lisa McGaha, Director of Student Financial Services, The Art Institute of Dallas, 8080 Park Lane, Dallas, TX 75231, 214-692-8080 Ext. 1258 or toll-free 800-275-4243. *Fax:* 214-692-6541. *E-mail:* lmcgaha@aii.edu.

THE ART INSTITUTE OF FORT LAUDERDALE

Fort Lauderdale, FL

CONTACT Office of Student Financial Services, The Art Institute of Fort Lauderdale, 1799 Southeast 17th Street Causeway, Fort Lauderdale, FL 33316-3000, 954-527-1799 or toll-free 800-275-7603.

THE ART INSTITUTE OF HOUSTON

Houston, TX

CONTACT Sara Benson, Director of Accounting and Financial Services, The Art Institute of Houston, 1900 Yorktown, Houston, TX 77056, 713-623-2040 Ext. 780 or toll-free 800-275-4244. *Fax:* 713-966-2700. *E-mail:* bensons@aii.edu.

THE ART INSTITUTE OF INDIANAPOLIS

Indianapolis, IN

CONTACT Financial Aid Office, The Art Institute of Indianapolis, 3500 Depauw Boulevard, Indianapolis, IN 46268, 866-441-9031.

THE ART INSTITUTE OF JACKSONVILLE
Jacksonville, FL

CONTACT Financial Aid Office, The Art Institute of Jacksonville, 8775 Baypine Road, Jacksonville, FL 32256, 904-732-9393 or toll-free 800-924-1589.

THE ART INSTITUTE OF LAS VEGAS
Henderson, NV

CONTACT Financial Aid Office, The Art Institute of Las Vegas, 2350 Corporate Circle Drive, Henderson, NV 89074, 702-369-9944.

THE ART INSTITUTE OF PHOENIX
Phoenix, AZ

ABOUT THE INSTITUTION Proprietary, coed. Awards: associate and bachelor's degrees. 7 undergraduate majors. Total enrollment: 1,055. Undergraduates: 1,055. Freshmen: 328.

GIFT AID (NEED-BASED) ***Scholarships, grants, and awards:*** Federal Pell, FSEOG, state, private, college/university gift aid from institutional funds.

LOANS ***Programs:*** FFEL (Subsidized and Unsubsidized Stafford, PLUS), Perkins, private alternative loans.

WORK-STUDY ***Federal work-study:*** Total amount: $42,632; 22 jobs averaging $2087.

APPLYING FOR FINANCIAL AID ***Required financial aid form:*** FAFSA.

CONTACT Dorena Spitler, Director of Student Financial Services, The Art Institute of Phoenix, 2233 West Dunlap Avenue, Phoenix, AZ 85021, 602-331-7500 Ext. 7510 or toll-free 800-474-2479. *Fax:* 602-331-5302. *E-mail:* aspitler@aii.edu.

THE ART INSTITUTE OF PITTSBURGH
Pittsburgh, PA

CONTACT Ms. Gayle J. Knight, Student Financial Services Director, The Art Institute of Pittsburgh, 526 Penn Avenue, Pittsburgh, PA 15222-3269, 412-263-6600 or toll-free 800-275-2470.

THE ART INSTITUTE OF PORTLAND
Portland, OR

Tuition & fees: $18,630 **Average undergraduate aid package: $8002**

ABOUT THE INSTITUTION Proprietary, coed. Awards: associate and bachelor's degrees. 7 undergraduate majors. Total enrollment: 1,614. Undergraduates: 1,614. Freshmen: 221. Federal methodology is used as a basis for awarding need-based institutional aid.

UNDERGRADUATE EXPENSES for 2006–07 ***Application fee:*** $50. ***Comprehensive fee:*** $26,880 includes full-time tuition ($18,630) and room and board ($8250). ***College room only:*** $5550. ***Part-time tuition:*** $414 per credit hour.

FRESHMAN FINANCIAL AID (Fall 2006, est.) 194 applied for aid; of those 96% were deemed to have need. 100% of freshmen with need received aid; of those 1% had need fully met. ***Average percent of need met:*** 1% (excluding resources awarded to replace EFC). ***Average financial aid package:*** $4759 (excluding resources awarded to replace EFC). 31% of all full-time freshmen had no need and received non-need-based gift aid.

UNDERGRADUATE FINANCIAL AID (Fall 2006, est.) 1,002 applied for aid; of those 89% were deemed to have need. 99% of undergraduates with need received aid; of those 1% had need fully met. ***Average percent of need met:*** 1% (excluding resources awarded to replace EFC). ***Average financial aid package:*** $8002 (excluding resources awarded to replace EFC). 3% of all full-time undergraduates had no need and received non-need-based gift aid.

GIFT AID (NEED-BASED) ***Total amount:*** $2,393,342 (87% federal, 12% institutional, 1% external sources). ***Receiving aid:*** Freshmen: 40% (82); All full-time undergraduates: 65% (705). ***Average award:*** Freshmen: $1901; Undergraduates: $1700. ***Scholarships, grants, and awards:*** Federal Pell, FSEOG, private, college/university gift aid from institutional funds, Bureau of Indian Affairs Grants.

GIFT AID (NON-NEED-BASED) ***Total amount:*** $922,495 (47% federal, 2% state, 40% institutional, 11% external sources). ***Receiving aid:*** Freshmen: 42% (87); Undergraduates: 13% (144). ***Average award:*** Freshmen: $1585; Undergraduates: $1973. ***Scholarships, grants, and awards by category:*** *Creative Arts/Performance:* 96 awards ($164,959 total): applied art and design, general creative arts/performance. *Special Characteristics:* 16 awards ($144,918 total): children of faculty/staff.

LOANS ***Student loans:*** $15,495,033 (35% need-based, 65% non-need-based). 82% of past graduating class borrowed through all loan programs. *Average indebtedness per student:* $39,434. ***Average need-based loan:*** Freshmen: $2418; Undergraduates: $4489. ***Parent loans:*** $5,318,038 (100% non-need-based). ***Programs:*** FFEL (Subsidized and Unsubsidized Stafford, PLUS), state, alternative loans.

WORK-STUDY ***Federal work-study:*** Total amount: $87,086; 28 jobs averaging $2585.

APPLYING FOR FINANCIAL AID ***Required financial aid forms:*** FAFSA, financial aid transcript (for transfers). ***Financial aid deadline (priority):*** 3/1. ***Notification date:*** Continuous beginning 1/1. Students must reply within 2 weeks of notification.

CONTACT Mr. Mickey Jacobson, Director of Student Financial Services, The Art Institute of Portland, 1122 Northwest Davis Street, Portland, OR 97209-2911, 503-228-6528 Ext. 4728 or toll-free 888-228-6528. *Fax:* 503-228-4227. *E-mail:* mjacobson@aii.edu.

THE ART INSTITUTE OF SEATTLE
Seattle, WA

CONTACT Shelly DuBois, Vice President/Director of Administrative and Financial Services, The Art Institute of Seattle, 2323 Elliott Avenue, Seattle, WA 98121, 206-448-0900 or toll-free 800-275-2471. *Fax:* 206-448-2501.

THE ART INSTITUTE OF TAMPA
Tampa, FL

CONTACT Financial Aid Office, The Art Institute of Tampa, 4401 North Himes Avenue, Suite 150, Tampa, FL 33614, 866-703-3277.

THE ART INSTITUTE OF TENNESSEE–NASHVILLE
Nashville, TN

CONTACT Financial Aid Office, The Art Institute of Tennessee–Nashville, 100 CNA Drive, Nashville, TN 37214, 866-747-5770.

THE ART INSTITUTE OF WASHINGTON
Arlington, VA

CONTACT Director of Student Financial Services, The Art Institute of Washington, 1820 North Fort Myer Drive, Arlington, VA 22209, 703-247-6849 or toll-free 877-303-3771. *Fax:* 703-247-6829.

THE ART INSTITUTES INTERNATIONAL MINNESOTA
Minneapolis, MN

CONTACT Tiffany Robb, Student Financial Planner, The Art Institutes International Minnesota, 825 2nd Avenue South, Minneapolis, MN 55402, 612-332-3361 Ext. 110 or toll-free 800-777-3643. *Fax:* 612-332-3934. *E-mail:* robbt@aii.edu.

ASBURY COLLEGE
Wilmore, KY

Tuition & fees: $21,286 **Average undergraduate aid package: $14,794**

ABOUT THE INSTITUTION Independent nondenominational, coed. Awards: bachelor's and master's degrees. 37 undergraduate majors. Total enrollment: 1,220. Undergraduates: 1,155. Freshmen: 276. Federal methodology is used as a basis for awarding need-based institutional aid.

UNDERGRADUATE EXPENSES for 2007–08 ***Application fee:*** $30. ***Comprehensive fee:*** $26,438 includes full-time tuition ($21,132), mandatory fees ($154), and room and board ($5152). ***College room only:*** $3024. ***Part-time tuition:*** $812 per semester hour.

FRESHMAN FINANCIAL AID (Fall 2006, est.) 251 applied for aid; of those 83% were deemed to have need. 100% of freshmen with need received aid; of those 33% had need fully met. ***Average percent of need met:*** 85% (excluding resources awarded to replace EFC). ***Average financial aid package:*** $15,680 (excluding resources awarded to replace EFC). 12% of all full-time freshmen had no need and received non-need-based gift aid.

UNDERGRADUATE FINANCIAL AID (Fall 2006, est.) 893 applied for aid; of those 86% were deemed to have need. 100% of undergraduates with need received aid; of those 27% had need fully met. ***Average percent of need met:*** 79% (excluding resources awarded to replace EFC). ***Average financial aid package:*** $14,794 (excluding resources awarded to replace EFC). 10% of all full-time undergraduates had no need and received non-need-based gift aid.

GIFT AID (NEED-BASED) ***Total amount:*** $9,065,218 (10% federal, 14% state, 71% institutional, 5% external sources). ***Receiving aid:*** Freshmen: 75% (206); All full-time undergraduates: 71% (755). ***Average award:*** Freshmen: $10,245; Undergraduates: $9248. ***Scholarships, grants, and awards:*** Federal Pell, FSEOG, state, private, college/university gift aid from institutional funds.

GIFT AID (NON-NEED-BASED) ***Total amount:*** $3,937,747 (3% state, 94% institutional, 3% external sources). ***Receiving aid:*** Freshmen: 35% (96); Undergraduates: 24% (259). ***Average award:*** Freshmen: $10,402; Undergraduates: $10,332. ***Scholarships, grants, and awards by category:*** *Academic Interests/Achievement:* general academic interests/achievements. *Creative Arts/Performance:* music. *Special Achievements/Activities:* leadership. *Special Characteristics:* children and siblings of alumni, children of faculty/staff, ethnic background, international students, siblings of current students. ***ROTC:*** Army cooperative, Air Force cooperative.

LOANS ***Student loans:*** $4,980,244 (91% need-based, 9% non-need-based). 72% of past graduating class borrowed through all loan programs. *Average indebtedness per student:* $24,739. ***Average need-based loan:*** Freshmen: $2620; Undergraduates: $3565. ***Parent loans:*** $1,326,108 (87% need-based, 13% non-need-based). ***Programs:*** FFEL (Subsidized and Unsubsidized Stafford, PLUS), Perkins, state, college/university, private alternative loans.

WORK-STUDY ***Federal work-study:*** Total amount: $141,199; jobs available (averaging $345). ***State or other work-study/employment:*** Total amount: $359,630 (100% need-based). Part-time jobs available (averaging $879).

ATHLETIC AWARDS Total amount: $5250 (29% need-based, 71% non-need-based).

APPLYING FOR FINANCIAL AID ***Required financial aid forms:*** FAFSA, institution's own form. ***Financial aid deadline (priority):*** 3/1. ***Notification date:*** Continuous beginning 2/15. Students must reply within 4 weeks of notification.

CONTACT Ronald Anderson, Director of Financial Aid, Asbury College, One Macklem Drive, Wilmore, KY 40390, 859-858-3511 Ext. 2195 or toll-free 800-888-1818. *Fax:* 859-858-3921. *E-mail:* ron.anderson@asbury.edu.

ASHFORD UNIVERSITY
Clinton, IA

Tuition & fees: $15,340 **Average undergraduate aid package: N/A**

ABOUT THE INSTITUTION Proprietary, coed. Awards: bachelor's and master's degrees. 32 undergraduate majors. Total enrollment: 3,836. Undergraduates: 3,485. Freshmen: 288. Federal methodology is used as a basis for awarding need-based institutional aid.

UNDERGRADUATE EXPENSES for 2006–07 ***Application fee:*** $20. ***Comprehensive fee:*** $21,140 includes full-time tuition ($15,340) and room and board ($5800). ***College room only:*** $2500. ***Part-time tuition:*** $448 per credit.

GIFT AID (NEED-BASED) ***Average award:*** Freshmen: $7683; Undergraduates: $7122. ***Scholarships, grants, and awards:*** Federal Pell, FSEOG, state, private, college/university gift aid from institutional funds.

GIFT AID (NON-NEED-BASED) ***Average award:*** Freshmen: $11,660; Undergraduates: $10,099. ***Scholarships, grants, and awards by category:*** *Academic Interests/Achievement:* general academic interests/achievements. *Special Characteristics:* children of faculty/staff, international students.

LOANS ***Student loans:*** 99% of past graduating class borrowed through all loan programs. *Average indebtedness per student:* $20,468. ***Average need-based loan:*** Freshmen: $2178; Undergraduates: $3492. ***Programs:*** Federal Direct (Subsidized and Unsubsidized Stafford, PLUS), FFEL (Subsidized and Unsubsidized Stafford, PLUS), Perkins.

WORK-STUDY ***Federal work-study:*** 55 jobs averaging $1650. ***State or other work-study/employment:*** 25 part-time jobs averaging $1650.

APPLYING FOR FINANCIAL AID ***Required financial aid forms:*** FAFSA, institution's own form. ***Financial aid deadline:*** Continuous. ***Notification date:*** Continuous beginning 3/15. Students must reply within 3 weeks of notification.

CONTACT Lisa Kramer, Director of Financial Aid, Ashford University, 400 North Bluff Boulevard, PO Box 2967, Clinton, IA 52733-2967, 563-242-4023 Ext. 1243 or toll-free 800-242-4153. *Fax:* 563-242-8684.

ASHLAND UNIVERSITY
Ashland, OH

ABOUT THE INSTITUTION Independent religious, coed. Awards: associate, bachelor's, master's, doctoral, and first professional degrees. 70 undergraduate majors. Total enrollment: 6,648. Undergraduates: 2,793. Freshmen: 564.

GIFT AID (NEED-BASED) ***Scholarships, grants, and awards:*** Federal Pell, FSEOG, state, private.

GIFT AID (NON-NEED-BASED) ***Scholarships, grants, and awards by category:*** *Academic Interests/Achievement:* general academic interests/achievements, mathematics, physical sciences, social sciences. *Creative Arts/Performance:* art/fine arts, music, theater/drama. *Special Characteristics:* children and siblings of alumni, children of faculty/staff, international students, relatives of clergy, religious affiliation.

LOANS ***Programs:*** Federal Direct (Subsidized and Unsubsidized Stafford, PLUS), Perkins, college/university.

WORK-STUDY ***Federal work-study:*** Total amount: $2,127,225; 1,155 jobs averaging $1841. ***State or other work-study/employment:*** Total amount: $651,443 (42% need-based, 58% non-need-based).

APPLYING FOR FINANCIAL AID ***Required financial aid forms:*** FAFSA, institution's own form.

CONTACT Mr. Stephen C. Howell, Director of Financial Aid, Ashland University, 401 College Avenue, Room 310, Ashland, OH 44805-3702, 419-289-5944 or toll-free 800-882-1548. *Fax:* 419-289-5976. *E-mail:* showell@ashland.edu.

ASPEN UNIVERSITY
Denver, CO

CONTACT Financial Aid Office, Aspen University, 501 South Cherry Street, Suite 350, Denver, CO 80246, 303-333-4224 or toll-free 800-441-4746 Ext. 177 (in-state).

ASSUMPTION COLLEGE
Worcester, MA

Tuition & fees: $26,060 **Average undergraduate aid package: $16,516**

ABOUT THE INSTITUTION Independent Roman Catholic, coed. Awards: bachelor's and master's degrees and post-master's certificates. 31 undergraduate majors. Total enrollment: 2,498. Undergraduates: 2,129. Freshmen: 675. Federal methodology is used as a basis for awarding need-based institutional aid.

UNDERGRADUATE EXPENSES for 2006–07 ***Application fee:*** $50. ***Comprehensive fee:*** $31,835 includes full-time tuition ($25,895), mandatory fees ($165), and room and board ($5775). ***College room only:*** $3395. Full-time tuition and fees vary according to course load and reciprocity agreements. ***Part-time tuition:*** $863 per credit hour. ***Part-time fees:*** $165 per year. Part-time tuition and fees vary according to course load. ***Payment plan:*** Installment.

FRESHMAN FINANCIAL AID (Fall 2006, est.) 588 applied for aid; of those 83% were deemed to have need. 100% of freshmen with need received aid; of those 20% had need fully met. ***Average percent of need met:*** 72% (excluding resources awarded to replace EFC). ***Average financial aid package:*** $16,233 (excluding resources awarded to replace EFC). 22% of all full-time freshmen had no need and received non-need-based gift aid.

UNDERGRADUATE FINANCIAL AID (Fall 2006, est.) 1,754 applied for aid; of those 86% were deemed to have need. 99% of undergraduates with need received aid; of those 20% had need fully met. ***Average percent of need met:*** 71% (excluding resources awarded to replace EFC). ***Average financial aid***

package: $16,516 (excluding resources awarded to replace EFC). 23% of all full-time undergraduates had no need and received non-need-based gift aid.

GIFT AID (NEED-BASED) ***Total amount:*** $17,810,940 (5% federal, 5% state, 87% institutional, 3% external sources). ***Receiving aid:*** Freshmen: 71% (477); All full-time undergraduates: 69% (1,469). ***Average award:*** Freshmen: $13,543; Undergraduates: $12,572. ***Scholarships, grants, and awards:*** Federal Pell, FSEOG, state, private, college/university gift aid from institutional funds.

GIFT AID (NON-NEED-BASED) ***Total amount:*** $4,148,062 (95% institutional, 5% external sources). ***Receiving aid:*** Freshmen: 9% (59); Undergraduates: 6% (135). ***Average award:*** Freshmen: $14,718; Undergraduates: $14,075. ***Scholarships, grants, and awards by category:*** *Academic Interests/Achievement:* 1,139 awards ($10,601,896 total): general academic interests/achievements. ***Tuition waivers:*** Full or partial for minority students, employees or children of employees. ***ROTC:*** Army cooperative, Air Force cooperative.

LOANS ***Student loans:*** $12,591,176 (65% need-based, 35% non-need-based). 76% of past graduating class borrowed through all loan programs. *Average indebtedness per student:* $21,304. ***Average need-based loan:*** Freshmen: $3123; Undergraduates: $4347. ***Parent loans:*** $8,123,615 (29% need-based, 71% non-need-based). ***Programs:*** FFEL (Subsidized and Unsubsidized Stafford, PLUS), Perkins, state, college/university.

WORK-STUDY ***Federal work-study:*** Total amount: $597,275; 390 jobs averaging $850.

ATHLETIC AWARDS Total amount: $778,651 (27% need-based, 73% non-need-based).

APPLYING FOR FINANCIAL AID ***Required financial aid form:*** FAFSA. ***Financial aid deadline:*** 2/1. ***Notification date:*** Continuous beginning 2/16. Students must reply by 5/1.

CONTACT Karen Puntillo, Director of Financial Aid, Assumption College, 500 Salisbury Street, Worcester, MA 01609-1296, 508-767-7157 or toll-free 888-882-7786. *Fax:* 508-767-7376. *E-mail:* fa@assumption.edu.

ATHENS STATE UNIVERSITY

Athens, AL

ABOUT THE INSTITUTION State-supported, coed. Awards: bachelor's degrees. 29 undergraduate majors. Total enrollment: 2,777. Undergraduates: 2,777.

GIFT AID (NEED-BASED) ***Scholarships, grants, and awards:*** Federal Pell, FSEOG, state, private, college/university gift aid from institutional funds.

GIFT AID (NON-NEED-BASED) ***Scholarships, grants, and awards by category:*** *Academic Interests/Achievement:* biological sciences, business, computer science, education, English, general academic interests/achievements, humanities, international studies, mathematics, physical sciences, religion/biblical studies, social sciences. *Creative Arts/Performance:* art/fine arts, journalism/publications. *Special Achievements/Activities:* cheerleading/drum major, general special achievements/activities, leadership. *Special Characteristics:* children and siblings of alumni, children of faculty/staff.

LOANS ***Programs:*** Federal Direct (Subsidized and Unsubsidized Stafford).

APPLYING FOR FINANCIAL AID ***Required financial aid form:*** FAFSA.

CONTACT Renee Stanford, Financial Aid Officer, Athens State University, 300 North Beaty Street, Athens, AL 35611, 256-233-8122 or toll-free 800-522-0272. *Fax:* 256-233-8178. *E-mail:* renee.stanford@athens.edu.

ATLANTA CHRISTIAN COLLEGE

East Point, GA

CONTACT Blair Walker, Director of Financial Aid, Atlanta Christian College, 2605 Ben Hill Road, East Point, GA 30344, 404-761-8861 or toll-free 800-776-1ACC. *Fax:* 404-669-2024. *E-mail:* blairw@acc.edu.

ATLANTIC COLLEGE

Guaynabo, PR

CONTACT Mrs. Velma Aponte, Financial Aid Coordinator, Atlantic College, Calle Colton #9, Guaynabo, PR 00970, 787-720-1092. *E-mail:* atlaneco@coqui.net.

ATLANTIC UNION COLLEGE

South Lancaster, MA

ABOUT THE INSTITUTION Independent Seventh-day Adventist, coed. Awards: associate, bachelor's, and master's degrees. 45 undergraduate majors. Total enrollment: 575. Undergraduates: 566. Freshmen: 103.

GIFT AID (NEED-BASED) ***Scholarships, grants, and awards:*** Federal Pell, FSEOG, state, private, college/university gift aid from institutional funds.

GIFT AID (NON-NEED-BASED) ***Scholarships, grants, and awards by category:*** *Academic Interests/Achievement:* business, computer science, education, English, general academic interests/achievements, health fields, mathematics, premedicine, religion/biblical studies. *Creative Arts/Performance:* music. *Special Achievements/Activities:* leadership. *Special Characteristics:* adult students, children of current students, children of faculty/staff, international students, out-of-state students, siblings of current students.

LOANS ***Programs:*** FFEL (Subsidized and Unsubsidized Stafford, PLUS), Perkins, Federal Nursing, state, college/university, TERI Loans, Signature Loans, Campus Door.

WORK-STUDY ***Federal work-study:*** Total amount: $114,648; 92 jobs averaging $1247. ***State or other work-study/employment:*** Total amount: $165,724 (29% need-based, 71% non-need-based). 45 part-time jobs averaging $576.

APPLYING FOR FINANCIAL AID ***Required financial aid form:*** FAFSA.

CONTACT Sandra Boucher, Director of Financial Aid, Atlantic Union College, PO Box 1000, South Lancaster, MA 01561-1000, 978-368-2284 or toll-free 800-282-2030. *Fax:* 978-368-2283. *E-mail:* sboucher@atlanticuc.edu.

AUBURN UNIVERSITY

Auburn University, AL

Tuition & fees (AL res): $5496 **Average undergraduate aid package: $7614**

ABOUT THE INSTITUTION State-supported, coed. Awards: bachelor's, master's, doctoral, and first professional degrees and post-master's certificates. 138 undergraduate majors. Total enrollment: 23,547. Undergraduates: 19,367. Freshmen: 4,092. Federal methodology is used as a basis for awarding need-based institutional aid.

UNDERGRADUATE EXPENSES for 2006–07 ***Application fee:*** $25. ***Tuition, state resident:*** full-time $5240; part-time $430 per semester hour. ***Tuition, nonresident:*** full-time $15,240; part-time $1290 per semester hour. ***Required fees:*** full-time $256; $128 per semester hour. ***College room and board:*** $7564; ***Room only:*** $3250.

FRESHMAN FINANCIAL AID (Fall 2005) 1910 applied for aid; of those 66% were deemed to have need. 94% of freshmen with need received aid; of those 14% had need fully met. ***Average percent of need met:*** 46% (excluding resources awarded to replace EFC). ***Average financial aid package:*** $7061 (excluding resources awarded to replace EFC). 9% of all full-time freshmen had no need and received non-need-based gift aid.

UNDERGRADUATE FINANCIAL AID (Fall 2005) 7,775 applied for aid; of those 77% were deemed to have need. 96% of undergraduates with need received aid; of those 11% had need fully met. ***Average percent of need met:*** 47% (excluding resources awarded to replace EFC). ***Average financial aid package:*** $7614 (excluding resources awarded to replace EFC). 4% of all full-time undergraduates had no need and received non-need-based gift aid.

GIFT AID (NEED-BASED) ***Total amount:*** $17,500,635 (47% federal, 9% state, 26% institutional, 18% external sources). ***Receiving aid:*** Freshmen: 20% (842); All full-time undergraduates: 20% (3,626). ***Average award:*** Freshmen: $4521; Undergraduates: $4513. ***Scholarships, grants, and awards:*** Federal Pell, FSEOG, state, private, college/university gift aid from institutional funds.

GIFT AID (NON-NEED-BASED) ***Total amount:*** $4,395,012 (9% state, 1% institutional, 90% external sources). ***Receiving aid:*** Freshmen: 2% (79); Undergraduates: 1% (241). ***Average award:*** Freshmen: $2764; Undergraduates: $3219. ***Scholarships, grants, and awards by category:*** *Academic Interests/Achievement:* agriculture, architecture, biological sciences, business, communication, computer science, education, engineering/technologies, English, foreign languages, general academic interests/achievements, health fields, home economics, humanities, international studies, mathematics, physical sciences, premedicine, social sciences. *Creative Arts/Performance:* applied art and design, art/fine arts, cinema/film/broadcasting, creative writing, journalism/publications, music, performing arts, theater/drama. *Special Achievements/Activities:* cheerleading/drum major, leadership, memberships. *Special Characteristics:* children and siblings of alumni, children of faculty/staff, children of union members/company employees, ethnic background, local/state students, married students, out-of-state students. ***ROTC:*** Army, Naval, Air Force.

LOANS ***Student loans:*** $44,009,456 (71% need-based, 29% non-need-based). 64% of past graduating class borrowed through all loan programs. *Average indebtedness per student:* $21,256. ***Average need-based loan:*** Freshmen: $2976; Undergraduates: $3967. ***Parent loans:*** $18,695,197 (31% need-based, 69% non-need-based). ***Programs:*** FFEL (Subsidized and Unsubsidized Stafford, PLUS), Perkins, college/university.

WORK-STUDY ***Federal work-study:*** Total amount: $1,213,562; 496 jobs averaging $2996.

ATHLETIC AWARDS Total amount: $7,042,486 (33% need-based, 67% non-need-based).

APPLYING FOR FINANCIAL AID ***Required financial aid forms:*** FAFSA, institution's own form. ***Financial aid deadline (priority):*** 3/1. ***Notification date:*** Continuous beginning 10/2. Students must reply within 2 weeks of notification.

CONTACT Mr. Mike Reynolds, Director of Student Financial Services, Auburn University, 203 Mary Martin Hall, Auburn University, AL 36849, 334-844-4634 or toll-free 800-AUBURN9 (in-state). *Fax:* 334-844-6085. *E-mail:* finaid7@auburn.edu.

AUBURN UNIVERSITY MONTGOMERY

Montgomery, AL

Tuition & fees (AL res): $5020 **Average undergraduate aid package: $5746**

ABOUT THE INSTITUTION State-supported, coed. Awards: bachelor's, master's, and doctoral degrees and post-master's certificates. 24 undergraduate majors. Total enrollment: 5,079. Undergraduates: 4,300. Freshmen: 654. Federal methodology is used as a basis for awarding need-based institutional aid.

UNDERGRADUATE EXPENSES for 2006–07 ***Application fee:*** $25. ***Tuition, state resident:*** full-time $4760; part-time $180 per semester hour. ***Tuition, nonresident:*** full-time $13,760; part-time $540 per semester hour. ***Required fees:*** full-time $260; $6 per semester hour or $40 per term part-time. Full-time tuition and fees vary according to course load. ***College room and board:*** $3050; ***Room only:*** $2890. Room and board charges vary according to housing facility. ***Payment plan:*** Deferred payment.

FRESHMAN FINANCIAL AID (Fall 2006, est.) 342 applied for aid; of those 77% were deemed to have need. 97% of freshmen with need received aid; of those 97% had need fully met. ***Average financial aid package:*** $4507 (excluding resources awarded to replace EFC).

UNDERGRADUATE FINANCIAL AID (Fall 2006, est.) 1,639 applied for aid; of those 79% were deemed to have need. 98% of undergraduates with need received aid; of those 96% had need fully met. ***Average financial aid package:*** $5746 (excluding resources awarded to replace EFC).

GIFT AID (NEED-BASED) ***Total amount:*** $6,669,236 (61% federal, 1% state, 38% institutional). ***Receiving aid:*** Freshmen: 34% (183); All full-time undergraduates: 32% (875). ***Average award:*** Freshmen: $3193; Undergraduates: $3367. ***Scholarships, grants, and awards:*** Federal Pell, FSEOG, state, private, college/university gift aid from institutional funds.

GIFT AID (NON-NEED-BASED) ***Scholarships, grants, and awards by category:*** *Academic Interests/Achievement:* 719 awards ($1,730,300 total): general academic interests/achievements. ***Tuition waivers:*** Full or partial for employees or children of employees. ***ROTC:*** Army, Air Force cooperative.

LOANS ***Student loans:*** $17,060,193 (100% need-based). *Average indebtedness per student:* $15,000. ***Average need-based loan:*** Freshmen: $2403; Undergraduates: $3590. ***Parent loans:*** $351,356 (100% need-based). ***Programs:*** FFEL (Subsidized and Unsubsidized Stafford, PLUS), Perkins.

WORK-STUDY ***Federal work-study:*** Total amount: $219,435; 69 jobs averaging $3366.

APPLYING FOR FINANCIAL AID ***Required financial aid form:*** FAFSA. ***Financial aid deadline (priority):*** 3/1. ***Notification date:*** 6/30. Students must reply within 3 weeks of notification.

CONTACT Anthony Richey, Senior Director of Financial Aid, Auburn University Montgomery, PO Box 244023, Montgomery, AL 36124-4023, 334-244-3571 or toll-free 800-227-2649 (in-state). *Fax:* 334-244-3913. *E-mail:* arichey@mail.aum.edu.

AUGSBURG COLLEGE

Minneapolis, MN

Tuition & fees: $23,422 **Average undergraduate aid package: $10,566**

ABOUT THE INSTITUTION Independent Lutheran, coed. Awards: bachelor's and master's degrees and post-bachelor's and post-master's certificates. 64 undergraduate majors. Total enrollment: 3,732. Undergraduates: 2,921. Freshmen: 401. Federal methodology is used as a basis for awarding need-based institutional aid.

UNDERGRADUATE EXPENSES for 2006–07 ***Application fee:*** $25. ***Comprehensive fee:*** $30,026 includes full-time tuition ($22,900), mandatory fees ($522), and room and board ($6604). ***College room only:*** $3396. Room and board charges vary according to board plan and housing facility. ***Part-time tuition:*** $2860 per course. ***Part-time fees:*** $90 per term. Part-time tuition and fees vary according to course load. ***Payment plan:*** Installment.

FRESHMAN FINANCIAL AID (Fall 2005) 267 applied for aid; of those 100% were deemed to have need. 100% of freshmen with need received aid; of those 28% had need fully met. ***Average percent of need met:*** 60% (excluding resources awarded to replace EFC). ***Average financial aid package:*** $12,862 (excluding resources awarded to replace EFC). 9% of all full-time freshmen had no need and received non-need-based gift aid.

UNDERGRADUATE FINANCIAL AID (Fall 2005) 1,786 applied for aid; of those 95% were deemed to have need. 100% of undergraduates with need received aid; of those 20% had need fully met. ***Average percent of need met:*** 49% (excluding resources awarded to replace EFC). ***Average financial aid package:*** $10,566 (excluding resources awarded to replace EFC). 8% of all full-time undergraduates had no need and received non-need-based gift aid.

GIFT AID (NEED-BASED) ***Total amount:*** $15,998,120 (15% federal, 11% state, 63% institutional, 11% external sources). ***Receiving aid:*** Freshmen: 78% (257); All full-time undergraduates: 68% (1,486). ***Average award:*** Freshmen: $12,106; Undergraduates: $9955. ***Scholarships, grants, and awards:*** Federal Pell, FSEOG, state, private, college/university gift aid from institutional funds, Federal Nursing.

GIFT AID (NON-NEED-BASED) ***Total amount:*** $2,514,339 (1% state, 95% institutional, 4% external sources). ***Receiving aid:*** Freshmen: 22% (74); Undergraduates: 16% (350). ***Average award:*** Freshmen: $8093; Undergraduates: $7759. ***Scholarships, grants, and awards by category:*** *Academic Interests/Achievement:* biological sciences, business, communication, computer science, education, English, foreign languages, general academic interests/achievements, health fields, international studies, mathematics, physical sciences, religion/biblical studies, social sciences. *Creative Arts/Performance:* music, performing arts, theater/drama. *Special Achievements/Activities:* community service, general special achievements/activities, junior miss, leadership, religious involvement. *Special Characteristics:* children and siblings of alumni, international students, members of minority groups, relatives of clergy, siblings of current students. ***Tuition waivers:*** Full or partial for children of alumni, employees or children of employees, senior citizens. ***ROTC:*** Army cooperative, Naval cooperative, Air Force cooperative.

LOANS ***Student loans:*** $26,844,143 (83% need-based, 17% non-need-based). 74% of past graduating class borrowed through all loan programs. *Average indebtedness per student:* $25,750. ***Average need-based loan:*** Freshmen: $3743; Undergraduates: $4890. ***Parent loans:*** $3,755,079 (26% need-based, 74% non-need-based). ***Programs:*** FFEL (Subsidized and Unsubsidized Stafford, PLUS), Perkins, Federal Nursing, state.

WORK-STUDY ***Federal work-study:*** Total amount: $255,300; 185 jobs averaging $1380. ***State or other work-study/employment:*** Total amount: $1,061,559 (78% need-based, 22% non-need-based). 415 part-time jobs averaging $2588.

APPLYING FOR FINANCIAL AID ***Required financial aid form:*** FAFSA. ***Financial aid deadline:*** 8/15. ***Notification date:*** Continuous. Students must reply within 3 weeks of notification.

CONTACT Mr. Paul L. Terrio, Director of Student Financial Services, Augsburg College, 2211 Riverside Avenue, Minneapolis, MN 55454-1351, 612-330-1049 or toll-free 800-788-5678. *Fax:* 612-330-1308. *E-mail:* terriop@augsburg.edu.

AUGUSTANA COLLEGE

Rock Island, IL

Tuition & fees: $24,924 **Average undergraduate aid package: $17,924**

ABOUT THE INSTITUTION Independent religious, coed. Awards: bachelor's degrees. 67 undergraduate majors. Total enrollment: 2,463. Undergraduates: 2,463. Freshmen: 691. Federal methodology is used as a basis for awarding need-based institutional aid.

UNDERGRADUATE EXPENSES for 2006–07 ***Application fee:*** $25. ***Comprehensive fee:*** $31,731 includes full-time tuition ($24,408), mandatory fees ($516), and room and board ($6807). ***College room only:*** $3447. Full-time tuition and fees vary according to course load. Room and board charges vary according to board plan and housing facility. ***Part-time tuition:*** $1020 per credit hour. ***Payment plans:*** Tuition prepayment, installment.

FRESHMAN FINANCIAL AID (Fall 2006, est.) 579 applied for aid; of those 81% were deemed to have need. 100% of freshmen with need received aid; of those 29% had need fully met. ***Average percent of need met:*** 85% (excluding resources awarded to replace EFC). ***Average financial aid package:*** $17,950 (excluding resources awarded to replace EFC). 16% of all full-time freshmen had no need and received non-need-based gift aid.

UNDERGRADUATE FINANCIAL AID (Fall 2006, est.) 1,915 applied for aid; of those 83% were deemed to have need. 99% of undergraduates with need received aid; of those 28% had need fully met. ***Average percent of need met:*** 84% (excluding resources awarded to replace EFC). ***Average financial aid package:*** $17,924 (excluding resources awarded to replace EFC). 12% of all full-time undergraduates had no need and received non-need-based gift aid.

GIFT AID (NEED-BASED) ***Total amount:*** $20,088,721 (6% federal, 15% state, 77% institutional, 2% external sources). ***Receiving aid:*** Freshmen: 24% (165); All full-time undergraduates: 64% (1,575). ***Average award:*** Freshmen: $13,092; Undergraduates: $12,689. ***Scholarships, grants, and awards:*** Federal Pell, FSEOG, state, private, college/university gift aid from institutional funds.

GIFT AID (NON-NEED-BASED) ***Total amount:*** $3,977,803 (95% institutional, 5% external sources). ***Receiving aid:*** Freshmen: 60% (416); Undergraduates: 56% (1,361). ***Average award:*** Freshmen: $10,403; Undergraduates: $8796. ***Scholarships, grants, and awards by category:*** *Academic Interests/Achievement:* 1,295 awards ($11,673,180 total): biological sciences, business, communication, education, general academic interests/achievements, mathematics, physical sciences, religion/biblical studies, social sciences. *Creative Arts/Performance:* 396 awards ($678,639 total): art/fine arts, creative writing, debating, music, theater/drama. *Special Characteristics:* 341 awards ($1,932,568 total): children and siblings of alumni, children of faculty/staff, international students, members of minority groups, religious affiliation, siblings of current students. ***Tuition waivers:*** Full or partial for employees or children of employees.

LOANS ***Student loans:*** $10,234,099 (100% need-based). 73% of past graduating class borrowed through all loan programs. *Average indebtedness per student:* $17,100. ***Average need-based loan:*** Freshmen: $3664; Undergraduates: $4300. ***Parent loans:*** $4,436,471 (100% need-based). ***Programs:*** FFEL (Subsidized and Unsubsidized Stafford, PLUS), Perkins.

WORK-STUDY ***Federal work-study:*** Total amount: $1,669,193; 1,008 jobs averaging $1656.

APPLYING FOR FINANCIAL AID ***Required financial aid forms:*** FAFSA, institution's own form. ***Financial aid deadline (priority):*** 3/15. ***Notification date:*** Continuous beginning 11/1. Students must reply by 5/1.

CONTACT Sue Standley, Director of Financial Aid, Augustana College, 639 38th Street, Rock Island, IL 61201-2296, 309-794-7207 or toll-free 800-798-8100. *Fax:* 309-794-7174. *E-mail:* suestandley@augustana.edu.

AUGUSTANA COLLEGE

Sioux Falls, SD

Tuition & fees: $19,986 **Average undergraduate aid package: $15,938**

ABOUT THE INSTITUTION Independent religious, coed. Awards: bachelor's and master's degrees. 52 undergraduate majors. Total enrollment: 1,768. Undergraduates: 1,747. Freshmen: 442. Federal methodology is used as a basis for awarding need-based institutional aid.

UNDERGRADUATE EXPENSES for 2006–07 ***Comprehensive fee:*** $25,650 includes full-time tuition ($19,750), mandatory fees ($236), and room and board ($5664). ***College room only:*** $2700. Room and board charges vary according to board plan and housing facility. ***Part-time tuition:*** $290 per credit. Part-time tuition and fees vary according to course load. ***Payment plan:*** Installment.

FRESHMAN FINANCIAL AID (Fall 2006, est.) 375 applied for aid; of those 83% were deemed to have need. 100% of freshmen with need received aid; of those 17% had need fully met. ***Average percent of need met:*** 95% (excluding resources awarded to replace EFC). ***Average financial aid package:*** $17,137 (excluding resources awarded to replace EFC). 27% of all full-time freshmen had no need and received non-need-based gift aid.

UNDERGRADUATE FINANCIAL AID (Fall 2006, est.) 1,319 applied for aid; of those 84% were deemed to have need. 100% of undergraduates with need received aid; of those 19% had need fully met. ***Average percent of need met:*** 88% (excluding resources awarded to replace EFC). ***Average financial aid package:*** $15,938 (excluding resources awarded to replace EFC). 31% of all full-time undergraduates had no need and received non-need-based gift aid.

GIFT AID (NEED-BASED) ***Total amount:*** $10,353,486 (14% federal, 79% institutional, 7% external sources). ***Receiving aid:*** Freshmen: 71% (312); All full-time undergraduates: 67% (1,104). ***Average award:*** Freshmen: $12,922; Undergraduates: $11,475. ***Scholarships, grants, and awards:*** Federal Pell, FSEOG, state, private, college/university gift aid from institutional funds, need-linked special talent scholarships and minority scholarships.

GIFT AID (NON-NEED-BASED) ***Total amount:*** $4,674,673 (3% state, 85% institutional, 12% external sources). ***Receiving aid:*** Freshmen: 69% (304); Undergraduates: 65% (1,079). ***Average award:*** Freshmen: $9269; Undergraduates: $7770. ***Scholarships, grants, and awards by category:*** *Academic Interests/Achievement:* biological sciences, business, communication, computer science, education, English, foreign languages, general academic interests/achievements, health fields, humanities, international studies, mathematics, physical sciences, premedicine, religion/biblical studies, social sciences. *Creative Arts/Performance:* art/fine arts, music, performing arts, theater/drama. *Special Achievements/Activities:* general special achievements/activities, leadership. *Special Characteristics:* children and siblings of alumni, children of current students, children of faculty/staff, ethnic background, international students, local/state students, members of minority groups, religious affiliation, siblings of current students, spouses of current students, veterans. ***Tuition waivers:*** Full or partial for employees or children of employees, adult students, senior citizens.

LOANS ***Student loans:*** $8,473,037 (64% need-based, 36% non-need-based). 79% of past graduating class borrowed through all loan programs. *Average indebtedness per student:* $26,006. ***Average need-based loan:*** Freshmen: $4739; Undergraduates: $5023. ***Parent loans:*** $1,654,643 (21% need-based, 79% non-need-based). ***Programs:*** FFEL (Subsidized and Unsubsidized Stafford, PLUS), Perkins, Federal Nursing, college/university, Minnesota SELF Loans, alternative loans.

WORK-STUDY ***Federal work-study:*** Total amount: $563,299; 417 jobs averaging $1311. ***State or other work-study/employment:*** Total amount: $109,088 (6% need-based, 94% non-need-based). 126 part-time jobs averaging $890.

ATHLETIC AWARDS Total amount: $1,933,630 (52% need-based, 48% non-need-based).

APPLYING FOR FINANCIAL AID ***Required financial aid form:*** FAFSA. ***Financial aid deadline (priority):*** 3/1. ***Notification date:*** Continuous beginning 4/1. Students must reply by 5/1 or within 3 weeks of notification.

CONTACT Ms. Brenda L. Murtha, Director of Financial Aid, Augustana College, 2001 South Summit Avenue, Sioux Falls, SD 57197, 605-274-5216 or toll-free 800-727-2844 Ext. 5516 (in-state), 800-727-2844 (out-of-state). *Fax:* 605-274-5295. *E-mail:* brenda.murtha@augie.edu.

AUGUSTA STATE UNIVERSITY

Augusta, GA

Tuition & fees (GA res): $3066 **Average undergraduate aid package: $12,338**

ABOUT THE INSTITUTION State-supported, coed. Awards: associate, bachelor's, and master's degrees and post-master's certificates. 33 undergraduate majors. Total enrollment: 6,552. Undergraduates: 5,707. Freshmen: 943. Federal methodology is used as a basis for awarding need-based institutional aid.

UNDERGRADUATE EXPENSES for 2006–07 ***Application fee:*** $20. ***Tuition, state resident:*** full-time $2560; part-time $107 per hour. ***Tuition, nonresident:*** full-time $10,242; part-time $427 per hour. ***College room and board: Room only:*** $4920. ***Payment plan:*** Guaranteed tuition.

FRESHMAN FINANCIAL AID (Fall 2005) 727 applied for aid; of those 81% were deemed to have need. 93% of freshmen with need received aid; of those .4% had need fully met. ***Average percent of need met:*** 70% (excluding resources awarded to replace EFC). ***Average financial aid package:*** $11,232 (excluding resources awarded to replace EFC). 35% of all full-time freshmen had no need and received non-need-based gift aid.

UNDERGRADUATE FINANCIAL AID (Fall 2005) 2,571 applied for aid; of those 80% were deemed to have need. 93% of undergraduates with need received

aid; of those 2% had need fully met. ***Average percent of need met:*** 70% (excluding resources awarded to replace EFC). ***Average financial aid package:*** $12,338 (excluding resources awarded to replace EFC). 20% of all full-time undergraduates had no need and received non-need-based gift aid.

GIFT AID (NEED-BASED) ***Total amount:*** $8,848,444 (100% federal). ***Receiving aid:*** Freshmen: 43% (381); All full-time undergraduates: 37% (1,352). ***Average award:*** Freshmen: $7082; Undergraduates: $7298. ***Scholarships, grants, and awards:*** Federal Pell, FSEOG, state, private, college/university gift aid from institutional funds.

GIFT AID (NON-NEED-BASED) ***Total amount:*** $7,269,176 (90% state, 5% institutional, 5% external sources). ***Receiving aid:*** Freshmen: 35% (311); Undergraduates: 20% (748). ***Average award:*** Freshmen: $518; Undergraduates: $520. ***Scholarships, grants, and awards by category:*** *Academic Interests/Achievement:* 77 awards ($95,326 total): biological sciences, business, communication, computer science, education, English, general academic interests/achievements, health fields, mathematics, military science, physical sciences, social sciences. *Creative Arts/Performance:* 67 awards ($37,692 total): art/fine arts, creative writing, general creative arts/performance, music, performing arts, theater/drama. *Special Achievements/Activities:* 19 awards ($27,015 total): community service, general special achievements/activities, hobbies/interests, leadership. *Special Characteristics:* 1,985 awards ($5,110,867 total): general special characteristics, handicapped students, local/state students. ***Tuition waivers:*** Full or partial for employees or children of employees, senior citizens. ***ROTC:*** Army.

LOANS ***Student loans:*** $13,352,400 (58% need-based, 42% non-need-based). 61% of past graduating class borrowed through all loan programs. *Average indebtedness per student:* $3191. ***Average need-based loan:*** Freshmen: $5636; Undergraduates: $7744. ***Parent loans:*** $305,770 (100% non-need-based). ***Programs:*** FFEL (Subsidized and Unsubsidized Stafford, PLUS), Perkins, state, college/university, alternative loans.

WORK-STUDY ***Federal work-study:*** Total amount: $149,214; 61 jobs averaging $2487. ***State or other work-study/employment:*** 267 part-time jobs averaging $1490.

ATHLETIC AWARDS Total amount: $592,810 (100% non-need-based).

APPLYING FOR FINANCIAL AID ***Required financial aid form:*** FAFSA. ***Financial aid deadline:*** 5/1 (priority: 4/15). ***Notification date:*** Continuous.

CONTACT Ms. Roxanne Padgett, Assistant Director of Financial Aid, Augusta State University, 2500 Walton Way, Augusta, GA 30904-2200, 706-737-1431 or toll-free 800-341-4373. *Fax:* 706-737-1777. *E-mail:* bpadgett@aug.edu.

AURORA UNIVERSITY

Aurora, IL

Tuition & fees: $16,850 **Average undergraduate aid package: $17,515**

ABOUT THE INSTITUTION Independent, coed. Awards: bachelor's, master's, and doctoral degrees and post-bachelor's and post-master's certificates. 32 undergraduate majors. Total enrollment: 3,791. Undergraduates: 1,974. Freshmen: 375. Federal methodology is used as a basis for awarding need-based institutional aid.

UNDERGRADUATE EXPENSES for 2007–08 ***Application fee:*** $25. ***Comprehensive fee:*** $23,884 includes full-time tuition ($16,750), mandatory fees ($100), and room and board ($7034). ***College room only:*** $3080. ***Part-time tuition:*** $510 per semester hour.

FRESHMAN FINANCIAL AID (Fall 2006, est.) 373 applied for aid; of those 78% were deemed to have need. 100% of freshmen with need received aid; of those 28% had need fully met. ***Average percent of need met:*** 89% (excluding resources awarded to replace EFC). ***Average financial aid package:*** $18,138 (excluding resources awarded to replace EFC). 20% of all full-time freshmen had no need and received non-need-based gift aid.

UNDERGRADUATE FINANCIAL AID (Fall 2006, est.) 1,685 applied for aid; of those 75% were deemed to have need. 99% of undergraduates with need received aid; of those 36% had need fully met. ***Average percent of need met:*** 88% (excluding resources awarded to replace EFC). ***Average financial aid package:*** $17,515 (excluding resources awarded to replace EFC). 22% of all full-time undergraduates had no need and received non-need-based gift aid.

GIFT AID (NEED-BASED) ***Total amount:*** $5,341,295 (30% federal, 61% state, 9% institutional). ***Receiving aid:*** Freshmen: 55% (206); All full-time undergraduates: 51% (878). ***Average award:*** Freshmen: $5950; Undergraduates: $5901. ***Scholarships, grants, and awards:*** Federal Pell, FSEOG, state, private, college/university gift aid from institutional funds.

GIFT AID (NON-NEED-BASED) ***Total amount:*** $11,161,175 (97% institutional, 3% external sources). ***Receiving aid:*** Freshmen: 78% (290); Undergraduates: 71% (1,226). ***Average award:*** Freshmen: $9510; Undergraduates: $8949. ***Scholarships, grants, and awards by category:*** *Academic Interests/Achievement:* 1,957 awards ($10,652,088 total): education, general academic interests/achievements, mathematics. *Creative Arts/Performance:* 30 awards ($23,750 total): music. *Special Achievements/Activities:* 160 awards ($352,442 total): general special achievements/activities. *Special Characteristics:* 236 awards ($399,157 total): children and siblings of alumni, children of educators, children of faculty/staff, out-of-state students, parents of current students, siblings of current students, spouses of current students. ***ROTC:*** Army cooperative.

LOANS ***Student loans:*** $7,979,815 (47% need-based, 53% non-need-based). 77% of past graduating class borrowed through all loan programs. *Average indebtedness per student:* $18,517. ***Average need-based loan:*** Freshmen: $2464; Undergraduates: $3822. ***Parent loans:*** $1,198,054 (100% non-need-based). ***Programs:*** FFEL (Subsidized and Unsubsidized Stafford, PLUS), Perkins, college/university.

WORK-STUDY ***Federal work-study:*** Total amount: $843,258; 565 jobs averaging $1511.

APPLYING FOR FINANCIAL AID ***Required financial aid form:*** FAFSA. ***Financial aid deadline (priority):*** 4/15. ***Notification date:*** Continuous beginning 3/1. Students must reply by 5/1.

CONTACT Heather Gutierrez, Dean of Student Financial Services, Aurora University, 347 South Gladstone Avenue, Aurora, IL 60506-4892, 630-844-5533 or toll-free 800-742-5281. *Fax:* 630-844-5535. *E-mail:* finaid@aurora.edu.

AUSTIN COLLEGE

Sherman, TX

Tuition & fees: $24,945 **Average undergraduate aid package: $22,532**

ABOUT THE INSTITUTION Independent Presbyterian, coed. Awards: bachelor's and master's degrees. 31 undergraduate majors. Total enrollment: 1,354. Undergraduates: 1,321. Freshmen: 340. Federal methodology is used as a basis for awarding need-based institutional aid.

UNDERGRADUATE EXPENSES for 2007–08 ***Application fee:*** $35. ***Comprehensive fee:*** $33,179 includes full-time tuition ($24,760), mandatory fees ($185), and room and board ($8234). ***Part-time tuition:*** $3590 per course.

FRESHMAN FINANCIAL AID (Fall 2006, est.) 247 applied for aid; of those 78% were deemed to have need. 100% of freshmen with need received aid; of those 100% had need fully met. ***Average percent of need met:*** 99% (excluding resources awarded to replace EFC). ***Average financial aid package:*** $24,107 (excluding resources awarded to replace EFC). 37% of all full-time freshmen had no need and received non-need-based gift aid.

UNDERGRADUATE FINANCIAL AID (Fall 2006, est.) 937 applied for aid; of those 81% were deemed to have need. 100% of undergraduates with need received aid; of those 100% had need fully met. ***Average percent of need met:*** 99% (excluding resources awarded to replace EFC). ***Average financial aid package:*** $22,532 (excluding resources awarded to replace EFC). 36% of all full-time undergraduates had no need and received non-need-based gift aid.

GIFT AID (NEED-BASED) ***Total amount:*** $10,127,179 (9% federal, 14% state, 75% institutional, 2% external sources). ***Receiving aid:*** Freshmen: 56% (192); All full-time undergraduates: 57% (759). ***Average award:*** Freshmen: $15,055; Undergraduates: $13,693. ***Scholarships, grants, and awards:*** Federal Pell, FSEOG, state, private, college/university gift aid from institutional funds.

GIFT AID (NON-NEED-BASED) ***Total amount:*** $5,675,678 (93% institutional, 7% external sources). ***Receiving aid:*** Freshmen: 25% (86); Undergraduates: 18% (236). ***Average award:*** Freshmen: $9591; Undergraduates: $9467. ***Scholarships, grants, and awards by category:*** *Academic Interests/Achievement:* biological sciences, business, communication, education, engineering/technologies, English, foreign languages, general academic interests/achievements, health fields, humanities, international studies, physical sciences, premedicine, religion/biblical studies, social sciences. *Creative Arts/Performance:* art/fine arts, music, theater/drama. *Special Achievements/Activities:* community service, general special achievements/activities, leadership, religious involvement. *Special Characteristics:* children of faculty/staff, ethnic background, first-generation college students, handicapped students, international students, local/state students, relatives of clergy.

LOANS ***Student loans:*** $8,606,301 (54% need-based, 46% non-need-based). ***Average need-based loan:*** Freshmen: $6660; Undergraduates: $6477. ***Parent***

loans: $8,187,831 (3% need-based, 97% non-need-based). ***Programs:*** FFEL (Subsidized and Unsubsidized Stafford, PLUS), Perkins, state, college/university, alternative loans through various sources.

WORK-STUDY ***Federal work-study:*** Total amount: $485,594; 319 jobs averaging $1524. ***State or other work-study/employment:*** Total amount: $309,026 (15% need-based, 85% non-need-based). 216 part-time jobs averaging $1430.

APPLYING FOR FINANCIAL AID ***Required financial aid forms:*** FAFSA, institution's own form. ***Financial aid deadline (priority):*** 4/1. ***Notification date:*** Continuous beginning 3/1. Students must reply by 5/1.

CONTACT Mrs. Laurie Coulter, Executive Director of Financial Aid, Austin College, 900 North Grand Avenue, Sherman, TX 75090, 903-813-2900 or toll-free 800-442-5363. *E-mail:* finaid@austincollege.edu.

AUSTIN GRADUATE SCHOOL OF THEOLOGY

Austin, TX

Tuition & fees: $6150 **Average undergraduate aid package: $6415**

ABOUT THE INSTITUTION Independent religious, coed. Awards: bachelor's and master's degrees. 1 undergraduate major. Total enrollment: 61. Undergraduates: 27. Federal methodology is used as a basis for awarding need-based institutional aid.

UNDERGRADUATE EXPENSES for 2006–07 ***Tuition:*** full-time $6150; part-time $615 per course. Full-time tuition and fees vary according to course load. Part-time tuition and fees vary according to course load. ***Payment plan:*** Installment.

UNDERGRADUATE FINANCIAL AID (Fall 2005) 6 applied for aid; of those 100% were deemed to have need. 100% of undergraduates with need received aid. ***Average percent of need met:*** 37% (excluding resources awarded to replace EFC). ***Average financial aid package:*** $6415 (excluding resources awarded to replace EFC).

GIFT AID (NEED-BASED) ***Total amount:*** $14,927 (91% federal, 9% institutional). ***Receiving aid:*** All full-time undergraduates: 67% (6). ***Average award:*** Undergraduates: $2488. ***Scholarships, grants, and awards:*** Federal Pell, FSEOG, college/university gift aid from institutional funds.

GIFT AID (NON-NEED-BASED) ***Receiving aid:*** Undergraduates: 11% (1). ***Scholarships, grants, and awards by category:*** *Academic Interests/Achievement:* 1 award ($1988 total): religion/biblical studies. ***Tuition waivers:*** Full or partial for employees or children of employees.

LOANS ***Student loans:*** $11,313 (82% need-based, 18% non-need-based). 50% of past graduating class borrowed through all loan programs. *Average indebtedness per student:* $11,625. ***Average need-based loan:*** Undergraduates: $3108. ***Programs:*** FFEL (Subsidized and Unsubsidized Stafford, PLUS).

WORK-STUDY ***Federal work-study:*** Total amount: $2457; 2 jobs averaging $1229.

APPLYING FOR FINANCIAL AID ***Required financial aid forms:*** FAFSA, institution's own form. ***Financial aid deadline:*** Continuous.

CONTACT David Arthur, Financial Aid Officer, Austin Graduate School of Theology, 1909 University Avenue, Austin, TX 78705-5610, 512-476-2772 Ext. 204 or toll-free 866-AUS-GRAD. *Fax:* 512-476-3919. *E-mail:* darthur@austingrad.edu.

AUSTIN PEAY STATE UNIVERSITY

Clarksville, TN

Tuition & fees (TN res): $4837 **Average undergraduate aid package: $6395**

ABOUT THE INSTITUTION State-supported, coed. Awards: associate, bachelor's, and master's degrees and post-bachelor's and post-master's certificates. 34 undergraduate majors. Total enrollment: 9,207. Undergraduates: 8,467. Freshmen: 1,292. Federal methodology is used as a basis for awarding need-based institutional aid.

UNDERGRADUATE EXPENSES for 2006–07 ***Application fee:*** $15. ***Tuition, state resident:*** full-time $3828; part-time $168 per credit hour. ***Tuition, nonresident:*** full-time $13,522; part-time $589 per credit hour. ***Required fees:*** full-time $1009; $39 per credit hour or $5 per term part-time. ***College room and board:*** $5190; ***Room only:*** $3200. Room and board charges vary according to board plan and housing facility. ***Payment plan:*** Installment.

FRESHMAN FINANCIAL AID (Fall 2005) 1136 applied for aid; of those 83% were deemed to have need. 99% of freshmen with need received aid. ***Average financial aid package:*** $6551 (excluding resources awarded to replace EFC). 14% of all full-time freshmen had no need and received non-need-based gift aid.

UNDERGRADUATE FINANCIAL AID (Fall 2005) 5,279 applied for aid; of those 88% were deemed to have need. 98% of undergraduates with need received aid. ***Average financial aid package:*** $6395 (excluding resources awarded to replace EFC). 7% of all full-time undergraduates had no need and received non-need-based gift aid.

GIFT AID (NEED-BASED) ***Total amount:*** $10,832,194 (82% federal, 18% state). ***Receiving aid:*** Freshmen: 38% (472); All full-time undergraduates: 43% (2,732). ***Average award:*** Freshmen: $4143; Undergraduates: $3641. ***Scholarships, grants, and awards:*** Federal Pell, FSEOG, state, private, college/university gift aid from institutional funds, corporate.

GIFT AID (NON-NEED-BASED) ***Total amount:*** $11,270,364 (41% state, 19% institutional, 40% external sources). ***Receiving aid:*** Freshmen: 59% (719); Undergraduates: 32% (2,012). ***Average award:*** Freshmen: $4514; Undergraduates: $4425. ***Scholarships, grants, and awards by category:*** *Academic Interests/Achievement:* 359 awards ($827,694 total): biological sciences, business, education, general academic interests/achievements, humanities, mathematics, military science, social sciences. *Creative Arts/Performance:* 325 awards ($308,696 total): art/fine arts, creative writing, debating, journalism/publications, music, theater/drama. *Special Achievements/Activities:* 81 awards ($186,803 total): general special achievements/activities, leadership. *Special Characteristics:* 68 awards ($96,000 total): children of educators, children of faculty/staff, general special characteristics, members of minority groups, veterans. ***Tuition waivers:*** Full or partial for employees or children of employees, senior citizens. ***ROTC:*** Army, Air Force cooperative.

LOANS ***Student loans:*** $24,687,030 (55% need-based, 45% non-need-based). ***Parent loans:*** $1,714,922 (100% non-need-based). ***Programs:*** FFEL (Subsidized and Unsubsidized Stafford, PLUS), Perkins.

WORK-STUDY ***Federal work-study:*** Total amount: $316,329; 518 jobs averaging $1207. ***State or other work-study/employment:*** Total amount: $530,631 (100% non-need-based). 315 part-time jobs averaging $1503.

ATHLETIC AWARDS Total amount: $1,145,050 (100% non-need-based).

APPLYING FOR FINANCIAL AID ***Required financial aid form:*** FAFSA. ***Financial aid deadline (priority):*** 3/1. ***Notification date:*** Continuous beginning 5/1. Students must reply within 2 weeks of notification.

CONTACT Greg Ross, Associate Director of Student Financial Aid, Austin Peay State University, PO Box 4546, Clarksville, TN 37044, 931-221-7907 or toll-free 800-844-2778 (out-of-state). *Fax:* 931-221-6329. *E-mail:* rossg@apsu.edu.

AVE MARIA COLLEGE

Ypsilanti, MI

CONTACT Mr. Bob Hickey, Director of Financial Aid, Ave Maria College, 300 West Forest Avenue, Ypsilanti, MI 48197, 734-337-4504 or toll-free 866-866-3030. *Fax:* 734-337-4140. *E-mail:* bhickey@avemaria.edu.

AVE MARIA UNIVERSITY

Naples, FL

CONTACT Financial Aid Office, Ave Maria University, 1025 Commons Circle, Naples, FL 34119, 239-280-2554 or toll-free 877-AVE-UNIV.

AVERETT UNIVERSITY

Danville, VA

Tuition & fees: $20,512 **Average undergraduate aid package: $14,561**

ABOUT THE INSTITUTION Independent religious, coed. Awards: associate, bachelor's, and master's degrees. 64 undergraduate majors. Total enrollment: 883. Undergraduates: 784. Freshmen: 161. Federal methodology is used as a basis for awarding need-based institutional aid.

UNDERGRADUATE EXPENSES for 2007–08 ***Comprehensive fee:*** $27,612 includes full-time tuition ($19,512), mandatory fees ($1000), and room and board ($7100). ***College room only:*** $4700. ***Part-time tuition:*** $390 per credit. ***Part-time fees:*** $250 per term.

FRESHMAN FINANCIAL AID (Fall 2006, est.) 151 applied for aid; of those 82% were deemed to have need. 100% of freshmen with need received aid; of those 20% had need fully met. ***Average percent of need met:*** 72% (excluding resources awarded to replace EFC). ***Average financial aid package:*** $12,837 (excluding resources awarded to replace EFC). 31% of all full-time freshmen had no need and received non-need-based gift aid.

UNDERGRADUATE FINANCIAL AID (Fall 2006, est.) 680 applied for aid; of those 89% were deemed to have need. 100% of undergraduates with need received aid; of those 22% had need fully met. ***Average percent of need met:*** 76% (excluding resources awarded to replace EFC). ***Average financial aid package:*** $14,561 (excluding resources awarded to replace EFC). 21% of all full-time undergraduates had no need and received non-need-based gift aid.

GIFT AID (NEED-BASED) ***Total amount:*** $6,797,880 (17% federal, 16% state, 59% institutional, 8% external sources). ***Receiving aid:*** Freshmen: 69% (122); All full-time undergraduates: 78% (602). ***Average award:*** Freshmen: $9236; Undergraduates: $10,839. ***Scholarships, grants, and awards:*** Federal Pell, FSEOG, state, private, college/university gift aid from institutional funds.

GIFT AID (NON-NEED-BASED) ***Total amount:*** $2,012,291 (19% state, 67% institutional, 14% external sources). ***Receiving aid:*** Freshmen: 12% (22); Undergraduates: 16% (120). ***Average award:*** Freshmen: $11,994; Undergraduates: $13,982. ***Scholarships, grants, and awards by category:*** *Academic Interests/Achievement:* 152 awards ($242,143 total): biological sciences, business, education, engineering/technologies, English, foreign languages, general academic interests/achievements, health fields, home economics, humanities, mathematics, physical sciences, premedicine, religion/biblical studies. *Creative Arts/Performance:* 17 awards ($12,035 total): art/fine arts, journalism/publications, music, theater/drama. *Special Achievements/Activities:* 7 awards ($10,177 total): general special achievements/activities, leadership, memberships, religious involvement. *Special Characteristics:* 217 awards ($185,913 total): adult students, children and siblings of alumni, children of union members/company employees, first-generation college students, general special characteristics, international students, local/state students, out-of-state students, relatives of clergy, religious affiliation.

LOANS ***Student loans:*** $4,742,574 (78% need-based, 22% non-need-based). 75% of past graduating class borrowed through all loan programs. *Average indebtedness per student:* $29,813. ***Average need-based loan:*** Freshmen: $4337; Undergraduates: $4446. ***Parent loans:*** $359,276 (100% need-based). ***Programs:*** FFEL (Subsidized and Unsubsidized Stafford, PLUS), Perkins, alternative loans.

WORK-STUDY ***Federal work-study:*** Total amount: $62,380; 134 jobs averaging $667.

APPLYING FOR FINANCIAL AID ***Required financial aid forms:*** FAFSA, state aid form. ***Financial aid deadline (priority):*** 4/1. ***Notification date:*** Continuous beginning 2/15. Students must reply within 2 weeks of notification.

CONTACT Carl Bradsher, Dean of Financial Assistance, Averett University, 420 West Main Street, Danville, VA 24541-3692, 434-791-5646 or toll-free 800-AVERETT. *Fax:* 434-791-5647. *E-mail:* carl.bradsher@averett.edu.

AVILA UNIVERSITY

Kansas City, MO

ABOUT THE INSTITUTION Independent Roman Catholic, coed. Awards: bachelor's and master's degrees. 32 undergraduate majors. Total enrollment: 1,683. Undergraduates: 1,130. Freshmen: 138.

GIFT AID (NEED-BASED) ***Scholarships, grants, and awards:*** Federal Pell, FSEOG, state, private, college/university gift aid from institutional funds.

GIFT AID (NON-NEED-BASED) ***Scholarships, grants, and awards by category:*** *Academic Interests/Achievement:* biological sciences, communication, general academic interests/achievements, humanities, premedicine. *Creative Arts/Performance:* art/fine arts, music, performing arts, theater/drama. *Special Characteristics:* children and siblings of alumni, children of current students, children of faculty/staff, religious affiliation, siblings of current students, spouses of current students.

LOANS ***Programs:*** FFEL (Subsidized and Unsubsidized Stafford, PLUS), Perkins.

WORK-STUDY ***Federal work-study:*** Total amount: $211,104; jobs available. ***State or other work-study/employment:*** Total amount: $96,239 (16% need-based, 84% non-need-based). Part-time jobs available.

APPLYING FOR FINANCIAL AID ***Required financial aid form:*** FAFSA.

CONTACT Kimberly Warren, Director of Financial Aid, Avila University, 11901 Wornall Road, Kansas City, MO 64145, 816-501-3782 or toll-free 800-GO-AVILA. *Fax:* 816-501-2462. *E-mail:* kimberly.warren@avila.edu.

AZUSA PACIFIC UNIVERSITY

Azusa, CA

Tuition & fees: $23,750 **Average undergraduate aid package: $19,785**

ABOUT THE INSTITUTION Independent nondenominational, coed. Awards: bachelor's, master's, doctoral, and first professional degrees. 37 undergraduate majors. Total enrollment: 8,128. Undergraduates: 4,722. Freshmen: 870. Federal methodology is used as a basis for awarding need-based institutional aid.

UNDERGRADUATE EXPENSES for 2006–07 ***Application fee:*** $45. ***Comprehensive fee:*** $31,078 includes full-time tuition ($23,050), mandatory fees ($700), and room and board ($7328). ***College room only:*** $3690. Full-time tuition and fees vary according to course load. Room and board charges vary according to board plan, housing facility, and student level. ***Part-time tuition:*** $960 per unit. Part-time tuition and fees vary according to course load. ***Payment plan:*** Installment.

FRESHMAN FINANCIAL AID (Fall 2005) 855 applied for aid; of those 61% were deemed to have need. 99% of freshmen with need received aid; of those 15% had need fully met. ***Average percent of need met:*** 57% (excluding resources awarded to replace EFC). ***Average financial aid package:*** $19,684 (excluding resources awarded to replace EFC). 30% of all full-time freshmen had no need and received non-need-based gift aid.

UNDERGRADUATE FINANCIAL AID (Fall 2005) 3,921 applied for aid; of those 62% were deemed to have need. 99% of undergraduates with need received aid; of those 17% had need fully met. ***Average percent of need met:*** 61% (excluding resources awarded to replace EFC). ***Average financial aid package:*** $19,785 (excluding resources awarded to replace EFC). 24% of all full-time undergraduates had no need and received non-need-based gift aid.

GIFT AID (NEED-BASED) ***Total amount:*** $22,058,103 (19% federal, 32% state, 44% institutional, 5% external sources). ***Receiving aid:*** Freshmen: 59% (504); All full-time undergraduates: 56% (2,201). ***Average award:*** Freshmen: $9418; Undergraduates: $9006. ***Scholarships, grants, and awards:*** Federal Pell, FSEOG, state, private, college/university gift aid from institutional funds, Federal Nursing.

GIFT AID (NON-NEED-BASED) ***Total amount:*** $5,811,163 (10% federal, 2% state, 77% institutional, 11% external sources). ***Receiving aid:*** Freshmen: 4% (31); Undergraduates: 3% (130). ***Average award:*** Freshmen: $4783; Undergraduates: $4741. ***Scholarships, grants, and awards by category:*** *Academic Interests/Achievement:* 8,663 awards ($9,988,677 total): biological sciences, computer science, general academic interests/achievements, health fields, religion/biblical studies. *Creative Arts/Performance:* 1,280 awards ($1,508,291 total): cinema/film/broadcasting, debating, music, theater/drama. *Special Achievements/Activities:* 149 awards ($272,036 total): cheerleading/drum major, leadership, religious involvement. *Special Characteristics:* 1,296 awards ($2,822,291 total): children of faculty/staff, ethnic background, international students, relatives of clergy, religious affiliation, siblings of current students. ***Tuition waivers:*** Full or partial for employees or children of employees. ***ROTC:*** Army cooperative.

LOANS ***Student loans:*** $12,937,427 (76% need-based, 24% non-need-based). 59% of past graduating class borrowed through all loan programs. *Average indebtedness per student:* $18,777. ***Average need-based loan:*** Freshmen: $7543; Undergraduates: $7888. ***Parent loans:*** $11,587,199 (53% need-based, 47% non-need-based). ***Programs:*** FFEL (Subsidized and Unsubsidized Stafford, PLUS), Perkins, Federal Nursing.

WORK-STUDY ***Federal work-study:*** Total amount: $1,131,476; 761 jobs averaging $1479.

ATHLETIC AWARDS Total amount: $2,060,549 (44% need-based, 56% non-need-based).

APPLYING FOR FINANCIAL AID ***Required financial aid forms:*** FAFSA, institution's own form. ***Financial aid deadline:*** 7/1 (priority: 3/2). ***Notification date:*** Continuous beginning 3/1. Students must reply within 3 weeks of notification.

CONTACT Todd Ross, Interim Director, Student Financial Services, Azusa Pacific University, 901 East Alosta Avenue, PO Box 7000, Azusa, CA 91702-7000, 626-812-3009 or toll-free 800-TALK-APU. *E-mail:* tross@apu.edu.

BABSON COLLEGE

Wellesley, MA

Tuition & fees: $34,112 **Average undergraduate aid package: $27,453**

ABOUT THE INSTITUTION Independent, coed. Awards: bachelor's and master's degrees and post-master's certificates. 24 undergraduate majors. Total enrollment: 3,359. Undergraduates: 1,776. Freshmen: 443. Both federal and institutional methodology are used as a basis for awarding need-based institutional aid.

UNDERGRADUATE EXPENSES for 2007–08 ***Application fee:*** $60. ***Comprehensive fee:*** $45,782 includes full-time tuition ($34,112) and room and board ($11,670). ***College room only:*** $7530.

FRESHMAN FINANCIAL AID (Fall 2006, est.) 230 applied for aid; of those 77% were deemed to have need. 100% of freshmen with need received aid; of those 84% had need fully met. ***Average percent of need met:*** 96% (excluding resources awarded to replace EFC). ***Average financial aid package:*** $26,179 (excluding resources awarded to replace EFC). 8% of all full-time freshmen had no need and received non-need-based gift aid.

UNDERGRADUATE FINANCIAL AID (Fall 2006, est.) 805 applied for aid; of those 91% were deemed to have need. 100% of undergraduates with need received aid; of those 84% had need fully met. ***Average percent of need met:*** 97% (excluding resources awarded to replace EFC). ***Average financial aid package:*** $27,453 (excluding resources awarded to replace EFC). 8% of all full-time undergraduates had no need and received non-need-based gift aid.

GIFT AID (NEED-BASED) ***Total amount:*** $16,174,914 (6% federal, 2% state, 92% institutional). ***Receiving aid:*** Freshmen: 37% (163); All full-time undergraduates: 40% (706). ***Average award:*** Freshmen: $21,793; Undergraduates: $22,064. ***Scholarships, grants, and awards:*** Federal Pell, FSEOG, state, college/university gift aid from institutional funds.

GIFT AID (NON-NEED-BASED) ***Total amount:*** $2,312,793 (87% institutional, 13% external sources). ***Receiving aid:*** Freshmen: 6% (26); Undergraduates: 5% (83). ***Average award:*** Freshmen: $15,692; Undergraduates: $14,504. ***Scholarships, grants, and awards by category:*** *Academic Interests/Achievement:* 124 awards ($1,780,000 total): general academic interests/achievements. *Special Achievements/Activities:* 140 awards ($2,030,000 total): leadership. ***ROTC:*** Army cooperative, Naval cooperative, Air Force cooperative.

LOANS ***Student loans:*** $5,971,362 (49% need-based, 51% non-need-based). 44% of past graduating class borrowed through all loan programs. *Average indebtedness per student:* $33,458. ***Average need-based loan:*** Freshmen: $2689; Undergraduates: $4003. ***Parent loans:*** $4,346,380 (100% non-need-based). ***Programs:*** FFEL (Subsidized and Unsubsidized Stafford, PLUS), Perkins, state.

WORK-STUDY ***Federal work-study:*** Total amount: $410,908; 264 jobs averaging $1556. ***State or other work-study/employment:*** Total amount: $1,021,200 (100% non-need-based). 617 part-time jobs averaging $1655.

APPLYING FOR FINANCIAL AID ***Required financial aid forms:*** FAFSA, CSS Financial Aid PROFILE, noncustodial (divorced/separated) parent's statement, business/farm supplement, federal income tax form(s), W-2 forms, verification worksheet. ***Financial aid deadline:*** 2/15 (priority: 2/15). ***Notification date:*** 4/1. Students must reply by 5/1.

CONTACT Ms. Melissa Shaak, Director of Financial Aid, Babson College, Hollister Hall, 3rd Floor, Babson Park, MA 02457-0310, 781-239-4219 or toll-free 800-488-3696. *Fax:* 781-239-5510. *E-mail:* shaak@babson.edu.

BACONE COLLEGE

Muskogee, OK

CONTACT Office of Financial Aid, Bacone College, 2299 Old Bacone Road, Muskogee, OK 74403-1597, 918-683-4581 Ext. 7298 or toll-free 888-682-5514 Ext. 7340. *Fax:* 918-682-5514. *E-mail:* financialaid@bacone.edu.

BAKER UNIVERSITY

Baldwin City, KS

Tuition & fees: $17,580 **Average undergraduate aid package: $14,231**

ABOUT THE INSTITUTION Independent United Methodist, coed. Awards: bachelor's degrees. 37 undergraduate majors. Total enrollment: 923. Undergraduates: 923. Freshmen: 236. Federal methodology is used as a basis for awarding need-based institutional aid.

UNDERGRADUATE EXPENSES for 2006–07 ***Comprehensive fee:*** $23,430 includes full-time tuition ($17,200), mandatory fees ($380), and room and board ($5850). ***College room only:*** $2660. Full-time tuition and fees vary according to location and program. Room and board charges vary according to board plan and housing facility. ***Part-time tuition:*** $515 per credit hour. ***Part-time fees:*** $45 per term. Part-time tuition and fees vary according to course load. ***Payment plan:*** Installment.

FRESHMAN FINANCIAL AID (Fall 2006, est.) 223 applied for aid; of those 83% were deemed to have need. 100% of freshmen with need received aid; of those 28% had need fully met. ***Average percent of need met:*** 85% (excluding resources awarded to replace EFC). ***Average financial aid package:*** $15,911 (excluding resources awarded to replace EFC). 22% of all full-time freshmen had no need and received non-need-based gift aid.

UNDERGRADUATE FINANCIAL AID (Fall 2006, est.) 823 applied for aid; of those 83% were deemed to have need. 100% of undergraduates with need received aid; of those 34% had need fully met. ***Average percent of need met:*** 85% (excluding resources awarded to replace EFC). ***Average financial aid package:*** $14,231 (excluding resources awarded to replace EFC). 22% of all full-time undergraduates had no need and received non-need-based gift aid.

GIFT AID (NEED-BASED) ***Total amount:*** $3,057,762 (24% federal, 25% state, 51% institutional). ***Receiving aid:*** Freshmen: 78% (183); All full-time undergraduates: 76% (669). ***Average award:*** Freshmen: $11,427; Undergraduates: $9492. ***Scholarships, grants, and awards:*** Federal Pell, FSEOG, state, private, college/university gift aid from institutional funds.

GIFT AID (NON-NEED-BASED) ***Total amount:*** $4,681,313 (1% federal, 91% institutional, 8% external sources). ***Receiving aid:*** Freshmen: 78% (183); Undergraduates: 76% (669). ***Average award:*** Freshmen: $7001; Undergraduates: $5909. ***Scholarships, grants, and awards by category:*** *Academic Interests/Achievement:* general academic interests/achievements. *Creative Arts/Performance:* art/fine arts, cinema/film/broadcasting, dance, debating, journalism/publications, music, theater/drama. *Special Achievements/Activities:* cheerleading/drum major, leadership, religious involvement. *Special Characteristics:* children and siblings of alumni, children of faculty/staff, ethnic background, international students, members of minority groups, out-of-state students, relatives of clergy. ***Tuition waivers:*** Full or partial for employees or children of employees, senior citizens. ***ROTC:*** Army cooperative, Air Force cooperative.

LOANS ***Student loans:*** $4,378,748 (55% need-based, 45% non-need-based). 88% of past graduating class borrowed through all loan programs. *Average indebtedness per student:* $25,844. ***Average need-based loan:*** Freshmen: $4125; Undergraduates: $7833. ***Parent loans:*** $1,435,371 (100% non-need-based). ***Programs:*** FFEL (Subsidized and Unsubsidized Stafford, PLUS), Perkins, college/university, alternative loans.

WORK-STUDY ***Federal work-study:*** Total amount: $404,435; jobs available. ***State or other work-study/employment:*** Total amount: $182,055 (100% non-need-based). Part-time jobs available.

ATHLETIC AWARDS Total amount: $1,347,860 (100% non-need-based).

APPLYING FOR FINANCIAL AID ***Required financial aid forms:*** FAFSA, institution's own form. ***Financial aid deadline (priority):*** 3/1. ***Notification date:*** Continuous. Students must reply by 5/1 or within 6 weeks of notification.

CONTACT Mrs. Jeanne Mott, Financial Aid Director, Baker University, Box 65, 618 8th Street, Baldwin City, KS 66006-0065, 785-594-4595 or toll-free 800-873-4282. *Fax:* 785-594-8358.

BALDWIN-WALLACE COLLEGE

Berea, OH

Tuition & fees: $21,236 **Average undergraduate aid package: $16,700**

ABOUT THE INSTITUTION Independent Methodist, coed. Awards: bachelor's and master's degrees. 62 undergraduate majors. Total enrollment: 4,365. Undergraduates: 3,625. Freshmen: 705. Federal methodology is used as a basis for awarding need-based institutional aid.

UNDERGRADUATE EXPENSES for 2006–07 ***Application fee:*** $25. ***Comprehensive fee:*** $28,210 includes full-time tuition ($21,236) and room and board ($6974). ***College room only:*** $3406. ***Part-time tuition:*** $674 per semester hour. Part-time tuition and fees vary according to class time. ***Payment plans:*** Installment, deferred payment.

FRESHMAN FINANCIAL AID (Fall 2006, est.) 682 applied for aid; of those 99% were deemed to have need. 100% of freshmen with need received aid; of those 61% had need fully met. ***Average percent of need met:*** 90% (excluding resources awarded to replace EFC). ***Average financial aid package:*** $18,198 (excluding resources awarded to replace EFC). 15% of all full-time freshmen had no need and received non-need-based gift aid.

UNDERGRADUATE FINANCIAL AID (Fall 2006, est.) 2,249 applied for aid; of those 90% were deemed to have need. 100% of undergraduates with need received aid; of those 61% had need fully met. ***Average percent of need met:*** 90% (excluding resources awarded to replace EFC). ***Average financial aid***

package: $16,700 (excluding resources awarded to replace EFC). 23% of all full-time undergraduates had no need and received non-need-based gift aid.

GIFT AID (NEED-BASED) ***Total amount:*** $23,264,882 (10% federal, 15% state, 73% institutional, 2% external sources). ***Receiving aid:*** Freshmen: 96% (672); All full-time undergraduates: 70% (2,034). ***Average award:*** Freshmen: $12,552; Undergraduates: $11,915. ***Scholarships, grants, and awards:*** Federal Pell, FSEOG, state, private, college/university gift aid from institutional funds.

GIFT AID (NON-NEED-BASED) ***Total amount:*** $7,364,733 (4% federal, 6% state, 81% institutional, 9% external sources). ***Receiving aid:*** Freshmen: 30% (213); Undergraduates: 22% (646). ***Average award:*** Freshmen: $8810; Undergraduates: $8560. ***Scholarships, grants, and awards by category:*** *Academic Interests/Achievement:* 2,115 awards ($14,156,916 total): general academic interests/achievements. *Creative Arts/Performance:* 147 awards ($352,900 total): music. *Special Achievements/Activities:* 173 awards ($448,500 total): leadership. *Special Characteristics:* 570 awards ($1,269,762 total): children and siblings of alumni, members of minority groups, religious affiliation, siblings of current students. ***Tuition waivers:*** Full or partial for children of alumni, employees or children of employees. ***ROTC:*** Air Force cooperative.

LOANS ***Student loans:*** $18,212,000 (57% need-based, 43% non-need-based). 95% of past graduating class borrowed through all loan programs. *Average indebtedness per student:* $17,849. ***Average need-based loan:*** Freshmen: $3640; Undergraduates: $3610. ***Parent loans:*** $5,719,000 (46% need-based, 54% non-need-based). ***Programs:*** FFEL (Subsidized and Unsubsidized Stafford, PLUS), Perkins.

WORK-STUDY ***Federal work-study:*** Total amount: $532,000; 779 jobs averaging $683. ***State or other work-study/employment:*** Total amount: $1,055,000 (44% need-based, 56% non-need-based). 779 part-time jobs averaging $858.

APPLYING FOR FINANCIAL AID ***Required financial aid form:*** FAFSA. ***Financial aid deadline:*** 9/1 (priority: 5/1). ***Notification date:*** Continuous beginning 2/14.

CONTACT Dr. George L. Rolleston, Director of Financial Aid, Baldwin-Wallace College, 275 Eastland Road, Berea, OH 44017-2088, 440-826-2108 or toll-free 877-BWAPPLY (in-state). *E-mail:* grollest@bw.edu.

BALL STATE UNIVERSITY

Muncie, IN

ABOUT THE INSTITUTION State-supported, coed. Awards: associate, bachelor's, master's, and doctoral degrees and post-bachelor's and post-master's certificates. 124 undergraduate majors. Total enrollment: 17,082. Undergraduates: 17,082. Freshmen: 3,995.

GIFT AID (NEED-BASED) ***Scholarships, grants, and awards:*** Federal Pell, FSEOG, state, private, college/university gift aid from institutional funds.

GIFT AID (NON-NEED-BASED) ***Scholarships, grants, and awards by category:*** *Academic Interests/Achievement:* architecture, biological sciences, business, communication, education, English, foreign languages, general academic interests/achievements, health fields, mathematics, social sciences. *Creative Arts/Performance:* art/fine arts, dance, general creative arts/performance, journalism/publications, music, theater/drama. *Special Achievements/Activities:* leadership. *Special Characteristics:* children and siblings of alumni, children of faculty/staff.

LOANS ***Programs:*** Federal Direct (Subsidized and Unsubsidized Stafford, PLUS), Perkins.

WORK-STUDY ***Federal work-study:*** Total amount: $2,596,590; 1,105 jobs averaging $2350. ***State or other work-study/employment:*** Total amount: $6,645,991 (11% need-based, 89% non-need-based). 4,763 part-time jobs averaging $1395.

APPLYING FOR FINANCIAL AID ***Required financial aid form:*** FAFSA.

CONTACT Robert Zellers, Director of Scholarships and Financial Aid, Ball State University, Lucina Hall, Room 202, Muncie, IN 47306-1099, 765-285-8898 or toll-free 800-482-4BSU. *Fax:* 765-285-2173. *E-mail:* finaid@bsu.edu.

BALTIMORE HEBREW UNIVERSITY

Baltimore, MD

CONTACT Ms. Yelena Feldman, Financial Aid Counselor, Baltimore Hebrew University, 5800 Park Heights Avenue, Baltimore, MD 21215-3996, 410-578-6913 or toll-free 888-248-7420 (out-of-state). *Fax:* 410-578-6940.

BAPTIST BIBLE COLLEGE

Springfield, MO

Tuition & fees: $13,460 **Average undergraduate aid package: N/A**

ABOUT THE INSTITUTION Independent Baptist, coed. Awards: associate, bachelor's, master's, and first professional degrees. 8 undergraduate majors. Total enrollment: 768. Undergraduates: 608. Freshmen: 142. Both federal and institutional methodology are used as a basis for awarding need-based institutional aid.

UNDERGRADUATE EXPENSES for 2006–07 ***Application fee:*** $40. ***Comprehensive fee:*** $18,960 includes full-time tuition ($13,460) and room and board ($5500). ***Payment plan:*** Installment.

GIFT AID (NEED-BASED) ***Total amount:*** $5,200,975 (17% federal, 83% institutional). ***Scholarships, grants, and awards:*** Federal Pell, FSEOG, private, college/university gift aid from institutional funds.

GIFT AID (NON-NEED-BASED) ***Scholarships, grants, and awards by category:*** *Academic Interests/Achievement:* 440 awards ($300,800 total): religion/biblical studies. *Creative Arts/Performance:* 7 awards ($4400 total): music. *Special Characteristics:* 85 awards ($66,454 total): children of faculty/staff, children of workers in trades, relatives of clergy, spouses of current students. ***Tuition waivers:*** Full or partial for employees or children of employees. ***ROTC:*** Army cooperative.

LOANS ***Student loans:*** $2,423,755 (100% need-based). ***Parent loans:*** $470,974 (100% need-based). ***Programs:*** FFEL (Subsidized and Unsubsidized Stafford, PLUS).

WORK-STUDY ***Federal work-study:*** Total amount: $52,736; 15 jobs averaging $3515.

APPLYING FOR FINANCIAL AID ***Required financial aid form:*** FAFSA. ***Financial aid deadline:*** Continuous. ***Notification date:*** Continuous. Students must reply within 2 weeks of notification.

CONTACT Bob Kotulski, Director of Financial Aid, Baptist Bible College, 628 East Kearney, Springfield, MO 65803-3498, 417-268-6036. *Fax:* 417-268-6694.

BAPTIST BIBLE COLLEGE OF PENNSYLVANIA

Clarks Summit, PA

CONTACT Mr. Thomas Pollock, Director of Student Financial Services, Baptist Bible College of Pennsylvania, 538 Venard Road, Clarks Summit, PA 18411, 570-586-2400 Ext. 9205 or toll-free 800-451-7664. *Fax:* 570-586-1753. *E-mail:* tpollock@bbc.edu.

THE BAPTIST COLLEGE OF FLORIDA

Graceville, FL

Tuition & fees: $7550 **Average undergraduate aid package: $6173**

ABOUT THE INSTITUTION Independent Southern Baptist, coed. Awards: associate and bachelor's degrees. 9 undergraduate majors. Total enrollment: 596. Undergraduates: 596. Freshmen: 42. Federal methodology is used as a basis for awarding need-based institutional aid.

UNDERGRADUATE EXPENSES for 2006–07 ***Application fee:*** $20. ***Comprehensive fee:*** $11,286 includes full-time tuition ($7200), mandatory fees ($350), and room and board ($3736). Full-time tuition and fees vary according to course load and location. Room and board charges vary according to board plan and housing facility. ***Part-time tuition:*** $240 per semester hour. ***Part-time fees:*** $175 per term. Part-time tuition and fees vary according to course load and location. ***Payment plan:*** Installment.

FRESHMAN FINANCIAL AID (Fall 2005) 29 applied for aid; of those 86% were deemed to have need. 100% of freshmen with need received aid; of those 4% had need fully met. ***Average percent of need met:*** 53% (excluding resources awarded to replace EFC). ***Average financial aid package:*** $5287 (excluding resources awarded to replace EFC). 38% of all full-time freshmen had no need and received non-need-based gift aid.

UNDERGRADUATE FINANCIAL AID (Fall 2005) 276 applied for aid; of those 94% were deemed to have need. 100% of undergraduates with need received aid; of those 7% had need fully met. ***Average percent of need met:*** 51% (excluding resources awarded to replace EFC). ***Average financial aid package:***

$6173 (excluding resources awarded to replace EFC). 14% of all full-time undergraduates had no need and received non-need-based gift aid.

GIFT AID (NEED-BASED) ***Total amount:*** $1,303,018 (51% federal, 23% state, 1% institutional, 25% external sources). ***Receiving aid:*** Freshmen: 60% (24); All full-time undergraduates: 82% (247). ***Average award:*** Freshmen: $3474; Undergraduates: $3882. ***Scholarships, grants, and awards:*** Federal Pell, FSEOG, state, private, college/university gift aid from institutional funds.

GIFT AID (NON-NEED-BASED) ***Total amount:*** $193,710 (41% state, 2% institutional, 57% external sources). ***Receiving aid:*** Undergraduates: 4% (13). ***Average award:*** Freshmen: $3145; Undergraduates: $3311. ***Scholarships, grants, and awards by category:*** *Academic Interests/Achievement:* 281 awards ($285,566 total): education, religion/biblical studies. *Creative Arts/Performance:* 11 awards ($5848 total): music. *Special Characteristics:* 289 awards ($289,268 total): children with a deceased or disabled parent, religious affiliation, spouses of current students. ***Tuition waivers:*** Full or partial for employees or children of employees.

LOANS ***Student loans:*** $1,248,270 (90% need-based, 10% non-need-based). 1% of past graduating class borrowed through all loan programs. *Average indebtedness per student:* $670. ***Average need-based loan:*** Freshmen: $2559; Undergraduates: $3365. ***Parent loans:*** $56,540 (35% need-based, 65% non-need-based). ***Programs:*** FFEL (Subsidized and Unsubsidized Stafford, PLUS).

WORK-STUDY ***Federal work-study:*** Total amount: $41,724; 40 jobs averaging $1253.

APPLYING FOR FINANCIAL AID ***Required financial aid forms:*** FAFSA, institution's own form, state aid form, business/farm supplement. ***Financial aid deadline:*** 4/15 (priority: 4/1). ***Notification date:*** Continuous beginning 6/15. Students must reply within 4 weeks of notification.

CONTACT Angela Rathel, Director of Financial Aid, The Baptist College of Florida, 5400 College Drive, Graceville, FL 32440-3306, 850-263-3261 Ext. 461 or toll-free 800-328-2660 Ext. 460. *Fax:* 850-263-2141. *E-mail:* finaid@baptistcollege.edu.

BAPTIST COLLEGE OF HEALTH SCIENCES

Memphis, TN

CONTACT Ms. Janet Bonney-Baker, Financial Aid Officer, Baptist College of Health Sciences, 1003 Monroe Avenue, Memphis, TN 38104, 901-227-6805 or toll-free 866-575-2247. *Fax:* 901-227-4311. *E-mail:* janet.bonney@bchs.edu.

BAPTIST MISSIONARY ASSOCIATION THEOLOGICAL SEMINARY

Jacksonville, TX

CONTACT Dr. Philip Attebery, Dean/Registrar, Baptist Missionary Association Theological Seminary, 1530 East Pine Street, Jacksonville, TX 75766-5407, 903-586-2501. *Fax:* 903-586-0378. *E-mail:* bmatsem@bmats.edu.

BAPTIST UNIVERSITY OF THE AMERICAS

San Antonio, TX

CONTACT Financial Aid Office, Baptist University of the Americas, 8019 South Pan Am Expressway, San Antonio, TX 78224-2701, 210-924-4338 or toll-free 800-721-1396.

BARCLAY COLLEGE

Haviland, KS

CONTACT Christina Foster, Financial Aid Coordinator, Barclay College, 607 North Kingman, Haviland, KS 67059, 800-862-0226. *Fax:* 620-862-5403. *E-mail:* financialaid@barclaycollege.edu.

BARD COLLEGE

Annandale-on-Hudson, NY

Tuition & fees: $34,080 **Average undergraduate aid package: $25,147**

ABOUT THE INSTITUTION Independent, coed. Awards: associate, bachelor's, master's, and doctoral degrees. 88 undergraduate majors. Total enrollment: 2,012. Undergraduates: 1,735. Freshmen: 498. Both federal and institutional methodology are used as a basis for awarding need-based institutional aid.

UNDERGRADUATE EXPENSES for 2006–07 ***Application fee:*** $50. ***Comprehensive fee:*** $43,930 includes full-time tuition ($34,080) and room and board ($9850). ***College room only:*** $4950. ***Part-time tuition:*** $1066 per credit. ***Part-time fees:*** $351 per term.

FRESHMAN FINANCIAL AID (Fall 2006, est.) 353 applied for aid; of those 88% were deemed to have need. 100% of freshmen with need received aid; of those 58% had need fully met. ***Average percent of need met:*** 86% (excluding resources awarded to replace EFC). ***Average financial aid package:*** $25,008 (excluding resources awarded to replace EFC). 2% of all full-time freshmen had no need and received non-need-based gift aid.

UNDERGRADUATE FINANCIAL AID (Fall 2006, est.) 1,118 applied for aid; of those 87% were deemed to have need. 100% of undergraduates with need received aid; of those 54% had need fully met. ***Average percent of need met:*** 88% (excluding resources awarded to replace EFC). ***Average financial aid package:*** $25,147 (excluding resources awarded to replace EFC). 4% of all full-time undergraduates had no need and received non-need-based gift aid.

GIFT AID (NEED-BASED) ***Total amount:*** $19,618,155 (6% federal, 3% state, 89% institutional, 2% external sources). ***Receiving aid:*** Freshmen: 60% (299); All full-time undergraduates: 57% (942). ***Average award:*** Freshmen: $21,873; Undergraduates: $20,829. ***Scholarships, grants, and awards:*** Federal Pell, FSEOG, state, private, college/university gift aid from institutional funds.

GIFT AID (NON-NEED-BASED) ***Total amount:*** $708,709 (2% state, 94% institutional, 4% external sources). ***Average award:*** Freshmen: $16,835; Undergraduates: $11,309. ***Scholarships, grants, and awards by category:*** *Academic Interests/Achievement:* 30 awards ($214,250 total): biological sciences, mathematics, physical sciences. *Special Achievements/Activities:* leadership. *Special Characteristics:* 21 awards ($470,000 total): children of educators, children of faculty/staff.

LOANS ***Student loans:*** $6,443,215 (81% need-based, 19% non-need-based). 65% of past graduating class borrowed through all loan programs. *Average indebtedness per student:* $18,345. ***Average need-based loan:*** Freshmen: $2512; Undergraduates: $3387. ***Parent loans:*** $4,629,018 (78% need-based, 22% non-need-based). ***Programs:*** FFEL (Subsidized and Unsubsidized Stafford, PLUS), Perkins, college/university loans from institutional funds (for international students only).

WORK-STUDY ***Federal work-study:*** Total amount: $958,775; 606 jobs averaging $1582. ***State or other work-study/employment:*** Total amount: $116,350 (100% need-based). 70 part-time jobs averaging $1650.

APPLYING FOR FINANCIAL AID ***Required financial aid forms:*** FAFSA, CSS Financial Aid PROFILE, state aid form, noncustodial (divorced/separated) parent's statement, business/farm supplement. ***Financial aid deadline:*** 2/15 (priority: 2/1). ***Notification date:*** 4/1. Students must reply by 5/1 or within 2 weeks of notification.

CONTACT Denise Ann Ackerman, Director of Financial Aid, Bard College, Annandale Road, Annandale-on-Hudson, NY 12504, 845-758-7525. *Fax:* 845-758-7336. *E-mail:* ackerman@bard.edu.

BARNARD COLLEGE

New York, NY

Tuition & fees: $33,078 **Average undergraduate aid package: $30,664**

ABOUT THE INSTITUTION Independent, women only. Awards: bachelor's degrees. 57 undergraduate majors. Total enrollment: 2,350. Undergraduates: 2,350. Freshmen: 556. Both federal and institutional methodology are used as a basis for awarding need-based institutional aid.

UNDERGRADUATE EXPENSES for 2006–07 ***Application fee:*** $55. ***Comprehensive fee:*** $44,470 includes full-time tuition ($31,714), mandatory fees ($1364), and room and board ($11,392). ***College room only:*** $6900. Room and board charges vary according to board plan and housing facility. ***Part-time tuition:*** $1060 per credit. ***Payment plans:*** Installment, deferred payment.

FRESHMAN FINANCIAL AID (Fall 2006, est.) 346 applied for aid; of those 75% were deemed to have need. 100% of freshmen with need received aid; of those 100% had need fully met. ***Average percent of need met:*** 100% (excluding resources awarded to replace EFC). ***Average financial aid package:*** $31,377 (excluding resources awarded to replace EFC).

UNDERGRADUATE FINANCIAL AID (Fall 2006, est.) 1,140 applied for aid; of those 87% were deemed to have need. 100% of undergraduates with need received aid; of those 100% had need fully met. ***Average percent of need met:***

100% (excluding resources awarded to replace EFC). ***Average financial aid package:*** $30,664 (excluding resources awarded to replace EFC).

GIFT AID (NEED-BASED) ***Total amount:*** $25,372,029 (7% federal, 6% state, 84% institutional, 3% external sources). ***Receiving aid:*** Freshmen: 45% (249); All full-time undergraduates: 42% (949). ***Average award:*** Freshmen: $29,341; Undergraduates: $26,861. ***Scholarships, grants, and awards:*** Federal Pell, FSEOG, state, private, college/university gift aid from institutional funds, ACG and SMART Grants (Federal).

GIFT AID (NON-NEED-BASED) ***Total amount:*** $501,822 (10% state, 90% external sources). ***Tuition waivers:*** Full or partial for employees or children of employees.

LOANS ***Student loans:*** $3,839,368 (89% need-based, 11% non-need-based). 48% of past graduating class borrowed through all loan programs. *Average indebtedness per student:* $19,400. ***Average need-based loan:*** Freshmen: $2469; Undergraduates: $3915. ***Parent loans:*** $6,523,491 (100% non-need-based). ***Programs:*** FFEL (Subsidized and Unsubsidized Stafford, PLUS), Perkins, state, college/university, alternative loans.

WORK-STUDY ***Federal work-study:*** Total amount: $576,047; 322 jobs averaging $1789. ***State or other work-study/employment:*** Total amount: $1,188,944 (69% need-based, 31% non-need-based). 704 part-time jobs averaging $1689.

APPLYING FOR FINANCIAL AID ***Required financial aid forms:*** FAFSA, institution's own form, CSS Financial Aid PROFILE, state aid form, noncustodial (divorced/separated) parent's statement, business/farm supplement, federal income tax form(s). ***Financial aid deadline:*** 2/1. ***Notification date:*** 4/1. Students must reply by 5/1.

CONTACT Dr. Alison Rabil, Director of Financial Aid, Barnard College, 3009 Broadway, New York, NY 10027-6598, 212-854-2154. *Fax:* 212-854-2902. *E-mail:* finaid@barnard.edu.

BARNES-JEWISH COLLEGE OF NURSING AND ALLIED HEALTH

St. Louis, MO

CONTACT Regina Blackshear, Chief Financial Aid Officer, Barnes-Jewish College of Nursing and Allied Health, 306 South Kingshighway, St. Louis, MO 63110-1091, 314-454-7770 or toll-free 800-832-9009 (in-state).

BARRY UNIVERSITY

Miami Shores, FL

CONTACT Mr. Dart Humeston, Assistant Dean of Enrollment Services/Director of Financial Aid, Barry University, 11300 Northeast Second Avenue, Miami Shores, FL 33161-6695, 305-899-3673 or toll-free 800-695-2279. *E-mail:* finaid@mail.barry.edu.

BARTON COLLEGE

Wilson, NC

Tuition & fees: $17,654 **Average undergraduate aid package: $15,760**

ABOUT THE INSTITUTION Independent religious, coed. Awards: bachelor's degrees and post-bachelor's certificates. 32 undergraduate majors. Total enrollment: 1,136. Undergraduates: 1,136. Freshmen: 220. Federal methodology is used as a basis for awarding need-based institutional aid.

UNDERGRADUATE EXPENSES for 2006–07 ***Application fee:*** $25. ***Comprehensive fee:*** $23,918 includes full-time tuition ($16,352), mandatory fees ($1302), and room and board ($6264). ***College room only:*** $3040. Full-time tuition and fees vary according to course load and program. Room and board charges vary according to housing facility. ***Part-time tuition:*** $696 per credit hour. Part-time tuition and fees vary according to course load and program. ***Payment plan:*** Installment.

FRESHMAN FINANCIAL AID (Fall 2006, est.) 191 applied for aid; of those 90% were deemed to have need. 100% of freshmen with need received aid; of those 15% had need fully met. ***Average percent of need met:*** 73% (excluding resources awarded to replace EFC). ***Average financial aid package:*** $16,697 (excluding resources awarded to replace EFC). 21% of all full-time freshmen had no need and received non-need-based gift aid.

UNDERGRADUATE FINANCIAL AID (Fall 2006, est.) 711 applied for aid; of those 93% were deemed to have need. 100% of undergraduates with need received aid; of those 16% had need fully met. ***Average percent of need met:*** 69% (excluding resources awarded to replace EFC). ***Average financial aid package:*** $15,760 (excluding resources awarded to replace EFC). 22% of all full-time undergraduates had no need and received non-need-based gift aid.

GIFT AID (NEED-BASED) ***Total amount:*** $2,350,666 (52% federal, 40% state, 4% institutional, 4% external sources). ***Receiving aid:*** Freshmen: 57% (124); All full-time undergraduates: 54% (482). ***Average award:*** Freshmen: $4602; Undergraduates: $4536. ***Scholarships, grants, and awards:*** Federal Pell, FSEOG, state, private, college/university gift aid from institutional funds.

GIFT AID (NON-NEED-BASED) ***Total amount:*** $5,686,887 (24% state, 72% institutional, 4% external sources). ***Receiving aid:*** Freshmen: 78% (170); Undergraduates: 73% (645). ***Average award:*** Freshmen: $5736; Undergraduates: $5324. ***Scholarships, grants, and awards by category:*** *Academic Interests/Achievement:* 1,182 awards ($2,375,672 total): biological sciences, business, communication, computer science, education, English, general academic interests/achievements, health fields, humanities, international studies, mathematics, physical sciences, religion/biblical studies, social sciences. *Creative Arts/Performance:* 10 awards ($6100 total): art/fine arts, music, theater/drama. *Special Achievements/Activities:* 22 awards ($37,530 total): general special achievements/activities, leadership, religious involvement. *Special Characteristics:* 149 awards ($485,650 total): adult students, children and siblings of alumni, children of faculty/staff, international students, local/state students, relatives of clergy, religious affiliation, siblings of current students, veterans. ***Tuition waivers:*** Full or partial for children of alumni, employees or children of employees, adult students, senior citizens.

LOANS ***Student loans:*** $5,928,164 (48% need-based, 52% non-need-based). 78% of past graduating class borrowed through all loan programs. *Average indebtedness per student:* $22,809. ***Average need-based loan:*** Freshmen: $3645; Undergraduates: $4748. ***Parent loans:*** $1,378,547 (100% non-need-based). ***Programs:*** FFEL (Subsidized and Unsubsidized Stafford, PLUS), Perkins, alternative loans.

WORK-STUDY ***Federal work-study:*** Total amount: $498,400; 438 jobs averaging $1138.

ATHLETIC AWARDS Total amount: $915,410 (100% non-need-based).

APPLYING FOR FINANCIAL AID ***Required financial aid form:*** FAFSA. ***Financial aid deadline (priority):*** 4/1. ***Notification date:*** Continuous beginning 2/1. Students must reply by 5/1 or within 2 weeks of notification.

CONTACT Ms. Bettie Westbrook, Director of Financial Aid, Barton College, Box 5000, Wilson, NC 27893, 252-399-6316 or toll-free 800-345-4973. *Fax:* 252-399-6572. *E-mail:* aid@barton.edu.

BASTYR UNIVERSITY

Kenmore, WA

Tuition & fees: $16,365 **Average undergraduate aid package: $17,600**

ABOUT THE INSTITUTION Independent, coed. Awards: bachelor's, master's, and first professional degrees and post-bachelor's, post-master's, and first professional certificates. 6 undergraduate majors. Total enrollment: 1,126. Undergraduates: 263. Entering class: 128. Federal methodology is used as a basis for awarding need-based institutional aid.

UNDERGRADUATE EXPENSES for 2007–08 ***Application fee:*** $60. ***Tuition:*** full-time $14,625; part-time $325 per credit.

UNDERGRADUATE FINANCIAL AID (Fall 2006, est.) 220 applied for aid; of those 89% were deemed to have need. 100% of undergraduates with need received aid. ***Average percent of need met:*** 50% (excluding resources awarded to replace EFC). ***Average financial aid package:*** $17,600 (excluding resources awarded to replace EFC).

GIFT AID (NEED-BASED) ***Total amount:*** $1,018,084 (31% federal, 33% state, 32% institutional, 4% external sources). ***Receiving aid:*** All full-time undergraduates: 76% (185). ***Average award:*** Undergraduates: $8750. ***Scholarships, grants, and awards:*** Federal Pell, FSEOG, state, private, college/university gift aid from institutional funds.

GIFT AID (NON-NEED-BASED) ***Scholarships, grants, and awards by category:*** *Academic Interests/Achievement:* health fields.

LOANS ***Student loans:*** $2,312,096 (100% need-based). 90% of past graduating class borrowed through all loan programs. *Average indebtedness per student:* $30,000. ***Average need-based loan:*** Undergraduates: $5500. ***Parent loans:*** $37,000 (100% need-based). ***Programs:*** FFEL (Subsidized and Unsubsidized Stafford, PLUS), Perkins.

WORK-STUDY ***Federal work-study:*** Total amount: $65,563; 40 jobs averaging $3000. ***State or other work-study/employment:*** Total amount: $36,429 (100% need-based). 31 part-time jobs averaging $3000.

APPLYING FOR FINANCIAL AID ***Required financial aid forms:*** FAFSA, institution's own form. ***Financial aid deadline (priority):*** 5/1. ***Notification date:*** Continuous beginning 5/15. Students must reply within 3 weeks of notification.

CONTACT Maria Rebecchi, Assistant Director of Financial Aid, Bastyr University, 14500 Juanita Drive NE, Kenmore, WA 98028-4966, 425-602-3081. *Fax:* 425-602-3090. *E-mail:* finaid@bastyr.edu.

BATES COLLEGE

Lewiston, ME

ABOUT THE INSTITUTION Independent, coed. Awards: bachelor's degrees. 36 undergraduate majors. Total enrollment: 1,744. Undergraduates: 1,744. Freshmen: 492.

GIFT AID (NEED-BASED) ***Scholarships, grants, and awards:*** Federal Pell, FSEOG, state, private, college/university gift aid from institutional funds.

LOANS ***Programs:*** FFEL (Subsidized and Unsubsidized Stafford, PLUS), Perkins, state.

WORK-STUDY ***Federal work-study:*** Total amount: $924,892; 573 jobs averaging $1614. ***State or other work-study/employment:*** Total amount: $116,000 (100% need-based). 71 part-time jobs averaging $1633.

APPLYING FOR FINANCIAL AID ***Required financial aid forms:*** FAFSA, CSS Financial Aid PROFILE, noncustodial (divorced/separated) parent's statement, business/farm supplement.

CONTACT Catherine D. Ganung, Director of Student Financial Services, Bates College, 44 Mountain Avenue, Lewiston, ME 04240, 207-786-6096. *Fax:* 207-786-8350. *E-mail:* cganung@bates.edu.

BAYAMÓN CENTRAL UNIVERSITY

Bayamón, PR

CONTACT Financial Aid Director, Bayamón Central University, PO Box 1725, Bayamón, PR 00960-1725, 787-786-3030 Ext. 2115. *Fax:* 787-785-4365.

BAYLOR UNIVERSITY

Waco, TX

Tuition & fees: $24,490 **Average undergraduate aid package: $15,882**

ABOUT THE INSTITUTION Independent Baptist, coed. Awards: bachelor's, master's, doctoral, and first professional degrees and post-master's certificates. 132 undergraduate majors. Total enrollment: 14,040. Undergraduates: 11,831. Freshmen: 2,783. Federal methodology is used as a basis for awarding need-based institutional aid.

UNDERGRADUATE EXPENSES for 2007–08 ***Application fee:*** $50. ***Comprehensive fee:*** $32,016 includes full-time tuition ($22,220), mandatory fees ($2270), and room and board ($7526). ***College room only:*** $3774.

FRESHMAN FINANCIAL AID (Fall 2006, est.) 1826 applied for aid; of those 74% were deemed to have need. 100% of freshmen with need received aid; of those 19% had need fully met. ***Average percent of need met:*** 64% (excluding resources awarded to replace EFC). ***Average financial aid package:*** $15,591 (excluding resources awarded to replace EFC). 41% of all full-time freshmen had no need and received non-need-based gift aid.

UNDERGRADUATE FINANCIAL AID (Fall 2006, est.) 6,880 applied for aid; of those 82% were deemed to have need. 99% of undergraduates with need received aid; of those 17% had need fully met. ***Average percent of need met:*** 63% (excluding resources awarded to replace EFC). ***Average financial aid package:*** $15,882 (excluding resources awarded to replace EFC). 33% of all full-time undergraduates had no need and received non-need-based gift aid.

GIFT AID (NEED-BASED) ***Total amount:*** $58,067,042 (11% federal, 18% state, 64% institutional, 7% external sources). ***Receiving aid:*** Freshmen: 47% (1,318); All full-time undergraduates: 46% (5,269). ***Average award:*** Freshmen: $11,582; Undergraduates: $11,376. ***Scholarships, grants, and awards:*** Federal Pell, FSEOG, state, college/university gift aid from institutional funds.

GIFT AID (NON-NEED-BASED) ***Total amount:*** $31,103,914 (87% institutional, 13% external sources). ***Receiving aid:*** Freshmen: 44% (1,214); Undergraduates: 37% (4,248). ***Average award:*** Freshmen: $7526; Undergraduates: $7598. ***Scholarships, grants, and awards by category:*** *Academic Interests/Achievement:* 9,936 awards ($46,200,816 total): business, communication, computer science, education, engineering/technologies, English, foreign languages, general academic interests/achievements, health fields, home economics, humanities, international studies, mathematics, military science, physical sciences, premedicine, religion/biblical studies, social sciences. *Creative Arts/Performance:* 560 awards ($1,815,094 total): art/fine arts, cinema/film/broadcasting, debating, journalism/publications, music, theater/drama. *Special Achievements/Activities:* 547 awards ($835,260 total): community service, leadership, religious involvement. *Special Characteristics:* 271 awards ($4,504,225 total): children of faculty/staff. ***ROTC:*** Air Force.

LOANS ***Student loans:*** $68,680,776 (66% need-based, 34% non-need-based). ***Average need-based loan:*** Freshmen: $1852; Undergraduates: $2500. ***Parent loans:*** $19,728,969 (26% need-based, 74% non-need-based). ***Programs:*** FFEL (Subsidized and Unsubsidized Stafford, PLUS), Perkins, Federal Nursing, state, college/university.

WORK-STUDY ***Federal work-study:*** Total amount: $8,135,024; 3,158 jobs averaging $2576. ***State or other work-study/employment:*** Part-time jobs available.

ATHLETIC AWARDS Total amount: $7,167,571 (28% need-based, 72% non-need-based).

APPLYING FOR FINANCIAL AID ***Required financial aid forms:*** FAFSA, state residency affirmation. ***Financial aid deadline (priority):*** 2/15. ***Notification date:*** Continuous beginning 3/15. Students must reply by 5/1 or within 2 weeks of notification.

CONTACT Office of Admission Services, Baylor University, PO Box 97056, Waco, TX 76798-7056, 254-710-3435 or toll-free 800-BAYLORU. *Fax:* 254-710-3436. *E-mail:* admissions@baylor.edu.

BAY PATH COLLEGE

Longmeadow, MA

CONTACT Phyllis Brand, Financial Aid Assistant, Bay Path College, 588 Longmeadow Street, Longmeadow, MA 01106-2292, 413-565-1261 or toll-free 800-782-7284 Ext. 1331. *Fax:* 413-565-1101. *E-mail:* pbrand@baypath.edu.

BEACON COLLEGE

Leesburg, FL

CONTACT Financial Aid Office, Beacon College, 105 East Main Street, Leesburg, FL 34748, 352-787-7660.

BEACON UNIVERSITY

Columbus, GA

Tuition & fees: N/R **Average undergraduate aid package: $7280**

ABOUT THE INSTITUTION Independent religious, coed. Awards: associate, bachelor's, master's, and doctoral degrees. 3 undergraduate majors. Total enrollment: 229. Undergraduates: 126. Federal methodology is used as a basis for awarding need-based institutional aid.

FRESHMAN FINANCIAL AID (Fall 2005) 10 applied for aid; of those 100% were deemed to have need. 100% of freshmen with need received aid; of those 100% had need fully met. ***Average percent of need met:*** 100% (excluding resources awarded to replace EFC). ***Average financial aid package:*** $5852 (excluding resources awarded to replace EFC).

UNDERGRADUATE FINANCIAL AID (Fall 2005) 37 applied for aid; of those 100% were deemed to have need. 100% of undergraduates with need received aid; of those 100% had need fully met. ***Average percent of need met:*** 100% (excluding resources awarded to replace EFC). ***Average financial aid package:*** $7280 (excluding resources awarded to replace EFC).

GIFT AID (NEED-BASED) ***Total amount:*** $3576 (87% federal, 13% state). ***Receiving aid:*** Freshmen: 60% (6); All full-time undergraduates: 73% (27). ***Average award:*** Freshmen: $2465; Undergraduates: $2840. ***Scholarships, grants, and awards:*** Federal Pell.

GIFT AID (NON-NEED-BASED) ***Receiving aid:*** Freshmen: 40% (4); Undergraduates: 46% (17). ***Tuition waivers:*** Full or partial for employees or children of employees.

LOANS ***Student loans:*** $3116 (100% need-based). 56% of past graduating class borrowed through all loan programs. *Average indebtedness per student:* $26,741. ***Average need-based loan:*** Freshmen: $3958; Undergraduates: $3922. ***Programs:*** FFEL (Subsidized and Unsubsidized Stafford, PLUS).

APPLYING FOR FINANCIAL AID ***Required financial aid forms:*** FAFSA, institution's own form. ***Financial aid deadline (priority):*** 7/1. ***Notification date:*** Continuous beginning 7/15. Students must reply within 2 weeks of notification.

CONTACT Mrs. Rita Roberts, Director of Student Financial Affairs, Beacon University, 6003 Veterans Parkway, Columbus, GA 31909-4663, 706-323-5364 Ext. 254. *Fax:* 706-323-5891. *E-mail:* rita.roberts@beacon.edu.

BECKER COLLEGE

Worcester, MA

Tuition & fees: $21,460 **Average undergraduate aid package: $9299**

ABOUT THE INSTITUTION Independent, coed. Awards: associate and bachelor's degrees (also includes Leicester, MA small town campus). 30 undergraduate majors. Total enrollment: 1,660. Undergraduates: 1,660. Freshmen: 496. Federal methodology is used as a basis for awarding need-based institutional aid.

UNDERGRADUATE EXPENSES for 2006–07 ***Application fee:*** $30. ***Comprehensive fee:*** $29,960 includes full-time tuition ($20,500), mandatory fees ($960), and room and board ($8500). Room and board charges vary according to board plan and housing facility. ***Part-time tuition:*** $855 per credit hour. Part-time tuition and fees vary according to program. ***Payment plan:*** Installment.

FRESHMAN FINANCIAL AID (Fall 2005) 429 applied for aid; of those 92% were deemed to have need. 99% of freshmen with need received aid; of those 9% had need fully met. ***Average percent of need met:*** 48% (excluding resources awarded to replace EFC). ***Average financial aid package:*** $9879 (excluding resources awarded to replace EFC). 17% of all full-time freshmen had no need and received non-need-based gift aid.

UNDERGRADUATE FINANCIAL AID (Fall 2005) 1,093 applied for aid; of those 91% were deemed to have need. 99% of undergraduates with need received aid; of those 8% had need fully met. ***Average percent of need met:*** 47% (excluding resources awarded to replace EFC). ***Average financial aid package:*** $9299 (excluding resources awarded to replace EFC). 13% of all full-time undergraduates had no need and received non-need-based gift aid.

GIFT AID (NEED-BASED) ***Total amount:*** $6,528,000 (25% federal, 9% state, 63% institutional, 3% external sources). ***Receiving aid:*** Freshmen: 81% (387); All full-time undergraduates: 80% (916). ***Average award:*** Freshmen: $7386; Undergraduates: $6723. ***Scholarships, grants, and awards:*** Federal Pell, FSEOG, state, private, college/university gift aid from institutional funds.

GIFT AID (NON-NEED-BASED) ***Total amount:*** $336,016 (2% federal, 7% state, 88% institutional, 3% external sources). ***Receiving aid:*** Freshmen: 3% (16); Undergraduates: 2% (24). ***Average award:*** Freshmen: $11,397; Undergraduates: $11,896. ***Scholarships, grants, and awards by category:*** *Academic Interests/Achievement:* 21 awards ($35,000 total): general academic interests/achievements. *Special Achievements/Activities:* general special achievements/activities, leadership. *Special Characteristics:* 42 awards ($267,180 total): children of faculty/staff, siblings of current students, twins. ***Tuition waivers:*** Full or partial for employees or children of employees, senior citizens. ***ROTC:*** Army cooperative, Naval cooperative, Air Force cooperative.

LOANS ***Student loans:*** $13,040,530 (72% need-based, 28% non-need-based). 98% of past graduating class borrowed through all loan programs. *Average indebtedness per student:* $32,121. ***Average need-based loan:*** Freshmen: $2306; Undergraduates: $2941. ***Parent loans:*** $3,114,125 (51% need-based, 49% non-need-based). ***Programs:*** FFEL (Subsidized and Unsubsidized Stafford, PLUS), state, alternative loans.

WORK-STUDY ***Federal work-study:*** Total amount: $305,250; 450 jobs averaging $879.

APPLYING FOR FINANCIAL AID ***Required financial aid form:*** FAFSA. ***Financial aid deadline (priority):*** 3/1. ***Notification date:*** Continuous. Students must reply within 2 weeks of notification.

CONTACT Denise Brindle, Director of Student Financial Services, Becker College, 61 Sever Street, PO Box 15071, Worcester, MA 01615-0071, 508-373-9430 Ext. 9430 or toll-free 877-5BECKER Ext. 245. *Fax:* 508-890-1511. *E-mail:* denise.brindle@becker.edu.

BEIS MEDRASH HEICHAL DOVID

Far Rockaway, NY

CONTACT Financial Aid Office, Beis Medrash Heichal Dovid, 257 Beach 17th Street, Far Rockaway, NY 11691, 718-868-2300.

BELHAVEN COLLEGE

Jackson, MS

ABOUT THE INSTITUTION Independent Presbyterian, coed. Awards: associate, bachelor's, and master's degrees. 26 undergraduate majors. Total enrollment: 2,575. Undergraduates: 2,215. Freshmen: 307.

GIFT AID (NEED-BASED) ***Scholarships, grants, and awards:*** Federal Pell, FSEOG, state, private, college/university gift aid from institutional funds.

GIFT AID (NON-NEED-BASED) ***Scholarships, grants, and awards by category:*** *Academic Interests/Achievement:* biological sciences, business, communication, computer science, education, English, foreign languages, general academic interests/achievements, humanities, mathematics, premedicine, religion/biblical studies, social sciences. *Creative Arts/Performance:* applied art and design, art/fine arts, creative writing, dance, journalism/publications, music, performing arts, theater/drama. *Special Achievements/Activities:* cheerleading/drum major, general special achievements/activities, junior miss, leadership. *Special Characteristics:* children of faculty/staff, general special characteristics, international students, local/state students, relatives of clergy, religious affiliation.

LOANS ***Programs:*** FFEL (Subsidized and Unsubsidized Stafford, PLUS), Perkins.

WORK-STUDY ***Federal work-study:*** Total amount: $179,789; 123 jobs averaging $1600.

APPLYING FOR FINANCIAL AID ***Required financial aid forms:*** FAFSA, state aid form.

CONTACT Ms. Linda Phillips, Assistant Vice President for Institutional Advancement, Belhaven College, 1500 Peachtree Street, Box 159, Jackson, MS 39202-1789, 601-968-5934 or toll-free 800-960-5940. *Fax:* 601-353-0701. *E-mail:* lphillips@belhaven.edu.

BELLARMINE UNIVERSITY

Louisville, KY

Tuition & fees: $24,150 **Average undergraduate aid package: $19,000**

ABOUT THE INSTITUTION Independent Roman Catholic, coed. Awards: bachelor's, master's, and doctoral degrees and post-bachelor's and post-master's certificates. 54 undergraduate majors. Total enrollment: 2,627. Undergraduates: 2,006. Freshmen: 432. Both federal and institutional methodology are used as a basis for awarding need-based institutional aid.

UNDERGRADUATE EXPENSES for 2006–07 ***Application fee:*** $25. ***Comprehensive fee:*** $31,030 includes full-time tuition ($23,300), mandatory fees ($850), and room and board ($6880). ***College room only:*** $3860. ***Part-time tuition:*** $550 per credit. ***Part-time fees:*** $35 per course.

FRESHMAN FINANCIAL AID (Fall 2006, est.) 362 applied for aid; of those 85% were deemed to have need. 100% of freshmen with need received aid; of those 29% had need fully met. ***Average percent of need met:*** 84% (excluding resources awarded to replace EFC). ***Average financial aid package:*** $19,416 (excluding resources awarded to replace EFC). 29% of all full-time freshmen had no need and received non-need-based gift aid.

UNDERGRADUATE FINANCIAL AID (Fall 2006, est.) 1,472 applied for aid; of those 79% were deemed to have need. 100% of undergraduates with need received aid; of those 26% had need fully met. ***Average percent of need met:*** 76% (excluding resources awarded to replace EFC). ***Average financial aid package:*** $19,000 (excluding resources awarded to replace EFC). 28% of all full-time undergraduates had no need and received non-need-based gift aid.

GIFT AID (NEED-BASED) ***Total amount:*** $14,016,598 (7% federal, 26% state, 61% institutional, 6% external sources). ***Receiving aid:*** Freshmen: 71% (306); All full-time undergraduates: 65% (1,154). ***Average award:*** Freshmen: $15,720; Undergraduates: $12,392. ***Scholarships, grants, and awards:*** Federal Pell, FSEOG, state, private, college/university gift aid from institutional funds.

GIFT AID (NON-NEED-BASED) ***Total amount:*** $6,350,566 (11% state, 81% institutional, 8% external sources). ***Receiving aid:*** Freshmen: 22% (94); Undergraduates: 18% (314). ***Average award:*** Freshmen: $11,737; Undergraduates: $9829. ***Scholarships, grants, and awards by category:*** *Academic Interests/Achievement:* biological sciences, business, education, general academic interests/achievements, health fields. *Creative Arts/Performance:* art/fine arts, music. *Special Achievements/Activities:* cheerleading/drum major, community service, general special achievements/activities, leadership, religious involvement. *Special Characteristics:* adult students, children of faculty/staff, ethnic background, international students, local/state students, out-of-state students, previous college experience. ***ROTC:*** Army cooperative, Air Force cooperative.

LOANS ***Student loans:*** $6,153,748 (79% need-based, 21% non-need-based). 65% of past graduating class borrowed through all loan programs. *Average indebtedness per student:* $15,295. ***Average need-based loan:*** Freshmen: $3065; Undergraduates: $4064. ***Parent loans:*** $1,996,345 (53% need-based, 47% non-need-based). ***Programs:*** FFEL (Subsidized and Unsubsidized Stafford, PLUS), Perkins, state, college/university.

WORK-STUDY ***Federal work-study:*** Total amount: $366,962; jobs available. ***State or other work-study/employment:*** Total amount: $12,500 (100% non-need-based). Part-time jobs available.

ATHLETIC AWARDS Total amount: $2,039,638 (39% need-based, 61% non-need-based).

APPLYING FOR FINANCIAL AID ***Required financial aid form:*** FAFSA. ***Financial aid deadline (priority):*** 3/1. ***Notification date:*** Continuous beginning 3/15. Students must reply by 5/1.

CONTACT Ms. Heather Boutell, Director of Financial Aid, Bellarmine University, 2001 Newburg Road, Louisville, KY 40205-0671, 502-452-8124 or toll-free 800-274-4723 Ext. 8131. *Fax:* 502-452-8002. *E-mail:* hboutell@bellarmine.edu.

BELLEVUE UNIVERSITY

Bellevue, NE

CONTACT Mr. Jon Dotterer, Director of Financial Aid, Bellevue University, 1000 Galvin Road South, Bellevue, NE 68005, 402-293-3762 or toll-free 800-756-7920. *Fax:* 402-293-2062.

BELLIN COLLEGE OF NURSING

Green Bay, WI

Tuition & fees: $15,839 **Average undergraduate aid package: $15,482**

ABOUT THE INSTITUTION Independent, coed, primarily women. Awards: bachelor's and master's degrees. 1 undergraduate major. Total enrollment: 239. Undergraduates: 216. Freshmen: 32. Federal methodology is used as a basis for awarding need-based institutional aid.

UNDERGRADUATE EXPENSES for 2006–07 ***Application fee:*** $30. ***Tuition:*** full-time $15,500; part-time $734 per credit. ***Required fees:*** full-time $339; $234 per semester hour. Full-time tuition and fees vary according to course level. Part-time tuition and fees vary according to course load. ***Payment plan:*** Installment.

UNDERGRADUATE FINANCIAL AID (Fall 2006, est.) 103 applied for aid; of those 90% were deemed to have need. 100% of undergraduates with need received aid; of those 11% had need fully met. ***Average percent of need met:*** 85% (excluding resources awarded to replace EFC). ***Average financial aid package:*** $15,482 (excluding resources awarded to replace EFC). 3% of all full-time undergraduates had no need and received non-need-based gift aid.

GIFT AID (NEED-BASED) ***Total amount:*** $547,686 (21% federal, 17% state, 48% institutional, 14% external sources). ***Receiving aid:*** All full-time undergraduates: 49% (91). ***Average award:*** Undergraduates: $4584. ***Scholarships, grants, and awards:*** Federal Pell, FSEOG, state, private, college/university gift aid from institutional funds.

GIFT AID (NON-NEED-BASED) ***Total amount:*** $22,719 (40% institutional, 60% external sources). ***Receiving aid:*** Undergraduates: 2% (3). ***Average award:*** Undergraduates: $1373. ***Scholarships, grants, and awards by category:*** *Academic Interests/Achievement:* 57 awards ($66,250 total): general academic interests/achievements. ***ROTC:*** Army cooperative.

LOANS ***Student loans:*** $1,638,456 (75% need-based, 25% non-need-based). 91% of past graduating class borrowed through all loan programs. *Average indebtedness per student:* $23,702. ***Average need-based loan:*** Undergraduates: $5029. ***Parent loans:*** $236,525 (45% need-based, 55% non-need-based). ***Programs:*** FFEL (Subsidized and Unsubsidized Stafford, PLUS), state.

WORK-STUDY ***Federal work-study:*** Total amount: $3924; 4 jobs averaging $981.

APPLYING FOR FINANCIAL AID ***Required financial aid form:*** FAFSA. ***Financial aid deadline (priority):*** 3/1. ***Notification date:*** 4/1. Students must reply within 2 weeks of notification.

CONTACT Ms. Lena C. Goodman, Director of Financial Aid, Bellin College of Nursing, 725 South Webster Avenue, PO Box 23400, Green Bay, WI 54305-3400, 920-433-5801 or toll-free 800-236-8707. *Fax:* 920-433-7416. *E-mail:* lena.goodman@bcon.edu.

BELMONT ABBEY COLLEGE

Belmont, NC

Tuition & fees: $17,302 **Average undergraduate aid package: $11,729**

ABOUT THE INSTITUTION Independent Roman Catholic, coed. Awards: bachelor's degrees. 23 undergraduate majors. Total enrollment: 1,110. Undergraduates: 1,110. Freshmen: 281. Federal methodology is used as a basis for awarding need-based institutional aid.

UNDERGRADUATE EXPENSES for 2006–07 ***Application fee:*** $35. ***Comprehensive fee:*** $26,732 includes full-time tuition ($16,870), mandatory fees ($432), and room and board ($9430). ***College room only:*** $5450. Full-time tuition and fees vary according to class time, course level, course load, location, program, reciprocity agreements, and student level. Room and board charges vary according to board plan, housing facility, location, and student level. ***Part-time tuition:*** $529 per credit hour. ***Part-time fees:*** $36 per credit. Part-time tuition and fees vary according to class time, course level, course load, location, reciprocity agreements, and student level. ***Payment plans:*** Installment, deferred payment.

FRESHMAN FINANCIAL AID (Fall 2006, est.) 232 applied for aid; of those 87% were deemed to have need. 63% of freshmen with need received aid; of those 26% had need fully met. ***Average percent of need met:*** 65% (excluding resources awarded to replace EFC). ***Average financial aid package:*** $13,461 (excluding resources awarded to replace EFC). 36% of all full-time freshmen had no need and received non-need-based gift aid.

UNDERGRADUATE FINANCIAL AID (Fall 2006, est.) 778 applied for aid; of those 90% were deemed to have need. 75% of undergraduates with need received aid; of those 19% had need fully met. ***Average percent of need met:*** 58% (excluding resources awarded to replace EFC). ***Average financial aid package:*** $11,729 (excluding resources awarded to replace EFC). 28% of all full-time undergraduates had no need and received non-need-based gift aid.

GIFT AID (NEED-BASED) ***Total amount:*** $6,372,566 (18% federal, 25% state, 46% institutional, 11% external sources). ***Receiving aid:*** Freshmen: 44% (125); All full-time undergraduates: 51% (520). ***Average award:*** Freshmen: $11,439; Undergraduates: $8736. ***Scholarships, grants, and awards:*** Federal Pell, FSEOG, state, private, college/university gift aid from institutional funds.

GIFT AID (NON-NEED-BASED) ***Total amount:*** $2,175,131 (11% state, 77% institutional, 12% external sources). ***Receiving aid:*** Freshmen: 9% (25); Undergraduates: 7% (69). ***Average award:*** Freshmen: $13,532; Undergraduates: $11,741. ***Scholarships, grants, and awards by category:*** *Academic Interests/Achievement:* 607 awards ($3,648,795 total): general academic interests/achievements. *Creative Arts/Performance:* 22 awards ($41,000 total): theater/drama. *Special Achievements/Activities:* 37 awards ($67,390 total): religious involvement. *Special Characteristics:* 22 awards ($143,566 total): children of faculty/staff. ***Tuition waivers:*** Full or partial for employees or children of employees, senior citizens. ***ROTC:*** Army cooperative, Air Force cooperative.

LOANS ***Student loans:*** $3,297,193 (82% need-based, 18% non-need-based). 70% of past graduating class borrowed through all loan programs. *Average indebtedness per student:* $16,608. ***Average need-based loan:*** Freshmen: $2245; Undergraduates: $3265. ***Parent loans:*** $6,033,015 (41% need-based, 59% non-need-based). ***Programs:*** Federal Direct (Subsidized and Unsubsidized Stafford, PLUS), Perkins.

WORK-STUDY ***Federal work-study:*** Total amount: $140,308; 104 jobs averaging $1733.

ATHLETIC AWARDS Total amount: $1,327,996 (44% need-based, 56% non-need-based).

APPLYING FOR FINANCIAL AID ***Required financial aid form:*** FAFSA. ***Financial aid deadline (priority):*** 4/1. ***Notification date:*** Continuous beginning 3/1. Students must reply within 2 weeks of notification.

CONTACT Ms. Julie Hodge, Associate Director of Financial Aid, Belmont Abbey College, 100 Belmont Mt. Holly Road, Belmont, NC 28012-1802, 704-825-6718 or toll-free 888-BAC-0110. *Fax:* 704-825-6882. *E-mail:* juliehodge@bac.edu.

BELMONT UNIVERSITY

Nashville, TN

Tuition & fees: $19,780 **Average undergraduate aid package: $10,159**

ABOUT THE INSTITUTION Independent Baptist, coed. Awards: bachelor's, master's, and doctoral degrees and post-master's certificates. 67 undergraduate majors. Total enrollment: 4,481. Undergraduates: 3,774. Freshmen: 767. Federal methodology is used as a basis for awarding need-based institutional aid.

UNDERGRADUATE EXPENSES for 2007–08 ***Application fee:*** $35. ***Comprehensive fee:*** $29,309 includes full-time tuition ($18,780), mandatory fees ($1000), and room and board ($9529). ***College room only:*** $6000. ***Part-time tuition:*** $720 per credit hour. ***Part-time fees:*** $340 per term.

FRESHMAN FINANCIAL AID (Fall 2005) 694 applied for aid; of those 56% were deemed to have need. 97% of freshmen with need received aid; of those 32% had need fully met. ***Average percent of need met:*** 87% (excluding resources awarded to replace EFC). ***Average financial aid package:*** $10,031 (excluding resources awarded to replace EFC). 54% of all full-time freshmen had no need and received non-need-based gift aid.

UNDERGRADUATE FINANCIAL AID (Fall 2005) 2,886 applied for aid; of those 60% were deemed to have need. 98% of undergraduates with need received aid; of those 26% had need fully met. ***Average percent of need met:*** 84% (excluding resources awarded to replace EFC). ***Average financial aid package:*** $10,159 (excluding resources awarded to replace EFC). 39% of all full-time undergraduates had no need and received non-need-based gift aid.

GIFT AID (NEED-BASED) ***Total amount:*** $8,553,008 (18% federal, 38% state, 36% institutional, 8% external sources). ***Receiving aid:*** Freshmen: 28% (215); All full-time undergraduates: 31% (1,078). ***Average award:*** Freshmen: $5339; Undergraduates: $4742. ***Scholarships, grants, and awards:*** Federal Pell, FSEOG, state, private, college/university gift aid from institutional funds.

GIFT AID (NON-NEED-BASED) ***Total amount:*** $7,085,845 (100% institutional). ***Receiving aid:*** Freshmen: 37% (284); Undergraduates: 26% (900). ***Average award:*** Freshmen: $5165; Undergraduates: $5248. ***Scholarships, grants, and awards by category:*** *Academic Interests/Achievement:* 939 awards ($5,013,763 total): general academic interests/achievements, religion/biblical studies. *Creative Arts/Performance:* 165 awards ($270,001 total): music. *Special Characteristics:* 42 awards ($566,604 total): children of faculty/staff. ***ROTC:*** Army cooperative, Naval cooperative.

LOANS ***Student loans:*** $14,064,748 (100% need-based). 55% of past graduating class borrowed through all loan programs. *Average indebtedness per student:* $10,200. ***Average need-based loan:*** Freshmen: $2678; Undergraduates: $4109. ***Parent loans:*** $10,700,523 (100% non-need-based). ***Programs:*** FFEL (Subsidized and Unsubsidized Stafford, PLUS), Perkins, college/university.

WORK-STUDY ***Federal work-study:*** Total amount: $197,142; 252 jobs averaging $789.

ATHLETIC AWARDS Total amount: $2,778,919 (100% non-need-based).

APPLYING FOR FINANCIAL AID ***Required financial aid form:*** FAFSA. ***Financial aid deadline (priority):*** 3/1. ***Notification date:*** Continuous beginning 3/15. Students must reply by 5/1 or within 2 weeks of notification.

CONTACT Mrs. Paula A. Gill, Director, Student Financial Services, Belmont University, 1900 Belmont Boulevard, Nashville, TN 37212-3757, 615-460-6403 or toll-free 800-56E-NROL. *E-mail:* gillp@mail.belmont.edu.

BELOIT COLLEGE

Beloit, WI

Tuition & fees: $28,350 **Average undergraduate aid package: $22,781**

ABOUT THE INSTITUTION Independent, coed. Awards: bachelor's degrees. 56 undergraduate majors. Total enrollment: 1,432. Undergraduates: 1,432. Freshmen: 347. Both federal and institutional methodology are used as a basis for awarding need-based institutional aid.

UNDERGRADUATE EXPENSES for 2006–07 ***Application fee:*** $35. ***Comprehensive fee:*** $34,512 includes full-time tuition ($28,130), mandatory fees ($220), and room and board ($6162). ***College room only:*** $3006. Room and board charges vary according to board plan. ***Part-time tuition:*** $3517 per course. ***Payment plan:*** Installment.

FRESHMAN FINANCIAL AID (Fall 2006, est.) 267 applied for aid; of those 76% were deemed to have need. 100% of freshmen with need received aid; of those 100% had need fully met. ***Average percent of need met:*** 100% (excluding resources awarded to replace EFC). ***Average financial aid package:*** $22,425 (excluding resources awarded to replace EFC). 34% of all full-time freshmen had no need and received non-need-based gift aid.

UNDERGRADUATE FINANCIAL AID (Fall 2006, est.) 960 applied for aid; of those 82% were deemed to have need. 100% of undergraduates with need received aid; of those 100% had need fully met. ***Average percent of need met:*** 100% (excluding resources awarded to replace EFC). ***Average financial aid package:*** $22,781 (excluding resources awarded to replace EFC). 30% of all full-time undergraduates had no need and received non-need-based gift aid.

GIFT AID (NEED-BASED) ***Total amount:*** $13,355,517 (6% federal, 2% state, 90% institutional, 2% external sources). ***Receiving aid:*** Freshmen: 57% (198); All full-time undergraduates: 58% (770). ***Average award:*** Freshmen: $17,026; Undergraduates: $17,897. ***Scholarships, grants, and awards:*** Federal Pell, FSEOG, state, private, college/university gift aid from institutional funds.

GIFT AID (NON-NEED-BASED) ***Total amount:*** $3,066,802 (1% federal, 1% state, 96% institutional, 2% external sources). ***Average award:*** Freshmen: $9926; Undergraduates: $11,972. ***Scholarships, grants, and awards by category:*** *Academic Interests/Achievement:* 514 awards ($5,366,301 total): general academic interests/achievements. *Creative Arts/Performance:* 58 awards ($185 total): music. *Special Achievements/Activities:* 30 awards ($105,250 total): community service, general special achievements/activities. *Special Characteristics:* 46 awards ($264,711 total): members of minority groups, siblings of current students. ***Tuition waivers:*** Full or partial for employees or children of employees.

LOANS ***Student loans:*** $6,555,610 (84% need-based, 16% non-need-based). 66% of past graduating class borrowed through all loan programs. *Average indebtedness per student:* $22,424. ***Average need-based loan:*** Freshmen: $4486; Undergraduates: $5678. ***Parent loans:*** $2,511,809 (100% non-need-based). ***Programs:*** FFEL (Subsidized and Unsubsidized Stafford, PLUS), Perkins, college/university.

WORK-STUDY ***Federal work-study:*** Total amount: $831,581; 519 jobs averaging $1602. ***State or other work-study/employment:*** Total amount: $605,899 (47% need-based, 53% non-need-based). 472 part-time jobs averaging $1283.

APPLYING FOR FINANCIAL AID ***Required financial aid forms:*** FAFSA, institution's own form. ***Financial aid deadline (priority):*** 3/1. ***Notification date:*** Continuous beginning 4/1. Students must reply by 5/1 or within 2 weeks of notification.

CONTACT Mr. Jon Urish, Senior Associate Director of Admissions and Financial Aid, Beloit College, 700 College Street, Beloit, WI 53511-5596, 800-356-0751 or toll-free 800-9-BELOIT. *Fax:* 608-363-2075. *E-mail:* urishj@beloit.edu.

BEMIDJI STATE UNIVERSITY

Bemidji, MN

Tuition & fees (MN res): $6690 **Average undergraduate aid package: $7856**

ABOUT THE INSTITUTION State-supported, coed. Awards: associate, bachelor's, and master's degrees. 72 undergraduate majors. Total enrollment: 4,918. Undergraduates: 4,388. Freshmen: 657. Federal methodology is used as a basis for awarding need-based institutional aid.

UNDERGRADUATE EXPENSES for 2006–07 ***Application fee:*** $20. ***Tuition, state resident:*** full-time $5900; part-time $199.50 per credit. ***Tuition, nonresident:*** full-time $5900; part-time $199.50 per credit. ***Required fees:*** full-time $790; $360.26 per term part-time. Full-time tuition and fees vary according to course load, program, and reciprocity agreements. Part-time tuition and fees vary according to course load, program, and reciprocity agreements. ***College room and board:*** $5860; ***Room only:*** $3628. Room and board charges vary according to board plan and housing facility. ***Payment plan:*** Installment.

FRESHMAN FINANCIAL AID (Fall 2006, est.) 514 applied for aid; of those 79% were deemed to have need. 98% of freshmen with need received aid; of those 20% had need fully met. ***Average percent of need met:*** 66% (excluding resources awarded to replace EFC). ***Average financial aid package:*** $6954 (excluding resources awarded to replace EFC). 15% of all full-time freshmen had no need and received non-need-based gift aid.

UNDERGRADUATE FINANCIAL AID (Fall 2006, est.) 2,578 applied for aid; of those 79% were deemed to have need. 99% of undergraduates with need received aid; of those 26% had need fully met. ***Average percent of need met:*** 72% (excluding resources awarded to replace EFC). ***Average financial aid package:*** $7856 (excluding resources awarded to replace EFC). 15% of all full-time undergraduates had no need and received non-need-based gift aid.

GIFT AID (NEED-BASED) ***Total amount:*** $7,867,029 (51% federal, 41% state, 1% institutional, 7% external sources). ***Receiving aid:*** Freshmen: 44% (284); All full-time undergraduates: 44% (1,521). ***Average award:*** Freshmen: $4819; Undergraduates: $4502. ***Scholarships, grants, and awards:*** Federal Pell, FSEOG, state, private, college/university gift aid from institutional funds.

GIFT AID (NON-NEED-BASED) ***Total amount:*** $4,165,870 (17% federal, 21% state, 45% institutional, 17% external sources). ***Receiving aid:*** Freshmen: 33% (210); Undergraduates: 34% (1,187). ***Average award:*** Freshmen: $7445; Undergraduates: $7179. ***Scholarships, grants, and awards by category:***

Academic Interests/Achievement: 471 awards ($484,795 total): general academic interests/achievements. *Creative Arts/Performance:* 44 awards ($88,300 total). *Special Characteristics:* 131 awards ($235,365 total): children and siblings of alumni, children of faculty/staff, international students, out-of-state students. ***Tuition waivers:*** Full or partial for employees or children of employees, senior citizens.

LOANS ***Student loans:*** $16,081,531 (41% need-based, 59% non-need-based). 74% of past graduating class borrowed through all loan programs. *Average indebtedness per student:* $18,850. ***Average need-based loan:*** Freshmen: $2635; Undergraduates: $3497. ***Parent loans:*** $428,971 (100% non-need-based). ***Programs:*** Federal Direct (Subsidized and Unsubsidized Stafford, PLUS), Perkins, state, Alaska Loans, Canada Student Loans, Norwest Collegiate Loans, CitiAssist Loans and other alternative loans.

WORK-STUDY ***Federal work-study:*** Total amount: $441,984; 238 jobs averaging $1857. ***State or other work-study/employment:*** Total amount: $1,847,444 (23% need-based, 77% non-need-based). 234 part-time jobs averaging $1805.

ATHLETIC AWARDS Total amount: $718,768 (100% non-need-based).

APPLYING FOR FINANCIAL AID ***Required financial aid forms:*** FAFSA, institution's own form. ***Financial aid deadline (priority):*** 5/15. ***Notification date:*** Continuous beginning 5/15.

CONTACT Financial Aid Office, Bemidji State University, 1500 Birchmont Drive, NE, Bemidji, MN 56601-2699, 218-755-2034 or toll-free 800-475-2001 (in-state), 800-652-9747 (out-of-state). *Fax:* 218-755-4361. *E-mail:* financialaid@bemidjistate.edu.

BENEDICT COLLEGE

Columbia, SC

CONTACT Assistant Director of Financial Aid, Benedict College, 1600 Harden Street, Columbia, SC 29204, 803-253-5105 or toll-free 800-868-6598 (in-state).

BENEDICTINE COLLEGE

Atchison, KS

ABOUT THE INSTITUTION Independent Roman Catholic, coed. Awards: associate, bachelor's, and master's degrees. 34 undergraduate majors. Total enrollment: 1,553. Undergraduates: 1,468. Freshmen: 360.

GIFT AID (NEED-BASED) ***Scholarships, grants, and awards:*** Federal Pell, FSEOG, state, private, college/university gift aid from institutional funds.

GIFT AID (NON-NEED-BASED) ***Scholarships, grants, and awards by category:*** *Academic Interests/Achievement:* general academic interests/achievements. *Creative Arts/Performance:* music, theater/drama. *Special Achievements/Activities:* general special achievements/activities. *Special Characteristics:* children of educators, ethnic background, general special characteristics, international students, local/state students, members of minority groups, out-of-state students, religious affiliation, veterans' children.

LOANS ***Programs:*** FFEL (Subsidized and Unsubsidized Stafford, PLUS), Perkins, alternative loans.

WORK-STUDY ***Federal work-study:*** Total amount: $305,701; 372 jobs averaging $822. ***State or other work-study/employment:*** Total amount: $39,966 (100% non-need-based). 73 part-time jobs averaging $547.

APPLYING FOR FINANCIAL AID ***Required financial aid form:*** FAFSA.

CONTACT Mr. Keith Jaloma, Assistant Dean of Enrollment Management/Director of Financial Aid, Benedictine College, 1020 North Second Street, Atchison, KS 66002-1499, 913-360-7484 or toll-free 800-467-5340. *Fax:* 913-367-5462. *E-mail:* kjaloma@benedictine.edu.

BENEDICTINE UNIVERSITY

Lisle, IL

Tuition & fees: $20,310 **Average undergraduate aid package: $11,980**

ABOUT THE INSTITUTION Independent Roman Catholic, coed. Awards: associate, bachelor's, master's, and doctoral degrees and post-bachelor's certificates. 51 undergraduate majors. Total enrollment: 3,900. Undergraduates: 2,657. Freshmen: 379. Federal methodology is used as a basis for awarding need-based institutional aid.

UNDERGRADUATE EXPENSES for 2006–07 ***Application fee:*** $40. ***Comprehensive fee:*** $27,010 includes full-time tuition ($19,800), mandatory fees ($510), and room and board ($6700). Full-time tuition and fees vary according to class time, degree level, and location. Room and board charges vary according to board plan and housing facility. ***Part-time tuition:*** $660 per credit hour. ***Part-time fees:*** $15 per credit hour. Part-time tuition and fees vary according to class time and degree level. ***Payment plans:*** Installment, deferred payment.

FRESHMAN FINANCIAL AID (Fall 2005) 252 applied for aid; of those 100% were deemed to have need. 99% of freshmen with need received aid; of those 38% had need fully met. ***Average percent of need met:*** 87% (excluding resources awarded to replace EFC). ***Average financial aid package:*** $13,630 (excluding resources awarded to replace EFC). 17% of all full-time freshmen had no need and received non-need-based gift aid.

UNDERGRADUATE FINANCIAL AID (Fall 2005) 1,135 applied for aid; of those 100% were deemed to have need. 98% of undergraduates with need received aid; of those 40% had need fully met. ***Average percent of need met:*** 85% (excluding resources awarded to replace EFC). ***Average financial aid package:*** $11,980 (excluding resources awarded to replace EFC). 18% of all full-time undergraduates had no need and received non-need-based gift aid.

GIFT AID (NEED-BASED) ***Total amount:*** $4,819,198 (36% federal, 57% state, 7% institutional). ***Receiving aid:*** Freshmen: 47% (144); All full-time undergraduates: 42% (640). ***Average award:*** Freshmen: $6897; Undergraduates: $6350. ***Scholarships, grants, and awards:*** Federal Pell, FSEOG, state, private, college/university gift aid from institutional funds.

GIFT AID (NON-NEED-BASED) ***Total amount:*** $7,991,778 (98% institutional, 2% external sources). ***Receiving aid:*** Freshmen: 80% (245); Undergraduates: 58% (886). ***Average award:*** Freshmen: $6305; Undergraduates: $6720. ***Scholarships, grants, and awards by category:*** *Academic Interests/Achievement:* general academic interests/achievements. *Creative Arts/Performance:* music. *Special Characteristics:* children and siblings of alumni, out-of-state students, previous college experience, siblings of current students. ***Tuition waivers:*** Full or partial for employees or children of employees. ***ROTC:*** Army cooperative.

LOANS ***Student loans:*** $10,415,179 (45% need-based, 55% non-need-based). ***Average need-based loan:*** Freshmen: $3383; Undergraduates: $4170. ***Parent loans:*** $8,699,214 (100% non-need-based). ***Programs:*** FFEL (Subsidized and Unsubsidized Stafford, PLUS), Perkins, alternative loans.

WORK-STUDY ***Federal work-study:*** Total amount: $193,161; jobs available.

APPLYING FOR FINANCIAL AID ***Required financial aid forms:*** FAFSA, institution's own form. ***Financial aid deadline:*** Continuous. ***Notification date:*** Continuous beginning 2/1. Students must reply within 2 weeks of notification.

CONTACT Diane Battistella, Director, Benedictine Central, Benedictine University, 5700 College Road, Lisle, IL 60532, 630-829-6415 or toll-free 888-829-6363 (out-of-state). *Fax:* 630-829-6456. *E-mail:* dbattistella@ben.edu.

BENNETT COLLEGE FOR WOMEN

Greensboro, NC

ABOUT THE INSTITUTION Independent United Methodist, women only. Awards: bachelor's degrees. 23 undergraduate majors. Total enrollment: 607. Undergraduates: 607. Freshmen: 193.

GIFT AID (NEED-BASED) ***Scholarships, grants, and awards:*** Federal Pell, FSEOG, state, private, college/university gift aid from institutional funds, United Negro College Fund, United Methodist Church Scholarships.

GIFT AID (NON-NEED-BASED) ***Scholarships, grants, and awards by category:*** *Academic Interests/Achievement:* business, general academic interests/achievements, mathematics. *Special Achievements/Activities:* general special achievements/activities. *Special Characteristics:* children of faculty/staff, relatives of clergy, religious affiliation.

LOANS ***Programs:*** FFEL (Subsidized and Unsubsidized Stafford, PLUS), Perkins.

WORK-STUDY ***Federal work-study:*** Total amount: $118,213; 82 jobs averaging $1800.

APPLYING FOR FINANCIAL AID ***Required financial aid forms:*** FAFSA, institution's own form, state aid form.

CONTACT Monty K. Hickman, Financial Aid Director, Bennett College For Women, 900 East Washington Street, Greensboro, NC 27401, 336-370-8677. *Fax:* 336-517-2204. *E-mail:* mhickman@bennett.edu.

BENNINGTON COLLEGE

Bennington, VT

Tuition & fees: $36,800 **Average undergraduate aid package: $26,894**

ABOUT THE INSTITUTION Independent, coed. Awards: bachelor's and master's degrees and post-bachelor's certificates. 85 undergraduate majors. Total enrollment: 657. Undergraduates: 523. Freshmen: 127. Federal methodology is used as a basis for awarding need-based institutional aid.

UNDERGRADUATE EXPENSES for 2007–08 ***Application fee:*** $60. ***Comprehensive fee:*** $46,180 includes full-time tuition ($35,850), mandatory fees ($950), and room and board ($9380). ***College room only:*** $5030.

FRESHMAN FINANCIAL AID (Fall 2006, est.) 95 applied for aid; of those 91% were deemed to have need. 97% of freshmen with need received aid; of those 5% had need fully met. ***Average percent of need met:*** 77% (excluding resources awarded to replace EFC). ***Average financial aid package:*** $24,825 (excluding resources awarded to replace EFC). 11% of all full-time freshmen had no need and received non-need-based gift aid.

UNDERGRADUATE FINANCIAL AID (Fall 2006, est.) 367 applied for aid; of those 94% were deemed to have need. 100% of undergraduates with need received aid; of those 7% had need fully met. ***Average percent of need met:*** 78% (excluding resources awarded to replace EFC). ***Average financial aid package:*** $26,894 (excluding resources awarded to replace EFC). 10% of all full-time undergraduates had no need and received non-need-based gift aid.

GIFT AID (NEED-BASED) ***Total amount:*** $7,650,863 (8% federal, 1% state, 87% institutional, 4% external sources). ***Receiving aid:*** Freshmen: 62% (79); All full-time undergraduates: 65% (337). ***Average award:*** Freshmen: $23,082; Undergraduates: $22,818. ***Scholarships, grants, and awards:*** Federal Pell, FSEOG, state, private, college/university gift aid from institutional funds.

GIFT AID (NON-NEED-BASED) ***Total amount:*** $300,514 (69% institutional, 31% external sources). ***Receiving aid:*** Undergraduates: 2% (10). ***Average award:*** Freshmen: $15,197; Undergraduates: $13,849. ***Scholarships, grants, and awards by category:*** *Academic Interests/Achievement:* general academic interests/achievements. *Creative Arts/Performance:* general creative arts/performance. *Special Achievements/Activities:* general special achievements/activities. *Special Characteristics:* children of educators, children of faculty/staff, general special characteristics.

LOANS ***Student loans:*** $2,143,479 (75% need-based, 25% non-need-based). 79% of past graduating class borrowed through all loan programs. *Average indebtedness per student:* $25,463. ***Average need-based loan:*** Freshmen: $2105; Undergraduates: $3805. ***Parent loans:*** $1,814,638 (48% need-based, 52% non-need-based). ***Programs:*** FFEL (Subsidized and Unsubsidized Stafford, PLUS), college/university.

WORK-STUDY ***Federal work-study:*** Total amount: $317,211; jobs available (averaging $1700). ***State or other work-study/employment:*** Total amount: $14,450 (100% need-based). Part-time jobs available (averaging $1700).

APPLYING FOR FINANCIAL AID ***Required financial aid forms:*** FAFSA, institution's own form, CSS Financial Aid PROFILE, noncustodial (divorced/separated) parent's statement, student and parent federal tax returns and W-2s. ***Financial aid deadline (priority):*** 3/1. ***Notification date:*** 4/1. Students must reply by 5/1 or within 2 weeks of notification.

CONTACT Meg Woolmington, Financial Aid Director, Bennington College, One College Drive, Bennington, VT 05201, 802-440-4325 or toll-free 800-833-6845. *Fax:* 802-440-4350. *E-mail:* finaid@bennington.edu.

BENTLEY COLLEGE

Waltham, MA

Tuition & fees: $30,044 **Average undergraduate aid package: $23,305**

ABOUT THE INSTITUTION Independent, coed. Awards: associate, bachelor's, and master's degrees and post-bachelor's and post-master's certificates. 14 undergraduate majors. Total enrollment: 5,497. Undergraduates: 4,241. Freshmen: 888. Both federal and institutional methodology are used as a basis for awarding need-based institutional aid.

UNDERGRADUATE EXPENSES for 2006–07 ***Application fee:*** $50. ***Comprehensive fee:*** $40,574 includes full-time tuition ($29,810), mandatory fees ($234), and room and board ($10,530). ***College room only:*** $6280. Full-time tuition and fees vary according to student level. Room and board charges vary according to board plan and housing facility. ***Part-time tuition:*** $1434 per course. ***Part-time fees:*** $10 per term. Part-time tuition and fees vary according to class time and student level. ***Payment plan:*** Installment.

FRESHMAN FINANCIAL AID (Fall 2005) 722 applied for aid; of those 74% were deemed to have need. 99% of freshmen with need received aid; of those 31% had need fully met. ***Average percent of need met:*** 93% (excluding resources awarded to replace EFC). ***Average financial aid package:*** $23,941 (excluding resources awarded to replace EFC). 13% of all full-time freshmen had no need and received non-need-based gift aid.

UNDERGRADUATE FINANCIAL AID (Fall 2005) 2,763 applied for aid; of those 75% were deemed to have need. 99% of undergraduates with need received aid; of those 30% had need fully met. ***Average percent of need met:*** 91% (excluding resources awarded to replace EFC). ***Average financial aid package:*** $23,305 (excluding resources awarded to replace EFC). 10% of all full-time undergraduates had no need and received non-need-based gift aid.

GIFT AID (NEED-BASED) ***Total amount:*** $27,564,144 (8% federal, 5% state, 87% institutional). ***Receiving aid:*** Freshmen: 48% (443); All full-time undergraduates: 42% (1,697). ***Average award:*** Freshmen: $17,665; Undergraduates: $16,550. ***Scholarships, grants, and awards:*** Federal Pell, FSEOG, state, private, college/university gift aid from institutional funds.

GIFT AID (NON-NEED-BASED) ***Total amount:*** $12,724,261 (92% institutional, 8% external sources). ***Receiving aid:*** Freshmen: 19% (176); Undergraduates: 14% (575). ***Average award:*** Freshmen: $12,719; Undergraduates: $12,234. ***Scholarships, grants, and awards by category:*** *Academic Interests/Achievement:* 901 awards ($10,742,682 total): general academic interests/achievements. *Special Achievements/Activities:* 19 awards ($141,650 total): community service. *Special Characteristics:* 34 awards ($558,676 total): international students, members of minority groups. ***Tuition waivers:*** Full or partial for employees or children of employees. ***ROTC:*** Army cooperative, Air Force cooperative.

LOANS ***Student loans:*** $21,500,527 (47% need-based, 53% non-need-based). 62% of past graduating class borrowed through all loan programs. *Average indebtedness per student:* $24,393. ***Average need-based loan:*** Freshmen: $3893; Undergraduates: $5099. ***Parent loans:*** $9,172,954 (100% non-need-based). ***Programs:*** FFEL (Subsidized and Unsubsidized Stafford, PLUS), Perkins, state.

WORK-STUDY ***Federal work-study:*** Total amount: $2,424,095; 1,434 jobs averaging $1485. ***State or other work-study/employment:*** Total amount: $865,494 (100% non-need-based). 537 part-time jobs averaging $2039.

ATHLETIC AWARDS Total amount: $1,816,126 (51% need-based, 49% non-need-based).

APPLYING FOR FINANCIAL AID ***Required financial aid forms:*** FAFSA, CSS Financial Aid PROFILE, noncustodial (divorced/separated) parent's statement, business/farm supplement, Federal tax returns, including all schedules for parents and student. ***Financial aid deadline:*** 2/1. ***Notification date:*** Continuous beginning 3/25.

CONTACT Ms. Donna Kendall, Director of Financial Aid, Bentley College, 175 Forest Street, Waltham, MA 02452-4705, 781-891-3441 or toll-free 800-523-2354. *Fax:* 781-891-2448. *E-mail:* finaid@bentley.edu.

BEREA COLLEGE

Berea, KY

Tuition & fees: $775 **Average undergraduate aid package: $28,059**

ABOUT THE INSTITUTION Independent, coed. Awards: bachelor's degrees. 52 undergraduate majors. Total enrollment: 1,576. Undergraduates: 1,576. Freshmen: 388. Federal methodology is used as a basis for awarding need-based institutional aid.

UNDERGRADUATE EXPENSES for 2006–07 includes mandatory fees ($775) and room and board ($5230). Financial aid is provided to all students for tuition costs.

FRESHMAN FINANCIAL AID (Fall 2006, est.) 383 applied for aid; of those 100% were deemed to have need. 100% of freshmen with need received aid; of those 8% had need fully met. ***Average percent of need met:*** 94% (excluding resources awarded to replace EFC). ***Average financial aid package:*** $28,683 (excluding resources awarded to replace EFC).

UNDERGRADUATE FINANCIAL AID (Fall 2006, est.) 1,520 applied for aid; of those 100% were deemed to have need. 100% of undergraduates with need received aid; of those 11% had need fully met. ***Average percent of need met:*** 92% (excluding resources awarded to replace EFC). ***Average financial aid package:*** $28,059 (excluding resources awarded to replace EFC).

GIFT AID (NEED-BASED) ***Total amount:*** $39,499,390 (11% federal, 7% state, 82% institutional). ***Receiving aid:*** Freshmen: 100% (383); All full-time undergraduates: 100% (1,520). ***Average award:*** Freshmen: $28,601; Undergraduates: $27,745. ***Scholarships, grants, and awards:*** Federal Pell, FSEOG, state, private, college/university gift aid from institutional funds.

LOANS ***Student loans:*** $1,326,758 (44% need-based, 56% non-need-based). 80% of past graduating class borrowed through all loan programs. *Average indebtedness per student:* $7638. ***Average need-based loan:*** Freshmen: $800; Undergraduates: $1445. ***Parent loans:*** $17,124 (100% need-based). ***Programs:*** FFEL (Subsidized and Unsubsidized Stafford, PLUS), Perkins, college/university.

WORK-STUDY ***Federal work-study:*** Total amount: $2,405,945; 1,201 jobs averaging $1585. ***State or other work-study/employment:*** Total amount: $505,105 (100% need-based). 319 part-time jobs averaging $1529.

APPLYING FOR FINANCIAL AID ***Required financial aid form:*** FAFSA. ***Financial aid deadline:*** 8/1 (priority: 4/15). ***Notification date:*** Continuous beginning 4/19.

CONTACT Bryan Erslan, Student Financial Aid Services, Berea College, CPO 2172, Berea, KY 40404, 859-985-3310 or toll-free 800-326-5948. *Fax:* 859-985-3914. *E-mail:* bryan_erslan@berea.edu.

BERKLEE COLLEGE OF MUSIC

Boston, MA

Tuition & fees: $29,331 **Average undergraduate aid package: $21,455**

ABOUT THE INSTITUTION Independent, coed. Awards: bachelor's degrees. 12 undergraduate majors. Total enrollment: 3,894. Undergraduates: 3,894. Federal methodology is used as a basis for awarding need-based institutional aid.

UNDERGRADUATE EXPENSES for 2006–07 ***Application fee:*** $150. ***Comprehensive fee:*** $41,881 includes full-time tuition ($23,450), mandatory fees ($5881), and room and board ($12,550). ***Part-time tuition:*** $675 per hour. ***Payment plans:*** Tuition prepayment, installment.

FRESHMAN FINANCIAL AID (Fall 2005) 646 applied for aid; of those 66% were deemed to have need. 100% of freshmen with need received aid. ***Average percent of need met:*** 67% (excluding resources awarded to replace EFC). ***Average financial aid package:*** $19,220 (excluding resources awarded to replace EFC).

UNDERGRADUATE FINANCIAL AID (Fall 2005) 2,923 applied for aid; of those 60% were deemed to have need. 99% of undergraduates with need received aid. ***Average percent of need met:*** 65% (excluding resources awarded to replace EFC). ***Average financial aid package:*** $21,455 (excluding resources awarded to replace EFC).

GIFT AID (NEED-BASED) ***Total amount:*** $5,533,091 (38% federal, 3% state, 30% institutional, 29% external sources). ***Receiving aid:*** Freshmen: 15% (129); All full-time undergraduates: 14% (595). ***Average award:*** Freshmen: $5954; Undergraduates: $5890. ***Scholarships, grants, and awards:*** Federal Pell, FSEOG, state, private, college/university gift aid from institutional funds.

GIFT AID (NON-NEED-BASED) ***Total amount:*** $10,264,047 (100% institutional). ***Receiving aid:*** Freshmen: 26% (219); Undergraduates: 17% (689). ***Average award:*** Freshmen: $7559; Undergraduates: $8918. ***Scholarships, grants, and awards by category:*** *Creative Arts/Performance:* 1,900 awards ($10,200,000 total): music. *Special Characteristics:* 29 awards ($441,618 total): children of faculty/staff. ***Tuition waivers:*** Full or partial for employees or children of employees.

LOANS ***Student loans:*** $33,867,131 (27% need-based, 73% non-need-based). ***Average need-based loan:*** Freshmen: $2991; Undergraduates: $4464. ***Parent loans:*** $11,211,775 (100% non-need-based). ***Programs:*** Federal Direct (Subsidized and Unsubsidized Stafford, PLUS), Perkins, state.

WORK-STUDY ***Federal work-study:*** Total amount: $460,600; 270 jobs averaging $1706. ***State or other work-study/employment:*** Total amount: $1,477,542 (100% non-need-based). Part-time jobs available.

APPLYING FOR FINANCIAL AID ***Required financial aid form:*** FAFSA. ***Financial aid deadline (priority):*** 3/1. ***Notification date:*** Continuous beginning 4/1. Students must reply within 3 weeks of notification.

CONTACT Julie Poorman, Director of Financial Aid, Berklee College of Music, 1140 Boylston Street, Boston, MA 02215-3693, 617-747-2274 or toll-free 800-BERKLEE. *Fax:* 617-747-2073. *E-mail:* jpoorman@berklee.edu.

BERNARD M. BARUCH COLLEGE OF THE CITY UNIVERSITY OF NEW YORK

New York, NY

ABOUT THE INSTITUTION State and locally supported, coed. Awards: bachelor's, master's, and doctoral degrees and post-master's certificates. 33 undergraduate majors. Total enrollment: 15,730. Undergraduates: 12,796. Freshmen: 1,508.

GIFT AID (NEED-BASED) ***Scholarships, grants, and awards:*** Federal Pell, FSEOG, state, college/university gift aid from institutional funds.

GIFT AID (NON-NEED-BASED) ***Scholarships, grants, and awards by category:*** *Academic Interests/Achievement:* general academic interests/achievements.

LOANS ***Programs:*** Federal Direct (Subsidized and Unsubsidized Stafford, PLUS), Perkins.

WORK-STUDY ***Federal work-study:*** Total amount: $300,000; 520 jobs available. ***State or other work-study/employment:*** Total amount: $500,000 (100% non-need-based). Part-time jobs available.

APPLYING FOR FINANCIAL AID ***Required financial aid forms:*** FAFSA, state aid form.

CONTACT Financial Aid Office, Bernard M. Baruch College of the City University of New York, 151 East 25th Street, Room 720, New York, NY 10010-5585, 646-312-1360. *Fax:* 646-312-1363. *E-mail:* financial_aid@baruch.cuny.edu.

BERRY COLLEGE

Mount Berry, GA

Tuition & fees: $18,950 **Average undergraduate aid package: $15,575**

ABOUT THE INSTITUTION Independent interdenominational, coed. Awards: bachelor's and master's degrees and post-master's certificates. 39 undergraduate majors. Total enrollment: 1,842. Undergraduates: 1,718. Freshmen: 428. Federal methodology is used as a basis for awarding need-based institutional aid.

UNDERGRADUATE EXPENSES for 2006–07 ***Application fee:*** $50. ***Comprehensive fee:*** $26,114 includes full-time tuition ($18,950) and room and board ($7164). ***College room only:*** $4024. Room and board charges vary according to board plan and housing facility. ***Payment plan:*** Installment.

FRESHMAN FINANCIAL AID (Fall 2006, est.) 366 applied for aid; of those 69% were deemed to have need. 100% of freshmen with need received aid; of those 27% had need fully met. ***Average percent of need met:*** 78% (excluding resources awarded to replace EFC). ***Average financial aid package:*** $14,621 (excluding resources awarded to replace EFC). 43% of all full-time freshmen had no need and received non-need-based gift aid.

UNDERGRADUATE FINANCIAL AID (Fall 2006, est.) 1,317 applied for aid; of those 77% were deemed to have need. 98% of undergraduates with need received aid; of those 24% had need fully met. ***Average percent of need met:*** 81% (excluding resources awarded to replace EFC). ***Average financial aid package:*** $15,575 (excluding resources awarded to replace EFC). 41% of all full-time undergraduates had no need and received non-need-based gift aid.

GIFT AID (NEED-BASED) ***Total amount:*** $11,298,839 (9% federal, 19% state, 68% institutional, 4% external sources). ***Receiving aid:*** Freshmen: 57% (251); All full-time undergraduates: 58% (987). ***Average award:*** Freshmen: $12,029; Undergraduates: $11,859. ***Scholarships, grants, and awards:*** Federal Pell, FSEOG, state, private, college/university gift aid from institutional funds.

GIFT AID (NON-NEED-BASED) ***Total amount:*** $6,694,778 (31% state, 62% institutional, 7% external sources). ***Receiving aid:*** Freshmen: 13% (56); Undergraduates: 11% (186). ***Average award:*** Freshmen: $16,532; Undergraduates: $14,526. ***Scholarships, grants, and awards by category:*** *Academic Interests/Achievement:* 1,090 awards ($6,043,407 total): agriculture, education, English, general academic interests/achievements, humanities, religion/biblical studies. *Creative Arts/Performance:* 160 awards ($265,890 total): art/fine arts, debating, journalism/publications, music, theater/drama. *Special Achievements/Activities:* 79 awards ($144,850 total): community service, religious involvement. *Special Characteristics:* 151 awards ($847,846 total): adult students, children of faculty/staff, ethnic background, local/state students, members of minority groups. ***Tuition waivers:*** Full or partial for employees or children of employees, senior citizens.

LOANS ***Student loans:*** $4,384,696 (68% need-based, 32% non-need-based). 65% of past graduating class borrowed through all loan programs. *Average indebtedness per student:* $13,882. ***Average need-based loan:*** Freshmen: $2175; Undergraduates: $2947. ***Parent loans:*** $4,730,303 (27% need-based, 73% non-need-based). ***Programs:*** FFEL (Subsidized and Unsubsidized Stafford, PLUS), Perkins, college/university.

WORK-STUDY ***Federal work-study:*** Total amount: $607,176; 384 jobs averaging $2178. ***State or other work-study/employment:*** Total amount: $4,339,651 (18% need-based, 82% non-need-based). 1,580 part-time jobs averaging $2785.

ATHLETIC AWARDS Total amount: $1,690,147 (25% need-based, 75% non-need-based).

APPLYING FOR FINANCIAL AID ***Required financial aid forms:*** FAFSA, institution's own form, state aid form. ***Financial aid deadline (priority):*** 4/1. ***Notification date:*** Continuous beginning 3/1. Students must reply by 5/1.

CONTACT J. Ron Elmore, Director of Financial Aid, Berry College, 2277 Martha Berry Highway, NW, Mount Berry, GA 30149-5007, 706-236-2276 or toll-free 800-237-7942. *Fax:* 706-290-2160. *E-mail:* wfron@berry.edu.

BETHANY COLLEGE

Lindsborg, KS

Tuition & fees: $17,110 **Average undergraduate aid package: $17,554**

ABOUT THE INSTITUTION Independent Lutheran, coed. Awards: bachelor's degrees. 41 undergraduate majors. Total enrollment: 554. Undergraduates: 554. Freshmen: 168. Federal methodology is used as a basis for awarding need-based institutional aid.

UNDERGRADUATE EXPENSES for 2007–08 ***Application fee:*** $20. ***Comprehensive fee:*** $22,610 includes full-time tuition ($16,900), mandatory fees ($210), and room and board ($5500). ***College room only:*** $3000. ***Part-time tuition:*** $300 per credit hour.

FRESHMAN FINANCIAL AID (Fall 2006, est.) 155 applied for aid; of those 90% were deemed to have need. 100% of freshmen with need received aid; of those 34% had need fully met. ***Average percent of need met:*** 91% (excluding resources awarded to replace EFC). ***Average financial aid package:*** $17,434 (excluding resources awarded to replace EFC). 3% of all full-time freshmen had no need and received non-need-based gift aid.

UNDERGRADUATE FINANCIAL AID (Fall 2006, est.) 475 applied for aid; of those 85% were deemed to have need. 100% of undergraduates with need received aid; of those 40% had need fully met. ***Average percent of need met:*** 92% (excluding resources awarded to replace EFC). ***Average financial aid package:*** $17,554 (excluding resources awarded to replace EFC). 6% of all full-time undergraduates had no need and received non-need-based gift aid.

GIFT AID (NEED-BASED) ***Total amount:*** $2,024,758 (35% federal, 27% state, 38% institutional). ***Receiving aid:*** Freshmen: 71% (119); All full-time undergraduates: 71% (342). ***Average award:*** Freshmen: $5822; Undergraduates: $5745. ***Scholarships, grants, and awards:*** Federal Pell, FSEOG, state, private, college/university gift aid from institutional funds.

GIFT AID (NON-NEED-BASED) ***Total amount:*** $432,426 (78% institutional, 22% external sources). ***Receiving aid:*** Freshmen: 16% (27); Undergraduates: 21% (102). ***Average award:*** Freshmen: $4700; Undergraduates: $7288. ***Scholarships, grants, and awards by category:*** *Academic Interests/Achievement:* 316 awards ($1,285,192 total): general academic interests/achievements. *Creative Arts/Performance:* 110 awards ($307,930 total): art/fine arts, music, theater/drama. *Special Achievements/Activities:* 15 awards ($27,250 total): cheerleading/drum major. *Special Characteristics:* 111 awards ($198,660 total): children and siblings of alumni, international students, relatives of clergy, religious affiliation.

LOANS ***Student loans:*** $2,841,057 (63% need-based, 37% non-need-based). 88% of past graduating class borrowed through all loan programs. *Average indebtedness per student:* $16,958. ***Average need-based loan:*** Freshmen: $4725; Undergraduates: $5149. ***Parent loans:*** $386,247 (100% non-need-based). ***Programs:*** FFEL (Subsidized and Unsubsidized Stafford, PLUS), Perkins, college/university.

WORK-STUDY ***Federal work-study:*** Total amount: $178,000; 115 jobs averaging $1500. ***State or other work-study/employment:*** Part-time jobs available.

ATHLETIC AWARDS Total amount: $949,905 (83% need-based, 17% non-need-based).

APPLYING FOR FINANCIAL AID ***Required financial aid form:*** FAFSA. ***Financial aid deadline:*** Continuous. ***Notification date:*** Continuous beginning 2/1. Students must reply within 3 weeks of notification.

CONTACT Ms. Brenda Meagher, Director of Financial Aid, Bethany College, 335 East Swensson, Lindsborg, KS 67456-1897, 785-227-3311 Ext. 8248 or toll-free 800-826-2281. *Fax:* 785-227-2004. *E-mail:* meagherb@bethanylb.edu.

BETHANY COLLEGE

Bethany, WV

Tuition & fees: $18,205 **Average undergraduate aid package: N/A**

ABOUT THE INSTITUTION Independent religious, coed. Awards: bachelor's degrees. 33 undergraduate majors. Total enrollment: 833. Undergraduates: 833. Freshmen: 213. Institutional methodology is used as a basis for awarding need-based institutional aid.

UNDERGRADUATE EXPENSES for 2007–08 ***Application fee:*** $25. ***Comprehensive fee:*** $25,975 includes full-time tuition ($18,205) and room and board ($7770). ***College room only:*** $4000.

GIFT AID (NEED-BASED) ***Total amount:*** $4,925,891 (27% federal, 7% state, 64% institutional, 2% external sources). ***Scholarships, grants, and awards:*** Federal Pell, FSEOG, state, private, college/university gift aid from institutional funds.

GIFT AID (NON-NEED-BASED) ***Total amount:*** $2,433,551 (5% state, 92% institutional, 3% external sources). ***Scholarships, grants, and awards by category:*** *Academic Interests/Achievement:* 32 awards ($2,020,678 total): general academic interests/achievements. *Creative Arts/Performance:* 6 awards ($3253 total): music. *Special Achievements/Activities:* 6 awards ($116,833 total): leadership, religious involvement. *Special Characteristics:* 207 awards ($445,575 total): children and siblings of alumni, children of faculty/staff, ethnic background, international students, relatives of clergy, religious affiliation.

LOANS ***Student loans:*** $3,518,320 (67% need-based, 33% non-need-based). 82% of past graduating class borrowed through all loan programs. *Average indebtedness per student:* $18,500. ***Parent loans:*** $1,598,221 (100% non-need-based). ***Programs:*** Federal Direct (Subsidized and Unsubsidized Stafford, PLUS), Perkins, alternative loans.

WORK-STUDY ***Federal work-study:*** Total amount: $683,134; 437 jobs averaging $1555. ***State or other work-study/employment:*** Total amount: $216,375 (100% non-need-based). 333 part-time jobs averaging $650.

APPLYING FOR FINANCIAL AID ***Required financial aid forms:*** FAFSA, institution's own form. ***Financial aid deadline:*** Continuous. ***Notification date:*** Continuous. Students must reply within 3 weeks of notification.

CONTACT Financial Aid Office, Bethany College, Main Street, Bethany, WV 26032, 304-829-7141 or toll-free 800-922-7611 (out-of-state).

BETHANY LUTHERAN COLLEGE

Mankato, MN

Tuition & fees: $17,760 **Average undergraduate aid package: $12,864**

ABOUT THE INSTITUTION Independent Lutheran, coed. Awards: associate and bachelor's degrees. 16 undergraduate majors. Total enrollment: 597. Undergraduates: 597. Freshmen: 212. Federal methodology is used as a basis for awarding need-based institutional aid.

UNDERGRADUATE EXPENSES for 2007–08 ***Comprehensive fee:*** $23,038 includes full-time tuition ($17,500), mandatory fees ($260), and room and board ($5278). ***College room only:*** $1988. ***Part-time tuition:*** $750 per credit. ***Part-time fees:*** $130 per term.

FRESHMAN FINANCIAL AID (Fall 2005) 123 applied for aid; of those 89% were deemed to have need. 100% of freshmen with need received aid; of those 27% had need fully met. ***Average percent of need met:*** 85% (excluding resources awarded to replace EFC). ***Average financial aid package:*** $12,114 (excluding resources awarded to replace EFC). 19% of all full-time freshmen had no need and received non-need-based gift aid.

UNDERGRADUATE FINANCIAL AID (Fall 2005) 487 applied for aid; of those 90% were deemed to have need. 100% of undergraduates with need received aid; of those 31% had need fully met. ***Average percent of need met:*** 86% (excluding resources awarded to replace EFC). ***Average financial aid package:*** $12,864 (excluding resources awarded to replace EFC). 16% of all full-time undergraduates had no need and received non-need-based gift aid.

GIFT AID (NEED-BASED) ***Total amount:*** $3,596,716 (15% federal, 18% state, 64% institutional, 3% external sources). ***Receiving aid:*** Freshmen: 77% (109); All full-time undergraduates: 81% (436). ***Average award:*** Freshmen: $9246; Undergraduates: $9250. ***Scholarships, grants, and awards:*** Federal Pell, FSEOG, state, private, college/university gift aid from institutional funds.

GIFT AID (NON-NEED-BASED) ***Total amount:*** $418,196 (3% state, 85% institutional, 12% external sources). ***Receiving aid:*** Freshmen: 9% (13); Undergraduates: 12% (63). ***Average award:*** Freshmen: $8327; Undergraduates: $7466. ***Scholarships, grants, and awards by category:*** *Creative Arts/Performance:* 99 awards ($196,289 total): art/fine arts, debating, journalism/publications, music, theater/drama. *Special Characteristics:* 34 awards ($419,960 total): children of faculty/staff. ***ROTC:*** Army cooperative.

LOANS ***Student loans:*** $2,610,316 (64% need-based, 36% non-need-based). 83% of past graduating class borrowed through all loan programs. *Average indebtedness per student:* $23,115. ***Average need-based loan:*** Freshmen: $3093; Undergraduates: $4042. ***Parent loans:*** $602,799 (26% need-based, 74% non-need-based). ***Programs:*** FFEL (Subsidized and Unsubsidized Stafford, PLUS), Perkins, state, alternative loans.

WORK-STUDY ***Federal work-study:*** Total amount: $36,807; 25 jobs averaging $1472. ***State or other work-study/employment:*** Total amount: $209,294 (47% need-based, 53% non-need-based). 268 part-time jobs averaging $781.

APPLYING FOR FINANCIAL AID ***Required financial aid forms:*** FAFSA, institution's own form, business/farm supplement, federal income tax form(s), W-2 forms. ***Financial aid deadline (priority):*** 4/15. ***Notification date:*** Continuous. Students must reply within 3 weeks of notification.

CONTACT Financial Aid Office, Bethany Lutheran College, 700 Luther Drive, Mankato, MN 56001-6163, 507-344-7328 or toll-free 800-944-3066 Ext. 331. *Fax:* 507-344-7376.

BETHANY UNIVERSITY

Scotts Valley, CA

CONTACT Deborah Snow, Financial Aid Director, Bethany University, 800 Bethany Drive, Scotts Valley, CA 95066-2820, 831-438-3800 Ext. 1477 or toll-free 800-843-9410. *Fax:* 831-461-1533.

BETH BENJAMIN ACADEMY OF CONNECTICUT

Stamford, CT

CONTACT Financial Aid Office, Beth Benjamin Academy of Connecticut, 132 Prospect Street, Stamford, CT 06901-1202, 203-325-4351.

BETHEL COLLEGE

Mishawaka, IN

Tuition & fees: $17,450 **Average undergraduate aid package: $13,025**

ABOUT THE INSTITUTION Independent religious, coed. Awards: associate, bachelor's, and master's degrees. 59 undergraduate majors. Total enrollment: 2,093. Undergraduates: 1,934. Freshmen: 288. Federal methodology is used as a basis for awarding need-based institutional aid.

UNDERGRADUATE EXPENSES for 2006–07 ***Application fee:*** $25. ***One-time required fee:*** $600. ***Comprehensive fee:*** $22,830 includes full-time tuition ($17,450) and room and board ($5380). ***Part-time tuition:*** $350 per hour.

FRESHMAN FINANCIAL AID (Fall 2006, est.) 246 applied for aid; of those 93% were deemed to have need. 100% of freshmen with need received aid; of those 5% had need fully met. ***Average percent of need met:*** 40% (excluding resources awarded to replace EFC). ***Average financial aid package:*** $14,632 (excluding resources awarded to replace EFC). 4% of all full-time freshmen had no need and received non-need-based gift aid.

UNDERGRADUATE FINANCIAL AID (Fall 2006, est.) 1,466 applied for aid; of those 81% were deemed to have need. 100% of undergraduates with need received aid; of those 54% had need fully met. ***Average percent of need met:*** 34% (excluding resources awarded to replace EFC). ***Average financial aid package:*** $13,025 (excluding resources awarded to replace EFC). 4% of all full-time undergraduates had no need and received non-need-based gift aid.

GIFT AID (NEED-BASED) ***Total amount:*** $5,512,562 (44% federal, 56% state). ***Receiving aid:*** Freshmen: 60% (179); All full-time undergraduates: 56% (834). ***Average award:*** Freshmen: $6968; Undergraduates: $6661. ***Scholarships, grants, and awards:*** Federal Pell, FSEOG, state, private, college/university gift aid from institutional funds, Federal Nursing.

GIFT AID (NON-NEED-BASED) ***Total amount:*** $6,212,038 (90% institutional, 10% external sources). ***Receiving aid:*** Freshmen: 73% (220); Undergraduates: 63% (940). ***Average award:*** Freshmen: $6195; Undergraduates: $7187. ***Scholarships, grants, and awards by category:*** *Academic Interests/Achievement:* 637 awards ($1,854,083 total): biological sciences, business, communication, computer science, education, English, general academic interests/achievements, health fields, mathematics, physical sciences, religion/biblical studies, social sciences. *Creative Arts/Performance:* 99 awards ($179,675 total): art/fine arts, journalism/publications, music, theater/drama. *Special Achievements/Activities:* 258 awards ($423,158 total): cheerleading/drum major, general special achievements/activities, leadership, religious involvement. *Special Characteristics:* 527 awards ($1,958,263 total): adult students, children of faculty/staff, international students, members of minority groups, relatives of clergy, religious affiliation, siblings of current students, spouses of current students. ***ROTC:*** Army cooperative, Air Force cooperative.

LOANS ***Student loans:*** $6,771,200 (88% need-based, 12% non-need-based). 83% of past graduating class borrowed through all loan programs. *Average indebtedness per student:* $16,337. ***Average need-based loan:*** Freshmen: $2540; Undergraduates: $3719. ***Parent loans:*** $739,572 (100% non-need-based). ***Programs:*** FFEL (Subsidized and Unsubsidized Stafford, PLUS), Perkins, college/university, GATE Loans.

WORK-STUDY ***Federal work-study:*** Total amount: $1,252,567; jobs available (averaging $2000). ***State or other work-study/employment:*** Total amount: $248,543 (100% non-need-based). Part-time jobs available (averaging $2000).

ATHLETIC AWARDS Total amount: $1,234,253 (100% non-need-based).

APPLYING FOR FINANCIAL AID ***Required financial aid forms:*** FAFSA, institution's own form. ***Financial aid deadline (priority):*** 3/1. ***Notification date:*** Continuous. Students must reply within 3 weeks of notification.

CONTACT Mr. Guy A. Fisher, Director of Financial Aid, Bethel College, 1001 West McKinley Avenue, Mishawaka, IN 46545-5591, 574-257-3316 or toll-free 800-422-4101. *Fax:* 574-257-3326. *E-mail:* fisherg@bethelcollege.edu.

BETHEL COLLEGE

North Newton, KS

Tuition & fees: $16,700 **Average undergraduate aid package: $16,476**

ABOUT THE INSTITUTION Independent religious, coed. Awards: bachelor's degrees. 27 undergraduate majors. Total enrollment: 539. Undergraduates: 539. Freshmen: 104. Federal methodology is used as a basis for awarding need-based institutional aid.

UNDERGRADUATE EXPENSES for 2006–07 ***Application fee:*** $20. ***Comprehensive fee:*** $22,800 includes full-time tuition ($16,700) and room and board ($6100). ***College room only:*** $3200. Full-time tuition and fees vary according to course load. Room and board charges vary according to board plan and housing facility. ***Part-time tuition:*** $590 per credit hour. Part-time tuition and fees vary according to course load. ***Payment plans:*** Installment, deferred payment.

FRESHMAN FINANCIAL AID (Fall 2005) 88 applied for aid; of those 99% were deemed to have need. 100% of freshmen with need received aid; of those 34% had need fully met. ***Average percent of need met:*** 94% (excluding resources awarded to replace EFC). ***Average financial aid package:*** $17,228 (excluding resources awarded to replace EFC). 8% of all full-time freshmen had no need and received non-need-based gift aid.

UNDERGRADUATE FINANCIAL AID (Fall 2005) 424 applied for aid; of those 100% were deemed to have need. 100% of undergraduates with need received aid; of those 35% had need fully met. ***Average percent of need met:*** 91% (excluding resources awarded to replace EFC). ***Average financial aid package:*** $16,476 (excluding resources awarded to replace EFC). 8% of all full-time undergraduates had no need and received non-need-based gift aid.

GIFT AID (NEED-BASED) ***Total amount:*** $1,205,902 (47% federal, 41% state, 12% institutional). ***Receiving aid:*** Freshmen: 70% (67); All full-time undergraduates: 62% (319). ***Average award:*** Freshmen: $4287; Undergraduates: $4787. ***Scholarships, grants, and awards:*** Federal Pell, FSEOG, state, college/university gift aid from institutional funds.

GIFT AID (NON-NEED-BASED) ***Total amount:*** $2,572,652 (83% institutional, 17% external sources). ***Receiving aid:*** Freshmen: 91% (87); Undergraduates: 75% (387). ***Average award:*** Freshmen: $10,059; Undergraduates: $8801. ***Scholarships, grants, and awards by category:*** *Academic Interests/Achievement:* 301 awards ($1,255,385 total): general academic interests/achievements. *Creative Arts/Performance:* 106 awards ($171,040 total): art/fine arts, debating, music, theater/drama. *Special Characteristics:* 662 awards ($884,451 total): children and siblings of alumni, children of faculty/staff, general special characteristics, international students, local/state students, previous college experience, relatives of clergy, religious affiliation. ***Tuition waivers:*** Full or partial for children of alumni, employees or children of employees, senior citizens.

LOANS ***Student loans:*** $2,748,285 (68% need-based, 32% non-need-based). 85% of past graduating class borrowed through all loan programs. *Average indebtedness per student:* $18,722. ***Average need-based loan:*** Freshmen: $3886; Undergraduates: $5482. ***Parent loans:*** $684,981 (100% non-need-based). ***Programs:*** FFEL (Subsidized and Unsubsidized Stafford, PLUS), Perkins.

WORK-STUDY ***Federal work-study:*** Total amount: $357,325; 267 jobs averaging $1338. ***State or other work-study/employment:*** Total amount: $198,622 (100% need-based). 207 part-time jobs averaging $899.

ATHLETIC AWARDS Total amount: $526,314 (100% non-need-based).

APPLYING FOR FINANCIAL AID ***Required financial aid form:*** FAFSA. ***Financial aid deadline (priority):*** 3/15. ***Notification date:*** Continuous. Students must reply by 5/1 or within 2 weeks of notification.

CONTACT Mr. Tony Graber, Financial Aid Director, Bethel College, 300 East 27th Street, North Newton, KS 67117, 316-284-5232 or toll-free 800-522-1887 Ext. 230. *Fax:* 316-284-5845. *E-mail:* tgraber@bethelks.edu.

BETHEL COLLEGE

McKenzie, TN

CONTACT Laura Bateman, Office of Financial Aid, Bethel College, 325 Cherry Avenue, McKenzie, TN 38201, 901-352-4007. *Fax:* 901-352-4069.

BETHEL UNIVERSITY

St. Paul, MN

Tuition & fees: $24,510 **Average undergraduate aid package: $16,609**

ABOUT THE INSTITUTION Independent religious, coed. Awards: associate, bachelor's, and master's degrees and post-bachelor's and post-master's certificates. 55 undergraduate majors. Total enrollment: 5,185. Undergraduates: 3,321. Freshmen: 674. Federal methodology is used as a basis for awarding need-based institutional aid.

UNDERGRADUATE EXPENSES for 2007–08 ***Application fee:*** $25. ***Comprehensive fee:*** $31,890 includes full-time tuition ($24,400), mandatory fees ($110), and room and board ($7380). ***College room only:*** $4400. ***Part-time tuition:*** $935 per credit.

FRESHMAN FINANCIAL AID (Fall 2006, est.) 522 applied for aid; of those 84% were deemed to have need. 100% of freshmen with need received aid; of those 19% had need fully met. ***Average percent of need met:*** 80% (excluding resources awarded to replace EFC). ***Average financial aid package:*** $17,120 (excluding resources awarded to replace EFC). 23% of all full-time freshmen had no need and received non-need-based gift aid.

UNDERGRADUATE FINANCIAL AID (Fall 2006, est.) 2,099 applied for aid; of those 85% were deemed to have need. 100% of undergraduates with need received aid; of those 23% had need fully met. ***Average percent of need met:*** 80% (excluding resources awarded to replace EFC). ***Average financial aid package:*** $16,609 (excluding resources awarded to replace EFC). 25% of all full-time undergraduates had no need and received non-need-based gift aid.

GIFT AID (NEED-BASED) ***Total amount:*** $17,320,000 (9% federal, 14% state, 70% institutional, 7% external sources). ***Receiving aid:*** Freshmen: 66% (439); All full-time undergraduates: 65% (1,770). ***Average award:*** Freshmen: $11,593; Undergraduates: $10,360. ***Scholarships, grants, and awards:*** Federal Pell, FSEOG, state, private, college/university gift aid from institutional funds.

GIFT AID (NON-NEED-BASED) ***Total amount:*** $3,220,000 (90% institutional, 10% external sources). ***Receiving aid:*** Freshmen: 6% (41); Undergraduates: 5% (130). ***Average award:*** Freshmen: $5194; Undergraduates: $4235. ***Scholarships, grants, and awards by category:*** *Academic Interests/Achievement:* 1,465 awards ($5,105,000 total): general academic interests/achievements. *Creative Arts/Performance:* 103 awards ($190,000 total): art/fine arts, debating, music, theater/drama. *Special Achievements/Activities:* 1,975 awards ($2,485,000 total): community service, junior miss, leadership, religious involvement. *Special Characteristics:* 1,200 awards ($3,616,000 total): children and siblings of alumni, children of faculty/staff, ethnic background, international students, members of minority groups, out-of-state students, relatives of clergy, religious affiliation. ***ROTC:*** Army cooperative, Air Force cooperative.

LOANS ***Student loans:*** $7,120,000 (100% need-based). 76% of past graduating class borrowed through all loan programs. *Average indebtedness per student:* $28,085. ***Average need-based loan:*** Freshmen: $3628; Undergraduates: $4298. ***Programs:*** FFEL (Subsidized and Unsubsidized Stafford, PLUS), Perkins, state, alternative loans.

WORK-STUDY ***Federal work-study:*** Total amount: $850,000; 385 jobs averaging $2200. ***State or other work-study/employment:*** Total amount: $3,180,000 (81% need-based, 19% non-need-based). 1,445 part-time jobs averaging $2200.

APPLYING FOR FINANCIAL AID ***Required financial aid forms:*** FAFSA, institution's own form. ***Financial aid deadline (priority):*** 4/15. ***Notification date:*** Continuous beginning 3/1. Students must reply by 5/1 or within 3 weeks of notification.

CONTACT Mr. Jeffrey D. Olson, Director of Financial Aid, Bethel University, 3900 Bethel Drive, St. Paul, MN 55112-6999, 651-638-6241 or toll-free 800-255-8706 Ext. 6242. *Fax:* 651-635-1491. *E-mail:* jeff-olson@bethel.edu.

BETHESDA CHRISTIAN UNIVERSITY

Anaheim, CA

Tuition & fees: N/R **Average undergraduate aid package: $5061**

ABOUT THE INSTITUTION Independent religious, coed. Awards: bachelor's, master's, and first professional degrees. 14 undergraduate majors. Total enrollment: 206. Undergraduates: 164. Freshmen: 32. Federal methodology is used as a basis for awarding need-based institutional aid.

FRESHMAN FINANCIAL AID (Fall 2005) 8 applied for aid; of those 100% were deemed to have need. 100% of freshmen with need received aid. ***Average financial aid package:*** $3381 (excluding resources awarded to replace EFC).

UNDERGRADUATE FINANCIAL AID (Fall 2005) 20 applied for aid; of those 100% were deemed to have need. 100% of undergraduates with need received aid. ***Average financial aid package:*** $5061 (excluding resources awarded to replace EFC).

GIFT AID (NEED-BASED) ***Total amount:*** $75,077 (100% federal). ***Receiving aid:*** Freshmen: 8; All full-time undergraduates: 2. ***Average award:*** Freshmen: $2114; Undergraduates: $3003. ***Scholarships, grants, and awards:*** Federal Pell, college/university gift aid from institutional funds.

GIFT AID (NON-NEED-BASED) ***Scholarships, grants, and awards by category:*** *Creative Arts/Performance:* music.

LOANS ***Student loans:*** $69,875 (100% need-based). 17% of past graduating class borrowed through all loan programs. *Average indebtedness per student:* $3250. ***Average need-based loan:*** Freshmen: $2406; Undergraduates: $3688. ***Programs:*** FFEL (Subsidized and Unsubsidized Stafford).

APPLYING FOR FINANCIAL AID ***Required financial aid forms:*** FAFSA, institution's own form. ***Financial aid deadline:*** Continuous. ***Notification date:*** Continuous beginning 9/15. Students must reply within 2 weeks of notification.

CONTACT Myongha Prince, Financial Aid Administrator, Bethesda Christian University, 730 North Euclid Street, Anaheim, CA 92801, 714-517-1945 Ext. 130. *Fax:* 714-517-1948. *E-mail:* financialaid@bcu.edu.

BETH HAMEDRASH SHAAREI YOSHER INSTITUTE

Brooklyn, NY

CONTACT Financial Aid Office, Beth HaMedrash Shaarei Yosher Institute, 4102-10 16th Avenue, Brooklyn, NY 11204, 718-854-2290.

BETH HATALMUD RABBINICAL COLLEGE

Brooklyn, NY

CONTACT Financial Aid Office, Beth Hatalmud Rabbinical College, 2127 82nd Street, Brooklyn, NY 11204, 718-259-2525.

BETH MEDRASH GOVOHA

Lakewood, NJ

CONTACT Financial Aid Office, Beth Medrash Govoha, 617 Sixth Street, Lakewood, NJ 08701-2797, 732-367-1060.

BETHUNE-COOKMAN COLLEGE

Daytona Beach, FL

Tuition & fees: $11,792 **Average undergraduate aid package: $14,166**

ABOUT THE INSTITUTION Independent Methodist, coed. Awards: bachelor's degrees. 37 undergraduate majors. Total enrollment: 3,112. Undergraduates: 3,093. Freshmen: 909. Federal methodology is used as a basis for awarding need-based institutional aid.

UNDERGRADUATE EXPENSES for 2006–07 ***Application fee:*** $25. ***Comprehensive fee:*** $18,998 includes full-time tuition ($11,792) and room and board ($7206). ***Part-time tuition:*** $487 per credit hour.

FRESHMAN FINANCIAL AID (Fall 2006, est.) 890 applied for aid; of those 99% were deemed to have need. 99% of freshmen with need received aid; of those 29% had need fully met. ***Average percent of need met:*** 68% (excluding resources awarded to replace EFC). ***Average financial aid package:*** $14,605 (excluding resources awarded to replace EFC). 3% of all full-time freshmen had no need and received non-need-based gift aid.

UNDERGRADUATE FINANCIAL AID (Fall 2006, est.) 2,905 applied for aid; of those 90% were deemed to have need. 98% of undergraduates with need received aid; of those 21% had need fully met. ***Average percent of need met:*** 64% (excluding resources awarded to replace EFC). ***Average financial aid package:*** $14,166 (excluding resources awarded to replace EFC). 3% of all full-time undergraduates had no need and received non-need-based gift aid.

GIFT AID (NEED-BASED) ***Total amount:*** $12,644,025 (59% federal, 13% state, 25% institutional, 3% external sources). ***Receiving aid:*** Freshmen: 76% (690); All full-time undergraduates: 71% (2,070). ***Average award:*** Freshmen: $6345; Undergraduates: $6603. ***Scholarships, grants, and awards:*** Federal Pell, FSEOG, state, private, college/university gift aid from institutional funds, United Negro College Fund, Federal Nursing.

GIFT AID (NON-NEED-BASED) ***Total amount:*** $6,179,895 (72% state, 28% institutional). ***Receiving aid:*** Freshmen: 11% (100); Undergraduates: 12% (341). ***Average award:*** Freshmen: $7720; Undergraduates: $8035. ***Scholarships, grants, and awards by category:*** *Academic Interests/Achievement:* 135 awards ($1,298,454 total): general academic interests/achievements. ***Tuition waivers:*** Full or partial for employees or children of employees. ***ROTC:*** Army cooperative, Air Force cooperative.

LOANS ***Student loans:*** $17,382,569 (46% need-based, 54% non-need-based). 85% of past graduating class borrowed through all loan programs. *Average indebtedness per student:* $32,500. ***Average need-based loan:*** Freshmen: $2640; Undergraduates: $3505. ***Parent loans:*** $4,355,026 (100% non-need-based). ***Programs:*** Federal Direct (Subsidized and Unsubsidized Stafford, PLUS), FFEL (Subsidized and Unsubsidized Stafford, PLUS).

WORK-STUDY ***Federal work-study:*** Total amount: $510,377; 300 jobs averaging $2000. ***State or other work-study/employment:*** Total amount: $269,616 (100% non-need-based). 125 part-time jobs averaging $2000.

ATHLETIC AWARDS Total amount: $3,170,799 (100% non-need-based).

APPLYING FOR FINANCIAL AID ***Required financial aid form:*** FAFSA. ***Financial aid deadline (priority):*** 4/1. ***Notification date:*** Continuous beginning 4/1. Students must reply within 3 weeks of notification.

CONTACT Mr. Joseph Coleman, Director of Financial Aid, Bethune-Cookman College, 640 Mary McLeod Bethune Boulevard, Daytona Beach, FL 32114-3099, 386-481-2626 or toll-free 800-448-0228. *Fax:* 386-481-2621. *E-mail:* colemanj@cookman.edu.

BEULAH HEIGHTS BIBLE COLLEGE

Atlanta, GA

ABOUT THE INSTITUTION Independent Pentecostal, coed. Awards: associate and bachelor's degrees. 2 undergraduate majors. Total enrollment: 620. Undergraduates: 620. Freshmen: 155.

GIFT AID (NEED-BASED) ***Scholarships, grants, and awards:*** Federal Pell, FSEOG, private, college/university gift aid from institutional funds.

GIFT AID (NON-NEED-BASED) ***Scholarships, grants, and awards by category:*** *Special Characteristics:* children of faculty/staff, general special characteristics, international students, married students, religious affiliation, spouses of current students.

LOANS ***Programs:*** FFEL (Subsidized and Unsubsidized Stafford, PLUS).

WORK-STUDY ***Federal work-study:*** Total amount: $45,724; 13 jobs averaging $3402.

APPLYING FOR FINANCIAL AID ***Required financial aid forms:*** FAFSA, institution's own form.

CONTACT Ms. Patricia Banks, Financial Aid Director, Beulah Heights Bible College, 892 Berne Street, SE, Atlanta, GA 30316, 404-627-2681 or toll-free 888-777-BHBC. *Fax:* 404-627-0702. *E-mail:* pat.banks@beulah.org.

BIOLA UNIVERSITY

La Mirada, CA

ABOUT THE INSTITUTION Independent interdenominational, coed. Awards: bachelor's, master's, doctoral, and first professional degrees. 39 undergraduate majors. Total enrollment: 5,752. Undergraduates: 3,924. Freshmen: 807.

GIFT AID (NEED-BASED) ***Scholarships, grants, and awards:*** Federal Pell, FSEOG, state, private, college/university gift aid from institutional funds.

GIFT AID (NON-NEED-BASED) ***Scholarships, grants, and awards by category:*** *Academic Interests/Achievement:* communication, general academic interests/achievements, health fields. *Creative Arts/Performance:* art/fine arts, debating, journalism/publications, music, performing arts, theater/drama. *Special Achievements/Activities:* community service. *Special Characteristics:* adult students, children of faculty/staff, ethnic background, international students, relatives of clergy.

LOANS ***Programs:*** FFEL (Subsidized and Unsubsidized Stafford, PLUS), Perkins, Federal Nursing, college/university, alternative loans.

APPLYING FOR FINANCIAL AID ***Required financial aid forms:*** FAFSA, state aid form.

CONTACT Financial Aid Office, Biola University, 13800 Biola Avenue, La Mirada, CA 90639-0001, 562-903-4742 or toll-free 800-652-4652. *Fax:* 562-906-4541. *E-mail:* finaid@biola.edu.

BIRMINGHAM-SOUTHERN COLLEGE

Birmingham, AL

Tuition & fees: $24,300 **Average undergraduate aid package: $22,166**

ABOUT THE INSTITUTION Independent Methodist, coed. Awards: bachelor's and master's degrees. 43 undergraduate majors. Total enrollment: 1,256. Undergraduates: 1,207. Freshmen: 292. Federal methodology is used as a basis for awarding need-based institutional aid.

UNDERGRADUATE EXPENSES for 2007–08 ***Application fee:*** $25. ***Comprehensive fee:*** $32,362 includes full-time tuition ($23,600), mandatory fees ($700), and room and board ($8062). ***College room only:*** $5000. ***Part-time tuition:*** $983 per credit hour.

FRESHMAN FINANCIAL AID (Fall 2006, est.) 183 applied for aid; of those 75% were deemed to have need. 100% of freshmen with need received aid; of those 35% had need fully met. ***Average percent of need met:*** 92% (excluding resources awarded to replace EFC). ***Average financial aid package:*** $23,562 (excluding resources awarded to replace EFC). 39% of all full-time freshmen had no need and received non-need-based gift aid.

UNDERGRADUATE FINANCIAL AID (Fall 2006, est.) 589 applied for aid; of those 79% were deemed to have need. 100% of undergraduates with need received aid; of those 40% had need fully met. ***Average percent of need met:*** 87% (excluding resources awarded to replace EFC). ***Average financial aid package:*** $22,166 (excluding resources awarded to replace EFC). 45% of all full-time undergraduates had no need and received non-need-based gift aid.

GIFT AID (NEED-BASED) ***Total amount:*** $4,449,167 (11% federal, 2% state, 79% institutional, 8% external sources). ***Receiving aid:*** Freshmen: 34% (98); All full-time undergraduates: 26% (309). ***Average award:*** Freshmen: $9378; Undergraduates: $7010. ***Scholarships, grants, and awards:*** Federal Pell, FSEOG, state, private, college/university gift aid from institutional funds.

GIFT AID (NON-NEED-BASED) ***Total amount:*** $5,049,993 (1% federal, 2% state, 84% institutional, 13% external sources). ***Receiving aid:*** Freshmen: 37% (108); Undergraduates: 29% (341). ***Average award:*** Freshmen: $10,852; Undergraduates: $9586. ***Scholarships, grants, and awards by category:*** *Academic Interests/Achievement:* 1,117 awards ($8,523,029 total): biological sciences, business, computer science, education, general academic interests/achievements, health fields, mathematics, physical sciences, premedicine. *Creative Arts/Performance:* 24 awards ($191,970 total): art/fine arts, dance, music, performing arts, theater/drama. *Special Achievements/Activities:* 219 awards ($558,779 total): junior miss, memberships, religious involvement. *Special Characteristics:* 81 awards ($478,005 total): children of faculty/staff, relatives of clergy, religious affiliation. ***ROTC:*** Army cooperative, Air Force cooperative.

LOANS ***Student loans:*** $2,399,220 (51% need-based, 49% non-need-based). 60% of past graduating class borrowed through all loan programs. ***Average need-based loan:*** Freshmen: $3587; Undergraduates: $4370. ***Parent loans:*** $1,321,705 (19% need-based, 81% non-need-based). ***Programs:*** FFEL (Subsidized and Unsubsidized Stafford, PLUS), Perkins, college/university.

WORK-STUDY ***Federal work-study:*** Total amount: $295,121; 154 jobs averaging $1916. ***State or other work-study/employment:*** Total amount: $400,456 (100% non-need-based). 275 part-time jobs averaging $1456.

ATHLETIC AWARDS Total amount: $2,991,676 (24% need-based, 76% non-need-based).

APPLYING FOR FINANCIAL AID ***Required financial aid forms:*** FAFSA, state aid form. ***Financial aid deadline (priority):*** 3/1. ***Notification date:*** Continuous beginning 3/1.

CONTACT Financial Aid Office, Birmingham-Southern College, 900 Arkadelphia Road, Box 549016, Birmingham, AL 35254, 205-226-4688 or toll-free 800-523-5793. *Fax:* 205-226-3082. *E-mail:* finaid@bsc.edu.

BIRTHINGWAY COLLEGE OF MIDWIFERY

Portland, OR

CONTACT Financial Aid Office, Birthingway College of Midwifery, 12113 SE Foster Road, Portland, OR 97299, 503-760-3131.

BLACKBURN COLLEGE

Carlinville, IL

CONTACT Mrs. Jane Kelsey, Financial Aid Administrator, Blackburn College, 700 College Avenue, Carlinville, IL 62626-1498, 217-854-3231 Ext. 4227 or toll-free 800-233-3550. *Fax:* 217-854-3731.

BLACK HILLS STATE UNIVERSITY

Spearfish, SD

Tuition & fees (SD res): $5335 **Average undergraduate aid package: $4337**

ABOUT THE INSTITUTION State-supported, coed. Awards: associate, bachelor's, and master's degrees and post-bachelor's and post-master's certificates. 47 undergraduate majors. Total enrollment: 3,896. Undergraduates: 3,733. Freshmen: 658. Federal methodology is used as a basis for awarding need-based institutional aid.

UNDERGRADUATE EXPENSES for 2006–07 ***Application fee:*** $20. ***Tuition, state resident:*** full-time $2541; part-time $79.40 per credit. ***Tuition, nonresident:*** full-time $8074; part-time $252.30 per credit. ***Required fees:*** full-time $2794; $87.30 per credit. Full-time tuition and fees vary according to course load and reciprocity agreements. Part-time tuition and fees vary according to course load and reciprocity agreements. ***College room and board:*** $3988; ***Room only:*** $2202. Room and board charges vary according to board plan and housing facility. ***Payment plans:*** Installment, deferred payment.

UNDERGRADUATE FINANCIAL AID (Fall 2005) ***Average financial aid package:*** $4337 (excluding resources awarded to replace EFC).

GIFT AID (NEED-BASED) ***Total amount:*** $3,446,097 (95% federal, 5% external sources). ***Scholarships, grants, and awards:*** Federal Pell, FSEOG, state, private, college/university gift aid from institutional funds.

GIFT AID (NON-NEED-BASED) ***Total amount:*** $982,881 (3% federal, 38% state, 59% external sources). ***Scholarships, grants, and awards by category:*** *Academic Interests/Achievement:* biological sciences, business, communication, computer science, education, English, foreign languages, general academic interests/achievements, health fields, humanities, mathematics, military science, physical sciences, social sciences. *Creative Arts/Performance:* art/fine arts, music, theater/drama. ***Tuition waivers:*** Full or partial for employees or children of employees, senior citizens. ***ROTC:*** Army.

LOANS ***Student loans:*** $12,870,389 (49% need-based, 51% non-need-based). 86% of past graduating class borrowed through all loan programs. *Average indebtedness per student:* $19,266. ***Parent loans:*** $612,558 (100% non-need-based). ***Programs:*** FFEL (Subsidized and Unsubsidized Stafford, PLUS), Perkins.

WORK-STUDY ***Federal work-study:*** Total amount: $334,053; 283 jobs averaging $1180. ***State or other work-study/employment:*** Total amount: $753,373 (100% non-need-based). 698 part-time jobs averaging $1079.

ATHLETIC AWARDS Total amount: $362,634 (100% non-need-based).

APPLYING FOR FINANCIAL AID ***Required financial aid form:*** FAFSA. ***Financial aid deadline (priority):*** 3/1. ***Notification date:*** Continuous beginning 5/1. Students must reply within 3 weeks of notification.

CONTACT Ms. Deb Henriksen, Director of Financial Aid, Black Hills State University, 1200 University Street, Box 9670, Spearfish, SD 57799-9670, 605-642-6581 or toll-free 800-255-2478. *Fax:* 605-642-6254. *E-mail:* debhenriksen@bhsu.edu.

BLESSING-RIEMAN COLLEGE OF NURSING

Quincy, IL

Tuition & fees: $17,300 **Average undergraduate aid package: N/A**

ABOUT THE INSTITUTION Independent, coed, primarily women. Awards: bachelor's degrees. 1 undergraduate major. Total enrollment: 214. Undergraduates: 214. Freshmen: 23. Federal methodology is used as a basis for awarding need-based institutional aid.

UNDERGRADUATE EXPENSES for 2006–07 ***Comprehensive fee:*** $23,850 includes full-time tuition ($16,800), mandatory fees ($500), and room and board ($6550). ***College room only:*** $3500. Full-time tuition and fees vary according to course load, location, and student level. Room and board charges vary according to board plan, location, and student level. ***Part-time tuition:*** $319 per credit hour. Part-time tuition and fees vary according to course load, location, and student level. ***Payment plan:*** Installment.

UNDERGRADUATE FINANCIAL AID (Fall 2006, est.) 91 applied for aid; of those 100% were deemed to have need. 100% of undergraduates with need received aid. ***Average percent of need met:*** 75% (excluding resources awarded to replace EFC).

GIFT AID (NEED-BASED) ***Total amount:*** $590,298 (14% federal, 17% state, 62% institutional, 7% external sources). ***Receiving aid:*** All full-time undergraduates: 90% (91). ***Scholarships, grants, and awards:*** Federal Pell, state, private, college/university gift aid from institutional funds.

GIFT AID (NON-NEED-BASED) ***Tuition waivers:*** Full or partial for employees or children of employees.

LOANS ***Student loans:*** $404,851 (100% need-based). 70% of past graduating class borrowed through all loan programs. *Average indebtedness per student:* $11,000. ***Parent loans:*** $15,600 (100% need-based). ***Programs:*** FFEL (Subsidized and Unsubsidized Stafford, PLUS), Federal Nursing, college/university.

APPLYING FOR FINANCIAL AID ***Required financial aid form:*** FAFSA. ***Financial aid deadline:*** Continuous.

CONTACT Ms. Sara Brehm, Financial Aid Officer, Blessing-Rieman College of Nursing, Broadway at 11th Street, Quincy, IL 62301, 217-223-8400 Ext. 6993 or toll-free 800-877-9140 Ext. 6964. *Fax:* 217-223-1781. *E-mail:* sbrehm@blessinghospital.org.

BLOOMFIELD COLLEGE

Bloomfield, NJ

Tuition & fees: $16,400 **Average undergraduate aid package: $15,048**

ABOUT THE INSTITUTION Independent religious, coed. Awards: bachelor's degrees. 56 undergraduate majors. Total enrollment: 2,084. Undergraduates: 2,084. Freshmen: 348. Federal methodology is used as a basis for awarding need-based institutional aid.

UNDERGRADUATE EXPENSES for 2006–07 ***Application fee:*** $40. ***Comprehensive fee:*** $24,500 includes full-time tuition ($16,100), mandatory fees ($300), and room and board ($8100). ***College room only:*** $4050. ***Part-time tuition:*** $1650 per course. ***Part-time fees:*** $50 per term. Part-time tuition and fees vary according to course load. ***Payment plans:*** Installment, deferred payment.

FRESHMAN FINANCIAL AID (Fall 2005) 401 applied for aid; of those 91% were deemed to have need. 99% of freshmen with need received aid; of those 57% had need fully met. ***Average percent of need met:*** 66% (excluding resources awarded to replace EFC). ***Average financial aid package:*** $15,269 (excluding resources awarded to replace EFC). 5% of all full-time freshmen had no need and received non-need-based gift aid.

UNDERGRADUATE FINANCIAL AID (Fall 2005) 1,591 applied for aid; of those 91% were deemed to have need. 100% of undergraduates with need received aid; of those 47% had need fully met. ***Average percent of need met:*** 62% (excluding resources awarded to replace EFC). ***Average financial aid package:*** $15,048 (excluding resources awarded to replace EFC). 3% of all full-time undergraduates had no need and received non-need-based gift aid.

GIFT AID (NEED-BASED) ***Total amount:*** $14,292,116 (26% federal, 52% state, 22% institutional). ***Receiving aid:*** Freshmen: 85% (343); All full-time undergraduates: 83% (1,359). ***Average award:*** Freshmen: $11,603; Undergraduates: $9557. ***Scholarships, grants, and awards:*** Federal Pell, FSEOG, state, private, college/university gift aid from institutional funds.

GIFT AID (NON-NEED-BASED) ***Total amount:*** $1,605,106 (1% state, 68% institutional, 31% external sources). ***Receiving aid:*** Freshmen: 26% (103);

Undergraduates: 22% (366). ***Average award:*** Freshmen: $5400; Undergraduates: $5524. ***Scholarships, grants, and awards by category:*** *Academic Interests/Achievement:* 140 awards ($648,855 total): biological sciences, business, computer science, education, English, general academic interests/achievements, health fields, humanities, mathematics, physical sciences, religion/biblical studies, social sciences. *Creative Arts/Performance:* applied art and design, art/fine arts, cinema/film/broadcasting, general creative arts/performance, music, performing arts, theater/drama. *Special Achievements/Activities:* 218 awards ($1,244,476 total): community service, general special achievements/activities. *Special Characteristics:* 81 awards ($127,453 total): adult students, children and siblings of alumni, general special characteristics, previous college experience. ***Tuition waivers:*** Full or partial for employees or children of employees, senior citizens. ***ROTC:*** Army cooperative.

LOANS ***Student loans:*** $8,082,580 (99% need-based, 1% non-need-based). 90% of past graduating class borrowed through all loan programs. *Average indebtedness per student:* $18,404. ***Average need-based loan:*** Freshmen: $2976; Undergraduates: $5063. ***Parent loans:*** $968,783 (100% need-based). ***Programs:*** FFEL (Subsidized and Unsubsidized Stafford, PLUS).

WORK-STUDY ***Federal work-study:*** Total amount: $533,463; 201 jobs averaging $1370. ***State or other work-study/employment:*** 23 part-time jobs averaging $7748.

ATHLETIC AWARDS Total amount: $894,083 (100% non-need-based).

APPLYING FOR FINANCIAL AID ***Required financial aid form:*** FAFSA. ***Financial aid deadline:*** 6/1 (priority: 3/15). ***Notification date:*** Continuous beginning 4/1. Students must reply by 3/15 or within 2 weeks of notification.

CONTACT Mr. Luis Gonzalez, Director of Financial Aid, Bloomfield College, Bloomfield College, 467 Franklin Street, Bloomfield, NJ 07003-9981, 973-748-9000 Ext. 212 or toll-free 800-848-4555 Ext. 230. *Fax:* 973-748-9735. *E-mail:* l_gonzalez@bloomfield.edu.

BLOOMSBURG UNIVERSITY OF PENNSYLVANIA

Bloomsburg, PA

Tuition & fees (PA res): $6412 **Average undergraduate aid package: $9752**

ABOUT THE INSTITUTION State-supported, coed. Awards: associate, bachelor's, master's, and doctoral degrees and post-bachelor's certificates. 51 undergraduate majors. Total enrollment: 8,723. Undergraduates: 7,877. Freshmen: 1,644. Federal methodology is used as a basis for awarding need-based institutional aid.

UNDERGRADUATE EXPENSES for 2006–07 ***Application fee:*** $30. ***Tuition, state resident:*** full-time $5038; part-time $210 per credit. ***Tuition, nonresident:*** full-time $12,598; part-time $525 per credit. ***Required fees:*** full-time $1374; $41 per credit or $66 per term part-time. Full-time tuition and fees vary according to course load. Part-time tuition and fees vary according to course load. ***College room and board:*** $5616; ***Room only:*** $3282. Room and board charges vary according to board plan and housing facility. ***Payment plan:*** Installment.

FRESHMAN FINANCIAL AID (Fall 2006, est.) 1419 applied for aid; of those 95% were deemed to have need. 95% of freshmen with need received aid; of those 90% had need fully met. ***Average percent of need met:*** 65% (excluding resources awarded to replace EFC). ***Average financial aid package:*** $9461 (excluding resources awarded to replace EFC). 2% of all full-time freshmen had no need and received non-need-based gift aid.

UNDERGRADUATE FINANCIAL AID (Fall 2006, est.) 6,348 applied for aid; of those 95% were deemed to have need. 94% of undergraduates with need received aid; of those 90% had need fully met. ***Average percent of need met:*** 65% (excluding resources awarded to replace EFC). ***Average financial aid package:*** $9752 (excluding resources awarded to replace EFC). 1% of all full-time undergraduates had no need and received non-need-based gift aid.

GIFT AID (NEED-BASED) ***Total amount:*** $13,466,756 (40% federal, 55% state, 2% institutional, 3% external sources). ***Receiving aid:*** Freshmen: 39% (632); All full-time undergraduates: 38% (2,759). ***Average award:*** Freshmen: $5685; Undergraduates: $4743. ***Scholarships, grants, and awards:*** Federal Pell, FSEOG, state, private, college/university gift aid from institutional funds, Federal ACG and Federal Smart Grants.

GIFT AID (NON-NEED-BASED) ***Total amount:*** $3,700,624 (28% federal, 11% state, 22% institutional, 39% external sources). ***Receiving aid:*** Freshmen: 24% (393); Undergraduates: 16% (1,149). ***Average award:*** Freshmen: $1839; Undergraduates: $2029. ***Scholarships, grants, and awards by category:*** *Academic Interests/Achievement:* 388 awards ($434,009 total): biological sciences, business, communication, computer science, education, English, foreign languages, general academic interests/achievements, health fields, humanities, international studies, mathematics, physical sciences, religion/biblical studies, social sciences. *Special Characteristics:* 214 awards ($776,045 total): children of faculty/staff, international students. ***Tuition waivers:*** Full or partial for minority students, employees or children of employees, senior citizens. ***ROTC:*** Army, Air Force cooperative.

LOANS ***Student loans:*** $26,145,596 (47% need-based, 53% non-need-based). 72% of past graduating class borrowed through all loan programs. *Average indebtedness per student:* $17,234. ***Average need-based loan:*** Freshmen: $2550; Undergraduates: $3608. ***Parent loans:*** $6,691,540 (100% non-need-based). ***Programs:*** FFEL (Subsidized and Unsubsidized Stafford, PLUS), Perkins, state, alternative loans.

WORK-STUDY ***Federal work-study:*** Total amount: $2,166,251; 809 jobs averaging $2678. ***State or other work-study/employment:*** Total amount: $2,700,101 (100% non-need-based). 839 part-time jobs averaging $3218.

ATHLETIC AWARDS Total amount: $495,375 (100% non-need-based).

APPLYING FOR FINANCIAL AID ***Required financial aid form:*** FAFSA. ***Financial aid deadline (priority):*** 3/15. ***Notification date:*** Continuous beginning 4/1.

CONTACT Mr. Thomas M. Lyons, Director of Financial Aid, Bloomsburg University of Pennsylvania, 119 Warren Student Services Center, 400 East 2nd Street, Bloomsburg, PA 17815-1301, 570-389-4279. *Fax:* 570-389-4795. *E-mail:* tlyons@bloomu.edu.

BLUEFIELD COLLEGE

Bluefield, VA

CONTACT Mrs. Debbie Checchio, Director of Financial Aid, Bluefield College, 3000 College Drive, Bluefield, VA 24605, 276-326-4215 or toll-free 800-872-0175. *Fax:* 276-326-4356. *E-mail:* dchecchio@bluefield.edu.

BLUEFIELD STATE COLLEGE

Bluefield, WV

Tuition & fees (WV res): $3648 **Average undergraduate aid package: $5800**

ABOUT THE INSTITUTION State-supported, coed. Awards: associate and bachelor's degrees. 28 undergraduate majors. Total enrollment: 1,788. Undergraduates: 1,788. Freshmen: 261. Federal methodology is used as a basis for awarding need-based institutional aid.

UNDERGRADUATE EXPENSES for 2006–07 ***Tuition, state resident:*** full-time $3648; part-time $153 per credit hour. ***Tuition, nonresident:*** full-time $7760; part-time $324 per credit hour.

FRESHMAN FINANCIAL AID (Fall 2006, est.) 360 applied for aid; of those 89% were deemed to have need. 100% of freshmen with need received aid; of those 58% had need fully met. ***Average percent of need met:*** 69% (excluding resources awarded to replace EFC). ***Average financial aid package:*** $5800 (excluding resources awarded to replace EFC). 12% of all full-time freshmen had no need and received non-need-based gift aid.

UNDERGRADUATE FINANCIAL AID (Fall 2006, est.) 1,250 applied for aid; of those 84% were deemed to have need. 100% of undergraduates with need received aid; of those 40% had need fully met. ***Average percent of need met:*** 69% (excluding resources awarded to replace EFC). ***Average financial aid package:*** $5800 (excluding resources awarded to replace EFC). 28% of all full-time undergraduates had no need and received non-need-based gift aid.

GIFT AID (NEED-BASED) ***Total amount:*** $4,290,000 (79% federal, 21% state). ***Receiving aid:*** Freshmen: 73% (320); All full-time undergraduates: 72% (1,050). ***Average award:*** Freshmen: $3100; Undergraduates: $3300. ***Scholarships, grants, and awards:*** Federal Pell, FSEOG, state.

GIFT AID (NON-NEED-BASED) ***Total amount:*** $1,600,000 (32% state, 22% institutional, 46% external sources). ***Receiving aid:*** Freshmen: 21% (90); Undergraduates: 2% (36). ***Average award:*** Freshmen: $1375; Undergraduates: $1375. ***Scholarships, grants, and awards by category:*** *Academic Interests/Achievement:* 420 awards ($360,000 total): engineering/technologies, general academic interests/achievements. *Special Achievements/Activities:* 11 awards ($4500 total): cheerleading/drum major, general special achievements/activities, junior miss, leadership. *Special Characteristics:* 3 awards ($1500 total): general special characteristics.

LOANS ***Student loans:*** $5,400,000 (56% need-based, 44% non-need-based). 54% of past graduating class borrowed through all loan programs. *Average indebtedness per student:* $17,500. ***Average need-based loan:*** Freshmen: $3400; Undergraduates: $3400. ***Parent loans:*** $180,000 (100% non-need-based). ***Programs:*** Federal Direct (Subsidized and Unsubsidized Stafford, PLUS), Perkins.

WORK-STUDY ***Federal work-study:*** Total amount: $110,000; 105 jobs averaging $1750. ***State or other work-study/employment:*** Total amount: $150,000 (100% non-need-based). 175 part-time jobs averaging $1900.

ATHLETIC AWARDS Total amount: $95,000 (100% non-need-based).

APPLYING FOR FINANCIAL AID ***Required financial aid forms:*** FAFSA, institution's own form. ***Financial aid deadline (priority):*** 3/1. ***Notification date:*** 6/1.

CONTACT Mr. Tom Ilse, Director of Financial Aid, Bluefield State College, 219 Rock Street, Bluefield, WV 24701-2198, 304-327-4020 or toll-free 800-344-8892 Ext. 4065 (in-state), 800-654-7798 Ext. 4065 (out-of-state). *Fax:* 304-325-7747. *E-mail:* tilse@bluefieldstate.edu.

BLUE MOUNTAIN COLLEGE

Blue Mountain, MS

Tuition & fees: $7490 **Average undergraduate aid package: $6763**

ABOUT THE INSTITUTION Independent Southern Baptist, coed. Awards: bachelor's degrees. 28 undergraduate majors. Total enrollment: 365. Undergraduates: 365. Freshmen: 45. Federal methodology is used as a basis for awarding need-based institutional aid.

UNDERGRADUATE EXPENSES for 2006–07 ***Application fee:*** $10. ***Comprehensive fee:*** $11,256 includes full-time tuition ($6900), mandatory fees ($590), and room and board ($3766). ***College room only:*** $1400. Full-time tuition and fees vary according to course load. Room and board charges vary according to board plan and gender. ***Part-time tuition:*** $230 per hour. ***Part-time fees:*** $80 per term. Part-time tuition and fees vary according to course load. ***Payment plan:*** Installment.

FRESHMAN FINANCIAL AID (Fall 2006, est.) 37 applied for aid; of those 100% were deemed to have need. 100% of freshmen with need received aid; of those 41% had need fully met. ***Average percent of need met:*** 96% (excluding resources awarded to replace EFC). ***Average financial aid package:*** $7589 (excluding resources awarded to replace EFC). 21% of all full-time freshmen had no need and received non-need-based gift aid.

UNDERGRADUATE FINANCIAL AID (Fall 2006, est.) 222 applied for aid; of those 79% were deemed to have need. 100% of undergraduates with need received aid; of those 64% had need fully met. ***Average percent of need met:*** 56% (excluding resources awarded to replace EFC). ***Average financial aid package:*** $6763 (excluding resources awarded to replace EFC). 48% of all full-time undergraduates had no need and received non-need-based gift aid.

GIFT AID (NEED-BASED) ***Total amount:*** $486,527 (99% federal, 1% state). ***Receiving aid:*** Freshmen: 79% (30); All full-time undergraduates: 41% (112). ***Average award:*** Freshmen: $2324; Undergraduates: $2967. ***Scholarships, grants, and awards:*** Federal Pell, FSEOG, state, private, college/university gift aid from institutional funds.

GIFT AID (NON-NEED-BASED) ***Total amount:*** $1,273,966 (23% state, 75% institutional, 2% external sources). ***Receiving aid:*** Freshmen: 95% (36); Undergraduates: 64% (175). ***Average award:*** Freshmen: $2944; Undergraduates: $3046. ***Scholarships, grants, and awards by category:*** *Academic Interests/Achievement:* biological sciences, business, education, English, general academic interests/achievements, mathematics, premedicine, religion/biblical studies, social sciences. *Creative Arts/Performance:* music, theater/drama. *Special Achievements/Activities:* leadership, memberships, religious involvement. *Special Characteristics:* children of faculty/staff. ***Tuition waivers:*** Full or partial for employees or children of employees.

LOANS ***Student loans:*** $1,087,512 (86% need-based, 14% non-need-based). 83% of past graduating class borrowed through all loan programs. *Average indebtedness per student:* $11,500. ***Average need-based loan:*** Freshmen: $2547; Undergraduates: $4286. ***Parent loans:*** $52,165 (100% non-need-based). ***Programs:*** FFEL (Subsidized and Unsubsidized Stafford, PLUS), Perkins.

WORK-STUDY ***Federal work-study:*** Total amount: $70,345; 52 jobs averaging $1400. ***State or other work-study/employment:*** Total amount: $61,845 (100% non-need-based). 46 part-time jobs averaging $1400.

ATHLETIC AWARDS Total amount: $175,259 (100% non-need-based).

APPLYING FOR FINANCIAL AID ***Required financial aid forms:*** FAFSA, institution's own form. ***Financial aid deadline (priority):*** 3/1. ***Notification date:*** Continuous. Students must reply within 2 weeks of notification.

CONTACT Joanna Fowler, Financial Aid Assistant, Blue Mountain College, PO Box 160, Blue Mountain, MS 38610-0160, 662-685-4771 Ext. 141 or toll-free 800-235-0136. *Fax:* 662-685-4776. *E-mail:* jfowler@bmc.edu.

BLUFFTON UNIVERSITY

Bluffton, OH

Tuition & fees: $20,570 **Average undergraduate aid package: $18,847**

ABOUT THE INSTITUTION Independent Mennonite, coed. Awards: bachelor's and master's degrees. 39 undergraduate majors. Total enrollment: 1,155. Undergraduates: 1,030. Freshmen: 244. Both federal and institutional methodology are used as a basis for awarding need-based institutional aid.

UNDERGRADUATE EXPENSES for 2006–07 ***Application fee:*** $20. ***Comprehensive fee:*** $27,652 includes full-time tuition ($20,170), mandatory fees ($400), and room and board ($7082). ***College room only:*** $3260. Full-time tuition and fees vary according to course load and program. Room and board charges vary according to board plan and housing facility. ***Part-time tuition:*** $840 per credit hour. Part-time tuition and fees vary according to course load and program. ***Payment plan:*** Installment.

FRESHMAN FINANCIAL AID (Fall 2006, est.) 229 applied for aid; of those 93% were deemed to have need. 100% of freshmen with need received aid; of those 63% had need fully met. ***Average percent of need met:*** 96% (excluding resources awarded to replace EFC). ***Average financial aid package:*** $19,980 (excluding resources awarded to replace EFC). 11% of all full-time freshmen had no need and received non-need-based gift aid.

UNDERGRADUATE FINANCIAL AID (Fall 2006, est.) 767 applied for aid; of those 93% were deemed to have need. 100% of undergraduates with need received aid; of those 41% had need fully met. ***Average percent of need met:*** 90% (excluding resources awarded to replace EFC). ***Average financial aid package:*** $18,847 (excluding resources awarded to replace EFC). 13% of all full-time undergraduates had no need and received non-need-based gift aid.

GIFT AID (NEED-BASED) ***Total amount:*** $9,284,194 (12% federal, 13% state, 68% institutional, 7% external sources). ***Receiving aid:*** Freshmen: 88% (214); All full-time undergraduates: 73% (715). ***Average award:*** Freshmen: $15,056; Undergraduates: $13,023. ***Scholarships, grants, and awards:*** Federal Pell, FSEOG, state, private, college/university gift aid from institutional funds.

GIFT AID (NON-NEED-BASED) ***Total amount:*** $1,476,176 (8% state, 73% institutional, 19% external sources). ***Receiving aid:*** Freshmen: 7% (16); Undergraduates: 6% (54). ***Average award:*** Freshmen: $7261; Undergraduates: $7161. ***Scholarships, grants, and awards by category:*** *Academic Interests/Achievement:* 476 awards ($3,565,727 total): general academic interests/achievements. *Creative Arts/Performance:* 30 awards ($30,000 total): art/fine arts, music. *Special Achievements/Activities:* 51 awards ($155,600 total): leadership. *Special Characteristics:* 402 awards ($1,164,091 total): children of faculty/staff, international students, members of minority groups, out-of-state students, relatives of clergy, religious affiliation. ***Tuition waivers:*** Full or partial for employees or children of employees.

LOANS ***Student loans:*** $6,550,284 (94% need-based, 6% non-need-based). 78% of past graduating class borrowed through all loan programs. *Average indebtedness per student:* $22,183. ***Average need-based loan:*** Freshmen: $3883; Undergraduates: $4618. ***Parent loans:*** $1,915,531 (66% need-based, 34% non-need-based). ***Programs:*** FFEL (Subsidized and Unsubsidized Stafford, PLUS), Perkins, alternative loans.

WORK-STUDY ***Federal work-study:*** Total amount: $932,166; 609 jobs averaging $1528. ***State or other work-study/employment:*** Total amount: $436,860 (50% need-based, 50% non-need-based). 267 part-time jobs averaging $1636.

APPLYING FOR FINANCIAL AID ***Required financial aid form:*** FAFSA. ***Financial aid deadline:*** 10/1 (priority: 5/1). ***Notification date:*** Continuous beginning 3/1. Students must reply within 3 weeks of notification.

CONTACT Lawrence Matthews, Director of Financial Aid, Bluffton University, 1 University Drive, Bluffton, OH 45817-2104, 419-358-3266 or toll-free 800-488-3257. *Fax:* 419-358-3073. *E-mail:* matthewsl@bluffton.edu.

BOB JONES UNIVERSITY

Greenville, SC

CONTACT Mr. Chris Baker, Director of Financial Aid, Bob Jones University, 1700 Wade Hampton Boulevard, Greenville, SC 29614, 803-242-5100 Ext. 3037 or toll-free 800-BJANDME.

BOISE BIBLE COLLEGE

Boise, ID

CONTACT Beth Turner, Financial Aid Counselor, Boise Bible College, 8695 West Marigold Street, Boise, ID 83714-1220, 208-376-7731 Ext. 12 or toll-free 800-893-7755. *Fax:* 208-376-7743. *E-mail:* betht@boisebible.edu.

BOISE STATE UNIVERSITY

Boise, ID

Tuition & fees (ID res): $4154 **Average undergraduate aid package: $8003**

ABOUT THE INSTITUTION State-supported, coed. Awards: associate, bachelor's, master's, and doctoral degrees. 97 undergraduate majors. Total enrollment: 188,265. Undergraduates: 17,040. Freshmen: 2,560. Federal methodology is used as a basis for awarding need-based institutional aid.

UNDERGRADUATE EXPENSES for 2006–07 ***Application fee:*** $40. ***Tuition, state resident:*** full-time $2670; part-time $143 per credit. ***Tuition, nonresident:*** full-time $7778; part-time $143 per credit. ***Required fees:*** full-time $1484; $68 per credit. Full-time tuition and fees vary according to reciprocity agreements. Part-time tuition and fees vary according to course load. ***College room and board:*** $5778. Room and board charges vary according to board plan and housing facility. ***Payment plan:*** Deferred payment.

FRESHMAN FINANCIAL AID (Fall 2006, est.) 1319 applied for aid; of those 74% were deemed to have need. 97% of freshmen with need received aid; of those 15% had need fully met. ***Average percent of need met:*** 62% (excluding resources awarded to replace EFC). ***Average financial aid package:*** $7554 (excluding resources awarded to replace EFC). 2% of all full-time freshmen had no need and received non-need-based gift aid.

UNDERGRADUATE FINANCIAL AID (Fall 2006, est.) 6,833 applied for aid; of those 80% were deemed to have need. 97% of undergraduates with need received aid; of those 16% had need fully met. ***Average percent of need met:*** 64% (excluding resources awarded to replace EFC). ***Average financial aid package:*** $8003 (excluding resources awarded to replace EFC). 1% of all full-time undergraduates had no need and received non-need-based gift aid.

GIFT AID (NEED-BASED) ***Total amount:*** $17,266,922 (77% federal, 5% state, 11% institutional, 7% external sources). ***Receiving aid:*** Freshmen: 46% (851); All full-time undergraduates: 41% (4,123). ***Average award:*** Freshmen: $3244; Undergraduates: $3414. ***Scholarships, grants, and awards:*** Federal Pell, FSEOG, state, private, college/university gift aid from institutional funds, Leveraged Educational Assistance Program (LEAP).

GIFT AID (NON-NEED-BASED) ***Total amount:*** $1,019,558 (1% federal, 23% state, 57% institutional, 19% external sources). ***Receiving aid:*** Freshmen: 6% (118); Undergraduates: 34% (3,391). ***Average award:*** Freshmen: $3616; Undergraduates: $2492. ***Scholarships, grants, and awards by category:*** *Academic Interests/Achievement:* 1,857 awards ($5,828,766 total): biological sciences, business, communication, computer science, education, engineering/technologies, English, foreign languages, general academic interests/achievements, health fields, humanities, international studies, mathematics, military science, physical sciences, premedicine, social sciences. *Creative Arts/Performance:* 212 awards ($252,478 total): art/fine arts, dance, debating, general creative arts/performance, journalism/publications, music, performing arts, theater/drama. *Special Achievements/Activities:* 188 awards ($170,053 total): cheerleading/drum major, community service, leadership, rodeo. *Special Characteristics:* 2,218 awards ($1,278,636 total): ethnic background, first-generation college students, general special characteristics, handicapped students, international students, local/state students, members of minority groups, out-of-state students, previous college experience, spouses of current students, veterans, veterans' children. ***Tuition waivers:*** Full or partial for employees or children of employees, senior citizens. ***ROTC:*** Army.

LOANS ***Student loans:*** $37,851,780 (82% need-based, 18% non-need-based). 64% of past graduating class borrowed through all loan programs. *Average indebtedness per student:* $20,004. ***Average need-based loan:*** Freshmen: $2779; Undergraduates: $4147. ***Parent loans:*** $1,122,184 (31% need-based, 69% non-need-based). ***Programs:*** Federal Direct (Subsidized and Unsubsidized Stafford, PLUS), Perkins, state, college/university, Alaska Loans.

WORK-STUDY ***Federal work-study:*** Total amount: $2,498,436; jobs available (averaging $4000). ***State or other work-study/employment:*** Total amount: $1,343,759 (100% need-based). Part-time jobs available (averaging $4000).

ATHLETIC AWARDS Total amount: $3,490,377 (76% need-based, 24% non-need-based).

APPLYING FOR FINANCIAL AID ***Required financial aid form:*** FAFSA. ***Financial aid deadline:*** 6/1 (priority: 2/15). ***Notification date:*** Continuous beginning 3/14. Students must reply by 6/1 or within 4 weeks of notification.

CONTACT Office of Financial Aid and Scholarships, Boise State University, Administration Building, Room 123, 1910 University Drive, Boise, ID 83725-1315, 208-426-1664 or toll-free 800-632-6586 (in-state), 800-824-7017 (out-of-state). *Fax:* 208-426-1305. *E-mail:* faquest@boisestate.edu.

BORICUA COLLEGE

New York, NY

Tuition & fees: N/R **Average undergraduate aid package: $5200**

ABOUT THE INSTITUTION Independent, coed. Awards: associate, bachelor's, and master's degrees. 7 undergraduate majors. Total enrollment: 1,520. Undergraduates: 1,468. Federal methodology is used as a basis for awarding need-based institutional aid.

FRESHMAN FINANCIAL AID (Fall 2005) 491 applied for aid; of those 99% were deemed to have need. 99% of freshmen with need received aid; of those 67% had need fully met. ***Average percent of need met:*** 67% (excluding resources awarded to replace EFC). ***Average financial aid package:*** $4987 (excluding resources awarded to replace EFC).

UNDERGRADUATE FINANCIAL AID (Fall 2005) 1,472 applied for aid; of those 99% were deemed to have need. 99% of undergraduates with need received aid; of those 41% had need fully met. ***Average percent of need met:*** 40% (excluding resources awarded to replace EFC). ***Average financial aid package:*** $5200 (excluding resources awarded to replace EFC). 1% of all full-time undergraduates had no need and received non-need-based gift aid.

GIFT AID (NEED-BASED) ***Total amount:*** $6,947,248 (49% federal, 49% state, 2% institutional). ***Receiving aid:*** Freshmen: 94% (483); All full-time undergraduates: 94% (1,443). ***Average award:*** Freshmen: $170; Undergraduates: $443. ***Scholarships, grants, and awards:*** Federal Pell, FSEOG, state, private, college/university gift aid from institutional funds.

GIFT AID (NON-NEED-BASED) ***Receiving aid:*** Freshmen: 1% (5); Undergraduates: 1% (19). ***Average award:*** Undergraduates: $700.

LOANS ***Student loans:*** $878,337 (100% need-based). ***Average need-based loan:*** Freshmen: $2870; Undergraduates: $3937. ***Programs:*** college/university.

WORK-STUDY ***Federal work-study:*** Total amount: $240,865; 121 jobs averaging $1900.

APPLYING FOR FINANCIAL AID ***Required financial aid forms:*** FAFSA, institution's own form, CSS Financial Aid PROFILE, state aid form. ***Financial aid deadline (priority):*** 3/1. ***Notification date:*** Continuous. Students must reply within 2 weeks of notification.

CONTACT Ms. Rosalia Cruz, Financial Aid Administrator, Boricua College, 3755 Broadway, New York, NY 10032-1560, 212-694-1000 Ext. 611. *Fax:* 212-694-1015. *E-mail:* rcruz@boricuacollege.edu.

BOSTON ARCHITECTURAL COLLEGE

Boston, MA

CONTACT Maureen Samways, Director of Financial Aid, Boston Architectural College, 320 Newbury Street, Boston, MA 02115, 617-585-0125 or toll-free 877-585-0100. *Fax:* 617-585-0131. *E-mail:* maureen.samways@the-bac.edu.

BOSTON BAPTIST COLLEGE

Boston, MA

CONTACT Curt A. Wiedenroth, Financial Aid Director, Boston Baptist College, 950 Metropolitan Avenue, Boston, MA 02136, 617-364-3510 or toll-free 888-235-2014 (out-of-state). *Fax:* 617-364-0723. *E-mail:* cw9083@aol.com.

BOSTON COLLEGE

Chestnut Hill, MA

Tuition & fees: $33,506 **Average undergraduate aid package: $25,967**

ABOUT THE INSTITUTION Independent Roman Catholic (Jesuit), coed. Awards: bachelor's, master's, doctoral, and first professional degrees and post-master's certificates (also offers continuing education program with significant enrollment not reflected in profile). 45 undergraduate majors. Total enrollment: 13,652. Undergraduates: 9,020. Freshmen: 2,284. Institutional methodology is used as a basis for awarding need-based institutional aid.

UNDERGRADUATE EXPENSES for 2006–07 ***Application fee:*** $70. ***Comprehensive fee:*** $44,944 includes full-time tuition ($33,000), mandatory fees ($506), and room and board ($11,438). ***College room only:*** $7338. Room and board charges vary according to housing facility. ***Payment plans:*** Tuition prepayment, installment.

FRESHMAN FINANCIAL AID (Fall 2006, est.) 1209 applied for aid; of those 79% were deemed to have need. 100% of freshmen with need received aid; of those 100% had need fully met. ***Average percent of need met:*** 100% (excluding resources awarded to replace EFC). ***Average financial aid package:*** $25,075 (excluding resources awarded to replace EFC). 1% of all full-time freshmen had no need and received non-need-based gift aid.

UNDERGRADUATE FINANCIAL AID (Fall 2006, est.) 4,301 applied for aid; of those 87% were deemed to have need. 100% of undergraduates with need received aid; of those 100% had need fully met. ***Average percent of need met:*** 100% (excluding resources awarded to replace EFC). ***Average financial aid package:*** $25,967 (excluding resources awarded to replace EFC). 2% of all full-time undergraduates had no need and received non-need-based gift aid.

GIFT AID (NEED-BASED) ***Total amount:*** $69,211,816 (6% federal, 2% state, 88% institutional, 4% external sources). ***Receiving aid:*** Freshmen: 37% (838); All full-time undergraduates: 36% (3,239). ***Average award:*** Freshmen: $21,589; Undergraduates: $21,368. ***Scholarships, grants, and awards:*** Federal Pell, FSEOG, state, private, college/university gift aid from institutional funds.

GIFT AID (NON-NEED-BASED) ***Total amount:*** $5,247,923 (20% federal, 56% institutional, 24% external sources). ***Receiving aid:*** Freshmen: 1% (23); Undergraduates: 1% (70). ***Average award:*** Freshmen: $16,326; Undergraduates: $15,259. ***Scholarships, grants, and awards by category:*** *Academic Interests/Achievement:* 89 awards ($21,981,135 total): general academic interests/achievements, military science. ***Tuition waivers:*** Full or partial for employees or children of employees. ***ROTC:*** Army cooperative, Naval cooperative, Air Force cooperative.

LOANS ***Student loans:*** $18,819,479 (85% need-based, 15% non-need-based). 61% of past graduating class borrowed through all loan programs. *Average indebtedness per student:* $19,137. ***Average need-based loan:*** Freshmen: $3792; Undergraduates: $4927. ***Parent loans:*** $44,872,791 (100% non-need-based). ***Programs:*** FFEL (Subsidized and Unsubsidized Stafford, PLUS), Perkins, Federal Nursing, state.

WORK-STUDY ***Federal work-study:*** Total amount: $6,255,615; 2,925 jobs averaging $2139.

ATHLETIC AWARDS Total amount: $11,445,601 (10% need-based, 90% non-need-based).

APPLYING FOR FINANCIAL AID ***Required financial aid forms:*** FAFSA, CSS Financial Aid PROFILE, noncustodial (divorced/separated) parent's statement, business/farm supplement, federal income tax form(s), W-2 forms. ***Financial aid deadline (priority):*** 2/1. ***Notification date:*** 4/1. Students must reply by 5/1.

CONTACT Office of Student Services, Boston College, Lyons Hall, Chestnut Hill, MA 02467, 800-294-0294 or toll-free 800-360-2522. *Fax:* 617-552-4889. *E-mail:* studentservices@bc.edu.

THE BOSTON CONSERVATORY

Boston, MA

ABOUT THE INSTITUTION Independent, coed. Awards: bachelor's and master's degrees and post-bachelor's and post-master's certificates. 9 undergraduate majors. Total enrollment: 518. Undergraduates: 423. Freshmen: 155.

GIFT AID (NEED-BASED) ***Scholarships, grants, and awards:*** Federal Pell, FSEOG, state, private, college/university gift aid from institutional funds.

GIFT AID (NON-NEED-BASED) ***Scholarships, grants, and awards by category:*** *Creative Arts/Performance:* dance, music, theater/drama.

LOANS ***Programs:*** FFEL (Subsidized and Unsubsidized Stafford, PLUS), college/university, alternative loans.

WORK-STUDY ***Federal work-study:*** Total amount: $127,000; 90 jobs averaging $1025. ***State or other work-study/employment:*** Total amount: $40,000 (100% need-based). 30 part-time jobs averaging $1335.

APPLYING FOR FINANCIAL AID ***Required financial aid forms:*** FAFSA, institution's own form.

CONTACT Jessica Raine, Financial Aid Assistant, The Boston Conservatory, 8 The Fenway, Boston, MA 02215, 617-912-9147. *Fax:* 617-536-1496. *E-mail:* jraine@bostonconservatory.edu.

BOSTON UNIVERSITY

Boston, MA

Tuition & fees: $33,792 **Average undergraduate aid package: $27,633**

ABOUT THE INSTITUTION Independent, coed. Awards: bachelor's, master's, doctoral, and first professional degrees and post-bachelor's, post-master's, and first professional certificates. 121 undergraduate majors. Total enrollment: 31,574. Undergraduates: 18,521. Freshmen: 4,124. Both federal and institutional methodology are used as a basis for awarding need-based institutional aid.

UNDERGRADUATE EXPENSES for 2006–07 ***Application fee:*** $75. ***Comprehensive fee:*** $44,272 includes full-time tuition ($33,330), mandatory fees ($462), and room and board ($10,480). ***College room only:*** $6760. Full-time tuition and fees vary according to class time and degree level. Room and board charges vary according to board plan and housing facility. ***Part-time tuition:*** $1042 per credit. ***Part-time fees:*** $40 per semester hour. Part-time tuition and fees vary according to class time, course load, and degree level. ***Payment plans:*** Tuition prepayment, installment.

FRESHMAN FINANCIAL AID (Fall 2005) 2708 applied for aid; of those 80% were deemed to have need. 100% of freshmen with need received aid; of those 55% had need fully met. ***Average percent of need met:*** 90% (excluding resources awarded to replace EFC). ***Average financial aid package:*** $27,009 (excluding resources awarded to replace EFC). 11% of all full-time freshmen had no need and received non-need-based gift aid.

UNDERGRADUATE FINANCIAL AID (Fall 2005) 8,295 applied for aid; of those 90% were deemed to have need. 100% of undergraduates with need received aid; of those 49% had need fully met. ***Average percent of need met:*** 90% (excluding resources awarded to replace EFC). ***Average financial aid package:*** $27,633 (excluding resources awarded to replace EFC). 9% of all full-time undergraduates had no need and received non-need-based gift aid.

GIFT AID (NEED-BASED) ***Total amount:*** $149,397,023 (7% federal, 2% state, 87% institutional, 4% external sources). ***Receiving aid:*** Freshmen: 44% (1,868); All full-time undergraduates: 38% (6,897). ***Average award:*** Freshmen: $19,149; Undergraduates: $18,831. ***Scholarships, grants, and awards:*** Federal Pell, FSEOG, state, private, college/university gift aid from institutional funds.

GIFT AID (NON-NEED-BASED) ***Total amount:*** $30,120,602 (10% federal, 77% institutional, 13% external sources). ***Receiving aid:*** Freshmen: 23% (948); Undergraduates: 11% (2,091). ***Average award:*** Freshmen: $15,849; Undergraduates: $16,606. ***Scholarships, grants, and awards by category:*** *Academic Interests/Achievement:* 2,442 awards ($33,889,142 total): education, engineering/technologies, foreign languages, general academic interests/achievements. *Creative Arts/Performance:* 196 awards ($1,312,640 total): art/fine arts, music, theater/drama. *Special Achievements/Activities:* 89 awards ($179,880 total): general special achievements/activities, leadership, memberships. *Special Characteristics:* 709 awards ($8,292,465 total): children and siblings of alumni, local/state students, relatives of clergy, religious affiliation. ***Tuition waivers:*** Full or partial for employees or children of employees, senior citizens. ***ROTC:*** Army, Naval, Air Force.

LOANS ***Student loans:*** $59,709,347 (66% need-based, 34% non-need-based). 57% of past graduating class borrowed through all loan programs. *Average indebtedness per student:* $21,196. ***Average need-based loan:*** Freshmen: $3593; Undergraduates: $4835. ***Parent loans:*** $48,089,445 (28% need-based, 72% non-need-based). ***Programs:*** Federal Direct (Subsidized and Unsubsidized Stafford, PLUS), Perkins, state, alternative loans.

WORK-STUDY ***Federal work-study:*** Total amount: $6,695,553; 3,820 jobs averaging $1753. ***State or other work-study/employment:*** Total amount: $1,858,715 (48% need-based, 52% non-need-based). 171 part-time jobs averaging $10,870.

ATHLETIC AWARDS Total amount: $8,755,602 (16% need-based, 84% non-need-based).

APPLYING FOR FINANCIAL AID ***Required financial aid forms:*** FAFSA, CSS Financial Aid PROFILE. ***Financial aid deadline (priority):*** 2/15. ***Notification date:*** Continuous beginning 2/15. Students must reply by 5/1 or within 2 weeks of notification.

CONTACT Christine McGuire, Director of Financial Assistance, Boston University, 881 Commonwealth Avenue, 5th Floor, Boston, MA 02215, 617-353-4176. *Fax:* 617-353-8200. *E-mail:* finaid@bu.edu.

BOWDOIN COLLEGE

Brunswick, ME

Tuition & fees: $34,640 **Average undergraduate aid package: $29,641**

ABOUT THE INSTITUTION Independent, coed. Awards: bachelor's degrees (SAT or ACT considered if submitted. Test scores are required for home-schooled applicants). 43 undergraduate majors. Total enrollment: 1,734. Undergraduates: 1,734. Freshmen: 474. Institutional methodology is used as a basis for awarding need-based institutional aid.

UNDERGRADUATE EXPENSES for 2006–07 ***Application fee:*** $60. ***Comprehensive fee:*** $43,950 includes full-time tuition ($34,280), mandatory fees ($360), and room and board ($9310). ***College room only:*** $4300. Room and board charges vary according to board plan. ***Payment plans:*** Installment, deferred payment.

FRESHMAN FINANCIAL AID (Fall 2006, est.) 251 applied for aid; of those 78% were deemed to have need. 100% of freshmen with need received aid; of those 100% had need fully met. ***Average percent of need met:*** 100% (excluding resources awarded to replace EFC). ***Average financial aid package:*** $29,899 (excluding resources awarded to replace EFC). 4% of all full-time freshmen had no need and received non-need-based gift aid.

UNDERGRADUATE FINANCIAL AID (Fall 2006, est.) 867 applied for aid; of those 85% were deemed to have need. 100% of undergraduates with need received aid; of those 100% had need fully met. ***Average percent of need met:*** 100% (excluding resources awarded to replace EFC). ***Average financial aid package:*** $29,641 (excluding resources awarded to replace EFC). 4% of all full-time undergraduates had no need and received non-need-based gift aid.

GIFT AID (NEED-BASED) ***Total amount:*** $18,706,095 (6% federal, 1% state, 90% institutional, 3% external sources). ***Receiving aid:*** Freshmen: 41% (196); All full-time undergraduates: 43% (734). ***Average award:*** Freshmen: $27,061; Undergraduates: $25,485. ***Scholarships, grants, and awards:*** Federal Pell, FSEOG, state, private, college/university gift aid from institutional funds.

GIFT AID (NON-NEED-BASED) ***Total amount:*** $537,968 (12% institutional, 88% external sources). ***Receiving aid:*** Undergraduates: 5. ***Average award:*** Freshmen: $1000; Undergraduates: $1000. ***Scholarships, grants, and awards by category:*** *Academic Interests/Achievement:* 65 awards ($65,000 total): general academic interests/achievements. *Special Achievements/Activities:* leadership. *Special Characteristics:* children of faculty/staff. ***Tuition waivers:*** Full or partial for employees or children of employees.

LOANS ***Student loans:*** $2,998,236 (68% need-based, 32% non-need-based). 63% of past graduating class borrowed through all loan programs. *Average indebtedness per student:* $16,160. ***Average need-based loan:*** Freshmen: $3326; Undergraduates: $3654. ***Programs:*** FFEL (Subsidized and Unsubsidized Stafford, PLUS), Perkins, state, college/university.

WORK-STUDY ***Federal work-study:*** Total amount: $302,070; 502 jobs averaging $602. ***State or other work-study/employment:*** Total amount: $753,475 (100% need-based). 659 part-time jobs averaging $1143.

APPLYING FOR FINANCIAL AID ***Required financial aid forms:*** FAFSA, institution's own form, CSS Financial Aid PROFILE, noncustodial (divorced/separated) parent's statement, business/farm supplement. ***Financial aid deadline:*** 2/15. ***Notification date:*** 4/5. Students must reply by 5/1 or within 1 week of notification.

CONTACT Mr. Stephen H. Joyce, Director of Student Aid, Bowdoin College, 5300 College Station, Brunswick, ME 04011-8444, 207-725-3273. *Fax:* 207-725-3864. *E-mail:* sjoyce@bowdoin.edu.

BOWIE STATE UNIVERSITY

Bowie, MD

Tuition & fees (MD res): $5730 **Average undergraduate aid package: $6943**

ABOUT THE INSTITUTION State-supported, coed. Awards: bachelor's, master's, and doctoral degrees and post-bachelor's certificates. 29 undergraduate majors. Total enrollment: 5,291. Undergraduates: 4,074. Freshmen: 789. Both federal and institutional methodology are used as a basis for awarding need-based institutional aid.

UNDERGRADUATE EXPENSES for 2006–07 ***Application fee:*** $40. ***Tuition, state resident:*** full-time $4286; part-time $189 per credit. ***Tuition, nonresident:*** full-time $13,804; part-time $581 per credit. ***Required fees:*** full-time $1444; $562 per term part-time. Part-time tuition and fees vary according to course load. ***College room and board:*** $5992; ***Room only:*** $3632. Room and board charges vary according to board plan and housing facility. ***Payment plans:*** Installment, deferred payment.

FRESHMAN FINANCIAL AID (Fall 2006, est.) 431 applied for aid; of those 97% were deemed to have need. 100% of freshmen with need received aid; of those 10% had need fully met. ***Average percent of need met:*** 43% (excluding resources awarded to replace EFC). ***Average financial aid package:*** $6396 (excluding resources awarded to replace EFC). 1% of all full-time freshmen had no need and received non-need-based gift aid.

UNDERGRADUATE FINANCIAL AID (Fall 2006, est.) 1,911 applied for aid; of those 98% were deemed to have need. 100% of undergraduates with need received aid; of those 9% had need fully met. ***Average percent of need met:*** 46% (excluding resources awarded to replace EFC). ***Average financial aid package:*** $6943 (excluding resources awarded to replace EFC). 1% of all full-time undergraduates had no need and received non-need-based gift aid.

GIFT AID (NEED-BASED) ***Total amount:*** $8,346,282 (45% federal, 37% state, 18% institutional). ***Receiving aid:*** Freshmen: 60% (327); All full-time undergraduates: 61% (1,492). ***Average award:*** Freshmen: $5507; Undergraduates: $5281. ***Scholarships, grants, and awards:*** Federal Pell, FSEOG, state, private, college/university gift aid from institutional funds.

GIFT AID (NON-NEED-BASED) ***Total amount:*** $3,502,744 (45% state, 42% institutional, 13% external sources). ***Receiving aid:*** Freshmen: 13% (73); Undergraduates: 10% (242). ***Average award:*** Freshmen: $1084; Undergraduates: $736. ***Scholarships, grants, and awards by category:*** *Academic Interests/Achievement:* 33 awards ($57,507 total): biological sciences, business, communication, computer science, engineering/technologies, mathematics, military science. *Creative Arts/Performance:* 69 awards ($103,550 total): applied art and design, art/fine arts, general creative arts/performance, music. *Special Characteristics:* 379 awards ($516,919 total): first-generation college students. ***Tuition waivers:*** Full or partial for employees or children of employees, senior citizens.

LOANS ***Student loans:*** $10,525,376 (52% need-based, 48% non-need-based). ***Average need-based loan:*** Freshmen: $2627; Undergraduates: $3548. ***Parent loans:*** $3,992,358 (100% non-need-based). ***Programs:*** Federal Direct (Subsidized and Unsubsidized Stafford, PLUS), Perkins.

WORK-STUDY ***Federal work-study:*** Total amount: $248,772; 104 jobs averaging $2392.

ATHLETIC AWARDS Total amount: $602,563 (100% non-need-based).

APPLYING FOR FINANCIAL AID ***Required financial aid form:*** FAFSA. ***Financial aid deadline (priority):*** 3/1. ***Notification date:*** Continuous beginning 4/15. Students must reply within 1 week of notification.

CONTACT Deborah Riley, Interim Financial Aid Director, Bowie State University, 14000 Jericho Park Road, Bowie, MD 20715, 301-860-3543 or toll-free 877-772-6943 (out-of-state). *Fax:* 301-860-3549. *E-mail:* driley@bowiestate.edu.

BOWLING GREEN STATE UNIVERSITY

Bowling Green, OH

Tuition & fees (OH res): $9060 **Average undergraduate aid package: $10,507**

ABOUT THE INSTITUTION State-supported, coed. Awards: bachelor's, master's, and doctoral degrees and post-master's certificates. 131 undergraduate majors. Total enrollment: 19,108. Undergraduates: 16,085. Freshmen: 3,598. Federal methodology is used as a basis for awarding need-based institutional aid.

UNDERGRADUATE EXPENSES for 2006–07 ***Application fee:*** $40. ***Tuition, state resident:*** full-time $7778; part-time $380 per credit hour. ***Tuition, nonresident:*** full-time $15,086; part-time $729 per credit hour. ***Required fees:*** full-time $1282; $64 per credit hour. Part-time tuition and fees vary according to course load. ***College room and board:*** $6684; ***Room only:*** $4084. Room and board charges vary according to board plan and housing facility. ***Payment plan:*** Installment.

FRESHMAN FINANCIAL AID (Fall 2005) 2904 applied for aid; of those 78% were deemed to have need. 96% of freshmen with need received aid; of those 20% had need fully met. ***Average percent of need met:*** 77% (excluding resources awarded to replace EFC). **Average financial aid package:** $10,288 (excluding resources awarded to replace EFC). 10% of all full-time freshmen had no need and received non-need-based gift aid.

UNDERGRADUATE FINANCIAL AID (Fall 2005) 10,477 applied for aid; of those 81% were deemed to have need. 98% of undergraduates with need received aid; of those 17% had need fully met. **Average percent of need met:** 77% (excluding resources awarded to replace EFC). **Average financial aid package:** $10,507 (excluding resources awarded to replace EFC). 10% of all full-time undergraduates had no need and received non-need-based gift aid.

GIFT AID (NEED-BASED) **Total amount:** $31,647,230 (33% federal, 13% state, 48% institutional, 6% external sources). **Receiving aid:** Freshmen: 46% (1,662); All full-time undergraduates: 37% (5,488). **Average award:** Freshmen: $6262; Undergraduates: $5625. **Scholarships, grants, and awards:** Federal Pell, FSEOG, state, private, college/university gift aid from institutional funds.

GIFT AID (NON-NEED-BASED) **Total amount:** $14,840,802 (1% federal, 18% state, 70% institutional, 11% external sources). **Receiving aid:** Freshmen: 7% (262); Undergraduates: 4% (591). **Average award:** Freshmen: $5077; Undergraduates: $4577. **Scholarships, grants, and awards by category:** *Academic Interests/Achievement:* biological sciences, business, communication, computer science, education, engineering/technologies, English, foreign languages, general academic interests/achievements, health fields, home economics, humanities, international studies, mathematics, military science, physical sciences, social sciences. *Creative Arts/Performance:* art/fine arts, cinema/film/broadcasting, creative writing, dance, debating, journalism/publications, music, performing arts, theater/drama. *Special Achievements/Activities:* general special achievements/activities, leadership. *Special Characteristics:* children and siblings of alumni, children of faculty/staff, general special characteristics, international students, members of minority groups. **Tuition waivers:** Full or partial for employees or children of employees, senior citizens. **ROTC:** Army, Air Force.

LOANS **Student loans:** $68,331,190 (77% need-based, 23% non-need-based). 74% of past graduating class borrowed through all loan programs. *Average indebtedness per student:* $22,929. **Average need-based loan:** Freshmen: $2646; Undergraduates: $3850. **Parent loans:** $16,742,282 (41% need-based, 59% non-need-based). **Programs:** Federal Direct (Subsidized and Unsubsidized Stafford, PLUS), Perkins, Federal Nursing, state, college/university, alternative loans.

WORK-STUDY **Federal work-study:** Total amount: $1,028,559; 900 jobs averaging $1143.

ATHLETIC AWARDS Total amount: $4,840,718 (29% need-based, 71% non-need-based).

APPLYING FOR FINANCIAL AID **Required financial aid form:** FAFSA. **Financial aid deadline:** Continuous. **Notification date:** Continuous beginning 4/15. Students must reply within 3 weeks of notification.

CONTACT Tina Coulter, Assistant Director, Office of Student Financial Aid, Bowling Green State University, 231 Administration Building, Bowling Green, OH 43403, 419-372-2651. *Fax:* 419-372-0404.

BRADLEY UNIVERSITY

Peoria, IL

Tuition & fees: $20,060 **Average undergraduate aid package: $13,037**

ABOUT THE INSTITUTION Independent, coed. Awards: bachelor's, master's, and first professional degrees. 74 undergraduate majors. Total enrollment: 6,126. Undergraduates: 5,315. Freshmen: 1,075. Federal methodology is used as a basis for awarding need-based institutional aid.

UNDERGRADUATE EXPENSES for 2006–07 **Application fee:** $35. **Comprehensive fee:** $26,810 includes full-time tuition ($19,900), mandatory fees ($160), and room and board ($6750). **College room only:** $3900. Full-time tuition and fees vary according to program and student level. Room and board charges vary according to board plan. **Part-time tuition:** $550 per credit. Part-time tuition and fees vary according to course load. **Payment plan:** Installment.

FRESHMAN FINANCIAL AID (Fall 2005) 931 applied for aid; of those 73% were deemed to have need. 100% of freshmen with need received aid; of those 51% had need fully met. **Average percent of need met:** 82% (excluding resources awarded to replace EFC). **Average financial aid package:** $13,984 (excluding resources awarded to replace EFC). 23% of all full-time freshmen had no need and received non-need-based gift aid.

UNDERGRADUATE FINANCIAL AID (Fall 2005) 4,220 applied for aid; of those 85% were deemed to have need. 100% of undergraduates with need received aid; of those 36% had need fully met. **Average percent of need met:** 80% (excluding resources awarded to replace EFC). **Average financial aid package:** $13,037 (excluding resources awarded to replace EFC). 20% of all full-time undergraduates had no need and received non-need-based gift aid.

GIFT AID (NEED-BASED) **Total amount:** $32,777,961 (9% federal, 20% state, 68% institutional, 3% external sources). **Receiving aid:** Freshmen: 65% (674); All full-time undergraduates: 68% (3,415). **Average award:** Freshmen: $10,648; Undergraduates: $8715. **Scholarships, grants, and awards:** Federal Pell, FSEOG, state, private, college/university gift aid from institutional funds.

GIFT AID (NON-NEED-BASED) **Total amount:** $7,047,345 (1% state, 93% institutional, 6% external sources). **Receiving aid:** Freshmen: 9% (95); Undergraduates: 7% (369). **Average award:** Freshmen: $9581; Undergraduates: $9556. **Scholarships, grants, and awards by category:** *Academic Interests/Achievement:* 3,009 awards ($19,766,240 total): general academic interests/achievements. *Creative Arts/Performance:* 206 awards ($241,990 total): art/fine arts, music, theater/drama. *Special Achievements/Activities:* 51 awards ($52,447 total): community service, leadership. *Special Characteristics:* 917 awards ($3,661,442 total): children and siblings of alumni, children of faculty/staff, members of minority groups. **Tuition waivers:** Full or partial for employees or children of employees, senior citizens. **ROTC:** Army cooperative.

LOANS **Student loans:** $24,232,594 (70% need-based, 30% non-need-based). 74% of past graduating class borrowed through all loan programs. *Average indebtedness per student:* $15,079. **Average need-based loan:** Freshmen: $3699; Undergraduates: $5718. **Parent loans:** $6,820,255 (29% need-based, 71% non-need-based). **Programs:** Federal Direct (Subsidized and Unsubsidized Stafford, PLUS), FFEL (PLUS), Perkins, Federal Nursing.

WORK-STUDY **Federal work-study:** Total amount: $1,805,290; 637 jobs averaging $1600.

ATHLETIC AWARDS Total amount: $1,989,552 (45% need-based, 55% non-need-based).

APPLYING FOR FINANCIAL AID **Required financial aid form:** FAFSA. **Financial aid deadline (priority):** 3/1. **Notification date:** Continuous. Students must reply within 3 weeks of notification.

CONTACT Mr. David L. Pardieck, Director of Financial Assistance, Bradley University, 1501 West Bradley Avenue, Peoria, IL 61625-0002, 309-677-3089 or toll-free 800-447-6460. *E-mail:* dlp@bradley.edu.

BRANDEIS UNIVERSITY

Waltham, MA

Tuition & fees: $34,035 **Average undergraduate aid package: $25,928**

ABOUT THE INSTITUTION Independent, coed. Awards: bachelor's, master's, and doctoral degrees and post-bachelor's certificates. 46 undergraduate majors. Total enrollment: 5,313. Undergraduates: 3,304. Freshmen: 765. Institutional methodology is used as a basis for awarding need-based institutional aid.

UNDERGRADUATE EXPENSES for 2006–07 **Application fee:** $55. **Comprehensive fee:** $43,498 includes full-time tuition ($32,951), mandatory fees ($1084), and room and board ($9463). **College room only:** $5315. Room and board charges vary according to board plan and housing facility. **Part-time tuition:** $1030 per credit. Part-time tuition and fees vary according to course load. **Payment plan:** Installment.

FRESHMAN FINANCIAL AID (Fall 2006, est.) 600 applied for aid; of those 70% were deemed to have need. 97% of freshmen with need received aid; of those 40% had need fully met. **Average percent of need met:** 84% (excluding resources awarded to replace EFC). **Average financial aid package:** $24,964 (excluding resources awarded to replace EFC). 26% of all full-time freshmen had no need and received non-need-based gift aid.

UNDERGRADUATE FINANCIAL AID (Fall 2006, est.) 1,937 applied for aid; of those 81% were deemed to have need. 99% of undergraduates with need received aid; of those 31% had need fully met. **Average percent of need met:** 85% (excluding resources awarded to replace EFC). **Average financial aid package:** $25,928 (excluding resources awarded to replace EFC). 22% of all full-time undergraduates had no need and received non-need-based gift aid.

GIFT AID (NEED-BASED) **Total amount:** $30,738,248 (6% federal, 2% state, 89% institutional, 3% external sources). **Receiving aid:** Freshmen: 52% (396); All full-time undergraduates: 46% (1,489). **Average award:** Freshmen: $22,011; Undergraduates: $20,643. **Scholarships, grants, and awards:** Federal Pell, FSEOG, state, private, college/university gift aid from institutional funds.

GIFT AID (NON-NEED-BASED) **Total amount:** $11,888,744 (91% institutional, 9% external sources). **Receiving aid:** Freshmen: 12% (91); Undergraduates: 5% (174). **Average award:** Freshmen: $19,861; Undergraduates: $19,915.

Scholarships, grants, and awards by category: *Academic Interests/Achievement:* general academic interests/achievements. ***Tuition waivers:*** Full or partial for employees or children of employees. ***ROTC:*** Army cooperative, Air Force cooperative.

LOANS ***Student loans:*** $12,067,546 (64% need-based, 36% non-need-based). 67% of past graduating class borrowed through all loan programs. *Average indebtedness per student:* $19,892. ***Average need-based loan:*** Freshmen: $4257; Undergraduates: $6024. ***Parent loans:*** $6,402,128 (25% need-based, 75% non-need-based). ***Programs:*** Federal Direct (Subsidized and Unsubsidized Stafford, PLUS), FFEL (Subsidized and Unsubsidized Stafford, PLUS), Perkins, state, college/university.

WORK-STUDY ***Federal work-study:*** Total amount: $1,336,317; jobs available. ***State or other work-study/employment:*** Total amount: $571,409 (26% need-based, 74% non-need-based). Part-time jobs available.

APPLYING FOR FINANCIAL AID ***Required financial aid forms:*** FAFSA, institution's own form, CSS Financial Aid PROFILE, noncustodial (divorced/separated) parent's statement, business/farm supplement. ***Financial aid deadline (priority):*** 1/15. ***Notification date:*** 4/1. Students must reply by 5/1.

CONTACT Peter Giumette, Student Financial Services, Brandeis University, 415 South Street, Usdan Student Center, Waltham, MA 02454-9110, 781-736-3700 or toll-free 800-622-0622 (out-of-state). *Fax:* 781-736-3719. *E-mail:* sfs@brandeis.edu.

BRENAU UNIVERSITY

Gainesville, GA

Tuition & fees: $17,700 **Average undergraduate aid package: $15,574**

ABOUT THE INSTITUTION Independent, undergraduate: women only; graduate: coed. Awards: bachelor's and master's degrees and post-master's certificates (also offers coed evening and weekend programs with significant enrollment not reflected in profile). 35 undergraduate majors. Total enrollment: 846. Undergraduates: 807. Freshmen: 219. Federal methodology is used as a basis for awarding need-based institutional aid.

UNDERGRADUATE EXPENSES for 2007–08 ***Application fee:*** $35. ***Comprehensive fee:*** $26,650 includes full-time tuition ($17,500), mandatory fees ($200), and room and board ($8950). ***Part-time tuition:*** $583 per hour. ***Part-time fees:*** $100 per term.

FRESHMAN FINANCIAL AID (Fall 2006, est.) 182 applied for aid; of those 88% were deemed to have need. 100% of freshmen with need received aid; of those 39% had need fully met. ***Average percent of need met:*** 86% (excluding resources awarded to replace EFC). ***Average financial aid package:*** $16,585 (excluding resources awarded to replace EFC). 27% of all full-time freshmen had no need and received non-need-based gift aid.

UNDERGRADUATE FINANCIAL AID (Fall 2006, est.) 600 applied for aid; of those 88% were deemed to have need. 100% of undergraduates with need received aid; of those 32% had need fully met. ***Average percent of need met:*** 79% (excluding resources awarded to replace EFC). ***Average financial aid package:*** $15,574 (excluding resources awarded to replace EFC). 25% of all full-time undergraduates had no need and received non-need-based gift aid.

GIFT AID (NEED-BASED) ***Total amount:*** $6,245,720 (15% federal, 21% state, 63% institutional, 1% external sources). ***Receiving aid:*** Freshmen: 73% (160); All full-time undergraduates: 70% (528). ***Average award:*** Freshmen: $14,334; Undergraduates: $12,514. ***Scholarships, grants, and awards:*** Federal Pell, FSEOG, state, private, college/university gift aid from institutional funds, Academic Competitiveness Grant, National Smart Grants.

GIFT AID (NON-NEED-BASED) ***Total amount:*** $2,733,281 (17% state, 82% institutional, 1% external sources). ***Receiving aid:*** Freshmen: 17% (37); Undergraduates: 11% (79). ***Average award:*** Freshmen: $12,519; Undergraduates: $10,634. ***Scholarships, grants, and awards by category:*** *Academic Interests/Achievement:* 417 awards ($2,367,645 total): biological sciences, business, communication, education, general academic interests/achievements, health fields, humanities. *Creative Arts/Performance:* 110 awards ($258,225 total): applied art and design, art/fine arts, cinema/film/broadcasting, creative writing, dance, journalism/publications, music, performing arts, theater/drama. *Special Achievements/Activities:* 65 awards ($390,989 total): general special achievements/activities, leadership. *Special Characteristics:* 12 awards ($112,855 total): children of faculty/staff, first-generation college students, general special characteristics, international students.

LOANS ***Student loans:*** $2,780,697 (50% need-based, 50% non-need-based). 56% of past graduating class borrowed through all loan programs. *Average indebtedness per student:* $16,426. ***Average need-based loan:*** Freshmen: $2325; Undergraduates: $3682. ***Parent loans:*** $422,897 (18% need-based, 82% non-need-based). ***Programs:*** FFEL (Subsidized and Unsubsidized Stafford, PLUS), Perkins, state.

WORK-STUDY ***Federal work-study:*** Total amount: $300,550; 151 jobs averaging $1990. ***State or other work-study/employment:*** Total amount: $3000 (100% non-need-based). 2 part-time jobs averaging $1500.

ATHLETIC AWARDS Total amount: $552,542 (48% need-based, 52% non-need-based).

APPLYING FOR FINANCIAL AID ***Required financial aid forms:*** FAFSA, state aid form. ***Financial aid deadline (priority):*** 4/1. ***Notification date:*** Continuous beginning 3/1.

CONTACT Pam Barrett, Director of Financial Aid, Brenau University, 500 Washington Street, SE, Gainesville, GA 30501-3697, 770-534-6152 or toll-free 800-252-5119. *Fax:* 770-538-4306. *E-mail:* pbarrett@brenau.edu.

BRESCIA UNIVERSITY

Owensboro, KY

CONTACT Martie Ruxer-Boyken, Director of Financial Aid, Brescia University, 717 Frederica Street, Owensboro, KY 42301-3023, 270-686-4290 or toll-free 877-273-7242. *Fax:* 270-686-4266. *E-mail:* martieb@brescia.edu.

BREVARD COLLEGE

Brevard, NC

Tuition & fees: $17,220 **Average undergraduate aid package: $16,300**

ABOUT THE INSTITUTION Independent United Methodist, coed. Awards: bachelor's degrees. 22 undergraduate majors. Total enrollment: 685. Undergraduates: 685. Freshmen: 232. Federal methodology is used as a basis for awarding need-based institutional aid.

UNDERGRADUATE EXPENSES for 2006–07 ***Application fee:*** $30. ***Comprehensive fee:*** $23,370 includes full-time tuition ($16,820), mandatory fees ($400), and room and board ($6150). Full-time tuition and fees vary according to course load. Room and board charges vary according to board plan and housing facility. ***Part-time tuition:*** $640 per credit hour. ***Part-time fees:*** $25 per term. Part-time tuition and fees vary according to course load. ***Payment plan:*** Installment.

FRESHMAN FINANCIAL AID (Fall 2005) 193 applied for aid; of those 85% were deemed to have need. 100% of freshmen with need received aid; of those 25% had need fully met. ***Average percent of need met:*** 78% (excluding resources awarded to replace EFC). ***Average financial aid package:*** $16,330 (excluding resources awarded to replace EFC). 31% of all full-time freshmen had no need and received non-need-based gift aid.

UNDERGRADUATE FINANCIAL AID (Fall 2005) 525 applied for aid; of those 86% were deemed to have need. 100% of undergraduates with need received aid; of those 30% had need fully met. ***Average percent of need met:*** 80% (excluding resources awarded to replace EFC). ***Average financial aid package:*** $16,300 (excluding resources awarded to replace EFC). 24% of all full-time undergraduates had no need and received non-need-based gift aid.

GIFT AID (NEED-BASED) ***Total amount:*** $3,450,000 (21% federal, 12% state, 64% institutional, 3% external sources). ***Receiving aid:*** Freshmen: 71% (164); All full-time undergraduates: 69% (450). ***Average award:*** Freshmen: $11,800; Undergraduates: $11,300. ***Scholarships, grants, and awards:*** Federal Pell, FSEOG, state, private, college/university gift aid from institutional funds.

GIFT AID (NON-NEED-BASED) ***Total amount:*** $1,385,000 (42% state, 51% institutional, 7% external sources). ***Receiving aid:*** Freshmen: 3% (8); Undergraduates: 5% (32). ***Average award:*** Freshmen: $4400; Undergraduates: $4200. ***Scholarships, grants, and awards by category:*** *Academic Interests/Achievement:* 330 awards ($935,000 total): biological sciences, business, education, English, general academic interests/achievements, health fields, mathematics, physical sciences, premedicine, religion/biblical studies, social sciences. *Creative Arts/Performance:* 80 awards ($145,800 total): art/fine arts, journalism/publications, music, theater/drama. *Special Achievements/Activities:* 100 awards ($75,000 total): cheerleading/drum major, community service, general special achievements/activities, hobbies/interests, leadership. *Special Characteristics:* 500 awards ($1,464,400 total): children of faculty/staff, local/state students, previous college experience, relatives of clergy, religious affiliation, siblings of current students, veterans' children. ***Tuition waivers:*** Full or partial for employees or children of employees, senior citizens.

LOANS ***Student loans:*** $2,793,000 (46% need-based, 54% non-need-based). 68% of past graduating class borrowed through all loan programs. *Average indebtedness per student:* $19,293. ***Average need-based loan:*** Freshmen: $2750; Undergraduates: $4500. ***Parent loans:*** $965,000 (40% need-based, 60% non-need-based). ***Programs:*** FFEL (Subsidized and Unsubsidized Stafford, PLUS), Perkins.

WORK-STUDY ***Federal work-study:*** Total amount: $41,000; 60 jobs averaging $1200. ***State or other work-study/employment:*** Total amount: $75,000 (100% non-need-based). 70 part-time jobs averaging $1100.

ATHLETIC AWARDS Total amount: $938,000 (55% need-based, 45% non-need-based).

APPLYING FOR FINANCIAL AID ***Required financial aid forms:*** FAFSA, state aid form. ***Financial aid deadline (priority):*** 4/15. ***Notification date:*** Continuous beginning 2/1. Students must reply within 4 weeks of notification.

CONTACT Ms. Lisanne J. Masterson, Director of Financial Aid, Brevard College, 1 Brevard College Drive, Brevard, NC 28712, 828-884-8287 or toll-free 800-527-9090. *Fax:* 828-884-3790. *E-mail:* finaid@brevard.edu.

BREWTON-PARKER COLLEGE

Mt. Vernon, GA

ABOUT THE INSTITUTION Independent Southern Baptist, coed. Awards: associate and bachelor's degrees. 31 undergraduate majors. Total enrollment: 1,119. Undergraduates: 1,119. Freshmen: 238.

GIFT AID (NEED-BASED) ***Scholarships, grants, and awards:*** Federal Pell, FSEOG, state, private, college/university gift aid from institutional funds, Georgia Baptist Funds; Ministerial Grants.

GIFT AID (NON-NEED-BASED) ***Scholarships, grants, and awards by category:*** *Academic Interests/Achievement:* biological sciences, business, communication, education, general academic interests/achievements, mathematics, religion/biblical studies. *Creative Arts/Performance:* art/fine arts, journalism/publications, music, theater/drama. *Special Achievements/Activities:* cheerleading/drum major, general special achievements/activities, leadership. *Special Characteristics:* children of faculty/staff, first-generation college students, general special characteristics, international students, local/state students, out-of-state students, relatives of clergy, religious affiliation.

LOANS ***Programs:*** FFEL (Subsidized and Unsubsidized Stafford, PLUS), Perkins.

APPLYING FOR FINANCIAL AID ***Required financial aid forms:*** FAFSA, state aid form.

CONTACT Ms. Rachel Jones, Assistant Director of Financial Aid, Brewton-Parker College, Financial Aid #2018, PO Box 197, Mt. Vernon, GA 30445-0197, 800-342-1087 Ext. 215 or toll-free 800-342-1087 Ext. 245. *Fax:* 912-583-3598. *E-mail:* finaid@bpc.edu.

BRIARCLIFFE COLLEGE

Bethpage, NY

CONTACT Johanna Kelly, Financial Aid Director, Briarcliffe College, 1055 Stewart Avenue, Bethpage, NY 11714, 516-918-3600 or toll-free 888-333-1150 (in-state).

BRIAR CLIFF UNIVERSITY

Sioux City, IA

CONTACT Financial Aid Office, Briar Cliff University, 3303 Rebecca Street, PO Box 2100, Sioux City, IA 51104-2100, 712-279-5200 or toll-free 800-662-3303 Ext. 5200. *Fax:* 712-279-5410.

BRIDGEWATER COLLEGE

Bridgewater, VA

Tuition & fees: $21,490 **Average undergraduate aid package: $18,227**

ABOUT THE INSTITUTION Independent religious, coed. Awards: bachelor's degrees. 34 undergraduate majors. Total enrollment: 1,514. Undergraduates: 1,514. Freshmen: 423. Federal methodology is used as a basis for awarding need-based institutional aid.

UNDERGRADUATE EXPENSES for 2007–08 ***Application fee:*** $30. ***Comprehensive fee:*** $30,800 includes full-time tuition ($21,490) and room and board ($9310). ***College room only:*** $4705. ***Part-time tuition:*** $700 per credit hour. ***Part-time fees:*** $30 per term.

FRESHMAN FINANCIAL AID (Fall 2006, est.) 365 applied for aid; of those 82% were deemed to have need. 100% of freshmen with need received aid; of those 31% had need fully met. ***Average percent of need met:*** 84% (excluding resources awarded to replace EFC). ***Average financial aid package:*** $18,869 (excluding resources awarded to replace EFC). 28% of all full-time freshmen had no need and received non-need-based gift aid.

UNDERGRADUATE FINANCIAL AID (Fall 2006, est.) 1,202 applied for aid; of those 84% were deemed to have need. 100% of undergraduates with need received aid; of those 33% had need fully met. ***Average percent of need met:*** 84% (excluding resources awarded to replace EFC). ***Average financial aid package:*** $18,227 (excluding resources awarded to replace EFC). 31% of all full-time undergraduates had no need and received non-need-based gift aid.

GIFT AID (NEED-BASED) ***Total amount:*** $13,954,984 (7% federal, 16% state, 74% institutional, 3% external sources). ***Receiving aid:*** Freshmen: 70% (298); All full-time undergraduates: 68% (1,012). ***Average award:*** Freshmen: $15,484; Undergraduates: $14,065. ***Scholarships, grants, and awards:*** Federal Pell, FSEOG, state, private, college/university gift aid from institutional funds.

GIFT AID (NON-NEED-BASED) ***Total amount:*** $4,572,555 (20% state, 79% institutional, 1% external sources). ***Receiving aid:*** Freshmen: 70% (297); Undergraduates: 67% (1,001). ***Average award:*** Freshmen: $7850; Undergraduates: $7838. ***Scholarships, grants, and awards by category:*** *Academic Interests/Achievement:* 1,015 awards ($8,523,620 total): general academic interests/achievements. *Creative Arts/Performance:* 36 awards ($32,579 total): music. *Special Characteristics:* 539 awards ($1,345,390 total): ethnic background, international students, out-of-state students, religious affiliation, siblings of current students.

LOANS ***Student loans:*** $7,829,458 (70% need-based, 30% non-need-based). 80% of past graduating class borrowed through all loan programs. *Average indebtedness per student:* $24,601. ***Average need-based loan:*** Freshmen: $4065; Undergraduates: $4840. ***Parent loans:*** $2,720,841 (78% need-based, 22% non-need-based). ***Programs:*** FFEL (Subsidized and Unsubsidized Stafford, PLUS), Perkins, GATE Loans.

WORK-STUDY ***Federal work-study:*** Total amount: $433,175; 390 jobs averaging $1110. ***State or other work-study/employment:*** Total amount: $88,497 (100% non-need-based). 106 part-time jobs averaging $835.

APPLYING FOR FINANCIAL AID ***Required financial aid forms:*** FAFSA, state aid form. ***Financial aid deadline (priority):*** 3/1. ***Notification date:*** Continuous beginning 3/15. Students must reply within 2 weeks of notification.

CONTACT Mr. J. Vern Fairchilds, Director of Financial Aid, Bridgewater College, College Box 27, Bridgewater, VA 22812-1599, 540-828-5376 or toll-free 800-759-8328. *Fax:* 540-828-5671. *E-mail:* vfairchi@bridgewater.edu.

BRIDGEWATER STATE COLLEGE

Bridgewater, MA

Tuition & fees (MA res): $5866 **Average undergraduate aid package: $6465**

ABOUT THE INSTITUTION State-supported, coed. Awards: bachelor's and master's degrees and post-bachelor's and post-master's certificates. 75 undergraduate majors. Total enrollment: 9,655. Undergraduates: 7,825. Freshmen: 1,361. Federal methodology is used as a basis for awarding need-based institutional aid.

UNDERGRADUATE EXPENSES for 2006–07 ***Application fee:*** $25. ***Tuition, state resident:*** full-time $910; part-time $38 per credit hour. ***Tuition, nonresident:*** full-time $7050; part-time $294 per credit hour. ***Required fees:*** full-time $4956; $203 per credit hour. ***College room and board:*** $6852. Room and board charges vary according to board plan and housing facility. ***Payment plan:*** Installment.

FRESHMAN FINANCIAL AID (Fall 2006, est.) 1076 applied for aid; of those 68% were deemed to have need. 98% of freshmen with need received aid. ***Average percent of need met:*** 49% (excluding resources awarded to replace EFC). ***Average financial aid package:*** $6067 (excluding resources awarded to replace EFC). 1% of all full-time freshmen had no need and received non-need-based gift aid.

UNDERGRADUATE FINANCIAL AID (Fall 2006, est.) 4,725 applied for aid; of those 71% were deemed to have need. 98% of undergraduates with need received aid. ***Average percent of need met:*** 56% (excluding resources awarded to replace EFC). ***Average financial aid package:*** $6465 (excluding resources awarded to replace EFC). 1% of all full-time undergraduates had no need and received non-need-based gift aid.

GIFT AID (NEED-BASED) ***Total amount:*** $8,244,698 (44% federal, 37% state, 19% institutional). ***Receiving aid:*** Freshmen: 43% (574); All full-time undergraduates: 40% (2,563). ***Average award:*** Freshmen: $3368; Undergraduates: $3640. ***Scholarships, grants, and awards:*** Federal Pell, FSEOG, state, private, college/university gift aid from institutional funds.

GIFT AID (NON-NEED-BASED) ***Total amount:*** $499,058 (49% state, 51% institutional). ***Receiving aid:*** Freshmen: 6; Undergraduates: 21. ***Average award:*** Freshmen: $5866; Undergraduates: $5280. ***Scholarships, grants, and awards by category:*** *Academic Interests/Achievement:* general academic interests/achievements. ***Tuition waivers:*** Full or partial for employees or children of employees. ***ROTC:*** Army cooperative, Air Force cooperative.

LOANS ***Student loans:*** $27,088,802 (41% need-based, 59% non-need-based). 56% of past graduating class borrowed through all loan programs. *Average indebtedness per student:* $16,634. ***Average need-based loan:*** Freshmen: $2526; Undergraduates: $3285. ***Parent loans:*** $1,858,968 (100% non-need-based). ***Programs:*** Federal Direct (Subsidized and Unsubsidized Stafford, PLUS), Perkins, state.

WORK-STUDY ***Federal work-study:*** Total amount: $575,000; 450 jobs averaging $1275.

APPLYING FOR FINANCIAL AID ***Required financial aid form:*** FAFSA. ***Financial aid deadline (priority):*** 3/1. ***Notification date:*** 3/15.

CONTACT Catherine M. Kedski, Office of Financial Aid, Bridgewater State College, Tillinghast Hall, Bridgewater, MA 02325-0001, 508-531-1341. *Fax:* 508-531-1728. *E-mail:* ckedski@bridgew.edu.

BRIGHAM YOUNG UNIVERSITY

Provo, UT

Tuition & fees: $7680 | **Average undergraduate aid package: $4067**

ABOUT THE INSTITUTION Independent religious, coed. Awards: bachelor's, master's, doctoral, and first professional degrees. 210 undergraduate majors. Total enrollment: 34,185. Undergraduates: 30,480. Freshmen: 4,606. Both federal and institutional methodology are used as a basis for awarding need-based institutional aid.

UNDERGRADUATE EXPENSES for 2007–08 ***Application fee:*** $30. ***Comprehensive fee:*** $14,140 includes full-time tuition ($7680) and room and board ($6460). Latter Day Saints full-time student $3840 per year.

FRESHMAN FINANCIAL AID (Fall 2005) 2303 applied for aid; of those 57% were deemed to have need. 84% of freshmen with need received aid. ***Average percent of need met:*** 22% (excluding resources awarded to replace EFC). ***Average financial aid package:*** $2331 (excluding resources awarded to replace EFC). 37% of all full-time freshmen had no need and received non-need-based gift aid.

UNDERGRADUATE FINANCIAL AID (Fall 2005) 18,140 applied for aid; of those 72% were deemed to have need. 93% of undergraduates with need received aid. ***Average percent of need met:*** 31% (excluding resources awarded to replace EFC). ***Average financial aid package:*** $4067 (excluding resources awarded to replace EFC). 38% of all full-time undergraduates had no need and received non-need-based gift aid.

GIFT AID (NEED-BASED) ***Total amount:*** $32,710,600 (94% federal, 6% institutional). ***Receiving aid:*** Freshmen: 10% (574); All full-time undergraduates: 28% (9,201). ***Average award:*** Freshmen: $1509; Undergraduates: $2364. ***Scholarships, grants, and awards:*** Federal Pell, state, private, college/university gift aid from institutional funds.

GIFT AID (NON-NEED-BASED) ***Total amount:*** $31,360,000 (83% institutional, 17% external sources). ***Receiving aid:*** Freshmen: 11% (611); Undergraduates: 16% (5,409). ***Average award:*** Freshmen: $2348; Undergraduates: $2410. ***Scholarships, grants, and awards by category:*** *Academic Interests/Achievement:* 12,300 awards ($29,653,000 total): agriculture, area/ethnic studies, biological sciences, business, communication, computer science, education, engineering/technologies, English, foreign languages, general academic interests/achievements, health fields, home economics, humanities, international studies, mathematics, military science, physical sciences, premedicine, religion/biblical studies, social sciences. *Creative Arts/Performance:* 380 awards ($376,000 total): applied art and design, art/fine arts, cinema/film/broadcasting, creative writing, dance, journalism/publications, music, performing arts, theater/drama. *Special Achievements/Activities:* cheerleading/drum major, community service, general special achievements/activities, leadership, memberships. *Special Characteristics:* adult students, ethnic background, general special characteristics, handicapped students, international students, local/state students, members of minority groups, out-of-state students, religious affiliation. ***ROTC:*** Army, Air Force.

LOANS ***Student loans:*** $30,830,449 (71% need-based, 29% non-need-based). 30% of past graduating class borrowed through all loan programs. *Average indebtedness per student:* $13,714. ***Average need-based loan:*** Freshmen: $822; Undergraduates: $1703. ***Parent loans:*** $2,193,248 (100% non-need-based). ***Programs:*** FFEL (Subsidized and Unsubsidized Stafford, PLUS), college/university.

WORK-STUDY ***State or other work-study/employment:*** Total amount: $180,000 (100% need-based). 74 part-time jobs averaging $2400.

ATHLETIC AWARDS Total amount: $3,105,922 (100% non-need-based).

APPLYING FOR FINANCIAL AID ***Required financial aid form:*** FAFSA. ***Financial aid deadline (priority):*** 4/20. ***Notification date:*** Continuous beginning 4/1.

CONTACT Paul R. Conrad, Director of Financial Aid, Brigham Young University, A-41 ASB, Provo, UT 84602, 801-422-7355. *Fax:* 801-422-0234. *E-mail:* paul_conrad@byu.edu.

BRIGHAM YOUNG UNIVERSITY–HAWAII

Laie, HI

Tuition & fees: $3040 | **Average undergraduate aid package: $11,000**

ABOUT THE INSTITUTION Independent Latter-day Saints, coed. Awards: associate and bachelor's degrees and post-bachelor's certificates. 51 undergraduate majors. Total enrollment: 2,473. Undergraduates: 2,473. Freshmen: 221. Institutional methodology is used as a basis for awarding need-based institutional aid.

UNDERGRADUATE EXPENSES for 2006–07 ***Application fee:*** $30. ***Comprehensive fee:*** $8210 includes full-time tuition ($3040) and room and board ($5170). Full-time tuition and fees vary according to course load. Room and board charges vary according to board plan and housing facility. ***Part-time tuition:*** $190 per credit. ***Payment plan:*** Installment.

FRESHMAN FINANCIAL AID (Fall 2006, est.) 185 applied for aid; of those 92% were deemed to have need. 96% of freshmen with need received aid; of those 55% had need fully met. ***Average percent of need met:*** 75% (excluding resources awarded to replace EFC). ***Average financial aid package:*** $4200 (excluding resources awarded to replace EFC). 33% of all full-time freshmen had no need and received non-need-based gift aid.

UNDERGRADUATE FINANCIAL AID (Fall 2006, est.) 2,230 applied for aid; of those 98% were deemed to have need. 91% of undergraduates with need received aid; of those 70% had need fully met. ***Average percent of need met:*** 75% (excluding resources awarded to replace EFC). ***Average financial aid package:*** $11,000 (excluding resources awarded to replace EFC). 7% of all full-time undergraduates had no need and received non-need-based gift aid.

GIFT AID (NEED-BASED) ***Total amount:*** $2,992,000 (58% federal, 27% institutional, 15% external sources). ***Receiving aid:*** Freshmen: 71% (150); All full-time undergraduates: 62% (1,400). ***Average award:*** Freshmen: $3500; Undergraduates: $5200. ***Scholarships, grants, and awards:*** Federal Pell, state, private, college/university gift aid from institutional funds.

GIFT AID (NON-NEED-BASED) ***Total amount:*** $1,620,000 (99% institutional, 1% external sources). ***Receiving aid:*** Freshmen: 19% (40); Undergraduates: 40% (900). ***Average award:*** Freshmen: $1500; Undergraduates: $1400. ***Scholarships, grants, and awards by category:*** *Academic Interests/Achievement:* area/ethnic studies, biological sciences, business, communication, computer science, education, English, foreign languages, general academic interests/achievements, humanities, international studies, mathematics, physical sciences, religion/biblical studies, social sciences. *Creative Arts/Performance:* art/fine arts, creative writing, journalism/publications, music, theater/drama. *Special Achievements/Activities:* cheerleading/drum major, community service, general special achievements/activities, junior miss, leadership, religious involvement. *Special Characteristics:* children and siblings of alumni, children of educators, children of faculty/staff, ethnic background, international students, local/state students, married students, members of minority groups, religious affiliation, veterans. ***Tuition waivers:*** Full or partial for employees or children of employees. ***ROTC:*** Army cooperative, Naval cooperative, Air Force cooperative.

LOANS ***Student loans:*** $1,974,000 (95% need-based, 5% non-need-based). 36% of past graduating class borrowed through all loan programs. *Average indebtedness per student:* $12,418. ***Average need-based loan:*** Freshmen: $2280;

Undergraduates: $3700. ***Parent loans:*** $40,000 (100% non-need-based). ***Programs:*** FFEL (Subsidized and Unsubsidized Stafford, PLUS), college/university.

WORK-STUDY ***State or other work-study/employment:*** Total amount: $9,857,000 (52% need-based, 48% non-need-based). Part-time jobs available.

ATHLETIC AWARDS Total amount: $496,000 (74% need-based, 26% non-need-based).

APPLYING FOR FINANCIAL AID ***Required financial aid form:*** FAFSA. ***Financial aid deadline:*** 3/31 (priority: 3/1). ***Notification date:*** Continuous beginning 6/30.

CONTACT Mr. Wes Duke, Director of Financial Aid, Brigham Young University–Hawaii, BYUH #1980, 55-220 Kulanui Street, Laie, HI 96762, 808-293-3530. *Fax:* 808-293-3349. *E-mail:* duekw@byuh.edu.

BROOKLYN COLLEGE OF THE CITY UNIVERSITY OF NEW YORK

Brooklyn, NY

CONTACT Sherwood Johnson, Director of Financial Aid, Brooklyn College of the City University of New York, 2900 Bedford Avenue, Brooklyn, NY 11210-2889, 718-951-5045. *Fax:* 718-951-4778. *E-mail:* sjohnson@brooklyn.cuny.edu.

BROOKS INSTITUTE OF PHOTOGRAPHY

Santa Barbara, CA

CONTACT Stacy Eymann, Brooks Institute of Photography, 801 Alston Road, Santa Barbara, CA 93108, 805-966-3888 or toll-free 888-304-3456 (out-of-state). *Fax:* 805-966-2909. *E-mail:* stacey.eymann@brooks.edu.

BROWN MACKIE COLLEGE–SAN DIEGO

San Diego, CA

See Argosy University, San Diego.

BROWN UNIVERSITY

Providence, RI

CONTACT Susan Farnum, Director of Financial Aid, Brown University, Box 1827, Providence, RI 02912, 401-863-2721. *Fax:* 401-863-7575. *E-mail:* susan_farnum@brown.edu.

BRYAN COLLEGE

Dayton, TN

Tuition & fees: $16,320 **Average undergraduate aid package: $12,203**

ABOUT THE INSTITUTION Independent interdenominational, coed. Awards: associate and bachelor's degrees. 39 undergraduate majors. Total enrollment: 920. Undergraduates: 906. Both federal and institutional methodology are used as a basis for awarding need-based institutional aid.

UNDERGRADUATE EXPENSES for 2007–08 ***Application fee:*** $30. ***Comprehensive fee:*** $20,860 includes full-time tuition ($16,200), mandatory fees ($120), and room and board ($4540).

FRESHMAN FINANCIAL AID (Fall 2006, est.) 158 applied for aid; of those 100% were deemed to have need. 100% of freshmen with need received aid; of those 44% had need fully met. ***Average percent of need met:*** 71% (excluding resources awarded to replace EFC). ***Average financial aid package:*** $14,284 (excluding resources awarded to replace EFC). 20% of all full-time freshmen had no need and received non-need-based gift aid.

UNDERGRADUATE FINANCIAL AID (Fall 2006, est.) 687 applied for aid; of those 100% were deemed to have need. 100% of undergraduates with need received aid; of those 34% had need fully met. ***Average percent of need met:*** 67% (excluding resources awarded to replace EFC). ***Average financial aid package:*** $12,203 (excluding resources awarded to replace EFC). 13% of all full-time undergraduates had no need and received non-need-based gift aid.

GIFT AID (NEED-BASED) ***Total amount:*** $3,524,096 (25% federal, 25% state, 45% institutional, 5% external sources). ***Receiving aid:*** Freshmen: 56% (110); All full-time undergraduates: 34% (293). ***Average award:*** Freshmen: $4671; Undergraduates: $4052. ***Scholarships, grants, and awards:*** Federal Pell, FSEOG, state, private, college/university gift aid from institutional funds.

GIFT AID (NON-NEED-BASED) ***Total amount:*** $696,361 (15% state, 81% institutional, 4% external sources). ***Receiving aid:*** Freshmen: 76% (150); Undergraduates: 60% (523). ***Average award:*** Freshmen: $6580; Undergraduates: $7356. ***Scholarships, grants, and awards by category:*** *Academic Interests/Achievement:* 332 awards ($926,750 total): biological sciences, business, communication, computer science, education, English, foreign languages, general academic interests/achievements, humanities, mathematics, physical sciences, premedicine, religion/biblical studies, social sciences. *Creative Arts/Performance:* 41 awards ($37,950 total): art/fine arts, journalism/publications, music, performing arts, theater/drama. *Special Achievements/Activities:* 63 awards ($51,551 total): cheerleading/drum major, community service, general special achievements/activities, leadership, religious involvement. *Special Characteristics:* 144 awards ($797,789 total): children and siblings of alumni, children of current students, children of educators, children of faculty/staff, general special characteristics, handicapped students, international students, local/state students, relatives of clergy, religious affiliation, spouses of current students.

LOANS ***Student loans:*** $3,227,196 (92% need-based, 8% non-need-based). 63% of past graduating class borrowed through all loan programs. *Average indebtedness per student:* $12,588. ***Average need-based loan:*** Freshmen: $4411; Undergraduates: $4183. ***Parent loans:*** $909,489 (83% need-based, 17% non-need-based). ***Programs:*** FFEL (Subsidized and Unsubsidized Stafford, PLUS), Perkins, state, college/university.

WORK-STUDY ***Federal work-study:*** Total amount: $339,629; 183 jobs averaging $1500.

ATHLETIC AWARDS Total amount: $770,434 (63% need-based, 37% non-need-based).

APPLYING FOR FINANCIAL AID ***Required financial aid forms:*** FAFSA, institution's own form. ***Financial aid deadline (priority):*** 2/15. ***Notification date:*** Continuous beginning 1/1. Students must reply within 2 weeks of notification.

CONTACT Michael Sapienza, Director of Financial Aid, Bryan College, PO Box 7000, Dayton, TN 37321-7000, 423-775-7339 or toll-free 800-277-9522. *Fax:* 423-775-7300. *E-mail:* finaid@bryan.edu.

BRYANT AND STRATTON COLLEGE

Cleveland, OH

CONTACT Bill Davenport, Financial Aid Supervisor, Bryant and Stratton College, 1700 East 13th Street, Cleveland, OH 44114-3203, 216-771-1700. *Fax:* 216-771-7787.

BRYANT AND STRATTON COLLEGE, WAUWATOSA CAMPUS

Wauwatosa, WI

CONTACT Financial Aid Office, Bryant and Stratton College, Wauwatosa Campus, 10950 W. Potter Road, Wauwatosa, WI 53226, 414-302-7000.

BRYANT UNIVERSITY

Smithfield, RI

Tuition & fees: $27,639 **Average undergraduate aid package: $15,707**

ABOUT THE INSTITUTION Independent, coed. Awards: bachelor's and master's degrees and post-master's certificates. 16 undergraduate majors. Total enrollment: 3,651. Undergraduates: 3,268. Freshmen: 810. Federal methodology is used as a basis for awarding need-based institutional aid.

UNDERGRADUATE EXPENSES for 2007–08 ***Application fee:*** $50. ***Comprehensive fee:*** $38,354 includes full-time tuition ($27,639) and room and board ($10,715). ***College room only:*** $6414. ***Part-time tuition:*** $987 per course.

FRESHMAN FINANCIAL AID (Fall 2006, est.) 635 applied for aid; of those 86% were deemed to have need. 100% of freshmen with need received aid; of those 16% had need fully met. ***Average percent of need met:*** 74% (excluding resources awarded to replace EFC). ***Average financial aid package:*** $16,731 (excluding resources awarded to replace EFC). 14% of all full-time freshmen had no need and received non-need-based gift aid.

UNDERGRADUATE FINANCIAL AID (Fall 2006, est.) 2,298 applied for aid; of those 91% were deemed to have need. 100% of undergraduates with need

received aid; of those 11% had need fully met. ***Average percent of need met:*** 73% (excluding resources awarded to replace EFC). ***Average financial aid package:*** $15,707 (excluding resources awarded to replace EFC). 11% of all full-time undergraduates had no need and received non-need-based gift aid.

GIFT AID (NEED-BASED) ***Total amount:*** $16,095,754 (7% federal, 3% state, 87% institutional, 3% external sources). ***Receiving aid:*** Freshmen: 57% (457); All full-time undergraduates: 55% (1,703). ***Average award:*** Freshmen: $10,446; Undergraduates: $9606. ***Scholarships, grants, and awards:*** Federal Pell, FSEOG, state, private, college/university gift aid from institutional funds.

GIFT AID (NON-NEED-BASED) ***Total amount:*** $11,312,623 (96% institutional, 4% external sources). ***Receiving aid:*** Freshmen: 40% (324); Undergraduates: 32% (993). ***Average award:*** Freshmen: $12,188; Undergraduates: $11,104. ***Scholarships, grants, and awards by category:*** *Academic Interests/Achievement:* 797 awards ($7,562,497 total): engineering/technologies, general academic interests/achievements. *Special Characteristics:* 150 awards ($1,583,894 total): children and siblings of alumni, local/state students, members of minority groups, siblings of current students. ***ROTC:*** Army.

LOANS ***Student loans:*** $21,666,780 (45% need-based, 55% non-need-based). 48% of past graduating class borrowed through all loan programs. *Average indebtedness per student:* $29,128. ***Average need-based loan:*** Freshmen: $3988; Undergraduates: $4120. ***Parent loans:*** $6,691,738 (11% need-based, 89% non-need-based). ***Programs:*** Federal Direct (Subsidized and Unsubsidized Stafford), FFEL (PLUS), Perkins, alternative loans.

WORK-STUDY ***Federal work-study:*** Total amount: $400,246; 431 jobs averaging $1168. ***State or other work-study/employment:*** Total amount: $793,749 (17% need-based, 83% non-need-based). 1,149 part-time jobs averaging $1534.

ATHLETIC AWARDS Total amount: $1,756,490 (53% need-based, 47% non-need-based).

APPLYING FOR FINANCIAL AID ***Required financial aid form:*** FAFSA. ***Financial aid deadline (priority):*** 2/15. ***Notification date:*** 3/24. Students must reply by 5/1.

CONTACT Mr. John B. Canning, Director of Financial Aid, Bryant University, Office of Financial Aid, 1150 Douglas Pike, Smithfield, RI 02917-1284, 401-232-6020 or toll-free 800-622-7001. *Fax:* 401-232-6293. *E-mail:* jcanning@bryant.edu.

BRYN ATHYN COLLEGE OF THE NEW CHURCH

Bryn Athyn, PA

CONTACT Les Alden, Business Manager, Bryn Athyn College of the New Church, Box 711, Bryn Athyn, PA 19009, 215-938-2635. *Fax:* 215-938-2616. *E-mail:* wlalden@newchurch.edu.

BRYN MAWR COLLEGE

Bryn Mawr, PA

Tuition & fees: $33,010 **Average undergraduate aid package: $29,169**

ABOUT THE INSTITUTION Independent, undergraduate: women only; graduate: coed. Awards: bachelor's, master's, and doctoral degrees and post-bachelor's certificates. 33 undergraduate majors. Total enrollment: 1,799. Undergraduates: 1,378. Freshmen: 358. Both federal and institutional methodology are used as a basis for awarding need-based institutional aid.

UNDERGRADUATE EXPENSES for 2006–07 ***Application fee:*** $50. ***Comprehensive fee:*** $43,560 includes full-time tuition ($32,230), mandatory fees ($780), and room and board ($10,550). ***College room only:*** $6030. ***Part-time tuition:*** $3990 per course.

FRESHMAN FINANCIAL AID (Fall 2006, est.) 267 applied for aid; of those 74% were deemed to have need. 100% of freshmen with need received aid; of those 100% had need fully met. ***Average percent of need met:*** 100% (excluding resources awarded to replace EFC). ***Average financial aid package:*** $26,815 (excluding resources awarded to replace EFC). 1% of all full-time freshmen had no need and received non-need-based gift aid.

UNDERGRADUATE FINANCIAL AID (Fall 2006, est.) 855 applied for aid; of those 83% were deemed to have need. 100% of undergraduates with need received aid; of those 100% had need fully met. ***Average percent of need met:*** 100% (excluding resources awarded to replace EFC). ***Average financial aid package:*** $29,169 (excluding resources awarded to replace EFC). 2% of all full-time undergraduates had no need and received non-need-based gift aid.

GIFT AID (NEED-BASED) ***Total amount:*** $17,442,577 (4% federal, 2% state, 92% institutional, 2% external sources). ***Receiving aid:*** Freshmen: 55% (198); All full-time undergraduates: 56% (706). ***Average award:*** Freshmen: $24,641; Undergraduates: $24,179. ***Scholarships, grants, and awards:*** Federal Pell, FSEOG, state, college/university gift aid from institutional funds.

GIFT AID (NON-NEED-BASED) ***Total amount:*** $445,361 (3% federal, 71% institutional, 26% external sources). ***Receiving aid:*** Freshmen: 3% (10); Undergraduates: 3% (43). ***Average award:*** Freshmen: $13,800; Undergraduates: $11,302. ***ROTC:*** Air Force cooperative.

LOANS ***Student loans:*** $3,797,555 (71% need-based, 29% non-need-based). 56% of past graduating class borrowed through all loan programs. *Average indebtedness per student:* $18,787. ***Average need-based loan:*** Freshmen: $3838; Undergraduates: $4817. ***Parent loans:*** $3,507,891 (100% non-need-based). ***Programs:*** FFEL (Subsidized and Unsubsidized Stafford, PLUS), Perkins.

WORK-STUDY ***Federal work-study:*** Total amount: $1,084,300; 610 jobs averaging $1849. ***State or other work-study/employment:*** Total amount: $171,591 (100% need-based). 73 part-time jobs averaging $1872.

APPLYING FOR FINANCIAL AID ***Required financial aid forms:*** FAFSA, CSS Financial Aid PROFILE, business/farm supplement, income tax form(s) student and parent tax returns. ***Financial aid deadline:*** 3/1. ***Notification date:*** 3/23. Students must reply by 5/1.

CONTACT Ethel M. Desmarais, Director of Financial Aid, Bryn Mawr College, 101 North Merion Avenue, Bryn Mawr, PA 19010-2899, 610-526-7922 or toll-free 800-BMC-1885 (out-of-state). *Fax:* 610-526-5249. *E-mail:* edesmara@brynmawr.edu.

BUCKNELL UNIVERSITY

Lewisburg, PA

Tuition & fees: $38,134 **Average undergraduate aid package: $23,400**

ABOUT THE INSTITUTION Independent, coed. Awards: bachelor's and master's degrees. 54 undergraduate majors. Total enrollment: 3,706. Undergraduates: 3,550. Freshmen: 923. Both federal and institutional methodology are used as a basis for awarding need-based institutional aid.

UNDERGRADUATE EXPENSES for 2007–08 ***Application fee:*** $60. ***Comprehensive fee:*** $46,186 includes full-time tuition ($37,934), mandatory fees ($200), and room and board ($8052). ***College room only:*** $4452.

FRESHMAN FINANCIAL AID (Fall 2006, est.) 529 applied for aid; of those 80% were deemed to have need. 100% of freshmen with need received aid; of those 100% had need fully met. ***Average percent of need met:*** 100% (excluding resources awarded to replace EFC). ***Average financial aid package:*** $24,500 (excluding resources awarded to replace EFC). 3% of all full-time freshmen had no need and received non-need-based gift aid.

UNDERGRADUATE FINANCIAL AID (Fall 2006, est.) 2,037 applied for aid; of those 83% were deemed to have need. 100% of undergraduates with need received aid; of those 100% had need fully met. ***Average percent of need met:*** 100% (excluding resources awarded to replace EFC). ***Average financial aid package:*** $23,400 (excluding resources awarded to replace EFC). 1% of all full-time undergraduates had no need and received non-need-based gift aid.

GIFT AID (NEED-BASED) ***Total amount:*** $34,232,450 (4% federal, 4% state, 89% institutional, 3% external sources). ***Receiving aid:*** Freshmen: 46% (421); All full-time undergraduates: 48% (1,686). ***Average award:*** Freshmen: $20,200; Undergraduates: $19,200. ***Scholarships, grants, and awards:*** Federal Pell, FSEOG, state, private, college/university gift aid from institutional funds.

GIFT AID (NON-NEED-BASED) ***Total amount:*** $1,008,400 (100% institutional). ***Receiving aid:*** Freshmen: 2% (22); Undergraduates: 2% (63). ***Average award:*** Freshmen: $11,408; Undergraduates: $13,837. ***Scholarships, grants, and awards by category:*** *Academic Interests/Achievement:* 27 awards ($279,500 total): business, engineering/technologies, general academic interests/achievements, physical sciences. *Creative Arts/Performance:* 53 awards ($331,000 total): art/fine arts, creative writing, dance, music, performing arts, theater/drama. *Special Achievements/Activities:* 25 awards ($886,107 total): general special achievements/activities, leadership. ***ROTC:*** Army.

LOANS ***Student loans:*** $11,500,000 (100% need-based). 65% of past graduating class borrowed through all loan programs. *Average indebtedness per student:* $17,500. ***Average need-based loan:*** Freshmen: $4200; Undergraduates: $5400. ***Parent loans:*** $7,302,300 (100% non-need-based). ***Programs:*** FFEL (Subsidized and Unsubsidized Stafford, PLUS), Perkins.

WORK-STUDY ***Federal work-study:*** Total amount: $1,309,000; 873 jobs averaging $1800. ***State or other work-study/employment:*** Total amount: $80,000 (100% need-based). 55 part-time jobs averaging $1500.

ATHLETIC AWARDS Total amount: $210,000 (100% non-need-based).

APPLYING FOR FINANCIAL AID ***Required financial aid forms:*** FAFSA, CSS Financial Aid PROFILE, noncustodial (divorced/separated) parent's statement. ***Financial aid deadline:*** 1/1. ***Notification date:*** 4/1. Students must reply by 5/1.

CONTACT Andrea Leithner, Director of Financial Aid, Bucknell University, Office of Financial Aid, Lewisburg, PA 17837, 570-577-1331. *Fax:* 570-577-1481. *E-mail:* finaid@bucknell.edu.

BUENA VISTA UNIVERSITY

Storm Lake, IA

Tuition & fees: $22,556 **Average undergraduate aid package: $22,457**

ABOUT THE INSTITUTION Independent religious, coed. Awards: bachelor's and master's degrees. 58 undergraduate majors. Total enrollment: 1,229. Undergraduates: 1,149. Freshmen: 266. Federal methodology is used as a basis for awarding need-based institutional aid.

UNDERGRADUATE EXPENSES for 2006–07 ***Application fee:*** $25. ***Comprehensive fee:*** $28,852 includes full-time tuition ($22,556) and room and board ($6296). Room and board charges vary according to board plan. ***Part-time tuition:*** $758 per semester hour.

FRESHMAN FINANCIAL AID (Fall 2006, est.) 255 applied for aid; of those 95% were deemed to have need. 100% of freshmen with need received aid; of those 24% had need fully met. ***Average percent of need met:*** 93% (excluding resources awarded to replace EFC). ***Average financial aid package:*** $23,280 (excluding resources awarded to replace EFC). 5% of all full-time freshmen had no need and received non-need-based gift aid.

UNDERGRADUATE FINANCIAL AID (Fall 2006, est.) 1,081 applied for aid; of those 95% were deemed to have need. 100% of undergraduates with need received aid; of those 31% had need fully met. ***Average percent of need met:*** 99% (excluding resources awarded to replace EFC). ***Average financial aid package:*** $22,457 (excluding resources awarded to replace EFC). 5% of all full-time undergraduates had no need and received non-need-based gift aid.

GIFT AID (NEED-BASED) ***Total amount:*** $10,974,215 (15% federal, 23% state, 62% institutional). ***Receiving aid:*** Freshmen: 89% (238); All full-time undergraduates: 91% (1,019). ***Average award:*** Freshmen: $10,089; Undergraduates: $9852. ***Scholarships, grants, and awards:*** Federal Pell, FSEOG, state, private, college/university gift aid from institutional funds.

GIFT AID (NON-NEED-BASED) ***Total amount:*** $4,728,907 (93% institutional, 7% external sources). ***Receiving aid:*** Freshmen: 55% (147); Undergraduates: 54% (601). ***Average award:*** Freshmen: $8671; Undergraduates: $7375. ***Scholarships, grants, and awards by category:*** *Academic Interests/Achievement:* 728 awards ($5,504,780 total): biological sciences, business, computer science, education, general academic interests/achievements, humanities, international studies, mathematics. *Creative Arts/Performance:* 85 awards ($119,077 total): art/fine arts, music, theater/drama. *Special Achievements/Activities:* 132 awards ($749,148 total): general special achievements/activities, leadership. *Special Characteristics:* 276 awards ($757,694 total): children of faculty/staff, ethnic background, international students, out-of-state students, religious affiliation, siblings of current students. ***Tuition waivers:*** Full or partial for employees or children of employees.

LOANS ***Student loans:*** $5,481,927 (78% need-based, 22% non-need-based). 94% of past graduating class borrowed through all loan programs. *Average indebtedness per student:* $29,578. ***Average need-based loan:*** Freshmen: $4078; Undergraduates: $4325. ***Programs:*** FFEL (Subsidized and Unsubsidized Stafford, PLUS), Perkins, college/university.

WORK-STUDY ***Federal work-study:*** Total amount: $667,424; 590 jobs averaging $1097. ***State or other work-study/employment:*** Total amount: $140,175 (100% non-need-based). 145 part-time jobs averaging $977.

APPLYING FOR FINANCIAL AID ***Required financial aid form:*** FAFSA. ***Financial aid deadline (priority):*** 6/1. ***Notification date:*** Continuous beginning 3/5. Students must reply by 5/1 or within 2 weeks of notification.

CONTACT Mrs. Leanne Valentine, Director of Financial Assistance, Buena Vista University, 610 West Fourth Street, Storm Lake, IA 50588, 712-749-2164 or toll-free 800-383-9600. *Fax:* 712-749-1451. *E-mail:* valentinel@bvu.edu.

BUFFALO STATE COLLEGE, STATE UNIVERSITY OF NEW YORK

Buffalo, NY

CONTACT Mr. Kent McGowan, Director of Financial Aid, Buffalo State College, State University of New York, 1300 Elmwood Avenue, Buffalo, NY 14222-1095, 716-878-4902. *Fax:* 716-878-4903.

BURLINGTON COLLEGE

Burlington, VT

Tuition & fees: $15,760 **Average undergraduate aid package: $10,029**

ABOUT THE INSTITUTION Independent, coed. Awards: associate and bachelor's degrees. 19 undergraduate majors. Total enrollment: 168. Undergraduates: 168. Freshmen: 19. Federal methodology is used as a basis for awarding need-based institutional aid.

UNDERGRADUATE EXPENSES for 2006–07 ***Application fee:*** $50. ***Tuition:*** full-time $15,760; part-time $515 per credit hour.

FRESHMAN FINANCIAL AID (Fall 2006, est.) 9 applied for aid; of those 67% were deemed to have need. 100% of freshmen with need received aid. ***Average percent of need met:*** 34% (excluding resources awarded to replace EFC). ***Average financial aid package:*** $7816 (excluding resources awarded to replace EFC). 20% of all full-time freshmen had no need and received non-need-based gift aid.

UNDERGRADUATE FINANCIAL AID (Fall 2006, est.) 77 applied for aid; of those 94% were deemed to have need. 99% of undergraduates with need received aid; of those 6% had need fully met. ***Average percent of need met:*** 48% (excluding resources awarded to replace EFC). ***Average financial aid package:*** $10,029 (excluding resources awarded to replace EFC). 5% of all full-time undergraduates had no need and received non-need-based gift aid.

GIFT AID (NEED-BASED) ***Total amount:*** $426,126 (51% federal, 44% state, 2% institutional, 3% external sources). ***Receiving aid:*** Freshmen: 20% (3); All full-time undergraduates: 52% (50). ***Average award:*** Freshmen: $6883; Undergraduates: $5640. ***Scholarships, grants, and awards:*** Federal Pell, FSEOG, state, private, college/university gift aid from institutional funds.

GIFT AID (NON-NEED-BASED) ***Total amount:*** $11,650 (13% institutional, 87% external sources). ***Average award:*** Freshmen: $2950; Undergraduates: $3570. ***Scholarships, grants, and awards by category:*** *Special Achievements/Activities:* general special achievements/activities.

LOANS ***Student loans:*** $953,403 (93% need-based, 7% non-need-based). 85% of past graduating class borrowed through all loan programs. *Average indebtedness per student:* $40,153. ***Average need-based loan:*** Freshmen: $3625; Undergraduates: $5590. ***Parent loans:*** $161,998 (55% need-based, 45% non-need-based). ***Programs:*** FFEL (Subsidized and Unsubsidized Stafford, PLUS), Perkins.

WORK-STUDY ***Federal work-study:*** Total amount: $61,584; 50 jobs averaging $1247.

APPLYING FOR FINANCIAL AID ***Required financial aid form:*** FAFSA. ***Financial aid deadline:*** Continuous. ***Notification date:*** Continuous beginning 4/1. Students must reply within 4 weeks of notification.

CONTACT Ms. Yvonne Whitaker, Office of Financial Aid Services, Burlington College, PO Box 2000, Winooski, VT 05404, 877-685-7787 or toll-free 800-862-9616. *Fax:* 802-654-3765. *E-mail:* bc@vsac.org.

BUTLER UNIVERSITY

Indianapolis, IN

Tuition & fees: $25,414 **Average undergraduate aid package: $18,743**

ABOUT THE INSTITUTION Independent, coed. Awards: bachelor's, master's, and first professional degrees. 52 undergraduate majors. Total enrollment: 4,437. Undergraduates: 3,652. Freshmen: 965. Federal methodology is used as a basis for awarding need-based institutional aid.

UNDERGRADUATE EXPENSES for 2006–07 ***Application fee:*** $35. ***Comprehensive fee:*** $33,944 includes full-time tuition ($24,710), mandatory fees ($704), and room and board ($8530). ***College room only:*** $4180. Full-time tuition and fees vary according to program. Room and board charges vary according to housing facility. ***Part-time tuition:*** $1030 per credit. Part-time tuition and fees vary according to program. ***Payment plan:*** Installment.

FRESHMAN FINANCIAL AID (Fall 2006, est.) 909 applied for aid; of those 70% were deemed to have need. 100% of freshmen with need received aid; of those 24% had need fully met. ***Average financial aid package:*** $20,264 (excluding resources awarded to replace EFC). 23% of all full-time freshmen had no need and received non-need-based gift aid.

UNDERGRADUATE FINANCIAL AID (Fall 2006, est.) 3,527 applied for aid; of those 69% were deemed to have need. 100% of undergraduates with need received aid; of those 19% had need fully met. ***Average financial aid package:*** $18,743 (excluding resources awarded to replace EFC). 24% of all full-time undergraduates had no need and received non-need-based gift aid.

GIFT AID (NEED-BASED) ***Total amount:*** $30,455,111 (5% federal, 11% state, 76% institutional, 8% external sources). ***Receiving aid:*** Freshmen: 62% (601); All full-time undergraduates: 61% (2,367). ***Average award:*** Freshmen: $15,348; Undergraduates: $13,520. ***Scholarships, grants, and awards:*** Federal Pell, FSEOG, state, private, college/university gift aid from institutional funds.

GIFT AID (NON-NEED-BASED) ***Total amount:*** $11,969,598 (77% institutional, 23% external sources). ***Receiving aid:*** Freshmen: 14% (134); Undergraduates: 11% (413). ***Average award:*** Freshmen: $11,663; Undergraduates: $10,467. ***Scholarships, grants, and awards by category:*** *Academic Interests/Achievement:* biological sciences, business, communication, computer science, education, engineering/technologies, English, foreign languages, general academic interests/achievements, humanities, international studies, mathematics, physical sciences, social sciences. *Creative Arts/Performance:* art/fine arts, cinema/film/broadcasting, dance, music, theater/drama. ***Tuition waivers:*** Full or partial for employees or children of employees. ***ROTC:*** Army, Air Force cooperative.

LOANS ***Student loans:*** $21,039,430 (82% need-based, 18% non-need-based). 62% of past graduating class borrowed through all loan programs. ***Average need-based loan:*** Freshmen: $4563; Undergraduates: $5920. ***Parent loans:*** $4,428,415 (18% need-based, 82% non-need-based). ***Programs:*** FFEL (Subsidized and Unsubsidized Stafford, PLUS), Perkins.

WORK-STUDY ***Federal work-study:*** Total amount: $241,000; jobs available. ***State or other work-study/employment:*** Part-time jobs available.

ATHLETIC AWARDS Total amount: $3,041,526 (27% need-based, 73% non-need-based).

APPLYING FOR FINANCIAL AID ***Required financial aid form:*** FAFSA. ***Financial aid deadline (priority):*** 3/1. ***Notification date:*** 3/15. Students must reply within 3 weeks of notification.

CONTACT Ms. Kristine Butz, Associate Director of Financial Aid, Butler University, 4600 Sunset Avenue, Indianapolis, IN 46208-3485, 317-940-8200 or toll-free 888-940-8100. *Fax:* 317-940-8250. *E-mail:* kbutz@butler.edu.

CABARRUS COLLEGE OF HEALTH SCIENCES

Concord, NC

Tuition & fees: $7700 **Average undergraduate aid package: N/A**

ABOUT THE INSTITUTION Independent, coed, primarily women. Awards: associate and bachelor's degrees. 6 undergraduate majors. Total enrollment: 334. Undergraduates: 334. Freshmen: 34. Federal methodology is used as a basis for awarding need-based institutional aid.

UNDERGRADUATE EXPENSES for 2006–07 ***Application fee:*** $35. ***Tuition:*** full-time $7700; part-time $250 per hour. Full-time tuition and fees vary according to course load.

GIFT AID (NEED-BASED) ***Total amount:*** $542,029 (39% federal, 42% state, 2% institutional, 17% external sources). ***Scholarships, grants, and awards:*** Federal Pell, FSEOG, state, private, college/university gift aid from institutional funds.

GIFT AID (NON-NEED-BASED) ***Total amount:*** $367,034 (77% state, 2% institutional, 21% external sources). ***Scholarships, grants, and awards by category:*** *Special Characteristics:* ethnic background, first-generation college students.

LOANS ***Student loans:*** $753,806 (42% need-based, 58% non-need-based). ***Parent loans:*** $35,098 (100% need-based). ***Programs:*** FFEL (Subsidized and Unsubsidized Stafford, PLUS), state.

WORK-STUDY ***Federal work-study:*** Total amount: $13,280; 20 jobs available. ***State or other work-study/employment:*** Total amount: $45,711 (7% need-based, 93% non-need-based).

APPLYING FOR FINANCIAL AID ***Required financial aid form:*** FAFSA. ***Financial aid deadline (priority):*** 4/15. ***Notification date:*** Continuous beginning 7/1. Students must reply within 2 weeks of notification.

CONTACT Valerie Richard, Director of Financial Aid, Cabarrus College of Health Sciences, 401 Medical Park Drive, Concord, NC 28025, 704-783-3507. *Fax:* 704-783-2077. *E-mail:* vrichard@northeastmedical.org.

CABRINI COLLEGE

Radnor, PA

Tuition & fees: $25,950 **Average undergraduate aid package: $17,029**

ABOUT THE INSTITUTION Independent Roman Catholic, coed. Awards: bachelor's and master's degrees and post-bachelor's certificates. 38 undergraduate majors. Total enrollment: 2,389. Undergraduates: 1,814. Freshmen: 530. Federal methodology is used as a basis for awarding need-based institutional aid.

UNDERGRADUATE EXPENSES for 2006–07 ***Application fee:*** $35. ***Comprehensive fee:*** $35,850 includes full-time tuition ($25,120), mandatory fees ($830), and room and board ($9900). Full-time tuition and fees vary according to location. Room and board charges vary according to board plan and housing facility. ***Part-time tuition:*** $410 per credit hour. ***Part-time fees:*** $45 per term. Part-time tuition and fees vary according to course load. ***Payment plan:*** Installment.

FRESHMAN FINANCIAL AID (Fall 2006, est.) 446 applied for aid; of those 86% were deemed to have need. 100% of freshmen with need received aid; of those 16% had need fully met. ***Average percent of need met:*** 71% (excluding resources awarded to replace EFC). ***Average financial aid package:*** $18,023 (excluding resources awarded to replace EFC). 26% of all full-time freshmen had no need and received non-need-based gift aid.

UNDERGRADUATE FINANCIAL AID (Fall 2006, est.) 1,309 applied for aid; of those 88% were deemed to have need. 100% of undergraduates with need received aid; of those 13% had need fully met. ***Average percent of need met:*** 68% (excluding resources awarded to replace EFC). ***Average financial aid package:*** $17,029 (excluding resources awarded to replace EFC). 26% of all full-time undergraduates had no need and received non-need-based gift aid.

GIFT AID (NEED-BASED) ***Total amount:*** $5,373,058 (21% federal, 28% state, 51% institutional). ***Receiving aid:*** Freshmen: 55% (292); All full-time undergraduates: 55% (886). ***Average award:*** Freshmen: $6668; Undergraduates: $5883. ***Scholarships, grants, and awards:*** Federal Pell, FSEOG, state, private, college/university gift aid from institutional funds.

GIFT AID (NON-NEED-BASED) ***Total amount:*** $12,984,340 (97% institutional, 3% external sources). ***Receiving aid:*** Freshmen: 70% (372); Undergraduates: 67% (1,091). ***Average award:*** Freshmen: $9400; Undergraduates: $8144. ***Scholarships, grants, and awards by category:*** *Academic Interests/Achievement:* general academic interests/achievements. *Special Characteristics:* children of faculty/staff, ethnic background. ***Tuition waivers:*** Full or partial for children of alumni, employees or children of employees, senior citizens. ***ROTC:*** Army cooperative, Air Force cooperative.

LOANS ***Student loans:*** $10,951,339 (36% need-based, 64% non-need-based). 74% of past graduating class borrowed through all loan programs. *Average indebtedness per student:* $17,515. ***Average need-based loan:*** Freshmen: $2913; Undergraduates: $3988. ***Parent loans:*** $5,809,168 (73% need-based, 27% non-need-based). ***Programs:*** FFEL (Subsidized and Unsubsidized Stafford, PLUS), Perkins, alternative loans.

WORK-STUDY ***Federal work-study:*** Total amount: $216,564; 176 jobs averaging $1504.

APPLYING FOR FINANCIAL AID ***Required financial aid form:*** FAFSA. ***Financial aid deadline:*** 4/15. ***Notification date:*** Continuous beginning 2/15.

CONTACT Mike Colahan, Director of Financial Aid, Cabrini College, 610 King of Prussia Road, Grace Hall, Radnor, PA 19087-3698, 610-902-8420 or toll-free 800-848-1003. *Fax:* 610-902-8426.

CALDWELL COLLEGE

Caldwell, NJ

CONTACT Ms. Lissa B. Anderson, Executive Director of Financial Aid, Caldwell College, Caldwell College, 9 Ryerson Avenue, Caldwell, NJ 07006, 973-618-3221 or toll-free 888-864-9516 (out-of-state). *E-mail:* landerson@caldwell.edu.

CALIFORNIA BAPTIST UNIVERSITY
Riverside, CA

ABOUT THE INSTITUTION Independent Southern Baptist, coed. Awards: bachelor's and master's degrees. 32 undergraduate majors. Total enrollment: 3,409. Undergraduates: 2,623. Freshmen: 439.

GIFT AID (NEED-BASED) ***Scholarships, grants, and awards:*** Federal Pell, FSEOG, state, private, college/university gift aid from institutional funds.

GIFT AID (NON-NEED-BASED) ***Scholarships, grants, and awards by category:*** *Academic Interests/Achievement:* general academic interests/achievements, religion/biblical studies. *Creative Arts/Performance:* art/fine arts, music, theater/drama. *Special Characteristics:* adult students, children and siblings of alumni, children of faculty/staff, relatives of clergy, siblings of current students.

LOANS ***Programs:*** FFEL (Subsidized and Unsubsidized Stafford, PLUS), Perkins, alternative loans.

WORK-STUDY ***Federal work-study:*** Total amount: $126,435; 149 jobs averaging $849.

APPLYING FOR FINANCIAL AID ***Required financial aid forms:*** FAFSA, state aid form.

CONTACT Ms. Bekah Reed, Senior Financial Aid Counselor, California Baptist University, 8432 Magnolia Avenue, Riverside, CA 92504-3297, 951-343-4236 or toll-free 877-228-8866. *Fax:* 951-343-4518. *E-mail:* eterry@calbaptist.edu.

CALIFORNIA CHRISTIAN COLLEGE
Fresno, CA

CONTACT Mindy Scroggins, Financial Aid Coordinator, California Christian College, 4881 East University, Fresno, CA 93703, 559-455-5580. *Fax:* 559-251-4231. *E-mail:* cccfadir@aol.com.

CALIFORNIA COAST UNIVERSITY
Santa Ana, CA

CONTACT Financial Aid Office, California Coast University, 700 North Main Street, Santa Ana, CA 92701, 714-547-9625 or toll-free 888-CCU-UNIV (out-of-state).

CALIFORNIA COLLEGE FOR HEALTH SCIENCES
Salt Lake City, UT

CONTACT Financial Aid Director, California College for Health Sciences, 2423 Hoover Avenue, National City, CA 91950-6605, 619-477-4800 or toll-free 800-791-7353. *Fax:* 619-477-5202.

CALIFORNIA COLLEGE OF THE ARTS
San Francisco, CA

Tuition & fees: $27,914 **Average undergraduate aid package: $19,275**

ABOUT THE INSTITUTION Independent, coed. Awards: bachelor's and master's degrees. 17 undergraduate majors. Total enrollment: 1,622. Undergraduates: 1,310. Freshmen: 184. Federal methodology is used as a basis for awarding need-based institutional aid.

UNDERGRADUATE EXPENSES for 2006–07 ***Application fee:*** $50. ***Comprehensive fee:*** $36,529 includes full-time tuition ($27,624), mandatory fees ($290), and room and board ($8615). Full-time tuition and fees vary according to course load. Room and board charges vary according to housing facility. ***Part-time tuition:*** $1151 per unit. Part-time tuition and fees vary according to course load. ***Payment plans:*** Installment, deferred payment.

FRESHMAN FINANCIAL AID (Fall 2006, est.) 147 applied for aid; of those 88% were deemed to have need. 100% of freshmen with need received aid; of those 9% had need fully met. ***Average percent of need met:*** 61% (excluding resources awarded to replace EFC). ***Average financial aid package:*** $18,881 (excluding resources awarded to replace EFC). 5% of all full-time freshmen had no need and received non-need-based gift aid.

UNDERGRADUATE FINANCIAL AID (Fall 2006, est.) 877 applied for aid; of those 92% were deemed to have need. 100% of undergraduates with need received aid; of those 4% had need fully met. ***Average percent of need met:*** 55% (excluding resources awarded to replace EFC). ***Average financial aid package:*** $19,275 (excluding resources awarded to replace EFC). 6% of all full-time undergraduates had no need and received non-need-based gift aid.

GIFT AID (NEED-BASED) ***Total amount:*** $10,936,908 (12% federal, 11% state, 75% institutional, 2% external sources). ***Receiving aid:*** Freshmen: 71% (129); All full-time undergraduates: 65% (802). ***Average award:*** Freshmen: $15,318; Undergraduates: $13,126. ***Scholarships, grants, and awards:*** Federal Pell, FSEOG, state, private, college/university gift aid from institutional funds.

GIFT AID (NON-NEED-BASED) ***Total amount:*** $427,250 (100% institutional). ***Receiving aid:*** Freshmen: 46% (83); Undergraduates: 29% (361). ***Average award:*** Freshmen: $5444; Undergraduates: $5695. ***Scholarships, grants, and awards by category:*** *Academic Interests/Achievement:* architecture, general academic interests/achievements. *Creative Arts/Performance:* applied art and design, art/fine arts, creative writing, general creative arts/performance. ***Tuition waivers:*** Full or partial for employees or children of employees.

LOANS ***Student loans:*** $8,939,873 (43% need-based, 57% non-need-based). 72% of past graduating class borrowed through all loan programs. *Average indebtedness per student:* $33,188. ***Average need-based loan:*** Freshmen: $2640; Undergraduates: $4856. ***Parent loans:*** $4,103,220 (100% non-need-based). ***Programs:*** FFEL (Subsidized and Unsubsidized Stafford, PLUS), Perkins, private education loans.

WORK-STUDY ***Federal work-study:*** Total amount: $1,533,822; 756 jobs averaging $2028. ***State or other work-study/employment:*** Total amount: $264,685 (100% non-need-based). 67 part-time jobs averaging $2474.

APPLYING FOR FINANCIAL AID ***Required financial aid form:*** FAFSA. ***Financial aid deadline (priority):*** 3/1. ***Notification date:*** Continuous beginning 4/1. Students must reply by 5/1 or within 3 weeks of notification.

CONTACT Financial Aid Office, California College of the Arts, 1111 Eighth Street, San Francisco, CA 94107, 415-703-9528 or toll-free 800-447-1ART. *Fax:* 415-551-9261. *E-mail:* finaid@ccac.edu.

CALIFORNIA DESIGN COLLEGE
Los Angeles, CA

CONTACT Mr. Jason F. Li, Director of Financial Aid, California Design College, 3440 Wilshire Boulevard, Seventh Floor, Los Angeles, CA 90010, 213-251-3636 Ext. 209 or toll-free 213-251-3636 (in-state), 877-468-6232 (out-of-state). *Fax:* 213-385-3545. *E-mail:* jason@cdc.edu.

CALIFORNIA INSTITUTE OF INTEGRAL STUDIES
San Francisco, CA

CONTACT Financial Aid Office, California Institute of Integral Studies, 1453 Mission Street, San Francisco, CA 94103, 415-575-6122. *Fax:* 415-575-1268. *E-mail:* finaid@ciis.edu.

CALIFORNIA INSTITUTE OF TECHNOLOGY
Pasadena, CA

Tuition & fees: $32,835 **Average undergraduate aid package: $25,923**

ABOUT THE INSTITUTION Independent, coed. Awards: bachelor's, master's, and doctoral degrees. 26 undergraduate majors. Total enrollment: 2,086. Undergraduates: 864. Freshmen: 214. Both federal and institutional methodology are used as a basis for awarding need-based institutional aid.

UNDERGRADUATE EXPENSES for 2007–08 ***Application fee:*** $60. ***Comprehensive fee:*** $42,375 includes full-time tuition ($29,940), mandatory fees ($2895), and room and board ($9540). ***College room only:*** $5370.

FRESHMAN FINANCIAL AID (Fall 2006, est.) 173 applied for aid; of those 75% were deemed to have need. 100% of freshmen with need received aid; of those 100% had need fully met. ***Average percent of need met:*** 100% (excluding resources awarded to replace EFC). ***Average financial aid package:*** $25,212 (excluding resources awarded to replace EFC). 5% of all full-time freshmen had no need and received non-need-based gift aid.

UNDERGRADUATE FINANCIAL AID (Fall 2006, est.) 572 applied for aid; of those 87% were deemed to have need. 100% of undergraduates with need received aid; of those 100% had need fully met. ***Average percent of need met:***

100% (excluding resources awarded to replace EFC). ***Average financial aid package:*** $25,923 (excluding resources awarded to replace EFC). 8% of all full-time undergraduates had no need and received non-need-based gift aid.

GIFT AID (NEED-BASED) ***Total amount:*** $11,692,627 (6% federal, 6% state, 84% institutional, 4% external sources). ***Receiving aid:*** Freshmen: 60% (129); All full-time undergraduates: 53% (454). ***Average award:*** Freshmen: $22,026; Undergraduates: $25,755. ***Scholarships, grants, and awards:*** Federal Pell, FSEOG, state, private, college/university gift aid from institutional funds.

GIFT AID (NON-NEED-BASED) ***Total amount:*** $2,784,445 (3% state, 76% institutional, 21% external sources). ***Receiving aid:*** Freshmen: 2% (5); Undergraduates: 4% (34). ***Average award:*** Freshmen: $28,315; Undergraduates: $29,177. ***Scholarships, grants, and awards by category:*** *Academic Interests/Achievement:* 73 awards ($2,129,898 total): general academic interests/achievements. ***ROTC:*** Army cooperative, Air Force cooperative.

LOANS ***Student loans:*** $764,910 (82% need-based, 18% non-need-based). 34% of past graduating class borrowed through all loan programs. *Average indebtedness per student:* $5156. ***Average need-based loan:*** Freshmen: $3106; Undergraduates: $2475. ***Parent loans:*** $549,574 (100% non-need-based). ***Programs:*** Federal Direct (Subsidized and Unsubsidized Stafford, PLUS), Perkins, college/university.

WORK-STUDY ***Federal work-study:*** Total amount: $543,269; 291 jobs averaging $1867. ***State or other work-study/employment:*** Total amount: $73,582 (100% need-based). 33 part-time jobs averaging $2230.

APPLYING FOR FINANCIAL AID ***Required financial aid forms:*** FAFSA, CSS Financial Aid PROFILE, state aid form, noncustodial (divorced/separated) parent's statement, business/farm supplement. ***Financial aid deadline (priority):*** 1/15. ***Notification date:*** 4/15. Students must reply by 5/1 or within 4 weeks of notification.

CONTACT David Busse, Interim Director of Financial Aid, California Institute of Technology, Financial Aid Office, MC 110-87, Pasadena, CA 91125-0001, 626-395-6280. *Fax:* 626-564-8136. *E-mail:* dbusse@caltech.edu.

CALIFORNIA INSTITUTE OF THE ARTS

Valencia, CA

Tuition & fees: $31,855 **Average undergraduate aid package: $27,631**

ABOUT THE INSTITUTION Independent, coed. Awards: bachelor's and master's degrees and post-bachelor's certificates. 23 undergraduate majors. Total enrollment: 1,349. Undergraduates: 839. Freshmen: 156. Federal methodology is used as a basis for awarding need-based institutional aid.

UNDERGRADUATE EXPENSES for 2007–08 ***Application fee:*** $70. ***Comprehensive fee:*** $39,855 includes full-time tuition ($31,290), mandatory fees ($565), and room and board ($8000). ***College room only:*** $4530.

FRESHMAN FINANCIAL AID (Fall 2006, est.) 116 applied for aid; of those 69% were deemed to have need. 98% of freshmen with need received aid; of those 1% had need fully met. ***Average percent of need met:*** 86% (excluding resources awarded to replace EFC). ***Average financial aid package:*** $26,334 (excluding resources awarded to replace EFC). 14% of all full-time freshmen had no need and received non-need-based gift aid.

UNDERGRADUATE FINANCIAL AID (Fall 2006, est.) 610 applied for aid; of those 80% were deemed to have need. 99% of undergraduates with need received aid; of those 9% had need fully met. ***Average percent of need met:*** 86% (excluding resources awarded to replace EFC). ***Average financial aid package:*** $27,631 (excluding resources awarded to replace EFC). 11% of all full-time undergraduates had no need and received non-need-based gift aid.

GIFT AID (NEED-BASED) ***Total amount:*** $5,797,170 (18% federal, 11% state, 70% institutional, 1% external sources). ***Receiving aid:*** Freshmen: 48% (75); All full-time undergraduates: 62% (469). ***Average award:*** Freshmen: $10,505; Undergraduates: $12,227. ***Scholarships, grants, and awards:*** Federal Pell, FSEOG, state, private, college/university gift aid from institutional funds.

GIFT AID (NON-NEED-BASED) ***Total amount:*** $363,162 (96% institutional, 4% external sources). ***Average award:*** Freshmen: $3523; Undergraduates: $4375. ***Scholarships, grants, and awards by category:*** *Creative Arts/Performance:* 83 awards ($363,162 total): applied art and design, art/fine arts, cinema/film/broadcasting, creative writing, dance, music, performing arts, theater/drama.

LOANS ***Student loans:*** $7,000,709 (91% need-based, 9% non-need-based). 72% of past graduating class borrowed through all loan programs. *Average indebtedness per student:* $30,051. ***Average need-based loan:*** Freshmen: $3925; Undergraduates: $5535. ***Parent loans:*** $1,466,568 (71% need-based, 29% non-need-based). ***Programs:*** FFEL (Subsidized and Unsubsidized Stafford, PLUS), Perkins, college/university.

WORK-STUDY ***Federal work-study:*** Total amount: $326,765; 178 jobs averaging $1836. ***State or other work-study/employment:*** Total amount: $27,200 (100% need-based). 16 part-time jobs averaging $1700.

APPLYING FOR FINANCIAL AID ***Required financial aid form:*** FAFSA. ***Financial aid deadline (priority):*** 3/2. ***Notification date:*** Continuous beginning 4/1. Students must reply by 5/1 or within 3 weeks of notification.

CONTACT Financial Aid Office, California Institute of the Arts, 24700 McBean Parkway, Valencia, CA 91355-2340, 661-253-7869 or toll-free 800-545-2787. *Fax:* 661-287-3816.

CALIFORNIA LUTHERAN UNIVERSITY

Thousand Oaks, CA

ABOUT THE INSTITUTION Independent Lutheran, coed. Awards: bachelor's, master's, and doctoral degrees and post-bachelor's and post-master's certificates. 51 undergraduate majors. Total enrollment: 3,298. Undergraduates: 2,128. Freshmen: 403.

GIFT AID (NEED-BASED) ***Scholarships, grants, and awards:*** Federal Pell, FSEOG, state, private, college/university gift aid from institutional funds.

GIFT AID (NON-NEED-BASED) ***Scholarships, grants, and awards by category:*** *Academic Interests/Achievement:* biological sciences, business, communication, computer science, education, English, foreign languages, general academic interests/achievements, humanities, international studies, mathematics, physical sciences, religion/biblical studies, social sciences. *Creative Arts/Performance:* art/fine arts, creative writing, journalism/publications, music, performing arts, theater/drama. *Special Achievements/Activities:* community service, general special achievements/activities, leadership, religious involvement. *Special Characteristics:* adult students, children and siblings of alumni, children of faculty/staff, ethnic background, first-generation college students, international students, relatives of clergy, religious affiliation.

LOANS ***Programs:*** FFEL (Subsidized and Unsubsidized Stafford, PLUS), Perkins.

APPLYING FOR FINANCIAL AID ***Required financial aid forms:*** FAFSA, loan application.

CONTACT Matthew Ward, Dean, Undergraduate Enrollment, California Lutheran University, 60 West Olsen Road, Thousand Oaks, CA 91360-2787, 805-493-3115 or toll-free 877-258-3678. *Fax:* 805-493-3114.

CALIFORNIA MARITIME ACADEMY

Vallejo, CA

CONTACT Financial Aid Manager, California Maritime Academy, 200 Maritime Academy Drive, Vallejo, CA 94590-0644, 707-654-1275 or toll-free 800-561-1945. *Fax:* 707-654-1007.

CALIFORNIA NATIONAL UNIVERSITY FOR ADVANCED STUDIES

Northridge, CA

CONTACT Office of Academic Affairs, California National University for Advanced Studies, 16909 Parthenia Street, North Hills, CA 91343, 800-782-2422 or toll-free 800-744-2822 (in-state).

CALIFORNIA POLYTECHNIC STATE UNIVERSITY, SAN LUIS OBISPO

San Luis Obispo, CA

Tuition & fees (CA res): $4350 **Average undergraduate aid package: $7456**

ABOUT THE INSTITUTION State-supported, coed. Awards: bachelor's and master's degrees. 60 undergraduate majors. Total enrollment: 18,722. Undergraduates: 17,777. Freshmen: 3,668. Federal methodology is used as a basis for awarding need-based institutional aid.

UNDERGRADUATE EXPENSES for 2006–07 ***Application fee:*** $55. ***Tuition, state resident:*** full-time $0. ***Tuition, nonresident:*** full-time $14,520; part-time $226 per unit. ***Required fees:*** full-time $4350; $982 per term part-time. Full-time tuition and fees vary according to course load and program. Part-time tuition and fees vary according to course load and program. ***College room and board:*** $8453; ***Room only:*** $4766. Room and board charges vary according to board plan and housing facility. ***Payment plan:*** Installment.

FRESHMAN FINANCIAL AID (Fall 2005) 2299 applied for aid; of those 46% were deemed to have need. 91% of freshmen with need received aid; of those 8% had need fully met. ***Average percent of need met:*** 57% (excluding resources awarded to replace EFC). ***Average financial aid package:*** $6058 (excluding resources awarded to replace EFC).

UNDERGRADUATE FINANCIAL AID (Fall 2005) 8,449 applied for aid; of those 67% were deemed to have need. 95% of undergraduates with need received aid; of those 7% had need fully met. ***Average percent of need met:*** 64% (excluding resources awarded to replace EFC). ***Average financial aid package:*** $7456 (excluding resources awarded to replace EFC).

GIFT AID (NEED-BASED) ***Total amount:*** $28,551,603 (32% federal, 42% state, 15% institutional, 11% external sources). ***Receiving aid:*** Freshmen: 19% (697); All full-time undergraduates: 23% (3,841). ***Average award:*** Freshmen: $1437; Undergraduates: $1794. ***Scholarships, grants, and awards:*** Federal Pell, FSEOG, state, private, college/university gift aid from institutional funds.

GIFT AID (NON-NEED-BASED) ***Receiving aid:*** Freshmen: 7% (262); Undergraduates: 4% (636). ***Scholarships, grants, and awards by category:*** *Academic Interests/Achievement:* agriculture, architecture, biological sciences, business, communication, computer science, education, engineering/technologies, English, foreign languages, general academic interests/achievements, health fields, home economics, humanities, international studies, library science, mathematics, military science, physical sciences, social sciences. *Creative Arts/Performance:* applied art and design, art/fine arts, cinema/film/broadcasting, creative writing, dance, debating, general creative arts/performance, journalism/publications, music, performing arts, theater/drama. *Special Achievements/Activities:* community service, leadership, rodeo. *Special Characteristics:* general special characteristics. ***Tuition waivers:*** Full or partial for employees or children of employees. ***ROTC:*** Army.

LOANS ***Student loans:*** $51,995,505 (37% need-based, 63% non-need-based). 34% of past graduating class borrowed through all loan programs. *Average indebtedness per student:* $14,032. ***Average need-based loan:*** Freshmen: $2418; Undergraduates: $3952. ***Parent loans:*** $18,897,552 (100% non-need-based). ***Programs:*** FFEL (Subsidized and Unsubsidized Stafford, PLUS), Perkins, college/university, alternative loans.

WORK-STUDY ***Federal work-study:*** Total amount: $608,622; jobs available.

ATHLETIC AWARDS Total amount: $3,284,409 (100% need-based).

APPLYING FOR FINANCIAL AID ***Required financial aid forms:*** FAFSA, institution's own form. ***Financial aid deadline:*** 6/30 (priority: 3/1). ***Notification date:*** Continuous beginning 4/15. Students must reply within 8 weeks of notification.

CONTACT Lois Kelly, Director, Financial Aid, California Polytechnic State University, San Luis Obispo, Cal Poly State University, San Luis Obispo, CA 93407, 805-756-5993. *Fax:* 805-756-7243. *E-mail:* lkelly@calpoly.edu.

CALIFORNIA STATE POLYTECHNIC UNIVERSITY, POMONA

Pomona, CA

CONTACT Diana Minor, Associate Director of Financial Aid, California State Polytechnic University, Pomona, 3801 West Temple Avenue, Pomona, CA 91768-2557, 909-869-3704. *Fax:* 909-869-4757. *E-mail:* dyminor@csupomona.edu.

CALIFORNIA STATE UNIVERSITY, BAKERSFIELD

Bakersfield, CA

ABOUT THE INSTITUTION State-supported, coed. Awards: bachelor's and master's degrees. 30 undergraduate majors. Total enrollment: 7,549. Undergraduates: 5,960. Freshmen: 782.

GIFT AID (NEED-BASED) ***Scholarships, grants, and awards:*** Federal Pell, FSEOG, state, private, college/university gift aid from institutional funds, Federal Nursing.

GIFT AID (NON-NEED-BASED) ***Scholarships, grants, and awards by category:*** *Academic Interests/Achievement:* architecture, biological sciences, business, communication, education, general academic interests/achievements, health fields, mathematics, physical sciences, social sciences. *Creative Arts/Performance:* art/fine arts, dance, music, theater/drama. *Special Achievements/Activities:* community service, general special achievements/activities. *Special Characteristics:* adult students, children of faculty/staff, children of union members/company employees, first-generation college students, general special characteristics, handicapped students.

LOANS ***Programs:*** Federal Direct (Subsidized and Unsubsidized Stafford, PLUS), Perkins, Federal Nursing, college/university.

APPLYING FOR FINANCIAL AID ***Required financial aid form:*** FAFSA.

CONTACT Mr. John Casdorph, Associate Director of Financial Aid, California State University, Bakersfield, 9001 Stockdale Highway, Bakersfield, CA 93311-1099, 661-664-3265 or toll-free 800-788-2782 (in-state). *Fax:* 661-665-6800. *E-mail:* jcasdorph@csub.edu.

CALIFORNIA STATE UNIVERSITY CHANNEL ISLANDS

Camarillo, CA

CONTACT Financial Aid Office, California State University Channel Islands, One University Drive, Camarillo, CA 93012, 805-437-8979.

CALIFORNIA STATE UNIVERSITY, CHICO

Chico, CA

Tuition & fees (CA res): $3412 **Average undergraduate aid package: $8508**

ABOUT THE INSTITUTION State-supported, coed. Awards: bachelor's and master's degrees and post-bachelor's and post-master's certificates. 120 undergraduate majors. Total enrollment: 16,250. Undergraduates: 14,927. Freshmen: 2,477. Federal methodology is used as a basis for awarding need-based institutional aid.

UNDERGRADUATE EXPENSES for 2006–07 ***Application fee:*** $55. ***Tuition, state resident:*** full-time $0. ***Tuition, nonresident:*** full-time $12,690; part-time $339 per unit. ***Required fees:*** full-time $3412; $446 per term part-time. Part-time tuition and fees vary according to course load. ***College room and board:*** $8314; ***Room only:*** $5772. Room and board charges vary according to board plan and housing facility. ***Payment plans:*** Installment, deferred payment.

FRESHMAN FINANCIAL AID (Fall 2005) 1469 applied for aid; of those 74% were deemed to have need. 93% of freshmen with need received aid; of those 24% had need fully met. ***Average percent of need met:*** 65% (excluding resources awarded to replace EFC). ***Average financial aid package:*** $8099 (excluding resources awarded to replace EFC). 12% of all full-time freshmen had no need and received non-need-based gift aid.

UNDERGRADUATE FINANCIAL AID (Fall 2005) 8,018 applied for aid; of those 87% were deemed to have need. 96% of undergraduates with need received aid; of those 23% had need fully met. ***Average percent of need met:*** 78% (excluding resources awarded to replace EFC). ***Average financial aid package:*** $8508 (excluding resources awarded to replace EFC). 9% of all full-time undergraduates had no need and received non-need-based gift aid.

GIFT AID (NEED-BASED) ***Total amount:*** $28,857,312 (50% federal, 50% state). ***Receiving aid:*** Freshmen: 27% (662); All full-time undergraduates: 33% (4,873). ***Average award:*** Freshmen: $7241; Undergraduates: $5920. ***Scholarships, grants, and awards:*** Federal Pell, FSEOG, state, private, college/university gift aid from institutional funds, United Negro College Fund.

GIFT AID (NON-NEED-BASED) ***Total amount:*** $2,031,723 (1% federal, 47% institutional, 52% external sources). ***Receiving aid:*** Freshmen: 21% (515); Undergraduates: 19% (2,756). ***Average award:*** Freshmen: $4635; Undergraduates: $5440. ***Scholarships, grants, and awards by category:*** *Academic Interests/Achievement:* agriculture, area/ethnic studies, biological sciences, business, communication, computer science, education, engineering/technologies, English, foreign languages, general academic interests/achievements, health fields, humanities, international studies, mathematics, physical sciences, social sciences. *Creative Arts/Performance:* applied art and design, art/fine arts, cinema/film/broadcasting, creative writing, dance, debating, general creative arts/performance, journalism/publications, music, performing arts, theater/drama. *Special Achievements/Activities:* community service, general special achievements/activities, hobbies/interests, leadership, memberships. *Special Characteristics:* adult students, children of faculty/staff, ethnic background, first-generation college students, handicapped students, international students, local/state students, married students, members of minority groups, out-of-state students. ***Tuition waivers:*** Full or partial for employees or children of employees, senior citizens.

LOANS ***Student loans:*** $31,758,300 (64% need-based, 36% non-need-based). ***Average need-based loan:*** Freshmen: $2541; Undergraduates: $4123. ***Parent loans:*** $3,108,187 (100% non-need-based). ***Programs:*** Federal Direct (Subsidized and Unsubsidized Stafford, PLUS), Perkins, college/university.

WORK-STUDY ***Federal work-study:*** Total amount: $5,567,136; 750 jobs averaging $2500.

ATHLETIC AWARDS Total amount: $433,843 (19% need-based, 81% non-need-based).

APPLYING FOR FINANCIAL AID ***Required financial aid forms:*** FAFSA, scholarship application form. ***Financial aid deadline:*** Continuous. ***Notification date:*** Continuous beginning 2/15.

CONTACT Yvonne Lydon, Administrative Support Coordinator, California State University, Chico, Financial Aid Office, Chico, CA 95929-0705, 530-898-6451 or toll-free 800-542-4426. *Fax:* 530-898-6883. *E-mail:* ylydon@csuchico.edu.

CALIFORNIA STATE UNIVERSITY, DOMINGUEZ HILLS

Carson, CA

Tuition & fees (CA res): $3051 **Average undergraduate aid package: $8239**

ABOUT THE INSTITUTION State-supported, coed. Awards: bachelor's and master's degrees. 70 undergraduate majors. Total enrollment: 12,068. Undergraduates: 8,925. Freshmen: 1,058. Federal methodology is used as a basis for awarding need-based institutional aid.

UNDERGRADUATE EXPENSES for 2007–08 ***Application fee:*** $55. ***Tuition, state resident:*** full-time $0. ***Tuition, nonresident:*** full-time $13,221; part-time $339 per unit. ***College room and board:*** $8690; ***Room only:*** $5990.

FRESHMAN FINANCIAL AID (Fall 2005) 542 applied for aid; of those 94% were deemed to have need. 100% of freshmen with need received aid; of those 5% had need fully met. ***Average percent of need met:*** 71% (excluding resources awarded to replace EFC). ***Average financial aid package:*** $7488 (excluding resources awarded to replace EFC). 2% of all full-time freshmen had no need and received non-need-based gift aid.

UNDERGRADUATE FINANCIAL AID (Fall 2005) 4,730 applied for aid; of those 94% were deemed to have need. 98% of undergraduates with need received aid; of those 5% had need fully met. ***Average percent of need met:*** 67% (excluding resources awarded to replace EFC). ***Average financial aid package:*** $8239 (excluding resources awarded to replace EFC). 1% of all full-time undergraduates had no need and received non-need-based gift aid.

GIFT AID (NEED-BASED) ***Total amount:*** $22,652,459 (48% federal, 50% state, 2% external sources). ***Receiving aid:*** Freshmen: 71% (500); All full-time undergraduates: 82% (4,355). ***Average award:*** Freshmen: $5637; Undergraduates: $4975. ***Scholarships, grants, and awards:*** Federal Pell, FSEOG, state, private, college/university gift aid from institutional funds.

GIFT AID (NON-NEED-BASED) ***Total amount:*** $674,996 (46% federal, 46% state, 4% institutional, 4% external sources). ***Receiving aid:*** Freshmen: 11% (79); Undergraduates: 6% (336). ***Average award:*** Freshmen: $3403; Undergraduates: $2669. ***Scholarships, grants, and awards by category:*** *Academic Interests/Achievement:* 505 awards ($873,420 total): general academic interests/achievements. *Special Characteristics:* 66 awards ($106,588 total): ethnic background, members of minority groups. ***ROTC:*** Army cooperative, Air Force cooperative.

LOANS ***Student loans:*** $13,416,256 (90% need-based, 10% non-need-based). *Average indebtedness per student:* $15,232. ***Average need-based loan:*** Freshmen: $2465; Undergraduates: $4258. ***Parent loans:*** $43,450 (70% need-based, 30% non-need-based). ***Programs:*** Federal Direct (Subsidized and Unsubsidized Stafford), FFEL (PLUS), Perkins.

WORK-STUDY ***Federal work-study:*** Total amount: $314,746; 240 jobs averaging $1312.

ATHLETIC AWARDS Total amount: $230,604 (78% need-based, 22% non-need-based).

APPLYING FOR FINANCIAL AID ***Required financial aid forms:*** FAFSA, institution's own form, state aid form. ***Financial aid deadline:*** 4/15 (priority: 3/2). ***Notification date:*** Continuous. Students must reply within 4 weeks of notification.

CONTACT Mrs. Delores S. Lee, Director of Financial Aid, California State University, Dominguez Hills, 1000 East Victoria Street, Carson, CA 90747-0001, 310-243-3691. *E-mail:* dslee@csudh.edu.

CALIFORNIA STATE UNIVERSITY, EAST BAY

Hayward, CA

Tuition & fees (CA res): $2916 **Average undergraduate aid package: $8671**

ABOUT THE INSTITUTION State-supported, coed. Awards: bachelor's and master's degrees and post-bachelor's certificates. 91 undergraduate majors. Total enrollment: 12,706. Undergraduates: 9,213. Freshmen: 883. Federal methodology is used as a basis for awarding need-based institutional aid.

UNDERGRADUATE EXPENSES for 2007–08 ***Application fee:*** $55. ***Tuition, state resident:*** full-time $0. ***Tuition, nonresident:*** full-time $8136. ***College room and board:*** $8939.

FRESHMAN FINANCIAL AID (Fall 2006, est.) 453 applied for aid; of those 90% were deemed to have need. 96% of freshmen with need received aid; of those 19% had need fully met. ***Average percent of need met:*** 73% (excluding resources awarded to replace EFC). ***Average financial aid package:*** $8400 (excluding resources awarded to replace EFC).

UNDERGRADUATE FINANCIAL AID (Fall 2006, est.) 3,716 applied for aid; of those 93% were deemed to have need. 98% of undergraduates with need received aid; of those 10% had need fully met. ***Average percent of need met:*** 67% (excluding resources awarded to replace EFC). ***Average financial aid package:*** $8671 (excluding resources awarded to replace EFC).

GIFT AID (NEED-BASED) ***Total amount:*** $24,189,551 (40% federal, 59% state, 1% external sources). ***Receiving aid:*** Freshmen: 40% (353); All full-time undergraduates: 39% (2,952). ***Average award:*** Freshmen: $7497; Undergraduates: $6591. ***Scholarships, grants, and awards:*** Federal Pell, FSEOG, state, private, college/university gift aid from institutional funds.

GIFT AID (NON-NEED-BASED) ***Scholarships, grants, and awards by category:*** *Academic Interests/Achievement:* general academic interests/achievements. *Creative Arts/Performance:* 5 awards ($4100 total): music.

LOANS ***Student loans:*** $15,622,845 (81% need-based, 19% non-need-based). 37% of past graduating class borrowed through all loan programs. *Average indebtedness per student:* $12,627. ***Average need-based loan:*** Freshmen: $3178; Undergraduates: $5818. ***Parent loans:*** $897,275 (20% need-based, 80% non-need-based). ***Programs:*** FFEL (Subsidized and Unsubsidized Stafford, PLUS), Perkins, college/university.

WORK-STUDY ***Federal work-study:*** Total amount: $585,000; jobs available.

ATHLETIC AWARDS Total amount: $3216 (100% need-based).

APPLYING FOR FINANCIAL AID ***Required financial aid form:*** FAFSA. ***Financial aid deadline (priority):*** 3/2. ***Notification date:*** Continuous beginning 5/31. Students must reply within 3 weeks of notification.

CONTACT Office of Financial Aid, California State University, East Bay, 25800 Carlos Bee Boulevard, Hayward, CA 94542-3028, 510-885-2784. *Fax:* 510-885-2161. *E-mail:* finaid@csueastbay.edu.

CALIFORNIA STATE UNIVERSITY, FRESNO

Fresno, CA

Tuition & fees (CA res): $3039 **Average undergraduate aid package: $6762**

ABOUT THE INSTITUTION State-supported, coed. Awards: bachelor's, master's, and doctoral degrees. 87 undergraduate majors. Total enrollment: 22,098. Undergraduates: 18,951. Freshmen: 2,602. Federal methodology is used as a basis for awarding need-based institutional aid.

UNDERGRADUATE EXPENSES for 2006–07 ***Application fee:*** $55. ***Tuition, state resident:*** full-time $0. ***Tuition, nonresident:*** full-time $13,209; part-time $339 per unit. ***Required fees:*** full-time $3039; $990 per term part-time. ***College room and board:*** $6880; ***Room only:*** $3700.

FRESHMAN FINANCIAL AID (Fall 2006, est.) 1493 applied for aid; of those 84% were deemed to have need. 88% of freshmen with need received aid; of those 24% had need fully met. ***Average percent of need met:*** 72% (excluding resources awarded to replace EFC). ***Average financial aid package:*** $6817 (excluding resources awarded to replace EFC). 3% of all full-time freshmen had no need and received non-need-based gift aid.

UNDERGRADUATE FINANCIAL AID (Fall 2006, est.) 10,977 applied for aid; of those 92% were deemed to have need. 90% of undergraduates with need received aid; of those 37% had need fully met. ***Average percent of need met:*** 73% (excluding resources awarded to replace EFC). ***Average financial aid***

package: $6762 (excluding resources awarded to replace EFC). 2% of all full-time undergraduates had no need and received non-need-based gift aid.

GIFT AID (NEED-BASED) ***Total amount:*** $49,813,295 (48% federal, 52% state). ***Receiving aid:*** Freshmen: 37% (925); All full-time undergraduates: 49% (7,418). ***Average award:*** Freshmen: $5792; Undergraduates: $6120. ***Scholarships, grants, and awards:*** Federal Pell, FSEOG, state, private, college/university gift aid from institutional funds.

GIFT AID (NON-NEED-BASED) ***Total amount:*** $4,699,257 (52% institutional, 48% external sources). ***Receiving aid:*** Freshmen: 8% (202); Undergraduates: 12% (1,836). ***Average award:*** Freshmen: $1758; Undergraduates: $2515. ***Scholarships, grants, and awards by category:*** *Academic Interests/Achievement:* 1,329 awards ($2,323,261 total): agriculture, area/ethnic studies, biological sciences, business, communication, education, engineering/technologies, English, foreign languages, general academic interests/achievements, health fields, humanities, mathematics, social sciences. *Creative Arts/Performance:* 239 awards ($196,755 total): art/fine arts, journalism/publications, music, theater/drama. *Special Achievements/Activities:* 33 awards ($37,200 total): community service. *Special Characteristics:* 4 awards ($5895 total): handicapped students, local/state students. ***ROTC:*** Army, Air Force.

LOANS ***Student loans:*** $28,569,955 (65% need-based, 35% non-need-based). 44% of past graduating class borrowed through all loan programs. *Average indebtedness per student:* $14,648. ***Average need-based loan:*** Freshmen: $2337; Undergraduates: $2458. ***Parent loans:*** $1,682,933 (100% non-need-based). ***Programs:*** FFEL (Subsidized and Unsubsidized Stafford, PLUS), Perkins, Federal Nursing, college/university.

WORK-STUDY ***Federal work-study:*** Total amount: $936,599; 340 jobs averaging $2754.

ATHLETIC AWARDS Total amount: $2,901,377 (100% non-need-based).

APPLYING FOR FINANCIAL AID ***Required financial aid form:*** FAFSA. ***Financial aid deadline (priority):*** 3/2. ***Notification date:*** Continuous beginning 4/1. Students must reply within 3 weeks of notification.

CONTACT Financial Aid Office, California State University, Fresno, 5150 North Maple Avenue, Mail Stop JA 64, Fresno, CA 93740, 559-278-2182. *Fax:* 559-278-4833.

CALIFORNIA STATE UNIVERSITY, FULLERTON

Fullerton, CA

Tuition & fees (CA res): $3030 **Average undergraduate aid package: $6675**

ABOUT THE INSTITUTION State-supported, coed. Awards: bachelor's and master's degrees. 88 undergraduate majors. Total enrollment: 35,921. Undergraduates: 30,606. Freshmen: 3,851. Federal methodology is used as a basis for awarding need-based institutional aid.

UNDERGRADUATE EXPENSES for 2006–07 ***Application fee:*** $55. ***Tuition, state resident:*** full-time $0. ***Tuition, nonresident:*** full-time $10,170; part-time $339 per unit. ***Required fees:*** full-time $3030; $987 per term part-time. Full-time tuition and fees vary according to course load. Part-time tuition and fees vary according to course load. ***College room and board:*** ***Room only:*** $4408. ***Payment plans:*** Installment, deferred payment.

FRESHMAN FINANCIAL AID (Fall 2006, est.) 2711 applied for aid; of those 70% were deemed to have need. 69% of freshmen with need received aid; of those 8% had need fully met. ***Average percent of need met:*** 60% (excluding resources awarded to replace EFC). ***Average financial aid package:*** $6358 (excluding resources awarded to replace EFC). 8% of all full-time freshmen had no need and received non-need-based gift aid.

UNDERGRADUATE FINANCIAL AID (Fall 2006, est.) 12,450 applied for aid; of those 79% were deemed to have need. 78% of undergraduates with need received aid; of those 11% had need fully met. ***Average percent of need met:*** 59% (excluding resources awarded to replace EFC). ***Average financial aid package:*** $6675 (excluding resources awarded to replace EFC). 7% of all full-time undergraduates had no need and received non-need-based gift aid.

GIFT AID (NEED-BASED) ***Total amount:*** $48,286,038 (46% federal, 52% state, 2% external sources). ***Receiving aid:*** Freshmen: 30% (1,134); All full-time undergraduates: 28% (6,158). ***Average award:*** Freshmen: $6278; Undergraduates: $5712. ***Scholarships, grants, and awards:*** Federal Pell, FSEOG, state, private, college/university gift aid from institutional funds.

GIFT AID (NON-NEED-BASED) ***Total amount:*** $916,135 (16% institutional, 84% external sources). ***Average award:*** Freshmen: $4619; Undergraduates: $4766. ***Scholarships, grants, and awards by category:*** *Academic Interests/Achievement:* 1,663 awards ($2,567,088 total): business, communication, engineering/technologies, general academic interests/achievements, humanities, mathematics, military science, social sciences. *Creative Arts/Performance:* 63 awards ($31,500 total): art/fine arts, music. *Special Achievements/Activities:* 75 awards ($192,760 total): general special achievements/activities, leadership. *Special Characteristics:* 43 awards ($185,692 total): general special characteristics. ***Tuition waivers:*** Full or partial for employees or children of employees, senior citizens. ***ROTC:*** Army.

LOANS ***Student loans:*** $37,936,472 (59% need-based, 41% non-need-based). 37% of past graduating class borrowed through all loan programs. *Average indebtedness per student:* $14,508. ***Average need-based loan:*** Freshmen: $2592; Undergraduates: $4137. ***Parent loans:*** $2,463,350 (100% non-need-based). ***Programs:*** FFEL (Subsidized and Unsubsidized Stafford, PLUS), Perkins, college/university.

WORK-STUDY ***Federal work-study:*** Total amount: $2,652,474; 960 jobs averaging $2763.

ATHLETIC AWARDS Total amount: $1,367,795 (15% need-based, 85% non-need-based).

APPLYING FOR FINANCIAL AID ***Required financial aid form:*** FAFSA. ***Financial aid deadline (priority):*** 3/2. ***Notification date:*** Continuous beginning 4/9. Students must reply within 3 weeks of notification.

CONTACT Ms. Deborah S. McCracken, Director of Financial Aid, California State University, Fullerton, 800 North State College Boulevard, Fullerton, CA 92831-3599, 714-278-3128. *Fax:* 714-278-1328. *E-mail:* dmccracken@fullerton.edu.

CALIFORNIA STATE UNIVERSITY, LONG BEACH

Long Beach, CA

CONTACT Office of Financial Aid, California State University, Long Beach, 1250 Bellflower Boulevard, Long Beach, CA 90840, 562-985-8403.

CALIFORNIA STATE UNIVERSITY, LOS ANGELES

Los Angeles, CA

Tuition & fees (CA res): $3080 **Average undergraduate aid package: $7672**

ABOUT THE INSTITUTION State-supported, coed. Awards: bachelor's, master's, and doctoral degrees. 63 undergraduate majors. Total enrollment: 20,565. Undergraduates: 15,352. Freshmen: 1,689. Federal methodology is used as a basis for awarding need-based institutional aid.

UNDERGRADUATE EXPENSES for 2006–07 ***Application fee:*** $55. ***Tuition, state resident:*** full-time $0. ***Tuition, nonresident:*** full-time $11,216; part-time $226 per unit. ***Required fees:*** full-time $3080; $673.75 per unit. Full-time tuition and fees vary according to course level. Part-time tuition and fees vary according to course level. ***College room and board:*** $7866. ***Payment plan:*** Installment.

FRESHMAN FINANCIAL AID (Fall 2006, est.) 1018 applied for aid; of those 91% were deemed to have need. 100% of freshmen with need received aid; of those 15% had need fully met. ***Average percent of need met:*** 73% (excluding resources awarded to replace EFC). ***Average financial aid package:*** $7927 (excluding resources awarded to replace EFC).

UNDERGRADUATE FINANCIAL AID (Fall 2006, est.) 7,436 applied for aid; of those 100% were deemed to have need. 79% of undergraduates with need received aid; of those 11% had need fully met. ***Average percent of need met:*** 65% (excluding resources awarded to replace EFC). ***Average financial aid package:*** $7672 (excluding resources awarded to replace EFC).

GIFT AID (NEED-BASED) ***Total amount:*** $38,590,432 (49% federal, 49% state, 2% institutional). ***Receiving aid:*** Freshmen: 75% (925); All full-time undergraduates: 52% (5,390). ***Average award:*** Freshmen: $6682; Undergraduates: $6130. ***Scholarships, grants, and awards:*** Federal Pell, FSEOG, state, private, college/university gift aid from institutional funds.

GIFT AID (NON-NEED-BASED) ***Scholarships, grants, and awards by category:*** *Academic Interests/Achievement:* biological sciences, business, communication, computer science, education, engineering/technologies, English, foreign languages, general academic interests/achievements, health fields, mathematics, physical sciences, social sciences. *Creative Arts/Performance:* art/fine arts, general creative arts/performance, journalism/publications, music, theater/

drama. *Special Achievements/Activities:* community service, general special achievements/activities. *Special Characteristics:* general special characteristics. ***Tuition waivers:*** Full or partial for employees or children of employees, senior citizens. ***ROTC:*** Army cooperative, Air Force cooperative.

LOANS ***Student loans:*** $7,555,868 (100% need-based). ***Average need-based loan:*** Freshmen: $2807; Undergraduates: $3990. ***Parent loans:*** $23,900 (100% need-based). ***Programs:*** Federal Direct (Subsidized and Unsubsidized Stafford), FFEL (PLUS), Perkins, Federal Nursing.

WORK-STUDY ***Federal work-study:*** Total amount: $833,726; 272 jobs averaging $4058.

ATHLETIC AWARDS Total amount: $235,087 (100% need-based).

APPLYING FOR FINANCIAL AID ***Required financial aid form:*** FAFSA. ***Financial aid deadline (priority):*** 3/2. ***Notification date:*** Continuous beginning 4/1.

CONTACT Lindy W. Fong, Director, Center for Student Financial Aid, California State University, Los Angeles, 5151 State University Drive, Los Angeles, CA 90032, 323-343-5808. *Fax:* 323-343-3166. *E-mail:* lfong@cslanet.calstatela.edu.

CALIFORNIA STATE UNIVERSITY, MONTEREY BAY

Seaside, CA

CONTACT Campus Service Center, California State University, Monterey Bay, 100 Campus Center, Seaside, CA 93955-8001, 831-582-4074. *Fax:* 831-582-3782.

CALIFORNIA STATE UNIVERSITY, NORTHRIDGE

Northridge, CA

Tuition & fees (CA res): $3042 **Average undergraduate aid package: $8382**

ABOUT THE INSTITUTION State-supported, coed. Awards: bachelor's and master's degrees. 47 undergraduate majors. Total enrollment: 34,560. Undergraduates: 28,281. Freshmen: 3,695. Federal methodology is used as a basis for awarding need-based institutional aid.

UNDERGRADUATE EXPENSES for 2006–07 ***Application fee:*** $55. ***Tuition, state resident:*** full-time $0. ***Tuition, nonresident:*** full-time $11,178; part-time $339 per unit. ***Required fees:*** full-time $3042; $1521 per term part-time. ***College room and board:*** $9328; ***Room only:*** $5155. Room and board charges vary according to board plan and housing facility.

FRESHMAN FINANCIAL AID (Fall 2005) 2339 applied for aid; of those 91% were deemed to have need. 100% of freshmen with need received aid. ***Average financial aid package:*** $7645 (excluding resources awarded to replace EFC). 4% of all full-time freshmen had no need and received non-need-based gift aid.

UNDERGRADUATE FINANCIAL AID (Fall 2005) 11,745 applied for aid; of those 94% were deemed to have need. 100% of undergraduates with need received aid. ***Average financial aid package:*** $8382 (excluding resources awarded to replace EFC). 3% of all full-time undergraduates had no need and received non-need-based gift aid.

GIFT AID (NEED-BASED) ***Total amount:*** $50,360,179 (63% federal, 37% state). ***Receiving aid:*** Freshmen: 51% (1,901); All full-time undergraduates: 46% (9,442). ***Average award:*** Freshmen: $4608; Undergraduates: $4744. ***Scholarships, grants, and awards:*** Federal Pell, FSEOG, state, private, college/university gift aid from institutional funds.

GIFT AID (NON-NEED-BASED) ***Total amount:*** $17,984,959 (88% state, 8% institutional, 4% external sources). ***Receiving aid:*** Freshmen: 43% (1,594); Undergraduates: 34% (7,111). ***Average award:*** Freshmen: $1478; Undergraduates: $1612. ***Scholarships, grants, and awards by category:*** *Academic Interests/Achievement:* business, communication, computer science, education, engineering/technologies, English, general academic interests/achievements, mathematics, social sciences. *Creative Arts/Performance:* journalism/publications, music. *Special Achievements/Activities:* leadership. ***Tuition waivers:*** Full or partial for employees or children of employees, senior citizens. ***ROTC:*** Army cooperative, Air Force cooperative.

LOANS ***Student loans:*** $45,998,948 (65% need-based, 35% non-need-based). 43% of past graduating class borrowed through all loan programs. *Average indebtedness per student:* $14,027. ***Average need-based loan:*** Freshmen: $2278; Undergraduates: $3861. ***Parent loans:*** $2,053,020 (100% non-need-based). ***Programs:*** FFEL (Subsidized and Unsubsidized Stafford, PLUS), Perkins.

WORK-STUDY ***Federal work-study:*** Total amount: $1,662,827; 859 jobs averaging $1823.

ATHLETIC AWARDS Total amount: $1,460,191 (100% non-need-based).

APPLYING FOR FINANCIAL AID ***Required financial aid forms:*** FAFSA, state aid form. ***Financial aid deadline (priority):*** 3/2. ***Notification date:*** Continuous beginning 4/1.

CONTACT Lili Vidal, Interim Director of Financial Aid and Scholarships, California State University, Northridge, 18111 Nordhoff Street, Northridge, CA 91330-8307, 818-677-4085. *Fax:* 818-677-3047. *E-mail:* financial.aid@csun.edu.

CALIFORNIA STATE UNIVERSITY, SACRAMENTO

Sacramento, CA

Tuition & fees (CA res): $3284 **Average undergraduate aid package: $8354**

ABOUT THE INSTITUTION State-supported, coed. Awards: bachelor's, master's, and doctoral degrees. 84 undergraduate majors. Total enrollment: 28,529. Undergraduates: 23,615. Freshmen: 2,655. Federal methodology is used as a basis for awarding need-based institutional aid.

UNDERGRADUATE EXPENSES for 2006–07 ***Application fee:*** $55. ***Tuition, state resident:*** full-time $0. ***Tuition, nonresident:*** full-time $12,690; part-time $339 per unit. ***Required fees:*** full-time $3284; $276 per term part-time. ***College room and board:*** $7966; ***Room only:*** $5250. Room and board charges vary according to board plan. ***Payment plan:*** Installment.

FRESHMAN FINANCIAL AID (Fall 2005) 1520 applied for aid; of those 77% were deemed to have need. 91% of freshmen with need received aid; of those 1% had need fully met. ***Average percent of need met:*** 58% (excluding resources awarded to replace EFC). ***Average financial aid package:*** $8096 (excluding resources awarded to replace EFC). 6% of all full-time freshmen had no need and received non-need-based gift aid.

UNDERGRADUATE FINANCIAL AID (Fall 2005) 10,826 applied for aid; of those 86% were deemed to have need. 92% of undergraduates with need received aid; of those 1% had need fully met. ***Average percent of need met:*** 61% (excluding resources awarded to replace EFC). ***Average financial aid package:*** $8354 (excluding resources awarded to replace EFC). 5% of all full-time undergraduates had no need and received non-need-based gift aid.

GIFT AID (NEED-BASED) ***Total amount:*** $44,146,605 (49% federal, 47% state, 1% institutional, 3% external sources). ***Receiving aid:*** Freshmen: 42% (865); All full-time undergraduates: 39% (6,890). ***Average award:*** Freshmen: $2274; Undergraduates: $2259. ***Scholarships, grants, and awards:*** Federal Pell, FSEOG, state, private, Federal Nursing.

GIFT AID (NON-NEED-BASED) ***Total amount:*** $4100 (100% institutional). ***Receiving aid:*** Undergraduates: 7. ***Average award:*** Freshmen: $6334; Undergraduates: $6078. ***Scholarships, grants, and awards by category:*** *Academic Interests/Achievement:* general academic interests/achievements. *Creative Arts/Performance:* general creative arts/performance. *Special Achievements/Activities:* general special achievements/activities. *Special Characteristics:* general special characteristics. ***Tuition waivers:*** Full or partial for employees or children of employees, senior citizens. ***ROTC:*** Army cooperative, Air Force.

LOANS ***Student loans:*** $40,001,353 (60% need-based, 40% non-need-based). 36% of past graduating class borrowed through all loan programs. *Average indebtedness per student:* $10,868. ***Average need-based loan:*** Freshmen: $2424; Undergraduates: $3803. ***Parent loans:*** $9,467,257 (100% non-need-based). ***Programs:*** Federal Direct (Subsidized and Unsubsidized Stafford), FFEL (PLUS), Perkins, Federal Nursing.

WORK-STUDY ***Federal work-study:*** Total amount: $1,043,593; 431 jobs averaging $2412.

ATHLETIC AWARDS Total amount: $2,538,642 (100% need-based).

APPLYING FOR FINANCIAL AID ***Required financial aid form:*** FAFSA. ***Financial aid deadline (priority):*** 3/2. ***Notification date:*** 4/1. Students must reply within 4 weeks of notification.

CONTACT Linda Joy Clemons, Financial Aid Director, California State University, Sacramento, 6000 J Street, Sacramento, CA 95819-6044, 916-278-6554. *Fax:* 916-278-6082. *E-mail:* ljclemons@csus.edu.

CALIFORNIA STATE UNIVERSITY, SAN BERNARDINO

San Bernardino, CA

Tuition & fees (CA res): $3398 **Average undergraduate aid package: $7648**

ABOUT THE INSTITUTION State-supported, coed. Awards: bachelor's and master's degrees. 51 undergraduate majors. Total enrollment: 16,479. Undergraduates: 12,926. Freshmen: 1,845. Federal methodology is used as a basis for awarding need-based institutional aid.

UNDERGRADUATE EXPENSES for 2006–07 ***Application fee:*** $55. ***Tuition, state resident:*** full-time $0. ***Tuition, nonresident:*** full-time $8136; part-time $226 per unit. Part-time tuition and fees vary according to course load. ***College room and board:*** $5886; ***Room only:*** $4376. Room and board charges vary according to board plan and housing facility.

FRESHMAN FINANCIAL AID (Fall 2006, est.) 1332 applied for aid; of those 83% were deemed to have need. 90% of freshmen with need received aid; of those 8% had need fully met. ***Average percent of need met:*** 63% (excluding resources awarded to replace EFC). ***Average financial aid package:*** $6927 (excluding resources awarded to replace EFC). 1% of all full-time freshmen had no need and received non-need-based gift aid.

UNDERGRADUATE FINANCIAL AID (Fall 2006, est.) 8,337 applied for aid; of those 89% were deemed to have need. 94% of undergraduates with need received aid; of those 11% had need fully met. ***Average percent of need met:*** 65% (excluding resources awarded to replace EFC). ***Average financial aid package:*** $7648 (excluding resources awarded to replace EFC). 1% of all full-time undergraduates had no need and received non-need-based gift aid.

GIFT AID (NEED-BASED) ***Total amount:*** $40,249,259 (47% federal, 49% state, 2% institutional, 2% external sources). ***Receiving aid:*** Freshmen: 52% (879); All full-time undergraduates: 53% (6,016). ***Average award:*** Freshmen: $6620; Undergraduates: $5927. ***Scholarships, grants, and awards:*** Federal Pell, FSEOG, state, college/university gift aid from institutional funds.

GIFT AID (NON-NEED-BASED) ***Total amount:*** $353,862 (22% federal, 5% state, 27% institutional, 46% external sources). ***Receiving aid:*** Freshmen: 2% (33); Undergraduates: 3% (306). ***Average award:*** Freshmen: $4045; Undergraduates: $2883. ***Scholarships, grants, and awards by category:*** *Academic Interests/Achievement:* 127 awards ($305,350 total): biological sciences, business, computer science, education, foreign languages, general academic interests/achievements, health fields. *Creative Arts/Performance:* 25 awards ($23,410 total): art/fine arts, music, theater/drama. *Special Achievements/Activities:* 36 awards ($36,000 total): community service, general special achievements/activities, hobbies/interests. *Special Characteristics:* 6 awards ($14,800 total): children of public servants, children with a deceased or disabled parent, ethnic background, first-generation college students, handicapped students. ***Tuition waivers:*** Full or partial for employees or children of employees. ***ROTC:*** Army, Air Force.

LOANS ***Student loans:*** $35,728,133 (100% need-based). 55% of past graduating class borrowed through all loan programs. *Average indebtedness per student:* $17,946. ***Average need-based loan:*** Freshmen: $2276; Undergraduates: $3845. ***Parent loans:*** $1,648,494 (100% non-need-based). ***Programs:*** Federal Direct (Subsidized and Unsubsidized Stafford), FFEL (PLUS), Perkins.

WORK-STUDY ***Federal work-study:*** Total amount: $1,102,176; 311 jobs averaging $3675. ***State or other work-study/employment:*** Part-time jobs available.

ATHLETIC AWARDS Total amount: $457,108 (100% non-need-based).

APPLYING FOR FINANCIAL AID ***Required financial aid forms:*** FAFSA, state aid form. ***Financial aid deadline (priority):*** 3/2. ***Notification date:*** Continuous beginning 4/1.

CONTACT Roseanna Ruiz, Director of Financial Aid, California State University, San Bernardino, 5500 University Parkway, San Bernardino, CA 92407-2397, 909-537-7651. *Fax:* 909-537-7024. *E-mail:* rruiz@csusb.edu.

CALIFORNIA STATE UNIVERSITY, SAN MARCOS

San Marcos, CA

ABOUT THE INSTITUTION State-supported, coed. Awards: bachelor's and master's degrees. 23 undergraduate majors. Total enrollment: 6,956. Undergraduates: 6,327. Freshmen: 804.

GIFT AID (NEED-BASED) ***Scholarships, grants, and awards:*** Federal Pell, FSEOG, state, private, college/university gift aid from institutional funds.

GIFT AID (NON-NEED-BASED) ***Scholarships, grants, and awards by category:*** *Academic Interests/Achievement:* general academic interests/achievements, mathematics.

LOANS ***Programs:*** Federal Direct (Subsidized and Unsubsidized Stafford, PLUS), Perkins, college/university.

APPLYING FOR FINANCIAL AID ***Required financial aid form:*** FAFSA.

CONTACT Addalou Davis, Director of Financial Aid, California State University, San Marcos, 333 South Twin Oaks Valley Road, San Marcos, CA 92096-0001, 760-750-4852. *Fax:* 760-750-3047. *E-mail:* finaid@csusm.edu.

CALIFORNIA STATE UNIVERSITY, STANISLAUS

Turlock, CA

Tuition & fees (CA res): $3043 **Average undergraduate aid package: $7923**

ABOUT THE INSTITUTION State-supported, coed. Awards: bachelor's and master's degrees. 35 undergraduate majors. Total enrollment: 8,374. Undergraduates: 6,671. Freshmen: 946. Federal methodology is used as a basis for awarding need-based institutional aid.

UNDERGRADUATE EXPENSES for 2006–07 ***Application fee:*** $55. ***Tuition, state resident:*** full-time $0. ***Tuition, nonresident:*** full-time $10,170; part-time $339 per unit. ***Required fees:*** full-time $3043; $862 per term part-time. ***College room and board:*** $7178; ***Room only:*** $4278. Room and board charges vary according to board plan and housing facility. ***Payment plans:*** Installment, deferred payment.

FRESHMAN FINANCIAL AID (Fall 2006, est.) 736 applied for aid; of those 77% were deemed to have need. 91% of freshmen with need received aid; of those 4% had need fully met. ***Average percent of need met:*** 68% (excluding resources awarded to replace EFC). ***Average financial aid package:*** $8537 (excluding resources awarded to replace EFC). 4% of all full-time freshmen had no need and received non-need-based gift aid.

UNDERGRADUATE FINANCIAL AID (Fall 2006, est.) 3,719 applied for aid; of those 88% were deemed to have need. 91% of undergraduates with need received aid; of those 4% had need fully met. ***Average percent of need met:*** 41% (excluding resources awarded to replace EFC). ***Average financial aid package:*** $7923 (excluding resources awarded to replace EFC). 2% of all full-time undergraduates had no need and received non-need-based gift aid.

GIFT AID (NEED-BASED) ***Total amount:*** $15,911,765 (49% federal, 50% state, 1% institutional). ***Receiving aid:*** Freshmen: 53% (449); All full-time undergraduates: 45% (2,074). ***Average award:*** Freshmen: $6116; Undergraduates: $6652. ***Scholarships, grants, and awards:*** Federal Pell, FSEOG, state, private, college/university gift aid from institutional funds.

GIFT AID (NON-NEED-BASED) ***Total amount:*** $912,518 (47% institutional, 53% external sources). ***Receiving aid:*** Freshmen: 3% (26); Undergraduates: 2% (103). ***Average award:*** Freshmen: $4056; Undergraduates: $1027. ***Scholarships, grants, and awards by category:*** *Academic Interests/Achievement:* 75 awards ($100,805 total): agriculture, area/ethnic studies, biological sciences, business, communication, computer science, education, English, foreign languages, general academic interests/achievements, health fields, humanities, international studies, mathematics, physical sciences, premedicine, social sciences. *Creative Arts/Performance:* 35 awards ($37,804 total): art/fine arts, music. *Special Achievements/Activities:* 104 awards ($278,413 total): community service, general special achievements/activities, leadership, memberships. *Special Characteristics:* 28 awards ($29,225 total): children of faculty/staff, ethnic background, first-generation college students, general special characteristics, local/state students, members of minority groups. ***Tuition waivers:*** Full or partial for employees or children of employees, adult students, senior citizens.

LOANS ***Student loans:*** $13,296,050 (72% need-based, 28% non-need-based). 19% of past graduating class borrowed through all loan programs. *Average indebtedness per student:* $8500. ***Average need-based loan:*** Freshmen: $2744; Undergraduates: $4283. ***Parent loans:*** $1,005,187 (100% non-need-based). ***Programs:*** FFEL (Subsidized and Unsubsidized Stafford, PLUS), Perkins, college/university.

WORK-STUDY ***Federal work-study:*** Total amount: $369,551; 152 jobs averaging $2431. ***State or other work-study/employment:*** Part-time jobs available.

ATHLETIC AWARDS Total amount: $288,417 (100% non-need-based).

APPLYING FOR FINANCIAL AID ***Required financial aid forms:*** FAFSA, state aid form. ***Financial aid deadline (priority):*** 3/2. ***Notification date:*** Continuous beginning 3/15. Students must reply within 3 weeks of notification.

CONTACT Mr. Matthew T. Sanchez, Director, Financial Aid/Scholarships Department, California State University, Stanislaus, 801 West Monte Vista Avenue, Turlock, CA 95382, 209-667-3336 or toll-free 800-300-7420 (in-state). *Fax:* 209-664-7064. *E-mail:* msanchez9@csustan.edu.

CALIFORNIA UNIVERSITY OF PENNSYLVANIA

California, PA

Tuition & fees (PA res): $6586 **Average undergraduate aid package: $8764**

ABOUT THE INSTITUTION State-supported, coed. Awards: associate, bachelor's, and master's degrees. 41 undergraduate majors. Total enrollment: 7,720. Undergraduates: 6,299. Freshmen: 1,273. Federal methodology is used as a basis for awarding need-based institutional aid.

UNDERGRADUATE EXPENSES for 2006–07 ***Application fee:*** $25. ***Tuition, state resident:*** full-time $5038; part-time $210 per credit. ***Tuition, nonresident:*** full-time $7558; part-time $315 per credit. ***Required fees:*** full-time $1548; $261 per course. Full-time tuition and fees vary according to location. Part-time tuition and fees vary according to location. ***College room and board:*** $8144; ***Room only:*** $5392. Room and board charges vary according to board plan and housing facility. ***Payment plan:*** Installment.

FRESHMAN FINANCIAL AID (Fall 2006, est.) 1066 applied for aid; of those 79% were deemed to have need. 99% of freshmen with need received aid; of those 5% had need fully met. ***Average percent of need met:*** 94% (excluding resources awarded to replace EFC). ***Average financial aid package:*** $7735 (excluding resources awarded to replace EFC). 22% of all full-time freshmen had no need and received non-need-based gift aid.

UNDERGRADUATE FINANCIAL AID (Fall 2006, est.) 4,756 applied for aid; of those 82% were deemed to have need. 99% of undergraduates with need received aid; of those 5% had need fully met. ***Average percent of need met:*** 98% (excluding resources awarded to replace EFC). ***Average financial aid package:*** $8764 (excluding resources awarded to replace EFC). 13% of all full-time undergraduates had no need and received non-need-based gift aid.

GIFT AID (NEED-BASED) ***Total amount:*** $14,204,000 (45% federal, 55% state). ***Receiving aid:*** Freshmen: 45% (564); All full-time undergraduates: 49% (2,759). ***Average award:*** Freshmen: $4642; Undergraduates: $4434. ***Scholarships, grants, and awards:*** Federal Pell, FSEOG, state, private, college/university gift aid from institutional funds, ACG (Academic Competitiveness Grant) National Science and Mathematics Access to Retain Talent.

GIFT AID (NON-NEED-BASED) ***Total amount:*** $2,527,000 (22% federal, 5% state, 42% institutional, 31% external sources). ***Receiving aid:*** Freshmen: 21% (259); Undergraduates: 13% (707). ***Average award:*** Freshmen: $2282; Undergraduates: $2991. ***Scholarships, grants, and awards by category:*** *Academic Interests/Achievement:* general academic interests/achievements. *Creative Arts/Performance:* general creative arts/performance. *Special Achievements/Activities:* general special achievements/activities. *Special Characteristics:* $2,527,000 total: ethnic background, international students, members of minority groups, veterans. ***Tuition waivers:*** Full or partial for employees or children of employees. ***ROTC:*** Army.

LOANS ***Student loans:*** $30,500,000 (48% need-based, 52% non-need-based). 79% of past graduating class borrowed through all loan programs. *Average indebtedness per student:* $21,860. ***Average need-based loan:*** Freshmen: $2792; Undergraduates: $3585. ***Parent loans:*** $4,450,000 (100% non-need-based). ***Programs:*** FFEL (Subsidized and Unsubsidized Stafford, PLUS), Perkins, college/university.

WORK-STUDY ***Federal work-study:*** Total amount: $475,000; jobs available. ***State or other work-study/employment:*** Total amount: $2,400,000 (100% non-need-based). Part-time jobs available.

ATHLETIC AWARDS Total amount: $926,000 (100% non-need-based).

APPLYING FOR FINANCIAL AID ***Required financial aid form:*** FAFSA. ***Financial aid deadline:*** Continuous. ***Notification date:*** Continuous. Students must reply within 2 weeks of notification.

CONTACT Financial Aid Office, California University of Pennsylvania, 250 University Avenue, California, PA 15419-1394, 724-938-4415.

CALUMET COLLEGE OF SAINT JOSEPH

Whiting, IN

Tuition & fees: $10,650 **Average undergraduate aid package: N/A**

ABOUT THE INSTITUTION Independent Roman Catholic, coed. Awards: associate, bachelor's, and master's degrees and post-bachelor's certificates. 28 undergraduate majors. Total enrollment: 1,252. Undergraduates: 1,091. Freshmen: 100. Federal methodology is used as a basis for awarding need-based institutional aid.

UNDERGRADUATE EXPENSES for 2006–07 ***Tuition:*** full-time $10,500; part-time $350 per credit hour.

FRESHMAN FINANCIAL AID (Fall 2005) 62 applied for aid; of those 79% were deemed to have need. 92% of freshmen with need received aid.

UNDERGRADUATE FINANCIAL AID (Fall 2005) 450 applied for aid; of those 84% were deemed to have need. 95% of undergraduates with need received aid.

GIFT AID (NEED-BASED) ***Total amount:*** $2,769,129 (44% federal, 39% state, 7% institutional, 10% external sources). ***Receiving aid:*** Freshmen: 58% (37); All full-time undergraduates: 56% (260). ***Scholarships, grants, and awards:*** Federal Pell, FSEOG, state, private, college/university gift aid from institutional funds, United Negro College Fund.

GIFT AID (NON-NEED-BASED) ***Total amount:*** $310,228 (100% institutional).

LOANS ***Student loans:*** $4,894,130 (47% need-based, 53% non-need-based). 79% of past graduating class borrowed through all loan programs. *Average indebtedness per student:* $22,800. ***Parent loans:*** $104,653 (100% need-based). ***Programs:*** FFEL (Subsidized and Unsubsidized Stafford, PLUS).

WORK-STUDY ***Federal work-study:*** Total amount: $70,332; 43 jobs averaging $1635. ***State or other work-study/employment:*** Total amount: $3696 (100% need-based). 2 part-time jobs averaging $1848.

ATHLETIC AWARDS Total amount: $521,219 (100% non-need-based).

APPLYING FOR FINANCIAL AID ***Required financial aid form:*** FAFSA. ***Financial aid deadline (priority):*** 3/1. ***Notification date:*** Continuous.

CONTACT Chuck Walz, Director of Admissions and Financial Aid, Calumet College of Saint Joseph, 2400 New York Avenue, Whiting, IN 46394, 219-473-4379 or toll-free 877-700-9100. *E-mail:* cwalz@ccsj.edu.

CALVARY BIBLE COLLEGE AND THEOLOGICAL SEMINARY

Kansas City, MO

ABOUT THE INSTITUTION Independent nondenominational, coed. Awards: associate, bachelor's, master's, and first professional degrees. 17 undergraduate majors. Total enrollment: 329. Undergraduates: 267. Freshmen: 47.

GIFT AID (NEED-BASED) ***Scholarships, grants, and awards:*** Federal Pell, FSEOG, private, college/university gift aid from institutional funds.

GIFT AID (NON-NEED-BASED) ***Scholarships, grants, and awards by category:*** *Academic Interests/Achievement:* general academic interests/achievements. *Special Achievements/Activities:* general special achievements/activities, religious involvement. *Special Characteristics:* children and siblings of alumni, children of educators, children of faculty/staff, relatives of clergy, siblings of current students, spouses of current students.

LOANS ***Programs:*** FFEL (Subsidized and Unsubsidized Stafford, PLUS), alternative loans.

APPLYING FOR FINANCIAL AID ***Required financial aid forms:*** FAFSA, institution's own form.

CONTACT Rachael Russiaky, Financial Aid Administrator, Calvary Bible College and Theological Seminary, 15800 Calvary Road, Kansas City, MO 64147-1341, 816-322-5152 Ext. 1323 or toll-free 800-326-3960. *Fax:* 816-331-4474. *E-mail:* finaid@calvary.edu.

CALVIN COLLEGE

Grand Rapids, MI

Tuition & fees: $20,470 **Average undergraduate aid package: $14,200**

ABOUT THE INSTITUTION Independent religious, coed. Awards: bachelor's and master's degrees and post-bachelor's certificates. 83 undergraduate majors.

Total enrollment: 4,187. Undergraduates: 4,130. Freshmen: 1,027. Both federal and institutional methodology are used as a basis for awarding need-based institutional aid.

UNDERGRADUATE EXPENSES for 2006–07 ***Application fee:*** $35. ***Comprehensive fee:*** $27,510 includes full-time tuition ($20,245), mandatory fees ($225), and room and board ($7040). ***College room only:*** $3830. Full-time tuition and fees vary according to program. Room and board charges vary according to board plan. ***Part-time tuition:*** $480 per credit hour. Part-time tuition and fees vary according to course load. ***Payment plans:*** Tuition prepayment, installment.

FRESHMAN FINANCIAL AID (Fall 2006, est.) 861 applied for aid; of those 76% were deemed to have need. 100% of freshmen with need received aid; of those 27% had need fully met. ***Average percent of need met:*** 85% (excluding resources awarded to replace EFC). ***Average financial aid package:*** $15,400 (excluding resources awarded to replace EFC). 29% of all full-time freshmen had no need and received non-need-based gift aid.

UNDERGRADUATE FINANCIAL AID (Fall 2006, est.) 2,994 applied for aid; of those 83% were deemed to have need. 100% of undergraduates with need received aid; of those 23% had need fully met. ***Average percent of need met:*** 80% (excluding resources awarded to replace EFC). ***Average financial aid package:*** $14,200 (excluding resources awarded to replace EFC). 29% of all full-time undergraduates had no need and received non-need-based gift aid.

GIFT AID (NEED-BASED) ***Total amount:*** $23,350,000 (10% federal, 12% state, 75% institutional, 3% external sources). ***Receiving aid:*** Freshmen: 64% (654); All full-time undergraduates: 63% (2,483). ***Average award:*** Freshmen: $10,300; Undergraduates: $9200. ***Scholarships, grants, and awards:*** Federal Pell, FSEOG, state, private, college/university gift aid from institutional funds.

GIFT AID (NON-NEED-BASED) ***Total amount:*** $6,850,000 (7% state, 89% institutional, 4% external sources). ***Receiving aid:*** Freshmen: 16% (166); Undergraduates: 12% (492). ***Average award:*** Freshmen: $4600; Undergraduates: $4200. ***Scholarships, grants, and awards by category:*** *Academic Interests/Achievement:* 3,490 awards ($9,600,000 total): biological sciences, business, communication, computer science, education, engineering/technologies, English, foreign languages, general academic interests/achievements, health fields, humanities, international studies, mathematics, physical sciences, premedicine, religion/biblical studies, social sciences. *Creative Arts/Performance:* 75 awards ($85,000 total): art/fine arts, music, performing arts, theater/drama. *Special Achievements/Activities:* 105 awards ($70,000 total): community service, religious involvement. *Special Characteristics:* 2,950 awards ($4,150,000 total): children and siblings of alumni, children of faculty/staff, children of union members/company employees, ethnic background, handicapped students, international students, members of minority groups, religious affiliation. ***Tuition waivers:*** Full or partial for employees or children of employees. ***ROTC:*** Army cooperative.

LOANS ***Student loans:*** $19,300,000 (68% need-based, 32% non-need-based). 66% of past graduating class borrowed through all loan programs. *Average indebtedness per student:* $21,600. ***Average need-based loan:*** Freshmen: $4200; Undergraduates: $6300. ***Parent loans:*** $1,250,000 (28% need-based, 72% non-need-based). ***Programs:*** Federal Direct (Subsidized and Unsubsidized Stafford, PLUS), Perkins, state, college/university, alternative educational loans.

WORK-STUDY ***Federal work-study:*** Total amount: $800,000; 710 jobs averaging $1140. ***State or other work-study/employment:*** Total amount: $1,390,000 (21% need-based, 79% non-need-based). 1,100 part-time jobs averaging $1200.

APPLYING FOR FINANCIAL AID ***Required financial aid form:*** FAFSA. ***Financial aid deadline (priority):*** 2/15. ***Notification date:*** Continuous beginning 3/15.

CONTACT Mr. Dave Brummel, Financial Aid Counselor, Calvin College, Spoelhof Center 356, 3201 Burton Street, SE, Grand Rapids, MI 49546-4388, 616-526-6134 or toll-free 800-688-0122. *Fax:* 616-526-6883. *E-mail:* dlbrum@calvin.edu.

CAMBRIDGE COLLEGE

Cambridge, MA

CONTACT Dr. Gerri Major, Director of Financial Aid, Cambridge College, 1000 Massachusetts Avenue, Cambridge, MA 02138, 617-868-1000 Ext. 137 or toll-free 800-877-4723. *Fax:* 617-349-3561. *E-mail:* gmajor@idea.cambridge.edu.

CAMERON UNIVERSITY

Lawton, OK

CONTACT Caryn Pacheco, Financial Aid Director, Cameron University, 2800 West Gore Boulevard, Lawton, OK 73505-6377, 580-581-2293 or toll-free 888-454-7600. *Fax:* 580-581-2556.

CAMPBELLSVILLE UNIVERSITY

Campbellsville, KY

Tuition & fees: $17,260 **Average undergraduate aid package: $13,127**

ABOUT THE INSTITUTION Independent religious, coed. Awards: associate, bachelor's, and master's degrees and post-bachelor's certificates. 54 undergraduate majors. Total enrollment: 2,376. Undergraduates: 1,988. Freshmen: 355. Federal methodology is used as a basis for awarding need-based institutional aid.

UNDERGRADUATE EXPENSES for 2007–08 ***Application fee:*** $20. ***Comprehensive fee:*** $23,490 includes full-time tuition ($16,880), mandatory fees ($380), and room and board ($6230). ***Part-time tuition:*** $703 per credit.

FRESHMAN FINANCIAL AID (Fall 2005) 301 applied for aid; of those 91% were deemed to have need. 100% of freshmen with need received aid; of those 27% had need fully met. ***Average percent of need met:*** 73% (excluding resources awarded to replace EFC). ***Average financial aid package:*** $13,932 (excluding resources awarded to replace EFC). 9% of all full-time freshmen had no need and received non-need-based gift aid.

UNDERGRADUATE FINANCIAL AID (Fall 2005) 1,101 applied for aid; of those 90% were deemed to have need. 100% of undergraduates with need received aid; of those 24% had need fully met. ***Average percent of need met:*** 74% (excluding resources awarded to replace EFC). ***Average financial aid package:*** $13,127 (excluding resources awarded to replace EFC). 16% of all full-time undergraduates had no need and received non-need-based gift aid.

GIFT AID (NEED-BASED) ***Total amount:*** $10,252,303 (16% federal, 35% state, 44% institutional, 5% external sources). ***Receiving aid:*** Freshmen: 77% (274); All full-time undergraduates: 81% (977). ***Average award:*** Freshmen: $10,680; Undergraduates: $9733. ***Scholarships, grants, and awards:*** Federal Pell, FSEOG, state, college/university gift aid from institutional funds.

GIFT AID (NON-NEED-BASED) ***Total amount:*** $1,917,764 (1% federal, 17% state, 74% institutional, 8% external sources). ***Receiving aid:*** Freshmen: 10% (36); Undergraduates: 9% (110). ***Average award:*** Freshmen: $9547; Undergraduates: $8949. ***Scholarships, grants, and awards by category:*** *Academic Interests/Achievement:* 469 awards ($2,376,144 total): biological sciences, business, communication, computer science, education, English, general academic interests/achievements, humanities, mathematics, physical sciences, premedicine, religion/biblical studies, social sciences. *Creative Arts/Performance:* 146 awards ($354,110 total): art/fine arts, journalism/publications, music, theater/drama. *Special Achievements/Activities:* 228 awards ($598,764 total): cheerleading/drum major, junior miss, leadership, religious involvement. *Special Characteristics:* 115 awards ($540,450 total): adult students, children of educators, international students, relatives of clergy, religious affiliation. ***ROTC:*** Army cooperative.

LOANS ***Student loans:*** $5,446,432 (76% need-based, 24% non-need-based). 76% of past graduating class borrowed through all loan programs. *Average indebtedness per student:* $17,083. ***Average need-based loan:*** Freshmen: $3134; Undergraduates: $3861. ***Parent loans:*** $1,160,929 (55% need-based, 45% non-need-based). ***Programs:*** FFEL (Subsidized and Unsubsidized Stafford, PLUS), Perkins, college/university.

WORK-STUDY ***Federal work-study:*** Total amount: $528,710; 328 jobs averaging $1320. ***State or other work-study/employment:*** Total amount: $128,472 (14% need-based, 86% non-need-based). 75 part-time jobs averaging $1925.

ATHLETIC AWARDS Total amount: $1,611,004 (56% need-based, 44% non-need-based).

APPLYING FOR FINANCIAL AID ***Required financial aid form:*** FAFSA. ***Financial aid deadline (priority):*** 3/1. ***Notification date:*** Continuous beginning 3/15. Students must reply within 3 weeks of notification.

CONTACT Mr. Aaron Gabehart, Financial Aid Counselor, Campbellsville University, 1 University Drive, Campbellsville, KY 42718, 270-789-5305 or toll-free 800-264-6014. *Fax:* 270-789-5060. *E-mail:* finaid@campbellsville.edu.

CAMPBELL UNIVERSITY

Buies Creek, NC

Tuition & fees: $18,598 **Average undergraduate aid package: $23,850**

ABOUT THE INSTITUTION Independent religious, coed. Awards: associate, bachelor's, master's, doctoral, and first professional degrees. 98 undergraduate majors. Total enrollment: 6,033. Undergraduates: 4,384. Freshmen: 820. Federal methodology is used as a basis for awarding need-based institutional aid.

UNDERGRADUATE EXPENSES for 2007–08 ***Application fee:*** $35. ***Comprehensive fee:*** $24,758 includes full-time tuition ($18,198), mandatory fees ($400), and room and board ($6160). ***Part-time tuition:*** $275 per credit hour.

FRESHMAN FINANCIAL AID (Fall 2006, est.) 716 applied for aid; of those 83% were deemed to have need. 100% of freshmen with need received aid; of those 100% had need fully met. ***Average percent of need met:*** 100% (excluding resources awarded to replace EFC). ***Average financial aid package:*** $25,545 (excluding resources awarded to replace EFC). 23% of all full-time freshmen had no need and received non-need-based gift aid.

UNDERGRADUATE FINANCIAL AID (Fall 2006, est.) 2,636 applied for aid; of those 85% were deemed to have need. 100% of undergraduates with need received aid; of those 100% had need fully met. ***Average percent of need met:*** 100% (excluding resources awarded to replace EFC). ***Average financial aid package:*** $23,850 (excluding resources awarded to replace EFC). 17% of all full-time undergraduates had no need and received non-need-based gift aid.

GIFT AID (NEED-BASED) ***Total amount:*** $18,024,370 (18% federal, 33% state, 46% institutional, 3% external sources). ***Receiving aid:*** Freshmen: 53% (432); All full-time undergraduates: 47% (1,615). ***Average award:*** Freshmen: $5459; Undergraduates: $4432. ***Scholarships, grants, and awards:*** Federal Pell, FSEOG, state, private, college/university gift aid from institutional funds.

GIFT AID (NON-NEED-BASED) ***Total amount:*** $8,989,818 (19% federal, 27% state, 49% institutional, 5% external sources). ***Receiving aid:*** Freshmen: 70% (575); Undergraduates: 61% (2,097). ***Average award:*** Freshmen: $6901; Undergraduates: $6127. ***Scholarships, grants, and awards by category:*** *Academic Interests/Achievement:* 1,575 awards ($9,240,096 total): general academic interests/achievements. *Creative Arts/Performance:* 73 awards ($73,560 total): art/fine arts, creative writing, journalism/publications, music, theater/drama. *Special Achievements/Activities:* 117 awards ($108,846 total): cheerleading/drum major, religious involvement. *Special Characteristics:* 113 awards ($820,547 total): children of faculty/staff. ***ROTC:*** Army.

LOANS ***Student loans:*** $19,191,238 (73% need-based, 27% non-need-based). 75% of past graduating class borrowed through all loan programs. *Average indebtedness per student:* $21,703. ***Average need-based loan:*** Freshmen: $2918; Undergraduates: $3957. ***Parent loans:*** $15,404,385 (73% need-based, 27% non-need-based). ***Programs:*** FFEL (Subsidized and Unsubsidized Stafford, PLUS), Perkins, state.

WORK-STUDY ***Federal work-study:*** Total amount: $1,144,865; 841 jobs averaging $1361. ***State or other work-study/employment:*** Total amount: $441,906 (100% non-need-based). 559 part-time jobs averaging $791.

ATHLETIC AWARDS Total amount: $2,478,280 (43% need-based, 57% non-need-based).

APPLYING FOR FINANCIAL AID ***Required financial aid form:*** FAFSA. ***Financial aid deadline (priority):*** 3/15. ***Notification date:*** Continuous beginning 3/1. Students must reply within 2 weeks of notification.

CONTACT Financial Aid Office, Campbell University, PO Box 36, Buies Creek, NC 27506, 910-893-1310 or toll-free 800-334-4111. *Fax:* 910-814-5788.

CANISIUS COLLEGE

Buffalo, NY

Tuition & fees: $24,937 **Average undergraduate aid package: $19,698**

ABOUT THE INSTITUTION Independent Roman Catholic (Jesuit), coed. Awards: bachelor's and master's degrees and post-master's certificates. 54 undergraduate majors. Total enrollment: 4,850. Undergraduates: 3,461. Freshmen: 755. Both federal and institutional methodology are used as a basis for awarding need-based institutional aid.

UNDERGRADUATE EXPENSES for 2006–07 ***Application fee:*** $40. ***One-time required fee:*** $125. ***Comprehensive fee:*** $34,417 includes full-time tuition ($23,930), mandatory fees ($1007), and room and board ($9480). ***College room only:*** $5620. Full-time tuition and fees vary according to course load. Room and board charges vary according to board plan and housing facility. ***Part-time tuition:*** $683 per credit hour. ***Part-time fees:*** $20.50 per credit; $18 per term. Part-time tuition and fees vary according to course load. ***Payment plans:*** Tuition prepayment, installment, deferred payment.

FRESHMAN FINANCIAL AID (Fall 2006, est.) 667 applied for aid; of those 90% were deemed to have need. 100% of freshmen with need received aid; of those 37% had need fully met. ***Average percent of need met:*** 86% (excluding resources awarded to replace EFC). ***Average financial aid package:*** $22,199 (excluding resources awarded to replace EFC). 18% of all full-time freshmen had no need and received non-need-based gift aid.

UNDERGRADUATE FINANCIAL AID (Fall 2006, est.) 2,655 applied for aid; of those 91% were deemed to have need. 100% of undergraduates with need received aid; of those 29% had need fully met. ***Average percent of need met:*** 79% (excluding resources awarded to replace EFC). ***Average financial aid package:*** $19,698 (excluding resources awarded to replace EFC). 20% of all full-time undergraduates had no need and received non-need-based gift aid.

GIFT AID (NEED-BASED) ***Total amount:*** $32,533,514 (9% federal, 13% state, 77% institutional, 1% external sources). ***Receiving aid:*** Freshmen: 80% (599); All full-time undergraduates: 75% (2,380). ***Average award:*** Freshmen: $16,455; Undergraduates: $14,111. ***Scholarships, grants, and awards:*** Federal Pell, FSEOG, state, private, college/university gift aid from institutional funds.

GIFT AID (NON-NEED-BASED) ***Total amount:*** $4,212,897 (5% federal, 2% state, 92% institutional, 1% external sources). ***Receiving aid:*** Freshmen: 19% (142); Undergraduates: 18% (567). ***Average award:*** Freshmen: $11,674; Undergraduates: $10,618. ***Scholarships, grants, and awards by category:*** *Academic Interests/Achievement:* 2,363 awards ($20,958,291 total): general academic interests/achievements. *Creative Arts/Performance:* 55 awards ($107,500 total): art/fine arts, music. *Special Achievements/Activities:* 63 awards ($125,415 total): community service, leadership, religious involvement. *Special Characteristics:* 470 awards ($2,513,458 total): children and siblings of alumni, children of educators, children of faculty/staff, international students, religious affiliation, siblings of current students, spouses of current students. ***Tuition waivers:*** Full or partial for children of alumni. ***ROTC:*** Army.

LOANS ***Student loans:*** $17,839,328 (68% need-based, 32% non-need-based). 75% of past graduating class borrowed through all loan programs. *Average indebtedness per student:* $24,386. ***Average need-based loan:*** Freshmen: $2982; Undergraduates: $4020. ***Parent loans:*** $7,279,418 (26% need-based, 74% non-need-based). ***Programs:*** FFEL (Subsidized and Unsubsidized Stafford, PLUS), Perkins, college/university.

WORK-STUDY ***Federal work-study:*** Total amount: $876,026; 584 jobs averaging $1396. ***State or other work-study/employment:*** Total amount: $86,477 (47% need-based, 53% non-need-based).

ATHLETIC AWARDS Total amount: $1,180,031 (55% need-based, 45% non-need-based).

APPLYING FOR FINANCIAL AID ***Required financial aid forms:*** FAFSA, state aid form. ***Financial aid deadline (priority):*** 2/15. ***Notification date:*** Continuous beginning 3/1. Students must reply by 5/1.

CONTACT Mr. Curtis Gaume, Director of Student Financial Aid, Canisius College, 2001 Main Street, Buffalo, NY 14208-1098, 716-888-2300 or toll-free 800-843-1517. *Fax:* 716-888-2377. *E-mail:* gaume@canisius.edu.

CAPELLA UNIVERSITY

Minneapolis, MN

CONTACT University Services, Capella University, 222 South Ninth Street, Minneapolis, MN 55402, 888-227-3552 or toll-free 888-CAPELLA.

CAPITAL UNIVERSITY

Columbus, OH

Tuition & fees: $25,100 **Average undergraduate aid package: $17,938**

ABOUT THE INSTITUTION Independent religious, coed. Awards: bachelor's, master's, and first professional degrees. 90 undergraduate majors. Total enrollment: 3,825. Undergraduates: 2,824. Freshmen: 696. Federal methodology is used as a basis for awarding need-based institutional aid.

UNDERGRADUATE EXPENSES for 2006–07 ***Application fee:*** $25. ***Comprehensive fee:*** $31,652 includes full-time tuition ($25,100) and room and board ($6552). Full-time tuition and fees vary according to course load, degree level, program, and student level. Room and board charges vary according to board plan and housing facility. ***Part-time tuition:*** $786 per credit hour. Part-time tuition and fees vary according to course load, degree level, program, and student level. ***Payment plan:*** Installment.

FRESHMAN FINANCIAL AID (Fall 2006, est.) 652 applied for aid; of those 87% were deemed to have need. 100% of freshmen with need received aid; of those 25% had need fully met. ***Average percent of need met:*** 88% (excluding resources awarded to replace EFC). ***Average financial aid package:*** $18,372 (excluding resources awarded to replace EFC). 19% of all full-time freshmen had no need and received non-need-based gift aid.

UNDERGRADUATE FINANCIAL AID (Fall 2006, est.) 1,979 applied for aid; of those 91% were deemed to have need. 100% of undergraduates with need received aid; of those 21% had need fully met. ***Average percent of need met:*** 80% (excluding resources awarded to replace EFC). ***Average financial aid package:*** $17,938 (excluding resources awarded to replace EFC). 21% of all full-time undergraduates had no need and received non-need-based gift aid.

GIFT AID (NEED-BASED) ***Total amount:*** $18,849,657 (10% federal, 7% state, 83% institutional). ***Receiving aid:*** Freshmen: 52% (360); All full-time undergraduates: 43% (986). ***Average award:*** Freshmen: $12,821; Undergraduates: $10,604. ***Scholarships, grants, and awards:*** Federal Pell, FSEOG, state, private, college/university gift aid from institutional funds.

GIFT AID (NON-NEED-BASED) ***Total amount:*** $4,416,013 (31% state, 28% institutional, 41% external sources). ***Receiving aid:*** Freshmen: 50% (345); Undergraduates: 76% (1,759). ***Average award:*** Freshmen: $10,867; Undergraduates: $8927. ***Scholarships, grants, and awards by category:*** *Academic Interests/Achievement:* general academic interests/achievements. *Creative Arts/Performance:* music. *Special Achievements/Activities:* hobbies/interests, leadership, religious involvement. *Special Characteristics:* children and siblings of alumni, children of faculty/staff, ethnic background, international students, members of minority groups, relatives of clergy, religious affiliation, siblings of current students. ***Tuition waivers:*** Full or partial for employees or children of employees, senior citizens. ***ROTC:*** Army, Air Force cooperative.

LOANS ***Student loans:*** $12,222,377 (52% need-based, 48% non-need-based). 78% of past graduating class borrowed through all loan programs. *Average indebtedness per student:* $25,171. ***Average need-based loan:*** Freshmen: $2950; Undergraduates: $4249. ***Parent loans:*** $18,337,745 (100% non-need-based). ***Programs:*** FFEL (Subsidized and Unsubsidized Stafford, PLUS), Perkins, Federal Nursing, state, college/university.

WORK-STUDY ***Federal work-study:*** Total amount: $1,888,815; jobs available. ***State or other work-study/employment:*** Part-time jobs available.

APPLYING FOR FINANCIAL AID ***Required financial aid form:*** FAFSA. ***Financial aid deadline (priority):*** 2/28. ***Notification date:*** Continuous beginning 3/1. Students must reply by 5/1.

CONTACT Pamela Varda, Office of Financial Aid, Capital University, 1 College and Main Street, Columbus, OH 43209-2394, 614-236-6511 or toll-free 800-289-6289. *Fax:* 614-236-6926. *E-mail:* finaid@capital.edu.

CAPITOL COLLEGE
Laurel, MD

ABOUT THE INSTITUTION Independent, coed. Awards: associate, bachelor's, and master's degrees and post-bachelor's certificates. 7 undergraduate majors. Total enrollment: 801. Undergraduates: 630. Freshmen: 61.

GIFT AID (NEED-BASED) ***Scholarships, grants, and awards:*** Federal Pell, FSEOG, state, private, college/university gift aid from institutional funds.

LOANS ***Programs:*** FFEL (Subsidized and Unsubsidized Stafford, PLUS), Perkins.

WORK-STUDY ***Federal work-study:*** Total amount: $68,528; 40 jobs averaging $2000. ***State or other work-study/employment:*** 30 part-time jobs averaging $3800.

APPLYING FOR FINANCIAL AID ***Required financial aid forms:*** FAFSA, institution's own form.

CONTACT Suzanne Thompson, Director of Financial Aid, Capitol College, 11301 Springfield Road, Laurel, MD 20708-9759, 301-369-2800 Ext. 3037 or toll-free 800-950-1992. *Fax:* 301-369-2328. *E-mail:* sthompson@capitol-college.edu.

CARDINAL STRITCH UNIVERSITY
Milwaukee, WI

CONTACT Financial Aid Director, Cardinal Stritch University, 6801 North Yates Road, Milwaukee, WI 53217-3985, 414-410-4000 or toll-free 800-347-8822 Ext. 4040.

CARIBBEAN UNIVERSITY
Bayamón, PR

CONTACT Financial Aid Office, Caribbean University, Box 493, Bayamón, PR 00960-0493, 787-780-0070.

CARLETON COLLEGE
Northfield, MN

Tuition & fees: $34,272 **Average undergraduate aid package: $29,116**

ABOUT THE INSTITUTION Independent, coed. Awards: bachelor's degrees. 35 undergraduate majors. Total enrollment: 1,980. Undergraduates: 1,980. Freshmen: 504. Both federal and institutional methodology are used as a basis for awarding need-based institutional aid.

UNDERGRADUATE EXPENSES for 2006–07 ***Application fee:*** $30. ***Comprehensive fee:*** $42,864 includes full-time tuition ($34,083), mandatory fees ($189), and room and board ($8592). ***College room only:*** $4299.

FRESHMAN FINANCIAL AID (Fall 2005) 380 applied for aid; of those 66% were deemed to have need. 100% of freshmen with need received aid; of those 100% had need fully met. ***Average percent of need met:*** 100% (excluding resources awarded to replace EFC). ***Average financial aid package:*** $28,714 (excluding resources awarded to replace EFC). 9% of all full-time freshmen had no need and received non-need-based gift aid.

UNDERGRADUATE FINANCIAL AID (Fall 2005) 1,659 applied for aid; of those 66% were deemed to have need. 100% of undergraduates with need received aid; of those 100% had need fully met. ***Average percent of need met:*** 100% (excluding resources awarded to replace EFC). ***Average financial aid package:*** $29,116 (excluding resources awarded to replace EFC). 8% of all full-time undergraduates had no need and received non-need-based gift aid.

GIFT AID (NEED-BASED) ***Total amount:*** $23,367,453 (3% federal, 2% state, 92% institutional, 3% external sources). ***Receiving aid:*** Freshmen: 50% (251); All full-time undergraduates: 56% (1,098). ***Average award:*** Freshmen: $24,799; Undergraduates: $23,279. ***Scholarships, grants, and awards:*** Federal Pell, FSEOG, state, private, college/university gift aid from institutional funds.

GIFT AID (NON-NEED-BASED) ***Total amount:*** $1,232,096 (2% federal, 53% institutional, 45% external sources). ***Receiving aid:*** Freshmen: 9% (47); Undergraduates: 10% (199). ***Average award:*** Freshmen: $2748; Undergraduates: $4365. ***Scholarships, grants, and awards by category:*** *Academic Interests/Achievement:* 285 awards ($645,041 total): general academic interests/achievements. *Creative Arts/Performance:* 2 awards ($1290 total): music.

LOANS ***Student loans:*** $4,951,364 (99% need-based, 1% non-need-based). 61% of past graduating class borrowed through all loan programs. *Average indebtedness per student:* $19,429. ***Average need-based loan:*** Freshmen: $3369; Undergraduates: $4739. ***Parent loans:*** $2,323,240 (100% non-need-based). ***Programs:*** FFEL (Subsidized and Unsubsidized Stafford, PLUS), Perkins, state, college/university.

WORK-STUDY ***Federal work-study:*** Total amount: $954,507; 391 jobs averaging $2473. ***State or other work-study/employment:*** Total amount: $2,794,115 (63% need-based, 37% non-need-based). 1,241 part-time jobs averaging $2335.

APPLYING FOR FINANCIAL AID ***Required financial aid forms:*** FAFSA, CSS Financial Aid PROFILE, noncustodial (divorced/separated) parent's statement, business/farm supplement. ***Financial aid deadline:*** 2/15 (priority: 2/15). ***Notification date:*** 4/1. Students must reply by 5/1 or within 2 weeks of notification.

CONTACT Mr. Rodney M. Oto, Director of Student Financial Services, Carleton College, One North College Street, Northfield, MN 55057-4001, 507-646-4138 or toll-free 800-995-2275. *Fax:* 507-646-4269.

CARLOS ALBIZU UNIVERSITY
San Juan, PR

CONTACT Financial Aid Office, Carlos Albizu University, 151 Tanca Street, San Juan, PR 00901, 787-725-6500.

CARLOS ALBIZU UNIVERSITY, MIAMI CAMPUS

Miami, FL

CONTACT Maria V. Chavez, Senior Financial Aid Officer, Carlos Albizu University, Miami Campus, 2173 Northwest 99th Avenue, Miami, FL 33172, 305-593-1223 Ext. 153 or toll-free 888-672-3246. *Fax:* 305-593-8902. *E-mail:* mchavez@albizu.edu.

CARLOW UNIVERSITY

Pittsburgh, PA

CONTACT Ms. Natalie Wilson, Director of Financial Aid, Carlow University, 3333 Fifth Avenue, Pittsburgh, PA 15213-3165, 412-578-6171 or toll-free 800-333-CARLOW.

CARNEGIE MELLON UNIVERSITY

Pittsburgh, PA

ABOUT THE INSTITUTION Independent, coed. Awards: bachelor's, master's, and doctoral degrees and post-master's certificates. 71 undergraduate majors. Total enrollment: 10,120. Undergraduates: 5,669. Freshmen: 1,428.

GIFT AID (NEED-BASED) ***Scholarships, grants, and awards:*** Federal Pell, FSEOG, state, private, college/university gift aid from institutional funds.

GIFT AID (NON-NEED-BASED) ***Scholarships, grants, and awards by category:*** *Academic Interests/Achievement:* general academic interests/achievements. *Creative Arts/Performance:* art/fine arts, music, theater/drama.

LOANS ***Programs:*** FFEL (Subsidized and Unsubsidized Stafford, PLUS), Perkins, GATE Loans.

WORK-STUDY ***Federal work-study:*** Total amount: $4,737,736; 2,012 jobs averaging $2355. ***State or other work-study/employment:*** 19 part-time jobs averaging $2247.

APPLYING FOR FINANCIAL AID ***Required financial aid forms:*** FAFSA, institution's own form, parent and student federal income tax returns, parents' W-2 forms.

CONTACT Linda M. Anderson, Director, Enrollment Services, Carnegie Mellon University, 5000 Forbes Avenue, Pittsburgh, PA 15213-3890, 412-268-8186. *Fax:* 412-268-8084. *E-mail:* thehub@andrew.cmu.edu.

CARROLL COLLEGE

Helena, MT

ABOUT THE INSTITUTION Independent Roman Catholic, coed. Awards: associate and bachelor's degrees. 56 undergraduate majors. Total enrollment: 1,452. Undergraduates: 1,452. Freshmen: 304.

GIFT AID (NEED-BASED) ***Scholarships, grants, and awards:*** Federal Pell, FSEOG, state, private, college/university gift aid from institutional funds.

GIFT AID (NON-NEED-BASED) ***Scholarships, grants, and awards by category:*** *Academic Interests/Achievement:* general academic interests/achievements. *Creative Arts/Performance:* debating, theater/drama. *Special Achievements/Activities:* general special achievements/activities, religious involvement. *Special Characteristics:* children of faculty/staff, children of union members/company employees, international students, siblings of current students, spouses of current students, veterans.

LOANS ***Programs:*** FFEL (Subsidized and Unsubsidized Stafford, PLUS), Perkins.

WORK-STUDY ***Federal work-study:*** Total amount: $1,015,746; 457 jobs averaging $2207. ***State or other work-study/employment:*** Total amount: $3856 (75% need-based, 25% non-need-based). 9 part-time jobs averaging $2411.

APPLYING FOR FINANCIAL AID ***Required financial aid form:*** FAFSA.

CONTACT Ms. Janet Riis, Director of Financial Aid, Carroll College, 1601 North Benton Avenue, Helena, MT 59625-0002, 406-447-5423 or toll-free 800-992-3648. *Fax:* 406-447-4533. *E-mail:* jriis@carroll.edu.

CARROLL COLLEGE

Waukesha, WI

Tuition & fees: $20,830 **Average undergraduate aid package: $14,979**

ABOUT THE INSTITUTION Independent Presbyterian, coed. Awards: bachelor's and master's degrees. 76 undergraduate majors. Total enrollment: 3,292. Undergraduates: 3,017. Freshmen: 685. Both federal and institutional methodology are used as a basis for awarding need-based institutional aid.

UNDERGRADUATE EXPENSES for 2007–08 ***Comprehensive fee:*** $27,180 includes full-time tuition ($20,400), mandatory fees ($430), and room and board ($6350). ***College room only:*** $3450. ***Part-time tuition:*** $250 per credit.

FRESHMAN FINANCIAL AID (Fall 2006, est.) 615 applied for aid; of those 77% were deemed to have need. 100% of freshmen with need received aid; of those 50% had need fully met. ***Average percent of need met:*** 100% (excluding resources awarded to replace EFC). ***Average financial aid package:*** $15,067 (excluding resources awarded to replace EFC). 26% of all full-time freshmen had no need and received non-need-based gift aid.

UNDERGRADUATE FINANCIAL AID (Fall 2006, est.) 2,326 applied for aid; of those 77% were deemed to have need. 100% of undergraduates with need received aid; of those 72% had need fully met. ***Average percent of need met:*** 100% (excluding resources awarded to replace EFC). ***Average financial aid package:*** $14,979 (excluding resources awarded to replace EFC). 27% of all full-time undergraduates had no need and received non-need-based gift aid.

GIFT AID (NEED-BASED) ***Total amount:*** $19,767,225 (9% federal, 9% state, 79% institutional, 3% external sources). ***Receiving aid:*** Freshmen: 70% (474); All full-time undergraduates: 73% (1,791). ***Average award:*** Freshmen: $11,657; Undergraduates: $10,566. ***Scholarships, grants, and awards:*** Federal Pell, FSEOG, state, private, college/university gift aid from institutional funds.

GIFT AID (NON-NEED-BASED) ***Total amount:*** $5,539,329 (2% federal, 1% state, 93% institutional, 4% external sources). ***Receiving aid:*** Freshmen: 70% (474); Undergraduates: 73% (1,791). ***Average award:*** Freshmen: $8675; Undergraduates: $7818. ***Scholarships, grants, and awards by category:*** *Academic Interests/Achievement:* 2,146 awards ($12,246,907 total): biological sciences, business, computer science, education, general academic interests/achievements, health fields, humanities, international studies, mathematics, physical sciences, premedicine, social sciences. *Creative Arts/Performance:* 109 awards ($170,330 total): art/fine arts, journalism/publications, music, performing arts, theater/drama. *Special Achievements/Activities:* 151 awards ($104,850 total): general special achievements/activities, junior miss, leadership, memberships, religious involvement. *Special Characteristics:* 1,182 awards ($1,233,650 total): adult students, children and siblings of alumni, children of current students, children of faculty/staff, general special characteristics, international students, siblings of current students, spouses of current students. ***ROTC:*** Army cooperative, Air Force cooperative.

LOANS ***Student loans:*** $14,248,940 (47% need-based, 53% non-need-based). 71% of past graduating class borrowed through all loan programs. *Average indebtedness per student:* $19,267. ***Average need-based loan:*** Freshmen: $1815; Undergraduates: $3072. ***Parent loans:*** $2,990,852 (75% need-based, 25% non-need-based). ***Programs:*** FFEL (Subsidized and Unsubsidized Stafford, PLUS), Perkins, state, college/university.

WORK-STUDY ***Federal work-study:*** Total amount: $1,157,176; 662 jobs averaging $1748. ***State or other work-study/employment:*** Total amount: $1,144,245 (100% non-need-based). 700 part-time jobs averaging $1635.

APPLYING FOR FINANCIAL AID ***Required financial aid form:*** FAFSA. ***Financial aid deadline:*** Continuous. ***Notification date:*** Continuous beginning 2/15. Students must reply by 5/1 or within 2 weeks of notification.

CONTACT Dawn Scott, Director of Financial Aid, Carroll College, 100 North East Avenue, Waukesha, WI 53186-5593, 262-524-7297 or toll-free 800-CARROLL. *Fax:* 262-951-3037. *E-mail:* dscott@cc.edu.

CARSON-NEWMAN COLLEGE

Jefferson City, TN

Tuition & fees: $16,060 **Average undergraduate aid package: $13,645**

ABOUT THE INSTITUTION Independent Southern Baptist, coed. Awards: associate, bachelor's, and master's degrees. 68 undergraduate majors. Total enrollment: 1,949. Undergraduates: 1,799. Freshmen: 438. Federal methodology is used as a basis for awarding need-based institutional aid.

UNDERGRADUATE EXPENSES for 2006–07 ***Application fee:*** $25. ***Comprehensive fee:*** $21,260 includes full-time tuition ($15,300), mandatory fees ($760), and room and board ($5200). ***College room only:*** $2250. ***Part-time tuition:*** $635 per semester hour.

FRESHMAN FINANCIAL AID (Fall 2006, est.) 408 applied for aid; of those 76% were deemed to have need. 100% of freshmen with need received aid; of those

33% had need fully met. ***Average percent of need met:*** 83% (excluding resources awarded to replace EFC). ***Average financial aid package:*** $14,645 (excluding resources awarded to replace EFC). 27% of all full-time freshmen had no need and received non-need-based gift aid.

UNDERGRADUATE FINANCIAL AID (Fall 2006, est.) 1,642 applied for aid; of those 76% were deemed to have need. 100% of undergraduates with need received aid; of those 29% had need fully met. ***Average percent of need met:*** 78% (excluding resources awarded to replace EFC). ***Average financial aid package:*** $13,645 (excluding resources awarded to replace EFC). 22% of all full-time undergraduates had no need and received non-need-based gift aid.

GIFT AID (NEED-BASED) ***Total amount:*** $11,892,340 (21% federal, 23% state, 53% institutional, 3% external sources). ***Receiving aid:*** Freshmen: 70% (307); All full-time undergraduates: 71% (1,224). ***Average award:*** Freshmen: $11,410; Undergraduates: $9650. ***Scholarships, grants, and awards:*** Federal Pell, FSEOG, state, private, college/university gift aid from institutional funds.

GIFT AID (NON-NEED-BASED) ***Total amount:*** $2,896,149 (7% federal, 21% state, 68% institutional, 4% external sources). ***Receiving aid:*** Freshmen: 69% (301); Undergraduates: 68% (1,185). ***Average award:*** Freshmen: $6050; Undergraduates: $5649. ***Scholarships, grants, and awards by category:*** *Academic Interests/Achievement:* biological sciences, business, education, general academic interests/achievements, home economics, mathematics, military science, religion/biblical studies. *Creative Arts/Performance:* art/fine arts, debating, journalism/publications, music. *Special Achievements/Activities:* leadership, memberships. *Special Characteristics:* children and siblings of alumni, members of minority groups, relatives of clergy, siblings of current students. ***ROTC:*** Army, Air Force cooperative.

LOANS ***Student loans:*** $6,046,621 (91% need-based, 9% non-need-based). 76% of past graduating class borrowed through all loan programs. *Average indebtedness per student:* $10,870. ***Average need-based loan:*** Freshmen: $2373; Undergraduates: $3663. ***Parent loans:*** $1,408,388 (84% need-based, 16% non-need-based). ***Programs:*** FFEL (Subsidized and Unsubsidized Stafford, PLUS), Perkins, state, college/university, alternative loans.

WORK-STUDY ***Federal work-study:*** Total amount: $477,398; jobs available. ***State or other work-study/employment:*** Total amount: $252,830 (62% need-based, 38% non-need-based). Part-time jobs available.

ATHLETIC AWARDS Total amount: $1,593,367 (68% need-based, 32% non-need-based).

APPLYING FOR FINANCIAL AID ***Required financial aid forms:*** FAFSA, institution's own form. ***Financial aid deadline (priority):*** 4/1. ***Notification date:*** Continuous. Students must reply within 2 weeks of notification.

CONTACT Danette Seale, Director of Financial Aid, Carson-Newman College, c/o Financial Aid, Jefferson City, TN 37760, 865-471-3247 or toll-free 800-678-9061. *Fax:* 865-471-3502. *E-mail:* dseale@cn.edu.

CARTHAGE COLLEGE

Kenosha, WI

Tuition & fees: $23,650 **Average undergraduate aid package: $15,224**

ABOUT THE INSTITUTION Independent religious, coed. Awards: bachelor's and master's degrees. 48 undergraduate majors. Total enrollment: 2,699. Undergraduates: 2,594. Freshmen: 598. Both federal and institutional methodology are used as a basis for awarding need-based institutional aid.

UNDERGRADUATE EXPENSES for 2006–07 ***Application fee:*** $25. ***Comprehensive fee:*** $30,450 includes full-time tuition ($23,650) and room and board ($6800). Room and board charges vary according to board plan. ***Part-time tuition:*** $345 per credit hour. Part-time tuition and fees vary according to class time and course load. ***Payment plan:*** Installment.

FRESHMAN FINANCIAL AID (Fall 2006, est.) 594 applied for aid; of those 80% were deemed to have need. 100% of freshmen with need received aid; of those 25% had need fully met. ***Average percent of need met:*** 69% (excluding resources awarded to replace EFC). ***Average financial aid package:*** $15,031 (excluding resources awarded to replace EFC). 25% of all full-time freshmen had no need and received non-need-based gift aid.

UNDERGRADUATE FINANCIAL AID (Fall 2006, est.) 1,878 applied for aid; of those 82% were deemed to have need. 100% of undergraduates with need received aid; of those 30% had need fully met. ***Average percent of need met:*** 71% (excluding resources awarded to replace EFC). ***Average financial aid package:*** $15,224 (excluding resources awarded to replace EFC). 28% of all full-time undergraduates had no need and received non-need-based gift aid.

GIFT AID (NEED-BASED) ***Total amount:*** $16,380,421 (7% federal, 5% state, 85% institutional, 3% external sources). ***Receiving aid:*** Freshmen: 73% (476); All full-time undergraduates: 69% (1,521). ***Average award:*** Freshmen: $11,259; Undergraduates: $10,654. ***Scholarships, grants, and awards:*** Federal Pell, FSEOG, state, private, college/university gift aid from institutional funds.

GIFT AID (NON-NEED-BASED) ***Total amount:*** $6,532,287 (1% federal, 94% institutional, 5% external sources). ***Receiving aid:*** Freshmen: 11% (73); Undergraduates: 10% (214). ***Average award:*** Freshmen: $12,500; Undergraduates: $11,784. ***Scholarships, grants, and awards by category:*** *Academic Interests/Achievement:* biological sciences, computer science, engineering/technologies, foreign languages, general academic interests/achievements, health fields, mathematics, physical sciences, premedicine. *Creative Arts/Performance:* applied art and design, art/fine arts, music, theater/drama. *Special Achievements/Activities:* general special achievements/activities, leadership, religious involvement. *Special Characteristics:* children and siblings of alumni, children of educators, children of faculty/staff, children of public servants, local/state students, members of minority groups, previous college experience, relatives of clergy, religious affiliation, siblings of current students. ***Tuition waivers:*** Full or partial for children of alumni, employees or children of employees. ***ROTC:*** Army cooperative, Air Force cooperative.

LOANS ***Student loans:*** $12,346,644 (68% need-based, 32% non-need-based). ***Average need-based loan:*** Freshmen: $4417; Undergraduates: $5608. ***Parent loans:*** $4,734,179 (40% need-based, 60% non-need-based). ***Programs:*** FFEL (Subsidized and Unsubsidized Stafford, PLUS), Perkins, state, college/university.

WORK-STUDY ***Federal work-study:*** Total amount: $126,029; jobs available (averaging $1200). ***State or other work-study/employment:*** Total amount: $145,875 (42% need-based, 58% non-need-based). Part-time jobs available.

APPLYING FOR FINANCIAL AID ***Required financial aid form:*** FAFSA. ***Financial aid deadline (priority):*** 2/15. ***Notification date:*** Continuous beginning 3/1.

CONTACT Robert Helgeson, Director of Student Financial Planning, Carthage College, 2001 Alford Park Drive, Kenosha, WI 53140, 262-551-6001 or toll-free 800-351-4058. *Fax:* 262-551-5762. *E-mail:* rhelgeson@carthage.edu.

CASCADE COLLEGE

Portland, OR

ABOUT THE INSTITUTION Independent religious, coed. Awards: bachelor's degrees. 9 undergraduate majors. Total enrollment: 295. Undergraduates: 295. Freshmen: 68.

GIFT AID (NEED-BASED) ***Scholarships, grants, and awards:*** Federal Pell, FSEOG, private, college/university gift aid from institutional funds.

GIFT AID (NON-NEED-BASED) ***Scholarships, grants, and awards by category:*** *Academic Interests/Achievement:* biological sciences, business, communication, education, English, general academic interests/achievements, international studies, religion/biblical studies. *Creative Arts/Performance:* journalism/publications, music, theater/drama. *Special Achievements/Activities:* general special achievements/activities, leadership, memberships. *Special Characteristics:* children and siblings of alumni, children of current students, children of faculty/staff, general special characteristics, international students, out-of-state students, parents of current students, siblings of current students, spouses of current students.

LOANS ***Programs:*** FFEL (Subsidized and Unsubsidized Stafford, PLUS), alternative loans.

WORK-STUDY ***Federal work-study:*** Total amount: $173,771; 87 jobs averaging $1997. ***State or other work-study/employment:*** Total amount: $20,000 (100% non-need-based). 11 part-time jobs averaging $1818.

APPLYING FOR FINANCIAL AID ***Required financial aid forms:*** FAFSA, institution's own form.

CONTACT Ms. Rebecca Lewis, Director of Financial Services, Cascade College, 9101 East Burnside Street, Portland, OR 97216-1515, 503-257-1218 or toll-free 800-550-7678. *Fax:* 503-257-1222. *E-mail:* jmurphy@cascade.edu.

CASE WESTERN RESERVE UNIVERSITY

Cleveland, OH

Tuition & fees: $31,738 **Average undergraduate aid package: $32,131**

ABOUT THE INSTITUTION Independent, coed. Awards: bachelor's, master's, doctoral, and first professional degrees. 63 undergraduate majors. Total enrollment: 9,592. Undergraduates: 4,080. Freshmen: 1,015. Both federal and institutional methodology are used as a basis for awarding need-based institutional aid.

UNDERGRADUATE EXPENSES for 2006–07 ***Comprehensive fee:*** $41,018 includes full-time tuition ($31,090), mandatory fees ($648), and room and board ($9280). ***College room only:*** $5440. Room and board charges vary according to board plan, housing facility, and student level. ***Part-time tuition:*** $1296 per credit hour. Part-time tuition and fees vary according to course load. ***Payment plan:*** Installment.

FRESHMAN FINANCIAL AID (Fall 2006, est.) 826 applied for aid; of those 79% were deemed to have need. 100% of freshmen with need received aid; of those 85% had need fully met. ***Average percent of need met:*** 92% (excluding resources awarded to replace EFC). ***Average financial aid package:*** $32,096 (excluding resources awarded to replace EFC). 24% of all full-time freshmen had no need and received non-need-based gift aid.

UNDERGRADUATE FINANCIAL AID (Fall 2006, est.) 2,669 applied for aid; of those 89% were deemed to have need. 98% of undergraduates with need received aid; of those 89% had need fully met. ***Average percent of need met:*** 94% (excluding resources awarded to replace EFC). ***Average financial aid package:*** $32,131 (excluding resources awarded to replace EFC). 31% of all full-time undergraduates had no need and received non-need-based gift aid.

GIFT AID (NEED-BASED) ***Total amount:*** $47,395,626 (7% federal, 5% state, 84% institutional, 4% external sources). ***Receiving aid:*** Freshmen: 64% (651); All full-time undergraduates: 60% (2,316). ***Average award:*** Freshmen: $23,700; Undergraduates: $20,941. ***Scholarships, grants, and awards:*** Federal Pell, FSEOG, state, private, college/university gift aid from institutional funds.

GIFT AID (NON-NEED-BASED) ***Total amount:*** $16,242,307 (5% state, 92% institutional, 3% external sources). ***Receiving aid:*** Freshmen: 54% (547); Undergraduates: 51% (1,945). ***Average award:*** Freshmen: $16,174; Undergraduates: $12,657. ***Scholarships, grants, and awards by category:*** *Academic Interests/Achievement:* 1,013 awards ($17,751,114 total): biological sciences, business, communication, computer science, engineering/technologies, English, general academic interests/achievements, health fields, humanities, international studies, mathematics, physical sciences, premedicine, religion/biblical studies, social sciences. *Creative Arts/Performance:* 44 awards ($108,400 total): art/fine arts, creative writing, dance, general creative arts/performance, music, theater/drama. *Special Achievements/Activities:* 79 awards ($229,175 total): leadership. *Special Characteristics:* 172 awards ($4,840,689 total): children of faculty/staff. ***Tuition waivers:*** Full or partial for employees or children of employees. ***ROTC:*** Army cooperative, Air Force cooperative.

LOANS ***Student loans:*** $29,057,800 (47% need-based, 53% non-need-based). 56% of past graduating class borrowed through all loan programs. *Average indebtedness per student:* $28,081. ***Average need-based loan:*** Freshmen: $4930; Undergraduates: $6241. ***Parent loans:*** $3,454,885 (86% need-based, 14% non-need-based). ***Programs:*** FFEL (Subsidized and Unsubsidized Stafford, PLUS), Perkins, Federal Nursing, state, college/university, alternative loans-Custom Signature.

WORK-STUDY ***Federal work-study:*** Total amount: $3,746,516; 2,113 jobs averaging $2576.

APPLYING FOR FINANCIAL AID ***Required financial aid forms:*** FAFSA, noncustodial (divorced/separated) parent's statement, business/farm supplement, income tax form(s), W-2 forms. ***Financial aid deadline (priority):*** 2/15. ***Notification date:*** Continuous beginning 3/15. Students must reply by 5/1 or within 2 weeks of notification.

CONTACT Ms. Nancy Issa, Associate Director of University Financial Aid, Case Western Reserve University, 10900 Euclid Avenue, Cleveland, OH 44106-7049, 216-368-4530. *Fax:* 216-368-5054. *E-mail:* nxi@po.cwru.edu.

CASTLETON STATE COLLEGE

Castleton, VT

CONTACT Audrey Reed, Director of Financial Aid, Castleton State College, Castleton, VT 05735, 802-468-1286 or toll-free 800-639-8521. *Fax:* 802-468-6470. *E-mail:* audrey.reed@castleton.edu.

CATAWBA COLLEGE

Salisbury, NC

Tuition & fees: $19,690 **Average undergraduate aid package: $14,811**

ABOUT THE INSTITUTION Independent religious, coed. Awards: bachelor's and master's degrees. 42 undergraduate majors. Total enrollment: 1,269. Undergraduates: 1,235. Freshmen: 244. Federal methodology is used as a basis for awarding need-based institutional aid.

UNDERGRADUATE EXPENSES for 2006–07 ***Application fee:*** $30. ***Comprehensive fee:*** $26,260 includes full-time tuition ($19,690) and room and board ($6570). Full-time tuition and fees vary according to class time. ***Part-time tuition:*** $525 per credit hour. Part-time tuition and fees vary according to class time, course load, and degree level. ***Payment plan:*** Installment.

FRESHMAN FINANCIAL AID (Fall 2006, est.) 205 applied for aid; of those 81% were deemed to have need. 100% of freshmen with need received aid; of those 34% had need fully met. ***Average percent of need met:*** 95% (excluding resources awarded to replace EFC). ***Average financial aid package:*** $18,096 (excluding resources awarded to replace EFC). 18% of all full-time freshmen had no need and received non-need-based gift aid.

UNDERGRADUATE FINANCIAL AID (Fall 2006, est.) 1,011 applied for aid; of those 84% were deemed to have need. 99% of undergraduates with need received aid; of those 29% had need fully met. ***Average percent of need met:*** 87% (excluding resources awarded to replace EFC). ***Average financial aid package:*** $14,811 (excluding resources awarded to replace EFC). 13% of all full-time undergraduates had no need and received non-need-based gift aid.

GIFT AID (NEED-BASED) ***Total amount:*** $2,265,409 (54% federal, 46% state). ***Receiving aid:*** Freshmen: 39% (94); All full-time undergraduates: 40% (482). ***Average award:*** Freshmen: $5357; Undergraduates: $4532. ***Scholarships, grants, and awards:*** Federal Pell, FSEOG, state, private, college/university gift aid from institutional funds.

GIFT AID (NON-NEED-BASED) ***Total amount:*** $7,765,522 (19% state, 77% institutional, 4% external sources). ***Receiving aid:*** Freshmen: 70% (166); Undergraduates: 69% (831). ***Average award:*** Freshmen: $9388; Undergraduates: $7529. ***Scholarships, grants, and awards by category:*** *Academic Interests/Achievement:* 893 awards ($4,712,230 total): education, general academic interests/achievements. *Creative Arts/Performance:* 116 awards ($202,475 total): music, theater/drama. *Special Characteristics:* children of faculty/staff. ***Tuition waivers:*** Full or partial for employees or children of employees. ***ROTC:*** Army cooperative.

LOANS ***Student loans:*** $4,808,915 (56% need-based, 44% non-need-based). 79% of past graduating class borrowed through all loan programs. *Average indebtedness per student:* $18,133. ***Average need-based loan:*** Freshmen: $4050; Undergraduates: $4231. ***Parent loans:*** $1,712,515 (100% non-need-based). ***Programs:*** FFEL (Subsidized and Unsubsidized Stafford, PLUS), Perkins, college/university, TERI Loans, Nellie Mae Loans, Advantage Loans, alternative loans, CitiAssist Loans, "Extra" loans.

WORK-STUDY ***Federal work-study:*** Total amount: $314,200; 191 jobs averaging $1645. ***State or other work-study/employment:*** Total amount: $321,086 (100% non-need-based). 210 part-time jobs averaging $1528.

ATHLETIC AWARDS Total amount: $1,992,327 (100% non-need-based).

APPLYING FOR FINANCIAL AID ***Required financial aid forms:*** FAFSA, state aid form. ***Financial aid deadline (priority):*** 3/15. ***Notification date:*** Continuous. Students must reply within 2 weeks of notification.

CONTACT Melanie McCulloh, Director of Scholarships and Financial Aid, Catawba College, 2300 West Innes Street, Salisbury, NC 28144-2488, 704-637-4416 or toll-free 800-CATAWBA. *Fax:* 704-637-4252. *E-mail:* mcmccull@catawba.edu.

THE CATHOLIC UNIVERSITY OF AMERICA

Washington, DC

Tuition & fees: $28,990 **Average undergraduate aid package: $17,620**

ABOUT THE INSTITUTION Independent religious, coed. Awards: bachelor's, master's, doctoral, and first professional degrees and post-master's certificates. 77 undergraduate majors. Total enrollment: 6,148. Undergraduates: 3,123. Freshmen: 857. Federal methodology is used as a basis for awarding need-based institutional aid.

UNDERGRADUATE EXPENSES for 2007–08 ***Application fee:*** $55. ***Comprehensive fee:*** $39,798 includes full-time tuition ($27,700), mandatory fees ($1290), and room and board ($10,808). ***College room only:*** $6224. ***Part-time tuition:*** $1045 per credit. ***Part-time fees:*** $655 per year.

FRESHMAN FINANCIAL AID (Fall 2006, est.) 650 applied for aid; of those 74% were deemed to have need. 100% of freshmen with need received aid; of those 55% had need fully met. ***Average percent of need met:*** 87% (excluding resources awarded to replace EFC). ***Average financial aid package:*** $19,157 (excluding resources awarded to replace EFC). 42% of all full-time freshmen had no need and received non-need-based gift aid.

UNDERGRADUATE FINANCIAL AID (Fall 2006, est.) 1,948 applied for aid; of those 79% were deemed to have need. 99% of undergraduates with need received aid; of those 54% had need fully met. ***Average percent of need met:*** 84% (excluding resources awarded to replace EFC). ***Average financial aid package:*** $17,620 (excluding resources awarded to replace EFC). 39% of all full-time undergraduates had no need and received non-need-based gift aid.

GIFT AID (NEED-BASED) ***Total amount:*** $19,016,948 (5% federal, 1% state, 91% institutional, 3% external sources). ***Receiving aid:*** Freshmen: 55% (474); All full-time undergraduates: 51% (1,469). ***Average award:*** Freshmen: $14,039; Undergraduates: $12,839. ***Scholarships, grants, and awards:*** Federal Pell, FSEOG, state, private, college/university gift aid from institutional funds, Federal Nursing, Commercial Loans.

GIFT AID (NON-NEED-BASED) ***Total amount:*** $10,445,285 (98% institutional, 2% external sources). ***Average award:*** Freshmen: $8849; Undergraduates: $9262. ***Scholarships, grants, and awards by category:*** *Academic Interests/Achievement:* general academic interests/achievements. *Creative Arts/Performance:* music, theater/drama. *Special Achievements/Activities:* general special achievements/activities. *Special Characteristics:* adult students, children of faculty/staff, ethnic background, first-generation college students, handicapped students, local/state students, religious affiliation, siblings of current students, twins. ***ROTC:*** Army cooperative, Naval cooperative, Air Force cooperative.

LOANS ***Student loans:*** $16,438,977 (83% need-based, 17% non-need-based). ***Average need-based loan:*** Freshmen: $4259; Undergraduates: $4674. ***Parent loans:*** $8,804,268 (75% need-based, 25% non-need-based). ***Programs:*** FFEL (Subsidized and Unsubsidized Stafford, PLUS), Perkins, Federal Nursing, college/university, commercial loans.

WORK-STUDY ***Federal work-study:*** Total amount: $1,938,627; jobs available.

APPLYING FOR FINANCIAL AID ***Required financial aid forms:*** FAFSA, Alumni and Parish Scholarship Application if appropriate. ***Financial aid deadline (priority):*** 3/1. ***Notification date:*** Continuous beginning 4/1. Students must reply by 5/1 or within 2 weeks of notification.

CONTACT Mr. Donald Bosse, Director of Financial Aid, The Catholic University of America, 620 Michigan Avenue, NE, 6 McMahon Hall, Washington, DC 20064, 202-319-5307 or toll-free 202-319-5305 (in-state), 800-673-2772 (out-of-state). *Fax:* 202-319-5573. *E-mail:* bosse@cua.edu.

CAZENOVIA COLLEGE

Cazenovia, NY

Tuition & fees: $21,490 | **Average undergraduate aid package: $16,990**

ABOUT THE INSTITUTION Independent, coed. Awards: associate and bachelor's degrees. 21 undergraduate majors. Total enrollment: 1,006. Undergraduates: 1,006. Freshmen: 258. Federal methodology is used as a basis for awarding need-based institutional aid.

UNDERGRADUATE EXPENSES for 2007–08 ***Application fee:*** $30. ***Comprehensive fee:*** $30,430 includes full-time tuition ($21,280), mandatory fees ($210), and room and board ($8940). ***Part-time tuition:*** $450 per credit. ***Part-time fees:*** $105 per term.

UNDERGRADUATE FINANCIAL AID (Fall 2006, est.) 747 applied for aid; of those 92% were deemed to have need. 100% of undergraduates with need received aid; of those 23% had need fully met. ***Average percent of need met:*** 72% (excluding resources awarded to replace EFC). ***Average financial aid package:*** $16,990 (excluding resources awarded to replace EFC). 10% of all full-time undergraduates had no need and received non-need-based gift aid.

GIFT AID (NEED-BASED) ***Total amount:*** $8,661,090 (13% federal, 18% state, 67% institutional, 2% external sources). ***Receiving aid:*** All full-time undergraduates: 83% (678). ***Average award:*** Undergraduates: $8000. ***Scholarships, grants, and awards:*** Federal Pell, FSEOG, state, private, college/university gift aid from institutional funds.

GIFT AID (NON-NEED-BASED) ***Total amount:*** $748,367 (2% federal, 5% state, 92% institutional, 1% external sources). ***Receiving aid:*** Undergraduates: 12% (102). ***Average award:*** Undergraduates: $8347. ***Scholarships, grants, and awards by category:*** *Academic Interests/Achievement:* general academic interests/achievements. ***ROTC:*** Army cooperative, Air Force cooperative.

LOANS ***Student loans:*** $6,449,503 (68% need-based, 32% non-need-based). 87% of past graduating class borrowed through all loan programs. *Average indebtedness per student:* $28,814. ***Average need-based loan:*** Undergraduates: $3698. ***Parent loans:*** $1,821,825 (41% need-based, 59% non-need-based). ***Programs:*** Federal Direct (Subsidized and Unsubsidized Stafford, PLUS).

WORK-STUDY ***Federal work-study:*** Total amount: $282,000; jobs available.

APPLYING FOR FINANCIAL AID ***Required financial aid forms:*** FAFSA, state aid form. ***Financial aid deadline (priority):*** 3/15. ***Notification date:*** Continuous beginning 11/1. Students must reply by 5/1 or within 2 weeks of notification.

CONTACT Christine L. Mandel, Director of Financial Aid, Cazenovia College, 3 Sullivan Street, Cazenovia, NY 13035, 315-655-7887 or toll-free 800-654-3210. *Fax:* 315-655-7219. *E-mail:* finaid@cazenovia.edu.

CEDAR CREST COLLEGE

Allentown, PA

Tuition & fees: $25,340 | **Average undergraduate aid package: $17,171**

ABOUT THE INSTITUTION Independent religious, women only. Awards: associate, bachelor's, and master's degrees and post-bachelor's certificates. 53 undergraduate majors. Total enrollment: 1,943. Undergraduates: 1,865. Freshmen: 263. Federal methodology is used as a basis for awarding need-based institutional aid.

UNDERGRADUATE EXPENSES for 2007–08 ***Application fee:*** $30. ***Comprehensive fee:*** $33,964 includes full-time tuition ($25,040), mandatory fees ($300), and room and board ($8624). ***Part-time tuition:*** $697 per credit.

FRESHMAN FINANCIAL AID (Fall 2006, est.) 236 applied for aid; of those 90% were deemed to have need. 100% of freshmen with need received aid; of those 13% had need fully met. ***Average percent of need met:*** 77% (excluding resources awarded to replace EFC). ***Average financial aid package:*** $18,901 (excluding resources awarded to replace EFC). 11% of all full-time freshmen had no need and received non-need-based gift aid.

UNDERGRADUATE FINANCIAL AID (Fall 2006, est.) 928 applied for aid; of those 91% were deemed to have need. 100% of undergraduates with need received aid; of those 16% had need fully met. ***Average percent of need met:*** 75% (excluding resources awarded to replace EFC). ***Average financial aid package:*** $17,171 (excluding resources awarded to replace EFC). 11% of all full-time undergraduates had no need and received non-need-based gift aid.

GIFT AID (NEED-BASED) ***Total amount:*** $11,940,799 (13% federal, 17% state, 65% institutional, 5% external sources). ***Receiving aid:*** Freshmen: 88% (212); All full-time undergraduates: 86% (813). ***Average award:*** Freshmen: $15,120; Undergraduates: $13,303. ***Scholarships, grants, and awards:*** Federal Pell, FSEOG, state, private, college/university gift aid from institutional funds, Federal Nursing.

GIFT AID (NON-NEED-BASED) ***Total amount:*** $1,285,668 (2% state, 70% institutional, 28% external sources). ***Receiving aid:*** Freshmen: 8% (19); Undergraduates: 9% (81). ***Average award:*** Freshmen: $14,744; Undergraduates: $13,345. ***Scholarships, grants, and awards by category:*** *Academic Interests/Achievement:* 335 awards ($3,127,666 total): general academic interests/achievements. *Creative Arts/Performance:* 126 awards ($183,971 total): art/fine arts, dance, performing arts, theater/drama. *Special Achievements/Activities:* 57 awards ($61,250 total): community service, general special achievements/activities, junior miss, leadership, memberships, religious involvement. *Special Characteristics:* 77 awards ($257,000 total): adult students, children and siblings of alumni, general special characteristics, previous college experience, relatives of clergy, religious affiliation, siblings of current students. ***ROTC:*** Army cooperative.

LOANS ***Student loans:*** $11,731,694 (74% need-based, 26% non-need-based). 99% of past graduating class borrowed through all loan programs. *Average indebtedness per student:* $28,730. ***Average need-based loan:*** Freshmen: $3140; Undergraduates: $4022. ***Parent loans:*** $1,966,717 (35% need-based, 65% non-need-based). ***Programs:*** FFEL (Subsidized and Unsubsidized Stafford, PLUS), Perkins, Federal Nursing, college/university.

WORK-STUDY ***Federal work-study:*** Total amount: $130,755; 104 jobs averaging $1257. ***State or other work-study/employment:*** Total amount: $646,660 (71% need-based, 29% non-need-based). 369 part-time jobs averaging $1752.

APPLYING FOR FINANCIAL AID ***Required financial aid forms:*** FAFSA, institution's own form. ***Financial aid deadline (priority):*** 5/1. ***Notification date:*** Continuous. Students must reply by 5/1.

CONTACT Ms. Lori Williams, Director of Financial Aid, Cedar Crest College, 100 College Drive, Allentown, PA 18104-6196, 610-740-3785 or toll-free 800-360-1222. *Fax:* 610-606-4653. *E-mail:* finaid@cedarcrest.edu.

CEDARVILLE UNIVERSITY

Cedarville, OH

Tuition & fees: $19,800 **Average undergraduate aid package: $16,048**

ABOUT THE INSTITUTION Independent Baptist, coed. Awards: bachelor's and master's degrees. 77 undergraduate majors. Total enrollment: 3,112. Undergraduates: 3,064. Freshmen: 713. Federal methodology is used as a basis for awarding need-based institutional aid.

UNDERGRADUATE EXPENSES for 2006–07 ***Application fee:*** $30. ***Comprehensive fee:*** $24,810 includes full-time tuition ($18,400), mandatory fees ($1400), and room and board ($5010). ***College room only:*** $2684. Room and board charges vary according to board plan. ***Part-time tuition:*** $575 per credit hour. Part-time tuition and fees vary according to course load. ***Payment plan:*** Installment.

FRESHMAN FINANCIAL AID (Fall 2006, est.) 742 applied for aid; of those 80% were deemed to have need. 98% of freshmen with need received aid; of those 50% had need fully met. ***Average percent of need met:*** 23% (excluding resources awarded to replace EFC). ***Average financial aid package:*** $15,654 (excluding resources awarded to replace EFC). 77% of all full-time freshmen had no need and received non-need-based gift aid.

UNDERGRADUATE FINANCIAL AID (Fall 2006, est.) 2,144 applied for aid; of those 83% were deemed to have need. 99% of undergraduates with need received aid; of those 50% had need fully met. ***Average percent of need met:*** 35% (excluding resources awarded to replace EFC). ***Average financial aid package:*** $16,048 (excluding resources awarded to replace EFC). 1% of all full-time undergraduates had no need and received non-need-based gift aid.

GIFT AID (NEED-BASED) ***Total amount:*** $3,614,601 (41% federal, 12% state, 44% institutional, 3% external sources). ***Receiving aid:*** Freshmen: 28% (243); All full-time undergraduates: 33% (954). ***Average award:*** Freshmen: $1391; Undergraduates: $1897. ***Scholarships, grants, and awards:*** Federal Pell, FSEOG, state, private, college/university gift aid from institutional funds.

GIFT AID (NON-NEED-BASED) ***Total amount:*** $9,686,317 (11% state, 63% institutional, 26% external sources). ***Receiving aid:*** Freshmen: 57% (500); Undergraduates: 46% (1,315). ***Average award:*** Freshmen: $8241; Undergraduates: $7890. ***Scholarships, grants, and awards by category:*** *Academic Interests/Achievement:* 950 awards ($1,796,182 total): general academic interests/achievements. *Creative Arts/Performance:* 75 awards ($112,805 total): debating, music. *Special Achievements/Activities:* 408 awards ($695,365 total): leadership. *Special Characteristics:* 225 awards ($2,318,866 total): children and siblings of alumni, children of faculty/staff, ethnic background, general special characteristics, religious affiliation, veterans. ***Tuition waivers:*** Full or partial for employees or children of employees, senior citizens. ***ROTC:*** Army cooperative, Air Force cooperative.

LOANS ***Student loans:*** $10,325,929 (55% need-based, 45% non-need-based). 66% of past graduating class borrowed through all loan programs. *Average indebtedness per student:* $21,746. ***Average need-based loan:*** Freshmen: $2595; Undergraduates: $3906. ***Parent loans:*** $9,640,902 (100% non-need-based). ***Programs:*** FFEL (Subsidized and Unsubsidized Stafford, PLUS), Perkins, Federal Nursing, college/university.

WORK-STUDY ***Federal work-study:*** Total amount: $348,401; 444 jobs averaging $785. ***State or other work-study/employment:*** Total amount: $1,308,026 (100% non-need-based). 1,417 part-time jobs averaging $974.

ATHLETIC AWARDS Total amount: $601,269 (100% non-need-based).

APPLYING FOR FINANCIAL AID ***Required financial aid form:*** FAFSA. ***Financial aid deadline (priority):*** 3/1. ***Notification date:*** Continuous beginning 3/1. Students must reply within 4 weeks of notification.

CONTACT Mr. Fred Merritt, Director of Financial Aid, Cedarville University, 251 North Main Street, Cedarville, OH 45314-0601, 937-766-7866 or toll-free 800-CEDARVILLE. *E-mail:* merrittf@cedarville.edu.

CENTENARY COLLEGE

Hackettstown, NJ

Tuition & fees: $22,415 **Average undergraduate aid package: $14,905**

ABOUT THE INSTITUTION Independent religious, coed. Awards: associate, bachelor's, and master's degrees and post-bachelor's certificates. 24 undergraduate majors. Total enrollment: 2,662. Undergraduates: 1,952. Freshmen: 304. Federal methodology is used as a basis for awarding need-based institutional aid.

UNDERGRADUATE EXPENSES for 2006–07 ***Application fee:*** $30. ***Comprehensive fee:*** $30,815 includes full-time tuition ($21,230), mandatory fees ($1185), and room and board ($8400). ***Part-time tuition:*** $420 per credit.

FRESHMAN FINANCIAL AID (Fall 2006, est.) 270 applied for aid; of those 83% were deemed to have need. 99% of freshmen with need received aid; of those 20% had need fully met. ***Average percent of need met:*** 69% (excluding resources awarded to replace EFC). ***Average financial aid package:*** $16,206 (excluding resources awarded to replace EFC). 9% of all full-time freshmen had no need and received non-need-based gift aid.

UNDERGRADUATE FINANCIAL AID (Fall 2006, est.) 1,655 applied for aid; of those 61% were deemed to have need. 99% of undergraduates with need received aid; of those 18% had need fully met. ***Average percent of need met:*** 67% (excluding resources awarded to replace EFC). ***Average financial aid package:*** $14,905 (excluding resources awarded to replace EFC). 2% of all full-time undergraduates had no need and received non-need-based gift aid.

GIFT AID (NEED-BASED) ***Total amount:*** $10,583,633 (11% federal, 25% state, 58% institutional, 6% external sources). ***Receiving aid:*** Freshmen: 61% (214); All full-time undergraduates: 52% (907). ***Average award:*** Freshmen: $13,182; Undergraduates: $11,484. ***Scholarships, grants, and awards:*** Federal Pell, FSEOG, state, private, college/university gift aid from institutional funds.

GIFT AID (NON-NEED-BASED) ***Total amount:*** $914,498 (79% institutional, 21% external sources). ***Receiving aid:*** Freshmen: 5% (19); Undergraduates: 4% (61). ***Average award:*** Freshmen: $17,711; Undergraduates: $17,711. ***Scholarships, grants, and awards by category:*** *Academic Interests/Achievement:* 636 awards ($3,653,964 total): general academic interests/achievements. *Special Achievements/Activities:* 96 awards ($405,600 total): leadership. *Special Characteristics:* 613 awards ($2,357,300 total): children and siblings of alumni, children of faculty/staff, ethnic background, general special characteristics, local/state students, out-of-state students, previous college experience, religious affiliation, siblings of current students.

LOANS ***Student loans:*** $10,524,111 (65% need-based, 35% non-need-based). 92% of past graduating class borrowed through all loan programs. *Average indebtedness per student:* $20,571. ***Average need-based loan:*** Freshmen: $3924; Undergraduates: $3924. ***Parent loans:*** $1,817,107 (47% need-based, 53% non-need-based). ***Programs:*** FFEL (Subsidized and Unsubsidized Stafford, PLUS), Perkins, state, NJ Class Loans.

WORK-STUDY ***Federal work-study:*** Total amount: $102,791; 223 jobs averaging $683. ***State or other work-study/employment:*** Total amount: $285,559 (52% need-based, 48% non-need-based). 286 part-time jobs averaging $780.

APPLYING FOR FINANCIAL AID ***Required financial aid form:*** FAFSA. ***Financial aid deadline (priority):*** 4/15. ***Notification date:*** Continuous beginning 3/7. Students must reply within 2 weeks of notification.

CONTACT Michael Corso, Director of Financial Aid, Centenary College, 400 Jefferson Street, Hackettstown, NJ 07840-2100, 908-852-1400 Ext. 2207 or toll-free 800-236-8679. *Fax:* 908-813-2632.

CENTENARY COLLEGE OF LOUISIANA

Shreveport, LA

Tuition & fees: $18,900 **Average undergraduate aid package: $16,783**

ABOUT THE INSTITUTION Independent United Methodist, coed. Awards: bachelor's and master's degrees. 66 undergraduate majors. Total enrollment: 1,044. Undergraduates: 904. Freshmen: 232. Federal methodology is used as a basis for awarding need-based institutional aid.

UNDERGRADUATE EXPENSES for 2006–07 ***Application fee:*** $30. ***Comprehensive fee:*** $25,680 includes full-time tuition ($18,900) and room and board ($6780). ***College room only:*** $3310. ***Part-time tuition:*** $630 per semester hour. ***Part-time fees:*** $50 per term.

FRESHMAN FINANCIAL AID (Fall 2006, est.) 198 applied for aid; of those 73% were deemed to have need. 100% of freshmen with need received aid; of those 31% had need fully met. ***Average percent of need met:*** 88% (excluding resources awarded to replace EFC). ***Average financial aid package:*** $17,119 (excluding resources awarded to replace EFC). 25% of all full-time freshmen had no need and received non-need-based gift aid.

UNDERGRADUATE FINANCIAL AID (Fall 2006, est.) 705 applied for aid; of those 72% were deemed to have need. 98% of undergraduates with need received aid; of those 37% had need fully met. ***Average percent of need met:*** 83% (excluding resources awarded to replace EFC). ***Average financial aid package:*** $16,783 (excluding resources awarded to replace EFC). 29% of all full-time undergraduates had no need and received non-need-based gift aid.

GIFT AID (NEED-BASED) ***Total amount:*** $5,971,924 (11% federal, 13% state, 74% institutional, 2% external sources). ***Receiving aid:*** Freshmen: 60% (144); All full-time undergraduates: 56% (496). ***Average award:*** Freshmen: $15,142; Undergraduates: $14,289. ***Scholarships, grants, and awards:*** Federal Pell, FSEOG, state, private, college/university gift aid from institutional funds.

GIFT AID (NON-NEED-BASED) ***Total amount:*** $3,909,517 (11% state, 87% institutional, 2% external sources). ***Receiving aid:*** Freshmen: 17% (40); Undergraduates: 16% (139). ***Average award:*** Freshmen: $10,061; Undergraduates: $10,070. ***Scholarships, grants, and awards by category:*** *Academic Interests/Achievement:* 656 awards ($534,952 total): biological sciences, business, communication, education, engineering/technologies, English, foreign languages, general academic interests/achievements, health fields, humanities, mathematics, physical sciences, premedicine, religion/biblical studies, social sciences. *Creative Arts/Performance:* 215 awards ($717,972 total): art/fine arts, dance, general creative arts/performance, music, performing arts, theater/drama. *Special Achievements/Activities:* 155 awards ($339,713 total): community service, general special achievements/activities, leadership, religious involvement. *Special Characteristics:* 130 awards ($519,275 total): children of educators, children of faculty/staff, ethnic background, general special characteristics, international students, local/state students, members of minority groups, out-of-state students, relatives of clergy, religious affiliation.

LOANS ***Student loans:*** $2,059,309 (54% need-based, 46% non-need-based). 51% of past graduating class borrowed through all loan programs. *Average indebtedness per student:* $17,300. ***Average need-based loan:*** Freshmen: $2857; Undergraduates: $4021. ***Parent loans:*** $2,428,061 (100% non-need-based). ***Programs:*** FFEL (Subsidized and Unsubsidized Stafford, PLUS), Perkins.

WORK-STUDY ***Federal work-study:*** Total amount: $265,747; 170 jobs averaging $1551. ***State or other work-study/employment:*** Total amount: $52,300 (100% non-need-based). 56 part-time jobs averaging $955.

ATHLETIC AWARDS Total amount: $2,489,413 (36% need-based, 64% non-need-based).

APPLYING FOR FINANCIAL AID ***Required financial aid forms:*** FAFSA, institution's own form. ***Financial aid deadline (priority):*** 2/15. ***Notification date:*** 3/15. Students must reply by 5/1.

CONTACT Ms. Mary Sue Rix, Director of Financial Aid, Centenary College of Louisiana, PO Box 41188, Shreveport, LA 71134-1188, 318-869-5137 or toll-free 800-234-4448. *Fax:* 318-841-7266. *E-mail:* msrix@centenary.edu.

CENTRAL BAPTIST COLLEGE

Conway, AR

CONTACT Christi Bell, Financial Aid Director, Central Baptist College, 1501 College Avenue, Conway, AR 72032-6470, 800-205-6872 Ext. 185 or toll-free 800-205-6872. *Fax:* 501-329-2941. *E-mail:* financialaid@cbc.edu.

CENTRAL BIBLE COLLEGE

Springfield, MO

CONTACT Rick Woolverton, Director of Financial Aid, Central Bible College, 3000 North Grant, Springfield, MO 65803-1096, 417-833-2551 or toll-free 800-831-4222 Ext. 1184. *Fax:* 417-833-2168.

CENTRAL CHRISTIAN COLLEGE OF KANSAS

McPherson, KS

CONTACT Mike Reimer, Financial Aid Director, Central Christian College of Kansas, 1200 South Main, PO Box 1403, McPherson, KS 67460, 620-241-0723 Ext. 333 or toll-free 800-835-0078 Ext. 337. *Fax:* 620-241-6032. *E-mail:* miker@centralchristian.edu.

CENTRAL CHRISTIAN COLLEGE OF THE BIBLE

Moberly, MO

ABOUT THE INSTITUTION Independent religious, coed. Awards: associate and bachelor's degrees. 7 undergraduate majors. Total enrollment: 531. Undergraduates: 531. Freshmen: 163.

GIFT AID (NEED-BASED) ***Scholarships, grants, and awards:*** Federal Pell, FSEOG, private, college/university gift aid from institutional funds.

GIFT AID (NON-NEED-BASED) ***Scholarships, grants, and awards by category:*** *Academic Interests/Achievement:* religion/biblical studies.

LOANS ***Programs:*** FFEL (Subsidized and Unsubsidized Stafford, PLUS), alternative loans.

CONTACT Rhonda J. Dunham, Financial Aid Director, Central Christian College of the Bible, 911 East Urbandale Drive, Moberly, MO 65270-1997, 660-263-3900 Ext. 121 or toll-free 888-263-3900 (in-state). *Fax:* 660-263-3936. *E-mail:* rdunham@cccb.edu.

CENTRAL COLLEGE

Pella, IA

Tuition & fees: $21,222 **Average undergraduate aid package: $18,016**

ABOUT THE INSTITUTION Independent religious, coed. Awards: bachelor's degrees. 35 undergraduate majors. Total enrollment: 1,606. Undergraduates: 1,606. Freshmen: 413. Federal methodology is used as a basis for awarding need-based institutional aid.

UNDERGRADUATE EXPENSES for 2006–07 ***Application fee:*** $25. ***Comprehensive fee:*** $28,446 includes full-time tuition ($20,972), mandatory fees ($250), and room and board ($7224). ***College room only:*** $3542. Room and board charges vary according to board plan. ***Part-time tuition:*** $728 per semester hour. Part-time tuition and fees vary according to course load. ***Payment plan:*** Installment.

FRESHMAN FINANCIAL AID (Fall 2006, est.) 395 applied for aid; of those 87% were deemed to have need. 100% of freshmen with need received aid; of those 20% had need fully met. ***Average percent of need met:*** 84% (excluding resources awarded to replace EFC). ***Average financial aid package:*** $18,228 (excluding resources awarded to replace EFC). 17% of all full-time freshmen had no need and received non-need-based gift aid.

UNDERGRADUATE FINANCIAL AID (Fall 2006, est.) 1,288 applied for aid; of those 89% were deemed to have need. 100% of undergraduates with need received aid; of those 20% had need fully met. ***Average percent of need met:*** 84% (excluding resources awarded to replace EFC). ***Average financial aid package:*** $18,016 (excluding resources awarded to replace EFC). 21% of all full-time undergraduates had no need and received non-need-based gift aid.

GIFT AID (NEED-BASED) ***Total amount:*** $14,415,478 (8% federal, 18% state, 71% institutional, 3% external sources). ***Receiving aid:*** Freshmen: 83% (343); All full-time undergraduates: 78% (1,141). ***Average award:*** Freshmen: $14,213; Undergraduates: $12,886. ***Scholarships, grants, and awards:*** Federal Pell, FSEOG, state, private, college/university gift aid from institutional funds.

GIFT AID (NON-NEED-BASED) ***Total amount:*** $3,183,379 (96% institutional, 4% external sources). ***Receiving aid:*** Freshmen: 12% (50); Undergraduates: 10% (142). ***Average award:*** Freshmen: $9175; Undergraduates: $8561. ***Scholarships, grants, and awards by category:*** *Academic Interests/Achievement:* biological sciences, business, communication, computer science, education, foreign languages, general academic interests/achievements, health fields, humanities, international studies, mathematics, physical sciences, religion/biblical studies. *Creative Arts/Performance:* art/fine arts, music, theater/drama. *Special Achievements/Activities:* religious involvement. *Special Characteristics:* children and siblings of alumni, children of current students, children of faculty/staff, general special characteristics, handicapped students, international students, members of minority groups, out-of-state students, previous college experience, religious affiliation, siblings of current students. ***Tuition waivers:*** Full or partial for employees or children of employees.

LOANS ***Student loans:*** $10,912,902 (59% need-based, 41% non-need-based). 87% of past graduating class borrowed through all loan programs. *Average indebtedness per student:* $23,490. ***Average need-based loan:*** Freshmen: $3086; Undergraduates: $4328. ***Parent loans:*** $1,545,213 (27% need-based, 73% non-need-based). ***Programs:*** Federal Direct (Subsidized and Unsubsidized Stafford, PLUS), Perkins, college/university, alternative loans.

WORK-STUDY ***Federal work-study:*** Total amount: $819,122; 758 jobs averaging $1039. ***State or other work-study/employment:*** Total amount: $608,179 (28% need-based, 72% non-need-based). 570 part-time jobs averaging $1067.

APPLYING FOR FINANCIAL AID ***Required financial aid form:*** FAFSA. ***Financial aid deadline (priority):*** 3/15. ***Notification date:*** Continuous beginning 3/15. Students must reply by 5/1 or within 2 weeks of notification.

CONTACT Ms. Jean Vander Wert, Director of Financial Aid, Central College, 812 University Street, Box 5800, Pella, IA 50219-1999, 641-628-5336 or toll-free 877-462-3687 (in-state), 877-462-3689 (out-of-state). *Fax:* 641-628-7199. *E-mail:* vanderwertj@central.edu.

CENTRAL CONNECTICUT STATE UNIVERSITY

New Britain, CT

ABOUT THE INSTITUTION State-supported, coed. Awards: bachelor's, master's, and doctoral degrees and post-bachelor's and post-master's certificates. 53 undergraduate majors. Total enrollment: 12,144. Undergraduates: 9,644. Freshmen: 1,294.

GIFT AID (NEED-BASED) ***Scholarships, grants, and awards:*** Federal Pell, FSEOG, state, private, college/university gift aid from institutional funds.

GIFT AID (NON-NEED-BASED) ***Scholarships, grants, and awards by category:*** *Academic Interests/Achievement:* general academic interests/achievements. *Special Characteristics:* members of minority groups.

LOANS ***Programs:*** Federal Direct (Subsidized and Unsubsidized Stafford, PLUS), FFEL (Subsidized and Unsubsidized Stafford, PLUS), Perkins.

WORK-STUDY ***Federal work-study:*** Total amount: $325,000; 289 jobs averaging $1990. ***State or other work-study/employment:*** 110 part-time jobs averaging $544.

APPLYING FOR FINANCIAL AID ***Required financial aid forms:*** FAFSA, institution's own form.

CONTACT Ms. Keri Lupachino, Assistant Director of Financial Aid, Central Connecticut State University, Memorial Hall, Room 103, 1615 Stanley Street, New Britain, CT 06050-4010, 860-832-2200 or toll-free 888-733-2278 (in-state). *Fax:* 860-832-1105. *E-mail:* lupachinok@ccsu.edu.

CENTRAL METHODIST UNIVERSITY

Fayette, MO

Tuition & fees: $17,160 **Average undergraduate aid package: $13,172**

ABOUT THE INSTITUTION Independent Methodist, coed. Awards: associate, bachelor's, and master's degrees. 47 undergraduate majors. Total enrollment: 841. Undergraduates: 841. Freshmen: 212. Federal methodology is used as a basis for awarding need-based institutional aid.

UNDERGRADUATE EXPENSES for 2007–08 ***Application fee:*** $20. ***Comprehensive fee:*** $22,880 includes full-time tuition ($16,430), mandatory fees ($730), and room and board ($5720). ***Part-time tuition:*** $170 per semester hour.

FRESHMAN FINANCIAL AID (Fall 2006, est.) 193 applied for aid; of those 62% were deemed to have need. 100% of freshmen with need received aid; of those 4% had need fully met. ***Average percent of need met:*** 54% (excluding resources awarded to replace EFC). ***Average financial aid package:*** $12,359 (excluding resources awarded to replace EFC). 5% of all full-time freshmen had no need and received non-need-based gift aid.

UNDERGRADUATE FINANCIAL AID (Fall 2006, est.) 796 applied for aid; of those 71% were deemed to have need. 100% of undergraduates with need received aid; of those 10% had need fully met. ***Average percent of need met:*** 57% (excluding resources awarded to replace EFC). ***Average financial aid package:*** $13,172 (excluding resources awarded to replace EFC). 2% of all full-time undergraduates had no need and received non-need-based gift aid.

GIFT AID (NEED-BASED) ***Total amount:*** $1,528,189 (63% federal, 36% state, 1% institutional). ***Receiving aid:*** Freshmen: 59% (120); All full-time undergraduates: 70% (563). ***Average award:*** Freshmen: $3847; Undergraduates: $3642. ***Scholarships, grants, and awards:*** Federal Pell, FSEOG, state, private, college/university gift aid from institutional funds.

GIFT AID (NON-NEED-BASED) ***Total amount:*** $5,175,339 (1% state, 97% institutional, 2% external sources). ***Receiving aid:*** Freshmen: 59% (120); Undergraduates: 70% (563). ***Average award:*** Freshmen: $7663; Undergraduates: $7883. ***Scholarships, grants, and awards by category:*** *Academic Interests/Achievement:* 532 awards ($1,773,465 total): biological sciences, business, communication, computer science, education, English, foreign languages, general academic interests/achievements, health fields, humanities, mathematics, physical sciences, premedicine, religion/biblical studies, social sciences. *Creative Arts/Performance:* 68 awards ($311,350 total): music, theater/drama. *Special Achievements/Activities:* 44 awards ($100,440 total): cheerleading/drum major, leadership, religious involvement. *Special Characteristics:* 295 awards ($500,886 total): children and siblings of alumni, children of faculty/staff, general special characteristics, international students, relatives of clergy, religious affiliation, siblings of current students, spouses of current students. ***ROTC:*** Army cooperative, Air Force cooperative.

LOANS ***Student loans:*** $2,376,032 (53% need-based, 47% non-need-based). 84% of past graduating class borrowed through all loan programs. *Average indebtedness per student:* $22,904. ***Average need-based loan:*** Freshmen: $3201; Undergraduates: $4952. ***Parent loans:*** $1,704,226 (100% non-need-based). ***Programs:*** FFEL (Subsidized and Unsubsidized Stafford, PLUS), Perkins, college/university.

WORK-STUDY ***Federal work-study:*** Total amount: $167,319; 145 jobs averaging $1000. ***State or other work-study/employment:*** Total amount: $95,475 (100% non-need-based). 90 part-time jobs averaging $1619.

ATHLETIC AWARDS Total amount: $2,494,130 (100% non-need-based).

APPLYING FOR FINANCIAL AID ***Required financial aid form:*** FAFSA. ***Financial aid deadline (priority):*** 3/15. ***Notification date:*** Continuous beginning 1/30. Students must reply within 2 weeks of notification.

CONTACT Linda Mackey, Director of Financial Assistance, Central Methodist University, 411 CMC Square, Fayette, MO 65248-1198, 660-248-6244 or toll-free 888-CMU-1854 (in-state). *Fax:* 660-248-6288. *E-mail:* lmackey@cmc.edu.

CENTRAL MICHIGAN UNIVERSITY

Mount Pleasant, MI

Tuition & fees (MI res): $6753 **Average undergraduate aid package: $10,212**

ABOUT THE INSTITUTION State-supported, coed. Awards: bachelor's, master's, and doctoral degrees and post-bachelor's and post-master's certificates. 117 undergraduate majors. Total enrollment: 26,710. Undergraduates: 20,129. Freshmen: 3,819. Federal methodology is used as a basis for awarding need-based institutional aid.

UNDERGRADUATE EXPENSES for 2006–07 ***Application fee:*** $35. ***Tuition, state resident:*** full-time $6753; part-time $225.11 per credit. ***Tuition, nonresident:*** full-time $15,915; part-time $530.50 per credit. Full-time tuition and fees vary according to student level. Part-time tuition and fees vary according to student level. ***College room and board:*** $6824; ***Room only:*** $3412. Room and board charges vary according to board plan, housing facility, location, and student level. Costs at Central Michigan University are based upon a guaranteed undergraduate tuition plan called the CMU Promise. The CMU Promise to new and transfer undergraduate students is one unchanging tuition rate for up to five years. In addition to fixing the cost of tuition, the CMU Promise guaranteed tuition program eliminates all former mandatory fees, so there are no added fees. The CMU Promise also guarantees that the room and board rate for residence halls will not increase for two years from the date of a student's admission to CMU. ***Payment plan:*** Installment.

FRESHMAN FINANCIAL AID (Fall 2006, est.) 2939 applied for aid; of those 67% were deemed to have need. 99% of freshmen with need received aid; of those 81% had need fully met. ***Average percent of need met:*** 100% (excluding resources awarded to replace EFC). ***Average financial aid package:*** $10,016 (excluding resources awarded to replace EFC). 16% of all full-time freshmen had no need and received non-need-based gift aid.

UNDERGRADUATE FINANCIAL AID (Fall 2006, est.) 12,438 applied for aid; of those 74% were deemed to have need. 99% of undergraduates with need received aid; of those 76% had need fully met. ***Average percent of need met:*** 95% (excluding resources awarded to replace EFC). ***Average financial aid package:*** $10,212 (excluding resources awarded to replace EFC). 10% of all full-time undergraduates had no need and received non-need-based gift aid.

GIFT AID (NEED-BASED) ***Total amount:*** $28,567,707 (48% federal, 21% state, 26% institutional, 5% external sources). ***Receiving aid:*** Freshmen: 46% (1,747); All full-time undergraduates: 39% (7,000). ***Average award:*** Freshmen: $5137; Undergraduates: $4090. ***Scholarships, grants, and awards:*** Federal Pell, FSEOG, state, private, college/university gift aid from institutional funds.

GIFT AID (NON-NEED-BASED) ***Total amount:*** $13,033,240 (7% federal, 29% state, 46% institutional, 18% external sources). ***Receiving aid:*** Freshmen: 7% (280); Undergraduates: 3% (572). ***Average award:*** Freshmen: $3488; Undergraduates: $3134. ***Scholarships, grants, and awards by category:*** *Academic Interests/Achievement:* 4,679 awards ($9,018,464 total): biological sciences, business, communication, computer science, education, engineering/technologies, English, foreign languages, general academic interests/achievements, health fields, humanities, mathematics, military science, physical sciences, social sciences. *Creative Arts/Performance:* 192 awards ($233,954 total): applied art and design, art/fine arts, cinema/film/broadcasting, creative writing, dance, journalism/publications, music, performing arts, theater/drama. *Special Achievements/Activities:* 315 awards ($229,263 total): leadership. *Special Characteristics:* 1,142 awards ($3,820,183 total): children and siblings of alumni, children of faculty/staff, children of union members/company employees, first-generation college students, international students, local/state students, members of minority groups, out-of-state students, veterans, veterans' children. ***Tuition waivers:*** Full or partial for children of alumni, employees or children of employees, senior citizens. ***ROTC:*** Army.

LOANS ***Student loans:*** $69,160,920 (70% need-based, 30% non-need-based). 65% of past graduating class borrowed through all loan programs. *Average indebtedness per student:* $17,365. ***Average need-based loan:*** Freshmen: $3842; Undergraduates: $5490. ***Parent loans:*** $33,222,102 (37% need-based, 63% non-need-based). ***Programs:*** Federal Direct (Subsidized and Unsubsidized Stafford, PLUS), Perkins, state, alternative loans.

WORK-STUDY ***Federal work-study:*** Total amount: $2,373,858; 1,088 jobs averaging $2182. ***State or other work-study/employment:*** Total amount: $6,567,578 (27% need-based, 73% non-need-based). 3,498 part-time jobs averaging $1878.

ATHLETIC AWARDS Total amount: $3,530,592 (30% need-based, 70% non-need-based).

APPLYING FOR FINANCIAL AID ***Required financial aid form:*** FAFSA. ***Financial aid deadline (priority):*** 3/1. ***Notification date:*** Continuous beginning 4/1.

CONTACT Mr. Michael Owens, Director of Scholarships and Financial Aid, Central Michigan University, WA 202, Mount Pleasant, MI 48859, 989-774-7428 or toll-free 888-292-5366. *Fax:* 989-774-3634. *E-mail:* owens1ma@cmich.edu.

CENTRAL MISSOURI STATE UNIVERSITY

Warrensburg, MO

See University of Central Missouri.

CENTRAL PENNSYLVANIA COLLEGE

Summerdale, PA

Tuition & fees: $12,165 **Average undergraduate aid package: N/A**

ABOUT THE INSTITUTION Proprietary, coed. Awards: associate and bachelor's degrees. 26 undergraduate majors. Total enrollment: 1,017. Undergraduates: 1,017. Freshmen: 211. Federal methodology is used as a basis for awarding need-based institutional aid.

UNDERGRADUATE EXPENSES for 2006–07 ***Comprehensive fee:*** $18,090 includes full-time tuition ($11,520), mandatory fees ($645), and room and board ($5925). ***College room only:*** $4725. Full-time tuition and fees vary according to course load and program. Room and board charges vary according to board plan and housing facility. ***Part-time tuition:*** $320 per credit hour. ***Part-time fees:*** $215 per term. Part-time tuition and fees vary according to course load and program. ***Payment plan:*** Deferred payment.

GIFT AID (NEED-BASED) ***Total amount:*** $3,124,291 (33% federal, 46% state, 16% institutional, 5% external sources). ***Scholarships, grants, and awards:*** Federal Pell, FSEOG, state, private, college/university gift aid from institutional funds.

GIFT AID (NON-NEED-BASED) ***Scholarships, grants, and awards by category:*** *Academic Interests/Achievement:* 5 awards ($37,500 total): general academic interests/achievements. *Special Achievements/Activities:* 60 awards ($50,000 total): leadership, memberships. *Special Characteristics:* 315 awards ($400,621 total): general special characteristics, out-of-state students. ***Tuition waivers:*** Full or partial for employees or children of employees.

LOANS ***Student loans:*** $5,980,929 (47% need-based, 53% non-need-based). ***Parent loans:*** $1,789,242 (100% need-based). ***Programs:*** FFEL (Subsidized and Unsubsidized Stafford, PLUS).

WORK-STUDY ***Federal work-study:*** Total amount: $85,365; 50 jobs averaging $1500.

APPLYING FOR FINANCIAL AID ***Required financial aid forms:*** FAFSA, institution's own form, state aid form, Federal Stafford Loan. ***Financial aid deadline:*** 5/1 (priority: 3/15). ***Notification date:*** Continuous beginning 1/1. Students must reply by 3/15 or within 2 weeks of notification.

CONTACT Kathy Shepard, Financial Aid Director, Central Pennsylvania College, College Hill and Valley Roads, Summerdale, PA 17093, 717-728-2261 or toll-free 800-759-2727 Ext. 2201. *Fax:* 717-728-2350. *E-mail:* financial-aid@centralpenn.edu.

CENTRAL STATE UNIVERSITY

Wilberforce, OH

Tuition & fees (OH res): $5294 **Average undergraduate aid package: N/A**

ABOUT THE INSTITUTION State-supported, coed. Awards: bachelor's and master's degrees and post-bachelor's certificates. 37 undergraduate majors. Total enrollment: 1,766. Undergraduates: 1,747. Freshmen: 546. Federal methodology is used as a basis for awarding need-based institutional aid.

UNDERGRADUATE EXPENSES for 2006–07 ***Application fee:*** $20. ***Tuition, state resident:*** full-time $5294; part-time $218 per credit hour. ***Tuition, nonresident:*** full-time $11,462; part-time $496 per credit hour. Full-time tuition and fees vary according to course load. ***College room and board:*** $7402; ***Room only:*** $3978. Room and board charges vary according to board plan. ***Payment plans:*** Installment, deferred payment.

FRESHMAN FINANCIAL AID (Fall 2006, est.) 515 applied for aid; of those 96% were deemed to have need. 99% of freshmen with need received aid. ***Average percent of need met:*** 90% (excluding resources awarded to replace EFC).

UNDERGRADUATE FINANCIAL AID (Fall 2006, est.) 1,470 applied for aid; of those 96% were deemed to have need. 99% of undergraduates with need received aid. ***Average percent of need met:*** 93% (excluding resources awarded to replace EFC).

GIFT AID (NEED-BASED) ***Total amount:*** $6,165,723 (72% federal, 17% state, 11% institutional). ***Receiving aid:*** Freshmen: 69% (366); All full-time undergraduates: 69% (1,061). ***Scholarships, grants, and awards:*** Federal Pell, FSEOG, state, private, college/university gift aid from institutional funds.

GIFT AID (NON-NEED-BASED) ***Total amount:*** $2,641,774 (68% institutional, 32% external sources). ***Receiving aid:*** Freshmen: 44% (233); Undergraduates: 41% (631). ***Scholarships, grants, and awards by category:*** *Academic Interests/Achievement:* 19 awards ($15,525 total): business, computer science, education, engineering/technologies, general academic interests/achievements, physical sciences. *Creative Arts/Performance:* 55 awards ($172,224 total): music. *Special Characteristics:* 42 awards ($157,377 total): children of faculty/staff, veterans, veterans' children. ***Tuition waivers:*** Full or partial for employees or children of employees, senior citizens. ***ROTC:*** Army.

LOANS ***Student loans:*** $8,965,369 (53% need-based, 47% non-need-based). ***Parent loans:*** $2,029,932 (100% non-need-based). ***Programs:*** FFEL (Subsidized and Unsubsidized Stafford, PLUS).

WORK-STUDY ***Federal work-study:*** Total amount: $585,460; jobs available.

ATHLETIC AWARDS Total amount: $298,485 (100% non-need-based).

APPLYING FOR FINANCIAL AID ***Required financial aid form:*** FAFSA. ***Financial aid deadline (priority):*** 2/15. ***Notification date:*** Continuous beginning 4/1. Students must reply within 2 weeks of notification.

CONTACT Veronica J. Leech, Director of Student Financial Aid, Central State University, PO Box 1004, Wilberforce, OH 45384, 937-376-6579 or toll-free 800-388-CSU1 (in-state).

CENTRAL WASHINGTON UNIVERSITY

Ellensburg, WA

Tuition & fees (WA res): $5238 **Average undergraduate aid package: $7775**

ABOUT THE INSTITUTION State-supported, coed. Awards: bachelor's and master's degrees and post-bachelor's certificates. 72 undergraduate majors. Total enrollment: 10,688. Undergraduates: 10,145. Freshmen: 1,480. Federal methodology is used as a basis for awarding need-based institutional aid.

UNDERGRADUATE EXPENSES for 2006–07 ***Application fee:*** $50. ***Tuition, state resident:*** full-time $4392; part-time $146 per credit. ***Tuition, nonresident:*** full-time $13,347; part-time $445 per credit. Part-time tuition and fees vary according to course load. ***College room and board:*** $7140. Room and board charges vary according to board plan and housing facility. ***Payment plan:*** Installment.

FRESHMAN FINANCIAL AID (Fall 2005) 819 applied for aid; of those 63% were deemed to have need. 95% of freshmen with need received aid; of those 28% had need fully met. ***Average percent of need met:*** 75% (excluding resources awarded to replace EFC). ***Average financial aid package:*** $7238 (excluding resources awarded to replace EFC). 1% of all full-time freshmen had no need and received non-need-based gift aid.

UNDERGRADUATE FINANCIAL AID (Fall 2005) 5,822 applied for aid; of those 74% were deemed to have need. 97% of undergraduates with need received

aid; of those 19% had need fully met. ***Average percent of need met:*** 69% (excluding resources awarded to replace EFC). ***Average financial aid package:*** $7775 (excluding resources awarded to replace EFC). 1% of all full-time undergraduates had no need and received non-need-based gift aid.

GIFT AID (NEED-BASED) ***Total amount:*** $19,078,424 (37% federal, 44% state, 8% institutional, 11% external sources). ***Receiving aid:*** Freshmen: 32% (359); All full-time undergraduates: 36% (3,061). ***Average award:*** Freshmen: $5070; Undergraduates: $5369. ***Scholarships, grants, and awards:*** Federal Pell, FSEOG, state, private, college/university gift aid from institutional funds, Title III grants, McNair scholarships, WA Regional Achievers Awards.

GIFT AID (NON-NEED-BASED) ***Total amount:*** $1,889,284 (2% state, 40% institutional, 58% external sources). ***Receiving aid:*** Undergraduates: 1. ***Average award:*** Freshmen: $507; Undergraduates: $452. ***Scholarships, grants, and awards by category:*** *Academic Interests/Achievement:* business, communication, computer science, education, engineering/technologies, English, foreign languages, general academic interests/achievements, health fields, international studies, mathematics, military science, physical sciences, premedicine. *Creative Arts/Performance:* applied art and design, art/fine arts, journalism/publications, music, performing arts, theater/drama. *Special Achievements/Activities:* community service, general special achievements/activities, hobbies/interests, leadership, memberships. *Special Characteristics:* adult students, children and siblings of alumni, general special characteristics, handicapped students, local/state students, previous college experience. ***Tuition waivers:*** Full or partial for employees or children of employees, senior citizens. ***ROTC:*** Army, Air Force.

LOANS ***Student loans:*** $27,076,523 (75% need-based, 25% non-need-based). 64% of past graduating class borrowed through all loan programs. *Average indebtedness per student:* $14,591. ***Average need-based loan:*** Freshmen: $3425; Undergraduates: $3890. ***Parent loans:*** $11,599,317 (46% need-based, 54% non-need-based). ***Programs:*** Federal Direct (Subsidized and Unsubsidized Stafford, PLUS), Perkins, state, college/university.

WORK-STUDY ***Federal work-study:*** Total amount: $525,919; 290 jobs averaging $2288. ***State or other work-study/employment:*** Total amount: $777,065 (100% need-based). 262 part-time jobs averaging $3319.

ATHLETIC AWARDS Total amount: $580,081 (67% need-based, 33% non-need-based).

APPLYING FOR FINANCIAL AID ***Required financial aid form:*** FAFSA. ***Financial aid deadline (priority):*** 3/1. ***Notification date:*** Continuous beginning 4/15. Students must reply within 4 weeks of notification.

CONTACT Ms. Agnes Canedo, Director of Financial Aid, Central Washington University, 400 East University Way, Ellensburg, WA 98926-7495, 509-963-3049 or toll-free 866-298-4968. *Fax:* 509-963-1788. *E-mail:* canedoa@cwu.edu.

CENTRAL YESHIVA TOMCHEI TMIMIM-LUBAVITCH

Brooklyn, NY

CONTACT Rabbi Moshe M. Gluckowsky, Director of Financial Aid, Central Yeshiva Tomchei Tmimim-Lubavitch, 841-853 Ocean Parkway, Brooklyn, NY 11230, 718-859-2277.

CENTRE COLLEGE

Danville, KY

Comprehensive fee: $33,000 **Average undergraduate aid package: $20,235**

ABOUT THE INSTITUTION Independent religious, coed. Awards: bachelor's degrees. 28 undergraduate majors. Total enrollment: 1,147. Undergraduates: 1,147. Freshmen: 327. Both federal and institutional methodology are used as a basis for awarding need-based institutional aid.

UNDERGRADUATE EXPENSES for 2006–07 ***Application fee:*** $40. ***Comprehensive fee:*** $33,000. Room and board charges vary according to board plan. ***Part-time tuition:*** $950 per credit hour. Part-time tuition and fees vary according to course load. ***Payment plan:*** Installment.

FRESHMAN FINANCIAL AID (Fall 2006, est.) 265 applied for aid; of those 79% were deemed to have need. 100% of freshmen with need received aid; of those 39% had need fully met. ***Average percent of need met:*** 91% (excluding resources awarded to replace EFC). ***Average financial aid package:*** $21,263 (excluding resources awarded to replace EFC). 31% of all full-time freshmen had no need and received non-need-based gift aid.

UNDERGRADUATE FINANCIAL AID (Fall 2006, est.) 827 applied for aid; of those 81% were deemed to have need. 100% of undergraduates with need received aid; of those 36% had need fully met. ***Average percent of need met:*** 88% (excluding resources awarded to replace EFC). ***Average financial aid package:*** $20,235 (excluding resources awarded to replace EFC). 36% of all full-time undergraduates had no need and received non-need-based gift aid.

GIFT AID (NEED-BASED) ***Total amount:*** $11,621,818 (6% federal, 19% state, 71% institutional, 4% external sources). ***Receiving aid:*** Freshmen: 64% (209); All full-time undergraduates: 58% (667). ***Average award:*** Freshmen: $19,218; Undergraduates: $17,424. ***Scholarships, grants, and awards:*** Federal Pell, FSEOG, state, private, college/university gift aid from institutional funds.

GIFT AID (NON-NEED-BASED) ***Total amount:*** $4,701,850 (12% state, 83% institutional, 5% external sources). ***Average award:*** Freshmen: $11,378; Undergraduates: $11,194. ***Scholarships, grants, and awards by category:*** *Academic Interests/Achievement:* 795 awards ($7,025,050 total): general academic interests/achievements. *Creative Arts/Performance:* 82 awards ($285,000 total): music, theater/drama. *Special Characteristics:* 159 awards ($1,130,387 total): children and siblings of alumni, children of faculty/staff, ethnic background, first-generation college students. ***Tuition waivers:*** Full or partial for children of alumni, employees or children of employees. ***ROTC:*** Army cooperative, Air Force cooperative.

LOANS ***Student loans:*** $2,789,016 (66% need-based, 34% non-need-based). 57% of past graduating class borrowed through all loan programs. *Average indebtedness per student:* $16,760. ***Average need-based loan:*** Freshmen: $3060; Undergraduates: $4225. ***Parent loans:*** $1,810,727 (100% non-need-based). ***Programs:*** FFEL (Subsidized and Unsubsidized Stafford, PLUS), Perkins, college/university.

WORK-STUDY ***Federal work-study:*** Total amount: $383,010; 285 jobs averaging $1360. ***State or other work-study/employment:*** Total amount: $77,660 (42% need-based, 58% non-need-based). 36 part-time jobs averaging $2120.

APPLYING FOR FINANCIAL AID ***Required financial aid forms:*** FAFSA, institution's own form. ***Financial aid deadline:*** 3/1. ***Notification date:*** 4/1. Students must reply by 5/1.

CONTACT Ms. Elaine Larson, Director of Student Financial Planning, Centre College, 600 West Walnut Street, Danville, KY 40422-1394, 859-238-5365 or toll-free 800-423-6236. *Fax:* 859-238-5373. *E-mail:* finaid@centre.edu.

CHADRON STATE COLLEGE

Chadron, NE

CONTACT Ms. Sherry Douglas, Director of Financial Aid, Chadron State College, 1000 Main Street, Chadron, NE 69337, 308-432-6230 or toll-free 800-242-3766 (in-state). *Fax:* 308-432-6229. *E-mail:* finaid@csc.edu.

CHAMBERLAIN COLLEGE OF NURSING

St. Louis, MO

CONTACT Financial Aid Counselor, Chamberlain College of Nursing, 6150 Oakland Avenue, St. Louis, MO 63139-3215, 314-768-5604 or toll-free 800-942-4310.

CHAMINADE UNIVERSITY OF HONOLULU

Honolulu, HI

ABOUT THE INSTITUTION Independent Roman Catholic, coed. Awards: associate, bachelor's, and master's degrees and post-bachelor's certificates. 22 undergraduate majors. Total enrollment: 1,810. Undergraduates: 1,106. Freshmen: 261.

GIFT AID (NEED-BASED) ***Scholarships, grants, and awards:*** Federal Pell, FSEOG, state, private, college/university gift aid from institutional funds.

GIFT AID (NON-NEED-BASED) ***Scholarships, grants, and awards by category:*** *Academic Interests/Achievement:* general academic interests/achievements.

LOANS ***Programs:*** FFEL (Subsidized and Unsubsidized Stafford, PLUS), Perkins, alternative loans.

APPLYING FOR FINANCIAL AID ***Required financial aid form:*** FAFSA.

CONTACT Mr. Eric Nemoto, Associate Dean of Enrollment Management, Chaminade University of Honolulu, 3140 Waialae Avenue, Honolulu, HI 96816-1578, 808-735-4780 or toll-free 800-735-3733 (out-of-state). *Fax:* 808-739-8362. *E-mail:* enemoto@chaminade.edu.

CHAMPLAIN COLLEGE

Burlington, VT

Tuition & fees: $22,550 **Average undergraduate aid package: $7596**

ABOUT THE INSTITUTION Independent, coed. Awards: associate, bachelor's, and master's degrees. 57 undergraduate majors. Total enrollment: 2,741. Undergraduates: 2,657. Freshmen: 531. Institutional methodology is used as a basis for awarding need-based institutional aid.

UNDERGRADUATE EXPENSES for 2007–08 ***Application fee:*** $40. ***Comprehensive fee:*** $33,460 includes full-time tuition ($22,550) and room and board ($10,910). ***College room only:*** $6510. ***Part-time tuition:*** $940 per credit.

FRESHMAN FINANCIAL AID (Fall 2006, est.) 398 applied for aid; of those 74% were deemed to have need. 100% of freshmen with need received aid. ***Average percent of need met:*** 58% (excluding resources awarded to replace EFC). ***Average financial aid package:*** $6658 (excluding resources awarded to replace EFC). 6% of all full-time freshmen had no need and received non-need-based gift aid.

UNDERGRADUATE FINANCIAL AID (Fall 2006, est.) 1,505 applied for aid; of those 99% were deemed to have need. 100% of undergraduates with need received aid. ***Average percent of need met:*** 63% (excluding resources awarded to replace EFC). ***Average financial aid package:*** $7596 (excluding resources awarded to replace EFC). 7% of all full-time undergraduates had no need and received non-need-based gift aid.

GIFT AID (NEED-BASED) ***Total amount:*** $4,007,268 (36% federal, 33% state, 25% institutional, 6% external sources). ***Receiving aid:*** Freshmen: 38% (187); All full-time undergraduates: 39% (748). ***Average award:*** Freshmen: $4392; Undergraduates: $4749. ***Scholarships, grants, and awards:*** Federal Pell, FSEOG, state, college/university gift aid from institutional funds.

GIFT AID (NON-NEED-BASED) ***Total amount:*** $378,100 (100% institutional). ***Receiving aid:*** Freshmen: 18% (91); Undergraduates: 11% (216). ***Average award:*** Freshmen: $4103; Undergraduates: $4022. ***ROTC:*** Army cooperative.

LOANS ***Student loans:*** $7,625,951 (63% need-based, 37% non-need-based). ***Average need-based loan:*** Freshmen: $3276; Undergraduates: $4120. ***Parent loans:*** $7,765,967 (100% need-based).

WORK-STUDY ***Federal work-study:*** Total amount: $528,111; 231 jobs averaging $1437.

APPLYING FOR FINANCIAL AID ***Required financial aid form:*** FAFSA. ***Financial aid deadline (priority):*** 3/1. ***Notification date:*** Continuous beginning 3/20.

CONTACT David B. Myette, Director of Financial Aid, Champlain College, 163 South Willard Street, Burlington, VT 05401, 802-865-6430 or toll-free 800-570-5858. *Fax:* 802-860-2775. *E-mail:* myette@champlain.edu.

CHAPMAN UNIVERSITY

Orange, CA

Tuition & fees: $30,748 **Average undergraduate aid package: $20,421**

ABOUT THE INSTITUTION Independent religious, coed. Awards: bachelor's, master's, and first professional degrees and post-bachelor's certificates. 54 undergraduate majors. Total enrollment: 5,908. Undergraduates: 4,086. Freshmen: 957. Both federal and institutional methodology are used as a basis for awarding need-based institutional aid.

UNDERGRADUATE EXPENSES for 2006–07 ***Application fee:*** $55. ***Comprehensive fee:*** $41,248 includes full-time tuition ($29,900), mandatory fees ($848), and room and board ($10,500). Room and board charges vary according to board plan and housing facility. ***Part-time tuition:*** $920 per credit. Part-time tuition and fees vary according to course load. ***Payment plans:*** Tuition prepayment, installment, deferred payment.

FRESHMAN FINANCIAL AID (Fall 2005) 676 applied for aid; of those 68% were deemed to have need. 100% of freshmen with need received aid; of those 100% had need fully met. ***Average percent of need met:*** 100% (excluding resources awarded to replace EFC). ***Average financial aid package:*** $22,931 (excluding resources awarded to replace EFC). 25% of all full-time freshmen had no need and received non-need-based gift aid.

UNDERGRADUATE FINANCIAL AID (Fall 2005) 3,575 applied for aid; of those 63% were deemed to have need. 100% of undergraduates with need received aid; of those 100% had need fully met. ***Average percent of need met:*** 100% (excluding resources awarded to replace EFC). ***Average financial aid package:*** $20,421 (excluding resources awarded to replace EFC). 24% of all full-time undergraduates had no need and received non-need-based gift aid.

GIFT AID (NEED-BASED) ***Total amount:*** $36,277,093 (8% federal, 13% state, 77% institutional, 2% external sources). ***Receiving aid:*** Freshmen: 60% (456); All full-time undergraduates: 59% (2,193). ***Average award:*** Freshmen: $19,801; Undergraduates: $16,900. ***Scholarships, grants, and awards:*** Federal Pell, FSEOG, state, private, college/university gift aid from institutional funds.

GIFT AID (NON-NEED-BASED) ***Total amount:*** $9,184,364 (99% institutional, 1% external sources). ***Average award:*** Freshmen: $19,855; Undergraduates: $15,888. ***Scholarships, grants, and awards by category:*** *Academic Interests/Achievement:* 115 awards ($177,500 total): biological sciences, physical sciences. *Creative Arts/Performance:* 304 awards ($1,247,505 total): art/fine arts, cinema/film/broadcasting, creative writing, dance, music, performing arts, theater/drama. *Special Characteristics:* 43 awards ($42,500 total): children and siblings of alumni. ***Tuition waivers:*** Full or partial for employees or children of employees. ***ROTC:*** Army cooperative, Air Force cooperative.

LOANS ***Student loans:*** $12,649,758 (91% need-based, 9% non-need-based). 64% of past graduating class borrowed through all loan programs. *Average indebtedness per student:* $22,277. ***Average need-based loan:*** Freshmen: $3932; Undergraduates: $4576. ***Parent loans:*** $9,881,274 (77% need-based, 23% non-need-based). ***Programs:*** FFEL (Subsidized and Unsubsidized Stafford, PLUS), Perkins, college/university.

WORK-STUDY ***Federal work-study:*** Total amount: $1,053,193; 667 jobs averaging $1579.

APPLYING FOR FINANCIAL AID ***Required financial aid forms:*** FAFSA, state aid form. ***Financial aid deadline (priority):*** 3/2. ***Notification date:*** Continuous beginning 3/15. Students must reply within 3 weeks of notification.

CONTACT Gregory L. Ball, Director of Financial Aid, Chapman University, One University Drive, Orange, CA 92866, 714-997-6741 or toll-free 888-CUAPPLY. *Fax:* 714-997-6743. *E-mail:* gball@chapman.edu.

CHARLES R. DREW UNIVERSITY OF MEDICINE AND SCIENCE

Los Angeles, CA

CONTACT Financial Aid Office, Charles R. Drew University of Medicine and Science, 1731 East 120th Street, Los Angeles, CA 90059, 323-563-4824. *Fax:* 323-569-0597.

CHARLESTON SOUTHERN UNIVERSITY

Charleston, SC

CONTACT Director of Financial Aid, Charleston Southern University, PO Box 118087, 9200 University Boulevard, Charleston, SC 29423-8087, 843-863-7050 or toll-free 800-947-7474. *Fax:* 843-863-7070.

CHARTER OAK STATE COLLEGE

New Britain, CT

CONTACT Velma Walters, Director, Financial Aid, Charter Oak State College, 55 Paul J. Manafort Drive, New Britain, CT 06053-2142, 860-832-3872. *Fax:* 860-832-3999. *E-mail:* sfa@charteroak.edu.

CHATHAM UNIVERSITY

Pittsburgh, PA

Tuition & fees: $24,808 **Average undergraduate aid package: $18,653**

ABOUT THE INSTITUTION Independent, undergraduate: women only; graduate: coed. Awards: bachelor's, master's, and doctoral degrees and post-bachelor's and post-master's certificates. 46 undergraduate majors. Total enrollment: 1,590. Undergraduates: 805. Freshmen: 147. Both federal and institutional methodology are used as a basis for awarding need-based institutional aid.

UNDERGRADUATE EXPENSES for 2006–07 ***Application fee:*** $35. ***Comprehensive fee:*** $32,394 includes full-time tuition ($24,014), mandatory fees ($794), and room and board ($7586). ***College room only:*** $3880. Full-time tuition and fees vary according to degree level. Room and board charges vary according to board plan and housing facility. ***Part-time tuition:*** $583 per credit. ***Part-time fees:*** $11 per credit. Part-time tuition and fees vary according to course load. ***Payment plan:*** Installment.

FRESHMAN FINANCIAL AID (Fall 2006, est.) 134 applied for aid; of those 89% were deemed to have need. 100% of freshmen with need received aid. ***Average percent of need met:*** 70% (excluding resources awarded to replace EFC). ***Average financial aid package:*** $21,400 (excluding resources awarded to replace EFC). 19% of all full-time freshmen had no need and received non-need-based gift aid.

UNDERGRADUATE FINANCIAL AID (Fall 2006, est.) 485 applied for aid; of those 94% were deemed to have need. 100% of undergraduates with need received aid. ***Average percent of need met:*** 60% (excluding resources awarded to replace EFC). ***Average financial aid package:*** $18,653 (excluding resources awarded to replace EFC). 7% of all full-time undergraduates had no need and received non-need-based gift aid.

GIFT AID (NEED-BASED) ***Total amount:*** $2,797,345 (22% federal, 26% state, 51% institutional, 1% external sources). ***Receiving aid:*** Freshmen: 81% (119); All full-time undergraduates: 88% (447). ***Average award:*** Freshmen: $7156; Undergraduates: $8140. ***Scholarships, grants, and awards:*** Federal Pell, FSEOG, state, private, college/university gift aid from institutional funds, United Negro College Fund.

GIFT AID (NON-NEED-BASED) ***Total amount:*** $3,581,193 (97% institutional, 3% external sources). ***Average award:*** Freshmen: $12,061; Undergraduates: $11,664. ***Scholarships, grants, and awards by category:*** *Academic Interests/Achievement:* 322 awards ($3,336,867 total): biological sciences, business, communication, education, English, general academic interests/achievements, international studies, mathematics, physical sciences, premedicine, social sciences. *Creative Arts/Performance:* 1 award ($1000 total): theater/drama. *Special Characteristics:* 23 awards ($41,000 total): children and siblings of alumni, children of faculty/staff, siblings of current students. ***Tuition waivers:*** Full or partial for employees or children of employees. ***ROTC:*** Army cooperative, Naval cooperative, Air Force cooperative.

LOANS ***Student loans:*** $3,704,636 (39% need-based, 61% non-need-based). 79% of past graduating class borrowed through all loan programs. *Average indebtedness per student:* $22,895. ***Average need-based loan:*** Freshmen: $3329; Undergraduates: $3550. ***Parent loans:*** $739,603 (40% need-based, 60% non-need-based). ***Programs:*** FFEL (Subsidized and Unsubsidized Stafford, PLUS), Perkins.

WORK-STUDY ***Federal work-study:*** Total amount: $312,065; 180 jobs averaging $2200. ***State or other work-study/employment:*** Total amount: $8500 (100% non-need-based). 25 part-time jobs averaging $1500.

APPLYING FOR FINANCIAL AID ***Required financial aid form:*** FAFSA. ***Financial aid deadline (priority):*** 5/1. ***Notification date:*** Continuous beginning 2/15. Students must reply by 5/1 or within 2 weeks of notification.

CONTACT Jennifer Burns, Director of Financial Aid, Chatham University, Woodland Road, Pittsburgh, PA 15232-2826, 800-837-1610 or toll-free 800-837-1290. *Fax:* 412-365-1643. *E-mail:* jburns@chatham.edu.

CHESTER COLLEGE OF NEW ENGLAND

Chester, NH

Tuition & fees: $15,930 **Average undergraduate aid package: $7200**

ABOUT THE INSTITUTION Independent, coed. Awards: bachelor's degrees. 6 undergraduate majors. Total enrollment: 205. Undergraduates: 205. Freshmen: 73. Federal methodology is used as a basis for awarding need-based institutional aid.

UNDERGRADUATE EXPENSES for 2007–08 ***Application fee:*** $35. ***Comprehensive fee:*** $23,780 includes full-time tuition ($15,400), mandatory fees ($530), and room and board ($7850). ***Part-time tuition:*** $640 per credit. ***Part-time fees:*** $265 per term.

FRESHMAN FINANCIAL AID (Fall 2006, est.) 73 applied for aid; of those 96% were deemed to have need. 100% of freshmen with need received aid. ***Average percent of need met:*** 23% (excluding resources awarded to replace EFC). ***Average financial aid package:*** $6692 (excluding resources awarded to replace EFC). 5% of all full-time freshmen had no need and received non-need-based gift aid.

UNDERGRADUATE FINANCIAL AID (Fall 2006, est.) 148 applied for aid; of those 95% were deemed to have need. 89% of undergraduates with need received aid. ***Average percent of need met:*** 25% (excluding resources awarded to replace EFC). ***Average financial aid package:*** $7200 (excluding resources awarded to replace EFC). 4% of all full-time undergraduates had no need and received non-need-based gift aid.

GIFT AID (NEED-BASED) ***Total amount:*** $271,795 (86% federal, 14% state). ***Receiving aid:*** Freshmen: 28% (21); All full-time undergraduates: 25% (57). ***Average award:*** Freshmen: $3282; Undergraduates: $2545. ***Scholarships, grants, and awards:*** Federal Pell, FSEOG, state, private, college/university gift aid from institutional funds.

GIFT AID (NON-NEED-BASED) ***Total amount:*** $687,718 (90% institutional, 10% external sources). ***Receiving aid:*** Freshmen: 79% (60); Undergraduates: 50% (112). ***Average award:*** Freshmen: $1375; Undergraduates: $2312. ***Scholarships, grants, and awards by category:*** *Academic Interests/Achievement:* 177 awards ($620,793 total): general academic interests/achievements. *Creative Arts/Performance:* applied art and design, art/fine arts, creative writing.

LOANS ***Student loans:*** $2,079,235 (31% need-based, 69% non-need-based). 90% of past graduating class borrowed through all loan programs. *Average indebtedness per student:* $32,915. ***Average need-based loan:*** Freshmen: $2062; Undergraduates: $3713. ***Parent loans:*** $600,668 (100% non-need-based). ***Programs:*** FFEL (Subsidized and Unsubsidized Stafford, PLUS), alternative loans.

WORK-STUDY ***Federal work-study:*** Total amount: $14,229.

APPLYING FOR FINANCIAL AID ***Required financial aid form:*** FAFSA. ***Financial aid deadline (priority):*** 3/15. ***Notification date:*** Continuous beginning 4/1. Students must reply within 2 weeks of notification.

CONTACT Jason Graves, Director of Financial Aid, Chester College of New England, 40 Chester Street, Chester, NH 03036-4331, 603-887-4401 Ext. 7404 or toll-free 800-974-6372. *Fax:* 603-887-1777. *E-mail:* financialaid@chestercollege.edu.

CHESTNUT HILL COLLEGE

Philadelphia, PA

Tuition & fees: $22,750 **Average undergraduate aid package: $17,024**

ABOUT THE INSTITUTION Independent Roman Catholic, coed, primarily women. Awards: associate, bachelor's, master's, and doctoral degrees and post-bachelor's and post-master's certificates (profile includes figures from both traditional and accelerated (part-time) programs). 37 undergraduate majors. Total enrollment: 1,918. Undergraduates: 1,154. Freshmen: 216. Federal methodology is used as a basis for awarding need-based institutional aid.

UNDERGRADUATE EXPENSES for 2006–07 ***Application fee:*** $35. ***Comprehensive fee:*** $30,700 includes full-time tuition ($22,750) and room and board ($7950). ***Part-time tuition:*** $500 per credit.

FRESHMAN FINANCIAL AID (Fall 2006, est.) 214 applied for aid; of those 91% were deemed to have need. 99% of freshmen with need received aid; of those 1% had need fully met. ***Average percent of need met:*** 21% (excluding resources awarded to replace EFC). ***Average financial aid package:*** $17,121 (excluding resources awarded to replace EFC). 16% of all full-time freshmen had no need and received non-need-based gift aid.

UNDERGRADUATE FINANCIAL AID (Fall 2006, est.) 645 applied for aid; of those 91% were deemed to have need. 94% of undergraduates with need received aid; of those 2% had need fully met. ***Average percent of need met:*** 23% (excluding resources awarded to replace EFC). ***Average financial aid package:*** $17,024 (excluding resources awarded to replace EFC). 13% of all full-time undergraduates had no need and received non-need-based gift aid.

GIFT AID (NEED-BASED) ***Total amount:*** $4,717,770 (34% federal, 39% state, 27% institutional). ***Receiving aid:*** Freshmen: 80% (173); All full-time undergraduates: 61% (555). ***Average award:*** Freshmen: $5667; Undergraduates: $6093. ***Scholarships, grants, and awards:*** Federal Pell, FSEOG, state, private, college/university gift aid from institutional funds.

GIFT AID (NON-NEED-BASED) ***Total amount:*** $5,817,416 (1% federal, 97% institutional, 2% external sources). ***Receiving aid:*** Freshmen: 87% (187); Undergraduates: 46% (413). ***Average award:*** Freshmen: $9246; Undergraduates: $8666. ***Scholarships, grants, and awards by category:*** *Special Achievements/Activities:* leadership. *Special Characteristics:* children and siblings of alumni, international students, religious affiliation.

LOANS ***Student loans:*** $12,824,564 (42% need-based, 58% non-need-based). 85% of past graduating class borrowed through all loan programs. *Average indebtedness per student:* $29,000. ***Average need-based loan:*** Freshmen: $3412; Undergraduates: $4012. ***Parent loans:*** $1,691,302 (100% non-need-based). ***Programs:*** FFEL (Subsidized and Unsubsidized Stafford, PLUS), Perkins.

WORK-STUDY ***Federal work-study:*** Total amount: $119,401; jobs available.

APPLYING FOR FINANCIAL AID ***Required financial aid form:*** FAFSA. ***Financial aid deadline:*** 3/15 (priority: 1/31). ***Notification date:*** Continuous beginning 1/31. Students must reply by 5/1 or within 2 weeks of notification.

CONTACT Nicholas Flocco, Director of Financial Aid, Chestnut Hill College, Chestnut Hill College, 9601 Germantown Avenue, Philadelphia, PA 19118-2693, 215-248-7192 or toll-free 800-248-0052 (out-of-state). *Fax:* 215-248-7217. *E-mail:* nfloccon@chc.edu.

CHEYNEY UNIVERSITY OF PENNSYLVANIA

Cheyney, PA

CONTACT Mr. James Brown, Director of Financial Aid, Cheyney University of Pennsylvania, 1837 University Circle, Cheyney, PA 19319, 610-399-2302 or toll-free 800-CHEYNEY. *Fax:* 610-399-2411. *E-mail:* jbrown@cheyney.edu.

CHICAGO STATE UNIVERSITY

Chicago, IL

CONTACT Director of Student Financial Aid, Chicago State University, 9501 South Martin Luther King Drive, Chicago, IL 60628, 773-995-2304.

CHOWAN UNIVERSITY

Murfreesboro, NC

ABOUT THE INSTITUTION Independent Baptist, coed. Awards: associate and bachelor's degrees. 37 undergraduate majors. Total enrollment: 800. Undergraduates: 800. Freshmen: 315.

GIFT AID (NEED-BASED) ***Scholarships, grants, and awards:*** Federal Pell, FSEOG, state, private, college/university gift aid from institutional funds.

GIFT AID (NON-NEED-BASED) ***Scholarships, grants, and awards by category:*** *Academic Interests/Achievement:* general academic interests/achievements. *Creative Arts/Performance:* music. *Special Achievements/Activities:* leadership. *Special Characteristics:* children of faculty/staff, first-generation college students, international students, local/state students, relatives of clergy, religious affiliation.

LOANS ***Programs:*** FFEL (Subsidized and Unsubsidized Stafford, PLUS), Perkins, state, alternative loans.

WORK-STUDY ***Federal work-study:*** Total amount: $176,055; 274 jobs averaging $642. ***State or other work-study/employment:*** 86 part-time jobs averaging $1550.

APPLYING FOR FINANCIAL AID ***Required financial aid form:*** FAFSA.

CONTACT Mrs. Stephanie W. Harrell, Director of Financial Aid, Chowan University, 200 Jones Drive, Murfreesboro, NC 27855, 252-398-1229 or toll-free 800-488-4101. *Fax:* 252-398-6513. *E-mail:* harres@chowan.edu.

CHRISTENDOM COLLEGE

Front Royal, VA

Tuition & fees: $16,740	Average undergraduate aid package: $12,785

ABOUT THE INSTITUTION Independent Roman Catholic, coed. Awards: associate, bachelor's, and master's degrees. 8 undergraduate majors. Total enrollment: 451. Undergraduates: 397. Freshmen: 96. Institutional methodology is used as a basis for awarding need-based institutional aid.

UNDERGRADUATE EXPENSES for 2006–07 ***Application fee:*** $25. ***Comprehensive fee:*** $22,806 includes full-time tuition ($16,290), mandatory fees ($450), and room and board ($6066). ***Payment plans:*** Tuition prepayment, installment.

FRESHMAN FINANCIAL AID (Fall 2006, est.) 57 applied for aid; of those 79% were deemed to have need. 100% of freshmen with need received aid; of those 100% had need fully met. ***Average percent of need met:*** 90% (excluding resources awarded to replace EFC). ***Average financial aid package:*** $13,500 (excluding resources awarded to replace EFC). 31% of all full-time freshmen had no need and received non-need-based gift aid.

UNDERGRADUATE FINANCIAL AID (Fall 2006, est.) 230 applied for aid; of those 84% were deemed to have need. 100% of undergraduates with need received aid; of those 100% had need fully met. ***Average percent of need met:*** 90% (excluding resources awarded to replace EFC). ***Average financial aid package:*** $12,785 (excluding resources awarded to replace EFC). 21% of all full-time undergraduates had no need and received non-need-based gift aid.

GIFT AID (NEED-BASED) ***Total amount:*** $1,293,004 (100% institutional). ***Receiving aid:*** Freshmen: 46% (44); All full-time undergraduates: 48% (190). ***Average award:*** Freshmen: $6080; Undergraduates: $6805. ***Scholarships, grants, and awards:*** private, college/university gift aid from institutional funds.

GIFT AID (NON-NEED-BASED) ***Total amount:*** $484,896 (85% institutional, 15% external sources). ***Average award:*** Freshmen: $6625; Undergraduates: $5025. ***Scholarships, grants, and awards by category:*** *Academic Interests/Achievement:* 139 awards ($617,600 total): general academic interests/achievements. ***Tuition waivers:*** Full or partial for employees or children of employees.

LOANS ***Student loans:*** $1,493,451 (62% need-based, 38% non-need-based). 60% of past graduating class borrowed through all loan programs. *Average indebtedness per student:* $16,180. ***Average need-based loan:*** Freshmen: $5445; Undergraduates: $5000. ***Programs:*** college/university.

WORK-STUDY ***State or other work-study/employment:*** Total amount: $248,300 (100% need-based). 130 part-time jobs averaging $1910.

APPLYING FOR FINANCIAL AID ***Required financial aid form:*** institution's own form. ***Financial aid deadline (priority):*** 4/1. ***Notification date:*** Continuous beginning 2/1. Students must reply within 4 weeks of notification.

CONTACT Mrs. Alisa Polk, Financial Aid Officer, Christendom College, 134 Christendom Drive, Front Royal, VA 22630-5103, 800-877-5456 Ext. 214 or toll-free 800-877-5456 Ext. 290. *Fax:* 540-636-1655. *E-mail:* apolk@christendom.edu.

CHRISTIAN BROTHERS UNIVERSITY

Memphis, TN

Tuition & fees: $20,080	Average undergraduate aid package: $15,808

ABOUT THE INSTITUTION Independent Roman Catholic, coed. Awards: bachelor's and master's degrees. 27 undergraduate majors. Total enrollment: 1,776. Undergraduates: 1,451. Freshmen: 282. Both federal and institutional methodology are used as a basis for awarding need-based institutional aid.

UNDERGRADUATE EXPENSES for 2006–07 ***Application fee:*** $25. ***Comprehensive fee:*** $25,730 includes full-time tuition ($19,560), mandatory fees ($520), and room and board ($5650). ***College room only:*** $2540. Full-time tuition and fees vary according to class time and course load. Room and board charges vary according to board plan and housing facility. ***Part-time tuition:*** $615 per credit hour. Part-time tuition and fees vary according to class time. ***Payment plans:*** Installment, deferred payment.

FRESHMAN FINANCIAL AID (Fall 2006, est.) 266 applied for aid; of those 72% were deemed to have need. 100% of freshmen with need received aid; of those 32% had need fully met. ***Average percent of need met:*** 99% (excluding resources awarded to replace EFC). ***Average financial aid package:*** $18,951 (excluding resources awarded to replace EFC). 24% of all full-time freshmen had no need and received non-need-based gift aid.

UNDERGRADUATE FINANCIAL AID (Fall 2006, est.) 1,025 applied for aid; of those 80% were deemed to have need. 100% of undergraduates with need received aid; of those 26% had need fully met. ***Average percent of need met:*** 82% (excluding resources awarded to replace EFC). ***Average financial aid package:*** $15,808 (excluding resources awarded to replace EFC). 22% of all full-time undergraduates had no need and received non-need-based gift aid.

GIFT AID (NEED-BASED) ***Total amount:*** $2,809,786 (59% federal, 41% state). ***Receiving aid:*** Freshmen: 35% (98); All full-time undergraduates: 36% (426). ***Average award:*** Freshmen: $5228; Undergraduates: $5810. ***Scholarships, grants, and awards:*** Federal Pell, FSEOG, state, private, college/university gift aid from institutional funds.

GIFT AID (NON-NEED-BASED) ***Total amount:*** $9,904,930 (16% state, 81% institutional, 3% external sources). ***Receiving aid:*** Freshmen: 67% (188); Undergraduates: 56% (658). ***Average award:*** Freshmen: $7796; Undergraduates: $9368. ***Scholarships, grants, and awards by category:*** *Academic Interests/Achievement:* 750 awards ($5,832,885 total): engineering/technologies, general academic interests/achievements. *Creative Arts/Performance:* 16 awards ($18,000 total): general creative arts/performance. *Special Achievements/Activities:* 102 awards ($431,060 total): general special achievements/activities, leadership. *Special Characteristics:* 562 awards ($1,709,906 total): children and siblings of alumni, general special characteristics, religious affiliation. ***Tuition waivers:*** Full or partial for children of alumni, employees or children of employees. ***ROTC:*** Army cooperative, Naval cooperative, Air Force cooperative.

LOANS ***Student loans:*** $6,033,984 (45% need-based, 55% non-need-based). 64% of past graduating class borrowed through all loan programs. *Average indebtedness per student:* $26,539. ***Average need-based loan:*** Freshmen: $2928;

Undergraduates: $4155. ***Parent loans:*** $634,471 (100% non-need-based). ***Programs:*** FFEL (Subsidized and Unsubsidized Stafford, PLUS), Perkins, college/university, alternative loans.

WORK-STUDY ***Federal work-study:*** Total amount: $275,950; 234 jobs averaging $1179. ***State or other work-study/employment:*** Total amount: $200,000 (100% non-need-based). 198 part-time jobs averaging $1010.

ATHLETIC AWARDS Total amount: $1,007,704 (100% non-need-based).

APPLYING FOR FINANCIAL AID ***Required financial aid form:*** FAFSA. ***Financial aid deadline (priority):*** 2/15. ***Notification date:*** Continuous beginning 2/28. Students must reply by 5/1 or within 2 weeks of notification.

CONTACT Mr. Jim Shannon, Student Financial Resources Director, Christian Brothers University, 650 East Parkway South, Memphis, TN 38104, 901-321-3305 or toll-free 800-288-7576. *E-mail:* jshannon@cbu.edu.

CHRISTIAN HERITAGE COLLEGE

El Cajon, CA

See San Diego Christian College.

CHRISTIAN LIFE COLLEGE

Mount Prospect, IL

CONTACT Jeanna Wilson, Office of Financial Aid, Christian Life College, 400 East Gregory Street, Mt. Prospect, IL 60056, 847-259-1840. *Fax:* 847-259-3888.

CHRISTOPHER NEWPORT UNIVERSITY

Newport News, VA

Tuition & fees (VA res): $9106 **Average undergraduate aid package: $6162**

ABOUT THE INSTITUTION State-supported, coed. Awards: bachelor's and master's degrees. 38 undergraduate majors. Total enrollment: 4,793. Undergraduates: 4,623. Freshmen: 1,174. Federal methodology is used as a basis for awarding need-based institutional aid.

UNDERGRADUATE EXPENSES for 2006–07 ***Application fee:*** $45. ***Tuition, state resident:*** full-time $6430; part-time $270 per credit hour. ***Tuition, nonresident:*** full-time $13,532; part-time $565 per credit hour. Full-time tuition and fees vary according to course load. Part-time tuition and fees vary according to course load. ***College room and board:*** $8100. Room and board charges vary according to board plan and housing facility. ***Payment plan:*** Installment.

FRESHMAN FINANCIAL AID (Fall 2005) 1029 applied for aid; of those 53% were deemed to have need. 89% of freshmen with need received aid; of those 24% had need fully met. ***Average percent of need met:*** 75% (excluding resources awarded to replace EFC). ***Average financial aid package:*** $5930 (excluding resources awarded to replace EFC). 8% of all full-time freshmen had no need and received non-need-based gift aid.

UNDERGRADUATE FINANCIAL AID (Fall 2005) 2,657 applied for aid; of those 61% were deemed to have need. 90% of undergraduates with need received aid; of those 30% had need fully met. ***Average percent of need met:*** 74% (excluding resources awarded to replace EFC). ***Average financial aid package:*** $6162 (excluding resources awarded to replace EFC). 8% of all full-time undergraduates had no need and received non-need-based gift aid.

GIFT AID (NEED-BASED) ***Total amount:*** $4,597,320 (30% federal, 68% state, 2% institutional). ***Receiving aid:*** Freshmen: 29% (357); All full-time undergraduates: 26% (1,085). ***Average award:*** Freshmen: $4187; Undergraduates: $4091. ***Scholarships, grants, and awards:*** Federal Pell, FSEOG, state, private, college/university gift aid from institutional funds.

GIFT AID (NON-NEED-BASED) ***Total amount:*** $1,164,012 (47% institutional, 53% external sources). ***Receiving aid:*** Freshmen: 12% (156); Undergraduates: 7% (290). ***Average award:*** Freshmen: $1496; Undergraduates: $1502. ***Scholarships, grants, and awards by category:*** *Academic Interests/Achievement:* 54 awards ($97,990 total): business, communication, computer science, education, English, foreign languages, general academic interests/achievements, humanities, mathematics, military science, religion/biblical studies. *Creative Arts/Performance:* 36 awards ($32,300 total): art/fine arts, music, theater/drama. *Special Achievements/Activities:* 347 awards ($419,588 total): general special achievements/activities, leadership. ***Tuition waivers:*** Full or partial for employees or children of employees, senior citizens. ***ROTC:*** Army.

LOANS ***Student loans:*** $10,544,345 (42% need-based, 58% non-need-based). 53% of past graduating class borrowed through all loan programs. *Average indebtedness per student:* $16,534. ***Average need-based loan:*** Freshmen: $2613; Undergraduates: $3236. ***Parent loans:*** $4,099,492 (100% non-need-based). ***Programs:*** FFEL (Subsidized and Unsubsidized Stafford, PLUS), state, college/university, alternative loans.

WORK-STUDY ***Federal work-study:*** Total amount: $119,581; 107 jobs averaging $1117. ***State or other work-study/employment:*** Total amount: $1,538,584 (100% non-need-based). 975 part-time jobs averaging $1578.

APPLYING FOR FINANCIAL AID ***Required financial aid form:*** FAFSA. ***Financial aid deadline (priority):*** 3/1. ***Notification date:*** Continuous beginning 2/1. Students must reply within 3 weeks of notification.

CONTACT Mary L. Wigginton, Director of Financial Aid, Christopher Newport University, 1 University Place, Newport News, VA 23606, 757-594-7278 or toll-free 800-333-4268. *Fax:* 757-594-7113.

CINCINNATI CHRISTIAN UNIVERSITY

Cincinnati, OH

ABOUT THE INSTITUTION Independent religious, coed. Awards: associate, bachelor's, master's, and first professional degrees. 12 undergraduate majors. Total enrollment: 1,125. Undergraduates: 841. Freshmen: 227.

GIFT AID (NEED-BASED) ***Scholarships, grants, and awards:*** Federal Pell, FSEOG, state, college/university gift aid from institutional funds.

GIFT AID (NON-NEED-BASED) ***Scholarships, grants, and awards by category:*** *Creative Arts/Performance:* music. *Special Characteristics:* children of current students, children of faculty/staff, international students, married students, parents of current students, siblings of current students, spouses of current students, twins.

LOANS ***Programs:*** FFEL (Subsidized and Unsubsidized Stafford, PLUS), alternative loans.

APPLYING FOR FINANCIAL AID ***Required financial aid forms:*** FAFSA, institution's own form, state aid form.

CONTACT Robbin D. Moore, Financial Aid Coordinator, Cincinnati Christian University, 2700 Glenway Avenue, Cincinnati, OH 45204-1799, 513-244-8450 or toll-free 800-949-4228 (in-state). *Fax:* 513-244-8140. *E-mail:* financialaid@ccuniversity.edu.

CIRCLEVILLE BIBLE COLLEGE

Circleville, OH

See Ohio Christian University.

THE CITADEL, THE MILITARY COLLEGE OF SOUTH CAROLINA

Charleston, SC

ABOUT THE INSTITUTION State-supported, coed. Awards: bachelor's and master's degrees and post-master's certificates. 23 undergraduate majors. Total enrollment: 3,386. Undergraduates: 2,113.

GIFT AID (NEED-BASED) ***Scholarships, grants, and awards:*** Federal Pell, FSEOG, state, private, college/university gift aid from institutional funds.

GIFT AID (NON-NEED-BASED) ***Scholarships, grants, and awards by category:*** *Academic Interests/Achievement:* biological sciences, business, engineering/technologies, general academic interests/achievements, humanities, military science, religion/biblical studies. *Creative Arts/Performance:* journalism/publications, music. *Special Achievements/Activities:* community service, leadership, religious involvement. *Special Characteristics:* children and siblings of alumni, children with a deceased or disabled parent, local/state students, out-of-state students.

LOANS ***Programs:*** Federal Direct (Subsidized and Unsubsidized Stafford, PLUS), Perkins, state, college/university.

WORK-STUDY ***Federal work-study:*** Total amount: $20,840; 21 jobs averaging $1121.

APPLYING FOR FINANCIAL AID ***Required financial aid form:*** FAFSA.

CONTACT Lt. Col. Hank M. Fuller, Director of Financial Aid and Scholarships, The Citadel, The Military College of South Carolina, 171 Moultrie Street, Charleston, SC 29409, 843-953-5187 or toll-free 800-868-1842. *Fax:* 843-953-6759. *E-mail:* fullerh@citadel.edu.

CITY COLLEGE OF THE CITY UNIVERSITY OF NEW YORK

New York, NY

Tuition & fees (NY res): $4359 Average undergraduate aid package: $8400

ABOUT THE INSTITUTION State and locally supported, coed. Awards: bachelor's, master's, and first professional degrees and post-master's certificates. 66 undergraduate majors. Total enrollment: 13,244. Undergraduates: 10,314. Freshmen: 1,564. Federal methodology is used as a basis for awarding need-based institutional aid.

UNDERGRADUATE EXPENSES for 2006–07 ***Application fee:*** $65. ***Tuition, state resident:*** full-time $4080; part-time $170 per credit. ***Tuition, nonresident:*** full-time $8640; part-time $360 per credit. Full-time tuition and fees vary according to class time, course load, and program. Part-time tuition and fees vary according to class time, course load, and program. ***College room and board: Room only:*** $9135. ***Payment plan:*** Deferred payment.

FRESHMAN FINANCIAL AID (Fall 2006, est.) 1329 applied for aid; of those 85% were deemed to have need. 90% of freshmen with need received aid; of those 75% had need fully met. ***Average percent of need met:*** 79% (excluding resources awarded to replace EFC). ***Average financial aid package:*** $7547 (excluding resources awarded to replace EFC). 23% of all full-time freshmen had no need and received non-need-based gift aid.

UNDERGRADUATE FINANCIAL AID (Fall 2006, est.) 6,212 applied for aid; of those 90% were deemed to have need. 95% of undergraduates with need received aid; of those 63% had need fully met. ***Average percent of need met:*** 77% (excluding resources awarded to replace EFC). ***Average financial aid package:*** $8400 (excluding resources awarded to replace EFC). 15% of all full-time undergraduates had no need and received non-need-based gift aid.

GIFT AID (NEED-BASED) ***Total amount:*** $32,759,300 (47% federal, 51% state, 2% institutional). ***Receiving aid:*** Freshmen: 58% (913); All full-time undergraduates: 69% (5,044). ***Average award:*** Freshmen: $5100; Undergraduates: $6005. ***Scholarships, grants, and awards:*** Federal Pell, FSEOG, state, private, college/university gift aid from institutional funds.

GIFT AID (NON-NEED-BASED) ***Total amount:*** $2,782,000 (11% state, 80% institutional, 9% external sources). ***Receiving aid:*** Freshmen: 27% (417); Undergraduates: 9% (653). ***Average award:*** Freshmen: $1830; Undergraduates: $2570. ***Scholarships, grants, and awards by category:*** *Academic Interests/Achievement:* architecture, area/ethnic studies, biological sciences, communication, computer science, education, engineering/technologies, English, foreign languages, general academic interests/achievements, humanities, international studies, mathematics, premedicine, social sciences. *Creative Arts/Performance:* applied art and design, art/fine arts, cinema/film/broadcasting, creative writing, general creative arts/performance, music, performing arts. *Special Achievements/Activities:* community service, general special achievements/activities, leadership. ***Tuition waivers:*** Full or partial for senior citizens. ***ROTC:*** Army cooperative, Air Force cooperative.

LOANS ***Student loans:*** $13,789,000 (95% need-based, 5% non-need-based). 33% of past graduating class borrowed through all loan programs. *Average indebtedness per student:* $16,080. ***Average need-based loan:*** Freshmen: $1600; Undergraduates: $3310. ***Parent loans:*** $166,000 (100% non-need-based). ***Programs:*** Federal Direct (Subsidized and Unsubsidized Stafford, PLUS), Perkins.

WORK-STUDY ***Federal work-study:*** Total amount: $2,355,000; 2,155 jobs averaging $1558.

APPLYING FOR FINANCIAL AID ***Required financial aid forms:*** FAFSA, state aid form. ***Financial aid deadline (priority):*** 4/1. ***Notification date:*** Continuous beginning 3/31.

CONTACT Thelma Mason, Director of Financial Aid, City College of the City University of New York, 160 Convent Avenue, Administration Building, Room 104, New York, NY 10031, 212-650-6656. *Fax:* 212-650-5829. *E-mail:* thelma@finance.ccny.cuny.edu.

CITY UNIVERSITY

Bellevue, WA

CONTACT Ms. Jean L. Roberts, Director of Student Financial Services, City University, 11900 Northeast 1st Street, Bellevue, WA 98005, 425-709-5251 or toll-free 888-42-CITYU. *Fax:* 425-709-5263. *E-mail:* jroberts@cityu.edu.

CLAFLIN UNIVERSITY

Orangeburg, SC

Tuition & fees: $11,764 Average undergraduate aid package: $10,917

ABOUT THE INSTITUTION Independent United Methodist, coed. Awards: bachelor's and master's degrees. 31 undergraduate majors. Total enrollment: 1,758. Undergraduates: 1,674. Freshmen: 400. Federal methodology is used as a basis for awarding need-based institutional aid.

UNDERGRADUATE EXPENSES for 2006–07 ***Application fee:*** $20. ***Comprehensive fee:*** $18,086 includes full-time tuition ($9862), mandatory fees ($1902), and room and board ($6322). ***College room only:*** $2816. Room and board charges vary according to housing facility. ***Part-time tuition:*** $411 per credit hour. ***Part-time fees:*** $68 per credit hour. ***Payment plan:*** Installment.

FRESHMAN FINANCIAL AID (Fall 2006, est.) 379 applied for aid; of those 97% were deemed to have need. 99% of freshmen with need received aid; of those 11% had need fully met. ***Average percent of need met:*** 59% (excluding resources awarded to replace EFC). ***Average financial aid package:*** $10,930 (excluding resources awarded to replace EFC). 24% of all full-time freshmen had no need and received non-need-based gift aid.

UNDERGRADUATE FINANCIAL AID (Fall 2006, est.) 1,517 applied for aid; of those 97% were deemed to have need. 100% of undergraduates with need received aid; of those 10% had need fully met. ***Average percent of need met:*** 56% (excluding resources awarded to replace EFC). ***Average financial aid package:*** $10,917 (excluding resources awarded to replace EFC). 19% of all full-time undergraduates had no need and received non-need-based gift aid.

GIFT AID (NEED-BASED) ***Total amount:*** $12,300,333 (38% federal, 38% state, 16% institutional, 8% external sources). ***Receiving aid:*** Freshmen: 87% (347); All full-time undergraduates: 87% (1,385). ***Average award:*** Freshmen: $8904; Undergraduates: $8220. ***Scholarships, grants, and awards:*** Federal Pell, FSEOG, state, private, college/university gift aid from institutional funds, United Negro College Fund.

GIFT AID (NON-NEED-BASED) ***Receiving aid:*** Freshmen: 10% (38); Undergraduates: 8% (128). ***Average award:*** Freshmen: $18,149; Undergraduates: $17,712. ***Scholarships, grants, and awards by category:*** *Academic Interests/Achievement:* general academic interests/achievements. *Creative Arts/Performance:* applied art and design, art/fine arts, music. *Special Achievements/Activities:* cheerleading/drum major. *Special Characteristics:* children of faculty/staff, relatives of clergy, religious affiliation. ***Tuition waivers:*** Full or partial for employees or children of employees. ***ROTC:*** Army cooperative.

LOANS ***Student loans:*** $10,799,660 (100% need-based). 83% of past graduating class borrowed through all loan programs. *Average indebtedness per student:* $19,993. ***Average need-based loan:*** Freshmen: $2666; Undergraduates: $3734. ***Parent loans:*** $639,412 (100% non-need-based). ***Programs:*** FFEL (Subsidized and Unsubsidized Stafford, PLUS), Perkins.

WORK-STUDY ***Federal work-study:*** Total amount: $221,114; jobs available.

ATHLETIC AWARDS Total amount: $312,821 (100% need-based).

APPLYING FOR FINANCIAL AID ***Required financial aid forms:*** FAFSA, institution's own form. ***Financial aid deadline:*** Continuous. ***Notification date:*** Continuous beginning 5/15. Students must reply within 2 weeks of notification.

CONTACT Ms. Yolanda Frazier, Interim Director of Financial Aid, Claflin University, Tingly Hall, Suite 12, 400 Magnolia Street, Orangeburg, SC 29115, 803-535-5720 or toll-free 800-922-1276 (in-state). *Fax:* 803-535-5383. *E-mail:* yfrazier@claflin.edu.

CLAREMONT McKENNA COLLEGE

Claremont, CA

Tuition & fees: $34,850 Average undergraduate aid package: $28,191

ABOUT THE INSTITUTION Independent, coed. Awards: bachelor's degrees. 83 undergraduate majors. Total enrollment: 1,153. Undergraduates: 1,153. Freshmen: 296. Institutional methodology is used as a basis for awarding need-based institutional aid.

UNDERGRADUATE EXPENSES for 2006–07 ***Application fee:*** $60. ***Comprehensive fee:*** $45,590 includes full-time tuition ($33,000), mandatory fees ($1850), and room and board ($10,740). ***College room only:*** $5420. Full-time tuition and fees vary according to reciprocity agreements. Room and board charges vary according to board plan and housing facility. Part-time tuition and fees vary according to reciprocity agreements. ***Payment plans:*** Tuition prepayment, installment.

FRESHMAN FINANCIAL AID (Fall 2006, est.) 170 applied for aid; of those 79% were deemed to have need. 100% of freshmen with need received aid; of those 100% had need fully met. ***Average percent of need met:*** 100% (excluding resources awarded to replace EFC). ***Average financial aid package:*** $29,432 (excluding resources awarded to replace EFC). 5% of all full-time freshmen had no need and received non-need-based gift aid.

UNDERGRADUATE FINANCIAL AID (Fall 2006, est.) 555 applied for aid; of those 95% were deemed to have need. 100% of undergraduates with need received aid; of those 99% had need fully met. ***Average percent of need met:*** 100% (excluding resources awarded to replace EFC). ***Average financial aid package:*** $28,191 (excluding resources awarded to replace EFC). 1% of all full-time undergraduates had no need and received non-need-based gift aid.

GIFT AID (NEED-BASED) ***Total amount:*** $13,488,117 (4% federal, 6% state, 87% institutional, 3% external sources). ***Receiving aid:*** Freshmen: 45% (133); All full-time undergraduates: 46% (524). ***Average award:*** Freshmen: $24,220; Undergraduates: $23,674. ***Scholarships, grants, and awards:*** Federal Pell, FSEOG, state, college/university gift aid from institutional funds.

GIFT AID (NON-NEED-BASED) ***Total amount:*** $787,995 (74% institutional, 26% external sources). ***Receiving aid:*** Freshmen: 21% (63); Undergraduates: 18% (210). ***Average award:*** Freshmen: $8439; Undergraduates: $8271. ***Scholarships, grants, and awards by category:*** *Academic Interests/Achievement:* general academic interests/achievements. *Special Achievements/Activities:* 22 awards ($10,000 total): leadership. ***Tuition waivers:*** Full or partial for employees or children of employees. ***ROTC:*** Army, Air Force cooperative.

LOANS ***Student loans:*** $2,866,235 (32% need-based, 68% non-need-based). 51% of past graduating class borrowed through all loan programs. *Average indebtedness per student:* $10,518. ***Average need-based loan:*** Freshmen: $3432; Undergraduates: $3604. ***Parent loans:*** $1,095,985 (100% non-need-based). ***Programs:*** FFEL (Subsidized and Unsubsidized Stafford, PLUS), Perkins, college/university.

WORK-STUDY ***Federal work-study:*** Total amount: $200,000; 280 jobs averaging $1000. ***State or other work-study/employment:*** Total amount: $910,000 (7% need-based, 93% non-need-based).

APPLYING FOR FINANCIAL AID ***Required financial aid forms:*** FAFSA, CSS Financial Aid PROFILE, noncustodial (divorced/separated) parent's statement, business/farm supplement. ***Notification date:*** 4/1. Students must reply by 5/1.

CONTACT Ms. Georgette R. DeVeres, Associate Vice President of Admission and Director of Financial Aid, Claremont McKenna College, 890 Columbia Avenue, Claremont, CA 91711, 909-621-8356. *Fax:* 909-621-8516. *E-mail:* gdeveres@cmc.edu.

CLARION UNIVERSITY OF PENNSYLVANIA

Clarion, PA

Tuition & fees (PA res): $6616 **Average undergraduate aid package: $7246**

ABOUT THE INSTITUTION State-supported, coed. Awards: associate, bachelor's, and master's degrees and post-master's certificates. 55 undergraduate majors. Total enrollment: 6,591. Undergraduates: 5,927. Freshmen: 1,399. Federal methodology is used as a basis for awarding need-based institutional aid.

UNDERGRADUATE EXPENSES for 2006–07 ***Application fee:*** $30. ***Tuition, state resident:*** full-time $5038; part-time $210 per credit. ***Tuition, nonresident:*** full-time $10,078; part-time $420 per credit. ***Required fees:*** full-time $1578; $74 per credit. ***College room and board:*** $5546; ***Room only:*** $3814.

FRESHMAN FINANCIAL AID (Fall 2006, est.) 1192 applied for aid; of those 81% were deemed to have need. 96% of freshmen with need received aid; of those 14% had need fully met. ***Average percent of need met:*** 61% (excluding resources awarded to replace EFC). ***Average financial aid package:*** $6629 (excluding resources awarded to replace EFC). 6% of all full-time freshmen had no need and received non-need-based gift aid.

UNDERGRADUATE FINANCIAL AID (Fall 2006, est.) 4,295 applied for aid; of those 84% were deemed to have need. 97% of undergraduates with need received aid; of those 17% had need fully met. ***Average percent of need met:*** 68% (excluding resources awarded to replace EFC). ***Average financial aid package:*** $7246 (excluding resources awarded to replace EFC). 6% of all full-time undergraduates had no need and received non-need-based gift aid.

GIFT AID (NEED-BASED) ***Total amount:*** $14,699,068 (36% federal, 50% state, 7% institutional, 7% external sources). ***Receiving aid:*** Freshmen: 57% (742); All full-time undergraduates: 53% (2,706). ***Average award:*** Freshmen: $5309; Undergraduates: $5054. ***Scholarships, grants, and awards:*** Federal Pell, FSEOG, state, private, college/university gift aid from institutional funds, United Negro College Fund.

GIFT AID (NON-NEED-BASED) ***Receiving aid:*** Freshmen: 20% (263); Undergraduates: 17% (857). ***Average award:*** Freshmen: $2042; Undergraduates: $2892. ***Scholarships, grants, and awards by category:*** *Academic Interests/Achievement:* biological sciences, business, communication, computer science, education, English, foreign languages, general academic interests/achievements, humanities, international studies, library science, mathematics, physical sciences, premedicine, social sciences. *Creative Arts/Performance:* art/fine arts, performing arts, theater/drama. *Special Achievements/Activities:* leadership. *Special Characteristics:* children of faculty/staff, ethnic background, local/state students, members of minority groups, veterans. ***ROTC:*** Army cooperative.

LOANS ***Student loans:*** $22,828,424 (47% need-based, 53% non-need-based). 77% of past graduating class borrowed through all loan programs. *Average indebtedness per student:* $18,628. ***Average need-based loan:*** Freshmen: $2507; Undergraduates: $3460. ***Parent loans:*** $3,721,969 (100% non-need-based). ***Programs:*** FFEL (Subsidized and Unsubsidized Stafford, PLUS), Perkins, college/university.

WORK-STUDY ***Federal work-study:*** Total amount: $495,626; 325 jobs averaging $1558. ***State or other work-study/employment:*** Total amount: $961,119 (100% non-need-based). 624 part-time jobs averaging $1661.

ATHLETIC AWARDS Total amount: $601,450 (100% need-based).

APPLYING FOR FINANCIAL AID ***Required financial aid form:*** FAFSA. ***Financial aid deadline (priority):*** 5/1. ***Notification date:*** Continuous beginning 3/1.

CONTACT Dr. Kenneth Grugel, Director of Financial Aid, Clarion University of Pennsylvania, 104 Egbert Hall, Clarion, PA 16214, 814-393-2315 or toll-free 800-672-7171. *Fax:* 814-393-2520. *E-mail:* maphillips@clarion.edu.

CLARK ATLANTA UNIVERSITY

Atlanta, GA

ABOUT THE INSTITUTION Independent United Methodist, coed. Awards: bachelor's, master's, and doctoral degrees and post-bachelor's and post-master's certificates. 47 undergraduate majors. Total enrollment: 4,514. Undergraduates: 3,681. Freshmen: 983.

GIFT AID (NEED-BASED) ***Scholarships, grants, and awards:*** Federal Pell, FSEOG, state, private, college/university gift aid from institutional funds, United Negro College Fund.

GIFT AID (NON-NEED-BASED) ***Scholarships, grants, and awards by category:*** *Academic Interests/Achievement:* general academic interests/achievements. *Creative Arts/Performance:* music. *Special Achievements/Activities:* general special achievements/activities, leadership. *Special Characteristics:* general special characteristics.

LOANS ***Programs:*** FFEL (Subsidized and Unsubsidized Stafford, PLUS), Perkins.

WORK-STUDY ***Federal work-study:*** Total amount: $842,633; 229 jobs averaging $1335.

APPLYING FOR FINANCIAL AID ***Required financial aid form:*** FAFSA.

CONTACT Office of Financial Aid, Clark Atlanta University, 223 James P. Brawley Drive, Atlanta, GA 30314, 404-880-8992 or toll-free 800-688-3228. *Fax:* 404-880-8070. *E-mail:* studentfinancialaid@cau.edu.

CLARKE COLLEGE

Dubuque, IA

Tuition & fees: $20,297 **Average undergraduate aid package: $17,276**

ABOUT THE INSTITUTION Independent Roman Catholic, coed. Awards: associate, bachelor's, and master's degrees. 42 undergraduate majors. Total enrollment: 1,201. Undergraduates: 1,006. Freshmen: 164. Federal methodology is used as a basis for awarding need-based institutional aid.

UNDERGRADUATE EXPENSES for 2006–07 ***Application fee:*** $25. ***Comprehensive fee:*** $26,871 includes full-time tuition ($19,682), mandatory fees ($615), and room and board ($6574). ***College room only:*** $3198. Room and board charges vary according to board plan and housing facility. ***Part-time tuition:*** $498 per credit hour. ***Payment plans:*** Installment, deferred payment.

FRESHMAN FINANCIAL AID (Fall 2006, est.) 157 applied for aid; of those 90% were deemed to have need. 100% of freshmen with need received aid; of those 25% had need fully met. ***Average percent of need met:*** 85% (excluding

resources awarded to replace EFC). ***Average financial aid package:*** $18,578 (excluding resources awarded to replace EFC). 9% of all full-time freshmen had no need and received non-need-based gift aid.

UNDERGRADUATE FINANCIAL AID (Fall 2006, est.) 791 applied for aid; of those 89% were deemed to have need. 100% of undergraduates with need received aid; of those 22% had need fully met. ***Average percent of need met:*** 85% (excluding resources awarded to replace EFC). ***Average financial aid package:*** $17,276 (excluding resources awarded to replace EFC). 9% of all full-time undergraduates had no need and received non-need-based gift aid.

GIFT AID (NEED-BASED) ***Total amount:*** $8,220,815 (12% federal, 16% state, 70% institutional, 2% external sources). ***Receiving aid:*** Freshmen: 89% (141); All full-time undergraduates: 86% (693). ***Average award:*** Freshmen: $15,185; Undergraduates: $13,295. ***Scholarships, grants, and awards:*** Federal Pell, FSEOG, state, private, college/university gift aid from institutional funds.

GIFT AID (NON-NEED-BASED) ***Total amount:*** $497,763 (95% institutional, 5% external sources). ***Receiving aid:*** Freshmen: 85% (135); Undergraduates: 79% (638). ***Average award:*** Freshmen: $10,518; Undergraduates: $13,319. ***Scholarships, grants, and awards by category:*** *Academic Interests/Achievement:* 536 awards ($2,656,675 total): computer science, foreign languages, general academic interests/achievements. *Creative Arts/Performance:* 81 awards ($170,115 total): art/fine arts, music, theater/drama. *Special Achievements/Activities:* 19 awards ($15,035 total): leadership. *Special Characteristics:* 625 awards ($1,019,682 total): children and siblings of alumni, children of faculty/staff, children with a deceased or disabled parent, general special characteristics, international students, local/state students, members of minority groups, relatives of clergy, religious affiliation, siblings of current students. ***Tuition waivers:*** Full or partial for children of alumni, employees or children of employees, adult students, senior citizens. ***ROTC:*** Army cooperative.

LOANS ***Student loans:*** $6,058,541 (53% need-based, 47% non-need-based). 80% of past graduating class borrowed through all loan programs. *Average indebtedness per student:* $22,268. ***Average need-based loan:*** Freshmen: $2953; Undergraduates: $4286. ***Parent loans:*** $564,511 (86% need-based, 14% non-need-based). ***Programs:*** FFEL (Subsidized and Unsubsidized Stafford, PLUS), Perkins, Federal Nursing, state, college/university, private loans.

WORK-STUDY ***Federal work-study:*** Total amount: $319,444; 271 jobs averaging $1173. ***State or other work-study/employment:*** Part-time jobs available.

APPLYING FOR FINANCIAL AID ***Required financial aid form:*** FAFSA. ***Financial aid deadline (priority):*** 4/15. ***Notification date:*** Continuous beginning 3/15. Students must reply by 5/1 or within 2 weeks of notification.

CONTACT Ann Heisler, Director of Financial Aid, Clarke College, 1550 Clarke Drive, Dubuque, IA 52001-3198, 563-588-6327 or toll-free 800-383-2345. *Fax:* 563-584-8666. *E-mail:* ann.heisler@clarke.edu.

CLARKSON COLLEGE

Omaha, NE

CONTACT Pam Shelton, Director of Financial Aid, Clarkson College, 101 South 42nd Street, Omaha, NE 68131-2739, 402-552-2749 or toll-free 800-647-5500. *Fax:* 402-552-6165. *E-mail:* shelton@clarksoncollege.edu.

CLARKSON UNIVERSITY

Potsdam, NY

Tuition & fees: $27,090 **Average undergraduate aid package: $19,993**

ABOUT THE INSTITUTION Independent, coed. Awards: bachelor's, master's, and doctoral degrees. 60 undergraduate majors. Total enrollment: 2,964. Undergraduates: 2,545. Freshmen: 646. Federal methodology is used as a basis for awarding need-based institutional aid.

UNDERGRADUATE EXPENSES for 2006–07 ***Application fee:*** $50. ***Comprehensive fee:*** $36,738 includes full-time tuition ($26,650), mandatory fees ($440), and room and board ($9648). ***College room only:*** $5058. Full-time tuition and fees vary according to course load. Room and board charges vary according to housing facility. ***Part-time tuition:*** $889 per credit. Part-time tuition and fees vary according to course load. ***Payment plans:*** Tuition prepayment, installment.

FRESHMAN FINANCIAL AID (Fall 2006, est.) 555 applied for aid; of those 88% were deemed to have need. 100% of freshmen with need received aid. ***Average percent of need met:*** 86% (excluding resources awarded to replace EFC). ***Average financial aid package:*** $22,513 (excluding resources awarded to replace EFC). 11% of all full-time freshmen had no need and received non-need-based gift aid.

UNDERGRADUATE FINANCIAL AID (Fall 2006, est.) 2,225 applied for aid; of those 92% were deemed to have need. 92% of undergraduates with need received aid. ***Average percent of need met:*** 86% (excluding resources awarded to replace EFC). ***Average financial aid package:*** $19,993 (excluding resources awarded to replace EFC). 7% of all full-time undergraduates had no need and received non-need-based gift aid.

GIFT AID (NEED-BASED) ***Total amount:*** $36,309,725 (7% federal, 6% state, 82% institutional, 5% external sources). ***Receiving aid:*** Freshmen: 48% (312); All full-time undergraduates: 62% (1,569). ***Average award:*** Freshmen: $10,084; Undergraduates: $15,358. ***Scholarships, grants, and awards:*** Federal Pell, FSEOG, state, private, college/university gift aid from institutional funds.

GIFT AID (NON-NEED-BASED) ***Total amount:*** $2,433,599 (23% state, 73% institutional, 4% external sources). ***Receiving aid:*** Freshmen: 12% (75); Undergraduates: 8% (210). ***Average award:*** Freshmen: $12,073; Undergraduates: $11,248. ***Scholarships, grants, and awards by category:*** *Academic Interests/Achievement:* 1,608 awards ($8,631,989 total): biological sciences, business, computer science, engineering/technologies, general academic interests/achievements, humanities, mathematics, military science, physical sciences. *Special Achievements/Activities:* 600 awards ($5,083,500 total): general special achievements/activities, leadership. *Special Characteristics:* 308 awards ($2,626,071 total): children of faculty/staff, general special characteristics, international students, local/state students, members of minority groups. ***Tuition waivers:*** Full or partial for employees or children of employees. ***ROTC:*** Army, Air Force.

LOANS ***Student loans:*** $19,695,865 (95% need-based, 5% non-need-based). 66% of past graduating class borrowed through all loan programs. *Average indebtedness per student:* $27,927. ***Average need-based loan:*** Freshmen: $4107; Undergraduates: $6500. ***Parent loans:*** $4,497,608 (88% need-based, 12% non-need-based). ***Programs:*** Federal Direct (Subsidized and Unsubsidized Stafford, PLUS), FFEL (Subsidized and Unsubsidized Stafford, PLUS), Perkins, college/university, alternative loans.

WORK-STUDY ***Federal work-study:*** Total amount: $1,594,381; 1,265 jobs averaging $1260. ***State or other work-study/employment:*** Total amount: $443,752 (64% need-based, 36% non-need-based). 174 part-time jobs averaging $2550.

ATHLETIC AWARDS Total amount: $1,347,768 (100% non-need-based).

APPLYING FOR FINANCIAL AID ***Required financial aid forms:*** FAFSA, institution's own form, state aid form. ***Financial aid deadline (priority):*** 2/15. ***Notification date:*** 3/19. Students must reply by 5/1 or within 2 weeks of notification.

CONTACT April L. Grant, Associate Director of Financial Aid, Clarkson University, Box 5615, Cubley-Reynolds, Potsdam, NY 13699-5615, 315-268-6413 or toll-free 800-527-6577. *E-mail:* agrant@clarkson.edu.

CLARK UNIVERSITY

Worcester, MA

Tuition & fees: $31,465 **Average undergraduate aid package: $24,072**

ABOUT THE INSTITUTION Independent, coed. Awards: bachelor's, master's, and doctoral degrees and post-bachelor's and post-master's certificates. 49 undergraduate majors. Total enrollment: 3,071. Undergraduates: 2,262. Freshmen: 567. Institutional methodology is used as a basis for awarding need-based institutional aid.

UNDERGRADUATE EXPENSES for 2006–07 ***Application fee:*** $50. ***Comprehensive fee:*** $37,365 includes full-time tuition ($31,200), mandatory fees ($265), and room and board ($5900). ***College room only:*** $3550. Room and board charges vary according to board plan and housing facility. ***Part-time tuition:*** $975 per credit hour. ***Payment plans:*** Tuition prepayment, installment.

FRESHMAN FINANCIAL AID (Fall 2006, est.) 419 applied for aid; of those 79% were deemed to have need. 98% of freshmen with need received aid; of those 67% had need fully met. ***Average percent of need met:*** 94% (excluding resources awarded to replace EFC). ***Average financial aid package:*** $24,072 (excluding resources awarded to replace EFC). 25% of all full-time freshmen had no need and received non-need-based gift aid.

UNDERGRADUATE FINANCIAL AID (Fall 2006, est.) 1,571 applied for aid; of those 79% were deemed to have need. 98% of undergraduates with need received aid; of those 67% had need fully met. ***Average percent of need met:*** 94% (excluding resources awarded to replace EFC). ***Average financial aid package:*** $24,072 (excluding resources awarded to replace EFC). 25% of all full-time undergraduates had no need and received non-need-based gift aid.

GIFT AID (NEED-BASED) ***Total amount:*** $19,481,543 (8% federal, 3% state, 89% institutional). ***Receiving aid:*** Freshmen: 57% (323); All full-time undergraduates: 57% (1,211). ***Average award:*** Freshmen: $19,164; Undergraduates: $19,164. ***Scholarships, grants, and awards:*** Federal Pell, FSEOG, state, college/university gift aid from institutional funds.

GIFT AID (NON-NEED-BASED) ***Total amount:*** $7,633,124 (100% institutional). ***Receiving aid:*** Freshmen: 30% (171); Undergraduates: 30% (641). ***Average award:*** Freshmen: $14,131; Undergraduates: $14,131. ***Scholarships, grants, and awards by category:*** *Academic Interests/Achievement:* general academic interests/achievements. *Special Achievements/Activities:* community service, general special achievements/activities. ***Tuition waivers:*** Full or partial for employees or children of employees. ***ROTC:*** Army cooperative, Naval cooperative, Air Force cooperative.

LOANS ***Student loans:*** $8,676,340 (68% need-based, 32% non-need-based). 88% of past graduating class borrowed through all loan programs. *Average indebtedness per student:* $19,125. ***Average need-based loan:*** Freshmen: $3555; Undergraduates: $3555. ***Parent loans:*** $4,648,192 (12% need-based, 88% non-need-based). ***Programs:*** FFEL (Subsidized and Unsubsidized Stafford, PLUS), Perkins, state.

WORK-STUDY ***Federal work-study:*** Total amount: $1,469,711; jobs available.

APPLYING FOR FINANCIAL AID ***Required financial aid forms:*** FAFSA, CSS Financial Aid PROFILE. ***Financial aid deadline:*** 2/1 (priority: 2/1). ***Notification date:*** 3/31. Students must reply by 5/1.

CONTACT Dr. Jeffrey J. Himmelberger, Coordinator, Clark University, 950 Main Street, Worcester, MA 01610-1477, 508-793-7374 or toll-free 800-GO-CLARK. *Fax:* 508-421-3764. *E-mail:* jhimmelberger@clarku.edu.

CLAYTON STATE UNIVERSITY

Morrow, GA

CONTACT Melody Hodge, Director of Financial Aid, Clayton State University, 5900 North Lee Street, Morrow, GA 30260, 770-961-3511. *Fax:* 770-960-4258. *E-mail:* financialaid@mail.clayton.edu.

CLEAR CREEK BAPTIST BIBLE COLLEGE

Pineville, KY

Tuition & fees: $5262 **Average undergraduate aid package: $4392**

ABOUT THE INSTITUTION Independent Southern Baptist, coed, primarily men. Awards: bachelor's degrees. 2 undergraduate majors. Total enrollment: 201. Undergraduates: 201. Both federal and institutional methodology are used as a basis for awarding need-based institutional aid.

UNDERGRADUATE EXPENSES for 2006–07 ***Application fee:*** $40. ***Comprehensive fee:*** $8572 includes full-time tuition ($4972), mandatory fees ($290), and room and board ($3310). ***College room only:*** $1870. ***Part-time tuition:*** $226 per semester hour. ***Part-time fees:*** $80 per term.

FRESHMAN FINANCIAL AID (Fall 2006, est.) 21 applied for aid; of those 81% were deemed to have need. 100% of freshmen with need received aid. ***Average percent of need met:*** 49% (excluding resources awarded to replace EFC). ***Average financial aid package:*** $4969 (excluding resources awarded to replace EFC). 19% of all full-time freshmen had no need and received non-need-based gift aid.

UNDERGRADUATE FINANCIAL AID (Fall 2006, est.) 168 applied for aid; of those 89% were deemed to have need. 100% of undergraduates with need received aid. ***Average percent of need met:*** 43% (excluding resources awarded to replace EFC). ***Average financial aid package:*** $4392 (excluding resources awarded to replace EFC). 14% of all full-time undergraduates had no need and received non-need-based gift aid.

GIFT AID (NEED-BASED) ***Total amount:*** $720,445 (62% federal, 4% state, 25% institutional, 9% external sources). ***Receiving aid:*** Freshmen: 81% (17); All full-time undergraduates: 75% (150). ***Scholarships, grants, and awards:*** Federal Pell, FSEOG, state, private, college/university gift aid from institutional funds.

GIFT AID (NON-NEED-BASED) ***Total amount:*** $85,753 (76% federal, 24% institutional). ***Receiving aid:*** Freshmen: 67% (14); Undergraduates: 20% (40). ***Average award:*** Freshmen: $450; Undergraduates: $411. ***Scholarships, grants, and awards by category:*** *Academic Interests/Achievement:* 8 awards ($3134 total): general academic interests/achievements. *Creative Arts/Performance:* 7 awards ($1400 total): music. *Special Characteristics:* 2 awards ($1006 total): handicapped students, international students.

WORK-STUDY ***Federal work-study:*** Total amount: $28,562; 22 jobs averaging $1298. ***State or other work-study/employment:*** Total amount: $9521 (100% need-based). 22 part-time jobs averaging $433.

APPLYING FOR FINANCIAL AID ***Required financial aid forms:*** FAFSA, institution's own form. ***Financial aid deadline (priority):*** 6/30. ***Notification date:*** 7/1.

CONTACT Mr. Sam Risner, Director of Financial Aid, Clear Creek Baptist Bible College, 300 Clear Creek Road, Pineville, KY 40977-9754, 606-337-3196 Ext. 142. *Fax:* 606-337-2372. *E-mail:* srisner@ccbbc.edu.

CLEARWATER CHRISTIAN COLLEGE

Clearwater, FL

Tuition & fees: $12,500 **Average undergraduate aid package: $9270**

ABOUT THE INSTITUTION Independent nondenominational, coed. Awards: associate and bachelor's degrees. 25 undergraduate majors. Total enrollment: 582. Undergraduates: 582. Freshmen: 149. Federal methodology is used as a basis for awarding need-based institutional aid.

UNDERGRADUATE EXPENSES for 2006–07 ***Application fee:*** $35. ***Comprehensive fee:*** $17,830 includes full-time tuition ($11,860), mandatory fees ($640), and room and board ($5330). ***Part-time tuition:*** $460 per hour.

FRESHMAN FINANCIAL AID (Fall 2006, est.) 224 applied for aid; of those 100% were deemed to have need. 55% of freshmen with need received aid; of those 4% had need fully met. ***Average percent of need met:*** 40% (excluding resources awarded to replace EFC). ***Average financial aid package:*** $8052 (excluding resources awarded to replace EFC).

UNDERGRADUATE FINANCIAL AID (Fall 2006, est.) 578 applied for aid; of those 100% were deemed to have need. 93% of undergraduates with need received aid; of those 3% had need fully met. ***Average percent of need met:*** 45% (excluding resources awarded to replace EFC). ***Average financial aid package:*** $9270 (excluding resources awarded to replace EFC).

GIFT AID (NEED-BASED) ***Total amount:*** $903,744 (81% federal, 15% state, 4% institutional). ***Receiving aid:*** Freshmen: 31% (70); All full-time undergraduates: 47% (272). ***Average award:*** Freshmen: $4728; Undergraduates: $4269. ***Scholarships, grants, and awards:*** Federal Pell, FSEOG, state, private, college/university gift aid from institutional funds.

GIFT AID (NON-NEED-BASED) ***Total amount:*** $2,544,715 (45% state, 48% institutional, 7% external sources). ***Receiving aid:*** Freshmen: 51% (114); Undergraduates: 79% (456). ***Scholarships, grants, and awards by category:*** *Academic Interests/Achievement:* 134 awards ($350,000 total): business, education, general academic interests/achievements, premedicine, religion/biblical studies. *Creative Arts/Performance:* 45 awards ($84,000 total): music. *Special Achievements/Activities:* 151 awards ($75,000 total): leadership. *Special Characteristics:* 145 awards ($310,000 total): children and siblings of alumni, ethnic background, religious affiliation, siblings of current students. ***ROTC:*** Army cooperative, Air Force cooperative.

LOANS ***Student loans:*** $1,474,991 (57% need-based, 43% non-need-based). 56% of past graduating class borrowed through all loan programs. *Average indebtedness per student:* $16,800. ***Average need-based loan:*** Freshmen: $2473; Undergraduates: $3559. ***Parent loans:*** $608,777 (100% non-need-based). ***Programs:*** FFEL (Subsidized and Unsubsidized Stafford, PLUS), state, alternative loans.

WORK-STUDY ***Federal work-study:*** Total amount: $27,000; 50 jobs averaging $670. ***State or other work-study/employment:*** Total amount: $15,000 (100% need-based). 20 part-time jobs averaging $612.

APPLYING FOR FINANCIAL AID ***Required financial aid forms:*** FAFSA, institution's own form, state aid form. ***Financial aid deadline (priority):*** 3/15. ***Notification date:*** Continuous beginning 1/1. Students must reply within 2 weeks of notification.

CONTACT Mrs. Ruth Strum, Director of Financial Aid, Clearwater Christian College, 3400 Gulf-to-Bay Boulevard, Clearwater, FL 33759-4595, 727-726-1153 Ext. 214 or toll-free 800-348-4463. *Fax:* 727-791-1347. *E-mail:* ruthstrum@clearwater.edu.

CLEARY UNIVERSITY

Ann Arbor, MI

Tuition & fees: $14,160 **Average undergraduate aid package: $10,287**

ABOUT THE INSTITUTION Independent, coed. Awards: associate, bachelor's, and master's degrees. 10 undergraduate majors. Total enrollment: 691. Undergraduates: 626. Federal methodology is used as a basis for awarding need-based institutional aid.

UNDERGRADUATE EXPENSES for 2007–08 ***Application fee:*** $25. ***Tuition:*** full-time $14,160; part-time $295 per quarter hour.

FRESHMAN FINANCIAL AID (Fall 2005) 34 applied for aid; of those 97% were deemed to have need. 100% of freshmen with need received aid; of those 6% had need fully met. ***Average percent of need met:*** 43% (excluding resources awarded to replace EFC). ***Average financial aid package:*** $11,255 (excluding resources awarded to replace EFC). 6% of all full-time freshmen had no need and received non-need-based gift aid.

UNDERGRADUATE FINANCIAL AID (Fall 2005) 299 applied for aid; of those 100% were deemed to have need. 100% of undergraduates with need received aid; of those 3% had need fully met. ***Average percent of need met:*** 42% (excluding resources awarded to replace EFC). ***Average financial aid package:*** $10,287 (excluding resources awarded to replace EFC). 10% of all full-time undergraduates had no need and received non-need-based gift aid.

GIFT AID (NEED-BASED) ***Total amount:*** $546,994 (56% federal, 42% state, 2% institutional). ***Receiving aid:*** Freshmen: 53% (26); All full-time undergraduates: 37% (200). ***Average award:*** Freshmen: $1069; Undergraduates: $1000. ***Scholarships, grants, and awards:*** Federal Pell, FSEOG, state, private, college/university gift aid from institutional funds.

GIFT AID (NON-NEED-BASED) ***Total amount:*** $32,145 (90% state, 10% institutional). ***Receiving aid:*** Freshmen: 10% (5); Undergraduates: 2% (12). ***Average award:*** Freshmen: $2970; Undergraduates: $2755. ***Scholarships, grants, and awards by category:*** *Academic Interests/Achievement:* 29 awards ($94,868 total): business, general academic interests/achievements. *Special Achievements/Activities:* 14 awards ($11,009 total): community service, general special achievements/activities. *Special Characteristics:* 45 awards ($207,015 total): adult students, children of faculty/staff.

LOANS ***Student loans:*** $2,890,507 (42% need-based, 58% non-need-based). ***Average need-based loan:*** Freshmen: $1024; Undergraduates: $1419. ***Parent loans:*** $147,149 (100% non-need-based). ***Programs:*** FFEL (Subsidized and Unsubsidized Stafford, PLUS).

WORK-STUDY ***Federal work-study:*** Total amount: $30,421; 15 jobs averaging $2028. ***State or other work-study/employment:*** Part-time jobs available.

APPLYING FOR FINANCIAL AID ***Required financial aid forms:*** FAFSA, institution's own form. ***Financial aid deadline (priority):*** 3/1. ***Notification date:*** Continuous beginning 5/1. Students must reply by 7/15 or within 2 weeks of notification.

CONTACT Vesta Smith-Campbell, Director of Financial Aid, Cleary University, 3750 Cleary Drive, Howell, MI 48843, 800-589-1979 Ext. 2234 or toll-free 888-5-CLEARY Ext. 2249. *Fax:* 517-552-8022. *E-mail:* vscampbell@cleary.edu.

CLEMSON UNIVERSITY

Clemson, SC

Tuition & fees (SC res): $9868 **Average undergraduate aid package: $9743**

ABOUT THE INSTITUTION State-supported, coed. Awards: bachelor's, master's, and doctoral degrees. 77 undergraduate majors. Total enrollment: 17,165. Undergraduates: 14,096. Freshmen: 2,903. Federal methodology is used as a basis for awarding need-based institutional aid.

UNDERGRADUATE EXPENSES for 2006–07 ***Application fee:*** $50. ***Tuition, state resident:*** full-time $9868; part-time $386 per hour. ***Tuition, nonresident:*** full-time $20,292; part-time $816 per hour. ***Required fees:*** $177 per term part-time. Full-time tuition and fees vary according to course load, degree level, and program. Part-time tuition and fees vary according to course load, degree level, and program. ***College room and board:*** $5874; ***Room only:*** $3500. Room and board charges vary according to board plan and housing facility. ***Payment plan:*** Installment.

FRESHMAN FINANCIAL AID (Fall 2006, est.) 1862 applied for aid; of those 66% were deemed to have need. 98% of freshmen with need received aid; of those 34% had need fully met. ***Average percent of need met:*** 72% (excluding resources awarded to replace EFC). ***Average financial aid package:*** $11,217 (excluding resources awarded to replace EFC). 24% of all full-time freshmen had no need and received non-need-based gift aid.

UNDERGRADUATE FINANCIAL AID (Fall 2006, est.) 6,987 applied for aid; of those 74% were deemed to have need. 97% of undergraduates with need received aid; of those 29% had need fully met. ***Average percent of need met:*** 62% (excluding resources awarded to replace EFC). ***Average financial aid package:*** $9743 (excluding resources awarded to replace EFC). 20% of all full-time undergraduates had no need and received non-need-based gift aid.

GIFT AID (NEED-BASED) ***Total amount:*** $11,786,413 (51% federal, 19% state, 16% institutional, 14% external sources). ***Receiving aid:*** Freshmen: 16% (463); All full-time undergraduates: 18% (2,336). ***Average award:*** Freshmen: $3753; Undergraduates: $3500. ***Scholarships, grants, and awards:*** Federal Pell, FSEOG, state, private, college/university gift aid from institutional funds, Federal Nursing.

GIFT AID (NON-NEED-BASED) ***Total amount:*** $44,238,779 (68% state, 21% institutional, 11% external sources). ***Receiving aid:*** Freshmen: 39% (1,100); Undergraduates: 25% (3,185). ***Average award:*** Freshmen: $2276; Undergraduates: $2045. ***Scholarships, grants, and awards by category:*** *Academic Interests/Achievement:* agriculture, architecture, biological sciences, business, communication, computer science, education, engineering/technologies, English, foreign languages, general academic interests/achievements, health fields, humanities, international studies, mathematics, military science, physical sciences, premedicine, social sciences. *Creative Arts/Performance:* applied art and design, art/fine arts, performing arts, theater/drama. *Special Achievements/Activities:* community service, general special achievements/activities, leadership. *Special Characteristics:* children of faculty/staff, ethnic background, local/state students, members of minority groups. ***Tuition waivers:*** Full or partial for senior citizens. ***ROTC:*** Army, Air Force.

LOANS ***Student loans:*** $57,311,645 (40% need-based, 60% non-need-based). ***Average need-based loan:*** Freshmen: $2874; Undergraduates: $4093. ***Parent loans:*** $12,160,748 (100% non-need-based). ***Programs:*** FFEL (Subsidized and Unsubsidized Stafford, PLUS), Perkins, state, college/university, private loans.

WORK-STUDY ***Federal work-study:*** Total amount: $1,583,689; 772 jobs averaging $2051. ***State or other work-study/employment:*** Total amount: $4,869,443 (100% non-need-based). 2,943 part-time jobs averaging $1655.

ATHLETIC AWARDS Total amount: $4,755,688 (100% non-need-based).

APPLYING FOR FINANCIAL AID ***Required financial aid form:*** FAFSA. ***Financial aid deadline (priority):*** 4/1. ***Notification date:*** Continuous beginning 4/15. Students must reply within 3 weeks of notification.

CONTACT Mr. Marvin G. Carmichael, Director of Financial Aid, Clemson University, G01 Sikes Hall, Clemson, SC 29634-5123, 864-656-2280. *Fax:* 864-656-1831. *E-mail:* finaid@clemson.edu.

THE CLEVELAND INSTITUTE OF ART

Cleveland, OH

Tuition & fees: N/R **Average undergraduate aid package: $16,642**

ABOUT THE INSTITUTION Independent, coed. Awards: bachelor's and master's degrees. 17 undergraduate majors. Total enrollment: 610. Undergraduates: 604. Freshmen: 123. Federal methodology is used as a basis for awarding need-based institutional aid.

UNDERGRADUATE EXPENSES for 2006–07 ***Application fee:*** $30. Contact Institute directly for tuition, fees, and room and board.

FRESHMAN FINANCIAL AID (Fall 2006, est.) 71 applied for aid; of those 89% were deemed to have need. 100% of freshmen with need received aid; of those 10% had need fully met. ***Average percent of need met:*** 55% (excluding resources awarded to replace EFC). ***Average financial aid package:*** $15,852 (excluding resources awarded to replace EFC). 21% of all full-time freshmen had no need and received non-need-based gift aid.

UNDERGRADUATE FINANCIAL AID (Fall 2006, est.) 424 applied for aid; of those 92% were deemed to have need. 100% of undergraduates with need received aid; of those 6% had need fully met. ***Average percent of need met:*** 52% (excluding resources awarded to replace EFC). ***Average financial aid package:*** $16,642 (excluding resources awarded to replace EFC). 17% of all full-time undergraduates had no need and received non-need-based gift aid.

GIFT AID (NEED-BASED) ***Total amount:*** $4,391,306 (12% federal, 12% state, 71% institutional, 5% external sources). ***Receiving aid:*** Freshmen: 79% (63); All full-time undergraduates: 82% (392). ***Average award:*** Freshmen: $11,603; Undergraduates: $11,176. ***Scholarships, grants, and awards:*** Federal Pell, FSEOG, state, private, college/university gift aid from institutional funds.

GIFT AID (NON-NEED-BASED) ***Total amount:*** $824,673 (4% state, 94% institutional, 2% external sources). ***Receiving aid:*** Freshmen: 5% (4); Undergraduates: 3% (15). ***Average award:*** Freshmen: $9657; Undergraduates: $13,412. ***Scholarships, grants, and awards by category:*** *Academic Interests/Achievement:* 30 awards ($62,280 total): general academic interests/achievements. *Creative Arts/Performance:* 445 awards ($3,010,088 total): art/fine arts.

LOANS ***Student loans:*** $5,287,680 (82% need-based, 18% non-need-based). 89% of past graduating class borrowed through all loan programs. *Average indebtedness per student:* $36,963. ***Average need-based loan:*** Freshmen: $3027; Undergraduates: $4438. ***Parent loans:*** $1,290,688 (62% need-based, 38% non-need-based). ***Programs:*** FFEL (Subsidized and Unsubsidized Stafford, PLUS), Perkins.

WORK-STUDY ***Federal work-study:*** Total amount: $228,451; 220 jobs averaging $1038.

APPLYING FOR FINANCIAL AID ***Required financial aid forms:*** FAFSA, institution's own form. ***Financial aid deadline (priority):*** 3/15. ***Notification date:*** Continuous beginning 3/16. Students must reply within 4 weeks of notification.

CONTACT Delores Hall, Assistant Director of Financial Aid, The Cleveland Institute of Art, 11141 East Boulevard, Cleveland, OH 44106-1700, 216-421-7425 or toll-free 800-223-4700. *Fax:* 216-754-3634. *E-mail:* financialaid@cia.edu.

CLEVELAND INSTITUTE OF MUSIC

Cleveland, OH

Tuition & fees: $29,034 **Average undergraduate aid package: $18,324**

ABOUT THE INSTITUTION Independent, coed. Awards: bachelor's, master's, and doctoral degrees and post-bachelor's certificates. 6 undergraduate majors. Total enrollment: 426. Undergraduates: 234. Freshmen: 67. Federal methodology is used as a basis for awarding need-based institutional aid.

UNDERGRADUATE EXPENSES for 2006–07 ***Application fee:*** $100. ***Comprehensive fee:*** $38,368 includes full-time tuition ($27,950), mandatory fees ($1084), and room and board ($9334). ***College room only:*** $5440. Room and board charges vary according to board plan. ***Part-time tuition:*** $1165 per credit hour. ***Payment plan:*** Installment.

FRESHMAN FINANCIAL AID (Fall 2006, est.) 50 applied for aid; of those 86% were deemed to have need. 100% of freshmen with need received aid; of those 23% had need fully met. ***Average percent of need met:*** 68% (excluding resources awarded to replace EFC). ***Average financial aid package:*** $18,481 (excluding resources awarded to replace EFC). 27% of all full-time freshmen had no need and received non-need-based gift aid.

UNDERGRADUATE FINANCIAL AID (Fall 2006, est.) 197 applied for aid; of those 79% were deemed to have need. 99% of undergraduates with need received aid; of those 18% had need fully met. ***Average percent of need met:*** 69% (excluding resources awarded to replace EFC). ***Average financial aid package:*** $18,324 (excluding resources awarded to replace EFC). 33% of all full-time undergraduates had no need and received non-need-based gift aid.

GIFT AID (NEED-BASED) ***Total amount:*** $2,029,485 (7% federal, 2% state, 85% institutional, 6% external sources). ***Receiving aid:*** Freshmen: 54% (43); All full-time undergraduates: 59% (154). ***Average award:*** Freshmen: $14,386; Undergraduates: $13,148. ***Scholarships, grants, and awards:*** Federal Pell, FSEOG, state, private, college/university gift aid from institutional funds.

GIFT AID (NON-NEED-BASED) ***Total amount:*** $1,075,379 (2% state, 86% institutional, 12% external sources). ***Receiving aid:*** Freshmen: 11% (9); Undergraduates: 9% (23). ***Average award:*** Freshmen: $15,475; Undergraduates: $13,345. ***Scholarships, grants, and awards by category:*** *Creative Arts/Performance:* music. ***Tuition waivers:*** Full or partial for employees or children of employees. ***ROTC:*** Army cooperative, Air Force cooperative.

LOANS ***Student loans:*** $1,160,816 (75% need-based, 25% non-need-based). 76% of past graduating class borrowed through all loan programs. *Average indebtedness per student:* $23,657. ***Average need-based loan:*** Freshmen: $4967; Undergraduates: $5680. ***Parent loans:*** $643,978 (49% need-based, 51% non-need-based). ***Programs:*** Federal Direct (Subsidized and Unsubsidized Stafford, PLUS), Perkins, college/university, private/alternative loans.

WORK-STUDY ***Federal work-study:*** Total amount: $92,555; 93 jobs averaging $995. ***State or other work-study/employment:*** Total amount: $25,749 (100% non-need-based). 31 part-time jobs averaging $831.

APPLYING FOR FINANCIAL AID ***Required financial aid form:*** FAFSA. ***Financial aid deadline:*** 2/15 (priority: 2/15). ***Notification date:*** 4/1. Students must reply by 5/1.

CONTACT Ms. Kristie Gripp, Director of Financial Aid, Cleveland Institute of Music, 11021 East Boulevard, Cleveland, OH 44106-1776, 216-791-5000 Ext. 262. *Fax:* 216-707-4519. *E-mail:* kxg26@cwru.edu.

CLEVELAND STATE UNIVERSITY

Cleveland, OH

Tuition & fees (OH res): $7920 **Average undergraduate aid package: $7679**

ABOUT THE INSTITUTION State-supported, coed. Awards: bachelor's, master's, doctoral, and first professional degrees and post-bachelor's and post-master's certificates. 83 undergraduate majors. Total enrollment: 15,483. Undergraduates: 9,878. Freshmen: 1,040. Federal methodology is used as a basis for awarding need-based institutional aid.

UNDERGRADUATE EXPENSES for 2006–07 ***Application fee:*** $30. ***Tuition, state resident:*** full-time $7920; part-time $330 per semester hour. ***Tuition, nonresident:*** full-time $10,664; part-time $444.30 per semester hour. Full-time tuition and fees vary according to program. Part-time tuition and fees vary according to program. ***College room and board:*** $7800; ***Room only:*** $5000. Room and board charges vary according to board plan and housing facility. ***Payment plan:*** Installment.

FRESHMAN FINANCIAL AID (Fall 2006, est.) 746 applied for aid; of those 87% were deemed to have need. 99% of freshmen with need received aid; of those 10% had need fully met. ***Average percent of need met:*** 46% (excluding resources awarded to replace EFC). ***Average financial aid package:*** $7508 (excluding resources awarded to replace EFC). 13% of all full-time freshmen had no need and received non-need-based gift aid.

UNDERGRADUATE FINANCIAL AID (Fall 2006, est.) 4,939 applied for aid; of those 90% were deemed to have need. 98% of undergraduates with need received aid; of those 9% had need fully met. ***Average percent of need met:*** 48% (excluding resources awarded to replace EFC). ***Average financial aid package:*** $7679 (excluding resources awarded to replace EFC). 12% of all full-time undergraduates had no need and received non-need-based gift aid.

GIFT AID (NEED-BASED) ***Total amount:*** $18,522,825 (55% federal, 18% state, 18% institutional, 9% external sources). ***Receiving aid:*** Freshmen: 60% (557); All full-time undergraduates: 52% (3,345). ***Average award:*** Freshmen: $6026; Undergraduates: $5189. ***Scholarships, grants, and awards:*** Federal Pell, FSEOG, state, private, college/university gift aid from institutional funds.

GIFT AID (NON-NEED-BASED) ***Total amount:*** $2,358,554 (8% state, 75% institutional, 17% external sources). ***Receiving aid:*** Freshmen: 4% (34); Undergraduates: 2% (124). ***Average award:*** Freshmen: $8088; Undergraduates: $8264. ***Scholarships, grants, and awards by category:*** *Academic Interests/Achievement:* engineering/technologies, general academic interests/achievements. *Creative Arts/Performance:* art/fine arts, creative writing, dance, music, theater/drama. *Special Achievements/Activities:* cheerleading/drum major. *Special Characteristics:* children and siblings of alumni, general special characteristics. ***Tuition waivers:*** Full or partial for employees or children of employees, senior citizens. ***ROTC:*** Army cooperative, Naval cooperative, Air Force cooperative.

LOANS ***Student loans:*** $40,022,223 (85% need-based, 15% non-need-based). ***Average need-based loan:*** Freshmen: $2713; Undergraduates: $4094. ***Parent loans:*** $7,896,894 (41% need-based, 59% non-need-based). ***Programs:*** FFEL (Subsidized and Unsubsidized Stafford, PLUS), Perkins, alternative.

WORK-STUDY ***Federal work-study:*** Total amount: $515,199; jobs available. ***State or other work-study/employment:*** Part-time jobs available.

ATHLETIC AWARDS Total amount: $2,020,960 (38% need-based, 62% non-need-based).

APPLYING FOR FINANCIAL AID ***Required financial aid forms:*** FAFSA, tax forms (for the base tax year), if selected for verification by Department of Education or the institution. ***Financial aid deadline (priority):*** 2/15. ***Notification date:*** Continuous beginning 3/15. Students must reply within 4 weeks of notification.

CONTACT Director of Financial Aid, Cleveland State University, 2121 Euclid Avenue, University Center, Room 560, Cleveland, OH 44115, 216-687-5594 or toll-free 888-CSU-OHIO.

COASTAL CAROLINA UNIVERSITY

Conway, SC

Tuition & fees (SC res): $7500 **Average undergraduate aid package: $7463**

ABOUT THE INSTITUTION State-supported, coed. Awards: bachelor's and master's degrees and post-bachelor's certificates. 31 undergraduate majors. Total enrollment: 8,049. Undergraduates: 6,660. Freshmen: 1,474. Federal methodology is used as a basis for awarding need-based institutional aid.

UNDERGRADUATE EXPENSES for 2006–07 ***Application fee:*** $45. ***Tuition, state resident:*** full-time $7420; part-time $315 per credit hour. ***Tuition, nonresident:*** full-time $16,110; part-time $675 per credit hour. Full-time tuition and fees vary according to course load. Part-time tuition and fees vary according to course load. ***College room and board:*** $6690; ***Room only:*** $4220. Room and board charges vary according to board plan and housing facility. ***Payment plans:*** Installment, deferred payment.

FRESHMAN FINANCIAL AID (Fall 2005) 1221 applied for aid; of those 71% were deemed to have need. 97% of freshmen with need received aid; of those 14% had need fully met. ***Average percent of need met:*** 47% (excluding resources awarded to replace EFC). ***Average financial aid package:*** $6479 (excluding resources awarded to replace EFC). 24% of all full-time freshmen had no need and received non-need-based gift aid.

UNDERGRADUATE FINANCIAL AID (Fall 2005) 4,341 applied for aid; of those 76% were deemed to have need. 98% of undergraduates with need received aid; of those 13% had need fully met. ***Average percent of need met:*** 50% (excluding resources awarded to replace EFC). ***Average financial aid package:*** $7463 (excluding resources awarded to replace EFC). 22% of all full-time undergraduates had no need and received non-need-based gift aid.

GIFT AID (NEED-BASED) ***Total amount:*** $4,917,794 (88% federal, 12% state). ***Receiving aid:*** Freshmen: 21% (315); All full-time undergraduates: 25% (1,436). ***Average award:*** Freshmen: $3032; Undergraduates: $3258. ***Scholarships, grants, and awards:*** Federal Pell, FSEOG, state, private, college/university gift aid from institutional funds.

GIFT AID (NON-NEED-BASED) ***Total amount:*** $8,625,454 (66% state, 14% institutional, 20% external sources). ***Receiving aid:*** Freshmen: 26% (390); Undergraduates: 15% (885). ***Average award:*** Freshmen: $8556; Undergraduates: $9004. ***Scholarships, grants, and awards by category:*** *Academic Interests/Achievement:* 993 awards ($2,546,465 total): biological sciences, business, education, general academic interests/achievements, humanities, mathematics. *Creative Arts/Performance:* 32 awards ($27,250 total): art/fine arts, music, theater/drama. *Special Characteristics:* 848 awards ($2,828,284 total): general special characteristics, international students, local/state students, out-of-state students, veterans' children. ***Tuition waivers:*** Full or partial for employees or children of employees, senior citizens.

LOANS ***Student loans:*** $26,363,242 (38% need-based, 62% non-need-based). 67% of past graduating class borrowed through all loan programs. *Average indebtedness per student:* $24,250. ***Average need-based loan:*** Freshmen: $5252; Undergraduates: $6590. ***Parent loans:*** $9,395,018 (100% non-need-based). ***Programs:*** FFEL (Subsidized and Unsubsidized Stafford, PLUS), Perkins, state.

WORK-STUDY ***Federal work-study:*** Total amount: $197,556; 152 jobs averaging $1300. ***State or other work-study/employment:*** Total amount: $1,052,361 (13% need-based, 87% non-need-based). 761 part-time jobs averaging $1760.

ATHLETIC AWARDS Total amount: $2,268,496 (100% non-need-based).

APPLYING FOR FINANCIAL AID ***Required financial aid form:*** FAFSA. ***Financial aid deadline (priority):*** 4/1. ***Notification date:*** Continuous beginning 3/1.

CONTACT Dawn Hitchcock, Interim Director of Financial Aid, Coastal Carolina University, PO Box 261954, Conway, SC 29528-6054, 843-349-2325 or toll-free 800-277-7000. *Fax:* 843-349-2347. *E-mail:* dawn@coastal.edu.

COE COLLEGE

Cedar Rapids, IA

Tuition & fees: $26,390 **Average undergraduate aid package: $21,859**

ABOUT THE INSTITUTION Independent religious, coed. Awards: bachelor's and master's degrees. 64 undergraduate majors. Total enrollment: 1,300. Undergraduates: 1,275. Freshmen: 276. Both federal and institutional methodology are used as a basis for awarding need-based institutional aid.

UNDERGRADUATE EXPENSES for 2007–08 ***Application fee:*** $30. ***Comprehensive fee:*** $32,990 includes full-time tuition ($26,100), mandatory fees ($290), and room and board ($6600). ***College room only:*** $2990. ***Part-time tuition:*** $3300 per course.

FRESHMAN FINANCIAL AID (Fall 2006, est.) 244 applied for aid; of those 85% were deemed to have need. 100% of freshmen with need received aid; of those 34% had need fully met. ***Average percent of need met:*** 96% (excluding resources awarded to replace EFC). ***Average financial aid package:*** $22,197 (excluding resources awarded to replace EFC). 24% of all full-time freshmen had no need and received non-need-based gift aid.

UNDERGRADUATE FINANCIAL AID (Fall 2006, est.) 1,055 applied for aid; of those 70% were deemed to have need. 100% of undergraduates with need received aid; of those 26% had need fully met. ***Average percent of need met:*** 94% (excluding resources awarded to replace EFC). ***Average financial aid package:*** $21,859 (excluding resources awarded to replace EFC). 39% of all full-time undergraduates had no need and received non-need-based gift aid.

GIFT AID (NEED-BASED) ***Total amount:*** $12,055,706 (9% federal, 15% state, 74% institutional, 2% external sources). ***Receiving aid:*** Freshmen: 76% (207); All full-time undergraduates: 60% (716). ***Average award:*** Freshmen: $15,937; Undergraduates: $14,717. ***Scholarships, grants, and awards:*** Federal Pell, FSEOG, state, private, college/university gift aid from institutional funds, ROTC.

GIFT AID (NON-NEED-BASED) ***Total amount:*** $5,292,148 (96% institutional, 4% external sources). ***Receiving aid:*** Freshmen: 28% (76); Undergraduates: 11% (130). ***Average award:*** Freshmen: $13,133; Undergraduates: $9785. ***Scholarships, grants, and awards by category:*** *Academic Interests/Achievement:* 1,115 awards ($8,840,910 total): biological sciences, business, foreign languages, general academic interests/achievements, physical sciences, premedicine. *Creative Arts/Performance:* 398 awards ($759,996 total): art/fine arts, creative writing, music, performing arts, theater/drama. *Special Characteristics:* 355 awards ($1,616,247 total): adult students, children and siblings of alumni, children of faculty/staff, international students, siblings of current students. ***ROTC:*** Army cooperative, Air Force cooperative.

LOANS ***Student loans:*** $8,770,429 (63% need-based, 37% non-need-based). 77% of past graduating class borrowed through all loan programs. *Average indebtedness per student:* $26,625. ***Average need-based loan:*** Freshmen: $5466; Undergraduates: $6810. ***Parent loans:*** $1,984,620 (19% need-based, 81% non-need-based). ***Programs:*** Federal Direct (Subsidized and Unsubsidized Stafford, PLUS), Perkins, college/university.

WORK-STUDY ***Federal work-study:*** Total amount: $490,300; jobs available (averaging $1200). ***State or other work-study/employment:*** Total amount: $201,600 (6% need-based, 94% non-need-based). Part-time jobs available (averaging $1200).

APPLYING FOR FINANCIAL AID ***Required financial aid form:*** FAFSA. ***Financial aid deadline (priority):*** 3/1. ***Notification date:*** Continuous beginning 3/15. Students must reply by 5/1 or within 2 weeks of notification.

CONTACT Ms. Barbara Hoffman, Director of Financial Aid, Coe College, 1220 1st Avenue, NE, Cedar Rapids, IA 52402-5070, 319-399-8540 or toll-free 877-225-5263. *Fax:* 319-399-8886.

COGSWELL POLYTECHNICAL COLLEGE

Sunnyvale, CA

Tuition & fees: $14,984 **Average undergraduate aid package: N/A**

ABOUT THE INSTITUTION Independent, coed, primarily men. Awards: bachelor's degrees. 7 undergraduate majors. Total enrollment: 287. Undergraduates: 287. Freshmen: 32. Federal methodology is used as a basis for awarding need-based institutional aid.

UNDERGRADUATE EXPENSES for 2006–07 ***Application fee:*** $55. ***Tuition:*** full-time $14,904; part-time $621 per credit. Full-time tuition and fees vary according to course load. Part-time tuition and fees vary according to course load. Room and board charges vary according to housing facility. ***Payment plan:*** Deferred payment.

FRESHMAN FINANCIAL AID (Fall 2005) 22 applied for aid; of those 59% were deemed to have need. 100% of freshmen with need received aid. 45% of all full-time freshmen had no need and received non-need-based gift aid.

UNDERGRADUATE FINANCIAL AID (Fall 2005) 116 applied for aid; of those 98% were deemed to have need. 100% of undergraduates with need received aid. 10% of all full-time undergraduates had no need and received non-need-based gift aid.

GIFT AID (NEED-BASED) ***Total amount:*** $308,142 (61% federal, 39% state). ***Receiving aid:*** Freshmen: 59% (13); All full-time undergraduates: 61% (71). ***Average award:*** Freshmen: $2410; Undergraduates: $3484. ***Scholarships, grants, and awards:*** Federal Pell, FSEOG, state, private, college/university gift aid from institutional funds.

GIFT AID (NON-NEED-BASED) ***Total amount:*** $69,649 (91% institutional, 9% external sources). ***Receiving aid:*** Freshmen: 36% (8); Undergraduates: 14% (16). ***Average award:*** Freshmen: $583; Undergraduates: $834. ***Scholarships, grants, and awards by category:*** *Academic Interests/Achievement:* 15 awards ($25,000 total): computer science, engineering/technologies. ***Tuition waivers:*** Full or partial for employees or children of employees.

LOANS ***Student loans:*** $967,816 (100% non-need-based). 100% of past graduating class borrowed through all loan programs. *Average indebtedness per student:*

$46,689. ***Average need-based loan:*** Freshmen: $2625; Undergraduates: $4472. ***Parent loans:*** $281,712 (100% non-need-based). ***Programs:*** FFEL (Subsidized and Unsubsidized Stafford, PLUS).

WORK-STUDY ***Federal work-study:*** Total amount: $25,729; 15 jobs averaging $3000.

APPLYING FOR FINANCIAL AID ***Required financial aid forms:*** FAFSA, state aid form. ***Financial aid deadline (priority):*** 3/1. ***Notification date:*** Continuous beginning 2/1. Students must reply within 4 weeks of notification.

CONTACT Andrew Hagedorn, Financial Aid Director, Cogswell Polytechnical College, 1175 Bordeaux Drive, Sunnyvale, CA 94089, 408-541-0100 Ext. 107 or toll-free 800-264-7955. *Fax:* 408-747-0766. *E-mail:* ahagedorn@cogswell.edu.

COKER COLLEGE

Hartsville, SC

CONTACT Betty Williams, Director of Financial Aid, Coker College, 300 East College Avenue, Hartsville, SC 29550, 843-383-8055 or toll-free 800-950-1908. *Fax:* 843-383-8056. *E-mail:* bwilliams@coker.edu.

THE COLBURN SCHOOL CONSERVATORY OF MUSIC

Los Angeles, CA

CONTACT Financial Aid Office, The Colburn School Conservatory of Music, 200 South Grand Avenue, Los Angeles, CA 90012, 213-621-2200.

COLBY COLLEGE

Waterville, ME

Comprehensive fee: $44,080 **Average undergraduate aid package: $29,908**

ABOUT THE INSTITUTION Independent, coed. Awards: bachelor's degrees. 41 undergraduate majors. Total enrollment: 1,865. Undergraduates: 1,865. Freshmen: 475. Both federal and institutional methodology are used as a basis for awarding need-based institutional aid.

UNDERGRADUATE EXPENSES for 2006–07 ***Application fee:*** $65. ***Comprehensive fee:*** $44,080.

FRESHMAN FINANCIAL AID (Fall 2006, est.) 251 applied for aid; of those 78% were deemed to have need. 100% of freshmen with need received aid; of those 100% had need fully met. ***Average percent of need met:*** 100% (excluding resources awarded to replace EFC). ***Average financial aid package:*** $30,042 (excluding resources awarded to replace EFC).

UNDERGRADUATE FINANCIAL AID (Fall 2006, est.) 795 applied for aid; of those 87% were deemed to have need. 100% of undergraduates with need received aid; of those 100% had need fully met. ***Average percent of need met:*** 100% (excluding resources awarded to replace EFC). ***Average financial aid package:*** $29,908 (excluding resources awarded to replace EFC).

GIFT AID (NEED-BASED) ***Total amount:*** $18,394,937 (4% federal, 1% state, 92% institutional, 3% external sources). ***Receiving aid:*** Freshmen: 40% (191); All full-time undergraduates: 35% (656). ***Average award:*** Freshmen: $28,236; Undergraduates: $28,041. ***Scholarships, grants, and awards:*** Federal Pell, FSEOG, state, private, college/university gift aid from institutional funds.

GIFT AID (NON-NEED-BASED) ***ROTC:*** Army cooperative.

LOANS ***Student loans:*** $3,455,172 (41% need-based, 59% non-need-based). 48% of past graduating class borrowed through all loan programs. *Average indebtedness per student:* $17,542. ***Average need-based loan:*** Freshmen: $3053; Undergraduates: $3423. ***Parent loans:*** $3,418,974 (100% non-need-based). ***Programs:*** Federal Direct (Subsidized and Unsubsidized Stafford, PLUS), FFEL (Subsidized and Unsubsidized Stafford, PLUS), Perkins, state, college/university, alternative loans.

WORK-STUDY ***Federal work-study:*** Total amount: $676,111; 441 jobs averaging $1533. ***State or other work-study/employment:*** Total amount: $162,165 (100% need-based). 98 part-time jobs averaging $1655.

APPLYING FOR FINANCIAL AID ***Required financial aid forms:*** FAFSA, either CSS PROFILE or Institutional Application. ***Financial aid deadline:*** 2/1. ***Notification date:*** 4/1. Students must reply by 5/1.

CONTACT Ms. Lucia Whittelsey, Director of Financial Aid, Colby College, 4850 Mayflower Hill, Waterville, ME 04901-8848, 207-859-4832 or toll-free 800-723-3032. *Fax:* 207-859-4828. *E-mail:* finaid@colby.edu.

COLBY-SAWYER COLLEGE

New London, NH

CONTACT Office of Financial Aid, Colby-Sawyer College, 541 Main Street, New London, NH 03257-7835, 603-526-3717 or toll-free 800-272-1015. *Fax:* 603-526-3452. *E-mail:* cscfinaid@colby-sawyer.edu.

COLEGIO BIBLICO PENTECOSTAL

St. Just, PR

CONTACT Mr. Eric Ayala, Director of Financial Aid, Colegio Biblico Pentecostal, PO Box 901, St. Just, PR 00978-0901, 787-761-0640.

COLEGIO PENTECOSTAL MIZPA

Río Piedras, PR

CONTACT Financial Aid Office, Colegio Pentecostal Mizpa, Bo Caimito Road 199, Apartado 20966, Río Piedras, PR 00928-0966, 787-720-4476.

COLEMAN COLLEGE

San Diego, CA

CONTACT Financial Aid Office, Coleman College, 7380 Parkway Drive, La Mesa, CA 91942, 619-465-3990. *Fax:* 619-465-0162. *E-mail:* faoffice@coleman.edu.

COLGATE UNIVERSITY

Hamilton, NY

Tuition & fees: $35,030 **Average undergraduate aid package: $31,355**

ABOUT THE INSTITUTION Independent, coed. Awards: bachelor's and master's degrees. 52 undergraduate majors. Total enrollment: 2,788. Undergraduates: 2,782. Freshmen: 744. Both federal and institutional methodology are used as a basis for awarding need-based institutional aid.

UNDERGRADUATE EXPENSES for 2006–07 ***Application fee:*** $55. ***Comprehensive fee:*** $43,560 includes full-time tuition ($34,795), mandatory fees ($235), and room and board ($8530). ***College room only:*** $4120. Full-time tuition and fees vary according to course load. Room and board charges vary according to board plan and housing facility. ***Part-time tuition:*** $4549 per course. Part-time tuition and fees vary according to course load. ***Payment plans:*** Tuition prepayment, installment, deferred payment.

FRESHMAN FINANCIAL AID (Fall 2006, est.) 310 applied for aid; of those 82% were deemed to have need. 100% of freshmen with need received aid; of those 100% had need fully met. ***Average percent of need met:*** 100% (excluding resources awarded to replace EFC). ***Average financial aid package:*** $33,221 (excluding resources awarded to replace EFC).

UNDERGRADUATE FINANCIAL AID (Fall 2006, est.) 1,182 applied for aid; of those 88% were deemed to have need. 100% of undergraduates with need received aid; of those 100% had need fully met. ***Average percent of need met:*** 100% (excluding resources awarded to replace EFC). ***Average financial aid package:*** $31,355 (excluding resources awarded to replace EFC).

GIFT AID (NEED-BASED) ***Total amount:*** $27,869,541 (4% federal, 2% state, 92% institutional, 2% external sources). ***Receiving aid:*** Freshmen: 34% (253); All full-time undergraduates: 36% (997). ***Average award:*** Freshmen: $29,089; Undergraduates: $27,261. ***Scholarships, grants, and awards:*** Federal Pell, FSEOG, state, college/university gift aid from institutional funds.

GIFT AID (NON-NEED-BASED) ***Tuition waivers:*** Full or partial for employees or children of employees. ***ROTC:*** Army cooperative.

LOANS ***Student loans:*** $3,733,496 (75% need-based, 25% non-need-based). 47% of past graduating class borrowed through all loan programs. *Average indebtedness per student:* $16,093. ***Average need-based loan:*** Freshmen: $2383; Undergraduates: $4421. ***Parent loans:*** $4,915,067 (100% non-need-based). ***Programs:*** FFEL (Subsidized and Unsubsidized Stafford, PLUS), Perkins.

WORK-STUDY ***Federal work-study:*** Total amount: $1,036,415; 473 jobs averaging $2123. ***State or other work-study/employment:*** Total amount: $592,619 (100% need-based). 325 part-time jobs averaging $1952.

ATHLETIC AWARDS Total amount: $3,626,978 (100% non-need-based).

APPLYING FOR FINANCIAL AID ***Required financial aid forms:*** CSS Financial Aid PROFILE, noncustodial (divorced/separated) parent's statement, business/farm supplement. ***Financial aid deadline:*** 1/15. ***Notification date:*** 4/1. Students must reply by 5/1 or within 2 weeks of notification.

CONTACT Financial Aid Office, Colgate University, 13 Oak Drive, Hamilton, NY 13346, 315-228-7431. *Fax:* 315-228-7050. *E-mail:* financialaid@colgate.edu.

COLLEGE FOR CREATIVE STUDIES

Detroit, MI

Tuition & fees: $26,375 **Average undergraduate aid package: N/A**

ABOUT THE INSTITUTION Independent, coed. Awards: bachelor's degrees. Total enrollment: 1,302. Undergraduates: 1,302. Freshmen: 197. Federal methodology is used as a basis for awarding need-based institutional aid.

UNDERGRADUATE EXPENSES for 2007–08 ***Application fee:*** $35. ***Tuition:*** full-time $25,230; part-time $841 per credit hour.

GIFT AID (NEED-BASED) ***Total amount:*** $3,245,905 (34% federal, 29% state, 34% institutional, 3% external sources). ***Scholarships, grants, and awards:*** Federal Pell, FSEOG, state, private, college/university gift aid from institutional funds.

GIFT AID (NON-NEED-BASED) ***Total amount:*** $4,564,617 (4% state, 90% institutional, 6% external sources). ***Scholarships, grants, and awards by category:*** *Creative Arts/Performance:* applied art and design, art/fine arts.

LOANS ***Student loans:*** $3,162,376 (100% need-based). 74% of past graduating class borrowed through all loan programs. *Average indebtedness per student:* $36,848. ***Parent loans:*** $2,557,304 (100% non-need-based). ***Programs:*** FFEL (Subsidized and Unsubsidized Stafford, PLUS), alternative loans.

WORK-STUDY ***Federal work-study:*** Total amount: $113,599; jobs available (averaging $1000). ***State or other work-study/employment:*** Total amount: $25,357 (100% need-based). Part-time jobs available (averaging $1000).

APPLYING FOR FINANCIAL AID ***Required financial aid form:*** FAFSA. ***Financial aid deadline (priority):*** 7/1. ***Notification date:*** Continuous beginning 3/15. Students must reply within 3 weeks of notification.

CONTACT Financial Aid Office, College for Creative Studies, 201 East Kirby, Detroit, MI 48202-4034, 313-664-7495 or toll-free 800-952-ARTS. *Fax:* 313-872-1521. *E-mail:* finaid@ccscad.edu.

COLLEGE MISERICORDIA

Dallas, PA

Tuition & fees: $20,860 **Average undergraduate aid package: $13,961**

ABOUT THE INSTITUTION Independent Roman Catholic, coed. Awards: bachelor's, master's, and doctoral degrees and post-bachelor's and post-master's certificates. 26 undergraduate majors. Total enrollment: 2,358. Undergraduates: 2,068. Freshmen: 318. Federal methodology is used as a basis for awarding need-based institutional aid.

UNDERGRADUATE EXPENSES for 2006–07 ***Application fee:*** $25. ***Comprehensive fee:*** $29,500 includes full-time tuition ($19,800), mandatory fees ($1060), and room and board ($8640). ***College room only:*** $4960. Room and board charges vary according to board plan and housing facility. ***Part-time tuition:*** $425 per credit. Part-time tuition and fees vary according to location. ***Payment plans:*** Installment, deferred payment.

FRESHMAN FINANCIAL AID (Fall 2006, est.) 299 applied for aid; of those 86% were deemed to have need. 100% of freshmen with need received aid; of those 16% had need fully met. ***Average percent of need met:*** 70% (excluding resources awarded to replace EFC). ***Average financial aid package:*** $14,324 (excluding resources awarded to replace EFC). 13% of all full-time freshmen had no need and received non-need-based gift aid.

UNDERGRADUATE FINANCIAL AID (Fall 2006, est.) 1,331 applied for aid; of those 89% were deemed to have need. 100% of undergraduates with need received aid; of those 22% had need fully met. ***Average percent of need met:*** 73% (excluding resources awarded to replace EFC). ***Average financial aid package:*** $13,961 (excluding resources awarded to replace EFC). 9% of all full-time undergraduates had no need and received non-need-based gift aid.

GIFT AID (NEED-BASED) ***Total amount:*** $11,947,235 (9% federal, 20% state, 70% institutional, 1% external sources). ***Receiving aid:*** Freshmen: 82% (254); All full-time undergraduates: 83% (1,172). ***Average award:*** Freshmen: $11,031; Undergraduates: $9979. ***Scholarships, grants, and awards:*** Federal Pell, FSEOG, state, private, college/university gift aid from institutional funds, Federal Nursing.

GIFT AID (NON-NEED-BASED) ***Total amount:*** $1,625,892 (96% institutional, 4% external sources). ***Receiving aid:*** Freshmen: 9% (29); Undergraduates: 12% (173). ***Average award:*** Freshmen: $5205; Undergraduates: $5616. ***Scholarships, grants, and awards by category:*** *Academic Interests/Achievement:* 1,031 awards ($4,306,515 total): business, computer science, education, general academic interests/achievements, health fields, physical sciences, social sciences. *Special Achievements/Activities:* 922 awards ($2,136,410 total): community service, general special achievements/activities, leadership. *Special Characteristics:* 568 awards ($1,237,423 total): children and siblings of alumni, children of current students, children of faculty/staff, general special characteristics, members of minority groups, out-of-state students, previous college experience, relatives of clergy, religious affiliation, siblings of current students. ***Tuition waivers:*** Full or partial for employees or children of employees. ***ROTC:*** Army cooperative, Air Force cooperative.

LOANS ***Student loans:*** $10,940,854 (71% need-based, 29% non-need-based). 74% of past graduating class borrowed through all loan programs. *Average indebtedness per student:* $22,437. ***Average need-based loan:*** Freshmen: $5607; Undergraduates: $6734. ***Parent loans:*** $3,028,991 (42% need-based, 58% non-need-based). ***Programs:*** FFEL (Subsidized and Unsubsidized Stafford, PLUS), Perkins, Federal Nursing, state.

WORK-STUDY ***Federal work-study:*** Total amount: $186,879; 130 jobs averaging $1400.

APPLYING FOR FINANCIAL AID ***Required financial aid forms:*** FAFSA, institution's own form. ***Financial aid deadline (priority):*** 3/1. ***Notification date:*** 3/15. Students must reply within 2 weeks of notification.

CONTACT Donna F. Cerza, Director of Financial Aid, College Misericordia, 301 Lake Street, Dallas, PA 18612-1098, 570-674-6280 or toll-free 866-262-6363 (in-state), 866-2626363 (out-of-state). *Fax:* 570-675-2441. *E-mail:* dcerza@misericordia.edu.

COLLEGE OF BIBLICAL STUDIES–HOUSTON

Houston, TX

CONTACT Financial Aid Office, College of Biblical Studies–Houston, 6000 Dale Carnegie Drive, Houston, TX 77036, 713-785-5995.

COLLEGE OF CHARLESTON

Charleston, SC

Tuition & fees (SC res): $7234 **Average undergraduate aid package: $10,379**

ABOUT THE INSTITUTION State-supported, coed. Awards: bachelor's and master's degrees (also offers graduate degree programs through University of Charleston, South Carolina). 43 undergraduate majors. Total enrollment: 11,218. Undergraduates: 9,820. Freshmen: 1,968. Federal methodology is used as a basis for awarding need-based institutional aid.

UNDERGRADUATE EXPENSES for 2006–07 ***Application fee:*** $45. ***Tuition, state resident:*** full-time $7234; part-time $301 per semester hour. ***Tuition, nonresident:*** full-time $16,800; part-time $700 per semester hour. Part-time tuition and fees vary according to course load. ***College room and board:*** $7596; ***Room only:*** $5216. Room and board charges vary according to board plan and housing facility. ***Payment plan:*** Installment.

FRESHMAN FINANCIAL AID (Fall 2006, est.) 1150 applied for aid; of those 59% were deemed to have need. 95% of freshmen with need received aid; of those 36% had need fully met. ***Average percent of need met:*** 66% (excluding resources awarded to replace EFC). ***Average financial aid package:*** $10,035 (excluding resources awarded to replace EFC). 13% of all full-time freshmen had no need and received non-need-based gift aid.

UNDERGRADUATE FINANCIAL AID (Fall 2006, est.) 4,700 applied for aid; of those 70% were deemed to have need. 96% of undergraduates with need received aid; of those 30% had need fully met. ***Average percent of need met:*** 65% (excluding resources awarded to replace EFC). ***Average financial aid package:*** $10,379 (excluding resources awarded to replace EFC). 10% of all full-time undergraduates had no need and received non-need-based gift aid.

GIFT AID (NEED-BASED) ***Total amount:*** $12,405,190 (36% federal, 43% state, 16% institutional, 5% external sources). ***Receiving aid:*** Freshmen: 24% (470); All full-time undergraduates: 22% (1,925). ***Average award:*** Freshmen: $2944;

Undergraduates: $2866. ***Scholarships, grants, and awards:*** Federal Pell, FSEOG, state, private, college/university gift aid from institutional funds.

GIFT AID (NON-NEED-BASED) ***Total amount:*** $17,356,146 (62% state, 31% institutional, 7% external sources). ***Receiving aid:*** Freshmen: 24% (479); Undergraduates: 15% (1,321). ***Average award:*** Freshmen: $10,995; Undergraduates: $10,544. ***Scholarships, grants, and awards by category:*** *Academic Interests/Achievement:* biological sciences, business, communication, computer science, education, engineering/technologies, English, foreign languages, general academic interests/achievements, health fields, humanities, mathematics, physical sciences, premedicine, social sciences. *Creative Arts/Performance:* art/fine arts, music, performing arts, theater/drama. *Special Characteristics:* general special characteristics. ***Tuition waivers:*** Full or partial for senior citizens. ***ROTC:*** Air Force cooperative.

LOANS ***Student loans:*** $22,966,585 (58% need-based, 42% non-need-based). 48% of past graduating class borrowed through all loan programs. *Average indebtedness per student:* $16,761. ***Average need-based loan:*** Freshmen: $2737; Undergraduates: $4080. ***Parent loans:*** $18,274,804 (46% need-based, 54% non-need-based). ***Programs:*** Federal Direct (Subsidized and Unsubsidized Stafford, PLUS), Perkins.

WORK-STUDY ***Federal work-study:*** Total amount: $459,474; jobs available. ***State or other work-study/employment:*** Total amount: $1,815,195 (100% non-need-based). Part-time jobs available.

ATHLETIC AWARDS Total amount: $2,311,285 (18% need-based, 82% non-need-based).

APPLYING FOR FINANCIAL AID ***Required financial aid form:*** FAFSA. ***Financial aid deadline (priority):*** 3/15. ***Notification date:*** Continuous beginning 4/10. Students must reply within 8 weeks of notification.

CONTACT Mr. Don Griggs, Financial Aid Director, College of Charleston, 66 George Street, Charleston, SC 29424, 843-953-5540 or toll-free 843-953-5670 (in-state). *Fax:* 843-953-7192.

COLLEGE OF MOUNT ST. JOSEPH

Cincinnati, OH

ABOUT THE INSTITUTION Independent Roman Catholic, coed. Awards: associate, bachelor's, master's, and doctoral degrees and post-bachelor's certificates. 39 undergraduate majors. Total enrollment: 2,259. Undergraduates: 1,916. Freshmen: 322.

GIFT AID (NEED-BASED) ***Scholarships, grants, and awards:*** Federal Pell, FSEOG, state, private, college/university gift aid from institutional funds.

GIFT AID (NON-NEED-BASED) ***Scholarships, grants, and awards by category:*** *Academic Interests/Achievement:* general academic interests/achievements. *Creative Arts/Performance:* art/fine arts, music. *Special Achievements/Activities:* community service, leadership. *Special Characteristics:* adult students, children and siblings of alumni, children of faculty/staff.

LOANS ***Programs:*** FFEL (Subsidized and Unsubsidized Stafford, PLUS), Perkins, Federal Nursing, state.

WORK-STUDY ***Federal work-study:*** Total amount: $174,000; 188 jobs averaging $1431. ***State or other work-study/employment:*** Total amount: $183,111 (100% need-based). 71 part-time jobs averaging $1397.

APPLYING FOR FINANCIAL AID ***Required financial aid form:*** FAFSA.

CONTACT Ms. Kathryn Kelly, Director of Student Administrative Services, College of Mount St. Joseph, 5701 Delhi Road, Cincinnati, OH 45233-1670, 513-244-4418 or toll-free 800-654-9314. *Fax:* 513-244-4201. *E-mail:* kathy_kelly@mail.msj.edu.

COLLEGE OF MOUNT SAINT VINCENT

Riverdale, NY

ABOUT THE INSTITUTION Independent, coed. Awards: associate, bachelor's, and master's degrees and post-master's certificates. 31 undergraduate majors. Total enrollment: 1,812. Undergraduates: 1,497. Freshmen: 391.

GIFT AID (NEED-BASED) ***Scholarships, grants, and awards:*** Federal Pell, FSEOG, state, private, college/university gift aid from institutional funds.

GIFT AID (NON-NEED-BASED) ***Scholarships, grants, and awards by category:*** *Academic Interests/Achievement:* general academic interests/achievements. *Special Achievements/Activities:* leadership. *Special Characteristics:* children and siblings of alumni, children of faculty/staff, siblings of current students.

LOANS ***Programs:*** FFEL (Subsidized and Unsubsidized Stafford, PLUS), Perkins.

APPLYING FOR FINANCIAL AID ***Required financial aid forms:*** FAFSA, state aid form.

CONTACT Ms. Monica Simotas, Director of Financial Aid, College of Mount Saint Vincent, 6301 Riverdale Avenue, Riverdale, NY 10471, 718-405-3290 or toll-free 800-665-CMSV. *Fax:* 718-405-3490. *E-mail:* msimotas@mountsaintvincent.edu.

THE COLLEGE OF NEW JERSEY

Ewing, NJ

Tuition & fees (NJ res): $10,553 **Average undergraduate aid package: $9207**

ABOUT THE INSTITUTION State-supported, coed. Awards: bachelor's and master's degrees and post-bachelor's and post-master's certificates. 53 undergraduate majors. Total enrollment: 6,934. Undergraduates: 6,094. Freshmen: 1,270. Federal methodology is used as a basis for awarding need-based institutional aid.

UNDERGRADUATE EXPENSES for 2006–07 ***Application fee:*** $60. ***Tuition, state resident:*** full-time $7615; part-time $269.75 per credit. ***Tuition, nonresident:*** full-time $14,161; part-time $501.40 per credit. ***Required fees:*** full-time $2938; $108.65 per credit. Part-time tuition and fees vary according to course load. ***College room and board:*** $8843; ***Room only:*** $6380. Room and board charges vary according to board plan. ***Payment plan:*** Installment.

FRESHMAN FINANCIAL AID (Fall 2006, est.) 1070 applied for aid; of those 57% were deemed to have need. 96% of freshmen with need received aid; of those 32% had need fully met. ***Average percent of need met:*** 51% (excluding resources awarded to replace EFC). ***Average financial aid package:*** $9805 (excluding resources awarded to replace EFC). 25% of all full-time freshmen had no need and received non-need-based gift aid.

UNDERGRADUATE FINANCIAL AID (Fall 2006, est.) 3,980 applied for aid; of those 65% were deemed to have need. 94% of undergraduates with need received aid; of those 25% had need fully met. ***Average percent of need met:*** 55% (excluding resources awarded to replace EFC). ***Average financial aid package:*** $9207 (excluding resources awarded to replace EFC). 21% of all full-time undergraduates had no need and received non-need-based gift aid.

GIFT AID (NEED-BASED) ***Total amount:*** $15,563,029 (16% federal, 43% state, 33% institutional, 8% external sources). ***Receiving aid:*** Freshmen: 16% (198); All full-time undergraduates: 16% (916). ***Average award:*** Freshmen: $13,735; Undergraduates: $9486. ***Scholarships, grants, and awards:*** Federal Pell, FSEOG, state, private, college/university gift aid from institutional funds.

GIFT AID (NON-NEED-BASED) ***Total amount:*** $9,779,482 (29% state, 61% institutional, 10% external sources). ***Receiving aid:*** Freshmen: 23% (297); Undergraduates: 16% (956). ***Average award:*** Freshmen: $6386; Undergraduates: $4106. ***Scholarships, grants, and awards by category:*** *Academic Interests/Achievement:* engineering/technologies, general academic interests/achievements, physical sciences. *Creative Arts/Performance:* art/fine arts, music. *Special Characteristics:* children with a deceased or disabled parent, members of minority groups. ***Tuition waivers:*** Full or partial for employees or children of employees, senior citizens. ***ROTC:*** Army cooperative, Air Force cooperative.

LOANS ***Student loans:*** $19,339,538 (73% need-based, 27% non-need-based). 54% of past graduating class borrowed through all loan programs. *Average indebtedness per student:* $19,459. ***Average need-based loan:*** Freshmen: $2917; Undergraduates: $4288. ***Parent loans:*** $4,813,461 (61% need-based, 39% non-need-based). ***Programs:*** FFEL (Subsidized and Unsubsidized Stafford, PLUS), Perkins, Federal Nursing.

WORK-STUDY ***Federal work-study:*** Total amount: $391,150; 319 jobs averaging $1226.

APPLYING FOR FINANCIAL AID ***Required financial aid form:*** FAFSA. ***Financial aid deadline:*** 10/1 (priority: 3/1). ***Notification date:*** Continuous beginning 6/1. Students must reply within 2 weeks of notification.

CONTACT Jamie Hightower, Director of Student Financial Services, The College of New Jersey, PO Box 7718, Ewing, NJ 08628, 609-771-2211 or toll-free 800-624-0967. *Fax:* 609-637-5154. *E-mail:* hightowe@tcnj.edu.

THE COLLEGE OF NEW ROCHELLE

New Rochelle, NY

Tuition & fees: $21,910 **Average undergraduate aid package: $19,677**

ABOUT THE INSTITUTION Independent, coed, primarily women. Awards: bachelor's and master's degrees and post-bachelor's and post-master's certificates (also offers a non-traditional adult program with significant enrollment not reflected in profile). 36 undergraduate majors. Total enrollment: 2,341. Undergraduates: 1,064. Freshmen: 130. Federal methodology is used as a basis for awarding need-based institutional aid.

UNDERGRADUATE EXPENSES for 2006–07 ***Application fee:*** $20. ***Comprehensive fee:*** $30,110 includes full-time tuition ($21,460), mandatory fees ($450), and room and board ($8200). Full-time tuition and fees vary according to course load and program. Room and board charges vary according to housing facility. ***Part-time tuition:*** $722 per credit. ***Part-time fees:*** $90 per term. Part-time tuition and fees vary according to course load. ***Payment plan:*** Installment.

FRESHMAN FINANCIAL AID (Fall 2005) 152 applied for aid; of those 97% were deemed to have need. 100% of freshmen with need received aid; of those 4% had need fully met. ***Average percent of need met:*** 85% (excluding resources awarded to replace EFC). ***Average financial aid package:*** $23,468 (excluding resources awarded to replace EFC). 8% of all full-time freshmen had no need and received non-need-based gift aid.

UNDERGRADUATE FINANCIAL AID (Fall 2005) 648 applied for aid; of those 96% were deemed to have need. 100% of undergraduates with need received aid; of those 5% had need fully met. ***Average percent of need met:*** 74% (excluding resources awarded to replace EFC). ***Average financial aid package:*** $19,677 (excluding resources awarded to replace EFC). 8% of all full-time undergraduates had no need and received non-need-based gift aid.

GIFT AID (NEED-BASED) ***Total amount:*** $9,840,945 (14% federal, 16% state, 60% institutional, 10% external sources). ***Receiving aid:*** Freshmen: 91% (143); All full-time undergraduates: 82% (577). ***Average award:*** Freshmen: $13,734; Undergraduates: $9470. ***Scholarships, grants, and awards:*** Federal Pell, FSEOG, state, private, college/university gift aid from institutional funds.

GIFT AID (NON-NEED-BASED) ***Total amount:*** $1,048,976 (1% state, 83% institutional, 16% external sources). ***Receiving aid:*** Freshmen: 51% (81); Undergraduates: 50% (351). ***Average award:*** Freshmen: $14,808; Undergraduates: $11,497. ***Scholarships, grants, and awards by category:*** *Academic Interests/Achievement:* 328 awards ($3,150,000 total): area/ethnic studies, biological sciences, business, communication, education, English, foreign languages, general academic interests/achievements, health fields, humanities, mathematics, physical sciences, premedicine, religion/biblical studies, social sciences. *Creative Arts/Performance:* 95 awards ($595,000 total): applied art and design, art/fine arts, cinema/film/broadcasting, creative writing, dance, debating, general creative arts/performance, journalism/publications, music, performing arts, theater/drama. *Special Achievements/Activities:* 60 awards ($325,000 total): community service, general special achievements/activities, hobbies/interests, junior miss, leadership, memberships, religious involvement. *Special Characteristics:* 80 awards ($450,000 total): children of current students, children of faculty/staff, general special characteristics, out-of-state students, parents of current students, previous college experience, siblings of current students, spouses of current students. ***Tuition waivers:*** Full or partial for employees or children of employees, senior citizens.

LOANS ***Student loans:*** $4,685,241 (65% need-based, 35% non-need-based). 83% of past graduating class borrowed through all loan programs. *Average indebtedness per student:* $26,486. ***Average need-based loan:*** Freshmen: $3316; Undergraduates: $4754. ***Parent loans:*** $357,438 (84% need-based, 16% non-need-based). ***Programs:*** Federal Direct (Subsidized and Unsubsidized Stafford), FFEL (PLUS), Perkins, Federal Nursing.

WORK-STUDY ***Federal work-study:*** Total amount: $1,146,672; 451 jobs averaging $2542. ***State or other work-study/employment:*** Part-time jobs available.

APPLYING FOR FINANCIAL AID ***Required financial aid forms:*** FAFSA, institution's own form, federal income tax form(s). ***Financial aid deadline:*** Continuous. ***Notification date:*** Continuous beginning 1/1. Students must reply within 2 weeks of notification.

CONTACT Anne Pelak, Director of Financial Aid, The College of New Rochelle, 29 Castle Place, New Rochelle, NY 10805-2339, 914-654-5225 or toll-free 800-933-5923. *Fax:* 914-654-5420. *E-mail:* apelak@cnr.edu.

COLLEGE OF NOTRE DAME OF MARYLAND

Baltimore, MD

Tuition & fees: N/R **Average undergraduate aid package: $17,950**

ABOUT THE INSTITUTION Independent Roman Catholic, undergraduate: women only; graduate: coed. Awards: bachelor's, master's, and doctoral degrees and post-bachelor's certificates. 33 undergraduate majors. Total enrollment: 3,307. Undergraduates: 1,686. Freshmen: 201. Federal methodology is used as a basis for awarding need-based institutional aid.

FRESHMAN FINANCIAL AID (Fall 2006, est.) 121 applied for aid; of those 89% were deemed to have need. 100% of freshmen with need received aid; of those 22% had need fully met. ***Average percent of need met:*** 78% (excluding resources awarded to replace EFC). ***Average financial aid package:*** $20,505 (excluding resources awarded to replace EFC). 10% of all full-time freshmen had no need and received non-need-based gift aid.

UNDERGRADUATE FINANCIAL AID (Fall 2006, est.) 490 applied for aid; of those 89% were deemed to have need. 100% of undergraduates with need received aid; of those 26% had need fully met. ***Average percent of need met:*** 72% (excluding resources awarded to replace EFC). ***Average financial aid package:*** $17,950 (excluding resources awarded to replace EFC). 8% of all full-time undergraduates had no need and received non-need-based gift aid.

GIFT AID (NEED-BASED) ***Total amount:*** $6,447,251 (13% federal, 18% state, 67% institutional, 2% external sources). ***Receiving aid:*** Freshmen: 84% (104); All full-time undergraduates: 68% (391). ***Average award:*** Freshmen: $9006; Undergraduates: $7862. ***Scholarships, grants, and awards:*** Federal Pell, FSEOG, state, private, college/university gift aid from institutional funds, ACG/SMART Grants.

GIFT AID (NON-NEED-BASED) ***Total amount:*** $1,350,291 (11% state, 85% institutional, 4% external sources). ***Receiving aid:*** Freshmen: 81% (100); Undergraduates: 63% (359). ***Average award:*** Freshmen: $9273; Undergraduates: $8992. ***Scholarships, grants, and awards by category:*** *Academic Interests/Achievement:* 181 awards ($1,901,812 total): general academic interests/achievements. *Creative Arts/Performance:* 63 awards ($287,000 total): art/fine arts, general creative arts/performance. *Special Achievements/Activities:* 162 awards ($1,109,870 total): community service, general special achievements/activities, leadership, memberships, religious involvement. *Special Characteristics:* 5 awards ($37,335 total): international students. ***Tuition waivers:*** Full or partial for employees or children of employees. ***ROTC:*** Army cooperative.

LOANS ***Student loans:*** $6,416,447 (87% need-based, 13% non-need-based). 78% of past graduating class borrowed through all loan programs. *Average indebtedness per student:* $21,681. ***Average need-based loan:*** Freshmen: $3775; Undergraduates: $4296. ***Parent loans:*** $1,104,472 (79% need-based, 21% non-need-based). ***Programs:*** FFEL (Subsidized and Unsubsidized Stafford, PLUS), Perkins.

WORK-STUDY ***Federal work-study:*** Total amount: $86,277; 74 jobs averaging $1166.

APPLYING FOR FINANCIAL AID ***Required financial aid form:*** FAFSA. ***Financial aid deadline (priority):*** 2/15. ***Notification date:*** Continuous beginning 3/1. Students must reply by 5/1.

CONTACT Zhanna Goltser, Director of Financial Aid, College of Notre Dame of Maryland, 4701 North Charles Street, Baltimore, MD 21210-2404, 410-532-5369 or toll-free 800-435-0200 (in-state), 800-435-0300 (out-of-state). *Fax:* 410-532-6287. *E-mail:* finaid@ndm.edu.

COLLEGE OF SAINT BENEDICT

Saint Joseph, MN

ABOUT THE INSTITUTION Independent Roman Catholic, coed, primarily women. Awards: bachelor's degrees (coordinate with Saint John's University for men). 49 undergraduate majors. Total enrollment: 2,059. Undergraduates: 2,059. Freshmen: 540.

GIFT AID (NEED-BASED) ***Scholarships, grants, and awards:*** Federal Pell, FSEOG, state, private, college/university gift aid from institutional funds.

GIFT AID (NON-NEED-BASED) ***Scholarships, grants, and awards by category:*** *Academic Interests/Achievement:* general academic interests/achievements, military science. *Creative Arts/Performance:* art/fine arts, music, theater/drama. *Special Achievements/Activities:* junior miss, memberships. *Special Characteristics:* ethnic background, international students.

LOANS ***Programs:*** FFEL (Subsidized and Unsubsidized Stafford, PLUS), Perkins, state, alternative loans.

WORK-STUDY ***Federal work-study:*** Total amount: $1,172,173; 600 jobs averaging $2000. ***State or other work-study/employment:*** Total amount: $1,500,529 (68% need-based, 32% non-need-based). 300 part-time jobs averaging $2000.

APPLYING FOR FINANCIAL AID ***Required financial aid forms:*** FAFSA, institution's own form.

CONTACT Ms. Jane Haugen, Executive Director of Financial Aid, College of Saint Benedict, 37 South College Avenue, Saint Joseph, MN 56374-2099, 320-363-5388 or toll-free 800-544-1489. *Fax:* 320-363-6099. *E-mail:* jhaugen@csbsju.edu.

COLLEGE OF ST. CATHERINE

St. Paul, MN

Tuition & fees: $22,880 **Average undergraduate aid package: $23,534**

ABOUT THE INSTITUTION Independent Roman Catholic, undergraduate: women only; graduate: coed. Awards: associate, bachelor's, master's, and doctoral degrees and post-bachelor's certificates. 76 undergraduate majors. Total enrollment: 5,246. Undergraduates: 3,831. Freshmen: 437. Federal methodology is used as a basis for awarding need-based institutional aid.

UNDERGRADUATE EXPENSES for 2006–07 ***Comprehensive fee:*** $29,312 includes full-time tuition ($22,620), mandatory fees ($260), and room and board ($6432). ***College room only:*** $3592. Full-time tuition and fees vary according to class time. Room and board charges vary according to board plan and housing facility. ***Part-time tuition:*** $754 per credit. Part-time tuition and fees vary according to class time.

FRESHMAN FINANCIAL AID (Fall 2006, est.) 336 applied for aid; of those 85% were deemed to have need. 99% of freshmen with need received aid; of those 1% had need fully met. ***Average percent of need met:*** 72% (excluding resources awarded to replace EFC). ***Average financial aid package:*** $25,793 (excluding resources awarded to replace EFC). 16% of all full-time freshmen had no need and received non-need-based gift aid.

UNDERGRADUATE FINANCIAL AID (Fall 2006, est.) 1,508 applied for aid; of those 87% were deemed to have need. 98% of undergraduates with need received aid; of those 14% had need fully met. ***Average percent of need met:*** 72% (excluding resources awarded to replace EFC). ***Average financial aid package:*** $23,534 (excluding resources awarded to replace EFC). 15% of all full-time undergraduates had no need and received non-need-based gift aid.

GIFT AID (NEED-BASED) ***Total amount:*** $12,113,827 (26% federal, 27% state, 46% institutional, 1% external sources). ***Receiving aid:*** Freshmen: 62% (228); All full-time undergraduates: 59% (1,047). ***Average award:*** Freshmen: $7952; Undergraduates: $7322. ***Scholarships, grants, and awards:*** Federal Pell, FSEOG, state, private, college/university gift aid from institutional funds, Federal Nursing.

GIFT AID (NON-NEED-BASED) ***Total amount:*** $9,038,342 (85% institutional, 15% external sources). ***Receiving aid:*** Freshmen: 62% (226); Undergraduates: 50% (882). ***Average award:*** Freshmen: $21,425; Undergraduates: $15,017. ***Scholarships, grants, and awards by category:*** *Academic Interests/Achievement:* business, education, English, foreign languages, general academic interests/achievements, health fields, home economics, humanities, mathematics, physical sciences, premedicine, social sciences. *Creative Arts/Performance:* art/fine arts, music. *Special Achievements/Activities:* community service, general special achievements/activities, leadership, memberships. *Special Characteristics:* adult students, children and siblings of alumni, children of educators, children of faculty/staff, ethnic background, general special characteristics, international students, local/state students, out-of-state students, religious affiliation, siblings of current students. ***Tuition waivers:*** Full or partial for employees or children of employees, senior citizens. ***ROTC:*** Army cooperative, Air Force cooperative.

LOANS ***Student loans:*** $28,850,313 (38% need-based, 62% non-need-based). 82% of past graduating class borrowed through all loan programs. *Average indebtedness per student:* $27,519. ***Average need-based loan:*** Freshmen: $3285; Undergraduates: $5008. ***Parent loans:*** $3,155,514 (100% non-need-based). ***Programs:*** FFEL (Subsidized and Unsubsidized Stafford, PLUS), Perkins, Federal Nursing, state, alternative loans.

WORK-STUDY ***Federal work-study:*** Total amount: $489,679; 500 jobs available. ***State or other work-study/employment:*** Total amount: $283,297 (94% need-based, 6% non-need-based). Part-time jobs available.

APPLYING FOR FINANCIAL AID ***Required financial aid forms:*** FAFSA, institution's own form. ***Financial aid deadline (priority):*** 4/15. ***Notification date:*** Continuous beginning 3/30. Students must reply within 2 weeks of notification.

CONTACT Sandy Sundstrom, Director of Financial Aid, College of St. Catherine, Mail #F-11, 2004 Randolph Avenue, St. Paul, MN 55105-1789, 651-690-6540 or toll-free 800-656-5283 (in-state). *Fax:* 651-690-6558.

COLLEGE OF ST. CATHERINE–MINNEAPOLIS

Minneapolis, MN

CONTACT Mr. Cal Mosley, Associate Dean/Director of Financial Aid, College of St. Catherine–Minneapolis, 601 25th Avenue South, Minneapolis, MN 55454, 651-690-8600 or toll-free 800-945-4599 Ext. 7800. *Fax:* 651-690-8119. *E-mail:* pajohnson@stkate.edu.

COLLEGE OF SAINT ELIZABETH

Morristown, NJ

Tuition & fees: $21,150 **Average undergraduate aid package: $18,190**

ABOUT THE INSTITUTION Independent Roman Catholic, undergraduate: women only; graduate: coed. Awards: bachelor's and master's degrees and post-bachelor's certificates (also offers coed adult undergraduate degree program and coed graduate programs). 25 undergraduate majors. Total enrollment: 1,982. Undergraduates: 1,260. Freshmen: 158. Both federal and institutional methodology are used as a basis for awarding need-based institutional aid.

UNDERGRADUATE EXPENSES for 2006–07 ***Application fee:*** $35. ***Comprehensive fee:*** $30,574 includes full-time tuition ($19,950), mandatory fees ($1200), and room and board ($9424). Full-time tuition and fees vary according to program. ***Part-time tuition:*** $623 per credit. ***Part-time fees:*** $140 per course. Part-time tuition and fees vary according to course load, location, and program. ***Payment plan:*** Installment.

FRESHMAN FINANCIAL AID (Fall 2006, est.) 153 applied for aid; of those 98% were deemed to have need. 100% of freshmen with need received aid; of those 14% had need fully met. ***Average percent of need met:*** 83% (excluding resources awarded to replace EFC). ***Average financial aid package:*** $18,092 (excluding resources awarded to replace EFC). 2% of all full-time freshmen had no need and received non-need-based gift aid.

UNDERGRADUATE FINANCIAL AID (Fall 2006, est.) 613 applied for aid; of those 85% were deemed to have need. 98% of undergraduates with need received aid; of those 17% had need fully met. ***Average percent of need met:*** 75% (excluding resources awarded to replace EFC). ***Average financial aid package:*** $18,190 (excluding resources awarded to replace EFC). 17% of all full-time undergraduates had no need and received non-need-based gift aid.

GIFT AID (NEED-BASED) ***Total amount:*** $7,406,761 (12% federal, 31% state, 56% institutional, 1% external sources). ***Receiving aid:*** Freshmen: 71% (112); All full-time undergraduates: 68% (483). ***Average award:*** Freshmen: $16,052; Undergraduates: $15,241. ***Scholarships, grants, and awards:*** Federal Pell, FSEOG, state, private, college/university gift aid from institutional funds.

GIFT AID (NON-NEED-BASED) ***Total amount:*** $1,438,045 (2% state, 96% institutional, 2% external sources). ***Receiving aid:*** Freshmen: 9% (14); Undergraduates: 9% (62). ***Average award:*** Freshmen: $22,287; Undergraduates: $12,926. ***Tuition waivers:*** Full or partial for children of alumni, employees or children of employees, senior citizens.

LOANS ***Student loans:*** $3,403,781 (72% need-based, 28% non-need-based). ***Average need-based loan:*** Freshmen: $2432; Undergraduates: $3792. ***Parent loans:*** $697,219 (43% need-based, 57% non-need-based). ***Programs:*** FFEL (Subsidized and Unsubsidized Stafford, PLUS), Perkins.

WORK-STUDY ***Federal work-study:*** Total amount: $75,000.

APPLYING FOR FINANCIAL AID ***Required financial aid form:*** FAFSA. ***Financial aid deadline (priority):*** 3/1. ***Notification date:*** Continuous beginning 11/15. Students must reply by 5/1 or within 2 weeks of notification.

CONTACT Vincent Tunstall, Director of Financial Aid, College of Saint Elizabeth, 2 Convent Road, Morristown, NJ 07960-6989, 973-290-4492 or toll-free 800-210-7900. *E-mail:* vtunstell@cse.edu.

COLLEGE OF ST. JOSEPH

Rutland, VT

Tuition & fees: $14,900 **Average undergraduate aid package: $12,702**

ABOUT THE INSTITUTION Independent Roman Catholic, coed. Awards: associate, bachelor's, and master's degrees and post-bachelor's certificates. 20

undergraduate majors. Total enrollment: 509. Undergraduates: 284. Freshmen: 41. Federal methodology is used as a basis for awarding need-based institutional aid.

UNDERGRADUATE EXPENSES for 2006–07 ***Application fee:*** $25. ***Comprehensive fee:*** $22,050 includes full-time tuition ($14,650), mandatory fees ($250), and room and board ($7150). Full-time tuition and fees vary according to program. Room and board charges vary according to housing facility. ***Part-time tuition:*** $245 per credit. ***Part-time fees:*** $45 per term. Part-time tuition and fees vary according to program. ***Payment plan:*** Installment.

FRESHMAN FINANCIAL AID (Fall 2006, est.) 39 applied for aid; of those 85% were deemed to have need. 100% of freshmen with need received aid; of those 9% had need fully met. ***Average percent of need met:*** 69% (excluding resources awarded to replace EFC). ***Average financial aid package:*** $13,043 (excluding resources awarded to replace EFC).

UNDERGRADUATE FINANCIAL AID (Fall 2006, est.) 176 applied for aid; of those 90% were deemed to have need. 99% of undergraduates with need received aid; of those 12% had need fully met. ***Average percent of need met:*** 66% (excluding resources awarded to replace EFC). ***Average financial aid package:*** $12,702 (excluding resources awarded to replace EFC).

GIFT AID (NEED-BASED) ***Total amount:*** $1,233,030 (26% federal, 20% state, 51% institutional, 3% external sources). ***Receiving aid:*** Freshmen: 33; All full-time undergraduates: 154. ***Average award:*** Freshmen: $9471; Undergraduates: $7722. ***Scholarships, grants, and awards:*** Federal Pell, FSEOG, state, private, college/university gift aid from institutional funds.

GIFT AID (NON-NEED-BASED) ***Total amount:*** $58,459 (96% institutional, 4% external sources). ***Receiving aid:*** Undergraduates: 3. ***Average award:*** Freshmen: $5917; Undergraduates: $4238. ***Scholarships, grants, and awards by category:*** *Academic Interests/Achievement:* 45 awards ($182,575 total): general academic interests/achievements. *Special Achievements/Activities:* 3 awards ($4000 total): community service, leadership. *Special Characteristics:* 51 awards ($98,830 total): general special characteristics, local/state students, previous college experience, religious affiliation. ***Tuition waivers:*** Full or partial for employees or children of employees, senior citizens.

LOANS ***Student loans:*** $1,072,058 (79% need-based, 21% non-need-based). *Average indebtedness per student:* $28,522. ***Average need-based loan:*** Freshmen: $2504; Undergraduates: $4548. ***Parent loans:*** $329,536 (34% need-based, 66% non-need-based). ***Programs:*** FFEL (Subsidized and Unsubsidized Stafford, PLUS), Perkins.

WORK-STUDY ***Federal work-study:*** Total amount: $35,500; 38 jobs averaging $980. ***State or other work-study/employment:*** Total amount: $89,000 (100% need-based). 77 part-time jobs averaging $945.

APPLYING FOR FINANCIAL AID ***Required financial aid forms:*** FAFSA, institution's own form. ***Financial aid deadline:*** Continuous. ***Notification date:*** Continuous beginning 3/15. Students must reply within 2 weeks of notification.

CONTACT Yvonne Payrits, Financial Aid Coordinator, College of St. Joseph, 71 Clement Road, Rutland, VT 05701-3899, 802-773-5900 Ext. 3218 or toll-free 877-270-9998 (in-state). *Fax:* 802-773-5900. *E-mail:* finaid@csj.edu.

COLLEGE OF SAINT MARY

Omaha, NE

Tuition & fees: $20,055 **Average undergraduate aid package: $12,301**

ABOUT THE INSTITUTION Independent Roman Catholic, women only. Awards: associate, bachelor's, and master's degrees. 27 undergraduate majors. Total enrollment: 960. Undergraduates: 921. Freshmen: 100. Federal methodology is used as a basis for awarding need-based institutional aid.

UNDERGRADUATE EXPENSES for 2007–08 ***Application fee:*** $30. ***Comprehensive fee:*** $26,307 includes full-time tuition ($19,635), mandatory fees ($420), and room and board ($6252). ***Part-time tuition:*** $651 per credit hour. ***Part-time fees:*** $14 per credit hour.

FRESHMAN FINANCIAL AID (Fall 2006, est.) 88 applied for aid; of those 91% were deemed to have need. 100% of freshmen with need received aid; of those 20% had need fully met. ***Average percent of need met:*** 69% (excluding resources awarded to replace EFC). ***Average financial aid package:*** $15,001 (excluding resources awarded to replace EFC). 18% of all full-time freshmen had no need and received non-need-based gift aid.

UNDERGRADUATE FINANCIAL AID (Fall 2006, est.) 644 applied for aid; of those 94% were deemed to have need. 100% of undergraduates with need received aid; of those 13% had need fully met. ***Average percent of need met:*** 61% (excluding resources awarded to replace EFC). ***Average financial aid package:*** $12,301 (excluding resources awarded to replace EFC). 11% of all full-time undergraduates had no need and received non-need-based gift aid.

GIFT AID (NEED-BASED) ***Total amount:*** $4,505,537 (32% federal, 4% state, 53% institutional, 11% external sources). ***Receiving aid:*** Freshmen: 79% (77); All full-time undergraduates: 81% (535). ***Average award:*** Freshmen: $11,613; Undergraduates: $7885. ***Scholarships, grants, and awards:*** Federal Pell, FSEOG, state, college/university gift aid from institutional funds.

GIFT AID (NON-NEED-BASED) ***Total amount:*** $1,149,462 (89% institutional, 11% external sources). ***Receiving aid:*** Freshmen: 7% (7); Undergraduates: 1% (8). ***Average award:*** Freshmen: $14,558; Undergraduates: $11,114. ***Scholarships, grants, and awards by category:*** *Academic Interests/Achievement:* general academic interests/achievements. *Creative Arts/Performance:* music. *Special Achievements/Activities:* community service, leadership. ***ROTC:*** Army cooperative, Air Force cooperative.

LOANS ***Student loans:*** $7,230,663 (81% need-based, 19% non-need-based). 90% of past graduating class borrowed through all loan programs. *Average indebtedness per student:* $18,047. ***Average need-based loan:*** Freshmen: $3752; Undergraduates: $5400. ***Parent loans:*** $948,706 (52% need-based, 48% non-need-based). ***Programs:*** FFEL (Subsidized and Unsubsidized Stafford, PLUS), Perkins, Federal Nursing.

WORK-STUDY ***Federal work-study:*** Total amount: $100,501; 129 jobs averaging $779. ***State or other work-study/employment:*** Total amount: $57,680 (100% need-based). Part-time jobs available.

ATHLETIC AWARDS Total amount: $232,352 (77% need-based, 23% non-need-based).

APPLYING FOR FINANCIAL AID ***Required financial aid form:*** FAFSA. ***Financial aid deadline (priority):*** 3/1. ***Notification date:*** Continuous beginning 3/1. Students must reply within 2 weeks of notification.

CONTACT Danni Warrick, Director of Financial Aid, College of Saint Mary, 7000 Mercy Road, Omaha, NE 68106, 402-399-2415 or toll-free 800-926-5534. *Fax:* 402-399-2480. *E-mail:* dwarrick@csm.edu.

THE COLLEGE OF SAINT ROSE

Albany, NY

Tuition & fees: $19,258 **Average undergraduate aid package: $7496**

ABOUT THE INSTITUTION Independent, coed. Awards: bachelor's and master's degrees and post-bachelor's and post-master's certificates. 42 undergraduate majors. Total enrollment: 5,062. Undergraduates: 3,116. Freshmen: 633. Federal methodology is used as a basis for awarding need-based institutional aid.

UNDERGRADUATE EXPENSES for 2006–07 ***Application fee:*** $35. ***Comprehensive fee:*** $27,374 includes full-time tuition ($18,672), mandatory fees ($586), and room and board ($8116). ***College room only:*** $3868. Full-time tuition and fees vary according to course load and program. Room and board charges vary according to board plan. ***Part-time tuition:*** $621 per credit hour. Part-time tuition and fees vary according to class time. ***Payment plan:*** Deferred payment.

FRESHMAN FINANCIAL AID (Fall 2006, est.) 614 applied for aid; of those 83% were deemed to have need. 100% of freshmen with need received aid; of those 5% had need fully met. ***Average percent of need met:*** 43% (excluding resources awarded to replace EFC). ***Average financial aid package:*** $7858 (excluding resources awarded to replace EFC). 11% of all full-time freshmen had no need and received non-need-based gift aid.

UNDERGRADUATE FINANCIAL AID (Fall 2006, est.) 2,581 applied for aid; of those 85% were deemed to have need. 99% of undergraduates with need received aid; of those 4% had need fully met. ***Average percent of need met:*** 42% (excluding resources awarded to replace EFC). ***Average financial aid package:*** $7496 (excluding resources awarded to replace EFC). 11% of all full-time undergraduates had no need and received non-need-based gift aid.

GIFT AID (NEED-BASED) ***Total amount:*** $20,859,475 (11% federal, 16% state, 53% institutional, 20% external sources). ***Receiving aid:*** Freshmen: 76% (478); All full-time undergraduates: 78% (2,069). ***Average award:*** Freshmen: $3753; Undergraduates: $3395. ***Scholarships, grants, and awards:*** Federal Pell, FSEOG, state, private, college/university gift aid from institutional funds.

GIFT AID (NON-NEED-BASED) ***Total amount:*** $2,340,956 (4% state, 71% institutional, 25% external sources). ***Average award:*** Freshmen: $2265; Undergraduates: $2219. ***Scholarships, grants, and awards by category:*** *Academic Interests/Achievement:* 684 awards ($2,593,711 total): business, education, engineering/technologies, English, foreign languages, general academic interests/achievements, mathematics, premedicine, social sciences. *Creative Arts/Performance:* art/fine arts, music. *Special Achievements/Activities:* community service. *Special Characteristics:* adult students, children and siblings of alumni, children of union members/company employees, ethnic background, general special characteristics, members of minority groups, siblings of current students, twins. ***Tuition waivers:*** Full or partial for employees or children of employees.

LOANS ***Student loans:*** $9,608,878 (67% need-based, 33% non-need-based). 83% of past graduating class borrowed through all loan programs. *Average indebtedness per student:* $24,732. ***Average need-based loan:*** Freshmen: $1206; Undergraduates: $1969. ***Parent loans:*** $5,119,569 (84% need-based, 16% non-need-based). ***Programs:*** FFEL (Subsidized and Unsubsidized Stafford, PLUS), Perkins.

WORK-STUDY ***Federal work-study:*** Total amount: $459,779; 406 jobs averaging $815. ***State or other work-study/employment:*** Total amount: $319,651 (81% need-based, 19% non-need-based). 83 part-time jobs averaging $892.

ATHLETIC AWARDS Total amount: $1,524,735 (68% need-based, 32% non-need-based).

APPLYING FOR FINANCIAL AID ***Required financial aid form:*** FAFSA. ***Financial aid deadline (priority):*** 3/1. ***Notification date:*** 3/15. Students must reply by 5/1 or within 2 weeks of notification.

CONTACT Steven Dwire, Director of Financial Aid, The College of Saint Rose, 432 Western Avenue, Albertus Hall, Room 206, Albany, NY 12203-1419, 518-458-4915 or toll-free 800-637-8556. *Fax:* 518-454-2802. *E-mail:* finaid@strose.edu.

THE COLLEGE OF ST. SCHOLASTICA

Duluth, MN

Tuition & fees: $23,574 **Average undergraduate aid package: $17,801**

ABOUT THE INSTITUTION Independent religious, coed. Awards: bachelor's, master's, and first professional degrees and post-bachelor's and post-master's certificates. 33 undergraduate majors. Total enrollment: 3,304. Undergraduates: 2,648. Freshmen: 499. Federal methodology is used as a basis for awarding need-based institutional aid.

UNDERGRADUATE EXPENSES for 2006–07 ***Application fee:*** $25. ***Comprehensive fee:*** $30,088 includes full-time tuition ($23,434), mandatory fees ($140), and room and board ($6514). ***College room only:*** $3708. Full-time tuition and fees vary according to class time. Room and board charges vary according to board plan and housing facility. ***Part-time tuition:*** $729 per credit hour. Part-time tuition and fees vary according to class time and course load. ***Payment plan:*** Installment.

FRESHMAN FINANCIAL AID (Fall 2006, est.) 432 applied for aid; of those 89% were deemed to have need. 99% of freshmen with need received aid; of those 16% had need fully met. ***Average percent of need met:*** 16% (excluding resources awarded to replace EFC). ***Average financial aid package:*** $18,298 (excluding resources awarded to replace EFC). 21% of all full-time freshmen had no need and received non-need-based gift aid.

UNDERGRADUATE FINANCIAL AID (Fall 2006, est.) 1,661 applied for aid; of those 91% were deemed to have need. 100% of undergraduates with need received aid; of those 12% had need fully met. ***Average percent of need met:*** 12% (excluding resources awarded to replace EFC). ***Average financial aid package:*** $17,801 (excluding resources awarded to replace EFC). 22% of all full-time undergraduates had no need and received non-need-based gift aid.

GIFT AID (NEED-BASED) ***Total amount:*** $7,074,788 (22% federal, 34% state, 44% institutional). ***Receiving aid:*** Freshmen: 62% (306); All full-time undergraduates: 60% (1,189). ***Average award:*** Freshmen: $6385; Undergraduates: $6048. ***Scholarships, grants, and awards:*** Federal Pell, FSEOG, state, private, college/university gift aid from institutional funds.

GIFT AID (NON-NEED-BASED) ***Total amount:*** $17,420,060 (3% federal, 93% institutional, 4% external sources). ***Receiving aid:*** Freshmen: 75% (368); Undergraduates: 71% (1,408). ***Average award:*** Freshmen: $12,352; Undergraduates: $10,746. ***Scholarships, grants, and awards by category:*** *Academic Interests/Achievement:* 1,676 awards ($13,462,495 total): general academic interests/achievements. *Creative Arts/Performance:* 8 awards ($9900 total): music. *Special Characteristics:* 962 awards ($3,572,870 total): children and siblings of alumni, children of faculty/staff, handicapped students, international students, members of minority groups, previous college experience, religious affiliation, siblings of current students. ***Tuition waivers:*** Full or partial for children of alumni, employees or children of employees, senior citizens. ***ROTC:*** Air Force cooperative.

LOANS ***Student loans:*** $13,850,386 (36% need-based, 64% non-need-based). 85% of past graduating class borrowed through all loan programs. *Average indebtedness per student:* $31,549. ***Average need-based loan:*** Freshmen: $3445; Undergraduates: $4435. ***Parent loans:*** $1,731,879 (100% non-need-based). ***Programs:*** FFEL (Subsidized and Unsubsidized Stafford, PLUS), Perkins, Federal Nursing, state, private supplemental loans.

WORK-STUDY ***Federal work-study:*** Total amount: $482,536; 228 jobs averaging $2116. ***State or other work-study/employment:*** Total amount: $769,515 (46% need-based, 54% non-need-based). 138 part-time jobs averaging $2544.

APPLYING FOR FINANCIAL AID ***Required financial aid forms:*** FAFSA, institution's own form. ***Financial aid deadline (priority):*** 3/15. ***Notification date:*** Continuous beginning 3/1. Students must reply by 5/1 or within 2 weeks of notification.

CONTACT Mr. Jon P. Erickson, Director of Financial Aid, The College of St. Scholastica, 1200 Kenwood Avenue, Duluth, MN 55811-4199, 218-723-6725 or toll-free 800-249-6412. *Fax:* 218-733-2229. *E-mail:* jerickso@css.edu.

THE COLLEGE OF SAINT THOMAS MORE

Fort Worth, TX

Tuition & fees: $12,000 **Average undergraduate aid package: $8560**

ABOUT THE INSTITUTION Independent religious, coed. Awards: associate and bachelor's degrees. 1 undergraduate major. Total enrollment: 53. Undergraduates: 53. Freshmen: 4. Federal methodology is used as a basis for awarding need-based institutional aid.

UNDERGRADUATE EXPENSES for 2007–08 ***Application fee:*** $35. ***Tuition:*** full-time $12,000; part-time $6000 per term.

FRESHMAN FINANCIAL AID (Fall 2005) 8 applied for aid; of those 75% were deemed to have need. 100% of freshmen with need received aid; of those 83% had need fully met. ***Average percent of need met:*** 85% (excluding resources awarded to replace EFC). ***Average financial aid package:*** $8600 (excluding resources awarded to replace EFC). 22% of all full-time freshmen had no need and received non-need-based gift aid.

UNDERGRADUATE FINANCIAL AID (Fall 2005) 26 applied for aid. of those 69% had need fully met. ***Average percent of need met:*** 85% (excluding resources awarded to replace EFC). ***Average financial aid package:*** $8560 (excluding resources awarded to replace EFC). 20% of all full-time undergraduates had no need and received non-need-based gift aid.

GIFT AID (NEED-BASED) ***Total amount:*** $90,856 (32% federal, 49% state, 15% institutional, 4% external sources). ***Receiving aid:*** Freshmen: 22% (2); All full-time undergraduates: 73% (22). ***Average award:*** Freshmen: $4250; Undergraduates: $3825. ***Scholarships, grants, and awards:*** Federal Pell, state, private, college/university gift aid from institutional funds.

GIFT AID (NON-NEED-BASED) ***Total amount:*** $6000 (100% institutional). ***Receiving aid:*** Freshmen: 22% (2); Undergraduates: 20% (6). ***Average award:*** Freshmen: $1000; Undergraduates: $1000. ***Scholarships, grants, and awards by category:*** *Academic Interests/Achievement:* 8 awards ($22,000 total): general academic interests/achievements. ***ROTC:*** Army cooperative.

LOANS ***Student loans:*** $42,250 (62% need-based, 38% non-need-based). 42% of past graduating class borrowed through all loan programs. *Average indebtedness per student:* $9250. ***Average need-based loan:*** Freshmen: $2625; Undergraduates: $4300. ***Parent loans:*** $4000 (100% non-need-based). ***Programs:*** FFEL (Subsidized and Unsubsidized Stafford, PLUS).

WORK-STUDY ***State or other work-study/employment:*** Total amount: $5200 (11% need-based, 89% non-need-based). 4 part-time jobs averaging $500.

APPLYING FOR FINANCIAL AID ***Required financial aid form:*** FAFSA. ***Financial aid deadline (priority):*** 4/15. ***Notification date:*** 6/1. Students must reply within 2 weeks of notification.

CONTACT Mary E. Swanson, Director of Financial Aid, The College of Saint Thomas More, 3020 Lubbock Street, Fort Worth, TX 76109-2323, 325-673-1934 or toll-free 800-583-6489 (out-of-state). *Fax:* 325-673-1934. *E-mail:* corkyswanson@suddenlink.net.

COLLEGE OF SANTA FE

Santa Fe, NM

ABOUT THE INSTITUTION Independent, coed. Awards: associate, bachelor's, and master's degrees. 43 undergraduate majors. Total enrollment: 2,004. Undergraduates: 1,362. Freshmen: 155.

GIFT AID (NEED-BASED) ***Scholarships, grants, and awards:*** Federal Pell, FSEOG, state, private, college/university gift aid from institutional funds.

GIFT AID (NON-NEED-BASED) ***Scholarships, grants, and awards by category:*** *Academic Interests/Achievement:* general academic interests/achievements. *Creative Arts/Performance:* applied art and design, art/fine arts, cinema/film/ broadcasting, creative writing, dance, general creative arts/performance, journalism/publications, music, performing arts, theater/drama. *Special Achievements/ Activities:* general special achievements/activities. *Special Characteristics:* children and siblings of alumni, general special characteristics.

LOANS ***Programs:*** FFEL (Subsidized and Unsubsidized Stafford, PLUS), Perkins, state, college/university.

WORK-STUDY ***Federal work-study:*** Total amount: $222,711; jobs available. ***State or other work-study/employment:*** Total amount: $189,257 (52% need-based, 48% non-need-based). Part-time jobs available.

APPLYING FOR FINANCIAL AID ***Required financial aid form:*** FAFSA.

CONTACT Ms. Jill Robertson, Director, Student Financial Services, College of Santa Fe, 1600 St. Michael's Drive, Santa Fe, NM 87505-7634, 505-473-6454 or toll-free 800-456-2673. *Fax:* 505-473-6464.

COLLEGE OF STATEN ISLAND OF THE CITY UNIVERSITY OF NEW YORK

Staten Island, NY

Tuition & fees (NY res): $4328 **Average undergraduate aid package: $6023**

ABOUT THE INSTITUTION State and locally supported, coed. Awards: associate, bachelor's, and master's degrees and post-master's certificates. 40 undergraduate majors. Total enrollment: 12,313. Undergraduates: 11,263. Freshmen: 2,281. Federal methodology is used as a basis for awarding need-based institutional aid.

UNDERGRADUATE EXPENSES for 2006–07 ***Application fee:*** $65. ***Tuition, state resident:*** full-time $4000; part-time $170 per credit. ***Tuition, nonresident:*** full-time $8640; part-time $360 per credit. ***Required fees:*** full-time $328; $100.50 per term part-time. Full-time tuition and fees vary according to course load. Part-time tuition and fees vary according to course load. ***Payment plan:*** Installment.

FRESHMAN FINANCIAL AID (Fall 2005) 1643 applied for aid; of those 68% were deemed to have need. 96% of freshmen with need received aid; of those 9% had need fully met. ***Average percent of need met:*** 60% (excluding resources awarded to replace EFC). ***Average financial aid package:*** $5790 (excluding resources awarded to replace EFC). 12% of all full-time freshmen had no need and received non-need-based gift aid.

UNDERGRADUATE FINANCIAL AID (Fall 2005) 5,552 applied for aid; of those 74% were deemed to have need. 97% of undergraduates with need received aid; of those 6% had need fully met. ***Average percent of need met:*** 57% (excluding resources awarded to replace EFC). ***Average financial aid package:*** $6023 (excluding resources awarded to replace EFC). 5% of all full-time undergraduates had no need and received non-need-based gift aid.

GIFT AID (NEED-BASED) ***Total amount:*** $21,881,944 (51% federal, 46% state, 3% external sources). ***Receiving aid:*** Freshmen: 51% (1,050); All full-time undergraduates: 50% (3,855). ***Average award:*** Freshmen: $5007; Undergraduates: $4978. ***Scholarships, grants, and awards:*** Federal Pell, FSEOG, state, private, college/university gift aid from institutional funds.

GIFT AID (NON-NEED-BASED) ***Total amount:*** $1,623,828 (3% federal, 49% state, 48% external sources). ***Receiving aid:*** Freshmen: 13% (276); Undergraduates: 6% (463). ***Average award:*** Freshmen: $1571; Undergraduates: $1918. ***Scholarships, grants, and awards by category:*** *Academic Interests/Achievement:* 162 awards ($252,206 total): biological sciences, business, computer science, education, engineering/technologies, general academic interests/achievements, health fields, international studies, mathematics, physical sciences, premedicine. *Creative Arts/Performance:* 4 awards ($4050 total): art/fine arts, music, theater/ drama. *Special Achievements/Activities:* 5 awards ($5500 total): community service, general special achievements/activities. *Special Characteristics:* 7 awards ($8500 total): children of public servants, children with a deceased or disabled parent, general special characteristics, handicapped students, international students, members of minority groups, public servants, spouses of deceased or disabled public servants, veterans' children. ***Tuition waivers:*** Full or partial for employees or children of employees, senior citizens.

LOANS ***Student loans:*** $6,828,910 (100% need-based). ***Average need-based loan:*** Freshmen: $2344; Undergraduates: $3690. ***Programs:*** Federal Direct (Subsidized and Unsubsidized Stafford, PLUS), Perkins.

WORK-STUDY ***Federal work-study:*** Total amount: $1,445,675; 337 jobs averaging $1300.

APPLYING FOR FINANCIAL AID ***Required financial aid forms:*** FAFSA, state aid form. ***Financial aid deadline (priority):*** 3/31. ***Notification date:*** Continuous beginning 4/30.

CONTACT Sherman Whipkey, Director of Financial Aid, College of Staten Island of the City University of New York, 2800 Victory Boulevard, 2A-401A, Staten Island, NY 10314-6600, 718-982-2030. *Fax:* 718-982-2037. *E-mail:* whipkey@mail.csi.cuny.edu.

COLLEGE OF THE ATLANTIC

Bar Harbor, ME

ABOUT THE INSTITUTION Independent, coed. Awards: bachelor's and master's degrees. 37 undergraduate majors. Total enrollment: 339. Undergraduates: 335. Freshmen: 73.

GIFT AID (NEED-BASED) ***Scholarships, grants, and awards:*** Federal Pell, FSEOG, state, private, college/university gift aid from institutional funds.

GIFT AID (NON-NEED-BASED) ***Scholarships, grants, and awards by category:*** *Academic Interests/Achievement:* general academic interests/achievements. *Special Achievements/Activities:* community service, general special achievements/ activities, leadership.

LOANS ***Programs:*** FFEL (Subsidized and Unsubsidized Stafford, PLUS), Perkins.

APPLYING FOR FINANCIAL AID ***Required financial aid forms:*** FAFSA, institution's own form, noncustodial (divorced/separated) parent's statement, financial aid transcript (for transfers).

CONTACT Bruce Hazam, Director of Financial Aid, College of the Atlantic, 105 Eden Street, Bar Harbor, ME 04609-1198, 207-288-5015 Ext. 232 or toll-free 800-528-0025. *Fax:* 207-288-4126. *E-mail:* bhazam@ecology.coa.edu.

COLLEGE OF THE HOLY CROSS

Worcester, MA

Tuition & fees: $33,313 **Average undergraduate aid package: $25,264**

ABOUT THE INSTITUTION Independent Roman Catholic (Jesuit), coed. Awards: bachelor's degrees (standardized tests are optional for admission to the College of Holy Cross). 33 undergraduate majors. Total enrollment: 2,821. Undergraduates: 2,821. Freshmen: 751. Both federal and institutional methodology are used as a basis for awarding need-based institutional aid.

UNDERGRADUATE EXPENSES for 2006–07 ***Application fee:*** $50. ***Comprehensive fee:*** $42,893 includes full-time tuition ($32,820), mandatory fees ($493), and room and board ($9580). ***College room only:*** $4790. Room and board charges vary according to board plan and housing facility. ***Payment plans:*** Tuition prepayment, installment.

FRESHMAN FINANCIAL AID (Fall 2006, est.) 532 applied for aid; of those 82% were deemed to have need. 99% of freshmen with need received aid; of those 100% had need fully met. ***Average percent of need met:*** 100% (excluding resources awarded to replace EFC). ***Average financial aid package:*** $23,745 (excluding resources awarded to replace EFC). 2% of all full-time freshmen had no need and received non-need-based gift aid.

UNDERGRADUATE FINANCIAL AID (Fall 2006, est.) 1,727 applied for aid; of those 90% were deemed to have need. 99% of undergraduates with need received aid; of those 100% had need fully met. ***Average percent of need met:*** 100% (excluding resources awarded to replace EFC). ***Average financial aid package:*** $25,264 (excluding resources awarded to replace EFC). 4% of all full-time undergraduates had no need and received non-need-based gift aid.

GIFT AID (NEED-BASED) ***Total amount:*** $22,301,691 (8% federal, 3% state, 80% institutional, 9% external sources). ***Receiving aid:*** Freshmen: 47% (351); All full-time undergraduates: 45% (1,265). ***Average award:*** Freshmen: $20,908; Undergraduates: $19,739. ***Scholarships, grants, and awards:*** Federal Pell, FSEOG, state, private, college/university gift aid from institutional funds.

GIFT AID (NON-NEED-BASED) ***Total amount:*** $2,605,164 (100% institutional). ***Receiving aid:*** Freshmen: 2% (14); Undergraduates: 9% (264). ***Average award:*** Freshmen: $24,525; Undergraduates: $20,900. ***Scholarships, grants, and awards by category:*** *Academic Interests/Achievement:* 138 awards ($2,235,224 total): general academic interests/achievements, humanities, military science. *Creative*

Arts/Performance: 5 awards ($160,000 total): music. *Special Characteristics:* 20 awards ($639,990 total): children of faculty/staff. ***Tuition waivers:*** Full or partial for employees or children of employees. ***ROTC:*** Army cooperative, Naval, Air Force cooperative.

LOANS ***Student loans:*** $7,698,507 (69% need-based, 31% non-need-based). *Average indebtedness per student:* $18,090. ***Average need-based loan:*** Freshmen: $4488; Undergraduates: $5056. ***Parent loans:*** $11,633,610 (100% non-need-based). ***Programs:*** FFEL (Subsidized and Unsubsidized Stafford, PLUS), Perkins, MEFA Loans.

WORK-STUDY ***Federal work-study:*** Total amount: $1,349,792; 934 jobs averaging $1459.

ATHLETIC AWARDS Total amount: $1,487,021 (30% need-based, 70% non-need-based).

APPLYING FOR FINANCIAL AID ***Required financial aid forms:*** FAFSA, CSS Financial Aid PROFILE, noncustodial (divorced/separated) parent's statement, business/farm supplement, federal income tax form(s). ***Financial aid deadline:*** 2/1. ***Notification date:*** 4/2. Students must reply by 5/1.

CONTACT Lynne Myers, Director of Financial Aid, College of the Holy Cross, One College Street, Worcester, MA 01610-2395, 508-793-2265 or toll-free 800-442-2421. *Fax:* 508-793-2527.

COLLEGE OF THE HUMANITIES AND SCIENCES, HARRISON MIDDLETON UNIVERSITY

Tempe, AZ

CONTACT Financial Aid Office, College of the Humanities and Sciences, Harrison Middleton University, 1105 East Broadway, Tempe, AZ 85282, 480-317-5955 or toll-free 877-248-6724.

COLLEGE OF THE OZARKS

Point Lookout, MO

Tuition & fees: N/R **Average undergraduate aid package: $17,013**

ABOUT THE INSTITUTION Independent Presbyterian, coed. Awards: bachelor's degrees. 95 undergraduate majors. Total enrollment: 1,345. Undergraduates: 1,345. Freshmen: 276. Federal methodology is used as a basis for awarding need-based institutional aid.

UNDERGRADUATE EXPENSES for 2007–08 ***Tuition:*** part-time $295 per credit hour. ***Required fees:*** $140 per term part-time.

FRESHMAN FINANCIAL AID (Fall 2005) 368 applied for aid; of those 92% were deemed to have need. 100% of freshmen with need received aid; of those 28% had need fully met. ***Average percent of need met:*** 84% (excluding resources awarded to replace EFC). ***Average financial aid package:*** $16,533 (excluding resources awarded to replace EFC). 12% of all full-time freshmen had no need and received non-need-based gift aid.

UNDERGRADUATE FINANCIAL AID (Fall 2005) 1,404 applied for aid; of those 92% were deemed to have need. 100% of undergraduates with need received aid; of those 39% had need fully met. ***Average percent of need met:*** 86% (excluding resources awarded to replace EFC). ***Average financial aid package:*** $17,013 (excluding resources awarded to replace EFC). 10% of all full-time undergraduates had no need and received non-need-based gift aid.

GIFT AID (NEED-BASED) ***Total amount:*** $15,521,131 (13% federal, 4% state, 82% institutional, 1% external sources). ***Receiving aid:*** Freshmen: 88% (340); All full-time undergraduates: 90% (1,296). ***Average award:*** Freshmen: $10,655; Undergraduates: $11,977. ***Scholarships, grants, and awards:*** Federal Pell, FSEOG, state, private, college/university gift aid from institutional funds.

GIFT AID (NON-NEED-BASED) ***Total amount:*** $2,798,958 (98% institutional, 2% external sources). ***Receiving aid:*** Freshmen: 12% (45); Undergraduates: 20% (282). ***Average award:*** Freshmen: $16,533; Undergraduates: $17,013. ***Scholarships, grants, and awards by category:*** *Academic Interests/Achievement:* general academic interests/achievements. ***ROTC:*** Army.

LOANS ***Student loans:*** $400,000 (100% non-need-based). 5% of past graduating class borrowed through all loan programs. *Average indebtedness per student:* $4648. ***Programs:*** alternative loans.

WORK-STUDY ***Federal work-study:*** Total amount: $2,030,034; 758 jobs averaging $2884. ***State or other work-study/employment:*** Total amount: $2,092,545 (22% need-based, 78% non-need-based). 723 part-time jobs averaging $2884.

ATHLETIC AWARDS Total amount: $169,975 (38% need-based, 62% non-need-based).

APPLYING FOR FINANCIAL AID ***Required financial aid forms:*** FAFSA, federal income tax form(s). ***Financial aid deadline (priority):*** 2/15. ***Notification date:*** 7/1.

CONTACT Kyla R. McCarty, Director of Financial Aid, College of the Ozarks, PO Box 17, Point Lookout, MO 65726, 417-334-6411 Ext. 4290 or toll-free 800-222-0525. *Fax:* 417-334-6737.

COLLEGE OF THE SOUTHWEST

Hobbs, NM

Tuition & fees: $10,500 **Average undergraduate aid package: $8390**

ABOUT THE INSTITUTION Independent, coed. Awards: bachelor's and master's degrees. 22 undergraduate majors. Total enrollment: 741. Undergraduates: 608. Freshmen: 90. Federal methodology is used as a basis for awarding need-based institutional aid.

UNDERGRADUATE EXPENSES for 2006–07 ***Application fee:*** $25. ***Comprehensive fee:*** $15,900 includes full-time tuition ($10,500) and room and board ($5400). Full-time tuition and fees vary according to course load. Room and board charges vary according to housing facility. ***Part-time tuition:*** $350 per hour. Part-time tuition and fees vary according to course load. ***Payment plan:*** Deferred payment.

FRESHMAN FINANCIAL AID (Fall 2006, est.) 49 applied for aid; of those 78% were deemed to have need. 100% of freshmen with need received aid; of those 45% had need fully met. ***Average percent of need met:*** 78% (excluding resources awarded to replace EFC). ***Average financial aid package:*** $11,144 (excluding resources awarded to replace EFC). 18% of all full-time freshmen had no need and received non-need-based gift aid.

UNDERGRADUATE FINANCIAL AID (Fall 2006, est.) 330 applied for aid; of those 76% were deemed to have need. 100% of undergraduates with need received aid; of those 47% had need fully met. ***Average percent of need met:*** 62% (excluding resources awarded to replace EFC). ***Average financial aid package:*** $8390 (excluding resources awarded to replace EFC). 22% of all full-time undergraduates had no need and received non-need-based gift aid.

GIFT AID (NEED-BASED) ***Total amount:*** $1,101,601 (64% federal, 36% state). ***Receiving aid:*** Freshmen: 59% (29); All full-time undergraduates: 59% (195). ***Average award:*** Freshmen: $5200; Undergraduates: $4303. ***Scholarships, grants, and awards:*** Federal Pell, FSEOG, state, private, college/university gift aid from institutional funds.

GIFT AID (NON-NEED-BASED) ***Total amount:*** $1,031,685 (91% institutional, 9% external sources). ***Receiving aid:*** Freshmen: 78% (38); Undergraduates: 76% (251). ***Average award:*** Freshmen: $5010; Undergraduates: $4020. ***Scholarships, grants, and awards by category:*** *Academic Interests/Achievement:* 73 awards ($98,100 total): biological sciences, business, education, English, general academic interests/achievements, humanities, mathematics, social sciences. *Creative Arts/Performance:* 18 awards ($14,500 total): debating, music, theater/drama. *Special Achievements/Activities:* 18 awards ($16,005 total): general special achievements/activities. *Special Characteristics:* 21 awards ($94,630 total): children of faculty/staff, first-generation college students, relatives of clergy. ***Tuition waivers:*** Full or partial for employees or children of employees.

LOANS ***Student loans:*** $2,871,293 (51% need-based, 49% non-need-based). 66% of past graduating class borrowed through all loan programs. *Average indebtedness per student:* $17,420. ***Average need-based loan:*** Freshmen: $2540; Undergraduates: $3863. ***Parent loans:*** $79,118 (100% non-need-based). ***Programs:*** FFEL (Subsidized and Unsubsidized Stafford, PLUS), state.

WORK-STUDY ***Federal work-study:*** Total amount: $48,316; 32 jobs averaging $1509. ***State or other work-study/employment:*** Total amount: $89,969 (69% need-based, 31% non-need-based). 42 part-time jobs averaging $1481.

ATHLETIC AWARDS Total amount: $361,042 (100% non-need-based).

APPLYING FOR FINANCIAL AID ***Required financial aid forms:*** FAFSA, institution's own form. ***Financial aid deadline:*** 8/1 (priority: 4/1). ***Notification date:*** Continuous beginning 4/1. Students must reply within 2 weeks of notification.

CONTACT Kerrie Mitchell, Senior Financial Aid Officer, College of the Southwest, 6610 Lovington Highway, Hobbs, NM 88240-9129, 505-392-6561 Ext. 1048 or toll-free 800-530-4400. *Fax:* 505-392-6006. *E-mail:* kmitchell@csw.edu.

COLLEGE OF VISUAL ARTS

St. Paul, MN

Tuition & fees: $21,684 **Average undergraduate aid package: $7915**

ABOUT THE INSTITUTION Independent, coed. Awards: bachelor's degrees. 7 undergraduate majors. Total enrollment: 172. Undergraduates: 172. Freshmen: 37. Federal methodology is used as a basis for awarding need-based institutional aid.

UNDERGRADUATE EXPENSES for 2007–08 ***Application fee:*** $40. ***Tuition:*** full-time $21,184; part-time $1057 per credit. ***Required fees:*** full-time $500; $50 per course.

FRESHMAN FINANCIAL AID (Fall 2006, est.) 37 applied for aid; of those 84% were deemed to have need. 100% of freshmen with need received aid; of those 3% had need fully met. ***Average percent of need met:*** 46% (excluding resources awarded to replace EFC). ***Average financial aid package:*** $8787 (excluding resources awarded to replace EFC). 15% of all full-time freshmen had no need and received non-need-based gift aid.

UNDERGRADUATE FINANCIAL AID (Fall 2006, est.) 161 applied for aid; of those 84% were deemed to have need. 99% of undergraduates with need received aid; of those 11% had need fully met. ***Average percent of need met:*** 55% (excluding resources awarded to replace EFC). ***Average financial aid package:*** $7915 (excluding resources awarded to replace EFC). 10% of all full-time undergraduates had no need and received non-need-based gift aid.

GIFT AID (NEED-BASED) ***Total amount:*** $625,343 (22% federal, 27% state, 48% institutional, 3% external sources). ***Receiving aid:*** Freshmen: 78% (31); All full-time undergraduates: 55% (100). ***Average award:*** Freshmen: $3599; Undergraduates: $2544. ***Scholarships, grants, and awards:*** Federal Pell, FSEOG, state, private, college/university gift aid from institutional funds.

GIFT AID (NON-NEED-BASED) ***Total amount:*** $67,706 (84% institutional, 16% external sources). ***Receiving aid:*** Freshmen: 18% (7); Undergraduates: 17% (31). ***Average award:*** Freshmen: $1089; Undergraduates: $1668. ***Scholarships, grants, and awards by category:*** *Academic Interests/Achievement:* 39 awards ($59,688 total): general academic interests/achievements. *Creative Arts/Performance:* 28 awards ($52,375 total): art/fine arts. *Special Characteristics:* children of faculty/staff.

LOANS ***Student loans:*** $1,659,473 (56% need-based, 44% non-need-based). 85% of past graduating class borrowed through all loan programs. ***Average need-based loan:*** Freshmen: $2618; Undergraduates: $2930. ***Parent loans:*** $224,712 (10% need-based, 90% non-need-based). ***Programs:*** FFEL (Subsidized and Unsubsidized Stafford, PLUS), state, alternative loans.

WORK-STUDY ***Federal work-study:*** Total amount: $35,496; 44 jobs averaging $806. ***State or other work-study/employment:*** Total amount: $61,440 (22% need-based, 78% non-need-based). 32 part-time jobs averaging $1920.

APPLYING FOR FINANCIAL AID ***Required financial aid forms:*** FAFSA, institution's own form. ***Financial aid deadline:*** 6/1 (priority: 4/1). ***Notification date:*** Continuous beginning 3/1.

CONTACT Susan Ant, Director of Financial Aid, College of Visual Arts, 344 Summit Avenue, St. Paul, MN 55102-2124, 651-224-3416 or toll-free 800-224-1536. *Fax:* 651-224-8854. *E-mail:* sant@cva.edu.

THE COLLEGE OF WILLIAM AND MARY

Williamsburg, VA

Tuition & fees (VA res): $8490 **Average undergraduate aid package: $12,252**

ABOUT THE INSTITUTION State-supported, coed. Awards: bachelor's, master's, doctoral, and first professional degrees and post-master's certificates. 44 undergraduate majors. Total enrollment: 7,709. Undergraduates: 5,734. Freshmen: 1,349. Federal methodology is used as a basis for awarding need-based institutional aid.

UNDERGRADUATE EXPENSES for 2006–07 ***Application fee:*** $60. ***Tuition, state resident:*** full-time $5180; part-time $196 per credit hour. ***Tuition, nonresident:*** full-time $21,600; part-time $750 per credit hour. Full-time tuition and fees vary according to program. Part-time tuition and fees vary according to program. ***College room and board:*** $6932; ***Room only:*** $4210. Room and board charges vary according to board plan and housing facility. ***Payment plan:*** Installment.

FRESHMAN FINANCIAL AID (Fall 2006, est.) 724 applied for aid; of those 46% were deemed to have need. 100% of freshmen with need received aid; of those 44% had need fully met. ***Average percent of need met:*** 84% (excluding resources awarded to replace EFC). ***Average financial aid package:*** $12,312 (excluding resources awarded to replace EFC). 2% of all full-time freshmen had no need and received non-need-based gift aid.

UNDERGRADUATE FINANCIAL AID (Fall 2006, est.) 2,649 applied for aid; of those 59% were deemed to have need. 100% of undergraduates with need received aid; of those 46% had need fully met. ***Average percent of need met:*** 84% (excluding resources awarded to replace EFC). ***Average financial aid package:*** $12,252 (excluding resources awarded to replace EFC). 5% of all full-time undergraduates had no need and received non-need-based gift aid.

GIFT AID (NEED-BASED) ***Total amount:*** $10,341,407 (14% federal, 31% state, 55% institutional). ***Receiving aid:*** Freshmen: 20% (248); All full-time undergraduates: 22% (1,266). ***Average award:*** Freshmen: $11,727; Undergraduates: $11,457. ***Scholarships, grants, and awards:*** Federal Pell, FSEOG, state, private, college/university gift aid from institutional funds.

GIFT AID (NON-NEED-BASED) ***Total amount:*** $5,351,410 (3% federal, 1% state, 43% institutional, 53% external sources). ***Receiving aid:*** Freshmen: 13% (162); Undergraduates: 9% (538). ***Average award:*** Freshmen: $7222; Undergraduates: $5222. ***Scholarships, grants, and awards by category:*** *Academic Interests/Achievement:* 12 awards ($180,000 total): general academic interests/achievements. *Creative Arts/Performance:* 10 awards ($25,000 total): music, theater/drama. ***Tuition waivers:*** Full or partial for employees or children of employees, senior citizens. ***ROTC:*** Army.

LOANS ***Student loans:*** $8,928,642 (38% need-based, 62% non-need-based). 32% of past graduating class borrowed through all loan programs. *Average indebtedness per student:* $14,524. ***Average need-based loan:*** Freshmen: $1722; Undergraduates: $2580. ***Parent loans:*** $6,415,638 (100% non-need-based). ***Programs:*** FFEL (Subsidized and Unsubsidized Stafford, PLUS), Perkins.

WORK-STUDY ***Federal work-study:*** Total amount: $119,248; 110 jobs averaging $1095.

ATHLETIC AWARDS Total amount: $4,617,211 (100% non-need-based).

APPLYING FOR FINANCIAL AID ***Required financial aid form:*** FAFSA. ***Financial aid deadline (priority):*** 2/15. ***Notification date:*** Continuous beginning 3/15. Students must reply by 5/1 or within 2 weeks of notification.

CONTACT Mr. Edward P. Irish, Director of Financial Aid, The College of William and Mary, PO Box 8795, Williamsburg, VA 23187, 757-221-2425. *Fax:* 757-221-2515. *E-mail:* epiris@wm.edu.

THE COLLEGE OF WOOSTER

Wooster, OH

Tuition & fees: $30,060 **Average undergraduate aid package: $24,981**

ABOUT THE INSTITUTION Independent religious, coed. Awards: bachelor's degrees. 45 undergraduate majors. Total enrollment: 1,819. Undergraduates: 1,819. Freshmen: 493. Both federal and institutional methodology are used as a basis for awarding need-based institutional aid.

UNDERGRADUATE EXPENSES for 2006–07 ***Application fee:*** $40. ***Comprehensive fee:*** $37,580 includes full-time tuition ($30,060) and room and board ($7520). ***College room only:*** $3420. Full-time tuition and fees vary according to course load and reciprocity agreements. Part-time tuition and fees vary according to course load. ***Payment plan:*** Installment.

FRESHMAN FINANCIAL AID (Fall 2006, est.) 353 applied for aid; of those 82% were deemed to have need. 100% of freshmen with need received aid; of those 92% had need fully met. ***Average percent of need met:*** 96% (excluding resources awarded to replace EFC). ***Average financial aid package:*** $25,922 (excluding resources awarded to replace EFC). 42% of all full-time freshmen had no need and received non-need-based gift aid.

UNDERGRADUATE FINANCIAL AID (Fall 2006, est.) 1,167 applied for aid; of those 87% were deemed to have need. 100% of undergraduates with need received aid; of those 88% had need fully met. ***Average percent of need met:*** 94% (excluding resources awarded to replace EFC). ***Average financial aid package:*** $24,981 (excluding resources awarded to replace EFC). 43% of all full-time undergraduates had no need and received non-need-based gift aid.

GIFT AID (NEED-BASED) ***Total amount:*** $19,012,549 (6% federal, 4% state, 88% institutional, 2% external sources). ***Receiving aid:*** Freshmen: 58% (288); All full-time undergraduates: 57% (1,010). ***Average award:*** Freshmen: $20,323; Undergraduates: $18,821. ***Scholarships, grants, and awards:*** Federal Pell, FSEOG, state, private, college/university gift aid from institutional funds.

GIFT AID (NON-NEED-BASED) ***Total amount:*** $11,045,230 (3% state, 96% institutional, 1% external sources). ***Receiving aid:*** Freshmen: 9% (44);

Undergraduates: 7% (127). ***Average award:*** Freshmen: $14,641; Undergraduates: $13,017. ***Scholarships, grants, and awards by category:*** *Academic Interests/Achievement:* 1,387 awards ($15,909,874 total): biological sciences, general academic interests/achievements, mathematics, physical sciences, social sciences. *Creative Arts/Performance:* 57 awards ($218,000 total): dance, music, theater/drama. *Special Achievements/Activities:* 229 awards ($1,012,159 total): community service, leadership, religious involvement. *Special Characteristics:* 209 awards ($3,911,016 total): children of faculty/staff, international students, local/state students, members of minority groups. ***Tuition waivers:*** Full or partial for employees or children of employees.

LOANS ***Student loans:*** $7,294,029 (67% need-based, 33% non-need-based). 58% of past graduating class borrowed through all loan programs. *Average indebtedness per student:* $23,527. ***Average need-based loan:*** Freshmen: $3631; Undergraduates: $4364. ***Parent loans:*** $2,905,023 (14% need-based, 86% non-need-based). ***Programs:*** Federal Direct (Subsidized and Unsubsidized Stafford, PLUS), Perkins.

WORK-STUDY ***Federal work-study:*** Total amount: $948,516. ***State or other work-study/employment:*** Total amount: $630,837 (23% need-based, 77% non-need-based).

APPLYING FOR FINANCIAL AID ***Required financial aid form:*** FAFSA. ***Financial aid deadline:*** 9/1 (priority: 2/15). ***Notification date:*** 3/15. Students must reply by 5/1 or within 4 weeks of notification.

CONTACT Office of Financial Aid, The College of Wooster, 1189 Beall Avenue, Wooster, OH 44691, 330-263-2317 or toll-free 800-877-9905. *Fax:* 330-263-2634. *E-mail:* financialaid@wooster.edu.

COLLINS COLLEGE: A SCHOOL OF DESIGN AND TECHNOLOGY

Tempe, AZ

ABOUT THE INSTITUTION Proprietary, coed. Awards: associate and bachelor's degrees. 6 undergraduate majors. Total enrollment: 1,690. Undergraduates: 1,690.

GIFT AID (NEED-BASED) ***Scholarships, grants, and awards:*** Federal Pell, FSEOG, state, private, college/university gift aid from institutional funds.

GIFT AID (NON-NEED-BASED) ***Scholarships, grants, and awards by category:*** *Creative Arts/Performance:* applied art and design.

LOANS ***Programs:*** FFEL (Subsidized and Unsubsidized Stafford, PLUS), college/university.

WORK-STUDY ***Federal work-study:*** Total amount: $212,862; 65 jobs averaging $3000. ***State or other work-study/employment:*** Total amount: $24,093 (100% need-based).

APPLYING FOR FINANCIAL AID ***Required financial aid forms:*** FAFSA, institution's own form.

CONTACT Carol Clapp, Director of Financial Aid, Collins College: A School of Design and Technology, 1140 South Priest Drive, Tempe, AZ 85281, 480-966-3000 Ext. 127 or toll-free 800-876-7070 (out-of-state). *Fax:* 480-446-1172. *E-mail:* cclapp@collinscollege.edu.

COLORADO CHRISTIAN UNIVERSITY

Lakewood, CO

CONTACT Mr. Steve Woodburn, Director of Financial Aid, Colorado Christian University, 180 South Garrison Street, Lakewood, CO 80226-7499, 303-963-3230 or toll-free 800-44-FAITH. *Fax:* 303-963-3231. *E-mail:* sfs@ccu.edu.

THE COLORADO COLLEGE

Colorado Springs, CO

Tuition & fees: $32,124 **Average undergraduate aid package: $29,982**

ABOUT THE INSTITUTION Independent, coed. Awards: bachelor's and master's degrees (master's degree in education only). 46 undergraduate majors. Total enrollment: 1,998. Undergraduates: 1,970. Freshmen: 492. Both federal and institutional methodology are used as a basis for awarding need-based institutional aid.

UNDERGRADUATE EXPENSES for 2006–07 ***Application fee:*** $50. ***Comprehensive fee:*** $40,176 includes full-time tuition ($32,124) and room and board ($8052). ***College room only:*** $4368. Room and board charges vary according to board plan. ***Payment plan:*** Installment.

FRESHMAN FINANCIAL AID (Fall 2006, est.) 211 applied for aid; of those 82% were deemed to have need. 100% of freshmen with need received aid; of those 56% had need fully met. ***Average percent of need met:*** 95% (excluding resources awarded to replace EFC). ***Average financial aid package:*** $28,705 (excluding resources awarded to replace EFC). 3% of all full-time freshmen had no need and received non-need-based gift aid.

UNDERGRADUATE FINANCIAL AID (Fall 2006, est.) 891 applied for aid; of those 89% were deemed to have need. 100% of undergraduates with need received aid; of those 55% had need fully met. ***Average percent of need met:*** 91% (excluding resources awarded to replace EFC). ***Average financial aid package:*** $29,982 (excluding resources awarded to replace EFC). 7% of all full-time undergraduates had no need and received non-need-based gift aid.

GIFT AID (NEED-BASED) ***Total amount:*** $18,460,294 (4% federal, 2% state, 92% institutional, 2% external sources). ***Receiving aid:*** Freshmen: 33% (161); All full-time undergraduates: 38% (745). ***Average award:*** Freshmen: $24,841; Undergraduates: $25,257. ***Scholarships, grants, and awards:*** Federal Pell, FSEOG, state, private, college/university gift aid from institutional funds.

GIFT AID (NON-NEED-BASED) ***Total amount:*** $4,117,843 (79% institutional, 21% external sources). ***Receiving aid:*** Freshmen: 5% (24); Undergraduates: 5% (89). ***Average award:*** Freshmen: $10,153; Undergraduates: $16,425. ***Scholarships, grants, and awards by category:*** *Academic Interests/Achievement:* 165 awards ($1,600,000 total): biological sciences, general academic interests/achievements, mathematics, physical sciences. ***Tuition waivers:*** Full or partial for employees or children of employees. ***ROTC:*** Army cooperative.

LOANS ***Student loans:*** $3,194,752 (61% need-based, 39% non-need-based). ***Average need-based loan:*** Freshmen: $3269; Undergraduates: $4379. ***Parent loans:*** $2,965,157 (19% need-based, 81% non-need-based). ***Programs:*** FFEL (Subsidized and Unsubsidized Stafford, PLUS), Perkins.

WORK-STUDY ***Federal work-study:*** Total amount: $433,191; 280 jobs averaging $1547. ***State or other work-study/employment:*** Total amount: $318,419 (68% need-based, 32% non-need-based). 193 part-time jobs averaging $1650.

ATHLETIC AWARDS Total amount: $1,210,265 (16% need-based, 84% non-need-based).

APPLYING FOR FINANCIAL AID ***Required financial aid forms:*** FAFSA, CSS Financial Aid PROFILE, noncustodial (divorced/separated) parent's statement, federal income tax form(s) for parents and student. ***Financial aid deadline:*** 2/15 (priority: 2/15). ***Notification date:*** 3/20. Students must reply by 5/1.

CONTACT Mr. James M. Swanson, Director of Financial Aid, The Colorado College, 14 East Cache La Poudre Street, Colorado Springs, CO 80903-3294, 719-389-6651 or toll-free 800-542-7214. *Fax:* 719-389-6173. *E-mail:* FinancialAid@ColoradoCollege.edu.

COLORADO SCHOOL OF MINES

Golden, CO

Tuition & fees (CO res): $9010 **Average undergraduate aid package: $14,800**

ABOUT THE INSTITUTION State-supported, coed. Awards: bachelor's, master's, doctoral, and first professional degrees. 16 undergraduate majors. Total enrollment: 4,056. Undergraduates: 3,223. Freshmen: 787. Federal methodology is used as a basis for awarding need-based institutional aid.

UNDERGRADUATE EXPENSES for 2006–07 ***Application fee:*** $45. ***Tuition, state resident:*** full-time $8088; part-time $300 per semester hour. ***Tuition, nonresident:*** full-time $20,624; part-time $687 per semester hour. ***Required fees:*** full-time $922; $60 per semester hour. Part-time tuition and fees vary according to course load. ***College room and board:*** $6880; ***Room only:*** $3600. Room and board charges vary according to board plan and housing facility. ***Payment plan:*** Installment.

FRESHMAN FINANCIAL AID (Fall 2006, est.) 645 applied for aid; of those 90% were deemed to have need. 100% of freshmen with need received aid; of those 81% had need fully met. ***Average percent of need met:*** 93% (excluding resources awarded to replace EFC). ***Average financial aid package:*** $14,800 (excluding resources awarded to replace EFC). 10% of all full-time freshmen had no need and received non-need-based gift aid.

UNDERGRADUATE FINANCIAL AID (Fall 2006, est.) 2,325 applied for aid; of those 90% were deemed to have need. 100% of undergraduates with need received aid; of those 83% had need fully met. ***Average percent of need met:*** 93% (excluding resources awarded to replace EFC). ***Average financial aid***

package: $14,800 (excluding resources awarded to replace EFC). 9% of all full-time undergraduates had no need and received non-need-based gift aid.

GIFT AID (NEED-BASED) ***Total amount:*** $8,794,000 (23% federal, 14% state, 53% institutional, 10% external sources). ***Receiving aid:*** Freshmen: 59% (510); All full-time undergraduates: 54% (1,660). ***Average award:*** Freshmen: $8100; Undergraduates: $8100. ***Scholarships, grants, and awards:*** Federal Pell, FSEOG, state, private, college/university gift aid from institutional funds.

GIFT AID (NON-NEED-BASED) ***Total amount:*** $3,052,000 (2% state, 69% institutional, 29% external sources). ***Receiving aid:*** Freshmen: 24% (210); Undergraduates: 59% (1,840). ***Average award:*** Freshmen: $5500; Undergraduates: $5500. ***Scholarships, grants, and awards by category:*** *Academic Interests/Achievement:* 350 awards ($1,100,000 total): business, computer science, engineering/technologies, general academic interests/achievements, mathematics, military science, physical sciences. *Creative Arts/Performance:* 42 awards ($58,000 total): music. *Special Characteristics:* 10 awards ($10,000 total): children and siblings of alumni. ***ROTC:*** Army.

LOANS ***Student loans:*** $8,850,000 (66% need-based, 34% non-need-based). 69% of past graduating class borrowed through all loan programs. *Average indebtedness per student:* $18,700. ***Average need-based loan:*** Freshmen: $4200; Undergraduates: $4200. ***Parent loans:*** $3,875,000 (100% non-need-based). ***Programs:*** FFEL (Subsidized and Unsubsidized Stafford, PLUS), Perkins, college/university.

WORK-STUDY ***Federal work-study:*** Total amount: $202,700; 164 jobs averaging $1200. ***State or other work-study/employment:*** Total amount: $668,000 (55% need-based, 45% non-need-based). 560 part-time jobs averaging $1200.

ATHLETIC AWARDS Total amount: $1,050,000 (66% need-based, 34% non-need-based).

APPLYING FOR FINANCIAL AID ***Required financial aid form:*** FAFSA. ***Financial aid deadline (priority):*** 3/1. ***Notification date:*** 3/15. Students must reply by 5/1 or within 2 weeks of notification.

CONTACT Mr. Roger A. Koester, Director of Financial Aid, Colorado School of Mines, 1500 Illinois Street, Golden, CO 80401-1887, 303-273-3220 or toll-free 800-446-9488 Ext. 3220 (out-of-state). *Fax:* 303-384-2252. *E-mail:* rkoester@mines.edu.

COLORADO STATE UNIVERSITY

Fort Collins, CO

Tuition & fees (CO res): $4717 Average undergraduate aid package: $8455

ABOUT THE INSTITUTION State-supported, coed. Awards: bachelor's, master's, doctoral, and first professional degrees. 118 undergraduate majors. Total enrollment: 26,723. Undergraduates: 21,283. Freshmen: 4,093. Federal methodology is used as a basis for awarding need-based institutional aid.

UNDERGRADUATE EXPENSES for 2006–07 ***Application fee:*** $50. ***Tuition, state resident:*** full-time $3466; part-time $192.55 per credit hour. ***Tuition, nonresident:*** full-time $14,994; part-time $833 per credit hour. ***Required fees:*** full-time $1251; $33.11 per term part-time. Full-time tuition and fees vary according to course load. Part-time tuition and fees vary according to course load. ***College room and board:*** $6602; ***Room only:*** $2980. Room and board charges vary according to board plan and housing facility. ***Payment plan:*** Installment.

FRESHMAN FINANCIAL AID (Fall 2005) 2224 applied for aid; of those 62% were deemed to have need. 100% of freshmen with need received aid; of those 38% had need fully met. ***Average percent of need met:*** 87% (excluding resources awarded to replace EFC). ***Average financial aid package:*** $7381 (excluding resources awarded to replace EFC). 8% of all full-time freshmen had no need and received non-need-based gift aid.

UNDERGRADUATE FINANCIAL AID (Fall 2005) 10,631 applied for aid; of those 69% were deemed to have need. 100% of undergraduates with need received aid; of those 45% had need fully met. ***Average percent of need met:*** 82% (excluding resources awarded to replace EFC). ***Average financial aid package:*** $8455 (excluding resources awarded to replace EFC). 6% of all full-time undergraduates had no need and received non-need-based gift aid.

GIFT AID (NEED-BASED) ***Total amount:*** $25,748,743 (46% federal, 20% state, 25% institutional, 9% external sources). ***Receiving aid:*** Freshmen: 27% (1,027); All full-time undergraduates: 26% (4,838). ***Average award:*** Freshmen: $6427; Undergraduates: $5465. ***Scholarships, grants, and awards:*** Federal Pell, FSEOG, state, private, college/university gift aid from institutional funds.

GIFT AID (NON-NEED-BASED) ***Total amount:*** $6,172,063 (17% federal, 2% state, 52% institutional, 29% external sources). ***Average award:*** Freshmen: $3222; Undergraduates: $2724. ***Scholarships, grants, and awards by category:*** *Academic Interests/Achievement:* 4,785 awards ($9,312,554 total): general academic interests/achievements. *Creative Arts/Performance:* 142 awards ($150,000 total): art/fine arts, creative writing, dance, music, theater/drama. *Special Achievements/Activities:* 244 awards ($634,553 total): general special achievements/activities. *Special Characteristics:* 500 awards ($970,489 total): children of faculty/staff, first-generation college students. ***Tuition waivers:*** Full or partial for employees or children of employees. ***ROTC:*** Army, Air Force.

LOANS ***Student loans:*** $52,362,775 (72% need-based, 28% non-need-based). 54% of past graduating class borrowed through all loan programs. *Average indebtedness per student:* $16,887. ***Average need-based loan:*** Freshmen: $3293; Undergraduates: $5403. ***Parent loans:*** $26,445,729 (55% need-based, 45% non-need-based). ***Programs:*** Federal Direct (Subsidized and Unsubsidized Stafford, PLUS), Perkins, college/university, alternative loans.

WORK-STUDY ***Federal work-study:*** Total amount: $845,243; 425 jobs averaging $1989. ***State or other work-study/employment:*** Total amount: $1,968,899 (72% need-based, 28% non-need-based). 1,055 part-time jobs averaging $1493.

ATHLETIC AWARDS Total amount: $3,734,421 (29% need-based, 71% non-need-based).

APPLYING FOR FINANCIAL AID ***Required financial aid form:*** FAFSA. ***Financial aid deadline (priority):*** 3/1. ***Notification date:*** Continuous beginning 3/1.

CONTACT Office of Student Financial Services, Colorado State University, Room 103, Administration Annex Building, Fort Collins, CO 80523-8024, 970-491-6321. *E-mail:* sfs@colostate.edu.

COLORADO STATE UNIVERSITY-PUEBLO

Pueblo, CO

Tuition & fees (CO res): $4190 Average undergraduate aid package: $7693

ABOUT THE INSTITUTION State-supported, coed. Awards: bachelor's and master's degrees. 65 undergraduate majors. Total enrollment: 6,205. Undergraduates: 5,087. Freshmen: 671. Federal methodology is used as a basis for awarding need-based institutional aid.

UNDERGRADUATE EXPENSES for 2006–07 ***Application fee:*** $25. ***Tuition, state resident:*** full-time $2975; part-time $124 per credit hour. ***Tuition, nonresident:*** full-time $13,543; part-time $564 per credit hour. ***Required fees:*** full-time $1215; $40 per credit hour. ***College room and board:*** $5810; ***Room only:*** $2960.

FRESHMAN FINANCIAL AID (Fall 2006, est.) 335 applied for aid; of those 80% were deemed to have need. 100% of freshmen with need received aid; of those 11% had need fully met. ***Average percent of need met:*** 65% (excluding resources awarded to replace EFC). ***Average financial aid package:*** $7264 (excluding resources awarded to replace EFC). 28% of all full-time freshmen had no need and received non-need-based gift aid.

UNDERGRADUATE FINANCIAL AID (Fall 2006, est.) 1,634 applied for aid; of those 85% were deemed to have need. 100% of undergraduates with need received aid; of those 8% had need fully met. ***Average percent of need met:*** 61% (excluding resources awarded to replace EFC). ***Average financial aid package:*** $7693 (excluding resources awarded to replace EFC). 24% of all full-time undergraduates had no need and received non-need-based gift aid.

GIFT AID (NEED-BASED) ***Total amount:*** $9,252,257 (54% federal, 24% state, 17% institutional, 5% external sources). ***Receiving aid:*** Freshmen: 60% (232); All full-time undergraduates: 61% (1,152). ***Average award:*** Freshmen: $5573; Undergraduates: $4913. ***Scholarships, grants, and awards:*** Federal Pell, FSEOG, state, private, college/university gift aid from institutional funds.

GIFT AID (NON-NEED-BASED) ***Total amount:*** $1,380,986 (1% state, 84% institutional, 15% external sources). ***Receiving aid:*** Freshmen: 3% (13); Undergraduates: 2% (40). ***Average award:*** Freshmen: $7749; Undergraduates: $7720. ***Scholarships, grants, and awards by category:*** *Academic Interests/Achievement:* 364 awards ($622,465 total): biological sciences, business, computer science, engineering/technologies, general academic interests/achievements, health fields, international studies, mathematics, premedicine, social sciences. *Creative Arts/Performance:* 204 awards ($414,997 total): applied art and design, art/fine arts, cinema/film/broadcasting, journalism/publications, music. *Special Achievements/Activities:* 21 awards ($28,500 total): community service, general special achievements/activities, leadership. *Special Characteristics:* 26 awards ($110,490 total): first-generation college students, general special characteristics. ***ROTC:*** Army.

LOANS ***Student loans:*** $16,434,038 (83% need-based, 17% non-need-based). 55% of past graduating class borrowed through all loan programs. *Average indebtedness per student:* $30. ***Average need-based loan:*** Freshmen: $2323;

Undergraduates: $3451. ***Parent loans:*** $6,066,124 (40% need-based, 60% non-need-based). ***Programs:*** FFEL (Subsidized and Unsubsidized Stafford, PLUS), Perkins.

WORK-STUDY ***Federal work-study:*** Total amount: $489,356; 247 jobs averaging $1981. ***State or other work-study/employment:*** Total amount: $997,126 (69% need-based, 31% non-need-based). 327 part-time jobs averaging $2100.

ATHLETIC AWARDS Total amount: $233,399 (96% need-based, 4% non-need-based).

APPLYING FOR FINANCIAL AID ***Required financial aid form:*** FAFSA. ***Financial aid deadline (priority):*** 3/1. ***Notification date:*** Continuous beginning 3/25. Students must reply within 3 weeks of notification.

CONTACT Sean McGiuney, Director of Student Financial Services, Colorado State University-Pueblo, 2200 Bonforte Boulevard, Pueblo, CO 81001-4901, 719-549-2753. *Fax:* 719-549-2088.

COLORADO TECHNICAL UNIVERSITY

Colorado Springs, CO

CONTACT Anne Marie Alba, Financial Aid Coordinator, Colorado Technical University, 4435 North Chestnut Street, Colorado Springs, CO 80907-3896, 719-598-0200. *Fax:* 719-598-3740.

COLORADO TECHNICAL UNIVERSITY DENVER CAMPUS

Greenwood Village, CO

CONTACT Ms. Natalie Dietsch, Financial Aid Manager, Colorado Technical University Denver Campus, 5775 Denver Tech Center Boulevard, Suite 100, Greenwood Village, CO 80111, 303-694-6600. *Fax:* 303-694-6673.

COLORADO TECHNICAL UNIVERSITY SIOUX FALLS CAMPUS

Sioux Falls, SD

CONTACT Vikki Van Hull, Financial Aid Officer, Colorado Technical University Sioux Falls Campus, 3901 West 59th Street, Sioux Falls, SD 57108, 605-361-0200 Ext. 140. *Fax:* 605-361-5954. *E-mail:* vvanhull@sf.coloradotech.edu.

COLUMBIA COLLEGE

Columbia, MO

Tuition & fees: $12,414 **Average undergraduate aid package: $12,096**

ABOUT THE INSTITUTION Independent religious, coed. Awards: associate, bachelor's, and master's degrees (offers continuing education program with significant enrollment not reflected in profile). 37 undergraduate majors. Total enrollment: 1,186. Undergraduates: 1,036. Freshmen: 191. Both federal and institutional methodology are used as a basis for awarding need-based institutional aid.

UNDERGRADUATE EXPENSES for 2006–07 ***Application fee:*** $25. ***Comprehensive fee:*** $17,578 includes full-time tuition ($12,414) and room and board ($5164). ***College room only:*** $3248. Full-time tuition and fees vary according to class time and course load. Room and board charges vary according to board plan. ***Part-time tuition:*** $266 per credit hour. Part-time tuition and fees vary according to class time, course load, and location. ***Payment plan:*** Deferred payment.

FRESHMAN FINANCIAL AID (Fall 2006, est.) 154 applied for aid; of those 72% were deemed to have need. 98% of freshmen with need received aid; of those 24% had need fully met. ***Average percent of need met:*** 67% (excluding resources awarded to replace EFC). ***Average financial aid package:*** $9448 (excluding resources awarded to replace EFC). 22% of all full-time freshmen had no need and received non-need-based gift aid.

UNDERGRADUATE FINANCIAL AID (Fall 2006, est.) 621 applied for aid; of those 72% were deemed to have need. 98% of undergraduates with need received aid; of those 29% had need fully met. ***Average percent of need met:*** 71% (excluding resources awarded to replace EFC). ***Average financial aid package:*** $12,096 (excluding resources awarded to replace EFC). 20% of all full-time undergraduates had no need and received non-need-based gift aid.

GIFT AID (NEED-BASED) ***Total amount:*** $1,151,111 (70% federal, 10% state, 20% institutional). ***Receiving aid:*** Freshmen: 58% (97); All full-time undergraduates: 44% (327). ***Average award:*** Freshmen: $2739; Undergraduates: $3364. ***Scholarships, grants, and awards:*** Federal Pell, FSEOG, state, private, college/university gift aid from institutional funds, VA, vocational rehabilitation.

GIFT AID (NON-NEED-BASED) ***Total amount:*** $4,375,398 (4% state, 89% institutional, 7% external sources). ***Receiving aid:*** Freshmen: 66% (109); Undergraduates: 56% (411). ***Average award:*** Freshmen: $6736; Undergraduates: $8759. ***Scholarships, grants, and awards by category:*** *Academic Interests/Achievement:* biological sciences, business, education, English, general academic interests/achievements, humanities, physical sciences, religion/biblical studies, social sciences. *Creative Arts/Performance:* applied art and design, art/fine arts, music. *Special Achievements/Activities:* leadership, memberships, religious involvement. *Special Characteristics:* children and siblings of alumni, children of current students, children of educators, children of faculty/staff, children of union members/company employees, children with a deceased or disabled parent, international students, local/state students, parents of current students, previous college experience, religious affiliation, siblings of current students, spouses of current students, veterans. ***Tuition waivers:*** Full or partial for children of alumni, employees or children of employees. ***ROTC:*** Army cooperative, Naval cooperative, Air Force cooperative.

LOANS ***Student loans:*** $3,367,352 (47% need-based, 53% non-need-based). 55% of past graduating class borrowed through all loan programs. *Average indebtedness per student:* $12,707. ***Average need-based loan:*** Freshmen: $2796; Undergraduates: $4291. ***Parent loans:*** $907,875 (100% non-need-based). ***Programs:*** Federal Direct (Subsidized and Unsubsidized Stafford, PLUS), Perkins.

WORK-STUDY ***Federal work-study:*** Total amount: $51,063; 92 jobs averaging $555.

ATHLETIC AWARDS Total amount: $742,667 (100% non-need-based).

APPLYING FOR FINANCIAL AID ***Required financial aid forms:*** FAFSA, institution's own form. ***Financial aid deadline (priority):*** 3/1. ***Notification date:*** Continuous beginning 3/15. Students must reply within 2 weeks of notification.

CONTACT Sharon Abernathy, Director of Financial Aid, Columbia College, 1001 Rogers Street, Columbia, MO 65216-0002, 573-875-7360 or toll-free 800-231-2391 Ext. 7366. *E-mail:* saabernathy@ccis.edu.

COLUMBIA COLLEGE

New York, NY

CONTACT Office of Financial Aid and Educational Financing, Columbia College, 407 Lerner Hall MC 2802, 1130 Amsterdam Avenue, New York, NY 10027, 212-854-3711. *Fax:* 212-854-8223. *E-mail:* ugrad-finaid@columbia.edu.

COLUMBIA COLLEGE

Caguas, PR

CONTACT Financial Aid Officer, Columbia College, Carr 183, Km 1.7, PO Box 8517, Caguas, PR 00726, 787-743-4041 Ext. 244 or toll-free 800-981-4877 Ext. 239 (in-state).

COLUMBIA COLLEGE

Columbia, SC

ABOUT THE INSTITUTION Independent United Methodist, undergraduate: women only; graduate: coed. Awards: bachelor's and master's degrees. 39 undergraduate majors. Total enrollment: 1,446. Undergraduates: 1,143. Freshmen: 259.

GIFT AID (NEED-BASED) ***Scholarships, grants, and awards:*** Federal Pell, FSEOG, state, private, college/university gift aid from institutional funds.

GIFT AID (NON-NEED-BASED) ***Scholarships, grants, and awards by category:*** *Academic Interests/Achievement:* biological sciences, business, communication, education, English, foreign languages, general academic interests/achievements, humanities, mathematics, religion/biblical studies. *Creative Arts/Performance:* applied art and design, art/fine arts, dance, music. *Special Achievements/Activities:* leadership. *Special Characteristics:* children of faculty/staff, relatives of clergy.

LOANS ***Programs:*** FFEL (Subsidized and Unsubsidized Stafford, PLUS), Perkins, state, South Carolina Teacher Loans, United Methodist Student Loans.

WORK-STUDY ***Federal work-study:*** Total amount: $285,246; 200 jobs averaging $1000. ***State or other work-study/employment:*** Total amount: $70,757 (100% need-based). Part-time jobs available.

APPLYING FOR FINANCIAL AID ***Required financial aid form:*** FAFSA.

CONTACT Anita Kaminer Elliott, Director of Financial Aid, Columbia College, 1301 Columbia College Drive, Columbia, SC 29203-5998, 803-786-3612 or toll-free 800-277-1301. *Fax:* 803-786-3560.

COLUMBIA COLLEGE CHICAGO

Chicago, IL

Tuition & fees: $16,788 **Average undergraduate aid package: N/A**

ABOUT THE INSTITUTION Independent, coed. Awards: bachelor's and master's degrees and post-bachelor's certificates. 42 undergraduate majors. Total enrollment: 11,499. Undergraduates: 10,771. Freshmen: 1,986. Both federal and institutional methodology are used as a basis for awarding need-based institutional aid.

UNDERGRADUATE EXPENSES for 2006–07 ***Application fee:*** $35. ***Comprehensive fee:*** $26,553 includes full-time tuition ($16,328), mandatory fees ($460), and room and board ($9765). ***College room only:*** $8265. ***Part-time tuition:*** $565 per credit hour.

FRESHMAN FINANCIAL AID (Fall 2006, est.) 1437 applied for aid; of those 88% were deemed to have need. 97% of freshmen with need received aid.

UNDERGRADUATE FINANCIAL AID (Fall 2006, est.) 6,342 applied for aid; of those 90% were deemed to have need. 98% of undergraduates with need received aid.

GIFT AID (NEED-BASED) ***Scholarships, grants, and awards:*** Federal Pell, FSEOG, state, private, college/university gift aid from institutional funds.

GIFT AID (NON-NEED-BASED) ***Total amount:*** $3,960,419 (82% institutional, 18% external sources). ***Scholarships, grants, and awards by category:*** *Academic Interests/Achievement:* business, communication, education, general academic interests/achievements. *Creative Arts/Performance:* applied art and design, art/fine arts, cinema/film/broadcasting, creative writing, dance, journalism/publications, music, performing arts, theater/drama. *Special Achievements/Activities:* leadership. *Special Characteristics:* children of faculty/staff, handicapped students.

LOANS ***Student loans:*** $59,820,237 (59% need-based, 41% non-need-based). ***Parent loans:*** $40,754,924 (100% need-based). ***Programs:*** Federal Direct (Subsidized and Unsubsidized Stafford, PLUS).

WORK-STUDY ***Federal work-study:*** Total amount: $1,470,774; jobs available. ***State or other work-study/employment:*** Part-time jobs available.

APPLYING FOR FINANCIAL AID ***Required financial aid forms:*** FAFSA, institution's own form. ***Financial aid deadline (priority):*** 8/15. ***Notification date:*** Continuous.

CONTACT Ms. Jennifer Waters, Executive Director of Student Financial Services, Columbia College Chicago, 600 South Michigan Avenue, Chicago, IL 60605-1996, 312-344-7831 or toll-free 312-663-1600 Ext. 7130 (in-state). *Fax:* 312-986-7008. *E-mail:* jwaters@colum.edu.

COLUMBIA COLLEGE HOLLYWOOD

Tarzana, CA

CONTACT Mr. Chris Freeman, Financial Aid Administrator, Columbia College Hollywood, 18618 Oxnard Street, Tarzana, CA 91356, 818-345-8414 Ext. 110 or toll-free 800-785-0585 (in-state). *Fax:* 818-345-9053. *E-mail:* finaid@columbiacollege.edu.

COLUMBIA INTERNATIONAL UNIVERSITY

Columbia, SC

Tuition & fees: $14,400 **Average undergraduate aid package: $9671**

ABOUT THE INSTITUTION Independent nondenominational, coed. Awards: associate, bachelor's, master's, doctoral, and first professional degrees and post-bachelor's certificates. 15 undergraduate majors. Total enrollment: 959. Undergraduates: 471. Freshmen: 91. Federal methodology is used as a basis for awarding need-based institutional aid.

UNDERGRADUATE EXPENSES for 2006–07 ***Application fee:*** $45. ***Comprehensive fee:*** $20,112 includes full-time tuition ($14,400) and room and board ($5712). Full-time tuition and fees vary according to course load. Room and board charges vary according to board plan. ***Part-time tuition:*** $600 per semester hour. Part-time tuition and fees vary according to course load. ***Payment plan:*** Installment.

FRESHMAN FINANCIAL AID (Fall 2005) 115 applied for aid; of those 84% were deemed to have need. 100% of freshmen with need received aid; of those 8% had need fully met. ***Average percent of need met:*** 72% (excluding resources awarded to replace EFC). ***Average financial aid package:*** $10,874 (excluding resources awarded to replace EFC).

UNDERGRADUATE FINANCIAL AID (Fall 2005) 397 applied for aid; of those 83% were deemed to have need. 100% of undergraduates with need received aid; of those 11% had need fully met. ***Average percent of need met:*** 69% (excluding resources awarded to replace EFC). ***Average financial aid package:*** $9671 (excluding resources awarded to replace EFC).

GIFT AID (NEED-BASED) ***Total amount:*** $1,086,271 (47% federal, 30% state, 23% institutional). ***Receiving aid:*** Freshmen: 73% (97); All full-time undergraduates: 77% (331). ***Average award:*** Freshmen: $3841; Undergraduates: $3796. ***Scholarships, grants, and awards:*** Federal Pell, FSEOG, state, private, college/university gift aid from institutional funds.

GIFT AID (NON-NEED-BASED) ***Total amount:*** $1,376,178 (28% state, 65% institutional, 7% external sources). ***Receiving aid:*** Freshmen: 55% (73); Undergraduates: 48% (207). ***Scholarships, grants, and awards by category:*** *Academic Interests/Achievement:* 179 awards ($398,681 total): business, communication, education, English, general academic interests/achievements, international studies, religion/biblical studies. *Creative Arts/Performance:* 10 awards ($6000 total): music, performing arts. *Special Achievements/Activities:* 178 awards ($481,560 total): general special achievements/activities, leadership. *Special Characteristics:* 171 awards ($201,374 total): children and siblings of alumni, ethnic background, international students, married students, relatives of clergy, religious affiliation, spouses of current students, veterans, veterans' children. ***Tuition waivers:*** Full or partial for employees or children of employees.

LOANS ***Student loans:*** $1,483,527 (62% need-based, 38% non-need-based). 68% of past graduating class borrowed through all loan programs. *Average indebtedness per student:* $21,678. ***Average need-based loan:*** Freshmen: $2691; Undergraduates: $3725. ***Parent loans:*** $615,268 (100% non-need-based). ***Programs:*** FFEL (Subsidized and Unsubsidized Stafford, PLUS).

WORK-STUDY ***Federal work-study:*** Total amount: $92,971; 76 jobs averaging $1223.

APPLYING FOR FINANCIAL AID ***Required financial aid forms:*** FAFSA, institution's own form. ***Financial aid deadline (priority):*** 1/31. ***Notification date:*** Continuous beginning 1/31. Students must reply by 6/1.

CONTACT Nicole Mathison, Office Manager, Columbia International University, 7435 Monticello Road, Columbia, SC 29203, 800-777-2227 Ext. 3036 or toll-free 800-777-2227 Ext. 3024. *Fax:* 803-223-2505. *E-mail:* nmathison@ciu.edu.

COLUMBIA UNION COLLEGE

Takoma Park, MD

CONTACT Elaine Oliver, Director, Financial Aid, Columbia Union College, 7600 Flower Avenue, Takoma Park, MD 20912, 301-891-4005 or toll-free 800-835-4212.

COLUMBIA UNIVERSITY, SCHOOL OF GENERAL STUDIES

New York, NY

Tuition & fees: $33,906 **Average undergraduate aid package: N/A**

ABOUT THE INSTITUTION Independent, coed. Awards: bachelor's degrees and post-bachelor's certificates. 45 undergraduate majors. Total enrollment: 1,260. Undergraduates: 1,260. Freshmen: 68. Both federal and institutional methodology are used as a basis for awarding need-based institutional aid.

UNDERGRADUATE EXPENSES for 2006–07 ***Application fee:*** $65. ***Comprehensive fee:*** $42,819 includes full-time tuition ($32,580), mandatory fees ($1326), and room and board ($8913). ***College room only:*** $5723. Full-time tuition and fees vary according to course load. Room and board charges vary according to board plan and housing facility. ***Part-time tuition:*** $1086 per credit. Part-time tuition and fees vary according to course load. ***Payment plans:*** Tuition prepayment, installment.

GIFT AID (NEED-BASED) ***Total amount:*** $7,371,130 (27% federal, 8% state, 64% institutional, 1% external sources). ***Scholarships, grants, and awards:*** Federal Pell, FSEOG, state, private, college/university gift aid from institutional funds.

GIFT AID (NON-NEED-BASED) ***Total amount:*** $1,662,616 (32% federal, 67% institutional, 1% external sources). ***Scholarships, grants, and awards by category:*** *Academic Interests/Achievement:* general academic interests/achievements. ***Tuition waivers:*** Full or partial for employees or children of employees. ***ROTC:*** Army cooperative, Air Force cooperative.

LOANS ***Student loans:*** $9,210,181 (56% need-based, 44% non-need-based). ***Parent loans:*** $2,916,229 (100% non-need-based). ***Programs:*** FFEL (Subsidized and Unsubsidized Stafford, PLUS), Perkins, college/university.

WORK-STUDY ***Federal work-study:*** Total amount: $521,578; 200 jobs averaging $2367.

APPLYING FOR FINANCIAL AID ***Required financial aid forms:*** FAFSA, institution's own form. ***Financial aid deadline (priority):*** 6/1. ***Notification date:*** Continuous. Students must reply within 2 weeks of notification.

CONTACT Student Financial Planning, Columbia University, School of General Studies, 208 Kent Hall, New York, NY 10027, 212-854-7040 or toll-free 800-895-1169 (out-of-state).

COLUMBIA UNIVERSITY, THE FU FOUNDATION SCHOOL OF ENGINEERING AND APPLIED SCIENCE

New York, NY

CONTACT Office of Financial Aid and Educational Financing, Columbia University, The Fu Foundation School of Engineering and Applied Science, 407 Lerner Hall, 1130 Amsterdam Avenue, New York, NY 10027, 212-854-3711. *Fax:* 212-854-8223. *E-mail:* ugrad-finaid@columbia.edu.

COLUMBUS COLLEGE OF ART & DESIGN

Columbus, OH

Tuition & fees: $21,346 **Average undergraduate aid package: $14,993**

ABOUT THE INSTITUTION Independent, coed. Awards: bachelor's degrees. 7 undergraduate majors. Total enrollment: 1,581. Undergraduates: 1,581. Freshmen: 350. Federal methodology is used as a basis for awarding need-based institutional aid.

UNDERGRADUATE EXPENSES for 2006–07 ***Application fee:*** $25. ***Comprehensive fee:*** $27,946 includes full-time tuition ($20,736), mandatory fees ($610), and room and board ($6600). Room and board charges vary according to housing facility and student level. ***Part-time tuition:*** $864 per credit. ***Part-time fees:*** $305 per term. Part-time tuition and fees vary according to course load. ***Payment plans:*** Installment, deferred payment.

FRESHMAN FINANCIAL AID (Fall 2005) 352 applied for aid; of those 86% were deemed to have need. 99% of freshmen with need received aid; of those 21% had need fully met. ***Average percent of need met:*** 67% (excluding resources awarded to replace EFC). ***Average financial aid package:*** $14,550 (excluding resources awarded to replace EFC). 20% of all full-time freshmen had no need and received non-need-based gift aid.

UNDERGRADUATE FINANCIAL AID (Fall 2005) 1,210 applied for aid; of those 88% were deemed to have need. 100% of undergraduates with need received aid; of those 20% had need fully met. ***Average percent of need met:*** 67% (excluding resources awarded to replace EFC). ***Average financial aid package:*** $14,993 (excluding resources awarded to replace EFC). 19% of all full-time undergraduates had no need and received non-need-based gift aid.

GIFT AID (NEED-BASED) ***Total amount:*** $11,058,112 (12% federal, 14% state, 70% institutional, 4% external sources). ***Receiving aid:*** Freshmen: 78% (299); All full-time undergraduates: 80% (1,057). ***Average award:*** Freshmen: $11,437; Undergraduates: $10,076. ***Scholarships, grants, and awards:*** Federal Pell, FSEOG, state, private, college/university gift aid from institutional funds.

GIFT AID (NON-NEED-BASED) ***Receiving aid:*** Freshmen: 8% (31); Undergraduates: 6% (73). ***Average award:*** Freshmen: $9305; Undergraduates: $10,251. ***Scholarships, grants, and awards by category:*** *Creative Arts/Performance:* 1,211 awards ($8,884,637 total): art/fine arts. *Special Characteristics:* 10 awards ($171,288 total): children of educators, children of faculty/staff, local/state students. ***Tuition waivers:*** Full or partial for employees or children of employees.

LOANS ***Student loans:*** $8,714,870 (74% need-based, 26% non-need-based). 92% of past graduating class borrowed through all loan programs. *Average indebtedness per student:* $31,288. ***Average need-based loan:*** Freshmen: $3833; Undergraduates: $5551. ***Parent loans:*** $1,964,673 (12% need-based, 88% non-need-based). ***Programs:*** FFEL (Subsidized and Unsubsidized Stafford, PLUS), Perkins, state.

WORK-STUDY ***Federal work-study:*** Total amount: $341,540; 148 jobs averaging $3250. ***State or other work-study/employment:*** 337 part-time jobs averaging $3000.

APPLYING FOR FINANCIAL AID ***Required financial aid forms:*** FAFSA, institution's own form, income tax forms, verification statement. ***Financial aid deadline (priority):*** 3/3. ***Notification date:*** 3/15. Students must reply within 2 weeks of notification.

CONTACT Mrs. Anna Schofield, Director of Financial Aid, Columbus College of Art & Design, 107 North Ninth Street, Columbus, OH 43215-1758, 614-224-9101 Ext. 3274 or toll-free 877-997-2223. *Fax:* 614-222-4034. *E-mail:* aschofield@ccad.edu.

COLUMBUS STATE UNIVERSITY

Columbus, GA

Tuition & fees (GA res): $3188 **Average undergraduate aid package: $3871**

ABOUT THE INSTITUTION State-supported, coed. Awards: associate, bachelor's, and master's degrees and post-bachelor's and post-master's certificates. 60 undergraduate majors. Total enrollment: 7,597. Undergraduates: 6,764. Freshmen: 1,167. Federal methodology is used as a basis for awarding need-based institutional aid.

UNDERGRADUATE EXPENSES for 2006–07 ***Application fee:*** $25. ***Tuition, state resident:*** full-time $2560; part-time $107 per semester hour. ***Tuition, nonresident:*** full-time $10,242; part-time $427 per semester hour. ***College room and board:*** $6284; ***Room only:*** $4320. Room and board charges vary according to board plan and location. ***Payment plan:*** Guaranteed tuition.

FRESHMAN FINANCIAL AID (Fall 2006, est.) 798 applied for aid; of those 61% were deemed to have need. 90% of freshmen with need received aid; of those 86% had need fully met. ***Average percent of need met:*** 61% (excluding resources awarded to replace EFC). ***Average financial aid package:*** $3524 (excluding resources awarded to replace EFC). 32% of all full-time freshmen had no need and received non-need-based gift aid.

UNDERGRADUATE FINANCIAL AID (Fall 2006, est.) 3,236 applied for aid; of those 71% were deemed to have need. 94% of undergraduates with need received aid; of those 68% had need fully met. ***Average percent of need met:*** 68% (excluding resources awarded to replace EFC). ***Average financial aid package:*** $3871 (excluding resources awarded to replace EFC). 25% of all full-time undergraduates had no need and received non-need-based gift aid.

GIFT AID (NEED-BASED) ***Total amount:*** $3,194,787 (96% federal, 2% institutional, 2% external sources). ***Receiving aid:*** Freshmen: 34% (353); All full-time undergraduates: 35% (1,616). ***Average award:*** Freshmen: $3298; Undergraduates: $3866. ***Scholarships, grants, and awards:*** Federal Pell, FSEOG, state, private, college/university gift aid from institutional funds.

GIFT AID (NON-NEED-BASED) ***Total amount:*** $4,347,037 (67% state, 19% institutional, 14% external sources). ***Receiving aid:*** Freshmen: 38% (389); Undergraduates: 36% (1,643). ***Average award:*** Freshmen: $1756; Undergraduates: $1724. ***Scholarships, grants, and awards by category:*** *Academic Interests/Achievement:* biological sciences, business, communication, computer science, education, English, general academic interests/achievements, health fields, humanities, international studies, military science, physical sciences. *Creative Arts/Performance:* art/fine arts, dance, music, performing arts, theater/drama. *Special Achievements/Activities:* cheerleading/drum major, community service, general special achievements/activities, leadership. ***Tuition waivers:*** Full or partial for employees or children of employees, senior citizens. ***ROTC:*** Army.

LOANS ***Student loans:*** $22,047,029 (50% need-based, 50% non-need-based). 73% of past graduating class borrowed through all loan programs. ***Average need-based loan:*** Freshmen: $2753; Undergraduates: $3656. ***Parent loans:*** $959,409 (100% need-based). ***Programs:*** Federal Direct (Subsidized and Unsubsidized Stafford, PLUS), Perkins, state, college/university.

WORK-STUDY ***Federal work-study:*** Total amount: $140,000; 80 jobs averaging $3000.

ATHLETIC AWARDS Total amount: $373,551 (100% non-need-based).

APPLYING FOR FINANCIAL AID ***Required financial aid form:*** FAFSA. ***Financial aid deadline (priority):*** 5/1. ***Notification date:*** Continuous beginning 5/1.

CONTACT Ms. Janis Bowles, Director of Financial Aid, Columbus State University, 4225 University Avenue, Columbus, GA 31907-5645, 706-568-2036 or toll-free 866-264-2035. *Fax:* 706-568-2230. *E-mail:* bowles_janis@colstate.edu.

CONCEPTION SEMINARY COLLEGE

Conception, MO

Tuition & fees: $13,024 **Average undergraduate aid package: $16,500**

ABOUT THE INSTITUTION Independent Roman Catholic, men only. Awards: bachelor's degrees. 1 undergraduate major. Total enrollment: 85. Undergraduates: 85. Freshmen: 13. Federal methodology is used as a basis for awarding need-based institutional aid.

UNDERGRADUATE EXPENSES for 2006–07 ***Comprehensive fee:*** $20,254 includes full-time tuition ($12,844), mandatory fees ($180), and room and board ($7230). ***College room only:*** $3228. ***Part-time tuition:*** $150 per credit. ***Payment plan:*** Installment.

FRESHMAN FINANCIAL AID (Fall 2005) 8 applied for aid; of those 88% were deemed to have need. 100% of freshmen with need received aid; of those 86% had need fully met. ***Average percent of need met:*** 94% (excluding resources awarded to replace EFC). ***Average financial aid package:*** $19,188 (excluding resources awarded to replace EFC). 15% of all full-time freshmen had no need and received non-need-based gift aid.

UNDERGRADUATE FINANCIAL AID (Fall 2005) 34 applied for aid; of those 88% were deemed to have need. 100% of undergraduates with need received aid; of those 53% had need fully met. ***Average percent of need met:*** 78% (excluding resources awarded to replace EFC). ***Average financial aid package:*** $16,500 (excluding resources awarded to replace EFC). 13% of all full-time undergraduates had no need and received non-need-based gift aid.

GIFT AID (NEED-BASED) ***Total amount:*** $95,044 (68% federal, 31% institutional, 1% external sources). ***Receiving aid:*** Freshmen: 15% (2); All full-time undergraduates: 17% (15). ***Average award:*** Freshmen: $6223; Undergraduates: $5825. ***Scholarships, grants, and awards:*** Federal Pell, FSEOG, private, college/university gift aid from institutional funds.

GIFT AID (NON-NEED-BASED) ***Total amount:*** $1,415,914 (2% institutional, 98% external sources). ***Receiving aid:*** Freshmen: 46% (6); Undergraduates: 17% (15). ***Average award:*** Freshmen: $450; Undergraduates: $1708. ***Scholarships, grants, and awards by category:*** *Academic Interests/Achievement:* 87 awards ($1,294,262 total): general academic interests/achievements. *Special Characteristics:* 87 awards ($1,294,262 total): religious affiliation. ***Tuition waivers:*** Full or partial for employees or children of employees.

LOANS ***Student loans:*** $92,998 (43% need-based, 57% non-need-based). 9% of past graduating class borrowed through all loan programs. *Average indebtedness per student:* $16,375. ***Average need-based loan:*** Undergraduates: $2254. ***Programs:*** FFEL (Subsidized and Unsubsidized Stafford, PLUS).

WORK-STUDY ***Federal work-study:*** Total amount: $9472; 13 jobs averaging $729. ***State or other work-study/employment:*** Total amount: $24,170 (100% non-need-based). 35 part-time jobs averaging $691.

APPLYING FOR FINANCIAL AID ***Required financial aid form:*** FAFSA. ***Financial aid deadline:*** Continuous. ***Notification date:*** Continuous beginning 6/1. Students must reply within 4 weeks of notification.

CONTACT Br. Justin Hernandez, PhD, Financial Aid Director, Conception Seminary College, PO Box 502, Conception, MO 64433-0502, 660-944-2851. *Fax:* 660-944-2829. *E-mail:* justin@conception.edu.

CONCORDIA COLLEGE

Selma, AL

CONTACT Financial Aid Office, Concordia College, 1804 Green Street, Selma, AL 36701, 334-874-5700. *Fax:* 334-874-3728.

CONCORDIA COLLEGE

Moorhead, MN

Tuition & fees: $20,980 **Average undergraduate aid package: $15,899**

ABOUT THE INSTITUTION Independent religious, coed. Awards: bachelor's and master's degrees. 81 undergraduate majors. Total enrollment: 2,764. Undergraduates: 2,759. Freshmen: 773. Federal methodology is used as a basis for awarding need-based institutional aid.

UNDERGRADUATE EXPENSES for 2006–07 ***Application fee:*** $20. ***Comprehensive fee:*** $26,070 includes full-time tuition ($20,816), mandatory fees ($164), and room and board ($5090). ***College room only:*** $2460. Room and board charges vary according to board plan and housing facility. ***Part-time tuition:*** $3273 per course. Part-time tuition and fees vary according to course load. ***Payment plan:*** Installment.

FRESHMAN FINANCIAL AID (Fall 2006, est.) 594 applied for aid; of those 80% were deemed to have need. 100% of freshmen with need received aid; of those 27% had need fully met. ***Average percent of need met:*** 90% (excluding resources awarded to replace EFC). ***Average financial aid package:*** $16,409 (excluding resources awarded to replace EFC). 27% of all full-time freshmen had no need and received non-need-based gift aid.

UNDERGRADUATE FINANCIAL AID (Fall 2006, est.) 2,232 applied for aid; of those 84% were deemed to have need. 100% of undergraduates with need received aid; of those 29% had need fully met. ***Average percent of need met:*** 86% (excluding resources awarded to replace EFC). ***Average financial aid package:*** $15,899 (excluding resources awarded to replace EFC). 28% of all full-time undergraduates had no need and received non-need-based gift aid.

GIFT AID (NEED-BASED) ***Total amount:*** $19,513,859 (12% federal, 14% state, 66% institutional, 8% external sources). ***Receiving aid:*** Freshmen: 66% (476); All full-time undergraduates: 68% (1,859). ***Average award:*** Freshmen: $11,755; Undergraduates: $10,465. ***Scholarships, grants, and awards:*** Federal Pell, FSEOG, state, private, college/university gift aid from institutional funds.

GIFT AID (NON-NEED-BASED) ***Total amount:*** $6,822,887 (81% institutional, 19% external sources). ***Receiving aid:*** Freshmen: 8% (59); Undergraduates: 7% (205). ***Average award:*** Freshmen: $11,518; Undergraduates: $10,705. ***Scholarships, grants, and awards by category:*** *Academic Interests/Achievement:* 2,229 awards ($12,243,232 total): general academic interests/achievements. *Creative Arts/Performance:* 197 awards ($422,917 total): debating, music, theater/drama. *Special Characteristics:* 168 awards ($1,528,213 total): international students, members of minority groups. ***Tuition waivers:*** Full or partial for employees or children of employees. ***ROTC:*** Army cooperative, Air Force cooperative.

LOANS ***Student loans:*** $15,517,964 (62% need-based, 38% non-need-based). 77% of past graduating class borrowed through all loan programs. *Average indebtedness per student:* $27,896. ***Average need-based loan:*** Freshmen: $3755; Undergraduates: $4808. ***Parent loans:*** $3,969,033 (21% need-based, 79% non-need-based). ***Programs:*** FFEL (Subsidized and Unsubsidized Stafford, PLUS), Perkins, state, college/university, alternative loans.

WORK-STUDY ***Federal work-study:*** Total amount: $660,518; 452 jobs averaging $1592. ***State or other work-study/employment:*** Total amount: $2,480,962 (66% need-based, 34% non-need-based). 1,034 part-time jobs averaging $977.

APPLYING FOR FINANCIAL AID ***Required financial aid forms:*** FAFSA, institution's own form. ***Financial aid deadline:*** Continuous. ***Notification date:*** Continuous beginning 3/1.

CONTACT Mrs. Jane Williams, Financial Aid Director, Concordia College, 901 South 8th Street, Moorhead, MN 56562, 218-299-3010 or toll-free 800-699-9897. *Fax:* 218-299-3025. *E-mail:* jwilliam@cord.edu.

CONCORDIA COLLEGE–NEW YORK

Bronxville, NY

CONTACT Mr. Ken Fick, Director of Financial Aid, Concordia College–New York, 171 White Plains Road, Bronxville, NY 10708, 914-337-9300 Ext. 2146 or toll-free 800-YES-COLLEGE. *Fax:* 914-395-4500. *E-mail:* financialaid@concordia-ny.edu.

CONCORDIA UNIVERSITY

Irvine, CA

Tuition & fees: $21,130 **Average undergraduate aid package: $20,751**

ABOUT THE INSTITUTION Independent religious, coed. Awards: bachelor's and master's degrees and post-bachelor's certificates (associate's degree for international students only). 23 undergraduate majors. Total enrollment: 2,317. Undergraduates: 1,348. Freshmen: 247. Federal methodology is used as a basis for awarding need-based institutional aid.

UNDERGRADUATE EXPENSES for 2006–07 ***Application fee:*** $50. ***Comprehensive fee:*** $28,190 includes full-time tuition ($21,130) and room and board ($7060). ***College room only:*** $4380. Room and board charges vary according to board plan. ***Part-time tuition:*** $600 per unit. Part-time tuition and fees vary according to course load. ***Payment plans:*** Installment, deferred payment.

FRESHMAN FINANCIAL AID (Fall 2006, est.) 240 applied for aid; of those 65% were deemed to have need. 99% of freshmen with need received aid; of those 17% had need fully met. ***Average percent of need met:*** 70% (excluding resources awarded to replace EFC). ***Average financial aid package:*** $22,802 (excluding resources awarded to replace EFC). 28% of all full-time freshmen had no need and received non-need-based gift aid.

UNDERGRADUATE FINANCIAL AID (Fall 2006, est.) 1,159 applied for aid; of those 70% were deemed to have need. 100% of undergraduates with need received aid; of those 21% had need fully met. ***Average percent of need met:*** 68% (excluding resources awarded to replace EFC). ***Average financial aid package:*** $20,751 (excluding resources awarded to replace EFC). 23% of all full-time undergraduates had no need and received non-need-based gift aid.

GIFT AID (NEED-BASED) ***Total amount:*** $8,334,643 (12% federal, 25% state, 62% institutional, 1% external sources). ***Receiving aid:*** Freshmen: 62% (152); All full-time undergraduates: 60% (750). ***Average award:*** Freshmen: $12,103; Undergraduates: $11,054. ***Scholarships, grants, and awards:*** Federal Pell, FSEOG, state, private, college/university gift aid from institutional funds.

GIFT AID (NON-NEED-BASED) ***Total amount:*** $2,376,134 (100% institutional). ***Receiving aid:*** Freshmen: 8% (20); Undergraduates: 8% (98). ***Average award:*** Freshmen: $7086; Undergraduates: $6513. ***Scholarships, grants, and awards by category:*** *Academic Interests/Achievement:* 890 awards ($3,774,634 total): general academic interests/achievements, religion/biblical studies, social sciences. *Creative Arts/Performance:* 133 awards ($293,532 total): applied art and design, music, theater/drama. *Special Achievements/Activities:* 33 awards ($109,750 total): general special achievements/activities. *Special Characteristics:* 301 awards ($944,951 total): children and siblings of alumni, children of faculty/staff, religious affiliation, siblings of current students. ***Tuition waivers:*** Full or partial for employees or children of employees.

LOANS ***Student loans:*** $5,769,734 (43% need-based, 57% non-need-based). 70% of past graduating class borrowed through all loan programs. *Average indebtedness per student:* $19,733. ***Average need-based loan:*** Freshmen: $2588; Undergraduates: $4089. ***Parent loans:*** $2,299,745 (100% non-need-based). ***Programs:*** FFEL (Subsidized and Unsubsidized Stafford, PLUS), alternative loan.

WORK-STUDY ***Federal work-study:*** Total amount: $101,346; 55 jobs averaging $1879. ***State or other work-study/employment:*** Total amount: $300,510 (100% need-based). 176 part-time jobs averaging $1674.

ATHLETIC AWARDS Total amount: $1,780,137 (50% need-based, 50% non-need-based).

APPLYING FOR FINANCIAL AID ***Required financial aid forms:*** FAFSA, institution's own form. ***Financial aid deadline:*** 4/1 (priority: 3/2). ***Notification date:*** Continuous. Students must reply within 4 weeks of notification.

CONTACT Lori McDonald, Director of Financial Aid, Concordia University, 1530 Concordia West, Irvine, CA 92612-3299, 949-854-8002 Ext. 1170 or toll-free 800-229-1200. *Fax:* 949-854-6709. *E-mail:* lori.mcdonald@cui.edu.

CONCORDIA UNIVERSITY

River Forest, IL

Tuition & fees: $21,320 **Average undergraduate aid package: $13,580**

ABOUT THE INSTITUTION Independent religious, coed. Awards: bachelor's, master's, and doctoral degrees and post-bachelor's and post-master's certificates. 54 undergraduate majors. Total enrollment: 3,710. Undergraduates: 1,074. Freshmen: 206. Federal methodology is used as a basis for awarding need-based institutional aid.

UNDERGRADUATE EXPENSES for 2007–08 ***Comprehensive fee:*** $28,312 includes full-time tuition ($20,900), mandatory fees ($420), and room and board ($6992). ***Part-time tuition:*** $650 per semester hour.

FRESHMAN FINANCIAL AID (Fall 2005) 197 applied for aid; of those 82% were deemed to have need. 100% of freshmen with need received aid; of those 38% had need fully met. ***Average percent of need met:*** 81% (excluding resources awarded to replace EFC). ***Average financial aid package:*** $13,800 (excluding resources awarded to replace EFC). 19% of all full-time freshmen had no need and received non-need-based gift aid.

UNDERGRADUATE FINANCIAL AID (Fall 2005) 872 applied for aid; of those 84% were deemed to have need. 100% of undergraduates with need received aid; of those 36% had need fully met. ***Average percent of need met:*** 80% (excluding resources awarded to replace EFC). ***Average financial aid package:*** $13,580 (excluding resources awarded to replace EFC). 19% of all full-time undergraduates had no need and received non-need-based gift aid.

GIFT AID (NEED-BASED) ***Total amount:*** $7,533,579 (14% federal, 18% state, 58% institutional, 10% external sources). ***Receiving aid:*** Freshmen: 72% (145); All full-time undergraduates: 69% (658). ***Average award:*** Freshmen: $10,518; Undergraduates: $8956. ***Scholarships, grants, and awards:*** Federal Pell, FSEOG, state, private, college/university gift aid from institutional funds.

GIFT AID (NON-NEED-BASED) ***Total amount:*** $2,849,425 (1% federal, 97% institutional, 2% external sources). ***Receiving aid:*** Freshmen: 29% (58); Undergraduates: 23% (219). ***Average award:*** Freshmen: $9192; Undergraduates: $8219. ***Scholarships, grants, and awards by category:*** *Academic Interests/Achievement:* biological sciences, business, communication, computer science, education, English, foreign languages, general academic interests/achievements, mathematics, religion/biblical studies. *Creative Arts/Performance:* art/fine arts, music. *Special Characteristics:* children and siblings of alumni, children of faculty/staff, international students, religious affiliation.

LOANS ***Student loans:*** $5,162,258 (94% need-based, 6% non-need-based). 87% of past graduating class borrowed through all loan programs. *Average indebtedness per student:* $15,426. ***Average need-based loan:*** Freshmen: $3200; Undergraduates: $3655. ***Parent loans:*** $938,352 (100% non-need-based). ***Programs:*** FFEL (Subsidized and Unsubsidized Stafford, PLUS), Perkins.

WORK-STUDY ***Federal work-study:*** Total amount: $110,966. ***State or other work-study/employment:*** Total amount: $55,990 (100% need-based).

APPLYING FOR FINANCIAL AID ***Required financial aid forms:*** FAFSA, institution's own form. ***Financial aid deadline:*** 4/1 (priority: 4/1). ***Notification date:*** Continuous beginning 2/24. Students must reply within 2 weeks of notification.

CONTACT Patricia Williamson, Director of Student Financial Planning, Concordia University, 7400 Augusta Street, River Forest, IL 60305-1499, 708-209-3261 or toll-free 800-285-2668. *Fax:* 708-209-3176. *E-mail:* patricia.williamson@cuchicago.edu.

CONCORDIA UNIVERSITY

Ann Arbor, MI

ABOUT THE INSTITUTION Independent religious, coed. Awards: associate, bachelor's, and master's degrees. 45 undergraduate majors. Total enrollment: 736. Undergraduates: 562. Freshmen: 112.

GIFT AID (NEED-BASED) ***Scholarships, grants, and awards:*** Federal Pell, FSEOG, state, private, college/university gift aid from institutional funds.

GIFT AID (NON-NEED-BASED) ***Scholarships, grants, and awards by category:*** *Academic Interests/Achievement:* general academic interests/achievements, religion/biblical studies. *Creative Arts/Performance:* art/fine arts, music, performing arts, theater/drama. *Special Achievements/Activities:* general special achievements/activities. *Special Characteristics:* children and siblings of alumni, children of faculty/staff, ethnic background, relatives of clergy, religious affiliation, siblings of current students.

LOANS ***Programs:*** FFEL (Subsidized and Unsubsidized Stafford, PLUS), Perkins.

WORK-STUDY ***Federal work-study:*** Total amount: $55,438; jobs available. ***State or other work-study/employment:*** Total amount: $17,903 (69% need-based, 31% non-need-based). Part-time jobs available.

APPLYING FOR FINANCIAL AID ***Required financial aid forms:*** FAFSA, institution's own form, tax returns.

CONTACT Sandy Tarbox, Financial Aid Office, Concordia University, 4090 Geddes Road, Ann Arbor, MI 48105-2797, 734-995-4622 or toll-free 800-253-0680. *Fax:* 734-995-4610. *E-mail:* sandy.tarbox@cuaa.edu.

CONCORDIA UNIVERSITY

Seward, NE

Tuition & fees: $19,790 **Average undergraduate aid package: $14,097**

ABOUT THE INSTITUTION Independent religious, coed. Awards: bachelor's and master's degrees. 73 undergraduate majors. Total enrollment: 1,251. Undergraduates: 1,107. Freshmen: 302. Federal methodology is used as a basis for awarding need-based institutional aid.

UNDERGRADUATE EXPENSES for 2007–08 ***Application fee:*** $25. ***Comprehensive fee:*** $24,860 includes full-time tuition ($19,670), mandatory fees ($120), and room and board ($5070). ***College room only:*** $2170. ***Part-time tuition:*** $610 per credit.

FRESHMAN FINANCIAL AID (Fall 2006, est.) 286 applied for aid; of those 84% were deemed to have need. 100% of freshmen with need received aid; of those 23% had need fully met. ***Average percent of need met:*** 74% (excluding resources awarded to replace EFC). ***Average financial aid package:*** $14,810 (excluding resources awarded to replace EFC). 21% of all full-time freshmen had no need and received non-need-based gift aid.

UNDERGRADUATE FINANCIAL AID (Fall 2006, est.) 941 applied for aid; of those 87% were deemed to have need. 100% of undergraduates with need received aid; of those 26% had need fully met. ***Average percent of need met:*** 74% (excluding resources awarded to replace EFC). ***Average financial aid package:*** $14,097 (excluding resources awarded to replace EFC). 20% of all full-time undergraduates had no need and received non-need-based gift aid.

GIFT AID (NEED-BASED) ***Total amount:*** $7,329,540 (12% federal, 1% state, 65% institutional, 22% external sources). ***Receiving aid:*** Freshmen: 78% (236); All full-time undergraduates: 76% (798). ***Average award:*** Freshmen: $9566; Undergraduates: $8935. ***Scholarships, grants, and awards:*** Federal Pell, FSEOG, state, private, college/university gift aid from institutional funds.

GIFT AID (NON-NEED-BASED) ***Total amount:*** $1,814,911 (100% institutional). ***Receiving aid:*** Freshmen: 14% (42); Undergraduates: 13% (135). ***Average award:*** Freshmen: $5847; Undergraduates: $5881. ***Scholarships, grants, and awards by category:*** *Academic Interests/Achievement:* biological sciences, business, communication, computer science, education, English, general academic interests/achievements, health fields, humanities, mathematics, physical sciences, premedicine, religion/biblical studies, social sciences. *Creative Arts/Performance:* art/fine arts, music, theater/drama. *Special Achievements/Activities:* memberships, religious involvement. *Special Characteristics:* children and siblings of alumni, children of educators, children of faculty/staff, international students, local/state students, members of minority groups. ***ROTC:*** Army cooperative, Air Force cooperative.

LOANS ***Student loans:*** $4,300,523 (54% need-based, 46% non-need-based). 76% of past graduating class borrowed through all loan programs. *Average indebtedness per student:* $18,923. ***Average need-based loan:*** Freshmen: $2921; Undergraduates: $3953. ***Parent loans:*** $2,842,450 (100% non-need-based). ***Programs:*** FFEL (Subsidized and Unsubsidized Stafford, PLUS), Perkins.

WORK-STUDY ***Federal work-study:*** Total amount: $101,788; 150 jobs averaging $679.

ATHLETIC AWARDS Total amount: $1,287,010 (73% need-based, 27% non-need-based).

APPLYING FOR FINANCIAL AID ***Required financial aid form:*** FAFSA. ***Financial aid deadline (priority):*** 3/1. ***Notification date:*** Continuous beginning 3/31. Students must reply within 4 weeks of notification.

CONTACT Mrs. Gloria F. Hennig, Director of Financial Aid, Concordia University, 800 North Columbia Avenue, Seward, NE 68434-1556, 800-535-5494. *Fax:* 402-643-3519. *E-mail:* gloria.hennig@cune.edu.

CONCORDIA UNIVERSITY

Portland, OR

CONTACT Mr. James W. Cullen, Director of Financial Aid, Concordia University, 2811 Northeast Holman Street, Portland, OR 97211-6099, 503-493-6508 or toll-free 800-321-9371. *Fax:* 503-280-8661. *E-mail:* jcullen@cu-portland.edu.

CONCORDIA UNIVERSITY AT AUSTIN

Austin, TX

Tuition & fees: $18,910 **Average undergraduate aid package: $15,201**

ABOUT THE INSTITUTION Independent religious, coed. Awards: associate, bachelor's, and master's degrees and post-bachelor's certificates. 21 undergraduate majors. Total enrollment: 1,254. Undergraduates: 1,164. Freshmen: 203. Federal methodology is used as a basis for awarding need-based institutional aid.

UNDERGRADUATE EXPENSES for 2007–08 ***Application fee:*** $25. ***Comprehensive fee:*** $26,210 includes full-time tuition ($18,600), mandatory fees ($310), and room and board ($7300). ***College room only:*** $4600. ***Part-time tuition:*** $620 per hour.

FRESHMAN FINANCIAL AID (Fall 2005) 183 applied for aid; of those 76% were deemed to have need. 100% of freshmen with need received aid; of those 27% had need fully met. ***Average percent of need met:*** 72% (excluding resources awarded to replace EFC). ***Average financial aid package:*** $14,034 (excluding resources awarded to replace EFC). 25% of all full-time freshmen had no need and received non-need-based gift aid.

UNDERGRADUATE FINANCIAL AID (Fall 2005) 637 applied for aid; of those 77% were deemed to have need. 100% of undergraduates with need received aid; of those 42% had need fully met. ***Average percent of need met:*** 80% (excluding resources awarded to replace EFC). ***Average financial aid package:*** $15,201 (excluding resources awarded to replace EFC). 17% of all full-time undergraduates had no need and received non-need-based gift aid.

GIFT AID (NEED-BASED) ***Total amount:*** $3,764,833 (22% federal, 25% state, 53% institutional). ***Receiving aid:*** Freshmen: 63% (123); All full-time undergraduates: 55% (401). ***Average award:*** Freshmen: $8884; Undergraduates: $8877. ***Scholarships, grants, and awards:*** Federal Pell, FSEOG, state, private, college/university gift aid from institutional funds, ACG/SMART Grants.

GIFT AID (NON-NEED-BASED) ***Total amount:*** $1,849,611 (2% federal, 8% state, 90% institutional). ***Receiving aid:*** Freshmen: 29% (57); Undergraduates: 28% (208). ***Average award:*** Freshmen: $7324; Undergraduates: $6858. ***Scholarships, grants, and awards by category:*** *Academic Interests/Achievement:* 282 awards ($1,557,540 total): biological sciences, business, education, general academic interests/achievements, international studies. *Creative Arts/Performance:* 10 awards ($24,225 total): music. *Special Achievements/Activities:* 151 awards ($838,487 total): leadership, religious involvement. *Special Characteristics:* 38 awards ($173,945 total): adult students, children and siblings of alumni, children of faculty/staff, religious affiliation. ***ROTC:*** Army cooperative, Air Force cooperative.

LOANS ***Student loans:*** $4,660,307 (100% need-based). 68% of past graduating class borrowed through all loan programs. *Average indebtedness per student:* $20,202. ***Average need-based loan:*** Freshmen: $4431; Undergraduates: $6452. ***Parent loans:*** $714,266 (100% need-based). ***Programs:*** FFEL (Subsidized and Unsubsidized Stafford, PLUS), state, private loans.

WORK-STUDY ***Federal work-study:*** Total amount: $78,831; 78 jobs averaging $1011. ***State or other work-study/employment:*** Total amount: $9924 (100% need-based). 6 part-time jobs averaging $1654.

APPLYING FOR FINANCIAL AID ***Required financial aid forms:*** FAFSA, institution's own form. ***Financial aid deadline (priority):*** 5/1. ***Notification date:*** Continuous beginning 2/15. Students must reply by 5/1 or within 2 weeks of notification.

CONTACT Cathy L. Schryer, Director of Student Financial Services, Concordia University at Austin, 3400 Interstate 35 North, Austin, TX 78705-2799, 512-486-1283 or toll-free 800-285-4252. *Fax:* 512-486-1350. *E-mail:* cathy.schryer@concordia.edu.

CONCORDIA UNIVERSITY, ST. PAUL

St. Paul, MN

Tuition & fees: $23,496 **Average undergraduate aid package: $13,035**

ABOUT THE INSTITUTION Independent religious, coed. Awards: associate, bachelor's, and master's degrees and post-bachelor's certificates. 43 undergraduate majors. Total enrollment: 2,046. Undergraduates: 1,683. Freshmen: 201. Federal methodology is used as a basis for awarding need-based institutional aid.

UNDERGRADUATE EXPENSES for 2007–08 ***Application fee:*** $30. ***Comprehensive fee:*** $30,272 includes full-time tuition ($23,496) and room and board ($6776). ***Part-time tuition:*** $490 per credit.

FRESHMAN FINANCIAL AID (Fall 2006, est.) 194 applied for aid; of those 89% were deemed to have need. 100% of freshmen with need received aid; of those 12% had need fully met. ***Average percent of need met:*** 76% (excluding resources awarded to replace EFC). ***Average financial aid package:*** $16,861 (excluding resources awarded to replace EFC). 11% of all full-time freshmen had no need and received non-need-based gift aid.

UNDERGRADUATE FINANCIAL AID (Fall 2006, est.) 1,083 applied for aid; of those 84% were deemed to have need. 100% of undergraduates with need received aid; of those 14% had need fully met. ***Average percent of need met:*** 64% (excluding resources awarded to replace EFC). ***Average financial aid package:*** $13,035 (excluding resources awarded to replace EFC). 8% of all full-time undergraduates had no need and received non-need-based gift aid.

GIFT AID (NEED-BASED) ***Total amount:*** $7,958,538 (15% federal, 16% state, 60% institutional, 9% external sources). ***Receiving aid:*** Freshmen: 86% (172); All full-time undergraduates: 55% (758). ***Average award:*** Freshmen: $13,297; Undergraduates: $10,438. ***Scholarships, grants, and awards:*** Federal Pell, FSEOG, state, private, college/university gift aid from institutional funds.

GIFT AID (NON-NEED-BASED) ***Total amount:*** $786,634 (2% state, 80% institutional, 18% external sources). ***Average award:*** Freshmen: $5548; Undergraduates: $5305. ***Scholarships, grants, and awards by category:*** *Academic Interests/Achievement:* 679 awards ($2,626,344 total): biological sciences, business, communication, English, general academic interests/achievements, mathematics, physical sciences, religion/biblical studies, social sciences. *Creative Arts/Performance:* 119 awards ($134,800 total): art/fine arts, journalism/publications, music, theater/drama. *Special Characteristics:* 223 awards ($367,707 total): children of faculty/staff, religious affiliation. ***ROTC:*** Army cooperative, Naval cooperative, Air Force cooperative.

LOANS ***Student loans:*** $8,662,483 (90% need-based, 10% non-need-based). 87% of past graduating class borrowed through all loan programs. *Average indebtedness per student:* $27,710. ***Average need-based loan:*** Freshmen: $3208; Undergraduates: $4203. ***Parent loans:*** $1,025,651 (84% need-based, 16% non-need-based). ***Programs:*** FFEL (Subsidized and Unsubsidized Stafford, PLUS), Perkins, state.

WORK-STUDY ***Federal work-study:*** Total amount: $229,849; 140 jobs averaging $1642. ***State or other work-study/employment:*** Total amount: $521,653 (100% need-based). 314 part-time jobs averaging $1661.

ATHLETIC AWARDS Total amount: $1,189,303 (76% need-based, 24% non-need-based).

APPLYING FOR FINANCIAL AID ***Required financial aid forms:*** FAFSA, institution's own form. ***Financial aid deadline (priority):*** 5/1. ***Notification date:*** Continuous. Students must reply within 3 weeks of notification.

CONTACT Brian Heinemann, Financial Aid Director, Concordia University, St. Paul, 275 North Syndicate Street, St. Paul, MN 55104-5494, 651-603-6300 or toll-free 800-333-4705. *Fax:* 651-641-8889. *E-mail:* heinemann@csp.edu.

CONCORDIA UNIVERSITY WISCONSIN

Mequon, WI

Tuition & fees: $18,140 **Average undergraduate aid package: $17,399**

ABOUT THE INSTITUTION Independent religious, coed. Awards: associate, bachelor's, master's, and doctoral degrees and post-bachelor's certificates. 62 undergraduate majors. Total enrollment: 5,574. Undergraduates: 3,782. Freshmen: 395. Federal methodology is used as a basis for awarding need-based institutional aid.

UNDERGRADUATE EXPENSES for 2006–07 ***Application fee:*** $35. ***Comprehensive fee:*** $25,000 includes full-time tuition ($18,050), mandatory fees ($90), and room and board ($6860). Full-time tuition and fees vary according to program. Room and board charges vary according to board plan. ***Part-time tuition:*** $752 per credit hour. Part-time tuition and fees vary according to class time and program. ***Payment plans:*** Guaranteed tuition, installment, deferred payment.

FRESHMAN FINANCIAL AID (Fall 2006, est.) 368 applied for aid; of those 82% were deemed to have need. 100% of freshmen with need received aid; of those 33% had need fully met. ***Average percent of need met:*** 77% (excluding resources awarded to replace EFC). ***Average financial aid package:*** $19,205 (excluding resources awarded to replace EFC). 17% of all full-time freshmen had no need and received non-need-based gift aid.

UNDERGRADUATE FINANCIAL AID (Fall 2006, est.) 1,953 applied for aid; of those 84% were deemed to have need. 99% of undergraduates with need received aid; of those 31% had need fully met. ***Average percent of need met:*** 70% (excluding resources awarded to replace EFC). ***Average financial aid package:*** $17,399 (excluding resources awarded to replace EFC). 12% of all full-time undergraduates had no need and received non-need-based gift aid.

GIFT AID (NEED-BASED) ***Total amount:*** $11,638,595 (18% federal, 8% state, 66% institutional, 8% external sources). ***Receiving aid:*** Freshmen: 73% (285); All full-time undergraduates: 62% (1,237). ***Average award:*** Freshmen: $10,404; Undergraduates: $8564. ***Scholarships, grants, and awards:*** Federal Pell, FSEOG, state, private, college/university gift aid from institutional funds.

GIFT AID (NON-NEED-BASED) ***Total amount:*** $3,783,198 (100% institutional). ***Receiving aid:*** Freshmen: 24% (95); Undergraduates: 20% (410). ***Average award:*** Freshmen: $8342; Undergraduates: $7362. ***Scholarships, grants, and awards by category:*** *Academic Interests/Achievement:* 1,950 awards ($1,865,231 total): general academic interests/achievements. *Creative Arts/Performance:* 52 awards ($49,150 total): music, performing arts. *Special Achievements/Activities:* 11 awards ($13,443 total): leadership. *Special Characteristics:* 544 awards ($10,413,306 total): children of faculty/staff, out-of-state students, religious affiliation. ***Tuition waivers:*** Full or partial for employees or children of employees.

LOANS ***Student loans:*** $19,723,570 (60% need-based, 40% non-need-based). 75% of past graduating class borrowed through all loan programs. *Average indebtedness per student:* $21,030. ***Average need-based loan:*** Freshmen: $4947; Undergraduates: $6394. ***Programs:*** Federal Direct (Subsidized and Unsubsidized Stafford, PLUS), FFEL (Subsidized and Unsubsidized Stafford, PLUS), Perkins, state.

WORK-STUDY ***Federal work-study:*** Total amount: $100,101; 82 jobs averaging $1700. ***State or other work-study/employment:*** 75 part-time jobs averaging $500.

APPLYING FOR FINANCIAL AID ***Required financial aid forms:*** FAFSA, institution's own form. ***Financial aid deadline (priority):*** 4/1. ***Notification date:*** Continuous beginning 1/15. Students must reply within 3 weeks of notification.

CONTACT Mr. Steven P. Taylor, Director of Financial Aid, Concordia University Wisconsin, 12800 North Lake Shore Drive, Mequon, WI 53097-2402, 262-243-4392 or toll-free 888-628-9472. *Fax:* 262-243-2636. *E-mail:* steve.taylor@cuw.edu.

CONCORD UNIVERSITY

Athens, WV

Tuition & fees (WV res): $4084 **Average undergraduate aid package: $7652**

ABOUT THE INSTITUTION State-supported, coed. Awards: associate, bachelor's, and master's degrees. 36 undergraduate majors. Total enrollment: 2,928. Undergraduates: 2,805. Freshmen: 603. Federal methodology is used as a basis for awarding need-based institutional aid.

UNDERGRADUATE EXPENSES for 2006–07 ***Tuition, state resident:*** full-time $4084; part-time $170 per credit hour. ***Tuition, nonresident:*** full-time $9218; part-time $385 per credit hour. Full-time tuition and fees vary according to course load. Part-time tuition and fees vary according to course load. ***College room and board:*** $6070; ***Room only:*** $3106. ***Payment plan:*** Installment.

FRESHMAN FINANCIAL AID (Fall 2005) 556 applied for aid; of those 77% were deemed to have need. 99% of freshmen with need received aid; of those 37% had need fully met. ***Average percent of need met:*** 100% (excluding resources awarded to replace EFC). ***Average financial aid package:*** $7384 (excluding resources awarded to replace EFC). 17% of all full-time freshmen had no need and received non-need-based gift aid.

UNDERGRADUATE FINANCIAL AID (Fall 2005) 1,959 applied for aid; of those 80% were deemed to have need. 99% of undergraduates with need received aid; of those 38% had need fully met. ***Average percent of need met:*** 97% (excluding resources awarded to replace EFC). ***Average financial aid package:*** $7652 (excluding resources awarded to replace EFC). 8% of all full-time undergraduates had no need and received non-need-based gift aid.

GIFT AID (NEED-BASED) ***Total amount:*** $4,671,964 (68% federal, 32% state). ***Receiving aid:*** Freshmen: 51% (305); All full-time undergraduates: 51% (1,170). ***Average award:*** Freshmen: $3898; Undergraduates: $4154. ***Scholarships, grants, and awards:*** Federal Pell, FSEOG, state, college/university gift aid from institutional funds.

GIFT AID (NON-NEED-BASED) ***Total amount:*** $4,629,267 (39% state, 47% institutional, 14% external sources). ***Receiving aid:*** Freshmen: 41% (246); Undergraduates: 25% (583). ***Average award:*** Freshmen: $2984; Undergraduates: $3179. ***Scholarships, grants, and awards by category:*** *Academic Interests/Achievement:* 596 awards ($1,288,569 total): business, communication, education, English, general academic interests/achievements, social sciences. *Creative Arts/Performance:* 66 awards ($133,500 total): art/fine arts, journalism/publications, music, theater/drama. *Special Achievements/Activities:* 281 awards ($134,295 total): community service, general special achievements/activities, leadership. ***Tuition waivers:*** Full or partial for adult students, senior citizens.

LOANS ***Student loans:*** $7,092,760 (93% need-based, 7% non-need-based). 79% of past graduating class borrowed through all loan programs. *Average indebtedness per student:* $12,989. ***Average need-based loan:*** Freshmen: $2465; Undergraduates: $3451. ***Parent loans:*** $1,004,859 (100% non-need-based). ***Programs:*** FFEL (Subsidized and Unsubsidized Stafford, PLUS), Perkins.

WORK-STUDY ***Federal work-study:*** Total amount: $491,923; 383 jobs averaging $1244. ***State or other work-study/employment:*** Total amount: $291,786 (100% non-need-based). 274 part-time jobs averaging $1003.

ATHLETIC AWARDS Total amount: $487,847 (100% non-need-based).

APPLYING FOR FINANCIAL AID ***Required financial aid forms:*** FAFSA, institution's own form, verification worksheet. ***Financial aid deadline (priority):*** 4/15. ***Notification date:*** Continuous. Students must reply within 2 weeks of notification.

CONTACT Patricia Harmon, Financial Aid Director, Concord University, PO Box 1000, Athens, WV 24712-1000, 304-384-6069 or toll-free 888-384-5249. *Fax:* 304-384-9044.

CONNECTICUT COLLEGE

New London, CT

Comprehensive fee: $44,240 **Average undergraduate aid package: $28,154**

ABOUT THE INSTITUTION Independent, coed. Awards: bachelor's and master's degrees. 56 undergraduate majors. Total enrollment: 1,886. Undergraduates: 1,872. Freshmen: 490. Both federal and institutional methodology are used as a basis for awarding need-based institutional aid.

UNDERGRADUATE EXPENSES for 2006–07 ***Application fee:*** $60. ***Comprehensive fee:*** $44,240. Full-time tuition and fees vary according to program. ***Part-time tuition:*** $1027 per credit hour. Part-time tuition and fees vary according to program. ***Payment plan:*** Installment.

FRESHMAN FINANCIAL AID (Fall 2006, est.) 263 applied for aid; of those 76% were deemed to have need. 100% of freshmen with need received aid; of those 100% had need fully met. ***Average percent of need met:*** 100% (excluding resources awarded to replace EFC). ***Average financial aid package:*** $27,578 (excluding resources awarded to replace EFC).

UNDERGRADUATE FINANCIAL AID (Fall 2006, est.) 888 applied for aid; of those 85% were deemed to have need. 100% of undergraduates with need received aid; of those 100% had need fully met. ***Average percent of need met:*** 100% (excluding resources awarded to replace EFC). ***Average financial aid package:*** $28,154 (excluding resources awarded to replace EFC).

GIFT AID (NEED-BASED) ***Total amount:*** $18,267,933 (4% federal, 3% state, 90% institutional, 3% external sources). ***Receiving aid:*** Freshmen: 37% (183); All full-time undergraduates: 36% (684). ***Average award:*** Freshmen: $25,966; Undergraduates: $26,024. ***Scholarships, grants, and awards:*** Federal Pell, FSEOG, state, college/university gift aid from institutional funds.

GIFT AID (NON-NEED-BASED) ***Total amount:*** $399,552 (100% external sources). ***Tuition waivers:*** Full or partial for employees or children of employees, senior citizens.

LOANS ***Student loans:*** $4,681,508 (52% need-based, 48% non-need-based). 38% of past graduating class borrowed through all loan programs. *Average indebtedness per student:* $22,160. ***Average need-based loan:*** Freshmen: $2933; Undergraduates: $4127. ***Parent loans:*** $4,955,741 (100% non-need-based). ***Programs:*** FFEL (Subsidized and Unsubsidized Stafford, PLUS), Perkins, college/university.

WORK-STUDY ***Federal work-study:*** Total amount: $834,606; 628 jobs averaging $1329. ***State or other work-study/employment:*** Total amount: $20,682 (100% need-based). 24 part-time jobs averaging $862.

APPLYING FOR FINANCIAL AID ***Required financial aid forms:*** FAFSA, CSS Financial Aid PROFILE, noncustodial (divorced/separated) parent's statement, business/farm supplement. ***Financial aid deadline:*** 2/1. ***Notification date:*** 4/1. Students must reply by 5/1 or within 2 weeks of notification.

CONTACT Ms. Elaine Solinga, Director of Financial Aid Services, Connecticut College, 270 Mohegan Avenue, New London, CT 06320-4196, 860-439-2058. *Fax:* 860-439-5357. *E-mail:* finaid@conncoll.edu.

CONSERVATORY OF MUSIC OF PUERTO RICO

San Juan, PR

CONTACT Mr. Jorge Medina, Director of Financial Aid, Conservatory of Music of Puerto Rico, 350 Rafael Lamar Street at FDR Avenue, San Juan, PR 00918, 787-751-0160 Ext. 230. *Fax:* 787-758-8268. *E-mail:* jmedina@cmpr.gobierno.pr.

CONVERSE COLLEGE

Spartanburg, SC

Tuition & fees: $22,234 **Average undergraduate aid package: $19,427**

ABOUT THE INSTITUTION Independent, undergraduate: women only; graduate: coed. Awards: bachelor's and master's degrees and post-master's certificates. 40 undergraduate majors. Total enrollment: 1,977. Undergraduates: 752. Freshmen: 162. Federal methodology is used as a basis for awarding need-based institutional aid.

UNDERGRADUATE EXPENSES for 2006–07 ***Application fee:*** $40. ***Comprehensive fee:*** $29,082 includes full-time tuition ($22,234) and room and board ($6848). ***Part-time tuition:*** $720 per credit hour. ***Part-time fees:*** $20 per term. ***Payment plan:*** Installment.

FRESHMAN FINANCIAL AID (Fall 2006, est.) 134 applied for aid; of those 83% were deemed to have need. 100% of freshmen with need received aid; of those 38% had need fully met. ***Average percent of need met:*** 88% (excluding resources awarded to replace EFC). ***Average financial aid package:*** $19,681 (excluding resources awarded to replace EFC). 29% of all full-time freshmen had no need and received non-need-based gift aid.

UNDERGRADUATE FINANCIAL AID (Fall 2006, est.) 446 applied for aid; of those 89% were deemed to have need. 100% of undergraduates with need received aid; of those 39% had need fully met. ***Average percent of need met:*** 87% (excluding resources awarded to replace EFC). ***Average financial aid package:*** $19,427 (excluding resources awarded to replace EFC). 30% of all full-time undergraduates had no need and received non-need-based gift aid.

GIFT AID (NEED-BASED) ***Total amount:*** $6,598,993 (10% federal, 22% state, 66% institutional, 2% external sources). ***Receiving aid:*** Freshmen: 69% (111); All full-time undergraduates: 68% (395). ***Average award:*** Freshmen: $16,853; Undergraduates: $16,419. ***Scholarships, grants, and awards:*** Federal Pell, FSEOG, state, private, college/university gift aid from institutional funds.

GIFT AID (NON-NEED-BASED) ***Total amount:*** $3,658,250 (22% state, 75% institutional, 3% external sources). ***Receiving aid:*** Freshmen: 22% (35); Undergraduates: 20% (119). ***Average award:*** Freshmen: $18,641; Undergraduates: $18,143. ***Scholarships, grants, and awards by category:*** *Academic Interests/Achievement:* 341 awards ($4,093,756 total): general academic interests/achievements. *Creative Arts/Performance:* 142 awards ($1,402,713 total): applied art and design, music, theater/drama. *Special Achievements/Activities:* 86 awards ($646,915 total): leadership. *Special Characteristics:* 60 awards ($111,592 total): children and siblings of alumni, children of faculty/staff. ***Tuition waivers:*** Full or partial for employees or children of employees, adult students, senior citizens. ***ROTC:*** Army cooperative.

LOANS ***Student loans:*** $2,844,467 (74% need-based, 26% non-need-based). 72% of past graduating class borrowed through all loan programs. *Average indebtedness per student:* $20,861. ***Average need-based loan:*** Freshmen: $3683; Undergraduates: $4190. ***Parent loans:*** $1,188,341 (14% need-based, 86% non-need-based). ***Programs:*** FFEL (Subsidized and Unsubsidized Stafford, PLUS), Perkins, state.

WORK-STUDY ***Federal work-study:*** Total amount: $215,900; 141 jobs averaging $1446. ***State or other work-study/employment:*** 60 part-time jobs averaging $1000.

ATHLETIC AWARDS Total amount: $316,151 (45% need-based, 55% non-need-based).

APPLYING FOR FINANCIAL AID ***Required financial aid form:*** FAFSA. ***Financial aid deadline (priority):*** 3/1. ***Notification date:*** Continuous beginning 3/15. Students must reply by 5/1 or within 2 weeks of notification.

CONTACT Ms. Margaret P. Collins, Director of Financial Assistance, Converse College, 580 East Main Street, Spartanburg, SC 29302-0006, 864-596-9019 or toll-free 800-766-1125. *Fax:* 864-596-9749. *E-mail:* peggy.collins@converse.edu.

COOPER UNION FOR THE ADVANCEMENT OF SCIENCE AND ART

New York, NY

Tuition & fees: $1550 **Average undergraduate aid package: $27,500**

ABOUT THE INSTITUTION Independent, coed. Awards: bachelor's degrees (also offers master's program primarily made up of currently-enrolled students). 8 undergraduate majors. Total enrollment: 968. Undergraduates: 920. Freshmen: 203. Both federal and institutional methodology are used as a basis for awarding need-based institutional aid.

UNDERGRADUATE EXPENSES for 2007–08 ***Application fee:*** $65. includes mandatory fees ($1550) and room and board ($13,500). ***College room only:*** $9500. All students are awarded full-tuition scholarships. Living expenses are subsidized by college-administered financial aid.

FRESHMAN FINANCIAL AID (Fall 2005) 155 applied for aid; of those 49% were deemed to have need. 100% of freshmen with need received aid; of those 75% had need fully met. ***Average percent of need met:*** 91% (excluding resources awarded to replace EFC). ***Average financial aid package:*** $27,500 (excluding resources awarded to replace EFC). 100% of all full-time freshmen had no need and received non-need-based gift aid.

UNDERGRADUATE FINANCIAL AID (Fall 2005) 300 applied for aid; of those 96% were deemed to have need. 100% of undergraduates with need received aid; of those 69% had need fully met. ***Average percent of need met:*** 93% (excluding resources awarded to replace EFC). ***Average financial aid package:*** $27,500 (excluding resources awarded to replace EFC). 100% of all full-time undergraduates had no need and received non-need-based gift aid.

GIFT AID (NEED-BASED) ***Total amount:*** $1,652,318 (29% federal, 27% state, 32% institutional, 12% external sources). ***Receiving aid:*** Freshmen: 34% (76); All full-time undergraduates: 31% (288). ***Average award:*** Freshmen: $3102; Undergraduates: $3115. ***Scholarships, grants, and awards:*** Federal Pell, FSEOG, state, private, college/university gift aid from institutional funds.

GIFT AID (NON-NEED-BASED) ***Total amount:*** $25,163,649 (100% institutional). ***Receiving aid:*** Freshmen: 34% (76); Undergraduates: 31% (288). ***Average award:*** Freshmen: $27,500; Undergraduates: $27,500. ***Scholarships, grants, and awards by category:*** *Academic Interests/Achievement:* 627 awards ($17,242,500 total): architecture, engineering/technologies. *Creative Arts/Performance:* 293 awards ($8,057,500 total): art/fine arts.

LOANS ***Student loans:*** $979,337 (84% need-based, 16% non-need-based). 30% of past graduating class borrowed through all loan programs. *Average indebtedness per student:* $3478. ***Average need-based loan:*** Freshmen: $2452; Undergraduates: $3437. ***Parent loans:*** $256,807 (60% need-based, 40% non-need-based). ***Programs:*** FFEL (Subsidized and Unsubsidized Stafford, PLUS), Perkins, college/university.

WORK-STUDY ***Federal work-study:*** Total amount: $47,223; 55 jobs averaging $859. ***State or other work-study/employment:*** Total amount: $469,797 (31% need-based, 69% non-need-based). 498 part-time jobs averaging $943.

APPLYING FOR FINANCIAL AID ***Required financial aid forms:*** FAFSA, CSS Financial Aid PROFILE. ***Financial aid deadline:*** 6/1 (priority: 4/15). ***Notification date:*** 6/1. Students must reply by 6/30 or within 2 weeks of notification.

CONTACT Ms. Mary Ruokonen, Director of Financial Aid, Cooper Union for the Advancement of Science and Art, 30 Cooper Square, New York, NY 10003-7120, 212-353-4130. *Fax:* 212-353-4343. *E-mail:* ruokon@cooper.edu.

COPPIN STATE UNIVERSITY

Baltimore, MD

Tuition & fees (MD res): $4910 **Average undergraduate aid package: $8593**

ABOUT THE INSTITUTION State-supported, coed. Awards: bachelor's and master's degrees. 26 undergraduate majors. Total enrollment: 4,003. Undergraduates: 3,092. Federal methodology is used as a basis for awarding need-based institutional aid.

UNDERGRADUATE EXPENSES for 2006–07 ***Application fee:*** $35. ***Tuition, state resident:*** full-time $3527; part-time $151 per credit. ***Tuition, nonresident:*** full-time $10,550; part-time $364 per credit. ***Required fees:*** full-time $1383; $180 per term part-time. Part-time tuition and fees vary according to course load. ***College room and board:*** $6511; ***Room only:*** $4082. Room and board charges vary according to board plan. ***Payment plan:*** Deferred payment.

FRESHMAN FINANCIAL AID (Fall 2006, est.) 412 applied for aid; of those 100% were deemed to have need. 90% of freshmen with need received aid; of those 12% had need fully met. ***Average percent of need met:*** 64% (excluding resources awarded to replace EFC). ***Average financial aid package:*** $7704 (excluding resources awarded to replace EFC). 1% of all full-time freshmen had no need and received non-need-based gift aid.

UNDERGRADUATE FINANCIAL AID (Fall 2006, est.) 2,156 applied for aid; of those 100% were deemed to have need. 93% of undergraduates with need received aid; of those 17% had need fully met. ***Average percent of need met:*** 72% (excluding resources awarded to replace EFC). ***Average financial aid package:*** $8593 (excluding resources awarded to replace EFC). 1% of all full-time undergraduates had no need and received non-need-based gift aid.

GIFT AID (NEED-BASED) ***Total amount:*** $39,396,612 (66% federal, 14% state, 20% institutional). ***Receiving aid:*** Freshmen: 62% (297); All full-time undergraduates: 64% (1,616). ***Average award:*** Freshmen: $5001; Undergraduates: $4836. ***Scholarships, grants, and awards:*** Federal Pell, FSEOG, state, private, college/university gift aid from institutional funds, Federal Nursing.

GIFT AID (NON-NEED-BASED) ***Total amount:*** $3,468,248 (77% state, 13% institutional, 10% external sources). ***Receiving aid:*** Freshmen: 10% (46); Undergraduates: 10% (243). ***Average award:*** Freshmen: $11,523; Undergraduates: $4169. ***Scholarships, grants, and awards by category:*** *Academic Interests/Achievement:* general academic interests/achievements. ***Tuition waivers:*** Full or partial for minority students, children of alumni, employees or children of employees, adult students, senior citizens. ***ROTC:*** Army.

LOANS ***Student loans:*** $21,341,255 (71% need-based, 29% non-need-based). 90% of past graduating class borrowed through all loan programs. *Average indebtedness per student:* $17,843. ***Average need-based loan:*** Freshmen: $3084; Undergraduates: $3875. ***Parent loans:*** $438,826 (100% non-need-based). ***Programs:*** Federal Direct (Subsidized and Unsubsidized Stafford), FFEL (PLUS), Perkins, alternative loans from lenders.

WORK-STUDY ***Federal work-study:*** Total amount: $2,831,564; 165 jobs averaging $2044.

ATHLETIC AWARDS Total amount: $657,733 (100% non-need-based).

APPLYING FOR FINANCIAL AID ***Required financial aid form:*** FAFSA. ***Financial aid deadline (priority):*** 3/1. ***Notification date:*** 4/15. Students must reply within 4 weeks of notification.

CONTACT Fay Tayree, Associate Director of Financial Aid, Coppin State University, 2500 West North Avenue, Baltimore, MD 21216-3698, 410-951-3636 or toll-free 800-635-3674. *Fax:* 410-951-3637. *E-mail:* ftayree@coppin.edu.

CORBAN COLLEGE

Salem, OR

Tuition & fees: $19,294 **Average undergraduate aid package: $12,148**

ABOUT THE INSTITUTION Independent religious, coed. Awards: associate, bachelor's, and master's degrees. 46 undergraduate majors. Total enrollment: 900. Undergraduates: 847. Freshmen: 188. Federal methodology is used as a basis for awarding need-based institutional aid.

UNDERGRADUATE EXPENSES for 2006–07 ***Application fee:*** $40. ***Comprehensive fee:*** $26,364 includes full-time tuition ($19,084), mandatory fees ($210), and room and board ($7070). Room and board charges vary according to board plan. ***Part-time tuition:*** $795 per credit. Part-time tuition and fees vary according to course load. ***Payment plan:*** Installment.

FRESHMAN FINANCIAL AID (Fall 2005) 188 applied for aid; of those 90% were deemed to have need. 100% of freshmen with need received aid; of those 10% had need fully met. ***Average percent of need met:*** 62% (excluding resources awarded to replace EFC). ***Average financial aid package:*** $11,964 (excluding resources awarded to replace EFC). 14% of all full-time freshmen had no need and received non-need-based gift aid.

UNDERGRADUATE FINANCIAL AID (Fall 2005) 611 applied for aid; of those 92% were deemed to have need. 100% of undergraduates with need received aid; of those 14% had need fully met. ***Average percent of need met:*** 62% (excluding resources awarded to replace EFC). ***Average financial aid package:*** $12,148 (excluding resources awarded to replace EFC). 14% of all full-time undergraduates had no need and received non-need-based gift aid.

GIFT AID (NEED-BASED) ***Total amount:*** $4,340,183 (13% federal, 5% state, 72% institutional, 10% external sources). ***Receiving aid:*** Freshmen: 85% (169); All full-time undergraduates: 86% (562). ***Average award:*** Freshmen: $9347; Undergraduates: $8797. ***Scholarships, grants, and awards:*** Federal Pell, FSEOG, state, private, college/university gift aid from institutional funds.

GIFT AID (NON-NEED-BASED) ***Total amount:*** $473,397 (83% institutional, 17% external sources). ***Receiving aid:*** Freshmen: 4% (8); Undergraduates: 7% (43). ***Average award:*** Freshmen: $9179; Undergraduates: $7729. ***Scholarships, grants, and awards by category:*** *Academic Interests/Achievement:* 413 awards ($1,529,760 total): general academic interests/achievements. *Creative Arts/Performance:* 26 awards ($37,525 total): music, performing arts. *Special Achievements/Activities:* 25 awards ($76,550 total): general special achievements/activities, hobbies/interests, leadership, memberships, religious involvement. *Special Characteristics:* 123 awards ($167,270 total): children and siblings of alumni, children of faculty/staff, international students, relatives of clergy, siblings of current students. ***Tuition waivers:*** Full or partial for employees or children of employees. ***ROTC:*** Army cooperative, Air Force cooperative.

LOANS ***Student loans:*** $4,145,883 (76% need-based, 24% non-need-based). 82% of past graduating class borrowed through all loan programs. *Average indebtedness per student:* $28,021. ***Average need-based loan:*** Freshmen: $2757;

Undergraduates: $3611. ***Parent loans:*** $804,287 (55% need-based, 45% non-need-based). ***Programs:*** Federal Direct (Subsidized and Unsubsidized Stafford, PLUS), Perkins, state, alternative loans.

WORK-STUDY ***Federal work-study:*** Total amount: $68,141; 150 jobs averaging $1109.

ATHLETIC AWARDS Total amount: $651,418 (79% need-based, 21% non-need-based).

APPLYING FOR FINANCIAL AID ***Required financial aid form:*** FAFSA. ***Financial aid deadline (priority):*** 2/15. ***Notification date:*** Continuous beginning 3/1. Students must reply within 4 weeks of notification.

CONTACT Nathan Warthan, Director of Financial Aid, Corban College, 5000 Deer Park Drive, SE, Salem, OR 97301-9392, 503-375-7006 or toll-free 800-845-3005 (out-of-state). *Fax:* 503-585-4316. *E-mail:* nwarthan@corban.edu.

CORCORAN COLLEGE OF ART AND DESIGN

Washington, DC

Tuition & fees: $24,489 **Average undergraduate aid package: $5394**

ABOUT THE INSTITUTION Independent, coed. Awards: associate, bachelor's, and master's degrees. 10 undergraduate majors. Total enrollment: 592. Undergraduates: 459. Freshmen: 39. Federal methodology is used as a basis for awarding need-based institutional aid.

UNDERGRADUATE EXPENSES for 2006–07 ***Application fee:*** $40. ***Comprehensive fee:*** $35,284 includes full-time tuition ($24,289), mandatory fees ($200), and room and board ($10,795). ***College room only:*** $8476. Full-time tuition and fees vary according to degree level. ***Part-time tuition:*** $810 per credit. ***Part-time fees:*** $200 per year. Part-time tuition and fees vary according to degree level. ***Payment plan:*** Installment.

FRESHMAN FINANCIAL AID (Fall 2005) 73 applied for aid; of those 100% were deemed to have need. 100% of freshmen with need received aid. ***Average percent of need met:*** 15% (excluding resources awarded to replace EFC). ***Average financial aid package:*** $5794 (excluding resources awarded to replace EFC). 5% of all full-time freshmen had no need and received non-need-based gift aid.

UNDERGRADUATE FINANCIAL AID (Fall 2005) 239 applied for aid; of those 100% were deemed to have need. 100% of undergraduates with need received aid. ***Average percent of need met:*** 26% (excluding resources awarded to replace EFC). ***Average financial aid package:*** $5394 (excluding resources awarded to replace EFC). 20% of all full-time undergraduates had no need and received non-need-based gift aid.

GIFT AID (NEED-BASED) ***Total amount:*** $608,134 (90% federal, 2% state, 8% institutional). ***Receiving aid:*** Freshmen: 73% (59); All full-time undergraduates: 60% (197). ***Average award:*** Freshmen: $4888; Undergraduates: $6508. ***Scholarships, grants, and awards:*** Federal Pell, FSEOG, state, college/university gift aid from institutional funds.

GIFT AID (NON-NEED-BASED) ***Total amount:*** $754,810 (1% state, 49% institutional, 50% external sources). ***Receiving aid:*** Freshmen: 44% (36); Undergraduates: 65% (212). ***Average award:*** Freshmen: $4800; Undergraduates: $4411. ***Scholarships, grants, and awards by category:*** *Academic Interests/Achievement:* 188 awards ($593,075 total): general academic interests/achievements. *Creative Arts/Performance:* 18 awards ($295,750 total): applied art and design. ***Tuition waivers:*** Full or partial for employees or children of employees.

LOANS ***Student loans:*** $2,921,493 (37% need-based, 63% non-need-based). 76% of past graduating class borrowed through all loan programs. *Average indebtedness per student:* $31,541. ***Average need-based loan:*** Freshmen: $3326; Undergraduates: $4439. ***Parent loans:*** $1,308,027 (100% non-need-based). ***Programs:*** FFEL (Subsidized and Unsubsidized Stafford, PLUS), Perkins.

WORK-STUDY ***Federal work-study:*** Total amount: $89,289; 128 jobs averaging $698.

APPLYING FOR FINANCIAL AID ***Required financial aid forms:*** FAFSA, institution's own form. ***Financial aid deadline (priority):*** 3/1. ***Notification date:*** Continuous beginning 4/1. Students must reply within 2 weeks of notification.

CONTACT Diane Morris, Financial Aid Director, Corcoran College of Art and Design, 500 17th Street, NW, Washington, DC 20006-4804, 202-639-1816 or toll-free 888-CORCORAN (out-of-state). *Fax:* 202-737-6921. *E-mail:* dmorris@corcoran.org.

CORNELL COLLEGE

Mount Vernon, IA

Tuition & fees: $24,800 **Average undergraduate aid package: $21,500**

ABOUT THE INSTITUTION Independent Methodist, coed. Awards: bachelor's degrees. 46 undergraduate majors. Total enrollment: 1,121. Undergraduates: 1,121. Freshmen: 248. Both federal and institutional methodology are used as a basis for awarding need-based institutional aid.

UNDERGRADUATE EXPENSES for 2006–07 ***Application fee:*** $30. ***Comprehensive fee:*** $31,460 includes full-time tuition ($24,620), mandatory fees ($180), and room and board ($6660). ***College room only:*** $3100. Full-time tuition and fees vary according to reciprocity agreements. Room and board charges vary according to board plan. ***Part-time tuition:*** $769 per credit hour. ***Part-time fees:*** $180 per year. Part-time tuition and fees vary according to course load. ***Payment plan:*** Installment.

FRESHMAN FINANCIAL AID (Fall 2006, est.) 212 applied for aid; of those 85% were deemed to have need. 100% of freshmen with need received aid; of those 77% had need fully met. ***Average percent of need met:*** 99% (excluding resources awarded to replace EFC). ***Average financial aid package:*** $22,080 (excluding resources awarded to replace EFC). 29% of all full-time freshmen had no need and received non-need-based gift aid.

UNDERGRADUATE FINANCIAL AID (Fall 2006, est.) 899 applied for aid; of those 89% were deemed to have need. 100% of undergraduates with need received aid; of those 45% had need fully met. ***Average percent of need met:*** 91% (excluding resources awarded to replace EFC). ***Average financial aid package:*** $21,500 (excluding resources awarded to replace EFC). 23% of all full-time undergraduates had no need and received non-need-based gift aid.

GIFT AID (NEED-BASED) ***Total amount:*** $13,590,691 (7% federal, 6% state, 84% institutional, 3% external sources). ***Receiving aid:*** Freshmen: 71% (181); All full-time undergraduates: 72% (800). ***Average award:*** Freshmen: $18,555; Undergraduates: $16,900. ***Scholarships, grants, and awards:*** Federal Pell, FSEOG, state, private, college/university gift aid from institutional funds.

GIFT AID (NON-NEED-BASED) ***Total amount:*** $3,059,752 (97% institutional, 3% external sources). ***Receiving aid:*** Freshmen: 62% (157); Undergraduates: 62% (691). ***Average award:*** Freshmen: $9985; Undergraduates: $11,345. ***Scholarships, grants, and awards by category:*** *Academic Interests/Achievement:* 396 awards ($5,087,203 total): general academic interests/achievements. *Creative Arts/Performance:* 126 awards ($760,565 total): art/fine arts, music, performing arts, theater/drama. *Special Achievements/Activities:* 321 awards ($2,181,956 total): community service, leadership, religious involvement. *Special Characteristics:* 197 awards ($2,231,295 total): children of educators, children of faculty/staff, ethnic background, international students, local/state students, members of minority groups, relatives of clergy, religious affiliation. ***Tuition waivers:*** Full or partial for employees or children of employees, adult students, senior citizens.

LOANS ***Student loans:*** $4,071,714 (69% need-based, 31% non-need-based). 66% of past graduating class borrowed through all loan programs. *Average indebtedness per student:* $24,622. ***Average need-based loan:*** Freshmen: $2850; Undergraduates: $3505. ***Parent loans:*** $979,822 (100% non-need-based). ***Programs:*** FFEL (Subsidized and Unsubsidized Stafford, PLUS), Perkins, state, college/university.

WORK-STUDY ***Federal work-study:*** Total amount: $488,023; 370 jobs averaging $850. ***State or other work-study/employment:*** Total amount: $212,485 (100% non-need-based). 264 part-time jobs averaging $800.

APPLYING FOR FINANCIAL AID ***Required financial aid forms:*** FAFSA, institution's own form, noncustodial (divorced/separated) parent's statement. ***Financial aid deadline:*** 3/1. ***Notification date:*** Continuous beginning 12/15. Students must reply by 5/1 or within 2 weeks of notification.

CONTACT Ms. Cindi P. Reints, Director of Financial Assistance, Cornell College, Wade House, 600 1st Street West, Mount Vernon, IA 52314-1098, 319-895-4216 or toll-free 800-747-1112. *Fax:* 319-895-4106. *E-mail:* creints@cornellcollege.edu.

CORNELL UNIVERSITY

Ithaca, NY

Tuition & fees: $32,981 **Average undergraduate aid package: $28,682**

ABOUT THE INSTITUTION Independent, coed. Awards: bachelor's, master's, doctoral, and first professional degrees. 156 undergraduate majors. Total enrollment: 19,639. Undergraduates: 13,562. Freshmen: 3,188. Institutional methodology is used as a basis for awarding need-based institutional aid.

UNDERGRADUATE EXPENSES for 2006–07 ***Application fee:*** $65. ***Comprehensive fee:*** $43,757 includes full-time tuition ($32,800), mandatory fees ($181), and room and board ($10,776). ***College room only:*** $6390. Room and board charges vary according to board plan and housing facility. ***Payment plan:*** Installment.

FRESHMAN FINANCIAL AID (Fall 2006, est.) 1933 applied for aid; of those 74% were deemed to have need. 100% of freshmen with need received aid; of those 100% had need fully met. ***Average percent of need met:*** 100% (excluding resources awarded to replace EFC). ***Average financial aid package:*** $28,929 (excluding resources awarded to replace EFC).

UNDERGRADUATE FINANCIAL AID (Fall 2006, est.) 6,993 applied for aid; of those 88% were deemed to have need. 100% of undergraduates with need received aid; of those 100% had need fully met. ***Average percent of need met:*** 100% (excluding resources awarded to replace EFC). ***Average financial aid package:*** $28,682 (excluding resources awarded to replace EFC).

GIFT AID (NEED-BASED) ***Total amount:*** $127,419,582 (7% federal, 5% state, 81% institutional, 7% external sources). ***Receiving aid:*** Freshmen: 42% (1,349); All full-time undergraduates: 43% (5,864). ***Average award:*** Freshmen: $22,992; Undergraduates: $21,184. ***Scholarships, grants, and awards:*** Federal Pell, FSEOG, state, private, college/university gift aid from institutional funds.

GIFT AID (NON-NEED-BASED) ***Tuition waivers:*** Full or partial for employees or children of employees. ***ROTC:*** Army, Air Force.

LOANS ***Student loans:*** $43,512,350 (100% need-based). 53% of past graduating class borrowed through all loan programs. *Average indebtedness per student:* $18,938. ***Average need-based loan:*** Freshmen: $5619; Undergraduates: $6529. ***Parent loans:*** $10,062,385 (100% need-based). ***Programs:*** Federal Direct (Subsidized and Unsubsidized Stafford, PLUS), FFEL (Subsidized and Unsubsidized Stafford, PLUS), Perkins, college/university, KeyBank Alternative Loans.

WORK-STUDY ***Federal work-study:*** Total amount: $8,117,258; 5,262 jobs averaging $1881. ***State or other work-study/employment:*** Total amount: $2,443,030 (100% need-based).

APPLYING FOR FINANCIAL AID ***Required financial aid forms:*** FAFSA, institution's own form, CSS Financial Aid PROFILE, noncustodial (divorced/separated) parent's statement, business/farm supplement, prior year tax return. ***Financial aid deadline:*** 2/11. ***Notification date:*** 4/1. Students must reply by 5/1 or within 2 weeks of notification.

CONTACT Mr. Thomas Keane, Director of Financial Aid and Student Employment, Cornell University, 410 Thurston Avenue, Ithaca, NY 14853-2488, 607-255-5147.

CORNERSTONE UNIVERSITY

Grand Rapids, MI

ABOUT THE INSTITUTION Independent nondenominational, coed. Awards: associate, bachelor's, master's, and first professional degrees. 52 undergraduate majors. Total enrollment: 2,509. Undergraduates: 1,981. Freshmen: 367.

GIFT AID (NEED-BASED) ***Scholarships, grants, and awards:*** Federal Pell, FSEOG, state, private, college/university gift aid from institutional funds.

GIFT AID (NON-NEED-BASED) ***Scholarships, grants, and awards by category:*** *Academic Interests/Achievement:* business, education, general academic interests/achievements, religion/biblical studies. *Creative Arts/Performance:* music. *Special Achievements/Activities:* leadership, religious involvement. *Special Characteristics:* children and siblings of alumni, children of faculty/staff, children of union members/company employees, ethnic background, general special characteristics, international students, members of minority groups, out-of-state students.

LOANS ***Programs:*** FFEL (Subsidized and Unsubsidized Stafford, PLUS), Perkins, state, college/university.

APPLYING FOR FINANCIAL AID ***Required financial aid form:*** FAFSA.

CONTACT Mr. Geoff Marsh, Director of Student Financial Services, Cornerstone University, 1001 East Beltline Avenue, NE, Grand Rapids, MI 49525-5897, 616-222-1424 or toll-free 800-787-9778. *Fax:* 616-222-1400. *E-mail:* geoff_a_marsh@cornerstone.edu.

CORNISH COLLEGE OF THE ARTS

Seattle, WA

CONTACT Sharron Starling, Office of Admissions, Cornish College of the Arts, 1000 Lenora Street, Seattle, WA 98121, 206-726-5017 or toll-free 800-726-ARTS. *Fax:* 206-720-1011. *E-mail:* admissions@cornish.edu.

COVENANT COLLEGE

Lookout Mountain, GA

CONTACT Mrs. Carolyn Hays, Assistant Director of Student Financial Planning, Covenant College, 14049 Scenic Highway, Lookout Mountain, GA 30750, 706-820-1560 Ext. 1150 or toll-free 888-451-2683. *Fax:* 706-820-2820. *E-mail:* hays@covenant.edu.

COX COLLEGE OF NURSING AND HEALTH SCIENCES

Springfield, MO

CONTACT Brenda Smith, Financial Aid Coordinator, Cox College of Nursing and Health Sciences, 1423 North Jefferson Avenue, Springfield, MO 65802, 417-269-3401 or toll-free 866-898-5355 (in-state). *Fax:* 417-269-3586. *E-mail:* bjsmit1@coxcollege.edu.

CREIGHTON UNIVERSITY

Omaha, NE

Tuition & fees: $25,126 **Average undergraduate aid package: $21,260**

ABOUT THE INSTITUTION Independent Roman Catholic (Jesuit), coed. Awards: associate, bachelor's, master's, doctoral, and first professional degrees. 46 undergraduate majors. Total enrollment: 6,981. Undergraduates: 4,075. Freshmen: 965. Federal methodology is used as a basis for awarding need-based institutional aid.

UNDERGRADUATE EXPENSES for 2006–07 ***Application fee:*** $40. ***Comprehensive fee:*** $32,968 includes full-time tuition ($24,166), mandatory fees ($960), and room and board ($7842). ***College room only:*** $4420. Full-time tuition and fees vary according to student level. Room and board charges vary according to board plan and housing facility. ***Part-time tuition:*** $756 per semester hour. ***Part-time fees:*** $78 per term. Part-time tuition and fees vary according to student level. ***Payment plan:*** Installment.

FRESHMAN FINANCIAL AID (Fall 2006, est.) 759 applied for aid; of those 77% were deemed to have need. 100% of freshmen with need received aid; of those 44% had need fully met. ***Average percent of need met:*** 92% (excluding resources awarded to replace EFC). ***Average financial aid package:*** $23,087 (excluding resources awarded to replace EFC). 32% of all full-time freshmen had no need and received non-need-based gift aid.

UNDERGRADUATE FINANCIAL AID (Fall 2006, est.) 2,525 applied for aid; of those 81% were deemed to have need. 99% of undergraduates with need received aid; of those 41% had need fully met. ***Average percent of need met:*** 91% (excluding resources awarded to replace EFC). ***Average financial aid package:*** $21,260 (excluding resources awarded to replace EFC). 33% of all full-time undergraduates had no need and received non-need-based gift aid.

GIFT AID (NEED-BASED) ***Total amount:*** $26,415,657 (10% federal, 1% state, 81% institutional, 8% external sources). ***Receiving aid:*** Freshmen: 60% (583); All full-time undergraduates: 52% (1,986). ***Average award:*** Freshmen: $14,853; Undergraduates: $13,066. ***Scholarships, grants, and awards:*** Federal Pell, FSEOG, state, private, college/university gift aid from institutional funds, Federal Nursing.

GIFT AID (NON-NEED-BASED) ***Total amount:*** $14,819,273 (94% institutional, 6% external sources). ***Receiving aid:*** Freshmen: 48% (459); Undergraduates: 38% (1,452). ***Average award:*** Freshmen: $9311; Undergraduates: $7406. ***Scholarships, grants, and awards by category:*** *Academic Interests/Achievement:* business, education, general academic interests/achievements, military science. *Creative Arts/Performance:* art/fine arts, creative writing, debating. *Special Characteristics:* children of faculty/staff, first-generation college students, handicapped students, local/state students, members of minority groups, religious affiliation, siblings of current students. ***Tuition waivers:*** Full or partial for employees or children of employees, adult students. ***ROTC:*** Army, Air Force cooperative.

LOANS ***Student loans:*** $18,315,158 (59% need-based, 41% non-need-based). 61% of past graduating class borrowed through all loan programs. *Average indebtedness per student:* $27,427. ***Average need-based loan:*** Freshmen: $5640; Undergraduates: $6701. ***Parent loans:*** $5,465,242 (100% non-need-based). ***Programs:*** FFEL (Subsidized and Unsubsidized Stafford, PLUS), Perkins, Federal Nursing, college/university.

WORK-STUDY ***Federal work-study:*** Total amount: $1,722,038; 1,045 jobs averaging $1648.

ATHLETIC AWARDS Total amount: $2,610,451 (26% need-based, 74% non-need-based).

APPLYING FOR FINANCIAL AID ***Required financial aid forms:*** FAFSA, institution's own form. ***Financial aid deadline (priority):*** 5/15. ***Notification date:*** Continuous. Students must reply within 4 weeks of notification.

CONTACT Sarah Sell, Assistant Director of Financial Aid, Creighton University, 2500 California Plaza, Omaha, NE 68178, 402-280-2731 or toll-free 800-282-5835. *Fax:* 402-280-2895. *E-mail:* sarahsell@creighton.edu.

CRICHTON COLLEGE

Memphis, TN

CONTACT Mrs. Dede Pirtle, Financial Aid Director, Crichton College, 255 North Highland, Memphis, TN 38111, 901-320-9700 Ext. 1030 or toll-free 800-960-9777. *Fax:* 901-320-9709. *E-mail:* dede@crichton.edu.

THE CRISWELL COLLEGE

Dallas, TX

CONTACT Kirk Spencer, Financial Aid Director, The Criswell College, 4010 Gaston Avenue, Dallas, TX 75246, 800-899-0012. *Fax:* 214-818-1310. *E-mail:* kspencer@criswell.edu.

CROSSROADS BIBLE COLLEGE

Indianapolis, IN

CONTACT Mrs. Phyllis Dodson, Director of Financial Aid, Crossroads Bible College, 601 North Shortridge Road, Indianapolis, IN 46219, 317-352-8736 Ext. 28 or toll-free 800-273-2224 Ext. 230. *Fax:* 317-352-9145.

CROSSROADS COLLEGE

Rochester, MN

CONTACT Polly Kellogg-Bradley, Director of Financial Aid, Crossroads College, 920 Mayowood Road SW, Rochester, MN 55902-2275, 507-535-3308 or toll-free 800-456-7651. *Fax:* 507-288-9046. *E-mail:* pkellogbradley@crossroadscollege.edu.

CROWN COLLEGE

St. Bonifacius, MN

Tuition & fees: $18,588 **Average undergraduate aid package: $12,720**

ABOUT THE INSTITUTION Independent religious, coed. Awards: associate, bachelor's, and master's degrees. 30 undergraduate majors. Total enrollment: 1,344. Undergraduates: 1,231. Freshmen: 156. Both federal and institutional methodology are used as a basis for awarding need-based institutional aid.

UNDERGRADUATE EXPENSES for 2007–08 ***Application fee:*** $35. ***Comprehensive fee:*** $25,510 includes full-time tuition ($18,588) and room and board ($6922). ***College room only:*** $3834. ***Part-time tuition:*** $777 per credit.

FRESHMAN FINANCIAL AID (Fall 2006, est.) 132 applied for aid; of those 87% were deemed to have need. 99% of freshmen with need received aid; of those 10% had need fully met. ***Average percent of need met:*** 59% (excluding resources awarded to replace EFC). ***Average financial aid package:*** $12,432 (excluding resources awarded to replace EFC). 10% of all full-time freshmen had no need and received non-need-based gift aid.

UNDERGRADUATE FINANCIAL AID (Fall 2006, est.) 560 applied for aid; of those 89% were deemed to have need. 99% of undergraduates with need received aid; of those 8% had need fully met. ***Average percent of need met:*** 61% (excluding resources awarded to replace EFC). ***Average financial aid package:*** $12,720 (excluding resources awarded to replace EFC). 7% of all full-time undergraduates had no need and received non-need-based gift aid.

GIFT AID (NEED-BASED) ***Total amount:*** $1,862,770 (40% federal, 39% state, 21% institutional). ***Receiving aid:*** Freshmen: 46% (72); All full-time undergraduates: 50% (356). ***Average award:*** Freshmen: $5224; Undergraduates: $5063. ***Scholarships, grants, and awards:*** Federal Pell, FSEOG, state, private, college/university gift aid from institutional funds.

GIFT AID (NON-NEED-BASED) ***Total amount:*** $2,651,685 (93% institutional, 7% external sources). ***Receiving aid:*** Freshmen: 70% (109); Undergraduates: 63% (452). ***Average award:*** Freshmen: $4080; Undergraduates: $3969. ***Scholarships, grants, and awards by category:*** *Academic Interests/Achievement:* 450 awards ($670,884 total): general academic interests/achievements. *Creative Arts/Performance:* 28 awards ($18,618 total): music. *Special Achievements/Activities:* 87 awards ($450,211 total): leadership. *Special Characteristics:* 141 awards ($515,279 total): children and siblings of alumni, children of faculty/staff, international students, members of minority groups, relatives of clergy, siblings of current students.

LOANS ***Student loans:*** $4,055,207 (46% need-based, 54% non-need-based). 88% of past graduating class borrowed through all loan programs. *Average indebtedness per student:* $30,444. ***Average need-based loan:*** Freshmen: $3355; Undergraduates: $4448. ***Parent loans:*** $906,980 (100% non-need-based). ***Programs:*** FFEL (Subsidized and Unsubsidized Stafford, PLUS), Perkins, state, SELF Loans, CitiAssist Loans, Signature Loans, Bremer Education Loans, U.S. Bank No Fee Educational Loans, Wells Fargo.

WORK-STUDY ***Federal work-study:*** Total amount: $401,371; 178 jobs averaging $2255. ***State or other work-study/employment:*** Total amount: $44,369 (100% need-based). 12 part-time jobs averaging $3697.

APPLYING FOR FINANCIAL AID ***Required financial aid forms:*** FAFSA, institution's own form. ***Financial aid deadline:*** 8/1 (priority: 4/5). ***Notification date:*** Continuous beginning 4/1. Students must reply within 3 weeks of notification.

CONTACT Cheryl Fernandez, Director of Financial Aid, Crown College, 8700 College View Drive, St. Bonifacius, MN 55375-9001, 952-446-4177 or toll-free 800-68-CROWN. *Fax:* 952-446-4178. *E-mail:* finaid@crown.edu.

THE CULINARY INSTITUTE OF AMERICA

Hyde Park, NY

Tuition & fees: $21,280 **Average undergraduate aid package: $11,507**

ABOUT THE INSTITUTION Independent, coed. Awards: bachelor's degrees. 2 undergraduate majors. Total enrollment: 2,742. Undergraduates: 2,742. Freshmen: 566. Federal methodology is used as a basis for awarding need-based institutional aid.

UNDERGRADUATE EXPENSES for 2006–07 ***Application fee:*** $30. ***Comprehensive fee:*** $28,450 includes full-time tuition ($20,300), mandatory fees ($980), and room and board ($7170). Full-time tuition and fees vary according to degree level. Room and board charges vary according to housing facility. ***Payment plan:*** Installment.

UNDERGRADUATE FINANCIAL AID (Fall 2005) 2,604 applied for aid; of those 90% were deemed to have need. 97% of undergraduates with need received aid; of those 5% had need fully met. ***Average percent of need met:*** 42% (excluding resources awarded to replace EFC). ***Average financial aid package:*** $11,507 (excluding resources awarded to replace EFC). 15% of all full-time undergraduates had no need and received non-need-based gift aid.

GIFT AID (NEED-BASED) ***Total amount:*** $11,904,229 (22% federal, 8% state, 65% institutional, 5% external sources). ***Receiving aid:*** All full-time undergraduates: 78% (2,023). ***Average award:*** Undergraduates: $3529. ***Scholarships, grants, and awards:*** Federal Pell, FSEOG, state, private, college/university gift aid from institutional funds.

GIFT AID (NON-NEED-BASED) ***Total amount:*** $2,869,897 (1% federal, 2% state, 97% institutional). ***Receiving aid:*** Undergraduates: 38% (1,000). ***Average award:*** Undergraduates: $2500. ***Scholarships, grants, and awards by category:*** *Academic Interests/Achievement:* 513 awards ($1,000,000 total): general academic interests/achievements. *Creative Arts/Performance:* 11 awards ($75,000 total): general creative arts/performance. *Special Achievements/Activities:* 10 awards ($50,000 total): general special achievements/activities. *Special Characteristics:* adult students, children and siblings of alumni, children of faculty/staff, general special characteristics, handicapped students, international students, members of minority groups, veterans. ***Tuition waivers:*** Full or partial for employees or children of employees.

LOANS ***Student loans:*** $29,990,114 (77% need-based, 23% non-need-based). 92% of past graduating class borrowed through all loan programs. *Average indebtedness per student:* $18,000. ***Average need-based loan:*** Undergraduates: $3495. ***Parent loans:*** $6,853,060 (100% non-need-based). ***Programs:*** FFEL (Subsidized and Unsubsidized Stafford, PLUS), Perkins, alternative loans.

WORK-STUDY ***Federal work-study:*** Total amount: $391,562; 900 jobs averaging $435.

APPLYING FOR FINANCIAL AID ***Required financial aid form:*** FAFSA. ***Financial aid deadline:*** 2/15. ***Notification date:*** Continuous beginning 4/15. Students must reply within 2 weeks of notification.

CONTACT Patricia A. Arcuri, Director of Financial Aid, The Culinary Institute of America, 1946 Campus Drive, Hyde Park, NY 12538-1499, 845-451-1243 or toll-free 800-CULINARY. *Fax:* 845-905-4030. *E-mail:* p_arcuri@culinary.edu.

CULVER-STOCKTON COLLEGE

Canton, MO

Tuition & fees: $16,600 **Average undergraduate aid package: $12,632**

ABOUT THE INSTITUTION Independent religious, coed. Awards: bachelor's degrees. 29 undergraduate majors. Total enrollment: 869. Undergraduates: 869. Freshmen: 212. Federal methodology is used as a basis for awarding need-based institutional aid.

UNDERGRADUATE EXPENSES for 2007–08 ***Application fee:*** $25. ***Comprehensive fee:*** $23,450 includes full-time tuition ($16,600) and room and board ($6850). ***College room only:*** $3100. ***Part-time tuition:*** $450 per credit hour. ***Part-time fees:*** $125 per term.

FRESHMAN FINANCIAL AID (Fall 2006, est.) 207 applied for aid; of those 88% were deemed to have need. 100% of freshmen with need received aid; of those 15% had need fully met. ***Average percent of need met:*** 72% (excluding resources awarded to replace EFC). ***Average financial aid package:*** $12,960 (excluding resources awarded to replace EFC). 13% of all full-time freshmen had no need and received non-need-based gift aid.

UNDERGRADUATE FINANCIAL AID (Fall 2006, est.) 754 applied for aid; of those 89% were deemed to have need. 100% of undergraduates with need received aid; of those 23% had need fully met. ***Average percent of need met:*** 73% (excluding resources awarded to replace EFC). ***Average financial aid package:*** $12,632 (excluding resources awarded to replace EFC). 11% of all full-time undergraduates had no need and received non-need-based gift aid.

GIFT AID (NEED-BASED) ***Total amount:*** $4,881,635 (18% federal, 7% state, 72% institutional, 3% external sources). ***Receiving aid:*** Freshmen: 86% (182); All full-time undergraduates: 87% (666). ***Average award:*** Freshmen: $9791; Undergraduates: $9012. ***Scholarships, grants, and awards:*** Federal Pell, FSEOG, state, private, college/university gift aid from institutional funds.

GIFT AID (NON-NEED-BASED) ***Total amount:*** $738,663 (1% state, 85% institutional, 14% external sources). ***Receiving aid:*** Freshmen: 9% (19); Undergraduates: 11% (86). ***Average award:*** Freshmen: $12,078; Undergraduates: $12,025. ***Scholarships, grants, and awards by category:*** *Academic Interests/Achievement:* 415 awards ($2,100,126 total): general academic interests/achievements, international studies. *Creative Arts/Performance:* 165 awards ($337,975 total): art/fine arts, debating, music, theater/drama. *Special Achievements/Activities:* 18 awards ($12,000 total): cheerleading/drum major, general special achievements/activities, leadership. *Special Characteristics:* 105 awards ($362,510 total): children and siblings of alumni, children of faculty/staff, international students, local/state students, religious affiliation.

LOANS ***Student loans:*** $5,026,755 (71% need-based, 29% non-need-based). 85% of past graduating class borrowed through all loan programs. *Average indebtedness per student:* $17,695. ***Average need-based loan:*** Freshmen: $3094; Undergraduates: $3958. ***Parent loans:*** $1,726,134 (40% need-based, 60% non-need-based). ***Programs:*** Federal Direct (Subsidized and Unsubsidized Stafford, PLUS), Perkins, Federal Nursing, state, college/university.

WORK-STUDY ***Federal work-study:*** Total amount: $76,307; 107 jobs averaging $1149. ***State or other work-study/employment:*** Total amount: $163,856 (28% need-based, 72% non-need-based). 92 part-time jobs averaging $1408.

ATHLETIC AWARDS Total amount: $1,315,400 (77% need-based, 23% non-need-based).

APPLYING FOR FINANCIAL AID ***Required financial aid form:*** FAFSA. ***Financial aid deadline:*** 6/15 (priority: 4/1). ***Notification date:*** Continuous beginning 2/15. Students must reply within 2 weeks of notification.

CONTACT Ms. Tina M. Wiseman, Director of Financial Aid, Culver-Stockton College, One College Hill, Canton, MO 63435, 573-288-63047 Ext. 6306 or toll-free 800-537-1883. *Fax:* 573-288-6308. *E-mail:* twiseman@culver.edu.

CUMBERLAND UNIVERSITY

Lebanon, TN

Tuition & fees: $15,510 **Average undergraduate aid package: $11,409**

ABOUT THE INSTITUTION Independent, coed. Awards: associate, bachelor's, and master's degrees. 37 undergraduate majors. Total enrollment: 1,345. Undergraduates: 1,037. Freshmen: 209. Both federal and institutional methodology are used as a basis for awarding need-based institutional aid.

UNDERGRADUATE EXPENSES for 2007–08 ***Application fee:*** $25. ***Comprehensive fee:*** $20,823 includes full-time tuition ($14,710), mandatory fees ($800), and room and board ($5313). ***College room only:*** $2174. ***Part-time tuition:*** $613 per hour. ***Part-time fees:*** $250 per term.

FRESHMAN FINANCIAL AID (Fall 2006, est.) 179 applied for aid; of those 83% were deemed to have need. 99% of freshmen with need received aid; of those 18% had need fully met. ***Average percent of need met:*** 57% (excluding resources awarded to replace EFC). ***Average financial aid package:*** $11,755 (excluding resources awarded to replace EFC). 19% of all full-time freshmen had no need and received non-need-based gift aid.

UNDERGRADUATE FINANCIAL AID (Fall 2006, est.) 800 applied for aid; of those 86% were deemed to have need. 99% of undergraduates with need received aid; of those 17% had need fully met. ***Average percent of need met:*** 59% (excluding resources awarded to replace EFC). ***Average financial aid package:*** $11,409 (excluding resources awarded to replace EFC). 16% of all full-time undergraduates had no need and received non-need-based gift aid.

GIFT AID (NEED-BASED) ***Total amount:*** $1,737,533 (65% federal, 35% state). ***Receiving aid:*** Freshmen: 39% (73); All full-time undergraduates: 35% (304). ***Average award:*** Freshmen: $5090; Undergraduates: $5375. ***Scholarships, grants, and awards:*** Federal Pell, FSEOG, state, private, college/university gift aid from institutional funds.

GIFT AID (NON-NEED-BASED) ***Total amount:*** $3,749,940 (31% state, 59% institutional, 10% external sources). ***Receiving aid:*** Freshmen: 75% (141); Undergraduates: 63% (552). ***Average award:*** Freshmen: $7910; Undergraduates: $7717. ***Scholarships, grants, and awards by category:*** *Academic Interests/Achievement:* 464 awards ($1,171,569 total): general academic interests/achievements. *Creative Arts/Performance:* 115 awards ($368,565 total): art/fine arts, music, performing arts, theater/drama. *Special Achievements/Activities:* 14 awards ($21,750 total): leadership. *Special Characteristics:* 6 awards ($67,925 total): children of faculty/staff. ***ROTC:*** Army.

LOANS ***Student loans:*** $3,724,097 (44% need-based, 56% non-need-based). 68% of past graduating class borrowed through all loan programs. *Average indebtedness per student:* $21,562. ***Average need-based loan:*** Freshmen: $2245; Undergraduates: $3757. ***Parent loans:*** $959,528 (100% non-need-based). ***Programs:*** FFEL (Subsidized and Unsubsidized Stafford, PLUS), Perkins, alternative loans.

WORK-STUDY ***Federal work-study:*** Total amount: $90,463; 120 jobs averaging $750. ***State or other work-study/employment:*** Total amount: $12,464 (100% non-need-based). 16 part-time jobs averaging $750.

ATHLETIC AWARDS Total amount: $2,758,997 (100% non-need-based).

APPLYING FOR FINANCIAL AID ***Required financial aid form:*** FAFSA. ***Financial aid deadline (priority):*** 2/15. ***Notification date:*** Continuous beginning 3/1. Students must reply within 2 weeks of notification.

CONTACT Ms. Beatrice LaChance, Director of Student Financial Services, Cumberland University, One Cumberland Square, Lebanon, TN 37087-3554, 615-444-2562 Ext. 1244 or toll-free 800-467-0562. *Fax:* 615-443-8424. *E-mail:* lvaughan@cumberland.edu.

CURRY COLLEGE

Milton, MA

Tuition & fees: $24,300 **Average undergraduate aid package: $15,183**

ABOUT THE INSTITUTION Independent, coed. Awards: bachelor's and master's degrees. 28 undergraduate majors. Total enrollment: 3,073. Undergraduates: 2,765. Freshmen: 586. Federal methodology is used as a basis for awarding need-based institutional aid.

UNDERGRADUATE EXPENSES for 2006–07 ***Application fee:*** $40. ***Comprehensive fee:*** $33,940 includes full-time tuition ($23,400), mandatory fees ($900), and room and board ($9640). ***College room only:*** $5640.

FRESHMAN FINANCIAL AID (Fall 2006, est.) 413 applied for aid; of those 99% were deemed to have need. 100% of freshmen with need received aid; of those 5% had need fully met. ***Average percent of need met:*** 64% (excluding resources awarded to replace EFC). ***Average financial aid package:*** $15,231 (excluding resources awarded to replace EFC). 4% of all full-time freshmen had no need and received non-need-based gift aid.

UNDERGRADUATE FINANCIAL AID (Fall 2006, est.) 1,367 applied for aid; of those 99% were deemed to have need. 100% of undergraduates with need received aid; of those 5% had need fully met. ***Average percent of need met:*** 66% (excluding resources awarded to replace EFC). ***Average financial aid package:*** $15,183 (excluding resources awarded to replace EFC). 2% of all full-time undergraduates had no need and received non-need-based gift aid.

GIFT AID (NEED-BASED) ***Total amount:*** $14,023,728 (12% federal, 7% state, 78% institutional, 3% external sources). ***Receiving aid:*** Freshmen: 67% (382); All full-time undergraduates: 61% (1,224). ***Average award:*** Freshmen: $11,009; Undergraduates: $10,463. ***Scholarships, grants, and awards:*** Federal Pell, FSEOG, state, private, college/university gift aid from institutional funds.

GIFT AID (NON-NEED-BASED) ***Total amount:*** $351,402 (58% institutional, 42% external sources). ***Receiving aid:*** Freshmen: 2; Undergraduates: 4. ***Average award:*** Freshmen: $3220; Undergraduates: $4946. ***Scholarships, grants, and awards by category:*** *Academic Interests/Achievement:* general academic interests/achievements. *Special Achievements/Activities:* leadership. ***ROTC:*** Army cooperative.

LOANS ***Student loans:*** $14,535,153 (36% need-based, 64% non-need-based). 58% of past graduating class borrowed through all loan programs. *Average indebtedness per student:* $27,145. ***Average need-based loan:*** Freshmen: $2629; Undergraduates: $3766. ***Parent loans:*** $5,398,955 (100% non-need-based). ***Programs:*** FFEL (Subsidized and Unsubsidized Stafford, PLUS), Perkins, state.

WORK-STUDY ***Federal work-study:*** Total amount: $798,797; jobs available. ***State or other work-study/employment:*** Total amount: $1000 (100% non-need-based).

APPLYING FOR FINANCIAL AID ***Required financial aid form:*** FAFSA. ***Financial aid deadline (priority):*** 3/1. ***Notification date:*** Continuous beginning 3/1.

CONTACT Stephanny Elias, Director of Student Financial Services, Curry College, 1071 Blue Hill Avenue, Milton, MA 02186-2395, 617-333-2354 or toll-free 800-669-0686. *Fax:* 617-333-2915. *E-mail:* fin-aid@curry.edu.

THE CURTIS INSTITUTE OF MUSIC

Philadelphia, PA

Tuition & fees: N/R **Average undergraduate aid package: $11,189**

ABOUT THE INSTITUTION Independent, coed. Awards: bachelor's and master's degrees. 5 undergraduate majors. Total enrollment: 160. Undergraduates: 144. Both federal and institutional methodology are used as a basis for awarding need-based institutional aid.

FRESHMAN FINANCIAL AID (Fall 2006, est.) 11 applied for aid; of those 100% were deemed to have need. 100% of freshmen with need received aid; of those 18% had need fully met. ***Average percent of need met:*** 76% (excluding resources awarded to replace EFC). ***Average financial aid package:*** $8496 (excluding resources awarded to replace EFC).

UNDERGRADUATE FINANCIAL AID (Fall 2006, est.) 60 applied for aid; of those 100% were deemed to have need. 100% of undergraduates with need received aid; of those 33% had need fully met. ***Average percent of need met:*** 90% (excluding resources awarded to replace EFC). ***Average financial aid package:*** $11,189 (excluding resources awarded to replace EFC).

GIFT AID (NEED-BASED) ***Total amount:*** $250,993 (13% federal, 81% institutional, 6% external sources). ***Receiving aid:*** Freshmen: 60% (9); All full-time undergraduates: 53% (46). ***Average award:*** Freshmen: $4368; Undergraduates: $5264. ***Scholarships, grants, and awards:*** Federal Pell, college/university gift aid from institutional funds.

LOANS ***Student loans:*** $252,625 (100% need-based). 52% of past graduating class borrowed through all loan programs. *Average indebtedness per student:* $18,192. ***Average need-based loan:*** Freshmen: $2625; Undergraduates: $4593. ***Programs:*** FFEL (Subsidized and Unsubsidized Stafford, PLUS), TERI Loans.

WORK-STUDY ***State or other work-study/employment:*** Total amount: $128,400 (100% need-based). 57 part-time jobs averaging $2253.

APPLYING FOR FINANCIAL AID ***Required financial aid forms:*** FAFSA, institution's own form, CSS Financial Aid PROFILE, noncustodial (divorced/separated) parent's statement, bank statements, tax returns. ***Financial aid deadline:*** 3/1. ***Notification date:*** 4/1. Students must reply by 5/1.

CONTACT Janice Miller, Director of Student Financial Assistance, The Curtis Institute of Music, 1726 Locust Street, Philadelphia, PA 19103-6107, 215-893-5252. *E-mail:* janice.miller@curtis.edu.

DAEMEN COLLEGE

Amherst, NY

ABOUT THE INSTITUTION Independent, coed. Awards: bachelor's, master's, and first professional degrees and post-bachelor's and post-master's certificates. 32 undergraduate majors. Total enrollment: 2,414. Undergraduates: 1,648. Freshmen: 370.

GIFT AID (NEED-BASED) ***Scholarships, grants, and awards:*** Federal Pell, FSEOG, state, private, college/university gift aid from institutional funds.

GIFT AID (NON-NEED-BASED) ***Scholarships, grants, and awards by category:*** *Academic Interests/Achievement:* general academic interests/achievements. *Creative Arts/Performance:* art/fine arts. *Special Characteristics:* children and siblings of alumni, children of faculty/staff, general special characteristics, siblings of current students.

LOANS ***Programs:*** FFEL (Subsidized and Unsubsidized Stafford, PLUS), Perkins, college/university, alternative loans.

WORK-STUDY ***Federal work-study:*** Total amount: $855,695; 290 jobs averaging $1067. ***State or other work-study/employment:*** Total amount: $73,400 (69% need-based, 31% non-need-based). 30 part-time jobs averaging $1163.

APPLYING FOR FINANCIAL AID ***Required financial aid forms:*** FAFSA, state aid form.

CONTACT Jeffrey Pagano, Director of Financial Aid, Daemen College, 4380 Main Street, Amherst, NY 14226-3592, 716-839-8254 or toll-free 800-462-7652. *Fax:* 716-839-8378. *E-mail:* jpagano@daemen.edu.

DAKOTA STATE UNIVERSITY

Madison, SD

Tuition & fees (SD res): $5699 **Average undergraduate aid package: $6360**

ABOUT THE INSTITUTION State-supported, coed. Awards: associate, bachelor's, and master's degrees. 30 undergraduate majors. Total enrollment: 2,392. Undergraduates: 2,144. Freshmen: 317. Federal methodology is used as a basis for awarding need-based institutional aid.

UNDERGRADUATE EXPENSES for 2006–07 ***Application fee:*** $20. ***Tuition, state resident:*** full-time $2382; part-time $79 per credit hour. ***Tuition, nonresident:*** full-time $3573; part-time $119 per credit hour. ***Required fees:*** full-time $3317; $89 per credit hour. Full-time tuition and fees vary according to location and reciprocity agreements. Part-time tuition and fees vary according to location and reciprocity agreements. ***College room and board:*** $3927; ***Room only:*** $1924. Room and board charges vary according to board plan and housing facility. ***Payment plans:*** Installment, deferred payment.

FRESHMAN FINANCIAL AID (Fall 2005) 252 applied for aid; of those 69% were deemed to have need. 99% of freshmen with need received aid; of those 16% had need fully met. ***Average percent of need met:*** 87% (excluding resources awarded to replace EFC). ***Average financial aid package:*** $5754 (excluding resources awarded to replace EFC). 25% of all full-time freshmen had no need and received non-need-based gift aid.

UNDERGRADUATE FINANCIAL AID (Fall 2005) 1,061 applied for aid; of those 74% were deemed to have need. 100% of undergraduates with need received aid; of those 22% had need fully met. ***Average percent of need met:*** 85% (excluding resources awarded to replace EFC). ***Average financial aid package:*** $6360 (excluding resources awarded to replace EFC). 22% of all full-time undergraduates had no need and received non-need-based gift aid.

GIFT AID (NEED-BASED) ***Total amount:*** $1,855,116 (75% federal, 14% institutional, 11% external sources). ***Receiving aid:*** Freshmen: 29% (83); All full-time undergraduates: 31% (373). ***Average award:*** Freshmen: $2947; Undergraduates: $3189. ***Scholarships, grants, and awards:*** Federal Pell, FSEOG, state, private, college/university gift aid from institutional funds.

GIFT AID (NON-NEED-BASED) ***Total amount:*** $233,584 (20% state, 44% institutional, 36% external sources). ***Receiving aid:*** Freshmen: 34% (100); Undergraduates: 23% (279). ***Average award:*** Freshmen: $4700; Undergraduates: $5817. ***Scholarships, grants, and awards by category:*** *Academic Interests/Achievement:* business, communication, computer science, education, English, general academic interests/achievements, mathematics. *Creative Arts/Performance:* music. *Special Achievements/Activities:* general special achievements/activities. *Special Characteristics:* children and siblings of alumni, ethnic background, local/state students, members of minority groups. ***Tuition waivers:*** Full or partial for employees or children of employees, senior citizens. ***ROTC:*** Army, Air Force cooperative.

LOANS ***Student loans:*** $6,480,609 (71% need-based, 29% non-need-based). 86% of past graduating class borrowed through all loan programs. *Average indebtedness per student:* $23,250. ***Average need-based loan:*** Freshmen: $3236; Undergraduates: $4745. ***Parent loans:*** $712,260 (71% need-based, 29% non-need-based). ***Programs:*** FFEL (Subsidized and Unsubsidized Stafford, PLUS), Perkins, alternative loans.

WORK-STUDY ***Federal work-study:*** Total amount: $325,174; 164 jobs averaging $1983. ***State or other work-study/employment:*** Total amount: $69,834 (100% non-need-based). 16 part-time jobs averaging $4365.

ATHLETIC AWARDS Total amount: $169,440 (71% need-based, 29% non-need-based).

APPLYING FOR FINANCIAL AID ***Required financial aid form:*** FAFSA. ***Financial aid deadline (priority):*** 3/1. ***Notification date:*** Continuous beginning 4/10. Students must reply within 2 weeks of notification.

CONTACT Denise Grayson, Financial Aid Director, Dakota State University, 103 Heston Hall, 820 North Washington Avenue, Madison, SD 57042-1799, 605-256-5158 or toll-free 888-DSU-9988. *Fax:* 605-256-5020. *E-mail:* fa@dsu.edu.

DAKOTA WESLEYAN UNIVERSITY

Mitchell, SD

Tuition & fees: $17,500 **Average undergraduate aid package: $12,000**

ABOUT THE INSTITUTION Independent United Methodist, coed. Awards: associate, bachelor's, and master's degrees. 43 undergraduate majors. Total enrollment: 776. Undergraduates: 735. Freshmen: 215. Federal methodology is used as a basis for awarding need-based institutional aid.

UNDERGRADUATE EXPENSES for 2007–08 ***Application fee:*** $25. ***Comprehensive fee:*** $22,900 includes full-time tuition ($17,500) and room and board ($5400). ***College room only:*** $2200. ***Part-time tuition:*** $367.50 per credit.

FRESHMAN FINANCIAL AID (Fall 2006, est.) 110 applied for aid; of those 95% were deemed to have need. 100% of freshmen with need received aid; of those 20% had need fully met. ***Average percent of need met:*** 60% (excluding resources awarded to replace EFC). ***Average financial aid package:*** $12,787 (excluding resources awarded to replace EFC).

UNDERGRADUATE FINANCIAL AID (Fall 2006, est.) 695 applied for aid; of those 96% were deemed to have need. 100% of undergraduates with need received aid; of those 8% had need fully met. ***Average percent of need met:*** 60% (excluding resources awarded to replace EFC). ***Average financial aid package:*** $12,000 (excluding resources awarded to replace EFC).

GIFT AID (NON-NEED-BASED) ***Total amount:*** $423,848 (2% federal, 84% institutional, 14% external sources). ***Receiving aid:*** Freshmen: 11% (13); Undergraduates: 6% (47).

LOANS ***Student loans:*** $5,594,888 (77% need-based, 23% non-need-based). 90% of past graduating class borrowed through all loan programs. *Average indebtedness per student:* $24,000. ***Average need-based loan:*** Freshmen: $2060; Undergraduates: $3726. ***Parent loans:*** $359,184 (47% need-based, 53% non-need-based). ***Programs:*** Private Alternative Loans: Methodist loan (for members of Methodist Church).

WORK-STUDY ***Federal work-study:*** Total amount: $104,099; 178 jobs averaging $1400. ***State or other work-study/employment:*** Total amount: $61,699 (89% need-based, 11% non-need-based). 6 part-time jobs averaging $1200.

ATHLETIC AWARDS Total amount: $1,375,826 (76% need-based, 24% non-need-based).

APPLYING FOR FINANCIAL AID ***Financial aid deadline (priority):*** 4/15. ***Notification date:*** Continuous beginning 3/1. Students must reply within 2 weeks of notification.

CONTACT Emily George, Administrative Assistant for Academic Affairs, Dakota Wesleyan University, 1200 West University Avenue, Mitchell, SD 57301, 605-995-2645 or toll-free 800-333-8506. *Fax:* 605-995-2609. *E-mail:* emgeorge@dwu.edu.

DALLAS BAPTIST UNIVERSITY

Dallas, TX

Tuition & fees: $13,650 **Average undergraduate aid package: $10,172**

ABOUT THE INSTITUTION Independent religious, coed. Awards: associate, bachelor's, and master's degrees and post-bachelor's certificates. 45 undergraduate majors. Total enrollment: 5,153. Undergraduates: 3,610. Freshmen: 360. Federal methodology is used as a basis for awarding need-based institutional aid.

UNDERGRADUATE EXPENSES for 2006–07 ***Application fee:*** $25. ***Comprehensive fee:*** $18,609 includes full-time tuition ($13,650) and room and board ($4959). ***College room only:*** $1990. Room and board charges vary according to board plan and housing facility. ***Part-time tuition:*** $455 per credit hour. ***Payment plan:*** Installment.

FRESHMAN FINANCIAL AID (Fall 2006, est.) 340 applied for aid; of those 65% were deemed to have need. 100% of freshmen with need received aid; of those 53% had need fully met. ***Average percent of need met:*** 83% (excluding resources awarded to replace EFC). ***Average financial aid package:*** $11,553 (excluding resources awarded to replace EFC). 25% of all full-time freshmen had no need and received non-need-based gift aid.

UNDERGRADUATE FINANCIAL AID (Fall 2006, est.) 1,807 applied for aid; of those 70% were deemed to have need. 99% of undergraduates with need received aid; of those 43% had need fully met. ***Average percent of need met:*** 75% (excluding resources awarded to replace EFC). ***Average financial aid package:*** $10,172 (excluding resources awarded to replace EFC). 17% of all full-time undergraduates had no need and received non-need-based gift aid.

GIFT AID (NEED-BASED) ***Total amount:*** $4,646,423 (52% federal, 48% state). ***Receiving aid:*** Freshmen: 44% (157); All full-time undergraduates: 39% (849). ***Average award:*** Freshmen: $2938; Undergraduates: $2949. ***Scholarships, grants, and awards:*** Federal Pell, FSEOG, state, private, college/university gift aid from institutional funds.

GIFT AID (NON-NEED-BASED) ***Total amount:*** $8,987,836 (72% institutional, 28% external sources). ***Receiving aid:*** Freshmen: 56% (203); Undergraduates: 44% (957). ***Average award:*** Freshmen: $5916; Undergraduates: $5902. ***Scholarships, grants, and awards by category:*** *Academic Interests/Achievement:* 1,375 awards ($2,983,783 total): business, communication, computer science, education, general academic interests/achievements, humanities, mathematics, premedicine, religion/biblical studies. *Creative Arts/Performance:* 73 awards ($1,733,875 total): music. *Special Achievements/Activities:* 1,187 awards ($3,078,754 total): community service, general special achievements/activities, leadership, memberships, religious involvement. *Special Characteristics:* 197 awards ($522,327 total): children of faculty/staff, general special characteristics, relatives of clergy, religious affiliation. ***Tuition waivers:*** Full or partial for employees or children of employees. ***ROTC:*** Army cooperative, Air Force cooperative.

LOANS ***Student loans:*** $13,729,985 (42% need-based, 58% non-need-based). 50% of past graduating class borrowed through all loan programs. *Average indebtedness per student:* $19,679. ***Average need-based loan:*** Freshmen: $2424; Undergraduates: $3479. ***Parent loans:*** $2,983,765 (100% non-need-based). ***Programs:*** FFEL (Subsidized and Unsubsidized Stafford, PLUS), Perkins, state, college/university.

WORK-STUDY ***Federal work-study:*** Total amount: $296,718; 164 jobs averaging $1923. ***State or other work-study/employment:*** Total amount: $34,221 (100% need-based). 63 part-time jobs averaging $557.

ATHLETIC AWARDS Total amount: $842,748 (100% non-need-based).

APPLYING FOR FINANCIAL AID ***Required financial aid forms:*** FAFSA, institution's own form. ***Financial aid deadline:*** Continuous. ***Notification date:*** Continuous.

CONTACT Mr. Donald Zackary, Director of Financial Aid, Dallas Baptist University, 3000 Mountain Creek Parkway, Dallas, TX 75211-9299, 214-333-5363 or toll-free 800-460-1328. *Fax:* 214-333-5586. *E-mail:* donz@dbu.edu.

DALLAS CHRISTIAN COLLEGE

Dallas, TX

ABOUT THE INSTITUTION Independent religious, coed. Awards: bachelor's degrees and post-bachelor's certificates. 3 undergraduate majors. Total enrollment: 366. Undergraduates: 366. Freshmen: 52.

GIFT AID (NEED-BASED) ***Scholarships, grants, and awards:*** Federal Pell, FSEOG, private, college/university gift aid from institutional funds.

GIFT AID (NON-NEED-BASED) ***Scholarships, grants, and awards by category:*** *Academic Interests/Achievement:* education, general academic interests/achievements, religion/biblical studies. *Creative Arts/Performance:* music. *Special Achievements/Activities:* general special achievements/activities, leadership. *Special Characteristics:* children of faculty/staff, general special characteristics, religious affiliation.

LOANS ***Programs:*** FFEL (Subsidized and Unsubsidized Stafford, PLUS).

WORK-STUDY ***Federal work-study:*** Total amount: $25,258; 36 jobs averaging $1404.

APPLYING FOR FINANCIAL AID ***Required financial aid forms:*** FAFSA, institution's own form.

CONTACT Robin L. Walker, Director of Student Financial Aid, Dallas Christian College, 2700 Christian Parkway, Dallas, TX 75234-7299, 972-241-3371 Ext. 105. *Fax:* 972-241-8021. *E-mail:* finaid@dallas.edu.

DALTON STATE COLLEGE

Dalton, GA

ABOUT THE INSTITUTION State-supported, coed. Awards: associate and bachelor's degrees. 64 undergraduate majors. Total enrollment: 4,349. Undergraduates: 4,349. Freshmen: 1,108.

GIFT AID (NEED-BASED) ***Scholarships, grants, and awards:*** Federal Pell, FSEOG, state, private, college/university gift aid from institutional funds.

GIFT AID (NON-NEED-BASED) ***Scholarships, grants, and awards by category:*** *Academic Interests/Achievement:* business, education, engineering/technologies, health fields, humanities. *Special Achievements/Activities:* hobbies/interests, memberships. *Special Characteristics:* adult students, children and siblings of alumni, children of faculty/staff.

LOANS ***Programs:*** FFEL (Subsidized and Unsubsidized Stafford, PLUS), state.

WORK-STUDY ***Federal work-study:*** Total amount: $82,639; 91 jobs averaging $1433. ***State or other work-study/employment:*** Total amount: $566,979 (41% need-based, 59% non-need-based). 98 part-time jobs averaging $3665.

APPLYING FOR FINANCIAL AID ***Required financial aid form:*** FAFSA.

CONTACT Dianne Cox, Director of Student Financial Aid, Dalton State College, 650 College Drive, Dalton, GA 30720, 706-272-4545 or toll-free 800-829-4436. *Fax:* 706-272-2458. *E-mail:* dcox@daltonstate.edu.

DANA COLLEGE

Blair, NE

Tuition & fees: $18,650 **Average undergraduate aid package: $16,241**

ABOUT THE INSTITUTION Independent religious, coed. Awards: bachelor's degrees. 41 undergraduate majors. Total enrollment: 601. Undergraduates: 601. Freshmen: 146. Federal methodology is used as a basis for awarding need-based institutional aid.

UNDERGRADUATE EXPENSES for 2006–07 ***Comprehensive fee:*** $24,040 includes full-time tuition ($17,850), mandatory fees ($800), and room and board ($5390). ***College room only:*** $2160. Room and board charges vary according to board plan and housing facility. ***Part-time tuition:*** $520 per semester hour. ***Part-time fees:*** $35 per term. Part-time tuition and fees vary according to course load. ***Payment plans:*** Installment, deferred payment.

FRESHMAN FINANCIAL AID (Fall 2006, est.) 142 applied for aid; of those 87% were deemed to have need. 100% of freshmen with need received aid; of those 29% had need fully met. ***Average percent of need met:*** 90% (excluding resources awarded to replace EFC). ***Average financial aid package:*** $16,516 (excluding resources awarded to replace EFC). 13% of all full-time freshmen had no need and received non-need-based gift aid.

UNDERGRADUATE FINANCIAL AID (Fall 2006, est.) 551 applied for aid; of those 87% were deemed to have need. 100% of undergraduates with need received aid; of those 30% had need fully met. ***Average percent of need met:*** 88% (excluding resources awarded to replace EFC). ***Average financial aid package:*** $16,241 (excluding resources awarded to replace EFC). 12% of all full-time undergraduates had no need and received non-need-based gift aid.

GIFT AID (NEED-BASED) ***Total amount:*** $1,357,042 (45% federal, 5% state, 50% institutional). ***Receiving aid:*** Freshmen: 39% (57); All full-time undergraduates: 48% (282). ***Average award:*** Freshmen: $4609; Undergraduates: $4473. ***Scholarships, grants, and awards:*** Federal Pell, FSEOG, state, private, college/university gift aid from institutional funds.

GIFT AID (NON-NEED-BASED) ***Total amount:*** $2,968,205 (94% institutional, 6% external sources). ***Receiving aid:*** Freshmen: 62% (91); Undergraduates: 59% (343). ***Average award:*** Freshmen: $4197; Undergraduates: $4500. ***Scholarships, grants, and awards by category:*** *Academic Interests/Achievement:* biological sciences, business, communication, education, English, foreign languages, general academic interests/achievements, health fields, international studies, mathematics, military science, premedicine, religion/biblical studies, social sciences. *Creative Arts/Performance:* applied art and design, art/fine arts, music, theater/drama. *Special Achievements/Activities:* general special achievements/activities, leadership, religious involvement. *Special Characteristics:* ethnic background, international students, local/state students, members of minority groups, out-of-state students, religious affiliation. ***Tuition waivers:*** Full or partial for children of alumni, employees or children of employees. ***ROTC:*** Army cooperative, Air Force cooperative.

LOANS ***Student loans:*** $2,263,822 (75% need-based, 25% non-need-based). 86% of past graduating class borrowed through all loan programs. *Average indebtedness per student:* $17,029. ***Average need-based loan:*** Freshmen: $4487; Undergraduates: $4578. ***Parent loans:*** $414,639 (100% non-need-based). ***Programs:*** FFEL (Subsidized and Unsubsidized Stafford, PLUS), Perkins.

WORK-STUDY ***Federal work-study:*** Total amount: $193,300; jobs available (averaging $1000). ***State or other work-study/employment:*** Part-time jobs available.

ATHLETIC AWARDS Total amount: $265,544 (100% non-need-based).

APPLYING FOR FINANCIAL AID ***Required financial aid forms:*** FAFSA, institution's own form. ***Financial aid deadline (priority):*** 3/15. ***Notification date:*** Continuous beginning 3/6. Students must reply within 3 weeks of notification.

CONTACT Rita McManigal, Director of Financial Aid, Dana College, 2848 College Drive, Blair, NE 68008-1099, 402-426-7227 or toll-free 800-444-3262. *Fax:* 402-426-7225. *E-mail:* rmcmanig@dana.edu.

DANIEL WEBSTER COLLEGE

Nashua, NH

Tuition & fees: $24,385 **Average undergraduate aid package: $15,371**

ABOUT THE INSTITUTION Independent, coed. Awards: associate and bachelor's degrees. 16 undergraduate majors. Total enrollment: 930. Undergraduates: 826. Freshmen: 229. Federal methodology is used as a basis for awarding need-based institutional aid.

UNDERGRADUATE EXPENSES for 2006–07 ***Application fee:*** $35. ***Comprehensive fee:*** $33,135 includes full-time tuition ($23,460), mandatory fees ($925), and room and board ($8750). ***College room only:*** $4360. Room and board charges vary according to housing facility. ***Part-time tuition:*** $978 per credit. ***Part-time fees:*** $260 per credit. ***Payment plan:*** Installment.

FRESHMAN FINANCIAL AID (Fall 2006, est.) ***Average percent of need met:*** 73% (excluding resources awarded to replace EFC). ***Average financial aid package:*** $16,187 (excluding resources awarded to replace EFC).

UNDERGRADUATE FINANCIAL AID (Fall 2006, est.) 567 applied for aid; of those 100% were deemed to have need. 100% of undergraduates with need received aid. ***Average percent of need met:*** 72% (excluding resources awarded to replace EFC). ***Average financial aid package:*** $15,371 (excluding resources awarded to replace EFC). 5% of all full-time undergraduates had no need and received non-need-based gift aid.

GIFT AID (NEED-BASED) ***Total amount:*** $2,873,895 (20% federal, 3% state, 75% institutional, 2% external sources). ***Receiving aid:*** Freshmen: 154; All full-time undergraduates: 74% (445). ***Average award:*** Freshmen: $5231; Undergraduates: $6114. ***Scholarships, grants, and awards:*** Federal Pell, FSEOG, state, private, college/university gift aid from institutional funds.

GIFT AID (NON-NEED-BASED) ***Total amount:*** $3,438,562 (100% institutional). ***Receiving aid:*** Freshmen: 155; Undergraduates: 73% (443). ***Average award:*** Freshmen: $8946; Undergraduates: $8287. ***Scholarships, grants, and awards by category:*** *Academic Interests/Achievement:* $2,856,250 total: business, computer science, engineering/technologies, general academic interests/achievements, social sciences. *Special Achievements/Activities:* 9 awards ($128,500 total): general special achievements/activities, leadership. ***Tuition waivers:*** Full or partial for employees or children of employees. ***ROTC:*** Army cooperative, Air Force cooperative.

LOANS ***Student loans:*** $2,417,695 (80% need-based, 20% non-need-based). 95% of past graduating class borrowed through all loan programs. *Average indebtedness per student:* $45,000. ***Average need-based loan:*** Freshmen: $3393;

Undergraduates: $4257. ***Parent loans:*** $3,546,223 (100% non-need-based). ***Programs:*** Federal Direct (Subsidized and Unsubsidized Stafford, PLUS), Perkins, Signature Loans.

WORK-STUDY ***Federal work-study:*** Total amount: $665,696; 369 jobs averaging $2000. ***State or other work-study/employment:*** Part-time jobs available.

APPLYING FOR FINANCIAL AID ***Required financial aid forms:*** FAFSA, institution's own form. ***Financial aid deadline (priority):*** 3/1. ***Notification date:*** Continuous beginning 4/1. Students must reply within 3 weeks of notification.

CONTACT Anne-Marie Caruso, Director of Financial Assistance, Daniel Webster College, 20 University Drive, Nashua, NH 03063-1300, 603-577-6590 or toll-free 800-325-6876. *Fax:* 603-577-6593. *E-mail:* caruso@dwc.edu.

DARKEI NOAM RABBINICAL COLLEGE

Brooklyn, NY

CONTACT Ms. Rivi Horowitz, Director of Financial Aid, Darkei Noam Rabbinical College, 2822 Avenue J, Brooklyn, NY 11219, 718-338-6464.

DARTMOUTH COLLEGE

Hanover, NH

Tuition & fees: $33,297 **Average undergraduate aid package: $31,840**

ABOUT THE INSTITUTION Independent, coed. Awards: bachelor's, master's, doctoral, and first professional degrees. 60 undergraduate majors. Total enrollment: 5,753. Undergraduates: 4,085. Freshmen: 1,086. Both federal and institutional methodology are used as a basis for awarding need-based institutional aid.

UNDERGRADUATE EXPENSES for 2007–08 ***Application fee:*** $70. ***Comprehensive fee:*** $43,137 includes full-time tuition ($33,297) and room and board ($9840). ***College room only:*** $5895.

FRESHMAN FINANCIAL AID (Fall 2005) 669 applied for aid; of those 77% were deemed to have need. 100% of freshmen with need received aid; of those 100% had need fully met. ***Average percent of need met:*** 100% (excluding resources awarded to replace EFC). ***Average financial aid package:*** $33,208 (excluding resources awarded to replace EFC). 1% of all full-time freshmen had no need and received non-need-based gift aid.

UNDERGRADUATE FINANCIAL AID (Fall 2005) 2,487 applied for aid; of those 84% were deemed to have need. 100% of undergraduates with need received aid; of those 100% had need fully met. ***Average percent of need met:*** 100% (excluding resources awarded to replace EFC). ***Average financial aid package:*** $31,840 (excluding resources awarded to replace EFC). 1% of all full-time undergraduates had no need and received non-need-based gift aid.

GIFT AID (NEED-BASED) ***Total amount:*** $53,382,926 (7% federal, 89% institutional, 4% external sources). ***Receiving aid:*** Freshmen: 46% (499); All full-time undergraduates: 49% (2,002). ***Average award:*** Freshmen: $30,303; Undergraduates: $27,843. ***Scholarships, grants, and awards:*** Federal Pell, FSEOG, state, college/university gift aid from institutional funds.

GIFT AID (NON-NEED-BASED) ***Total amount:*** $805,665 (19% federal, 1% institutional, 80% external sources). ***Average award:*** Freshmen: $450; Undergraduates: $465. ***ROTC:*** Army cooperative.

LOANS ***Student loans:*** $10,997,691 (65% need-based, 35% non-need-based). 52% of past graduating class borrowed through all loan programs. *Average indebtedness per student:* $21,561. ***Average need-based loan:*** Freshmen: $3201; Undergraduates: $4270. ***Parent loans:*** $6,510,472 (100% non-need-based). ***Programs:*** FFEL (Subsidized and Unsubsidized Stafford, PLUS), Perkins, college/university.

WORK-STUDY ***Federal work-study:*** Total amount: $2,698,516; 1,393 jobs averaging $1937. ***State or other work-study/employment:*** Total amount: $759,225 (100% need-based). 431 part-time jobs averaging $1761.

APPLYING FOR FINANCIAL AID ***Required financial aid forms:*** FAFSA, CSS Financial Aid PROFILE, noncustodial (divorced/separated) parent's statement, business/farm supplement, W-2 forms, federal income tax form(s). ***Financial aid deadline:*** 2/1. ***Notification date:*** 4/2. Students must reply by 5/1.

CONTACT Ms. Virginia S. Hazen, Director of Financial Aid, Dartmouth College, 6024 McNutt Hall, Hanover, NH 03755, 603-646-2451 or toll-free 603-646-2875 (in-state). *Fax:* 603-646-1414. *E-mail:* virginia.s.hazen@dartmouth.edu.

DAVENPORT UNIVERSITY

Dearborn, MI

ABOUT THE INSTITUTION Independent, coed. Awards: associate, bachelor's, and master's degrees and post-bachelor's certificates. 26 undergraduate majors. Total enrollment: 12,617. Undergraduates: 11,954. Freshmen: 1,230.

GIFT AID (NEED-BASED) ***Scholarships, grants, and awards:*** Federal Pell, FSEOG, state, private, college/university gift aid from institutional funds.

GIFT AID (NON-NEED-BASED) ***Scholarships, grants, and awards by category:*** *Special Characteristics:* children of faculty/staff.

LOANS ***Programs:*** FFEL (Subsidized and Unsubsidized Stafford, PLUS), alternative loans.

APPLYING FOR FINANCIAL AID ***Required financial aid forms:*** FAFSA, scholarship app., if applicable.

CONTACT Mrs. Susan Crkovski, Executive Director of Financial Aid, Davenport University, 4801 Oakman Boulevard, Dearborn, MI 48126-3799, 313-581-4400 Ext. 217 or toll-free 800-632-9569. *Fax:* 313-581-1955. *E-mail:* susan.crkovski@davenport.edu.

DAVENPORT UNIVERSITY

Flint, MI

CONTACT Ms. Rita Miller, Director of Financial Aid, Davenport University, 3488 North Jennings Road, Flint, MI 48504-1700, 810-789-2200 or toll-free 800-727-1443. *Fax:* 810-789-2266. *E-mail:* flrmiller@dcb.edu.

DAVENPORT UNIVERSITY

Gaylord, MI

CONTACT Office of Financial Aid, Davenport University, 80 Livingston Boulevard, Gaylord, MI 49735, 989-705-3720 or toll-free 800-632-9569. *Fax:* 989-705-3727.

DAVENPORT UNIVERSITY

Grand Rapids, MI

CONTACT Mary Kay Bethune, Vice President for Financial Aid, Davenport University, 415 East Fulton Street, Grand Rapids, MI 49503, 616-451-3511 or toll-free 800-632-9569. *E-mail:* marykay.bethune@davenport.edu.

DAVENPORT UNIVERSITY

Holland, MI

CONTACT Office of Financial Aid, Davenport University, 643 South Waverly Road, Holland, MI 49423, 616-395-4600 or toll-free 800-632-9569. *Fax:* 616-395-4698.

DAVENPORT UNIVERSITY

Kalamazoo, MI

CONTACT Ms. Linda Reischer, Director of Financial Aid, Davenport University, 4123 West Main Street, Kalamazoo, MI 49006-2791, 269-552-3320 or toll-free 800-632-9569. *Fax:* 269-552-3305. *E-mail:* linda.reischer@davenport.edu.

DAVENPORT UNIVERSITY

Lansing, MI

CONTACT Libby Jean, Acting Director of Financial Aid, Davenport University, 220 East Kalamazoo Street, Lansing, MI 48933-2197, 517-484-2600 Ext. 8226 or toll-free 800-632-9569. *Fax:* 517-484-1132. *E-mail:* libby.jean@davenport.edu.

DAVENPORT UNIVERSITY

Lapeer, MI

CONTACT Office of Financial Aid, Davenport University, 550 Lake Drive, Suite B, Lapeer, MI 48446, 810-664-9655 or toll-free 800-632-9569. *Fax:* 810-664-1912.

DAVENPORT UNIVERSITY

Traverse City, MI

ABOUT THE INSTITUTION Independent, coed. Awards: associate, bachelor's, and master's degrees and post-bachelor's certificates. Total enrollment: 12,822. Undergraduates: 12,066. Freshmen: 1,231.

GIFT AID (NEED-BASED) ***Scholarships, grants, and awards:*** Federal Pell, FSEOG, state, private, college/university gift aid from institutional funds, State of MI Nursing Scholarships.

LOANS ***Programs:*** FFEL (Subsidized and Unsubsidized Stafford, PLUS), state.

APPLYING FOR FINANCIAL AID ***Required financial aid form:*** FAFSA.

CONTACT Office of Financial Aid, Davenport University, 2200 Dendrinos Drive, Suite 110, Traverse City, MI 49684, 231-995-1740 or toll-free 866-925-3884 (out-of-state). *Fax:* 231-995-1743.

DAVENPORT UNIVERSITY

Warren, MI

CONTACT Ms. Carol Agee, Director of Financial Aid, Davenport University, 27500 Dequindre Road, Warren, MI 48092-5209, 586-558-8700 Ext. 230 or toll-free 800-632-9569. *Fax:* 586-558-7528. *E-mail:* carol.agee@davenport.edu.

DAVID N. MYERS UNIVERSITY

Cleveland, OH

See Myers University.

DAVIDSON COLLEGE

Davidson, NC

Tuition & fees: $30,194 **Average undergraduate aid package: $19,045**

ABOUT THE INSTITUTION Independent Presbyterian, coed. Awards: bachelor's degrees. 21 undergraduate majors. Total enrollment: 1,667. Undergraduates: 1,667. Freshmen: 461. Both federal and institutional methodology are used as a basis for awarding need-based institutional aid.

UNDERGRADUATE EXPENSES for 2006–07 ***Application fee:*** $50. ***Comprehensive fee:*** $38,784 includes full-time tuition ($29,119), mandatory fees ($1075), and room and board ($8590).

FRESHMAN FINANCIAL AID (Fall 2005) 228 applied for aid; of those 65% were deemed to have need. 100% of freshmen with need received aid; of those 100% had need fully met. ***Average percent of need met:*** 100% (excluding resources awarded to replace EFC). ***Average financial aid package:*** $19,379 (excluding resources awarded to replace EFC). 13% of all full-time freshmen had no need and received non-need-based gift aid.

UNDERGRADUATE FINANCIAL AID (Fall 2005) 704 applied for aid; of those 81% were deemed to have need. 100% of undergraduates with need received aid; of those 100% had need fully met. ***Average percent of need met:*** 100% (excluding resources awarded to replace EFC). ***Average financial aid package:*** $19,045 (excluding resources awarded to replace EFC). 11% of all full-time undergraduates had no need and received non-need-based gift aid.

GIFT AID (NEED-BASED) ***Total amount:*** $11,008,700 (4% federal, 5% state, 91% institutional). ***Receiving aid:*** Freshmen: 31% (142); All full-time undergraduates: 32% (540). ***Average award:*** Freshmen: $17,300; Undergraduates: $16,383. ***Scholarships, grants, and awards:*** Federal Pell, FSEOG, state, private, college/university gift aid from institutional funds, need-linked special talent scholarships.

GIFT AID (NON-NEED-BASED) ***Total amount:*** $5,044,201 (8% federal, 7% state, 68% institutional, 17% external sources). ***Receiving aid:*** Freshmen: 6% (28); Undergraduates: 6% (99). ***Average award:*** Freshmen: $10,515; Undergraduates: $9650. ***Scholarships, grants, and awards by category:*** *Academic Interests/Achievement:* 227 awards ($2,876,297 total): biological sciences, education, foreign languages, general academic interests/achievements, mathematics, physical sciences, premedicine. *Creative Arts/Performance:* 37 awards ($232,100 total): art/fine arts, creative writing, music, theater/drama. *Special Achievements/Activities:* 43 awards ($616,265 total): community service, general special achievements/activities, leadership, religious involvement. *Special Characteristics:* 98 awards ($1,314,990 total): children of faculty/staff, general special characteristics, relatives of clergy. ***ROTC:*** Army, Air Force cooperative.

LOANS ***Student loans:*** $4,177,829 (30% need-based, 70% non-need-based). 33% of past graduating class borrowed through all loan programs. *Average indebtedness per student:* $26,130. ***Average need-based loan:*** Freshmen: $3406; Undergraduates: $4090. ***Parent loans:*** $2,784,761 (100% non-need-based). ***Programs:*** FFEL (Subsidized and Unsubsidized Stafford, PLUS), Perkins, alternative loans.

WORK-STUDY ***Federal work-study:*** Total amount: $305,700; 204 jobs averaging $1693. ***State or other work-study/employment:*** Total amount: $350,800 (87% need-based, 13% non-need-based). 221 part-time jobs averaging $1719.

ATHLETIC AWARDS Total amount: $2,465,400 (100% non-need-based).

APPLYING FOR FINANCIAL AID ***Required financial aid forms:*** FAFSA, CSS Financial Aid PROFILE, noncustodial (divorced/separated) parent's statement, business/farm supplement, parent and student tax returns and W-2 forms; corporate tax returns, if applicable. ***Financial aid deadline (priority):*** 2/15. ***Notification date:*** 4/1. Students must reply by 5/1.

CONTACT Kathleen Stevenson, Senior Associate Dean of Admission and Financial Aid, Davidson College, 413 North Main Street, Box 7157, Davidson, NC 28035-7157, 704-894-2232 or toll-free 800-768-0380. *Fax:* 704-894-2845. *E-mail:* kastevenson@davidson.edu.

DAVIS & ELKINS COLLEGE

Elkins, WV

Tuition & fees: $17,730 **Average undergraduate aid package: $12,846**

ABOUT THE INSTITUTION Independent Presbyterian, coed. Awards: associate and bachelor's degrees. 48 undergraduate majors. Total enrollment: 636. Undergraduates: 636. Freshmen: 121. Federal methodology is used as a basis for awarding need-based institutional aid.

UNDERGRADUATE EXPENSES for 2006–07 ***Application fee:*** $35. ***Comprehensive fee:*** $24,030 includes full-time tuition ($17,210), mandatory fees ($520), and room and board ($6300). Full-time tuition and fees vary according to course load. Room and board charges vary according to board plan. ***Part-time tuition:*** $555 per credit hour. Part-time tuition and fees vary according to course load. ***Payment plan:*** Installment.

FRESHMAN FINANCIAL AID (Fall 2005) 78 applied for aid; of those 100% were deemed to have need. 100% of freshmen with need received aid; of those 27% had need fully met. ***Average percent of need met:*** 74% (excluding resources awarded to replace EFC). ***Average financial aid package:*** $13,003 (excluding resources awarded to replace EFC). 22% of all full-time freshmen had no need and received non-need-based gift aid.

UNDERGRADUATE FINANCIAL AID (Fall 2005) 431 applied for aid; of those 100% were deemed to have need. 100% of undergraduates with need received aid; of those 22% had need fully met. ***Average percent of need met:*** 71% (excluding resources awarded to replace EFC). ***Average financial aid package:*** $12,846 (excluding resources awarded to replace EFC). 20% of all full-time undergraduates had no need and received non-need-based gift aid.

GIFT AID (NEED-BASED) ***Total amount:*** $1,439,624 (67% federal, 18% state, 6% institutional, 9% external sources). ***Receiving aid:*** Freshmen: 49% (50); All full-time undergraduates: 55% (322). ***Average award:*** Freshmen: $4373; Undergraduates: $4247. ***Scholarships, grants, and awards:*** Federal Pell, FSEOG, state, private, college/university gift aid from institutional funds.

GIFT AID (NON-NEED-BASED) ***Total amount:*** $2,603,147 (11% state, 81% institutional, 8% external sources). ***Receiving aid:*** Freshmen: 76% (78); Undergraduates: 74% (431). ***Average award:*** Freshmen: $4649; Undergraduates: $5476. ***Scholarships, grants, and awards by category:*** *Academic Interests/Achievement:* 808 awards ($1,743,722 total): biological sciences, business, computer science, education, engineering/technologies, general academic interests/achievements, health fields, physical sciences, religion/biblical studies. *Creative Arts/Performance:* 60 awards ($109,100 total): art/fine arts, music, performing arts, theater/drama. *Special Achievements/Activities:* 64 awards ($62,500 total): leadership, religious involvement. *Special Characteristics:* 337 awards ($520,482 total): children of faculty/staff, first-generation college students, local/state students, religious affiliation. ***Tuition waivers:*** Full or partial for employees or children of employees.

LOANS ***Student loans:*** $4,089,354 (34% need-based, 66% non-need-based). 79% of past graduating class borrowed through all loan programs. *Average indebtedness per student:* $23,973. ***Average need-based loan:*** Freshmen: $4178; Undergraduates: $4388. ***Parent loans:*** $338,982 (100% non-need-based). ***Programs:*** FFEL (Subsidized and Unsubsidized Stafford, PLUS), Perkins, college/university.

WORK-STUDY ***Federal work-study:*** Total amount: $255,651; 176 jobs averaging $1453. ***State or other work-study/employment:*** Total amount: $57,100 (100% non-need-based). 37 part-time jobs averaging $1543.

ATHLETIC AWARDS Total amount: $640,427 (100% non-need-based).

APPLYING FOR FINANCIAL AID ***Required financial aid form:*** FAFSA. ***Financial aid deadline:*** Continuous. ***Notification date:*** Continuous. Students must reply within 2 weeks of notification.

CONTACT Susan M. George, Director of Financial Planning, Davis & Elkins College, 100 Campus Drive, Elkins, WV 26241-3996, 304-637-1373 or toll-free 800-624-3157 Ext. 1230. *Fax:* 304-637-1986. *E-mail:* ssw@davisandelkins.edu.

DAVIS COLLEGE

Johnson City, NY

CONTACT Mr. James P. Devine, Financial Aid Director, Davis College, PO Box 601, Bible School Park, NY 13737-0601, 607-729-1581 Ext. 401 or toll-free 800-331-4137 Ext. 406. *Fax:* 607-770-6886. *E-mail:* financialaid@practical.edu.

DEACONESS COLLEGE OF NURSING

St. Louis, MO

See Chamberlain College of Nursing.

DEFIANCE COLLEGE

Defiance, OH

ABOUT THE INSTITUTION Independent religious, coed. Awards: associate, bachelor's, and master's degrees. 38 undergraduate majors. Total enrollment: 930. Undergraduates: 827. Freshmen: 244.

GIFT AID (NEED-BASED) ***Scholarships, grants, and awards:*** Federal Pell, FSEOG, state, private, college/university gift aid from institutional funds.

GIFT AID (NON-NEED-BASED) ***Scholarships, grants, and awards by category:*** *Academic Interests/Achievement:* biological sciences, business, communication, computer science, education, general academic interests/achievements, humanities, mathematics, physical sciences, premedicine, religion/biblical studies, social sciences. *Special Achievements/Activities:* community service, general special achievements/activities, leadership, religious involvement. *Special Characteristics:* children of faculty/staff, children with a deceased or disabled parent, first-generation college students, general special characteristics, international students, local/state students, members of minority groups, out-of-state students, previous college experience, relatives of clergy, religious affiliation.

LOANS ***Programs:*** FFEL (Subsidized and Unsubsidized Stafford, PLUS), Perkins, alternative loans.

WORK-STUDY ***Federal work-study:*** Total amount: $88,429; 138 jobs averaging $640. ***State or other work-study/employment:*** Total amount: $123,311 (100% non-need-based). 154 part-time jobs averaging $800.

APPLYING FOR FINANCIAL AID ***Required financial aid form:*** FAFSA.

CONTACT Ms. Amy Francis, Director of Financial Aid, Defiance College, 701 North Clinton Street, Defiance, OH 43512-1610, 419-784-4010 Ext. 376 or toll-free 800-520-4632 Ext. 2359.

DELAWARE STATE UNIVERSITY

Dover, DE

CONTACT Associate Director of Financial Aid, Delaware State University, 1200 North DuPont Highway, Dover, DE 19901-2277, 302-857-6250 or toll-free 800-845-2544.

DELAWARE VALLEY COLLEGE

Doylestown, PA

Tuition & fees: $23,110 **Average undergraduate aid package: $17,242**

ABOUT THE INSTITUTION Independent, coed. Awards: associate, bachelor's, and master's degrees and post-bachelor's certificates. 28 undergraduate majors. Total enrollment: 2,035. Undergraduates: 1,959. Freshmen: 447. Federal methodology is used as a basis for awarding need-based institutional aid.

UNDERGRADUATE EXPENSES for 2007–08 ***Application fee:*** $35. ***Comprehensive fee:*** $32,075 includes full-time tuition ($23,110) and room and board ($8965). ***College room only:*** $4064. ***Part-time tuition:*** $630 per credit.

FRESHMAN FINANCIAL AID (Fall 2006, est.) 407 applied for aid; of those 87% were deemed to have need. 100% of freshmen with need received aid; of those 21% had need fully met. ***Average percent of need met:*** 73% (excluding resources awarded to replace EFC). ***Average financial aid package:*** $15,663 (excluding resources awarded to replace EFC). 17% of all full-time freshmen had no need and received non-need-based gift aid.

UNDERGRADUATE FINANCIAL AID (Fall 2006, est.) 1,462 applied for aid; of those 86% were deemed to have need. 99% of undergraduates with need received aid; of those 17% had need fully met. ***Average percent of need met:*** 83% (excluding resources awarded to replace EFC). ***Average financial aid package:*** $17,242 (excluding resources awarded to replace EFC). 17% of all full-time undergraduates had no need and received non-need-based gift aid.

GIFT AID (NEED-BASED) ***Total amount:*** $15,671,718 (8% federal, 12% state, 78% institutional, 2% external sources). ***Receiving aid:*** Freshmen: 79% (354); All full-time undergraduates: 75% (1,203). ***Average award:*** Freshmen: $13,700; Undergraduates: $13,027. ***Scholarships, grants, and awards:*** Federal Pell, FSEOG, state, private, college/university gift aid from institutional funds.

GIFT AID (NON-NEED-BASED) ***Total amount:*** $2,725,088 (2% state, 84% institutional, 14% external sources). ***Receiving aid:*** Freshmen: 17% (75); Undergraduates: 17% (274). ***Average award:*** Freshmen: $10,085; Undergraduates: $8886. ***Scholarships, grants, and awards by category:*** *Academic Interests/Achievement:* 352 awards ($3,274,304 total): general academic interests/achievements. *Creative Arts/Performance:* 36 awards ($17,200 total): music. *Special Achievements/Activities:* 1 award ($1000 total): memberships. *Special Characteristics:* 1 award ($1000 total): handicapped students.

LOANS ***Student loans:*** $10,445,482 (39% need-based, 61% non-need-based). 68% of past graduating class borrowed through all loan programs. *Average indebtedness per student:* $17,482. ***Average need-based loan:*** Freshmen: $2846; Undergraduates: $4024. ***Parent loans:*** $4,363,791 (33% need-based, 67% non-need-based). ***Programs:*** FFEL (Subsidized and Unsubsidized Stafford, PLUS), Perkins, state, alternative loans.

WORK-STUDY ***Federal work-study:*** Total amount: $190,000; 111 jobs averaging $1621.

APPLYING FOR FINANCIAL AID ***Required financial aid form:*** FAFSA. ***Financial aid deadline (priority):*** 4/1. ***Notification date:*** Continuous beginning 2/15. Students must reply by 5/1.

CONTACT Mr. Robert Sauer, Director of Student Financial Aid, Delaware Valley College, 700 East Butler Avenue, Doylestown, PA 18901-2697, 215-489-2297 or toll-free 800-2DELVAL (in-state). *E-mail:* finaid@devalcol.edu.

DELTA STATE UNIVERSITY

Cleveland, MS

CONTACT Ms. Ann Margaret Mullins, Director of Student Financial Assistance, Delta State University, PO Box 3154, Cleveland, MS 38733-0001, 662-846-4670 or toll-free 800-468-6378. *E-mail:* amullins@deltastate.edu.

DENISON UNIVERSITY

Granville, OH

Tuition & fees: $30,660 **Average undergraduate aid package: $26,424**

ABOUT THE INSTITUTION Independent, coed. Awards: bachelor's degrees. 39 undergraduate majors. Total enrollment: 2,263. Undergraduates: 2,263. Freshmen: 573. Federal methodology is used as a basis for awarding need-based institutional aid.

UNDERGRADUATE EXPENSES for 2006–07 ***Application fee:*** $40. ***Comprehensive fee:*** $39,220 includes full-time tuition ($29,860), mandatory fees ($800), and room and board ($8560). ***College room only:*** $4740. Room and board charges vary according to housing facility. ***Part-time tuition:*** $930 per semester hour. Part-time tuition and fees vary according to course load. ***Payment plan:*** Installment.

FRESHMAN FINANCIAL AID (Fall 2006, est.) 349 applied for aid; of those 70% were deemed to have need. 100% of freshmen with need received aid; of those 64% had need fully met. ***Average percent of need met:*** 94% (excluding

resources awarded to replace EFC). ***Average financial aid package:*** $25,983 (excluding resources awarded to replace EFC). 52% of all full-time freshmen had no need and received non-need-based gift aid.

UNDERGRADUATE FINANCIAL AID (Fall 2006, est.) 1,211 applied for aid; of those 81% were deemed to have need. 100% of undergraduates with need received aid; of those 56% had need fully met. ***Average percent of need met:*** 94% (excluding resources awarded to replace EFC). ***Average financial aid package:*** $26,424 (excluding resources awarded to replace EFC). 54% of all full-time undergraduates had no need and received non-need-based gift aid.

GIFT AID (NEED-BASED) ***Total amount:*** $18,141,093 (6% federal, 1% state, 93% institutional). ***Receiving aid:*** Freshmen: 43% (244); All full-time undergraduates: 46% (976). ***Average award:*** Freshmen: $20,901; Undergraduates: $20,424. ***Scholarships, grants, and awards:*** Federal Pell, FSEOG, state, private, college/university gift aid from institutional funds.

GIFT AID (NON-NEED-BASED) ***Total amount:*** $18,554,430 (5% state, 91% institutional, 4% external sources). ***Receiving aid:*** Freshmen: 38% (220); Undergraduates: 42% (889). ***Average award:*** Freshmen: $13,983; Undergraduates: $13,233. ***Scholarships, grants, and awards by category:*** *Academic Interests/Achievement:* 2,020 awards ($25,645,441 total): biological sciences, communication, English, foreign languages, general academic interests/achievements, humanities, physical sciences. *Creative Arts/Performance:* 115 awards ($159,399 total): art/fine arts, dance, music, theater/drama. *Special Achievements/Activities:* 14 awards ($25,600 total): leadership. *Special Characteristics:* 14 awards ($8250 total): members of minority groups. ***Tuition waivers:*** Full or partial for employees or children of employees. ***ROTC:*** Army cooperative.

LOANS ***Student loans:*** $4,778,043 (92% need-based, 8% non-need-based). 47% of past graduating class borrowed through all loan programs. *Average indebtedness per student:* $15,263. ***Average need-based loan:*** Freshmen: $3731; Undergraduates: $4688. ***Parent loans:*** $3,057,353 (100% non-need-based). ***Programs:*** Federal Direct (Subsidized and Unsubsidized Stafford, PLUS), Perkins, college/university.

WORK-STUDY ***Federal work-study:*** Total amount: $900,194; 479 jobs averaging $1820. ***State or other work-study/employment:*** Total amount: $2,712,376 (100% non-need-based). 1,198 part-time jobs averaging $2040.

APPLYING FOR FINANCIAL AID ***Required financial aid form:*** FAFSA. ***Financial aid deadline (priority):*** 2/15. ***Notification date:*** 3/30. Students must reply by 5/1 or within 2 weeks of notification.

CONTACT Ms. Nancy Hoover, Director of Financial Aid, Denison University, PO Box M, Granville, OH 43023-0613, 740-587-6279 or toll-free 800-DENISON. *Fax:* 740-587-5706. *E-mail:* hoover@denison.edu.

DePAUL UNIVERSITY

Chicago, IL

ABOUT THE INSTITUTION Independent Roman Catholic, coed. Awards: bachelor's, master's, doctoral, and first professional degrees and post-bachelor's and post-master's certificates. 100 undergraduate majors. Total enrollment: 23,149. Undergraduates: 14,893. Freshmen: 2,537.

GIFT AID (NEED-BASED) ***Scholarships, grants, and awards:*** Federal Pell, FSEOG, state, private, college/university gift aid from institutional funds, United Negro College Fund.

GIFT AID (NON-NEED-BASED) ***Scholarships, grants, and awards by category:*** *Academic Interests/Achievement:* biological sciences, business, computer science, education, general academic interests/achievements. *Creative Arts/Performance:* art/fine arts, debating, music, performing arts, theater/drama. *Special Achievements/Activities:* community service. *Special Characteristics:* children of faculty/staff.

LOANS ***Programs:*** Federal Direct (Subsidized and Unsubsidized Stafford, PLUS), Perkins.

WORK-STUDY ***Federal work-study:*** Total amount: $2,200,000; 890 jobs averaging $2472. ***State or other work-study/employment:*** Total amount: $4,140,000 (31% need-based, 69% non-need-based). Part-time jobs available.

APPLYING FOR FINANCIAL AID ***Required financial aid form:*** FAFSA.

CONTACT Christopher Rone, Associate Director of Financial Aid, DePaul University, 1 East Jackson Boulevard, Suite 9000, Chicago, IL 60604-2287, 773-325-7815. *Fax:* 773-325-7746.

DePAUW UNIVERSITY

Greencastle, IN

ABOUT THE INSTITUTION Independent religious, coed. Awards: bachelor's degrees. 45 undergraduate majors. Total enrollment: 2,326. Undergraduates: 2,326. Freshmen: 596.

GIFT AID (NEED-BASED) ***Scholarships, grants, and awards:*** Federal Pell, FSEOG, state, private, college/university gift aid from institutional funds.

GIFT AID (NON-NEED-BASED) ***Scholarships, grants, and awards by category:*** *Academic Interests/Achievement:* biological sciences, business, communication, computer science, foreign languages, general academic interests/achievements, humanities, international studies, mathematics, physical sciences. *Creative Arts/Performance:* art/fine arts, cinema/film/broadcasting, journalism/publications, music. *Special Achievements/Activities:* community service, leadership. *Special Characteristics:* children and siblings of alumni, children of faculty/staff, ethnic background, international students, members of minority groups, relatives of clergy, religious affiliation.

LOANS ***Programs:*** FFEL (Subsidized and Unsubsidized Stafford, PLUS), Perkins, college/university, alternative loans.

WORK-STUDY ***Federal work-study:*** Total amount: $986,013; 698 jobs averaging $1412. ***State or other work-study/employment:*** Total amount: $20,800 (45% need-based, 55% non-need-based). 17 part-time jobs averaging $1224.

APPLYING FOR FINANCIAL AID ***Required financial aid forms:*** FAFSA, institution's own form.

CONTACT Joanne L. Haymaker, Associate Director of Financial Aid, DePauw University, 313 South Locust Street, Greencastle, IN 46135-0037, 765-658-4030 or toll-free 800-447-2495. *Fax:* 765-658-4177. *E-mail:* jhaymaker@depauw.edu.

DeSALES UNIVERSITY

Center Valley, PA

Tuition & fees: $22,000 **Average undergraduate aid package: $15,648**

ABOUT THE INSTITUTION Independent Roman Catholic, coed. Awards: bachelor's and master's degrees and post-bachelor's and post-master's certificates. 38 undergraduate majors. Total enrollment: 2,936. Undergraduates: 2,126. Freshmen: 392. Federal methodology is used as a basis for awarding need-based institutional aid.

UNDERGRADUATE EXPENSES for 2006–07 ***Application fee:*** $30. ***One-time required fee:*** $200. ***Comprehensive fee:*** $30,250 includes full-time tuition ($21,200), mandatory fees ($800), and room and board ($8250). Room and board charges vary according to board plan and housing facility. ***Part-time tuition:*** $880 per credit. ***Payment plans:*** Installment, deferred payment.

FRESHMAN FINANCIAL AID (Fall 2006, est.) 369 applied for aid; of those 78% were deemed to have need. 98% of freshmen with need received aid; of those 54% had need fully met. ***Average percent of need met:*** 56% (excluding resources awarded to replace EFC). ***Average financial aid package:*** $15,566 (excluding resources awarded to replace EFC). 25% of all full-time freshmen had no need and received non-need-based gift aid.

UNDERGRADUATE FINANCIAL AID (Fall 2006, est.) 1,257 applied for aid; of those 77% were deemed to have need. 96% of undergraduates with need received aid; of those 50% had need fully met. ***Average percent of need met:*** 84% (excluding resources awarded to replace EFC). ***Average financial aid package:*** $15,648 (excluding resources awarded to replace EFC). 20% of all full-time undergraduates had no need and received non-need-based gift aid.

GIFT AID (NEED-BASED) ***Total amount:*** $12,987,011 (5% federal, 13% state, 80% institutional, 2% external sources). ***Receiving aid:*** Freshmen: 58% (229); All full-time undergraduates: 54% (770). ***Average award:*** Freshmen: $8317; Undergraduates: $9027. ***Scholarships, grants, and awards:*** Federal Pell, FSEOG, state, private, college/university gift aid from institutional funds.

GIFT AID (NON-NEED-BASED) ***Total amount:*** $2,132,831 (1% federal, 96% institutional, 3% external sources). ***Receiving aid:*** Freshmen: 70% (276); Undergraduates: 63% (903). ***Average award:*** Freshmen: $6055; Undergraduates: $5680. ***Scholarships, grants, and awards by category:*** *Academic Interests/Achievement:* 309 awards ($358,000 total): biological sciences, business, communication, computer science, education, English, foreign languages, general academic interests/achievements, health fields, humanities, mathematics, military science, physical sciences, premedicine, religion/biblical studies, social sciences. *Creative Arts/Performance:* 123 awards ($209,500 total): cinema/film/

broadcasting, creative writing, dance, general creative arts/performance, music, performing arts, theater/drama. *Special Achievements/Activities:* 504 awards ($3,218,200 total): general special achievements/activities, leadership. *Special Characteristics:* 76 awards ($890,149 total): children of educators, children of faculty/staff, relatives of clergy, religious affiliation, siblings of current students. ***Tuition waivers:*** Full or partial for employees or children of employees, senior citizens. ***ROTC:*** Army cooperative.

LOANS ***Student loans:*** $9,214,541 (89% need-based, 11% non-need-based). 72% of past graduating class borrowed through all loan programs. *Average indebtedness per student:* $13,977. ***Average need-based loan:*** Freshmen: $2904; Undergraduates: $4175. ***Parent loans:*** $4,857,364 (82% need-based, 18% non-need-based). ***Programs:*** FFEL (Subsidized and Unsubsidized Stafford, PLUS), Perkins, Federal Nursing, alternative loans.

WORK-STUDY ***Federal work-study:*** Total amount: $335,125; 324 jobs averaging $631. ***State or other work-study/employment:*** Total amount: $384,250 (65% need-based, 35% non-need-based). 234 part-time jobs averaging $631.

APPLYING FOR FINANCIAL AID ***Required financial aid forms:*** FAFSA, institution's own form, state aid form. ***Financial aid deadline (priority):*** 2/1. ***Notification date:*** Continuous beginning 2/15. Students must reply within 2 weeks of notification.

CONTACT Mr. Peter Rautzhan, Director of Admissions and Financial Aid, DeSales University, 2755 Station Avenue, Center Valley, PA 18034-9568, 610-282-1100 Ext. 1332 or toll-free 877-4DESALES (in-state), 800-228-5114 (out-of-state). *Fax:* 610-282-0131. *E-mail:* peter.rautzhan@desales.edu.

DESIGN INSTITUTE OF SAN DIEGO

San Diego, CA

CONTACT Financial Aid Office, Design Institute of San Diego, 8555 Commerce Avenue, San Diego, CA 92121, 858-566-1200 or toll-free 800-619-4337.

DeVRY INSTITUTE OF TECHNOLOGY

Long Island City, NY

CONTACT Elvira Senese, Dean of Student Finance, DeVry Institute of Technology, 30-20 Thomson Avenue, Long Island City, NY 11101, 718-472-2728. *Fax:* 718-269-4284.

DeVRY UNIVERSITY

Mesa, AZ

CONTACT Financial Aid Office, DeVry University, 1201 South Alma School Road, Mesa, AZ 85210-2011, 480-827-1511.

DeVRY UNIVERSITY

Phoenix, AZ

CONTACT Kathy Wyse, Dean of Student Finance, DeVry University, 2149 West Dunlap Avenue, Phoenix, AZ 85021-2995, 602-870-9222. *Fax:* 602-870-1209.

DeVRY UNIVERSITY

Elk Grove, CA

CONTACT Financial Aid Office, DeVry University, Sacramento Center, 2218 Kausen Drive, Elk Grove, CA 95758, 916-478-2847 or toll-free 866-573-3879.

DeVRY UNIVERSITY

Fremont, CA

CONTACT Kim Kane, Director of Student Finance, DeVry University, 6600 Dumbarton Circle, Fremont, CA 94555, 510-574-1100. *Fax:* 510-742-0868.

DeVRY UNIVERSITY

Irvine, CA

CONTACT Financial Aid Office, DeVry University, 3333 Michelson Drive, Suite 420, Irvine, CA 92612-1682, 949-752-5631.

DeVRY UNIVERSITY

Long Beach, CA

CONTACT Kathy Odom, Director of Financial Aid, DeVry University, 3880 Kilroy Airport Way, Long Beach, CA 90806, 562-427-0861. *Fax:* 562-989-1578.

DeVRY UNIVERSITY

Pomona, CA

CONTACT Kathy Odom, Director of Financial Aid, DeVry University, 901 Corporate Center Drive, Pomona, CA 91768-2642, 909-622-8866. *Fax:* 909-623-5666.

DeVRY UNIVERSITY

San Diego, CA

CONTACT Financial Aid Office, DeVry University, 2655 Camino Del Rio North, Suite 201, San Diego, CA 92108-1633, 619-683-2446.

DeVRY UNIVERSITY

San Francisco, CA

CONTACT Financial Aid Office, DeVry University, 455 Market Street, Suite 1650, San Francisco, CA 94105-2472, 415-243-8787.

DeVRY UNIVERSITY

West Hills, CA

CONTACT Ann Logan, Dean of Student Finance, DeVry University, 22801 Roscoe Boulevard, West Hills, CA 91304, 818-932-3001 or toll-free 888-610-0800. *Fax:* 818-932-3131.

DeVRY UNIVERSITY

Broomfield, CO

CONTACT Terry Bargas, Director of Financial Aid, DeVry University, 925 South Niagara Street, Denver, CO 80224, 303-329-3340. *Fax:* 303-321-3412.

DeVRY UNIVERSITY

Colorado Springs, CO

CONTACT Carol Oppman, Director of Financial Aid, DeVry University, 225 South Union Boulevard, Colorado Springs, CO 80910, 719-632-3000 or toll-free 866-338-7934. *Fax:* 719-632-1909.

DeVRY UNIVERSITY

Westminster, CO

CONTACT Office of Financial Aid, DeVry University, 1870 West 122nd Avenue, Westminster, CO 80234-2010, 303-280-7400.

DeVRY UNIVERSITY

Miami, FL

CONTACT Financial Aid Office, DeVry University, 200 South Biscayne Boulevard, Suite 500, Miami, FL 33131-5351, 786-425-1113.

DeVRY UNIVERSITY

Miramar, FL

CONTACT Office of Financial Aid, DeVry University, 2300 Southwest 145th Avenue, Miramar, FL 33027, 954-499-9700.

DeVRY UNIVERSITY

Orlando, FL

CONTACT Estrella Velazquez-Domenech, Director of Student Finance, DeVry University, 4000 Millenia Boulevard, Orlando, FL 32839, 407-345-2816. *Fax:* 407-355-4855.

DeVRY UNIVERSITY
Tampa, FL

CONTACT Financial Aid Office, DeVry University, 3030 North Rocky Point Drive West, Suite 100, Tampa, FL 33607-5901, 813-288-8994.

DeVRY UNIVERSITY
Alpharetta, GA

CONTACT David Pickett, Assistant Director of Financial Aid, DeVry University, 2555 Northwinds Parkway, Alpharetta, GA 30004, 770-521-4900 or toll-free 800-346-5420. *Fax:* 770-664-8024.

DeVRY UNIVERSITY
Atlanta, GA

CONTACT Financial Aid Office, DeVry University, Fifteen Piedmont Center, Plaza Level 100, Atlanta, GA 30305-1543, 404-296-7400.

DeVRY UNIVERSITY
Decatur, GA

CONTACT Robin Winston, Director of Financial Aid, DeVry University, 250 North Arcadia Avenue, Decatur, GA 30030-2198, 404-292-7900. *Fax:* 404-292-2321.

DeVRY UNIVERSITY
Duluth, GA

CONTACT Financial Aid Office, DeVry University, 3505 Koger Boulevard, Suite 170, Duluth, GA 30096-7671, 678-380-9780.

DeVRY UNIVERSITY
Addison, IL

CONTACT Sejal Amin, Director of Student Finance, DeVry University, 1221 North Swift Road, Addison, IL 60101-6106, 630-953-1300 or toll-free 800-346-5420.

DeVRY UNIVERSITY
Chicago, IL

CONTACT Milena Dobrina, Director of Financial Aid, DeVry University, 3300 North Campbell Avenue, Chicago, IL 60618-5994, 773-929-8500. *Fax:* 773-348-1780.

DeVRY UNIVERSITY
Elgin, IL

CONTACT Financial Aid Office, DeVry University, 385 Airport Road, Elgin, IL 60123-9341, 847-622-1135.

DeVRY UNIVERSITY
Gurnee, IL

CONTACT Financial Aid Office, DeVry University, 1075 Tri-State Parkway, Suite 800, Gurnee, IL 60031-9126, 847-855-2649 or toll-free 866-563-3879.

DeVRY UNIVERSITY
Naperville, IL

CONTACT Financial Aid Office, DeVry University, 2056 Westings Avenue, Suite 40, Naperville, IL 60563-2361, 630-428-9086 or toll-free 877-496-9050.

DeVRY UNIVERSITY
Oakbrook Terrace, IL

CONTACT Financial Aid Office, DeVry University, One Tower Lane, Oakbrook Terrace, IL 60181, 630-574-1960.

DeVRY UNIVERSITY
Tinley Park, IL

CONTACT Director of Student Finance, DeVry University, 18624 West Creek Drive, Tinley Park, IL 60477, 708-342-3300. *Fax:* 708-342-3120.

DeVRY UNIVERSITY
Indianapolis, IN

CONTACT Financial Aid Office, DeVry University, 9100 Keystone Crossing, Suite 350, Indianapolis, IN 46240-2158, 317-581-8854.

DeVRY UNIVERSITY
Merrillville, IN

CONTACT Financial Aid Office, DeVry University, Twin Towers, 1000 East 80th Place, Suite 222 Mall, Merrillville, IN 46410-5673, 219-736-7440.

DeVRY UNIVERSITY
Bethesda, MD

CONTACT Financial Aid Office, DeVry University, 4550 Montgomery Avenue. Suite 100 North, Bethesda, MD 20814-3304, 301-652-8477.

DeVRY UNIVERSITY
Edina, MN

CONTACT Financial Aid Office, DeVry University, 7700 France Avenue South, Suite 575, Edina, MN 55435, 952-838-1860.

DeVRY UNIVERSITY
Kansas City, MO

CONTACT Maureen Kelly, Senior Associate Director of Financial Aid, DeVry University, 11224 Holmes Street, Kansas City, MO 64131-3698, 816-941-0430.

DeVRY UNIVERSITY
Kansas City, MO

CONTACT Financial Aid Office, DeVry University, City Center Square, 1100 Main Street, Suite 118, Kansas City, MO 64105-2112, 816-221-1300.

DeVRY UNIVERSITY
St. Louis, MO

CONTACT Financial Aid Office, DeVry University, 1801 Park 270 Drive, Suite 260, St. Louis, MO 63146-4020, 314-542-4222.

DeVRY UNIVERSITY
Henderson, NV

CONTACT Financial Aid Office, DeVry University, 2490 Paseo Verde Parkway, Suite 150, Henderson, NV 89074-7120, 702-933-9700.

DeVRY UNIVERSITY
North Brunswick, NJ

CONTACT Albert Cama, Director of Financial Aid, DeVry University, 630 US Highway 1, North Brunswick, NJ 08902, 732-435-4880. *Fax:* 732-435-4867.

DeVRY UNIVERSITY
Charlotte, NC

CONTACT Financial Aid Office, DeVry University, 4521 Sharon Road, Suite 145, Charlotte, NC 28211-3627, 704-362-2345.

DeVRY UNIVERSITY
Cleveland, OH

CONTACT Financial Aid Office, DeVry University, 200 Public Square, Suite 150, Cleveland, OH 44114-2301, 216-781-8000.

DeVRY UNIVERSITY
Columbus, OH

CONTACT Cynthia Price, Director of Financial Aid, DeVry University, 1350 Alum Creek Drive, Columbus, OH 43209-2705, 614-253-7291. *Fax:* 614-252-4108.

DeVRY UNIVERSITY
Seven Hills, OH

CONTACT Financial Aid Office, DeVry University, The Genesis Building, 6000 Lombardo Center, Seven Hills, OH 44131-6907, 216-328-8754 or toll-free 866-453-3879.

DeVRY UNIVERSITY
Portland, OR

CONTACT Financial Aid Office, DeVry University, Peterkort Center II, 9755 SW Barnes Road, Suite 150, Portland, OR 97225-6651, 503-296-7468.

DeVRY UNIVERSITY
Chesterbrook, PA

CONTACT Financial Aid Office, DeVry University, 701 Lee Road, Suite 103, Chesterbrook, PA 19087-5612, 610-889-9980.

DeVRY UNIVERSITY
Fort Washington, PA

CONTACT Financial Aid Office, DeVry University, 1140 Virginia Drive, Fort Washington, PA 19034, 215-591-5700.

DeVRY UNIVERSITY
Pittsburgh, PA

CONTACT Financial Aid Office, DeVry University, FreeMarkets Center, 210 Sixth Avenue, Suite 200, Pittsburgh, PA 15222-9123, 412-642-9072 or toll-free 866-77DEVRY.

DeVRY UNIVERSITY
Memphis, TN

CONTACT Financial Aid Office, DeVry University, PennMarc Centre, 6401 Poplar Avenue, Suite 600, Memphis, TN 38119, 901-537-2560 or toll-free 888-563-3879.

DeVRY UNIVERSITY
Houston, TX

CONTACT Financial Aid Office, DeVry University, 11125 Equity Drive, Houston, TX 77041, 713-850-0888 or toll-free 866-703-3879.

DeVRY UNIVERSITY
Irving, TX

CONTACT Tommy Sims, Financial Aid Officer, DeVry University, 4800 Regent Boulevard, Irving, TX 75063-2440, 972-929-6777.

DeVRY UNIVERSITY
Plano, TX

CONTACT Financial Aid Office, DeVry University, Plano Corporate Center II, 2301 West Plano Parkway, Suite 101, Plano, TX 75075-8435, 972-943-8041.

DeVRY UNIVERSITY
Arlington, VA

CONTACT Roberta McDevitt, Director of Student Finance, DeVry University, 2341 Jefferson Davis Highway, Arlington, VA 22202, 866-338-7932. *Fax:* 703-414-4040.

DeVRY UNIVERSITY
McLean, VA

CONTACT Financial Aid Office, DeVry University, 1751 Pinnacle Drive, Suite 250, McLean, VA 22102-3832, 703-556-9669.

DeVRY UNIVERSITY
Bellevue, WA

CONTACT Financial Aid Office, DeVry University, 500 108th Avenue NE, Suite 320, Bellevue, WA 98004-5519, 425-455-2242.

DeVRY UNIVERSITY
Federal Way, WA

CONTACT Diane Rooney, Assistant Director of Student Finance, DeVry University, 3600 South 344th Way, Federal Way, WA 98001, 253-943-2800. *Fax:* 253-943-5503.

DeVRY UNIVERSITY
Milwaukee, WI

CONTACT Financial Aid Office, DeVry University, 100 East Wisconsin Avenue, Suite 2550, Milwaukee, WI 53202-4107, 414-278-7677.

DeVRY UNIVERSITY
Waukesha, WI

CONTACT Financial Aid Office, DeVry University, 20935 Swenson Drive, Suite 450, Waukesha, WI 53186-4047, 262-798-9889.

DeVRY UNIVERSITY ONLINE
Oakbrook Terrace, IL

CONTACT Financial Aid Office, DeVry University Online, One Tower Lane, Suite 1000, Oakbrook Terrace, IL 60181, 630-574-1960 or toll-free 866-338-7934.

DICKINSON COLLEGE
Carlisle, PA

Tuition & fees: $35,784 **Average undergraduate aid package: $26,239**

ABOUT THE INSTITUTION Independent, coed. Awards: bachelor's degrees. 46 undergraduate majors. Total enrollment: 2,400. Undergraduates: 2,400. Freshmen: 618. Both federal and institutional methodology are used as a basis for awarding need-based institutional aid.

UNDERGRADUATE EXPENSES for 2007–08 ***Application fee:*** $60. ***Comprehensive fee:*** $44,764 includes full-time tuition ($35,450), mandatory fees ($334), and room and board ($8980). ***College room only:*** $4630. ***Part-time tuition:*** $4430 per course. ***Part-time fees:*** $42 per course.

FRESHMAN FINANCIAL AID (Fall 2006, est.) 382 applied for aid; of those 77% were deemed to have need. 100% of freshmen with need received aid; of those 88% had need fully met. ***Average percent of need met:*** 97% (excluding resources awarded to replace EFC). ***Average financial aid package:*** $26,916 (excluding resources awarded to replace EFC). 6% of all full-time freshmen had no need and received non-need-based gift aid.

UNDERGRADUATE FINANCIAL AID (Fall 2006, est.) 1,337 applied for aid; of those 85% were deemed to have need. 100% of undergraduates with need received aid; of those 71% had need fully met. ***Average percent of need met:*** 96% (excluding resources awarded to replace EFC). ***Average financial aid***

package: $26,239 (excluding resources awarded to replace EFC). 10% of all full-time undergraduates had no need and received non-need-based gift aid.

GIFT AID (NEED-BASED) ***Total amount:*** $24,232,643 (5% federal, 3% state, 89% institutional, 3% external sources). ***Receiving aid:*** Freshmen: 45% (279); All full-time undergraduates: 46% (1,081). ***Average award:*** Freshmen: $24,201; Undergraduates: $22,749. ***Scholarships, grants, and awards:*** Federal Pell, FSEOG, state, private, college/university gift aid from institutional funds.

GIFT AID (NON-NEED-BASED) ***Total amount:*** $4,422,574 (13% federal, 1% state, 73% institutional, 13% external sources). ***Receiving aid:*** Freshmen: 6% (35); Undergraduates: 5% (129). ***Average award:*** Freshmen: $10,317; Undergraduates: $11,527. ***Scholarships, grants, and awards by category:*** *Academic Interests/Achievement:* 470 awards ($6,437,097 total): general academic interests/achievements, military science. *Special Achievements/Activities:* general special achievements/activities, leadership. *Special Characteristics:* 39 awards ($1,000,022 total): children and siblings of alumni, children of faculty/staff, international students. ***ROTC:*** Army.

LOANS ***Student loans:*** $7,227,074 (61% need-based, 39% non-need-based). 69% of past graduating class borrowed through all loan programs. *Average indebtedness per student:* $19,413. ***Average need-based loan:*** Freshmen: $3809; Undergraduates: $4683. ***Parent loans:*** $5,197,477 (16% need-based, 84% non-need-based). ***Programs:*** FFEL (Subsidized and Unsubsidized Stafford, PLUS), Perkins, college/university.

WORK-STUDY ***Federal work-study:*** Total amount: $1,478,832; 782 jobs averaging $1891. ***State or other work-study/employment:*** Total amount: $508,040 (61% need-based, 39% non-need-based). 165 part-time jobs averaging $3079.

APPLYING FOR FINANCIAL AID ***Required financial aid forms:*** FAFSA, CSS Financial Aid PROFILE, state aid form, noncustodial (divorced/separated) parent's statement, business/farm supplement. ***Financial aid deadline:*** 2/1 (priority: 11/15). ***Notification date:*** 3/31. Students must reply by 5/1 or within 2 weeks of notification.

CONTACT Judith B. Carter, Director of Financial Aid, Dickinson College, PO Box 1773, Carlisle, PA 17013-2896, 717-245-1308 or toll-free 800-644-1773. *Fax:* 717-245-1972. *E-mail:* finaid@dickinson.edu.

DICKINSON STATE UNIVERSITY

Dickinson, ND

Tuition & fees (ND res): $5295 Average undergraduate aid package: $5174

ABOUT THE INSTITUTION State-supported, coed. Awards: associate and bachelor's degrees. 43 undergraduate majors. Total enrollment: 2,572. Undergraduates: 2,572. Freshmen: 358. Federal methodology is used as a basis for awarding need-based institutional aid.

UNDERGRADUATE EXPENSES for 2006–07 ***Application fee:*** $35. ***Tuition, state resident:*** full-time $4470; part-time $186.25 per credit. ***Tuition, nonresident:*** full-time $10,560; part-time $440 per credit. Full-time tuition and fees vary according to location, program, and reciprocity agreements. Part-time tuition and fees vary according to course load, location, program, and reciprocity agreements. ***College room and board:*** $3882. Room and board charges vary according to board plan.

FRESHMAN FINANCIAL AID (Fall 2005) 343 applied for aid. of those 20% had need fully met. ***Average percent of need met:*** 42% (excluding resources awarded to replace EFC). ***Average financial aid package:*** $4910 (excluding resources awarded to replace EFC). 32% of all full-time freshmen had no need and received non-need-based gift aid.

UNDERGRADUATE FINANCIAL AID (Fall 2005) 1,495 applied for aid. of those 19% had need fully met. ***Average percent of need met:*** 49% (excluding resources awarded to replace EFC). ***Average financial aid package:*** $5174 (excluding resources awarded to replace EFC). 29% of all full-time undergraduates had no need and received non-need-based gift aid.

GIFT AID (NEED-BASED) ***Total amount:*** $3,007,891 (72% federal, 3% state, 18% institutional, 7% external sources). ***Receiving aid:*** Freshmen: 62% (236); All full-time undergraduates: 58% (970). ***Average award:*** Freshmen: $2561; Undergraduates: $2480. ***Scholarships, grants, and awards:*** Federal Pell, FSEOG, state, college/university gift aid from institutional funds, National Guard tuition waivers, staff waivers.

GIFT AID (NON-NEED-BASED) ***Total amount:*** $213,830 (67% institutional, 33% external sources). ***Receiving aid:*** Freshmen: 1; Undergraduates: 3. ***Average award:*** Freshmen: $1096; Undergraduates: $1123. ***Scholarships, grants, and awards by category:*** *Academic Interests/Achievement:* agriculture, biological sciences, business, communication, computer science, education, English, foreign languages, general academic interests/achievements, health fields, humanities, mathematics, physical sciences, premedicine, social sciences. *Creative Arts/Performance:* art/fine arts, creative writing, journalism/publications, music, theater/drama. *Special Achievements/Activities:* cheerleading/drum major, leadership, rodeo. *Special Characteristics:* children of faculty/staff, children with a deceased or disabled parent, ethnic background, general special characteristics, international students, members of minority groups, veterans, veterans' children. ***Tuition waivers:*** Full or partial for minority students, children of alumni, employees or children of employees, senior citizens.

LOANS ***Student loans:*** $7,796,445 (52% need-based, 48% non-need-based). ***Average need-based loan:*** Freshmen: $2352; Undergraduates: $3217. ***Parent loans:*** $186,730 (100% non-need-based). ***Programs:*** FFEL (Subsidized and Unsubsidized Stafford, PLUS), Perkins, Federal Nursing, state, college/university, Alaska Loans, alternative loans.

WORK-STUDY ***Federal work-study:*** Total amount: $186,357; jobs available. ***State or other work-study/employment:*** Part-time jobs available.

ATHLETIC AWARDS Total amount: $188,146 (69% need-based, 31% non-need-based).

APPLYING FOR FINANCIAL AID ***Required financial aid form:*** FAFSA. ***Financial aid deadline (priority):*** 3/15. ***Notification date:*** 6/5. Students must reply within 2 weeks of notification.

CONTACT Ms. Sandy Klein, Director of Financial Aid, Dickinson State University, 291 Campus Drive, Dickinson, ND 58601-4896, 701-483-2371 or toll-free 800-279-4295. *Fax:* 701-483-2720. *E-mail:* sandy.klein@dsu.nodak.edu.

DIGIPEN INSTITUTE OF TECHNOLOGY

Redmond, WA

CONTACT Financial Aid Office, DigiPen Institute of Technology, 5001 150th Avenue, NE, Redmond, WA 98052, 425-558-0299.

DILLARD UNIVERSITY

New Orleans, LA

CONTACT Mrs. Cynthia Thornton, Director of Financial Aid, Dillard University, 2601 Gentilly Boulevard, New Orleans, LA 70122-3097, 504-816-4677 or toll-free 800-716-8353 (in-state), 800-216-6637 (out-of-state). *Fax:* 504-816-4353. *E-mail:* cthornton@dillard.edu.

DOANE COLLEGE

Crete, NE

Tuition & fees: $19,150 Average undergraduate aid package: $18,997

ABOUT THE INSTITUTION Independent religious, coed. Awards: bachelor's and master's degrees (non-traditional undergraduate programs and graduate programs offered at Lincoln campus). 40 undergraduate majors. Total enrollment: 922. Undergraduates: 922. Freshmen: 247. Federal methodology is used as a basis for awarding need-based institutional aid.

UNDERGRADUATE EXPENSES for 2007–08 ***Application fee:*** $15. ***Comprehensive fee:*** $24,560 includes full-time tuition ($18,800), mandatory fees ($350), and room and board ($5410). ***College room only:*** $1950. ***Part-time tuition:*** $630 per credit hour. ***Part-time fees:*** $125 per term.

FRESHMAN FINANCIAL AID (Fall 2006, est.) 230 applied for aid; of those 85% were deemed to have need. 100% of freshmen with need received aid; of those 77% had need fully met. ***Average percent of need met:*** 98% (excluding resources awarded to replace EFC). ***Average financial aid package:*** $18,590 (excluding resources awarded to replace EFC). 6% of all full-time freshmen had no need and received non-need-based gift aid.

UNDERGRADUATE FINANCIAL AID (Fall 2006, est.) 806 applied for aid; of those 88% were deemed to have need. 100% of undergraduates with need received aid; of those 7% had need fully met. ***Average percent of need met:*** 99% (excluding resources awarded to replace EFC). ***Average financial aid package:*** $18,997 (excluding resources awarded to replace EFC). 8% of all full-time undergraduates had no need and received non-need-based gift aid.

GIFT AID (NEED-BASED) ***Total amount:*** $4,433,134 (24% federal, 6% state, 58% institutional, 12% external sources). ***Receiving aid:*** Freshmen: 78% (192); All full-time undergraduates: 75% (683). ***Average award:*** Freshmen: $13,047; Undergraduates: $11,327. ***Scholarships, grants, and awards:*** Federal Pell, FSEOG, state, private, college/university gift aid from institutional funds.

GIFT AID (NON-NEED-BASED) ***Total amount:*** $3,185,538 (100% institutional). ***Receiving aid:*** Freshmen: 2% (6); Undergraduates: 4% (32). ***Average award:*** Freshmen: $11,155; Undergraduates: $7594. ***Scholarships, grants, and awards by category:*** *Creative Arts/Performance:* art/fine arts, debating, music, theater/drama. *Special Characteristics:* religious affiliation, siblings of current students. ***ROTC:*** Army cooperative, Air Force cooperative.

LOANS ***Student loans:*** $3,282,202 (69% need-based, 31% non-need-based). 87% of past graduating class borrowed through all loan programs. *Average indebtedness per student:* $13,647. ***Average need-based loan:*** Freshmen: $3297; Undergraduates: $4244. ***Parent loans:*** $2,553,462 (100% non-need-based). ***Programs:*** FFEL (Subsidized and Unsubsidized Stafford, PLUS), Perkins.

WORK-STUDY ***Federal work-study:*** Total amount: $348,973; jobs available. ***State or other work-study/employment:*** Total amount: $140,542 (100% non-need-based). Part-time jobs available.

ATHLETIC AWARDS Total amount: $1,591,986 (56% need-based, 44% non-need-based).

APPLYING FOR FINANCIAL AID ***Required financial aid form:*** FAFSA. ***Financial aid deadline (priority):*** 3/1. ***Notification date:*** Continuous beginning 3/1. Students must reply within 2 weeks of notification.

CONTACT Ms. Janet Dodson, Director of Financial Aid, Doane College, 1014 Boswell Avenue, Crete, NE 68333-2430, 402-826-8260 or toll-free 800-333-6263. *Fax:* 402-826-8600. *E-mail:* janet.dodson@doane.edu.

DOMINICAN COLLEGE

Orangeburg, NY

Tuition & fees: $18,610 **Average undergraduate aid package: $13,144**

ABOUT THE INSTITUTION Independent, coed. Awards: associate, bachelor's, master's, and doctoral degrees. 35 undergraduate majors. Total enrollment: 1,856. Undergraduates: 1,690. Freshmen: 306. Federal methodology is used as a basis for awarding need-based institutional aid.

UNDERGRADUATE EXPENSES for 2006–07 ***Application fee:*** $35. ***Comprehensive fee:*** $27,590 includes full-time tuition ($17,930), mandatory fees ($680), and room and board ($8980). ***Part-time tuition:*** $536 per credit. ***Part-time fees:*** $165 per term. ***Payment plans:*** Installment, deferred payment.

FRESHMAN FINANCIAL AID (Fall 2006, est.) 290 applied for aid; of those 88% were deemed to have need. 98% of freshmen with need received aid; of those 12% had need fully met. ***Average percent of need met:*** 58% (excluding resources awarded to replace EFC). ***Average financial aid package:*** $12,675 (excluding resources awarded to replace EFC). 14% of all full-time freshmen had no need and received non-need-based gift aid.

UNDERGRADUATE FINANCIAL AID (Fall 2006, est.) 1,052 applied for aid; of those 88% were deemed to have need. 100% of undergraduates with need received aid; of those 13% had need fully met. ***Average percent of need met:*** 61% (excluding resources awarded to replace EFC). ***Average financial aid package:*** $13,144 (excluding resources awarded to replace EFC). 10% of all full-time undergraduates had no need and received non-need-based gift aid.

GIFT AID (NEED-BASED) ***Total amount:*** $9,723,383 (19% federal, 17% state, 59% institutional, 5% external sources). ***Receiving aid:*** Freshmen: 81% (245); All full-time undergraduates: 70% (818). ***Average award:*** Freshmen: $10,656; Undergraduates: $10,097. ***Scholarships, grants, and awards:*** Federal Pell, FSEOG, state, private, college/university gift aid from institutional funds.

GIFT AID (NON-NEED-BASED) ***Total amount:*** $11,822 (100% institutional). ***Receiving aid:*** Freshmen: 9% (26); Undergraduates: 8% (90). ***Average award:*** Freshmen: $14,177; Undergraduates: $11,822. ***Scholarships, grants, and awards by category:*** *Academic Interests/Achievement:* 836 awards ($6,035,457 total): education, general academic interests/achievements, health fields. *Special Characteristics:* 16 awards ($104,694 total): children of faculty/staff, general special characteristics, relatives of clergy. ***Tuition waivers:*** Full or partial for employees or children of employees, senior citizens.

LOANS ***Student loans:*** $8,232,325 (100% need-based). 73% of past graduating class borrowed through all loan programs. *Average indebtedness per student:* $23,091. ***Average need-based loan:*** Freshmen: $2499; Undergraduates: $3778. ***Parent loans:*** $2,675,535 (100% need-based). ***Programs:*** FFEL (Subsidized and Unsubsidized Stafford, PLUS), Perkins, Federal Nursing.

WORK-STUDY ***Federal work-study:*** Total amount: $321,083; 228 jobs averaging $1408. ***State or other work-study/employment:*** Total amount: $8000 (100% need-based). 4 part-time jobs averaging $2000.

ATHLETIC AWARDS Total amount: $1,195,706 (100% need-based).

APPLYING FOR FINANCIAL AID ***Required financial aid form:*** FAFSA. ***Financial aid deadline (priority):*** 2/15. ***Notification date:*** Continuous beginning 2/15. Students must reply within 4 weeks of notification.

CONTACT Ms. Eileen Felske, Director of Financial Aid, Dominican College, 470 Western Highway, Orangeburg, NY 10962-1210, 845-359-7800 Ext. 225 or toll-free 866-432-4636. *Fax:* 845-359-2313. *E-mail:* eileen.felske@dc.edu.

DOMINICAN UNIVERSITY

River Forest, IL

Tuition & fees: $21,250 **Average undergraduate aid package: $16,344**

ABOUT THE INSTITUTION Independent Roman Catholic, coed. Awards: bachelor's and master's degrees and post-master's certificates. 46 undergraduate majors. Total enrollment: 3,292. Undergraduates: 1,462. Freshmen: 362. Federal methodology is used as a basis for awarding need-based institutional aid.

UNDERGRADUATE EXPENSES for 2006–07 ***Application fee:*** $25. ***Comprehensive fee:*** $27,870 includes full-time tuition ($21,150), mandatory fees ($100), and room and board ($6620). Full-time tuition and fees vary according to program. Room and board charges vary according to board plan and housing facility. ***Part-time tuition:*** $705 per semester hour. ***Part-time fees:*** $10 per course. Part-time tuition and fees vary according to location and program. ***Payment plan:*** Installment.

FRESHMAN FINANCIAL AID (Fall 2006, est.) 356 applied for aid; of those 88% were deemed to have need. 99% of freshmen with need received aid; of those 14% had need fully met. ***Average percent of need met:*** 77% (excluding resources awarded to replace EFC). ***Average financial aid package:*** $16,458 (excluding resources awarded to replace EFC). 12% of all full-time freshmen had no need and received non-need-based gift aid.

UNDERGRADUATE FINANCIAL AID (Fall 2006, est.) 1,077 applied for aid; of those 90% were deemed to have need. 99% of undergraduates with need received aid; of those 17% had need fully met. ***Average percent of need met:*** 78% (excluding resources awarded to replace EFC). ***Average financial aid package:*** $16,344 (excluding resources awarded to replace EFC). 17% of all full-time undergraduates had no need and received non-need-based gift aid.

GIFT AID (NEED-BASED) ***Total amount:*** $12,086,212 (12% federal, 23% state, 64% institutional, 1% external sources). ***Receiving aid:*** Freshmen: 86% (312); All full-time undergraduates: 80% (950). ***Average award:*** Freshmen: $13,109; Undergraduates: $12,456. ***Scholarships, grants, and awards:*** Federal Pell, FSEOG, state, private, college/university gift aid from institutional funds.

GIFT AID (NON-NEED-BASED) ***Total amount:*** $1,637,874 (1% federal, 96% institutional, 3% external sources). ***Receiving aid:*** Freshmen: 9% (34); Undergraduates: 8% (96). ***Average award:*** Freshmen: $8813; Undergraduates: $10,690. ***Scholarships, grants, and awards by category:*** *Academic Interests/Achievement:* 754 awards ($4,967,525 total): general academic interests/achievements, physical sciences. *Special Achievements/Activities:* 38 awards ($121,750 total): leadership. *Special Characteristics:* 115 awards ($262,501 total): children and siblings of alumni, children of faculty/staff, international students, siblings of current students, twins. ***Tuition waivers:*** Full or partial for children of alumni, employees or children of employees.

LOANS ***Student loans:*** $5,908,531 (73% need-based, 27% non-need-based). 58% of past graduating class borrowed through all loan programs. *Average indebtedness per student:* $16,137. ***Average need-based loan:*** Freshmen: $2566; Undergraduates: $3823. ***Parent loans:*** $1,338,208 (28% need-based, 72% non-need-based). ***Programs:*** FFEL (Subsidized and Unsubsidized Stafford, PLUS), Perkins.

WORK-STUDY ***Federal work-study:*** Total amount: $723,439; 326 jobs averaging $1865. ***State or other work-study/employment:*** Total amount: $378,261 (13% need-based, 87% non-need-based). 181 part-time jobs averaging $1975.

APPLYING FOR FINANCIAL AID ***Required financial aid form:*** FAFSA. ***Financial aid deadline (priority):*** 6/1. ***Notification date:*** Continuous beginning 3/1. Students must reply within 2 weeks of notification.

CONTACT Michael Shields, Director of Financial Aid, Dominican University, 7900 West Division Street, River Forest, IL 60305-1099, 708-524-6807 or toll-free 800-828-8475. *Fax:* 708-366-6478. *E-mail:* mshields@dom.edu.

DOMINICAN UNIVERSITY OF CALIFORNIA

San Rafael, CA

ABOUT THE INSTITUTION Independent religious, coed. Awards: bachelor's and master's degrees and post-bachelor's certificates. 28 undergraduate majors. Total enrollment: 2,045. Undergraduates: 1,468. Freshmen: 267.

GIFT AID (NEED-BASED) ***Scholarships, grants, and awards:*** Federal Pell, FSEOG, state, private, college/university gift aid from institutional funds, Federal Nursing.

GIFT AID (NON-NEED-BASED) ***Scholarships, grants, and awards by category:*** *Academic Interests/Achievement:* general academic interests/achievements. *Creative Arts/Performance:* music. *Special Achievements/Activities:* community service, general special achievements/activities. *Special Characteristics:* adult students, children and siblings of alumni, children of faculty/staff, ethnic background, first-generation college students, international students, local/state students, members of minority groups, out-of-state students.

LOANS ***Programs:*** FFEL (Subsidized and Unsubsidized Stafford, PLUS), Perkins, private loans.

WORK-STUDY ***Federal work-study:*** Total amount: $693,184; 284 jobs averaging $2431. ***State or other work-study/employment:*** Total amount: $206,998 (71% need-based, 29% non-need-based). 24 part-time jobs averaging $7751.

APPLYING FOR FINANCIAL AID ***Required financial aid forms:*** FAFSA, institution's own form, state aid form.

CONTACT Audrey Tanne, Assistant Vice President for Financial Aid and Student Services, Dominican University of California, 50 Acacia Avenue, San Rafael, CA 94901-2298, 415-257-1321 or toll-free 888-323-6763. *Fax:* 415-485-3294. *E-mail:* atanner@dominican.edu.

DORDT COLLEGE

Sioux Center, IA

Tuition & fees: $18,660 **Average undergraduate aid package: $16,350**

ABOUT THE INSTITUTION Independent Christian Reformed, coed. Awards: associate, bachelor's, and master's degrees. 86 undergraduate majors. Total enrollment: 1,261. Undergraduates: 1,259. Freshmen: 337. Federal methodology is used as a basis for awarding need-based institutional aid.

UNDERGRADUATE EXPENSES for 2006–07 ***Application fee:*** $25. ***Comprehensive fee:*** $23,820 includes full-time tuition ($18,400), mandatory fees ($260), and room and board ($5160). ***College room only:*** $2720. Full-time tuition and fees vary according to course load. Room and board charges vary according to board plan and housing facility. ***Part-time tuition:*** $770 per credit hour. ***Part-time fees:*** $120 per term. ***Payment plan:*** Installment.

FRESHMAN FINANCIAL AID (Fall 2006, est.) 328 applied for aid; of those 85% were deemed to have need. 100% of freshmen with need received aid; of those 18% had need fully met. ***Average percent of need met:*** 88% (excluding resources awarded to replace EFC). ***Average financial aid package:*** $16,682 (excluding resources awarded to replace EFC). 18% of all full-time freshmen had no need and received non-need-based gift aid.

UNDERGRADUATE FINANCIAL AID (Fall 2006, est.) 1,050 applied for aid; of those 88% were deemed to have need. 100% of undergraduates with need received aid; of those 14% had need fully met. ***Average percent of need met:*** 86% (excluding resources awarded to replace EFC). ***Average financial aid package:*** $16,350 (excluding resources awarded to replace EFC). 20% of all full-time undergraduates had no need and received non-need-based gift aid.

GIFT AID (NEED-BASED) ***Total amount:*** $8,821,621 (9% federal, 12% state, 71% institutional, 8% external sources). ***Receiving aid:*** Freshmen: 81% (278); All full-time undergraduates: 78% (920). ***Average award:*** Freshmen: $10,338; Undergraduates: $9137. ***Scholarships, grants, and awards:*** Federal Pell, FSEOG, state, private, college/university gift aid from institutional funds.

GIFT AID (NON-NEED-BASED) ***Total amount:*** $1,366,740 (91% institutional, 9% external sources). ***Average award:*** Freshmen: $10,573; Undergraduates: $8771. ***Scholarships, grants, and awards by category:*** *Academic Interests/Achievement:* agriculture, biological sciences, business, communication, computer science, education, engineering/technologies, English, foreign languages, general academic interests/achievements, humanities, mathematics, physical sciences, premedicine, religion/biblical studies, social sciences. *Creative Arts/Performance:* journalism/publications, music, theater/drama. *Special Achievements/Activities:* general special achievements/activities, leadership. *Special Characteristics:* children and siblings of alumni, children of faculty/staff, general special characteristics, handicapped students, international students, local/state students, members of minority groups, out-of-state students, religious affiliation. ***Tuition waivers:*** Full or partial for employees or children of employees, senior citizens.

LOANS ***Student loans:*** $6,258,369 (92% need-based, 8% non-need-based). 80% of past graduating class borrowed through all loan programs. *Average indebtedness per student:* $19,157. ***Average need-based loan:*** Freshmen: $4364; Undergraduates: $4624. ***Parent loans:*** $2,074,388 (89% need-based, 11% non-need-based). ***Programs:*** FFEL (Subsidized and Unsubsidized Stafford, PLUS), Perkins, state, college/university, alternative loans.

WORK-STUDY ***Federal work-study:*** Total amount: $633,950; 525 jobs averaging $1300. ***State or other work-study/employment:*** Total amount: $809,530 (73% need-based, 27% non-need-based). 505 part-time jobs averaging $1300.

ATHLETIC AWARDS Total amount: $602,475 (77% need-based, 23% non-need-based).

APPLYING FOR FINANCIAL AID ***Required financial aid forms:*** FAFSA, institution's own form. ***Financial aid deadline (priority):*** 4/1. ***Notification date:*** Continuous beginning 3/5. Students must reply within 3 weeks of notification.

CONTACT Michael Epema, Director of Financial Aid, Dordt College, 498 4th Avenue NE, Sioux Center, IA 51250-1697, 712-722-6087 Ext. 6082 or toll-free 800-343-6738. *Fax:* 712-722-1967.

DOWLING COLLEGE

Oakdale, NY

Tuition & fees: $18,430 **Average undergraduate aid package: $13,546**

ABOUT THE INSTITUTION Independent, coed. Awards: bachelor's, master's, and doctoral degrees and post-bachelor's and post-master's certificates. 52 undergraduate majors. Total enrollment: 5,546. Undergraduates: 3,052. Freshmen: 443. Federal methodology is used as a basis for awarding need-based institutional aid.

UNDERGRADUATE EXPENSES for 2006–07 ***Application fee:*** $25. ***Comprehensive fee:*** $27,418 includes full-time tuition ($17,340), mandatory fees ($1090), and room and board ($8988). Full-time tuition and fees vary according to course load and degree level. Room and board charges vary according to housing facility and location. ***Part-time tuition:*** $578 per credit. Part-time tuition and fees vary according to course load and degree level. ***Payment plans:*** Installment, deferred payment.

FRESHMAN FINANCIAL AID (Fall 2006, est.) 343 applied for aid; of those 82% were deemed to have need. 98% of freshmen with need received aid; of those 4% had need fully met. ***Average percent of need met:*** 78% (excluding resources awarded to replace EFC). ***Average financial aid package:*** $12,734 (excluding resources awarded to replace EFC). 19% of all full-time freshmen had no need and received non-need-based gift aid.

UNDERGRADUATE FINANCIAL AID (Fall 2006, est.) 1,662 applied for aid; of those 85% were deemed to have need. 99% of undergraduates with need received aid; of those 13% had need fully met. ***Average percent of need met:*** 79% (excluding resources awarded to replace EFC). ***Average financial aid package:*** $13,546 (excluding resources awarded to replace EFC). 14% of all full-time undergraduates had no need and received non-need-based gift aid.

GIFT AID (NEED-BASED) ***Total amount:*** $10,276,607 (26% federal, 30% state, 43% institutional, 1% external sources). ***Receiving aid:*** Freshmen: 65% (275); All full-time undergraduates: 63% (1,392). ***Average award:*** Freshmen: $4926; Undergraduates: $4487. ***Scholarships, grants, and awards:*** Federal Pell, FSEOG, state, private, college/university gift aid from institutional funds.

GIFT AID (NON-NEED-BASED) ***Total amount:*** $1,740,965 (2% federal, 7% state, 91% institutional). ***Average award:*** Freshmen: $4334; Undergraduates: $4861. ***Scholarships, grants, and awards by category:*** *Academic Interests/Achievement:* business, education, general academic interests/achievements. *Special Achievements/Activities:* general special achievements/activities. *Special Characteristics:* children and siblings of alumni, children of educators, children of faculty/staff, children of public servants, children of union members/company employees, children of workers in trades, first-generation college students, general special characteristics, local/state students, public servants. ***Tuition waivers:*** Full or partial for minority students, children of alumni, employees or children of employees, adult students, senior citizens. ***ROTC:*** Air Force cooperative.

LOANS ***Student loans:*** $12,548,606 (84% need-based, 16% non-need-based). 61% of past graduating class borrowed through all loan programs. *Average indebtedness per student:* $22,735. ***Average need-based loan:*** Freshmen: $2913;

Undergraduates: $3902. ***Parent loans:*** $1,975,985 (70% need-based, 30% non-need-based). ***Programs:*** Federal Direct (Subsidized and Unsubsidized Stafford, PLUS), FFEL (PLUS), Perkins, alternative loans.

WORK-STUDY ***Federal work-study:*** Total amount: $318,000; jobs available. ***State or other work-study/employment:*** Part-time jobs available.

ATHLETIC AWARDS Total amount: $2,018,314 (41% need-based, 59% non-need-based).

APPLYING FOR FINANCIAL AID ***Required financial aid forms:*** FAFSA, institution's own form, state aid form. ***Financial aid deadline (priority):*** 4/1. ***Notification date:*** Continuous beginning 2/1.

CONTACT Lisa Kandell, Director of Enrollment Services/Financial Aid, Dowling College, Idle Hour Boulevard, Oakdale, NY 11769-1999, 631-244-3385 or toll-free 800-DOWLING. *Fax:* 631-563-3827. *E-mail:* kandelll@dowling.edu.

DRAKE UNIVERSITY

Des Moines, IA

Tuition & fees: $22,682 **Average undergraduate aid package: $18,450**

ABOUT THE INSTITUTION Independent, coed. Awards: bachelor's, master's, doctoral, and first professional degrees and post-master's certificates. 66 undergraduate majors. Total enrollment: 5,366. Undergraduates: 3,255. Freshmen: 781. Federal methodology is used as a basis for awarding need-based institutional aid.

UNDERGRADUATE EXPENSES for 2006–07 ***Application fee:*** $25. ***Comprehensive fee:*** $29,182 includes full-time tuition ($22,270), mandatory fees ($412), and room and board ($6500). ***College room only:*** $3190. Full-time tuition and fees vary according to class time, course load, and student level. Room and board charges vary according to board plan. ***Part-time tuition:*** $430 per hour. ***Part-time fees:*** $40 per semester hour. Part-time tuition and fees vary according to class time. ***Payment plan:*** Installment.

FRESHMAN FINANCIAL AID (Fall 2006, est.) 632 applied for aid; of those 76% were deemed to have need. 100% of freshmen with need received aid; of those 31% had need fully met. ***Average percent of need met:*** 83% (excluding resources awarded to replace EFC). ***Average financial aid package:*** $18,860 (excluding resources awarded to replace EFC). 31% of all full-time freshmen had no need and received non-need-based gift aid.

UNDERGRADUATE FINANCIAL AID (Fall 2006, est.) 2,201 applied for aid; of those 82% were deemed to have need. 100% of undergraduates with need received aid; of those 31% had need fully met. ***Average percent of need met:*** 82% (excluding resources awarded to replace EFC). ***Average financial aid package:*** $18,450 (excluding resources awarded to replace EFC). 32% of all full-time undergraduates had no need and received non-need-based gift aid.

GIFT AID (NEED-BASED) ***Total amount:*** $20,659,122 (10% federal, 9% state, 78% institutional, 3% external sources). ***Receiving aid:*** Freshmen: 61% (474); All full-time undergraduates: 60% (1,773). ***Average award:*** Freshmen: $12,422; Undergraduates: $11,490. ***Scholarships, grants, and awards:*** Federal Pell, FSEOG, state, private, college/university gift aid from institutional funds.

GIFT AID (NON-NEED-BASED) ***Total amount:*** $11,695,788 (2% federal, 94% institutional, 4% external sources). ***Receiving aid:*** Freshmen: 14% (111); Undergraduates: 11% (340). ***Average award:*** Freshmen: $9593; Undergraduates: $9780. ***Scholarships, grants, and awards by category:*** *Academic Interests/Achievement:* 2,264 awards ($18,176,304 total): general academic interests/achievements. *Creative Arts/Performance:* 262 awards ($785,292 total): art/fine arts, music, theater/drama. *Special Characteristics:* 310 awards ($1,017,809 total): children and siblings of alumni, ethnic background, members of minority groups. ***Tuition waivers:*** Full or partial for children of alumni, employees or children of employees, senior citizens. ***ROTC:*** Army, Air Force cooperative.

LOANS ***Student loans:*** $25,817,396 (47% need-based, 53% non-need-based). 77% of past graduating class borrowed through all loan programs. *Average indebtedness per student:* $26,482. ***Average need-based loan:*** Freshmen: $4617; Undergraduates: $5404. ***Parent loans:*** $24,677,112 (13% need-based, 87% non-need-based). ***Programs:*** FFEL (Subsidized and Unsubsidized Stafford, PLUS), Perkins, college/university.

WORK-STUDY ***Federal work-study:*** Total amount: $2,311,776; 1,509 jobs averaging $1533. ***State or other work-study/employment:*** Part-time jobs available.

ATHLETIC AWARDS Total amount: $2,834,161 (27% need-based, 73% non-need-based).

APPLYING FOR FINANCIAL AID ***Required financial aid form:*** FAFSA. ***Financial aid deadline (priority):*** 3/1. ***Notification date:*** Continuous beginning 3/1. Students must reply by 5/1 or within 3 weeks of notification.

CONTACT Office of Student Financial Planning, Drake University, 2507 University Avenue, Des Moines, IA 50311-4516, 800-44-DRAKE Ext. 2905 or toll-free 800-44DRAKE Ext. 3181. *Fax:* 515-271-4042.

DREW UNIVERSITY

Madison, NJ

Tuition & fees: $33,068 **Average undergraduate aid package: $23,242**

ABOUT THE INSTITUTION Independent religious, coed. Awards: bachelor's, master's, doctoral, and first professional degrees and post-bachelor's certificates. 30 undergraduate majors. Total enrollment: 2,647. Undergraduates: 1,656. Freshmen: 481. Institutional methodology is used as a basis for awarding need-based institutional aid.

UNDERGRADUATE EXPENSES for 2006–07 ***Application fee:*** $50. ***Comprehensive fee:*** $42,068 includes full-time tuition ($32,508), mandatory fees ($560), and room and board ($9000). ***College room only:*** $5818. Full-time tuition and fees vary according to course load. Room and board charges vary according to board plan and housing facility. ***Part-time tuition:*** $1354 per credit. ***Part-time fees:*** $23.30 per credit. Part-time tuition and fees vary according to course load. ***Payment plans:*** Tuition prepayment, installment, deferred payment.

FRESHMAN FINANCIAL AID (Fall 2005) 291 applied for aid; of those 69% were deemed to have need. 99% of freshmen with need received aid; of those 26% had need fully met. ***Average percent of need met:*** 78% (excluding resources awarded to replace EFC). ***Average financial aid package:*** $23,523 (excluding resources awarded to replace EFC). 28% of all full-time freshmen had no need and received non-need-based gift aid.

UNDERGRADUATE FINANCIAL AID (Fall 2005) 966 applied for aid; of those 78% were deemed to have need. 99% of undergraduates with need received aid; of those 32% had need fully met. ***Average percent of need met:*** 82% (excluding resources awarded to replace EFC). ***Average financial aid package:*** $23,242 (excluding resources awarded to replace EFC). 28% of all full-time undergraduates had no need and received non-need-based gift aid.

GIFT AID (NEED-BASED) ***Total amount:*** $13,071,994 (7% federal, 12% state, 78% institutional, 3% external sources). ***Receiving aid:*** Freshmen: 51% (199); All full-time undergraduates: 48% (736). ***Average award:*** Freshmen: $19,064; Undergraduates: $17,761. ***Scholarships, grants, and awards:*** Federal Pell, FSEOG, state, private, college/university gift aid from institutional funds.

GIFT AID (NON-NEED-BASED) ***Total amount:*** $6,140,846 (5% state, 92% institutional, 3% external sources). ***Receiving aid:*** Freshmen: 9% (37); Undergraduates: 7% (103). ***Average award:*** Freshmen: $11,368; Undergraduates: $12,240. ***Scholarships, grants, and awards by category:*** *Academic Interests/Achievement:* 991 awards ($9,200,516 total): general academic interests/achievements. *Creative Arts/Performance:* 16 awards ($155,000 total): general creative arts/performance. *Special Characteristics:* 35 awards ($245,038 total): general special characteristics. ***Tuition waivers:*** Full or partial for employees or children of employees, senior citizens.

LOANS ***Student loans:*** $3,909,975 (75% need-based, 25% non-need-based). 59% of past graduating class borrowed through all loan programs. *Average indebtedness per student:* $18,275. ***Average need-based loan:*** Freshmen: $3639; Undergraduates: $4920. ***Parent loans:*** $7,597,120 (23% need-based, 77% non-need-based). ***Programs:*** FFEL (Subsidized and Unsubsidized Stafford, PLUS), Perkins, state.

WORK-STUDY ***Federal work-study:*** Total amount: $374,831; 300 jobs averaging $1249. ***State or other work-study/employment:*** Total amount: $261,128 (70% need-based, 30% non-need-based). 31 part-time jobs averaging $8423.

APPLYING FOR FINANCIAL AID ***Required financial aid forms:*** FAFSA, CSS Financial Aid PROFILE. ***Financial aid deadline:*** 2/15. ***Notification date:*** 3/30. Students must reply by 5/1.

CONTACT Renee Volak, Acting Director of Financial Assistance, Drew University, 36 Madison Avenue, Madison, NJ 07940-1493, 973-408-3112. *Fax:* 973-408-3188.

DREXEL UNIVERSITY

Philadelphia, PA

ABOUT THE INSTITUTION Independent, coed. Awards: associate, bachelor's, master's, doctoral, and first professional degrees and post-bachelor's, post-master's, and first professional certificates. 55 undergraduate majors. Total enrollment: 19,882. Undergraduates: 12,908.

GIFT AID (NEED-BASED) ***Scholarships, grants, and awards:*** Federal Pell, FSEOG, state, private, college/university gift aid from institutional funds, United Negro College Fund.

GIFT AID (NON-NEED-BASED) ***Scholarships, grants, and awards by category:*** *Academic Interests/Achievement:* general academic interests/achievements. *Creative Arts/Performance:* dance, music, performing arts, theater/drama. *Special Achievements/Activities:* cheerleading/drum major. *Special Characteristics:* children and siblings of alumni, siblings of current students, twins.

LOANS ***Programs:*** FFEL (Subsidized and Unsubsidized Stafford, PLUS), Perkins, college/university.

WORK-STUDY ***Federal work-study:*** Total amount: $4,998,860; jobs available.

APPLYING FOR FINANCIAL AID ***Required financial aid form:*** FAFSA.

CONTACT Melissa Englund, Director of Financial Aid, Drexel University, 3141 Chestnut Street, Main Building, Room 106, Philadelphia, PA 19104-2875, 215-895-2537 or toll-free 800-2-DREXEL. *Fax:* 215-895-6903.

DRURY UNIVERSITY

Springfield, MO

Tuition & fees: $15,512 **Average undergraduate aid package: $7689**

ABOUT THE INSTITUTION Independent, coed. Awards: bachelor's and master's degrees (also offers evening program with significant enrollment not reflected in profile). 58 undergraduate majors. Total enrollment: 2,053. Undergraduates: 1,606. Freshmen: 398. Federal methodology is used as a basis for awarding need-based institutional aid.

UNDERGRADUATE EXPENSES for 2006–07 ***Application fee:*** $25. ***Comprehensive fee:*** $21,302 includes full-time tuition ($15,173), mandatory fees ($339), and room and board ($5790). Room and board charges vary according to board plan and housing facility. ***Part-time tuition:*** $500 per semester hour. ***Payment plans:*** Tuition prepayment, installment, deferred payment.

FRESHMAN FINANCIAL AID (Fall 2006, est.) 363 applied for aid; of those 95% were deemed to have need. 100% of freshmen with need received aid; of those 84% had need fully met. ***Average percent of need met:*** 83% (excluding resources awarded to replace EFC). ***Average financial aid package:*** $7428 (excluding resources awarded to replace EFC). 16% of all full-time freshmen had no need and received non-need-based gift aid.

UNDERGRADUATE FINANCIAL AID (Fall 2006, est.) 1,523 applied for aid; of those 95% were deemed to have need. 100% of undergraduates with need received aid; of those 91% had need fully met. ***Average percent of need met:*** 84% (excluding resources awarded to replace EFC). ***Average financial aid package:*** $7689 (excluding resources awarded to replace EFC). 15% of all full-time undergraduates had no need and received non-need-based gift aid.

GIFT AID (NEED-BASED) ***Total amount:*** $7,649,609 (8% federal, 9% state, 61% institutional, 22% external sources). ***Receiving aid:*** Freshmen: 82% (327); All full-time undergraduates: 90% (1,393). ***Average award:*** Freshmen: $5979; Undergraduates: $6842. ***Scholarships, grants, and awards:*** Federal Pell, FSEOG, state, private, college/university gift aid from institutional funds.

GIFT AID (NON-NEED-BASED) ***Total amount:*** $1,783,444 (21% state, 72% institutional, 7% external sources). ***Receiving aid:*** Freshmen: 84% (332); Undergraduates: 89% (1,379). ***Average award:*** Freshmen: $3163; Undergraduates: $3197. ***Scholarships, grants, and awards by category:*** *Academic Interests/Achievement:* 1,492 awards ($2,617,446 total): architecture, biological sciences, business, communication, education, English, general academic interests/achievements, health fields, humanities, mathematics, physical sciences, premedicine, social sciences. *Creative Arts/Performance:* 139 awards ($272,684 total): art/fine arts, creative writing, music, theater/drama. *Special Achievements/Activities:* 574 awards ($218,420 total): cheerleading/drum major, leadership, religious involvement. *Special Characteristics:* 39 awards ($43,876 total): children and siblings of alumni, children of faculty/staff, relatives of clergy, religious affiliation. ***Tuition waivers:*** Full or partial for children of alumni, employees or children of employees, senior citizens. ***ROTC:*** Army cooperative.

LOANS ***Student loans:*** $17,798,031 (95% need-based, 5% non-need-based). 55% of past graduating class borrowed through all loan programs. *Average indebtedness per student:* $17,885. ***Average need-based loan:*** Freshmen: $4125; Undergraduates: $5494. ***Parent loans:*** $1,008,584 (100% need-based). ***Programs:*** FFEL (Subsidized and Unsubsidized Stafford, PLUS), Perkins.

WORK-STUDY ***Federal work-study:*** Total amount: $347,854; jobs available. ***State or other work-study/employment:*** Total amount: $17,421,320 (99% need-based, 1% non-need-based). 91 part-time jobs averaging $2000.

ATHLETIC AWARDS Total amount: $838,651 (29% need-based, 71% non-need-based).

APPLYING FOR FINANCIAL AID ***Required financial aid forms:*** FAFSA, institution's own form. ***Financial aid deadline (priority):*** 3/15. ***Notification date:*** Continuous beginning 3/15. Students must reply within 2 weeks of notification.

CONTACT Ms. Annette Avery, Director of Financial Aid, Drury University, 900 North Benton Avenue, Springfield, MO 65802-3791, 417-873-7312 or toll-free 800-922-2274. *Fax:* 417-873-6906. *E-mail:* aavery@drury.edu.

DUKE UNIVERSITY

Durham, NC

Tuition & fees: $33,963 **Average undergraduate aid package: $29,449**

ABOUT THE INSTITUTION Independent religious, coed. Awards: bachelor's, master's, doctoral, and first professional degrees and post-bachelor's and post-master's certificates. 45 undergraduate majors. Total enrollment: 13,373. Undergraduates: 6,330. Freshmen: 1,683. Both federal and institutional methodology are used as a basis for awarding need-based institutional aid.

UNDERGRADUATE EXPENSES for 2006–07 ***Application fee:*** $75. ***Comprehensive fee:*** $43,115 includes full-time tuition ($32,845), mandatory fees ($1118), and room and board ($9152). ***College room only:*** $4950.

FRESHMAN FINANCIAL AID (Fall 2006, est.) 798 applied for aid; of those 86% were deemed to have need. 100% of freshmen with need received aid; of those 100% had need fully met. ***Average percent of need met:*** 100% (excluding resources awarded to replace EFC). ***Average financial aid package:*** $28,996 (excluding resources awarded to replace EFC). 2% of all full-time freshmen had no need and received non-need-based gift aid.

UNDERGRADUATE FINANCIAL AID (Fall 2006, est.) 2,803 applied for aid; of those 90% were deemed to have need. 100% of undergraduates with need received aid; of those 100% had need fully met. ***Average percent of need met:*** 100% (excluding resources awarded to replace EFC). ***Average financial aid package:*** $29,449 (excluding resources awarded to replace EFC). 4% of all full-time undergraduates had no need and received non-need-based gift aid.

GIFT AID (NEED-BASED) ***Total amount:*** $59,169,189 (6% federal, 3% state, 85% institutional, 6% external sources). ***Receiving aid:*** Freshmen: 40% (665); All full-time undergraduates: 38% (2,422). ***Average award:*** Freshmen: $25,835; Undergraduates: $25,184. ***Scholarships, grants, and awards:*** Federal Pell, FSEOG, state, private, college/university gift aid from institutional funds.

GIFT AID (NON-NEED-BASED) ***Total amount:*** $9,559,731 (9% state, 68% institutional, 23% external sources). ***Receiving aid:*** Freshmen: 4% (63); Undergraduates: 3% (180). ***Average award:*** Freshmen: $32,337; Undergraduates: $24,869. ***Scholarships, grants, and awards by category:*** *Academic Interests/Achievement:* 114 awards ($3,852,672 total): general academic interests/achievements, mathematics. *Creative Arts/Performance:* creative writing. *Special Achievements/Activities:* 66 awards ($2,358,998 total): general special achievements/activities, leadership. *Special Characteristics:* 38 awards ($1,268,146 total): children and siblings of alumni, ethnic background, local/state students. ***ROTC:*** Army, Naval, Air Force.

LOANS ***Student loans:*** $14,642,236 (79% need-based, 21% non-need-based). 40% of past graduating class borrowed through all loan programs. *Average indebtedness per student:* $23,499. ***Average need-based loan:*** Freshmen: $2842; Undergraduates: $3970. ***Parent loans:*** $10,037,754 (57% need-based, 43% non-need-based). ***Programs:*** FFEL (Subsidized and Unsubsidized Stafford, PLUS), Perkins, college/university, alternative loans from private sources.

WORK-STUDY ***Federal work-study:*** Total amount: $3,264,699; 1,768 jobs averaging $1846. ***State or other work-study/employment:*** Total amount: $1,142,773 (57% need-based, 43% non-need-based). 725 part-time jobs averaging $1577.

ATHLETIC AWARDS Total amount: $10,417,987 (20% need-based, 80% non-need-based).

APPLYING FOR FINANCIAL AID ***Required financial aid forms:*** FAFSA, CSS Financial Aid PROFILE, noncustodial (divorced/separated) parent's statement, business/farm supplement, income tax form(s). ***Financial aid deadline:*** 2/1. ***Notification date:*** 4/1. Students must reply by 5/1.

CONTACT Jim Belvin, Director, Duke University, 2122 Campus Drive, Box 90397, Durham, NC 27708-0397, 919-684-6225. *Fax:* 919-660-9811. *E-mail:* finaid@duke.edu.

DUQUESNE UNIVERSITY

Pittsburgh, PA

Tuition & fees: $22,665 **Average undergraduate aid package: $15,204**

ABOUT THE INSTITUTION Independent Roman Catholic, coed. Awards: bachelor's, master's, doctoral, and first professional degrees and post-bachelor's and post-master's certificates. 74 undergraduate majors. Total enrollment: 10,110. Undergraduates: 5,678. Freshmen: 1,325. Federal methodology is used as a basis for awarding need-based institutional aid.

UNDERGRADUATE EXPENSES for 2006–07 ***Application fee:*** $50. ***Comprehensive fee:*** $30,961 includes full-time tuition ($20,855), mandatory fees ($1810), and room and board ($8296). ***College room only:*** $4526. Full-time tuition and fees vary according to program. Room and board charges vary according to board plan and housing facility. ***Part-time tuition:*** $678 per credit. ***Part-time fees:*** $71 per credit. Part-time tuition and fees vary according to program. ***Payment plan:*** Installment.

FRESHMAN FINANCIAL AID (Fall 2006, est.) 1154 applied for aid; of those 80% were deemed to have need. 100% of freshmen with need received aid; of those 60% had need fully met. ***Average percent of need met:*** 90% (excluding resources awarded to replace EFC). ***Average financial aid package:*** $15,268 (excluding resources awarded to replace EFC). 42% of all full-time freshmen had no need and received non-need-based gift aid.

UNDERGRADUATE FINANCIAL AID (Fall 2006, est.) 4,111 applied for aid; of those 85% were deemed to have need. 100% of undergraduates with need received aid; of those 59% had need fully met. ***Average percent of need met:*** 89% (excluding resources awarded to replace EFC). ***Average financial aid package:*** $15,204 (excluding resources awarded to replace EFC). 31% of all full-time undergraduates had no need and received non-need-based gift aid.

GIFT AID (NEED-BASED) ***Total amount:*** $35,836,015 (9% federal, 19% state, 64% institutional, 8% external sources). ***Receiving aid:*** Freshmen: 70% (924); All full-time undergraduates: 64% (3,383). ***Average award:*** Freshmen: $11,279; Undergraduates: $11,403. ***Scholarships, grants, and awards:*** Federal Pell, FSEOG, state, private, college/university gift aid from institutional funds, United Negro College Fund.

GIFT AID (NON-NEED-BASED) ***Total amount:*** $9,908,438 (1% state, 91% institutional, 8% external sources). ***Receiving aid:*** Freshmen: 68% (902); Undergraduates: 53% (2,796). ***Average award:*** Freshmen: $6592; Undergraduates: $7858. ***Scholarships, grants, and awards by category:*** *Academic Interests/Achievement:* 4,784 awards ($19,480,004 total): general academic interests/achievements. *Creative Arts/Performance:* 220 awards ($1,419,199 total): dance, music. *Special Characteristics:* 763 awards ($9,377,212 total): children and siblings of alumni, children of faculty/staff, general special characteristics, international students, members of minority groups, relatives of clergy, religious affiliation. ***Tuition waivers:*** Full or partial for employees or children of employees, senior citizens. ***ROTC:*** Army, Naval cooperative, Air Force cooperative.

LOANS ***Student loans:*** $37,023,630 (88% need-based, 12% non-need-based). 80% of past graduating class borrowed through all loan programs. *Average indebtedness per student:* $27,080. ***Average need-based loan:*** Freshmen: $3355; Undergraduates: $4364. ***Parent loans:*** $11,088,672 (81% need-based, 19% non-need-based). ***Programs:*** FFEL (Subsidized and Unsubsidized Stafford, PLUS), Perkins, Federal Nursing, private alternative loans.

WORK-STUDY ***Federal work-study:*** Total amount: $4,569,512; 1,539 jobs averaging $2559.

ATHLETIC AWARDS Total amount: $3,589,625 (49% need-based, 51% non-need-based).

APPLYING FOR FINANCIAL AID ***Required financial aid forms:*** FAFSA, institution's own form. ***Financial aid deadline:*** 5/1. ***Notification date:*** Continuous beginning 3/1. Students must reply by 5/1 or within 3 weeks of notification.

CONTACT Mr. Richard C. Esposito, Director of Financial Aid, Duquesne University, 600 Forbes Avenue, Pittsburgh, PA 15282-0299, 412-396-6607 or toll-free 800-456-0590. *Fax:* 412-396-5284. *E-mail:* esposito@duq.edu.

D'YOUVILLE COLLEGE

Buffalo, NY

Tuition & fees: $17,000 **Average undergraduate aid package: $13,295**

ABOUT THE INSTITUTION Independent, coed. Awards: bachelor's, master's, doctoral, and first professional degrees and post-bachelor's and post-master's certificates. 33 undergraduate majors. Total enrollment: 3,024. Undergraduates: 1,620. Freshmen: 229. Federal methodology is used as a basis for awarding need-based institutional aid.

UNDERGRADUATE EXPENSES for 2006–07 ***Application fee:*** $25. ***Comprehensive fee:*** $25,300 includes full-time tuition ($16,800), mandatory fees ($200), and room and board ($8300). ***College room only:*** $6800. Full-time tuition and fees vary according to course level, degree level, and program. Room and board charges vary according to board plan and housing facility. ***Part-time tuition:*** $460 per credit hour. ***Part-time fees:*** $100 per term. Part-time tuition and fees vary according to course load. ***Payment plans:*** Guaranteed tuition, tuition prepayment, installment, deferred payment.

FRESHMAN FINANCIAL AID (Fall 2005) 164 applied for aid; of those 90% were deemed to have need. 100% of freshmen with need received aid; of those 30% had need fully met. ***Average percent of need met:*** 83% (excluding resources awarded to replace EFC). ***Average financial aid package:*** $13,639 (excluding resources awarded to replace EFC). 10% of all full-time freshmen had no need and received non-need-based gift aid.

UNDERGRADUATE FINANCIAL AID (Fall 2005) 989 applied for aid; of those 90% were deemed to have need. 99% of undergraduates with need received aid; of those 23% had need fully met. ***Average percent of need met:*** 73% (excluding resources awarded to replace EFC). ***Average financial aid package:*** $13,295 (excluding resources awarded to replace EFC). 15% of all full-time undergraduates had no need and received non-need-based gift aid.

GIFT AID (NEED-BASED) ***Total amount:*** $9,517,710 (19% federal, 23% state, 53% institutional, 5% external sources). ***Receiving aid:*** Freshmen: 89% (147); All full-time undergraduates: 79% (864). ***Average award:*** Freshmen: $9657; Undergraduates: $8380. ***Scholarships, grants, and awards:*** Federal Pell, FSEOG, state, private, college/university gift aid from institutional funds.

GIFT AID (NON-NEED-BASED) ***Total amount:*** $1,383,749 (3% state, 88% institutional, 9% external sources). ***Receiving aid:*** Freshmen: 7% (11); Undergraduates: 6% (66). ***Average award:*** Freshmen: $13,145; Undergraduates: $9979. ***Scholarships, grants, and awards by category:*** *Academic Interests/Achievement:* 345 awards ($755,120 total): biological sciences, business, education, English, general academic interests/achievements, health fields, humanities, international studies, premedicine, social sciences. *Special Characteristics:* 61 awards ($354,198 total): children and siblings of alumni, children of faculty/staff. ***Tuition waivers:*** Full or partial for children of alumni, employees or children of employees, senior citizens. ***ROTC:*** Army cooperative.

LOANS ***Student loans:*** $11,457,787 (77% need-based, 23% non-need-based). 80% of past graduating class borrowed through all loan programs. *Average indebtedness per student:* $26,897. ***Average need-based loan:*** Freshmen: $3930; Undergraduates: $5317. ***Parent loans:*** $454,801 (41% need-based, 59% non-need-based). ***Programs:*** FFEL (Subsidized and Unsubsidized Stafford, PLUS), Perkins, Federal Nursing, college/university.

WORK-STUDY ***Federal work-study:*** Total amount: $332,898; jobs available (averaging $2000). ***State or other work-study/employment:*** 72 part-time jobs averaging $2000.

APPLYING FOR FINANCIAL AID ***Required financial aid form:*** FAFSA. ***Financial aid deadline (priority):*** 3/1. ***Notification date:*** Continuous beginning 3/30. Students must reply within 2 weeks of notification.

CONTACT Ms. Lorraine A. Metz, Director of Financial Aid, D'Youville College, 320 Porter Avenue, Buffalo, NY 14201-1084, 716-829-7500 or toll-free 800-777-3921. *Fax:* 716-829-7779. *E-mail:* metzla@dyc.edu.

EARLHAM COLLEGE

Richmond, IN

CONTACT Mr. Robert W. Arnold, Director of Financial Aid, Earlham College, National Road West, Richmond, IN 47374-4095, 765-983-1217 or toll-free 800-327-5426. *Fax:* 765-983-1299.

EAST CAROLINA UNIVERSITY

Greenville, NC

ABOUT THE INSTITUTION State-supported, coed. Awards: bachelor's, master's, doctoral, and first professional degrees and post-master's certificates. 91 undergraduate majors. Total enrollment: 24,351. Undergraduates: 18,587. Freshmen: 3,457.

GIFT AID (NEED-BASED) ***Scholarships, grants, and awards:*** Federal Pell, FSEOG, state, private, college/university gift aid from institutional funds.

GIFT AID (NON-NEED-BASED) ***Scholarships, grants, and awards by category:*** *Academic Interests/Achievement:* biological sciences, business, education, general academic interests/achievements, health fields, home economics, humanities, military science. *Creative Arts/Performance:* applied art and design, art/fine arts, music. *Special Achievements/Activities:* leadership. *Special Characteristics:* adult students, children of faculty/staff, ethnic background, handicapped students, local/state students.

LOANS ***Programs:*** FFEL (Subsidized and Unsubsidized Stafford, PLUS), Perkins, Federal Nursing.

WORK-STUDY ***Federal work-study:*** Total amount: $623,581; 382 jobs averaging $1584. ***State or other work-study/employment:*** Total amount: $940,697 (100% need-based). 127 part-time jobs averaging $7344.

APPLYING FOR FINANCIAL AID ***Required financial aid form:*** FAFSA.

CONTACT Rose Mary Stelma, Director, Student Financial Aid, East Carolina University, Office of Financial Aid, East 5th Street, Greenville, NC 27858-4353, 252-328-6610. *Fax:* 252-328-4347. *E-mail:* pattersonba@ecu.edu.

EAST CENTRAL UNIVERSITY

Ada, OK

Tuition & fees (OK res): $3496 Average undergraduate aid package: $6628

ABOUT THE INSTITUTION State-supported, coed. Awards: bachelor's and master's degrees. 81 undergraduate majors. Total enrollment: 4,506. Undergraduates: 3,761. Freshmen: 615. Federal methodology is used as a basis for awarding need-based institutional aid.

UNDERGRADUATE EXPENSES for 2006–07 ***Application fee:*** $20. ***Tuition, state resident:*** full-time $2,422; part-time $80.75 per semester hour. ***Tuition, nonresident:*** full-time $7,402; part-time $246.75 per semester hour. ***Required fees:*** full-time $1074; $34.50 per semester hour or $36 per term part-time. Full-time tuition and fees vary according to course load. Part-time tuition and fees vary according to course load. ***College room and board:*** $3190; ***Room only:*** $1200. Room and board charges vary according to board plan and housing facility.

FRESHMAN FINANCIAL AID (Fall 2006, est.) 463 applied for aid; of those 84% were deemed to have need. 99% of freshmen with need received aid; of those 35% had need fully met. ***Average percent of need met:*** 50% (excluding resources awarded to replace EFC). ***Average financial aid package:*** $4466 (excluding resources awarded to replace EFC). 12% of all full-time freshmen had no need and received non-need-based gift aid.

UNDERGRADUATE FINANCIAL AID (Fall 2006, est.) 2,343 applied for aid; of those 87% were deemed to have need. 98% of undergraduates with need received aid; of those 37% had need fully met. ***Average percent of need met:*** 70% (excluding resources awarded to replace EFC). ***Average financial aid package:*** $6628 (excluding resources awarded to replace EFC). 7% of all full-time undergraduates had no need and received non-need-based gift aid.

GIFT AID (NEED-BASED) ***Total amount:*** $8,751,822 (69% federal, 31% state). ***Receiving aid:*** Freshmen: 45% (263); All full-time undergraduates: 48% (1,455). ***Average award:*** Freshmen: $3247; Undergraduates: $3140. ***Scholarships, grants, and awards:*** Federal Pell, FSEOG, state, private, college/university gift aid from institutional funds.

GIFT AID (NON-NEED-BASED) ***Total amount:*** $3,105,772 (32% institutional, 68% external sources). ***Receiving aid:*** Freshmen: 57% (332); Undergraduates: 50% (1,529). ***Average award:*** Freshmen: $950; Undergraduates: $927. ***Scholarships, grants, and awards by category:*** *Academic Interests/Achievement:* 680 awards ($487,806 total): communication, general academic interests/achievements. *Creative Arts/Performance:* 114 awards ($180,016 total): music, theater/drama. *Special Achievements/Activities:* 8 awards ($3650 total): cheerleading/drum major. *Special Characteristics:* 375 awards ($851,772 total): children of faculty/staff, general special characteristics, members of minority groups, out-of-state students, previous college experience, veterans, veterans' children. ***Tuition waivers:*** Full or partial for employees or children of employees, senior citizens.

LOANS ***Student loans:*** $9,468,845 (60% need-based, 40% non-need-based). 50% of past graduating class borrowed through all loan programs. *Average indebtedness per student:* $12,196. ***Average need-based loan:*** Freshmen: $2143; Undergraduates: $3418. ***Parent loans:*** $188,038 (100% non-need-based). ***Programs:*** FFEL (Subsidized and Unsubsidized Stafford, PLUS), Perkins, college/university.

WORK-STUDY ***Federal work-study:*** Total amount: $411,210; 209 jobs averaging $1967. ***State or other work-study/employment:*** Total amount: $271,852 (100% non-need-based). 309 part-time jobs averaging $880.

ATHLETIC AWARDS Total amount: $767,666 (100% non-need-based).

APPLYING FOR FINANCIAL AID ***Required financial aid form:*** FAFSA. ***Financial aid deadline (priority):*** 3/1. ***Notification date:*** Continuous beginning 4/15. Students must reply within 2 weeks of notification.

CONTACT Marcia Carter, Director of Financial Aid, East Central University, 1100 East 14th, Ada, OK 74820-6899, 580-332-8000 Ext. 242. *Fax:* 580-436-5612.

EASTERN CONNECTICUT STATE UNIVERSITY

Willimantic, CT

CONTACT Assistant to the Director of Financial Aid, Eastern Connecticut State University, 83 Windham Street, Willimantic, CT 06226-2295, 860-465-4428 or toll-free 877-353-3278. *Fax:* 860-465-4440.

EASTERN ILLINOIS UNIVERSITY

Charleston, IL

Tuition & fees (IL res): $7069 Average undergraduate aid package: $10,902

ABOUT THE INSTITUTION State-supported, coed. Awards: bachelor's and master's degrees and post-bachelor's and post-master's certificates. 42 undergraduate majors. Total enrollment: 12,349. Undergraduates: 10,592. Freshmen: 1,773. Federal methodology is used as a basis for awarding need-based institutional aid.

UNDERGRADUATE EXPENSES for 2006–07 ***Application fee:*** $30. ***Tuition, state resident:*** full-time $5207; part-time $174 per credit hour. ***Tuition, nonresident:*** full-time $15,620; part-time $521 per credit hour. ***Required fees:*** full-time $1862; $66 per credit hour. Full-time tuition and fees vary according to course load. Part-time tuition and fees vary according to course load. ***College room and board:*** $6660. Room and board charges vary according to board plan and housing facility. ***Payment plan:*** Installment.

FRESHMAN FINANCIAL AID (Fall 2006, est.) 1480 applied for aid; of those 70% were deemed to have need. 92% of freshmen with need received aid; of those 76% had need fully met. ***Average percent of need met:*** 16% (excluding resources awarded to replace EFC). ***Average financial aid package:*** $11,249 (excluding resources awarded to replace EFC). 6% of all full-time freshmen had no need and received non-need-based gift aid.

UNDERGRADUATE FINANCIAL AID (Fall 2006, est.) 6,725 applied for aid; of those 75% were deemed to have need. 95% of undergraduates with need received aid; of those 75% had need fully met. ***Average percent of need met:*** 18% (excluding resources awarded to replace EFC). ***Average financial aid package:*** $10,902 (excluding resources awarded to replace EFC). 4% of all full-time undergraduates had no need and received non-need-based gift aid.

GIFT AID (NEED-BASED) ***Total amount:*** $18,144,490 (33% federal, 52% state, 10% institutional, 5% external sources). ***Receiving aid:*** Freshmen: 24% (430); All full-time undergraduates: 24% (2,247). ***Average award:*** Freshmen: $2890; Undergraduates: $3072. ***Scholarships, grants, and awards:*** Federal Pell, FSEOG, state, private, college/university gift aid from institutional funds.

GIFT AID (NON-NEED-BASED) ***Total amount:*** $4,378,438 (4% federal, 30% state, 50% institutional, 16% external sources). ***Receiving aid:*** Freshmen: 30% (543); Undergraduates: 26% (2,419). ***Average award:*** Freshmen: $8164; Undergraduates: $8404. ***Tuition waivers:*** Full or partial for employees or children of employees. ***ROTC:*** Army.

LOANS ***Student loans:*** $30,166,237 (76% need-based, 24% non-need-based). 63% of past graduating class borrowed through all loan programs. *Average indebtedness per student:* $16,890. ***Average need-based loan:*** Freshmen: $2389; Undergraduates: $3450. ***Parent loans:*** $6,388,444 (100% need-based). ***Programs:*** Federal Direct (Subsidized and Unsubsidized Stafford, PLUS), Perkins.

WORK-STUDY ***Federal work-study:*** Total amount: $665,477; 447 jobs averaging $1489. ***State or other work-study/employment:*** Total amount: $12,669 (42% need-based, 58% non-need-based). Part-time jobs available.

ATHLETIC AWARDS Total amount: $2,509,593 (29% need-based, 71% non-need-based).

APPLYING FOR FINANCIAL AID ***Required financial aid form:*** FAFSA. ***Financial aid deadline (priority):*** 3/1. ***Notification date:*** Continuous beginning 3/1. Students must reply within 2 weeks of notification.

CONTACT Tracy L. Hall, Assistant Director of Financial Aid, Eastern Illinois University, 600 Lincoln Avenue, Charleston, IL 61920-3099, 217-581-7511 or toll-free 800-252-5711. *Fax:* 217-581-6422. *E-mail:* cstlh@eiu.edu.

EASTERN KENTUCKY UNIVERSITY

Richmond, KY

Tuition & fees (KY res): $5192 Average undergraduate aid package: $7762

ABOUT THE INSTITUTION State-supported, coed. Awards: associate, bachelor's, and master's degrees and post-bachelor's and post-master's certificates. 135 undergraduate majors. Total enrollment: 15,763. Undergraduates: 13,623. Freshmen: 2,487. Federal methodology is used as a basis for awarding need-based institutional aid.

UNDERGRADUATE EXPENSES for 2006–07 ***Application fee:*** $30. ***Tuition, state resident:*** full-time $5192; part-time $216 per credit hour. ***Tuition, nonresident:*** full-time $14,538; part-time $606 per credit hour. Part-time tuition and fees vary according to course load. ***College room and board:*** $5392; ***Room only:*** $2792. Room and board charges vary according to board plan and housing facility. ***Payment plan:*** Deferred payment.

FRESHMAN FINANCIAL AID (Fall 2006, est.) 1954 applied for aid; of those 71% were deemed to have need. 99% of freshmen with need received aid; of those 13% had need fully met. ***Average percent of need met:*** 89% (excluding resources awarded to replace EFC). ***Average financial aid package:*** $7545 (excluding resources awarded to replace EFC). 34% of all full-time freshmen had no need and received non-need-based gift aid.

UNDERGRADUATE FINANCIAL AID (Fall 2006, est.) 7,817 applied for aid; of those 78% were deemed to have need. 97% of undergraduates with need received aid; of those 12% had need fully met. ***Average percent of need met:*** 87% (excluding resources awarded to replace EFC). ***Average financial aid package:*** $7762 (excluding resources awarded to replace EFC). 24% of all full-time undergraduates had no need and received non-need-based gift aid.

GIFT AID (NEED-BASED) ***Total amount:*** $29,498,336 (46% federal, 29% state, 25% institutional). ***Receiving aid:*** Freshmen: 45% (1,095); All full-time undergraduates: 40% (4,295). ***Average award:*** Freshmen: $4473; Undergraduates: $4397. ***Scholarships, grants, and awards:*** Federal Pell, FSEOG, state, private, college/university gift aid from institutional funds, Federal Nursing.

GIFT AID (NON-NEED-BASED) ***Total amount:*** $12,239,288 (29% state, 70% institutional, 1% external sources). ***Receiving aid:*** Freshmen: 45% (1,105); Undergraduates: 27% (2,949). ***Average award:*** Freshmen: $1630; Undergraduates: $1854. ***Scholarships, grants, and awards by category:*** *Academic Interests/Achievement:* 1,257 awards ($5,545,371 total): general academic interests/achievements. *Creative Arts/Performance:* 148 awards ($254,504 total): music. *Special Achievements/Activities:* 17 awards ($13,250 total). *Special Characteristics:* 295 awards ($553,984 total): children and siblings of alumni, children of faculty/staff, members of minority groups. ***Tuition waivers:*** Full or partial for employees or children of employees, senior citizens. ***ROTC:*** Army, Air Force cooperative.

LOANS ***Student loans:*** $49,844,918 (81% need-based, 19% non-need-based). 48% of past graduating class borrowed through all loan programs. *Average indebtedness per student:* $14,257. ***Average need-based loan:*** Freshmen: $2131; Undergraduates: $3317. ***Parent loans:*** $15,201,096 (58% need-based, 42% non-need-based). ***Programs:*** FFEL (Subsidized and Unsubsidized Stafford, PLUS), Perkins, college/university.

WORK-STUDY ***Federal work-study:*** Total amount: $3,678,426; 1,000 jobs averaging $1800. ***State or other work-study/employment:*** Total amount: $2,517,354 (100% non-need-based). 1,000 part-time jobs averaging $1800.

ATHLETIC AWARDS Total amount: $2,967,734 (40% need-based, 60% non-need-based).

APPLYING FOR FINANCIAL AID ***Required financial aid form:*** FAFSA. ***Financial aid deadline (priority):*** 3/15. ***Notification date:*** Continuous beginning 4/1.

CONTACT Financial Aid Office Staff, Eastern Kentucky University, 521 Lancaster Avenue, SSB CPO 59, Richmond, KY 40475-3102, 859-622-2361 or toll-free 800-465-9191 (in-state). *Fax:* 859-622-2019. *E-mail:* finaid@eku.edu.

EASTERN MENNONITE UNIVERSITY

Harrisonburg, VA

CONTACT Ms. Renee Leap, Assistant Director of Financial Assistance, Eastern Mennonite University, 1200 Park Road, Harrisonburg, VA 22802-2462, 540-432-4138 or toll-free 800-368-2665. *Fax:* 540-432-4081. *E-mail:* leapr@emu.edu.

EASTERN MICHIGAN UNIVERSITY

Ypsilanti, MI

Tuition & fees (MI res): $6935 Average undergraduate aid package: $6584

ABOUT THE INSTITUTION State-supported, coed. Awards: bachelor's, master's, and doctoral degrees and post-bachelor's and post-master's certificates. 132 undergraduate majors. Total enrollment: 22,821. Undergraduates: 18,172. Freshmen: 2,347. Federal methodology is used as a basis for awarding need-based institutional aid.

UNDERGRADUATE EXPENSES for 2006–07 ***Application fee:*** $30. ***Tuition, state resident:*** full-time $5835; part-time $194.50 per credit hour. ***Tuition, nonresident:*** full-time $17,190; part-time $573 per credit hour. ***Required fees:*** full-time $1100; $34 per credit hour or $40 per term part-time. ***College room and board:*** $6610; ***Room only:*** $3104. Room and board charges vary according to board plan, housing facility, and location. ***Payment plan:*** Installment.

FRESHMAN FINANCIAL AID (Fall 2005) 1816 applied for aid; of those 74% were deemed to have need. 95% of freshmen with need received aid; of those 4% had need fully met. ***Average percent of need met:*** 62% (excluding resources awarded to replace EFC). ***Average financial aid package:*** $6949 (excluding resources awarded to replace EFC). 14% of all full-time freshmen had no need and received non-need-based gift aid.

UNDERGRADUATE FINANCIAL AID (Fall 2005) 8,718 applied for aid; of those 79% were deemed to have need. 97% of undergraduates with need received aid; of those 2% had need fully met. ***Average percent of need met:*** 58% (excluding resources awarded to replace EFC). ***Average financial aid package:*** $6584 (excluding resources awarded to replace EFC). 8% of all full-time undergraduates had no need and received non-need-based gift aid.

GIFT AID (NEED-BASED) ***Total amount:*** $14,143,849 (85% federal, 7% state, 8% institutional). ***Receiving aid:*** Freshmen: 37% (851); All full-time undergraduates: 29% (3,877). ***Average award:*** Freshmen: $3473; Undergraduates: $3117. ***Scholarships, grants, and awards:*** Federal Pell, FSEOG, state, private, college/university gift aid from institutional funds.

GIFT AID (NON-NEED-BASED) ***Total amount:*** $17,920,029 (15% state, 40% institutional, 45% external sources). ***Receiving aid:*** Freshmen: 33% (763); Undergraduates: 16% (2,099). ***Average award:*** Freshmen: $2787; Undergraduates: $2856. ***Scholarships, grants, and awards by category:*** *Academic Interests/Achievement:* 3,771 awards ($8,974,945 total): agriculture, architecture, biological sciences, business, communication, computer science, education, engineering/technologies, English, foreign languages, general academic interests/achievements, health fields, home economics, humanities, mathematics, physical sciences, religion/biblical studies, social sciences. *Creative Arts/Performance:* 132 awards ($110,350 total): applied art and design, art/fine arts, cinema/film/broadcasting, creative writing, dance, debating, general creative arts/performance, music, performing arts, theater/drama. *Special Achievements/Activities:* 186 awards ($165,766 total): general special achievements/activities, leadership, memberships, religious involvement. *Special Characteristics:* 220 awards ($1,553,801 total): children and siblings of alumni, ethnic background, international students, members of minority groups, out-of-state students, previous college experience, religious affiliation. ***Tuition waivers:*** Full or partial for employees or children of employees. ***ROTC:*** Army, Naval cooperative, Air Force cooperative.

LOANS ***Student loans:*** $69,862,798 (41% need-based, 59% non-need-based). 56% of past graduating class borrowed through all loan programs. *Average indebtedness per student:* $22,757. ***Average need-based loan:*** Freshmen: $2770; Undergraduates: $3900. ***Parent loans:*** $9,946,393 (100% non-need-based). ***Programs:*** FFEL (Subsidized and Unsubsidized Stafford, PLUS), Perkins, college/university, alternative (private) loans.

WORK-STUDY ***Federal work-study:*** Total amount: $1,009,178; 561 jobs averaging $1799. ***State or other work-study/employment:*** Total amount: $395,684 (100% need-based). 224 part-time jobs averaging $1766.

ATHLETIC AWARDS Total amount: $4,734,579 (100% non-need-based).

APPLYING FOR FINANCIAL AID ***Required financial aid form:*** FAFSA. ***Financial aid deadline:*** Continuous. ***Notification date:*** 3/15.

CONTACT Ms. Bernice A. Lindke, Associate Vice President, Enrollment Services, Eastern Michigan University, 403 Pierce Hall, Ypsilanti, MI 48197, 734-487-1048 or toll-free 800-GO TO EMU. *Fax:* 734-487-4281. *E-mail:* bernice.lindke@emich.edu.

EASTERN NAZARENE COLLEGE

Quincy, MA

CONTACT Financial Aid Department, Eastern Nazarene College, 23 East Elm Avenue, Quincy, MA 02170, 617-745-3712 or toll-free 800-88-ENC88. *Fax:* 617-745-3929. *E-mail:* finaid@enc.edu.

EASTERN NEW MEXICO UNIVERSITY

Portales, NM

CONTACT Ms. Patricia Willis, Financial Aid Specialist, Eastern New Mexico University, Station 54, Portales, NM 88130, 505-562-2194 or toll-free 800-367-3668. *Fax:* 505-562-2198. *E-mail:* pat.willis@enmu.edu.

EASTERN OREGON UNIVERSITY

La Grande, OR

CONTACT Mr. Eric Bucks, Director of Financial Aid, Eastern Oregon University, One University Boulevard, La Grande, OR 97850-2899, 541-962-3550 or toll-free 800-452-8639 (in-state), 800-452-3393 (out-of-state). *Fax:* 541-962-3661. *E-mail:* eric.bucks@eou.edu.

EASTERN UNIVERSITY

St. Davids, PA

CONTACT Financial Aid Office, Eastern University, 1300 Eagle Road, St. Davids, PA 19087-3696, 610-341-5842 or toll-free 800-452-0996. *Fax:* 610-341-1492. *E-mail:* finaid@eastern.edu.

EASTERN WASHINGTON UNIVERSITY

Cheney, WA

ABOUT THE INSTITUTION State-supported, coed. Awards: bachelor's, master's, and doctoral degrees. 109 undergraduate majors. Total enrollment: 11,161. Undergraduates: 11,161.

GIFT AID (NEED-BASED) ***Scholarships, grants, and awards:*** Federal Pell, FSEOG, state, private, college/university gift aid from institutional funds.

GIFT AID (NON-NEED-BASED) ***Scholarships, grants, and awards by category:*** *Academic Interests/Achievement:* biological sciences, business, computer science, education, engineering/technologies, English, foreign languages, general academic interests/achievements, health fields, mathematics, physical sciences, social sciences. *Creative Arts/Performance:* art/fine arts, cinema/film/broadcasting, creative writing, journalism/publications, music, theater/drama. *Special Characteristics:* children and siblings of alumni, children of union members/company employees, ethnic background, handicapped students, local/state students.

LOANS ***Programs:*** FFEL (Subsidized and Unsubsidized Stafford, PLUS), Perkins.

APPLYING FOR FINANCIAL AID ***Required financial aid form:*** FAFSA.

CONTACT Bruce DeFrates, Financial Aid Director, Eastern Washington University, 102 Sutton Hall, Cheney, WA 99004-2447, 509-359-2314. *Fax:* 509-359-4330. *E-mail:* finaid@mail.ewu.edu.

EAST STROUDSBURG UNIVERSITY OF PENNSYLVANIA

East Stroudsburg, PA

ABOUT THE INSTITUTION State-supported, coed. Awards: associate, bachelor's, and master's degrees. 50 undergraduate majors. Total enrollment: 7,013. Undergraduates: 5,890. Freshmen: 1,248.

GIFT AID (NEED-BASED) ***Scholarships, grants, and awards:*** Federal Pell, FSEOG, state, private, college/university gift aid from institutional funds.

GIFT AID (NON-NEED-BASED) ***Scholarships, grants, and awards by category:*** *Academic Interests/Achievement:* biological sciences, business, communication, computer science, education, English, foreign languages, general academic interests/achievements, health fields, mathematics, physical sciences, social sciences. *Creative Arts/Performance:* applied art and design, music, theater/drama. *Special Achievements/Activities:* general special achievements/activities. *Special Characteristics:* adult students, handicapped students, international students, members of minority groups.

LOANS ***Programs:*** FFEL (Subsidized and Unsubsidized Stafford, PLUS), Perkins, alternative loans.

APPLYING FOR FINANCIAL AID ***Required financial aid form:*** FAFSA.

CONTACT Georgia K. Prell, Director of Enrollment Services, East Stroudsburg University of Pennsylvania, 200 Prospect Street, East Stroudsburg, PA 18301-2999, 570-422-2820 or toll-free 877-230-5547. *Fax:* 570-422-2849.

EAST TENNESSEE STATE UNIVERSITY

Johnson City, TN

Tuition & fees (TN res): $4637 Average undergraduate aid package: $4711

ABOUT THE INSTITUTION State-supported, coed. Awards: associate, bachelor's, master's, doctoral, and first professional degrees and post-bachelor's and post-master's certificates. 38 undergraduate majors. Total enrollment: 12,390. Undergraduates: 10,204. Freshmen: 1,740. Federal methodology is used as a basis for awarding need-based institutional aid.

UNDERGRADUATE EXPENSES for 2006–07 ***Application fee:*** $15. ***Tuition, state resident:*** full-time $3828; part-time $168 per hour. ***Tuition, nonresident:*** full-time $13,522; part-time $589 per hour. ***Required fees:*** full-time $809; $70 per hour. Full-time tuition and fees vary according to course load and program. ***College room and board:*** $5024; ***Room only:*** $2426. Room and board charges vary according to board plan and housing facility. ***Payment plans:*** Installment, deferred payment.

FRESHMAN FINANCIAL AID (Fall 2006, est.) 1515 applied for aid; of those 75% were deemed to have need. 98% of freshmen with need received aid; of those 33% had need fully met. ***Average percent of need met:*** 82% (excluding resources awarded to replace EFC). ***Average financial aid package:*** $7402 (excluding resources awarded to replace EFC). 9% of all full-time freshmen had no need and received non-need-based gift aid.

UNDERGRADUATE FINANCIAL AID (Fall 2006, est.) 7,086 applied for aid; of those 72% were deemed to have need. 97% of undergraduates with need received aid; of those 45% had need fully met. ***Average percent of need met:*** 81% (excluding resources awarded to replace EFC). ***Average financial aid package:*** $4711 (excluding resources awarded to replace EFC). 12% of all full-time undergraduates had no need and received non-need-based gift aid.

GIFT AID (NEED-BASED) ***Total amount:*** $25,550,012 (41% federal, 59% state). ***Receiving aid:*** Freshmen: 56% (968); All full-time undergraduates: 44% (3,725). ***Average award:*** Freshmen: $4654; Undergraduates: $3123. ***Scholarships, grants, and awards:*** Federal Pell, FSEOG, state, private, college/university gift aid from institutional funds, Federal Nursing.

GIFT AID (NON-NEED-BASED) ***Total amount:*** $7,747,643 (5% federal, 12% state, 59% institutional, 24% external sources). ***Receiving aid:*** Freshmen: 20% (340); Undergraduates: 17% (1,435). ***Average award:*** Freshmen: $3760; Undergraduates: $3003. ***Scholarships, grants, and awards by category:*** *Academic Interests/Achievement:* biological sciences, business, computer science, education, engineering/technologies, English, general academic interests/achievements, health fields, mathematics, military science, social sciences. *Creative Arts/Performance:* art/fine arts, journalism/publications, music, theater/drama. *Special Achievements/Activities:* leadership, memberships. *Special Characteristics:* children of union members/company employees, members of minority groups. ***Tuition waivers:*** Full or partial for employees or children of employees, senior citizens. ***ROTC:*** Army.

LOANS ***Student loans:*** $34,309,979 (59% need-based, 41% non-need-based). 29% of past graduating class borrowed through all loan programs. *Average indebtedness per student:* $19,707. ***Average need-based loan:*** Freshmen: $1521; Undergraduates: $3296. ***Parent loans:*** $3,139,058 (100% non-need-based). ***Programs:*** FFEL (Subsidized and Unsubsidized Stafford, PLUS), Perkins, Federal Nursing, college/university.

WORK-STUDY ***Federal work-study:*** Total amount: $2,975,128; 1,674 jobs averaging $1272. ***State or other work-study/employment:*** Total amount: $399,238 (100% non-need-based). 412 part-time jobs averaging $1189.

ATHLETIC AWARDS Total amount: $2,020,819 (100% non-need-based).

APPLYING FOR FINANCIAL AID ***Required financial aid form:*** FAFSA. ***Financial aid deadline (priority):*** 4/15. ***Notification date:*** Continuous beginning 5/1. Students must reply within 3 weeks of notification.

CONTACT Cindy A. Johnson, Assistant Director of Financial Aid, East Tennessee State University, PO Box 70722, Johnson City, TN 37614, 423-439-4300 or toll-free 800-462-3878.

EAST TEXAS BAPTIST UNIVERSITY

Marshall, TX

Tuition & fees: $13,700 **Average undergraduate aid package: $11,418**

ABOUT THE INSTITUTION Independent Baptist, coed. Awards: associate and bachelor's degrees. 44 undergraduate majors. Total enrollment: 1,365. Undergraduates: 1,365. Freshmen: 342. Federal methodology is used as a basis for awarding need-based institutional aid.

UNDERGRADUATE EXPENSES for 2006–07 ***Application fee:*** $25. ***Comprehensive fee:*** $17,890 includes full-time tuition ($13,700) and room and board ($4190). Room and board charges vary according to board plan and housing facility. ***Part-time tuition:*** $475 per credit hour. ***Payment plans:*** Guaranteed tuition, installment.

FRESHMAN FINANCIAL AID (Fall 2006, est.) 325 applied for aid; of those 75% were deemed to have need. 92% of freshmen with need received aid; of those 29% had need fully met. ***Average percent of need met:*** 83% (excluding resources awarded to replace EFC). ***Average financial aid package:*** $11,566 (excluding resources awarded to replace EFC). 16% of all full-time freshmen had no need and received non-need-based gift aid.

UNDERGRADUATE FINANCIAL AID (Fall 2006, est.) 1,101 applied for aid; of those 79% were deemed to have need. 89% of undergraduates with need received aid; of those 25% had need fully met. ***Average percent of need met:*** 89% (excluding resources awarded to replace EFC). ***Average financial aid package:*** $11,418 (excluding resources awarded to replace EFC). 11% of all full-time undergraduates had no need and received non-need-based gift aid.

GIFT AID (NEED-BASED) ***Total amount:*** $3,525,154 (48% federal, 52% state). ***Receiving aid:*** Freshmen: 66% (225); All full-time undergraduates: 64% (774). ***Average award:*** Freshmen: $5897; Undergraduates: $6060. ***Scholarships, grants, and awards:*** Federal Pell, FSEOG, state, private, college/university gift aid from institutional funds.

GIFT AID (NON-NEED-BASED) ***Total amount:*** $6,412,173 (90% institutional, 10% external sources). ***Receiving aid:*** Freshmen: 66% (225); Undergraduates: 64% (774). ***Average award:*** Freshmen: $6960; Undergraduates: $7318. ***Scholarships, grants, and awards by category:*** *Academic Interests/Achievement:* biological sciences, business, communication, computer science, education, English, foreign languages, general academic interests/achievements, health fields, mathematics, physical sciences, religion/biblical studies. *Creative Arts/Performance:* music, theater/drama. *Special Achievements/Activities:* cheerleading/drum major, general special achievements/activities, leadership, religious involvement. *Special Characteristics:* children and siblings of alumni, children of educators, children of faculty/staff, general special characteristics, international students, local/state students, previous college experience, religious affiliation, siblings of current students, twins. ***Tuition waivers:*** Full or partial for employees or children of employees.

LOANS ***Student loans:*** $5,940,540 (45% need-based, 55% non-need-based). 85% of past graduating class borrowed through all loan programs. *Average indebtedness per student:* $18,551. ***Average need-based loan:*** Freshmen: $2404; Undergraduates: $3471. ***Parent loans:*** $714,762 (100% non-need-based). ***Programs:*** FFEL (Subsidized and Unsubsidized Stafford, PLUS), Perkins, state, college/university.

WORK-STUDY ***Federal work-study:*** Total amount: $170,396; 144 jobs averaging $1108. ***State or other work-study/employment:*** Total amount: $382,905 (7% need-based, 93% non-need-based). 303 part-time jobs averaging $1099.

APPLYING FOR FINANCIAL AID ***Required financial aid forms:*** FAFSA, institution's own form. ***Financial aid deadline (priority):*** 6/1. ***Notification date:*** Continuous. Students must reply within 3 weeks of notification.

CONTACT Katherine Evans, Director of Financial Aid, East Texas Baptist University, 1209 North Grove Street, Marshall, TX 75670-1498, 903-923-2137 or toll-free 800-804-ETBU. *Fax:* 903-934-8120.

EAST-WEST UNIVERSITY

Chicago, IL

CONTACT Financial Aid Office, East-West University, 816 South Michigan Avenue, Chicago, IL 60605-2103, 312-939-0111 Ext. 1809.

ECKERD COLLEGE

St. Petersburg, FL

ABOUT THE INSTITUTION Independent Presbyterian, coed. Awards: bachelor's degrees. 36 undergraduate majors. Total enrollment: 1,845. Undergraduates: 1,845. Freshmen: 546.

GIFT AID (NEED-BASED) ***Scholarships, grants, and awards:*** Federal Pell, FSEOG, state, private, college/university gift aid from institutional funds.

GIFT AID (NON-NEED-BASED) ***Scholarships, grants, and awards by category:*** *Academic Interests/Achievement:* general academic interests/achievements. *Creative Arts/Performance:* art/fine arts, creative writing, music, theater/drama. *Special Achievements/Activities:* community service, leadership. *Special Characteristics:* children of faculty/staff, international students, local/state students, religious affiliation.

LOANS ***Programs:*** FFEL (Subsidized and Unsubsidized Stafford, PLUS), Perkins, college/university.

WORK-STUDY ***Federal work-study:*** Total amount: $1,370,018; 661 jobs averaging $2000. ***State or other work-study/employment:*** Total amount: $141,755 (100% non-need-based). 75 part-time jobs averaging $1500.

APPLYING FOR FINANCIAL AID ***Required financial aid form:*** FAFSA.

CONTACT Dr. Pat Garrett Watkins, Director of Financial Aid, Eckerd College, 4200 54th Avenue, South, St. Petersburg, FL 33711, 727-864-8334 or toll-free 800-456-9009. *Fax:* 727-866-2304. *E-mail:* watkinpe@eckerd.edu.

EDGEWOOD COLLEGE

Madison, WI

Tuition & fees: $19,080 **Average undergraduate aid package: $12,859**

ABOUT THE INSTITUTION Independent Roman Catholic, coed. Awards: associate, bachelor's, master's, and doctoral degrees. 41 undergraduate majors. Total enrollment: 2,565. Undergraduates: 1,989. Freshmen: 296. Federal methodology is used as a basis for awarding need-based institutional aid.

UNDERGRADUATE EXPENSES for 2007–08 ***Application fee:*** $25. ***Comprehensive fee:*** $25,615 includes full-time tuition ($19,080) and room and board ($6535). ***College room only:*** $3335. ***Part-time tuition:*** $601 per credit.

FRESHMAN FINANCIAL AID (Fall 2005) 268 applied for aid; of those 82% were deemed to have need. 100% of freshmen with need received aid; of those 21% had need fully met. ***Average percent of need met:*** 82% (excluding resources awarded to replace EFC). ***Average financial aid package:*** $13,363 (excluding resources awarded to replace EFC). 22% of all full-time freshmen had no need and received non-need-based gift aid.

UNDERGRADUATE FINANCIAL AID (Fall 2005) 1,164 applied for aid; of those 85% were deemed to have need. 100% of undergraduates with need received aid; of those 18% had need fully met. ***Average percent of need met:*** 72% (excluding resources awarded to replace EFC). ***Average financial aid package:*** $12,859 (excluding resources awarded to replace EFC). 21% of all full-time undergraduates had no need and received non-need-based gift aid.

GIFT AID (NEED-BASED) ***Total amount:*** $8,308,919 (16% federal, 17% state, 58% institutional, 9% external sources). ***Receiving aid:*** Freshmen: 71% (216); All full-time undergraduates: 66% (939). ***Average award:*** Freshmen: $9730; Undergraduates: $8043. ***Scholarships, grants, and awards:*** Federal Pell, FSEOG, state, private, college/university gift aid from institutional funds.

GIFT AID (NON-NEED-BASED) ***Total amount:*** $1,443,819 (1% federal, 1% state, 74% institutional, 24% external sources). ***Receiving aid:*** Freshmen: 5% (16); Undergraduates: 5% (65). ***Average award:*** Freshmen: $8688; Undergraduates: $9742. ***Scholarships, grants, and awards by category:*** *Academic Interests/Achievement:* foreign languages, general academic interests/achievements. *Creative Arts/Performance:* art/fine arts, creative writing, music, performing arts, theater/drama. *Special Achievements/Activities:* community service, hobbies/interests, leadership. *Special Characteristics:* first-generation college students, handicapped students, local/state students, members of minority groups, religious affiliation.

LOANS ***Student loans:*** $10,125,300 (67% need-based, 33% non-need-based). 68% of past graduating class borrowed through all loan programs. *Average indebtedness per student:* $24,727. ***Average need-based loan:*** Freshmen: $2935; Undergraduates: $4360. ***Parent loans:*** $1,635,289 (36% need-based, 64% non-need-based). ***Programs:*** FFEL (Subsidized and Unsubsidized Stafford, PLUS), Perkins, state, college/university.

WORK-STUDY ***Federal work-study:*** Total amount: $580,886; 334 jobs averaging $1676. ***State or other work-study/employment:*** Total amount: $1,662,465 (43% need-based, 57% non-need-based). 656 part-time jobs averaging $1667.

APPLYING FOR FINANCIAL AID ***Required financial aid forms:*** FAFSA, institution's own form. ***Financial aid deadline (priority):*** 3/15. ***Notification date:*** 3/30. Students must reply within 2 weeks of notification.

CONTACT Kari Gribble, Director for Financial Aid, Edgewood College, 1000 Edgewood College Drive, Madison, WI 53711-1997, 608-663-2206 or toll-free 800-444-4861 Ext. 2294.

EDINBORO UNIVERSITY OF PENNSYLVANIA

Edinboro, PA

ABOUT THE INSTITUTION State-supported, coed. Awards: associate, bachelor's, and master's degrees and post-bachelor's and post-master's certificates. 55 undergraduate majors. Total enrollment: 7,579. Undergraduates: 6,443. Freshmen: 1,266.

GIFT AID (NEED-BASED) ***Scholarships, grants, and awards:*** Federal Pell, FSEOG, state, private, college/university gift aid from institutional funds.

GIFT AID (NON-NEED-BASED) ***Scholarships, grants, and awards by category:*** *Academic Interests/Achievement:* biological sciences, business, communication, computer science, education, engineering/technologies, English, foreign languages, general academic interests/achievements, health fields, humanities, mathematics, military science, physical sciences, premedicine, religion/biblical studies, social sciences. *Creative Arts/Performance:* art/fine arts, cinema/film/broadcasting, journalism/publications, music. *Special Achievements/Activities:* general special achievements/activities. *Special Characteristics:* adult students, children and siblings of alumni, children of faculty/staff, children of union members/company employees, children with a deceased or disabled parent, first-generation college students, general special characteristics, handicapped students, international students, local/state students, members of minority groups, out-of-state students, religious affiliation, veterans, veterans' children.

LOANS ***Programs:*** FFEL (Subsidized and Unsubsidized Stafford, PLUS), Perkins, Federal Nursing, college/university.

APPLYING FOR FINANCIAL AID ***Required financial aid form:*** FAFSA.

CONTACT Ms. Dorothy Body, Assistant Vice President for Student Financial Support and Services, Edinboro University of Pennsylvania, Hamilton Hall, Edinboro, PA 16444, 814-732-5555 Ext. 266 or toll-free 888-846-2676 (in-state), 800-626-2203 (out-of-state). *Fax:* 814-732-2129. *E-mail:* dbody@edinboro.edu.

EDWARD WATERS COLLEGE

Jacksonville, FL

CONTACT Gabriel Mbomeh, Director of Financial Aid, Edward Waters College, 1658 Kings Road, Jacksonville, FL 32209-6199, 904-366-2528 or toll-free 888-898-3191.

ELECTRONIC DATA PROCESSING COLLEGE OF PUERTO RICO

Hato Rey, PR

CONTACT Dean of Financial Aid, Electronic Data Processing College of Puerto Rico, PO Box 192303, San Juan, PR 00919-2303, 787-765-3560 Ext. 4713. *Fax:* 787-765-2650.

ELECTRONIC DATA PROCESSING COLLEGE OF PUERTO RICO–SAN SEBASTIAN

San Sebastian, PR

CONTACT Financial Aid Office, Electronic Data Processing College of Puerto Rico–San Sebastian, Avenue Betances #49, San Sebastian, PR 00685, 787-896-2137.

ELIZABETH CITY STATE UNIVERSITY

Elizabeth City, NC

CONTACT Assistant Director of Financial Aid, Elizabeth City State University, 1704 Weeksville Road, Campus Box 914, Elizabeth City, NC 27909-7806, 252-335-3285 or toll-free 800-347-3278. *Fax:* 252-335-3716.

ELIZABETHTOWN COLLEGE

Elizabethtown, PA

Tuition & fees: $29,000 **Average undergraduate aid package: $18,309**

ABOUT THE INSTITUTION Independent religious, coed. Awards: associate, bachelor's, and master's degrees and post-bachelor's certificates. 50 undergraduate majors. Total enrollment: 2,366. Undergraduates: 1,991. Freshmen: 529. Both federal and institutional methodology are used as a basis for awarding need-based institutional aid.

UNDERGRADUATE EXPENSES for 2007–08 ***Application fee:*** $30. ***Comprehensive fee:*** $36,600 includes full-time tuition ($29,000) and room and board ($7600). ***College room only:*** $3800.

FRESHMAN FINANCIAL AID (Fall 2006, est.) 459 applied for aid; of those 79% were deemed to have need. 100% of freshmen with need received aid; of those 27% had need fully met. ***Average percent of need met:*** 83% (excluding resources awarded to replace EFC). ***Average financial aid package:*** $17,642 (excluding resources awarded to replace EFC). 30% of all full-time freshmen had no need and received non-need-based gift aid.

UNDERGRADUATE FINANCIAL AID (Fall 2006, est.) 1,607 applied for aid; of those 86% were deemed to have need. 100% of undergraduates with need received aid; of those 25% had need fully met. ***Average percent of need met:*** 83% (excluding resources awarded to replace EFC). ***Average financial aid package:*** $18,309 (excluding resources awarded to replace EFC). 25% of all full-time undergraduates had no need and received non-need-based gift aid.

GIFT AID (NEED-BASED) ***Total amount:*** $19,670,238 (4% federal, 12% state, 77% institutional, 7% external sources). ***Receiving aid:*** Freshmen: 66% (362); All full-time undergraduates: 69% (1,364). ***Average award:*** Freshmen: $14,541; Undergraduates: $14,199. ***Scholarships, grants, and awards:*** Federal Pell, FSEOG, state, private, college/university gift aid from institutional funds.

GIFT AID (NON-NEED-BASED) ***Total amount:*** $6,655,590 (83% institutional, 17% external sources). ***Receiving aid:*** Freshmen: 12% (67); Undergraduates: 10% (190). ***Average award:*** Freshmen: $14,320; Undergraduates: $13,604. ***Scholarships, grants, and awards by category:*** *Academic Interests/Achievement:* biological sciences, business, communication, computer science, education, engineering/technologies, English, foreign languages, general academic interests/achievements, health fields, humanities, international studies, mathematics, physical sciences, premedicine, religion/biblical studies, social sciences. *Creative Arts/Performance:* art/fine arts, music, performing arts, theater/drama. *Special Achievements/Activities:* religious involvement. *Special Characteristics:* children of faculty/staff, international students, local/state students, members of minority groups, religious affiliation, siblings of current students.

LOANS ***Student loans:*** $11,748,146 (58% need-based, 42% non-need-based). ***Average need-based loan:*** Freshmen: $2769; Undergraduates: $4008. ***Parent loans:*** $5,208,824 (21% need-based, 79% non-need-based). ***Programs:*** FFEL (Subsidized and Unsubsidized Stafford, PLUS), Perkins, state, college/university.

WORK-STUDY ***Federal work-study:*** Total amount: $1,153,724; 924 jobs averaging $1249.

APPLYING FOR FINANCIAL AID ***Required financial aid forms:*** FAFSA, institution's own form, state aid form, federal income tax form(s), W-2 forms. ***Financial aid deadline (priority):*** 3/15. ***Notification date:*** Continuous beginning 3/15. Students must reply by 5/1 or within 2 weeks of notification.

CONTACT Ms. Elizabeth K. McCloud, Director of Financial Aid, Elizabethtown College, 1 Alpha Drive, Elizabethtown, PA 17022-2298, 717-361-1404. *Fax:* 717-361-1514. *E-mail:* mcclouek@etown.edu.

ELMHURST COLLEGE

Elmhurst, IL

Tuition & fees: $24,660 **Average undergraduate aid package: $15,692**

ABOUT THE INSTITUTION Independent religious, coed. Awards: bachelor's and master's degrees. 67 undergraduate majors. Total enrollment: 3,107. Undergraduates: 2,841. Freshmen: 485. Federal methodology is used as a basis for awarding need-based institutional aid.

UNDERGRADUATE EXPENSES for 2007–08 ***Comprehensive fee:*** $31,824 includes full-time tuition ($24,600), mandatory fees ($60), and room and board ($7164). ***College room only:*** $4200. ***Part-time tuition:*** $700 per semester hour. ***Part-time fees:*** $30 per term.

FRESHMAN FINANCIAL AID (Fall 2006, est.) 413 applied for aid; of those 84% were deemed to have need. 100% of freshmen with need received aid; of those 27% had need fully met. ***Average percent of need met:*** 90% (excluding resources awarded to replace EFC). ***Average financial aid package:*** $17,669 (excluding resources awarded to replace EFC). 19% of all full-time freshmen had no need and received non-need-based gift aid.

UNDERGRADUATE FINANCIAL AID (Fall 2006, est.) 2,138 applied for aid; of those 75% were deemed to have need. 100% of undergraduates with need received aid; of those 36% had need fully met. ***Average percent of need met:*** 88% (excluding resources awarded to replace EFC). ***Average financial aid package:*** $15,692 (excluding resources awarded to replace EFC). 21% of all full-time undergraduates had no need and received non-need-based gift aid.

GIFT AID (NEED-BASED) ***Total amount:*** $22,355,854 (9% federal, 18% state, 72% institutional, 1% external sources). ***Receiving aid:*** Freshmen: 65% (316); All full-time undergraduates: 62% (1,565). ***Average award:*** Freshmen: $8509; Undergraduates: $7870. ***Scholarships, grants, and awards:*** Federal Pell, FSEOG, state, private, college/university gift aid from institutional funds.

GIFT AID (NON-NEED-BASED) ***Total amount:*** $5,786,568 (1% state, 98% institutional, 1% external sources). ***Receiving aid:*** Freshmen: 22% (107); Undergraduates: 12% (291). ***Average award:*** Freshmen: $8517; Undergraduates: $8662. ***Scholarships, grants, and awards by category:*** *Academic Interests/Achievement:* 1,253 awards ($6,043,970 total): biological sciences, business, communication, computer science, education, English, foreign languages, general academic interests/achievements, health fields, humanities, mathematics, physical sciences, premedicine, religion/biblical studies. *Creative Arts/Performance:* 81 awards ($230,466 total): art/fine arts, music, theater/drama. *Special Achievements/Activities:* community service. *Special Characteristics:* 327 awards ($770,640 total): children and siblings of alumni, children of current students, ethnic background, members of minority groups, religious affiliation, siblings of current students, spouses of current students. ***ROTC:*** Army cooperative, Air Force cooperative.

LOANS ***Student loans:*** $13,877,336 (45% need-based, 55% non-need-based). 78% of past graduating class borrowed through all loan programs. *Average indebtedness per student:* $17,244. ***Average need-based loan:*** Freshmen: $3007; Undergraduates: $3937. ***Parent loans:*** $3,737,414 (33% need-based, 67% non-need-based). ***Programs:*** Federal Direct (Subsidized and Unsubsidized Stafford, PLUS), Perkins, alternative loans.

WORK-STUDY ***Federal work-study:*** Total amount: $296,594; 334 jobs averaging $823. ***State or other work-study/employment:*** Total amount: $523,168 (100% non-need-based). 299 part-time jobs averaging $1492.

APPLYING FOR FINANCIAL AID ***Required financial aid form:*** FAFSA. ***Financial aid deadline (priority):*** 4/15. ***Notification date:*** Continuous beginning 3/1. Students must reply within 3 weeks of notification.

CONTACT Ruth A. Pusich, Director of Financial Aid, Elmhurst College, Goebel Hall 106A, 190 Prospect Avenue, Elmhurst, IL 60126-3296, 630-617-3080 or toll-free 800-697-1871 (out-of-state). *Fax:* 630-617-5188. *E-mail:* ruthp@elmhurst.edu.

ELMIRA COLLEGE

Elmira, NY

Tuition & fees: $30,050 **Average undergraduate aid package: $23,500**

ABOUT THE INSTITUTION Independent, coed. Awards: bachelor's and master's degrees. 67 undergraduate majors. Total enrollment: 1,853. Undergraduates: 1,484. Freshmen: 323. Federal methodology is used as a basis for awarding need-based institutional aid.

UNDERGRADUATE EXPENSES for 2006–07 ***Application fee:*** $50. ***Comprehensive fee:*** $39,150 includes full-time tuition ($29,000), mandatory fees ($1050), and room and board ($9100). ***Part-time tuition:*** $270 per credit. ***Payment plans:*** Tuition prepayment, installment.

FRESHMAN FINANCIAL AID (Fall 2006, est.) 283 applied for aid; of those 91% were deemed to have need. 100% of freshmen with need received aid; of those 15% had need fully met. ***Average percent of need met:*** 82% (excluding resources awarded to replace EFC). ***Average financial aid package:*** $24,400 (excluding resources awarded to replace EFC). 24% of all full-time freshmen had no need and received non-need-based gift aid.

UNDERGRADUATE FINANCIAL AID (Fall 2006, est.) 1,013 applied for aid; of those 92% were deemed to have need. 100% of undergraduates with need received aid; of those 14% had need fully met. ***Average percent of need met:*** 81% (excluding resources awarded to replace EFC). ***Average financial aid package:*** $23,500 (excluding resources awarded to replace EFC). 21% of all full-time undergraduates had no need and received non-need-based gift aid.

GIFT AID (NEED-BASED) ***Total amount:*** $16,447,104 (7% federal, 6% state, 84% institutional, 3% external sources). ***Receiving aid:*** Freshmen: 76% (258); All full-time undergraduates: 76% (932). ***Average award:*** Freshmen: $20,000; Undergraduates: $17,900. ***Scholarships, grants, and awards:*** Federal Pell, FSEOG, state, private, college/university gift aid from institutional funds.

GIFT AID (NON-NEED-BASED) ***Total amount:*** $3,922,491 (1% state, 95% institutional, 4% external sources). ***Receiving aid:*** Freshmen: 9% (30); Undergraduates: 8% (92). ***Average award:*** Freshmen: $15,000; Undergraduates: $17,000. ***Scholarships, grants, and awards by category:*** *Academic Interests/Achievement:* 794 awards ($9,772,324 total): general academic interests/achievements. *Special Achievements/Activities:* 116 awards ($475,060 total): leadership. *Special Characteristics:* 139 awards ($1,473,476 total): children of faculty/staff, international students, local/state students, previous college experience, siblings of current students. ***Tuition waivers:*** Full or partial for employees or children of employees. ***ROTC:*** Army, Air Force cooperative.

LOANS ***Student loans:*** $10,005,425 (68% need-based, 32% non-need-based). 80% of past graduating class borrowed through all loan programs. *Average indebtedness per student:* $29,058. ***Average need-based loan:*** Freshmen: $4870; Undergraduates: $6090. ***Parent loans:*** $2,734,551 (34% need-based, 66% non-need-based). ***Programs:*** FFEL (Subsidized and Unsubsidized Stafford, PLUS), Perkins, college/university, GATE Loans, alternative loans.

WORK-STUDY ***Federal work-study:*** Total amount: $408,766; 409 jobs averaging $1000. ***State or other work-study/employment:*** Total amount: $274,675 (43% need-based, 57% non-need-based). 228 part-time jobs averaging $1200.

APPLYING FOR FINANCIAL AID ***Required financial aid forms:*** FAFSA, state aid form. ***Financial aid deadline (priority):*** 2/1. ***Notification date:*** Continuous beginning 2/15. Students must reply by 5/1 or within 3 weeks of notification.

CONTACT Kathleen L. Cohen, Dean of Financial Aid, Elmira College, Hamilton Hall, One Park Place, Elmira, NY 14901-2099, 607-735-1728 or toll-free 800-935-6472. *Fax:* 607-735-1718. *E-mail:* kcohen@elmira.edu.

ELMS COLLEGE

Chicopee, MA

ABOUT THE INSTITUTION Independent Roman Catholic, coed, primarily women. Awards: associate, bachelor's, and master's degrees and post-bachelor's certificates. 42 undergraduate majors. Total enrollment: 1,234. Undergraduates: 1,066. Freshmen: 145.

GIFT AID (NEED-BASED) ***Scholarships, grants, and awards:*** Federal Pell, FSEOG, state, private, college/university gift aid from institutional funds.

GIFT AID (NON-NEED-BASED) ***Scholarships, grants, and awards by category:*** *Academic Interests/Achievement:* general academic interests/achievements. *Special Characteristics:* children of faculty/staff, general special characteristics, religious affiliation.

LOANS ***Programs:*** FFEL (Subsidized and Unsubsidized Stafford, PLUS), Perkins, state, alternative loans, MEFA Loans, Signature Loans.

APPLYING FOR FINANCIAL AID ***Required financial aid forms:*** FAFSA, institution's own form.

CONTACT Ms. April Arcouette, Assistant Director of Student Financial Aid Services, Elms College, 291 Springfield Street, Chicopee, MA 01013-2839, 413-265-2249 or toll-free 800-255-ELMS. *Fax:* 413-265-2671. *E-mail:* arcouettea@elms.edu.

ELON UNIVERSITY

Elon, NC

Tuition & fees: $20,441 **Average undergraduate aid package: $12,794**

ABOUT THE INSTITUTION Independent religious, coed. Awards: bachelor's, master's, doctoral, and first professional degrees. 51 undergraduate majors.

Total enrollment: 5,230. Undergraduates: 4,849. Freshmen: 1,283. Institutional methodology is used as a basis for awarding need-based institutional aid.

UNDERGRADUATE EXPENSES for 2006–07 ***Application fee:*** $40. ***Comprehensive fee:*** $27,291 includes full-time tuition ($20,171), mandatory fees ($270), and room and board ($6850). Room and board charges vary according to board plan and housing facility. ***Part-time tuition:*** $634 per hour. ***Part-time fees:*** $135 per term. Part-time tuition and fees vary according to course load. ***Payment plan:*** Installment.

FRESHMAN FINANCIAL AID (Fall 2006, est.) 707 applied for aid; of those 61% were deemed to have need. 99% of freshmen with need received aid. ***Average percent of need met:*** 69% (excluding resources awarded to replace EFC). ***Average financial aid package:*** $11,903 (excluding resources awarded to replace EFC). 20% of all full-time freshmen had no need and received non-need-based gift aid.

UNDERGRADUATE FINANCIAL AID (Fall 2006, est.) 2,134 applied for aid; of those 72% were deemed to have need. 99% of undergraduates with need received aid. ***Average percent of need met:*** 70% (excluding resources awarded to replace EFC). ***Average financial aid package:*** $12,794 (excluding resources awarded to replace EFC). 20% of all full-time undergraduates had no need and received non-need-based gift aid.

GIFT AID (NEED-BASED) ***Total amount:*** $10,624,998 (11% federal, 31% state, 56% institutional, 2% external sources). ***Receiving aid:*** Freshmen: 28% (358); All full-time undergraduates: 29% (1,361). ***Average award:*** Freshmen: $7588; Undergraduates: $7384. ***Scholarships, grants, and awards:*** Federal Pell, FSEOG, state, private, college/university gift aid from institutional funds.

GIFT AID (NON-NEED-BASED) ***Total amount:*** $5,257,748 (30% state, 67% institutional, 3% external sources). ***Receiving aid:*** Freshmen: 3% (39); Undergraduates: 3% (136). ***Average award:*** Freshmen: $4602; Undergraduates: $4431. ***Scholarships, grants, and awards by category:*** *Academic Interests/Achievement:* 1,408 awards ($6,201,957 total): biological sciences, business, communication, computer science, education, engineering/technologies, general academic interests/achievements, mathematics, military science, physical sciences, premedicine, religion/biblical studies, social sciences. *Creative Arts/Performance:* 175 awards ($150,154 total): art/fine arts, journalism/publications, music, performing arts, theater/drama. *Special Achievements/Activities:* 31 awards ($42,750 total): community service, general special achievements/activities, leadership, religious involvement. *Special Characteristics:* 101 awards ($771,257 total): children of faculty/staff, first-generation college students, relatives of clergy. ***Tuition waivers:*** Full or partial for employees or children of employees. ***ROTC:*** Army, Air Force cooperative.

LOANS ***Student loans:*** $13,822,145 (43% need-based, 57% non-need-based). 46% of past graduating class borrowed through all loan programs. *Average indebtedness per student:* $21,991. ***Average need-based loan:*** Freshmen: $2422; Undergraduates: $3723. ***Parent loans:*** $9,282,041 (35% need-based, 65% non-need-based). ***Programs:*** FFEL (Subsidized and Unsubsidized Stafford, PLUS), Perkins, state, college/university, alternative loans.

WORK-STUDY ***Federal work-study:*** Total amount: $2,115,411; 887 jobs averaging $2286.

ATHLETIC AWARDS Total amount: $4,176,104 (45% need-based, 55% non-need-based).

APPLYING FOR FINANCIAL AID ***Required financial aid forms:*** FAFSA, institution's own form, CSS Financial Aid PROFILE. ***Financial aid deadline (priority):*** 3/15. ***Notification date:*** 3/30.

CONTACT Patrick Murphy, Director of Financial Planning, Elon University, 2725 Campus Box, Elon, NC 27244, 336-278-7640 or toll-free 800-334-8448. *Fax:* 336-278-7639. *E-mail:* finaid@elon.edu.

EMBRY-RIDDLE AERONAUTICAL UNIVERSITY

Prescott, AZ

Tuition & fees: $26,130 **Average undergraduate aid package: $15,248**

ABOUT THE INSTITUTION Independent, coed. Awards: bachelor's and master's degrees. 11 undergraduate majors. Total enrollment: 1,674. Undergraduates: 1,630. Freshmen: 403. Federal methodology is used as a basis for awarding need-based institutional aid.

UNDERGRADUATE EXPENSES for 2007–08 ***Application fee:*** $50. ***Comprehensive fee:*** $33,344 includes full-time tuition ($25,400), mandatory fees ($730), and room and board ($7214). ***College room only:*** $3990. ***Part-time tuition:*** $1060 per credit hour.

FRESHMAN FINANCIAL AID (Fall 2006, est.) 355 applied for aid; of those 80% were deemed to have need. 100% of freshmen with need received aid. ***Average financial aid package:*** $13,951 (excluding resources awarded to replace EFC).

UNDERGRADUATE FINANCIAL AID (Fall 2006, est.) 1,119 applied for aid; of those 85% were deemed to have need. 100% of undergraduates with need received aid. ***Average financial aid package:*** $15,248 (excluding resources awarded to replace EFC).

GIFT AID (NEED-BASED) ***Total amount:*** $13,466,080 (10% federal, 64% institutional, 26% external sources). ***Receiving aid:*** Freshmen: 70% (282); All full-time undergraduates: 62% (914). ***Average award:*** Freshmen: $9321; Undergraduates: $8702. ***Scholarships, grants, and awards:*** Federal Pell, FSEOG, state, private, college/university gift aid from institutional funds.

GIFT AID (NON-NEED-BASED) ***Scholarships, grants, and awards by category:*** *Academic Interests/Achievement:* 555 awards ($3,127,776 total): general academic interests/achievements. *Special Achievements/Activities:* 21 awards ($95,300 total): leadership. *Special Characteristics:* 79 awards ($729,413 total): children and siblings of alumni, children of faculty/staff. ***ROTC:*** Army, Air Force.

LOANS ***Student loans:*** $12,594,016 (100% need-based). 82% of past graduating class borrowed through all loan programs. *Average indebtedness per student:* $49,037. ***Average need-based loan:*** Freshmen: $3554; Undergraduates: $4700. ***Parent loans:*** $5,718,902 (100% need-based). ***Programs:*** FFEL (Subsidized and Unsubsidized Stafford, PLUS), Perkins.

WORK-STUDY ***Federal work-study:*** Total amount: $54,160; 92 jobs averaging $465. ***State or other work-study/employment:*** Total amount: $1,100,853 (100% need-based). 523 part-time jobs averaging $1721.

ATHLETIC AWARDS Total amount: $700,195 (100% need-based).

APPLYING FOR FINANCIAL AID ***Required financial aid form:*** FAFSA. ***Financial aid deadline:*** Continuous. ***Notification date:*** Continuous beginning 3/1. Students must reply within 4 weeks of notification.

CONTACT Mr. Dan Lupin, Director of Financial Aid, Embry-Riddle Aeronautical University, 3700 Willow Creek Road, Prescott, AZ 86301-3720, 928-777-3765 or toll-free 800-888-3728. *Fax:* 928-777-3893. *E-mail:* lupind@erau.edu.

EMBRY-RIDDLE AERONAUTICAL UNIVERSITY

Daytona Beach, FL

Tuition & fees: $26,496 **Average undergraduate aid package: $13,821**

ABOUT THE INSTITUTION Independent, coed. Awards: bachelor's and master's degrees. 19 undergraduate majors. Total enrollment: 4,863. Undergraduates: 4,473. Freshmen: 1,113. Federal methodology is used as a basis for awarding need-based institutional aid.

UNDERGRADUATE EXPENSES for 2007–08 ***Application fee:*** $50. ***Comprehensive fee:*** $35,646 includes full-time tuition ($25,400), mandatory fees ($1096), and room and board ($9150). ***College room only:*** $4750. ***Part-time tuition:*** $1060 per credit hour.

FRESHMAN FINANCIAL AID (Fall 2006, est.) 960 applied for aid; of those 83% were deemed to have need. 100% of freshmen with need received aid. ***Average financial aid package:*** $13,913 (excluding resources awarded to replace EFC).

UNDERGRADUATE FINANCIAL AID (Fall 2006, est.) 3,045 applied for aid; of those 86% were deemed to have need. 100% of undergraduates with need received aid. ***Average financial aid package:*** $13,821 (excluding resources awarded to replace EFC).

GIFT AID (NEED-BASED) ***Total amount:*** $31,056,147 (12% federal, 12% state, 52% institutional, 24% external sources). ***Receiving aid:*** Freshmen: 72% (798); All full-time undergraduates: 59% (2,449). ***Average award:*** Freshmen: $9031; Undergraduates: $7748. ***Scholarships, grants, and awards:*** Federal Pell, FSEOG, state, private, college/university gift aid from institutional funds.

GIFT AID (NON-NEED-BASED) ***Scholarships, grants, and awards by category:*** *Academic Interests/Achievement:* 1,869 awards ($9,061,315 total): general academic interests/achievements. *Special Achievements/Activities:* 66 awards ($164,910 total): leadership. *Special Characteristics:* 137 awards ($1,484,203 total): children and siblings of alumni, children of faculty/staff, siblings of current students. ***ROTC:*** Army, Naval, Air Force.

LOANS ***Student loans:*** $35,942,093 (100% need-based). 74% of past graduating class borrowed through all loan programs. *Average indebtedness per student:* $52,495. ***Average need-based loan:*** Freshmen: $3470; Undergraduates: $4678. ***Parent loans:*** $13,524,021 (100% need-based). ***Programs:*** FFEL (Subsidized and Unsubsidized Stafford, PLUS), Perkins.

WORK-STUDY ***Federal work-study:*** Total amount: $226,318; 191 jobs averaging $1027. ***State or other work-study/employment:*** Total amount: $3,106,434 (100% need-based). 1,285 part-time jobs averaging $2209.

ATHLETIC AWARDS Total amount: $1,503,909 (100% need-based).

APPLYING FOR FINANCIAL AID ***Required financial aid form:*** FAFSA. ***Financial aid deadline:*** Continuous. ***Notification date:*** Continuous beginning 3/1. Students must reply within 4 weeks of notification.

CONTACT Barbara Dryden, Director of Financial Aid, Embry-Riddle Aeronautical University, 600 South Clyde Morris Boulevard, Daytona Beach, FL 32114-3900, 800-943-6279 or toll-free 800-862-2416. *Fax:* 386-226-6307. *E-mail:* barbara.dryden@erau.edu.

EMBRY-RIDDLE AERONAUTICAL UNIVERSITY WORLDWIDE

Daytona Beach, FL

Tuition & fees: $4584 **Average undergraduate aid package: $5119**

ABOUT THE INSTITUTION Independent, coed. Awards: associate, bachelor's, and master's degrees (programs offered at 100 military bases worldwide). 4 undergraduate majors. Total enrollment: 16,826. Undergraduates: 12,782. Freshmen: 469. Federal methodology is used as a basis for awarding need-based institutional aid.

UNDERGRADUATE EXPENSES for 2007–08 ***Application fee:*** $50. ***Tuition:*** full-time $4584; part-time $191 per credit hour.

FRESHMAN FINANCIAL AID (Fall 2006, est.) 10 applied for aid; of those 90% were deemed to have need. 100% of freshmen with need received aid. ***Average financial aid package:*** $5294 (excluding resources awarded to replace EFC).

UNDERGRADUATE FINANCIAL AID (Fall 2006, est.) 469 applied for aid; of those 100% were deemed to have need. 97% of undergraduates with need received aid. ***Average financial aid package:*** $5119 (excluding resources awarded to replace EFC).

GIFT AID (NEED-BASED) ***Total amount:*** $2,902,301 (58% federal, 39% state, 1% institutional, 2% external sources). ***Receiving aid:*** Freshmen: 11% (7); All full-time undergraduates: 13% (292). ***Average award:*** Freshmen: $3834; Undergraduates: $3312. ***Scholarships, grants, and awards:*** Federal Pell, state, private, college/university gift aid from institutional funds.

GIFT AID (NON-NEED-BASED) ***Scholarships, grants, and awards by category:*** *Academic Interests/Achievement:* 21 awards ($11,566 total): general academic interests/achievements. *Special Achievements/Activities:* 64 awards ($10,114 total): leadership. *Special Characteristics:* 21 awards ($35,709 total): children of faculty/staff.

LOANS ***Student loans:*** $8,498,094 (100% need-based). 24% of past graduating class borrowed through all loan programs. *Average indebtedness per student:* $24,494. ***Average need-based loan:*** Freshmen: $2964; Undergraduates: $3501. ***Parent loans:*** $28,101 (100% need-based). ***Programs:*** FFEL (Subsidized and Unsubsidized Stafford, PLUS).

APPLYING FOR FINANCIAL AID ***Required financial aid form:*** FAFSA. ***Financial aid deadline:*** Continuous. ***Notification date:*** Continuous beginning 3/1. Students must reply within 4 weeks of notification.

CONTACT Barbara Dryden, Director of Financial Aid, Embry-Riddle Aeronautical University Worldwide, 600 South Clyde Morris Boulevard, Daytona Beach, FL 32114-3900, 800-943-6279 or toll-free 800-522-6787. *Fax:* 386-226-6307. *E-mail:* barbara.dryden@erau.edu.

EMERSON COLLEGE

Boston, MA

Tuition & fees: $25,894 **Average undergraduate aid package: $13,777**

ABOUT THE INSTITUTION Independent, coed. Awards: bachelor's, master's, and doctoral degrees. 29 undergraduate majors. Total enrollment: 4,324. Undergraduates: 3,402. Freshmen: 727. Both federal and institutional methodology are used as a basis for awarding need-based institutional aid.

UNDERGRADUATE EXPENSES for 2006–07 ***Application fee:*** $60. ***Comprehensive fee:*** $36,764 includes full-time tuition ($25,248), mandatory fees ($646), and room and board ($10,870). ***Part-time tuition:*** $789 per credit hour. ***Payment plan:*** Installment.

FRESHMAN FINANCIAL AID (Fall 2005) 567 applied for aid; of those 72% were deemed to have need. 100% of freshmen with need received aid; of those 96% had need fully met. ***Average percent of need met:*** 76% (excluding resources awarded to replace EFC). ***Average financial aid package:*** $13,502 (excluding resources awarded to replace EFC). 28% of all full-time freshmen had no need and received non-need-based gift aid.

UNDERGRADUATE FINANCIAL AID (Fall 2005) 1,994 applied for aid; of those 82% were deemed to have need. 100% of undergraduates with need received aid; of those 84% had need fully met. ***Average percent of need met:*** 67% (excluding resources awarded to replace EFC). ***Average financial aid package:*** $13,777 (excluding resources awarded to replace EFC). 19% of all full-time undergraduates had no need and received non-need-based gift aid.

GIFT AID (NEED-BASED) ***Total amount:*** $15,346,906 (9% federal, 3% state, 83% institutional, 5% external sources). ***Receiving aid:*** Freshmen: 46% (331); All full-time undergraduates: 41% (1,274). ***Average award:*** Freshmen: $12,062; Undergraduates: $11,525. ***Scholarships, grants, and awards:*** Federal Pell, FSEOG, state, private, college/university gift aid from institutional funds.

GIFT AID (NON-NEED-BASED) ***Total amount:*** $1,741,174 (86% institutional, 14% external sources). ***Receiving aid:*** Freshmen: 2% (15); Undergraduates: 1% (36). ***Average award:*** Freshmen: $11,251; Undergraduates: $14,443. ***Scholarships, grants, and awards by category:*** *Academic Interests/Achievement:* 322 awards ($2,796,821 total): general academic interests/achievements. *Creative Arts/Performance:* 44 awards ($190,600 total): performing arts. ***Tuition waivers:*** Full or partial for employees or children of employees.

LOANS ***Student loans:*** $22,437,716 (60% need-based, 40% non-need-based). 61% of past graduating class borrowed through all loan programs. *Average indebtedness per student:* $25,108. ***Average need-based loan:*** Freshmen: $3131; Undergraduates: $4323. ***Parent loans:*** $9,129,079 (34% need-based, 66% non-need-based). ***Programs:*** FFEL (Subsidized and Unsubsidized Stafford, PLUS), Perkins, state.

WORK-STUDY ***Federal work-study:*** Total amount: $752,000; 405 jobs averaging $2000. ***State or other work-study/employment:*** Total amount: $794,987 (71% need-based, 29% non-need-based). 47 part-time jobs averaging $9409.

APPLYING FOR FINANCIAL AID ***Required financial aid forms:*** FAFSA, CSS Financial Aid PROFILE, noncustodial (divorced/separated) parent's statement, business/farm supplement, income tax returns. ***Financial aid deadline (priority):*** 3/1. ***Notification date:*** 4/1. Students must reply by 5/1 or within 3 weeks of notification.

CONTACT Michelle Smith, Director, Office of Student Financial Services, Emerson College, 120 Boylston Street, Boston, MA 02116-4624, 617-824-8655. *Fax:* 617-824-8619. *E-mail:* finaid@emerson.edu.

EMMANUEL COLLEGE

Franklin Springs, GA

CONTACT Mary Beadles, Director of Financial Aid, Emmanuel College, PO Box 129, Franklin Springs, GA 30639-0129, 706-245-2844 or toll-free 800-860-8800 (in-state). *Fax:* 706-245-4424. *E-mail:* mbeadles@emmanuel-college.edu.

EMMANUEL COLLEGE

Boston, MA

Tuition & fees: $24,200 **Average undergraduate aid package: $17,211**

ABOUT THE INSTITUTION Independent Roman Catholic, coed. Awards: bachelor's and master's degrees and post-master's certificates. 35 undergraduate majors. Total enrollment: 2,340. Undergraduates: 2,156. Freshmen: 467. Federal methodology is used as a basis for awarding need-based institutional aid.

UNDERGRADUATE EXPENSES for 2006–07 ***Application fee:*** $40. ***Comprehensive fee:*** $34,600 includes full-time tuition ($23,800), mandatory fees ($400), and room and board ($10,400). Full-time tuition and fees vary according to course load, degree level, and program. Room and board charges vary according to housing facility. ***Part-time tuition:*** $744 per credit. Part-time tuition and fees vary according to program. ***Payment plan:*** Installment.

FRESHMAN FINANCIAL AID (Fall 2006, est.) 405 applied for aid; of those 88% were deemed to have need. 100% of freshmen with need received aid; of those

36% had need fully met. ***Average percent of need met:*** 68% (excluding resources awarded to replace EFC). ***Average financial aid package:*** $17,636 (excluding resources awarded to replace EFC). 9% of all full-time freshmen had no need and received non-need-based gift aid.

UNDERGRADUATE FINANCIAL AID (Fall 2006, est.) 1,412 applied for aid; of those 87% were deemed to have need. 100% of undergraduates with need received aid; of those 32% had need fully met. ***Average percent of need met:*** 71% (excluding resources awarded to replace EFC). ***Average financial aid package:*** $17,211 (excluding resources awarded to replace EFC). 21% of all full-time undergraduates had no need and received non-need-based gift aid.

GIFT AID (NEED-BASED) ***Total amount:*** $9,459,115 (15% federal, 10% state, 73% institutional, 2% external sources). ***Receiving aid:*** Freshmen: 66% (308); All full-time undergraduates: 62% (974). ***Average award:*** Freshmen: $11,109; Undergraduates: $9823. ***Scholarships, grants, and awards:*** Federal Pell, FSEOG, state, private, college/university gift aid from institutional funds.

GIFT AID (NON-NEED-BASED) ***Total amount:*** $6,948,390 (92% institutional, 8% external sources). ***Receiving aid:*** Freshmen: 30% (141); Undergraduates: 29% (449). ***Average award:*** Freshmen: $10,167; Undergraduates: $11,848. ***Scholarships, grants, and awards by category:*** *Academic Interests/Achievement:* 555 awards ($5,936,152 total): biological sciences, education, engineering/technologies, foreign languages, general academic interests/achievements, health fields, humanities, mathematics, physical sciences, religion/biblical studies, social sciences. *Creative Arts/Performance:* 1 award ($3375 total): general creative arts/performance. *Special Achievements/Activities:* 31 awards ($77,500 total): community service. *Special Characteristics:* 176 awards ($627,531 total): children and siblings of alumni, children of educators, children of faculty/staff, children of union members/company employees, ethnic background, general special characteristics, handicapped students, international students, local/state students, religious affiliation, siblings of current students. ***Tuition waivers:*** Full or partial for employees or children of employees. ***ROTC:*** Army cooperative.

LOANS ***Student loans:*** $6,514,199 (75% need-based, 25% non-need-based). 73% of past graduating class borrowed through all loan programs. *Average indebtedness per student:* $18,637. ***Average need-based loan:*** Freshmen: $3259; Undergraduates: $4424. ***Parent loans:*** $5,031,702 (100% non-need-based). ***Programs:*** FFEL (Subsidized and Unsubsidized Stafford, PLUS), Perkins, state, alternative loans.

WORK-STUDY ***Federal work-study:*** Total amount: $450,000; 485 jobs averaging $927. ***State or other work-study/employment:*** Total amount: $300,000 (100% non-need-based). 300 part-time jobs averaging $1000.

APPLYING FOR FINANCIAL AID ***Required financial aid forms:*** FAFSA, institution's own form. ***Financial aid deadline (priority):*** 4/1. ***Notification date:*** Continuous. Students must reply within 2 weeks of notification.

CONTACT Jennifer Porter, Director of Student Financial Services, Emmanuel College, 400 The Fenway, Boston, MA 02115, 617-735-9938. *Fax:* 617-735-9939. *E-mail:* porterj@emmanuel.edu.

EMMAUS BIBLE COLLEGE

Dubuque, IA

Tuition & fees: N/R **Average undergraduate aid package: $5216**

ABOUT THE INSTITUTION Independent nondenominational, coed. Awards: associate and bachelor's degrees. 5 undergraduate majors. Total enrollment: 296. Undergraduates: 296. Freshmen: 59. Federal methodology is used as a basis for awarding need-based institutional aid.

FRESHMAN FINANCIAL AID (Fall 2005) 99 applied for aid; of those 62% were deemed to have need. 84% of freshmen with need received aid. ***Average percent of need met:*** 56% (excluding resources awarded to replace EFC). ***Average financial aid package:*** $4780 (excluding resources awarded to replace EFC).

UNDERGRADUATE FINANCIAL AID (Fall 2005) 212 applied for aid; of those 68% were deemed to have need. 86% of undergraduates with need received aid. ***Average percent of need met:*** 74% (excluding resources awarded to replace EFC). ***Average financial aid package:*** $5216 (excluding resources awarded to replace EFC).

GIFT AID (NEED-BASED) ***Total amount:*** $708,208 (49% federal, 30% institutional, 21% external sources). ***Receiving aid:*** Freshmen: 42% (51); All full-time undergraduates: 43% (115). ***Average award:*** Freshmen: $2687; Undergraduates: $2852. ***Scholarships, grants, and awards:*** Federal Pell, FSEOG, state, private, college/university gift aid from institutional funds.

GIFT AID (NON-NEED-BASED) ***Receiving aid:*** Freshmen: 24% (29); Undergraduates: 34% (91). ***Scholarships, grants, and awards by category:*** *Academic Interests/Achievement:* 93 awards ($60,850 total): general academic interests/achievements. *Creative Arts/Performance:* 4 awards ($800 total). *Special Achievements/Activities:* 34 awards ($93,021 total): leadership, religious involvement. *Special Characteristics:* 11 awards ($71,228 total): children of faculty/staff. ***Tuition waivers:*** Full or partial for employees or children of employees.

LOANS ***Student loans:*** $935,073 (48% need-based, 52% non-need-based). 66% of past graduating class borrowed through all loan programs. ***Average need-based loan:*** Freshmen: $3119; Undergraduates: $3652. ***Parent loans:*** $56,990 (100% need-based). ***Programs:*** FFEL (Subsidized and Unsubsidized Stafford, PLUS).

APPLYING FOR FINANCIAL AID ***Notification date:*** Continuous.

CONTACT Steve Seeman, Financial Aid Director, Emmaus Bible College, 2570 Asbury Road, Dubuque, IA 52001-3097, 800-397-2425 Ext. 1309 or toll-free 800-397-2425. *Fax:* 563-588-1216. *E-mail:* financialaid@emmaus.edu.

EMORY & HENRY COLLEGE

Emory, VA

Tuition & fees: $20,860 **Average undergraduate aid package: $17,585**

ABOUT THE INSTITUTION Independent United Methodist, coed. Awards: bachelor's and master's degrees. 37 undergraduate majors. Total enrollment: 1,051. Undergraduates: 996. Freshmen: 282. Federal methodology is used as a basis for awarding need-based institutional aid.

UNDERGRADUATE EXPENSES for 2006–07 ***Application fee:*** $30. ***Comprehensive fee:*** $28,220 includes full-time tuition ($20,860) and room and board ($7360). ***College room only:*** $3640. Full-time tuition and fees vary according to course load and degree level. Room and board charges vary according to board plan. ***Part-time tuition:*** $870 per hour. Part-time tuition and fees vary according to course load and degree level. ***Payment plan:*** Installment.

FRESHMAN FINANCIAL AID (Fall 2006, est.) 243 applied for aid; of those 95% were deemed to have need. 100% of freshmen with need received aid; of those 30% had need fully met. ***Average percent of need met:*** 91% (excluding resources awarded to replace EFC). ***Average financial aid package:*** $19,173 (excluding resources awarded to replace EFC). 22% of all full-time freshmen had no need and received non-need-based gift aid.

UNDERGRADUATE FINANCIAL AID (Fall 2006, est.) 775 applied for aid; of those 96% were deemed to have need. 100% of undergraduates with need received aid; of those 27% had need fully met. ***Average percent of need met:*** 83% (excluding resources awarded to replace EFC). ***Average financial aid package:*** $17,585 (excluding resources awarded to replace EFC). 23% of all full-time undergraduates had no need and received non-need-based gift aid.

GIFT AID (NEED-BASED) ***Total amount:*** $10,544,104 (9% federal, 14% state, 73% institutional, 4% external sources). ***Receiving aid:*** Freshmen: 82% (230); All full-time undergraduates: 75% (739). ***Average award:*** Freshmen: $15,547; Undergraduates: $13,791. ***Scholarships, grants, and awards:*** Federal Pell, FSEOG, state, private, college/university gift aid from institutional funds.

GIFT AID (NON-NEED-BASED) ***Total amount:*** $2,104,569 (15% state, 83% institutional, 2% external sources). ***Receiving aid:*** Freshmen: 77% (217); Undergraduates: 34% (338). ***Average award:*** Freshmen: $8025; Undergraduates: $4780. ***Tuition waivers:*** Full or partial for employees or children of employees.

LOANS ***Student loans:*** $3,179,941 (93% need-based, 7% non-need-based). 79% of past graduating class borrowed through all loan programs. *Average indebtedness per student:* $13,312. ***Average need-based loan:*** Freshmen: $2891; Undergraduates: $3493. ***Programs:*** FFEL (Subsidized and Unsubsidized Stafford, PLUS), Perkins.

WORK-STUDY ***Federal work-study:*** Total amount: $615,393.

APPLYING FOR FINANCIAL AID ***Required financial aid forms:*** FAFSA, state aid form. ***Financial aid deadline (priority):*** 4/1. ***Notification date:*** Continuous beginning 2/1. Students must reply within 2 weeks of notification.

CONTACT Scarlett Cortner, Coordinator of Financial Aid, Emory & Henry College, PO Box 947, Emory, VA 24327-0010, 276-944-6115 or toll-free 800-848-5493. *Fax:* 276-944-6884. *E-mail:* sblevins@ehc.edu.

EMORY UNIVERSITY

Atlanta, GA

Tuition & fees: $34,336 **Average undergraduate aid package: $27,971**

ABOUT THE INSTITUTION Independent Methodist, coed. Awards: associate, bachelor's, master's, doctoral, and first professional degrees (enrollment figures include Emory University, Oxford College; application data for main campus only). 57 undergraduate majors. Total enrollment: 12,338. Undergraduates: 6,646. Freshmen: 1,665. Both federal and institutional methodology are used as a basis for awarding need-based institutional aid.

UNDERGRADUATE EXPENSES for 2007–08 ***Application fee:*** $50. ***Comprehensive fee:*** $45,356 includes full-time tuition ($33,900), mandatory fees ($436), and room and board ($11,020). ***Part-time tuition:*** $1413 per hour.

FRESHMAN FINANCIAL AID (Fall 2006, est.) 852 applied for aid; of those 76% were deemed to have need. 100% of freshmen with need received aid; of those 100% had need fully met. ***Average percent of need met:*** 100% (excluding resources awarded to replace EFC). ***Average financial aid package:*** $27,760 (excluding resources awarded to replace EFC). 16% of all full-time freshmen had no need and received non-need-based gift aid.

UNDERGRADUATE FINANCIAL AID (Fall 2006, est.) 3,004 applied for aid; of those 84% were deemed to have need. 100% of undergraduates with need received aid; of those 100% had need fully met. ***Average percent of need met:*** 100% (excluding resources awarded to replace EFC). ***Average financial aid package:*** $27,971 (excluding resources awarded to replace EFC). 16% of all full-time undergraduates had no need and received non-need-based gift aid.

GIFT AID (NEED-BASED) ***Total amount:*** $50,476,434 (6% federal, 5% state, 86% institutional, 3% external sources). ***Receiving aid:*** Freshmen: 37% (622); All full-time undergraduates: 35% (2,414). ***Average award:*** Freshmen: $26,544; Undergraduates: $27,011. ***Scholarships, grants, and awards:*** Federal Pell, FSEOG, state, private, college/university gift aid from institutional funds.

GIFT AID (NON-NEED-BASED) ***Total amount:*** $11,795,580 (18% state, 72% institutional, 10% external sources). ***Receiving aid:*** Freshmen: 5% (84); Undergraduates: 4% (248). ***Average award:*** Freshmen: $13,012; Undergraduates: $17,013. ***Scholarships, grants, and awards by category:*** *Academic Interests/Achievement:* 734 awards ($12,148,175 total): general academic interests/achievements. *Creative Arts/Performance:* 6 awards ($152,040 total): debating, music, performing arts. *Special Achievements/Activities:* 1 award ($1300 total): memberships. *Special Characteristics:* 1,651 awards ($17,883,667 total): children of faculty/staff, local/state students, relatives of clergy, religious affiliation, veterans. ***ROTC:*** Army cooperative, Naval cooperative, Air Force cooperative.

LOANS ***Student loans:*** $15,160,773 (54% need-based, 46% non-need-based). 39% of past graduating class borrowed through all loan programs. *Average indebtedness per student:* $24,272. ***Average need-based loan:*** Freshmen: $1815; Undergraduates: $3291. ***Parent loans:*** $11,201,781 (100% non-need-based). ***Programs:*** FFEL (Subsidized and Unsubsidized Stafford, PLUS), Perkins, Federal Nursing, state, college/university.

WORK-STUDY ***Federal work-study:*** Total amount: $3,286,885; 1,802 jobs averaging $1880. ***State or other work-study/employment:*** Total amount: $573,166 (62% need-based, 38% non-need-based). 98 part-time jobs averaging $6020.

APPLYING FOR FINANCIAL AID ***Required financial aid forms:*** FAFSA, CSS Financial Aid PROFILE, noncustodial (divorced/separated) parent's statement. ***Financial aid deadline:*** 3/1 (priority: 2/15). ***Notification date:*** 4/2. Students must reply within 4 weeks of notification.

CONTACT Julia Padgett, Director of Financial Aid, Emory University, 200 Dowman Drive, Boisfeuillet Jones Center, Suite 300, Atlanta, GA 30322-1100, 404-727-6039 or toll-free 800-727-6036. *Fax:* 404-727-6709. *E-mail:* finaid@emory.edu.

EMPORIA STATE UNIVERSITY

Emporia, KS

Tuition & fees (KS res): $3586 **Average undergraduate aid package: $5955**

ABOUT THE INSTITUTION State-supported, coed. Awards: bachelor's, master's, and doctoral degrees and post-bachelor's and post-master's certificates. 33 undergraduate majors. Total enrollment: 6,473. Undergraduates: 4,458. Freshmen: 769. Federal methodology is used as a basis for awarding need-based institutional aid.

UNDERGRADUATE EXPENSES for 2006–07 ***Application fee:*** $30. ***Tuition, state resident:*** full-time $2862; part-time $95 per credit hour. ***Tuition, nonresident:*** full-time $10,214; part-time $340 per credit hour. ***Required fees:*** full-time $724; $44 per credit hour. Full-time tuition and fees vary according to degree level. Part-time tuition and fees vary according to degree level. ***College room and board:*** $5170; ***Room only:*** $2552. Room and board charges vary according to board plan and housing facility. ***Payment plans:*** Installment, deferred payment.

FRESHMAN FINANCIAL AID (Fall 2005) 606 applied for aid; of those 69% were deemed to have need. 100% of freshmen with need received aid; of those 26% had need fully met. ***Average percent of need met:*** 65% (excluding resources awarded to replace EFC). ***Average financial aid package:*** $4880 (excluding resources awarded to replace EFC). 21% of all full-time freshmen had no need and received non-need-based gift aid.

UNDERGRADUATE FINANCIAL AID (Fall 2005) 2,899 applied for aid; of those 76% were deemed to have need. 100% of undergraduates with need received aid; of those 26% had need fully met. ***Average percent of need met:*** 67% (excluding resources awarded to replace EFC). ***Average financial aid package:*** $5955 (excluding resources awarded to replace EFC). 9% of all full-time undergraduates had no need and received non-need-based gift aid.

GIFT AID (NEED-BASED) ***Total amount:*** $6,111,697 (66% federal, 9% state, 14% institutional, 11% external sources). ***Receiving aid:*** Freshmen: 40% (288); All full-time undergraduates: 38% (1,430). ***Average award:*** Freshmen: $1923; Undergraduates: $2192. ***Scholarships, grants, and awards:*** Federal Pell, FSEOG, state, private, college/university gift aid from institutional funds, Jones Foundation Grants.

GIFT AID (NON-NEED-BASED) ***Total amount:*** $1,285,648 (1% federal, 10% state, 61% institutional, 28% external sources). ***Receiving aid:*** Freshmen: 41% (296); Undergraduates: 28% (1,059). ***Average award:*** Freshmen: $1013; Undergraduates: $849. ***Scholarships, grants, and awards by category:*** *Academic Interests/Achievement:* 1,485 awards ($1,118,082 total): biological sciences, business, communication, computer science, education, engineering/technologies, English, foreign languages, general academic interests/achievements, health fields, humanities, library science, mathematics, physical sciences, premedicine, social sciences. *Creative Arts/Performance:* 271 awards ($227,357 total): art/fine arts, creative writing, debating, music, theater/drama. *Special Achievements/Activities:* 12 awards ($3494 total): memberships. *Special Characteristics:* 26 awards ($20,679 total): children and siblings of alumni, children of faculty/staff, children of union members/company employees, handicapped students, international students, members of minority groups, religious affiliation, veterans, veterans' children. ***Tuition waivers:*** Full or partial for employees or children of employees, senior citizens.

LOANS ***Student loans:*** $14,574,706 (67% need-based, 33% non-need-based). 70% of past graduating class borrowed through all loan programs. *Average indebtedness per student:* $16,005. ***Average need-based loan:*** Freshmen: $2465; Undergraduates: $2765. ***Parent loans:*** $1,204,521 (17% need-based, 83% non-need-based). ***Programs:*** FFEL (Subsidized and Unsubsidized Stafford, PLUS), Perkins, Alaska Loans, alternative loans.

WORK-STUDY ***Federal work-study:*** Total amount: $423,916; 198 jobs averaging $2140. ***State or other work-study/employment:*** Total amount: $42,588 (25% need-based, 75% non-need-based). 29 part-time jobs averaging $1465.

ATHLETIC AWARDS Total amount: $925,371 (40% need-based, 60% non-need-based).

APPLYING FOR FINANCIAL AID ***Required financial aid forms:*** FAFSA, state aid form. ***Financial aid deadline (priority):*** 3/15. ***Notification date:*** Continuous. Students must reply within 2 weeks of notification.

CONTACT Elaine Henrie, Director of Financial Aid, Emporia State University, 1200 Commercial Street, Campus Box 4038, Emporia, KS 66801-5087, 620-341-5457 or toll-free 877-GOTOESU (in-state), 877-468-6378 (out-of-state). *Fax:* 620-341-6088. *E-mail:* ehenrie@emporia.edu.

ENDICOTT COLLEGE

Beverly, MA

Tuition & fees: $21,374 **Average undergraduate aid package: $13,249**

ABOUT THE INSTITUTION Independent, coed. Awards: associate, bachelor's, and master's degrees. 22 undergraduate majors. Total university enrollment: 3,810. Total unit enrollment: 1,721. Undergraduates: 1,721. Freshmen: 529. Federal methodology is used as a basis for awarding need-based institutional aid.

UNDERGRADUATE EXPENSES for 2006–07 ***Application fee:*** $40. ***Comprehensive fee:*** $31,628 includes full-time tuition ($21,074), mandatory fees ($300), and room and board ($10,254). ***College room only:*** $7188. Full-time tuition and fees vary according to student level. Room and board charges vary according to board plan and housing facility. ***Part-time tuition:*** $646 per credit. ***Part-time fees:*** $200 per term. Part-time tuition and fees vary according to student level. ***Payment plan:*** Installment.

FRESHMAN FINANCIAL AID (Fall 2006, est.) 459 applied for aid; of those 73% were deemed to have need. 99% of freshmen with need received aid; of those 11% had need fully met. ***Average percent of need met:*** 56% (excluding resources awarded to replace EFC). ***Average financial aid package:*** $12,557 (excluding resources awarded to replace EFC). 15% of all full-time freshmen had no need and received non-need-based gift aid.

UNDERGRADUATE FINANCIAL AID (Fall 2006, est.) 1,473 applied for aid; of those 72% were deemed to have need. 100% of undergraduates with need received aid; of those 13% had need fully met. ***Average percent of need met:*** 58% (excluding resources awarded to replace EFC). ***Average financial aid package:*** $13,249 (excluding resources awarded to replace EFC). 15% of all full-time undergraduates had no need and received non-need-based gift aid.

GIFT AID (NEED-BASED) ***Total amount:*** $9,654,380 (7% federal, 3% state, 90% institutional). ***Receiving aid:*** Freshmen: 47% (253); All full-time undergraduates: 46% (804). ***Average award:*** Freshmen: $6494; Undergraduates: $6517. ***Scholarships, grants, and awards:*** Federal Pell, FSEOG, state, private, college/university gift aid from institutional funds.

GIFT AID (NON-NEED-BASED) ***Total amount:*** $2,054,801 (84% institutional, 16% external sources). ***Receiving aid:*** Freshmen: 40% (214); Undergraduates: 32% (568). ***Average award:*** Freshmen: $5349; Undergraduates: $6083. ***Scholarships, grants, and awards by category:*** *Academic Interests/Achievement:* 763 awards ($3,809,017 total): business, education, general academic interests/achievements, health fields. *Creative Arts/Performance:* 6 awards ($3500 total): art/fine arts. *Special Achievements/Activities:* 15 awards ($30,500 total): community service, general special achievements/activities, leadership, religious involvement. *Special Characteristics:* 140 awards ($500,427 total): children and siblings of alumni, children of educators, general special characteristics, international students, local/state students, religious affiliation. ***Tuition waivers:*** Full or partial for employees or children of employees. ***ROTC:*** Army cooperative, Air Force cooperative.

LOANS ***Student loans:*** $5,439,693 (72% need-based, 28% non-need-based). 67% of past graduating class borrowed through all loan programs. *Average indebtedness per student:* $27,725. ***Average need-based loan:*** Freshmen: $2854; Undergraduates: $3967. ***Parent loans:*** $10,693,687 (100% non-need-based). ***Programs:*** FFEL (Subsidized and Unsubsidized Stafford, PLUS), Perkins, college/university.

WORK-STUDY ***Federal work-study:*** Total amount: $203,850; 361 jobs averaging $1500.

APPLYING FOR FINANCIAL AID ***Required financial aid forms:*** FAFSA, institution's own form. ***Financial aid deadline (priority):*** 3/15. ***Notification date:*** Continuous beginning 3/15. Students must reply within 2 weeks of notification.

CONTACT Ms. Marcia Toomey, Director of Financial Aid, Endicott College, 376 Hale Street, Beverly, MA 01915-2096, 978-232-2060 or toll-free 800-325-1114 (out-of-state). *Fax:* 978-232-2085. *E-mail:* mtoomey@endicott.edu.

ERSKINE COLLEGE

Due West, SC

Tuition & fees: $20,275 **Average undergraduate aid package: $19,100**

ABOUT THE INSTITUTION Independent religious, coed. Awards: bachelor's, master's, doctoral, and first professional degrees. 30 undergraduate majors. Total enrollment: 925. Undergraduates: 601. Freshmen: 178. Both federal and institutional methodology are used as a basis for awarding need-based institutional aid.

UNDERGRADUATE EXPENSES for 2006–07 ***Application fee:*** $25. ***Comprehensive fee:*** $27,226 includes full-time tuition ($18,840), mandatory fees ($1435), and room and board ($6951). Room and board charges vary according to board plan and housing facility. ***Part-time tuition:*** $698 per semester hour. ***Payment plan:*** Installment.

FRESHMAN FINANCIAL AID (Fall 2005) 166 applied for aid; of those 100% were deemed to have need. 100% of freshmen with need received aid; of those 49% had need fully met. ***Average percent of need met:*** 89% (excluding resources awarded to replace EFC). ***Average financial aid package:*** $19,100 (excluding resources awarded to replace EFC). 27% of all full-time freshmen had no need and received non-need-based gift aid.

UNDERGRADUATE FINANCIAL AID (Fall 2005) 543 applied for aid; of those 92% were deemed to have need. 100% of undergraduates with need received aid; of those 52% had need fully met. ***Average percent of need met:*** 87% (excluding resources awarded to replace EFC). ***Average financial aid package:*** $19,100 (excluding resources awarded to replace EFC). 22% of all full-time undergraduates had no need and received non-need-based gift aid.

GIFT AID (NEED-BASED) ***Total amount:*** $2,631,312 (18% federal, 30% state, 52% institutional). ***Receiving aid:*** Freshmen: 87% (158); All full-time undergraduates: 69% (412). ***Average award:*** Freshmen: $10,000; Undergraduates: $10,000. ***Scholarships, grants, and awards:*** Federal Pell, FSEOG, state, private, college/university gift aid from institutional funds.

GIFT AID (NON-NEED-BASED) ***Total amount:*** $5,596,783 (22% state, 74% institutional, 4% external sources). ***Receiving aid:*** Freshmen: 91% (164); Undergraduates: 83% (495). ***Average award:*** Freshmen: $9850; Undergraduates: $10,210. ***Scholarships, grants, and awards by category:*** *Academic Interests/Achievement:* 180 awards ($1,478,500 total): biological sciences, business, education, English, foreign languages, general academic interests/achievements, mathematics, premedicine, religion/biblical studies, social sciences. *Creative Arts/Performance:* 20 awards ($100,000 total): music, theater/drama. *Special Achievements/Activities:* 18 awards ($20,000 total): general special achievements/activities, leadership, memberships. *Special Characteristics:* 75 awards ($450,000 total): children and siblings of alumni, children of faculty/staff, children with a deceased or disabled parent, ethnic background, first-generation college students, members of minority groups, out-of-state students, relatives of clergy, religious affiliation, siblings of current students. ***Tuition waivers:*** Full or partial for children of alumni, employees or children of employees.

LOANS ***Student loans:*** $1,950,123 (41% need-based, 59% non-need-based). 77% of past graduating class borrowed through all loan programs. *Average indebtedness per student:* $16,940. ***Average need-based loan:*** Freshmen: $2950; Undergraduates: $3760. ***Parent loans:*** $475,139 (100% non-need-based). ***Programs:*** FFEL (Subsidized and Unsubsidized Stafford, PLUS), Perkins, college/university, teacher loans.

WORK-STUDY ***Federal work-study:*** Total amount: $91,665; 211 jobs averaging $950. ***State or other work-study/employment:*** Total amount: $37,445 (100% non-need-based). 110 part-time jobs averaging $1220.

ATHLETIC AWARDS Total amount: $699,413 (100% non-need-based).

APPLYING FOR FINANCIAL AID ***Required financial aid forms:*** FAFSA, institution's own form. ***Financial aid deadline (priority):*** 4/1. ***Notification date:*** Continuous beginning 12/15. Students must reply within 2 weeks of notification.

CONTACT Allison Sullivan, Director of Financial Aid, Erskine College, PO Box 337, Due West, SC 29639, 864-379-8832 or toll-free 800-241-8721. *Fax:* 864-379-2172. *E-mail:* sullivan@erskine.edu.

ESCUELA DE ARTES PLASTICAS DE PUERTO RICO

San Juan, PR

CONTACT Ms. Marion E. Muñoz, Financial Aid Administrator, Escuela de Artes Plasticas de Puerto Rico, PO Box 9021112, San Juan, PR 00902-1112, 787-725-8120 Ext. 231. *Fax:* 787-725-8111. *E-mail:* mmunoz@coqui.net.

EUGENE BIBLE COLLEGE

Eugene, OR

Tuition & fees: $8720 **Average undergraduate aid package: $8900**

ABOUT THE INSTITUTION Independent religious, coed. Awards: bachelor's degrees. 7 undergraduate majors. Total enrollment: 222. Undergraduates: 222. Freshmen: 61. Both federal and institutional methodology are used as a basis for awarding need-based institutional aid.

UNDERGRADUATE EXPENSES for 2006–07 ***Application fee:*** $30. ***Comprehensive fee:*** $13,525 includes full-time tuition ($7800), mandatory fees ($920), and room and board ($4805).

FRESHMAN FINANCIAL AID (Fall 2006, est.) 49% of freshmen with need received aid. ***Average percent of need met:*** 31% (excluding resources awarded to replace EFC). ***Average financial aid package:*** $8811 (excluding resources awarded to replace EFC). 3% of all full-time freshmen had no need and received non-need-based gift aid.

UNDERGRADUATE FINANCIAL AID (Fall 2006, est.) 140 applied for aid; of those 100% were deemed to have need. 100% of undergraduates with need received aid; of those 1% had need fully met. ***Average percent of need met:*** 42% (excluding resources awarded to replace EFC). ***Average financial aid package:*** $8900 (excluding resources awarded to replace EFC). 1% of all full-time undergraduates had no need and received non-need-based gift aid.

GIFT AID (NEED-BASED) ***Total amount:*** $227,746 (97% federal, 3% institutional). ***Receiving aid:*** Freshmen: 17% (6); All full-time undergraduates: 59% (85). ***Average award:*** Freshmen: $3090; Undergraduates: $3500. ***Scholarships, grants, and awards:*** Federal Pell, FSEOG, private, college/university gift aid from institutional funds.

GIFT AID (NON-NEED-BASED) ***Total amount:*** $52,890 (52% institutional, 48% external sources). ***Receiving aid:*** Freshmen: 29% (10); Undergraduates: 33% (47). ***Average award:*** Freshmen: $100; Undergraduates: $100. ***Scholarships, grants, and awards by category:*** *Academic Interests/Achievement:* general academic interests/achievements, religion/biblical studies. *Creative Arts/Performance:* music. *Special Achievements/Activities:* 2 awards ($5500 total): community service, general special achievements/activities, hobbies/interests, leadership, religious involvement. *Special Characteristics:* 56 awards ($35,400 total): general special characteristics, international students, married students, out-of-state students, relatives of clergy, spouses of current students, veterans, veterans' children.

LOANS ***Student loans:*** $1,075,925 (46% need-based, 54% non-need-based). 82% of past graduating class borrowed through all loan programs. *Average indebtedness per student:* $10,550. ***Average need-based loan:*** Freshmen: $2625; Undergraduates: $3850. ***Parent loans:*** $201,254 (100% non-need-based). ***Programs:*** FFEL (Subsidized and Unsubsidized Stafford, PLUS), college/university, Key Alternative Loans.

WORK-STUDY ***Federal work-study:*** Total amount: $13,125; 6 jobs averaging $2123. ***State or other work-study/employment:*** Total amount: $50,025 (100% non-need-based). 23 part-time jobs averaging $2175.

ATHLETIC AWARDS Total amount: $3000 (100% non-need-based).

APPLYING FOR FINANCIAL AID ***Required financial aid forms:*** FAFSA, institution's own form, CSS Financial Aid PROFILE. ***Financial aid deadline:*** 9/1 (priority: 3/1). ***Notification date:*** Continuous beginning 4/1. Students must reply by 9/1.

CONTACT Mrs. Rulena Mellor, Financial Aid Director, Eugene Bible College, 2155 Bailey Hill Road, Eugene, OR 97405-1194, 541-485-1780 Ext. 125 or toll-free 800-322-2638. *Fax:* 541-343-5801. *E-mail:* finaid@ebc.edu.

EUGENE LANG COLLEGE THE NEW SCHOOL FOR LIBERAL ARTS

New York, NY

Tuition & fees: $29,210 **Average undergraduate aid package: $19,478**

ABOUT THE INSTITUTION Independent, coed. Awards: bachelor's degrees. 21 undergraduate majors. Total enrollment: 1,164. Undergraduates: 1,164. Freshmen: 283. Federal methodology is used as a basis for awarding need-based institutional aid.

UNDERGRADUATE EXPENSES for 2006–07 ***Application fee:*** $50. ***Comprehensive fee:*** $40,960 includes full-time tuition ($28,600), mandatory fees ($610), and room and board ($11,750). ***College room only:*** $8750. Full-time tuition and fees vary according to program. Room and board charges vary according to board plan and housing facility. ***Part-time tuition:*** $976 per credit. Part-time tuition and fees vary according to course load, program, and reciprocity agreements. ***Payment plan:*** Installment.

FRESHMAN FINANCIAL AID (Fall 2006, est.) 245 applied for aid; of those 71% were deemed to have need. 100% of freshmen with need received aid; of those 9% had need fully met. ***Average percent of need met:*** 79% (excluding resources awarded to replace EFC). ***Average financial aid package:*** $25,068 (excluding resources awarded to replace EFC).

UNDERGRADUATE FINANCIAL AID (Fall 2006, est.) 839 applied for aid; of those 81% were deemed to have need. 100% of undergraduates with need received aid; of those 15% had need fully met. ***Average percent of need met:*** 80% (excluding resources awarded to replace EFC). ***Average financial aid package:*** $19,478 (excluding resources awarded to replace EFC).

GIFT AID (NEED-BASED) ***Total amount:*** $10,123,018 (7% federal, 4% state, 89% institutional). ***Receiving aid:*** Freshmen: 166. ***Average award:*** Freshmen: $18,770; Undergraduates: $15,393. ***Scholarships, grants, and awards:*** Federal Pell, FSEOG, state, private, college/university gift aid from institutional funds.

GIFT AID (NON-NEED-BASED) ***Total amount:*** $352,250 (100% institutional). ***Receiving aid:*** Freshmen: 55; Undergraduates: 184. ***Average award:*** Freshmen: $2539; Undergraduates: $2153. ***Scholarships, grants, and awards by category:*** *Academic Interests/Achievement:* general academic interests/achievements. *Special Achievements/Activities:* general special achievements/activities. ***Tuition waivers:*** Full or partial for employees or children of employees.

LOANS ***Student loans:*** $3,185,188 (71% need-based, 29% non-need-based). 74% of past graduating class borrowed through all loan programs. *Average indebtedness per student:* $21,293. ***Average need-based loan:*** Freshmen: $3247; Undergraduates: $4281. ***Parent loans:*** $2,718,671 (100% non-need-based). ***Programs:*** FFEL (Subsidized and Unsubsidized Stafford), Perkins, college/university.

WORK-STUDY ***Federal work-study:*** Total amount: $209,105; jobs available. ***State or other work-study/employment:*** Part-time jobs available.

APPLYING FOR FINANCIAL AID ***Required financial aid forms:*** FAFSA, state aid form. ***Financial aid deadline:*** Continuous. ***Notification date:*** Continuous. Students must reply within 4 weeks of notification.

CONTACT Financial Aid Counselor, Eugene Lang College The New School for Liberal Arts, 65 West 11th Street, New York, NY 10011, 212-229-5665 or toll-free 877-528-3321.

EUREKA COLLEGE

Eureka, IL

Tuition & fees: $14,180 **Average undergraduate aid package: $11,297**

ABOUT THE INSTITUTION Independent religious, coed. Awards: bachelor's degrees. 42 undergraduate majors. Total enrollment: 516. Undergraduates: 516. Freshmen: 138. Federal methodology is used as a basis for awarding need-based institutional aid.

UNDERGRADUATE EXPENSES for 2006–07 ***Comprehensive fee:*** $20,400 includes full-time tuition ($13,760), mandatory fees ($420), and room and board ($6220). Full-time tuition and fees vary according to course load and program. Room and board charges vary according to board plan and housing facility. ***Part-time tuition:*** $390 per semester hour. Part-time tuition and fees vary according to course load and program. ***Payment plan:*** Installment.

FRESHMAN FINANCIAL AID (Fall 2006, est.) 126 applied for aid; of those 71% were deemed to have need. 100% of freshmen with need received aid; of those 34% had need fully met. ***Average percent of need met:*** 70% (excluding resources awarded to replace EFC). ***Average financial aid package:*** $12,570 (excluding resources awarded to replace EFC). 26% of all full-time freshmen had no need and received non-need-based gift aid.

UNDERGRADUATE FINANCIAL AID (Fall 2006, est.) 500 applied for aid; of those 79% were deemed to have need. 100% of undergraduates with need received aid; of those 20% had need fully met. ***Average percent of need met:*** 76% (excluding resources awarded to replace EFC). ***Average financial aid package:*** $11,297 (excluding resources awarded to replace EFC). 30% of all full-time undergraduates had no need and received non-need-based gift aid.

GIFT AID (NEED-BASED) ***Total amount:*** $3,674,003 (18% federal, 37% state, 43% institutional, 2% external sources). ***Receiving aid:*** Freshmen: 66% (90); All full-time undergraduates: 70% (395). ***Average award:*** Freshmen: $12,570; Undergraduates: $11,297. ***Scholarships, grants, and awards:*** Federal Pell, FSEOG, state, private, college/university gift aid from institutional funds.

GIFT AID (NON-NEED-BASED) ***Total amount:*** $771,858 (9% state, 91% institutional). ***Average award:*** Freshmen: $3966; Undergraduates: $5104. ***Scholarships, grants, and awards by category:*** *Academic Interests/Achievement:* 395 awards ($2,273,075 total): general academic interests/achievements. *Creative Arts/Performance:* 64 awards ($61,875 total): art/fine arts, music, performing arts, theater/drama. *Special Achievements/Activities:* 20 awards ($271,507 total): leadership. *Special Characteristics:* 78 awards ($134,052 total): children of faculty/staff, religious affiliation, siblings of current students. ***Tuition waivers:*** Full or partial for children of alumni, employees or children of employees, adult students, senior citizens.

LOANS ***Student loans:*** $2,409,738 (58% need-based, 42% non-need-based). 86% of past graduating class borrowed through all loan programs. *Average indebtedness per student:* $14,727. ***Average need-based loan:*** Freshmen: $2901;

Undergraduates: $2989. ***Parent loans:*** $598,160 (100% non-need-based). ***Programs:*** FFEL (Subsidized and Unsubsidized Stafford, PLUS), Perkins, college/university, alternative loans.

WORK-STUDY ***Federal work-study:*** Total amount: $100,318; 93 jobs averaging $1078. ***State or other work-study/employment:*** Total amount: $81,735 (100% non-need-based). 61 part-time jobs averaging $1340.

ATHLETIC AWARDS Total amount: $710,081 (4% need-based, 96% non-need-based).

APPLYING FOR FINANCIAL AID ***Required financial aid form:*** FAFSA. ***Financial aid deadline (priority):*** 4/15. ***Notification date:*** 5/1. Students must reply within 2 weeks of notification.

CONTACT Ms. Ellen Rigsby, Assistant Dean and Director of Financial Aid, Eureka College, 300 East College Avenue, Eureka, IL 61530, 309-467-6311 or toll-free 888-4-EUREKA. *Fax:* 309-467-6897. *E-mail:* eraid@eureka.edu.

EVANGEL UNIVERSITY

Springfield, MO

Tuition & fees: $14,300 **Average undergraduate aid package: $8409**

ABOUT THE INSTITUTION Independent religious, coed. Awards: associate, bachelor's, and master's degrees. 56 undergraduate majors. Total enrollment: 1,721. Undergraduates: 1,640. Freshmen: 367. Federal methodology is used as a basis for awarding need-based institutional aid.

UNDERGRADUATE EXPENSES for 2007–08 ***Application fee:*** $25. ***Comprehensive fee:*** $19,420 includes full-time tuition ($13,530), mandatory fees ($770), and room and board ($5120). ***College room only:*** $2580. ***Part-time tuition:*** $528 per credit hour. ***Part-time fees:*** $384 per term.

FRESHMAN FINANCIAL AID (Fall 2006, est.) 326 applied for aid; of those 82% were deemed to have need. 96% of freshmen with need received aid; of those 8% had need fully met. ***Average percent of need met:*** 38% (excluding resources awarded to replace EFC). ***Average financial aid package:*** $7940 (excluding resources awarded to replace EFC). 24% of all full-time freshmen had no need and received non-need-based gift aid.

UNDERGRADUATE FINANCIAL AID (Fall 2006, est.) 1,460 applied for aid; of those 86% were deemed to have need. 96% of undergraduates with need received aid; of those 10% had need fully met. ***Average percent of need met:*** 41% (excluding resources awarded to replace EFC). ***Average financial aid package:*** $8409 (excluding resources awarded to replace EFC). 19% of all full-time undergraduates had no need and received non-need-based gift aid.

GIFT AID (NEED-BASED) ***Total amount:*** $4,191,154 (47% federal, 1% state, 32% institutional, 20% external sources). ***Receiving aid:*** Freshmen: 54% (232); All full-time undergraduates: 58% (1,007). ***Average award:*** Freshmen: $5772; Undergraduates: $5535. ***Scholarships, grants, and awards:*** Federal Pell, FSEOG, state, college/university gift aid from institutional funds.

GIFT AID (NON-NEED-BASED) ***Total amount:*** $859,523 (66% institutional, 34% external sources). ***Receiving aid:*** Freshmen: 4% (19); Undergraduates: 4% (64). ***Average award:*** Freshmen: $5373; Undergraduates: $7259. ***Scholarships, grants, and awards by category:*** *Academic Interests/Achievement:* 817 awards ($1,731,462 total): business, communication, computer science, education, engineering/technologies, English, foreign languages, general academic interests/achievements, humanities, mathematics, physical sciences, premedicine, religion/biblical studies, social sciences. *Creative Arts/Performance:* 160 awards ($290,255 total): art/fine arts, debating, music. *Special Achievements/Activities:* 528 awards ($1,644,319 total): cheerleading/drum major, general special achievements/activities, leadership, religious involvement. *Special Characteristics:* 309 awards ($1,527,282 total): children of faculty/staff, general special characteristics, religious affiliation. ***ROTC:*** Army.

LOANS ***Student loans:*** $11,455,140 (74% need-based, 26% non-need-based). 98% of past graduating class borrowed through all loan programs. *Average indebtedness per student:* $22,105. ***Average need-based loan:*** Freshmen: $2876; Undergraduates: $4025. ***Parent loans:*** $2,395,342 (40% need-based, 60% non-need-based). ***Programs:*** FFEL (Subsidized and Unsubsidized Stafford, PLUS), Perkins, college/university.

WORK-STUDY ***Federal work-study:*** Total amount: $290,609; 358 jobs averaging $949. ***State or other work-study/employment:*** Total amount: $100,181 (74% need-based, 26% non-need-based). 89 part-time jobs averaging $663.

ATHLETIC AWARDS Total amount: $1,406,611 (72% need-based, 28% non-need-based).

APPLYING FOR FINANCIAL AID ***Required financial aid form:*** FAFSA. ***Financial aid deadline (priority):*** 3/1. ***Notification date:*** Continuous beginning 4/1. Students must reply within 4 weeks of notification.

CONTACT Mrs. Kathy White, Director of Financial Aid, Evangel University, 1111 North Glenstone Avenue, Springfield, MO 65802-2191, 417-865-2811 Ext. 7264 or toll-free 800-382-6435 (in-state). *E-mail:* whitek@evangel.edu.

EVERGLADES UNIVERSITY

Boca Raton, FL

CONTACT Fred Pfeffer, Financial Aid Office, Everglades University, 1500 Northwest 49th Street, Fort Lauderdale, FL 33309, 888-772-6077. *Fax:* 954-772-2695. *E-mail:* fredp@evergladesuniversity.edu.

EVERGLADES UNIVERSITY

Orlando, FL

CONTACT Financial Aid Office, Everglades University, 5600 Lake Underhill Road, Orlando, FL 32807, 407-277-0311.

EVERGLADES UNIVERSITY

Sarasota, FL

CONTACT Financial Aid Office, Everglades University, 6151 Lake Osprey Drive, Sarasota, FL 34240, 941-907-2262 or toll-free 866-907-2262.

THE EVERGREEN STATE COLLEGE

Olympia, WA

ABOUT THE INSTITUTION State-supported, coed. Awards: bachelor's and master's degrees. 23 undergraduate majors. Total enrollment: 4,416. Undergraduates: 4,124. Freshmen: 583.

GIFT AID (NEED-BASED) ***Scholarships, grants, and awards:*** Federal Pell, FSEOG, state, private, college/university gift aid from institutional funds.

GIFT AID (NON-NEED-BASED) ***Scholarships, grants, and awards by category:*** *Academic Interests/Achievement:* general academic interests/achievements. *Creative Arts/Performance:* applied art and design, art/fine arts, creative writing. *Special Achievements/Activities:* community service, general special achievements/activities. *Special Characteristics:* adult students, first-generation college students, members of minority groups.

LOANS ***Programs:*** FFEL (Subsidized and Unsubsidized Stafford, PLUS), Perkins, college/university.

APPLYING FOR FINANCIAL AID ***Required financial aid forms:*** FAFSA, institution's own form.

CONTACT Financial Aid Office, The Evergreen State College, 2700 Evergreen Parkway NW, Olympia, WA 98505, 360-867-6205. *Fax:* 360-866-6576.

EXCELSIOR COLLEGE

Albany, NY

Tuition & fees: N/R **Average undergraduate aid package: N/A**

ABOUT THE INSTITUTION Independent, coed. Awards: associate, bachelor's, and master's degrees and post-bachelor's certificates (offers only external degree programs). 42 undergraduate majors. Total enrollment: 30,680. Undergraduates: 29,989. Both federal and institutional methodology are used as a basis for awarding need-based institutional aid.

UNDERGRADUATE EXPENSES for 2006–07 ***Application fee:*** $75. ***Tuition:*** part-time $275 per credit hour. ***Required fees:*** $515 per year part-time. ***Payment plan:*** Installment.

GIFT AID (NEED-BASED) ***Total amount:*** $303,902 (47% state, 50% institutional, 3% external sources). ***Scholarships, grants, and awards:*** state, private, college/university gift aid from institutional funds.

GIFT AID (NON-NEED-BASED) ***Total amount:*** $192,827 (100% external sources). ***Scholarships, grants, and awards by category:*** *Academic Interests/Achievement:* general academic interests/achievements. *Special Characteristics:* 1,139 awards ($1,209,319 total): veterans, veterans' children. ***Tuition waivers:*** Full or partial for employees or children of employees.

LOANS ***Student loans:*** $2,060,269 (100% non-need-based). 1% of past graduating class borrowed through all loan programs. *Average indebtedness per student:* $5410. ***Programs:*** alternative loans, PLATO Loans, Excel, CitiAssist, KeyBank.

APPLYING FOR FINANCIAL AID ***Required financial aid form:*** institution's own form. ***Financial aid deadline (priority):*** 7/1. ***Notification date:*** Continuous.

CONTACT Donna L. Cooper, Director of Financial Aid, Excelsior College, 7 Columbia Circle, Albany, NY 12203-5159, 518-464-8500 or toll-free 888-647-2388. *Fax:* 518-464-8777.

FAIRFIELD UNIVERSITY

Fairfield, CT

Tuition & fees: $31,955 **Average undergraduate aid package: $19,101**

ABOUT THE INSTITUTION Independent Roman Catholic (Jesuit), coed. Awards: bachelor's and master's degrees and post-master's certificates. 35 undergraduate majors. Total enrollment: 5,091. Undergraduates: 4,008. Freshmen: 899. Federal methodology is used as a basis for awarding need-based institutional aid.

UNDERGRADUATE EXPENSES for 2006–07 ***Application fee:*** $55. ***Comprehensive fee:*** $41,935 includes full-time tuition ($31,450), mandatory fees ($505), and room and board ($9980). ***College room only:*** $5980. Room and board charges vary according to board plan and housing facility. ***Part-time tuition:*** $410 per credit. ***Part-time fees:*** $60 per term. Part-time tuition and fees vary according to course load and program. ***Payment plan:*** Installment.

FRESHMAN FINANCIAL AID (Fall 2006, est.) 640 applied for aid; of those 80% were deemed to have need. 99% of freshmen with need received aid; of those 29% had need fully met. ***Average percent of need met:*** 72% (excluding resources awarded to replace EFC). ***Average financial aid package:*** $22,654 (excluding resources awarded to replace EFC). 7% of all full-time freshmen had no need and received non-need-based gift aid.

UNDERGRADUATE FINANCIAL AID (Fall 2006, est.) 2,104 applied for aid; of those 80% were deemed to have need. 99% of undergraduates with need received aid; of those 26% had need fully met. ***Average percent of need met:*** 66% (excluding resources awarded to replace EFC). ***Average financial aid package:*** $19,101 (excluding resources awarded to replace EFC). 7% of all full-time undergraduates had no need and received non-need-based gift aid.

GIFT AID (NEED-BASED) ***Total amount:*** $21,856,123 (8% federal, 1% state, 91% institutional). ***Receiving aid:*** Freshmen: 49% (442); All full-time undergraduates: 42% (1,485). ***Average award:*** Freshmen: $18,453; Undergraduates: $14,078. ***Scholarships, grants, and awards:*** Federal Pell, FSEOG, state, private, college/university gift aid from institutional funds, United Negro College Fund.

GIFT AID (NON-NEED-BASED) ***Total amount:*** $7,118,812 (91% institutional, 9% external sources). ***Receiving aid:*** Freshmen: 18% (159); Undergraduates: 14% (476). ***Average award:*** Freshmen: $11,870; Undergraduates: $11,304. ***Scholarships, grants, and awards by category:*** *Academic Interests/Achievement:* 620 awards ($7,386,547 total): biological sciences, business, education, engineering/technologies, foreign languages, general academic interests/achievements, physical sciences. *Creative Arts/Performance:* 12 awards ($21,320 total): art/fine arts, music, performing arts. *Special Achievements/Activities:* 30 awards ($139,900 total): religious involvement. *Special Characteristics:* 6 awards ($72,052 total): children and siblings of alumni, ethnic background, first-generation college students, members of minority groups, religious affiliation. ***Tuition waivers:*** Full or partial for employees or children of employees. ***ROTC:*** Army cooperative, Air Force cooperative.

LOANS ***Student loans:*** $21,019,081 (34% need-based, 66% non-need-based). 60% of past graduating class borrowed through all loan programs. *Average indebtedness per student:* $28,751. ***Average need-based loan:*** Freshmen: $3365; Undergraduates: $4061. ***Parent loans:*** $7,762,500 (100% non-need-based). ***Programs:*** FFEL (Subsidized and Unsubsidized Stafford, PLUS), Perkins, Federal Nursing, alternative loans.

WORK-STUDY ***Federal work-study:*** Total amount: $794,798; 416 jobs averaging $1316.

ATHLETIC AWARDS Total amount: $3,461,822 (100% non-need-based).

APPLYING FOR FINANCIAL AID ***Required financial aid forms:*** FAFSA, CSS Financial Aid PROFILE, business/farm supplement. ***Financial aid deadline:*** 2/15 (priority: 2/15). ***Notification date:*** 4/1. Students must reply by 5/1.

CONTACT Mr. Erin Chiaro, Director of Financial Aid, Fairfield University, 1073 North Benson Road, Fairfield, CT 06824-5195, 203-254-4125. *Fax:* 203-254-4008. *E-mail:* echiaro@mail.fairfield.edu.

FAIRLEIGH DICKINSON UNIVERSITY, COLLEGE AT FLORHAM

Madison, NJ

CONTACT Financial Aid Office, Fairleigh Dickinson University, College at Florham, 285 Madison Avenue, Madison, NJ 07940-1099, 973-443-8700 or toll-free 800-338-8803.

FAIRLEIGH DICKINSON UNIVERSITY, METROPOLITAN CAMPUS

Teaneck, NJ

CONTACT Financial Aid Office, Fairleigh Dickinson University, Metropolitan Campus, 100 River Road, Teaneck, NJ 07666-1914, 201-692-2363 or toll-free 800-338-8803.

FAIRMONT STATE UNIVERSITY

Fairmont, WV

ABOUT THE INSTITUTION State-supported, coed. Awards: associate, bachelor's, and master's degrees. 60 undergraduate majors. Total enrollment: 7,417. Undergraduates: 7,067. Freshmen: 1,266.

GIFT AID (NEED-BASED) ***Scholarships, grants, and awards:*** Federal Pell, FSEOG, state, private, college/university gift aid from institutional funds.

GIFT AID (NON-NEED-BASED) ***Scholarships, grants, and awards by category:*** *Academic Interests/Achievement:* architecture, business, communication, computer science, education, engineering/technologies, English, foreign languages, general academic interests/achievements, health fields, home economics, humanities, mathematics, physical sciences, social sciences. *Creative Arts/Performance:* art/fine arts, debating, music, theater/drama. *Special Achievements/Activities:* cheerleading/drum major. *Special Characteristics:* children and siblings of alumni, general special characteristics, international students, local/state students, members of minority groups, out-of-state students.

LOANS ***Programs:*** Federal Direct (Subsidized and Unsubsidized Stafford, PLUS), Perkins.

APPLYING FOR FINANCIAL AID ***Required financial aid forms:*** FAFSA, state aid form.

CONTACT Sandra K. Oerly-Bennett, Director of Financial Aid and Scholarships, Fairmont State University, 1201 Locust Avenue, Fairmont, WV 26554, 304-367-4213 or toll-free 800-641-5678. *Fax:* 304-367-4584. *E-mail:* financialaid@fairmontstate.edu.

FAITH BAPTIST BIBLE COLLEGE AND THEOLOGICAL SEMINARY

Ankeny, IA

ABOUT THE INSTITUTION Independent religious, coed. Awards: associate, bachelor's, master's, and first professional degrees. 10 undergraduate majors. Total enrollment: 404. Undergraduates: 319. Freshmen: 87.

GIFT AID (NEED-BASED) ***Scholarships, grants, and awards:*** Federal Pell, state, private, college/university gift aid from institutional funds.

GIFT AID (NON-NEED-BASED) ***Scholarships, grants, and awards by category:*** *Academic Interests/Achievement:* general academic interests/achievements. *Creative Arts/Performance:* music. *Special Achievements/Activities:* leadership. *Special Characteristics:* children of faculty/staff, relatives of clergy.

LOANS ***Programs:*** FFEL (Subsidized and Unsubsidized Stafford, PLUS).

APPLYING FOR FINANCIAL AID ***Required financial aid form:*** FAFSA.

CONTACT Mr. Breck Appell, Director of Financial Assistance, Faith Baptist Bible College and Theological Seminary, 1900 Northwest 4th Street, Ankeny, IA 50021-2152, 515-964-0601 or toll-free 888-FAITH 4U. *Fax:* 515-964-1638.

FARMINGDALE STATE COLLEGE

Farmingdale, NY

CONTACT Dionne Walker-Belgrave, Assistant Director of Financial Aid, Farmingdale State College, 2350 Broadhollow Road, Route 110, Farmingdale, NY 11735, 631-420-2328 or toll-free 877-4-FARMINGDALE. *Fax:* 631-420-3662.

FASHION INSTITUTE OF TECHNOLOGY

New York, NY

Tuition & fees (NY res): $4770 **Average undergraduate aid package: $8365**

ABOUT THE INSTITUTION State and locally supported, coed, primarily women. Awards: associate, bachelor's, and master's degrees. 21 undergraduate majors. Total enrollment: 10,010. Undergraduates: 9,825. Freshmen: 946. Federal methodology is used as a basis for awarding need-based institutional aid.

UNDERGRADUATE EXPENSES for 2007–08 ***Application fee:*** $40. ***Tuition, state resident:*** full-time $4350; part-time $181 per credit. ***Tuition, nonresident:*** full-time $10,610; part-time $442 per credit. ***Required fees:*** full-time $420; $30 per term part-time. ***College room and board:*** $11,213; ***Room only:*** $7823.

FRESHMAN FINANCIAL AID (Fall 2006, est.) 746 applied for aid; of those 61% were deemed to have need. 99% of freshmen with need received aid; of those 17% had need fully met. ***Average percent of need met:*** 70% (excluding resources awarded to replace EFC). ***Average financial aid package:*** $7947 (excluding resources awarded to replace EFC). 6% of all full-time freshmen had no need and received non-need-based gift aid.

UNDERGRADUATE FINANCIAL AID (Fall 2006, est.) 4,572 applied for aid; of those 67% were deemed to have need. 98% of undergraduates with need received aid; of those 13% had need fully met. ***Average percent of need met:*** 65% (excluding resources awarded to replace EFC). ***Average financial aid package:*** $8365 (excluding resources awarded to replace EFC). 2% of all full-time undergraduates had no need and received non-need-based gift aid.

GIFT AID (NEED-BASED) ***Total amount:*** $9,787,834 (54% federal, 38% state, 8% institutional). ***Receiving aid:*** Freshmen: 36% (332); All full-time undergraduates: 32% (2,263). ***Average award:*** Freshmen: $4041; Undergraduates: $3926. ***Scholarships, grants, and awards:*** Federal Pell, FSEOG, state, private, college/university gift aid from institutional funds.

GIFT AID (NON-NEED-BASED) ***Total amount:*** $996,341 (8% institutional, 92% external sources). ***Receiving aid:*** Freshmen: 12% (109); Undergraduates: 4% (260). ***Average award:*** Freshmen: $1777; Undergraduates: $1563. ***Scholarships, grants, and awards by category:*** *Creative Arts/Performance:* 153 awards ($74,750 total): applied art and design.

LOANS ***Student loans:*** $20,855,309 (39% need-based, 61% non-need-based). 39% of past graduating class borrowed through all loan programs. *Average indebtedness per student:* $12,869. ***Average need-based loan:*** Freshmen: $2652; Undergraduates: $3630. ***Parent loans:*** $4,801,935 (100% non-need-based). ***Programs:*** FFEL (Subsidized and Unsubsidized Stafford, PLUS), Perkins, alternative loans.

WORK-STUDY ***Federal work-study:*** Total amount: $1,369,161; 644 jobs averaging $2126.

APPLYING FOR FINANCIAL AID ***Required financial aid forms:*** FAFSA, state aid form. ***Financial aid deadline (priority):*** 2/15. ***Notification date:*** Continuous beginning 4/15. Students must reply within 2 weeks of notification.

CONTACT Financial Aid Office, Fashion Institute of Technology, Seventh Avenue at 27th Street, New York, NY 10001-5992, 212-217-7439 or toll-free 800-GOTOFIT (out-of-state).

FAULKNER UNIVERSITY

Montgomery, AL

Tuition & fees: $11,565 **Average undergraduate aid package: $7100**

ABOUT THE INSTITUTION Independent religious, coed. Awards: associate, bachelor's, master's, and first professional degrees. 48 undergraduate majors. Total enrollment: 2,625. Undergraduates: 2,212. Freshmen: 240. Federal methodology is used as a basis for awarding need-based institutional aid.

UNDERGRADUATE EXPENSES for 2007–08 ***Application fee:*** $10. ***Comprehensive fee:*** $16,965 includes full-time tuition ($11,540), mandatory fees ($25), and room and board ($5400). ***College room only:*** $2500. ***Part-time tuition:*** $400 per semester hour.

FRESHMAN FINANCIAL AID (Fall 2006, est.) 190 applied for aid; of those 78% were deemed to have need. 100% of freshmen with need received aid; of those 12% had need fully met. ***Average percent of need met:*** 60% (excluding resources awarded to replace EFC). ***Average financial aid package:*** $5800 (excluding resources awarded to replace EFC). 6% of all full-time freshmen had no need and received non-need-based gift aid.

UNDERGRADUATE FINANCIAL AID (Fall 2006, est.) 1,443 applied for aid; of those 78% were deemed to have need. 100% of undergraduates with need received aid; of those 11% had need fully met. ***Average percent of need met:*** 61% (excluding resources awarded to replace EFC). ***Average financial aid package:*** $7100 (excluding resources awarded to replace EFC). 3% of all full-time undergraduates had no need and received non-need-based gift aid.

GIFT AID (NEED-BASED) ***Total amount:*** $4,700,000 (100% federal). ***Receiving aid:*** Freshmen: 50% (105); All full-time undergraduates: 50% (799). ***Average award:*** Freshmen: $3600; Undergraduates: $3800. ***Scholarships, grants, and awards:*** Federal Pell, FSEOG, state, private, college/university gift aid from institutional funds.

GIFT AID (NON-NEED-BASED) ***Total amount:*** $3,440,000 (18% state, 76% institutional, 6% external sources). ***Receiving aid:*** Freshmen: 43% (90); Undergraduates: 43% (686). ***Average award:*** Freshmen: $2400; Undergraduates: $2800. ***Scholarships, grants, and awards by category:*** *Academic Interests/Achievement:* 329 awards ($1,111,600 total): general academic interests/achievements, religion/biblical studies. *Creative Arts/Performance:* 34 awards ($64,300 total): journalism/publications, music, theater/drama. *Special Achievements/Activities:* 191 awards ($253,786 total): cheerleading/drum major, leadership, religious involvement. *Special Characteristics:* 409 awards ($286,742 total): adult students, children and siblings of alumni, children of faculty/staff, relatives of clergy, religious affiliation, siblings of current students. ***ROTC:*** Army cooperative, Air Force cooperative.

LOANS ***Student loans:*** $18,600,000 (49% need-based, 51% non-need-based). 90% of past graduating class borrowed through all loan programs. *Average indebtedness per student:* $18,900. ***Average need-based loan:*** Freshmen: $2625; Undergraduates: $5500. ***Parent loans:*** $690,000 (100% non-need-based). ***Programs:*** FFEL (Subsidized and Unsubsidized Stafford, PLUS), Perkins.

WORK-STUDY ***Federal work-study:*** Total amount: $200,000; 132 jobs averaging $1515. ***State or other work-study/employment:*** Total amount: $2900 (100% non-need-based). 4 part-time jobs averaging $725.

ATHLETIC AWARDS Total amount: $1,100,000 (100% non-need-based).

APPLYING FOR FINANCIAL AID ***Required financial aid forms:*** FAFSA, institution's own form, state aid form. ***Financial aid deadline (priority):*** 5/1.

CONTACT William G. Jackson II, Director of Financial Aid, Faulkner University, 5345 Atlanta Highway, Montgomery, AL 36109-3398, 334-386-7195 or toll-free 800-879-9816. *Fax:* 334-386-7201.

FAYETTEVILLE STATE UNIVERSITY

Fayetteville, NC

CONTACT Lois L. McKoy, Director of Financial Aid, Fayetteville State University, 1200 Murchison Road, Fayetteville, NC 28301-4298, 910-672-1325 or toll-free 800-222-2594. *Fax:* 910-672-1423. *E-mail:* lmckoy@uncfsu.edu.

FELICIAN COLLEGE

Lodi, NJ

Tuition & fees: $19,950 **Average undergraduate aid package: $14,340**

ABOUT THE INSTITUTION Independent Roman Catholic, coed. Awards: associate, bachelor's, and master's degrees. 40 undergraduate majors. Total enrollment: 1,992. Undergraduates: 1,867. Freshmen: 267. Federal methodology is used as a basis for awarding need-based institutional aid.

UNDERGRADUATE EXPENSES for 2007–08 ***Application fee:*** $30. ***Comprehensive fee:*** $27,382 includes full-time tuition ($18,900), mandatory fees ($1050), and room and board ($7432). ***Part-time tuition:*** $625 per credit.

FRESHMAN FINANCIAL AID (Fall 2005) 231 applied for aid; of those 55% were deemed to have need. 100% of freshmen with need received aid; of those 13% had need fully met. ***Average percent of need met:*** 85% (excluding resources awarded to replace EFC). ***Average financial aid package:*** $14,340 (excluding resources awarded to replace EFC). 34% of all full-time freshmen had no need and received non-need-based gift aid.

UNDERGRADUATE FINANCIAL AID (Fall 2005) 1,060 applied for aid; of those 89% were deemed to have need. 100% of undergraduates with need received aid; of those 13% had need fully met. ***Average percent of need met:*** 85% (excluding resources awarded to replace EFC). ***Average financial aid package:*** $14,340 (excluding resources awarded to replace EFC). 18% of all full-time undergraduates had no need and received non-need-based gift aid.

GIFT AID (NEED-BASED) ***Total amount:*** $4,120,645 (31% federal, 68% state, 1% institutional). ***Receiving aid:*** Freshmen: 31% (83); All full-time undergraduates: 50% (612). ***Average award:*** Freshmen: $6500; Undergraduates: $6500. ***Scholarships, grants, and awards:*** Federal Pell, FSEOG, state, private, college/university gift aid from institutional funds.

GIFT AID (NON-NEED-BASED) ***Total amount:*** $1,688,018 (91% institutional, 9% external sources). ***Receiving aid:*** Freshmen: 9% (25); Undergraduates: 15% (188). ***Average award:*** Freshmen: $4642; Undergraduates: $4642. ***Scholarships, grants, and awards by category:*** *Academic Interests/Achievement:* 124 awards ($224,000 total): area/ethnic studies, biological sciences, business, computer science, education, English, general academic interests/achievements, health fields, mathematics, premedicine, religion/biblical studies, social sciences.

LOANS ***Student loans:*** $7,758,674 (37% need-based, 63% non-need-based). 57% of past graduating class borrowed through all loan programs. *Average indebtedness per student:* $19,500. ***Average need-based loan:*** Freshmen: $3500; Undergraduates: $4300. ***Parent loans:*** $1,869,000 (100% non-need-based). ***Programs:*** FFEL (Subsidized and Unsubsidized Stafford, PLUS), state.

WORK-STUDY ***Federal work-study:*** Total amount: $35,020; jobs available. ***State or other work-study/employment:*** Total amount: $180,000 (100% non-need-based).

ATHLETIC AWARDS Total amount: $1,185,680 (100% non-need-based).

APPLYING FOR FINANCIAL AID ***Required financial aid form:*** FAFSA. ***Financial aid deadline:*** Continuous. ***Notification date:*** Continuous beginning 4/1.

CONTACT Norma Betz, Financial Aid Director, Felician College, 262 South Main Street, Lodi, NJ 07644, 201-559-6040. *Fax:* 201-559-6188. *E-mail:* betzn@inet.felician.edu.

FERRIS STATE UNIVERSITY

Big Rapids, MI

Tuition & fees (MI res): $7342 **Average undergraduate aid package: $8000**

ABOUT THE INSTITUTION State-supported, coed. Awards: associate, bachelor's, master's, and first professional degrees (Associate). 93 undergraduate majors. Total enrollment: 12,575. Undergraduates: 11,409. Freshmen: 1,980. Federal methodology is used as a basis for awarding need-based institutional aid.

UNDERGRADUATE EXPENSES for 2006–07 ***Application fee:*** $30. ***Tuition, state resident:*** full-time $7200; part-time $270 per credit hour. ***Tuition, nonresident:*** full-time $14,640; part-time $530 per credit hour. Full-time tuition and fees vary according to reciprocity agreements. ***College room and board:*** $7220; ***Room only:*** $3668. Room and board charges vary according to board plan and housing facility. ***Payment plans:*** Installment, deferred payment.

FRESHMAN FINANCIAL AID (Fall 2005) 2030 applied for aid; of those 86% were deemed to have need. 77% of freshmen with need received aid; of those 11% had need fully met. ***Average percent of need met:*** 70% (excluding resources awarded to replace EFC). ***Average financial aid package:*** $7000 (excluding resources awarded to replace EFC). 7% of all full-time freshmen had no need and received non-need-based gift aid.

UNDERGRADUATE FINANCIAL AID (Fall 2005) 8,417 applied for aid; of those 86% were deemed to have need. 81% of undergraduates with need received aid; of those 10% had need fully met. ***Average percent of need met:*** 75% (excluding resources awarded to replace EFC). ***Average financial aid package:*** $8000 (excluding resources awarded to replace EFC). 4% of all full-time undergraduates had no need and received non-need-based gift aid.

GIFT AID (NEED-BASED) ***Total amount:*** $14,221,087 (71% federal, 20% state, 9% institutional). ***Receiving aid:*** Freshmen: 35% (775); All full-time undergraduates: 44% (3,913). ***Average award:*** Freshmen: $3000; Undergraduates: $3500. ***Scholarships, grants, and awards:*** Federal Pell, FSEOG, state, private, college/university gift aid from institutional funds.

GIFT AID (NON-NEED-BASED) ***Total amount:*** $9,492,816 (31% state, 53% institutional, 16% external sources). ***Receiving aid:*** Freshmen: 24% (528); Undergraduates: 10% (921). ***Average award:*** Freshmen: $2000; Undergraduates: $2000. ***Scholarships, grants, and awards by category:*** *Academic Interests/Achievement:* 1,350 awards ($2,000,000 total): general academic interests/achievements. *Creative Arts/Performance:* 175 awards ($87,500 total): debating, general creative arts/performance, journalism/publications, music, theater/drama. *Special Characteristics:* 450 awards ($1,195,000 total): children of faculty/staff, general special characteristics. ***Tuition waivers:*** Full or partial for employees or children of employees. ***ROTC:*** Army cooperative.

LOANS ***Student loans:*** $64,705,720 (47% need-based, 53% non-need-based). 85% of past graduating class borrowed through all loan programs. *Average indebtedness per student:* $15,000. ***Average need-based loan:*** Freshmen: $2000; Undergraduates: $3500. ***Parent loans:*** $5,051,604 (100% non-need-based). ***Programs:*** Federal Direct (Subsidized and Unsubsidized Stafford, PLUS), Perkins, Federal Nursing, college/university, alternative loans.

WORK-STUDY ***Federal work-study:*** Total amount: $800,912; 566 jobs averaging $1030. ***State or other work-study/employment:*** Total amount: $253,495 (100% need-based). 120 part-time jobs averaging $1820.

ATHLETIC AWARDS Total amount: $1,505,836 (100% non-need-based).

APPLYING FOR FINANCIAL AID ***Required financial aid form:*** FAFSA. ***Financial aid deadline (priority):*** 3/1. ***Notification date:*** Continuous beginning 4/1. Students must reply within 2 weeks of notification.

CONTACT Sara Dew, Interim Director of Financial Aid, Ferris State University, 1201 South State Street, CSS 101, Big Rapids, MI 49307-2020, 231-591-2110 or toll-free 800-433-7747. *Fax:* 231-591-2950. *E-mail:* dews@ferris.edu.

FERRUM COLLEGE

Ferrum, VA

ABOUT THE INSTITUTION Independent United Methodist, coed. Awards: bachelor's degrees. 33 undergraduate majors. Total enrollment: 1,060. Undergraduates: 1,060. Freshmen: 426.

GIFT AID (NEED-BASED) ***Scholarships, grants, and awards:*** Federal Pell, FSEOG, state, private, college/university gift aid from institutional funds.

GIFT AID (NON-NEED-BASED) ***Scholarships, grants, and awards by category:*** *Academic Interests/Achievement:* general academic interests/achievements. *Creative Arts/Performance:* art/fine arts, performing arts, theater/drama. *Special Achievements/Activities:* community service, general special achievements/activities, leadership, religious involvement. *Special Characteristics:* adult students, children and siblings of alumni, children of educators, children of faculty/staff, international students, local/state students, out-of-state students, relatives of clergy, religious affiliation, siblings of current students.

LOANS ***Programs:*** FFEL (Subsidized and Unsubsidized Stafford, PLUS), Perkins, alternative loans.

APPLYING FOR FINANCIAL AID ***Required financial aid forms:*** FAFSA, state aid form.

CONTACT Heather Hollandsworth, Associate Director of Financial Aid, Ferrum College, PO Box 1000, Spilman-Daniel House, Ferrum, VA 24088-9001, 540-365-4282 or toll-free 800-868-9797. *Fax:* 540-365-4266.

FINLANDIA UNIVERSITY

Hancock, MI

ABOUT THE INSTITUTION Independent religious, coed. Awards: associate and bachelor's degrees. 15 undergraduate majors. Total enrollment: 584. Undergraduates: 584. Freshmen: 119.

GIFT AID (NEED-BASED) ***Scholarships, grants, and awards:*** Federal Pell, FSEOG, state, private, college/university gift aid from institutional funds.

GIFT AID (NON-NEED-BASED) ***Scholarships, grants, and awards by category:*** *Creative Arts/Performance:* art/fine arts, general creative arts/performance. *Special Achievements/Activities:* community service, general special achievements/activities, leadership, religious involvement. *Special Characteristics:* children of current students, children of faculty/staff, first-generation college students, international students, religious affiliation, siblings of current students, spouses of current students, twins.

LOANS ***Programs:*** FFEL (Subsidized and Unsubsidized Stafford, PLUS), state, private loan program.

APPLYING FOR FINANCIAL AID ***Required financial aid forms:*** FAFSA, institution's own form.

CONTACT Sandy Turnquist, Director of Financial Aid, Finlandia University, 601 Quincy Street, Hancock, MI 49930, 906-487-7240 or toll-free 877-202-5491. *Fax:* 906-487-7509. *E-mail:* sandy.turnquist@finlandia.edu.

FISK UNIVERSITY

Nashville, TN

CONTACT Director of Financial Aid, Fisk University, 1000 17th Avenue North, Nashville, TN 37208-3051, 615-329-8585 or toll-free 800-443-FISK. *Fax:* 615-329-8774.

FITCHBURG STATE COLLEGE
Fitchburg, MA

Tuition & fees (MA res): $5542 **Average undergraduate aid package: $6559**

ABOUT THE INSTITUTION State-supported, coed. Awards: bachelor's and master's degrees and post-bachelor's and post-master's certificates. 58 undergraduate majors. Total enrollment: 5,508. Undergraduates: 3,768. Freshmen: 738. Federal methodology is used as a basis for awarding need-based institutional aid.

UNDERGRADUATE EXPENSES for 2006–07 ***Application fee:*** $10. ***Tuition, state resident:*** full-time $970; part-time $40.42 per credit. ***Tuition, nonresident:*** full-time $7050; part-time $293.75 per credit. ***Required fees:*** full-time $4572; $191 per credit. Full-time tuition and fees vary according to reciprocity agreements. Part-time tuition and fees vary according to course load and reciprocity agreements. ***College room and board:*** $6486. Room and board charges vary according to board plan and student level. ***Payment plan:*** Installment.

FRESHMAN FINANCIAL AID (Fall 2005) 606 applied for aid; of those 53% were deemed to have need. 98% of freshmen with need received aid; of those 94% had need fully met. ***Average percent of need met:*** 94% (excluding resources awarded to replace EFC). ***Average financial aid package:*** $6167 (excluding resources awarded to replace EFC). 3% of all full-time freshmen had no need and received non-need-based gift aid.

UNDERGRADUATE FINANCIAL AID (Fall 2005) 2,480 applied for aid; of those 55% were deemed to have need. 97% of undergraduates with need received aid; of those 94% had need fully met. ***Average percent of need met:*** 94% (excluding resources awarded to replace EFC). ***Average financial aid package:*** $6559 (excluding resources awarded to replace EFC). 1% of all full-time undergraduates had no need and received non-need-based gift aid.

GIFT AID (NEED-BASED) ***Total amount:*** $4,745,741 (39% federal, 39% state, 22% institutional). ***Receiving aid:*** Freshmen: 39% (262); All full-time undergraduates: 37% (1,074). ***Average award:*** Freshmen: $3214; Undergraduates: $3265. ***Scholarships, grants, and awards:*** Federal Pell, FSEOG, state, private, college/university gift aid from institutional funds.

GIFT AID (NON-NEED-BASED) ***Total amount:*** $914,978 (14% state, 54% institutional, 32% external sources). ***Receiving aid:*** Freshmen: 17% (114); Undergraduates: 10% (295). ***Average award:*** Freshmen: $1641; Undergraduates: $1573. ***Scholarships, grants, and awards by category:*** *Academic Interests/Achievement:* 246 awards ($474,170 total): biological sciences, business, communication, computer science, education, English, general academic interests/achievements, health fields, mathematics, social sciences. *Special Achievements/Activities:* 65 awards ($260,260 total): general special achievements/activities, leadership. *Special Characteristics:* 23 awards ($14,760 total): adult students, children and siblings of alumni. ***Tuition waivers:*** Full or partial for employees or children of employees, senior citizens. ***ROTC:*** Air Force cooperative.

LOANS ***Student loans:*** $6,845,140 (51% need-based, 49% non-need-based). 28% of past graduating class borrowed through all loan programs. *Average indebtedness per student:* $13,228. ***Average need-based loan:*** Freshmen: $2017; Undergraduates: $2659. ***Parent loans:*** $982,205 (100% non-need-based). ***Programs:*** Federal Direct (Subsidized and Unsubsidized Stafford, PLUS), Perkins, Federal Nursing, state.

WORK-STUDY ***Federal work-study:*** Total amount: $211,406; 204 jobs averaging $1050.

APPLYING FOR FINANCIAL AID ***Required financial aid form:*** FAFSA. ***Financial aid deadline (priority):*** 3/1. ***Notification date:*** Continuous beginning 3/15. Students must reply within 2 weeks of notification.

CONTACT Pamela McCafferty, Director of Financial Aid, Fitchburg State College, 160 Pearl Street, Fitchburg, MA 01420-2697, 978-665-3156 or toll-free 800-705-9692. *Fax:* 978-665-3559. *E-mail:* finaid@fsc.edu.

FIVE TOWNS COLLEGE
Dix Hills, NY

Tuition & fees: $17,085 **Average undergraduate aid package: $8100**

ABOUT THE INSTITUTION Independent, coed. Awards: associate, bachelor's, master's, and doctoral degrees. 19 undergraduate majors. Total enrollment: 1,254. Undergraduates: 1,195. Freshmen: 291. Federal methodology is used as a basis for awarding need-based institutional aid.

UNDERGRADUATE EXPENSES for 2007–08 ***Application fee:*** $35. ***Comprehensive fee:*** $33,885 includes full-time tuition ($16,400), mandatory fees ($685), and room and board ($16,800). ***Part-time tuition:*** $685 per credit.

FRESHMAN FINANCIAL AID (Fall 2006, est.) 353 applied for aid; of those 77% were deemed to have need. 100% of freshmen with need received aid; of those 56% had need fully met. ***Average percent of need met:*** 48% (excluding resources awarded to replace EFC). ***Average financial aid package:*** $5350 (excluding resources awarded to replace EFC).

UNDERGRADUATE FINANCIAL AID (Fall 2006, est.) 870 applied for aid; of those 90% were deemed to have need. 100% of undergraduates with need received aid; of those 56% had need fully met. ***Average percent of need met:*** 48% (excluding resources awarded to replace EFC). ***Average financial aid package:*** $8100 (excluding resources awarded to replace EFC).

GIFT AID (NEED-BASED) ***Total amount:*** $4,277,000 (24% federal, 35% state, 41% institutional). ***Receiving aid:*** Freshmen: 54% (245); All full-time undergraduates: 64% (710). ***Average award:*** Freshmen: $6500; Undergraduates: $6000. ***Scholarships, grants, and awards:*** Federal Pell, FSEOG, state, private, college/university gift aid from institutional funds.

GIFT AID (NON-NEED-BASED) ***Total amount:*** $102,000 (100% external sources). ***Receiving aid:*** Freshmen: 7% (34); Undergraduates: 9% (100). ***Scholarships, grants, and awards by category:*** *Academic Interests/Achievement:* 320 awards ($1,300,000 total): business, education, general academic interests/achievements. *Creative Arts/Performance:* 140 awards ($400,000 total): cinema/film/broadcasting, music, theater/drama.

LOANS ***Student loans:*** $7,000,000 (43% need-based, 57% non-need-based). 79% of past graduating class borrowed through all loan programs. *Average indebtedness per student:* $18,000. ***Average need-based loan:*** Freshmen: $2625; Undergraduates: $4300. ***Parent loans:*** $3,800,000 (100% non-need-based). ***Programs:*** Federal Direct (Subsidized and Unsubsidized Stafford, PLUS).

WORK-STUDY ***Federal work-study:*** Total amount: $110,000; 100 jobs averaging $1100.

APPLYING FOR FINANCIAL AID ***Required financial aid forms:*** FAFSA, institution's own form, state aid form. ***Financial aid deadline (priority):*** 3/31. ***Notification date:*** Continuous beginning 5/1. Students must reply within 4 weeks of notification.

CONTACT Ms. Mary Venezia, Financial Aid/Director, Five Towns College, 305 North Service Road, Dix Hills, NY 11746-6055, 631-656-2113. *Fax:* 631-656-2191. *E-mail:* mvenezia@ftc.edu.

FLAGLER COLLEGE
St. Augustine, FL

Tuition & fees: $11,200 **Average undergraduate aid package: $12,280**

ABOUT THE INSTITUTION Independent, coed. Awards: bachelor's degrees. 23 undergraduate majors. Total enrollment: 2,253. Undergraduates: 2,253. Freshmen: 489. Federal methodology is used as a basis for awarding need-based institutional aid.

UNDERGRADUATE EXPENSES for 2007–08 ***Application fee:*** $40. ***Comprehensive fee:*** $18,000 includes full-time tuition ($11,200) and room and board ($6800). ***Part-time tuition:*** $375 per credit.

FRESHMAN FINANCIAL AID (Fall 2006, est.) 326 applied for aid; of those 66% were deemed to have need. 98% of freshmen with need received aid; of those 8% had need fully met. ***Average percent of need met:*** 80% (excluding resources awarded to replace EFC). ***Average financial aid package:*** $11,858 (excluding resources awarded to replace EFC). 1% of all full-time freshmen had no need and received non-need-based gift aid.

UNDERGRADUATE FINANCIAL AID (Fall 2006, est.) 1,330 applied for aid; of those 72% were deemed to have need. 99% of undergraduates with need received aid; of those 16% had need fully met. ***Average percent of need met:*** 80% (excluding resources awarded to replace EFC). ***Average financial aid package:*** $12,280 (excluding resources awarded to replace EFC). 4% of all full-time undergraduates had no need and received non-need-based gift aid.

GIFT AID (NEED-BASED) ***Total amount:*** $4,133,096 (24% federal, 68% state, 4% institutional, 4% external sources). ***Receiving aid:*** Freshmen: 18% (85); All full-time undergraduates: 21% (473). ***Average award:*** Freshmen: $3746; Undergraduates: $3366. ***Scholarships, grants, and awards:*** Federal Pell, FSEOG, state, private, college/university gift aid from institutional funds.

GIFT AID (NON-NEED-BASED) ***Total amount:*** $4,566,342 (91% state, 6% institutional, 3% external sources). ***Receiving aid:*** Freshmen: 35% (168);

Undergraduates: 31% (717). ***Average award:*** Freshmen: $3436; Undergraduates: $3268. ***Scholarships, grants, and awards by category:*** *Academic Interests/Achievement:* 47 awards ($94,912 total): business, communication, education, English, foreign languages, general academic interests/achievements, humanities, religion/biblical studies, social sciences. *Creative Arts/Performance:* 4 awards ($6500 total): applied art and design, art/fine arts, cinema/film/broadcasting, performing arts, theater/drama. *Special Achievements/Activities:* 71 awards ($174,197 total): general special achievements/activities, leadership, memberships, religious involvement. *Special Characteristics:* 72 awards ($223,561 total): children of faculty/staff, ethnic background, first-generation college students, general special characteristics, local/state students, members of minority groups, out-of-state students.

LOANS ***Student loans:*** $5,500,826 (70% need-based, 30% non-need-based). *Average indebtedness per student:* $15,535. ***Average need-based loan:*** Freshmen: $2816; Undergraduates: $4060. ***Parent loans:*** $1,310,965 (50% need-based, 50% non-need-based). ***Programs:*** Federal Direct (Subsidized and Unsubsidized Stafford, PLUS), Perkins.

WORK-STUDY ***Federal work-study:*** Total amount: $152,100; 162 jobs averaging $1018. ***State or other work-study/employment:*** Total amount: $58,300 (12% need-based, 88% non-need-based). 124 part-time jobs averaging $750.

ATHLETIC AWARDS Total amount: $525,690 (28% need-based, 72% non-need-based).

APPLYING FOR FINANCIAL AID ***Required financial aid forms:*** FAFSA, institution's own form. ***Financial aid deadline (priority):*** 4/1. ***Notification date:*** Continuous beginning 3/1. Students must reply within 2 weeks of notification.

CONTACT Ms. Sheia Pleasant, Assistant Director of Financial Aid, Flagler College, PO Box 1027, St. Augustine, FL 32085-1027, 904-819-6225 or toll-free 800-304-4208. *Fax:* 904-819-6453. *E-mail:* spleasant@flagler.edu.

FLORIDA AGRICULTURAL AND MECHANICAL UNIVERSITY

Tallahassee, FL

ABOUT THE INSTITUTION State-supported, coed. Awards: associate, bachelor's, master's, doctoral, and first professional degrees. 84 undergraduate majors. Total enrollment: 13,064. Undergraduates: 10,576. Freshmen: 2,001.

GIFT AID (NEED-BASED) ***Scholarships, grants, and awards:*** Federal Pell, FSEOG, state, private, college/university gift aid from institutional funds, United Negro College Fund, Federal Nursing.

GIFT AID (NON-NEED-BASED) ***Scholarships, grants, and awards by category:*** *Academic Interests/Achievement:* agriculture, business, engineering/technologies, general academic interests/achievements, health fields.

LOANS ***Programs:*** Federal Direct (Subsidized and Unsubsidized Stafford, PLUS), Perkins.

APPLYING FOR FINANCIAL AID ***Required financial aid form:*** FAFSA.

CONTACT Dr. Joel V. Harrell, Director of Student Financial Aid, Florida Agricultural and Mechanical University, 101 Foote-Hilyer Administration Center, Tallahassee, FL 32307, 850-599-3730. *E-mail:* joel.harrell@famu.edu.

FLORIDA ATLANTIC UNIVERSITY

Boca Raton, FL

Tuition & fees (FL res): $3327 Average undergraduate aid package: $7498

ABOUT THE INSTITUTION State-supported, coed. Awards: associate, bachelor's, master's, and doctoral degrees and post-master's certificates. 62 undergraduate majors. Total enrollment: 25,385. Undergraduates: 21,139. Freshmen: 2,312. Federal methodology is used as a basis for awarding need-based institutional aid.

UNDERGRADUATE EXPENSES for 2006–07 ***Application fee:*** $30. ***Tuition, state resident:*** full-time $3327; part-time $110.90 per credit hour. ***Tuition, nonresident:*** full-time $16,391; part-time $546.36 per credit hour. Full-time tuition and fees vary according to course load. Part-time tuition and fees vary according to course load. ***College room and board:*** $8280. Room and board charges vary according to board plan and housing facility. ***Payment plans:*** Tuition prepayment, installment, deferred payment.

FRESHMAN FINANCIAL AID (Fall 2006, est.) 1769 applied for aid; of those 50% were deemed to have need. 97% of freshmen with need received aid; of those 20% had need fully met. ***Average percent of need met:*** 94% (excluding resources awarded to replace EFC). ***Average financial aid package:*** $7750 (excluding resources awarded to replace EFC). 4% of all full-time freshmen had no need and received non-need-based gift aid.

UNDERGRADUATE FINANCIAL AID (Fall 2006, est.) 8,577 applied for aid; of those 62% were deemed to have need. 96% of undergraduates with need received aid; of those 16% had need fully met. ***Average percent of need met:*** 76% (excluding resources awarded to replace EFC). ***Average financial aid package:*** $7498 (excluding resources awarded to replace EFC). 3% of all full-time undergraduates had no need and received non-need-based gift aid.

GIFT AID (NEED-BASED) ***Total amount:*** $32,152,869 (40% federal, 50% state, 3% institutional, 7% external sources). ***Receiving aid:*** Freshmen: 37% (789); All full-time undergraduates: 37% (4,310). ***Average award:*** Freshmen: $7092; Undergraduates: $5748. ***Scholarships, grants, and awards:*** Federal Pell, FSEOG, state, private, college/university gift aid from institutional funds, Federal Nursing.

GIFT AID (NON-NEED-BASED) ***Average award:*** Freshmen: $2319; Undergraduates: $2388. ***Scholarships, grants, and awards by category:*** *Academic Interests/Achievement:* business, engineering/technologies, general academic interests/achievements, physical sciences, social sciences. *Creative Arts/Performance:* music, performing arts. ***Tuition waivers:*** Full or partial for employees or children of employees, senior citizens. ***ROTC:*** Army cooperative, Air Force cooperative.

LOANS ***Student loans:*** $20,224,491 (100% need-based). ***Average need-based loan:*** Freshmen: $2462; Undergraduates: $3854. ***Parent loans:*** $2,400,067 (100% non-need-based). ***Programs:*** FFEL (Subsidized and Unsubsidized Stafford, PLUS), Perkins, college/university.

WORK-STUDY ***Federal work-study:*** Total amount: $582,342; 179 jobs averaging $2900. ***State or other work-study/employment:*** Total amount: $15,000 (100% need-based). Part-time jobs available.

ATHLETIC AWARDS Total amount: $2,480,207 (100% need-based).

APPLYING FOR FINANCIAL AID ***Required financial aid form:*** FAFSA. ***Financial aid deadline (priority):*** 3/1. ***Notification date:*** Continuous beginning 5/1. Students must reply within 3 weeks of notification.

CONTACT Carole Pfeilsticker, Director of Student Financial Aid, Florida Atlantic University, 777 Glades Road, Student Services Building, Room 227, Boca Raton, FL 33431-0991, 561-297-3528 or toll-free 800-299-4FAU. *E-mail:* pfeilsti@fau.edu.

FLORIDA ATLANTIC UNIVERSITY, JUPITER CAMPUS

Jupiter, FL

CONTACT Financial Aid Office, Florida Atlantic University, Jupiter Campus, 5353 Parkside Drive, Jupiter, FL 33458, 561-799-8500 or toll-free 561-799-8502 (in-state).

FLORIDA CHRISTIAN COLLEGE

Kissimmee, FL

ABOUT THE INSTITUTION Independent religious, coed. Awards: associate and bachelor's degrees. 3 undergraduate majors. Total enrollment: 259. Undergraduates: 259.

GIFT AID (NEED-BASED) ***Scholarships, grants, and awards:*** Federal Pell, FSEOG, state, private, college/university gift aid from institutional funds.

GIFT AID (NON-NEED-BASED) ***Scholarships, grants, and awards by category:*** *Academic Interests/Achievement:* education, religion/biblical studies. *Creative Arts/Performance:* music. *Special Characteristics:* children and siblings of alumni, children of faculty/staff, relatives of clergy, religious affiliation, spouses of current students.

LOANS ***Programs:*** FFEL (Subsidized and Unsubsidized Stafford, PLUS), alternative loans, Sallie Mae Loans.

WORK-STUDY ***Federal work-study:*** Total amount: $41,917; 38 jobs averaging $1103.

APPLYING FOR FINANCIAL AID ***Required financial aid forms:*** FAFSA, institution's own form.

CONTACT Ms. Sandra Peppard, Director of Student Financial Aid, Florida Christian College, 1011 Bill Beck Boulevard, Kissimmee, FL 34744-5301, 407-847-8966 Ext. 365 or toll-free 888-GO-TO-FCC (in-state). *Fax:* 407-847-3925. *E-mail:* sandi.peppard@fcc.edu.

FLORIDA COLLEGE
Temple Terrace, FL

Tuition & fees: $11,380 **Average undergraduate aid package: $2629**

ABOUT THE INSTITUTION Independent, coed. Awards: associate and bachelor's degrees. 3 undergraduate majors. Total enrollment: 513. Undergraduates: 513. Freshmen: 229. Both federal and institutional methodology are used as a basis for awarding need-based institutional aid.

UNDERGRADUATE EXPENSES for 2006–07 ***Application fee:*** $25. ***Comprehensive fee:*** $16,840 includes full-time tuition ($10,680), mandatory fees ($700), and room and board ($5460). Room and board charges vary according to board plan and housing facility. ***Part-time tuition:*** $430 per semester hour. ***Part-time fees:*** $275 per term. ***Payment plan:*** Installment.

FRESHMAN FINANCIAL AID (Fall 2005) 204 applied for aid; of those 58% were deemed to have need. 100% of freshmen with need received aid; of those 15% had need fully met. ***Average percent of need met:*** 15% (excluding resources awarded to replace EFC). ***Average financial aid package:*** $3961 (excluding resources awarded to replace EFC). 40% of all full-time freshmen had no need and received non-need-based gift aid.

UNDERGRADUATE FINANCIAL AID (Fall 2005) 442 applied for aid; of those 62% were deemed to have need. 100% of undergraduates with need received aid; of those 19% had need fully met. ***Average percent of need met:*** 19% (excluding resources awarded to replace EFC). ***Average financial aid package:*** $2629 (excluding resources awarded to replace EFC). 34% of all full-time undergraduates had no need and received non-need-based gift aid.

GIFT AID (NEED-BASED) ***Total amount:*** $1,219,967 (22% federal, 2% state, 10% institutional, 66% external sources). ***Receiving aid:*** Freshmen: 21% (46); All full-time undergraduates: 21% (105). ***Average award:*** Freshmen: $1801; Undergraduates: $2099. ***Scholarships, grants, and awards:*** Federal Pell, FSEOG, state, private, college/university gift aid from institutional funds.

GIFT AID (NON-NEED-BASED) ***Total amount:*** $1,179,138 (44% state, 43% institutional, 13% external sources). ***Receiving aid:*** Freshmen: 21% (45); Undergraduates: 21% (105). ***Average award:*** Freshmen: $894; Undergraduates: $852. ***Scholarships, grants, and awards by category:*** *Academic Interests/Achievement:* general academic interests/achievements. *Creative Arts/Performance:* debating, journalism/publications, music, theater/drama. *Special Characteristics:* children of educators, children of faculty/staff. ***Tuition waivers:*** Full or partial for employees or children of employees. ***ROTC:*** Army cooperative, Air Force cooperative.

LOANS ***Student loans:*** $1,649,747 (70% need-based, 30% non-need-based). 41% of past graduating class borrowed through all loan programs. *Average indebtedness per student:* $7574. ***Average need-based loan:*** Freshmen: $1703; Undergraduates: $1947. ***Parent loans:*** $1,196,648 (100% non-need-based). ***Programs:*** FFEL (Subsidized and Unsubsidized Stafford, PLUS), Perkins.

WORK-STUDY ***Federal work-study:*** Total amount: $19,399; jobs available. ***State or other work-study/employment:*** Total amount: $197,582 (100% non-need-based). Part-time jobs available.

ATHLETIC AWARDS Total amount: $216,006 (100% non-need-based).

APPLYING FOR FINANCIAL AID ***Required financial aid form:*** FAFSA. ***Financial aid deadline:*** 8/1 (priority: 4/1). ***Notification date:*** Continuous. Students must reply within 2 weeks of notification.

CONTACT Lisa McClister, Financial Aid Officer, Florida College, 119 North Glen Arven Avenue, Temple Terrace, FL 33617, 813-849-6720 or toll-free 800-326-7655. *Fax:* 813-899-6772. *E-mail:* mcclisterl@floridacollege.edu.

FLORIDA GULF COAST UNIVERSITY
Fort Myers, FL

Tuition & fees (FL res): $3730 **Average undergraduate aid package: $6878**

ABOUT THE INSTITUTION State-supported, coed. Awards: associate, bachelor's, and master's degrees. 25 undergraduate majors. Total enrollment: 8,292. Undergraduates: 7,121. Freshmen: 1,634. Federal methodology is used as a basis for awarding need-based institutional aid.

UNDERGRADUATE EXPENSES for 2006–07 ***Application fee:*** $30. ***Tuition, state resident:*** full-time $3550; part-time $74 per credit. ***Tuition, nonresident:*** full-time $16,260; part-time $452 per credit. ***Required fees:*** full-time $180; $7 per credit or $105 per year part-time. Full-time tuition and fees vary according to course load. Part-time tuition and fees vary according to course load. ***College room and board:*** $7740; ***Room only:*** $4240. Room and board charges vary according to board plan.

FRESHMAN FINANCIAL AID (Fall 2006, est.) 1257 applied for aid; of those 45% were deemed to have need. 100% of freshmen with need received aid; of those 11% had need fully met. ***Average percent of need met:*** 64% (excluding resources awarded to replace EFC). ***Average financial aid package:*** $6099 (excluding resources awarded to replace EFC). 6% of all full-time freshmen had no need and received non-need-based gift aid.

UNDERGRADUATE FINANCIAL AID (Fall 2006, est.) 3,972 applied for aid; of those 48% were deemed to have need. 100% of undergraduates with need received aid; of those 12% had need fully met. ***Average percent of need met:*** 68% (excluding resources awarded to replace EFC). ***Average financial aid package:*** $6878 (excluding resources awarded to replace EFC). 4% of all full-time undergraduates had no need and received non-need-based gift aid.

GIFT AID (NEED-BASED) ***Total amount:*** $9,452,837 (33% federal, 34% state, 27% institutional, 6% external sources). ***Receiving aid:*** Freshmen: 23% (349); All full-time undergraduates: 24% (1,300). ***Average award:*** Freshmen: $3327; Undergraduates: $3388. ***Scholarships, grants, and awards:*** Federal Pell, FSEOG, state, private, college/university gift aid from institutional funds.

GIFT AID (NON-NEED-BASED) ***Total amount:*** $6,162,202 (70% state, 23% institutional, 7% external sources). ***Receiving aid:*** Freshmen: 28% (429); Undergraduates: 33% (1,778). ***Average award:*** Freshmen: $2468; Undergraduates: $2061. ***Scholarships, grants, and awards by category:*** *Academic Interests/Achievement:* biological sciences, business, education, engineering/technologies, general academic interests/achievements, health fields, humanities, mathematics, physical sciences, religion/biblical studies, social sciences. *Creative Arts/Performance:* art/fine arts, music. *Special Achievements/Activities:* community service, leadership. *Special Characteristics:* adult students, ethnic background, handicapped students, international students, local/state students, members of minority groups, out-of-state students. ***Tuition waivers:*** Full or partial for employees or children of employees, senior citizens.

LOANS ***Student loans:*** $11,717,418 (75% need-based, 25% non-need-based). 41% of past graduating class borrowed through all loan programs. *Average indebtedness per student:* $11,332. ***Average need-based loan:*** Freshmen: $2851; Undergraduates: $4887. ***Programs:*** FFEL (Subsidized and Unsubsidized Stafford, PLUS), state.

WORK-STUDY ***Federal work-study:*** Total amount: $90,207; 64 jobs averaging $1409. ***State or other work-study/employment:*** Total amount: $1,694,440 (100% need-based). 855 part-time jobs averaging $198.

APPLYING FOR FINANCIAL AID ***Required financial aid forms:*** FAFSA, institution's own form. ***Financial aid deadline:*** 3/15 (priority: 1/1). ***Notification date:*** Continuous beginning 2/15. Students must reply within 4 weeks of notification.

CONTACT Jorge Lopez-Rosado, Director, Student Financial Services, Florida Gulf Coast University, 10501 FGCU Boulevard South, Fort Myers, FL 33965, 239-590-1210 or toll-free 888-889-1095. *Fax:* 239-590-7923. *E-mail:* faso@fgcu.edu.

FLORIDA INSTITUTE OF TECHNOLOGY
Melbourne, FL

Tuition & fees: $27,540 **Average undergraduate aid package: $22,448**

ABOUT THE INSTITUTION Independent, coed. Awards: bachelor's, master's, and doctoral degrees and post-master's certificates. 47 undergraduate majors. Total enrollment: 4,741. Undergraduates: 2,365. Freshmen: 597. Federal methodology is used as a basis for awarding need-based institutional aid.

UNDERGRADUATE EXPENSES for 2006–07 ***Application fee:*** $50. ***Comprehensive fee:*** $34,940 includes full-time tuition ($27,540) and room and board ($7400). ***College room only:*** $4200. Full-time tuition and fees vary according to course load and program. Room and board charges vary according to board plan and housing facility. ***Part-time tuition:*** $835 per credit hour. Part-time tuition and fees vary according to course load and program. ***Payment plan:*** Installment.

FRESHMAN FINANCIAL AID (Fall 2006, est.) 450 applied for aid; of those 82% were deemed to have need. 100% of freshmen with need received aid; of those 32% had need fully met. ***Average percent of need met:*** 84% (excluding resources awarded to replace EFC). ***Average financial aid package:*** $22,383 (excluding resources awarded to replace EFC). 25% of all full-time freshmen had no need and received non-need-based gift aid.

UNDERGRADUATE FINANCIAL AID (Fall 2006, est.) 1,578 applied for aid; of those 88% were deemed to have need. 100% of undergraduates with need

received aid; of those 29% had need fully met. ***Average percent of need met:*** 82% (excluding resources awarded to replace EFC). ***Average financial aid package:*** $22,448 (excluding resources awarded to replace EFC). 25% of all full-time undergraduates had no need and received non-need-based gift aid.

GIFT AID (NEED-BASED) ***Total amount:*** $19,429,226 (13% federal, 14% state, 71% institutional, 2% external sources). ***Receiving aid:*** Freshmen: 62% (369); All full-time undergraduates: 62% (1,377). ***Average award:*** Freshmen: $15,263; Undergraduates: $14,270. ***Scholarships, grants, and awards:*** Federal Pell, FSEOG, state, private, college/university gift aid from institutional funds.

GIFT AID (NON-NEED-BASED) ***Total amount:*** $6,149,155 (14% federal, 12% state, 73% institutional, 1% external sources). ***Receiving aid:*** Freshmen: 55% (330); Undergraduates: 50% (1,111). ***Average award:*** Freshmen: $8249; Undergraduates: $7991. ***Scholarships, grants, and awards by category:*** *Academic Interests/Achievement:* 1,569 awards ($11,248,722 total): general academic interests/achievements, military science. *Special Characteristics:* 255 awards ($1,307,617 total): children and siblings of alumni, children of faculty/staff, general special characteristics, previous college experience. ***Tuition waivers:*** Full or partial for employees or children of employees, senior citizens. ***ROTC:*** Army.

LOANS ***Student loans:*** $14,557,969 (90% need-based, 10% non-need-based). 66% of past graduating class borrowed through all loan programs. *Average indebtedness per student:* $25,768. ***Average need-based loan:*** Freshmen: $3936; Undergraduates: $4810. ***Parent loans:*** $3,396,254 (91% need-based, 9% non-need-based). ***Programs:*** FFEL (Subsidized and Unsubsidized Stafford, PLUS), Perkins, college/university, alternative loans.

WORK-STUDY ***Federal work-study:*** Total amount: $865,553; 599 jobs averaging $1445. ***State or other work-study/employment:*** Total amount: $14,203 (100% need-based). 5 part-time jobs averaging $2841.

ATHLETIC AWARDS Total amount: $2,088,500 (56% need-based, 44% non-need-based).

APPLYING FOR FINANCIAL AID ***Required financial aid forms:*** FAFSA, state aid form. ***Financial aid deadline (priority):*** 3/15. ***Notification date:*** Continuous beginning 2/15. Students must reply by 5/1 or within 4 weeks of notification.

CONTACT Jean Maltese, Financial Aid Administrative Clerk, Florida Institute of Technology, 150 West University Boulevard, Melbourne, FL 32901-6975, 321-674-8070 or toll-free 800-888-4348. *Fax:* 321-724-2778. *E-mail:* dtouma@fit.edu.

FLORIDA INTERNATIONAL UNIVERSITY

Miami, FL

CONTACT Maria A. Tolon, Associate Director, Financial Aid, Florida International University, University Park PC 125, Miami, FL 33199, 305-348-2340. *Fax:* 305-348-2346. *E-mail:* tolonm@fiu.edu.

FLORIDA MEMORIAL COLLEGE

Miami-Dade, FL

CONTACT Brian Phillip, Director of Financial Aid, Florida Memorial College, 15800 Northwest 42nd Avenue, Miami, FL 33054, 305-626-3745 or toll-free 800-822-1362. *Fax:* 305-626-3106.

FLORIDA METROPOLITAN UNIVERSITY–BRANDON CAMPUS

Tampa, FL

CONTACT Ms. Ginger Waymire, Director of Financial Aid, Florida Metropolitan University–Brandon Campus, 3924 Coconut Palm Drive, Tampa, FL 33619, 813-621-0041 Ext. 118 or toll-free 877-338-0068. *Fax:* 813-621-6283. *E-mail:* gwaymire@cci.edu.

FLORIDA METROPOLITAN UNIVERSITY–JACKSONVILLE CAMPUS

Jacksonville, FL

CONTACT Financial Aid Office, Florida Metropolitan University–Jacksonville Campus, 8226 Phillips Highway, Jacksonville, FL 32256, 904-731-4949 or toll-free 888-741-4271.

FLORIDA METROPOLITAN UNIVERSITY–LAKELAND CAMPUS

Lakeland, FL

CONTACT Brian Jones, Senior Finance Officer, Florida Metropolitan University–Lakeland Campus, Office of Financial Aid, 995 East Memorial Boulevard, Lakeland, FL 33801, 863-686-1444 Ext. 118 or toll-free 877-225-0014 (in-state). *Fax:* 863-682-1077.

FLORIDA METROPOLITAN UNIVERSITY–MELBOURNE CAMPUS

Melbourne, FL

CONTACT Ronda Nabb-Landolfi, Director of Student Financial Aid, Florida Metropolitan University–Melbourne Campus, 2401 North Harbor City Boulevard, Melbourne, FL 32935-6657, 321-253-2929 Ext. 19.

FLORIDA METROPOLITAN UNIVERSITY–NORTH ORLANDO CAMPUS

Orlando, FL

CONTACT Ms. Linda Kaisrlik, Director of Student Finance, Florida Metropolitan University–North Orlando Campus, 5421 Diplomat Circle, Orlando, FL 32810-5674, 407-628-5870 Ext. 118 or toll-free 800-628-5870.

FLORIDA METROPOLITAN UNIVERSITY–PINELLAS CAMPUS

Clearwater, FL

Tuition & fees: $15,120 **Average undergraduate aid package: $7500**

ABOUT THE INSTITUTION Proprietary, coed. Awards: associate, bachelor's, and master's degrees. 6 undergraduate majors. Total enrollment: 1,201. Undergraduates: 1,057. Federal methodology is used as a basis for awarding need-based institutional aid.

UNDERGRADUATE EXPENSES for 2006–07 ***Application fee:*** $25. ***Tuition:*** full-time $13,680; part-time $285 per credit. ***Required fees:*** full-time $1440; $60 per term. Full-time tuition and fees vary according to program. Part-time tuition and fees vary according to program. ***Payment plans:*** Installment, deferred payment.

FRESHMAN FINANCIAL AID (Fall 2006, est.) 126 applied for aid; of those 96% were deemed to have need. 100% of freshmen with need received aid. ***Average percent of need met:*** 88% (excluding resources awarded to replace EFC). ***Average financial aid package:*** $6625 (excluding resources awarded to replace EFC).

UNDERGRADUATE FINANCIAL AID (Fall 2006, est.) 476 applied for aid; of those 100% were deemed to have need. 100% of undergraduates with need received aid. ***Average percent of need met:*** 95% (excluding resources awarded to replace EFC). ***Average financial aid package:*** $7500 (excluding resources awarded to replace EFC).

GIFT AID (NEED-BASED) ***Total amount:*** $17,430 (23% federal, 7% state, 43% institutional, 27% external sources). ***Receiving aid:*** Freshmen: 96% (121). ***Average award:*** Freshmen: $2700; Undergraduates: $2700. ***Scholarships, grants, and awards:*** Federal Pell, FSEOG, state, private, college/university gift aid from institutional funds.

GIFT AID (NON-NEED-BASED) ***Total amount:*** $7500 (100% institutional). ***Receiving aid:*** Freshmen: 96% (121); Undergraduates: 83% (476). ***Scholarships, grants, and awards by category:*** *Academic Interests/Achievement:* business, computer science, general academic interests/achievements, health fields. ***Tuition waivers:*** Full or partial for employees or children of employees.

LOANS ***Student loans:*** $11,369,000 (43% need-based, 57% non-need-based). 80% of past graduating class borrowed through all loan programs. *Average indebtedness per student:* $45,000. ***Parent loans:*** $35,000 (100% non-need-based). ***Programs:*** FFEL (Subsidized and Unsubsidized Stafford, PLUS), Signature Loans; career training; NLSC.

WORK-STUDY ***Federal work-study:*** Total amount: $80,000; 6 jobs averaging $9000.

APPLYING FOR FINANCIAL AID ***Required financial aid form:*** FAFSA. ***Financial aid deadline:*** Continuous. ***Notification date:*** Continuous.

CONTACT Ms. Rebeca Handsaker, Director of Student Finance, Florida Metropolitan University–Pinellas Campus, 2471 North McMullen Booth Road, Clearwater, FL 33759, 727-725-2688 Ext. 166 or toll-free 800-353-FMUS. *Fax:* 727-796-3406.

FLORIDA METROPOLITAN UNIVERSITY–POMPANO BEACH CAMPUS

Pompano Beach, FL

CONTACT Sharon Scheible, Director of Student Financial Aid, Florida Metropolitan University–Pompano Beach Campus, 1040 Bayview Drive, Fort Lauderdale, FL 33304-2522, 954-568-1600 Ext. 52 or toll-free 800-468-0168. *Fax:* 954-564-5283. *E-mail:* scheible@cci.edu.

FLORIDA METROPOLITAN UNIVERSITY–SOUTH ORLANDO CAMPUS

Orlando, FL

CONTACT Sherri Williams, Director of Financial Aid, Florida Metropolitan University–South Orlando Campus, 2411 Sand Lake Road, Orlando, FL 32809, 407-851-2525 or toll-free 888-471-4270 (out-of-state).

FLORIDA METROPOLITAN UNIVERSITY–TAMPA CAMPUS

Tampa, FL

Tuition & fees: N/R **Average undergraduate aid package: $6625**

ABOUT THE INSTITUTION Proprietary, coed. Awards: associate, bachelor's, and master's degrees. 10 undergraduate majors. Total enrollment: 1,390. Undergraduates: 1,281. Freshmen: 167. Federal methodology is used as a basis for awarding need-based institutional aid.

FRESHMAN FINANCIAL AID (Fall 2006, est.) 385 applied for aid; of those 100% were deemed to have need. 100% of freshmen with need received aid; of those 58% had need fully met. ***Average percent of need met:*** 83% (excluding resources awarded to replace EFC). ***Average financial aid package:*** $6625 (excluding resources awarded to replace EFC).

UNDERGRADUATE FINANCIAL AID (Fall 2006, est.) 1,054 applied for aid; of those 100% were deemed to have need. 100% of undergraduates with need received aid; of those 81% had need fully met. ***Average percent of need met:*** 83% (excluding resources awarded to replace EFC). ***Average financial aid package:*** $6625 (excluding resources awarded to replace EFC).

GIFT AID (NEED-BASED) ***Total amount:*** $3,695,233 (97% federal, 3% state). ***Receiving aid:*** Freshmen: 64% (288); All full-time undergraduates: 81% (1,001). ***Average award:*** Freshmen: $1350; Undergraduates: $1350. ***Scholarships, grants, and awards:*** Federal Pell, FSEOG, state, private, college/university gift aid from institutional funds.

GIFT AID (NON-NEED-BASED) ***Receiving aid:*** Freshmen: 54% (243); Undergraduates: 75% (930). ***Tuition waivers:*** Full or partial for employees or children of employees.

LOANS ***Student loans:*** $10,121,333 (56% need-based, 44% non-need-based). 81% of past graduating class borrowed through all loan programs. *Average indebtedness per student:* $12,000. ***Average need-based loan:*** Freshmen: $2625; Undergraduates: $2625. ***Parent loans:*** $429,000 (100% non-need-based). ***Programs:*** FFEL (Subsidized and Unsubsidized Stafford, PLUS).

WORK-STUDY ***Federal work-study:*** Total amount: $101,000; 25 jobs averaging $4000.

APPLYING FOR FINANCIAL AID ***Required financial aid form:*** FAFSA. ***Financial aid deadline:*** Continuous. ***Notification date:*** Continuous.

CONTACT Mr. Rod Kirkwood, Financial Aid Director, Florida Metropolitan University–Tampa Campus, 3319 West Hillsborough Avenue, Tampa, FL 33614, 813-879-6000 Ext. 145. *Fax:* 813-871-2483. *E-mail:* rkirkwoo@cci.edu.

FLORIDA SOUTHERN COLLEGE

Lakeland, FL

ABOUT THE INSTITUTION Independent religious, coed. Awards: bachelor's and master's degrees. 57 undergraduate majors. Total enrollment: 1,873. Undergraduates: 1,753. Freshmen: 443.

GIFT AID (NEED-BASED) ***Scholarships, grants, and awards:*** Federal Pell, FSEOG, state, private, college/university gift aid from institutional funds.

GIFT AID (NON-NEED-BASED) ***Scholarships, grants, and awards by category:*** *Academic Interests/Achievement:* agriculture, biological sciences, business, communication, education, general academic interests/achievements, physical sciences, religion/biblical studies, social sciences. *Creative Arts/Performance:* art/fine arts, music, theater/drama. *Special Achievements/Activities:* community service, general special achievements/activities, leadership. *Special Characteristics:* children and siblings of alumni, children of faculty/staff, general special characteristics, local/state students, out-of-state students, relatives of clergy, siblings of current students.

LOANS ***Programs:*** FFEL (Subsidized and Unsubsidized Stafford, PLUS), Perkins.

WORK-STUDY ***Federal work-study:*** Total amount: $436,601; 356 jobs averaging $1226. ***State or other work-study/employment:*** Total amount: $169,162 (81% need-based, 19% non-need-based). 73 part-time jobs averaging $1871.

APPLYING FOR FINANCIAL AID ***Required financial aid forms:*** FAFSA, institution's own form.

CONTACT David M. Bodwell, Financial Aid Director, Florida Southern College, 111 Lake Hollingsworth Drive, Lakeland, FL 33801-5698, 863-680-4140 or toll-free 800-274-4131. *Fax:* 863-680-4567. *E-mail:* dbodwell@flsouthern.edu.

FLORIDA STATE UNIVERSITY

Tallahassee, FL

Tuition & fees (FL res): $3307 **Average undergraduate aid package: $8890**

ABOUT THE INSTITUTION State-supported, coed. Awards: associate, bachelor's, master's, doctoral, and first professional degrees and post-bachelor's and post-master's certificates. 157 undergraduate majors. Total enrollment: 39,973. Undergraduates: 31,347. Freshmen: 6,219. Federal methodology is used as a basis for awarding need-based institutional aid.

UNDERGRADUATE EXPENSES for 2006–07 ***Application fee:*** $30. ***Tuition, state resident:*** full-time $3307; part-time $110.23 per credit hour. ***Tuition, nonresident:*** full-time $16,439; part-time $547.95 per credit hour. Full-time tuition and fees vary according to location. Part-time tuition and fees vary according to location. ***College room and board:*** $7078; ***Room only:*** $3780. Room and board charges vary according to board plan and housing facility. ***Payment plans:*** Tuition prepayment, installment.

FRESHMAN FINANCIAL AID (Fall 2006, est.) 3927 applied for aid; of those 51% were deemed to have need. 100% of freshmen with need received aid; of those 72% had need fully met. ***Average percent of need met:*** 62% (excluding resources awarded to replace EFC). ***Average financial aid package:*** $8483 (excluding resources awarded to replace EFC). 6% of all full-time freshmen had no need and received non-need-based gift aid.

UNDERGRADUATE FINANCIAL AID (Fall 2006, est.) 15,027 applied for aid; of those 55% were deemed to have need. 100% of undergraduates with need received aid; of those 78% had need fully met. ***Average percent of need met:*** 67% (excluding resources awarded to replace EFC). ***Average financial aid package:*** $8890 (excluding resources awarded to replace EFC). 4% of all full-time undergraduates had no need and received non-need-based gift aid.

GIFT AID (NEED-BASED) ***Total amount:*** $56,093,645 (37% federal, 34% state, 26% institutional, 3% external sources). ***Receiving aid:*** Freshmen: 18% (1,119); All full-time undergraduates: 17% (4,720). ***Average award:*** Freshmen: $3509; Undergraduates: $3444. ***Scholarships, grants, and awards:*** Federal Pell, FSEOG, state, private, college/university gift aid from institutional funds, Federal ACG and Federal SMART Grants.

GIFT AID (NON-NEED-BASED) ***Total amount:*** $47,000,857 (80% state, 16% institutional, 4% external sources). ***Receiving aid:*** Freshmen: 29% (1,820); Undergraduates: 20% (5,624). ***Average award:*** Freshmen: $2282; Undergraduates: $2009. ***Scholarships, grants, and awards by category:*** *Academic Interests/Achievement:* general academic interests/achievements. *Creative Arts/Performance:* cinema/film/broadcasting, dance, music, theater/drama. *Special*

Characteristics: local/state students. ***Tuition waivers:*** Full or partial for employees or children of employees, senior citizens. ***ROTC:*** Army, Naval cooperative, Air Force.

LOANS ***Student loans:*** $65,927,898 (57% need-based, 43% non-need-based). 50% of past graduating class borrowed through all loan programs. *Average indebtedness per student:* $13,290. ***Average need-based loan:*** Freshmen: $2222; Undergraduates: $3370. ***Parent loans:*** $10,830,356 (20% need-based, 80% non-need-based). ***Programs:*** FFEL (Subsidized and Unsubsidized Stafford, PLUS), Perkins, college/university.

WORK-STUDY ***Federal work-study:*** Total amount: $1,293,870; 841 jobs averaging $1538. ***State or other work-study/employment:*** Part-time jobs available.

ATHLETIC AWARDS Total amount: $483,181 (59% need-based, 41% non-need-based).

APPLYING FOR FINANCIAL AID ***Required financial aid form:*** FAFSA. ***Financial aid deadline:*** Continuous. ***Notification date:*** Continuous beginning 3/1.

CONTACT Darryl Marshall, Director of Financial Aid, Florida State University, University Center A4400, Tallahassee, FL 32306-2430, 850-644-5716. *Fax:* 850-644-6404. *E-mail:* ofacs@admin.fsu.edu.

FONTBONNE UNIVERSITY

St. Louis, MO

CONTACT Financial Aid Office, Fontbonne University, 6800 Wydown Boulevard, St. Louis, MO 63105-3098, 314-889-1414. *Fax:* 314-889-1451.

FORDHAM UNIVERSITY

New York, NY

ABOUT THE INSTITUTION Independent Roman Catholic (Jesuit), coed. Awards: bachelor's, master's, doctoral, and first professional degrees and post-master's certificates (branch locations at Rose Hill and Lincoln Center). 94 undergraduate majors. Total enrollment: 14,732. Undergraduates: 7,701. Freshmen: 1,722.

GIFT AID (NEED-BASED) ***Scholarships, grants, and awards:*** Federal Pell, FSEOG, state, private, college/university gift aid from institutional funds.

GIFT AID (NON-NEED-BASED) ***Scholarships, grants, and awards by category:*** *Academic Interests/Achievement:* communication, foreign languages, general academic interests/achievements. *Creative Arts/Performance:* music. *Special Achievements/Activities:* general special achievements/activities. *Special Characteristics:* children and siblings of alumni, children of faculty/staff, children of union members/company employees, children with a deceased or disabled parent, handicapped students, veterans, veterans' children.

LOANS ***Programs:*** FFEL (Subsidized and Unsubsidized Stafford, PLUS), Perkins.

APPLYING FOR FINANCIAL AID ***Required financial aid forms:*** FAFSA, CSS Financial Aid PROFILE, noncustodial (divorced/separated) parent's statement, business/farm supplement.

CONTACT Calvin Brian Ghanoo, Senior Associate Director of Student Financial Services, Fordham University, 441 East Fordham Road, Thebaud Hall, New York, NY 10458, 718-817-3800 or toll-free 800-FORDHAM. *E-mail:* ghanoo@fordham.edu.

FORT HAYS STATE UNIVERSITY

Hays, KS

ABOUT THE INSTITUTION State-supported, coed. Awards: associate, bachelor's, and master's degrees and post-master's certificates. 55 undergraduate majors. Total enrollment: 7,403. Undergraduates: 5,920. Freshmen: 904.

GIFT AID (NEED-BASED) ***Scholarships, grants, and awards:*** Federal Pell, FSEOG, state, private, college/university gift aid from institutional funds, athletic.

GIFT AID (NON-NEED-BASED) ***Scholarships, grants, and awards by category:*** *Academic Interests/Achievement:* agriculture, biological sciences, business, communication, computer science, education, engineering/technologies, English, foreign languages, general academic interests/achievements, health fields, humanities, international studies, library science, mathematics, physical sciences, premedicine, social sciences. *Creative Arts/Performance:* applied art and design, art/fine arts, cinema/film/broadcasting, creative writing, debating, journalism/publications, music, performing arts, theater/drama. *Special Achievements/Activities:* cheerleading/drum major, rodeo. *Special Characteristics:* adult students, members of minority groups.

LOANS ***Programs:*** FFEL (Subsidized and Unsubsidized Stafford, PLUS), Perkins, college/university.

APPLYING FOR FINANCIAL AID ***Required financial aid forms:*** FAFSA, state aid form.

CONTACT Craig Karlin, Director of Financial Assistance, Fort Hays State University, Custer Hall, Room 306, 600 Park Street, Hays, KS 67601, 785-628-4408 or toll-free 800-628-FHSU. *Fax:* 785-628-4014. *E-mail:* finaid@fhsu.edu.

FORT LEWIS COLLEGE

Durango, CO

Tuition & fees (CO res): $5973 **Average undergraduate aid package: $7142**

ABOUT THE INSTITUTION State-supported, coed. Awards: bachelor's degrees. 56 undergraduate majors. Total enrollment: 3,907. Undergraduates: 3,907. Freshmen: 910. Federal methodology is used as a basis for awarding need-based institutional aid.

UNDERGRADUATE EXPENSES for 2006–07 ***Application fee:*** $30. ***Tuition, state resident:*** full-time $5102; part-time $210 per credit hour. ***Tuition, nonresident:*** full-time $13,190; part-time $659 per credit hour. ***Required fees:*** full-time $871; $44.25 per credit hour. Full-time tuition and fees vary according to reciprocity agreements. Part-time tuition and fees vary according to course load and reciprocity agreements. ***College room and board:*** $6468; ***Room only:*** $3420. Room and board charges vary according to board plan and housing facility.

FRESHMAN FINANCIAL AID (Fall 2005) 581 applied for aid; of those 67% were deemed to have need. 97% of freshmen with need received aid; of those 18% had need fully met. ***Average percent of need met:*** 66% (excluding resources awarded to replace EFC). ***Average financial aid package:*** $6164 (excluding resources awarded to replace EFC). 10% of all full-time freshmen had no need and received non-need-based gift aid.

UNDERGRADUATE FINANCIAL AID (Fall 2005) 2,220 applied for aid; of those 77% were deemed to have need. 97% of undergraduates with need received aid; of those 18% had need fully met. ***Average percent of need met:*** 71% (excluding resources awarded to replace EFC). ***Average financial aid package:*** $7142 (excluding resources awarded to replace EFC). 6% of all full-time undergraduates had no need and received non-need-based gift aid.

GIFT AID (NEED-BASED) ***Total amount:*** $6,607,543 (61% federal, 13% state, 20% institutional, 6% external sources). ***Receiving aid:*** Freshmen: 24% (215); All full-time undergraduates: 29% (1,039). ***Average award:*** Freshmen: $4076; Undergraduates: $4103. ***Scholarships, grants, and awards:*** Federal Pell, FSEOG, state, private, college/university gift aid from institutional funds.

GIFT AID (NON-NEED-BASED) ***Total amount:*** $1,176,735 (1% federal, 1% state, 66% institutional, 32% external sources). ***Receiving aid:*** Freshmen: 22% (190); Undergraduates: 17% (595). ***Average award:*** Freshmen: $1841; Undergraduates: $1927. ***Scholarships, grants, and awards by category:*** *Academic Interests/Achievement:* 327 awards ($450,602 total): agriculture, area/ethnic studies, biological sciences, business, communication, computer science, education, English, general academic interests/achievements, humanities, mathematics, physical sciences, social sciences. *Creative Arts/Performance:* 49 awards ($27,635 total): art/fine arts, music, performing arts, theater/drama. *Special Achievements/Activities:* 90 awards ($234,166 total): general special achievements/activities, leadership. *Special Characteristics:* 190 awards ($185,986 total): children and siblings of alumni, children of faculty/staff, ethnic background, first-generation college students, general special characteristics, handicapped students, international students, local/state students, out-of-state students, veterans' children. ***Tuition waivers:*** Full or partial for minority students, employees or children of employees.

LOANS ***Student loans:*** $8,229,196 (78% need-based, 22% non-need-based). ***Average need-based loan:*** Freshmen: $2569; Undergraduates: $3722. ***Parent loans:*** $1,840,802 (62% need-based, 38% non-need-based). ***Programs:*** FFEL (Subsidized and Unsubsidized Stafford, PLUS), Perkins, college/university.

WORK-STUDY ***Federal work-study:*** Total amount: $191,958; 147 jobs averaging $2500. ***State or other work-study/employment:*** Total amount: $746,441 (63% need-based, 37% non-need-based). 152 part-time jobs averaging $2400.

ATHLETIC AWARDS Total amount: $641,168 (42% need-based, 58% non-need-based).

APPLYING FOR FINANCIAL AID ***Required financial aid form:*** FAFSA. ***Financial aid deadline (priority):*** 2/15. ***Notification date:*** Continuous beginning 3/15. Students must reply within 2 weeks of notification.

CONTACT Ms. Elaine Redwine, Director of Financial Aid, Fort Lewis College, 1000 Rim Drive, Durango, CO 81301-3999, 970-247-7464. *Fax:* 970-247-7108. *E-mail:* redwine_e@fortlewis.edu.

FORT VALLEY STATE UNIVERSITY

Fort Valley, GA

CONTACT Financial Aid Director, Fort Valley State University, PO Box 4129, Fort Valley, GA 31030-3298, 478-825-6182 or toll-free 800-248-7343. *Fax:* 478-825-6976.

FRAMINGHAM STATE COLLEGE

Framingham, MA

Tuition & fees (MA res): $5449 **Average undergraduate aid package: $6449**

ABOUT THE INSTITUTION State-supported, coed. Awards: bachelor's and master's degrees and post-bachelor's certificates. 89 undergraduate majors. Total enrollment: 5,861. Undergraduates: 3,829. Freshmen: 718. Federal methodology is used as a basis for awarding need-based institutional aid.

UNDERGRADUATE EXPENSES for 2006–07 ***Application fee:*** $25. ***Tuition, state resident:*** full-time $970. ***Tuition, nonresident:*** full-time $7050. Full-time tuition and fees vary according to class time. Part-time tuition and fees vary according to class time and course load. ***College room and board:*** $6699; ***Room only:*** $4339. Room and board charges vary according to board plan and housing facility. ***Payment plan:*** Installment.

FRESHMAN FINANCIAL AID (Fall 2005) 562 applied for aid; of those 60% were deemed to have need. 100% of freshmen with need received aid; of those 57% had need fully met. ***Average percent of need met:*** 79% (excluding resources awarded to replace EFC). ***Average financial aid package:*** $6424 (excluding resources awarded to replace EFC). 3% of all full-time freshmen had no need and received non-need-based gift aid.

UNDERGRADUATE FINANCIAL AID (Fall 2005) 2,043 applied for aid; of those 64% were deemed to have need. 100% of undergraduates with need received aid; of those 67% had need fully met. ***Average percent of need met:*** 81% (excluding resources awarded to replace EFC). ***Average financial aid package:*** $6449 (excluding resources awarded to replace EFC). 4% of all full-time undergraduates had no need and received non-need-based gift aid.

GIFT AID (NEED-BASED) ***Total amount:*** $3,829,186 (36% federal, 15% state, 45% institutional, 4% external sources). ***Receiving aid:*** Freshmen: 38% (271); All full-time undergraduates: 34% (1,036). ***Average award:*** Freshmen: $3596; Undergraduates: $3485. ***Scholarships, grants, and awards:*** Federal Pell, FSEOG, state, private, college/university gift aid from institutional funds.

GIFT AID (NON-NEED-BASED) ***Total amount:*** $283,519 (9% state, 37% institutional, 54% external sources). ***Receiving aid:*** Freshmen: 2% (14); Undergraduates: 1% (33). ***Average award:*** Freshmen: $1930; Undergraduates: $2043. ***Scholarships, grants, and awards by category:*** *Academic Interests/Achievement:* biological sciences, education, general academic interests/achievements, home economics, physical sciences. *Special Characteristics:* children of faculty/staff, children of public servants, children of union members/company employees, local/state students, veterans. ***Tuition waivers:*** Full or partial for employees or children of employees, senior citizens. ***ROTC:*** Army cooperative.

LOANS ***Student loans:*** $8,623,967 (54% need-based, 46% non-need-based). 62% of past graduating class borrowed through all loan programs. *Average indebtedness per student:* $15,328. ***Average need-based loan:*** Freshmen: $2812; Undergraduates: $2889. ***Parent loans:*** $2,083,465 (24% need-based, 76% non-need-based). ***Programs:*** FFEL (Subsidized and Unsubsidized Stafford, PLUS), Perkins, state.

WORK-STUDY ***Federal work-study:*** Total amount: $143,297; jobs available.

APPLYING FOR FINANCIAL AID ***Required financial aid form:*** FAFSA. ***Financial aid deadline (priority):*** 3/1. ***Notification date:*** Continuous beginning 4/15. Students must reply by 5/1 or within 2 weeks of notification.

CONTACT Financial Aid Office, Framingham State College, 100 State Street, PO Box 9101, Framingham, MA 01701-9101, 508-626-4534. *Fax:* 508-626-4598.

FRANCISCAN UNIVERSITY OF STEUBENVILLE

Steubenville, OH

CONTACT John Herrmann, Director of Student Financial Services, Franciscan University of Steubenville, 1235 University Boulevard, Steubenville, OH 43952-1763, 740-283-6211 or toll-free 800-783-6220. *Fax:* 740-284-5469. *E-mail:* jherrmann@franciscan.edu.

FRANCIS MARION UNIVERSITY

Florence, SC

Tuition & fees (SC res): $7038 **Average undergraduate aid package: N/A**

ABOUT THE INSTITUTION State-supported, coed. Awards: bachelor's and master's degrees. 30 undergraduate majors. Total enrollment: 4,075. Undergraduates: 3,514. Freshmen: 797. Federal methodology is used as a basis for awarding need-based institutional aid.

UNDERGRADUATE EXPENSES for 2007–08 ***Application fee:*** $30. ***Tuition, state resident:*** full-time $6803; part-time $340 per credit hour. ***Tuition, nonresident:*** full-time $13,606; part-time $680 per credit hour. ***Required fees:*** full-time $235; $7.25 per credit hour. ***College room and board:*** $5860; ***Room only:*** $3260.

FRESHMAN FINANCIAL AID (Fall 2005) 674 applied for aid; of those 88% were deemed to have need. 96% of freshmen with need received aid. 3% of all full-time freshmen had no need and received non-need-based gift aid.

UNDERGRADUATE FINANCIAL AID (Fall 2005) 2,876 applied for aid; of those 91% were deemed to have need. 97% of undergraduates with need received aid. 5% of all full-time undergraduates had no need and received non-need-based gift aid.

GIFT AID (NEED-BASED) ***Total amount:*** $4,809,751 (87% federal, 13% state). ***Receiving aid:*** Freshmen: 51% (406); All full-time undergraduates: 51% (1,568). ***Scholarships, grants, and awards:*** Federal Pell, FSEOG, state, private, Federal ACG and SMART Grants.

GIFT AID (NON-NEED-BASED) ***Total amount:*** $6,576,548 (76% state, 12% institutional, 12% external sources). ***Receiving aid:*** Freshmen: 56% (450); Undergraduates: 37% (1,138). ***Scholarships, grants, and awards by category:*** *Academic Interests/Achievement:* biological sciences, business, education, English, general academic interests/achievements, health fields, humanities, mathematics, premedicine, social sciences. *Creative Arts/Performance:* art/fine arts, music, theater/drama. *Special Achievements/Activities:* cheerleading/drum major. *Special Characteristics:* adult students, children and siblings of alumni, children of faculty/staff, handicapped students, international students, out-of-state students, spouses of deceased or disabled public servants, veterans, veterans' children.

LOANS ***Student loans:*** $14,203,658 (51% need-based, 49% non-need-based). *Average indebtedness per student:* $20,640. ***Parent loans:*** $749,744 (100% non-need-based). ***Programs:*** FFEL (Subsidized and Unsubsidized Stafford, PLUS), Perkins, state.

WORK-STUDY ***Federal work-study:*** Total amount: $152,000; 142 jobs averaging $1447. ***State or other work-study/employment:*** Total amount: $474,770 (100% non-need-based). 145 part-time jobs available.

ATHLETIC AWARDS Total amount: $479,605 (100% non-need-based).

APPLYING FOR FINANCIAL AID ***Required financial aid form:*** FAFSA. ***Financial aid deadline (priority):*** 3/1. ***Notification date:*** 4/1.

CONTACT Kim Ellisor, Director of Financial Assistance, Francis Marion University, PO Box 100547, Florence, SC 29501-0547, 843-661-1190 or toll-free 800-368-7551.

FRANKLIN & MARSHALL COLLEGE

Lancaster, PA

Tuition & fees: $34,450 **Average undergraduate aid package: $26,165**

ABOUT THE INSTITUTION Independent, coed. Awards: bachelor's degrees. 38 undergraduate majors. Total enrollment: 2,028. Undergraduates: 2,028. Freshmen: 524. Both federal and institutional methodology are used as a basis for awarding need-based institutional aid.

UNDERGRADUATE EXPENSES for 2006–07 ***Application fee:*** $50. ***Comprehensive fee:*** $42,990 includes full-time tuition ($34,400), mandatory fees ($50), and room and board ($8540). ***College room only:*** $5560. Full-time tuition and fees vary according to reciprocity agreements. Room and board charges vary according to board plan, housing facility, and location. ***Part-time tuition:*** $4300 per course. ***Payment plans:*** Installment, deferred payment.

FRESHMAN FINANCIAL AID (Fall 2006, est.) 453 applied for aid; of those 69% were deemed to have need. 100% of freshmen with need received aid; of those 100% had need fully met. ***Average percent of need met:*** 100% (excluding resources awarded to replace EFC). ***Average financial aid package:*** $28,961 (excluding resources awarded to replace EFC). 26% of all full-time freshmen had no need and received non-need-based gift aid.

UNDERGRADUATE FINANCIAL AID (Fall 2006, est.) 1,161 applied for aid; of those 78% were deemed to have need. 99% of undergraduates with need received aid; of those 31% had need fully met. ***Average percent of need met:*** 96% (excluding resources awarded to replace EFC). ***Average financial aid package:*** $26,165 (excluding resources awarded to replace EFC). 25% of all full-time undergraduates had no need and received non-need-based gift aid.

GIFT AID (NEED-BASED) ***Total amount:*** $17,223,529 (4% federal, 4% state, 92% institutional). ***Receiving aid:*** Freshmen: 56% (292); All full-time undergraduates: 42% (825). ***Average award:*** Freshmen: $25,917; Undergraduates: $21,407. ***Scholarships, grants, and awards:*** Federal Pell, FSEOG, state, private, college/university gift aid from institutional funds.

GIFT AID (NON-NEED-BASED) ***Total amount:*** $3,691,953 (91% institutional, 9% external sources). ***Receiving aid:*** Freshmen: 4% (21); Undergraduates: 3% (54). ***Average award:*** Freshmen: $12,211; Undergraduates: $14,084. ***Scholarships, grants, and awards by category:*** *Academic Interests/Achievement:* 638 awards ($5,591,728 total): general academic interests/achievements. *Creative Arts/Performance:* 39 awards ($97,500 total): music. *Special Characteristics:* 79 awards: children of faculty/staff, members of minority groups. ***Tuition waivers:*** Full or partial for employees or children of employees.

LOANS ***Student loans:*** $6,859,182 (46% need-based, 54% non-need-based). 59% of past graduating class borrowed through all loan programs. *Average indebtedness per student:* $23,043. ***Average need-based loan:*** Freshmen: $3553; Undergraduates: $5294. ***Parent loans:*** $4,819,885 (100% non-need-based). ***Programs:*** FFEL (Subsidized and Unsubsidized Stafford, PLUS), Perkins, college/university.

WORK-STUDY ***Federal work-study:*** Total amount: $342,746. ***State or other work-study/employment:*** Total amount: $860,195 (100% non-need-based). 141 part-time jobs averaging $1875.

APPLYING FOR FINANCIAL AID ***Required financial aid forms:*** FAFSA, institution's own form, CSS Financial Aid PROFILE, noncustodial (divorced/separated) parent's statement, business/farm supplement, federal income tax form(s), W-2 forms. ***Financial aid deadline:*** 3/1 (priority: 2/1). ***Notification date:*** 3/15. Students must reply by 5/1.

CONTACT Mr. Christopher K. Hanlon, Director of Student Aid, Franklin & Marshall College, PO Box 3003, Lancaster, PA 17604-3003, 717-291-3991. *Fax:* 717-291-4389. *E-mail:* chris.hanlon@fandm.edu.

FRANKLIN COLLEGE

Franklin, IN

Tuition & fees: $20,325 **Average undergraduate aid package: $16,712**

ABOUT THE INSTITUTION Independent religious, coed. Awards: bachelor's degrees. 32 undergraduate majors. Total enrollment: 1,013. Undergraduates: 1,013. Freshmen: 277. Federal methodology is used as a basis for awarding need-based institutional aid.

UNDERGRADUATE EXPENSES for 2006–07 ***Application fee:*** $30. ***Comprehensive fee:*** $26,295 includes full-time tuition ($20,150), mandatory fees ($175), and room and board ($5970). ***College room only:*** $3480. Room and board charges vary according to board plan and housing facility. ***Part-time tuition:*** $280 per credit hour. Part-time tuition and fees vary according to course load. ***Payment plan:*** Installment.

FRESHMAN FINANCIAL AID (Fall 2006, est.) 271 applied for aid; of those 88% were deemed to have need. 100% of freshmen with need received aid; of those 19% had need fully met. ***Average percent of need met:*** 87% (excluding resources awarded to replace EFC). ***Average financial aid package:*** $16,994 (excluding resources awarded to replace EFC). 21% of all full-time freshmen had no need and received non-need-based gift aid.

UNDERGRADUATE FINANCIAL AID (Fall 2006, est.) 885 applied for aid; of those 88% were deemed to have need. 99% of undergraduates with need received aid; of those 21% had need fully met. ***Average percent of need met:*** 87% (excluding resources awarded to replace EFC). ***Average financial aid package:*** $16,712 (excluding resources awarded to replace EFC). 19% of all full-time undergraduates had no need and received non-need-based gift aid.

GIFT AID (NEED-BASED) ***Total amount:*** $9,949,326 (10% federal, 28% state, 58% institutional, 4% external sources). ***Receiving aid:*** Freshmen: 78% (237); All full-time undergraduates: 80% (769). ***Average award:*** Freshmen: $13,532; Undergraduates: $12,769. ***Scholarships, grants, and awards:*** Federal Pell, FSEOG, state, private, college/university gift aid from institutional funds.

GIFT AID (NON-NEED-BASED) ***Total amount:*** $2,101,172 (2% state, 82% institutional, 16% external sources). ***Receiving aid:*** Freshmen: 12% (35); Undergraduates: 13% (129). ***Average award:*** Freshmen: $9234; Undergraduates: $11,968. ***Scholarships, grants, and awards by category:*** *Academic Interests/Achievement:* general academic interests/achievements. *Creative Arts/Performance:* art/fine arts, journalism/publications, music, performing arts, theater/drama. *Special Characteristics:* children and siblings of alumni, children of faculty/staff, ethnic background, members of minority groups, out-of-state students, religious affiliation, siblings of current students. ***Tuition waivers:*** Full or partial for employees or children of employees, senior citizens. ***ROTC:*** Army cooperative.

LOANS ***Student loans:*** $5,049,246 (67% need-based, 33% non-need-based). 99% of past graduating class borrowed through all loan programs. *Average indebtedness per student:* $32,778. ***Average need-based loan:*** Freshmen: $3270; Undergraduates: $4065. ***Parent loans:*** $1,645,071 (14% need-based, 86% non-need-based). ***Programs:*** FFEL (Subsidized and Unsubsidized Stafford, PLUS), Perkins, college/university.

WORK-STUDY ***Federal work-study:*** Total amount: $155,104; jobs available. ***State or other work-study/employment:*** Total amount: $81,100 (69% need-based, 31% non-need-based).

APPLYING FOR FINANCIAL AID ***Required financial aid forms:*** FAFSA, institution's own form. ***Financial aid deadline:*** 3/1. ***Notification date:*** 4/1. Students must reply by 5/1 or within 4 weeks of notification.

CONTACT Elizabeth Sappenfield, Director of Financial Aid, Franklin College, 101 Branigin Boulevard, Franklin, IN 46131-2598, 317-738-8075 or toll-free 800-852-0232. *Fax:* 317-738-8072. *E-mail:* finaid@franklincollege.edu.

FRANKLIN PIERCE UNIVERSITY

Rindge, NH

Tuition & fees: $25,300 **Average undergraduate aid package: $16,346**

ABOUT THE INSTITUTION Independent, coed. Awards: bachelor's degrees (profile does not reflect significant enrollment at 6 continuing education sites; master's degree is only offered at these sites). 50 undergraduate majors. Total enrollment: 1,704. Undergraduates: 1,704. Freshmen: 554. Federal methodology is used as a basis for awarding need-based institutional aid.

UNDERGRADUATE EXPENSES for 2006–07 ***Comprehensive fee:*** $33,500 includes full-time tuition ($24,300), mandatory fees ($1000), and room and board ($8200). ***College room only:*** $4600. ***Part-time tuition:*** $810 per credit.

FRESHMAN FINANCIAL AID (Fall 2006, est.) 398 applied for aid; of those 87% were deemed to have need. 100% of freshmen with need received aid; of those 11% had need fully met. ***Average percent of need met:*** 64% (excluding resources awarded to replace EFC). ***Average financial aid package:*** $15,089 (excluding resources awarded to replace EFC). 19% of all full-time freshmen had no need and received non-need-based gift aid.

UNDERGRADUATE FINANCIAL AID (Fall 2006, est.) 1,306 applied for aid; of those 91% were deemed to have need. 100% of undergraduates with need received aid; of those 11% had need fully met. ***Average percent of need met:*** 67% (excluding resources awarded to replace EFC). ***Average financial aid package:*** $16,346 (excluding resources awarded to replace EFC). 19% of all full-time undergraduates had no need and received non-need-based gift aid.

GIFT AID (NEED-BASED) ***Total amount:*** $12,986,099 (9% federal, 1% state, 89% institutional, 1% external sources). ***Receiving aid:*** Freshmen: 67% (340); All full-time undergraduates: 73% (1,160). ***Average award:*** Freshmen: $12,044; Undergraduates: $11,888. ***Scholarships, grants, and awards:*** Federal Pell, FSEOG, state, private, college/university gift aid from institutional funds, United Negro College Fund.

GIFT AID (NON-NEED-BASED) ***Total amount:*** $2,665,231 (99% institutional, 1% external sources). ***Receiving aid:*** Freshmen: 6% (29); Undergraduates: 6% (92). ***Average award:*** Freshmen: $10,786; Undergraduates: $11,589. ***Scholarships, grants, and awards by category:*** *Academic Interests/Achievement:* 1,330 awards ($9,605,692 total): communication, general academic interests/achievements. *Creative Arts/Performance:* 19 awards ($37,000 total): performing arts, theater/drama. *Special Achievements/Activities:* general special achievements/activities, leadership. *Special Characteristics:* adult students, children and siblings of alumni, children of current students, children of educators, children of faculty/staff, general special characteristics, international students, local/state students, married students, parents of current students, siblings of current students, spouses of current students. ***ROTC:*** Army cooperative, Air Force cooperative.

LOANS ***Student loans:*** $13,444,424 (69% need-based, 31% non-need-based). 80% of past graduating class borrowed through all loan programs. *Average*

indebtedness per student: $28,036. ***Average need-based loan:*** Freshmen: $2875; Undergraduates: $4486. ***Parent loans:*** $3,888,309 (46% need-based, 54% non-need-based). ***Programs:*** FFEL (Subsidized and Unsubsidized Stafford, PLUS), Perkins.

WORK-STUDY ***Federal work-study:*** Total amount: $635,492; 758 jobs averaging $1467. ***State or other work-study/employment:*** Total amount: $300,690 (34% need-based, 66% non-need-based). 183 part-time jobs averaging $2128.

ATHLETIC AWARDS Total amount: $1,100,978 (39% need-based, 61% non-need-based).

APPLYING FOR FINANCIAL AID ***Required financial aid form:*** FAFSA. ***Financial aid deadline (priority):*** 3/1. ***Notification date:*** Continuous beginning 4/1.

CONTACT Kenneth Ferreira, Executive Director of SFS, Franklin Pierce University, 20 College Road, Rindge, NH 03461-0060, 603-899-4180 or toll-free 800-437-0048. *Fax:* 603-899-4372. *E-mail:* ferreirak@fpc.edu.

FRANKLIN UNIVERSITY

Columbus, OH

CONTACT Ms. Marlowe Collier, Financial Aid Assistant, Franklin University, 201 South Grant Avenue, Columbus, OH 43215-5399, 614-797-4700 or toll-free 877-341-6300. *Fax:* 614-220-8931. *E-mail:* finaid@franklin.edu.

FREED-HARDEMAN UNIVERSITY

Henderson, TN

Tuition & fees: $13,192 **Average undergraduate aid package: $11,176**

ABOUT THE INSTITUTION Independent religious, coed. Awards: bachelor's and master's degrees and post-master's certificates. 53 undergraduate majors. Total enrollment: 1,969. Undergraduates: 1,473. Freshmen: 361. Federal methodology is used as a basis for awarding need-based institutional aid.

UNDERGRADUATE EXPENSES for 2006–07 ***Comprehensive fee:*** $19,752 includes full-time tuition ($11,100), mandatory fees ($2092), and room and board ($6560). ***College room only:*** $3700. Full-time tuition and fees vary according to course load and degree level. Room and board charges vary according to board plan and housing facility. ***Part-time tuition:*** $370 per semester hour. ***Part-time fees:*** $80 per semester hour. Part-time tuition and fees vary according to course load and degree level. ***Payment plans:*** Tuition prepayment, installment.

FRESHMAN FINANCIAL AID (Fall 2006, est.) 319 applied for aid; of those 85% were deemed to have need. 100% of freshmen with need received aid; of those 29% had need fully met. ***Average percent of need met:*** 72% (excluding resources awarded to replace EFC). ***Average financial aid package:*** $11,541 (excluding resources awarded to replace EFC). 22% of all full-time freshmen had no need and received non-need-based gift aid.

UNDERGRADUATE FINANCIAL AID (Fall 2006, est.) 1,209 applied for aid; of those 85% were deemed to have need. 100% of undergraduates with need received aid; of those 18% had need fully met. ***Average percent of need met:*** 62% (excluding resources awarded to replace EFC). ***Average financial aid package:*** $11,176 (excluding resources awarded to replace EFC). 21% of all full-time undergraduates had no need and received non-need-based gift aid.

GIFT AID (NEED-BASED) ***Total amount:*** $7,054,267 (19% federal, 21% state, 57% institutional, 3% external sources). ***Receiving aid:*** Freshmen: 74% (266); All full-time undergraduates: 70% (947). ***Average award:*** Freshmen: $9082; Undergraduates: $8050. ***Scholarships, grants, and awards:*** Federal Pell, FSEOG, state, private, college/university gift aid from institutional funds.

GIFT AID (NON-NEED-BASED) ***Total amount:*** $2,329,665 (24% state, 72% institutional, 4% external sources). ***Receiving aid:*** Freshmen: 17% (61); Undergraduates: 11% (148). ***Average award:*** Freshmen: $11,257; Undergraduates: $11,239. ***Scholarships, grants, and awards by category:*** *Academic Interests/Achievement:* biological sciences, business, computer science, education, engineering/technologies, English, general academic interests/achievements, humanities, mathematics, physical sciences, premedicine, religion/biblical studies. *Creative Arts/Performance:* art/fine arts, cinema/film/broadcasting, journalism/publications, music, performing arts, theater/drama. *Special Achievements/Activities:* leadership. *Special Characteristics:* adult students, children of faculty/staff. ***Tuition waivers:*** Full or partial for employees or children of employees, senior citizens.

LOANS ***Student loans:*** $9,078,788 (73% need-based, 27% non-need-based). 81% of past graduating class borrowed through all loan programs. *Average indebtedness per student:* $30,584. ***Average need-based loan:*** Freshmen: $3025; Undergraduates: $4109. ***Parent loans:*** $3,211,903 (39% need-based, 61% non-need-based). ***Programs:*** FFEL (Subsidized and Unsubsidized Stafford, PLUS), Perkins, alternative loans.

WORK-STUDY ***Federal work-study:*** Total amount: $435,056; jobs available. ***State or other work-study/employment:*** Part-time jobs available.

ATHLETIC AWARDS Total amount: $1,080,659 (40% need-based, 60% non-need-based).

APPLYING FOR FINANCIAL AID ***Required financial aid form:*** FAFSA. ***Financial aid deadline (priority):*** 3/1. ***Notification date:*** Continuous beginning 3/1. Students must reply within 4 weeks of notification.

CONTACT Larry Cyr, Director of Financial Aid, Freed-Hardeman University, 158 East Main Street, Henderson, TN 38340-2399, 731-989-6662 or toll-free 800-630-3480. *Fax:* 731-989-6775. *E-mail:* lcyr@fhu.edu.

FREE WILL BAPTIST BIBLE COLLEGE

Nashville, TN

Tuition & fees: $11,166 **Average undergraduate aid package: N/A**

ABOUT THE INSTITUTION Independent Free Will Baptist, coed. Awards: associate and bachelor's degrees. 12 undergraduate majors. Total enrollment: 383. Undergraduates: 383. Freshmen: 75. Federal methodology is used as a basis for awarding need-based institutional aid.

UNDERGRADUATE EXPENSES for 2006–07 ***Application fee:*** $35. ***Comprehensive fee:*** $15,874 includes full-time tuition ($10,470), mandatory fees ($696), and room and board ($4708). ***Part-time tuition:*** $349 per semester hour.

GIFT AID (NEED-BASED) ***Total amount:*** $971,312 (34% federal, 4% state, 44% institutional, 18% external sources). ***Scholarships, grants, and awards:*** Federal Pell, FSEOG, state, private, college/university gift aid from institutional funds.

GIFT AID (NON-NEED-BASED) ***Total amount:*** $89,825 (100% state). ***Scholarships, grants, and awards by category:*** *Special Characteristics:* 46 awards ($100,781 total): children of faculty/staff, international students, married students, relatives of clergy, veterans, veterans' children. ***ROTC:*** Army cooperative, Air Force cooperative.

LOANS ***Student loans:*** $1,599,280 (51% need-based, 49% non-need-based). 70% of past graduating class borrowed through all loan programs. *Average indebtedness per student:* $14,509. ***Parent loans:*** $483,755 (100% non-need-based). ***Programs:*** FFEL (Subsidized and Unsubsidized Stafford, PLUS), alternative loans.

WORK-STUDY ***Federal work-study:*** Total amount: $22,343; 16 jobs averaging $1397. ***State or other work-study/employment:*** Total amount: $138,075 (100% non-need-based). 90 part-time jobs averaging $1447.

APPLYING FOR FINANCIAL AID ***Required financial aid forms:*** FAFSA, institution's own form. ***Financial aid deadline (priority):*** 4/15. ***Notification date:*** Continuous beginning 7/1.

CONTACT Jeff Caudill, Director of Enrollment Services, Free Will Baptist Bible College, 3606 West End Avenue, Nashville, TN 37205, 615-844-5000 or toll-free 800-763-9222. *Fax:* 615-269-6028. *E-mail:* jcaudill@fwbbc.edu.

FRESNO PACIFIC UNIVERSITY

Fresno, CA

Tuition & fees: $20,790 **Average undergraduate aid package: $16,270**

ABOUT THE INSTITUTION Independent religious, coed. Awards: associate, bachelor's, and master's degrees. 42 undergraduate majors. Total enrollment: 2,324. Undergraduates: 1,565. Freshmen: 201. Federal methodology is used as a basis for awarding need-based institutional aid.

UNDERGRADUATE EXPENSES for 2006–07 ***Application fee:*** $40. ***Comprehensive fee:*** $26,780 includes full-time tuition ($20,550), mandatory fees ($240), and room and board ($5990). ***College room only:*** $3400. Full-time tuition and fees vary according to program. Room and board charges vary according to board plan and housing facility. ***Part-time tuition:*** $735 per unit. Part-time tuition and fees vary according to program. ***Payment plan:*** Installment.

FRESHMAN FINANCIAL AID (Fall 2005) 193 applied for aid; of those 83% were deemed to have need. 100% of freshmen with need received aid; of those 15% had need fully met. ***Average percent of need met:*** 71% (excluding resources awarded to replace EFC). ***Average financial aid package:*** $17,037 (excluding resources awarded to replace EFC).

UNDERGRADUATE FINANCIAL AID (Fall 2005) 1,111 applied for aid; of those 83% were deemed to have need. 100% of undergraduates with need received aid; of those 16% had need fully met. ***Average percent of need met:*** 64% (excluding resources awarded to replace EFC). ***Average financial aid package:*** $16,270 (excluding resources awarded to replace EFC).

GIFT AID (NEED-BASED) ***Total amount:*** $12,434,077 (15% federal, 40% state, 45% institutional). ***Receiving aid:*** Freshmen: 80% (157); All full-time undergraduates: 65% (825). ***Average award:*** Freshmen: $12,578; Undergraduates: $10,489. ***Scholarships, grants, and awards:*** Federal Pell, FSEOG, state, private, college/university gift aid from institutional funds.

GIFT AID (NON-NEED-BASED) ***Total amount:*** $1,093,744 (54% institutional, 46% external sources). ***Receiving aid:*** Freshmen: 35% (69); Undergraduates: 25% (319). ***Scholarships, grants, and awards by category:*** *Academic Interests/Achievement:* general academic interests/achievements, humanities, religion/biblical studies, social sciences. *Creative Arts/Performance:* art/fine arts, journalism/publications, music, theater/drama. *Special Achievements/Activities:* general special achievements/activities, leadership, memberships, religious involvement. *Special Characteristics:* children of faculty/staff, ethnic background, international students, members of minority groups, religious affiliation. ***Tuition waivers:*** Full or partial for employees or children of employees, senior citizens.

LOANS ***Student loans:*** $7,071,897 (100% need-based). 99% of past graduating class borrowed through all loan programs. *Average indebtedness per student:* $15,588. ***Average need-based loan:*** Freshmen: $2593; Undergraduates: $4248. ***Parent loans:*** $1,149,893 (100% need-based). ***Programs:*** FFEL (Subsidized and Unsubsidized Stafford, PLUS), Perkins, private alternative loans.

WORK-STUDY ***Federal work-study:*** Total amount: $1,359,778; 468 jobs averaging $2733. ***State or other work-study/employment:*** Part-time jobs available.

ATHLETIC AWARDS Total amount: $1,411,369 (100% need-based).

APPLYING FOR FINANCIAL AID ***Required financial aid forms:*** FAFSA, institution's own form. ***Financial aid deadline (priority):*** 3/2. ***Notification date:*** Continuous beginning 2/21. Students must reply by 7/30 or within 3 weeks of notification.

CONTACT April Powell, Associate Director of Financial Aid, Fresno Pacific University, 1717 South Chestnut Avenue, #2004, Fresno, CA 93702, 559-453-7137 or toll-free 800-660-6089 (in-state). *Fax:* 559-453-5595. *E-mail:* sfs@fresno.edu.

FRIENDS UNIVERSITY

Wichita, KS

Tuition & fees: N/R **Average undergraduate aid package: $11,219**

ABOUT THE INSTITUTION Independent, coed. Awards: associate, bachelor's, and master's degrees. 59 undergraduate majors. Total enrollment: 3,190. Undergraduates: 2,629. Federal methodology is used as a basis for awarding need-based institutional aid.

FRESHMAN FINANCIAL AID (Fall 2006, est.) 209 applied for aid; of those 90% were deemed to have need. 99% of freshmen with need received aid; of those 33% had need fully met. ***Average percent of need met:*** 76% (excluding resources awarded to replace EFC). ***Average financial aid package:*** $12,727 (excluding resources awarded to replace EFC). 21% of all full-time freshmen had no need and received non-need-based gift aid.

UNDERGRADUATE FINANCIAL AID (Fall 2006, est.) 1,290 applied for aid; of those 90% were deemed to have need. 99% of undergraduates with need received aid; of those 24% had need fully met. ***Average percent of need met:*** 66% (excluding resources awarded to replace EFC). ***Average financial aid package:*** $11,219 (excluding resources awarded to replace EFC). 16% of all full-time undergraduates had no need and received non-need-based gift aid.

GIFT AID (NEED-BASED) ***Total amount:*** $7,641,384 (32% federal, 13% state, 42% institutional, 13% external sources). ***Receiving aid:*** Freshmen: 72% (184); All full-time undergraduates: 73% (1,033). ***Average award:*** Freshmen: $8876; Undergraduates: $7092. ***Scholarships, grants, and awards:*** Federal Pell, FSEOG, state, private, college/university gift aid from institutional funds.

GIFT AID (NON-NEED-BASED) ***Total amount:*** $1,298,116 (70% institutional, 30% external sources). ***Receiving aid:*** Freshmen: 7% (17); Undergraduates: 5% (70). ***Average award:*** Freshmen: $7928; Undergraduates: $7792. ***Scholarships, grants, and awards by category:*** *Academic Interests/Achievement:* 785 awards ($2,693,825 total): biological sciences, business, communication, computer science, education, English, foreign languages, general academic interests/achievements, health fields, humanities, mathematics, physical sciences, premedicine, religion/biblical studies, social sciences. *Creative Arts/Performance:* 237 awards ($450,299 total): applied art and design, art/fine arts, dance, music, performing arts, theater/drama. *Special Achievements/Activities:* 114 awards ($54,500 total): cheerleading/drum major, junior miss, leadership, religious involvement. *Special Characteristics:* 150 awards ($140,100 total): children and siblings of alumni, international students, out-of-state students, relatives of clergy, religious affiliation.

LOANS ***Student loans:*** $11,523,119 (84% need-based, 16% non-need-based). 88% of past graduating class borrowed through all loan programs. *Average indebtedness per student:* $17,750. ***Average need-based loan:*** Freshmen: $2953; Undergraduates: $4098. ***Parent loans:*** $891,138 (100% non-need-based). ***Programs:*** FFEL (Subsidized and Unsubsidized Stafford, PLUS), Perkins, college/university.

WORK-STUDY ***Federal work-study:*** Total amount: $267,548; 239 jobs averaging $1221. ***State or other work-study/employment:*** Total amount: $453,373 (100% non-need-based). 185 part-time jobs averaging $1608.

ATHLETIC AWARDS Total amount: $895,590 (75% need-based, 25% non-need-based).

APPLYING FOR FINANCIAL AID ***Required financial aid forms:*** FAFSA, institution's own form. ***Financial aid deadline (priority):*** 3/15. ***Notification date:*** Continuous beginning 3/1. Students must reply within 3 weeks of notification.

CONTACT Brandon Pierce, Director of Financial Aid, Friends University, 2100 University Street, Wichita, KS 67213, 316-295-5658 or toll-free 800-577-2233. *Fax:* 316-295-5703. *E-mail:* piercb@friends.edu.

FROSTBURG STATE UNIVERSITY

Frostburg, MD

Tuition & fees (MD res): $6550 **Average undergraduate aid package: $7488**

ABOUT THE INSTITUTION State-supported, coed. Awards: bachelor's and master's degrees and post-bachelor's and post-master's certificates. 46 undergraduate majors. Total enrollment: 4,910. Undergraduates: 4,252. Freshmen: 1,013. Both federal and institutional methodology are used as a basis for awarding need-based institutional aid.

UNDERGRADUATE EXPENSES for 2007–08 ***Application fee:*** $30. ***Tuition, state resident:*** full-time $5000; part-time $207 per credit hour. ***Tuition, nonresident:*** full-time $14,612; part-time $411 per credit hour. ***Required fees:*** full-time $1550; $74 per credit hour or $9 per term part-time. ***College room and board:*** $6746; ***Room only:*** $3340.

FRESHMAN FINANCIAL AID (Fall 2006, est.) 840 applied for aid; of those 66% were deemed to have need. 96% of freshmen with need received aid; of those 27% had need fully met. ***Average percent of need met:*** 68% (excluding resources awarded to replace EFC). ***Average financial aid package:*** $7494 (excluding resources awarded to replace EFC). 13% of all full-time freshmen had no need and received non-need-based gift aid.

UNDERGRADUATE FINANCIAL AID (Fall 2006, est.) 3,023 applied for aid; of those 69% were deemed to have need. 100% of undergraduates with need received aid; of those 26% had need fully met. ***Average percent of need met:*** 7% (excluding resources awarded to replace EFC). ***Average financial aid package:*** $7488 (excluding resources awarded to replace EFC). 9% of all full-time undergraduates had no need and received non-need-based gift aid.

GIFT AID (NEED-BASED) ***Total amount:*** $8,185,063 (41% federal, 44% state, 11% institutional, 4% external sources). ***Receiving aid:*** Freshmen: 42% (453); All full-time undergraduates: 34% (1,595). ***Average award:*** Freshmen: $5537; Undergraduates: $4792. ***Scholarships, grants, and awards:*** Federal Pell, FSEOG, state, private, college/university gift aid from institutional funds.

GIFT AID (NON-NEED-BASED) ***Total amount:*** $2,537,560 (15% state, 76% institutional, 9% external sources). ***Receiving aid:*** Freshmen: 20% (210); Undergraduates: 13% (593). ***Average award:*** Freshmen: $2410; Undergraduates: $2349. ***Scholarships, grants, and awards by category:*** *Academic Interests/Achievement:* 756 awards ($1,480,699 total): biological sciences, business, communication, computer science, education, engineering/technologies, English, foreign languages, general academic interests/achievements, health fields, humanities, international studies, mathematics, physical sciences, premedicine, social sciences. *Creative Arts/Performance:* 105 awards ($101,775 total): art/fine arts, creative writing, dance, journalism/publications, music, performing arts, theater/drama. *Special Achievements/Activities:* 21 awards ($26,600 total): community service, leadership. *Special Characteristics:* 130 awards ($131,750 total): adult students, children of union members/company employees, international students, local/state students, out-of-state students, veterans, veterans' children.

LOANS ***Student loans:*** $15,772,170 (45% need-based, 55% non-need-based). 64% of past graduating class borrowed through all loan programs. *Average*

indebtedness per student: $11,423. ***Average need-based loan:*** Freshmen: $2338; Undergraduates: $3336. ***Parent loans:*** $3,724,866 (100% non-need-based). ***Programs:*** FFEL (Subsidized and Unsubsidized Stafford, PLUS), Perkins.

WORK-STUDY ***Federal work-study:*** Total amount: $104,970; 242 jobs averaging $1000. ***State or other work-study/employment:*** Total amount: $465,307 (100% non-need-based). 518 part-time jobs averaging $519.

APPLYING FOR FINANCIAL AID ***Required financial aid form:*** FAFSA. ***Financial aid deadline (priority):*** 3/1. ***Notification date:*** Continuous beginning 3/15. Students must reply within 3 weeks of notification.

CONTACT Mrs. Angela Hovatter, Director of Financial Aid, Frostburg State University, 101 Braddock Road, Frostburg, MD 21532-1099, 301-687-4301. *Fax:* 301-687-7074.

FURMAN UNIVERSITY

Greenville, SC

Tuition & fees: $28,840 **Average undergraduate aid package: $23,132**

ABOUT THE INSTITUTION Independent, coed. Awards: bachelor's and master's degrees and post-bachelor's certificates. 48 undergraduate majors. Total enrollment: 3,010. Undergraduates: 2,759. Freshmen: 687. Both federal and institutional methodology are used as a basis for awarding need-based institutional aid.

UNDERGRADUATE EXPENSES for 2006–07 ***Application fee:*** $50. ***Comprehensive fee:*** $36,392 includes full-time tuition ($28,352), mandatory fees ($488), and room and board ($7552). ***College room only:*** $3968. Room and board charges vary according to board plan and housing facility. ***Part-time tuition:*** $886 per credit hour. Part-time tuition and fees vary according to course load. ***Payment plan:*** Installment.

FRESHMAN FINANCIAL AID (Fall 2006, est.) 397 applied for aid; of those 72% were deemed to have need. 100% of freshmen with need received aid; of those 36% had need fully met. ***Average percent of need met:*** 87% (excluding resources awarded to replace EFC). ***Average financial aid package:*** $24,282 (excluding resources awarded to replace EFC). 32% of all full-time freshmen had no need and received non-need-based gift aid.

UNDERGRADUATE FINANCIAL AID (Fall 2006, est.) 1,332 applied for aid; of those 81% were deemed to have need. 100% of undergraduates with need received aid; of those 49% had need fully met. ***Average percent of need met:*** 83% (excluding resources awarded to replace EFC). ***Average financial aid package:*** $23,132 (excluding resources awarded to replace EFC). 31% of all full-time undergraduates had no need and received non-need-based gift aid.

GIFT AID (NEED-BASED) ***Total amount:*** $17,337,009 (10% federal, 8% state, 77% institutional, 5% external sources). ***Receiving aid:*** Freshmen: 42% (287); All full-time undergraduates: 40% (1,066). ***Average award:*** Freshmen: $21,688; Undergraduates: $19,792. ***Scholarships, grants, and awards:*** Federal Pell, FSEOG, state, private, college/university gift aid from institutional funds, Smart, ACG.

GIFT AID (NON-NEED-BASED) ***Total amount:*** $14,967,099 (24% state, 69% institutional, 7% external sources). ***Receiving aid:*** Freshmen: 36% (248); Undergraduates: 34% (897). ***Average award:*** Freshmen: $11,556; Undergraduates: $11,228. ***Scholarships, grants, and awards by category:*** *Academic Interests/Achievement:* 2,801 awards ($14,044,969 total): area/ethnic studies, biological sciences, business, communication, computer science, education, engineering/technologies, English, foreign languages, general academic interests/achievements, health fields, humanities, international studies, mathematics, military science, physical sciences, premedicine, religion/biblical studies, social sciences. *Creative Arts/Performance:* 323 awards ($1,234,364 total): art/fine arts, creative writing, music, theater/drama. *Special Achievements/Activities:* 32 awards ($140,869 total): community service, leadership, religious involvement. *Special Characteristics:* 1,237 awards ($7,640,692 total): children of faculty/staff, ethnic background, international students, local/state students, relatives of clergy, religious affiliation, veterans. ***Tuition waivers:*** Full or partial for employees or children of employees. ***ROTC:*** Army.

LOANS ***Student loans:*** $7,094,284 (75% need-based, 25% non-need-based). 47% of past graduating class borrowed through all loan programs. *Average indebtedness per student:* $24,538. ***Average need-based loan:*** Freshmen: $2961; Undergraduates: $2049. ***Parent loans:*** $2,386,177 (70% need-based, 30% non-need-based). ***Programs:*** FFEL (Subsidized and Unsubsidized Stafford, PLUS), Perkins, state, alternative loans.

WORK-STUDY ***Federal work-study:*** Total amount: $630,894; 452 jobs averaging $1453.

ATHLETIC AWARDS Total amount: $5,573,272 (26% need-based, 74% non-need-based).

APPLYING FOR FINANCIAL AID ***Required financial aid forms:*** FAFSA, institution's own form, state aid form, South Carolina residents must complete required SC forms. ***Financial aid deadline:*** 1/15. ***Notification date:*** 3/15. Students must reply by 5/1.

CONTACT Martin Carney, Director of Financial Aid, Furman University, 3300 Poinsett Highway, Greenville, SC 29613, 864-294-2204. *Fax:* 864-294-3127. *E-mail:* martin.carney@furman.edu.

GALLAUDET UNIVERSITY

Washington, DC

Tuition & fees: N/R **Average undergraduate aid package: $11,462**

ABOUT THE INSTITUTION Independent, coed. Awards: bachelor's, master's, and doctoral degrees and post-bachelor's certificates (undergraduate programs are open primarily to the hearing-impaired). 52 undergraduate majors. Total enrollment: 1,834. Undergraduates: 1,207. Freshmen: 227. Federal methodology is used as a basis for awarding need-based institutional aid.

FRESHMAN FINANCIAL AID (Fall 2006, est.) 169 applied for aid; of those 89% were deemed to have need. 97% of freshmen with need received aid; of those 36% had need fully met. ***Average percent of need met:*** 61% (excluding resources awarded to replace EFC). ***Average financial aid package:*** $11,139 (excluding resources awarded to replace EFC). 9% of all full-time freshmen had no need and received non-need-based gift aid.

UNDERGRADUATE FINANCIAL AID (Fall 2006, est.) 988 applied for aid; of those 90% were deemed to have need. 97% of undergraduates with need received aid; of those 36% had need fully met. ***Average percent of need met:*** 60% (excluding resources awarded to replace EFC). ***Average financial aid package:*** $11,462 (excluding resources awarded to replace EFC). 3% of all full-time undergraduates had no need and received non-need-based gift aid.

GIFT AID (NEED-BASED) ***Total amount:*** $11,668,071 (11% federal, 68% state, 19% institutional, 2% external sources). ***Receiving aid:*** Freshmen: 71% (146); All full-time undergraduates: 68% (857). ***Average award:*** Freshmen: $10,579; Undergraduates: $10,692. ***Scholarships, grants, and awards:*** Federal Pell, FSEOG, state, private, college/university gift aid from institutional funds.

GIFT AID (NON-NEED-BASED) ***Total amount:*** $1,386,523 (78% state, 19% institutional, 3% external sources). ***Receiving aid:*** Freshmen: 25% (52); Undergraduates: 24% (298). ***Average award:*** Freshmen: $4406; Undergraduates: $5016. ***Scholarships, grants, and awards by category:*** *Academic Interests/Achievement:* general academic interests/achievements. *Special Characteristics:* children of educators, children of faculty/staff, handicapped students, international students. ***Tuition waivers:*** Full or partial for employees or children of employees.

LOANS ***Student loans:*** $2,057,509 (95% need-based, 5% non-need-based). 65% of past graduating class borrowed through all loan programs. *Average indebtedness per student:* $14,071. ***Average need-based loan:*** Freshmen: $2168; Undergraduates: $2898. ***Parent loans:*** $395,911 (90% need-based, 10% non-need-based). ***Programs:*** FFEL (Subsidized and Unsubsidized Stafford, PLUS), Perkins.

WORK-STUDY ***Federal work-study:*** Total amount: $43,031; 41 jobs averaging $1050.

APPLYING FOR FINANCIAL AID ***Required financial aid forms:*** FAFSA, institution's own form. ***Financial aid deadline (priority):*** 7/1. ***Notification date:*** Continuous beginning 4/1. Students must reply within 4 weeks of notification.

CONTACT Mrs. Nancy C. Goodman, Director of Financial Aid, Gallaudet University, 800 Florida Avenue, NE, Washington, DC 20002-3695, 202-651-5290 or toll-free 800-995-0550 (out-of-state). *Fax:* 202-651-5740.

GANNON UNIVERSITY

Erie, PA

Tuition & fees: $19,996 **Average undergraduate aid package: $16,261**

ABOUT THE INSTITUTION Independent Roman Catholic, coed. Awards: bachelor's, master's, and doctoral degrees and post-bachelor's and post-master's certificates (associate). 65 undergraduate majors. Total enrollment: 3,815. Undergraduates: 2,675. Freshmen: 615. Federal methodology is used as a basis for awarding need-based institutional aid.

UNDERGRADUATE EXPENSES for 2006–07 ***Application fee:*** $25. ***Comprehensive fee:*** $27,876 includes full-time tuition ($19,500), mandatory fees ($496), and room and board ($7880). ***College room only:*** $4310. Full-time tuition and fees vary according to class time and program. Room and board charges vary according to board plan and housing facility. ***Part-time tuition:*** $605 per credit hour. ***Part-time fees:*** $16 per credit hour. Part-time tuition and fees vary according to class time and program. ***Payment plans:*** Installment, deferred payment.

FRESHMAN FINANCIAL AID (Fall 2006, est.) 573 applied for aid; of those 87% were deemed to have need. 100% of freshmen with need received aid; of those 35% had need fully met. ***Average percent of need met:*** 81% (excluding resources awarded to replace EFC). ***Average financial aid package:*** $16,413 (excluding resources awarded to replace EFC). 15% of all full-time freshmen had no need and received non-need-based gift aid.

UNDERGRADUATE FINANCIAL AID (Fall 2006, est.) 2,093 applied for aid; of those 88% were deemed to have need. 99% of undergraduates with need received aid; of those 39% had need fully met. ***Average percent of need met:*** 80% (excluding resources awarded to replace EFC). ***Average financial aid package:*** $16,261 (excluding resources awarded to replace EFC). 15% of all full-time undergraduates had no need and received non-need-based gift aid.

GIFT AID (NEED-BASED) ***Total amount:*** $21,843,909 (11% federal, 21% state, 65% institutional, 3% external sources). ***Receiving aid:*** Freshmen: 81% (490); All full-time undergraduates: 81% (1,820). ***Average award:*** Freshmen: $13,074; Undergraduates: $12,339. ***Scholarships, grants, and awards:*** Federal Pell, FSEOG, state, private, college/university gift aid from institutional funds, Federal Nursing.

GIFT AID (NON-NEED-BASED) ***Total amount:*** $2,192,694 (1% state, 95% institutional, 4% external sources). ***Receiving aid:*** Freshmen: 10% (60); Undergraduates: 15% (331). ***Average award:*** Freshmen: $7271; Undergraduates: $6488. ***Scholarships, grants, and awards by category:*** *Academic Interests/Achievement:* 1,174 awards ($6,590,531 total): biological sciences, business, education, engineering/technologies, English, foreign languages, general academic interests/achievements, humanities, international studies, mathematics, premedicine, religion/biblical studies, social sciences. *Creative Arts/Performance:* 69 awards ($120,000 total): music, performing arts, theater/drama. *Special Achievements/Activities:* 1,510 awards ($2,195,409 total): community service, leadership. *Special Characteristics:* 592 awards ($924,187 total): adult students, ethnic background, international students, members of minority groups, religious affiliation. ***Tuition waivers:*** Full or partial for employees or children of employees, senior citizens. ***ROTC:*** Army.

LOANS ***Student loans:*** $9,502,247 (67% need-based, 33% non-need-based). 83% of past graduating class borrowed through all loan programs. *Average indebtedness per student:* $20,423. ***Average need-based loan:*** Freshmen: $2575; Undergraduates: $3971. ***Parent loans:*** $3,361,863 (100% non-need-based). ***Programs:*** FFEL (Subsidized and Unsubsidized Stafford, PLUS), Perkins, Federal Nursing.

WORK-STUDY ***Federal work-study:*** Total amount: $522,478; 545 jobs averaging $1583. ***State or other work-study/employment:*** Total amount: $380,953 (100% non-need-based). 189 part-time jobs averaging $1166.

ATHLETIC AWARDS Total amount: $2,629,086 (64% need-based, 36% non-need-based).

APPLYING FOR FINANCIAL AID ***Required financial aid forms:*** FAFSA, institution's own form. ***Financial aid deadline (priority):*** 3/15. ***Notification date:*** Continuous beginning 11/1. Students must reply within 4 weeks of notification.

CONTACT Ms. Sharon Krahe, Director of Financial Aid, Gannon University, 109 University Square, Erie, PA 16541, 814-871-7670 or toll-free 800-GANNONU. *Fax:* 814-871-5826. *E-mail:* krahe001@gannon.edu.

GARDNER-WEBB UNIVERSITY

Boiling Springs, NC

Tuition & fees: $17,590 **Average undergraduate aid package: $14,100**

ABOUT THE INSTITUTION Independent Baptist, coed. Awards: associate, bachelor's, master's, doctoral, and first professional degrees. 53 undergraduate majors. Total enrollment: 3,840. Undergraduates: 2,659. Freshmen: 405. Both federal and institutional methodology are used as a basis for awarding need-based institutional aid.

UNDERGRADUATE EXPENSES for 2006–07 ***Application fee:*** $40. ***Comprehensive fee:*** $23,330 includes full-time tuition ($17,040), mandatory fees ($550), and room and board ($5740). ***College room only:*** $2950. Room and board charges vary according to board plan and housing facility. ***Part-time tuition:*** $305 per credit hour. Part-time tuition and fees vary according to course load. ***Payment plan:*** Installment.

FRESHMAN FINANCIAL AID (Fall 2006, est.) 338 applied for aid; of those 87% were deemed to have need. 100% of freshmen with need received aid; of those 25% had need fully met. ***Average percent of need met:*** 72% (excluding resources awarded to replace EFC). ***Average financial aid package:*** $14,568 (excluding resources awarded to replace EFC).

UNDERGRADUATE FINANCIAL AID (Fall 2006, est.) 1,103 applied for aid; of those 89% were deemed to have need. 100% of undergraduates with need received aid; of those 24% had need fully met. ***Average percent of need met:*** 68% (excluding resources awarded to replace EFC). ***Average financial aid package:*** $14,100 (excluding resources awarded to replace EFC).

GIFT AID (NEED-BASED) ***Total amount:*** $7,854,287 (22% federal, 41% state, 31% institutional, 6% external sources). ***Receiving aid:*** Freshmen: 220; All full-time undergraduates: 737. ***Average award:*** Freshmen: $6031; Undergraduates: $5436. ***Scholarships, grants, and awards:*** Federal Pell, FSEOG, state, private, college/university gift aid from institutional funds.

GIFT AID (NON-NEED-BASED) ***Total amount:*** $1,629,428 (18% state, 77% institutional, 5% external sources). ***Receiving aid:*** Freshmen: 175; Undergraduates: 609. ***Average award:*** Freshmen: $4798; Undergraduates: $4843. ***Scholarships, grants, and awards by category:*** *Academic Interests/Achievement:* biological sciences, business, communication, computer science, education, English, foreign languages, general academic interests/achievements, health fields, humanities, mathematics, physical sciences, premedicine, religion/biblical studies, social sciences. *Creative Arts/Performance:* music, theater/drama. *Special Achievements/Activities:* cheerleading/drum major, religious involvement. *Special Characteristics:* children of faculty/staff, handicapped students, local/state students, members of minority groups, out-of-state students, previous college experience, relatives of clergy. ***Tuition waivers:*** Full or partial for employees or children of employees, senior citizens. ***ROTC:*** Army.

LOANS ***Student loans:*** $5,922,125 (94% need-based, 6% non-need-based). ***Average need-based loan:*** Freshmen: $3151; Undergraduates: $3916. ***Parent loans:*** $2,220,403 (84% need-based, 16% non-need-based). ***Programs:*** FFEL (Subsidized and Unsubsidized Stafford, PLUS), Perkins, Federal Nursing, state, college/university, alternative loans.

WORK-STUDY ***Federal work-study:*** Total amount: $290,636; jobs available. ***State or other work-study/employment:*** Total amount: $313,457 (75% need-based, 25% non-need-based). Part-time jobs available.

ATHLETIC AWARDS Total amount: $4,082,497 (50% need-based, 50% non-need-based).

APPLYING FOR FINANCIAL AID ***Required financial aid forms:*** FAFSA, state aid form. ***Financial aid deadline (priority):*** 3/15. ***Notification date:*** Continuous beginning 3/1. Students must reply within 4 weeks of notification.

CONTACT Debra Hintz, Assistant Vice President of Financial Planning, Gardner-Webb University, PO Box 955, Boiling Springs, NC 28017, 704-406-4243 or toll-free 800-253-6472. *Fax:* 704-406-4102. *E-mail:* bkirkland@gardner-webb.edu.

GENEVA COLLEGE

Beaver Falls, PA

Tuition & fees: $19,430 **Average undergraduate aid package: $15,111**

ABOUT THE INSTITUTION Independent religious, coed. Awards: associate, bachelor's, and master's degrees. 38 undergraduate majors. Total enrollment: 1,952. Undergraduates: 1,659. Freshmen: 296. Both federal and institutional methodology are used as a basis for awarding need-based institutional aid.

UNDERGRADUATE EXPENSES for 2007–08 ***Application fee:*** $40. ***Comprehensive fee:*** $26,630 includes full-time tuition ($19,430) and room and board ($7200). ***Part-time tuition:*** $650 per credit.

FRESHMAN FINANCIAL AID (Fall 2006, est.) 264 applied for aid; of those 89% were deemed to have need. 100% of freshmen with need received aid; of those 23% had need fully met. ***Average percent of need met:*** 83% (excluding resources awarded to replace EFC). ***Average financial aid package:*** $15,277 (excluding resources awarded to replace EFC). 15% of all full-time freshmen had no need and received non-need-based gift aid.

UNDERGRADUATE FINANCIAL AID (Fall 2006, est.) 1,222 applied for aid; of those 91% were deemed to have need. 99% of undergraduates with need received aid; of those 25% had need fully met. ***Average percent of need met:*** 81% (excluding resources awarded to replace EFC). ***Average financial aid***

package: $15,111 (excluding resources awarded to replace EFC). 14% of all full-time undergraduates had no need and received non-need-based gift aid.

GIFT AID (NEED-BASED) ***Total amount:*** $11,467,046 (13% federal, 22% state, 61% institutional, 4% external sources). ***Receiving aid:*** Freshmen: 83% (234); All full-time undergraduates: 79% (1,091). ***Average award:*** Freshmen: $11,677; Undergraduates: $11,031. ***Scholarships, grants, and awards:*** Federal Pell, FSEOG, state, private, college/university gift aid from institutional funds.

GIFT AID (NON-NEED-BASED) ***Total amount:*** $1,367,831 (5% state, 88% institutional, 7% external sources). ***Receiving aid:*** Freshmen: 10% (29); Undergraduates: 9% (123). ***Average award:*** Freshmen: $9109; Undergraduates: $8823. ***Scholarships, grants, and awards by category:*** *Academic Interests/Achievement:* engineering/technologies, general academic interests/achievements, religion/biblical studies. *Creative Arts/Performance:* music. *Special Characteristics:* children of faculty/staff, religious affiliation. ***ROTC:*** Army cooperative.

LOANS ***Student loans:*** $8,055,108 (69% need-based, 31% non-need-based). 96% of past graduating class borrowed through all loan programs. *Average indebtedness per student:* $26,034. ***Average need-based loan:*** Freshmen: $3356; Undergraduates: $3988. ***Parent loans:*** $1,646,497 (31% need-based, 69% non-need-based). ***Programs:*** FFEL (Subsidized and Unsubsidized Stafford, PLUS), Perkins.

WORK-STUDY ***Federal work-study:*** Total amount: $226,213; jobs available (averaging $2000).

ATHLETIC AWARDS Total amount: $598,343 (77% need-based, 23% non-need-based).

APPLYING FOR FINANCIAL AID ***Required financial aid form:*** FAFSA. ***Financial aid deadline (priority):*** 3/15. ***Notification date:*** Continuous. Students must reply within 4 weeks of notification.

CONTACT Mr. Steve Bell, Director of Financial Aid, Geneva College, 3200 College Avenue, Beaver Falls, PA 15010-3599, 800-847-8255. *Fax:* 724-847-6776. *E-mail:* financialaid@geneva.edu.

GEORGE FOX UNIVERSITY

Newberg, OR

Tuition & fees: $23,790 **Average undergraduate aid package: $16,709**

ABOUT THE INSTITUTION Independent Friends, coed. Awards: bachelor's, master's, doctoral, and first professional degrees and post-bachelor's certificates. 62 undergraduate majors. Total enrollment: 3,252. Undergraduates: 1,864. Freshmen: 416. Both federal and institutional methodology are used as a basis for awarding need-based institutional aid.

UNDERGRADUATE EXPENSES for 2007–08 ***Application fee:*** $40. ***Comprehensive fee:*** $31,390 includes full-time tuition ($23,470), mandatory fees ($320), and room and board ($7600). ***College room only:*** $4280. ***Part-time tuition:*** $730 per hour.

FRESHMAN FINANCIAL AID (Fall 2006, est.) 406 applied for aid; of those 87% were deemed to have need. 100% of freshmen with need received aid; of those 16% had need fully met. ***Average percent of need met:*** 70% (excluding resources awarded to replace EFC). ***Average financial aid package:*** $16,623 (excluding resources awarded to replace EFC). 17% of all full-time freshmen had no need and received non-need-based gift aid.

UNDERGRADUATE FINANCIAL AID (Fall 2006, est.) 1,555 applied for aid; of those 83% were deemed to have need. 98% of undergraduates with need received aid; of those 20% had need fully met. ***Average percent of need met:*** 63% (excluding resources awarded to replace EFC). ***Average financial aid package:*** $16,709 (excluding resources awarded to replace EFC). 16% of all full-time undergraduates had no need and received non-need-based gift aid.

GIFT AID (NEED-BASED) ***Total amount:*** $14,318,377 (6% federal, 7% state, 82% institutional, 5% external sources). ***Receiving aid:*** Freshmen: 79% (326); All full-time undergraduates: 69% (1,115). ***Average award:*** Freshmen: $13,512; Undergraduates: $12,755. ***Scholarships, grants, and awards:*** Federal Pell, FSEOG, state, private, college/university gift aid from institutional funds.

GIFT AID (NON-NEED-BASED) ***Total amount:*** $1,801,327 (1% federal, 82% institutional, 17% external sources). ***Receiving aid:*** Freshmen: 31% (129); Undergraduates: 19% (316). ***Average award:*** Freshmen: $5547; Undergraduates: $5273. ***Scholarships, grants, and awards by category:*** *Academic Interests/Achievement:* 166 awards ($189,000 total): biological sciences, education, general academic interests/achievements, mathematics, physical sciences, religion/biblical studies. *Creative Arts/Performance:* 101 awards ($140,780 total): art/fine arts, debating, music, theater/drama. *Special Achievements/Activities:* 278 awards ($423,926 total): leadership, religious involvement. *Special Characteristics:* 484 awards ($1,984,148 total): children and siblings of alumni, children of faculty/staff, ethnic background, international students, members of minority groups, out-of-state students, relatives of clergy, religious affiliation. ***ROTC:*** Air Force cooperative.

LOANS ***Student loans:*** $4,331,983 (53% need-based, 47% non-need-based). 78% of past graduating class borrowed through all loan programs. *Average indebtedness per student:* $17,903. ***Average need-based loan:*** Freshmen: $2725; Undergraduates: $3941. ***Parent loans:*** $20,477,330 (91% need-based, 9% non-need-based). ***Programs:*** Federal Direct (Subsidized and Unsubsidized Stafford, PLUS), FFEL (Subsidized and Unsubsidized Stafford, PLUS), Perkins, Alaska Loans, alternative loans.

WORK-STUDY ***Federal work-study:*** Total amount: $310,586; 640 jobs averaging $2089. ***State or other work-study/employment:*** Total amount: $2,002,131 (100% need-based). Part-time jobs available.

APPLYING FOR FINANCIAL AID ***Required financial aid forms:*** FAFSA, state aid form. ***Financial aid deadline (priority):*** 2/1. ***Notification date:*** Continuous beginning 3/1. Students must reply by 5/1 or within 4 weeks of notification.

CONTACT James Oshiro, Associate Director of Financial Services, George Fox University, 414 North Meridian Street, Newberg, OR 97132-2697, 503-554-2290 or toll-free 800-765-4369. *Fax:* 503-554-3880. *E-mail:* sfs@georgefox.edu.

GEORGE MASON UNIVERSITY

Fairfax, VA

Tuition & fees (VA res): $6408 **Average undergraduate aid package: $8341**

ABOUT THE INSTITUTION State-supported, coed. Awards: bachelor's, master's, doctoral, and first professional degrees and post-bachelor's certificates. 47 undergraduate majors. Total enrollment: 29,889. Undergraduates: 18,221. Freshmen: 2,458. Federal methodology is used as a basis for awarding need-based institutional aid.

UNDERGRADUATE EXPENSES for 2006–07 ***Application fee:*** $70. ***Tuition, state resident:*** full-time $4752; part-time $198 per credit. ***Tuition, nonresident:*** full-time $16,896; part-time $704 per credit. ***Required fees:*** full-time $1656; $69 per credit. Full-time tuition and fees vary according to course load. Part-time tuition and fees vary according to course load. ***College room and board:*** $6750; ***Room only:*** $3850. Room and board charges vary according to board plan and housing facility. ***Payment plans:*** Installment, deferred payment.

FRESHMAN FINANCIAL AID (Fall 2006, est.) 1518 applied for aid; of those 59% were deemed to have need. 97% of freshmen with need received aid; of those 14% had need fully met. ***Average percent of need met:*** 67% (excluding resources awarded to replace EFC). ***Average financial aid package:*** $8397 (excluding resources awarded to replace EFC). 3% of all full-time freshmen had no need and received non-need-based gift aid.

UNDERGRADUATE FINANCIAL AID (Fall 2006, est.) 7,333 applied for aid; of those 71% were deemed to have need. 97% of undergraduates with need received aid; of those 16% had need fully met. ***Average percent of need met:*** 69% (excluding resources awarded to replace EFC). ***Average financial aid package:*** $8341 (excluding resources awarded to replace EFC). 2% of all full-time undergraduates had no need and received non-need-based gift aid.

GIFT AID (NEED-BASED) ***Total amount:*** $19,664,718 (46% federal, 46% state, 8% institutional). ***Receiving aid:*** Freshmen: 27% (646); All full-time undergraduates: 26% (3,582). ***Average award:*** Freshmen: $5341; Undergraduates: $5078. ***Scholarships, grants, and awards:*** Federal Pell, FSEOG, state, private, college/university gift aid from institutional funds.

GIFT AID (NON-NEED-BASED) ***Total amount:*** $4,561,138 (62% institutional, 38% external sources). ***Receiving aid:*** Freshmen: 11% (258); Undergraduates: 5% (762). ***Average award:*** Freshmen: $6566; Undergraduates: $4627. ***Scholarships, grants, and awards by category:*** *Academic Interests/Achievement:* 722 awards ($2,814,772 total): general academic interests/achievements. *Creative Arts/Performance:* general creative arts/performance. *Special Characteristics:* general special characteristics. ***Tuition waivers:*** Full or partial for employees or children of employees, senior citizens. ***ROTC:*** Army, Naval cooperative, Air Force cooperative.

LOANS ***Student loans:*** $39,990,282 (61% need-based, 39% non-need-based). 48% of past graduating class borrowed through all loan programs. *Average indebtedness per student:* $15,791. ***Average need-based loan:*** Freshmen: $2724; Undergraduates: $3871. ***Parent loans:*** $7,642,216 (27% need-based, 73% non-need-based). ***Programs:*** FFEL (Subsidized and Unsubsidized Stafford, PLUS), Perkins, Federal Nursing.

WORK-STUDY ***Federal work-study:*** Total amount: $1,399,523; 675 jobs averaging $2073.

ATHLETIC AWARDS Total amount: $2,686,865 (100% non-need-based).

APPLYING FOR FINANCIAL AID ***Required financial aid form:*** FAFSA. ***Financial aid deadline (priority):*** 3/1. ***Notification date:*** Continuous beginning 4/1. Students must reply within 3 weeks of notification.

CONTACT Office of Student Financial Aid, George Mason University, Mail Stop 3B5, Fairfax, VA 22030-4444, 703-993-2353. *Fax:* 703-993-2350. *E-mail:* finaid@gmu.edu.

GEORGE MEANY CENTER FOR LABOR STUDIES-THE NATIONAL LABOR COLLEGE

Silver Spring, MD

CONTACT Financial Aid Office, George Meany Center for Labor Studies-The National Labor College, 10000 New Hampshire Avenue, Silver Spring, MD 20903, 301-431-6400 or toll-free 800-GMC-4CDP.

GEORGETOWN COLLEGE

Georgetown, KY

Tuition & fees: $22,360 **Average undergraduate aid package: $19,510**

ABOUT THE INSTITUTION Independent religious, coed. Awards: bachelor's and master's degrees and post-master's certificates. 32 undergraduate majors. Total enrollment: 1,910. Undergraduates: 1,407. Freshmen: 364. Federal methodology is used as a basis for awarding need-based institutional aid.

UNDERGRADUATE EXPENSES for 2007–08 ***Application fee:*** $30. ***Comprehensive fee:*** $28,740 includes full-time tuition ($22,360) and room and board ($6380). ***College room only:*** $3080. ***Part-time tuition:*** $930 per hour.

FRESHMAN FINANCIAL AID (Fall 2006, est.) 314 applied for aid; of those 81% were deemed to have need. 100% of freshmen with need received aid; of those 48% had need fully met. ***Average percent of need met:*** 91% (excluding resources awarded to replace EFC). ***Average financial aid package:*** $19,525 (excluding resources awarded to replace EFC). 30% of all full-time freshmen had no need and received non-need-based gift aid.

UNDERGRADUATE FINANCIAL AID (Fall 2006, est.) 1,065 applied for aid; of those 84% were deemed to have need. 100% of undergraduates with need received aid; of those 50% had need fully met. ***Average percent of need met:*** 90% (excluding resources awarded to replace EFC). ***Average financial aid package:*** $19,510 (excluding resources awarded to replace EFC). 33% of all full-time undergraduates had no need and received non-need-based gift aid.

GIFT AID (NEED-BASED) ***Total amount:*** $10,959,596 (8% federal, 18% state, 71% institutional, 3% external sources). ***Receiving aid:*** Freshmen: 70% (254); All full-time undergraduates: 68% (893). ***Average award:*** Freshmen: $17,164; Undergraduates: $16,170. ***Scholarships, grants, and awards:*** Federal Pell, FSEOG, state, private, college/university gift aid from institutional funds.

GIFT AID (NON-NEED-BASED) ***Total amount:*** $5,581,086 (32% state, 66% institutional, 2% external sources). ***Receiving aid:*** Freshmen: 38% (139); Undergraduates: 30% (401). ***Average award:*** Freshmen: $8951; Undergraduates: $8866. ***Scholarships, grants, and awards by category:*** *Academic Interests/Achievement:* 789 awards ($6,064,415 total): general academic interests/achievements. *Creative Arts/Performance:* 138 awards ($188,168 total): art/fine arts, music, performing arts, theater/drama. *Special Achievements/Activities:* 280 awards ($469,185 total): junior miss, leadership, religious involvement. *Special Characteristics:* 301 awards ($460,967 total): children of faculty/staff, local/state students, relatives of clergy, religious affiliation. ***ROTC:*** Army cooperative, Air Force cooperative.

LOANS ***Student loans:*** $5,064,505 (48% need-based, 52% non-need-based). 59% of past graduating class borrowed through all loan programs. *Average indebtedness per student:* $17,326. ***Average need-based loan:*** Freshmen: $3188; Undergraduates: $4451. ***Parent loans:*** $1,776,160 (100% non-need-based). ***Programs:*** FFEL (Subsidized and Unsubsidized Stafford, PLUS), Perkins, college/university.

WORK-STUDY ***Federal work-study:*** Total amount: $558,412; 503 jobs averaging $1110. ***State or other work-study/employment:*** Part-time jobs available.

ATHLETIC AWARDS Total amount: $1,336,395 (37% need-based, 63% non-need-based).

APPLYING FOR FINANCIAL AID ***Required financial aid forms:*** FAFSA, institution's own form. ***Financial aid deadline (priority):*** 2/15. ***Notification date:*** Continuous beginning 3/1. Students must reply by 5/1.

CONTACT Rhyan Conyers, Director of Financial Planning, Georgetown College, 400 East College Street, Georgetown, KY 40324-1696, 502-863-8027 or toll-free 800-788-9985. *E-mail:* financialaid@georgetowncollege.edu.

GEORGETOWN UNIVERSITY

Washington, DC

Tuition & fees: $35,568 **Average undergraduate aid package: $27,317**

ABOUT THE INSTITUTION Independent Roman Catholic (Jesuit), coed. Awards: bachelor's, master's, doctoral, and first professional degrees. 46 undergraduate majors. Total enrollment: 14,148. Undergraduates: 6,853. Freshmen: 1,588. Both federal and institutional methodology are used as a basis for awarding need-based institutional aid.

UNDERGRADUATE EXPENSES for 2007–08 ***Application fee:*** $65. ***Comprehensive fee:*** $47,714 includes full-time tuition ($35,568) and room and board ($12,146). ***College room only:*** $8092. ***Part-time tuition:*** $1482 per credit hour.

FRESHMAN FINANCIAL AID (Fall 2006, est.) 803 applied for aid; of those 75% were deemed to have need. 99% of freshmen with need received aid; of those 100% had need fully met. ***Average percent of need met:*** 100% (excluding resources awarded to replace EFC). ***Average financial aid package:*** $27,330 (excluding resources awarded to replace EFC).

UNDERGRADUATE FINANCIAL AID (Fall 2006, est.) 3,006 applied for aid; of those 87% were deemed to have need. 98% of undergraduates with need received aid; of those 100% had need fully met. ***Average percent of need met:*** 100% (excluding resources awarded to replace EFC). ***Average financial aid package:*** $27,317 (excluding resources awarded to replace EFC). 1% of all full-time undergraduates had no need and received non-need-based gift aid.

GIFT AID (NEED-BASED) ***Total amount:*** $58,580,000 (6% federal, 89% institutional, 5% external sources). ***Receiving aid:*** Freshmen: 38% (583); All full-time undergraduates: 36% (2,342). ***Average award:*** Freshmen: $22,822; Undergraduates: $21,041. ***Scholarships, grants, and awards:*** Federal Pell, FSEOG, state, private, college/university gift aid from institutional funds.

GIFT AID (NON-NEED-BASED) ***Total amount:*** $2,505,000 (52% federal, 4% institutional, 44% external sources). ***Receiving aid:*** Freshmen: 7; Undergraduates: 17. ***Average award:*** Undergraduates: $25,743. ***Scholarships, grants, and awards by category:*** *Special Characteristics:* children of faculty/staff. ***ROTC:*** Army, Naval cooperative, Air Force cooperative.

LOANS ***Student loans:*** $20,500,000 (50% need-based, 50% non-need-based). 46% of past graduating class borrowed through all loan programs. *Average indebtedness per student:* $24,816. ***Average need-based loan:*** Freshmen: $1702; Undergraduates: $3600. ***Parent loans:*** $17,296,588 (100% non-need-based). ***Programs:*** FFEL (Subsidized and Unsubsidized Stafford, PLUS), Perkins, Federal Nursing.

WORK-STUDY ***Federal work-study:*** Total amount: $6,000,000; 1,828 jobs averaging $3000.

ATHLETIC AWARDS Total amount: $5,250,000 (26% need-based, 74% non-need-based).

APPLYING FOR FINANCIAL AID ***Required financial aid forms:*** FAFSA, CSS Financial Aid PROFILE, noncustodial (divorced/separated) parent's statement, business/farm supplement. ***Financial aid deadline:*** 2/1. ***Notification date:*** 4/1. Students must reply by 5/1 or within 2 weeks of notification.

CONTACT Ms. Patricia A. McWade, Dean of Student Financial Services, Georgetown University, 37th and O Street, NW, Box 1252, Washington, DC 20057, 202-687-4547. *Fax:* 202-687-6542. *E-mail:* mcwadep@georgetown.edu.

THE GEORGE WASHINGTON UNIVERSITY

Washington, DC

Tuition & fees: $39,240 **Average undergraduate aid package: $33,196**

ABOUT THE INSTITUTION Independent, coed. Awards: associate, bachelor's, master's, doctoral, and first professional degrees and post-bachelor's and post-master's certificates. 82 undergraduate majors. Total enrollment: 24,531. Undergraduates: 10,813. Freshmen: 2,454. Both federal and institutional methodology are used as a basis for awarding need-based institutional aid.

UNDERGRADUATE EXPENSES for 2007–08 ***Application fee:*** $70. ***Comprehensive fee:*** $50,760 includes full-time tuition ($39,210), mandatory fees ($30), and room and board ($11,520). ***College room only:*** $8020. ***Part-time tuition:*** $1090 per credit hour.

FRESHMAN FINANCIAL AID (Fall 2005) 1313 applied for aid; of those 77% were deemed to have need. 96% of freshmen with need received aid; of those 65% had need fully met. ***Average percent of need met:*** 91% (excluding resources awarded to replace EFC). ***Average financial aid package:*** $34,139 (excluding resources awarded to replace EFC). 18% of all full-time freshmen had no need and received non-need-based gift aid.

UNDERGRADUATE FINANCIAL AID (Fall 2005) 4,932 applied for aid; of those 86% were deemed to have need. 98% of undergraduates with need received aid; of those 65% had need fully met. ***Average percent of need met:*** 91% (excluding resources awarded to replace EFC). ***Average financial aid package:*** $33,196 (excluding resources awarded to replace EFC). 24% of all full-time undergraduates had no need and received non-need-based gift aid.

GIFT AID (NEED-BASED) ***Total amount:*** $90,306,269 (5% federal, 92% institutional, 3% external sources). ***Receiving aid:*** Freshmen: 39% (939); All full-time undergraduates: 41% (3,915). ***Average award:*** Freshmen: $21,467; Undergraduates: $19,828. ***Scholarships, grants, and awards:*** Federal Pell, FSEOG, state, college/university gift aid from institutional funds.

GIFT AID (NON-NEED-BASED) ***Total amount:*** $20,147,853 (100% institutional). ***Receiving aid:*** Freshmen: 13% (302); Undergraduates: 12% (1,206). ***Average award:*** Freshmen: $22,544; Undergraduates: $19,290. ***Scholarships, grants, and awards by category:*** *Academic Interests/Achievement:* engineering/technologies, general academic interests/achievements, mathematics. *Creative Arts/Performance:* debating, music, performing arts, theater/drama. ***ROTC:*** Army cooperative, Naval, Air Force cooperative.

LOANS ***Student loans:*** $35,412,046 (100% need-based). 50% of past graduating class borrowed through all loan programs. *Average indebtedness per student:* $29,304. ***Average need-based loan:*** Freshmen: $5078; Undergraduates: $6806. ***Parent loans:*** $28,255,063 (99% need-based, 1% non-need-based). ***Programs:*** FFEL (Subsidized and Unsubsidized Stafford, PLUS), Perkins.

WORK-STUDY ***Federal work-study:*** Total amount: $3,910,264; jobs available. ***State or other work-study/employment:*** Part-time jobs available.

ATHLETIC AWARDS Total amount: $5,046,090 (12% need-based, 88% non-need-based).

APPLYING FOR FINANCIAL AID ***Required financial aid forms:*** FAFSA, CSS Financial Aid PROFILE. ***Financial aid deadline:*** 2/1 (priority: 2/1). ***Notification date:*** Continuous beginning 3/24. Students must reply by 5/1.

CONTACT Dan Small, Director of Student Financial Assistance, The George Washington University, 2121 Eye Street, NW, Rice Hall, 3rd Floor, Washington, DC 20052, 202-994-6620 or toll-free 800-447-3765. *Fax:* 202-994-0906. *E-mail:* finaid@gwu.edu.

GEORGIA COLLEGE & STATE UNIVERSITY

Milledgeville, GA

Tuition & fees (GA res): $4424 Average undergraduate aid package: $5338

ABOUT THE INSTITUTION State-supported, coed. Awards: bachelor's and master's degrees and post-master's certificates. 34 undergraduate majors. Total enrollment: 6,041. Undergraduates: 5,141. Freshmen: 1,066. Federal methodology is used as a basis for awarding need-based institutional aid.

UNDERGRADUATE EXPENSES for 2006–07 ***Application fee:*** $25. ***Tuition, state resident:*** full-time $3642. ***Tuition, nonresident:*** full-time $14,570. ***College room and board:*** $7116; ***Room only:*** $3800. Room and board charges vary according to board plan and housing facility. ***Payment plan:*** Guaranteed tuition.

FRESHMAN FINANCIAL AID (Fall 2005) 994 applied for aid; of those 36% were deemed to have need. 99% of freshmen with need received aid; of those 3% had need fully met. ***Average percent of need met:*** 31% (excluding resources awarded to replace EFC). ***Average financial aid package:*** $5253 (excluding resources awarded to replace EFC). 5% of all full-time freshmen had no need and received non-need-based gift aid.

UNDERGRADUATE FINANCIAL AID (Fall 2005) 3,949 applied for aid; of those 41% were deemed to have need. 97% of undergraduates with need received aid; of those 1% had need fully met. ***Average percent of need met:*** 41% (excluding resources awarded to replace EFC). ***Average financial aid package:*** $5338 (excluding resources awarded to replace EFC). 2% of all full-time undergraduates had no need and received non-need-based gift aid.

GIFT AID (NEED-BASED) ***Total amount:*** $2,376,245 (99% federal, 1% state). ***Receiving aid:*** Freshmen: 12% (121); All full-time undergraduates: 16% (699). ***Average award:*** Freshmen: $2898; Undergraduates: $2859. ***Scholarships, grants, and awards:*** Federal Pell, FSEOG, state, college/university gift aid from institutional funds.

GIFT AID (NON-NEED-BASED) ***Total amount:*** $11,543,839 (91% state, 5% institutional, 4% external sources). ***Receiving aid:*** Freshmen: 35% (356); Undergraduates: 36% (1,532). ***Average award:*** Freshmen: $1447; Undergraduates: $1439. ***Scholarships, grants, and awards by category:*** *Academic Interests/Achievement:* business, computer science, education, English, foreign languages, general academic interests/achievements, health fields, humanities, international studies, mathematics, physical sciences, social sciences. *Creative Arts/Performance:* applied art and design, art/fine arts, creative writing, debating, journalism/publications, music, performing arts, theater/drama. *Special Achievements/Activities:* community service, general special achievements/activities, leadership. *Special Characteristics:* children of faculty/staff, children with a deceased or disabled parent, handicapped students, international students, local/state students, members of minority groups, out-of-state students, religious affiliation. ***Tuition waivers:*** Full or partial for employees or children of employees, senior citizens. ***ROTC:*** Army cooperative.

LOANS ***Student loans:*** $10,994,036 (54% need-based, 46% non-need-based). 57% of past graduating class borrowed through all loan programs. *Average indebtedness per student:* $15,128. ***Average need-based loan:*** Freshmen: $2306; Undergraduates: $2291. ***Parent loans:*** $1,530,855 (100% non-need-based). ***Programs:*** Federal Direct (PLUS), FFEL (Subsidized and Unsubsidized Stafford, PLUS), Perkins, state, college/university.

WORK-STUDY ***Federal work-study:*** Total amount: $142,099; 155 jobs averaging $1211.

ATHLETIC AWARDS Total amount: $554,163 (100% non-need-based).

APPLYING FOR FINANCIAL AID ***Required financial aid form:*** FAFSA. ***Financial aid deadline:*** Continuous. ***Notification date:*** Continuous beginning 3/1. Students must reply within 2 weeks of notification.

CONTACT Mrs. Cathy Crawley, Associate Director of Financial Aid, Georgia College & State University, Campus Box 30, Milledgeville, GA 31061, 478-445-5149 or toll-free 800-342-0471 (in-state). *Fax:* 478-445-0729. *E-mail:* cathy.crawley@gcsu.edu.

GEORGIA INSTITUTE OF TECHNOLOGY

Atlanta, GA

Tuition & fees (GA res): $4926 Average undergraduate aid package: $9033

ABOUT THE INSTITUTION State-supported, coed. Awards: bachelor's, master's, and doctoral degrees. 34 undergraduate majors. Total enrollment: 17,936. Undergraduates: 12,361. Freshmen: 2,837. Federal methodology is used as a basis for awarding need-based institutional aid.

UNDERGRADUATE EXPENSES for 2006–07 ***Application fee:*** $50. ***Tuition, state resident:*** full-time $3892; part-time $163 per hour. ***Tuition, nonresident:*** full-time $19,238; part-time $803 per hour. ***Required fees:*** full-time $1034; $517 per term part-time. Full-time tuition and fees vary according to course load, reciprocity agreements, and student level. Part-time tuition and fees vary according to course load, reciprocity agreements, and student level. ***College room and board:*** $7094; ***Room only:*** $4192. Room and board charges vary according to board plan and housing facility. ***Payment plan:*** Guaranteed tuition.

FRESHMAN FINANCIAL AID (Fall 2006, est.) 2226 applied for aid; of those 41% were deemed to have need. 97% of freshmen with need received aid; of those 53% had need fully met. ***Average percent of need met:*** 51% (excluding resources awarded to replace EFC). ***Average financial aid package:*** $9901 (excluding resources awarded to replace EFC). 35% of all full-time freshmen had no need and received non-need-based gift aid.

UNDERGRADUATE FINANCIAL AID (Fall 2006, est.) 6,983 applied for aid; of those 53% were deemed to have need. 96% of undergraduates with need received aid; of those 47% had need fully met. ***Average percent of need met:*** 51% (excluding resources awarded to replace EFC). ***Average financial aid package:*** $9033 (excluding resources awarded to replace EFC). 17% of all full-time undergraduates had no need and received non-need-based gift aid.

GIFT AID (NEED-BASED) ***Total amount:*** $20,657,996 (29% federal, 33% state, 34% institutional, 4% external sources). ***Receiving aid:*** Freshmen: 18% (511); All full-time undergraduates: 18% (2,112). ***Average award:*** Freshmen: $5707; Undergraduates: $4860. ***Scholarships, grants, and awards:*** Federal Pell, FSEOG, state, private, college/university gift aid from institutional funds.

GIFT AID (NON-NEED-BASED) ***Total amount:*** $20,322,602 (1% federal, 82% state, 10% institutional, 7% external sources). ***Receiving aid:*** Freshmen: 23% (658); Undergraduates: 17% (1,908). ***Average award:*** Freshmen: $5429; Undergraduates: $5195. ***Scholarships, grants, and awards by category:*** *Academic Interests/Achievement:* 1,633 awards ($5,771,624 total): architecture, biological sciences, computer science, engineering/technologies, general academic interests/achievements, physical sciences. *Special Achievements/Activities:* 218 awards ($1,978,547 total): leadership. *Special Characteristics:* 329 awards ($784,501 total): children of faculty/staff, children of union members/company employees, ethnic background, general special characteristics, handicapped students, local/state students, members of minority groups, out-of-state students. ***ROTC:*** Army, Naval, Air Force.

LOANS ***Student loans:*** $25,874,600 (67% need-based, 33% non-need-based). 49% of past graduating class borrowed through all loan programs. *Average indebtedness per student:* $14,895. ***Average need-based loan:*** Freshmen: $3316; Undergraduates: $3847. ***Parent loans:*** $15,363,798 (52% need-based, 48% non-need-based). ***Programs:*** FFEL (Subsidized and Unsubsidized Stafford, PLUS), Perkins, college/university.

WORK-STUDY ***Federal work-study:*** Total amount: $357,008; 237 jobs averaging $2150.

ATHLETIC AWARDS Total amount: $4,676,697 (32% need-based, 68% non-need-based).

APPLYING FOR FINANCIAL AID ***Required financial aid forms:*** FAFSA, institution's own form. ***Financial aid deadline:*** 3/1 (priority: 3/1). ***Notification date:*** Continuous beginning 4/1. Students must reply by 5/1.

CONTACT Ms. Marie Mons, Director of Student Financial Planning and Services, Georgia Institute of Technology, 225 North Avenue, NW, Atlanta, GA 30332-0460, 404-894-4160. *Fax:* 404-894-7412. *E-mail:* marie.mons@finaid.gatech.edu.

GEORGIAN COURT UNIVERSITY

Lakewood, NJ

CONTACT Carol Straus, Director of Financial Aid, Georgian Court University, 900 Lakewood Avenue, Lakewood, NJ 08701-2697, 732-364-2200 Ext. 2258 or toll-free 800-458-8422. *Fax:* 732-987-2012. *E-mail:* financialaid@georgian.edu.

GEORGIA SOUTHERN UNIVERSITY

Statesboro, GA

Tuition & fees (GA res): $4082 Average undergraduate aid package: $6711

ABOUT THE INSTITUTION State-supported, coed. Awards: bachelor's, master's, and doctoral degrees and post-master's certificates. 79 undergraduate majors. Total enrollment: 16,425. Undergraduates: 14,483. Freshmen: 2,750. Federal methodology is used as a basis for awarding need-based institutional aid.

UNDERGRADUATE EXPENSES for 2007–08 ***Application fee:*** $30. ***Tuition, state resident:*** full-time $2958. ***Tuition, nonresident:*** full-time $11,830. ***College room and board:*** $6860; ***Room only:*** $4340.

FRESHMAN FINANCIAL AID (Fall 2005) 2898 applied for aid; of those 49% were deemed to have need. 99% of freshmen with need received aid; of those 23% had need fully met. ***Average percent of need met:*** 67% (excluding resources awarded to replace EFC). ***Average financial aid package:*** $6377 (excluding resources awarded to replace EFC). 3% of all full-time freshmen had no need and received non-need-based gift aid.

UNDERGRADUATE FINANCIAL AID (Fall 2005) 11,221 applied for aid; of those 58% were deemed to have need. 97% of undergraduates with need received aid; of those 17% had need fully met. ***Average percent of need met:*** 62% (excluding resources awarded to replace EFC). ***Average financial aid package:*** $6711 (excluding resources awarded to replace EFC). 2% of all full-time undergraduates had no need and received non-need-based gift aid.

GIFT AID (NEED-BASED) ***Total amount:*** $22,596,272 (49% federal, 47% state, 1% institutional, 3% external sources). ***Receiving aid:*** Freshmen: 43% (1,336); All full-time undergraduates: 39% (5,089). ***Average award:*** Freshmen: $5068; Undergraduates: $4455. ***Scholarships, grants, and awards:*** Federal Pell, FSEOG, state, private, college/university gift aid from institutional funds, Georgia HOPE Scholarships, Federal work study.

GIFT AID (NON-NEED-BASED) ***Total amount:*** $11,992,177 (93% state, 4% institutional, 3% external sources). ***Receiving aid:*** Freshmen: 6% (179); Undergraduates: 3% (427). ***Average award:*** Freshmen: $1595; Undergraduates: $1469. ***Scholarships, grants, and awards by category:*** *Academic Interests/Achievement:* 579 awards ($750,902 total): biological sciences, business, communication, education, engineering/technologies, English, foreign languages, general academic interests/achievements, health fields, humanities, international studies, mathematics, military science, social sciences. *Creative Arts/Performance:* 68 awards ($69,000 total): art/fine arts, cinema/film/broadcasting, general creative arts/performance, music, theater/drama. *Special Achievements/Activities:* 236 awards ($111,039 total): community service, junior miss, leadership, memberships. *Special Characteristics:* 18 awards ($60,021 total): children and siblings of alumni, children of public servants, first-generation college students, handicapped students, married students, members of minority groups. ***ROTC:*** Army.

LOANS ***Student loans:*** $37,837,466 (70% need-based, 30% non-need-based). 66% of past graduating class borrowed through all loan programs. *Average indebtedness per student:* $18,146. ***Average need-based loan:*** Freshmen: $2438; Undergraduates: $3905. ***Parent loans:*** $6,931,319 (51% need-based, 49% non-need-based). ***Programs:*** Federal Direct (Subsidized and Unsubsidized Stafford, PLUS), Perkins, Service-Cancelable State Direct Student Loans, external alternative loans.

WORK-STUDY ***Federal work-study:*** Total amount: $241,687; 182 jobs averaging $1328.

ATHLETIC AWARDS Total amount: $1,720,866 (52% need-based, 48% non-need-based).

APPLYING FOR FINANCIAL AID ***Required financial aid form:*** FAFSA. ***Financial aid deadline (priority):*** 4/20. ***Notification date:*** Continuous beginning 4/20.

CONTACT Ms. Elise Boyett, Associate Director of Financial Aid, Georgia Southern University, Box 8065, Statesboro, GA 30460-8065, 912-681-5413. *Fax:* 912-681-0573. *E-mail:* eboyett@georgiasouthern.edu.

GEORGIA SOUTHWESTERN STATE UNIVERSITY

Americus, GA

ABOUT THE INSTITUTION State-supported, coed. Awards: associate, bachelor's, and master's degrees and post-master's certificates. 64 undergraduate majors. Total enrollment: 2,457. Undergraduates: 2,222. Freshmen: 441.

GIFT AID (NEED-BASED) ***Scholarships, grants, and awards:*** Federal Pell, FSEOG, state, private, college/university gift aid from institutional funds.

GIFT AID (NON-NEED-BASED) ***Scholarships, grants, and awards by category:*** *Academic Interests/Achievement:* general academic interests/achievements. *Creative Arts/Performance:* art/fine arts, music. *Special Achievements/Activities:* leadership.

LOANS ***Programs:*** FFEL (Subsidized and Unsubsidized Stafford, PLUS), Perkins, state, college/university.

WORK-STUDY ***Federal work-study:*** Total amount: $114,458; 82 jobs averaging $1396. ***State or other work-study/employment:*** Part-time jobs available.

APPLYING FOR FINANCIAL AID ***Required financial aid forms:*** FAFSA, institution's own form.

CONTACT Ms. Freida Jones, Director of Financial Aid, Georgia Southwestern State University, 800 Georgia Southwestern State University Drive, Americus, GA 31709-4693, 229-928-1378 or toll-free 800-338-0082. *Fax:* 229-931-2061.

GEORGIA STATE UNIVERSITY

Atlanta, GA

CONTACT Financial Aid Office, Georgia State University, 102 Sparks Hall, Atlanta, GA 30303, 404-651-2227.

GETTYSBURG COLLEGE

Gettysburg, PA

ABOUT THE INSTITUTION Independent religious, coed. Awards: bachelor's degrees. 83 undergraduate majors. Total enrollment: 2,689. Undergraduates: 2,689. Freshmen: 730.

GIFT AID (NEED-BASED) ***Scholarships, grants, and awards:*** Federal Pell, FSEOG, state, private, college/university gift aid from institutional funds.

GIFT AID (NON-NEED-BASED) ***Scholarships, grants, and awards by category:*** *Academic Interests/Achievement:* general academic interests/achievements. *Creative Arts/Performance:* music.

LOANS ***Programs:*** FFEL (Subsidized and Unsubsidized Stafford, PLUS), Perkins, college/university.

WORK-STUDY ***Federal work-study:*** Total amount: $509,230; 546 jobs averaging $933. ***State or other work-study/employment:*** Total amount: $644,862 (14% need-based, 86% non-need-based). 732 part-time jobs averaging $838.

APPLYING FOR FINANCIAL AID ***Required financial aid forms:*** FAFSA, CSS Financial Aid PROFILE, business/farm supplement, income tax form(s) and verification worksheet.

CONTACT Timothy A. Opgenorth, Director of Financial Aid, Gettysburg College, 300 North Washington Street, Box 438, Gettysburg, PA 17325, 717-337-6611 or toll-free 800-431-0803. *Fax:* 717-337-8555. *E-mail:* finaid@gettysburg.edu.

GLENVILLE STATE COLLEGE

Glenville, WV

Tuition & fees (WV res): $4042 **Average undergraduate aid package: $8791**

ABOUT THE INSTITUTION State-supported, coed. Awards: associate and bachelor's degrees. 31 undergraduate majors. Total enrollment: 1,381. Undergraduates: 1,381. Freshmen: 268. Federal methodology is used as a basis for awarding need-based institutional aid.

UNDERGRADUATE EXPENSES for 2006–07 ***Tuition, state resident:*** full-time $3882; part-time $161.75 per credit hour. ***Tuition, nonresident:*** full-time $9294; part-time $387.25 per credit hour. Full-time tuition and fees vary according to location and program. Part-time tuition and fees vary according to course load, location, and program. ***College room and board:*** $5370; ***Room only:*** $2600. Room and board charges vary according to housing facility. ***Payment plan:*** Installment.

FRESHMAN FINANCIAL AID (Fall 2006, est.) 250 applied for aid; of those 89% were deemed to have need. 99% of freshmen with need received aid; of those 17% had need fully met. ***Average percent of need met:*** 70% (excluding resources awarded to replace EFC). ***Average financial aid package:*** $7903 (excluding resources awarded to replace EFC). 7% of all full-time freshmen had no need and received non-need-based gift aid.

UNDERGRADUATE FINANCIAL AID (Fall 2006, est.) 975 applied for aid; of those 89% were deemed to have need. 99% of undergraduates with need received aid; of those 24% had need fully met. ***Average percent of need met:*** 76% (excluding resources awarded to replace EFC). ***Average financial aid package:*** $8791 (excluding resources awarded to replace EFC). 6% of all full-time undergraduates had no need and received non-need-based gift aid.

GIFT AID (NEED-BASED) ***Total amount:*** $3,176,435 (65% federal, 34% state, 1% institutional). ***Receiving aid:*** Freshmen: 62% (165); All full-time undergraduates: 59% (652). ***Average award:*** Freshmen: $4463; Undergraduates: $4644. ***Scholarships, grants, and awards:*** Federal Pell, FSEOG, state, private, college/university gift aid from institutional funds.

GIFT AID (NON-NEED-BASED) ***Total amount:*** $1,059,216 (54% state, 22% institutional, 24% external sources). ***Receiving aid:*** Freshmen: 52% (140); Undergraduates: 37% (406). ***Average award:*** Freshmen: $1722; Undergraduates: $1843. ***Scholarships, grants, and awards by category:*** *Academic Interests/Achievement:* 175 awards ($236,756 total): biological sciences, business, education, English, general academic interests/achievements, mathematics, social sciences. *Creative Arts/Performance:* 18 awards ($31,519 total): journalism/publications, music. *Special Characteristics:* 2 awards ($2000 total): first-generation college students, veterans' children. ***Tuition waivers:*** Full or partial for senior citizens.

LOANS ***Student loans:*** $3,762,246 (60% need-based, 40% non-need-based). 71% of past graduating class borrowed through all loan programs. *Average indebtedness per student:* $17,057. ***Average need-based loan:*** Freshmen: $2334; Undergraduates: $3386. ***Parent loans:*** $364,930 (100% non-need-based). ***Programs:*** Federal Direct (Subsidized and Unsubsidized Stafford, PLUS).

WORK-STUDY ***Federal work-study:*** Total amount: $137,056; 102 jobs averaging $1343. ***State or other work-study/employment:*** Total amount: $287,599 (100% non-need-based). 261 part-time jobs averaging $718.

ATHLETIC AWARDS Total amount: $372,520 (100% non-need-based).

APPLYING FOR FINANCIAL AID ***Required financial aid form:*** FAFSA. ***Financial aid deadline (priority):*** 2/1. ***Notification date:*** Continuous beginning 3/1. Students must reply within 3 weeks of notification.

CONTACT Ms. Karen Lay, Director of Financial Aid, Glenville State College, 200 High Street, Glenville, WV 26351-1200, 304-462-4103 Ext. 5 or toll-free 800-924-2010 (in-state). *Fax:* 304-462-4407. *E-mail:* karen.lay@glenville.edu.

GLOBE INSTITUTE OF TECHNOLOGY

New York, NY

CONTACT Office of Admissions, Globe Institute of Technology, 291 Broadway, 2nd Floor, New York, NY 10007, 212-349-4330 or toll-free 877-394-5623. *Fax:* 212-227-5920. *E-mail:* admission@globe.edu.

GODDARD COLLEGE

Plainfield, VT

Tuition & fees: $11,442 **Average undergraduate aid package: $6350**

ABOUT THE INSTITUTION Independent, coed. Awards: bachelor's and master's degrees. 5 undergraduate majors. Total enrollment: 560. Undergraduates: 165. Freshmen: 7. Federal methodology is used as a basis for awarding need-based institutional aid.

UNDERGRADUATE EXPENSES for 2006–07 ***Application fee:*** $40. ***Tuition:*** full-time $10,444. ***Payment plan:*** Installment.

FRESHMAN FINANCIAL AID (Fall 2006, est.) 14 applied for aid; of those 79% were deemed to have need. 82% of freshmen with need received aid. ***Average percent of need met:*** 28% (excluding resources awarded to replace EFC). ***Average financial aid package:*** $4672 (excluding resources awarded to replace EFC). 2% of all full-time freshmen had no need and received non-need-based gift aid.

UNDERGRADUATE FINANCIAL AID (Fall 2006, est.) 211 applied for aid; of those 94% were deemed to have need. 92% of undergraduates with need received aid; of those 1% had need fully met. ***Average percent of need met:*** 36% (excluding resources awarded to replace EFC). ***Average financial aid package:*** $6350 (excluding resources awarded to replace EFC). 1% of all full-time undergraduates had no need and received non-need-based gift aid.

GIFT AID (NEED-BASED) ***Total amount:*** $492,117 (72% federal, 12% state, 16% external sources). ***Receiving aid:*** Freshmen: 8% (5); All full-time undergraduates: 40% (131). ***Average award:*** Freshmen: $3220; Undergraduates: $3756. ***Scholarships, grants, and awards:*** Federal Pell, FSEOG, state, private, college/university gift aid from institutional funds.

GIFT AID (NON-NEED-BASED) ***Total amount:*** $27,183 (100% external sources). ***Receiving aid:*** Undergraduates: 1. ***Average award:*** Freshmen: $7348; Undergraduates: $5524. ***Tuition waivers:*** Full or partial for employees or children of employees.

LOANS ***Student loans:*** $1,256,632 (96% need-based, 4% non-need-based). 81% of past graduating class borrowed through all loan programs. *Average indebtedness per student:* $23,054. ***Average need-based loan:*** Freshmen: $2883; Undergraduates: $3973. ***Parent loans:*** $69,061 (70% need-based, 30% non-need-based). ***Programs:*** FFEL (Subsidized and Unsubsidized Stafford, PLUS), Perkins, college/university.

APPLYING FOR FINANCIAL AID ***Required financial aid form:*** FAFSA. ***Financial aid deadline:*** Continuous. ***Notification date:*** Continuous. Students must reply within 2 weeks of notification.

CONTACT Beverly Jene, Director of Financial Aid, Goddard College, 123 Pitkin Road, Plainfield, VT 05667, 802-454-8311 Ext. 324 or toll-free 800-906-8312 Ext. 243. *Fax:* 802-454-1029. *E-mail:* beverly.jene@goddard.edu.

GOD'S BIBLE SCHOOL AND COLLEGE

Cincinnati, OH

CONTACT Mrs. Lori Waggoner, Financial Aid Director, God's Bible School and College, 1810 Young Street, Cincinnati, OH 45202-6899, 513-721-7944 Ext. 205 or toll-free 800-486-4637. *Fax:* 513-721-1357. *E-mail:* lwaggoner@gbs.edu.

GOLDEN GATE UNIVERSITY

San Francisco, CA

CONTACT Ken Walsh, Associate Director of Financial Services, Golden Gate University, 536 Mission Street, San Francisco, CA 94105-2968, 415-442-7262 or toll-free 800-448-4968. *Fax:* 415-442-7819. *E-mail:* kwalsh@ggu.edu.

GOLDEY-BEACOM COLLEGE
Wilmington, DE

CONTACT Jane H. Lysle, Dean of Enrollment Management, Goldey-Beacom College, 4701 Limestone Road, Wilmington, DE 19808-1999, 302-225-6274 or toll-free 800-833-4877. *Fax:* 302-998-8631. *E-mail:* lyslej@goldey.gbc.edu.

GONZAGA UNIVERSITY
Spokane, WA

Tuition & fees: $25,012 **Average undergraduate aid package: $18,004**

ABOUT THE INSTITUTION Independent Roman Catholic, coed. Awards: bachelor's, master's, doctoral, and first professional degrees and post-master's certificates. 51 undergraduate majors. Total enrollment: 6,610. Undergraduates: 4,275. Freshmen: 977. Federal methodology is used as a basis for awarding need-based institutional aid.

UNDERGRADUATE EXPENSES for 2006–07 ***Application fee:*** $45. ***Comprehensive fee:*** $32,232 includes full-time tuition ($24,590), mandatory fees ($422), and room and board ($7220). ***College room only:*** $3560. Room and board charges vary according to board plan and housing facility. ***Part-time tuition:*** $715 per credit. ***Part-time fees:*** $45 per term. ***Payment plans:*** Installment, deferred payment.

FRESHMAN FINANCIAL AID (Fall 2005) 813 applied for aid; of those 70% were deemed to have need. 100% of freshmen with need received aid; of those 27% had need fully met. ***Average percent of need met:*** 93% (excluding resources awarded to replace EFC). ***Average financial aid package:*** $18,076 (excluding resources awarded to replace EFC). 38% of all full-time freshmen had no need and received non-need-based gift aid.

UNDERGRADUATE FINANCIAL AID (Fall 2005) 3,014 applied for aid; of those 80% were deemed to have need. 100% of undergraduates with need received aid; of those 32% had need fully met. ***Average percent of need met:*** 88% (excluding resources awarded to replace EFC). ***Average financial aid package:*** $18,004 (excluding resources awarded to replace EFC). 34% of all full-time undergraduates had no need and received non-need-based gift aid.

GIFT AID (NEED-BASED) ***Total amount:*** $25,140,753 (9% federal, 8% state, 78% institutional, 5% external sources). ***Receiving aid:*** Freshmen: 57% (566); All full-time undergraduates: 59% (2,317). ***Average award:*** Freshmen: $13,219; Undergraduates: $12,467. ***Scholarships, grants, and awards:*** Federal Pell, FSEOG, state, private, college/university gift aid from institutional funds, United Negro College Fund, Federal Nursing.

GIFT AID (NON-NEED-BASED) ***Total amount:*** $12,627,260 (86% institutional, 14% external sources). ***Receiving aid:*** Freshmen: 19% (188); Undergraduates: 22% (871). ***Average award:*** Freshmen: $7857; Undergraduates: $7204. ***Scholarships, grants, and awards by category:*** *Academic Interests/Achievement:* 146 awards ($394,141 total): business, engineering/technologies, military science. *Creative Arts/Performance:* 75 awards ($121,300 total): debating, music. *Special Achievements/Activities:* 116 awards ($329,000 total): leadership, memberships. *Special Characteristics:* 342 awards ($2,385,116 total): children and siblings of alumni, children of faculty/staff, international students, members of minority groups, siblings of current students. ***Tuition waivers:*** Full or partial for employees or children of employees. ***ROTC:*** Army.

LOANS ***Student loans:*** $16,664,659 (70% need-based, 30% non-need-based). 66% of past graduating class borrowed through all loan programs. *Average indebtedness per student:* $23,416. ***Average need-based loan:*** Freshmen: $3696; Undergraduates: $5362. ***Parent loans:*** $6,601,961 (79% need-based, 21% non-need-based). ***Programs:*** FFEL (Subsidized and Unsubsidized Stafford, PLUS), Perkins, Federal Nursing, state, college/university.

WORK-STUDY ***Federal work-study:*** Total amount: $1,591,241; 447 jobs averaging $3560. ***State or other work-study/employment:*** Total amount: $1,787,880 (100% need-based). 369 part-time jobs averaging $4845.

ATHLETIC AWARDS Total amount: $2,401,341 (17% need-based, 83% non-need-based).

APPLYING FOR FINANCIAL AID ***Required financial aid form:*** FAFSA. ***Financial aid deadline (priority):*** 2/1. ***Notification date:*** Continuous beginning 3/1. Students must reply by 5/1 or within 3 weeks of notification.

CONTACT Darlene Hendrickson, Director of Operations for Financial Aid, Gonzaga University, 502 East Boone Avenue, Spokane, WA 99258-0072, 509-323-6568 or toll-free 800-322-2584 Ext. 6572. *Fax:* 509-323-5816. *E-mail:* hendrickson@gonzaga.edu.

GORDON COLLEGE
Wenham, MA

ABOUT THE INSTITUTION Independent nondenominational, coed. Awards: bachelor's and master's degrees. 32 undergraduate majors. Total enrollment: 1,660. Undergraduates: 1,528. Freshmen: 382.

GIFT AID (NEED-BASED) ***Scholarships, grants, and awards:*** Federal Pell, FSEOG, state, private, college/university gift aid from institutional funds.

GIFT AID (NON-NEED-BASED) ***Scholarships, grants, and awards by category:*** *Academic Interests/Achievement:* general academic interests/achievements. *Creative Arts/Performance:* music. *Special Achievements/Activities:* leadership. *Special Characteristics:* children and siblings of alumni, relatives of clergy.

LOANS ***Programs:*** FFEL (Subsidized and Unsubsidized Stafford, PLUS), Perkins, state, college/university.

WORK-STUDY ***Federal work-study:*** Total amount: $856,414; 151 jobs averaging $1503.

APPLYING FOR FINANCIAL AID ***Required financial aid forms:*** FAFSA, CSS Financial Aid PROFILE, state aid form.

CONTACT Barbara Layne, Associate Vice President and Student Services, Gordon College, 255 Grapevine Road, Wenham, MA 01984-1899, 978-867-4246 or toll-free 866-464-6736. *Fax:* 978-867-4657. *E-mail:* blayne@hope.gordon.edu.

GOSHEN COLLEGE
Goshen, IN

ABOUT THE INSTITUTION Independent Mennonite, coed. Awards: bachelor's degrees. 48 undergraduate majors. Total enrollment: 951. Undergraduates: 951. Freshmen: 209.

GIFT AID (NEED-BASED) ***Scholarships, grants, and awards:*** Federal Pell, FSEOG, state, private, college/university gift aid from institutional funds.

GIFT AID (NON-NEED-BASED) ***Scholarships, grants, and awards by category:*** *Academic Interests/Achievement:* business, communication, education, general academic interests/achievements. *Creative Arts/Performance:* music. *Special Characteristics:* international students.

LOANS ***Programs:*** Federal Direct (Subsidized and Unsubsidized Stafford, PLUS), Perkins, Federal Nursing, college/university.

WORK-STUDY ***Federal work-study:*** Total amount: $475,593; 614 jobs averaging $775. ***State or other work-study/employment:*** Total amount: $22,354 (95% need-based, 5% non-need-based). 16 part-time jobs averaging $1320.

APPLYING FOR FINANCIAL AID ***Required financial aid forms:*** FAFSA, institution's own form.

CONTACT Mr. Galen Graber, Director of Enrollment, Goshen College, 1700 South Main Street, Goshen, IN 46526-4794, 574-535-7525 or toll-free 800-348-7422. *Fax:* 574-535-7654.

GOUCHER COLLEGE
Baltimore, MD

Tuition & fees: $29,325 **Average undergraduate aid package: $19,917**

ABOUT THE INSTITUTION Independent, coed. Awards: bachelor's and master's degrees and post-bachelor's certificates. 31 undergraduate majors. Total enrollment: 2,310. Undergraduates: 1,446. Freshmen: 451. Both federal and institutional methodology are used as a basis for awarding need-based institutional aid.

UNDERGRADUATE EXPENSES for 2006–07 ***Application fee:*** $40. ***Comprehensive fee:*** $38,250 includes full-time tuition ($28,900), mandatory fees ($425), and room and board ($8925). ***College room only:*** $3125. Room and board charges vary according to board plan and housing facility. ***Part-time tuition:*** $1000 per credit. ***Payment plans:*** Tuition prepayment, installment.

FRESHMAN FINANCIAL AID (Fall 2005) 241 applied for aid; of those 73% were deemed to have need. 99% of freshmen with need received aid; of those 23% had need fully met. ***Average percent of need met:*** 82% (excluding resources awarded to replace EFC). ***Average financial aid package:*** $19,796 (excluding resources awarded to replace EFC). 33% of all full-time freshmen had no need and received non-need-based gift aid.

UNDERGRADUATE FINANCIAL AID (Fall 2005) 859 applied for aid; of those 82% were deemed to have need. 100% of undergraduates with need received aid; of those 24% had need fully met. ***Average percent of need met:*** 82% (excluding resources awarded to replace EFC). ***Average financial aid package:***

$19,917 (excluding resources awarded to replace EFC). 31% of all full-time undergraduates had no need and received non-need-based gift aid.

GIFT AID (NEED-BASED) ***Total amount:*** $10,818,313 (6% federal, 6% state, 83% institutional, 5% external sources). ***Receiving aid:*** Freshmen: 47% (167); All full-time undergraduates: 52% (668). ***Average award:*** Freshmen: $16,645; Undergraduates: $16,078. ***Scholarships, grants, and awards:*** Federal Pell, FSEOG, state, private, college/university gift aid from institutional funds.

GIFT AID (NON-NEED-BASED) ***Total amount:*** $4,358,456 (1% state, 78% institutional, 21% external sources). ***Receiving aid:*** Freshmen: 7% (25); Undergraduates: 6% (83). ***Average award:*** Freshmen: $13,952; Undergraduates: $13,674. ***Scholarships, grants, and awards by category:*** *Creative Arts/Performance:* 11 awards ($55,000 total): art/fine arts, dance, music, performing arts, theater/drama. ***Tuition waivers:*** Full or partial for employees or children of employees, adult students, senior citizens. ***ROTC:*** Army cooperative.

LOANS ***Student loans:*** $5,209,520 (63% need-based, 37% non-need-based). 62% of past graduating class borrowed through all loan programs. *Average indebtedness per student:* $17,097. ***Average need-based loan:*** Freshmen: $4070; Undergraduates: $4912. ***Parent loans:*** $3,901,598 (26% need-based, 74% non-need-based). ***Programs:*** FFEL (Subsidized and Unsubsidized Stafford, PLUS), Perkins, college/university.

WORK-STUDY ***Federal work-study:*** Total amount: $300,383; 297 jobs averaging $1225. ***State or other work-study/employment:*** Total amount: $1200 (100% non-need-based). 1 part-time job averaging $1200.

APPLYING FOR FINANCIAL AID ***Required financial aid forms:*** FAFSA, CSS Financial Aid PROFILE. ***Financial aid deadline (priority):*** 2/15. ***Notification date:*** 4/1. Students must reply by 5/1 or within 2 weeks of notification.

CONTACT Sharon Hassan, Director of Student Financial Aid, Goucher College, 1021 Dulaney Valley Road, Baltimore, MD 21204-2794, 410-337-6141 or toll-free 800-468-2437. *Fax:* 410-337-6504.

GOVERNORS STATE UNIVERSITY

University Park, IL

CONTACT Financial Aid Office, Governors State University, One University Parkway, University Park, IL 60466-0975, 708-534-4480.

GRACE BIBLE COLLEGE

Grand Rapids, MI

Tuition & fees: $11,290 **Average undergraduate aid package: $7762**

ABOUT THE INSTITUTION Independent religious, coed. Awards: associate and bachelor's degrees. 21 undergraduate majors. Total enrollment: 173. Undergraduates: 173. Freshmen: 42. Federal methodology is used as a basis for awarding need-based institutional aid.

UNDERGRADUATE EXPENSES for 2006–07 ***Comprehensive fee:*** $17,860 includes full-time tuition ($10,770), mandatory fees ($520), and room and board ($6570). ***College room only:*** $2860. Room and board charges vary according to housing facility. ***Part-time tuition:*** $450 per semester hour. Part-time tuition and fees vary according to course load. ***Payment plan:*** Installment.

FRESHMAN FINANCIAL AID (Fall 2006, est.) 40 applied for aid; of those 80% were deemed to have need. 100% of freshmen with need received aid; of those 6% had need fully met. ***Average percent of need met:*** 56% (excluding resources awarded to replace EFC). ***Average financial aid package:*** $6864 (excluding resources awarded to replace EFC). 2% of all full-time freshmen had no need and received non-need-based gift aid.

UNDERGRADUATE FINANCIAL AID (Fall 2006, est.) 145 applied for aid; of those 86% were deemed to have need. 99% of undergraduates with need received aid; of those 8% had need fully met. ***Average percent of need met:*** 57% (excluding resources awarded to replace EFC). ***Average financial aid package:*** $7762 (excluding resources awarded to replace EFC). 2% of all full-time undergraduates had no need and received non-need-based gift aid.

GIFT AID (NEED-BASED) ***Total amount:*** $551,119 (34% federal, 36% state, 24% institutional, 6% external sources). ***Receiving aid:*** Freshmen: 73% (32); All full-time undergraduates: 70% (112). ***Average award:*** Freshmen: $5784; Undergraduates: $5532. ***Scholarships, grants, and awards:*** Federal Pell, FSEOG, state, private, college/university gift aid from institutional funds.

GIFT AID (NON-NEED-BASED) ***Total amount:*** $83,445 (18% state, 56% institutional, 26% external sources). ***Receiving aid:*** Freshmen: 2% (1); Undergraduates: 1% (2). ***Average award:*** Freshmen: $1750; Undergraduates: $1375. ***Scholarships, grants, and awards by category:*** *Academic Interests/Achievement:* 67 awards ($78,775 total): general academic interests/achievements. *Creative Arts/Performance:* 16 awards ($11,125 total): music. *Special Characteristics:* 21 awards ($81,250 total): children of faculty/staff, general special characteristics, relatives of clergy. ***Tuition waivers:*** Full or partial for employees or children of employees. ***ROTC:*** Army cooperative.

LOANS ***Student loans:*** $807,432 (59% need-based, 41% non-need-based). 67% of past graduating class borrowed through all loan programs. *Average indebtedness per student:* $13,640. ***Average need-based loan:*** Freshmen: $2017; Undergraduates: $3350. ***Parent loans:*** $119,855 (30% need-based, 70% non-need-based). ***Programs:*** FFEL (Subsidized and Unsubsidized Stafford, PLUS).

WORK-STUDY ***Federal work-study:*** Total amount: $29,833; 37 jobs averaging $806. ***State or other work-study/employment:*** Total amount: $7045 (100% need-based). 19 part-time jobs averaging $371.

APPLYING FOR FINANCIAL AID ***Required financial aid form:*** FAFSA. ***Financial aid deadline (priority):*** 2/28. ***Notification date:*** Continuous beginning 5/15.

CONTACT Mr. Daniel Wait, Director of Financial Aid, Grace Bible College, 1011 Aldon Street, SW, PO Box 910, Grand Rapids, MI 49509-1921, 616-538-2330 or toll-free 800-968-1887. *Fax:* 616-538-0599.

GRACE COLLEGE

Winona Lake, IN

Tuition & fees: $17,350 **Average undergraduate aid package: $14,540**

ABOUT THE INSTITUTION Independent religious, coed. Awards: associate, bachelor's, master's, doctoral, and first professional degrees. 39 undergraduate majors. Total enrollment: 1,291. Undergraduates: 1,179. Freshmen: 276. Federal methodology is used as a basis for awarding need-based institutional aid.

UNDERGRADUATE EXPENSES for 2006–07 ***Application fee:*** $30. ***Comprehensive fee:*** $23,710 includes full-time tuition ($16,950), mandatory fees ($400), and room and board ($6360). ***College room only:*** $3280. Room and board charges vary according to board plan and housing facility. ***Part-time tuition:*** $320 per credit. ***Part-time fees:*** $280 per year. Part-time tuition and fees vary according to course load. ***Payment plan:*** Installment.

FRESHMAN FINANCIAL AID (Fall 2006, est.) 231 applied for aid; of those 86% were deemed to have need. 99% of freshmen with need received aid; of those 37% had need fully met. ***Average percent of need met:*** 87% (excluding resources awarded to replace EFC). ***Average financial aid package:*** $15,011 (excluding resources awarded to replace EFC). 21% of all full-time freshmen had no need and received non-need-based gift aid.

UNDERGRADUATE FINANCIAL AID (Fall 2006, est.) 719 applied for aid; of those 87% were deemed to have need. 100% of undergraduates with need received aid; of those 33% had need fully met. ***Average percent of need met:*** 85% (excluding resources awarded to replace EFC). ***Average financial aid package:*** $14,540 (excluding resources awarded to replace EFC). 21% of all full-time undergraduates had no need and received non-need-based gift aid.

GIFT AID (NEED-BASED) ***Total amount:*** $4,955,059 (16% federal, 26% state, 51% institutional, 7% external sources). ***Receiving aid:*** Freshmen: 79% (198); All full-time undergraduates: 77% (609). ***Average award:*** Freshmen: $10,753; Undergraduates: $9121. ***Scholarships, grants, and awards:*** Federal Pell, FSEOG, state, private, college/university gift aid from institutional funds.

GIFT AID (NON-NEED-BASED) ***Total amount:*** $1,072,718 (3% state, 80% institutional, 17% external sources). ***Receiving aid:*** Freshmen: 16% (39); Undergraduates: 10% (79). ***Average award:*** Freshmen: $17,036; Undergraduates: $15,009. ***Scholarships, grants, and awards by category:*** *Academic Interests/Achievement:* 36 awards ($28,615 total): business. *Creative Arts/Performance:* 58 awards ($79,575 total): applied art and design, art/fine arts, music, theater/drama. *Special Achievements/Activities:* junior miss. *Special Characteristics:* 209 awards ($704,788 total): children of faculty/staff, ethnic background, relatives of clergy, religious affiliation. ***Tuition waivers:*** Full or partial for employees or children of employees.

LOANS ***Student loans:*** $5,059,182 (73% need-based, 27% non-need-based). 72% of past graduating class borrowed through all loan programs. *Average indebtedness per student:* $18,017. ***Average need-based loan:*** Freshmen: $4689; Undergraduates: $5890. ***Parent loans:*** $4,927,631 (21% need-based, 79% non-need-based). ***Programs:*** FFEL (Subsidized and Unsubsidized Stafford, PLUS), Perkins.

WORK-STUDY ***Federal work-study:*** Total amount: $315,283.

ATHLETIC AWARDS Total amount: $755,110 (56% need-based, 44% non-need-based).

APPLYING FOR FINANCIAL AID ***Required financial aid form:*** FAFSA. ***Financial aid deadline (priority):*** 3/10. ***Notification date:*** Continuous beginning 3/1.

CONTACT Gretchen Bailey, Senior Financial Aid Advisor, Grace College, 200 Seminary Drive, Winona Lake, IN 46590-1294, 574-372-5100 or toll-free 800-54-GRACE Ext. 6412 (in-state), 800-54 GRACE Ext. 6412 (out-of-state). *Fax:* 574-372-5144. *E-mail:* baileyga@grace.edu.

GRACELAND UNIVERSITY

Lamoni, IA

Tuition & fees: $17,900 **Average undergraduate aid package: $15,976**

ABOUT THE INSTITUTION Independent Community of Christ, coed. Awards: bachelor's and master's degrees and post-master's certificates. 54 undergraduate majors. Total enrollment: 2,116. Undergraduates: 1,820. Freshmen: 250. Federal methodology is used as a basis for awarding need-based institutional aid.

UNDERGRADUATE EXPENSES for 2007–08 ***Application fee:*** $50. ***Comprehensive fee:*** $23,900 includes full-time tuition ($17,700), mandatory fees ($200), and room and board ($6000). ***College room only:*** $2400. ***Part-time tuition:*** $560 per semester hour.

FRESHMAN FINANCIAL AID (Fall 2006, est.) 216 applied for aid; of those 86% were deemed to have need. 95% of freshmen with need received aid; of those 37% had need fully met. ***Average percent of need met:*** 91% (excluding resources awarded to replace EFC). ***Average financial aid package:*** $18,449 (excluding resources awarded to replace EFC). 25% of all full-time freshmen had no need and received non-need-based gift aid.

UNDERGRADUATE FINANCIAL AID (Fall 2006, est.) 995 applied for aid; of those 87% were deemed to have need. 95% of undergraduates with need received aid; of those 29% had need fully met. ***Average percent of need met:*** 83% (excluding resources awarded to replace EFC). ***Average financial aid package:*** $15,976 (excluding resources awarded to replace EFC). 20% of all full-time undergraduates had no need and received non-need-based gift aid.

GIFT AID (NEED-BASED) ***Total amount:*** $8,249,637 (19% federal, 7% state, 68% institutional, 6% external sources). ***Receiving aid:*** Freshmen: 66% (174); All full-time undergraduates: 60% (784). ***Average award:*** Freshmen: $14,546; Undergraduates: $11,725. ***Scholarships, grants, and awards:*** Federal Pell, FSEOG, state, private, college/university gift aid from institutional funds.

GIFT AID (NON-NEED-BASED) ***Total amount:*** $3,026,559 (3% federal, 89% institutional, 8% external sources). ***Receiving aid:*** Freshmen: 35% (93); Undergraduates: 30% (385). ***Average award:*** Freshmen: $10,102; Undergraduates: $10,454. ***Scholarships, grants, and awards by category:*** *Academic Interests/Achievement:* 922 awards ($3,819,882 total): computer science, engineering/technologies, English, general academic interests/achievements, physical sciences. *Creative Arts/Performance:* 323 awards ($644,829 total): applied art and design, creative writing, music, theater/drama. *Special Achievements/Activities:* 186 awards ($315,796 total): cheerleading/drum major, general special achievements/activities, leadership, religious involvement. *Special Characteristics:* 1,515 awards ($4,176,146 total): children and siblings of alumni, children of faculty/staff, children of public servants, first-generation college students, general special characteristics, international students, local/state students, members of minority groups, religious affiliation.

LOANS ***Student loans:*** $7,680,730 (69% need-based, 31% non-need-based). 90% of past graduating class borrowed through all loan programs. *Average indebtedness per student:* $26,892. ***Average need-based loan:*** Freshmen: $4223; Undergraduates: $5081. ***Parent loans:*** $673,566 (26% need-based, 74% non-need-based). ***Programs:*** Federal Direct (Subsidized and Unsubsidized Stafford, PLUS), Perkins, state, college/university.

WORK-STUDY ***Federal work-study:*** Total amount: $517,036; 335 jobs averaging $1543. ***State or other work-study/employment:*** Total amount: $409,438 (18% need-based, 82% non-need-based). 384 part-time jobs averaging $1066.

ATHLETIC AWARDS Total amount: $1,353,758 (71% need-based, 29% non-need-based).

APPLYING FOR FINANCIAL AID ***Required financial aid form:*** FAFSA. ***Financial aid deadline:*** Continuous. ***Notification date:*** Continuous beginning 2/1. Students must reply within 2 weeks of notification.

CONTACT Mrs. Sherry Mesle-Morain, Director of Financial Aid, Graceland University, 1 University Place, Lamoni, IA 50140, 641-784-5140 or toll-free 866-GRACELAND. *Fax:* 641-784-5488. *E-mail:* smorain@graceland.edu.

GRACE UNIVERSITY

Omaha, NE

Tuition & fees: $13,970 **Average undergraduate aid package: $9152**

ABOUT THE INSTITUTION Independent interdenominational, coed. Awards: associate, bachelor's, and master's degrees. 39 undergraduate majors. Total enrollment: 513. Undergraduates: 427. Freshmen: 122. Federal methodology is used as a basis for awarding need-based institutional aid.

UNDERGRADUATE EXPENSES for 2006–07 ***Application fee:*** $35. ***Comprehensive fee:*** $19,320 includes full-time tuition ($13,700), mandatory fees ($270), and room and board ($5350). ***College room only:*** $2450. Room and board charges vary according to board plan and student level. ***Part-time tuition:*** $390 per credit hour. ***Part-time fees:*** $35 per term. Part-time tuition and fees vary according to course load. ***Payment plan:*** Installment.

FRESHMAN FINANCIAL AID (Fall 2006, est.) 57 applied for aid; of those 89% were deemed to have need. 100% of freshmen with need received aid; of those 18% had need fully met. ***Average percent of need met:*** 67% (excluding resources awarded to replace EFC). ***Average financial aid package:*** $10,631 (excluding resources awarded to replace EFC). 16% of all full-time freshmen had no need and received non-need-based gift aid.

UNDERGRADUATE FINANCIAL AID (Fall 2006, est.) 262 applied for aid; of those 92% were deemed to have need. 100% of undergraduates with need received aid; of those 11% had need fully met. ***Average percent of need met:*** 57% (excluding resources awarded to replace EFC). ***Average financial aid package:*** $9152 (excluding resources awarded to replace EFC). 13% of all full-time undergraduates had no need and received non-need-based gift aid.

GIFT AID (NEED-BASED) ***Total amount:*** $1,344,666 (26% federal, 4% state, 55% institutional, 15% external sources). ***Receiving aid:*** Freshmen: 84% (51); All full-time undergraduates: 81% (224). ***Average award:*** Freshmen: $7321; Undergraduates: $5497. ***Scholarships, grants, and awards:*** Federal Pell, FSEOG, state, private, college/university gift aid from institutional funds.

GIFT AID (NON-NEED-BASED) ***Total amount:*** $217,463 (80% institutional, 20% external sources). ***Receiving aid:*** Freshmen: 13% (8); Undergraduates: 7% (19). ***Average award:*** Freshmen: $7595; Undergraduates: $7631. ***Scholarships, grants, and awards by category:*** *Academic Interests/Achievement:* 22 awards ($25,300 total): business, education, general academic interests/achievements, health fields, international studies, religion/biblical studies. *Creative Arts/Performance:* 9 awards ($9520 total): cinema/film/broadcasting, music. *Special Achievements/Activities:* 239 awards ($730,037 total): general special achievements/activities, leadership, religious involvement. *Special Characteristics:* 110 awards ($141,376 total): adult students, children and siblings of alumni, children of current students, children of faculty/staff, ethnic background, general special characteristics, international students, local/state students, married students, members of minority groups, out-of-state students, previous college experience, relatives of clergy, religious affiliation, siblings of current students, spouses of current students. ***Tuition waivers:*** Full or partial for children of alumni, employees or children of employees, senior citizens. ***ROTC:*** Army cooperative, Air Force cooperative.

LOANS ***Student loans:*** $1,647,711 (86% need-based, 14% non-need-based). 94% of past graduating class borrowed through all loan programs. *Average indebtedness per student:* $17,823. ***Average need-based loan:*** Freshmen: $3021; Undergraduates: $4042. ***Parent loans:*** $510,393 (51% need-based, 49% non-need-based). ***Programs:*** FFEL (Subsidized and Unsubsidized Stafford, PLUS).

WORK-STUDY ***Federal work-study:*** Total amount: $94,788; 85 jobs averaging $1103. ***State or other work-study/employment:*** Total amount: $33,300 (46% need-based, 54% non-need-based).

APPLYING FOR FINANCIAL AID ***Required financial aid forms:*** FAFSA, institution's own form. ***Financial aid deadline (priority):*** 3/1. ***Notification date:*** 3/1. Students must reply within 2 weeks of notification.

CONTACT Office of Financial Aid, Grace University, 1311 South Ninth Street, Omaha, NE 68108-3629, 402-449-2810 or toll-free 800-383-1422. *Fax:* 402-341-9587. *E-mail:* gufinaid@graceu.edu.

GRAMBLING STATE UNIVERSITY

Grambling, LA

ABOUT THE INSTITUTION State-supported, coed. Awards: associate, bachelor's, master's, and doctoral degrees. 51 undergraduate majors. Total enrollment: 5,065. Undergraduates: 4,584. Freshmen: 1,137.

GIFT AID (NEED-BASED) ***Scholarships, grants, and awards:*** Federal Pell, FSEOG, state.

GIFT AID (NON-NEED-BASED) ***Scholarships, grants, and awards by category:*** *Academic Interests/Achievement:* biological sciences, business, communication, computer science, education, engineering/technologies, English, foreign languages, general academic interests/achievements, health fields, home economics, humanities, mathematics, military science, physical sciences, premedicine, social sciences. *Creative Arts/Performance:* dance, general creative arts/performance, music, performing arts, theater/drama. *Special Achievements/Activities:* cheerleading/drum major, junior miss, leadership. *Special Characteristics:* children and siblings of alumni, children of faculty/staff, children of public servants, ethnic background, international students, local/state students, members of minority groups, out-of-state students, public servants, veterans, veterans' children.

LOANS ***Programs:*** FFEL (Subsidized and Unsubsidized Stafford, PLUS), alternative loans.

WORK-STUDY ***Federal work-study:*** Total amount: $753,810; 788 jobs averaging $957. ***State or other work-study/employment:*** Total amount: $75,000 (100% non-need-based). 72 part-time jobs averaging $1030.

APPLYING FOR FINANCIAL AID ***Required financial aid form:*** FAFSA.

CONTACT Mrs. Anne Rugege, Assistant Director of Student Financial Aid and Scholarships, Grambling State University, PO Box 629, Grambling, LA 71245, 318-274-6415. *Fax:* 318-274-3358.

GRAND CANYON UNIVERSITY

Phoenix, AZ

CONTACT Director of Financial Aid, Grand Canyon University, 3300 West Camelback Road, PO Box 11097, Phoenix, AZ 85017-3030, 800-800-9776 Ext. 2885 or toll-free 800-800-9776 (in-state). *Fax:* 602-589-2044.

GRAND VALLEY STATE UNIVERSITY

Allendale, MI

Tuition & fees (MI res): $6588 **Average undergraduate aid package: $7753**

ABOUT THE INSTITUTION State-supported, coed. Awards: bachelor's and master's degrees and post-bachelor's and post-master's certificates. 122 undergraduate majors. Total enrollment: 23,295. Undergraduates: 19,578. Freshmen: 3,562. Federal methodology is used as a basis for awarding need-based institutional aid.

UNDERGRADUATE EXPENSES for 2006–07 ***Application fee:*** $30. ***Tuition, state resident:*** full-time $6588; part-time $287 per credit hour. ***Tuition, nonresident:*** full-time $12,510; part-time $532 per credit hour. Full-time tuition and fees vary according to program and student level. Part-time tuition and fees vary according to course load, program, and student level. ***College room and board:*** $6600; ***Room only:*** $4700. Room and board charges vary according to board plan, housing facility, and location. ***Payment plans:*** Installment, deferred payment.

FRESHMAN FINANCIAL AID (Fall 2006, est.) 3248 applied for aid; of those 62% were deemed to have need. 100% of freshmen with need received aid; of those 100% had need fully met. ***Average percent of need met:*** 100% (excluding resources awarded to replace EFC). ***Average financial aid package:*** $8416 (excluding resources awarded to replace EFC). 26% of all full-time freshmen had no need and received non-need-based gift aid.

UNDERGRADUATE FINANCIAL AID (Fall 2006, est.) 14,050 applied for aid; of those 68% were deemed to have need. 100% of undergraduates with need received aid; of those 81% had need fully met. ***Average percent of need met:*** 81% (excluding resources awarded to replace EFC). ***Average financial aid package:*** $7753 (excluding resources awarded to replace EFC). 17% of all full-time undergraduates had no need and received non-need-based gift aid.

GIFT AID (NEED-BASED) ***Total amount:*** $29,695,637 (43% federal, 26% state, 31% institutional). ***Receiving aid:*** Freshmen: 57% (1,973); All full-time undergraduates: 54% (9,308). ***Average award:*** Freshmen: $4203; Undergraduates: $3116. ***Scholarships, grants, and awards:*** Federal Pell, FSEOG, state, private, college/university gift aid from institutional funds, Federal Nursing.

GIFT AID (NON-NEED-BASED) ***Total amount:*** $16,212,198 (23% state, 56% institutional, 21% external sources). ***Receiving aid:*** Freshmen: 55% (1,912); Undergraduates: 13% (2,223). ***Average award:*** Freshmen: $3308; Undergraduates: $3132. ***Scholarships, grants, and awards by category:*** *Academic Interests/Achievement:* 800 awards ($2,505,000 total): general academic interests/achievements. *Creative Arts/Performance:* 190 awards ($210,000 total): art/fine arts, music, theater/drama. *Special Characteristics:* 1,150 awards ($4,300,000 total): children of faculty/staff, children of union members/company employees, handicapped students, local/state students, members of minority groups, out-of-state students. ***Tuition waivers:*** Full or partial for employees or children of employees.

LOANS ***Student loans:*** $89,860,000 (46% need-based, 54% non-need-based). 78% of past graduating class borrowed through all loan programs. *Average indebtedness per student:* $18,003. ***Average need-based loan:*** Freshmen: $2854; Undergraduates: $3813. ***Parent loans:*** $6,200,000 (100% non-need-based). ***Programs:*** Federal Direct (Subsidized and Unsubsidized Stafford, PLUS), Perkins, Federal Nursing, state.

WORK-STUDY ***Federal work-study:*** Total amount: $1,051,897; 865 jobs averaging $1200. ***State or other work-study/employment:*** Total amount: $9,120,000 (4% need-based, 96% non-need-based). 261 part-time jobs averaging $1340.

ATHLETIC AWARDS Total amount: $2,300,380 (100% non-need-based).

APPLYING FOR FINANCIAL AID ***Required financial aid form:*** FAFSA. ***Financial aid deadline (priority):*** 3/1. ***Notification date:*** 4/1. Students must reply by 5/1.

CONTACT Mr. Ken Fridsma, Director of Financial Aid, Grand Valley State University, 100 Student Services Building, Allendale, MI 49401-9403, 616-331-3234 or toll-free 800-748-0246. *Fax:* 616-331-3180. *E-mail:* fridsmak@gvsu.edu.

GRAND VIEW COLLEGE

Des Moines, IA

Tuition & fees: $16,940 **Average undergraduate aid package: $11,398**

ABOUT THE INSTITUTION Independent religious, coed. Awards: associate and bachelor's degrees and post-bachelor's certificates. 29 undergraduate majors. Total enrollment: 1,707. Undergraduates: 1,707. Freshmen: 200. Federal methodology is used as a basis for awarding need-based institutional aid.

UNDERGRADUATE EXPENSES for 2006–07 ***Application fee:*** $35. ***Comprehensive fee:*** $22,536 includes full-time tuition ($16,570), mandatory fees ($370), and room and board ($5596). Full-time tuition and fees vary according to class time. Room and board charges vary according to board plan and housing facility. ***Part-time tuition:*** $450 per hour. Part-time tuition and fees vary according to class time. ***Payment plan:*** Installment.

FRESHMAN FINANCIAL AID (Fall 2005) 205 applied for aid; of those 82% were deemed to have need. 100% of freshmen with need received aid; of those 14% had need fully met. ***Average percent of need met:*** 73% (excluding resources awarded to replace EFC). ***Average financial aid package:*** $11,811 (excluding resources awarded to replace EFC). 25% of all full-time freshmen had no need and received non-need-based gift aid.

UNDERGRADUATE FINANCIAL AID (Fall 2005) 1,333 applied for aid; of those 86% were deemed to have need. 100% of undergraduates with need received aid; of those 15% had need fully met. ***Average percent of need met:*** 68% (excluding resources awarded to replace EFC). ***Average financial aid package:*** $11,398 (excluding resources awarded to replace EFC). 19% of all full-time undergraduates had no need and received non-need-based gift aid.

GIFT AID (NEED-BASED) ***Total amount:*** $9,232,656 (18% federal, 32% state, 45% institutional, 5% external sources). ***Receiving aid:*** Freshmen: 77% (167); All full-time undergraduates: 83% (1,135). ***Average award:*** Freshmen: $9629; Undergraduates: $8071. ***Scholarships, grants, and awards:*** Federal Pell, FSEOG, state, private, college/university gift aid from institutional funds, Federal ACG and SMART.

GIFT AID (NON-NEED-BASED) ***Total amount:*** $1,399,012 (5% federal, 6% state, 79% institutional, 10% external sources). ***Receiving aid:*** Freshmen: 8% (18); Undergraduates: 7% (95). ***Average award:*** Freshmen: $11,682; Undergraduates: $10,532. ***Scholarships, grants, and awards by category:*** *Academic Interests/Achievement:* 1,205 awards ($4,106,092 total): general academic interests/achievements. *Creative Arts/Performance:* 59 awards ($65,570 total): art/fine arts, music, theater/drama. *Special Achievements/Activities:* 1 award ($500 total): junior miss. *Special Characteristics:* 135 awards ($478,056 total): children and siblings of alumni, children of educators, children of faculty/staff. ***Tuition waivers:*** Full or partial for employees or children of employees, senior citizens. ***ROTC:*** Army cooperative, Air Force cooperative.

LOANS ***Student loans:*** $12,583,520 (64% need-based, 36% non-need-based). ***Average need-based loan:*** Freshmen: $2701; Undergraduates: $3761. ***Parent loans:*** $482,829 (20% need-based, 80% non-need-based). ***Programs:*** FFEL (Subsidized and Unsubsidized Stafford, PLUS), Perkins, Federal Nursing.

WORK-STUDY ***Federal work-study:*** Total amount: $111,336; 207 jobs averaging $538. ***State or other work-study/employment:*** Total amount: $905 (100% need-based). 1 part-time job averaging $905.

ATHLETIC AWARDS Total amount: $552,256 (56% need-based, 44% non-need-based).

APPLYING FOR FINANCIAL AID ***Required financial aid form:*** FAFSA. ***Financial aid deadline (priority):*** 3/1. ***Notification date:*** Continuous beginning 3/15. Students must reply by 5/1 or within 4 weeks of notification.

CONTACT Michele Dunne, Director of Financial Aid, Grand View College, 1200 Grandview Avenue, Des Moines, IA 50316-1599, 515-263-2820 or toll-free 800-444-6083 Ext. 2810. *Fax:* 515-263-6191. *E-mail:* mdunne@gvc.edu.

GRATZ COLLEGE
Melrose Park, PA

CONTACT Karen West, Student Financial Services Adviser, Gratz College, 7605 Old York Road, Melrose Park, PA 19027, 215-635-7300 Ext. 163 or toll-free 800-475-4635 Ext. 140 (out-of-state). *Fax:* 215-635-7320.

GREAT LAKES CHRISTIAN COLLEGE
Lansing, MI

CONTACT Financial Aid Officer, Great Lakes Christian College, 6211 West Willow Highway, Lansing, MI 48917-1299, 517-321-0242 or toll-free 800-YES-GLCC.

GREEN MOUNTAIN COLLEGE
Poultney, VT

Tuition & fees: $23,329 **Average undergraduate aid package: $19,273**

ABOUT THE INSTITUTION Independent, coed. Awards: bachelor's and master's degrees. 24 undergraduate majors. Total enrollment: 759. Undergraduates: 729. Freshmen: 217. Federal methodology is used as a basis for awarding need-based institutional aid.

UNDERGRADUATE EXPENSES for 2006–07 ***Application fee:*** $30. ***Comprehensive fee:*** $31,755 includes full-time tuition ($22,662), mandatory fees ($667), and room and board ($8426). ***College room only:*** $5076. Full-time tuition and fees vary according to course load. Room and board charges vary according to housing facility. ***Part-time tuition:*** $756 per credit hour. Part-time tuition and fees vary according to course load. ***Payment plan:*** Installment.

FRESHMAN FINANCIAL AID (Fall 2006, est.) 186 applied for aid; of those 91% were deemed to have need. 100% of freshmen with need received aid; of those 22% had need fully met. ***Average percent of need met:*** 73% (excluding resources awarded to replace EFC). ***Average financial aid package:*** $18,730 (excluding resources awarded to replace EFC). 9% of all full-time freshmen had no need and received non-need-based gift aid.

UNDERGRADUATE FINANCIAL AID (Fall 2006, est.) 606 applied for aid; of those 92% were deemed to have need. 100% of undergraduates with need received aid; of those 26% had need fully met. ***Average percent of need met:*** 75% (excluding resources awarded to replace EFC). ***Average financial aid package:*** $19,273 (excluding resources awarded to replace EFC). 11% of all full-time undergraduates had no need and received non-need-based gift aid.

GIFT AID (NEED-BASED) ***Total amount:*** $6,881,525 (17% federal, 4% state, 76% institutional, 3% external sources). ***Receiving aid:*** Freshmen: 77% (169); All full-time undergraduates: 74% (538). ***Average award:*** Freshmen: $14,428; Undergraduates: $13,230. ***Scholarships, grants, and awards:*** Federal Pell, FSEOG, state, private, college/university gift aid from institutional funds.

GIFT AID (NON-NEED-BASED) ***Total amount:*** $727,730 (96% institutional, 4% external sources). ***Receiving aid:*** Freshmen: 6% (14); Undergraduates: 5% (38). ***Average award:*** Freshmen: $10,260; Undergraduates: $13,733. ***Scholarships, grants, and awards by category:*** *Academic Interests/Achievement:* 23 awards ($44,250 total): biological sciences, business, education, English, general academic interests/achievements, social sciences. *Creative Arts/Performance:* 20 awards ($41,500 total): art/fine arts, music, performing arts, theater/drama. *Special Achievements/Activities:* 72 awards ($141,850 total): community service, leadership, religious involvement. *Special Characteristics:* 57 awards ($213,219 total): children and siblings of alumni, children of current students, international students, local/state students, parents of current students, relatives of clergy, religious affiliation, siblings of current students. ***Tuition waivers:*** Full or partial for employees or children of employees.

LOANS ***Student loans:*** $5,506,790 (71% need-based, 29% non-need-based). 76% of past graduating class borrowed through all loan programs. *Average indebtedness per student:* $28,026. ***Average need-based loan:*** Freshmen: $4050; Undergraduates: $6394. ***Parent loans:*** $1,789,441 (51% need-based, 49% non-need-based). ***Programs:*** FFEL (Subsidized and Unsubsidized Stafford, PLUS).

WORK-STUDY ***Federal work-study:*** Total amount: $152,819; 101 jobs averaging $1500. ***State or other work-study/employment:*** Total amount: $308,595 (69% need-based, 31% non-need-based). 132 part-time jobs averaging $1500.

APPLYING FOR FINANCIAL AID ***Required financial aid form:*** FAFSA. ***Financial aid deadline (priority):*** 3/1. ***Notification date:*** Continuous beginning 1/1. Students must reply by 5/1 or within 4 weeks of notification.

CONTACT Wendy J. Ellis, Director of Financial Aid, Green Mountain College, One College Circle, Poultney, VT 05764-1199, 800-776-6675 Ext. 8210 or toll-free 800-776-6675 (out-of-state). *Fax:* 802-287-8099. *E-mail:* ellisw@greenmtn.edu.

GREENSBORO COLLEGE
Greensboro, NC

CONTACT Mr. Ron Elmore, Director of Financial Aid, Greensboro College, 815 West Market Street, Greensboro, NC 27401-1875, 336-272-7102 Ext. 339 or toll-free 800-346-8226. *Fax:* 336-271-6634. *E-mail:* relmore@gborocollege.edu.

GREENVILLE COLLEGE
Greenville, IL

ABOUT THE INSTITUTION Independent Free Methodist, coed. Awards: bachelor's and master's degrees. 51 undergraduate majors. Total enrollment: 1,451. Undergraduates: 1,322. Freshmen: 299.

GIFT AID (NEED-BASED) ***Scholarships, grants, and awards:*** Federal Pell, FSEOG, state, private, college/university gift aid from institutional funds.

GIFT AID (NON-NEED-BASED) ***Scholarships, grants, and awards by category:*** *Academic Interests/Achievement:* biological sciences, business, education, engineering/technologies, general academic interests/achievements, mathematics, physical sciences, religion/biblical studies. *Creative Arts/Performance:* applied art and design, art/fine arts, music, performing arts. *Special Achievements/Activities:* leadership, memberships, religious involvement. *Special Characteristics:* children and siblings of alumni, children of faculty/staff, international students, local/state students, out-of-state students, relatives of clergy, religious affiliation, siblings of current students.

LOANS ***Programs:*** FFEL (Subsidized and Unsubsidized Stafford, PLUS), Perkins, college/university.

WORK-STUDY ***Federal work-study:*** Total amount: $289,000; 212 jobs averaging $1390. ***State or other work-study/employment:*** Total amount: $23,000 (100% non-need-based). 26 part-time jobs averaging $827.

APPLYING FOR FINANCIAL AID ***Required financial aid form:*** FAFSA.

CONTACT Mr. Karl Somerville, Director of Financial Aid, Greenville College, 315 East College Avenue, Greenville, IL 62246-0159, 618-664-7110 or toll-free 800-345-4440. *Fax:* 618-664-9841. *E-mail:* karl.somerville@greenville.edu.

GRINNELL COLLEGE
Grinnell, IA

Tuition & fees: $29,030 **Average undergraduate aid package: $25,972**

ABOUT THE INSTITUTION Independent, coed. Awards: bachelor's degrees. 24 undergraduate majors. Total enrollment: 1,589. Undergraduates: 1,589. Freshmen: 405. Institutional methodology is used as a basis for awarding need-based institutional aid.

UNDERGRADUATE EXPENSES for 2006–07 ***Application fee:*** $30. ***Comprehensive fee:*** $36,730 includes full-time tuition ($28,566), mandatory fees ($464), and room and board ($7700). ***College room only:*** $3600. Room and board charges vary according to board plan and housing facility. ***Part-time tuition:*** $893 per credit hour. ***Payment plans:*** Tuition prepayment, installment.

FRESHMAN FINANCIAL AID (Fall 2006, est.) 302 applied for aid; of those 79% were deemed to have need. 100% of freshmen with need received aid; of those 100% had need fully met. ***Average percent of need met:*** 100% (excluding resources awarded to replace EFC). ***Average financial aid package:*** $26,136 (excluding resources awarded to replace EFC). 27% of all full-time freshmen had no need and received non-need-based gift aid.

UNDERGRADUATE FINANCIAL AID (Fall 2006, est.) 981 applied for aid; of those 88% were deemed to have need. 100% of undergraduates with need received aid; of those 100% had need fully met. ***Average percent of need met:*** 100% (excluding resources awarded to replace EFC). ***Average financial aid package:*** $25,972 (excluding resources awarded to replace EFC). 33% of all full-time undergraduates had no need and received non-need-based gift aid.

GIFT AID (NEED-BASED) ***Total amount:*** $16,448,044 (4% federal, 1% state, 92% institutional, 3% external sources). ***Receiving aid:*** Freshmen: 57% (232); All full-time undergraduates: 55% (850). ***Average award:*** Freshmen: $19,411; Undergraduates: $19,317. ***Scholarships, grants, and awards:*** Federal Pell, FSEOG, state, private, college/university gift aid from institutional funds.

GIFT AID (NON-NEED-BASED) ***Total amount:*** $6,763,736 (90% institutional, 10% external sources). ***Receiving aid:*** Freshmen: 11% (46); Undergraduates: 8% (131). ***Average award:*** Freshmen: $8777; Undergraduates: $10,463. ***Scholarships, grants, and awards by category:*** *Academic Interests/Achievement:* 623 awards ($6,067,223 total): general academic interests/achievements. ***Tuition waivers:*** Full or partial for employees or children of employees.

LOANS ***Student loans:*** $3,585,800 (91% need-based, 9% non-need-based). 57% of past graduating class borrowed through all loan programs. *Average indebtedness per student:* $17,975. ***Average need-based loan:*** Freshmen: $4835; Undergraduates: $5553. ***Programs:*** FFEL (Subsidized and Unsubsidized Stafford, PLUS), Perkins, college/university.

WORK-STUDY ***Federal work-study:*** Total amount: $702,520; 411 jobs averaging $1709. ***State or other work-study/employment:*** Total amount: $612,428 (37% need-based, 63% non-need-based). 332 part-time jobs averaging $1845.

APPLYING FOR FINANCIAL AID ***Required financial aid forms:*** FAFSA, institution's own form, noncustodial (divorced/separated) parent's statement. ***Financial aid deadline:*** 2/1. ***Notification date:*** 4/1. Students must reply by 5/1.

CONTACT Mr. Arnold Woods, Director of Student Financial Aid, Grinnell College, 1103 Park Street, Grinnell, IA 50112-1690, 641-269-3250 or toll-free 800-247-0113. *Fax:* 641-269-4937. *E-mail:* woods@grinnell.edu.

GROVE CITY COLLEGE

Grove City, PA

Tuition & fees: $10,962 **Average undergraduate aid package: $5232**

ABOUT THE INSTITUTION Independent Presbyterian, coed. Awards: bachelor's degrees. 45 undergraduate majors. Total enrollment: 2,489. Undergraduates: 2,489. Freshmen: 674. Institutional methodology is used as a basis for awarding need-based institutional aid.

UNDERGRADUATE EXPENSES for 2006–07 ***Application fee:*** $50. ***Comprehensive fee:*** $16,728 includes full-time tuition ($10,962) and room and board ($5766). Full-time tuition and fees vary according to course load. Room and board charges vary according to housing facility. ***Part-time tuition:*** $350 per credit. ***Payment plan:*** Installment.

FRESHMAN FINANCIAL AID (Fall 2006, est.) 399 applied for aid; of those 72% were deemed to have need. 100% of freshmen with need received aid; of those 14% had need fully met. ***Average percent of need met:*** 56% (excluding resources awarded to replace EFC). ***Average financial aid package:*** $5187 (excluding resources awarded to replace EFC). 28% of all full-time freshmen had no need and received non-need-based gift aid.

UNDERGRADUATE FINANCIAL AID (Fall 2006, est.) 1,103 applied for aid; of those 81% were deemed to have need. 97% of undergraduates with need received aid; of those 9% had need fully met. ***Average percent of need met:*** 51% (excluding resources awarded to replace EFC). ***Average financial aid package:*** $5232 (excluding resources awarded to replace EFC). 32% of all full-time undergraduates had no need and received non-need-based gift aid.

GIFT AID (NEED-BASED) ***Total amount:*** $4,576,595 (23% state, 65% institutional, 12% external sources). ***Receiving aid:*** Freshmen: 42% (286); All full-time undergraduates: 33% (823). ***Average award:*** Freshmen: $5171; Undergraduates: $5545. ***Scholarships, grants, and awards:*** state, private, college/university gift aid from institutional funds.

GIFT AID (NON-NEED-BASED) ***Total amount:*** $1,731,375 (4% state, 45% institutional, 51% external sources). ***Receiving aid:*** Freshmen: 6% (39); Undergraduates: 3% (73). ***Average award:*** Freshmen: $5108; Undergraduates: $6440. ***Scholarships, grants, and awards by category:*** *Academic Interests/Achievement:* 559 awards ($1,171,426 total): biological sciences, business, communication, education, engineering/technologies, English, foreign languages, general academic interests/achievements, physical sciences, religion/biblical studies, social sciences. *Creative Arts/Performance:* 14 awards ($28,800 total): creative writing, music. *Special Achievements/Activities:* 21 awards ($44,500 total): general special achievements/activities, leadership, memberships, religious involvement. *Special Characteristics:* 10 awards ($36,600 total): ethnic background, general special characteristics, members of minority groups. ***Tuition waivers:*** Full or partial for employees or children of employees. ***ROTC:*** Army cooperative.

LOANS ***Student loans:*** $8,506,249 (35% need-based, 65% non-need-based). 68% of past graduating class borrowed through all loan programs. *Average indebtedness per student:* $22,532. ***Average need-based loan:*** Freshmen: $30; Undergraduates: $8. ***Programs:*** alternative loans.

WORK-STUDY ***State or other work-study/employment:*** Total amount: $3000 (100% non-need-based). 18 part-time jobs averaging $600.

APPLYING FOR FINANCIAL AID ***Required financial aid forms:*** institution's own form, state aid form. ***Financial aid deadline:*** 4/15. ***Notification date:*** Continuous beginning 3/20.

CONTACT Thomas G. Ball, Director of Financial Aid, Grove City College, 100 Campus Drive, Grove City, PA 16127-2104, 724-458-3300. *Fax:* 724-450-4040. *E-mail:* financialaid@gcc.edu.

GUILFORD COLLEGE

Greensboro, NC

Tuition & fees: $23,020 **Average undergraduate aid package: $11,661**

ABOUT THE INSTITUTION Independent religious, coed. Awards: bachelor's degrees. 37 undergraduate majors. Total enrollment: 2,687. Undergraduates: 2,687. Freshmen: 466. Federal methodology is used as a basis for awarding need-based institutional aid.

UNDERGRADUATE EXPENSES for 2006–07 ***Application fee:*** $25. ***Comprehensive fee:*** $29,710 includes full-time tuition ($22,690), mandatory fees ($330), and room and board ($6690). Room and board charges vary according to board plan and housing facility. ***Part-time tuition:*** $698 per credit hour. ***Part-time fees:*** $330 per year. Part-time tuition and fees vary according to course load. ***Payment plan:*** Installment.

FRESHMAN FINANCIAL AID (Fall 2006, est.) 315 applied for aid; of those 74% were deemed to have need. 100% of freshmen with need received aid; of those 27% had need fully met. ***Average percent of need met:*** 87% (excluding resources awarded to replace EFC). ***Average financial aid package:*** $17,950 (excluding resources awarded to replace EFC). 19% of all full-time freshmen had no need and received non-need-based gift aid.

UNDERGRADUATE FINANCIAL AID (Fall 2006, est.) 1,201 applied for aid; of those 87% were deemed to have need. 99% of undergraduates with need received aid; of those 18% had need fully met. ***Average percent of need met:*** 67% (excluding resources awarded to replace EFC). ***Average financial aid package:*** $11,661 (excluding resources awarded to replace EFC). 26% of all full-time undergraduates had no need and received non-need-based gift aid.

GIFT AID (NEED-BASED) ***Total amount:*** $15,496,058 (21% federal, 22% state, 54% institutional, 3% external sources). ***Receiving aid:*** Freshmen: 57% (233); All full-time undergraduates: 65% (999). ***Average award:*** Freshmen: $13,772; Undergraduates: $8325. ***Scholarships, grants, and awards:*** Federal Pell, FSEOG, state, private, college/university gift aid from institutional funds.

GIFT AID (NON-NEED-BASED) ***Total amount:*** $952,711 (8% state, 88% institutional, 4% external sources). ***Receiving aid:*** Freshmen: 29% (119); Undergraduates: 49% (758). ***Average award:*** Freshmen: $8116; Undergraduates: $7006. ***Scholarships, grants, and awards by category:*** *Academic Interests/Achievement:* 1,215 awards ($4,750,175 total): biological sciences, general academic interests/achievements. *Creative Arts/Performance:* 36 awards ($42,780 total): music, theater/drama. *Special Achievements/Activities:* 25 awards ($75,525 total): religious involvement. *Special Characteristics:* 310 awards ($554,173 total): children of faculty/staff, first-generation college students, local/state students. ***Tuition waivers:*** Full or partial for employees or children of employees. ***ROTC:*** Army cooperative, Naval cooperative, Air Force cooperative.

LOANS ***Student loans:*** $10,322,519 (97% need-based, 3% non-need-based). 68% of past graduating class borrowed through all loan programs. *Average indebtedness per student:* $22,130. ***Average need-based loan:*** Freshmen: $4695; Undergraduates: $4145. ***Parent loans:*** $1,493,293 (96% need-based, 4% non-need-based). ***Programs:*** FFEL (Subsidized and Unsubsidized Stafford, PLUS), Perkins, college/university.

WORK-STUDY ***Federal work-study:*** Total amount: $282,312; 225 jobs averaging $278. ***State or other work-study/employment:*** Total amount: $157,850 (86% need-based, 14% non-need-based). 173 part-time jobs averaging $1200.

APPLYING FOR FINANCIAL AID ***Required financial aid forms:*** FAFSA, noncustodial (divorced/separated) parent's statement, business/farm supplement. ***Financial aid deadline (priority):*** 3/1. ***Notification date:*** Continuous beginning 2/1. Students must reply within 2 weeks of notification.

CONTACT Mr. Anthony E. Gurley, Director of Student Financial Services, Guilford College, 5800 West Friendly Avenue, Greensboro, NC 27410, 336-316-2142 or toll-free 800-992-7759. *Fax:* 336-316-2942. *E-mail:* agurley@guilford.edu.

GUSTAVUS ADOLPHUS COLLEGE

St. Peter, MN

Tuition & fees: $28,515 **Average undergraduate aid package: $18,100**

ABOUT THE INSTITUTION Independent religious, coed. Awards: bachelor's degrees. 64 undergraduate majors. Total enrollment: 2,618. Undergraduates: 2,618. Freshmen: 685. Both federal and institutional methodology are used as a basis for awarding need-based institutional aid.

UNDERGRADUATE EXPENSES for 2007–08 ***Comprehensive fee:*** $32,790 includes full-time tuition ($28,125), mandatory fees ($390), and room and board ($4275). ***College room only:*** $2500. ***Part-time tuition:*** $3840 per course.

FRESHMAN FINANCIAL AID (Fall 2005) 575 applied for aid; of those 79% were deemed to have need. 100% of freshmen with need received aid. ***Average percent of need met:*** 92% (excluding resources awarded to replace EFC). ***Average financial aid package:*** $19,800 (excluding resources awarded to replace EFC). 37% of all full-time freshmen had no need and received non-need-based gift aid.

UNDERGRADUATE FINANCIAL AID (Fall 2005) 1,976 applied for aid; of those 83% were deemed to have need. 100% of undergraduates with need received aid. ***Average percent of need met:*** 89% (excluding resources awarded to replace EFC). ***Average financial aid package:*** $18,100 (excluding resources awarded to replace EFC). 28% of all full-time undergraduates had no need and received non-need-based gift aid.

GIFT AID (NEED-BASED) ***Total amount:*** $21,804,903 (8% federal, 11% state, 77% institutional, 4% external sources). ***Receiving aid:*** Freshmen: 64% (453); All full-time undergraduates: 64% (1,639). ***Average award:*** Freshmen: $16,500; Undergraduates: $14,100. ***Scholarships, grants, and awards:*** Federal Pell, FSEOG, state, private, college/university gift aid from institutional funds.

GIFT AID (NON-NEED-BASED) ***Total amount:*** $5,562,200 (1% federal, 90% institutional, 9% external sources). ***Receiving aid:*** Freshmen: 46% (325); Undergraduates: 55% (1,412). ***Average award:*** Freshmen: $7200; Undergraduates: $6000. ***Scholarships, grants, and awards by category:*** *Academic Interests/Achievement:* 415 awards ($2,275,815 total): general academic interests/achievements. *Creative Arts/Performance:* 75 awards ($190,000 total): art/fine arts, debating, music, theater/drama. *Special Achievements/Activities:* 220 awards ($165,000 total): community service, junior miss, leadership. *Special Characteristics:* 127 awards ($150,000 total): children and siblings of alumni, ethnic background, first-generation college students, international students, members of minority groups, out-of-state students, parents of current students, siblings of current students. ***ROTC:*** Army cooperative.

LOANS ***Student loans:*** $14,040,000 (51% need-based, 49% non-need-based). 71% of past graduating class borrowed through all loan programs. *Average indebtedness per student:* $21,300. ***Average need-based loan:*** Freshmen: $4500; Undergraduates: $4900. ***Parent loans:*** $2,301,000 (14% need-based, 86% non-need-based). ***Programs:*** Federal Direct (Subsidized and Unsubsidized Stafford, PLUS), Perkins, state, GATE Loans.

WORK-STUDY ***Federal work-study:*** Total amount: $717,066; 1,000 jobs averaging $1200. ***State or other work-study/employment:*** Total amount: $1,057,934 (60% need-based, 40% non-need-based). 516 part-time jobs averaging $1000.

APPLYING FOR FINANCIAL AID ***Required financial aid forms:*** FAFSA, institution's own form, CSS Financial Aid PROFILE. ***Financial aid deadline:*** 4/1 (priority: 2/15). ***Notification date:*** Continuous beginning 11/20. Students must reply by 5/1 or within 2 weeks of notification.

CONTACT Mary Booker, Director of Financial Aid, Gustavus Adolphus College, 500 West College Avenue, St. Peter, MN 56082-1498, 507-933-7527 or toll-free 800-GUSTAVU(S). *Fax:* 507-933-7727. *E-mail:* financial_aid@gustavus.edu.

GUTENBERG COLLEGE

Eugene, OR

CONTACT Financial Aid Office, Gutenberg College, 1883 University Street, Eugene, OR 97403, 541-683-5141.

GWYNEDD-MERCY COLLEGE

Gwynedd Valley, PA

Tuition & fees: $21,000 **Average undergraduate aid package: $12,676**

ABOUT THE INSTITUTION Independent Roman Catholic, coed. Awards: associate, bachelor's, and master's degrees and post-bachelor's and post-master's certificates. 36 undergraduate majors. Total enrollment: 2,727. Undergraduates: 2,135. Freshmen: 271. Federal methodology is used as a basis for awarding need-based institutional aid.

UNDERGRADUATE EXPENSES for 2007–08 ***Application fee:*** $25. ***Comprehensive fee:*** $29,600 includes full-time tuition ($20,500), mandatory fees ($500), and room and board ($8600). ***Part-time tuition:*** $475 per credit. ***Part-time fees:*** $10 per credit.

FRESHMAN FINANCIAL AID (Fall 2006, est.) 265 applied for aid; of those 85% were deemed to have need. 100% of freshmen with need received aid; of those 15% had need fully met. ***Average percent of need met:*** 74% (excluding resources awarded to replace EFC). ***Average financial aid package:*** $12,895 (excluding resources awarded to replace EFC). 19% of all full-time freshmen had no need and received non-need-based gift aid.

UNDERGRADUATE FINANCIAL AID (Fall 2006, est.) 1,170 applied for aid; of those 84% were deemed to have need. 97% of undergraduates with need received aid; of those 16% had need fully met. ***Average percent of need met:*** 70% (excluding resources awarded to replace EFC). ***Average financial aid package:*** $12,676 (excluding resources awarded to replace EFC). 19% of all full-time undergraduates had no need and received non-need-based gift aid.

GIFT AID (NEED-BASED) ***Total amount:*** $9,447,350 (11% federal, 18% state, 64% institutional, 7% external sources). ***Receiving aid:*** Freshmen: 78% (223); All full-time undergraduates: 72% (941). ***Average award:*** Freshmen: $10,670; Undergraduates: $9909. ***Scholarships, grants, and awards:*** Federal Pell, FSEOG, state, private, college/university gift aid from institutional funds.

GIFT AID (NON-NEED-BASED) ***Total amount:*** $2,016,220 (4% state, 90% institutional, 6% external sources). ***Receiving aid:*** Freshmen: 64% (183); Undergraduates: 55% (720). ***Average award:*** Freshmen: $12,304; Undergraduates: $11,601. ***Scholarships, grants, and awards by category:*** *Academic Interests/Achievement:* 590 awards ($3,638,169 total): general academic interests/achievements. *Special Achievements/Activities:* 180 awards ($655,100 total): general special achievements/activities. *Special Characteristics:* 14 awards ($25,300 total): children and siblings of alumni, siblings of current students.

LOANS ***Student loans:*** $7,755,541 (60% need-based, 40% non-need-based). 85% of past graduating class borrowed through all loan programs. *Average indebtedness per student:* $18,877. ***Average need-based loan:*** Freshmen: $2461; Undergraduates: $3333. ***Parent loans:*** $1,994,017 (19% need-based, 81% non-need-based). ***Programs:*** FFEL (Subsidized and Unsubsidized Stafford, PLUS), Perkins, Federal Nursing, alternative loans.

WORK-STUDY ***Federal work-study:*** Total amount: $115,130; 185 jobs averaging $813. ***State or other work-study/employment:*** Total amount: $15,700 (100% need-based). 10 part-time jobs averaging $1450.

APPLYING FOR FINANCIAL AID ***Required financial aid forms:*** FAFSA, institution's own form. ***Financial aid deadline (priority):*** 3/1. ***Notification date:*** Continuous beginning 3/1. Students must reply by 5/1.

CONTACT Sr. Barbara A. Kaufmann, Director of Student Financial Aid, Gwynedd-Mercy College, PO Box 901, Gwynedd Valley, PA 19437-0901, 215-641-5570 or toll-free 800-DIAL-GMC (in-state). *Fax:* 215-641-5556.

HAMILTON COLLEGE

Clinton, NY

Tuition & fees: $34,980 **Average undergraduate aid package: $29,148**

ABOUT THE INSTITUTION Independent, coed. Awards: bachelor's degrees. 46 undergraduate majors. Total enrollment: 1,821. Undergraduates: 1,821. Freshmen: 501. Both federal and institutional methodology are used as a basis for awarding need-based institutional aid.

UNDERGRADUATE EXPENSES for 2006–07 ***Application fee:*** $50. ***Comprehensive fee:*** $43,890 includes full-time tuition ($34,780), mandatory fees ($200), and room and board ($8910). ***College room only:*** $4860. Room and board charges vary according to board plan. ***Payment plan:*** Installment.

FRESHMAN FINANCIAL AID (Fall 2006, est.) 293 applied for aid; of those 80% were deemed to have need. 100% of freshmen with need received aid; of those 100% had need fully met. ***Average percent of need met:*** 100% (excluding resources awarded to replace EFC). ***Average financial aid package:*** $30,355 (excluding resources awarded to replace EFC). 3% of all full-time freshmen had no need and received non-need-based gift aid.

UNDERGRADUATE FINANCIAL AID (Fall 2006, est.) 1,026 applied for aid; of those 87% were deemed to have need. 100% of undergraduates with need received aid; of those 100% had need fully met. ***Average percent of need met:*** 100% (excluding resources awarded to replace EFC). ***Average financial aid package:*** $29,148 (excluding resources awarded to replace EFC). 4% of all full-time undergraduates had no need and received non-need-based gift aid.

GIFT AID (NEED-BASED) ***Total amount:*** $21,915,383 (4% federal, 4% state, 90% institutional, 2% external sources). ***Receiving aid:*** Freshmen: 46% (230); All full-time undergraduates: 49% (881). ***Average award:*** Freshmen: $24,368; Undergraduates: $22,565. ***Scholarships, grants, and awards:*** Federal Pell, FSEOG, state, private, college/university gift aid from institutional funds.

GIFT AID (NON-NEED-BASED) ***Total amount:*** $1,511,444 (3% state, 67% institutional, 30% external sources). ***Receiving aid:*** Freshmen: 1% (4); Undergraduates: 2% (29). ***Average award:*** Freshmen: $8280; Undergraduates: $11,264. ***Scholarships, grants, and awards by category:*** *Academic Interests/Achievement:* general academic interests/achievements. *Creative Arts/Performance:* general creative arts/performance. *Special Achievements/Activities:* general special achievements/activities. *Special Characteristics:* general special characteristics. ***Tuition waivers:*** Full or partial for employees or children of employees. ***ROTC:*** Army cooperative, Air Force cooperative.

LOANS ***Student loans:*** $2,558,991 (99% need-based, 1% non-need-based). 48% of past graduating class borrowed through all loan programs. *Average indebtedness per student:* $19,371. ***Average need-based loan:*** Freshmen: $2481; Undergraduates: $3514. ***Programs:*** FFEL (Subsidized and Unsubsidized Stafford, PLUS), Perkins.

WORK-STUDY ***Federal work-study:*** Total amount: $678,726; jobs available (averaging $1600). ***State or other work-study/employment:*** Total amount: $120,000 (100% need-based).

APPLYING FOR FINANCIAL AID ***Required financial aid forms:*** FAFSA, institution's own form, CSS Financial Aid PROFILE, state aid form, noncustodial (divorced/separated) parent's statement, business/farm supplement. ***Financial aid deadline:*** 1/1 (priority: 1/1). ***Notification date:*** 4/1. Students must reply by 5/1.

CONTACT Colleen Seymour, Office Assistant, Hamilton College, 198 College Hill Road, Clinton, NY 13323, 800-859-4413 or toll-free 800-843-2655. *Fax:* 315-859-4457. *E-mail:* finaid@hamilton.edu.

HAMILTON TECHNICAL COLLEGE

Davenport, IA

CONTACT Ms. Lisa Boyd, Executive Vice President/Director of Financial Aid, Hamilton Technical College, 1011 East 53rd Street, Davenport, IA 52807-2653, 563-386-3570 Ext. 33. *Fax:* 563-386-6756.

HAMLINE UNIVERSITY

St. Paul, MN

ABOUT THE INSTITUTION Independent religious, coed. Awards: bachelor's, master's, doctoral, and first professional degrees and post-bachelor's certificates. 61 undergraduate majors. Total enrollment: 4,575. Undergraduates: 2,012. Freshmen: 424.

GIFT AID (NEED-BASED) ***Scholarships, grants, and awards:*** Federal Pell, FSEOG, state, private, college/university gift aid from institutional funds.

GIFT AID (NON-NEED-BASED) ***Scholarships, grants, and awards by category:*** *Academic Interests/Achievement:* area/ethnic studies, biological sciences, communication, English, foreign languages, general academic interests/achievements, health fields, physical sciences, premedicine. *Creative Arts/Performance:* art/fine arts, creative writing, music, theater/drama. *Special Achievements/Activities:* junior miss. *Special Characteristics:* children with a deceased or disabled parent, ethnic background, general special characteristics, international students, local/state students, members of minority groups.

LOANS ***Programs:*** FFEL (Subsidized and Unsubsidized Stafford, PLUS), Perkins.

CONTACT Ms. Cheryl Anderson-Dooley, Associate Director, Financial Aid, Hamline University, 1536 Hewitt Avenue, MS C1915, St. Paul, MN 55104, 651-523-2280 or toll-free 800-753-9753. *Fax:* 651-523-2585. *E-mail:* cdooley@gw.hamline.edu.

HAMPDEN-SYDNEY COLLEGE

Hampden-Sydney, VA

Tuition & fees: $27,732 **Average undergraduate aid package: $19,427**

ABOUT THE INSTITUTION Independent religious, men only. Awards: bachelor's degrees. 28 undergraduate majors. Total enrollment: 1,106. Undergraduates: 1,106. Freshmen: 345. Both federal and institutional methodology are used as a basis for awarding need-based institutional aid.

UNDERGRADUATE EXPENSES for 2007–08 ***Application fee:*** $30. ***Comprehensive fee:*** $36,403 includes full-time tuition ($26,676), mandatory fees ($1056), and room and board ($8671). ***College room only:*** $3608. ***Part-time tuition:*** $852 per credit hour.

FRESHMAN FINANCIAL AID (Fall 2006, est.) 243 applied for aid; of those 68% were deemed to have need. 100% of freshmen with need received aid; of those 37% had need fully met. ***Average percent of need met:*** 87% (excluding resources awarded to replace EFC). ***Average financial aid package:*** $18,564 (excluding resources awarded to replace EFC). 54% of all full-time freshmen had no need and received non-need-based gift aid.

UNDERGRADUATE FINANCIAL AID (Fall 2006, est.) 692 applied for aid; of those 76% were deemed to have need. 100% of undergraduates with need received aid; of those 30% had need fully met. ***Average percent of need met:*** 85% (excluding resources awarded to replace EFC). ***Average financial aid package:*** $19,427 (excluding resources awarded to replace EFC). 52% of all full-time undergraduates had no need and received non-need-based gift aid.

GIFT AID (NEED-BASED) ***Total amount:*** $7,934,044 (5% federal, 12% state, 80% institutional, 3% external sources). ***Receiving aid:*** Freshmen: 51% (165); All full-time undergraduates: 49% (521). ***Average award:*** Freshmen: $15,298; Undergraduates: $15,228. ***Scholarships, grants, and awards:*** Federal Pell, FSEOG, state, private, college/university gift aid from institutional funds.

GIFT AID (NON-NEED-BASED) ***Total amount:*** $5,484,140 (20% state, 72% institutional, 8% external sources). ***Receiving aid:*** Freshmen: 14% (45); Undergraduates: 10% (109). ***Average award:*** Freshmen: $20,292; Undergraduates: $16,999. ***Scholarships, grants, and awards by category:*** *Academic Interests/Achievement:* 392 awards ($4,511,380 total): biological sciences, education, general academic interests/achievements, health fields, premedicine, religion/biblical studies. *Creative Arts/Performance:* 1 award ($5000 total): music. *Special Achievements/Activities:* 370 awards ($996,500 total): general special achievements/activities, leadership. *Special Characteristics:* 32 awards ($445,633 total): children of educators, children of faculty/staff, out-of-state students, religious affiliation. ***ROTC:*** Army cooperative.

LOANS ***Student loans:*** $4,804,120 (44% need-based, 56% non-need-based). 53% of past graduating class borrowed through all loan programs. *Average indebtedness per student:* $16,244. ***Average need-based loan:*** Freshmen: $3165; Undergraduates: $4243. ***Parent loans:*** $8,763,502 (15% need-based, 85% non-need-based). ***Programs:*** FFEL (Subsidized and Unsubsidized Stafford, PLUS), Perkins, college/university.

WORK-STUDY ***Federal work-study:*** Total amount: $461,175; 248 jobs averaging $1859.

APPLYING FOR FINANCIAL AID ***Required financial aid forms:*** FAFSA, CSS Financial Aid PROFILE. ***Financial aid deadline (priority):*** 3/1. ***Notification date:*** Continuous. Students must reply by 5/1 or within 2 weeks of notification.

CONTACT Mrs. Lynn Clements, Assistant Director of Financial Aid, Hampden-Sydney College, PO Box 726, Hampden-Sydney, VA 23943-0667, 434-223-6119 or toll-free 800-755-0733. *Fax:* 434-223-6075. *E-mail:* lclements@hsc.edu.

HAMPSHIRE COLLEGE

Amherst, MA

Tuition & fees: $34,605 **Average undergraduate aid package: $27,990**

ABOUT THE INSTITUTION Independent, coed. Awards: bachelor's degrees. 46 undergraduate majors. Total enrollment: 1,448. Undergraduates: 1,448. Freshmen: 392. Institutional methodology is used as a basis for awarding need-based institutional aid.

UNDERGRADUATE EXPENSES for 2006–07 ***Application fee:*** $55. ***Comprehensive fee:*** $43,635 includes full-time tuition ($33,855), mandatory fees ($750), and room and board ($9030). ***College room only:*** $5759. Room and board charges vary according to board plan. ***Payment plan:*** Installment.

FRESHMAN FINANCIAL AID (Fall 2006, est.) 271 applied for aid; of those 81% were deemed to have need. 100% of freshmen with need received aid; of those 80% had need fully met. ***Average percent of need met:*** 99% (excluding resources awarded to replace EFC). ***Average financial aid package:*** $28,725 (excluding resources awarded to replace EFC). 17% of all full-time freshmen had no need and received non-need-based gift aid.

UNDERGRADUATE FINANCIAL AID (Fall 2006, est.) 894 applied for aid; of those 91% were deemed to have need. 100% of undergraduates with need received aid; of those 80% had need fully met. ***Average percent of need met:*** 97% (excluding resources awarded to replace EFC). ***Average financial aid package:*** $27,990 (excluding resources awarded to replace EFC). 13% of all full-time undergraduates had no need and received non-need-based gift aid.

GIFT AID (NEED-BASED) ***Total amount:*** $18,342,520 (5% federal, 93% institutional, 2% external sources). ***Receiving aid:*** Freshmen: 56% (220); All full-time undergraduates: 57% (817). ***Average award:*** Freshmen: $24,000; Undergraduates: $22,100. ***Scholarships, grants, and awards:*** Federal Pell, FSEOG, state, private, college/university gift aid from institutional funds.

GIFT AID (NON-NEED-BASED) ***Total amount:*** $1,195,630 (1% state, 82% institutional, 17% external sources). ***Receiving aid:*** Freshmen: 31% (122); Undergraduates: 20% (284). ***Average award:*** Freshmen: $6225; Undergraduates: $4880. ***Scholarships, grants, and awards by category:*** *Academic Interests/Achievement:* 472 awards ($2,095,500 total): general academic interests/achievements, international studies, physical sciences, social sciences. *Creative Arts/Performance:* 1 award ($3500 total): creative writing. *Special Achievements/Activities:* 54 awards ($250,200 total): community service, leadership. *Special Characteristics:* 12 awards ($360,800 total): children of faculty/staff. ***Tuition waivers:*** Full or partial for employees or children of employees. ***ROTC:*** Army cooperative.

LOANS ***Student loans:*** $3,030,676 (93% need-based, 7% non-need-based). 59% of past graduating class borrowed through all loan programs. *Average indebtedness per student:* $22,830. ***Average need-based loan:*** Freshmen: $2625; Undergraduates: $3490. ***Parent loans:*** $4,214,470 (71% need-based, 29% non-need-based). ***Programs:*** Federal Direct (Subsidized and Unsubsidized Stafford), FFEL (PLUS), Perkins.

WORK-STUDY ***Federal work-study:*** Total amount: $1,275,780; 585 jobs averaging $2300. ***State or other work-study/employment:*** Total amount: $594,655 (75% need-based, 25% non-need-based). 284 part-time jobs averaging $2300.

APPLYING FOR FINANCIAL AID ***Required financial aid forms:*** FAFSA, CSS Financial Aid PROFILE, noncustodial (divorced/separated) parent's statement. ***Financial aid deadline (priority):*** 2/1. ***Notification date:*** 4/1. Students must reply by 5/1 or within 2 weeks of notification.

CONTACT Ms. Kathleen Methot, Director of Financial Aid, Hampshire College, 893 West Street, Amherst, MA 01002, 413-559-5484 or toll-free 877-937-4267 (out-of-state). *Fax:* 413-559-5585. *E-mail:* sfs@hampshire.edu.

HAMPTON UNIVERSITY

Hampton, VA

ABOUT THE INSTITUTION Independent, coed. Awards: associate, bachelor's, master's, doctoral, and first professional degrees. 83 undergraduate majors. Total enrollment: 6,152. Undergraduates: 5,135. Freshmen: 1,133.

GIFT AID (NEED-BASED) ***Scholarships, grants, and awards:*** Federal Pell, FSEOG, state, private, college/university gift aid from institutional funds, Federal Nursing.

GIFT AID (NON-NEED-BASED) ***Scholarships, grants, and awards by category:*** *Academic Interests/Achievement:* general academic interests/achievements. *Creative Arts/Performance:* music. *Special Characteristics:* international students, members of minority groups.

LOANS ***Programs:*** FFEL (Subsidized and Unsubsidized Stafford, PLUS), Perkins, Federal Nursing, college/university.

WORK-STUDY ***Federal work-study:*** Total amount: $319,803; 378 jobs averaging $1800.

APPLYING FOR FINANCIAL AID ***Required financial aid form:*** FAFSA.

CONTACT Marcia Boyd, Director, Financial Aid, Hampton University, Hampton University, Office of Financial Aid and Scholarships, Hampton, VA 23668, 757-727-5332 or toll-free 800-624-3328. *Fax:* 757-728-6567. *E-mail:* marcia.boyd@hamptonu.edu.

HANNIBAL-LaGRANGE COLLEGE

Hannibal, MO

ABOUT THE INSTITUTION Independent Southern Baptist, coed. Awards: associate and bachelor's degrees. 43 undergraduate majors. Total enrollment: 1,091. Undergraduates: 1,091. Freshmen: 132.

GIFT AID (NEED-BASED) ***Scholarships, grants, and awards:*** Federal Pell, FSEOG, state, private.

GIFT AID (NON-NEED-BASED) ***Scholarships, grants, and awards by category:*** *Academic Interests/Achievement:* general academic interests/achievements, religion/biblical studies. *Creative Arts/Performance:* art/fine arts, journalism/publications, music, performing arts, theater/drama. *Special Characteristics:* children of faculty/staff, public servants, relatives of clergy, religious affiliation.

LOANS ***Programs:*** FFEL (Subsidized and Unsubsidized Stafford, PLUS), Perkins.

WORK-STUDY ***Federal work-study:*** 85 jobs averaging $550. ***State or other work-study/employment:*** Total amount: $28,875 (100% non-need-based).

APPLYING FOR FINANCIAL AID ***Required financial aid forms:*** FAFSA, institution's own form.

CONTACT Amy Blackwell, Director of Financial Aid, Hannibal-LaGrange College, 2800 Palmyra Road, Hannibal, MO 63401-1940, 573-221-3675 Ext. 279 or toll-free 800-HLG-1119. *Fax:* 573-221-6594.

HANOVER COLLEGE

Hanover, IN

Tuition & fees: $22,700 **Average undergraduate aid package: $17,526**

ABOUT THE INSTITUTION Independent Presbyterian, coed. Awards: bachelor's degrees. 29 undergraduate majors. Total enrollment: 975. Undergraduates: 975. Freshmen: 230. Federal methodology is used as a basis for awarding need-based institutional aid.

UNDERGRADUATE EXPENSES for 2006–07 ***Application fee:*** $35. ***Comprehensive fee:*** $29,500 includes full-time tuition ($22,200), mandatory fees ($500), and room and board ($6800). ***College room only:*** $3250. Full-time tuition and fees vary according to reciprocity agreements. Room and board charges vary according to housing facility and location. ***Part-time tuition:*** $2468 per unit. Part-time tuition and fees vary according to course load and reciprocity agreements. ***Payment plan:*** Installment.

FRESHMAN FINANCIAL AID (Fall 2005) 215 applied for aid; of those 82% were deemed to have need. 100% of freshmen with need received aid; of those 49% had need fully met. ***Average percent of need met:*** 88% (excluding resources awarded to replace EFC). ***Average financial aid package:*** $16,949 (excluding resources awarded to replace EFC). 32% of all full-time freshmen had no need and received non-need-based gift aid.

UNDERGRADUATE FINANCIAL AID (Fall 2005) 898 applied for aid; of those 86% were deemed to have need. 100% of undergraduates with need received aid; of those 38% had need fully met. ***Average percent of need met:*** 73% (excluding resources awarded to replace EFC). ***Average financial aid package:*** $17,526 (excluding resources awarded to replace EFC). 22% of all full-time undergraduates had no need and received non-need-based gift aid.

GIFT AID (NEED-BASED) ***Total amount:*** $10,406,446 (4% federal, 14% state, 82% institutional). ***Receiving aid:*** Freshmen: 66% (176); All full-time undergraduates: 76% (768). ***Average award:*** Freshmen: $14,440; Undergraduates: $14,912. ***Scholarships, grants, and awards:*** Federal Pell, state, private, college/university gift aid from institutional funds.

GIFT AID (NON-NEED-BASED) ***Total amount:*** $3,759,271 (75% institutional, 25% external sources). ***Receiving aid:*** Freshmen: 20% (52); Undergraduates: 14% (144). ***Average award:*** Freshmen: $14,724; Undergraduates: $14,839. ***Scholarships, grants, and awards by category:*** *Academic Interests/Achievement:* general academic interests/achievements. *Creative Arts/Performance:* 44 awards ($98,500 total): music, theater/drama. *Special Characteristics:* children and siblings of alumni, children of faculty/staff, international students, members of minority groups, out-of-state students, religious affiliation, siblings of current students. ***Tuition waivers:*** Full or partial for employees or children of employees, senior citizens.

LOANS ***Student loans:*** $3,086,649 (58% need-based, 42% non-need-based). 62% of past graduating class borrowed through all loan programs. *Average indebtedness per student:* $18,181. ***Average need-based loan:*** Freshmen: $2553; Undergraduates: $3378. ***Parent loans:*** $1,620,130 (19% need-based, 81% non-need-based). ***Programs:*** FFEL (Subsidized and Unsubsidized Stafford, PLUS), college/university.

APPLYING FOR FINANCIAL AID ***Required financial aid form:*** FAFSA. ***Financial aid deadline (priority):*** 3/1. ***Notification date:*** Continuous beginning 3/1. Students must reply by 5/1.

CONTACT Jon Riester, Director of Financial Aid, Hanover College, PO Box 108, Hanover, IN 47243-0108, 800-213-2178. *Fax:* 812-866-7098. *E-mail:* finaid@hanover.edu.

HARDING UNIVERSITY

Searcy, AR

Tuition & fees: $11,650 **Average undergraduate aid package: $9418**

ABOUT THE INSTITUTION Independent religious, coed. Awards: bachelor's and master's degrees. 96 undergraduate majors. Total enrollment: 6,085. Undergraduates: 4,029. Freshmen: 911. Federal methodology is used as a basis for awarding need-based institutional aid.

UNDERGRADUATE EXPENSES for 2006–07 ***Application fee:*** $35. ***Comprehensive fee:*** $17,092 includes full-time tuition ($11,250), mandatory fees ($400), and room and board ($5442). ***College room only:*** $2700. Full-time tuition and fees vary according to course load. Room and board charges vary according to board plan and housing facility. ***Part-time tuition:*** $375 per semester hour. ***Part-time fees:*** $20 per semester hour. Part-time tuition and fees vary according to course load. ***Payment plans:*** Tuition prepayment, installment.

FRESHMAN FINANCIAL AID (Fall 2006, est.) 669 applied for aid; of those 68% were deemed to have need. 100% of freshmen with need received aid; of those 31% had need fully met. ***Average percent of need met:*** 76% (excluding resources awarded to replace EFC). ***Average financial aid package:*** $9911 (excluding resources awarded to replace EFC). 43% of all full-time freshmen had no need and received non-need-based gift aid.

UNDERGRADUATE FINANCIAL AID (Fall 2006, est.) 2,732 applied for aid; of those 73% were deemed to have need. 99% of undergraduates with need received aid; of those 25% had need fully met. ***Average percent of need met:*** 70% (excluding resources awarded to replace EFC). ***Average financial aid package:*** $9418 (excluding resources awarded to replace EFC). 31% of all full-time undergraduates had no need and received non-need-based gift aid.

GIFT AID (NEED-BASED) ***Total amount:*** $8,308,858 (38% federal, 7% state, 51% institutional, 4% external sources). ***Receiving aid:*** Freshmen: 47% (428); All full-time undergraduates: 45% (1,701). ***Average award:*** Freshmen: $6397; Undergraduates: $5228. ***Scholarships, grants, and awards:*** Federal Pell, FSEOG, state, private, college/university gift aid from institutional funds.

GIFT AID (NON-NEED-BASED) ***Total amount:*** $6,929,277 (8% state, 68% institutional, 24% external sources). ***Receiving aid:*** Freshmen: 9% (83); Undergraduates: 7% (254). ***Average award:*** Freshmen: $3515; Undergraduates: $3565. ***Scholarships, grants, and awards by category:*** *Academic Interests/Achievement:* 1,999 awards ($5,563,638 total): communication, computer science, engineering/technologies, English, general academic interests/achievements, health fields. *Creative Arts/Performance:* 226 awards ($197,032 total): art/fine arts, cinema/film/broadcasting, debating, journalism/publications, music. *Special Achievements/Activities:* 116 awards ($104,016 total): cheerleading/drum major, leadership, religious involvement. *Special Characteristics:* 471 awards ($2,012,880 total): children with a deceased or disabled parent, international students, siblings of current students. ***Tuition waivers:*** Full or partial for employees or children of employees, senior citizens. ***ROTC:*** Army cooperative.

LOANS ***Student loans:*** $19,588,159 (59% need-based, 41% non-need-based). 72% of past graduating class borrowed through all loan programs. *Average indebtedness per student:* $28,717. ***Average need-based loan:*** Freshmen: $3902; Undergraduates: $4756. ***Parent loans:*** $6,119,422 (19% need-based, 81% non-need-based). ***Programs:*** FFEL (Subsidized and Unsubsidized Stafford, PLUS), Perkins, Federal Nursing, state, college/university.

WORK-STUDY ***Federal work-study:*** Total amount: $424,807; 499 jobs averaging $854. ***State or other work-study/employment:*** Total amount: $871,239 (11% need-based, 89% non-need-based). 954 part-time jobs averaging $944.

ATHLETIC AWARDS Total amount: $1,586,706 (23% need-based, 77% non-need-based).

APPLYING FOR FINANCIAL AID ***Required financial aid form:*** FAFSA. ***Financial aid deadline (priority):*** 4/15. ***Notification date:*** Continuous beginning 2/15. Students must reply within 2 weeks of notification.

CONTACT Dr. Jonathan C. Roberts, Director of Student Financial Services, Harding University, Box 12282, Searcy, AR 72149-2282, 501-279-4257 or toll-free 800-477-4407. *Fax:* 501-279-4129. *E-mail:* jroberts@harding.edu.

HARDIN-SIMMONS UNIVERSITY

Abilene, TX

Tuition & fees: $16,946 **Average undergraduate aid package: $13,152**

ABOUT THE INSTITUTION Independent Baptist, coed. Awards: bachelor's, master's, doctoral, and first professional degrees and post-bachelor's certificates. 73 undergraduate majors. Total enrollment: 2,372. Undergraduates: 1,942. Freshmen: 400. Federal methodology is used as a basis for awarding need-based institutional aid.

UNDERGRADUATE EXPENSES for 2007–08 ***Application fee:*** $50. ***Comprehensive fee:*** $21,896 includes full-time tuition ($16,050), mandatory fees ($896), and room and board ($4950). ***College room only:*** $2602. ***Part-time tuition:*** $535 per semester hour. ***Part-time fees:*** $105 per term.

FRESHMAN FINANCIAL AID (Fall 2006, est.) 394 applied for aid; of those 71% were deemed to have need. 100% of freshmen with need received aid; of those 15% had need fully met. ***Average percent of need met:*** 57% (excluding resources awarded to replace EFC). ***Average financial aid package:*** $12,172 (excluding resources awarded to replace EFC). 15% of all full-time freshmen had no need and received non-need-based gift aid.

UNDERGRADUATE FINANCIAL AID (Fall 2006, est.) 1,659 applied for aid; of those 72% were deemed to have need. 100% of undergraduates with need received aid; of those 20% had need fully met. ***Average percent of need met:*** 65% (excluding resources awarded to replace EFC). ***Average financial aid package:*** $13,152 (excluding resources awarded to replace EFC). 12% of all full-time undergraduates had no need and received non-need-based gift aid.

GIFT AID (NEED-BASED) ***Total amount:*** $10,529,581 (18% federal, 27% state, 49% institutional, 6% external sources). ***Receiving aid:*** Freshmen: 54% (216); All full-time undergraduates: 51% (884). ***Average award:*** Freshmen: $5661; Undergraduates: $6463. ***Scholarships, grants, and awards:*** Federal Pell, FSEOG, state, private, college/university gift aid from institutional funds, Academic Competitiveness Grant, National SMART Grants.

GIFT AID (NON-NEED-BASED) ***Receiving aid:*** Freshmen: 56% (223); Undergraduates: 57% (990). ***Average award:*** Freshmen: $3660; Undergraduates: $3689. ***Scholarships, grants, and awards by category:*** *Academic Interests/Achievement:* 1,214 awards ($3,184,570 total): biological sciences, business, communication, education, English, foreign languages, general academic interests/achievements, health fields, humanities, mathematics, physical sciences, premedicine, religion/biblical studies, social sciences. *Creative Arts/Performance:* 146 awards ($237,595 total): art/fine arts, creative writing, journalism/publications, music, theater/drama. *Special Achievements/Activities:* 259 awards ($251,368 total): general special achievements/activities, junior miss, leadership. *Special Characteristics:* 274 awards ($726,166 total): children of faculty/staff, ethnic background, general special characteristics, local/state students, out-of-state students, public servants, relatives of clergy, religious affiliation, siblings of current students.

LOANS ***Student loans:*** $14,031,234 (39% need-based, 61% non-need-based). 74% of past graduating class borrowed through all loan programs. *Average indebtedness per student:* $24,837. ***Average need-based loan:*** Freshmen: $2252; Undergraduates: $4049. ***Parent loans:*** $1,102,093 (100% non-need-based). ***Programs:*** FFEL (Subsidized and Unsubsidized Stafford, PLUS), Perkins, state, college/university.

WORK-STUDY ***Federal work-study:*** Total amount: $247,046; 183 jobs averaging $1350. ***State or other work-study/employment:*** Total amount: $536,376 (4% need-based, 96% non-need-based). 381 part-time jobs averaging $1408.

APPLYING FOR FINANCIAL AID ***Required financial aid form:*** FAFSA. ***Financial aid deadline (priority):*** 3/15. ***Notification date:*** Continuous beginning 1/1.

CONTACT Jim Jones, Director of Financial Aid, Hardin-Simmons University, PO Box 16050, Abilene, TX 79698-6050, 325-670-5891 or toll-free 877-464-7889. *Fax:* 325-670-5822. *E-mail:* jjones@hsutx.edu.

HARRINGTON COLLEGE OF DESIGN

Chicago, IL

CONTACT Ms. Renee Darosky, Director of Financial Aid, Harrington College of Design, 410 South Michigan Avenue, Chicago, IL 60605-1496, 312-939-4975 or toll-free 877-939-4975. *Fax:* 312-697-8058. *E-mail:* financialaid@interiordesign.edu.

HARRISBURG UNIVERSITY OF SCIENCE AND TECHNOLOGY

Harrisburg, PA

CONTACT Financial Aid Office, Harrisburg University of Science and Technology, 215 Market Street, Harrisburg, PA 17101, 717-901-5100 or toll-free 866-HBG-UNIV.

HARRIS-STOWE STATE UNIVERSITY

St. Louis, MO

ABOUT THE INSTITUTION State-supported, coed. Awards: bachelor's degrees and post-bachelor's certificates. 17 undergraduate majors. Total enrollment: 1,868. Undergraduates: 1,868. Freshmen: 413.

GIFT AID (NEED-BASED) ***Scholarships, grants, and awards:*** Federal Pell, FSEOG, state, private, college/university gift aid from institutional funds.

GIFT AID (NON-NEED-BASED) ***Scholarships, grants, and awards by category:*** *Academic Interests/Achievement:* general academic interests/achievements. *Creative Arts/Performance:* music, theater/drama.

LOANS ***Programs:*** FFEL (Subsidized and Unsubsidized Stafford, PLUS), college/university.

APPLYING FOR FINANCIAL AID ***Required financial aid forms:*** FAFSA, institution's own form.

CONTACT Regina Blackshear, Director of Financial Aid, Harris-Stowe State University, 3026 Laclede Avenue, St. Louis, MO 63103-2136, 314-340-3502. *Fax:* 314-340-3503.

HARTWICK COLLEGE

Oneonta, NY

CONTACT Kathleen Ryan-O'Neill, Director, Financial Aid Department, Hartwick College, One Hartwick Drive, Oneonta, NY 13820, 607-431-4158 or toll-free 888-HARTWICK (out-of-state). *Fax:* 607-431-4006. *E-mail:* oneillk@hartwick.edu.

HARVARD UNIVERSITY

Cambridge, MA

Tuition & fees: $33,709 **Average undergraduate aid package: $33,625**

ABOUT THE INSTITUTION Independent, coed. Awards: bachelor's, master's, doctoral, and first professional degrees. 141 undergraduate majors. Total enrollment: 19,538. Undergraduates: 6,715. Freshmen: 1,686. Both federal and institutional methodology are used as a basis for awarding need-based institutional aid.

UNDERGRADUATE EXPENSES for 2006–07 ***Application fee:*** $65. ***Comprehensive fee:*** $43,655 includes full-time tuition ($30,275), mandatory fees ($3434), and room and board ($9946). ***College room only:*** $5328.

FRESHMAN FINANCIAL AID (Fall 2006, est.) 1071 applied for aid; of those 82% were deemed to have need. 100% of freshmen with need received aid; of those 100% had need fully met. ***Average percent of need met:*** 100% (excluding resources awarded to replace EFC). ***Average financial aid package:*** $35,036 (excluding resources awarded to replace EFC).

UNDERGRADUATE FINANCIAL AID (Fall 2006, est.) 3,715 applied for aid; of those 89% were deemed to have need. 100% of undergraduates with need received aid; of those 100% had need fully met. ***Average percent of need met:*** 100% (excluding resources awarded to replace EFC). ***Average financial aid package:*** $33,625 (excluding resources awarded to replace EFC).

GIFT AID (NEED-BASED) ***Total amount:*** $101,681,075 (5% federal, 1% state, 89% institutional, 5% external sources). ***Receiving aid:*** Freshmen: 53% (873); All full-time undergraduates: 49% (3,295). ***Average award:*** Freshmen: $33,015; Undergraduates: $30,803. ***Scholarships, grants, and awards:*** Federal Pell, FSEOG, state, private, college/university gift aid from institutional funds.

GIFT AID (NON-NEED-BASED) ***Total amount:*** $5,212,627 (23% federal, 77% external sources). ***ROTC:*** Army cooperative, Naval cooperative, Air Force cooperative.

LOANS ***Student loans:*** $5,524,125 (65% need-based, 35% non-need-based). 42% of past graduating class borrowed through all loan programs. *Average indebtedness per student:* $9717. ***Average need-based loan:*** Freshmen: $3425; Undergraduates: $3922. ***Parent loans:*** $13,431,463 (100% non-need-based). ***Programs:*** Federal Direct (Subsidized and Unsubsidized Stafford, PLUS), Perkins, state, college/university.

WORK-STUDY ***Federal work-study:*** Total amount: $2,990,982; 998 jobs averaging $2530. ***State or other work-study/employment:*** Total amount: $4,057,274 (81% need-based, 19% non-need-based). 1,600 part-time jobs averaging $2421.

APPLYING FOR FINANCIAL AID ***Required financial aid forms:*** FAFSA, CSS Financial Aid PROFILE, noncustodial (divorced/separated) parent's statement, business/farm supplement, income tax form(s). ***Financial aid deadline (priority):*** 2/1. ***Notification date:*** 4/1. Students must reply by 5/1 or within 2 weeks of notification.

CONTACT Financial Aid Office, Harvard University, 86 Brattle Street, Cambridge, MA 02138, 617-495-1581. *Fax:* 617-496-0256.

HARVEY MUDD COLLEGE

Claremont, CA

Tuition & fees: $34,670 **Average undergraduate aid package: $27,752**

ABOUT THE INSTITUTION Independent, coed. Awards: bachelor's and master's degrees. 6 undergraduate majors. Total enrollment: 729. Undergraduates: 729. Freshmen: 180. Both federal and institutional methodology are used as a basis for awarding need-based institutional aid.

UNDERGRADUATE EXPENSES for 2007–08 ***Application fee:*** $50. ***Comprehensive fee:*** $46,082 includes full-time tuition ($34,670) and room and board ($11,412). ***College room only:*** $5729.

FRESHMAN FINANCIAL AID (Fall 2006, est.) 131 applied for aid; of those 88% were deemed to have need. 100% of freshmen with need received aid; of those 100% had need fully met. ***Average percent of need met:*** 100% (excluding resources awarded to replace EFC). ***Average financial aid package:*** $30,439 (excluding resources awarded to replace EFC). 21% of all full-time freshmen had no need and received non-need-based gift aid.

UNDERGRADUATE FINANCIAL AID (Fall 2006, est.) 465 applied for aid; of those 84% were deemed to have need. 100% of undergraduates with need received aid; of those 100% had need fully met. ***Average percent of need met:*** 100% (excluding resources awarded to replace EFC). ***Average financial aid package:*** $27,752 (excluding resources awarded to replace EFC). 20% of all full-time undergraduates had no need and received non-need-based gift aid.

GIFT AID (NEED-BASED) ***Total amount:*** $9,442,822 (5% federal, 8% state, 87% institutional). ***Receiving aid:*** Freshmen: 60% (108); All full-time undergraduates: 51% (376). ***Average award:*** Freshmen: $27,963; Undergraduates: $24,359. ***Scholarships, grants, and awards:*** Federal Pell, FSEOG, state, private, college/university gift aid from institutional funds.

GIFT AID (NON-NEED-BASED) ***Total amount:*** $1,490,025 (2% state, 49% institutional, 49% external sources). ***Receiving aid:*** Freshmen: 23% (41); Undergraduates: 24% (181). ***Average award:*** Freshmen: $10,911; Undergraduates: $6843. ***Scholarships, grants, and awards by category:*** *Academic Interests/Achievement:* 271 awards ($2,290,838 total): general academic interests/achievements. ***ROTC:*** Army cooperative, Air Force.

LOANS ***Student loans:*** $1,860,232 (65% need-based, 35% non-need-based). 57% of past graduating class borrowed through all loan programs. *Average indebtedness per student:* $18,288. ***Average need-based loan:*** Freshmen: $3486; Undergraduates: $4280. ***Parent loans:*** $1,972,973 (100% non-need-based). ***Programs:*** FFEL (Subsidized and Unsubsidized Stafford, PLUS), Perkins, college/university, alternative loans.

WORK-STUDY ***Federal work-study:*** Total amount: $429,832; 224 jobs averaging $1919. ***State or other work-study/employment:*** Total amount: $24,575 (100% need-based). 13 part-time jobs averaging $1890.

APPLYING FOR FINANCIAL AID ***Required financial aid forms:*** FAFSA, CSS Financial Aid PROFILE, state aid form, noncustodial (divorced/separated) parent's statement, business/farm supplement. ***Financial aid deadline:*** 2/1. ***Notification date:*** 4/1. Students must reply by 5/1 or within 2 weeks of notification.

CONTACT Gilma Lopez, Office of Financial Aid, Harvey Mudd College, 301 Platt Boulevard, Claremont, CA 91711-5994, 909-621-8055. *Fax:* 909-607-7046. *E-mail:* financial_aid@hmc.edu.

HASKELL INDIAN NATIONS UNIVERSITY

Lawrence, KS

CONTACT Reta Beaver, Director of Financial Aid, Haskell Indian Nations University, 155 Indian Avenue, Box 5027, Lawrence, KS 66046-4800, 785-749-8468. *Fax:* 785-832-6617.

HASTINGS COLLEGE

Hastings, NE

Tuition & fees: $18,302 **Average undergraduate aid package: $11,739**

ABOUT THE INSTITUTION Independent Presbyterian, coed. Awards: bachelor's and master's degrees. 81 undergraduate majors. Total enrollment: 1,137. Undergraduates: 1,093. Freshmen: 263. Federal methodology is used as a basis for awarding need-based institutional aid.

UNDERGRADUATE EXPENSES for 2006–07 ***Application fee:*** $20. ***Comprehensive fee:*** $23,450 includes full-time tuition ($17,572), mandatory fees ($730), and room and board ($5148). ***College room only:*** $2200. Full-time tuition and fees vary according to course level and program. Room and board charges vary according to board plan and housing facility. ***Part-time tuition:*** $728 per semester hour. ***Part-time fees:*** $193 per term. Part-time tuition and fees vary according to course level, course load, and program. ***Payment plans:*** Installment, deferred payment.

FRESHMAN FINANCIAL AID (Fall 2005) 258 applied for aid; of those 85% were deemed to have need. 100% of freshmen with need received aid; of those 32% had need fully met. ***Average percent of need met:*** 79% (excluding resources awarded to replace EFC). ***Average financial aid package:*** $12,216 (excluding resources awarded to replace EFC). 22% of all full-time freshmen had no need and received non-need-based gift aid.

UNDERGRADUATE FINANCIAL AID (Fall 2005) 944 applied for aid; of those 88% were deemed to have need. 100% of undergraduates with need received aid; of those 29% had need fully met. ***Average percent of need met:*** 75% (excluding resources awarded to replace EFC). ***Average financial aid package:*** $11,739 (excluding resources awarded to replace EFC). 22% of all full-time undergraduates had no need and received non-need-based gift aid.

GIFT AID (NEED-BASED) ***Total amount:*** $5,377,931 (19% federal, 3% state, 69% institutional, 9% external sources). ***Receiving aid:*** Freshmen: 77% (220); All full-time undergraduates: 75% (825). ***Average award:*** Freshmen: $9885; Undergraduates: $8412. ***Scholarships, grants, and awards:*** Federal Pell, FSEOG, state, private, college/university gift aid from institutional funds.

GIFT AID (NON-NEED-BASED) ***Total amount:*** $2,056,390 (78% institutional, 22% external sources). ***Receiving aid:*** Freshmen: 17% (48); Undergraduates: 12% (136). ***Average award:*** Freshmen: $9024; Undergraduates: $8577. ***Scholarships, grants, and awards by category:*** *Academic Interests/Achievement:* communication, general academic interests/achievements, religion/biblical studies. *Creative Arts/Performance:* art/fine arts, debating, music, performing arts, theater/drama. *Special Characteristics:* adult students, children of educators, children of faculty/staff, relatives of clergy, religious affiliation, siblings of current students. ***Tuition waivers:*** Full or partial for adult students.

LOANS ***Student loans:*** $4,183,979 (73% need-based, 27% non-need-based). 90% of past graduating class borrowed through all loan programs. *Average indebtedness per student:* $17,634. ***Average need-based loan:*** Freshmen: $3074; Undergraduates: $4122. ***Parent loans:*** $2,047,844 (41% need-based, 59% non-need-based). ***Programs:*** FFEL (Subsidized and Unsubsidized Stafford, PLUS), Perkins, college/university.

WORK-STUDY ***Federal work-study:*** Total amount: $68,355; jobs available (averaging $600). ***State or other work-study/employment:*** Total amount: $116,277 (36% need-based, 64% non-need-based). Part-time jobs available.

ATHLETIC AWARDS Total amount: $2,174,810 (72% need-based, 28% non-need-based).

APPLYING FOR FINANCIAL AID ***Required financial aid forms:*** FAFSA, institution's own form. ***Financial aid deadline:*** 9/1 (priority: 5/1). ***Notification date:*** Continuous. Students must reply within 2 weeks of notification.

CONTACT Mr. Ian Roberts, Associate Vice President-Administration, Hastings College, 7th and Turner, Hastings, NE 68901, 402-461-7455 or toll-free 800-532-7642. *Fax:* 402-461-7714. *E-mail:* iroberts@hastings.edu.

HAVERFORD COLLEGE

Haverford, PA

Tuition & fees: $33,710 **Average undergraduate aid package: $28,881**

ABOUT THE INSTITUTION Independent, coed. Awards: bachelor's degrees. 44 undergraduate majors. Total enrollment: 1,168. Undergraduates: 1,168. Freshmen: 314. Institutional methodology is used as a basis for awarding need-based institutional aid.

UNDERGRADUATE EXPENSES for 2006–07 ***Application fee:*** $60. ***Comprehensive fee:*** $44,100 includes full-time tuition ($33,394), mandatory fees ($316), and room and board ($10,390). ***College room only:*** $5870. ***Payment plan:*** Installment.

FRESHMAN FINANCIAL AID (Fall 2006, est.) 166 applied for aid; of those 80% were deemed to have need. 100% of freshmen with need received aid; of those 100% had need fully met. ***Average percent of need met:*** 100% (excluding resources awarded to replace EFC). ***Average financial aid package:*** $28,531 (excluding resources awarded to replace EFC).

UNDERGRADUATE FINANCIAL AID (Fall 2006, est.) 566 applied for aid; of those 88% were deemed to have need. 100% of undergraduates with need received aid; of those 100% had need fully met. ***Average percent of need met:*** 100% (excluding resources awarded to replace EFC). ***Average financial aid package:*** $28,881 (excluding resources awarded to replace EFC).

GIFT AID (NEED-BASED) ***Total amount:*** $12,330,791 (4% federal, 1% state, 91% institutional, 4% external sources). ***Receiving aid:*** Freshmen: 39% (123); All full-time undergraduates: 40% (462). ***Average award:*** Freshmen: $27,533; Undergraduates: $26,349. ***Scholarships, grants, and awards:*** Federal Pell, FSEOG, state, private, college/university gift aid from institutional funds.

GIFT AID (NON-NEED-BASED) ***Tuition waivers:*** Full or partial for employees or children of employees.

LOANS ***Student loans:*** $1,706,118 (70% need-based, 30% non-need-based). 39% of past graduating class borrowed through all loan programs. *Average indebtedness per student:* $15,875. ***Average need-based loan:*** Freshmen: $2861; Undergraduates: $4135. ***Parent loans:*** $2,520,428 (100% non-need-based). ***Programs:*** FFEL (Subsidized and Unsubsidized Stafford, PLUS), Perkins.

WORK-STUDY ***Federal work-study:*** Total amount: $253,067; jobs available. ***State or other work-study/employment:*** Total amount: $588,514 (28% need-based, 72% non-need-based). Part-time jobs available.

APPLYING FOR FINANCIAL AID ***Required financial aid forms:*** FAFSA, CSS Financial Aid PROFILE, state aid form, noncustodial (divorced/separated) parent's statement, business/farm supplement. ***Financial aid deadline:*** 1/31. ***Notification date:*** 4/15. Students must reply by 5/1.

CONTACT Mr. David J. Hoy, Director of Financial Aid Office, Haverford College, 370 Lancaster Avenue, Haverford, PA 19041-1392, 610-896-1350. *Fax:* 610-896-1338. *E-mail:* finaid@haverford.edu.

HAWAI'I PACIFIC UNIVERSITY

Honolulu, HI

Tuition & fees: $13,080 **Average undergraduate aid package: $12,326**

ABOUT THE INSTITUTION Independent, coed. Awards: associate, bachelor's, and master's degrees and post-bachelor's and post-master's certificates. 55 undergraduate majors. Total enrollment: 8,080. Undergraduates: 6,856. Freshmen: 661. Federal methodology is used as a basis for awarding need-based institutional aid.

UNDERGRADUATE EXPENSES for 2007–08 ***Application fee:*** $50. ***Comprehensive fee:*** $23,640 includes full-time tuition ($13,000), mandatory fees ($80), and room and board ($10,560). ***Part-time tuition:*** $254 per credit.

FRESHMAN FINANCIAL AID (Fall 2006, est.) 515 applied for aid; of those 57% were deemed to have need. 93% of freshmen with need received aid; of those 18% had need fully met. ***Average percent of need met:*** 78% (excluding resources awarded to replace EFC). ***Average financial aid package:*** $11,390 (excluding resources awarded to replace EFC). 10% of all full-time freshmen had no need and received non-need-based gift aid.

UNDERGRADUATE FINANCIAL AID (Fall 2006, est.) 2,640 applied for aid; of those 60% were deemed to have need. 97% of undergraduates with need received aid; of those 24% had need fully met. ***Average percent of need met:*** 77% (excluding resources awarded to replace EFC). ***Average financial aid package:*** $12,326 (excluding resources awarded to replace EFC). 8% of all full-time undergraduates had no need and received non-need-based gift aid.

GIFT AID (NEED-BASED) ***Total amount:*** $3,233,539 (100% federal). ***Receiving aid:*** Freshmen: 19% (120); All full-time undergraduates: 18% (706). ***Average award:*** Freshmen: $3776; Undergraduates: $3891. ***Scholarships, grants, and awards:*** Federal Pell, FSEOG, state, private, college/university gift aid from institutional funds.

GIFT AID (NON-NEED-BASED) ***Total amount:*** $10,239,964 (78% institutional, 22% external sources). ***Receiving aid:*** Freshmen: 17% (111); Undergraduates: 11% (440). ***Average award:*** Freshmen: $600; Undergraduates: $2770. ***Scholarships, grants, and awards by category:*** *Academic Interests/Achievement:* 112 awards ($537,174 total): biological sciences, business, communication, general academic interests/achievements, health fields, social sciences. *Creative Arts/Performance:* 122 awards ($1,146,712 total): dance, journalism/publications, music. *Special Achievements/Activities:* 102 awards ($834,364 total): cheerleading/drum major, hobbies/interests, leadership, memberships, religious involvement. *Special Characteristics:* 710 awards ($4,807,194 total): ethnic background, international students, local/state students, out-of-state students, previous college experience, relatives of clergy, religious affiliation. ***ROTC:*** Army cooperative, Air Force cooperative.

LOANS ***Student loans:*** $18,380,814 (100% need-based). 36% of past graduating class borrowed through all loan programs. *Average indebtedness per student:* $17,125. ***Average need-based loan:*** Freshmen: $5110; Undergraduates: $6578. ***Parent loans:*** $8,490,691 (100% need-based). ***Programs:*** FFEL (Subsidized and Unsubsidized Stafford, PLUS), Perkins, Federal Nursing.

WORK-STUDY ***Federal work-study:*** Total amount: $621,629; 253 jobs averaging $2250.

ATHLETIC AWARDS Total amount: $1,357,852 (100% non-need-based).

APPLYING FOR FINANCIAL AID ***Required financial aid form:*** FAFSA. ***Financial aid deadline (priority):*** 3/1. ***Notification date:*** Continuous beginning 4/1. Students must reply within 3 weeks of notification.

CONTACT Adam Hatch, Director of Financial Aid, Hawai'i Pacific University, 1164 Bishop Street, Suite 201, Honolulu, HI 96813-2785, 808-544-0253 or toll-free 866-225-5478 (out-of-state). *Fax:* 808-544-0884. *E-mail:* financialaid@hpu.edu.

HAWAI'I THEOLOGICAL SEMINARY

Honolulu, HI

CONTACT Mr. Jon Rawlings, Executive Vice President, Hawai'i Theological Seminary, 20 Dowsett Avenue, Honolulu, HI 96817, 808-595-4247. *Fax:* 808-595-4779. *E-mail:* icgs@hawaii.rr.com.

HEBREW COLLEGE

Newton Centre, MA

CONTACT Ms. Norma Frankel, Registrar, Hebrew College, 160 Herrick Road, Newton Centre, MA 02459, 617-559-8612 or toll-free 800-866-4814 Ext. 8619. *Fax:* 617-559-8601.

HEBREW THEOLOGICAL COLLEGE

Skokie, IL

CONTACT Ms. Rhoda Morris, Financial Aid Administrator, Hebrew Theological College, 7135 Carpenter Road, Skokie, IL 60077-3263, 847-982-2500. *Fax:* 847-674-6381.

HEIDELBERG COLLEGE

Tiffin, OH

Tuition & fees: $18,618 **Average undergraduate aid package: $15,397**

ABOUT THE INSTITUTION Independent religious, coed. Awards: bachelor's and master's degrees. 46 undergraduate majors. Total enrollment: 1,569. Undergraduates: 1,330. Freshmen: 274. Federal methodology is used as a basis for awarding need-based institutional aid.

UNDERGRADUATE EXPENSES for 2007–08 ***Application fee:*** $25. ***Comprehensive fee:*** $26,520 includes full-time tuition ($18,190), mandatory fees ($428), and room and board ($7902). ***College room only:*** $3740.

FRESHMAN FINANCIAL AID (Fall 2006, est.) 259 applied for aid; of those 89% were deemed to have need. 100% of freshmen with need received aid; of those 18% had need fully met. ***Average percent of need met:*** 81% (excluding resources awarded to replace EFC). ***Average financial aid package:*** $16,443 (excluding resources awarded to replace EFC). 7% of all full-time freshmen had no need and received non-need-based gift aid.

UNDERGRADUATE FINANCIAL AID (Fall 2006, est.) 896 applied for aid; of those 90% were deemed to have need. 100% of undergraduates with need received aid; of those 18% had need fully met. ***Average percent of need met:*** 83% (excluding resources awarded to replace EFC). ***Average financial aid package:*** $15,397 (excluding resources awarded to replace EFC). 13% of all full-time undergraduates had no need and received non-need-based gift aid.

GIFT AID (NEED-BASED) ***Total amount:*** $9,221,725 (14% federal, 15% state, 68% institutional, 3% external sources). ***Receiving aid:*** Freshmen: 85% (230); All full-time undergraduates: 77% (804). ***Average award:*** Freshmen: $10,900; Undergraduates: $10,823. ***Scholarships, grants, and awards:*** Federal Pell, FSEOG, state, private, college/university gift aid from institutional funds.

GIFT AID (NON-NEED-BASED) ***Total amount:*** $1,193,924 (13% state, 83% institutional, 4% external sources). ***Receiving aid:*** Freshmen: 77% (209); Undergraduates: 45% (467). ***Average award:*** Freshmen: $5026; Undergraduates: $5797. ***Scholarships, grants, and awards by category:*** *Academic Interests/Achievement:* 579 awards ($2,509,085 total): general academic interests/achievements, mathematics, physical sciences. *Creative Arts/Performance:* 55 awards ($107,225 total): music. *Special Achievements/Activities:* religious involvement. *Special Characteristics:* 157 awards ($551,102 total): children of faculty/staff, out-of-state students, relatives of clergy, religious affiliation. ***ROTC:*** Army cooperative, Air Force cooperative.

LOANS ***Student loans:*** $4,854,452 (76% need-based, 24% non-need-based). 74% of past graduating class borrowed through all loan programs. *Average indebtedness per student:* $30,979. ***Average need-based loan:*** Freshmen: $3574; Undergraduates: $4237. ***Parent loans:*** $919,760 (86% need-based, 14% non-need-based). ***Programs:*** FFEL (Subsidized and Unsubsidized Stafford, PLUS), Perkins.

WORK-STUDY ***Federal work-study:*** Total amount: $576,040; 560 jobs averaging $1028. ***State or other work-study/employment:*** Total amount: $32,445 (63% need-based, 37% non-need-based). 11 part-time jobs averaging $3040.

APPLYING FOR FINANCIAL AID ***Required financial aid form:*** FAFSA. ***Financial aid deadline (priority):*** 3/1. ***Notification date:*** Continuous beginning 3/1. Students must reply within 2 weeks of notification.

CONTACT Ms. Juli L. Weininger, Director of Financial Aid, Heidelberg College, 310 East Market Street, Tiffin, OH 44883-2462, 419-448-2293 or toll-free 800-434-3352. *Fax:* 419-448-2296.

HELLENIC COLLEGE

Brookline, MA

Tuition & fees: $16,515 **Average undergraduate aid package: $9200**

ABOUT THE INSTITUTION Independent Greek Orthodox, coed. Awards: bachelor's degrees (also offers graduate degree programs through Holy Cross Greek Orthodox School of Theology). 6 undergraduate majors. Total enrollment: 191. Undergraduates: 82. Freshmen: 19. Both federal and institutional methodology are used as a basis for awarding need-based institutional aid.

UNDERGRADUATE EXPENSES for 2006–07 ***Application fee:*** $50. ***Comprehensive fee:*** $26,885 includes full-time tuition ($16,210), mandatory fees ($305), and room and board ($10,370). ***Part-time tuition:*** $675 per credit.

FRESHMAN FINANCIAL AID (Fall 2005) 21 applied for aid; of those 100% were deemed to have need. 100% of freshmen with need received aid. ***Average percent of need met:*** 80% (excluding resources awarded to replace EFC). ***Average financial aid package:*** $9700 (excluding resources awarded to replace EFC). 3% of all full-time freshmen had no need and received non-need-based gift aid.

UNDERGRADUATE FINANCIAL AID (Fall 2005) 69 applied for aid; of those 97% were deemed to have need. 100% of undergraduates with need received aid. ***Average percent of need met:*** 80% (excluding resources awarded to replace EFC). ***Average financial aid package:*** $9200 (excluding resources awarded to replace EFC). 4% of all full-time undergraduates had no need and received non-need-based gift aid.

GIFT AID (NEED-BASED) ***Total amount:*** $2,020,000 (4% federal, 1% state, 86% institutional, 9% external sources). ***Receiving aid:*** Freshmen: 70% (21); All full-time undergraduates: 93% (67). ***Average award:*** Freshmen: $9700; Undergraduates: $10,100. ***Scholarships, grants, and awards:*** Federal Pell, FSEOG, state, private, college/university gift aid from institutional funds.

GIFT AID (NON-NEED-BASED) ***Average award:*** Freshmen: $2600; Undergraduates: $1100. ***Scholarships, grants, and awards by category:*** *Academic Interests/Achievement:* religion/biblical studies. *Special Achievements/Activities:* religious involvement.

LOANS ***Student loans:*** $436,798 (100% need-based). 65% of past graduating class borrowed through all loan programs. *Average indebtedness per student:* $7300. ***Average need-based loan:*** Freshmen: $2625; Undergraduates: $5500. ***Parent loans:*** $28,400 (100% need-based). ***Programs:*** FFEL (Subsidized and Unsubsidized Stafford, PLUS), state.

WORK-STUDY ***Federal work-study:*** Total amount: $24,200; 9 jobs averaging $720. ***State or other work-study/employment:*** Total amount: $6000 (100% need-based).

APPLYING FOR FINANCIAL AID ***Required financial aid forms:*** FAFSA, institution's own form. ***Financial aid deadline (priority):*** 4/1. ***Notification date:*** Continuous. Students must reply within 2 weeks of notification.

CONTACT George A. Georgenes, Director of Financial Aid and Housing, Hellenic College, 50 Goddard Avenue, Brookline, MA 02146-7496, 617-731-3500 Ext. 1297 or toll-free 866-424-2338. *Fax:* 617-850-1465. *E-mail:* ggeorgenes@hchc.edu.

HENDERSON STATE UNIVERSITY

Arkadelphia, AR

CONTACT Ms. Jo Holland, Director of Financial Aid, Henderson State University, Box 7812, 1100 Henderson Street, Arkadelphia, AR 71999-0001, 870-230-5094 or toll-free 800-228-7333. *Fax:* 870-230-5144. *E-mail:* hollanj@hsu.edu.

HENDRIX COLLEGE

Conway, AR

Tuition & fees: $22,916 **Average undergraduate aid package: $16,968**

ABOUT THE INSTITUTION Independent United Methodist, coed. Awards: bachelor's and master's degrees. 26 undergraduate majors. Total enrollment: 1,095. Undergraduates: 1,088. Freshmen: 396. Federal methodology is used as a basis for awarding need-based institutional aid.

UNDERGRADUATE EXPENSES for 2006–07 ***Application fee:*** $40. ***Comprehensive fee:*** $29,654 includes full-time tuition ($22,616), mandatory fees ($300), and room and board ($6738). ***College room only:*** $3008. Full-time tuition and fees vary according to course load. Room and board charges vary according to board plan and housing facility. ***Part-time tuition:*** $716 per credit hour. Part-time tuition and fees vary according to course load. ***Payment plan:*** Installment.

FRESHMAN FINANCIAL AID (Fall 2006, est.) 329 applied for aid; of those 70% were deemed to have need. 100% of freshmen with need received aid; of those 44% had need fully met. ***Average percent of need met:*** 84% (excluding resources awarded to replace EFC). ***Average financial aid package:*** $18,394 (excluding resources awarded to replace EFC). 41% of all full-time freshmen had no need and received non-need-based gift aid.

UNDERGRADUATE FINANCIAL AID (Fall 2006, est.) 820 applied for aid; of those 77% were deemed to have need. 100% of undergraduates with need received aid; of those 35% had need fully met. ***Average percent of need met:*** 80% (excluding resources awarded to replace EFC). ***Average financial aid package:*** $16,968 (excluding resources awarded to replace EFC). 41% of all full-time undergraduates had no need and received non-need-based gift aid.

GIFT AID (NEED-BASED) ***Total amount:*** $7,629,955 (10% federal, 7% state, 81% institutional, 2% external sources). ***Receiving aid:*** Freshmen: 59% (231); All full-time undergraduates: 57% (617). ***Average award:*** Freshmen: $14,979; Undergraduates: $12,719. ***Scholarships, grants, and awards:*** Federal Pell, FSEOG, state, private, college/university gift aid from institutional funds.

GIFT AID (NON-NEED-BASED) ***Total amount:*** $5,738,525 (11% state, 86% institutional, 3% external sources). ***Receiving aid:*** Freshmen: 18% (69); Undergraduates: 12% (136). ***Average award:*** Freshmen: $17,554; Undergraduates: $16,110. ***Scholarships, grants, and awards by category:*** *Academic Interests/Achievement:* 906 awards ($6,390,895 total): general academic interests/achievements. *Creative Arts/Performance:* 121 awards ($155,500 total): art/fine arts, dance, music, theater/drama. *Special Achievements/Activities:* 766 awards ($1,986,024 total): community service, general special achievements/activities, leadership, religious involvement. *Special Characteristics:* 54 awards ($784,957 total): children of educators, children of faculty/staff, international students, previous college experience, relatives of clergy. ***Tuition waivers:*** Full or partial for employees or children of employees. ***ROTC:*** Army cooperative.

LOANS ***Student loans:*** $4,051,904 (65% need-based, 35% non-need-based). 80% of past graduating class borrowed through all loan programs. *Average indebtedness per student:* $16,360. ***Average need-based loan:*** Freshmen: $3428; Undergraduates: $4352. ***Parent loans:*** $4,111,199 (22% need-based, 78% non-need-based). ***Programs:*** FFEL (Subsidized and Unsubsidized Stafford, PLUS), Perkins, United Methodist Loan.

WORK-STUDY ***Federal work-study:*** Total amount: $571,619; 420 jobs averaging $1360. ***State or other work-study/employment:*** Total amount: $215,620 (11% need-based, 89% non-need-based). 188 part-time jobs averaging $1146.

APPLYING FOR FINANCIAL AID ***Required financial aid forms:*** FAFSA, state aid form. ***Financial aid deadline (priority):*** 2/15. ***Notification date:*** Continuous beginning 2/16. Students must reply by 5/1.

CONTACT Mark Bandré, Director of Financial Aid, Hendrix College, 1600 Washington Avenue, Conway, AR 72032, 501-450-1368 or toll-free 800-277-9017. *Fax:* 501-450-3871. *E-mail:* bandre@hendrix.edu.

HERITAGE BIBLE COLLEGE

Dunn, NC

Tuition & fees: $4200 **Average undergraduate aid package: $4250**

ABOUT THE INSTITUTION Independent Pentecostal Free Will Baptist, coed. Awards: associate and bachelor's degrees. 3 undergraduate majors. Total enrollment: 114. Undergraduates: 114. Freshmen: 25. Federal methodology is used as a basis for awarding need-based institutional aid.

UNDERGRADUATE EXPENSES for 2007–08 ***Application fee:*** $25. ***Comprehensive fee:*** $6600 includes full-time tuition ($3600), mandatory fees ($600), and room and board ($2400). ***College room only:*** $1440. ***Part-time tuition:*** $150 per credit. ***Part-time fees:*** $150 per term.

FRESHMAN FINANCIAL AID (Fall 2005) 17 applied for aid; of those 100% were deemed to have need. 100% of freshmen with need received aid. ***Average financial aid package:*** $4250 (excluding resources awarded to replace EFC).

UNDERGRADUATE FINANCIAL AID (Fall 2005) 116 applied for aid; of those 79% were deemed to have need. 100% of undergraduates with need received aid. ***Average financial aid package:*** $4250 (excluding resources awarded to replace EFC).

GIFT AID (NEED-BASED) ***Total amount:*** $272,100 (82% federal, 18% institutional). ***Receiving aid:*** Freshmen: 82% (14); All full-time undergraduates: 49% (57). ***Average award:*** Freshmen: $250; Undergraduates: $250. ***Scholarships, grants, and awards:*** Federal Pell, FSEOG, private, college/university gift aid from institutional funds.

LOANS ***Student loans:*** $297,237 (100% need-based). 46% of past graduating class borrowed through all loan programs. *Average indebtedness per student:* $14,554. ***Average need-based loan:*** Freshmen: $2625; Undergraduates: $3500. ***Programs:*** FFEL (Subsidized and Unsubsidized Stafford, PLUS).

WORK-STUDY ***Federal work-study:*** Total amount: $7250; 3 jobs averaging $300.

APPLYING FOR FINANCIAL AID ***Required financial aid forms:*** FAFSA, institution's own form, verification documents. ***Financial aid deadline:*** 9/28 (priority: 4/30). ***Notification date:*** Continuous beginning 5/25. Students must reply within 4 weeks of notification.

CONTACT Mrs. Laurie Minard, Director of Financial Aid, Heritage Bible College, Box 1628, Dunn, NC 28335, 800-297-6351 Ext. 226 or toll-free 800-297-6351 Ext. 230. *Fax:* 910-892-1809. *E-mail:* lminard@heritagebiblecollege.edu.

HERITAGE CHRISTIAN UNIVERSITY

Florence, AL

ABOUT THE INSTITUTION Independent religious, coed, primarily men. Awards: associate, bachelor's, and master's degrees. 1 undergraduate major. Total enrollment: 112. Undergraduates: 93. Freshmen: 2.

GIFT AID (NEED-BASED) ***Scholarships, grants, and awards:*** Federal Pell, FSEOG, college/university gift aid from institutional funds.

GIFT AID (NON-NEED-BASED) ***Scholarships, grants, and awards by category:*** *Academic Interests/Achievement:* general academic interests/achievements. *Special Characteristics:* children and siblings of alumni, children of educators, children of faculty/staff, spouses of current students.

LOANS ***Programs:*** FFEL (Subsidized and Unsubsidized Stafford, PLUS).

APPLYING FOR FINANCIAL AID ***Required financial aid forms:*** FAFSA, federal income tax form(s).

CONTACT Angie Horton, Financial Aid Counselor, Heritage Christian University, PO Box HCU, Florence, AL 35630, 800-367-3565 Ext. 24 or toll-free 800-367-3565. *Fax:* 256-766-9289. *E-mail:* ahorton@hcu.edu.

HERITAGE UNIVERSITY

Toppenish, WA

CONTACT Mr. Norberto Espindola, Director of Enrollment Management Services, Heritage University, 3240 Fort Road, Toppenish, WA 98948-9599, 509-865-8500 or toll-free 888-272-6190 (in-state). *Fax:* 509-865-8659. *E-mail:* financial_aid@heritage.edu.

HIGH POINT UNIVERSITY

High Point, NC

CONTACT Dana D. Kelly, Director of Financial Aid, High Point University, Box 3232, University Station, 833 Montlieu Avenue, High Point, NC 27262, 336-841-9128 or toll-free 800-345-6993. *Fax:* 336-884-0221. *E-mail:* dkelly@highpoint.edu.

HILBERT COLLEGE

Hamburg, NY

Tuition & fees: $15,700 **Average undergraduate aid package: $10,601**

ABOUT THE INSTITUTION Independent, coed. Awards: associate and bachelor's degrees. 13 undergraduate majors. Total enrollment: 1,064. Undergraduates: 1,064. Freshmen: 157. Federal methodology is used as a basis for awarding need-based institutional aid.

UNDERGRADUATE EXPENSES for 2006–07 ***Application fee:*** $20. ***Comprehensive fee:*** $21,600 includes full-time tuition ($15,100), mandatory fees ($600), and room and board ($5900). ***College room only:*** $2600. Full-time tuition and fees vary according to course load. Room and board charges vary according to board plan and housing facility. ***Part-time tuition:*** $350 per credit hour. ***Part-time fees:*** $13 per credit hour; $55 per term. Part-time tuition and fees vary according to course load. ***Payment plans:*** Installment, deferred payment.

FRESHMAN FINANCIAL AID (Fall 2006, est.) 169 applied for aid; of those 88% were deemed to have need. 100% of freshmen with need received aid; of those 23% had need fully met. ***Average percent of need met:*** 74% (excluding resources awarded to replace EFC). ***Average financial aid package:*** $10,917 (excluding resources awarded to replace EFC). 12% of all full-time freshmen had no need and received non-need-based gift aid.

UNDERGRADUATE FINANCIAL AID (Fall 2006, est.) 797 applied for aid; of those 89% were deemed to have need. 100% of undergraduates with need received aid; of those 29% had need fully met. ***Average percent of need met:*** 74% (excluding resources awarded to replace EFC). ***Average financial aid package:*** $10,601 (excluding resources awarded to replace EFC). 13% of all full-time undergraduates had no need and received non-need-based gift aid.

GIFT AID (NEED-BASED) ***Total amount:*** $4,676,362 (24% federal, 29% state, 37% institutional, 10% external sources). ***Receiving aid:*** Freshmen: 85% (145); All full-time undergraduates: 84% (690). ***Average award:*** Freshmen: $7834; Undergraduates: $6380. ***Scholarships, grants, and awards:*** Federal Pell, FSEOG, state, private, college/university gift aid from institutional funds.

GIFT AID (NON-NEED-BASED) ***Total amount:*** $481,080 (11% state, 44% institutional, 45% external sources). ***Receiving aid:*** Freshmen: 6% (10); Undergraduates: 5% (44). ***Average award:*** Freshmen: $11,210; Undergraduates: $9997. ***Scholarships, grants, and awards by category:*** *Academic Interests/Achievement:* 84 awards ($153,000 total): general academic interests/achievements. *Special Achievements/Activities:* 40 awards ($54,000 total): leadership. *Special Characteristics:* 42 awards ($38,000 total): children and siblings of alumni, members of minority groups, siblings of current students. ***Tuition waivers:*** Full or partial for children of alumni, employees or children of employees, senior citizens. ***ROTC:*** Army cooperative.

LOANS ***Student loans:*** $6,496,956 (69% need-based, 31% non-need-based). 91% of past graduating class borrowed through all loan programs. *Average indebtedness per student:* $22,282. ***Average need-based loan:*** Freshmen: $3578; Undergraduates: $4758. ***Parent loans:*** $805,086 (33% need-based, 67% non-need-based). ***Programs:*** FFEL (Subsidized and Unsubsidized Stafford, PLUS), Perkins, alternative loans.

WORK-STUDY ***Federal work-study:*** Total amount: $88,101; 54 jobs averaging $1665.

APPLYING FOR FINANCIAL AID ***Required financial aid form:*** FAFSA. ***Financial aid deadline:*** 5/1 (priority: 3/1). ***Notification date:*** Continuous beginning 3/15. Students must reply within 2 weeks of notification.

CONTACT Beverly Chudy, Director of Financial Aid, Hilbert College, 5200 South Park Avenue, Hamburg, NY 14075-1597, 716-649-7900 Ext. 207. *Fax:* 716-649-1152. *E-mail:* bchudy@hilbert.edu.

HILLSDALE COLLEGE

Hillsdale, MI

Tuition & fees: $18,260 **Average undergraduate aid package: $15,000**

ABOUT THE INSTITUTION Independent, coed. Awards: bachelor's degrees. 43 undergraduate majors. Total enrollment: 1,346. Undergraduates: 1,346. Freshmen: 381. Both federal and institutional methodology are used as a basis for awarding need-based institutional aid.

UNDERGRADUATE EXPENSES for 2006–07 ***Application fee:*** $35. ***Comprehensive fee:*** $25,290 includes full-time tuition ($17,850), mandatory fees ($410), and room and board ($7030). ***College room only:*** $3530. Room and board charges vary according to board plan. ***Part-time tuition:*** $700 per semester hour. ***Payment plans:*** Tuition prepayment, installment, deferred payment.

FRESHMAN FINANCIAL AID (Fall 2006, est.) 209 applied for aid; of those 87% were deemed to have need. 100% of freshmen with need received aid; of those 34% had need fully met. ***Average percent of need met:*** 70% (excluding resources awarded to replace EFC). ***Average financial aid package:*** $13,750 (excluding resources awarded to replace EFC). 25% of all full-time freshmen had no need and received non-need-based gift aid.

UNDERGRADUATE FINANCIAL AID (Fall 2006, est.) 600 applied for aid; of those 87% were deemed to have need. 100% of undergraduates with need received aid; of those 48% had need fully met. ***Average percent of need met:*** 80% (excluding resources awarded to replace EFC). ***Average financial aid package:*** $15,000 (excluding resources awarded to replace EFC). 26% of all full-time undergraduates had no need and received non-need-based gift aid.

GIFT AID (NEED-BASED) ***Total amount:*** $7,452,000 (5% state, 95% institutional). ***Receiving aid:*** Freshmen: 51% (182); All full-time undergraduates: 40% (521). ***Average award:*** Freshmen: $7800; Undergraduates: $8500. ***Scholarships, grants, and awards:*** state, private, college/university gift aid from institutional funds.

GIFT AID (NON-NEED-BASED) ***Total amount:*** $2,616,000 (12% state, 75% institutional, 13% external sources). ***Receiving aid:*** Freshmen: 31% (110); Undergraduates: 26% (344). ***Average award:*** Freshmen: $5500; Undergraduates: $7750. ***Scholarships, grants, and awards by category:*** *Academic Interests/Achievement:* 670 awards ($2,200,000 total): biological sciences, business, education, English, foreign languages, general academic interests/achievements, health fields, humanities, international studies, mathematics, physical sciences, premedicine, religion/biblical studies, social sciences. *Creative Arts/Performance:* 55 awards ($120,000 total): art/fine arts, debating, journalism/publications, music, theater/drama. *Special Achievements/Activities:* 240 awards ($1,200,000 total): community service, general special achievements/activities, leadership. *Special Characteristics:* 38 awards ($330,000 total): children of faculty/staff, international students. ***Tuition waivers:*** Full or partial for children of alumni, employees or children of employees.

LOANS ***Student loans:*** $5,237,000 (42% need-based, 58% non-need-based). 65% of past graduating class borrowed through all loan programs. *Average indebtedness per student:* $16,000. ***Average need-based loan:*** Freshmen: $4000; Undergraduates: $3000. ***Programs:*** college/university, alternative loans.

ATHLETIC AWARDS Total amount: $2,050,000 (100% non-need-based).

APPLYING FOR FINANCIAL AID ***Required financial aid forms:*** institution's own form, noncustodial (divorced/separated) parent's statement, business/farm supplement. ***Financial aid deadline:*** 4/1 (priority: 2/1). ***Notification date:*** Continuous beginning 1/20. Students must reply by 5/1 or within 3 weeks of notification.

CONTACT Mr. Rich Moeggengberg, Director of Student Financial Aid, Hillsdale College, 33 East College Street, Hillsdale, MI 49242-1298, 517-607-2550. *Fax:* 517-607-2298. *E-mail:* rich.moeggenbeng@hillsdale.edu.

HILLSDALE FREE WILL BAPTIST COLLEGE

Moore, OK

CONTACT Ms. Pamela Thompson, Director of Admissions and Financial Aid, Hillsdale Free Will Baptist College, PO Box 7208, Moore, OK 73153-1208, 405-912-9006. *Fax:* 405-912-9050. *E-mail:* pamthompson@hc.edu.

HIRAM COLLEGE

Hiram, OH

CONTACT Ann Marie Gruber, Associate Director of Financial Aid, Hiram College, Box 67, Hiram, OH 44234-0067, 330-569-5107 or toll-free 800-362-5280. *Fax:* 330-569-5499.

HOBART AND WILLIAM SMITH COLLEGES

Geneva, NY

Tuition & fees: $34,688 **Average undergraduate aid package: $25,059**

ABOUT THE INSTITUTION Independent, coed. Awards: bachelor's degrees. 54 undergraduate majors. Total enrollment: 1,883. Undergraduates: 1,868. Freshmen: 545. Both federal and institutional methodology are used as a basis for awarding need-based institutional aid.

UNDERGRADUATE EXPENSES for 2006–07 ***Application fee:*** $45. ***Comprehensive fee:*** $43,516 includes full-time tuition ($33,730), mandatory fees ($958), and room and board ($8828). Room and board charges vary according to board plan. ***Payment plans:*** Tuition prepayment, installment.

FRESHMAN FINANCIAL AID (Fall 2006, est.) 423 applied for aid; of those 80% were deemed to have need. 99% of freshmen with need received aid; of those 81% had need fully met. ***Average percent of need met:*** 88% (excluding resources awarded to replace EFC). ***Average financial aid package:*** $25,182 (excluding resources awarded to replace EFC). 23% of all full-time freshmen had no need and received non-need-based gift aid.

UNDERGRADUATE FINANCIAL AID (Fall 2006, est.) 1,403 applied for aid; of those 84% were deemed to have need. 100% of undergraduates with need received aid; of those 80% had need fully met. ***Average percent of need met:*** 80% (excluding resources awarded to replace EFC). ***Average financial aid package:*** $25,059 (excluding resources awarded to replace EFC). 19% of all full-time undergraduates had no need and received non-need-based gift aid.

GIFT AID (NEED-BASED) ***Total amount:*** $24,465,029 (7% federal, 6% state, 83% institutional, 4% external sources). ***Receiving aid:*** Freshmen: 56% (335); All full-time undergraduates: 64% (1,159). ***Average award:*** Freshmen: $22,316; Undergraduates: $21,122. ***Scholarships, grants, and awards:*** Federal Pell, FSEOG, state, private, college/university gift aid from institutional funds, Federal ACG and SMART Grants.

GIFT AID (NON-NEED-BASED) ***Total amount:*** $4,802,256 (1% state, 90% institutional, 9% external sources). ***Receiving aid:*** Freshmen: 9% (51); Undergraduates: 8% (151). ***Average award:*** Freshmen: $18,384; Undergraduates: $17,900. ***Scholarships, grants, and awards by category:*** *Academic Interests/Achievement:* 86 awards ($1,181,500 total): general academic interests/achievements. *Creative Arts/Performance:* 13 awards ($161,000 total): art/fine arts, creative writing, dance, music, performing arts. *Special Achievements/Activities:* 32 awards ($325,000 total): leadership. ***Tuition waivers:*** Full or partial for employees or children of employees.

LOANS ***Student loans:*** $8,863,984 (65% need-based, 35% non-need-based). 64% of past graduating class borrowed through all loan programs. *Average indebtedness per student:* $25,913. ***Average need-based loan:*** Freshmen: $2495; Undergraduates: $3670. ***Parent loans:*** $5,896,347 (29% need-based, 71% non-need-based). ***Programs:*** FFEL (Subsidized and Unsubsidized Stafford, PLUS), Perkins.

WORK-STUDY ***Federal work-study:*** Total amount: $1,569,766; 911 jobs averaging $1725. ***State or other work-study/employment:*** Total amount: $934,432 (12% need-based, 88% non-need-based). 447 part-time jobs averaging $2110.

APPLYING FOR FINANCIAL AID ***Required financial aid forms:*** FAFSA, CSS Financial Aid PROFILE, state aid form, noncustodial (divorced/separated) parent's statement, income tax form(s). ***Financial aid deadline:*** 3/15 (priority: 2/15). ***Notification date:*** 4/1. Students must reply by 5/1 or within 3 weeks of notification.

CONTACT Beth Turner, Director of Financial Aid, Hobart and William Smith Colleges, Geneva, NY 14456-3397, 315-781-3315 or toll-free 800-245-0100. *Fax:* 315-781-3655. *E-mail:* finaid@hws.edu.

HOBE SOUND BIBLE COLLEGE

Hobe Sound, FL

CONTACT Director of Financial Aid, Hobe Sound Bible College, PO Box 1065, Hobe Sound, FL 33475-1065, 561-546-5534 or toll-free 800-881-5534. *Fax:* 561-545-1422.

HOFSTRA UNIVERSITY

Hempstead, NY

Tuition & fees: $24,830 **Average undergraduate aid package: $17,353**

ABOUT THE INSTITUTION Independent, coed. Awards: bachelor's, master's, doctoral, and first professional degrees and post-bachelor's and post-master's certificates. 128 undergraduate majors. Total enrollment: 12,550. Undergraduates: 8,498. Freshmen: 1,716. Federal methodology is used as a basis for awarding need-based institutional aid.

UNDERGRADUATE EXPENSES for 2006–07 ***Application fee:*** $50. ***Comprehensive fee:*** $34,630 includes full-time tuition ($23,800), mandatory fees ($1030), and room and board ($9800). ***College room only:*** $6500. Full-time tuition and fees vary according to course load and program. Room and board charges vary according to board plan and housing facility. ***Part-time tuition:*** $735 per credit hour. ***Part-time fees:*** $155 per term. Part-time tuition and fees vary according to course load and program. ***Payment plans:*** Installment, deferred payment.

FRESHMAN FINANCIAL AID (Fall 2005) 1393 applied for aid; of those 80% were deemed to have need. 98% of freshmen with need received aid; of those 10% had need fully met. ***Average percent of need met:*** 48% (excluding resources awarded to replace EFC). ***Average financial aid package:*** $15,404 (excluding resources awarded to replace EFC). 21% of all full-time freshmen had no need and received non-need-based gift aid.

UNDERGRADUATE FINANCIAL AID (Fall 2005) 5,657 applied for aid; of those 81% were deemed to have need. 99% of undergraduates with need received aid; of those 17% had need fully met. ***Average percent of need met:*** 51% (excluding resources awarded to replace EFC). ***Average financial aid package:*** $17,353 (excluding resources awarded to replace EFC). 17% of all full-time undergraduates had no need and received non-need-based gift aid.

GIFT AID (NEED-BASED) ***Total amount:*** $29,832,989 (19% federal, 22% state, 56% institutional, 3% external sources). ***Receiving aid:*** Freshmen: 54% (949); All full-time undergraduates: 49% (3,897). ***Average award:*** Freshmen: $8338; Undergraduates: $7551. ***Scholarships, grants, and awards:*** Federal Pell, FSEOG, state, private, college/university gift aid from institutional funds.

GIFT AID (NON-NEED-BASED) ***Total amount:*** $11,761,164 (3% federal, 2% state, 90% institutional, 5% external sources). ***Receiving aid:*** Freshmen: 6% (98); Undergraduates: 4% (325). ***Average award:*** Freshmen: $6687; Undergraduates: $6528. ***Scholarships, grants, and awards by category:*** *Academic Interests/Achievement:* 3,326 awards ($22,128,265 total): communication, general academic interests/achievements. *Creative Arts/Performance:* 163 awards ($335,519 total): art/fine arts, dance, music, theater/drama. *Special Achievements/Activities:* 112 awards ($241,288 total): general special achievements/activities, leadership. *Special Characteristics:* 133 awards ($304,621 total): children and siblings of alumni, children of union members/company employees, general special characteristics, handicapped students, public servants. ***Tuition waivers:*** Full or partial for employees or children of employees, senior citizens. ***ROTC:*** Army.

LOANS ***Student loans:*** $49,677,118 (68% need-based, 32% non-need-based). 52% of past graduating class borrowed through all loan programs. *Average indebtedness per student:* $31,196. ***Average need-based loan:*** Freshmen: $2625; Undergraduates: $4269. ***Parent loans:*** $35,491,947 (42% need-based, 58% non-need-based). ***Programs:*** FFEL (Subsidized and Unsubsidized Stafford, PLUS), Perkins.

WORK-STUDY ***Federal work-study:*** Total amount: $995,368; 565 jobs averaging $1762. ***State or other work-study/employment:*** Total amount: $4,811,134 (21% need-based, 79% non-need-based). 2,071 part-time jobs averaging $2323.

ATHLETIC AWARDS Total amount: $6,970,658 (40% need-based, 60% non-need-based).

APPLYING FOR FINANCIAL AID ***Required financial aid forms:*** FAFSA, state aid form. ***Financial aid deadline (priority):*** 2/15. ***Notification date:*** Continuous beginning 3/15. Students must reply within 2 weeks of notification.

CONTACT Sandra Filby, Associate Director of Financial Aid, Hofstra University, 126 Hofstra University, Hempstead, NY 11549, 516-463-4335 or toll-free 800-HOFSTRA. *Fax:* 516-463-4936. *E-mail:* sandra.a.filbry@hofstra.edu.

HOLLINS UNIVERSITY

Roanoke, VA

ABOUT THE INSTITUTION Independent, undergraduate: women only; graduate: coed. Awards: bachelor's and master's degrees and post-master's certificates. 30 undergraduate majors. Total enrollment: 1,061. Undergraduates: 799. Freshmen: 194.

GIFT AID (NEED-BASED) ***Scholarships, grants, and awards:*** Federal Pell, FSEOG, state, private, college/university gift aid from institutional funds.

GIFT AID (NON-NEED-BASED) ***Scholarships, grants, and awards by category:*** *Academic Interests/Achievement:* general academic interests/achievements. *Creative Arts/Performance:* art/fine arts, creative writing, dance, music. *Special Achievements/Activities:* community service, leadership. *Special Characteristics:* children and siblings of alumni, international students, local/state students, out-of-state students, veterans.

LOANS ***Programs:*** Federal Direct (Subsidized and Unsubsidized Stafford, PLUS), Perkins, college/university, Key Alternative Loans, PLATO Loans, CitiAssist Loans, GATE Loans, Sallie Mae Loans, OneChoice loans.

WORK-STUDY ***Federal work-study:*** Total amount: $586,965; 278 jobs averaging $2111. ***State or other work-study/employment:*** Total amount: $167,600 (100% non-need-based). 86 part-time jobs averaging $1948.

APPLYING FOR FINANCIAL AID ***Required financial aid forms:*** FAFSA, state aid form.

CONTACT Mrs. Amy J. Moore, Director of Scholarships and Financial Assistance, Hollins University, PO Box 9718, Roanoke, VA 24020-1688, 540-362-6332 or toll-free 800-456-9595. *Fax:* 540-362-6093. *E-mail:* amoore@hollins.edu.

HOLY FAMILY UNIVERSITY

Philadelphia, PA

CONTACT Financial Aid Office, Holy Family University, Grant and Frankford Avenues, Philadelphia, PA 19114-2094, 215-637-5538 or toll-free 800-637-1191. *Fax:* 215-599-1694. *E-mail:* hfcfinaid@holyfamily.edu.

HOLY NAMES UNIVERSITY

Oakland, CA

Tuition & fees: $22,710 **Average undergraduate aid package: $15,554**

ABOUT THE INSTITUTION Independent Roman Catholic, coed, primarily women. Awards: bachelor's and master's degrees and post-bachelor's certificates. 26 undergraduate majors. Total enrollment: 1,048. Undergraduates: 620. Freshmen: 86. Federal methodology is used as a basis for awarding need-based institutional aid.

UNDERGRADUATE EXPENSES for 2006–07 ***Application fee:*** $50. ***Comprehensive fee:*** $30,710 includes full-time tuition ($22,470), mandatory fees ($240), and room and board ($8000). ***College room only:*** $4200. Full-time tuition and fees vary according to course load. Room and board charges vary according to board plan. ***Part-time tuition:*** $750 per unit. ***Part-time fees:*** $120 per term. ***Payment plan:*** Installment.

FRESHMAN FINANCIAL AID (Fall 2006, est.) 72 applied for aid; of those 97% were deemed to have need. 89% of freshmen with need received aid; of those 15% had need fully met. ***Average percent of need met:*** 28% (excluding resources awarded to replace EFC). ***Average financial aid package:*** $18,950 (excluding resources awarded to replace EFC). 29% of all full-time freshmen had no need and received non-need-based gift aid.

UNDERGRADUATE FINANCIAL AID (Fall 2006, est.) 373 applied for aid; of those 66% were deemed to have need. 70% of undergraduates with need received aid; of those 33% had need fully met. ***Average percent of need met:*** 43% (excluding resources awarded to replace EFC). ***Average financial aid package:*** $15,554 (excluding resources awarded to replace EFC). 18% of all full-time undergraduates had no need and received non-need-based gift aid.

GIFT AID (NEED-BASED) ***Total amount:*** $4,826,119 (15% federal, 22% state, 55% institutional, 8% external sources). ***Receiving aid:*** Freshmen: 75% (62); All full-time undergraduates: 37% (156). ***Average award:*** Freshmen: $16,491; Undergraduates: $13,258. ***Scholarships, grants, and awards:*** Federal Pell, FSEOG, state, private, college/university gift aid from institutional funds.

GIFT AID (NON-NEED-BASED) ***Total amount:*** $622,489 (7% federal, 4% state, 79% institutional, 10% external sources). ***Receiving aid:*** Freshmen: 11% (9); Undergraduates: 10% (41). ***Average award:*** Freshmen: $10,821; Undergraduates: $10,557. ***Scholarships, grants, and awards by category:*** *Academic Interests/Achievement:* 97 awards ($677,787 total): general academic interests/achievements. *Creative Arts/Performance:* 11 awards ($260,096 total): music. *Special Achievements/Activities:* 10 awards ($8500 total): community service. *Special Characteristics:* 35 awards ($141,005 total): children and siblings of alumni, ethnic background, international students, religious affiliation. ***Tuition waivers:*** Full or partial for employees or children of employees. ***ROTC:*** Army cooperative, Air Force cooperative.

LOANS ***Student loans:*** $3,518,359 (81% need-based, 19% non-need-based). 50% of past graduating class borrowed through all loan programs. *Average indebtedness per student:* $10,500. ***Average need-based loan:*** Freshmen: $3122; Undergraduates: $4154. ***Parent loans:*** $1,417,054 (50% need-based, 50% non-need-based). ***Programs:*** FFEL (Subsidized and Unsubsidized Stafford, PLUS), Perkins, alternative loans.

WORK-STUDY ***Federal work-study:*** Total amount: $46,664; 50 jobs averaging $1699. ***State or other work-study/employment:*** 53 part-time jobs averaging $1750.

ATHLETIC AWARDS Total amount: $956,070 (58% need-based, 42% non-need-based).

APPLYING FOR FINANCIAL AID ***Required financial aid forms:*** FAFSA, institution's own form, state aid form, merit scholarship application. ***Financial aid deadline:*** 6/30 (priority: 3/2). ***Notification date:*** Continuous beginning 2/15. Students must reply by 5/1 or within 2 weeks of notification.

CONTACT Christina Miller, Director of Financial Aid, Holy Names University, 3500 Mountain Boulevard, Oakland, CA 94619-1699, 510-436-1327 or toll-free 800-430-1321. *Fax:* 510-436-1199. *E-mail:* miller@hnu.edu.

HOOD COLLEGE

Frederick, MD

Tuition & fees: $23,655 **Average undergraduate aid package: $19,463**

ABOUT THE INSTITUTION Independent, coed. Awards: bachelor's and master's degrees and post-bachelor's certificates (also offers adult program with significant enrollment not reflected in profile). 27 undergraduate majors. Total enrollment: 2,248. Undergraduates: 1,274. Freshmen: 278. Federal methodology is used as a basis for awarding need-based institutional aid.

UNDERGRADUATE EXPENSES for 2006–07 ***Application fee:*** $35. ***Comprehensive fee:*** $31,790 includes full-time tuition ($23,320), mandatory fees ($335), and room and board ($8135). ***College room only:*** $4250. Full-time tuition and fees vary according to course load. Room and board charges vary according to board plan. ***Part-time tuition:*** $670 per credit. ***Part-time fees:*** $105 per term. Part-time tuition and fees vary according to course load. ***Payment plans:*** Tuition prepayment, installment, deferred payment.

FRESHMAN FINANCIAL AID (Fall 2006, est.) 242 applied for aid; of those 82% were deemed to have need. 100% of freshmen with need received aid; of those 42% had need fully met. ***Average percent of need met:*** 90% (excluding resources awarded to replace EFC). ***Average financial aid package:*** $21,864 (excluding resources awarded to replace EFC). 26% of all full-time freshmen had no need and received non-need-based gift aid.

UNDERGRADUATE FINANCIAL AID (Fall 2006, est.) 984 applied for aid; of those 88% were deemed to have need. 99% of undergraduates with need received aid; of those 38% had need fully met. ***Average percent of need met:*** 86% (excluding resources awarded to replace EFC). ***Average financial aid package:*** $19,463 (excluding resources awarded to replace EFC). 21% of all full-time undergraduates had no need and received non-need-based gift aid.

GIFT AID (NEED-BASED) ***Total amount:*** $13,431,742 (10% federal, 13% state, 71% institutional, 6% external sources). ***Receiving aid:*** Freshmen: 71% (197); All full-time undergraduates: 78% (846). ***Average award:*** Freshmen: $16,093; Undergraduates: $15,948. ***Scholarships, grants, and awards:*** Federal Pell, FSEOG, state, private, college/university gift aid from institutional funds.

GIFT AID (NON-NEED-BASED) ***Total amount:*** $3,623,741 (2% federal, 6% state, 82% institutional, 10% external sources). ***Receiving aid:*** Freshmen: 22% (62); Undergraduates: 21% (228). ***Average award:*** Freshmen: $14,493; Undergraduates: $14,203. ***Scholarships, grants, and awards by category:*** *Academic Interests/Achievement:* general academic interests/achievements. *Creative Arts/Performance:* creative writing. *Special Achievements/Activities:* community service, leadership, memberships. *Special Characteristics:* children and siblings of alumni, children of faculty/staff, ethnic background, international students, previous college experience, siblings of current students. ***Tuition waivers:*** Full or partial for children of alumni, employees or children of employees, adult students. ***ROTC:*** Army cooperative.

LOANS ***Student loans:*** $5,194,964 (66% need-based, 34% non-need-based). 86% of past graduating class borrowed through all loan programs. *Average indebtedness per student:* $21,112. ***Average need-based loan:*** Freshmen: $3632; Undergraduates: $4297. ***Parent loans:*** $1,734,850 (100% non-need-based). ***Programs:*** Federal Direct (Subsidized and Unsubsidized Stafford, PLUS), FFEL (Subsidized and Unsubsidized Stafford, PLUS), Perkins.

WORK-STUDY ***Federal work-study:*** Total amount: $324,818; 191 jobs averaging $1700. ***State or other work-study/employment:*** Total amount: $198,175 (73% need-based, 27% non-need-based). 120 part-time jobs averaging $1650.

APPLYING FOR FINANCIAL AID ***Required financial aid form:*** FAFSA. ***Financial aid deadline (priority):*** 2/15. ***Notification date:*** Continuous beginning 3/1. Students must reply by 5/1 or within 3 weeks of notification.

CONTACT Ronald L. Shunk, Director of Financial Aid, Hood College, 401 Rosemont Avenue, Frederick, MD 21701-8575, 301-696-3411 or toll-free 800-922-1599. *Fax:* 301-696-3812. *E-mail:* finaid@hood.edu.

HOPE COLLEGE

Holland, MI

Tuition & fees: $22,570 **Average undergraduate aid package: $18,771**

ABOUT THE INSTITUTION Independent religious, coed. Awards: bachelor's degrees. 84 undergraduate majors. Total enrollment: 3,203. Undergraduates: 3,203. Freshmen: 778. Federal methodology is used as a basis for awarding need-based institutional aid.

UNDERGRADUATE EXPENSES for 2006–07 ***Application fee:*** $35. ***Comprehensive fee:*** $29,552 includes full-time tuition ($22,430), mandatory fees ($140), and room and board ($6982). Full-time tuition and fees vary according to course load. Room and board charges vary according to board plan. ***Payment plan:*** Installment.

FRESHMAN FINANCIAL AID (Fall 2006, est.) 613 applied for aid; of those 72% were deemed to have need. 100% of freshmen with need received aid; of those 28% had need fully met. ***Average percent of need met:*** 85% (excluding resources awarded to replace EFC). ***Average financial aid package:*** $18,879 (excluding resources awarded to replace EFC). 34% of all full-time freshmen had no need and received non-need-based gift aid.

UNDERGRADUATE FINANCIAL AID (Fall 2006, est.) 2,040 applied for aid; of those 79% were deemed to have need. 100% of undergraduates with need received aid; of those 34% had need fully met. ***Average percent of need met:*** 85% (excluding resources awarded to replace EFC). ***Average financial aid package:*** $18,771 (excluding resources awarded to replace EFC). 31% of all full-time undergraduates had no need and received non-need-based gift aid.

GIFT AID (NEED-BASED) ***Total amount:*** $17,547,640 (7% federal, 12% state, 79% institutional, 2% external sources). ***Receiving aid:*** Freshmen: 50% (372); All full-time undergraduates: 49% (1,364). ***Average award:*** Freshmen: $14,799; Undergraduates: $13,521. ***Scholarships, grants, and awards:*** Federal Pell, FSEOG, state, private, college/university gift aid from institutional funds.

GIFT AID (NON-NEED-BASED) ***Total amount:*** $8,852,182 (1% federal, 14% state, 75% institutional, 10% external sources). ***Receiving aid:*** Freshmen: 51% (383); Undergraduates: 43% (1,207). ***Average award:*** Freshmen: $6994; Undergraduates: $6975. ***Scholarships, grants, and awards by category:*** *Academic Interests/Achievement:* 2,020 awards ($12,638,144 total): general academic interests/achievements. *Creative Arts/Performance:* 129 awards ($313,437 total): art/fine arts, creative writing, dance, music, theater/drama. ***ROTC:*** Army cooperative.

LOANS ***Student loans:*** $12,912,433 (44% need-based, 56% non-need-based). 67% of past graduating class borrowed through all loan programs. *Average indebtedness per student:* $23,324. ***Average need-based loan:*** Freshmen: $3220; Undergraduates: $4517. ***Parent loans:*** $2,628,278 (100% non-need-based). ***Programs:*** Federal Direct (Subsidized and Unsubsidized Stafford, PLUS), Perkins, state, college/university.

WORK-STUDY ***Federal work-study:*** Total amount: $324,506; 240 jobs averaging $1352. ***State or other work-study/employment:*** Total amount: $1,613,434 (60% need-based, 40% non-need-based). 530 part-time jobs averaging $1818.

APPLYING FOR FINANCIAL AID ***Required financial aid forms:*** FAFSA, institution's own form. ***Financial aid deadline (priority):*** 3/1. ***Notification date:*** Continuous beginning 3/15. Students must reply by 5/1 or within 2 weeks of notification.

CONTACT Ms. Phyllis Hooyman, Director of Financial Aid, Hope College, 141 East 12th Street, PO Box 9000, Holland, MI 49422-9000, 616-395-7765 or toll-free 800-968-7850. *Fax:* 616-395-7160. *E-mail:* hooyman@hope.edu.

HOPE INTERNATIONAL UNIVERSITY

Fullerton, CA

CONTACT Mr. Mai Bui, Director of Financial Aid, Hope International University, 2500 East Nutwood Avenue, Fullerton, CA 92831, 714-879-3901 or toll-free 800-762-1294. *Fax:* 714-526-0231. *E-mail:* mbui@hiu.edu.

HOUGHTON COLLEGE

Houghton, NY

Tuition & fees: $20,400 **Average undergraduate aid package: $15,808**

ABOUT THE INSTITUTION Independent Wesleyan, coed. Awards: associate, bachelor's, and master's degrees. 52 undergraduate majors. Total enrollment: 1,432. Undergraduates: 1,418. Freshmen: 307. Both federal and institutional methodology are used as a basis for awarding need-based institutional aid.

UNDERGRADUATE EXPENSES for 2006–07 ***Application fee:*** $40. ***Comprehensive fee:*** $27,080 includes full-time tuition ($20,400) and room and board ($6680). ***College room only:*** $3500. Full-time tuition and fees vary according to class time, program, and reciprocity agreements. Room and board charges vary according to board plan and housing facility. ***Part-time tuition:*** $850 per credit. ***Payment plan:*** Installment.

FRESHMAN FINANCIAL AID (Fall 2006, est.) 356 applied for aid; of those 94% were deemed to have need. 99% of freshmen with need received aid; of those 13% had need fully met. ***Average percent of need met:*** 56% (excluding resources awarded to replace EFC). ***Average financial aid package:*** $13,883 (excluding resources awarded to replace EFC). 7% of all full-time freshmen had no need and received non-need-based gift aid.

UNDERGRADUATE FINANCIAL AID (Fall 2006, est.) 1,089 applied for aid; of those 93% were deemed to have need. 100% of undergraduates with need received aid; of those 22% had need fully met. ***Average percent of need met:*** 70% (excluding resources awarded to replace EFC). ***Average financial aid package:*** $15,808 (excluding resources awarded to replace EFC). 9% of all full-time undergraduates had no need and received non-need-based gift aid.

GIFT AID (NEED-BASED) ***Total amount:*** $9,363,759 (13% federal, 13% state, 69% institutional, 5% external sources). ***Receiving aid:*** Freshmen: 90% (330); All full-time undergraduates: 89% (1,002). ***Average award:*** Freshmen: $10,338; Undergraduates: $10,212. ***Scholarships, grants, and awards:*** Federal Pell, FSEOG, state, private, college/university gift aid from institutional funds, United Negro College Fund.

GIFT AID (NON-NEED-BASED) ***Total amount:*** $783,303 (8% state, 82% institutional, 10% external sources). ***Receiving aid:*** Freshmen: 4% (16); Undergraduates: 6% (72). ***Average award:*** Freshmen: $18,574; Undergraduates: $18,634. ***Scholarships, grants, and awards by category:*** *Academic Interests/Achievement:* 662 awards ($2,667,208 total): general academic interests/achievements. *Creative Arts/Performance:* 97 awards ($187,699 total): art/fine arts, music. *Special Achievements/Activities:* 322 awards ($272,643 total): religious involvement. *Special Characteristics:* 614 awards ($2,098,660 total): children and siblings of alumni, children of faculty/staff, international students, local/state students, relatives of clergy, religious affiliation, siblings of current students. ***Tuition waivers:*** Full or partial for employees or children of employees, senior citizens. ***ROTC:*** Army cooperative.

LOANS ***Student loans:*** $11,297,915 (54% need-based, 46% non-need-based). 72% of past graduating class borrowed through all loan programs. *Average indebtedness per student:* $24,125. ***Average need-based loan:*** Freshmen: $4096;

Undergraduates: $5488. ***Parent loans:*** $2,034,982 (72% need-based, 28% non-need-based). ***Programs:*** FFEL (Subsidized and Unsubsidized Stafford, PLUS), Perkins, college/university, alternative loans.

WORK-STUDY ***Federal work-study:*** Total amount: $1,205,424; 766 jobs averaging $1757. ***State or other work-study/employment:*** Part-time jobs available.

ATHLETIC AWARDS Total amount: $583,490 (82% need-based, 18% non-need-based).

APPLYING FOR FINANCIAL AID ***Required financial aid forms:*** FAFSA, state aid form. ***Financial aid deadline (priority):*** 3/1. ***Notification date:*** Continuous beginning 3/15. Students must reply within 4 weeks of notification.

CONTACT Mr. Troy Martin, Director of Financial Aid, Houghton College, One Willard Avenue, Houghton, NY 14744, 716-567-9328 or toll-free 800-777-2556. *Fax:* 716-567-9610. *E-mail:* troy.martin@houghton.edu.

HOUSTON BAPTIST UNIVERSITY

Houston, TX

Tuition & fees: $17,716 **Average undergraduate aid package: $13,838**

ABOUT THE INSTITUTION Independent Baptist, coed. Awards: associate, bachelor's, and master's degrees and post-bachelor's and post-master's certificates. 65 undergraduate majors. Total enrollment: 2,143. Undergraduates: 1,815. Freshmen: 229. Federal methodology is used as a basis for awarding need-based institutional aid.

UNDERGRADUATE EXPENSES for 2007–08 ***Application fee:*** $25. ***Comprehensive fee:*** $22,711 includes full-time tuition ($17,446), mandatory fees ($270), and room and board ($4995). ***College room only:*** $2460. ***Part-time tuition:*** $630 per credit hour.

FRESHMAN FINANCIAL AID (Fall 2006, est.) 120 applied for aid; of those 88% were deemed to have need. 100% of freshmen with need received aid; of those 18% had need fully met. ***Average percent of need met:*** 64% (excluding resources awarded to replace EFC). ***Average financial aid package:*** $13,128 (excluding resources awarded to replace EFC). 31% of all full-time freshmen had no need and received non-need-based gift aid.

UNDERGRADUATE FINANCIAL AID (Fall 2006, est.) 1,053 applied for aid; of those 84% were deemed to have need. 100% of undergraduates with need received aid; of those 15% had need fully met. ***Average percent of need met:*** 61% (excluding resources awarded to replace EFC). ***Average financial aid package:*** $13,838 (excluding resources awarded to replace EFC). 23% of all full-time undergraduates had no need and received non-need-based gift aid.

GIFT AID (NEED-BASED) ***Total amount:*** $6,547,776 (30% federal, 35% state, 33% institutional, 2% external sources). ***Receiving aid:*** Freshmen: 53% (102); All full-time undergraduates: 52% (814). ***Average award:*** Freshmen: $8494; Undergraduates: $7826. ***Scholarships, grants, and awards:*** Federal Pell, FSEOG, state, private, college/university gift aid from institutional funds.

GIFT AID (NON-NEED-BASED) ***Total amount:*** $2,236,601 (96% institutional, 4% external sources). ***Receiving aid:*** Freshmen: 24% (46); Undergraduates: 17% (270). ***Average award:*** Freshmen: $5825; Undergraduates: $6233. ***Scholarships, grants, and awards by category:*** *Academic Interests/Achievement:* 775 awards ($3,484,083 total): general academic interests/achievements, health fields, religion/biblical studies. *Creative Arts/Performance:* 125 awards ($324,991 total): art/fine arts, music. *Special Achievements/Activities:* 12 awards ($31,200 total): cheerleading/drum major, general special achievements/activities. *Special Characteristics:* 84 awards ($361,339 total): children and siblings of alumni, children of faculty/staff, general special characteristics, relatives of clergy, siblings of current students. ***ROTC:*** Army cooperative.

LOANS ***Student loans:*** $7,138,982 (79% need-based, 21% non-need-based). 83% of past graduating class borrowed through all loan programs. *Average indebtedness per student:* $17,256. ***Average need-based loan:*** Freshmen: $2774; Undergraduates: $3569. ***Parent loans:*** $4,027,172 (38% need-based, 62% non-need-based). ***Programs:*** FFEL (Subsidized and Unsubsidized Stafford, PLUS), state, alternative loans.

WORK-STUDY ***Federal work-study:*** Total amount: $888,955; 602 jobs averaging $1477.

ATHLETIC AWARDS Total amount: $1,309,243 (22% need-based, 78% non-need-based).

APPLYING FOR FINANCIAL AID ***Required financial aid form:*** FAFSA. ***Financial aid deadline:*** 4/15 (priority: 3/1). ***Notification date:*** Continuous beginning 3/1.

CONTACT Allison Sullivan, Director of Student Aid Programs, Houston Baptist University, 109 Administration Building, 7502 Fondren Road, Houston, TX 77074-3298, 281-649-3471 or toll-free 800-696-3210. *Fax:* 281-649-3298. *E-mail:* sullivan@erskine.edu.

HOWARD PAYNE UNIVERSITY

Brownwood, TX

CONTACT Glenda Huff, Director of Financial Aid, Howard Payne University, 1000 Fisk Avenue, Brownwood, TX 76801, 325-649-8014 or toll-free 800-880-4478. *Fax:* 325-649-8901. *E-mail:* ghuff@hputx.edu.

HOWARD UNIVERSITY

Washington, DC

ABOUT THE INSTITUTION Independent, coed. Awards: bachelor's, master's, doctoral, and first professional degrees and post-master's and first professional certificates. 64 undergraduate majors. Total enrollment: 10,623. Undergraduates: 7,112. Freshmen: 1,451.

GIFT AID (NEED-BASED) ***Scholarships, grants, and awards:*** Federal Pell, FSEOG, state, private, college/university gift aid from institutional funds, Federal Nursing.

GIFT AID (NON-NEED-BASED) ***Scholarships, grants, and awards by category:*** *Creative Arts/Performance:* art/fine arts, dance, music.

LOANS ***Programs:*** Federal Direct (Subsidized and Unsubsidized Stafford, PLUS), FFEL (Subsidized and Unsubsidized Stafford, PLUS), Perkins, Federal Nursing, district, college/university.

APPLYING FOR FINANCIAL AID ***Required financial aid form:*** FAFSA.

CONTACT Mr. Steven G. Johnson, Director of Financial Aid and Scholarships, Howard University, 2400 Sixth Street, NW, Washington, DC 20059-0002, 202-806-2762 or toll-free 800-HOWARD-U. *Fax:* 202-806-2818.

HUMBOLDT STATE UNIVERSITY

Arcata, CA

ABOUT THE INSTITUTION State-supported, coed. Awards: bachelor's and master's degrees. 78 undergraduate majors. Total enrollment: 7,435. Undergraduates: 6,466. Freshmen: 958.

GIFT AID (NEED-BASED) ***Scholarships, grants, and awards:*** Federal Pell, FSEOG, state, private, college/university gift aid from institutional funds.

GIFT AID (NON-NEED-BASED) ***Scholarships, grants, and awards by category:*** *Academic Interests/Achievement:* general academic interests/achievements.

LOANS ***Programs:*** Federal Direct (Subsidized and Unsubsidized Stafford, PLUS), Perkins.

APPLYING FOR FINANCIAL AID ***Required financial aid form:*** FAFSA.

CONTACT Kim Coughlin-Lamphear, Director of Financial Aid, Humboldt State University, 1 Harpst Street, Arcata, CA 95521-8299, 707-826-4321. *E-mail:* coughlin@humboldt.edu.

HUMPHREYS COLLEGE

Stockton, CA

CONTACT Judi LaFeber, Director of Financial Aid, Humphreys College, 6650 Inglewood Avenue, Stockton, CA 95207-3896, 209-478-0800. *Fax:* 209-478-8721.

HUNTER COLLEGE OF THE CITY UNIVERSITY OF NEW YORK

New York, NY

CONTACT Kevin McGowan, Director of Financial Aid, Hunter College of the City University of New York, 695 Park Avenue, New York, NY 10021-5085, 212-772-4820.

HUNTINGDON COLLEGE

Montgomery, AL

CONTACT Belinda Goris, Student Financial Aid Director, Huntingdon College, 1500 East Fairview Avenue, Montgomery, AL 36106-2148, 334-833-4519 or toll-free 800-763-0313. *E-mail:* bgoris@huntingdon.edu.

HUNTINGTON UNIVERSITY

Huntington, IN

Tuition & fees: $19,430 **Average undergraduate aid package: $13,300**

ABOUT THE INSTITUTION Independent religious, coed. Awards: associate, bachelor's, and master's degrees. 58 undergraduate majors. Total enrollment: 1,084. Undergraduates: 997. Freshmen: 252. Federal methodology is used as a basis for awarding need-based institutional aid.

UNDERGRADUATE EXPENSES for 2007–08 ***Application fee:*** $20. ***Comprehensive fee:*** $26,160 includes full-time tuition ($18,980), mandatory fees ($450), and room and board ($6730). ***Part-time tuition:*** $570 per semester hour. ***Part-time fees:*** $22 per semester hour.

FRESHMAN FINANCIAL AID (Fall 2006, est.) 215 applied for aid; of those 89% were deemed to have need. 100% of freshmen with need received aid; of those 17% had need fully met. ***Average percent of need met:*** 78% (excluding resources awarded to replace EFC). ***Average financial aid package:*** $14,555 (excluding resources awarded to replace EFC). 15% of all full-time freshmen had no need and received non-need-based gift aid.

UNDERGRADUATE FINANCIAL AID (Fall 2006, est.) 723 applied for aid; of those 87% were deemed to have need. 100% of undergraduates with need received aid; of those 16% had need fully met. ***Average percent of need met:*** 73% (excluding resources awarded to replace EFC). ***Average financial aid package:*** $13,300 (excluding resources awarded to replace EFC). 14% of all full-time undergraduates had no need and received non-need-based gift aid.

GIFT AID (NEED-BASED) ***Total amount:*** $5,840,818 (12% federal, 24% state, 57% institutional, 7% external sources). ***Receiving aid:*** Freshmen: 78% (187); All full-time undergraduates: 66% (572). ***Average award:*** Freshmen: $12,059; Undergraduates: $10,849. ***Scholarships, grants, and awards:*** Federal Pell, FSEOG, state, private, college/university gift aid from institutional funds.

GIFT AID (NON-NEED-BASED) ***Total amount:*** $1,016,431 (1% state, 84% institutional, 15% external sources). ***Receiving aid:*** Freshmen: 20% (48); Undergraduates: 16% (142). ***Average award:*** Freshmen: $7514; Undergraduates: $6635. ***Scholarships, grants, and awards by category:*** *Academic Interests/Achievement:* 452 awards ($1,514,320 total): general academic interests/achievements. *Creative Arts/Performance:* 75 awards ($91,900 total): art/fine arts, journalism/publications, music, theater/drama. *Special Achievements/Activities:* 7 awards ($4100 total): cheerleading/drum major. *Special Characteristics:* 556 awards ($1,617,306 total): children and siblings of alumni, children of current students, children of faculty/staff, international students, parents of current students, relatives of clergy, religious affiliation, siblings of current students, spouses of current students.

LOANS ***Student loans:*** $4,607,824 (68% need-based, 32% non-need-based). 66% of past graduating class borrowed through all loan programs. *Average indebtedness per student:* $23,005. ***Average need-based loan:*** Freshmen: $3606; Undergraduates: $4379. ***Parent loans:*** $1,072,947 (34% need-based, 66% non-need-based). ***Programs:*** FFEL (Subsidized and Unsubsidized Stafford, PLUS), Perkins.

WORK-STUDY ***Federal work-study:*** Total amount: $379,996; 192 jobs averaging $1877.

ATHLETIC AWARDS Total amount: $755,244 (60% need-based, 40% non-need-based).

APPLYING FOR FINANCIAL AID ***Required financial aid form:*** FAFSA. ***Financial aid deadline (priority):*** 3/1. ***Notification date:*** Continuous beginning 3/1. Students must reply by 5/1 or within 2 weeks of notification.

CONTACT Mrs. Cindy Kreps, Financial Aid Secretary, Huntington University, 2303 College Avenue, Huntington, IN 46750, 260-359-4015 or toll-free 800-642-6493. *Fax:* 260-358-3699. *E-mail:* ckreps@huntington.edu.

HUSSIAN SCHOOL OF ART

Philadelphia, PA

CONTACT Ms. Susan Cohen, Financial Aid and Placement Director, Hussian School of Art, 1118 Market Street, Philadelphia, PA 19107-3679, 215-981-0900.

HUSSON COLLEGE

Bangor, ME

Tuition & fees: $11,770 **Average undergraduate aid package: $9569**

ABOUT THE INSTITUTION Independent, coed. Awards: associate, bachelor's, and master's degrees and post-bachelor's and post-master's certificates. 28 undergraduate majors. Total enrollment: 2,242. Undergraduates: 1,984. Freshmen: 284. Federal methodology is used as a basis for awarding need-based institutional aid.

UNDERGRADUATE EXPENSES for 2006–07 ***Application fee:*** $25. ***Comprehensive fee:*** $18,010 includes full-time tuition ($11,520), mandatory fees ($250), and room and board ($6240). Full-time tuition and fees vary according to class time. ***Part-time tuition:*** $384 per credit hour. Part-time tuition and fees vary according to class time and course load. ***Payment plans:*** Tuition prepayment, installment.

FRESHMAN FINANCIAL AID (Fall 2006, est.) 392 applied for aid; of those 91% were deemed to have need. 97% of freshmen with need received aid; of those 8% had need fully met. ***Average percent of need met:*** 75% (excluding resources awarded to replace EFC). ***Average financial aid package:*** $10,374 (excluding resources awarded to replace EFC). 27% of all full-time freshmen had no need and received non-need-based gift aid.

UNDERGRADUATE FINANCIAL AID (Fall 2006, est.) 1,293 applied for aid; of those 90% were deemed to have need. 99% of undergraduates with need received aid; of those 9% had need fully met. ***Average percent of need met:*** 71% (excluding resources awarded to replace EFC). ***Average financial aid package:*** $9569 (excluding resources awarded to replace EFC). 18% of all full-time undergraduates had no need and received non-need-based gift aid.

GIFT AID (NEED-BASED) ***Total amount:*** $7,334,229 (37% federal, 12% state, 42% institutional, 9% external sources). ***Receiving aid:*** Freshmen: 67% (331); All full-time undergraduates: 72% (1,019). ***Average award:*** Freshmen: $7955; Undergraduates: $6545. ***Scholarships, grants, and awards:*** Federal Pell, FSEOG, state, private, college/university gift aid from institutional funds.

GIFT AID (NON-NEED-BASED) ***Total amount:*** $585,695 (81% institutional, 19% external sources). ***Receiving aid:*** Freshmen: 2% (12); Undergraduates: 2% (34). ***Average award:*** Freshmen: $4908; Undergraduates: $7750. ***Scholarships, grants, and awards by category:*** *Academic Interests/Achievement:* 152 awards ($15,897 total): business, computer science, education, general academic interests/achievements, health fields. *Special Achievements/Activities:* general special achievements/activities, leadership. *Special Characteristics:* children of union members/company employees. ***Tuition waivers:*** Full or partial for employees or children of employees, senior citizens. ***ROTC:*** Army cooperative, Naval cooperative.

LOANS ***Student loans:*** $9,999,998 (68% need-based, 32% non-need-based). 88% of past graduating class borrowed through all loan programs. *Average indebtedness per student:* $19,380. ***Average need-based loan:*** Freshmen: $2282; Undergraduates: $3377. ***Parent loans:*** $1,405,055 (36% need-based, 64% non-need-based). ***Programs:*** FFEL (Subsidized and Unsubsidized Stafford, PLUS), Perkins, state, alternative loans.

WORK-STUDY ***Federal work-study:*** Total amount: $630,503; 635 jobs averaging $1350.

APPLYING FOR FINANCIAL AID ***Required financial aid forms:*** FAFSA, state aid form. ***Financial aid deadline (priority):*** 4/15. ***Notification date:*** Continuous beginning 2/15. Students must reply by 5/1 or within 2 weeks of notification.

CONTACT Linda B. Conant, Director of Financial Aid, Husson College, One College Circle, Bangor, ME 04401, 207-941-7156 or toll-free 800-4-HUSSON. *Fax:* 207-973-1038. *E-mail:* conantl@husson.edu.

HUSTON-TILLOTSON UNIVERSITY

Austin, TX

CONTACT Anthony P. Barrientez, Director of Financial Aid, Huston-Tillotson University, 900 Chicon Street, Austin, TX 78702, 512-505-3031.

IDAHO STATE UNIVERSITY

Pocatello, ID

Tuition & fees (ID res): $4190 **Average undergraduate aid package: $5731**

ABOUT THE INSTITUTION State-supported, coed. Awards: bachelor's, master's, doctoral, and first professional degrees and post-bachelor's, post-master's, and first professional certificates. 100 undergraduate majors. Total enrollment: 12,679. Undergraduates: 10,640. Freshmen: 1,331. Federal methodology is used as a basis for awarding need-based institutional aid.

UNDERGRADUATE EXPENSES for 2007–08 ***Application fee:*** $40. ***Tuition, state resident:*** full-time $2689; part-time $214 per credit hour. ***Tuition, nonresident:*** full-time $10,959; part-time $329 per credit hour. ***College room and board:*** $4950; ***Room only:*** $2250.

FRESHMAN FINANCIAL AID (Fall 2005) 758 applied for aid; of those 72% were deemed to have need. 97% of freshmen with need received aid; of those 11% had need fully met. ***Average percent of need met:*** 53% (excluding resources awarded to replace EFC). ***Average financial aid package:*** $4067 (excluding resources awarded to replace EFC). 29% of all full-time freshmen had no need and received non-need-based gift aid.

UNDERGRADUATE FINANCIAL AID (Fall 2005) 5,698 applied for aid; of those 89% were deemed to have need. 96% of undergraduates with need received aid; of those 6% had need fully met. ***Average percent of need met:*** 52% (excluding resources awarded to replace EFC). ***Average financial aid package:*** $5731 (excluding resources awarded to replace EFC). 12% of all full-time undergraduates had no need and received non-need-based gift aid.

GIFT AID (NEED-BASED) ***Total amount:*** $14,712,322 (99% federal, 1% state). ***Receiving aid:*** Freshmen: 33% (316); All full-time undergraduates: 48% (3,452). ***Average award:*** Freshmen: $2656; Undergraduates: $3041. ***Scholarships, grants, and awards:*** Federal Pell, FSEOG, state, private.

GIFT AID (NON-NEED-BASED) ***Total amount:*** $7,832,653 (4% federal, 10% state, 40% institutional, 46% external sources). ***Receiving aid:*** Freshmen: 40% (384); Undergraduates: 25% (1,795). ***Average award:*** Freshmen: $2291; Undergraduates: $2352. ***Scholarships, grants, and awards by category:*** *Academic Interests/Achievement:* 2,770 awards ($2,964,955 total): biological sciences, business, communication, computer science, education, engineering/technologies, English, foreign languages, general academic interests/achievements, health fields, home economics, humanities, international studies, mathematics, military science, physical sciences, premedicine, religion/biblical studies, social sciences. *Creative Arts/Performance:* 274 awards ($151,835 total): art/fine arts, debating, music, performing arts, theater/drama. *Special Achievements/Activities:* 125 awards ($61,432 total): general special achievements/activities, junior miss, leadership, memberships, rodeo. *Special Characteristics:* 1,440 awards ($695,482 total): children and siblings of alumni, children of faculty/staff, first-generation college students, handicapped students, local/state students, members of minority groups, out-of-state students. ***ROTC:*** Army cooperative.

LOANS ***Student loans:*** $39,730,138 (55% need-based, 45% non-need-based). 71% of past graduating class borrowed through all loan programs. *Average indebtedness per student:* $20,253. ***Average need-based loan:*** Freshmen: $2122; Undergraduates: $3689. ***Parent loans:*** $582,682 (100% non-need-based). ***Programs:*** Federal Direct (Subsidized and Unsubsidized Stafford, PLUS), Perkins.

WORK-STUDY ***Federal work-study:*** Total amount: $913,276; 901 jobs averaging $2370. ***State or other work-study/employment:*** Total amount: $436,767 (100% need-based). 817 part-time jobs averaging $1150.

ATHLETIC AWARDS Total amount: $2,602,533 (1% need-based, 99% non-need-based).

APPLYING FOR FINANCIAL AID ***Required financial aid form:*** FAFSA. ***Financial aid deadline:*** Continuous. ***Notification date:*** Continuous beginning 4/1.

CONTACT Mr. Doug Severs, Director of Financial Aid, Idaho State University, 921 S. 8th Avenue, Stop 8077, Pocatello, ID 83209, 208-282-2981. *Fax:* 208-282-4755. *E-mail:* sevedoug@isu.edu.

ILLINOIS COLLEGE

Jacksonville, IL

Tuition & fees: $17,100 **Average undergraduate aid package: $13,570**

ABOUT THE INSTITUTION Independent interdenominational, coed. Awards: bachelor's degrees. 44 undergraduate majors. Total enrollment: 1,023. Undergraduates: 1,023. Freshmen: 293. Federal methodology is used as a basis for awarding need-based institutional aid.

UNDERGRADUATE EXPENSES for 2006–07 ***Comprehensive fee:*** $23,830 includes full-time tuition ($17,100) and room and board ($6730). ***College room only:*** $2800. ***Part-time tuition:*** $715 per credit hour. ***Payment plans:*** Installment, deferred payment.

FRESHMAN FINANCIAL AID (Fall 2006, est.) 272 applied for aid; of those 92% were deemed to have need. 100% of freshmen with need received aid; of those 61% had need fully met. ***Average percent of need met:*** 91% (excluding resources awarded to replace EFC). ***Average financial aid package:*** $13,253 (excluding resources awarded to replace EFC). 23% of all full-time freshmen had no need and received non-need-based gift aid.

UNDERGRADUATE FINANCIAL AID (Fall 2006, est.) 914 applied for aid; of those 85% were deemed to have need. 100% of undergraduates with need received aid; of those 34% had need fully met. ***Average percent of need met:*** 91% (excluding resources awarded to replace EFC). ***Average financial aid package:*** $13,570 (excluding resources awarded to replace EFC). 22% of all full-time undergraduates had no need and received non-need-based gift aid.

GIFT AID (NEED-BASED) ***Total amount:*** $7,472,445 (11% federal, 26% state, 61% institutional, 2% external sources). ***Receiving aid:*** Freshmen: 62% (181); All full-time undergraduates: 65% (652). ***Average award:*** Freshmen: $6176; Undergraduates: $6292. ***Scholarships, grants, and awards:*** Federal Pell, FSEOG, state, private, college/university gift aid from institutional funds.

GIFT AID (NON-NEED-BASED) ***Total amount:*** $1,791,122 (94% institutional, 6% external sources). ***Receiving aid:*** Freshmen: 85% (249); Undergraduates: 62% (622). ***Average award:*** Freshmen: $6489; Undergraduates: $5587. ***Scholarships, grants, and awards by category:*** *Academic Interests/Achievement:* 634 awards ($3,564,423 total): general academic interests/achievements. *Creative Arts/Performance:* 58 awards ($47,085 total): art/fine arts, music, theater/drama. *Special Characteristics:* 190 awards ($759,270 total): children of faculty/staff, ethnic background, international students, members of minority groups, out-of-state students, previous college experience, religious affiliation. ***Tuition waivers:*** Full or partial for employees or children of employees.

LOANS ***Student loans:*** $4,391,838 (59% need-based, 41% non-need-based). 77% of past graduating class borrowed through all loan programs. *Average indebtedness per student:* $17,733. ***Average need-based loan:*** Freshmen: $3563; Undergraduates: $4229. ***Parent loans:*** $1,197,555 (100% non-need-based). ***Programs:*** FFEL (Subsidized and Unsubsidized Stafford, PLUS), Perkins.

WORK-STUDY ***Federal work-study:*** Total amount: $674,525; 513 jobs averaging $1315. ***State or other work-study/employment:*** Total amount: $276,547 (100% non-need-based). 362 part-time jobs averaging $764.

APPLYING FOR FINANCIAL AID ***Required financial aid form:*** FAFSA. ***Financial aid deadline (priority):*** 3/1. ***Notification date:*** Continuous beginning 3/7. Students must reply within 2 weeks of notification.

CONTACT Kate Taylor, Director of Financial Aid, Illinois College, 1101 West College Avenue, Jacksonville, IL 62650-2299, 217-245-3035 or toll-free 866-464-5265. *Fax:* 217-245-3274. *E-mail:* finaid@hilltop.ic.edu.

THE ILLINOIS INSTITUTE OF ART–CHICAGO

Chicago, IL

CONTACT Director of Student Financial Services, The Illinois Institute of Art–Chicago, 350 North Orleans Street, Suite 136, Chicago, IL 60654-1593, 800-351-3450.

THE ILLINOIS INSTITUTE OF ART–SCHAUMBURG

Schaumburg, IL

CONTACT Financial Aid Office, The Illinois Institute of Art–Schaumburg, 1000 North Plaza Drive, Schaumburg, IL 60173, 800-314-3450.

ILLINOIS INSTITUTE OF TECHNOLOGY

Chicago, IL

Tuition & fees: $24,113 **Average undergraduate aid package: $21,490**

ABOUT THE INSTITUTION Independent, coed. Awards: bachelor's, master's, doctoral, and first professional degrees and post-bachelor's certificates. 31 undergraduate majors. Total enrollment: 6,795. Undergraduates: 2,353. Freshmen: 484. Federal methodology is used as a basis for awarding need-based institutional aid.

UNDERGRADUATE EXPENSES for 2006–07 ***Application fee:*** $30. ***Comprehensive fee:*** $32,162 includes full-time tuition ($23,329), mandatory fees ($784), and room and board ($8049). ***College room only:*** $4212. Room and board charges vary according to board plan and housing facility. ***Part-time tuition:*** $727 per credit hour. ***Part-time fees:*** $7 per credit hour; $250 per term. Part-time tuition and fees vary according to course load. ***Payment plan:*** Installment.

FRESHMAN FINANCIAL AID (Fall 2005) 357 applied for aid; of those 84% were deemed to have need. 100% of freshmen with need received aid; of those 21% had need fully met. ***Average percent of need met:*** 87% (excluding resources awarded to replace EFC). ***Average financial aid package:*** $22,239 (excluding resources awarded to replace EFC). 26% of all full-time freshmen had no need and received non-need-based gift aid.

UNDERGRADUATE FINANCIAL AID (Fall 2005) 1,325 applied for aid; of those 89% were deemed to have need. 100% of undergraduates with need received aid; of those 19% had need fully met. ***Average percent of need met:*** 85% (excluding resources awarded to replace EFC). ***Average financial aid package:*** $21,490 (excluding resources awarded to replace EFC). 38% of all full-time undergraduates had no need and received non-need-based gift aid.

GIFT AID (NEED-BASED) ***Total amount:*** $14,973,572 (14% federal, 12% state, 73% institutional, 1% external sources). ***Receiving aid:*** Freshmen: 72% (298); All full-time undergraduates: 58% (1,158). ***Average award:*** Freshmen: $15,245; Undergraduates: $13,162. ***Scholarships, grants, and awards:*** Federal Pell, FSEOG, state, private, college/university gift aid from institutional funds.

GIFT AID (NON-NEED-BASED) ***Total amount:*** $8,851,089 (9% federal, 90% institutional, 1% external sources). ***Receiving aid:*** Freshmen: 12% (49); Undergraduates: 7% (136). ***Average award:*** Freshmen: $10,605; Undergraduates: $9684. ***Scholarships, grants, and awards by category:*** *Academic Interests/Achievement:* 1,967 awards ($28,273,773 total): architecture, biological sciences, business, communication, computer science, engineering/technologies, general academic interests/achievements, humanities, mathematics, military science, physical sciences, premedicine, social sciences. *Special Achievements/Activities:* 136 awards ($1,226,915 total): general special achievements/activities, leadership. *Special Characteristics:* 345 awards ($2,432,796 total): children and siblings of alumni, children of faculty/staff, ethnic background, international students. ***Tuition waivers:*** Full or partial for employees or children of employees. ***ROTC:*** Army, Naval, Air Force.

LOANS ***Student loans:*** $7,458,243 (73% need-based, 27% non-need-based). 50% of past graduating class borrowed through all loan programs. *Average indebtedness per student:* $20,155. ***Average need-based loan:*** Freshmen: $3426; Undergraduates: $4319. ***Parent loans:*** $3,832,473 (36% need-based, 64% non-need-based). ***Programs:*** FFEL (Subsidized and Unsubsidized Stafford, PLUS), Perkins, college/university.

WORK-STUDY ***Federal work-study:*** Total amount: $724,397; 394 jobs averaging $1839.

ATHLETIC AWARDS Total amount: $673,863 (39% need-based, 61% non-need-based).

APPLYING FOR FINANCIAL AID ***Required financial aid form:*** FAFSA. ***Financial aid deadline (priority):*** 4/15. ***Notification date:*** Continuous beginning 3/1. Students must reply by 5/1 or within 2 weeks of notification.

CONTACT Virginia Foster, Director of Financial Aid, Illinois Institute of Technology, 3300 South Federal Street, Chicago, IL 60616, 312-567-7219 or toll-free 800-448-2329 (out-of-state). *Fax:* 312-567-3982. *E-mail:* finaid@iit.edu.

ILLINOIS STATE UNIVERSITY

Normal, IL

Tuition & fees (IL res): $8040 **Average undergraduate aid package: $9515**

ABOUT THE INSTITUTION State-supported, coed. Awards: bachelor's, master's, and doctoral degrees and post-bachelor's and post-master's certificates. 61 undergraduate majors. Total enrollment: 20,521. Undergraduates: 17,885. Freshmen: 3,200. Federal methodology is used as a basis for awarding need-based institutional aid.

UNDERGRADUATE EXPENSES for 2006–07 ***Application fee:*** $40. ***Tuition, state resident:*** full-time $6150; part-time $205 per credit hour. ***Tuition, nonresident:*** full-time $12,840; part-time $428 per credit hour. ***Required fees:*** full-time $1,890; $52.45 per credit hour or $786.75 per term part-time. Full-time tuition and fees vary according to course load. Part-time tuition and fees vary according to course load. ***College room and board:*** $6148; ***Room only:*** $3200. Room and board charges vary according to board plan. ***Payment plans:*** Guaranteed tuition, installment.

FRESHMAN FINANCIAL AID (Fall 2006, est.) 2396 applied for aid; of those 62% were deemed to have need. 92% of freshmen with need received aid; of those 44% had need fully met. ***Average percent of need met:*** 79% (excluding resources awarded to replace EFC). ***Average financial aid package:*** $8714 (excluding resources awarded to replace EFC). 2% of all full-time freshmen had no need and received non-need-based gift aid.

UNDERGRADUATE FINANCIAL AID (Fall 2006, est.) 11,081 applied for aid; of those 70% were deemed to have need. 94% of undergraduates with need received aid; of those 45% had need fully met. ***Average percent of need met:*** 82% (excluding resources awarded to replace EFC). ***Average financial aid package:*** $9515 (excluding resources awarded to replace EFC). 2% of all full-time undergraduates had no need and received non-need-based gift aid.

GIFT AID (NEED-BASED) ***Total amount:*** $35,329,645 (33% federal, 53% state, 12% institutional, 2% external sources). ***Receiving aid:*** Freshmen: 26% (834); All full-time undergraduates: 28% (4,606). ***Average award:*** Freshmen: $7658; Undergraduates: $7434. ***Scholarships, grants, and awards:*** Federal Pell, FSEOG, state, private, college/university gift aid from institutional funds, Federal Nursing.

GIFT AID (NON-NEED-BASED) ***Total amount:*** $6,835,081 (12% federal, 53% state, 22% institutional, 13% external sources). ***Receiving aid:*** Freshmen: 20% (653); Undergraduates: 11% (1,895). ***Average award:*** Freshmen: $2533; Undergraduates: $3795. ***Scholarships, grants, and awards by category:*** *Academic Interests/Achievement:* 401 awards ($1,479,480 total): agriculture, biological sciences, business, communication, computer science, education, engineering/technologies, English, foreign languages, general academic interests/achievements, health fields, home economics, humanities, international studies, library science, mathematics, military science, physical sciences, premedicine, social sciences. *Creative Arts/Performance:* 174 awards ($191,139 total): applied art and design, art/fine arts, cinema/film/broadcasting, creative writing, debating, general creative arts/performance, music, performing arts, theater/drama. *Special Achievements/Activities:* 1 award ($1000 total): community service, leadership. *Special Characteristics:* 381 awards ($1,318,687 total): children of faculty/staff, children of union members/company employees, children with a deceased or disabled parent, first-generation college students, general special characteristics, members of minority groups, previous college experience. ***Tuition waivers:*** Full or partial for minority students, employees or children of employees, senior citizens. ***ROTC:*** Army.

LOANS ***Student loans:*** $53,012,622 (60% need-based, 40% non-need-based). 55% of past graduating class borrowed through all loan programs. *Average indebtedness per student:* $17,015. ***Average need-based loan:*** Freshmen: $4336; Undergraduates: $5240. ***Parent loans:*** $15,156,487 (21% need-based, 79% non-need-based). ***Programs:*** Federal Direct (Subsidized and Unsubsidized Stafford, PLUS), Perkins, Federal Nursing, college/university.

WORK-STUDY ***Federal work-study:*** Total amount: $1,154,467; 658 jobs averaging $1937. ***State or other work-study/employment:*** Total amount: $194,435 (46% need-based, 54% non-need-based). 43 part-time jobs averaging $2299.

ATHLETIC AWARDS Total amount: $3,035,416 (19% need-based, 81% non-need-based).

APPLYING FOR FINANCIAL AID ***Required financial aid form:*** FAFSA. ***Financial aid deadline (priority):*** 3/1.

CONTACT Mr. David Krueger, Assistant Director of Financial Aid, Illinois State University, Campus Box 2320, Normal, IL 61790-2320, 309-438-2231 or toll-free 800-366-2478 (in-state). *E-mail:* askfao@ilstu.edu.

ILLINOIS WESLEYAN UNIVERSITY

Bloomington, IL

Tuition & fees: $30,750 **Average undergraduate aid package: $21,417**

ABOUT THE INSTITUTION Independent, coed. Awards: bachelor's degrees. 52 undergraduate majors. Total enrollment: 2,144. Undergraduates: 2,144. Freshmen: 552. Both federal and institutional methodology are used as a basis for awarding need-based institutional aid.

UNDERGRADUATE EXPENSES for 2007–08 ***Comprehensive fee:*** $37,780 includes full-time tuition ($30,580), mandatory fees ($170), and room and board ($7030). ***College room only:*** $4330. ***Part-time tuition:*** $3823 per course.

FRESHMAN FINANCIAL AID (Fall 2006, est.) 444 applied for aid; of those 76% were deemed to have need. 100% of freshmen with need received aid; of those 53% had need fully met. ***Average percent of need met:*** 92% (excluding resources awarded to replace EFC). ***Average financial aid package:*** $20,928 (excluding resources awarded to replace EFC). 28% of all full-time freshmen had no need and received non-need-based gift aid.

UNDERGRADUATE FINANCIAL AID (Fall 2006, est.) 1,448 applied for aid; of those 83% were deemed to have need. 100% of undergraduates with need received aid; of those 37% had need fully met. ***Average percent of need met:*** 92% (excluding resources awarded to replace EFC). ***Average financial aid package:*** $21,417 (excluding resources awarded to replace EFC). 31% of all full-time undergraduates had no need and received non-need-based gift aid.

GIFT AID (NEED-BASED) ***Total amount:*** $17,157,627 (4% federal, 12% state, 82% institutional, 2% external sources). ***Receiving aid:*** Freshmen: 61% (339); All full-time undergraduates: 56% (1,197). ***Average award:*** Freshmen: $16,195; Undergraduates: $15,206. ***Scholarships, grants, and awards:*** Federal Pell, FSEOG, state, private, college/university gift aid from institutional funds.

GIFT AID (NON-NEED-BASED) ***Total amount:*** $8,160,990 (99% institutional, 1% external sources). ***Receiving aid:*** Freshmen: 7% (38); Undergraduates: 6% (124). ***Average award:*** Freshmen: $8062; Undergraduates: $8691. ***Scholarships, grants, and awards by category:*** *Academic Interests/Achievement:* 595 awards ($5,771,276 total): general academic interests/achievements. *Creative Arts/Performance:* 153 awards ($1,716,540 total): art/fine arts, music, theater/drama. *Special Characteristics:* 53 awards ($803,894 total): children of faculty/staff, international students. ***ROTC:*** Army cooperative.

LOANS ***Student loans:*** $8,808,448 (59% need-based, 41% non-need-based). 67% of past graduating class borrowed through all loan programs. *Average indebtedness per student:* $21,794. ***Average need-based loan:*** Freshmen: $4439; Undergraduates: $5370. ***Parent loans:*** $3,218,897 (100% non-need-based). ***Programs:*** FFEL (Subsidized and Unsubsidized Stafford, PLUS), Perkins, Federal Nursing, college/university.

WORK-STUDY ***Federal work-study:*** Total amount: $380,269; 263 jobs averaging $2151. ***State or other work-study/employment:*** Total amount: $1,518,307 (77% need-based, 23% non-need-based). 531 part-time jobs averaging $2140.

APPLYING FOR FINANCIAL AID ***Required financial aid forms:*** FAFSA, institution's own form, CSS Financial Aid PROFILE, business/farm supplement. ***Financial aid deadline:*** 3/1 (priority: 3/1). ***Notification date:*** Continuous beginning 2/15. Students must reply by 5/1 or within 3 weeks of notification.

CONTACT Mr. Scott Seibring, Director of Financial Aid, Illinois Wesleyan University, 1312 North Park Street, PO Box 2900, Bloomington, IL 61702-2900, 309-556-3096 or toll-free 800-332-2498. *Fax:* 309-556-3833. *E-mail:* seibring@iwu.edu.

IMMACULATA UNIVERSITY

Immaculata, PA

CONTACT Mr. Peter Lysionek, Director of Student Financial Aid, Immaculata University, 1145 King Road, Box 500, Immaculata, PA 19345, 610-647-4400 Ext. 3026 or toll-free 877-428-6328. *Fax:* 610-640-0836. *E-mail:* plysionek@immaculata.edu.

INDIANA STATE UNIVERSITY

Terre Haute, IN

Tuition & fees (IN res): $6436 **Average undergraduate aid package: $7410**

ABOUT THE INSTITUTION State-supported, coed. Awards: associate, bachelor's, master's, and doctoral degrees and post-bachelor's and post-master's certificates. 76 undergraduate majors. Total enrollment: 10,568. Undergraduates: 8,537. Freshmen: 1,703. Federal methodology is used as a basis for awarding need-based institutional aid.

UNDERGRADUATE EXPENSES for 2006–07 ***Application fee:*** $25. ***Tuition, state resident:*** full-time $6102; part-time $220 per credit hour. ***Tuition, nonresident:*** full-time $13,518; part-time $476 per credit hour. ***Required fees:*** full-time $334; $167 per term part-time. Full-time tuition and fees vary according to course load. ***College room and board:*** $6294; ***Room only:*** $3339. Room and board charges vary according to board plan, housing facility, and student level. ***Payment plans:*** Installment, deferred payment.

FRESHMAN FINANCIAL AID (Fall 2005) 1417 applied for aid; of those 73% were deemed to have need. 94% of freshmen with need received aid; of those 16% had need fully met. ***Average percent of need met:*** 73% (excluding resources awarded to replace EFC). ***Average financial aid package:*** $6329 (excluding resources awarded to replace EFC). 8% of all full-time freshmen had no need and received non-need-based gift aid.

UNDERGRADUATE FINANCIAL AID (Fall 2005) 6,041 applied for aid; of those 74% were deemed to have need. 95% of undergraduates with need received aid; of those 19% had need fully met. ***Average percent of need met:*** 79% (excluding resources awarded to replace EFC). ***Average financial aid package:*** $7410 (excluding resources awarded to replace EFC). 9% of all full-time undergraduates had no need and received non-need-based gift aid.

GIFT AID (NEED-BASED) ***Total amount:*** $13,965,484 (49% federal, 45% state, 4% institutional, 2% external sources). ***Receiving aid:*** Freshmen: 35% (576); All full-time undergraduates: 35% (2,674). ***Average award:*** Freshmen: $4687; Undergraduates: $4837. ***Scholarships, grants, and awards:*** Federal Pell, FSEOG, state, private, college/university gift aid from institutional funds.

GIFT AID (NON-NEED-BASED) ***Total amount:*** $7,854,833 (32% state, 46% institutional, 22% external sources). ***Receiving aid:*** Freshmen: 28% (456); Undergraduates: 21% (1,609). ***Average award:*** Freshmen: $3175; Undergraduates: $2884. ***Scholarships, grants, and awards by category:*** *Academic Interests/Achievement:* 565 awards ($1,591,862 total): general academic interests/achievements. *Creative Arts/Performance:* 107 awards ($173,400 total): art/fine arts, performing arts. *Special Characteristics:* 114 awards ($144,182 total): children and siblings of alumni, children of faculty/staff, children with a deceased or disabled parent, members of minority groups, veterans' children. ***Tuition waivers:*** Full or partial for employees or children of employees, senior citizens. ***ROTC:*** Army, Air Force.

LOANS ***Student loans:*** $29,275,897 (49% need-based, 51% non-need-based). 62% of past graduating class borrowed through all loan programs. *Average indebtedness per student:* $22,724. ***Average need-based loan:*** Freshmen: $2736; Undergraduates: $3899. ***Parent loans:*** $5,064,723 (100% non-need-based). ***Programs:*** FFEL (Subsidized and Unsubsidized Stafford, PLUS), Perkins.

WORK-STUDY ***Federal work-study:*** Total amount: $331,965; 269 jobs averaging $1244. ***State or other work-study/employment:*** Part-time jobs available.

ATHLETIC AWARDS Total amount: $2,621,726 (100% non-need-based).

APPLYING FOR FINANCIAL AID ***Required financial aid form:*** FAFSA. ***Financial aid deadline:*** 3/1 (priority: 3/1). ***Notification date:*** Continuous beginning 4/15.

CONTACT Brenda Hall, Senior Associate Director, Indiana State University, Tirey Hall, Room 150, Terre Haute, IN 47809-1401, 812-237-2215 or toll-free 800-742-0891. *Fax:* 812-237-4330. *E-mail:* finaid@indstate.edu.

INDIANA TECH

Fort Wayne, IN

CONTACT Financial Aid Office, Indiana Tech, 1600 East Washington Boulevard, Fort Wayne, IN 46803-1297, 800-937-2448 or toll-free 888-666-TECH (out-of-state). *Fax:* 219-422-1578.

INDIANA UNIVERSITY BLOOMINGTON

Bloomington, IN

Tuition & fees (IN res): $7460 **Average undergraduate aid package: $7463**

ABOUT THE INSTITUTION State-supported, coed. Awards: associate, bachelor's, master's, doctoral, and first professional degrees and post-bachelor's and post-master's certificates. 140 undergraduate majors. Total enrollment: 38,247. Undergraduates: 29,828. Freshmen: 7,259. Federal methodology is used as a basis for awarding need-based institutional aid.

UNDERGRADUATE EXPENSES for 2006–07 ***Application fee:*** $50. ***Tuition, state resident:*** full-time $6657; part-time $207.83 per credit hour. ***Tuition, nonresident:*** full-time $19,669; part-time $614.75 per credit hour. Full-time tuition and fees vary according to location and program. Part-time tuition and fees vary according to course load, location, and program. ***College room and board:*** $6352; ***Room only:*** $3872. Room and board charges vary according to board plan and housing facility. ***Payment plan:*** Deferred payment.

FRESHMAN FINANCIAL AID (Fall 2006, est.) 4755 applied for aid; of those 63% were deemed to have need. 97% of freshmen with need received aid; of those 26% had need fully met. ***Average percent of need met:*** 66% (excluding resources awarded to replace EFC). ***Average financial aid package:*** $7369 (excluding resources awarded to replace EFC). 25% of all full-time freshmen had no need and received non-need-based gift aid.

UNDERGRADUATE FINANCIAL AID (Fall 2006, est.) 15,604 applied for aid; of those 69% were deemed to have need. 97% of undergraduates with need received aid; of those 20% had need fully met. ***Average percent of need met:*** 67% (excluding resources awarded to replace EFC). ***Average financial aid package:*** $7463 (excluding resources awarded to replace EFC). 19% of all full-time undergraduates had no need and received non-need-based gift aid.

GIFT AID (NEED-BASED) ***Total amount:*** $51,206,814 (30% federal, 33% state, 32% institutional, 5% external sources). ***Receiving aid:*** Freshmen: 33% (2,379); All full-time undergraduates: 28% (7,923). ***Average award:*** Freshmen: $7463; Undergraduates: $6828. ***Scholarships, grants, and awards:*** Federal Pell, FSEOG, state, private, college/university gift aid from institutional funds.

GIFT AID (NON-NEED-BASED) ***Total amount:*** $32,947,931 (3% federal, 5% state, 79% institutional, 13% external sources). ***Receiving aid:*** Freshmen: 7% (488); Undergraduates: 4% (1,190). ***Average award:*** Freshmen: $4981; Undergraduates: $4435. ***Scholarships, grants, and awards by category:*** *Academic Interests/Achievement:* general academic interests/achievements. *Creative Arts/Performance:* general creative arts/performance. *Special Achievements/Activities:* general special achievements/activities. *Special Characteristics:* general special characteristics. ***Tuition waivers:*** Full or partial for employees or children of employees. ***ROTC:*** Army, Air Force.

LOANS ***Student loans:*** $93,691,639 (54% need-based, 46% non-need-based). 53% of past graduating class borrowed through all loan programs. *Average indebtedness per student:* $19,756. ***Average need-based loan:*** Freshmen: $2897; Undergraduates: $4003. ***Parent loans:*** $33,662,263 (21% need-based, 79% non-need-based). ***Programs:*** FFEL (Subsidized and Unsubsidized Stafford, PLUS), Perkins, Federal Nursing, college/university.

WORK-STUDY ***Federal work-study:*** Total amount: $1,634,240; 1,016 jobs averaging $1456. ***State or other work-study/employment:*** Total amount: $26,077 (59% need-based, 41% non-need-based).

ATHLETIC AWARDS Total amount: $7,082,525 (26% need-based, 74% non-need-based).

APPLYING FOR FINANCIAL AID ***Required financial aid form:*** FAFSA. ***Financial aid deadline (priority):*** 3/1. ***Notification date:*** Continuous beginning 4/1.

CONTACT Susan Pugh, Director of the Office of Student Financial Assistance, Indiana University Bloomington, Franklin Hall, Room 208, 601 E Kirkwood, Bloomington, IN 47405, 812-855-0321. *Fax:* 812-855-7615. *E-mail:* rsvposfa@indiana.edu.

INDIANA UNIVERSITY EAST

Richmond, IN

Tuition & fees (IN res): $5040 Average undergraduate aid package: $6467

ABOUT THE INSTITUTION State-supported, coed. Awards: associate and bachelor's degrees and post-bachelor's certificates. 21 undergraduate majors. Total enrollment: 2,246. Undergraduates: 2,194. Freshmen: 281. Federal methodology is used as a basis for awarding need-based institutional aid.

UNDERGRADUATE EXPENSES for 2006–07 ***Application fee:*** $25. ***Tuition, state resident:*** full-time $4697; part-time $156.55 per credit hour. ***Tuition, nonresident:*** full-time $11,655; part-time $388.50 per credit hour. Full-time tuition and fees vary according to course load, program, and reciprocity agreements. Part-time tuition and fees vary according to course load, program, and reciprocity agreements. ***Payment plan:*** Deferred payment.

FRESHMAN FINANCIAL AID (Fall 2006, est.) 200 applied for aid; of those 80% were deemed to have need. 97% of freshmen with need received aid; of those 10% had need fully met. ***Average percent of need met:*** 58% (excluding resources awarded to replace EFC). ***Average financial aid package:*** $5559 (excluding resources awarded to replace EFC). 5% of all full-time freshmen had no need and received non-need-based gift aid.

UNDERGRADUATE FINANCIAL AID (Fall 2006, est.) 1,024 applied for aid; of those 85% were deemed to have need. 99% of undergraduates with need received aid; of those 9% had need fully met. ***Average percent of need met:*** 60% (excluding resources awarded to replace EFC). ***Average financial aid package:*** $6467 (excluding resources awarded to replace EFC). 3% of all full-time undergraduates had no need and received non-need-based gift aid.

GIFT AID (NEED-BASED) ***Total amount:*** $4,101,881 (60% federal, 30% state, 7% institutional, 3% external sources). ***Receiving aid:*** Freshmen: 63% (142); All full-time undergraduates: 62% (730). ***Average award:*** Freshmen: $4791; Undergraduates: $4833. ***Scholarships, grants, and awards:*** Federal Pell, FSEOG, state, private, college/university gift aid from institutional funds.

GIFT AID (NON-NEED-BASED) ***Total amount:*** $306,746 (44% federal, 9% state, 15% institutional, 32% external sources). ***Receiving aid:*** Freshmen: 3% (7); Undergraduates: 2% (27). ***Average award:*** Freshmen: $1054; Undergraduates: $961. ***Scholarships, grants, and awards by category:*** *Academic Interests/Achievement:* general academic interests/achievements. *Creative Arts/Performance:* general creative arts/performance. *Special Achievements/Activities:* general special achievements/activities. *Special Characteristics:* general special characteristics. ***Tuition waivers:*** Full or partial for employees or children of employees.

LOANS ***Student loans:*** $6,112,376 (80% need-based, 20% non-need-based). 71% of past graduating class borrowed through all loan programs. *Average indebtedness per student:* $25,402. ***Average need-based loan:*** Freshmen: $2195; Undergraduates: $3278. ***Parent loans:*** $70,794 (16% need-based, 84% non-need-based). ***Programs:*** FFEL (Subsidized and Unsubsidized Stafford, PLUS), Perkins, Federal Nursing, college/university.

WORK-STUDY ***Federal work-study:*** Total amount: $130,684; 42 jobs averaging $3168.

ATHLETIC AWARDS Total amount: $7520 (100% need-based).

APPLYING FOR FINANCIAL AID ***Required financial aid forms:*** FAFSA, institution's own form. ***Financial aid deadline (priority):*** 3/1. ***Notification date:*** Continuous beginning 5/1. Students must reply within 2 weeks of notification.

CONTACT William Gill, Financial Aid Director, Indiana University East, 2325 Chester Boulevard, Whitewater Hall, Richmond, IN 47374-1289, 765-973-8231 or toll-free 800-959-EAST. *Fax:* 765-973-8288.

INDIANA UNIVERSITY KOKOMO

Kokomo, IN

Tuition & fees (IN res): $5072 Average undergraduate aid package: $5508

ABOUT THE INSTITUTION State-supported, coed. Awards: associate, bachelor's, and master's degrees and post-bachelor's certificates. 17 undergraduate majors. Total enrollment: 2,734. Undergraduates: 2,604. Freshmen: 385. Federal methodology is used as a basis for awarding need-based institutional aid.

UNDERGRADUATE EXPENSES for 2006–07 ***Application fee:*** $30. ***Tuition, state resident:*** full-time $4694; part-time $156.45 per credit hour. ***Tuition, nonresident:*** full-time $11,648; part-time $388.25 per credit hour. Full-time tuition and fees vary according to course load and program. Part-time tuition and fees vary according to course load and program. ***Payment plan:*** Deferred payment.

FRESHMAN FINANCIAL AID (Fall 2006, est.) 267 applied for aid; of those 71% were deemed to have need. 91% of freshmen with need received aid; of those 13% had need fully met. ***Average percent of need met:*** 53% (excluding resources awarded to replace EFC). ***Average financial aid package:*** $4465 (excluding resources awarded to replace EFC). 10% of all full-time freshmen had no need and received non-need-based gift aid.

UNDERGRADUATE FINANCIAL AID (Fall 2006, est.) 1,019 applied for aid; of those 78% were deemed to have need. 95% of undergraduates with need received aid; of those 10% had need fully met. ***Average percent of need met:*** 60% (excluding resources awarded to replace EFC). ***Average financial aid package:*** $5508 (excluding resources awarded to replace EFC). 6% of all full-time undergraduates had no need and received non-need-based gift aid.

GIFT AID (NEED-BASED) ***Total amount:*** $3,458,149 (57% federal, 35% state, 5% institutional, 3% external sources). ***Receiving aid:*** Freshmen: 43% (142); All full-time undergraduates: 43% (589). ***Average award:*** Freshmen: $4404; Undergraduates: $4636. ***Scholarships, grants, and awards:*** Federal Pell, FSEOG, state, private, college/university gift aid from institutional funds.

GIFT AID (NON-NEED-BASED) ***Total amount:*** $638,494 (44% federal, 21% state, 19% institutional, 16% external sources). ***Receiving aid:*** Freshmen: 4% (14); Undergraduates: 3% (39). ***Average award:*** Freshmen: $1523; Undergraduates: $1288. ***Scholarships, grants, and awards by category:*** *Academic Interests/Achievement:* general academic interests/achievements. *Special Characteristics:* general special characteristics. ***Tuition waivers:*** Full or partial for employees or children of employees. ***ROTC:*** Army cooperative.

LOANS ***Student loans:*** $6,546,345 (68% need-based, 32% non-need-based). 57% of past graduating class borrowed through all loan programs. *Average indebtedness per student:* $19,667. ***Average need-based loan:*** Freshmen: $2244; Undergraduates: $3325. ***Parent loans:*** $128,897 (24% need-based, 76% non-need-based). ***Programs:*** FFEL (Subsidized and Unsubsidized Stafford, PLUS), Perkins, Federal Nursing, college/university.

WORK-STUDY ***Federal work-study:*** Total amount: $134,792; 78 jobs averaging $1495.

APPLYING FOR FINANCIAL AID ***Required financial aid forms:*** FAFSA, institution's own form. ***Financial aid deadline:*** 3/1. ***Notification date:*** Continuous beginning 5/1. Students must reply within 4 weeks of notification.

CONTACT Jolane Rohr, Director of Financial Aid, Indiana University Kokomo, 2300 South Washington Street, PO Box 9003, Kelley Student Center, Room 230, Kokomo, IN 46904-9003, 765-455-9216 or toll-free 888-875-4485. *Fax:* 765-455-9537.

INDIANA UNIVERSITY NORTHWEST

Gary, IN

Tuition & fees (IN res): $5142 **Average undergraduate aid package: $7259**

ABOUT THE INSTITUTION State-supported, coed. Awards: associate, bachelor's, and master's degrees and post-bachelor's certificates. 44 undergraduate majors. Total enrollment: 4,819. Undergraduates: 4,229. Freshmen: 680. Federal methodology is used as a basis for awarding need-based institutional aid.

UNDERGRADUATE EXPENSES for 2006–07 ***Application fee:*** $25. ***Tuition, state resident:*** full-time $4710; part-time $157 per credit hour. ***Tuition, nonresident:*** full-time $11,654; part-time $388.45 per credit hour. Full-time tuition and fees vary according to course load and program. Part-time tuition and fees vary according to course load and program. ***Payment plans:*** Installment, deferred payment.

FRESHMAN FINANCIAL AID (Fall 2006, est.) 434 applied for aid; of those 77% were deemed to have need. 93% of freshmen with need received aid; of those 9% had need fully met. ***Average percent of need met:*** 54% (excluding resources awarded to replace EFC). ***Average financial aid package:*** $6046 (excluding resources awarded to replace EFC). 5% of all full-time freshmen had no need and received non-need-based gift aid.

UNDERGRADUATE FINANCIAL AID (Fall 2006, est.) 1,898 applied for aid; of those 84% were deemed to have need. 96% of undergraduates with need received aid; of those 10% had need fully met. ***Average percent of need met:*** 61% (excluding resources awarded to replace EFC). ***Average financial aid package:*** $7259 (excluding resources awarded to replace EFC). 4% of all full-time undergraduates had no need and received non-need-based gift aid.

GIFT AID (NEED-BASED) ***Total amount:*** $7,298,406 (61% federal, 35% state, 3% institutional, 1% external sources). ***Receiving aid:*** Freshmen: 41% (231); All full-time undergraduates: 47% (1,163). ***Average award:*** Freshmen: $4785; Undergraduates: $5247. ***Scholarships, grants, and awards:*** Federal Pell, FSEOG, state, private, college/university gift aid from institutional funds, Federal Nursing.

GIFT AID (NON-NEED-BASED) ***Total amount:*** $780,204 (18% federal, 9% state, 61% institutional, 12% external sources). ***Receiving aid:*** Freshmen: 2% (11); Undergraduates: 1% (34). ***Average award:*** Freshmen: $4460; Undergraduates: $3804. ***Scholarships, grants, and awards by category:*** *Academic Interests/Achievement:* general academic interests/achievements. *Creative Arts/Performance:* general creative arts/performance. *Special Achievements/Activities:* general special achievements/activities. *Special Characteristics:* general special characteristics. ***Tuition waivers:*** Full or partial for employees or children of employees, senior citizens. ***ROTC:*** Army.

LOANS ***Student loans:*** $13,787,001 (77% need-based, 23% non-need-based). 66% of past graduating class borrowed through all loan programs. *Average indebtedness per student:* $20,622. ***Average need-based loan:*** Freshmen: $2294; Undergraduates: $3212. ***Parent loans:*** $197,339 (21% need-based, 79% non-need-based). ***Programs:*** FFEL (Subsidized and Unsubsidized Stafford, PLUS), Perkins, college/university.

WORK-STUDY ***Federal work-study:*** Total amount: $1,558,568; 491 jobs averaging $2690.

ATHLETIC AWARDS Total amount: $8900 (54% need-based, 46% non-need-based).

APPLYING FOR FINANCIAL AID ***Required financial aid forms:*** FAFSA, institution's own form. ***Financial aid deadline (priority):*** 3/1. ***Notification date:*** Continuous beginning 5/1. Students must reply within 2 weeks of notification.

CONTACT Harold Burtley, Director of Scholarships and Financial Aid, Indiana University Northwest, 3400 Broadway, Hawthorn Hall, Room 111, Gary, IN 46408-1197, 877-280-4593 or toll-free 800-968-7486. *Fax:* 219-981-5622.

INDIANA UNIVERSITY OF PENNSYLVANIA

Indiana, PA

Tuition & fees (PA res): $6390 **Average undergraduate aid package: $7549**

ABOUT THE INSTITUTION State-supported, coed. Awards: associate, bachelor's, master's, and doctoral degrees and post-bachelor's and post-master's certificates. 74 undergraduate majors. Total enrollment: 14,248. Undergraduates: 11,976. Freshmen: 2,568. Federal methodology is used as a basis for awarding need-based institutional aid.

UNDERGRADUATE EXPENSES for 2006–07 ***Application fee:*** $35. ***Tuition, state resident:*** full-time $5038; part-time $210 per credit. ***Tuition, nonresident:*** full-time $12,598; part-time $525 per credit. ***Required fees:*** full-time $1352; $21 per credit or $167 per term part-time. Full-time tuition and fees vary according to course load, location, and reciprocity agreements. Part-time tuition and fees vary according to course load, location, and reciprocity agreements. ***College room and board:*** $5162; ***Room only:*** $3150. Room and board charges vary according to board plan, housing facility, and location. ***Payment plans:*** Installment, deferred payment.

FRESHMAN FINANCIAL AID (Fall 2005) 2220 applied for aid; of those 76% were deemed to have need. 99% of freshmen with need received aid; of those 20% had need fully met. ***Average percent of need met:*** 80% (excluding resources awarded to replace EFC). ***Average financial aid package:*** $8137 (excluding resources awarded to replace EFC). 6% of all full-time freshmen had no need and received non-need-based gift aid.

UNDERGRADUATE FINANCIAL AID (Fall 2005) 9,185 applied for aid; of those 77% were deemed to have need. 99% of undergraduates with need received aid; of those 19% had need fully met. ***Average percent of need met:*** 75% (excluding resources awarded to replace EFC). ***Average financial aid package:*** $7549 (excluding resources awarded to replace EFC). 4% of all full-time undergraduates had no need and received non-need-based gift aid.

GIFT AID (NEED-BASED) ***Total amount:*** $21,955,035 (50% federal, 50% state). ***Receiving aid:*** Freshmen: 52% (1,277); All full-time undergraduates: 47% (5,185). ***Average award:*** Freshmen: $4294; Undergraduates: $4034. ***Scholarships, grants, and awards:*** Federal Pell, FSEOG, state, private, college/university gift aid from institutional funds.

GIFT AID (NON-NEED-BASED) ***Total amount:*** $5,828,453 (1% state, 47% institutional, 52% external sources). ***Receiving aid:*** Freshmen: 26% (637); Undergraduates: 14% (1,535). ***Average award:*** Freshmen: $1549; Undergraduates: $2337. ***Scholarships, grants, and awards by category:*** *Academic Interests/Achievement:* 1,213 awards ($2,249,051 total): area/ethnic studies, biological sciences, business, communication, computer science, education, engineering/technologies, English, foreign languages, general academic interests/achievements, health fields, home economics, humanities, international studies, mathematics, physical sciences, premedicine, social sciences. *Creative Arts/Performance:* applied art and design, art/fine arts, dance, general creative arts/performance, journalism/publications, music, performing arts, theater/drama. *Special Achievements/Activities:* community service, general special achievements/activities, hobbies/interests, leadership. *Special Characteristics:* 764 awards ($2,073,140 total): adult students, children of faculty/staff, ethnic background, international students. ***Tuition waivers:*** Full or partial for minority students, employees or children of employees. ***ROTC:*** Army.

LOANS ***Student loans:*** $46,594,001 (49% need-based, 51% non-need-based). 79% of past graduating class borrowed through all loan programs. *Average indebtedness per student:* $21,716. ***Average need-based loan:*** Freshmen: $2997; Undergraduates: $3583. ***Parent loans:*** $7,802,697 (100% non-need-based). ***Programs:*** FFEL (Subsidized and Unsubsidized Stafford, PLUS), Perkins, alternative loans/private loans.

WORK-STUDY ***Federal work-study:*** Total amount: $4,910,352; 1,326 jobs averaging $1305. ***State or other work-study/employment:*** Total amount: $1,046,844 (100% non-need-based). 1,315 part-time jobs averaging $1393.

ATHLETIC AWARDS Total amount: $717,989 (100% non-need-based).

APPLYING FOR FINANCIAL AID ***Required financial aid form:*** FAFSA. ***Financial aid deadline:*** 4/15. ***Notification date:*** Continuous beginning 3/15.

CONTACT Mrs. Patricia C. McCarthy, Director of Financial Aid, Indiana University of Pennsylvania, 213 Clark Hall, 1090 South Drive, Indiana, PA 15705, 724-357-2218 or toll-free 800-442-6830. *Fax:* 724-357-2094. *E-mail:* mccarthy@iup.edu.

INDIANA UNIVERSITY–PURDUE UNIVERSITY FORT WAYNE

Fort Wayne, IN

ABOUT THE INSTITUTION State-supported, coed. Awards: associate, bachelor's, and master's degrees and post-bachelor's certificates. 97 undergraduate majors. Total enrollment: 11,672. Undergraduates: 10,890. Freshmen: 1,882.

GIFT AID (NEED-BASED) ***Scholarships, grants, and awards:*** Federal Pell, FSEOG, state, private, college/university gift aid from institutional funds.

GIFT AID (NON-NEED-BASED) ***Scholarships, grants, and awards by category:*** *Academic Interests/Achievement:* biological sciences, business, communication, computer science, education, engineering/technologies, English, foreign languages, general academic interests/achievements, health fields, humanities, mathematics, physical sciences, premedicine, social sciences. *Creative Arts/Performance:* art/fine arts, music, theater/drama. *Special Characteristics:* children and siblings of alumni, children of faculty/staff, children with a deceased or disabled parent, handicapped students, local/state students, spouses of deceased or disabled public servants.

LOANS ***Programs:*** FFEL (Subsidized and Unsubsidized Stafford, PLUS), Perkins.

APPLYING FOR FINANCIAL AID ***Required financial aid form:*** FAFSA.

CONTACT Mr. Joel Wenger, Director of Financial Aid, Indiana University–Purdue University Fort Wayne, 2101 East Coliseum Boulevard, Fort Wayne, IN 46805-1499, 260-481-6130 or toll-free 800-324-4739 (in-state). *E-mail:* wengerj@ipfw.edu.

INDIANA UNIVERSITY–PURDUE UNIVERSITY INDIANAPOLIS

Indianapolis, IN

Tuition & fees (IN res): $6524 **Average undergraduate aid package: $7246**

ABOUT THE INSTITUTION State-supported, coed. Awards: associate, bachelor's, master's, doctoral, and first professional degrees and post-bachelor's certificates. 77 undergraduate majors. Total enrollment: 29,764. Undergraduates: 21,193. Freshmen: 2,792. Federal methodology is used as a basis for awarding need-based institutional aid.

UNDERGRADUATE EXPENSES for 2006–07 ***Application fee:*** $50. ***Tuition, state resident:*** full-time $5924; part-time $197.46 per credit hour. ***Tuition, nonresident:*** full-time $16,766; part-time $558.86 per credit hour. Full-time tuition and fees vary according to course load and program. Part-time tuition and fees vary according to course load and program. ***College room and board:*** $4834; ***Room only:*** $2434. Room and board charges vary according to board plan and housing facility. ***Payment plans:*** Installment, deferred payment.

FRESHMAN FINANCIAL AID (Fall 2006, est.) 2015 applied for aid; of those 79% were deemed to have need. 96% of freshmen with need received aid; of those 8% had need fully met. ***Average percent of need met:*** 51% (excluding resources awarded to replace EFC). ***Average financial aid package:*** $6378 (excluding resources awarded to replace EFC). 10% of all full-time freshmen had no need and received non-need-based gift aid.

UNDERGRADUATE FINANCIAL AID (Fall 2006, est.) 10,140 applied for aid; of those 84% were deemed to have need. 94% of undergraduates with need received aid; of those 7% had need fully met. ***Average percent of need met:*** 52% (excluding resources awarded to replace EFC). ***Average financial aid package:*** $7246 (excluding resources awarded to replace EFC). 6% of all full-time undergraduates had no need and received non-need-based gift aid.

GIFT AID (NEED-BASED) ***Total amount:*** $36,883,357 (47% federal, 40% state, 10% institutional, 3% external sources). ***Receiving aid:*** Freshmen: 49% (1,244); All full-time undergraduates: 44% (6,044). ***Average award:*** Freshmen: $5723; Undergraduates: $5656. ***Scholarships, grants, and awards:*** Federal Pell, FSEOG, state, private, college/university gift aid from institutional funds.

GIFT AID (NON-NEED-BASED) ***Total amount:*** $6,126,646 (12% federal, 13% state, 56% institutional, 19% external sources). ***Receiving aid:*** Freshmen: 4% (98); Undergraduates: 3% (354). ***Average award:*** Freshmen: $3368; Undergraduates: $3191. ***Scholarships, grants, and awards by category:*** *Academic Interests/Achievement:* general academic interests/achievements. *Creative Arts/Performance:* general creative arts/performance. *Special Achievements/Activities:* general special achievements/activities. *Special Characteristics:* general special characteristics. ***Tuition waivers:*** Full or partial for employees or children of employees. ***ROTC:*** Army, Naval cooperative, Air Force cooperative.

LOANS ***Student loans:*** $71,059,080 (75% need-based, 25% non-need-based). 67% of past graduating class borrowed through all loan programs. *Average indebtedness per student:* $22,542. ***Average need-based loan:*** Freshmen: $2374; Undergraduates: $3817. ***Parent loans:*** $3,346,093 (29% need-based, 71% non-need-based). ***Programs:*** FFEL (Subsidized and Unsubsidized Stafford, PLUS), Perkins, Federal Nursing, college/university.

WORK-STUDY ***Federal work-study:*** Total amount: $2,120,847; 813 jobs averaging $3350. ***State or other work-study/employment:*** Total amount: $55,158 (79% need-based, 21% non-need-based).

ATHLETIC AWARDS Total amount: $1,309,073 (39% need-based, 61% non-need-based).

APPLYING FOR FINANCIAL AID ***Required financial aid form:*** FAFSA. ***Financial aid deadline (priority):*** 3/1. ***Notification date:*** Continuous beginning 4/1.

CONTACT Kathy Purris, Director of Financial Aid Services, Indiana University–Purdue University Indianapolis, 425 North University Boulevard, Cavanaugh Hall, Room 103, Indianapolis, IN 46202-5145, 317-274-4162. *Fax:* 317-274-5930.

INDIANA UNIVERSITY SOUTH BEND

South Bend, IN

Tuition & fees (IN res): $5232 **Average undergraduate aid package: $6198**

ABOUT THE INSTITUTION State-supported, coed. Awards: associate, bachelor's, and master's degrees and post-bachelor's certificates. 53 undergraduate majors. Total enrollment: 7,420. Undergraduates: 6,371. Freshmen: 994. Federal methodology is used as a basis for awarding need-based institutional aid.

UNDERGRADUATE EXPENSES for 2006–07 ***Application fee:*** $45. ***Tuition, state resident:*** full-time $4826; part-time $160.85 per credit hour. ***Tuition, nonresident:*** full-time $12,612; part-time $420.40 per credit hour. Full-time tuition and fees vary according to course load and program. Part-time tuition and fees vary according to course load and program. ***Payment plan:*** Deferred payment.

FRESHMAN FINANCIAL AID (Fall 2006, est.) 595 applied for aid; of those 75% were deemed to have need. 94% of freshmen with need received aid; of those 9% had need fully met. ***Average percent of need met:*** 52% (excluding resources awarded to replace EFC). ***Average financial aid package:*** $4808 (excluding resources awarded to replace EFC). 5% of all full-time freshmen had no need and received non-need-based gift aid.

UNDERGRADUATE FINANCIAL AID (Fall 2006, est.) 2,702 applied for aid; of those 80% were deemed to have need. 95% of undergraduates with need received aid; of those 12% had need fully met. ***Average percent of need met:*** 59% (excluding resources awarded to replace EFC). ***Average financial aid package:*** $6198 (excluding resources awarded to replace EFC). 3% of all full-time undergraduates had no need and received non-need-based gift aid.

GIFT AID (NEED-BASED) ***Total amount:*** $9,106,464 (55% federal, 34% state, 7% institutional, 4% external sources). ***Receiving aid:*** Freshmen: 44% (341); All full-time undergraduates: 45% (1,594). ***Average award:*** Freshmen: $4553; Undergraduates: $4947. ***Scholarships, grants, and awards:*** Federal Pell, FSEOG, state, private, college/university gift aid from institutional funds.

GIFT AID (NON-NEED-BASED) ***Total amount:*** $1,095,148 (31% federal, 14% state, 32% institutional, 23% external sources). ***Receiving aid:*** Freshmen: 2% (12); Undergraduates: 2% (83). ***Average award:*** Freshmen: $2131; Undergraduates: $2800. ***Scholarships, grants, and awards by category:*** *Academic Interests/Achievement:* general academic interests/achievements. *Creative Arts/Performance:* general creative arts/performance. *Special Achievements/Activities:* general special achievements/activities. *Special Characteristics:* general special characteristics. ***Tuition waivers:*** Full or partial for employees or children of employees. ***ROTC:*** Army cooperative, Naval cooperative, Air Force cooperative.

LOANS ***Student loans:*** $14,995,706 (74% need-based, 26% non-need-based). 66% of past graduating class borrowed through all loan programs. *Average indebtedness per student:* $19,139. ***Average need-based loan:*** Freshmen: $2103; Undergraduates: $3301. ***Parent loans:*** $686,283 (19% need-based, 81% non-need-based). ***Programs:*** FFEL (Subsidized and Unsubsidized Stafford, PLUS), Perkins, Federal Nursing, college/university.

WORK-STUDY ***Federal work-study:*** Total amount: $356,754; 178 jobs averaging $2299. ***State or other work-study/employment:*** Total amount: $10,520 (100% need-based).

ATHLETIC AWARDS Total amount: $125,236 (51% need-based, 49% non-need-based).

APPLYING FOR FINANCIAL AID ***Required financial aid forms:*** FAFSA, institution's own form. ***Financial aid deadline:*** 3/1. ***Notification date:*** Continuous beginning 5/1.

CONTACT Bev Cooper, Financial Aid Director, Indiana University South Bend, 1700 Mishawaka Avenue, PO Box 7111, South Bend, IN 46634-7111, 574-520-4357 or toll-free 877-GO-2-IUSB. *Fax:* 574-520-5561. *E-mail:* beacoope@iusb.edu.

INDIANA UNIVERSITY SOUTHEAST

New Albany, IN

Tuition & fees (IN res): $5118 **Average undergraduate aid package: $5624**

ABOUT THE INSTITUTION State-supported, coed. Awards: associate, bachelor's, and master's degrees and post-bachelor's certificates. 37 undergraduate majors. Total enrollment: 6,183. Undergraduates: 5,365. Freshmen: 838. Federal methodology is used as a basis for awarding need-based institutional aid.

UNDERGRADUATE EXPENSES for 2006–07 ***Application fee:*** $30. ***Tuition, state resident:*** full-time $4698; part-time $157 per credit hour. ***Tuition, nonresident:*** full-time $11,655; part-time $388.50 per credit hour. Full-time tuition and fees vary according to course load, program, and reciprocity agreements. Part-time tuition and fees vary according to course load, program, and reciprocity agreements. ***Payment plan:*** Deferred payment.

FRESHMAN FINANCIAL AID (Fall 2006, est.) 531 applied for aid; of those 73% were deemed to have need. 93% of freshmen with need received aid; of those 13% had need fully met. ***Average percent of need met:*** 56% (excluding resources awarded to replace EFC). ***Average financial aid package:*** $4487 (excluding resources awarded to replace EFC). 7% of all full-time freshmen had no need and received non-need-based gift aid.

UNDERGRADUATE FINANCIAL AID (Fall 2006, est.) 2,226 applied for aid; of those 80% were deemed to have need. 95% of undergraduates with need received aid; of those 10% had need fully met. ***Average percent of need met:*** 59% (excluding resources awarded to replace EFC). ***Average financial aid package:*** $5624 (excluding resources awarded to replace EFC). 5% of all full-time undergraduates had no need and received non-need-based gift aid.

GIFT AID (NEED-BASED) ***Total amount:*** $6,586,584 (57% federal, 30% state, 9% institutional, 4% external sources). ***Receiving aid:*** Freshmen: 40% (288); All full-time undergraduates: 39% (1,253). ***Average award:*** Freshmen: $4496; Undergraduates: $4581. ***Scholarships, grants, and awards:*** Federal Pell, FSEOG, state, private, college/university gift aid from institutional funds.

GIFT AID (NON-NEED-BASED) ***Total amount:*** $834,337 (15% federal, 16% state, 39% institutional, 30% external sources). ***Receiving aid:*** Freshmen: 3% (24); Undergraduates: 2% (67). ***Average award:*** Freshmen: $1442; Undergraduates: $1600. ***Scholarships, grants, and awards by category:*** *Academic Interests/Achievement:* general academic interests/achievements. *Creative Arts/Performance:* general creative arts/performance. *Special Achievements/Activities:* general special achievements/activities. *Special Characteristics:* general special characteristics. ***Tuition waivers:*** Full or partial for employees or children of employees. ***ROTC:*** Army, Naval.

LOANS ***Student loans:*** $12,667,269 (74% need-based, 26% non-need-based). 57% of past graduating class borrowed through all loan programs. *Average indebtedness per student:* $16,676. ***Average need-based loan:*** Freshmen: $2258; Undergraduates: $3589. ***Parent loans:*** $235,953 (20% need-based, 80% non-need-based). ***Programs:*** FFEL (Subsidized and Unsubsidized Stafford, PLUS), Perkins, Federal Nursing, college/university.

WORK-STUDY ***Federal work-study:*** Total amount: $423,741; 230 jobs averaging $2046. ***State or other work-study/employment:*** Total amount: $738 (100% need-based).

ATHLETIC AWARDS Total amount: $73,523 (92% need-based, 8% non-need-based).

APPLYING FOR FINANCIAL AID ***Required financial aid form:*** FAFSA. ***Financial aid deadline (priority):*** 3/1. ***Notification date:*** Continuous beginning 5/1. Students must reply within 3 weeks of notification.

CONTACT Brittany Hubbard, Director of Financial Aid, Indiana University Southeast, University Center, South Room 105, New Albany, IN 47150, 812-941-2246 or toll-free 800-852-8835 (in-state). *Fax:* 812-941-2546. *E-mail:* mibarlow@ius.edu.

INDIANA WESLEYAN UNIVERSITY

Marion, IN

CONTACT Director of Financial Aid, Indiana Wesleyan University, 4201 South Washington Street, Marion, IN 46953-4999, 765-677-2116 or toll-free 800-332-6901. *Fax:* 765-677-2809.

INSTITUTE OF COMPUTER TECHNOLOGY

Los Angeles, CA

See LA College International.

INTER AMERICAN UNIVERSITY OF PUERTO RICO, AGUADILLA CAMPUS

Aguadilla, PR

CONTACT Mr. Juan Gonzalez, Director of Financial Aid, Inter American University of Puerto Rico, Aguadilla Campus, PO Box 20000, Aguadilla, PR 00605, 787-891-0925 Ext. 2108. *Fax:* 787-882-3020.

INTER AMERICAN UNIVERSITY OF PUERTO RICO, ARECIBO CAMPUS

Arecibo, PR

CONTACT Ramón O. de Jesús, Financial Aid Director, Inter American University of Puerto Rico, Arecibo Campus, PO Box 4050, Arecibo, PR 00614-4050, 787-878-5475 Ext. 2275. *Fax:* 787-880-1624.

INTER AMERICAN UNIVERSITY OF PUERTO RICO, BARRANQUITAS CAMPUS

Barranquitas, PR

CONTACT Mr. Eduardo Fontánez Colón, Financial Aid Officer, Inter American University of Puerto Rico, Barranquitas Campus, Box 517, Barranquitas, PR 00794, 787-857-3600 Ext. 2049. *Fax:* 787-857-2244.

INTER AMERICAN UNIVERSITY OF PUERTO RICO, BAYAMÓN CAMPUS

Bayamón, PR

CONTACT Financial Aid Office, Inter American University of Puerto Rico, Bayamón Campus, 500 Road 830, Bayamon, PR 00957, 787-279-1912 Ext. 2025.

INTER AMERICAN UNIVERSITY OF PUERTO RICO, FAJARDO CAMPUS

Fajardo, PR

CONTACT Financial Aid Director, Inter American University of Puerto Rico, Fajardo Campus, Call Box 700003, Fajardo, PR 00738-7003, 787-863-2390 Ext. 2208.

INTER AMERICAN UNIVERSITY OF PUERTO RICO, GUAYAMA CAMPUS

Guayama, PR

ABOUT THE INSTITUTION Independent, coed. Awards: associate, bachelor's, and master's degrees. 15 undergraduate majors. Total enrollment: 2,270. Undergraduates: 2,221.

GIFT AID (NEED-BASED) ***Scholarships, grants, and awards:*** Federal Pell, FSEOG, state, college/university gift aid from institutional funds, Federal Nursing.

LOANS ***Programs:*** Federal Direct (Subsidized and Unsubsidized Stafford, PLUS), Perkins, Federal Nursing.

APPLYING FOR FINANCIAL AID ***Required financial aid form:*** FAFSA.

CONTACT Sr. Jose A. Vechini, Director of Financial Aid Office, Inter American University of Puerto Rico, Guayama Campus, Call Box 10004, Guyama, PR 00785, 787-864-2222 Ext. 2206 or toll-free 787-864-2222 Ext. 2243 (in-state). *Fax:* 787-864-8232. *E-mail:* javechi@inter.edu.

INTER AMERICAN UNIVERSITY OF PUERTO RICO, METROPOLITAN CAMPUS

San Juan, PR

CONTACT Mrs. Luz M. Medina, Acting Director of Financial Aid, Inter American University of Puerto Rico, Metropolitan Campus, PO Box 191293, San Juan, PR 00919-1293, 787-758-2891. *Fax:* 787-250-0782.

INTER AMERICAN UNIVERSITY OF PUERTO RICO, PONCE CAMPUS

Mercedita, PR

CONTACT Financial Aid Officer, Inter American University of Puerto Rico, Ponce Campus, Street #1, Km 123.2, Mercedita, PR 00715-2201, 787-284-1912 Ext. 2015.

INTER AMERICAN UNIVERSITY OF PUERTO RICO, SAN GERMÁN CAMPUS

San Germán, PR

CONTACT Ms. María I. Lugo, Financial Aid Director, Inter American University of Puerto Rico, San Germán Campus, PO Box 5100, San Germán, PR 00683-5008, 787-264-1912 Ext. 7252. *Fax:* 787-892-6350.

INTERIOR DESIGNERS INSTITUTE

Newport Beach, CA

CONTACT Office of Financial Aid, Interior Designers Institute, 1061 Camelback Road, Newport Beach, CA 92660, 949-675-4451.

INTERNATIONAL ACADEMY OF DESIGN & TECHNOLOGY

Tampa, FL

CONTACT Financial Aid Office, International Academy of Design & Technology, 5225 Memorial Highway, Tampa, FL 33634-7350, 813-881-0007 or toll-free 800-ACADEMY. *Fax:* 813-881-3440.

INTERNATIONAL ACADEMY OF DESIGN & TECHNOLOGY

Chicago, IL

CONTACT Barbara Williams, Financial Aid Director, International Academy of Design & Technology, 1 North State Street, Suite 400, Chicago, IL 60602, 312-980-9200 or toll-free 877-ACADEMY (out-of-state). *Fax:* 312-541-3929.

INTERNATIONAL ACADEMY OF DESIGN & TECHNOLOGY

Fairmont, WV

CONTACT Financial Aid Office, International Academy of Design & Technology, 2000 Green River Drive, Fairmont, WV 26554-9790, 304-534-5677 or toll-free 888-406-8324.

INTERNATIONAL BAPTIST COLLEGE

Tempe, AZ

CONTACT Financial Aid Office, International Baptist College, 2150 East Southern Avenue, Tempe, AZ 85282, 480-838-7070 or toll-free 800-422-4858. *Fax:* 480-838-5432.

INTERNATIONAL COLLEGE

Naples, FL

ABOUT THE INSTITUTION Independent, coed. Awards: associate, bachelor's, and master's degrees. 13 undergraduate majors. Total enrollment: 1,640. Undergraduates: 1,454. Freshmen: 129.

GIFT AID (NEED-BASED) ***Scholarships, grants, and awards:*** Federal Pell, FSEOG, state, private, college/university gift aid from institutional funds.

GIFT AID (NON-NEED-BASED) ***Scholarships, grants, and awards by category:*** *Special Achievements/Activities:* general special achievements/activities.

LOANS ***Programs:*** FFEL (Subsidized and Unsubsidized Stafford, PLUS).

WORK-STUDY ***Federal work-study:*** Total amount: $108,924; 48 jobs averaging $2269.

APPLYING FOR FINANCIAL AID ***Required financial aid form:*** FAFSA.

CONTACT Mr. Joe Gilchrist, Vice President of Student Financial Assistance, International College, 2655 Northbrooke Drive, Naples, FL 34119, 239-513-1122 Ext. 116 or toll-free 800-466-8017. *Fax:* 239-513-9579. *E-mail:* jgilchrist@internationalcollege.edu.

INTERNATIONAL COLLEGE AND GRADUATE SCHOOL

Honolulu, HI

See Hawai'i Theological Seminary.

INTERNATIONAL IMPORT-EXPORT INSTITUTE

Phoenix, AZ

CONTACT Financial Aid Office, International Import-Export Institute, 2432 West Peoria Avenue, Suite 1026, Phoenix, AZ 85029, 602-648-5750 or toll-free 800-474-8013.

IONA COLLEGE

New Rochelle, NY

Tuition & fees: $23,218 **Average undergraduate aid package: $14,433**

ABOUT THE INSTITUTION Independent religious, coed. Awards: bachelor's and master's degrees and post-bachelor's and post-master's certificates. 58 undergraduate majors. Total enrollment: 4,242. Undergraduates: 3,451. Freshmen: 910. Federal methodology is used as a basis for awarding need-based institutional aid.

UNDERGRADUATE EXPENSES for 2006–07 ***Application fee:*** $50. ***Comprehensive fee:*** $33,216 includes full-time tuition ($21,518), mandatory fees ($1700), and room and board ($9998). Full-time tuition and fees vary according to class time. Room and board charges vary according to housing facility. ***Part-time tuition:*** $714 per credit. ***Part-time fees:*** $400 per term. Part-time tuition and fees vary according to class time and course load. ***Payment plan:*** Installment.

FRESHMAN FINANCIAL AID (Fall 2006, est.) 896 applied for aid; of those 76% were deemed to have need. 100% of freshmen with need received aid; of those 20% had need fully met. ***Average percent of need met:*** 21% (excluding resources awarded to replace EFC). ***Average financial aid package:*** $15,293 (excluding resources awarded to replace EFC). 23% of all full-time freshmen had no need and received non-need-based gift aid.

UNDERGRADUATE FINANCIAL AID (Fall 2006, est.) 3,073 applied for aid; of those 78% were deemed to have need. 99% of undergraduates with need received aid; of those 21% had need fully met. ***Average percent of need met:*** 22% (excluding resources awarded to replace EFC). ***Average financial aid package:*** $14,433 (excluding resources awarded to replace EFC). 20% of all full-time undergraduates had no need and received non-need-based gift aid.

GIFT AID (NEED-BASED) ***Total amount:*** $6,774,680 (36% federal, 56% state, 4% institutional, 4% external sources). ***Receiving aid:*** Freshmen: 57% (516); All full-time undergraduates: 34% (1,090). ***Average award:*** Freshmen: $2689; Undergraduates: $3055. ***Scholarships, grants, and awards:*** Federal Pell, FSEOG, state, private, college/university gift aid from institutional funds.

GIFT AID (NON-NEED-BASED) ***Total amount:*** $22,460,375 (98% institutional, 2% external sources). ***Receiving aid:*** Freshmen: 75% (678); Undergraduates:

71% (2,311). ***Average award:*** Freshmen: $10,605; Undergraduates: $10,297. ***Scholarships, grants, and awards by category:*** *Academic Interests/Achievement:* 2,812 awards ($21,149,615 total): general academic interests/achievements. *Creative Arts/Performance:* 31 awards ($95,700 total): music. *Special Characteristics:* 237 awards ($964,623 total): children and siblings of alumni, children of faculty/staff, religious affiliation, siblings of current students. ***Tuition waivers:*** Full or partial for employees or children of employees, senior citizens. ***ROTC:*** Army cooperative, Air Force cooperative.

LOANS ***Student loans:*** $14,792,589 (39% need-based, 61% non-need-based). 66% of past graduating class borrowed through all loan programs. *Average indebtedness per student:* $19,457. ***Average need-based loan:*** Freshmen: $1612; Undergraduates: $2200. ***Parent loans:*** $6,856,902 (100% non-need-based). ***Programs:*** FFEL (Subsidized and Unsubsidized Stafford, PLUS), Perkins, alternative loans.

WORK-STUDY ***Federal work-study:*** Total amount: $564,029; 417 jobs averaging $753. ***State or other work-study/employment:*** Total amount: $350,000 (100% non-need-based). 258 part-time jobs averaging $906.

ATHLETIC AWARDS Total amount: $2,335,000 (100% non-need-based).

APPLYING FOR FINANCIAL AID ***Required financial aid forms:*** FAFSA, institution's own form, state aid form. ***Financial aid deadline:*** 4/15 (priority: 2/15). ***Notification date:*** Continuous beginning 12/20. Students must reply by 5/1 or within 2 weeks of notification.

CONTACT Mary Grant, Director of Financial Aid, Iona College, 715 North Avenue, New Rochelle, NY 10801-1890, 914-633-2676 or toll-free 800-231-IONA (in-state). *Fax:* 914-633-2486.

IOWA STATE UNIVERSITY OF SCIENCE AND TECHNOLOGY

Ames, IA

CONTACT Roberta Johnson, Director of Financial Aid, Iowa State University of Science and Technology, 0210 Beardshear Hall, Ames, IA 50011, 515-294-2223 or toll-free 800-262-3810. *Fax:* 515-294-3622. *E-mail:* rljohns@iastate.edu.

IOWA WESLEYAN COLLEGE

Mount Pleasant, IA

Tuition & fees: $18,870 **Average undergraduate aid package: $12,513**

ABOUT THE INSTITUTION Independent United Methodist, coed. Awards: bachelor's degrees. 40 undergraduate majors. Total enrollment: 849. Undergraduates: 849. Freshmen: 118. Federal methodology is used as a basis for awarding need-based institutional aid.

UNDERGRADUATE EXPENSES for 2007–08 ***Comprehensive fee:*** $24,750 includes full-time tuition ($18,870) and room and board ($5880). ***College room only:*** $2430. ***Part-time tuition:*** $465 per credit hour.

FRESHMAN FINANCIAL AID (Fall 2006, est.) 107 applied for aid; of those 74% were deemed to have need. 100% of freshmen with need received aid; of those 54% had need fully met. ***Average percent of need met:*** 91% (excluding resources awarded to replace EFC). ***Average financial aid package:*** $16,253 (excluding resources awarded to replace EFC). 9% of all full-time freshmen had no need and received non-need-based gift aid.

UNDERGRADUATE FINANCIAL AID (Fall 2006, est.) 611 applied for aid; of those 96% were deemed to have need. 100% of undergraduates with need received aid; of those 41% had need fully met. ***Average percent of need met:*** 87% (excluding resources awarded to replace EFC). ***Average financial aid package:*** $12,513 (excluding resources awarded to replace EFC). 5% of all full-time undergraduates had no need and received non-need-based gift aid.

GIFT AID (NEED-BASED) ***Total amount:*** $4,499,701 (25% federal, 18% state, 55% institutional, 2% external sources). ***Receiving aid:*** Freshmen: 67% (79); All full-time undergraduates: 91% (586). ***Average award:*** Freshmen: $9970; Undergraduates: $7672. ***Scholarships, grants, and awards:*** Federal Pell, FSEOG, state, private, college/university gift aid from institutional funds.

GIFT AID (NON-NEED-BASED) ***Total amount:*** $1,541,582 (9% state, 90% institutional, 1% external sources). ***Receiving aid:*** Freshmen: 67% (79); Undergraduates: 91% (586). ***Average award:*** Freshmen: $10,411; Undergraduates: $7821. ***Scholarships, grants, and awards by category:*** *Academic Interests/Achievement:* 248 awards ($964,222 total): general academic interests/achievements. *Creative Arts/Performance:* 42 awards ($90,067 total): art/fine arts, music. *Special Achievements/Activities:* 148 awards ($403,110 total): cheerleading/drum major, community service, leadership, religious involvement. *Special Characteristics:* 358 awards ($1,589,989 total): children and siblings of alumni, children of faculty/staff, international students, out-of-state students, relatives of clergy, religious affiliation.

LOANS ***Student loans:*** $4,934,483 (56% need-based, 44% non-need-based). 90% of past graduating class borrowed through all loan programs. *Average indebtedness per student:* $20,794. ***Average need-based loan:*** Freshmen: $2600; Undergraduates: $5000. ***Parent loans:*** $509,818 (30% need-based, 70% non-need-based). ***Programs:*** FFEL (Subsidized and Unsubsidized Stafford, PLUS), Perkins, state, alternative loans.

WORK-STUDY ***Federal work-study:*** Total amount: $78,703; 85 jobs averaging $1000. ***State or other work-study/employment:*** Total amount: $88,221 (60% need-based, 40% non-need-based). 47 part-time jobs averaging $1000.

ATHLETIC AWARDS Total amount: $1,500,593 (75% need-based, 25% non-need-based).

APPLYING FOR FINANCIAL AID ***Required financial aid form:*** FAFSA. ***Financial aid deadline (priority):*** 4/1. ***Notification date:*** Continuous beginning 3/1. Students must reply within 3 weeks of notification.

CONTACT Melissa Kilbride, Director of Financial Aid, Iowa Wesleyan College, 601 North Main Street, Mount Pleasant, IA 52641-1398, 319-385-6242 or toll-free 800-582-2383 Ext. 6231. *Fax:* 319-385-6203. *E-mail:* mkilbride@iwc.edu.

ITHACA COLLEGE

Ithaca, NY

Tuition & fees: $26,832 **Average undergraduate aid package: $22,694**

ABOUT THE INSTITUTION Independent, coed. Awards: bachelor's, master's, and doctoral degrees. 105 undergraduate majors. Total enrollment: 6,409. Undergraduates: 6,028. Freshmen: 1,522. Institutional methodology is used as a basis for awarding need-based institutional aid.

UNDERGRADUATE EXPENSES for 2006–07 ***Application fee:*** $60. ***Comprehensive fee:*** $37,146 includes full-time tuition ($26,832) and room and board ($10,314). ***College room only:*** $5388. ***Part-time tuition:*** $894 per credit hour. ***Payment plan:*** Installment.

FRESHMAN FINANCIAL AID (Fall 2006, est.) 1233 applied for aid; of those 91% were deemed to have need. 100% of freshmen with need received aid; of those 52% had need fully met. ***Average percent of need met:*** 88% (excluding resources awarded to replace EFC). ***Average financial aid package:*** $22,875 (excluding resources awarded to replace EFC). 9% of all full-time freshmen had no need and received non-need-based gift aid.

UNDERGRADUATE FINANCIAL AID (Fall 2006, est.) 4,469 applied for aid; of those 91% were deemed to have need. 100% of undergraduates with need received aid; of those 44% had need fully met. ***Average percent of need met:*** 86% (excluding resources awarded to replace EFC). ***Average financial aid package:*** $22,694 (excluding resources awarded to replace EFC). 11% of all full-time undergraduates had no need and received non-need-based gift aid.

GIFT AID (NEED-BASED) ***Total amount:*** $56,788,821 (6% federal, 6% state, 85% institutional, 3% external sources). ***Receiving aid:*** Freshmen: 65% (994); All full-time undergraduates: 64% (3,766). ***Average award:*** Freshmen: $15,749; Undergraduates: $15,057. ***Scholarships, grants, and awards:*** Federal Pell, FSEOG, state, private, college/university gift aid from institutional funds.

GIFT AID (NON-NEED-BASED) ***Total amount:*** $10,351,960 (1% federal, 1% state, 91% institutional, 7% external sources). ***Receiving aid:*** Freshmen: 21% (313); Undergraduates: 15% (864). ***Average award:*** Freshmen: $9713; Undergraduates: $10,463. ***Scholarships, grants, and awards by category:*** *Academic Interests/Achievement:* 2,014 awards ($16,687,116 total): communication, general academic interests/achievements. *Creative Arts/Performance:* 24 awards ($290,388 total): dance, journalism/publications, music, performing arts, theater/drama. *Special Achievements/Activities:* 108 awards ($642,000 total): leadership. *Special Characteristics:* 300 awards ($301,000 total): children and siblings of alumni, siblings of current students. ***Tuition waivers:*** Full or partial for employees or children of employees. ***ROTC:*** Army cooperative, Air Force cooperative.

LOANS ***Student loans:*** $24,024,381 (87% need-based, 13% non-need-based). ***Average need-based loan:*** Freshmen: $5638; Undergraduates: $5933. ***Parent loans:*** $22,805,124 (26% need-based, 74% non-need-based). ***Programs:*** FFEL (Subsidized and Unsubsidized Stafford, PLUS), Perkins, alternative loans.

WORK-STUDY ***Federal work-study:*** Total amount: $975,000; jobs available. ***State or other work-study/employment:*** Total amount: $9,637,245 (62% need-based, 38% non-need-based). Part-time jobs available.

APPLYING FOR FINANCIAL AID ***Required financial aid forms:*** FAFSA, CSS PROFILE required of early decision applicants; deadline Nov. 1. ***Financial aid deadline (priority):*** 2/1. ***Notification date:*** Continuous beginning 2/15.

CONTACT Mr. Larry Chambers, Director of Financial Aid, Ithaca College, 350 Egbert Hall, Ithaca, NY 14850, 800-429-4275 or toll-free 800-429-4274. *Fax:* 607-274-1895. *E-mail:* finaid@ithaca.edu.

ITT TECHNICAL INSTITUTE

Tempe, AZ

CONTACT Financial Aid Office, ITT Technical Institute, 5005 S. Wendler Drive, Tempe, AZ 85282, 602-437-7500 or toll-free 800-879-4881.

ITT TECHNICAL INSTITUTE

Clovis, CA

CONTACT Financial Aid Office, ITT Technical Institute, 362 N. Clovis Avenue, Clovis, CA 93612, 559-325-5400.

ITT TECHNICAL INSTITUTE

Lexington, KY

CONTACT Financial Aid Office, ITT Technical Institute, 2473 Fortune Drive, Suite 180, Lexington, KY 40509, 859-246-3300.

ITT TECHNICAL INSTITUTE

Oklahoma City, OK

CONTACT Financial Aid Office, ITT Technical Institute, 50 Penn Place Office Tower, 1900 Northwest Expressway, Suite 305R, Oklahoma City, OK 73118, 405-810-4100 or toll-free 800-518-1612 (in-state).

JACKSON STATE UNIVERSITY

Jackson, MS

Tuition & fees (MS res): $4224 **Average undergraduate aid package: N/A**

ABOUT THE INSTITUTION State-supported, coed. Awards: bachelor's, master's, and doctoral degrees and post-master's certificates. 61 undergraduate majors. Total enrollment: 8,256. Undergraduates: 6,523. Freshmen: 898. Federal methodology is used as a basis for awarding need-based institutional aid.

UNDERGRADUATE EXPENSES for 2006–07 ***Tuition, state resident:*** full-time $4224; part-time $174 per credit hour. ***Tuition, nonresident:*** full-time $9540; part-time $394 per credit hour. ***College room and board:*** $5212; ***Room only:*** $3116. Room and board charges vary according to board plan. ***Payment plan:*** Installment.

GIFT AID (NEED-BASED) ***Scholarships, grants, and awards:*** Federal Pell, FSEOG, state, private, college/university gift aid from institutional funds.

GIFT AID (NON-NEED-BASED) ***Scholarships, grants, and awards by category:*** *Academic Interests/Achievement:* general academic interests/achievements. *Creative Arts/Performance:* music. *Special Achievements/Activities:* leadership. *Special Characteristics:* children of faculty/staff. ***Tuition waivers:*** Full or partial for children of alumni, employees or children of employees. ***ROTC:*** Army.

LOANS ***Programs:*** FFEL (Subsidized and Unsubsidized Stafford, PLUS), Perkins.

APPLYING FOR FINANCIAL AID ***Required financial aid forms:*** FAFSA, institution's own form, state aid form. ***Financial aid deadline (priority):*** 4/15. ***Notification date:*** Continuous.

CONTACT B. J. Moncure, Director of Financial Aid, Jackson State University, 1400 J.R. Lynch Street, PO Box 17065, Jackson, MS 39217, 601-979-2227 or toll-free 800-682-5390 (in-state), 800-848-6817 (out-of-state). *Fax:* 601-979-2237.

JACKSONVILLE STATE UNIVERSITY

Jacksonville, AL

Tuition & fees (AL res): $5070 **Average undergraduate aid package: $6675**

ABOUT THE INSTITUTION State-supported, coed. Awards: bachelor's and master's degrees and post-master's certificates. 58 undergraduate majors. Total enrollment: 8,957. Undergraduates: 7,311. Freshmen: 1,144. Federal methodology is used as a basis for awarding need-based institutional aid.

UNDERGRADUATE EXPENSES for 2006–07 ***Application fee:*** $20. ***Tuition, state resident:*** full-time $5070; part-time $169 per credit hour. ***Tuition, nonresident:*** full-time $10,140; part-time $338 per credit hour. ***College room and board:*** $3764. Room and board charges vary according to board plan and housing facility.

FRESHMAN FINANCIAL AID (Fall 2005) of those 60% had need fully met. ***Average percent of need met:*** 25% (excluding resources awarded to replace EFC). ***Average financial aid package:*** $6675 (excluding resources awarded to replace EFC). 16% of all full-time freshmen had no need and received non-need-based gift aid.

UNDERGRADUATE FINANCIAL AID (Fall 2005) of those 62% had need fully met. ***Average percent of need met:*** 40% (excluding resources awarded to replace EFC). ***Average financial aid package:*** $6675 (excluding resources awarded to replace EFC). 14% of all full-time undergraduates had no need and received non-need-based gift aid.

GIFT AID (NEED-BASED) ***Total amount:*** $17,922,416 (47% federal, 1% state, 27% institutional, 25% external sources). ***Receiving aid:*** Freshmen: 32% (352); All full-time undergraduates: 23% (1,326). ***Average award:*** Freshmen: $3646; Undergraduates: $3745. ***Scholarships, grants, and awards:*** Federal Pell, FSEOG, state, private, college/university gift aid from institutional funds, Federal Nursing.

GIFT AID (NON-NEED-BASED) ***Receiving aid:*** Freshmen: 32% (352); Undergraduates: 23% (1,326). ***Average award:*** Freshmen: $1200; Undergraduates: $1200. ***Scholarships, grants, and awards by category:*** *Academic Interests/Achievement:* biological sciences, business, communication, computer science, education, English, health fields, home economics, humanities, mathematics, military science, physical sciences, social sciences. *Creative Arts/Performance:* art/fine arts, journalism/publications, music, theater/drama. *Special Achievements/Activities:* general special achievements/activities. ***Tuition waivers:*** Full or partial for employees or children of employees. ***ROTC:*** Army.

LOANS ***Student loans:*** $34,192,293 (62% need-based, 38% non-need-based). 47% of past graduating class borrowed through all loan programs. *Average indebtedness per student:* $17,125. ***Average need-based loan:*** Freshmen: $2625; Undergraduates: $5670. ***Parent loans:*** $756,000 (100% non-need-based). ***Programs:*** FFEL (Subsidized and Unsubsidized Stafford, PLUS), college/university.

WORK-STUDY ***Federal work-study:*** Total amount: $434,953; 380 jobs averaging $1164. ***State or other work-study/employment:*** Total amount: $1,302,222 (100% non-need-based). 517 part-time jobs averaging $2518.

ATHLETIC AWARDS Total amount: $2,597,913 (100% non-need-based).

APPLYING FOR FINANCIAL AID ***Required financial aid forms:*** FAFSA, institution's own form. ***Financial aid deadline (priority):*** 3/15. ***Notification date:*** Continuous beginning 5/15. Students must reply within 2 weeks of notification.

CONTACT Mrs. Vicki Adams, Director of Financial Aid, Jacksonville State University, 700 Pelham Road North, Jacksonville, AL 36265-9982, 256-782-5006 Ext. 8399 or toll-free 800-231-5291. *Fax:* 256-782-5476. *E-mail:* finaid@jsu.edu.

JACKSONVILLE UNIVERSITY

Jacksonville, FL

ABOUT THE INSTITUTION Independent, coed. Awards: bachelor's and master's degrees and first professional certificates. 58 undergraduate majors. Total enrollment: 3,093. Undergraduates: 2,699. Freshmen: 498.

GIFT AID (NEED-BASED) ***Scholarships, grants, and awards:*** Federal Pell, FSEOG, state, private, college/university gift aid from institutional funds.

GIFT AID (NON-NEED-BASED) ***Scholarships, grants, and awards by category:*** *Academic Interests/Achievement:* business, general academic interests/achievements. *Creative Arts/Performance:* general creative arts/performance. *Special Achievements/Activities:* general special achievements/activities. *Special Characteristics:* children of educators, children of faculty/staff, international students.

LOANS ***Programs:*** FFEL (Subsidized and Unsubsidized Stafford, PLUS), Perkins, college/university, Navy ROTC.

WORK-STUDY ***Federal work-study:*** Total amount: $535,315; 250 jobs averaging $2000.

APPLYING FOR FINANCIAL AID ***Required financial aid form:*** FAFSA.

CONTACT Mrs. Catherine Huntress, Director of Student Financial Assistance, Jacksonville University, 2800 University Boulevard North, Jacksonville, FL 32211, 904-256-7060 or toll-free 800-225-2027. *Fax:* 904-256-7148. *E-mail:* chuntres@ju.edu.

JAMES MADISON UNIVERSITY

Harrisonburg, VA

Tuition & fees (VA res): $6290 **Average undergraduate aid package: $7683**

ABOUT THE INSTITUTION State-supported, coed. Awards: bachelor's, master's, and doctoral degrees (also offers specialist in education degree). 46 undergraduate majors. Total enrollment: 17,393. Undergraduates: 16,013. Freshmen: 3,748. Federal methodology is used as a basis for awarding need-based institutional aid.

UNDERGRADUATE EXPENSES for 2006–07 ***Application fee:*** $40. ***Tuition, state resident:*** full-time $6290; part-time $208 per credit hour. ***Tuition, nonresident:*** full-time $16,236; part-time $539 per credit hour. Part-time tuition and fees vary according to course load. ***College room and board:*** $6756; ***Room only:*** $3508. Room and board charges vary according to board plan and housing facility. ***Payment plan:*** Installment.

FRESHMAN FINANCIAL AID (Fall 2006, est.) 2743 applied for aid; of those 49% were deemed to have need. 85% of freshmen with need received aid; of those 93% had need fully met. ***Average percent of need met:*** 42% (excluding resources awarded to replace EFC). ***Average financial aid package:*** $6693 (excluding resources awarded to replace EFC). 3% of all full-time freshmen had no need and received non-need-based gift aid.

UNDERGRADUATE FINANCIAL AID (Fall 2006, est.) 11,993 applied for aid; of those 61% were deemed to have need. 62% of undergraduates with need received aid; of those 75% had need fully met. ***Average percent of need met:*** 50% (excluding resources awarded to replace EFC). ***Average financial aid package:*** $7683 (excluding resources awarded to replace EFC). 1% of all full-time undergraduates had no need and received non-need-based gift aid.

GIFT AID (NEED-BASED) ***Total amount:*** $12,891,220 (32% federal, 36% state, 18% institutional, 14% external sources). ***Receiving aid:*** Freshmen: 16% (583); All full-time undergraduates: 12% (1,878). ***Average award:*** Freshmen: $5749; Undergraduates: $5739. ***Scholarships, grants, and awards:*** Federal Pell, FSEOG, state, private, college/university gift aid from institutional funds.

GIFT AID (NON-NEED-BASED) ***Total amount:*** $2,563,460 (5% state, 77% institutional, 18% external sources). ***Receiving aid:*** Freshmen: 13% (484); Undergraduates: 7% (1,133). ***Average award:*** Freshmen: $2253; Undergraduates: $2059. ***Scholarships, grants, and awards by category:*** *Academic Interests/Achievement:* 691 awards ($931,636 total): architecture, biological sciences, business, computer science, education, engineering/technologies, English, general academic interests/achievements, health fields, humanities, international studies, mathematics, military science, physical sciences, premedicine, religion/biblical studies, social sciences. *Creative Arts/Performance:* 156 awards ($153,055 total): art/fine arts, cinema/film/broadcasting, dance, journalism/publications, music, theater/drama. *Special Achievements/Activities:* 105 awards ($67,520 total): cheerleading/drum major, general special achievements/activities, leadership. *Special Characteristics:* 42 awards ($61,930 total): children and siblings of alumni, children of faculty/staff, handicapped students, international students, out-of-state students, siblings of current students. ***Tuition waivers:*** Full or partial for employees or children of employees, senior citizens. ***ROTC:*** Army, Air Force cooperative.

LOANS ***Student loans:*** $45,780,716 (41% need-based, 59% non-need-based). 68% of past graduating class borrowed through all loan programs. *Average indebtedness per student:* $11,932. ***Average need-based loan:*** Freshmen: $3024; Undergraduates: $3772. ***Parent loans:*** $27,406,664 (100% non-need-based). ***Programs:*** FFEL (Subsidized and Unsubsidized Stafford, PLUS), Perkins.

WORK-STUDY ***Federal work-study:*** Total amount: $2,809,563; 1,545 jobs averaging $1830. ***State or other work-study/employment:*** Total amount: $4,626,864 (100% non-need-based). 2,460 part-time jobs averaging $1881.

ATHLETIC AWARDS Total amount: $3,610,021 (100% non-need-based).

APPLYING FOR FINANCIAL AID ***Required financial aid form:*** FAFSA. ***Financial aid deadline (priority):*** 3/1. ***Notification date:*** Continuous beginning 4/1. Students must reply within 4 weeks of notification.

CONTACT Lisa L. Turner, Director of Financial Aid and Scholarships, James Madison University, Warren Hall B504, MSC 3519, Harrisonburg, VA 22807, 540-568-7820.

JAMESTOWN COLLEGE

Jamestown, ND

Tuition & fees: $11,235 **Average undergraduate aid package: $7939**

ABOUT THE INSTITUTION Independent Presbyterian, coed. Awards: bachelor's degrees. 43 undergraduate majors. Total enrollment: 996. Undergraduates: 996. Freshmen: 242. Both federal and institutional methodology are used as a basis for awarding need-based institutional aid.

UNDERGRADUATE EXPENSES for 2007–08 ***Application fee:*** $20. ***Comprehensive fee:*** $15,855 includes full-time tuition ($11,235) and room and board ($4620). ***College room only:*** $1970. ***Part-time tuition:*** $310 per credit. ***Part-time fees:*** $200 per year.

FRESHMAN FINANCIAL AID (Fall 2006, est.) 229 applied for aid; of those 93% were deemed to have need. 100% of freshmen with need received aid; of those 26% had need fully met. ***Average percent of need met:*** 66% (excluding resources awarded to replace EFC). ***Average financial aid package:*** $7744 (excluding resources awarded to replace EFC). 19% of all full-time freshmen had no need and received non-need-based gift aid.

UNDERGRADUATE FINANCIAL AID (Fall 2006, est.) 897 applied for aid; of those 86% were deemed to have need. 100% of undergraduates with need received aid; of those 22% had need fully met. ***Average percent of need met:*** 64% (excluding resources awarded to replace EFC). ***Average financial aid package:*** $7939 (excluding resources awarded to replace EFC). 17% of all full-time undergraduates had no need and received non-need-based gift aid.

GIFT AID (NEED-BASED) ***Total amount:*** $3,265,927 (31% federal, 3% state, 58% institutional, 8% external sources). ***Receiving aid:*** Freshmen: 89% (212); All full-time undergraduates: 84% (763). ***Average award:*** Freshmen: $5784; Undergraduates: $5004. ***Scholarships, grants, and awards:*** Federal Pell, FSEOG, state, private, college/university gift aid from institutional funds, Federal Nursing, National Smart Grant, Academic Competitiveness Grant (ACG).

GIFT AID (NON-NEED-BASED) ***Total amount:*** $705,925 (1% state, 87% institutional, 12% external sources). ***Receiving aid:*** Freshmen: 17% (40); Undergraduates: 9% (80). ***Average award:*** Freshmen: $7330; Undergraduates: $8246. ***Scholarships, grants, and awards by category:*** *Academic Interests/Achievement:* 354 awards ($1,170,057 total): general academic interests/achievements, physical sciences. *Creative Arts/Performance:* 15 awards ($29,250 total): art/fine arts, music, theater/drama. *Special Achievements/Activities:* 25 awards ($12,350 total): leadership. *Special Characteristics:* 77 awards ($176,129 total): children of faculty/staff, general special characteristics, international students, relatives of clergy, religious affiliation, spouses of current students.

LOANS ***Student loans:*** $4,751,135 (62% need-based, 38% non-need-based). 92% of past graduating class borrowed through all loan programs. *Average indebtedness per student:* $21,879. ***Average need-based loan:*** Freshmen: $2665; Undergraduates: $3695. ***Parent loans:*** $393,614 (26% need-based, 74% non-need-based). ***Programs:*** FFEL (Subsidized and Unsubsidized Stafford, PLUS), Perkins, college/university, alternative loans.

WORK-STUDY ***Federal work-study:*** Total amount: $246,193; 268 jobs averaging $918. ***State or other work-study/employment:*** Total amount: $38,173 (100% non-need-based). 51 part-time jobs averaging $748.

ATHLETIC AWARDS Total amount: $661,599 (76% need-based, 24% non-need-based).

APPLYING FOR FINANCIAL AID ***Required financial aid form:*** FAFSA. ***Financial aid deadline (priority):*** 3/15. ***Notification date:*** Continuous beginning 4/1. Students must reply within 6 weeks of notification.

CONTACT Margery Michael, Director of Financial Aid, Jamestown College, 6085 College Lane, Jamestown, ND 58405, 701-252-3467 Ext. 2556 or toll-free 800-336-2554. *Fax:* 701-253-4318. *E-mail:* mmichael@jc.edu.

JARVIS CHRISTIAN COLLEGE

Hawkins, TX

Tuition & fees: N/R **Average undergraduate aid package: $13,600**

ABOUT THE INSTITUTION Independent religious, coed. Awards: bachelor's degrees. 23 undergraduate majors. Total enrollment: 675. Undergraduates: 675. Freshmen: 113. Federal methodology is used as a basis for awarding need-based institutional aid.

UNDERGRADUATE EXPENSES for 2007–08 ***Application fee:*** $25. ***Tuition:*** part-time $300 per hour. ***Required fees:*** $385 per term part-time.

FRESHMAN FINANCIAL AID (Fall 2005) 108 applied for aid; of those 87% were deemed to have need. 98% of freshmen with need received aid; of those 100% had need fully met. ***Average percent of need met:*** 97% (excluding resources awarded to replace EFC). ***Average financial aid package:*** $12,800 (excluding resources awarded to replace EFC). 8% of all full-time freshmen had no need and received non-need-based gift aid.

UNDERGRADUATE FINANCIAL AID (Fall 2005) 591 applied for aid; of those 93% were deemed to have need. 98% of undergraduates with need received aid; of those 94% had need fully met. ***Average percent of need met:*** 94% (excluding resources awarded to replace EFC). ***Average financial aid package:*** $13,600 (excluding resources awarded to replace EFC). 8% of all full-time undergraduates had no need and received non-need-based gift aid.

GIFT AID (NEED-BASED) ***Total amount:*** $5,576,142 (34% federal, 16% state, 50% external sources). ***Receiving aid:*** Freshmen: 78% (84); All full-time undergraduates: 89% (529). ***Average award:*** Freshmen: $3200; Undergraduates: $3200. ***Scholarships, grants, and awards:*** Federal Pell, FSEOG, state, private, college/university gift aid from institutional funds, United Negro College Fund.

GIFT AID (NON-NEED-BASED) ***Total amount:*** $1,419,409 (81% institutional, 19% external sources). ***Receiving aid:*** Freshmen: 24% (26); Undergraduates: 32% (193). ***Average award:*** Freshmen: $11,000; Undergraduates: $12,500. ***Scholarships, grants, and awards by category:*** *Academic Interests/Achievement:* 127 awards ($1,154,409 total): education, general academic interests/achievements. *Special Characteristics:* religious affiliation.

LOANS ***Student loans:*** $2,285,000 (61% need-based, 39% non-need-based). 90% of past graduating class borrowed through all loan programs. *Average indebtedness per student:* $14,500. ***Average need-based loan:*** Freshmen: $2625; Undergraduates: $4400. ***Parent loans:*** $821,560 (100% non-need-based). ***Programs:*** FFEL (Subsidized and Unsubsidized Stafford, PLUS), Perkins.

WORK-STUDY ***Federal work-study:*** Total amount: $205,000; 160 jobs available. ***State or other work-study/employment:*** Total amount: $4800 (100% need-based). 4 part-time jobs averaging $4800.

ATHLETIC AWARDS Total amount: $871,960 (100% non-need-based).

APPLYING FOR FINANCIAL AID ***Required financial aid form:*** FAFSA. ***Financial aid deadline (priority):*** 4/1. ***Notification date:*** Continuous beginning 5/1. Students must reply within 2 weeks of notification.

CONTACT Kenon Woods, Assistant Director of Financial Aid, Jarvis Christian College, PO Box 1470, Hawkins, TX 75765, 903-769-5733. *Fax:* 903-769-4842. *E-mail:* kenon_woods@jarvis.edu.

JEFFERSON COLLEGE OF HEALTH SCIENCES

Roanoke, VA

ABOUT THE INSTITUTION Independent, coed. Awards: associate and bachelor's degrees. 13 undergraduate majors. Total enrollment: 697. Undergraduates: 697. Freshmen: 77.

GIFT AID (NEED-BASED) ***Scholarships, grants, and awards:*** Federal Pell, FSEOG, state, private, college/university gift aid from institutional funds.

GIFT AID (NON-NEED-BASED) ***Scholarships, grants, and awards by category:*** *Academic Interests/Achievement:* biological sciences, health fields. *Special Characteristics:* local/state students.

LOANS ***Programs:*** FFEL (Subsidized and Unsubsidized Stafford, PLUS), alternative loans.

WORK-STUDY ***Federal work-study:*** Total amount: $261,453; 185 jobs averaging $1414. ***State or other work-study/employment:*** Total amount: $5581 (69% need-based, 31% non-need-based).

APPLYING FOR FINANCIAL AID ***Required financial aid forms:*** FAFSA, state aid form.

CONTACT Debra A. Johnson, Director of Financial Aid, Jefferson College of Health Sciences, 920 South Jefferson Street, PO Box 13186, Roanoke, VA 24031-3186, 540-985-8492 or toll-free 888-985-8483. *Fax:* 540-224-6916. *E-mail:* djohnson@jchs.edu.

THE JEWISH THEOLOGICAL SEMINARY

New York, NY

CONTACT Linda Levine, Registrar/Director of Financial Aid, The Jewish Theological Seminary, 3080 Broadway, New York, NY 10027-4649, 212-678-8007. *Fax:* 212-678-8947. *E-mail:* financialaid@jtsa.edu.

JOHN BROWN UNIVERSITY

Siloam Springs, AR

ABOUT THE INSTITUTION Independent interdenominational, coed. Awards: bachelor's and master's degrees. 59 undergraduate majors. Total enrollment: 1,882. Undergraduates: 1,682. Freshmen: 326.

GIFT AID (NEED-BASED) ***Scholarships, grants, and awards:*** Federal Pell, FSEOG, state, private, college/university gift aid from institutional funds.

GIFT AID (NON-NEED-BASED) ***Scholarships, grants, and awards by category:*** *Academic Interests/Achievement:* general academic interests/achievements. *Creative Arts/Performance:* journalism/publications, music. *Special Achievements/Activities:* cheerleading/drum major, leadership. *Special Characteristics:* children and siblings of alumni, children of educators, children of faculty/staff, ethnic background, international students, members of minority groups, relatives of clergy, siblings of current students.

LOANS ***Programs:*** FFEL (Subsidized and Unsubsidized Stafford, PLUS), Perkins, state.

WORK-STUDY ***Federal work-study:*** Total amount: $428,930; 297 jobs averaging $1362. ***State or other work-study/employment:*** Total amount: $329,330 (71% need-based, 29% non-need-based). 255 part-time jobs averaging $1318.

APPLYING FOR FINANCIAL AID ***Required financial aid forms:*** FAFSA, institution's own form.

CONTACT Mrs. Emily Nichols, Assistant Director of Student Financial Aid, John Brown University, 2000 West University Street, Siloam Springs, AR 72761-2121, 479-524-7115 or toll-free 877-JBU-INFO. *Fax:* 479-524-7405. *E-mail:* emnichols@jbu.edu.

JOHN CARROLL UNIVERSITY

University Heights, OH

CONTACT Financial Aid Counselor, John Carroll University, 20700 North Park Boulevard, University Heights, OH 44118-4581, 216-397-4248. *Fax:* 216-397-3098. *E-mail:* jcuofa@jcu.edu.

JOHN F. KENNEDY UNIVERSITY

Pleasant Hill, CA

ABOUT THE INSTITUTION Independent, coed. Awards: bachelor's, master's, doctoral, and first professional degrees and post-bachelor's certificates. 6 undergraduate majors. Total enrollment: 1,653. Undergraduates: 197.

GIFT AID (NEED-BASED) ***Scholarships, grants, and awards:*** Federal Pell, FSEOG, state, private, college/university gift aid from institutional funds.

LOANS ***Programs:*** FFEL (Subsidized and Unsubsidized Stafford, PLUS), Perkins, college/university.

APPLYING FOR FINANCIAL AID ***Required financial aid forms:*** FAFSA, institution's own form.

CONTACT Mindy Bergeron, Director of Financial Aid, John F. Kennedy University, 100 Ellinwood Way, Pleasant Hill, CA 94523, 925-969-3385 or toll-free 800-696-JFKU. *Fax:* 925-969-3390. *E-mail:* bergeron@jfku.edu.

JOHN JAY COLLEGE OF CRIMINAL JUSTICE OF THE CITY UNIVERSITY OF NEW YORK

New York, NY

Tuition & fees: N/R **Average undergraduate aid package: $6900**

ABOUT THE INSTITUTION State and locally supported, coed. Awards: associate, bachelor's, master's, and doctoral degrees and post-bachelor's certificates. 15 undergraduate majors. Total enrollment: 14,051. Undergraduates: 12,276. Federal methodology is used as a basis for awarding need-based institutional aid.

FRESHMAN FINANCIAL AID (Fall 2005) 2409 applied for aid; of those 89% were deemed to have need. 93% of freshmen with need received aid. ***Average percent of need met:*** 85% (excluding resources awarded to replace EFC). ***Average financial aid package:*** $6900 (excluding resources awarded to replace EFC).

UNDERGRADUATE FINANCIAL AID (Fall 2005) 8,377 applied for aid; of those 89% were deemed to have need. ***Average percent of need met:*** 85% (excluding resources awarded to replace EFC). ***Average financial aid package:*** $6900 (excluding resources awarded to replace EFC).

GIFT AID (NEED-BASED) ***Total amount:*** $39,249,628 (50% federal, 49% state, 1% external sources). ***Receiving aid:*** Freshmen: 67% (1,798); All full-time undergraduates: 80% (7,446). ***Average award:*** Freshmen: $2800; Undergraduates: $3600. ***Scholarships, grants, and awards:*** Federal Pell, FSEOG, state, college/university gift aid from institutional funds.

GIFT AID (NON-NEED-BASED) ***Scholarships, grants, and awards by category:*** *Academic Interests/Achievement:* general academic interests/achievements. ***ROTC:*** Air Force cooperative.

LOANS ***Student loans:*** $18,767,785 (91% need-based, 9% non-need-based). 48% of past graduating class borrowed through all loan programs. *Average indebtedness per student:* $14,000. ***Average need-based loan:*** Undergraduates: $1800. ***Parent loans:*** $715,102 (100% need-based). ***Programs:*** Federal Direct (Subsidized and Unsubsidized Stafford, PLUS), Perkins, alternative loans.

WORK-STUDY ***Federal work-study:*** Total amount: $394,639; 442 jobs averaging $1064. ***State or other work-study/employment:*** Part-time jobs available.

APPLYING FOR FINANCIAL AID ***Required financial aid form:*** FAFSA. ***Financial aid deadline (priority):*** 6/1. ***Notification date:*** Continuous. Students must reply within 2 weeks of notification.

CONTACT Alikham Morgan, Director of Financial Aid, John Jay College of Criminal Justice of the City University of New York, 445 West 59th Street, New York, NY 10019-1093, 212-237-8156 or toll-free 877-JOHNJAY. *Fax:* 212-237-8936. *E-mail:* amnrgan@jjay.cuny.edu.

THE JOHNS HOPKINS UNIVERSITY

Baltimore, MD

Tuition & fees: $33,900 **Average undergraduate aid package: $31,176**

ABOUT THE INSTITUTION Independent, coed. Awards: bachelor's, master's, doctoral, and first professional degrees and post-bachelor's and post-master's certificates. 59 undergraduate majors. Total enrollment: 6,124. Undergraduates: 4,478. Freshmen: 1,207. Both federal and institutional methodology are used as a basis for awarding need-based institutional aid.

UNDERGRADUATE EXPENSES for 2006–07 ***Application fee:*** $60. ***One-time required fee:*** $500. ***Comprehensive fee:*** $44,522 includes full-time tuition ($33,900) and room and board ($10,622). ***College room only:*** $6096. Room and board charges vary according to board plan and housing facility. ***Part-time tuition:*** $1130 per credit.

FRESHMAN FINANCIAL AID (Fall 2006, est.) 822 applied for aid; of those 70% were deemed to have need. 98% of freshmen with need received aid; of those 100% had need fully met. ***Average percent of need met:*** 100% (excluding resources awarded to replace EFC). ***Average financial aid package:*** $31,612 (excluding resources awarded to replace EFC). 1% of all full-time freshmen had no need and received non-need-based gift aid.

UNDERGRADUATE FINANCIAL AID (Fall 2006, est.) 2,445 applied for aid; of those 84% were deemed to have need. 97% of undergraduates with need received aid; of those 100% had need fully met. ***Average percent of need met:*** 100% (excluding resources awarded to replace EFC). ***Average financial aid package:*** $31,176 (excluding resources awarded to replace EFC). 2% of all full-time undergraduates had no need and received non-need-based gift aid.

GIFT AID (NEED-BASED) ***Total amount:*** $43,708,881 (5% federal, 2% state, 89% institutional, 4% external sources). ***Receiving aid:*** Freshmen: 42% (512); All full-time undergraduates: 40% (1,744). ***Average award:*** Freshmen: $23,188; Undergraduates: $19,363. ***Scholarships, grants, and awards:*** Federal Pell, FSEOG, state, private, college/university gift aid from institutional funds.

GIFT AID (NON-NEED-BASED) ***Total amount:*** $3,815,330 (13% federal, 11% state, 59% institutional, 17% external sources). ***Receiving aid:*** Freshmen: 9% (114); Undergraduates: 10% (441). ***Average award:*** Freshmen: $24,817; Undergraduates: $16,691. ***Scholarships, grants, and awards by category:*** *Academic Interests/Achievement:* 78 awards ($1,708,987 total): engineering/technologies, general academic interests/achievements. *Special Characteristics:* 56 awards ($1,106,850 total): children of faculty/staff. ***Tuition waivers:*** Full or partial for employees or children of employees. ***ROTC:*** Army, Air Force cooperative.

LOANS ***Student loans:*** $11,647,084 (86% need-based, 14% non-need-based). 53% of past graduating class borrowed through all loan programs. *Average indebtedness per student:* $16,932. ***Average need-based loan:*** Freshmen: $2625; Undergraduates: $3136. ***Parent loans:*** $10,695,548 (65% need-based, 35% non-need-based). ***Programs:*** Federal Direct (Subsidized and Unsubsidized Stafford), FFEL (Subsidized and Unsubsidized Stafford, PLUS), Perkins, college/university.

WORK-STUDY ***Federal work-study:*** Total amount: $3,752,184; 1,553 jobs averaging $2416. ***State or other work-study/employment:*** Part-time jobs available.

ATHLETIC AWARDS Total amount: $1,112,876 (20% need-based, 80% non-need-based).

APPLYING FOR FINANCIAL AID ***Required financial aid forms:*** FAFSA, CSS Financial Aid PROFILE, noncustodial (divorced/separated) parent's statement, business/farm supplement, prior and current year federal income tax form(s). ***Financial aid deadline:*** 3/1 (priority: 3/1). ***Notification date:*** 4/1. Students must reply by 5/1 or within 2 weeks of notification.

CONTACT Dr. Ellen Frishberg, University Director of Student Financial Services, The Johns Hopkins University, 146 Garland Hall, Baltimore, MD 21218, 410-516-8028. *Fax:* 410-516-6015. *E-mail:* efrish@jhu.edu.

JOHNSON & WALES UNIVERSITY

Denver, CO

ABOUT THE INSTITUTION Independent, coed. Awards: associate and bachelor's degrees. 18 undergraduate majors. Total enrollment: 1,543. Undergraduates: 1,543. Freshmen: 404.

GIFT AID (NEED-BASED) ***Scholarships, grants, and awards:*** Federal Pell, FSEOG, state, private, college/university gift aid from institutional funds.

GIFT AID (NON-NEED-BASED) ***Scholarships, grants, and awards by category:*** *Academic Interests/Achievement:* general academic interests/achievements. *Special Achievements/Activities:* memberships. *Special Characteristics:* children of faculty/staff.

LOANS ***Programs:*** FFEL (Subsidized and Unsubsidized Stafford, PLUS), Perkins, state, college/university.

WORK-STUDY ***Federal work-study:*** Total amount: $612,560; jobs available.

APPLYING FOR FINANCIAL AID ***Required financial aid forms:*** FAFSA, CSS Financial Aid PROFILE.

CONTACT Ms. Lynn Robinson, Director of Financial Aid, Johnson & Wales University, 8 Abbott Park Place, Providence, RI 02903, 401-598-4648 or toll-free 877-598-3368. *Fax:* 401-598-1040. *E-mail:* fp@jwu.edu.

JOHNSON & WALES UNIVERSITY

North Miami, FL

ABOUT THE INSTITUTION Independent, coed. Awards: associate and bachelor's degrees. 16 undergraduate majors. Total enrollment: 2,215. Undergraduates: 2,215. Freshmen: 650.

GIFT AID (NON-NEED-BASED) ***Scholarships, grants, and awards by category:*** *Academic Interests/Achievement:* general academic interests/achievements. *Special Achievements/Activities:* memberships. *Special Characteristics:* children of faculty/staff.

LOANS ***Programs:*** FFEL (Subsidized and Unsubsidized Stafford, PLUS), Perkins, state, college/university.

WORK-STUDY ***Federal work-study:*** Total amount: $1,575,542; jobs available. ***State or other work-study/employment:*** Total amount: $8150 (100% need-based). Part-time jobs available.

APPLYING FOR FINANCIAL AID ***Required financial aid forms:*** FAFSA, CSS Financial Aid PROFILE.

CONTACT Ms. Lynn Robinson, Director of Financial Aid, Johnson & Wales University, 8 Abbott Park Place, Providence, RI 02903, 401-598-4648 or toll-free 800-232-2433. *Fax:* 401-598-1040. *E-mail:* fp@jwu.edu.

JOHNSON & WALES UNIVERSITY

Charlotte, NC

ABOUT THE INSTITUTION Independent, coed. Awards: associate and bachelor's degrees. 13 undergraduate majors. Total enrollment: 2,493. Undergraduates: 2,493. Freshmen: 771.

GIFT AID (NEED-BASED) ***Scholarships, grants, and awards:*** Federal Pell, FSEOG, state, private, college/university gift aid from institutional funds.

GIFT AID (NON-NEED-BASED) ***Scholarships, grants, and awards by category:*** *Academic Interests/Achievement:* general academic interests/achievements. *Special Achievements/Activities:* memberships. *Special Characteristics:* children of faculty/staff.

LOANS ***Programs:*** FFEL (Subsidized and Unsubsidized Stafford, PLUS), Perkins, state, college/university.

WORK-STUDY ***Federal work-study:*** Total amount: $1,159,980; jobs available.

APPLYING FOR FINANCIAL AID ***Required financial aid forms:*** FAFSA, CSS Financial Aid PROFILE.

CONTACT Ms. Lynn Robinson, Director of Financial Aid, Johnson & Wales University, 8 Abbott Park Place, Providence, RI 02903, 401-598-1648 or toll-free 866-598-2427. *Fax:* 401-598-4751. *E-mail:* fp@jwu.edu.

JOHNSON & WALES UNIVERSITY

Providence, RI

ABOUT THE INSTITUTION Independent, coed. Awards: associate, bachelor's, master's, and doctoral degrees (branch locations in Charleston, SC; Denver, CO; North Miami, FL; Norfolk, VA; Gothenberg, Sweden). 38 undergraduate majors. Total enrollment: 10,310. Undergraduates: 9,349. Freshmen: 2,470.

GIFT AID (NEED-BASED) ***Scholarships, grants, and awards:*** Federal Pell, FSEOG, state, private, college/university gift aid from institutional funds.

GIFT AID (NON-NEED-BASED) ***Scholarships, grants, and awards by category:*** *Academic Interests/Achievement:* general academic interests/achievements. *Special Achievements/Activities:* memberships. *Special Characteristics:* children of faculty/staff.

LOANS ***Programs:*** FFEL (Subsidized and Unsubsidized Stafford, PLUS), Perkins, state, college/university.

WORK-STUDY ***Federal work-study:*** Total amount: $3,966,982; jobs available.

APPLYING FOR FINANCIAL AID ***Required financial aid forms:*** FAFSA, CSS Financial Aid PROFILE.

CONTACT Ms. Lynn Robinson, Director of Financial Aid, Johnson & Wales University, 8 Abbott Park Place, Providence, RI 02903, 401-598-4648 or toll-free 800-598-1000 (in-state), 800-342-5598 (out-of-state). *Fax:* 401-598-1040.

JOHNSON BIBLE COLLEGE

Knoxville, TN

Tuition & fees: $6830 **Average undergraduate aid package: $5049**

ABOUT THE INSTITUTION Independent religious, coed. Awards: associate, bachelor's, and master's degrees. 6 undergraduate majors. Total enrollment: 889. Undergraduates: 756. Freshmen: 147. Federal methodology is used as a basis for awarding need-based institutional aid.

UNDERGRADUATE EXPENSES for 2006–07 ***Application fee:*** $35. ***Comprehensive fee:*** $11,320 includes full-time tuition ($6100), mandatory fees ($730), and room and board ($4490). ***College room only:*** $2190. Room and board charges vary according to board plan and housing facility. ***Part-time tuition:*** $254 per semester hour. ***Part-time fees:*** $30.42 per semester hour. Part-time tuition and fees vary according to course load. ***Payment plan:*** Installment.

FRESHMAN FINANCIAL AID (Fall 2005) 183 applied for aid; of those 79% were deemed to have need. 100% of freshmen with need received aid. ***Average percent of need met:*** 63% (excluding resources awarded to replace EFC). ***Average financial aid package:*** $5047 (excluding resources awarded to replace EFC).

UNDERGRADUATE FINANCIAL AID (Fall 2005) 786 applied for aid; of those 86% were deemed to have need. 100% of undergraduates with need received aid. ***Average percent of need met:*** 65% (excluding resources awarded to replace EFC). ***Average financial aid package:*** $5049 (excluding resources awarded to replace EFC).

GIFT AID (NEED-BASED) ***Total amount:*** $4,939,977 (12% federal, 5% state, 83% institutional). ***Receiving aid:*** Freshmen: 78% (143); All full-time undergraduates: 79% (653). ***Average award:*** Freshmen: $2491; Undergraduates: $2577. ***Scholarships, grants, and awards:*** Federal Pell, FSEOG, state, private, college/university gift aid from institutional funds.

GIFT AID (NON-NEED-BASED) ***Total amount:*** $431,354 (100% external sources). ***Receiving aid:*** Freshmen: 43% (79); Undergraduates: 33% (274). ***Scholarships, grants, and awards by category:*** *Academic Interests/Achievement:* 586 awards ($965,604 total): communication, education, general academic interests/achievements, religion/biblical studies. *Creative Arts/Performance:* 9 awards ($6750 total): art/fine arts, general creative arts/performance, music. *Special Achievements/Activities:* 186 awards ($67,050 total): community service, general special achievements/activities, leadership, religious involvement. *Special Characteristics:* 241 awards ($271,775 total): children of current students, children of educators, children of faculty/staff, ethnic background, general special characteristics, international students, married students, members of minority groups, parents of current students, relatives of clergy, religious affiliation, siblings of current students, spouses of current students. ***Tuition waivers:*** Full or partial for employees or children of employees.

LOANS ***Student loans:*** $1,701,559 (54% need-based, 46% non-need-based). 56% of past graduating class borrowed through all loan programs. *Average indebtedness per student:* $11,425. ***Average need-based loan:*** Freshmen: $2043; Undergraduates: $2581. ***Parent loans:*** $421,295 (100% non-need-based). ***Programs:*** FFEL (Subsidized and Unsubsidized Stafford, PLUS), college/university, alternative loans.

WORK-STUDY ***Federal work-study:*** Total amount: $146,235; 125 jobs averaging $820.

APPLYING FOR FINANCIAL AID ***Required financial aid forms:*** FAFSA, institution's own form. ***Financial aid deadline (priority):*** 5/1. ***Notification date:*** Continuous beginning 5/15. Students must reply within 2 weeks of notification.

CONTACT Mrs. Janette Overton, Financial Aid Director, Johnson Bible College, 7900 Johnson Drive, Knoxville, TN 37998, 865-251-2303 Ext. 2292 or toll-free 800-827-2122. *Fax:* 865-251-2337. *E-mail:* joverton@jbc.edu.

JOHNSON C. SMITH UNIVERSITY

Charlotte, NC

Tuition & fees: $15,004 **Average undergraduate aid package: $9725**

ABOUT THE INSTITUTION Independent, coed. Awards: bachelor's degrees. 37 undergraduate majors. Total enrollment: 1,470. Undergraduates: 1,470. Freshmen: 507. Federal methodology is used as a basis for awarding need-based institutional aid.

UNDERGRADUATE EXPENSES for 2006–07 ***Application fee:*** $25. ***Comprehensive fee:*** $20,844 includes full-time tuition ($12,725), mandatory fees ($2279), and room and board ($5840). ***College room only:*** $3361. Full-time tuition and fees vary according to course load. Room and board charges vary according to board plan and housing facility. ***Part-time tuition:*** $361 per credit hour. ***Part-time fees:*** $314 per term. Part-time tuition and fees vary according to course load. ***Payment plan:*** Installment.

FRESHMAN FINANCIAL AID (Fall 2006, est.) 445 applied for aid; of those 90% were deemed to have need. 100% of freshmen with need received aid; of those 5% had need fully met. ***Average percent of need met:*** 40% (excluding resources awarded to replace EFC). ***Average financial aid package:*** $7625 (excluding resources awarded to replace EFC).

UNDERGRADUATE FINANCIAL AID (Fall 2006, est.) 1,239 applied for aid; of those 77% were deemed to have need. 100% of undergraduates with need received aid; of those 3% had need fully met. ***Average percent of need met:*** 60% (excluding resources awarded to replace EFC). ***Average financial aid package:*** $9725 (excluding resources awarded to replace EFC).

GIFT AID (NEED-BASED) ***Total amount:*** $5,390,016 (54% federal, 21% state, 18% institutional, 7% external sources). ***Receiving aid:*** Freshmen: 71% (359); All full-time undergraduates: 65% (927). ***Average award:*** Freshmen: $3000; Undergraduates: $3000. ***Scholarships, grants, and awards:*** Federal Pell, FSEOG, state, private, college/university gift aid from institutional funds, United Negro College Fund.

GIFT AID (NON-NEED-BASED) ***Receiving aid:*** Freshmen: 20% (100); Undergraduates: 13% (185). ***Scholarships, grants, and awards by category:*** *Academic Interests/Achievement:* computer science, general academic interests/achievements, mathematics. *Creative Arts/Performance:* music. *Special Achievements/Activities:* community service, general special achievements/activities, leadership. *Special Characteristics:* children of faculty/staff, ethnic background, siblings of current students. ***Tuition waivers:*** Full or partial for employees or children of employees. ***ROTC:*** Army, Air Force cooperative.

LOANS ***Student loans:*** $9,500,000 (100% need-based). 90% of past graduating class borrowed through all loan programs. *Average indebtedness per student:* $25,000. ***Average need-based loan:*** Freshmen: $2625; Undergraduates: $5500. ***Parent loans:*** $7,400,000 (100% need-based). ***Programs:*** Federal Direct (Subsidized and Unsubsidized Stafford, PLUS), FFEL (PLUS), Perkins, alternative loans.

WORK-STUDY ***Federal work-study:*** Total amount: $450,000; jobs available.

ATHLETIC AWARDS Total amount: $825,000 (100% need-based).

APPLYING FOR FINANCIAL AID ***Required financial aid form:*** FAFSA. ***Financial aid deadline:*** Continuous. ***Notification date:*** Continuous beginning 3/1. Students must reply within 2 weeks of notification.

CONTACT Ms. Cynthia Anderson, Director of Financial Aid, Johnson C. Smith University, 100 Beatties Ford Road, Charlotte, NC 28216, 704-378-1035 or toll-free 800-782-7303. *Fax:* 704-378-1292.

JOHNSON STATE COLLEGE

Johnson, VT

CONTACT Ms. Kimberly Goodell, Financial Aid Officer, Johnson State College, 337 College Hill, Johnson, VT 05656-9405, 802-635-2356 or toll-free 800-635-2356. *Fax:* 802-635-1463. *E-mail:* goodellk@badger.jsc.vsc.edu.

JOHN WESLEY COLLEGE

High Point, NC

CONTACT Mrs. Shirley Carter, Director of Financial Aid, John Wesley College, 2314 North Centennial Street, High Point, NC 27265-3197, 336-889-2262. *Fax:* 336-889-2261. *E-mail:* scarter@johnwesley.edu.

JONES COLLEGE

Jacksonville, FL

CONTACT Mrs. Becky Davis, Director of Financial Assistance, Jones College, 5353 Arlington Expressway, Jacksonville, FL 32211-5540, 904-743-1122. *Fax:* 904-743-4446.

JONES COLLEGE

Miami, FL

CONTACT Financial Aid Office, Jones College, 11430 North Kendall Drive, Suite 200, Miami, FL 33176, 305-275-9996.

JONES INTERNATIONAL UNIVERSITY

Centennial, CO

CONTACT Steve Bidwell, Director of Financial And Accounting, Jones International University, 9697 East Mineral Avenue, Englewood, CO 80112, 303-784-8284 or toll-free 800-811-5663. *Fax:* 303-784-8524. *E-mail:* marketing@ jonesknowledge.com.

JUDSON COLLEGE

Marion, AL

Tuition & fees: $10,710 **Average undergraduate aid package: $11,075**

ABOUT THE INSTITUTION Independent Baptist, women only. Awards: bachelor's degrees. 23 undergraduate majors. Total enrollment: 305. Undergraduates: 305. Freshmen: 67. Both federal and institutional methodology are used as a basis for awarding need-based institutional aid.

UNDERGRADUATE EXPENSES for 2006–07 ***Application fee:*** $30. ***Comprehensive fee:*** $17,274 includes full-time tuition ($9800), mandatory fees ($910), and room and board ($6564). Full-time tuition and fees vary according to course load. ***Part-time tuition:*** $319 per semester hour. ***Part-time fees:*** $20 per hour. Part-time tuition and fees vary according to course load. ***Payment plan:*** Installment.

FRESHMAN FINANCIAL AID (Fall 2006, est.) 62 applied for aid; of those 92% were deemed to have need. 100% of freshmen with need received aid; of those 7% had need fully met. ***Average percent of need met:*** 74% (excluding resources awarded to replace EFC). ***Average financial aid package:*** $11,256 (excluding resources awarded to replace EFC). 9% of all full-time freshmen had no need and received non-need-based gift aid.

UNDERGRADUATE FINANCIAL AID (Fall 2006, est.) 192 applied for aid; of those 91% were deemed to have need. 100% of undergraduates with need received aid; of those 21% had need fully met. ***Average percent of need met:*** 79% (excluding resources awarded to replace EFC). ***Average financial aid package:*** $11,075 (excluding resources awarded to replace EFC). 15% of all full-time undergraduates had no need and received non-need-based gift aid.

GIFT AID (NEED-BASED) ***Total amount:*** $1,176,550 (26% federal, 6% state, 59% institutional, 9% external sources). ***Receiving aid:*** Freshmen: 84% (56); All full-time undergraduates: 72% (168). ***Average award:*** Freshmen: $8077; Undergraduates: $7245. ***Scholarships, grants, and awards:*** Federal Pell, FSEOG, state, private, college/university gift aid from institutional funds, Federal ACG and SMART Grants.

GIFT AID (NON-NEED-BASED) ***Total amount:*** $41,398 (32% state, 40% institutional, 28% external sources). ***Receiving aid:*** Freshmen: 10% (7); Undergraduates: 9% (22). ***Average award:*** Freshmen: $2956; Undergraduates: $5321. ***Scholarships, grants, and awards by category:*** *Academic Interests/Achievement:* 50 awards ($200,000 total): general academic interests/achievements. *Creative Arts/Performance:* 22 awards ($18,150 total): art/fine arts, music. *Special Achievements/Activities:* 6 awards ($3500 total): general special achievements/activities, junior miss. *Special Characteristics:* 32 awards ($106,000 total): children of educators, children of faculty/staff, relatives of clergy, religious affiliation. ***Tuition waivers:*** Full or partial for employees or children of employees. ***ROTC:*** Army cooperative.

LOANS ***Student loans:*** $656,659 (65% need-based, 35% non-need-based). 76% of past graduating class borrowed through all loan programs. *Average indebtedness per student:* $15,917. ***Average need-based loan:*** Freshmen: $2790; Undergraduates: $3671. ***Parent loans:*** $192,155 (93% need-based, 7% non-need-based). ***Programs:*** FFEL (Subsidized and Unsubsidized Stafford, PLUS), Perkins, college/university.

WORK-STUDY ***Federal work-study:*** Total amount: $92,270; 58 jobs averaging $1590. ***State or other work-study/employment:*** Total amount: $68,831 (89% need-based, 11% non-need-based). 63 part-time jobs averaging $1093.

ATHLETIC AWARDS Total amount: $101,000 (79% need-based, 21% non-need-based).

APPLYING FOR FINANCIAL AID ***Required financial aid forms:*** FAFSA, institution's own form, state aid form. ***Financial aid deadline (priority):*** 3/1. ***Notification date:*** Continuous beginning 3/15. Students must reply within 2 weeks of notification.

CONTACT Mrs. Doris A. Wilson, Director of Financial Aid, Judson College, PO Box 120, Marion, AL 36756, 334-683-5157 or toll-free 800-447-9472. *Fax:* 334-683-5282. *E-mail:* dwilson@judson.edu.

JUDSON COLLEGE

Elgin, IL

Tuition & fees: $20,420 **Average undergraduate aid package: $12,036**

ABOUT THE INSTITUTION Independent Baptist, coed. Awards: bachelor's and master's degrees. 48 undergraduate majors. Total enrollment: 1,243. Undergraduates: 1,180. Freshmen: 160. Federal methodology is used as a basis for awarding need-based institutional aid.

UNDERGRADUATE EXPENSES for 2007–08 ***Application fee:*** $35. ***Comprehensive fee:*** $27,620 includes full-time tuition ($20,100), mandatory fees ($320), and room and board ($7200). ***Part-time tuition:*** $670 per credit hour.

FRESHMAN FINANCIAL AID (Fall 2005) 100 applied for aid; of those 85% were deemed to have need. 99% of freshmen with need received aid; of those 2% had need fully met. ***Average percent of need met:*** 38% (excluding resources awarded to replace EFC). ***Average financial aid package:*** $12,149 (excluding resources awarded to replace EFC). 9% of all full-time freshmen had no need and received non-need-based gift aid.

UNDERGRADUATE FINANCIAL AID (Fall 2005) 689 applied for aid; of those 86% were deemed to have need. 99% of undergraduates with need received aid; of those 2% had need fully met. ***Average percent of need met:*** 36% (excluding resources awarded to replace EFC). ***Average financial aid package:*** $12,036 (excluding resources awarded to replace EFC). 7% of all full-time undergraduates had no need and received non-need-based gift aid.

GIFT AID (NEED-BASED) ***Total amount:*** $4,767,805 (17% federal, 21% state, 59% institutional, 3% external sources). ***Receiving aid:*** Freshmen: 73% (78); All full-time undergraduates: 71% (533). ***Average award:*** Freshmen: $5999; Undergraduates: $5954. ***Scholarships, grants, and awards:*** Federal Pell, FSEOG, state, private, college/university gift aid from institutional funds.

GIFT AID (NON-NEED-BASED) ***Total amount:*** $641,963 (1% state, 90% institutional, 9% external sources). ***Receiving aid:*** Freshmen: 57% (61); Undergraduates: 45% (339). ***Average award:*** Freshmen: $8049; Undergraduates: $4405. ***Scholarships, grants, and awards by category:*** *Academic Interests/Achievement:* general academic interests/achievements. *Creative Arts/Performance:* art/fine arts, music. *Special Achievements/Activities:* leadership. ***ROTC:*** Army cooperative.

LOANS ***Student loans:*** $6,442,457 (83% need-based, 17% non-need-based). 77% of past graduating class borrowed through all loan programs. *Average indebtedness per student:* $21,960. ***Average need-based loan:*** Freshmen: $3043; Undergraduates: $3777. ***Parent loans:*** $557,715 (100% non-need-based). ***Programs:*** Federal Direct (Subsidized and Unsubsidized Stafford, PLUS), Perkins.

WORK-STUDY ***Federal work-study:*** Total amount: $265,479; jobs available (averaging $1600). ***State or other work-study/employment:*** Part-time jobs available.

ATHLETIC AWARDS Total amount: $745,530 (66% need-based, 34% non-need-based).

APPLYING FOR FINANCIAL AID ***Required financial aid form:*** FAFSA. ***Financial aid deadline:*** Continuous. ***Notification date:*** Continuous. Students must reply within 4 weeks of notification.

CONTACT Michael Davis, Director of Financial Aid, Judson College, 1151 North State Street, Elgin, IL 60123-1498, 847-628-2532 or toll-free 800-879-5376. *Fax:* 847-628-2533. *E-mail:* mdavis@judsoncollege.edu.

THE JUILLIARD SCHOOL

New York, NY

CONTACT Mary K. Gray, Associate Dean for Admissions, The Juilliard School, 60 Lincoln Center Plaza, New York, NY 10023, 212-799-5000 Ext. 223. *Fax:* 212-769-6420.

JUNIATA COLLEGE

Huntingdon, PA

Tuition & fees: $28,920 **Average undergraduate aid package: $21,974**

ABOUT THE INSTITUTION Independent religious, coed. Awards: bachelor's degrees. 87 undergraduate majors. Total enrollment: 1,460. Undergraduates: 1,460. Freshmen: 383. Federal methodology is used as a basis for awarding need-based institutional aid.

UNDERGRADUATE EXPENSES for 2007–08 ***Application fee:*** $30. ***Comprehensive fee:*** $36,960 includes full-time tuition ($28,250), mandatory fees ($670), and room and board ($8040). ***College room only:*** $4220. ***Part-time tuition:*** $1120 per credit hour.

FRESHMAN FINANCIAL AID (Fall 2006, est.) 312 applied for aid; of those 81% were deemed to have need. 100% of freshmen with need received aid; of those 23% had need fully met. ***Average percent of need met:*** 85% (excluding resources awarded to replace EFC). ***Average financial aid package:*** $22,124 (excluding resources awarded to replace EFC). 30% of all full-time freshmen had no need and received non-need-based gift aid.

UNDERGRADUATE FINANCIAL AID (Fall 2006, est.) 1,217 applied for aid; of those 87% were deemed to have need. 100% of undergraduates with need received aid; of those 23% had need fully met. ***Average percent of need met:*** 86% (excluding resources awarded to replace EFC). ***Average financial aid package:*** $21,974 (excluding resources awarded to replace EFC). 26% of all full-time undergraduates had no need and received non-need-based gift aid.

GIFT AID (NEED-BASED) ***Total amount:*** $16,350,726 (6% federal, 12% state, 78% institutional, 4% external sources). ***Receiving aid:*** Freshmen: 65% (236); All full-time undergraduates: 71% (1,021). ***Average award:*** Freshmen: $17,293; Undergraduates: $16,339. ***Scholarships, grants, and awards:*** Federal Pell, FSEOG, state, private, college/university gift aid from institutional funds.

GIFT AID (NON-NEED-BASED) ***Total amount:*** $4,714,039 (2% state, 98% institutional). ***Receiving aid:*** Freshmen: 65% (235); Undergraduates: 65% (928). ***Average award:*** Freshmen: $11,792; Undergraduates: $12,609. ***Scholarships, grants, and awards by category:*** *Academic Interests/Achievement:* business, general academic interests/achievements, premedicine. *Creative Arts/Performance:* general creative arts/performance. *Special Achievements/Activities:* community service, leadership. *Special Characteristics:* adult students, children and siblings of alumni, children of faculty/staff, ethnic background, international students, religious affiliation.

LOANS ***Student loans:*** $6,433,290 (95% need-based, 5% non-need-based). 71% of past graduating class borrowed through all loan programs. *Average indebtedness per student:* $23,405. ***Average need-based loan:*** Freshmen: $3642; Undergraduates: $4775. ***Parent loans:*** $3,978,189 (98% need-based, 2% non-need-based). ***Programs:*** FFEL (Subsidized and Unsubsidized Stafford, PLUS), Perkins.

WORK-STUDY ***Federal work-study:*** Total amount: $730,370; jobs available. ***State or other work-study/employment:*** Total amount: $906,400 (51% need-based, 49% non-need-based). 378 part-time jobs averaging $665.

APPLYING FOR FINANCIAL AID ***Required financial aid form:*** FAFSA. ***Financial aid deadline:*** 3/1 (priority: 3/1). ***Notification date:*** Continuous beginning 2/1. Students must reply by 5/1 or within 2 weeks of notification.

CONTACT Vincent P. Frank, Director of Student Financial Planning, Juniata College, 1700 Moore Street, Huntingdon, PA 16652-2119, 814-641-3140 or toll-free 877-JUNIATA. *Fax:* 814-641-5311. *E-mail:* frankv@juniata.edu.

KALAMAZOO COLLEGE

Kalamazoo, MI

Tuition & fees: $27,054 **Average undergraduate aid package: $22,820**

ABOUT THE INSTITUTION Independent religious, coed. Awards: bachelor's degrees. 24 undergraduate majors. Total enrollment: 1,345. Undergraduates: 1,345. Freshmen: 390. Both federal and institutional methodology are used as a basis for awarding need-based institutional aid.

UNDERGRADUATE EXPENSES for 2006–07 ***Application fee:*** $35. ***Comprehensive fee:*** $33,969 includes full-time tuition ($27,054) and room and board ($6915). ***College room only:*** $3372. Room and board charges vary according to board plan. ***Payment plan:*** Installment.

FRESHMAN FINANCIAL AID (Fall 2006, est.) 276 applied for aid; of those 70% were deemed to have need. 100% of freshmen with need received aid; of those 76% had need fully met. ***Average financial aid package:*** $22,830 (excluding resources awarded to replace EFC). 48% of all full-time freshmen had no need and received non-need-based gift aid.

UNDERGRADUATE FINANCIAL AID (Fall 2006, est.) 845 applied for aid; of those 79% were deemed to have need. 100% of undergraduates with need received aid. ***Average financial aid package:*** $22,820 (excluding resources awarded to replace EFC). 38% of all full-time undergraduates had no need and received non-need-based gift aid.

GIFT AID (NEED-BASED) ***Total amount:*** $9,683,249 (7% federal, 8% state, 85% institutional). ***Receiving aid:*** Freshmen: 51% (193); All full-time undergraduates: 51% (667). ***Average award:*** Freshmen: $17,945; Undergraduates: $16,095. ***Scholarships, grants, and awards:*** Federal Pell, FSEOG, state, private, college/university gift aid from institutional funds.

GIFT AID (NON-NEED-BASED) ***Total amount:*** $8,238,066 (8% state, 77% institutional, 15% external sources). ***Receiving aid:*** Freshmen: 51% (192); Undergraduates: 50% (655). ***Average award:*** Freshmen: $9675; Undergraduates: $9290. ***Scholarships, grants, and awards by category:*** *Academic Interests/Achievement:* biological sciences, English, foreign languages, general academic interests/achievements, mathematics, physical sciences, social sciences. *Creative Arts/Performance:* art/fine arts, cinema/film/broadcasting, music, theater/drama. *Special Achievements/Activities:* general special achievements/activities. ***Tuition waivers:*** Full or partial for employees or children of employees. ***ROTC:*** Army cooperative.

LOANS ***Student loans:*** $4,418,695 (57% need-based, 43% non-need-based). 67% of past graduating class borrowed through all loan programs. *Average indebtedness per student:* $25,000. ***Average need-based loan:*** Freshmen: $3884; Undergraduates: $5329. ***Parent loans:*** $1,765,134 (100% non-need-based). ***Programs:*** Federal Direct (Subsidized and Unsubsidized Stafford, PLUS), Perkins, state.

WORK-STUDY ***Federal work-study:*** Total amount: $340,000; 394 jobs averaging $1583. ***State or other work-study/employment:*** Total amount: $6500 (100% need-based). 9 part-time jobs averaging $836.

APPLYING FOR FINANCIAL AID ***Required financial aid forms:*** FAFSA, institution's own form. ***Financial aid deadline (priority):*** 2/15. ***Notification date:*** 3/21. Students must reply by 5/1.

CONTACT Judy Clark, Associate Director of Financial Aid, Kalamazoo College, 1200 Academy Street, Kalamazoo, MI 49006-3295, 269-337-7192 or toll-free 800-253-3602. *Fax:* 269-337-7390.

KANSAS CITY ART INSTITUTE

Kansas City, MO

ABOUT THE INSTITUTION Independent, coed. Awards: bachelor's degrees. 12 undergraduate majors. Total enrollment: 674. Undergraduates: 674. Freshmen: 139.

GIFT AID (NEED-BASED) ***Scholarships, grants, and awards:*** Federal Pell, FSEOG, state, private, college/university gift aid from institutional funds.

GIFT AID (NON-NEED-BASED) ***Scholarships, grants, and awards by category:*** *Creative Arts/Performance:* art/fine arts.

LOANS ***Programs:*** FFEL (Subsidized and Unsubsidized Stafford, PLUS), Perkins, alternative loans.

WORK-STUDY ***Federal work-study:*** Total amount: $123,614; 124 jobs averaging $997. ***State or other work-study/employment:*** Total amount: $30,000 (3% need-based, 97% non-need-based). 30 part-time jobs averaging $1000.

APPLYING FOR FINANCIAL AID ***Required financial aid form:*** FAFSA.

CONTACT Ms. Christal D. Williams, Director of Financial Aid, Kansas City Art Institute, 4415 Warwick Boulevard, Kansas City, MO 64111-1874, 816-802-3448 or toll-free 800-522-5224. *Fax:* 816-802-3453. *E-mail:* cdwilliams@kcai.edu.

KANSAS STATE UNIVERSITY

Manhattan, KS

ABOUT THE INSTITUTION State-supported, coed. Awards: associate, bachelor's, master's, doctoral, and first professional degrees. 78 undergraduate majors. Total enrollment: 23,141. Undergraduates: 18,761. Freshmen: 3,385.

GIFT AID (NEED-BASED) ***Scholarships, grants, and awards:*** Federal Pell, FSEOG, state, private, college/university gift aid from institutional funds.

GIFT AID (NON-NEED-BASED) ***Scholarships, grants, and awards by category:*** *Academic Interests/Achievement:* agriculture, architecture, biological sciences, business, communication, computer science, education, engineering/technologies, English, foreign languages, general academic interests/achievements, health fields, home economics, humanities, mathematics, military science, physical sciences, premedicine, social sciences. *Creative Arts/Performance:* art/fine arts, debating, music, theater/drama. *Special Achievements/Activities:* general special achievements/activities, leadership. *Special Characteristics:* adult students, children and siblings of alumni, general special characteristics.

LOANS ***Programs:*** FFEL (Subsidized and Unsubsidized Stafford, PLUS), Perkins, college/university, alternative student loans.

APPLYING FOR FINANCIAL AID ***Required financial aid form:*** FAFSA.

CONTACT Mr. Larry Moeder, Director of Admissions and Student Financial Assistance, Kansas State University, 104 Fairchild Hall, Manhattan, KS 66506, 785-532-6420 or toll-free 800-432-8270 (in-state). *E-mail:* larrym@ksu.edu.

KANSAS WESLEYAN UNIVERSITY

Salina, KS

CONTACT Mrs. Glenna Alexander, Director of Financial Assistance, Kansas Wesleyan University, 100 East Claflin, Salina, KS 67401-6196, 785-827-5541 Ext. 1130 or toll-free 800-874-1154 Ext. 1285. *Fax:* 785-827-0927. *E-mail:* kglennaa@acck.edu.

KEAN UNIVERSITY

Union, NJ

Tuition & fees (NJ res): $8036 **Average undergraduate aid package: $7931**

ABOUT THE INSTITUTION State-supported, coed. Awards: bachelor's and master's degrees and post-bachelor's and post-master's certificates. 48 undergraduate majors. Total enrollment: 13,050. Undergraduates: 9,990. Freshmen: 1,422. Federal methodology is used as a basis for awarding need-based institutional aid.

UNDERGRADUATE EXPENSES for 2006–07 ***Application fee:*** $50. ***Tuition, state resident:*** full-time $5243; part-time $174.75 per credit. ***Tuition, nonresident:*** full-time $8070; part-time $269 per credit. ***Required fees:*** full-time $2793; $93.85 per credit. Part-time tuition and fees vary according to course load. ***College room and board:*** $8880; ***Room only:*** $6180. Room and board charges vary according to board plan and housing facility. ***Payment plans:*** Installment, deferred payment.

FRESHMAN FINANCIAL AID (Fall 2006, est.) 1156 applied for aid; of those 74% were deemed to have need. 97% of freshmen with need received aid; of those 9% had need fully met. ***Average percent of need met:*** 54% (excluding resources awarded to replace EFC). ***Average financial aid package:*** $7154 (excluding resources awarded to replace EFC). 4% of all full-time freshmen had no need and received non-need-based gift aid.

UNDERGRADUATE FINANCIAL AID (Fall 2006, est.) 5,438 applied for aid; of those 78% were deemed to have need. 96% of undergraduates with need received aid; of those 15% had need fully met. ***Average percent of need met:*** 55% (excluding resources awarded to replace EFC). ***Average financial aid package:*** $7931 (excluding resources awarded to replace EFC). 2% of all full-time undergraduates had no need and received non-need-based gift aid.

GIFT AID (NEED-BASED) ***Total amount:*** $17,543,545 (45% federal, 47% state, 7% institutional, 1% external sources). ***Receiving aid:*** Freshmen: 59% (822); All full-time undergraduates: 53% (4,006). ***Average award:*** Freshmen: $6433; Undergraduates: $6159. ***Scholarships, grants, and awards:*** Federal Pell, FSEOG, state, private, college/university gift aid from institutional funds.

GIFT AID (NON-NEED-BASED) ***Total amount:*** $84,000 (100% state). ***Average award:*** Freshmen: $2132; Undergraduates: $2219. ***Scholarships, grants, and awards by category:*** *Academic Interests/Achievement:* 1,193 awards ($1,678,048 total): business, education, general academic interests/achievements, health fields, humanities, international studies. *Creative Arts/Performance:* 22 awards ($115,335 total): applied art and design, art/fine arts, music, theater/drama. *Special Achievements/Activities:* community service, leadership. *Special Characteristics:* 160 awards ($321,531 total): general special characteristics. ***Tuition waivers:*** Full or partial for employees or children of employees, senior citizens. ***ROTC:*** Army cooperative, Air Force cooperative.

LOANS ***Student loans:*** $32,361,132 (47% need-based, 53% non-need-based). 75% of past graduating class borrowed through all loan programs. *Average indebtedness per student:* $20,037. ***Average need-based loan:*** Freshmen: $2670; Undergraduates: $3846. ***Parent loans:*** $3,735,738 (100% non-need-based). ***Programs:*** Federal Direct (Subsidized and Unsubsidized Stafford, PLUS), Perkins.

WORK-STUDY ***Federal work-study:*** Total amount: $275,209; 250 jobs averaging $1985.

APPLYING FOR FINANCIAL AID ***Required financial aid form:*** FAFSA. ***Financial aid deadline:*** 3/15. ***Notification date:*** Continuous beginning 3/15. Students must reply by 5/1.

CONTACT Office of Financial Aid, Kean University, 1000 Morris Avenue, Union, NJ 07083, 908-737-3190. *Fax:* 908-737-3200.

KEENE STATE COLLEGE

Keene, NH

Tuition & fees (NH res): $7822 **Average undergraduate aid package: $7802**

ABOUT THE INSTITUTION State-supported, coed. Awards: bachelor's and master's degrees and post-bachelor's and post-master's certificates. 87 undergraduate majors. Total enrollment: 4,940. Undergraduates: 4,767. Freshmen: 1,141. Federal methodology is used as a basis for awarding need-based institutional aid.

UNDERGRADUATE EXPENSES for 2006–07 ***Application fee:*** $35. ***Tuition, state resident:*** full-time $5780; part-time $241 per credit. ***Tuition, nonresident:*** full-time $13,050; part-time $544 per credit. ***Required fees:*** full-time $2042; $80 per credit. Part-time tuition and fees vary according to course load and degree level. ***College room and board:*** $7026; ***Room only:*** $4700. Room and board charges vary according to board plan and housing facility. ***Payment plan:*** Installment.

FRESHMAN FINANCIAL AID (Fall 2005) 823 applied for aid; of those 66% were deemed to have need. 98% of freshmen with need received aid; of those 20% had need fully met. ***Average percent of need met:*** 67% (excluding resources awarded to replace EFC). ***Average financial aid package:*** $7331 (excluding resources awarded to replace EFC). 9% of all full-time freshmen had no need and received non-need-based gift aid.

UNDERGRADUATE FINANCIAL AID (Fall 2005) 2,985 applied for aid; of those 72% were deemed to have need. 99% of undergraduates with need received aid; of those 23% had need fully met. ***Average percent of need met:*** 71% (excluding resources awarded to replace EFC). ***Average financial aid package:*** $7802 (excluding resources awarded to replace EFC). 8% of all full-time undergraduates had no need and received non-need-based gift aid.

GIFT AID (NEED-BASED) ***Total amount:*** $6,068,123 (35% federal, 8% state, 47% institutional, 10% external sources). ***Receiving aid:*** Freshmen: 34% (341); All full-time undergraduates: 34% (1,385). ***Average award:*** Freshmen: $4501; Undergraduates: $4241. ***Scholarships, grants, and awards:*** Federal Pell, FSEOG, state, private, college/university gift aid from institutional funds.

GIFT AID (NON-NEED-BASED) ***Total amount:*** $2,730,932 (1% state, 76% institutional, 23% external sources). ***Receiving aid:*** Freshmen: 16% (158); Undergraduates: 13% (518). ***Average award:*** Freshmen: $2257; Undergraduates: $2658. ***Scholarships, grants, and awards by category:*** *Academic Interests/Achievement:* 568 awards ($1,266,061 total): general academic interests/achievements. *Creative Arts/Performance:* 24 awards ($69,400 total): applied art and design, art/fine arts, cinema/film/broadcasting, dance, general creative arts/performance, music, theater/drama. *Special Achievements/Activities:* 11 awards ($30,700 total): general special achievements/activities. ***Tuition waivers:*** Full or partial for employees or children of employees, senior citizens. ***ROTC:*** Air Force cooperative.

LOANS ***Student loans:*** $19,565,890 (38% need-based, 62% non-need-based). 75% of past graduating class borrowed through all loan programs. *Average indebtedness per student:* $20,992. ***Average need-based loan:*** Freshmen: $2935; Undergraduates: $3753. ***Parent loans:*** $5,867,082 (100% non-need-based). ***Programs:*** FFEL (Subsidized and Unsubsidized Stafford, PLUS), Perkins, college/university.

WORK-STUDY ***Federal work-study:*** Total amount: $2,090,383; 604 jobs averaging $870. ***State or other work-study/employment:*** Total amount: $458,458 (100% non-need-based). 522 part-time jobs averaging $878.

APPLYING FOR FINANCIAL AID ***Required financial aid form:*** FAFSA. ***Financial aid deadline:*** 3/1. ***Notification date:*** Continuous beginning 12/1. Students must reply within 4 weeks of notification.

CONTACT Ms. Patricia Blodgett, Director of Student Financial Management, Keene State College, 229 Main Street, Keene, NH 03435-2606, 603-358-2280 or toll-free 800-572-1909. *Fax:* 603-358-2794. *E-mail:* pblodget@keene.edu.

KEHILATH YAKOV RABBINICAL SEMINARY

Brooklyn, NY

CONTACT Financial Aid Office, Kehilath Yakov Rabbinical Seminary, 206 Wilson Street, Brooklyn, NY 11211-7207, 718-963-1212.

KEISER UNIVERSITY

Fort Lauderdale, FL

CONTACT Mr. Fred Pfeffer, Director of Student Financial Services, Keiser University, 1500 Northwest 49th Street, Fort Lauderdale, FL 33309, 954-351-4036 or toll-free 800-749-4456 (out-of-state). *Fax:* 954-489-2974.

KENDALL COLLEGE

Chicago, IL

CONTACT Cynthia Sabo, Director of Financial Aid, Kendall College, 2408 Orrington Avenue, Evanston, IL 60201, 847-448-2349 or toll-free 866-667-3344 (in-state), 877-588-8860 (out-of-state). *Fax:* 847-448-2403.

KENNESAW STATE UNIVERSITY

Kennesaw, GA

ABOUT THE INSTITUTION State-supported, coed. Awards: bachelor's and master's degrees. 44 undergraduate majors. Total enrollment: 19,854. Undergraduates: 17,708. Freshmen: 2,405.

GIFT AID (NEED-BASED) ***Scholarships, grants, and awards:*** Federal Pell, FSEOG, state, private, college/university gift aid from institutional funds.

GIFT AID (NON-NEED-BASED) ***Scholarships, grants, and awards by category:*** *Academic Interests/Achievement:* biological sciences, business, communication, computer science, education, English, foreign languages, general academic interests/achievements, health fields, humanities, international studies, mathematics, physical sciences, premedicine, social sciences. *Creative Arts/Performance:* music, performing arts, theater/drama. *Special Achievements/Activities:* community service, leadership, memberships. *Special Characteristics:* children and siblings of alumni, children of union members/company employees, children of workers in trades, ethnic background, general special characteristics, handicapped students, international students, local/state students, members of minority groups, religious affiliation, veterans' children.

LOANS ***Programs:*** FFEL (Subsidized and Unsubsidized Stafford, PLUS), Perkins, Federal Nursing, state.

WORK-STUDY ***Federal work-study:*** Total amount: $378,558; 325 jobs averaging $1112.

APPLYING FOR FINANCIAL AID ***Required financial aid forms:*** FAFSA, state aid form.

CONTACT Mr. Michael C. Roberts, Director of Student Financial Aid, Kennesaw State University, 1000 Chastain Road, Kennesaw, GA 30144-5591, 770-499-3240. *Fax:* 770-423-6708. *E-mail:* finaid@kennesaw.edu.

KENT STATE UNIVERSITY

Kent, OH

Tuition & fees (OH res): $8430 **Average undergraduate aid package: $7685**

ABOUT THE INSTITUTION State-supported, coed. Awards: associate, bachelor's, master's, and doctoral degrees and post-bachelor's and post-master's certificates. 125 undergraduate majors. Total enrollment: 22,697. Undergraduates: 18,136. Freshmen: 3,696. Federal methodology is used as a basis for awarding need-based institutional aid.

UNDERGRADUATE EXPENSES for 2006–07 ***Application fee:*** $30. ***Tuition, state resident:*** full-time $8430; part-time $384 per credit hour. ***Tuition, nonresident:*** full-time $15,862; part-time $722 per credit hour. Full-time tuition and fees vary according to course load, program, and reciprocity agreements. Part-time tuition and fees vary according to course load, program, and reciprocity agreements. ***College room and board:*** $6880; ***Room only:*** $4200. Room and board charges vary according to board plan and housing facility. ***Payment plans:*** Tuition prepayment, installment, deferred payment.

FRESHMAN FINANCIAL AID (Fall 2006, est.) 2885 applied for aid; of those 80% were deemed to have need. 100% of freshmen with need received aid; of those 14% had need fully met. ***Average percent of need met:*** 59% (excluding resources awarded to replace EFC). ***Average financial aid package:*** $7972 (excluding resources awarded to replace EFC). 14% of all full-time freshmen had no need and received non-need-based gift aid.

UNDERGRADUATE FINANCIAL AID (Fall 2006, est.) 10,787 applied for aid; of those 84% were deemed to have need. 100% of undergraduates with need received aid; of those 14% had need fully met. ***Average percent of need met:*** 58% (excluding resources awarded to replace EFC). ***Average financial aid package:*** $7685 (excluding resources awarded to replace EFC). 10% of all full-time undergraduates had no need and received non-need-based gift aid.

GIFT AID (NEED-BASED) ***Total amount:*** $33,402,358 (45% federal, 17% state, 33% institutional, 5% external sources). ***Receiving aid:*** Freshmen: 50% (1,806); All full-time undergraduates: 40% (6,271). ***Average award:*** Freshmen: $5725; Undergraduates: $5051. ***Scholarships, grants, and awards:*** Federal Pell, FSEOG, state, private, college/university gift aid from institutional funds.

GIFT AID (NON-NEED-BASED) ***Total amount:*** $7,915,137 (5% federal, 10% state, 75% institutional, 10% external sources). ***Receiving aid:*** Freshmen: 9% (333); Undergraduates: 4% (644). ***Average award:*** Freshmen: $3788; Undergraduates: $3874. ***Scholarships, grants, and awards by category:*** *Academic Interests/Achievement:* architecture, area/ethnic studies, biological sciences, business, communication, computer science, education, English, general academic interests/achievements, health fields, international studies, library science, mathematics, military science, physical sciences, social sciences. *Creative Arts/Performance:* art/fine arts, journalism/publications, music, theater/drama. *Special Achievements/Activities:* community service, general special achievements/activities, leadership. *Special Characteristics:* adult students, children and siblings of alumni, children of faculty/staff, children of union members/company employees, children with a deceased or disabled parent, ethnic background, handicapped students, international students, members of minority groups, out-of-state students. ***Tuition waivers:*** Full or partial for employees or children of employees, senior citizens. ***ROTC:*** Army, Air Force.

LOANS ***Student loans:*** $71,646,938 (83% need-based, 17% non-need-based). 72% of past graduating class borrowed through all loan programs. *Average indebtedness per student:* $22,230. ***Average need-based loan:*** Freshmen: $3436; Undergraduates: $4075. ***Parent loans:*** $52,273,736 (27% need-based, 73% non-need-based). ***Programs:*** Federal Direct (Subsidized and Unsubsidized Stafford, PLUS), Perkins, Federal Nursing, state, college/university, alternative loans.

WORK-STUDY ***Federal work-study:*** Total amount: $1,325,516; 1,042 jobs averaging $2316.

ATHLETIC AWARDS Total amount: $4,041,982 (60% need-based, 40% non-need-based).

APPLYING FOR FINANCIAL AID ***Required financial aid forms:*** FAFSA, University Scholarship Application. ***Financial aid deadline (priority):*** 3/1. ***Notification date:*** 3/15. Students must reply within 2 weeks of notification.

CONTACT Constance Dubick, Associate Director of Student Financial Aid, Kent State University, 103 Michael Schwartz Center, PO Box 5190, Kent, OH 44242-0001, 330-672-2972 or toll-free 800-988-KENT. *Fax:* 330-672-4014. *E-mail:* cdubick@kent.edu.

KENTUCKY CHRISTIAN UNIVERSITY

Grayson, KY

Tuition & fees: $12,630 **Average undergraduate aid package: $10,772**

ABOUT THE INSTITUTION Independent religious, coed. Awards: associate, bachelor's, and master's degrees. 13 undergraduate majors. Total enrollment: 556. Undergraduates: 538. Freshmen: 125. Federal methodology is used as a basis for awarding need-based institutional aid.

UNDERGRADUATE EXPENSES for 2006–07 ***Application fee:*** $30. ***Comprehensive fee:*** $17,254 includes full-time tuition ($12,480), mandatory fees ($150), and room and board ($4624). Room and board charges vary according to board plan and housing facility. ***Part-time tuition:*** $390 per credit hour. ***Payment plan:*** Installment.

FRESHMAN FINANCIAL AID (Fall 2006, est.) 114 applied for aid; of those 89% were deemed to have need. 100% of freshmen with need received aid; of those 11% had need fully met. ***Average percent of need met:*** 64% (excluding resources awarded to replace EFC). ***Average financial aid package:*** $10,633 (excluding resources awarded to replace EFC). 14% of all full-time freshmen had no need and received non-need-based gift aid.

UNDERGRADUATE FINANCIAL AID (Fall 2006, est.) 498 applied for aid; of those 86% were deemed to have need. 100% of undergraduates with need received aid; of those 18% had need fully met. ***Average percent of need met:*** 63% (excluding resources awarded to replace EFC). ***Average financial aid package:*** $10,772 (excluding resources awarded to replace EFC). 18% of all full-time undergraduates had no need and received non-need-based gift aid.

GIFT AID (NEED-BASED) ***Total amount:*** $1,824,912 (41% federal, 33% state, 26% institutional). ***Receiving aid:*** Freshmen: 74% (87); All full-time undergraduates: 64% (348). ***Average award:*** Freshmen: $5315; Undergraduates: $4988. ***Scholarships, grants, and awards:*** Federal Pell, FSEOG, state, private, college/university gift aid from institutional funds, Federal ACG.

GIFT AID (NON-NEED-BASED) ***Total amount:*** $2,080,303 (10% state, 71% institutional, 19% external sources). ***Receiving aid:*** Freshmen: 86% (101); Undergraduates: 78% (426). ***Average award:*** Freshmen: $2907; Undergraduates: $5456. ***Scholarships, grants, and awards by category:*** *Academic Interests/Achievement:* 509 awards ($1,076,450 total): business, education, general academic interests/achievements, religion/biblical studies. *Creative Arts/Performance:* 36 awards ($108,372 total): debating, music, performing arts, theater/drama. *Special Achievements/Activities:* 37 awards ($42,955 total): community service, general special achievements/activities, leadership, religious involvement. *Special Characteristics:* 50 awards ($259,632 total): children and siblings of alumni, children of faculty/staff, general special characteristics, international students, members of minority groups, religious affiliation.

LOANS ***Student loans:*** $2,764,452 (51% need-based, 49% non-need-based). 84% of past graduating class borrowed through all loan programs. *Average indebtedness per student:* $19,200. ***Average need-based loan:*** Freshmen: $2672; Undergraduates: $3739. ***Parent loans:*** $438,904 (100% non-need-based). ***Programs:*** FFEL (Subsidized and Unsubsidized Stafford, PLUS), Perkins.

WORK-STUDY ***Federal work-study:*** Total amount: $411,225; 217 jobs averaging $1895. ***State or other work-study/employment:*** Total amount: $70,525 (100% non-need-based). 40 part-time jobs averaging $1763.

APPLYING FOR FINANCIAL AID ***Required financial aid form:*** FAFSA. ***Financial aid deadline (priority):*** 3/1. ***Notification date:*** Continuous beginning 3/15. Students must reply within 2 weeks of notification.

CONTACT Mrs. Jennie M. Bender, Director of Financial Aid, Kentucky Christian University, 100 Academic Parkway, Grayson, KY 41143-2205, 606-474-3226 or toll-free 800-522-3181. *Fax:* 606-474-3155. *E-mail:* jbender@kcu.edu.

KENTUCKY MOUNTAIN BIBLE COLLEGE

Vancleve, KY

CONTACT Ms. Sara Klopping, Director of Financial Aid, Kentucky Mountain Bible College, PO Box 10, Vancleve, KY 41385-0010, 800-879-KMBC Ext. 142 or toll-free 800-879-KMBC Ext. 130 (in-state), 800-879-KMBC Ext. 136 (out-of-state). *Fax:* 606-693-0495.

KENTUCKY STATE UNIVERSITY

Frankfort, KY

ABOUT THE INSTITUTION State-related, coed. Awards: associate, bachelor's, and master's degrees. 31 undergraduate majors. Total enrollment: 2,500. Undergraduates: 2,340. Freshmen: 542.

GIFT AID (NEED-BASED) ***Scholarships, grants, and awards:*** Federal Pell, FSEOG, state, private, college/university gift aid from institutional funds, Federal Nursing.

GIFT AID (NON-NEED-BASED) ***Scholarships, grants, and awards by category:*** *Academic Interests/Achievement:* general academic interests/achievements, mathematics. *Creative Arts/Performance:* art/fine arts, music. *Special Characteristics:* adult students, children with a deceased or disabled parent, handicapped students.

LOANS ***Programs:*** Federal Direct (Subsidized and Unsubsidized Stafford, PLUS), Perkins.

WORK-STUDY ***Federal work-study:*** Total amount: $715,502; 500 jobs available.

APPLYING FOR FINANCIAL AID ***Required financial aid form:*** FAFSA.

CONTACT Myrna C. Bryant, Assistant Director of Financial Aid, Kentucky State University, 400 East Main Street, Frankfort, KY 40601, 502-597-6025 or toll-free 800-633-9415 (in-state), 800-325-1716 (out-of-state). *E-mail:* myrna.bryant@kysu.edu.

KENTUCKY WESLEYAN COLLEGE

Owensboro, KY

Tuition & fees: $13,600 **Average undergraduate aid package: $12,583**

ABOUT THE INSTITUTION Independent Methodist, coed. Awards: bachelor's degrees. 41 undergraduate majors. Total enrollment: 968. Undergraduates: 968. Freshmen: 327. Federal methodology is used as a basis for awarding need-based institutional aid.

UNDERGRADUATE EXPENSES for 2006–07 ***Comprehensive fee:*** $19,350 includes full-time tuition ($13,200), mandatory fees ($400), and room and board ($5750). ***College room only:*** $2600. Full-time tuition and fees vary according to course load. ***Part-time tuition:*** $400 per credit hour. ***Part-time fees:*** $25 per term. Part-time tuition and fees vary according to course load. ***Payment plans:*** Installment, deferred payment.

FRESHMAN FINANCIAL AID (Fall 2006, est.) 324 applied for aid; of those 89% were deemed to have need. 100% of freshmen with need received aid; of those 19% had need fully met. ***Average percent of need met:*** 71% (excluding resources awarded to replace EFC). ***Average financial aid package:*** $12,462 (excluding resources awarded to replace EFC). 16% of all full-time freshmen had no need and received non-need-based gift aid.

UNDERGRADUATE FINANCIAL AID (Fall 2006, est.) 872 applied for aid; of those 89% were deemed to have need. 100% of undergraduates with need received aid; of those 23% had need fully met. ***Average percent of need met:*** 73% (excluding resources awarded to replace EFC). ***Average financial aid package:*** $12,583 (excluding resources awarded to replace EFC). 16% of all full-time undergraduates had no need and received non-need-based gift aid.

GIFT AID (NEED-BASED) ***Total amount:*** $7,828,782 (14% federal, 31% state, 50% institutional, 5% external sources). ***Receiving aid:*** Freshmen: 84% (288); All full-time undergraduates: 83% (770). ***Average award:*** Freshmen: $10,263;

Undergraduates: $10,086. ***Scholarships, grants, and awards:*** Federal Pell, FSEOG, state, private, college/university gift aid from institutional funds.

GIFT AID (NON-NEED-BASED) ***Total amount:*** $1,635,245 (14% state, 80% institutional, 6% external sources). ***Receiving aid:*** Freshmen: 11% (38); Undergraduates: 12% (108). ***Average award:*** Freshmen: $9654; Undergraduates: $10,597. ***Scholarships, grants, and awards by category:*** *Academic Interests/Achievement:* 907 awards ($3,093,882 total): general academic interests/achievements. *Creative Arts/Performance:* 69 awards ($83,295 total): art/fine arts, music, theater/drama. *Special Achievements/Activities:* 82 awards ($165,000 total): junior miss, leadership. *Special Characteristics:* 237 awards ($385,612 total): children and siblings of alumni, children of faculty/staff, children of union members/company employees, general special characteristics, out-of-state students, relatives of clergy, religious affiliation, siblings of current students. ***Tuition waivers:*** Full or partial for children of alumni, employees or children of employees, senior citizens. ***ROTC:*** Army cooperative.

LOANS ***Student loans:*** $3,144,302 (71% need-based, 29% non-need-based). 87% of past graduating class borrowed through all loan programs. *Average indebtedness per student:* $15,428. ***Average need-based loan:*** Freshmen: $2649; Undergraduates: $3125. ***Parent loans:*** $591,390 (37% need-based, 63% non-need-based). ***Programs:*** FFEL (Subsidized and Unsubsidized Stafford, PLUS), Perkins, alternative loans.

WORK-STUDY ***Federal work-study:*** Total amount: $157,222; 173 jobs averaging $893.

APPLYING FOR FINANCIAL AID ***Required financial aid form:*** FAFSA. ***Financial aid deadline (priority):*** 3/15. ***Notification date:*** Continuous beginning 2/15. Students must reply by 5/1 or within 2 weeks of notification.

CONTACT Mary Jo Harper, Director of Financial Aid, Kentucky Wesleyan College, 3000 Frederica Street, Owensboro, KY 42301, 270-852-3130 or toll-free 800-999-0592 (in-state), 800-990-0592 (out-of-state). *Fax:* 270-926-3196. *E-mail:* mharper@kwc.edu.

KENYON COLLEGE

Gambier, OH

Tuition & fees: $36,050 **Average undergraduate aid package: $27,275**

ABOUT THE INSTITUTION Independent, coed. Awards: bachelor's degrees. 54 undergraduate majors. Total enrollment: 1,661. Undergraduates: 1,661. Freshmen: 440. Both federal and institutional methodology are used as a basis for awarding need-based institutional aid.

UNDERGRADUATE EXPENSES for 2006–07 ***Application fee:*** $50. ***Comprehensive fee:*** $41,950 includes full-time tuition ($34,990), mandatory fees ($1060), and room and board ($5900). ***College room only:*** $2780. Room and board charges vary according to housing facility. ***Payment plan:*** Installment.

FRESHMAN FINANCIAL AID (Fall 2006, est.) 255 applied for aid; of those 71% were deemed to have need. 100% of freshmen with need received aid; of those 59% had need fully met. ***Average percent of need met:*** 98% (excluding resources awarded to replace EFC). ***Average financial aid package:*** $26,300 (excluding resources awarded to replace EFC). 26% of all full-time freshmen had no need and received non-need-based gift aid.

UNDERGRADUATE FINANCIAL AID (Fall 2006, est.) 895 applied for aid; of those 83% were deemed to have need. 99% of undergraduates with need received aid; of those 48% had need fully met. ***Average percent of need met:*** 98% (excluding resources awarded to replace EFC). ***Average financial aid package:*** $27,275 (excluding resources awarded to replace EFC). 23% of all full-time undergraduates had no need and received non-need-based gift aid.

GIFT AID (NEED-BASED) ***Total amount:*** $17,055,304 (4% federal, 2% state, 88% institutional, 6% external sources). ***Receiving aid:*** Freshmen: 38% (174); All full-time undergraduates: 41% (715). ***Average award:*** Freshmen: $24,681; Undergraduates: $23,853. ***Scholarships, grants, and awards:*** Federal Pell, FSEOG, state, private, college/university gift aid from institutional funds.

GIFT AID (NON-NEED-BASED) ***Total amount:*** $3,294,413 (7% state, 73% institutional, 20% external sources). ***Receiving aid:*** Freshmen: 16% (75); Undergraduates: 14% (249). ***Average award:*** Freshmen: $11,919; Undergraduates: $12,212. ***Scholarships, grants, and awards by category:*** *Academic Interests/Achievement:* 347 awards ($2,906,850 total): general academic interests/achievements. *Special Characteristics:* 41 awards ($525,500 total): ethnic background, first-generation college students. ***Tuition waivers:*** Full or partial for employees or children of employees.

LOANS ***Student loans:*** $5,204,869 (54% need-based, 46% non-need-based). 60% of past graduating class borrowed through all loan programs. *Average indebtedness per student:* $20,627. ***Average need-based loan:*** Freshmen: $2862; Undergraduates: $4110. ***Parent loans:*** $3,494,736 (9% need-based, 91% non-need-based). ***Programs:*** FFEL (Subsidized and Unsubsidized Stafford, PLUS), Perkins, college/university.

WORK-STUDY ***Federal work-study:*** Total amount: $135,351; 306 jobs averaging $575. ***State or other work-study/employment:*** Total amount: $355,840 (59% need-based, 41% non-need-based). 194 part-time jobs averaging $545.

APPLYING FOR FINANCIAL AID ***Required financial aid forms:*** FAFSA, CSS Financial Aid PROFILE, noncustodial (divorced/separated) parent's statement, income tax form(s). ***Financial aid deadline (priority):*** 2/15. ***Notification date:*** 4/1. Students must reply by 5/1.

CONTACT Mr. Craig Daugherty, Director of Financial Aid, Kenyon College, Stephens Hall, Gambier, OH 43022-9623, 740-427-5430 or toll-free 800-848-2468. *Fax:* 740-427-5240. *E-mail:* daugherty@kenyon.edu.

KETTERING UNIVERSITY

Flint, MI

Tuition & fees: $24,908 **Average undergraduate aid package: $13,586**

ABOUT THE INSTITUTION Independent, coed. Awards: bachelor's and master's degrees. 22 undergraduate majors. Total enrollment: 2,809. Undergraduates: 2,290. Freshmen: 398. Federal methodology is used as a basis for awarding need-based institutional aid.

UNDERGRADUATE EXPENSES for 2006–07 ***Application fee:*** $35. ***Comprehensive fee:*** $30,598 includes full-time tuition ($24,512), mandatory fees ($396), and room and board ($5690). ***College room only:*** $3600. Full-time tuition and fees vary according to student level. ***Part-time tuition:*** $766 per credit hour. ***Payment plan:*** Installment.

FRESHMAN FINANCIAL AID (Fall 2005) 450 applied for aid; of those 89% were deemed to have need. 100% of freshmen with need received aid; of those 12% had need fully met. ***Average percent of need met:*** 48% (excluding resources awarded to replace EFC). ***Average financial aid package:*** $15,433 (excluding resources awarded to replace EFC). 16% of all full-time freshmen had no need and received non-need-based gift aid.

UNDERGRADUATE FINANCIAL AID (Fall 2005) 1,789 applied for aid; of those 92% were deemed to have need. 100% of undergraduates with need received aid; of those 10% had need fully met. ***Average percent of need met:*** 52% (excluding resources awarded to replace EFC). ***Average financial aid package:*** $13,586 (excluding resources awarded to replace EFC). 18% of all full-time undergraduates had no need and received non-need-based gift aid.

GIFT AID (NEED-BASED) ***Total amount:*** $18,096,773 (9% federal, 10% state, 78% institutional, 3% external sources). ***Receiving aid:*** Freshmen: 75% (372); All full-time undergraduates: 59% (1,419). ***Average award:*** Freshmen: $12,078; Undergraduates: $9388. ***Scholarships, grants, and awards:*** Federal Pell, FSEOG, state, private, college/university gift aid from institutional funds.

GIFT AID (NON-NEED-BASED) ***Total amount:*** $3,791,464 (6% state, 85% institutional, 9% external sources). ***Receiving aid:*** Freshmen: 60% (299); Undergraduates: 50% (1,204). ***Average award:*** Freshmen: $9078; Undergraduates: $6915. ***Scholarships, grants, and awards by category:*** *Academic Interests/Achievement:* 1,640 awards ($10,591,918 total): business, computer science, engineering/technologies, general academic interests/achievements, mathematics, physical sciences. *Special Achievements/Activities:* 42 awards ($182,000 total): general special achievements/activities, memberships. *Special Characteristics:* 219 awards ($908,086 total): children and siblings of alumni, children of faculty/staff, members of minority groups, siblings of current students. ***Tuition waivers:*** Full or partial for employees or children of employees.

LOANS ***Student loans:*** $23,546,334 (68% need-based, 32% non-need-based). 80% of past graduating class borrowed through all loan programs. *Average indebtedness per student:* $47,487. ***Average need-based loan:*** Freshmen: $2525; Undergraduates: $3921. ***Parent loans:*** $1,419,759 (52% need-based, 48% non-need-based). ***Programs:*** FFEL (Subsidized and Unsubsidized Stafford, PLUS), state, alternative loans.

WORK-STUDY ***Federal work-study:*** Total amount: $337,625; 233 jobs averaging $907. ***State or other work-study/employment:*** Total amount: $29,000 (100% need-based). 63 part-time jobs averaging $356.

APPLYING FOR FINANCIAL AID ***Required financial aid form:*** FAFSA. ***Financial aid deadline (priority):*** 2/14. ***Notification date:*** Continuous beginning 2/15. Students must reply within 2 weeks of notification.

CONTACT Diane Bice, Director of Financial Aid, Kettering University, 1700 West Third Avenue, Flint, MI 48504-4898, 800-955-4464 Ext. 7859 or toll-free 800-955-4464 Ext. 7865 (in-state), 800-955-4464 (out-of-state). *Fax:* 810-762-9807. *E-mail:* finaid@kettering.edu.

KEUKA COLLEGE

Keuka Park, NY

Tuition & fees: $19,120 **Average undergraduate aid package: $16,358**

ABOUT THE INSTITUTION Independent religious, coed. Awards: bachelor's and master's degrees. 34 undergraduate majors. Total enrollment: 1,521. Undergraduates: 1,373. Freshmen: 254. Federal methodology is used as a basis for awarding need-based institutional aid.

UNDERGRADUATE EXPENSES for 2006–07 ***Application fee:*** $30. ***Comprehensive fee:*** $27,330 includes full-time tuition ($18,850), mandatory fees ($270), and room and board ($8210). ***College room only:*** $3900. Full-time tuition and fees vary according to program. Room and board charges vary according to board plan and housing facility. ***Part-time tuition:*** $650 per credit hour. Part-time tuition and fees vary according to program. ***Payment plan:*** Installment.

FRESHMAN FINANCIAL AID (Fall 2006, est.) 228 applied for aid; of those 93% were deemed to have need. 100% of freshmen with need received aid; of those 29% had need fully met. ***Average percent of need met:*** 82% (excluding resources awarded to replace EFC). ***Average financial aid package:*** $18,135 (excluding resources awarded to replace EFC). 9% of all full-time freshmen had no need and received non-need-based gift aid.

UNDERGRADUATE FINANCIAL AID (Fall 2006, est.) 1,066 applied for aid; of those 93% were deemed to have need. 100% of undergraduates with need received aid; of those 28% had need fully met. ***Average percent of need met:*** 79% (excluding resources awarded to replace EFC). ***Average financial aid package:*** $16,358 (excluding resources awarded to replace EFC). 8% of all full-time undergraduates had no need and received non-need-based gift aid.

GIFT AID (NEED-BASED) ***Total amount:*** $10,225,453 (13% federal, 18% state, 67% institutional, 2% external sources). ***Receiving aid:*** Freshmen: 90% (211); All full-time undergraduates: 89% (958). ***Average award:*** Freshmen: $12,925; Undergraduates: $10,800. ***Scholarships, grants, and awards:*** Federal Pell, FSEOG, state, college/university gift aid from institutional funds.

GIFT AID (NON-NEED-BASED) ***Total amount:*** $1,021,728 (6% state, 91% institutional, 3% external sources). ***Receiving aid:*** Freshmen: 13% (30); Undergraduates: 8% (91). ***Average award:*** Freshmen: $12,517; Undergraduates: $13,693. ***Scholarships, grants, and awards by category:*** *Academic Interests/Achievement:* general academic interests/achievements, international studies. *Special Achievements/Activities:* community service, general special achievements/activities, leadership. *Special Characteristics:* children and siblings of alumni, children of faculty/staff, international students, siblings of current students. ***Tuition waivers:*** Full or partial for employees or children of employees.

LOANS ***Student loans:*** $9,504,550 (74% need-based, 26% non-need-based). 97% of past graduating class borrowed through all loan programs. *Average indebtedness per student:* $18,645. ***Average need-based loan:*** Freshmen: $5093; Undergraduates: $6075. ***Parent loans:*** $1,037,731 (42% need-based, 58% non-need-based). ***Programs:*** FFEL (Subsidized and Unsubsidized Stafford, PLUS), Perkins.

WORK-STUDY ***Federal work-study:*** Total amount: $446,971; 401 jobs averaging $1365. ***State or other work-study/employment:*** Total amount: $250,030 (20% need-based, 80% non-need-based). 261 part-time jobs averaging $1083.

APPLYING FOR FINANCIAL AID ***Required financial aid form:*** FAFSA. ***Financial aid deadline:*** Continuous. ***Notification date:*** Continuous beginning 3/1. Students must reply by 5/1 or within 2 weeks of notification.

CONTACT Jennifer Bates, Director of Financial Aid, Keuka College, Financial Aid Office, Keuka Park, NY 14478-0098, 315-279-5232 or toll-free 800-33-KEUKA. *Fax:* 315-536-5327. *E-mail:* jbates@mail.keuka.edu.

KING COLLEGE

Bristol, TN

Tuition & fees: $19,262 **Average undergraduate aid package: $13,924**

ABOUT THE INSTITUTION Independent religious, coed. Awards: bachelor's and master's degrees. 49 undergraduate majors. Total enrollment: 1,271. Undergraduates: 1,122. Freshmen: 207. Federal methodology is used as a basis for awarding need-based institutional aid.

UNDERGRADUATE EXPENSES for 2006–07 ***Application fee:*** $20. ***Comprehensive fee:*** $25,770 includes full-time tuition ($18,156), mandatory fees ($1106), and room and board ($6508). ***College room only:*** $3200. Full-time tuition and fees vary according to course load and program. Room and board charges vary according to board plan. ***Part-time tuition:*** $600 per credit hour. Part-time tuition and fees vary according to course load and program. ***Payment plan:*** Installment.

FRESHMAN FINANCIAL AID (Fall 2006, est.) 196 applied for aid; of those 86% were deemed to have need. 100% of freshmen with need received aid; of those 33% had need fully met. ***Average percent of need met:*** 81% (excluding resources awarded to replace EFC). ***Average financial aid package:*** $16,372 (excluding resources awarded to replace EFC). 14% of all full-time freshmen had no need and received non-need-based gift aid.

UNDERGRADUATE FINANCIAL AID (Fall 2006, est.) 890 applied for aid; of those 87% were deemed to have need. 99% of undergraduates with need received aid; of those 24% had need fully met. ***Average percent of need met:*** 93% (excluding resources awarded to replace EFC). ***Average financial aid package:*** $13,924 (excluding resources awarded to replace EFC). 17% of all full-time undergraduates had no need and received non-need-based gift aid.

GIFT AID (NEED-BASED) ***Total amount:*** $7,078,543 (14% federal, 14% state, 61% institutional, 11% external sources). ***Receiving aid:*** Freshmen: 82% (169); All full-time undergraduates: 72% (745). ***Average award:*** Freshmen: $14,631; Undergraduates: $11,168. ***Scholarships, grants, and awards:*** Federal Pell, FSEOG, state, private, college/university gift aid from institutional funds.

GIFT AID (NON-NEED-BASED) ***Total amount:*** $2,035,843 (21% state, 53% institutional, 26% external sources). ***Receiving aid:*** Freshmen: 25% (51); Undergraduates: 14% (143). ***Average award:*** Freshmen: $11,730; Undergraduates: $9251. ***Scholarships, grants, and awards by category:*** *Academic Interests/Achievement:* 494 awards ($3,715,170 total): general academic interests/achievements. *Creative Arts/Performance:* 48 awards ($96,650 total): music, performing arts, theater/drama. *Special Achievements/Activities:* 294 awards ($2,050,214 total): general special achievements/activities. *Special Characteristics:* 58 awards ($537,215 total): children of faculty/staff, members of minority groups, relatives of clergy. ***Tuition waivers:*** Full or partial for employees or children of employees, senior citizens.

LOANS ***Student loans:*** $4,262,866 (76% need-based, 24% non-need-based). 89% of past graduating class borrowed through all loan programs. *Average indebtedness per student:* $18,635. ***Average need-based loan:*** Freshmen: $2941; Undergraduates: $4582. ***Parent loans:*** $919,115 (45% need-based, 55% non-need-based). ***Programs:*** FFEL (Subsidized and Unsubsidized Stafford, PLUS), Perkins, college/university.

WORK-STUDY ***Federal work-study:*** Total amount: $59,956; 86 jobs averaging $649. ***State or other work-study/employment:*** Part-time jobs available.

ATHLETIC AWARDS Total amount: $1,999,438 (65% need-based, 35% non-need-based).

APPLYING FOR FINANCIAL AID ***Required financial aid form:*** FAFSA. ***Financial aid deadline (priority):*** 3/1. ***Notification date:*** Continuous beginning 3/1. Students must reply within 2 weeks of notification.

CONTACT Brenda L. Clark, Director of Financial Aid, King College, 1350 King College Road, Bristol, TN 37620-2699, 423-652-4728 or toll-free 800-362-0014. *Fax:* 423-652-6039. *E-mail:* blclark@king.edu.

THE KING'S COLLEGE

New York, NY

CONTACT Financial Aid Office, The King's College, 350 Fifth Avenue, 15th Floor Empire State Building, New York, NY 10118, 212-659-7200 or toll-free 888-969-7200 Ext. 3610.

KING'S COLLEGE

Wilkes-Barre, PA

Tuition & fees: $22,280 **Average undergraduate aid package: $14,822**

ABOUT THE INSTITUTION Independent Roman Catholic, coed. Awards: associate, bachelor's, and master's degrees and post-bachelor's certificates. 40

undergraduate majors. Total enrollment: 2,386. Undergraduates: 2,127. Freshmen: 481. Federal methodology is used as a basis for awarding need-based institutional aid.

UNDERGRADUATE EXPENSES for 2006–07 ***Application fee:*** $30. ***Comprehensive fee:*** $30,870 includes full-time tuition ($22,280) and room and board ($8590). ***College room only:*** $3980. Room and board charges vary according to board plan and housing facility. ***Part-time tuition:*** $445 per credit hour. ***Payment plans:*** Installment, deferred payment.

FRESHMAN FINANCIAL AID (Fall 2006, est.) 453 applied for aid; of those 85% were deemed to have need. 99% of freshmen with need received aid; of those 18% had need fully met. ***Average percent of need met:*** 69% (excluding resources awarded to replace EFC). ***Average financial aid package:*** $15,246 (excluding resources awarded to replace EFC). 11% of all full-time freshmen had no need and received non-need-based gift aid.

UNDERGRADUATE FINANCIAL AID (Fall 2006, est.) 1,646 applied for aid; of those 88% were deemed to have need. 99% of undergraduates with need received aid; of those 17% had need fully met. ***Average percent of need met:*** 69% (excluding resources awarded to replace EFC). ***Average financial aid package:*** $14,822 (excluding resources awarded to replace EFC). 18% of all full-time undergraduates had no need and received non-need-based gift aid.

GIFT AID (NEED-BASED) ***Total amount:*** $17,915,655 (8% federal, 17% state, 73% institutional, 2% external sources). ***Receiving aid:*** Freshmen: 55% (266); All full-time undergraduates: 53% (968). ***Average award:*** Freshmen: $4640; Undergraduates: $5565. ***Scholarships, grants, and awards:*** Federal Pell, FSEOG, state, private, college/university gift aid from institutional funds.

GIFT AID (NON-NEED-BASED) ***Total amount:*** $2,836,471 (3% federal, 96% institutional, 1% external sources). ***Receiving aid:*** Freshmen: 46% (222); Undergraduates: 42% (769). ***Average award:*** Freshmen: $8004; Undergraduates: $8151. ***Scholarships, grants, and awards by category:*** *Academic Interests/Achievement:* 979 awards ($9,260,601 total): biological sciences, business, communication, computer science, education, English, foreign languages, general academic interests/achievements, health fields, humanities, mathematics, physical sciences, premedicine, religion/biblical studies, social sciences. *Special Achievements/Activities:* 465 awards ($2,495,929 total): community service, general special achievements/activities, leadership. *Special Characteristics:* 181 awards ($1,278,753 total): children of educators, children of faculty/staff, international students, members of minority groups, relatives of clergy, siblings of current students. ***Tuition waivers:*** Full or partial for employees or children of employees, senior citizens. ***ROTC:*** Army.

LOANS ***Student loans:*** $7,701,046 (92% need-based, 8% non-need-based). 74% of past graduating class borrowed through all loan programs. *Average indebtedness per student:* $25,391. ***Average need-based loan:*** Freshmen: $3496; Undergraduates: $4286. ***Parent loans:*** $4,567,605 (85% need-based, 15% non-need-based). ***Programs:*** FFEL (Subsidized and Unsubsidized Stafford, PLUS), Perkins, alternative loans.

WORK-STUDY ***Federal work-study:*** Total amount: $293,397; 300 jobs averaging $977. ***State or other work-study/employment:*** Total amount: $248,633 (100% non-need-based). 245 part-time jobs averaging $1013.

APPLYING FOR FINANCIAL AID ***Required financial aid forms:*** FAFSA, institution's own form. ***Financial aid deadline (priority):*** 2/15. ***Notification date:*** Continuous beginning 3/1. Students must reply by 5/1 or within 2 weeks of notification.

CONTACT Ellen E. McGuire, Director of Financial Aid, King's College, 133 North River Street, Wilkes-Barre, PA 18711-0801, 570-208-5868 or toll-free 888-KINGSPA. *Fax:* 570-208-6015. *E-mail:* finaid@kings.edu.

THE KING'S COLLEGE AND SEMINARY

Van Nuys, CA

CONTACT Financial Aid Office, The King's College and Seminary, 14800 Sherman Way, Van Nuys, CA 91405-8040, 818-779-8040 or toll-free 888-779-8040 (in-state).

KNOX COLLEGE

Galesburg, IL

Tuition & fees: $27,900 **Average undergraduate aid package: $22,477**

ABOUT THE INSTITUTION Independent, coed. Awards: bachelor's degrees. 33 undergraduate majors. Total enrollment: 1,351. Undergraduates: 1,351. Freshmen: 407. Both federal and institutional methodology are used as a basis for awarding need-based institutional aid.

UNDERGRADUATE EXPENSES for 2006–07 ***Application fee:*** $40. ***Comprehensive fee:*** $33,825 includes full-time tuition ($27,606), mandatory fees ($294), and room and board ($5925). ***College room only:*** $2865. Room and board charges vary according to board plan. ***Part-time tuition:*** $921 per credit. Part-time tuition and fees vary according to course load. ***Payment plan:*** Installment.

FRESHMAN FINANCIAL AID (Fall 2006, est.) 336 applied for aid; of those 84% were deemed to have need. 100% of freshmen with need received aid; of those 32% had need fully met. ***Average percent of need met:*** 94% (excluding resources awarded to replace EFC). ***Average financial aid package:*** $22,948 (excluding resources awarded to replace EFC). 27% of all full-time freshmen had no need and received non-need-based gift aid.

UNDERGRADUATE FINANCIAL AID (Fall 2006, est.) 1,003 applied for aid; of those 87% were deemed to have need. 100% of undergraduates with need received aid; of those 36% had need fully met. ***Average percent of need met:*** 94% (excluding resources awarded to replace EFC). ***Average financial aid package:*** $22,477 (excluding resources awarded to replace EFC). 30% of all full-time undergraduates had no need and received non-need-based gift aid.

GIFT AID (NEED-BASED) ***Total amount:*** $14,804,429 (7% federal, 8% state, 82% institutional, 3% external sources). ***Receiving aid:*** Freshmen: 69% (283); All full-time undergraduates: 66% (871). ***Average award:*** Freshmen: $17,720; Undergraduates: $16,886. ***Scholarships, grants, and awards:*** Federal Pell, FSEOG, state, private, college/university gift aid from institutional funds.

GIFT AID (NON-NEED-BASED) ***Total amount:*** $4,121,535 (98% institutional, 2% external sources). ***Receiving aid:*** Freshmen: 17% (68); Undergraduates: 17% (229). ***Average award:*** Freshmen: $10,144; Undergraduates: $10,314. ***Scholarships, grants, and awards by category:*** *Academic Interests/Achievement:* general academic interests/achievements, mathematics. *Creative Arts/Performance:* art/fine arts, creative writing, dance, music, theater/drama. *Special Achievements/Activities:* community service. ***Tuition waivers:*** Full or partial for employees or children of employees.

LOANS ***Student loans:*** $5,422,532 (64% need-based, 36% non-need-based). 79% of past graduating class borrowed through all loan programs. *Average indebtedness per student:* $22,860. ***Average need-based loan:*** Freshmen: $4564; Undergraduates: $5234. ***Parent loans:*** $2,474,907 (100% non-need-based). ***Programs:*** Federal Direct (Subsidized and Unsubsidized Stafford, PLUS), Perkins, college/university, private loans.

WORK-STUDY ***Federal work-study:*** Total amount: $1,150,046; 662 jobs averaging $1737. ***State or other work-study/employment:*** Total amount: $155,411 (87% need-based, 13% non-need-based). 94 part-time jobs averaging $1653.

APPLYING FOR FINANCIAL AID ***Required financial aid forms:*** FAFSA, institution's own form, income tax form(s). ***Financial aid deadline (priority):*** 2/1. ***Notification date:*** Continuous beginning 3/15. Students must reply by 5/1 or within 2 weeks of notification.

CONTACT Ms. Teresa K. Jackson, Director of Financial Aid, Knox College, 2 East South Street, Galesburg, IL 61401, 309-341-7130 or toll-free 800-678-KNOX. *Fax:* 309-341-7070. *E-mail:* tjackson@knox.edu.

KOL YAAKOV TORAH CENTER

Monsey, NY

CONTACT Office of Financial Aid, Kol Yaakov Torah Center, 29 West Maple Avenue, Monsey, NY 10952-2954, 914-425-3863.

KUTZTOWN UNIVERSITY OF PENNSYLVANIA

Kutztown, PA

Tuition & fees (PA res): $6619 **Average undergraduate aid package: $6653**

ABOUT THE INSTITUTION State-supported, coed. Awards: bachelor's and master's degrees and post-bachelor's certificates. 62 undergraduate majors. Total enrollment: 10,193. Undergraduates: 9,189. Freshmen: 1,936. Federal methodology is used as a basis for awarding need-based institutional aid.

UNDERGRADUATE EXPENSES for 2006–07 ***Application fee:*** $35. ***Tuition, state resident:*** full-time $5038; part-time $210 per credit. ***Tuition, nonresident:*** full-time $12,598; part-time $525 per credit. ***Required fees:*** full-time $1581;

$44.25 per credit or $31 per term part-time. ***College room and board:*** $6208; ***Room only:*** $4144. Room and board charges vary according to board plan and housing facility. ***Payment plans:*** Installment, deferred payment.

FRESHMAN FINANCIAL AID (Fall 2006, est.) 1707 applied for aid; of those 70% were deemed to have need. 100% of freshmen with need received aid; of those 50% had need fully met. ***Average percent of need met:*** 52% (excluding resources awarded to replace EFC). ***Average financial aid package:*** $5905 (excluding resources awarded to replace EFC). 4% of all full-time freshmen had no need and received non-need-based gift aid.

UNDERGRADUATE FINANCIAL AID (Fall 2006, est.) 6,881 applied for aid; of those 71% were deemed to have need. 100% of undergraduates with need received aid; of those 52% had need fully met. ***Average percent of need met:*** 59% (excluding resources awarded to replace EFC). ***Average financial aid package:*** $6653 (excluding resources awarded to replace EFC). 3% of all full-time undergraduates had no need and received non-need-based gift aid.

GIFT AID (NEED-BASED) ***Total amount:*** $14,903,356 (37% federal, 53% state, 5% institutional, 5% external sources). ***Receiving aid:*** Freshmen: 42% (817); All full-time undergraduates: 40% (3,391). ***Average award:*** Freshmen: $4850; Undergraduates: $4533. ***Scholarships, grants, and awards:*** Federal Pell, FSEOG, state, private, college/university gift aid from institutional funds.

GIFT AID (NON-NEED-BASED) ***Total amount:*** $1,013,495 (21% federal, 26% state, 18% institutional, 35% external sources). ***Receiving aid:*** Freshmen: 1% (25); Undergraduates: 2% (142). ***Average award:*** Freshmen: $1696; Undergraduates: $1955. ***Scholarships, grants, and awards by category:*** *Academic Interests/Achievement:* 361 awards ($852,491 total): business, communication, computer science, education, English, foreign languages, general academic interests/achievements, humanities, library science, mathematics, physical sciences. *Creative Arts/Performance:* 20 awards ($21,077 total): applied art and design, art/fine arts, dance, music, theater/drama. *Special Achievements/Activities:* 113 awards ($45,008 total): general special achievements/activities, leadership, religious involvement. *Special Characteristics:* 108 awards ($412,037 total): children of faculty/staff, children of union members/company employees, handicapped students. ***Tuition waivers:*** Full or partial for employees or children of employees, senior citizens. ***ROTC:*** Army cooperative.

LOANS ***Student loans:*** $32,579,937 (62% need-based, 38% non-need-based). 81% of past graduating class borrowed through all loan programs. *Average indebtedness per student:* $15,559. ***Average need-based loan:*** Freshmen: $2491; Undergraduates: $3558. ***Parent loans:*** $9,044,109 (31% need-based, 69% non-need-based). ***Programs:*** FFEL (Subsidized and Unsubsidized Stafford, PLUS), Perkins.

WORK-STUDY ***Federal work-study:*** Total amount: $432,583; 425 jobs averaging $1017. ***State or other work-study/employment:*** Part-time jobs available.

ATHLETIC AWARDS Total amount: $504,150 (52% need-based, 48% non-need-based).

APPLYING FOR FINANCIAL AID ***Required financial aid form:*** FAFSA. ***Financial aid deadline (priority):*** 2/15. ***Notification date:*** Continuous beginning 3/30. Students must reply by 5/1 or within 4 weeks of notification.

CONTACT Ms. Anita Faust, Director of Financial Aid, Kutztown University of Pennsylvania, 209A Stratton Administration Center, Kutztown, PA 19530-0730, 610-683-4077 or toll-free 877-628-1915. *Fax:* 610-683-1380. *E-mail:* faust@kutztown.edu.

KUYPER COLLEGE

Grand Rapids, MI

Tuition & fees: $12,725 **Average undergraduate aid package: $10,860**

ABOUT THE INSTITUTION Independent religious, coed. Awards: associate and bachelor's degrees and post-bachelor's certificates. 21 undergraduate majors. Total enrollment: 290. Undergraduates: 290. Freshmen: 51. Federal methodology is used as a basis for awarding need-based institutional aid.

UNDERGRADUATE EXPENSES for 2007–08 ***Application fee:*** $25. ***Comprehensive fee:*** $18,425 includes full-time tuition ($12,200), mandatory fees ($525), and room and board ($5700). ***Part-time tuition:*** $585 per credit hour.

FRESHMAN FINANCIAL AID (Fall 2006, est.) 42 applied for aid; of those 81% were deemed to have need. 100% of freshmen with need received aid; of those 18% had need fully met. ***Average percent of need met:*** 68% (excluding resources awarded to replace EFC). ***Average financial aid package:*** $8557 (excluding resources awarded to replace EFC). 17% of all full-time freshmen had no need and received non-need-based gift aid.

UNDERGRADUATE FINANCIAL AID (Fall 2006, est.) 215 applied for aid; of those 65% were deemed to have need. 97% of undergraduates with need received aid; of those 18% had need fully met. ***Average percent of need met:*** 71% (excluding resources awarded to replace EFC). ***Average financial aid package:*** $10,860 (excluding resources awarded to replace EFC). 34% of all full-time undergraduates had no need and received non-need-based gift aid.

GIFT AID (NEED-BASED) ***Total amount:*** $1,005,514 (24% federal, 29% state, 47% institutional). ***Receiving aid:*** Freshmen: 74% (34); All full-time undergraduates: 61% (134). ***Average award:*** Freshmen: $7039; Undergraduates: $5824. ***Scholarships, grants, and awards:*** Federal Pell, FSEOG, state, private, college/university gift aid from institutional funds.

GIFT AID (NON-NEED-BASED) ***Total amount:*** $129,218 (9% state, 87% institutional, 4% external sources). ***Receiving aid:*** Freshmen: 2% (1); Undergraduates: 1% (2). ***Average award:*** Freshmen: $2731; Undergraduates: $1550. ***Scholarships, grants, and awards by category:*** *Academic Interests/Achievement:* 84 awards ($97,693 total): general academic interests/achievements. *Special Achievements/Activities:* 19 awards ($44,000 total): leadership, religious involvement. *Special Characteristics:* 41 awards ($259,056 total): children of faculty/staff, international students, members of minority groups.

LOANS ***Student loans:*** $985,499 (65% need-based, 35% non-need-based). 48% of past graduating class borrowed through all loan programs. *Average indebtedness per student:* $12,900. ***Average need-based loan:*** Freshmen: $2150; Undergraduates: $3328. ***Parent loans:*** $21,400 (100% need-based). ***Programs:*** FFEL (Subsidized and Unsubsidized Stafford, PLUS), alternative loans.

WORK-STUDY ***Federal work-study:*** Total amount: $33,382; 29 jobs averaging $1141. ***State or other work-study/employment:*** Total amount: $218,935 (3% need-based, 97% non-need-based). 75 part-time jobs averaging $3000.

APPLYING FOR FINANCIAL AID ***Required financial aid forms:*** FAFSA, institution's own form. ***Financial aid deadline (priority):*** 3/1. ***Notification date:*** Continuous beginning 3/20. Students must reply within 2 weeks of notification.

CONTACT Ms. Agnes Russell, Director of Financial Aid, Kuyper College, 3333 East Beltline NE, Grand Rapids, MI 49525-9749, 616-222-3000 Ext. 656 or toll-free 800-511-3749. *Fax:* 616-222-3045. *E-mail:* arussell@kuyper.edu.

LABORATORY INSTITUTE OF MERCHANDISING

New York, NY

Tuition & fees: $17,700 **Average undergraduate aid package: $6015**

ABOUT THE INSTITUTION Proprietary, coed, primarily women. Awards: associate and bachelor's degrees. 2 undergraduate majors. Total enrollment: 970. Undergraduates: 970. Freshmen: 242. Federal methodology is used as a basis for awarding need-based institutional aid.

UNDERGRADUATE EXPENSES for 2006–07 ***Application fee:*** $40. ***Comprehensive fee:*** $30,700 includes full-time tuition ($17,250), mandatory fees ($450), and room and board ($13,000). ***Part-time tuition:*** $545 per credit. ***Part-time fees:*** $112.50 per term.

FRESHMAN FINANCIAL AID (Fall 2006, est.) 175 applied for aid; of those 97% were deemed to have need. 100% of freshmen with need received aid. ***Average financial aid package:*** $5260 (excluding resources awarded to replace EFC). 10% of all full-time freshmen had no need and received non-need-based gift aid.

UNDERGRADUATE FINANCIAL AID (Fall 2006, est.) 719 applied for aid; of those 80% were deemed to have need. 100% of undergraduates with need received aid. ***Average financial aid package:*** $6015 (excluding resources awarded to replace EFC). 8% of all full-time undergraduates had no need and received non-need-based gift aid.

GIFT AID (NEED-BASED) ***Total amount:*** $2,279,004 (31% federal, 28% state, 36% institutional, 5% external sources). ***Receiving aid:*** Freshmen: 40% (96); All full-time undergraduates: 46% (433). ***Average award:*** Freshmen: $4325; Undergraduates: $3916. ***Scholarships, grants, and awards:*** Federal Pell, FSEOG, state, private, college/university gift aid from institutional funds.

GIFT AID (NON-NEED-BASED) ***Total amount:*** $250,202 (14% state, 86% institutional). ***Receiving aid:*** Freshmen: 18% (43); Undergraduates: 10% (99). ***Average award:*** Freshmen: $2598; Undergraduates: $2675. ***Scholarships, grants, and awards by category:*** *Academic Interests/Achievement:* 145 awards ($318,500 total): general academic interests/achievements. *Special Achievements/Activities:* 2 awards ($6312 total): memberships. *Special Characteristics:* 3 awards ($14,625 total): local/state students.

LOANS ***Student loans:*** $5,532,868 (35% need-based, 65% non-need-based). 91% of past graduating class borrowed through all loan programs. *Average indebtedness per student:* $17,662. ***Average need-based loan:*** Freshmen: $2347; Undergraduates: $3833. ***Parent loans:*** $4,640,218 (100% non-need-based). ***Programs:*** Federal Direct (Subsidized and Unsubsidized Stafford, PLUS), FFEL (PLUS), state.

WORK-STUDY ***Federal work-study:*** Total amount: $52,000; 22 jobs averaging $1601.

APPLYING FOR FINANCIAL AID ***Required financial aid forms:*** FAFSA, institution's own form. ***Financial aid deadline:*** Continuous. ***Notification date:*** Continuous beginning 2/15. Students must reply by 5/1 or within 2 weeks of notification.

CONTACT Mr. Christopher Barto, Director of Financial Aid, Laboratory Institute of Merchandising, 12 East 53rd Street, New York, NY 10022-5268, 212-752-1530 or toll-free 800-677-1323. *Fax:* 212-317-8602. *E-mail:* cbarto@limcollege.edu.

LA COLLEGE INTERNATIONAL

Los Angeles, CA

CONTACT Office of Financial Aid, LA College International, 3200 Wilshire Boulevard, Los Angeles, CA 90010, 213-381-3333 or toll-free 800-57 GO ICT (in-state). *Fax:* 213-383-9369.

LAFAYETTE COLLEGE

Easton, PA

CONTACT Arlinda DeNardo, Director Financial Aid, Lafayette College, 107 Markle Hall, Easton, PA 18042-1777, 610-330-5055. *Fax:* 610-330-5758. *E-mail:* denardoa@lafayette.edu.

LaGRANGE COLLEGE

LaGrange, GA

Tuition & fees: $18,575 **Average undergraduate aid package: $13,999**

ABOUT THE INSTITUTION Independent United Methodist, coed. Awards: associate, bachelor's, and master's degrees. 33 undergraduate majors. Total enrollment: 1,136. Undergraduates: 1,058. Freshmen: 270. Federal methodology is used as a basis for awarding need-based institutional aid.

UNDERGRADUATE EXPENSES for 2007–08 ***Application fee:*** $30. ***Comprehensive fee:*** $26,173 includes full-time tuition ($18,500), mandatory fees ($75), and room and board ($7598). ***Part-time tuition:*** $762 per hour.

FRESHMAN FINANCIAL AID (Fall 2006, est.) 174 applied for aid; of those 83% were deemed to have need. 100% of freshmen with need received aid; of those 33% had need fully met. ***Average percent of need met:*** 80% (excluding resources awarded to replace EFC). ***Average financial aid package:*** $13,841 (excluding resources awarded to replace EFC). 18% of all full-time freshmen had no need and received non-need-based gift aid.

UNDERGRADUATE FINANCIAL AID (Fall 2006, est.) 786 applied for aid; of those 84% were deemed to have need. 99% of undergraduates with need received aid; of those 29% had need fully met. ***Average percent of need met:*** 75% (excluding resources awarded to replace EFC). ***Average financial aid package:*** $13,999 (excluding resources awarded to replace EFC). 14% of all full-time undergraduates had no need and received non-need-based gift aid.

GIFT AID (NEED-BASED) ***Total amount:*** $6,029,228 (16% federal, 22% state, 58% institutional, 4% external sources). ***Receiving aid:*** Freshmen: 55% (144); All full-time undergraduates: 67% (652). ***Average award:*** Freshmen: $11,809; Undergraduates: $10,233. ***Scholarships, grants, and awards:*** Federal Pell, FSEOG, state, private, college/university gift aid from institutional funds.

GIFT AID (NON-NEED-BASED) ***Total amount:*** $2,492,144 (21% state, 72% institutional, 7% external sources). ***Receiving aid:*** Freshmen: 13% (33); Undergraduates: 13% (123). ***Average award:*** Freshmen: $7924; Undergraduates: $7624. ***Scholarships, grants, and awards by category:*** *Academic Interests/Achievement:* religion/biblical studies. *Creative Arts/Performance:* music, theater/drama. *Special Achievements/Activities:* leadership. *Special Characteristics:* children of faculty/staff, ethnic background, first-generation college students, relatives of clergy, religious affiliation.

LOANS ***Student loans:*** $4,132,405 (75% need-based, 25% non-need-based). 63% of past graduating class borrowed through all loan programs. *Average indebtedness per student:* $19,596. ***Average need-based loan:*** Freshmen: $2438; Undergraduates: $3615. ***Parent loans:*** $1,270,763 (21% need-based, 79% non-need-based). ***Programs:*** FFEL (Subsidized and Unsubsidized Stafford, PLUS), Perkins, state.

WORK-STUDY ***Federal work-study:*** Total amount: $72,260; jobs available. ***State or other work-study/employment:*** Total amount: $305,422 (30% need-based, 70% non-need-based).

APPLYING FOR FINANCIAL AID ***Required financial aid forms:*** FAFSA, state aid form. ***Financial aid deadline (priority):*** 4/1. ***Notification date:*** Continuous beginning 3/15. Students must reply by 8/15 or within 2 weeks of notification.

CONTACT Michelle Reeves, Assistant Director, LaGrange College, 601 Broad Street, LaGrange, GA 30240-2999, 888-253-9918 or toll-free 800-593-2885. *Fax:* 706-880-8348. *E-mail:* ssmith@lagrange.edu.

LAGUNA COLLEGE OF ART & DESIGN

Laguna Beach, CA

CONTACT Christopher Brown, Director of Student Services, Laguna College of Art & Design, 2222 Laguna Canyon Road, Laguna Beach, CA 92651-1136, 949-376-6000 or toll-free 800-255-0762. *Fax:* 949-497-5220. *E-mail:* cbrown@lagunacollege.edu.

LAKE ERIE COLLEGE

Painesville, OH

CONTACT Patricia Canfield, Director of Financial Aid, Lake Erie College, 391 West Washington Street, Painesville, OH 44077-3389, 440-375-7100 or toll-free 800-916-0904. *Fax:* 440-375-7005.

LAKE FOREST COLLEGE

Lake Forest, IL

Tuition & fees: $29,164 **Average undergraduate aid package: $23,024**

ABOUT THE INSTITUTION Independent, coed. Awards: bachelor's and master's degrees. 32 undergraduate majors. Total enrollment: 1,448. Undergraduates: 1,422. Freshmen: 386. Both federal and institutional methodology are used as a basis for awarding need-based institutional aid.

UNDERGRADUATE EXPENSES for 2006–07 ***Application fee:*** $40. ***One-time required fee:*** $200. ***Comprehensive fee:*** $36,124 includes full-time tuition ($28,700), mandatory fees ($464), and room and board ($6960). ***College room only:*** $3500. Full-time tuition and fees vary according to course load. Room and board charges vary according to housing facility. ***Part-time tuition:*** $3590 per course. Part-time tuition and fees vary according to course load. ***Payment plan:*** Installment.

FRESHMAN FINANCIAL AID (Fall 2006, est.) 350 applied for aid; of those 85% were deemed to have need. 100% of freshmen with need received aid; of those 100% had need fully met. ***Average percent of need met:*** 100% (excluding resources awarded to replace EFC). ***Average financial aid package:*** $21,963 (excluding resources awarded to replace EFC). 12% of all full-time freshmen had no need and received non-need-based gift aid.

UNDERGRADUATE FINANCIAL AID (Fall 2006, est.) 1,278 applied for aid; of those 83% were deemed to have need. 100% of undergraduates with need received aid; of those 100% had need fully met. ***Average percent of need met:*** 100% (excluding resources awarded to replace EFC). ***Average financial aid package:*** $23,024 (excluding resources awarded to replace EFC). 15% of all full-time undergraduates had no need and received non-need-based gift aid.

GIFT AID (NEED-BASED) ***Total amount:*** $19,989,796 (7% federal, 7% state, 83% institutional, 3% external sources). ***Receiving aid:*** Freshmen: 77% (299); All full-time undergraduates: 76% (1,057). ***Average award:*** Freshmen: $18,827; Undergraduates: $18,769. ***Scholarships, grants, and awards:*** Federal Pell, FSEOG, state, private, college/university gift aid from institutional funds.

GIFT AID (NON-NEED-BASED) ***Total amount:*** $2,350,966 (97% institutional, 3% external sources). ***Average award:*** Freshmen: $10,848; Undergraduates: $11,319. ***Scholarships, grants, and awards by category:*** *Academic Interests/Achievement:* 795 awards ($8,407,638 total): biological sciences, foreign languages, general academic interests/achievements, physical sciences. *Creative Arts/Performance:* 206 awards ($651,500 total): art/fine arts, creative writing, music, theater/drama. *Special Achievements/Activities:* 129 awards ($401,000 total): leadership. *Special Characteristics:* 53 awards ($639,900 total): children and siblings of alumni, general special characteristics, previous college experience. ***Tuition waivers:*** Full or partial for employees or children of employees.

LOANS ***Student loans:*** $6,385,291 (70% need-based, 30% non-need-based). 63% of past graduating class borrowed through all loan programs. *Average indebtedness per student:* $19,976. ***Average need-based loan:*** Freshmen: $3938; Undergraduates: $5181. ***Parent loans:*** $1,772,409 (100% non-need-based). ***Programs:*** FFEL (Subsidized and Unsubsidized Stafford, PLUS), Perkins, college/university, alternative loans.

WORK-STUDY ***Federal work-study:*** Total amount: $937,427; 549 jobs averaging $1707.

APPLYING FOR FINANCIAL AID ***Required financial aid forms:*** FAFSA, institution's own form, federal 1040. ***Financial aid deadline (priority):*** 3/1. ***Notification date:*** Continuous beginning 3/1. Students must reply by 5/1 or within 3 weeks of notification.

CONTACT Mr. Jerry Cebrzynski, Director of Financial Aid, Lake Forest College, 555 North Sheridan Road, Lake Forest, IL 60045-2399, 847-735-5104 or toll-free 800-828-4751. *Fax:* 847-735-6271. *E-mail:* cebrzynski@lakeforest.edu.

LAKELAND COLLEGE

Sheboygan, WI

Tuition & fees: $17,595 **Average undergraduate aid package: $11,728**

ABOUT THE INSTITUTION Independent religious, coed. Awards: bachelor's and master's degrees. 29 undergraduate majors. Total enrollment: 4,047. Undergraduates: 3,298. Freshmen: 220. Federal methodology is used as a basis for awarding need-based institutional aid.

UNDERGRADUATE EXPENSES for 2007–08 ***Application fee:*** $20. ***Comprehensive fee:*** $23,740 includes full-time tuition ($16,845), mandatory fees ($750), and room and board ($6145). ***Part-time tuition:*** $1686 per course.

FRESHMAN FINANCIAL AID (Fall 2006, est.) 259 applied for aid; of those 83% were deemed to have need. 99% of freshmen with need received aid; of those 22% had need fully met. ***Average percent of need met:*** 77% (excluding resources awarded to replace EFC). ***Average financial aid package:*** $13,183 (excluding resources awarded to replace EFC). 16% of all full-time freshmen had no need and received non-need-based gift aid.

UNDERGRADUATE FINANCIAL AID (Fall 2006, est.) 1,180 applied for aid; of those 85% were deemed to have need. 98% of undergraduates with need received aid; of those 24% had need fully met. ***Average percent of need met:*** 71% (excluding resources awarded to replace EFC). ***Average financial aid package:*** $11,728 (excluding resources awarded to replace EFC). 16% of all full-time undergraduates had no need and received non-need-based gift aid.

GIFT AID (NEED-BASED) ***Total amount:*** $8,049,138 (20% federal, 12% state, 61% institutional, 7% external sources). ***Receiving aid:*** Freshmen: 62% (211); All full-time undergraduates: 64% (874). ***Average award:*** Freshmen: $9944; Undergraduates: $8474. ***Scholarships, grants, and awards:*** Federal Pell, FSEOG, state, private, college/university gift aid from institutional funds, Federal ACG and Federal SMART Grants.

GIFT AID (NON-NEED-BASED) ***Total amount:*** $1,498,706 (1% state, 92% institutional, 7% external sources). ***Receiving aid:*** Freshmen: 5% (18); Undergraduates: 5% (67). ***Average award:*** Freshmen: $7853; Undergraduates: $8747. ***Scholarships, grants, and awards by category:*** *Academic Interests/Achievement:* 431 awards ($2,380,180 total): business, engineering/technologies, English, general academic interests/achievements, religion/biblical studies. *Creative Arts/Performance:* 19 awards ($35,000 total): art/fine arts, creative writing, journalism/publications, music, performing arts. *Special Achievements/Activities:* 40 awards ($54,000 total): community service, leadership, religious involvement. *Special Characteristics:* 107 awards ($470,658 total): children and siblings of alumni, children of faculty/staff, religious affiliation, siblings of current students.

LOANS ***Student loans:*** $11,356,010 (75% need-based, 25% non-need-based). ***Average need-based loan:*** Freshmen: $3003; Undergraduates: $4198. ***Parent loans:*** $681,402 (35% need-based, 65% non-need-based). ***Programs:*** FFEL (Subsidized and Unsubsidized Stafford, PLUS), Perkins, alternative loans.

WORK-STUDY ***Federal work-study:*** Total amount: $390,065; 200 jobs averaging $1650. ***State or other work-study/employment:*** Total amount: $202,016 (12% need-based, 88% non-need-based). 160 part-time jobs averaging $1650.

APPLYING FOR FINANCIAL AID ***Required financial aid forms:*** FAFSA, institution's own form. ***Financial aid deadline:*** 7/1 (priority: 3/31). ***Notification date:*** Continuous beginning 3/1. Students must reply within 2 weeks of notification.

CONTACT Ms. Patty Taylor, Director of Financial Aid, Lakeland College, PO Box 359, Sheboygan, WI 53082-0359, 920-565-1214 or toll-free 800-242-3347 (in-state). *Fax:* 920-565-1470.

LAKE SUPERIOR STATE UNIVERSITY

Sault Sainte Marie, MI

Tuition & fees (MI res): $6698 **Average undergraduate aid package: $8157**

ABOUT THE INSTITUTION State-supported, coed. Awards: associate, bachelor's, and master's degrees. 63 undergraduate majors. Total enrollment: 2,919. Undergraduates: 2,916. Freshmen: 492. Both federal and institutional methodology are used as a basis for awarding need-based institutional aid.

UNDERGRADUATE EXPENSES for 2006–07 ***Application fee:*** $35. ***Tuition, state resident:*** full-time $6628; part-time $273.25 per credit hour. ***Tuition, nonresident:*** full-time $13,186; part-time $546.50 per credit hour. Full-time tuition and fees vary according to reciprocity agreements. Part-time tuition and fees vary according to course load and reciprocity agreements. ***College room and board:*** $6836. Room and board charges vary according to board plan and housing facility. ***Payment plans:*** Installment, deferred payment.

FRESHMAN FINANCIAL AID (Fall 2005) 481 applied for aid; of those 100% were deemed to have need. 100% of freshmen with need received aid; of those 54% had need fully met. ***Average percent of need met:*** 77% (excluding resources awarded to replace EFC). ***Average financial aid package:*** $8436 (excluding resources awarded to replace EFC). 12% of all full-time freshmen had no need and received non-need-based gift aid.

UNDERGRADUATE FINANCIAL AID (Fall 2005) 2,115 applied for aid; of those 100% were deemed to have need. 100% of undergraduates with need received aid; of those 49% had need fully met. ***Average percent of need met:*** 75% (excluding resources awarded to replace EFC). ***Average financial aid package:*** $8157 (excluding resources awarded to replace EFC). 7% of all full-time undergraduates had no need and received non-need-based gift aid.

GIFT AID (NEED-BASED) ***Total amount:*** $2,911,100 (74% federal, 23% state, 3% institutional). ***Receiving aid:*** Freshmen: 41% (209); All full-time undergraduates: 34% (832). ***Average award:*** Freshmen: $3725; Undergraduates: $3407. ***Scholarships, grants, and awards:*** Federal Pell, FSEOG, state, private, college/university gift aid from institutional funds, Federal Nursing, third party payments.

GIFT AID (NON-NEED-BASED) ***Total amount:*** $3,514,446 (2% federal, 33% state, 47% institutional, 18% external sources). ***Receiving aid:*** Freshmen: 72% (369); Undergraduates: 50% (1,232). ***Average award:*** Freshmen: $2718; Undergraduates: $2734. ***Tuition waivers:*** Full or partial for minority students, children of alumni, employees or children of employees, senior citizens.

LOANS ***Student loans:*** $10,284,864 (100% need-based). 63% of past graduating class borrowed through all loan programs. *Average indebtedness per student:* $19,825. ***Average need-based loan:*** Freshmen: $3807; Undergraduates: $4787. ***Parent loans:*** $1,565,000 (100% need-based). ***Programs:*** Federal Direct (Subsidized and Unsubsidized Stafford, PLUS), Perkins, Federal Nursing, state.

WORK-STUDY ***Federal work-study:*** Total amount: $512,254; jobs available. ***State or other work-study/employment:*** Total amount: $204,833 (100% need-based). Part-time jobs available.

ATHLETIC AWARDS Total amount: $841,891 (100% non-need-based).

APPLYING FOR FINANCIAL AID ***Required financial aid form:*** FAFSA. ***Financial aid deadline (priority):*** 2/21. ***Notification date:*** Continuous. Students must reply within 3 weeks of notification.

CONTACT Deborah Faust, Director of Financial Aid, Lake Superior State University, 650 West Easterday Avenue, Sault Sainte Marie, MI 49783, 906-635-2678 or toll-free 888-800-LSSU Ext. 2231. *Fax:* 906-635-6669. *E-mail:* finaid@lssu.edu.

LAKEVIEW COLLEGE OF NURSING

Danville, IL

CONTACT Director of Financial Aid, Lakeview College of Nursing, 903 North Logan Avenue, Danville, IL 61832, 217-443-5238 or toll-free 217-443-5238 Ext. 5454 (in-state).

LAMAR UNIVERSITY

Beaumont, TX

Tuition & fees (TX res): $4080 **Average undergraduate aid package: $1343**

ABOUT THE INSTITUTION State-supported, coed. Awards: associate, bachelor's, master's, and doctoral degrees. 102 undergraduate majors. Total enrollment: 10,595. Undergraduates: 9,684. Freshmen: 1,683. Federal methodology is used as a basis for awarding need-based institutional aid.

UNDERGRADUATE EXPENSES for 2006–07 ***Tuition, state resident:*** full-time $2880. ***Tuition, nonresident:*** full-time $9504. Full-time tuition and fees vary according to course load. Part-time tuition and fees vary according to course load. ***College room and board:*** $5888; ***Room only:*** $3990. Room and board charges vary according to board plan and housing facility. ***Payment plan:*** Installment.

FRESHMAN FINANCIAL AID (Fall 2006, est.) 1030 applied for aid; of those 63% were deemed to have need. 95% of freshmen with need received aid; of those 17% had need fully met. ***Average percent of need met:*** 60% (excluding resources awarded to replace EFC). ***Average financial aid package:*** $1391 (excluding resources awarded to replace EFC). 40% of all full-time freshmen had no need and received non-need-based gift aid.

UNDERGRADUATE FINANCIAL AID (Fall 2006, est.) 4,559 applied for aid; of those 78% were deemed to have need. 91% of undergraduates with need received aid; of those 7% had need fully met. ***Average percent of need met:*** 45% (excluding resources awarded to replace EFC). ***Average financial aid package:*** $1343 (excluding resources awarded to replace EFC). 16% of all full-time undergraduates had no need and received non-need-based gift aid.

GIFT AID (NEED-BASED) ***Total amount:*** $14,904,597 (62% federal, 36% state, 2% institutional). ***Scholarships, grants, and awards:*** Federal Pell, FSEOG, state, college/university gift aid from institutional funds.

GIFT AID (NON-NEED-BASED) ***Total amount:*** $2,098,107 (52% institutional, 48% external sources). ***Receiving aid:*** Freshmen: 14% (200); Undergraduates: 9% (573). ***Average award:*** Freshmen: $900; Undergraduates: $900. ***Scholarships, grants, and awards by category:*** *Academic Interests/Achievement:* general academic interests/achievements. *Creative Arts/Performance:* general creative arts/performance. *Special Achievements/Activities:* general special achievements/activities.

LOANS ***Student loans:*** $21,141,277 (53% need-based, 47% non-need-based). 20% of past graduating class borrowed through all loan programs. *Average indebtedness per student:* $7408. ***Parent loans:*** $1,075,647 (100% need-based). ***Programs:*** FFEL (Subsidized and Unsubsidized Stafford, PLUS), Perkins, state, college/university.

WORK-STUDY ***Federal work-study:*** Total amount: $1,066,578; 261 jobs averaging $3651. ***State or other work-study/employment:*** Total amount: $74,726 (100% need-based). 23 part-time jobs averaging $3230.

ATHLETIC AWARDS Total amount: $215,628 (100% non-need-based).

APPLYING FOR FINANCIAL AID ***Required financial aid forms:*** FAFSA, institution's own form. ***Financial aid deadline (priority):*** 4/1. ***Notification date:*** Continuous beginning 5/1. Students must reply within 2 weeks of notification.

CONTACT Financial Aid Department, Lamar University, PO Box 10042, Beaumont, TX 77710, 409-880-8450. *Fax:* 409-880-8934. *E-mail:* finaid@hal.lamar.edu.

LAMBUTH UNIVERSITY

Jackson, TN

Tuition & fees: $17,400 — **Average undergraduate aid package: $17,187**

ABOUT THE INSTITUTION Independent United Methodist, coed. Awards: bachelor's degrees. 70 undergraduate majors. Total enrollment: 749. Undergraduates: 749. Freshmen: 166. Federal methodology is used as a basis for awarding need-based institutional aid.

UNDERGRADUATE EXPENSES for 2007–08 ***Application fee:*** $25. ***Comprehensive fee:*** $24,560 includes full-time tuition ($17,000), mandatory fees ($400), and room and board ($7160). ***College room only:*** $3410. ***Part-time tuition:*** $705 per credit hour. ***Part-time fees:*** $200 per term.

FRESHMAN FINANCIAL AID (Fall 2006, est.) 160 applied for aid; of those 80% were deemed to have need. 100% of freshmen with need received aid; of those 36% had need fully met. ***Average percent of need met:*** 81% (excluding resources awarded to replace EFC). ***Average financial aid package:*** $18,465 (excluding resources awarded to replace EFC). 15% of all full-time freshmen had no need and received non-need-based gift aid.

UNDERGRADUATE FINANCIAL AID (Fall 2006, est.) 651 applied for aid; of those 84% were deemed to have need. 100% of undergraduates with need received aid; of those 34% had need fully met. ***Average percent of need met:*** 78% (excluding resources awarded to replace EFC). ***Average financial aid package:*** $17,187 (excluding resources awarded to replace EFC). 15% of all full-time undergraduates had no need and received non-need-based gift aid.

GIFT AID (NEED-BASED) ***Total amount:*** $5,620,088 (14% federal, 25% state, 58% institutional, 3% external sources). ***Receiving aid:*** Freshmen: 74% (123); All full-time undergraduates: 72% (511). ***Average award:*** Freshmen: $12,920; Undergraduates: $10,969. ***Scholarships, grants, and awards:*** Federal Pell, FSEOG, state, private, college/university gift aid from institutional funds.

GIFT AID (NON-NEED-BASED) ***Total amount:*** $1,732,157 (15% state, 78% institutional, 7% external sources). ***Receiving aid:*** Freshmen: 15% (25); Undergraduates: 10% (72). ***Average award:*** Freshmen: $4838; Undergraduates: $7719. ***Scholarships, grants, and awards by category:*** *Academic Interests/Achievement:* biological sciences, business, communication, computer science, education, English, foreign languages, general academic interests/achievements, home economics, humanities, international studies, mathematics, physical sciences, premedicine, religion/biblical studies, social sciences. *Creative Arts/Performance:* dance, music, theater/drama. *Special Achievements/Activities:* cheerleading/drum major. *Special Characteristics:* children and siblings of alumni, children of faculty/staff, relatives of clergy, religious affiliation.

LOANS ***Student loans:*** $2,494,057 (73% need-based, 27% non-need-based). 65% of past graduating class borrowed through all loan programs. *Average indebtedness per student:* $19,008. ***Average need-based loan:*** Freshmen: $2341; Undergraduates: $3812. ***Parent loans:*** $350,500 (31% need-based, 69% non-need-based). ***Programs:*** FFEL (Subsidized and Unsubsidized Stafford, PLUS), Perkins, United Methodist Student Loans.

WORK-STUDY ***Federal work-study:*** Total amount: $127,004; 124 jobs averaging $1024. ***State or other work-study/employment:*** Total amount: $23,252 (8% need-based, 92% non-need-based). 25 part-time jobs averaging $930.

ATHLETIC AWARDS Total amount: $2,356,701 (57% need-based, 43% non-need-based).

APPLYING FOR FINANCIAL AID ***Required financial aid form:*** FAFSA. ***Financial aid deadline (priority):*** 2/15. ***Notification date:*** Continuous beginning 3/1. Students must reply by 5/1 or within 2 weeks of notification.

CONTACT Ms. Melissa Boyd, Director of Scholarships and Financial Aid, Lambuth University, 705 Lambuth Boulevard, Jackson, TN 38301, 731-425-3332 or toll-free 800-526-2884. *Fax:* 731-425-3496. *E-mail:* boyd-m@lambuth.edu.

LANCASTER BIBLE COLLEGE

Lancaster, PA

Tuition & fees: $13,800 — **Average undergraduate aid package: $10,551**

ABOUT THE INSTITUTION Independent nondenominational, coed. Awards: associate, bachelor's, and master's degrees and post-bachelor's certificates. 17 undergraduate majors. Total enrollment: 958. Undergraduates: 786. Freshmen: 109. Federal methodology is used as a basis for awarding need-based institutional aid.

UNDERGRADUATE EXPENSES for 2006–07 ***Application fee:*** $25. ***Comprehensive fee:*** $19,780 includes full-time tuition ($13,200), mandatory fees ($600), and room and board ($5980). ***College room only:*** $2620. Room and board charges vary according to board plan. ***Part-time tuition:*** $440 per credit. ***Part-time fees:*** $20 per credit. ***Payment plan:*** Installment.

FRESHMAN FINANCIAL AID (Fall 2006, est.) 92 applied for aid; of those 91% were deemed to have need. 100% of freshmen with need received aid; of those 10% had need fully met. ***Average percent of need met:*** 67% (excluding resources awarded to replace EFC). ***Average financial aid package:*** $10,582 (excluding resources awarded to replace EFC). 16% of all full-time freshmen had no need and received non-need-based gift aid.

UNDERGRADUATE FINANCIAL AID (Fall 2006, est.) 485 applied for aid; of those 91% were deemed to have need. 100% of undergraduates with need received aid; of those 14% had need fully met. ***Average percent of need met:*** 71% (excluding resources awarded to replace EFC). ***Average financial aid package:*** $10,551 (excluding resources awarded to replace EFC). 14% of all full-time undergraduates had no need and received non-need-based gift aid.

GIFT AID (NEED-BASED) ***Total amount:*** $2,688,159 (18% federal, 26% state, 50% institutional, 6% external sources). ***Receiving aid:*** Freshmen: 76% (81); All full-time undergraduates: 76% (406). ***Average award:*** Freshmen: $8250; Undergraduates: $6691. ***Scholarships, grants, and awards:*** Federal Pell, FSEOG, state, private, college/university gift aid from institutional funds, Office of Vocational Rehabilitation, Blindness and Visual Services Awards.

GIFT AID (NON-NEED-BASED) ***Total amount:*** $502,693 (86% institutional, 14% external sources). ***Receiving aid:*** Freshmen: 65% (69); Undergraduates: 60%

(323). ***Average award:*** Freshmen: $4807; Undergraduates: $4018. ***Scholarships, grants, and awards by category:*** *Academic Interests/Achievement:* 214 awards ($426,479 total): general academic interests/achievements. *Creative Arts/Performance:* 8 awards ($25,052 total): general creative arts/performance, music. *Special Achievements/Activities:* 87 awards ($80,400 total): general special achievements/activities, leadership, religious involvement. *Special Characteristics:* 311 awards ($1,214,970 total): adult students, children and siblings of alumni, children of current students, children of faculty/staff, international students, married students, previous college experience, relatives of clergy, religious affiliation, siblings of current students, spouses of current students. ***Tuition waivers:*** Full or partial for children of alumni, employees or children of employees, senior citizens.

LOANS ***Student loans:*** $2,348,991 (82% need-based, 18% non-need-based). 82% of past graduating class borrowed through all loan programs. *Average indebtedness per student:* $19,229. ***Average need-based loan:*** Freshmen: $2598; Undergraduates: $3753. ***Parent loans:*** $786,164 (41% need-based, 59% non-need-based). ***Programs:*** FFEL (Subsidized and Unsubsidized Stafford, PLUS), Perkins, state, alternative loans.

WORK-STUDY ***Federal work-study:*** Total amount: $104,312; 97 jobs averaging $2000.

APPLYING FOR FINANCIAL AID ***Required financial aid forms:*** FAFSA, state aid form. ***Financial aid deadline (priority):*** 5/1. ***Notification date:*** Continuous beginning 3/15. Students must reply within 3 weeks of notification.

CONTACT Karen Fox, Director of Financial Aid, Lancaster Bible College, PO Box 83403, Lancaster, PA 17608-3403, 717-560-8254 Ext. 5352 or toll-free 866-LBC4YOU. *Fax:* 717-560-8216. *E-mail:* kfox@lbc.edu.

LANDER UNIVERSITY

Greenwood, SC

CONTACT Director of Financial Aid, Lander University, 320 Stanley Avenue, Greenwood, SC 29649, 864-388-8340 or toll-free 888-452-6337. *Fax:* 864-388-8811. *E-mail:* fhardin@lander.edu.

LANE COLLEGE

Jackson, TN

CONTACT Ms. Ursula Singleton, Director of Financial Aid, Lane College, 545 Lane Avenue, Jackson, TN 38301, 731-426-7536 or toll-free 800-960-7533. *Fax:* 731-426-7652. *E-mail:* fao@lanecollege.edu.

LANGSTON UNIVERSITY

Langston, OK

CONTACT Yvonne Maxwell, Director of Financial Aid, Langston University, Page Hall, Room 311, Langston, OK 73050, 405-466-3282 or toll-free 405-466-3428 (in-state). *Fax:* 405-466-2986. *E-mail:* ymaxwell@lunet.edu.

LA ROCHE COLLEGE

Pittsburgh, PA

Tuition & fees: $18,220 | **Average undergraduate aid package: $11,056**

ABOUT THE INSTITUTION Independent religious, coed. Awards: associate, bachelor's, and master's degrees. 34 undergraduate majors. Total enrollment: 1,533. Undergraduates: 1,367. Freshmen: 263. Federal methodology is used as a basis for awarding need-based institutional aid.

UNDERGRADUATE EXPENSES for 2006–07 ***Application fee:*** $50. ***Comprehensive fee:*** $25,784 includes full-time tuition ($17,620), mandatory fees ($600), and room and board ($7564). ***College room only:*** $4738. Full-time tuition and fees vary according to program. Room and board charges vary according to board plan. ***Part-time tuition:*** $528 per credit. ***Part-time fees:*** $14 per credit; $50 per term. Part-time tuition and fees vary according to program. ***Payment plan:*** Installment.

FRESHMAN FINANCIAL AID (Fall 2006, est.) 248 applied for aid; of those 100% were deemed to have need. 100% of freshmen with need received aid. ***Average percent of need met:*** 87% (excluding resources awarded to replace EFC). ***Average financial aid package:*** $14,598 (excluding resources awarded to replace EFC). 35% of all full-time freshmen had no need and received non-need-based gift aid.

UNDERGRADUATE FINANCIAL AID (Fall 2006, est.) 1,033 applied for aid; of those 100% were deemed to have need. 100% of undergraduates with need received aid. ***Average percent of need met:*** 85% (excluding resources awarded to replace EFC). ***Average financial aid package:*** $11,056 (excluding resources awarded to replace EFC). 23% of all full-time undergraduates had no need and received non-need-based gift aid.

GIFT AID (NEED-BASED) ***Total amount:*** $3,669,459 (28% federal, 45% state, 27% institutional). ***Receiving aid:*** Freshmen: 64% (161); All full-time undergraduates: 53% (582). ***Average award:*** Freshmen: $5379; Undergraduates: $5188. ***Scholarships, grants, and awards:*** Federal Pell, FSEOG, state, private, college/university gift aid from institutional funds.

GIFT AID (NON-NEED-BASED) ***Total amount:*** $5,438,885 (99% institutional, 1% external sources). ***Receiving aid:*** Freshmen: 95% (238); Undergraduates: 59% (649). ***Average award:*** Freshmen: $9712; Undergraduates: $8132. ***Scholarships, grants, and awards by category:*** *Creative Arts/Performance:* 2 awards ($650 total): applied art and design. ***Tuition waivers:*** Full or partial for employees or children of employees, senior citizens. ***ROTC:*** Army cooperative, Air Force cooperative.

LOANS ***Student loans:*** $6,124,704 (57% need-based, 43% non-need-based). 80% of past graduating class borrowed through all loan programs. *Average indebtedness per student:* $18,000. ***Average need-based loan:*** Freshmen: $2886; Undergraduates: $4668. ***Parent loans:*** $1,930,610 (100% non-need-based). ***Programs:*** FFEL (Subsidized and Unsubsidized Stafford, PLUS), Perkins, state.

WORK-STUDY ***Federal work-study:*** Total amount: $265,808; 185 jobs averaging $2000.

APPLYING FOR FINANCIAL AID ***Required financial aid form:*** FAFSA. ***Financial aid deadline:*** 5/1 (priority: 5/1). ***Notification date:*** Continuous beginning 3/15. Students must reply within 2 weeks of notification.

CONTACT Mrs. Sharon Platt, Director of Financial Aid, La Roche College, 9000 Babcock Boulevard, Pittsburgh, PA 15237-5898, 412-536-1120 or toll-free 800-838-4LRC. *Fax:* 412-536-1072. *E-mail:* sharon.platt@laroche.edu.

LA SALLE UNIVERSITY

Philadelphia, PA

CONTACT Robert G. Voss, Dean of Admission and Financial Aid, La Salle University, 1900 West Olney Avenue, Philadelphia, PA 19141-1199, 215-951-1500 or toll-free 800-328-1910.

LASELL COLLEGE

Newton, MA

ABOUT THE INSTITUTION Independent, coed. Awards: bachelor's and master's degrees. 28 undergraduate majors. Total enrollment: 1,253. Undergraduates: 1,216. Freshmen: 374.

GIFT AID (NEED-BASED) ***Scholarships, grants, and awards:*** Federal Pell, FSEOG, state, private, college/university gift aid from institutional funds.

GIFT AID (NON-NEED-BASED) ***Scholarships, grants, and awards by category:*** *Academic Interests/Achievement:* general academic interests/achievements. *Special Achievements/Activities:* community service, general special achievements/activities. *Special Characteristics:* children and siblings of alumni, children of faculty/staff, siblings of current students, twins.

LOANS ***Programs:*** FFEL (Subsidized and Unsubsidized Stafford, PLUS), Perkins, state, alternative loans.

WORK-STUDY ***Federal work-study:*** Total amount: $290,500; 632 jobs averaging $2000.

APPLYING FOR FINANCIAL AID ***Required financial aid forms:*** FAFSA, institution's own form.

CONTACT Michele R. Kosboth, Director of Student Financial Planning, Lasell College, 1844 Commonwealth Avenue, Newton, MA 02466-2709, 617-243-2227 or toll-free 888-LASELL-4. *Fax:* 617-243-2326. *E-mail:* finaid@lasell.edu.

LA SIERRA UNIVERSITY

Riverside, CA

Tuition & fees: $21,846 | **Average undergraduate aid package: $15,006**

ABOUT THE INSTITUTION Independent Seventh-day Adventist, coed. Awards: bachelor's, master's, and doctoral degrees and post-bachelor's and post-master's certificates. 33 undergraduate majors. Total enrollment: 1,896. Undergraduates: 1,578. Freshmen: 323. Federal methodology is used as a basis for awarding need-based institutional aid.

UNDERGRADUATE EXPENSES for 2007–08 ***Application fee:*** $30. ***Comprehensive fee:*** $28,176 includes full-time tuition ($21,060), mandatory fees ($786), and room and board ($6330). ***Part-time tuition:*** $585 per unit.

FRESHMAN FINANCIAL AID (Fall 2005) 310 applied for aid; of those 89% were deemed to have need. 100% of freshmen with need received aid; of those 12% had need fully met. ***Average percent of need met:*** 65% (excluding resources awarded to replace EFC). ***Average financial aid package:*** $14,520 (excluding resources awarded to replace EFC). 25% of all full-time freshmen had no need and received non-need-based gift aid.

UNDERGRADUATE FINANCIAL AID (Fall 2005) 1,114 applied for aid; of those 91% were deemed to have need. 100% of undergraduates with need received aid; of those 12% had need fully met. ***Average percent of need met:*** 64% (excluding resources awarded to replace EFC). ***Average financial aid package:*** $15,006 (excluding resources awarded to replace EFC). 26% of all full-time undergraduates had no need and received non-need-based gift aid.

GIFT AID (NEED-BASED) ***Total amount:*** $11,577,602 (17% federal, 28% state, 42% institutional, 13% external sources). ***Receiving aid:*** Freshmen: 73% (276); All full-time undergraduates: 69% (1,001). ***Average award:*** Freshmen: $12,599; Undergraduates: $11,281. ***Scholarships, grants, and awards:*** Federal Pell, FSEOG, state, private, college/university gift aid from institutional funds.

GIFT AID (NON-NEED-BASED) ***Total amount:*** $2,924,320 (75% institutional, 25% external sources). ***Average award:*** Freshmen: $6615; Undergraduates: $5847. ***Scholarships, grants, and awards by category:*** *Academic Interests/Achievement:* general academic interests/achievements. *Creative Arts/Performance:* music, theater/drama. *Special Achievements/Activities:* leadership. *Special Characteristics:* adult students, children of faculty/staff, relatives of clergy, religious affiliation, siblings of current students.

LOANS ***Student loans:*** $8,396,402 (90% need-based, 10% non-need-based). 77% of past graduating class borrowed through all loan programs. *Average indebtedness per student:* $28,876. ***Average need-based loan:*** Freshmen: $2706; Undergraduates: $4856. ***Parent loans:*** $2,489,337 (84% need-based, 16% non-need-based). ***Programs:*** FFEL (Subsidized and Unsubsidized Stafford, PLUS), Perkins.

WORK-STUDY ***Federal work-study:*** Total amount: $622,445; 269 jobs averaging $2314.

APPLYING FOR FINANCIAL AID ***Required financial aid forms:*** FAFSA, state aid form. ***Financial aid deadline (priority):*** 3/2. ***Notification date:*** Continuous beginning 4/15. Students must reply by 9/1.

CONTACT Financial Aid Office, La Sierra University, 4500 Riverwalk Parkway, Riverside, CA 92515, 951-785-2175 or toll-free 800-874-5587. *Fax:* 951-785-2942. *E-mail:* sfs@lasierra.edu.

LAURA AND ALVIN SIEGAL COLLEGE OF JUDAIC STUDIES

Beachwood, OH

ABOUT THE INSTITUTION Independent, coed. Awards: bachelor's and master's degrees. 7 undergraduate majors. Total enrollment: 146. Undergraduates: 11. Freshmen: 1.

GIFT AID (NEED-BASED) ***Scholarships, grants, and awards:*** college/university gift aid from institutional funds.

GIFT AID (NON-NEED-BASED) ***Scholarships, grants, and awards by category:*** *Academic Interests/Achievement:* education, religion/biblical studies.

APPLYING FOR FINANCIAL AID ***Required financial aid form:*** institution's own form.

CONTACT Ruth Kronick, Director of Student Services, Laura and Alvin Siegal College of Judaic Studies, 26500 Shaker Boulevard, Cleveland, OH 44122, 216-464-4050 Ext. 101 or toll-free 888-336-2257. *Fax:* 216-464-5278. *E-mail:* rkronick@siegalcollege.edu.

LAWRENCE TECHNOLOGICAL UNIVERSITY

Southfield, MI

Tuition & fees: $19,443 | **Average undergraduate aid package: $14,891**

ABOUT THE INSTITUTION Independent, coed. Awards: associate, bachelor's, master's, and doctoral degrees. 34 undergraduate majors. Total enrollment: 4,049. Undergraduates: 2,680. Freshmen: 329. Federal methodology is used as a basis for awarding need-based institutional aid.

UNDERGRADUATE EXPENSES for 2006–07 ***Application fee:*** $30. ***Comprehensive fee:*** $26,709 includes full-time tuition ($19,073), mandatory fees ($370), and room and board ($7266). ***College room only:*** $5286. ***Part-time tuition:*** $635 per credit hour. ***Part-time fees:*** $185 per term.

FRESHMAN FINANCIAL AID (Fall 2005) 295 applied for aid; of those 72% were deemed to have need. 100% of freshmen with need received aid; of those 26% had need fully met. ***Average percent of need met:*** 72% (excluding resources awarded to replace EFC). ***Average financial aid package:*** $14,255 (excluding resources awarded to replace EFC). 18% of all full-time freshmen had no need and received non-need-based gift aid.

UNDERGRADUATE FINANCIAL AID (Fall 2005) 1,455 applied for aid; of those 70% were deemed to have need. 100% of undergraduates with need received aid; of those 19% had need fully met. ***Average percent of need met:*** 69% (excluding resources awarded to replace EFC). ***Average financial aid package:*** $14,891 (excluding resources awarded to replace EFC). 18% of all full-time undergraduates had no need and received non-need-based gift aid.

GIFT AID (NEED-BASED) ***Total amount:*** $7,747,521 (20% federal, 26% state, 52% institutional, 2% external sources). ***Receiving aid:*** Freshmen: 65% (201); All full-time undergraduates: 57% (921). ***Average award:*** Freshmen: $7640; Undergraduates: $7180. ***Scholarships, grants, and awards:*** Federal Pell, FSEOG, state, private, college/university gift aid from institutional funds, Michigan National Guard and ROTC.

GIFT AID (NON-NEED-BASED) ***Total amount:*** $2,501,531 (1% federal, 9% state, 86% institutional, 4% external sources). ***Receiving aid:*** Freshmen: 49% (152); Undergraduates: 36% (578). ***Average award:*** Freshmen: $6570; Undergraduates: $6648. ***Scholarships, grants, and awards by category:*** *Academic Interests/Achievement:* 1,342 awards ($6,479,459 total): architecture, business, computer science, education, engineering/technologies, general academic interests/achievements, humanities, international studies, mathematics, military science, physical sciences. *Special Achievements/Activities:* general special achievements/activities. *Special Characteristics:* 72 awards ($480,598 total): children of faculty/staff, members of minority groups. ***ROTC:*** Army cooperative, Naval cooperative, Air Force cooperative.

LOANS ***Student loans:*** $8,647,743 (94% need-based, 6% non-need-based). 58% of past graduating class borrowed through all loan programs. *Average indebtedness per student:* $29,224. ***Average need-based loan:*** Freshmen: $2704; Undergraduates: $4199. ***Parent loans:*** $5,925,036 (78% need-based, 22% non-need-based). ***Programs:*** FFEL (Subsidized and Unsubsidized Stafford, PLUS), Perkins, state, college/university, alternative loans.

WORK-STUDY ***Federal work-study:*** Total amount: $1,108,995; 140 jobs averaging $4000. ***State or other work-study/employment:*** Total amount: $59,303 (100% need-based). 18 part-time jobs averaging $2000.

APPLYING FOR FINANCIAL AID ***Required financial aid form:*** FAFSA. ***Financial aid deadline (priority):*** 4/1. ***Notification date:*** Continuous beginning 4/1. Students must reply within 2 weeks of notification.

CONTACT Mr. Mark Martin, Director of Financial Aid, Lawrence Technological University, 21000 West Ten Mile Road, Southfield, MI 48075-1058, 248-204-2126 or toll-free 800-225-5588. *Fax:* 248-204-2124. *E-mail:* m_martin@ltu.edu.

LAWRENCE UNIVERSITY

Appleton, WI

Tuition & fees: $29,598 | **Average undergraduate aid package: $23,900**

ABOUT THE INSTITUTION Independent, coed. Awards: bachelor's degrees. 58 undergraduate majors. Total enrollment: 1,480. Undergraduates: 1,480. Freshmen: 372. Institutional methodology is used as a basis for awarding need-based institutional aid.

UNDERGRADUATE EXPENSES for 2006–07 ***Application fee:*** $40. ***Comprehensive fee:*** $36,480 includes full-time tuition ($29,376), mandatory fees ($222), and room and board ($6882). ***College room only:*** $2934.

FRESHMAN FINANCIAL AID (Fall 2006, est.) 289 applied for aid; of those 88% were deemed to have need. 100% of freshmen with need received aid; of those 79% had need fully met. ***Average percent of need met:*** 94% (excluding resources awarded to replace EFC). ***Average financial aid package:*** $23,800 (excluding resources awarded to replace EFC). 26% of all full-time freshmen had no need and received non-need-based gift aid.

UNDERGRADUATE FINANCIAL AID (Fall 2006, est.) 1,060 applied for aid; of those 89% were deemed to have need. 100% of undergraduates with need

received aid; of those 94% had need fully met. ***Average percent of need met:*** 96% (excluding resources awarded to replace EFC). ***Average financial aid package:*** $23,900 (excluding resources awarded to replace EFC). 26% of all full-time undergraduates had no need and received non-need-based gift aid.

GIFT AID (NEED-BASED) ***Total amount:*** $14,993,396 (7% federal, 5% state, 85% institutional, 3% external sources). ***Receiving aid:*** Freshmen: 68% (253); All full-time undergraduates: 66% (939). ***Average award:*** Freshmen: $17,350; Undergraduates: $16,300. ***Scholarships, grants, and awards:*** Federal Pell, FSEOG, state, private, college/university gift aid from institutional funds.

GIFT AID (NON-NEED-BASED) ***Total amount:*** $4,153,460 (96% institutional, 4% external sources). ***Average award:*** Freshmen: $10,480; Undergraduates: $9707. ***Scholarships, grants, and awards by category:*** *Academic Interests/Achievement:* 681 awards ($5,396,831 total): general academic interests/achievements. *Creative Arts/Performance:* 233 awards ($1,326,271 total): music. *Special Characteristics:* 134 awards ($677,676 total): children and siblings of alumni, members of minority groups.

LOANS ***Student loans:*** $6,194,945 (80% need-based, 20% non-need-based). 70% of past graduating class borrowed through all loan programs. *Average indebtedness per student:* $22,626. ***Average need-based loan:*** Freshmen: $4360; Undergraduates: $6150. ***Parent loans:*** $2,318,383 (100% non-need-based). ***Programs:*** Federal Direct (Subsidized and Unsubsidized Stafford, PLUS), FFEL (PLUS), Perkins, alternative loans.

WORK-STUDY ***Federal work-study:*** Total amount: $1,565,260; 670 jobs averaging $2295. ***State or other work-study/employment:*** Total amount: $902,732 (32% need-based, 68% non-need-based). 363 part-time jobs averaging $2465.

APPLYING FOR FINANCIAL AID ***Required financial aid forms:*** FAFSA, institution's own form, signed copies of 2006 federal tax returns and W-2 for parents and students. ***Financial aid deadline (priority):*** 3/15. ***Notification date:*** Continuous beginning 3/15. Students must reply by 5/1.

CONTACT Mrs. Sara Beth Holman, Director of Financial Aid, Lawrence University, PO Box 599, Appleton, WI 54912-0599, 920-832-6583 or toll-free 800-227-0982. *Fax:* 920-832-6582. *E-mail:* sara.b.holman@lawrence.edu.

LEBANON VALLEY COLLEGE

Annville, PA

Tuition & fees: $26,385 **Average undergraduate aid package: $19,056**

ABOUT THE INSTITUTION Independent United Methodist, coed. Awards: associate, bachelor's, master's, and first professional degrees and post-bachelor's certificates. 53 undergraduate majors. Total enrollment: 1,961. Undergraduates: 1,804. Freshmen: 447. Federal methodology is used as a basis for awarding need-based institutional aid.

UNDERGRADUATE EXPENSES for 2006–07 ***Application fee:*** $30. ***Comprehensive fee:*** $33,500 includes full-time tuition ($25,710), mandatory fees ($675), and room and board ($7115). ***College room only:*** $3475. Room and board charges vary according to board plan and housing facility. ***Part-time tuition:*** $455 per credit. Part-time tuition and fees vary according to class time and degree level. ***Payment plans:*** Tuition prepayment, installment.

FRESHMAN FINANCIAL AID (Fall 2006, est.) 413 applied for aid; of those 87% were deemed to have need. 100% of freshmen with need received aid; of those 35% had need fully met. ***Average percent of need met:*** 87% (excluding resources awarded to replace EFC). ***Average financial aid package:*** $18,510 (excluding resources awarded to replace EFC). 16% of all full-time freshmen had no need and received non-need-based gift aid.

UNDERGRADUATE FINANCIAL AID (Fall 2006, est.) 1,439 applied for aid; of those 87% were deemed to have need. 100% of undergraduates with need received aid; of those 33% had need fully met. ***Average percent of need met:*** 87% (excluding resources awarded to replace EFC). ***Average financial aid package:*** $19,056 (excluding resources awarded to replace EFC). 19% of all full-time undergraduates had no need and received non-need-based gift aid.

GIFT AID (NEED-BASED) ***Total amount:*** $16,447,671 (5% federal, 13% state, 82% institutional). ***Receiving aid:*** Freshmen: 80% (356); All full-time undergraduates: 76% (1,235). ***Average award:*** Freshmen: $15,830; Undergraduates: $16,038. ***Scholarships, grants, and awards:*** Federal Pell, FSEOG, state, private, college/university gift aid from institutional funds, Federal Academic Competitiveness Grant (ACG).

GIFT AID (NON-NEED-BASED) ***Total amount:*** $5,055,044 (2% state, 84% institutional, 14% external sources). ***Receiving aid:*** Freshmen: 12% (54); Undergraduates: 9% (148). ***Average award:*** Freshmen: $10,976; Undergraduates: $10,607. ***Scholarships, grants, and awards by category:*** *Academic Interests/Achievement:* 1,324 awards ($13,734,052 total): biological sciences, general academic interests/achievements. *Creative Arts/Performance:* 42 awards ($53,180 total): music. *Special Achievements/Activities:* 103 awards ($52,250 total): general special achievements/activities, junior miss. *Special Characteristics:* 185 awards ($987,607 total): children and siblings of alumni, children of faculty/staff, ethnic background, international students. ***Tuition waivers:*** Full or partial for employees or children of employees, senior citizens.

LOANS ***Student loans:*** $11,426,528 (38% need-based, 62% non-need-based). 83% of past graduating class borrowed through all loan programs. *Average indebtedness per student:* $28,051. ***Average need-based loan:*** Freshmen: $3422; Undergraduates: $4098. ***Parent loans:*** $5,658,310 (100% non-need-based). ***Programs:*** FFEL (Subsidized and Unsubsidized Stafford, PLUS), Perkins.

WORK-STUDY ***Federal work-study:*** Total amount: $1,214,884; 804 jobs averaging $1196.

APPLYING FOR FINANCIAL AID ***Required financial aid forms:*** FAFSA, institution's own form. ***Financial aid deadline (priority):*** 3/1. ***Notification date:*** Continuous beginning 3/1. Students must reply by 5/1 or within 2 weeks of notification.

CONTACT Kendra M. Feigert, Director of Financial Aid, Lebanon Valley College, 101 North College Avenue, Annville, PA 17003, 866-582-4236 or toll-free 866-LVC-4ADM. *Fax:* 717-867-6027. *E-mail:* feigert@lvc.edu.

LEES-MCRAE COLLEGE

Banner Elk, NC

CONTACT Lester McKenzie, Assistant Dean of Students for Financial Aid, Lees-McRae College, PO Box 128, Banner Elk, NC 28604-0128, 828-898-8793 or toll-free 800-280-4562. *Fax:* 828-898-8814. *E-mail:* mckenzie@lmc.edu.

LEE UNIVERSITY

Cleveland, TN

Tuition & fees: $10,258 **Average undergraduate aid package: $8301**

ABOUT THE INSTITUTION Independent religious, coed. Awards: bachelor's and master's degrees. 33 undergraduate majors. Total enrollment: 4,012. Undergraduates: 3,724. Freshmen: 812. Federal methodology is used as a basis for awarding need-based institutional aid.

UNDERGRADUATE EXPENSES for 2006–07 ***Application fee:*** $25. ***Comprehensive fee:*** $15,282 includes full-time tuition ($9888), mandatory fees ($370), and room and board ($5024). ***College room only:*** $2434. Room and board charges vary according to board plan and housing facility. ***Part-time tuition:*** $412 per credit hour. ***Payment plan:*** Deferred payment.

FRESHMAN FINANCIAL AID (Fall 2006, est.) 609 applied for aid; of those 75% were deemed to have need. 98% of freshmen with need received aid; of those 26% had need fully met. ***Average percent of need met:*** 62% (excluding resources awarded to replace EFC). ***Average financial aid package:*** $8591 (excluding resources awarded to replace EFC). 29% of all full-time freshmen had no need and received non-need-based gift aid.

UNDERGRADUATE FINANCIAL AID (Fall 2006, est.) 2,588 applied for aid; of those 81% were deemed to have need. 98% of undergraduates with need received aid; of those 17% had need fully met. ***Average percent of need met:*** 53% (excluding resources awarded to replace EFC). ***Average financial aid package:*** $8301 (excluding resources awarded to replace EFC). 26% of all full-time undergraduates had no need and received non-need-based gift aid.

GIFT AID (NEED-BASED) ***Total amount:*** $9,690,820 (35% federal, 22% state, 40% institutional, 3% external sources). ***Receiving aid:*** Freshmen: 5% (40); All full-time undergraduates: 51% (1,708). ***Average award:*** Freshmen: $7583; Undergraduates: $6173. ***Scholarships, grants, and awards:*** Federal Pell, FSEOG, state, private, college/university gift aid from institutional funds.

GIFT AID (NON-NEED-BASED) ***Total amount:*** $4,884,820 (20% state, 74% institutional, 6% external sources). ***Receiving aid:*** Freshmen: 11% (93); Undergraduates: 6% (217). ***Average award:*** Freshmen: $8136; Undergraduates: $7616. ***Scholarships, grants, and awards by category:*** *Academic Interests/Achievement:* 1,119 awards ($5,757,468 total): biological sciences, business, communication, education, general academic interests/achievements, religion/biblical studies. *Creative Arts/Performance:* 222 awards ($245,220 total): music, theater/drama. *Special Achievements/Activities:* 457 awards ($648,783 total): cheerleading/drum major, leadership, religious involvement. *Special Characteristics:*

650 awards ($1,791,056 total): children of faculty/staff, local/state students, siblings of current students, spouses of current students. ***Tuition waivers:*** Full or partial for employees or children of employees.

LOANS ***Student loans:*** $14,182,380 (75% need-based, 25% non-need-based). 70% of past graduating class borrowed through all loan programs. *Average indebtedness per student:* $27,308. ***Average need-based loan:*** Freshmen: $2781; Undergraduates: $3939. ***Parent loans:*** $2,806,121 (37% need-based, 63% non-need-based). ***Programs:*** FFEL (Subsidized and Unsubsidized Stafford, PLUS), Perkins, college/university.

WORK-STUDY ***Federal work-study:*** Total amount: $293,024; 200 jobs averaging $1465. ***State or other work-study/employment:*** Total amount: $600,000 (100% non-need-based). 350 part-time jobs averaging $1714.

ATHLETIC AWARDS Total amount: $1,337,260 (34% need-based, 66% non-need-based).

APPLYING FOR FINANCIAL AID ***Required financial aid forms:*** FAFSA, institution's own form. ***Financial aid deadline (priority):*** 3/15. ***Notification date:*** Continuous beginning 2/1. Students must reply within 3 weeks of notification.

CONTACT Mr. Michael Ellis, Director of Student Financial Aid, Lee University, 1120 North Ocoee Street, Cleveland, TN 37320-3450, 423-614-8300 or toll-free 800-533-9930. *Fax:* 423-614-8308. *E-mail:* finaid@leeuniversity.edu.

LEHIGH UNIVERSITY

Bethlehem, PA

Tuition & fees: $33,770 **Average undergraduate aid package: $26,584**

ABOUT THE INSTITUTION Independent, coed. Awards: bachelor's, master's, and doctoral degrees and post-bachelor's and post-master's certificates. 77 undergraduate majors. Total enrollment: 6,858. Undergraduates: 4,743. Freshmen: 1,217. Institutional methodology is used as a basis for awarding need-based institutional aid.

UNDERGRADUATE EXPENSES for 2006–07 ***Application fee:*** $65. ***Comprehensive fee:*** $42,690 includes full-time tuition ($33,470), mandatory fees ($300), and room and board ($8920). ***College room only:*** $5100. Room and board charges vary according to board plan and student level. ***Part-time tuition:*** $1395 per credit. ***Payment plans:*** Tuition prepayment, installment.

FRESHMAN FINANCIAL AID (Fall 2006, est.) 801 applied for aid; of those 75% were deemed to have need. 100% of freshmen with need received aid; of those 52% had need fully met. ***Average percent of need met:*** 96% (excluding resources awarded to replace EFC). ***Average financial aid package:*** $26,697 (excluding resources awarded to replace EFC). 8% of all full-time freshmen had no need and received non-need-based gift aid.

UNDERGRADUATE FINANCIAL AID (Fall 2006, est.) 2,619 applied for aid; of those 86% were deemed to have need. 99% of undergraduates with need received aid; of those 51% had need fully met. ***Average percent of need met:*** 96% (excluding resources awarded to replace EFC). ***Average financial aid package:*** $26,584 (excluding resources awarded to replace EFC). 6% of all full-time undergraduates had no need and received non-need-based gift aid.

GIFT AID (NEED-BASED) ***Total amount:*** $42,301,099 (5% federal, 3% state, 92% institutional). ***Receiving aid:*** Freshmen: 45% (545); All full-time undergraduates: 43% (1,992). ***Average award:*** Freshmen: $22,960; Undergraduates: $21,794. ***Scholarships, grants, and awards:*** Federal Pell, FSEOG, state, private, college/university gift aid from institutional funds, United Negro College Fund.

GIFT AID (NON-NEED-BASED) ***Total amount:*** $7,215,331 (1% state, 74% institutional, 25% external sources). ***Receiving aid:*** Freshmen: 7% (89); Undergraduates: 7% (342). ***Average award:*** Freshmen: $11,165; Undergraduates: $10,204. ***Scholarships, grants, and awards by category:*** *Academic Interests/Achievement:* 461 awards ($4,908,055 total): communication, general academic interests/achievements, military science. *Creative Arts/Performance:* 18 awards ($36,000 total): general creative arts/performance, music, performing arts, theater/drama. *Special Achievements/Activities:* general special achievements/activities. ***Tuition waivers:*** Full or partial for employees or children of employees, senior citizens. ***ROTC:*** Army.

LOANS ***Student loans:*** $20,350,892 (44% need-based, 56% non-need-based). 53% of past graduating class borrowed through all loan programs. *Average indebtedness per student:* $25,603. ***Average need-based loan:*** Freshmen: $2912; Undergraduates: $4367. ***Parent loans:*** $8,674,400 (100% non-need-based). ***Programs:*** FFEL (Subsidized and Unsubsidized Stafford, PLUS), Perkins, college/university, alternative loans.

WORK-STUDY ***Federal work-study:*** Total amount: $1,971,871; 1,259 jobs averaging $1566. ***State or other work-study/employment:*** Total amount: $772,711 (11% need-based, 89% non-need-based). 156 part-time jobs averaging $4413.

ATHLETIC AWARDS Total amount: $2,538,115 (52% need-based, 48% non-need-based).

APPLYING FOR FINANCIAL AID ***Required financial aid forms:*** FAFSA, CSS Financial Aid PROFILE, noncustodial (divorced/separated) parent's statement, business/farm supplement. ***Financial aid deadline:*** 2/1. ***Notification date:*** 3/30. Students must reply by 5/1 or within 3 weeks of notification.

CONTACT Linda F. Bell, Director of Financial Aid, Lehigh University, 218 West Packer Avenue, Bethlehem, PA 18015-3094, 610-758-3181. *Fax:* 610-758-6211. *E-mail:* lfn0@lehigh.edu.

LEHMAN COLLEGE OF THE CITY UNIVERSITY OF NEW YORK

Bronx, NY

Tuition & fees (NY res): $4290 **Average undergraduate aid package: $3537**

ABOUT THE INSTITUTION State and locally supported, coed. Awards: bachelor's and master's degrees and post-master's certificates. 53 undergraduate majors. Total enrollment: 10,814. Undergraduates: 8,747. Freshmen: 932. Federal methodology is used as a basis for awarding need-based institutional aid.

UNDERGRADUATE EXPENSES for 2006–07 ***Application fee:*** $65. ***Tuition, state resident:*** full-time $4000; part-time $170 per credit. ***Tuition, nonresident:*** full-time $10,800; part-time $360 per credit.

FRESHMAN FINANCIAL AID (Fall 2006, est.) 697 applied for aid; of those 100% were deemed to have need. 100% of freshmen with need received aid; of those 2% had need fully met. ***Average percent of need met:*** 74% (excluding resources awarded to replace EFC). ***Average financial aid package:*** $3524 (excluding resources awarded to replace EFC). 7% of all full-time freshmen had no need and received non-need-based gift aid.

UNDERGRADUATE FINANCIAL AID (Fall 2006, est.) 4,275 applied for aid; of those 99% were deemed to have need. 100% of undergraduates with need received aid; of those 3% had need fully met. ***Average percent of need met:*** 68% (excluding resources awarded to replace EFC). ***Average financial aid package:*** $3537 (excluding resources awarded to replace EFC). 2% of all full-time undergraduates had no need and received non-need-based gift aid.

GIFT AID (NEED-BASED) ***Total amount:*** $24,718,176 (56% federal, 43% state, 1% institutional). ***Receiving aid:*** Freshmen: 80% (634); All full-time undergraduates: 77% (3,927). ***Average award:*** Freshmen: $1531; Undergraduates: $1361. ***Scholarships, grants, and awards:*** Federal Pell, FSEOG, state, college/university gift aid from institutional funds.

GIFT AID (NON-NEED-BASED) ***Total amount:*** $783,906 (9% state, 23% institutional, 68% external sources). ***Receiving aid:*** Freshmen: 36% (285); Undergraduates: 11% (585). ***Average award:*** Freshmen: $1219; Undergraduates: $1400. ***ROTC:*** Army cooperative.

LOANS ***Student loans:*** $6,561,368 (100% need-based). 37% of past graduating class borrowed through all loan programs. *Average indebtedness per student:* $10,500. ***Average need-based loan:*** Freshmen: $1440; Undergraduates: $1559. ***Programs:*** Federal Direct (Subsidized and Unsubsidized Stafford, PLUS), Perkins.

WORK-STUDY ***Federal work-study:*** Total amount: $1,918,159; 510 jobs averaging $950.

APPLYING FOR FINANCIAL AID ***Required financial aid forms:*** FAFSA, state aid form. ***Financial aid deadline:*** Continuous. ***Notification date:*** Continuous beginning 3/1.

CONTACT David Martinez, Director of Financial Aid, Lehman College of the City University of New York, 250 Bedford Park Boulevard West, Bronx, NY 10468-1589, 718-960-8545 or toll-free 877-Lehman1 (out-of-state). *Fax:* 718-960-8328. *E-mail:* idmlc@cunyvm.cuny.edu.

LE MOYNE COLLEGE

Syracuse, NY

Tuition & fees: $22,580 **Average undergraduate aid package: $16,821**

ABOUT THE INSTITUTION Independent Roman Catholic (Jesuit), coed. Awards: bachelor's and master's degrees and post-bachelor's and post-master's certificates. 54 undergraduate majors. Total enrollment: 3,536. Undergraduates: 2,771. Freshmen: 545. Both federal and institutional methodology are used as a basis for awarding need-based institutional aid.

UNDERGRADUATE EXPENSES for 2006–07 ***Application fee:*** $35. ***Comprehensive fee:*** $31,200 includes full-time tuition ($21,860), mandatory fees ($720), and room and board ($8620). ***College room only:*** $5450. Room and board charges vary according to board plan and housing facility. ***Part-time tuition:*** $464 per credit hour. Part-time tuition and fees vary according to class time. ***Payment plans:*** Installment, deferred payment.

FRESHMAN FINANCIAL AID (Fall 2005) 472 applied for aid; of those 88% were deemed to have need. 100% of freshmen with need received aid; of those 37% had need fully met. ***Average percent of need met:*** 85% (excluding resources awarded to replace EFC). ***Average financial aid package:*** $18,423 (excluding resources awarded to replace EFC). 13% of all full-time freshmen had no need and received non-need-based gift aid.

UNDERGRADUATE FINANCIAL AID (Fall 2005) 2,088 applied for aid; of those 89% were deemed to have need. 100% of undergraduates with need received aid; of those 28% had need fully met. ***Average percent of need met:*** 78% (excluding resources awarded to replace EFC). ***Average financial aid package:*** $16,821 (excluding resources awarded to replace EFC). 10% of all full-time undergraduates had no need and received non-need-based gift aid.

GIFT AID (NEED-BASED) ***Total amount:*** $22,926,077 (10% federal, 15% state, 72% institutional, 3% external sources). ***Receiving aid:*** Freshmen: 80% (417); All full-time undergraduates: 79% (1,841). ***Average award:*** Freshmen: $15,453; Undergraduates: $12,945. ***Scholarships, grants, and awards:*** Federal Pell, FSEOG, state, private, college/university gift aid from institutional funds.

GIFT AID (NON-NEED-BASED) ***Total amount:*** $2,962,970 (3% state, 95% institutional, 2% external sources). ***Receiving aid:*** Freshmen: 50% (259); Undergraduates: 42% (972). ***Average award:*** Freshmen: $11,627; Undergraduates: $9415. ***Scholarships, grants, and awards by category:*** *Academic Interests/Achievement:* 336 awards ($4,249,232 total): general academic interests/achievements. *Special Achievements/Activities:* 516 awards ($3,071,900 total): leadership. *Special Characteristics:* 109 awards ($376,750 total): children and siblings of alumni, members of minority groups. ***Tuition waivers:*** Full or partial for employees or children of employees. ***ROTC:*** Army cooperative, Air Force cooperative.

LOANS ***Student loans:*** $10,759,129 (94% need-based, 6% non-need-based). 87% of past graduating class borrowed through all loan programs. *Average indebtedness per student:* $18,360. ***Average need-based loan:*** Freshmen: $3091; Undergraduates: $4423. ***Parent loans:*** $4,448,816 (85% need-based, 15% non-need-based). ***Programs:*** FFEL (Subsidized and Unsubsidized Stafford, PLUS), Perkins.

WORK-STUDY ***Federal work-study:*** Total amount: $316,648; 263 jobs averaging $832.

ATHLETIC AWARDS Total amount: $1,250,074 (76% need-based, 24% non-need-based).

APPLYING FOR FINANCIAL AID ***Required financial aid forms:*** FAFSA, institution's own form, state aid form. ***Financial aid deadline (priority):*** 2/1. ***Notification date:*** 3/15. Students must reply by 5/1 or within 2 weeks of notification.

CONTACT Mr. William Cheetham, Director of Financial Aid, Le Moyne College, Financial Aid Office, Syracuse, NY 13214-1301, 315-445-4400 or toll-free 800-333-4733. *Fax:* 315-445-4182. *E-mail:* cheethwc@lemoyne.edu.

LeMOYNE-OWEN COLLEGE

Memphis, TN

Tuition & fees: $10,318 **Average undergraduate aid package: $9309**

ABOUT THE INSTITUTION Independent religious, coed. Awards: bachelor's degrees and post-bachelor's certificates. 20 undergraduate majors. Total enrollment: 714. Undergraduates: 714. Freshmen: 89. Federal methodology is used as a basis for awarding need-based institutional aid.

UNDERGRADUATE EXPENSES for 2006–07 ***Application fee:*** $25. ***Comprehensive fee:*** $14,886 includes full-time tuition ($10,098), mandatory fees ($220), and room and board ($4568). ***College room only:*** $2258. Room and board charges vary according to board plan. ***Part-time tuition:*** $421 per credit hour. ***Payment plan:*** Installment.

FRESHMAN FINANCIAL AID (Fall 2005) 109 applied for aid; of those 98% were deemed to have need. 94% of freshmen with need received aid; of those 4% had need fully met. ***Average percent of need met:*** 43% (excluding resources awarded to replace EFC). ***Average financial aid package:*** $7197 (excluding resources awarded to replace EFC). 9% of all full-time freshmen had no need and received non-need-based gift aid.

UNDERGRADUATE FINANCIAL AID (Fall 2005) 581 applied for aid; of those 96% were deemed to have need. 97% of undergraduates with need received aid; of those 6% had need fully met. ***Average percent of need met:*** 55% (excluding resources awarded to replace EFC). ***Average financial aid package:*** $9309 (excluding resources awarded to replace EFC). 6% of all full-time undergraduates had no need and received non-need-based gift aid.

GIFT AID (NEED-BASED) ***Total amount:*** $4,365,989 (50% federal, 22% state, 21% institutional, 7% external sources). ***Receiving aid:*** Freshmen: 80% (96); All full-time undergraduates: 85% (508). ***Average award:*** Freshmen: $5395; Undergraduates: $6792. ***Scholarships, grants, and awards:*** Federal Pell, FSEOG, state, private, college/university gift aid from institutional funds, United Negro College Fund.

GIFT AID (NON-NEED-BASED) ***Total amount:*** $334,734 (4% state, 77% institutional, 19% external sources). ***Receiving aid:*** Freshmen: 3% (4); Undergraduates: 4% (24). ***Average award:*** Freshmen: $6696; Undergraduates: $8050. ***Scholarships, grants, and awards by category:*** *Academic Interests/Achievement:* 115 awards ($571,740 total): general academic interests/achievements. *Creative Arts/Performance:* 19 awards ($136,687 total): journalism/publications, music. *Special Characteristics:* 9 awards ($59,508 total): children of faculty/staff. ***Tuition waivers:*** Full or partial for employees or children of employees. ***ROTC:*** Army cooperative, Air Force cooperative.

LOANS ***Student loans:*** $3,623,322 (96% need-based, 4% non-need-based). 62% of past graduating class borrowed through all loan programs. *Average indebtedness per student:* $13,354. ***Average need-based loan:*** Freshmen: $2221; Undergraduates: $3090. ***Parent loans:*** $340,521 (67% need-based, 33% non-need-based). ***Programs:*** FFEL (Subsidized and Unsubsidized Stafford, PLUS).

WORK-STUDY ***Federal work-study:*** Total amount: $265,264; 205 jobs averaging $1294.

ATHLETIC AWARDS Total amount: $329,281 (71% need-based, 29% non-need-based).

APPLYING FOR FINANCIAL AID ***Required financial aid forms:*** FAFSA, institution's own form. ***Financial aid deadline (priority):*** 4/1. ***Notification date:*** Continuous beginning 5/1. Students must reply within 2 weeks of notification.

CONTACT Phyllis Nettles Torry, Director of Student Financial Services, LeMoyne-Owen College, 807 Walker Avenue, Memphis, TN 38126-6595, 901-435-1550. *Fax:* 901-435-1574. *E-mail:* phyllis_torry@loc.edu.

LENOIR-RHYNE COLLEGE

Hickory, NC

CONTACT Mrs. Rachel Nichols, Dean of Admissions and Financial Aid, Lenoir-Rhyne College, PO Box 7227, Hickory, NC 28603, 828-328-7300 or toll-free 800-277-5721. *Fax:* 828-328-7039. *E-mail:* admission@lrc.edu.

LESLEY UNIVERSITY

Cambridge, MA

Tuition & fees: $25,850 **Average undergraduate aid package: $16,022**

ABOUT THE INSTITUTION Independent, coed. Awards: associate, bachelor's, master's, and doctoral degrees and post-bachelor's and post-master's certificates. 22 undergraduate majors. Total enrollment: 6,539. Undergraduates: 1,351. Freshmen: 307. Both federal and institutional methodology are used as a basis for awarding need-based institutional aid.

UNDERGRADUATE EXPENSES for 2007–08 ***Application fee:*** $40. ***Comprehensive fee:*** $37,950 includes full-time tuition ($25,600), mandatory fees ($250), and room and board ($12,100). ***College room only:*** $6800.

FRESHMAN FINANCIAL AID (Fall 2006, est.) 291 applied for aid; of those 72% were deemed to have need. 100% of freshmen with need received aid; of those 7% had need fully met. ***Average percent of need met:*** 70% (excluding resources awarded to replace EFC). ***Average financial aid package:*** $20,175 (excluding resources awarded to replace EFC). 13% of all full-time freshmen had no need and received non-need-based gift aid.

UNDERGRADUATE FINANCIAL AID (Fall 2006, est.) 814 applied for aid; of those 87% were deemed to have need. 94% of undergraduates with need received aid; of those 7% had need fully met. ***Average percent of need met:*** 70% (excluding resources awarded to replace EFC). ***Average financial aid***

package: $16,022 (excluding resources awarded to replace EFC). 8% of all full-time undergraduates had no need and received non-need-based gift aid.

GIFT AID (NEED-BASED) ***Total amount:*** $6,581,229 (17% federal, 8% state, 66% institutional, 9% external sources). ***Receiving aid:*** Freshmen: 62% (202); All full-time undergraduates: 62% (667). ***Average award:*** Freshmen: $15,135; Undergraduates: $11,536. ***Scholarships, grants, and awards:*** Federal Pell, FSEOG, state, private, college/university gift aid from institutional funds.

GIFT AID (NON-NEED-BASED) ***Total amount:*** $3,861,672 (100% institutional). ***Receiving aid:*** Freshmen: 13% (42); Undergraduates: 8% (90). ***Average award:*** Freshmen: $8075; Undergraduates: $6686. ***Scholarships, grants, and awards by category:*** *Academic Interests/Achievement:* 7 awards ($166,218 total): general academic interests/achievements. *Creative Arts/Performance:* 17 awards ($30,000 total): art/fine arts. *Special Achievements/Activities:* 184 awards ($1,370,500 total): general special achievements/activities. *Special Characteristics:* 34 awards ($278,613 total): ethnic background, local/state students, members of minority groups.

LOANS ***Student loans:*** $7,708,669 (50% need-based, 50% non-need-based). 91% of past graduating class borrowed through all loan programs. *Average indebtedness per student:* $15,000. ***Average need-based loan:*** Freshmen: $3292; Undergraduates: $3286. ***Parent loans:*** $1,956,282 (100% non-need-based). ***Programs:*** FFEL (Subsidized and Unsubsidized Stafford, PLUS), Perkins, state.

WORK-STUDY ***Federal work-study:*** Total amount: $450,000; 261 jobs averaging $1724. ***State or other work-study/employment:*** 122 part-time jobs averaging $2000.

APPLYING FOR FINANCIAL AID ***Required financial aid forms:*** FAFSA, institution's own form. ***Financial aid deadline (priority):*** 3/15. ***Notification date:*** Continuous beginning 3/15.

CONTACT Scott A. Jewell, Director of Financial Aid, Lesley University, 29 Everett Street, Cambridge, MA 02138-2790, 617-349-8714 or toll-free 800-999-1959 Ext. 8800. *Fax:* 617-349-8717. *E-mail:* sjewell@lesley.edu.

LeTOURNEAU UNIVERSITY

Longview, TX

Tuition & fees: $16,920 **Average undergraduate aid package: $11,386**

ABOUT THE INSTITUTION Independent nondenominational, coed. Awards: associate, bachelor's, and master's degrees. 41 undergraduate majors. Total enrollment: 3,975. Undergraduates: 3,635. Freshmen: 334. Federal methodology is used as a basis for awarding need-based institutional aid.

UNDERGRADUATE EXPENSES for 2006–07 ***Application fee:*** $25. ***Comprehensive fee:*** $23,490 includes full-time tuition ($16,720), mandatory fees ($200), and room and board ($6570). Room and board charges vary according to board plan. ***Part-time tuition:*** $296 per hour. Part-time tuition and fees vary according to course load. ***Payment plan:*** Installment.

FRESHMAN FINANCIAL AID (Fall 2005) 265 applied for aid; of those 84% were deemed to have need. 100% of freshmen with need received aid; of those 15% had need fully met. ***Average percent of need met:*** 70% (excluding resources awarded to replace EFC). ***Average financial aid package:*** $11,611 (excluding resources awarded to replace EFC). 21% of all full-time freshmen had no need and received non-need-based gift aid.

UNDERGRADUATE FINANCIAL AID (Fall 2005) 1,066 applied for aid; of those 85% were deemed to have need. 100% of undergraduates with need received aid; of those 16% had need fully met. ***Average percent of need met:*** 69% (excluding resources awarded to replace EFC). ***Average financial aid package:*** $11,386 (excluding resources awarded to replace EFC). 17% of all full-time undergraduates had no need and received non-need-based gift aid.

GIFT AID (NEED-BASED) ***Total amount:*** $8,864,624 (28% federal, 17% state, 51% institutional, 4% external sources). ***Receiving aid:*** Freshmen: 70% (222); All full-time undergraduates: 61% (852). ***Average award:*** Freshmen: $8422; Undergraduates: $7816. ***Scholarships, grants, and awards:*** Federal Pell, FSEOG, state, private, college/university gift aid from institutional funds.

GIFT AID (NON-NEED-BASED) ***Total amount:*** $1,035,060 (1% federal, 1% state, 93% institutional, 5% external sources). ***Receiving aid:*** Freshmen: 58% (183); Undergraduates: 30% (424). ***Average award:*** Freshmen: $1177; Undergraduates: $4102. ***Scholarships, grants, and awards by category:*** *Academic Interests/Achievement:* general academic interests/achievements. *Special Achievements/Activities:* general special achievements/activities. *Special Characteristics:* children of faculty/staff, international students, local/state students, relatives of clergy, spouses of current students. ***Tuition waivers:*** Full or partial for employees or children of employees.

LOANS ***Student loans:*** $21,462,236 (53% need-based, 47% non-need-based). 94% of past graduating class borrowed through all loan programs. ***Average need-based loan:*** Freshmen: $2856; Undergraduates: $3981. ***Parent loans:*** $4,555,185 (77% need-based, 23% non-need-based). ***Programs:*** FFEL (Subsidized and Unsubsidized Stafford, PLUS), Perkins, state.

WORK-STUDY ***Federal work-study:*** Total amount: $176,424; jobs available. ***State or other work-study/employment:*** Total amount: $20,000 (100% need-based). Part-time jobs available.

APPLYING FOR FINANCIAL AID ***Required financial aid form:*** FAFSA. ***Financial aid deadline (priority):*** 2/1. ***Notification date:*** Continuous beginning 3/1. Students must reply within 3 weeks of notification.

CONTACT Ms. Denise Welch, Director of Financial Aid, LeTourneau University, 2100 South Mobberly Avenue, PO Box 7001, Longview, TX 75607, 903-233-4350 or toll-free 800-759-8811. *Fax:* 903-233-4302. *E-mail:* finaid@letu.edu.

LEWIS & CLARK COLLEGE

Portland, OR

Tuition & fees: $29,772 **Average undergraduate aid package: $25,018**

ABOUT THE INSTITUTION Independent, coed. Awards: bachelor's, master's, doctoral, and first professional degrees and post-master's certificates. 29 undergraduate majors. Total enrollment: 3,641. Undergraduates: 1,985. Freshmen: 509. Federal methodology is used as a basis for awarding need-based institutional aid.

UNDERGRADUATE EXPENSES for 2006–07 ***Application fee:*** $50. ***One-time required fee:*** $3876. ***Comprehensive fee:*** $37,820 includes full-time tuition ($29,556), mandatory fees ($216), and room and board ($8048). ***College room only:*** $4172. ***Part-time tuition:*** $1489 per credit hour.

FRESHMAN FINANCIAL AID (Fall 2006, est.) 366 applied for aid; of those 74% were deemed to have need. 100% of freshmen with need received aid; of those 49% had need fully met. ***Average percent of need met:*** 91% (excluding resources awarded to replace EFC). ***Average financial aid package:*** $26,051 (excluding resources awarded to replace EFC). 24% of all full-time freshmen had no need and received non-need-based gift aid.

UNDERGRADUATE FINANCIAL AID (Fall 2006, est.) 1,306 applied for aid; of those 83% were deemed to have need. 100% of undergraduates with need received aid; of those 46% had need fully met. ***Average percent of need met:*** 91% (excluding resources awarded to replace EFC). ***Average financial aid package:*** $25,018 (excluding resources awarded to replace EFC). 24% of all full-time undergraduates had no need and received non-need-based gift aid.

GIFT AID (NEED-BASED) ***Total amount:*** $15,823,085 (7% federal, 2% state, 90% institutional, 1% external sources). ***Receiving aid:*** Freshmen: 49% (251); All full-time undergraduates: 53% (1,023). ***Average award:*** Freshmen: $21,903; Undergraduates: $21,444. ***Scholarships, grants, and awards:*** Federal Pell, FSEOG, state, private, college/university gift aid from institutional funds.

GIFT AID (NON-NEED-BASED) ***Total amount:*** $7,055,811 (87% institutional, 13% external sources). ***Receiving aid:*** Freshmen: 3% (17); Undergraduates: 2% (44). ***Average award:*** Freshmen: $7844; Undergraduates: $6942. ***Scholarships, grants, and awards by category:*** *Academic Interests/Achievement:* 672 awards ($5,319,792 total): general academic interests/achievements. *Creative Arts/Performance:* 39 awards ($143,878 total): debating, music. *Special Achievements/Activities:* 97 awards ($483,000 total): community service.

LOANS ***Student loans:*** $7,289,683 (65% need-based, 35% non-need-based). 56% of past graduating class borrowed through all loan programs. *Average indebtedness per student:* $19,489. ***Average need-based loan:*** Freshmen: $4005; Undergraduates: $5290. ***Parent loans:*** $937,373 (29% need-based, 71% non-need-based). ***Programs:*** Federal Direct (Subsidized and Unsubsidized Stafford, PLUS), state.

WORK-STUDY ***Federal work-study:*** Total amount: $1,503,300; 674 jobs averaging $2034.

APPLYING FOR FINANCIAL AID ***Required financial aid form:*** FAFSA. ***Financial aid deadline (priority):*** 3/1. ***Notification date:*** Continuous beginning 3/1. Students must reply by 5/1.

CONTACT Glendi Gaddis, Director of Student Financial Services, Lewis & Clark College, Templeton Student Center, MS 56, Portland, OR 97219-7899, 503-768-7096 or toll-free 800-444-4111. *Fax:* 503-768-7074. *E-mail:* sfs@lclark.edu.

LEWIS-CLARK STATE COLLEGE

Lewiston, ID

Tuition & fees (ID res): $3897 **Average undergraduate aid package: $5445**

ABOUT THE INSTITUTION State-supported, coed. Awards: associate and bachelor's degrees. 50 undergraduate majors. Total enrollment: 3,394. Undergraduates: 3,394. Freshmen: 482. Federal methodology is used as a basis for awarding need-based institutional aid.

UNDERGRADUATE EXPENSES for 2006–07 ***Application fee:*** $35. ***Tuition, state resident:*** full-time $3897; part-time $194 per credit. ***Tuition, nonresident:*** full-time $10,841; part-time $194 per credit. Full-time tuition and fees vary according to course load and reciprocity agreements. ***College room and board:*** $4670; ***Room only:*** $2200. Room and board charges vary according to board plan and housing facility. ***Payment plan:*** Deferred payment.

FRESHMAN FINANCIAL AID (Fall 2005) 351 applied for aid; of those 81% were deemed to have need. 94% of freshmen with need received aid; of those 8% had need fully met. ***Average percent of need met:*** 12% (excluding resources awarded to replace EFC). ***Average financial aid package:*** $3659 (excluding resources awarded to replace EFC). 14% of all full-time freshmen had no need and received non-need-based gift aid.

UNDERGRADUATE FINANCIAL AID (Fall 2005) 1,624 applied for aid; of those 87% were deemed to have need. 98% of undergraduates with need received aid; of those 12% had need fully met. ***Average percent of need met:*** 12% (excluding resources awarded to replace EFC). ***Average financial aid package:*** $5445 (excluding resources awarded to replace EFC). 9% of all full-time undergraduates had no need and received non-need-based gift aid.

GIFT AID (NEED-BASED) ***Total amount:*** $4,628,915 (85% federal, 1% state, 7% institutional, 7% external sources). ***Receiving aid:*** Freshmen: 42% (178); All full-time undergraduates: 49% (1,003). ***Average award:*** Freshmen: $2757; Undergraduates: $3118. ***Scholarships, grants, and awards:*** Federal Pell, FSEOG, state, private, college/university gift aid from institutional funds.

GIFT AID (NON-NEED-BASED) ***Total amount:*** $527,567 (71% institutional, 29% external sources). ***Receiving aid:*** Freshmen: 25% (107); Undergraduates: 12% (251). ***Average award:*** Freshmen: $1964; Undergraduates: $2360. ***Scholarships, grants, and awards by category:*** *Academic Interests/Achievement:* 61 awards ($121,467 total): biological sciences, business, education, English, general academic interests/achievements, health fields, humanities, mathematics, physical sciences, social sciences. *Creative Arts/Performance:* 12 awards ($22,084 total): art/fine arts, creative writing, debating, music, theater/drama. *Special Achievements/Activities:* 126 awards ($74,340 total): community service, general special achievements/activities, junior miss, leadership, rodeo. *Special Characteristics:* 225 awards ($551,868 total): ethnic background, first-generation college students, general special characteristics, local/state students, members of minority groups, out-of-state students, previous college experience. ***Tuition waivers:*** Full or partial for employees or children of employees, senior citizens. ***ROTC:*** Army, Air Force cooperative.

LOANS ***Student loans:*** $8,700,766 (68% need-based, 32% non-need-based). 61% of past graduating class borrowed through all loan programs. ***Average need-based loan:*** Freshmen: $2269; Undergraduates: $3633. ***Parent loans:*** $501,731 (100% non-need-based). ***Programs:*** FFEL (Subsidized and Unsubsidized Stafford, PLUS), Perkins, Federal Nursing.

WORK-STUDY ***Federal work-study:*** Total amount: $127,492; 121 jobs averaging $1054. ***State or other work-study/employment:*** Total amount: $103,847 (86% need-based, 14% non-need-based). 79 part-time jobs averaging $1315.

ATHLETIC AWARDS Total amount: $877,187 (100% non-need-based).

APPLYING FOR FINANCIAL AID ***Required financial aid form:*** FAFSA. ***Financial aid deadline (priority):*** 3/1. ***Notification date:*** Continuous beginning 4/15. Students must reply within 2 weeks of notification.

CONTACT Ms. Laura Hughes, Director of Financial Aid, Lewis-Clark State College, 500 8th Avenue, Lewiston, ID 83501-2698, 208-792-2224 or toll-free 800-933-LCSC Ext. 2210. *Fax:* 208-792-2063. *E-mail:* lhughes@lcsc.edu.

LEWIS UNIVERSITY

Romeoville, IL

CONTACT Ms. Janeen Decharinte, Director of Financial Aid, Lewis University, One University Parkway, Romeoville, IL 60446, 815-836-5262 or toll-free 800-897-9000. *Fax:* 815-836-5135. *E-mail:* decharja@lewisu.edu.

LEXINGTON COLLEGE

Chicago, IL

Tuition & fees: $17,810 **Average undergraduate aid package: $9200**

ABOUT THE INSTITUTION Independent, women only. Awards: associate and bachelor's degrees. 12 undergraduate majors. Total enrollment: 57. Undergraduates: 57. Freshmen: 17. Federal methodology is used as a basis for awarding need-based institutional aid.

UNDERGRADUATE EXPENSES for 2006–07 ***Application fee:*** $30. ***Tuition:*** full-time $17,000; part-time $566 per credit hour. ***Required fees:*** full-time $810; $300 per term part-time. ***Payment plans:*** Guaranteed tuition, installment.

FRESHMAN FINANCIAL AID (Fall 2006, est.) 27 applied for aid; of those 100% were deemed to have need. 100% of freshmen with need received aid; of those 4% had need fully met. ***Average percent of need met:*** 91% (excluding resources awarded to replace EFC). ***Average financial aid package:*** $13,850 (excluding resources awarded to replace EFC).

UNDERGRADUATE FINANCIAL AID (Fall 2006, est.) 55 applied for aid; of those 93% were deemed to have need. 98% of undergraduates with need received aid. ***Average percent of need met:*** 94% (excluding resources awarded to replace EFC). ***Average financial aid package:*** $9200 (excluding resources awarded to replace EFC).

GIFT AID (NEED-BASED) ***Total amount:*** $515,049 (23% federal, 25% state, 41% institutional, 11% external sources). ***Receiving aid:*** Freshmen: 100% (27); All full-time undergraduates: 91% (50). ***Average award:*** Freshmen: $11,500; Undergraduates: $7900. ***Scholarships, grants, and awards:*** Federal Pell, FSEOG, state, private, college/university gift aid from institutional funds, ACG Academic Competitiveness Grant.

GIFT AID (NON-NEED-BASED) ***Tuition waivers:*** Full or partial for employees or children of employees.

LOANS ***Student loans:*** $194,040 (100% need-based). 90% of past graduating class borrowed through all loan programs. *Average indebtedness per student:* $25,000. ***Average need-based loan:*** Freshmen: $2625; Undergraduates: $6625. ***Parent loans:*** $58,548 (100% need-based). ***Programs:*** FFEL (Subsidized and Unsubsidized Stafford, PLUS), Sallie Mae Signature Student Loans, alternative loans.

WORK-STUDY ***Federal work-study:*** Total amount: $5721; 6 jobs averaging $5721.

APPLYING FOR FINANCIAL AID ***Required financial aid form:*** FAFSA. ***Financial aid deadline:*** 10/1 (priority: 5/15). ***Notification date:*** Continuous.

CONTACT Maria Lebron-Cardona, Director of Financial Aid, Lexington College, 310 South Peoria Street, Suite 512, Chicago, IL 60607, 312-226-6294 Ext. 227. *Fax:* 312-226-6405. *E-mail:* finaid@lexingtoncollege.edu.

LIBERTY UNIVERSITY

Lynchburg, VA

CONTACT Rhonda Allbeck, Director, Financial Aid Office, Liberty University, 1971 University Boulevard, Lynchburg, VA 24502, 434-582-2288 or toll-free 800-543-5317. *Fax:* 434-582-2053. *E-mail:* rfallbeck@liberty.edu.

LIFE PACIFIC COLLEGE

San Dimas, CA

CONTACT Mrs. Becky Huyck, Director of Financial Aid, Life Pacific College, 1100 Covina Boulevard, San Dimas, CA 91773-3298, 909-599-5433 Ext. 319 or toll-free 877-886-5433 Ext. 314. *Fax:* 909-599-6690. *E-mail:* bhuyck@lifepacific.edu.

LIFE UNIVERSITY

Marietta, GA

Tuition & fees: $5823 **Average undergraduate aid package: $4800**

ABOUT THE INSTITUTION Independent, coed. Awards: associate, bachelor's, master's, and first professional degrees. 5 undergraduate majors. Total enrollment: 1,662. Undergraduates: 495. Freshmen: 41. Federal methodology is used as a basis for awarding need-based institutional aid.

UNDERGRADUATE EXPENSES for 2006–07 ***Application fee:*** $50. ***Comprehensive fee:*** $17,823 includes full-time tuition ($5508), mandatory fees ($315), and room and board ($12,000). Full-time tuition and fees vary according to course load and degree level. ***Part-time tuition:*** $153 per credit hour. ***Part-time fees:*** $105 per term. Part-time tuition and fees vary according to course load and degree level.

FRESHMAN FINANCIAL AID (Fall 2006, est.) 79 applied for aid; of those 81% were deemed to have need. 98% of freshmen with need received aid; of those 10% had need fully met. ***Average percent of need met:*** 10% (excluding resources awarded to replace EFC). ***Average financial aid package:*** $5800 (excluding resources awarded to replace EFC).

UNDERGRADUATE FINANCIAL AID (Fall 2006, est.) 312 applied for aid; of those 88% were deemed to have need. 97% of undergraduates with need received aid; of those 9% had need fully met. ***Average percent of need met:*** 9% (excluding resources awarded to replace EFC). ***Average financial aid package:*** $4800 (excluding resources awarded to replace EFC). 1% of all full-time undergraduates had no need and received non-need-based gift aid.

GIFT AID (NEED-BASED) ***Total amount:*** $600,000 (100% federal). ***Receiving aid:*** Freshmen: 35% (39); All full-time undergraduates: 33% (132). ***Average award:*** Freshmen: $4000; Undergraduates: $3700. ***Scholarships, grants, and awards:*** Federal Pell, FSEOG, state, private, college/university gift aid from institutional funds.

GIFT AID (NON-NEED-BASED) ***Total amount:*** $277,000 (70% state, 26% institutional, 4% external sources). ***Receiving aid:*** Freshmen: 28% (31); Undergraduates: 51% (206). ***Average award:*** Undergraduates: $3300. ***Scholarships, grants, and awards by category:*** *Academic Interests/Achievement:* 14 awards ($61,750 total): general academic interests/achievements. ***Tuition waivers:*** Full or partial for employees or children of employees.

LOANS ***Student loans:*** $2,100,000 (52% need-based, 48% non-need-based). 100% of past graduating class borrowed through all loan programs. *Average indebtedness per student:* $30,000. ***Average need-based loan:*** Freshmen: $3000; Undergraduates: $3200. ***Parent loans:*** $47,000 (100% non-need-based). ***Programs:*** FFEL (Subsidized and Unsubsidized Stafford, PLUS), Perkins, college/university, alternative loans.

WORK-STUDY ***Federal work-study:*** Total amount: $170,000; 111 jobs averaging $2100.

ATHLETIC AWARDS Total amount: $30,000 (100% non-need-based).

APPLYING FOR FINANCIAL AID ***Required financial aid forms:*** FAFSA, institution's own form. ***Financial aid deadline (priority):*** 3/1. ***Notification date:*** Continuous beginning 5/1.

CONTACT Michelle Nixon, Director of Financial Aid, Life University, 1269 Barclay Circle, Marietta, GA 30060, 770-426-2901 or toll-free 800-543-3202 (in-state). *Fax:* 770-426-2926. *E-mail:* finaid@life.edu.

LIMESTONE COLLEGE

Gaffney, SC

Tuition & fees: $15,900 **Average undergraduate aid package: $10,813**

ABOUT THE INSTITUTION Independent, coed. Awards: associate and bachelor's degrees. 45 undergraduate majors. Total enrollment: 728. Undergraduates: 728. Freshmen: 188. Federal methodology is used as a basis for awarding need-based institutional aid.

UNDERGRADUATE EXPENSES for 2007–08 ***Application fee:*** $25. ***Comprehensive fee:*** $22,100 includes full-time tuition ($15,900) and room and board ($6200). ***Part-time tuition:*** $662 per credit hour.

FRESHMAN FINANCIAL AID (Fall 2005) 164 applied for aid; of those 88% were deemed to have need. 100% of freshmen with need received aid; of those 19% had need fully met. ***Average percent of need met:*** 60% (excluding resources awarded to replace EFC). ***Average financial aid package:*** $10,738 (excluding resources awarded to replace EFC). 28% of all full-time freshmen had no need and received non-need-based gift aid.

UNDERGRADUATE FINANCIAL AID (Fall 2005) 642 applied for aid; of those 90% were deemed to have need. 100% of undergraduates with need received aid; of those 18% had need fully met. ***Average percent of need met:*** 60% (excluding resources awarded to replace EFC). ***Average financial aid package:*** $10,813 (excluding resources awarded to replace EFC). 18% of all full-time undergraduates had no need and received non-need-based gift aid.

GIFT AID (NEED-BASED) ***Total amount:*** $3,648,861 (28% federal, 24% state, 45% institutional, 3% external sources). ***Receiving aid:*** Freshmen: 79% (143); All full-time undergraduates: 87% (565). ***Average award:*** Freshmen: $8592; Undergraduates: $7807. ***Scholarships, grants, and awards:*** Federal Pell, FSEOG, state, private, college/university gift aid from institutional funds.

GIFT AID (NON-NEED-BASED) ***Total amount:*** $679,398 (29% state, 68% institutional, 3% external sources). ***Receiving aid:*** Freshmen: 9% (17); Undergraduates: 10% (66). ***Average award:*** Freshmen: $7335; Undergraduates: $8131. ***Scholarships, grants, and awards by category:*** *Academic Interests/Achievement:* 363 awards ($711,615 total): biological sciences, business, communication, computer science, education, English, general academic interests/achievements, humanities, mathematics, physical sciences, religion/biblical studies, social sciences. *Creative Arts/Performance:* 36 awards ($77,200 total): art/fine arts, music, performing arts, theater/drama. *Special Achievements/Activities:* 318 awards ($463,525 total): cheerleading/drum major, leadership, religious involvement. *Special Characteristics:* 477 awards ($738,898 total): children and siblings of alumni, children of faculty/staff, first-generation college students, local/state students, out-of-state students, siblings of current students. ***ROTC:*** Army cooperative.

LOANS ***Student loans:*** $3,842,852 (76% need-based, 24% non-need-based). 100% of past graduating class borrowed through all loan programs. *Average indebtedness per student:* $16,761. ***Average need-based loan:*** Freshmen: $2253; Undergraduates: $3309. ***Parent loans:*** $772,956 (44% need-based, 56% non-need-based). ***Programs:*** FFEL (Subsidized and Unsubsidized Stafford, PLUS), Perkins.

WORK-STUDY ***Federal work-study:*** Total amount: $238,905; 129 jobs averaging $2500. ***State or other work-study/employment:*** Total amount: $46,000 (31% need-based, 69% non-need-based). 25 part-time jobs averaging $1000.

ATHLETIC AWARDS Total amount: $1,227,981 (78% need-based, 22% non-need-based).

APPLYING FOR FINANCIAL AID ***Required financial aid form:*** FAFSA. ***Financial aid deadline (priority):*** 2/1. ***Notification date:*** Continuous beginning 1/15. Students must reply within 3 weeks of notification.

CONTACT Mrs. Lauren Mack, Director of Financial Aid, Limestone College, 1115 College Drive, Gaffney, SC 29340-3799, 864-488-4567 or toll-free 800-795-7151 Ext. 554. *Fax:* 864-487-8706. *E-mail:* lmack@limestone.edu.

LINCOLN CHRISTIAN COLLEGE

Lincoln, IL

Tuition & fees: $11,100 **Average undergraduate aid package: $8000**

ABOUT THE INSTITUTION Independent religious, coed. Awards: associate and bachelor's degrees. 13 undergraduate majors. Total enrollment: 708. Undergraduates: 708. Freshmen: 182. Federal methodology is used as a basis for awarding need-based institutional aid.

UNDERGRADUATE EXPENSES for 2006–07 ***Application fee:*** $20. ***Comprehensive fee:*** $15,680 includes full-time tuition ($11,100) and room and board ($4580). ***Part-time tuition:*** $370 per semester hour. ***Payment plans:*** Installment, deferred payment.

FRESHMAN FINANCIAL AID (Fall 2005) 180 applied for aid; of those 73% were deemed to have need. 100% of freshmen with need received aid. ***Average percent of need met:*** 80% (excluding resources awarded to replace EFC). ***Average financial aid package:*** $7500 (excluding resources awarded to replace EFC). 9% of all full-time freshmen had no need and received non-need-based gift aid.

UNDERGRADUATE FINANCIAL AID (Fall 2005) 648 applied for aid; of those 83% were deemed to have need. 100% of undergraduates with need received aid. ***Average percent of need met:*** 80% (excluding resources awarded to replace EFC). ***Average financial aid package:*** $8000 (excluding resources awarded to replace EFC). 6% of all full-time undergraduates had no need and received non-need-based gift aid.

GIFT AID (NEED-BASED) ***Total amount:*** $2,083,723 (35% federal, 51% state, 14% institutional). ***Scholarships, grants, and awards:*** Federal Pell, FSEOG, state.

GIFT AID (NON-NEED-BASED) ***Total amount:*** $619,376 (26% institutional, 74% external sources). ***Scholarships, grants, and awards by category:*** *Academic Interests/Achievement:* 43 awards ($148,539 total): general academic interests/achievements. *Special Achievements/Activities:* 32 awards ($58,975 total): community service, leadership. *Special Characteristics:* 20 awards ($149,204 total): children of faculty/staff. ***Tuition waivers:*** Full or partial for employees or children of employees.

LOANS ***Student loans:*** $2,366,862 (60% need-based, 40% non-need-based). 73% of past graduating class borrowed through all loan programs. *Average indebtedness per student:* $16,379. ***Parent loans:*** $376,132 (100% non-need-based). ***Programs:*** FFEL (Subsidized and Unsubsidized Stafford, PLUS), Perkins, college/university.

WORK-STUDY ***Federal work-study:*** Total amount: $68,281; 67 jobs averaging $1020. ***State or other work-study/employment:*** Total amount: $165,573 (100% non-need-based). 141 part-time jobs averaging $1175.

APPLYING FOR FINANCIAL AID ***Required financial aid form:*** FAFSA. ***Financial aid deadline:*** Continuous. ***Notification date:*** Continuous beginning 3/1. Students must reply within 2 weeks of notification.

CONTACT Nancy Siddens, Co-Director of Financial Aid, Lincoln Christian College, 100 Campus View Drive, Lincoln, IL 62656, 217-732-3168 Ext. 2250 or toll-free 888-522-5228. *Fax:* 217-732-4199. *E-mail:* finaid@lccs.edu.

LINCOLN MEMORIAL UNIVERSITY

Harrogate, TN

CONTACT Celena Rader-Lombdin, Director of Financial Aid, Lincoln Memorial University, Cumberland Gap Parkway, Harrogate, TN 37752-1901, 423-869-6465 or toll-free 800-325-0900. *Fax:* 423-869-6347. *E-mail:* clambdin@lmunet.edu.

LINCOLN UNIVERSITY

Jefferson City, MO

ABOUT THE INSTITUTION State-supported, coed. Awards: associate, bachelor's, and master's degrees and post-master's certificates. 41 undergraduate majors. Total enrollment: 3,224. Undergraduates: 2,927. Freshmen: 563.

GIFT AID (NEED-BASED) ***Scholarships, grants, and awards:*** Federal Pell, FSEOG, state, private, college/university gift aid from institutional funds, Federal Nursing.

GIFT AID (NON-NEED-BASED) ***Scholarships, grants, and awards by category:*** *Academic Interests/Achievement:* agriculture, education, general academic interests/achievements, military science. *Creative Arts/Performance:* art/fine arts, journalism/publications, music.

LOANS ***Programs:*** FFEL (Subsidized and Unsubsidized Stafford, PLUS).

WORK-STUDY ***Federal work-study:*** Total amount: $192,396; 241 jobs averaging $1200. ***State or other work-study/employment:*** Total amount: $151,000 (100% non-need-based). 40 part-time jobs averaging $1000.

APPLYING FOR FINANCIAL AID ***Required financial aid forms:*** FAFSA, institution's own form.

CONTACT Mr. Alfred Robinson, Director of Financial Aid, Lincoln University, 820 Chestnut Street, Jefferson City, MO 65102-0029, 573-681-6156 or toll-free 800-521-5052. *Fax:* 573-681-5871.

LINCOLN UNIVERSITY

Lincoln University, PA

Tuition & fees (PA res): $7892 **Average undergraduate aid package: $6203**

ABOUT THE INSTITUTION State-related, coed. Awards: bachelor's and master's degrees. 45 undergraduate majors. Total enrollment: 2,423. Undergraduates: 1,860. Freshmen: 656. Federal methodology is used as a basis for awarding need-based institutional aid.

UNDERGRADUATE EXPENSES for 2006–07 ***Application fee:*** $20. ***Tuition, state resident:*** full-time $5420; part-time $226 per credit hour. ***Tuition, nonresident:*** full-time $9224; part-time $384 per credit hour. ***Required fees:*** full-time $2472; $92 per credit hour. Part-time tuition and fees vary according to course load. ***College room and board:*** $7142; ***Room only:*** $3822. Room and board charges vary according to board plan. ***Payment plans:*** Installment, deferred payment.

FRESHMAN FINANCIAL AID (Fall 2006, est.) 633 applied for aid; of those 93% were deemed to have need. 100% of freshmen with need received aid; of those 35% had need fully met. ***Average percent of need met:*** 45% (excluding resources awarded to replace EFC). ***Average financial aid package:*** $7550 (excluding resources awarded to replace EFC). 4% of all full-time freshmen had no need and received non-need-based gift aid.

UNDERGRADUATE FINANCIAL AID (Fall 2006, est.) 1,694 applied for aid; of those 93% were deemed to have need. 99% of undergraduates with need received aid; of those 35% had need fully met. ***Average percent of need met:*** 47% (excluding resources awarded to replace EFC). ***Average financial aid package:*** $6203 (excluding resources awarded to replace EFC). 5% of all full-time undergraduates had no need and received non-need-based gift aid.

GIFT AID (NEED-BASED) ***Total amount:*** $6,568,777 (66% federal, 26% state, 1% institutional, 7% external sources). ***Receiving aid:*** Freshmen: 68% (447); All full-time undergraduates: 66% (1,200). ***Average award:*** Freshmen: $6047; Undergraduates: $4551. ***Scholarships, grants, and awards:*** Federal Pell, FSEOG, state, private, college/university gift aid from institutional funds, United Negro College Fund.

GIFT AID (NON-NEED-BASED) ***Total amount:*** $3,403,590 (4% federal, 4% state, 85% institutional, 7% external sources). ***Receiving aid:*** Freshmen: 34% (220); Undergraduates: 31% (558). ***Average award:*** Freshmen: $9215; Undergraduates: $7933. ***Scholarships, grants, and awards by category:*** *Academic Interests/Achievement:* 500 awards ($1,783,351 total): biological sciences, business, communication, computer science, education, English, general academic interests/achievements, humanities, mathematics, physical sciences, social sciences. *Creative Arts/Performance:* 3 awards ($1696 total): music. *Special Achievements/Activities:* 60 awards ($80,322 total): general special achievements/activities. *Special Characteristics:* 213 awards ($607,861 total): children and siblings of alumni, children of faculty/staff, international students. ***Tuition waivers:*** Full or partial for employees or children of employees. ***ROTC:*** Army cooperative, Air Force cooperative.

LOANS ***Student loans:*** $12,413,282 (79% need-based, 21% non-need-based). 82% of past graduating class borrowed through all loan programs. *Average indebtedness per student:* $28,858. ***Average need-based loan:*** Freshmen: $2701; Undergraduates: $3223. ***Parent loans:*** $3,689,943 (100% non-need-based). ***Programs:*** FFEL (Subsidized and Unsubsidized Stafford, PLUS), Perkins.

WORK-STUDY ***Federal work-study:*** Total amount: $279,226; 231 jobs averaging $1221.

APPLYING FOR FINANCIAL AID ***Required financial aid form:*** FAFSA. ***Financial aid deadline:*** 5/1 (priority: 5/1). ***Notification date:*** Continuous beginning 5/1. Students must reply within 2 weeks of notification.

CONTACT Thelma Ross, Director of Financial Aid, Lincoln University, PO Box 179, 1570 Baltimore Pike, Lincoln University, PA 19352, 484-365-7583 or toll-free 800-790-0191. *Fax:* 484-365-8198. *E-mail:* tross@lincoln.edu.

LINDENWOOD UNIVERSITY

St. Charles, MO

Tuition & fees: $12,700 **Average undergraduate aid package: N/A**

ABOUT THE INSTITUTION Independent Presbyterian, coed. Awards: bachelor's and master's degrees and post-master's certificates (education specialist). 87 undergraduate majors. Total enrollment: 9,525. Undergraduates: 6,068. Freshmen: 871. Federal methodology is used as a basis for awarding need-based institutional aid.

UNDERGRADUATE EXPENSES for 2007–08 ***Application fee:*** $30. ***Comprehensive fee:*** $18,900 includes full-time tuition ($12,400), mandatory fees ($300), and room and board ($6200). ***College room only:*** $3100. ***Part-time tuition:*** $350 per credit hour.

GIFT AID (NEED-BASED) ***Total amount:*** $22,039,722 (18% federal, 8% state, 74% institutional). ***Scholarships, grants, and awards:*** Federal Pell, FSEOG, state, private, college/university gift aid from institutional funds.

GIFT AID (NON-NEED-BASED) ***Total amount:*** $9,804,406 (2% state, 96% institutional, 2% external sources). ***Scholarships, grants, and awards by category:*** *Academic Interests/Achievement:* biological sciences, business, communication, computer science, education, engineering/technologies, English, foreign languages, general academic interests/achievements, health fields, humanities, international studies, library science, mathematics, military science, physical sciences, premedicine, social sciences. *Creative Arts/Performance:* applied art and design, art/fine arts, cinema/film/broadcasting, dance, general creative arts/performance, music, performing arts, theater/drama. *Special Achievements/Activities:* cheerleading/drum major, community service, general special achievements/activities, junior miss, leadership. ***ROTC:*** Army, Air Force cooperative.

LOANS ***Student loans:*** $20,245,825 (60% need-based, 40% non-need-based). ***Parent loans:*** $2,757,171 (100% non-need-based). ***Programs:*** FFEL (Subsidized and Unsubsidized Stafford, PLUS), Perkins.

WORK-STUDY ***Federal work-study:*** Total amount: $445,352; jobs available (averaging $1800). ***State or other work-study/employment:*** Total amount: $5,356,700 (66% need-based, 34% non-need-based). Part-time jobs available.

APPLYING FOR FINANCIAL AID ***Required financial aid form:*** FAFSA. ***Financial aid deadline (priority):*** 3/15. ***Notification date:*** Continuous. Students must reply within 1 week of notification.

CONTACT Lori Bode, Director of Financial Aid, Lindenwood University, 209 South Kingshighway, St. Charles, MO 63301-1695, 636-949-4925. *Fax:* 636-949-4924.

LINDSEY WILSON COLLEGE

Columbia, KY

Tuition & fees: $15,806 **Average undergraduate aid package: $10,801**

ABOUT THE INSTITUTION Independent United Methodist, coed. Awards: associate, bachelor's, and master's degrees. 36 undergraduate majors. Total enrollment: 1,832. Undergraduates: 1,620. Freshmen: 423. Federal methodology is used as a basis for awarding need-based institutional aid.

UNDERGRADUATE EXPENSES for 2007–08 ***Comprehensive fee:*** $22,346 includes full-time tuition ($15,576), mandatory fees ($230), and room and board ($6540). ***Part-time tuition:*** $649 per credit hour.

FRESHMAN FINANCIAL AID (Fall 2006, est.) 383 applied for aid; of those 93% were deemed to have need. 100% of freshmen with need received aid; of those 26% had need fully met. ***Average financial aid package:*** $12,636 (excluding resources awarded to replace EFC).

UNDERGRADUATE FINANCIAL AID (Fall 2006, est.) 1,507 applied for aid; of those 93% were deemed to have need. 98% of undergraduates with need received aid; of those 24% had need fully met. ***Average financial aid package:*** $10,801 (excluding resources awarded to replace EFC).

GIFT AID (NEED-BASED) ***Total amount:*** $14,073,783 (24% federal, 34% state, 39% institutional, 3% external sources). ***Receiving aid:*** Freshmen: 93% (356); All full-time undergraduates: 91% (1,374). ***Average award:*** Freshmen: $12,493; Undergraduates: $11,463. ***Scholarships, grants, and awards:*** Federal Pell, FSEOG, state, private, college/university gift aid from institutional funds.

GIFT AID (NON-NEED-BASED) ***Total amount:*** $509,502 (2% state, 95% institutional, 3% external sources). ***Scholarships, grants, and awards by category:*** *Academic Interests/Achievement:* biological sciences, business, education, English, general academic interests/achievements, mathematics, premedicine, religion/biblical studies. *Creative Arts/Performance:* $218,560 total: applied art and design, music. *Special Achievements/Activities:* cheerleading/drum major, general special achievements/activities, junior miss, leadership, religious involvement. *Special Characteristics:* children and siblings of alumni, children of faculty/staff, relatives of clergy, religious affiliation.

LOANS ***Student loans:*** $9,786,929 (100% need-based). 99% of past graduating class borrowed through all loan programs. *Average indebtedness per student:* $14,712. ***Average need-based loan:*** Freshmen: $3798; Undergraduates: $3666. ***Parent loans:*** $250,014 (100% need-based). ***Programs:*** FFEL (Subsidized and Unsubsidized Stafford, PLUS), Perkins, college/university.

WORK-STUDY ***Federal work-study:*** Total amount: $266,798; 179 jobs averaging $1404. ***State or other work-study/employment:*** Total amount: $19,648 (24% need-based, 76% non-need-based). Part-time jobs available.

ATHLETIC AWARDS Total amount: $2,114,066 (38% need-based, 62% non-need-based).

APPLYING FOR FINANCIAL AID ***Required financial aid form:*** FAFSA. ***Financial aid deadline (priority):*** 4/1. ***Notification date:*** Continuous beginning 4/15. Students must reply within 2 weeks of notification.

CONTACT Ms. Marilyn D. Radford, Assistant Director of Student Financial Services, Lindsey Wilson College, 210 Lindsey Wilson Street, Columbia, KY 42728-1298, 270-384-8022 or toll-free 800-264-0138. *Fax:* 270-384-8591. *E-mail:* radfordm@lindsey.edu.

LINFIELD COLLEGE

McMinnville, OR

Tuition & fees: $24,174 **Average undergraduate aid package: $18,300**

ABOUT THE INSTITUTION Independent American Baptist Churches in the USA, coed. Awards: bachelor's degrees. 34 undergraduate majors. Total enrollment: 1,754. Undergraduates: 1,754. Freshmen: 449. Federal methodology is used as a basis for awarding need-based institutional aid.

UNDERGRADUATE EXPENSES for 2006–07 ***Application fee:*** $40. ***Comprehensive fee:*** $31,254 includes full-time tuition ($23,930), mandatory fees ($244), and room and board ($7080). ***College room only:*** $3760. Room and board charges vary according to board plan and housing facility. ***Part-time tuition:*** $745 per credit. ***Part-time fees:*** $72 per term. Part-time tuition and fees vary according to course load. ***Payment plan:*** Installment.

FRESHMAN FINANCIAL AID (Fall 2006, est.) 275 applied for aid; of those 100% were deemed to have need. 85% of freshmen with need received aid; of those 44% had need fully met. ***Average percent of need met:*** 86% (excluding resources awarded to replace EFC). ***Average financial aid package:*** $18,758 (excluding resources awarded to replace EFC). 28% of all full-time freshmen had no need and received non-need-based gift aid.

UNDERGRADUATE FINANCIAL AID (Fall 2006, est.) 1,074 applied for aid; of those 100% were deemed to have need. 100% of undergraduates with need received aid; of those 36% had need fully met. ***Average percent of need met:*** 85% (excluding resources awarded to replace EFC). ***Average financial aid package:*** $18,300 (excluding resources awarded to replace EFC). 23% of all full-time undergraduates had no need and received non-need-based gift aid.

GIFT AID (NEED-BASED) ***Total amount:*** $13,536,810 (9% federal, 2% state, 82% institutional, 7% external sources). ***Receiving aid:*** Freshmen: 49% (221); All full-time undergraduates: 53% (882). ***Average award:*** Freshmen: $8304; Undergraduates: $7317. ***Scholarships, grants, and awards:*** Federal Pell, FSEOG, state, private, college/university gift aid from institutional funds.

GIFT AID (NON-NEED-BASED) ***Total amount:*** $4,232,100 (95% institutional, 5% external sources). ***Receiving aid:*** Freshmen: 33% (148); Undergraduates: 40% (666). ***Average award:*** Freshmen: $10,013; Undergraduates: $9215. ***Scholarships, grants, and awards by category:*** *Academic Interests/Achievement:* 156 awards ($501,950 total): general academic interests/achievements. *Creative Arts/Performance:* 47 awards ($91,000 total): debating, music. *Special Achievements/Activities:* 42 awards ($66,750 total): leadership. *Special Characteristics:* 49 awards ($843,635 total): children of faculty/staff. ***Tuition waivers:*** Full or partial for employees or children of employees, senior citizens. ***ROTC:*** Air Force cooperative.

LOANS ***Student loans:*** $8,124,658 (93% need-based, 7% non-need-based). 75% of past graduating class borrowed through all loan programs. *Average indebtedness per student:* $25,447. ***Average need-based loan:*** Freshmen: $3382; Undergraduates: $4020. ***Parent loans:*** $2,662,825 (100% non-need-based). ***Programs:*** FFEL (Subsidized and Unsubsidized Stafford, PLUS), Perkins, college/university, alternative loans.

WORK-STUDY ***Federal work-study:*** Total amount: $1,384,097; 713 jobs averaging $1941. ***State or other work-study/employment:*** Total amount: $497,938 (100% non-need-based). 656 part-time jobs averaging $760.

APPLYING FOR FINANCIAL AID ***Required financial aid form:*** FAFSA. ***Financial aid deadline (priority):*** 2/1. ***Notification date:*** 4/1. Students must reply by 5/1.

CONTACT Crisanne Werner, Associate Director of Financial Aid, Linfield College, A484 900 Southeast Baker Street, McMinnville, OR 97128-6894, 503-883-2225 or toll-free 800-640-2287. *Fax:* 503-883-2486. *E-mail:* finaid@linfield.edu.

LIPSCOMB UNIVERSITY

Nashville, TN

Tuition & fees: $15,566 **Average undergraduate aid package: $12,752**

ABOUT THE INSTITUTION Independent religious, coed. Awards: bachelor's, master's, and first professional degrees. 58 undergraduate majors. Total enrollment: 2,563. Undergraduates: 2,289. Freshmen: 573. Federal methodology is used as a basis for awarding need-based institutional aid.

UNDERGRADUATE EXPENSES for 2006–07 ***Application fee:*** $25. ***Comprehensive fee:*** $22,296 includes full-time tuition ($14,896), mandatory fees ($670), and room and board ($6730). Full-time tuition and fees vary according to class time and degree level. Room and board charges vary according to board plan and housing facility. ***Part-time tuition:*** $575 per hour. ***Part-time fees:*** $670 per year. Part-time tuition and fees vary according to class time and degree level. ***Payment plans:*** Installment, deferred payment.

FRESHMAN FINANCIAL AID (Fall 2006, est.) 550 applied for aid; of those 66% were deemed to have need. 100% of freshmen with need received aid; of those 28% had need fully met. ***Average percent of need met:*** 67% (excluding resources awarded to replace EFC). ***Average financial aid package:*** $12,485 (excluding resources awarded to replace EFC). 29% of all full-time freshmen had no need and received non-need-based gift aid.

UNDERGRADUATE FINANCIAL AID (Fall 2006, est.) 1,960 applied for aid; of those 59% were deemed to have need. 100% of undergraduates with need received aid; of those 33% had need fully met. ***Average percent of need met:***

67% (excluding resources awarded to replace EFC). ***Average financial aid package:*** $12,752 (excluding resources awarded to replace EFC). 30% of all full-time undergraduates had no need and received non-need-based gift aid.

GIFT AID (NEED-BASED) ***Total amount:*** $9,571,937 (13% federal, 23% state, 57% institutional, 7% external sources). ***Receiving aid:*** Freshmen: 25% (144); All full-time undergraduates: 21% (439). ***Average award:*** Freshmen: $4154; Undergraduates: $4390. ***Scholarships, grants, and awards:*** Federal Pell, FSEOG, state, private, college/university gift aid from institutional funds.

GIFT AID (NON-NEED-BASED) ***Total amount:*** $4,958,598 (23% state, 68% institutional, 9% external sources). ***Receiving aid:*** Freshmen: 56% (322); Undergraduates: 42% (886). ***Average award:*** Freshmen: $6074; Undergraduates: $6304. ***Scholarships, grants, and awards by category:*** *Academic Interests/Achievement:* biological sciences, business, communication, education, engineering/technologies, English, general academic interests/achievements, home economics, mathematics, premedicine, religion/biblical studies. *Creative Arts/Performance:* art/fine arts, journalism/publications, music, theater/drama. *Special Achievements/Activities:* cheerleading/drum major, community service, general special achievements/activities, leadership, religious involvement. *Special Characteristics:* adult students, children and siblings of alumni, children of educators, children of faculty/staff, children with a deceased or disabled parent, international students, members of minority groups, relatives of clergy. ***Tuition waivers:*** Full or partial for minority students, employees or children of employees. ***ROTC:*** Army cooperative, Air Force cooperative.

LOANS ***Student loans:*** $3,767,206 (100% need-based). 49% of past graduating class borrowed through all loan programs. *Average indebtedness per student:* $25,589. ***Average need-based loan:*** Freshmen: $3165; Undergraduates: $4372. ***Parent loans:*** $3,687,708 (73% need-based, 27% non-need-based). ***Programs:*** FFEL (Subsidized and Unsubsidized Stafford, PLUS), Perkins, Federal Nursing.

WORK-STUDY ***Federal work-study:*** Total amount: $278,678; jobs available.

ATHLETIC AWARDS Total amount: $1,843,594 (46% need-based, 54% non-need-based).

APPLYING FOR FINANCIAL AID ***Required financial aid form:*** FAFSA. ***Financial aid deadline (priority):*** 3/1. ***Notification date:*** Continuous beginning 3/15.

CONTACT Mrs. Karita McCaleb Waters, Director of Financial Aid, Lipscomb University, 3901 Granny White Pike, Nashville, TN 37204-3951, 615-966-1791 or toll-free 877-582-4766. *Fax:* 615-966-7640. *E-mail:* karita.waters@lipscomb.edu.

LIVINGSTONE COLLEGE

Salisbury, NC

CONTACT Mrs. Terry Jefferies, Financial Aid Director, Livingstone College, 701 West Monroe Street, Price Building, Salisbury, NC 28144-5298, 704-216-6069 or toll-free 800-835-3435. *Fax:* 704-216-6319. *E-mail:* tjefferies@livingstone.edu.

LOCK HAVEN UNIVERSITY OF PENNSYLVANIA

Lock Haven, PA

Tuition & fees (PA res): $6445   Average undergraduate aid package: $11,600

ABOUT THE INSTITUTION State-supported, coed. Awards: associate, bachelor's, and master's degrees. 56 undergraduate majors. Total enrollment: 5,175. Undergraduates: 4,890. Freshmen: 1,093. Federal methodology is used as a basis for awarding need-based institutional aid.

UNDERGRADUATE EXPENSES for 2006–07 ***Application fee:*** $25. ***Tuition, state resident:*** full-time $5038; part-time $210 per credit. ***Tuition, nonresident:*** full-time $10,598; part-time $442 per credit. ***Required fees:*** full-time $1407; $53 per credit or $31 per term part-time. Full-time tuition and fees vary according to course load and location. Part-time tuition and fees vary according to course load and location. ***College room and board:*** $6060; ***Room only:*** $3328. Room and board charges vary according to board plan and housing facility. ***Payment plans:*** Installment, deferred payment.

FRESHMAN FINANCIAL AID (Fall 2006, est.) 738 applied for aid; of those 77% were deemed to have need. 100% of freshmen with need received aid; of those 19% had need fully met. ***Average percent of need met:*** 64% (excluding resources awarded to replace EFC). ***Average financial aid package:*** $9852 (excluding resources awarded to replace EFC). 1% of all full-time freshmen had no need and received non-need-based gift aid.

UNDERGRADUATE FINANCIAL AID (Fall 2006, est.) 3,067 applied for aid; of those 77% were deemed to have need. 100% of undergraduates with need received aid; of those 19% had need fully met. ***Average percent of need met:*** 64% (excluding resources awarded to replace EFC). ***Average financial aid package:*** $11,600 (excluding resources awarded to replace EFC). 1% of all full-time undergraduates had no need and received non-need-based gift aid.

GIFT AID (NEED-BASED) ***Total amount:*** $10,651,904 (43% federal, 52% state, 1% institutional, 4% external sources). ***Receiving aid:*** Freshmen: 41% (439); All full-time undergraduates: 41% (1,831). ***Average award:*** Freshmen: $4575; Undergraduates: $4785. ***Scholarships, grants, and awards:*** Federal Pell, FSEOG, state, private, college/university gift aid from institutional funds.

GIFT AID (NON-NEED-BASED) ***Total amount:*** $949,482 (12% institutional, 88% external sources). ***Receiving aid:*** Freshmen: 2% (21); Undergraduates: 2% (85). ***Average award:*** Freshmen: $1605; Undergraduates: $1800. ***Scholarships, grants, and awards by category:*** *Academic Interests/Achievement:* 195 awards ($164,183 total): biological sciences, communication, education, English, foreign languages, general academic interests/achievements, international studies, library science, mathematics, physical sciences, social sciences. *Creative Arts/Performance:* 7 awards ($10,410 total): art/fine arts, journalism/publications, music. *Special Achievements/Activities:* 12 awards ($12,500 total): leadership, memberships. *Special Characteristics:* 94 awards ($398,200 total): handicapped students, local/state students, members of minority groups, previous college experience. ***Tuition waivers:*** Full or partial for minority students, employees or children of employees, senior citizens. ***ROTC:*** Army.

LOANS ***Student loans:*** $23,759,390 (100% need-based). 85% of past graduating class borrowed through all loan programs. *Average indebtedness per student:* $21,340. ***Average need-based loan:*** Freshmen: $2625; Undergraduates: $4500. ***Parent loans:*** $3,654,081 (100% non-need-based). ***Programs:*** FFEL (Subsidized and Unsubsidized Stafford, PLUS), Perkins.

WORK-STUDY ***Federal work-study:*** Total amount: $325,160; 253 jobs averaging $1174. ***State or other work-study/employment:*** Total amount: $779,650 (100% need-based). 951 part-time jobs averaging $711.

ATHLETIC AWARDS Total amount: $614,007 (100% non-need-based).

APPLYING FOR FINANCIAL AID ***Required financial aid form:*** FAFSA. ***Financial aid deadline:*** 3/15 (priority: 3/15). ***Notification date:*** Continuous beginning 3/1. Students must reply by 5/1 or within 2 weeks of notification.

CONTACT James Theeuwes, Director, Financial Services, Lock Haven University of Pennsylvania, Russell Hall 118, Lock Haven, PA 17745-2390, 570-893-2344 or toll-free 800-332-8900 (in-state), 800-233-8978 (out-of-state). *Fax:* 570-893-2918. *E-mail:* jtheeuwe@lhup.edu.

LOGAN UNIVERSITY-COLLEGE OF CHIROPRACTIC

Chesterfield, MO

CONTACT Linda K. Haman, Director of Financial Aid, Logan University-College of Chiropractic, 1851 Schoettler Road, PO Box 1065, Chesterfield, MO 63006-1065, 636-227-2100 Ext. 141 or toll-free 800-533-9210.

LOMA LINDA UNIVERSITY

Loma Linda, CA

CONTACT Verdell Schaefer, Director of Financial Aid, Loma Linda University, 11139 Anderson Street, Loma Linda, CA 92350, 909-558-4509. *Fax:* 909-558-4879. *E-mail:* finaid@univ.llu.edu.

LONG ISLAND UNIVERSITY, BROOKLYN CAMPUS

Brooklyn, NY

ABOUT THE INSTITUTION Independent, coed. Awards: associate, bachelor's, master's, doctoral, and first professional degrees and post-bachelor's, post-master's, and first professional certificates. 64 undergraduate majors. Total enrollment: 8,144. Undergraduates: 5,331. Freshmen: 1,086.

GIFT AID (NEED-BASED) ***Scholarships, grants, and awards:*** Federal Pell, FSEOG, state, private, college/university gift aid from institutional funds, Scholarships for Disadvantaged Students (Nursing and Pharmacy).

GIFT AID (NON-NEED-BASED) ***Scholarships, grants, and awards by category:*** *Academic Interests/Achievement:* communication, education, general academic interests/achievements, health fields. *Creative Arts/Performance:* art/fine arts, cinema/film/broadcasting, dance, music. *Special Achievements/Activities:* cheerleading/drum major, general special achievements/activities, leadership. *Special Characteristics:* children and siblings of alumni, children of faculty/staff, ethnic background, first-generation college students, general special characteristics, international students.

LOANS ***Programs:*** Federal Direct (Subsidized and Unsubsidized Stafford, PLUS), Perkins, Federal Health Professions Student Loans, alternative loans.

WORK-STUDY ***Federal work-study:*** Total amount: $1,707,332; jobs available. ***State or other work-study/employment:*** Part-time jobs available.

APPLYING FOR FINANCIAL AID ***Required financial aid form:*** FAFSA.

CONTACT Ms. Rose Iannicelli, Dean of Financial Services, Long Island University, Brooklyn Campus, 1 University Plaza, Brooklyn, NY 11201-8423, 718-488-1037 or toll-free 800-LIU-PLAN. *Fax:* 718-488-3343.

LONG ISLAND UNIVERSITY, C.W. POST CAMPUS

Brookville, NY

CONTACT Office of Financial Assistance, Long Island University, C.W. Post Campus, 720 Northern Boulevard, Brookville, NY 11548-1300, 516-299-2338 or toll-free 800-LIU-PLAN. *Fax:* 516-299-3833. *E-mail:* finaid@cwpost.liu.edu.

LONGWOOD UNIVERSITY

Farmville, VA

Tuition & fees (VA res): $7589 **Average undergraduate aid package: $8502**

ABOUT THE INSTITUTION State-supported, coed. Awards: bachelor's and master's degrees. 74 undergraduate majors. Total enrollment: 4,479. Undergraduates: 3,787. Freshmen: 990. Federal methodology is used as a basis for awarding need-based institutional aid.

UNDERGRADUATE EXPENSES for 2006–07 ***Application fee:*** $40. ***Tuition, state resident:*** full-time $3960; part-time $132 per credit hour. ***Tuition, nonresident:*** full-time $11,580; part-time $366 per credit hour. Full-time tuition and fees vary according to course load. Part-time tuition and fees vary according to course load. ***College room and board:*** $6058; ***Room only:*** $3622. Room and board charges vary according to board plan, housing facility, and location. ***Payment plan:*** Installment.

FRESHMAN FINANCIAL AID (Fall 2006, est.) 686 applied for aid; of those 62% were deemed to have need. 100% of freshmen with need received aid; of those 27% had need fully met. ***Average percent of need met:*** 74% (excluding resources awarded to replace EFC). ***Average financial aid package:*** $8094 (excluding resources awarded to replace EFC). 33% of all full-time freshmen had no need and received non-need-based gift aid.

UNDERGRADUATE FINANCIAL AID (Fall 2006, est.) 2,335 applied for aid; of those 66% were deemed to have need. 100% of undergraduates with need received aid; of those 42% had need fully met. ***Average percent of need met:*** 83% (excluding resources awarded to replace EFC). ***Average financial aid package:*** $8502 (excluding resources awarded to replace EFC). 27% of all full-time undergraduates had no need and received non-need-based gift aid.

GIFT AID (NEED-BASED) ***Total amount:*** $6,915,967 (26% federal, 50% state, 18% institutional, 6% external sources). ***Receiving aid:*** Freshmen: 42% (407); All full-time undergraduates: 39% (1,412). ***Average award:*** Freshmen: $5053; Undergraduates: $4935. ***Scholarships, grants, and awards:*** Federal Pell, FSEOG, state, private, college/university gift aid from institutional funds.

GIFT AID (NON-NEED-BASED) ***Total amount:*** $3,533,306 (1% federal, 18% state, 22% institutional, 59% external sources). ***Receiving aid:*** Freshmen: 6% (57); Undergraduates: 8% (307). ***Average award:*** Freshmen: $4279; Undergraduates: $5777. ***Scholarships, grants, and awards by category:*** *Academic Interests/Achievement:* 224 awards ($254,509 total): biological sciences, business, computer science, education, English, general academic interests/achievements, humanities, mathematics, social sciences. *Creative Arts/Performance:* 34 awards ($25,416 total): art/fine arts, general creative arts/performance, music, theater/drama. *Special Achievements/Activities:* 12 awards ($28,683 total): memberships. *Special Characteristics:* 20 awards ($33,944 total): children and siblings of alumni, general special characteristics, local/state students. ***Tuition waivers:*** Full or partial for senior citizens. ***ROTC:*** Army.

LOANS ***Student loans:*** $11,685,113 (51% need-based, 49% non-need-based). ***Average need-based loan:*** Freshmen: $3184; Undergraduates: $4068. ***Parent loans:*** $10,049,601 (11% need-based, 89% non-need-based). ***Programs:*** FFEL (Subsidized and Unsubsidized Stafford, PLUS), Perkins, college/university, private/alternative loans.

WORK-STUDY ***Federal work-study:*** Total amount: $310,094; jobs available (averaging $1500). ***State or other work-study/employment:*** Total amount: $367,566 (100% non-need-based). Part-time jobs available (averaging $1500).

ATHLETIC AWARDS Total amount: $1,460,150 (28% need-based, 72% non-need-based).

APPLYING FOR FINANCIAL AID ***Required financial aid form:*** FAFSA. ***Financial aid deadline (priority):*** 3/1. ***Notification date:*** Continuous beginning 4/1. Students must reply within 2 weeks of notification.

CONTACT Kevin Messenger, Operations Manager, Longwood University, 201 High Street, Farmville, VA 23909, 434-395-2214 or toll-free 800-281-4677. *Fax:* 434-395-2829. *E-mail:* messengerkc@longwood.edu.

LORAS COLLEGE

Dubuque, IA

Tuition & fees: $22,053 **Average undergraduate aid package: $19,655**

ABOUT THE INSTITUTION Independent Roman Catholic, coed. Awards: associate, bachelor's, and master's degrees. 54 undergraduate majors. Total enrollment: 1,673. Undergraduates: 1,591. Freshmen: 403. Federal methodology is used as a basis for awarding need-based institutional aid.

UNDERGRADUATE EXPENSES for 2006–07 ***Application fee:*** $25. ***Comprehensive fee:*** $28,358 includes full-time tuition ($20,890), mandatory fees ($1163), and room and board ($6305). ***College room only:*** $3220. Full-time tuition and fees vary according to course load and degree level. Room and board charges vary according to board plan and housing facility. ***Part-time tuition:*** $425 per credit. ***Payment plan:*** Installment.

FRESHMAN FINANCIAL AID (Fall 2006, est.) 377 applied for aid; of those 96% were deemed to have need. 100% of freshmen with need received aid; of those 33% had need fully met. ***Average percent of need met:*** 85% (excluding resources awarded to replace EFC). ***Average financial aid package:*** $16,791 (excluding resources awarded to replace EFC). 21% of all full-time freshmen had no need and received non-need-based gift aid.

UNDERGRADUATE FINANCIAL AID (Fall 2006, est.) 1,298 applied for aid; of those 90% were deemed to have need. 99% of undergraduates with need received aid; of those 33% had need fully met. ***Average percent of need met:*** 88% (excluding resources awarded to replace EFC). ***Average financial aid package:*** $19,655 (excluding resources awarded to replace EFC). 32% of all full-time undergraduates had no need and received non-need-based gift aid.

GIFT AID (NEED-BASED) ***Total amount:*** $12,674,893 (8% federal, 15% state, 77% institutional). ***Receiving aid:*** Freshmen: 76% (305); All full-time undergraduates: 67% (1,035). ***Average award:*** Freshmen: $8192; Undergraduates: $8170. ***Scholarships, grants, and awards:*** Federal Pell, FSEOG, state, college/university gift aid from institutional funds.

GIFT AID (NON-NEED-BASED) ***Total amount:*** $5,494,477 (1% state, 95% institutional, 4% external sources). ***Receiving aid:*** Freshmen: 64% (259); Undergraduates: 66% (1,010). ***Average award:*** Freshmen: $9050; Undergraduates: $8289. ***Scholarships, grants, and awards by category:*** *Academic Interests/Achievement:* 1,320 awards ($8,157,000 total): engineering/technologies, general academic interests/achievements, physical sciences. *Creative Arts/Performance:* 56 awards ($52,450 total): music. *Special Achievements/Activities:* memberships, religious involvement. *Special Characteristics:* 379 awards ($354,528 total): children and siblings of alumni, siblings of current students. ***Tuition waivers:*** Full or partial for employees or children of employees, senior citizens. ***ROTC:*** Army cooperative.

LOANS ***Student loans:*** $9,037,381 (52% need-based, 48% non-need-based). 86% of past graduating class borrowed through all loan programs. *Average indebtedness per student:* $28,800. ***Average need-based loan:*** Freshmen: $3705; Undergraduates: $4405. ***Parent loans:*** $961,546 (100% non-need-based). ***Programs:*** FFEL (Subsidized and Unsubsidized Stafford, PLUS), Perkins, college/university.

WORK-STUDY ***Federal work-study:*** Total amount: $203,361; 280 jobs averaging $942. ***State or other work-study/employment:*** Total amount: $551,468 (100% non-need-based). 254 part-time jobs averaging $2581.

APPLYING FOR FINANCIAL AID ***Required financial aid form:*** FAFSA. ***Financial aid deadline (priority):*** 4/15. ***Notification date:*** Continuous beginning 3/6. Students must reply within 3 weeks of notification.

CONTACT Ms. Julie A. Dunn, Director of Financial Planning, Loras College, 1450 Alta Vista Street, Dubuque, IA 52004-0178, 563-588-7136 or toll-free 800-245-6727. *Fax:* 563-588-7119. *E-mail:* Julie.Dunn@loras.edu.

LOUISIANA COLLEGE

Pineville, LA

CONTACT Shelley Jinks, Financial Aid Director, Louisiana College, 1140 College Drive, Pineville, LA 71359-0001, 318-487-7386 or toll-free 800-487-1906. *Fax:* 318-487-7449. *E-mail:* jinks@lacollege.edu.

LOUISIANA STATE UNIVERSITY AND AGRICULTURAL AND MECHANICAL COLLEGE

Baton Rouge, LA

Tuition & fees (LA res): $4449   Average undergraduate aid package: $8011

ABOUT THE INSTITUTION State-supported, coed. Awards: bachelor's, master's, doctoral, and first professional degrees and post-master's certificates. 69 undergraduate majors. Total enrollment: 29,925. Undergraduates: 24,583. Freshmen: 4,508. Federal methodology is used as a basis for awarding need-based institutional aid.

UNDERGRADUATE EXPENSES for 2006–07 ***Application fee:*** $40. ***Tuition, state resident:*** full-time $2981. ***Tuition, nonresident:*** full-time $11,281. Part-time tuition and fees vary according to course load. ***College room and board:*** $6498; ***Room only:*** $3930. Room and board charges vary according to board plan and housing facility. ***Payment plan:*** Deferred payment.

FRESHMAN FINANCIAL AID (Fall 2005) 2694 applied for aid; of those 63% were deemed to have need. 99% of freshmen with need received aid; of those 18% had need fully met. ***Average percent of need met:*** 62% (excluding resources awarded to replace EFC). ***Average financial aid package:*** $7644 (excluding resources awarded to replace EFC). 16% of all full-time freshmen had no need and received non-need-based gift aid.

UNDERGRADUATE FINANCIAL AID (Fall 2005) 12,618 applied for aid; of those 71% were deemed to have need. 96% of undergraduates with need received aid; of those 14% had need fully met. ***Average percent of need met:*** 58% (excluding resources awarded to replace EFC). ***Average financial aid package:*** $8011 (excluding resources awarded to replace EFC). 11% of all full-time undergraduates had no need and received non-need-based gift aid.

GIFT AID (NEED-BASED) ***Total amount:*** $37,120,682 (35% federal, 38% state, 24% institutional, 3% external sources). ***Receiving aid:*** Freshmen: 32% (1,619); All full-time undergraduates: 30% (7,281). ***Average award:*** Freshmen: $5649; Undergraduates: $5230. ***Scholarships, grants, and awards:*** Federal Pell, FSEOG, state, private, college/university gift aid from institutional funds.

GIFT AID (NON-NEED-BASED) ***Total amount:*** $46,919,923 (2% federal, 69% state, 25% institutional, 4% external sources). ***Receiving aid:*** Freshmen: 2% (76); Undergraduates: 1% (209). ***Average award:*** Freshmen: $3570; Undergraduates: $4003. ***Scholarships, grants, and awards by category:*** *Academic Interests/Achievement:* 1,018 awards ($1,844,547 total): agriculture, architecture, biological sciences, business, communication, computer science, education, engineering/technologies, English, foreign languages, general academic interests/achievements, home economics, humanities, mathematics, military science, physical sciences, premedicine. *Creative Arts/Performance:* 267 awards ($1,244,673 total): applied art and design, art/fine arts, journalism/publications, music, performing arts, theater/drama. *Special Achievements/Activities:* leadership. *Special Characteristics:* 386 awards ($2,027,035 total): children and siblings of alumni, children with a deceased or disabled parent, general special characteristics. ***Tuition waivers:*** Full or partial for children of alumni, employees or children of employees. ***ROTC:*** Army, Naval cooperative, Air Force.

LOANS ***Student loans:*** $49,169,190 (72% need-based, 28% non-need-based). 44% of past graduating class borrowed through all loan programs. *Average indebtedness per student:* $16,354. ***Average need-based loan:*** Freshmen: $2437; Undergraduates: $3904. ***Parent loans:*** $11,323,551 (30% need-based, 70% non-need-based). ***Programs:*** FFEL (Subsidized and Unsubsidized Stafford, PLUS).

WORK-STUDY ***Federal work-study:*** Total amount: $1,483,370; 774 jobs averaging $1300. ***State or other work-study/employment:*** Total amount: $12,737,505 (25% need-based, 75% non-need-based). 4,929 part-time jobs averaging $1934.

ATHLETIC AWARDS Total amount: $6,346,235 (32% need-based, 68% non-need-based).

APPLYING FOR FINANCIAL AID ***Required financial aid forms:*** FAFSA, institution's own form. ***Financial aid deadline (priority):*** 3/1. ***Notification date:*** 3/1. Students must reply within 2 weeks of notification.

CONTACT Mary G. Parker, Director of Student Aid and Scholarships, Louisiana State University and Agricultural and Mechanical College, LSU 208 Coates Hall, Baton Rouge, LA 70803-3103, 225-578-3113. *Fax:* 225-578-9460. *E-mail:* financialaid@lsu.edu.

LOUISIANA STATE UNIVERSITY HEALTH SCIENCES CENTER

New Orleans, LA

CONTACT Mr. Patrick Gorman, Director of Financial Aid, Louisiana State University Health Sciences Center, 433 Bolivar Street, New Orleans, LA 70112, 504-568-4821. *Fax:* 504-599-1390.

LOUISIANA STATE UNIVERSITY IN SHREVEPORT

Shreveport, LA

CONTACT Office of Student Financial Aid, Louisiana State University in Shreveport, One University Place, Shreveport, LA 71115-2399, 318-797-5363 or toll-free 800-229-5957 (in-state). *Fax:* 318-797-5366.

LOUISIANA TECH UNIVERSITY

Ruston, LA

Tuition & fees (LA res): $4502   Average undergraduate aid package: $5944

ABOUT THE INSTITUTION State-supported, coed. Awards: associate, bachelor's, master's, and doctoral degrees and first professional certificates. 79 undergraduate majors. Total enrollment: 11,203. Undergraduates: 9,000. Freshmen: 1,706. Both federal and institutional methodology are used as a basis for awarding need-based institutional aid.

UNDERGRADUATE EXPENSES for 2006–07 ***Application fee:*** $20. ***Tuition, state resident:*** full-time $4502. ***Tuition, nonresident:*** full-time $9407. Full-time tuition and fees vary according to course load, location, and program. Part-time tuition and fees vary according to course load, location, and program. ***College room and board:*** $4365; ***Room only:*** $2310. Room and board charges vary according to board plan and housing facility. ***Payment plans:*** Installment, deferred payment.

FRESHMAN FINANCIAL AID (Fall 2005) 1249 applied for aid; of those 59% were deemed to have need. 98% of freshmen with need received aid; of those 24% had need fully met. ***Average percent of need met:*** 63% (excluding resources awarded to replace EFC). ***Average financial aid package:*** $5520 (excluding resources awarded to replace EFC). 37% of all full-time freshmen had no need and received non-need-based gift aid.

UNDERGRADUATE FINANCIAL AID (Fall 2005) 4,467 applied for aid; of those 65% were deemed to have need. 94% of undergraduates with need received aid; of those 16% had need fully met. ***Average percent of need met:*** 57% (excluding resources awarded to replace EFC). ***Average financial aid package:*** $5944 (excluding resources awarded to replace EFC). 26% of all full-time undergraduates had no need and received non-need-based gift aid.

GIFT AID (NEED-BASED) ***Total amount:*** $14,006,976 (48% federal, 33% state, 14% institutional, 5% external sources). ***Receiving aid:*** Freshmen: 41% (679); All full-time undergraduates: 32% (2,401). ***Average award:*** Freshmen: $4510; Undergraduates: $4482. ***Scholarships, grants, and awards:*** Federal Pell, FSEOG, state, private, college/university gift aid from institutional funds.

GIFT AID (NON-NEED-BASED) ***Total amount:*** $10,653,073 (61% state, 29% institutional, 10% external sources). ***Receiving aid:*** Freshmen: 9% (157); Undergraduates: 5% (387). ***Average award:*** Freshmen: $5197; Undergraduates: $5280. ***Scholarships, grants, and awards by category:*** *Academic Interests/Achievement:* 1,269 awards ($3,018,154 total): agriculture, architecture, biological sciences, business, computer science, education, engineering/technologies, English, foreign languages, general academic interests/achievements, health fields, home economics, humanities, library science, mathematics, military science, physical sciences, social sciences. *Creative Arts/Performance:* 491 awards ($555,876 total): debating, journalism/publications, music, performing arts, theater/drama. *Special Achievements/Activities:* 77 awards ($111,725 total):

cheerleading/drum major. *Special Characteristics:* 475 awards ($1,871,794 total): children of faculty/staff, children with a deceased or disabled parent, out-of-state students, public servants, spouses of deceased or disabled public servants. ***Tuition waivers:*** Full or partial for children of alumni, employees or children of employees, senior citizens. ***ROTC:*** Army cooperative, Naval.

LOANS ***Student loans:*** $22,094,783 (66% need-based, 34% non-need-based). 65% of past graduating class borrowed through all loan programs. *Average indebtedness per student:* $17,142. ***Average need-based loan:*** Freshmen: $1932; Undergraduates: $2734. ***Parent loans:*** $2,313,097 (23% need-based, 77% non-need-based). ***Programs:*** FFEL (Subsidized and Unsubsidized Stafford, PLUS), Perkins, state.

WORK-STUDY ***Federal work-study:*** Total amount: $464,334; 355 jobs averaging $1308. ***State or other work-study/employment:*** Total amount: $1,779,217 (100% need-based). 1,297 part-time jobs averaging $1372.

ATHLETIC AWARDS Total amount: $2,242,361 (43% need-based, 57% non-need-based).

APPLYING FOR FINANCIAL AID ***Required financial aid forms:*** FAFSA, institution's own form. ***Financial aid deadline:*** Continuous. ***Notification date:*** Continuous beginning 4/1. Students must reply within 4 weeks of notification.

CONTACT Financial Aid Office, Louisiana Tech University, PO Box 7925, Ruston, LA 71272, 318-257-2641 or toll-free 800-528-3241. *Fax:* 318-257-2628. *E-mail:* techaid@ltfa.latech.edu.

LOURDES COLLEGE

Sylvania, OH

Tuition & fees: $13,200 **Average undergraduate aid package: $9373**

ABOUT THE INSTITUTION Independent Roman Catholic, coed. Awards: associate, bachelor's, and master's degrees. 21 undergraduate majors. Total enrollment: 1,881. Undergraduates: 1,733. Freshmen: 124. Both federal and institutional methodology are used as a basis for awarding need-based institutional aid.

UNDERGRADUATE EXPENSES for 2006–07 ***Application fee:*** $25. ***Tuition:*** full-time $11,700; part-time $390 per credit hour. ***Required fees:*** full-time $1500; $50 per credit hour. Full-time tuition and fees vary according to course load and location. Part-time tuition and fees vary according to course load and location. ***Payment plans:*** Installment, deferred payment.

FRESHMAN FINANCIAL AID (Fall 2006, est.) 92 applied for aid; of those 79% were deemed to have need. 100% of freshmen with need received aid. ***Average financial aid package:*** $9530 (excluding resources awarded to replace EFC).

UNDERGRADUATE FINANCIAL AID (Fall 2006, est.) 799 applied for aid; of those 83% were deemed to have need. 100% of undergraduates with need received aid. ***Average financial aid package:*** $9373 (excluding resources awarded to replace EFC).

GIFT AID (NEED-BASED) ***Total amount:*** $4,598,328 (46% federal, 38% state, 12% institutional, 4% external sources). ***Receiving aid:*** Freshmen: 47% (51); All full-time undergraduates: 57% (491). ***Average award:*** Freshmen: $6901; Undergraduates: $5570. ***Scholarships, grants, and awards:*** Federal Pell, FSEOG, state, private, college/university gift aid from institutional funds.

GIFT AID (NON-NEED-BASED) ***Receiving aid:*** Freshmen: 68% (73); Undergraduates: 77% (661). ***Scholarships, grants, and awards by category:*** *Academic Interests/Achievement:* 300 awards ($238,753 total): general academic interests/achievements. *Creative Arts/Performance:* art/fine arts, music. *Special Achievements/Activities:* general special achievements/activities. *Special Characteristics:* children of faculty/staff, local/state students, members of minority groups, out-of-state students, previous college experience. ***Tuition waivers:*** Full or partial for employees or children of employees, senior citizens. ***ROTC:*** Army cooperative, Air Force cooperative.

LOANS ***Student loans:*** $8,530,658 (100% need-based). ***Average need-based loan:*** Freshmen: $2557; Undergraduates: $3800. ***Parent loans:*** $604,843 (100% need-based). ***Programs:*** FFEL (Subsidized and Unsubsidized Stafford, PLUS), Perkins, state, college/university, alternative loans.

WORK-STUDY ***Federal work-study:*** Total amount: $130,183; 77 jobs averaging $1691.

APPLYING FOR FINANCIAL AID ***Required financial aid form:*** FAFSA. ***Financial aid deadline (priority):*** 3/1. ***Notification date:*** Continuous beginning 3/1. Students must reply within 4 weeks of notification.

CONTACT Greg Guzman, Director of Financial Aid, Lourdes College, 6832 Convent Boulevard, Sylvania, OH 43560-2898, 419-824-3732 or toll-free 800-878-3210 Ext. 1299. *Fax:* 419-882-3987. *E-mail:* finaid@lourdes.edu.

LOYOLA COLLEGE IN MARYLAND

Baltimore, MD

Tuition & fees: $31,715 **Average undergraduate aid package: $20,830**

ABOUT THE INSTITUTION Independent Roman Catholic (Jesuit), coed. Awards: bachelor's, master's, and doctoral degrees and post-master's certificates. 32 undergraduate majors. Total enrollment: 6,035. Undergraduates: 3,502. Freshmen: 946. Institutional methodology is used as a basis for awarding need-based institutional aid.

UNDERGRADUATE EXPENSES for 2006–07 ***Application fee:*** $50. ***Comprehensive fee:*** $41,293 includes full-time tuition ($30,615), mandatory fees ($1100), and room and board ($9578). ***College room only:*** $7578. Full-time tuition and fees vary according to student level. Room and board charges vary according to board plan. ***Part-time tuition:*** $510 per credit. ***Part-time fees:*** $25 per term.

FRESHMAN FINANCIAL AID (Fall 2006, est.) 635 applied for aid; of those 70% were deemed to have need. 100% of freshmen with need received aid; of those 93% had need fully met. ***Average percent of need met:*** 96% (excluding resources awarded to replace EFC). ***Average financial aid package:*** $21,900 (excluding resources awarded to replace EFC). 11% of all full-time freshmen had no need and received non-need-based gift aid.

UNDERGRADUATE FINANCIAL AID (Fall 2006, est.) 1,903 applied for aid; of those 77% were deemed to have need. 100% of undergraduates with need received aid; of those 95% had need fully met. ***Average percent of need met:*** 98% (excluding resources awarded to replace EFC). ***Average financial aid package:*** $20,830 (excluding resources awarded to replace EFC). 12% of all full-time undergraduates had no need and received non-need-based gift aid.

GIFT AID (NEED-BASED) ***Total amount:*** $24,646,395 (6% federal, 3% state, 88% institutional, 3% external sources). ***Receiving aid:*** Freshmen: 44% (414); All full-time undergraduates: 39% (1,353). ***Average award:*** Freshmen: $13,860; Undergraduates: $12,870. ***Scholarships, grants, and awards:*** Federal Pell, FSEOG, state, private, college/university gift aid from institutional funds.

GIFT AID (NON-NEED-BASED) ***Total amount:*** $5,529,626 (9% federal, 1% state, 80% institutional, 10% external sources). ***Receiving aid:*** Freshmen: 19% (180); Undergraduates: 14% (498). ***Average award:*** Freshmen: $11,200; Undergraduates: $11,240. ***Scholarships, grants, and awards by category:*** *Academic Interests/Achievement:* 605 awards ($6,655,445 total): general academic interests/achievements. *Special Characteristics:* 117 awards ($1,611,750 total): members of minority groups. ***Tuition waivers:*** Full or partial for employees or children of employees. ***ROTC:*** Army, Air Force cooperative.

LOANS ***Student loans:*** $13,463,270 (49% need-based, 51% non-need-based). 78% of past graduating class borrowed through all loan programs. *Average indebtedness per student:* $16,073. ***Average need-based loan:*** Freshmen: $5790; Undergraduates: $5710. ***Parent loans:*** $11,733,166 (100% non-need-based). ***Programs:*** Federal Direct (Subsidized and Unsubsidized Stafford), FFEL (PLUS), Perkins, college/university.

WORK-STUDY ***Federal work-study:*** Total amount: $977,075; 493 jobs averaging $1980. ***State or other work-study/employment:*** Total amount: $672,465 (65% need-based, 35% non-need-based). 86 part-time jobs averaging $7820.

ATHLETIC AWARDS Total amount: $3,969,758 (26% need-based, 74% non-need-based).

APPLYING FOR FINANCIAL AID ***Required financial aid forms:*** FAFSA, CSS Financial Aid PROFILE, noncustodial (divorced/separated) parent's statement, business/farm supplement. ***Financial aid deadline:*** 2/15. ***Notification date:*** 4/1. Students must reply by 5/1.

CONTACT Mr. Mark Lindenmeyer, Director of Financial Aid, Loyola College in Maryland, 4501 North Charles Street, Baltimore, MD 21210-2699, 410-617-2576 or toll-free 800-221-9107 Ext. 2252 (in-state). *Fax:* 410-617-5149. *E-mail:* lindenmeyer@loyola.edu.

LOYOLA MARYMOUNT UNIVERSITY

Los Angeles, CA

CONTACT Financial Aid Office, Loyola Marymount University, One LMU Drive, Los Angeles, CA 90045-8350, 310-338-2753 or toll-free 800-LMU-INFO. *E-mail:* finaid@lmu.edu.

LOYOLA UNIVERSITY CHICAGO

Chicago, IL

Tuition & fees: $27,966 **Average undergraduate aid package: $21,689**

ABOUT THE INSTITUTION Independent Roman Catholic (Jesuit), coed. Awards: bachelor's, master's, doctoral, and first professional degrees and post-bachelor's and post-master's certificates (also offers adult part-time program with significant enrollment not reflected in profile). 51 undergraduate majors. Total enrollment: 15,194. Undergraduates: 9,725. Freshmen: 2,134. Federal methodology is used as a basis for awarding need-based institutional aid.

UNDERGRADUATE EXPENSES for 2007–08 ***Application fee:*** $25. ***Comprehensive fee:*** $37,896 includes full-time tuition ($27,200), mandatory fees ($766), and room and board ($9930). ***College room only:*** $6680. ***Part-time tuition:*** $550 per semester hour. ***Part-time fees:*** $80 per semester hour.

FRESHMAN FINANCIAL AID (Fall 2006, est.) 1825 applied for aid; of those 84% were deemed to have need. 100% of freshmen with need received aid; of those 8% had need fully met. ***Average percent of need met:*** 78% (excluding resources awarded to replace EFC). ***Average financial aid package:*** $21,722 (excluding resources awarded to replace EFC). 16% of all full-time freshmen had no need and received non-need-based gift aid.

UNDERGRADUATE FINANCIAL AID (Fall 2006, est.) 7,036 applied for aid; of those 88% were deemed to have need. 100% of undergraduates with need received aid; of those 8% had need fully met. ***Average percent of need met:*** 77% (excluding resources awarded to replace EFC). ***Average financial aid package:*** $21,689 (excluding resources awarded to replace EFC). 10% of all full-time undergraduates had no need and received non-need-based gift aid.

GIFT AID (NEED-BASED) ***Total amount:*** $87,063,597 (9% federal, 13% state, 75% institutional, 3% external sources). ***Receiving aid:*** Freshmen: 70% (1,491); All full-time undergraduates: 65% (5,835). ***Average award:*** Freshmen: $14,896; Undergraduates: $13,608. ***Scholarships, grants, and awards:*** Federal Pell, FSEOG, state, private, college/university gift aid from institutional funds.

GIFT AID (NON-NEED-BASED) ***Total amount:*** $6,255,622 (93% institutional, 7% external sources). ***Receiving aid:*** Freshmen: 6% (125); Undergraduates: 5% (480). ***Average award:*** Freshmen: $6048; Undergraduates: $6245. ***Scholarships, grants, and awards by category:*** *Academic Interests/Achievement:* 4,124 awards ($30,709,280 total): general academic interests/achievements. *Creative Arts/Performance:* 43 awards ($121,937 total): art/fine arts, debating, journalism/publications, music, theater/drama. *Special Achievements/Activities:* 133 awards ($569,768 total): community service, general special achievements/activities, leadership, memberships. *Special Characteristics:* 1,578 awards ($3,834,357 total): adult students, general special characteristics, religious affiliation. ***ROTC:*** Army cooperative, Naval cooperative, Air Force cooperative.

LOANS ***Student loans:*** $67,100,155 (75% need-based, 25% non-need-based). 67% of past graduating class borrowed through all loan programs. *Average indebtedness per student:* $25,470. ***Average need-based loan:*** Freshmen: $3041; Undergraduates: $4497. ***Parent loans:*** $14,036,542 (42% need-based, 58% non-need-based). ***Programs:*** FFEL (Subsidized and Unsubsidized Stafford, PLUS), Perkins, Federal Nursing.

WORK-STUDY ***Federal work-study:*** Total amount: $8,872,363; 4,249 jobs averaging $2088.

ATHLETIC AWARDS Total amount: $3,018,101 (67% need-based, 33% non-need-based).

APPLYING FOR FINANCIAL AID ***Required financial aid form:*** FAFSA. ***Financial aid deadline:*** Continuous. ***Notification date:*** Continuous beginning 2/15. Students must reply within 3 weeks of notification.

CONTACT Mr. Eric Weems, Director of Financial Aid, Loyola University Chicago, 6525 North Sheridan Road, Sullivan Center, Chicago, IL 60626, 773-508-3155 or toll-free 800-262-2373. *Fax:* 773-508-3177. *E-mail:* lufinaid@luc.edu.

LOYOLA UNIVERSITY NEW ORLEANS

New Orleans, LA

Tuition & fees: $26,508 **Average undergraduate aid package: $23,188**

ABOUT THE INSTITUTION Independent Roman Catholic (Jesuit), coed. Awards: bachelor's, master's, and first professional degrees and post-bachelor's and post-master's certificates. 49 undergraduate majors. Total enrollment: 4,604. Undergraduates: 2,991. Freshmen: 520. Federal methodology is used as a basis for awarding need-based institutional aid.

UNDERGRADUATE EXPENSES for 2007–08 ***Application fee:*** $20. ***Comprehensive fee:*** $35,658 includes full-time tuition ($25,632), mandatory fees ($876), and room and board ($9150). ***College room only:*** $5488. ***Part-time tuition:*** $731 per credit hour.

FRESHMAN FINANCIAL AID (Fall 2006, est.) 418 applied for aid; of those 83% were deemed to have need. 100% of freshmen with need received aid; of those 37% had need fully met. ***Average percent of need met:*** 80% (excluding resources awarded to replace EFC). ***Average financial aid package:*** $23,346 (excluding resources awarded to replace EFC). 29% of all full-time freshmen had no need and received non-need-based gift aid.

UNDERGRADUATE FINANCIAL AID (Fall 2006, est.) 1,673 applied for aid; of those 83% were deemed to have need. 100% of undergraduates with need received aid; of those 40% had need fully met. ***Average percent of need met:*** 81% (excluding resources awarded to replace EFC). ***Average financial aid package:*** $23,188 (excluding resources awarded to replace EFC). 38% of all full-time undergraduates had no need and received non-need-based gift aid.

GIFT AID (NEED-BASED) ***Total amount:*** $18,421,499 (11% federal, 6% state, 81% institutional, 2% external sources). ***Receiving aid:*** Freshmen: 56% (293); All full-time undergraduates: 45% (1,181). ***Average award:*** Freshmen: $16,998; Undergraduates: $15,704. ***Scholarships, grants, and awards:*** Federal Pell, FSEOG, private, college/university gift aid from institutional funds.

GIFT AID (NON-NEED-BASED) ***Total amount:*** $15,018,657 (6% state, 91% institutional, 3% external sources). ***Receiving aid:*** Freshmen: 13% (70); Undergraduates: 9% (246). ***Average award:*** Freshmen: $13,408; Undergraduates: $11,793. ***Scholarships, grants, and awards by category:*** *Academic Interests/Achievement:* 766 awards ($6,926,625 total): general academic interests/achievements. *Creative Arts/Performance:* general creative arts/performance. *Special Characteristics:* 49 awards ($805,156 total): children of faculty/staff. ***ROTC:*** Army cooperative, Naval cooperative, Air Force cooperative.

LOANS ***Student loans:*** $6,880,096 (85% need-based, 15% non-need-based). 61% of past graduating class borrowed through all loan programs. ***Average need-based loan:*** Freshmen: $4954; Undergraduates: $5963. ***Parent loans:*** $3,347,686 (27% need-based, 73% non-need-based). ***Programs:*** FFEL (Subsidized and Unsubsidized Stafford, PLUS), Perkins.

WORK-STUDY ***Federal work-study:*** Total amount: $1,023,189; 764 jobs averaging $1858.

ATHLETIC AWARDS Total amount: $467,920 (28% need-based, 72% non-need-based).

APPLYING FOR FINANCIAL AID ***Required financial aid form:*** FAFSA. ***Financial aid deadline:*** 6/1 (priority: 2/15). ***Notification date:*** 3/1. Students must reply by 5/1 or within 2 weeks of notification.

CONTACT Catherine Simoneaux, Director of Scholarships and Financial Aid, Loyola University New Orleans, 6363 St. Charles Avenue, Box 206, New Orleans, LA 70118-6195, 504-865-3231 or toll-free 800-4-LOYOLA. *Fax:* 504-865-3233. *E-mail:* finaid@loyno.edu.

LUBBOCK CHRISTIAN UNIVERSITY

Lubbock, TX

Tuition & fees: $14,290 **Average undergraduate aid package: $11,564**

ABOUT THE INSTITUTION Independent religious, coed. Awards: bachelor's, master's, and first professional degrees. 44 undergraduate majors. Total enrollment: 2,076. Undergraduates: 1,832. Freshmen: 320. Federal methodology is used as a basis for awarding need-based institutional aid.

UNDERGRADUATE EXPENSES for 2007–08 ***Application fee:*** $25. ***Comprehensive fee:*** $19,040 includes full-time tuition ($13,134), mandatory fees ($1156), and room and board ($4750). ***Part-time tuition:*** $421 per semester hour. ***Part-time fees:*** $431 per term.

FRESHMAN FINANCIAL AID (Fall 2006, est.) 234 applied for aid; of those 85% were deemed to have need. 100% of freshmen with need received aid; of those 15% had need fully met. ***Average percent of need met:*** 74% (excluding resources awarded to replace EFC). ***Average financial aid package:*** $11,506 (excluding resources awarded to replace EFC). 20% of all full-time freshmen had no need and received non-need-based gift aid.

UNDERGRADUATE FINANCIAL AID (Fall 2006, est.) 981 applied for aid; of those 87% were deemed to have need. 100% of undergraduates with need received aid; of those 11% had need fully met. ***Average percent of need met:*** 72% (excluding resources awarded to replace EFC). ***Average financial aid package:*** $11,564 (excluding resources awarded to replace EFC). 20% of all full-time undergraduates had no need and received non-need-based gift aid.

GIFT AID (NEED-BASED) ***Total amount:*** $7,047,252 (28% federal, 33% state, 32% institutional, 7% external sources). ***Receiving aid:*** Freshmen: 78% (200); All full-time undergraduates: 75% (831). ***Average award:*** Freshmen: $8233; Undergraduates: $7772. ***Scholarships, grants, and awards:*** Federal Pell, FSEOG, state, college/university gift aid from institutional funds.

GIFT AID (NON-NEED-BASED) ***Total amount:*** $1,055,360 (1% state, 80% institutional, 19% external sources). ***Receiving aid:*** Freshmen: 9% (23); Undergraduates: 7% (72). ***Average award:*** Freshmen: $10,363; Undergraduates: $10,268. ***Scholarships, grants, and awards by category:*** *Academic Interests/Achievement:* agriculture, business, communication, computer science, education, English, foreign languages, general academic interests/achievements, humanities, physical sciences, religion/biblical studies, social sciences. *Creative Arts/Performance:* art/fine arts, journalism/publications, music, performing arts, theater/drama. *Special Achievements/Activities:* 48 awards ($45,100 total): cheerleading/drum major, leadership. *Special Characteristics:* 43 awards ($330,306 total): children of faculty/staff, general special characteristics. ***ROTC:*** Army cooperative, Air Force cooperative.

LOANS ***Student loans:*** $11,212,455 (75% need-based, 25% non-need-based). 81% of past graduating class borrowed through all loan programs. *Average indebtedness per student:* $22,814. ***Average need-based loan:*** Freshmen: $2917; Undergraduates: $3649. ***Parent loans:*** $2,586,906 (29% need-based, 71% non-need-based). ***Programs:*** FFEL (Subsidized and Unsubsidized Stafford, PLUS), Perkins, state.

WORK-STUDY ***Federal work-study:*** Total amount: $880,568; 883 jobs averaging $2000. ***State or other work-study/employment:*** Total amount: $25,747 (49% need-based, 51% non-need-based). 111 part-time jobs averaging $232.

ATHLETIC AWARDS Total amount: $4,704,751 (91% need-based, 9% non-need-based).

APPLYING FOR FINANCIAL AID ***Required financial aid forms:*** FAFSA, institution's own form. ***Financial aid deadline (priority):*** 6/1. ***Notification date:*** Continuous beginning 3/1.

CONTACT Amy Hardesty, Financial Aid Director, Lubbock Christian University, 5601 19th Street, Lubbock, TX 79407, 806-720-7176 or toll-free 800-933-7601. *Fax:* 806-720-7185. *E-mail:* amy.hardesty@lcu.edu.

LUTHER COLLEGE

Decorah, IA

Tuition & fees: $26,380 **Average undergraduate aid package: $20,916**

ABOUT THE INSTITUTION Independent religious, coed. Awards: bachelor's degrees. 41 undergraduate majors. Total enrollment: 2,504. Undergraduates: 2,504. Freshmen: 612. Federal methodology is used as a basis for awarding need-based institutional aid.

UNDERGRADUATE EXPENSES for 2006–07 ***Application fee:*** $25. ***Comprehensive fee:*** $30,670 includes full-time tuition ($26,380) and room and board ($4290). ***College room only:*** $2100. Full-time tuition and fees vary according to course load. Room and board charges vary according to board plan and housing facility. ***Part-time tuition:*** $924 per semester hour. Part-time tuition and fees vary according to course load. ***Payment plan:*** Installment.

FRESHMAN FINANCIAL AID (Fall 2006, est.) 514 applied for aid; of those 84% were deemed to have need. 100% of freshmen with need received aid; of those 41% had need fully met. ***Average percent of need met:*** 93% (excluding resources awarded to replace EFC). ***Average financial aid package:*** $22,101 (excluding resources awarded to replace EFC). 13% of all full-time freshmen had no need and received non-need-based gift aid.

UNDERGRADUATE FINANCIAL AID (Fall 2006, est.) 2,030 applied for aid; of those 84% were deemed to have need. 100% of undergraduates with need received aid; of those 35% had need fully met. ***Average percent of need met:*** 89% (excluding resources awarded to replace EFC). ***Average financial aid package:*** $20,916 (excluding resources awarded to replace EFC). 12% of all full-time undergraduates had no need and received non-need-based gift aid.

GIFT AID (NEED-BASED) ***Total amount:*** $22,990,464 (8% federal, 7% state, 81% institutional, 4% external sources). ***Receiving aid:*** Freshmen: 70% (430); All full-time undergraduates: 70% (1,694). ***Average award:*** Freshmen: $15,477; Undergraduates: $13,579. ***Scholarships, grants, and awards:*** Federal Pell, FSEOG, state, private, college/university gift aid from institutional funds.

GIFT AID (NON-NEED-BASED) ***Total amount:*** $902,959 (1% federal, 93% institutional, 6% external sources). ***Receiving aid:*** Freshmen: 12% (74); Undergraduates: 8% (203). ***Average award:*** Freshmen: $8270; Undergraduates: $7604. ***Scholarships, grants, and awards by category:*** *Academic Interests/Achievement:* 1,651 awards ($10,950,750 total): general academic interests/achievements. *Creative Arts/Performance:* 854 awards ($1,975,000 total): music. *Special Characteristics:* 650 awards ($880,765 total): children and siblings of alumni, members of minority groups, religious affiliation. ***Tuition waivers:*** Full or partial for employees or children of employees.

LOANS ***Student loans:*** $7,994,921 (88% need-based, 12% non-need-based). 82% of past graduating class borrowed through all loan programs. *Average indebtedness per student:* $18,271. ***Average need-based loan:*** Freshmen: $4559; Undergraduates: $5205. ***Parent loans:*** $6,373,355 (27% need-based, 73% non-need-based). ***Programs:*** Federal Direct (Subsidized and Unsubsidized Stafford, PLUS), Perkins, college/university.

WORK-STUDY ***Federal work-study:*** Total amount: $1,558,289; 943 jobs averaging $1652. ***State or other work-study/employment:*** Total amount: $1,024,457 (24% need-based, 76% non-need-based). 1,029 part-time jobs averaging $996.

APPLYING FOR FINANCIAL AID ***Required financial aid forms:*** FAFSA, institution's own form. ***Financial aid deadline (priority):*** 3/1. ***Notification date:*** Continuous beginning 3/15. Students must reply by 5/1.

CONTACT Ms. Janice Cordell, Director of Student Financial Planning, Luther College, 700 College Drive, Decorah, IA 52101-1045, 563-387-1018 or toll-free 800-458-8437. *E-mail:* cordellj@luther.edu.

LUTHER RICE UNIVERSITY

Lithonia, GA

CONTACT Gary W. Cooke, Director of Financial Aid, Luther Rice University, 3038 Evans Mill Road, Lithonia, GA 30038-2418, 770-484-1204 Ext. 241 or toll-free 800-442-1577. *Fax:* 678-990-5388. *E-mail:* gcooke@lrs.edu.

LYCOMING COLLEGE

Williamsport, PA

Tuition & fees: $25,605 **Average undergraduate aid package: $19,152**

ABOUT THE INSTITUTION Independent United Methodist, coed. Awards: bachelor's degrees. 49 undergraduate majors. Total enrollment: 1,430. Undergraduates: 1,430. Freshmen: 375. Federal methodology is used as a basis for awarding need-based institutional aid.

UNDERGRADUATE EXPENSES for 2006–07 ***Application fee:*** $35. ***Comprehensive fee:*** $32,431 includes full-time tuition ($25,120), mandatory fees ($485), and room and board ($6826). ***College room only:*** $3490. Full-time tuition and fees vary according to course load. Room and board charges vary according to housing facility. ***Part-time tuition:*** $785 per credit hour. Part-time tuition and fees vary according to course load. ***Payment plan:*** Installment.

FRESHMAN FINANCIAL AID (Fall 2006, est.) 344 applied for aid; of those 89% were deemed to have need. 100% of freshmen with need received aid; of those 12% had need fully met. ***Average percent of need met:*** 75% (excluding resources awarded to replace EFC). ***Average financial aid package:*** $19,798 (excluding resources awarded to replace EFC). 14% of all full-time freshmen had no need and received non-need-based gift aid.

UNDERGRADUATE FINANCIAL AID (Fall 2006, est.) 1,246 applied for aid; of those 91% were deemed to have need. 100% of undergraduates with need received aid; of those 15% had need fully met. ***Average percent of need met:*** 76% (excluding resources awarded to replace EFC). ***Average financial aid package:*** $19,152 (excluding resources awarded to replace EFC). 14% of all full-time undergraduates had no need and received non-need-based gift aid.

GIFT AID (NEED-BASED) ***Total amount:*** $16,127,113 (7% federal, 13% state, 77% institutional, 3% external sources). ***Receiving aid:*** Freshmen: 81% (305); All full-time undergraduates: 82% (1,136). ***Average award:*** Freshmen: $16,092; Undergraduates: $14,788. ***Scholarships, grants, and awards:*** Federal Pell, FSEOG, state, private, college/university gift aid from institutional funds.

GIFT AID (NON-NEED-BASED) ***Total amount:*** $2,418,829 (1% state, 93% institutional, 6% external sources). ***Receiving aid:*** Freshmen: 7% (27); Undergraduates: 8% (105). ***Average award:*** Freshmen: $9168; Undergraduates: $9266. ***Scholarships, grants, and awards by category:*** *Academic Interests/Achievement:* 772 awards ($6,323,955 total): biological sciences, business, communication, computer science, education, English, foreign languages, general academic interests/achievements, health fields, humanities, international studies, mathematics, physical sciences, premedicine, religion/biblical studies, social sciences. *Creative Arts/Performance:* 175 awards ($327,550 total): art/fine arts, creative writing, music, theater/drama. *Special Achievements/Activities:* 55 awards

($95,375 total): general special achievements/activities, leadership. *Special Characteristics:* 50 awards ($1,057,587 total): children of educators, children of faculty/staff, relatives of clergy. ***Tuition waivers:*** Full or partial for employees or children of employees. ***ROTC:*** Army cooperative.

LOANS *Student loans:* $8,416,610 (67% need-based, 33% non-need-based). 79% of past graduating class borrowed through all loan programs. *Average indebtedness per student:* $23,343. ***Average need-based loan:*** Freshmen: $3497; Undergraduates: $4474. ***Parent loans:*** $4,993,381 (79% need-based, 21% non-need-based). ***Programs:*** FFEL (Subsidized and Unsubsidized Stafford, PLUS), Perkins, college/university.

WORK-STUDY *Federal work-study:* Total amount: $421,067; 489 jobs averaging $1201. ***State or other work-study/employment:*** Part-time jobs available.

APPLYING FOR FINANCIAL AID *Required financial aid forms:* FAFSA, institution's own form, state aid form. ***Financial aid deadline (priority):*** 3/1. ***Notification date:*** Continuous beginning 3/1. Students must reply by 5/1.

CONTACT Mrs. Jamie Lowthert, Director of Financial Aid, Lycoming College, 700 College Place, Long Hall, Williamsport, PA 17701-5192, 570-321-4040 or toll-free 800-345-3920 Ext. 4026. *Fax:* 570-321-4993. *E-mail:* lowthert@lycoming.edu.

LYME ACADEMY COLLEGE OF FINE ARTS

Old Lyme, CT

Tuition & fees: N/R **Average undergraduate aid package: $7801**

ABOUT THE INSTITUTION Independent, coed. Awards: bachelor's degrees. 3 undergraduate majors. Total enrollment: 160. Undergraduates: 160. Freshmen: 14. Both federal and institutional methodology are used as a basis for awarding need-based institutional aid.

FRESHMAN FINANCIAL AID (Fall 2006, est.) 17 applied for aid; of those 76% were deemed to have need. 100% of freshmen with need received aid. ***Average financial aid package:*** $10,749 (excluding resources awarded to replace EFC). 18% of all full-time freshmen had no need and received non-need-based gift aid.

UNDERGRADUATE FINANCIAL AID (Fall 2006, est.) 79 applied for aid; of those 86% were deemed to have need. 100% of undergraduates with need received aid. ***Average financial aid package:*** $7801 (excluding resources awarded to replace EFC). 6% of all full-time undergraduates had no need and received non-need-based gift aid.

GIFT AID (NEED-BASED) *Total amount:* $548,829 (21% federal, 13% state, 55% institutional, 11% external sources). ***Receiving aid:*** Freshmen: 76% (13); All full-time undergraduates: 83% (68). ***Average award:*** Freshmen: $8473; Undergraduates: $7801. ***Scholarships, grants, and awards:*** Federal Pell, FSEOG, state, private, college/university gift aid from institutional funds.

GIFT AID (NON-NEED-BASED) *Total amount:* $47,500 (100% institutional). ***Receiving aid:*** Freshmen: 76% (13); Undergraduates: 6% (5). ***Average award:*** Freshmen: $7667; Undergraduates: $3909. ***Scholarships, grants, and awards by category:*** *Creative Arts/Performance:* 76 awards ($359,000 total): art/fine arts.

LOANS *Student loans:* $604,189 (100% need-based). 75% of past graduating class borrowed through all loan programs. ***Average need-based loan:*** Freshmen: $2625; Undergraduates: $3593. ***Parent loans:*** $193,113 (100% need-based). ***Programs:*** FFEL (Subsidized and Unsubsidized Stafford, PLUS), Nellie Mae Loans, EXCEL Loans, TERI Loans, Connecticut Student Loan Foundation FFELP loans, alternative loans.

WORK-STUDY *Federal work-study:* Total amount: $5666; 9 jobs averaging $629. ***State or other work-study/employment:*** Total amount: $3668 (100% need-based). 2 part-time jobs averaging $1834.

APPLYING FOR FINANCIAL AID *Required financial aid forms:* FAFSA, CSS Financial Aid PROFILE, business/farm supplement. ***Financial aid deadline:*** Continuous. ***Notification date:*** Continuous beginning 3/1. Students must reply within 2 weeks of notification.

CONTACT Mr. James Falconer, Director of Financial Aid, Lyme Academy College of Fine Arts, 84 Lyme Street, Old Lyme, CT 06371, 860-434-5232 Ext. 114. *Fax:* 860-434-8725. *E-mail:* jfalconer@lymeacademy.edu.

LYNCHBURG COLLEGE

Lynchburg, VA

ABOUT THE INSTITUTION Independent religious, coed. Awards: bachelor's and master's degrees. 47 undergraduate majors. Total enrollment: 2,398. Undergraduates: 2,053. Freshmen: 553.

GIFT AID (NEED-BASED) *Scholarships, grants, and awards:* Federal Pell, FSEOG, state, college/university gift aid from institutional funds.

GIFT AID (NON-NEED-BASED) *Scholarships, grants, and awards by category:* *Academic Interests/Achievement:* general academic interests/achievements. *Creative Arts/Performance:* music. *Special Achievements/Activities:* community service, leadership. *Special Characteristics:* children of faculty/staff.

LOANS *Programs:* FFEL (Subsidized and Unsubsidized Stafford, PLUS), Perkins.

WORK-STUDY *Federal work-study:* Total amount: $200,000; 352 jobs averaging $1088. ***State or other work-study/employment:*** Total amount: $635,913 (25% need-based, 75% non-need-based). 465 part-time jobs averaging $1373.

APPLYING FOR FINANCIAL AID *Required financial aid forms:* FAFSA, state aid form.

CONTACT Mrs. Michelle Davis, Director of Financial Aid, Lynchburg College, 1501 Lakeside Drive, Lynchburg, VA 24501-3199, 434-544-8228 or toll-free 800-426-8101. *Fax:* 434-544-8653.

LYNDON STATE COLLEGE

Lyndonville, VT

Tuition & fees (VT res): $6828 **Average undergraduate aid package: N/A**

ABOUT THE INSTITUTION State-supported, coed. Awards: associate, bachelor's, and master's degrees. 31 undergraduate majors. Total enrollment: 1,412. Undergraduates: 1,342. Freshmen: 352. Federal methodology is used as a basis for awarding need-based institutional aid.

UNDERGRADUATE EXPENSES for 2006–07 *Application fee:* $35. ***Tuition, state resident:*** full-time $6648; part-time $277 per credit hour. ***Tuition, nonresident:*** full-time $14,376; part-time $599 per credit hour. ***Required fees:*** full-time $180; $8 per credit hour. Full-time tuition and fees vary according to course load. Part-time tuition and fees vary according to course load. ***College room and board:*** $6942; ***Room only:*** $4134. Room and board charges vary according to board plan and housing facility. ***Payment plan:*** Installment.

FRESHMAN FINANCIAL AID (Fall 2005) 314 applied for aid; of those 79% were deemed to have need. 100% of freshmen with need received aid; of those 17% had need fully met. ***Average percent of need met:*** 64% (excluding resources awarded to replace EFC). ***Average financial aid package:*** $8843 (excluding resources awarded to replace EFC). 25% of all full-time freshmen had no need and received non-need-based gift aid.

GIFT AID (NEED-BASED) *Total amount:* $3,610,484 (41% federal, 21% state, 24% institutional, 14% external sources). ***Receiving aid:*** Freshmen: 50% (169). ***Average award:*** Freshmen: $4117. ***Scholarships, grants, and awards:*** Federal Pell, FSEOG, state, private, college/university gift aid from institutional funds.

GIFT AID (NON-NEED-BASED) *Total amount:* $198,156 (82% institutional, 18% external sources). ***Receiving aid:*** Freshmen: 53% (180). ***Average award:*** Freshmen: $1913. ***Tuition waivers:*** Full or partial for employees or children of employees. ***ROTC:*** Air Force cooperative.

LOANS *Student loans:* $7,332,024 (85% need-based, 15% non-need-based). ***Average need-based loan:*** Freshmen: $2912. ***Parent loans:*** $2,765,043 (64% need-based, 36% non-need-based). ***Programs:*** FFEL (Subsidized and Unsubsidized Stafford, PLUS), Perkins.

WORK-STUDY *Federal work-study:* Total amount: $413,375. ***State or other work-study/employment:*** Total amount: $350,000 (100% non-need-based).

APPLYING FOR FINANCIAL AID *Required financial aid form:* FAFSA. ***Financial aid deadline (priority):*** 2/15. ***Notification date:*** Continuous beginning 2/1. Students must reply within 2 weeks of notification.

CONTACT Student Services Center, Student Services Consultant, Lyndon State College, 1001 College Road, Lyndonville, VT 05851, 802-626-6396 or toll-free 800-225-1998. *Fax:* 802-626-9770. *E-mail:* financialaid@lyndonstate.edu.

LYNN UNIVERSITY

Boca Raton, FL

ABOUT THE INSTITUTION Independent, coed. Awards: bachelor's, master's, and doctoral degrees and post-bachelor's and post-master's certificates. 15 undergraduate majors. Total enrollment: 2,715. Undergraduates: 2,300. Freshmen: 564.

GIFT AID (NEED-BASED) ***Scholarships, grants, and awards:*** Federal Pell, FSEOG, state, private, college/university gift aid from institutional funds.

GIFT AID (NON-NEED-BASED) ***Scholarships, grants, and awards by category:*** *Academic Interests/Achievement:* business, communication, general academic interests/achievements. *Creative Arts/Performance:* music. *Special Achievements/Activities:* leadership, religious involvement. *Special Characteristics:* children of faculty/staff, siblings of current students.

LOANS ***Programs:*** FFEL (Subsidized and Unsubsidized Stafford, PLUS), Perkins, state, college/university.

APPLYING FOR FINANCIAL AID ***Required financial aid forms:*** FAFSA, institution's own form.

CONTACT William Healy, Director of Student Financial Services, Lynn University, 3601 North Military Trail, Boca Raton, FL 33431-5598, 561-237-7814 or toll-free 800-888-LYNN (in-state), 800-888-5966 (out-of-state). *Fax:* 561-237-7189. *E-mail:* whealy@lynn.edu.

LYON COLLEGE

Batesville, AR

Tuition & fees: $15,960 **Average undergraduate aid package: $13,927**

ABOUT THE INSTITUTION Independent Presbyterian, coed. Awards: bachelor's degrees. 18 undergraduate majors. Total enrollment: 489. Undergraduates: 489. Freshmen: 128. Both federal and institutional methodology are used as a basis for awarding need-based institutional aid.

UNDERGRADUATE EXPENSES for 2007–08 ***Application fee:*** $25. ***Comprehensive fee:*** $22,604 includes full-time tuition ($15,466), mandatory fees ($494), and room and board ($6644). ***College room only:*** $2734. ***Part-time tuition:*** $644 per credit hour.

FRESHMAN FINANCIAL AID (Fall 2006, est.) 108 applied for aid; of those 82% were deemed to have need. 100% of freshmen with need received aid; of those 44% had need fully met. ***Average percent of need met:*** 84% (excluding resources awarded to replace EFC). ***Average financial aid package:*** $13,452 (excluding resources awarded to replace EFC). 25% of all full-time freshmen had no need and received non-need-based gift aid.

UNDERGRADUATE FINANCIAL AID (Fall 2006, est.) 386 applied for aid; of those 84% were deemed to have need. 100% of undergraduates with need received aid; of those 29% had need fully met. ***Average percent of need met:*** 78% (excluding resources awarded to replace EFC). ***Average financial aid package:*** $13,927 (excluding resources awarded to replace EFC). 28% of all full-time undergraduates had no need and received non-need-based gift aid.

GIFT AID (NEED-BASED) ***Total amount:*** $2,928,214 (20% federal, 11% state, 65% institutional, 4% external sources). ***Receiving aid:*** Freshmen: 70% (89); All full-time undergraduates: 70% (322). ***Average award:*** Freshmen: $11,269; Undergraduates: $10,263. ***Scholarships, grants, and awards:*** Federal Pell, FSEOG, state, private, college/university gift aid from institutional funds, United Negro College Fund.

GIFT AID (NON-NEED-BASED) ***Total amount:*** $1,451,882 (18% state, 78% institutional, 4% external sources). ***Receiving aid:*** Freshmen: 24% (31); Undergraduates: 15% (69). ***Average award:*** Freshmen: $11,045; Undergraduates: $11,549. ***Scholarships, grants, and awards by category:*** *Academic Interests/Achievement:* 460 awards ($1,888,896 total): general academic interests/achievements. *Creative Arts/Performance:* 29 awards ($57,450 total): art/fine arts, music, theater/drama. *Special Achievements/Activities:* 18 awards ($70,000 total): leadership. *Special Characteristics:* 16 awards ($113,445 total): children of faculty/staff, ethnic background, local/state students, members of minority groups, religious affiliation.

LOANS ***Student loans:*** $1,879,433 (78% need-based, 22% non-need-based). 91% of past graduating class borrowed through all loan programs. *Average indebtedness per student:* $15,495. ***Average need-based loan:*** Freshmen: $3179; Undergraduates: $4744. ***Parent loans:*** $599,911 (30% need-based, 70% non-need-based). ***Programs:*** FFEL (Subsidized and Unsubsidized Stafford, PLUS), Perkins.

WORK-STUDY ***Federal work-study:*** Total amount: $101,754; 114 jobs averaging $1085. ***State or other work-study/employment:*** Total amount: $5000 (100% non-need-based). 5 part-time jobs averaging $1000.

ATHLETIC AWARDS Total amount: $921,575 (39% need-based, 61% non-need-based).

APPLYING FOR FINANCIAL AID ***Required financial aid form:*** FAFSA. ***Financial aid deadline (priority):*** 3/15. ***Notification date:*** Continuous beginning 3/1. Students must reply by 8/15.

CONTACT Ms. Louise Strauser, Assistant Director of Student Financial Assistance, Lyon College, 2300 Highland Road, Batesville, AR 72501, 870-698-4257 or toll-free 800-423-2542. *Fax:* 870-793-1791. *E-mail:* financialaid@lyon.edu.

MACALESTER COLLEGE

St. Paul, MN

ABOUT THE INSTITUTION Independent Presbyterian, coed. Awards: bachelor's degrees. 38 undergraduate majors. Total enrollment: 1,918. Undergraduates: 1,918. Freshmen: 501.

GIFT AID (NEED-BASED) ***Scholarships, grants, and awards:*** Federal Pell, FSEOG, state, private, college/university gift aid from institutional funds.

GIFT AID (NON-NEED-BASED) ***Scholarships, grants, and awards by category:*** *Academic Interests/Achievement:* general academic interests/achievements. *Special Characteristics:* ethnic background.

LOANS ***Programs:*** FFEL (Subsidized and Unsubsidized Stafford, PLUS), Perkins, state.

WORK-STUDY ***Federal work-study:*** Total amount: $500,972; 315 jobs averaging $1591. ***State or other work-study/employment:*** Total amount: $1,896,965 (98% need-based, 2% non-need-based). 936 part-time jobs averaging $2026.

APPLYING FOR FINANCIAL AID ***Required financial aid forms:*** FAFSA, CSS Financial Aid PROFILE, noncustodial (divorced/separated) parent's statement.

CONTACT Financial Aid Office, Macalester College, 1600 Grand Avenue, St. Paul, MN 55105, 651-696-6214 or toll-free 800-231-7974. *Fax:* 651-696-6866. *E-mail:* finaid@macalester.edu.

MACHZIKEI HADATH RABBINICAL COLLEGE

Brooklyn, NY

CONTACT Rabbi Baruch Rozmarin, Director of Financial Aid, Machzikei Hadath Rabbinical College, 5407 16th Avenue, Brooklyn, NY 11204-1805, 718-854-8777.

MacMURRAY COLLEGE

Jacksonville, IL

Tuition & fees: $16,730 **Average undergraduate aid package: $12,981**

ABOUT THE INSTITUTION Independent United Methodist, coed. Awards: associate and bachelor's degrees. 39 undergraduate majors. Total enrollment: 699. Undergraduates: 699. Freshmen: 163. Federal methodology is used as a basis for awarding need-based institutional aid.

UNDERGRADUATE EXPENSES for 2007–08 ***Comprehensive fee:*** $22,896 includes full-time tuition ($16,400), mandatory fees ($330), and room and board ($6166). ***College room only:*** $2900. ***Part-time tuition:*** $400 per credit. ***Part-time fees:*** $111 per term.

FRESHMAN FINANCIAL AID (Fall 2005) 158 applied for aid; of those 91% were deemed to have need. 100% of freshmen with need received aid; of those 23% had need fully met. ***Average percent of need met:*** 75% (excluding resources awarded to replace EFC). ***Average financial aid package:*** $12,291 (excluding resources awarded to replace EFC). 9% of all full-time freshmen had no need and received non-need-based gift aid.

UNDERGRADUATE FINANCIAL AID (Fall 2005) 629 applied for aid; of those 91% were deemed to have need. 100% of undergraduates with need received aid; of those 23% had need fully met. ***Average percent of need met:*** 77% (excluding resources awarded to replace EFC). ***Average financial aid package:*** $12,981 (excluding resources awarded to replace EFC). 9% of all full-time undergraduates had no need and received non-need-based gift aid.

GIFT AID (NEED-BASED) ***Total amount:*** $5,660,745 (19% federal, 26% state, 53% institutional, 2% external sources). ***Receiving aid:*** Freshmen: 91% (143); All full-time undergraduates: 90% (568). ***Average award:*** Freshmen: $9150;

Undergraduates: $8856. ***Scholarships, grants, and awards:*** Federal Pell, FSEOG, state, private, college/university gift aid from institutional funds.

GIFT AID (NON-NEED-BASED) ***Total amount:*** $569,692 (1% federal, 1% state, 92% institutional, 6% external sources). ***Receiving aid:*** Freshmen: 9% (14); Undergraduates: 7% (43). ***Average award:*** Freshmen: $14,408; Undergraduates: $12,062. ***Scholarships, grants, and awards by category:*** *Academic Interests/Achievement:* 200 awards ($6,106,118 total): biological sciences, education, English, foreign languages, general academic interests/achievements, health fields, physical sciences, religion/biblical studies, social sciences. *Creative Arts/Performance:* 24 awards ($44,125 total): art/fine arts, music, theater/drama. *Special Achievements/Activities:* 42 awards ($65,210 total): leadership, religious involvement. *Special Characteristics:* 129 awards ($364,447 total): children and siblings of alumni, children of faculty/staff, international students, out-of-state students, previous college experience, religious affiliation, siblings of current students.

LOANS ***Student loans:*** $4,475,657 (77% need-based, 23% non-need-based). 95% of past graduating class borrowed through all loan programs. *Average indebtedness per student:* $22,487. ***Average need-based loan:*** Freshmen: $3900; Undergraduates: $4778. ***Parent loans:*** $591,765 (43% need-based, 57% non-need-based). ***Programs:*** FFEL (Subsidized and Unsubsidized Stafford, PLUS), Perkins.

WORK-STUDY ***Federal work-study:*** Total amount: $57,530; 91 jobs averaging $671. ***State or other work-study/employment:*** Total amount: $91,716 (100% non-need-based). 115 part-time jobs averaging $797.

APPLYING FOR FINANCIAL AID ***Required financial aid form:*** FAFSA. ***Financial aid deadline (priority):*** 5/31. ***Notification date:*** Continuous. Students must reply within 2 weeks of notification.

CONTACT Dena Dobson, Director of Financial Aid, MacMurray College, 447 East College Avenue, Jacksonville, IL 62650, 217-479-7041 or toll-free 800-252-7485 (in-state). *Fax:* 217-291-0702. *E-mail:* dena.dobson@mac.edu.

MACON STATE COLLEGE

Macon, GA

Tuition & fees (GA res): $1792 **Average undergraduate aid package: $5984**

ABOUT THE INSTITUTION State-supported, coed. Awards: associate and bachelor's degrees. 58 undergraduate majors. Total enrollment: 6,244. Undergraduates: 6,244. Freshmen: 1,117. Federal methodology is used as a basis for awarding need-based institutional aid.

UNDERGRADUATE EXPENSES for 2007–08 ***Application fee:*** $20. ***Tuition, state resident:*** full-time $1604; part-time $68 per credit hour. ***Tuition, nonresident:*** full-time $6412; part-time $268 per credit hour. ***Required fees:*** full-time $188; $94 per term part-time.

FRESHMAN FINANCIAL AID (Fall 2005) 100% of freshmen with need received aid; of those 10% had need fully met. ***Average financial aid package:*** $5334 (excluding resources awarded to replace EFC). 30% of all full-time freshmen had no need and received non-need-based gift aid.

UNDERGRADUATE FINANCIAL AID (Fall 2005) 100% of undergraduates with need received aid; of those 3% had need fully met. ***Average percent of need met:*** 46% (excluding resources awarded to replace EFC). ***Average financial aid package:*** $5984 (excluding resources awarded to replace EFC). 21% of all full-time undergraduates had no need and received non-need-based gift aid.

GIFT AID (NEED-BASED) ***Total amount:*** $5,416,682 (99% federal, 1% state). ***Receiving aid:*** Freshmen: 45% (322); All full-time undergraduates: 44% (1,095). ***Average award:*** Freshmen: $3152; Undergraduates: $3031. ***Scholarships, grants, and awards:*** Federal Pell, FSEOG, state, college/university gift aid from institutional funds, Georgia HOPE Scholarships.

GIFT AID (NON-NEED-BASED) ***Total amount:*** $2,930,386 (99% state, 1% external sources). ***Receiving aid:*** Freshmen: 33% (235); Undergraduates: 22% (543). ***Average award:*** Freshmen: $1871; Undergraduates: $1826. ***Scholarships, grants, and awards by category:*** *Academic Interests/Achievement:* 77 awards ($68,875 total): biological sciences, business, communication, education, engineering/technologies, general academic interests/achievements, health fields, social sciences. *Creative Arts/Performance:* 3 awards ($2250 total): journalism/publications. *Special Characteristics:* 6 awards ($6400 total): local/state students.

LOANS ***Student loans:*** $8,434,786 (51% need-based, 49% non-need-based). ***Average need-based loan:*** Freshmen: $2158; Undergraduates: $2749. ***Parent loans:*** $74,213 (100% non-need-based). ***Programs:*** FFEL (Subsidized and Unsubsidized Stafford, PLUS), state.

WORK-STUDY ***Federal work-study:*** Total amount: $167,541; 106 jobs available. ***State or other work-study/employment:*** Part-time jobs available.

APPLYING FOR FINANCIAL AID ***Required financial aid forms:*** FAFSA, state aid form. ***Financial aid deadline (priority):*** 4/1. ***Notification date:*** Continuous beginning 4/15.

CONTACT Office of Financial Aid, Macon State College, 100 College Station Drive, Macon, GA 31206, 478-471-2717 or toll-free 800-272-7619 Ext. 2800. *Fax:* 478-471-2790. *E-mail:* fainfo@mail.maconstate.edu.

MADONNA UNIVERSITY

Livonia, MI

CONTACT Financial Aid Secretary, Madonna University, 36600 Schoolcraft Road, Livonia, MI 48150-1173, 734-432-5663 or toll-free 800-852-4951.

MAGDALEN COLLEGE

Warner, NH

Tuition & fees: N/R **Average undergraduate aid package: $12,590**

ABOUT THE INSTITUTION Independent Roman Catholic, coed. Awards: associate and bachelor's degrees. 1 undergraduate major. Total enrollment: 73. Undergraduates: 73. Freshmen: 28. Institutional methodology is used as a basis for awarding need-based institutional aid.

FRESHMAN FINANCIAL AID (Fall 2006, est.) 15 applied for aid; of those 100% were deemed to have need. 100% of freshmen with need received aid; of those 100% had need fully met. ***Average percent of need met:*** 100% (excluding resources awarded to replace EFC). ***Average financial aid package:*** $16,118 (excluding resources awarded to replace EFC).

UNDERGRADUATE FINANCIAL AID (Fall 2006, est.) 38 applied for aid; of those 100% were deemed to have need. 100% of undergraduates with need received aid; of those 100% had need fully met. ***Average percent of need met:*** 100% (excluding resources awarded to replace EFC). ***Average financial aid package:*** $12,590 (excluding resources awarded to replace EFC).

GIFT AID (NEED-BASED) ***Total amount:*** $114,600 (98% institutional, 2% external sources). ***Receiving aid:*** Freshmen: 71% (15); All full-time undergraduates: 58% (38). ***Average award:*** Freshmen: $4150; Undergraduates: $2210. ***Scholarships, grants, and awards:*** private, college/university gift aid from institutional funds.

GIFT AID (NON-NEED-BASED) ***Total amount:*** $146,500 (98% institutional, 2% external sources). ***Tuition waivers:*** Full or partial for employees or children of employees.

LOANS ***Student loans:*** $430,199 (57% need-based, 43% non-need-based). 40% of past graduating class borrowed through all loan programs. *Average indebtedness per student:* $16,500. ***Programs:*** college/university, alternative loans.

WORK-STUDY ***State or other work-study/employment:*** Total amount: $29,200 (51% need-based, 49% non-need-based). 16 part-time jobs averaging $888.

APPLYING FOR FINANCIAL AID ***Required financial aid form:*** institution's own form. ***Financial aid deadline:*** Continuous. ***Notification date:*** 7/1. Students must reply within 4 weeks of notification.

CONTACT Gail Crowdes, Assistant to Executive Vice President, Magdalen College, 511 Kearsarge Mountain Road, Warner, NH 03278, 603-456-2656 or toll-free 877-498-1723 (out-of-state). *Fax:* 603-456-2660. *E-mail:* gcrowdes@magdalen.edu.

MAGNOLIA BIBLE COLLEGE

Kosciusko, MS

CONTACT Allen Coker, Financial Aid Director, Magnolia Bible College, PO Box 1109, Kosciusko, MS 39090-1109, 662-289-2896 or toll-free 800-748-8655 (in-state). *Fax:* 662-289-1850. *E-mail:* acoker@magnolia.edu.

MAHARISHI UNIVERSITY OF MANAGEMENT

Fairfield, IA

Tuition & fees: $24,430 **Average undergraduate aid package: $23,963**

ABOUT THE INSTITUTION Independent, coed. Awards: bachelor's, master's, and doctoral degrees and post-bachelor's certificates. 10 undergraduate majors. Total enrollment: 931. Undergraduates: 284. Freshmen: 32. Federal methodology is used as a basis for awarding need-based institutional aid.

UNDERGRADUATE EXPENSES for 2006–07 ***Application fee:*** $15. ***Comprehensive fee:*** $30,430 includes full-time tuition ($24,000), mandatory fees ($430), and room and board ($6000). ***Part-time tuition:*** $350 per credit hour.

FRESHMAN FINANCIAL AID (Fall 2006, est.) 42 applied for aid; of those 95% were deemed to have need. 100% of freshmen with need received aid; of those 25% had need fully met. ***Average percent of need met:*** 89% (excluding resources awarded to replace EFC). ***Average financial aid package:*** $23,963 (excluding resources awarded to replace EFC).

UNDERGRADUATE FINANCIAL AID (Fall 2006, est.) 150 applied for aid; of those 99% were deemed to have need. 100% of undergraduates with need received aid; of those 22% had need fully met. ***Average percent of need met:*** 89% (excluding resources awarded to replace EFC). ***Average financial aid package:*** $23,963 (excluding resources awarded to replace EFC). 3% of all full-time undergraduates had no need and received non-need-based gift aid.

GIFT AID (NEED-BASED) ***Total amount:*** $2,623,774 (20% federal, 7% state, 72% institutional, 1% external sources). ***Receiving aid:*** Freshmen: 93% (40); All full-time undergraduates: 92% (148). ***Average award:*** Freshmen: $15,138; Undergraduates: $14,082. ***Scholarships, grants, and awards:*** Federal Pell, FSEOG, state, private, college/university gift aid from institutional funds.

GIFT AID (NON-NEED-BASED) ***Total amount:*** $11,494 (100% institutional). ***Receiving aid:*** Undergraduates: 7% (11). ***Average award:*** Undergraduates: $9300. ***Scholarships, grants, and awards by category:*** *Academic Interests/Achievement:* 9 awards ($75,497 total): general academic interests/achievements. *Creative Arts/Performance:* 7 awards ($6050 total): creative writing, music. *Special Characteristics:* 47 awards ($353,612 total): children of faculty/staff, ethnic background, veterans, veterans' children.

LOANS ***Student loans:*** $1,653,214 (79% need-based, 21% non-need-based). 83% of past graduating class borrowed through all loan programs. *Average indebtedness per student:* $26,800. ***Average need-based loan:*** Freshmen: $6625; Undergraduates: $8281. ***Parent loans:*** $39,066 (100% non-need-based). ***Programs:*** FFEL (Subsidized and Unsubsidized Stafford, PLUS), Perkins, college/university, alternative loans.

WORK-STUDY ***Federal work-study:*** Total amount: $170,655; 120 jobs averaging $1422. ***State or other work-study/employment:*** Total amount: $19,100 (100% need-based). 7 part-time jobs averaging $2729.

APPLYING FOR FINANCIAL AID ***Required financial aid form:*** FAFSA. ***Financial aid deadline:*** Continuous. ***Notification date:*** Continuous beginning 2/15.

CONTACT Mr. Bill Christensen, Director of Financial Aid, Maharishi University of Management, 1000 North 4th Street, DB 1127, Fairfield, IA 52557-1127, 641-472-1156 or toll-free 800-369-6480. *Fax:* 641-472-1133. *E-mail:* bchrist@mum.edu.

MAINE COLLEGE OF ART

Portland, ME

Tuition & fees: $26,060 **Average undergraduate aid package: $13,894**

ABOUT THE INSTITUTION Independent, coed. Awards: bachelor's and master's degrees. 9 undergraduate majors. Total enrollment: 409. Undergraduates: 381. Freshmen: 71. Federal methodology is used as a basis for awarding need-based institutional aid.

UNDERGRADUATE EXPENSES for 2007–08 ***Application fee:*** $40. ***Comprehensive fee:*** $35,330 includes full-time tuition ($25,410), mandatory fees ($650), and room and board ($9270).

FRESHMAN FINANCIAL AID (Fall 2005) 70 applied for aid; of those 87% were deemed to have need. 100% of freshmen with need received aid; of those 3% had need fully met. ***Average percent of need met:*** 53% (excluding resources awarded to replace EFC). ***Average financial aid package:*** $13,152 (excluding resources awarded to replace EFC). 20% of all full-time freshmen had no need and received non-need-based gift aid.

UNDERGRADUATE FINANCIAL AID (Fall 2005) 323 applied for aid; of those 90% were deemed to have need. 100% of undergraduates with need received aid; of those 10% had need fully met. ***Average percent of need met:*** 56% (excluding resources awarded to replace EFC). ***Average financial aid package:*** $13,894 (excluding resources awarded to replace EFC). 12% of all full-time undergraduates had no need and received non-need-based gift aid.

GIFT AID (NEED-BASED) ***Total amount:*** $3,020,561 (16% federal, 3% state, 78% institutional, 3% external sources). ***Receiving aid:*** Freshmen: 80% (61); All full-time undergraduates: 85% (290). ***Average award:*** Freshmen: $9965; Undergraduates: $10,174. ***Scholarships, grants, and awards:*** Federal Pell, FSEOG, state, private, college/university gift aid from institutional funds.

GIFT AID (NON-NEED-BASED) ***Total amount:*** $541,750 (91% institutional, 9% external sources). ***Receiving aid:*** Freshmen: 1% (1); Undergraduates: 5% (16). ***Average award:*** Freshmen: $4367; Undergraduates: $6860. ***Scholarships, grants, and awards by category:*** *Creative Arts/Performance:* 614 awards ($1,456,533 total): art/fine arts. *Special Characteristics:* 1 award ($24,670 total): children of faculty/staff.

LOANS ***Student loans:*** $3,243,074 (75% need-based, 25% non-need-based). 80% of past graduating class borrowed through all loan programs. *Average indebtedness per student:* $33,350. ***Average need-based loan:*** Freshmen: $2860; Undergraduates: $3965. ***Parent loans:*** $914,978 (49% need-based, 51% non-need-based). ***Programs:*** FFEL (Subsidized and Unsubsidized Stafford, PLUS), Perkins, alternative loans.

WORK-STUDY ***Federal work-study:*** Total amount: $104,677; 54 jobs averaging $2151.

APPLYING FOR FINANCIAL AID ***Required financial aid form:*** FAFSA. ***Financial aid deadline (priority):*** 3/1. ***Notification date:*** Continuous beginning 3/15. Students must reply within 2 weeks of notification.

CONTACT Michelle A. Leclerc, Director of Financial Aid, Maine College of Art, 97 Spring Street, Portland, ME 04101-3987, 207-775-3052 or toll-free 800-639-4808. *Fax:* 207-772-5069. *E-mail:* mleclerc@meca.edu.

MAINE MARITIME ACADEMY

Castine, ME

Tuition & fees (ME res): $8195 **Average undergraduate aid package: $13,822**

ABOUT THE INSTITUTION State-supported, coed, primarily men. Awards: associate, bachelor's, and master's degrees. 11 undergraduate majors. Total enrollment: 858. Undergraduates: 836. Freshmen: 239. Federal methodology is used as a basis for awarding need-based institutional aid.

UNDERGRADUATE EXPENSES for 2006–07 ***Application fee:*** $15. ***Tuition, state resident:*** full-time $6800; part-time $245 per credit hour. ***Tuition, nonresident:*** full-time $13,110; part-time $435 per credit hour. Full-time tuition and fees vary according to course load and program. Part-time tuition and fees vary according to course load and program. ***College room and board:*** $7050; ***Room only:*** $2540. Room and board charges vary according to board plan. ***Payment plan:*** Installment.

FRESHMAN FINANCIAL AID (Fall 2005) 154 applied for aid; of those 83% were deemed to have need. 100% of freshmen with need received aid; of those 12% had need fully met. ***Average percent of need met:*** 63% (excluding resources awarded to replace EFC). ***Average financial aid package:*** $6911 (excluding resources awarded to replace EFC). 12% of all full-time freshmen had no need and received non-need-based gift aid.

UNDERGRADUATE FINANCIAL AID (Fall 2005) 691 applied for aid; of those 89% were deemed to have need. 100% of undergraduates with need received aid; of those 13% had need fully met. ***Average percent of need met:*** 56% (excluding resources awarded to replace EFC). ***Average financial aid package:*** $13,822 (excluding resources awarded to replace EFC). 10% of all full-time undergraduates had no need and received non-need-based gift aid.

GIFT AID (NEED-BASED) ***Total amount:*** $1,662,309 (40% federal, 18% state, 28% institutional, 14% external sources). ***Receiving aid:*** Freshmen: 51% (111); All full-time undergraduates: 61% (480). ***Average award:*** Freshmen: $3842; Undergraduates: $4861. ***Scholarships, grants, and awards:*** Federal Pell, FSEOG, state, private, college/university gift aid from institutional funds.

GIFT AID (NON-NEED-BASED) ***Total amount:*** $774,774 (45% federal, 2% state, 44% institutional, 9% external sources). ***Receiving aid:*** Freshmen: 22% (48); Undergraduates: 18% (146). ***Average award:*** Freshmen: $2500; Undergraduates: $2500. ***Scholarships, grants, and awards by category:*** *Academic Interests/Achievement:* 162 awards ($338,425 total): biological sciences, business, engineering/technologies, general academic interests/achievements. *Special Characteristics:* 8 awards ($44,140 total): children of faculty/staff. ***ROTC:*** Army, Naval.

LOANS ***Student loans:*** $5,637,087 (42% need-based, 58% non-need-based). 82% of past graduating class borrowed through all loan programs. *Average indebtedness per student:* $26,508. ***Average need-based loan:*** Freshmen: $3993;

Undergraduates: $4875. ***Parent loans:*** $986,230 (27% need-based, 73% non-need-based). ***Programs:*** FFEL (Subsidized and Unsubsidized Stafford, PLUS), Perkins, college/university, alternative loans.

WORK-STUDY ***Federal work-study:*** Total amount: $117,791; 178 jobs averaging $662.

APPLYING FOR FINANCIAL AID ***Required financial aid form:*** FAFSA. ***Financial aid deadline (priority):*** 4/15. ***Notification date:*** Continuous beginning 4/1. Students must reply within 4 weeks of notification.

CONTACT Ms. Holly Bayle, Assistant Director of Financial Aid, Maine Maritime Academy, Pleasant Street, Castine, ME 04420, 207-326-2205 or toll-free 800-464-6565 (in-state), 800-227-8465 (out-of-state). *Fax:* 207-326-2515. *E-mail:* bbayle@mma.edu.

MALONE COLLEGE

Canton, OH

Tuition & fees: $17,790 **Average undergraduate aid package: $12,794**

ABOUT THE INSTITUTION Independent religious, coed. Awards: bachelor's and master's degrees and post-bachelor's certificates. 43 undergraduate majors. Total enrollment: 2,296. Undergraduates: 1,960. Freshmen: 345. Federal methodology is used as a basis for awarding need-based institutional aid.

UNDERGRADUATE EXPENSES for 2006–07 ***Application fee:*** $20. ***Comprehensive fee:*** $24,190 includes full-time tuition ($17,520), mandatory fees ($270), and room and board ($6400). ***College room only:*** $3300. Room and board charges vary according to board plan. ***Part-time tuition:*** $330 per semester hour. ***Part-time fees:*** $67.50 per term. Part-time tuition and fees vary according to course load. ***Payment plan:*** Installment.

FRESHMAN FINANCIAL AID (Fall 2006, est.) 307 applied for aid; of those 87% were deemed to have need. 100% of freshmen with need received aid; of those 15% had need fully met. ***Average percent of need met:*** 72% (excluding resources awarded to replace EFC). ***Average financial aid package:*** $13,770 (excluding resources awarded to replace EFC). 13% of all full-time freshmen had no need and received non-need-based gift aid.

UNDERGRADUATE FINANCIAL AID (Fall 2006, est.) 1,407 applied for aid; of those 88% were deemed to have need. 100% of undergraduates with need received aid; of those 17% had need fully met. ***Average percent of need met:*** 70% (excluding resources awarded to replace EFC). ***Average financial aid package:*** $12,794 (excluding resources awarded to replace EFC). 11% of all full-time undergraduates had no need and received non-need-based gift aid.

GIFT AID (NEED-BASED) ***Total amount:*** $9,487,202 (18% federal, 21% state, 53% institutional, 8% external sources). ***Receiving aid:*** Freshmen: 78% (267); All full-time undergraduates: 72% (1,228). ***Average award:*** Freshmen: $10,204; Undergraduates: $8846. ***Scholarships, grants, and awards:*** Federal Pell, FSEOG, state, private, college/university gift aid from institutional funds.

GIFT AID (NON-NEED-BASED) ***Total amount:*** $1,625,306 (18% state, 70% institutional, 12% external sources). ***Receiving aid:*** Freshmen: 75% (256); Undergraduates: 70% (1,183). ***Average award:*** Freshmen: $5412; Undergraduates: $4894. ***Scholarships, grants, and awards by category:*** *Academic Interests/Achievement:* 753 awards ($3,606,322 total): biological sciences, business, communication, computer science, education, English, foreign languages, general academic interests/achievements, health fields, humanities, international studies, mathematics, physical sciences, premedicine, religion/biblical studies, social sciences. *Creative Arts/Performance:* 87 awards ($101,250 total): debating, journalism/publications, music, theater/drama. *Special Achievements/Activities:* 167 awards ($263,231 total): community service, junior miss, leadership, religious involvement. *Special Characteristics:* 288 awards ($892,381 total): children and siblings of alumni, children of faculty/staff, international students, parents of current students, relatives of clergy, religious affiliation, siblings of current students, spouses of current students. ***Tuition waivers:*** Full or partial for employees or children of employees, senior citizens. ***ROTC:*** Army cooperative, Air Force cooperative.

LOANS ***Student loans:*** $9,641,384 (88% need-based, 12% non-need-based). 77% of past graduating class borrowed through all loan programs. *Average indebtedness per student:* $20,505. ***Average need-based loan:*** Freshmen: $3308; Undergraduates: $4309. ***Parent loans:*** $1,771,848 (85% need-based, 15% non-need-based). ***Programs:*** FFEL (Subsidized and Unsubsidized Stafford, PLUS), Perkins, state, college/university, alternative loans.

WORK-STUDY ***Federal work-study:*** Total amount: $585,978; 300 jobs averaging $1953. ***State or other work-study/employment:*** Total amount: $165,918 (71% need-based, 29% non-need-based). 66 part-time jobs averaging $2553.

ATHLETIC AWARDS Total amount: $1,628,396 (73% need-based, 27% non-need-based).

APPLYING FOR FINANCIAL AID ***Required financial aid form:*** FAFSA. ***Financial aid deadline:*** 7/31 (priority: 3/1). ***Notification date:*** Continuous beginning 3/1. Students must reply within 2 weeks of notification.

CONTACT Pamela Pustay, Director of Financial Aid, Malone College, 515 25th Street, NW, Canton, OH 44709-3897, 330-471-8162 or toll-free 800-521-1146. *Fax:* 330-471-8478. *E-mail:* ppustay@malone.edu.

MANCHESTER COLLEGE

North Manchester, IN

Tuition & fees: $21,700 **Average undergraduate aid package: $18,984**

ABOUT THE INSTITUTION Independent religious, coed. Awards: associate, bachelor's, and master's degrees. 59 undergraduate majors. Total enrollment: 1,056. Undergraduates: 1,056. Freshmen: 311. Federal methodology is used as a basis for awarding need-based institutional aid.

UNDERGRADUATE EXPENSES for 2007–08 ***Application fee:*** $25. ***Comprehensive fee:*** $29,150 includes full-time tuition ($21,000), mandatory fees ($700), and room and board ($7450). ***College room only:*** $4500. ***Part-time tuition:*** $670 per credit hour.

FRESHMAN FINANCIAL AID (Fall 2006, est.) 285 applied for aid; of those 89% were deemed to have need. 100% of freshmen with need received aid; of those 35% had need fully met. ***Average percent of need met:*** 93% (excluding resources awarded to replace EFC). ***Average financial aid package:*** $20,858 (excluding resources awarded to replace EFC). 17% of all full-time freshmen had no need and received non-need-based gift aid.

UNDERGRADUATE FINANCIAL AID (Fall 2006, est.) 922 applied for aid; of those 88% were deemed to have need. 100% of undergraduates with need received aid; of those 30% had need fully met. ***Average percent of need met:*** 95% (excluding resources awarded to replace EFC). ***Average financial aid package:*** $18,984 (excluding resources awarded to replace EFC). 13% of all full-time undergraduates had no need and received non-need-based gift aid.

GIFT AID (NEED-BASED) ***Total amount:*** $11,578,209 (7% federal, 22% state, 71% institutional). ***Receiving aid:*** Freshmen: 83% (253); All full-time undergraduates: 82% (815). ***Average award:*** Freshmen: $15,245; Undergraduates: $13,833. ***Scholarships, grants, and awards:*** Federal Pell, FSEOG, state, private, college/university gift aid from institutional funds.

GIFT AID (NON-NEED-BASED) ***Total amount:*** $2,285,866 (4% federal, 5% state, 91% institutional). ***Receiving aid:*** Freshmen: 58% (176); Undergraduates: 60% (602). ***Average award:*** Freshmen: $11,143; Undergraduates: $8698. ***Scholarships, grants, and awards by category:*** *Academic Interests/Achievement:* business, English, foreign languages, general academic interests/achievements, humanities. *Special Characteristics:* children and siblings of alumni, ethnic background, international students, members of minority groups, previous college experience, religious affiliation.

LOANS ***Student loans:*** $5,219,343 (90% need-based, 10% non-need-based). 68% of past graduating class borrowed through all loan programs. *Average indebtedness per student:* $19,929. ***Average need-based loan:*** Freshmen: $4173; Undergraduates: $3694. ***Parent loans:*** $2,379,343 (91% need-based, 9% non-need-based). ***Programs:*** FFEL (Subsidized and Unsubsidized Stafford, PLUS), Perkins.

WORK-STUDY ***Federal work-study:*** Total amount: $795,069; jobs available (averaging $1500). ***State or other work-study/employment:*** Total amount: $614,314 (67% need-based, 33% non-need-based). Part-time jobs available.

APPLYING FOR FINANCIAL AID ***Required financial aid form:*** FAFSA. ***Financial aid deadline (priority):*** 3/1. ***Notification date:*** Continuous beginning 3/1. Students must reply within 2 weeks of notification.

CONTACT Ms. Gina Voelz, Director of Financial Aid, Manchester College, 604 East College Avenue, North Manchester, IN 46962-1225, 260-982-5066 or toll-free 800-852-3648. *Fax:* 260-982-5121. *E-mail:* glvoelz@manchester.edu.

MANHATTAN CHRISTIAN COLLEGE

Manhattan, KS

Tuition & fees: N/R **Average undergraduate aid package: $9597**

ABOUT THE INSTITUTION Independent religious, coed. Awards: associate and bachelor's degrees. 9 undergraduate majors. Total enrollment: 331. Undergraduates: 331. Freshmen: 83. Federal methodology is used as a basis for awarding need-based institutional aid.

FRESHMAN FINANCIAL AID (Fall 2006, est.) 70 applied for aid; of those 74% were deemed to have need. 100% of freshmen with need received aid; of those 44% had need fully met. ***Average percent of need met:*** 75% (excluding resources awarded to replace EFC). ***Average financial aid package:*** $12,249 (excluding resources awarded to replace EFC). 34% of all full-time freshmen had no need and received non-need-based gift aid.

UNDERGRADUATE FINANCIAL AID (Fall 2006, est.) 356 applied for aid; of those 75% were deemed to have need. 100% of undergraduates with need received aid; of those 17% had need fully met. ***Average percent of need met:*** 73% (excluding resources awarded to replace EFC). ***Average financial aid package:*** $9597 (excluding resources awarded to replace EFC). 28% of all full-time undergraduates had no need and received non-need-based gift aid.

GIFT AID (NEED-BASED) ***Total amount:*** $470,595 (69% federal, 31% state). ***Receiving aid:*** Freshmen: 46% (36); All full-time undergraduates: 36% (131). ***Average award:*** Freshmen: $3059; Undergraduates: $3592. ***Scholarships, grants, and awards:*** Federal Pell, FSEOG, state, private, college/university gift aid from institutional funds.

GIFT AID (NON-NEED-BASED) ***Total amount:*** $1,128,819 (68% institutional, 32% external sources). ***Receiving aid:*** Freshmen: 66% (52); Undergraduates: 72% (266). ***Average award:*** Freshmen: $3884; Undergraduates: $3777. ***Scholarships, grants, and awards by category:*** *Academic Interests/Achievement:* 225 awards ($646,309 total): general academic interests/achievements, religion/biblical studies. *Creative Arts/Performance:* music. *Special Achievements/Activities:* 12 awards ($70,303 total): leadership. *Special Characteristics:* 9 awards ($53,889 total): children of faculty/staff. ***Tuition waivers:*** Full or partial for employees or children of employees, senior citizens. ***ROTC:*** Army cooperative, Air Force cooperative.

LOANS ***Student loans:*** $1,461,908 (57% need-based, 43% non-need-based). 67% of past graduating class borrowed through all loan programs. *Average indebtedness per student:* $12,046. ***Average need-based loan:*** Freshmen: $2759; Undergraduates: $3628. ***Parent loans:*** $371,402 (100% non-need-based). ***Programs:*** FFEL (Subsidized and Unsubsidized Stafford, PLUS), Perkins.

WORK-STUDY ***Federal work-study:*** Total amount: $72,414; 65 jobs averaging $1114.

APPLYING FOR FINANCIAL AID ***Required financial aid forms:*** FAFSA, state aid form. ***Financial aid deadline (priority):*** 4/1. ***Notification date:*** Continuous beginning 3/5. Students must reply within 2 weeks of notification.

CONTACT Mrs. Margaret Carlisle, Director of Financial Aid, Manhattan Christian College, 1415 Anderson Avenue, Manhattan, KS 66502-4081, 785-539-3571 or toll-free 877-246-4622. *E-mail:* carlisle@mccks.edu.

MANHATTAN COLLEGE

Riverdale, NY

Tuition & fees: $21,550 **Average undergraduate aid package: $16,440**

ABOUT THE INSTITUTION Independent religious, coed. Awards: bachelor's and master's degrees and post-master's certificates. 41 undergraduate majors. Total enrollment: 3,357. Undergraduates: 3,021. Freshmen: 707. Federal methodology is used as a basis for awarding need-based institutional aid.

UNDERGRADUATE EXPENSES for 2006–07 ***Application fee:*** $50. ***Comprehensive fee:*** $30,875 includes full-time tuition ($20,350), mandatory fees ($1200), and room and board ($9325). ***Part-time tuition:*** $585 per credit hour.

FRESHMAN FINANCIAL AID (Fall 2006, est.) 527 applied for aid; of those 76% were deemed to have need. 99% of freshmen with need received aid; of those 23% had need fully met. ***Average percent of need met:*** 78% (excluding resources awarded to replace EFC). ***Average financial aid package:*** $16,225 (excluding resources awarded to replace EFC). 17% of all full-time freshmen had no need and received non-need-based gift aid.

UNDERGRADUATE FINANCIAL AID (Fall 2006, est.) 2,253 applied for aid; of those 79% were deemed to have need. 100% of undergraduates with need received aid; of those 23% had need fully met. ***Average percent of need met:*** 78% (excluding resources awarded to replace EFC). ***Average financial aid package:*** $16,440 (excluding resources awarded to replace EFC). 22% of all full-time undergraduates had no need and received non-need-based gift aid.

GIFT AID (NEED-BASED) ***Total amount:*** $16,369,865 (12% federal, 16% state, 70% institutional, 2% external sources). ***Receiving aid:*** Freshmen: 50% (379); All full-time undergraduates: 60% (1,705). ***Average award:*** Freshmen: $11,643; Undergraduates: $11,042. ***Scholarships, grants, and awards:*** Federal Pell, FSEOG, state, private, college/university gift aid from institutional funds.

GIFT AID (NON-NEED-BASED) ***Total amount:*** $4,127,122 (3% state, 92% institutional, 5% external sources). ***Receiving aid:*** Freshmen: 14% (104); Undergraduates: 15% (427). ***Average award:*** Freshmen: $9019; Undergraduates: $7969. ***Scholarships, grants, and awards by category:*** *Academic Interests/Achievement:* biological sciences, business, computer science, foreign languages, general academic interests/achievements, mathematics, military science. *Creative Arts/Performance:* music. *Special Achievements/Activities:* community service, leadership. *Special Characteristics:* children of faculty/staff. ***ROTC:*** Army cooperative, Air Force.

LOANS ***Student loans:*** $14,517,130 (73% need-based, 27% non-need-based). 67% of past graduating class borrowed through all loan programs. *Average indebtedness per student:* $35,130. ***Average need-based loan:*** Freshmen: $5518; Undergraduates: $8064. ***Parent loans:*** $7,472,777 (36% need-based, 64% non-need-based). ***Programs:*** Federal Direct (Subsidized and Unsubsidized Stafford, PLUS), FFEL (Subsidized and Unsubsidized Stafford, PLUS), Perkins.

WORK-STUDY ***Federal work-study:*** Total amount: $560,000; 501 jobs averaging $1118. ***State or other work-study/employment:*** Total amount: $200,000 (100% non-need-based). 224 part-time jobs averaging $893.

ATHLETIC AWARDS Total amount: $2,594,482 (43% need-based, 57% non-need-based).

APPLYING FOR FINANCIAL AID ***Required financial aid forms:*** FAFSA, institution's own form, state aid form. ***Financial aid deadline (priority):*** 3/1. ***Notification date:*** 4/1. Students must reply by 5/1.

CONTACT Mr. Edward Keough, Director of Student Financial Services, Manhattan College, 4513 Manhattan College Parkway, Riverdale, NY 10471, 718-862-7100 or toll-free 800-622-9235 (in-state). *Fax:* 718-862-8027. *E-mail:* finaid@manhattan.edu.

MANHATTAN SCHOOL OF MUSIC

New York, NY

ABOUT THE INSTITUTION Independent, coed. Awards: bachelor's, master's, and doctoral degrees and post-bachelor's and post-master's certificates. 6 undergraduate majors. Total enrollment: 823. Undergraduates: 379. Freshmen: 79.

GIFT AID (NEED-BASED) ***Scholarships, grants, and awards:*** Federal Pell, FSEOG, state, private, college/university gift aid from institutional funds.

GIFT AID (NON-NEED-BASED) ***Scholarships, grants, and awards by category:*** *Creative Arts/Performance:* music.

LOANS ***Programs:*** FFEL (Subsidized and Unsubsidized Stafford, PLUS), Perkins.

APPLYING FOR FINANCIAL AID ***Required financial aid forms:*** FAFSA, institution's own form, CSS Financial Aid PROFILE, verification worksheet.

CONTACT Ms. Amy Anderson, Assistant Dean of Admission and Financial Aid, Manhattan School of Music, 120 Claremont Avenue, New York, NY 10027-4698, 212-749-2802 Ext. 4501. *Fax:* 212-749-3025. *E-mail:* aanderson@msmnyc.edu.

MANHATTANVILLE COLLEGE

Purchase, NY

Tuition & fees: $30,776 **Average undergraduate aid package: $24,548**

ABOUT THE INSTITUTION Independent, coed. Awards: bachelor's and master's degrees. 42 undergraduate majors. Total enrollment: 2,974. Undergraduates: 1,830. Freshmen: 503. Federal methodology is used as a basis for awarding need-based institutional aid.

UNDERGRADUATE EXPENSES for 2007–08 ***Application fee:*** $55. ***Comprehensive fee:*** $43,016 includes full-time tuition ($29,636), mandatory fees ($1140), and room and board ($12,240). ***College room only:*** $7270. ***Part-time tuition:*** $655 per credit. ***Part-time fees:*** $40 per semester hour.

FRESHMAN FINANCIAL AID (Fall 2005) 406 applied for aid; of those 91% were deemed to have need. 99% of freshmen with need received aid; of those 15% had need fully met. ***Average percent of need met:*** 81% (excluding resources awarded to replace EFC). ***Average financial aid package:*** $25,039 (excluding resources awarded to replace EFC). 20% of all full-time freshmen had no need and received non-need-based gift aid.

UNDERGRADUATE FINANCIAL AID (Fall 2005) 1,302 applied for aid; of those 90% were deemed to have need. 100% of undergraduates with need received

aid; of those 18% had need fully met. ***Average percent of need met:*** 79% (excluding resources awarded to replace EFC). ***Average financial aid package:*** $24,548 (excluding resources awarded to replace EFC). 22% of all full-time undergraduates had no need and received non-need-based gift aid.

GIFT AID (NEED-BASED) ***Total amount:*** $10,481,061 (12% federal, 14% state, 74% institutional). ***Receiving aid:*** Freshmen: 62% (312); All full-time undergraduates: 57% (966). ***Average award:*** Freshmen: $13,619; Undergraduates: $12,366. ***Scholarships, grants, and awards:*** Federal Pell, FSEOG, state, private, college/university gift aid from institutional funds.

GIFT AID (NON-NEED-BASED) ***Total amount:*** $14,305,075 (98% institutional, 2% external sources). ***Receiving aid:*** Freshmen: 59% (301); Undergraduates: 57% (973). ***Average award:*** Freshmen: $8505; Undergraduates: $8325. ***Scholarships, grants, and awards by category:*** *Academic Interests/Achievement:* 1,605 awards ($12,604,278 total): general academic interests/achievements, mathematics. *Creative Arts/Performance:* 68 awards ($660,062 total): dance, performing arts. *Special Achievements/Activities:* 83 awards ($158,500 total): community service, leadership. *Special Characteristics:* 20 awards ($161,460 total): previous college experience.

LOANS ***Student loans:*** $12,002,203 (69% need-based, 31% non-need-based). 67% of past graduating class borrowed through all loan programs. *Average indebtedness per student:* $23,253. ***Average need-based loan:*** Freshmen: $3142; Undergraduates: $4183. ***Parent loans:*** $3,217,496 (100% non-need-based). ***Programs:*** FFEL (Subsidized and Unsubsidized Stafford, PLUS), Perkins.

WORK-STUDY ***Federal work-study:*** Total amount: $299,887; 305 jobs averaging $1075. ***State or other work-study/employment:*** Total amount: $625,539 (100% need-based). 651 part-time jobs averaging $1500.

APPLYING FOR FINANCIAL AID ***Required financial aid forms:*** FAFSA, state aid form. ***Financial aid deadline (priority):*** 3/1. ***Notification date:*** Continuous. Students must reply by 5/1 or within 2 weeks of notification.

CONTACT Maria A. Barlaam, Director of Financial Aid, Manhattanville College, 2900 Purchase Street, Purchase, NY 10577-2132, 914-323-5357 or toll-free 800-328-4553. *Fax:* 914-323-5382. *E-mail:* barlaamm@mville.edu.

MANNES COLLEGE THE NEW SCHOOL FOR MUSIC

New York, NY

Tuition & fees: $28,210 **Average undergraduate aid package: $12,162**

ABOUT THE INSTITUTION Independent, coed. Awards: bachelor's and master's degrees and post-bachelor's certificates. 7 undergraduate majors. Total enrollment: 385. Undergraduates: 201. Freshmen: 73. Federal methodology is used as a basis for awarding need-based institutional aid.

UNDERGRADUATE EXPENSES for 2007–08 ***Application fee:*** $100. ***Comprehensive fee:*** $39,960 includes full-time tuition ($27,600), mandatory fees ($610), and room and board ($11,750). ***College room only:*** $8750. ***Part-time tuition:*** $912 per credit hour.

FRESHMAN FINANCIAL AID (Fall 2006, est.) 21 applied for aid; of those 86% were deemed to have need. 89% of freshmen with need received aid; of those 12% had need fully met. ***Average percent of need met:*** 57% (excluding resources awarded to replace EFC). ***Average financial aid package:*** $11,396 (excluding resources awarded to replace EFC). 29% of all full-time freshmen had no need and received non-need-based gift aid.

UNDERGRADUATE FINANCIAL AID (Fall 2006, est.) 116 applied for aid; of those 43% were deemed to have need. 92% of undergraduates with need received aid; of those 35% had need fully met. ***Average percent of need met:*** 34% (excluding resources awarded to replace EFC). ***Average financial aid package:*** $12,162 (excluding resources awarded to replace EFC). 30% of all full-time undergraduates had no need and received non-need-based gift aid.

GIFT AID (NEED-BASED) ***Total amount:*** $211,906 (34% federal, 19% state, 47% institutional). ***Receiving aid:*** Freshmen: 33% (8); All full-time undergraduates: 14% (19). ***Average award:*** Freshmen: $3116; Undergraduates: $4335. ***Scholarships, grants, and awards:*** Federal Pell, FSEOG, state, private, college/university gift aid from institutional funds.

GIFT AID (NON-NEED-BASED) ***Total amount:*** $1,066,122 (100% institutional). ***Receiving aid:*** Freshmen: 29% (7); Undergraduates: 30% (39). ***Average award:*** Freshmen: $11,993; Undergraduates: $9876. ***Scholarships, grants, and awards by category:*** *Academic Interests/Achievement:* general academic interests/achievements. *Creative Arts/Performance:* music. *Special Achievements/Activities:* general special achievements/activities.

LOANS ***Student loans:*** $539,523 (37% need-based, 63% non-need-based). 60% of past graduating class borrowed through all loan programs. *Average indebtedness per student:* $18,025. ***Average need-based loan:*** Freshmen: $2625; Undergraduates: $3884. ***Parent loans:*** $260,547 (100% non-need-based). ***Programs:*** FFEL (Subsidized and Unsubsidized Stafford, PLUS), Perkins, college/university.

WORK-STUDY ***Federal work-study:*** Total amount: $23,500; jobs available.

APPLYING FOR FINANCIAL AID ***Required financial aid forms:*** FAFSA, state aid form. ***Financial aid deadline:*** Continuous. ***Notification date:*** 3/1. Students must reply within 4 weeks of notification.

CONTACT Financial Aid Counselor, Mannes College The New School for Music, 150 West 85th Street, New York, NY 10024-4402, 212-580-0210 or toll-free 800-292-3040. *Fax:* 212-580-1738.

MANSFIELD UNIVERSITY OF PENNSYLVANIA

Mansfield, PA

Tuition & fees (PA res): $6676 **Average undergraduate aid package: $5120**

ABOUT THE INSTITUTION State-supported, coed. Awards: associate, bachelor's, and master's degrees. 82 undergraduate majors. Total enrollment: 3,360. Undergraduates: 2,936. Freshmen: 616. Federal methodology is used as a basis for awarding need-based institutional aid.

UNDERGRADUATE EXPENSES for 2006–07 ***Application fee:*** $25. ***Tuition, state resident:*** full-time $5038. ***Tuition, nonresident:*** full-time $12,598. Part-time tuition and fees vary according to course load. ***College room and board:*** $5934. Room and board charges vary according to board plan. ***Payment plans:*** Installment, deferred payment.

FRESHMAN FINANCIAL AID (Fall 2005) of those 4% had need fully met. ***Average percent of need met:*** 68% (excluding resources awarded to replace EFC). ***Average financial aid package:*** $5303 (excluding resources awarded to replace EFC). 8% of all full-time freshmen had no need and received non-need-based gift aid.

UNDERGRADUATE FINANCIAL AID (Fall 2005) of those 3% had need fully met. ***Average percent of need met:*** 48% (excluding resources awarded to replace EFC). ***Average financial aid package:*** $5120 (excluding resources awarded to replace EFC). 6% of all full-time undergraduates had no need and received non-need-based gift aid.

GIFT AID (NEED-BASED) ***Total amount:*** $6,366,748 (52% federal, 47% state, 1% external sources). ***Receiving aid:*** Freshmen: 47% (316); All full-time undergraduates: 49% (1,317). ***Average award:*** Freshmen: $4065; Undergraduates: $4025. ***Scholarships, grants, and awards:*** Federal Pell, FSEOG, state, private, college/university gift aid from institutional funds, United Negro College Fund, Federal Nursing.

GIFT AID (NON-NEED-BASED) ***Total amount:*** $1,661,209 (7% federal, 9% state, 39% institutional, 45% external sources). ***Receiving aid:*** Freshmen: 19% (128); Undergraduates: 12% (324). ***Average award:*** Freshmen: $1858; Undergraduates: $2075. ***Scholarships, grants, and awards by category:*** *Academic Interests/Achievement:* biological sciences, communication, education, general academic interests/achievements, health fields, mathematics, physical sciences. *Creative Arts/Performance:* art/fine arts, journalism/publications, music. *Special Characteristics:* local/state students, members of minority groups. ***Tuition waivers:*** Full or partial for employees or children of employees, senior citizens.

LOANS ***Student loans:*** $16,582,471 (44% need-based, 56% non-need-based). 74% of past graduating class borrowed through all loan programs. *Average indebtedness per student:* $19,262. ***Average need-based loan:*** Freshmen: $2733; Undergraduates: $3709. ***Parent loans:*** $1,695,886 (100% non-need-based). ***Programs:*** FFEL (Subsidized and Unsubsidized Stafford, PLUS), Perkins, Federal Nursing, state.

WORK-STUDY ***Federal work-study:*** Total amount: $333,356; jobs available. ***State or other work-study/employment:*** Total amount: $609,898 (100% non-need-based). Part-time jobs available.

ATHLETIC AWARDS Total amount: $358,746 (100% non-need-based).

APPLYING FOR FINANCIAL AID ***Required financial aid forms:*** FAFSA, institution's own form. ***Financial aid deadline (priority):*** 3/15. ***Notification date:*** Continuous beginning 3/15. Students must reply within 2 weeks of notification.

CONTACT Ms. Darcie Stephens, Director of Financial Aid, Mansfield University of Pennsylvania, 109 South Hall, Mansfield, PA 16933, 570-662-4854 or toll-free 800-577-6826. *Fax:* 570-662-4136.

MAPLE SPRINGS BAPTIST BIBLE COLLEGE AND SEMINARY

Capitol Heights, MD

CONTACT Ms. Fannie G. Thompson, Director of Business Affairs, Maple Springs Baptist Bible College and Seminary, 4130 Belt Road, Capitol Heights, MD 20743, 301-736-3631. *Fax:* 301-735-6507.

MARANATHA BAPTIST BIBLE COLLEGE

Watertown, WI

Tuition & fees: $9030 **Average undergraduate aid package: $6765**

ABOUT THE INSTITUTION Independent Baptist, coed. Awards: associate, bachelor's, and master's degrees. 19 undergraduate majors. Total enrollment: 876. Undergraduates: 811. Freshmen: 212. Federal methodology is used as a basis for awarding need-based institutional aid.

UNDERGRADUATE EXPENSES for 2006–07 ***Application fee:*** $50. ***Comprehensive fee:*** $14,180 includes full-time tuition ($8160), mandatory fees ($870), and room and board ($5150). ***Part-time tuition:*** $255 per semester hour.

FRESHMAN FINANCIAL AID (Fall 2005) 187 applied for aid; of those 87% were deemed to have need. 100% of freshmen with need received aid; of those 4% had need fully met. ***Average percent of need met:*** 55% (excluding resources awarded to replace EFC). ***Average financial aid package:*** $6084 (excluding resources awarded to replace EFC). 5% of all full-time freshmen had no need and received non-need-based gift aid.

UNDERGRADUATE FINANCIAL AID (Fall 2005) 642 applied for aid; of those 90% were deemed to have need. 100% of undergraduates with need received aid; of those 3% had need fully met. ***Average percent of need met:*** 57% (excluding resources awarded to replace EFC). ***Average financial aid package:*** $6765 (excluding resources awarded to replace EFC). 5% of all full-time undergraduates had no need and received non-need-based gift aid.

GIFT AID (NEED-BASED) ***Total amount:*** $1,186,704 (66% federal, 13% state, 14% institutional, 7% external sources). ***Receiving aid:*** Freshmen: 48% (97); All full-time undergraduates: 38% (281). ***Average award:*** Freshmen: $2878; Undergraduates: $3221. ***Scholarships, grants, and awards:*** Federal Pell, FSEOG, state, private, college/university gift aid from institutional funds.

GIFT AID (NON-NEED-BASED) ***Total amount:*** $92,123 (24% state, 38% institutional, 38% external sources). ***Receiving aid:*** Freshmen: 5% (10); Undergraduates: 2% (17). ***Average award:*** Freshmen: $950; Undergraduates: $1078. ***Scholarships, grants, and awards by category:*** *Academic Interests/Achievement:* 49 awards ($42,100 total): business, general academic interests/achievements, religion/biblical studies. *Special Characteristics:* 115 awards ($216,419 total): children and siblings of alumni, children of educators, children of faculty/staff, relatives of clergy, spouses of current students. ***ROTC:*** Army.

LOANS ***Student loans:*** $1,946,635 (92% need-based, 8% non-need-based). 64% of past graduating class borrowed through all loan programs. *Average indebtedness per student:* $13,689. ***Average need-based loan:*** Freshmen: $2468; Undergraduates: $3454. ***Parent loans:*** $459,294 (74% need-based, 26% non-need-based). ***Programs:*** FFEL (Subsidized and Unsubsidized Stafford, PLUS), state, alternative loans.

WORK-STUDY ***State or other work-study/employment:*** Total amount: $1,549,519 (100% need-based). 278 part-time jobs averaging $3162.

APPLYING FOR FINANCIAL AID ***Required financial aid form:*** FAFSA. ***Financial aid deadline (priority):*** 3/1. ***Notification date:*** Continuous. Students must reply within 2 weeks of notification.

CONTACT Mr. Bruce Roth, Associate Director of Financial Aid, Maranatha Baptist Bible College, 745 West Main Street, Watertown, WI 53094, 920-206-2318 or toll-free 800-622-2947. *Fax:* 920-261-9109. *E-mail:* financialaid@mbbc.edu.

MARIAN COLLEGE

Indianapolis, IN

ABOUT THE INSTITUTION Independent Roman Catholic, coed. Awards: associate, bachelor's, and master's degrees. 36 undergraduate majors. Total enrollment: 1,796. Undergraduates: 1,779. Freshmen: 280.

GIFT AID (NEED-BASED) ***Scholarships, grants, and awards:*** Federal Pell, FSEOG, state, private, college/university gift aid from institutional funds.

GIFT AID (NON-NEED-BASED) ***Scholarships, grants, and awards by category:*** *Academic Interests/Achievement:* area/ethnic studies, general academic interests/achievements, religion/biblical studies. *Creative Arts/Performance:* applied art and design, art/fine arts, music, performing arts, theater/drama. *Special Achievements/Activities:* community service, religious involvement. *Special Characteristics:* adult students, children and siblings of alumni, children of faculty/staff, international students, members of minority groups, religious affiliation, siblings of current students, spouses of current students.

LOANS ***Programs:*** FFEL (Subsidized and Unsubsidized Stafford, PLUS), Perkins, college/university.

WORK-STUDY ***Federal work-study:*** Total amount: $213,826; 200 jobs averaging $1500. ***State or other work-study/employment:*** Total amount: $69,960 (100% non-need-based). Part-time jobs available.

APPLYING FOR FINANCIAL AID ***Required financial aid forms:*** FAFSA, institution's own form.

CONTACT Mr. John E. Shelton, Dean of Financial Aid, Marian College, 3200 Cold Spring Road, Indianapolis, IN 46222-1997, 317-955-6040 or toll-free 800-772-7264 (in-state). *Fax:* 317-955-6424. *E-mail:* jshelton@marian.edu.

MARIAN COLLEGE OF FOND DU LAC

Fond du Lac, WI

Tuition & fees: $17,625 **Average undergraduate aid package: $17,973**

ABOUT THE INSTITUTION Independent Roman Catholic, coed. Awards: bachelor's, master's, and doctoral degrees. 50 undergraduate majors. Total enrollment: 3,040. Undergraduates: 2,126. Freshmen: 245. Federal methodology is used as a basis for awarding need-based institutional aid.

UNDERGRADUATE EXPENSES for 2006–07 ***Application fee:*** $20. ***Comprehensive fee:*** $22,825 includes full-time tuition ($17,300), mandatory fees ($325), and room and board ($5200). ***College room only:*** $3420. Full-time tuition and fees vary according to class time, course load, and program. Room and board charges vary according to board plan and housing facility. ***Part-time tuition:*** $290 per credit. ***Part-time fees:*** $80 per term. Part-time tuition and fees vary according to class time, course load, and program. ***Payment plan:*** Installment.

FRESHMAN FINANCIAL AID (Fall 2006, est.) 242 applied for aid; of those 88% were deemed to have need. 100% of freshmen with need received aid; of those 32% had need fully met. ***Average percent of need met:*** 86% (excluding resources awarded to replace EFC). ***Average financial aid package:*** $18,191 (excluding resources awarded to replace EFC). 12% of all full-time freshmen had no need and received non-need-based gift aid.

UNDERGRADUATE FINANCIAL AID (Fall 2006, est.) 1,307 applied for aid; of those 85% were deemed to have need. 100% of undergraduates with need received aid; of those 41% had need fully met. ***Average percent of need met:*** 90% (excluding resources awarded to replace EFC). ***Average financial aid package:*** $17,973 (excluding resources awarded to replace EFC). 14% of all full-time undergraduates had no need and received non-need-based gift aid.

GIFT AID (NEED-BASED) ***Total amount:*** $10,638,708 (16% federal, 14% state, 69% institutional, 1% external sources). ***Receiving aid:*** Freshmen: 86% (211); All full-time undergraduates: 77% (1,070). ***Average award:*** Freshmen: $10,532; Undergraduates: $9656. ***Scholarships, grants, and awards:*** Federal Pell, FSEOG, state, private, college/university gift aid from institutional funds, endowed scholarships.

GIFT AID (NON-NEED-BASED) ***Total amount:*** $1,041,845 (1% state, 94% institutional, 5% external sources). ***Receiving aid:*** Freshmen: 84% (206); Undergraduates: 76% (1,055). ***Average award:*** Freshmen: $4747; Undergraduates: $4311. ***Scholarships, grants, and awards by category:*** *Academic Interests/Achievement:* 1,269 awards ($4,585,813 total): general academic interests/achievements. *Creative Arts/Performance:* 43 awards ($60,000 total): music. *Special Characteristics:* 82 awards ($345,496 total): children of faculty/staff, children with a deceased or disabled parent, siblings of current students. ***Tuition waivers:*** Full or partial for employees or children of employees, senior citizens. ***ROTC:*** Army.

LOANS ***Student loans:*** $9,236,342 (75% need-based, 25% non-need-based). 90% of past graduating class borrowed through all loan programs. *Average indebtedness per student:* $21,500. ***Average need-based loan:*** Freshmen: $3379; Undergraduates: $5079. ***Parent loans:*** $1,183,229 (66% need-based, 34% non-need-based). ***Programs:*** FFEL (Subsidized and Unsubsidized Stafford, PLUS), Perkins, Federal Nursing.

WORK-STUDY ***Federal work-study:*** Total amount: $1,281,100; 682 jobs averaging $1878. ***State or other work-study/employment:*** Total amount: $418,980 (100% non-need-based). 378 part-time jobs averaging $800.

APPLYING FOR FINANCIAL AID ***Required financial aid forms:*** FAFSA, institution's own form. ***Financial aid deadline (priority):*** 3/1. ***Notification date:*** Continuous. Students must reply within 4 weeks of notification.

CONTACT Ms. Debra E. McKinney, Director of Financial Aid, Marian College of Fond du Lac, 45 South National Avenue, Fond du Lac, WI 54935-4699, 920-923-7614 or toll-free 800-2-MARIAN Ext. 7652 (in-state). *Fax:* 920-923-8767. *E-mail:* dmckinney@mariancollege.edu.

MARIETTA COLLEGE

Marietta, OH

CONTACT Mr. Gary Craig, Dean of Enrollment, Marietta College, 215 Fifth Street, Marietta, OH 45750-4000, 740-376-4712 or toll-free 800-331-7896. *Fax:* 740-376-4990. *E-mail:* finaid@marietta.edu.

MARIST COLLEGE

Poughkeepsie, NY

Tuition & fees: $22,576 **Average undergraduate aid package: $13,925**

ABOUT THE INSTITUTION Independent, coed. Awards: bachelor's and master's degrees. 50 undergraduate majors. Total enrollment: 5,877. Undergraduates: 5,023. Freshmen: 1,038. Federal methodology is used as a basis for awarding need-based institutional aid.

UNDERGRADUATE EXPENSES for 2006–07 ***Application fee:*** $40. ***Comprehensive fee:*** $32,366 includes full-time tuition ($22,066), mandatory fees ($510), and room and board ($9790). ***College room only:*** $6260. Room and board charges vary according to board plan and housing facility. ***Part-time tuition:*** $510 per credit. ***Part-time fees:*** $70 per term. ***Payment plan:*** Installment.

FRESHMAN FINANCIAL AID (Fall 2006, est.) 849 applied for aid; of those 71% were deemed to have need. 100% of freshmen with need received aid; of those 21% had need fully met. ***Average percent of need met:*** 72% (excluding resources awarded to replace EFC). ***Average financial aid package:*** $14,291 (excluding resources awarded to replace EFC). 31% of all full-time freshmen had no need and received non-need-based gift aid.

UNDERGRADUATE FINANCIAL AID (Fall 2006, est.) 3,459 applied for aid; of those 99% were deemed to have need. 79% of undergraduates with need received aid; of those 18% had need fully met. ***Average percent of need met:*** 68% (excluding resources awarded to replace EFC). ***Average financial aid package:*** $13,925 (excluding resources awarded to replace EFC). 21% of all full-time undergraduates had no need and received non-need-based gift aid.

GIFT AID (NEED-BASED) ***Total amount:*** $24,719,800 (9% federal, 12% state, 76% institutional, 3% external sources). ***Receiving aid:*** Freshmen: 58% (605); All full-time undergraduates: 58% (2,586). ***Average award:*** Freshmen: $10,598; Undergraduates: $9492. ***Scholarships, grants, and awards:*** Federal Pell, FSEOG, state, private, college/university gift aid from institutional funds.

GIFT AID (NON-NEED-BASED) ***Total amount:*** $7,351,419 (2% state, 95% institutional, 3% external sources). ***Receiving aid:*** Freshmen: 46% (475); Undergraduates: 33% (1,473). ***Average award:*** Freshmen: $6539; Undergraduates: $6088. ***Scholarships, grants, and awards by category:*** *Academic Interests/Achievement:* general academic interests/achievements. *Creative Arts/Performance:* debating, music. *Special Achievements/Activities:* general special achievements/activities. ***Tuition waivers:*** Full or partial for employees or children of employees. ***ROTC:*** Army.

LOANS ***Student loans:*** $25,461,547 (42% need-based, 58% non-need-based). 64% of past graduating class borrowed through all loan programs. *Average indebtedness per student:* $28,450. ***Average need-based loan:*** Freshmen: $3350; Undergraduates: $4728. ***Parent loans:*** $8,475,478 (100% non-need-based). ***Programs:*** FFEL (Subsidized and Unsubsidized Stafford, PLUS), Perkins, alternative loans, Key Alternative Loans, CitiAssist Loans, TERI Loans, Signature Loans, EXCEL Loans.

WORK-STUDY ***Federal work-study:*** Total amount: $1,984,683; 649 jobs averaging $1969. ***State or other work-study/employment:*** Total amount: $801,500 (100% non-need-based). 605 part-time jobs averaging $1000.

ATHLETIC AWARDS Total amount: $2,649,315 (20% need-based, 80% non-need-based).

APPLYING FOR FINANCIAL AID ***Required financial aid forms:*** FAFSA, institution's own form. ***Financial aid deadline:*** 5/1 (priority: 2/15). ***Notification date:*** Continuous beginning 3/15. Students must reply by 5/1 or within 2 weeks of notification.

CONTACT Joseph R. Weglarz, Executive Director, Student Financial Services, Marist College, 3399 North Road, Poughkeepsie, NY 12601, 845-575-3230 or toll-free 800-436-5483. *Fax:* 845-575-3099. *E-mail:* joseph.weglarz@marist.edu.

MARLBORO COLLEGE

Marlboro, VT

ABOUT THE INSTITUTION Independent, coed. Awards: bachelor's, master's, and first professional degrees. 77 undergraduate majors. Total enrollment: 400. Undergraduates: 329. Freshmen: 90.

GIFT AID (NEED-BASED) ***Scholarships, grants, and awards:*** Federal Pell, FSEOG, state, private, college/university gift aid from institutional funds.

GIFT AID (NON-NEED-BASED) ***Scholarships, grants, and awards by category:*** *Academic Interests/Achievement:* general academic interests/achievements. *Special Achievements/Activities:* community service.

LOANS ***Programs:*** FFEL (Subsidized and Unsubsidized Stafford, PLUS), state.

WORK-STUDY ***Federal work-study:*** Total amount: $329,924; 244 jobs averaging $2050. ***State or other work-study/employment:*** Total amount: $60,150 (100% non-need-based). 2 part-time jobs averaging $2000.

APPLYING FOR FINANCIAL AID ***Required financial aid form:*** FAFSA.

CONTACT Alan E. Young, Dean of Enrollment Management, Marlboro College, South Road, PO Box A, Marlboro, VT 05344-0300, 802-258-9261 or toll-free 800-343-0049. *Fax:* 802-258-9300. *E-mail:* finaid@marlboro.edu.

MARQUETTE UNIVERSITY

Milwaukee, WI

Tuition & fees: $25,074 **Average undergraduate aid package: $18,248**

ABOUT THE INSTITUTION Independent Roman Catholic (Jesuit), coed. Awards: associate, bachelor's, master's, doctoral, and first professional degrees and post-master's certificates. 85 undergraduate majors. Total enrollment: 11,548. Undergraduates: 8,048. Freshmen: 1,854. Federal methodology is used as a basis for awarding need-based institutional aid.

UNDERGRADUATE EXPENSES for 2006–07 ***Application fee:*** $30. ***Comprehensive fee:*** $33,194 includes full-time tuition ($24,670), mandatory fees ($404), and room and board ($8120). ***College room only:*** $5278. Full-time tuition and fees vary according to course load and program. Room and board charges vary according to board plan and housing facility. ***Part-time tuition:*** $725 per credit. ***Part-time fees:*** $725 per credit. Part-time tuition and fees vary according to program. ***Payment plan:*** Installment.

FRESHMAN FINANCIAL AID (Fall 2006, est.) 1443 applied for aid; of those 77% were deemed to have need. 100% of freshmen with need received aid; of those 37% had need fully met. ***Average percent of need met:*** 77% (excluding resources awarded to replace EFC). ***Average financial aid package:*** $18,761 (excluding resources awarded to replace EFC). 12% of all full-time freshmen had no need and received non-need-based gift aid.

UNDERGRADUATE FINANCIAL AID (Fall 2006, est.) 5,476 applied for aid; of those 83% were deemed to have need. 97% of undergraduates with need received aid; of those 36% had need fully met. ***Average percent of need met:*** 77% (excluding resources awarded to replace EFC). ***Average financial aid package:*** $18,248 (excluding resources awarded to replace EFC). 7% of all full-time undergraduates had no need and received non-need-based gift aid.

GIFT AID (NEED-BASED) ***Total amount:*** $45,792,707 (10% federal, 8% state, 77% institutional, 5% external sources). ***Receiving aid:*** Freshmen: 54% (995); All full-time undergraduates: 52% (3,915). ***Average award:*** Freshmen: $13,196; Undergraduates: $11,619. ***Scholarships, grants, and awards:*** Federal Pell, FSEOG, state, private, college/university gift aid from institutional funds.

GIFT AID (NON-NEED-BASED) ***Total amount:*** $22,439,773 (1% state, 75% institutional, 24% external sources). ***Receiving aid:*** Freshmen: 6% (114); Undergraduates: 5% (392). ***Average award:*** Freshmen: $8651; Undergraduates: $8242. ***Scholarships, grants, and awards by category:*** *Academic Interests/Achievement:* biological sciences, business, communication, engineering/technologies, foreign languages, general academic interests/achievements, health fields, mathematics. *Special Characteristics:* 168 awards ($3,948,647 total):

children of faculty/staff. ***Tuition waivers:*** Full or partial for employees or children of employees, adult students, senior citizens. ***ROTC:*** Army, Naval, Air Force.

LOANS ***Student loans:*** $34,662,125 (87% need-based, 13% non-need-based). 65% of past graduating class borrowed through all loan programs. *Average indebtedness per student:* $25,753. ***Average need-based loan:*** Freshmen: $4299; Undergraduates: $5367. ***Parent loans:*** $16,448,821 (81% need-based, 19% non-need-based). ***Programs:*** Federal Direct (Subsidized and Unsubsidized Stafford, PLUS), Perkins, Federal Nursing, state, college/university, alternative loans.

WORK-STUDY ***Federal work-study:*** Total amount: $1,648,022; 894 jobs averaging $2500. ***State or other work-study/employment:*** Total amount: $4,424,837 (100% non-need-based). Part-time jobs available.

ATHLETIC AWARDS Total amount: $2,819,128 (15% need-based, 85% non-need-based).

APPLYING FOR FINANCIAL AID ***Required financial aid form:*** FAFSA. ***Financial aid deadline:*** Continuous. ***Notification date:*** Continuous beginning 3/21. Students must reply by 5/1 or within 3 weeks of notification.

CONTACT Daniel L. Goyette, Director of Financial Aid, Marquette University, Office of Student Financial Aid, 1212 Building, Room 415, Milwaukee, WI 53201-1881, 414-288-7390 or toll-free 800-222-6544. *Fax:* 414-288-1718. *E-mail:* financialaid@marquette.edu.

MARSHALL UNIVERSITY

Huntington, WV

ABOUT THE INSTITUTION State-supported, coed. Awards: associate, bachelor's, master's, doctoral, and first professional degrees and post-master's certificates. 46 undergraduate majors. Total enrollment: 13,936. Undergraduates: 9,723. Freshmen: 1,542.

GIFT AID (NEED-BASED) ***Scholarships, grants, and awards:*** Federal Pell, FSEOG, state, private, college/university gift aid from institutional funds.

GIFT AID (NON-NEED-BASED) ***Scholarships, grants, and awards by category:*** *Academic Interests/Achievement:* general academic interests/achievements. *Creative Arts/Performance:* applied art and design, art/fine arts, cinema/film/broadcasting, creative writing, dance, debating, general creative arts/performance, journalism/publications, music, performing arts, theater/drama. *Special Characteristics:* children of faculty/staff.

LOANS ***Programs:*** Federal Direct (Subsidized and Unsubsidized Stafford, PLUS), Perkins, state, college/university, alternative loans through outside sources.

WORK-STUDY ***Federal work-study:*** Total amount: $632,497; 359 jobs averaging $1761. ***State or other work-study/employment:*** Total amount: $349,745 (100% non-need-based). 58 part-time jobs averaging $6030.

APPLYING FOR FINANCIAL AID ***Required financial aid form:*** FAFSA.

CONTACT Ms. Nadine A. Hamrick, Associate Director of Student Financial Aid, Marshall University, One John Marshall Drive, Huntington, WV 25755, 304-696-2277 or toll-free 800-642-3499 (in-state). *Fax:* 304-696-3242. *E-mail:* hamrick@marshall.edu.

MARS HILL COLLEGE

Mars Hill, NC

CONTACT Myrtle Martin, Director of Financial Aid, Mars Hill College, PO Box 370, Mars Hill, NC 28754, 828-689-1123 or toll-free 866-MHC-4-YOU. *Fax:* 828-689-1300.

MARTIN LUTHER COLLEGE

New Ulm, MN

Tuition & fees: $9850 **Average undergraduate aid package: $7789**

ABOUT THE INSTITUTION Independent religious, coed. Awards: bachelor's degrees. 6 undergraduate majors. Total enrollment: 820. Undergraduates: 786. Freshmen: 166. Federal methodology is used as a basis for awarding need-based institutional aid.

UNDERGRADUATE EXPENSES for 2007–08 ***Application fee:*** $25. ***Comprehensive fee:*** $13,675 includes full-time tuition ($9850) and room and board ($3825). ***Part-time tuition:*** $200 per credit hour.

FRESHMAN FINANCIAL AID (Fall 2005) 137 applied for aid; of those 88% were deemed to have need. 100% of freshmen with need received aid; of those 18% had need fully met. ***Average percent of need met:*** 82% (excluding resources awarded to replace EFC). ***Average financial aid package:*** $8790 (excluding resources awarded to replace EFC). 5% of all full-time freshmen had no need and received non-need-based gift aid.

UNDERGRADUATE FINANCIAL AID (Fall 2005) 727 applied for aid; of those 86% were deemed to have need. 99% of undergraduates with need received aid; of those 43% had need fully met. ***Average percent of need met:*** 87% (excluding resources awarded to replace EFC). ***Average financial aid package:*** $7789 (excluding resources awarded to replace EFC). 4% of all full-time undergraduates had no need and received non-need-based gift aid.

GIFT AID (NEED-BASED) ***Total amount:*** $2,548,692 (19% federal, 9% state, 47% institutional, 25% external sources). ***Receiving aid:*** Freshmen: 81% (120); All full-time undergraduates: 77% (615). ***Average award:*** Freshmen: $3010; Undergraduates: $3209. ***Scholarships, grants, and awards:*** Federal Pell, FSEOG, state, private, college/university gift aid from institutional funds.

GIFT AID (NON-NEED-BASED) ***Total amount:*** $335,285 (100% institutional). ***Receiving aid:*** Freshmen: 46% (69); Undergraduates: 45% (359). ***Average award:*** Freshmen: $500; Undergraduates: $555. ***Scholarships, grants, and awards by category:*** *Academic Interests/Achievement:* general academic interests/achievements. *Creative Arts/Performance:* music. *Special Achievements/Activities:* general special achievements/activities. *Special Characteristics:* general special characteristics.

LOANS ***Student loans:*** $2,254,546 (77% need-based, 23% non-need-based). 60% of past graduating class borrowed through all loan programs. *Average indebtedness per student:* $15,315. ***Average need-based loan:*** Freshmen: $1861; Undergraduates: $2379. ***Parent loans:*** $244,442 (100% non-need-based). ***Programs:*** FFEL (Subsidized and Unsubsidized Stafford, PLUS), Perkins, state, college/university.

WORK-STUDY ***Federal work-study:*** Total amount: $74,161; jobs available.

APPLYING FOR FINANCIAL AID ***Required financial aid forms:*** FAFSA, institution's own form. ***Financial aid deadline:*** 4/15. ***Notification date:*** Continuous beginning 4/1. Students must reply by 8/15.

CONTACT Mr. Gene Slettedahl, Director of Financial Aid, Martin Luther College, 1995 Luther Court, New Ulm, MN 56073, 507-354-8221 Ext. 225. *Fax:* 507-354-8225. *E-mail:* slettega@mlc-wels.edu.

MARTIN METHODIST COLLEGE

Pulaski, TN

CONTACT Ms. Anita Beecham, Financial Aid Assistant, Martin Methodist College, 433 West Madison Street, Pulaski, TN 38478-2716, 931-363-9808 or toll-free 800-467-1273. *Fax:* 931-363-9818. *E-mail:* abeecham@martinmethodist.edu.

MARTIN UNIVERSITY

Indianapolis, IN

Tuition & fees: $12,170 **Average undergraduate aid package: $8779**

ABOUT THE INSTITUTION Independent, coed. Awards: bachelor's and master's degrees. 28 undergraduate majors. Total enrollment: 571. Undergraduates: 465. Freshmen: 49. Federal methodology is used as a basis for awarding need-based institutional aid.

UNDERGRADUATE EXPENSES for 2006–07 ***Application fee:*** $25. ***Tuition:*** full-time $11,850; part-time $395 per credit. ***Required fees:*** full-time $320; $160 per term part-time. ***Payment plan:*** Installment.

FRESHMAN FINANCIAL AID (Fall 2005) 100% of freshmen with need received aid; of those 38% had need fully met. ***Average percent of need met:*** 72% (excluding resources awarded to replace EFC). ***Average financial aid package:*** $7346 (excluding resources awarded to replace EFC).

UNDERGRADUATE FINANCIAL AID (Fall 2005) 351 applied for aid; of those 97% were deemed to have need. 100% of undergraduates with need received aid; of those 6% had need fully met. ***Average percent of need met:*** 78% (excluding resources awarded to replace EFC). ***Average financial aid package:*** $8779 (excluding resources awarded to replace EFC).

GIFT AID (NEED-BASED) ***Total amount:*** $2,052,808 (52% federal, 45% state, 2% institutional, 1% external sources). ***Receiving aid:*** Freshmen: 81% (35); All full-time undergraduates: 85% (329). ***Average award:*** Freshmen: $6147; Undergraduates: $6705. ***Scholarships, grants, and awards:*** Federal Pell, FSEOG, state, private, college/university gift aid from institutional funds.

GIFT AID (NON-NEED-BASED) ***Receiving aid:*** Freshmen: 35% (15); Undergraduates: 5% (21). ***Tuition waivers:*** Full or partial for employees or children of employees, senior citizens.

LOANS ***Student loans:*** $21,619,533 (9% need-based, 91% non-need-based). 94% of past graduating class borrowed through all loan programs. *Average indebtedness per student:* $27,193. ***Average need-based loan:*** Freshmen: $2625; Undergraduates: $3192. ***Programs:*** FFEL (Subsidized and Unsubsidized Stafford, PLUS), Charles E. Schell Foundation loans.

WORK-STUDY ***Federal work-study:*** Total amount: $23,000.

APPLYING FOR FINANCIAL AID ***Required financial aid form:*** FAFSA. ***Financial aid deadline:*** Continuous. ***Notification date:*** Continuous.

CONTACT Pertrina P. Briggs, Director of Financial Aid, Martin University, 2171 Avondale Place, PO Box 18567, Indianapolis, IN 46218-3867, 317-543-3670. *Fax:* 317-543-4790. *E-mail:* pbriggs@martin.edu.

MARY BALDWIN COLLEGE

Staunton, VA

Tuition & fees: $21,450 **Average undergraduate aid package: $20,510**

ABOUT THE INSTITUTION Independent, coed, primarily women. Awards: bachelor's and master's degrees. 30 undergraduate majors. Total enrollment: 1,755. Undergraduates: 1,563. Freshmen: 284. Federal methodology is used as a basis for awarding need-based institutional aid.

UNDERGRADUATE EXPENSES for 2006–07 ***Application fee:*** $35. ***Comprehensive fee:*** $27,550 includes full-time tuition ($21,250), mandatory fees ($200), and room and board ($6100). ***College room only:*** $3890. Full-time tuition and fees vary according to degree level. Room and board charges vary according to housing facility. ***Part-time tuition:*** $355 per credit hour. Part-time tuition and fees vary according to degree level. ***Payment plan:*** Installment.

FRESHMAN FINANCIAL AID (Fall 2006, est.) 218 applied for aid; of those 89% were deemed to have need. 96% of freshmen with need received aid; of those 62% had need fully met. ***Average percent of need met:*** 93% (excluding resources awarded to replace EFC). ***Average financial aid package:*** $23,300 (excluding resources awarded to replace EFC). 17% of all full-time freshmen had no need and received non-need-based gift aid.

UNDERGRADUATE FINANCIAL AID (Fall 2006, est.) 894 applied for aid; of those 89% were deemed to have need. 98% of undergraduates with need received aid; of those 52% had need fully met. ***Average percent of need met:*** 89% (excluding resources awarded to replace EFC). ***Average financial aid package:*** $20,510 (excluding resources awarded to replace EFC). 21% of all full-time undergraduates had no need and received non-need-based gift aid.

GIFT AID (NEED-BASED) ***Total amount:*** $8,713,389 (16% federal, 21% state, 58% institutional, 5% external sources). ***Receiving aid:*** Freshmen: 75% (179); All full-time undergraduates: 73% (759). ***Average award:*** Freshmen: $10,487; Undergraduates: $9521. ***Scholarships, grants, and awards:*** Federal Pell, FSEOG, state, private, college/university gift aid from institutional funds.

GIFT AID (NON-NEED-BASED) ***Total amount:*** $1,079,417 (17% state, 65% institutional, 18% external sources). ***Receiving aid:*** Freshmen: 79% (187); Undergraduates: 74% (773). ***Average award:*** Freshmen: $13,453; Undergraduates: $12,866. ***Scholarships, grants, and awards by category:*** *Academic Interests/Achievement:* 1,090 awards ($5,531,321 total): general academic interests/achievements. *Special Achievements/Activities:* 39 awards ($79,540 total): leadership. *Special Characteristics:* 28 awards ($214,267 total): children of educators, children of faculty/staff. ***Tuition waivers:*** Full or partial for employees or children of employees. ***ROTC:*** Army, Naval cooperative, Air Force cooperative.

LOANS ***Student loans:*** $6,248,516 (93% need-based, 7% non-need-based). 77% of past graduating class borrowed through all loan programs. *Average indebtedness per student:* $23,598. ***Average need-based loan:*** Freshmen: $1888; Undergraduates: $3313. ***Parent loans:*** $2,823,906 (96% need-based, 4% non-need-based). ***Programs:*** FFEL (Subsidized and Unsubsidized Stafford, PLUS), Perkins, alternative loans.

WORK-STUDY ***Federal work-study:*** Total amount: $552,663; 310 jobs averaging $1782. ***State or other work-study/employment:*** Total amount: $109,056 (78% need-based, 22% non-need-based). 85 part-time jobs averaging $1283.

APPLYING FOR FINANCIAL AID ***Required financial aid forms:*** FAFSA, state aid form (for VA residents only). ***Financial aid deadline:*** 4/15. ***Notification date:*** Continuous. Students must reply within 3 weeks of notification.

CONTACT Lisa Branson, Executive Director of Admissions and Financial Aid, Mary Baldwin College, Office of Financial Aid and Student Campus Employment, Staunton, VA 24401, 540-887-7022 or toll-free 800-468-2262. *Fax:* 540-887-7229. *E-mail:* lbranson@mbc.edu.

MARYGROVE COLLEGE

Detroit, MI

CONTACT Mr. Donald Hurt, Director of Financial Aid, Marygrove College, 8425 West McNichols Road, Detroit, MI 48221-2599, 313-862-8000 Ext. 436 or toll-free 866-313-1297.

MARYLAND INSTITUTE COLLEGE OF ART

Baltimore, MD

CONTACT Ms. Diane Prengaman, Associate Vice President for Financial Aid, Maryland Institute College of Art, 1300 Mount Royal Avenue, Baltimore, MD 21217, 410-225-2285. *Fax:* 410-225-2337. *E-mail:* dprengam@mica.edu.

MARYLHURST UNIVERSITY

Marylhurst, OR

CONTACT Marlena McKee-Flores, Office of Financial Aid, Marylhurst University, 17600 Pacific Highway, PO Box 261, Marylhurst, OR 97036, 503-699-6253 or toll-free 800-634-9982. *Fax:* 503-635-6585. *E-mail:* finaid@marylhurst.edu.

MARYMOUNT MANHATTAN COLLEGE

New York, NY

Tuition & fees: $19,638 **Average undergraduate aid package: N/A**

ABOUT THE INSTITUTION Independent, coed. Awards: bachelor's degrees. 20 undergraduate majors. Total enrollment: 1,938. Undergraduates: 1,938. Freshmen: 454. Federal methodology is used as a basis for awarding need-based institutional aid.

UNDERGRADUATE EXPENSES for 2006–07 ***Application fee:*** $60. ***Comprehensive fee:*** $31,728 includes full-time tuition ($18,748), mandatory fees ($890), and room and board ($12,090). ***College room only:*** $10,090. ***Part-time tuition:*** $598 per credit. ***Part-time fees:*** $393 per term.

FRESHMAN FINANCIAL AID (Fall 2006, est.) 337 applied for aid; of those 78% were deemed to have need. 100% of freshmen with need received aid; of those 8% had need fully met. ***Average percent of need met:*** 52% (excluding resources awarded to replace EFC). 19% of all full-time freshmen had no need and received non-need-based gift aid.

UNDERGRADUATE FINANCIAL AID (Fall 2006, est.) 1,200 applied for aid; of those 80% were deemed to have need. 99% of undergraduates with need received aid; of those 10% had need fully met. ***Average percent of need met:*** 43% (excluding resources awarded to replace EFC). 11% of all full-time undergraduates had no need and received non-need-based gift aid.

GIFT AID (NEED-BASED) ***Total amount:*** $7,099,251 (19% federal, 12% state, 67% institutional, 2% external sources). ***Receiving aid:*** Freshmen: 57% (247); All full-time undergraduates: 56% (871). ***Average award:*** Freshmen: $11,278; Undergraduates: $10,849. ***Scholarships, grants, and awards:*** Federal Pell, FSEOG, state, private, college/university gift aid from institutional funds.

GIFT AID (NON-NEED-BASED) ***Total amount:*** $1,533,259 (98% institutional, 2% external sources). ***Receiving aid:*** Freshmen: 2% (8); Undergraduates: 3% (42). ***Average award:*** Freshmen: $4760; Undergraduates: $4632. ***Scholarships, grants, and awards by category:*** *Academic Interests/Achievement:* general academic interests/achievements. *Creative Arts/Performance:* dance, performing arts, theater/drama.

LOANS ***Student loans:*** $8,448,072 (76% need-based, 24% non-need-based). 65% of past graduating class borrowed through all loan programs. *Average indebtedness per student:* $17,125. ***Average need-based loan:*** Freshmen: $2539; Undergraduates: $3698. ***Parent loans:*** $16,004,229 (51% need-based, 49% non-need-based). ***Programs:*** FFEL (Subsidized and Unsubsidized Stafford, PLUS).

WORK-STUDY ***Federal work-study:*** Total amount: $111,693; jobs available. ***State or other work-study/employment:*** Total amount: $37,231 (100% need-based). Part-time jobs available.

APPLYING FOR FINANCIAL AID ***Required financial aid form:*** FAFSA. ***Financial aid deadline (priority):*** 3/15. ***Notification date:*** Continuous.

CONTACT Miss Christina Bennett, Marymount Manhattan College, 221 East 71st Street, New York, NY 10021-4597, 212-517-0400 or toll-free 800-MARYMOUNT (out-of-state).

MARYMOUNT UNIVERSITY

Arlington, VA

Tuition & fees: $19,199 **Average undergraduate aid package: $13,381**

ABOUT THE INSTITUTION Independent religious, coed. Awards: bachelor's, master's, and doctoral degrees and post-bachelor's and post-master's certificates (Associate). 37 undergraduate majors. Total enrollment: 3,604. Undergraduates: 2,300. Freshmen: 371. Both federal and institutional methodology are used as a basis for awarding need-based institutional aid.

UNDERGRADUATE EXPENSES for 2006–07 ***Application fee:*** $40. ***Comprehensive fee:*** $27,411 includes full-time tuition ($19,048), mandatory fees ($151), and room and board ($8212). ***Part-time tuition:*** $620 per credit hour. ***Part-time fees:*** $6.30 per credit hour. ***Payment plan:*** Installment.

FRESHMAN FINANCIAL AID (Fall 2006, est.) 296 applied for aid; of those 78% were deemed to have need. 98% of freshmen with need received aid; of those 17% had need fully met. ***Average percent of need met:*** 78% (excluding resources awarded to replace EFC). ***Average financial aid package:*** $15,233 (excluding resources awarded to replace EFC). 24% of all full-time freshmen had no need and received non-need-based gift aid.

UNDERGRADUATE FINANCIAL AID (Fall 2006, est.) 1,388 applied for aid; of those 80% were deemed to have need. 98% of undergraduates with need received aid; of those 13% had need fully met. ***Average percent of need met:*** 70% (excluding resources awarded to replace EFC). ***Average financial aid package:*** $13,381 (excluding resources awarded to replace EFC). 17% of all full-time undergraduates had no need and received non-need-based gift aid.

GIFT AID (NEED-BASED) ***Total amount:*** $6,166,948 (23% federal, 1% state, 76% institutional). ***Receiving aid:*** Freshmen: 53% (193); All full-time undergraduates: 42% (819). ***Average award:*** Freshmen: $8407; Undergraduates: $7259. ***Scholarships, grants, and awards:*** Federal Pell, FSEOG, state, private, college/university gift aid from institutional funds.

GIFT AID (NON-NEED-BASED) ***Total amount:*** $8,218,602 (1% federal, 24% state, 75% institutional). ***Receiving aid:*** Freshmen: 48% (176); Undergraduates: 39% (761). ***Average award:*** Freshmen: $7241; Undergraduates: $8518. ***Scholarships, grants, and awards by category:*** *Academic Interests/Achievement:* 519 awards ($4,529,500 total): general academic interests/achievements. *Special Achievements/Activities:* 66 awards ($85,124 total): community service, leadership, memberships. *Special Characteristics:* 95 awards ($523,130 total): children and siblings of alumni, children of current students, children of faculty/staff, parents of current students, siblings of current students. ***Tuition waivers:*** Full or partial for children of alumni, employees or children of employees, senior citizens. ***ROTC:*** Army cooperative.

LOANS ***Student loans:*** $9,593,919 (38% need-based, 62% non-need-based). 69% of past graduating class borrowed through all loan programs. *Average indebtedness per student:* $24,661. ***Average need-based loan:*** Freshmen: $2703; Undergraduates: $3869. ***Parent loans:*** $3,619,722 (100% non-need-based). ***Programs:*** Federal Direct (Subsidized and Unsubsidized Stafford), FFEL (Subsidized and Unsubsidized Stafford, PLUS), Perkins.

WORK-STUDY ***Federal work-study:*** Total amount: $401,141; 233 jobs averaging $1722.

APPLYING FOR FINANCIAL AID ***Required financial aid form:*** FAFSA. ***Financial aid deadline (priority):*** 3/1. ***Notification date:*** Continuous beginning 3/15. Students must reply within 2 weeks of notification.

CONTACT Ms. Debbie A. Raines, Director of Financial Aid, Marymount University, 2807 North Glebe Road, Arlington, VA 22207-4299, 703-284-1530 or toll-free 800-548-7638. *Fax:* 703-516-4771. *E-mail:* admissions@marymount.edu.

MARYVILLE COLLEGE

Maryville, TN

ABOUT THE INSTITUTION Independent Presbyterian, coed. Awards: bachelor's degrees. 50 undergraduate majors. Total enrollment: 1,155. Undergraduates: 1,155. Freshmen: 297.

GIFT AID (NEED-BASED) ***Scholarships, grants, and awards:*** Federal Pell, FSEOG, state, private, college/university gift aid from institutional funds.

GIFT AID (NON-NEED-BASED) ***Scholarships, grants, and awards by category:*** *Academic Interests/Achievement:* general academic interests/achievements. *Creative Arts/Performance:* art/fine arts, music, theater/drama. *Special Achievements/Activities:* community service, leadership. *Special Characteristics:* children and siblings of alumni, children of faculty/staff, local/state students, members of minority groups, religious affiliation.

LOANS ***Programs:*** FFEL (Subsidized and Unsubsidized Stafford, PLUS), Perkins, state, college/university.

WORK-STUDY ***Federal work-study:*** Total amount: $645,567; 441 jobs averaging $1464. ***State or other work-study/employment:*** Total amount: $286,443 (83% need-based, 17% non-need-based). 162 part-time jobs averaging $1768.

APPLYING FOR FINANCIAL AID ***Required financial aid form:*** FAFSA.

CONTACT Mr. Richard Brand, Director of Financial Aid, Maryville College, 502 East Lamar Alexander Parkway, Maryville, TN 37804-5907, 865-981-8100 or toll-free 800-597-2687. *E-mail:* richard.brand@maryvillecollege.edu.

MARYVILLE UNIVERSITY OF SAINT LOUIS

St. Louis, MO

Tuition & fees: $18,120 **Average undergraduate aid package: $13,522**

ABOUT THE INSTITUTION Independent, coed. Awards: bachelor's, master's, and doctoral degrees. 48 undergraduate majors. Total enrollment: 3,333. Undergraduates: 2,748. Freshmen: 292. Both federal and institutional methodology are used as a basis for awarding need-based institutional aid.

UNDERGRADUATE EXPENSES for 2006–07 ***Application fee:*** $25. ***Comprehensive fee:*** $25,840 includes full-time tuition ($17,800), mandatory fees ($320), and room and board ($7720). ***College room only:*** $6800. Full-time tuition and fees vary according to course load. Room and board charges vary according to housing facility. ***Part-time tuition:*** $540 per credit hour. ***Part-time fees:*** $80 per term. Part-time tuition and fees vary according to class time. ***Payment plan:*** Deferred payment.

FRESHMAN FINANCIAL AID (Fall 2006, est.) 270 applied for aid; of those 82% were deemed to have need. 100% of freshmen with need received aid; of those 13% had need fully met. ***Average percent of need met:*** 71% (excluding resources awarded to replace EFC). ***Average financial aid package:*** $13,980 (excluding resources awarded to replace EFC). 20% of all full-time freshmen had no need and received non-need-based gift aid.

UNDERGRADUATE FINANCIAL AID (Fall 2006, est.) 1,541 applied for aid; of those 86% were deemed to have need. 100% of undergraduates with need received aid; of those 12% had need fully met. ***Average percent of need met:*** 65% (excluding resources awarded to replace EFC). ***Average financial aid package:*** $13,522 (excluding resources awarded to replace EFC). 21% of all full-time undergraduates had no need and received non-need-based gift aid.

GIFT AID (NEED-BASED) ***Total amount:*** $9,671,011 (15% federal, 7% state, 75% institutional, 3% external sources). ***Receiving aid:*** Freshmen: 76% (221); All full-time undergraduates: 73% (1,224). ***Average award:*** Freshmen: $8974; Undergraduates: $7384. ***Scholarships, grants, and awards:*** Federal Pell, FSEOG, state, private, college/university gift aid from institutional funds, Federal Academic Competitiveness Grant and Federal Smart Grant.

GIFT AID (NON-NEED-BASED) ***Total amount:*** $2,125,800 (2% state, 93% institutional, 5% external sources). ***Receiving aid:*** Freshmen: 69% (199); Undergraduates: 16% (261). ***Average award:*** Freshmen: $7123; Undergraduates: $3366. ***Scholarships, grants, and awards by category:*** *Academic Interests/Achievement:* 1,556 awards ($7,875,572 total): biological sciences, business, education, general academic interests/achievements, health fields. *Creative Arts/Performance:* 36 awards ($74,750 total): art/fine arts. *Special Achievements/Activities:* 262 awards ($182,000 total): community service, general special achievements/activities, leadership. *Special Characteristics:* 42 awards ($40,553 total): children and siblings of alumni, children of current students, children of faculty/staff, ethnic background, general special characteristics, members of minority groups, parents of current students, siblings of current students, spouses of current students, twins. ***Tuition waivers:*** Full or partial for employees or children of employees, senior citizens. ***ROTC:*** Army cooperative.

LOANS ***Student loans:*** $15,163,165 (69% need-based, 31% non-need-based). 69% of past graduating class borrowed through all loan programs. *Average indebtedness per student:* $23,560. ***Average need-based loan:*** Freshmen: $3374; Undergraduates: $5656. ***Parent loans:*** $3,691,126 (41% need-based, 59% non-need-based). ***Programs:*** Federal Direct (Subsidized and Unsubsidized Stafford, PLUS), Perkins, Sallie Mae Signature Loans, KeyBank Loans, TERI Loans, CitiAssist Loans, MOHELA ED Cash Loans, Wells Fargo Loans, Nelnet.

WORK-STUDY ***Federal work-study:*** Total amount: $233,589; 205 jobs averaging $1140. ***State or other work-study/employment:*** Total amount: $381,184 (82% need-based, 18% non-need-based). 110 part-time jobs averaging $2028.

APPLYING FOR FINANCIAL AID ***Required financial aid form:*** FAFSA. ***Financial aid deadline (priority):*** 3/1. ***Notification date:*** Continuous beginning 3/15. Students must reply by 5/1 or within 2 weeks of notification.

CONTACT Ms. Martha Harbaugh, Director of Financial Aid, Maryville University of Saint Louis, 650 Maryville University Drive, St. Louis, MO 63141-7299, 800-627-9855 Ext. 9360 or toll-free 800-627-9855. *Fax:* 314-529-9199. *E-mail:* fin_aid@maryville.edu.

MARYWOOD UNIVERSITY

Scranton, PA

Tuition & fees: $24,090 **Average undergraduate aid package: $16,952**

ABOUT THE INSTITUTION Independent Roman Catholic, coed. Awards: associate, bachelor's, master's, and doctoral degrees and post-bachelor's and post-master's certificates. 86 undergraduate majors. Total enrollment: 3,180. Undergraduates: 1,896. Freshmen: 392. Federal methodology is used as a basis for awarding need-based institutional aid.

UNDERGRADUATE EXPENSES for 2007–08 ***Application fee:*** $30. ***Comprehensive fee:*** $34,500 includes full-time tuition ($23,040), mandatory fees ($1050), and room and board ($10,410). ***College room only:*** $5980. ***Part-time tuition:*** $550 per credit. ***Part-time fees:*** $200 per term.

FRESHMAN FINANCIAL AID (Fall 2006, est.) 360 applied for aid; of those 89% were deemed to have need. 100% of freshmen with need received aid; of those 17% had need fully met. ***Average percent of need met:*** 77% (excluding resources awarded to replace EFC). ***Average financial aid package:*** $17,301 (excluding resources awarded to replace EFC). 15% of all full-time freshmen had no need and received non-need-based gift aid.

UNDERGRADUATE FINANCIAL AID (Fall 2006, est.) 1,543 applied for aid; of those 92% were deemed to have need. 99% of undergraduates with need received aid; of those 16% had need fully met. ***Average percent of need met:*** 73% (excluding resources awarded to replace EFC). ***Average financial aid package:*** $16,952 (excluding resources awarded to replace EFC). 16% of all full-time undergraduates had no need and received non-need-based gift aid.

GIFT AID (NEED-BASED) ***Total amount:*** $17,581,022 (12% federal, 17% state, 69% institutional, 2% external sources). ***Receiving aid:*** Freshmen: 83% (319); All full-time undergraduates: 81% (1,402). ***Average award:*** Freshmen: $13,245; Undergraduates: $12,214. ***Scholarships, grants, and awards:*** Federal Pell, FSEOG, state, private, college/university gift aid from institutional funds, Federal Nursing, Federal ACG, SMART, Disadvantaged Student Scholarship.

GIFT AID (NON-NEED-BASED) ***Total amount:*** $3,048,687 (92% institutional, 8% external sources). ***Receiving aid:*** Freshmen: 10% (39); Undergraduates: 6% (112). ***Average award:*** Freshmen: $11,208; Undergraduates: $8818. ***Scholarships, grants, and awards by category:*** *Academic Interests/Achievement:* 121 awards ($830,614 total): business, communication, education, foreign languages, general academic interests/achievements, health fields, mathematics, religion/biblical studies. *Creative Arts/Performance:* 33 awards ($36,100 total): art/fine arts, cinema/film/broadcasting, journalism/publications, music, performing arts, theater/drama. *Special Achievements/Activities:* 158 awards ($723,389 total): community service, general special achievements/activities, leadership. *Special Characteristics:* 59 awards: adult students, children and siblings of alumni, children of current students, children of faculty/staff, children of workers in trades, ethnic background, general special characteristics, international students, local/state students, religious affiliation, siblings of current students, spouses of current students. ***ROTC:*** Army cooperative, Air Force cooperative.

LOANS ***Student loans:*** $12,731,991 (72% need-based, 28% non-need-based). 58% of past graduating class borrowed through all loan programs. *Average indebtedness per student:* $34,364. ***Average need-based loan:*** Freshmen: $2922; Undergraduates: $4332. ***Parent loans:*** $2,615,277 (31% need-based, 69% non-need-based). ***Programs:*** FFEL (Subsidized and Unsubsidized Stafford, PLUS), Perkins, state.

WORK-STUDY ***Federal work-study:*** Total amount: $432,975; 643 jobs averaging $1724. ***State or other work-study/employment:*** Total amount: $432,975 (100% need-based).

APPLYING FOR FINANCIAL AID ***Required financial aid form:*** FAFSA. ***Financial aid deadline:*** Continuous. ***Notification date:*** Continuous beginning 3/1. Students must reply by 5/1 or within 3 weeks of notification.

CONTACT Mr. Stanley F. Skrutski, Director of Financial Aid, Marywood University, 2300 Adams Avenue, Scranton, PA 18509-1598, 570-348-6225 or toll-free 800-346-5014. *Fax:* 570-961-4739. *E-mail:* skrutski@ac.marywood.edu.

MASSACHUSETTS COLLEGE OF ART

Boston, MA

Tuition & fees (MA res): $7200 **Average undergraduate aid package: $8278**

ABOUT THE INSTITUTION State-supported, coed. Awards: bachelor's and master's degrees and post-bachelor's certificates. 17 undergraduate majors. Total enrollment: 2,286. Undergraduates: 2,136. Freshmen: 338. Federal methodology is used as a basis for awarding need-based institutional aid.

UNDERGRADUATE EXPENSES for 2006–07 ***Application fee:*** $65. ***Tuition, state resident:*** full-time $7200. ***Tuition, nonresident:*** full-time $20,600. ***College room and board:*** $11,090. Room and board charges vary according to housing facility. ***Payment plan:*** Installment.

FRESHMAN FINANCIAL AID (Fall 2006, est.) 286 applied for aid; of those 73% were deemed to have need. 100% of freshmen with need received aid. ***Average financial aid package:*** $6696 (excluding resources awarded to replace EFC).

UNDERGRADUATE FINANCIAL AID (Fall 2006, est.) 1,132 applied for aid; of those 79% were deemed to have need. 100% of undergraduates with need received aid. ***Average financial aid package:*** $8278 (excluding resources awarded to replace EFC).

GIFT AID (NEED-BASED) ***Total amount:*** $3,047,756 (44% federal, 37% state, 19% institutional). ***Receiving aid:*** Freshmen: 33% (111); All full-time undergraduates: 35% (526). ***Average award:*** Freshmen: $5497; Undergraduates: $5541. ***Scholarships, grants, and awards:*** Federal Pell, FSEOG, state, private, college/university gift aid from institutional funds.

GIFT AID (NON-NEED-BASED) ***Total amount:*** $554,208 (100% external sources). ***Receiving aid:*** Freshmen: 21% (72); Undergraduates: 11% (167). ***Scholarships, grants, and awards by category:*** *Special Characteristics:* children of faculty/staff, children of union members/company employees, veterans. ***Tuition waivers:*** Full or partial for employees or children of employees.

LOANS ***Student loans:*** $8,742,883 (43% need-based, 57% non-need-based). ***Average need-based loan:*** Freshmen: $2785; Undergraduates: $4050. ***Parent loans:*** $14,430,608 (100% non-need-based). ***Programs:*** Federal Direct (Subsidized and Unsubsidized Stafford, PLUS), FFEL (Subsidized and Unsubsidized Stafford, PLUS), Perkins, state, college/university, alternative loans.

WORK-STUDY ***Federal work-study:*** Total amount: $161,000; 221 jobs averaging $750.

APPLYING FOR FINANCIAL AID ***Required financial aid form:*** FAFSA. ***Financial aid deadline (priority):*** 3/1. ***Notification date:*** Continuous beginning 3/1. Students must reply within 3 weeks of notification.

CONTACT Laura Hofeldt, Director of Student Financial Assistance, Massachusetts College of Art, 621 Huntington Avenue, Boston, MA 02115-5882, 617-879-7846. *Fax:* 617-879-7880. *E-mail:* lhofeldt@massart.edu.

MASSACHUSETTS COLLEGE OF LIBERAL ARTS

North Adams, MA

Tuition & fees (MA res): $6326 **Average undergraduate aid package: $7415**

ABOUT THE INSTITUTION State-supported, coed. Awards: bachelor's and master's degrees and post-bachelor's certificates. 41 undergraduate majors. Total enrollment: 1,805. Undergraduates: 1,454. Freshmen: 304. Federal methodology is used as a basis for awarding need-based institutional aid.

UNDERGRADUATE EXPENSES for 2006–07 ***Application fee:*** $25. ***Tuition, state resident:*** full-time $1030; part-time $42.92 per credit. ***Tuition, nonresident:*** full-time $9975; part-time $415.63 per credit. ***College room and board:*** $6542; ***Room only:*** $3504.

FRESHMAN FINANCIAL AID (Fall 2006, est.) 292 applied for aid; of those 75% were deemed to have need. 96% of freshmen with need received aid; of those 38% had need fully met. ***Average percent of need met:*** 55% (excluding resources awarded to replace EFC). ***Average financial aid package:*** $7131 (excluding resources awarded to replace EFC). 22% of all full-time freshmen had no need and received non-need-based gift aid.

UNDERGRADUATE FINANCIAL AID (Fall 2006, est.) 1,119 applied for aid; of those 77% were deemed to have need. 96% of undergraduates with need

received aid; of those 45% had need fully met. ***Average percent of need met:*** 65% (excluding resources awarded to replace EFC). ***Average financial aid package:*** $7415 (excluding resources awarded to replace EFC). 19% of all full-time undergraduates had no need and received non-need-based gift aid.

GIFT AID (NEED-BASED) ***Total amount:*** $3,107,952 (38% federal, 25% state, 34% institutional, 3% external sources). ***Receiving aid:*** Freshmen: 50% (149); All full-time undergraduates: 46% (580). ***Average award:*** Freshmen: $4849; Undergraduates: $4576. ***Scholarships, grants, and awards:*** Federal Pell, FSEOG, state, private, college/university gift aid from institutional funds.

GIFT AID (NON-NEED-BASED) ***Total amount:*** $415,336 (6% state, 56% institutional, 38% external sources). ***Receiving aid:*** Freshmen: 33% (100); Undergraduates: 24% (306). ***Average award:*** Freshmen: $4298; Undergraduates: $5614. ***Scholarships, grants, and awards by category:*** *Academic Interests/Achievement:* 164 awards ($309,119 total): biological sciences, business, communication, computer science, education, English, general academic interests/achievements, health fields, humanities, mathematics, physical sciences, social sciences. *Creative Arts/Performance:* 22 awards ($26,320 total): applied art and design, art/fine arts, cinema/film/broadcasting, journalism/publications, music, performing arts, theater/drama. *Special Achievements/Activities:* 10 awards ($5585 total): general special achievements/activities, leadership, memberships. *Special Characteristics:* 67 awards ($84,339 total): first-generation college students, handicapped students, local/state students, out-of-state students.

LOANS ***Student loans:*** $5,916,497 (68% need-based, 32% non-need-based). 75% of past graduating class borrowed through all loan programs. *Average indebtedness per student:* $18,628. ***Average need-based loan:*** Freshmen: $2732; Undergraduates: $3392. ***Parent loans:*** $1,037,823 (10% need-based, 90% non-need-based). ***Programs:*** FFEL (Subsidized and Unsubsidized Stafford, PLUS), Perkins, state.

WORK-STUDY ***Federal work-study:*** Total amount: $266,837; 169 jobs averaging $1531. ***State or other work-study/employment:*** Total amount: $688,692 (100% non-need-based). 434 part-time jobs averaging $1541.

APPLYING FOR FINANCIAL AID ***Required financial aid forms:*** FAFSA, institution's own form. ***Financial aid deadline (priority):*** 3/1. ***Notification date:*** Continuous beginning 3/1. Students must reply by 5/1 or within 2 weeks of notification.

CONTACT Elizabeth M. Petri, Director of Financial Aid, Massachusetts College of Liberal Arts, 375 Church Street, Eldridge Hall, Room 112, North Adams, MA 01247, 413-662-5219 or toll-free 800-292-6632 (in-state). *E-mail:* epetri@mcla.edu.

MASSACHUSETTS COLLEGE OF PHARMACY AND HEALTH SCIENCES

Boston, MA

Tuition & fees: $21,880 **Average undergraduate aid package: $10,375**

ABOUT THE INSTITUTION Independent, coed. Awards: bachelor's, master's, doctoral, and first professional degrees and post-bachelor's certificates. 10 undergraduate majors. Total enrollment: 3,298. Undergraduates: 2,187. Freshmen: 511. Federal methodology is used as a basis for awarding need-based institutional aid.

UNDERGRADUATE EXPENSES for 2006–07 ***Application fee:*** $70. ***Comprehensive fee:*** $33,180 includes full-time tuition ($21,200), mandatory fees ($680), and room and board ($11,300). Full-time tuition and fees vary according to course load, program, and student level. ***Part-time tuition:*** $780 per credit hour. ***Part-time fees:*** $165 per term. ***Payment plan:*** Installment.

FRESHMAN FINANCIAL AID (Fall 2006, est.) 445 applied for aid; of those 88% were deemed to have need. 100% of freshmen with need received aid; of those 8% had need fully met. ***Average percent of need met:*** 50% (excluding resources awarded to replace EFC). ***Average financial aid package:*** $13,333 (excluding resources awarded to replace EFC). 20% of all full-time freshmen had no need and received non-need-based gift aid.

UNDERGRADUATE FINANCIAL AID (Fall 2006, est.) 1,885 applied for aid; of those 91% were deemed to have need. 99% of undergraduates with need received aid; of those 5% had need fully met. ***Average percent of need met:*** 35% (excluding resources awarded to replace EFC). ***Average financial aid package:*** $10,375 (excluding resources awarded to replace EFC). 11% of all full-time undergraduates had no need and received non-need-based gift aid.

GIFT AID (NEED-BASED) ***Total amount:*** $9,164,413 (19% federal, 6% state, 69% institutional, 6% external sources). ***Receiving aid:*** Freshmen: 71% (350); All full-time undergraduates: 68% (1,330). ***Average award:*** Freshmen: $9530; Undergraduates: $6791. ***Scholarships, grants, and awards:*** Federal Pell, FSEOG, state, private, college/university gift aid from institutional funds.

GIFT AID (NON-NEED-BASED) ***Total amount:*** $903,179 (94% institutional, 6% external sources). ***Receiving aid:*** Freshmen: 4% (19); Undergraduates: 2% (32). ***Average award:*** Freshmen: $13,078; Undergraduates: $15,391. ***Scholarships, grants, and awards by category:*** *Academic Interests/Achievement:* general academic interests/achievements. *Special Characteristics:* children of faculty/staff. ***Tuition waivers:*** Full or partial for employees or children of employees.

LOANS ***Student loans:*** $36,547,738 (78% need-based, 22% non-need-based). 76% of past graduating class borrowed through all loan programs. *Average indebtedness per student:* $54,495. ***Average need-based loan:*** Freshmen: $4446; Undergraduates: $4967. ***Parent loans:*** $2,333,791 (57% need-based, 43% non-need-based). ***Programs:*** FFEL (Subsidized and Unsubsidized Stafford, PLUS), Perkins, state.

WORK-STUDY ***Federal work-study:*** Total amount: $414,446; jobs available.

APPLYING FOR FINANCIAL AID ***Required financial aid form:*** FAFSA. ***Financial aid deadline (priority):*** 3/15. ***Notification date:*** Continuous beginning 2/20. Students must reply by 5/1 or within 2 weeks of notification.

CONTACT Ms. Carrie Glass, Director of Student Financial Services, Massachusetts College of Pharmacy and Health Sciences, 179 Longwood Avenue, Boston, MA 02115-5896, 617-732-2199 or toll-free 617-732-2850 (in-state), 800-225-5506 (out-of-state). *Fax:* 617-732-2082. *E-mail:* carrie.glass@mcphs.edu.

MASSACHUSETTS INSTITUTE OF TECHNOLOGY

Cambridge, MA

Tuition & fees: $33,600 **Average undergraduate aid package: $29,831**

ABOUT THE INSTITUTION Independent, coed. Awards: bachelor's, master's, and doctoral degrees. 33 undergraduate majors. Total enrollment: 10,253. Undergraduates: 4,127. Freshmen: 1,002. Institutional methodology is used as a basis for awarding need-based institutional aid.

UNDERGRADUATE EXPENSES for 2006–07 ***Application fee:*** $65. ***Comprehensive fee:*** $43,550 includes full-time tuition ($33,400), mandatory fees ($200), and room and board ($9950). ***College room only:*** $5600. Room and board charges vary according to board plan and housing facility. ***Part-time tuition:*** $525 per unit. Part-time tuition and fees vary according to course load. ***Payment plan:*** Installment.

FRESHMAN FINANCIAL AID (Fall 2005) 780 applied for aid; of those 81% were deemed to have need. 100% of freshmen with need received aid; of those 100% had need fully met. ***Average percent of need met:*** 100% (excluding resources awarded to replace EFC). ***Average financial aid package:*** $30,466 (excluding resources awarded to replace EFC).

UNDERGRADUATE FINANCIAL AID (Fall 2005) 2,868 applied for aid; of those 86% were deemed to have need. 100% of undergraduates with need received aid; of those 100% had need fully met. ***Average percent of need met:*** 100% (excluding resources awarded to replace EFC). ***Average financial aid package:*** $29,831 (excluding resources awarded to replace EFC).

GIFT AID (NEED-BASED) ***Total amount:*** $62,963,224 (7% federal, 86% institutional, 7% external sources). ***Receiving aid:*** Freshmen: 61% (607); All full-time undergraduates: 60% (2,385). ***Average award:*** Freshmen: $27,516; Undergraduates: $26,013. ***Scholarships, grants, and awards:*** Federal Pell, FSEOG, state, private, college/university gift aid from institutional funds.

GIFT AID (NON-NEED-BASED) ***Total amount:*** $3,699,952 (24% federal, 76% external sources). ***Tuition waivers:*** Full or partial for employees or children of employees. ***ROTC:*** Army, Naval, Air Force.

LOANS ***Student loans:*** $8,802,858 (84% need-based, 16% non-need-based). 45% of past graduating class borrowed through all loan programs. *Average indebtedness per student:* $17,956. ***Average need-based loan:*** Freshmen: $3556; Undergraduates: $4010. ***Parent loans:*** $7,241,694 (100% non-need-based). ***Programs:*** Federal Direct (Subsidized and Unsubsidized Stafford, PLUS), Perkins, college/university.

WORK-STUDY ***Federal work-study:*** Total amount: $2,779,220; 981 jobs averaging $2569. ***State or other work-study/employment:*** Total amount: $2,396,258 (73% need-based, 27% non-need-based). 1,040 part-time jobs averaging $2284.

APPLYING FOR FINANCIAL AID ***Required financial aid forms:*** FAFSA, CSS Financial Aid PROFILE, noncustodial (divorced/separated) parent's statement, business/farm supplement, parents' complete federal income returns from prior year and W2s. ***Financial aid deadline:*** 2/15 (priority: 2/15). ***Notification date:*** 3/20. Students must reply by 5/1.

CONTACT Elizabeth Hicks, Student Financial Services, Massachusetts Institute of Technology, 77 Massachusetts Avenue, Room 11-320, Cambridge, MA 02139-4307, 617-253-4971. *Fax:* 617-253-9859. *E-mail:* finaid@mit.edu.

MASSACHUSETTS MARITIME ACADEMY

Buzzards Bay, MA

ABOUT THE INSTITUTION State-supported, coed, primarily men. Awards: bachelor's and master's degrees and first professional certificates. 8 undergraduate majors. Total enrollment: 1,008. Undergraduates: 969. Freshmen: 266.

GIFT AID (NEED-BASED) ***Scholarships, grants, and awards:*** Federal Pell, FSEOG, state, private, college/university gift aid from institutional funds.

GIFT AID (NON-NEED-BASED) ***Scholarships, grants, and awards by category:*** *Academic Interests/Achievement:* general academic interests/achievements. *Creative Arts/Performance:* theater/drama. *Special Achievements/Activities:* leadership. *Special Characteristics:* children and siblings of alumni, children of faculty/staff, international students, veterans.

LOANS ***Programs:*** Federal Direct (Subsidized and Unsubsidized Stafford, PLUS).

WORK-STUDY ***Federal work-study:*** Total amount: $89,583; 147 jobs averaging $1233.

APPLYING FOR FINANCIAL AID ***Required financial aid forms:*** FAFSA, institution's own form.

CONTACT Mrs. Elizabeth Benway, Director of Financial Aid, Massachusetts Maritime Academy, 101 Academy Drive, Buzzards Bay, MA 02532, 508-830-5086 or toll-free 800-544-3411. *Fax:* 508-830-5077. *E-mail:* ebenway@maritime.edu.

THE MASTER'S COLLEGE AND SEMINARY

Santa Clarita, CA

ABOUT THE INSTITUTION Independent nondenominational, coed. Awards: bachelor's, master's, doctoral, and first professional degrees and first professional certificates. 47 undergraduate majors. Total enrollment: 1,521. Undergraduates: 1,130. Freshmen: 189.

GIFT AID (NEED-BASED) ***Scholarships, grants, and awards:*** Federal Pell, FSEOG, state, private, college/university gift aid from institutional funds.

GIFT AID (NON-NEED-BASED) ***Scholarships, grants, and awards by category:*** *Academic Interests/Achievement:* biological sciences, business, education, general academic interests/achievements, mathematics, physical sciences, religion/biblical studies, social sciences. *Creative Arts/Performance:* music. *Special Achievements/Activities:* leadership. *Special Characteristics:* children and siblings of alumni, children of faculty/staff, general special characteristics, international students, relatives of clergy.

LOANS ***Programs:*** FFEL (Subsidized and Unsubsidized Stafford, PLUS), Perkins, alternative loans.

WORK-STUDY ***Federal work-study:*** Total amount: $108,000; 45 jobs averaging $2666. ***State or other work-study/employment:*** Total amount: $1,045,019 (74% need-based, 26% non-need-based). Part-time jobs available.

APPLYING FOR FINANCIAL AID ***Required financial aid forms:*** FAFSA, institution's own form, state aid form.

CONTACT Gary Edwards, Director of Financial Aid, The Master's College and Seminary, 21726 Placerita Canyon Road, Santa Clarita, CA 91321-1200, 661-259-3540 Ext. 3391 or toll-free 800-568-6248. *Fax:* 661-362-2693. *E-mail:* gedwards@masters.edu.

MAYVILLE STATE UNIVERSITY

Mayville, ND

Tuition & fees (ND res): $5257 **Average undergraduate aid package: $4622**

ABOUT THE INSTITUTION State-supported, coed. Awards: associate and bachelor's degrees. 37 undergraduate majors. Total enrollment: 832. Undergraduates: 832. Freshmen: 134. Federal methodology is used as a basis for awarding need-based institutional aid.

UNDERGRADUATE EXPENSES for 2006–07 ***Application fee:*** $35. ***Tuition, state resident:*** full-time $3614; part-time $150.58 per credit hour. ***Tuition, nonresident:*** full-time $5421; part-time $225.88 per credit hour. ***Required fees:*** full-time $1643; $68.45 per hour. Full-time tuition and fees vary according to course load and reciprocity agreements. Part-time tuition and fees vary according to course load and reciprocity agreements. ***College room and board:*** $3884; ***Room only:*** $1576. Room and board charges vary according to board plan and housing facility. ***Payment plan:*** Installment.

FRESHMAN FINANCIAL AID (Fall 2006, est.) 124 applied for aid; of those 99% were deemed to have need. 100% of freshmen with need received aid; of those 40% had need fully met. ***Average percent of need met:*** 45% (excluding resources awarded to replace EFC). ***Average financial aid package:*** $4039 (excluding resources awarded to replace EFC). 49% of all full-time freshmen had no need and received non-need-based gift aid.

UNDERGRADUATE FINANCIAL AID (Fall 2006, est.) 469 applied for aid; of those 79% were deemed to have need. 99% of undergraduates with need received aid; of those 41% had need fully met. ***Average percent of need met:*** 46% (excluding resources awarded to replace EFC). ***Average financial aid package:*** $4622 (excluding resources awarded to replace EFC). 32% of all full-time undergraduates had no need and received non-need-based gift aid.

GIFT AID (NEED-BASED) ***Total amount:*** $834,681 (74% federal, 5% state, 11% institutional, 10% external sources). ***Receiving aid:*** Freshmen: 67% (92); All full-time undergraduates: 59% (300). ***Average award:*** Freshmen: $2130; Undergraduates: $2243. ***Scholarships, grants, and awards:*** Federal Pell, FSEOG, state, private, college/university gift aid from institutional funds.

GIFT AID (NON-NEED-BASED) ***Total amount:*** $83,859 (4% state, 57% institutional, 39% external sources). ***Receiving aid:*** Freshmen: 10% (14); Undergraduates: 6% (31). ***Average award:*** Freshmen: $795; Undergraduates: $653. ***Scholarships, grants, and awards by category:*** *Academic Interests/Achievement:* 120 awards ($66,000 total): biological sciences, business, education, English, general academic interests/achievements, library science, mathematics, physical sciences. *Creative Arts/Performance:* 60 awards ($12,000 total): music, theater/drama. *Special Characteristics:* 52 awards ($84,600 total): children of faculty/staff, international students, local/state students, members of minority groups, out-of-state students. ***Tuition waivers:*** Full or partial for minority students, senior citizens. ***ROTC:*** Army cooperative, Air Force cooperative.

LOANS ***Student loans:*** $2,743,281 (60% need-based, 40% non-need-based). *Average indebtedness per student:* $15,758. ***Average need-based loan:*** Freshmen: $2319; Undergraduates: $3246. ***Parent loans:*** $179,767 (20% need-based, 80% non-need-based). ***Programs:*** FFEL (Subsidized and Unsubsidized Stafford, PLUS), Perkins, college/university.

WORK-STUDY ***Federal work-study:*** Total amount: $58,049; 50 jobs averaging $1200.

ATHLETIC AWARDS Total amount: $233,330 (40% need-based, 60% non-need-based).

APPLYING FOR FINANCIAL AID ***Required financial aid form:*** FAFSA. ***Financial aid deadline:*** Continuous. ***Notification date:*** Continuous beginning 5/1. Students must reply within 2 weeks of notification.

CONTACT Ms. Shirley Hanson, Director of Financial Aid, Mayville State University, 330 3rd Street NE, Mayville, ND 58257-1299, 701-788-4767 or toll-free 800-437-4104. *Fax:* 701-788-4818. *E-mail:* s_hanson@mayvillestate.edu.

McDANIEL COLLEGE

Westminster, MD

Tuition & fees: $27,280 **Average undergraduate aid package: $21,474**

ABOUT THE INSTITUTION Independent, coed. Awards: bachelor's and master's degrees. 28 undergraduate majors. Total enrollment: 3,671. Undergraduates: 1,771. Freshmen: 476. Both federal and institutional methodology are used as a basis for awarding need-based institutional aid.

UNDERGRADUATE EXPENSES for 2006–07 ***Application fee:*** $50. ***Comprehensive fee:*** $33,180 includes full-time tuition ($26,980), mandatory fees ($300), and room and board ($5900). ***College room only:*** $3200. Room and board charges vary according to board plan and housing facility. ***Part-time tuition:*** $843 per credit. ***Part-time fees:*** $150 per term. Part-time tuition and fees vary according to reciprocity agreements. ***Payment plan:*** Installment.

FRESHMAN FINANCIAL AID (Fall 2005) 375 applied for aid; of those 85% were deemed to have need. 99% of freshmen with need received aid; of those 30% had need fully met. ***Average percent of need met:*** 96% (excluding resources awarded to replace EFC). ***Average financial aid package:*** $21,013 (excluding resources awarded to replace EFC). 33% of all full-time freshmen had no need and received non-need-based gift aid.

UNDERGRADUATE FINANCIAL AID (Fall 2005) 1,246 applied for aid; of those 85% were deemed to have need. 99% of undergraduates with need received aid; of those 30% had need fully met. ***Average percent of need met:*** 95% (excluding resources awarded to replace EFC). ***Average financial aid package:*** $21,474 (excluding resources awarded to replace EFC). 27% of all full-time undergraduates had no need and received non-need-based gift aid.

GIFT AID (NEED-BASED) ***Total amount:*** $15,674,640 (6% federal, 12% state, 82% institutional). ***Receiving aid:*** Freshmen: 66% (310); All full-time undergraduates: 60% (1,025). ***Average award:*** Freshmen: $9568; Undergraduates: $9374. ***Scholarships, grants, and awards:*** Federal Pell, FSEOG, state, private, college/university gift aid from institutional funds.

GIFT AID (NON-NEED-BASED) ***Total amount:*** $6,679,067 (5% state, 90% institutional, 5% external sources). ***Average award:*** Freshmen: $11,387; Undergraduates: $11,416. ***Scholarships, grants, and awards by category:*** *Academic Interests/Achievement:* 1,257 awards ($12,424,853 total): general academic interests/achievements. *Special Achievements/Activities:* 6 awards ($12,000 total): junior miss, leadership. *Special Characteristics:* 342 awards ($571,800 total): local/state students, previous college experience, siblings of current students. ***Tuition waivers:*** Full or partial for employees or children of employees. ***ROTC:*** Army.

LOANS ***Student loans:*** $6,927,251 (48% need-based, 52% non-need-based). 64% of past graduating class borrowed through all loan programs. *Average indebtedness per student:* $22,753. ***Average need-based loan:*** Freshmen: $3984; Undergraduates: $4637. ***Parent loans:*** $2,784,154 (100% non-need-based). ***Programs:*** FFEL (Subsidized and Unsubsidized Stafford, PLUS), Perkins, college/university.

WORK-STUDY ***Federal work-study:*** Total amount: $160,517; 220 jobs averaging $729. ***State or other work-study/employment:*** Total amount: $196,906 (100% non-need-based). 263 part-time jobs averaging $749.

APPLYING FOR FINANCIAL AID ***Required financial aid forms:*** FAFSA, institution's own form, federal income tax form(s). ***Financial aid deadline (priority):*** 3/1. ***Notification date:*** Continuous beginning 3/1. Students must reply by 5/1 or within 2 weeks of notification.

CONTACT Financial Aid Office, McDaniel College, 2 College Hill, Westminster, MD 21157-4390, 410-857-2233 or toll-free 800-638-5005. *Fax:* 410-857-2729. *E-mail:* finaid@mcdaniel.edu.

McKENDREE COLLEGE

Lebanon, IL

Tuition & fees: $18,900 **Average undergraduate aid package: $15,361**

ABOUT THE INSTITUTION Independent religious, coed. Awards: bachelor's and master's degrees. 50 undergraduate majors. Total enrollment: 3,212. Undergraduates: 2,399. Freshmen: 344. Federal methodology is used as a basis for awarding need-based institutional aid.

UNDERGRADUATE EXPENSES for 2006–07 ***Application fee:*** $40. ***Comprehensive fee:*** $26,280 includes full-time tuition ($18,300), mandatory fees ($600), and room and board ($7380). ***College room only:*** $3900. ***Part-time tuition:*** $615 per hour.

FRESHMAN FINANCIAL AID (Fall 2006, est.) 327 applied for aid; of those 91% were deemed to have need. 100% of freshmen with need received aid; of those 44% had need fully met. ***Average percent of need met:*** 91% (excluding resources awarded to replace EFC). ***Average financial aid package:*** $17,910 (excluding resources awarded to replace EFC). 13% of all full-time freshmen had no need and received non-need-based gift aid.

UNDERGRADUATE FINANCIAL AID (Fall 2006, est.) 1,396 applied for aid; of those 90% were deemed to have need. 99% of undergraduates with need received aid; of those 33% had need fully met. ***Average percent of need met:*** 82% (excluding resources awarded to replace EFC). ***Average financial aid package:*** $15,361 (excluding resources awarded to replace EFC). 19% of all full-time undergraduates had no need and received non-need-based gift aid.

GIFT AID (NEED-BASED) ***Total amount:*** $14,099,778 (12% federal, 23% state, 59% institutional, 6% external sources). ***Receiving aid:*** Freshmen: 86% (296); All full-time undergraduates: 76% (1,210). ***Average award:*** Freshmen: $15,376; Undergraduates: $12,462. ***Scholarships, grants, and awards:*** Federal Pell, FSEOG, state, private, college/university gift aid from institutional funds.

GIFT AID (NON-NEED-BASED) ***Total amount:*** $2,939,978 (2% state, 81% institutional, 17% external sources). ***Receiving aid:*** Freshmen: 19% (64); Undergraduates: 12% (189). ***Average award:*** Freshmen: $17,059; Undergraduates: $11,382. ***Scholarships, grants, and awards by category:*** *Academic Interests/Achievement:* 883 awards ($4,197,363 total): biological sciences, business, general academic interests/achievements, religion/biblical studies. *Creative Arts/Performance:* 150 awards ($391,905 total): music. *Special Achievements/Activities:* 47 awards ($99,731 total): cheerleading/drum major, community service, leadership. *Special Characteristics:* 217 awards ($822,710 total): children of faculty/staff, general special characteristics, out-of-state students, religious affiliation. ***ROTC:*** Army cooperative, Air Force cooperative.

LOANS ***Student loans:*** $8,227,013 (60% need-based, 40% non-need-based). 57% of past graduating class borrowed through all loan programs. *Average indebtedness per student:* $18,956. ***Average need-based loan:*** Freshmen: $2364; Undergraduates: $3473. ***Parent loans:*** $2,859,068 (26% need-based, 74% non-need-based). ***Programs:*** FFEL (Subsidized and Unsubsidized Stafford, PLUS), Perkins.

WORK-STUDY ***Federal work-study:*** Total amount: $622,315; 439 jobs averaging $1678. ***State or other work-study/employment:*** Total amount: $369,986 (4% need-based, 96% non-need-based). 264 part-time jobs averaging $1434.

ATHLETIC AWARDS Total amount: $2,543,378 (52% need-based, 48% non-need-based).

APPLYING FOR FINANCIAL AID ***Required financial aid forms:*** FAFSA, institution's own form. ***Financial aid deadline (priority):*** 5/31. ***Notification date:*** Continuous beginning 3/1.

CONTACT James A. Myers, Director of Financial Aid, McKendree College, 701 College Road, Lebanon, IL 62254-1299, 618-537-6529 or toll-free 800-232-7228 Ext. 6831. *Fax:* 618-537-6530. *E-mail:* jamyers@mckendree.edu.

McMURRY UNIVERSITY

Abilene, TX

Tuition & fees: $16,300 **Average undergraduate aid package: $15,725**

ABOUT THE INSTITUTION Independent United Methodist, coed. Awards: bachelor's degrees. 46 undergraduate majors. Total enrollment: 1,385. Undergraduates: 1,385. Freshmen: 307. Federal methodology is used as a basis for awarding need-based institutional aid.

UNDERGRADUATE EXPENSES for 2007–08 ***Application fee:*** $20. ***Comprehensive fee:*** $22,725 includes full-time tuition ($16,100), mandatory fees ($200), and room and board ($6425). ***College room only:*** $3128. ***Part-time tuition:*** $500 per semester hour.

FRESHMAN FINANCIAL AID (Fall 2006, est.) 291 applied for aid; of those 87% were deemed to have need. 100% of freshmen with need received aid; of those 17% had need fully met. ***Average percent of need met:*** 89% (excluding resources awarded to replace EFC). ***Average financial aid package:*** $19,763 (excluding resources awarded to replace EFC). 9% of all full-time freshmen had no need and received non-need-based gift aid.

UNDERGRADUATE FINANCIAL AID (Fall 2006, est.) 1,051 applied for aid; of those 89% were deemed to have need. 100% of undergraduates with need received aid; of those 17% had need fully met. ***Average percent of need met:*** 86% (excluding resources awarded to replace EFC). ***Average financial aid package:*** $15,725 (excluding resources awarded to replace EFC). 8% of all full-time undergraduates had no need and received non-need-based gift aid.

GIFT AID (NEED-BASED) ***Total amount:*** $8,032,715 (24% federal, 27% state, 45% institutional, 4% external sources). ***Receiving aid:*** Freshmen: 80% (243); All full-time undergraduates: 77% (881). ***Average award:*** Freshmen: $9297; Undergraduates: $8043. ***Scholarships, grants, and awards:*** Federal Pell, FSEOG, state, private, college/university gift aid from institutional funds.

GIFT AID (NON-NEED-BASED) ***Total amount:*** $2,491,030 (6% federal, 13% state, 80% institutional, 1% external sources). ***Receiving aid:*** Freshmen: 44% (135); Undergraduates: 44% (502). ***Average award:*** Freshmen: $3788; Undergraduates: $3874. ***Scholarships, grants, and awards by category:*** *Academic Interests/Achievement:* 872 awards ($2,773,800 total): biological sciences, business, communication, computer science, education, English, general academic interests/achievements, mathematics, physical sciences, premedicine, religion/biblical studies, social sciences. *Creative Arts/Performance:* 33 awards ($62,964 total): art/fine arts, music, theater/drama. *Special Achievements/Activities:* 58 awards ($65,300 total): general special achievements/activities, junior miss. *Special Characteristics:* 466 awards ($2,826,673 total): children of faculty/staff, ethnic background, international students, local/state students, out-of-state students, previous college experience, relatives of clergy, religious affiliation, veterans. ***ROTC:*** Air Force cooperative.

LOANS ***Student loans:*** $7,739,397 (42% need-based, 58% non-need-based). 78% of past graduating class borrowed through all loan programs. *Average*

indebtedness per student: $22,446. ***Average need-based loan:*** Freshmen: $3052; Undergraduates: $4100. ***Parent loans:*** $1,169,306 (100% non-need-based). ***Programs:*** FFEL (Subsidized and Unsubsidized Stafford, PLUS), Perkins, state, alternative loan, United Methodist Loan, Bonner Price Loan.

WORK-STUDY ***Federal work-study:*** Total amount: $402,048; 241 jobs averaging $885. ***State or other work-study/employment:*** Total amount: $170,067 (31% need-based, 69% non-need-based). 164 part-time jobs averaging $927.

APPLYING FOR FINANCIAL AID ***Required financial aid form:*** FAFSA. ***Financial aid deadline (priority):*** 3/15. ***Notification date:*** Continuous beginning 2/1. Students must reply within 3 weeks of notification.

CONTACT Rachel Atkins, Director of Financial Aid, McMurry University, Box 908, McMurry Station, Abilene, TX 79697, 325-793-4709 or toll-free 800-477-0077. *Fax:* 325-793-4718. *E-mail:* atkinsr@mcmurryadm.mcm.edu.

McNEESE STATE UNIVERSITY

Lake Charles, LA

CONTACT Ms. Taina J. Savoit, Director of Financial Aid, McNeese State University, PO Box 93260, Lake Charles, LA 70609-3260, 337-475-5065 or toll-free 800-622-3352. *Fax:* 337-475-5068. *E-mail:* tsavoit@mail.mcneese.edu.

McPHERSON COLLEGE

McPherson, KS

CONTACT Ms. Carol L. Williams, Director of Admissions and Financial Aid, McPherson College, PO Box 1402, McPherson, KS 67460-1402, 316-241-0731 Ext. 1270 or toll-free 800-365-7402. *Fax:* 316-241-8443. *E-mail:* williamc@mcpherson.edu.

MEDAILLE COLLEGE

Buffalo, NY

Tuition & fees: $15,780 **Average undergraduate aid package: $14,000**

ABOUT THE INSTITUTION Independent, coed. Awards: associate, bachelor's, and master's degrees. 29 undergraduate majors. Total enrollment: 2,971. Undergraduates: 1,707. Freshmen: 330. Federal methodology is used as a basis for awarding need-based institutional aid.

UNDERGRADUATE EXPENSES for 2006–07 ***Application fee:*** $25. ***Comprehensive fee:*** $23,804 includes full-time tuition ($15,780) and room and board ($8024). Full-time tuition and fees vary according to location. Room and board charges vary according to housing facility. ***Part-time tuition:*** $560 per credit hour. Part-time tuition and fees vary according to course load. ***Payment plan:*** Installment.

FRESHMAN FINANCIAL AID (Fall 2006, est.) 200 applied for aid; of those 100% were deemed to have need. 100% of freshmen with need received aid; of those 10% had need fully met. ***Average percent of need met:*** 70% (excluding resources awarded to replace EFC). ***Average financial aid package:*** $13,500 (excluding resources awarded to replace EFC). 9% of all full-time freshmen had no need and received non-need-based gift aid.

UNDERGRADUATE FINANCIAL AID (Fall 2006, est.) 1,500 applied for aid; of those 100% were deemed to have need. 100% of undergraduates with need received aid; of those 3% had need fully met. ***Average percent of need met:*** 70% (excluding resources awarded to replace EFC). ***Average financial aid package:*** $14,000 (excluding resources awarded to replace EFC). 3% of all full-time undergraduates had no need and received non-need-based gift aid.

GIFT AID (NEED-BASED) ***Total amount:*** $6,942,408 (22% federal, 25% state, 52% institutional, 1% external sources). ***Receiving aid:*** Freshmen: 89% (190); All full-time undergraduates: 95% (1,500). ***Average award:*** Freshmen: $2000; Undergraduates: $3000. ***Scholarships, grants, and awards:*** Federal Pell, FSEOG, state, college/university gift aid from institutional funds.

GIFT AID (NON-NEED-BASED) ***Total amount:*** $20,000 (100% institutional). ***Receiving aid:*** Freshmen: 89% (190); Undergraduates: 32% (500). ***Average award:*** Freshmen: $3000; Undergraduates: $2000. ***Scholarships, grants, and awards by category:*** *Academic Interests/Achievement:* general academic interests/achievements. *Special Characteristics:* adult students. ***Tuition waivers:*** Full or partial for employees or children of employees, adult students, senior citizens. ***ROTC:*** Army cooperative.

LOANS ***Student loans:*** $11,942,732 (100% need-based). 75% of past graduating class borrowed through all loan programs. *Average indebtedness per student:* $23,000. ***Average need-based loan:*** Freshmen: $2625; Undergraduates: $5500. ***Parent loans:*** $1,494,107 (100% need-based). ***Programs:*** FFEL (Subsidized and Unsubsidized Stafford, PLUS).

WORK-STUDY ***Federal work-study:*** Total amount: $200,000; 150 jobs averaging $1500.

APPLYING FOR FINANCIAL AID ***Required financial aid forms:*** FAFSA, institution's own form, state aid form. ***Financial aid deadline (priority):*** 4/1. ***Notification date:*** Continuous. Students must reply within 2 weeks of notification.

CONTACT Ms. Catherine Buzonsky, Director of Financial Aid, Medaille College, 18 Agassiz Circle, Buffalo, NY 14214-2695, 716-880-2179 or toll-free 800-292-1582 (in-state). *Fax:* 716-884-0291. *E-mail:* cbuzanski@madaille.edu.

MEDCENTER ONE COLLEGE OF NURSING

Bismarck, ND

Tuition & fees: $10,017 **Average undergraduate aid package: $13,343**

ABOUT THE INSTITUTION Independent, coed, primarily women. Awards: bachelor's degrees. 1 undergraduate major. Total enrollment: 93. Undergraduates: 93. Both federal and institutional methodology are used as a basis for awarding need-based institutional aid.

UNDERGRADUATE EXPENSES for 2007–08 ***Application fee:*** $40. ***Tuition:*** full-time $9258; part-time $385.75 per credit. ***Required fees:*** full-time $759; $15.01 per credit or $199.50 per term part-time.

UNDERGRADUATE FINANCIAL AID (Fall 2005) 75 applied for aid; of those 85% were deemed to have need. 100% of undergraduates with need received aid; of those 69% had need fully met. ***Average percent of need met:*** 92% (excluding resources awarded to replace EFC). ***Average financial aid package:*** $13,343 (excluding resources awarded to replace EFC). 7% of all full-time undergraduates had no need and received non-need-based gift aid.

GIFT AID (NEED-BASED) ***Total amount:*** $142,732 (77% federal, 9% state, 8% institutional, 6% external sources). ***Receiving aid:*** All full-time undergraduates: 46% (42). ***Average award:*** Undergraduates: $3172. ***Scholarships, grants, and awards:*** Federal Pell, FSEOG, state, private, college/university gift aid from institutional funds.

GIFT AID (NON-NEED-BASED) ***Total amount:*** $12,138 (31% institutional, 69% external sources). ***Receiving aid:*** Undergraduates: 13% (12). ***Average award:*** Undergraduates: $200. ***Scholarships, grants, and awards by category:*** *Academic Interests/Achievement:* 12 awards ($6150 total): general academic interests/achievements, health fields. *Special Achievements/Activities:* 15 awards ($1500 total): memberships. *Special Characteristics:* 7 awards ($4772 total): children and siblings of alumni, general special characteristics, local/state students.

LOANS ***Student loans:*** $1,147,137 (17% need-based, 83% non-need-based). 96% of past graduating class borrowed through all loan programs. *Average indebtedness per student:* $24,471. ***Average need-based loan:*** Undergraduates: $3706. ***Parent loans:*** $6000 (100% non-need-based). ***Programs:*** FFEL (Subsidized and Unsubsidized Stafford, PLUS), Perkins, Federal Nursing, college/university.

WORK-STUDY ***Federal work-study:*** Total amount: $5937; 6 jobs averaging $990.

APPLYING FOR FINANCIAL AID ***Required financial aid forms:*** FAFSA, institution's own form, institutional scholarship application form. ***Financial aid deadline (priority):*** 3/15. ***Notification date:*** Continuous beginning 5/1. Students must reply within 2 weeks of notification.

CONTACT Ms. Janell Thomas, Financial Aid Director, Medcenter One College of Nursing, 512 North 7th Street, Bismarck, ND 58501-4494, 701-323-6270. *Fax:* 701-323-6967. *E-mail:* jthomas@mohs.org.

MEDCENTRAL COLLEGE OF NURSING

Mansfield, OH

CONTACT Financial Aid Office, MedCentral College of Nursing, 335 Glessner Avenue, Mansfield, OH 44903, 419-520-2600 or toll-free 877-656-4360.

MEDGAR EVERS COLLEGE OF THE CITY UNIVERSITY OF NEW YORK

Brooklyn, NY

Tuition & fees (NY res): $4230 **Average undergraduate aid package: N/A**

ABOUT THE INSTITUTION State and locally supported, coed. Awards: associate and bachelor's degrees. 19 undergraduate majors. Total enrollment: 5,562. Undergraduates: 5,562. Freshmen: 943. Federal methodology is used as a basis for awarding need-based institutional aid.

UNDERGRADUATE EXPENSES for 2006–07 ***Application fee:*** $60. ***Tuition, state resident:*** full-time $4000; part-time $170 per credit. ***Tuition, nonresident:*** full-time $8640; part-time $360 per credit. ***Required fees:*** full-time $230; $89 per term part-time. ***Payment plans:*** Installment, deferred payment.

GIFT AID (NEED-BASED) ***Total amount:*** $15,688,748 (55% federal, 44% state, 1% institutional). ***Receiving aid:*** Freshmen: 73% (507); All full-time undergraduates: 71% (2,228). ***Scholarships, grants, and awards:*** Federal Pell, FSEOG, state, private, college/university gift aid from institutional funds, Thurgood Marshall Scholarship.

GIFT AID (NON-NEED-BASED) ***Total amount:*** $20,500 (100% external sources). ***Receiving aid:*** Freshmen: 2; Undergraduates: 1% (17). ***Scholarships, grants, and awards by category:*** *Academic Interests/Achievement:* 17 awards ($10,128 total): general academic interests/achievements.

LOANS ***Student loans:*** $935,394 (91% need-based, 9% non-need-based). ***Programs:*** Federal Direct (Subsidized and Unsubsidized Stafford, PLUS), FFEL (Subsidized and Unsubsidized Stafford, PLUS), Perkins.

WORK-STUDY ***Federal work-study:*** Total amount: $1,121,836; 218 jobs averaging $1144.

APPLYING FOR FINANCIAL AID ***Required financial aid forms:*** FAFSA, state aid form, University Financial Aid Information Supplemental Request (FASIR). ***Financial aid deadline (priority):*** 4/1. ***Notification date:*** Continuous beginning 9/1.

CONTACT Conley James, Director of Financial Aid (Acting), Medgar Evers College of the City University of New York, 1650 Bedford Avenue, Brooklyn, NY 11225, 718-270-6038. *Fax:* 718-270-6194. *E-mail:* conley@mec.cuny.edu.

MEDICAL COLLEGE OF GEORGIA

Augusta, GA

Tuition & fees (GA res): $4288 **Average undergraduate aid package: $10,059**

ABOUT THE INSTITUTION State-supported, coed. Awards: bachelor's, master's, doctoral, and first professional degrees and post-bachelor's certificates. 10 undergraduate majors. Total enrollment: 2,227. Undergraduates: 648. Federal methodology is used as a basis for awarding need-based institutional aid.

UNDERGRADUATE EXPENSES for 2007–08 ***Application fee:*** $30. ***Tuition, state resident:*** full-time $3820; part-time $160 per credit hour. ***Tuition, nonresident:*** full-time $15,280; part-time $637 per credit hour. ***College room and board:*** ***Room only:*** $2556.

UNDERGRADUATE FINANCIAL AID (Fall 2006, est.) 262 applied for aid; of those 79% were deemed to have need. 90% of undergraduates with need received aid; of those 10% had need fully met. ***Average percent of need met:*** 51% (excluding resources awarded to replace EFC). ***Average financial aid package:*** $10,059 (excluding resources awarded to replace EFC). 28% of all full-time undergraduates had no need and received non-need-based gift aid.

GIFT AID (NEED-BASED) ***Total amount:*** $1,269,487 (26% federal, 62% state, 8% institutional, 4% external sources). ***Receiving aid:*** All full-time undergraduates: 47% (157). ***Average award:*** Undergraduates: $5549. ***Scholarships, grants, and awards:*** Federal Pell, FSEOG, state, private, college/university gift aid from institutional funds, Federal Nursing.

GIFT AID (NON-NEED-BASED) ***Total amount:*** $755,631 (96% state, 4% external sources). ***Receiving aid:*** Undergraduates: 4% (13). ***Average award:*** Undergraduates: $6501. ***Scholarships, grants, and awards by category:*** *Academic Interests/Achievement:* 734 awards ($7,661,590 total): health fields. *Special Characteristics:* 172 awards ($165,300 total): religious affiliation.

LOANS ***Student loans:*** $2,712,683 (77% need-based, 23% non-need-based). 66% of past graduating class borrowed through all loan programs. *Average indebtedness per student:* $10,365. ***Average need-based loan:*** Undergraduates: $7017. ***Parent loans:*** $165,792 (50% need-based, 50% non-need-based). ***Programs:*** FFEL (Subsidized and Unsubsidized Stafford, PLUS), Perkins, Federal Nursing, state, college/university.

WORK-STUDY ***Federal work-study:*** Total amount: $23,264; 21 jobs averaging $1108.

APPLYING FOR FINANCIAL AID ***Required financial aid forms:*** FAFSA, institution's own form, state aid form. ***Financial aid deadline (priority):*** 3/31. ***Notification date:*** Continuous beginning 4/30. Students must reply within 2 weeks of notification.

CONTACT Dr. Beverly Boggs, Director of Student Financial Aid, Medical College of Georgia, 2013 Administration Building, 1120 Fifteenth Street, Augusta, GA 30912-7320, 706-721-4901 or toll-free 800-519-3388 (in-state). *Fax:* 706-721-9407. *E-mail:* osfa@mail.mcg.edu.

MEDICAL UNIVERSITY OF SOUTH CAROLINA

Charleston, SC

CONTACT William H. Vandiver, Associate Director for Financial Aid Services, Medical University of South Carolina, 45 Courtenay Drive, PO Box 250176, Charleston, SC 29425, 843-792-2536. *Fax:* 843-792-2060. *E-mail:* vandivew@musc.edu.

MEMPHIS COLLEGE OF ART

Memphis, TN

Tuition & fees: $20,660 **Average undergraduate aid package: $8781**

ABOUT THE INSTITUTION Independent, coed. Awards: bachelor's and master's degrees. 20 undergraduate majors. Total enrollment: 308. Undergraduates: 289. Freshmen: 63. Both federal and institutional methodology are used as a basis for awarding need-based institutional aid.

UNDERGRADUATE EXPENSES for 2007–08 ***Application fee:*** $25. ***Tuition:*** full-time $20,100; part-time $2625 per course. ***Required fees:*** full-time $560; $560 per term part-time.

FRESHMAN FINANCIAL AID (Fall 2006, est.) 59 applied for aid; of those 86% were deemed to have need. 100% of freshmen with need received aid; of those 29% had need fully met. ***Average percent of need met:*** 75% (excluding resources awarded to replace EFC). ***Average financial aid package:*** $6625 (excluding resources awarded to replace EFC). 19% of all full-time freshmen had no need and received non-need-based gift aid.

UNDERGRADUATE FINANCIAL AID (Fall 2006, est.) 214 applied for aid; of those 93% were deemed to have need. 100% of undergraduates with need received aid; of those 22% had need fully met. ***Average percent of need met:*** 75% (excluding resources awarded to replace EFC). ***Average financial aid package:*** $8781 (excluding resources awarded to replace EFC). 13% of all full-time undergraduates had no need and received non-need-based gift aid.

GIFT AID (NEED-BASED) ***Total amount:*** $752,881 (61% federal, 25% state, 6% institutional, 8% external sources). ***Receiving aid:*** Freshmen: 52% (33); All full-time undergraduates: 48% (119). ***Average award:*** Freshmen: $3600; Undergraduates: $3600. ***Scholarships, grants, and awards:*** Federal Pell, FSEOG, state, private, college/university gift aid from institutional funds.

GIFT AID (NON-NEED-BASED) ***Total amount:*** $1,335,069 (9% state, 91% institutional). ***Receiving aid:*** Freshmen: 76% (48); Undergraduates: 73% (180). ***Average award:*** Freshmen: $7492; Undergraduates: $4905. ***Scholarships, grants, and awards by category:*** *Academic Interests/Achievement:* 277 awards ($1,143,224 total): general academic interests/achievements. *Creative Arts/Performance:* 36 awards ($81,075 total): applied art and design, art/fine arts. *Special Characteristics:* 14 awards ($10,000 total): previous college experience.

LOANS ***Student loans:*** $2,482,521 (33% need-based, 67% non-need-based). 90% of past graduating class borrowed through all loan programs. *Average indebtedness per student:* $34,360. ***Average need-based loan:*** Freshmen: $2625; Undergraduates: $4281. ***Parent loans:*** $973,918 (100% non-need-based). ***Programs:*** Federal Direct (Subsidized and Unsubsidized Stafford, PLUS), FFEL (Subsidized and Unsubsidized Stafford, PLUS), Perkins, college/university.

WORK-STUDY ***Federal work-study:*** Total amount: $85,850; 86 jobs averaging $998. ***State or other work-study/employment:*** Total amount: $27,300 (100% non-need-based). 28 part-time jobs averaging $975.

APPLYING FOR FINANCIAL AID ***Required financial aid form:*** FAFSA. ***Financial aid deadline (priority):*** 3/1. ***Notification date:*** Continuous beginning 4/1. Students must reply within 3 weeks of notification.

CONTACT Kara Ziegemeier, Director of Financial Aid, Memphis College of Art, 1930 Poplar Avenue, Memphis, TN 38104-2764, 901-272-5136 or toll-free 800-727-1088. *Fax:* 901-272-5134. *E-mail:* kziegemeier@mca.edu.

MENLO COLLEGE

Atherton, CA

Tuition & fees: $26,220 **Average undergraduate aid package: $19,677**

ABOUT THE INSTITUTION Independent, coed. Awards: bachelor's degrees. 3 undergraduate majors. Total enrollment: 769. Undergraduates: 769. Freshmen: 183. Federal methodology is used as a basis for awarding need-based institutional aid.

UNDERGRADUATE EXPENSES for 2006–07 ***Application fee:*** $40. ***Comprehensive fee:*** $36,020 includes full-time tuition ($25,920), mandatory fees ($300), and room and board ($9800). Full-time tuition and fees vary according to program. Room and board charges vary according to housing facility. ***Part-time tuition:*** $1080 per unit. Part-time tuition and fees vary according to course load and program. ***Payment plan:*** Installment.

FRESHMAN FINANCIAL AID (Fall 2006, est.) 109 applied for aid; of those 91% were deemed to have need. 100% of freshmen with need received aid; of those 5% had need fully met. ***Average percent of need met:*** 69% (excluding resources awarded to replace EFC). ***Average financial aid package:*** $21,120 (excluding resources awarded to replace EFC). 28% of all full-time freshmen had no need and received non-need-based gift aid.

UNDERGRADUATE FINANCIAL AID (Fall 2006, est.) 429 applied for aid; of those 92% were deemed to have need. 100% of undergraduates with need received aid; of those 9% had need fully met. ***Average percent of need met:*** 70% (excluding resources awarded to replace EFC). ***Average financial aid package:*** $19,677 (excluding resources awarded to replace EFC). 26% of all full-time undergraduates had no need and received non-need-based gift aid.

GIFT AID (NEED-BASED) ***Total amount:*** $6,385,350 (10% federal, 12% state, 74% institutional, 4% external sources). ***Receiving aid:*** Freshmen: 55% (98); All full-time undergraduates: 59% (385). ***Average award:*** Freshmen: $18,928; Undergraduates: $16,643. ***Scholarships, grants, and awards:*** Federal Pell, FSEOG, state, college/university gift aid from institutional funds, Federal ACG Grants.

GIFT AID (NON-NEED-BASED) ***Total amount:*** $1,625,217 (1% state, 93% institutional, 6% external sources). ***Receiving aid:*** Freshmen: 3% (5); Undergraduates: 3% (20). ***Average award:*** Freshmen: $9665; Undergraduates: $10,355. ***Scholarships, grants, and awards by category:*** *Academic Interests/Achievement:* 496 awards ($4,051,273 total): general academic interests/achievements. *Special Achievements/Activities:* 386 awards ($3,424,173 total): community service. ***Tuition waivers:*** Full or partial for employees or children of employees. ***ROTC:*** Army cooperative.

LOANS ***Student loans:*** $2,841,527 (76% need-based, 24% non-need-based). 60% of past graduating class borrowed through all loan programs. *Average indebtedness per student:* $26,243. ***Average need-based loan:*** Freshmen: $1918; Undergraduates: $3285. ***Parent loans:*** $802,745 (87% need-based, 13% non-need-based). ***Programs:*** FFEL (Subsidized and Unsubsidized Stafford, PLUS).

WORK-STUDY ***Federal work-study:*** Total amount: $218,417; 237 jobs averaging $1000.

APPLYING FOR FINANCIAL AID ***Required financial aid forms:*** FAFSA, state aid form. ***Financial aid deadline (priority):*** 3/2. ***Notification date:*** Continuous beginning 3/15.

CONTACT Elinore Burkhardt, Director of Financial Aid, Menlo College, 1000 El Camino Real, Atherton, CA 94027-4301, 650-543-3880 or toll-free 800-556-3656. *Fax:* 650-543-4103.

MERCER UNIVERSITY

Macon, GA

Tuition & fees: $25,256 **Average undergraduate aid package: $24,969**

ABOUT THE INSTITUTION Independent Baptist, coed. Awards: bachelor's, master's, doctoral, and first professional degrees and post-bachelor's, post-master's, and first professional certificates. 49 undergraduate majors. Total enrollment: 5,090. Undergraduates: 2,301. Freshmen: 567. Federal methodology is used as a basis for awarding need-based institutional aid.

UNDERGRADUATE EXPENSES for 2006–07 ***Application fee:*** $50. ***Comprehensive fee:*** $32,966 includes full-time tuition ($25,056), mandatory fees ($200), and room and board ($7710). ***College room only:*** $3710. Full-time tuition and fees vary according to class time, course load, and location. Room and board charges vary according to board plan, housing facility, and location. ***Part-time tuition:*** $835 per credit hour. ***Part-time fees:*** $6.50 per credit hour. Part-time tuition and fees vary according to class time, course load, and location. ***Payment plan:*** Installment.

FRESHMAN FINANCIAL AID (Fall 2006, est.) 490 applied for aid; of those 79% were deemed to have need. 100% of freshmen with need received aid; of those 61% had need fully met. ***Average percent of need met:*** 96% (excluding resources awarded to replace EFC). ***Average financial aid package:*** $26,194 (excluding resources awarded to replace EFC). 31% of all full-time freshmen had no need and received non-need-based gift aid.

UNDERGRADUATE FINANCIAL AID (Fall 2006, est.) 1,759 applied for aid; of those 82% were deemed to have need. 100% of undergraduates with need received aid; of those 50% had need fully met. ***Average percent of need met:*** 89% (excluding resources awarded to replace EFC). ***Average financial aid package:*** $24,969 (excluding resources awarded to replace EFC). 33% of all full-time undergraduates had no need and received non-need-based gift aid.

GIFT AID (NEED-BASED) ***Total amount:*** $21,276,910 (10% federal, 11% state, 75% institutional, 4% external sources). ***Receiving aid:*** Freshmen: 68% (385); All full-time undergraduates: 64% (1,435). ***Average award:*** Freshmen: $17,758; Undergraduates: $15,497. ***Scholarships, grants, and awards:*** Federal Pell, FSEOG, state, college/university gift aid from institutional funds, Federal Nursing.

GIFT AID (NON-NEED-BASED) ***Total amount:*** $13,757,910 (17% state, 77% institutional, 6% external sources). ***Receiving aid:*** Freshmen: 25% (140); Undergraduates: 19% (425). ***Average award:*** Freshmen: $16,945; Undergraduates: $16,275. ***Scholarships, grants, and awards by category:*** *Academic Interests/Achievement:* 2,517 awards ($13,700,276 total): biological sciences, business, education, engineering/technologies, English, foreign languages, general academic interests/achievements, international studies, military science, religion/biblical studies. *Creative Arts/Performance:* 141 awards ($500,872 total): art/fine arts, debating, music, theater/drama. *Special Achievements/Activities:* 31 awards ($209,687 total): community service, general special achievements/activities, junior miss, memberships. *Special Characteristics:* 2,542 awards ($13,423,139 total): adult students, children of faculty/staff, children of public servants, children of union members/company employees, general special characteristics, international students, local/state students, members of minority groups, relatives of clergy, religious affiliation, siblings of current students. ***Tuition waivers:*** Full or partial for employees or children of employees. ***ROTC:*** Army.

LOANS ***Student loans:*** $10,431,867 (64% need-based, 36% non-need-based). 67% of past graduating class borrowed through all loan programs. *Average indebtedness per student:* $22,529. ***Average need-based loan:*** Freshmen: $5021; Undergraduates: $7381. ***Parent loans:*** $2,482,660 (28% need-based, 72% non-need-based). ***Programs:*** Federal Direct (Subsidized and Unsubsidized Stafford, PLUS), Perkins, Federal Nursing, college/university.

WORK-STUDY ***Federal work-study:*** Total amount: $946,700; 448 jobs averaging $2013. ***State or other work-study/employment:*** Total amount: $2500 (100% non-need-based).

ATHLETIC AWARDS Total amount: $2,989,977 (21% need-based, 79% non-need-based).

APPLYING FOR FINANCIAL AID ***Required financial aid forms:*** FAFSA, institution's own form, state aid form (for GA residents only). ***Financial aid deadline (priority):*** 4/1. ***Notification date:*** Continuous beginning 3/15. Students must reply within 2 weeks of notification.

CONTACT Ms. Carol Williams, Associate Vice President, Financial Planning, Mercer University, 1400 Coleman Avenue, Macon, GA 31207-0003, 478-301-2670 or toll-free 800-840-8577. *Fax:* 478-301-2671. *E-mail:* williams_ck@mercer.edu.

MERCY COLLEGE

Dobbs Ferry, NY

CONTACT Director of Financial Aid, Mercy College, 28 Wells Avenue, 5th Floor, Yonkers, NY 00701, 800-MERCY-NY. *Fax:* 914-375-8582. *E-mail:* @mercy.edu.

MERCY COLLEGE OF HEALTH SCIENCES

Des Moines, IA

CONTACT Lisa Croat, Financial Aid Assistant Coordinator, Mercy College of Health Sciences, 928 Sixth Avenue, Des Moines, IA 50309, 515-643-6720 or toll-free 800-637-2994. *Fax:* 515-643-6702. *E-mail:* lcroat@mercydesmoines.org.

MERCYHURST COLLEGE

Erie, PA

ABOUT THE INSTITUTION Independent Roman Catholic, coed. Awards: associate, bachelor's, and master's degrees and post-bachelor's certificates. 107 undergraduate majors. Total enrollment: 4,155. Undergraduates: 3,856. Freshmen: 677.

GIFT AID (NEED-BASED) ***Scholarships, grants, and awards:*** Federal Pell, FSEOG, state, private, college/university gift aid from institutional funds.

GIFT AID (NON-NEED-BASED) ***Scholarships, grants, and awards by category:*** *Academic Interests/Achievement:* general academic interests/achievements, physical sciences, premedicine, social sciences. *Creative Arts/Performance:* applied art and design, art/fine arts, dance, music. *Special Achievements/Activities:* community service, general special achievements/activities, leadership, religious involvement. *Special Characteristics:* adult students, children and siblings of alumni, children of faculty/staff, local/state students.

LOANS ***Programs:*** FFEL (Subsidized and Unsubsidized Stafford, PLUS), Perkins, college/university.

WORK-STUDY ***Federal work-study:*** Total amount: $362,626; 248 jobs averaging $1400. ***State or other work-study/employment:*** Total amount: $1,676,056 (79% need-based, 21% non-need-based). 1,404 part-time jobs averaging $1202.

APPLYING FOR FINANCIAL AID ***Required financial aid forms:*** FAFSA, institution's own form.

CONTACT Dan Shumate, Interim Director, Financial Aid, Mercyhurst College, 501 East 38th Street, Erie, PA 16546, 814-824-2288 or toll-free 800-825-1926 Ext. 2202. *Fax:* 814-824-2438. *E-mail:* dshumate@mercyhurst.edu.

MEREDITH COLLEGE

Raleigh, NC

Tuition & fees: $21,200 **Average undergraduate aid package: $15,027**

ABOUT THE INSTITUTION Independent, undergraduate: women only; graduate: coed. Awards: bachelor's and master's degrees and post-bachelor's certificates. 57 undergraduate majors. Total enrollment: 2,139. Undergraduates: 1,990. Freshmen: 456. Federal methodology is used as a basis for awarding need-based institutional aid.

UNDERGRADUATE EXPENSES for 2006–07 ***Application fee:*** $40. ***Comprehensive fee:*** $27,140 includes full-time tuition ($21,150), mandatory fees ($50), and room and board ($5940). ***Part-time tuition:*** $555 per credit hour. ***Part-time fees:*** $25 per term. ***Payment plan:*** Installment.

FRESHMAN FINANCIAL AID (Fall 2006, est.) 350 applied for aid; of those 84% were deemed to have need. 100% of freshmen with need received aid; of those 21% had need fully met. ***Average percent of need met:*** 76% (excluding resources awarded to replace EFC). ***Average financial aid package:*** $14,731 (excluding resources awarded to replace EFC). 13% of all full-time freshmen had no need and received non-need-based gift aid.

UNDERGRADUATE FINANCIAL AID (Fall 2006, est.) 1,280 applied for aid; of those 86% were deemed to have need. 100% of undergraduates with need received aid; of those 15% had need fully met. ***Average percent of need met:*** 73% (excluding resources awarded to replace EFC). ***Average financial aid package:*** $15,027 (excluding resources awarded to replace EFC). 7% of all full-time undergraduates had no need and received non-need-based gift aid.

GIFT AID (NEED-BASED) ***Total amount:*** $12,268,982 (11% federal, 30% state, 49% institutional, 10% external sources). ***Receiving aid:*** Freshmen: 65% (293); All full-time undergraduates: 65% (1,088). ***Average award:*** Freshmen: $11,824; Undergraduates: $11,150. ***Scholarships, grants, and awards:*** Federal Pell, FSEOG, state, private, college/university gift aid from institutional funds.

GIFT AID (NON-NEED-BASED) ***Total amount:*** $2,910,927 (36% state, 53% institutional, 11% external sources). ***Receiving aid:*** Freshmen: 8% (36); Undergraduates: 5% (89). ***Average award:*** Freshmen: $5496; Undergraduates: $5564. ***Scholarships, grants, and awards by category:*** *Academic Interests/Achievement:* 517 awards: biological sciences, business, computer science, education, English, foreign languages, general academic interests/achievements, mathematics, physical sciences, religion/biblical studies. *Creative Arts/Performance:* 63 awards ($114,925 total): applied art and design, art/fine arts, creative writing, music. *Special Achievements/Activities:* 20 awards ($62,050 total): community service, leadership. *Special Characteristics:* 78 awards ($222,670 total): adult students, children of faculty/staff, ethnic background, first-generation college students, international students, members of minority groups, out-of-state students, previous college experience, religious affiliation. ***Tuition waivers:*** Full or partial for employees or children of employees. ***ROTC:*** Army cooperative, Air Force cooperative.

LOANS ***Student loans:*** $9,322,338 (82% need-based, 18% non-need-based). 63% of past graduating class borrowed through all loan programs. *Average indebtedness per student:* $18,962. ***Average need-based loan:*** Freshmen: $2621; Undergraduates: $3909. ***Parent loans:*** $3,284,002 (31% need-based, 69% non-need-based). ***Programs:*** FFEL (Subsidized and Unsubsidized Stafford, PLUS), Perkins, college/university.

WORK-STUDY ***Federal work-study:*** Total amount: $170,066; 132 jobs averaging $1284. ***State or other work-study/employment:*** Total amount: $407,925 (99% need-based, 1% non-need-based). 316 part-time jobs averaging $1292.

APPLYING FOR FINANCIAL AID ***Required financial aid form:*** FAFSA. ***Financial aid deadline (priority):*** 2/15. ***Notification date:*** Continuous beginning 3/15. Students must reply by 5/1 or within 2 weeks of notification.

CONTACT Mr. Kevin Michaelsen, Director of Financial Assistance, Meredith College, 3800 Hillsborough Street, Raleigh, NC 27607-5298, 919-760-8565 or toll-free 800-MEREDITH. *Fax:* 919-760-2375. *E-mail:* michaelsen@meredith.edu.

MERRIMACK COLLEGE

North Andover, MA

ABOUT THE INSTITUTION Independent Roman Catholic, coed. Awards: associate, bachelor's, and master's degrees. 41 undergraduate majors. Total enrollment: 2,251. Undergraduates: 2,213. Freshmen: 535.

GIFT AID (NEED-BASED) ***Scholarships, grants, and awards:*** Federal Pell, FSEOG, state, private, college/university gift aid from institutional funds.

GIFT AID (NON-NEED-BASED) ***Scholarships, grants, and awards by category:*** *Academic Interests/Achievement:* general academic interests/achievements. *Creative Arts/Performance:* theater/drama. *Special Achievements/Activities:* leadership. *Special Characteristics:* children and siblings of alumni, children of faculty/staff, relatives of clergy, siblings of current students.

LOANS ***Programs:*** FFEL (Subsidized and Unsubsidized Stafford, PLUS), Perkins, state, college/university, MEFA Loans, alternative loans.

WORK-STUDY ***Federal work-study:*** Total amount: $165,245; 138 jobs averaging $1200. ***State or other work-study/employment:*** Total amount: $821,249 (100% non-need-based). 410 part-time jobs averaging $2000.

APPLYING FOR FINANCIAL AID ***Required financial aid forms:*** FAFSA, noncustodial (divorced/separated) parent's statement, business/farm supplement.

CONTACT Christine A. Mordach, Director of Student Financial Aid and Scholarships, Merrimack College, 315 Turnpike Street, North Andover, MA 01845, 978-837-5186. *Fax:* 978-837-5067. *E-mail:* christine.mordach@merrimack.edu.

MESA STATE COLLEGE

Grand Junction, CO

Tuition & fees (CO res): $3840 **Average undergraduate aid package: $7081**

ABOUT THE INSTITUTION State-supported, coed. Awards: associate, bachelor's, and master's degrees. 67 undergraduate majors. Total enrollment: 5,938. Undergraduates: 5,854. Freshmen: 1,240. Federal methodology is used as a basis for awarding need-based institutional aid.

UNDERGRADUATE EXPENSES for 2007–08 ***Application fee:*** $30. ***Tuition, state resident:*** full-time $3614; part-time $139.02 per hour. ***Tuition, nonresident:*** full-time $11,193; part-time $430.50 per hour. ***Required fees:*** full-time $226; $8.15 per hour. ***College room and board:*** $7214; ***Room only:*** $3708.

FRESHMAN FINANCIAL AID (Fall 2006, est.) 934 applied for aid; of those 90% were deemed to have need. 100% of freshmen with need received aid; of those 15% had need fully met. ***Average percent of need met:*** 46% (excluding

resources awarded to replace EFC). ***Average financial aid package:*** $6576 (excluding resources awarded to replace EFC). 4% of all full-time freshmen had no need and received non-need-based gift aid.

UNDERGRADUATE FINANCIAL AID (Fall 2006, est.) 3,614 applied for aid; of those 90% were deemed to have need. 100% of undergraduates with need received aid; of those 13% had need fully met. ***Average percent of need met:*** 49% (excluding resources awarded to replace EFC). ***Average financial aid package:*** $7081 (excluding resources awarded to replace EFC). 5% of all full-time undergraduates had no need and received non-need-based gift aid.

GIFT AID (NEED-BASED) ***Total amount:*** $7,524,970 (71% federal, 29% state). ***Receiving aid:*** Freshmen: 49% (551); All full-time undergraduates: 49% (2,126). ***Average award:*** Freshmen: $3903; Undergraduates: $4104. ***Scholarships, grants, and awards:*** Federal Pell, FSEOG, state, private, college/university gift aid from institutional funds.

GIFT AID (NON-NEED-BASED) ***Total amount:*** $1,488,344 (9% federal, 3% state, 78% institutional, 10% external sources). ***Receiving aid:*** Freshmen: 19% (212); Undergraduates: 14% (590). ***Average award:*** Freshmen: $2354; Undergraduates: $2354. ***Scholarships, grants, and awards by category:*** *Academic Interests/Achievement:* 698 awards ($828,986 total): biological sciences, business, communication, computer science, education, engineering/technologies, English, general academic interests/achievements, health fields, humanities, mathematics, physical sciences, social sciences. *Creative Arts/Performance:* 47 awards ($19,873 total): art/fine arts, creative writing, journalism/publications, music, theater/drama. *Special Achievements/Activities:* general special achievements/activities, hobbies/interests. *Special Characteristics:* 112 awards ($137,866 total): first-generation college students, international students, local/state students, members of minority groups, out-of-state students.

LOANS ***Student loans:*** $14,402,018 (55% need-based, 45% non-need-based). 53% of past graduating class borrowed through all loan programs. *Average indebtedness per student:* $18,353. ***Average need-based loan:*** Freshmen: $2320; Undergraduates: $3126. ***Parent loans:*** $2,094,509 (100% non-need-based). ***Programs:*** FFEL (Subsidized and Unsubsidized Stafford, PLUS), Perkins.

WORK-STUDY ***Federal work-study:*** Total amount: $187,486; 189 jobs averaging $1428. ***State or other work-study/employment:*** Total amount: $645,207 (76% need-based, 24% non-need-based). 394 part-time jobs averaging $1669.

ATHLETIC AWARDS Total amount: $653,342 (100% non-need-based).

APPLYING FOR FINANCIAL AID ***Required financial aid form:*** FAFSA. ***Financial aid deadline (priority):*** 3/1. ***Notification date:*** Continuous beginning 4/1. Students must reply within 5 weeks of notification.

CONTACT Mr. Curt Martin, Director of Financial Aid, Mesa State College, 1100 North Avenue, Grand Junction, CO 81501-3122, 970-248-1396 or toll-free 800-982-MESA. *Fax:* 970-248-1191. *E-mail:* cmartin@mesastate.edu.

MESIVTA OF EASTERN PARKWAY RABBINICAL SEMINARY

Brooklyn, NY

CONTACT Rabbi Joseph Halberstadt, Dean, Mesivta of Eastern Parkway Rabbinical Seminary, 510 Dahill Road, Brooklyn, NY 11218-5559, 718-438-1002.

MESIVTA TIFERETH JERUSALEM OF AMERICA

New York, NY

CONTACT Rabbi Dickstein, Director of Financial Aid, Mesivta Tifereth Jerusalem of America, 141 East Broadway, New York, NY 10002-6301, 212-964-2830.

MESIVTA TORAH VODAATH RABBINICAL SEMINARY

Brooklyn, NY

CONTACT Mrs. Kayla Goldring, Director of Financial Aid, Mesivta Torah Vodaath Rabbinical Seminary, 425 East Ninth Street, Brooklyn, NY 11218-5209, 718-941-8000.

MESSENGER COLLEGE

Joplin, MO

Tuition & fees: $5860 **Average undergraduate aid package: $6000**

ABOUT THE INSTITUTION Independent Pentecostal, coed. Awards: associate and bachelor's degrees. 13 undergraduate majors. Total enrollment: 96. Undergraduates: 96. Freshmen: 19. Federal methodology is used as a basis for awarding need-based institutional aid.

UNDERGRADUATE EXPENSES for 2006–07 ***Application fee:*** $35. ***Comprehensive fee:*** $9760 includes full-time tuition ($5250), mandatory fees ($610), and room and board ($3900). Room and board charges vary according to housing facility. ***Part-time tuition:*** $175 per credit hour. ***Part-time fees:*** $26 per credit hour. ***Payment plan:*** Installment.

FRESHMAN FINANCIAL AID (Fall 2005) 22 applied for aid; of those 95% were deemed to have need. 100% of freshmen with need received aid. ***Average percent of need met:*** 45% (excluding resources awarded to replace EFC). ***Average financial aid package:*** $5600 (excluding resources awarded to replace EFC).

UNDERGRADUATE FINANCIAL AID (Fall 2005) 107 applied for aid; of those 96% were deemed to have need. 100% of undergraduates with need received aid. ***Average percent of need met:*** 48% (excluding resources awarded to replace EFC). ***Average financial aid package:*** $6000 (excluding resources awarded to replace EFC).

GIFT AID (NEED-BASED) ***Total amount:*** $203,585 (93% federal, 4% institutional, 3% external sources). ***Receiving aid:*** Freshmen: 60% (15); All full-time undergraduates: 78% (90). ***Average award:*** Freshmen: $2607; Undergraduates: $3000. ***Scholarships, grants, and awards:*** Federal Pell, FSEOG, private.

GIFT AID (NON-NEED-BASED) ***Scholarships, grants, and awards by category:*** *Academic Interests/Achievement:* 7 awards ($2438 total): education, general academic interests/achievements, religion/biblical studies. *Special Achievements/Activities:* 5 awards ($1238 total): religious involvement. *Special Characteristics:* religious affiliation. ***Tuition waivers:*** Full or partial for employees or children of employees.

LOANS ***Student loans:*** $312,209 (100% need-based). 90% of past graduating class borrowed through all loan programs. *Average indebtedness per student:* $19,342. ***Average need-based loan:*** Freshmen: $2100; Undergraduates: $2900. ***Parent loans:*** $13,901 (100% need-based). ***Programs:*** FFEL (Subsidized and Unsubsidized Stafford, PLUS).

WORK-STUDY ***Federal work-study:*** Total amount: $8875; 18 jobs averaging $493.

APPLYING FOR FINANCIAL AID ***Required financial aid form:*** FAFSA. ***Financial aid deadline:*** Continuous. ***Notification date:*** Continuous.

CONTACT Susan Aleckson, Financial Aid Director, Messenger College, 300 East 50th Street, Joplin, MO 64804, 417-624-7070 Ext. 308 or toll-free 800-385-8940 (in-state). *Fax:* 417-624-5070.

MESSIAH COLLEGE

Grantham, PA

Tuition & fees: $23,290 **Average undergraduate aid package: $11,017**

ABOUT THE INSTITUTION Independent interdenominational, coed. Awards: bachelor's degrees. 64 undergraduate majors. Total enrollment: 2,854. Undergraduates: 2,854. Freshmen: 736. Federal methodology is used as a basis for awarding need-based institutional aid.

UNDERGRADUATE EXPENSES for 2006–07 ***Application fee:*** $30. ***Comprehensive fee:*** $30,350 includes full-time tuition ($22,600), mandatory fees ($690), and room and board ($7060). ***College room only:*** $3680. Room and board charges vary according to board plan, housing facility, and location. ***Part-time tuition:*** $950 per credit. ***Part-time fees:*** $28 per credit. ***Payment plan:*** Installment.

FRESHMAN FINANCIAL AID (Fall 2005) 605 applied for aid; of those 80% were deemed to have need. 100% of freshmen with need received aid; of those 26% had need fully met. ***Average percent of need met:*** 63% (excluding resources awarded to replace EFC). ***Average financial aid package:*** $12,349 (excluding resources awarded to replace EFC). 18% of all full-time freshmen had no need and received non-need-based gift aid.

UNDERGRADUATE FINANCIAL AID (Fall 2005) 2,279 applied for aid; of those 86% were deemed to have need. 100% of undergraduates with need received aid; of those 27% had need fully met. ***Average percent of need met:*** 61%

(excluding resources awarded to replace EFC). ***Average financial aid package:*** $11,017 (excluding resources awarded to replace EFC). 19% of all full-time undergraduates had no need and received non-need-based gift aid.

GIFT AID (NEED-BASED) ***Total amount:*** $17,899,135 (8% federal, 12% state, 76% institutional, 4% external sources). ***Receiving aid:*** Freshmen: 60% (424); All full-time undergraduates: 63% (1,807). ***Average award:*** Freshmen: $4742; Undergraduates: $3910. ***Scholarships, grants, and awards:*** Federal Pell, FSEOG, state, private, college/university gift aid from institutional funds.

GIFT AID (NON-NEED-BASED) ***Total amount:*** $6,225,625 (94% institutional, 6% external sources). ***Receiving aid:*** Freshmen: 64% (454); Undergraduates: 60% (1,708). ***Average award:*** Freshmen: $8095; Undergraduates: $7726. ***Scholarships, grants, and awards by category:*** *Academic Interests/Achievement:* general academic interests/achievements. *Creative Arts/Performance:* art/fine arts, music, theater/drama. *Special Achievements/Activities:* leadership. *Special Characteristics:* adult students, children and siblings of alumni, children of faculty/staff, relatives of clergy, religious affiliation, siblings of current students, spouses of current students. ***Tuition waivers:*** Full or partial for minority students, children of alumni, employees or children of employees, adult students, senior citizens.

LOANS ***Student loans:*** $14,097,072 (68% need-based, 32% non-need-based). 70% of past graduating class borrowed through all loan programs. *Average indebtedness per student:* $27,322. ***Average need-based loan:*** Freshmen: $2069; Undergraduates: $3010. ***Parent loans:*** $4,093,912 (40% need-based, 60% non-need-based). ***Programs:*** Federal Direct (Subsidized and Unsubsidized Stafford, PLUS), Perkins, Federal Nursing.

WORK-STUDY ***Federal work-study:*** Total amount: $1,435,213; 754 jobs averaging $1866. ***State or other work-study/employment:*** Total amount: $1,793,083 (40% need-based, 60% non-need-based). 919 part-time jobs averaging $2052.

APPLYING FOR FINANCIAL AID ***Required financial aid form:*** FAFSA. ***Financial aid deadline (priority):*** 4/1. ***Notification date:*** Continuous beginning 3/15. Students must reply by 5/1 or within 4 weeks of notification.

CONTACT Mr. Michael Strite, Assistant Director of Financial Aid, Messiah College, PO Box 3006, One College Avenue, Grantham, PA 17027, 717-691-6007 or toll-free 800-233-4220. *Fax:* 717-796-4791. *E-mail:* mstrite@messiah.edu.

METHODIST UNIVERSITY

Fayetteville, NC

Tuition & fees: $20,080 **Average undergraduate aid package: $15,882**

ABOUT THE INSTITUTION Independent United Methodist, coed. Awards: associate, bachelor's, and master's degrees. 56 undergraduate majors. Total enrollment: 2,082. Undergraduates: 1,996. Freshmen: 485. Federal methodology is used as a basis for awarding need-based institutional aid.

UNDERGRADUATE EXPENSES for 2007–08 ***Application fee:*** $25. ***Comprehensive fee:*** $27,630 includes full-time tuition ($20,080) and room and board ($7550). ***College room only:*** $3800. ***Part-time tuition:*** $605 per semester hour.

FRESHMAN FINANCIAL AID (Fall 2005) 385 applied for aid; of those 76% were deemed to have need. 100% of freshmen with need received aid; of those 45% had need fully met. ***Average percent of need met:*** 77% (excluding resources awarded to replace EFC). ***Average financial aid package:*** $18,377 (excluding resources awarded to replace EFC). 21% of all full-time freshmen had no need and received non-need-based gift aid.

UNDERGRADUATE FINANCIAL AID (Fall 2005) 1,635 applied for aid; of those 75% were deemed to have need. 100% of undergraduates with need received aid; of those 41% had need fully met. ***Average percent of need met:*** 75% (excluding resources awarded to replace EFC). ***Average financial aid package:*** $15,882 (excluding resources awarded to replace EFC). 15% of all full-time undergraduates had no need and received non-need-based gift aid.

GIFT AID (NEED-BASED) ***Total amount:*** $8,798,303 (20% federal, 14% state, 66% institutional). ***Receiving aid:*** Freshmen: 73% (282); All full-time undergraduates: 67% (1,124). ***Average award:*** Freshmen: $8308; Undergraduates: $6659. ***Scholarships, grants, and awards:*** Federal Pell, FSEOG, state, private, college/university gift aid from institutional funds.

GIFT AID (NON-NEED-BASED) ***Total amount:*** $6,899,013 (30% federal, 25% state, 33% institutional, 12% external sources). ***Receiving aid:*** Freshmen: 55% (214); Undergraduates: 59% (985). ***Average award:*** Freshmen: $6489; Undergraduates: $6607. ***Scholarships, grants, and awards by category:*** *Academic Interests/Achievement:* 592 awards ($3,009,063 total): English, general academic interests/achievements. *Creative Arts/Performance:* 110 awards ($84,840 total): debating, music, theater/drama. *Special Achievements/Activities:* 36 awards ($13,000 total): cheerleading/drum major, leadership. *Special Characteristics:* 328 awards ($556,089 total): children and siblings of alumni, children of faculty/staff, relatives of clergy, religious affiliation. ***ROTC:*** Army, Air Force cooperative.

LOANS ***Student loans:*** $11,212,843 (40% need-based, 60% non-need-based). 79% of past graduating class borrowed through all loan programs. *Average indebtedness per student:* $26,640. ***Average need-based loan:*** Freshmen: $2446; Undergraduates: $3575. ***Parent loans:*** $3,927,407 (100% non-need-based). ***Programs:*** FFEL (Subsidized and Unsubsidized Stafford, PLUS), Perkins.

WORK-STUDY ***Federal work-study:*** Total amount: $165,205; 817 jobs averaging $200. ***State or other work-study/employment:*** Total amount: $55,068 (100% non-need-based). 121 part-time jobs averaging $797.

APPLYING FOR FINANCIAL AID ***Required financial aid form:*** FAFSA. ***Financial aid deadline:*** Continuous. ***Notification date:*** Continuous beginning 3/6. Students must reply within 2 weeks of notification.

CONTACT Financial Aid Office, Methodist University, 5400 Ramsey Street, Fayetteville, NC 28311-1420, 910-630-7307 or toll-free 800-488-7110 Ext. 7027. *Fax:* 910-630-7285.

METROPOLITAN COLLEGE OF NEW YORK

New York, NY

CONTACT Rosibel Gomez, Financial Aid Director, Metropolitan College of New York, 75 Varick Street, New York, NY 10013-1919, 212-343-1234 Ext. 5004 or toll-free 800-33-THINK Ext. 5001 (in-state). *Fax:* 212-343-7399.

METROPOLITAN STATE COLLEGE OF DENVER

Denver, CO

Tuition & fees (CO res): $3431 **Average undergraduate aid package: $6852**

ABOUT THE INSTITUTION State-supported, coed. Awards: bachelor's degrees. 49 undergraduate majors. Total enrollment: 20,761. Undergraduates: 20,761. Freshmen: 2,490. Federal methodology is used as a basis for awarding need-based institutional aid.

UNDERGRADUATE EXPENSES for 2006–07 ***Application fee:*** $25. ***Tuition, state resident:*** full-time $2,839. ***Tuition, nonresident:*** full-time $10,249. Full-time tuition and fees vary according to course load and location. Part-time tuition and fees vary according to course load and location. ***Payment plans:*** Installment, deferred payment.

FRESHMAN FINANCIAL AID (Fall 2005) 1268 applied for aid; of those 66% were deemed to have need. 82% of freshmen with need received aid; of those 1% had need fully met. ***Average percent of need met:*** 51% (excluding resources awarded to replace EFC). ***Average financial aid package:*** $4922 (excluding resources awarded to replace EFC). 5% of all full-time freshmen had no need and received non-need-based gift aid.

UNDERGRADUATE FINANCIAL AID (Fall 2005) 7,559 applied for aid; of those 77% were deemed to have need. 91% of undergraduates with need received aid; of those 3% had need fully met. ***Average percent of need met:*** 59% (excluding resources awarded to replace EFC). ***Average financial aid package:*** $6852 (excluding resources awarded to replace EFC). 11% of all full-time undergraduates had no need and received non-need-based gift aid.

GIFT AID (NEED-BASED) ***Total amount:*** $19,812,312 (64% federal, 23% state, 11% institutional, 2% external sources). ***Receiving aid:*** Freshmen: 27% (532); All full-time undergraduates: 31% (3,798). ***Average award:*** Freshmen: $3806; Undergraduates: $4301. ***Scholarships, grants, and awards:*** Federal Pell, FSEOG, state, private, college/university gift aid from institutional funds.

GIFT AID (NON-NEED-BASED) ***Total amount:*** $966,863 (3% federal, 9% state, 67% institutional, 21% external sources). ***Receiving aid:*** Freshmen: 27% (532); Undergraduates: 31% (3,798). ***Average award:*** Freshmen: $1889; Undergraduates: $1920. ***Scholarships, grants, and awards by category:*** *Academic Interests/Achievement:* 1,303 awards ($1,776,264 total): biological sciences, business, communication, computer science, education, engineering/technologies, English, foreign languages, general academic interests/achievements, health fields, humanities, mathematics, physical sciences, social sciences. *Creative Arts/Performance:* 61 awards ($49,895 total): art/fine arts, music, theater/drama. *Special Achievements/Activities:* 51 awards ($109,551 total): general special achievements/activities. ***Tuition waivers:*** Full or partial for senior citizens. ***ROTC:*** Army cooperative, Air Force cooperative.

LOANS ***Student loans:*** $47,234,865 (85% need-based, 15% non-need-based). 52% of past graduating class borrowed through all loan programs. *Average indebtedness per student:* $23,678. ***Average need-based loan:*** Freshmen: $2479; Undergraduates: $3990. ***Parent loans:*** $2,071,995 (51% need-based, 49% non-need-based). ***Programs:*** FFEL (Subsidized and Unsubsidized Stafford, PLUS), Perkins.

WORK-STUDY ***Federal work-study:*** Total amount: $615,670; 149 jobs averaging $4132. ***State or other work-study/employment:*** Total amount: $1,671,720 (77% need-based, 23% non-need-based). 474 part-time jobs averaging $3699.

ATHLETIC AWARDS Total amount: $950,129 (28% need-based, 72% non-need-based).

APPLYING FOR FINANCIAL AID ***Required financial aid form:*** FAFSA. ***Financial aid deadline:*** Continuous. ***Notification date:*** Continuous beginning 4/1.

CONTACT Office of Financial Aid, Metropolitan State College of Denver, PO Box 173362, Denver, CO 80217-3362, 303-556-8593. *Fax:* 303-556-4927.

METROPOLITAN STATE UNIVERSITY

St. Paul, MN

CONTACT Mr. Michael Uran, Director of Financial Aid, Metropolitan State University, Founder's Hall, Room 105, 700 East 7th Street, St. Paul, MN 55106-5000, 651-793-1414. *E-mail:* finaid@metrostate.edu.

MIAMI INTERNATIONAL UNIVERSITY OF ART & DESIGN

Miami, FL

CONTACT Mitzie Forrest, Financial Aid Director, Miami International University of Art & Design, 1737 Bayshore Drive, Miami, FL 33132, 800-225-9023 Ext. 125 or toll-free 800-225-9023. *Fax:* 305-374-7946.

MIAMI UNIVERSITY

Oxford, OH

Tuition & fees (OH res): $10,502 Average undergraduate aid package: $17,573

ABOUT THE INSTITUTION State-related, coed. Awards: associate, bachelor's, master's, and doctoral degrees and post-master's certificates. 111 undergraduate majors. Total enrollment: 16,329. Undergraduates: 14,551. Freshmen: 3,560. Federal methodology is used as a basis for awarding need-based institutional aid.

UNDERGRADUATE EXPENSES for 2006–07 ***Application fee:*** $45. ***Tuition, state resident:*** full-time $8496; part-time $349 per credit hour. ***Tuition, nonresident:*** full-time $21,011; part-time $884 per credit hour. ***Required fees:*** full-time $2006; $43 per credit hour. ***College room and board:*** $8140; ***Room only:*** $4160. Room and board charges vary according to board plan and housing facility. ***Payment plan:*** Installment.

FRESHMAN FINANCIAL AID (Fall 2006, est.) 2400 applied for aid; of those 68% were deemed to have need. 100% of freshmen with need received aid; of those 36% had need fully met. ***Average percent of need met:*** 74% (excluding resources awarded to replace EFC). ***Average financial aid package:*** $17,660 (excluding resources awarded to replace EFC). 35% of all full-time freshmen had no need and received non-need-based gift aid.

UNDERGRADUATE FINANCIAL AID (Fall 2006, est.) 7,506 applied for aid; of those 78% were deemed to have need. 100% of undergraduates with need received aid; of those 30% had need fully met. ***Average percent of need met:*** 74% (excluding resources awarded to replace EFC). ***Average financial aid package:*** $17,573 (excluding resources awarded to replace EFC). 39% of all full-time undergraduates had no need and received non-need-based gift aid.

GIFT AID (NEED-BASED) ***Total amount:*** $12,150,952 (37% federal, 8% state, 55% institutional). ***Receiving aid:*** Freshmen: 16% (600); All full-time undergraduates: 17% (2,364). ***Average award:*** Freshmen: $6158; Undergraduates: $4685. ***Scholarships, grants, and awards:*** Federal Pell, FSEOG, state, private, college/university gift aid from institutional funds.

GIFT AID (NON-NEED-BASED) ***Total amount:*** $143,576,872 (97% institutional, 3% external sources). ***Receiving aid:*** Freshmen: 41% (1,487); Undergraduates: 38% (5,382). ***Average award:*** Freshmen: $11,363; Undergraduates: $11,864. ***Scholarships, grants, and awards by category:*** *Academic Interests/Achievement:* architecture, education, engineering/technologies, general academic interests/achievements. *Creative Arts/Performance:* art/fine arts, music, theater/drama. *Special Achievements/Activities:* general special achievements/activities, leadership. *Special Characteristics:* children of faculty/staff, local/state students, members of minority groups, out-of-state students. ***Tuition waivers:*** Full or partial for employees or children of employees. ***ROTC:*** Army cooperative, Naval, Air Force.

LOANS ***Student loans:*** $51,032,977 (32% need-based, 68% non-need-based). 52% of past graduating class borrowed through all loan programs. *Average indebtedness per student:* $22,255. ***Average need-based loan:*** Freshmen: $2826; Undergraduates: $3939. ***Parent loans:*** $17,927,997 (100% non-need-based). ***Programs:*** Federal Direct (Subsidized and Unsubsidized Stafford, PLUS), Perkins, Federal Nursing, college/university, bank education loans.

WORK-STUDY ***Federal work-study:*** Total amount: $2,053,433; 951 jobs averaging $1650.

ATHLETIC AWARDS Total amount: $6,418,058 (100% non-need-based).

APPLYING FOR FINANCIAL AID ***Required financial aid form:*** FAFSA. ***Financial aid deadline (priority):*** 2/15. ***Notification date:*** Continuous beginning 3/20. Students must reply by 5/1 or within 3 weeks of notification.

CONTACT Chuck Knepfle, Office of Student Financial Aid, Miami University, Campus Avenue Building, Oxford, OH 45056-3427, 513-529-8734. *Fax:* 513-529-8713. *E-mail:* financialaid@muohio.edu.

MICHIGAN JEWISH INSTITUTE

Oak Park, MI

CONTACT Financial Aid Office, Michigan Jewish Institute, 25401 Coolidge Highway, Oak Park, MI 48237-1304, 248-414-6900.

MICHIGAN STATE UNIVERSITY

East Lansing, MI

Tuition & fees (MI res): $8843 Average undergraduate aid package: $9307

ABOUT THE INSTITUTION State-supported, coed. Awards: bachelor's, master's, doctoral, and first professional degrees and post-master's certificates. 130 undergraduate majors. Total enrollment: 45,520. Undergraduates: 35,821. Freshmen: 7,440. Federal methodology is used as a basis for awarding need-based institutional aid.

UNDERGRADUATE EXPENSES for 2006–07 ***Application fee:*** $35. ***Tuition, state resident:*** full-time $7665; part-time $234.75 per credit hour. ***Tuition, nonresident:*** full-time $20,310; part-time $656.25 per credit hour. ***Required fees:*** full-time $1178; $422 per term part-time. Full-time tuition and fees vary according to course load, degree level, program, and student level. Part-time tuition and fees vary according to course load, degree level, program, and student level. ***College room and board:*** $6044; ***Room only:*** $2618. Room and board charges vary according to board plan and housing facility. ***Payment plan:*** Deferred payment.

FRESHMAN FINANCIAL AID (Fall 2006, est.) 5080 applied for aid; of those 61% were deemed to have need. 100% of freshmen with need received aid; of those 41% had need fully met. ***Average percent of need met:*** 82% (excluding resources awarded to replace EFC). ***Average financial aid package:*** $9798 (excluding resources awarded to replace EFC). 11% of all full-time freshmen had no need and received non-need-based gift aid.

UNDERGRADUATE FINANCIAL AID (Fall 2006, est.) 19,179 applied for aid; of those 69% were deemed to have need. 99% of undergraduates with need received aid; of those 30% had need fully met. ***Average percent of need met:*** 75% (excluding resources awarded to replace EFC). ***Average financial aid package:*** $9307 (excluding resources awarded to replace EFC). 6% of all full-time undergraduates had no need and received non-need-based gift aid.

GIFT AID (NEED-BASED) ***Total amount:*** $46,283,773 (47% federal, 53% institutional). ***Receiving aid:*** Freshmen: 23% (1,681); All full-time undergraduates: 24% (7,712). ***Average award:*** Freshmen: $6149; Undergraduates: $5489. ***Scholarships, grants, and awards:*** Federal Pell, FSEOG, state, private, college/university gift aid from institutional funds, United Negro College Fund.

GIFT AID (NON-NEED-BASED) ***Total amount:*** $76,326,648 (3% federal, 55% state, 24% institutional, 18% external sources). ***Receiving aid:*** Freshmen: 36% (2,645); Undergraduates: 24% (7,965). ***Average award:*** Freshmen: $3886; Undergraduates: $5241. ***Scholarships, grants, and awards by category:*** *Academic Interests/Achievement:* agriculture, architecture, biological sciences, business, communication, computer science, education, engineering/technologies, English, foreign languages, general academic interests/achievements, health fields, international studies, mathematics, military science, physical sciences, social sciences. *Creative Arts/Performance:* creative writing, debating, journalism/publications, music, performing arts, theater/drama. *Special Achievements/Activities:* community service, hobbies/interests, junior miss, leadership, memberships, rodeo. *Special Characteristics:* children and siblings of alumni, children of faculty/staff, children of union members/company employees, ethnic background, first-generation college students, handicapped students, international students, local/state students, members of minority groups, out-of-state students, public servants, religious affiliation, spouses of deceased or disabled public servants, veterans, veterans' children. ***Tuition waivers:*** Full or partial for employees or children of employees. ***ROTC:*** Army, Air Force.

LOANS ***Student loans:*** $105,906,404 (47% need-based, 53% non-need-based). 56% of past graduating class borrowed through all loan programs. *Average indebtedness per student:* $22,147. ***Average need-based loan:*** Freshmen: $2619; Undergraduates: $4016. ***Parent loans:*** $47,230,689 (100% non-need-based). ***Programs:*** FFEL (Subsidized and Unsubsidized Stafford, PLUS), Perkins, state, college/university.

WORK-STUDY ***Federal work-study:*** Total amount: $2,823,617; 1,700 jobs averaging $1500. ***State or other work-study/employment:*** Total amount: $412,090 (100% need-based). 320 part-time jobs averaging $900.

ATHLETIC AWARDS Total amount: $7,342,971 (37% need-based, 63% non-need-based).

APPLYING FOR FINANCIAL AID ***Required financial aid form:*** FAFSA. ***Financial aid deadline:*** Continuous. ***Notification date:*** Continuous beginning 3/15. Students must reply within 4 weeks of notification.

CONTACT Mr. Keith Williams, Associate Director, Michigan State University, 252 Student Services Building, East Lansing, MI 48824-1113, 517-353-5940. *Fax:* 517-432-1155. *E-mail:* willi398@msu.edu.

MICHIGAN TECHNOLOGICAL UNIVERSITY

Houghton, MI

Tuition & fees (MI res): $8910 **Average undergraduate aid package: $9065**

ABOUT THE INSTITUTION State-supported, coed. Awards: associate, bachelor's, master's, and doctoral degrees and post-bachelor's certificates. 88 undergraduate majors. Total enrollment: 6,550. Undergraduates: 5,634. Freshmen: 1,169. Federal methodology is used as a basis for awarding need-based institutional aid.

UNDERGRADUATE EXPENSES for 2006–07 ***Application fee:*** $40. ***Tuition, state resident:*** full-time $8271; part-time $275.70 per credit hour. ***Tuition, nonresident:*** full-time $20,040; part-time $668 per credit hour. ***Required fees:*** full-time $639; $319.54 per term part-time. Full-time tuition and fees vary according to course load and program. Part-time tuition and fees vary according to course load and program. ***College room and board:*** $6840; ***Room only:*** $3461. Room and board charges vary according to board plan and housing facility. ***Payment plans:*** Installment, deferred payment.

FRESHMAN FINANCIAL AID (Fall 2006, est.) 885 applied for aid; of those 69% were deemed to have need. 100% of freshmen with need received aid; of those 33% had need fully met. ***Average percent of need met:*** 82% (excluding resources awarded to replace EFC). ***Average financial aid package:*** $10,177 (excluding resources awarded to replace EFC). 31% of all full-time freshmen had no need and received non-need-based gift aid.

UNDERGRADUATE FINANCIAL AID (Fall 2006, est.) 3,989 applied for aid; of those 72% were deemed to have need. 100% of undergraduates with need received aid; of those 36% had need fully met. ***Average percent of need met:*** 76% (excluding resources awarded to replace EFC). ***Average financial aid package:*** $9065 (excluding resources awarded to replace EFC). 28% of all full-time undergraduates had no need and received non-need-based gift aid.

GIFT AID (NEED-BASED) ***Total amount:*** $15,596,363 (25% federal, 17% state, 48% institutional, 10% external sources). ***Receiving aid:*** Freshmen: 52% (602); All full-time undergraduates: 50% (2,565). ***Average award:*** Freshmen: $7052; Undergraduates: $7088. ***Scholarships, grants, and awards:*** Federal Pell, FSEOG, state, private, college/university gift aid from institutional funds.

GIFT AID (NON-NEED-BASED) ***Total amount:*** $6,929,360 (13% state, 57% institutional, 30% external sources). ***Receiving aid:*** Freshmen: 47% (543); Undergraduates: 35% (1,816). ***Average award:*** Freshmen: $2945; Undergraduates: $2424. ***Scholarships, grants, and awards by category:*** *Academic Interests/Achievement:* 1,561 awards ($6,397,998 total): biological sciences, business, communication, computer science, education, engineering/technologies, general academic interests/achievements, humanities, mathematics, physical sciences, premedicine, social sciences. *Special Achievements/Activities:* 25 awards ($10,000 total): leadership. *Special Characteristics:* 2,399 awards ($3,817,044 total): children and siblings of alumni, children of faculty/staff, ethnic background, general special characteristics, international students, local/state students, members of minority groups, out-of-state students, previous college experience. ***Tuition waivers:*** Full or partial for children of alumni, employees or children of employees, senior citizens. ***ROTC:*** Army, Air Force.

LOANS ***Student loans:*** $22,860,006 (80% need-based, 20% non-need-based). 63% of past graduating class borrowed through all loan programs. *Average indebtedness per student:* $13,807. ***Average need-based loan:*** Freshmen: $3009; Undergraduates: $4069. ***Parent loans:*** $3,535,738 (65% need-based, 35% non-need-based). ***Programs:*** Federal Direct (Subsidized and Unsubsidized Stafford, PLUS), Perkins, state, college/university, external private loans.

WORK-STUDY ***Federal work-study:*** Total amount: $324,080; 218 jobs averaging $1487. ***State or other work-study/employment:*** Total amount: $3,670,447 (5% need-based, 95% non-need-based). 2,497 part-time jobs averaging $1600.

ATHLETIC AWARDS Total amount: $1,774,470 (29% need-based, 71% non-need-based).

APPLYING FOR FINANCIAL AID ***Required financial aid form:*** FAFSA. ***Financial aid deadline (priority):*** 2/16. ***Notification date:*** Continuous beginning 3/1. Students must reply within 4 weeks of notification.

CONTACT Adrene Remali, Business Systems Analyst, Michigan Technological University, 1400 Townsend Drive, Houghton, MI 49931-1295, 906-487-3222 or toll-free 888-MTU-1885. *Fax:* 906-487-3042. *E-mail:* adrene@mtu.edu.

MID-AMERICA CHRISTIAN UNIVERSITY

Oklahoma City, OK

CONTACT Mr. Todd Martin, Director of Financial Aid, Mid-America Christian University, 3500 Southwest 119th Street, Oklahoma City, OK 73170-4504, 405-691-3800. *Fax:* 405-692-3165. *E-mail:* tmartin@mabc.edu.

MIDAMERICA NAZARENE UNIVERSITY

Olathe, KS

ABOUT THE INSTITUTION Independent religious, coed. Awards: associate, bachelor's, and master's degrees. 40 undergraduate majors. Total enrollment: 1,779. Undergraduates: 1,357. Freshmen: 216.

GIFT AID (NEED-BASED) ***Scholarships, grants, and awards:*** Federal Pell, FSEOG, state, private, college/university gift aid from institutional funds.

GIFT AID (NON-NEED-BASED) ***Scholarships, grants, and awards by category:*** *Academic Interests/Achievement:* agriculture, general academic interests/achievements, health fields. *Creative Arts/Performance:* cinema/film/broadcasting, music. *Special Achievements/Activities:* cheerleading/drum major, leadership. *Special Characteristics:* children of faculty/staff, general special characteristics, relatives of clergy, religious affiliation.

LOANS ***Programs:*** FFEL (Subsidized and Unsubsidized Stafford, PLUS), Perkins, Federal Nursing.

WORK-STUDY ***Federal work-study:*** Total amount: $19,650; jobs available.

APPLYING FOR FINANCIAL AID ***Required financial aid forms:*** FAFSA, institution's own form.

CONTACT Rhonda L. Cole, Director of Student Financial Services, MidAmerica Nazarene University, 2030 East College Way, Olathe, KS 66062-1899, 913-791-3298 or toll-free 800-800-8887. *Fax:* 913-791-3482. *E-mail:* rcole@mnu.edu.

MID-CONTINENT UNIVERSITY

Mayfield, KY

CONTACT Kent Youngblood, Director of Financial Aid, Mid-Continent University, 99 Powell Road East, Mayfield, KY 42066, 270-251-9400 Ext. 260. *Fax:* 270-251-9475. *E-mail:* kyoungblood@midcontinent.edu.

MIDDLEBURY COLLEGE

Middlebury, VT

Comprehensive fee: $44,330 **Average undergraduate aid package: $28,413**

ABOUT THE INSTITUTION Independent, coed. Awards: bachelor's, master's, and doctoral degrees. 44 undergraduate majors. Total enrollment: 2,406.

Undergraduates: 2,406. Freshmen: 563. Both federal and institutional methodology are used as a basis for awarding need-based institutional aid.

UNDERGRADUATE EXPENSES for 2006–07 ***Application fee:*** $65. ***Comprehensive fee:*** $44,330. ***Payment plan:*** Tuition prepayment.

FRESHMAN FINANCIAL AID (Fall 2005) 342 applied for aid; of those 78% were deemed to have need. 100% of freshmen with need received aid; of those 100% had need fully met. ***Average percent of need met:*** 100% (excluding resources awarded to replace EFC). ***Average financial aid package:*** $29,286 (excluding resources awarded to replace EFC).

UNDERGRADUATE FINANCIAL AID (Fall 2005) 1,198 applied for aid; of those 88% were deemed to have need. 100% of undergraduates with need received aid; of those 100% had need fully met. ***Average percent of need met:*** 100% (excluding resources awarded to replace EFC). ***Average financial aid package:*** $28,413 (excluding resources awarded to replace EFC).

GIFT AID (NEED-BASED) ***Total amount:*** $21,229,548 (3% federal, 1% state, 96% institutional). ***Receiving aid:*** Freshmen: 48% (266); All full-time undergraduates: 44% (1,055). ***Average award:*** Freshmen: $26,202; Undergraduates: $24,845. ***Scholarships, grants, and awards:*** Federal Pell, FSEOG, state, private, college/university gift aid from institutional funds.

GIFT AID (NON-NEED-BASED) ***Tuition waivers:*** Full or partial for employees or children of employees. ***ROTC:*** Army cooperative.

LOANS ***Student loans:*** $4,174,613 (62% need-based, 38% non-need-based). 39% of past graduating class borrowed through all loan programs. *Average indebtedness per student:* $12,322. ***Average need-based loan:*** Freshmen: $3899; Undergraduates: $4504. ***Parent loans:*** $3,688,135 (100% non-need-based). ***Programs:*** Federal Direct (Subsidized and Unsubsidized Stafford, PLUS), Perkins, college/university.

WORK-STUDY ***Federal work-study:*** Total amount: $598,698; jobs available. ***State or other work-study/employment:*** Total amount: $297,666 (100% need-based). Part-time jobs available.

APPLYING FOR FINANCIAL AID ***Required financial aid forms:*** FAFSA, institution's own form, CSS Financial Aid PROFILE, federal income tax return. ***Financial aid deadline:*** 1/1 (priority: 11/15). ***Notification date:*** 4/1. Students must reply by 5/1.

CONTACT Marguerite Corbin, Financial Aid Assistant, Middlebury College, Emma Willard House, Middlebury, VT 05753, 802-443-5158. *E-mail:* financialaid@middlebury.edu.

MIDDLE TENNESSEE STATE UNIVERSITY

Murfreesboro, TN

Tuition & fees (TN res): $4670 **Average undergraduate aid package: $4118**

ABOUT THE INSTITUTION State-supported, coed. Awards: bachelor's, master's, and doctoral degrees and post-bachelor's and post-master's certificates. 61 undergraduate majors. Total enrollment: 22,863. Undergraduates: 20,643. Freshmen: 3,373. Federal methodology is used as a basis for awarding need-based institutional aid.

UNDERGRADUATE EXPENSES for 2006–07 ***Application fee:*** $25. ***Tuition, state resident:*** full-time $3678; part-time $161 per semester hour. ***Tuition, nonresident:*** full-time $12,990; part-time $565 per semester hour. Part-time tuition and fees vary according to course load. ***College room and board:*** $5626; ***Room only:*** $3478. Room and board charges vary according to board plan and housing facility. ***Payment plan:*** Deferred payment.

FRESHMAN FINANCIAL AID (Fall 2006, est.) 3348 applied for aid; of those 59% were deemed to have need. 99% of freshmen with need received aid; of those 57% had need fully met. ***Average percent of need met:*** 83% (excluding resources awarded to replace EFC). ***Average financial aid package:*** $7800 (excluding resources awarded to replace EFC). 36% of all full-time freshmen had no need and received non-need-based gift aid.

UNDERGRADUATE FINANCIAL AID (Fall 2006, est.) 14,437 applied for aid; of those 62% were deemed to have need. 97% of undergraduates with need received aid; of those 65% had need fully met. ***Average percent of need met:*** 79% (excluding resources awarded to replace EFC). ***Average financial aid package:*** $4118 (excluding resources awarded to replace EFC). 23% of all full-time undergraduates had no need and received non-need-based gift aid.

GIFT AID (NEED-BASED) ***Total amount:*** $21,036,716 (70% federal, 21% state, 9% external sources). ***Receiving aid:*** Freshmen: 30% (1,008); All full-time undergraduates: 27% (4,775). ***Average award:*** Freshmen: $2405; Undergraduates: $2033. ***Scholarships, grants, and awards:*** Federal Pell, FSEOG, state, private, college/university gift aid from institutional funds.

GIFT AID (NON-NEED-BASED) ***Total amount:*** $33,693,345 (69% state, 17% institutional, 14% external sources). ***Receiving aid:*** Freshmen: 46% (1,562); Undergraduates: 25% (4,293). ***Average award:*** Freshmen: $5157; Undergraduates: $3358. ***Scholarships, grants, and awards by category:*** *Academic Interests/Achievement:* 795 awards ($945,487 total): agriculture, biological sciences, business, communication, computer science, education, engineering/technologies, English, foreign languages, general academic interests/achievements, health fields, home economics, humanities, international studies, mathematics, military science, physical sciences, premedicine, social sciences. *Creative Arts/Performance:* 533 awards ($355,974 total): dance, debating, journalism/publications, music, theater/drama. *Special Achievements/Activities:* 1,922 awards ($4,412,738 total): cheerleading/drum major, general special achievements/activities, leadership. *Special Characteristics:* 874 awards ($1,555,931 total): adult students, local/state students, members of minority groups. ***Tuition waivers:*** Full or partial for employees or children of employees, senior citizens. ***ROTC:*** Army, Air Force cooperative.

LOANS ***Student loans:*** $55,404,909 (100% need-based). 8% of past graduating class borrowed through all loan programs. *Average indebtedness per student:* $21,301. ***Average need-based loan:*** Freshmen: $1515; Undergraduates: $4370. ***Parent loans:*** $8,417,203 (100% non-need-based). ***Programs:*** FFEL (Subsidized and Unsubsidized Stafford, PLUS), Perkins, college/university.

WORK-STUDY ***Federal work-study:*** Total amount: $274,408; 249 jobs averaging $1102.

ATHLETIC AWARDS Total amount: $4,668,982 (100% non-need-based).

APPLYING FOR FINANCIAL AID ***Required financial aid form:*** FAFSA. ***Financial aid deadline (priority):*** 5/15. ***Notification date:*** Continuous beginning 4/15. Students must reply within 2 weeks of notification.

CONTACT David Hutton, Financial Aid Director, Middle Tennessee State University, 218 Cope Administration Building, Murfreesboro, TN 37132, 615-898-2830 or toll-free 800-331-MTSU (in-state), 800-433-MTSU (out-of-state). *Fax:* 615-898-5167.

MIDLAND LUTHERAN COLLEGE

Fremont, NE

ABOUT THE INSTITUTION Independent Lutheran, coed. Awards: associate and bachelor's degrees. 57 undergraduate majors. Total enrollment: 909. Undergraduates: 909. Freshmen: 249.

GIFT AID (NEED-BASED) ***Scholarships, grants, and awards:*** Federal Pell, FSEOG, state, private, college/university gift aid from institutional funds.

GIFT AID (NON-NEED-BASED) ***Scholarships, grants, and awards by category:*** *Academic Interests/Achievement:* general academic interests/achievements. *Creative Arts/Performance:* art/fine arts, debating, journalism/publications, music, theater/drama. *Special Achievements/Activities:* community service, general special achievements/activities, leadership, religious involvement. *Special Characteristics:* children and siblings of alumni, handicapped students, international students, members of minority groups, religious affiliation, siblings of current students.

LOANS ***Programs:*** FFEL (Subsidized and Unsubsidized Stafford, PLUS), Perkins, college/university.

APPLYING FOR FINANCIAL AID ***Required financial aid form:*** FAFSA.

CONTACT Mr. Doug G. Watson, Associate Vice President, Midland Lutheran College, 900 North Clarkson Street, Fremont, NE 68025-4200, 402-721-5480 Ext. 6521 or toll-free 800-642-8382 Ext. 6501. *Fax:* 402-721-6513. *E-mail:* watson@mlc.edu.

MIDSTATE COLLEGE

Peoria, IL

CONTACT Janet Ozuna, Director of Financial Aid/Business Manager, Midstate College, 411 West Northmoor Road, Peoria, IL 61614, 309-692-4092. *Fax:* 309-692-3893.

MIDWAY COLLEGE

Midway, KY

ABOUT THE INSTITUTION Independent religious, women only. Awards: associate and bachelor's degrees. 20 undergraduate majors. Total enrollment: 1,316. Undergraduates: 1,316. Freshmen: 153.

GIFT AID (NEED-BASED) ***Scholarships, grants, and awards:*** Federal Pell, FSEOG, state, private, college/university gift aid from institutional funds.

GIFT AID (NON-NEED-BASED) ***Scholarships, grants, and awards by category:*** *Academic Interests/Achievement:* agriculture, business, general academic interests/achievements, health fields, premedicine. *Creative Arts/Performance:* art/fine arts, music. *Special Achievements/Activities:* general special achievements/activities, junior miss, leadership, religious involvement. *Special Characteristics:* children and siblings of alumni, children of faculty/staff, members of minority groups, relatives of clergy, religious affiliation, veterans.

LOANS ***Programs:*** FFEL (Subsidized and Unsubsidized Stafford, PLUS), Perkins, college/university.

APPLYING FOR FINANCIAL AID ***Required financial aid forms:*** FAFSA, institution's own form.

CONTACT Katie Valentine, Director of Financial Aid, Midway College, 512 East Stephens Street, Midway, KY 40347-1120, 859-846-5410 or toll-free 800-755-0031. *Fax:* 859-846-5751. *E-mail:* kvalentine@midway.edu.

MIDWESTERN STATE UNIVERSITY

Wichita Falls, TX

Tuition & fees (TX res): $4716 **Average undergraduate aid package: $6606**

ABOUT THE INSTITUTION State-supported, coed. Awards: associate, bachelor's, and master's degrees and post-bachelor's certificates. 58 undergraduate majors. Total enrollment: 6,042. Undergraduates: 5,367. Freshmen: 681. Federal methodology is used as a basis for awarding need-based institutional aid.

UNDERGRADUATE EXPENSES for 2007–08 ***Application fee:*** $25. ***Tuition, state resident:*** full-time $1500; part-time $50 per credit hour. ***Tuition, nonresident:*** full-time $2400; part-time $80 per credit hour. ***Required fees:*** full-time $3216; $232.25 per credit hour. ***College room and board:*** $5220; ***Room only:*** $2660.

FRESHMAN FINANCIAL AID (Fall 2006, est.) 603 applied for aid; of those 48% were deemed to have need. 99% of freshmen with need received aid; of those 18% had need fully met. ***Average percent of need met:*** 66% (excluding resources awarded to replace EFC). ***Average financial aid package:*** $6190 (excluding resources awarded to replace EFC). 26% of all full-time freshmen had no need and received non-need-based gift aid.

UNDERGRADUATE FINANCIAL AID (Fall 2006, est.) 3,025 applied for aid; of those 63% were deemed to have need. 99% of undergraduates with need received aid; of those 21% had need fully met. ***Average percent of need met:*** 69% (excluding resources awarded to replace EFC). ***Average financial aid package:*** $6606 (excluding resources awarded to replace EFC). 18% of all full-time undergraduates had no need and received non-need-based gift aid.

GIFT AID (NEED-BASED) ***Total amount:*** $7,164,952 (61% federal, 27% state, 8% institutional, 4% external sources). ***Receiving aid:*** Freshmen: 37% (242); All full-time undergraduates: 40% (1,562). ***Average award:*** Freshmen: $4524; Undergraduates: $4117. ***Scholarships, grants, and awards:*** Federal Pell, FSEOG, state, private, college/university gift aid from institutional funds.

GIFT AID (NON-NEED-BASED) ***Total amount:*** $1,157,411 (7% federal, 1% state, 70% institutional, 22% external sources). ***Receiving aid:*** Freshmen: 1% (6); Undergraduates: 1% (32). ***Average award:*** Freshmen: $1310; Undergraduates: $1415. ***Scholarships, grants, and awards by category:*** *Academic Interests/Achievement:* business, communication, computer science, education, engineering/technologies, English, general academic interests/achievements, health fields, mathematics, social sciences. *Creative Arts/Performance:* art/fine arts, general creative arts/performance, music, theater/drama. *Special Achievements/Activities:* cheerleading/drum major, general special achievements/activities, leadership, memberships. *Special Characteristics:* children of faculty/staff, general special characteristics, handicapped students, international students, out-of-state students, veterans. ***ROTC:*** Air Force cooperative.

LOANS ***Student loans:*** $12,589,724 (75% need-based, 25% non-need-based). 54% of past graduating class borrowed through all loan programs. *Average indebtedness per student:* $17,882. ***Average need-based loan:*** Freshmen: $2668; Undergraduates: $3442. ***Parent loans:*** $3,339,619 (39% need-based, 61% non-need-based). ***Programs:*** Federal Direct (Subsidized and Unsubsidized Stafford, PLUS), FFEL (Subsidized and Unsubsidized Stafford, PLUS), Perkins, state, college/university, alternative private loans.

WORK-STUDY ***Federal work-study:*** Total amount: $109,224; 33 jobs averaging $3310. ***State or other work-study/employment:*** Total amount: $43,675 (100% need-based). 14 part-time jobs averaging $3120.

ATHLETIC AWARDS Total amount: $485,563 (41% need-based, 59% non-need-based).

APPLYING FOR FINANCIAL AID ***Required financial aid forms:*** FAFSA, institution's own form. ***Financial aid deadline (priority):*** 5/1. ***Notification date:*** Continuous.

CONTACT Ms. Kathy Pennartz, Director of Financial Aid, Midwestern State University, 3410 Taft Boulevard, Wichita Falls, TX 76308-2099, 940-397-4214 or toll-free 800-842-1922. *Fax:* 940-397-4852. *E-mail:* financial-aid@mwsu.edu.

MIDWESTERN UNIVERSITY, GLENDALE CAMPUS

Glendale, AZ

Tuition & fees: N/R **Average undergraduate aid package: $10,131**

ABOUT THE INSTITUTION Independent, coed. Awards: bachelor's, master's, and doctoral degrees and post-bachelor's certificates. 1 undergraduate major. Total enrollment: 1,117. Undergraduates: 20. Federal methodology is used as a basis for awarding need-based institutional aid.

UNDERGRADUATE FINANCIAL AID (Fall 2006, est.) 67 applied for aid; of those 99% were deemed to have need. 100% of undergraduates with need received aid; of those 2% had need fully met. ***Average percent of need met:*** 32% (excluding resources awarded to replace EFC). ***Average financial aid package:*** $10,131 (excluding resources awarded to replace EFC).

GIFT AID (NEED-BASED) ***Total amount:*** $198,481 (93% federal, 3% state, 4% external sources). ***Receiving aid:*** All full-time undergraduates: 49% (36). ***Average award:*** Undergraduates: $5513. ***Scholarships, grants, and awards:*** Federal Pell, FSEOG, state, private, college/university gift aid from institutional funds.

GIFT AID (NON-NEED-BASED) ***Total amount:*** $128,412 (18% federal, 57% state, 7% institutional, 18% external sources). ***Receiving aid:*** Undergraduates: 20% (15). ***Scholarships, grants, and awards by category:*** *Academic Interests/Achievement:* 1 award ($5000 total): health fields.

LOANS ***Student loans:*** $1,496,625 (22% need-based, 78% non-need-based). 89% of past graduating class borrowed through all loan programs. *Average indebtedness per student:* $49,834. ***Average need-based loan:*** Undergraduates: $4375. ***Parent loans:*** $18,372 (100% non-need-based). ***Programs:*** FFEL (Subsidized and Unsubsidized Stafford, PLUS), Perkins, alternative loans.

WORK-STUDY ***Federal work-study:*** Total amount: $27,795; 18 jobs averaging $1544.

APPLYING FOR FINANCIAL AID ***Required financial aid forms:*** FAFSA, institution's own form. ***Financial aid deadline:*** Continuous. ***Notification date:*** Continuous beginning 6/1. Students must reply within 2 weeks of notification.

CONTACT Lesa Stanford, Administrative Assistant, Office of Student Financial Services, Midwestern University, Glendale Campus, 19555 North 59th Avenue, Glendale, AZ 85308, 623-572-3321 or toll-free 888-247-9277 (in-state), 888-247-9271 (out-of-state). *Fax:* 623-572-3283. *E-mail:* az_fin_aid@arizona.midwestern.edu.

MIDWEST UNIVERSITY

Wentzville, MO

CONTACT Financial Aid Office, Midwest University, PO Box 365, 851 Parr Road, Wentzville, MO 63385, 636-327-4645.

MIDWIVES COLLEGE OF UTAH

Orem, UT

CONTACT Financial Aid Office, Midwives College of Utah, 560 South State Street, Suite B2, Orem, UT 84058, 801-764-9068 or toll-free 866-764-9068.

MILES COLLEGE

Fairfield, AL

CONTACT P. N. Lanier, Financial Aid Administrator, Miles College, PO Box 3800, Birmingham, AL 35208, 205-929-1663 or toll-free 800-445-0708. *Fax:* 205-929-1668. *E-mail:* pnlani@netscape.net.

MILLERSVILLE UNIVERSITY OF PENNSYLVANIA

Millersville, PA

Tuition & fees (PA res): $6398 **Average undergraduate aid package: $6861**

ABOUT THE INSTITUTION State-supported, coed. Awards: associate, bachelor's, and master's degrees and post-bachelor's and post-master's certificates. 48 undergraduate majors. Total enrollment: 8,194. Undergraduates: 7,206. Freshmen: 1,363. Federal methodology is used as a basis for awarding need-based institutional aid.

UNDERGRADUATE EXPENSES for 2006–07 ***Application fee:*** $35. ***Tuition, state resident:*** full-time $5038; part-time $210 per credit. ***Tuition, nonresident:*** full-time $12,598; part-time $525 per credit. ***Required fees:*** full-time $1360; $52 per credit or $31 per term part-time. Full-time tuition and fees vary according to degree level. Part-time tuition and fees vary according to course load and degree level. ***College room and board:*** $6566; ***Room only:*** $4000. Room and board charges vary according to board plan. ***Payment plan:*** Installment.

FRESHMAN FINANCIAL AID (Fall 2005) 1127 applied for aid; of those 62% were deemed to have need. 98% of freshmen with need received aid; of those 19% had need fully met. ***Average percent of need met:*** 76% (excluding resources awarded to replace EFC). ***Average financial aid package:*** $6744 (excluding resources awarded to replace EFC). 4% of all full-time freshmen had no need and received non-need-based gift aid.

UNDERGRADUATE FINANCIAL AID (Fall 2005) 4,735 applied for aid; of those 68% were deemed to have need. 98% of undergraduates with need received aid; of those 27% had need fully met. ***Average percent of need met:*** 85% (excluding resources awarded to replace EFC). ***Average financial aid package:*** $6861 (excluding resources awarded to replace EFC). 3% of all full-time undergraduates had no need and received non-need-based gift aid.

GIFT AID (NEED-BASED) ***Total amount:*** $10,034,215 (35% federal, 54% state, 7% institutional, 4% external sources). ***Receiving aid:*** Freshmen: 42% (545); All full-time undergraduates: 38% (2,409). ***Average award:*** Freshmen: $4610; Undergraduates: $3991. ***Scholarships, grants, and awards:*** Federal Pell, FSEOG, state, private, college/university gift aid from institutional funds, SICO Scholarships.

GIFT AID (NON-NEED-BASED) ***Total amount:*** $2,531,015 (12% state, 38% institutional, 50% external sources). ***Receiving aid:*** Freshmen: 14% (185); Undergraduates: 8% (485). ***Average award:*** Freshmen: $2960; Undergraduates: $2356. ***Scholarships, grants, and awards by category:*** *Academic Interests/Achievement:* 414 awards ($993,373 total): biological sciences, business, communication, computer science, education, English, foreign languages, general academic interests/achievements, health fields, humanities, mathematics, physical sciences, social sciences. *Creative Arts/Performance:* 21 awards ($16,228 total): art/fine arts, music. *Special Achievements/Activities:* 2 awards ($2380 total): community service. *Special Characteristics:* 122 awards ($509,404 total): children of union members/company employees, international students. ***ROTC:*** Army.

LOANS ***Student loans:*** $22,549,742 (48% need-based, 52% non-need-based). 46% of past graduating class borrowed through all loan programs. *Average indebtedness per student:* $17,885. ***Average need-based loan:*** Freshmen: $2584; Undergraduates: $3641. ***Parent loans:*** $4,454,667 (100% non-need-based). ***Programs:*** FFEL (Subsidized and Unsubsidized Stafford, PLUS), Perkins, college/university.

WORK-STUDY ***Federal work-study:*** Total amount: $333,860; 371 jobs averaging $900. ***State or other work-study/employment:*** Total amount: $2,120,079 (100% non-need-based). 1,664 part-time jobs averaging $1274.

ATHLETIC AWARDS Total amount: $290,307 (16% need-based, 84% non-need-based).

APPLYING FOR FINANCIAL AID ***Required financial aid form:*** FAFSA. ***Financial aid deadline:*** 3/15. ***Notification date:*** Continuous beginning 3/19. Students must reply within 2 weeks of notification.

CONTACT Mr. Dwight Horsey, Director of Financial Aid, Millersville University of Pennsylvania, PO Box 1002, Millersville, PA 17551-0302, 717-872-3026 or toll-free 800-MU-ADMIT (out-of-state). *Fax:* 717-871-2248. *E-mail:* dwight.horsey@millersville.edu.

MILLIGAN COLLEGE

Milligan College, TN

Tuition & fees: $18,320 **Average undergraduate aid package: $14,512**

ABOUT THE INSTITUTION Independent Christian, coed. Awards: bachelor's and master's degrees. 26 undergraduate majors. Total enrollment: 951. Undergraduates: 746. Freshmen: 166. Federal methodology is used as a basis for awarding need-based institutional aid.

UNDERGRADUATE EXPENSES for 2006–07 ***Application fee:*** $30. ***Comprehensive fee:*** $23,350 includes full-time tuition ($17,800), mandatory fees ($520), and room and board ($5030). ***College room only:*** $2550. Full-time tuition and fees vary according to course load. Room and board charges vary according to board plan and housing facility. ***Part-time tuition:*** $305 per credit. ***Part-time fees:*** $259 per term. Part-time tuition and fees vary according to course load. ***Payment plan:*** Installment.

FRESHMAN FINANCIAL AID (Fall 2005) 160 applied for aid; of those 89% were deemed to have need. 99% of freshmen with need received aid; of those 50% had need fully met. ***Average percent of need met:*** 54% (excluding resources awarded to replace EFC). ***Average financial aid package:*** $14,551 (excluding resources awarded to replace EFC). 15% of all full-time freshmen had no need and received non-need-based gift aid.

UNDERGRADUATE FINANCIAL AID (Fall 2005) 632 applied for aid; of those 93% were deemed to have need. 99% of undergraduates with need received aid; of those 49% had need fully met. ***Average percent of need met:*** 51% (excluding resources awarded to replace EFC). ***Average financial aid package:*** $14,512 (excluding resources awarded to replace EFC). 12% of all full-time undergraduates had no need and received non-need-based gift aid.

GIFT AID (NEED-BASED) ***Total amount:*** $4,589,348 (13% federal, 13% state, 61% institutional, 13% external sources). ***Receiving aid:*** Freshmen: 26% (47); All full-time undergraduates: 30% (214). ***Average award:*** Freshmen: $3801; Undergraduates: $4025. ***Scholarships, grants, and awards:*** Federal Pell, FSEOG, state, private, college/university gift aid from institutional funds.

GIFT AID (NON-NEED-BASED) ***Total amount:*** $716,906 (15% state, 73% institutional, 12% external sources). ***Receiving aid:*** Freshmen: 79% (141); Undergraduates: 83% (586). ***Average award:*** Freshmen: $5662; Undergraduates: $5980. ***Scholarships, grants, and awards by category:*** *Academic Interests/Achievement:* 364 awards ($1,712,038 total): communication, computer science, general academic interests/achievements, health fields, mathematics, religion/biblical studies. *Creative Arts/Performance:* 31 awards ($29,625 total): art/fine arts, music. *Special Achievements/Activities:* 83 awards ($137,670 total): cheerleading/drum major, community service. *Special Characteristics:* 18 awards ($216,320 total): children of faculty/staff. ***Tuition waivers:*** Full or partial for employees or children of employees. ***ROTC:*** Army cooperative.

LOANS ***Student loans:*** $6,167,475 (92% need-based, 8% non-need-based). 70% of past graduating class borrowed through all loan programs. *Average indebtedness per student:* $18,500. ***Average need-based loan:*** Freshmen: $2824; Undergraduates: $4098. ***Parent loans:*** $1,042,567 (87% need-based, 13% non-need-based). ***Programs:*** FFEL (Subsidized and Unsubsidized Stafford, PLUS), Perkins, Signature Loans.

WORK-STUDY ***Federal work-study:*** Total amount: $77,493; 112 jobs averaging $870. ***State or other work-study/employment:*** Total amount: $133,479 (63% need-based, 37% non-need-based). 194 part-time jobs averaging $861.

ATHLETIC AWARDS Total amount: $1,200,844 (90% need-based, 10% non-need-based).

APPLYING FOR FINANCIAL AID ***Required financial aid form:*** FAFSA. ***Financial aid deadline (priority):*** 3/1. ***Notification date:*** Continuous beginning 3/4. Students must reply within 2 weeks of notification.

CONTACT Diane Keasling, Coordinator Financial Aid, Milligan College, PO Box 250, Milligan College, TN 37682, 423-461-8968 or toll-free 800-262-8337 (in-state). *Fax:* 423-929-2368. *E-mail:* dlkeasling@milligan.edu.

MILLIKIN UNIVERSITY

Decatur, IL

CONTACT Director of Financial Aid, Millikin University, 1184 West Main Street, Decatur, IL 62522-2084, 217-424-6343 or toll-free 800-373-7733. *Fax:* 217-425-4669.

MILLSAPS COLLEGE

Jackson, MS

Tuition & fees: $23,352 **Average undergraduate aid package: $18,892**

ABOUT THE INSTITUTION Independent United Methodist, coed. Awards: bachelor's and master's degrees. 27 undergraduate majors. Total enrollment: 1,084. Undergraduates: 1,003. Freshmen: 232. Federal methodology is used as a basis for awarding need-based institutional aid.

UNDERGRADUATE EXPENSES for 2007–08 ***Comprehensive fee:*** $31,720 includes full-time tuition ($21,900), mandatory fees ($1452), and room and board ($8368). ***College room only:*** $4708. ***Part-time tuition:*** $680 per credit hour. ***Part-time fees:*** $32 per credit hour.

FRESHMAN FINANCIAL AID (Fall 2006, est.) 180 applied for aid; of those 71% were deemed to have need. 100% of freshmen with need received aid; of those 41% had need fully met. ***Average percent of need met:*** 90% (excluding resources awarded to replace EFC). ***Average financial aid package:*** $18,462 (excluding resources awarded to replace EFC). 42% of all full-time freshmen had no need and received non-need-based gift aid.

UNDERGRADUATE FINANCIAL AID (Fall 2006, est.) 658 applied for aid; of those 81% were deemed to have need. 100% of undergraduates with need received aid; of those 29% had need fully met. ***Average percent of need met:*** 83% (excluding resources awarded to replace EFC). ***Average financial aid package:*** $18,892 (excluding resources awarded to replace EFC). 41% of all full-time undergraduates had no need and received non-need-based gift aid.

GIFT AID (NEED-BASED) ***Total amount:*** $8,243,267 (23% federal, 3% state, 67% institutional, 7% external sources). ***Receiving aid:*** Freshmen: 55% (127); All full-time undergraduates: 55% (530). ***Average award:*** Freshmen: $16,156; Undergraduates: $15,617. ***Scholarships, grants, and awards:*** Federal Pell, FSEOG, state, private, college/university gift aid from institutional funds.

GIFT AID (NON-NEED-BASED) ***Total amount:*** $5,552,803 (5% state, 90% institutional, 5% external sources). ***Receiving aid:*** Freshmen: 16% (38); Undergraduates: 10% (96). ***Average award:*** Freshmen: $15,604; Undergraduates: $14,212. ***Scholarships, grants, and awards by category:*** *Academic Interests/Achievement:* 845 awards ($7,135,701 total): business, general academic interests/achievements. *Creative Arts/Performance:* 78 awards ($129,516 total): art/fine arts, music, theater/drama. *Special Achievements/Activities:* 837 awards ($7,100,976 total): community service, general special achievements/activities, hobbies/interests, leadership, religious involvement. *Special Characteristics:* 68 awards ($276,268 total): adult students, children of faculty/staff, ethnic background, first-generation college students, members of minority groups, relatives of clergy, religious affiliation. ***ROTC:*** Army cooperative.

LOANS ***Student loans:*** $3,701,302 (60% need-based, 40% non-need-based). 59% of past graduating class borrowed through all loan programs. *Average indebtedness per student:* $21,495. ***Average need-based loan:*** Freshmen: $2686; Undergraduates: $3805. ***Parent loans:*** $1,129,476 (9% need-based, 91% non-need-based). ***Programs:*** FFEL (Subsidized and Unsubsidized Stafford, PLUS), Perkins, college/university.

WORK-STUDY ***Federal work-study:*** Total amount: $197,095; 293 jobs averaging $1256. ***State or other work-study/employment:*** Part-time jobs available.

APPLYING FOR FINANCIAL AID ***Required financial aid forms:*** FAFSA, institution's own form. ***Financial aid deadline (priority):*** 3/1. ***Notification date:*** Continuous beginning 3/15. Students must reply by 5/1 or within 2 weeks of notification.

CONTACT Patrick James, Director of Financial Aid, Millsaps College, 1701 North State Street, Jackson, MS 39210-0001, 601-974-1220 or toll-free 800-352-1050. *Fax:* 601-974-1224. *E-mail:* jamespg@millsaps.edu.

MILLS COLLEGE

Oakland, CA

Tuition & fees: $33,024 **Average undergraduate aid package: $24,002**

ABOUT THE INSTITUTION Independent, undergraduate: women only; graduate: coed. Awards: bachelor's, master's, and doctoral degrees and post-bachelor's certificates. 38 undergraduate majors. Total enrollment: 1,410. Undergraduates: 927. Freshmen: 200. Both federal and institutional methodology are used as a basis for awarding need-based institutional aid.

UNDERGRADUATE EXPENSES for 2006–07 ***Application fee:*** $40. ***Comprehensive fee:*** $43,264 includes full-time tuition ($30,300), mandatory fees ($2724), and room and board ($10,240). ***College room only:*** $5460. Full-time tuition and fees vary according to course load. Room and board charges vary according to board plan and housing facility. ***Part-time tuition:*** $5090 per course. Part-time tuition and fees vary according to course load. ***Payment plan:*** Installment.

GIFT AID (NEED-BASED) ***Total amount:*** $9,668,325 (12% federal, 17% state, 69% institutional, 2% external sources). ***Receiving aid:*** Freshmen: 76% (158); All full-time undergraduates: 82% (723). ***Average award:*** Freshmen: $20,108; Undergraduates: $18,210. ***Scholarships, grants, and awards:*** Federal Pell, FSEOG, state, private, college/university gift aid from institutional funds.

GIFT AID (NON-NEED-BASED) ***Total amount:*** $623,215 (3% state, 95% institutional, 2% external sources). ***Receiving aid:*** Freshmen: 45% (93); Undergraduates: 60% (533). ***Average award:*** Freshmen: $9876; Undergraduates: $8100. ***Scholarships, grants, and awards by category:*** *Academic Interests/Achievement:* biological sciences, computer science, general academic interests/achievements, mathematics, physical sciences, premedicine. *Creative Arts/Performance:* art/fine arts, music. *Special Characteristics:* children of faculty/staff. ***Tuition waivers:*** Full or partial for employees or children of employees.

LOANS ***Student loans:*** $4,315,942 (95% need-based, 5% non-need-based). 76% of past graduating class borrowed through all loan programs. *Average indebtedness per student:* $19,206. ***Average need-based loan:*** Freshmen: $3885; Undergraduates: $5490. ***Parent loans:*** $957,056 (87% need-based, 13% non-need-based). ***Programs:*** FFEL (Subsidized and Unsubsidized Stafford, PLUS), Perkins, college/university.

APPLYING FOR FINANCIAL AID ***Required financial aid forms:*** FAFSA, institution's own form, state aid form, noncustodial (divorced/separated) parent's statement. ***Financial aid deadline:*** 2/15 (priority: 2/15). ***Notification date:*** Continuous beginning 3/1. Students must reply by 5/1 or within 2 weeks of notification.

CONTACT The M Center/Financial Aid, Mills College, 5000 MacArthur Boulevard, Oakland, CA 94613, 510-430-2000 or toll-free 800-87-MILLS. *E-mail:* mcenter-finaid@mills.edu.

MILWAUKEE INSTITUTE OF ART AND DESIGN

Milwaukee, WI

CONTACT Mr. Lloyd Mueller, Director of Financial Aid, Milwaukee Institute of Art and Design, 273 East Erie Street, Milwaukee, WI 53202-6003, 414-291-3272 or toll-free 888-749-MIAD. *Fax:* 414-291-8077. *E-mail:* llmuelle@miad.edu.

MILWAUKEE SCHOOL OF ENGINEERING

Milwaukee, WI

Tuition & fees: $25,980 **Average undergraduate aid package: $16,915**

ABOUT THE INSTITUTION Independent, coed. Awards: bachelor's and master's degrees. 14 undergraduate majors. Total enrollment: 2,427. Undergraduates: 2,203. Freshmen: 560. Federal methodology is used as a basis for awarding need-based institutional aid.

UNDERGRADUATE EXPENSES for 2007–08 ***Application fee:*** $25. ***Comprehensive fee:*** $32,481 includes full-time tuition ($25,980) and room and board ($6501). ***College room only:*** $4170. ***Part-time tuition:*** $450 per quarter hour.

FRESHMAN FINANCIAL AID (Fall 2005) 407 applied for aid; of those 85% were deemed to have need. 99% of freshmen with need received aid; of those 15% had need fully met. ***Average percent of need met:*** 74% (excluding resources awarded to replace EFC). ***Average financial aid package:*** $16,759 (excluding resources awarded to replace EFC). 22% of all full-time freshmen had no need and received non-need-based gift aid.

UNDERGRADUATE FINANCIAL AID (Fall 2005) 1,594 applied for aid; of those 90% were deemed to have need. 100% of undergraduates with need received aid; of those 18% had need fully met. ***Average percent of need met:*** 72% (excluding resources awarded to replace EFC). ***Average financial aid package:*** $16,915 (excluding resources awarded to replace EFC). 16% of all full-time undergraduates had no need and received non-need-based gift aid.

GIFT AID (NEED-BASED) ***Total amount:*** $19,691,509 (7% federal, 9% state, 80% institutional, 4% external sources). ***Receiving aid:*** Freshmen: 78% (344); All full-time undergraduates: 79% (1,431). ***Average award:*** Freshmen: $13,744; Undergraduates: $13,221. ***Scholarships, grants, and awards:*** Federal Pell, FSEOG, state, private, college/university gift aid from institutional funds.

GIFT AID (NON-NEED-BASED) ***Total amount:*** $3,757,737 (1% state, 92% institutional, 7% external sources). ***Receiving aid:*** Freshmen: 9% (39); Undergraduates: 9% (156). ***Average award:*** Freshmen: $13,410; Undergraduates: $14,159. ***Scholarships, grants, and awards by category:*** *Academic Interests/Achievement:* 2,191 awards ($14,982,203 total): business, communication, computer science, engineering/technologies, health fields. *Special Characteristics:* 24 awards ($408,193 total): children of faculty/staff. ***ROTC:*** Army cooperative, Naval cooperative, Air Force cooperative.

LOANS ***Student loans:*** $15,272,353 (68% need-based, 32% non-need-based). 86% of past graduating class borrowed through all loan programs. *Average indebtedness per student:* $34,862. ***Average need-based loan:*** Freshmen: $2944; Undergraduates: $3951. ***Parent loans:*** $3,088,961 (40% need-based, 60% non-need-based). ***Programs:*** FFEL (Subsidized and Unsubsidized Stafford, PLUS), Perkins, state, college/university.

WORK-STUDY ***Federal work-study:*** Total amount: $270,502; 208 jobs averaging $1300.

APPLYING FOR FINANCIAL AID ***Required financial aid form:*** FAFSA. ***Financial aid deadline (priority):*** 3/15. ***Notification date:*** Continuous beginning 3/1. Students must reply within 2 weeks of notification.

CONTACT Steve Midthun, Director of Financial Aid, Milwaukee School of Engineering, 1025 North Broadway Street, Milwaukee, WI 53202-3109, 414-277-7223 or toll-free 800-332-6763. *Fax:* 414-277-6952. *E-mail:* finaid@msoe.edu.

MINNEAPOLIS COLLEGE OF ART AND DESIGN

Minneapolis, MN

CONTACT Laura Link, Director of Financial Aid, Minneapolis College of Art and Design, 2501 Stevens Avenue South, Minneapolis, MN 55404-4347, 612-874-3733 or toll-free 800-874-6223. *Fax:* 612-874-3701. *E-mail:* laura_link@mead.edu.

MINNESOTA SCHOOL OF BUSINESS

Rochester, MN

CONTACT Financial Aid Office, Minnesota School of Business, 2521 Pennington Drive, NW, Rochester, MN 55901, 507-536-9500 or toll-free 888-662-8772.

MINNESOTA STATE UNIVERSITY MANKATO

Mankato, MN

Tuition & fees (MN res): $5840 **Average undergraduate aid package: $7058**

ABOUT THE INSTITUTION State-supported, coed. Awards: associate, bachelor's, and master's degrees and post-master's certificates. 127 undergraduate majors. Total enrollment: 14,148. Undergraduates: 12,534. Freshmen: 2,163. Federal methodology is used as a basis for awarding need-based institutional aid.

UNDERGRADUATE EXPENSES for 2006–07 ***Application fee:*** $20. ***Tuition, state resident:*** full-time $5104; part-time $204.10 per credit. ***Tuition, nonresident:*** full-time $10,932; part-time $436 per credit. ***Required fees:*** full-time $736; $30.56 per credit. Full-time tuition and fees vary according to course load and reciprocity agreements. Part-time tuition and fees vary according to course load and reciprocity agreements. ***College room and board:*** $5099. Room and board charges vary according to board plan. ***Payment plan:*** Installment.

FRESHMAN FINANCIAL AID (Fall 2006, est.) 1754 applied for aid; of those 62% were deemed to have need. 99% of freshmen with need received aid; of those 39% had need fully met. ***Average percent of need met:*** 75% (excluding resources awarded to replace EFC). ***Average financial aid package:*** $6719 (excluding resources awarded to replace EFC). 5% of all full-time freshmen had no need and received non-need-based gift aid.

UNDERGRADUATE FINANCIAL AID (Fall 2006, est.) 8,423 applied for aid; of those 66% were deemed to have need. 99% of undergraduates with need received aid; of those 44% had need fully met. ***Average percent of need met:*** 79% (excluding resources awarded to replace EFC). ***Average financial aid package:*** $7058 (excluding resources awarded to replace EFC). 3% of all full-time undergraduates had no need and received non-need-based gift aid.

GIFT AID (NEED-BASED) ***Total amount:*** $16,605,899 (49% federal, 44% state, 6% institutional, 1% external sources). ***Receiving aid:*** Freshmen: 32% (688); All full-time undergraduates: 33% (3,632). ***Average award:*** Freshmen: $4138; Undergraduates: $3849. ***Scholarships, grants, and awards:*** Federal Pell, FSEOG, state, private, college/university gift aid from institutional funds.

GIFT AID (NON-NEED-BASED) ***Total amount:*** $3,882,545 (31% federal, 5% state, 35% institutional, 29% external sources). ***Receiving aid:*** Freshmen: 15% (321); Undergraduates: 9% (966). ***Average award:*** Freshmen: $2147; Undergraduates: $2924. ***Scholarships, grants, and awards by category:*** *Academic Interests/Achievement:* business, computer science, engineering/technologies, general academic interests/achievements, mathematics, physical sciences. *Creative Arts/Performance:* applied art and design, art/fine arts, creative writing, debating, music, theater/drama. *Special Achievements/Activities:* community service, leadership. *Special Characteristics:* children of union members/company employees, local/state students, out-of-state students. ***Tuition waivers:*** Full or partial for employees or children of employees, senior citizens. ***ROTC:*** Army.

LOANS ***Student loans:*** $52,655,418 (61% need-based, 39% non-need-based). 73% of past graduating class borrowed through all loan programs. *Average indebtedness per student:* $20,826. ***Average need-based loan:*** Freshmen: $3025; Undergraduates: $3936. ***Parent loans:*** $3,539,876 (100% non-need-based). ***Programs:*** FFEL (Subsidized and Unsubsidized Stafford, PLUS), Perkins, state, SELF Loans.

WORK-STUDY ***Federal work-study:*** Total amount: $684,402; 317 jobs averaging $2980. ***State or other work-study/employment:*** Total amount: $3,068,406 (30% need-based, 70% non-need-based). 342 part-time jobs averaging $3045.

ATHLETIC AWARDS Total amount: $1,413,252 (25% need-based, 75% non-need-based).

APPLYING FOR FINANCIAL AID ***Required financial aid forms:*** FAFSA, SELF or Alternative Loan Application or PLUS Application. ***Financial aid deadline (priority):*** 3/15. ***Notification date:*** Continuous beginning 3/30. Students must reply within 2 weeks of notification.

CONTACT Financial Aid Office, Minnesota State University Mankato, Student Financial Services, 117 Centennial Student Union, Mankato, MN 56001, 507-389-1866 or toll-free 800-722-0544. *Fax:* 507-389-2227. *E-mail:* campushub@mnsu.edu.

MINNESOTA STATE UNIVERSITY MOORHEAD

Moorhead, MN

CONTACT Ms. Carolyn Zehren, Director of Financial Aid, Minnesota State University Moorhead, 1104 7th Avenue South, Moorhead, MN 56563-0002, 218-477-2251 or toll-free 800-593-7246. *Fax:* 218-477-2058. *E-mail:* zehren@mnstate.edu.

MINOT STATE UNIVERSITY

Minot, ND

Tuition & fees (ND res): $4492 **Average undergraduate aid package: $4931**

ABOUT THE INSTITUTION State-supported, coed. Awards: associate, bachelor's, and master's degrees and post-master's certificates. 58 undergraduate majors. Total enrollment: 3,712. Undergraduates: 3,433. Freshmen: 483. Federal methodology is used as a basis for awarding need-based institutional aid.

UNDERGRADUATE EXPENSES for 2006–07 ***Application fee:*** $35. ***Tuition, state resident:*** full-time $3790; part-time $187 per credit hour. ***Tuition, nonresident:*** full-time $10,116; part-time $450.74 per credit hour. ***Required fees:*** full-time $702; $29 per credit hour. Full-time tuition and fees vary according to class time, course load, location, program, and reciprocity agreements. Part-time tuition and fees vary according to class time, location, program, and reciprocity agreements. ***College room and board:*** $5294; ***Room only:*** $2600. Room and board charges vary according to board plan and housing facility. ***Payment plan:*** Installment.

FRESHMAN FINANCIAL AID (Fall 2005) 424 applied for aid; of those 77% were deemed to have need. 95% of freshmen with need received aid; of those 33% had need fully met. ***Average financial aid package:*** $4019 (excluding resources awarded to replace EFC). 24% of all full-time freshmen had no need and received non-need-based gift aid.

UNDERGRADUATE FINANCIAL AID (Fall 2005) 1,833 applied for aid; of those 83% were deemed to have need. 98% of undergraduates with need received aid; of those 24% had need fully met. ***Average financial aid package:*** $4931 (excluding resources awarded to replace EFC). 21% of all full-time undergraduates had no need and received non-need-based gift aid.

GIFT AID (NEED-BASED) ***Total amount:*** $3,969,388 (64% federal, 5% state, 7% institutional, 24% external sources). ***Receiving aid:*** Freshmen: 51% (251); All full-time undergraduates: 49% (1,051). ***Average award:*** Freshmen: $2724; Undergraduates: $3022. ***Scholarships, grants, and awards:*** Federal Pell, FSEOG, state, private, college/university gift aid from institutional funds, Federal Nursing.

GIFT AID (NON-NEED-BASED) ***Total amount:*** $1,120,242 (2% federal, 1% state, 21% institutional, 76% external sources). ***Receiving aid:*** Freshmen: 11% (54); Undergraduates: 9% (205). ***Average award:*** Freshmen: $980; Undergraduates: $927. ***Scholarships, grants, and awards by category:*** *Academic Interests/Achievement:* 1,155 awards ($735,555 total): business, communication, computer science, education, English, general academic interests/achievements, health fields, humanities, mathematics, social sciences. *Creative Arts/Performance:* $122,181 total: music, theater/drama. *Special Characteristics:* 154 awards ($301,083 total): ethnic background, international students, local/state students, members of minority groups, out-of-state students, veterans, veterans' children. ***Tuition waivers:*** Full or partial for minority students, children of alumni, employees or children of employees.

LOANS ***Student loans:*** $9,848,620 (71% need-based, 29% non-need-based). 97% of past graduating class borrowed through all loan programs. *Average indebtedness per student:* $16,354. ***Average need-based loan:*** Freshmen: $2295; Undergraduates: $3523. ***Parent loans:*** $224,943 (25% need-based, 75% non-need-based). ***Programs:*** FFEL (Subsidized and Unsubsidized Stafford, PLUS), Perkins, Federal Nursing, college/university.

WORK-STUDY ***Federal work-study:*** Total amount: $203,023; 142 jobs averaging $1779.

ATHLETIC AWARDS Total amount: $249,159 (27% need-based, 73% non-need-based).

APPLYING FOR FINANCIAL AID ***Required financial aid form:*** FAFSA. ***Financial aid deadline (priority):*** 3/15. ***Notification date:*** Continuous beginning 4/1. Students must reply within 2 weeks of notification.

CONTACT Mr. Dale Gehring, Director of Financial Aid, Minot State University, 500 University Avenue, West, Minot, ND 58707-0002, 701-858-3862 or toll-free 800-777-0750 Ext. 3350. *Fax:* 701-858-4310. *E-mail:* dale.gehring@minotstateu.edu.

MIRRER YESHIVA

Brooklyn, NY

CONTACT Financial Aid Office, Mirrer Yeshiva, 1795 Ocean Parkway, Brooklyn, NY 11223-2010, 718-645-0536.

MISSISSIPPI COLLEGE

Clinton, MS

CONTACT Mary Givhan, Director of Financial Aid, Mississippi College, PO Box 4035, Clinton, MS 39058, 601-925-3319 or toll-free 800-738-1236. *E-mail:* givhan@mc.edu.

MISSISSIPPI STATE UNIVERSITY

Mississippi State, MS

Tuition & fees (MS res): $4596 **Average undergraduate aid package: $8286**

ABOUT THE INSTITUTION State-supported, coed. Awards: bachelor's, master's, doctoral, and first professional degrees and post-master's certificates. 71 undergraduate majors. Total enrollment: 16,206. Undergraduates: 12,630. Freshmen: 1,911. Federal methodology is used as a basis for awarding need-based institutional aid.

UNDERGRADUATE EXPENSES for 2006–07 ***Application fee:*** $25. ***Tuition, state resident:*** full-time $4596; part-time $189.75 per hour. ***Tuition, nonresident:*** full-time $10,552; part-time $438 per hour. Part-time tuition and fees vary according to course load. ***College room and board:*** $6331; ***Room only:*** $3296. Room and board charges vary according to board plan, housing facility, and student level.

FRESHMAN FINANCIAL AID (Fall 2005) 1400 applied for aid; of those 84% were deemed to have need. 96% of freshmen with need received aid; of those 22% had need fully met. ***Average percent of need met:*** 62% (excluding resources awarded to replace EFC). ***Average financial aid package:*** $7106 (excluding resources awarded to replace EFC). 26% of all full-time freshmen had no need and received non-need-based gift aid.

UNDERGRADUATE FINANCIAL AID (Fall 2005) 7,746 applied for aid; of those 85% were deemed to have need. 97% of undergraduates with need received aid; of those 33% had need fully met. ***Average percent of need met:*** 66% (excluding resources awarded to replace EFC). ***Average financial aid package:*** $8286 (excluding resources awarded to replace EFC). 15% of all full-time undergraduates had no need and received non-need-based gift aid.

GIFT AID (NEED-BASED) ***Total amount:*** $27,934,620 (60% federal, 10% state, 13% institutional, 17% external sources). ***Receiving aid:*** Freshmen: 56% (1,075); All full-time undergraduates: 47% (5,791). ***Average award:*** Freshmen: $4512; Undergraduates: $4295. ***Scholarships, grants, and awards:*** Federal Pell, FSEOG, state, private, college/university gift aid from institutional funds, United Negro College Fund.

GIFT AID (NON-NEED-BASED) ***Total amount:*** $12,353,640 (28% state, 47% institutional, 25% external sources). ***Receiving aid:*** Freshmen: 12% (232); Undergraduates: 6% (731). ***Average award:*** Freshmen: $2845; Undergraduates: $2554. ***Scholarships, grants, and awards by category:*** *Academic Interests/Achievement:* agriculture, architecture, area/ethnic studies, biological sciences, business, communication, computer science, education, engineering/technologies, English, foreign languages, general academic interests/achievements, health fields, home economics, humanities, international studies, library science, mathematics, military science, physical sciences, premedicine, religion/biblical studies, social sciences. *Creative Arts/Performance:* applied art and design, art/fine arts, cinema/film/broadcasting, creative writing, dance, debating, general creative arts/performance, journalism/publications, music, performing arts, theater/drama. *Special Achievements/Activities:* cheerleading/drum major, general special achievements/activities, leadership, memberships. *Special Characteristics:* adult students, children and siblings of alumni, children of educators, children of faculty/staff, children of public servants, first-generation college students, handicapped students, local/state students, out-of-state students, previous college experience, spouses of deceased or disabled public servants. ***Tuition waivers:*** Full or partial for children of alumni, employees or children of employees, senior citizens. ***ROTC:*** Army, Air Force.

LOANS ***Student loans:*** $55,625,553 (80% need-based, 20% non-need-based). 43% of past graduating class borrowed through all loan programs. *Average indebtedness per student:* $19,780. ***Average need-based loan:*** Freshmen: $2948; Undergraduates: $3999. ***Parent loans:*** $3,624,024 (26% need-based, 74% non-need-based). ***Programs:*** FFEL (Subsidized and Unsubsidized Stafford, PLUS), Perkins, college/university.

WORK-STUDY ***Federal work-study:*** Total amount: $2,325,625; 726 jobs averaging $2658.

ATHLETIC AWARDS Total amount: $2,861,916 (100% non-need-based).

APPLYING FOR FINANCIAL AID ***Required financial aid forms:*** FAFSA, state grant/scholarship application. ***Financial aid deadline (priority):*** 4/1. ***Notification date:*** Continuous beginning 12/1. Students must reply by 5/1.

CONTACT Mr. Bruce Crain, Director of Financial Aid, Mississippi State University, PO Box 6035, Mississippi State, MS 39762, 662-325-2450. *Fax:* 662-325-0702. *E-mail:* financialaid@saffairs.msstate.edu.

MISSISSIPPI UNIVERSITY FOR WOMEN

Columbus, MS

CONTACT Frank McClinton, Director of Financial Aid, Mississippi University for Women, 1100 College Street, MUW 1614, Columbus, MS 39701-4044, 662-329-7114 or toll-free 877-GO 2 THE W. *Fax:* 662-329-7325. *E-mail:* fmcclinton@muw.edu.

MISSISSIPPI VALLEY STATE UNIVERSITY

Itta Bena, MS

CONTACT Mr. Darrell G. Boyd, Director of Student Financial Aid, Mississippi Valley State University, 14000 Highway 82W #7268, Itta Bena, MS 38941-1400, 662-254-3765 or toll-free 800-844-6885 (in-state). *Fax:* 662-254-3759. *E-mail:* dboyd@mvsu.edu.

MISSOURI BAPTIST UNIVERSITY

St. Louis, MO

Tuition & fees: $14,810 **Average undergraduate aid package: $8120**

ABOUT THE INSTITUTION Independent Southern Baptist, coed. Awards: associate, bachelor's, and master's degrees and post-bachelor's certificates. 33 undergraduate majors. Total enrollment: 4,511. Undergraduates: 3,496. Freshmen: 195. Both federal and institutional methodology are used as a basis for awarding need-based institutional aid.

UNDERGRADUATE EXPENSES for 2006–07 ***Application fee:*** $30. ***Comprehensive fee:*** $20,800 includes full-time tuition ($14,140), mandatory fees ($670), and room and board ($5990). Full-time tuition and fees vary according to course load and location. Room and board charges vary according to housing facility. ***Part-time tuition:*** $490 per credit. ***Part-time fees:*** $11 per credit; $25 per term. Part-time tuition and fees vary according to course load and location. ***Payment plan:*** Installment.

UNDERGRADUATE FINANCIAL AID (Fall 2005) 1,509 applied for aid; of those 100% were deemed to have need. 100% of undergraduates with need received aid. ***Average percent of need met:*** 27% (excluding resources awarded to replace EFC). ***Average financial aid package:*** $8120 (excluding resources awarded to replace EFC). 7% of all full-time undergraduates had no need and received non-need-based gift aid.

GIFT AID (NEED-BASED) ***Total amount:*** $2,023,821 (58% federal, 14% state, 28% institutional). ***Receiving aid:*** All full-time undergraduates: 60% (980). ***Average award:*** Undergraduates: $5116. ***Scholarships, grants, and awards:*** Federal Pell, FSEOG, state, private, college/university gift aid from institutional funds.

GIFT AID (NON-NEED-BASED) ***Total amount:*** $1,666,173 (2% state, 80% institutional, 18% external sources). ***Receiving aid:*** Undergraduates: 14% (228). ***Average award:*** Undergraduates: $3004. ***Scholarships, grants, and awards by category:*** *Academic Interests/Achievement:* 428 awards ($1,560,262 total): general academic interests/achievements, religion/biblical studies. *Creative Arts/Performance:* 66 awards ($115,470 total): music, theater/drama. *Special Achievements/Activities:* 275 awards ($240,882 total): cheerleading/drum major, religious involvement. *Special Characteristics:* 189 awards ($667,034 total): children and siblings of alumni, children of current students, children of faculty/staff, parents of current students, public servants, relatives of clergy, religious affiliation, siblings of current students. ***Tuition waivers:*** Full or partial for children of alumni, employees or children of employees, senior citizens. ***ROTC:*** Army cooperative.

LOANS ***Student loans:*** $5,503,610 (58% need-based, 42% non-need-based). 58% of past graduating class borrowed through all loan programs. *Average indebtedness per student:* $18,358. ***Average need-based loan:*** Undergraduates: $3959. ***Parent loans:*** $522,773 (100% need-based). ***Programs:*** FFEL (Subsidized and Unsubsidized Stafford, PLUS).

WORK-STUDY ***Federal work-study:*** Total amount: $83,256; 68 jobs averaging $1224. ***State or other work-study/employment:*** Total amount: $50,913 (100% need-based). 15 part-time jobs averaging $3394.

ATHLETIC AWARDS Total amount: $3,850,368 (100% non-need-based).

APPLYING FOR FINANCIAL AID ***Required financial aid forms:*** FAFSA, institution's own form. ***Financial aid deadline (priority):*** 4/1. ***Notification date:*** Continuous beginning 4/15. Students must reply within 2 weeks of notification.

CONTACT Laurie Wallace, Director of Financial Services, Missouri Baptist University, One College Park Drive, St. Louis, MO 63141, 314-392-2366 or toll-free 877-434-1115 Ext. 2290. *Fax:* 314-434-7596. *E-mail:* wallace@mobap.edu.

MISSOURI SOUTHERN STATE UNIVERSITY

Joplin, MO

CONTACT Mr. James E. Gilbert, Director of Financial Aid, Missouri Southern State University, 3950 East Newman Road, Joplin, MO 64801-1595, 417-625-9325 or toll-free 866-818-MSSU. *Fax:* 417-625-3121. *E-mail:* gilbert-j@mssu.edu.

MISSOURI STATE UNIVERSITY

Springfield, MO

Tuition & fees (MO res): $5738 **Average undergraduate aid package: $6093**

ABOUT THE INSTITUTION State-supported, coed. Awards: bachelor's, master's, and doctoral degrees and post-bachelor's and post-master's certificates. 91 undergraduate majors. Total enrollment: 19,218. Undergraduates: 16,234. Freshmen: 2,775. Federal methodology is used as a basis for awarding need-based institutional aid.

UNDERGRADUATE EXPENSES for 2007–08 ***Application fee:*** $30. ***Tuition, state resident:*** full-time $5190; part-time $173 per credit hour. ***Tuition, nonresident:*** full-time $10,110; part-time $337 per credit hour. ***College room and board:*** $5358; ***Room only:*** $3600.

FRESHMAN FINANCIAL AID (Fall 2006, est.) 2028 applied for aid; of those 63% were deemed to have need. 99% of freshmen with need received aid; of those 24% had need fully met. ***Average percent of need met:*** 62% (excluding resources awarded to replace EFC). ***Average financial aid package:*** $5921 (excluding resources awarded to replace EFC). 40% of all full-time freshmen had no need and received non-need-based gift aid.

UNDERGRADUATE FINANCIAL AID (Fall 2006, est.) 9,140 applied for aid; of those 73% were deemed to have need. 97% of undergraduates with need received aid; of those 22% had need fully met. ***Average percent of need met:*** 58% (excluding resources awarded to replace EFC). ***Average financial aid package:*** $6093 (excluding resources awarded to replace EFC). 33% of all full-time undergraduates had no need and received non-need-based gift aid.

GIFT AID (NEED-BASED) ***Total amount:*** $19,723,153 (50% federal, 12% state, 30% institutional, 8% external sources). ***Receiving aid:*** Freshmen: 42% (1,002); All full-time undergraduates: 41% (4,472). ***Average award:*** Freshmen: $4907; Undergraduates: $4437. ***Scholarships, grants, and awards:*** Federal Pell, FSEOG, state, private, college/university gift aid from institutional funds.

GIFT AID (NON-NEED-BASED) ***Total amount:*** $11,463,880 (11% state, 77% institutional, 12% external sources). ***Receiving aid:*** Freshmen: 8% (184); Undergraduates: 4% (478). ***Average award:*** Freshmen: $8663; Undergraduates: $7908. ***Scholarships, grants, and awards by category:*** *Academic Interests/Achievement:* 6,888 awards ($10,500,000 total): agriculture, biological sciences, business, communication, computer science, education, foreign languages, general academic interests/achievements, health fields, home economics, mathematics, military science, physical sciences, premedicine, religion/biblical studies, social sciences. *Creative Arts/Performance:* applied art and design, art/fine arts, dance, debating, general creative arts/performance, journalism/publications, music, performing arts, theater/drama. *Special Achievements/Activities:* cheerleading/drum major, general special achievements/activities, hobbies/interests, memberships, rodeo. *Special Characteristics:* adult students, children and siblings of alumni, children of faculty/staff, ethnic background, first-generation college students, general special characteristics, handicapped students, international students, members of minority groups, out-of-state students, spouses of deceased or disabled public servants, veterans. ***ROTC:*** Army.

LOANS ***Student loans:*** $43,167,837 (66% need-based, 34% non-need-based). 66% of past graduating class borrowed through all loan programs. *Average indebtedness per student:* $16,003. ***Average need-based loan:*** Freshmen: $2613; Undergraduates: $3703. ***Parent loans:*** $20,201,930 (18% need-based, 82% non-need-based). ***Programs:*** FFEL (Subsidized and Unsubsidized Stafford, PLUS), Perkins, college/university.

WORK-STUDY ***Federal work-study:*** Total amount: $489,032; 449 jobs averaging $1748. ***State or other work-study/employment:*** 1,336 part-time jobs averaging $2924.

ATHLETIC AWARDS Total amount: $3,391,737 (23% need-based, 77% non-need-based).

APPLYING FOR FINANCIAL AID ***Required financial aid form:*** FAFSA. ***Financial aid deadline (priority):*** 3/30. ***Notification date:*** Continuous.

CONTACT David G. King, Assistant Director of Financial Aid, Missouri State University, 901 South National Avenue, Springfield, MO 65804, 417-836-5262 or toll-free 800-492-7900.

MISSOURI TECH

St. Louis, MO

CONTACT Director of Financial Aid, Missouri Tech, 1167 Corporate Lake Drive, St. Louis, MO 63132-1716, 314-569-3600. *Fax:* 314-569-1167. *E-mail:* contact@motech.edu.

MISSOURI VALLEY COLLEGE

Marshall, MO

Tuition & fees: $15,450 **Average undergraduate aid package: $12,450**

ABOUT THE INSTITUTION Independent religious, coed. Awards: associate and bachelor's degrees. 40 undergraduate majors. Total enrollment: 1,606. Undergraduates: 1,606. Freshmen: 375. Federal methodology is used as a basis for awarding need-based institutional aid.

UNDERGRADUATE EXPENSES for 2007–08 ***Application fee:*** $15. ***Comprehensive fee:*** $21,300 includes full-time tuition ($14,950), mandatory fees ($500), and room and board ($5850). ***College room only:*** $3000. ***Part-time tuition:*** $350 per credit hour.

FRESHMAN FINANCIAL AID (Fall 2006, est.) 343 applied for aid; of those 80% were deemed to have need. 100% of freshmen with need received aid; of those 36% had need fully met. ***Average percent of need met:*** 80% (excluding resources awarded to replace EFC). ***Average financial aid package:*** $12,150 (excluding resources awarded to replace EFC). 32% of all full-time freshmen had no need and received non-need-based gift aid.

UNDERGRADUATE FINANCIAL AID (Fall 2006, est.) 1,262 applied for aid; of those 80% were deemed to have need. 100% of undergraduates with need received aid; of those 36% had need fully met. ***Average percent of need met:*** 80% (excluding resources awarded to replace EFC). ***Average financial aid package:*** $12,450 (excluding resources awarded to replace EFC). 32% of all full-time undergraduates had no need and received non-need-based gift aid.

GIFT AID (NEED-BASED) ***Total amount:*** $8,988,345 (23% federal, 7% state, 70% institutional). ***Receiving aid:*** Freshmen: 68% (275); All full-time undergraduates: 68% (1,009). ***Average award:*** Freshmen: $10,492; Undergraduates: $10,301. ***Scholarships, grants, and awards:*** Federal Pell, FSEOG, state, private, college/university gift aid from institutional funds.

GIFT AID (NON-NEED-BASED) ***Total amount:*** $622,762 (62% institutional, 38% external sources). ***Receiving aid:*** Freshmen: 68% (275); Undergraduates: 68% (1,009). ***Average award:*** Freshmen: $8240; Undergraduates: $7974. ***Scholarships, grants, and awards by category:*** *Academic Interests/Achievement:* 220 awards ($284,180 total): biological sciences, business, communication, computer science, education, English, humanities, mathematics, military science, physical sciences, premedicine, social sciences. *Creative Arts/Performance:* 51 awards ($131,802 total): dance, journalism/publications, music, performing arts, theater/drama. *Special Achievements/Activities:* 35 awards ($48,353 total): cheerleading/drum major, community service, general special achievements/activities, hobbies/interests, junior miss, leadership, rodeo. *Special Characteristics:* 34 awards ($136,152 total): children and siblings of alumni, children of faculty/staff. ***ROTC:*** Army.

LOANS ***Student loans:*** $5,018,018 (54% need-based, 46% non-need-based). 77% of past graduating class borrowed through all loan programs. *Average indebtedness per student:* $14,200. ***Average need-based loan:*** Freshmen: $2422; Undergraduates: $3624. ***Parent loans:*** $585,627 (100% non-need-based). ***Programs:*** FFEL (Subsidized and Unsubsidized Stafford, PLUS), Perkins.

WORK-STUDY ***Federal work-study:*** Total amount: $224,478; 164 jobs averaging $1312. ***State or other work-study/employment:*** Total amount: $684,030 (100% non-need-based). 573 part-time jobs averaging $1259.

ATHLETIC AWARDS Total amount: $6,474,193 (100% need-based).

APPLYING FOR FINANCIAL AID ***Required financial aid form:*** FAFSA. ***Financial aid deadline:*** 9/15 (priority: 3/15). ***Notification date:*** Continuous beginning 10/1. Students must reply within 4 weeks of notification.

CONTACT Charles Mayfield, Director of Financial Aid, Missouri Valley College, 500 East College, Marshall, MO 65340-3197, 660-831-4176. *Fax:* 660-831-4003. *E-mail:* mayfieldb@moval.edu.

MISSOURI WESTERN STATE UNIVERSITY

St. Joseph, MO

CONTACT Angela Beam, Director of Financial Aid, Missouri Western State University, 4525 Downs Drive, St. Joseph, MO 64507-2294, 816-271-4361 or toll-free 800-662-7041 Ext. 60. *Fax:* 816-271-5833.

MITCHELL COLLEGE

New London, CT

CONTACT Jacklyn Stoltz, Director of Financial Aid, Mitchell College, 437 Pequot Avenue, New London, CT 06320-4498, 800-443-2811. *Fax:* 860-444-1209. *E-mail:* stoltz_j@mitchell.edu.

MOLLOY COLLEGE

Rockville Centre, NY

Tuition & fees: $17,310 **Average undergraduate aid package: $11,026**

ABOUT THE INSTITUTION Independent, coed. Awards: associate, bachelor's, and master's degrees and post-master's certificates. 44 undergraduate majors. Total enrollment: 3,673. Undergraduates: 2,834. Freshmen: 278. Federal methodology is used as a basis for awarding need-based institutional aid.

UNDERGRADUATE EXPENSES for 2006–07 ***Application fee:*** $30. ***Tuition:*** full-time $16,560; part-time $550 per credit. ***Payment plan:*** Installment.

FRESHMAN FINANCIAL AID (Fall 2006, est.) 229 applied for aid; of those 80% were deemed to have need. 100% of freshmen with need received aid; of those 22% had need fully met. ***Average percent of need met:*** 63% (excluding resources awarded to replace EFC). ***Average financial aid package:*** $11,788 (excluding resources awarded to replace EFC). 19% of all full-time freshmen had no need and received non-need-based gift aid.

UNDERGRADUATE FINANCIAL AID (Fall 2006, est.) 1,641 applied for aid; of those 84% were deemed to have need. 100% of undergraduates with need received aid; of those 18% had need fully met. ***Average percent of need met:*** 57% (excluding resources awarded to replace EFC). ***Average financial aid package:*** $11,026 (excluding resources awarded to replace EFC). 15% of all full-time undergraduates had no need and received non-need-based gift aid.

GIFT AID (NEED-BASED) ***Total amount:*** $8,899,639 (27% federal, 30% state, 40% institutional, 3% external sources). ***Receiving aid:*** Freshmen: 77% (176); All full-time undergraduates: 75% (1,232). ***Average award:*** Freshmen: $8031; Undergraduates: $6588. ***Scholarships, grants, and awards:*** Federal Pell, FSEOG, state, private, college/university gift aid from institutional funds.

GIFT AID (NON-NEED-BASED) ***Total amount:*** $1,088,987 (9% state, 83% institutional, 8% external sources). ***Receiving aid:*** Freshmen: 7% (15); Undergraduates: 5% (84). ***Average award:*** Freshmen: $10,622; Undergraduates: $11,380. ***Scholarships, grants, and awards by category:*** *Academic Interests/Achievement:* 653 awards ($2,235,727 total): biological sciences, business, communication, education, English, general academic interests/achievements, health fields, mathematics. *Creative Arts/Performance:* 43 awards ($93,624 total): art/fine arts, music, performing arts. *Special Achievements/Activities:* 161 awards ($273,500 total): community service, memberships, religious involvement. *Special Characteristics:* 169 awards ($887,436 total): children and siblings of alumni, children of faculty/staff, ethnic background, siblings of current students. ***Tuition waivers:*** Full or partial for employees or children of employees. ***ROTC:*** Army cooperative, Naval cooperative, Air Force cooperative.

LOANS ***Student loans:*** $18,267,298 (80% need-based, 20% non-need-based). 70% of past graduating class borrowed through all loan programs. *Average indebtedness per student:* $23,000. ***Average need-based loan:*** Freshmen: $4214; Undergraduates: $5481. ***Parent loans:*** $4,491,081 (46% need-based, 54% non-need-based). ***Programs:*** FFEL (Subsidized and Unsubsidized Stafford, PLUS), Perkins, Federal Nursing, alternative loans.

WORK-STUDY ***Federal work-study:*** Total amount: $610,074; 428 jobs averaging $1997.

ATHLETIC AWARDS Total amount: $1,157,252 (69% need-based, 31% non-need-based).

APPLYING FOR FINANCIAL AID ***Required financial aid forms:*** FAFSA, state aid form. ***Financial aid deadline:*** 5/1 (priority: 5/1). ***Notification date:*** 3/1. Students must reply within 5 weeks of notification.

CONTACT Ana C. Lockward, Director of Financial Aid, Molloy College, 1000 Hempstead Avenue, PO Box 5002, Rockville Centre, NY 11571, 516-678-5000 Ext. 6221 or toll-free 888-4MOLLOY. *Fax:* 516-256-2292. *E-mail:* alockward@molloy.edu.

MONMOUTH COLLEGE

Monmouth, IL

CONTACT Ms. Jayne Whiteside, Director of Financial Aid, Monmouth College, 700 East Broadway, Monmouth, IL 61462-1998, 309-457-2129 or toll-free 800-747-2687. *Fax:* 309-457-2152. *E-mail:* jayne@monm.edu.

MONMOUTH UNIVERSITY

West Long Branch, NJ

Tuition & fees: $21,868 **Average undergraduate aid package: $16,739**

ABOUT THE INSTITUTION Independent, coed. Awards: associate, bachelor's, and master's degrees and post-master's certificates. 28 undergraduate majors. Total enrollment: 6,399. Undergraduates: 4,621. Freshmen: 960. Federal methodology is used as a basis for awarding need-based institutional aid.

UNDERGRADUATE EXPENSES for 2006–07 ***Application fee:*** $50. ***Comprehensive fee:*** $30,340 includes full-time tuition ($21,248), mandatory fees ($620), and room and board ($8472). ***College room only:*** $4754. Room and board charges vary according to board plan and housing facility. ***Part-time tuition:*** $615 per credit hour. ***Part-time fees:*** $155 per term. ***Payment plan:*** Installment.

FRESHMAN FINANCIAL AID (Fall 2006, est.) 797 applied for aid; of those 75% were deemed to have need. 99% of freshmen with need received aid; of those 23% had need fully met. ***Average percent of need met:*** 79% (excluding resources awarded to replace EFC). ***Average financial aid package:*** $12,409 (excluding resources awarded to replace EFC). 33% of all full-time freshmen had no need and received non-need-based gift aid.

UNDERGRADUATE FINANCIAL AID (Fall 2006, est.) 3,153 applied for aid; of those 80% were deemed to have need. 100% of undergraduates with need received aid; of those 18% had need fully met. ***Average percent of need met:*** 76% (excluding resources awarded to replace EFC). ***Average financial aid package:*** $16,739 (excluding resources awarded to replace EFC). 33% of all full-time undergraduates had no need and received non-need-based gift aid.

GIFT AID (NEED-BASED) ***Total amount:*** $10,390,544 (31% federal, 63% state, 6% institutional). ***Receiving aid:*** Freshmen: 21% (203); All full-time undergraduates: 34% (1,425). ***Average award:*** Freshmen: $11,245; Undergraduates: $7515. ***Scholarships, grants, and awards:*** Federal Pell, FSEOG, state, private, college/university gift aid from institutional funds, Federal Nursing.

GIFT AID (NON-NEED-BASED) ***Total amount:*** $20,738,999 (96% institutional, 4% external sources). ***Receiving aid:*** Freshmen: 56% (535); Undergraduates: 54% (2,255). ***Average award:*** Freshmen: $6553; Undergraduates: $5526. ***Scholarships, grants, and awards by category:*** *Academic Interests/Achievement:* 3,943 awards ($23,416,050 total): business, communication, computer science, education, general academic interests/achievements, health fields, humanities, international studies, mathematics, social sciences. *Special Achievements/Activities:* 5 awards ($5000 total): leadership. *Special Characteristics:* 223 awards ($674,682 total): adult students, children and siblings of alumni, children of faculty/staff, children of public servants, first-generation college students, general special characteristics, international students, local/state students, members of minority groups, out-of-state students, previous college experience, veterans. ***Tuition waivers:*** Full or partial for employees or children of employees, senior citizens. ***ROTC:*** Air Force cooperative.

LOANS ***Student loans:*** $31,756,343 (33% need-based, 67% non-need-based). 76% of past graduating class borrowed through all loan programs. *Average indebtedness per student:* $53,092. ***Average need-based loan:*** Freshmen: $3243; Undergraduates: $4631. ***Parent loans:*** $7,100,554 (100% non-need-based). ***Programs:*** Federal Direct (Subsidized and Unsubsidized Stafford, PLUS), FFEL (PLUS), Perkins, state, college/university, alternative/private loans.

WORK-STUDY ***Federal work-study:*** Total amount: $450,000; 549 jobs averaging $1200.

ATHLETIC AWARDS Total amount: $2,871,330 (100% non-need-based).

APPLYING FOR FINANCIAL AID ***Required financial aid form:*** FAFSA. ***Financial aid deadline:*** Continuous. ***Notification date:*** Continuous beginning 2/1. Students must reply within 2 weeks of notification.

CONTACT Ms. Claire Alasio, Associate Vice President for Enrollment Management, Monmouth University, 400 Cedar Avenue, West Long Branch, NJ 07764-1898, 732-571-3463 or toll-free 800-543-9671. *Fax:* 732-923-4791. *E-mail:* finaid@monmouth.edu.

MONROE COLLEGE

Bronx, NY

Tuition & fees: $10,200 **Average undergraduate aid package: $9832**

ABOUT THE INSTITUTION Proprietary, coed. Awards: associate, bachelor's, and master's degrees. 8 undergraduate majors. Total enrollment: 4,361. Undergraduates: 4,253. Freshmen: 864. Federal methodology is used as a basis for awarding need-based institutional aid.

UNDERGRADUATE EXPENSES for 2006–07 ***Application fee:*** $35. ***Comprehensive fee:*** $20,320 includes full-time tuition ($9600), mandatory fees ($600), and room and board ($10,120). Room and board charges vary according to board plan. ***Part-time tuition:*** $400 per credit hour. ***Part-time fees:*** $150 per term. ***Payment plan:*** Installment.

FRESHMAN FINANCIAL AID (Fall 2005) 771 applied for aid; of those 97% were deemed to have need. 100% of freshmen with need received aid; of those 31% had need fully met. ***Average percent of need met:*** 92% (excluding resources awarded to replace EFC). ***Average financial aid package:*** $9905 (excluding resources awarded to replace EFC).

UNDERGRADUATE FINANCIAL AID (Fall 2005) 3,269 applied for aid; of those 96% were deemed to have need. 100% of undergraduates with need received aid; of those 37% had need fully met. ***Average percent of need met:*** 91% (excluding resources awarded to replace EFC). ***Average financial aid package:*** $9832 (excluding resources awarded to replace EFC).

GIFT AID (NEED-BASED) ***Total amount:*** $35,180,668 (46% federal, 48% state, 6% institutional). ***Receiving aid:*** Freshmen: 78% (605); All full-time undergraduates: 78% (2,569). ***Average award:*** Freshmen: $6300; Undergraduates: $6237. ***Scholarships, grants, and awards:*** Federal Pell, FSEOG, state, private, college/university gift aid from institutional funds.

GIFT AID (NON-NEED-BASED) ***Total amount:*** $535,783 (100% external sources). ***Receiving aid:*** Freshmen: 13% (99); Undergraduates: 22% (714). ***Tuition waivers:*** Full or partial for employees or children of employees.

LOANS ***Student loans:*** $23,263,064 (100% need-based). 40% of past graduating class borrowed through all loan programs. *Average indebtedness per student:* $6240. ***Average need-based loan:*** Freshmen: $4350; Undergraduates: $4100. ***Parent loans:*** $427,264 (100% need-based). ***Programs:*** FFEL (Subsidized and Unsubsidized Stafford, PLUS), college/university.

WORK-STUDY ***Federal work-study:*** Total amount: $933,335; 234 jobs averaging $4000.

ATHLETIC AWARDS Total amount: $194,697 (100% non-need-based).

APPLYING FOR FINANCIAL AID ***Required financial aid forms:*** FAFSA, state aid form. ***Financial aid deadline:*** Continuous. ***Notification date:*** Continuous beginning 3/1.

CONTACT Howard Leslie, Dean of Student Financial Services, Monroe College, 434 Main Street, New Rochelle, NY 10468, 914-740-6864 or toll-free 800-55MONROE. *Fax:* 914-632-5794. *E-mail:* hleslie@monroecollege.edu.

MONROE COLLEGE

New Rochelle, NY

Tuition & fees: N/R **Average undergraduate aid package: $11,230**

ABOUT THE INSTITUTION Proprietary, coed. Awards: associate, bachelor's, and master's degrees. 7 undergraduate majors. Total enrollment: 1,781. Undergraduates: 1,781. Freshmen: 490. Federal methodology is used as a basis for awarding need-based institutional aid.

FRESHMAN FINANCIAL AID (Fall 2005) 405 applied for aid; of those 90% were deemed to have need. 100% of freshmen with need received aid; of those 40% had need fully met. ***Average percent of need met:*** 89% (excluding resources awarded to replace EFC). ***Average financial aid package:*** $10,480 (excluding resources awarded to replace EFC).

UNDERGRADUATE FINANCIAL AID (Fall 2005) 1,189 applied for aid; of those 89% were deemed to have need. 100% of undergraduates with need received

aid; of those 47% had need fully met. ***Average percent of need met:*** 93% (excluding resources awarded to replace EFC). ***Average financial aid package:*** $11,230 (excluding resources awarded to replace EFC).

GIFT AID (NEED-BASED) ***Total amount:*** $11,273,387 (39% federal, 37% state, 24% institutional). ***Receiving aid:*** Freshmen: 57% (266); All full-time undergraduates: 52% (758). ***Average award:*** Freshmen: $6300; Undergraduates: $6237. ***Scholarships, grants, and awards:*** Federal Pell, FSEOG, state, private, college/university gift aid from institutional funds, county scholarships.

GIFT AID (NON-NEED-BASED) ***Total amount:*** $320,071 (100% external sources). ***Receiving aid:*** Freshmen: 26% (121); Undergraduates: 25% (362).

LOANS ***Student loans:*** $10,204,346 (100% need-based). 15% of past graduating class borrowed through all loan programs. *Average indebtedness per student:* $7300. ***Average need-based loan:*** Freshmen: $4350; Undergraduates: $4100. ***Parent loans:*** $1,887,894 (100% need-based). ***Programs:*** FFEL (Subsidized and Unsubsidized Stafford, PLUS), college/university.

WORK-STUDY ***Federal work-study:*** Total amount: $334,307; 69 jobs averaging $4845.

ATHLETIC AWARDS Total amount: $46,921 (100% non-need-based).

APPLYING FOR FINANCIAL AID ***Required financial aid forms:*** FAFSA, state aid form. ***Financial aid deadline:*** Continuous. ***Notification date:*** Continuous beginning 3/1.

CONTACT Ms. Erdene Kims, Director of Financial Aid Compliance, Monroe College, Monroe College Way, Bronx, NY 10468, 718-933-6700 or toll-free 800-55MONROE. *E-mail:* ekims@monroecoll.edu.

MONTANA STATE UNIVERSITY

Bozeman, MT

Tuition & fees (MT res): $5673 **Average undergraduate aid package: $7444**

ABOUT THE INSTITUTION State-supported, coed. Awards: bachelor's, master's, and doctoral degrees and post-master's certificates. 55 undergraduate majors. Total enrollment: 12,338. Undergraduates: 10,832. Freshmen: 2,216. Federal methodology is used as a basis for awarding need-based institutional aid.

UNDERGRADUATE EXPENSES for 2006–07 ***Application fee:*** $30. ***Tuition, state resident:*** full-time $5673. ***Tuition, nonresident:*** full-time $15,522. Full-time tuition and fees vary according to course load. Part-time tuition and fees vary according to course load. ***College room and board:*** $6450. Room and board charges vary according to board plan and housing facility. ***Payment plans:*** Installment, deferred payment.

FRESHMAN FINANCIAL AID (Fall 2005) 1791 applied for aid; of those 59% were deemed to have need. 96% of freshmen with need received aid; of those 12% had need fully met. ***Average percent of need met:*** 52% (excluding resources awarded to replace EFC). ***Average financial aid package:*** $6808 (excluding resources awarded to replace EFC). 9% of all full-time freshmen had no need and received non-need-based gift aid.

UNDERGRADUATE FINANCIAL AID (Fall 2005) 7,413 applied for aid; of those 66% were deemed to have need. 97% of undergraduates with need received aid; of those 11% had need fully met. ***Average percent of need met:*** 61% (excluding resources awarded to replace EFC). ***Average financial aid package:*** $7444 (excluding resources awarded to replace EFC). 6% of all full-time undergraduates had no need and received non-need-based gift aid.

GIFT AID (NEED-BASED) ***Total amount:*** $13,943,199 (59% federal, 6% state, 16% institutional, 19% external sources). ***Receiving aid:*** Freshmen: 36% (759); All full-time undergraduates: 36% (3,388). ***Average award:*** Freshmen: $4052; Undergraduates: $4214. ***Scholarships, grants, and awards:*** Federal Pell, FSEOG, state, private, college/university gift aid from institutional funds, Federal Nursing.

GIFT AID (NON-NEED-BASED) ***Total amount:*** $5,466,770 (100% external sources). ***Receiving aid:*** Freshmen: 17% (351); Undergraduates: 10% (938). ***Average award:*** Freshmen: $2217; Undergraduates: $4911. ***Scholarships, grants, and awards by category:*** *Academic Interests/Achievement:* agriculture, architecture, area/ethnic studies, biological sciences, business, communication, computer science, education, engineering/technologies, English, foreign languages, general academic interests/achievements, health fields, home economics, humanities, mathematics, military science, physical sciences, social sciences. *Creative Arts/Performance:* art/fine arts, cinema/film/broadcasting, dance, music, theater/drama. *Special Achievements/Activities:* general special achievements/activities. *Special Characteristics:* general special characteristics. ***Tuition waivers:*** Full or partial for minority students, employees or children of employees, senior citizens. ***ROTC:*** Army, Air Force.

LOANS ***Student loans:*** $34,505,179 (57% need-based, 43% non-need-based). 65% of past graduating class borrowed through all loan programs. *Average indebtedness per student:* $18,081. ***Average need-based loan:*** Freshmen: $3293; Undergraduates: $4292. ***Parent loans:*** $10,282,774 (18% need-based, 82% non-need-based). ***Programs:*** Federal Direct (Subsidized and Unsubsidized Stafford, PLUS), Perkins, Federal Nursing, college/university.

WORK-STUDY ***Federal work-study:*** Total amount: $446,604; 353 jobs averaging $1781. ***State or other work-study/employment:*** Total amount: $339,847 (100% need-based). 282 part-time jobs averaging $1792.

ATHLETIC AWARDS Total amount: $2,963,521 (87% need-based, 13% non-need-based).

APPLYING FOR FINANCIAL AID ***Required financial aid form:*** FAFSA. ***Financial aid deadline (priority):*** 3/1. ***Notification date:*** Continuous beginning 4/1. Students must reply within 3 weeks of notification.

CONTACT Brandi Payne, Director of Financial Aid Services, Montana State University, Strand Union Building, Room 135, PO Box 174160, Bozeman, MT 59717-4160, 406-994-2845 or toll-free 888-MSU-CATS. *Fax:* 406-994-6962.

MONTANA STATE UNIVERSITY–BILLINGS

Billings, MT

Tuition & fees (MT res): $5055 **Average undergraduate aid package: $9363**

ABOUT THE INSTITUTION State-supported, coed. Awards: associate, bachelor's, and master's degrees and post-bachelor's and post-master's certificates. 75 undergraduate majors. Total enrollment: 4,799. Undergraduates: 4,312. Freshmen: 759. Federal methodology is used as a basis for awarding need-based institutional aid.

UNDERGRADUATE EXPENSES for 2006–07 ***Application fee:*** $30. ***Tuition, state resident:*** full-time $3951; part-time $141 per credit hour. ***Tuition, nonresident:*** full-time $13,305; part-time $371 per credit hour. Full-time tuition and fees vary according to course load, degree level, and location. Part-time tuition and fees vary according to course load, degree level, and location. ***College room and board:*** $4310. Room and board charges vary according to board plan and housing facility. ***Payment plan:*** Installment.

FRESHMAN FINANCIAL AID (Fall 2005) 676 applied for aid; of those 87% were deemed to have need. 89% of freshmen with need received aid; of those 19% had need fully met. ***Average percent of need met:*** 51% (excluding resources awarded to replace EFC). ***Average financial aid package:*** $7208 (excluding resources awarded to replace EFC). 5% of all full-time freshmen had no need and received non-need-based gift aid.

UNDERGRADUATE FINANCIAL AID (Fall 2005) 2,791 applied for aid; of those 97% were deemed to have need. 85% of undergraduates with need received aid; of those 30% had need fully met. ***Average percent of need met:*** 65% (excluding resources awarded to replace EFC). ***Average financial aid package:*** $9363 (excluding resources awarded to replace EFC). 4% of all full-time undergraduates had no need and received non-need-based gift aid.

GIFT AID (NEED-BASED) ***Total amount:*** $6,181,192 (78% federal, 5% state, 11% institutional, 6% external sources). ***Receiving aid:*** Freshmen: 59% (451); All full-time undergraduates: 64% (2,066). ***Average award:*** Freshmen: $4436; Undergraduates: $2707. ***Scholarships, grants, and awards:*** Federal Pell, FSEOG, state, private, college/university gift aid from institutional funds.

GIFT AID (NON-NEED-BASED) ***Total amount:*** $379,286 (73% institutional, 27% external sources). ***Receiving aid:*** Freshmen: 33% (249); Undergraduates: 34% (1,091). ***Average award:*** Freshmen: $4206; Undergraduates: $9609. ***Scholarships, grants, and awards by category:*** *Academic Interests/Achievement:* biological sciences, business, communication, computer science, education, engineering/technologies, English, general academic interests/achievements, health fields, humanities, mathematics, physical sciences, premedicine, social sciences. *Creative Arts/Performance:* art/fine arts, music, theater/drama. *Special Achievements/Activities:* cheerleading/drum major, general special achievements/activities. *Special Characteristics:* adult students, children and siblings of alumni, children of faculty/staff, children of union members/company employees, ethnic background, first-generation college students, local/state students, members of minority groups, out-of-state students, veterans. ***Tuition waivers:*** Full or partial for minority students, employees or children of employees, senior citizens.

LOANS ***Student loans:*** $17,177,372 (54% need-based, 46% non-need-based). 70% of past graduating class borrowed through all loan programs. *Average indebtedness per student:* $15,461. ***Average need-based loan:*** Freshmen: $3189;

Undergraduates: $3025. ***Parent loans:*** $1,345,713 (100% non-need-based). ***Programs:*** FFEL (Subsidized and Unsubsidized Stafford, PLUS), Perkins, college/university.

WORK-STUDY ***Federal work-study:*** Total amount: $183,245; 141 jobs averaging $1299. ***State or other work-study/employment:*** Total amount: $147,379 (100% need-based). 105 part-time jobs averaging $1404.

ATHLETIC AWARDS Total amount: $862,793 (97% need-based, 3% non-need-based).

APPLYING FOR FINANCIAL AID ***Required financial aid form:*** FAFSA. ***Financial aid deadline (priority):*** 3/1. ***Notification date:*** Continuous beginning 4/1. Students must reply within 3 weeks of notification.

CONTACT Judy Chapman, Director of Financial Aid, Montana State University–Billings, 1500 University Drive, Billings, MT 59101, 406-657-2188 or toll-free 800-565-6782. *Fax:* 406-657-1789. *E-mail:* jchapman@msubillings.edu.

MONTANA STATE UNIVERSITY–NORTHERN

Havre, MT

CONTACT Kris Dramstad, Director of Financial Aid, Montana State University–Northern, PO Box 7751, Havre, MT 59501, 406-265-3787 or toll-free 800-662-6132 (in-state).

MONTANA TECH OF THE UNIVERSITY OF MONTANA

Butte, MT

Tuition & fees (MT res): $5605 **Average undergraduate aid package: $7000**

ABOUT THE INSTITUTION State-supported, coed. Awards: associate, bachelor's, and master's degrees and post-bachelor's certificates. 53 undergraduate majors. Total enrollment: 2,951. Undergraduates: 2,850. Freshmen: 463. Federal methodology is used as a basis for awarding need-based institutional aid.

UNDERGRADUATE EXPENSES for 2006–07 ***Application fee:*** $30. ***Tuition, state resident:*** full-time $5605; part-time $270 per credit hour. ***Tuition, nonresident:*** full-time $14,766; part-time $651 per credit hour. ***Required fees:*** $50 per credit or $58 per credit. Full-time tuition and fees vary according to course level, course load, and degree level. Part-time tuition and fees vary according to course level, course load, and degree level. ***College room and board:*** $5594; ***Room only:*** $2410. Room and board charges vary according to board plan. ***Payment plans:*** Installment, deferred payment.

FRESHMAN FINANCIAL AID (Fall 2006, est.) 200 applied for aid; of those 75% were deemed to have need. 93% of freshmen with need received aid; of those 50% had need fully met. ***Average percent of need met:*** 65% (excluding resources awarded to replace EFC). ***Average financial aid package:*** $5000 (excluding resources awarded to replace EFC). 9% of all full-time freshmen had no need and received non-need-based gift aid.

UNDERGRADUATE FINANCIAL AID (Fall 2006, est.) 1,500 applied for aid; of those 87% were deemed to have need. 92% of undergraduates with need received aid; of those 58% had need fully met. ***Average percent of need met:*** 70% (excluding resources awarded to replace EFC). ***Average financial aid package:*** $7000 (excluding resources awarded to replace EFC). 5% of all full-time undergraduates had no need and received non-need-based gift aid.

GIFT AID (NEED-BASED) ***Total amount:*** $2,584,155 (88% federal, 6% state, 4% institutional, 2% external sources). ***Receiving aid:*** Freshmen: 29% (100); All full-time undergraduates: 47% (900). ***Average award:*** Freshmen: $1000; Undergraduates: $1000. ***Scholarships, grants, and awards:*** Federal Pell, FSEOG, state, private, college/university gift aid from institutional funds.

GIFT AID (NON-NEED-BASED) ***Total amount:*** $1,250,000 (68% institutional, 32% external sources). ***Receiving aid:*** Freshmen: 9% (30); Undergraduates: 5% (100). ***Average award:*** Freshmen: $2500; Undergraduates: $4000. ***Scholarships, grants, and awards by category:*** *Academic Interests/Achievement:* 350 awards ($600,000 total): business, computer science, engineering/technologies, general academic interests/achievements, health fields, mathematics, physical sciences. *Special Achievements/Activities:* $50,000 total: general special achievements/activities. *Special Characteristics:* $50,000 total: general special characteristics. ***Tuition waivers:*** Full or partial for employees or children of employees. ***ROTC:*** Army.

LOANS ***Student loans:*** $6,100,000 (54% need-based, 46% non-need-based). 75% of past graduating class borrowed through all loan programs. *Average indebtedness per student:* $20,000. ***Average need-based loan:*** Freshmen: $2500; Undergraduates: $5000. ***Parent loans:*** $575,000 (100% need-based). ***Programs:*** FFEL (Subsidized and Unsubsidized Stafford, PLUS), Perkins, college/university.

WORK-STUDY ***Federal work-study:*** Total amount: $150,000; 100 jobs averaging $2000. ***State or other work-study/employment:*** Total amount: $15,000 (100% need-based). 25 part-time jobs averaging $2000.

ATHLETIC AWARDS Total amount: $650,000 (100% non-need-based).

APPLYING FOR FINANCIAL AID ***Required financial aid forms:*** FAFSA, institution's own form. ***Financial aid deadline (priority):*** 3/1. ***Notification date:*** Continuous beginning 3/15. Students must reply within 3 weeks of notification.

CONTACT Mike Richardson, Director of Financial Aid, Montana Tech of The University of Montana, West Park Street, Butte, MT 59701-8997, 406-496-4212 or toll-free 800-445-TECH Ext. 1. *Fax:* 406-496-4705.

MONTCLAIR STATE UNIVERSITY

Montclair, NJ

Tuition & fees (NJ res): $8404 **Average undergraduate aid package: $7465**

ABOUT THE INSTITUTION State-supported, coed. Awards: bachelor's, master's, and doctoral degrees and post-bachelor's and post-master's certificates. 46 undergraduate majors. Total enrollment: 16,076. Undergraduates: 12,365. Freshmen: 2,043. Federal methodology is used as a basis for awarding need-based institutional aid.

UNDERGRADUATE EXPENSES for 2006–07 ***Application fee:*** $55. ***Tuition, state resident:*** full-time $6028; part-time $200.92 per credit. ***Tuition, nonresident:*** full-time $11,382; part-time $379.34 per credit. ***Required fees:*** full-time $2376; $77.66 per credit or $23 per term part-time. ***College room and board:*** $8988; ***Room only:*** $5998. Room and board charges vary according to board plan and housing facility. ***Payment plan:*** Installment.

FRESHMAN FINANCIAL AID (Fall 2006, est.) 1280 applied for aid; of those 73% were deemed to have need. 91% of freshmen with need received aid; of those 39% had need fully met. ***Average percent of need met:*** 63% (excluding resources awarded to replace EFC). ***Average financial aid package:*** $5982 (excluding resources awarded to replace EFC). 2% of all full-time freshmen had no need and received non-need-based gift aid.

UNDERGRADUATE FINANCIAL AID (Fall 2006, est.) 6,469 applied for aid; of those 82% were deemed to have need. 95% of undergraduates with need received aid; of those 38% had need fully met. ***Average percent of need met:*** 64% (excluding resources awarded to replace EFC). ***Average financial aid package:*** $7465 (excluding resources awarded to replace EFC). 3% of all full-time undergraduates had no need and received non-need-based gift aid.

GIFT AID (NEED-BASED) ***Total amount:*** $20,885,753 (45% federal, 55% state). ***Receiving aid:*** Freshmen: 19% (381); All full-time undergraduates: 27% (2,750). ***Average award:*** Freshmen: $6851; Undergraduates: $6560. ***Scholarships, grants, and awards:*** Federal Pell, FSEOG, state, college/university gift aid from institutional funds.

GIFT AID (NON-NEED-BASED) ***Total amount:*** $5,267,317 (17% state, 68% institutional, 15% external sources). ***Receiving aid:*** Freshmen: 5% (103); Undergraduates: 5% (475). ***Average award:*** Freshmen: $5403; Undergraduates: $4531. ***Scholarships, grants, and awards by category:*** *Academic Interests/Achievement:* 982 awards ($3,165,232 total): biological sciences, business, communication, education, English, foreign languages, general academic interests/achievements, home economics, humanities, international studies, mathematics, physical sciences, religion/biblical studies, social sciences. *Creative Arts/Performance:* 69 awards ($87,682 total): art/fine arts, cinema/film/broadcasting, dance, music, performing arts, theater/drama. *Special Achievements/Activities:* 138 awards ($417,751 total): community service, general special achievements/activities, leadership. *Special Characteristics:* 6 awards ($71,648 total): children and siblings of alumni, international students. ***Tuition waivers:*** Full or partial for employees or children of employees, senior citizens. ***ROTC:*** Air Force cooperative.

LOANS ***Student loans:*** $33,240,404 (61% need-based, 39% non-need-based). ***Average need-based loan:*** Freshmen: $2690; Undergraduates: $3971. ***Parent loans:*** $6,469,250 (100% non-need-based). ***Programs:*** FFEL (Subsidized and Unsubsidized Stafford, PLUS), Perkins, state, private educational loans.

WORK-STUDY ***Federal work-study:*** Total amount: $377,756; 414 jobs averaging $913. ***State or other work-study/employment:*** Total amount: $1,567,755 (100% non-need-based). 1,249 part-time jobs averaging $1256.

APPLYING FOR FINANCIAL AID ***Required financial aid form:*** FAFSA. ***Financial aid deadline (priority):*** 3/1. ***Notification date:*** Continuous beginning 4/1. Students must reply within 2 weeks of notification.

CONTACT Frank A. Cuozzo, Director of Financial Aid, Montclair State University, College Hall, Room 222, Upper Montclair, NJ 07043, 973-655-7022 or toll-free 800-331-9205. *Fax:* 973-655-7712. *E-mail:* cuozzof@mail.montclair.edu.

MONTREAT COLLEGE

Montreat, NC

Tuition & fees: $16,182 **Average undergraduate aid package: $14,051**

ABOUT THE INSTITUTION Independent religious, coed. Awards: associate, bachelor's, and master's degrees. 14 undergraduate majors. Total enrollment: 1,039. Undergraduates: 959. Freshmen: 236. Federal methodology is used as a basis for awarding need-based institutional aid.

UNDERGRADUATE EXPENSES for 2006–07 ***Application fee:*** $30. ***Comprehensive fee:*** $21,440 includes full-time tuition ($16,182) and room and board ($5258). Room and board charges vary according to board plan. ***Part-time tuition:*** $480 per credit hour. ***Payment plan:*** Installment.

FRESHMAN FINANCIAL AID (Fall 2006, est.) 130 applied for aid; of those 57% were deemed to have need. 100% of freshmen with need received aid. ***Average percent of need met:*** 84% (excluding resources awarded to replace EFC). ***Average financial aid package:*** $14,051 (excluding resources awarded to replace EFC). 100% of all full-time freshmen had no need and received non-need-based gift aid.

UNDERGRADUATE FINANCIAL AID (Fall 2006, est.) 427 applied for aid; of those 59% were deemed to have need. 100% of undergraduates with need received aid. ***Average percent of need met:*** 81% (excluding resources awarded to replace EFC). ***Average financial aid package:*** $14,051 (excluding resources awarded to replace EFC). 100% of all full-time undergraduates had no need and received non-need-based gift aid.

GIFT AID (NEED-BASED) ***Total amount:*** $4,215,588 (33% federal, 17% state, 43% institutional, 7% external sources). ***Receiving aid:*** Freshmen: 55% (74); All full-time undergraduates: 55% (252). ***Average award:*** Freshmen: $5310; Undergraduates: $5310. ***Scholarships, grants, and awards:*** Federal Pell, FSEOG, state, private, college/university gift aid from institutional funds.

GIFT AID (NON-NEED-BASED) ***Total amount:*** $451,250 (100% state). ***Receiving aid:*** Freshmen: 53% (71); Undergraduates: 54% (247). ***Average award:*** Freshmen: $5276; Undergraduates: $5276. ***Scholarships, grants, and awards by category:*** *Academic Interests/Achievement:* general academic interests/achievements. *Creative Arts/Performance:* art/fine arts, music, theater/drama. *Special Achievements/Activities:* leadership. *Special Characteristics:* 10 awards ($91,435 total): children of faculty/staff, first-generation college students, international students. ***Tuition waivers:*** Full or partial for employees or children of employees.

LOANS ***Student loans:*** $1,495,743 (68% need-based, 32% non-need-based). 73% of past graduating class borrowed through all loan programs. *Average indebtedness per student:* $17,682. ***Average need-based loan:*** Freshmen: $3071; Undergraduates: $3071. ***Parent loans:*** $559,760 (100% non-need-based). ***Programs:*** FFEL (Subsidized and Unsubsidized Stafford, PLUS), Perkins.

WORK-STUDY ***Federal work-study:*** Total amount: $108,718; 76 jobs averaging $1431. ***State or other work-study/employment:*** Total amount: $53,120 (100% non-need-based). 35 part-time jobs averaging $1518.

ATHLETIC AWARDS Total amount: $475,666 (100% non-need-based).

APPLYING FOR FINANCIAL AID ***Required financial aid form:*** FAFSA. ***Financial aid deadline (priority):*** 4/1. ***Notification date:*** Continuous beginning 4/1. Students must reply within 2 weeks of notification.

CONTACT Financial Aid Office, Montreat College, PO Box 1267, Montreat, NC 28757, 828-669-8012 Ext. 3790 or toll-free 800-622-6968 (in-state). *Fax:* 828-669-0120. *E-mail:* financialaid@montreat.edu.

MONTSERRAT COLLEGE OF ART

Beverly, MA

ABOUT THE INSTITUTION Independent, coed. Awards: bachelor's degrees and post-bachelor's certificates. 10 undergraduate majors. Total enrollment: 308. Undergraduates: 308. Freshmen: 75.

GIFT AID (NEED-BASED) ***Scholarships, grants, and awards:*** Federal Pell, FSEOG, state, private, college/university gift aid from institutional funds.

GIFT AID (NON-NEED-BASED) ***Scholarships, grants, and awards by category:*** *Creative Arts/Performance:* applied art and design, art/fine arts. *Special Characteristics:* siblings of current students.

LOANS ***Programs:*** FFEL (Subsidized and Unsubsidized Stafford, PLUS), state, alternative loans.

WORK-STUDY ***Federal work-study:*** Total amount: $96,097; 65 jobs averaging $847.

APPLYING FOR FINANCIAL AID ***Required financial aid form:*** FAFSA.

CONTACT Creda Carney, Director of Financial Aid, Montserrat College of Art, 23 Essex Street, PO Box 26, Beverly, MA 01915, 978-922-8222 Ext. 1155 or toll-free 800-836-0487. *Fax:* 978-922-4268. *E-mail:* finaid@montserrat.edu.

MOODY BIBLE INSTITUTE

Chicago, IL

CONTACT Daniel R. Ward, Director of Financial Aid, Moody Bible Institute, 820 North LaSalle Boulevard, Chicago, IL 60610-3284, 312-329-4178 or toll-free 800-967-4MBI. *Fax:* 312-329-4197. *E-mail:* daniel.ward@moody.edu.

MOORE COLLEGE OF ART & DESIGN

Philadelphia, PA

Tuition & fees: $26,154 **Average undergraduate aid package: $14,823**

ABOUT THE INSTITUTION Independent, women only. Awards: bachelor's degrees and post-bachelor's certificates. 10 undergraduate majors. Total enrollment: 542. Undergraduates: 507. Freshmen: 119. Federal methodology is used as a basis for awarding need-based institutional aid.

UNDERGRADUATE EXPENSES for 2007–08 ***Application fee:*** $40. ***Comprehensive fee:*** $36,060 includes full-time tuition ($25,290), mandatory fees ($864), and room and board ($9906). ***College room only:*** $5964. ***Part-time tuition:*** $1054 per credit. ***Part-time fees:*** $355 per term.

FRESHMAN FINANCIAL AID (Fall 2006, est.) 110 applied for aid; of those 95% were deemed to have need. 100% of freshmen with need received aid; of those 2% had need fully met. ***Average percent of need met:*** 42% (excluding resources awarded to replace EFC). ***Average financial aid package:*** $14,091 (excluding resources awarded to replace EFC). 21% of all full-time freshmen had no need and received non-need-based gift aid.

UNDERGRADUATE FINANCIAL AID (Fall 2006, est.) 383 applied for aid; of those 93% were deemed to have need. 100% of undergraduates with need received aid; of those 3% had need fully met. ***Average percent of need met:*** 45% (excluding resources awarded to replace EFC). ***Average financial aid package:*** $14,823 (excluding resources awarded to replace EFC). 20% of all full-time undergraduates had no need and received non-need-based gift aid.

GIFT AID (NEED-BASED) ***Total amount:*** $4,074,111 (19% federal, 14% state, 60% institutional, 7% external sources). ***Receiving aid:*** Freshmen: 78% (103); All full-time undergraduates: 78% (354). ***Average award:*** Freshmen: $10,745; Undergraduates: $10,180. ***Scholarships, grants, and awards:*** Federal Pell, FSEOG, state, private, college/university gift aid from institutional funds.

GIFT AID (NON-NEED-BASED) ***Total amount:*** $564,449 (94% institutional, 6% external sources). ***Receiving aid:*** Freshmen: 2% (2); Undergraduates: 2% (7). ***Average award:*** Freshmen: $7575; Undergraduates: $9729. ***Scholarships, grants, and awards by category:*** *Academic Interests/Achievement:* 522 awards ($2,377,916 total): general academic interests/achievements. *Special Achievements/Activities:* 37 awards ($143,000 total): leadership.

LOANS ***Student loans:*** $5,214,945 (86% need-based, 14% non-need-based). 75% of past graduating class borrowed through all loan programs. *Average indebtedness per student:* $36,778. ***Average need-based loan:*** Freshmen: $3018; Undergraduates: $4355. ***Parent loans:*** $2,215,701 (62% need-based, 38% non-need-based). ***Programs:*** FFEL (Subsidized and Unsubsidized Stafford, PLUS), Perkins.

WORK-STUDY ***Federal work-study:*** Total amount: $112,449; 87 jobs averaging $1500. ***State or other work-study/employment:*** Part-time jobs available.

APPLYING FOR FINANCIAL AID ***Required financial aid form:*** FAFSA. ***Financial aid deadline (priority):*** 3/1. ***Notification date:*** Continuous beginning 2/15. Students must reply within 2 weeks of notification.

CONTACT Rochelle Iannuzzi, Director of Financial Aid, Moore College of Art & Design, 20th and the Parkway, Philadelphia, PA 19103-1179, 215-965-4042 or toll-free 800-523-2025. *Fax:* 215-568-1773. *E-mail:* riannuzzi@moore.edu.

MORAVIAN COLLEGE

Bethlehem, PA

Tuition & fees: $26,775 **Average undergraduate aid package: $18,154**

ABOUT THE INSTITUTION Independent religious, coed. Awards: bachelor's, master's, and first professional degrees and post-bachelor's certificates. 61 undergraduate majors. Total enrollment: 1,965. Undergraduates: 1,764. Freshmen: 375. Both federal and institutional methodology are used as a basis for awarding need-based institutional aid.

UNDERGRADUATE EXPENSES for 2006–07 ***Application fee:*** $40. ***Comprehensive fee:*** $34,535 includes full-time tuition ($26,300), mandatory fees ($475), and room and board ($7760). ***College room only:*** $4360. Room and board charges vary according to board plan and housing facility. ***Part-time tuition:*** $822 per credit hour. Part-time tuition and fees vary according to class time. ***Payment plan:*** Installment.

FRESHMAN FINANCIAL AID (Fall 2006, est.) 329 applied for aid; of those 84% were deemed to have need. 100% of freshmen with need received aid; of those 18% had need fully met. ***Average percent of need met:*** 81% (excluding resources awarded to replace EFC). ***Average financial aid package:*** $18,668 (excluding resources awarded to replace EFC). 21% of all full-time freshmen had no need and received non-need-based gift aid.

UNDERGRADUATE FINANCIAL AID (Fall 2006, est.) 1,256 applied for aid; of those 89% were deemed to have need. 100% of undergraduates with need received aid; of those 19% had need fully met. ***Average percent of need met:*** 75% (excluding resources awarded to replace EFC). ***Average financial aid package:*** $18,154 (excluding resources awarded to replace EFC). 21% of all full-time undergraduates had no need and received non-need-based gift aid.

GIFT AID (NEED-BASED) ***Total amount:*** $14,245,294 (7% federal, 12% state, 78% institutional, 3% external sources). ***Receiving aid:*** Freshmen: 74% (276); All full-time undergraduates: 74% (1,104). ***Average award:*** Freshmen: $14,066; Undergraduates: $13,070. ***Scholarships, grants, and awards:*** Federal Pell, FSEOG, state, private, college/university gift aid from institutional funds.

GIFT AID (NON-NEED-BASED) ***Total amount:*** $2,872,274 (2% federal, 89% institutional, 9% external sources). ***Receiving aid:*** Freshmen: 8% (29); Undergraduates: 7% (102). ***Average award:*** Freshmen: $11,686; Undergraduates: $13,068. ***Scholarships, grants, and awards by category:*** *Academic Interests/Achievement:* 1,359 awards ($3,644,123 total): biological sciences, business, computer science, foreign languages, general academic interests/achievements, health fields, mathematics, physical sciences. *Creative Arts/Performance:* 18 awards ($45,000 total): music. *Special Achievements/Activities:* 44 awards ($90,400 total): leadership, religious involvement. *Special Characteristics:* 224 awards ($942,622 total): adult students, children and siblings of alumni, children of educators, children of faculty/staff, ethnic background, international students, relatives of clergy, religious affiliation. ***Tuition waivers:*** Full or partial for children of alumni, employees or children of employees. ***ROTC:*** Army cooperative.

LOANS ***Student loans:*** $10,919,579 (64% need-based, 36% non-need-based). ***Average need-based loan:*** Freshmen: $3409; Undergraduates: $4288. ***Parent loans:*** $4,320,866 (34% need-based, 66% non-need-based). ***Programs:*** FFEL (Subsidized and Unsubsidized Stafford, PLUS), Perkins.

WORK-STUDY ***Federal work-study:*** Total amount: $1,400,000; 905 jobs averaging $1464. ***State or other work-study/employment:*** Total amount: $279,750 (2% need-based, 98% non-need-based). 269 part-time jobs averaging $1092.

APPLYING FOR FINANCIAL AID ***Required financial aid forms:*** FAFSA, CSS Financial Aid PROFILE, state aid form, noncustodial (divorced/separated) parent's statement, business/farm supplement. ***Financial aid deadline (priority):*** 2/14. ***Notification date:*** 3/31. Students must reply by 5/1 or within 2 weeks of notification.

CONTACT Mr. Stephen C. Cassel, Director of Financial Aid, Moravian College, 1200 Main Street, Bethlehem, PA 18018-6650, 610-861-1330 or toll-free 800-441-3191. *Fax:* 610-861-1346. *E-mail:* cassels@moravian.edu.

MOREHEAD STATE UNIVERSITY

Morehead, KY

Tuition & fees (KY res): $4870 **Average undergraduate aid package: $8141**

ABOUT THE INSTITUTION State-supported, coed. Awards: associate, bachelor's, and master's degrees and post-master's certificates. 49 undergraduate majors. Total enrollment: 9,025. Undergraduates: 7,512. Freshmen: 1,306. Federal methodology is used as a basis for awarding need-based institutional aid.

UNDERGRADUATE EXPENSES for 2006–07 ***Tuition, state resident:*** full-time $4870; part-time $205 per credit hour. ***Tuition, nonresident:*** full-time $12,950; part-time $540 per credit hour. Full-time tuition and fees vary according to course load and reciprocity agreements. ***College room and board:*** $5208. Room and board charges vary according to board plan and housing facility. ***Payment plans:*** Installment, deferred payment.

FRESHMAN FINANCIAL AID (Fall 2006, est.) 1101 applied for aid; of those 79% were deemed to have need. 99% of freshmen with need received aid; of those 35% had need fully met. ***Average percent of need met:*** 83% (excluding resources awarded to replace EFC). ***Average financial aid package:*** $7517 (excluding resources awarded to replace EFC). 15% of all full-time freshmen had no need and received non-need-based gift aid.

UNDERGRADUATE FINANCIAL AID (Fall 2006, est.) 4,675 applied for aid; of those 84% were deemed to have need. 99% of undergraduates with need received aid; of those 36% had need fully met. ***Average percent of need met:*** 83% (excluding resources awarded to replace EFC). ***Average financial aid package:*** $8141 (excluding resources awarded to replace EFC). 11% of all full-time undergraduates had no need and received non-need-based gift aid.

GIFT AID (NEED-BASED) ***Total amount:*** $13,540,026 (75% federal, 24% state, 1% institutional). ***Receiving aid:*** Freshmen: 43% (547); All full-time undergraduates: 48% (2,737). ***Average award:*** Freshmen: $4388; Undergraduates: $4353. ***Scholarships, grants, and awards:*** Federal Pell, FSEOG, state, private, college/university gift aid from institutional funds.

GIFT AID (NON-NEED-BASED) ***Total amount:*** $9,621,901 (41% state, 51% institutional, 8% external sources). ***Receiving aid:*** Freshmen: 56% (706); Undergraduates: 37% (2,117). ***Average award:*** Freshmen: $4476; Undergraduates: $3647. ***Scholarships, grants, and awards by category:*** *Academic Interests/Achievement:* 1,653 awards ($4,044,210 total): agriculture, biological sciences, business, communication, education, English, general academic interests/achievements, health fields, humanities, physical sciences, social sciences. *Creative Arts/Performance:* 142 awards ($213,594 total): art/fine arts, cinema/film/broadcasting, debating, journalism/publications, music, theater/drama. *Special Achievements/Activities:* 90 awards ($68,825 total): cheerleading/drum major, leadership. *Special Characteristics:* 391 awards ($438,429 total): adult students, children and siblings of alumni, local/state students, members of minority groups, out-of-state students. ***Tuition waivers:*** Full or partial for children of alumni, employees or children of employees, senior citizens. ***ROTC:*** Army.

LOANS ***Student loans:*** $20,752,947 (51% need-based, 49% non-need-based). 70% of past graduating class borrowed through all loan programs. *Average indebtedness per student:* $18,167. ***Average need-based loan:*** Freshmen: $2390; Undergraduates: $3324. ***Parent loans:*** $2,043,967 (100% non-need-based). ***Programs:*** Federal Direct (Subsidized and Unsubsidized Stafford, PLUS), FFEL (Subsidized and Unsubsidized Stafford, PLUS), Perkins, college/university.

WORK-STUDY ***Federal work-study:*** Total amount: $592,483; 438 jobs averaging $1353. ***State or other work-study/employment:*** Total amount: $1,257,389 (100% non-need-based). 701 part-time jobs averaging $1572.

ATHLETIC AWARDS Total amount: $1,141,419 (100% non-need-based).

APPLYING FOR FINANCIAL AID ***Required financial aid forms:*** FAFSA, institution's own form. ***Financial aid deadline (priority):*** 3/15. ***Notification date:*** Continuous.

CONTACT Carol Becker, Director of Financial Aid, Morehead State University, 100 Admissions Center, Morehead, KY 40351, 606-783-2011 or toll-free 800-585-6781. *Fax:* 606-783-2293. *E-mail:* c.becker@moreheadstate.edu.

MOREHOUSE COLLEGE

Atlanta, GA

CONTACT James A. Stotts, Director of Financial Aid, Morehouse College, 830 Westview Drive, SW, Atlanta, GA 30314, 404-681-2800 Ext. 2638 or toll-free 800-851-1254. *Fax:* 404-215-2711. *E-mail:* jstotts@morehouse.edu.

MORGAN STATE UNIVERSITY

Baltimore, MD

CONTACT Director of Financial Aid, Morgan State University, 1700 East Cold Spring Lane, Baltimore, MD 21251, 443-885-3170 or toll-free 800-332-6674.

MORNINGSIDE COLLEGE
Sioux City, IA

Tuition & fees: $19,902 **Average undergraduate aid package: $16,302**

ABOUT THE INSTITUTION Independent religious, coed. Awards: bachelor's and master's degrees. 43 undergraduate majors. Total enrollment: 1,722. Undergraduates: 1,232. Freshmen: 332. Federal methodology is used as a basis for awarding need-based institutional aid.

UNDERGRADUATE EXPENSES for 2006–07 ***Application fee:*** $25. ***Comprehensive fee:*** $26,129 includes full-time tuition ($18,932), mandatory fees ($970), and room and board ($6227). ***College room only:*** $3213. Full-time tuition and fees vary according to program. Room and board charges vary according to housing facility. ***Part-time tuition:*** $580 per semester hour. Part-time tuition and fees vary according to course load. ***Payment plan:*** Installment.

FRESHMAN FINANCIAL AID (Fall 2005) 301 applied for aid; of those 93% were deemed to have need. 100% of freshmen with need received aid; of those 64% had need fully met. ***Average percent of need met:*** 77% (excluding resources awarded to replace EFC). ***Average financial aid package:*** $16,962 (excluding resources awarded to replace EFC). 9% of all full-time freshmen had no need and received non-need-based gift aid.

UNDERGRADUATE FINANCIAL AID (Fall 2005) 1,012 applied for aid; of those 92% were deemed to have need. 100% of undergraduates with need received aid; of those 62% had need fully met. ***Average percent of need met:*** 77% (excluding resources awarded to replace EFC). ***Average financial aid package:*** $16,302 (excluding resources awarded to replace EFC). 12% of all full-time undergraduates had no need and received non-need-based gift aid.

GIFT AID (NEED-BASED) ***Total amount:*** $4,516,795 (30% federal, 45% state, 25% institutional). ***Receiving aid:*** Freshmen: 73% (225); All full-time undergraduates: 69% (735). ***Average award:*** Freshmen: $5939; Undergraduates: $5702. ***Scholarships, grants, and awards:*** Federal Pell, FSEOG, state, private, college/university gift aid from institutional funds.

GIFT AID (NON-NEED-BASED) ***Total amount:*** $7,436,288 (2% state, 91% institutional, 7% external sources). ***Receiving aid:*** Freshmen: 90% (279); Undergraduates: 84% (899). ***Average award:*** Freshmen: $7503; Undergraduates: $6130. ***Scholarships, grants, and awards by category:*** *Academic Interests/Achievement:* 712 awards ($2,810,469 total): general academic interests/achievements. *Creative Arts/Performance:* 268 awards ($676,925 total): art/fine arts, cinema/film/broadcasting, journalism/publications, music, theater/drama. *Special Achievements/Activities:* 299 awards ($653,809 total): cheerleading/drum major, community service, leadership. *Special Characteristics:* 1,114 awards ($1,733,089 total): children of faculty/staff, international students, out-of-state students. ***Tuition waivers:*** Full or partial for children of alumni, employees or children of employees, senior citizens. ***ROTC:*** Army cooperative.

LOANS ***Student loans:*** $8,759,072 (40% need-based, 60% non-need-based). 91% of past graduating class borrowed through all loan programs. *Average indebtedness per student:* $26,816. ***Average need-based loan:*** Freshmen: $3228; Undergraduates: $3585. ***Parent loans:*** $363,677 (100% non-need-based). ***Programs:*** FFEL (Subsidized and Unsubsidized Stafford, PLUS), Perkins, state, college/university, private loans.

WORK-STUDY ***Federal work-study:*** Total amount: $348,577; 300 jobs averaging $1161. ***State or other work-study/employment:*** Total amount: $364,680 (100% non-need-based). 1 part-time job averaging $580.

ATHLETIC AWARDS Total amount: $1,377,047 (100% non-need-based).

APPLYING FOR FINANCIAL AID ***Required financial aid form:*** FAFSA. ***Financial aid deadline (priority):*** 3/1. ***Notification date:*** 3/31.

CONTACT Karen Gagnon, Director of Student Financial Planning, Morningside College, 1501 Morningside Avenue, Sioux City, IA 51106, 712-274-5272 or toll-free 800-831-0806 Ext. 5111. *Fax:* 712-274-5605. *E-mail:* gagnon@morningside.edu.

MORRIS COLLEGE
Sumter, SC

CONTACT Ms. Sandra S. Gibson, Director of Financial Aid, Morris College, 100 West College Street, Sumter, SC 29150-3599, 803-934-3238 or toll-free 866-853-1345. *Fax:* 803-773-3687.

MORRISON UNIVERSITY
Reno, NV

CONTACT Kim Droniak, Financial Aid Administrator, Morrison University, 140 Washington Street, Reno, NV 89503-5600, 775-850-0700 or toll-free 800-369-6144. *Fax:* 775-850-0711.

MOUNTAIN STATE UNIVERSITY
Beckley, WV

Tuition & fees: $7800 **Average undergraduate aid package: $6259**

ABOUT THE INSTITUTION Independent, coed. Awards: associate, bachelor's, and master's degrees and post-master's certificates. 61 undergraduate majors. Total enrollment: 4,420. Undergraduates: 3,921. Freshmen: 421. Federal methodology is used as a basis for awarding need-based institutional aid.

UNDERGRADUATE EXPENSES for 2006–07 ***Application fee:*** $25. ***Comprehensive fee:*** $13,436 includes full-time tuition ($6000), mandatory fees ($1800), and room and board ($5636). ***College room only:*** $2810. Full-time tuition and fees vary according to program. Room and board charges vary according to board plan. ***Part-time tuition:*** $200 per credit. ***Part-time fees:*** $60 per credit. Part-time tuition and fees vary according to program. ***Payment plan:*** Installment.

FRESHMAN FINANCIAL AID (Fall 2005) 226 applied for aid; of those 88% were deemed to have need. 100% of freshmen with need received aid; of those 3% had need fully met. ***Average percent of need met:*** 36% (excluding resources awarded to replace EFC). ***Average financial aid package:*** $4844 (excluding resources awarded to replace EFC).

UNDERGRADUATE FINANCIAL AID (Fall 2005) 2,006 applied for aid; of those 95% were deemed to have need. 100% of undergraduates with need received aid; of those 4% had need fully met. ***Average percent of need met:*** 47% (excluding resources awarded to replace EFC). ***Average financial aid package:*** $6259 (excluding resources awarded to replace EFC). 1% of all full-time undergraduates had no need and received non-need-based gift aid.

GIFT AID (NEED-BASED) ***Total amount:*** $6,164,442 (83% federal, 13% state, 1% institutional, 3% external sources). ***Receiving aid:*** Freshmen: 64% (166); All full-time undergraduates: 43% (1,247). ***Average award:*** Freshmen: $3330; Undergraduates: $3520. ***Scholarships, grants, and awards:*** Federal Pell, FSEOG, state, private, college/university gift aid from institutional funds, Federal Nursing.

GIFT AID (NON-NEED-BASED) ***Total amount:*** $387,627 (55% state, 45% institutional). ***Receiving aid:*** Freshmen: 6% (15); Undergraduates: 2% (66). ***Average award:*** Undergraduates: $4283. ***Scholarships, grants, and awards by category:*** *Academic Interests/Achievement:* 36 awards ($163,485 total): general academic interests/achievements. *Special Achievements/Activities:* 7 awards ($5000 total): cheerleading/drum major. ***Tuition waivers:*** Full or partial for employees or children of employees, senior citizens.

LOANS ***Student loans:*** $22,053,592 (47% need-based, 53% non-need-based). 86% of past graduating class borrowed through all loan programs. *Average indebtedness per student:* $29,045. ***Average need-based loan:*** Freshmen: $2520; Undergraduates: $4361. ***Parent loans:*** $271,843 (100% non-need-based). ***Programs:*** FFEL (Subsidized and Unsubsidized Stafford, PLUS), private education loans.

WORK-STUDY ***Federal work-study:*** Total amount: $202,147; 151 jobs averaging $1339.

ATHLETIC AWARDS Total amount: $388,362 (100% non-need-based).

APPLYING FOR FINANCIAL AID ***Required financial aid form:*** FAFSA. ***Financial aid deadline:*** Continuous. ***Notification date:*** Continuous. Students must reply within 2 weeks of notification.

CONTACT Sandra Richmond, Director of Financial Aid, Mountain State University, PO Box 9003, Beckley, WV 25802-9003, 304-929-1595 or toll-free 800-766-6067 Ext. 1433. *Fax:* 304-929-1390. *E-mail:* srichmond@mountainstate.edu.

MOUNT ALOYSIUS COLLEGE
Cresson, PA

Tuition & fees: $15,350 **Average undergraduate aid package: $8300**

ABOUT THE INSTITUTION Independent Roman Catholic, coed. Awards: associate, bachelor's, and master's degrees. 34 undergraduate majors. Total enrollment: 1,587. Undergraduates: 1,520. Freshmen: 322. Federal methodology is used as a basis for awarding need-based institutional aid.

UNDERGRADUATE EXPENSES for 2006–07 ***Application fee:*** $30. ***Comprehensive fee:*** $21,820 includes full-time tuition ($14,800), mandatory fees ($550), and room and board ($6470). ***College room only:*** $3270. Full-time tuition and fees vary according to class time, course load, and program. Room and board charges vary according to board plan. ***Part-time tuition:*** $450 per credit. ***Part-time fees:*** $150 per term. Part-time tuition and fees vary according to class time, course load, and program. ***Payment plan:*** Installment.

FRESHMAN FINANCIAL AID (Fall 2005) 293 applied for aid; of those 84% were deemed to have need. 100% of freshmen with need received aid. ***Average percent of need met:*** 24% (excluding resources awarded to replace EFC). ***Average financial aid package:*** $10,845 (excluding resources awarded to replace EFC). 16% of all full-time freshmen had no need and received non-need-based gift aid.

UNDERGRADUATE FINANCIAL AID (Fall 2005) 1,230 applied for aid; of those 97% were deemed to have need. 100% of undergraduates with need received aid. ***Average percent of need met:*** 26% (excluding resources awarded to replace EFC). ***Average financial aid package:*** $8300 (excluding resources awarded to replace EFC). 3% of all full-time undergraduates had no need and received non-need-based gift aid.

GIFT AID (NEED-BASED) ***Total amount:*** $8,167,827 (25% federal, 35% state, 38% institutional, 2% external sources). ***Receiving aid:*** Freshmen: 84% (245); All full-time undergraduates: 97% (1,189). ***Average award:*** Freshmen: $3200; Undergraduates: $2690. ***Scholarships, grants, and awards:*** Federal Pell, FSEOG, state, private, college/university gift aid from institutional funds.

GIFT AID (NON-NEED-BASED) ***Receiving aid:*** Freshmen: 16% (48); Undergraduates: 3% (41). ***Average award:*** Freshmen: $2600; Undergraduates: $2100. ***Scholarships, grants, and awards by category:*** *Creative Arts/Performance:* 23 awards ($18,500 total): music, performing arts. *Special Achievements/Activities:* 32 awards ($241,000 total): leadership. *Special Characteristics:* 84 awards ($50,000 total): children of current students, parents of current students, religious affiliation, siblings of current students, spouses of current students, twins. ***Tuition waivers:*** Full or partial for employees or children of employees.

LOANS ***Student loans:*** $6,766,478 (100% need-based). 72% of past graduating class borrowed through all loan programs. *Average indebtedness per student:* $23,458. ***Average need-based loan:*** Freshmen: $2720; Undergraduates: $3400. ***Parent loans:*** $1,896,157 (100% need-based). ***Programs:*** FFEL (Subsidized and Unsubsidized Stafford, PLUS), Perkins, Federal Nursing, alternative loans.

WORK-STUDY ***Federal work-study:*** Total amount: $277,717; 169 jobs averaging $1640.

ATHLETIC AWARDS Total amount: $11,600 (100% need-based).

APPLYING FOR FINANCIAL AID ***Required financial aid form:*** FAFSA. ***Financial aid deadline (priority):*** 2/15. ***Notification date:*** Continuous beginning 3/15. Students must reply within 4 weeks of notification.

CONTACT Mrs. Stacy L. Schenk, Director of Financial Aid, Mount Aloysius College, 7373 Admiral Peary Highway, Cresson, PA 16630-1900, 814-886-6357 or toll-free 888-823-2220. *Fax:* 814-886-6463. *E-mail:* sschenk@mtaloy.edu.

MOUNT ANGEL SEMINARY

Saint Benedict, OR

CONTACT Dorene Preis, Director of Student Financial Aid/Registrar, Mount Angel Seminary, 1 Abbey Drive, Saint Benedict, OR 97373, 503-845-3951. *Fax:* 503-845-3126. *E-mail:* dpreis@mtangel.edu.

MOUNT CARMEL COLLEGE OF NURSING

Columbus, OH

CONTACT Carol Graham, Director of Financial Aid, Mount Carmel College of Nursing, 127 South Davis Avenue, Columbus, OH 43222, 614-234-5800 Ext. 5177. *E-mail:* cgraham@mchs.com.

MOUNT HOLYOKE COLLEGE

South Hadley, MA

Tuition & fees: $34,266 **Average undergraduate aid package: $28,464**

ABOUT THE INSTITUTION Independent, women only. Awards: bachelor's and master's degrees and post-bachelor's certificates. 47 undergraduate majors. Total enrollment: 2,153. Undergraduates: 2,149. Freshmen: 556. Both federal and institutional methodology are used as a basis for awarding need-based institutional aid.

UNDERGRADUATE EXPENSES for 2006–07 ***Application fee:*** $60. ***Comprehensive fee:*** $44,306 includes full-time tuition ($34,090), mandatory fees ($176), and room and board ($10,040). ***College room only:*** $5130. Room and board charges vary according to board plan and housing facility. ***Part-time tuition:*** $1065 per credit hour. ***Payment plans:*** Tuition prepayment, installment, deferred payment.

FRESHMAN FINANCIAL AID (Fall 2006, est.) 392 applied for aid; of those 73% were deemed to have need. 100% of freshmen with need received aid; of those 100% had need fully met. ***Average percent of need met:*** 100% (excluding resources awarded to replace EFC). ***Average financial aid package:*** $30,145 (excluding resources awarded to replace EFC). 7% of all full-time freshmen had no need and received non-need-based gift aid.

UNDERGRADUATE FINANCIAL AID (Fall 2006, est.) 1,502 applied for aid; of those 89% were deemed to have need. 100% of undergraduates with need received aid; of those 100% had need fully met. ***Average percent of need met:*** 100% (excluding resources awarded to replace EFC). ***Average financial aid package:*** $28,464 (excluding resources awarded to replace EFC). 6% of all full-time undergraduates had no need and received non-need-based gift aid.

GIFT AID (NEED-BASED) ***Total amount:*** $30,454,037 (5% federal, 1% state, 92% institutional, 2% external sources). ***Receiving aid:*** Freshmen: 51% (284); All full-time undergraduates: 57% (1,273). ***Average award:*** Freshmen: $27,034; Undergraduates: $23,948. ***Scholarships, grants, and awards:*** Federal Pell, FSEOG, state, private, college/university gift aid from institutional funds.

GIFT AID (NON-NEED-BASED) ***Total amount:*** $2,645,662 (81% institutional, 19% external sources). ***Average award:*** Freshmen: $16,951; Undergraduates: $13,632. ***Scholarships, grants, and awards by category:*** *Academic Interests/Achievement:* 144 awards ($1,963,008 total): general academic interests/achievements. *Special Characteristics:* 25 awards ($816,898 total): children of faculty/staff. ***Tuition waivers:*** Full or partial for employees or children of employees. ***ROTC:*** Army cooperative, Air Force cooperative.

LOANS ***Student loans:*** $8,420,392 (82% need-based, 18% non-need-based). 70% of past graduating class borrowed through all loan programs. *Average indebtedness per student:* $23,900. ***Average need-based loan:*** Freshmen: $2908; Undergraduates: $4529. ***Parent loans:*** $6,081,771 (100% non-need-based). ***Programs:*** Federal Direct (Subsidized and Unsubsidized Stafford, PLUS), Perkins, state, college/university.

WORK-STUDY ***Federal work-study:*** Total amount: $1,248,001; 833 jobs averaging $1580. ***State or other work-study/employment:*** Total amount: $609,412 (100% need-based). 407 part-time jobs averaging $1625.

APPLYING FOR FINANCIAL AID ***Required financial aid forms:*** FAFSA, CSS Financial Aid PROFILE, noncustodial (divorced/separated) parent's statement, business/farm supplement, federal income tax form(s), W-2 forms. ***Financial aid deadline:*** 3/1 (priority: 2/15). ***Notification date:*** 4/1. Students must reply by 5/1.

CONTACT Ms. Kathy Blaisdell, Director of Student Financial Services, Mount Holyoke College, 50 College Street, South Hadley, MA 01075-1492, 413-538-2291. *Fax:* 413-538-2512. *E-mail:* kblaisde@mtholyoke.edu.

MOUNT IDA COLLEGE

Newton, MA

Tuition & fees: $21,330 **Average undergraduate aid package: $12,066**

ABOUT THE INSTITUTION Independent, coed. Awards: associate and bachelor's degrees. 24 undergraduate majors. Total enrollment: 1,367. Undergraduates: 1,367. Freshmen: 441. Federal methodology is used as a basis for awarding need-based institutional aid.

UNDERGRADUATE EXPENSES for 2007–08 ***Application fee:*** $35. ***Comprehensive fee:*** $31,965 includes full-time tuition ($21,115), mandatory fees ($215), and room and board ($10,635). ***Part-time tuition:*** $525 per credit hour. ***Part-time fees:*** $15 per credit.

FRESHMAN FINANCIAL AID (Fall 2006, est.) 370 applied for aid; of those 88% were deemed to have need. 100% of freshmen with need received aid; of those 9% had need fully met. ***Average percent of need met:*** 53% (excluding resources awarded to replace EFC). ***Average financial aid package:*** $11,513 (excluding resources awarded to replace EFC). 40% of all full-time freshmen had no need and received non-need-based gift aid.

UNDERGRADUATE FINANCIAL AID (Fall 2006, est.) 1,067 applied for aid; of those 90% were deemed to have need. 100% of undergraduates with need received aid; of those 6% had need fully met. ***Average percent of need met:*** 51% (excluding resources awarded to replace EFC). ***Average financial aid package:*** $12,066 (excluding resources awarded to replace EFC). 24% of all full-time undergraduates had no need and received non-need-based gift aid.

GIFT AID (NEED-BASED) ***Total amount:*** $8,425,031 (17% federal, 7% state, 74% institutional, 2% external sources). ***Receiving aid:*** Freshmen: 59% (321); All full-time undergraduates: 75% (949). ***Average award:*** Freshmen: $9118; Undergraduates: $8624. ***Scholarships, grants, and awards:*** Federal Pell, FSEOG, state, private, college/university gift aid from institutional funds.

GIFT AID (NON-NEED-BASED) ***Total amount:*** $994,568 (2% state, 96% institutional, 2% external sources). ***Receiving aid:*** Freshmen: 5% (26); Undergraduates: 3% (44). ***Average award:*** Freshmen: $6303; Undergraduates: $7994. ***Scholarships, grants, and awards by category:*** *Creative Arts/Performance:* 65 awards ($72,500 total): applied art and design, art/fine arts, general creative arts/performance. *Special Achievements/Activities:* 953 awards ($4,234,305 total): community service, general special achievements/activities, leadership.

LOANS ***Student loans:*** $11,853,474 (73% need-based, 27% non-need-based). 72% of past graduating class borrowed through all loan programs. ***Average need-based loan:*** Freshmen: $2296; Undergraduates: $3389. ***Parent loans:*** $3,486,911 (52% need-based, 48% non-need-based). ***Programs:*** FFEL (Subsidized and Unsubsidized Stafford, PLUS), state, alternative loans.

WORK-STUDY ***Federal work-study:*** Total amount: $300,049; 299 jobs averaging $1613. ***State or other work-study/employment:*** Total amount: $253,300 (100% non-need-based). 126 part-time jobs averaging $2010.

APPLYING FOR FINANCIAL AID ***Required financial aid form:*** FAFSA. ***Financial aid deadline (priority):*** 5/1. ***Notification date:*** Continuous beginning 2/1.

CONTACT Linda Mularczyk, Director of Financial Aid, Mount Ida College, 777 Dedham Street, Newton, MA 02459-3310, 617-928-4099. *Fax:* 617-332-7869. *E-mail:* finserv@mountida.edu.

MOUNT MARTY COLLEGE

Yankton, SD

Tuition & fees: $16,582 **Average undergraduate aid package: $13,253**

ABOUT THE INSTITUTION Independent Roman Catholic, coed. Awards: associate, bachelor's, and master's degrees and post-bachelor's certificates. 31 undergraduate majors. Total enrollment: 1,220. Undergraduates: 1,083. Freshmen: 152. Federal methodology is used as a basis for awarding need-based institutional aid.

UNDERGRADUATE EXPENSES for 2006–07 ***Application fee:*** $35. ***Comprehensive fee:*** $21,540 includes full-time tuition ($14,752), mandatory fees ($1830), and room and board ($4958). Full-time tuition and fees vary according to course load and location. ***Part-time tuition:*** $239 per credit hour. ***Part-time fees:*** $25 per credit hour. Part-time tuition and fees vary according to course load and location. ***Payment plan:*** Installment.

FRESHMAN FINANCIAL AID (Fall 2005) 116 applied for aid; of those 94% were deemed to have need. 100% of freshmen with need received aid; of those 17% had need fully met. ***Average percent of need met:*** 78% (excluding resources awarded to replace EFC). ***Average financial aid package:*** $14,336 (excluding resources awarded to replace EFC). 8% of all full-time freshmen had no need and received non-need-based gift aid.

UNDERGRADUATE FINANCIAL AID (Fall 2005) 495 applied for aid; of those 92% were deemed to have need. 100% of undergraduates with need received aid; of those 20% had need fully met. ***Average percent of need met:*** 75% (excluding resources awarded to replace EFC). ***Average financial aid package:*** $13,253 (excluding resources awarded to replace EFC). 10% of all full-time undergraduates had no need and received non-need-based gift aid.

GIFT AID (NEED-BASED) ***Total amount:*** $3,386,099 (24% federal, 1% state, 67% institutional, 8% external sources). ***Receiving aid:*** Freshmen: 92% (108); All full-time undergraduates: 87% (450). ***Average award:*** Freshmen: $10,431; Undergraduates: $8552. ***Scholarships, grants, and awards:*** Federal Pell, FSEOG, state, private, college/university gift aid from institutional funds.

GIFT AID (NON-NEED-BASED) ***Total amount:*** $221,842 (2% state, 82% institutional, 16% external sources). ***Receiving aid:*** Freshmen: 90% (106); Undergraduates: 79% (405). ***Average award:*** Freshmen: $10,402; Undergraduates: $9217. ***Scholarships, grants, and awards by category:*** *Academic Interests/Achievement:* 435 awards ($1,126,364 total): general academic interests/achievements. *Creative Arts/Performance:* 64 awards ($36,970 total): creative writing, music, theater/drama. *Special Achievements/Activities:* 141 awards ($256,708 total): leadership, memberships, religious involvement. *Special Characteristics:* 71 awards ($265,056 total): children of current students, children of faculty/staff, international students, parents of current students, religious affiliation, siblings of current students, spouses of current students. ***ROTC:*** Army cooperative.

LOANS ***Student loans:*** $3,965,867 (65% need-based, 35% non-need-based). 85% of past graduating class borrowed through all loan programs. *Average indebtedness per student:* $26,304. ***Average need-based loan:*** Freshmen: $3284; Undergraduates: $4632. ***Parent loans:*** $1,038,132 (6% need-based, 94% non-need-based). ***Programs:*** FFEL (Subsidized and Unsubsidized Stafford, PLUS), Perkins, Federal Nursing.

WORK-STUDY ***Federal work-study:*** Total amount: $267,144; 237 jobs averaging $1000. ***State or other work-study/employment:*** Total amount: $71,633 (100% non-need-based). 61 part-time jobs averaging $1000.

ATHLETIC AWARDS Total amount: $477,565 (25% need-based, 75% non-need-based).

APPLYING FOR FINANCIAL AID ***Required financial aid forms:*** FAFSA, institution's own form. ***Financial aid deadline (priority):*** 3/1. ***Notification date:*** Continuous beginning 3/15. Students must reply within 2 weeks of notification.

CONTACT Mr. Ken Kocer, Director of Financial Assistance, Mount Marty College, 1105 West 8th Street, Yankton, SD 57078-3724, 605-668-1589 or toll-free 800-658-4552. *Fax:* 605-668-1585. *E-mail:* kkocer@mtmc.edu.

MOUNT MARY COLLEGE

Milwaukee, WI

Tuition & fees: $19,204 **Average undergraduate aid package: $11,918**

ABOUT THE INSTITUTION Independent Roman Catholic, undergraduate: women only; graduate: coed. Awards: bachelor's and master's degrees and post-bachelor's certificates. 53 undergraduate majors. Total enrollment: 1,732. Undergraduates: 1,459. Freshmen: 139. Federal methodology is used as a basis for awarding need-based institutional aid.

UNDERGRADUATE EXPENSES for 2007–08 ***Application fee:*** $25. ***Comprehensive fee:*** $25,399 includes full-time tuition ($18,994), mandatory fees ($210), and room and board ($6195). ***Part-time tuition:*** $510 per credit. ***Part-time fees:*** $57.50 per term.

FRESHMAN FINANCIAL AID (Fall 2006, est.) 97 applied for aid; of those 91% were deemed to have need. 99% of freshmen with need received aid; of those 8% had need fully met. ***Average percent of need met:*** 66% (excluding resources awarded to replace EFC). ***Average financial aid package:*** $13,647 (excluding resources awarded to replace EFC). 20% of all full-time freshmen had no need and received non-need-based gift aid.

UNDERGRADUATE FINANCIAL AID (Fall 2006, est.) 661 applied for aid; of those 89% were deemed to have need. 98% of undergraduates with need received aid; of those 13% had need fully met. ***Average percent of need met:*** 60% (excluding resources awarded to replace EFC). ***Average financial aid package:*** $11,918 (excluding resources awarded to replace EFC). 16% of all full-time undergraduates had no need and received non-need-based gift aid.

GIFT AID (NEED-BASED) ***Total amount:*** $6,364,179 (22% federal, 18% state, 59% institutional, 1% external sources). ***Receiving aid:*** Freshmen: 66% (87); All full-time undergraduates: 63% (570). ***Average award:*** Freshmen: $9911; Undergraduates: $7891. ***Scholarships, grants, and awards:*** Federal Pell, FSEOG, state, private, college/university gift aid from institutional funds, Metropolitan Milwaukee Association of Commerce Awards.

GIFT AID (NON-NEED-BASED) ***Total amount:*** $882,120 (2% state, 97% institutional, 1% external sources). ***Receiving aid:*** Freshmen: 3% (4); Undergraduates: 5% (42). ***Average award:*** Freshmen: $6200; Undergraduates: $8949. ***Scholarships, grants, and awards by category:*** *Academic Interests/Achievement:* 266 awards ($838,899 total): business, communication, education, English, general academic interests/achievements, health fields, home economics, humanities, mathematics, physical sciences, social sciences. *Creative Arts/Performance:* 31 awards ($29,398 total): applied art and design, art/fine arts, music. *Special Achievements/Activities:* 15 awards ($47,030 total): general special achievements/activities, leadership. *Special Characteristics:* 36 awards ($296,228 total): children of faculty/staff, international students, parents of current students, siblings of current students. ***ROTC:*** Army cooperative.

LOANS ***Student loans:*** $8,003,761 (79% need-based, 21% non-need-based). 78% of past graduating class borrowed through all loan programs. *Average*

indebtedness per student: $18,125. ***Average need-based loan:*** Freshmen: $2861; Undergraduates: $3799. ***Parent loans:*** $721,458 (40% need-based, 60% non-need-based). ***Programs:*** FFEL (Subsidized and Unsubsidized Stafford, PLUS), Perkins, state.

WORK-STUDY ***Federal work-study:*** Total amount: $180,000; 288 jobs averaging $1325. ***State or other work-study/employment:*** Total amount: $224,000 (100% non-need-based). 180 part-time jobs averaging $1250.

APPLYING FOR FINANCIAL AID ***Required financial aid form:*** FAFSA. ***Financial aid deadline (priority):*** 3/1. ***Notification date:*** Continuous. Students must reply within 2 weeks of notification.

CONTACT Debra Duff, Director of Financial Aid, Mount Mary College, 2900 North Menomonee River Parkway, Milwaukee, WI 53222-4597, 414-256-1258. *Fax:* 414-443-3602. *E-mail:* finaid@mtmary.edu.

MOUNT MERCY COLLEGE

Cedar Rapids, IA

Tuition & fees: $18,930 **Average undergraduate aid package: $15,214**

ABOUT THE INSTITUTION Independent Roman Catholic, coed. Awards: bachelor's degrees. 35 undergraduate majors. Total university enrollment: 151. Total unit enrollment: 1,482. Undergraduates: 1,482. Freshmen: 181. Federal methodology is used as a basis for awarding need-based institutional aid.

UNDERGRADUATE EXPENSES for 2006–07 ***Application fee:*** $20. ***Comprehensive fee:*** $24,900 includes full-time tuition ($18,930) and room and board ($5970). Full-time tuition and fees vary according to course load. Room and board charges vary according to board plan and housing facility. ***Part-time tuition:*** $525 per credit hour. Part-time tuition and fees vary according to course load. ***Payment plan:*** Installment.

FRESHMAN FINANCIAL AID (Fall 2006, est.) 174 applied for aid; of those 87% were deemed to have need. 99% of freshmen with need received aid; of those 47% had need fully met. ***Average percent of need met:*** 84% (excluding resources awarded to replace EFC). ***Average financial aid package:*** $16,355 (excluding resources awarded to replace EFC). 16% of all full-time freshmen had no need and received non-need-based gift aid.

UNDERGRADUATE FINANCIAL AID (Fall 2006, est.) 925 applied for aid; of those 88% were deemed to have need. 97% of undergraduates with need received aid; of those 37% had need fully met. ***Average percent of need met:*** 77% (excluding resources awarded to replace EFC). ***Average financial aid package:*** $15,214 (excluding resources awarded to replace EFC). 18% of all full-time undergraduates had no need and received non-need-based gift aid.

GIFT AID (NEED-BASED) ***Total amount:*** $8,696,397 (13% federal, 27% state, 55% institutional, 5% external sources). ***Receiving aid:*** Freshmen: 84% (151); All full-time undergraduates: 80% (790). ***Average award:*** Freshmen: $11,861; Undergraduates: $10,164. ***Scholarships, grants, and awards:*** Federal Pell, FSEOG, state, college/university gift aid from institutional funds.

GIFT AID (NON-NEED-BASED) ***Total amount:*** $1,525,788 (93% institutional, 7% external sources). ***Receiving aid:*** Freshmen: 9% (17); Undergraduates: 8% (75). ***Average award:*** Freshmen: $13,435; Undergraduates: $10,414. ***Scholarships, grants, and awards by category:*** *Academic Interests/Achievement:* 1,030 awards ($5,723,647 total): general academic interests/achievements. *Creative Arts/Performance:* 53 awards ($55,475 total): art/fine arts, music, theater/drama. *Special Achievements/Activities:* 240 awards ($260,250 total): leadership. *Special Characteristics:* 23 awards ($14,125 total): previous college experience. ***Tuition waivers:*** Full or partial for employees or children of employees.

LOANS ***Student loans:*** $7,905,858 (65% need-based, 35% non-need-based). 89% of past graduating class borrowed through all loan programs. *Average indebtedness per student:* $27,083. ***Average need-based loan:*** Freshmen: $4221; Undergraduates: $5289. ***Parent loans:*** $363,094 (24% need-based, 76% non-need-based). ***Programs:*** Federal Direct (Subsidized and Unsubsidized Stafford, PLUS), Perkins, state, college/university.

WORK-STUDY ***Federal work-study:*** Total amount: $404,294; 285 jobs averaging $1419. ***State or other work-study/employment:*** Total amount: $243,925 (25% need-based, 75% non-need-based). 127 part-time jobs averaging $1921.

APPLYING FOR FINANCIAL AID ***Required financial aid form:*** FAFSA. ***Financial aid deadline (priority):*** 3/1. ***Notification date:*** Continuous beginning 3/15. Students must reply by 5/1 or within 3 weeks of notification.

CONTACT Aaron Steffens, Director of Financial Aid, Mount Mercy College, 1330 Elmhurst Drive NE, Cedar Rapids, IA 52402-4797, 319-368-6467 or toll-free 800-248-4504. *Fax:* 319-364-3546. *E-mail:* steffens@mtmercy.edu.

MOUNT OLIVE COLLEGE

Mount Olive, NC

Tuition & fees: $13,126 **Average undergraduate aid package: $7296**

ABOUT THE INSTITUTION Independent Free Will Baptist, coed. Awards: associate and bachelor's degrees. 22 undergraduate majors. Total enrollment: 3,155. Undergraduates: 3,155. Freshmen: 274. Both federal and institutional methodology are used as a basis for awarding need-based institutional aid.

UNDERGRADUATE EXPENSES for 2007–08 ***Application fee:*** $20. ***Comprehensive fee:*** $18,426 includes full-time tuition ($13,126) and room and board ($5300). ***College room only:*** $2200. ***Part-time tuition:*** $250 per credit hour.

FRESHMAN FINANCIAL AID (Fall 2005) 342 applied for aid; of those 69% were deemed to have need. 95% of freshmen with need received aid; of those 22% had need fully met. ***Average percent of need met:*** 66% (excluding resources awarded to replace EFC). ***Average financial aid package:*** $7843 (excluding resources awarded to replace EFC). 10% of all full-time freshmen had no need and received non-need-based gift aid.

UNDERGRADUATE FINANCIAL AID (Fall 2005) 1,941 applied for aid; of those 79% were deemed to have need. 98% of undergraduates with need received aid; of those 20% had need fully met. ***Average percent of need met:*** 67% (excluding resources awarded to replace EFC). ***Average financial aid package:*** $7296 (excluding resources awarded to replace EFC). 11% of all full-time undergraduates had no need and received non-need-based gift aid.

GIFT AID (NEED-BASED) ***Total amount:*** $7,500,424 (34% federal, 58% state, 2% institutional, 6% external sources). ***Receiving aid:*** Freshmen: 38% (222); All full-time undergraduates: 51% (1,461). ***Average award:*** Freshmen: $6186; Undergraduates: $4972. ***Scholarships, grants, and awards:*** Federal Pell, FSEOG, state, private, college/university gift aid from institutional funds.

GIFT AID (NON-NEED-BASED) ***Total amount:*** $1,441,404 (1% federal, 52% state, 4% institutional, 43% external sources). ***Receiving aid:*** Freshmen: 5% (27); Undergraduates: 4% (117). ***Average award:*** Freshmen: $3349; Undergraduates: $4602. ***Scholarships, grants, and awards by category:*** *Academic Interests/Achievement:* 63 awards ($218,526 total): general academic interests/achievements, mathematics. *Creative Arts/Performance:* 53 awards ($84,955 total): art/fine arts, music. *Special Achievements/Activities:* 144 awards ($272,701 total): leadership. *Special Characteristics:* 47 awards ($129,839 total): children of faculty/staff, religious affiliation.

LOANS ***Student loans:*** $9,091,320 (47% need-based, 53% non-need-based). 67% of past graduating class borrowed through all loan programs. *Average indebtedness per student:* $9786. ***Average need-based loan:*** Freshmen: $2136; Undergraduates: $2833. ***Parent loans:*** $257,645 (22% need-based, 78% non-need-based). ***Programs:*** FFEL (Subsidized Stafford, PLUS), Perkins, Federal Nursing, state.

WORK-STUDY ***Federal work-study:*** Total amount: $122,241; 120 jobs averaging $719.

ATHLETIC AWARDS Total amount: $752,555 (57% need-based, 43% non-need-based).

APPLYING FOR FINANCIAL AID ***Required financial aid forms:*** FAFSA, state aid form. ***Financial aid deadline (priority):*** 3/1. ***Notification date:*** Continuous beginning 2/14.

CONTACT Ms. Karen Britt Statler, Director of Financial Aid, Mount Olive College, 634 Henderson Street, Mount Olive, NC 28365, 919-658-2502 Ext. 3006 or toll-free 800-653-0854 (in-state). *Fax:* 919-658-9816.

MOUNT SAINT MARY COLLEGE

Newburgh, NY

Tuition & fees: $18,290 **Average undergraduate aid package: $11,048**

ABOUT THE INSTITUTION Independent, coed. Awards: bachelor's and master's degrees. 35 undergraduate majors. Total enrollment: 2,601. Undergraduates: 2,043. Freshmen: 405. Federal methodology is used as a basis for awarding need-based institutional aid.

UNDERGRADUATE EXPENSES for 2006–07 ***Application fee:*** $35. ***Comprehensive fee:*** $27,330 includes full-time tuition ($17,730), mandatory fees ($560), and room and board ($9040). ***College room only:*** $5050. Full-time tuition and fees vary according to degree level. Room and board charges vary according to board plan, housing facility, and student level. ***Part-time tuition:*** $591 per credit hour. ***Part-time fees:*** $40 per term. Part-time tuition and fees vary according to degree level. ***Payment plan:*** Installment.

FRESHMAN FINANCIAL AID (Fall 2006, est.) 356 applied for aid; of those 83% were deemed to have need. 99% of freshmen with need received aid; of those 10% had need fully met. ***Average percent of need met:*** 53% (excluding resources awarded to replace EFC). ***Average financial aid package:*** $11,817 (excluding resources awarded to replace EFC). 18% of all full-time freshmen had no need and received non-need-based gift aid.

UNDERGRADUATE FINANCIAL AID (Fall 2006, est.) 1,423 applied for aid; of those 85% were deemed to have need. 99% of undergraduates with need received aid; of those 10% had need fully met. ***Average percent of need met:*** 54% (excluding resources awarded to replace EFC). ***Average financial aid package:*** $11,048 (excluding resources awarded to replace EFC). 16% of all full-time undergraduates had no need and received non-need-based gift aid.

GIFT AID (NEED-BASED) ***Total amount:*** $7,944,513 (21% federal, 25% state, 51% institutional, 3% external sources). ***Receiving aid:*** Freshmen: 66% (266); All full-time undergraduates: 62% (1,049). ***Average award:*** Freshmen: $9486; Undergraduates: $7522. ***Scholarships, grants, and awards:*** Federal Pell, FSEOG, state, private, college/university gift aid from institutional funds, Federal Nursing.

GIFT AID (NON-NEED-BASED) ***Total amount:*** $1,114,060 (1% federal, 13% state, 81% institutional, 5% external sources). ***Receiving aid:*** Freshmen: 4% (15); Undergraduates: 3% (50). ***Average award:*** Freshmen: $12,821; Undergraduates: $12,421. ***Scholarships, grants, and awards by category:*** *Academic Interests/Achievement:* 456 awards ($2,754,600 total): general academic interests/achievements. *Special Characteristics:* 18 awards ($202,756 total): children of faculty/staff. ***Tuition waivers:*** Full or partial for employees or children of employees.

LOANS ***Student loans:*** $13,013,010 (71% need-based, 29% non-need-based). 79% of past graduating class borrowed through all loan programs. *Average indebtedness per student:* $20,000. ***Average need-based loan:*** Freshmen: $2934; Undergraduates: $4554. ***Parent loans:*** $2,050,298 (7% need-based, 93% non-need-based). ***Programs:*** FFEL (Subsidized and Unsubsidized Stafford, PLUS), Perkins, Federal Nursing.

WORK-STUDY ***Federal work-study:*** Total amount: $348,366; 283 jobs averaging $1417. ***State or other work-study/employment:*** Total amount: $86,352 (49% need-based, 51% non-need-based). 24 part-time jobs averaging $1396.

APPLYING FOR FINANCIAL AID ***Required financial aid form:*** FAFSA. ***Financial aid deadline (priority):*** 2/15. ***Notification date:*** Continuous beginning 4/1. Students must reply within 2 weeks of notification.

CONTACT Michelle Taylor, Director of Financial Aid, Mount Saint Mary College, 330 Powell Avenue, Newburgh, NY 12550-3494, 845-561-0800 or toll-free 888-937-6762. *Fax:* 845-569-3302. *E-mail:* taylor@msmc.edu.

MOUNT ST. MARY'S COLLEGE

Los Angeles, CA

Tuition & fees: $24,150 **Average undergraduate aid package: N/A**

ABOUT THE INSTITUTION Independent Roman Catholic, coed, primarily women. Awards: associate, bachelor's, and master's degrees and post-bachelor's certificates. 40 undergraduate majors. Total enrollment: 2,384. Undergraduates: 1,921. Freshmen: 411. Federal methodology is used as a basis for awarding need-based institutional aid.

UNDERGRADUATE EXPENSES for 2006–07 ***Application fee:*** $40. ***Comprehensive fee:*** $32,897 includes full-time tuition ($23,380), mandatory fees ($770), and room and board ($8747). ***Part-time tuition:*** $900 per unit.

GIFT AID (NEED-BASED) ***Total amount:*** $12,873,322 (15% federal, 31% state, 52% institutional, 2% external sources). ***Scholarships, grants, and awards:*** Federal Pell, FSEOG, state, private, college/university gift aid from institutional funds.

GIFT AID (NON-NEED-BASED) ***Total amount:*** $2,033,019 (100% institutional). ***Scholarships, grants, and awards by category:*** *Academic Interests/Achievement:* biological sciences, education, general academic interests/achievements. *Creative Arts/Performance:* music. *Special Achievements/Activities:* community service, leadership. *Special Characteristics:* children and siblings of alumni.

LOANS ***Student loans:*** $8,135,703 (95% need-based, 5% non-need-based). ***Programs:*** FFEL (Subsidized and Unsubsidized Stafford, PLUS), Federal Nursing, college/university.

WORK-STUDY ***Federal work-study:*** Total amount: $627,642; 248 jobs averaging $2531. ***State or other work-study/employment:*** Total amount: $51,750 (92% need-based, 8% non-need-based). 22 part-time jobs averaging $3352.

APPLYING FOR FINANCIAL AID ***Required financial aid forms:*** FAFSA, institution's own form, state aid form. ***Financial aid deadline:*** 5/15 (priority: 3/2). ***Notification date:*** Continuous beginning 12/1. Students must reply by 5/1.

CONTACT La Royce Dodd, Financial Aid Director, Mount St. Mary's College, 12001 Chalon Road, Los Angeles, CA 90049, 310-954-4192 or toll-free 800-999-9893.

MOUNT ST. MARY'S UNIVERSITY

Emmitsburg, MD

Tuition & fees: $25,890 **Average undergraduate aid package: $16,185**

ABOUT THE INSTITUTION Independent Roman Catholic, coed. Awards: bachelor's, master's, and first professional degrees and post-bachelor's and post-master's certificates. 28 undergraduate majors. Total enrollment: 2,186. Undergraduates: 1,695. Freshmen: 426. Federal methodology is used as a basis for awarding need-based institutional aid.

UNDERGRADUATE EXPENSES for 2007–08 ***Application fee:*** $35. ***Comprehensive fee:*** $35,020 includes full-time tuition ($25,290), mandatory fees ($600), and room and board ($9130). ***College room only:*** $4600. ***Part-time tuition:*** $845 per credit hour.

FRESHMAN FINANCIAL AID (Fall 2006, est.) 351 applied for aid; of those 79% were deemed to have need. 100% of freshmen with need received aid; of those 26% had need fully met. ***Average percent of need met:*** 75% (excluding resources awarded to replace EFC). ***Average financial aid package:*** $15,682 (excluding resources awarded to replace EFC). 31% of all full-time freshmen had no need and received non-need-based gift aid.

UNDERGRADUATE FINANCIAL AID (Fall 2006, est.) 1,141 applied for aid; of those 80% were deemed to have need. 100% of undergraduates with need received aid; of those 29% had need fully met. ***Average percent of need met:*** 76% (excluding resources awarded to replace EFC). ***Average financial aid package:*** $16,185 (excluding resources awarded to replace EFC). 35% of all full-time undergraduates had no need and received non-need-based gift aid.

GIFT AID (NEED-BASED) ***Total amount:*** $10,314,270 (8% federal, 11% state, 79% institutional, 2% external sources). ***Receiving aid:*** Freshmen: 65% (279); All full-time undergraduates: 59% (906). ***Average award:*** Freshmen: $12,274; Undergraduates: $12,344. ***Scholarships, grants, and awards:*** Federal Pell, FSEOG, state, private, college/university gift aid from institutional funds.

GIFT AID (NON-NEED-BASED) ***Total amount:*** $6,250,922 (3% federal, 4% state, 89% institutional, 4% external sources). ***Receiving aid:*** Freshmen: 15% (63); Undergraduates: 13% (202). ***Average award:*** Freshmen: $13,276; Undergraduates: $13,888. ***Scholarships, grants, and awards by category:*** *Academic Interests/Achievement:* 1,123 awards ($9,370,233 total): general academic interests/achievements. *Creative Arts/Performance:* 18 awards ($36,100 total): art/fine arts. *Special Characteristics:* 202 awards ($608,435 total): children of educators, children of faculty/staff, members of minority groups, siblings of current students. ***ROTC:*** Army cooperative.

LOANS ***Student loans:*** $7,436,280 (55% need-based, 45% non-need-based). 71% of past graduating class borrowed through all loan programs. *Average indebtedness per student:* $20,703. ***Average need-based loan:*** Freshmen: $3485; Undergraduates: $4347. ***Parent loans:*** $3,499,312 (25% need-based, 75% non-need-based). ***Programs:*** FFEL (Subsidized and Unsubsidized Stafford, PLUS), Perkins.

WORK-STUDY ***Federal work-study:*** Total amount: $403,900; 198 jobs averaging $1465. ***State or other work-study/employment:*** Total amount: $251,088 (66% need-based, 34% non-need-based). 32 part-time jobs averaging $6910.

ATHLETIC AWARDS Total amount: $2,123,109 (34% need-based, 66% non-need-based).

APPLYING FOR FINANCIAL AID ***Required financial aid forms:*** FAFSA, institution's own form. ***Financial aid deadline:*** 2/15. ***Notification date:*** Continuous beginning 2/15. Students must reply by 5/1.

CONTACT Mr. David C. Reeder, Director of Financial Aid, Mount St. Mary's University, 16300 Old Emmitsburg Road, Emmitsburg, MD 21727-7799, 301-447-5207 or toll-free 800-448-4347. *Fax:* 301-447-5755. *E-mail:* reeder@msmary.edu.

MT. SIERRA COLLEGE

Monrovia, CA

CONTACT Financial Aid Office, Mt. Sierra College, 101 East Huntington Drive, Monrovia, CA 91016, 888-828-8800 or toll-free 888-828-8800.

MOUNT UNION COLLEGE

Alliance, OH

Tuition & fees: $20,970 **Average undergraduate aid package: $15,618**

ABOUT THE INSTITUTION Independent United Methodist, coed. Awards: bachelor's degrees. 43 undergraduate majors. Total enrollment: 2,193. Undergraduates: 2,193. Freshmen: 636. Federal methodology is used as a basis for awarding need-based institutional aid.

UNDERGRADUATE EXPENSES for 2006–07 ***Comprehensive fee:*** $27,320 includes full-time tuition ($20,720), mandatory fees ($250), and room and board ($6350). ***College room only:*** $2850. Room and board charges vary according to board plan and housing facility. ***Part-time tuition:*** $870 per semester hour. ***Part-time fees:*** $50 per term. ***Payment plans:*** Tuition prepayment, installment.

FRESHMAN FINANCIAL AID (Fall 2005) 473 applied for aid; of those 86% were deemed to have need. 100% of freshmen with need received aid; of those 21% had need fully met. ***Average percent of need met:*** 79% (excluding resources awarded to replace EFC). ***Average financial aid package:*** $15,665 (excluding resources awarded to replace EFC). 19% of all full-time freshmen had no need and received non-need-based gift aid.

UNDERGRADUATE FINANCIAL AID (Fall 2005) 1,697 applied for aid; of those 91% were deemed to have need. 100% of undergraduates with need received aid; of those 22% had need fully met. ***Average percent of need met:*** 79% (excluding resources awarded to replace EFC). ***Average financial aid package:*** $15,618 (excluding resources awarded to replace EFC). 19% of all full-time undergraduates had no need and received non-need-based gift aid.

GIFT AID (NEED-BASED) ***Total amount:*** $17,248,275 (10% federal, 13% state, 74% institutional, 3% external sources). ***Receiving aid:*** Freshmen: 79% (406); All full-time undergraduates: 80% (1,537). ***Average award:*** Freshmen: $11,573; Undergraduates: $11,015. ***Scholarships, grants, and awards:*** Federal Pell, FSEOG, state, private, college/university gift aid from institutional funds.

GIFT AID (NON-NEED-BASED) ***Total amount:*** $2,548,805 (16% state, 78% institutional, 6% external sources). ***Receiving aid:*** Freshmen: 9% (46); Undergraduates: 7% (134). ***Average award:*** Freshmen: $9488; Undergraduates: $9748. ***Scholarships, grants, and awards by category:*** *Academic Interests/Achievement:* 1,089 awards ($5,832,460 total): general academic interests/achievements. *Creative Arts/Performance:* 131 awards ($348,604 total): art/fine arts, cinema/film/broadcasting, debating, journalism/publications, music, theater/drama. *Special Characteristics:* 169 awards ($934,847 total): children and siblings of alumni, children of faculty/staff, ethnic background, international students, relatives of clergy. ***Tuition waivers:*** Full or partial for children of alumni, employees or children of employees, adult students. ***ROTC:*** Army cooperative, Air Force cooperative.

LOANS ***Student loans:*** $11,590,469 (71% need-based, 29% non-need-based). 82% of past graduating class borrowed through all loan programs. *Average indebtedness per student:* $18,627. ***Average need-based loan:*** Freshmen: $4580; Undergraduates: $4934. ***Parent loans:*** $2,881,781 (33% need-based, 67% non-need-based). ***Programs:*** FFEL (Subsidized and Unsubsidized Stafford, PLUS), Perkins, alternative loans.

WORK-STUDY ***Federal work-study:*** Total amount: $182,189; 1,176 jobs averaging $248. ***State or other work-study/employment:*** Total amount: $383,610 (24% need-based, 76% non-need-based). 324 part-time jobs averaging $1186.

APPLYING FOR FINANCIAL AID ***Required financial aid form:*** FAFSA. ***Financial aid deadline:*** Continuous. ***Notification date:*** Continuous beginning 3/15. Students must reply within 4 weeks of notification.

CONTACT Mrs. Sandra S. Pittenger, Director of Student Financial Services, Mount Union College, 1972 Clark Avenue, Alliance, OH 44601-3993, 330-823-2674 or toll-free 800-334-6682 (in-state), 800-992-6682 (out-of-state). *Fax:* 330-829-2814. *E-mail:* pittenss@muc.edu.

MOUNT VERNON NAZARENE UNIVERSITY

Mount Vernon, OH

Tuition & fees: $18,064 **Average undergraduate aid package: $13,283**

ABOUT THE INSTITUTION Independent Nazarene, coed. Awards: associate, bachelor's, and master's degrees. 64 undergraduate majors. Total enrollment: 2,670. Undergraduates: 2,171. Freshmen: 347. Federal methodology is used as a basis for awarding need-based institutional aid.

UNDERGRADUATE EXPENSES for 2007–08 ***Application fee:*** $25. ***Comprehensive fee:*** $23,350 includes full-time tuition ($17,544), mandatory fees ($520), and room and board ($5286). ***College room only:*** $2954. ***Part-time tuition:*** $626 per semester hour. ***Part-time fees:*** $18 per semester hour.

FRESHMAN FINANCIAL AID (Fall 2006, est.) 346 applied for aid; of those 82% were deemed to have need. 100% of freshmen with need received aid; of those 16% had need fully met. ***Average percent of need met:*** 78% (excluding resources awarded to replace EFC). ***Average financial aid package:*** $13,706 (excluding resources awarded to replace EFC). 11% of all full-time freshmen had no need and received non-need-based gift aid.

UNDERGRADUATE FINANCIAL AID (Fall 2006, est.) 1,354 applied for aid; of those 75% were deemed to have need. 100% of undergraduates with need received aid; of those 17% had need fully met. ***Average percent of need met:*** 84% (excluding resources awarded to replace EFC). ***Average financial aid package:*** $13,283 (excluding resources awarded to replace EFC). 7% of all full-time undergraduates had no need and received non-need-based gift aid.

GIFT AID (NEED-BASED) ***Total amount:*** $8,436,454 (20% federal, 19% state, 52% institutional, 9% external sources). ***Receiving aid:*** Freshmen: 82% (283); All full-time undergraduates: 52% (1,006). ***Average award:*** Freshmen: $8698; Undergraduates: $7434. ***Scholarships, grants, and awards:*** Federal Pell, FSEOG, state, private, college/university gift aid from institutional funds.

GIFT AID (NON-NEED-BASED) ***Total amount:*** $1,969,392 (52% state, 37% institutional, 11% external sources). ***Receiving aid:*** Freshmen: 9% (31); Undergraduates: 5% (91). ***Average award:*** Freshmen: $3519; Undergraduates: $2886. ***Scholarships, grants, and awards by category:*** *Academic Interests/Achievement:* business, computer science, education, general academic interests/achievements, health fields, home economics, physical sciences, religion/biblical studies. *Creative Arts/Performance:* music. *Special Achievements/Activities:* general special achievements/activities, junior miss, religious involvement. *Special Characteristics:* children of faculty/staff, international students, local/state students, members of minority groups, relatives of clergy, religious affiliation, siblings of current students, spouses of current students, veterans, veterans' children.

LOANS ***Student loans:*** $11,944,665 (62% need-based, 38% non-need-based). 79% of past graduating class borrowed through all loan programs. *Average indebtedness per student:* $21,719. ***Average need-based loan:*** Freshmen: $3403; Undergraduates: $4140. ***Parent loans:*** $2,235,088 (37% need-based, 63% non-need-based). ***Programs:*** FFEL (Subsidized and Unsubsidized Stafford, PLUS), Perkins, alternative loans.

WORK-STUDY ***Federal work-study:*** Total amount: $255,296; 176 jobs averaging $1450. ***State or other work-study/employment:*** Total amount: $581,027 (37% need-based, 63% non-need-based). 380 part-time jobs averaging $1529.

ATHLETIC AWARDS Total amount: $524,948 (66% need-based, 34% non-need-based).

APPLYING FOR FINANCIAL AID ***Required financial aid forms:*** FAFSA, institution's own form. ***Financial aid deadline (priority):*** 3/15. ***Notification date:*** Continuous beginning 3/1. Students must reply within 2 weeks of notification.

CONTACT Steve Tracht, Associate Director of Student Financial Planning, Mount Vernon Nazarene University, 800 Martinsburg Road, Mount Vernon, OH 43050-9500, 740-392-6868 Ext. 4521 or toll-free 866-462-6868. *Fax:* 740-393-0511. *E-mail:* stracht@mvnu.edu.

MUHLENBERG COLLEGE

Allentown, PA

CONTACT Mr. Greg Mitton, Director of Financial Aid, Muhlenberg College, 2400 Chew Street, Allentown, PA 18104-5586, 484-664-3175. *Fax:* 484-664-3234. *E-mail:* mitton@muhlenberg.edu.

MULTNOMAH BIBLE COLLEGE AND BIBLICAL SEMINARY

Portland, OR

CONTACT Mr. David Allen, Director of Financial Aid, Multnomah Bible College and Biblical Seminary, 8435 Northeast Glisan Street, Portland, OR 97220-5898, 503-251-5335 or toll-free 800-275-4672. *Fax:* 503-254-1268.

MURRAY STATE UNIVERSITY

Murray, KY

Tuition & fees (KY res): $5418 **Average undergraduate aid package: $4615**

ABOUT THE INSTITUTION State-supported, coed. Awards: bachelor's and master's degrees and post-master's certificates. 112 undergraduate majors. Total enrollment: 10,298. Undergraduates: 8,601. Freshmen: 1,403. Federal methodology is used as a basis for awarding need-based institutional aid.

UNDERGRADUATE EXPENSES for 2007–08 ***Application fee:*** $30. ***Tuition, state resident:*** full-time $4650; part-time $194 per hour. ***Tuition, nonresident:*** full-time $6728; part-time $268 per hour. ***Required fees:*** full-time $768; $32 per hour. ***College room and board:*** $5670; ***Room only:*** $3036.

FRESHMAN FINANCIAL AID (Fall 2006, est.) 1112 applied for aid; of those 60% were deemed to have need. 94% of freshmen with need received aid; of those 94% had need fully met. ***Average percent of need met:*** 92% (excluding resources awarded to replace EFC). ***Average financial aid package:*** $4595 (excluding resources awarded to replace EFC). 36% of all full-time freshmen had no need and received non-need-based gift aid.

UNDERGRADUATE FINANCIAL AID (Fall 2006, est.) 6,014 applied for aid; of those 56% were deemed to have need. 92% of undergraduates with need received aid; of those 98% had need fully met. ***Average percent of need met:*** 87% (excluding resources awarded to replace EFC). ***Average financial aid package:*** $4615 (excluding resources awarded to replace EFC). 34% of all full-time undergraduates had no need and received non-need-based gift aid.

GIFT AID (NEED-BASED) ***Total amount:*** $11,604,345 (62% federal, 17% state, 12% institutional, 9% external sources). ***Receiving aid:*** Freshmen: 34% (470); All full-time undergraduates: 30% (2,107). ***Average award:*** Freshmen: $2570; Undergraduates: $2183. ***Scholarships, grants, and awards:*** Federal Pell, FSEOG, state, private, college/university gift aid from institutional funds.

GIFT AID (NON-NEED-BASED) ***Total amount:*** $10,079,313 (43% state, 39% institutional, 18% external sources). ***Receiving aid:*** Freshmen: 23% (315); Undergraduates: 21% (1,487). ***Average award:*** Freshmen: $2520; Undergraduates: $2554. ***Scholarships, grants, and awards by category:*** *Academic Interests/Achievement:* 4,251 awards ($4,820,800 total): agriculture, biological sciences, business, communication, computer science, education, engineering/technologies, English, foreign languages, general academic interests/achievements, health fields, humanities, international studies, library science, mathematics. *Creative Arts/Performance:* 182 awards ($110,012 total): applied art and design, art/fine arts, creative writing, dance, debating, general creative arts/performance, journalism/publications, music, theater/drama. *Special Achievements/Activities:* 819 awards ($800,959 total): cheerleading/drum major, general special achievements/activities, junior miss, leadership, rodeo. *Special Characteristics:* 2,369 awards ($9,276,858 total): adult students, children and siblings of alumni, children of faculty/staff, general special characteristics, handicapped students, international students, local/state students, members of minority groups, out-of-state students. ***ROTC:*** Army cooperative.

LOANS ***Student loans:*** $23,318,480 (59% need-based, 41% non-need-based). 95% of past graduating class borrowed through all loan programs. *Average indebtedness per student:* $15,010. ***Average need-based loan:*** Freshmen: $1853; Undergraduates: $1957. ***Parent loans:*** $1,693,826 (100% non-need-based). ***Programs:*** FFEL (Subsidized and Unsubsidized Stafford, PLUS), Perkins, Federal Nursing, state, college/university.

WORK-STUDY ***Federal work-study:*** Total amount: $573,120; 462 jobs averaging $1297. ***State or other work-study/employment:*** Total amount: $4,073,868 (100% non-need-based). 2,035 part-time jobs averaging $1590.

ATHLETIC AWARDS Total amount: $2,420,009 (30% need-based, 70% non-need-based).

APPLYING FOR FINANCIAL AID ***Required financial aid forms:*** FAFSA, institution's own form. ***Financial aid deadline (priority):*** 4/1. ***Notification date:*** Continuous beginning 4/15.

CONTACT Charles Vinson, Director of Student Financial Aid, Murray State University, B2 Sparks Hall, Murray, KY 42071-0009, 270-809-2546 or toll-free 800-272-4678. *Fax:* 270-809-3116. *E-mail:* charles.vinson@murraystate.edu.

MUSICIANS INSTITUTE

Hollywood, CA

CONTACT Director of Financial Aid, Musicians Institute, 1655 North McCadden Place, Hollywood, CA 90028, 323-462-1384 or toll-free 800-255-PLAY.

MUSKINGUM COLLEGE

New Concord, OH

CONTACT Mr. Jeff Zellers, Dean of Enrollment, Muskingum College, 163 Stormont Street, New Concord, OH 43762, 740-826-8139 or toll-free 800-752-6082. *Fax:* 740-826-8100. *E-mail:* jzellers@muskingum.edu.

MYERS UNIVERSITY

Cleveland, OH

Tuition & fees: N/R **Average undergraduate aid package: $9526**

ABOUT THE INSTITUTION Independent, coed. Awards: associate, bachelor's, and master's degrees. 14 undergraduate majors. Total enrollment: 1,177. Undergraduates: 1,096. Freshmen: 115. Federal methodology is used as a basis for awarding need-based institutional aid.

FRESHMAN FINANCIAL AID (Fall 2005) 72 applied for aid; of those 82% were deemed to have need. 100% of freshmen with need received aid; of those 17% had need fully met. ***Average percent of need met:*** 69% (excluding resources awarded to replace EFC). ***Average financial aid package:*** $9923 (excluding resources awarded to replace EFC). 4% of all full-time freshmen had no need and received non-need-based gift aid.

UNDERGRADUATE FINANCIAL AID (Fall 2005) 421 applied for aid; of those 93% were deemed to have need. 100% of undergraduates with need received aid; of those 15% had need fully met. ***Average percent of need met:*** 67% (excluding resources awarded to replace EFC). ***Average financial aid package:*** $9526 (excluding resources awarded to replace EFC). 1% of all full-time undergraduates had no need and received non-need-based gift aid.

GIFT AID (NEED-BASED) ***Total amount:*** $3,335,536 (49% federal, 34% state, 13% institutional, 4% external sources). ***Receiving aid:*** Freshmen: 75% (57); All full-time undergraduates: 78% (352). ***Average award:*** Freshmen: $5687; Undergraduates: $4812. ***Scholarships, grants, and awards:*** Federal Pell, FSEOG, state, private, college/university gift aid from institutional funds, United Negro College Fund.

GIFT AID (NON-NEED-BASED) ***Total amount:*** $41,750 (20% state, 80% institutional). ***Receiving aid:*** Freshmen: 58% (44); Undergraduates: 64% (288). ***Average award:*** Freshmen: $3500; Undergraduates: $4000. ***Scholarships, grants, and awards by category:*** *Academic Interests/Achievement:* 7 awards ($11,200 total): business, general academic interests/achievements. *Special Achievements/Activities:* 34 awards ($21,500 total): leadership.

LOANS ***Student loans:*** $6,380,984 (91% need-based, 9% non-need-based). 81% of past graduating class borrowed through all loan programs. *Average indebtedness per student:* $31,429. ***Average need-based loan:*** Freshmen: $1737; Undergraduates: $2761. ***Parent loans:*** $114,515 (67% need-based, 33% non-need-based). ***Programs:*** FFEL (Subsidized and Unsubsidized Stafford, PLUS), Perkins.

WORK-STUDY ***Federal work-study:*** Total amount: $79,772; 118 jobs averaging $670.

ATHLETIC AWARDS Total amount: $307,442 (100% need-based).

APPLYING FOR FINANCIAL AID ***Required financial aid forms:*** FAFSA, institution's own form. ***Financial aid deadline (priority):*** 3/15. ***Notification date:*** Continuous beginning 4/1. Students must reply within 3 weeks of notification.

CONTACT Miria Batig, Director of Financial Aid, Myers University, 3921 Chester Avenue, Cleveland, OH 44114, 216-361-2739 or toll-free 877-366-9377. *Fax:* 216-361-9096. *E-mail:* mbatig@myers.edu.

NAROPA UNIVERSITY
Boulder, CO

Tuition & fees: $19,426 **Average undergraduate aid package: $21,838**

ABOUT THE INSTITUTION Independent, coed. Awards: bachelor's, master's, and first professional degrees. 11 undergraduate majors. Total enrollment: 1,136. Undergraduates: 473. Freshmen: 55. Federal methodology is used as a basis for awarding need-based institutional aid.

UNDERGRADUATE EXPENSES for 2006–07 ***Application fee:*** $50. ***Comprehensive fee:*** $26,320 includes full-time tuition ($19,426) and room and board ($6894). ***College room only:*** $4050. Full-time tuition and fees vary according to course load. Room and board charges vary according to board plan. ***Part-time tuition:*** $630 per semester hour. ***Part-time fees:*** $288 per term. Part-time tuition and fees vary according to course load. ***Payment plan:*** Installment.

FRESHMAN FINANCIAL AID (Fall 2006, est.) 40 applied for aid; of those 95% were deemed to have need. 97% of freshmen with need received aid. ***Average percent of need met:*** 95% (excluding resources awarded to replace EFC). ***Average financial aid package:*** $18,795 (excluding resources awarded to replace EFC).

UNDERGRADUATE FINANCIAL AID (Fall 2006, est.) 307 applied for aid; of those 99% were deemed to have need. 99% of undergraduates with need received aid. ***Average percent of need met:*** 89% (excluding resources awarded to replace EFC). ***Average financial aid package:*** $21,838 (excluding resources awarded to replace EFC).

GIFT AID (NEED-BASED) ***Total amount:*** $3,070,036 (20% federal, 79% institutional, 1% external sources). ***Receiving aid:*** Freshmen: 52% (28); All full-time undergraduates: 63% (259). ***Average award:*** Freshmen: $11,036; Undergraduates: $11,670. ***Scholarships, grants, and awards:*** Federal Pell, FSEOG, private, college/university gift aid from institutional funds.

GIFT AID (NON-NEED-BASED) ***Tuition waivers:*** Full or partial for employees or children of employees.

LOANS ***Student loans:*** $2,134,803 (100% need-based). ***Average need-based loan:*** Freshmen: $3546; Undergraduates: $4643. ***Parent loans:*** $743,921 (100% need-based). ***Programs:*** FFEL (Subsidized and Unsubsidized Stafford, PLUS), Perkins.

WORK-STUDY ***Federal work-study:*** Total amount: $761,470; 216 jobs averaging $3525. ***State or other work-study/employment:*** Total amount: $16,900 (100% need-based). 6 part-time jobs averaging $2817.

APPLYING FOR FINANCIAL AID ***Required financial aid form:*** FAFSA. ***Financial aid deadline (priority):*** 3/1. ***Notification date:*** Continuous beginning 3/1. Students must reply within 4 weeks of notification.

CONTACT Financial Aid Office, Naropa University, 2130 Arapahoe Avenue, Boulder, CO 80302-6697, 303-546-3534 or toll-free 800-772-0410 (out-of-state). *E-mail:* finaid@naropa.edu.

NATIONAL AMERICAN UNIVERSITY
Colorado Springs, CO

CONTACT Financial Aid Coordinator, National American University, 2577 North Chelton Road, Colorado Springs, CO 80909, 719-471-4205.

NATIONAL AMERICAN UNIVERSITY
Denver, CO

CONTACT Cheryl Schunneman, Director of Financial Aid, National American University, 321 Kansas City Street, Rapid City, SD 57701, 605-394-4800.

NATIONAL AMERICAN UNIVERSITY
Roseville, MN

CONTACT Financial Aid Office, National American University, 1500 West Highway 36, Roseville, MN 55113-4035, 651-644-1265.

NATIONAL AMERICAN UNIVERSITY
Kansas City, MO

CONTACT Mary Anderson, Coordinator of Financial Aid, National American University, 4200 Blue Ridge, Kansas City, MO 64133, 816-353-4554. *Fax:* 816-353-1176.

NATIONAL AMERICAN UNIVERSITY
Albuquerque, NM

CONTACT Director of Financial Aid, National American University, 321 Kansas City Street, Rapid City, SD 57701, 605-394-4800 or toll-free 800-843-8892.

NATIONAL AMERICAN UNIVERSITY
Rapid City, SD

CONTACT Financial Aid Director, National American University, PO Box 1780, Rapid City, SD 57709-1780, 605-721-5213 or toll-free 800-843-8892.

NATIONAL AMERICAN UNIVERSITY–SIOUX FALLS BRANCH
Sioux Falls, SD

CONTACT Ms. Rhonda Kohnen, Financial Aid Coordinator, National American University–Sioux Falls Branch, 2801 South Kiwanis Avenue, Suite 100, Sioux Falls, SD 57105-4293, 605-334-5430 or toll-free 800-388-5430 (out-of-state). *Fax:* 605-334-1575. *E-mail:* rkohnen@national.edu.

THE NATIONAL HISPANIC UNIVERSITY
San Jose, CA

Tuition & fees: N/R **Average undergraduate aid package: N/A**

ABOUT THE INSTITUTION Independent, coed. Awards: associate and bachelor's degrees and post-bachelor's certificates. 5 undergraduate majors. Total enrollment: 469. Undergraduates: 293. Freshmen: 34. Federal methodology is used as a basis for awarding need-based institutional aid.

FRESHMAN FINANCIAL AID (Fall 2005) 72 applied for aid; of those 97% were deemed to have need. 100% of freshmen with need received aid. ***Average percent of need met:*** 25% (excluding resources awarded to replace EFC).

UNDERGRADUATE FINANCIAL AID (Fall 2005) 200 applied for aid; of those 92% were deemed to have need. 98% of undergraduates with need received aid. ***Average percent of need met:*** 30% (excluding resources awarded to replace EFC). 5% of all full-time undergraduates had no need and received non-need-based gift aid.

GIFT AID (NEED-BASED) ***Total amount:*** $1,007,560 (52% federal, 14% state, 30% institutional, 4% external sources). ***Receiving aid:*** Freshmen: 96% (70); All full-time undergraduates: 75% (170). ***Average award:*** Freshmen: $1900; Undergraduates: $2500. ***Scholarships, grants, and awards:*** Federal Pell, FSEOG, state, private, college/university gift aid from institutional funds.

GIFT AID (NON-NEED-BASED) ***Total amount:*** $235,691 (100% institutional). ***Receiving aid:*** Undergraduates: 11% (25). ***Average award:*** Undergraduates: $3000. ***Scholarships, grants, and awards by category:*** *Academic Interests/Achievement:* business, computer science, education. *Special Characteristics:* veterans, veterans' children.

LOANS ***Student loans:*** $461,141 (65% need-based, 35% non-need-based). ***Average need-based loan:*** Undergraduates: $3300. ***Programs:*** FFEL (Subsidized and Unsubsidized Stafford, PLUS).

WORK-STUDY ***Federal work-study:*** Total amount: $32,500; 3 jobs averaging $3000.

APPLYING FOR FINANCIAL AID ***Required financial aid form:*** FAFSA. ***Financial aid deadline:*** Continuous. ***Notification date:*** Continuous beginning 6/1. Students must reply by 8/1 or within 2 weeks of notification.

CONTACT Takeo Kubo, Director of Financial Aid and Scholarship, The National Hispanic University, 14271 Story Road, San Jose, CA 95127-3823, 408-273-2708. *Fax:* 408-254-1369. *E-mail:* tkubo@nhu.edu.

NATIONAL-LOUIS UNIVERSITY
Chicago, IL

CONTACT Toni Todd, Student Finance Officer, National-Louis University, 1000 Capitol Drive, Wheeling, IL 60090, 847-465-0575 Ext. 5350 or toll-free 888-NLU-TODAY (in-state), 800-443-5522 (out-of-state).

NATIONAL UNIVERSITY
La Jolla, CA

Tuition & fees: $9132 **Average undergraduate aid package: $9389**

ABOUT THE INSTITUTION Independent, coed. Awards: associate, bachelor's, and master's degrees and post-bachelor's certificates. 45 undergraduate majors. Total enrollment: 25,992. Undergraduates: 7,068. Freshmen: 757. Federal methodology is used as a basis for awarding need-based institutional aid.

UNDERGRADUATE EXPENSES for 2006–07 ***Application fee:*** $60. ***Tuition:*** full-time $9072; part-time $1134 per course. Full-time tuition and fees vary according to course load. Part-time tuition and fees vary according to course load.

FRESHMAN FINANCIAL AID (Fall 2005) 263 applied for aid; of those 100% were deemed to have need. 32% of freshmen with need received aid. ***Average percent of need met:*** 87% (excluding resources awarded to replace EFC). ***Average financial aid package:*** $7033 (excluding resources awarded to replace EFC).

UNDERGRADUATE FINANCIAL AID (Fall 2005) 822 applied for aid; of those 100% were deemed to have need. 61% of undergraduates with need received aid; of those 1% had need fully met. ***Average percent of need met:*** 84% (excluding resources awarded to replace EFC). ***Average financial aid package:*** $9389 (excluding resources awarded to replace EFC). 1% of all full-time undergraduates had no need and received non-need-based gift aid.

GIFT AID (NEED-BASED) ***Total amount:*** $2,419,256 (63% federal, 29% state, 8% institutional). ***Receiving aid:*** Freshmen: 7% (37); All full-time undergraduates: 16% (226). ***Average award:*** Freshmen: $7980; Undergraduates: $8694. ***Scholarships, grants, and awards:*** Federal Pell, FSEOG, state, college/university gift aid from institutional funds.

GIFT AID (NON-NEED-BASED) ***Total amount:*** $101,007 (100% institutional). ***Receiving aid:*** Freshmen: 15% (84); Undergraduates: 35% (505). ***Average award:*** Undergraduates: $6667. ***Scholarships, grants, and awards by category:*** *Academic Interests/Achievement:* general academic interests/achievements. *Special Achievements/Activities:* leadership. ***Tuition waivers:*** Full or partial for employees or children of employees. ***ROTC:*** Army cooperative, Air Force cooperative.

LOANS ***Student loans:*** $59,830,053 (44% need-based, 56% non-need-based). 41% of past graduating class borrowed through all loan programs. *Average indebtedness per student:* $32,312. ***Average need-based loan:*** Freshmen: $4420; Undergraduates: $7704. ***Parent loans:*** $63,762 (100% need-based). ***Programs:*** FFEL (Subsidized and Unsubsidized Stafford, PLUS), Perkins, college/university.

APPLYING FOR FINANCIAL AID ***Required financial aid forms:*** FAFSA, institution's own form. ***Financial aid deadline:*** Continuous. ***Notification date:*** Continuous beginning 6/30.

CONTACT Valerie Ryan, Financial Aid Office, National University, 11255 North Torrey Pines Road, La Jolla, CA 92037-1011, 858-642-8500 or toll-free 800-NAT-UNIV. *Fax:* 858-642-8720. *E-mail:* vryan@nu.edu.

NAZARENE BIBLE COLLEGE
Colorado Springs, CO

Tuition & fees: $8400 **Average undergraduate aid package: N/A**

ABOUT THE INSTITUTION Independent religious, coed. Awards: associate and bachelor's degrees. 6 undergraduate majors. Total enrollment: 808. Undergraduates: 808. Freshmen: 21. Federal methodology is used as a basis for awarding need-based institutional aid.

UNDERGRADUATE EXPENSES for 2007–08 ***Tuition:*** full-time $8100; part-time $300 per credit hour.

FRESHMAN FINANCIAL AID (Fall 2005) 6 applied for aid; of those 100% were deemed to have need. 100% of freshmen with need received aid.

UNDERGRADUATE FINANCIAL AID (Fall 2005) 121 applied for aid; of those 100% were deemed to have need. 100% of undergraduates with need received aid.

GIFT AID (NEED-BASED) ***Total amount:*** $685,884 (79% federal, 19% institutional, 2% external sources). ***Receiving aid:*** Freshmen: 100% (6); All full-time undergraduates: 79% (110). ***Scholarships, grants, and awards:*** Federal Pell, FSEOG, college/university gift aid from institutional funds.

GIFT AID (NON-NEED-BASED) ***Receiving aid:*** Freshmen: 100% (6); Undergraduates: 79% (110). ***Scholarships, grants, and awards by category:*** *Academic Interests/Achievement:* 70 awards ($29,810 total): religion/biblical studies.

LOANS ***Student loans:*** $1,799,137 (58% need-based, 42% non-need-based). 83% of past graduating class borrowed through all loan programs. *Average indebtedness per student:* $19,908. ***Parent loans:*** $8600 (100% non-need-based). ***Programs:*** FFEL (Subsidized and Unsubsidized Stafford, PLUS), Perkins, college/university.

WORK-STUDY ***Federal work-study:*** Total amount: $19,015; 5 jobs averaging $3800.

APPLYING FOR FINANCIAL AID ***Required financial aid form:*** FAFSA. ***Financial aid deadline:*** Continuous. ***Notification date:*** Continuous beginning 2/1.

CONTACT Mr. Malcolm Britton, Director of Financial Aid, Nazarene Bible College, 1111 Academy Park Loop, Colorado Springs, CO 80910-3717, 719-884-5051 or toll-free 800-873-3873. *Fax:* 719-884-5199.

NAZARETH COLLEGE OF ROCHESTER
Rochester, NY

Tuition & fees: $21,640 **Average undergraduate aid package: $15,214**

ABOUT THE INSTITUTION Independent, coed. Awards: bachelor's, master's, and doctoral degrees and post-master's certificates. 72 undergraduate majors. Total enrollment: 3,179. Undergraduates: 2,148. Freshmen: 481. Both federal and institutional methodology are used as a basis for awarding need-based institutional aid.

UNDERGRADUATE EXPENSES for 2006–07 ***Application fee:*** $40. ***Comprehensive fee:*** $30,720 includes full-time tuition ($20,656), mandatory fees ($984), and room and board ($9080). ***College room only:*** $4960. Room and board charges vary according to board plan and housing facility. ***Part-time tuition:*** $493 per credit hour. ***Payment plan:*** Installment.

FRESHMAN FINANCIAL AID (Fall 2006, est.) 442 applied for aid; of those 83% were deemed to have need. 99% of freshmen with need received aid; of those 14% had need fully met. ***Average percent of need met:*** 77% (excluding resources awarded to replace EFC). ***Average financial aid package:*** $16,446 (excluding resources awarded to replace EFC). 22% of all full-time freshmen had no need and received non-need-based gift aid.

UNDERGRADUATE FINANCIAL AID (Fall 2006, est.) 1,731 applied for aid; of those 88% were deemed to have need. 100% of undergraduates with need received aid; of those 20% had need fully met. ***Average percent of need met:*** 73% (excluding resources awarded to replace EFC). ***Average financial aid package:*** $15,214 (excluding resources awarded to replace EFC). 19% of all full-time undergraduates had no need and received non-need-based gift aid.

GIFT AID (NEED-BASED) ***Total amount:*** $15,957,353 (10% federal, 15% state, 71% institutional, 4% external sources). ***Receiving aid:*** Freshmen: 76% (366); All full-time undergraduates: 77% (1,511). ***Average award:*** Freshmen: $11,753; Undergraduates: $10,701. ***Scholarships, grants, and awards:*** Federal Pell, FSEOG, state, private, college/university gift aid from institutional funds.

GIFT AID (NON-NEED-BASED) ***Total amount:*** $4,278,803 (5% state, 81% institutional, 14% external sources). ***Receiving aid:*** Freshmen: 14% (67); Undergraduates: 10% (199). ***Average award:*** Freshmen: $9781; Undergraduates: $9213. ***Scholarships, grants, and awards by category:*** *Academic Interests/Achievement:* 932 awards ($6,750,628 total): general academic interests/achievements. *Creative Arts/Performance:* 136 awards ($323,950 total): art/fine arts, music, theater/drama. *Special Characteristics:* 28 awards ($493,598 total): children and siblings of alumni, children of faculty/staff, siblings of current students. ***Tuition waivers:*** Full or partial for minority students, children of alumni, employees or children of employees. ***ROTC:*** Army cooperative, Air Force cooperative.

LOANS ***Student loans:*** $14,571,128 (68% need-based, 32% non-need-based). 77% of past graduating class borrowed through all loan programs. *Average indebtedness per student:* $26,795. ***Average need-based loan:*** Freshmen: $2941; Undergraduates: $4502. ***Parent loans:*** $4,211,629 (34% need-based, 66% non-need-based). ***Programs:*** FFEL (Subsidized and Unsubsidized Stafford, PLUS), Perkins.

WORK-STUDY ***Federal work-study:*** Total amount: $1,166,801; 1,093 jobs averaging $959.

APPLYING FOR FINANCIAL AID ***Required financial aid form:*** FAFSA. ***Financial aid deadline:*** 5/1 (priority: 2/15). ***Notification date:*** Continuous beginning 2/20. Students must reply by 5/1 or within 2 weeks of notification.

CONTACT Dr. Bruce C. Woolley, Director of Financial Aid, Nazareth College of Rochester, 4245 East Avenue, Rochester, NY 14618-3790, 585-389-2310 or toll-free 800-462-3944 (in-state). *Fax:* 585-389-2317. *E-mail:* bwoolle5@naz.edu.

NEBRASKA CHRISTIAN COLLEGE

Norfolk, NE

CONTACT Linda Bigbee, Director of Financial Aid, Nebraska Christian College, 1800 Syracuse Avenue, Norfolk, NE 68701-2458, 402-379-5017. *Fax:* 402-379-5100. *E-mail:* lbigbee@nechristian.edu.

NEBRASKA METHODIST COLLEGE

Omaha, NE

Tuition & fees: $13,230 **Average undergraduate aid package: $6789**

ABOUT THE INSTITUTION Independent religious, coed, primarily women. Awards: associate, bachelor's, and master's degrees and post-master's certificates. 6 undergraduate majors. Total enrollment: 512. Undergraduates: 446. Freshmen: 20. Federal methodology is used as a basis for awarding need-based institutional aid.

UNDERGRADUATE EXPENSES for 2007–08 ***Application fee:*** $25. ***Tuition:*** full-time $12,630; part-time $421 per credit hour. ***Required fees:*** full-time $600; $20 per credit hour.

FRESHMAN FINANCIAL AID (Fall 2005) 22 applied for aid; of those 86% were deemed to have need. 95% of freshmen with need received aid; of those 56% had need fully met. ***Average percent of need met:*** 67% (excluding resources awarded to replace EFC). ***Average financial aid package:*** $7001 (excluding resources awarded to replace EFC). 27% of all full-time freshmen had no need and received non-need-based gift aid.

UNDERGRADUATE FINANCIAL AID (Fall 2005) 170 applied for aid; of those 84% were deemed to have need. 99% of undergraduates with need received aid; of those 19% had need fully met. ***Average percent of need met:*** 56% (excluding resources awarded to replace EFC). ***Average financial aid package:*** $6789 (excluding resources awarded to replace EFC). 24% of all full-time undergraduates had no need and received non-need-based gift aid.

GIFT AID (NEED-BASED) ***Total amount:*** $1,228,257 (31% federal, 6% state, 44% institutional, 19% external sources). ***Receiving aid:*** Freshmen: 57% (17); All full-time undergraduates: 60% (118). ***Average award:*** Freshmen: $5056; Undergraduates: $3752. ***Scholarships, grants, and awards:*** Federal Pell, FSEOG, state, private, college/university gift aid from institutional funds.

GIFT AID (NON-NEED-BASED) ***Total amount:*** $324,404 (73% institutional, 27% external sources). ***Receiving aid:*** Freshmen: 3% (1); Undergraduates: 4% (7). ***Average award:*** Freshmen: $7059; Undergraduates: $8642. ***Scholarships, grants, and awards by category:*** *Academic Interests/Achievement:* 256 awards ($544,441 total): general academic interests/achievements. ***ROTC:*** Army cooperative, Air Force cooperative.

LOANS ***Student loans:*** $3,660,103 (65% need-based, 35% non-need-based). 66% of past graduating class borrowed through all loan programs. *Average indebtedness per student:* $24,901. ***Average need-based loan:*** Freshmen: $2356; Undergraduates: $3855. ***Parent loans:*** $268,402 (24% need-based, 76% non-need-based). ***Programs:*** FFEL (Subsidized and Unsubsidized Stafford, PLUS), Perkins, Federal Nursing, college/university, alternative loans.

WORK-STUDY ***Federal work-study:*** Total amount: $4339; jobs available (averaging $2400). ***State or other work-study/employment:*** Total amount: $8937 (19% need-based, 81% non-need-based).

APPLYING FOR FINANCIAL AID ***Required financial aid forms:*** FAFSA, institution's own form. ***Financial aid deadline (priority):*** 5/1. ***Notification date:*** Continuous. Students must reply within 3 weeks of notification.

CONTACT Ms. Brenda Boyd, Director of Financial Aid, Nebraska Methodist College, The Josie Harper Campus, 720 North 87th Street, Omaha, NE 68114-3426, 402-354-7225 or toll-free 800-335-5510. *Fax:* 402-354-7020. *E-mail:* brenda.boyd@methodistcollege.edu.

NEBRASKA WESLEYAN UNIVERSITY

Lincoln, NE

Tuition & fees: $19,302 **Average undergraduate aid package: $13,419**

ABOUT THE INSTITUTION Independent United Methodist, coed. Awards: bachelor's and master's degrees and post-master's certificates. 50 undergraduate majors. Total enrollment: 2,068. Undergraduates: 1,864. Freshmen: 414. Federal methodology is used as a basis for awarding need-based institutional aid.

UNDERGRADUATE EXPENSES for 2006–07 ***Application fee:*** $20. ***Comprehensive fee:*** $24,467 includes full-time tuition ($18,980), mandatory fees ($322), and room and board ($5165). Full-time tuition and fees vary according to class time, course load, degree level, location, and program. Room and board charges vary according to board plan and housing facility. ***Part-time tuition:*** $715 per credit hour. Part-time tuition and fees vary according to class time, course load, degree level, location, and program. ***Payment plans:*** Installment, deferred payment.

FRESHMAN FINANCIAL AID (Fall 2006, est.) 362 applied for aid; of those 78% were deemed to have need. 100% of freshmen with need received aid; of those 25% had need fully met. ***Average percent of need met:*** 71% (excluding resources awarded to replace EFC). ***Average financial aid package:*** $14,117 (excluding resources awarded to replace EFC). 29% of all full-time freshmen had no need and received non-need-based gift aid.

UNDERGRADUATE FINANCIAL AID (Fall 2006, est.) 1,319 applied for aid; of those 84% were deemed to have need. 100% of undergraduates with need received aid; of those 20% had need fully met. ***Average percent of need met:*** 68% (excluding resources awarded to replace EFC). ***Average financial aid package:*** $13,419 (excluding resources awarded to replace EFC). 24% of all full-time undergraduates had no need and received non-need-based gift aid.

GIFT AID (NEED-BASED) ***Total amount:*** $9,873,229 (11% federal, 2% state, 84% institutional, 3% external sources). ***Receiving aid:*** Freshmen: 68% (280); All full-time undergraduates: 67% (1,083). ***Average award:*** Freshmen: $10,511; Undergraduates: $9075. ***Scholarships, grants, and awards:*** Federal Pell, FSEOG, state, private, college/university gift aid from institutional funds.

GIFT AID (NON-NEED-BASED) ***Total amount:*** $2,958,934 (95% institutional, 5% external sources). ***Receiving aid:*** Freshmen: 11% (44); Undergraduates: 8% (123). ***Average award:*** Freshmen: $7234; Undergraduates: $6446. ***Scholarships, grants, and awards by category:*** *Academic Interests/Achievement:* 391 awards ($2,313,047 total): general academic interests/achievements. *Creative Arts/Performance:* 153 awards ($181,225 total): art/fine arts, music, theater/drama. *Special Characteristics:* 93 awards ($223,700 total): children of faculty/staff, members of minority groups, relatives of clergy, siblings of current students. ***Tuition waivers:*** Full or partial for employees or children of employees, adult students, senior citizens. ***ROTC:*** Army cooperative, Air Force cooperative.

LOANS ***Student loans:*** $5,875,291 (76% need-based, 24% non-need-based). 79% of past graduating class borrowed through all loan programs. *Average indebtedness per student:* $18,944. ***Average need-based loan:*** Freshmen: $3600; Undergraduates: $4427. ***Parent loans:*** $3,623,846 (41% need-based, 59% non-need-based). ***Programs:*** FFEL (Subsidized and Unsubsidized Stafford, PLUS), Perkins.

WORK-STUDY ***Federal work-study:*** Total amount: $110,000; 164 jobs averaging $670. ***State or other work-study/employment:*** Total amount: $514,659 (34% need-based, 66% non-need-based). 457 part-time jobs averaging $1125.

APPLYING FOR FINANCIAL AID ***Required financial aid form:*** FAFSA. ***Financial aid deadline:*** Continuous. ***Notification date:*** Continuous beginning 3/1. Students must reply within 4 weeks of notification.

CONTACT Mr. Thomas J. Ochsner, Director of Scholarships and Financial Aid, Nebraska Wesleyan University, 5000 Saint Paul Avenue, Lincoln, NE 68504, 402-465-2212 or toll-free 800-541-3818. *Fax:* 402-465-2179. *E-mail:* tjo@nebrwesleyan.edu.

NER ISRAEL RABBINICAL COLLEGE

Baltimore, MD

CONTACT Mr. Moshe Pelberg, Financial Aid Administrator, Ner Israel Rabbinical College, 400 Mount Wilson Lane, Baltimore, MD 21208, 410-484-7200.

NEUMANN COLLEGE

Aston, PA

Tuition & fees: $18,632 **Average undergraduate aid package: $17,000**

ABOUT THE INSTITUTION Independent Roman Catholic, coed. Awards: associate, bachelor's, and master's degrees. 18 undergraduate majors. Total enrollment: 2,969. Undergraduates: 2,418. Freshmen: 544. Federal methodology is used as a basis for awarding need-based institutional aid.

UNDERGRADUATE EXPENSES for 2006–07 ***Application fee:*** $35. ***Comprehensive fee:*** $27,050 includes full-time tuition ($17,992), mandatory fees ($640), and room and board ($8418). ***College room only:*** $4998. ***Part-time tuition:*** $411 per credit.

FRESHMAN FINANCIAL AID (Fall 2006, est.) 490 applied for aid; of those 100% were deemed to have need. 100% of freshmen with need received aid; of those 65% had need fully met. ***Average percent of need met:*** 65% (excluding resources awarded to replace EFC). ***Average financial aid package:*** $17,000 (excluding resources awarded to replace EFC).

UNDERGRADUATE FINANCIAL AID (Fall 2006, est.) 1,600 applied for aid; of those 100% were deemed to have need. 100% of undergraduates with need received aid; of those 60% had need fully met. ***Average percent of need met:*** 65% (excluding resources awarded to replace EFC). ***Average financial aid package:*** $17,000 (excluding resources awarded to replace EFC).

GIFT AID (NEED-BASED) ***Total amount:*** $16,027,500 (12% federal, 14% state, 72% institutional, 2% external sources). ***Receiving aid:*** Freshmen: 83% (450); All full-time undergraduates: 78% (1,472). ***Average award:*** Freshmen: $17,000; Undergraduates: $17,000. ***Scholarships, grants, and awards:*** Federal Pell, FSEOG, state, private, college/university gift aid from institutional funds.

GIFT AID (NON-NEED-BASED) ***Receiving aid:*** Freshmen: 55% (300); Undergraduates: 51% (950). ***Scholarships, grants, and awards by category:*** *Creative Arts/Performance:* 1 award ($1000 total): music. *Special Characteristics:* 29 awards ($254,386 total): children of faculty/staff. ***ROTC:*** Army cooperative.

LOANS ***Student loans:*** $15,720,500 (100% need-based). 80% of past graduating class borrowed through all loan programs. *Average indebtedness per student:* $20,000. ***Average need-based loan:*** Freshmen: $1200; Undergraduates: $1200. ***Parent loans:*** $3,930,600 (100% need-based). ***Programs:*** Federal Direct (Subsidized and Unsubsidized Stafford, PLUS), FFEL (Subsidized and Unsubsidized Stafford, PLUS), Perkins, Federal Nursing.

WORK-STUDY ***Federal work-study:*** Total amount: $200,000; 120 jobs averaging $1200. ***State or other work-study/employment:*** Part-time jobs available.

APPLYING FOR FINANCIAL AID ***Required financial aid form:*** FAFSA. ***Financial aid deadline:*** Continuous.

CONTACT Katherine Markert, Director of Financial Aid, Neumann College, One Neumann Drive, Aston, PA 19014-1298, 610-558-5519 or toll-free 800-963-8626.

NEUMONT UNIVERSITY

Salt Lake City, UT

CONTACT Financial Aid Office, Neumont University, 2755 East Cottonwood Parkway, Suite 600, Salt Lake City, UT 84121, 801-438-1100 or toll-free 866-622-3448.

NEVADA STATE COLLEGE AT HENDERSON

Henderson, NV

CONTACT Financial Aid Office, Nevada State College at Henderson, 1125 Nevada State Drive, Henderson, NV 89015, 702-992-2000.

NEWBERRY COLLEGE

Newberry, SC

ABOUT THE INSTITUTION Independent Evangelical Lutheran, coed. Awards: bachelor's degrees. 36 undergraduate majors. Total enrollment: 851. Undergraduates: 851. Freshmen: 265.

GIFT AID (NEED-BASED) ***Scholarships, grants, and awards:*** Federal Pell, FSEOG, state, private, college/university gift aid from institutional funds.

GIFT AID (NON-NEED-BASED) ***Scholarships, grants, and awards by category:*** *Academic Interests/Achievement:* biological sciences, business, communication, education, foreign languages, general academic interests/achievements, humanities, mathematics, physical sciences, religion/biblical studies, social sciences. *Creative Arts/Performance:* music, theater/drama. *Special Achievements/Activities:* cheerleading/drum major, religious involvement. *Special Characteristics:* children and siblings of alumni, children of faculty/staff, international students, local/state students, relatives of clergy, religious affiliation, siblings of current students.

LOANS ***Programs:*** FFEL (Subsidized and Unsubsidized Stafford, PLUS), Perkins, state.

WORK-STUDY ***Federal work-study:*** Total amount: $43,687; 52 jobs averaging $804. ***State or other work-study/employment:*** Total amount: $23,838 (100% non-need-based). 45 part-time jobs averaging $518.

APPLYING FOR FINANCIAL AID ***Required financial aid forms:*** FAFSA, institution's own form.

CONTACT Mrs. Susanne Nelson, Director of Financial Aid, Newberry College, 2100 College Street, Newberry, SC 29108, 803-321-5127 or toll-free 800-845-4955 Ext. 5127. *Fax:* 803-321-5627. *E-mail:* susanne.nelson@newberry.edu.

NEWBURY COLLEGE

Brookline, MA

CONTACT Financial Aid Office, Newbury College, 129 Fisher Avenue, Brookline, MA 02445-5796, 617-730-7101 or toll-free 800-NEWBURY. *Fax:* 617-731-9618.

NEW COLLEGE OF CALIFORNIA

San Francisco, CA

CONTACT Director of Student Financial Aid, New College of California, 50 Fell Street, San Francisco, CA 94102-5206, 415-241-1300 Ext. 338 or toll-free 888-437-3460.

NEW COLLEGE OF FLORIDA

Sarasota, FL

Tuition & fees (area res): $3850 **Average undergraduate aid package: $12,018**

ABOUT THE INSTITUTION State-supported, coed. Awards: bachelor's degrees. 38 undergraduate majors. Total enrollment: 746. Undergraduates: 746. Freshmen: 175. Federal methodology is used as a basis for awarding need-based institutional aid.

UNDERGRADUATE EXPENSES for 2007–08 ***Application fee:*** $30. ***Tuition, area resident:*** full-time $3850. ***Tuition, nonresident:*** full-time $20,575. ***College room and board:*** $7080; ***Room only:*** $4590.

FRESHMAN FINANCIAL AID (Fall 2006, est.) 125 applied for aid; of those 59% were deemed to have need. 100% of freshmen with need received aid; of those 72% had need fully met. ***Average percent of need met:*** 92% (excluding resources awarded to replace EFC). ***Average financial aid package:*** $11,662 (excluding resources awarded to replace EFC). 58% of all full-time freshmen had no need and received non-need-based gift aid.

UNDERGRADUATE FINANCIAL AID (Fall 2006, est.) 411 applied for aid; of those 68% were deemed to have need. 100% of undergraduates with need received aid; of those 66% had need fully met. ***Average percent of need met:*** 92% (excluding resources awarded to replace EFC). ***Average financial aid package:*** $12,018 (excluding resources awarded to replace EFC). 50% of all full-time undergraduates had no need and received non-need-based gift aid.

GIFT AID (NEED-BASED) ***Total amount:*** $1,873,905 (26% federal, 34% state, 37% institutional, 3% external sources). ***Receiving aid:*** Freshmen: 42% (74); All full-time undergraduates: 37% (277). ***Average award:*** Freshmen: $8350; Undergraduates: $7620. ***Scholarships, grants, and awards:*** Federal Pell, FSEOG, state, private, college/university gift aid from institutional funds, Federal Academic Competitiveness Grant.

GIFT AID (NON-NEED-BASED) ***Total amount:*** $2,331,850 (52% state, 45% institutional, 3% external sources). ***Receiving aid:*** Freshmen: 10% (18); Undergraduates: 7% (52). ***Average award:*** Freshmen: $3277; Undergraduates: $3410. ***Scholarships, grants, and awards by category:*** *Academic Interests/Achievement:* 500 awards ($1,079,453 total): general academic interests/achievements. *Special Achievements/Activities:* 57 awards ($381,250 total): general special achievements/activities. *Special Characteristics:* 88 awards ($602,107 total): out-of-state students.

LOANS ***Student loans:*** $1,070,926 (82% need-based, 18% non-need-based). 26% of past graduating class borrowed through all loan programs. *Average indebtedness per student:* $15,334. ***Average need-based loan:*** Freshmen: $2085; Undergraduates: $3708. ***Parent loans:*** $370,644 (28% need-based, 72% non-need-based). ***Programs:*** FFEL (Subsidized and Unsubsidized Stafford, PLUS), alternative loans.

WORK-STUDY ***Federal work-study:*** Total amount: $64,913; 20 jobs averaging $3246. ***State or other work-study/employment:*** Total amount: $158,185 (100% need-based). 53 part-time jobs averaging $2985.

APPLYING FOR FINANCIAL AID ***Required financial aid form:*** FAFSA. ***Financial aid deadline (priority):*** 2/15. ***Notification date:*** Continuous beginning 3/15. Students must reply by 5/1 or within 4 weeks of notification.

CONTACT Monica Baldwin, Director of Financial Aid, New College of Florida, 5800 Bay Shore Rd., PME 119, Sarasota, FL 34243-2109, 941-487-5001. *Fax:* 941-487-5011. *E-mail:* ncfinaid@ncf.edu.

NEW ENGLAND COLLEGE

Henniker, NH

Tuition & fees: N/R **Average undergraduate aid package: $21,733**

ABOUT THE INSTITUTION Independent, coed. Awards: associate, bachelor's, and master's degrees. 39 undergraduate majors. Total enrollment: 1,340. Undergraduates: 1,065. Freshmen: 326. Both federal and institutional methodology are used as a basis for awarding need-based institutional aid.

UNDERGRADUATE EXPENSES for 2007–08 ***Application fee:*** $30.

FRESHMAN FINANCIAL AID (Fall 2006, est.) 271 applied for aid; of those 88% were deemed to have need. 100% of freshmen with need received aid; of those 25% had need fully met. ***Average percent of need met:*** 82% (excluding resources awarded to replace EFC). ***Average financial aid package:*** $21,543 (excluding resources awarded to replace EFC). 21% of all full-time freshmen had no need and received non-need-based gift aid.

UNDERGRADUATE FINANCIAL AID (Fall 2006, est.) 813 applied for aid; of those 89% were deemed to have need. 100% of undergraduates with need received aid; of those 32% had need fully met. ***Average percent of need met:*** 84% (excluding resources awarded to replace EFC). ***Average financial aid package:*** $21,733 (excluding resources awarded to replace EFC). 16% of all full-time undergraduates had no need and received non-need-based gift aid.

GIFT AID (NEED-BASED) ***Total amount:*** $8,535,547 (11% federal, 1% state, 87% institutional, 1% external sources). ***Receiving aid:*** Freshmen: 72% (235); All full-time undergraduates: 71% (699). ***Average award:*** Freshmen: $12,739; Undergraduates: $11,647. ***Scholarships, grants, and awards:*** Federal Pell, FSEOG, state, private, college/university gift aid from institutional funds.

GIFT AID (NON-NEED-BASED) ***Total amount:*** $1,455,283 (99% institutional, 1% external sources). ***Receiving aid:*** Freshmen: 5% (17); Undergraduates: 5% (48). ***Average award:*** Freshmen: $9235; Undergraduates: $9166. ***Scholarships, grants, and awards by category:*** *Academic Interests/Achievement:* 971 awards ($7,069,155 total): biological sciences, business, communication, computer science, education, engineering/technologies, English, general academic interests/achievements, humanities, international studies, mathematics, social sciences. *Creative Arts/Performance:* 21 awards ($230,364 total): applied art and design, art/fine arts, creative writing, theater/drama. *Special Achievements/Activities:* 36 awards ($294,600 total): community service, leadership. *Special Characteristics:* 109 awards ($1,114,561 total): children and siblings of alumni, children of educators, children of faculty/staff, ethnic background, international students, local/state students, parents of current students, siblings of current students. ***ROTC:*** Army cooperative, Air Force cooperative.

LOANS ***Student loans:*** $7,112,575 (90% need-based, 10% non-need-based). 70% of past graduating class borrowed through all loan programs. *Average indebtedness per student:* $32,476. ***Average need-based loan:*** Freshmen: $9163; Undergraduates: $10,952. ***Parent loans:*** $2,481,103 (83% need-based, 17% non-need-based). ***Programs:*** FFEL (Subsidized and Unsubsidized Stafford, PLUS), Perkins, state.

WORK-STUDY ***Federal work-study:*** Total amount: $499,228; 296 jobs averaging $1687. ***State or other work-study/employment:*** Total amount: $64,092 (75% need-based, 25% non-need-based). Part-time jobs available.

APPLYING FOR FINANCIAL AID ***Required financial aid forms:*** FAFSA, institution's own form. ***Financial aid deadline (priority):*** 4/1. ***Notification date:*** Continuous beginning 1/2. Students must reply within 2 weeks of notification.

CONTACT Shannon Carroll, Student Financial Services, New England College, 7 Main Street, Henniker, NH 03242-3293, 603-428-2226 or toll-free 800-521-7642. *Fax:* 603-428-2404.

NEW ENGLAND CONSERVATORY OF MUSIC

Boston, MA

CONTACT Kenneth T. Ferreira Jr., Director of Financial Aid, New England Conservatory of Music, 290 Huntington Avenue, Boston, MA 02115, 617-585-1110. *Fax:* 617-585-1115. *E-mail:* kferreira@newenglandconservatory.edu.

THE NEW ENGLAND INSTITUTE OF ART

Brookline, MA

CONTACT Ms. Merry Kerber, Director of Financial Aid, The New England Institute of Art, 142 Berkeley Street, Boston, MA 02116-5100, 617-267-7910 or toll-free 800-903=4425 (in-state).

NEW ENGLAND SCHOOL OF COMMUNICATIONS

Bangor, ME

Tuition & fees: $10,270 **Average undergraduate aid package: $2511**

ABOUT THE INSTITUTION Independent, coed. Awards: associate and bachelor's degrees. 20 undergraduate majors. Total enrollment: 306. Undergraduates: 306. Freshmen: 117. Federal methodology is used as a basis for awarding need-based institutional aid.

UNDERGRADUATE EXPENSES for 2007–08 ***Application fee:*** $15. ***Comprehensive fee:*** $16,770 includes full-time tuition ($9990), mandatory fees ($280), and room and board ($6500). ***Part-time tuition:*** $330 per credit.

GIFT AID (NEED-BASED) ***Receiving aid:*** Freshmen: 38% (51); All full-time undergraduates: 36% (109). ***Average award:*** Freshmen: $1980; Undergraduates: $1900. ***Scholarships, grants, and awards:*** Federal Pell, state, private, college/university gift aid from institutional funds.

GIFT AID (NON-NEED-BASED) ***Receiving aid:*** Freshmen: 12% (17); Undergraduates: 8% (25). ***Scholarships, grants, and awards by category:*** *Academic Interests/Achievement:* 25 awards ($21,000 total): communication. *Special Achievements/Activities:* general special achievements/activities. ***ROTC:*** Army cooperative.

LOANS ***Student loans:*** 93% of past graduating class borrowed through all loan programs. *Average indebtedness per student:* $20,000. ***Average need-based loan:*** Freshmen: $2625; Undergraduates: $4500. ***Programs:*** FFEL (Subsidized and Unsubsidized Stafford, PLUS), alternative loans.

APPLYING FOR FINANCIAL AID ***Required financial aid form:*** FAFSA. ***Financial aid deadline (priority):*** 5/1. ***Notification date:*** Continuous beginning 5/1. Students must reply within 4 weeks of notification.

CONTACT Ms. Nicole Rediker, Director of Financial Aid, New England School of Communications, One College Circle, Bangor, ME 04401, 888-877-1876. *Fax:* 207-947-3987.

NEW HAMPSHIRE INSTITUTE OF ART

Manchester, NH

ABOUT THE INSTITUTION Proprietary, coed. Awards: bachelor's degrees. 1 undergraduate major. Total enrollment: 281. Undergraduates: 281. Freshmen: 107.

GIFT AID (NEED-BASED) ***Scholarships, grants, and awards:*** Federal Pell, FSEOG, state, private, college/university gift aid from institutional funds.

GIFT AID (NON-NEED-BASED) ***Scholarships, grants, and awards by category:*** *Creative Arts/Performance:* art/fine arts.

LOANS ***Programs:*** FFEL (Subsidized and Unsubsidized Stafford, PLUS), alternative loans.

APPLYING FOR FINANCIAL AID ***Required financial aid form:*** FAFSA.

CONTACT Linda Lavallee, Director of Financial Aid, New Hampshire Institute of Art, 148 Concord Street, Manchester, NH 03104-4858, 603-623-0313 Ext. 577 or toll-free 866-241-4918 (in-state). *Fax:* 603-647-0658. *E-mail:* llavallee@nhia.edu.

NEW JERSEY CITY UNIVERSITY

Jersey City, NJ

Tuition & fees (NJ res): $7536 **Average undergraduate aid package: $7549**

ABOUT THE INSTITUTION State-supported, coed. Awards: bachelor's and master's degrees and post-master's certificates. 27 undergraduate majors. Total enrollment: 8,523. Undergraduates: 6,158. Freshmen: 818. Federal methodology is used as a basis for awarding need-based institutional aid.

UNDERGRADUATE EXPENSES for 2006–07 ***Application fee:*** $35. ***Tuition, state resident:*** full-time $5600; part-time $186.65 per credit. ***Tuition, nonresident:*** full-time $11,400; part-time $380 per credit. ***Required fees:*** full-time $1,936; $64.55 per credit. Full-time tuition and fees vary according to course load. Part-time tuition and fees vary according to course load. ***College room and board:*** $7880; ***Room only:*** $5000. ***Payment plan:*** Deferred payment.

FRESHMAN FINANCIAL AID (Fall 2005) 512 applied for aid; of those 85% were deemed to have need. 94% of freshmen with need received aid; of those 10% had need fully met. ***Average percent of need met:*** 65% (excluding resources awarded to replace EFC). ***Average financial aid package:*** $7496 (excluding resources awarded to replace EFC). 2% of all full-time freshmen had no need and received non-need-based gift aid.

UNDERGRADUATE FINANCIAL AID (Fall 2005) 3,449 applied for aid; of those 93% were deemed to have need. 95% of undergraduates with need received aid; of those 11% had need fully met. ***Average percent of need met:*** 63% (excluding resources awarded to replace EFC). ***Average financial aid package:*** $7549 (excluding resources awarded to replace EFC). 1% of all full-time undergraduates had no need and received non-need-based gift aid.

GIFT AID (NEED-BASED) ***Total amount:*** $14,298,087 (52% federal, 48% state). ***Receiving aid:*** Freshmen: 52% (313); All full-time undergraduates: 54% (2,272). ***Average award:*** Freshmen: $6795; Undergraduates: $5990. ***Scholarships, grants, and awards:*** Federal Pell, FSEOG, state, private, college/university gift aid from institutional funds, United Negro College Fund.

GIFT AID (NON-NEED-BASED) ***Total amount:*** $775,879 (7% state, 90% institutional, 3% external sources). ***Receiving aid:*** Freshmen: 10% (58); Undergraduates: 6% (249). ***Average award:*** Freshmen: $3028; Undergraduates: $3671. ***Scholarships, grants, and awards by category:*** *Academic Interests/Achievement:* biological sciences, business, communication, education, general academic interests/achievements, mathematics. *Creative Arts/Performance:* art/fine arts, dance, music. ***Tuition waivers:*** Full or partial for senior citizens.

LOANS ***Student loans:*** $14,243,151 (59% need-based, 41% non-need-based). 73% of past graduating class borrowed through all loan programs. *Average indebtedness per student:* $26,344. ***Average need-based loan:*** Freshmen: $2671; Undergraduates: $3680. ***Parent loans:*** $544,070 (100% non-need-based). ***Programs:*** FFEL (Subsidized and Unsubsidized Stafford, PLUS), Perkins, state.

WORK-STUDY ***Federal work-study:*** Total amount: $1,096,687; jobs available.

APPLYING FOR FINANCIAL AID ***Required financial aid form:*** FAFSA. ***Financial aid deadline (priority):*** 4/15. ***Notification date:*** 5/1.

CONTACT Ms. Carmen Panlilio, Assistant Vice President for Admissions and Financial Aid, New Jersey City University, 2039 Kennedy Boulevard, Jersey City, NJ 07305-1597, 201-200-3173 or toll-free 888-441-NJCU.

NEW JERSEY INSTITUTE OF TECHNOLOGY

Newark, NJ

CONTACT Ms. Kathy Bialk, Director of Financial Aid, New Jersey Institute of Technology, University Heights, Newark, NJ 07102, 973-596-3478 or toll-free 800-925-NJIT. *Fax:* 973-802-1854. *E-mail:* kathy.j.bialk@njit.edu.

NEW LIFE THEOLOGICAL SEMINARY

Charlotte, NC

CONTACT Financial Aid Office, New Life Theological Seminary, PO Box 790106, Charlotte, NC 28206-7901, 704-334-6882.

NEWMAN UNIVERSITY

Wichita, KS

Tuition & fees: $17,308 **Average undergraduate aid package: $10,323**

ABOUT THE INSTITUTION Independent Roman Catholic, coed. Awards: associate, bachelor's, and master's degrees. 36 undergraduate majors. Total enrollment: 2,104. Undergraduates: 1,631. Freshmen: 162. Federal methodology is used as a basis for awarding need-based institutional aid.

UNDERGRADUATE EXPENSES for 2006–07 ***Application fee:*** $20. ***Comprehensive fee:*** $22,680 includes full-time tuition ($17,008), mandatory fees ($300), and room and board ($5372). Full-time tuition and fees vary according to location and program. Room and board charges vary according to housing facility. ***Part-time tuition:*** $567 per credit hour. ***Part-time fees:*** $10 per credit hour. Part-time tuition and fees vary according to location and program. ***Payment plan:*** Installment.

FRESHMAN FINANCIAL AID (Fall 2005) 223 applied for aid; of those 48% were deemed to have need. 100% of freshmen with need received aid; of those 20% had need fully met. ***Average percent of need met:*** 62% (excluding resources awarded to replace EFC). ***Average financial aid package:*** $10,739 (excluding resources awarded to replace EFC). 8% of all full-time freshmen had no need and received non-need-based gift aid.

UNDERGRADUATE FINANCIAL AID (Fall 2005) 1,249 applied for aid; of those 72% were deemed to have need. 100% of undergraduates with need received aid; of those 13% had need fully met. ***Average percent of need met:*** 56% (excluding resources awarded to replace EFC). ***Average financial aid package:*** $10,323 (excluding resources awarded to replace EFC). 6% of all full-time undergraduates had no need and received non-need-based gift aid.

GIFT AID (NEED-BASED) ***Total amount:*** $1,977,960 (65% federal, 35% state). ***Receiving aid:*** Freshmen: 34% (75); All full-time undergraduates: 55% (698). ***Average award:*** Freshmen: $3684; Undergraduates: $3891. ***Scholarships, grants, and awards:*** Federal Pell, FSEOG, state, private, college/university gift aid from institutional funds.

GIFT AID (NON-NEED-BASED) ***Total amount:*** $4,386,756 (93% institutional, 7% external sources). ***Receiving aid:*** Freshmen: 48% (106); Undergraduates: 63% (792). ***Average award:*** Freshmen: $2734; Undergraduates: $2313. ***Scholarships, grants, and awards by category:*** *Academic Interests/Achievement:* 893 awards ($2,401,510 total): general academic interests/achievements. *Creative Arts/Performance:* 38 awards ($88,575 total): art/fine arts, journalism/publications, music, theater/drama. *Special Achievements/Activities:* 122 awards ($324,700 total): community service, leadership, memberships, religious involvement. *Special Characteristics:* 399 awards ($821,531 total): children and siblings of alumni, children of faculty/staff, first-generation college students, international students, siblings of current students. ***Tuition waivers:*** Full or partial for employees or children of employees.

LOANS ***Student loans:*** $10,834,657 (41% need-based, 59% non-need-based). 76% of past graduating class borrowed through all loan programs. *Average indebtedness per student:* $20,504. ***Average need-based loan:*** Freshmen: $2190; Undergraduates: $3899. ***Parent loans:*** $874,441 (100% non-need-based). ***Programs:*** FFEL (Subsidized and Unsubsidized Stafford, PLUS), Perkins.

WORK-STUDY ***Federal work-study:*** Total amount: $109,291; 102 jobs averaging $1071. ***State or other work-study/employment:*** Total amount: $171,817 (100% non-need-based). 149 part-time jobs averaging $1153.

ATHLETIC AWARDS Total amount: $1,091,228 (100% non-need-based).

APPLYING FOR FINANCIAL AID ***Required financial aid forms:*** FAFSA, institution's own form. ***Financial aid deadline (priority):*** 3/1. ***Notification date:*** Continuous.

CONTACT Victoria Tillotson, Financial Aid Counselor, Newman University, 3100 McCormick Avenue, Wichita, KS 67213, 316-942-4291 Ext. 2103 or toll-free 877-NEWMANU Ext. 2144. *Fax:* 316-942-4483.

NEW MEXICO HIGHLANDS UNIVERSITY

Las Vegas, NM

CONTACT Eileen Sedillo, Director, Financial Aid & Scholarship, New Mexico Highlands University, Box 9000, Las Vegas, NM 87701, 505-454-3430 or toll-free 800-338-6648. *Fax:* 505-454-3398. *E-mail:* sedillo_e@nmhu.edu.

NEW MEXICO INSTITUTE OF MINING AND TECHNOLOGY

Socorro, NM

CONTACT Ms. Annette Kaus, Director of Financial Aid, New Mexico Institute of Mining and Technology, Financial Aid Office, 801 Leroy Place, Socorro, NM 87801, 505-835-5333 or toll-free 800-428-TECH. *Fax:* 505-835-5959. *E-mail:* akaus@admin.nmt.edu.

NEW MEXICO STATE UNIVERSITY

Las Cruces, NM

Tuition & fees (NM res): $4230 **Average undergraduate aid package: $7438**

ABOUT THE INSTITUTION State-supported, coed. Awards: associate, bachelor's, master's, and doctoral degrees and post-master's certificates. 82 undergraduate majors. Total enrollment: 16,415. Undergraduates: 13,210. Freshmen: 1,946. Federal methodology is used as a basis for awarding need-based institutional aid.

UNDERGRADUATE EXPENSES for 2006–07 ***Application fee:*** $15. ***Tuition, state resident:*** full-time $3164; part-time $163.25 per credit. ***Tuition, nonresident:*** full-time $12,738; part-time $550.25 per credit. ***College room and board:*** $5576; ***Room only:*** $3226. Room and board charges vary according to board plan and gender. ***Payment plans:*** Installment, deferred payment.

FRESHMAN FINANCIAL AID (Fall 2006, est.) 1515 applied for aid; of those 80% were deemed to have need. 95% of freshmen with need received aid; of those 13% had need fully met. ***Average percent of need met:*** 53% (excluding resources awarded to replace EFC). ***Average financial aid package:*** $6405 (excluding resources awarded to replace EFC). 28% of all full-time freshmen had no need and received non-need-based gift aid.

UNDERGRADUATE FINANCIAL AID (Fall 2006, est.) 7,203 applied for aid; of those 86% were deemed to have need. 92% of undergraduates with need received aid; of those 12% had need fully met. ***Average percent of need met:*** 58% (excluding resources awarded to replace EFC). ***Average financial aid package:*** $7438 (excluding resources awarded to replace EFC). 20% of all full-time undergraduates had no need and received non-need-based gift aid.

GIFT AID (NEED-BASED) ***Total amount:*** $26,385,859 (59% federal, 32% state, 5% institutional, 4% external sources). ***Receiving aid:*** Freshmen: 49% (1,041); All full-time undergraduates: 45% (4,976). ***Average award:*** Freshmen: $5069; Undergraduates: $5137. ***Scholarships, grants, and awards:*** Federal Pell, FSEOG, state, private, college/university gift aid from institutional funds.

GIFT AID (NON-NEED-BASED) ***Total amount:*** $8,349,922 (88% state, 9% institutional, 3% external sources). ***Receiving aid:*** Freshmen: 5% (112); Undergraduates: 3% (312). ***Average award:*** Freshmen: $3688; Undergraduates: $3413. ***Scholarships, grants, and awards by category:*** *Academic Interests/Achievement:* agriculture, biological sciences, business, communication, computer science, education, engineering/technologies, English, foreign languages, general academic interests/achievements, health fields, home economics, humanities, mathematics, military science, physical sciences, social sciences. *Creative Arts/Performance:* applied art and design, art/fine arts, general creative arts/performance, journalism/publications, music, performing arts, theater/drama. *Special Achievements/Activities:* leadership, rodeo. *Special Characteristics:* adult students, children and siblings of alumni, children of faculty/staff, children of public servants, children of union members/company employees, children of workers in trades, children with a deceased or disabled parent, ethnic background, handicapped students, international students, local/state students, married students, members of minority groups, out-of-state students, previous college experience, spouses of current students, veterans, veterans' children. ***Tuition waivers:*** Full or partial for employees or children of employees, senior citizens. ***ROTC:*** Army, Air Force.

LOANS ***Student loans:*** $20,129,572 (83% need-based, 17% non-need-based). ***Average need-based loan:*** Freshmen: $3157; Undergraduates: $4375. ***Parent loans:*** $671,348 (31% need-based, 69% non-need-based). ***Programs:*** FFEL (Subsidized and Unsubsidized Stafford, PLUS), Perkins, state.

WORK-STUDY ***Federal work-study:*** Total amount: $978,967; 479 jobs averaging $1854. ***State or other work-study/employment:*** Total amount: $1,731,586 (75% need-based, 25% non-need-based). 546 part-time jobs averaging $1873.

ATHLETIC AWARDS Total amount: $2,142,436 (26% need-based, 74% non-need-based).

APPLYING FOR FINANCIAL AID ***Required financial aid forms:*** FAFSA, institution's own form. ***Financial aid deadline (priority):*** 3/1.

CONTACT Mr. Tyler Pruett, Director of Financial Aid, New Mexico State University, Box 30001, Department 5100, Las Cruces, NM 88003-8001, 505-646-4105 or toll-free 800-662-6678. *Fax:* 505-646-7381.

NEW ORLEANS BAPTIST THEOLOGICAL SEMINARY

New Orleans, LA

CONTACT Financial Aid Office, New Orleans Baptist Theological Seminary, 3939 Gentilly Boulevard, New Orleans, LA 70126-4858, 504-282-4455 Ext. 3348 or toll-free 800-662-8701. *E-mail:* financialaid@nobts.edu.

NEW SAINT ANDREWS COLLEGE

Moscow, ID

CONTACT Financial Aid Office, New Saint Andrews College, PO Box 9025, Moscow, ID 83843, 208-882-1566.

THE NEW SCHOOL FOR GENERAL STUDIES

New York, NY

CONTACT Financial Aid Counselor, The New School for General Studies, 65 Fifth Avenue, New York, NY 10003, 212-229-8930 or toll-free 800-862-5039 (out-of-state). *Fax:* 212-229-5919.

THE NEW SCHOOL FOR JAZZ AND CONTEMPORARY MUSIC

New York, NY

Tuition & fees: $28,210 **Average undergraduate aid package: $11,713**

ABOUT THE INSTITUTION Independent, coed. 1 undergraduate major. Total enrollment: 260. Undergraduates: 260. Freshmen: 51.

UNDERGRADUATE EXPENSES for 2007–08 ***Application fee:*** $100. ***Comprehensive fee:*** $39,960 includes full-time tuition ($27,600), mandatory fees ($610), and room and board ($11,750). ***College room only:*** $8750. ***Part-time tuition:*** $900 per credit hour.

FRESHMAN FINANCIAL AID (Fall 2006, est.) 30 applied for aid; of those 100% were deemed to have need. 100% of freshmen with need received aid; of those 13% had need fully met. ***Average percent of need met:*** 69% (excluding resources awarded to replace EFC). ***Average financial aid package:*** $9918 (excluding resources awarded to replace EFC). 26% of all full-time freshmen had no need and received non-need-based gift aid.

UNDERGRADUATE FINANCIAL AID (Fall 2006, est.) 127 applied for aid; of those 100% were deemed to have need. 100% of undergraduates with need received aid; of those 10% had need fully met. ***Average percent of need met:*** 71% (excluding resources awarded to replace EFC). ***Average financial aid package:*** $11,713 (excluding resources awarded to replace EFC). 43% of all full-time undergraduates had no need and received non-need-based gift aid.

GIFT AID (NEED-BASED) ***Total amount:*** $1,936,140 (10% federal, 3% state, 87% institutional). ***Receiving aid:*** Freshmen: 14% (7); All full-time undergraduates: 11% (27). ***Average award:*** Freshmen: $5213; Undergraduates: $5191. ***Scholarships, grants, and awards:*** Federal Pell, FSEOG, state, private, college/university gift aid from institutional funds.

GIFT AID (NON-NEED-BASED) ***Total amount:*** $89,650 (100% institutional). ***Receiving aid:*** Freshmen: 42% (21); Undergraduates: 47% (111). ***Average award:*** Freshmen: $9923; Undergraduates: $9104.

LOANS ***Student loans:*** $1,504,066 (57% need-based, 43% non-need-based). 45% of past graduating class borrowed through all loan programs. *Average indebtedness per student:* $28,106. ***Average need-based loan:*** Freshmen: $1953; Undergraduates: $3482. ***Parent loans:*** $720,973 (100% non-need-based). ***Programs:*** FFEL (Subsidized and Unsubsidized Stafford, PLUS), Perkins.

WORK-STUDY ***Federal work-study:*** Total amount: $106,540.

APPLYING FOR FINANCIAL AID ***Required financial aid form:*** FAFSA. ***Financial aid deadline:*** Continuous. ***Notification date:*** Students must reply within 4 weeks of notification.

CONTACT Financial Aid Office, The New School for Jazz and Contemporary Music, 55 West 13th Street, 5th Floor, New York, NY 10011, 212-229-5896.

NEWSCHOOL OF ARCHITECTURE & DESIGN

San Diego, CA

CONTACT Ms. Cara E. Baker, Director of Financial Aid, Newschool of Architecture & Design, 1249 F Street, San Diego, CA 92101-6634, 619-235-4100 Ext. 103. *Fax:* 619-235-4651. *E-mail:* cbaker@newschoolarch.edu.

NEW YORK INSTITUTE OF TECHNOLOGY

Old Westbury, NY

Tuition & fees: $20,358 **Average undergraduate aid package: $15,531**

ABOUT THE INSTITUTION Independent, coed. Awards: associate, bachelor's, master's, doctoral, and first professional degrees and post-bachelor's and post-master's certificates. 70 undergraduate majors. Total enrollment: 11,404. Undergraduates: 6,751. Freshmen: 937. Federal methodology is used as a basis for awarding need-based institutional aid.

UNDERGRADUATE EXPENSES for 2006–07 ***Application fee:*** $50. ***Comprehensive fee:*** $31,810 includes full-time tuition ($19,818), mandatory fees ($540), and room and board ($11,452). Full-time tuition and fees vary according to course load and program. Room and board charges vary according to board plan, housing facility, and location. ***Part-time tuition:*** $668 per credit. ***Part-time fees:*** $230 per term. Part-time tuition and fees vary according to course load. ***Payment plan:*** Installment.

FRESHMAN FINANCIAL AID (Fall 2005) 1120 applied for aid; of those 86% were deemed to have need. 99% of freshmen with need received aid. ***Average financial aid package:*** $12,061 (excluding resources awarded to replace EFC). 15% of all full-time freshmen had no need and received non-need-based gift aid.

UNDERGRADUATE FINANCIAL AID (Fall 2005) 3,414 applied for aid; of those 88% were deemed to have need. 99% of undergraduates with need received aid. ***Average financial aid package:*** $15,531 (excluding resources awarded to replace EFC). 12% of all full-time undergraduates had no need and received non-need-based gift aid.

GIFT AID (NEED-BASED) ***Total amount:*** $14,982,956 (41% federal, 37% state, 22% institutional). ***Receiving aid:*** Freshmen: 51% (646); All full-time undergraduates: 52% (2,079). ***Average award:*** Freshmen: $3475; Undergraduates: $4873. ***Scholarships, grants, and awards:*** Federal Pell, FSEOG, state, private, college/university gift aid from institutional funds.

GIFT AID (NON-NEED-BASED) ***Total amount:*** $13,200,217 (1% state, 99% institutional). ***Receiving aid:*** Freshmen: 71% (900); Undergraduates: 64% (2,581). ***Average award:*** Freshmen: $7518; Undergraduates: $9407. ***Scholarships, grants, and awards by category:*** *Academic Interests/Achievement:* general academic interests/achievements. *Special Characteristics:* children and siblings of alumni, children of educators, children of faculty/staff, children of public servants, local/state students, previous college experience, public servants, spouses of deceased or disabled public servants, veterans. ***Tuition waivers:*** Full or partial for employees or children of employees, senior citizens. ***ROTC:*** Army, Air Force.

LOANS ***Student loans:*** $31,074,538 (36% need-based, 64% non-need-based). 75% of past graduating class borrowed through all loan programs. *Average indebtedness per student:* $17,125. ***Average need-based loan:*** Freshmen: $2880; Undergraduates: $4667. ***Parent loans:*** $7,566,012 (100% non-need-based). ***Programs:*** FFEL (Subsidized and Unsubsidized Stafford, PLUS), Perkins, Federal Nursing, alternative loans.

WORK-STUDY ***Federal work-study:*** Total amount: $692,697; jobs available. ***State or other work-study/employment:*** Total amount: $454,216 (100% non-need-based). Part-time jobs available.

ATHLETIC AWARDS Total amount: $1,651,342 (100% non-need-based).

APPLYING FOR FINANCIAL AID ***Required financial aid form:*** FAFSA. ***Financial aid deadline (priority):*** 2/1. ***Notification date:*** Continuous beginning 2/15. Students must reply by 5/1 or within 2 weeks of notification.

CONTACT Doreen Meyer, Director of Financial Aid Office, New York Institute of Technology, PO Box 8000, Old Westbury, NY 11568-8000, 516-686-1083 or toll-free 800-345-NYIT. *Fax:* 516-686-7997. *E-mail:* dmeyer@nyit.edu.

NEW YORK SCHOOL OF INTERIOR DESIGN

New York, NY

Tuition & fees: $20,750 **Average undergraduate aid package: $6500**

ABOUT THE INSTITUTION Independent, coed, primarily women. Awards: associate, bachelor's, and master's degrees. 1 undergraduate major. Total enrollment: 736. Undergraduates: 718. Freshmen: 10. Federal methodology is used as a basis for awarding need-based institutional aid.

UNDERGRADUATE EXPENSES for 2007–08 ***Application fee:*** $50. ***Tuition:*** full-time $20,460; part-time $620 per credit. ***Required fees:*** full-time $290; $145 per term part-time.

UNDERGRADUATE FINANCIAL AID (Fall 2006, est.) 66 applied for aid; of those 85% were deemed to have need. 100% of undergraduates with need received aid; of those 9% had need fully met. ***Average percent of need met:*** 50% (excluding resources awarded to replace EFC). ***Average financial aid package:*** $6500 (excluding resources awarded to replace EFC).

GIFT AID (NEED-BASED) ***Total amount:*** $276,105 (31% federal, 34% state, 35% institutional). ***Receiving aid:*** All full-time undergraduates: 31% (50). ***Average award:*** Undergraduates: $2384. ***Scholarships, grants, and awards:*** Federal Pell, FSEOG, state, college/university gift aid from institutional funds.

GIFT AID (NON-NEED-BASED) ***Total amount:*** $74,000 (100% institutional).

LOANS ***Student loans:*** $998,147 (40% need-based, 60% non-need-based). 15% of past graduating class borrowed through all loan programs. *Average indebtedness per student:* $30,000. ***Average need-based loan:*** Undergraduates: $3000. ***Parent loans:*** $649,406 (100% need-based). ***Programs:*** FFEL (Subsidized and Unsubsidized Stafford, PLUS).

WORK-STUDY ***Federal work-study:*** Total amount: $33,203.

APPLYING FOR FINANCIAL AID ***Required financial aid forms:*** FAFSA, institution's own form. ***Financial aid deadline (priority):*** 5/1. ***Notification date:*** Continuous. Students must reply within 2 weeks of notification.

CONTACT Nina Bunchuk, Director of Financial Aid, New York School of Interior Design, 170 East 70th Street, New York, NY 10021-5110, 212-472-1500 Ext. 212 or toll-free 800-336-9743 Ext. 204. *Fax:* 212-472-1867. *E-mail:* nina@nysid.edu.

NEW YORK UNIVERSITY

New York, NY

Tuition & fees: $33,420 **Average undergraduate aid package: $20,707**

ABOUT THE INSTITUTION Independent, coed. Awards: associate, bachelor's, master's, doctoral, and first professional degrees and post-bachelor's, post-master's, and first professional certificates. 116 undergraduate majors. Total enrollment: 40,870. Undergraduates: 20,965. Freshmen: 4,740. Federal methodology is used as a basis for awarding need-based institutional aid.

UNDERGRADUATE EXPENSES for 2006–07 ***Application fee:*** $65. ***Comprehensive fee:*** $45,200 includes full-time tuition ($31,534), mandatory fees ($1886), and room and board ($11,780). Full-time tuition and fees vary according to program. Room and board charges vary according to board plan and housing facility. ***Part-time tuition:*** $929 per credit. ***Part-time fees:*** $56 per credit; $299 per term. Part-time tuition and fees vary according to program. ***Payment plans:*** Installment, deferred payment.

FRESHMAN FINANCIAL AID (Fall 2006, est.) 3094 applied for aid; of those 80% were deemed to have need. 100% of freshmen with need received aid. ***Average percent of need met:*** 65% (excluding resources awarded to replace EFC). ***Average financial aid package:*** $20,643 (excluding resources awarded to replace EFC). 9% of all full-time freshmen had no need and received non-need-based gift aid.

UNDERGRADUATE FINANCIAL AID (Fall 2006, est.) 11,800 applied for aid; of those 85% were deemed to have need. 99% of undergraduates with need received aid. ***Average percent of need met:*** 66% (excluding resources awarded to replace EFC). ***Average financial aid package:*** $20,707 (excluding resources awarded to replace EFC). 9% of all full-time undergraduates had no need and received non-need-based gift aid.

GIFT AID (NEED-BASED) ***Total amount:*** $130,758,304 (12% federal, 8% state, 75% institutional, 5% external sources). ***Receiving aid:*** Freshmen: 50% (2,272); All full-time undergraduates: 48% (9,292). ***Average award:*** Freshmen: $14,374; Undergraduates: $14,207. ***Scholarships, grants, and awards:*** Federal Pell, FSEOG, state, private, college/university gift aid from institutional funds.

GIFT AID (NON-NEED-BASED) ***Total amount:*** $16,935,825 (86% institutional, 14% external sources). ***Average award:*** Freshmen: $6930; Undergraduates: $7087. ***Scholarships, grants, and awards by category:*** *Academic Interests/Achievement:* 1,820 awards ($12,899,190 total): general academic interests/achievements. ***Tuition waivers:*** Full or partial for employees or children of employees. ***ROTC:*** Army cooperative, Naval cooperative.

LOANS ***Student loans:*** $99,662,764 (87% need-based, 13% non-need-based). 61% of past graduating class borrowed through all loan programs. *Average indebtedness per student:* $34,417. ***Average need-based loan:*** Freshmen: $4449; Undergraduates: $5149. ***Parent loans:*** $86,240,039 (81% need-based, 19% non-need-based). ***Programs:*** FFEL (Subsidized and Unsubsidized Stafford, PLUS), Perkins, Federal Nursing.

WORK-STUDY ***Federal work-study:*** Total amount: $5,005,757; 2,539 jobs averaging $1972.

APPLYING FOR FINANCIAL AID ***Required financial aid forms:*** FAFSA, state aid form. ***Financial aid deadline (priority):*** 2/15. ***Notification date:*** 4/1. Students must reply by 5/1.

CONTACT Financial Aid Office, New York University, 25 West Fourth Street, New York, NY 10012-1199, 212-998-4444. *Fax:* 212-995-4661. *E-mail:* financial.aid@nyu.edu.

NIAGARA UNIVERSITY

Niagara Falls, NY

Tuition & fees: $21,240 **Average undergraduate aid package: $16,286**

ABOUT THE INSTITUTION Independent religious, coed. Awards: associate, bachelor's, and master's degrees and post-master's certificates. 56 undergraduate majors. Total enrollment: 3,881. Undergraduates: 2,967. Freshmen: 709. Federal methodology is used as a basis for awarding need-based institutional aid.

UNDERGRADUATE EXPENSES for 2006–07 ***Application fee:*** $30. ***Comprehensive fee:*** $30,090 includes full-time tuition ($20,400), mandatory fees ($840), and room and board ($8850). ***Part-time tuition:*** $680 per credit hour. ***Payment plans:*** Installment, deferred payment.

FRESHMAN FINANCIAL AID (Fall 2006, est.) 670 applied for aid; of those 89% were deemed to have need. 98% of freshmen with need received aid; of those 49% had need fully met. ***Average percent of need met:*** 81% (excluding resources awarded to replace EFC). ***Average financial aid package:*** $17,508 (excluding resources awarded to replace EFC). 16% of all full-time freshmen had no need and received non-need-based gift aid.

UNDERGRADUATE FINANCIAL AID (Fall 2006, est.) 2,405 applied for aid; of those 91% were deemed to have need. 98% of undergraduates with need received aid; of those 40% had need fully met. ***Average percent of need met:*** 79% (excluding resources awarded to replace EFC). ***Average financial aid package:*** $16,286 (excluding resources awarded to replace EFC). 19% of all full-time undergraduates had no need and received non-need-based gift aid.

GIFT AID (NEED-BASED) ***Total amount:*** $30,734,247 (9% federal, 12% state, 77% institutional, 2% external sources). ***Receiving aid:*** Freshmen: 81% (577); All full-time undergraduates: 75% (2,114). ***Average award:*** Freshmen: $11,650; Undergraduates: $9299. ***Scholarships, grants, and awards:*** Federal Pell, FSEOG, state, private, college/university gift aid from institutional funds.

GIFT AID (NON-NEED-BASED) ***Total amount:*** $4,781,899 (5% federal, 2% state, 92% institutional, 1% external sources). ***Receiving aid:*** Freshmen: 16% (111); Undergraduates: 17% (477). ***Average award:*** Freshmen: $9121; Undergraduates: $8376. ***Scholarships, grants, and awards by category:*** *Academic Interests/Achievement:* 2,650 awards ($19,954,218 total): general academic interests/achievements. *Creative Arts/Performance:* 51 awards ($185,108 total): theater/drama. *Special Achievements/Activities:* 10 awards ($18,000 total): community service. *Special Characteristics:* 92 awards ($1,603,040 total): children of faculty/staff, relatives of clergy. ***Tuition waivers:*** Full or partial for employees or children of employees, senior citizens. ***ROTC:*** Army.

LOANS ***Student loans:*** $14,770,050 (95% need-based, 5% non-need-based). 80% of past graduating class borrowed through all loan programs. *Average indebtedness per student:* $21,594. ***Average need-based loan:*** Freshmen: $3705; Undergraduates: $4410. ***Parent loans:*** $4,242,244 (89% need-based, 11% non-need-based). ***Programs:*** FFEL (Subsidized and Unsubsidized Stafford, PLUS), Perkins, Federal Nursing, college/university.

WORK-STUDY ***Federal work-study:*** Total amount: $1,292,040; 455 jobs averaging $2701. ***State or other work-study/employment:*** Total amount: $134,085 (100% non-need-based). 43 part-time jobs averaging $2848.

ATHLETIC AWARDS Total amount: $3,277,163 (32% need-based, 68% non-need-based).

APPLYING FOR FINANCIAL AID ***Required financial aid forms:*** FAFSA, state aid form. ***Financial aid deadline (priority):*** 2/15. ***Notification date:*** Continuous beginning 3/15. Students must reply within 3 weeks of notification.

CONTACT Mrs. Maureen E. Salfi, Director of Financial Aid, Niagara University, Financial Aid Office, Niagara University, NY 14109, 716-286-8686 or toll-free 800-462-2111. *Fax:* 716-286-8678. *E-mail:* finaid@niagara.edu.

NICHOLLS STATE UNIVERSITY

Thibodaux, LA

Tuition & fees (LA res): $3470 **Average undergraduate aid package: $5612**

ABOUT THE INSTITUTION State-supported, coed. Awards: associate, bachelor's, and master's degrees and post-master's certificates. 52 undergraduate majors. Total enrollment: 6,805. Undergraduates: 6,130. Freshmen: 1,119. Federal methodology is used as a basis for awarding need-based institutional aid.

UNDERGRADUATE EXPENSES for 2006–07 ***Application fee:*** $20. ***Tuition, state resident:*** full-time $2230; part-time $278.50 per credit hour. ***Tuition, nonresident:*** full-time $7679; part-time $278.50 per credit hour. Part-time tuition and fees vary according to course load. ***College room and board:*** $4038. Room and board charges vary according to board plan and housing facility. ***Payment plans:*** Installment, deferred payment.

FRESHMAN FINANCIAL AID (Fall 2005) 1073 applied for aid; of those 53% were deemed to have need. 99% of freshmen with need received aid; of those 67% had need fully met. ***Average percent of need met:*** 86% (excluding resources awarded to replace EFC). ***Average financial aid package:*** $5235 (excluding resources awarded to replace EFC). 4% of all full-time freshmen had no need and received non-need-based gift aid.

UNDERGRADUATE FINANCIAL AID (Fall 2005) 4,525 applied for aid; of those 61% were deemed to have need. 99% of undergraduates with need received aid; of those 62% had need fully met. ***Average percent of need met:*** 85% (excluding resources awarded to replace EFC). ***Average financial aid package:*** $5612 (excluding resources awarded to replace EFC). 2% of all full-time undergraduates had no need and received non-need-based gift aid.

GIFT AID (NEED-BASED) ***Total amount:*** $8,116,740 (82% federal, 14% state, 2% institutional, 2% external sources). ***Receiving aid:*** Freshmen: 42% (498); All full-time undergraduates: 41% (2,265). ***Average award:*** Freshmen: $3176; Undergraduates: $3136. ***Scholarships, grants, and awards:*** Federal Pell, FSEOG, state, private, college/university gift aid from institutional funds.

GIFT AID (NON-NEED-BASED) ***Total amount:*** $4,765,260 (80% state, 10% institutional, 10% external sources). ***Receiving aid:*** Freshmen: 19% (225); Undergraduates: 10% (563). ***Average award:*** Freshmen: $3215; Undergraduates: $3076. ***Scholarships, grants, and awards by category:*** *Academic Interests/Achievement:* 177 awards ($458,745 total): general academic interests/achievements. *Creative Arts/Performance:* music. *Special Characteristics:* 531 awards ($1,176,442 total): children of faculty/staff, general special characteristics, members of minority groups, public servants. ***Tuition waivers:*** Full or partial for employees or children of employees.

LOANS ***Student loans:*** $12,555,071 (44% need-based, 56% non-need-based). 56% of past graduating class borrowed through all loan programs. *Average indebtedness per student:* $14,095. ***Average need-based loan:*** Freshmen: $2184; Undergraduates: $3108. ***Parent loans:*** $506,100 (8% need-based, 92% non-need-based). ***Programs:*** FFEL (Subsidized and Unsubsidized Stafford, PLUS), Perkins.

WORK-STUDY ***Federal work-study:*** Total amount: $250,732; 233 jobs averaging $1092. ***State or other work-study/employment:*** Total amount: $1,112,419 (5% need-based, 95% non-need-based). 526 part-time jobs averaging $1785.

ATHLETIC AWARDS Total amount: $907,915 (26% need-based, 74% non-need-based).

APPLYING FOR FINANCIAL AID ***Required financial aid forms:*** FAFSA, institution's own form, state aid form, noncustodial (divorced/separated) parent's statement. ***Financial aid deadline:*** 5/1 (priority: 4/17). ***Notification date:*** Continuous. Students must reply within 2 weeks of notification.

CONTACT Colette Lagarde, Office of Financial Aid, Nicholls State University, East Elkins Hall, PO Box 2005, Thibodaux, LA 70310, 985-448-4048 or toll-free 877-NICHOLLS. *Fax:* 985-448-4124. *E-mail:* colette.lagarde@nicholls.edu.

NICHOLS COLLEGE

Dudley, MA

Tuition & fees: $23,900 **Average undergraduate aid package: $16,008**

ABOUT THE INSTITUTION Independent, coed. Awards: associate, bachelor's, and master's degrees. 14 undergraduate majors. Total enrollment: 1,470. Undergraduates: 1,215. Freshmen: 347. Federal methodology is used as a basis for awarding need-based institutional aid.

UNDERGRADUATE EXPENSES for 2006–07 ***Application fee:*** $25. ***Comprehensive fee:*** $32,700 includes full-time tuition ($23,600), mandatory fees ($300), and room and board ($8800). ***College room only:*** $4800. ***Part-time tuition:*** $245 per credit hour. Part-time tuition and fees vary according to class time and course load. ***Payment plan:*** Installment.

FRESHMAN FINANCIAL AID (Fall 2005) 266 applied for aid; of those 77% were deemed to have need. 99% of freshmen with need received aid; of those 26% had need fully met. ***Average percent of need met:*** 70% (excluding resources awarded to replace EFC). ***Average financial aid package:*** $16,272 (excluding resources awarded to replace EFC). 14% of all full-time freshmen had no need and received non-need-based gift aid.

UNDERGRADUATE FINANCIAL AID (Fall 2005) 973 applied for aid; of those 67% were deemed to have need. 98% of undergraduates with need received aid; of those 30% had need fully met. ***Average percent of need met:*** 73% (excluding resources awarded to replace EFC). ***Average financial aid package:*** $16,008 (excluding resources awarded to replace EFC). 17% of all full-time undergraduates had no need and received non-need-based gift aid.

GIFT AID (NEED-BASED) ***Total amount:*** $6,380,123 (10% federal, 6% state, 78% institutional, 6% external sources). ***Receiving aid:*** Freshmen: 71% (201); All full-time undergraduates: 57% (624). ***Average award:*** Freshmen: $11,478; Undergraduates: $10,000. ***Scholarships, grants, and awards:*** Federal Pell, FSEOG, state, private, college/university gift aid from institutional funds.

GIFT AID (NON-NEED-BASED) ***Total amount:*** $1,289,784 (83% institutional, 17% external sources). ***Receiving aid:*** Freshmen: 3% (8); Undergraduates: 3% (29). ***Average award:*** Freshmen: $11,780; Undergraduates: $11,731. ***Scholarships, grants, and awards by category:*** *Academic Interests/Achievement:* 505 awards ($3,300,095 total): general academic interests/achievements. *Special Achievements/Activities:* 8 awards ($17,500 total): community service, general special achievements/activities, leadership. *Special Characteristics:* 46 awards ($262,529 total): children and siblings of alumni, children of faculty/staff, siblings of current students. ***Tuition waivers:*** Full or partial for employees or children of employees, senior citizens. ***ROTC:*** Army cooperative.

LOANS ***Student loans:*** $6,160,862 (68% need-based, 32% non-need-based). 61% of past graduating class borrowed through all loan programs. *Average indebtedness per student:* $27,483. ***Average need-based loan:*** Freshmen: $5344; Undergraduates: $6270. ***Parent loans:*** $2,753,053 (39% need-based, 61% non-need-based). ***Programs:*** FFEL (Subsidized and Unsubsidized Stafford, PLUS), state.

WORK-STUDY ***Federal work-study:*** Total amount: $446,254; 240 jobs averaging $1729.

APPLYING FOR FINANCIAL AID ***Required financial aid form:*** FAFSA. ***Financial aid deadline (priority):*** 3/1. ***Notification date:*** Continuous beginning 2/25. Students must reply within 2 weeks of notification.

CONTACT Ms. Kathleen A. Goozey, Associate Director of Financial Aid, Nichols College, PO Box 5000, Dudley, MA 01571, 508-213-2276 or toll-free 800-470-3379. *Fax:* 508-943-9885. *E-mail:* kathleen.goozey@nichols.edu.

NORFOLK STATE UNIVERSITY

Norfolk, VA

CONTACT Mrs. Estherine Harding, Director of Financial Aid, Norfolk State University, 700 Park Avenue, Norfolk, VA 23504-3907, 757-823-8381. *Fax:* 757-823-9059. *E-mail:* ejharding@nsu.edu.

NORTH CAROLINA AGRICULTURAL AND TECHNICAL STATE UNIVERSITY

Greensboro, NC

Tuition & fees (NC res): $3872 **Average undergraduate aid package: $5898**

ABOUT THE INSTITUTION State-supported, coed. Awards: bachelor's, master's, and doctoral degrees. 59 undergraduate majors. Total enrollment: 11,098. Undergraduates: 9,687. Freshmen: 2,094. Federal methodology is used as a basis for awarding need-based institutional aid.

UNDERGRADUATE EXPENSES for 2006–07 ***Application fee:*** $45. ***One-time required fee:*** $10. ***Tuition, state resident:*** full-time $1994. ***Tuition, nonresident:*** full-time $11,436. Full-time tuition and fees vary according to student level. Part-time tuition and fees vary according to student level. ***College room and board:*** $6686. Room and board charges vary according to board plan and housing facility. ***Payment plan:*** Installment.

FRESHMAN FINANCIAL AID (Fall 2005) 2717 applied for aid; of those 86% were deemed to have need. 98% of freshmen with need received aid; of those 4% had need fully met. ***Average percent of need met:*** 50% (excluding resources awarded to replace EFC). ***Average financial aid package:*** $5720 (excluding resources awarded to replace EFC). 1% of all full-time freshmen had no need and received non-need-based gift aid.

UNDERGRADUATE FINANCIAL AID (Fall 2005) 7,873 applied for aid; of those 87% were deemed to have need. 96% of undergraduates with need received aid; of those 7% had need fully met. ***Average percent of need met:*** 50% (excluding resources awarded to replace EFC). ***Average financial aid package:*** $5898 (excluding resources awarded to replace EFC). 3% of all full-time undergraduates had no need and received non-need-based gift aid.

GIFT AID (NEED-BASED) ***Total amount:*** $23,885,165 (58% federal, 42% state). ***Receiving aid:*** Freshmen: 61% (1,777); All full-time undergraduates: 54% (4,886). ***Average award:*** Freshmen: $4181; Undergraduates: $4028. ***Scholarships, grants, and awards:*** Federal Pell, FSEOG, state, private, college/university gift aid from institutional funds, United Negro College Fund.

GIFT AID (NON-NEED-BASED) ***Total amount:*** $23,412,049 (1% federal, 14% state, 16% institutional, 69% external sources). ***Receiving aid:*** Freshmen: 37% (1,065); Undergraduates: 28% (2,588). ***Average award:*** Freshmen: $3998; Undergraduates: $4466. ***Scholarships, grants, and awards by category:*** *Academic Interests/Achievement:* military science. *Creative Arts/Performance:* music, theater/drama. *Special Characteristics:* ethnic background, handicapped students, members of minority groups. ***Tuition waivers:*** Full or partial for senior citizens. ***ROTC:*** Army, Air Force.

LOANS ***Student loans:*** $30,776,581 (100% need-based). 75% of past graduating class borrowed through all loan programs. *Average indebtedness per student:* $20,052. ***Average need-based loan:*** Freshmen: $4457; Undergraduates: $7202. ***Parent loans:*** $8,834,537 (100% non-need-based). ***Programs:*** Federal Direct (Subsidized and Unsubsidized Stafford, PLUS), Perkins, state, alternative loans.

WORK-STUDY ***Federal work-study:*** Total amount: $383,037; jobs available. ***State or other work-study/employment:*** Part-time jobs available.

ATHLETIC AWARDS Total amount: $1,764,816 (100% non-need-based).

APPLYING FOR FINANCIAL AID ***Required financial aid form:*** FAFSA. ***Financial aid deadline (priority):*** 3/15. ***Notification date:*** Continuous beginning 4/1.

CONTACT Mrs. Sherri Avent, Director of Student Financial Aid, North Carolina Agricultural and Technical State University, 1601 East Market Street, Dowdy Administration Building, Greensboro, NC 27411, 336-334-7973 or toll-free 800-443-8964 (in-state). *Fax:* 336-334-7954.

NORTH CAROLINA CENTRAL UNIVERSITY

Durham, NC

CONTACT Sharon J. Oliver, Director of Scholarships and Student Aid, North Carolina Central University, 106 Student Services Building, Durham, NC 27707-3129, 919-530-7412 or toll-free 877-667-7533.

NORTH CAROLINA SCHOOL OF THE ARTS

Winston-Salem, NC

Tuition & fees (NC res): $4891 **Average undergraduate aid package: $11,056**

ABOUT THE INSTITUTION State-supported, coed. Awards: bachelor's and master's degrees and post-master's certificates. 9 undergraduate majors. Total enrollment: 845. Undergraduates: 727. Freshmen: 184. Federal methodology is used as a basis for awarding need-based institutional aid.

UNDERGRADUATE EXPENSES for 2006–07 ***Application fee:*** $50. ***Tuition, state resident:*** full-time $3074. ***Tuition, nonresident:*** full-time $14,354. Full-time tuition and fees vary according to program. Part-time tuition and fees vary according to course load. ***College room and board:*** $6139; ***Room only:*** $3189. Room and board charges vary according to board plan and housing facility. ***Payment plan:*** Installment.

FRESHMAN FINANCIAL AID (Fall 2005) 118 applied for aid; of those 75% were deemed to have need. 100% of freshmen with need received aid; of those 8% had need fully met. ***Average percent of need met:*** 70% (excluding resources awarded to replace EFC). ***Average financial aid package:*** $9884 (excluding resources awarded to replace EFC). 13% of all full-time freshmen had no need and received non-need-based gift aid.

UNDERGRADUATE FINANCIAL AID (Fall 2005) 480 applied for aid; of those 78% were deemed to have need. 100% of undergraduates with need received aid; of those 11% had need fully met. ***Average percent of need met:*** 79% (excluding resources awarded to replace EFC). ***Average financial aid package:*** $11,056 (excluding resources awarded to replace EFC). 15% of all full-time undergraduates had no need and received non-need-based gift aid.

GIFT AID (NEED-BASED) ***Total amount:*** $1,656,208 (31% federal, 30% state, 36% institutional, 3% external sources). ***Receiving aid:*** Freshmen: 46% (81); All full-time undergraduates: 49% (351). ***Average award:*** Freshmen: $4768; Undergraduates: $4718. ***Scholarships, grants, and awards:*** Federal Pell, FSEOG, state, private, college/university gift aid from institutional funds.

GIFT AID (NON-NEED-BASED) ***Total amount:*** $252,854 (6% state, 76% institutional, 18% external sources). ***Receiving aid:*** Undergraduates: 1% (7). ***Average award:*** Freshmen: $1469; Undergraduates: $2192. ***Scholarships, grants, and awards by category:*** *Creative Arts/Performance:* applied art and design, cinema/film/broadcasting, dance, music, performing arts, theater/drama.

LOANS ***Student loans:*** $2,698,869 (67% need-based, 33% non-need-based). 69% of past graduating class borrowed through all loan programs. *Average indebtedness per student:* $20,574. ***Average need-based loan:*** Freshmen: $2914; Undergraduates: $3918. ***Parent loans:*** $1,745,257 (48% need-based, 52% non-need-based). ***Programs:*** Federal Direct (Subsidized and Unsubsidized Stafford, PLUS), Perkins.

WORK-STUDY ***Federal work-study:*** Total amount: $51,086; 119 jobs averaging $429.

APPLYING FOR FINANCIAL AID ***Required financial aid form:*** FAFSA. ***Financial aid deadline (priority):*** 3/1. ***Notification date:*** Continuous beginning 4/10. Students must reply within 2 weeks of notification.

CONTACT Jane C. Kamiab, Director of Financial Aid, North Carolina School of the Arts, 1533 South Main Street, Winston-Salem, NC 27127, 336-770-3297. *Fax:* 336-770-1489.

NORTH CAROLINA STATE UNIVERSITY

Raleigh, NC

Tuition & fees (NC res): $5117 **Average undergraduate aid package: $8925**

ABOUT THE INSTITUTION State-supported, coed. Awards: associate, bachelor's, master's, doctoral, and first professional degrees and first professional certificates. 121 undergraduate majors. Total enrollment: 31,130. Undergraduates: 23,730. Freshmen: 4,693. Federal methodology is used as a basis for awarding need-based institutional aid.

UNDERGRADUATE EXPENSES for 2007–08 ***Application fee:*** $60. ***Tuition, state resident:*** full-time $3760. ***Tuition, nonresident:*** full-time $15,958. ***College room and board:*** $7373; ***Room only:*** $4460.

FRESHMAN FINANCIAL AID (Fall 2006, est.) 3145 applied for aid; of those 61% were deemed to have need. 98% of freshmen with need received aid; of those 38% had need fully met. ***Average percent of need met:*** 80% (excluding resources awarded to replace EFC). ***Average financial aid package:*** $8588 (excluding resources awarded to replace EFC). 27% of all full-time freshmen had no need and received non-need-based gift aid.

UNDERGRADUATE FINANCIAL AID (Fall 2006, est.) 11,088 applied for aid; of those 71% were deemed to have need. 97% of undergraduates with need received aid; of those 42% had need fully met. ***Average percent of need met:*** 79% (excluding resources awarded to replace EFC). ***Average financial aid package:*** $8925 (excluding resources awarded to replace EFC). 22% of all full-time undergraduates had no need and received non-need-based gift aid.

GIFT AID (NEED-BASED) ***Total amount:*** $50,703,405 (25% federal, 20% state, 48% institutional, 7% external sources). ***Receiving aid:*** Freshmen: 39% (1,816); All full-time undergraduates: 36% (7,228). ***Average award:*** Freshmen: $7163; Undergraduates: $6908. ***Scholarships, grants, and awards:*** Federal Pell, FSEOG, state, private, college/university gift aid from institutional funds.

GIFT AID (NON-NEED-BASED) ***Total amount:*** $15,018,978 (4% state, 61% institutional, 35% external sources). ***Receiving aid:*** Freshmen: 3% (163); Undergraduates: 2% (472). ***Average award:*** Freshmen: $6733; Undergraduates: $7558. ***Scholarships, grants, and awards by category:*** *Academic Interests/Achievement:* agriculture, biological sciences, business, education, engineering/technologies, general academic interests/achievements, humanities, mathematics, physical sciences, social sciences. ***ROTC:*** Army, Naval, Air Force.

LOANS ***Student loans:*** $42,945,948 (52% need-based, 48% non-need-based). 48% of past graduating class borrowed through all loan programs. *Average indebtedness per student:* $14,719. ***Average need-based loan:*** Freshmen: $2109; Undergraduates: $2946. ***Parent loans:*** $14,701,013 (15% need-based, 85% non-need-based). ***Programs:*** FFEL (Subsidized and Unsubsidized Stafford, PLUS), Perkins, state, college/university.

WORK-STUDY ***Federal work-study:*** Total amount: $735,123; 735 jobs averaging $1055. ***State or other work-study/employment:*** Total amount: $1,404,958 (42% need-based, 58% non-need-based). 220 part-time jobs averaging $7040.

ATHLETIC AWARDS Total amount: $4,977,796 (34% need-based, 66% non-need-based).

APPLYING FOR FINANCIAL AID ***Required financial aid forms:*** FAFSA, institution's own form. ***Financial aid deadline (priority):*** 3/1. ***Notification date:*** Continuous beginning 3/1.

CONTACT Ms. Julia Rice Mallette, Director of Scholarships and Financial Aid, North Carolina State University, 2016 Harris Hall, Box 7302, Raleigh, NC 27695-7302, 919-515-2334. *Fax:* 919-515-8422. *E-mail:* julie_mallette@ncsu.edu.

NORTH CAROLINA WESLEYAN COLLEGE

Rocky Mount, NC

CONTACT Director of Financial Aid, North Carolina Wesleyan College, 3400 North Wesleyan Boulevard, Rocky Mount, NC 27804, 252-985-5290 or toll-free 800-488-6292.

NORTH CENTRAL COLLEGE

Naperville, IL

Tuition & fees: $23,115 **Average undergraduate aid package: $17,034**

ABOUT THE INSTITUTION Independent United Methodist, coed. Awards: bachelor's and master's degrees and post-bachelor's certificates. 63 undergraduate majors. Total enrollment: 2,556. Undergraduates: 2,236. Freshmen: 470. Federal methodology is used as a basis for awarding need-based institutional aid.

UNDERGRADUATE EXPENSES for 2006–07 ***Application fee:*** $25. ***Comprehensive fee:*** $30,555 includes full-time tuition ($22,710), mandatory fees ($405), and room and board ($7440). Room and board charges vary according to housing facility. ***Part-time tuition:*** $570 per semester hour. ***Part-time fees:*** $20 per term. Part-time tuition and fees vary according to course load. ***Payment plan:*** Installment.

FRESHMAN FINANCIAL AID (Fall 2006, est.) 414 applied for aid; of those 81% were deemed to have need. 100% of freshmen with need received aid; of those 29% had need fully met. ***Average percent of need met:*** 85% (excluding resources awarded to replace EFC). ***Average financial aid package:*** $18,433 (excluding resources awarded to replace EFC). 23% of all full-time freshmen had no need and received non-need-based gift aid.

UNDERGRADUATE FINANCIAL AID (Fall 2006, est.) 1,544 applied for aid; of those 85% were deemed to have need. 100% of undergraduates with need received aid; of those 21% had need fully met. ***Average percent of need met:*** 77% (excluding resources awarded to replace EFC). ***Average financial aid package:*** $17,034 (excluding resources awarded to replace EFC). 25% of all full-time undergraduates had no need and received non-need-based gift aid.

GIFT AID (NEED-BASED) ***Total amount:*** $16,734,158 (7% federal, 17% state, 74% institutional, 2% external sources). ***Receiving aid:*** Freshmen: 71% (336); All full-time undergraduates: 64% (1,283). ***Average award:*** Freshmen: $14,919;

Undergraduates: $12,493. ***Scholarships, grants, and awards:*** Federal Pell, FSEOG, state, private, college/university gift aid from institutional funds.

GIFT AID (NON-NEED-BASED) ***Total amount:*** $5,295,388 (97% institutional, 3% external sources). ***Receiving aid:*** Freshmen: 12% (57); Undergraduates: 8% (158). ***Average award:*** Freshmen: $7776; Undergraduates: $6464. ***Scholarships, grants, and awards by category:*** *Academic Interests/Achievement:* 1,441 awards ($11,627,535 total): biological sciences, business, communication, computer science, education, English, foreign languages, general academic interests/achievements, humanities, international studies, mathematics, physical sciences, premedicine, religion/biblical studies, social sciences. *Creative Arts/Performance:* 180 awards ($360,160 total): art/fine arts, cinema/film/broadcasting, debating, journalism/publications, music, theater/drama. *Special Achievements/Activities:* 55 awards ($77,041 total): community service, religious involvement. *Special Characteristics:* 117 awards ($1,145,555 total): adult students, children of faculty/staff, general special characteristics, international students, relatives of clergy. ***Tuition waivers:*** Full or partial for employees or children of employees, senior citizens. ***ROTC:*** Army cooperative, Air Force cooperative.

LOANS ***Student loans:*** $9,377,676 (67% need-based, 33% non-need-based). 69% of past graduating class borrowed through all loan programs. *Average indebtedness per student:* $21,078. ***Average need-based loan:*** Freshmen: $2187; Undergraduates: $3347. ***Parent loans:*** $2,547,487 (20% need-based, 80% non-need-based). ***Programs:*** FFEL (Subsidized and Unsubsidized Stafford, PLUS), Perkins, state, college/university.

WORK-STUDY ***Federal work-study:*** Total amount: $286,433; 196 jobs averaging $884. ***State or other work-study/employment:*** Total amount: $244,119 (38% need-based, 62% non-need-based). Part-time jobs available.

APPLYING FOR FINANCIAL AID ***Required financial aid forms:*** FAFSA, institution's own form, federal income tax form(s). ***Financial aid deadline:*** Continuous. ***Notification date:*** Continuous beginning 3/1. Students must reply within 4 weeks of notification.

CONTACT Marty Rossman, Director of Financial Aid, North Central College, 30 North Brainard Street, Naperville, IL 60540, 630-637-5600 or toll-free 800-411-1861. *Fax:* 630-637-5608. *E-mail:* mprossman@noctrl.edu.

NORTH CENTRAL UNIVERSITY

Minneapolis, MN

CONTACT Mrs. Donna Jager, Director of Financial Aid, North Central University, 910 Elliot Avenue, Minneapolis, MN 55404-1322, 612-343-4485 or toll-free 800-289-6222. *Fax:* 612-343-8067. *E-mail:* finaid@northcentral.edu.

NORTH DAKOTA STATE UNIVERSITY

Fargo, ND

Tuition & fees (ND res): $5722 **Average undergraduate aid package: $4604**

ABOUT THE INSTITUTION State-supported, coed. Awards: bachelor's, master's, doctoral, and first professional degrees and post-master's certificates. 95 undergraduate majors. Total enrollment: 12,258. Undergraduates: 10,596. Freshmen: 2,073. Federal methodology is used as a basis for awarding need-based institutional aid.

UNDERGRADUATE EXPENSES for 2006–07 ***Application fee:*** $35. ***One-time required fee:*** $45. ***Tuition, state resident:*** full-time $4774; part-time $198.92 per credit. ***Tuition, nonresident:*** full-time $12,747; part-time $531.11 per credit. ***Required fees:*** full-time $948; $38.99 per credit. Full-time tuition and fees vary according to reciprocity agreements. Part-time tuition and fees vary according to course load and reciprocity agreements. ***College room and board:*** $5477; ***Room only:*** $2277. Room and board charges vary according to board plan and housing facility. ***Payment plan:*** Installment.

FRESHMAN FINANCIAL AID (Fall 2005) 1997 applied for aid; of those 95% were deemed to have need. 98% of freshmen with need received aid; of those 40% had need fully met. ***Average percent of need met:*** 33% (excluding resources awarded to replace EFC). ***Average financial aid package:*** $4106 (excluding resources awarded to replace EFC). 21% of all full-time freshmen had no need and received non-need-based gift aid.

UNDERGRADUATE FINANCIAL AID (Fall 2005) 7,345 applied for aid; of those 88% were deemed to have need. 91% of undergraduates with need received aid; of those 34% had need fully met. ***Average percent of need met:*** 32% (excluding resources awarded to replace EFC). ***Average financial aid package:*** $4604 (excluding resources awarded to replace EFC). 19% of all full-time undergraduates had no need and received non-need-based gift aid.

GIFT AID (NEED-BASED) ***Total amount:*** $9,636,667 (61% federal, 4% state, 23% institutional, 12% external sources). ***Receiving aid:*** Freshmen: 51% (1,128); All full-time undergraduates: 40% (3,434). ***Average award:*** Freshmen: $2223; Undergraduates: $2500. ***Scholarships, grants, and awards:*** Federal Pell, FSEOG, state, private, college/university gift aid from institutional funds, diversity waivers.

GIFT AID (NON-NEED-BASED) ***Total amount:*** $3,779,981 (3% state, 72% institutional, 25% external sources). ***Receiving aid:*** Freshmen: 10% (220); Undergraduates: 8% (689). ***Average award:*** Freshmen: $2377; Undergraduates: $2309. ***Scholarships, grants, and awards by category:*** *Academic Interests/Achievement:* 2,600 awards ($3,673,253 total): agriculture, architecture, biological sciences, business, communication, computer science, education, engineering/technologies, English, general academic interests/achievements, health fields, home economics, humanities, mathematics, military science, physical sciences, premedicine, social sciences. *Creative Arts/Performance:* 106 awards ($73,923 total): art/fine arts, debating, journalism/publications, music, theater/drama. *Special Achievements/Activities:* memberships, religious involvement. *Special Characteristics:* 774 awards ($1,329,577 total): children of faculty/staff, ethnic background. ***Tuition waivers:*** Full or partial for minority students, children of alumni, employees or children of employees, senior citizens. ***ROTC:*** Army, Air Force.

LOANS ***Student loans:*** $43,161,148 (57% need-based, 43% non-need-based). 56% of past graduating class borrowed through all loan programs. *Average indebtedness per student:* $23,197. ***Average need-based loan:*** Freshmen: $2887; Undergraduates: $3757. ***Parent loans:*** $1,703,496 (19% need-based, 81% non-need-based). ***Programs:*** FFEL (Subsidized and Unsubsidized Stafford, PLUS), Perkins, Federal Nursing, alternative loans.

WORK-STUDY ***Federal work-study:*** Total amount: $704,697; 672 jobs averaging $1660.

ATHLETIC AWARDS Total amount: $314,608 (13% need-based, 87% non-need-based).

APPLYING FOR FINANCIAL AID ***Required financial aid form:*** FAFSA. ***Financial aid deadline (priority):*** 3/15. ***Notification date:*** Continuous.

CONTACT Jeanne Enebo, Director of Financial Aid, North Dakota State University, PO Box 5315, Fargo, ND 58105, 701-231-7537 or toll-free 800-488-NDSU. *Fax:* 701-231-6126. *E-mail:* j.enebo@ndsu.edu.

NORTHEASTERN ILLINOIS UNIVERSITY

Chicago, IL

Tuition & fees (IL res): $6261 **Average undergraduate aid package: $7231**

ABOUT THE INSTITUTION State-supported, coed. Awards: bachelor's and master's degrees. 42 undergraduate majors. Total enrollment: 12,056. Undergraduates: 9,257. Freshmen: 1,114. Federal methodology is used as a basis for awarding need-based institutional aid.

UNDERGRADUATE EXPENSES for 2006–07 ***Application fee:*** $25. ***Tuition, state resident:*** full-time $5250; part-time $175 per credit hour. ***Tuition, nonresident:*** full-time $10,500; part-time $350 per credit hour. ***Required fees:*** full-time $1011; $34 per credit hour. Full-time tuition and fees vary according to student level.

FRESHMAN FINANCIAL AID (Fall 2006, est.) 773 applied for aid; of those 74% were deemed to have need. 96% of freshmen with need received aid; of those 3% had need fully met. ***Average percent of need met:*** 58% (excluding resources awarded to replace EFC). ***Average financial aid package:*** $6599 (excluding resources awarded to replace EFC). 2% of all full-time freshmen had no need and received non-need-based gift aid.

UNDERGRADUATE FINANCIAL AID (Fall 2006, est.) 3,271 applied for aid; of those 81% were deemed to have need. 97% of undergraduates with need received aid; of those 12% had need fully met. ***Average percent of need met:*** 62% (excluding resources awarded to replace EFC). ***Average financial aid package:*** $7231 (excluding resources awarded to replace EFC). 2% of all full-time undergraduates had no need and received non-need-based gift aid.

GIFT AID (NEED-BASED) ***Total amount:*** $16,008,885 (52% federal, 48% state). ***Receiving aid:*** Freshmen: 51% (520); All full-time undergraduates: 43% (2,247). ***Average award:*** Freshmen: $6216; Undergraduates: $5665. ***Scholarships, grants, and awards:*** Federal Pell, FSEOG, state, private, college/university gift aid from institutional funds, Federal ACG and SMART Grants.

GIFT AID (NON-NEED-BASED) ***Total amount:*** $2,036,314 (2% federal, 70% state, 15% institutional, 13% external sources). ***Receiving aid:*** Freshmen: 2%

(23); Undergraduates: 4% (185). ***Average award:*** Freshmen: $1772; Undergraduates: $1818. ***Scholarships, grants, and awards by category:*** *Academic Interests/Achievement:* 399 awards ($508,914 total): biological sciences, business, communication, computer science, education, English, foreign languages, general academic interests/achievements, mathematics, physical sciences, social sciences. *Creative Arts/Performance:* 106 awards ($182,335 total): art/fine arts, creative writing, dance, journalism/publications, music, performing arts, theater/drama. *Special Achievements/Activities:* 7 awards ($14,676 total): general special achievements/activities, leadership. *Special Characteristics:* 78 awards ($84,237 total): adult students, children of faculty/staff, general special characteristics. ***Tuition waivers:*** Full or partial for employees or children of employees. ***ROTC:*** Army cooperative, Air Force cooperative.

LOANS ***Student loans:*** $9,108,088 (62% need-based, 38% non-need-based). 8% of past graduating class borrowed through all loan programs. *Average indebtedness per student:* $12,569. ***Average need-based loan:*** Freshmen: $2531; Undergraduates: $3853. ***Parent loans:*** $122,304 (100% non-need-based). ***Programs:*** FFEL (Subsidized and Unsubsidized Stafford, PLUS), Perkins.

WORK-STUDY ***Federal work-study:*** Total amount: $521,704; 230 jobs averaging $2268. ***State or other work-study/employment:*** Total amount: $911,103 (100% non-need-based). 429 part-time jobs averaging $2124.

APPLYING FOR FINANCIAL AID ***Required financial aid forms:*** FAFSA, institution's own form. ***Financial aid deadline (priority):*** 3/1. ***Notification date:*** Continuous beginning 4/15. Students must reply within 3 weeks of notification.

CONTACT Financial Aid Office, Northeastern Illinois University, 5500 North St. Louis Avenue, Chicago, IL 60625, 773-442-5000. *Fax:* 773-442-5040. *E-mail:* financialaid@neiu.edu.

NORTHEASTERN STATE UNIVERSITY

Tahlequah, OK

Tuition & fees (OK res): $3489 **Average undergraduate aid package: $7570**

ABOUT THE INSTITUTION State-supported, coed. Awards: bachelor's, master's, and first professional degrees. 65 undergraduate majors. Total enrollment: 9,540. Undergraduates: 8,499. Freshmen: 1,202. Federal methodology is used as a basis for awarding need-based institutional aid.

UNDERGRADUATE EXPENSES for 2006–07 ***Tuition, state resident:*** full-time $2700. ***Tuition, nonresident:*** full-time $7800. Full-time tuition and fees vary according to course level, course load, and location. Part-time tuition and fees vary according to course level and course load. ***College room and board:*** $3600. Room and board charges vary according to board plan and housing facility.

FRESHMAN FINANCIAL AID (Fall 2006, est.) 815 applied for aid; of those 74% were deemed to have need. 96% of freshmen with need received aid; of those 66% had need fully met. ***Average percent of need met:*** 68% (excluding resources awarded to replace EFC). ***Average financial aid package:*** $5854 (excluding resources awarded to replace EFC). 31% of all full-time freshmen had no need and received non-need-based gift aid.

UNDERGRADUATE FINANCIAL AID (Fall 2006, est.) 4,890 applied for aid; of those 85% were deemed to have need. 95% of undergraduates with need received aid; of those 70% had need fully met. ***Average percent of need met:*** 64% (excluding resources awarded to replace EFC). ***Average financial aid package:*** $7570 (excluding resources awarded to replace EFC). 19% of all full-time undergraduates had no need and received non-need-based gift aid.

GIFT AID (NEED-BASED) ***Total amount:*** $17,979,506 (70% federal, 15% state, 2% institutional, 13% external sources). ***Receiving aid:*** Freshmen: 40% (411); All full-time undergraduates: 46% (2,907). ***Average award:*** Freshmen: $3802; Undergraduates: $3916. ***Scholarships, grants, and awards:*** Federal Pell, FSEOG, state, private, college/university gift aid from institutional funds.

GIFT AID (NON-NEED-BASED) ***Total amount:*** $3,574,244 (49% state, 6% institutional, 45% external sources). ***Receiving aid:*** Freshmen: 39% (396); Undergraduates: 57% (3,585). ***Average award:*** Freshmen: $948; Undergraduates: $705. ***Scholarships, grants, and awards by category:*** *Academic Interests/Achievement:* 940 awards ($1,569,907 total): biological sciences, business, communication, computer science, education, English, foreign languages, general academic interests/achievements, health fields, home economics, humanities, library science, mathematics, physical sciences, premedicine, social sciences. *Creative Arts/Performance:* 223 awards ($206,489 total): applied art and design, art/fine arts, dance, debating, journalism/publications, music, performing arts, theater/drama. *Special Achievements/Activities:* 25 awards ($25,340 total): cheerleading/drum major, community service, junior miss, leadership. *Special Characteristics:* 85 awards ($64,110 total): children and siblings of alumni, children of faculty/staff, children with a deceased or disabled parent, spouses of deceased or disabled public servants. ***Tuition waivers:*** Full or partial for employees or children of employees, senior citizens. ***ROTC:*** Army.

LOANS ***Student loans:*** $23,928,127 (60% need-based, 40% non-need-based). 61% of past graduating class borrowed through all loan programs. *Average indebtedness per student:* $18,981. ***Average need-based loan:*** Freshmen: $2467; Undergraduates: $4017. ***Parent loans:*** $685,775 (94% need-based, 6% non-need-based). ***Programs:*** FFEL (Subsidized and Unsubsidized Stafford, PLUS), Perkins, college/university.

WORK-STUDY ***Federal work-study:*** Total amount: $398,954; 384 jobs averaging $2027. ***State or other work-study/employment:*** Total amount: $1,777,632 (100% non-need-based). 768 part-time jobs averaging $3000.

ATHLETIC AWARDS Total amount: $1,112,030 (100% non-need-based).

APPLYING FOR FINANCIAL AID ***Required financial aid forms:*** FAFSA, institution's own form. ***Financial aid deadline (priority):*** 4/1. ***Notification date:*** Continuous beginning 2/1. Students must reply within 2 weeks of notification.

CONTACT Teri Cochran, Director of Student Financial Services, Northeastern State University, 715 North Grand Avenue, Tahlequah, OK 74464-2399, 918-456-5511 Ext. 3410 or toll-free 800-722-9614 (in-state). *Fax:* 918-458-2510. *E-mail:* kindlet@nsuok.edu.

NORTHEASTERN UNIVERSITY

Boston, MA

Tuition & fees: $30,309 **Average undergraduate aid package: $16,433**

ABOUT THE INSTITUTION Independent, coed. Awards: bachelor's, master's, doctoral, and first professional degrees and post-master's certificates. 83 undergraduate majors. Total enrollment: 20,605. Undergraduates: 15,195. Freshmen: 2,955. Both federal and institutional methodology are used as a basis for awarding need-based institutional aid.

UNDERGRADUATE EXPENSES for 2006–07 ***Application fee:*** $75. ***Comprehensive fee:*** $41,279 includes full-time tuition ($29,910), mandatory fees ($399), and room and board ($10,970). ***College room only:*** $5840. Room and board charges vary according to board plan and housing facility. ***Payment plan:*** Installment.

FRESHMAN FINANCIAL AID (Fall 2006, est.) 2303 applied for aid; of those 79% were deemed to have need. 100% of freshmen with need received aid; of those 17% had need fully met. ***Average percent of need met:*** 64% (excluding resources awarded to replace EFC). ***Average financial aid package:*** $17,553 (excluding resources awarded to replace EFC). 28% of all full-time freshmen had no need and received non-need-based gift aid.

UNDERGRADUATE FINANCIAL AID (Fall 2006, est.) 10,450 applied for aid; of those 85% were deemed to have need. 99% of undergraduates with need received aid; of those 16% had need fully met. ***Average percent of need met:*** 60% (excluding resources awarded to replace EFC). ***Average financial aid package:*** $16,433 (excluding resources awarded to replace EFC). 23% of all full-time undergraduates had no need and received non-need-based gift aid.

GIFT AID (NEED-BASED) ***Total amount:*** $94,884,208 (8% federal, 2% state, 86% institutional, 4% external sources). ***Receiving aid:*** Freshmen: 60% (1,761); All full-time undergraduates: 55% (8,318). ***Average award:*** Freshmen: $13,660; Undergraduates: $11,654. ***Scholarships, grants, and awards:*** Federal Pell, FSEOG, state, private, college/university gift aid from institutional funds, Federal Nursing.

GIFT AID (NON-NEED-BASED) ***Total amount:*** $31,381,733 (91% institutional, 9% external sources). ***Receiving aid:*** Freshmen: 8% (222); Undergraduates: 6% (869). ***Average award:*** Freshmen: $12,281; Undergraduates: $12,975. ***Scholarships, grants, and awards by category:*** *Academic Interests/Achievement:* 5,093 awards ($42,647,920 total): engineering/technologies, general academic interests/achievements. *Creative Arts/Performance:* 18 awards ($183,337 total): music. *Special Characteristics:* 62 awards ($324,375 total): international students. ***Tuition waivers:*** Full or partial for employees or children of employees, senior citizens. ***ROTC:*** Army, Naval cooperative, Air Force cooperative.

LOANS ***Student loans:*** $108,194,621 (65% need-based, 35% non-need-based). ***Average need-based loan:*** Freshmen: $3715; Undergraduates: $4836. ***Parent loans:*** $23,367,606 (38% need-based, 62% non-need-based). ***Programs:*** FFEL (Subsidized and Unsubsidized Stafford, PLUS), Perkins, Federal Nursing, state, MEFA, TERI, Massachusetts No-Interest Loans (NIL), CitiAssist.

WORK-STUDY ***Federal work-study:*** Total amount: $6,791,547; 3,479 jobs averaging $1448. ***State or other work-study/employment:*** Total amount: $3,092,772 (100% need-based).

ATHLETIC AWARDS Total amount: $8,794,705 (34% need-based, 66% non-need-based).

APPLYING FOR FINANCIAL AID ***Required financial aid forms:*** FAFSA, CSS Financial Aid PROFILE. ***Financial aid deadline (priority):*** 2/15. ***Notification date:*** Continuous beginning 2/15. Students must reply by 5/1.

CONTACT Mr. M. Seamus Harreys, Dean of Student Financial Services, Northeastern University, 360 Huntington Avenue, Boston, MA 02115, 617-373-3190. *Fax:* 617-373-8735. *E-mail:* sfs@neu.edu.

NORTHERN ARIZONA UNIVERSITY

Flagstaff, AZ

Tuition & fees (AZ res): $4546 **Average undergraduate aid package: $7885**

ABOUT THE INSTITUTION State-supported, coed. Awards: bachelor's, master's, doctoral, and first professional degrees and post-bachelor's and post-master's certificates. 105 undergraduate majors. Total enrollment: 20,562. Undergraduates: 14,526. Freshmen: 2,846. Federal methodology is used as a basis for awarding need-based institutional aid.

UNDERGRADUATE EXPENSES for 2006–07 ***Application fee:*** $25. ***Tuition, state resident:*** full-time $4376; part-time $270 per credit hour. ***Tuition, nonresident:*** full-time $13,316; part-time $596 per credit hour. Full-time tuition and fees vary according to program. Part-time tuition and fees vary according to program. ***College room and board:*** $6260; ***Room only:*** $3452. Room and board charges vary according to board plan and housing facility. ***Payment plan:*** Installment.

FRESHMAN FINANCIAL AID (Fall 2006, est.) 1959 applied for aid; of those 59% were deemed to have need. 95% of freshmen with need received aid; of those 20% had need fully met. ***Average percent of need met:*** 67% (excluding resources awarded to replace EFC). ***Average financial aid package:*** $7537 (excluding resources awarded to replace EFC). 25% of all full-time freshmen had no need and received non-need-based gift aid.

UNDERGRADUATE FINANCIAL AID (Fall 2006, est.) 8,182 applied for aid; of those 74% were deemed to have need. 97% of undergraduates with need received aid; of those 17% had need fully met. ***Average percent of need met:*** 64% (excluding resources awarded to replace EFC). ***Average financial aid package:*** $7885 (excluding resources awarded to replace EFC). 16% of all full-time undergraduates had no need and received non-need-based gift aid.

GIFT AID (NEED-BASED) ***Total amount:*** $32,239,349 (44% federal, 1% state, 42% institutional, 13% external sources). ***Receiving aid:*** Freshmen: 26% (680); All full-time undergraduates: 33% (3,981). ***Average award:*** Freshmen: $5053; Undergraduates: $4110. ***Scholarships, grants, and awards:*** Federal Pell, FSEOG, state, private, college/university gift aid from institutional funds, Federal Nursing.

GIFT AID (NON-NEED-BASED) ***Total amount:*** $10,014,157 (4% federal, 73% institutional, 23% external sources). ***Receiving aid:*** Freshmen: 26% (673); Undergraduates: 21% (2,452). ***Average award:*** Freshmen: $3140; Undergraduates: $3122. ***Scholarships, grants, and awards by category:*** *Academic Interests/Achievement:* 1,175 awards ($1,747,271 total): area/ethnic studies, biological sciences, business, communication, computer science, education, engineering/technologies, English, foreign languages, general academic interests/achievements, health fields, home economics, humanities, international studies, library science, mathematics, military science, physical sciences, premedicine, religion/biblical studies, social sciences. *Creative Arts/Performance:* 312 awards ($952,609 total): art/fine arts, cinema/film/broadcasting, creative writing, debating, journalism/publications, music, performing arts, theater/drama. *Special Characteristics:* 4,365 awards ($12,985,613 total): children and siblings of alumni, children of educators, children of faculty/staff, children of public servants, first-generation college students, general special characteristics, handicapped students, international students, local/state students, out-of-state students, spouses of deceased or disabled public servants. ***Tuition waivers:*** Full or partial for employees or children of employees. ***ROTC:*** Army, Air Force.

LOANS ***Student loans:*** $45,305,022 (83% need-based, 17% non-need-based). 59% of past graduating class borrowed through all loan programs. *Average indebtedness per student:* $17,563. ***Average need-based loan:*** Freshmen: $2131; Undergraduates: $3676. ***Parent loans:*** $12,507,093 (59% need-based, 41% non-need-based). ***Programs:*** Federal Direct (Subsidized and Unsubsidized Stafford, PLUS), Perkins, Federal Nursing, college/university.

WORK-STUDY ***Federal work-study:*** Total amount: $750,807; 414 jobs averaging $1695. ***State or other work-study/employment:*** Total amount: $6,144,496 (52% need-based, 48% non-need-based). 3,172 part-time jobs averaging $1810.

ATHLETIC AWARDS Total amount: $3,124,268 (35% need-based, 65% non-need-based).

APPLYING FOR FINANCIAL AID ***Required financial aid form:*** FAFSA. ***Financial aid deadline (priority):*** 2/14. ***Notification date:*** Continuous beginning 3/15.

CONTACT Jack Edwards, Director, Financial Aid, Northern Arizona University, Box 4108, Flagstaff, AZ 86011-4108, 928-523-1383 or toll-free 888-MORE-NAU. *Fax:* 928-523-1551.

NORTHERN ILLINOIS UNIVERSITY

De Kalb, IL

Tuition & fees (IL res): $7125 **Average undergraduate aid package: $10,337**

ABOUT THE INSTITUTION State-supported, coed. Awards: bachelor's, master's, doctoral, and first professional degrees. 61 undergraduate majors. Total enrollment: 25,313. Undergraduates: 18,816. Freshmen: 3,282. Federal methodology is used as a basis for awarding need-based institutional aid.

UNDERGRADUATE EXPENSES for 2006–07 ***Tuition, state resident:*** full-time $5670; part-time $189 per credit hour. ***Tuition, nonresident:*** full-time $11,100; part-time $370 per credit hour. ***Required fees:*** full-time $1455; $60.63 per credit hour. Part-time tuition and fees vary according to course load. ***College room and board:*** $6848. Room and board charges vary according to board plan and housing facility. ***Payment plan:*** Installment.

FRESHMAN FINANCIAL AID (Fall 2005) 2698 applied for aid; of those 70% were deemed to have need. 96% of freshmen with need received aid; of those 22% had need fully met. ***Average percent of need met:*** 67% (excluding resources awarded to replace EFC). ***Average financial aid package:*** $8830 (excluding resources awarded to replace EFC). 2% of all full-time freshmen had no need and received non-need-based gift aid.

UNDERGRADUATE FINANCIAL AID (Fall 2005) 12,720 applied for aid; of those 71% were deemed to have need. 97% of undergraduates with need received aid; of those 18% had need fully met. ***Average percent of need met:*** 68% (excluding resources awarded to replace EFC). ***Average financial aid package:*** $10,337 (excluding resources awarded to replace EFC). 3% of all full-time undergraduates had no need and received non-need-based gift aid.

GIFT AID (NEED-BASED) ***Total amount:*** $34,475,584 (41% federal, 59% state). ***Receiving aid:*** Freshmen: 34% (1,086); All full-time undergraduates: 33% (5,477). ***Average award:*** Freshmen: $6351; Undergraduates: $4332. ***Scholarships, grants, and awards:*** Federal Pell, FSEOG, state, private, college/university gift aid from institutional funds, United Negro College Fund, Federal Nursing.

GIFT AID (NON-NEED-BASED) ***Total amount:*** $9,734,448 (9% federal, 60% state, 15% institutional, 16% external sources). ***Receiving aid:*** Freshmen: 19% (588); Undergraduates: 16% (2,717). ***Average award:*** Freshmen: $947; Undergraduates: $1096. ***Scholarships, grants, and awards by category:*** *Academic Interests/Achievement:* biological sciences, business, communication, computer science, education, engineering/technologies, English, foreign languages, general academic interests/achievements, health fields, humanities, international studies, mathematics, physical sciences, social sciences. *Creative Arts/Performance:* applied art and design, art/fine arts, creative writing, dance, debating, journalism/publications, music, performing arts, theater/drama. *Special Achievements/Activities:* leadership. *Special Characteristics:* adult students, children of faculty/staff, ethnic background, international students, members of minority groups, veterans. ***Tuition waivers:*** Full or partial for minority students, employees or children of employees. ***ROTC:*** Army, Air Force cooperative.

LOANS ***Student loans:*** $65,544,718 (50% need-based, 50% non-need-based). 38% of past graduating class borrowed through all loan programs. *Average indebtedness per student:* $19,764. ***Average need-based loan:*** Freshmen: $2408; Undergraduates: $4027. ***Parent loans:*** $14,530,476 (100% non-need-based). ***Programs:*** FFEL (Subsidized and Unsubsidized Stafford, PLUS), Perkins.

WORK-STUDY ***Federal work-study:*** Total amount: $841,213; 545 jobs averaging $1543. ***State or other work-study/employment:*** Part-time jobs available.

ATHLETIC AWARDS Total amount: $4,250,671 (100% non-need-based).

APPLYING FOR FINANCIAL AID ***Required financial aid forms:*** FAFSA, institution's own form. ***Financial aid deadline (priority):*** 3/1. ***Notification date:*** Continuous beginning 3/24. Students must reply within 2 weeks of notification.

CONTACT Ms. Kathleen D. Brunson, Director of Student Financial Aid, Northern Illinois University, De Kalb, IL 60115-2854, 815-753-1395 or toll-free 800-892-3050 (in-state). *Fax:* 815-753-9475.

NORTHERN KENTUCKY UNIVERSITY

Highland Heights, KY

CONTACT Mr. Robert F. Sprague, Director of Student Financial Assistance, Northern Kentucky University, 416 Administrative Center, Nunn Drive, Highland Heights, KY 41099, 859-572-5143 or toll-free 800-637-9948. *Fax:* 859-572-6997. *E-mail:* ofa@nku.edu.

NORTHERN MICHIGAN UNIVERSITY

Marquette, MI

Tuition & fees (MI res): $6141 Average undergraduate aid package: $6971

ABOUT THE INSTITUTION State-supported, coed. Awards: associate, bachelor's, and master's degrees and post-bachelor's and post-master's certificates. 110 undergraduate majors. Total enrollment: 9,353. Undergraduates: 8,702. Freshmen: 1,389. Federal methodology is used as a basis for awarding need-based institutional aid.

UNDERGRADUATE EXPENSES for 2006–07 ***Application fee:*** $30. ***Tuition, state resident:*** full-time $5592; part-time $233 per credit hour. ***Tuition, nonresident:*** full-time $9528; part-time $397 per credit hour. ***Required fees:*** full-time $549; $30.26 per term part-time. Full-time tuition and fees vary according to location. Part-time tuition and fees vary according to location. ***College room and board:*** $6874; ***Room only:*** $3366. Room and board charges vary according to board plan and housing facility. ***Payment plans:*** Installment, deferred payment.

FRESHMAN FINANCIAL AID (Fall 2005) 1668 applied for aid; of those 62% were deemed to have need. 97% of freshmen with need received aid; of those 22% had need fully met. ***Average percent of need met:*** 66% (excluding resources awarded to replace EFC). ***Average financial aid package:*** $6674 (excluding resources awarded to replace EFC). 10% of all full-time freshmen had no need and received non-need-based gift aid.

UNDERGRADUATE FINANCIAL AID (Fall 2005) 6,800 applied for aid; of those 66% were deemed to have need. 97% of undergraduates with need received aid; of those 17% had need fully met. ***Average percent of need met:*** 67% (excluding resources awarded to replace EFC). ***Average financial aid package:*** $6971 (excluding resources awarded to replace EFC). 5% of all full-time undergraduates had no need and received non-need-based gift aid.

GIFT AID (NEED-BASED) ***Total amount:*** $10,865,419 (75% federal, 9% state, 14% institutional, 2% external sources). ***Receiving aid:*** Freshmen: 35% (626); All full-time undergraduates: 36% (2,798). ***Average award:*** Freshmen: $2986; Undergraduates: $3292. ***Scholarships, grants, and awards:*** Federal Pell, FSEOG, state, private, college/university gift aid from institutional funds, Federal Nursing.

GIFT AID (NON-NEED-BASED) ***Total amount:*** $10,939,834 (27% state, 49% institutional, 24% external sources). ***Receiving aid:*** Freshmen: 32% (559); Undergraduates: 19% (1,502). ***Average award:*** Freshmen: $2958; Undergraduates: $2506. ***Scholarships, grants, and awards by category:*** *Academic Interests/Achievement:* 257 awards ($267,809 total): biological sciences, business, communication, computer science, education, engineering/technologies, English, foreign languages, general academic interests/achievements, health fields, international studies, mathematics, military science, physical sciences, premedicine, social sciences. *Creative Arts/Performance:* 65 awards ($44,256 total): applied art and design, music, theater/drama. *Special Achievements/Activities:* 153 awards ($81,500 total): leadership, memberships. *Special Characteristics:* 924 awards ($3,258,776 total): children of faculty/staff, children of union members/company employees, members of minority groups, out-of-state students. ***Tuition waivers:*** Full or partial for employees or children of employees, senior citizens. ***ROTC:*** Army.

LOANS ***Student loans:*** $33,887,553 (50% need-based, 50% non-need-based). 63% of past graduating class borrowed through all loan programs. *Average indebtedness per student:* $15,799. ***Average need-based loan:*** Freshmen: $2836; Undergraduates: $3648. ***Parent loans:*** $2,820,857 (100% non-need-based). ***Programs:*** Federal Direct (Subsidized and Unsubsidized Stafford, PLUS), Perkins, state, alternative loans.

WORK-STUDY ***Federal work-study:*** Total amount: $688,986; 507 jobs averaging $1149. ***State or other work-study/employment:*** Total amount: $280,558 (100% need-based). 189 part-time jobs averaging $1331.

ATHLETIC AWARDS Total amount: $1,813,351 (100% non-need-based).

APPLYING FOR FINANCIAL AID ***Required financial aid form:*** FAFSA. ***Financial aid deadline (priority):*** 3/1. ***Notification date:*** Continuous beginning 4/1. Students must reply within 2 weeks of notification.

CONTACT Michael Rotundo, Director of Financial Aid, Northern Michigan University, 1401 Presque Isle Avenue, Marquette, MI 49855, 906-227-1575 or toll-free 800-682-9797. *Fax:* 906-227-2321. *E-mail:* mrotundo@nmu.edu.

NORTHERN STATE UNIVERSITY

Aberdeen, SD

Tuition & fees (SD res): $4962 Average undergraduate aid package: $7318

ABOUT THE INSTITUTION State-supported, coed. Awards: associate, bachelor's, and master's degrees and post-bachelor's certificates. 52 undergraduate majors. Total enrollment: 2,407. Undergraduates: 2,183. Freshmen: 376. Federal methodology is used as a basis for awarding need-based institutional aid.

UNDERGRADUATE EXPENSES for 2006–07 ***Application fee:*** $15. ***Tuition, state resident:*** full-time $2382; part-time $79.40 per credit hour. ***Tuition, nonresident:*** full-time $7589; part-time $252.30 per credit hour. ***Required fees:*** full-time $2580; $86 per credit hour. Full-time tuition and fees vary according to course level, course load, and reciprocity agreements. Part-time tuition and fees vary according to course level, course load, and reciprocity agreements. ***College room and board:*** $4102; ***Room only:*** $2145. Room and board charges vary according to board plan. ***Payment plan:*** Installment.

FRESHMAN FINANCIAL AID (Fall 2006, est.) 282 applied for aid; of those 76% were deemed to have need. 100% of freshmen with need received aid; of those 100% had need fully met. ***Average financial aid package:*** $6627 (excluding resources awarded to replace EFC). 12% of all full-time freshmen had no need and received non-need-based gift aid.

UNDERGRADUATE FINANCIAL AID (Fall 2006, est.) 1,165 applied for aid; of those 78% were deemed to have need. 99% of undergraduates with need received aid; of those 100% had need fully met. ***Average financial aid package:*** $7318 (excluding resources awarded to replace EFC). 7% of all full-time undergraduates had no need and received non-need-based gift aid.

GIFT AID (NEED-BASED) ***Total amount:*** $2,171,713 (93% federal, 7% state). ***Receiving aid:*** Freshmen: 52% (190); All full-time undergraduates: 45% (696). ***Average award:*** Freshmen: $2305; Undergraduates: $2467. ***Scholarships, grants, and awards:*** Federal Pell, FSEOG, state, private, college/university gift aid from institutional funds.

GIFT AID (NON-NEED-BASED) ***Total amount:*** $1,120,297 (8% state, 60% institutional, 32% external sources). ***Receiving aid:*** Freshmen: 45% (164); Undergraduates: 38% (581). ***Average award:*** Freshmen: $2915; Undergraduates: $2353. ***Scholarships, grants, and awards by category:*** *Academic Interests/Achievement:* 244 awards ($156,269 total): biological sciences, business, education, English, foreign languages, general academic interests/achievements, humanities, international studies, mathematics, physical sciences, social sciences. *Creative Arts/Performance:* 113 awards ($58,310 total): art/fine arts, music, theater/drama. *Special Achievements/Activities:* 20 awards ($6825 total): leadership.

LOANS ***Student loans:*** $8,154,189 (52% need-based, 48% non-need-based). 80% of past graduating class borrowed through all loan programs. *Average indebtedness per student:* $21,123. ***Average need-based loan:*** Freshmen: $3293; Undergraduates: $3491. ***Parent loans:*** $405,051 (100% non-need-based). ***Programs:*** FFEL (Subsidized and Unsubsidized Stafford, PLUS), Perkins, college/university, SELF Loans, alternative loans.

WORK-STUDY ***Federal work-study:*** Total amount: $512,800; 350 jobs averaging $1631. ***State or other work-study/employment:*** Total amount: $437,610 (100% non-need-based). 424 part-time jobs averaging $1032.

ATHLETIC AWARDS Total amount: $523,438 (100% non-need-based).

APPLYING FOR FINANCIAL AID ***Required financial aid form:*** FAFSA. ***Financial aid deadline (priority):*** 3/1. ***Notification date:*** 4/15. Students must reply within 2 weeks of notification.

CONTACT Ms. Sharon Kienow, Director of Financial Aid, Northern State University, 1200 South Jay Street, Aberdeen, SD 57401-7198, 605-626-2640 or toll-free 800-678-5330. *Fax:* 605-626-2587. *E-mail:* kienows@northern.edu.

NORTH GEORGIA COLLEGE & STATE UNIVERSITY

Dahlonega, GA

Tuition & fees (GA res): $3452 **Average undergraduate aid package: $5782**

ABOUT THE INSTITUTION State-supported, coed. Awards: associate, bachelor's, and master's degrees and post-bachelor's and post-master's certificates. 48 undergraduate majors. Total enrollment: 4,922. Undergraduates: 4,356. Freshmen: 877. Federal methodology is used as a basis for awarding need-based institutional aid.

UNDERGRADUATE EXPENSES for 2006–07 ***Application fee:*** $25. ***Tuition, state resident:*** full-time $2560; part-time $107 per semester hour. ***Tuition, nonresident:*** full-time $10,242; part-time $427 per semester hour. ***Required fees:*** full-time $892; $434 per term part-time. Part-time tuition and fees vary according to course load. ***College room and board:*** $4780; ***Room only:*** $2384. Room and board charges vary according to board plan and housing facility. ***Payment plan:*** Guaranteed tuition.

UNDERGRADUATE FINANCIAL AID (Fall 2005) 3,622 applied for aid; of those 50% were deemed to have need. 100% of undergraduates with need received aid; of those 78% had need fully met. ***Average percent of need met:*** 90% (excluding resources awarded to replace EFC). ***Average financial aid package:*** $5782 (excluding resources awarded to replace EFC). 71% of all full-time undergraduates had no need and received non-need-based gift aid.

GIFT AID (NEED-BASED) ***Total amount:*** $413,047 (51% federal, 6% state, 36% institutional, 7% external sources). ***Receiving aid:*** All full-time undergraduates: 41% (1,800). ***Average award:*** Undergraduates: $1100. ***Scholarships, grants, and awards:*** Federal Pell, FSEOG, state, private, college/university gift aid from institutional funds.

GIFT AID (NON-NEED-BASED) ***Total amount:*** $7,712,665 (97% state, 2% institutional, 1% external sources). ***Receiving aid:*** Undergraduates: 40% (1,750). ***Scholarships, grants, and awards by category:*** *Academic Interests/Achievement:* biological sciences, business, education, English, general academic interests/achievements, health fields, humanities, mathematics, military science, physical sciences, premedicine. *Creative Arts/Performance:* applied art and design, general creative arts/performance, music. *Special Achievements/Activities:* cheerleading/drum major, community service, general special achievements/activities, leadership. *Special Characteristics:* general special characteristics. ***Tuition waivers:*** Full or partial for employees or children of employees, senior citizens. ***ROTC:*** Army.

LOANS ***Student loans:*** $7,597,620 (45% need-based, 55% non-need-based). 42% of past graduating class borrowed through all loan programs. *Average indebtedness per student:* $9852. ***Average need-based loan:*** Undergraduates: $3500. ***Parent loans:*** $264,693 (100% need-based). ***Programs:*** FFEL (Subsidized and Unsubsidized Stafford, PLUS), Perkins, state, college/university.

WORK-STUDY ***Federal work-study:*** Total amount: $71,132; jobs available. ***State or other work-study/employment:*** Total amount: $90,000 (56% need-based, 44% non-need-based).

ATHLETIC AWARDS Total amount: $400,664 (100% non-need-based).

APPLYING FOR FINANCIAL AID ***Required financial aid form:*** FAFSA. ***Financial aid deadline (priority):*** 5/1. ***Notification date:*** Continuous beginning 3/15. Students must reply within 3 weeks of notification.

CONTACT Jill Royner, Director, Financial Aid, North Georgia College & State University, 82 College Circle, Dahlonega, GA 30597-1001, 706-864-1688 or toll-free 800-498-9581. *Fax:* 706-864-1411. *E-mail:* jproyner@ngcsu.edu.

NORTH GREENVILLE UNIVERSITY

Tigerville, SC

Tuition & fees: $11,180 **Average undergraduate aid package: N/A**

ABOUT THE INSTITUTION Independent Southern Baptist, coed. Awards: associate and bachelor's degrees. 30 undergraduate majors. Total enrollment: 1,948. Undergraduates: 1,882. Federal methodology is used as a basis for awarding need-based institutional aid.

UNDERGRADUATE EXPENSES for 2006–07 ***Application fee:*** $25. ***Tuition:*** full-time $11,180.

GIFT AID (NEED-BASED) ***Total amount:*** $12,162,304 (15% federal, 24% state, 56% institutional, 5% external sources). ***Scholarships, grants, and awards:*** Federal Pell, FSEOG, state, private, college/university gift aid from institutional funds.

GIFT AID (NON-NEED-BASED) ***Total amount:*** $3,297,025 (100% state). ***Scholarships, grants, and awards by category:*** *Academic Interests/Achievement:* biological sciences, communication, education, general academic interests/achievements, military science, religion/biblical studies. *Creative Arts/Performance:* journalism/publications, music, theater/drama. *Special Achievements/Activities:* $4900 total. *Special Characteristics:* $225,000 total: children of faculty/staff. ***ROTC:*** Army cooperative.

LOANS ***Student loans:*** $5,153,010 (66% need-based, 34% non-need-based). ***Parent loans:*** $1,327,000 (100% need-based). ***Programs:*** FFEL (Subsidized and Unsubsidized Stafford, PLUS), Perkins, state.

WORK-STUDY ***Federal work-study:*** Total amount: $163,800; 164 jobs averaging $1000. ***State or other work-study/employment:*** Total amount: $137,500 (100% need-based). 138 part-time jobs averaging $1000.

ATHLETIC AWARDS Total amount: $950,000 (100% need-based).

APPLYING FOR FINANCIAL AID ***Required financial aid form:*** FAFSA. ***Financial aid deadline:*** Continuous.

CONTACT Mike Jordan, Director of Financial Aid, North Greenville University, PO Box 1892, Tigerville, SC 29688, 864-977-7058 or toll-free 800-468-6642 Ext. 7001. *Fax:* 864-977-7177. *E-mail:* mjordan@ngu.edu.

NORTHLAND COLLEGE

Ashland, WI

Tuition & fees: $21,901 **Average undergraduate aid package: $16,008**

ABOUT THE INSTITUTION Independent religious, coed. Awards: bachelor's degrees. 54 undergraduate majors. Total enrollment: 692. Undergraduates: 692. Freshmen: 181. Federal methodology is used as a basis for awarding need-based institutional aid.

UNDERGRADUATE EXPENSES for 2007–08 ***Comprehensive fee:*** $28,061 includes full-time tuition ($21,300), mandatory fees ($601), and room and board ($6160). ***College room only:*** $2490. ***Part-time tuition:*** $410 per credit.

FRESHMAN FINANCIAL AID (Fall 2006, est.) 175 applied for aid; of those 89% were deemed to have need. 100% of freshmen with need received aid; of those 18% had need fully met. ***Average percent of need met:*** 85% (excluding resources awarded to replace EFC). ***Average financial aid package:*** $17,050 (excluding resources awarded to replace EFC). 14% of all full-time freshmen had no need and received non-need-based gift aid.

UNDERGRADUATE FINANCIAL AID (Fall 2006, est.) 632 applied for aid; of those 88% were deemed to have need. 100% of undergraduates with need received aid; of those 20% had need fully met. ***Average percent of need met:*** 78% (excluding resources awarded to replace EFC). ***Average financial aid package:*** $16,008 (excluding resources awarded to replace EFC). 16% of all full-time undergraduates had no need and received non-need-based gift aid.

GIFT AID (NEED-BASED) ***Total amount:*** $6,079,047 (14% federal, 5% state, 78% institutional, 3% external sources). ***Receiving aid:*** Freshmen: 84% (152); All full-time undergraduates: 84% (538). ***Average award:*** Freshmen: $15,082; Undergraduates: $10,824. ***Scholarships, grants, and awards:*** Federal Pell, FSEOG, state, private, college/university gift aid from institutional funds, Bureau of Indian Affairs Grants.

GIFT AID (NON-NEED-BASED) ***Total amount:*** $653,998 (97% institutional, 3% external sources). ***Receiving aid:*** Freshmen: 1% (1); Undergraduates: 3% (20). ***Average award:*** Freshmen: $7503; Undergraduates: $6314. ***Scholarships, grants, and awards by category:*** *Academic Interests/Achievement:* 345 awards ($2,255,116 total): general academic interests/achievements. *Creative Arts/Performance:* 31 awards ($30,850 total): art/fine arts, music. *Special Achievements/Activities:* 32 awards ($58,750 total): leadership. *Special Characteristics:* 26 awards ($33,400 total): ethnic background.

LOANS ***Student loans:*** $3,746,842 (54% need-based, 46% non-need-based). 81% of past graduating class borrowed through all loan programs. *Average indebtedness per student:* $20,911. ***Average need-based loan:*** Freshmen: $3932; Undergraduates: $4484. ***Parent loans:*** $1,720,886 (81% need-based, 19% non-need-based). ***Programs:*** Federal Direct (Subsidized and Unsubsidized Stafford, PLUS), FFEL (Subsidized and Unsubsidized Stafford, PLUS), Perkins.

WORK-STUDY ***Federal work-study:*** Total amount: $461,899; 334 jobs averaging $1383. ***State or other work-study/employment:*** Total amount: $332,448 (79% need-based, 21% non-need-based). 256 part-time jobs averaging $1021.

APPLYING FOR FINANCIAL AID ***Required financial aid form:*** FAFSA. ***Financial aid deadline (priority):*** 4/15. ***Notification date:*** Continuous beginning 3/1. Students must reply by 5/1 or within 4 weeks of notification.

CONTACT Tracy K. Steine, Director of Financial Aid, Northland College, 1411 Ellis Avenue, Ashland, WI 54806, 715-682-1255 or toll-free 800-753-1840 (in-state), 800-753-1040 (out-of-state). *Fax:* 715-682-1308. *E-mail:* tsteine@northland.edu.

NORTH PARK UNIVERSITY

Chicago, IL

CONTACT Dr. Lucy Shaker, Director of Financial Aid, North Park University, 3225 West Foster Avenue, Chicago, IL 60625-4895, 773-244-5526 or toll-free 800-888-NPC8. *Fax:* 773-244-4953.

NORTHWEST CHRISTIAN COLLEGE

Eugene, OR

Tuition & fees: $19,890 **Average undergraduate aid package: $16,807**

ABOUT THE INSTITUTION Independent Christian, coed. Awards: associate, bachelor's, and master's degrees and post-bachelor's certificates. 14 undergraduate majors. Total enrollment: 480. Undergraduates: 387. Freshmen: 66. Federal methodology is used as a basis for awarding need-based institutional aid.

UNDERGRADUATE EXPENSES for 2006–07 ***Comprehensive fee:*** $26,314 includes full-time tuition ($19,890) and room and board ($6424). ***College room only:*** $2800. Full-time tuition and fees vary according to course load and program. Room and board charges vary according to board plan and housing facility. ***Part-time tuition:*** $663 per credit. Part-time tuition and fees vary according to course load and program. ***Payment plans:*** Installment, deferred payment.

FRESHMAN FINANCIAL AID (Fall 2006, est.) 64 applied for aid; of those 88% were deemed to have need. 100% of freshmen with need received aid; of those 20% had need fully met. ***Average percent of need met:*** 73% (excluding resources awarded to replace EFC). ***Average financial aid package:*** $15,379 (excluding resources awarded to replace EFC). 12% of all full-time freshmen had no need and received non-need-based gift aid.

UNDERGRADUATE FINANCIAL AID (Fall 2006, est.) 273 applied for aid; of those 91% were deemed to have need. 100% of undergraduates with need received aid; of those 21% had need fully met. ***Average percent of need met:*** 75% (excluding resources awarded to replace EFC). ***Average financial aid package:*** $16,807 (excluding resources awarded to replace EFC). 8% of all full-time undergraduates had no need and received non-need-based gift aid.

GIFT AID (NEED-BASED) ***Total amount:*** $2,859,539 (15% federal, 6% state, 56% institutional, 23% external sources). ***Receiving aid:*** Freshmen: 85% (56); All full-time undergraduates: 89% (248). ***Average award:*** Freshmen: $12,418; Undergraduates: $12,492. ***Scholarships, grants, and awards:*** Federal Pell, FSEOG, state, private, college/university gift aid from institutional funds.

GIFT AID (NON-NEED-BASED) ***Total amount:*** $152,276 (70% institutional, 30% external sources). ***Receiving aid:*** Freshmen: 11% (7); Undergraduates: 5% (15). ***Average award:*** Freshmen: $11,079; Undergraduates: $11,252. ***Scholarships, grants, and awards by category:*** *Academic Interests/Achievement:* general academic interests/achievements. *Creative Arts/Performance:* general creative arts/performance, music. *Special Achievements/Activities:* general special achievements/activities, leadership, religious involvement. *Special Characteristics:* children of faculty/staff, relatives of clergy, religious affiliation. ***Tuition waivers:*** Full or partial for employees or children of employees. ***ROTC:*** Army cooperative.

LOANS ***Student loans:*** $1,496,263 (78% need-based, 22% non-need-based). 75% of past graduating class borrowed through all loan programs. *Average indebtedness per student:* $14,415. ***Average need-based loan:*** Freshmen: $2723; Undergraduates: $3950. ***Parent loans:*** $496,008 (64% need-based, 36% non-need-based). ***Programs:*** FFEL (Subsidized and Unsubsidized Stafford, PLUS), Perkins.

WORK-STUDY ***Federal work-study:*** Total amount: $219,837; jobs available. ***State or other work-study/employment:*** Total amount: $23,125 (89% need-based, 11% non-need-based). Part-time jobs available.

ATHLETIC AWARDS Total amount: $214,750 (79% need-based, 21% non-need-based).

APPLYING FOR FINANCIAL AID ***Financial aid deadline (priority):*** 3/1. ***Notification date:*** Continuous beginning 4/1.

CONTACT Scott Palmer, Financial Aid Information Specialist, Northwest Christian College, 828 East 11th Avenue, Eugene, OR 97401-3727, 541-684-7291 or toll-free 877-463-6622. *Fax:* 541-684-7323. *E-mail:* spalmer@nwcc.edu.

NORTHWEST COLLEGE OF ART

Poulsbo, WA

CONTACT Ms. Kim Y. Perigard, Director of Financial Aid, Northwest College of Art, 16464 State Highway 305, Poulsbo, WA 98370, 360-779-9993 or toll-free 800-769-ARTS.

NORTHWESTERN COLLEGE

Orange City, IA

Tuition & fees: $18,296 **Average undergraduate aid package: $15,040**

ABOUT THE INSTITUTION Independent religious, coed. Awards: bachelor's degrees. 38 undergraduate majors. Total enrollment: 1,342. Undergraduates: 1,342. Freshmen: 363. Federal methodology is used as a basis for awarding need-based institutional aid.

UNDERGRADUATE EXPENSES for 2006–07 ***Application fee:*** $25. ***Comprehensive fee:*** $23,506 includes full-time tuition ($18,296) and room and board ($5210). ***College room only:*** $2386. Room and board charges vary according to housing facility. Part-time tuition and fees vary according to course load. ***Payment plans:*** Tuition prepayment, installment.

FRESHMAN FINANCIAL AID (Fall 2006, est.) 344 applied for aid; of those 85% were deemed to have need. 97% of freshmen with need received aid; of those 35% had need fully met. ***Average percent of need met:*** 91% (excluding resources awarded to replace EFC). ***Average financial aid package:*** $14,480 (excluding resources awarded to replace EFC). 20% of all full-time freshmen had no need and received non-need-based gift aid.

UNDERGRADUATE FINANCIAL AID (Fall 2006, est.) 1,168 applied for aid; of those 86% were deemed to have need. 98% of undergraduates with need received aid; of those 46% had need fully met. ***Average percent of need met:*** 96% (excluding resources awarded to replace EFC). ***Average financial aid package:*** $15,040 (excluding resources awarded to replace EFC). 20% of all full-time undergraduates had no need and received non-need-based gift aid.

GIFT AID (NEED-BASED) ***Total amount:*** $5,466,372 (22% federal, 33% state, 45% institutional). ***Receiving aid:*** Freshmen: 78% (283); All full-time undergraduates: 69% (882). ***Average award:*** Freshmen: $5284; Undergraduates: $6134. ***Scholarships, grants, and awards:*** Federal Pell, FSEOG, state, private, college/university gift aid from institutional funds.

GIFT AID (NON-NEED-BASED) ***Total amount:*** $6,349,170 (1% federal, 1% state, 92% institutional, 6% external sources). ***Receiving aid:*** Freshmen: 69% (250); Undergraduates: 71% (907). ***Average award:*** Freshmen: $5041; Undergraduates: $5176. ***Scholarships, grants, and awards by category:*** *Academic Interests/Achievement:* biological sciences, business, communication, computer science, education, engineering/technologies, English, foreign languages, general academic interests/achievements, health fields, humanities, mathematics, physical sciences, premedicine, religion/biblical studies, social sciences. *Creative Arts/Performance:* art/fine arts, journalism/publications, music, theater/drama. *Special Characteristics:* adult students, children and siblings of alumni, children of faculty/staff, ethnic background, first-generation college students, handicapped students, international students, religious affiliation, siblings of current students. ***Tuition waivers:*** Full or partial for employees or children of employees.

LOANS ***Student loans:*** $8,051,523 (47% need-based, 53% non-need-based). 85% of past graduating class borrowed through all loan programs. *Average indebtedness per student:* $23,143. ***Average need-based loan:*** Freshmen: $3189; Undergraduates: $4033. ***Parent loans:*** $1,312,501 (100% non-need-based). ***Programs:*** FFEL (Subsidized and Unsubsidized Stafford, PLUS), Perkins, college/university, alternative loans.

WORK-STUDY ***Federal work-study:*** Total amount: $321,365; 305 jobs averaging $1100. ***State or other work-study/employment:*** Total amount: $763,012 (100% non-need-based). 695 part-time jobs averaging $1100.

ATHLETIC AWARDS Total amount: $1,252,307 (100% non-need-based).

APPLYING FOR FINANCIAL AID ***Required financial aid form:*** FAFSA. ***Financial aid deadline (priority):*** 4/1. ***Notification date:*** Continuous beginning 3/15. Students must reply within 3 weeks of notification.

CONTACT Mr. Gerry Korver, Director of Financial Aid, Northwestern College, 101 Seventh Street, SW, Orange City, IA 51041-1996, 712-707-7131 or toll-free 800-747-4757. *Fax:* 712-707-7164.

NORTHWESTERN COLLEGE

St. Paul, MN

Tuition & fees: $20,990 **Average undergraduate aid package: $14,551**

ABOUT THE INSTITUTION Independent nondenominational, coed. Awards: associate, bachelor's, and master's degrees. 45 undergraduate majors. Total enrollment: 1,781. Undergraduates: 1,781. Freshmen: 487. Federal methodology is used as a basis for awarding need-based institutional aid.

UNDERGRADUATE EXPENSES for 2007–08 ***Application fee:*** $30. ***Comprehensive fee:*** $27,740 includes full-time tuition ($20,990) and room and board ($6750). ***College room only:*** $3800. ***Part-time tuition:*** $895 per credit.

FRESHMAN FINANCIAL AID (Fall 2005) 459 applied for aid; of those 84% were deemed to have need. 100% of freshmen with need received aid; of those 9% had need fully met. ***Average percent of need met:*** 71% (excluding resources awarded to replace EFC). ***Average financial aid package:*** $14,142 (excluding resources awarded to replace EFC). 16% of all full-time freshmen had no need and received non-need-based gift aid.

UNDERGRADUATE FINANCIAL AID (Fall 2005) 1,679 applied for aid; of those 84% were deemed to have need. 100% of undergraduates with need received aid; of those 11% had need fully met. ***Average percent of need met:*** 75% (excluding resources awarded to replace EFC). ***Average financial aid package:*** $14,551 (excluding resources awarded to replace EFC). 14% of all full-time undergraduates had no need and received non-need-based gift aid.

GIFT AID (NEED-BASED) ***Total amount:*** $8,940,565 (19% federal, 21% state, 60% institutional). ***Receiving aid:*** Freshmen: 82% (385); All full-time undergraduates: 82% (1,411). ***Average award:*** Freshmen: $11,069; Undergraduates: $10,377. ***Scholarships, grants, and awards:*** Federal Pell, FSEOG, state, private, college/university gift aid from institutional funds.

GIFT AID (NON-NEED-BASED) ***Total amount:*** $6,407,414 (92% institutional, 8% external sources). ***Receiving aid:*** Freshmen: 73% (342); Undergraduates: 69% (1,196). ***Average award:*** Freshmen: $4670; Undergraduates: $5088. ***Scholarships, grants, and awards by category:*** *Academic Interests/Achievement:* 720 awards ($2,024,639 total): biological sciences, general academic interests/achievements. *Creative Arts/Performance:* 147 awards ($171,775 total): music, theater/drama. *Special Achievements/Activities:* 165 awards ($266,812 total): leadership. *Special Characteristics:* 646 awards ($2,740,812 total): children of faculty/staff, ethnic background, international students, relatives of clergy, siblings of current students. ***ROTC:*** Army cooperative, Air Force cooperative.

LOANS ***Student loans:*** $11,383,752 (55% need-based, 45% non-need-based). 78% of past graduating class borrowed through all loan programs. *Average indebtedness per student:* $22,650. ***Average need-based loan:*** Freshmen: $3458; Undergraduates: $4389. ***Parent loans:*** $3,950,674 (100% non-need-based). ***Programs:*** FFEL (Subsidized and Unsubsidized Stafford, PLUS), Perkins, state.

WORK-STUDY ***Federal work-study:*** Total amount: $447,046; 227 jobs averaging $1969. ***State or other work-study/employment:*** Total amount: $556,792 (100% need-based). 323 part-time jobs averaging $1723.

APPLYING FOR FINANCIAL AID ***Required financial aid forms:*** FAFSA, institution's own form. ***Financial aid deadline:*** 5/1 (priority: 3/1). ***Notification date:*** Continuous beginning 3/1. Students must reply within 2 weeks of notification.

CONTACT Mr. Richard L. Blatchley, Director of Financial Aid, Northwestern College, 3003 Snelling Avenue North, St. Paul, MN 55113-1598, 651-631-5321 or toll-free 800-827-6827. *Fax:* 651-628-3332. *E-mail:* rlb@nwc.edu.

NORTHWESTERN OKLAHOMA STATE UNIVERSITY

Alva, OK

Tuition & fees (OK res): $3450 **Average undergraduate aid package: $5512**

ABOUT THE INSTITUTION State-supported, coed. Awards: bachelor's and master's degrees and post-bachelor's and post-master's certificates. 37 undergraduate majors. Total enrollment: 2,024. Undergraduates: 1,778. Freshmen: 261. Both federal and institutional methodology are used as a basis for awarding need-based institutional aid.

UNDERGRADUATE EXPENSES for 2006–07 ***Application fee:*** $15. ***Tuition, state resident:*** full-time $3450; part-time $115 per credit hour. ***Tuition, nonresident:*** full-time $8550; part-time $285 per credit hour. Full-time tuition and fees vary according to course load, location, and program. Part-time tuition and fees vary according to course load, location, and program. ***College room and board:*** $3310; ***Room only:*** $1250. Room and board charges vary according to board plan. ***Payment plan:*** Installment.

FRESHMAN FINANCIAL AID (Fall 2005) 194 applied for aid; of those 68% were deemed to have need. 100% of freshmen with need received aid; of those 52% had need fully met. ***Average percent of need met:*** 65% (excluding resources awarded to replace EFC). ***Average financial aid package:*** $4786 (excluding resources awarded to replace EFC). 30% of all full-time freshmen had no need and received non-need-based gift aid.

UNDERGRADUATE FINANCIAL AID (Fall 2005) 954 applied for aid; of those 78% were deemed to have need. 100% of undergraduates with need received aid; of those 48% had need fully met. ***Average percent of need met:*** 68% (excluding resources awarded to replace EFC). ***Average financial aid package:*** $5512 (excluding resources awarded to replace EFC). 16% of all full-time undergraduates had no need and received non-need-based gift aid.

GIFT AID (NEED-BASED) ***Total amount:*** $2,961,419 (70% federal, 24% state, 6% institutional). ***Receiving aid:*** Freshmen: 42% (115); All full-time undergraduates: 46% (604). ***Average award:*** Freshmen: $3931; Undergraduates: $3817. ***Scholarships, grants, and awards:*** Federal Pell, FSEOG, state, college/university gift aid from institutional funds.

GIFT AID (NON-NEED-BASED) ***Total amount:*** $735,708 (27% state, 38% institutional, 35% external sources). ***Receiving aid:*** Freshmen: 9% (24); Undergraduates: 5% (65). ***Average award:*** Freshmen: $1055; Undergraduates: $1106. ***Scholarships, grants, and awards by category:*** *Academic Interests/Achievement:* 295 awards ($352,630 total): agriculture, biological sciences, business, communication, computer science, education, English, foreign languages, general academic interests/achievements, health fields, humanities, international studies, library science, mathematics, physical sciences, premedicine, social sciences. *Creative Arts/Performance:* 100 awards ($66,117 total): art/fine arts, cinema/film/broadcasting, dance, debating, general creative arts/performance, journalism/publications, music, theater/drama. *Special Achievements/Activities:* 72 awards ($86,066 total): cheerleading/drum major, general special achievements/activities, leadership, memberships, rodeo. *Special Characteristics:* 43 awards ($56,832 total): children and siblings of alumni, children of faculty/staff. ***Tuition waivers:*** Full or partial for employees or children of employees, senior citizens.

LOANS ***Student loans:*** $3,910,779 (62% need-based, 38% non-need-based). 58% of past graduating class borrowed through all loan programs. *Average indebtedness per student:* $11,478. ***Average need-based loan:*** Freshmen: $1951; Undergraduates: $3293. ***Parent loans:*** $114,752 (100% non-need-based). ***Programs:*** FFEL (Subsidized and Unsubsidized Stafford, PLUS), Perkins.

WORK-STUDY ***Federal work-study:*** Total amount: $164,754; 148 jobs averaging $1113. ***State or other work-study/employment:*** Total amount: $169,236 (100% non-need-based). 191 part-time jobs averaging $886.

ATHLETIC AWARDS Total amount: $230,963 (49% need-based, 51% non-need-based).

APPLYING FOR FINANCIAL AID ***Required financial aid forms:*** FAFSA, institutional scholarship application form. ***Financial aid deadline (priority):*** 3/1. ***Notification date:*** Continuous beginning 6/1. Students must reply by 8/15.

CONTACT Irala K. Magee, Director of Financial Aid, Northwestern Oklahoma State University, 709 Oklahoma Boulevard, Alva, OK 73717-2799, 580-327-1700 Ext. 8542. *Fax:* 580-327-8177. *E-mail:* ikmagee@nwosu.edu.

NORTHWESTERN STATE UNIVERSITY OF LOUISIANA

Natchitoches, LA

Tuition & fees (LA res): $3553 **Average undergraduate aid package: $5318**

ABOUT THE INSTITUTION State-supported, coed. Awards: associate, bachelor's, and master's degrees and post-master's certificates. 52 undergraduate majors. Total enrollment: 9,431. Undergraduates: 8,248. Freshmen: 1,379. Both federal and institutional methodology are used as a basis for awarding need-based institutional aid.

UNDERGRADUATE EXPENSES for 2006–07 ***Application fee:*** $20. ***Tuition, state resident:*** full-time $2240; part-time $288 per credit. ***Tuition, nonresident:*** full-time $8318; part-time $543 per credit. Full-time tuition and fees vary according to course load. Part-time tuition and fees vary according to course load. ***College room and board:*** $4686; ***Room only:*** $2816. Room and board charges vary according to board plan, housing facility, and location. ***Payment plan:*** Installment.

FRESHMAN FINANCIAL AID (Fall 2005) 1171 applied for aid; of those 84% were deemed to have need. 97% of freshmen with need received aid; of those 34% had need fully met. ***Average percent of need met:*** 50% (excluding resources awarded to replace EFC). ***Average financial aid package:*** $4308 (excluding resources awarded to replace EFC). 21% of all full-time freshmen had no need and received non-need-based gift aid.

UNDERGRADUATE FINANCIAL AID (Fall 2005) 4,963 applied for aid; of those 88% were deemed to have need. 96% of undergraduates with need received aid; of those 22% had need fully met. ***Average percent of need met:*** 39% (excluding resources awarded to replace EFC). ***Average financial aid package:*** $5318 (excluding resources awarded to replace EFC). 21% of all full-time undergraduates had no need and received non-need-based gift aid.

GIFT AID (NEED-BASED) ***Total amount:*** $10,630,807 (99% federal, 1% state). ***Receiving aid:*** Freshmen: 46% (658); All full-time undergraduates: 45% (2,902). ***Average award:*** Freshmen: $3156; Undergraduates: $3149. ***Scholarships, grants, and awards:*** Federal Pell, FSEOG, state, private, college/university gift aid from institutional funds, United Negro College Fund, Federal Nursing, third party scholarships.

GIFT AID (NON-NEED-BASED) ***Total amount:*** $8,314,259 (59% state, 21% institutional, 20% external sources). ***Receiving aid:*** Freshmen: 26% (373); Undergraduates: 20% (1,301). ***Average award:*** Freshmen: $4686; Undergraduates: $4027. ***Scholarships, grants, and awards by category:*** *Academic Interests/Achievement:* 1,987 awards ($1,640,339 total): biological sciences, education, engineering/technologies, general academic interests/achievements, humanities, mathematics, physical sciences. *Creative Arts/Performance:* 520 awards ($554,737 total): art/fine arts, cinema/film/broadcasting, creative writing, dance, general creative arts/performance, journalism/publications, music, performing arts, theater/drama. *Special Achievements/Activities:* 161 awards ($129,501 total): cheerleading/drum major, general special achievements/activities, leadership, memberships. *Special Characteristics:* 681 awards ($2,226,787 total): adult students, children of faculty/staff, children of public servants, general special characteristics, international students, out-of-state students, public servants, veterans, veterans' children. ***Tuition waivers:*** Full or partial for employees or children of employees, senior citizens. ***ROTC:*** Army.

LOANS ***Student loans:*** $24,198,919 (52% need-based, 48% non-need-based). 72% of past graduating class borrowed through all loan programs. *Average indebtedness per student:* $18,812. ***Average need-based loan:*** Freshmen: $3700; Undergraduates: $5155. ***Parent loans:*** $331,000 (100% non-need-based). ***Programs:*** FFEL (Subsidized and Unsubsidized Stafford, PLUS), Perkins, alternative loans.

WORK-STUDY ***Federal work-study:*** Total amount: $288,932; 301 jobs averaging $960. ***State or other work-study/employment:*** Total amount: $801,442 (100% non-need-based). 678 part-time jobs averaging $1182.

ATHLETIC AWARDS Total amount: $1,782,334 (100% non-need-based).

APPLYING FOR FINANCIAL AID ***Required financial aid forms:*** FAFSA, institution's own form. ***Financial aid deadline (priority):*** 5/1. ***Notification date:*** Continuous beginning 5/1. Students must reply within 4 weeks of notification.

CONTACT Mrs. Misti Adams, Director of Financial Aid, Northwestern State University of Louisiana, 103 Roy Hall, Natchitoches, LA 71497, 318-357-5961 or toll-free 800-327-1903. *Fax:* 318-357-5488. *E-mail:* nsufinaid@nsula.edu.

NORTHWESTERN UNIVERSITY

Evanston, IL

ABOUT THE INSTITUTION Independent, coed. Awards: bachelor's, master's, doctoral, and first professional degrees and post-master's certificates. 112 undergraduate majors. Total enrollment: 17,460. Undergraduates: 8,153. Freshmen: 2,062.

GIFT AID (NEED-BASED) ***Scholarships, grants, and awards:*** Federal Pell, FSEOG, state, private, college/university gift aid from institutional funds, United Negro College Fund.

GIFT AID (NON-NEED-BASED) ***Scholarships, grants, and awards by category:*** *Creative Arts/Performance:* music. *Special Achievements/Activities:* general special achievements/activities. *Special Characteristics:* international students.

LOANS ***Programs:*** FFEL (Subsidized and Unsubsidized Stafford, PLUS), Perkins, college/university.

WORK-STUDY ***Federal work-study:*** Total amount: $2,300,000; 1,126 jobs averaging $2041. ***State or other work-study/employment:*** Total amount: $2,135,106 (100% need-based). 1,046 part-time jobs averaging $2041.

APPLYING FOR FINANCIAL AID ***Required financial aid forms:*** FAFSA, institution's own form, CSS Financial Aid PROFILE, noncustodial (divorced/separated) parent's statement, business/farm supplement, parent and student federal tax returns.

CONTACT Coordinator of Financial Aid, Northwestern University, PO Box 3060, 1801 Hinman Avenue, Evanston, IL 60204-3060, 847-491-8000. *E-mail:* newstudentaid@northwestern.edu.

NORTHWEST MISSOURI STATE UNIVERSITY

Maryville, MO

CONTACT Mr. Del Morley, Director of Financial Assistance, Northwest Missouri State University, 800 University Drive, Maryville, MO 64468-6001, 660-562-1138 or toll-free 800-633-1175.

NORTHWEST NAZARENE UNIVERSITY

Nampa, ID

Tuition & fees: $19,970 **Average undergraduate aid package: $13,180**

ABOUT THE INSTITUTION Independent religious, coed. Awards: bachelor's and master's degrees. 64 undergraduate majors. Total enrollment: 1,749. Undergraduates: 1,225. Freshmen: 292. Federal methodology is used as a basis for awarding need-based institutional aid.

UNDERGRADUATE EXPENSES for 2007–08 ***Application fee:*** $25. ***Comprehensive fee:*** $25,270 includes full-time tuition ($19,700), mandatory fees ($270), and room and board ($5300). ***Part-time tuition:*** $853 per credit.

FRESHMAN FINANCIAL AID (Fall 2006, est.) 234 applied for aid; of those 78% were deemed to have need. 99% of freshmen with need received aid; of those 17% had need fully met. ***Average percent of need met:*** 71% (excluding resources awarded to replace EFC). ***Average financial aid package:*** $12,801 (excluding resources awarded to replace EFC). 30% of all full-time freshmen had no need and received non-need-based gift aid.

UNDERGRADUATE FINANCIAL AID (Fall 2006, est.) 863 applied for aid; of those 84% were deemed to have need. 100% of undergraduates with need received aid; of those 20% had need fully met. ***Average percent of need met:*** 75% (excluding resources awarded to replace EFC). ***Average financial aid package:*** $13,180 (excluding resources awarded to replace EFC). 29% of all full-time undergraduates had no need and received non-need-based gift aid.

GIFT AID (NEED-BASED) ***Total amount:*** $5,378,115 (19% federal, 1% state, 69% institutional, 11% external sources). ***Receiving aid:*** Freshmen: 58% (154); All full-time undergraduates: 58% (599). ***Average award:*** Freshmen: $6020; Undergraduates: $5331. ***Scholarships, grants, and awards:*** Federal Pell, FSEOG, state, private, college/university gift aid from institutional funds.

GIFT AID (NON-NEED-BASED) ***Total amount:*** $1,334,762 (1% federal, 2% state, 85% institutional, 12% external sources). ***Receiving aid:*** Freshmen: 67% (178); Undergraduates: 64% (666). ***Average award:*** Freshmen: $4314; Undergraduates: $3837. ***Scholarships, grants, and awards by category:*** *Academic Interests/Achievement:* 447 awards ($1,126,832 total): biological sciences, business, computer science, education, English, general academic interests/achievements, health fields, mathematics, military science, physical sciences, premedicine, religion/biblical studies, social sciences. *Creative Arts/Performance:* 54 awards ($38,625 total): art/fine arts, debating, general creative arts/performance, journalism/publications, music, performing arts, theater/drama. *Special Achievements/Activities:* 6 awards ($2350 total): cheerleading/drum major, general special achievements/activities, leadership, religious involvement. *Special Characteristics:* 659 awards ($2,524,230 total): children and siblings of alumni, children of educators, children of faculty/staff, ethnic background, international students, members of minority groups, out-of-state students, relatives of clergy, religious affiliation, siblings of current students, veterans. ***ROTC:*** Army.

LOANS ***Student loans:*** $6,845,061 (73% need-based, 27% non-need-based). 77% of past graduating class borrowed through all loan programs. *Average indebtedness per student:* $25,301. ***Average need-based loan:*** Freshmen: $2809;

Undergraduates: $4101. ***Parent loans:*** $2,248,829 (81% need-based, 19% non-need-based). ***Programs:*** FFEL (Subsidized and Unsubsidized Stafford, PLUS), Perkins, college/university.

WORK-STUDY ***Federal work-study:*** Total amount: $227,049; 160 jobs averaging $1419.

ATHLETIC AWARDS Total amount: $1,034,678 (71% need-based, 29% non-need-based).

APPLYING FOR FINANCIAL AID ***Required financial aid forms:*** FAFSA, institution's own form. ***Financial aid deadline (priority):*** 3/1. ***Notification date:*** Continuous beginning 4/1. Students must reply within 3 weeks of notification.

CONTACT Mr. Wes Maggard, Director of Financial Aid, Northwest Nazarene University, 623 Holly Street, Nampa, ID 83686, 208-467-8774 or toll-free 877-668-4968. *Fax:* 208-467-8375. *E-mail:* mwmaggard@nnu.edu.

NORTHWEST UNIVERSITY

Kirkland, WA

Tuition & fees: $19,762 **Average undergraduate aid package: $12,826**

ABOUT THE INSTITUTION Independent religious, coed. Awards: associate, bachelor's, and master's degrees. 36 undergraduate majors. Total enrollment: 1,265. Undergraduates: 1,141. Freshmen: 170. Federal methodology is used as a basis for awarding need-based institutional aid.

UNDERGRADUATE EXPENSES for 2007–08 ***Application fee:*** $30. ***Comprehensive fee:*** $26,340 includes full-time tuition ($19,520), mandatory fees ($242), and room and board ($6578). ***Part-time tuition:*** $820 per credit. ***Part-time fees:*** $242 per year.

FRESHMAN FINANCIAL AID (Fall 2006, est.) 144 applied for aid; of those 91% were deemed to have need. 98% of freshmen with need received aid; of those 24% had need fully met. ***Average percent of need met:*** 73% (excluding resources awarded to replace EFC). ***Average financial aid package:*** $13,577 (excluding resources awarded to replace EFC). 14% of all full-time freshmen had no need and received non-need-based gift aid.

UNDERGRADUATE FINANCIAL AID (Fall 2006, est.) 889 applied for aid; of those 88% were deemed to have need. 99% of undergraduates with need received aid; of those 17% had need fully met. ***Average percent of need met:*** 63% (excluding resources awarded to replace EFC). ***Average financial aid package:*** $12,826 (excluding resources awarded to replace EFC). 16% of all full-time undergraduates had no need and received non-need-based gift aid.

GIFT AID (NEED-BASED) ***Total amount:*** $5,260,123 (18% federal, 17% state, 60% institutional, 5% external sources). ***Receiving aid:*** Freshmen: 76% (129); All full-time undergraduates: 74% (766). ***Average award:*** Freshmen: $10,065; Undergraduates: $8769. ***Scholarships, grants, and awards:*** Federal Pell, FSEOG, state, private, college/university gift aid from institutional funds.

GIFT AID (NON-NEED-BASED) ***Total amount:*** $714,745 (1% state, 95% institutional, 4% external sources). ***Receiving aid:*** Freshmen: 11% (18); Undergraduates: 7% (70). ***Average award:*** Freshmen: $6825; Undergraduates: $9876. ***Scholarships, grants, and awards by category:*** *Academic Interests/Achievement:* 301 awards ($999,088 total): general academic interests/achievements. *Creative Arts/Performance:* 120 awards ($275,131 total): debating, music, performing arts, theater/drama. *Special Characteristics:* 194 awards ($803,493 total): children of current students, children of faculty/staff, general special characteristics, international students, married students, parents of current students, relatives of clergy, religious affiliation, siblings of current students, spouses of current students. ***ROTC:*** Army cooperative.

LOANS ***Student loans:*** $6,862,460 (67% need-based, 33% non-need-based). 83% of past graduating class borrowed through all loan programs. *Average indebtedness per student:* $20,133. ***Average need-based loan:*** Freshmen: $2884; Undergraduates: $3943. ***Parent loans:*** $1,312,785 (31% need-based, 69% non-need-based). ***Programs:*** FFEL (Subsidized and Unsubsidized Stafford, PLUS), Perkins, state, alternative loans.

WORK-STUDY ***Federal work-study:*** Total amount: $125,581; 69 jobs averaging $2555. ***State or other work-study/employment:*** Total amount: $134,056 (100% need-based). 37 part-time jobs averaging $3893.

ATHLETIC AWARDS Total amount: $555,593 (52% need-based, 48% non-need-based).

APPLYING FOR FINANCIAL AID ***Required financial aid forms:*** FAFSA, institution's own form. ***Financial aid deadline:*** 8/1 (priority: 3/1). ***Notification date:*** Continuous beginning 3/3. Students must reply within 4 weeks of notification.

CONTACT Ms. Lana J. Walter, Director of Financial Aid, Northwest University, PO Box 579, Kirkland, WA 98083-0579, 425-889-5336 or toll-free 800-669-3781. *Fax:* 425-889-5224. *E-mail:* lana.walter@northwestu.edu.

NORTHWOOD UNIVERSITY

Midland, MI

Tuition & fees: $16,455 **Average undergraduate aid package: $13,375**

ABOUT THE INSTITUTION Independent, coed. Awards: associate, bachelor's, and master's degrees. 15 undergraduate majors. Total enrollment: 4,125. Undergraduates: 3,802. Freshmen: 504. Federal methodology is used as a basis for awarding need-based institutional aid.

UNDERGRADUATE EXPENSES for 2007–08 ***Application fee:*** $25. ***Comprehensive fee:*** $23,649 includes full-time tuition ($15,825), mandatory fees ($630), and room and board ($7194). ***College room only:*** $3474. ***Part-time tuition:*** $330 per credit hour.

FRESHMAN FINANCIAL AID (Fall 2006, est.) 400 applied for aid; of those 86% were deemed to have need. 100% of freshmen with need received aid; of those 29% had need fully met. ***Average percent of need met:*** 56% (excluding resources awarded to replace EFC). ***Average financial aid package:*** $14,665 (excluding resources awarded to replace EFC). 25% of all full-time freshmen had no need and received non-need-based gift aid.

UNDERGRADUATE FINANCIAL AID (Fall 2006, est.) 1,353 applied for aid; of those 85% were deemed to have need. 100% of undergraduates with need received aid; of those 28% had need fully met. ***Average percent of need met:*** 54% (excluding resources awarded to replace EFC). ***Average financial aid package:*** $13,375 (excluding resources awarded to replace EFC). 26% of all full-time undergraduates had no need and received non-need-based gift aid.

GIFT AID (NEED-BASED) ***Total amount:*** $9,153,581 (16% federal, 22% state, 59% institutional, 3% external sources). ***Receiving aid:*** Freshmen: 58% (294); All full-time undergraduates: 50% (963). ***Average award:*** Freshmen: $5446; Undergraduates: $5002. ***Scholarships, grants, and awards:*** Federal Pell, FSEOG, state, private, college/university gift aid from institutional funds.

GIFT AID (NON-NEED-BASED) ***Total amount:*** $3,872,318 (8% state, 88% institutional, 4% external sources). ***Receiving aid:*** Freshmen: 25% (124); Undergraduates: 24% (460). ***Average award:*** Freshmen: $6580; Undergraduates: $5398. ***Scholarships, grants, and awards by category:*** *Academic Interests/Achievement:* 1,252 awards ($6,470,674 total): business, general academic interests/achievements. *Special Achievements/Activities:* 239 awards ($401,452 total): cheerleading/drum major, leadership, memberships. *Special Characteristics:* 142 awards ($671,904 total): children and siblings of alumni, children of faculty/staff, siblings of current students.

LOANS ***Student loans:*** $9,054,075 (59% need-based, 41% non-need-based). 63% of past graduating class borrowed through all loan programs. *Average indebtedness per student:* $23,445. ***Average need-based loan:*** Freshmen: $2387; Undergraduates: $3588. ***Parent loans:*** $1,491,668 (28% need-based, 72% non-need-based). ***Programs:*** FFEL (Subsidized and Unsubsidized Stafford, PLUS), state.

WORK-STUDY ***Federal work-study:*** Total amount: $673,308; 399 jobs averaging $1726. ***State or other work-study/employment:*** Total amount: $273,340 (100% need-based). 160 part-time jobs averaging $1708.

ATHLETIC AWARDS Total amount: $1,912,225 (40% need-based, 60% non-need-based).

APPLYING FOR FINANCIAL AID ***Required financial aid form:*** FAFSA. ***Financial aid deadline:*** Continuous. ***Notification date:*** Continuous beginning 3/1.

CONTACT Terri Mieler, Director of Financial Aid, Northwood University, 4000 Whiting Drive, Midland, MI 48640-2398, 989-837-4301 or toll-free 800-457-7878. *Fax:* 989-837-4130. *E-mail:* mieler@northwood.edu.

NORTHWOOD UNIVERSITY, FLORIDA CAMPUS

West Palm Beach, FL

Tuition & fees: $16,455 **Average undergraduate aid package: $13,923**

ABOUT THE INSTITUTION Independent, coed. Awards: associate and bachelor's degrees. 12 undergraduate majors. Total enrollment: 911. Undergraduates: 911. Freshmen: 127. Both federal and institutional methodology are used as a basis for awarding need-based institutional aid.

UNDERGRADUATE EXPENSES for 2007–08 ***Application fee:*** $25. ***Comprehensive fee:*** $24,222 includes full-time tuition ($15,825), mandatory fees ($630), and room and board ($7767). ***College room only:*** $4104. ***Part-time tuition:*** $330 per credit hour.

FRESHMAN FINANCIAL AID (Fall 2006, est.) 73 applied for aid; of those 82% were deemed to have need. 100% of freshmen with need received aid; of those 23% had need fully met. ***Average percent of need met:*** 65% (excluding resources awarded to replace EFC). ***Average financial aid package:*** $13,772 (excluding resources awarded to replace EFC). 17% of all full-time freshmen had no need and received non-need-based gift aid.

UNDERGRADUATE FINANCIAL AID (Fall 2006, est.) 301 applied for aid; of those 85% were deemed to have need. 100% of undergraduates with need received aid; of those 18% had need fully met. ***Average percent of need met:*** 61% (excluding resources awarded to replace EFC). ***Average financial aid package:*** $13,923 (excluding resources awarded to replace EFC). 22% of all full-time undergraduates had no need and received non-need-based gift aid.

GIFT AID (NEED-BASED) ***Total amount:*** $2,192,172 (20% federal, 7% state, 70% institutional, 3% external sources). ***Receiving aid:*** Freshmen: 38% (48); All full-time undergraduates: 30% (201). ***Average award:*** Freshmen: $6635; Undergraduates: $6423. ***Scholarships, grants, and awards:*** Federal Pell, FSEOG, state, private, college/university gift aid from institutional funds.

GIFT AID (NON-NEED-BASED) ***Total amount:*** $1,328,565 (6% state, 91% institutional, 3% external sources). ***Receiving aid:*** Freshmen: 11% (14); Undergraduates: 10% (65). ***Average award:*** Freshmen: $5237; Undergraduates: $4641. ***Scholarships, grants, and awards by category:*** *Academic Interests/Achievement:* 575 awards ($1,713,308 total): business, general academic interests/achievements. *Special Achievements/Activities:* 46 awards ($48,616 total): memberships. *Special Characteristics:* 34 awards ($105,698 total): children and siblings of alumni, children of faculty/staff, siblings of current students.

LOANS ***Student loans:*** $1,844,215 (65% need-based, 35% non-need-based). 50% of past graduating class borrowed through all loan programs. *Average indebtedness per student:* $21,654. ***Average need-based loan:*** Freshmen: $2489; Undergraduates: $3707. ***Parent loans:*** $836,372 (39% need-based, 61% non-need-based). ***Programs:*** FFEL (Subsidized and Unsubsidized Stafford, PLUS).

WORK-STUDY ***Federal work-study:*** Total amount: $210,000; 102 jobs averaging $2059.

ATHLETIC AWARDS Total amount: $1,053,037 (23% need-based, 77% non-need-based).

APPLYING FOR FINANCIAL AID ***Required financial aid forms:*** FAFSA, state aid form. ***Financial aid deadline:*** Continuous. ***Notification date:*** Continuous beginning 3/1.

CONTACT Ms. Teresa A. Palmer, Director of Financial Aid, Northwood University, Florida Campus, 2600 North Military Trail, West Palm Beach, FL 33409-2911, 561-478-5590 or toll-free 800-458-8325. *Fax:* 561-681-7990. *E-mail:* palmer@northwood.edu.

NORTHWOOD UNIVERSITY, TEXAS CAMPUS

Cedar Hill, TX

Tuition & fees: $16,455 **Average undergraduate aid package: $14,327**

ABOUT THE INSTITUTION Independent, coed. Awards: associate and bachelor's degrees. 13 undergraduate majors. Total enrollment: 979. Undergraduates: 979. Freshmen: 120. Federal methodology is used as a basis for awarding need-based institutional aid.

UNDERGRADUATE EXPENSES for 2007–08 ***Application fee:*** $25. ***Comprehensive fee:*** $23,343 includes full-time tuition ($15,825), mandatory fees ($630), and room and board ($6888). ***College room only:*** $3720. ***Part-time tuition:*** $330 per credit hour.

FRESHMAN FINANCIAL AID (Fall 2006, est.) 112 applied for aid; of those 88% were deemed to have need. 100% of freshmen with need received aid; of those 19% had need fully met. ***Average percent of need met:*** 62% (excluding resources awarded to replace EFC). ***Average financial aid package:*** $15,449 (excluding resources awarded to replace EFC). 22% of all full-time freshmen had no need and received non-need-based gift aid.

UNDERGRADUATE FINANCIAL AID (Fall 2006, est.) 396 applied for aid; of those 88% were deemed to have need. 100% of undergraduates with need received aid; of those 18% had need fully met. ***Average percent of need met:*** 60% (excluding resources awarded to replace EFC). ***Average financial aid package:*** $14,327 (excluding resources awarded to replace EFC). 24% of all full-time undergraduates had no need and received non-need-based gift aid.

GIFT AID (NEED-BASED) ***Total amount:*** $2,992,968 (22% federal, 75% institutional, 3% external sources). ***Receiving aid:*** Freshmen: 63% (76); All full-time undergraduates: 65% (319). ***Average award:*** Freshmen: $5261; Undergraduates: $4926. ***Scholarships, grants, and awards:*** Federal Pell, FSEOG, private, college/university gift aid from institutional funds.

GIFT AID (NON-NEED-BASED) ***Total amount:*** $1,498,438 (97% institutional, 3% external sources). ***Receiving aid:*** Freshmen: 80% (96); Undergraduates: 64% (314). ***Average award:*** Freshmen: $6780; Undergraduates: $5549. ***Scholarships, grants, and awards by category:*** *Academic Interests/Achievement:* 465 awards ($2,921,137 total): business, general academic interests/achievements. *Special Achievements/Activities:* 135 awards ($234,872 total): general special achievements/activities, memberships. *Special Characteristics:* 15 awards ($65,364 total): children and siblings of alumni, children of faculty/staff, siblings of current students.

LOANS ***Student loans:*** $2,277,672 (78% need-based, 22% non-need-based). 76% of past graduating class borrowed through all loan programs. *Average indebtedness per student:* $16,206. ***Average need-based loan:*** Freshmen: $2524; Undergraduates: $3702. ***Parent loans:*** $755,870 (29% need-based, 71% non-need-based). ***Programs:*** FFEL (Subsidized and Unsubsidized Stafford, PLUS).

WORK-STUDY ***Federal work-study:*** Total amount: $490,392; 235 jobs averaging $2057.

ATHLETIC AWARDS Total amount: $644,526 (44% need-based, 56% non-need-based).

APPLYING FOR FINANCIAL AID ***Required financial aid form:*** FAFSA. ***Financial aid deadline:*** Continuous. ***Notification date:*** Continuous beginning 3/1.

CONTACT Michael Rhodes, Director of Financial Aid, Northwood University, Texas Campus, 1114 West FM 1382, Cedar Hill, TX 75104, 972-293-5479 or toll-free 800-927-9663. *Fax:* 972-293-7196. *E-mail:* rhodes@northwood.edu.

NORWICH UNIVERSITY

Northfield, VT

CONTACT Director of Student Financial Planning, Norwich University, 158 Harmon Drive, Northfield, VT 05663, 802-485-2015 or toll-free 800-468-6679.

NOTRE DAME COLLEGE

South Euclid, OH

CONTACT Ms. Mary E. McCrystal, Financial Aid Director, Notre Dame College, 4545 College Road, South Euclid, OH 44121-4293, 216-381-1680 Ext. 263 or toll-free 800-632-1680. *Fax:* 216-381-3802. *E-mail:* mmccrystal@ndc.edu.

NOTRE DAME DE NAMUR UNIVERSITY

Belmont, CA

CONTACT Ms. Kathleen Kelly, Director of Financial Aid, Notre Dame de Namur University, 1500 Ralston Avenue, Belmont, CA 94002, 650-508-3509 or toll-free 800-263-0545.

NOVA SOUTHEASTERN UNIVERSITY

Fort Lauderdale, FL

Tuition & fees: $18,650 **Average undergraduate aid package: $15,100**

ABOUT THE INSTITUTION Independent, coed. Awards: associate, bachelor's, master's, doctoral, and first professional degrees and post-master's and first professional certificates. 32 undergraduate majors. Total enrollment: 25,960. Undergraduates: 5,413. Freshmen: 516. Federal methodology is used as a basis for awarding need-based institutional aid.

UNDERGRADUATE EXPENSES for 2006–07 ***Application fee:*** $50. ***Comprehensive fee:*** $24,662 includes full-time tuition ($18,150), mandatory fees ($500), and room and board ($6012). ***College room only:*** $3612. Full-time tuition and fees vary according to class time and program. Room and board charges vary according to board plan and housing facility. ***Part-time tuition:*** $605 per credit hour. Part-time tuition and fees vary according to class time, course load, and program. ***Payment plans:*** Installment, deferred payment.

FRESHMAN FINANCIAL AID (Fall 2006, est.) 406 applied for aid; of those 91% were deemed to have need. 100% of freshmen with need received aid; of those

6% had need fully met. ***Average financial aid package:*** $15,322 (excluding resources awarded to replace EFC). 15% of all full-time freshmen had no need and received non-need-based gift aid.

UNDERGRADUATE FINANCIAL AID (Fall 2006, est.) 2,913 applied for aid; of those 93% were deemed to have need. 99% of undergraduates with need received aid; of those 4% had need fully met. ***Average percent of need met:*** 69% (excluding resources awarded to replace EFC). ***Average financial aid package:*** $15,100 (excluding resources awarded to replace EFC). 11% of all full-time undergraduates had no need and received non-need-based gift aid.

GIFT AID (NEED-BASED) ***Total amount:*** $18,520,925 (38% federal, 46% state, 16% institutional). ***Receiving aid:*** Freshmen: 69% (327); All full-time undergraduates: 70% (2,450). ***Average award:*** Freshmen: $5862; Undergraduates: $6334. ***Scholarships, grants, and awards:*** Federal Pell, FSEOG, state, private, college/university gift aid from institutional funds.

GIFT AID (NON-NEED-BASED) ***Total amount:*** $11,795,771 (22% state, 77% institutional, 1% external sources). ***Receiving aid:*** Freshmen: 52% (246); Undergraduates: 33% (1,147). ***Average award:*** Freshmen: $3347; Undergraduates: $3568. ***Scholarships, grants, and awards by category:*** *Academic Interests/Achievement:* 2,115 awards ($4,580,680 total): general academic interests/achievements. *Special Achievements/Activities:* 32 awards ($98,643 total): leadership. *Special Characteristics:* 48 awards ($365,215 total): children of faculty/staff. ***Tuition waivers:*** Full or partial for employees or children of employees.

LOANS ***Student loans:*** $34,871,372 (44% need-based, 56% non-need-based). 69% of past graduating class borrowed through all loan programs. *Average indebtedness per student:* $31,368. ***Average need-based loan:*** Freshmen: $3170; Undergraduates: $5326. ***Parent loans:*** $1,489,333 (92% need-based, 8% non-need-based). ***Programs:*** FFEL (Subsidized and Unsubsidized Stafford, PLUS), Perkins, college/university.

WORK-STUDY ***Federal work-study:*** Total amount: $1,980,554; 1,163 jobs averaging $3068. ***State or other work-study/employment:*** Total amount: $808,687 (100% non-need-based). 250 part-time jobs averaging $2950.

ATHLETIC AWARDS Total amount: $2,145,941 (100% non-need-based).

APPLYING FOR FINANCIAL AID ***Required financial aid forms:*** FAFSA, institution's own form. ***Financial aid deadline (priority):*** 4/15. ***Notification date:*** Continuous beginning 3/15. Students must reply within 4 weeks of notification.

CONTACT Etta Fleischer, Associate Vice President for Student Financial Services and Registration (Interim), Nova Southeastern University, 3301 College Avenue, Fort Lauderdale, FL 33314, 954-262-7439 or toll-free 800-541-NOVA. *Fax:* 954-262-3967. *E-mail:* ettaf@nova.edu.

NYACK COLLEGE

Nyack, NY

Tuition & fees: $15,400 **Average undergraduate aid package: $14,285**

ABOUT THE INSTITUTION Independent religious, coed. Awards: associate, bachelor's, master's, and first professional degrees. 28 undergraduate majors. Total enrollment: 3,063. Undergraduates: 1,970. Freshmen: 329. Federal methodology is used as a basis for awarding need-based institutional aid.

UNDERGRADUATE EXPENSES for 2006–07 ***Application fee:*** $25. ***Comprehensive fee:*** $23,000 includes full-time tuition ($15,400) and room and board ($7600). ***Part-time tuition:*** $640 per credit.

FRESHMAN FINANCIAL AID (Fall 2005) 284 applied for aid; of those 94% were deemed to have need. 100% of freshmen with need received aid; of those 20% had need fully met. ***Average percent of need met:*** 64% (excluding resources awarded to replace EFC). ***Average financial aid package:*** $13,872 (excluding resources awarded to replace EFC). 14% of all full-time freshmen had no need and received non-need-based gift aid.

UNDERGRADUATE FINANCIAL AID (Fall 2005) 1,200 applied for aid; of those 94% were deemed to have need. 100% of undergraduates with need received aid; of those 20% had need fully met. ***Average percent of need met:*** 65% (excluding resources awarded to replace EFC). ***Average financial aid package:*** $14,285 (excluding resources awarded to replace EFC). 14% of all full-time undergraduates had no need and received non-need-based gift aid.

GIFT AID (NEED-BASED) ***Total amount:*** $10,109,009 (25% federal, 21% state, 52% institutional, 2% external sources). ***Receiving aid:*** Freshmen: 83% (264); All full-time undergraduates: 83% (1,112). ***Average award:*** Freshmen: $9590; Undergraduates: $8910. ***Scholarships, grants, and awards:*** Federal Pell, FSEOG, state, private, college/university gift aid from institutional funds.

GIFT AID (NON-NEED-BASED) ***Total amount:*** $1,083,859 (3% state, 97% institutional). ***Receiving aid:*** Freshmen: 4% (14); Undergraduates: 4% (50). ***Average award:*** Freshmen: $5998; Undergraduates: $7356. ***Scholarships, grants, and awards by category:*** *Academic Interests/Achievement:* 317 awards ($647,032 total): general academic interests/achievements. *Creative Arts/Performance:* 88 awards ($196,175 total): journalism/publications, music, performing arts, theater/drama. *Special Achievements/Activities:* 1,197 awards ($1,519,850 total): general special achievements/activities, leadership, religious involvement. *Special Characteristics:* 989 awards ($2,284,185 total): children and siblings of alumni, children of faculty/staff, general special characteristics, international students, local/state students, out-of-state students, relatives of clergy, religious affiliation, spouses of current students.

LOANS ***Student loans:*** $10,741,760 (83% need-based, 17% non-need-based). 80% of past graduating class borrowed through all loan programs. *Average indebtedness per student:* $19,351. ***Average need-based loan:*** Freshmen: $3968; Undergraduates: $5096. ***Parent loans:*** $1,878,201 (61% need-based, 39% non-need-based). ***Programs:*** FFEL (Subsidized and Unsubsidized Stafford, PLUS), Perkins.

WORK-STUDY ***Federal work-study:*** Total amount: $283,862; 221 jobs averaging $1284. ***State or other work-study/employment:*** Total amount: $61,311 (100% need-based). 46 part-time jobs averaging $1332.

ATHLETIC AWARDS Total amount: $1,220,038 (70% need-based, 30% non-need-based).

APPLYING FOR FINANCIAL AID ***Required financial aid forms:*** FAFSA, state aid form. ***Financial aid deadline (priority):*** 3/1. ***Notification date:*** Continuous. Students must reply by 5/1 or within 4 weeks of notification.

CONTACT Andres Valenzuela, Director of Student Financial Services, Nyack College, 1 South Boulevard, Nyack, NY 10960-3698, 845-358-1710 or toll-free 800-33-NYACK. *Fax:* 845-358-7016. *E-mail:* sfs@nyack.edu.

OAK HILLS CHRISTIAN COLLEGE

Bemidji, MN

CONTACT Daniel Hovestol, Financial Aid Director, Oak Hills Christian College, 1600 Oak Hills Road, SW, Bemidji, MN 56601-8832, 218-751-8671 Ext. 1220 or toll-free 888-751-8670 Ext. 285. *Fax:* 218-444-1311. *E-mail:* ohfinaid@oakhills.edu.

OAKLAND CITY UNIVERSITY

Oakland City, IN

CONTACT Mrs. Caren K. Richeson, Director of Financial Aid, Oakland City University, 138 North Lucretia Street, Oakland City, IN 47660-1099, 812-749-1224 or toll-free 800-737-5125. *Fax:* 812-749-1438.

OAKLAND UNIVERSITY

Rochester, MI

CONTACT Ms. Cindy Hermsen, Director of Financial Aid, Oakland University, 120 North Foundation Hall, Rochester, MI 48309-4481, 248-370-2550 or toll-free 800-OAK-UNIV. *E-mail:* finaid@oakland.edu.

OAKWOOD COLLEGE

Huntsville, AL

CONTACT Financial Aid Director, Oakwood College, 7000 Adventist Boulevard, Huntsville, AL 35896, 256-726-7210 or toll-free 800-358-3978 (in-state).

OBERLIN COLLEGE

Oberlin, OH

Tuition & fees: $34,426 **Average undergraduate aid package: $24,255**

ABOUT THE INSTITUTION Independent, coed. Awards: bachelor's and master's degrees and post-bachelor's certificates. 54 undergraduate majors. Total enrollment: 2,841. Undergraduates: 2,829. Freshmen: 715. Both federal and institutional methodology are used as a basis for awarding need-based institutional aid.

UNDERGRADUATE EXPENSES for 2006–07 ***Application fee:*** $35. ***Comprehensive fee:*** $43,146 includes full-time tuition ($34,216), mandatory fees ($210), and

room and board ($8720). ***College room only:*** $4580. Full-time tuition and fees vary according to course load. Room and board charges vary according to board plan and housing facility. ***Part-time tuition:*** $1420 per credit. Part-time tuition and fees vary according to course load. ***Payment plan:*** Installment.

FRESHMAN FINANCIAL AID (Fall 2006, est.) 475 applied for aid; of those 80% were deemed to have need. 100% of freshmen with need received aid; of those 100% had need fully met. ***Average percent of need met:*** 100% (excluding resources awarded to replace EFC). ***Average financial aid package:*** $22,919 (excluding resources awarded to replace EFC). 20% of all full-time freshmen had no need and received non-need-based gift aid.

UNDERGRADUATE FINANCIAL AID (Fall 2006, est.) 1,752 applied for aid; of those 88% were deemed to have need. 100% of undergraduates with need received aid; of those 100% had need fully met. ***Average percent of need met:*** 100% (excluding resources awarded to replace EFC). ***Average financial aid package:*** $24,255 (excluding resources awarded to replace EFC). 13% of all full-time undergraduates had no need and received non-need-based gift aid.

GIFT AID (NEED-BASED) ***Total amount:*** $35,784,594 (4% federal, 1% state, 90% institutional, 5% external sources). ***Receiving aid:*** Freshmen: 45% (326); All full-time undergraduates: 51% (1,408). ***Average award:*** Freshmen: $17,372; Undergraduates: $18,807. ***Scholarships, grants, and awards:*** Federal Pell, FSEOG, state, private, college/university gift aid from institutional funds.

GIFT AID (NON-NEED-BASED) ***Total amount:*** $4,206,835 (88% institutional, 12% external sources). ***Receiving aid:*** Freshmen: 29% (208); Undergraduates: 29% (806). ***Average award:*** Freshmen: $11,190; Undergraduates: $10,409. ***Scholarships, grants, and awards by category:*** *Academic Interests/Achievement:* 546 awards ($5,178,325 total): general academic interests/achievements, physical sciences. *Creative Arts/Performance:* 441 awards ($4,734,509 total): music. ***Tuition waivers:*** Full or partial for employees or children of employees.

LOANS ***Student loans:*** $7,661,140 (92% need-based, 8% non-need-based). 60% of past graduating class borrowed through all loan programs. *Average indebtedness per student:* $16,922. ***Average need-based loan:*** Freshmen: $3984; Undergraduates: $4423. ***Parent loans:*** $3,891,336 (65% need-based, 35% non-need-based). ***Programs:*** FFEL (Subsidized and Unsubsidized Stafford, PLUS), Perkins, college/university.

WORK-STUDY ***Federal work-study:*** Total amount: $2,255,648; jobs available (averaging $1650). ***State or other work-study/employment:*** Part-time jobs available (averaging $1650).

APPLYING FOR FINANCIAL AID ***Required financial aid forms:*** FAFSA, CSS Financial Aid PROFILE, noncustodial (divorced/separated) parent's statement. ***Financial aid deadline (priority):*** 1/15. ***Notification date:*** 4/1. Students must reply by 5/1 or within 2 weeks of notification.

CONTACT Robert Reddy, Office of Financial Aid, Oberlin College, Carnegie Building 123, 52 West Lorain Street, Oberlin, OH 44074, 800-693-3173 or toll-free 800-622-OBIE. *Fax:* 440-775-8249. *E-mail:* financial.aid@oberlin.edu.

OCCIDENTAL COLLEGE

Los Angeles, CA

ABOUT THE INSTITUTION Independent, coed. Awards: bachelor's and master's degrees. 31 undergraduate majors. Total enrollment: 1,825. Undergraduates: 1,804. Freshmen: 458.

GIFT AID (NEED-BASED) ***Scholarships, grants, and awards:*** Federal Pell, FSEOG, state, private, college/university gift aid from institutional funds.

GIFT AID (NON-NEED-BASED) ***Scholarships, grants, and awards by category:*** *Academic Interests/Achievement:* general academic interests/achievements. *Creative Arts/Performance:* music. *Special Achievements/Activities:* general special achievements/activities, leadership. *Special Characteristics:* children of educators, children of faculty/staff.

LOANS ***Programs:*** FFEL (Subsidized and Unsubsidized Stafford, PLUS), Perkins, college/university.

WORK-STUDY ***Federal work-study:*** Total amount: $938,311; 684 jobs averaging $2325. ***State or other work-study/employment:*** Total amount: $296,115 (38% need-based, 62% non-need-based). 96 part-time jobs averaging $2299.

APPLYING FOR FINANCIAL AID ***Required financial aid forms:*** FAFSA, CSS Financial Aid PROFILE, state aid form, noncustodial (divorced/separated) parent's statement, business/farm supplement, income tax form(s), W-2 forms.

CONTACT Maureen McRae Levy, Director of Financial Aid, Occidental College, 1600 Campus Road, Los Angeles, CA 90041, 323-259-2548 or toll-free 800-825-5262. *Fax:* 323-341-4961. *E-mail:* finaid@oxy.edu.

OGLALA LAKOTA COLLEGE

Kyle, SD

CONTACT Financial Aid Director, Oglala Lakota College, 490 Piya Wiconi Road, Kyle, SD 57752-0490, 605-455-6000.

OGLETHORPE UNIVERSITY

Atlanta, GA

Tuition & fees: $23,510 **Average undergraduate aid package: $20,753**

ABOUT THE INSTITUTION Independent, coed. Awards: bachelor's and master's degrees. 33 undergraduate majors. Total enrollment: 1,030. Undergraduates: 985. Freshmen: 186. Federal methodology is used as a basis for awarding need-based institutional aid.

UNDERGRADUATE EXPENSES for 2006–07 ***Application fee:*** $35. ***Comprehensive fee:*** $31,510 includes full-time tuition ($23,310), mandatory fees ($200), and room and board ($8000). Room and board charges vary according to board plan and housing facility. ***Part-time tuition:*** $945 per credit hour. Part-time tuition and fees vary according to program. ***Payment plans:*** Tuition prepayment, installment.

FRESHMAN FINANCIAL AID (Fall 2005) 154 applied for aid; of those 86% were deemed to have need. 100% of freshmen with need received aid; of those 15% had need fully met. ***Average percent of need met:*** 76% (excluding resources awarded to replace EFC). ***Average financial aid package:*** $21,503 (excluding resources awarded to replace EFC). 26% of all full-time freshmen had no need and received non-need-based gift aid.

UNDERGRADUATE FINANCIAL AID (Fall 2005) 584 applied for aid; of those 88% were deemed to have need. 100% of undergraduates with need received aid; of those 9% had need fully met. ***Average percent of need met:*** 72% (excluding resources awarded to replace EFC). ***Average financial aid package:*** $20,753 (excluding resources awarded to replace EFC). 31% of all full-time undergraduates had no need and received non-need-based gift aid.

GIFT AID (NEED-BASED) ***Total amount:*** $8,333,481 (7% federal, 12% state, 80% institutional, 1% external sources). ***Receiving aid:*** Freshmen: 72% (133); All full-time undergraduates: 60% (508). ***Average award:*** Freshmen: $18,497; Undergraduates: $15,974. ***Scholarships, grants, and awards:*** Federal Pell, FSEOG, state, private, college/university gift aid from institutional funds.

GIFT AID (NON-NEED-BASED) ***Total amount:*** $3,197,825 (13% state, 87% institutional). ***Receiving aid:*** Freshmen: 71% (132); Undergraduates: 55% (462). ***Average award:*** Freshmen: $11,336; Undergraduates: $10,542. ***Scholarships, grants, and awards by category:*** *Academic Interests/Achievement:* general academic interests/achievements. *Creative Arts/Performance:* journalism/publications, music, performing arts, theater/drama. *Special Achievements/Activities:* community service, religious involvement. *Special Characteristics:* children of faculty/staff, siblings of current students. ***Tuition waivers:*** Full or partial for employees or children of employees.

LOANS ***Student loans:*** $4,096,375 (80% need-based, 20% non-need-based). 58% of past graduating class borrowed through all loan programs. *Average indebtedness per student:* $17,024. ***Average need-based loan:*** Freshmen: $2923; Undergraduates: $4626. ***Parent loans:*** $1,253,819 (100% non-need-based). ***Programs:*** Federal Direct (Subsidized and Unsubsidized Stafford, PLUS), FFEL (Subsidized and Unsubsidized Stafford, PLUS), Perkins.

WORK-STUDY ***Federal work-study:*** Total amount: $28,950; jobs available.

APPLYING FOR FINANCIAL AID ***Required financial aid forms:*** FAFSA, institution's own form, state aid form, noncustodial (divorced/separated) parent's statement. ***Financial aid deadline (priority):*** 3/1. ***Notification date:*** 4/1. Students must reply by 5/1 or within 3 weeks of notification.

CONTACT Ms. Meg McGinnis, Director of Financial Aid, Oglethorpe University, 4484 Peachtree Road NE, Atlanta, GA 30319, 404-364-8366 or toll-free 800-428-4484.

OHIO CHRISTIAN UNIVERSITY

Circleville, OH

Tuition & fees: N/R **Average undergraduate aid package: $10,000**

ABOUT THE INSTITUTION Independent religious, coed. Awards: associate and bachelor's degrees. 12 undergraduate majors. Total enrollment: 317. Undergraduates: 317. Freshmen: 45. Both federal and institutional methodology are used as a basis for awarding need-based institutional aid.

FRESHMAN FINANCIAL AID (Fall 2006, est.) 170 applied for aid; of those 88% were deemed to have need. 100% of freshmen with need received aid; of those 50% had need fully met. ***Average percent of need met:*** 50% (excluding resources awarded to replace EFC). ***Average financial aid package:*** $10,000 (excluding resources awarded to replace EFC).

UNDERGRADUATE FINANCIAL AID (Fall 2006, est.) 463 applied for aid; of those 85% were deemed to have need. 100% of undergraduates with need received aid; of those 51% had need fully met. ***Average percent of need met:*** 50% (excluding resources awarded to replace EFC). ***Average financial aid package:*** $10,000 (excluding resources awarded to replace EFC).

GIFT AID (NEED-BASED) ***Total amount:*** $1,175,000 (64% federal, 32% state, 4% external sources). ***Receiving aid:*** Freshmen: 66% (115); All full-time undergraduates: 58% (275). ***Scholarships, grants, and awards:*** Federal Pell, FSEOG, state, private, college/university gift aid from institutional funds.

GIFT AID (NON-NEED-BASED) ***Total amount:*** $885,000 (35% state, 65% institutional). ***Receiving aid:*** Freshmen: 86% (150); Undergraduates: 83% (395). ***Scholarships, grants, and awards by category:*** *Academic Interests/Achievement:* business, education, general academic interests/achievements, health fields, religion/biblical studies. *Creative Arts/Performance:* music. *Special Achievements/Activities:* leadership. *Special Characteristics:* 100 awards ($125,000 total): adult students, children of faculty/staff, international students, out-of-state students, relatives of clergy, religious affiliation, siblings of current students, veterans, veterans' children.

LOANS ***Student loans:*** $3,250,000 (38% need-based, 62% non-need-based). 90% of past graduating class borrowed through all loan programs. *Average indebtedness per student:* $22,000. ***Average need-based loan:*** Freshmen: $2500; Undergraduates: $4500. ***Parent loans:*** $108,000 (100% non-need-based). ***Programs:*** FFEL (Subsidized and Unsubsidized Stafford, PLUS), college/university, state nursing loans.

WORK-STUDY ***Federal work-study:*** Total amount: $85,000; 75 jobs averaging $1133. ***State or other work-study/employment:*** Part-time jobs available.

ATHLETIC AWARDS Total amount: $33,000 (100% non-need-based).

APPLYING FOR FINANCIAL AID ***Required financial aid form:*** FAFSA. ***Financial aid deadline (priority):*** 3/31. ***Notification date:*** 6/1. Students must reply within 2 weeks of notification.

CONTACT Michael Fracassa, Director of Financial Services, Ohio Christian University, 1476 Lancaster Pike, PO Box 458, Circleville, OH 43113-9487, 740-477-7758 or toll-free 800-701-0222. *Fax:* 740-477-5921. *E-mail:* mfracassa@ohiochristian.edu.

OHIO DOMINICAN UNIVERSITY

Columbus, OH

CONTACT Ms. Cynthia A. Hahn, Director of Financial Aid, Ohio Dominican University, 1216 Sunbury Road, Columbus, OH 43219, 614-251-4778 or toll-free 800-854-2670. *Fax:* 614-251-4456. *E-mail:* fin-aid@ohiodominican.edu.

OHIO NORTHERN UNIVERSITY

Ada, OH

ABOUT THE INSTITUTION Independent religious, coed. Awards: bachelor's, master's, and first professional degrees and post-bachelor's certificates. 111 undergraduate majors. Total enrollment: 3,620. Undergraduates: 2,612. Freshmen: 760.

GIFT AID (NEED-BASED) ***Scholarships, grants, and awards:*** Federal Pell, FSEOG, state, private, college/university gift aid from institutional funds.

GIFT AID (NON-NEED-BASED) ***Scholarships, grants, and awards by category:*** *Academic Interests/Achievement:* biological sciences, business, communication, computer science, education, engineering/technologies, English, foreign languages, general academic interests/achievements, health fields, humanities, international studies, mathematics, physical sciences, premedicine, religion/biblical studies, social sciences. *Creative Arts/Performance:* applied art and design, art/fine arts, creative writing, dance, journalism/publications, music, performing arts, theater/drama. *Special Achievements/Activities:* community service, general special achievements/activities, junior miss, leadership. *Special Characteristics:* children of faculty/staff, international students, relatives of clergy, religious affiliation, siblings of current students.

LOANS ***Programs:*** FFEL (Subsidized and Unsubsidized Stafford, PLUS), Perkins, Federal Nursing, college/university.

WORK-STUDY ***Federal work-study:*** Total amount: $2,901,445; 1,349 jobs averaging $2151. ***State or other work-study/employment:*** Total amount: $220,745 (45% need-based, 55% non-need-based). 96 part-time jobs averaging $2299.

APPLYING FOR FINANCIAL AID ***Required financial aid forms:*** FAFSA, institution's own form.

CONTACT Craig Sneider, Director of Financial Aid, Ohio Northern University, 525 South Main Street, Ada, OH 45810, 419-772-2272 or toll-free 888-408-4ONU. *Fax:* 419-772-2313. *E-mail:* c-sneider@onu.edu.

THE OHIO STATE UNIVERSITY

Columbus, OH

Tuition & fees (OH res): $8559 Average undergraduate aid package: $10,149

ABOUT THE INSTITUTION State-supported, coed. Awards: associate, bachelor's, master's, doctoral, and first professional degrees and post-bachelor's and post-master's certificates. 170 undergraduate majors. Total enrollment: 51,818. Undergraduates: 38,479. Freshmen: 6,280. Federal methodology is used as a basis for awarding need-based institutional aid.

UNDERGRADUATE EXPENSES for 2006–07 ***Application fee:*** $40. ***Tuition, state resident:*** full-time $8298. ***Tuition, nonresident:*** full-time $20,193. Full-time tuition and fees vary according to course load, program, reciprocity agreements, and student level. Part-time tuition and fees vary according to course load, program, reciprocity agreements, and student level. ***College room and board:*** $6720. Room and board charges vary according to board plan and housing facility. ***Payment plan:*** Installment.

FRESHMAN FINANCIAL AID (Fall 2006, est.) 4994 applied for aid; of those 66% were deemed to have need. 100% of freshmen with need received aid; of those 30% had need fully met. ***Average percent of need met:*** 73% (excluding resources awarded to replace EFC). ***Average financial aid package:*** $10,391 (excluding resources awarded to replace EFC). 34% of all full-time freshmen had no need and received non-need-based gift aid.

UNDERGRADUATE FINANCIAL AID (Fall 2006, est.) 23,464 applied for aid; of those 78% were deemed to have need. 100% of undergraduates with need received aid; of those 22% had need fully met. ***Average percent of need met:*** 67% (excluding resources awarded to replace EFC). ***Average financial aid package:*** $10,149 (excluding resources awarded to replace EFC). 19% of all full-time undergraduates had no need and received non-need-based gift aid.

GIFT AID (NEED-BASED) ***Total amount:*** $92,802,662 (25% federal, 11% state, 59% institutional, 5% external sources). ***Receiving aid:*** Freshmen: 48% (2,940); All full-time undergraduates: 42% (14,658). ***Average award:*** Freshmen: $7913; Undergraduates: $6525. ***Scholarships, grants, and awards:*** Federal Pell, FSEOG, state, private, college/university gift aid from institutional funds.

GIFT AID (NON-NEED-BASED) ***Total amount:*** $39,975,124 (11% state, 76% institutional, 13% external sources). ***Receiving aid:*** Freshmen: 4% (220); Undergraduates: 2% (625). ***Average award:*** Freshmen: $4038; Undergraduates: $4209. ***Scholarships, grants, and awards by category:*** *Academic Interests/Achievement:* agriculture, architecture, area/ethnic studies, biological sciences, business, communication, computer science, education, engineering/technologies, English, foreign languages, general academic interests/achievements, health fields, home economics, humanities, international studies, mathematics, military science, physical sciences, premedicine, social sciences. *Creative Arts/Performance:* creative writing, dance, journalism/publications, music, performing arts, theater/drama. *Special Achievements/Activities:* cheerleading/drum major, hobbies/interests, leadership, memberships. *Special Characteristics:* adult students, children and siblings of alumni, children of faculty/staff, children of public servants, children of union members/company employees, children of workers in trades, children with a deceased or disabled parent, ethnic background, handicapped students, members of minority groups, out-of-state students, previous college experience. ***Tuition waivers:*** Full or partial for employees or children of employees, senior citizens. ***ROTC:*** Army, Naval, Air Force.

LOANS ***Student loans:*** $150,489,848 (69% need-based, 31% non-need-based). 56% of past graduating class borrowed through all loan programs. *Average indebtedness per student:* $18,130. ***Average need-based loan:*** Freshmen: $3334;

Undergraduates: $4539. ***Parent loans:*** $48,629,357 (100% non-need-based). ***Programs:*** Federal Direct (Subsidized and Unsubsidized Stafford, PLUS), Perkins, Federal Nursing, college/university.

WORK-STUDY ***Federal work-study:*** Total amount: $9,246,427; 2,009 jobs averaging $3292. ***State or other work-study/employment:*** Total amount: $491,197 (58% need-based, 42% non-need-based).

ATHLETIC AWARDS Total amount: $11,435,005 (100% non-need-based).

APPLYING FOR FINANCIAL AID ***Required financial aid form:*** FAFSA. ***Financial aid deadline (priority):*** 3/1. ***Notification date:*** 4/5. Students must reply by 5/1 or within 4 weeks of notification.

CONTACT Ms. Julia Benz, Director of Student Financial Aid, The Ohio State University, Lincoln Tower, Suite 1100, 1800 Cannon Drive, Columbus, OH 43210-1230, 614-292-3600. *Fax:* 614-292-9264. *E-mail:* sfa-finaid@osu.edu.

OHIO UNIVERSITY

Athens, OH

Tuition & fees (OH res): $8847 **Average undergraduate aid package: $6785**

ABOUT THE INSTITUTION State-supported, coed. Awards: associate, bachelor's, master's, doctoral, and first professional degrees. 173 undergraduate majors. Total enrollment: 20,593. Undergraduates: 17,176. Freshmen: 4,075. Federal methodology is used as a basis for awarding need-based institutional aid.

UNDERGRADUATE EXPENSES for 2006–07 ***Application fee:*** $45. ***Tuition, state resident:*** full-time $8847; part-time $277 per quarter hour. ***Tuition, nonresident:*** full-time $17,811; part-time $572 per quarter hour. ***College room and board:*** $7839; ***Room only:*** $4008. Room and board charges vary according to board plan. ***Payment plan:*** Installment.

FRESHMAN FINANCIAL AID (Fall 2006, est.) 3548 applied for aid; of those 61% were deemed to have need. 93% of freshmen with need received aid; of those 14% had need fully met. ***Average percent of need met:*** 49% (excluding resources awarded to replace EFC). ***Average financial aid package:*** $5985 (excluding resources awarded to replace EFC). 19% of all full-time freshmen had no need and received non-need-based gift aid.

UNDERGRADUATE FINANCIAL AID (Fall 2006, est.) 11,644 applied for aid; of those 68% were deemed to have need. 94% of undergraduates with need received aid; of those 16% had need fully met. ***Average percent of need met:*** 53% (excluding resources awarded to replace EFC). ***Average financial aid package:*** $6785 (excluding resources awarded to replace EFC). 12% of all full-time undergraduates had no need and received non-need-based gift aid.

GIFT AID (NEED-BASED) ***Total amount:*** $14,401,614 (59% federal, 17% state, 24% institutional). ***Receiving aid:*** Freshmen: 20% (832); All full-time undergraduates: 21% (3,306). ***Average award:*** Freshmen: $5438; Undergraduates: $4513. ***Scholarships, grants, and awards:*** Federal Pell, FSEOG, state, college/university gift aid from institutional funds.

GIFT AID (NON-NEED-BASED) ***Total amount:*** $20,675,045 (5% state, 80% institutional, 15% external sources). ***Receiving aid:*** Freshmen: 28% (1,125); Undergraduates: 18% (2,892). ***Average award:*** Freshmen: $3786; Undergraduates: $3920. ***Scholarships, grants, and awards by category:*** *Academic Interests/Achievement:* area/ethnic studies, biological sciences, business, communication, computer science, education, engineering/technologies, English, foreign languages, general academic interests/achievements, health fields, home economics, humanities, international studies, mathematics, military science, physical sciences, premedicine, social sciences. *Creative Arts/Performance:* applied art and design, art/fine arts, cinema/film/broadcasting, dance, debating, journalism/publications, music, performing arts, theater/drama. *Special Characteristics:* children of faculty/staff, members of minority groups. ***Tuition waivers:*** Full or partial for employees or children of employees. ***ROTC:*** Army, Air Force.

LOANS ***Student loans:*** $57,131,769 (43% need-based, 57% non-need-based). 63% of past graduating class borrowed through all loan programs. *Average indebtedness per student:* $19,194. ***Average need-based loan:*** Freshmen: $2778; Undergraduates: $4067. ***Parent loans:*** $21,072,380 (100% non-need-based). ***Programs:*** Federal Direct (Subsidized and Unsubsidized Stafford, PLUS), Perkins, state, college/university.

WORK-STUDY ***Federal work-study:*** Total amount: $1,139,769; jobs available. ***State or other work-study/employment:*** Total amount: $11,835,653 (100% non-need-based). Part-time jobs available.

ATHLETIC AWARDS Total amount: $5,228,794 (100% non-need-based).

APPLYING FOR FINANCIAL AID ***Required financial aid form:*** FAFSA. ***Financial aid deadline (priority):*** 3/15. ***Notification date:*** 3/15.

CONTACT Ms. Sondra Williams, Director of Financial Aid, Ohio University, 020 Chubb Hall, Athens, OH 45701-2979, 740-593-4141. *Fax:* 740-593-4140. *E-mail:* willias1@ohio.edu.

OHIO UNIVERSITY–CHILLICOTHE

Chillicothe, OH

Tuition & fees: N/R **Average undergraduate aid package: $7411**

ABOUT THE INSTITUTION State-supported, coed. Awards: associate, bachelor's, and master's degrees (offers first 2 years of most bachelor's degree programs available at the main campus in Athens; also offers several bachelor's degree programs that can be completed at this campus and several programs exclusive to this campus; also offers some graduate programs). 14 undergraduate majors. Total enrollment: 2,000. Undergraduates: 1,960. Federal methodology is used as a basis for awarding need-based institutional aid.

UNDERGRADUATE EXPENSES for 2006–07 ***Application fee:*** $20. ***Tuition, state resident:*** part-time $153 per hour. ***Tuition, nonresident:*** part-time $297 per hour. Full-time tuition and fees vary according to student level. Part-time tuition and fees vary according to student level.

FRESHMAN FINANCIAL AID (Fall 2006, est.) 189 applied for aid; of those 80% were deemed to have need. 95% of freshmen with need received aid; of those 10% had need fully met. ***Average percent of need met:*** 57% (excluding resources awarded to replace EFC). ***Average financial aid package:*** $6119 (excluding resources awarded to replace EFC). 5% of all full-time freshmen had no need and received non-need-based gift aid.

UNDERGRADUATE FINANCIAL AID (Fall 2006, est.) 949 applied for aid; of those 87% were deemed to have need. 96% of undergraduates with need received aid; of those 7% had need fully met. ***Average percent of need met:*** 56% (excluding resources awarded to replace EFC). ***Average financial aid package:*** $7411 (excluding resources awarded to replace EFC). 2% of all full-time undergraduates had no need and received non-need-based gift aid.

GIFT AID (NEED-BASED) ***Total amount:*** $3,431,885 (71% federal, 23% state, 6% institutional). ***Receiving aid:*** Freshmen: 58% (114); All full-time undergraduates: 61% (637). ***Average award:*** Freshmen: $5119; Undergraduates: $4973. ***Scholarships, grants, and awards:*** Federal Pell, FSEOG, state, college/university gift aid from institutional funds.

GIFT AID (NON-NEED-BASED) ***Total amount:*** $315,855 (7% state, 50% institutional, 43% external sources). ***Receiving aid:*** Freshmen: 14% (27); Undergraduates: 7% (73). ***Average award:*** Freshmen: $2677; Undergraduates: $2403. ***Scholarships, grants, and awards by category:*** *Academic Interests/Achievement:* area/ethnic studies, biological sciences, business, communication, computer science, education, engineering/technologies, English, foreign languages, general academic interests/achievements, health fields, home economics, humanities, international studies, mathematics, military science, physical sciences, premedicine, social sciences. *Creative Arts/Performance:* applied art and design, art/fine arts, cinema/film/broadcasting, dance, debating, journalism/publications, music, performing arts, theater/drama. *Special Characteristics:* children of faculty/staff, members of minority groups. ***ROTC:*** Army cooperative, Air Force cooperative.

LOANS ***Student loans:*** $5,689,759 (51% need-based, 49% non-need-based). 63% of past graduating class borrowed through all loan programs. *Average indebtedness per student:* $19,194. ***Average need-based loan:*** Freshmen: $2510; Undergraduates: $3725. ***Parent loans:*** $104,691 (100% non-need-based). ***Programs:*** Federal Direct (Subsidized and Unsubsidized Stafford, PLUS), Perkins, state, college/university.

WORK-STUDY ***Federal work-study:*** Total amount: $109,791; jobs available. ***State or other work-study/employment:*** Part-time jobs available.

APPLYING FOR FINANCIAL AID ***Required financial aid form:*** FAFSA. ***Financial aid deadline (priority):*** 3/15. ***Notification date:*** 3/15.

CONTACT Ms. Sondra Williams, Director of Financial Aid, Ohio University–Chillicothe, 020 Chubb Hall, Athens, OH 45701-2979, 740-593-4141 or toll-free 877-462-6824 (in-state). *Fax:* 740-593-4140. *E-mail:* willias1@ohio.edu.

OHIO UNIVERSITY–EASTERN

St. Clairsville, OH

Tuition & fees: N/R **Average undergraduate aid package: $6679**

ABOUT THE INSTITUTION State-supported, coed. Awards: associate and bachelor's degrees (also offers some graduate courses). 77 undergraduate majors. Total enrollment: 1,118. Undergraduates: 931. Freshmen: 210. Federal methodology is used as a basis for awarding need-based institutional aid.

FRESHMAN FINANCIAL AID (Fall 2006, est.) 132 applied for aid; of those 82% were deemed to have need. 94% of freshmen with need received aid; of those 15% had need fully met. ***Average percent of need met:*** 61% (excluding resources awarded to replace EFC). ***Average financial aid package:*** $5953 (excluding resources awarded to replace EFC). 5% of all full-time freshmen had no need and received non-need-based gift aid.

UNDERGRADUATE FINANCIAL AID (Fall 2006, est.) 418 applied for aid; of those 82% were deemed to have need. 94% of undergraduates with need received aid; of those 15% had need fully met. ***Average percent of need met:*** 60% (excluding resources awarded to replace EFC). ***Average financial aid package:*** $6679 (excluding resources awarded to replace EFC). 4% of all full-time undergraduates had no need and received non-need-based gift aid.

GIFT AID (NEED-BASED) ***Total amount:*** $1,230,750 (71% federal, 22% state, 7% institutional). ***Receiving aid:*** Freshmen: 56% (77); All full-time undergraduates: 47% (231). ***Average award:*** Freshmen: $5432; Undergraduates: $5001. ***Scholarships, grants, and awards:*** Federal Pell, FSEOG, state, college/university gift aid from institutional funds.

GIFT AID (NON-NEED-BASED) ***Total amount:*** $268,180 (9% state, 79% institutional, 12% external sources). ***Receiving aid:*** Freshmen: 27% (37); Undergraduates: 18% (87). ***Average award:*** Freshmen: $863; Undergraduates: $2153. ***Scholarships, grants, and awards by category:*** *Academic Interests/Achievement:* area/ethnic studies, biological sciences, business, communication, computer science, education, engineering/technologies, English, foreign languages, general academic interests/achievements, health fields, home economics, humanities, international studies, mathematics, military science, physical sciences, premedicine, social sciences. *Creative Arts/Performance:* applied art and design, art/fine arts, cinema/film/broadcasting, dance, debating, journalism/publications, music, performing arts, theater/drama. *Special Characteristics:* children of faculty/staff, members of minority groups.

LOANS ***Student loans:*** $1,713,029 (59% need-based, 41% non-need-based). 63% of past graduating class borrowed through all loan programs. *Average indebtedness per student:* $19,194. ***Average need-based loan:*** Freshmen: $2533; Undergraduates: $3901. ***Parent loans:*** $30,706 (100% non-need-based). ***Programs:*** Federal Direct (Subsidized and Unsubsidized Stafford, PLUS), Perkins, state, college/university.

WORK-STUDY ***Federal work-study:*** Total amount: $37,286; jobs available. ***State or other work-study/employment:*** Part-time jobs available.

APPLYING FOR FINANCIAL AID ***Required financial aid form:*** FAFSA. ***Financial aid deadline (priority):*** 3/15. ***Notification date:*** 3/15.

CONTACT Ms. Sondra Williams, Director of Financial Aid, Ohio University–Eastern, 020 Chubb Hall, Athens, OH 45701-2979, 740-593-4141 or toll-free 800-648-3331 (in-state). *Fax:* 740-593-4140. *E-mail:* willias1@ohio.edu.

OHIO UNIVERSITY–LANCASTER

Lancaster, OH

Tuition & fees: N/R | **Average undergraduate aid package: $6389**

ABOUT THE INSTITUTION State-supported, coed. Awards: associate, bachelor's, and master's degrees. 20 undergraduate majors. Total enrollment: 1,744. Undergraduates: 1,617. Freshmen: 308. Federal methodology is used as a basis for awarding need-based institutional aid.

FRESHMAN FINANCIAL AID (Fall 2006, est.) 294 applied for aid; of those 66% were deemed to have need. 90% of freshmen with need received aid; of those 11% had need fully met. ***Average percent of need met:*** 54% (excluding resources awarded to replace EFC). ***Average financial aid package:*** $5490 (excluding resources awarded to replace EFC). 8% of all full-time freshmen had no need and received non-need-based gift aid.

UNDERGRADUATE FINANCIAL AID (Fall 2006, est.) 929 applied for aid; of those 77% were deemed to have need. 92% of undergraduates with need received aid; of those 10% had need fully met. ***Average percent of need met:*** 54% (excluding resources awarded to replace EFC). ***Average financial aid package:*** $6389 (excluding resources awarded to replace EFC). 6% of all full-time undergraduates had no need and received non-need-based gift aid.

GIFT AID (NEED-BASED) ***Total amount:*** $2,422,131 (68% federal, 23% state, 9% institutional). ***Receiving aid:*** Freshmen: 44% (138); All full-time undergraduates: 52% (489). ***Average award:*** Freshmen: $4870; Undergraduates: $4716. ***Scholarships, grants, and awards:*** Federal Pell, FSEOG, state, college/university gift aid from institutional funds.

GIFT AID (NON-NEED-BASED) ***Total amount:*** $453,005 (5% state, 69% institutional, 26% external sources). ***Receiving aid:*** Freshmen: 10% (31); Undergraduates: 10% (92). ***Average award:*** Freshmen: $3439; Undergraduates: $2907. ***Scholarships, grants, and awards by category:*** *Academic Interests/Achievement:* area/ethnic studies, biological sciences, business, communication, computer science, education, engineering/technologies, English, foreign languages, general academic interests/achievements, health fields, home economics, humanities, international studies, mathematics, military science, physical sciences, premedicine, social sciences. *Creative Arts/Performance:* applied art and design, art/fine arts, cinema/film/broadcasting, dance, debating, journalism/publications, music, performing arts, theater/drama. *Special Characteristics:* children of faculty/staff, members of minority groups. ***ROTC:*** Army cooperative, Air Force cooperative.

LOANS ***Student loans:*** $4,173,537 (51% need-based, 49% non-need-based). 63% of past graduating class borrowed through all loan programs. *Average indebtedness per student:* $19,194. ***Average need-based loan:*** Freshmen: $2778; Undergraduates: $4067. ***Parent loans:*** $61,426 (100% non-need-based). ***Programs:*** Federal Direct (Subsidized and Unsubsidized Stafford, PLUS), Perkins, state, college/university.

WORK-STUDY ***Federal work-study:*** Total amount: $81,982; jobs available. ***State or other work-study/employment:*** Part-time jobs available.

APPLYING FOR FINANCIAL AID ***Required financial aid form:*** FAFSA. ***Financial aid deadline (priority):*** 3/15. ***Notification date:*** 3/15.

CONTACT Ms. Sondra Williams, Director of Financial Aid, Ohio University–Lancaster, 020 Chubb Hall, Athens, OH 45701-2979, 740-593-4141 or toll-free 888-446-4468 Ext. 215. *Fax:* 740-593-4140. *E-mail:* willias1@ohio.edu.

OHIO UNIVERSITY–SOUTHERN CAMPUS

Ironton, OH

Tuition & fees: N/R | **Average undergraduate aid package: $7340**

ABOUT THE INSTITUTION State-supported, coed. Awards: associate, bachelor's, and master's degrees. 20 undergraduate majors. Total enrollment: 1,746. Undergraduates: 1,630. Freshmen: 348. Federal methodology is used as a basis for awarding need-based institutional aid.

FRESHMAN FINANCIAL AID (Fall 2006, est.) 276 applied for aid; of those 88% were deemed to have need. 95% of freshmen with need received aid; of those 9% had need fully met. ***Average percent of need met:*** 58% (excluding resources awarded to replace EFC). ***Average financial aid package:*** $6495 (excluding resources awarded to replace EFC). 4% of all full-time freshmen had no need and received non-need-based gift aid.

UNDERGRADUATE FINANCIAL AID (Fall 2006, est.) 1,156 applied for aid; of those 90% were deemed to have need. 97% of undergraduates with need received aid; of those 8% had need fully met. ***Average percent of need met:*** 57% (excluding resources awarded to replace EFC). ***Average financial aid package:*** $7340 (excluding resources awarded to replace EFC). 3% of all full-time undergraduates had no need and received non-need-based gift aid.

GIFT AID (NEED-BASED) ***Total amount:*** $4,227,384 (73% federal, 21% state, 6% institutional). ***Receiving aid:*** Freshmen: 70% (200); All full-time undergraduates: 65% (829). ***Average award:*** Freshmen: $5262; Undergraduates: $4853. ***Scholarships, grants, and awards:*** Federal Pell, FSEOG, state, college/university gift aid from institutional funds.

GIFT AID (NON-NEED-BASED) ***Total amount:*** $354,796 (11% state, 71% institutional, 18% external sources). ***Receiving aid:*** Freshmen: 11% (32); Undergraduates: 11% (136). ***Average award:*** Freshmen: $2748; Undergraduates: $2097. ***Scholarships, grants, and awards by category:*** *Academic Interests/Achievement:* area/ethnic studies, biological sciences, business, communication, computer science, education, engineering/technologies, English, foreign languages, general academic interests/achievements, health fields, home economics, humanities, international studies, mathematics, military science, physical sciences, premedicine, social sciences. *Creative Arts/Performance:* applied art and design, art/fine arts, cinema/film/broadcasting, dance, debating, journalism/publications, music, performing arts, theater/drama. *Special Characteristics:* children of faculty/staff, members of minority groups. ***Tuition waivers:*** Full or partial for employees or children of employees, senior citizens.

LOANS ***Student loans:*** $6,242,497 (55% need-based, 45% non-need-based). 63% of past graduating class borrowed through all loan programs. *Average*

indebtedness per student: $19,194. ***Average need-based loan:*** Freshmen: $2674; Undergraduates: $3769. ***Parent loans:*** $72,910 (100% non-need-based). ***Programs:*** Federal Direct (Subsidized and Unsubsidized Stafford, PLUS), Perkins, state, college/university.

WORK-STUDY ***Federal work-study:*** Total amount: $128,415; jobs available. ***State or other work-study/employment:*** Part-time jobs available.

APPLYING FOR FINANCIAL AID ***Required financial aid form:*** FAFSA. ***Financial aid deadline (priority):*** 3/15. ***Notification date:*** 3/15.

CONTACT Ms. Sondra Williams, Director of Financial Aid, Ohio University–Southern Campus, 020 Chubb Hall, Athens, OH 45701-2979, 740-593-4141 or toll-free 800-626-0513. *Fax:* 740-593-4140. *E-mail:* willias1@ohio.edu.

OHIO UNIVERSITY–ZANESVILLE

Zanesville, OH

Tuition & fees (OH res): $4596 **Average undergraduate aid package: $6827**

ABOUT THE INSTITUTION State-supported, coed. Awards: associate, bachelor's, and master's degrees (offers first 2 years of most bachelor's degree programs available at the main campus in Athens; also offers several bachelor's degree programs that can be completed at this campus; also offers some graduate courses). 9 undergraduate majors. Total enrollment: 1,679. Undergraduates: 1,679. Freshmen: 248. Federal methodology is used as a basis for awarding need-based institutional aid.

UNDERGRADUATE EXPENSES for 2006–07 ***Application fee:*** $20. ***Tuition, state resident:*** full-time $4596; part-time $144 per quarter hour. ***Tuition, nonresident:*** full-time $8919. Full-time tuition and fees vary according to student level. Part-time tuition and fees vary according to student level. ***Payment plan:*** Installment.

FRESHMAN FINANCIAL AID (Fall 2006, est.) 213 applied for aid; of those 84% were deemed to have need. 93% of freshmen with need received aid; of those 17% had need fully met. ***Average percent of need met:*** 62% (excluding resources awarded to replace EFC). ***Average financial aid package:*** $5862 (excluding resources awarded to replace EFC). 5% of all full-time freshmen had no need and received non-need-based gift aid.

UNDERGRADUATE FINANCIAL AID (Fall 2006, est.) 980 applied for aid; of those 85% were deemed to have need. 94% of undergraduates with need received aid; of those 12% had need fully met. ***Average percent of need met:*** 58% (excluding resources awarded to replace EFC). ***Average financial aid package:*** $6827 (excluding resources awarded to replace EFC). 4% of all full-time undergraduates had no need and received non-need-based gift aid.

GIFT AID (NEED-BASED) ***Total amount:*** $2,975,124 (70% federal, 21% state, 9% institutional). ***Receiving aid:*** Freshmen: 56% (120); All full-time undergraduates: 55% (577). ***Average award:*** Freshmen: $5033; Undergraduates: $4814. ***Scholarships, grants, and awards:*** Federal Pell, FSEOG, state, college/university gift aid from institutional funds.

GIFT AID (NON-NEED-BASED) ***Total amount:*** $629,001 (5% state, 76% institutional, 19% external sources). ***Receiving aid:*** Freshmen: 24% (51); Undergraduates: 16% (170). ***Average award:*** Freshmen: $4224; Undergraduates: $3238. ***Scholarships, grants, and awards by category:*** *Academic Interests/Achievement:* area/ethnic studies, biological sciences, business, communication, computer science, education, engineering/technologies, English, foreign languages, general academic interests/achievements, health fields, home economics, humanities, international studies, mathematics, military science, physical sciences, premedicine, social sciences. *Creative Arts/Performance:* applied art and design, art/fine arts, cinema/film/broadcasting, dance, debating, journalism/publications, music, performing arts, theater/drama. *Special Characteristics:* children of faculty/staff, members of minority groups. ***Tuition waivers:*** Full or partial for employees or children of employees, senior citizens.

LOANS ***Student loans:*** $4,684,318 (55% need-based, 45% non-need-based). 63% of past graduating class borrowed through all loan programs. *Average indebtedness per student:* $19,194. ***Average need-based loan:*** Freshmen: $2519; Undergraduates: $3908. ***Parent loans:*** $51,707 (100% non-need-based). ***Programs:*** Federal Direct (Subsidized and Unsubsidized Stafford, PLUS), Perkins, state, college/university.

WORK-STUDY ***Federal work-study:*** Total amount: $101,265; jobs available. ***State or other work-study/employment:*** Part-time jobs available.

APPLYING FOR FINANCIAL AID ***Required financial aid form:*** FAFSA. ***Financial aid deadline (priority):*** 3/15. ***Notification date:*** 3/15.

CONTACT Ms. Sondra Williams, Director of Financial Aid, Ohio University–Zanesville, 020 Chubb Hall, Athens, OH 45701-2979, 740-593-4141. *Fax:* 740-593-4140. *E-mail:* willias1@ohio.edu.

OHIO VALLEY UNIVERSITY

Vienna, WV

Tuition & fees: $14,262 **Average undergraduate aid package: $10,500**

ABOUT THE INSTITUTION Independent religious, coed. Awards: associate and bachelor's degrees. 19 undergraduate majors. Total enrollment: 527. Undergraduates: 527. Freshmen: 95. Federal methodology is used as a basis for awarding need-based institutional aid.

UNDERGRADUATE EXPENSES for 2006–07 ***Application fee:*** $20. ***Comprehensive fee:*** $20,122 includes full-time tuition ($12,750), mandatory fees ($1512), and room and board ($5860). ***College room only:*** $3200. Full-time tuition and fees vary according to course load. Room and board charges vary according to board plan. ***Part-time tuition:*** $465 per credit hour. ***Part-time fees:*** $63 per credit hour. Part-time tuition and fees vary according to course load. ***Payment plan:*** Installment.

FRESHMAN FINANCIAL AID (Fall 2006, est.) 94 applied for aid; of those 88% were deemed to have need. 100% of freshmen with need received aid. ***Average percent of need met:*** 65% (excluding resources awarded to replace EFC). ***Average financial aid package:*** $9500 (excluding resources awarded to replace EFC).

UNDERGRADUATE FINANCIAL AID (Fall 2006, est.) 436 applied for aid; of those 88% were deemed to have need. 100% of undergraduates with need received aid. ***Average percent of need met:*** 68% (excluding resources awarded to replace EFC). ***Average financial aid package:*** $10,500 (excluding resources awarded to replace EFC). 18% of all full-time undergraduates had no need and received non-need-based gift aid.

GIFT AID (NEED-BASED) ***Total amount:*** $693,000 (83% federal, 17% state). ***Receiving aid:*** Freshmen: 33% (34); All full-time undergraduates: 57% (308). ***Average award:*** Freshmen: $2600; Undergraduates: $3144. ***Scholarships, grants, and awards:*** Federal Pell, FSEOG, state, private, college/university gift aid from institutional funds.

GIFT AID (NON-NEED-BASED) ***Total amount:*** $1,127,000 (4% state, 91% institutional, 5% external sources). ***Receiving aid:*** Freshmen: 81% (83); Undergraduates: 71% (385). ***Average award:*** Freshmen: $4500; Undergraduates: $5700. ***Scholarships, grants, and awards by category:*** *Academic Interests/Achievement:* 191 awards ($271,431 total): education, English, general academic interests/achievements, religion/biblical studies. *Creative Arts/Performance:* 31 awards ($35,850 total): general creative arts/performance, journalism/publications, music, performing arts, theater/drama. *Special Achievements/Activities:* 48 awards ($52,361 total): community service, general special achievements/activities, leadership, religious involvement. *Special Characteristics:* 190 awards ($567,325 total): adult students, children of faculty/staff, ethnic background, general special characteristics, international students, local/state students, relatives of clergy, religious affiliation. ***Tuition waivers:*** Full or partial for employees or children of employees, senior citizens. ***ROTC:*** Air Force cooperative.

LOANS ***Student loans:*** $3,054,000 (56% need-based, 44% non-need-based). 90% of past graduating class borrowed through all loan programs. *Average indebtedness per student:* $15,000. ***Average need-based loan:*** Freshmen: $2625; Undergraduates: $4250. ***Parent loans:*** $720,000 (100% non-need-based). ***Programs:*** FFEL (Subsidized and Unsubsidized Stafford, PLUS), Perkins.

WORK-STUDY ***Federal work-study:*** Total amount: $80,000; 139 jobs averaging $1000. ***State or other work-study/employment:*** Total amount: $30,000 (100% non-need-based). 83 part-time jobs averaging $1000.

ATHLETIC AWARDS Total amount: $820,000 (100% non-need-based).

APPLYING FOR FINANCIAL AID ***Required financial aid form:*** FAFSA. ***Financial aid deadline (priority):*** 3/1. ***Notification date:*** Continuous beginning 6/30. Students must reply within 4 weeks of notification.

CONTACT Dennis Cox, Director of Financial Aid, Ohio Valley University, 1 Campus View Drive, Vienna, WV 26105-8000, 304-865-6081 or toll-free 877-446-8668 Ext. 6200 (out-of-state). *Fax:* 304-865-6001. *E-mail:* dennis.cox@ovc.edu.

OHIO WESLEYAN UNIVERSITY

Delaware, OH

Tuition & fees: $30,290 **Average undergraduate aid package: $20,854**

ABOUT THE INSTITUTION Independent United Methodist, coed. Awards: bachelor's degrees. 90 undergraduate majors. Total enrollment: 1,935. Undergraduates: 1,935. Freshmen: 565. Federal methodology is used as a basis for awarding need-based institutional aid.

UNDERGRADUATE EXPENSES for 2006–07 ***Application fee:*** $35. ***Comprehensive fee:*** $38,080 includes full-time tuition ($29,870), mandatory fees ($420), and room and board ($7790). ***College room only:*** $3880. Room and board charges vary according to board plan. ***Part-time tuition:*** $3250 per course. ***Payment plan:*** Installment.

FRESHMAN FINANCIAL AID (Fall 2006, est.) 420 applied for aid; of those 84% were deemed to have need. 100% of freshmen with need received aid; of those 30% had need fully met. ***Average percent of need met:*** 85% (excluding resources awarded to replace EFC). ***Average financial aid package:*** $21,893 (excluding resources awarded to replace EFC). 40% of all full-time freshmen had no need and received non-need-based gift aid.

UNDERGRADUATE FINANCIAL AID (Fall 2006, est.) 1,274 applied for aid; of those 85% were deemed to have need. 100% of undergraduates with need received aid; of those 28% had need fully met. ***Average percent of need met:*** 82% (excluding resources awarded to replace EFC). ***Average financial aid package:*** $20,854 (excluding resources awarded to replace EFC). 41% of all full-time undergraduates had no need and received non-need-based gift aid.

GIFT AID (NEED-BASED) ***Total amount:*** $18,319,286 (7% federal, 7% state, 84% institutional, 2% external sources). ***Receiving aid:*** Freshmen: 59% (351); All full-time undergraduates: 56% (1,085). ***Average award:*** Freshmen: $15,595; Undergraduates: $14,473. ***Scholarships, grants, and awards:*** Federal Pell, FSEOG, state, private, college/university gift aid from institutional funds.

GIFT AID (NON-NEED-BASED) ***Total amount:*** $10,573,635 (3% state, 96% institutional, 1% external sources). ***Receiving aid:*** Freshmen: 8% (48); Undergraduates: 6% (123). ***Average award:*** Freshmen: $11,747; Undergraduates: $11,439. ***Scholarships, grants, and awards by category:*** *Academic Interests/Achievement:* 949 awards ($18,687,367 total): area/ethnic studies, biological sciences, business, communication, computer science, education, engineering/technologies, English, foreign languages, general academic interests/achievements, health fields, humanities, international studies, mathematics, physical sciences, premedicine, religion/biblical studies, social sciences. *Creative Arts/Performance:* 44 awards ($1,232,072 total): art/fine arts, dance, music, theater/drama. *Special Achievements/Activities:* 42 awards ($605,581 total): community service, leadership, religious involvement. *Special Characteristics:* 735 awards ($10,269,965 total): children and siblings of alumni, children of faculty/staff, ethnic background, international students, local/state students, members of minority groups, out-of-state students, relatives of clergy, religious affiliation. ***Tuition waivers:*** Full or partial for children of alumni, employees or children of employees. ***ROTC:*** Army cooperative, Air Force cooperative.

LOANS ***Student loans:*** $6,337,598 (71% need-based, 29% non-need-based). 60% of past graduating class borrowed through all loan programs. *Average indebtedness per student:* $22,619. ***Average need-based loan:*** Freshmen: $3245; Undergraduates: $3525. ***Parent loans:*** $3,014,540 (100% non-need-based). ***Programs:*** FFEL (Subsidized and Unsubsidized Stafford, PLUS), Perkins, state, college/university.

WORK-STUDY ***Federal work-study:*** Total amount: $1,148,971; 800 jobs averaging $1436. ***State or other work-study/employment:*** Total amount: $273,725 (30% need-based, 70% non-need-based). 302 part-time jobs averaging $906.

APPLYING FOR FINANCIAL AID ***Required financial aid forms:*** FAFSA, institution's own form. ***Financial aid deadline:*** 5/1 (priority: 3/1). ***Notification date:*** Continuous beginning 2/1. Students must reply by 5/1 or within 2 weeks of notification.

CONTACT Mr. Gregory W. Matthews, Director of Financial Aid, Ohio Wesleyan University, 61 South Sandusky Street, Delaware, OH 43015, 740-368-3050 or toll-free 800-922-8953. *Fax:* 740-368-3066. *E-mail:* owfinaid@owu.edu.

OHR HAMEIR THEOLOGICAL SEMINARY

Peekskill, NY

CONTACT Financial Aid Office, Ohr Hameir Theological Seminary, Furnace Woods Road, Peekskill, NY 10566, 914-736-1500.

OHR SOMAYACH/JOSEPH TANENBAUM EDUCATIONAL CENTER

Monsey, NY

CONTACT Financial Aid Office, Ohr Somayach/Joseph Tanenbaum Educational Center, PO Box 334244, Route 306, Monsey, NY 10952-0334, 914-425-1370.

OKLAHOMA BAPTIST UNIVERSITY

Shawnee, OK

Tuition & fees: $14,666 **Average undergraduate aid package: $11,873**

ABOUT THE INSTITUTION Independent Southern Baptist, coed. Awards: bachelor's and master's degrees. 100 undergraduate majors. Total enrollment: 1,883. Undergraduates: 1,866. Freshmen: 411. Federal methodology is used as a basis for awarding need-based institutional aid.

UNDERGRADUATE EXPENSES for 2006–07 ***Application fee:*** $25. ***Comprehensive fee:*** $18,996 includes full-time tuition ($13,654), mandatory fees ($1012), and room and board ($4330). ***College room only:*** $1930. Full-time tuition and fees vary according to course load. Room and board charges vary according to board plan and housing facility. Part-time tuition and fees vary according to course load. ***Payment plan:*** Installment.

FRESHMAN FINANCIAL AID (Fall 2005) 298 applied for aid; of those 85% were deemed to have need. 100% of freshmen with need received aid; of those 44% had need fully met. ***Average percent of need met:*** 67% (excluding resources awarded to replace EFC). ***Average financial aid package:*** $12,627 (excluding resources awarded to replace EFC). 13% of all full-time freshmen had no need and received non-need-based gift aid.

UNDERGRADUATE FINANCIAL AID (Fall 2005) 1,054 applied for aid; of those 98% were deemed to have need. 99% of undergraduates with need received aid; of those 44% had need fully met. ***Average percent of need met:*** 72% (excluding resources awarded to replace EFC). ***Average financial aid package:*** $11,873 (excluding resources awarded to replace EFC). 16% of all full-time undergraduates had no need and received non-need-based gift aid.

GIFT AID (NEED-BASED) ***Total amount:*** $2,165,114 (56% federal, 29% state, 15% institutional). ***Receiving aid:*** Freshmen: 64% (238); All full-time undergraduates: 57% (926). ***Average award:*** Freshmen: $3848; Undergraduates: $3718. ***Scholarships, grants, and awards:*** Federal Pell, FSEOG, state, private, college/university gift aid from institutional funds.

GIFT AID (NON-NEED-BASED) ***Total amount:*** $7,680,050 (1% state, 82% institutional, 17% external sources). ***Receiving aid:*** Freshmen: 65% (243); Undergraduates: 56% (900). ***Average award:*** Freshmen: $5878; Undergraduates: $5240. ***Scholarships, grants, and awards by category:*** *Academic Interests/Achievement:* general academic interests/achievements, religion/biblical studies. *Creative Arts/Performance:* art/fine arts, music, performing arts. *Special Achievements/Activities:* leadership, religious involvement. *Special Characteristics:* children and siblings of alumni, children of faculty/staff, general special characteristics, local/state students, out-of-state students, relatives of clergy, religious affiliation. ***Tuition waivers:*** Full or partial for employees or children of employees, senior citizens. ***ROTC:*** Air Force cooperative.

LOANS ***Student loans:*** $3,876,919 (61% need-based, 39% non-need-based). 58% of past graduating class borrowed through all loan programs. *Average indebtedness per student:* $16,614. ***Average need-based loan:*** Freshmen: $3205; Undergraduates: $3869. ***Parent loans:*** $1,711,402 (100% non-need-based). ***Programs:*** FFEL (Subsidized and Unsubsidized Stafford, PLUS), Perkins.

WORK-STUDY ***Federal work-study:*** Total amount: $161,742; 303 jobs averaging $834. ***State or other work-study/employment:*** Total amount: $538,258 (100% non-need-based). Part-time jobs available.

ATHLETIC AWARDS Total amount: $1,579,272 (100% non-need-based).

APPLYING FOR FINANCIAL AID ***Required financial aid forms:*** FAFSA, institution's own form. ***Financial aid deadline (priority):*** 3/1. ***Notification date:*** Continuous. Students must reply by 5/1 or within 2 weeks of notification.

CONTACT Student Financial Services, Oklahoma Baptist University, 500 West University, Shawnee, OK 74804, 405-878-2016 or toll-free 800-654-3285.

OKLAHOMA CHRISTIAN UNIVERSITY

Oklahoma City, OK

CONTACT Missi Bryant, Director of Financial Services, Oklahoma Christian University, Box 11000, Oklahoma City, OK 73136-1100, 405-425-5190 or toll-free 800-877-5010 (in-state). *Fax:* 405-425-5197. *E-mail:* missi.bryant@oc.edu.

OKLAHOMA CITY UNIVERSITY

Oklahoma City, OK

CONTACT Denise Flis, Financial Aid Director, Oklahoma City University, 2501 North Blackwelder, Oklahoma City, OK 73106-1493, 405-208-5848 or toll-free 800-633-7242. *Fax:* 405-208-5466. *E-mail:* dflis@okcu.edu.

OKLAHOMA PANHANDLE STATE UNIVERSITY

Goodwell, OK

Tuition & fees (OK res): $3521 **Average undergraduate aid package: N/A**

ABOUT THE INSTITUTION State-supported, coed. Awards: associate and bachelor's degrees. 32 undergraduate majors. Total enrollment: 1,136. Undergraduates: 1,136. Freshmen: 255. Both federal and institutional methodology are used as a basis for awarding need-based institutional aid.

UNDERGRADUATE EXPENSES for 2006–07 ***Tuition, state resident:*** full-time $2274; part-time $75.80 per hour. ***Tuition, nonresident:*** full-time $2274; part-time $75.80 per hour. ***Required fees:*** full-time $1247; $34.50 per hour or $61 per term part-time. Full-time tuition and fees vary according to course level and program. Part-time tuition and fees vary according to course level. ***College room and board:*** $3200; ***Room only:*** $900. Room and board charges vary according to board plan, housing facility, and student level. ***Payment plan:*** Installment.

GIFT AID (NEED-BASED) ***Total amount:*** $2,361,171 (60% federal, 13% state, 15% institutional, 12% external sources). ***Scholarships, grants, and awards:*** Federal Pell, FSEOG, state, private, college/university gift aid from institutional funds.

GIFT AID (NON-NEED-BASED) ***Scholarships, grants, and awards by category:*** *Academic Interests/Achievement:* agriculture, education, English, general academic interests/achievements, health fields, mathematics, physical sciences. *Creative Arts/Performance:* art/fine arts, debating, music, performing arts, theater/drama. *Special Achievements/Activities:* cheerleading/drum major, general special achievements/activities, rodeo. *Special Characteristics:* children of faculty/staff, general special characteristics, local/state students, out-of-state students, veterans, veterans' children. ***Tuition waivers:*** Full or partial for employees or children of employees.

LOANS ***Student loans:*** $2,100,116 (100% need-based). ***Parent loans:*** $61,721 (100% need-based). ***Programs:*** FFEL (Subsidized and Unsubsidized Stafford, PLUS), Perkins.

WORK-STUDY ***Federal work-study:*** Total amount: $42,237; 37 jobs averaging $1142. ***State or other work-study/employment:*** Total amount: $345,382 (100% need-based). 218 part-time jobs averaging $1669.

ATHLETIC AWARDS Total amount: $327,133 (100% need-based).

APPLYING FOR FINANCIAL AID ***Required financial aid form:*** FAFSA. ***Financial aid deadline (priority):*** 3/15. ***Notification date:*** 5/1. Students must reply by 8/1.

CONTACT Ms. Mary Ellen Riley, Director of Financial Aid, Oklahoma Panhandle State University, PO Box 430, Goodwell, OK 73939-0430, 580-349-2611 Ext. 324 or toll-free 800-664-6778. *E-mail:* mriley@opsu.edu.

OKLAHOMA STATE UNIVERSITY

Stillwater, OK

Tuition & fees (OK res): $4996 **Average undergraduate aid package: $9296**

ABOUT THE INSTITUTION State-supported, coed. Awards: bachelor's, master's, doctoral, and first professional degrees and post-master's certificates. 80 undergraduate majors. Total enrollment: 23,307. Undergraduates: 18,737. Freshmen: 3,236. Federal methodology is used as a basis for awarding need-based institutional aid.

UNDERGRADUATE EXPENSES for 2006–07 ***Application fee:*** $40. ***Tuition, state resident:*** full-time $3,262; part-time $108.75 per credit hour. ***Tuition, nonresident:*** full-time $11,835; part-time $394.50 per credit hour. ***Required fees:*** full-time $1,734; $57.81 per credit hour. Full-time tuition and fees vary according to program and student level. Part-time tuition and fees vary according to program and student level. ***College room and board:*** $6015; ***Room only:*** $3015. Room and board charges vary according to board plan and housing facility. ***Payment plan:*** Installment.

FRESHMAN FINANCIAL AID (Fall 2006, est.) 2011 applied for aid; of those 72% were deemed to have need. 97% of freshmen with need received aid; of those 18% had need fully met. ***Average percent of need met:*** 75% (excluding resources awarded to replace EFC). ***Average financial aid package:*** $9112 (excluding resources awarded to replace EFC). 34% of all full-time freshmen had no need and received non-need-based gift aid.

UNDERGRADUATE FINANCIAL AID (Fall 2006, est.) 10,899 applied for aid; of those 79% were deemed to have need. 96% of undergraduates with need received aid; of those 18% had need fully met. ***Average percent of need met:*** 73% (excluding resources awarded to replace EFC). ***Average financial aid package:*** $9296 (excluding resources awarded to replace EFC). 23% of all full-time undergraduates had no need and received non-need-based gift aid.

GIFT AID (NEED-BASED) ***Total amount:*** $29,687,577 (49% federal, 29% state, 11% institutional, 11% external sources). ***Receiving aid:*** Freshmen: 33% (1,016); All full-time undergraduates: 35% (6,004). ***Average award:*** Freshmen: $4700; Undergraduates: $4117. ***Scholarships, grants, and awards:*** Federal Pell, FSEOG, state, private, college/university gift aid from institutional funds.

GIFT AID (NON-NEED-BASED) ***Total amount:*** $11,533,615 (28% federal, 12% state, 32% institutional, 28% external sources). ***Receiving aid:*** Freshmen: 29% (885); Undergraduates: 21% (3,595). ***Average award:*** Freshmen: $3341; Undergraduates: $3241. ***Scholarships, grants, and awards by category:*** *Academic Interests/Achievement:* agriculture, architecture, area/ethnic studies, biological sciences, business, communication, computer science, education, engineering/technologies, English, foreign languages, general academic interests/achievements, home economics, humanities, international studies, mathematics, military science, physical sciences, premedicine, social sciences. *Creative Arts/Performance:* art/fine arts, creative writing, general creative arts/performance, journalism/publications, music, theater/drama. *Special Achievements/Activities:* cheerleading/drum major, community service, general special achievements/activities, leadership, memberships, rodeo. *Special Characteristics:* adult students, children and siblings of alumni, ethnic background, first-generation college students, general special characteristics, handicapped students, out-of-state students, previous college experience. ***Tuition waivers:*** Full or partial for children of alumni. ***ROTC:*** Army, Air Force.

LOANS ***Student loans:*** $51,335,020 (55% need-based, 45% non-need-based). 59% of past graduating class borrowed through all loan programs. ***Average need-based loan:*** Freshmen: $2672; Undergraduates: $4061. ***Parent loans:*** $27,774,242 (19% need-based, 81% non-need-based). ***Programs:*** Federal Direct (Subsidized and Unsubsidized Stafford, PLUS), Perkins, college/university.

WORK-STUDY ***Federal work-study:*** Total amount: $586,076; 329 jobs averaging $1786. ***State or other work-study/employment:*** Total amount: $7,909,617 (100% non-need-based). 3,739 part-time jobs averaging $2115.

ATHLETIC AWARDS Total amount: $2,840,973 (42% need-based, 58% non-need-based).

APPLYING FOR FINANCIAL AID ***Required financial aid forms:*** FAFSA, combined scholarship/admissions application. ***Financial aid deadline:*** Continuous. ***Notification date:*** Continuous beginning 4/1. Students must reply within 4 weeks of notification.

CONTACT Office of Scholarships and Financial Aid, Oklahoma State University, 119 Student Union, Stillwater, OK 74078-5061, 405-744-6604 or toll-free 800-233-5019 Ext. 1 (in-state), 800-852-1255 (out-of-state). *Fax:* 405-744-6438. *E-mail:* finaid@okstate.edu.

OKLAHOMA WESLEYAN UNIVERSITY

Bartlesville, OK

CONTACT Lee Kanakis, Director of Financial Aid, Oklahoma Wesleyan University, 2201 Silver Lake Road, Bartlesville, OK 74006, 918-335-6282 or toll-free 866-222-8226 (in-state). *Fax:* 918-335-6811. *E-mail:* financialaid@okwu.edu.

OLD DOMINION UNIVERSITY
Norfolk, VA

CONTACT Betty Diamond, Director of Student Financial Aid, Old Dominion University, 121 Rollins Hall, Norfolk, VA 23529, 757-683-3690 or toll-free 800-348-7926. *E-mail:* bdiamond@odu.edu.

OLIVET COLLEGE
Olivet, MI

Tuition & fees: $17,594 **Average undergraduate aid package: $12,816**

ABOUT THE INSTITUTION Independent religious, coed. Awards: bachelor's and master's degrees. 38 undergraduate majors. Total enrollment: 1,069. Undergraduates: 1,023. Freshmen: 198. Federal methodology is used as a basis for awarding need-based institutional aid.

UNDERGRADUATE EXPENSES for 2006–07 ***Application fee:*** $25. ***Comprehensive fee:*** $23,654 includes full-time tuition ($16,968), mandatory fees ($626), and room and board ($6060). ***College room only:*** $3270. Full-time tuition and fees vary according to reciprocity agreements. Room and board charges vary according to board plan and housing facility. ***Part-time tuition:*** $550 per credit. Part-time tuition and fees vary according to course load and reciprocity agreements. ***Payment plan:*** Installment.

FRESHMAN FINANCIAL AID (Fall 2005) 267 applied for aid; of those 94% were deemed to have need. 100% of freshmen with need received aid; of those 11% had need fully met. ***Average percent of need met:*** 80% (excluding resources awarded to replace EFC). ***Average financial aid package:*** $12,733 (excluding resources awarded to replace EFC). 15% of all full-time freshmen had no need and received non-need-based gift aid.

UNDERGRADUATE FINANCIAL AID (Fall 2005) 927 applied for aid; of those 95% were deemed to have need. 99% of undergraduates with need received aid; of those 14% had need fully met. ***Average percent of need met:*** 79% (excluding resources awarded to replace EFC). ***Average financial aid package:*** $12,816 (excluding resources awarded to replace EFC). 12% of all full-time undergraduates had no need and received non-need-based gift aid.

GIFT AID (NEED-BASED) ***Total amount:*** $8,312,417 (21% federal, 17% state, 60% institutional, 2% external sources). ***Receiving aid:*** Freshmen: 84% (250); All full-time undergraduates: 87% (872). ***Average award:*** Freshmen: $10,012; Undergraduates: $9079. ***Scholarships, grants, and awards:*** Federal Pell, FSEOG, state, private, college/university gift aid from institutional funds.

GIFT AID (NON-NEED-BASED) ***Total amount:*** $1,023,030 (4% state, 89% institutional, 7% external sources). ***Receiving aid:*** Freshmen: 4% (11); Undergraduates: 4% (45). ***Average award:*** Freshmen: $9131; Undergraduates: $9445. ***Scholarships, grants, and awards by category:*** *Academic Interests/Achievement:* 503 awards ($2,234,852 total): business, communication, education, English, foreign languages, general academic interests/achievements. *Creative Arts/Performance:* 50 awards ($97,050 total): art/fine arts, journalism/publications, music. *Special Achievements/Activities:* 138 awards ($641,200 total): community service, leadership, memberships. *Special Characteristics:* 390 awards ($1,796,073 total): children and siblings of alumni, children of faculty/staff, international students, religious affiliation, siblings of current students. ***Tuition waivers:*** Full or partial for employees or children of employees.

LOANS ***Student loans:*** $6,013,583 (78% need-based, 22% non-need-based). 89% of past graduating class borrowed through all loan programs. *Average indebtedness per student:* $23,258. ***Average need-based loan:*** Freshmen: $2452; Undergraduates: $3593. ***Parent loans:*** $315,736 (31% need-based, 69% non-need-based). ***Programs:*** FFEL (Subsidized and Unsubsidized Stafford, PLUS), Perkins, state, Key Alternative Loans, CitiAssist Loans MI-Loan, Signature Loan.

WORK-STUDY ***Federal work-study:*** Total amount: $176,843; 175 jobs averaging $1017. ***State or other work-study/employment:*** Total amount: $337,805 (100% need-based). 260 part-time jobs averaging $1135.

APPLYING FOR FINANCIAL AID ***Required financial aid form:*** FAFSA. ***Financial aid deadline:*** Continuous. ***Notification date:*** Continuous beginning 3/1.

CONTACT Mr. Douglas Gilbertson, Director of Financial Services, Olivet College, 320 South Main Street, Olivet, MI 49076-9701, 269-749-7102 Ext. 7102 or toll-free 800-456-7189. *Fax:* 269-749-3821. *E-mail:* dgilbertson@olivetcollege.edu.

OLIVET NAZARENE UNIVERSITY
Bourbonnais, IL

ABOUT THE INSTITUTION Independent religious, coed. Awards: associate, bachelor's, and master's degrees. 77 undergraduate majors. Total enrollment: 4,364. Undergraduates: 2,633. Freshmen: 703.

GIFT AID (NEED-BASED) ***Scholarships, grants, and awards:*** Federal Pell, FSEOG, state, private, college/university gift aid from institutional funds.

GIFT AID (NON-NEED-BASED) ***Scholarships, grants, and awards by category:*** *Academic Interests/Achievement:* general academic interests/achievements, military science. *Creative Arts/Performance:* art/fine arts, music, performing arts, theater/drama. *Special Achievements/Activities:* cheerleading/drum major, leadership, religious involvement. *Special Characteristics:* children of current students, children of educators, children of faculty/staff, general special characteristics, international students, parents of current students, relatives of clergy, siblings of current students, spouses of current students.

LOANS ***Programs:*** FFEL (Subsidized and Unsubsidized Stafford, PLUS), Perkins, alternative loans.

WORK-STUDY ***Federal work-study:*** Total amount: $225,300; 267 jobs averaging $716. ***State or other work-study/employment:*** Total amount: $771,716 (100% need-based). 787 part-time jobs averaging $980.

CONTACT Mr. Greg Bruner, Financial Aid Director, Olivet Nazarene University, One University Avenue, Bourbonnais, IL 60914, 815-939-5249 or toll-free 800-648-1463. *Fax:* 815-939-5074. *E-mail:* gbruner@olivet.edu.

O'MORE COLLEGE OF DESIGN
Franklin, TN

CONTACT Office of Financial Aid, O'More College of Design, 423 South Margin Street, Franklin, TN 37064-2816, 615-794-4254 Ext. 30.

ORAL ROBERTS UNIVERSITY
Tulsa, OK

Tuition & fees: $17,400 **Average undergraduate aid package: $18,350**

ABOUT THE INSTITUTION Independent interdenominational, coed. Awards: bachelor's, master's, doctoral, and first professional degrees. 78 undergraduate majors. Total enrollment: 3,244. Undergraduates: 2,758. Freshmen: 553. Federal methodology is used as a basis for awarding need-based institutional aid.

UNDERGRADUATE EXPENSES for 2007–08 ***Application fee:*** $35. ***Comprehensive fee:*** $24,750 includes full-time tuition ($17,000), mandatory fees ($400), and room and board ($7350). ***Part-time tuition:*** $710 per credit hour.

FRESHMAN FINANCIAL AID (Fall 2006, est.) 393 applied for aid; of those 88% were deemed to have need. 100% of freshmen with need received aid; of those 50% had need fully met. ***Average percent of need met:*** 99% (excluding resources awarded to replace EFC). ***Average financial aid package:*** $18,541 (excluding resources awarded to replace EFC). 20% of all full-time freshmen had no need and received non-need-based gift aid.

UNDERGRADUATE FINANCIAL AID (Fall 2006, est.) 1,895 applied for aid; of those 89% were deemed to have need. 100% of undergraduates with need received aid; of those 46% had need fully met. ***Average percent of need met:*** 96% (excluding resources awarded to replace EFC). ***Average financial aid package:*** $18,350 (excluding resources awarded to replace EFC). 19% of all full-time undergraduates had no need and received non-need-based gift aid.

GIFT AID (NEED-BASED) ***Total amount:*** $4,953,527 (62% federal, 9% state, 11% institutional, 18% external sources). ***Receiving aid:*** Freshmen: 74% (343); All full-time undergraduates: 70% (1,681). ***Average award:*** Freshmen: $8996; Undergraduates: $8598. ***Scholarships, grants, and awards:*** Federal Pell, FSEOG, state, private, college/university gift aid from institutional funds.

GIFT AID (NON-NEED-BASED) ***Total amount:*** $2,866,534 (2% state, 94% institutional, 4% external sources). ***Receiving aid:*** Freshmen: 22% (103); Undergraduates: 24% (590). ***Average award:*** Freshmen: $5925; Undergraduates: $6993. ***Scholarships, grants, and awards by category:*** *Academic Interests/Achievement:* 1,504 awards ($6,526,699 total): biological sciences, business, communication, education, engineering/technologies, general academic interests/achievements, health fields, religion/biblical studies. *Creative Arts/Performance:* 263 awards ($569,637 total): applied art and design, art/fine arts, cinema/film/broadcasting, journalism/publications, music. *Special Achievements/Activities:* 480 awards ($887,157 total): cheerleading/drum major, community service, general special achievements/activities, leadership, memberships, religious involvement. *Special Characteristics:* 1,605 awards ($4,166,293 total): children and siblings of alumni, children of faculty/staff, general special characteristics, international students, relatives of clergy, siblings of current students. ***ROTC:*** Air Force cooperative.

LOANS ***Student loans:*** $14,019,782 (74% need-based, 26% non-need-based). 69% of past graduating class borrowed through all loan programs. *Average indebtedness per student:* $32,978. ***Average need-based loan:*** Freshmen: $9325; Undergraduates: $10,304. ***Parent loans:*** $5,108,133 (100% need-based). ***Programs:*** FFEL (Subsidized and Unsubsidized Stafford, PLUS), Perkins.

WORK-STUDY ***Federal work-study:*** Total amount: $693,531; 313 jobs averaging $1590. ***State or other work-study/employment:*** Total amount: $278,706 (100% need-based). 750 part-time jobs averaging $1500.

ATHLETIC AWARDS Total amount: $3,353,041 (100% need-based).

APPLYING FOR FINANCIAL AID ***Required financial aid form:*** FAFSA. ***Financial aid deadline (priority):*** 3/15. ***Notification date:*** Students must reply by 7/15.

CONTACT Scott Carr, Director of Financial Aid, Oral Roberts University, PO Box 700540, Tulsa, OK 74170-0540, 918-495-6510 or toll-free 800-678-8876. *Fax:* 918-495-6803. *E-mail:* finaid@oru.edu.

OREGON COLLEGE OF ART & CRAFT

Portland, OR

Tuition & fees: $17,900 **Average undergraduate aid package: $18,130**

ABOUT THE INSTITUTION Independent, coed. Awards: bachelor's degrees and post-bachelor's certificates. 2 undergraduate majors. Total enrollment: 153. Undergraduates: 153. Freshmen: 8. Both federal and institutional methodology are used as a basis for awarding need-based institutional aid.

UNDERGRADUATE EXPENSES for 2006–07 ***Application fee:*** $35. ***Tuition:*** full-time $16,900; part-time $2214 per course. ***Required fees:*** full-time $1000; $50 per course.

FRESHMAN FINANCIAL AID (Fall 2005) 6 applied for aid; of those 100% were deemed to have need. 100% of freshmen with need received aid; of those 17% had need fully met. ***Average percent of need met:*** 60% (excluding resources awarded to replace EFC). ***Average financial aid package:*** $11,743 (excluding resources awarded to replace EFC).

UNDERGRADUATE FINANCIAL AID (Fall 2005) 75 applied for aid; of those 100% were deemed to have need. 100% of undergraduates with need received aid; of those 3% had need fully met. ***Average percent of need met:*** 68% (excluding resources awarded to replace EFC). ***Average financial aid package:*** $18,130 (excluding resources awarded to replace EFC). 2% of all full-time undergraduates had no need and received non-need-based gift aid.

GIFT AID (NEED-BASED) ***Total amount:*** $516,395 (41% federal, 18% state, 32% institutional, 9% external sources). ***Receiving aid:*** Freshmen: 50% (4); All full-time undergraduates: 73% (69). ***Average award:*** Freshmen: $1475; Undergraduates: $6763. ***Scholarships, grants, and awards:*** Federal Pell, FSEOG, state, private, college/university gift aid from institutional funds.

GIFT AID (NON-NEED-BASED) ***Total amount:*** $32,783 (44% institutional, 56% external sources). ***Receiving aid:*** Freshmen: 12% (1); Undergraduates: 2% (2). ***Average award:*** Undergraduates: $5000. ***Scholarships, grants, and awards by category:*** *Creative Arts/Performance:* 5 awards ($10,000 total): art/fine arts.

LOANS ***Student loans:*** $871,145 (81% need-based, 19% non-need-based). 80% of past graduating class borrowed through all loan programs. *Average indebtedness per student:* $32,000. ***Average need-based loan:*** Freshmen: $2625; Undergraduates: $3980. ***Parent loans:*** $54,000 (68% need-based, 32% non-need-based). ***Programs:*** FFEL (Subsidized and Unsubsidized Stafford, PLUS), state, alternative loans.

WORK-STUDY ***Federal work-study:*** Total amount: $18,361; 40 jobs averaging $459. ***State or other work-study/employment:*** Total amount: $32,441 (98% need-based, 2% non-need-based). 49 part-time jobs averaging $622.

APPLYING FOR FINANCIAL AID ***Required financial aid form:*** FAFSA. ***Financial aid deadline (priority):*** 3/1. ***Notification date:*** Continuous. Students must reply by 9/1.

CONTACT Lisa Newman, Director of Financial Aid, Oregon College of Art & Craft, 8245 Southwest Barnes Road, Portland, OR 97225, 503-297-5544 Ext. 124 or toll-free 800-390-0632 Ext. 129. *Fax:* 503-297-9651. *E-mail:* lnewman@ocac.edu.

OREGON HEALTH & SCIENCE UNIVERSITY

Portland, OR

Tuition & fees (OR res): $11,540 **Average undergraduate aid package: $11,238**

ABOUT THE INSTITUTION State-related, coed. Awards: bachelor's, master's, doctoral, and first professional degrees and post-bachelor's, post-master's, and first professional certificates. 2 undergraduate majors. Total enrollment: 2,418. Undergraduates: 597. Federal methodology is used as a basis for awarding need-based institutional aid.

UNDERGRADUATE EXPENSES for 2006–07 ***Application fee:*** $125. ***Tuition, state resident:*** full-time $8880; part-time $185 per credit. ***Tuition, nonresident:*** full-time $20,688; part-time $431 per credit. ***Required fees:*** full-time $2660; $1644 per year part-time.

UNDERGRADUATE FINANCIAL AID (Fall 2006, est.) 294 applied for aid; of those 94% were deemed to have need. 99% of undergraduates with need received aid; of those 8% had need fully met. ***Average percent of need met:*** 48% (excluding resources awarded to replace EFC). ***Average financial aid package:*** $11,238 (excluding resources awarded to replace EFC). 2% of all full-time undergraduates had no need and received non-need-based gift aid.

GIFT AID (NEED-BASED) ***Total amount:*** $1,654,459 (37% federal, 13% state, 18% institutional, 32% external sources). ***Receiving aid:*** All full-time undergraduates: 46% (162). ***Average award:*** Undergraduates: $7550. ***Scholarships, grants, and awards:*** Federal Pell, FSEOG, state, private, college/university gift aid from institutional funds, Health Profession Scholarships.

GIFT AID (NON-NEED-BASED) ***Total amount:*** $67,455 (14% federal, 3% state, 40% institutional, 43% external sources). ***Receiving aid:*** Undergraduates: 2% (7). ***Average award:*** Undergraduates: $5675. ***Scholarships, grants, and awards by category:*** *Academic Interests/Achievement:* 143 awards ($1,133,859 total): health fields. ***ROTC:*** Army cooperative.

LOANS ***Student loans:*** $6,294,504 (80% need-based, 20% non-need-based). ***Average need-based loan:*** Undergraduates: $6442. ***Parent loans:*** $834,259 (60% need-based, 40% non-need-based). ***Programs:*** Federal Direct (Subsidized and Unsubsidized Stafford, PLUS), Perkins, Federal Nursing, state, college/university, alternative loans.

WORK-STUDY ***Federal work-study:*** Total amount: $17,860; 13 jobs averaging $1375.

CONTACT Ms. Cherie Honnell, Director of Financial Aid/Registrar, Oregon Health & Science University, 3181 SW Sam Jackson Park Road, L-109, Portland, OR 97239-3089, 503-494-7800. *Fax:* 503-494-4629. *E-mail:* finaid@ohsu.edu.

OREGON INSTITUTE OF TECHNOLOGY

Klamath Falls, OR

CONTACT Tracey Lehman, Financial Aid Director, Oregon Institute of Technology, 3201 Campus Drive, Klamath Falls, OR 97601-8801, 541-885-1280 or toll-free 800-422-2017 (in-state), 800-343-6653 (out-of-state). *Fax:* 541-885-1024. *E-mail:* marquitt@oit.edu.

OREGON STATE UNIVERSITY

Corvallis, OR

Tuition & fees (OR res): $5643 **Average undergraduate aid package: $9022**

ABOUT THE INSTITUTION State-supported, coed. Awards: bachelor's, master's, doctoral, and first professional degrees and post-bachelor's certificates. 113 undergraduate majors. Total enrollment: 19,362. Undergraduates: 15,829. Freshmen: 2,945. Federal methodology is used as a basis for awarding need-based institutional aid.

UNDERGRADUATE EXPENSES for 2006–07 ***Application fee:*** $50. ***Tuition, state resident:*** full-time $4320; part-time $120 per credit. ***Tuition, nonresident:*** full-time $16,236; part-time $451 per credit. Part-time tuition and fees vary according to course load. ***College room and board:*** $7344. Room and board charges vary according to board plan and housing facility. ***Payment plan:*** Deferred payment.

FRESHMAN FINANCIAL AID (Fall 2005) 2165 applied for aid; of those 65% were deemed to have need. 97% of freshmen with need received aid; of those 28% had need fully met. ***Average percent of need met:*** 71% (excluding resources awarded to replace EFC). ***Average financial aid package:*** $9095 (excluding resources awarded to replace EFC). 1% of all full-time freshmen had no need and received non-need-based gift aid.

UNDERGRADUATE FINANCIAL AID (Fall 2005) 9,085 applied for aid; of those 74% were deemed to have need. 98% of undergraduates with need received aid; of those 22% had need fully met. ***Average percent of need met:*** 68% (excluding resources awarded to replace EFC). ***Average financial aid package:*** $9022 (excluding resources awarded to replace EFC). 1% of all full-time undergraduates had no need and received non-need-based gift aid.

GIFT AID (NEED-BASED) ***Total amount:*** $23,966,637 (54% federal, 14% state, 22% institutional, 10% external sources). ***Receiving aid:*** Freshmen: 37% (1,068); All full-time undergraduates: 35% (4,764). ***Average award:*** Freshmen: $2249; Undergraduates: $2466. ***Scholarships, grants, and awards:*** Federal Pell, FSEOG, state, private, college/university gift aid from institutional funds.

GIFT AID (NON-NEED-BASED) ***Total amount:*** $7,088,539 (1% federal, 65% institutional, 34% external sources). ***Receiving aid:*** Freshmen: 2% (55); Undergraduates: 1% (184). ***Average award:*** Freshmen: $2470; Undergraduates: $2556. ***Scholarships, grants, and awards by category:*** *Academic Interests/Achievement:* general academic interests/achievements. *Creative Arts/Performance:* music. *Special Achievements/Activities:* general special achievements/activities. *Special Characteristics:* general special characteristics. ***Tuition waivers:*** Full or partial for employees or children of employees. ***ROTC:*** Army, Naval, Air Force.

LOANS ***Student loans:*** $54,050,912 (78% need-based, 22% non-need-based). 60% of past graduating class borrowed through all loan programs. *Average indebtedness per student:* $19,550. ***Average need-based loan:*** Freshmen: $2188; Undergraduates: $3108. ***Parent loans:*** $24,382,619 (47% need-based, 53% non-need-based). ***Programs:*** Federal Direct (Subsidized and Unsubsidized Stafford, PLUS), Perkins, college/university.

WORK-STUDY ***Federal work-study:*** Total amount: $3,986,339; jobs available.

ATHLETIC AWARDS Total amount: $5,983,521 (29% need-based, 71% non-need-based).

APPLYING FOR FINANCIAL AID ***Required financial aid form:*** FAFSA. ***Financial aid deadline:*** 5/1 (priority: 2/28). ***Notification date:*** Continuous beginning 4/1. Students must reply within 4 weeks of notification.

CONTACT Emilio Vejil, Director, Financial Aid, Oregon State University, 218 Kerr Administration Building, Corvallis, OR 97331-2120, 541-737-2241 or toll-free 800-291-4192 (in-state).

OREGON STATE UNIVERSITY–CASCADES

Bend, OR

CONTACT Financial Aid Office, Oregon State University–Cascades, 2600 NW College Way, Bend, OR 97701, 541-322-3100.

OTIS COLLEGE OF ART AND DESIGN

Los Angeles, CA

Tuition & fees: $28,346 **Average undergraduate aid package: $19,067**

ABOUT THE INSTITUTION Independent, coed. Awards: bachelor's and master's degrees. 10 undergraduate majors. Total enrollment: 1,125. Undergraduates: 1,073. Freshmen: 161. Federal methodology is used as a basis for awarding need-based institutional aid.

UNDERGRADUATE EXPENSES for 2007–08 ***Application fee:*** $50. ***Tuition:*** full-time $27,796; part-time $945 per credit.

FRESHMAN FINANCIAL AID (Fall 2005) 153 applied for aid; of those 86% were deemed to have need. 100% of freshmen with need received aid; of those 1% had need fully met. ***Average percent of need met:*** 40% (excluding resources awarded to replace EFC). ***Average financial aid package:*** $18,367 (excluding resources awarded to replace EFC). 9% of all full-time freshmen had no need and received non-need-based gift aid.

UNDERGRADUATE FINANCIAL AID (Fall 2005) 825 applied for aid; of those 93% were deemed to have need. 100% of undergraduates with need received aid; of those 2% had need fully met. ***Average percent of need met:*** 49% (excluding resources awarded to replace EFC). ***Average financial aid package:*** $19,067 (excluding resources awarded to replace EFC). 5% of all full-time undergraduates had no need and received non-need-based gift aid.

GIFT AID (NEED-BASED) ***Total amount:*** $8,038,151 (19% federal, 21% state, 59% institutional, 1% external sources). ***Receiving aid:*** Freshmen: 79% (132); All full-time undergraduates: 75% (770). ***Average award:*** Freshmen: $12,128; Undergraduates: $11,363. ***Scholarships, grants, and awards:*** Federal Pell, FSEOG, state, private, college/university gift aid from institutional funds.

GIFT AID (NON-NEED-BASED) ***Total amount:*** $509,967 (89% institutional, 11% external sources). ***Receiving aid:*** Freshmen: 9% (15); Undergraduates: 5% (54). ***Average award:*** Freshmen: $5466; Undergraduates: $4338. ***Scholarships, grants, and awards by category:*** *Academic Interests/Achievement:* 100 awards ($431,550 total): general academic interests/achievements. *Creative Arts/Performance:* applied art and design, art/fine arts.

LOANS ***Student loans:*** $5,623,657 (94% need-based, 6% non-need-based). 63% of past graduating class borrowed through all loan programs. *Average indebtedness per student:* $44,706. ***Average need-based loan:*** Freshmen: $2450; Undergraduates: $3711. ***Parent loans:*** $953,749 (83% need-based, 17% non-need-based). ***Programs:*** FFEL (Subsidized and Unsubsidized Stafford, PLUS), Perkins.

WORK-STUDY ***Federal work-study:*** Total amount: $183,331; 170 jobs averaging $2145. ***State or other work-study/employment:*** Total amount: $6994 (100% non-need-based). 11 part-time jobs averaging $1166.

APPLYING FOR FINANCIAL AID ***Required financial aid forms:*** FAFSA, institution's own form. ***Financial aid deadline (priority):*** 2/15. ***Notification date:*** 3/1. Students must reply within 2 weeks of notification.

CONTACT Nasreen Zia, Associate Director of Financial Aid, Otis College of Art and Design, 9045 Lincoln Boulevard, Los Angeles, CA 90045-9785, 310-665-6883 or toll-free 800-527-OTIS. *Fax:* 310-665-6884. *E-mail:* nzia@otis.edu.

OTTAWA UNIVERSITY

Ottawa, KS

CONTACT Financial Aid Coordinator, Ottawa University, 1001 South Cedar, Ottawa, KS 66067-3399, 785-242-5200 or toll-free 800-755-5200 Ext. 5559. *E-mail:* finaid@ottawa.edu.

OTTERBEIN COLLEGE

Westerville, OH

CONTACT Mr. Thomas V. Yarnell, Director of Financial Aid, Otterbein College, One Otterbein College, Clippinger Hall, Westerville, OH 43081-2006, 614-823-1502 or toll-free 800-488-8144. *Fax:* 614-823-1200. *E-mail:* tyarnell@otterbein.edu.

OUACHITA BAPTIST UNIVERSITY

Arkadelphia, AR

Tuition & fees: $17,950 **Average undergraduate aid package: $15,215**

ABOUT THE INSTITUTION Independent Baptist, coed. Awards: associate and bachelor's degrees. 54 undergraduate majors. Total enrollment: 1,452. Undergraduates: 1,452. Freshmen: 367. Federal methodology is used as a basis for awarding need-based institutional aid.

UNDERGRADUATE EXPENSES for 2007–08 ***Application fee:*** $50. ***Comprehensive fee:*** $23,350 includes full-time tuition ($17,560), mandatory fees ($390), and room and board ($5400). ***Part-time tuition:*** $490 per semester hour.

FRESHMAN FINANCIAL AID (Fall 2006, est.) 284 applied for aid; of those 79% were deemed to have need. 100% of freshmen with need received aid; of those 43% had need fully met. ***Average percent of need met:*** 80% (excluding resources awarded to replace EFC). ***Average financial aid package:*** $14,767 (excluding resources awarded to replace EFC). 26% of all full-time freshmen had no need and received non-need-based gift aid.

UNDERGRADUATE FINANCIAL AID (Fall 2006, est.) 922 applied for aid; of those 82% were deemed to have need. 100% of undergraduates with need received aid; of those 48% had need fully met. ***Average percent of need met:*** 85% (excluding resources awarded to replace EFC). ***Average financial aid package:*** $15,215 (excluding resources awarded to replace EFC). 30% of all full-time undergraduates had no need and received non-need-based gift aid.

GIFT AID (NEED-BASED) ***Total amount:*** $8,050,061 (11% federal, 5% state, 79% institutional, 5% external sources). ***Receiving aid:*** Freshmen: 60% (219); All full-time undergraduates: 54% (747). ***Average award:*** Freshmen: $10,625; Undergraduates: $8068. ***Scholarships, grants, and awards:*** Federal Pell, FSEOG, state, private, college/university gift aid from institutional funds.

GIFT AID (NON-NEED-BASED) ***Total amount:*** $4,406,638 (8% state, 76% institutional, 16% external sources). ***Receiving aid:*** Freshmen: 20% (73); Undergraduates: 17% (229). ***Average award:*** Freshmen: $8081; Undergraduates: $7353. ***Scholarships, grants, and awards by category:*** *Academic Interests/Achievement:* 420 awards ($1,062,404 total): area/ethnic studies, biological sciences, business, communication, computer science, education, engineering/technologies, English, foreign languages, general academic interests/achievements, health fields, home economics, humanities, international studies, mathematics, physical sciences, premedicine, religion/biblical studies, social sciences. *Creative Arts/Performance:* 200 awards ($839,200 total): art/fine arts, journalism/publications, music, performing arts, theater/drama. *Special Achievements/Activities:* 723 awards ($3,917,810 total): general special achievements/activities. *Special Characteristics:* 788 awards ($4,680,308 total): children and siblings of alumni, children of faculty/staff, ethnic background, first-generation college students, general special characteristics, handicapped students, international students, local/state students, married students, members of minority groups, out-of-state students, previous college experience, relatives of clergy, religious affiliation, twins. ***ROTC:*** Army.

LOANS ***Student loans:*** $3,571,305 (56% need-based, 44% non-need-based). 49% of past graduating class borrowed through all loan programs. *Average indebtedness per student:* $13,504. ***Average need-based loan:*** Freshmen: $2964; Undergraduates: $3911. ***Parent loans:*** $1,548,213 (18% need-based, 82% non-need-based). ***Programs:*** FFEL (Subsidized and Unsubsidized Stafford, PLUS), Perkins, state, college/university, alternative loans.

WORK-STUDY ***Federal work-study:*** Total amount: $454,264; 316 jobs averaging $1493. ***State or other work-study/employment:*** Total amount: $357,298 (7% need-based, 93% non-need-based). 228 part-time jobs averaging $1632.

ATHLETIC AWARDS Total amount: $2,013,805 (42% need-based, 58% non-need-based).

APPLYING FOR FINANCIAL AID ***Required financial aid form:*** FAFSA. ***Financial aid deadline:*** 6/1 (priority: 2/15). ***Notification date:*** Continuous beginning 11/1. Students must reply by 5/1.

CONTACT Mr. Lane Smith, Director of Financial Aid, Ouachita Baptist University, Box 3774, Arkadelphia, AR 71998-0001, 870-245-5570 or toll-free 800-342-5628 (in-state). *Fax:* 870-245-5318. *E-mail:* smithl@obu.edu.

OUR LADY OF HOLY CROSS COLLEGE

New Orleans, LA

ABOUT THE INSTITUTION Independent Roman Catholic, coed. Awards: associate, bachelor's, and master's degrees and post-bachelor's certificates. 25 undergraduate majors. Total enrollment: 1,446. Undergraduates: 1,316. Freshmen: 124.

GIFT AID (NEED-BASED) ***Scholarships, grants, and awards:*** Federal Pell, FSEOG, state, private, college/university gift aid from institutional funds, Federal Nursing.

GIFT AID (NON-NEED-BASED) ***Scholarships, grants, and awards by category:*** *Academic Interests/Achievement:* general academic interests/achievements. *Special Characteristics:* children of faculty/staff, general special characteristics, relatives of clergy, religious affiliation.

LOANS ***Programs:*** FFEL (Subsidized and Unsubsidized Stafford, PLUS).

WORK-STUDY ***Federal work-study:*** Total amount: $94,887; 38 jobs averaging $2499.

APPLYING FOR FINANCIAL AID ***Required financial aid forms:*** FAFSA, institution's own form.

CONTACT Mrs. Johnell S. Armer, Director of Financial Aid, Our Lady of Holy Cross College, 4123 Woodland Drive, New Orleans, LA 70131-7399, 504-398-2165 or toll-free 800-259-7744 Ext. 175. *Fax:* 504-391-2421. *E-mail:* jarmer@olhcc.edu.

OUR LADY OF THE LAKE COLLEGE

Baton Rouge, LA

CONTACT Sharon Butler, Director of Financial Aid, Our Lady of the Lake College, 7434 Perkins Road, Baton Rouge, LA 70808, 225-768-1701 or toll-free 877-242-3509. *Fax:* 225-768-1726.

OUR LADY OF THE LAKE UNIVERSITY OF SAN ANTONIO

San Antonio, TX

CONTACT Leah Garza, Director of Financial Aid, Our Lady of the Lake University of San Antonio, 411 Southwest 24th Street, San Antonio, TX 78207-4689, 210-434-6711 Ext. 2299 or toll-free 800-436-6558. *Fax:* 210-431-3958.

OZARK CHRISTIAN COLLEGE

Joplin, MO

CONTACT Jill Kaminsky, Application Processor, Ozark Christian College, 1111 North Main Street, Joplin, MO 64801-4804, 417-624-2518 Ext. 2017 or toll-free 800-299-4622. *Fax:* 417-624-0090. *E-mail:* finaid@occ.edu.

PACE UNIVERSITY

New York, NY

CONTACT Mark Stephens, Pace University, 861 Bedford Road, Pleasantville, NY 10570, 212-773-3501 or toll-free 800-874-7223. *E-mail:* mstephens@pace.edu.

PACIFIC ISLANDS BIBLE COLLEGE

Mangilao, GU

CONTACT Financial Aid Office, Pacific Islands Bible College, PO Box 22619, Guam Main Facility, GU 96921-2619, 671-734-1812.

PACIFIC LUTHERAN UNIVERSITY

Tacoma, WA

Tuition & fees: $23,450 **Average undergraduate aid package: $23,185**

ABOUT THE INSTITUTION Independent religious, coed. Awards: bachelor's and master's degrees and post-bachelor's and post-master's certificates. 60 undergraduate majors. Total enrollment: 3,640. Undergraduates: 3,340. Freshmen: 670. Federal methodology is used as a basis for awarding need-based institutional aid.

UNDERGRADUATE EXPENSES for 2006–07 ***Application fee:*** $40. ***Comprehensive fee:*** $30,590 includes full-time tuition ($23,450) and room and board ($7140). ***College room only:*** $3510. Full-time tuition and fees vary according to course load. Room and board charges vary according to board plan and housing facility. ***Part-time tuition:*** $731 per semester hour. Part-time tuition and fees vary according to course load. ***Payment plan:*** Installment.

FRESHMAN FINANCIAL AID (Fall 2006, est.) 616 applied for aid; of those 79% were deemed to have need. 99% of freshmen with need received aid; of those 43% had need fully met. ***Average percent of need met:*** 93% (excluding resources awarded to replace EFC). ***Average financial aid package:*** $22,190 (excluding resources awarded to replace EFC). 26% of all full-time freshmen had no need and received non-need-based gift aid.

UNDERGRADUATE FINANCIAL AID (Fall 2006, est.) 2,526 applied for aid; of those 83% were deemed to have need. 99% of undergraduates with need received aid; of those 33% had need fully met. ***Average percent of need met:*** 89% (excluding resources awarded to replace EFC). ***Average financial aid package:*** $23,185 (excluding resources awarded to replace EFC). 26% of all full-time undergraduates had no need and received non-need-based gift aid.

GIFT AID (NEED-BASED) ***Total amount:*** $22,265,296 (12% federal, 13% state, 70% institutional, 5% external sources). ***Receiving aid:*** Freshmen: 53% (367); All full-time undergraduates: 50% (1,565). ***Average award:*** Freshmen: $13,778; Undergraduates: $12,136. ***Scholarships, grants, and awards:*** Federal Pell, FSEOG, state, private, college/university gift aid from institutional funds, Federal Nursing.

GIFT AID (NON-NEED-BASED) ***Total amount:*** $13,619,288 (1% state, 82% institutional, 17% external sources). ***Receiving aid:*** Freshmen: 50% (346); Undergraduates: 36% (1,118). ***Average award:*** Freshmen: $10,254; Undergraduates: $8909. ***Scholarships, grants, and awards by category:*** *Academic Interests/Achievement:* 1,819 awards ($15,096,882 total): general academic interests/achievements. *Creative Arts/Performance:* 211 awards ($773,183 total): art/fine arts, dance, debating, general creative arts/performance, music, theater/drama. *Special Achievements/Activities:* 30 awards ($59,850 total): leadership. *Special*

Characteristics: 535 awards ($2,225,666 total): children and siblings of alumni, children of educators, children of faculty/staff, international students, previous college experience, relatives of clergy. ***Tuition waivers:*** Full or partial for employees or children of employees. ***ROTC:*** Army.

LOANS ***Student loans:*** $16,334,227 (86% need-based, 14% non-need-based). 72% of past graduating class borrowed through all loan programs. *Average indebtedness per student:* $22,101. ***Average need-based loan:*** Freshmen: $5155; Undergraduates: $7712. ***Parent loans:*** $6,049,629 (64% need-based, 36% non-need-based). ***Programs:*** FFEL (Subsidized and Unsubsidized Stafford, PLUS), Perkins, Federal Nursing, state, college/university.

WORK-STUDY ***Federal work-study:*** Total amount: $1,100,000; 590 jobs averaging $1864. ***State or other work-study/employment:*** Total amount: $3,800,000 (34% need-based, 66% non-need-based). 255 part-time jobs averaging $5098.

APPLYING FOR FINANCIAL AID ***Required financial aid form:*** FAFSA. ***Financial aid deadline (priority):*** 3/1. ***Notification date:*** Continuous beginning 3/15. Students must reply by 5/1 or within 4 weeks of notification.

CONTACT Ms. Joan Riley, Associate Director, Systems, Pacific Lutheran University, Tacoma, WA 98447, 253-535-7168 or toll-free 800-274-6758. *Fax:* 253-535-8406. *E-mail:* rileyjo@plu.edu.

PACIFIC NORTHWEST COLLEGE OF ART

Portland, OR

Tuition & fees: $18,208 **Average undergraduate aid package: $11,845**

ABOUT THE INSTITUTION Independent, coed. Awards: bachelor's degrees. 9 undergraduate majors. Total enrollment: 293. Undergraduates: 293. Federal methodology is used as a basis for awarding need-based institutional aid.

UNDERGRADUATE EXPENSES for 2006–07 ***Application fee:*** $35. ***Comprehensive fee:*** $24,508 includes full-time tuition ($17,480), mandatory fees ($728), and room and board ($6300). Full-time tuition and fees vary according to course load. Room and board charges vary according to housing facility. ***Part-time tuition:*** $728 per semester hour. ***Part-time fees:*** $28 per semester hour. Part-time tuition and fees vary according to course load.

FRESHMAN FINANCIAL AID (Fall 2006, est.) 33 applied for aid; of those 88% were deemed to have need. 100% of freshmen with need received aid; of those 7% had need fully met. ***Average percent of need met:*** 57% (excluding resources awarded to replace EFC). ***Average financial aid package:*** $11,185 (excluding resources awarded to replace EFC). 3% of all full-time freshmen had no need and received non-need-based gift aid.

UNDERGRADUATE FINANCIAL AID (Fall 2006, est.) 264 applied for aid; of those 90% were deemed to have need. 100% of undergraduates with need received aid; of those 5% had need fully met. ***Average percent of need met:*** 54% (excluding resources awarded to replace EFC). ***Average financial aid package:*** $11,845 (excluding resources awarded to replace EFC). 3% of all full-time undergraduates had no need and received non-need-based gift aid.

GIFT AID (NEED-BASED) ***Total amount:*** $1,585,561 (31% federal, 11% state, 58% institutional). ***Receiving aid:*** Freshmen: 64% (23); All full-time undergraduates: 77% (225). ***Average award:*** Freshmen: $4899; Undergraduates: $4699. ***Scholarships, grants, and awards:*** Federal Pell, FSEOG, state, private, college/university gift aid from institutional funds.

GIFT AID (NON-NEED-BASED) ***Total amount:*** $394,873 (86% institutional, 14% external sources). ***Receiving aid:*** Freshmen: 42% (15); Undergraduates: 31% (91). ***Average award:*** Freshmen: $5000; Undergraduates: $2442. ***Scholarships, grants, and awards by category:*** *Academic Interests/Achievement:* general academic interests/achievements. *Creative Arts/Performance:* art/fine arts. ***Tuition waivers:*** Full or partial for employees or children of employees.

LOANS ***Student loans:*** $1,787,104 (56% need-based, 44% non-need-based). 73% of past graduating class borrowed through all loan programs. *Average indebtedness per student:* $22,155. ***Average need-based loan:*** Freshmen: $2520; Undergraduates: $4040. ***Parent loans:*** $666,808 (100% non-need-based). ***Programs:*** FFEL (Subsidized and Unsubsidized Stafford, PLUS).

WORK-STUDY ***Federal work-study:*** Total amount: $36,124; 33 jobs averaging $1200. ***State or other work-study/employment:*** Total amount: $24,894 (100% non-need-based). 33 part-time jobs averaging $1200.

APPLYING FOR FINANCIAL AID ***Required financial aid form:*** FAFSA. ***Financial aid deadline (priority):*** 3/1. ***Notification date:*** Continuous beginning 4/1. Students must reply within 2 weeks of notification.

CONTACT Peggy Burgus, Director of Financial Aid, Pacific Northwest College of Art, 1241 Northwest Johnson Street, Portland, OR 97209, 503-821-8976. *Fax:* 503-821-8978.

PACIFIC OAKS COLLEGE

Pasadena, CA

Tuition & fees: $19,140 **Average undergraduate aid package: N/A**

ABOUT THE INSTITUTION Independent, coed, primarily women. Awards: bachelor's and master's degrees and post-bachelor's and post-master's certificates. 6 undergraduate majors. Total enrollment: 1,028. Undergraduates: 257. Entering class: 55. Federal methodology is used as a basis for awarding need-based institutional aid.

UNDERGRADUATE EXPENSES for 2007–08 ***Application fee:*** $55. ***Tuition:*** full-time $19,080; part-time $795 per unit. ***Required fees:*** full-time $60; $30 per term part-time.

GIFT AID (NEED-BASED) ***Total amount:*** $440,178 (56% federal, 36% state, 6% institutional, 2% external sources). ***Scholarships, grants, and awards:*** Federal Pell, FSEOG, state, private, college/university gift aid from institutional funds.

LOANS ***Student loans:*** $2,052,951 (100% need-based). ***Parent loans:*** $41,000 (100% need-based). ***Programs:*** FFEL (Subsidized and Unsubsidized Stafford, PLUS), Perkins.

WORK-STUDY ***Federal work-study:*** Total amount: $36,150; 11 jobs averaging $5000.

APPLYING FOR FINANCIAL AID ***Required financial aid forms:*** FAFSA, institution's own form. ***Financial aid deadline (priority):*** 4/15. ***Notification date:*** Continuous beginning 5/1.

CONTACT Rosie Tristan, Financial Aid Specialist, Pacific Oaks College, 5 Westmoreland Place, Pasadena, CA 91103, 626-397-1350 or toll-free 800-684-0900. *Fax:* 626-577-6144. *E-mail:* financial@pacificoaks.edu.

PACIFIC UNION COLLEGE

Angwin, CA

Tuition & fees: $20,265 **Average undergraduate aid package: $10,958**

ABOUT THE INSTITUTION Independent Seventh-day Adventist, coed. Awards: associate, bachelor's, and master's degrees. 67 undergraduate majors. Total enrollment: 1,397. Undergraduates: 1,394. Freshmen: 265. Federal methodology is used as a basis for awarding need-based institutional aid.

UNDERGRADUATE EXPENSES for 2006–07 ***Application fee:*** $30. ***Comprehensive fee:*** $25,917 includes full-time tuition ($20,130), mandatory fees ($135), and room and board ($5652). ***College room only:*** $3447. Full-time tuition and fees vary according to course load. ***Part-time tuition:*** $584 per quarter hour. ***Part-time fees:*** $45 per term. Part-time tuition and fees vary according to course load. ***Payment plans:*** Guaranteed tuition, installment.

FRESHMAN FINANCIAL AID (Fall 2006, est.) 218 applied for aid; of those 67% were deemed to have need. 100% of freshmen with need received aid; of those 27% had need fully met. ***Average percent of need met:*** 69% (excluding resources awarded to replace EFC). ***Average financial aid package:*** $11,652 (excluding resources awarded to replace EFC). 6% of all full-time freshmen had no need and received non-need-based gift aid.

UNDERGRADUATE FINANCIAL AID (Fall 2006, est.) 1,028 applied for aid; of those 64% were deemed to have need. 100% of undergraduates with need received aid; of those 27% had need fully met. ***Average percent of need met:*** 72% (excluding resources awarded to replace EFC). ***Average financial aid package:*** $10,958 (excluding resources awarded to replace EFC). 3% of all full-time undergraduates had no need and received non-need-based gift aid.

GIFT AID (NEED-BASED) ***Total amount:*** $11,844,179 (13% federal, 19% state, 51% institutional, 17% external sources). ***Receiving aid:*** Freshmen: 66% (147); All full-time undergraduates: 61% (658). ***Average award:*** Freshmen: $7940; Undergraduates: $6424. ***Scholarships, grants, and awards:*** Federal Pell, FSEOG, state, private, college/university gift aid from institutional funds.

GIFT AID (NON-NEED-BASED) ***Total amount:*** $2,406,271 (44% institutional, 56% external sources). ***Receiving aid:*** Freshmen: 64% (141); Undergraduates: 57% (619). ***Average award:*** Freshmen: $6523; Undergraduates: $7606. ***Scholarships, grants, and awards by category:*** *Academic Interests/Achievement:* education. *Special Achievements/Activities:* community service, general special achievements/activities, leadership, religious involvement. *Special Characteristics:* $50,000 total: siblings of current students. ***Tuition waivers:*** Full or partial for employees or children of employees, senior citizens.

LOANS ***Student loans:*** $7,685,642 (54% need-based, 46% non-need-based). 49% of past graduating class borrowed through all loan programs. *Average indebtedness per student:* $17,000. ***Parent loans:*** $961,751 (100% need-based). ***Programs:*** FFEL (Subsidized and Unsubsidized Stafford, PLUS), Perkins, college/university.

WORK-STUDY ***Federal work-study:*** Total amount: $159,000; 196 jobs averaging $861.

APPLYING FOR FINANCIAL AID ***Required financial aid forms:*** FAFSA, institution's own form, state aid form. ***Financial aid deadline (priority):*** 3/2. ***Notification date:*** Continuous beginning 5/1. Students must reply within 3 weeks of notification.

CONTACT Glen Bobst Jr., Director of Student Financial Services, Pacific Union College, One Angwin Avenue, Angwin, CA 94508, 707-965-7321 or toll-free 800-862-7080. *Fax:* 707-965-6595. *E-mail:* gbobst@puc.edu.

PACIFIC UNIVERSITY

Forest Grove, OR

ABOUT THE INSTITUTION Independent, coed. Awards: bachelor's, master's, doctoral, and first professional degrees. 49 undergraduate majors. Total enrollment: 2,790. Undergraduates: 1,347. Freshmen: 360.

GIFT AID (NEED-BASED) ***Scholarships, grants, and awards:*** Federal Pell, FSEOG, state, private, college/university gift aid from institutional funds.

GIFT AID (NON-NEED-BASED) ***Scholarships, grants, and awards by category:*** *Academic Interests/Achievement:* business, education, English, foreign languages, general academic interests/achievements, humanities, mathematics, physical sciences, social sciences. *Creative Arts/Performance:* art/fine arts, debating, journalism/publications, music, theater/drama. *Special Achievements/Activities:* community service, memberships. *Special Characteristics:* children and siblings of alumni, children of faculty/staff, general special characteristics, international students, relatives of clergy.

LOANS ***Programs:*** Federal Direct (Subsidized and Unsubsidized Stafford, PLUS), Perkins, alternative loans.

WORK-STUDY ***Federal work-study:*** Total amount: $1,080,374; 639 jobs averaging $1663. ***State or other work-study/employment:*** Total amount: $283,080 (38% need-based, 62% non-need-based). 171 part-time jobs averaging $516.

APPLYING FOR FINANCIAL AID ***Required financial aid form:*** FAFSA.

CONTACT Dala Ramsey, Director of Financial Aid, Pacific University, 2043 College Way, Forest Grove, OR 97116-1797, 503-352-2871 or toll-free 877-722-8648. *Fax:* 503-352-2950. *E-mail:* dramsey@pacificu.edu.

PAIER COLLEGE OF ART, INC.

Hamden, CT

CONTACT Mr. John DeRose, Director of Financial Aid, Paier College of Art, Inc., 20 Gorham Avenue, Hamden, CT 06514-3902, 203-287-3034. *Fax:* 203-287-3021. *E-mail:* paier.art@snet.net.

PAINE COLLEGE

Augusta, GA

CONTACT Ms. Gerri Bogan, Director of Financial Aid, Paine College, 1235 15th Street, Augusta, GA 30901, 706-821-8262 or toll-free 800-476-7703. *Fax:* 706-821-8691. *E-mail:* bogang@mail.paine.edu.

PALM BEACH ATLANTIC UNIVERSITY

West Palm Beach, FL

Tuition & fees: $18,740 **Average undergraduate aid package: $2448**

ABOUT THE INSTITUTION Independent nondenominational, coed. Awards: associate, bachelor's, master's, and first professional degrees. 46 undergraduate majors. Total enrollment: 3,264. Undergraduates: 2,524. Freshmen: 400. Federal methodology is used as a basis for awarding need-based institutional aid.

UNDERGRADUATE EXPENSES for 2006–07 ***Application fee:*** $25. ***Comprehensive fee:*** $25,520 includes full-time tuition ($18,500), mandatory fees ($240), and room and board ($6780). ***College room only:*** $3750. Full-time tuition and fees vary according to course load, degree level, location, program, and reciprocity agreements. Room and board charges vary according to board plan and housing facility. ***Part-time tuition:*** $455 per credit. ***Part-time fees:*** $90 per term. Part-time tuition and fees vary according to course load, degree level, location, program, and reciprocity agreements. ***Payment plan:*** Installment.

FRESHMAN FINANCIAL AID (Fall 2005) 380 applied for aid; of those 75% were deemed to have need. 100% of freshmen with need received aid; of those 48% had need fully met. ***Average percent of need met:*** 66% (excluding resources awarded to replace EFC). ***Average financial aid package:*** $2540 (excluding resources awarded to replace EFC). 21% of all full-time freshmen had no need and received non-need-based gift aid.

UNDERGRADUATE FINANCIAL AID (Fall 2005) 1,976 applied for aid; of those 43% were deemed to have need. 62% of undergraduates with need received aid; of those 99% had need fully met. ***Average percent of need met:*** 32% (excluding resources awarded to replace EFC). ***Average financial aid package:*** $2448 (excluding resources awarded to replace EFC). 15% of all full-time undergraduates had no need and received non-need-based gift aid.

GIFT AID (NEED-BASED) ***Total amount:*** $3,683,961 (58% federal, 9% state, 33% institutional). ***Receiving aid:*** Freshmen: 35% (156); All full-time undergraduates: 7% (171). ***Average award:*** Freshmen: $1911; Undergraduates: $2145. ***Scholarships, grants, and awards:*** Federal Pell, FSEOG, state, private, college/university gift aid from institutional funds.

GIFT AID (NON-NEED-BASED) ***Total amount:*** $14,014,228 (40% state, 51% institutional, 9% external sources). ***Receiving aid:*** Freshmen: 62% (280); Undergraduates: 23% (517). ***Average award:*** Freshmen: $4799; Undergraduates: $1846. ***Scholarships, grants, and awards by category:*** *Academic Interests/Achievement:* 1,575 awards ($4,391,657 total): general academic interests/achievements. *Creative Arts/Performance:* 124 awards ($308,994 total): dance, music, theater/drama. *Special Achievements/Activities:* 353 awards ($323,800 total): religious involvement. *Special Characteristics:* 119 awards ($688,441 total): children and siblings of alumni, children of current students, children of educators, children of faculty/staff, previous college experience, relatives of clergy, siblings of current students, spouses of current students. ***Tuition waivers:*** Full or partial for employees or children of employees.

LOANS ***Student loans:*** $10,451,029 (48% need-based, 52% non-need-based). 55% of past graduating class borrowed through all loan programs. *Average indebtedness per student:* $24,393. ***Average need-based loan:*** Freshmen: $2367; Undergraduates: $3213. ***Parent loans:*** $3,843,069 (100% non-need-based). ***Programs:*** FFEL (Subsidized and Unsubsidized Stafford, PLUS).

WORK-STUDY ***Federal work-study:*** Total amount: $522,596; 267 jobs averaging $2027.

ATHLETIC AWARDS Total amount: $626,749 (100% non-need-based).

APPLYING FOR FINANCIAL AID ***Required financial aid form:*** FAFSA. ***Financial aid deadline:*** 8/1 (priority: 2/1). ***Notification date:*** Continuous beginning 2/15. Students must reply within 1 week of notification.

CONTACT Becky Moore, Interim Director, Financial Aid, Palm Beach Atlantic University, PO Box 24708, West Palm Beach, FL 33416-4708, 561-803-2127 or toll-free 800-238-3998. *Fax:* 561-803-2130. *E-mail:* becky_moore@pba.edu.

PALMER COLLEGE OF CHIROPRACTIC

Davenport, IA

Tuition & fees: $6416 **Average undergraduate aid package: N/A**

ABOUT THE INSTITUTION Independent, coed. Awards: associate, master's, and first professional degrees. 2 undergraduate majors. Total enrollment: 1,505. Undergraduates: 92. Freshmen: 24. Federal methodology is used as a basis for awarding need-based institutional aid.

UNDERGRADUATE EXPENSES for 2006–07 ***Application fee:*** $50. ***Tuition:*** full-time $6060; part-time $152 per credit. ***Required fees:*** full-time $356; $100 per term part-time.

FRESHMAN FINANCIAL AID (Fall 2006, est.) 69 applied for aid; of those 97% were deemed to have need. 100% of freshmen with need received aid; of those 81% had need fully met. ***Average percent of need met:*** 43% (excluding resources awarded to replace EFC). ***Average financial aid package:*** $6498 (excluding resources awarded to replace EFC).

GIFT AID (NEED-BASED) ***Total amount:*** $230,114 (91% federal, 7% institutional, 2% external sources). ***Receiving aid:*** Freshmen: 41% (38). ***Average award:*** Freshmen: $4050. ***Scholarships, grants, and awards:*** Federal Pell, FSEOG, state, private, college/university gift aid from institutional funds.

GIFT AID (NON-NEED-BASED) ***Scholarships, grants, and awards by category:*** *Academic Interests/Achievement:* biological sciences, general academic interests/achievements, health fields. ***Tuition waivers:*** Full or partial for employees or children of employees.

LOANS ***Student loans:*** $740,874 (100% need-based). 74% of past graduating class borrowed through all loan programs. *Average indebtedness per student:* $10,895. ***Average need-based loan:*** Freshmen: $4000. ***Programs:*** FFEL (Subsidized and Unsubsidized Stafford, PLUS), Perkins, state.

WORK-STUDY ***Federal work-study:*** Total amount: $8,800; 4 jobs averaging $2200.

APPLYING FOR FINANCIAL AID ***Required financial aid form:*** FAFSA. ***Financial aid deadline:*** Continuous. ***Notification date:*** Continuous beginning 1/3. Students must reply within 4 weeks of notification.

CONTACT Sue McCabe, Financial Planning Office, Palmer College of Chiropractic, 1000 Brady Street, Davenport, IA 52803, 563-884-5888 or toll-free 800-722-3648. *Fax:* 563-884-5299. *E-mail:* sue.mccabe@palmer.edu.

PARK UNIVERSITY

Parkville, MO

CONTACT Ms. Cathy Colapietro, Director of Student Financial Services, Park University, 8700 NW River Park Drive, Parkville, MO 64152, 816-584-6728 or toll-free 800-745-7275. *Fax:* 816-741-9668.

PARSONS THE NEW SCHOOL FOR DESIGN

New York, NY

Tuition & fees: $30,930 **Average undergraduate aid package: $9940**

ABOUT THE INSTITUTION Independent, coed. Awards: associate, bachelor's, and master's degrees. 12 undergraduate majors. Total enrollment: 3,598. Undergraduates: 3,180. Freshmen: 488. Federal methodology is used as a basis for awarding need-based institutional aid.

UNDERGRADUATE EXPENSES for 2007–08 ***Application fee:*** $50. ***Comprehensive fee:*** $42,680 includes full-time tuition ($30,270), mandatory fees ($660), and room and board ($11,750). ***College room only:*** $8750.

FRESHMAN FINANCIAL AID (Fall 2006, est.) 282 applied for aid; of those 85% were deemed to have need. 98% of freshmen with need received aid; of those 18% had need fully met. ***Average percent of need met:*** 52% (excluding resources awarded to replace EFC). ***Average financial aid package:*** $10,471 (excluding resources awarded to replace EFC). 33% of all full-time freshmen had no need and received non-need-based gift aid.

UNDERGRADUATE FINANCIAL AID (Fall 2006, est.) 1,590 applied for aid; of those 89% were deemed to have need. 100% of undergraduates with need received aid; of those 14% had need fully met. ***Average percent of need met:*** 53% (excluding resources awarded to replace EFC). ***Average financial aid package:*** $9940 (excluding resources awarded to replace EFC). 31% of all full-time undergraduates had no need and received non-need-based gift aid.

GIFT AID (NEED-BASED) ***Total amount:*** $19,180,482 (10% federal, 5% state, 85% institutional). ***Receiving aid:*** Freshmen: 45% (228); All full-time undergraduates: 44% (1,318). ***Average award:*** Freshmen: $9802; Undergraduates: $9708. ***Scholarships, grants, and awards:*** Federal Pell, FSEOG, state, private, college/university gift aid from institutional funds.

GIFT AID (NON-NEED-BASED) ***Total amount:*** $4,846,513 (100% institutional). ***Receiving aid:*** Freshmen: 45% (228); Undergraduates: 44% (1,318). ***Average award:*** Freshmen: $4145; Undergraduates: $4436. ***Scholarships, grants, and awards by category:*** *Academic Interests/Achievement:* general academic interests/achievements. *Creative Arts/Performance:* general creative arts/performance. *Special Achievements/Activities:* general special achievements/activities.

LOANS ***Student loans:*** $12,333,314 (38% need-based, 62% non-need-based). 75% of past graduating class borrowed through all loan programs. *Average indebtedness per student:* $42,784. ***Average need-based loan:*** Freshmen: $2699; Undergraduates: $3389. ***Parent loans:*** $5,639,565 (100% non-need-based). ***Programs:*** FFEL (Subsidized and Unsubsidized Stafford, PLUS), Perkins, college/university.

WORK-STUDY ***Federal work-study:*** Total amount: $720,409; jobs available. ***State or other work-study/employment:*** Part-time jobs available.

APPLYING FOR FINANCIAL AID ***Required financial aid form:*** FAFSA. ***Financial aid deadline:*** Continuous. ***Notification date:*** Continuous. Students must reply within 4 weeks of notification.

CONTACT Financial Aid Counselor, Parsons The New School for Design, 66 Fifth Avenue, New York, NY 10011, 212-229-8930 or toll-free 877-528-3321.

PATRICK HENRY COLLEGE

Purcellville, VA

CONTACT Financial Aid Office, Patrick Henry College, One Patrick Henry Circle, Purcellville, VA 20132, 540-338-1776.

PATTEN UNIVERSITY

Oakland, CA

CONTACT Mr. Robert A. Olivera, Dean of Enrollment Services, Patten University, 2433 Coolidge Avenue, Oakland, CA 94601-2699, 510-261-8500 Ext. 783. *Fax:* 510-534-8969. *E-mail:* oliverob@patten.edu.

PAUL QUINN COLLEGE

Dallas, TX

CONTACT Khaleelah Ali, Assistant Director of Financial Aid, Paul Quinn College, 3837 Simpson Stuart Road, Dallas, TX 75241, 214-302-3530 or toll-free 800-237-2648. *Fax:* 214-302-3535. *E-mail:* kali@pqc.edu.

PAUL SMITH'S COLLEGE OF ARTS AND SCIENCES

Paul Smiths, NY

Tuition & fees: $19,500 **Average undergraduate aid package: $15,008**

ABOUT THE INSTITUTION Independent, coed. Awards: associate and bachelor's degrees. 13 undergraduate majors. Total enrollment: 870. Undergraduates: 870. Federal methodology is used as a basis for awarding need-based institutional aid.

UNDERGRADUATE EXPENSES for 2007–08 ***Application fee:*** $30. ***Comprehensive fee:*** $27,300 includes full-time tuition ($17,750), mandatory fees ($1750), and room and board ($7800). ***Part-time tuition:*** $500 per credit hour.

FRESHMAN FINANCIAL AID (Fall 2005) 301 applied for aid; of those 93% were deemed to have need. 100% of freshmen with need received aid; of those 16% had need fully met. ***Average percent of need met:*** 69% (excluding resources awarded to replace EFC). ***Average financial aid package:*** $14,752 (excluding resources awarded to replace EFC). 7% of all full-time freshmen had no need and received non-need-based gift aid.

UNDERGRADUATE FINANCIAL AID (Fall 2005) 806 applied for aid; of those 92% were deemed to have need. 100% of undergraduates with need received aid; of those 17% had need fully met. ***Average percent of need met:*** 71% (excluding resources awarded to replace EFC). ***Average financial aid package:*** $15,008 (excluding resources awarded to replace EFC). 8% of all full-time undergraduates had no need and received non-need-based gift aid.

GIFT AID (NEED-BASED) ***Total amount:*** $7,207,566 (13% federal, 18% state, 64% institutional, 5% external sources). ***Receiving aid:*** Freshmen: 90% (278); All full-time undergraduates: 89% (731). ***Average award:*** Freshmen: $7316; Undergraduates: $6707. ***Scholarships, grants, and awards:*** Federal Pell, FSEOG, state, private, college/university gift aid from institutional funds.

GIFT AID (NON-NEED-BASED) ***Total amount:*** $363,753 (80% institutional, 20% external sources). ***Receiving aid:*** Freshmen: 8% (24); Undergraduates: 7% (55). ***Average award:*** Freshmen: $5695; Undergraduates: $3178. ***Scholarships, grants, and awards by category:*** *Academic Interests/Achievement:* general academic interests/achievements.

LOANS ***Student loans:*** $5,766,387 (83% need-based, 17% non-need-based). 90% of past graduating class borrowed through all loan programs. *Average indebtedness per student:* $6625. ***Average need-based loan:*** Freshmen: $3227; Undergraduates: $4347. ***Parent loans:*** $2,719,421 (100% need-based). ***Programs:*** FFEL (Subsidized and Unsubsidized Stafford, PLUS), Perkins.

WORK-STUDY ***Federal work-study:*** Total amount: $1,332,615; 735 jobs averaging $1813.

ATHLETIC AWARDS Total amount: $4000 (100% need-based).

APPLYING FOR FINANCIAL AID ***Required financial aid forms:*** FAFSA, state aid form. ***Financial aid deadline (priority):*** 3/3. ***Notification date:*** Continuous. Students must reply within 4 weeks of notification.

CONTACT Mary Ellen Chamberlain, Director of Financial Aid, Paul Smith's College of Arts and Sciences, Routes 86 and 30, PO Box 265, Paul Smiths, NY 12970, 518-327-6220 or toll-free 800-421-2605. *Fax:* 518-327-6055. *E-mail:* mchamberlain@paulsmiths.edu.

PEABODY CONSERVATORY OF MUSIC OF THE JOHNS HOPKINS UNIVERSITY

Baltimore, MD

Tuition & fees: $29,990 **Average undergraduate aid package: $8999**

ABOUT THE INSTITUTION Independent, coed. Awards: bachelor's, master's, and doctoral degrees and post-bachelor's certificates. 8 undergraduate majors. Total enrollment: 675. Undergraduates: 335. Freshmen: 99. Federal methodology is used as a basis for awarding need-based institutional aid.

UNDERGRADUATE EXPENSES for 2006–07 ***Application fee:*** $100. ***Comprehensive fee:*** $39,490 includes full-time tuition ($29,630), mandatory fees ($360), and room and board ($9500). Full-time tuition and fees vary according to program. Room and board charges vary according to board plan. ***Part-time tuition:*** $840 per semester hour. Part-time tuition and fees vary according to course load. ***Payment plan:*** Installment.

FRESHMAN FINANCIAL AID (Fall 2005) 68 applied for aid; of those 82% were deemed to have need. 89% of freshmen with need received aid; of those 4% had need fully met. ***Average percent of need met:*** 45% (excluding resources awarded to replace EFC). ***Average financial aid package:*** $11,012 (excluding resources awarded to replace EFC). 7% of all full-time freshmen had no need and received non-need-based gift aid.

UNDERGRADUATE FINANCIAL AID (Fall 2005) 200 applied for aid; of those 90% were deemed to have need. 94% of undergraduates with need received aid; of those 4% had need fully met. ***Average percent of need met:*** 34% (excluding resources awarded to replace EFC). ***Average financial aid package:*** $8999 (excluding resources awarded to replace EFC). 4% of all full-time undergraduates had no need and received non-need-based gift aid.

GIFT AID (NEED-BASED) ***Total amount:*** $1,256,277 (18% federal, 4% state, 78% institutional). ***Receiving aid:*** Freshmen: 43% (39); All full-time undergraduates: 43% (132). ***Average award:*** Freshmen: $6335; Undergraduates: $7339. ***Scholarships, grants, and awards:*** Federal Pell, FSEOG, state, private, college/university gift aid from institutional funds.

GIFT AID (NON-NEED-BASED) ***Total amount:*** $1,234,475 (1% state, 98% institutional, 1% external sources). ***Receiving aid:*** Freshmen: 19% (17); Undergraduates: 30% (94). ***Average award:*** Freshmen: $11,833; Undergraduates: $10,653. ***Scholarships, grants, and awards by category:*** *Creative Arts/Performance:* 170 awards ($1,213,175 total): music.

LOANS ***Student loans:*** $1,676,910 (48% need-based, 52% non-need-based). 47% of past graduating class borrowed through all loan programs. *Average indebtedness per student:* $19,196. ***Average need-based loan:*** Freshmen: $4509; Undergraduates: $5610. ***Parent loans:*** $872,973 (100% non-need-based). ***Programs:*** Federal Direct (Subsidized and Unsubsidized Stafford), FFEL (PLUS), Perkins, college/university.

WORK-STUDY ***Federal work-study:*** Total amount: $218,753; 114 jobs averaging $1919. ***State or other work-study/employment:*** Total amount: $96,213 (100% non-need-based). 103 part-time jobs averaging $934.

APPLYING FOR FINANCIAL AID ***Required financial aid form:*** FAFSA. ***Financial aid deadline (priority):*** 3/1. ***Notification date:*** 4/1. Students must reply within 2 weeks of notification.

CONTACT Rebecca Polgar, Financial Aid Officer, Peabody Conservatory of Music of The Johns Hopkins University, 1 East Mount Vernon Place, Baltimore, MD 21202-2397, 410-659-8100 Ext. 3023 or toll-free 800-368-2521 (out-of-state). *Fax:* 410-659-8102. *E-mail:* finaid@peabody.jhu.edu.

PEACE COLLEGE

Raleigh, NC

ABOUT THE INSTITUTION Independent religious, women only. Awards: bachelor's degrees. 13 undergraduate majors. Total enrollment: 651. Undergraduates: 651. Freshmen: 153.

GIFT AID (NEED-BASED) ***Scholarships, grants, and awards:*** Federal Pell, FSEOG, state, private, college/university gift aid from institutional funds, Federal Nursing.

GIFT AID (NON-NEED-BASED) ***Scholarships, grants, and awards by category:*** *Academic Interests/Achievement:* general academic interests/achievements. *Creative Arts/Performance:* art/fine arts, music, theater/drama. *Special Characteristics:* children of faculty/staff, relatives of clergy.

LOANS ***Programs:*** FFEL (Subsidized and Unsubsidized Stafford, PLUS), alternative loans.

WORK-STUDY ***Federal work-study:*** Total amount: $266,351; 204 jobs averaging $1306. ***State or other work-study/employment:*** Total amount: $22,816 (21% need-based, 79% non-need-based). 14 part-time jobs averaging $1630.

APPLYING FOR FINANCIAL AID ***Required financial aid form:*** FAFSA.

CONTACT Angela Kirkley, Director of Financial Aid, Peace College, 15 East Peace Street, Raleigh, NC 27604, 919-508-2249 or toll-free 800-PEACE-47. *Fax:* 919-508-2325. *E-mail:* akirkley@peace.edu.

PEIRCE COLLEGE

Philadelphia, PA

Tuition & fees: $13,240 **Average undergraduate aid package: $4206**

ABOUT THE INSTITUTION Independent, coed. Awards: associate and bachelor's degrees and post-bachelor's certificates. 19 undergraduate majors. Total enrollment: 2,179. Undergraduates: 2,179. Freshmen: 130. Federal methodology is used as a basis for awarding need-based institutional aid.

UNDERGRADUATE EXPENSES for 2006–07 ***Application fee:*** $50. ***Tuition:*** full-time $12,240; part-time $408 per credit hour. ***Required fees:*** full-time $1000; $100 per course. Full-time tuition and fees vary according to course load. Part-time tuition and fees vary according to course load. ***Payment plan:*** Installment.

FRESHMAN FINANCIAL AID (Fall 2005) 60 applied for aid; of those 100% were deemed to have need. 100% of freshmen with need received aid; of those 95% had need fully met. ***Average percent of need met:*** 82% (excluding resources awarded to replace EFC). ***Average financial aid package:*** $4611 (excluding resources awarded to replace EFC). 1% of all full-time freshmen had no need and received non-need-based gift aid.

UNDERGRADUATE FINANCIAL AID (Fall 2005) 560 applied for aid; of those 100% were deemed to have need. 100% of undergraduates with need received aid; of those 95% had need fully met. ***Average percent of need met:*** 68% (excluding resources awarded to replace EFC). ***Average financial aid package:*** $4206 (excluding resources awarded to replace EFC). 6% of all full-time undergraduates had no need and received non-need-based gift aid.

GIFT AID (NEED-BASED) ***Total amount:*** $3,750,664 (60% federal, 37% state, 3% institutional). ***Receiving aid:*** Freshmen: 4% (3); All full-time undergraduates: 6% (51). ***Average award:*** Freshmen: $3600; Undergraduates: $2193. ***Scholarships, grants, and awards:*** Federal Pell, FSEOG, state, private, college/university gift aid from institutional funds.

GIFT AID (NON-NEED-BASED) ***Total amount:*** $701,502 (100% institutional). ***Receiving aid:*** Freshmen: 16% (12); Undergraduates: 11% (90). ***Average award:*** Freshmen: $1516; Undergraduates: $2311. ***Scholarships, grants, and awards by category:*** *Academic Interests/Achievement:* 44 awards ($87,271 total): general academic interests/achievements. *Special Achievements/Activities:* 15 awards ($15,251 total): community service, leadership, memberships. *Special Characteristics:* 127 awards ($157,098 total): children and siblings of alumni, children of public servants, parents of current students, previous college experience, public servants, siblings of current students, spouses of current students. ***Tuition waivers:*** Full or partial for children of alumni, employees or children of employees.

LOANS ***Student loans:*** $9,668,845 (48% need-based, 52% non-need-based). 80% of past graduating class borrowed through all loan programs. *Average indebtedness per student:* $15,662. ***Average need-based loan:*** Freshmen: $2000; Undergraduates: $3000. ***Parent loans:*** $103,279 (100% need-based). ***Programs:*** FFEL (Subsidized and Unsubsidized Stafford, PLUS).

WORK-STUDY ***Federal work-study:*** Total amount: $140,835; 35 jobs averaging $2175. ***State or other work-study/employment:*** Total amount: $73,880 (100% need-based).

APPLYING FOR FINANCIAL AID ***Required financial aid form:*** FAFSA. ***Financial aid deadline (priority):*** 6/1. ***Notification date:*** 6/15. Students must reply within 3 weeks of notification.

CONTACT Lisa A. Gargiulo, Student Financial Services Manager, Peirce College, 1420 Pine Street, Philadelphia, PA 19102, 215-670-9370 or toll-free 888-467-3472. *Fax:* 215-545-3671. *E-mail:* lagargiulo@peirce.edu.

PENN STATE ABINGTON

Abington, PA

Tuition & fees (PA res): $10,520 Average undergraduate aid package: $10,768

ABOUT THE INSTITUTION State-related, coed. Awards: associate and bachelor's degrees. 119 undergraduate majors. Total enrollment: 3,141. Undergraduates: 3,141. Freshmen: 869. Federal methodology is used as a basis for awarding need-based institutional aid.

UNDERGRADUATE EXPENSES for 2006–07 ***Application fee:*** $50. ***Tuition, state resident:*** full-time $10,008; part-time $405 per credit hour. ***Tuition, nonresident:*** full-time $15,284; part-time $637 per credit hour. ***Required fees:*** full-time $512; $86 per term part-time. Full-time tuition and fees vary according to course level, location, program, and student level. Part-time tuition and fees vary according to course level, course load, location, program, and student level. ***Payment plan:*** Deferred payment.

FRESHMAN FINANCIAL AID (Fall 2005) 633 applied for aid; of those 80% were deemed to have need. 99% of freshmen with need received aid; of those 5% had need fully met. ***Average percent of need met:*** 69% (excluding resources awarded to replace EFC). ***Average financial aid package:*** $10,118 (excluding resources awarded to replace EFC). 8% of all full-time freshmen had no need and received non-need-based gift aid.

UNDERGRADUATE FINANCIAL AID (Fall 2005) 1,788 applied for aid; of those 80% were deemed to have need. 99% of undergraduates with need received aid; of those 6% had need fully met. ***Average percent of need met:*** 68% (excluding resources awarded to replace EFC). ***Average financial aid package:*** $10,768 (excluding resources awarded to replace EFC). 5% of all full-time undergraduates had no need and received non-need-based gift aid.

GIFT AID (NEED-BASED) ***Total amount:*** $7,303,549 (42% federal, 38% state, 20% institutional). ***Receiving aid:*** Freshmen: 55% (417); All full-time undergraduates: 51% (1,164). ***Average award:*** Freshmen: $5771; Undergraduates: $5254. ***Scholarships, grants, and awards:*** Federal Pell, FSEOG, state, private, college/university gift aid from institutional funds.

GIFT AID (NON-NEED-BASED) ***Total amount:*** $1,901,230 (50% institutional, 50% external sources). ***Receiving aid:*** Freshmen: 40% (299); Undergraduates: 26% (596). ***Average award:*** Freshmen: $1459; Undergraduates: $1856. ***Scholarships, grants, and awards by category:*** *Academic Interests/Achievement:* general academic interests/achievements. *Special Characteristics:* general special characteristics. ***Tuition waivers:*** Full or partial for employees or children of employees, senior citizens. ***ROTC:*** Army cooperative, Air Force cooperative.

LOANS ***Student loans:*** $7,284,161 (61% need-based, 39% non-need-based). 66% of past graduating class borrowed through all loan programs. *Average indebtedness per student:* $23,500. ***Average need-based loan:*** Freshmen: $2512; Undergraduates: $3440. ***Parent loans:*** $1,624,410 (100% non-need-based). ***Programs:*** FFEL (Subsidized and Unsubsidized Stafford, PLUS), Perkins, college/university, private loans.

WORK-STUDY ***Federal work-study:*** Total amount: $95,109; 77 jobs averaging $1222. ***State or other work-study/employment:*** Part-time jobs available.

APPLYING FOR FINANCIAL AID ***Required financial aid form:*** FAFSA. ***Financial aid deadline (priority):*** 2/15. ***Notification date:*** Continuous.

CONTACT Debbie Meditz, Assistant Student Aid Coordinator, Penn State Abington, 106 Sutherland Building, 1600 Woodland Road, Abington, PA 19001, 215-881-7348. *Fax:* 215-881-7655. *E-mail:* dlm175@psu.edu.

PENN STATE ALTOONA

Altoona, PA

Tuition & fees (PA res): $10,958 Average undergraduate aid package: $13,597

ABOUT THE INSTITUTION State-related, coed. Awards: associate and bachelor's degrees. 123 undergraduate majors. Total enrollment: 3,833. Undergraduates: 3,833. Freshmen: 1,484. Federal methodology is used as a basis for awarding need-based institutional aid.

UNDERGRADUATE EXPENSES for 2006–07 ***Application fee:*** $50. ***Tuition, state resident:*** full-time $10,446; part-time $435 per credit hour. ***Tuition, nonresident:*** full-time $15,994; part-time $666 per credit hour. ***Required fees:*** full-time $512; $86 per term part-time. Full-time tuition and fees vary according to course level, location, program, and student level. Part-time tuition and fees vary according to course level, course load, location, program, and student level. ***College room and board:*** $6850; ***Room only:*** $3620. Room and board charges vary according to board plan and housing facility. ***Payment plan:*** Deferred payment.

FRESHMAN FINANCIAL AID (Fall 2005) 1026 applied for aid; of those 79% were deemed to have need. 99% of freshmen with need received aid; of those 6% had need fully met. ***Average percent of need met:*** 64% (excluding resources awarded to replace EFC). ***Average financial aid package:*** $12,860 (excluding resources awarded to replace EFC). 3% of all full-time freshmen had no need and received non-need-based gift aid.

UNDERGRADUATE FINANCIAL AID (Fall 2005) 2,685 applied for aid; of those 82% were deemed to have need. 99% of undergraduates with need received aid; of those 9% had need fully met. ***Average percent of need met:*** 68% (excluding resources awarded to replace EFC). ***Average financial aid package:*** $13,597 (excluding resources awarded to replace EFC). 2% of all full-time undergraduates had no need and received non-need-based gift aid.

GIFT AID (NEED-BASED) ***Total amount:*** $9,062,398 (41% federal, 49% state, 10% institutional). ***Receiving aid:*** Freshmen: 46% (553); All full-time undergraduates: 49% (1,601). ***Average award:*** Freshmen: $4634; Undergraduates: $4593. ***Scholarships, grants, and awards:*** Federal Pell, FSEOG, state, private, college/university gift aid from institutional funds.

GIFT AID (NON-NEED-BASED) ***Total amount:*** $2,211,187 (63% institutional, 37% external sources). ***Receiving aid:*** Freshmen: 29% (352); Undergraduates: 27% (896). ***Average award:*** Freshmen: $2319; Undergraduates: $4411. ***Scholarships, grants, and awards by category:*** *Academic Interests/Achievement:* general academic interests/achievements. *Special Characteristics:* general special characteristics. ***Tuition waivers:*** Full or partial for employees or children of employees, senior citizens. ***ROTC:*** Army, Air Force.

LOANS ***Student loans:*** $12,080,523 (64% need-based, 36% non-need-based). 66% of past graduating class borrowed through all loan programs. *Average indebtedness per student:* $23,500. ***Average need-based loan:*** Freshmen: $2786; Undergraduates: $3603. ***Parent loans:*** $6,251,532 (100% non-need-based). ***Programs:*** FFEL (Subsidized and Unsubsidized Stafford, PLUS), Perkins, college/university, private loans.

WORK-STUDY ***Federal work-study:*** Total amount: $498,872; 291 jobs averaging $1698. ***State or other work-study/employment:*** Part-time jobs available.

APPLYING FOR FINANCIAL AID ***Required financial aid form:*** FAFSA. ***Financial aid deadline (priority):*** 2/15. ***Notification date:*** Continuous.

CONTACT Mr. David Pearlman, Assistant Director of Student Affairs, Penn State Altoona, W111 Smith Building, Altoona, PA 16601-3760, 814-949-5055 or toll-free 800-848-9843. *Fax:* 814-949-5536. *E-mail:* dpp1@psu.edu.

PENN STATE BERKS

Reading, PA

Tuition & fees (PA res): $10,958 Average undergraduate aid package: $12,355

ABOUT THE INSTITUTION State-related, coed. Awards: associate and bachelor's degrees. 127 undergraduate majors. Total enrollment: 2,660. Undergraduates: 2,631. Freshmen: 961. Federal methodology is used as a basis for awarding need-based institutional aid.

UNDERGRADUATE EXPENSES for 2006–07 ***Application fee:*** $50. ***Tuition, state resident:*** full-time $10,446; part-time $435 per credit. ***Tuition, nonresident:*** full-time $15,994; part-time $666 per credit. ***Required fees:*** full-time $512; $86 per term part-time. Full-time tuition and fees vary according to course level, course load, and student level. Part-time tuition and fees vary according to course level and student level. ***College room and board:*** $7490; ***Room only:*** $4260. Room and board charges vary according to board plan and housing facility. ***Payment plan:*** Deferred payment.

FRESHMAN FINANCIAL AID (Fall 2005) 685 applied for aid; of those 70% were deemed to have need. 99% of freshmen with need received aid; of those 6% had need fully met. ***Average percent of need met:*** 61% (excluding resources awarded to replace EFC). ***Average financial aid package:*** $11,482 (excluding resources awarded to replace EFC). 4% of all full-time freshmen had no need and received non-need-based gift aid.

UNDERGRADUATE FINANCIAL AID (Fall 2005) 1,624 applied for aid; of those 73% were deemed to have need. 99% of undergraduates with need received aid; of those 7% had need fully met. ***Average percent of need met:*** 64% (excluding resources awarded to replace EFC). ***Average financial aid package:*** $12,355 (excluding resources awarded to replace EFC). 4% of all full-time undergraduates had no need and received non-need-based gift aid.

GIFT AID (NEED-BASED) ***Total amount:*** $4,521,893 (36% federal, 46% state, 18% institutional). ***Receiving aid:*** Freshmen: 35% (301); All full-time undergraduates: 37% (784). ***Average award:*** Freshmen: $4934; Undergraduates: $4696. ***Scholarships, grants, and awards:*** Federal Pell, FSEOG, state, private, college/university gift aid from institutional funds.

GIFT AID (NON-NEED-BASED) ***Total amount:*** $1,385,417 (58% institutional, 42% external sources). ***Receiving aid:*** Freshmen: 22% (190); Undergraduates: 23% (481). ***Average award:*** Freshmen: $2995; Undergraduates: $2737. ***Scholarships, grants, and awards by category:*** *Academic Interests/Achievement:* general academic interests/achievements. *Special Characteristics:* general special characteristics. ***Tuition waivers:*** Full or partial for employees or children of employees, senior citizens. ***ROTC:*** Army cooperative.

LOANS ***Student loans:*** $6,620,149 (59% need-based, 41% non-need-based). 66% of past graduating class borrowed through all loan programs. *Average indebtedness per student:* $23,500. ***Average need-based loan:*** Freshmen: $2829; Undergraduates: $3503. ***Parent loans:*** $3,738,832 (100% non-need-based). ***Programs:*** FFEL (Subsidized and Unsubsidized Stafford, PLUS), Perkins, college/university, private loans.

WORK-STUDY ***Federal work-study:*** Total amount: $73,953; 68 jobs averaging $1068. ***State or other work-study/employment:*** Part-time jobs available.

APPLYING FOR FINANCIAL AID ***Required financial aid form:*** FAFSA. ***Financial aid deadline (priority):*** 2/15. ***Notification date:*** Continuous.

CONTACT Maryann Hubick, Financial Aid Coordinator, Penn State Berks, Perkins Student Center, Room 6, Reading, PA 19610-6009, 610-396-6071. *Fax:* 610-396-6077. *E-mail:* mxh61@psu.edu.

PENN STATE ERIE, THE BEHREND COLLEGE

Erie, PA

Tuition & fees (PA res): $10,958 Average undergraduate aid package: $14,321

ABOUT THE INSTITUTION State-related, coed. Awards: associate, bachelor's, and master's degrees. 131 undergraduate majors. Total enrollment: 3,839. Undergraduates: 3,675. Freshmen: 1,027. Federal methodology is used as a basis for awarding need-based institutional aid.

UNDERGRADUATE EXPENSES for 2006–07 ***Application fee:*** $50. ***Tuition, state resident:*** full-time $10,446; part-time $435 per credit. ***Tuition, nonresident:*** full-time $15,994; part-time $666 per credit. ***Required fees:*** full-time $512; $86 per term part-time. Full-time tuition and fees vary according to course level, location, program, and student level. Part-time tuition and fees vary according to course level, course load, location, program, and student level. ***College room and board:*** $6850; ***Room only:*** $3620. Room and board charges vary according to board plan and housing facility. ***Payment plan:*** Deferred payment.

FRESHMAN FINANCIAL AID (Fall 2005) 736 applied for aid; of those 81% were deemed to have need. 99% of freshmen with need received aid; of those 10% had need fully met. ***Average percent of need met:*** 70% (excluding resources awarded to replace EFC). ***Average financial aid package:*** $13,641 (excluding resources awarded to replace EFC). 5% of all full-time freshmen had no need and received non-need-based gift aid.

UNDERGRADUATE FINANCIAL AID (Fall 2005) 2,619 applied for aid; of those 83% were deemed to have need. 99% of undergraduates with need received aid; of those 11% had need fully met. ***Average percent of need met:*** 72% (excluding resources awarded to replace EFC). ***Average financial aid package:*** $14,321 (excluding resources awarded to replace EFC). 6% of all full-time undergraduates had no need and received non-need-based gift aid.

GIFT AID (NEED-BASED) ***Total amount:*** $8,555,877 (34% federal, 51% state, 15% institutional). ***Receiving aid:*** Freshmen: 48% (397); All full-time undergraduates: 49% (1,503). ***Average award:*** Freshmen: $4390; Undergraduates: $4390. ***Scholarships, grants, and awards:*** Federal Pell, FSEOG, state, private, college/university gift aid from institutional funds.

GIFT AID (NON-NEED-BASED) ***Total amount:*** $2,904,709 (59% institutional, 41% external sources). ***Receiving aid:*** Freshmen: 33% (278); Undergraduates: 29% (897). ***Average award:*** Freshmen: $2737; Undergraduates: $3361. ***Scholarships, grants, and awards by category:*** *Academic Interests/Achievement:* general academic interests/achievements. *Special Characteristics:* general special characteristics. ***Tuition waivers:*** Full or partial for employees or children of employees, senior citizens. ***ROTC:*** Army cooperative.

LOANS ***Student loans:*** $12,164,609 (68% need-based, 32% non-need-based). 66% of past graduating class borrowed through all loan programs. *Average indebtedness per student:* $23,500. ***Average need-based loan:*** Freshmen: $2996; Undergraduates: $4128. ***Parent loans:*** $6,403,326 (100% non-need-based). ***Programs:*** FFEL (Subsidized and Unsubsidized Stafford, PLUS), Perkins, college/university, private loans.

WORK-STUDY ***Federal work-study:*** Total amount: $326,899; 260 jobs averaging $1410. ***State or other work-study/employment:*** Total amount: $5610 (100% need-based). 52 part-time jobs averaging $5226.

APPLYING FOR FINANCIAL AID ***Required financial aid form:*** FAFSA. ***Financial aid deadline (priority):*** 2/15. ***Notification date:*** Continuous.

CONTACT Ms. Jane Brady, Assistant Director of Admissions and Financial Aid, Penn State Erie, The Behrend College, 5091 Station Road, Erie, PA 16563, 814-898-6162 or toll-free 866-374-3378. *Fax:* 814-898-7595. *E-mail:* jub9@psu.edu.

PENN STATE HARRISBURG

Middletown, PA

Tuition & fees (PA res): $10,948 Average undergraduate aid package: $13,849

ABOUT THE INSTITUTION State-related, coed. Awards: associate, bachelor's, master's, and doctoral degrees and post-bachelor's certificates. 33 undergraduate majors. Total enrollment: 3,799. Undergraduates: 2,259. Freshmen: 339. Federal methodology is used as a basis for awarding need-based institutional aid.

UNDERGRADUATE EXPENSES for 2006–07 ***Application fee:*** $50. ***Tuition, state resident:*** full-time $10,446; part-time $435 per credit. ***Tuition, nonresident:*** full-time $15,994; part-time $666 per credit. ***Required fees:*** full-time $502; $84 per term part-time. Full-time tuition and fees vary according to course level, location, program, and student level. Part-time tuition and fees vary according to course level, course load, location, program, and student level. ***College room and board:*** $8430; ***Room only:*** $5200. Room and board charges vary according to board plan and housing facility. ***Payment plan:*** Deferred payment.

FRESHMAN FINANCIAL AID (Fall 2005) 179 applied for aid; of those 77% were deemed to have need. 99% of freshmen with need received aid; of those 7% had need fully met. ***Average percent of need met:*** 64% (excluding resources awarded to replace EFC). ***Average financial aid package:*** $14,019 (excluding resources awarded to replace EFC). 5% of all full-time freshmen had no need and received non-need-based gift aid.

UNDERGRADUATE FINANCIAL AID (Fall 2005) 1,231 applied for aid; of those 82% were deemed to have need. 99% of undergraduates with need received aid; of those 11% had need fully met. ***Average percent of need met:*** 68% (excluding resources awarded to replace EFC). ***Average financial aid package:*** $13,849 (excluding resources awarded to replace EFC). 4% of all full-time undergraduates had no need and received non-need-based gift aid.

GIFT AID (NEED-BASED) ***Total amount:*** $4,794,822 (44% federal, 43% state, 13% institutional). ***Receiving aid:*** Freshmen: 42% (92); All full-time undergraduates: 47% (741). ***Average award:*** Freshmen: $4842; Undergraduates: $4700. ***Scholarships, grants, and awards:*** Federal Pell, FSEOG, state, private, college/university gift aid from institutional funds.

GIFT AID (NON-NEED-BASED) ***Total amount:*** $1,025,206 (60% institutional, 40% external sources). ***Receiving aid:*** Freshmen: 40% (86); Undergraduates: 28% (436). ***Average award:*** Freshmen: $6481; Undergraduates: $5930. ***Scholarships, grants, and awards by category:*** *Academic Interests/Achievement:* general academic interests/achievements. *Special Characteristics:* general special characteristics. ***Tuition waivers:*** Full or partial for employees or children of employees, senior citizens. ***ROTC:*** Army cooperative.

LOANS ***Student loans:*** $8,062,779 (58% need-based, 42% non-need-based). 66% of past graduating class borrowed through all loan programs. *Average indebtedness per student:* $23,500. ***Average need-based loan:*** Freshmen: $2796; Undergraduates: $4455. ***Parent loans:*** $1,354,203 (100% non-need-based). ***Programs:*** FFEL (Subsidized and Unsubsidized Stafford, PLUS), Perkins, college/university, private loans.

WORK-STUDY ***Federal work-study:*** Total amount: $69,888; 56 jobs averaging $1237. ***State or other work-study/employment:*** Part-time jobs available.

APPLYING FOR FINANCIAL AID ***Required financial aid form:*** FAFSA. ***Financial aid deadline (priority):*** 2/15. ***Notification date:*** Continuous.

CONTACT Ms. Carolyn Julian, Student Aid Adviser, Penn State Harrisburg, W112 Olmstead, 777 West Harrisburg Pike, Middletown, PA 17057-4898, 717-948-6307 or toll-free 800-222-2056. *Fax:* 717-948-6008. *E-mail:* czb3@psu.edu.

PENN STATE UNIVERSITY PARK

State College, PA

Tuition & fees (PA res): $12,164 Average undergraduate aid package: $15,295

ABOUT THE INSTITUTION State-related, coed. Awards: associate, bachelor's, master's, and doctoral degrees and post-bachelor's certificates. 123 undergraduate majors. Total enrollment: 42,914. Undergraduates: 36,613. Freshmen: 8,039. Federal methodology is used as a basis for awarding need-based institutional aid.

UNDERGRADUATE EXPENSES for 2006–07 ***Application fee:*** $50. ***Tuition, state resident:*** full-time $11,646; part-time $485 per credit hour. ***Tuition, nonresident:*** full-time $22,194; part-time $925 per credit hour. ***College room and board:*** $6850; ***Room only:*** $3620.

FRESHMAN FINANCIAL AID (Fall 2005) 4980 applied for aid; of those 64% were deemed to have need. 97% of freshmen with need received aid; of those 10% had need fully met. ***Average percent of need met:*** 67% (excluding resources awarded to replace EFC). ***Average financial aid package:*** $14,778 (excluding resources awarded to replace EFC). 13% of all full-time freshmen had no need and received non-need-based gift aid.

UNDERGRADUATE FINANCIAL AID (Fall 2005) 22,011 applied for aid; of those 74% were deemed to have need. 98% of undergraduates with need received aid; of those 12% had need fully met. ***Average percent of need met:*** 70% (excluding resources awarded to replace EFC). ***Average financial aid package:*** $15,295 (excluding resources awarded to replace EFC). 12% of all full-time undergraduates had no need and received non-need-based gift aid.

GIFT AID (NEED-BASED) ***Total amount:*** $66,636,124 (31% federal, 38% state, 31% institutional). ***Receiving aid:*** Freshmen: 26% (1,678); All full-time undergraduates: 29% (9,524). ***Average award:*** Freshmen: $5037; Undergraduates: $4695. ***Scholarships, grants, and awards:*** Federal Pell, FSEOG, state, private, college/university gift aid from institutional funds.

GIFT AID (NON-NEED-BASED) ***Total amount:*** $33,773,672 (65% institutional, 35% external sources). ***Receiving aid:*** Freshmen: 28% (1,840); Undergraduates: 24% (7,927). ***Average award:*** Freshmen: $3571; Undergraduates: $4341. ***Scholarships, grants, and awards by category:*** *Academic Interests/Achievement:* general academic interests/achievements. *Special Characteristics:* general special characteristics. ***ROTC:*** Army, Naval, Air Force.

LOANS ***Student loans:*** $94,897,086 (64% need-based, 36% non-need-based). 66% of past graduating class borrowed through all loan programs. *Average indebtedness per student:* $23,500. ***Average need-based loan:*** Freshmen: $2752; Undergraduates: $4259. ***Parent loans:*** $68,350,980 (100% non-need-based). ***Programs:*** FFEL (Subsidized and Unsubsidized Stafford, PLUS), Perkins, college/university, alternative loans.

WORK-STUDY ***Federal work-study:*** Total amount: $1,932,729; 1,331 jobs averaging $1443. ***State or other work-study/employment:*** Total amount: $7588 (100% need-based). 9 part-time jobs averaging $843.

ATHLETIC AWARDS Total amount: $9,478,943 (100% non-need-based).

APPLYING FOR FINANCIAL AID ***Required financial aid form:*** FAFSA. ***Financial aid deadline (priority):*** 2/15. ***Notification date:*** Continuous.

CONTACT Ms. Anna Griswold, Assistant Vice Provost for Student Aid, Penn State University Park, 311 Shields Building, University Park, PA 16802, 814-863-0507. *Fax:* 814-863-0322. *E-mail:* amg5@psu.edu.

PENNSYLVANIA COLLEGE OF ART & DESIGN

Lancaster, PA

CONTACT J. David Hershey, Registrar/Director of Financial Aid, Pennsylvania College of Art & Design, 204 North Prince Street, PO Box 59, Lancaster, PA 17608-0059, 717-396-7833 Ext. 13. *Fax:* 717-396-1339. *E-mail:* finaid@psad.edu.

PENNSYLVANIA COLLEGE OF TECHNOLOGY

Williamsport, PA

Tuition & fees (PA res): $10,620 Average undergraduate aid package: $10,831

ABOUT THE INSTITUTION State-related, coed. Awards: associate and bachelor's degrees. 108 undergraduate majors. Total enrollment: 6,569. Undergraduates: 6,569. Freshmen: 1,589. Federal methodology is used as a basis for awarding need-based institutional aid.

UNDERGRADUATE EXPENSES for 2006–07 ***Application fee:*** $50. ***Tuition, state resident:*** full-time $9030; part-time $301 per credit. ***Tuition, nonresident:*** full-time $11,760; part-time $392 per credit. Full-time tuition and fees vary according to course load and program. Part-time tuition and fees vary according to course load and program. ***College room and board:*** $7300; ***Room only:*** $4600. Room and board charges vary according to board plan, housing facility, and location. ***Payment plan:*** Deferred payment.

UNDERGRADUATE FINANCIAL AID (Fall 2005) ***Average percent of need met:*** 76% (excluding resources awarded to replace EFC). ***Average financial aid package:*** $10,831 (excluding resources awarded to replace EFC).

GIFT AID (NEED-BASED) ***Total amount:*** $21,745,441 (24% federal, 38% state, 3% institutional, 35% external sources). ***Average award:*** Undergraduates: $2479. ***Scholarships, grants, and awards:*** Federal Pell, FSEOG, state, private, college/university gift aid from institutional funds.

GIFT AID (NON-NEED-BASED) ***Tuition waivers:*** Full or partial for employees or children of employees. ***ROTC:*** Army cooperative.

LOANS ***Student loans:*** $32,512,742 (100% need-based). ***Parent loans:*** $10,757,119 (100% need-based). ***Programs:*** FFEL (Subsidized and Unsubsidized Stafford, PLUS).

WORK-STUDY ***Federal work-study:*** Total amount: $363,390; 242 jobs averaging $1502. ***State or other work-study/employment:*** Total amount: $462,657 (100% need-based). 331 part-time jobs averaging $1398.

APPLYING FOR FINANCIAL AID ***Required financial aid forms:*** FAFSA, institution's own form. ***Financial aid deadline (priority):*** 4/1. ***Notification date:*** Continuous beginning 6/1. Students must reply within 2 weeks of notification.

CONTACT Dennis L. Correll, Director of Financial Aid, Pennsylvania College of Technology, One College Avenue, DIF 108, Williamsport, PA 17701, 570-326-4766 or toll-free 800-367-9222 (in-state). *Fax:* 570-321-5552. *E-mail:* dcorrell@pct.edu.

PEPPERDINE UNIVERSITY

Malibu, CA

ABOUT THE INSTITUTION Independent religious, coed. Awards: bachelor's, master's, doctoral, and first professional degrees and post-master's certificates. 43 undergraduate majors. Total enrollment: 7,593. Undergraduates: 3,297. Freshmen: 706.

GIFT AID (NEED-BASED) ***Scholarships, grants, and awards:*** Federal Pell, FSEOG, state, private, college/university gift aid from institutional funds.

GIFT AID (NON-NEED-BASED) ***Scholarships, grants, and awards by category:*** *Academic Interests/Achievement:* biological sciences, business, communication, education, general academic interests/achievements, humanities, international studies, religion/biblical studies, social sciences. *Creative Arts/Performance:* art/fine arts, debating, journalism/publications, music, performing arts, theater/drama. *Special Characteristics:* general special characteristics.

LOANS ***Programs:*** FFEL (Subsidized and Unsubsidized Stafford, PLUS), Perkins, college/university.

WORK-STUDY ***Federal work-study:*** Total amount: $1,068,000; 785 jobs averaging $1809. ***State or other work-study/employment:*** Total amount: $628,590 (15% need-based, 85% non-need-based). 284 part-time jobs averaging $1999.

APPLYING FOR FINANCIAL AID ***Required financial aid forms:*** FAFSA, institution's own form.

CONTACT Janet Lockhart, Director of Financial Assistance, Pepperdine University, 24255 Pacific Coast Highway, Malibu, CA 90263-4301, 310-506-4301. *Fax:* 310-506-4746. *E-mail:* finaid2@pepperdine.edu.

PERU STATE COLLEGE

Peru, NE

CONTACT Diana Lind, Director of Financial Aid, Peru State College, PO Box 10, Peru, NE 68421, 402-872-2228 or toll-free 800-742-4412 (in-state). *Fax:* 402-872-2419. *E-mail:* finaid@oakmail.peru.edu.

PFEIFFER UNIVERSITY

Misenheimer, NC

Tuition & fees: $16,450 **Average undergraduate aid package: $11,351**

ABOUT THE INSTITUTION Independent United Methodist, coed. Awards: bachelor's and master's degrees. 45 undergraduate majors. Total enrollment: 2,116. Undergraduates: 1,133. Freshmen: 230. Institutional methodology is used as a basis for awarding need-based institutional aid.

UNDERGRADUATE EXPENSES for 2006–07 ***Application fee:*** $25. ***Comprehensive fee:*** $23,100 includes full-time tuition ($16,450) and room and board ($6650). ***College room only:*** $3910. Full-time tuition and fees vary according to course load. Room and board charges vary according to housing facility. ***Part-time tuition:*** $375 per credit hour. Part-time tuition and fees vary according to course load. ***Payment plan:*** Installment.

FRESHMAN FINANCIAL AID (Fall 2005) 197 applied for aid; of those 85% were deemed to have need. 100% of freshmen with need received aid; of those 22% had need fully met. ***Average percent of need met:*** 77% (excluding resources awarded to replace EFC). ***Average financial aid package:*** $12,245 (excluding resources awarded to replace EFC). 15% of all full-time freshmen had no need and received non-need-based gift aid.

UNDERGRADUATE FINANCIAL AID (Fall 2005) 918 applied for aid; of those 87% were deemed to have need. 100% of undergraduates with need received aid; of those 20% had need fully met. ***Average percent of need met:*** 76% (excluding resources awarded to replace EFC). ***Average financial aid package:*** $11,351 (excluding resources awarded to replace EFC). 12% of all full-time undergraduates had no need and received non-need-based gift aid.

GIFT AID (NEED-BASED) ***Total amount:*** $6,603,090 (19% federal, 31% state, 44% institutional, 6% external sources). ***Receiving aid:*** Freshmen: 85% (168); All full-time undergraduates: 86% (785). ***Average award:*** Freshmen: $9999; Undergraduates: $8498. ***Scholarships, grants, and awards:*** Federal Pell, FSEOG, state, private, college/university gift aid from institutional funds, United Negro College Fund.

GIFT AID (NON-NEED-BASED) ***Total amount:*** $746,926 (33% state, 56% institutional, 11% external sources). ***Receiving aid:*** Freshmen: 12% (23); Undergraduates: 9% (85). ***Average award:*** Freshmen: $10,745; Undergraduates: $10,102. ***Scholarships, grants, and awards by category:*** *Academic Interests/Achievement:* 413 awards ($2,077,508 total): general academic interests/achievements. *Creative Arts/Performance:* 42 awards ($46,845 total): music. *Special Achievements/Activities:* 13 awards ($12,500 total): leadership, religious involvement. *Special Characteristics:* 10 awards ($91,942 total): children and siblings of alumni, children of educators, children of faculty/staff. ***Tuition waivers:*** Full or partial for employees or children of employees. ***ROTC:*** Army cooperative.

LOANS ***Student loans:*** $5,586,399 (67% need-based, 33% non-need-based). 71% of past graduating class borrowed through all loan programs. *Average indebtedness per student:* $17,350. ***Average need-based loan:*** Freshmen: $2512; Undergraduates: $3462. ***Parent loans:*** $938,143 (25% need-based, 75% non-need-based). ***Programs:*** FFEL (Subsidized and Unsubsidized Stafford, PLUS), Perkins, state, college/university.

WORK-STUDY ***Federal work-study:*** Total amount: $155,564; 233 jobs averaging $668.

ATHLETIC AWARDS Total amount: $595,032 (74% need-based, 26% non-need-based).

APPLYING FOR FINANCIAL AID ***Required financial aid forms:*** FAFSA, state aid form, noncustodial (divorced/separated) parent's statement. ***Financial aid deadline (priority):*** 4/15. ***Notification date:*** Continuous beginning 3/1.

CONTACT Amy Brown, Director of Financial Aid, Pfeiffer University, PO Box 960, Misenheimer, NC 28109, 704-463-1360 Ext. 3046 or toll-free 800-338-2060. *Fax:* 704-463-1363. *E-mail:* amy.brown@pfeiffer.edu.

PHILADELPHIA BIBLICAL UNIVERSITY

Langhorne, PA

Tuition & fees: $15,875 **Average undergraduate aid package: $13,833**

ABOUT THE INSTITUTION Independent nondenominational, coed. Awards: bachelor's, master's, and first professional degrees. 11 undergraduate majors. Total enrollment: 1,389. Undergraduates: 1,058. Freshmen: 192. Federal methodology is used as a basis for awarding need-based institutional aid.

UNDERGRADUATE EXPENSES for 2006–07 ***Application fee:*** $25. ***Comprehensive fee:*** $22,425 includes full-time tuition ($15,555), mandatory fees ($320), and room and board ($6550). ***College room only:*** $3400. Full-time tuition and fees vary according to course load, location, and program. Room and board charges vary according to board plan, housing facility, and location. ***Part-time tuition:*** $469 per credit. Part-time tuition and fees vary according to course load, location, and program. ***Payment plan:*** Installment.

FRESHMAN FINANCIAL AID (Fall 2006, est.) 165 applied for aid; of those 81% were deemed to have need. 100% of freshmen with need received aid; of those 25% had need fully met. ***Average percent of need met:*** 78% (excluding resources awarded to replace EFC). ***Average financial aid package:*** $13,605 (excluding resources awarded to replace EFC). 28% of all full-time freshmen had no need and received non-need-based gift aid.

UNDERGRADUATE FINANCIAL AID (Fall 2006, est.) 715 applied for aid; of those 90% were deemed to have need. 100% of undergraduates with need received aid; of those 28% had need fully met. ***Average percent of need met:*** 78% (excluding resources awarded to replace EFC). ***Average financial aid package:*** $13,833 (excluding resources awarded to replace EFC). 20% of all full-time undergraduates had no need and received non-need-based gift aid.

GIFT AID (NEED-BASED) ***Total amount:*** $7,023,075 (15% federal, 14% state, 68% institutional, 3% external sources). ***Receiving aid:*** Freshmen: 69% (132); All full-time undergraduates: 72% (626). ***Average award:*** Freshmen: $10,585; Undergraduates: $9857. ***Scholarships, grants, and awards:*** Federal Pell, FSEOG, state, private, college/university gift aid from institutional funds.

GIFT AID (NON-NEED-BASED) ***Total amount:*** $1,711,503 (3% federal, 1% state, 93% institutional, 3% external sources). ***Receiving aid:*** Freshmen: 7% (13); Undergraduates: 6% (52). ***Average award:*** Freshmen: $9399; Undergraduates: $8789. ***Scholarships, grants, and awards by category:*** *Academic Interests/Achievement:* 458 awards ($2,850,000 total): general academic interests/achievements. *Creative Arts/Performance:* 39 awards ($60,000 total): music. *Special Achievements/Activities:* general special achievements/activities, leadership, religious involvement. *Special Characteristics:* 162 awards ($730,933 total): children and siblings of alumni, children of faculty/staff, international students, relatives of clergy, siblings of current students. ***Tuition waivers:*** Full or partial for children of alumni, employees or children of employees. ***ROTC:*** Air Force cooperative.

LOANS ***Student loans:*** $4,946,244 (68% need-based, 32% non-need-based). ***Average need-based loan:*** Freshmen: $3757; Undergraduates: $4844. ***Parent loans:*** $818,210 (39% need-based, 61% non-need-based). ***Programs:*** Federal Direct (Subsidized and Unsubsidized Stafford, PLUS).

WORK-STUDY ***Federal work-study:*** Total amount: $115,070; 111 jobs averaging $1072.

APPLYING FOR FINANCIAL AID ***Required financial aid form:*** FAFSA. ***Financial aid deadline (priority):*** 5/1. ***Notification date:*** Continuous beginning 3/15.

CONTACT William Kellaris, Director of Financial Aid, Philadelphia Biblical University, 200 Manor Avenue, Langhorne, PA 19047-2990, 215-702-4243 or toll-free 800-366-0049. *E-mail:* bkellaris@pbu.edu.

PHILADELPHIA UNIVERSITY

Philadelphia, PA

Tuition & fees: $23,818 **Average undergraduate aid package: $16,592**

ABOUT THE INSTITUTION Independent, coed. Awards: associate, bachelor's, master's, and doctoral degrees and post-bachelor's and post-master's certificates. 32 undergraduate majors. Total enrollment: 3,256. Undergraduates: 2,747. Freshmen: 709. Federal methodology is used as a basis for awarding need-based institutional aid.

UNDERGRADUATE EXPENSES for 2006–07 ***Application fee:*** $35. ***One-time required fee:*** $100. ***Comprehensive fee:*** $32,030 includes full-time tuition ($23,748), mandatory fees ($70), and room and board ($8212). ***College room only:*** $4046. Full-time tuition and fees vary according to program. Room and board charges vary according to board plan and housing facility. ***Part-time tuition:*** $767 per credit. Part-time tuition and fees vary according to class time and program. ***Payment plans:*** Installment, deferred payment.

FRESHMAN FINANCIAL AID (Fall 2006, est.) 623 applied for aid; of those 82% were deemed to have need. 100% of freshmen with need received aid; of those 12% had need fully met. ***Average percent of need met:*** 77% (excluding resources awarded to replace EFC). ***Average financial aid package:*** $17,838 (excluding resources awarded to replace EFC). 26% of all full-time freshmen had no need and received non-need-based gift aid.

UNDERGRADUATE FINANCIAL AID (Fall 2006, est.) 1,985 applied for aid; of those 85% were deemed to have need. 100% of undergraduates with need received aid; of those 9% had need fully met. ***Average percent of need met:*** 72% (excluding resources awarded to replace EFC). ***Average financial aid package:*** $16,592 (excluding resources awarded to replace EFC). 27% of all full-time undergraduates had no need and received non-need-based gift aid.

GIFT AID (NEED-BASED) ***Total amount:*** $17,430,099 (10% federal, 10% state, 78% institutional, 2% external sources). ***Receiving aid:*** Freshmen: 72% (513); All full-time undergraduates: 68% (1,689). ***Average award:*** Freshmen: $12,750; Undergraduates: $10,870. ***Scholarships, grants, and awards:*** Federal Pell, FSEOG, state, private, college/university gift aid from institutional funds, gifts scholarships from outside sources (non-endowed) for which university chooses recipients.

GIFT AID (NON-NEED-BASED) ***Total amount:*** $2,923,624 (96% institutional, 4% external sources). ***Receiving aid:*** Freshmen: 5% (34); Undergraduates: 4% (91). ***Average award:*** Freshmen: $4762; Undergraduates: $4164. ***Scholarships, grants, and awards by category:*** *Academic Interests/Achievement:* 2,165 awards ($8,871,858 total): general academic interests/achievements. ***Tuition waivers:*** Full or partial for employees or children of employees.

LOANS ***Student loans:*** $14,898,790 (79% need-based, 21% non-need-based). 74% of past graduating class borrowed through all loan programs. *Average indebtedness per student:* $27,991. ***Average need-based loan:*** Freshmen: $3152; Undergraduates: $4228. ***Parent loans:*** $8,816,759 (33% need-based, 67% non-need-based). ***Programs:*** FFEL (Subsidized and Unsubsidized Stafford, PLUS), Perkins, private loans.

WORK-STUDY ***Federal work-study:*** Total amount: $2,133,964; 992 jobs averaging $2000. ***State or other work-study/employment:*** Total amount: $323,780 (80% need-based, 20% non-need-based). Part-time jobs available.

ATHLETIC AWARDS Total amount: $1,691,982 (50% need-based, 50% non-need-based).

APPLYING FOR FINANCIAL AID ***Required financial aid form:*** FAFSA. ***Financial aid deadline:*** 4/15. ***Notification date:*** Continuous beginning 2/10. Students must reply by 5/1 or within 3 weeks of notification.

CONTACT Ms. Lisa J. Cooper, Director of Financial Aid, Philadelphia University, School House Lane and Henry Avenue, Philadelphia, PA 19144-5497, 215-951-2940. *Fax:* 215-951-2907.

PHILANDER SMITH COLLEGE

Little Rock, AR

CONTACT Director of Financial Aid, Philander Smith College, 812 West 13th Street, Little Rock, AR 72202-3799, 501-370-5270 or toll-free 800-446-6772.

PIEDMONT BAPTIST COLLEGE

Winston-Salem, NC

CONTACT Ronnie Mathis, Director of Financial Aid, Piedmont Baptist College, 716 Franklin Street, Winston-Salem, NC 27101-5197, 336-725-8344 Ext. 2322 or toll-free 800-937-5097. *Fax:* 336-725-5522. *E-mail:* mathisr@pbc.edu.

PIEDMONT COLLEGE

Demorest, GA

Tuition & fees: $16,500 **Average undergraduate aid package: $13,026**

ABOUT THE INSTITUTION Independent religious, coed. Awards: bachelor's and master's degrees and post-master's certificates. 32 undergraduate majors. Total enrollment: 2,118. Undergraduates: 949. Freshmen: 180. Both federal and institutional methodology are used as a basis for awarding need-based institutional aid.

UNDERGRADUATE EXPENSES for 2007–08 ***Comprehensive fee:*** $22,500 includes full-time tuition ($16,500) and room and board ($6000). ***Part-time tuition:*** $688 per semester hour.

FRESHMAN FINANCIAL AID (Fall 2006, est.) 146 applied for aid; of those 84% were deemed to have need. 96% of freshmen with need received aid; of those 40% had need fully met. ***Average percent of need met:*** 71% (excluding resources awarded to replace EFC). ***Average financial aid package:*** $15,249 (excluding resources awarded to replace EFC). 13% of all full-time freshmen had no need and received non-need-based gift aid.

UNDERGRADUATE FINANCIAL AID (Fall 2006, est.) 672 applied for aid; of those 84% were deemed to have need. 100% of undergraduates with need received aid; of those 20% had need fully met. ***Average percent of need met:*** 69% (excluding resources awarded to replace EFC). ***Average financial aid package:*** $13,026 (excluding resources awarded to replace EFC). 8% of all full-time undergraduates had no need and received non-need-based gift aid.

GIFT AID (NEED-BASED) ***Total amount:*** $1,954,628 (56% federal, 42% institutional, 2% external sources). ***Receiving aid:*** Freshmen: 47% (81); All full-time undergraduates: 40% (319). ***Average award:*** Freshmen: $552; Undergraduates: $4562. ***Scholarships, grants, and awards:*** Federal Pell, FSEOG, state, private, college/university gift aid from institutional funds.

GIFT AID (NON-NEED-BASED) ***Total amount:*** $5,615,012 (41% state, 55% institutional, 4% external sources). ***Receiving aid:*** Freshmen: 67% (117); Undergraduates: 69% (556). ***Average award:*** Freshmen: $8381; Undergraduates: $8097. ***Scholarships, grants, and awards by category:*** *Academic Interests/Achievement:* 586 awards ($1,597,320 total): biological sciences, education, English, foreign languages, general academic interests/achievements, health fields, humanities, mathematics, premedicine, religion/biblical studies. *Creative Arts/Performance:* 56 awards ($65,320 total): art/fine arts, music, theater/drama. *Special Achievements/Activities:* 221 awards ($814,696 total): leadership. *Special Characteristics:* 298 awards ($2,010,640 total): adult students, children of faculty/staff, international students, out-of-state students.

LOANS ***Student loans:*** $3,457,730 (58% need-based, 42% non-need-based). 68% of past graduating class borrowed through all loan programs. *Average indebtedness per student:* $15,537. ***Average need-based loan:*** Freshmen: $2455; Undergraduates: $3477. ***Parent loans:*** $852,333 (100% non-need-based). ***Programs:*** Federal Direct (Subsidized and Unsubsidized Stafford, PLUS), state.

WORK-STUDY ***Federal work-study:*** Total amount: $106,224; 106 jobs averaging $1220. ***State or other work-study/employment:*** Total amount: $343,776 (35% need-based, 65% non-need-based). 163 part-time jobs averaging $1024.

APPLYING FOR FINANCIAL AID ***Required financial aid forms:*** FAFSA, state aid form. ***Financial aid deadline (priority):*** 5/1. ***Notification date:*** Continuous. Students must reply within 2 weeks of notification.

CONTACT Mrs. Kim Lovell, Director of Financial Aid, Piedmont College, PO Box 10, Demorest, GA 30535-0010, 706-778-3000 Ext. 1191 or toll-free 800-277-7020. *Fax:* 706-776-2811. *E-mail:* klovell@piedmont.edu.

PIKEVILLE COLLEGE

Pikeville, KY

Tuition & fees: $12,750 **Average undergraduate aid package: $13,340**

ABOUT THE INSTITUTION Independent religious, coed. Awards: associate, bachelor's, and first professional degrees and post-bachelor's certificates. 25 undergraduate majors. Total enrollment: 1,098. Undergraduates: 795. Freshmen: 222. Federal methodology is used as a basis for awarding need-based institutional aid.

UNDERGRADUATE EXPENSES for 2006–07 ***Comprehensive fee:*** $17,750 includes full-time tuition ($12,750) and room and board ($5000). ***Part-time tuition:*** $531 per credit hour. ***Payment plan:*** Installment.

FRESHMAN FINANCIAL AID (Fall 2006, est.) 219 applied for aid; of those 100% were deemed to have need. 100% of freshmen with need received aid; of those 62% had need fully met. ***Average percent of need met:*** 90% (excluding resources awarded to replace EFC). ***Average financial aid package:*** $13,656 (excluding resources awarded to replace EFC).

UNDERGRADUATE FINANCIAL AID (Fall 2006, est.) 727 applied for aid; of those 100% were deemed to have need. 100% of undergraduates with need received aid; of those 67% had need fully met. ***Average percent of need met:*** 91% (excluding resources awarded to replace EFC). ***Average financial aid package:*** $13,340 (excluding resources awarded to replace EFC).

GIFT AID (NEED-BASED) ***Total amount:*** $6,791,581 (25% federal, 34% state, 37% institutional, 4% external sources). ***Receiving aid:*** Freshmen: 98% (218); All full-time undergraduates: 97% (721). ***Average award:*** Freshmen: $11,693; Undergraduates: $11,041. ***Scholarships, grants, and awards:*** Federal Pell, FSEOG, state, private, college/university gift aid from institutional funds.

GIFT AID (NON-NEED-BASED) ***Tuition waivers:*** Full or partial for employees or children of employees, senior citizens.

LOANS ***Student loans:*** $2,410,494 (100% need-based). 60% of past graduating class borrowed through all loan programs. *Average indebtedness per student:*

$11,973. ***Average need-based loan:*** Freshmen: $2292; Undergraduates: $3301. ***Parent loans:*** $206,068 (100% need-based). ***Programs:*** FFEL (Subsidized and Unsubsidized Stafford, PLUS), Perkins, college/university.

WORK-STUDY ***Federal work-study:*** Total amount: $350,666; 285 jobs averaging $1383.

ATHLETIC AWARDS Total amount: $1,296,606 (100% need-based).

APPLYING FOR FINANCIAL AID ***Required financial aid forms:*** FAFSA, institution's own form. ***Financial aid deadline (priority):*** 3/15. ***Notification date:*** Continuous beginning 1/15. Students must reply by 5/1.

CONTACT Melinda Lynch, Dean of Admissions and Student Financial Services, Pikeville College, 147 Sycamore Street, Pikeville, KY 41501, 606-218-5251 or toll-free 866-232-7700. *Fax:* 606-218-5255. *E-mail:* finaid@pc.edu.

PILLSBURY BAPTIST BIBLE COLLEGE

Owatonna, MN

CONTACT Financial Aid Administrator, Pillsbury Baptist Bible College, 315 South Grove Street, Owatonna, MN 55060-3097, 507-451-2710 or toll-free 800-747-4557. *Fax:* 507-451-6459. *E-mail:* pbbc@pillsbury.edu.

PINE MANOR COLLEGE

Chestnut Hill, MA

CONTACT Ms. Nancy Amaral, Director of Financial Aid, Pine Manor College, 400 Heath Street, Chestnut Hill, MA 02467, 617-731-7129 or toll-free 800-762-1357. *Fax:* 617-731-7102. *E-mail:* finaid@pmc.edu.

PITTSBURG STATE UNIVERSITY

Pittsburg, KS

Tuition & fees (KS res): $3790 **Average undergraduate aid package: $7107**

ABOUT THE INSTITUTION State-supported, coed. Awards: bachelor's and master's degrees (associate, specialist in education). 66 undergraduate majors. Total enrollment: 6,859. Undergraduates: 5,747. Freshmen: 864. Federal methodology is used as a basis for awarding need-based institutional aid.

UNDERGRADUATE EXPENSES for 2006–07 ***Application fee:*** $30. ***Tuition, state resident:*** full-time $3036; part-time $101 per credit hour. ***Tuition, nonresident:*** full-time $10,366; part-time $346 per credit hour. ***Required fees:*** full-time $754; $34 per credit hour. ***College room and board:*** $4844. Room and board charges vary according to board plan and housing facility. ***Payment plan:*** Installment.

FRESHMAN FINANCIAL AID (Fall 2006, est.) 735 applied for aid; of those 69% were deemed to have need. 99% of freshmen with need received aid; of those 14% had need fully met. ***Average percent of need met:*** 89% (excluding resources awarded to replace EFC). ***Average financial aid package:*** $6431 (excluding resources awarded to replace EFC). 9% of all full-time freshmen had no need and received non-need-based gift aid.

UNDERGRADUATE FINANCIAL AID (Fall 2006, est.) 3,740 applied for aid; of those 79% were deemed to have need. 98% of undergraduates with need received aid; of those 14% had need fully met. ***Average percent of need met:*** 85% (excluding resources awarded to replace EFC). ***Average financial aid package:*** $7107 (excluding resources awarded to replace EFC). 8% of all full-time undergraduates had no need and received non-need-based gift aid.

GIFT AID (NEED-BASED) ***Total amount:*** $8,988,270 (57% federal, 7% state, 15% institutional, 21% external sources). ***Receiving aid:*** Freshmen: 45% (425); All full-time undergraduates: 45% (2,315). ***Average award:*** Freshmen: $3834; Undergraduates: $3619. ***Scholarships, grants, and awards:*** Federal Pell, FSEOG, state, private, college/university gift aid from institutional funds.

GIFT AID (NON-NEED-BASED) ***Total amount:*** $1,501,824 (1% federal, 69% institutional, 30% external sources). ***Receiving aid:*** Freshmen: 15% (144); Undergraduates: 7% (355). ***Average award:*** Freshmen: $1656; Undergraduates: $2044. ***Scholarships, grants, and awards by category:*** *Academic Interests/Achievement:* 1,806 awards ($1,894,664 total): biological sciences, business, communication, computer science, education, engineering/technologies, English, foreign languages, general academic interests/achievements, health fields, home economics, mathematics, military science, physical sciences, social sciences. *Creative Arts/Performance:* 210 awards ($187,758 total): music. *Special Characteristics:* 141 awards ($64,175 total): children and siblings of alumni, general special characteristics. ***Tuition waivers:*** Full or partial for employees or children of employees. ***ROTC:*** Army.

LOANS ***Student loans:*** $12,942,421 (73% need-based, 27% non-need-based). 94% of past graduating class borrowed through all loan programs. *Average indebtedness per student:* $11,502. ***Average need-based loan:*** Freshmen: $2678; Undergraduates: $3764. ***Parent loans:*** $1,464,579 (4% need-based, 96% non-need-based). ***Programs:*** FFEL (Subsidized and Unsubsidized Stafford, PLUS), Perkins, Federal Nursing, college/university.

WORK-STUDY ***Federal work-study:*** Total amount: $430,941; 264 jobs averaging $1053. ***State or other work-study/employment:*** Total amount: $1,562,120 (27% need-based, 73% non-need-based). 1,027 part-time jobs averaging $1444.

ATHLETIC AWARDS Total amount: $953,733 (52% need-based, 48% non-need-based).

APPLYING FOR FINANCIAL AID ***Required financial aid form:*** FAFSA. ***Financial aid deadline (priority):*** 3/1. ***Notification date:*** Continuous. Students must reply within 2 weeks of notification.

CONTACT Marilyn Haverly, Director of Student Financial Assistance, Pittsburg State University, 1701 South Broadway, Pittsburg, KS 66762-5880, 620-235-4238 or toll-free 800-854-7488 Ext. 1. *Fax:* 620-235-4078. *E-mail:* mhaverly@pittstate.edu.

PITZER COLLEGE

Claremont, CA

Tuition & fees: $34,038 **Average undergraduate aid package: $30,802**

ABOUT THE INSTITUTION Independent, coed. Awards: bachelor's degrees. 53 undergraduate majors. Total enrollment: 958. Undergraduates: 958. Freshmen: 229. Both federal and institutional methodology are used as a basis for awarding need-based institutional aid.

UNDERGRADUATE EXPENSES for 2006–07 ***Application fee:*** $50. ***Comprehensive fee:*** $43,708 includes full-time tuition ($31,000), mandatory fees ($3038), and room and board ($9670). ***College room only:*** $6120. Full-time tuition and fees vary according to course load. Room and board charges vary according to board plan. ***Part-time tuition:*** $3875 per course. Part-time tuition and fees vary according to course load. ***Payment plans:*** Installment, deferred payment.

FRESHMAN FINANCIAL AID (Fall 2006, est.) 106 applied for aid; of those 78% were deemed to have need. 98% of freshmen with need received aid; of those 100% had need fully met. ***Average percent of need met:*** 100% (excluding resources awarded to replace EFC). ***Average financial aid package:*** $30,194 (excluding resources awarded to replace EFC). 7% of all full-time freshmen had no need and received non-need-based gift aid.

UNDERGRADUATE FINANCIAL AID (Fall 2006, est.) 398 applied for aid; of those 87% were deemed to have need. 99% of undergraduates with need received aid; of those 100% had need fully met. ***Average percent of need met:*** 100% (excluding resources awarded to replace EFC). ***Average financial aid package:*** $30,802 (excluding resources awarded to replace EFC). 5% of all full-time undergraduates had no need and received non-need-based gift aid.

GIFT AID (NEED-BASED) ***Total amount:*** $9,121,098 (9% federal, 10% state, 79% institutional, 2% external sources). ***Receiving aid:*** Freshmen: 34% (79); All full-time undergraduates: 36% (334). ***Average award:*** Freshmen: $26,228; Undergraduates: $25,672. ***Scholarships, grants, and awards:*** Federal Pell, FSEOG, state, private, college/university gift aid from institutional funds.

GIFT AID (NON-NEED-BASED) ***Total amount:*** $446,716 (3% state, 66% institutional, 31% external sources). ***Receiving aid:*** Freshmen: 1; Undergraduates: 4. ***Average award:*** Freshmen: $4781; Undergraduates: $6589. ***Scholarships, grants, and awards by category:*** *Academic Interests/Achievement:* 98 awards ($640,000 total): general academic interests/achievements. *Special Achievements/Activities:* community service, leadership. *Special Characteristics:* 37 awards ($180,000 total): adult students, members of minority groups. ***Tuition waivers:*** Full or partial for employees or children of employees. ***ROTC:*** Army cooperative, Air Force cooperative.

LOANS ***Student loans:*** $2,271,286 (81% need-based, 19% non-need-based). 42% of past graduating class borrowed through all loan programs. *Average indebtedness per student:* $20,701. ***Average need-based loan:*** Freshmen: $2920; Undergraduates: $4059. ***Parent loans:*** $1,051,786 (49% need-based, 51% non-need-based). ***Programs:*** FFEL (Subsidized and Unsubsidized Stafford, PLUS), Perkins, college/university.

WORK-STUDY ***Federal work-study:*** Total amount: $744,843; 298 jobs averaging $2499.

APPLYING FOR FINANCIAL AID ***Required financial aid forms:*** FAFSA, CSS Financial Aid PROFILE, state aid form, noncustodial (divorced/separated) parent's statement, business/farm supplement. ***Financial aid deadline:*** 2/1. ***Notification date:*** 4/1. Students must reply by 5/1.

CONTACT Margaret Carothers, Director of Financial Aid, Pitzer College, 1050 North Mills Avenue, Claremont, CA 91711-6101, 909-621-8208 or toll-free 800-748-9371. *Fax:* 909-607-1205. *E-mail:* margaret_carothers@pitzer.edu.

PLYMOUTH STATE UNIVERSITY

Plymouth, NH

ABOUT THE INSTITUTION State-supported, coed. Awards: bachelor's and master's degrees and post-bachelor's and post-master's certificates. 43 undergraduate majors. Total enrollment: 5,872. Undergraduates: 4,297. Freshmen: 1,021.

GIFT AID (NEED-BASED) ***Scholarships, grants, and awards:*** Federal Pell, FSEOG, state, private, college/university gift aid from institutional funds.

GIFT AID (NON-NEED-BASED) ***Scholarships, grants, and awards by category:*** *Academic Interests/Achievement:* business, communication, education, English, general academic interests/achievements, health fields, mathematics, physical sciences, social sciences. *Creative Arts/Performance:* creative writing, dance, music, theater/drama. *Special Characteristics:* children of faculty/staff, international students.

LOANS ***Programs:*** FFEL (Subsidized and Unsubsidized Stafford, PLUS), Perkins.

APPLYING FOR FINANCIAL AID ***Required financial aid form:*** FAFSA.

CONTACT June Schlabach, Director of Financial Aid, Plymouth State University, 17 High Street, MSC 18, Plymouth, NH 03264-1595, 603-535-2338 or toll-free 800-842-6900. *Fax:* 603-535-2627. *E-mail:* jlschlabach@plymouth.edu.

POINT LOMA NAZARENE UNIVERSITY

San Diego, CA

Tuition & fees: $23,730 | **Average undergraduate aid package: $16,100**

ABOUT THE INSTITUTION Independent Nazarene, coed. Awards: bachelor's and master's degrees. 55 undergraduate majors. Total enrollment: 3,437. Undergraduates: 2,383. Freshmen: 538. Federal methodology is used as a basis for awarding need-based institutional aid.

UNDERGRADUATE EXPENSES for 2007–08 ***Application fee:*** $50. ***Comprehensive fee:*** $31,200 includes full-time tuition ($23,200), mandatory fees ($530), and room and board ($7470). ***Part-time tuition:*** $900 per unit. ***Part-time fees:*** $20 per unit.

FRESHMAN FINANCIAL AID (Fall 2006, est.) 370 applied for aid; of those 75% were deemed to have need. 100% of freshmen with need received aid; of those 23% had need fully met. ***Average percent of need met:*** 65% (excluding resources awarded to replace EFC). ***Average financial aid package:*** $14,630 (excluding resources awarded to replace EFC). 22% of all full-time freshmen had no need and received non-need-based gift aid.

UNDERGRADUATE FINANCIAL AID (Fall 2006, est.) 1,572 applied for aid; of those 82% were deemed to have need. 100% of undergraduates with need received aid; of those 27% had need fully met. ***Average percent of need met:*** 71% (excluding resources awarded to replace EFC). ***Average financial aid package:*** $16,100 (excluding resources awarded to replace EFC). 28% of all full-time undergraduates had no need and received non-need-based gift aid.

GIFT AID (NON-NEED-BASED) ***Total amount:*** $3,869,530 (2% state, 75% institutional, 23% external sources). ***Receiving aid:*** Freshmen: 6% (27); Undergraduates: 6% (116). ***Average award:*** Freshmen: $9093; Undergraduates: $9732. ***Scholarships, grants, and awards by category:*** *Academic Interests/Achievement:* biological sciences, business, communication, education, engineering/technologies, general academic interests/achievements, health fields, home economics, humanities, mathematics, religion/biblical studies, social sciences. *Creative Arts/Performance:* art/fine arts, debating, music, theater/drama. ***ROTC:*** Army cooperative, Naval cooperative, Air Force cooperative.

LOANS ***Student loans:*** $9,584,975 (70% need-based, 30% non-need-based). ***Average need-based loan:*** Freshmen: $3226; Undergraduates: $5416. ***Parent loans:*** $5,878,941 (45% need-based, 55% non-need-based). ***Programs:*** FFEL (Subsidized and Unsubsidized Stafford, PLUS), Perkins, Federal Nursing, state.

WORK-STUDY ***Federal work-study:*** Total amount: $1,474,618.

ATHLETIC AWARDS Total amount: $1,575,275 (46% need-based, 54% non-need-based).

APPLYING FOR FINANCIAL AID ***Required financial aid forms:*** FAFSA, institution's own form. ***Financial aid deadline (priority):*** 3/2. ***Notification date:*** Continuous beginning 3/1.

CONTACT Student Financial Services, Point Loma Nazarene University, 3900 Lomaland Drive, San Diego, CA 92106, 619-849-2538 or toll-free 800-733-7770. *Fax:* 619-849-7017.

POINT PARK UNIVERSITY

Pittsburgh, PA

CONTACT Sandra M. Cronin, Director of Financial Aid, Point Park University, 201 Wood Street, Pittsburgh, PA 15222-1984, 412-392-3930 or toll-free 800-321-0129. *E-mail:* scronin@pointpark.edu.

POLYTECHNIC UNIVERSITY, BROOKLYN CAMPUS

Brooklyn, NY

Tuition & fees: $29,789 | **Average undergraduate aid package: $22,221**

ABOUT THE INSTITUTION Independent, coed. Awards: bachelor's, master's, and doctoral degrees and post-bachelor's certificates. 15 undergraduate majors. Total enrollment: 2,919. Undergraduates: 1,480. Freshmen: 381. Federal methodology is used as a basis for awarding need-based institutional aid.

UNDERGRADUATE EXPENSES for 2006–07 ***Application fee:*** $50. ***Comprehensive fee:*** $38,289 includes full-time tuition ($28,745), mandatory fees ($1044), and room and board ($8500). ***College room only:*** $6500. Full-time tuition and fees vary according to course load. Room and board charges vary according to housing facility. ***Part-time tuition:*** $915 per credit. ***Part-time fees:*** $382 per year. Part-time tuition and fees vary according to course load. ***Payment plans:*** Guaranteed tuition, installment, deferred payment.

FRESHMAN FINANCIAL AID (Fall 2006, est.) 379 applied for aid; of those 78% were deemed to have need. 100% of freshmen with need received aid; of those 69% had need fully met. ***Average percent of need met:*** 93% (excluding resources awarded to replace EFC). ***Average financial aid package:*** $23,011 (excluding resources awarded to replace EFC). 21% of all full-time freshmen had no need and received non-need-based gift aid.

UNDERGRADUATE FINANCIAL AID (Fall 2006, est.) 1,367 applied for aid; of those 80% were deemed to have need. 100% of undergraduates with need received aid; of those 63% had need fully met. ***Average percent of need met:*** 91% (excluding resources awarded to replace EFC). ***Average financial aid package:*** $22,221 (excluding resources awarded to replace EFC). 18% of all full-time undergraduates had no need and received non-need-based gift aid.

GIFT AID (NEED-BASED) ***Total amount:*** $7,580,846 (36% federal, 32% state, 32% institutional). ***Receiving aid:*** Freshmen: 63% (241); All full-time undergraduates: 66% (930). ***Average award:*** Freshmen: $8413; Undergraduates: $8027. ***Scholarships, grants, and awards:*** Federal Pell, FSEOG, state, private, college/university gift aid from institutional funds, United Negro College Fund.

GIFT AID (NON-NEED-BASED) ***Total amount:*** $17,462,584 (1% state, 96% institutional, 3% external sources). ***Receiving aid:*** Freshmen: 69% (262); Undergraduates: 61% (855). ***Average award:*** Freshmen: $17,066; Undergraduates: $16,342. ***Scholarships, grants, and awards by category:*** *Academic Interests/Achievement:* computer science, engineering/technologies, general academic interests/achievements. *Special Characteristics:* members of minority groups. ***Tuition waivers:*** Full or partial for employees or children of employees. ***ROTC:*** Army cooperative, Air Force cooperative.

LOANS ***Student loans:*** $6,550,666 (54% need-based, 46% non-need-based). 75% of past graduating class borrowed through all loan programs. *Average indebtedness per student:* $25,012. ***Average need-based loan:*** Freshmen: $2917; Undergraduates: $4133. ***Parent loans:*** $1,084,375 (100% non-need-based). ***Programs:*** FFEL (Subsidized and Unsubsidized Stafford, PLUS), Perkins, college/university, alternative loans.

WORK-STUDY ***Federal work-study:*** Total amount: $379,268; 211 jobs averaging $1797.

APPLYING FOR FINANCIAL AID ***Required financial aid forms:*** FAFSA, state aid form. ***Financial aid deadline:*** Continuous. ***Notification date:*** Continuous beginning 2/15. Students must reply by 5/1 or within 2 weeks of notification.

CONTACT Mr. Nicholas Simos, Director of Financial Aid Services, Polytechnic University, Brooklyn Campus, 6 Metrotech Center, Brooklyn, NY 11201-2990, 718-260-3025 or toll-free 800-POLYTECH. *Fax:* 718-260-3062.

POLYTECHNIC UNIVERSITY OF PUERTO RICO

Hato Rey, PR

CONTACT Lidia L. Cruz, Financial Aid Administrator, Polytechnic University of Puerto Rico, 377 Ponce de Leon Avenue, Hato Rey, PR 00919, 787-754-8000 Ext. 253. *Fax:* 787-766-1163.

POMONA COLLEGE

Claremont, CA

Tuition & fees: $31,865 **Average undergraduate aid package: $32,100**

ABOUT THE INSTITUTION Independent, coed. Awards: bachelor's degrees. 53 undergraduate majors. Total enrollment: 1,545. Undergraduates: 1,545. Freshmen: 379. Both federal and institutional methodology are used as a basis for awarding need-based institutional aid.

UNDERGRADUATE EXPENSES for 2006–07 ***Application fee:*** $60. ***Comprehensive fee:*** $43,156 includes full-time tuition ($31,580), mandatory fees ($285), and room and board ($11,291). Room and board charges vary according to board plan. ***Payment plan:*** Installment.

FRESHMAN FINANCIAL AID (Fall 2006, est.) 249 applied for aid; of those 76% were deemed to have need. 100% of freshmen with need received aid; of those 100% had need fully met. ***Average percent of need met:*** 100% (excluding resources awarded to replace EFC). ***Average financial aid package:*** $32,250 (excluding resources awarded to replace EFC).

UNDERGRADUATE FINANCIAL AID (Fall 2006, est.) 1,000 applied for aid; of those 81% were deemed to have need. 100% of undergraduates with need received aid; of those 100% had need fully met. ***Average percent of need met:*** 100% (excluding resources awarded to replace EFC). ***Average financial aid package:*** $32,100 (excluding resources awarded to replace EFC).

GIFT AID (NEED-BASED) ***Total amount:*** $22,544,664 (3% federal, 4% state, 90% institutional, 3% external sources). ***Receiving aid:*** Freshmen: 50% (188); All full-time undergraduates: 53% (811). ***Average award:*** Freshmen: $29,000; Undergraduates: $27,800. ***Scholarships, grants, and awards:*** Federal Pell, FSEOG, state, private, college/university gift aid from institutional funds.

GIFT AID (NON-NEED-BASED) ***Total amount:*** $936,000 (100% external sources). ***Tuition waivers:*** Full or partial for employees or children of employees. ***ROTC:*** Army cooperative, Air Force cooperative.

LOANS ***Student loans:*** $2,401,659 (94% need-based, 6% non-need-based). 55% of past graduating class borrowed through all loan programs. *Average indebtedness per student:* $11,250. ***Average need-based loan:*** Freshmen: $2000; Undergraduates: $2800. ***Parent loans:*** $2,580,990 (100% non-need-based). ***Programs:*** FFEL (Subsidized and Unsubsidized Stafford, PLUS), Perkins, college/university.

WORK-STUDY ***Federal work-study:*** Total amount: $240,000; 203 jobs averaging $1180. ***State or other work-study/employment:*** Total amount: $1,347,000 (65% need-based, 35% non-need-based). 527 part-time jobs averaging $1650.

APPLYING FOR FINANCIAL AID ***Required financial aid forms:*** FAFSA, CSS Financial Aid PROFILE, state aid form, noncustodial (divorced/separated) parent's statement, business/farm supplement. ***Financial aid deadline:*** 2/1. ***Notification date:*** 4/10. Students must reply by 5/1.

CONTACT Patricia A. Coye, Director of Financial Aid, Pomona College, 550 North College Avenue, Room 117, Claremont, CA 91711, 909-621-8205. *Fax:* 909-607-7941. *E-mail:* financial_aid@pomadm.pomona.edu.

PONTIFICAL CATHOLIC UNIVERSITY OF PUERTO RICO

Ponce, PR

ABOUT THE INSTITUTION Independent Roman Catholic, coed. Awards: associate, bachelor's, master's, doctoral, and first professional degrees (branch locations in Arecibo, Guayana, Mayagüez). 65 undergraduate majors. Total enrollment: 7,412. Undergraduates: 5,261. Freshmen: 1,115.

GIFT AID (NEED-BASED) ***Scholarships, grants, and awards:*** Federal Pell, FSEOG, state, private, college/university gift aid from institutional funds, Scholarships for Disadvantaged Students (SDS).

GIFT AID (NON-NEED-BASED) ***Scholarships, grants, and awards by category:*** *Academic Interests/Achievement:* general academic interests/achievements. *Creative Arts/Performance:* music, performing arts, theater/drama. *Special Characteristics:* children of faculty/staff, first-generation college students, spouses of current students, veterans, veterans' children.

LOANS ***Programs:*** FFEL (Subsidized and Unsubsidized Stafford, PLUS), Perkins.

WORK-STUDY ***Federal work-study:*** Total amount: $1,445,724; 1,100 jobs averaging $750. ***State or other work-study/employment:*** Total amount: $40,000 (100% non-need-based). Part-time jobs available.

APPLYING FOR FINANCIAL AID ***Required financial aid forms:*** FAFSA, institution's own form, noncustodial (divorced/separated) parent's statement.

CONTACT Mrs. Margaret Alustiza, Director of Financial Aid, Pontifical Catholic University of Puerto Rico, 2250 Las Americas Avenue, Suite 549, Ponce, PR 00717-0777, 787-841-2000 Ext. 1065 or toll-free 800-981-5040. *Fax:* 787-651-2041. *E-mail:* malustiza@pucpr.edu.

PONTIFICAL COLLEGE JOSEPHINUM

Columbus, OH

CONTACT Marky Leichtnam, Financial Aid Director, Pontifical College Josephinum, 7625 North High Street, Columbus, OH 43235-1498, 614-985-2212 or toll-free 888-252-5812. *Fax:* 614-885-2307. *E-mail:* mleichtnam@pcj.edu.

PORTLAND STATE UNIVERSITY

Portland, OR

Tuition & fees (OR res): $5600 **Average undergraduate aid package: $7762**

ABOUT THE INSTITUTION State-supported, coed. Awards: bachelor's, master's, and doctoral degrees and post-bachelor's certificates. 63 undergraduate majors. Total enrollment: 24,254. Undergraduates: 17,998. Freshmen: 1,460. Federal methodology is used as a basis for awarding need-based institutional aid.

UNDERGRADUATE EXPENSES for 2006–07 ***Application fee:*** $50. ***One-time required fee:*** $150. ***Tuition, state resident:*** full-time $4320; part-time $96 per credit. ***Tuition, nonresident:*** full-time $16,155; part-time $96 per credit. ***Required fees:*** full-time $1280; $23 per credit or $58.50 per term part-time. Full-time tuition and fees vary according to program. ***College room and board:*** $8940; ***Room only:*** $6300. Room and board charges vary according to board plan and housing facility. ***Payment plan:*** Installment.

FRESHMAN FINANCIAL AID (Fall 2006, est.) 882 applied for aid; of those 75% were deemed to have need. 99% of freshmen with need received aid; of those 11% had need fully met. ***Average percent of need met:*** 50% (excluding resources awarded to replace EFC). ***Average financial aid package:*** $6323 (excluding resources awarded to replace EFC). 2% of all full-time freshmen had no need and received non-need-based gift aid.

UNDERGRADUATE FINANCIAL AID (Fall 2006, est.) 7,224 applied for aid; of those 86% were deemed to have need. 99% of undergraduates with need received aid; of those 11% had need fully met. ***Average percent of need met:*** 55% (excluding resources awarded to replace EFC). ***Average financial aid package:*** $7762 (excluding resources awarded to replace EFC). 2% of all full-time undergraduates had no need and received non-need-based gift aid.

GIFT AID (NEED-BASED) ***Total amount:*** $24,414,281 (68% federal, 21% state, 4% institutional, 7% external sources). ***Receiving aid:*** Freshmen: 31% (399); All full-time undergraduates: 35% (3,903). ***Average award:*** Freshmen: $4920; Undergraduates: $4895. ***Scholarships, grants, and awards:*** Federal Pell, FSEOG, state, private, college/university gift aid from institutional funds, United Negro College Fund.

GIFT AID (NON-NEED-BASED) ***Total amount:*** $1,926,487 (77% institutional, 23% external sources). ***Receiving aid:*** Freshmen: 9% (114); Undergraduates: 4% (397). ***Average award:*** Freshmen: $2754; Undergraduates: $3418. ***Scholarships, grants, and awards by category:*** *Academic Interests/Achievement:* architecture, area/ethnic studies, business, computer science, education, engineering/technologies, foreign languages, general academic interests/achievements, humanities, international studies, physical sciences, social sciences. *Creative Arts/Performance:* art/fine arts, general creative arts/performance, music, theater/drama. *Special Achievements/Activities:* community service, general special achievements/activities, leadership, memberships. *Special Characteristics:* adult students, ethnic background, handicapped students, international students, members of minority groups, out-of-state students. ***Tuition waivers:*** Full or partial for minority students, employees or children of employees, senior citizens. ***ROTC:*** Army, Air Force cooperative.

LOANS ***Student loans:*** $59,018,763 (100% need-based). 78% of past graduating class borrowed through all loan programs. *Average indebtedness per student:* $17,629. ***Average need-based loan:*** Freshmen: $2759; Undergraduates: $4242. ***Parent loans:*** $3,883,124 (100% need-based). ***Programs:*** Federal Direct (Subsidized and Unsubsidized Stafford, PLUS), FFEL (Subsidized and Unsubsidized Stafford, PLUS), Perkins.

WORK-STUDY ***Federal work-study:*** Total amount: $2,696,292; 1,983 jobs averaging $1360.

ATHLETIC AWARDS Total amount: $1,910,213 (100% need-based).

APPLYING FOR FINANCIAL AID ***Required financial aid form:*** FAFSA. ***Financial aid deadline:*** Continuous. ***Notification date:*** Continuous. Students must reply within 4 weeks of notification.

CONTACT Phillip Rodgers, Director of Financial Aid, Portland State University, PO Box 751, Portland, OR 97207-0751, 800-547-8887. *Fax:* 503-725-5965. *E-mail:* askfa@pdx.edu.

POST UNIVERSITY

Waterbury, CT

CONTACT Patricia Del Buono, Associate Director of Financial Aid, Post University, 800 Country Club Road, Waterbury, CT 06723-2540, 203-596-4526 or toll-free 800-345-2562. *Fax:* 203-756-5810. *E-mail:* pdelbuono@teikyopost.edu.

POTOMAC COLLEGE

Washington, DC

CONTACT Phyllis Crews, Financial Aid Counselor, Potomac College, 4000 Chesapeake Street NW, Washington, DC 20016, 202-686-0876 or toll-free 888-686-0876. *Fax:* 202-686-0818. *E-mail:* pcrews@potomac.edu.

PRAIRIE VIEW A&M UNIVERSITY

Prairie View, TX

CONTACT Mr. A. D. James Jr., Executive Director, Student Financial Services and Scholarships, Prairie View A&M University, PO Box 2967, Prairie View, TX 77446-2967, 936-857-2423. *Fax:* 936-857-2425. *E-mail:* ad_james@pvamu.edu.

PRATT INSTITUTE

Brooklyn, NY

CONTACT Karen Price-Scott, Director of Financial Aid, Pratt Institute, 200 Willoughby Avenue, Brooklyn, NY 11205-3899, 718-636-3519 or toll-free 800-331-0834. *Fax:* 718-636-3739. *E-mail:* kpricesc@pratt.edu.

PRESBYTERIAN COLLEGE

Clinton, SC

CONTACT Ms. Judi Gillespie, Director of Financial Aid, Presbyterian College, 503 South Broad Street, Clinton, SC 29325, 864-833-8287 or toll-free 800-476-7272. *Fax:* 864-833-8481. *E-mail:* jgillesp@admin.presby.edu.

PRESCOTT COLLEGE

Prescott, AZ

ABOUT THE INSTITUTION Independent, coed. Awards: bachelor's, master's, and doctoral degrees and post-bachelor's certificates. 49 undergraduate majors. Total enrollment: 1,053. Undergraduates: 758. Freshmen: 56.

GIFT AID (NEED-BASED) ***Scholarships, grants, and awards:*** Federal Pell, FSEOG, state, private, college/university gift aid from institutional funds.

LOANS ***Programs:*** FFEL (Subsidized and Unsubsidized Stafford, PLUS), Perkins, state.

APPLYING FOR FINANCIAL AID ***Required financial aid form:*** FAFSA.

CONTACT Financial Aid Office, Prescott College, 220 Grove Avenue, Prescott, AZ 86301-2990, 928-350-1111 or toll-free 800-628-6364. *Fax:* 928-776-5225. *E-mail:* finaid@prescott.edu.

PRESENTATION COLLEGE

Aberdeen, SD

ABOUT THE INSTITUTION Independent Roman Catholic, coed. Awards: associate and bachelor's degrees. 14 undergraduate majors. Total enrollment: 786. Undergraduates: 786. Freshmen: 94.

GIFT AID (NEED-BASED) ***Scholarships, grants, and awards:*** Federal Pell, FSEOG, private, college/university gift aid from institutional funds.

GIFT AID (NON-NEED-BASED) ***Scholarships, grants, and awards by category:*** *Special Achievements/Activities:* community service, general special achievements/activities, leadership, religious involvement. *Special Characteristics:* children of faculty/staff.

LOANS ***Programs:*** FFEL (Subsidized and Unsubsidized Stafford, PLUS), Perkins, state, college/university.

WORK-STUDY ***Federal work-study:*** Total amount: $54,225; 42 jobs averaging $1500. ***State or other work-study/employment:*** Total amount: $37,634 (100% need-based). 19 part-time jobs averaging $1500.

APPLYING FOR FINANCIAL AID ***Required financial aid forms:*** FAFSA, state aid form.

CONTACT Ms. Valerie Weisser, Director of Financial Aid, Presentation College, 1500 North Main Street, Aberdeen, SD 57401-1299, 605-229-8427 or toll-free 800-437-6060. *Fax:* 605-229-8537. *E-mail:* weisserv@presentation.edu.

PRINCETON UNIVERSITY

Princeton, NJ

Tuition & fees: $33,000 **Average undergraduate aid package: $28,792**

ABOUT THE INSTITUTION Independent, coed. Awards: bachelor's, master's, and doctoral degrees. 35 undergraduate majors. Total enrollment: 7,242. Undergraduates: 4,923. Freshmen: 1,228. Both federal and institutional methodology are used as a basis for awarding need-based institutional aid.

UNDERGRADUATE EXPENSES for 2007–08 ***Application fee:*** $65. ***Comprehensive fee:*** $43,980 includes full-time tuition ($33,000) and room and board ($10,980). ***College room only:*** $5980.

FRESHMAN FINANCIAL AID (Fall 2005) 784 applied for aid; of those 86% were deemed to have need. 100% of freshmen with need received aid; of those 100% had need fully met. ***Average percent of need met:*** 100% (excluding resources awarded to replace EFC). ***Average financial aid package:*** $29,443 (excluding resources awarded to replace EFC).

UNDERGRADUATE FINANCIAL AID (Fall 2005) 2,651 applied for aid; of those 91% were deemed to have need. 100% of undergraduates with need received aid; of those 100% had need fully met. ***Average percent of need met:*** 100% (excluding resources awarded to replace EFC). ***Average financial aid package:*** $28,792 (excluding resources awarded to replace EFC).

GIFT AID (NEED-BASED) ***Total amount:*** $65,120,800 (3% federal, 1% state, 91% institutional, 5% external sources). ***Receiving aid:*** Freshmen: 55% (675); All full-time undergraduates: 51% (2,405). ***Average award:*** Freshmen: $28,209; Undergraduates: $27,077. ***Scholarships, grants, and awards:*** Federal Pell, FSEOG, state, private, college/university gift aid from institutional funds.

GIFT AID (NON-NEED-BASED) ***ROTC:*** Army, Air Force cooperative.

LOANS ***Student loans:*** 26% of past graduating class borrowed through all loan programs. *Average indebtedness per student:* $4965. ***Programs:*** FFEL (Subsidized and Unsubsidized Stafford, PLUS), Perkins, college/university.

WORK-STUDY ***Federal work-study:*** Total amount: $998,400; 763 jobs averaging $1308. ***State or other work-study/employment:*** Total amount: $1,189,100 (100% need-based). 948 part-time jobs averaging $1254.

APPLYING FOR FINANCIAL AID ***Required financial aid forms:*** FAFSA, institution's own form. ***Financial aid deadline (priority):*** 2/1. ***Notification date:*** 4/1. Students must reply by 5/1.

CONTACT Robin Moscato, Director of Financial Aid, Princeton University, Box 591, Princeton, NJ 08542, 609-258-3330. *Fax:* 609-258-0336. *E-mail:* moscato@princeton.edu.

PRINCIPIA COLLEGE

Elsah, IL

ABOUT THE INSTITUTION Independent Christian Science, coed. Awards: bachelor's degrees. 28 undergraduate majors. Total enrollment: 542. Undergraduates: 542. Freshmen: 139.

GIFT AID (NEED-BASED) ***Scholarships, grants, and awards:*** private, college/university gift aid from institutional funds.

GIFT AID (NON-NEED-BASED) ***Scholarships, grants, and awards by category:*** *Academic Interests/Achievement:* general academic interests/achievements. *Special Characteristics:* children and siblings of alumni, children of faculty/staff.

LOANS ***Programs:*** college/university.

WORK-STUDY ***State or other work-study/employment:*** Total amount: $242,599 (100% need-based). 185 part-time jobs averaging $1368.

APPLYING FOR FINANCIAL AID ***Required financial aid forms:*** institution's own form, CSS Financial Aid PROFILE, income tax form(s).

CONTACT Sarah E. McGuigan, Director of Financial Aid, Principia College, 1 Maybeck Place, Elsah, IL 62028-9799, 618-374-5186 or toll-free 800-277-4648 Ext. 2802. *Fax:* 618-374-5906. *E-mail:* finaid@prin.edu.

PROVIDENCE COLLEGE

Providence, RI

Tuition & fees: $27,345 **Average undergraduate aid package: $17,906**

ABOUT THE INSTITUTION Independent Roman Catholic, coed. Awards: associate, bachelor's, and master's degrees. 39 undergraduate majors. Total enrollment: 4,835. Undergraduates: 3,998. Freshmen: 1,027. Both federal and institutional methodology are used as a basis for awarding need-based institutional aid.

UNDERGRADUATE EXPENSES for 2006–07 ***Application fee:*** $55. ***Comprehensive fee:*** $37,110 includes full-time tuition ($26,780), mandatory fees ($565), and room and board ($9765). ***College room only:*** $5365. Room and board charges vary according to board plan and housing facility. ***Part-time tuition:*** $250 per credit. ***Payment plan:*** Installment.

FRESHMAN FINANCIAL AID (Fall 2005) 776 applied for aid; of those 74% were deemed to have need. 100% of freshmen with need received aid; of those 21% had need fully met. ***Average percent of need met:*** 88% (excluding resources awarded to replace EFC). ***Average financial aid package:*** $18,901 (excluding resources awarded to replace EFC). 8% of all full-time freshmen had no need and received non-need-based gift aid.

UNDERGRADUATE FINANCIAL AID (Fall 2005) 2,915 applied for aid; of those 81% were deemed to have need. 97% of undergraduates with need received aid; of those 15% had need fully met. ***Average percent of need met:*** 86% (excluding resources awarded to replace EFC). ***Average financial aid package:*** $17,906 (excluding resources awarded to replace EFC). 10% of all full-time undergraduates had no need and received non-need-based gift aid.

GIFT AID (NEED-BASED) ***Total amount:*** $23,751,400 (7% federal, 2% state, 87% institutional, 4% external sources). ***Receiving aid:*** Freshmen: 52% (530); All full-time undergraduates: 56% (2,222). ***Average award:*** Freshmen: $11,260; Undergraduates: $11,945. ***Scholarships, grants, and awards:*** Federal Pell, FSEOG, state, private, college/university gift aid from institutional funds, Federal Academic Competitiveness Grant Federal Smart Grant.

GIFT AID (NON-NEED-BASED) ***Total amount:*** $7,382,710 (93% institutional, 7% external sources). ***Receiving aid:*** Freshmen: 8% (83); Undergraduates: 12% (467). ***Average award:*** Freshmen: $19,500; Undergraduates: $12,000. ***Scholarships, grants, and awards by category:*** *Academic Interests/Achievement:* 400 awards ($3,750,000 total): business, general academic interests/achievements, military science, premedicine. *Creative Arts/Performance:* 5 awards ($15,000 total): theater/drama. *Special Achievements/Activities:* 20 awards ($100,000 total): community service. ***Tuition waivers:*** Full or partial for employees or children of employees, senior citizens. ***ROTC:*** Army.

LOANS ***Student loans:*** $20,082,000 (63% need-based, 37% non-need-based). 65% of past graduating class borrowed through all loan programs. ***Average need-based loan:*** Freshmen: $3625; Undergraduates: $6150. ***Parent loans:*** $9,339,700 (100% non-need-based). ***Programs:*** Federal Direct (Subsidized and Unsubsidized Stafford, PLUS), FFEL (Subsidized and Unsubsidized Stafford, PLUS), Perkins.

WORK-STUDY ***Federal work-study:*** Total amount: $800,000; 700 jobs averaging $1800. ***State or other work-study/employment:*** Total amount: $805,000 (100% non-need-based). 700 part-time jobs averaging $1800.

ATHLETIC AWARDS Total amount: $6,065,451 (16% need-based, 84% non-need-based).

APPLYING FOR FINANCIAL AID ***Required financial aid forms:*** FAFSA, CSS Financial Aid PROFILE, business/farm supplement. ***Financial aid deadline:*** 2/1. ***Notification date:*** 4/1. Students must reply by 5/1.

CONTACT Ms. Sandra J. Oliveira, Executive Director of Financial Aid, Providence College, River Avenue and Eaton Street, Providence, RI 02918, 401-865-2286 or toll-free 800-721-6444. *Fax:* 401-865-1186. *E-mail:* solivei6@providence.edu.

PURCHASE COLLEGE, STATE UNIVERSITY OF NEW YORK

Purchase, NY

Tuition & fees (NY res): $5709 **Average undergraduate aid package: $8654**

ABOUT THE INSTITUTION State-supported, coed. Awards: bachelor's and master's degrees and post-master's certificates. 29 undergraduate majors. Total enrollment: 3,901. Undergraduates: 3,754. Freshmen: 680. Federal methodology is used as a basis for awarding need-based institutional aid.

UNDERGRADUATE EXPENSES for 2006–07 ***Application fee:*** $40. ***Tuition, state resident:*** full-time $4350; part-time $181 per credit. ***Tuition, nonresident:*** full-time $10,610; part-time $442 per credit. ***Required fees:*** full-time $1359; $56.01 per credit or $5 per term part-time. ***College room and board:*** $9078; ***Room only:*** $5528.

FRESHMAN FINANCIAL AID (Fall 2006, est.) 521 applied for aid; of those 69% were deemed to have need. 100% of freshmen with need received aid; of those 11% had need fully met. ***Average percent of need met:*** 57% (excluding resources awarded to replace EFC). ***Average financial aid package:*** $7357 (excluding resources awarded to replace EFC). 24% of all full-time freshmen had no need and received non-need-based gift aid.

UNDERGRADUATE FINANCIAL AID (Fall 2006, est.) 2,197 applied for aid; of those 76% were deemed to have need. 100% of undergraduates with need received aid; of those 16% had need fully met. ***Average percent of need met:*** 63% (excluding resources awarded to replace EFC). ***Average financial aid package:*** $8654 (excluding resources awarded to replace EFC). 21% of all full-time undergraduates had no need and received non-need-based gift aid.

GIFT AID (NEED-BASED) ***Total amount:*** $6,740,092 (51% federal, 46% state, 1% institutional, 2% external sources). ***Receiving aid:*** Freshmen: 44% (296); All full-time undergraduates: 43% (1,392). ***Average award:*** Freshmen: $4694; Undergraduates: $4745. ***Scholarships, grants, and awards:*** Federal Pell, FSEOG, state, private, college/university gift aid from institutional funds.

GIFT AID (NON-NEED-BASED) ***Total amount:*** $1,158,966 (6% state, 90% institutional, 4% external sources). ***Receiving aid:*** Freshmen: 1% (4); Undergraduates: 1% (44). ***Average award:*** Freshmen: $10,423; Undergraduates: $12,164. ***Scholarships, grants, and awards by category:*** *Academic Interests/Achievement:* 235 awards ($379,353 total): area/ethnic studies, biological sciences, computer science, English, general academic interests/achievements, humanities, mathematics, social sciences. *Creative Arts/Performance:* 291 awards ($639,779 total): art/fine arts, cinema/film/broadcasting, creative writing, dance, general creative arts/performance, music, performing arts, theater/drama.

LOANS ***Student loans:*** $9,986,054 (69% need-based, 31% non-need-based). 70% of past graduating class borrowed through all loan programs. *Average indebtedness per student:* $16,058. ***Average need-based loan:*** Freshmen: $3414; Undergraduates: $4492. ***Parent loans:*** $5,600,262 (20% need-based, 80% non-need-based). ***Programs:*** FFEL (Subsidized and Unsubsidized Stafford, PLUS), Perkins.

WORK-STUDY ***Federal work-study:*** Total amount: $223,228; 212 jobs averaging $1115. ***State or other work-study/employment:*** Total amount: $390,000 (42% need-based, 58% non-need-based). 250 part-time jobs averaging $1100.

APPLYING FOR FINANCIAL AID ***Required financial aid forms:*** FAFSA, state aid form (for NY residents only). ***Financial aid deadline (priority):*** 3/15. ***Notification date:*** Continuous beginning 3/1. Students must reply within 2 weeks of notification.

CONTACT Ms. Emilie B. Devine, Associate Dean of Financial Aid, Purchase College, State University of New York, 735 Anderson Hill Road, Purchase, NY 10577-1400, 914-251-6352. *Fax:* 914-251-6356. *E-mail:* emilie.devine@purchase.edu.

PURDUE UNIVERSITY

West Lafayette, IN

Tuition & fees (IN res): $7096 **Average undergraduate aid package: $12,131**

ABOUT THE INSTITUTION State-supported, coed. Awards: associate, bachelor's, master's, doctoral, and first professional degrees. 84 undergraduate majors. Total enrollment: 39,228. Undergraduates: 31,290. Freshmen: 7,389. Federal methodology is used as a basis for awarding need-based institutional aid.

UNDERGRADUATE EXPENSES for 2006–07 ***Application fee:*** $30. ***Tuition, state resident:*** full-time $7096; part-time $254.15 per credit. ***Tuition, nonresident:*** full-time $21,266; part-time $706.25 per credit. ***College room and board:*** $7546.

FRESHMAN FINANCIAL AID (Fall 2006, est.) 5311 applied for aid; of those 61% were deemed to have need. 100% of freshmen with need received aid; of those 33% had need fully met. ***Average percent of need met:*** 92% (excluding resources awarded to replace EFC). ***Average financial aid package:*** $12,578 (excluding resources awarded to replace EFC). 18% of all full-time freshmen had no need and received non-need-based gift aid.

UNDERGRADUATE FINANCIAL AID (Fall 2006, est.) 18,363 applied for aid; of those 68% were deemed to have need. 100% of undergraduates with need received aid; of those 36% had need fully met. ***Average percent of need met:*** 92% (excluding resources awarded to replace EFC). ***Average financial aid package:*** $12,131 (excluding resources awarded to replace EFC). 13% of all full-time undergraduates had no need and received non-need-based gift aid.

GIFT AID (NEED-BASED) ***Total amount:*** $72,147,673 (36% federal, 28% state, 36% institutional). ***Receiving aid:*** Freshmen: 16% (1,166); All full-time undergraduates: 15% (4,345). ***Average award:*** Freshmen: $10,231; Undergraduates: $8893. ***Scholarships, grants, and awards:*** Federal Pell, FSEOG, state, private, college/university gift aid from institutional funds, Academic Competitiveness Grant (ACG); National SMART Grant Program.

GIFT AID (NON-NEED-BASED) ***Total amount:*** $10,780,119 (100% external sources). ***Receiving aid:*** Freshmen: 11% (791); Undergraduates: 6% (1,876). ***Average award:*** Freshmen: $15,005; Undergraduates: $12,116. ***Scholarships, grants, and awards by category:*** *Academic Interests/Achievement:* agriculture, computer science, education, engineering/technologies, general academic interests/achievements, health fields, humanities, mathematics, military science, physical sciences. *Creative Arts/Performance:* music. *Special Achievements/Activities:* leadership. *Special Characteristics:* children of faculty/staff. ***ROTC:*** Army, Naval, Air Force.

LOANS ***Student loans:*** $115,043,399 (55% need-based, 45% non-need-based). 47% of past graduating class borrowed through all loan programs. *Average indebtedness per student:* $20,102. ***Average need-based loan:*** Freshmen: $3555; Undergraduates: $4405. ***Parent loans:*** $147,765,709 (16% need-based, 84% non-need-based). ***Programs:*** FFEL (Subsidized and Unsubsidized Stafford, PLUS), Perkins, college/university.

WORK-STUDY ***Federal work-study:*** Total amount: $2,074,010; 1,176 jobs averaging $1764.

ATHLETIC AWARDS Total amount: $6,226,586 (100% non-need-based).

APPLYING FOR FINANCIAL AID ***Required financial aid form:*** FAFSA. ***Financial aid deadline (priority):*** 3/1. ***Notification date:*** 4/15.

CONTACT Division of Financial Aid, Purdue University, Schleman Hall of Student Services, Room 305, 475 Stadium Mall Drive, West Lafayette, IN 47907-2050, 765-494-5083. *Fax:* 765-496-3918. *E-mail:* bcjoerschke@purdue.edu.

PURDUE UNIVERSITY CALUMET
Hammond, IN

Tuition & fees (IN res): $5467 Average undergraduate aid package: $5926

ABOUT THE INSTITUTION State-supported, coed. Awards: associate, bachelor's, and master's degrees and post-bachelor's certificates. 62 undergraduate majors. Total enrollment: 9,303. Undergraduates: 8,387. Freshmen: 1,290. Federal methodology is used as a basis for awarding need-based institutional aid.

UNDERGRADUATE EXPENSES for 2006–07 ***Tuition, state resident:*** full-time $4961; part-time $168 per credit hour. ***Tuition, nonresident:*** full-time $11,654; part-time $391 per credit hour. ***Required fees:*** full-time $506; $18.40 per credit hour. Full-time tuition and fees vary according to program. Part-time tuition and fees vary according to course load and program. ***College room and board: Room only:*** $4150. Room and board charges vary according to housing facility. ***Payment plan:*** Deferred payment.

FRESHMAN FINANCIAL AID (Fall 2005) 870 applied for aid; of those 76% were deemed to have need. 90% of freshmen with need received aid; of those .2% had need fully met. ***Average percent of need met:*** 18% (excluding resources awarded to replace EFC). ***Average financial aid package:*** $4968 (excluding resources awarded to replace EFC). 7% of all full-time freshmen had no need and received non-need-based gift aid.

UNDERGRADUATE FINANCIAL AID (Fall 2005) 3,555 applied for aid; of those 82% were deemed to have need. 92% of undergraduates with need received aid; of those 1% had need fully met. ***Average percent of need met:*** 20% (excluding resources awarded to replace EFC). ***Average financial aid package:*** $5926 (excluding resources awarded to replace EFC). 4% of all full-time undergraduates had no need and received non-need-based gift aid.

GIFT AID (NEED-BASED) ***Total amount:*** $10,445,471 (63% federal, 37% state). ***Receiving aid:*** Freshmen: 38% (411); All full-time undergraduates: 37% (1,872). ***Average award:*** Freshmen: $4417; Undergraduates: $4567. ***Scholarships, grants, and awards:*** Federal Pell, FSEOG, state, private, college/university gift aid from institutional funds.

GIFT AID (NON-NEED-BASED) ***Total amount:*** $1,580,184 (25% state, 52% institutional, 23% external sources). ***Receiving aid:*** Freshmen: 12% (136); Undergraduates: 9% (454). ***Average award:*** Freshmen: $1440; Undergraduates: $1660. ***Scholarships, grants, and awards by category:*** *Academic Interests/Achievement:* 602 awards ($924,207 total): general academic interests/achievements. ***Tuition waivers:*** Full or partial for employees or children of employees, senior citizens.

LOANS ***Student loans:*** $18,207,125 (94% need-based, 6% non-need-based). 54% of past graduating class borrowed through all loan programs. *Average indebtedness per student:* $15,833. ***Average need-based loan:*** Freshmen: $2188; Undergraduates: $3069. ***Parent loans:*** $1,447,179 (100% non-need-based). ***Programs:*** Federal Direct (Subsidized and Unsubsidized Stafford, PLUS), Perkins.

WORK-STUDY ***Federal work-study:*** Total amount: $229,929; 83 jobs averaging $2770. ***State or other work-study/employment:*** Part-time jobs available.

ATHLETIC AWARDS Total amount: $49,525 (100% non-need-based).

APPLYING FOR FINANCIAL AID ***Required financial aid form:*** FAFSA. ***Financial aid deadline (priority):*** 3/10. ***Notification date:*** Continuous beginning 5/1. Students must reply within 2 weeks of notification.

CONTACT Ms. Chris Strug, Assistant Director of Financial Aid, Purdue University Calumet, 2200 169th Street, Hammond, IN 46323-2094, 219-989-2301 or toll-free 800-447-8738 (in-state). *Fax:* 219-989-2141. *E-mail:* finaid@calumet.purdue.edu.

PURDUE UNIVERSITY NORTH CENTRAL
Westville, IN

CONTACT Gerald Lewis, Director of Financial Aid, Purdue University North Central, 1401 South US Highway 421, Westville, IN 46391-9528, 219-785-5279 Ext. 5502 or toll-free 800-872-1231 (in-state). *Fax:* 219-785-5538.

QUEENS COLLEGE OF THE CITY UNIVERSITY OF NEW YORK
Flushing, NY

CONTACT Office of Financial Aid Services, Queens College of the City University of New York, 65-30 Kissena Boulevard, Flushing, NY 11367-1597, 718-997-5100.

QUEENS UNIVERSITY OF CHARLOTTE
Charlotte, NC

CONTACT Lauren H. Mack, Director of Financial Aid, Queens University of Charlotte, 1900 Selwyn Avenue, Charlotte, NC 28274-0002, 704-337-2230 or toll-free 800-849-0202. *Fax:* 704-337-2416. *E-mail:* mackl@queens.edu.

QUINCY UNIVERSITY
Quincy, IL

ABOUT THE INSTITUTION Independent Roman Catholic, coed. Awards: associate, bachelor's, and master's degrees. 40 undergraduate majors. Total enrollment: 1,250. Undergraduates: 1,005. Freshmen: 162.

GIFT AID (NEED-BASED) ***Scholarships, grants, and awards:*** Federal Pell, FSEOG, state, private, college/university gift aid from institutional funds.

GIFT AID (NON-NEED-BASED) ***Scholarships, grants, and awards by category:*** *Academic Interests/Achievement:* biological sciences, business, communication, computer science, education, English, general academic interests/achievements, health fields, international studies, mathematics, premedicine, religion/biblical studies, social sciences. *Creative Arts/Performance:* art/fine arts, cinema/film/broadcasting, music. *Special Achievements/Activities:* community service, leadership. *Special Characteristics:* children of faculty/staff.

LOANS *Programs:* FFEL (Subsidized and Unsubsidized Stafford, PLUS), Perkins.

APPLYING FOR FINANCIAL AID *Required financial aid form:* FAFSA.

CONTACT Shann Doerr, Director of Financial Aid, Quincy University, 1800 College Avenue, Quincy, IL 62301-2699, 217-228-5260 or toll-free 800-688-4295. *Fax:* 217-228-5635. *E-mail:* doerrsh@quincy.edu.

QUINNIPIAC UNIVERSITY

Hamden, CT

Tuition & fees: $28,720 **Average undergraduate aid package: $15,338**

ABOUT THE INSTITUTION Independent, coed. Awards: bachelor's, master's, doctoral, and first professional degrees and post-bachelor's certificates. 60 undergraduate majors. Total enrollment: 7,341. Undergraduates: 5,821. Freshmen: 1,426. Federal methodology is used as a basis for awarding need-based institutional aid.

UNDERGRADUATE EXPENSES for 2007–08 *Application fee:* $45. ***Comprehensive fee:*** $39,920 includes full-time tuition ($27,600), mandatory fees ($1120), and room and board ($11,200). ***Part-time tuition:*** $640 per credit. ***Part-time fees:*** $30 per credit.

FRESHMAN FINANCIAL AID (Fall 2006, est.) 1106 applied for aid; of those 76% were deemed to have need. 100% of freshmen with need received aid; of those 14% had need fully met. ***Average percent of need met:*** 66% (excluding resources awarded to replace EFC). ***Average financial aid package:*** $15,201 (excluding resources awarded to replace EFC). 12% of all full-time freshmen had no need and received non-need-based gift aid.

UNDERGRADUATE FINANCIAL AID (Fall 2006, est.) 3,814 applied for aid; of those 82% were deemed to have need. 99% of undergraduates with need received aid; of those 14% had need fully met. ***Average percent of need met:*** 65% (excluding resources awarded to replace EFC). ***Average financial aid package:*** $15,338 (excluding resources awarded to replace EFC). 11% of all full-time undergraduates had no need and received non-need-based gift aid.

GIFT AID (NEED-BASED) *Total amount:* $25,217,004 (8% federal, 10% state, 77% institutional, 5% external sources). ***Receiving aid:*** Freshmen: 59% (834); All full-time undergraduates: 56% (3,053). ***Average award:*** Freshmen: $11,233; Undergraduates: $10,400. ***Scholarships, grants, and awards:*** Federal Pell, FSEOG, state, private, college/university gift aid from institutional funds.

GIFT AID (NON-NEED-BASED) *Total amount:* $10,786,474 (98% institutional, 2% external sources). ***Receiving aid:*** Freshmen: 23% (331); Undergraduates: 20% (1,103). ***Average award:*** Freshmen: $7853; Undergraduates: $7181. ***Scholarships, grants, and awards by category:*** *Academic Interests/Achievement:* 1,223 awards ($8,221,658 total): general academic interests/achievements. *Special Achievements/Activities:* 9 awards ($74,000 total): leadership. *Special Characteristics:* 544 awards ($2,480,978 total): children of faculty/staff, international students, members of minority groups, siblings of current students. ***ROTC:*** Army cooperative, Air Force cooperative.

LOANS *Student loans:* $26,238,760 (76% need-based, 24% non-need-based). 68% of past graduating class borrowed through all loan programs. *Average indebtedness per student:* $31,070. ***Average need-based loan:*** Freshmen: $2984; Undergraduates: $4210. ***Parent loans:*** $12,703,526 (100% non-need-based). ***Programs:*** FFEL (Subsidized and Unsubsidized Stafford, PLUS), Perkins, Federal Nursing.

WORK-STUDY *Federal work-study:* Total amount: $3,038,883; 1,482 jobs averaging $1963. ***State or other work-study/employment:*** Total amount: $44,225 (100% need-based). 34 part-time jobs averaging $1519.

ATHLETIC AWARDS Total amount: $5,647,561 (100% non-need-based).

APPLYING FOR FINANCIAL AID *Required financial aid form:* FAFSA. ***Financial aid deadline (priority):*** 3/1. ***Notification date:*** Continuous beginning 3/1. Students must reply by 5/1 or within 2 weeks of notification.

CONTACT Mr. Dominic Yoia, Senior Director of Financial Aid, Quinnipiac University, 275 Mount Carmel Avenue, Hamden, CT 06518, 203-582-5224 or toll-free 800-462-1944 (out-of-state). *Fax:* 203-582-5238. *E-mail:* finaid@quinnipiac.edu.

RABBI JACOB JOSEPH SCHOOL

Edison, NJ

CONTACT Financial Aid Office, Rabbi Jacob Joseph School, One Plainfield Ave, Edison, NJ 08817, 908-985-6533.

RABBINICAL ACADEMY MESIVTA RABBI CHAIM BERLIN

Brooklyn, NY

CONTACT Office of Financial Aid, Rabbinical Academy Mesivta Rabbi Chaim Berlin, 1605 Coney Island Avenue, Brooklyn, NY 11230-4715, 718-377-0777.

RABBINICAL COLLEGE BETH SHRAGA

Monsey, NY

CONTACT Financial Aid Office, Rabbinical College Beth Shraga, 28 Saddle River Road, Monsey, NY 10952-3035, 914-356-1980.

RABBINICAL COLLEGE BOBOVER YESHIVA B'NEI ZION

Brooklyn, NY

CONTACT Financial Aid Office, Rabbinical College Bobover Yeshiva B'nei Zion, 1577 48th Street, Brooklyn, NY 11219, 718-438-2018.

RABBINICAL COLLEGE CH'SAN SOFER

Brooklyn, NY

CONTACT Financial Aid Office, Rabbinical College Ch'san Sofer, 1876 50th Street, Brooklyn, NY 11204, 718-236-1171.

RABBINICAL COLLEGE OF AMERICA

Morristown, NJ

CONTACT Financial Aid Office, Rabbinical College of America, 226 Sussex Avenue, Morristown, NJ 07960, 973-267-9404. *Fax:* 973-267-5208.

RABBINICAL COLLEGE OF LONG ISLAND

Long Beach, NY

CONTACT Rabbi Cone, Financial Aid Administrator, Rabbinical College of Long Island, 201 Magnolia Boulevard, Long Beach, NY 11561-3305, 516-431-7414.

RABBINICAL COLLEGE OF OHR SHIMON YISROEL

Brooklyn, NY

CONTACT Financial Aid Office, Rabbinical College of Ohr Shimon Yisroel, 215-217 Hewes Street, Brooklyn, NY 11211, 718-855-4092.

RABBINICAL COLLEGE OF TELSHE

Wickliffe, OH

CONTACT Financial Aid Office, Rabbinical College of Telshe, 28400 Euclid Avenue, Wickliffe, OH 44092-2523, 216-943-5300.

RABBINICAL SEMINARY ADAS YEREIM

Brooklyn, NY

CONTACT Mr. Israel Weingarten, Financial Aid Administrator, Rabbinical Seminary Adas Yereim, 185 Wilson Street, Brooklyn, NY 11211-7206, 718-388-1751.

RABBINICAL SEMINARY M'KOR CHAIM

Brooklyn, NY

CONTACT Financial Aid Office, Rabbinical Seminary M'kor Chaim, 1571 55th Street, Brooklyn, NY 11219, 718-851-0183.

RABBINICAL SEMINARY OF AMERICA

Flushing, NY

CONTACT Ms. Leah Eisenstein, Director of Financial Aid, Rabbinical Seminary of America, 92-15 69th Avenue, Forest Hills, NY 11375, 718-268-4700. *Fax:* 718-268-4684.

RADFORD UNIVERSITY

Radford, VA

Tuition & fees (VA res): $5746 Average undergraduate aid package: $7768

ABOUT THE INSTITUTION State-supported, coed. Awards: bachelor's and master's degrees and post-master's certificates. 42 undergraduate majors. Total enrollment: 9,220. Undergraduates: 8,155. Freshmen: 1,733. Federal methodology is used as a basis for awarding need-based institutional aid.

UNDERGRADUATE EXPENSES for 2006–07 ***Application fee:*** $50. ***Tuition, state resident:*** full-time $3728; part-time $154.92 per credit hour. ***Tuition, nonresident:*** full-time $11,476; part-time $477.92 per credit hour. ***Required fees:*** full-time $2018; $84.08 per credit hour. ***College room and board:*** $6218. Room and board charges vary according to board plan and housing facility. ***Payment plan:*** Installment.

FRESHMAN FINANCIAL AID (Fall 2006, est.) 1128 applied for aid; of those 55% were deemed to have need. 95% of freshmen with need received aid; of those 32% had need fully met. ***Average percent of need met:*** 76% (excluding resources awarded to replace EFC). ***Average financial aid package:*** $7407 (excluding resources awarded to replace EFC). 4% of all full-time freshmen had no need and received non-need-based gift aid.

UNDERGRADUATE FINANCIAL AID (Fall 2006, est.) 4,534 applied for aid; of those 67% were deemed to have need. 95% of undergraduates with need received aid; of those 47% had need fully met. ***Average percent of need met:*** 77% (excluding resources awarded to replace EFC). ***Average financial aid package:*** $7768 (excluding resources awarded to replace EFC). 3% of all full-time undergraduates had no need and received non-need-based gift aid.

GIFT AID (NEED-BASED) ***Total amount:*** $11,772,755 (37% federal, 46% state, 9% institutional, 8% external sources). ***Receiving aid:*** Freshmen: 20% (377); All full-time undergraduates: 23% (1,858). ***Average award:*** Freshmen: $5804; Undergraduates: $5187. ***Scholarships, grants, and awards:*** Federal Pell, FSEOG, state, private, college/university gift aid from institutional funds.

GIFT AID (NON-NEED-BASED) ***Receiving aid:*** Freshmen: 11% (212); Undergraduates: 7% (602). ***Average award:*** Freshmen: $3786; Undergraduates: $3244. ***Scholarships, grants, and awards by category:*** *Academic Interests/Achievement:* 337 awards ($700,785 total): area/ethnic studies, biological sciences, business, communication, computer science, education, English, general academic interests/achievements, health fields, humanities, library science, mathematics, military science, physical sciences, premedicine, social sciences. *Creative Arts/Performance:* 41 awards ($61,959 total): applied art and design, art/fine arts, cinema/film/broadcasting, dance, music, theater/drama. *Special Achievements/Activities:* 1 award ($550 total): leadership. *Special Characteristics:* 2 awards ($6085 total): children of faculty/staff. ***Tuition waivers:*** Full or partial for employees or children of employees, senior citizens. ***ROTC:*** Army.

LOANS ***Student loans:*** $9,509,547 (100% need-based). *Average indebtedness per student:* $14,729. ***Average need-based loan:*** Freshmen: $2696; Undergraduates: $3764. ***Parent loans:*** $1,982,627 (100% need-based). ***Programs:*** FFEL (Subsidized and Unsubsidized Stafford, PLUS), Perkins, Federal Nursing, state, college/university.

WORK-STUDY ***Federal work-study:*** Total amount: $601,224; 461 jobs averaging $1258. ***State or other work-study/employment:*** Total amount: $585,030 (100% need-based). 720 part-time jobs averaging $2241.

ATHLETIC AWARDS Total amount: $1,593,784 (31% need-based, 69% non-need-based).

APPLYING FOR FINANCIAL AID ***Required financial aid form:*** FAFSA. ***Financial aid deadline (priority):*** 3/1. ***Notification date:*** 4/15. Students must reply within 2 weeks of notification.

CONTACT Mrs. Barbara Porter, Director of Financial Aid, Radford University, PO Box 6905, Radford, VA 24142, 540-831-5408 or toll-free 800-890-4265. *Fax:* 540-831-5138. *E-mail:* bporter@radford.edu.

RAMAPO COLLEGE OF NEW JERSEY

Mahwah, NJ

Tuition & fees (NJ res): $9496 Average undergraduate aid package: $9965

ABOUT THE INSTITUTION State-supported, coed. Awards: bachelor's and master's degrees. 39 undergraduate majors. Total enrollment: 5,499. Undergraduates: 5,188. Freshmen: 814. Federal methodology is used as a basis for awarding need-based institutional aid.

UNDERGRADUATE EXPENSES for 2006–07 ***Application fee:*** $55. ***Tuition, state resident:*** full-time $6579; part-time $205.60 per credit. ***Tuition, nonresident:*** full-time $11,890; part-time $371.55 per credit. ***Required fees:*** full-time $2917; $91.15 per credit. ***College room and board:*** $9924; ***Room only:*** $7220. Room and board charges vary according to board plan and housing facility. ***Payment plan:*** Installment.

FRESHMAN FINANCIAL AID (Fall 2006, est.) 638 applied for aid; of those 68% were deemed to have need. 97% of freshmen with need received aid; of those 17% had need fully met. ***Average percent of need met:*** 78% (excluding resources awarded to replace EFC). ***Average financial aid package:*** $10,943 (excluding resources awarded to replace EFC). 14% of all full-time freshmen had no need and received non-need-based gift aid.

UNDERGRADUATE FINANCIAL AID (Fall 2006, est.) 2,828 applied for aid; of those 76% were deemed to have need. 97% of undergraduates with need received aid; of those 5% had need fully met. ***Average percent of need met:*** 72% (excluding resources awarded to replace EFC). ***Average financial aid package:*** $9965 (excluding resources awarded to replace EFC). 12% of all full-time undergraduates had no need and received non-need-based gift aid.

GIFT AID (NEED-BASED) ***Total amount:*** $7,670,908 (41% federal, 50% state, 9% institutional). ***Receiving aid:*** Freshmen: 24% (198); All full-time undergraduates: 24% (1,061). ***Average award:*** Freshmen: $10,362; Undergraduates: $7349. ***Scholarships, grants, and awards:*** Federal Pell, FSEOG, state, private, college/university gift aid from institutional funds.

GIFT AID (NON-NEED-BASED) ***Total amount:*** $6,118,755 (12% state, 78% institutional, 10% external sources). ***Receiving aid:*** Freshmen: 19% (154); Undergraduates: 14% (604). ***Average award:*** Freshmen: $10,849; Undergraduates: $9295. ***Scholarships, grants, and awards by category:*** *Academic Interests/Achievement:* 643 awards ($5,281,331 total): general academic interests/achievements. *Special Characteristics:* 76 awards ($1,199,235 total): international students, out-of-state students. ***Tuition waivers:*** Full or partial for employees or children of employees, senior citizens. ***ROTC:*** Air Force cooperative.

LOANS ***Student loans:*** $19,320,472 (38% need-based, 62% non-need-based). 37% of past graduating class borrowed through all loan programs. *Average indebtedness per student:* $15,937. ***Average need-based loan:*** Freshmen: $2612; Undergraduates: $3746. ***Parent loans:*** $9,415,999 (100% non-need-based). ***Programs:*** Federal Direct (Subsidized and Unsubsidized Stafford, PLUS), Perkins, state.

WORK-STUDY ***Federal work-study:*** Total amount: $252,951; 137 jobs averaging $1846. ***State or other work-study/employment:*** Total amount: $1,225,087 (100% non-need-based). 655 part-time jobs averaging $1870.

APPLYING FOR FINANCIAL AID ***Required financial aid form:*** FAFSA. ***Financial aid deadline (priority):*** 3/1. ***Notification date:*** Continuous beginning 4/1. Students must reply by 5/1 or within 2 weeks of notification.

CONTACT Bernice Mulch, Assistant Director of Financial Aid, Ramapo College of New Jersey, 505 Ramapo Valley Road, Mahwah, NJ 07430-1680, 201-684-7252 or toll-free 800-9RAMAPO (in-state). *Fax:* 201-684-7085. *E-mail:* finaid@ramapo.edu.

RANDOLPH COLLEGE

Lynchburg, VA

Tuition & fees: $24,410 Average undergraduate aid package: $23,411

ABOUT THE INSTITUTION Independent Methodist, coed. Awards: bachelor's degrees. 37 undergraduate majors. Total enrollment: 715. Undergraduates: 706. Freshmen: 187. Federal methodology is used as a basis for awarding need-based institutional aid.

UNDERGRADUATE EXPENSES for 2006–07 ***Application fee:*** $35. ***Comprehensive fee:*** $33,210 includes full-time tuition ($23,900), mandatory fees ($510), and room and board ($8800). ***Part-time tuition:*** $995 per semester hour. ***Part-time fees:*** $52.50 per term. Part-time tuition and fees vary according to course load. ***Payment plan:*** Installment.

FRESHMAN FINANCIAL AID (Fall 2006, est.) 153 applied for aid; of those 84% were deemed to have need. 100% of freshmen with need received aid; of those 46% had need fully met. ***Average percent of need met:*** 92% (excluding resources awarded to replace EFC). ***Average financial aid package:*** $23,152 (excluding resources awarded to replace EFC). 32% of all full-time freshmen had no need and received non-need-based gift aid.

UNDERGRADUATE FINANCIAL AID (Fall 2006, est.) 483 applied for aid; of those 88% were deemed to have need. 100% of undergraduates with need received aid; of those 34% had need fully met. ***Average percent of need met:*** 89% (excluding resources awarded to replace EFC). ***Average financial aid package:*** $23,411 (excluding resources awarded to replace EFC). 34% of all full-time undergraduates had no need and received non-need-based gift aid.

GIFT AID (NEED-BASED) ***Total amount:*** $7,425,678 (8% federal, 6% state, 83% institutional, 3% external sources). ***Receiving aid:*** Freshmen: 68% (128); All full-time undergraduates: 65% (423). ***Average award:*** Freshmen: $18,189; Undergraduates: $17,618. ***Scholarships, grants, and awards:*** Federal Pell, FSEOG, state, private, college/university gift aid from institutional funds.

GIFT AID (NON-NEED-BASED) ***Total amount:*** $3,719,832 (5% state, 93% institutional, 2% external sources). ***Receiving aid:*** Freshmen: 11% (21); Undergraduates: 8% (50). ***Average award:*** Freshmen: $16,051; Undergraduates: $14,696. ***Scholarships, grants, and awards by category:*** *Academic Interests/Achievement:* 473 awards ($5,248,826 total): biological sciences, education, English, general academic interests/achievements, mathematics, physical sciences, premedicine, social sciences. *Creative Arts/Performance:* 10 awards ($23,000 total): art/fine arts, creative writing, music, theater/drama. *Special Achievements/Activities:* 132 awards ($1,173,817 total): community service, general special achievements/activities, leadership, religious involvement. *Special Characteristics:* 163 awards ($1,347,154 total): adult students, children of faculty/staff, international students, local/state students, relatives of clergy, religious affiliation, twins. ***Tuition waivers:*** Full or partial for employees or children of employees, adult students.

LOANS ***Student loans:*** $3,927,357 (64% need-based, 36% non-need-based). 71% of past graduating class borrowed through all loan programs. *Average indebtedness per student:* $26,650. ***Average need-based loan:*** Freshmen: $4974; Undergraduates: $5684. ***Parent loans:*** $781,124 (20% need-based, 80% non-need-based). ***Programs:*** FFEL (Subsidized and Unsubsidized Stafford, PLUS), Perkins.

WORK-STUDY ***Federal work-study:*** Total amount: $146,141; 78 jobs averaging $1860. ***State or other work-study/employment:*** Total amount: $458,410 (61% need-based, 39% non-need-based). 290 part-time jobs averaging $1070.

APPLYING FOR FINANCIAL AID ***Required financial aid forms:*** FAFSA, state aid form. ***Financial aid deadline (priority):*** 3/1. ***Notification date:*** Continuous beginning 3/1. Students must reply by 5/1 or within 2 weeks of notification.

CONTACT Katherine E. Cooper, Director of Financial Planning and Assistance, Randolph College, 2500 Rivermont Avenue, Lynchburg, VA 24503-1526, 434-947-8128 or toll-free 800-745-7692. *Fax:* 434-947-8996. *E-mail:* kcooper@randolphcollege.edu.

RANDOLPH-MACON COLLEGE

Ashland, VA

ABOUT THE INSTITUTION Independent United Methodist, coed. Awards: bachelor's degrees. 30 undergraduate majors. Total enrollment: 1,146. Undergraduates: 1,146. Freshmen: 398.

GIFT AID (NEED-BASED) ***Scholarships, grants, and awards:*** Federal Pell, FSEOG, state, private, college/university gift aid from institutional funds.

GIFT AID (NON-NEED-BASED) ***Scholarships, grants, and awards by category:*** *Academic Interests/Achievement:* general academic interests/achievements, premedicine. *Special Achievements/Activities:* general special achievements/activities. *Special Characteristics:* children and siblings of alumni, children of faculty/staff, relatives of clergy, siblings of current students.

LOANS ***Programs:*** FFEL (Subsidized and Unsubsidized Stafford, PLUS), Perkins, college/university.

WORK-STUDY ***Federal work-study:*** Total amount: $351,306; 194 jobs averaging $1811.

APPLYING FOR FINANCIAL AID ***Required financial aid forms:*** FAFSA, state aid form.

CONTACT Ms. Mary Neal, Director of Financial Aid, Randolph-Macon College, PO Box 5005, Ashland, VA 23005-5505, 804-752-7259 or toll-free 800-888-1762. *Fax:* 804-752-3719. *E-mail:* mneal@rmc.edu.

REED COLLEGE

Portland, OR

Tuition & fees: $34,530 **Average undergraduate aid package: $27,257**

ABOUT THE INSTITUTION Independent, coed. Awards: bachelor's and master's degrees. 29 undergraduate majors. Total enrollment: 1,436. Undergraduates: 1,407. Freshmen: 376. Both federal and institutional methodology are used as a basis for awarding need-based institutional aid.

UNDERGRADUATE EXPENSES for 2006–07 ***Application fee:*** $40. ***Comprehensive fee:*** $43,530 includes full-time tuition ($34,300), mandatory fees ($230), and room and board ($9000). ***College room only:*** $4660. Room and board charges vary according to board plan and housing facility. ***Part-time tuition:*** $5800 per course. Part-time tuition and fees vary according to course load. ***Payment plan:*** Installment.

FRESHMAN FINANCIAL AID (Fall 2006, est.) 224 applied for aid; of those 79% were deemed to have need. 93% of freshmen with need received aid; of those 96% had need fully met. ***Average percent of need met:*** 100% (excluding resources awarded to replace EFC). ***Average financial aid package:*** $28,205 (excluding resources awarded to replace EFC).

UNDERGRADUATE FINANCIAL AID (Fall 2006, est.) 773 applied for aid; of those 90% were deemed to have need. 95% of undergraduates with need received aid; of those 98% had need fully met. ***Average percent of need met:*** 100% (excluding resources awarded to replace EFC). ***Average financial aid package:*** $27,257 (excluding resources awarded to replace EFC).

GIFT AID (NEED-BASED) ***Total amount:*** $15,154,318 (6% federal, 1% state, 91% institutional, 2% external sources). ***Receiving aid:*** Freshmen: 43% (153); All full-time undergraduates: 49% (620). ***Average award:*** Freshmen: $27,387; Undergraduates: $24,493. ***Scholarships, grants, and awards:*** Federal Pell, FSEOG, state, private, college/university gift aid from institutional funds.

GIFT AID (NON-NEED-BASED) ***Total amount:*** $51,085 (100% external sources). ***Tuition waivers:*** Full or partial for employees or children of employees.

LOANS ***Student loans:*** $3,086,967 (89% need-based, 11% non-need-based). 61% of past graduating class borrowed through all loan programs. *Average indebtedness per student:* $17,175. ***Average need-based loan:*** Freshmen: $2684; Undergraduates: $4280. ***Parent loans:*** $2,200,284 (100% non-need-based). ***Programs:*** FFEL (Subsidized and Unsubsidized Stafford, PLUS), Perkins.

WORK-STUDY ***Federal work-study:*** Total amount: $285,850; 422 jobs averaging $700. ***State or other work-study/employment:*** Total amount: $25,900 (100% need-based). 32 part-time jobs averaging $678.

APPLYING FOR FINANCIAL AID ***Required financial aid forms:*** FAFSA, institution's own form, CSS Financial Aid PROFILE, noncustodial (divorced/separated) parent's statement. ***Financial aid deadline:*** 2/1 (priority: 1/15). ***Notification date:*** 4/1. Students must reply by 5/1 or within 2 weeks of notification.

CONTACT Leslie Limper, Financial Aid Director, Reed College, 3203 Southeast Woodstock Boulevard, Portland, OR 97202-8199, 503-777-7223 or toll-free 800-547-4750 (out-of-state). *Fax:* 503-788-6682. *E-mail:* financial.aid@reed.edu.

REGENT UNIVERSITY

Virginia Beach, VA

CONTACT Financial Aid Office, Regent University, 1000 Regent University Drive, Virginia Beach, VA 23464-9800, 757-226-4000 or toll-free 800-373-5504.

REGIONS UNIVERSITY

Montgomery, AL

CONTACT Rosemary Kennington, Financial Aid Director, Regions University, 1200 Taylor Road, Montgomery, AL 36117, 334-387-3877 Ext. 7527 or toll-free 800-351-4040 Ext. 213. *Fax:* 334-387-3878. *E-mail:* financialaid@southernchristian.edu.

REGIS COLLEGE
Weston, MA

Tuition & fees: $23,680 **Average undergraduate aid package: $21,149**

ABOUT THE INSTITUTION Independent Roman Catholic, coed. Awards: associate, bachelor's, and master's degrees and post-master's certificates. 23 undergraduate majors. Total enrollment: 1,314. Undergraduates: 859. Freshmen: 171. Both federal and institutional methodology are used as a basis for awarding need-based institutional aid.

UNDERGRADUATE EXPENSES for 2006–07 ***Application fee:*** $50. ***Comprehensive fee:*** $34,260 includes full-time tuition ($23,680) and room and board ($10,580). ***College room only:*** $5370. Full-time tuition and fees vary according to course load. ***Part-time tuition:*** $585 per credit. Part-time tuition and fees vary according to class time. ***Payment plan:*** Installment.

FRESHMAN FINANCIAL AID (Fall 2006, est.) 159 applied for aid; of those 91% were deemed to have need. 100% of freshmen with need received aid; of those 16% had need fully met. ***Average percent of need met:*** 59% (excluding resources awarded to replace EFC). ***Average financial aid package:*** $22,545 (excluding resources awarded to replace EFC). 11% of all full-time freshmen had no need and received non-need-based gift aid.

UNDERGRADUATE FINANCIAL AID (Fall 2006, est.) 579 applied for aid; of those 93% were deemed to have need. 99% of undergraduates with need received aid; of those 13% had need fully met. ***Average percent of need met:*** 60% (excluding resources awarded to replace EFC). ***Average financial aid package:*** $21,149 (excluding resources awarded to replace EFC). 11% of all full-time undergraduates had no need and received non-need-based gift aid.

GIFT AID (NEED-BASED) ***Total amount:*** $8,489,487 (12% federal, 6% state, 80% institutional, 2% external sources). ***Receiving aid:*** Freshmen: 76% (130); All full-time undergraduates: 73% (484). ***Average award:*** Freshmen: $11,779; Undergraduates: $11,022. ***Scholarships, grants, and awards:*** Federal Pell, FSEOG, state, private, college/university gift aid from institutional funds.

GIFT AID (NON-NEED-BASED) ***Receiving aid:*** Freshmen: 53% (91); Undergraduates: 42% (280). ***Average award:*** Freshmen: $8526; Undergraduates: $8314. ***Scholarships, grants, and awards by category:*** *Academic Interests/Achievement:* 211 awards ($2,237,000 total): general academic interests/achievements. *Special Achievements/Activities:* 121 awards ($588,800 total): community service, leadership. *Special Characteristics:* 51 awards ($187,416 total): adult students, children of faculty/staff, international students, relatives of clergy, religious affiliation, siblings of current students. ***Tuition waivers:*** Full or partial for employees or children of employees.

LOANS ***Student loans:*** $4,289,478 (100% need-based). 90% of past graduating class borrowed through all loan programs. *Average indebtedness per student:* $23,472. ***Average need-based loan:*** Freshmen: $4284; Undergraduates: $5117. ***Parent loans:*** $1,463,558 (100% non-need-based). ***Programs:*** FFEL (Subsidized and Unsubsidized Stafford, PLUS), Perkins, state.

WORK-STUDY ***Federal work-study:*** Total amount: $724,565; 400 jobs averaging $2000. ***State or other work-study/employment:*** Total amount: $50,000 (100% non-need-based). 34 part-time jobs averaging $1500.

APPLYING FOR FINANCIAL AID ***Required financial aid forms:*** FAFSA, institution's own form. ***Financial aid deadline (priority):*** 2/15. ***Notification date:*** Continuous beginning 3/15. Students must reply by 5/1 or within 2 weeks of notification.

CONTACT Dee J. Ludwick, Director of Financial Aid, Regis College, Box 81, 235 Wellesley Street, Weston, MA 02493, 781-768-7180 or toll-free 866-438-7344. *Fax:* 781-768-7225. *E-mail:* finaid@regiscollege.edu.

REGIS UNIVERSITY
Denver, CO

Tuition & fees: $26,900 **Average undergraduate aid package: $17,572**

ABOUT THE INSTITUTION Independent Roman Catholic (Jesuit), coed. Awards: bachelor's, master's, and doctoral degrees. 33 undergraduate majors. Total enrollment: 16,004. Undergraduates: 8,119. Freshmen: 529. Federal methodology is used as a basis for awarding need-based institutional aid.

UNDERGRADUATE EXPENSES for 2007–08 ***Application fee:*** $40. ***Comprehensive fee:*** $35,730 includes full-time tuition ($26,600), mandatory fees ($300), and room and board ($8830). ***College room only:*** $5050. ***Part-time tuition:*** $831 per hour. ***Part-time fees:*** $240 per year.

FRESHMAN FINANCIAL AID (Fall 2005) 390 applied for aid; of those 59% were deemed to have need. 100% of freshmen with need received aid; of those 47% had need fully met. ***Average percent of need met:*** 77% (excluding resources awarded to replace EFC). ***Average financial aid package:*** $17,806 (excluding resources awarded to replace EFC). 15% of all full-time freshmen had no need and received non-need-based gift aid.

UNDERGRADUATE FINANCIAL AID (Fall 2005) 1,271 applied for aid; of those 64% were deemed to have need. 100% of undergraduates with need received aid; of those 34% had need fully met. ***Average percent of need met:*** 75% (excluding resources awarded to replace EFC). ***Average financial aid package:*** $17,572 (excluding resources awarded to replace EFC). 10% of all full-time undergraduates had no need and received non-need-based gift aid.

GIFT AID (NEED-BASED) ***Total amount:*** $11,070,171 (12% federal, 16% state, 63% institutional, 9% external sources). ***Receiving aid:*** Freshmen: 58% (230); All full-time undergraduates: 56% (775). ***Average award:*** Freshmen: $14,757; Undergraduates: $13,330. ***Scholarships, grants, and awards:*** Federal Pell, FSEOG, state, private, college/university gift aid from institutional funds, ACG/SMART Grants.

GIFT AID (NON-NEED-BASED) ***Total amount:*** $4,478,090 (1% state, 93% institutional, 6% external sources). ***Receiving aid:*** Freshmen: 57% (225); Undergraduates: 40% (550). ***Average award:*** Freshmen: $9977; Undergraduates: $9113. ***Scholarships, grants, and awards by category:*** *Academic Interests/Achievement:* biological sciences, general academic interests/achievements, physical sciences. *Creative Arts/Performance:* 6 awards ($66,600 total): debating. *Special Achievements/Activities:* 8 awards ($4000 total): leadership. *Special Characteristics:* children of faculty/staff, ethnic background, local/state students, members of minority groups. ***ROTC:*** Army cooperative, Air Force cooperative.

LOANS ***Student loans:*** $5,323,495 (75% need-based, 25% non-need-based). ***Average need-based loan:*** Freshmen: $1505; Undergraduates: $2452. ***Parent loans:*** $4,680,393 (27% need-based, 73% non-need-based). ***Programs:*** FFEL (Subsidized and Unsubsidized Stafford, PLUS), Perkins, Federal Nursing.

WORK-STUDY ***Federal work-study:*** Total amount: $390,848; 320 jobs averaging $1256. ***State or other work-study/employment:*** Total amount: $1,071,907 (44% need-based, 56% non-need-based). 423 part-time jobs averaging $2307.

ATHLETIC AWARDS Total amount: $1,836,107 (48% need-based, 52% non-need-based).

APPLYING FOR FINANCIAL AID ***Required financial aid form:*** FAFSA. ***Financial aid deadline (priority):*** 3/1. ***Notification date:*** Continuous beginning 3/15.

CONTACT Ellie Miller, Director of Financial Aid, Regis University, 3333 Regis Boulevard, Denver, CO 80221-1099, 303-964-5758 or toll-free 800-388-2366 Ext. 4900. *Fax:* 303-964-5449. *E-mail:* emiller@regis.edu.

REINHARDT COLLEGE
Waleska, GA

Tuition & fees: $14,970 **Average undergraduate aid package: $2608**

ABOUT THE INSTITUTION Independent religious, coed. Awards: associate and bachelor's degrees. 22 undergraduate majors. Total enrollment: 1,060. Undergraduates: 1,060. Freshmen: 265. Federal methodology is used as a basis for awarding need-based institutional aid.

UNDERGRADUATE EXPENSES for 2007–08 ***Application fee:*** $25. ***Comprehensive fee:*** $20,988 includes full-time tuition ($14,800), mandatory fees ($170), and room and board ($6018). ***Part-time tuition:*** $495 per hour. ***Part-time fees:*** $85 per term.

FRESHMAN FINANCIAL AID (Fall 2006, est.) 184 applied for aid; of those 70% were deemed to have need. 77% of freshmen with need received aid; of those 72% had need fully met. ***Average percent of need met:*** 31% (excluding resources awarded to replace EFC). ***Average financial aid package:*** $2421 (excluding resources awarded to replace EFC). 59% of all full-time freshmen had no need and received non-need-based gift aid.

UNDERGRADUATE FINANCIAL AID (Fall 2006, est.) 608 applied for aid; of those 51% were deemed to have need. 95% of undergraduates with need received aid; of those 38% had need fully met. ***Average percent of need met:*** 42% (excluding resources awarded to replace EFC). ***Average financial aid package:*** $2608 (excluding resources awarded to replace EFC). 43% of all full-time undergraduates had no need and received non-need-based gift aid.

GIFT AID (NEED-BASED) ***Total amount:*** $1,141,447 (77% federal, 22% institutional, 1% external sources). ***Receiving aid:*** Freshmen: 29% (74); All full-time undergraduates: 23% (213). ***Average award:*** Freshmen: $1104;

Undergraduates: $1392. ***Scholarships, grants, and awards:*** Federal Pell, FSEOG, state, private, college/university gift aid from institutional funds.

GIFT AID (NON-NEED-BASED) ***Total amount:*** $6,134,219 (36% state, 62% institutional, 2% external sources). ***Receiving aid:*** Freshmen: 39% (98); Undergraduates: 16% (146). ***Average award:*** Freshmen: $1400; Undergraduates: $2860. ***Scholarships, grants, and awards by category:*** *Academic Interests/Achievement:* general academic interests/achievements. *Creative Arts/Performance:* art/fine arts, music. *Special Achievements/Activities:* religious involvement. *Special Characteristics:* children of faculty/staff.

LOANS ***Student loans:*** $1,828,796 (75% need-based, 25% non-need-based). ***Average need-based loan:*** Freshmen: $2900; Undergraduates: $4212. ***Parent loans:*** $1,319,552 (100% non-need-based). ***Programs:*** FFEL (Subsidized and Unsubsidized Stafford, PLUS), alternative loans.

WORK-STUDY ***Federal work-study:*** Total amount: $57,399; 68 jobs averaging $1138. ***State or other work-study/employment:*** Total amount: $53,000 (100% non-need-based). 156 part-time jobs averaging $909.

ATHLETIC AWARDS Total amount: $824,863 (100% non-need-based).

APPLYING FOR FINANCIAL AID ***Required financial aid forms:*** FAFSA, institution's own form, state aid form. ***Financial aid deadline (priority):*** 5/1. ***Notification date:*** Continuous beginning 3/15. Students must reply within 2 weeks of notification.

CONTACT Robert Gregory, Director of Financial Aid, Reinhardt College, 7300 Reinhardt College Circle, Waleska, GA 30183-2981, 770-720-5532 or toll-free 87-REINHARDT. *Fax:* 770-720-9126.

REMINGTON COLLEGE–COLORADO SPRINGS CAMPUS

Colorado Springs, CO

CONTACT Financial Aid Office, Remington College–Colorado Springs Campus, 6050 Erin Park Drive, #250, Colorado Springs, CO 80918, 719-532-1234.

REMINGTON COLLEGE–DENVER CAMPUS

Lakewood, CO

CONTACT Robert J. Lantzy, Director of Financial Services, Remington College–Denver Campus, 11011 West Sixth Avenue, Lakewood, CO 80215, 303-445-0500 or toll-free 800-999-5181. *Fax:* 303-445-0090. *E-mail:* rlantzy@edamerica.com.

REMINGTON COLLEGE–HONOLULU CAMPUS

Honolulu, HI

CONTACT Financial Aid Office, Remington College–Honolulu Campus, 1111 Bishop Street, Suite 400, Honolulu, HI 96813, 808-942-1000.

REMINGTON COLLEGE–SAN DIEGO CAMPUS

San Diego, CA

CONTACT Financial Aid Office, Remington College–San Diego Campus, 123 Camino de la Reina, North Building, Suite 100, San Diego, CA 92108, 619-686-8600 or toll-free 800-214-7001.

REMINGTON COLLEGE–TEMPE CAMPUS

Tempe, AZ

CONTACT Financial Aid Office, Remington College–Tempe Campus, 875 West Elliot Road, Suite 216, Tempe, AZ 85284, 480-834-1000 or toll-free 800-395-4322.

RENSSELAER POLYTECHNIC INSTITUTE

Troy, NY

Tuition & fees: $33,496 **Average undergraduate aid package: $26,650**

ABOUT THE INSTITUTION Independent, coed. Awards: bachelor's, master's, and doctoral degrees. 51 undergraduate majors. Total enrollment: 7,433. Undergraduates: 5,193. Freshmen: 1,270. Federal methodology is used as a basis for awarding need-based institutional aid.

UNDERGRADUATE EXPENSES for 2006–07 ***Application fee:*** $70. ***Comprehensive fee:*** $43,411 includes full-time tuition ($32,600), mandatory fees ($896), and room and board ($9915). ***College room only:*** $5568. Room and board charges vary according to board plan. ***Part-time tuition:*** $1019 per credit hour. ***Payment plan:*** Installment.

FRESHMAN FINANCIAL AID (Fall 2006, est.) 1034 applied for aid; of those 81% were deemed to have need. 100% of freshmen with need received aid; of those 50% had need fully met. ***Average percent of need met:*** 89% (excluding resources awarded to replace EFC). ***Average financial aid package:*** $27,220 (excluding resources awarded to replace EFC). 33% of all full-time freshmen had no need and received non-need-based gift aid.

UNDERGRADUATE FINANCIAL AID (Fall 2006, est.) 3,884 applied for aid; of those 89% were deemed to have need. 100% of undergraduates with need received aid; of those 49% had need fully met. ***Average percent of need met:*** 86% (excluding resources awarded to replace EFC). ***Average financial aid package:*** $26,650 (excluding resources awarded to replace EFC). 24% of all full-time undergraduates had no need and received non-need-based gift aid.

GIFT AID (NEED-BASED) ***Total amount:*** $72,055,696 (9% federal, 6% state, 83% institutional, 2% external sources). ***Receiving aid:*** Freshmen: 66% (837); All full-time undergraduates: 67% (3,455). ***Average award:*** Freshmen: $21,248; Undergraduates: $20,345. ***Scholarships, grants, and awards:*** Federal Pell, FSEOG, state, private, college/university gift aid from institutional funds, Gates Millennium Scholarships.

GIFT AID (NON-NEED-BASED) ***Total amount:*** $17,223,857 (10% federal, 87% institutional, 3% external sources). ***Receiving aid:*** Freshmen: 19% (241); Undergraduates: 12% (610). ***Average award:*** Freshmen: $15,939; Undergraduates: $15,000. ***Scholarships, grants, and awards by category:*** *Academic Interests/Achievement:* general academic interests/achievements, humanities, mathematics, military science. *Creative Arts/Performance:* general creative arts/performance. *Special Achievements/Activities:* general special achievements/activities. *Special Characteristics:* children and siblings of alumni, children of faculty/staff, ethnic background, general special characteristics, members of minority groups. ***Tuition waivers:*** Full or partial for employees or children of employees. ***ROTC:*** Army cooperative, Naval, Air Force.

LOANS ***Student loans:*** $32,000,000 (75% need-based, 25% non-need-based). 75% of past graduating class borrowed through all loan programs. *Average indebtedness per student:* $27,235. ***Average need-based loan:*** Freshmen: $6000; Undergraduates: $7000. ***Parent loans:*** $10,000,000 (80% need-based, 20% non-need-based). ***Programs:*** FFEL (Subsidized and Unsubsidized Stafford, PLUS), Perkins, college/university.

WORK-STUDY ***Federal work-study:*** Total amount: $1,200,000; 1,122 jobs averaging $1969.

ATHLETIC AWARDS Total amount: $910,710 (100% non-need-based).

APPLYING FOR FINANCIAL AID ***Required financial aid forms:*** FAFSA, state aid form. ***Financial aid deadline (priority):*** 2/15. ***Notification date:*** 3/25.

CONTACT Mr. James Stevenson, Director of Financial Aid, Rensselaer Polytechnic Institute, Financial Aid Building, 110 8th Street, Troy, NY 12180-3590, 518-276-6813 or toll-free 800-448-6562. *Fax:* 518-276-4797. *E-mail:* stevej@rpi.edu.

RESEARCH COLLEGE OF NURSING

Kansas City, MO

CONTACT Ms. Stacie Withers, Financial Aid Director, Research College of Nursing, 2300 East Meyer Boulevard, Kansas City, MO 64132, 816-276-4728 or toll-free 800-842-6776. *Fax:* 816-276-3526. *E-mail:* stacie.withers@hcamidwest.com.

RHODE ISLAND COLLEGE

Providence, RI

CONTACT Office of Financial Aid, Rhode Island College, 600 Mount Pleasant Avenue, Providence, RI 02908, 401-456-8033 or toll-free 800-669-5760.

RHODE ISLAND SCHOOL OF DESIGN

Providence, RI

CONTACT Mr. Peter R. Riefler, Director of Financial Aid, Rhode Island School of Design, 2 College Street, Providence, RI 02903-2784, 401-454-6636 or toll-free 800-364-7473. *Fax:* 401-454-6412. *E-mail:* priefler@risd.edu.

RHODES COLLEGE

Memphis, TN

Tuition & fees: $29,112 **Average undergraduate aid package: $25,184**

ABOUT THE INSTITUTION Independent Presbyterian, coed. Awards: bachelor's and master's degrees (master's degree in accounting only). 33 undergraduate majors. Total enrollment: 1,696. Undergraduates: 1,687. Freshmen: 452. Institutional methodology is used as a basis for awarding need-based institutional aid.

UNDERGRADUATE EXPENSES for 2006–07 ***Application fee:*** $45. ***Comprehensive fee:*** $36,292 includes full-time tuition ($28,802), mandatory fees ($310), and room and board ($7180). ***Part-time tuition:*** $1120 per credit hour.

FRESHMAN FINANCIAL AID (Fall 2006, est.) 309 applied for aid; of those 69% were deemed to have need. 99% of freshmen with need received aid; of those 55% had need fully met. ***Average percent of need met:*** 89% (excluding resources awarded to replace EFC). ***Average financial aid package:*** $25,656 (excluding resources awarded to replace EFC). 36% of all full-time freshmen had no need and received non-need-based gift aid.

UNDERGRADUATE FINANCIAL AID (Fall 2006, est.) 918 applied for aid; of those 73% were deemed to have need. 98% of undergraduates with need received aid; of those 43% had need fully met. ***Average percent of need met:*** 84% (excluding resources awarded to replace EFC). ***Average financial aid package:*** $25,184 (excluding resources awarded to replace EFC). 39% of all full-time undergraduates had no need and received non-need-based gift aid.

GIFT AID (NEED-BASED) ***Total amount:*** $10,178,516 (6% federal, 9% state, 80% institutional, 5% external sources). ***Receiving aid:*** Freshmen: 46% (208); All full-time undergraduates: 39% (640). ***Average award:*** Freshmen: $18,011; Undergraduates: $15,889. ***Scholarships, grants, and awards:*** Federal Pell, FSEOG, state, private, college/university gift aid from institutional funds.

GIFT AID (NON-NEED-BASED) ***Total amount:*** $8,572,168 (1% federal, 5% state, 89% institutional, 5% external sources). ***Receiving aid:*** Freshmen: 12% (52); Undergraduates: 9% (146). ***Average award:*** Freshmen: $10,210; Undergraduates: $10,421. ***Scholarships, grants, and awards by category:*** *Academic Interests/Achievement:* 785 awards ($7,065,788 total): business, general academic interests/achievements, humanities. *Creative Arts/Performance:* 36 awards ($360,000 total): art/fine arts, music, theater/drama. *Special Achievements/Activities:* 77 awards ($303,900 total): community service. *Special Characteristics:* 46 awards ($574,151 total): children of faculty/staff, ethnic background, relatives of clergy, religious affiliation. ***ROTC:*** Army cooperative, Air Force cooperative.

LOANS ***Student loans:*** $3,903,888 (56% need-based, 44% non-need-based). 40% of past graduating class borrowed through all loan programs. *Average indebtedness per student:* $23,710. ***Average need-based loan:*** Freshmen: $3912; Undergraduates: $5819. ***Parent loans:*** $2,897,071 (9% need-based, 91% non-need-based). ***Programs:*** FFEL (Subsidized and Unsubsidized Stafford, PLUS), Perkins.

WORK-STUDY ***Federal work-study:*** Total amount: $275,310; 204 jobs averaging $1501. ***State or other work-study/employment:*** Total amount: $626,632 (40% need-based, 60% non-need-based). 263 part-time jobs averaging $1340.

APPLYING FOR FINANCIAL AID ***Required financial aid forms:*** FAFSA, CSS Financial Aid PROFILE, noncustodial (divorced/separated) parent's statement. ***Financial aid deadline:*** 3/1 (priority: 3/1). ***Notification date:*** Students must reply by 5/1 or within 2 weeks of notification.

CONTACT Forrest M. Stuart, Director of Financial Aid, Rhodes College, 2000 North Parkway, Memphis, TN 38112-1690, 901-843-3810 or toll-free 800-844-5969 (out-of-state). *Fax:* 901-843-3435. *E-mail:* stuart@rhodes.edu.

RICE UNIVERSITY

Houston, TX

Tuition & fees: $28,900 **Average undergraduate aid package: $22,048**

ABOUT THE INSTITUTION Independent, coed. Awards: bachelor's, master's, and doctoral degrees. 59 undergraduate majors. Total enrollment: 5,119. Undergraduates: 3,049. Freshmen: 713. Both federal and institutional methodology are used as a basis for awarding need-based institutional aid.

UNDERGRADUATE EXPENSES for 2007–08 ***Application fee:*** $50. ***Comprehensive fee:*** $39,150 includes full-time tuition ($28,400), mandatory fees ($500), and room and board ($10,250). ***College room only:*** $6750. ***Part-time tuition:*** $1184 per credit hour.

FRESHMAN FINANCIAL AID (Fall 2006, est.) 510 applied for aid; of those 52% were deemed to have need. 100% of freshmen with need received aid; of those 100% had need fully met. ***Average percent of need met:*** 100% (excluding resources awarded to replace EFC). ***Average financial aid package:*** $23,754 (excluding resources awarded to replace EFC). 14% of all full-time freshmen had no need and received non-need-based gift aid.

UNDERGRADUATE FINANCIAL AID (Fall 2006, est.) 1,556 applied for aid; of those 69% were deemed to have need. 100% of undergraduates with need received aid; of those 99% had need fully met. ***Average percent of need met:*** 99% (excluding resources awarded to replace EFC). ***Average financial aid package:*** $22,048 (excluding resources awarded to replace EFC). 21% of all full-time undergraduates had no need and received non-need-based gift aid.

GIFT AID (NEED-BASED) ***Total amount:*** $18,260,573 (6% federal, 12% state, 79% institutional, 3% external sources). ***Receiving aid:*** Freshmen: 37% (263); All full-time undergraduates: 36% (1,078). ***Average award:*** Freshmen: $20,150; Undergraduates: $16,871. ***Scholarships, grants, and awards:*** Federal Pell, FSEOG, state, private, college/university gift aid from institutional funds.

GIFT AID (NON-NEED-BASED) ***Total amount:*** $7,735,541 (3% state, 66% institutional, 31% external sources). ***Receiving aid:*** Freshmen: 10% (69); Undergraduates: 9% (261). ***Average award:*** Freshmen: $6538; Undergraduates: $4355. ***Scholarships, grants, and awards by category:*** *Academic Interests/Achievement:* architecture, area/ethnic studies, biological sciences, computer science, engineering/technologies, English, foreign languages, general academic interests/achievements, humanities, international studies, mathematics, physical sciences, social sciences. *Creative Arts/Performance:* applied art and design, art/fine arts, creative writing, debating, journalism/publications, music, performing arts. *Special Achievements/Activities:* community service, general special achievements/activities, leadership. *Special Characteristics:* children and siblings of alumni, children of faculty/staff, ethnic background, general special characteristics, international students. ***ROTC:*** Army cooperative, Naval, Air Force cooperative.

LOANS ***Student loans:*** $2,921,020 (51% need-based, 49% non-need-based). 41% of past graduating class borrowed through all loan programs. *Average indebtedness per student:* $15,873. ***Average need-based loan:*** Freshmen: $1216; Undergraduates: $3192. ***Parent loans:*** $4,735,071 (100% non-need-based). ***Programs:*** FFEL (Subsidized and Unsubsidized Stafford, PLUS), Perkins, state.

WORK-STUDY ***Federal work-study:*** Total amount: $1,062,599; jobs available (averaging $1800). ***State or other work-study/employment:*** Total amount: $5100 (100% need-based). Part-time jobs available.

ATHLETIC AWARDS Total amount: $6,774,081 (10% need-based, 90% non-need-based).

APPLYING FOR FINANCIAL AID ***Required financial aid forms:*** FAFSA, CSS Financial Aid PROFILE, noncustodial (divorced/separated) parent's statement, business/farm supplement, tax returns and W-2s. ***Financial aid deadline (priority):*** 3/1. ***Notification date:*** Continuous beginning 3/1. Students must reply by 5/1.

CONTACT Office of Student Financial Services, Rice University, 116 Allen Center, MS 12, 6100 Main Street, Houston, TX 77005, 713-348-4958 or toll-free 800-527-OWLS. *Fax:* 713-348-2139.

THE RICHARD STOCKTON COLLEGE OF NEW JERSEY

Pomona, NJ

Tuition & fees (NJ res): $9058 **Average undergraduate aid package: $12,053**

ABOUT THE INSTITUTION State-supported, coed. Awards: bachelor's and master's degrees and post-bachelor's certificates. 31 undergraduate majors. Total enrollment: 7,212. Undergraduates: 6,726. Freshmen: 808. Federal methodology is used as a basis for awarding need-based institutional aid.

UNDERGRADUATE EXPENSES for 2006–07 ***Application fee:*** $50. ***Tuition, state resident:*** full-time $5,938; part-time $185.55 per credit. ***Tuition, nonresident:***

full-time $10,230; part-time $319.70 per credit. ***Required fees:*** full-time $3120; $97.50 per credit. ***College room and board:*** $8446; ***Room only:*** $5,790. Room and board charges vary according to board plan and housing facility. ***Payment plans:*** Installment, deferred payment.

FRESHMAN FINANCIAL AID (Fall 2006, est.) 662 applied for aid; of those 72% were deemed to have need. 100% of freshmen with need received aid; of those 49% had need fully met. ***Average percent of need met:*** 80% (excluding resources awarded to replace EFC). ***Average financial aid package:*** $11,840 (excluding resources awarded to replace EFC). 10% of all full-time freshmen had no need and received non-need-based gift aid.

UNDERGRADUATE FINANCIAL AID (Fall 2006, est.) 4,181 applied for aid; of those 77% were deemed to have need. 99% of undergraduates with need received aid; of those 43% had need fully met. ***Average percent of need met:*** 77% (excluding resources awarded to replace EFC). ***Average financial aid package:*** $12,053 (excluding resources awarded to replace EFC). 5% of all full-time undergraduates had no need and received non-need-based gift aid.

GIFT AID (NEED-BASED) ***Total amount:*** $13,074,150 (42% federal, 47% state, 10% institutional, 1% external sources). ***Receiving aid:*** Freshmen: 30% (240); All full-time undergraduates: 30% (1,700). ***Average award:*** Freshmen: $7104; Undergraduates: $6129. ***Scholarships, grants, and awards:*** Federal Pell, FSEOG, state, college/university gift aid from institutional funds.

GIFT AID (NON-NEED-BASED) ***Total amount:*** $1,191,285 (15% state, 69% institutional, 16% external sources). ***Receiving aid:*** Freshmen: 25% (197); Undergraduates: 12% (672). ***Average award:*** Freshmen: $3427; Undergraduates: $2287. ***Scholarships, grants, and awards by category:*** *Academic Interests/Achievement:* 129 awards ($186,675 total): area/ethnic studies, biological sciences, business, computer science, education, general academic interests/achievements, health fields, humanities, mathematics, physical sciences, social sciences. *Creative Arts/Performance:* 14 awards ($11,250 total): applied art and design, art/fine arts, creative writing, dance, journalism/publications, music, performing arts, theater/drama. *Special Achievements/Activities:* 10 awards ($9500 total): community service, general special achievements/activities, leadership. *Special Characteristics:* 29 awards ($38,000 total): adult students, children of faculty/staff, children of union members/company employees, ethnic background, first-generation college students, general special characteristics, international students, local/state students, members of minority groups, previous college experience. ***Tuition waivers:*** Full or partial for employees or children of employees, senior citizens.

LOANS ***Student loans:*** $26,058,769 (72% need-based, 28% non-need-based). ***Average need-based loan:*** Freshmen: $2368; Undergraduates: $3773. ***Parent loans:*** $4,192,919 (49% need-based, 51% non-need-based). ***Programs:*** FFEL (Subsidized and Unsubsidized Stafford, PLUS), Perkins, state.

WORK-STUDY ***Federal work-study:*** Total amount: $283,453; 207 jobs averaging $1648. ***State or other work-study/employment:*** Total amount: $1,047,368 (100% non-need-based). 699 part-time jobs averaging $1498.

APPLYING FOR FINANCIAL AID ***Required financial aid form:*** FAFSA. ***Financial aid deadline (priority):*** 3/1. ***Notification date:*** Continuous beginning 4/1. Students must reply within 2 weeks of notification.

CONTACT Ms. Jeanne L. Lewis, Director of Financial Aid, The Richard Stockton College of New Jersey, Jimmie Leeds Road, Pomona, NJ 08240-9988, 609-652-4203. *Fax:* 609-626-5517. *E-mail:* iaprod91@stockton.edu.

RIDER UNIVERSITY

Lawrenceville, NJ

ABOUT THE INSTITUTION Independent, coed. Awards: associate, bachelor's, and master's degrees and post-master's certificates. 59 undergraduate majors. Total enrollment: 5,790. Undergraduates: 4,586. Freshmen: 1,028.

GIFT AID (NEED-BASED) ***Scholarships, grants, and awards:*** Federal Pell, FSEOG, state, private, college/university gift aid from institutional funds.

GIFT AID (NON-NEED-BASED) ***Scholarships, grants, and awards by category:*** *Academic Interests/Achievement:* general academic interests/achievements. *Creative Arts/Performance:* theater/drama. *Special Characteristics:* members of minority groups.

LOANS ***Programs:*** FFEL (Subsidized and Unsubsidized Stafford, PLUS), Perkins, state, college/university, alternative loans.

WORK-STUDY ***Federal work-study:*** Total amount: $3,792,721; 1,779 jobs averaging $2087.

APPLYING FOR FINANCIAL AID ***Required financial aid form:*** FAFSA.

CONTACT John J. Williams, Student Financial Services Office, Rider University, 2083 Lawrenceville Road, Lawrenceville, NJ 08648-3001, 609-896-5360 or toll-free 800-257-9026. *Fax:* 609-219-4487. *E-mail:* finaid@rider.edu.

RINGLING COLLEGE OF ART AND DESIGN

Sarasota, FL

Tuition & fees: $23,125 **Average undergraduate aid package: $9791**

ABOUT THE INSTITUTION Independent, coed. Awards: bachelor's degrees. 6 undergraduate majors. Total enrollment: 1,090. Undergraduates: 1,090. Freshmen: 243. Federal methodology is used as a basis for awarding need-based institutional aid.

UNDERGRADUATE EXPENSES for 2006–07 ***Application fee:*** $35. ***Comprehensive fee:*** $33,124 includes full-time tuition ($22,700), mandatory fees ($425), and room and board ($9999). ***College room only:*** $5272. Full-time tuition and fees vary according to course load, program, and student level. Room and board charges vary according to board plan and housing facility. ***Part-time tuition:*** $1070 per credit hour. Part-time tuition and fees vary according to course load, program, and student level. ***Payment plan:*** Installment.

FRESHMAN FINANCIAL AID (Fall 2006, est.) 165 applied for aid; of those 88% were deemed to have need. 100% of freshmen with need received aid; of those 3% had need fully met. ***Average percent of need met:*** 29% (excluding resources awarded to replace EFC). ***Average financial aid package:*** $8366 (excluding resources awarded to replace EFC). 8% of all full-time freshmen had no need and received non-need-based gift aid.

UNDERGRADUATE FINANCIAL AID (Fall 2006, est.) 737 applied for aid; of those 90% were deemed to have need. 100% of undergraduates with need received aid; of those 5% had need fully met. ***Average percent of need met:*** 25% (excluding resources awarded to replace EFC). ***Average financial aid package:*** $9791 (excluding resources awarded to replace EFC). 9% of all full-time undergraduates had no need and received non-need-based gift aid.

GIFT AID (NEED-BASED) ***Total amount:*** $7,863,153 (13% federal, 22% state, 13% institutional, 52% external sources). ***Receiving aid:*** Freshmen: 39% (124); All full-time undergraduates: 53% (556). ***Average award:*** Freshmen: $6613; Undergraduates: $6853. ***Scholarships, grants, and awards:*** Federal Pell, FSEOG, state, private.

GIFT AID (NON-NEED-BASED) ***Total amount:*** $351,484 (74% state, 26% institutional). ***Receiving aid:*** Freshmen: 2% (5); Undergraduates: 1% (12). ***Average award:*** Freshmen: $12,133; Undergraduates: $14,656. ***Scholarships, grants, and awards by category:*** *Academic Interests/Achievement:* general academic interests/achievements. *Creative Arts/Performance:* applied art and design, art/fine arts. ***Tuition waivers:*** Full or partial for employees or children of employees.

LOANS ***Student loans:*** $9,798,502 (84% need-based, 16% non-need-based). 75% of past graduating class borrowed through all loan programs. *Average indebtedness per student:* $71,865. ***Average need-based loan:*** Freshmen: $2514; Undergraduates: $3770. ***Parent loans:*** $4,491,623 (64% need-based, 36% non-need-based). ***Programs:*** FFEL (Subsidized and Unsubsidized Stafford, PLUS), alternative loans.

WORK-STUDY ***Federal work-study:*** Total amount: $369,894; 99 jobs averaging $1876. ***State or other work-study/employment:*** Part-time jobs available.

APPLYING FOR FINANCIAL AID ***Required financial aid form:*** FAFSA. ***Financial aid deadline (priority):*** 3/1. ***Notification date:*** Continuous beginning 3/15. Students must reply within 4 weeks of notification.

CONTACT Micah Jordan, Financial Aid Assistant Director, Ringling College of Art and Design, 2700 North Tamiami Trail, Sarasota, FL 34243, 941-359-7533 or toll-free 800-255-7695. *Fax:* 941-359-6107. *E-mail:* finaid@ringling.edu.

RIPON COLLEGE

Ripon, WI

Tuition & fees: $22,437 **Average undergraduate aid package: $19,019**

ABOUT THE INSTITUTION Independent, coed. Awards: bachelor's degrees. 38 undergraduate majors. Total enrollment: 977. Undergraduates: 977. Freshmen: 264. Federal methodology is used as a basis for awarding need-based institutional aid.

UNDERGRADUATE EXPENSES for 2006–07 ***Application fee:*** $30. ***Comprehensive fee:*** $28,497 includes full-time tuition ($22,162), mandatory fees ($275), and

room and board ($6060). ***College room only:*** $3030. ***Part-time tuition:*** $890 per credit. ***Payment plans:*** Guaranteed tuition, installment.

FRESHMAN FINANCIAL AID (Fall 2006, est.) 253 applied for aid; of those 85% were deemed to have need. 100% of freshmen with need received aid; of those 48% had need fully met. ***Average percent of need met:*** 94% (excluding resources awarded to replace EFC). ***Average financial aid package:*** $19,019 (excluding resources awarded to replace EFC). 24% of all full-time freshmen had no need and received non-need-based gift aid.

UNDERGRADUATE FINANCIAL AID (Fall 2006, est.) 890 applied for aid; of those 85% were deemed to have need. 100% of undergraduates with need received aid; of those 39% had need fully met. ***Average percent of need met:*** 92% (excluding resources awarded to replace EFC). ***Average financial aid package:*** $19,019 (excluding resources awarded to replace EFC). 21% of all full-time undergraduates had no need and received non-need-based gift aid.

GIFT AID (NEED-BASED) ***Total amount:*** $10,841,734 (9% federal, 8% state, 65% institutional, 18% external sources). ***Receiving aid:*** Freshmen: 82% (216); All full-time undergraduates: 79% (752). ***Average award:*** Freshmen: $14,967; Undergraduates: $14,459. ***Scholarships, grants, and awards:*** Federal Pell, FSEOG, state, private, college/university gift aid from institutional funds.

GIFT AID (NON-NEED-BASED) ***Total amount:*** $4,719,667 (38% institutional, 62% external sources). ***Receiving aid:*** Freshmen: 17% (45); Undergraduates: 13% (124). ***Average award:*** Freshmen: $16,923; Undergraduates: $17,580. ***Scholarships, grants, and awards by category:*** *Academic Interests/Achievement:* 506 awards ($4,328,673 total): biological sciences, business, computer science, education, English, foreign languages, general academic interests/achievements, humanities, mathematics, military science, physical sciences, premedicine, religion/biblical studies, social sciences. *Creative Arts/Performance:* 104 awards ($309,500 total): art/fine arts, debating, music, theater/drama. *Special Achievements/Activities:* 159 awards ($633,500 total): general special achievements/activities, leadership, memberships. *Special Characteristics:* 313 awards ($1,663,852 total): children and siblings of alumni, children of faculty/staff, general special characteristics, international students, local/state students, members of minority groups, out-of-state students, previous college experience, religious affiliation, siblings of current students. ***Tuition waivers:*** Full or partial for children of alumni, employees or children of employees. ***ROTC:*** Army.

LOANS ***Student loans:*** $5,619,129 (59% need-based, 41% non-need-based). 84% of past graduating class borrowed through all loan programs. *Average indebtedness per student:* $19,468. ***Average need-based loan:*** Freshmen: $4059; Undergraduates: $4750. ***Parent loans:*** $2,309,403 (12% need-based, 88% non-need-based). ***Programs:*** FFEL (Subsidized and Unsubsidized Stafford, PLUS), Perkins, alternative loans.

WORK-STUDY ***Federal work-study:*** Total amount: $519,153; 348 jobs averaging $1492. ***State or other work-study/employment:*** Total amount: $613,483 (3% need-based, 97% non-need-based). 345 part-time jobs averaging $1727.

APPLYING FOR FINANCIAL AID ***Required financial aid form:*** FAFSA. ***Financial aid deadline (priority):*** 3/1. ***Notification date:*** Continuous. Students must reply within 2 weeks of notification.

CONTACT Steven M. Schuetz, Dean of Admission and Financial Aid, Ripon College, 300 Seward Street, Ripon, WI 54971, 920-748-8185 or toll-free 800-947-4766. *Fax:* 920-748-8335. *E-mail:* financialaid@ripon.edu.

RIVIER COLLEGE

Nashua, NH

Tuition & fees: $21,695 **Average undergraduate aid package: $14,606**

ABOUT THE INSTITUTION Independent Roman Catholic, coed. Awards: associate, bachelor's, and master's degrees and post-bachelor's and post-master's certificates. 41 undergraduate majors. Total enrollment: 2,320. Undergraduates: 1,462. Freshmen: 276. Federal methodology is used as a basis for awarding need-based institutional aid.

UNDERGRADUATE EXPENSES for 2007–08 ***Application fee:*** $25. ***Comprehensive fee:*** $29,637 includes full-time tuition ($20,970), mandatory fees ($725), and room and board ($7942).

FRESHMAN FINANCIAL AID (Fall 2005) 215 applied for aid; of those 92% were deemed to have need. 99% of freshmen with need received aid; of those 25% had need fully met. ***Average percent of need met:*** 71% (excluding resources awarded to replace EFC). ***Average financial aid package:*** $15,011 (excluding resources awarded to replace EFC). 16% of all full-time freshmen had no need and received non-need-based gift aid.

UNDERGRADUATE FINANCIAL AID (Fall 2005) 810 applied for aid; of those 91% were deemed to have need. 100% of undergraduates with need received aid; of those 33% had need fully met. ***Average percent of need met:*** 74% (excluding resources awarded to replace EFC). ***Average financial aid package:*** $14,606 (excluding resources awarded to replace EFC). 16% of all full-time undergraduates had no need and received non-need-based gift aid.

GIFT AID (NEED-BASED) ***Total amount:*** $5,870,821 (13% federal, 3% state, 78% institutional, 6% external sources). ***Receiving aid:*** Freshmen: 82% (193); All full-time undergraduates: 80% (700). ***Average award:*** Freshmen: $9532; Undergraduates: $8193. ***Scholarships, grants, and awards:*** Federal Pell, FSEOG, state, private, college/university gift aid from institutional funds.

GIFT AID (NON-NEED-BASED) ***Total amount:*** $726,854 (90% institutional, 10% external sources). ***Receiving aid:*** Freshmen: 5% (11); Undergraduates: 4% (39). ***Average award:*** Freshmen: $13,275; Undergraduates: $11,974. ***Scholarships, grants, and awards by category:*** *Academic Interests/Achievement:* biological sciences, business, communication, computer science, education, English, foreign languages, general academic interests/achievements, humanities, mathematics, premedicine, social sciences. *Creative Arts/Performance:* applied art and design, art/fine arts, journalism/publications. *Special Achievements/Activities:* general special achievements/activities. *Special Characteristics:* children and siblings of alumni, children of current students, international students, siblings of current students. ***ROTC:*** Air Force cooperative.

LOANS ***Student loans:*** $9,630,554 (64% need-based, 36% non-need-based). 87% of past graduating class borrowed through all loan programs. *Average indebtedness per student:* $25,959. ***Average need-based loan:*** Freshmen: $5241; Undergraduates: $6666. ***Parent loans:*** $2,020,183 (42% need-based, 58% non-need-based). ***Programs:*** FFEL (Subsidized and Unsubsidized Stafford, PLUS), Perkins, state.

WORK-STUDY ***Federal work-study:*** Total amount: $435,340; 393 jobs averaging $1107. ***State or other work-study/employment:*** Total amount: $199,546 (100% non-need-based). 153 part-time jobs averaging $1304.

APPLYING FOR FINANCIAL AID ***Required financial aid form:*** FAFSA. ***Financial aid deadline (priority):*** 3/1. ***Notification date:*** Continuous beginning 3/1. Students must reply within 3 weeks of notification.

CONTACT Valerie Patnaude, Director of Financial Aid, Rivier College, 420 Main Street, Nashua, NH 03060-5086, 603-897-8533 or toll-free 800-44RIVIER. *Fax:* 603-897-8810. *E-mail:* vpatnaude@rivier.edu.

ROANOKE BIBLE COLLEGE

Elizabeth City, NC

Tuition & fees: $9915 **Average undergraduate aid package: $6520**

ABOUT THE INSTITUTION Independent Christian, coed. Awards: associate and bachelor's degrees. 3 undergraduate majors. Total enrollment: 156. Undergraduates: 156. Freshmen: 24. Federal methodology is used as a basis for awarding need-based institutional aid.

UNDERGRADUATE EXPENSES for 2007–08 ***Application fee:*** $25. ***Comprehensive fee:*** $15,635 includes full-time tuition ($9440), mandatory fees ($475), and room and board ($5720). ***College room only:*** $3120. ***Part-time tuition:*** $295 per credit hour. ***Part-time fees:*** $12 per credit hour.

FRESHMAN FINANCIAL AID (Fall 2005) 28 applied for aid; of those 93% were deemed to have need. 100% of freshmen with need received aid; of those 4% had need fully met. ***Average percent of need met:*** 74% (excluding resources awarded to replace EFC). ***Average financial aid package:*** $4827 (excluding resources awarded to replace EFC). 7% of all full-time freshmen had no need and received non-need-based gift aid.

UNDERGRADUATE FINANCIAL AID (Fall 2005) 155 applied for aid; of those 88% were deemed to have need. 100% of undergraduates with need received aid; of those 9% had need fully met. ***Average percent of need met:*** 73% (excluding resources awarded to replace EFC). ***Average financial aid package:*** $6520 (excluding resources awarded to replace EFC). 10% of all full-time undergraduates had no need and received non-need-based gift aid.

GIFT AID (NEED-BASED) ***Total amount:*** $597,882 (40% federal, 58% institutional, 2% external sources). ***Receiving aid:*** Freshmen: 90% (26); All full-time undergraduates: 86% (137). ***Average award:*** Freshmen: $2887; Undergraduates: $3743. ***Scholarships, grants, and awards:*** Federal Pell, FSEOG, state, private, college/university gift aid from institutional funds.

GIFT AID (NON-NEED-BASED) ***Total amount:*** $57,659 (96% institutional, 4% external sources). ***Receiving aid:*** Freshmen: 10% (3); Undergraduates: 5% (8). ***Average award:*** Freshmen: $1655; Undergraduates: $1554. ***Scholarships, grants,***

and awards by category: *Academic Interests/Achievement:* 27 awards ($89,240 total): general academic interests/achievements, religion/biblical studies. *Special Achievements/Activities:* 18 awards ($15,491 total): general special achievements/activities, religious involvement. *Special Characteristics:* 63 awards ($66,424 total): children and siblings of alumni, children of faculty/staff, general special characteristics, handicapped students, international students, married students, spouses of current students.

LOANS ***Student loans:*** $953,541 (77% need-based, 23% non-need-based). 79% of past graduating class borrowed through all loan programs. *Average indebtedness per student:* $19,486. ***Average need-based loan:*** Freshmen: $2375; Undergraduates: $1684. ***Parent loans:*** $84,100 (49% need-based, 51% non-need-based). ***Programs:*** FFEL (Subsidized and Unsubsidized Stafford, PLUS), alternative loans.

WORK-STUDY ***Federal work-study:*** Total amount: $13,930; 21 jobs averaging $677.

APPLYING FOR FINANCIAL AID ***Required financial aid forms:*** FAFSA, institution's own form. ***Financial aid deadline (priority):*** 3/15. ***Notification date:*** Continuous beginning 4/1. Students must reply within 2 weeks of notification.

CONTACT Lisa W. Pipkin, Financial Aid Administrator, Roanoke Bible College, 715 North Poindexter Street, Elizabeth City, NC 27909, 252-334-2020 or toll-free 800-RBC-8980. *Fax:* 252-334-2064. *E-mail:* lwp@roanokebible.edu.

ROANOKE COLLEGE

Salem, VA

Tuition & fees: $24,653 **Average undergraduate aid package: $19,945**

ABOUT THE INSTITUTION Independent religious, coed. Awards: bachelor's degrees. 30 undergraduate majors. Total enrollment: 1,970. Undergraduates: 1,970. Freshmen: 505. Federal methodology is used as a basis for awarding need-based institutional aid.

UNDERGRADUATE EXPENSES for 2006–07 ***Application fee:*** $30. ***Comprehensive fee:*** $32,805 includes full-time tuition ($24,048), mandatory fees ($605), and room and board ($8152). ***College room only:*** $3802. Room and board charges vary according to housing facility. ***Part-time tuition:*** $1145 per course. ***Payment plan:*** Installment.

FRESHMAN FINANCIAL AID (Fall 2006, est.) 370 applied for aid; of those 99% were deemed to have need. 99% of freshmen with need received aid; of those 23% had need fully met. ***Average percent of need met:*** 92% (excluding resources awarded to replace EFC). ***Average financial aid package:*** $21,013 (excluding resources awarded to replace EFC). 23% of all full-time freshmen had no need and received non-need-based gift aid.

UNDERGRADUATE FINANCIAL AID (Fall 2006, est.) 1,458 applied for aid; of those 93% were deemed to have need. 100% of undergraduates with need received aid; of those 30% had need fully met. ***Average percent of need met:*** 90% (excluding resources awarded to replace EFC). ***Average financial aid package:*** $19,945 (excluding resources awarded to replace EFC). 23% of all full-time undergraduates had no need and received non-need-based gift aid.

GIFT AID (NEED-BASED) ***Total amount:*** $18,069,842 (5% federal, 11% state, 81% institutional, 3% external sources). ***Receiving aid:*** Freshmen: 57% (290); All full-time undergraduates: 61% (1,131). ***Average award:*** Freshmen: $17,925; Undergraduates: $16,115. ***Scholarships, grants, and awards:*** Federal Pell, FSEOG, state, private, college/university gift aid from institutional funds.

GIFT AID (NON-NEED-BASED) ***Total amount:*** $6,517,644 (12% state, 86% institutional, 2% external sources). ***Receiving aid:*** Freshmen: 65% (328); Undergraduates: 48% (890). ***Average award:*** Freshmen: $9117; Undergraduates: $10,537. ***Scholarships, grants, and awards by category:*** *Academic Interests/Achievement:* general academic interests/achievements. *Creative Arts/Performance:* art/fine arts, music. *Special Characteristics:* local/state students, members of minority groups, religious affiliation. ***Tuition waivers:*** Full or partial for employees or children of employees, senior citizens.

LOANS ***Student loans:*** $8,117,155 (89% need-based, 11% non-need-based). 74% of past graduating class borrowed through all loan programs. *Average indebtedness per student:* $21,807. ***Average need-based loan:*** Freshmen: $3333; Undergraduates: $4234. ***Parent loans:*** $2,767,199 (80% need-based, 20% non-need-based). ***Programs:*** FFEL (Subsidized and Unsubsidized Stafford, PLUS), Perkins, college/university, alternative loans.

WORK-STUDY ***Federal work-study:*** Total amount: $827,211; 620 jobs averaging $1409.

APPLYING FOR FINANCIAL AID ***Required financial aid forms:*** FAFSA, state aid form. ***Financial aid deadline (priority):*** 3/1. ***Notification date:*** Continuous beginning 11/1. Students must reply within 2 weeks of notification.

CONTACT Mr. Thomas S. Blair Jr., Director of Financial Aid, Roanoke College, 221 College Lane, Salem, VA 24153-3794, 540-375-2235 or toll-free 800-388-2276. *E-mail:* finaid@roanoke.edu.

ROBERT MORRIS COLLEGE

Chicago, IL

ABOUT THE INSTITUTION Independent, coed. Awards: associate, bachelor's, and master's degrees. 24 undergraduate majors. Total enrollment: 4,701. Undergraduates: 4,512. Freshmen: 1,008.

GIFT AID (NEED-BASED) ***Scholarships, grants, and awards:*** Federal Pell, FSEOG, state, private, college/university gift aid from institutional funds.

GIFT AID (NON-NEED-BASED) ***Scholarships, grants, and awards by category:*** *Academic Interests/Achievement:* business, computer science, general academic interests/achievements, health fields. *Creative Arts/Performance:* applied art and design, journalism/publications. *Special Achievements/Activities:* community service, general special achievements/activities. *Special Characteristics:* children of faculty/staff, general special characteristics, out-of-state students, veterans.

LOANS ***Programs:*** FFEL (Subsidized and Unsubsidized Stafford, PLUS), Perkins.

WORK-STUDY ***Federal work-study:*** Total amount: $133,494; 177 jobs averaging $792.

APPLYING FOR FINANCIAL AID ***Required financial aid form:*** FAFSA.

CONTACT Gabriel Hennessey, Assistant Director of Financial Services, Robert Morris College, 401 South State Street, Suite 140, Chicago, IL 60605, 312-935-4075 or toll-free 800-RMC-5960. *Fax:* 312-935-4074. *E-mail:* ghennessey@robertmorris.edu.

ROBERT MORRIS UNIVERSITY

Moon Township, PA

Tuition & fees: $16,290 **Average undergraduate aid package: $14,486**

ABOUT THE INSTITUTION Independent, coed. Awards: bachelor's, master's, and doctoral degrees and post-bachelor's certificates. 37 undergraduate majors. Total enrollment: 5,065. Undergraduates: 3,945. Freshmen: 658. Federal methodology is used as a basis for awarding need-based institutional aid.

UNDERGRADUATE EXPENSES for 2006–07 ***Application fee:*** $30. ***Comprehensive fee:*** $24,700 includes full-time tuition ($16,290) and room and board ($8410). ***College room only:*** $4890. Full-time tuition and fees vary according to program. Room and board charges vary according to board plan and housing facility. ***Part-time tuition:*** $545 per credit. ***Part-time fees:*** $150 per term. Part-time tuition and fees vary according to course load and program. ***Payment plans:*** Installment, deferred payment.

FRESHMAN FINANCIAL AID (Fall 2006, est.) 599 applied for aid; of those 85% were deemed to have need. 100% of freshmen with need received aid; of those 31% had need fully met. ***Average percent of need met:*** 75% (excluding resources awarded to replace EFC). ***Average financial aid package:*** $14,295 (excluding resources awarded to replace EFC). 20% of all full-time freshmen had no need and received non-need-based gift aid.

UNDERGRADUATE FINANCIAL AID (Fall 2006, est.) 2,612 applied for aid; of those 89% were deemed to have need. 100% of undergraduates with need received aid; of those 28% had need fully met. ***Average percent of need met:*** 73% (excluding resources awarded to replace EFC). ***Average financial aid package:*** $14,486 (excluding resources awarded to replace EFC). 19% of all full-time undergraduates had no need and received non-need-based gift aid.

GIFT AID (NEED-BASED) ***Total amount:*** $15,295,650 (19% federal, 35% state, 44% institutional, 2% external sources). ***Receiving aid:*** Freshmen: 76% (494); All full-time undergraduates: 71% (2,136). ***Average award:*** Freshmen: $8336; Undergraduates: $7629. ***Scholarships, grants, and awards:*** Federal Pell, FSEOG, state, private, college/university gift aid from institutional funds.

GIFT AID (NON-NEED-BASED) ***Total amount:*** $2,708,603 (2% federal, 3% state, 88% institutional, 7% external sources). ***Receiving aid:*** Freshmen: 6% (40); Undergraduates: 4% (127). ***Average award:*** Freshmen: $10,470; Undergraduates: $10,130. ***Scholarships, grants, and awards by category:*** *Academic Interests/Achievement:* general academic interests/achievements. *Creative Arts/Performance:* general creative arts/performance. *Special Achievements/Activities:* general special achievements/activities. *Special Characteristics:* children of faculty/staff, ethnic background, members of minority groups, out-of-state students. ***Tuition waivers:*** Full or partial for employees or children of employees. ***ROTC:*** Army, Air Force cooperative.

LOANS ***Student loans:*** $27,264,503 (73% need-based, 27% non-need-based). ***Average need-based loan:*** Freshmen: $5252; Undergraduates: $6552. ***Parent loans:*** $4,837,747 (43% need-based, 57% non-need-based). ***Programs:*** FFEL (Subsidized and Unsubsidized Stafford, PLUS), Perkins, alternative private loans.

WORK-STUDY ***Federal work-study:*** Total amount: $3,391,311; jobs available. ***State or other work-study/employment:*** Part-time jobs available.

ATHLETIC AWARDS Total amount: $2,677,539 (57% need-based, 43% non-need-based).

APPLYING FOR FINANCIAL AID ***Required financial aid form:*** FAFSA. ***Financial aid deadline:*** Continuous. ***Notification date:*** Continuous beginning 3/15. Students must reply within 2 weeks of notification.

CONTACT Ms. Stephanie Thompson, Director, Financial Aid, Robert Morris University, 6001 University Boulevard, Moon Township, PA 15108-1189, 412-299-2450 or toll-free 800-762-0097. *Fax:* 412-262-8601. *E-mail:* finaid@rmu.edu.

ROBERTS WESLEYAN COLLEGE

Rochester, NY

Tuition & fees: $21,656 **Average undergraduate aid package: $16,768**

ABOUT THE INSTITUTION Independent religious, coed. Awards: associate, bachelor's, and master's degrees. 55 undergraduate majors. Total enrollment: 1,903. Undergraduates: 1,346. Freshmen: 246. Federal methodology is used as a basis for awarding need-based institutional aid.

UNDERGRADUATE EXPENSES for 2007–08 ***Application fee:*** $35. ***Comprehensive fee:*** $29,430 includes full-time tuition ($20,564), mandatory fees ($1092), and room and board ($7774). ***College room only:*** $5388. ***Part-time tuition:*** $450 per credit.

FRESHMAN FINANCIAL AID (Fall 2006, est.) 194 applied for aid; of those 93% were deemed to have need. 100% of freshmen with need received aid; of those 25% had need fully met. ***Average percent of need met:*** 80% (excluding resources awarded to replace EFC). ***Average financial aid package:*** $17,964 (excluding resources awarded to replace EFC). 14% of all full-time freshmen had no need and received non-need-based gift aid.

UNDERGRADUATE FINANCIAL AID (Fall 2006, est.) 912 applied for aid; of those 93% were deemed to have need. 100% of undergraduates with need received aid; of those 22% had need fully met. ***Average percent of need met:*** 76% (excluding resources awarded to replace EFC). ***Average financial aid package:*** $16,768 (excluding resources awarded to replace EFC). 13% of all full-time undergraduates had no need and received non-need-based gift aid.

GIFT AID (NEED-BASED) ***Total amount:*** $9,196,444 (16% federal, 18% state, 56% institutional, 10% external sources). ***Receiving aid:*** Freshmen: 86% (181); All full-time undergraduates: 86% (844). ***Average award:*** Freshmen: $12,539; Undergraduates: $10,601. ***Scholarships, grants, and awards:*** Federal Pell, FSEOG, state, private, college/university gift aid from institutional funds.

GIFT AID (NON-NEED-BASED) ***Total amount:*** $1,147,927 (4% state, 62% institutional, 34% external sources). ***Receiving aid:*** Freshmen: 10% (22); Undergraduates: 6% (61). ***Average award:*** Freshmen: $7482; Undergraduates: $10,285. ***Scholarships, grants, and awards by category:*** *Academic Interests/Achievement:* 287 awards ($1,198,815 total): general academic interests/achievements. *Creative Arts/Performance:* 156 awards ($289,550 total): art/fine arts, music. *Special Achievements/Activities:* 629 awards ($503,692 total): general special achievements/activities, leadership. *Special Characteristics:* 591 awards ($1,171,711 total): children and siblings of alumni, children of faculty/staff, international students, out-of-state students, relatives of clergy, religious affiliation, siblings of current students. ***ROTC:*** Army cooperative, Air Force cooperative.

LOANS ***Student loans:*** $7,163,837 (81% need-based, 19% non-need-based). ***Average need-based loan:*** Freshmen: $5177; Undergraduates: $5787. ***Parent loans:*** $2,868,441 (49% need-based, 51% non-need-based). ***Programs:*** FFEL (Subsidized and Unsubsidized Stafford, PLUS), Perkins.

WORK-STUDY ***Federal work-study:*** Total amount: $230,000; 700 jobs averaging $1000. ***State or other work-study/employment:*** Total amount: $154,300 (65% need-based, 35% non-need-based). 50 part-time jobs averaging $1800.

ATHLETIC AWARDS Total amount: $671,650 (69% need-based, 31% non-need-based).

APPLYING FOR FINANCIAL AID ***Required financial aid forms:*** FAFSA, state aid form. ***Financial aid deadline (priority):*** 3/15. ***Notification date:*** Continuous beginning 3/15. Students must reply by 5/1 or within 2 weeks of notification.

CONTACT Financial Aid Office, Roberts Wesleyan College, 2301 Westside Drive, Rochester, NY 14624-1997, 585-594-6150 or toll-free 800-777-4RWC. *E-mail:* finaid@roberts.edu.

ROCHESTER COLLEGE

Rochester Hills, MI

CONTACT Burt Rutledge, Director of Financial Aid, Rochester College, 800 West Avon Road, Rochester Hills, MI 48307, 248-218-2028 or toll-free 800-521-6010. *Fax:* 248-218-2035. *E-mail:* brutledge@rc.edu.

ROCHESTER INSTITUTE OF TECHNOLOGY

Rochester, NY

Tuition & fees: $25,011 **Average undergraduate aid package: $17,100**

ABOUT THE INSTITUTION Independent, coed. Awards: associate, bachelor's, master's, and doctoral degrees and post-bachelor's and post-master's certificates. 112 undergraduate majors. Total enrollment: 15,557. Undergraduates: 13,140. Freshmen: 2,374. Both federal and institutional methodology are used as a basis for awarding need-based institutional aid.

UNDERGRADUATE EXPENSES for 2006–07 ***Application fee:*** $50. ***Comprehensive fee:*** $33,759 includes full-time tuition ($24,627), mandatory fees ($384), and room and board ($8748). ***College room only:*** $5034. Full-time tuition and fees vary according to course load, program, and student level. Room and board charges vary according to board plan and housing facility. ***Part-time tuition:*** $547 per credit hour. ***Part-time fees:*** $38 per term. Part-time tuition and fees vary according to class time, course load, program, and student level. ***Payment plans:*** Tuition prepayment, installment, deferred payment.

FRESHMAN FINANCIAL AID (Fall 2005) 1910 applied for aid; of those 83% were deemed to have need. 100% of freshmen with need received aid; of those 83% had need fully met. ***Average percent of need met:*** 88% (excluding resources awarded to replace EFC). ***Average financial aid package:*** $17,600 (excluding resources awarded to replace EFC). 11% of all full-time freshmen had no need and received non-need-based gift aid.

UNDERGRADUATE FINANCIAL AID (Fall 2005) 7,950 applied for aid; of those 88% were deemed to have need. 100% of undergraduates with need received aid; of those 83% had need fully met. ***Average percent of need met:*** 88% (excluding resources awarded to replace EFC). ***Average financial aid package:*** $17,100 (excluding resources awarded to replace EFC). 9% of all full-time undergraduates had no need and received non-need-based gift aid.

GIFT AID (NEED-BASED) ***Total amount:*** $75,582,000 (12% federal, 11% state, 74% institutional, 3% external sources). ***Receiving aid:*** Freshmen: 68% (1,510); All full-time undergraduates: 62% (6,615). ***Average award:*** Freshmen: $11,500; Undergraduates: $11,300. ***Scholarships, grants, and awards:*** Federal Pell, FSEOG, state, private, college/university gift aid from institutional funds, NACME.

GIFT AID (NON-NEED-BASED) ***Total amount:*** $20,167,100 (10% federal, 29% state, 49% institutional, 12% external sources). ***Receiving aid:*** Freshmen: 20% (440); Undergraduates: 21% (2,260). ***Average award:*** Freshmen: $6500; Undergraduates: $6200. ***Scholarships, grants, and awards by category:*** *Academic Interests/Achievement:* 3,000 awards ($19,500,000 total): biological sciences, business, communication, computer science, engineering/technologies, general academic interests/achievements, health fields, international studies, mathematics, military science, physical sciences, premedicine, social sciences. *Creative Arts/Performance:* 300 awards ($1,800,000 total): applied art and design, art/fine arts, cinema/film/broadcasting. *Special Achievements/Activities:* 200 awards ($1,200,000 total): community service, leadership. *Special Characteristics:* children of faculty/staff, international students, members of minority groups, veterans. ***Tuition waivers:*** Full or partial for employees or children of employees. ***ROTC:*** Army, Naval cooperative, Air Force.

LOANS ***Student loans:*** $66,004,900 (57% need-based, 43% non-need-based). ***Average need-based loan:*** Freshmen: $5000; Undergraduates: $5400. ***Parent loans:*** $14,094,900 (40% need-based, 60% non-need-based). ***Programs:*** Federal Direct (Subsidized and Unsubsidized Stafford, PLUS), Perkins, alternative loans, RIT loans.

WORK-STUDY ***Federal work-study:*** Total amount: $2,800,000; 2,060 jobs averaging $1360. ***State or other work-study/employment:*** Total amount: $8,400,000 (100% non-need-based). 4,700 part-time jobs averaging $1780.

APPLYING FOR FINANCIAL AID ***Required financial aid form:*** FAFSA. ***Financial aid deadline (priority):*** 3/1. ***Notification date:*** Continuous beginning 3/15. Students must reply by 5/1 or within 2 weeks of notification.

CONTACT Mrs. Verna Hazen, Assistant Vice President, Financial Aid and Scholarships, Rochester Institute of Technology, Office of Financial Aid and Scholarships, 56 Lomb Drive, Rochester, NY 14623-5604, 585-475-5520. *Fax:* 585-475-7270. *E-mail:* verna.hazen@rit.edu.

ROCKFORD COLLEGE

Rockford, IL

CONTACT Mrs. Stacey Zimmerman, Financial Aid Specialist, Rockford College, 5050 East State Street, Rockford, IL 61108, 815-226-3396 or toll-free 800-892-2984. *Fax:* 815-394-5174.

ROCKHURST UNIVERSITY

Kansas City, MO

Tuition & fees: $22,990 **Average undergraduate aid package: $20,314**

ABOUT THE INSTITUTION Independent Roman Catholic (Jesuit), coed. Awards: bachelor's, master's, and doctoral degrees and post-bachelor's certificates. 31 undergraduate majors. Total enrollment: 3,066. Undergraduates: 2,222. Freshmen: 396. Federal methodology is used as a basis for awarding need-based institutional aid.

UNDERGRADUATE EXPENSES for 2007–08 ***Application fee:*** $25. ***Comprehensive fee:*** $29,190 includes full-time tuition ($22,000), mandatory fees ($990), and room and board ($6200). ***Part-time tuition:*** $733 per credit hour. ***Part-time fees:*** $30 per term.

FRESHMAN FINANCIAL AID (Fall 2006, est.) 394 applied for aid; of those 94% were deemed to have need. 100% of freshmen with need received aid; of those 27% had need fully met. ***Average percent of need met:*** 99% (excluding resources awarded to replace EFC). ***Average financial aid package:*** $20,426 (excluding resources awarded to replace EFC). 4% of all full-time freshmen had no need and received non-need-based gift aid.

UNDERGRADUATE FINANCIAL AID (Fall 2006, est.) 1,407 applied for aid; of those 85% were deemed to have need. 97% of undergraduates with need received aid; of those 18% had need fully met. ***Average percent of need met:*** 92% (excluding resources awarded to replace EFC). ***Average financial aid package:*** $20,314 (excluding resources awarded to replace EFC). 9% of all full-time undergraduates had no need and received non-need-based gift aid.

GIFT AID (NEED-BASED) ***Total amount:*** $10,063,761 (10% federal, 6% state, 81% institutional, 3% external sources). ***Receiving aid:*** Freshmen: 56% (221); All full-time undergraduates: 50% (745). ***Average award:*** Freshmen: $5150; Undergraduates: $5608. ***Scholarships, grants, and awards:*** Federal Pell, FSEOG, state, private, college/university gift aid from institutional funds.

GIFT AID (NON-NEED-BASED) ***Total amount:*** $6,120,251 (3% state, 95% institutional, 2% external sources). ***Receiving aid:*** Freshmen: 93% (369); Undergraduates: 78% (1,147). ***Average award:*** Freshmen: $10,780; Undergraduates: $10,787. ***Scholarships, grants, and awards by category:*** *Academic Interests/Achievement:* 1,132 awards ($8,028,487 total): biological sciences, business, communication, computer science, English, foreign languages, general academic interests/achievements, health fields, humanities, mathematics, physical sciences, premedicine, religion/biblical studies, social sciences. *Creative Arts/Performance:* 32 awards ($34,500 total): creative writing, music, performing arts, theater/drama. *Special Achievements/Activities:* 118 awards ($189,000 total): community service, leadership. *Special Characteristics:* 173 awards ($545,740 total): children and siblings of alumni, children of faculty/staff, siblings of current students. ***ROTC:*** Army cooperative.

LOANS ***Student loans:*** $4,516,326 (59% need-based, 41% non-need-based). 67% of past graduating class borrowed through all loan programs. *Average indebtedness per student:* $17,525. ***Average need-based loan:*** Freshmen: $2423; Undergraduates: $3356. ***Parent loans:*** $1,151,977 (52% need-based, 48% non-need-based). ***Programs:*** FFEL (Subsidized and Unsubsidized Stafford, PLUS), Perkins.

WORK-STUDY ***Federal work-study:*** Total amount: $284,432; 170 jobs averaging $1500. ***State or other work-study/employment:*** Total amount: $100,615 (32% need-based, 68% non-need-based). 110 part-time jobs averaging $1200.

ATHLETIC AWARDS Total amount: $1,988,462 (33% need-based, 67% non-need-based).

APPLYING FOR FINANCIAL AID ***Required financial aid form:*** FAFSA. ***Financial aid deadline:*** 6/30 (priority: 3/1). ***Notification date:*** Continuous beginning 1/30. Students must reply by 6/1 or within 4 weeks of notification.

CONTACT Ms. Carla Boren, Director of Financial Aid, Rockhurst University, 1100 Rockhurst Road, Kansas City, MO 64110-2561, 816-501-4600 or toll-free 800-842-6776. *Fax:* 816-501-2291. *E-mail:* carla.boren@rockhurst.edu.

ROCKY MOUNTAIN COLLEGE

Billings, MT

CONTACT Lisa Browning, Financial Aid Director, Rocky Mountain College, 1511 Poly Drive, Billings, MT 59102-1796, 406-657-1031 or toll-free 800-877-6259. *Fax:* 406-238-7351. *E-mail:* browninl@rocky.edu.

ROCKY MOUNTAIN COLLEGE OF ART & DESIGN

Lakewood, CO

ABOUT THE INSTITUTION Proprietary, coed. Awards: bachelor's degrees. 7 undergraduate majors. Total enrollment: 454. Undergraduates: 454. Freshmen: 83.

GIFT AID (NEED-BASED) ***Scholarships, grants, and awards:*** Federal Pell, FSEOG, state, private, college/university gift aid from institutional funds.

GIFT AID (NON-NEED-BASED) ***Scholarships, grants, and awards by category:*** *Academic Interests/Achievement:* general academic interests/achievements. *Creative Arts/Performance:* applied art and design, art/fine arts. *Special Characteristics:* children of faculty/staff.

LOANS ***Programs:*** FFEL (Subsidized and Unsubsidized Stafford, PLUS), alternative loans.

APPLYING FOR FINANCIAL AID ***Required financial aid forms:*** FAFSA, state aid form.

CONTACT David Nelson, Director of Financial Aid, Rocky Mountain College of Art & Design, 1600 Pierce Street, Lakewood, CO 80214, 303-225-8551 or toll-free 800-888-ARTS. *Fax:* 303-567-7200. *E-mail:* dnelson@rmcad.edu.

ROGERS STATE UNIVERSITY

Claremore, OK

CONTACT Cynthia Hoyt, Director of Financial Aid, Rogers State University, 1701 West Will Rogers Boulevard, Claremore, OK 74017-3252, 918-343-7553 or toll-free 800-256-7511. *Fax:* 918-343-7598. *E-mail:* finaid@rsu.edu.

ROGER WILLIAMS UNIVERSITY

Bristol, RI

ABOUT THE INSTITUTION Independent, coed. Awards: associate, bachelor's, master's, and first professional degrees. 47 undergraduate majors. Total enrollment: 5,172. Undergraduates: 4,348. Freshmen: 1,028.

GIFT AID (NEED-BASED) ***Scholarships, grants, and awards:*** Federal Pell, FSEOG, state, private, college/university gift aid from institutional funds.

GIFT AID (NON-NEED-BASED) ***Scholarships, grants, and awards by category:*** *Academic Interests/Achievement:* general academic interests/achievements.

LOANS ***Programs:*** FFEL (Subsidized and Unsubsidized Stafford, PLUS), Perkins, state.

WORK-STUDY ***Federal work-study:*** Total amount: $696,179; 715 jobs averaging $1813. ***State or other work-study/employment:*** Total amount: $874,300 (92% need-based, 8% non-need-based). 490 part-time jobs averaging $1693.

APPLYING FOR FINANCIAL AID ***Required financial aid forms:*** FAFSA, CSS Financial Aid PROFILE.

CONTACT Ms. Tracy DaCosta, Associate Dean of Enrollment Management, Roger Williams University, 1 Old Ferry Road, Bristol, RI 02809, 401-254-3100 or toll-free 800-458-7144 (out-of-state). *Fax:* 401-254-5376. *E-mail:* tdacosta@rwu.edu.

ROLLINS COLLEGE

Winter Park, FL

Tuition & fees: $30,860 **Average undergraduate aid package: $29,865**

ABOUT THE INSTITUTION Independent, coed. Awards: bachelor's and master's degrees. 32 undergraduate majors. Total enrollment: 2,454. Undergraduates: 1,720. Freshmen: 501. Federal methodology is used as a basis for awarding need-based institutional aid.

UNDERGRADUATE EXPENSES for 2006–07 ***Application fee:*** $40. ***Comprehensive fee:*** $40,486 includes full-time tuition ($30,420), mandatory fees ($440), and room and board ($9626). ***College room only:*** $5650. ***Payment plan:*** Installment.

FRESHMAN FINANCIAL AID (Fall 2006, est.) 244 applied for aid; of those 85% were deemed to have need. 100% of freshmen with need received aid; of those 32% had need fully met. ***Average percent of need met:*** 91% (excluding resources awarded to replace EFC). ***Average financial aid package:*** $30,213 (excluding resources awarded to replace EFC). 11% of all full-time freshmen had no need and received non-need-based gift aid.

UNDERGRADUATE FINANCIAL AID (Fall 2006, est.) 806 applied for aid; of those 89% were deemed to have need. 100% of undergraduates with need received aid; of those 44% had need fully met. ***Average percent of need met:*** 93% (excluding resources awarded to replace EFC). ***Average financial aid package:*** $29,865 (excluding resources awarded to replace EFC). 13% of all full-time undergraduates had no need and received non-need-based gift aid.

GIFT AID (NEED-BASED) ***Total amount:*** $16,302,833 (7% federal, 17% state, 75% institutional, 1% external sources). ***Receiving aid:*** Freshmen: 40% (202); All full-time undergraduates: 41% (701). ***Average award:*** Freshmen: $25,398; Undergraduates: $25,100. ***Scholarships, grants, and awards:*** Federal Pell, FSEOG, state, private, college/university gift aid from institutional funds.

GIFT AID (NON-NEED-BASED) ***Total amount:*** $5,256,480 (38% state, 60% institutional, 2% external sources). ***Receiving aid:*** Freshmen: 4% (22); Undergraduates: 3% (56). ***Average award:*** Freshmen: $10,945; Undergraduates: $11,384. ***Scholarships, grants, and awards by category:*** *Academic Interests/Achievement:* 470 awards ($5,137,034 total): computer science, engineering/technologies, general academic interests/achievements, mathematics, physical sciences. *Creative Arts/Performance:* 73 awards ($350,237 total): art/fine arts, music, theater/drama. ***Tuition waivers:*** Full or partial for employees or children of employees.

LOANS ***Student loans:*** $3,404,772 (85% need-based, 15% non-need-based). 43% of past graduating class borrowed through all loan programs. *Average indebtedness per student:* $21,540. ***Average need-based loan:*** Freshmen: $3940; Undergraduates: $4331. ***Parent loans:*** $1,937,979 (47% need-based, 53% non-need-based). ***Programs:*** Federal Direct (Subsidized and Unsubsidized Stafford, PLUS), Perkins, college/university.

WORK-STUDY ***Federal work-study:*** Total amount: $356,443; jobs available.

ATHLETIC AWARDS Total amount: $2,673,421 (10% need-based, 90% non-need-based).

APPLYING FOR FINANCIAL AID ***Required financial aid forms:*** FAFSA, institution's own form. ***Financial aid deadline:*** 3/1 (priority: 3/1). ***Notification date:*** Continuous beginning 3/1.

CONTACT Mr. Phil Asbury, Director of Student Financial Aid, Rollins College, 1000 Holt Avenue, #2721, Winter Park, FL 32789-4499, 407-646-2395. *Fax:* 407-646-2173. *E-mail:* pasbury@rollins.edu.

ROOSEVELT UNIVERSITY

Chicago, IL

ABOUT THE INSTITUTION Independent, coed. Awards: bachelor's, master's, and doctoral degrees and post-bachelor's and post-master's certificates. 86 undergraduate majors. Total enrollment: 7,186. Undergraduates: 3,975. Freshmen: 337.

GIFT AID (NEED-BASED) ***Scholarships, grants, and awards:*** Federal Pell, FSEOG, state, private, college/university gift aid from institutional funds.

GIFT AID (NON-NEED-BASED) ***Scholarships, grants, and awards by category:*** *Academic Interests/Achievement:* general academic interests/achievements. *Creative Arts/Performance:* music, theater/drama. *Special Achievements/Activities:* general special achievements/activities. *Special Characteristics:* general special characteristics.

LOANS ***Programs:*** FFEL (Subsidized and Unsubsidized Stafford, PLUS).

APPLYING FOR FINANCIAL AID ***Required financial aid forms:*** FAFSA, institution's own form.

CONTACT Mr. Walter J. H. O'Neill, Director of Financial Aid, Roosevelt University, 430 South Michigan Avenue, Chicago, IL 60605-1394, 312-341-2090 or toll-free 877-APPLYRU. *Fax:* 312-341-3545. *E-mail:* woneill@roosevelt.edu.

ROSE-HULMAN INSTITUTE OF TECHNOLOGY

Terre Haute, IN

Tuition & fees: $28,995 **Average undergraduate aid package: $22,011**

ABOUT THE INSTITUTION Independent, coed, primarily men. Awards: bachelor's and master's degrees. 16 undergraduate majors. Total enrollment: 1,963. Undergraduates: 1,862. Freshmen: 525. Federal methodology is used as a basis for awarding need-based institutional aid.

UNDERGRADUATE EXPENSES for 2006–07 ***Application fee:*** $40. ***Comprehensive fee:*** $36,864 includes full-time tuition ($28,530), mandatory fees ($465), and room and board ($7869). ***College room only:*** $4491. Full-time tuition and fees vary according to course load. Room and board charges vary according to board plan. ***Part-time tuition:*** $831 per credit. Part-time tuition and fees vary according to course load. ***Payment plans:*** Tuition prepayment, installment.

FRESHMAN FINANCIAL AID (Fall 2006, est.) 461 applied for aid; of those 83% were deemed to have need. 100% of freshmen with need received aid; of those 7% had need fully met. ***Average percent of need met:*** 85% (excluding resources awarded to replace EFC). ***Average financial aid package:*** $25,411 (excluding resources awarded to replace EFC). 27% of all full-time freshmen had no need and received non-need-based gift aid.

UNDERGRADUATE FINANCIAL AID (Fall 2006, est.) 1,496 applied for aid; of those 83% were deemed to have need. 100% of undergraduates with need received aid; of those 11% had need fully met. ***Average percent of need met:*** 79% (excluding resources awarded to replace EFC). ***Average financial aid package:*** $22,011 (excluding resources awarded to replace EFC). 30% of all full-time undergraduates had no need and received non-need-based gift aid.

GIFT AID (NEED-BASED) ***Total amount:*** $18,933,250 (5% federal, 8% state, 66% institutional, 21% external sources). ***Receiving aid:*** Freshmen: 73% (383); All full-time undergraduates: 67% (1,228). ***Average award:*** Freshmen: $17,689; Undergraduates: $15,387. ***Scholarships, grants, and awards:*** Federal Pell, FSEOG, state, college/university gift aid from institutional funds.

GIFT AID (NON-NEED-BASED) ***Total amount:*** $6,019,944 (77% institutional, 23% external sources). ***Average award:*** Freshmen: $8609; Undergraduates: $8343. ***Tuition waivers:*** Full or partial for employees or children of employees. ***ROTC:*** Army, Air Force.

LOANS ***Student loans:*** $15,681,715 (88% need-based, 12% non-need-based). 74% of past graduating class borrowed through all loan programs. *Average indebtedness per student:* $29,491. ***Average need-based loan:*** Freshmen: $7830; Undergraduates: $6945. ***Parent loans:*** $5,916,040 (85% need-based, 15% non-need-based). ***Programs:*** Federal Direct (Subsidized and Unsubsidized Stafford, PLUS), Perkins.

WORK-STUDY ***Federal work-study:*** Total amount: $742,291; 470 jobs averaging $1579. ***State or other work-study/employment:*** Total amount: $960,555 (89% need-based, 11% non-need-based). 612 part-time jobs averaging $1569.

APPLYING FOR FINANCIAL AID ***Required financial aid form:*** FAFSA. ***Financial aid deadline (priority):*** 3/1. ***Notification date:*** 3/10.

CONTACT Melinda L. Middleton, Director of Financial Aid, Rose-Hulman Institute of Technology, 5500 Wabash Avenue, Box #5, Terre Haute, IN 47803, 812-877-8259 or toll-free 800-248-7448. *Fax:* 812-877-8746. *E-mail:* melinda.middleton@rose-hulman.edu.

ROSEMONT COLLEGE

Rosemont, PA

Tuition & fees: $22,835 **Average undergraduate aid package: $17,605**

ABOUT THE INSTITUTION Independent Roman Catholic, undergraduate: women only; graduate: coed. Awards: bachelor's and master's degrees and post-bachelor's certificates. 24 undergraduate majors. Total enrollment: 995. Undergraduates: 578. Freshmen: 70. Federal methodology is used as a basis for awarding need-based institutional aid.

UNDERGRADUATE EXPENSES for 2007–08 ***Application fee:*** $35. ***Comprehensive fee:*** $32,035 includes full-time tuition ($21,630), mandatory fees ($1205), and room and board ($9200). ***Part-time tuition:*** $830 per credit. ***Part-time fees:*** $310 per credit.

FRESHMAN FINANCIAL AID (Fall 2006, est.) 67 applied for aid; of those 82% were deemed to have need. 100% of freshmen with need received aid; of those 13% had need fully met. ***Average percent of need met:*** 65% (excluding resources awarded to replace EFC). ***Average financial aid package:*** $16,135 (excluding resources awarded to replace EFC). 23% of all full-time freshmen had no need and received non-need-based gift aid.

UNDERGRADUATE FINANCIAL AID (Fall 2006, est.) 315 applied for aid; of those 88% were deemed to have need. 100% of undergraduates with need received aid; of those 21% had need fully met. ***Average percent of need met:*** 73% (excluding resources awarded to replace EFC). ***Average financial aid package:*** $17,605 (excluding resources awarded to replace EFC). 18% of all full-time undergraduates had no need and received non-need-based gift aid.

GIFT AID (NEED-BASED) ***Total amount:*** $3,920,503 (12% federal, 16% state, 68% institutional, 4% external sources). ***Receiving aid:*** Freshmen: 77% (55); All full-time undergraduates: 79% (275). ***Average award:*** Freshmen: $13,687; Undergraduates: $14,536. ***Scholarships, grants, and awards:*** Federal Pell, FSEOG, state, private, college/university gift aid from institutional funds.

GIFT AID (NON-NEED-BASED) ***Total amount:*** $980,428 (1% state, 94% institutional, 5% external sources). ***Receiving aid:*** Freshmen: 8% (6); Undergraduates: 12% (40). ***Average award:*** Freshmen: $13,053; Undergraduates: $14,468. ***Scholarships, grants, and awards by category:*** *Academic Interests/Achievement:* 191 awards ($1,536,054 total): general academic interests/achievements. *Creative Arts/Performance:* 2 awards ($4450 total): art/fine arts. *Special Achievements/Activities:* 264 awards ($835,507 total): community service, general special achievements/activities, religious involvement. *Special Characteristics:* 52 awards ($292,150 total): children and siblings of alumni, children of educators, children of faculty/staff, relatives of clergy, religious affiliation, siblings of current students. ***ROTC:*** Army cooperative.

LOANS ***Student loans:*** $2,035,479 (72% need-based, 28% non-need-based). 78% of past graduating class borrowed through all loan programs. *Average indebtedness per student:* $23,091. ***Average need-based loan:*** Freshmen: $2376; Undergraduates: $3487. ***Parent loans:*** $636,069 (61% need-based, 39% non-need-based). ***Programs:*** FFEL (Subsidized and Unsubsidized Stafford, PLUS), Perkins.

WORK-STUDY ***Federal work-study:*** Total amount: $108,559; 97 jobs averaging $1259. ***State or other work-study/employment:*** Total amount: $7000 (100% non-need-based). 7 part-time jobs averaging $1000.

APPLYING FOR FINANCIAL AID ***Required financial aid form:*** FAFSA. ***Financial aid deadline (priority):*** 2/15. ***Notification date:*** Continuous beginning 3/15. Students must reply by 5/1 or within 4 weeks of notification.

CONTACT Melissa Walsh, Director of Financial Aid, Rosemont College, 1400 Montgomery Avenue, Rosemont, PA 19010, 610-527-0200 Ext. 2220 or toll-free 800-331-0708. *Fax:* 610-527-0341. *E-mail:* mwalsh@rosemont.edu.

ROWAN UNIVERSITY

Glassboro, NJ

Tuition & fees (NJ res): $9330 **Average undergraduate aid package: $6073**

ABOUT THE INSTITUTION State-supported, coed. Awards: bachelor's, master's, and doctoral degrees. 38 undergraduate majors. Total enrollment: 9,578. Undergraduates: 8,430. Freshmen: 1,218. Federal methodology is used as a basis for awarding need-based institutional aid.

UNDERGRADUATE EXPENSES for 2006–07 ***Application fee:*** $50. ***Tuition, state resident:*** full-time $6798; part-time $262 per credit hour. ***Tuition, nonresident:*** full-time $13,598; part-time $524 per credit hour. ***Required fees:*** full-time $2532; $108.60 per credit hour. Full-time tuition and fees vary according to degree level. Part-time tuition and fees vary according to degree level. ***College room and board:*** $8742. Room and board charges vary according to board plan and housing facility. ***Payment plan:*** Deferred payment.

FRESHMAN FINANCIAL AID (Fall 2006, est.) 1228 applied for aid; of those 90% were deemed to have need. 92% of freshmen with need received aid; of those 35% had need fully met. ***Average percent of need met:*** 65% (excluding resources awarded to replace EFC). ***Average financial aid package:*** $6584 (excluding resources awarded to replace EFC).

UNDERGRADUATE FINANCIAL AID (Fall 2006, est.) 7,082 applied for aid; of those 90% were deemed to have need. 93% of undergraduates with need received aid; of those 38% had need fully met. ***Average percent of need met:*** 64% (excluding resources awarded to replace EFC). ***Average financial aid package:*** $6073 (excluding resources awarded to replace EFC). 1% of all full-time undergraduates had no need and received non-need-based gift aid.

GIFT AID (NEED-BASED) ***Total amount:*** $19,826,912 (29% federal, 42% state, 25% institutional, 4% external sources). ***Receiving aid:*** Freshmen: 53% (665); All full-time undergraduates: 46% (3,303). ***Average award:*** Freshmen: $6113; Undergraduates: $5810. ***Scholarships, grants, and awards:*** Federal Pell, FSEOG, state, private, college/university gift aid from institutional funds.

GIFT AID (NON-NEED-BASED) ***Total amount:*** $91,986 (66% institutional, 34% external sources). ***Receiving aid:*** Freshmen: 52% (653); Undergraduates: 43% (3,061). ***Average award:*** Undergraduates: $2826. ***Scholarships, grants, and awards by category:*** *Academic Interests/Achievement:* general academic interests/achievements. *Creative Arts/Performance:* general creative arts/performance, music. *Special Characteristics:* handicapped students, international students, members of minority groups. ***ROTC:*** Army cooperative.

LOANS ***Student loans:*** $34,048,754 (100% need-based). *Average indebtedness per student:* $16,253. ***Average need-based loan:*** Freshmen: $2314; Undergraduates: $3575. ***Parent loans:*** $18,330,795 (100% need-based). ***Programs:*** Federal Direct (Subsidized and Unsubsidized Stafford, PLUS), state.

WORK-STUDY ***Federal work-study:*** Total amount: $954,516; 751 jobs averaging $1271. ***State or other work-study/employment:*** Total amount: $2,018,964 (100% need-based). 597 part-time jobs averaging $3382.

APPLYING FOR FINANCIAL AID ***Required financial aid form:*** FAFSA. ***Financial aid deadline:*** Continuous. ***Notification date:*** Continuous beginning 3/15.

CONTACT Luis Tavarez, Director of Financial Aid, Rowan University, 201 Mullica Hill Road, Savitz Hall, Glassboro, NJ 08028-1701, 856-256-4276 or toll-free 800-447-1165 (in-state). *Fax:* 856-256-4413. *E-mail:* tavarez@rowan.edu.

RUSH UNIVERSITY

Chicago, IL

CONTACT Mr. Robert A. Dame, Director of Student Financial Aid, Rush University, 600 South Paulina Street, Suite 440, Chicago, IL 60612-3832, 312-942-6256. *Fax:* 312-942-2219.

RUSSELL SAGE COLLEGE

Troy, NY

Tuition & fees: $24,670 **Average undergraduate aid package: N/A**

ABOUT THE INSTITUTION Independent, women only. Awards: bachelor's degrees. 26 undergraduate majors. Total enrollment: 800. Undergraduates: 800. Freshmen: 113. Both federal and institutional methodology are used as a basis for awarding need-based institutional aid.

UNDERGRADUATE EXPENSES for 2006–07 ***Application fee:*** $30. ***Comprehensive fee:*** $33,190 includes full-time tuition ($23,800), mandatory fees ($870), and room and board ($8520). ***College room only:*** $4430. ***Part-time tuition:*** $795 per credit hour. ***Payment plans:*** Installment, deferred payment.

FRESHMAN FINANCIAL AID (Fall 2006, est.) 113 applied for aid; of those 91% were deemed to have need. 100% of freshmen with need received aid; of those 2% had need fully met. 5% of all full-time freshmen had no need and received non-need-based gift aid.

UNDERGRADUATE FINANCIAL AID (Fall 2006, est.) 750 applied for aid; of those 88% were deemed to have need. 100% of undergraduates with need received aid; of those .3% had need fully met. 4% of all full-time undergraduates had no need and received non-need-based gift aid.

GIFT AID (NEED-BASED) ***Total amount:*** $4,916,493 (19% federal, 27% state, 51% institutional, 3% external sources). ***Receiving aid:*** Freshmen: 52% (59); All full-time undergraduates: 53% (405). ***Scholarships, grants, and awards:*** Federal Pell, FSEOG, state, private, college/university gift aid from institutional funds, Federal Nursing.

GIFT AID (NON-NEED-BASED) ***Total amount:*** $4,988,023 (99% institutional, 1% external sources). ***Receiving aid:*** Freshmen: 84% (95); Undergraduates: 74% (563). ***Average award:*** Freshmen: $10,800; Undergraduates: $9451. ***Scholarships, grants, and awards by category:*** *Academic Interests/Achievement:* 426 awards ($4,257,625 total): general academic interests/achievements. *Creative Arts/Performance:* 2 awards ($10,000 total): theater/drama. *Special Achievements/Activities:* 10 awards ($20,000 total): community service, general special achievements/activities, leadership. *Special Characteristics:* 39 awards ($121,459 total): children and siblings of alumni, children of faculty/staff, siblings of current students, spouses of current students. ***Tuition waivers:*** Full or partial for employees or children of employees. ***ROTC:*** Army cooperative, Air Force cooperative.

LOANS ***Student loans:*** $4,355,994 (60% need-based, 40% non-need-based). 92% of past graduating class borrowed through all loan programs. *Average indebtedness per student:* $26,000. ***Parent loans:*** $2,878,596 (62% need-based, 38% non-need-based). ***Programs:*** FFEL (Subsidized and Unsubsidized Stafford, PLUS), Perkins.

WORK-STUDY ***Federal work-study:*** Total amount: $250,511; 432 jobs averaging $1500. ***State or other work-study/employment:*** Total amount: $131,200 (100% non-need-based). 91 part-time jobs averaging $1200.

APPLYING FOR FINANCIAL AID ***Required financial aid forms:*** FAFSA, state aid form. ***Financial aid deadline (priority):*** 3/1. ***Notification date:*** Continuous beginning 3/1. Students must reply within 2 weeks of notification.

CONTACT James Dease, Associate Vice President for Student Services, Russell Sage College, 45 Ferry Street, Troy, NY 12180, 518-244-2062 or toll-free 888-VERY-SAGE (in-state), 888-VERY SAGE (out-of-state). *Fax:* 518-244-2460. *E-mail:* deasej@sage.edu.

RUST COLLEGE

Holly Springs, MS

CONTACT Mrs. Helen L. Street, Director of Financial Aid, Rust College, 150 Rust Avenue, Holly Springs, MS 38635, 662-252-8000 Ext. 4061 or toll-free 888-886-8492 Ext. 4065. *Fax:* 662-252-8895.

RUTGERS, THE STATE UNIVERSITY OF NEW JERSEY, CAMDEN

Camden, NJ

Tuition & fees (NJ res): $9758 **Average undergraduate aid package: $11,175**

ABOUT THE INSTITUTION State-supported, coed. Awards: bachelor's, master's, and first professional degrees. 33 undergraduate majors. Total enrollment: 5,165. Undergraduates: 3,694. Freshmen: 398. Federal methodology is used as a basis for awarding need-based institutional aid.

UNDERGRADUATE EXPENSES for 2006–07 ***Application fee:*** $60. ***Tuition, state resident:*** full-time $7923; part-time $255 per credit hour. ***Tuition, nonresident:*** full-time $16,428; part-time $533 per credit hour. ***College room and board:*** $8596; ***Room only:*** $6136.

FRESHMAN FINANCIAL AID (Fall 2006, est.) 346 applied for aid; of those 71% were deemed to have need. 98% of freshmen with need received aid; of those 50% had need fully met. ***Average percent of need met:*** 70% (excluding resources awarded to replace EFC). ***Average financial aid package:*** $11,846 (excluding resources awarded to replace EFC). 3% of all full-time freshmen had no need and received non-need-based gift aid.

UNDERGRADUATE FINANCIAL AID (Fall 2006, est.) 2,294 applied for aid; of those 79% were deemed to have need. 98% of undergraduates with need received aid; of those 46% had need fully met. ***Average percent of need met:*** 73% (excluding resources awarded to replace EFC). ***Average financial aid package:*** $11,175 (excluding resources awarded to replace EFC). 4% of all full-time undergraduates had no need and received non-need-based gift aid.

GIFT AID (NEED-BASED) ***Total amount:*** $11,702,453 (29% federal, 50% state, 19% institutional, 2% external sources). ***Receiving aid:*** Freshmen: 41% (164); All full-time undergraduates: 44% (1,254). ***Average award:*** Freshmen: $8710; Undergraduates: $7882. ***Scholarships, grants, and awards:*** Federal Pell, FSEOG, state, private, college/university gift aid from institutional funds, Federal Nursing.

GIFT AID (NON-NEED-BASED) ***Total amount:*** $890,851 (9% state, 84% institutional, 7% external sources). ***Receiving aid:*** Freshmen: 29% (115); Undergraduates: 19% (540). ***Average award:*** Freshmen: $7958; Undergraduates: $3598. ***Scholarships, grants, and awards by category:*** *Academic Interests/Achievement:* 512 awards ($1,593,836 total): general academic interests/achievements. *Creative Arts/Performance:* general creative arts/performance. *Special Characteristics:* 42 awards ($217,119 total): children of faculty/staff. ***ROTC:*** Army cooperative, Air Force cooperative.

LOANS ***Student loans:*** $16,514,691 (77% need-based, 23% non-need-based). 67% of past graduating class borrowed through all loan programs. *Average indebtedness per student:* $18,645. ***Average need-based loan:*** Freshmen: $2898; Undergraduates: $4109. ***Parent loans:*** $652,051 (63% need-based, 37% non-need-based). ***Programs:*** Federal Direct (Subsidized and Unsubsidized Stafford, PLUS), Perkins, state, college/university.

WORK-STUDY ***Federal work-study:*** Total amount: $566,644; 330 jobs averaging $1780. ***State or other work-study/employment:*** Total amount: $746,768 (100% non-need-based).

ATHLETIC AWARDS Total amount: $2000 (100% need-based).

APPLYING FOR FINANCIAL AID ***Required financial aid form:*** FAFSA. ***Financial aid deadline (priority):*** 3/15. ***Notification date:*** Continuous beginning 2/3. Students must reply within 2 weeks of notification.

CONTACT Ms. Marlene Martin, Assistant Funds Manager, Rutgers, The State University of New Jersey, Camden, 620 George Street, New Brunswick, NJ 08901, 732-932-7868. *E-mail:* mgmartin@rci.rutgers.edu.

RUTGERS, THE STATE UNIVERSITY OF NEW JERSEY, NEWARK

Newark, NJ

Tuition & fees (NJ res): $9534 **Average undergraduate aid package: $11,311**

ABOUT THE INSTITUTION State-supported, coed. Awards: bachelor's, master's, doctoral, and first professional degrees. 51 undergraduate majors. Total enrollment: 10,203. Undergraduates: 6,503. Freshmen: 911. Federal methodology is used as a basis for awarding need-based institutional aid.

UNDERGRADUATE EXPENSES for 2006–07 ***Application fee:*** $60. ***Tuition, state resident:*** full-time $7923; part-time $255 per credit hour. ***Tuition, nonresident:*** full-time $16,428; part-time $533 per credit hour. ***College room and board:*** $9535; ***Room only:*** $6057. Room and board charges vary according to board plan and housing facility. ***Payment plan:*** Installment.

FRESHMAN FINANCIAL AID (Fall 2006, est.) 703 applied for aid; of those 80% were deemed to have need. 96% of freshmen with need received aid; of those 31% had need fully met. ***Average percent of need met:*** 82% (excluding resources awarded to replace EFC). ***Average financial aid package:*** $11,960 (excluding resources awarded to replace EFC). 1% of all full-time freshmen had no need and received non-need-based gift aid.

UNDERGRADUATE FINANCIAL AID (Fall 2006, est.) 3,726 applied for aid; of those 87% were deemed to have need. 98% of undergraduates with need received aid; of those 28% had need fully met. ***Average percent of need met:*** 81% (excluding resources awarded to replace EFC). ***Average financial aid package:*** $11,311 (excluding resources awarded to replace EFC). 3% of all full-time undergraduates had no need and received non-need-based gift aid.

GIFT AID (NEED-BASED) ***Total amount:*** $23,342,073 (31% federal, 51% state, 17% institutional, 1% external sources). ***Receiving aid:*** Freshmen: 47% (420); All full-time undergraduates: 50% (2,457). ***Average award:*** Freshmen: $9095; Undergraduates: $8358. ***Scholarships, grants, and awards:*** Federal Pell, FSEOG, state, private, college/university gift aid from institutional funds.

GIFT AID (NON-NEED-BASED) ***Total amount:*** $1,116,144 (6% state, 88% institutional, 6% external sources). ***Receiving aid:*** Freshmen: 20% (176); Undergraduates: 16% (809). ***Average award:*** Freshmen: $6188; Undergraduates: $3286. ***Scholarships, grants, and awards by category:*** *Academic Interests/Achievement:* 853 awards ($2,738,824 total): general academic interests/achievements. *Creative Arts/Performance:* general creative arts/performance. *Special Characteristics:* 21 awards ($136,843 total): children of faculty/staff. ***Tuition waivers:*** Full or partial for employees or children of employees. ***ROTC:*** Army, Air Force.

LOANS ***Student loans:*** $20,821,435 (85% need-based, 15% non-need-based). 89% of past graduating class borrowed through all loan programs. *Average indebtedness per student:* $17,143. ***Average need-based loan:*** Freshmen: $3532; Undergraduates: $4438. ***Parent loans:*** $613,973 (61% need-based, 39% non-need-based). ***Programs:*** Federal Direct (Subsidized and Unsubsidized Stafford, PLUS), Perkins, state, college/university.

WORK-STUDY ***Federal work-study:*** Total amount: $1,304,156; 673 jobs averaging $1930. ***State or other work-study/employment:*** Total amount: $1,382,629 (100% non-need-based).

ATHLETIC AWARDS Total amount: $106,338 (68% need-based, 32% non-need-based).

APPLYING FOR FINANCIAL AID ***Required financial aid form:*** FAFSA. ***Financial aid deadline (priority):*** 3/15. ***Notification date:*** Continuous beginning 2/1. Students must reply within 2 weeks of notification.

CONTACT Ms. Marlene Martin, Assistant Funds Manager, Rutgers, The State University of New Jersey, Newark, 620 George Street, New Brunswick, NJ 08901, 732-932-7868. *E-mail:* mgmartin@rci.rutgers.edu.

RUTGERS, THE STATE UNIVERSITY OF NEW JERSEY, NEW BRUNSWICK

New Brunswick, NJ

Tuition & fees (NJ res): $9958 **Average undergraduate aid package: $12,536**

ABOUT THE INSTITUTION State-supported, coed. Awards: bachelor's, master's, doctoral, and first professional degrees and post-master's certificates. 122 undergraduate majors. Total enrollment: 34,392. Undergraduates: 26,691. Freshmen: 5,274. Federal methodology is used as a basis for awarding need-based institutional aid.

UNDERGRADUATE EXPENSES for 2006–07 ***Application fee:*** $60. ***Tuition, state resident:*** full-time $7923; part-time $255 per credit hour. ***Tuition, nonresident:*** full-time $16,428; part-time $533 per credit hour. Part-time tuition and fees vary according to course level. ***College room and board:*** $9312; ***Room only:*** $5682. Room and board charges vary according to board plan and housing facility. ***Payment plan:*** Installment.

FRESHMAN FINANCIAL AID (Fall 2006, est.) 4043 applied for aid; of those 69% were deemed to have need. 97% of freshmen with need received aid; of those 40% had need fully met. ***Average percent of need met:*** 68% (excluding resources awarded to replace EFC). ***Average financial aid package:*** $12,573 (excluding resources awarded to replace EFC). 5% of all full-time freshmen had no need and received non-need-based gift aid.

UNDERGRADUATE FINANCIAL AID (Fall 2006, est.) 16,095 applied for aid; of those 78% were deemed to have need. 99% of undergraduates with need received aid; of those 38% had need fully met. ***Average percent of need met:*** 70% (excluding resources awarded to replace EFC). ***Average financial aid package:*** $12,536 (excluding resources awarded to replace EFC). 7% of all full-time undergraduates had no need and received non-need-based gift aid.

GIFT AID (NEED-BASED) ***Total amount:*** $77,955,479 (27% federal, 48% state, 23% institutional, 2% external sources). ***Receiving aid:*** Freshmen: 31% (1,620); All full-time undergraduates: 32% (7,831). ***Average award:*** Freshmen: $9530; Undergraduates: $8890. ***Scholarships, grants, and awards:*** Federal Pell, FSEOG, state, private, college/university gift aid from institutional funds.

GIFT AID (NON-NEED-BASED) ***Total amount:*** $9,015,878 (16% state, 73% institutional, 11% external sources). ***Receiving aid:*** Freshmen: 30% (1,603); Undergraduates: 25% (6,081). ***Average award:*** Freshmen: $6655; Undergraduates: $2592. ***Scholarships, grants, and awards by category:*** *Academic Interests/Achievement:* 5,560 awards ($21,410,325 total): general academic interests/achievements. *Creative Arts/Performance:* 67 awards ($138,847 total): general creative arts/performance. *Special Characteristics:* 442 awards ($3,109,869 total): children of faculty/staff. ***Tuition waivers:*** Full or partial for employees or children of employees. ***ROTC:*** Army, Air Force.

LOANS ***Student loans:*** $108,012,841 (78% need-based, 22% non-need-based). 65% of past graduating class borrowed through all loan programs. *Average indebtedness per student:* $16,283. ***Average need-based loan:*** Freshmen: $3199; Undergraduates: $4262. ***Parent loans:*** $9,607,432 (66% need-based, 34% non-need-based). ***Programs:*** Federal Direct (Subsidized and Unsubsidized Stafford, PLUS), Perkins, Federal Nursing, state, college/university.

WORK-STUDY ***Federal work-study:*** Total amount: $4,946,829; 2,646 jobs averaging $1903. ***State or other work-study/employment:*** Total amount: $11,168,622 (100% non-need-based).

ATHLETIC AWARDS Total amount: $6,182,246 (48% need-based, 52% non-need-based).

APPLYING FOR FINANCIAL AID ***Required financial aid form:*** FAFSA. ***Financial aid deadline (priority):*** 3/15. ***Notification date:*** Continuous beginning 2/1. Students must reply within 2 weeks of notification.

CONTACT Ms. Marlene Martin, Assistant Funds Manager, Rutgers, The State University of New Jersey, New Brunswick, 620 George Street, New Brunswick, NJ 08901, 732-932-7868. *E-mail:* mgmartin@rci.rutgers.edu.

SACRED HEART MAJOR SEMINARY

Detroit, MI

CONTACT Financial Aid Office, Sacred Heart Major Seminary, 2701 Chicago Boulevard, Detroit, MI 48206-1799, 313-883-8500. *Fax:* 313-868-6440.

SACRED HEART UNIVERSITY

Fairfield, CT

Tuition & fees: $25,400 **Average undergraduate aid package: $16,025**

ABOUT THE INSTITUTION Independent Roman Catholic, coed. Awards: associate, bachelor's, master's, and doctoral degrees and post-bachelor's and post-master's certificates (also offers part-time program with significant enrollment not reflected in profile). 67 undergraduate majors. Total enrollment: 5,756. Undergraduates: 4,203. Freshmen: 931. Both federal and institutional methodology are used as a basis for awarding need-based institutional aid.

UNDERGRADUATE EXPENSES for 2006–07 ***Application fee:*** $50. ***Comprehensive fee:*** $35,720 includes full-time tuition ($25,300), mandatory fees ($100), and room and board ($10,320). ***College room only:*** $7638. Full-time tuition and fees vary according to program. Room and board charges vary according to board plan and housing facility. ***Part-time tuition:*** $410 per credit. ***Part-time fees:*** $76 per term. Part-time tuition and fees vary according to program. ***Payment plan:*** Installment.

FRESHMAN FINANCIAL AID (Fall 2006, est.) 785 applied for aid; of those 79% were deemed to have need. 99% of freshmen with need received aid; of those 32% had need fully met. ***Average percent of need met:*** 69% (excluding resources awarded to replace EFC). ***Average financial aid package:*** $16,090 (excluding resources awarded to replace EFC). 23% of all full-time freshmen had no need and received non-need-based gift aid.

UNDERGRADUATE FINANCIAL AID (Fall 2006, est.) 2,859 applied for aid; of those 80% were deemed to have need. 98% of undergraduates with need received aid; of those 31% had need fully met. ***Average percent of need met:*** 70% (excluding resources awarded to replace EFC). ***Average financial aid package:*** $16,025 (excluding resources awarded to replace EFC). 20% of all full-time undergraduates had no need and received non-need-based gift aid.

GIFT AID (NEED-BASED) ***Total amount:*** $19,602,235 (8% federal, 10% state, 74% institutional, 8% external sources). ***Receiving aid:*** Freshmen: 65% (606); All full-time undergraduates: 64% (2,176). ***Average award:*** Freshmen: $10,541; Undergraduates: $10,080. ***Scholarships, grants, and awards:*** Federal Pell, FSEOG, state, private, college/university gift aid from institutional funds, Federal Nursing.

GIFT AID (NON-NEED-BASED) ***Total amount:*** $3,045,938 (1% federal, 70% institutional, 29% external sources). ***Receiving aid:*** Freshmen: 5% (49); Undergraduates: 4% (149). ***Average award:*** Freshmen: $11,421; Undergraduates: $11,125. ***Scholarships, grants, and awards by category:*** *Academic Interests/Achievement:* 1,734 awards ($6,183,456 total): biological sciences, business, computer science, education, English, general academic interests/achievements, health fields, humanities, mathematics, physical sciences, premedicine. *Creative Arts/Performance:* 103 awards ($128,950 total): applied art and design, art/fine arts, creative writing, music. *Special Achievements/Activities:* 240 awards ($483,287 total): community service, general special achievements/activities, leadership, religious involvement. *Special Characteristics:* children of faculty/staff, ethnic background, handicapped students, members of minority groups, religious affiliation, siblings of current students, twins. ***Tuition waivers:*** Full or partial for employees or children of employees. ***ROTC:*** Army.

LOANS ***Student loans:*** $25,196,741 (57% need-based, 43% non-need-based). 87% of past graduating class borrowed through all loan programs. *Average indebtedness per student:* $21,166. ***Average need-based loan:*** Freshmen: $5648; Undergraduates: $6565. ***Parent loans:*** $8,328,371 (40% need-based, 60% non-need-based). ***Programs:*** FFEL (Subsidized and Unsubsidized Stafford, PLUS), Perkins, state.

WORK-STUDY ***Federal work-study:*** Total amount: $578,297; 449 jobs averaging $1287. ***State or other work-study/employment:*** Total amount: $1,308,381 (26% need-based, 74% non-need-based). 284 part-time jobs averaging $1129.

ATHLETIC AWARDS Total amount: $5,271,759 (50% need-based, 50% non-need-based).

APPLYING FOR FINANCIAL AID ***Required financial aid forms:*** FAFSA, CSS Financial Aid PROFILE. ***Financial aid deadline (priority):*** 2/15. ***Notification date:*** Continuous beginning 3/1. Students must reply within 2 weeks of notification.

CONTACT Ms. Julie B. Savino, Dean of University Financial Assistance, Sacred Heart University, 5151 Park Avenue, Fairfield, CT 06825, 203-371-7980. *Fax:* 203-365-7608. *E-mail:* savinoj@sacredheart.edu.

SAGE COLLEGE OF ALBANY

Albany, NY

Tuition & fees: $17,670 **Average undergraduate aid package: N/A**

ABOUT THE INSTITUTION Independent, coed. Awards: associate and bachelor's degrees. 23 undergraduate majors. Total enrollment: 1,074. Undergraduates: 1,074. Freshmen: 105. Federal methodology is used as a basis for awarding need-based institutional aid.

UNDERGRADUATE EXPENSES for 2006–07 ***Application fee:*** $30. ***Comprehensive fee:*** $26,190 includes full-time tuition ($16,800), mandatory fees ($870), and room and board ($8520). ***College room only:*** $4430. ***Part-time tuition:*** $560 per credit hour. ***Payment plans:*** Installment, deferred payment.

FRESHMAN FINANCIAL AID (Fall 2006, est.) 104 applied for aid; of those 87% were deemed to have need. 100% of freshmen with need received aid. 3% of all full-time freshmen had no need and received non-need-based gift aid.

UNDERGRADUATE FINANCIAL AID (Fall 2006, est.) 521 applied for aid; of those 85% were deemed to have need. 100% of undergraduates with need received aid. 6% of all full-time undergraduates had no need and received non-need-based gift aid.

GIFT AID (NEED-BASED) ***Total amount:*** $2,942,115 (22% federal, 31% state, 47% institutional). ***Receiving aid:*** Freshmen: 53% (56); All full-time undergraduates: 49% (265). ***Scholarships, grants, and awards:*** Federal Pell, FSEOG, state, private, college/university gift aid from institutional funds.

GIFT AID (NON-NEED-BASED) ***Total amount:*** $1,361,050 (98% institutional, 2% external sources). ***Receiving aid:*** Freshmen: 45% (47); Undergraduates: 52% (284). ***Average award:*** Freshmen: $5000; Undergraduates: $5450. ***Scholarships, grants, and awards by category:*** *Academic Interests/Achievement:* 319 awards ($1,136,000 total): general academic interests/achievements. *Creative Arts/Performance:* 16 awards ($42,000 total): art/fine arts. *Special Achievements/Activities:* 14 awards ($12,375 total): community service. *Special Characteristics:* 10 awards ($122,898 total): children of faculty/staff. ***Tuition waivers:*** Full or partial for employees or children of employees.

LOANS ***Student loans:*** $3,625,536 (47% need-based, 53% non-need-based). 93% of past graduating class borrowed through all loan programs. *Average indebtedness per student:* $18,000. ***Parent loans:*** $691,361 (37% need-based, 63% non-need-based). ***Programs:*** FFEL (Subsidized and Unsubsidized Stafford, PLUS), Perkins, alternative loans.

WORK-STUDY ***Federal work-study:*** Total amount: $98,900; 210 jobs averaging $1500. ***State or other work-study/employment:*** Total amount: $18,092 (100% non-need-based). 19 part-time jobs averaging $1200.

APPLYING FOR FINANCIAL AID ***Required financial aid forms:*** FAFSA, state aid form. ***Financial aid deadline (priority):*** 3/1. ***Notification date:*** Continuous beginning 3/1. Students must reply within 2 weeks of notification.

CONTACT James K. Dease, Associate Vice President for Student Service, Sage College of Albany, 45 Ferry Street, Troy, NY 12180, 518-244-4525 or toll-free 888-VERY-SAGE. *Fax:* 518-244-2460. *E-mail:* deasej@sage.edu.

SAGINAW VALLEY STATE UNIVERSITY

University Center, MI

CONTACT Robert Lemuel, Director of Scholarships and Financial Aid, Saginaw Valley State University, 7400 Bay Road, University Center, MI 48710, 989-964-4103 or toll-free 800-968-9500. *Fax:* 989-790-0180.

ST. AMBROSE UNIVERSITY

Davenport, IA

Tuition & fees: N/R **Average undergraduate aid package: $17,638**

ABOUT THE INSTITUTION Independent Roman Catholic, coed. Awards: bachelor's, master's, and doctoral degrees and post-bachelor's and post-master's certificates. 72 undergraduate majors. Total enrollment: 3,780. Undergraduates: 2,829. Freshmen: 510. Federal methodology is used as a basis for awarding need-based institutional aid.

UNDERGRADUATE EXPENSES for 2007–08 ***Application fee:*** $25. ***Tuition:*** part-time $640 per semester hour.

FRESHMAN FINANCIAL AID (Fall 2006, est.) 505 applied for aid; of those 70% were deemed to have need. 100% of freshmen with need received aid; of those 32% had need fully met. ***Average percent of need met:*** 15% (excluding resources awarded to replace EFC). ***Average financial aid package:*** $17,551 (excluding resources awarded to replace EFC). 30% of all full-time freshmen had no need and received non-need-based gift aid.

UNDERGRADUATE FINANCIAL AID (Fall 2006, est.) 2,281 applied for aid; of those 73% were deemed to have need. 99% of undergraduates with need received aid; of those 33% had need fully met. ***Average percent of need met:*** 15% (excluding resources awarded to replace EFC). ***Average financial aid package:*** $17,638 (excluding resources awarded to replace EFC). 25% of all full-time undergraduates had no need and received non-need-based gift aid.

GIFT AID (NEED-BASED) ***Total amount:*** $16,021,567 (12% federal, 15% state, 71% institutional, 2% external sources). ***Receiving aid:*** Freshmen: 70% (352); All full-time undergraduates: 69% (1,616). ***Average award:*** Freshmen: $9673; Undergraduates: $8990. ***Scholarships, grants, and awards:*** Federal Pell, FSEOG, state, private, college/university gift aid from institutional funds.

GIFT AID (NON-NEED-BASED) ***Total amount:*** $4,376,460 (1% state, 98% institutional, 1% external sources). ***Receiving aid:*** Freshmen: 34% (173); Undergraduates: 24% (553). ***Average award:*** Freshmen: $6893; Undergraduates: $6457. ***Scholarships, grants, and awards by category:*** *Academic Interests/Achievement:* 1,635 awards ($8,223,177 total): general academic interests/achievements, international studies. *Creative Arts/Performance:* 134 awards ($274,969 total): art/fine arts, dance, theater/drama. *Special Characteristics:* 66 awards ($58,400 total): children of faculty/staff, international students, members of minority groups.

LOANS ***Student loans:*** $22,348,399 (91% need-based, 9% non-need-based). 82% of past graduating class borrowed through all loan programs. *Average indebtedness per student:* $30,541. ***Average need-based loan:*** Freshmen: $2715; Undergraduates: $4077. ***Parent loans:*** $2,102,624 (74% need-based, 26% non-need-based). ***Programs:*** FFEL (Subsidized and Unsubsidized Stafford, PLUS), Perkins.

WORK-STUDY ***Federal work-study:*** Total amount: $750,809; 540 jobs averaging $1450. ***State or other work-study/employment:*** Total amount: $186,320 (69% need-based, 31% non-need-based). 152 part-time jobs averaging $1378.

ATHLETIC AWARDS Total amount: $1,774,562 (68% need-based, 32% non-need-based).

APPLYING FOR FINANCIAL AID ***Required financial aid form:*** FAFSA. ***Financial aid deadline (priority):*** 3/15. ***Notification date:*** Continuous beginning 2/1. Students must reply within 2 weeks of notification.

CONTACT Ms. Julie Haack, Director of Financial Aid, St. Ambrose University, 518 West Locust Street, Davenport, IA 52803, 563-333-6314 or toll-free 800-383-2627. *Fax:* 563-333-6243. *E-mail:* haackjuliea@sau.edu.

ST. ANDREWS PRESBYTERIAN COLLEGE

Laurinburg, NC

Tuition & fees: $17,162 **Average undergraduate aid package: $13,232**

ABOUT THE INSTITUTION Independent Presbyterian, coed. Awards: bachelor's degrees. 23 undergraduate majors. Total enrollment: 808. Undergraduates: 808. Freshmen: 196. Federal methodology is used as a basis for awarding need-based institutional aid.

UNDERGRADUATE EXPENSES for 2006–07 ***Application fee:*** $30. ***Comprehensive fee:*** $24,702 includes full-time tuition ($17,162) and room and board ($7540). Full-time tuition and fees vary according to location. Room and board charges vary according to housing facility. ***Part-time tuition:*** $410 per credit. Part-time tuition and fees vary according to location. Room, board, and fees are no longer listed separately; all are included in the room and board costs. ***Payment plan:*** Installment.

FRESHMAN FINANCIAL AID (Fall 2006, est.) 147 applied for aid; of those 80% were deemed to have need. 100% of freshmen with need received aid; of those 27% had need fully met. ***Average percent of need met:*** 72% (excluding resources awarded to replace EFC). ***Average financial aid package:*** $12,778 (excluding resources awarded to replace EFC). 40% of all full-time freshmen had no need and received non-need-based gift aid.

UNDERGRADUATE FINANCIAL AID (Fall 2006, est.) 551 applied for aid; of those 83% were deemed to have need. 100% of undergraduates with need received aid; of those 27% had need fully met. ***Average percent of need met:*** 75% (excluding resources awarded to replace EFC). ***Average financial aid package:*** $13,232 (excluding resources awarded to replace EFC). 38% of all full-time undergraduates had no need and received non-need-based gift aid.

GIFT AID (NEED-BASED) ***Total amount:*** $3,728,190 (18% federal, 21% state, 50% institutional, 11% external sources). ***Receiving aid:*** Freshmen: 57% (118); All full-time undergraduates: 60% (453). ***Average award:*** Freshmen: $9794; Undergraduates: $9477. ***Scholarships, grants, and awards:*** Federal Pell, FSEOG, state, private, college/university gift aid from institutional funds.

GIFT AID (NON-NEED-BASED) ***Total amount:*** $2,115,303 (12% state, 82% institutional, 6% external sources). ***Receiving aid:*** Freshmen: 11% (22); Undergraduates: 9% (71). ***Average award:*** Freshmen: $9164; Undergraduates: $8833. ***Scholarships, grants, and awards by category:*** *Academic Interests/Achievement:* 643 awards ($2,897,217 total): general academic interests/achievements. *Creative Arts/Performance:* 22 awards ($23,750 total): performing arts. *Special Achievements/Activities:* 75 awards ($96,854 total): general special achievements/activities, leadership. ***Tuition waivers:*** Full or partial for employees or children of employees, adult students, senior citizens.

LOANS ***Student loans:*** $2,621,096 (70% need-based, 30% non-need-based). 58% of past graduating class borrowed through all loan programs. *Average indebtedness per student:* $18,951. ***Average need-based loan:*** Freshmen: $3049; Undergraduates: $3972. ***Parent loans:*** $2,232,883 (34% need-based, 66% non-need-based). ***Programs:*** FFEL (Subsidized and Unsubsidized Stafford, PLUS).

WORK-STUDY ***Federal work-study:*** Total amount: $281,452; 274 jobs averaging $1800. ***State or other work-study/employment:*** Total amount: $12,388 (7% need-based, 93% non-need-based). 30 part-time jobs averaging $1800.

ATHLETIC AWARDS Total amount: $951,347 (63% need-based, 37% non-need-based).

APPLYING FOR FINANCIAL AID ***Required financial aid forms:*** FAFSA, state aid form. ***Financial aid deadline:*** Continuous. ***Notification date:*** Continuous beginning 2/1. Students must reply within 2 weeks of notification.

CONTACT Kimberly Driggers, Director of Student Financial Planning, St. Andrews Presbyterian College, 1700 Dogwood Mile, Laurinburg, NC 28352, 910-277-5562 or toll-free 800-763-0198. *Fax:* 910-277-5206.

SAINT ANSELM COLLEGE

Manchester, NH

Tuition & fees: N/R **Average undergraduate aid package: $20,040**

ABOUT THE INSTITUTION Independent Roman Catholic, coed. Awards: bachelor's degrees. 29 undergraduate majors. Total enrollment: 1,986. Undergraduates: 1,986. Freshmen: 519. Both federal and institutional methodology are used as a basis for awarding need-based institutional aid.

FRESHMAN FINANCIAL AID (Fall 2006, est.) 490 applied for aid; of those 82% were deemed to have need. 100% of freshmen with need received aid; of those 29% had need fully met. ***Average percent of need met:*** 87% (excluding resources awarded to replace EFC). ***Average financial aid package:*** $19,996 (excluding resources awarded to replace EFC). 6% of all full-time freshmen had no need and received non-need-based gift aid.

UNDERGRADUATE FINANCIAL AID (Fall 2006, est.) 1,572 applied for aid; of those 86% were deemed to have need. 100% of undergraduates with need received aid; of those 25% had need fully met. ***Average percent of need met:*** 86% (excluding resources awarded to replace EFC). ***Average financial aid package:*** $20,040 (excluding resources awarded to replace EFC). 15% of all full-time undergraduates had no need and received non-need-based gift aid.

GIFT AID (NEED-BASED) ***Total amount:*** $17,999,796 (5% federal, 1% state, 91% institutional, 3% external sources). ***Receiving aid:*** Freshmen: 71% (402); All full-time undergraduates: 70% (1,342). ***Average award:*** Freshmen: $15,632; Undergraduates: $13,855. ***Scholarships, grants, and awards:*** Federal Pell, FSEOG, state, private, college/university gift aid from institutional funds.

GIFT AID (NON-NEED-BASED) ***Total amount:*** $2,365,305 (94% institutional, 6% external sources). ***Receiving aid:*** Freshmen: 52% (294); Undergraduates: 41% (782). ***Average award:*** Freshmen: $12,510; Undergraduates: $8851. ***Scholarships, grants, and awards by category:*** *Academic Interests/Achievement:* 768 awards ($4,404,100 total): general academic interests/achievements. *Special Characteristics:* 153 awards ($1,991,627 total): children of educators, children of faculty/staff, siblings of current students. ***ROTC:*** Army cooperative, Air Force cooperative.

LOANS ***Student loans:*** $15,694,496 (53% need-based, 47% non-need-based). 77% of past graduating class borrowed through all loan programs. *Average indebtedness per student:* $27,300. ***Average need-based loan:*** Freshmen: $3900; Undergraduates: $5695. ***Parent loans:*** $5,071,240 (14% need-based, 86% non-need-based). ***Programs:*** FFEL (Subsidized and Unsubsidized Stafford, PLUS), Perkins, GATE Loans.

WORK-STUDY ***Federal work-study:*** Total amount: $1,523,688; 1,094 jobs averaging $1393. ***State or other work-study/employment:*** Total amount: $16,000 (100% non-need-based). 8 part-time jobs averaging $2000.

ATHLETIC AWARDS Total amount: $681,465 (13% need-based, 87% non-need-based).

APPLYING FOR FINANCIAL AID ***Required financial aid forms:*** FAFSA, CSS Financial Aid PROFILE. ***Financial aid deadline:*** 3/15 (priority: 3/15). ***Notification date:*** Continuous beginning 3/1. Students must reply by 5/1 or within 2 weeks of notification.

CONTACT Elizabeth Keuffel, Director of Financial Aid, Saint Anselm College, 100 Saint Anselm Drive, Manchester, NH 03102-1310, 603-641-7110 or toll-free 888-4ANSELM. *Fax:* 603-656-6015. *E-mail:* financial_aid@anselm.edu.

SAINT ANTHONY COLLEGE OF NURSING

Rockford, IL

Tuition & fees: $17,336 **Average undergraduate aid package: $14,518**

ABOUT THE INSTITUTION Independent Roman Catholic, coed, primarily women. Awards: bachelor's degrees. 1 undergraduate major. Total enrollment: 161. Undergraduates: 146. Federal methodology is used as a basis for awarding need-based institutional aid.

UNDERGRADUATE EXPENSES for 2007–08 ***Application fee:*** $50. ***Tuition:*** full-time $17,220; part-time $539 per credit.

UNDERGRADUATE FINANCIAL AID (Fall 2006, est.) 144 applied for aid; of those 100% were deemed to have need. 100% of undergraduates with need received aid. ***Average percent of need met:*** 50% (excluding resources awarded to replace EFC). ***Average financial aid package:*** $14,518 (excluding resources awarded to replace EFC).

GIFT AID (NEED-BASED) ***Total amount:*** $528,857 (28% federal, 64% state, 4% institutional, 4% external sources). ***Receiving aid:*** All full-time undergraduates: 67% (112). ***Average award:*** Undergraduates: $4722. ***Scholarships, grants, and awards:*** Federal Pell, state, private, college/university gift aid from institutional funds.

GIFT AID (NON-NEED-BASED) ***Receiving aid:*** Undergraduates: 44% (74).

LOANS ***Student loans:*** $791,650 (56% need-based, 44% non-need-based). 87% of past graduating class borrowed through all loan programs. *Average indebtedness per student:* $21,000. ***Average need-based loan:*** Undergraduates: $7996. ***Parent loans:*** $159,898 (100% non-need-based). ***Programs:*** FFEL (Subsidized and Unsubsidized Stafford, PLUS), alternative loans.

APPLYING FOR FINANCIAL AID ***Required financial aid forms:*** FAFSA, institution's own form. ***Financial aid deadline (priority):*** 5/1. ***Notification date:*** 7/1.

CONTACT Serrita Woods, Financial Aid Officer, Saint Anthony College of Nursing, 5658 East State Street, Rockford, IL 61108-2468, 815-395-5089. *Fax:* 815-395-2275. *E-mail:* serritawoods@sacn.edu.

ST. AUGUSTINE COLLEGE

Chicago, IL

CONTACT Mrs. Maria Zambonino, Director of Financial Aid, St. Augustine College, 1345 W Angyle, Chicago, IL 60640, 773-878-3813. *Fax:* 773-878-9032. *E-mail:* mzambonino@hotmail.com.

SAINT AUGUSTINE'S COLLEGE

Raleigh, NC

CONTACT Ms. Wanda C. White, Director of Financial Aid, Saint Augustine's College, 1315 Oakwood Avenue, Raleigh, NC 27610-2298, 919-516-4131 or toll-free 800-948-1126. *Fax:* 919-516-4338. *E-mail:* wwhite@es.st-aug.edu.

ST. BONAVENTURE UNIVERSITY

St. Bonaventure, NY

ABOUT THE INSTITUTION Independent religious, coed. Awards: bachelor's and master's degrees and post-bachelor's and post-master's certificates. 59 undergraduate majors. Total enrollment: 2,614. Undergraduates: 2,141. Freshmen: 478.

GIFT AID (NEED-BASED) ***Scholarships, grants, and awards:*** Federal Pell, FSEOG, state, private, college/university gift aid from institutional funds.

GIFT AID (NON-NEED-BASED) ***Scholarships, grants, and awards by category:*** *Academic Interests/Achievement:* business, general academic interests/ achievements. *Creative Arts/Performance:* journalism/publications, music, performing arts. *Special Characteristics:* children of faculty/staff, local/state students, members of minority groups, relatives of clergy, religious affiliation, siblings of current students.

LOANS ***Programs:*** FFEL (Subsidized and Unsubsidized Stafford, PLUS), Perkins, college/university.

WORK-STUDY ***Federal work-study:*** Total amount: $817,058; 525 jobs averaging $1200. ***State or other work-study/employment:*** Part-time jobs available.

APPLYING FOR FINANCIAL AID ***Required financial aid forms:*** FAFSA, institution's own form, state aid form.

CONTACT Ms. Elizabeth T. Rankin, Director of Financial Aid, St. Bonaventure University, Route 417, St. Bonaventure, NY 14778-2284, 716-375-2528 or toll-free 800-462-5050. *Fax:* 716-375-2087. *E-mail:* erankin@sbu.edu.

ST. CHARLES BORROMEO SEMINARY, OVERBROOK

Wynnewood, PA

CONTACT Ms. Bonnie L. Behm, Coordinator of Financial Aid, St. Charles Borromeo Seminary, Overbrook, 100 East Wynnewood Road, Wynnewood, PA 19096-3099, 610-785-6582. *Fax:* 610-667-3971. *E-mail:* finaid.scs@erols.com.

ST. CLOUD STATE UNIVERSITY

St. Cloud, MN

Tuition & fees (MN res): $5718 **Average undergraduate aid package: $10,772**

ABOUT THE INSTITUTION State-supported, coed. Awards: associate, bachelor's, and master's degrees and post-bachelor's certificates. 139 undergraduate majors. Total enrollment: 15,964. Undergraduates: 14,486. Freshmen: 2,152. Federal methodology is used as a basis for awarding need-based institutional aid.

UNDERGRADUATE EXPENSES for 2006–07 ***Application fee:*** $20. ***Tuition, state resident:*** full-time $5045; part-time $169 per credit. ***Tuition, nonresident:*** full-time $10,952; part-time $365 per credit. ***Required fees:*** full-time $673; $27 per credit. Full-time tuition and fees vary according to course load and reciprocity agreements. Part-time tuition and fees vary according to course load and reciprocity agreements. ***College room and board:*** $5194. Room and board charges vary according to board plan and housing facility. ***Payment plan:*** Installment.

FRESHMAN FINANCIAL AID (Fall 2006, est.) 1642 applied for aid; of those 69% were deemed to have need. 100% of freshmen with need received aid; of those 75% had need fully met. ***Average percent of need met:*** 75% (excluding resources awarded to replace EFC). ***Average financial aid package:*** $10,698 (excluding resources awarded to replace EFC). 4% of all full-time freshmen had no need and received non-need-based gift aid.

UNDERGRADUATE FINANCIAL AID (Fall 2006, est.) 7,654 applied for aid; of those 71% were deemed to have need. 100% of undergraduates with need received aid; of those 62% had need fully met. ***Average percent of need met:*** 62% (excluding resources awarded to replace EFC). ***Average financial aid package:*** $10,772 (excluding resources awarded to replace EFC). 2% of all full-time undergraduates had no need and received non-need-based gift aid.

GIFT AID (NEED-BASED) ***Total amount:*** $18,838,352 (51% federal, 39% state, 6% institutional, 4% external sources). ***Receiving aid:*** Freshmen: 39% (880); All full-time undergraduates: 36% (4,194). ***Average award:*** Freshmen: $4562; Undergraduates: $4492. ***Scholarships, grants, and awards:*** Federal Pell, FSEOG, state, private, college/university gift aid from institutional funds.

GIFT AID (NON-NEED-BASED) ***Total amount:*** $2,929,529 (24% federal, 12% state, 39% institutional, 25% external sources). ***Receiving aid:*** Freshmen: 6% (128); Undergraduates: 4% (444). ***Average award:*** Freshmen: $2030; Undergraduates: $1605. ***Scholarships, grants, and awards by category:*** *Academic Interests/ Achievement:* biological sciences, business, communication, computer science, education, engineering/technologies, English, general academic interests/ achievements, health fields, international studies, mathematics, physical sciences, social sciences. *Creative Arts/Performance:* applied art and design, art/fine arts, cinema/film/broadcasting, creative writing, journalism/publications, music, performing arts, theater/drama. *Special Achievements/Activities:* community service, general special achievements/activities. *Special Characteristics:* children of faculty/staff, children of union members/company employees, local/state students, members of minority groups, out-of-state students. ***Tuition waivers:*** Full or partial for employees or children of employees, senior citizens. ***ROTC:*** Army.

LOANS ***Student loans:*** $75,672,075 (46% need-based, 54% non-need-based). 69% of past graduating class borrowed through all loan programs. *Average indebtedness per student:* $21,869. ***Average need-based loan:*** Freshmen: $4928; Undergraduates: $5872. ***Parent loans:*** $18,860,386 (3% need-based, 97% non-need-based). ***Programs:*** FFEL (Subsidized and Unsubsidized Stafford, PLUS), Perkins, state.

WORK-STUDY ***Federal work-study:*** Total amount: $719,830; jobs available. ***State or other work-study/employment:*** Total amount: $1,349,549 (100% need-based). Part-time jobs available.

ATHLETIC AWARDS Total amount: $1,239,224 (22% need-based, 78% non-need-based).

APPLYING FOR FINANCIAL AID ***Required financial aid forms:*** FAFSA, institution's own form. ***Financial aid deadline:*** Continuous. ***Notification date:*** Continuous beginning 6/15.

CONTACT Frank P. Morrissey, Associate Director of Scholarships and Financial Aid, St. Cloud State University, 106 Administrative Services, 720 4th Avenue South, St. Cloud, MN 56301-4498, 320-308-2047 or toll-free 877-654-7278. *Fax:* 320-308-5424. *E-mail:* fpmorrissey@stcloudstate.edu.

ST. EDWARD'S UNIVERSITY

Austin, TX

Tuition & fees: $20,400 **Average undergraduate aid package: $15,238**

ABOUT THE INSTITUTION Independent Roman Catholic, coed. Awards: bachelor's and master's degrees and post-bachelor's certificates. 49 undergraduate majors. Total enrollment: 5,224. Undergraduates: 4,229. Freshmen: 714. Federal methodology is used as a basis for awarding need-based institutional aid.

UNDERGRADUATE EXPENSES for 2007–08 ***Application fee:*** $45. ***Comprehensive fee:*** $27,860 includes full-time tuition ($20,400) and room and board ($7460). ***College room only:*** $4310. ***Part-time tuition:*** $680 per credit hour.

FRESHMAN FINANCIAL AID (Fall 2006, est.) 579 applied for aid; of those 72% were deemed to have need. 100% of freshmen with need received aid; of those 36% had need fully met. ***Average percent of need met:*** 81% (excluding resources awarded to replace EFC). ***Average financial aid package:*** $16,278 (excluding resources awarded to replace EFC). 17% of all full-time freshmen had no need and received non-need-based gift aid.

UNDERGRADUATE FINANCIAL AID (Fall 2006, est.) 2,408 applied for aid; of those 80% were deemed to have need. 99% of undergraduates with need received aid; of those 33% had need fully met. ***Average percent of need met:*** 75% (excluding resources awarded to replace EFC). ***Average financial aid package:*** $15,238 (excluding resources awarded to replace EFC). 12% of all full-time undergraduates had no need and received non-need-based gift aid.

GIFT AID (NEED-BASED) ***Total amount:*** $20,443,397 (18% federal, 21% state, 61% institutional). ***Receiving aid:*** Freshmen: 57% (395); All full-time undergraduates: 54% (1,749). ***Average award:*** Freshmen: $9929; Undergraduates: $10,137. ***Scholarships, grants, and awards:*** Federal Pell, FSEOG, state, private, college/ university gift aid from institutional funds, endowed scholarships.

GIFT AID (NON-NEED-BASED) ***Total amount:*** $4,571,781 (83% institutional, 17% external sources). ***Receiving aid:*** Freshmen: 34% (237); Undergraduates: 23% (738). ***Average award:*** Freshmen: $8000; Undergraduates: $6692. ***Scholarships, grants, and awards by category:*** *Academic Interests/Achievement:* 1,346 awards ($7,298,949 total): biological sciences, business, communication, computer science, education, English, foreign languages, general academic interests/achievements, humanities, international studies, mathematics, military science, physical sciences, religion/biblical studies, social sciences. *Creative Arts/Performance:* 40 awards ($91,651 total): theater/drama. *Special Achievements/ Activities:* 78 awards ($144,157 total): cheerleading/drum major, community service, general special achievements/activities, leadership. *Special Characteristics:* 50 awards ($702,175 total): adult students, children of faculty/staff, religious affiliation. ***ROTC:*** Army cooperative, Air Force cooperative.

LOANS ***Student loans:*** $23,305,866 (31% need-based, 69% non-need-based). 71% of past graduating class borrowed through all loan programs. *Average indebtedness per student:* $25,832. ***Average need-based loan:*** Freshmen: $4819; Undergraduates: $5151. ***Parent loans:*** $4,357,785 (100% non-need-based). ***Programs:*** FFEL (Subsidized and Unsubsidized Stafford, PLUS), Perkins, state, alternative loans.

WORK-STUDY ***Federal work-study:*** Total amount: $320,669; 182 jobs averaging $1762. ***State or other work-study/employment:*** Total amount: $34,789 (100% need-based). 19 part-time jobs averaging $1831.

ATHLETIC AWARDS Total amount: $1,661,541 (100% non-need-based).

APPLYING FOR FINANCIAL AID ***Required financial aid form:*** FAFSA. ***Financial aid deadline (priority):*** 3/1. ***Notification date:*** Continuous beginning 2/15. Students must reply by 5/1 or within 2 weeks of notification.

CONTACT Office of Student Financial Services, St. Edward's University, 3001 South Congress Avenue, Austin, TX 78704, 512-448-8523 or toll-free 800-555-0164. *Fax:* 512-416-5837. *E-mail:* seu.finaid@stedwards.edu.

ST. FRANCIS COLLEGE

Brooklyn Heights, NY

Tuition & fees: $14,020 **Average undergraduate aid package: $9300**

ABOUT THE INSTITUTION Independent Roman Catholic, coed. Awards: associate, bachelor's, and master's degrees. 35 undergraduate majors. Total enrollment: 2,258. Undergraduates: 2,251. Freshmen: 483. Federal methodology is used as a basis for awarding need-based institutional aid.

UNDERGRADUATE EXPENSES for 2006–07 ***Application fee:*** $35. ***Tuition:*** full-time $13,500; part-time $480 per credit. ***Required fees:*** full-time $520; $140 per term part-time. Full-time tuition and fees vary according to course level, course load, degree level, program, and student level. Part-time tuition and fees vary according to course level, course load, degree level, program, and student level. ***Payment plans:*** Installment, deferred payment.

FRESHMAN FINANCIAL AID (Fall 2006, est.) 453 applied for aid; of those 100% were deemed to have need. 100% of freshmen with need received aid; of those 15% had need fully met. ***Average percent of need met:*** 57% (excluding resources awarded to replace EFC). ***Average financial aid package:*** $9100 (excluding resources awarded to replace EFC).

UNDERGRADUATE FINANCIAL AID (Fall 2006, est.) 1,747 applied for aid; of those 96% were deemed to have need. 100% of undergraduates with need received aid; of those 26% had need fully met. ***Average percent of need met:*** 64% (excluding resources awarded to replace EFC). ***Average financial aid package:*** $9300 (excluding resources awarded to replace EFC).

GIFT AID (NEED-BASED) ***Total amount:*** $10,699,899 (36% federal, 28% state, 36% institutional). ***Receiving aid:*** Freshmen: 64% (303); All full-time undergraduates: 72% (1,393). ***Average award:*** Freshmen: $6800; Undergraduates: $6640. ***Scholarships, grants, and awards:*** Federal Pell, FSEOG, state, college/university gift aid from institutional funds.

GIFT AID (NON-NEED-BASED) ***Receiving aid:*** Freshmen: 39% (185); Undergraduates: 28% (546). ***Scholarships, grants, and awards by category:*** *Academic Interests/Achievement:* 827 awards ($4,976,000 total): general academic interests/achievements. *Special Characteristics:* children of public servants, handicapped students, public servants. ***Tuition waivers:*** Full or partial for employees or children of employees. ***ROTC:*** Army cooperative, Air Force cooperative.

LOANS ***Student loans:*** $5,750,000 (100% need-based). ***Average need-based loan:*** Freshmen: $2625; Undergraduates: $7700. ***Parent loans:*** $1,500,000 (100% need-based). ***Programs:*** FFEL (Subsidized and Unsubsidized Stafford, PLUS), Perkins.

WORK-STUDY ***Federal work-study:*** Total amount: $152,999; 161 jobs averaging $2200.

ATHLETIC AWARDS Total amount: $812,052 (100% need-based).

APPLYING FOR FINANCIAL AID ***Required financial aid forms:*** FAFSA, state aid form. ***Financial aid deadline (priority):*** 2/15. ***Notification date:*** Continuous. Students must reply within 2 weeks of notification.

CONTACT Joseph Cummings, Director of Student Financial Services, St. Francis College, 180 Remsen Street, Brooklyn Heights, NY 11201-4398, 718-489-5390. *Fax:* 718-522-1274. *E-mail:* jcummings@stfranciscollege.edu.

SAINT FRANCIS MEDICAL CENTER COLLEGE OF NURSING

Peoria, IL

Tuition & fees: $13,720 **Average undergraduate aid package: $12,953**

ABOUT THE INSTITUTION Independent Roman Catholic, coed, primarily women. Awards: bachelor's and master's degrees. 1 undergraduate major. Total enrollment: 347. Undergraduates: 270. Federal methodology is used as a basis for awarding need-based institutional aid.

UNDERGRADUATE EXPENSES for 2006–07 ***Application fee:*** $50. ***Tuition:*** full-time $13,200; part-time $440 per semester hour. ***Required fees:*** full-time $520; $250 per term part-time. Full-time tuition and fees vary according to course load. Part-time tuition and fees vary according to course load. ***Payment plan:*** Installment.

UNDERGRADUATE FINANCIAL AID (Fall 2006, est.) 196 applied for aid; of those 82% were deemed to have need. 100% of undergraduates with need received aid; of those 12% had need fully met. ***Average percent of need met:*** 76% (excluding resources awarded to replace EFC). ***Average financial aid package:*** $12,953 (excluding resources awarded to replace EFC). 25% of all full-time undergraduates had no need and received non-need-based gift aid.

GIFT AID (NEED-BASED) ***Total amount:*** $1,124,877 (17% federal, 53% state, 27% institutional, 3% external sources). ***Receiving aid:*** All full-time undergraduates: 66% (157). ***Average award:*** Undergraduates: $5361. ***Scholarships, grants, and awards:*** Federal Pell, state, private, college/university gift aid from institutional funds.

GIFT AID (NON-NEED-BASED) ***Total amount:*** $402,072 (15% state, 73% institutional, 12% external sources). ***Receiving aid:*** Undergraduates: 3% (7). ***Average award:*** Undergraduates: $4537. ***Scholarships, grants, and awards by category:*** *Academic Interests/Achievement:* 133 awards ($51,750 total): general academic interests/achievements, health fields. ***Tuition waivers:*** Full or partial for employees or children of employees.

LOANS ***Student loans:*** $1,289,123 (81% need-based, 19% non-need-based). ***Average need-based loan:*** Undergraduates: $7682. ***Parent loans:*** $59,856 (35% need-based, 65% non-need-based). ***Programs:*** FFEL (Subsidized and Unsubsidized Stafford, PLUS), college/university.

APPLYING FOR FINANCIAL AID ***Required financial aid forms:*** FAFSA, institution's own form. ***Financial aid deadline (priority):*** 3/1. ***Notification date:*** Continuous beginning 5/1.

CONTACT Ms. Nancy Perryman, Coordinator Student Finance, Financial Assistance, Saint Francis Medical Center College of Nursing, 511 Northeast Greenleaf Street, Peoria, IL 61603-3783, 309-655-4119. *E-mail:* nancy.s.perryman@osfhealthcare.org.

SAINT FRANCIS UNIVERSITY

Loretto, PA

Tuition & fees: $22,224 **Average undergraduate aid package: $17,459**

ABOUT THE INSTITUTION Independent Roman Catholic, coed. Awards: associate, bachelor's, and master's degrees. 71 undergraduate majors. Total enrollment: 2,014. Undergraduates: 1,410. Freshmen: 364. Federal methodology is used as a basis for awarding need-based institutional aid.

UNDERGRADUATE EXPENSES for 2006–07 ***Application fee:*** $30. ***Comprehensive fee:*** $29,864 includes full-time tuition ($21,174), mandatory fees ($1050), and room and board ($7640). ***College room only:*** $3840. Full-time tuition and fees vary according to course load and program. Room and board charges vary according to board plan and housing facility. ***Part-time tuition:*** $661 per credit. ***Part-time fees:*** $332 per credit; $30 per term. Part-time tuition and fees vary according to class time. ***Payment plan:*** Installment.

FRESHMAN FINANCIAL AID (Fall 2006, est.) 379 applied for aid; of those 92% were deemed to have need. 100% of freshmen with need received aid; of those 22% had need fully met. ***Average percent of need met:*** 73% (excluding resources awarded to replace EFC). ***Average financial aid package:*** $16,603 (excluding resources awarded to replace EFC). 10% of all full-time freshmen had no need and received non-need-based gift aid.

UNDERGRADUATE FINANCIAL AID (Fall 2006, est.) 1,270 applied for aid; of those 90% were deemed to have need. 99% of undergraduates with need received aid; of those 34% had need fully met. ***Average percent of need met:*** 76% (excluding resources awarded to replace EFC). ***Average financial aid package:*** $17,459 (excluding resources awarded to replace EFC). 14% of all full-time undergraduates had no need and received non-need-based gift aid.

GIFT AID (NEED-BASED) ***Total amount:*** $13,580,458 (10% federal, 18% state, 68% institutional, 4% external sources). ***Receiving aid:*** Freshmen: 88% (349); All full-time undergraduates: 84% (1,128). ***Average award:*** Freshmen: $13,688; Undergraduates: $13,786. ***Scholarships, grants, and awards:*** Federal Pell, FSEOG, state, private, college/university gift aid from institutional funds.

GIFT AID (NON-NEED-BASED) ***Total amount:*** $2,259,931 (3% state, 94% institutional, 3% external sources). ***Receiving aid:*** Freshmen: 16% (63); Undergraduates: 12% (166). ***Average award:*** Freshmen: $10,587; Undergraduates: $13,211. ***Scholarships, grants, and awards by category:*** *Academic Interests/Achievement:* 732 awards ($4,039,077 total): general academic interests/achievements, religion/biblical studies, social sciences. *Creative Arts/Performance:* 33 awards ($32,000 total): art/fine arts, music. *Special Achievements/Activities:* 37 awards ($60,285 total): cheerleading/drum major, religious involvement. *Special Characteristics:* 234 awards ($1,610,836 total): adult students, children of educators, children of faculty/staff, international students, previous college experience, siblings of current students. ***Tuition waivers:*** Full or partial for employees or children of employees. ***ROTC:*** Army cooperative.

LOANS ***Student loans:*** $9,447,415 (65% need-based, 35% non-need-based). 93% of past graduating class borrowed through all loan programs. *Average indebtedness per student:* $15,600. ***Average need-based loan:*** Freshmen: $2785; Undergraduates: $4458. ***Parent loans:*** $2,385,267 (37% need-based, 63% non-need-based). ***Programs:*** FFEL (Subsidized and Unsubsidized Stafford, PLUS), Perkins, private alternative loans for lenders such as: Citibank, Wells Fargo, etc.

WORK-STUDY ***Federal work-study:*** Total amount: $751,422; 693 jobs averaging $906. ***State or other work-study/employment:*** Total amount: $31,000 (42% need-based, 58% non-need-based).

ATHLETIC AWARDS Total amount: $3,345,424 (62% need-based, 38% non-need-based).

APPLYING FOR FINANCIAL AID ***Required financial aid form:*** FAFSA. ***Financial aid deadline:*** Continuous. ***Notification date:*** Continuous beginning 3/1. Students must reply by 5/1.

CONTACT Shane Himes, Financial Aid Counselor, Saint Francis University, PO Box 600, Loretto, PA 15931, 814-472-3010 or toll-free 800-342-5732. *Fax:* 814-472-3999. *E-mail:* shimos@francis.edu.

ST. GREGORY'S UNIVERSITY

Shawnee, OK

Tuition & fees: $13,772 **Average undergraduate aid package: $10,686**

ABOUT THE INSTITUTION Independent Roman Catholic, coed. Awards: associate and bachelor's degrees. 46 undergraduate majors. Total enrollment: 860. Undergraduates: 823. Freshmen: 100. Federal methodology is used as a basis for awarding need-based institutional aid.

UNDERGRADUATE EXPENSES for 2006–07 ***Application fee:*** $25. ***Comprehensive fee:*** $19,408 includes full-time tuition ($12,922), mandatory fees ($850), and room and board ($5636). ***College room only:*** $3200. Room and board charges vary according to board plan. ***Part-time tuition:*** $430 per hour. ***Part-time fees:*** $35 per hour. Part-time tuition and fees vary according to course load and reciprocity agreements. ***Payment plans:*** Installment, deferred payment.

FRESHMAN FINANCIAL AID (Fall 2005) 70 applied for aid; of those 90% were deemed to have need. 100% of freshmen with need received aid; of those 17% had need fully met. ***Average percent of need met:*** 68% (excluding resources awarded to replace EFC). ***Average financial aid package:*** $10,686 (excluding resources awarded to replace EFC). 9% of all full-time freshmen had no need and received non-need-based gift aid.

UNDERGRADUATE FINANCIAL AID (Fall 2005) 555 applied for aid; of those 94% were deemed to have need. 99% of undergraduates with need received aid; of those 12% had need fully met. ***Average percent of need met:*** 69% (excluding resources awarded to replace EFC). ***Average financial aid package:*** $10,686 (excluding resources awarded to replace EFC). 9% of all full-time undergraduates had no need and received non-need-based gift aid.

GIFT AID (NEED-BASED) ***Total amount:*** $2,092,536 (44% federal, 16% state, 36% institutional, 4% external sources). ***Receiving aid:*** Freshmen: 41% (33); All full-time undergraduates: 38% (271). ***Average award:*** Freshmen: $6883; Undergraduates: $6883. ***Scholarships, grants, and awards:*** Federal Pell, FSEOG, state, private, college/university gift aid from institutional funds.

GIFT AID (NON-NEED-BASED) ***Total amount:*** $362,393 (90% institutional, 10% external sources). ***Receiving aid:*** Freshmen: 77% (62); Undergraduates: 70% (498). ***Average award:*** Freshmen: $1500; Undergraduates: $1500. ***Scholarships, grants, and awards by category:*** *Academic Interests/Achievement:* 231 awards ($811,210 total): general academic interests/achievements. *Creative Arts/Performance:* 34 awards ($40,474 total): art/fine arts, dance, journalism/publications, music, theater/drama. *Special Achievements/Activities:* 8 awards ($10,187 total): religious involvement. *Special Characteristics:* 159 awards ($90,116 total): ethnic background, handicapped students, international students, religious affiliation. ***Tuition waivers:*** Full or partial for employees or children of employees, senior citizens. ***ROTC:*** Air Force cooperative.

LOANS ***Student loans:*** $4,558,996 (71% need-based, 29% non-need-based). 72% of past graduating class borrowed through all loan programs. *Average indebtedness per student:* $10,160. ***Average need-based loan:*** Freshmen: $3720; Undergraduates: $3720. ***Parent loans:*** $265,859 (58% need-based, 42% non-need-based). ***Programs:*** FFEL (Subsidized and Unsubsidized Stafford, PLUS), Perkins, alternative loans.

WORK-STUDY ***Federal work-study:*** Total amount: $32,942; 38 jobs averaging $867. ***State or other work-study/employment:*** Total amount: $61,230 (100% non-need-based). 24 part-time jobs averaging $2551.

ATHLETIC AWARDS Total amount: $1,225,623 (62% need-based, 38% non-need-based).

APPLYING FOR FINANCIAL AID ***Required financial aid forms:*** FAFSA, institution's own form. ***Financial aid deadline:*** Continuous. ***Notification date:*** Continuous beginning 2/15. Students must reply within 2 weeks of notification.

CONTACT Matt McCoin, Director of Financial Aid, St. Gregory's University, 1900 West MacArthur Drive, Shawnee, OK 74804, 405-878-5412 or toll-free 888-STGREGS. *Fax:* 405-878-5403. *E-mail:* mdmccoin@stgregorys.edu.

ST. JOHN FISHER COLLEGE

Rochester, NY

Tuition & fees: $20,710 **Average undergraduate aid package: $16,711**

ABOUT THE INSTITUTION Independent religious, coed. Awards: bachelor's and master's degrees and post-bachelor's and post-master's certificates. 37 undergraduate majors. Total enrollment: 3,704. Undergraduates: 2,793. Freshmen: 563. Federal methodology is used as a basis for awarding need-based institutional aid.

UNDERGRADUATE EXPENSES for 2006–07 ***Application fee:*** $30. ***Comprehensive fee:*** $29,590 includes full-time tuition ($20,450), mandatory fees ($260), and room and board ($8880). ***College room only:*** $5720. Room and board charges vary according to board plan. ***Part-time tuition:*** $555 per credit. ***Part-time fees:*** $25 per term. Part-time tuition and fees vary according to course load. ***Payment plans:*** Installment, deferred payment.

FRESHMAN FINANCIAL AID (Fall 2006, est.) 543 applied for aid; of those 83% were deemed to have need. 100% of freshmen with need received aid; of those 11% had need fully met. ***Average percent of need met:*** 85% (excluding resources awarded to replace EFC). ***Average financial aid package:*** $17,458 (excluding resources awarded to replace EFC). 18% of all full-time freshmen had no need and received non-need-based gift aid.

UNDERGRADUATE FINANCIAL AID (Fall 2006, est.) 2,530 applied for aid; of those 71% were deemed to have need. 95% of undergraduates with need received aid; of those 71% had need fully met. ***Average percent of need met:*** 79% (excluding resources awarded to replace EFC). ***Average financial aid package:*** $16,711 (excluding resources awarded to replace EFC). 28% of all full-time undergraduates had no need and received non-need-based gift aid.

GIFT AID (NEED-BASED) ***Total amount:*** $20,083,095 (12% federal, 19% state, 68% institutional, 1% external sources). ***Receiving aid:*** Freshmen: 80% (450); All full-time undergraduates: 65% (1,665). ***Average award:*** Freshmen: $12,846; Undergraduates: $10,741. ***Scholarships, grants, and awards:*** Federal Pell, FSEOG, state, private, college/university gift aid from institutional funds, Federal Nursing.

GIFT AID (NON-NEED-BASED) ***Total amount:*** $4,195,080 (1% state, 97% institutional, 2% external sources). ***Receiving aid:*** Freshmen: 62% (348); Undergraduates: 47% (1,218). ***Average award:*** Freshmen: $7308; Undergraduates: $5105. ***Scholarships, grants, and awards by category:*** *Academic Interests/Achievement:* 1,063 awards ($7,916,650 total): biological sciences, business, English, foreign languages, general academic interests/achievements, humanities, mathematics, physical sciences. *Special Achievements/Activities:* 120 awards ($1,037,465 total): community service. *Special Characteristics:* 125 awards ($1,124,775 total): children and siblings of alumni, ethnic background, first-generation college students, local/state students, members of minority groups. ***Tuition waivers:*** Full or partial for employees or children of employees. ***ROTC:*** Army cooperative, Air Force cooperative.

LOANS ***Student loans:*** $28,374,930 (70% need-based, 30% non-need-based). 87% of past graduating class borrowed through all loan programs. *Average indebtedness per student:* $31,206. ***Average need-based loan:*** Freshmen: $4483;

Undergraduates: $6770. ***Parent loans:*** $8,093,324 (41% need-based, 59% non-need-based). ***Programs:*** FFEL (Subsidized and Unsubsidized Stafford, PLUS), Perkins.

WORK-STUDY ***Federal work-study:*** Total amount: $300,000; 1,493 jobs averaging $1500.

APPLYING FOR FINANCIAL AID ***Required financial aid forms:*** FAFSA, state aid form. ***Financial aid deadline (priority):*** 2/15. ***Notification date:*** Continuous beginning 3/21. Students must reply by 5/1 or within 3 weeks of notification.

CONTACT Mrs. Angela Monnat, Director of Financial Aid, St. John Fisher College, 3690 East Avenue, Rochester, NY 14618-3597, 585-385-8042 or toll-free 800-444-4640. *Fax:* 585-385-8044. *E-mail:* amonnat@sjfc.edu.

ST. JOHN'S COLLEGE

Springfield, IL

CONTACT Mary M. Deatherage, Financial Aid Officer, St. John's College, 421 North Ninth Street, Springfield, IL 62702, 217-544-6464 Ext. 44705. *Fax:* 217-757-6870. *E-mail:* mdeather@st-johns.org.

ST. JOHN'S COLLEGE

Annapolis, MD

Tuition & fees: $34,506 **Average undergraduate aid package: $26,029**

ABOUT THE INSTITUTION Independent, coed. Awards: bachelor's and master's degrees. 3 undergraduate majors. Total enrollment: 600. Undergraduates: 510. Freshmen: 148. Both federal and institutional methodology are used as a basis for awarding need-based institutional aid.

UNDERGRADUATE EXPENSES for 2006–07 ***Comprehensive fee:*** $42,776 includes full-time tuition ($34,306), mandatory fees ($200), and room and board ($8270). Room and board charges vary according to board plan. ***Payment plan:*** Installment.

FRESHMAN FINANCIAL AID (Fall 2006, est.) 108 applied for aid; of those 82% were deemed to have need. 100% of freshmen with need received aid; of those 70% had need fully met. ***Average percent of need met:*** 96% (excluding resources awarded to replace EFC). ***Average financial aid package:*** $27,149 (excluding resources awarded to replace EFC).

UNDERGRADUATE FINANCIAL AID (Fall 2006, est.) 357 applied for aid; of those 84% were deemed to have need. 100% of undergraduates with need received aid; of those 92% had need fully met. ***Average percent of need met:*** 97% (excluding resources awarded to replace EFC). ***Average financial aid package:*** $26,029 (excluding resources awarded to replace EFC).

GIFT AID (NEED-BASED) ***Total amount:*** $5,825,033 (7% federal, 2% state, 89% institutional, 2% external sources). ***Receiving aid:*** Freshmen: 55% (82); All full-time undergraduates: 55% (278). ***Average award:*** Freshmen: $21,369; Undergraduates: $19,352. ***Scholarships, grants, and awards:*** Federal Pell, FSEOG, state, college/university gift aid from institutional funds.

GIFT AID (NON-NEED-BASED) ***Total amount:*** $35,550 (34% state, 66% external sources). ***Tuition waivers:*** Full or partial for employees or children of employees.

LOANS ***Student loans:*** $2,424,188 (90% need-based, 10% non-need-based). ***Average need-based loan:*** Freshmen: $4951; Undergraduates: $7288. ***Parent loans:*** $5,734,133 (77% need-based, 23% non-need-based). ***Programs:*** FFEL (Subsidized and Unsubsidized Stafford, PLUS), Perkins, college/university.

WORK-STUDY ***Federal work-study:*** Total amount: $450,031; 177 jobs averaging $2543. ***State or other work-study/employment:*** Part-time jobs available.

APPLYING FOR FINANCIAL AID ***Required financial aid forms:*** FAFSA, CSS Financial Aid PROFILE, noncustodial (divorced/separated) parent's statement, business/farm supplement. ***Financial aid deadline (priority):*** 2/15. ***Notification date:*** Continuous. Students must reply by 5/5.

CONTACT Ms. Paula Abernethy, Director of Financial Aid, St. John's College, PO Box 2800, Annapolis, MD 21404, 410-626-2502 or toll-free 800-727-9238. *Fax:* 410-626-2885. *E-mail:* paula.abernethy@sjca.edu.

ST. JOHN'S COLLEGE

Santa Fe, NM

Tuition & fees: $36,596 **Average undergraduate aid package: $24,858**

ABOUT THE INSTITUTION Independent, coed. Awards: bachelor's and master's degrees. 22 undergraduate majors. Total enrollment: 520. Undergraduates: 434. Freshmen: 120. Both federal and institutional methodology are used as a basis for awarding need-based institutional aid.

UNDERGRADUATE EXPENSES for 2007–08 ***Comprehensive fee:*** $45,280 includes full-time tuition ($36,346), mandatory fees ($250), and room and board ($8684).

FRESHMAN FINANCIAL AID (Fall 2006, est.) 71 applied for aid; of those 89% were deemed to have need. 100% of freshmen with need received aid; of those 95% had need fully met. ***Average percent of need met:*** 97% (excluding resources awarded to replace EFC). ***Average financial aid package:*** $24,205 (excluding resources awarded to replace EFC).

UNDERGRADUATE FINANCIAL AID (Fall 2006, est.) 287 applied for aid; of those 95% were deemed to have need. 100% of undergraduates with need received aid; of those 96% had need fully met. ***Average percent of need met:*** 95% (excluding resources awarded to replace EFC). ***Average financial aid package:*** $24,858 (excluding resources awarded to replace EFC). 1% of all full-time undergraduates had no need and received non-need-based gift aid.

GIFT AID (NEED-BASED) ***Total amount:*** $5,363,425 (9% federal, 2% state, 89% institutional). ***Receiving aid:*** Freshmen: 47% (57); All full-time undergraduates: 63% (273). ***Average award:*** Freshmen: $19,744; Undergraduates: $18,247. ***Scholarships, grants, and awards:*** Federal Pell, FSEOG, state, college/university gift aid from institutional funds.

GIFT AID (NON-NEED-BASED) ***Total amount:*** $148,067 (100% external sources). ***Receiving aid:*** Freshmen: 6% (7); Undergraduates: 3% (11). ***Average award:*** Undergraduates: $1500. ***Scholarships, grants, and awards by category:*** *Special Characteristics:* 18 awards ($201,996 total): children of faculty/staff.

LOANS ***Student loans:*** $2,035,076 (60% need-based, 40% non-need-based). 81% of past graduating class borrowed through all loan programs. *Average indebtedness per student:* $28,770. ***Average need-based loan:*** Freshmen: $3380; Undergraduates: $5885. ***Parent loans:*** $1,726,082 (100% non-need-based). ***Programs:*** FFEL (Subsidized and Unsubsidized Stafford, PLUS), Perkins, college/university.

WORK-STUDY ***Federal work-study:*** Total amount: $332,594; 193 jobs averaging $2350. ***State or other work-study/employment:*** Total amount: $45,000 (60% need-based, 40% non-need-based). 14 part-time jobs averaging $2290.

APPLYING FOR FINANCIAL AID ***Required financial aid forms:*** FAFSA, CSS Financial Aid PROFILE, noncustodial (divorced/separated) parent's statement, business/farm supplement. ***Financial aid deadline:*** 2/15. ***Notification date:*** Continuous beginning 12/1. Students must reply by 5/1 or within 2 weeks of notification.

CONTACT Michael Rodriguez, Director of Financial Aid, St. John's College, 1160 Camino Cruz Blanca, Santa Fe, NM 87505, 505-984-6058 or toll-free 800-331-5232. *Fax:* 505-984-6003. *E-mail:* faid@mail.sjcsf.edu.

SAINT JOHN'S UNIVERSITY

Collegeville, MN

Tuition & fees: $24,924 **Average undergraduate aid package: $18,898**

ABOUT THE INSTITUTION Independent Roman Catholic, coed, primarily men. Awards: bachelor's, master's, and first professional degrees (coordinate with College of Saint Benedict for women). 48 undergraduate majors. Total enrollment: 2,044. Undergraduates: 1,919. Freshmen: 506. Federal methodology is used as a basis for awarding need-based institutional aid.

UNDERGRADUATE EXPENSES for 2006–07 ***Comprehensive fee:*** $31,420 includes full-time tuition ($24,448), mandatory fees ($476), and room and board ($6496). ***College room only:*** $3262. Room and board charges vary according to board plan and housing facility. ***Part-time tuition:*** $1020 per credit. ***Part-time fees:*** $238 per term. Part-time tuition and fees vary according to course load. ***Payment plans:*** Tuition prepayment, installment.

FRESHMAN FINANCIAL AID (Fall 2006, est.) 377 applied for aid; of those 73% were deemed to have need. 100% of freshmen with need received aid; of those 46% had need fully met. ***Average percent of need met:*** 94% (excluding resources awarded to replace EFC). ***Average financial aid package:*** $20,993 (excluding resources awarded to replace EFC). 42% of all full-time freshmen had no need and received non-need-based gift aid.

UNDERGRADUATE FINANCIAL AID (Fall 2006, est.) 1,266 applied for aid; of those 82% were deemed to have need. 100% of undergraduates with need received aid; of those 39% had need fully met. ***Average percent of need met:*** 87% (excluding resources awarded to replace EFC). ***Average financial aid***

package: $18,898 (excluding resources awarded to replace EFC). 38% of all full-time undergraduates had no need and received non-need-based gift aid.

GIFT AID (NEED-BASED) ***Total amount:*** $13,689,956 (9% federal, 11% state, 77% institutional, 3% external sources). ***Receiving aid:*** Freshmen: 54% (275); All full-time undergraduates: 54% (1,019). ***Average award:*** Freshmen: $15,711; Undergraduates: $13,358. ***Scholarships, grants, and awards:*** Federal Pell, FSEOG, state, private, college/university gift aid from institutional funds.

GIFT AID (NON-NEED-BASED) ***Total amount:*** $7,792,594 (92% institutional, 8% external sources). ***Receiving aid:*** Freshmen: 53% (266); Undergraduates: 50% (933). ***Average award:*** Freshmen: $10,075; Undergraduates: $8472. ***Scholarships, grants, and awards by category:*** *Academic Interests/Achievement:* 1,607 awards ($12,464,595 total): general academic interests/achievements. *Creative Arts/Performance:* 157 awards ($244,375 total): art/fine arts, music, theater/drama. *Special Characteristics:* 79 awards ($1,619,253 total): international students. ***Tuition waivers:*** Full or partial for employees or children of employees. ***ROTC:*** Army.

LOANS ***Student loans:*** $7,517,644 (87% need-based, 13% non-need-based). 74% of past graduating class borrowed through all loan programs. *Average indebtedness per student:* $25,407. ***Average need-based loan:*** Freshmen: $4066; Undergraduates: $4491. ***Parent loans:*** $2,617,376 (76% need-based, 24% non-need-based). ***Programs:*** FFEL (Subsidized and Unsubsidized Stafford, PLUS), Perkins, state, SELF Loans, alternative loans.

WORK-STUDY ***Federal work-study:*** Total amount: $855,049; 313 jobs averaging $2732. ***State or other work-study/employment:*** Total amount: $1,587,452 (63% need-based, 37% non-need-based). 731 part-time jobs averaging $2172.

APPLYING FOR FINANCIAL AID ***Required financial aid forms:*** FAFSA, institution's own form, federal income tax form(s). ***Financial aid deadline (priority):*** 3/15. ***Notification date:*** Continuous beginning 3/15. Students must reply by 5/1 or within 3 weeks of notification.

CONTACT Ms. Mary Dehler, Associate Director of Financial Aid, Saint John's University, PO Box 5000, Collegeville, MN 56321-5000, 320-363-3664 or toll-free 800-544-1489. *Fax:* 320-363-3102. *E-mail:* mdehler@csbsju.edu.

ST. JOHN'S UNIVERSITY

Queens, NY

ABOUT THE INSTITUTION Independent religious, coed. Awards: associate, bachelor's, master's, doctoral, and first professional degrees and post-bachelor's and post-master's certificates. 105 undergraduate majors. Total enrollment: 20,069. Undergraduates: 14,983. Freshmen: 3,266.

GIFT AID (NEED-BASED) ***Scholarships, grants, and awards:*** Federal Pell, FSEOG, state, private, college/university gift aid from institutional funds.

GIFT AID (NON-NEED-BASED) ***Scholarships, grants, and awards by category:*** *Academic Interests/Achievement:* biological sciences, business, communication, computer science, education, general academic interests/achievements, health fields, mathematics, military science. *Creative Arts/Performance:* art/fine arts, cinema/film/broadcasting, dance, debating, journalism/publications, music. *Special Achievements/Activities:* cheerleading/drum major, community service, general special achievements/activities, hobbies/interests, leadership, religious involvement. *Special Characteristics:* children of faculty/staff, general special characteristics, local/state students, relatives of clergy, religious affiliation.

LOANS ***Programs:*** FFEL (Subsidized and Unsubsidized Stafford, PLUS), Perkins.

APPLYING FOR FINANCIAL AID ***Required financial aid form:*** FAFSA.

CONTACT Mr. Jorge Rodriguez, Assistant Vice President/Executive Director of Financial Aid, St. John's University, 8000 Utopia Parkway, Queens, NY 11439, 718-990-2000 or toll-free 888-9STJOHNS (in-state), 888-9ST JOHNS (out-of-state). *Fax:* 718-990-5945. *E-mail:* financialaid@stjohns.edu.

ST. JOHN VIANNEY COLLEGE SEMINARY

Miami, FL

CONTACT Ms. Bonnie DeAngulo, Director of Financial Aid, St. John Vianney College Seminary, 2900 Southwest 87th Avenue, Miami, FL 33165-3244, 305-223-4561 Ext. 10.

SAINT JOSEPH COLLEGE

West Hartford, CT

CONTACT Mr. Philip T. Malinoski, Student Financial Services Director, Saint Joseph College, 1678 Asylum Avenue, West Hartford, CT 06117, 860-231-5319 or toll-free 866-442-8752. *E-mail:* pmalinoski@sjc.edu.

SAINT JOSEPH'S COLLEGE

Rensselaer, IN

Tuition & fees: $20,960 **Average undergraduate aid package: $18,976**

ABOUT THE INSTITUTION Independent Roman Catholic, coed. Awards: associate, bachelor's, and master's degrees. 33 undergraduate majors. Total university enrollment: 9. Total unit enrollment: 1,031. Undergraduates: 1,030. Freshmen: 237. Federal methodology is used as a basis for awarding need-based institutional aid.

UNDERGRADUATE EXPENSES for 2006–07 ***Application fee:*** $25. ***Comprehensive fee:*** $27,680 includes full-time tuition ($20,800), mandatory fees ($160), and room and board ($6720). Full-time tuition and fees vary according to reciprocity agreements. Room and board charges vary according to housing facility. ***Part-time tuition:*** $700 per credit. Part-time tuition and fees vary according to course load and reciprocity agreements. ***Payment plan:*** Installment.

FRESHMAN FINANCIAL AID (Fall 2005) 227 applied for aid; of those 87% were deemed to have need. 100% of freshmen with need received aid; of those 36% had need fully met. ***Average percent of need met:*** 82% (excluding resources awarded to replace EFC). ***Average financial aid package:*** $17,773 (excluding resources awarded to replace EFC). 12% of all full-time freshmen had no need and received non-need-based gift aid.

UNDERGRADUATE FINANCIAL AID (Fall 2005) 763 applied for aid; of those 83% were deemed to have need. 100% of undergraduates with need received aid; of those 36% had need fully met. ***Average percent of need met:*** 84% (excluding resources awarded to replace EFC). ***Average financial aid package:*** $18,976 (excluding resources awarded to replace EFC). 14% of all full-time undergraduates had no need and received non-need-based gift aid.

GIFT AID (NEED-BASED) ***Total amount:*** $6,337,883 (11% federal, 24% state, 63% institutional, 2% external sources). ***Receiving aid:*** Freshmen: 84% (195); All full-time undergraduates: 71% (626). ***Average award:*** Freshmen: $12,365; Undergraduates: $12,234. ***Scholarships, grants, and awards:*** Federal Pell, FSEOG, state, private, college/university gift aid from institutional funds.

GIFT AID (NON-NEED-BASED) ***Total amount:*** $1,185,468 (89% institutional, 11% external sources). ***Receiving aid:*** Freshmen: 26% (61); Undergraduates: 18% (159). ***Average award:*** Freshmen: $10,386; Undergraduates: $10,042. ***Scholarships, grants, and awards by category:*** *Academic Interests/Achievement:* 390 awards ($2,598,164 total): general academic interests/achievements. *Creative Arts/Performance:* 145 awards ($271,987 total): cinema/film/broadcasting, music, theater/drama. *Special Achievements/Activities:* 14 awards ($19,250 total): cheerleading/drum major. *Special Characteristics:* 112 awards ($450,174 total): children and siblings of alumni, children of faculty/staff, siblings of current students. ***Tuition waivers:*** Full or partial for minority students, children of alumni, employees or children of employees.

LOANS ***Student loans:*** $4,410,549 (63% need-based, 37% non-need-based). 80% of past graduating class borrowed through all loan programs. *Average indebtedness per student:* $22,603. ***Average need-based loan:*** Freshmen: $3232; Undergraduates: $4299. ***Parent loans:*** $1,288,289 (28% need-based, 72% non-need-based). ***Programs:*** FFEL (Subsidized and Unsubsidized Stafford, PLUS), Perkins.

WORK-STUDY ***Federal work-study:*** Total amount: $82,328; 111 jobs averaging $742.

ATHLETIC AWARDS Total amount: $2,323,887 (59% need-based, 41% non-need-based).

APPLYING FOR FINANCIAL AID ***Required financial aid form:*** FAFSA. ***Financial aid deadline (priority):*** 3/1. ***Notification date:*** Continuous. Students must reply by 5/1 or within 2 weeks of notification.

CONTACT Debra Sizemore, Director of Student Financial Services, Saint Joseph's College, US Highway 231, PO Box 971, Rensselaer, IN 47978, 219-866-6163 or toll-free 800-447-8781 (out-of-state). *Fax:* 219-866-6144. *E-mail:* debbie@saintjoe.edu.

ST. JOSEPH'S COLLEGE, NEW YORK

Brooklyn, NY

Tuition & fees: $12,946 **Average undergraduate aid package: $10,500**

ABOUT THE INSTITUTION Independent, coed. Awards: bachelor's and master's degrees. 22 undergraduate majors. Total enrollment: 1,310. Undergraduates: 1,087. Freshmen: 166. Federal methodology is used as a basis for awarding need-based institutional aid.

UNDERGRADUATE EXPENSES for 2006–07 ***Application fee:*** $25. ***Tuition:*** full-time $12,564; part-time $404 per credit. ***Payment plan:*** Installment.

FRESHMAN FINANCIAL AID (Fall 2006, est.) 155 applied for aid; of those 92% were deemed to have need. 100% of freshmen with need received aid; of those 70% had need fully met. ***Average percent of need met:*** 87% (excluding resources awarded to replace EFC). ***Average financial aid package:*** $11,500 (excluding resources awarded to replace EFC). 18% of all full-time freshmen had no need and received non-need-based gift aid.

UNDERGRADUATE FINANCIAL AID (Fall 2006, est.) 660 applied for aid; of those 87% were deemed to have need. 100% of undergraduates with need received aid; of those 61% had need fully met. ***Average percent of need met:*** 74% (excluding resources awarded to replace EFC). ***Average financial aid package:*** $10,500 (excluding resources awarded to replace EFC). 18% of all full-time undergraduates had no need and received non-need-based gift aid.

GIFT AID (NEED-BASED) ***Total amount:*** $3,656,817 (33% federal, 36% state, 31% institutional). ***Receiving aid:*** Freshmen: 86% (142); All full-time undergraduates: 84% (575). ***Average award:*** Freshmen: $9200; Undergraduates: $6200. ***Scholarships, grants, and awards:*** Federal Pell, FSEOG, state, private, college/university gift aid from institutional funds.

GIFT AID (NON-NEED-BASED) ***Total amount:*** $1,186,818 (1% state, 95% institutional, 4% external sources). ***Receiving aid:*** Freshmen: 67% (112); Undergraduates: 71% (484). ***Average award:*** Freshmen: $5800; Undergraduates: $4800. ***Scholarships, grants, and awards by category:*** *Academic Interests/Achievement:* 484 awards ($1,400,000 total): general academic interests/achievements. *Special Characteristics:* 15 awards ($67,000 total): children and siblings of alumni, children of faculty/staff. ***Tuition waivers:*** Full or partial for employees or children of employees.

LOANS ***Student loans:*** $3,346,232 (44% need-based, 56% non-need-based). 52% of past graduating class borrowed through all loan programs. *Average indebtedness per student:* $17,978. ***Average need-based loan:*** Freshmen: $2550; Undergraduates: $3750. ***Parent loans:*** $493,488 (100% non-need-based). ***Programs:*** FFEL (Subsidized and Unsubsidized Stafford, PLUS), Perkins.

WORK-STUDY ***Federal work-study:*** Total amount: $119,222; 75 jobs averaging $1700. ***State or other work-study/employment:*** Total amount: $13,973 (100% non-need-based). 6 part-time jobs averaging $1700.

APPLYING FOR FINANCIAL AID ***Required financial aid forms:*** FAFSA, institution's own form, state aid form. ***Financial aid deadline (priority):*** 2/25. ***Notification date:*** Continuous beginning 3/15. Students must reply by 5/1 or within 2 weeks of notification.

CONTACT Ms. Carol Sullivan, Executive Director of Financial Aid, St. Joseph's College, New York, 245 Clinton Avenue, Brooklyn, NY 11205-3688, 718-636-6808. *Fax:* 718-636-6827. *E-mail:* csullivan@sjcny.edu.

SAINT JOSEPH'S COLLEGE OF MAINE

Standish, ME

Tuition & fees: $21,760 **Average undergraduate aid package: $17,297**

ABOUT THE INSTITUTION Independent religious, coed. Awards: bachelor's and master's degrees (profile does not include enrollment in distance learning master's program). 40 undergraduate majors. Total enrollment: 1,050. Undergraduates: 1,050. Freshmen: 364. Both federal and institutional methodology are used as a basis for awarding need-based institutional aid.

UNDERGRADUATE EXPENSES for 2006–07 ***Application fee:*** $50. ***Comprehensive fee:*** $30,790 includes full-time tuition ($21,000), mandatory fees ($760), and room and board ($9030). Full-time tuition and fees vary according to program. ***Part-time tuition:*** $375 per credit. ***Part-time fees:*** $65 per term. Part-time tuition and fees vary according to course load, degree level, and program. ***Payment plan:*** Installment.

FRESHMAN FINANCIAL AID (Fall 2006, est.) 335 applied for aid; of those 91% were deemed to have need. 100% of freshmen with need received aid; of those 33% had need fully met. ***Average percent of need met:*** 82% (excluding resources awarded to replace EFC). ***Average financial aid package:*** $17,642 (excluding resources awarded to replace EFC). 17% of all full-time freshmen had no need and received non-need-based gift aid.

UNDERGRADUATE FINANCIAL AID (Fall 2006, est.) 893 applied for aid; of those 91% were deemed to have need. 100% of undergraduates with need received aid; of those 37% had need fully met. ***Average percent of need met:*** 81% (excluding resources awarded to replace EFC). ***Average financial aid package:*** $17,297 (excluding resources awarded to replace EFC). 19% of all full-time undergraduates had no need and received non-need-based gift aid.

GIFT AID (NEED-BASED) ***Total amount:*** $9,208,164 (9% federal, 4% state, 79% institutional, 8% external sources). ***Receiving aid:*** Freshmen: 84% (304); All full-time undergraduates: 79% (805). ***Average award:*** Freshmen: $12,771; Undergraduates: $11,394. ***Scholarships, grants, and awards:*** Federal Pell, FSEOG, state, private, college/university gift aid from institutional funds, Federal Nursing.

GIFT AID (NON-NEED-BASED) ***Total amount:*** $1,960,235 (87% institutional, 13% external sources). ***Receiving aid:*** Freshmen: 10% (38); Undergraduates: 9% (93). ***Average award:*** Freshmen: $12,868; Undergraduates: $13,201. ***Scholarships, grants, and awards by category:*** *Academic Interests/Achievement:* 795 awards ($4,786,911 total): general academic interests/achievements. *Special Achievements/Activities:* 171 awards ($1,598,455 total): community service, religious involvement. *Special Characteristics:* 34 awards: children of faculty/staff, siblings of current students, spouses of current students. ***Tuition waivers:*** Full or partial for employees or children of employees. ***ROTC:*** Army cooperative.

LOANS ***Student loans:*** $8,150,261 (57% need-based, 43% non-need-based). 95% of past graduating class borrowed through all loan programs. *Average indebtedness per student:* $34,488. ***Average need-based loan:*** Freshmen: $4678; Undergraduates: $6042. ***Parent loans:*** $2,493,187 (31% need-based, 69% non-need-based). ***Programs:*** FFEL (Subsidized and Unsubsidized Stafford, PLUS), Perkins, Federal Nursing, state.

WORK-STUDY ***Federal work-study:*** Total amount: $562,765; 403 jobs averaging $1396.

APPLYING FOR FINANCIAL AID ***Required financial aid forms:*** FAFSA, institution's own form. ***Financial aid deadline (priority):*** 3/1. ***Notification date:*** Continuous beginning 3/1. Students must reply by 5/1 or within 3 weeks of notification.

CONTACT Office of Financial Aid, Saint Joseph's College of Maine, 278 Whites Bridge Road, Standish, ME 04084-5263, 800-752-1266 or toll-free 800-338-7057. *Fax:* 207-893-6699. *E-mail:* finaid@sjcme.edu.

ST. JOSEPH'S COLLEGE, SUFFOLK CAMPUS

Patchogue, NY

Tuition & fees: $13,610 **Average undergraduate aid package: $5829**

ABOUT THE INSTITUTION Independent, coed. Awards: bachelor's and master's degrees. 34 undergraduate majors. Total enrollment: 3,833. Undergraduates: 3,798. Freshmen: 439. Federal methodology is used as a basis for awarding need-based institutional aid.

UNDERGRADUATE EXPENSES for 2006–07 ***Application fee:*** $25. ***Tuition:*** full-time $13,168; part-time $426 per credit. ***Required fees:*** full-time $442; $13 per credit or $207 per term part-time. Part-time tuition and fees vary according to course load. ***Payment plan:*** Installment.

FRESHMAN FINANCIAL AID (Fall 2006, est.) 398 applied for aid; of those 92% were deemed to have need. 100% of freshmen with need received aid; of those 68% had need fully met. ***Average percent of need met:*** 28% (excluding resources awarded to replace EFC). ***Average financial aid package:*** $7433 (excluding resources awarded to replace EFC). 26% of all full-time freshmen had no need and received non-need-based gift aid.

UNDERGRADUATE FINANCIAL AID (Fall 2006, est.) 2,383 applied for aid; of those 90% were deemed to have need. 100% of undergraduates with need received aid; of those 66% had need fully met. ***Average percent of need met:*** 32% (excluding resources awarded to replace EFC). ***Average financial aid package:*** $5829 (excluding resources awarded to replace EFC). 20% of all full-time undergraduates had no need and received non-need-based gift aid.

GIFT AID (NEED-BASED) ***Total amount:*** $8,224,307 (23% federal, 38% state, 39% institutional). ***Receiving aid:*** Freshmen: 85% (368); All full-time undergraduates: 74% (2,147). ***Average award:*** Freshmen: $4106; Undergraduates: $3645. ***Scholarships, grants, and awards:*** Federal Pell, FSEOG, state, private, college/university gift aid from institutional funds.

GIFT AID (NON-NEED-BASED) ***Total amount:*** $3,248,832 (1% state, 96% institutional, 3% external sources). ***Receiving aid:*** Freshmen: 30% (130); Undergraduates: 20% (588). ***Average award:*** Freshmen: $6160; Undergraduates: $5380. ***Scholarships, grants, and awards by category:*** *Academic Interests/Achievement:* 588 awards ($3,119,809 total): general academic interests/achievements. ***Tuition waivers:*** Full or partial for employees or children of employees, senior citizens. ***ROTC:*** Army cooperative, Air Force cooperative.

LOANS ***Student loans:*** $14,344,910 (46% need-based, 54% non-need-based). 74% of past graduating class borrowed through all loan programs. *Average indebtedness per student:* $17,806. ***Average need-based loan:*** Freshmen: $2493; Undergraduates: $4095. ***Parent loans:*** $6,221,806 (100% non-need-based). ***Programs:*** FFEL (Subsidized and Unsubsidized Stafford, PLUS), Perkins.

WORK-STUDY ***Federal work-study:*** Total amount: $146,965; 61 jobs averaging $2409. ***State or other work-study/employment:*** Total amount: $291,493 (100% non-need-based). 106 part-time jobs averaging $2750.

APPLYING FOR FINANCIAL AID ***Required financial aid forms:*** FAFSA, institution's own form, state aid form. ***Financial aid deadline (priority):*** 2/25. ***Notification date:*** 4/1. Students must reply within 3 weeks of notification.

CONTACT Joan Farley, Director of Financial Aid, St. Joseph's College, Suffolk Campus, 155 West Roe Boulevard, Patchogue, NY 11772-2399, 631-447-3214 or toll-free 866-AT ST JOE (in-state). *Fax:* 631-447-1734. *E-mail:* jfarley@sjcny.edu.

SAINT JOSEPH SEMINARY COLLEGE

Saint Benedict, LA

CONTACT Betty Anne Burns, Financial Aid Officer, Saint Joseph Seminary College, Saint Benedict, LA 70457, 985-867-2229. *Fax:* 985-867-2270.

SAINT JOSEPH'S UNIVERSITY

Philadelphia, PA

ABOUT THE INSTITUTION Independent Roman Catholic (Jesuit), coed. Awards: associate, bachelor's, master's, and doctoral degrees and post-bachelor's and post-master's certificates. 53 undergraduate majors. Total enrollment: 7,535. Undergraduates: 4,932. Freshmen: 1,024.

GIFT AID (NEED-BASED) ***Scholarships, grants, and awards:*** Federal Pell, FSEOG, state, private, college/university gift aid from institutional funds.

GIFT AID (NON-NEED-BASED) ***Scholarships, grants, and awards by category:*** *Academic Interests/Achievement:* general academic interests/achievements. *Creative Arts/Performance:* debating, theater/drama. *Special Characteristics:* members of minority groups.

LOANS ***Programs:*** FFEL (Subsidized and Unsubsidized Stafford, PLUS), Perkins.

WORK-STUDY ***Federal work-study:*** Total amount: $500,000; 350 jobs averaging $949.

APPLYING FOR FINANCIAL AID ***Required financial aid form:*** FAFSA.

CONTACT Eileen M. Tucker, Director of Financial Assistance, Saint Joseph's University, 5600 City Avenue, Philadelphia, PA 19131-1395, 610-660-1556 or toll-free 888-BEAHAWK (in-state). *Fax:* 610-660-1342. *E-mail:* tucker@sju.edu.

ST. LAWRENCE UNIVERSITY

Canton, NY

Tuition & fees: $33,910 | **Average undergraduate aid package: $32,471**

ABOUT THE INSTITUTION Independent, coed. Awards: bachelor's and master's degrees and post-master's certificates. 39 undergraduate majors. Total enrollment: 2,303. Undergraduates: 2,182. Freshmen: 611. Both federal and institutional methodology are used as a basis for awarding need-based institutional aid.

UNDERGRADUATE EXPENSES for 2006–07 ***Application fee:*** $50. ***Comprehensive fee:*** $42,540 includes full-time tuition ($33,690), mandatory fees ($220), and room and board ($8630). ***College room only:*** $4640. Room and board charges vary according to board plan. ***Part-time tuition:*** $4212 per course. ***Payment plans:*** Installment, deferred payment.

FRESHMAN FINANCIAL AID (Fall 2006, est.) 442 applied for aid; of those 86% were deemed to have need. 100% of freshmen with need received aid; of those 60% had need fully met. ***Average percent of need met:*** 95% (excluding resources awarded to replace EFC). ***Average financial aid package:*** $33,307 (excluding resources awarded to replace EFC). 15% of all full-time freshmen had no need and received non-need-based gift aid.

UNDERGRADUATE FINANCIAL AID (Fall 2006, est.) 1,648 applied for aid; of those 90% were deemed to have need. 93% of undergraduates with need received aid; of those 54% had need fully met. ***Average percent of need met:*** 94% (excluding resources awarded to replace EFC). ***Average financial aid package:*** $32,471 (excluding resources awarded to replace EFC). 13% of all full-time undergraduates had no need and received non-need-based gift aid.

GIFT AID (NEED-BASED) ***Total amount:*** $30,625,081 (6% federal, 5% state, 86% institutional, 3% external sources). ***Receiving aid:*** Freshmen: 62% (376); All full-time undergraduates: 64% (1,363). ***Average award:*** Freshmen: $23,701; Undergraduates: $22,070. ***Scholarships, grants, and awards:*** Federal Pell, FSEOG, state, college/university gift aid from institutional funds.

GIFT AID (NON-NEED-BASED) ***Total amount:*** $3,321,081 (98% institutional, 2% external sources). ***Receiving aid:*** Freshmen: 10% (62); Undergraduates: 7% (159). ***Average award:*** Freshmen: $10,429; Undergraduates: $9897. ***Scholarships, grants, and awards by category:*** *Academic Interests/Achievement:* 715 awards ($10,524,209 total): general academic interests/achievements. *Special Achievements/Activities:* 41 awards ($307,500 total): community service. *Special Characteristics:* 313 awards ($781,250 total): children and siblings of alumni, siblings of current students. ***Tuition waivers:*** Full or partial for employees or children of employees. ***ROTC:*** Army cooperative, Air Force cooperative.

LOANS ***Student loans:*** $11,941,967 (41% need-based, 59% non-need-based). 72% of past graduating class borrowed through all loan programs. *Average indebtedness per student:* $28,611. ***Average need-based loan:*** Freshmen: $2473; Undergraduates: $3770. ***Parent loans:*** $4,580,652 (100% need-based). ***Programs:*** FFEL (Subsidized and Unsubsidized Stafford, PLUS), Perkins, college/university.

WORK-STUDY ***Federal work-study:*** Total amount: $1,204,913; 883 jobs averaging $1360. ***State or other work-study/employment:*** Total amount: $605,179 (100% non-need-based). 445 part-time jobs averaging $1365.

ATHLETIC AWARDS Total amount: $1,418,360 (100% non-need-based).

APPLYING FOR FINANCIAL AID ***Required financial aid forms:*** FAFSA, institution's own form, noncustodial (divorced/separated) parent's statement, income tax returns/w2s. ***Financial aid deadline:*** 2/15. ***Notification date:*** 3/30. Students must reply by 5/1 or within 2 weeks of notification.

CONTACT Mrs. Patricia J. B. Farmer, Director of Financial Aid, St. Lawrence University, Payson Hall, Park Street, Canton, NY 13617-1455, 315-229-5265 or toll-free 800-285-1856. *Fax:* 315-229-5502. *E-mail:* pfarmer@stlawu.edu.

SAINT LEO UNIVERSITY

Saint Leo, FL

Tuition & fees: $16,420 | **Average undergraduate aid package: $15,550**

ABOUT THE INSTITUTION Independent Roman Catholic, coed. Awards: associate, bachelor's, and master's degrees. 25 undergraduate majors. Total enrollment: 2,774. Undergraduates: 1,514. Freshmen: 417. Federal methodology is used as a basis for awarding need-based institutional aid.

UNDERGRADUATE EXPENSES for 2007–08 ***Application fee:*** $35. ***Comprehensive fee:*** $24,522 includes full-time tuition ($16,420) and room and board ($8102).

FRESHMAN FINANCIAL AID (Fall 2006, est.) 368 applied for aid; of those 73% were deemed to have need. 100% of freshmen with need received aid; of those 34% had need fully met. ***Average percent of need met:*** 79% (excluding resources awarded to replace EFC). ***Average financial aid package:*** $14,430 (excluding resources awarded to replace EFC). 4% of all full-time freshmen had no need and received non-need-based gift aid.

UNDERGRADUATE FINANCIAL AID (Fall 2006, est.) 1,229 applied for aid; of those 77% were deemed to have need. 98% of undergraduates with need received aid; of those 39% had need fully met. ***Average percent of need met:*** 82% (excluding resources awarded to replace EFC). ***Average financial aid package:*** $15,550 (excluding resources awarded to replace EFC). 4% of all full-time undergraduates had no need and received non-need-based gift aid.

GIFT AID (NEED-BASED) ***Total amount:*** $11,088,087 (10% federal, 22% state, 65% institutional, 3% external sources). ***Receiving aid:*** Freshmen: 65% (268); All full-time undergraduates: 64% (929). ***Average award:*** Freshmen: $10,042; Undergraduates: $10,606. ***Scholarships, grants, and awards:*** Federal Pell, FSEOG, state, private, college/university gift aid from institutional funds, United Negro College Fund.

GIFT AID (NON-NEED-BASED) ***Total amount:*** $1,410,494 (67% state, 17% institutional, 16% external sources). ***Receiving aid:*** Freshmen: 10% (40); Undergraduates: 8% (119). ***Average award:*** Freshmen: $1000; Undergraduates: $3464. ***ROTC:*** Army cooperative, Air Force cooperative.

LOANS ***Student loans:*** $6,756,044 (65% need-based, 35% non-need-based). 67% of past graduating class borrowed through all loan programs. *Average indebtedness per student:* $15,300. ***Average need-based loan:*** Freshmen: $2481; Undergraduates: $3515. ***Parent loans:*** $1,943,721 (41% need-based, 59% non-need-based). ***Programs:*** FFEL (Subsidized and Unsubsidized Stafford, PLUS), Perkins.

WORK-STUDY ***Federal work-study:*** Total amount: $1,504,600; 560 jobs averaging $2323.

ATHLETIC AWARDS Total amount: $1,210,473 (60% need-based, 40% non-need-based).

APPLYING FOR FINANCIAL AID ***Required financial aid form:*** FAFSA. ***Financial aid deadline (priority):*** 4/1. ***Notification date:*** Continuous beginning 1/31.

CONTACT Office of Student Financial Services, Saint Leo University, PO Box 6665, MC 2228, Saint Leo, FL 33574-6665, 800-240-7658 or toll-free 800-334-5532. *Fax:* 352-588-8403. *E-mail:* finaid@saintleo.edu.

ST. LOUIS CHRISTIAN COLLEGE

Florissant, MO

Tuition & fees: N/R **Average undergraduate aid package: $8190**

ABOUT THE INSTITUTION Independent Christian, coed. Awards: associate and bachelor's degrees. 6 undergraduate majors. Total enrollment: 213. Undergraduates: 213. Freshmen: 26. Federal methodology is used as a basis for awarding need-based institutional aid.

FRESHMAN FINANCIAL AID (Fall 2006, est.) 61 applied for aid; of those 72% were deemed to have need. 100% of freshmen with need received aid; of those 23% had need fully met. ***Average percent of need met:*** 73% (excluding resources awarded to replace EFC). ***Average financial aid package:*** $9620 (excluding resources awarded to replace EFC). 28% of all full-time freshmen had no need and received non-need-based gift aid.

UNDERGRADUATE FINANCIAL AID (Fall 2006, est.) 323 applied for aid; of those 88% were deemed to have need. 100% of undergraduates with need received aid; of those 19% had need fully met. ***Average percent of need met:*** 72% (excluding resources awarded to replace EFC). ***Average financial aid package:*** $8190 (excluding resources awarded to replace EFC). 22% of all full-time undergraduates had no need and received non-need-based gift aid.

GIFT AID (NEED-BASED) ***Total amount:*** $1,416,159 (25% federal, 72% institutional, 3% external sources). ***Receiving aid:*** Freshmen: 72% (44); All full-time undergraduates: 87% (282). ***Average award:*** Freshmen: $8486; Undergraduates: $6483. ***Scholarships, grants, and awards:*** Federal Pell, FSEOG, private, college/university gift aid from institutional funds.

GIFT AID (NON-NEED-BASED) ***Total amount:*** $425,955 (85% institutional, 15% external sources). ***Average award:*** Freshmen: $6916; Undergraduates: $5260. ***Scholarships, grants, and awards by category:*** *Academic Interests/Achievement:* 14 awards ($21,000 total). *Special Characteristics:* 3 awards ($14,000 total): children of faculty/staff, general special characteristics. ***Tuition waivers:*** Full or partial for employees or children of employees.

LOANS ***Student loans:*** $1,112,816 (94% need-based, 6% non-need-based). 80% of past graduating class borrowed through all loan programs. *Average indebtedness per student:* $13,968. ***Average need-based loan:*** Freshmen: $1134; Undergraduates: $2701. ***Parent loans:*** $74,700 (45% need-based, 55% non-need-based). ***Programs:*** FFEL (Subsidized and Unsubsidized Stafford, PLUS).

WORK-STUDY ***Federal work-study:*** Total amount: $14,700; 13 jobs averaging $1100. ***State or other work-study/employment:*** Total amount: $130,000 (100% non-need-based). 20 part-time jobs averaging $5000.

APPLYING FOR FINANCIAL AID ***Required financial aid form:*** FAFSA. ***Notification date:*** Continuous.

CONTACT Mrs. Catherine Wilhoit, Director of Financial Aid, St. Louis Christian College, 1360 Grandview Drive, Florissant, MO 63033-6499, 314-837-6777 Ext. 1101 or toll-free 800-887-SLCC. *Fax:* 314-837-8291.

ST. LOUIS COLLEGE OF PHARMACY

St. Louis, MO

ABOUT THE INSTITUTION Independent, coed. Awards: master's and first professional degrees. 1 undergraduate major. Total enrollment: 1,126.

GIFT AID (NEED-BASED) ***Scholarships, grants, and awards:*** Federal Pell, FSEOG, state, private, college/university gift aid from institutional funds.

GIFT AID (NON-NEED-BASED) ***Scholarships, grants, and awards by category:*** *Academic Interests/Achievement:* general academic interests/achievements. *Special Achievements/Activities:* community service, leadership. *Special Characteristics:* children of faculty/staff, local/state students.

LOANS ***Programs:*** FFEL (Subsidized and Unsubsidized Stafford, PLUS), Perkins, Federal Health Professions Loan.

WORK-STUDY ***Federal work-study:*** Total amount: $126,321; 105 jobs averaging $1200.

APPLYING FOR FINANCIAL AID ***Required financial aid forms:*** FAFSA, institution's own form.

CONTACT Mr. David Rice, Director of Financial Aid, St. Louis College of Pharmacy, 4588 Parkview Place, St. Louis, MO 63110, 314-446-8320 or toll-free 800-278-5267 (in-state). *Fax:* 314-446-8310. *E-mail:* drice@stlcop.edu.

SAINT LOUIS UNIVERSITY

St. Louis, MO

Tuition & fees: $26,648 **Average undergraduate aid package: $19,034**

ABOUT THE INSTITUTION Independent Roman Catholic (Jesuit), coed. Awards: bachelor's, master's, doctoral, and first professional degrees and post-bachelor's and post-master's certificates. 72 undergraduate majors. Total enrollment: 12,034. Undergraduates: 7,479. Freshmen: 1,721. Federal methodology is used as a basis for awarding need-based institutional aid.

UNDERGRADUATE EXPENSES for 2006–07 ***Application fee:*** $25. ***Comprehensive fee:*** $34,878 includes full-time tuition ($26,250), mandatory fees ($398), and room and board ($8230). ***College room only:*** $4700. Full-time tuition and fees vary according to location and program. Room and board charges vary according to board plan, housing facility, and location. ***Part-time tuition:*** $915 per credit hour. ***Part-time fees:*** $120 per term. Part-time tuition and fees vary according to location and program. ***Payment plan:*** Installment.

FRESHMAN FINANCIAL AID (Fall 2005) 1192 applied for aid; of those 80% were deemed to have need. 100% of freshmen with need received aid; of those 15% had need fully met. ***Average percent of need met:*** 63% (excluding resources awarded to replace EFC). ***Average financial aid package:*** $19,061 (excluding resources awarded to replace EFC). 30% of all full-time freshmen had no need and received non-need-based gift aid.

UNDERGRADUATE FINANCIAL AID (Fall 2005) 4,729 applied for aid; of those 84% were deemed to have need. 100% of undergraduates with need received aid; of those 15% had need fully met. ***Average percent of need met:*** 60% (excluding resources awarded to replace EFC). ***Average financial aid package:*** $19,034 (excluding resources awarded to replace EFC). 25% of all full-time undergraduates had no need and received non-need-based gift aid.

GIFT AID (NEED-BASED) ***Total amount:*** $47,901,917 (10% federal, 6% state, 81% institutional, 3% external sources). ***Receiving aid:*** Freshmen: 61% (918); All full-time undergraduates: 57% (3,800). ***Average award:*** Freshmen: $13,351; Undergraduates: $11,796. ***Scholarships, grants, and awards:*** Federal Pell, FSEOG, state, private, college/university gift aid from institutional funds, Federal Nursing.

GIFT AID (NON-NEED-BASED) ***Total amount:*** $17,451,555 (2% state, 83% institutional, 15% external sources). ***Receiving aid:*** Freshmen: 8% (121); Undergraduates: 7% (485). ***Average award:*** Freshmen: $9321; Undergraduates: $8589. ***Scholarships, grants, and awards by category:*** *Academic Interests/Achievement:* 4,485 awards ($35,035,120 total): area/ethnic studies, biological sciences, business, communication, computer science, education, engineering/technologies, English, foreign languages, general academic interests/achievements, health fields, humanities, international studies, mathematics, military science, physical sciences, premedicine, religion/biblical studies, social sciences. *Creative Arts/Performance:* 107 awards ($103,350 total): art/fine arts, music, performing arts, theater/drama. *Special Achievements/Activities:* 398 awards ($4,442,586 total): cheerleading/drum major, community service, general special achievements/activities, leadership, memberships. *Special Characteristics:* 1,241 awards ($13,224,685 total): children of faculty/staff, first-generation college students, general special characteristics, international students, members of minority groups, previous college experience, siblings of current students. ***Tuition waivers:*** Full or partial for employees or children of employees. ***ROTC:*** Army cooperative, Air Force.

LOANS ***Student loans:*** $37,638,316 (42% need-based, 58% non-need-based). 68% of past graduating class borrowed through all loan programs. *Average indebtedness per student:* $34,539. ***Average need-based loan:*** Freshmen: $3368; Undergraduates: $4598. ***Parent loans:*** $13,483,978 (100% non-need-based). ***Programs:*** FFEL (Subsidized and Unsubsidized Stafford, PLUS), Perkins, Federal Nursing.

WORK-STUDY ***Federal work-study:*** Total amount: $1,171,239; 650 jobs averaging $1499. ***State or other work-study/employment:*** Total amount: $811,087 (13% need-based, 87% non-need-based). 64 part-time jobs averaging $2100.

ATHLETIC AWARDS Total amount: $3,030,983 (33% need-based, 67% non-need-based).

APPLYING FOR FINANCIAL AID ***Required financial aid form:*** FAFSA. ***Financial aid deadline (priority):*** 3/1. ***Notification date:*** Continuous beginning 3/1. Students must reply by 5/1 or within 4 weeks of notification.

CONTACT Cari Wickliffe, Director of Scholarship and Financial Aid, Saint Louis University, 221 North Grand Boulevard, Room 121, St. Louis, MO 63103-2097, 314-977-2350 or toll-free 800-758-3678 (out-of-state). *Fax:* 314-977-3437. *E-mail:* wicklics@slu.edu.

SAINT LUKE'S COLLEGE

Kansas City, MO

CONTACT Jeff Gannon, Director of Financial Aid, Saint Luke's College, 8320 Ward Parkway, Suite 300, Kansas City, MO 64114, 816-932-2194. *Fax:* 816-932-9064. *E-mail:* jgannon@saint-lukes.org.

SAINT MARTIN'S UNIVERSITY

Lacey, WA

ABOUT THE INSTITUTION Independent Roman Catholic, coed. Awards: bachelor's and master's degrees and post-bachelor's certificates. 31 undergraduate majors. Total enrollment: 1,463. Undergraduates: 1,180. Freshmen: 172.

GIFT AID (NEED-BASED) ***Scholarships, grants, and awards:*** Federal Pell, FSEOG, state, private, college/university gift aid from institutional funds.

GIFT AID (NON-NEED-BASED) ***Scholarships, grants, and awards by category:*** *Academic Interests/Achievement:* business, education, engineering/technologies, general academic interests/achievements, humanities. *Creative Arts/Performance:* music, performing arts, theater/drama. *Special Achievements/Activities:* community service, leadership, memberships. *Special Characteristics:* children and siblings of alumni, children of current students, children of faculty/staff, ethnic background, general special characteristics, international students, local/state students, members of minority groups, religious affiliation, siblings of current students, spouses of current students.

LOANS ***Programs:*** Federal Direct (Subsidized and Unsubsidized Stafford), FFEL (PLUS), Perkins, college/university.

WORK-STUDY ***Federal work-study:*** Total amount: $435,168; 191 jobs averaging $1875. ***State or other work-study/employment:*** Total amount: $964,444 (89% need-based, 11% non-need-based). 175 part-time jobs averaging $1893.

APPLYING FOR FINANCIAL AID ***Required financial aid forms:*** FAFSA, admissions application.

CONTACT Director of Financial Aid (Interim), Saint Martin's University, 5300 Pacific Avenue, SE, Lacey, WA 98503-1297, 360-438-4463 or toll-free 800-368-8803. *Fax:* 360-459-4124. *E-mail:* rwonderly@stmartins.edu.

SAINT MARY-OF-THE-WOODS COLLEGE

Saint Mary-of-the-Woods, IN

Tuition & fees: $20,180 **Average undergraduate aid package: $17,140**

ABOUT THE INSTITUTION Independent Roman Catholic, undergraduate: women only; graduate: coed. Awards: associate, bachelor's, and master's degrees and post-bachelor's and post-master's certificates (also offers external degree program with significant enrollment not reflected in profile). 61 undergraduate majors. Total enrollment: 1,668. Undergraduates: 1,540. Freshmen: 118. Federal methodology is used as a basis for awarding need-based institutional aid.

UNDERGRADUATE EXPENSES for 2007–08 ***Application fee:*** $30. ***Comprehensive fee:*** $27,560 includes full-time tuition ($19,530), mandatory fees ($650), and room and board ($7380). ***College room only:*** $2880. ***Part-time tuition:*** $370 per hour. ***Part-time fees:*** $120 per year.

UNDERGRADUATE FINANCIAL AID (Fall 2005) 83 applied for aid; of those 100% were deemed to have need. 100% of undergraduates with need received aid. ***Average percent of need met:*** 80% (excluding resources awarded to replace EFC). ***Average financial aid package:*** $17,140 (excluding resources awarded to replace EFC).

GIFT AID (NEED-BASED) ***Total amount:*** $5,080,779 (22% federal, 29% state, 45% institutional, 4% external sources). ***Receiving aid:*** All full-time undergraduates: 88% (75). ***Average award:*** Undergraduates: $5420. ***Scholarships, grants, and awards:*** Federal Pell, FSEOG, state, private, college/university gift aid from institutional funds.

GIFT AID (NON-NEED-BASED) ***Scholarships, grants, and awards by category:*** *Academic Interests/Achievement:* general academic interests/achievements. *Creative Arts/Performance:* applied art and design, art/fine arts, creative writing, dance, general creative arts/performance, journalism/publications, music, performing arts, theater/drama. *Special Achievements/Activities:* community service, general special achievements/activities, leadership, memberships, religious involvement. *Special Characteristics:* adult students, children and siblings of alumni, children of current students, children of faculty/staff, ethnic background, first-generation college students, general special characteristics, international students, local/state students, members of minority groups, out-of-state students, parents of current students, religious affiliation, siblings of current students, spouses of current students. ***ROTC:*** Army cooperative, Air Force cooperative.

LOANS ***Student loans:*** 89% of past graduating class borrowed through all loan programs. *Average indebtedness per student:* $20,180. ***Average need-based loan:*** Undergraduates: $2939. ***Parent loans:*** $1,513,076 (100% need-based). ***Programs:*** Federal Direct (Subsidized and Unsubsidized Stafford, PLUS), FFEL (Subsidized and Unsubsidized Stafford, PLUS), Perkins, college/university, Signature Loans.

WORK-STUDY ***Federal work-study:*** Total amount: $124,111; 93 jobs averaging $1334.

ATHLETIC AWARDS Total amount: $226,456 (100% need-based).

APPLYING FOR FINANCIAL AID ***Required financial aid form:*** FAFSA. ***Financial aid deadline:*** Continuous.

CONTACT Ms. Jan Benton, Director of Financial Aid, Saint Mary-of-the-Woods College, 106 Guerin Hall, Saint Mary-of-the-Woods, IN 47876, 812-535-5106 or toll-free 800-926-SMWC. *Fax:* 812-535-4900. *E-mail:* jbenton@smwc.edu.

SAINT MARY'S COLLEGE

Notre Dame, IN

Tuition & fees: $26,872 **Average undergraduate aid package: $20,191**

ABOUT THE INSTITUTION Independent Roman Catholic, women only. Awards: bachelor's degrees. 36 undergraduate majors. Total enrollment: 1,527. Undergraduates: 1,527. Freshmen: 426. Both federal and institutional methodology are used as a basis for awarding need-based institutional aid.

UNDERGRADUATE EXPENSES for 2007–08 ***Application fee:*** $30. ***Comprehensive fee:*** $35,550 includes full-time tuition ($26,282), mandatory fees ($590), and room and board ($8678). ***College room only:*** $5346. ***Part-time tuition:*** $1039 per semester hour.

FRESHMAN FINANCIAL AID (Fall 2005) 339 applied for aid; of those 78% were deemed to have need. 100% of freshmen with need received aid; of those 47% had need fully met. ***Average percent of need met:*** 81% (excluding resources awarded to replace EFC). ***Average financial aid package:*** $19,709 (excluding resources awarded to replace EFC). 29% of all full-time freshmen had no need and received non-need-based gift aid.

UNDERGRADUATE FINANCIAL AID (Fall 2005) 1,119 applied for aid; of those 82% were deemed to have need. 100% of undergraduates with need received aid; of those 41% had need fully met. ***Average percent of need met:*** 81% (excluding resources awarded to replace EFC). ***Average financial aid package:*** $20,191 (excluding resources awarded to replace EFC). 25% of all full-time undergraduates had no need and received non-need-based gift aid.

GIFT AID (NEED-BASED) ***Total amount:*** $7,447,260 (10% federal, 13% state, 77% institutional). ***Receiving aid:*** Freshmen: 49% (207); All full-time undergraduates: 50% (744). ***Average award:*** Freshmen: $9435; Undergraduates: $10,010. ***Scholarships, grants, and awards:*** Federal Pell, FSEOG, state, private, college/university gift aid from institutional funds.

GIFT AID (NON-NEED-BASED) ***Total amount:*** $8,595,226 (85% institutional, 15% external sources). ***Receiving aid:*** Freshmen: 21% (89); Undergraduates: 13% (195). ***Average award:*** Freshmen: $8048; Undergraduates: $7237. ***Scholarships, grants, and awards by category:*** *Academic Interests/Achievement:* general academic interests/achievements. *Creative Arts/Performance:* art/fine arts, music, theater/drama. *Special Achievements/Activities:* community service. *Special Characteristics:* children of faculty/staff, siblings of current students. ***ROTC:*** Army cooperative, Naval cooperative, Air Force cooperative.

LOANS ***Student loans:*** $7,081,574 (44% need-based, 56% non-need-based). 68% of past graduating class borrowed through all loan programs. *Average indebtedness per student:* $35,143. ***Average need-based loan:*** Freshmen: $2332; Undergraduates: $4544. ***Parent loans:*** $3,880,815 (100% non-need-based). ***Programs:*** FFEL (Subsidized and Unsubsidized Stafford, PLUS), Perkins, college/university.

WORK-STUDY ***Federal work-study:*** Total amount: $513,524; 344 jobs averaging $1451. ***State or other work-study/employment:*** Total amount: $1,320,242 (39% need-based, 61% non-need-based). 923 part-time jobs averaging $3854.

APPLYING FOR FINANCIAL AID ***Required financial aid forms:*** FAFSA, CSS Financial Aid PROFILE. ***Financial aid deadline (priority):*** 3/1. ***Notification date:*** Continuous beginning 12/15. Students must reply by 5/1.

CONTACT Kathleen M. Brown, Director of Financial Aid, Saint Mary's College, 141 Le Mans Hall, Notre Dame, IN 46556, 574-284-4557 or toll-free 800-551-7621. *Fax:* 574-284-4707. *E-mail:* kbrown@saintmarys.edu.

SAINT MARY'S COLLEGE OF CALIFORNIA

Moraga, CA

Tuition & fees: $29,050 **Average undergraduate aid package: $21,717**

ABOUT THE INSTITUTION Independent Roman Catholic, coed. Awards: bachelor's, master's, and doctoral degrees. 69 undergraduate majors. Total enrollment: 3,962. Undergraduates: 2,835. Freshmen: 610. Federal methodology is used as a basis for awarding need-based institutional aid.

UNDERGRADUATE EXPENSES for 2006–07 ***Application fee:*** $55. ***Comprehensive fee:*** $39,616 includes full-time tuition ($28,900), mandatory fees ($150), and room and board ($10,566). ***College room only:*** $5926. Full-time tuition and fees vary according to course load. Room and board charges vary according to board plan and housing facility. ***Part-time tuition:*** $3615 per course. Part-time tuition and fees vary according to course load. ***Payment plan:*** Installment.

FRESHMAN FINANCIAL AID (Fall 2006, est.) 573 applied for aid; of those 81% were deemed to have need. 99% of freshmen with need received aid; of those 6% had need fully met. ***Average percent of need met:*** 68% (excluding resources awarded to replace EFC). ***Average financial aid package:*** $20,431 (excluding resources awarded to replace EFC). 5% of all full-time freshmen had no need and received non-need-based gift aid.

UNDERGRADUATE FINANCIAL AID (Fall 2006, est.) 1,686 applied for aid; of those 85% were deemed to have need. 99% of undergraduates with need received aid; of those 9% had need fully met. ***Average percent of need met:*** 69% (excluding resources awarded to replace EFC). ***Average financial aid package:*** $21,717 (excluding resources awarded to replace EFC). 4% of all full-time undergraduates had no need and received non-need-based gift aid.

GIFT AID (NEED-BASED) ***Total amount:*** $22,140,514 (10% federal, 20% state, 67% institutional, 3% external sources). ***Receiving aid:*** Freshmen: 66% (405); All full-time undergraduates: 52% (1,257). ***Average award:*** Freshmen: $16,014; Undergraduates: $15,833. ***Scholarships, grants, and awards:*** Federal Pell, FSEOG, state, private, college/university gift aid from institutional funds.

GIFT AID (NON-NEED-BASED) ***Total amount:*** $1,257,670 (95% institutional, 5% external sources). ***Receiving aid:*** Freshmen: 20% (120); Undergraduates: 15% (373). ***Average award:*** Freshmen: $10,286; Undergraduates: $8895. ***Scholarships, grants, and awards by category:*** *Academic Interests/Achievement:* 334 awards ($2,378,019 total): general academic interests/achievements. *Special Achievements/Activities:* 68 awards ($470,851 total): memberships. *Special Characteristics:* 67 awards ($1,404,855 total): children and siblings of alumni, children of educators, children of faculty/staff, general special characteristics, relatives of clergy. ***Tuition waivers:*** Full or partial for employees or children of employees. ***ROTC:*** Army cooperative, Air Force cooperative.

LOANS ***Student loans:*** $11,459,056 (79% need-based, 21% non-need-based). 65% of past graduating class borrowed through all loan programs. *Average indebtedness per student:* $23,402. ***Average need-based loan:*** Freshmen: $3067; Undergraduates: $4178. ***Parent loans:*** $8,288,158 (44% need-based, 56% non-need-based). ***Programs:*** FFEL (Subsidized and Unsubsidized Stafford, PLUS), Perkins.

WORK-STUDY ***Federal work-study:*** Total amount: $1,124,736; 506 jobs averaging $2220.

ATHLETIC AWARDS Total amount: $5,672,408 (27% need-based, 73% non-need-based).

APPLYING FOR FINANCIAL AID ***Required financial aid forms:*** FAFSA, state aid form. ***Financial aid deadline (priority):*** 2/15. ***Notification date:*** Continuous beginning 3/30. Students must reply by 5/1 or within 2 weeks of notification.

CONTACT Linda Judge, Director of Financial Aid, Saint Mary's College of California, PO Box 4530, Moraga, CA 94575, 925-631-4370 or toll-free 800-800-4SMC. *Fax:* 925-376-2965. *E-mail:* finaid@stmarys-ca.edu.

ST. MARY'S COLLEGE OF MARYLAND

St. Mary's City, MD

Tuition & fees (MD res): $11,989 **Average undergraduate aid package: $6500**

ABOUT THE INSTITUTION State-supported, coed. Awards: bachelor's degrees. 23 undergraduate majors. Total enrollment: 1,957. Undergraduates: 1,948. Freshmen: 429. Federal methodology is used as a basis for awarding need-based institutional aid.

UNDERGRADUATE EXPENSES for 2007–08 ***Application fee:*** $40. ***Tuition, state resident:*** full-time $9973; part-time $160 per credit. ***Tuition, nonresident:*** full-time $20,307; part-time $160 per credit. ***College room and board:*** $8855; ***Room only:*** $5060.

FRESHMAN FINANCIAL AID (Fall 2005) 344 applied for aid; of those 64% were deemed to have need. 100% of freshmen with need received aid. ***Average percent of need met:*** 59% (excluding resources awarded to replace EFC). ***Average financial aid package:*** $7500 (excluding resources awarded to replace EFC). 32% of all full-time freshmen had no need and received non-need-based gift aid.

UNDERGRADUATE FINANCIAL AID (Fall 2005) 1,124 applied for aid; of those 73% were deemed to have need. 100% of undergraduates with need received aid. ***Average percent of need met:*** 62% (excluding resources awarded to replace EFC). ***Average financial aid package:*** $6500 (excluding resources awarded to replace EFC). 24% of all full-time undergraduates had no need and received non-need-based gift aid.

GIFT AID (NEED-BASED) ***Total amount:*** $3,838,451 (17% federal, 28% state, 45% institutional, 10% external sources). ***Receiving aid:*** Freshmen: 17% (85); All full-time undergraduates: 19% (340). ***Average award:*** Freshmen: $3000; Undergraduates: $4000. ***Scholarships, grants, and awards:*** Federal Pell, FSEOG, state, private, college/university gift aid from institutional funds.

GIFT AID (NON-NEED-BASED) ***Total amount:*** $3,743,502 (16% state, 70% institutional, 14% external sources). ***Receiving aid:*** Freshmen: 17% (85); Undergraduates: 19% (340). ***Average award:*** Freshmen: $3000; Undergraduates: $4000. ***Scholarships, grants, and awards by category:*** *Academic Interests/Achievement:* 795 awards ($2,609,626 total): general academic interests/achievements. *Special Characteristics:* 166 awards ($636,532 total): children and siblings of alumni, children of faculty/staff.

LOANS ***Student loans:*** $4,565,192 (45% need-based, 55% non-need-based). 69% of past graduating class borrowed through all loan programs. *Average indebtedness per student:* $17,125. ***Average need-based loan:*** Freshmen: $2625; Undergraduates: $5500. ***Parent loans:*** $5,828,327 (100% non-need-based). ***Programs:*** FFEL (Subsidized and Unsubsidized Stafford, PLUS), Perkins.

WORK-STUDY ***Federal work-study:*** Total amount: $102,007; 108 jobs averaging $800. ***State or other work-study/employment:*** Part-time jobs available.

APPLYING FOR FINANCIAL AID ***Required financial aid form:*** FAFSA. ***Financial aid deadline:*** 3/1. ***Notification date:*** 4/1. Students must reply by 5/1.

CONTACT Tim Wolfe, Director of Financial Aid, St. Mary's College of Maryland, 18952 East Fisher Road, St. Mary's City, MD 20686-3001, 240-895-3000 or toll-free 800-492-7181. *Fax:* 240-895-4959. *E-mail:* tawolfe@smcm.edu.

SAINT MARY'S UNIVERSITY OF MINNESOTA

Winona, MN

Tuition & fees: $22,398 **Average undergraduate aid package: $15,570**

ABOUT THE INSTITUTION Independent Roman Catholic, coed. Awards: bachelor's, master's, and doctoral degrees and post-bachelor's and post-master's certificates. 61 undergraduate majors. Total enrollment: 5,566. Undergraduates: 1,818. Freshmen: 378. Federal methodology is used as a basis for awarding need-based institutional aid.

UNDERGRADUATE EXPENSES for 2007–08 ***Application fee:*** $25. ***Comprehensive fee:*** $28,528 includes full-time tuition ($21,918), mandatory fees ($480), and room and board ($6130). ***College room only:*** $3430. ***Part-time tuition:*** $730 per credit. ***Part-time fees:*** $460 per year.

FRESHMAN FINANCIAL AID (Fall 2006, est.) 339 applied for aid; of those 81% were deemed to have need. 100% of freshmen with need received aid; of those 60% had need fully met. ***Average percent of need met:*** 85% (excluding resources awarded to replace EFC). ***Average financial aid package:*** $15,830 (excluding resources awarded to replace EFC). 21% of all full-time freshmen had no need and received non-need-based gift aid.

UNDERGRADUATE FINANCIAL AID (Fall 2006, est.) 1,047 applied for aid; of those 85% were deemed to have need. 100% of undergraduates with need received aid; of those 63% had need fully met. ***Average percent of need met:*** 81% (excluding resources awarded to replace EFC). ***Average financial aid package:*** $15,570 (excluding resources awarded to replace EFC). 23% of all full-time undergraduates had no need and received non-need-based gift aid.

GIFT AID (NEED-BASED) ***Total amount:*** $10,393,951 (8% federal, 9% state, 81% institutional, 2% external sources). ***Receiving aid:*** Freshmen: 73% (276); All full-time undergraduates: 68% (888). ***Average award:*** Freshmen: $11,390; Undergraduates: $10,405. ***Scholarships, grants, and awards:*** Federal Pell, FSEOG, state.

GIFT AID (NON-NEED-BASED) ***Average award:*** Freshmen: $6444; Undergraduates: $6553. ***Scholarships, grants, and awards by category:*** *Academic Interests/Achievement:* general academic interests/achievements. *Creative Arts/Performance:* music, theater/drama. *Special Achievements/Activities:* leadership. *Special Characteristics:* children and siblings of alumni, children of faculty/staff, members of minority groups. ***ROTC:*** Army cooperative.

LOANS ***Student loans:*** $5,491,058 (100% need-based). 74% of past graduating class borrowed through all loan programs. *Average indebtedness per student:* $28,500. ***Average need-based loan:*** Freshmen: $3237; Undergraduates: $4041. ***Parent loans:*** $1,665,792 (100% need-based). ***Programs:*** FFEL (Subsidized and Unsubsidized Stafford, PLUS), Perkins, state, Signature Loans.

WORK-STUDY ***Federal work-study:*** Total amount: $300,943; 223 jobs averaging $1280. ***State or other work-study/employment:*** Total amount: $504,332 (100% need-based). 382 part-time jobs averaging $1079.

APPLYING FOR FINANCIAL AID ***Required financial aid forms:*** FAFSA, donor form. ***Financial aid deadline (priority):*** 3/15. ***Notification date:*** Continuous beginning 2/1. Students must reply within 2 weeks of notification.

CONTACT Ms. Jayne P. Wobig, Director of Financial Aid, Saint Mary's University of Minnesota, 700 Terrace Heights, #5, Winona, MN 55987-1399, 507-457-1437 or toll-free 800-635-5987. *Fax:* 507-457-6698. *E-mail:* jwobig@smumn.edu.

ST. MARY'S UNIVERSITY OF SAN ANTONIO

San Antonio, TX

CONTACT Mr. David R. Krause, Director of Financial Assistance, St. Mary's University of San Antonio, One Camino Santa Maria, San Antonio, TX 78228-8541, 210-436-3141 or toll-free 800-FOR-STMU. *Fax:* 210-431-2221. *E-mail:* dkrause@alvin.stmarytx.edu.

SAINT MICHAEL'S COLLEGE

Colchester, VT

Tuition & fees: $28,515 **Average undergraduate aid package: $21,672**

ABOUT THE INSTITUTION Independent Roman Catholic, coed. Awards: bachelor's and master's degrees and post-bachelor's and post-master's certificates. 35 undergraduate majors. Total enrollment: 2,437. Undergraduates: 1,992. Freshmen: 577. Both federal and institutional methodology are used as a basis for awarding need-based institutional aid.

UNDERGRADUATE EXPENSES for 2006–07 ***Application fee:*** $50. ***Comprehensive fee:*** $35,505 includes full-time tuition ($28,280), mandatory fees ($235), and room and board ($6990). Room and board charges vary according to housing facility. ***Part-time tuition:*** $945 per credit hour. ***Payment plan:*** Installment.

FRESHMAN FINANCIAL AID (Fall 2006, est.) 459 applied for aid; of those 84% were deemed to have need. 100% of freshmen with need received aid; of those 14% had need fully met. ***Average percent of need met:*** 82% (excluding resources awarded to replace EFC). ***Average financial aid package:*** $24,067 (excluding resources awarded to replace EFC). 28% of all full-time freshmen had no need and received non-need-based gift aid.

UNDERGRADUATE FINANCIAL AID (Fall 2006, est.) 1,438 applied for aid; of those 87% were deemed to have need. 100% of undergraduates with need received aid; of those 23% had need fully met. ***Average percent of need met:*** 79% (excluding resources awarded to replace EFC). ***Average financial aid package:*** $21,672 (excluding resources awarded to replace EFC). 20% of all full-time undergraduates had no need and received non-need-based gift aid.

GIFT AID (NEED-BASED) ***Total amount:*** $18,629,166 (7% federal, 3% state, 86% institutional, 4% external sources). ***Receiving aid:*** Freshmen: 66% (380); All full-time undergraduates: 63% (1,212). ***Average award:*** Freshmen: $15,918; Undergraduates: $14,884. ***Scholarships, grants, and awards:*** Federal Pell, FSEOG, state, private, college/university gift aid from institutional funds.

GIFT AID (NON-NEED-BASED) ***Total amount:*** $2,396,925 (95% institutional, 5% external sources). ***Receiving aid:*** Freshmen: 7% (41); Undergraduates: 7% (135). ***Average award:*** Freshmen: $3419; Undergraduates: $6050. ***Scholarships, grants, and awards by category:*** *Academic Interests/Achievement:* general academic interests/achievements. *Creative Arts/Performance:* art/fine arts. *Special Characteristics:* local/state students, members of minority groups, out-of-state students, religious affiliation, siblings of current students. ***Tuition waivers:*** Full or partial for employees or children of employees. ***ROTC:*** Army cooperative, Air Force cooperative.

LOANS ***Student loans:*** $10,459,312 (62% need-based, 38% non-need-based). 73% of past graduating class borrowed through all loan programs. *Average indebtedness per student:* $22,264. ***Average need-based loan:*** Freshmen: $3808; Undergraduates: $4488. ***Parent loans:*** $6,495,375 (100% non-need-based). ***Programs:*** FFEL (Subsidized and Unsubsidized Stafford, PLUS), Perkins.

WORK-STUDY ***Federal work-study:*** Total amount: $407,373; 489 jobs averaging $833. ***State or other work-study/employment:*** Total amount: $374,089 (100% need-based). 499 part-time jobs averaging $750.

ATHLETIC AWARDS Total amount: $712,575 (100% non-need-based).

APPLYING FOR FINANCIAL AID ***Required financial aid forms:*** FAFSA, federal income tax forms (student and parent). ***Financial aid deadline (priority):*** 3/15. ***Notification date:*** 4/1. Students must reply by 5/1 or within 2 weeks of notification.

CONTACT Mrs. Nelberta B. Lunde, Director of New Student Aid and Scholarships, Saint Michael's College, Winooski Park, Colchester, VT 05439, 802-654-3243 or toll-free 800-762-8000. *Fax:* 802-654-2591. *E-mail:* finaid@smcvt.edu.

ST. NORBERT COLLEGE

De Pere, WI

Tuition & fees: $23,497 **Average undergraduate aid package: $17,303**

ABOUT THE INSTITUTION Independent Roman Catholic, coed. Awards: bachelor's and master's degrees. 31 undergraduate majors. Total enrollment: 2,072. Undergraduates: 2,015. Freshmen: 552. Federal methodology is used as a basis for awarding need-based institutional aid.

UNDERGRADUATE EXPENSES for 2006–07 ***Application fee:*** $25. ***Comprehensive fee:*** $29,816 includes full-time tuition ($23,097), mandatory fees ($400), and room and board ($6319). ***College room only:*** $3349. Full-time tuition and fees vary according to course load. Room and board charges vary according to board plan, housing facility, and student level. ***Part-time tuition:*** $722 per credit. Part-time tuition and fees vary according to course load. ***Payment plans:*** Installment, deferred payment.

FRESHMAN FINANCIAL AID (Fall 2006, est.) 465 applied for aid; of those 78% were deemed to have need. 100% of freshmen with need received aid; of those 38% had need fully met. ***Average percent of need met:*** 92% (excluding resources awarded to replace EFC). ***Average financial aid package:*** $17,598 (excluding resources awarded to replace EFC). 29% of all full-time freshmen had no need and received non-need-based gift aid.

UNDERGRADUATE FINANCIAL AID (Fall 2006, est.) 1,519 applied for aid; of those 82% were deemed to have need. 100% of undergraduates with need received aid; of those 43% had need fully met. ***Average percent of need met:*** 90% (excluding resources awarded to replace EFC). ***Average financial aid***

package: $17,303 (excluding resources awarded to replace EFC). 31% of all full-time undergraduates had no need and received non-need-based gift aid.

GIFT AID (NEED-BASED) ***Total amount:*** $15,757,199 (7% federal, 8% state, 79% institutional, 6% external sources). ***Receiving aid:*** Freshmen: 64% (353); All full-time undergraduates: 62% (1,208). ***Average award:*** Freshmen: $13,541; Undergraduates: $12,337. ***Scholarships, grants, and awards:*** Federal Pell, FSEOG, state, private, college/university gift aid from institutional funds.

GIFT AID (NON-NEED-BASED) ***Total amount:*** $4,856,752 (1% federal, 89% institutional, 10% external sources). ***Receiving aid:*** Freshmen: 2% (13); Undergraduates: 2% (39). ***Average award:*** Freshmen: $7520; Undergraduates: $7341. ***Scholarships, grants, and awards by category:*** *Academic Interests/Achievement:* 1,283 awards ($8,898,037 total): general academic interests/achievements. *Creative Arts/Performance:* 73 awards ($113,200 total): art/fine arts, music, theater/drama. *Special Achievements/Activities:* 169 awards ($587,000 total): general special achievements/activities. *Special Characteristics:* 164 awards ($1,495,321 total): children of faculty/staff, children with a deceased or disabled parent, ethnic background, international students. ***Tuition waivers:*** Full or partial for employees or children of employees. ***ROTC:*** Army.

LOANS ***Student loans:*** $10,848,796 (93% need-based, 7% non-need-based). 65% of past graduating class borrowed through all loan programs. *Average indebtedness per student:* $24,808. ***Average need-based loan:*** Freshmen: $3420; Undergraduates: $4723. ***Parent loans:*** $2,285,912 (72% need-based, 28% non-need-based). ***Programs:*** Federal Direct (Subsidized and Unsubsidized Stafford, PLUS), Perkins, college/university.

WORK-STUDY ***Federal work-study:*** Total amount: $489,892; 329 jobs averaging $1489. ***State or other work-study/employment:*** Total amount: $1,405,254 (56% need-based, 44% non-need-based). 743 part-time jobs averaging $1891.

APPLYING FOR FINANCIAL AID ***Required financial aid forms:*** FAFSA, institution's own form. ***Financial aid deadline (priority):*** 3/1. ***Notification date:*** Continuous beginning 3/15. Students must reply within 2 weeks of notification.

CONTACT Mr. Jeffrey A. Zahn, Director of Financial Aid, St. Norbert College, 100 Grant Street, De Pere, WI 54115-2099, 920-403-3071 or toll-free 800-236-4878. *Fax:* 920-403-3062. *E-mail:* jeff.zahn@snc.edu.

ST. OLAF COLLEGE

Northfield, MN

Tuition & fees: $30,600 **Average undergraduate aid package: $15,990**

ABOUT THE INSTITUTION Independent Lutheran, coed. Awards: bachelor's degrees. 50 undergraduate majors. Total enrollment: 3,041. Undergraduates: 3,041. Freshmen: 793. Both federal and institutional methodology are used as a basis for awarding need-based institutional aid.

UNDERGRADUATE EXPENSES for 2007–08 ***Application fee:*** $40. ***Comprehensive fee:*** $38,500 includes full-time tuition ($30,600) and room and board ($7900). ***College room only:*** $3650. ***Part-time tuition:*** $955 per credit hour.

FRESHMAN FINANCIAL AID (Fall 2006, est.) 625 applied for aid; of those 82% were deemed to have need. 100% of freshmen with need received aid; of those 100% had need fully met. ***Average percent of need met:*** 100% (excluding resources awarded to replace EFC). ***Average financial aid package:*** $22,416 (excluding resources awarded to replace EFC). 18% of all full-time freshmen had no need and received non-need-based gift aid.

UNDERGRADUATE FINANCIAL AID (Fall 2006, est.) 2,182 applied for aid; of those 88% were deemed to have need. 100% of undergraduates with need received aid; of those 100% had need fully met. ***Average percent of need met:*** 100% (excluding resources awarded to replace EFC). ***Average financial aid package:*** $15,990 (excluding resources awarded to replace EFC). 18% of all full-time undergraduates had no need and received non-need-based gift aid.

GIFT AID (NEED-BASED) ***Total amount:*** $31,067,543 (5% federal, 5% state, 86% institutional, 4% external sources). ***Receiving aid:*** Freshmen: 64% (511); All full-time undergraduates: 65% (1,910). ***Average award:*** Freshmen: $16,844; Undergraduates: $15,990. ***Scholarships, grants, and awards:*** Federal Pell, FSEOG, state, private, college/university gift aid from institutional funds.

GIFT AID (NON-NEED-BASED) ***Total amount:*** $4,417,438 (90% institutional, 10% external sources). ***Receiving aid:*** Freshmen: 31% (249); Undergraduates: 26% (775). ***Average award:*** Freshmen: $7954; Undergraduates: $7208. ***Scholarships, grants, and awards by category:*** *Academic Interests/Achievement:* 1,213 awards ($7,822,250 total): general academic interests/achievements. *Creative Arts/Performance:* 188 awards ($622,000 total): music. *Special Achievements/Activities:* 200 awards ($698,495 total): community service, religious involvement. *Special Characteristics:* 20 awards ($256,650 total): international students.

LOANS ***Student loans:*** $12,369,043 (66% need-based, 34% non-need-based). 62% of past graduating class borrowed through all loan programs. *Average indebtedness per student:* $23,993. ***Average need-based loan:*** Freshmen: $3820; Undergraduates: $4931. ***Parent loans:*** $10,962,203 (100% non-need-based). ***Programs:*** FFEL (Subsidized and Unsubsidized Stafford, PLUS), Perkins, Federal Nursing, state, college/university.

WORK-STUDY ***Federal work-study:*** Total amount: $2,003,885; 1,123 jobs averaging $1887. ***State or other work-study/employment:*** Total amount: $2,025,000 (85% need-based, 15% non-need-based). 806 part-time jobs averaging $1725.

APPLYING FOR FINANCIAL AID ***Required financial aid forms:*** FAFSA, CSS Financial Aid PROFILE, business/farm supplement, St. Olaf noncustodial form. ***Financial aid deadline:*** 4/15 (priority: 1/15). ***Notification date:*** Continuous beginning 3/1. Students must reply by 5/1 or within 2 weeks of notification.

CONTACT Ms. Katharine Ruby, Director of Financial Aid, St. Olaf College, 1520 Saint Olaf Avenue, Northfield, MN 55057-1098, 507-646-3019 or toll-free 800-800-3025. *E-mail:* ruby@stolaf.edu.

SAINT PAUL'S COLLEGE

Lawrenceville, VA

CONTACT Office of Financial Aid, Saint Paul's College, 115 College Drive, Lawrenceville, VA 23868-1202, 434-848-6495 or toll-free 800-678-7071. *Fax:* 434-848-6498. *E-mail:* aid@saintpauls.edu.

ST. PETERSBURG THEOLOGICAL SEMINARY

St. Petersburg, FL

CONTACT Financial Aid Office, St. Petersburg Theological Seminary, 10830 Navajo Drive, St. Petersburg, FL 33708, 727-399-0276.

SAINT PETER'S COLLEGE

Jersey City, NJ

CONTACT Director of Financial Aid, Saint Peter's College, 2641 Kennedy Boulevard, Jersey City, NJ 07306, 201-915-4929 or toll-free 888-SPC-9933. *Fax:* 201-434-6878.

ST. THOMAS AQUINAS COLLEGE

Sparkill, NY

CONTACT Margaret McGrail, Director of Financial Aid, St. Thomas Aquinas College, 125 Route 340, Sparkill, NY 10976, 914-398-4097 or toll-free 800-999-STAC.

ST. THOMAS UNIVERSITY

Miami Gardens, FL

ABOUT THE INSTITUTION Independent Roman Catholic, coed. Awards: bachelor's, master's, and first professional degrees and post-bachelor's and post-master's certificates. 28 undergraduate majors. Total enrollment: 2,517. Undergraduates: 1,155. Freshmen: 248.

GIFT AID (NEED-BASED) ***Scholarships, grants, and awards:*** Federal Pell, FSEOG, state, private, college/university gift aid from institutional funds.

GIFT AID (NON-NEED-BASED) ***Scholarships, grants, and awards by category:*** *Academic Interests/Achievement:* general academic interests/achievements.

LOANS ***Programs:*** FFEL (Subsidized and Unsubsidized Stafford, PLUS), Perkins.

WORK-STUDY ***Federal work-study:*** Total amount: $441,077; 227 jobs averaging $2325. ***State or other work-study/employment:*** 47 part-time jobs averaging $3277.

APPLYING FOR FINANCIAL AID ***Required financial aid forms:*** FAFSA, state aid form.

CONTACT Ms. Anh Do, Director of Financial Aid, St. Thomas University, 16400 Northwest 32nd Avenue, Miami, FL 33054-6459, 305-628-6547 or toll-free 800-367-9010. *Fax:* 305-628-6754. *E-mail:* ado@stu.edu.

SAINT VINCENT COLLEGE

Latrobe, PA

Tuition & fees: $23,000 **Average undergraduate aid package: $18,515**

ABOUT THE INSTITUTION Independent Roman Catholic, coed. Awards: bachelor's and master's degrees and post-bachelor's certificates. 44 undergraduate majors. Total enrollment: 1,818. Undergraduates: 1,652. Freshmen: 437. Federal methodology is used as a basis for awarding need-based institutional aid.

UNDERGRADUATE EXPENSES for 2006–07 ***Application fee:*** $25. ***Comprehensive fee:*** $30,242 includes full-time tuition ($22,350), mandatory fees ($650), and room and board ($7242). ***College room only:*** $3700. Room and board charges vary according to board plan and student level. ***Part-time tuition:*** $699 per credit. ***Part-time fees:*** $45 per term. ***Payment plan:*** Installment.

FRESHMAN FINANCIAL AID (Fall 2006, est.) 411 applied for aid; of those 85% were deemed to have need. 100% of freshmen with need received aid; of those 21% had need fully met. ***Average percent of need met:*** 85% (excluding resources awarded to replace EFC). ***Average financial aid package:*** $19,109 (excluding resources awarded to replace EFC). 19% of all full-time freshmen had no need and received non-need-based gift aid.

UNDERGRADUATE FINANCIAL AID (Fall 2006, est.) 1,314 applied for aid; of those 88% were deemed to have need. 100% of undergraduates with need received aid; of those 23% had need fully met. ***Average percent of need met:*** 82% (excluding resources awarded to replace EFC). ***Average financial aid package:*** $18,515 (excluding resources awarded to replace EFC). 18% of all full-time undergraduates had no need and received non-need-based gift aid.

GIFT AID (NEED-BASED) ***Total amount:*** $13,840,606 (9% federal, 20% state, 69% institutional, 2% external sources). ***Receiving aid:*** Freshmen: 80% (351); All full-time undergraduates: 74% (1,158). ***Average award:*** Freshmen: $15,249; Undergraduates: $13,671. ***Scholarships, grants, and awards:*** Federal Pell, FSEOG, state, private, college/university gift aid from institutional funds, United Negro College Fund.

GIFT AID (NON-NEED-BASED) ***Total amount:*** $4,083,003 (100% institutional). ***Receiving aid:*** Freshmen: 79% (347); Undergraduates: 63% (980). ***Average award:*** Freshmen: $8927; Undergraduates: $8270. ***Scholarships, grants, and awards by category:*** *Academic Interests/Achievement:* 1,150 awards ($8,053,940 total): biological sciences, business, computer science, general academic interests/achievements, mathematics, physical sciences, social sciences. *Creative Arts/Performance:* music. *Special Achievements/Activities:* 1,325 awards ($2,202,875 total): leadership. *Special Characteristics:* 262 awards ($978,787 total): children of faculty/staff, international students, members of minority groups, out-of-state students, veterans, veterans' children. ***Tuition waivers:*** Full or partial for employees or children of employees, senior citizens. ***ROTC:*** Air Force cooperative.

LOANS ***Student loans:*** $7,857,066 (49% need-based, 51% non-need-based). ***Average need-based loan:*** Freshmen: $2810; Undergraduates: $3291. ***Parent loans:*** $2,634,611 (100% non-need-based). ***Programs:*** FFEL (Subsidized and Unsubsidized Stafford, PLUS), Perkins.

WORK-STUDY ***Federal work-study:*** Total amount: $608,415; 181 jobs averaging $1000. ***State or other work-study/employment:*** Total amount: $33,677 (100% need-based). 578 part-time jobs averaging $975.

ATHLETIC AWARDS Total amount: $1,319,797 (55% need-based, 45% non-need-based).

APPLYING FOR FINANCIAL AID ***Required financial aid forms:*** FAFSA, state aid form. ***Financial aid deadline:*** 5/1 (priority: 3/1). ***Notification date:*** Continuous beginning 3/1. Students must reply within 2 weeks of notification.

CONTACT Kimberly Woodley, Director of Financial Aid, Saint Vincent College, 300 Fraser Purchase Road, Latrobe, PA 15650, 724-537-4540 or toll-free 800-782-5549. *Fax:* 724-532-5069. *E-mail:* admission@stvincent.edu.

SAINT XAVIER UNIVERSITY

Chicago, IL

Tuition & fees: $19,860 **Average undergraduate aid package: $16,795**

ABOUT THE INSTITUTION Independent Roman Catholic, coed. Awards: bachelor's and master's degrees and post-bachelor's and post-master's certificates. 39 undergraduate majors. Total enrollment: 5,657. Undergraduates: 3,316. Freshmen: 532. Federal methodology is used as a basis for awarding need-based institutional aid.

UNDERGRADUATE EXPENSES for 2006–07 ***Application fee:*** $25. ***Comprehensive fee:*** $27,274 includes full-time tuition ($19,640), mandatory fees ($220), and room and board ($7414). ***College room only:*** $4230. Full-time tuition and fees vary according to course load. Room and board charges vary according to board plan and housing facility. ***Part-time tuition:*** $658 per credit hour. ***Part-time fees:*** $130 per year. Part-time tuition and fees vary according to course load. ***Payment plan:*** Installment.

FRESHMAN FINANCIAL AID (Fall 2006, est.) 505 applied for aid; of those 87% were deemed to have need. 100% of freshmen with need received aid; of those 21% had need fully met. ***Average percent of need met:*** 88% (excluding resources awarded to replace EFC). ***Average financial aid package:*** $18,973 (excluding resources awarded to replace EFC). 16% of all full-time freshmen had no need and received non-need-based gift aid.

UNDERGRADUATE FINANCIAL AID (Fall 2006, est.) 2,317 applied for aid; of those 89% were deemed to have need. 100% of undergraduates with need received aid; of those 23% had need fully met. ***Average percent of need met:*** 83% (excluding resources awarded to replace EFC). ***Average financial aid package:*** $16,795 (excluding resources awarded to replace EFC). 18% of all full-time undergraduates had no need and received non-need-based gift aid.

GIFT AID (NEED-BASED) ***Total amount:*** $24,031,308 (16% federal, 29% state, 49% institutional, 6% external sources). ***Receiving aid:*** Freshmen: 82% (438); All full-time undergraduates: 79% (2,056). ***Average award:*** Freshmen: $13,123; Undergraduates: $9701. ***Scholarships, grants, and awards:*** Federal Pell, FSEOG, state, private, college/university gift aid from institutional funds, United Negro College Fund, Federal Nursing.

GIFT AID (NON-NEED-BASED) ***Total amount:*** $4,445,332 (5% state, 65% institutional, 30% external sources). ***Receiving aid:*** Freshmen: 79% (422); Undergraduates: 76% (1,964). ***Average award:*** Freshmen: $7532; Undergraduates: $4821. ***Scholarships, grants, and awards by category:*** *Academic Interests/Achievement:* 2,908 awards ($11,141,651 total): general academic interests/achievements. *Creative Arts/Performance:* 65 awards ($207,654 total): music. *Special Achievements/Activities:* leadership. *Special Characteristics:* 121 awards ($1,238,030 total): children of faculty/staff. ***Tuition waivers:*** Full or partial for employees or children of employees, senior citizens. ***ROTC:*** Air Force cooperative.

LOANS ***Student loans:*** $18,180,535 (86% need-based, 14% non-need-based). 88% of past graduating class borrowed through all loan programs. *Average indebtedness per student:* $18,730. ***Average need-based loan:*** Freshmen: $2698; Undergraduates: $3744. ***Parent loans:*** $2,103,903 (31% need-based, 69% non-need-based). ***Programs:*** FFEL (Subsidized and Unsubsidized Stafford, PLUS), Perkins.

WORK-STUDY ***Federal work-study:*** Total amount: $3,616,284; 1,427 jobs averaging $2653. ***State or other work-study/employment:*** Total amount: $340,270 (73% need-based, 27% non-need-based). 33 part-time jobs averaging $6315.

ATHLETIC AWARDS Total amount: $1,703,828 (70% need-based, 30% non-need-based).

APPLYING FOR FINANCIAL AID ***Required financial aid form:*** FAFSA. ***Financial aid deadline (priority):*** 3/1. ***Notification date:*** Continuous beginning 2/15. Students must reply by 5/1 or within 2 weeks of notification.

CONTACT Ms. Susan Swisher, Assistant Vice President for Student Financial Services, Saint Xavier University, 3700 West 103rd Street, Chicago, IL 60655-3105, 773-298-3070 or toll-free 800-462-9288. *Fax:* 773-779-3084. *E-mail:* swisher@sxu.edu.

SALEM COLLEGE

Winston-Salem, NC

CONTACT Director of Financial Aid, Salem College, PO Box 10548, Winston-Salem, NC 27108, 336-721-2808 or toll-free 800-327-2536. *Fax:* 336-917-5584.

SALEM INTERNATIONAL UNIVERSITY

Salem, WV

ABOUT THE INSTITUTION Independent, coed. Awards: associate, bachelor's, and master's degrees. 27 undergraduate majors. Total enrollment: 786. Undergraduates: 420. Freshmen: 65.

GIFT AID (NEED-BASED) ***Scholarships, grants, and awards:*** Federal Pell, FSEOG, state, private, college/university gift aid from institutional funds.

GIFT AID (NON-NEED-BASED) ***Scholarships, grants, and awards by category:*** *Academic Interests/Achievement:* business, education, general academic interests/achievements, humanities. *Special Characteristics:* out-of-state students, religious affiliation.

LOANS ***Programs:*** FFEL (Subsidized and Unsubsidized Stafford, PLUS), Perkins, alternative educational Loans.

WORK-STUDY ***Federal work-study:*** Total amount: $126,535; 106 jobs averaging $650. ***State or other work-study/employment:*** Total amount: $22,785 (100% non-need-based). 25 part-time jobs averaging $911.

APPLYING FOR FINANCIAL AID ***Required financial aid form:*** FAFSA.

CONTACT Mrs. Charlotte Lake, Director of Financial Aid, Salem International University, 223 West Main Street, Salem, WV 26426-0500, 304-326-1303 or toll-free 800-283-4562. *Fax:* 304-326-1509. *E-mail:* lake@salemiu.edu.

SALEM STATE COLLEGE

Salem, MA

CONTACT Mary Benda, Director of Financial Aid, Salem State College, 352 Lafayette Street, Salem, MA 01970-5353, 978-542-6139. *Fax:* 978-542-6876.

SALISBURY UNIVERSITY

Salisbury, MD

Tuition & fees (MD res): $6412 **Average undergraduate aid package: $7046**

ABOUT THE INSTITUTION State-supported, coed. Awards: bachelor's and master's degrees and post-bachelor's certificates. 42 undergraduate majors. Total enrollment: 7,383. Undergraduates: 6,791. Freshmen: 1,033. Federal methodology is used as a basis for awarding need-based institutional aid.

UNDERGRADUATE EXPENSES for 2006–07 ***Application fee:*** $45. ***Tuition, state resident:*** full-time $4814; part-time $200 per credit hour. ***Tuition, nonresident:*** full-time $12,708; part-time $529 per credit hour. ***Required fees:*** full-time $1598; $52 per credit hour. ***College room and board:*** $7058; ***Room only:*** $3732. Room and board charges vary according to board plan and housing facility. ***Payment plan:*** Installment.

FRESHMAN FINANCIAL AID (Fall 2005) 733 applied for aid; of those 54% were deemed to have need. 95% of freshmen with need received aid; of those 22% had need fully met. ***Average percent of need met:*** 65% (excluding resources awarded to replace EFC). ***Average financial aid package:*** $6519 (excluding resources awarded to replace EFC). 23% of all full-time freshmen had no need and received non-need-based gift aid.

UNDERGRADUATE FINANCIAL AID (Fall 2005) 3,432 applied for aid; of those 66% were deemed to have need. 99% of undergraduates with need received aid; of those 24% had need fully met. ***Average percent of need met:*** 66% (excluding resources awarded to replace EFC). ***Average financial aid package:*** $7046 (excluding resources awarded to replace EFC). 15% of all full-time undergraduates had no need and received non-need-based gift aid.

GIFT AID (NEED-BASED) ***Total amount:*** $7,753,413 (35% federal, 39% state, 19% institutional, 7% external sources). ***Receiving aid:*** Freshmen: 32% (308); All full-time undergraduates: 28% (1,615). ***Average award:*** Freshmen: $5875; Undergraduates: $4682. ***Scholarships, grants, and awards:*** Federal Pell, FSEOG, state, college/university gift aid from institutional funds.

GIFT AID (NON-NEED-BASED) ***Total amount:*** $2,466,025 (4% federal, 30% state, 32% institutional, 34% external sources). ***Average award:*** Freshmen: $4145; Undergraduates: $3211. ***Scholarships, grants, and awards by category:*** *Academic Interests/Achievement:* 931 awards ($1,207,246 total): biological sciences, business, communication, computer science, education, English, foreign languages, general academic interests/achievements, health fields, humanities, mathematics, physical sciences, premedicine, social sciences. *Creative Arts/Performance:* 4 awards ($2200 total): applied art and design, music. *Special Characteristics:* 4 awards ($7000 total): children and siblings of alumni, first-generation college students. ***Tuition waivers:*** Full or partial for employees or children of employees, senior citizens. ***ROTC:*** Army cooperative.

LOANS ***Student loans:*** $16,099,414 (68% need-based, 32% non-need-based). 51% of past graduating class borrowed through all loan programs. *Average indebtedness per student:* $18,330. ***Average need-based loan:*** Freshmen: $2162; Undergraduates: $3329. ***Parent loans:*** $13,030,671 (56% need-based, 44% non-need-based). ***Programs:*** Federal Direct (Subsidized and Unsubsidized Stafford, PLUS), Perkins.

WORK-STUDY ***Federal work-study:*** Total amount: $131,248; 64 jobs averaging $2004. ***State or other work-study/employment:*** 70 part-time jobs averaging $1875.

APPLYING FOR FINANCIAL AID ***Required financial aid form:*** FAFSA. ***Financial aid deadline (priority):*** 2/1. ***Notification date:*** Continuous beginning 4/1. Students must reply by 5/1.

CONTACT Ms. Elizabeth B. Zimmerman, Director of Financial Aid, Salisbury University, 1101 Camden Avenue, Salisbury, MD 21801-6837, 410-543-6165 or toll-free 888-543-0148. *E-mail:* ebzimmerman@salisbury.edu.

SALVE REGINA UNIVERSITY

Newport, RI

Tuition & fees: $25,175 **Average undergraduate aid package: $17,467**

ABOUT THE INSTITUTION Independent Roman Catholic, coed. Awards: associate, bachelor's, master's, and doctoral degrees and post-bachelor's and post-master's certificates. 47 undergraduate majors. Total enrollment: 2,589. Undergraduates: 2,090. Freshmen: 567. Both federal and institutional methodology are used as a basis for awarding need-based institutional aid.

UNDERGRADUATE EXPENSES for 2006–07 ***Application fee:*** $40. ***Comprehensive fee:*** $34,975 includes full-time tuition ($24,975), mandatory fees ($200), and room and board ($9800). Room and board charges vary according to board plan and housing facility. ***Part-time tuition:*** $833 per credit. ***Part-time fees:*** $40 per term. Part-time tuition and fees vary according to course load. ***Payment plan:*** Installment.

FRESHMAN FINANCIAL AID (Fall 2006, est.) 491 applied for aid; of those 86% were deemed to have need. 98% of freshmen with need received aid; of those 11% had need fully met. ***Average percent of need met:*** 75% (excluding resources awarded to replace EFC). ***Average financial aid package:*** $18,616 (excluding resources awarded to replace EFC). 14% of all full-time freshmen had no need and received non-need-based gift aid.

UNDERGRADUATE FINANCIAL AID (Fall 2006, est.) 1,677 applied for aid; of those 86% were deemed to have need. 95% of undergraduates with need received aid; of those 12% had need fully met. ***Average percent of need met:*** 70% (excluding resources awarded to replace EFC). ***Average financial aid package:*** $17,467 (excluding resources awarded to replace EFC). 15% of all full-time undergraduates had no need and received non-need-based gift aid.

GIFT AID (NEED-BASED) ***Total amount:*** $16,856,630 (5% federal, 2% state, 89% institutional, 4% external sources). ***Receiving aid:*** Freshmen: 70% (396); All full-time undergraduates: 62% (1,288). ***Average award:*** Freshmen: $15,635; Undergraduates: $13,219. ***Scholarships, grants, and awards:*** Federal Pell, FSEOG, state, private, college/university gift aid from institutional funds.

GIFT AID (NON-NEED-BASED) ***Total amount:*** $1,375,195 (1% state, 82% institutional, 17% external sources). ***Receiving aid:*** Freshmen: 2% (14); Undergraduates: 2% (50). ***Scholarships, grants, and awards by category:*** *Academic Interests/Achievement:* 588 awards ($4,036,786 total): general academic interests/achievements. ***Tuition waivers:*** Full or partial for employees or children of employees. ***ROTC:*** Army cooperative.

LOANS ***Student loans:*** $13,203,115 (63% need-based, 37% non-need-based). 76% of past graduating class borrowed through all loan programs. *Average indebtedness per student:* $24,631. ***Average need-based loan:*** Freshmen: $3065; Undergraduates: $4438. ***Parent loans:*** $6,644,528 (34% need-based, 66% non-need-based). ***Programs:*** FFEL (Subsidized and Unsubsidized Stafford, PLUS), Perkins, Federal Nursing, college/university, alternative loans.

WORK-STUDY ***Federal work-study:*** Total amount: $392,908; 454 jobs averaging $865. ***State or other work-study/employment:*** Total amount: $327,490 (4% need-based, 96% non-need-based). 203 part-time jobs averaging $1613.

APPLYING FOR FINANCIAL AID ***Required financial aid forms:*** FAFSA, CSS Financial Aid PROFILE, business/farm supplement, non-custodial statement. ***Financial aid deadline (priority):*** 3/1. ***Notification date:*** Continuous beginning 2/15. Students must reply by 5/1 or within 2 weeks of notification.

CONTACT Aida Mirante, Director of Financial Aid, Salve Regina University, 100 Ochre Point Avenue, Newport, RI 02840-4192, 401-341-2901 or toll-free 888-GO SALVE. *Fax:* 401-341-2928. *E-mail:* financial_aid@salve.edu.

SAMFORD UNIVERSITY

Birmingham, AL

Tuition & fees: $16,000 **Average undergraduate aid package: $11,977**

ABOUT THE INSTITUTION Independent Baptist, coed. Awards: associate, bachelor's, master's, doctoral, and first professional degrees and post-master's certificates. 68 undergraduate majors. Total enrollment: 4,478. Undergraduates: 2,882. Freshmen: 648. Federal methodology is used as a basis for awarding need-based institutional aid.

UNDERGRADUATE EXPENSES for 2006–07 ***Application fee:*** $35. ***Comprehensive fee:*** $22,060 includes full-time tuition ($16,000) and room and board ($6060). ***College room only:*** $2970. Full-time tuition and fees vary according to course load. Room and board charges vary according to board plan and housing facility. ***Part-time tuition:*** $535 per hour. Part-time tuition and fees vary according to course load.

FRESHMAN FINANCIAL AID (Fall 2005) 450 applied for aid; of those 58% were deemed to have need. 100% of freshmen with need received aid; of those 27% had need fully met. ***Average percent of need met:*** 75% (excluding resources awarded to replace EFC). ***Average financial aid package:*** $12,642 (excluding resources awarded to replace EFC). 26% of all full-time freshmen had no need and received non-need-based gift aid.

UNDERGRADUATE FINANCIAL AID (Fall 2005) 1,500 applied for aid; of those 70% were deemed to have need. 99% of undergraduates with need received aid; of those 27% had need fully met. ***Average percent of need met:*** 70% (excluding resources awarded to replace EFC). ***Average financial aid package:*** $11,977 (excluding resources awarded to replace EFC). 23% of all full-time undergraduates had no need and received non-need-based gift aid.

GIFT AID (NEED-BASED) ***Total amount:*** $6,276,533 (20% federal, 2% state, 63% institutional, 15% external sources). ***Receiving aid:*** Freshmen: 32% (246); All full-time undergraduates: 34% (937). ***Average award:*** Freshmen: $8898; Undergraduates: $6615. ***Scholarships, grants, and awards:*** Federal Pell, FSEOG, state, private, college/university gift aid from institutional funds.

GIFT AID (NON-NEED-BASED) ***Total amount:*** $4,421,219 (2% state, 67% institutional, 31% external sources). ***Average award:*** Freshmen: $4056; Undergraduates: $4713. ***Scholarships, grants, and awards by category:*** *Academic Interests/Achievement:* 369 awards ($1,467,392 total): general academic interests/achievements. *Creative Arts/Performance:* 39 awards ($68,600 total): music. *Special Characteristics:* 125 awards ($913,250 total): children of faculty/staff, relatives of clergy. ***Tuition waivers:*** Full or partial for employees or children of employees. ***ROTC:*** Army cooperative, Air Force.

LOANS ***Student loans:*** $7,753,017 (45% need-based, 55% non-need-based). 46% of past graduating class borrowed through all loan programs. *Average indebtedness per student:* $18,501. ***Average need-based loan:*** Freshmen: $2175; Undergraduates: $3487. ***Parent loans:*** $6,207,500 (100% non-need-based). ***Programs:*** FFEL (Subsidized and Unsubsidized Stafford, PLUS), Perkins, college/university.

WORK-STUDY ***Federal work-study:*** Total amount: $924,272; 606 jobs averaging $1800. ***State or other work-study/employment:*** Total amount: $531,311 (49% need-based, 51% non-need-based). 750 part-time jobs averaging $692.

ATHLETIC AWARDS Total amount: $3,613,071 (27% need-based, 73% non-need-based).

APPLYING FOR FINANCIAL AID ***Required financial aid form:*** FAFSA. ***Financial aid deadline (priority):*** 3/1. ***Notification date:*** 4/1.

CONTACT Ms. Lissa Burleson, Director of Financial Aid, Samford University, 800 Lakeshore Drive, Birmingham, AL 35229-0002, 205-726-2860 or toll-free 800-888-7218. *Fax:* 205-726-2738. *E-mail:* lrburles@samford.edu.

SAM HOUSTON STATE UNIVERSITY

Huntsville, TX

Tuition & fees (TX res): $4896 **Average undergraduate aid package: $6116**

ABOUT THE INSTITUTION State-supported, coed. Awards: bachelor's, master's, and doctoral degrees. 96 undergraduate majors. Total enrollment: 15,935. Undergraduates: 13,761. Freshmen: 2,224. Federal methodology is used as a basis for awarding need-based institutional aid.

UNDERGRADUATE EXPENSES for 2006–07 ***Application fee:*** $35. ***Tuition, state resident:*** full-time $3600. ***Tuition, nonresident:*** full-time $11,850. Full-time tuition and fees vary according to course load. Part-time tuition and fees vary according to course load. ***College room and board:*** $5880; ***Room only:*** $3640. Room and board charges vary according to board plan and housing facility. ***Payment plan:*** Installment.

FRESHMAN FINANCIAL AID (Fall 2005) 1546 applied for aid; of those 89% were deemed to have need. 98% of freshmen with need received aid; of those 3% had need fully met. ***Average percent of need met:*** 48% (excluding resources awarded to replace EFC). ***Average financial aid package:*** $5658 (excluding resources awarded to replace EFC). 13% of all full-time freshmen had no need and received non-need-based gift aid.

UNDERGRADUATE FINANCIAL AID (Fall 2005) 7,441 applied for aid; of those 86% were deemed to have need. 88% of undergraduates with need received aid; of those 7% had need fully met. ***Average percent of need met:*** 50% (excluding resources awarded to replace EFC). ***Average financial aid package:*** $6116 (excluding resources awarded to replace EFC). 7% of all full-time undergraduates had no need and received non-need-based gift aid.

GIFT AID (NEED-BASED) ***Total amount:*** $18,653,043 (51% federal, 40% state, 9% institutional). ***Receiving aid:*** Freshmen: 34% (730); All full-time undergraduates: 38% (4,308). ***Average award:*** Freshmen: $4194; Undergraduates: $3495. ***Scholarships, grants, and awards:*** Federal Pell, FSEOG, state, private, college/university gift aid from institutional funds.

GIFT AID (NON-NEED-BASED) ***Total amount:*** $1,903,421 (100% external sources). ***Receiving aid:*** Freshmen: 33% (718); Undergraduates: 17% (1,954). ***Average award:*** Freshmen: $2174; Undergraduates: $1862. ***Scholarships, grants, and awards by category:*** *Academic Interests/Achievement:* agriculture, biological sciences, business, communication, computer science, education, engineering/technologies, English, foreign languages, general academic interests/achievements, home economics, humanities, library science, mathematics, military science, physical sciences, social sciences. *Special Achievements/Activities:* cheerleading/drum major, general special achievements/activities, leadership, rodeo. *Special Characteristics:* general special characteristics, handicapped students. ***Tuition waivers:*** Full or partial for employees or children of employees. ***ROTC:*** Army.

LOANS ***Student loans:*** $36,355,033 (46% need-based, 54% non-need-based). 62% of past graduating class borrowed through all loan programs. *Average indebtedness per student:* $16,948. ***Average need-based loan:*** Freshmen: $2282; Undergraduates: $3515. ***Parent loans:*** $4,723,644 (100% non-need-based). ***Programs:*** FFEL (Subsidized and Unsubsidized Stafford, PLUS), Perkins.

WORK-STUDY ***Federal work-study:*** Total amount: $287,851; 211 jobs averaging $1364. ***State or other work-study/employment:*** Total amount: $87,204 (100% need-based). 156 part-time jobs averaging $558.

ATHLETIC AWARDS Total amount: $1,862,529 (100% non-need-based).

APPLYING FOR FINANCIAL AID ***Required financial aid forms:*** FAFSA, institution's own form. ***Financial aid deadline (priority):*** 5/31. ***Notification date:*** Continuous beginning 3/1. Students must reply within 4 weeks of notification.

CONTACT Patricia Mabry, Director of Financial Aid, Sam Houston State University, Box 2328, Huntsville, TX 77341-2328, 936-294-1774 or toll-free 866-232-7528 Ext. 1828. *Fax:* 936-294-3668.

SAMUEL MERRITT COLLEGE

Oakland, CA

ABOUT THE INSTITUTION Independent, coed, primarily women. Awards: bachelor's, master's, doctoral, and first professional degrees (bachelor's degree offered jointly with Saint Mary's College of California). 1 undergraduate major. Total enrollment: 1,178. Undergraduates: 403. Entering class: 16.

GIFT AID (NEED-BASED) ***Scholarships, grants, and awards:*** Federal Pell, FSEOG, state, private, college/university gift aid from institutional funds, Federal Nursing.

LOANS ***Programs:*** FFEL (Subsidized and Unsubsidized Stafford, PLUS), Perkins, Federal Nursing, college/university.

APPLYING FOR FINANCIAL AID ***Required financial aid form:*** FAFSA.

CONTACT Anne-Marie Larroque, Assistant Director, Financial Aid Office, Samuel Merritt College, 450 30th Street, Room 2850, Oakland, CA 94609, 510-869-6193 or toll-free 800-607-MERRITT. *Fax:* 510-869-1529. *E-mail:* alarroque@samuelmerritt.edu.

SAN DIEGO CHRISTIAN COLLEGE

El Cajon, CA

ABOUT THE INSTITUTION Independent nondenominational, coed. Awards: bachelor's degrees and post-bachelor's certificates. 29 undergraduate majors. Total enrollment: 543. Undergraduates: 502. Freshmen: 120.

GIFT AID (NEED-BASED) ***Scholarships, grants, and awards:*** Federal Pell, FSEOG, state, private, college/university gift aid from institutional funds.

GIFT AID (NON-NEED-BASED) ***Scholarships, grants, and awards by category:*** *Academic Interests/Achievement:* general academic interests/achievements. *Creative Arts/Performance:* music, performing arts, theater/drama. *Special Achievements/Activities:* leadership, religious involvement. *Special Characteristics:* children of faculty/staff, international students, out-of-state students, relatives of clergy, religious affiliation, siblings of current students.

LOANS ***Programs:*** FFEL (Subsidized and Unsubsidized Stafford, PLUS), Perkins.

WORK-STUDY ***Federal work-study:*** Total amount: $29,908; 20 jobs averaging $1495. ***State or other work-study/employment:*** Total amount: $19,126 (100% need-based). 12 part-time jobs averaging $1594.

APPLYING FOR FINANCIAL AID ***Required financial aid forms:*** FAFSA, institution's own form, state aid form.

CONTACT Nancy DeMars, Director of Financial Aid, San Diego Christian College, 2100 Greenfield Drive, El Cajon, CA 92019, 619-590-1786 Ext. 3 or toll-free 800-676-2242. *Fax:* 619-590-2186. *E-mail:* ndemars@sdcc.edu.

SAN DIEGO STATE UNIVERSITY

San Diego, CA

Tuition & fees (CA res): $3160 Average undergraduate aid package: $7300

ABOUT THE INSTITUTION State-supported, coed. Awards: bachelor's, master's, and doctoral degrees and post-bachelor's and post-master's certificates. 106 undergraduate majors. Total enrollment: 34,305. Undergraduates: 28,527. Freshmen: 5,124. Federal methodology is used as a basis for awarding need-based institutional aid.

UNDERGRADUATE EXPENSES for 2006–07 ***Application fee:*** $55. ***Tuition, state resident:*** full-time $0. ***Tuition, nonresident:*** full-time $10,170; part-time $339 per unit. ***Required fees:*** full-time $3160; $1033 per term part-time. Full-time tuition and fees vary according to degree level. Part-time tuition and fees vary according to course load and degree level. ***College room and board:*** $10,093. Room and board charges vary according to board plan and housing facility. ***Payment plan:*** Installment.

FRESHMAN FINANCIAL AID (Fall 2006, est.) 2850 applied for aid; of those 63% were deemed to have need. 96% of freshmen with need received aid; of those 17% had need fully met. ***Average percent of need met:*** 66% (excluding resources awarded to replace EFC). ***Average financial aid package:*** $5800 (excluding resources awarded to replace EFC). 2% of all full-time freshmen had no need and received non-need-based gift aid.

UNDERGRADUATE FINANCIAL AID (Fall 2006, est.) 14,420 applied for aid; of those 78% were deemed to have need. 97% of undergraduates with need received aid; of those 17% had need fully met. ***Average percent of need met:*** 70% (excluding resources awarded to replace EFC). ***Average financial aid package:*** $7300 (excluding resources awarded to replace EFC). 2% of all full-time undergraduates had no need and received non-need-based gift aid.

GIFT AID (NEED-BASED) ***Total amount:*** $49,021,000 (44% federal, 28% state, 28% institutional). ***Receiving aid:*** Freshmen: 28% (1,150); All full-time undergraduates: 35% (8,060). ***Average award:*** Freshmen: $7000; Undergraduates: $5800. ***Scholarships, grants, and awards:*** Federal Pell, FSEOG, state, private, college/university gift aid from institutional funds, Federal Nursing.

GIFT AID (NON-NEED-BASED) ***Total amount:*** $5,844,600 (39% federal, 1% state, 19% institutional, 41% external sources). ***Receiving aid:*** Freshmen: 17% (690); Undergraduates: 7% (1,650). ***Average award:*** Freshmen: $2100; Undergraduates: $1700. ***Scholarships, grants, and awards by category:*** *Academic Interests/Achievement:* general academic interests/achievements. *Creative Arts/Performance:* art/fine arts, creative writing, dance, journalism/publications, music, performing arts, theater/drama. *Special Achievements/Activities:* community service, leadership. *Special Characteristics:* children and siblings of alumni, children of faculty/staff, children of public servants, handicapped students, local/state students. ***Tuition waivers:*** Full or partial for employees or children of employees. ***ROTC:*** Army, Naval, Air Force.

LOANS ***Student loans:*** $72,737,200 (65% need-based, 35% non-need-based). 48% of past graduating class borrowed through all loan programs. *Average indebtedness per student:* $14,700. ***Average need-based loan:*** Freshmen: $2300; Undergraduates: $4000. ***Parent loans:*** $68,594,100 (17% need-based, 83% non-need-based). ***Programs:*** Federal Direct (Subsidized and Unsubsidized Stafford, PLUS), Perkins, college/university.

WORK-STUDY ***Federal work-study:*** Total amount: $1,509,000; 840 jobs averaging $1876.

ATHLETIC AWARDS Total amount: $4,428,500 (100% non-need-based).

APPLYING FOR FINANCIAL AID ***Required financial aid forms:*** FAFSA, state aid form. ***Financial aid deadline:*** 3/2. ***Notification date:*** Continuous beginning 2/14.

CONTACT Ms. Chrys Dutton, Director of Financial Aid and Scholarships, San Diego State University, 5500 Campanile Drive, SSW-3605, San Diego, CA 92182-7436, 619-594-6323.

SAN FRANCISCO ART INSTITUTE

San Francisco, CA

Tuition & fees: $27,235 Average undergraduate aid package: $24,880

ABOUT THE INSTITUTION Independent, coed. Awards: bachelor's and master's degrees and post-bachelor's certificates. 8 undergraduate majors. Total enrollment: 652. Undergraduates: 420. Freshmen: 69. Federal methodology is used as a basis for awarding need-based institutional aid.

UNDERGRADUATE EXPENSES for 2006–07 ***Application fee:*** $65. ***Tuition:*** full-time $27,200; part-time $1175 per unit. ***Required fees:*** full-time $35; $175 per semester hour. Part-time tuition and fees vary according to course load. Room and board charges vary according to housing facility. ***Payment plan:*** Deferred payment.

FRESHMAN FINANCIAL AID (Fall 2006, est.) 38 applied for aid; of those 89% were deemed to have need. 100% of freshmen with need received aid; of those 9% had need fully met. ***Average percent of need met:*** 73% (excluding resources awarded to replace EFC). ***Average financial aid package:*** $24,054 (excluding resources awarded to replace EFC). 12% of all full-time freshmen had no need and received non-need-based gift aid.

UNDERGRADUATE FINANCIAL AID (Fall 2006, est.) 205 applied for aid; of those 92% were deemed to have need. 99% of undergraduates with need received aid; of those 6% had need fully met. ***Average percent of need met:*** 72% (excluding resources awarded to replace EFC). ***Average financial aid package:*** $24,880 (excluding resources awarded to replace EFC). 16% of all full-time undergraduates had no need and received non-need-based gift aid.

GIFT AID (NEED-BASED) ***Total amount:*** $2,591,368 (20% federal, 10% state, 65% institutional, 5% external sources). ***Receiving aid:*** Freshmen: 83% (34); All full-time undergraduates: 62% (183). ***Average award:*** Freshmen: $12,690; Undergraduates: $11,441. ***Scholarships, grants, and awards:*** Federal Pell, FSEOG, state, college/university gift aid from institutional funds.

GIFT AID (NON-NEED-BASED) ***Total amount:*** $485,829 (1% federal, 73% institutional, 26% external sources). ***Receiving aid:*** Undergraduates: 1% (2). ***Average award:*** Freshmen: $37,126; Undergraduates: $24,787. ***Scholarships, grants, and awards by category:*** *Creative Arts/Performance:* 156 awards ($1,020,997 total): art/fine arts. ***Tuition waivers:*** Full or partial for employees or children of employees.

LOANS ***Student loans:*** $4,415,212 (80% need-based, 20% non-need-based). ***Average need-based loan:*** Freshmen: $8078; Undergraduates: $10,694. ***Parent loans:*** $2,073,999 (48% need-based, 52% non-need-based). ***Programs:*** Federal Direct (Subsidized and Unsubsidized Stafford, PLUS), alternative loans.

WORK-STUDY ***Federal work-study:*** Total amount: $744,473; jobs available.

APPLYING FOR FINANCIAL AID ***Required financial aid form:*** FAFSA. ***Financial aid deadline:*** Continuous. ***Notification date:*** Continuous beginning 3/31. Students must reply within 3 weeks of notification.

CONTACT Erin Zagaski, Interim Director of Financial Aid, San Francisco Art Institute, 800 Chestnut Street, San Francisco, CA 94133-2299, 415-749-4513 or toll-free 800-345-SFAI. *Fax:* 415-351-3503.

SAN FRANCISCO CONSERVATORY OF MUSIC

San Francisco, CA

CONTACT Doris Howard, Financial Aid Manager, San Francisco Conservatory of Music, 1201 Ortega Street, San Francisco, CA 94122-4411, 415-759-3414. *Fax:* 415-759-3499.

SAN FRANCISCO STATE UNIVERSITY

San Francisco, CA

Tuition & fees (CA res): $3166 Average undergraduate aid package: $8441

ABOUT THE INSTITUTION State-supported, coed. Awards: bachelor's, master's, and doctoral degrees and post-bachelor's certificates. 91 undergraduate majors. Total enrollment: 29,628. Undergraduates: 23,843. Freshmen: 3,258. Federal methodology is used as a basis for awarding need-based institutional aid.

UNDERGRADUATE EXPENSES for 2006–07 ***Application fee:*** $55. ***Tuition, state resident:*** full-time $0. ***Tuition, nonresident:*** full-time $10,170; part-time $339 per unit. ***Required fees:*** full-time $3166; $323 per term part-time. Full-time tuition and fees vary according to degree level. Part-time tuition and fees vary according to degree level. ***College room and board:*** $9544; ***Room only:*** $6202. Room and board charges vary according to board plan and housing facility. ***Payment plan:*** Installment.

FRESHMAN FINANCIAL AID (Fall 2006, est.) 2582 applied for aid; of those 78% were deemed to have need. 92% of freshmen with need received aid; of those 8% had need fully met. ***Average percent of need met:*** 62% (excluding resources awarded to replace EFC). ***Average financial aid package:*** $7532 (excluding resources awarded to replace EFC). 2% of all full-time freshmen had no need and received non-need-based gift aid.

UNDERGRADUATE FINANCIAL AID (Fall 2006, est.) 9,948 applied for aid; of those 86% were deemed to have need. 95% of undergraduates with need received aid; of those 8% had need fully met. ***Average percent of need met:*** 65% (excluding resources awarded to replace EFC). ***Average financial aid package:*** $8441 (excluding resources awarded to replace EFC). 1% of all full-time undergraduates had no need and received non-need-based gift aid.

GIFT AID (NEED-BASED) ***Total amount:*** $45,670,061 (47% federal, 49% state, 1% institutional, 3% external sources). ***Receiving aid:*** Freshmen: 35% (1,317); All full-time undergraduates: 36% (6,058). ***Average award:*** Freshmen: $6341; Undergraduates: $5711. ***Scholarships, grants, and awards:*** Federal Pell, FSEOG, state, private, college/university gift aid from institutional funds.

GIFT AID (NON-NEED-BASED) ***Total amount:*** $546,834 (25% institutional, 75% external sources). ***Receiving aid:*** Freshmen: 8% (295); Undergraduates: 4% (692). ***Average award:*** Freshmen: $1939; Undergraduates: $1841. ***Tuition waivers:*** Full or partial for employees or children of employees, senior citizens. ***ROTC:*** Army cooperative, Naval cooperative, Air Force cooperative.

LOANS ***Student loans:*** $43,666,906 (90% need-based, 10% non-need-based). 41% of past graduating class borrowed through all loan programs. *Average indebtedness per student:* $15,288. ***Average need-based loan:*** Freshmen: $1715; Undergraduates: $2995. ***Parent loans:*** $14,401,113 (64% need-based, 36% non-need-based). ***Programs:*** Federal Direct (Subsidized and Unsubsidized Stafford), FFEL (PLUS), Perkins.

WORK-STUDY ***Federal work-study:*** Total amount: $1,500,000; 600 jobs averaging $2500.

ATHLETIC AWARDS Total amount: $258,277 (44% need-based, 56% non-need-based).

APPLYING FOR FINANCIAL AID ***Required financial aid form:*** FAFSA. ***Financial aid deadline (priority):*** 3/2. ***Notification date:*** Continuous beginning 1/31. Students must reply within 3 weeks of notification.

CONTACT Barbara Hubler, Director of Financial Aid, San Francisco State University, 1600 Holloway Avenue, San Francisco, CA 94132-1722, 415-338-7000. *E-mail:* finaid@sfsu.edu.

SAN JOSE STATE UNIVERSITY

San Jose, CA

Tuition & fees: N/R Average undergraduate aid package: $9822

ABOUT THE INSTITUTION State-supported, coed. Awards: bachelor's and master's degrees. 89 undergraduate majors. Total enrollment: 29,604. Undergraduates: 22,521. Freshmen: 2,722. Federal methodology is used as a basis for awarding need-based institutional aid.

UNDERGRADUATE EXPENSES for 2006–07 ***Application fee:*** $55. ***Tuition, nonresident:*** full-time $10,170; part-time $339 per unit. Full-time tuition and fees vary according to course load. Part-time tuition and fees vary according to course load. ***College room and board:*** $9096; ***Room only:*** $5640. Room and board charges vary according to board plan and housing facility. ***Payment plan:*** Installment.

FRESHMAN FINANCIAL AID (Fall 2005) 1714 applied for aid; of those 75% were deemed to have need. 93% of freshmen with need received aid; of those 2% had need fully met. ***Average percent of need met:*** 85% (excluding resources awarded to replace EFC). ***Average financial aid package:*** $9797 (excluding resources awarded to replace EFC). 1% of all full-time freshmen had no need and received non-need-based gift aid.

UNDERGRADUATE FINANCIAL AID (Fall 2005) 8,810 applied for aid; of those 100% were deemed to have need. 90% of undergraduates with need received aid; of those 3% had need fully met. ***Average percent of need met:*** 83% (excluding resources awarded to replace EFC). ***Average financial aid package:*** $9822 (excluding resources awarded to replace EFC). 2% of all full-time undergraduates had no need and received non-need-based gift aid.

GIFT AID (NEED-BASED) ***Total amount:*** $40,824,873 (46% federal, 42% state, 5% institutional, 7% external sources). ***Receiving aid:*** Freshmen: 36% (937); All full-time undergraduates: 34% (6,338). ***Average award:*** Freshmen: $5930; Undergraduates: $7347. ***Scholarships, grants, and awards:*** Federal Pell, FSEOG, state, private, college/university gift aid from institutional funds.

GIFT AID (NON-NEED-BASED) ***Total amount:*** $278,087 (30% institutional, 70% external sources). ***Average award:*** Freshmen: $1524; Undergraduates: $1901. ***Scholarships, grants, and awards by category:*** *Academic Interests/Achievement:* 115 awards ($120,246 total): general academic interests/achievements. ***Tuition waivers:*** Full or partial for employees or children of employees. ***ROTC:*** Army, Air Force.

LOANS ***Student loans:*** $26,350,528 (100% need-based). 50% of past graduating class borrowed through all loan programs. *Average indebtedness per student:* $18,521. ***Average need-based loan:*** Freshmen: $2996; Undergraduates: $4214. ***Parent loans:*** $2,286,131 (100% need-based). ***Programs:*** FFEL (Subsidized and Unsubsidized Stafford, PLUS), Perkins, college/university.

WORK-STUDY ***Federal work-study:*** Total amount: $16,146,719.

ATHLETIC AWARDS Total amount: $858,784 (100% need-based).

APPLYING FOR FINANCIAL AID ***Required financial aid form:*** FAFSA. ***Financial aid deadline (priority):*** 3/2. ***Notification date:*** Continuous beginning 4/1.

CONTACT Colleen S. Brown, Director of Financial Aid, San Jose State University, One Washington Square, Student Services Center 200, San Jose, CA 95192-0036, 408-924-6060. *E-mail:* brownc@sjsu.edu.

SANTA CLARA UNIVERSITY

Santa Clara, CA

Tuition & fees: $30,900 Average undergraduate aid package: $19,689

ABOUT THE INSTITUTION Independent Roman Catholic (Jesuit), coed. Awards: bachelor's, master's, doctoral, and first professional degrees and post-bachelor's, post-master's, and first professional certificates. 43 undergraduate majors. Total enrollment: 7,952. Undergraduates: 4,613. Freshmen: 1,339. Both federal and institutional methodology are used as a basis for awarding need-based institutional aid.

UNDERGRADUATE EXPENSES for 2006–07 ***Application fee:*** $55. ***Comprehensive fee:*** $41,280 includes full-time tuition ($30,900) and room and board ($10,380). Room and board charges vary according to board plan, housing facility, and student level. ***Part-time tuition:*** $1030 per unit. Part-time tuition and fees vary according to course load. ***Payment plans:*** Tuition prepayment, installment, deferred payment.

FRESHMAN FINANCIAL AID (Fall 2006, est.) 759 applied for aid; of those 61% were deemed to have need. 98% of freshmen with need received aid; of those 74% had need fully met. ***Average percent of need met:*** 71% (excluding resources awarded to replace EFC). ***Average financial aid package:*** $18,545 (excluding resources awarded to replace EFC). 29% of all full-time freshmen had no need and received non-need-based gift aid.

UNDERGRADUATE FINANCIAL AID (Fall 2006, est.) 3,021 applied for aid; of those 75% were deemed to have need. 82% of undergraduates with need received aid; of those 69% had need fully met. ***Average percent of need met:*** 68% (excluding resources awarded to replace EFC). ***Average financial aid package:*** $19,689 (excluding resources awarded to replace EFC). 21% of all full-time undergraduates had no need and received non-need-based gift aid.

GIFT AID (NEED-BASED) ***Total amount:*** $27,070,114 (7% federal, 16% state, 74% institutional, 3% external sources). ***Receiving aid:*** Freshmen: 28% (375); All full-time undergraduates: 33% (1,624). ***Average award:*** Freshmen: $14,486; Undergraduates: $15,209. ***Scholarships, grants, and awards:*** Federal Pell, FSEOG, state, private, college/university gift aid from institutional funds.

GIFT AID (NON-NEED-BASED) ***Total amount:*** $16,023,581 (91% institutional, 9% external sources). ***Receiving aid:*** Freshmen: 16% (214); Undergraduates: 11% (534). ***Average award:*** Freshmen: $9794; Undergraduates: $9728. ***Scholarships, grants, and awards by category:*** *Academic Interests/Achievement:* 2,225 awards ($22,352,076 total): business, engineering/technologies, general academic interests/achievements, military science. *Creative Arts/Performance:* 81 awards ($186,583 total): dance, debating, music, theater/drama. *Special Characteristics:* 93 awards ($2,315,670 total): children and siblings of alumni, children of faculty/staff, children with a deceased or disabled parent, handicapped students. ***Tuition waivers:*** Full or partial for employees or children of employees. ***ROTC:*** Army, Air Force cooperative.

LOANS ***Student loans:*** $13,055,712 (50% need-based, 50% non-need-based). 49% of past graduating class borrowed through all loan programs. *Average indebtedness per student:* $17,527. ***Average need-based loan:*** Freshmen: $3951; Undergraduates: $5747. ***Parent loans:*** $17,079,198 (100% non-need-based). ***Programs:*** Federal Direct (Subsidized and Unsubsidized Stafford, PLUS), Perkins, alternative private loans.

WORK-STUDY ***Federal work-study:*** Total amount: $1,309,306; 343 jobs averaging $2470.

ATHLETIC AWARDS Total amount: $3,209,244 (100% non-need-based).

APPLYING FOR FINANCIAL AID ***Required financial aid forms:*** FAFSA, CSS Financial Aid PROFILE. ***Financial aid deadline (priority):*** 2/1. ***Notification date:*** 4/1. Students must reply by 5/1 or within 2 weeks of notification.

CONTACT Marta I. Chaskelmann, Assistant Director, Technical Services, Santa Clara University, 500 El Camino Real, Santa Clara, CA 95053, 408-551-6088. *Fax:* 408-551-6085. *E-mail:* mchaskelmann@scu.edu.

SARAH LAWRENCE COLLEGE

Bronxville, NY

Tuition & fees: $36,088 **Average undergraduate aid package: $26,435**

ABOUT THE INSTITUTION Independent, coed. Awards: bachelor's and master's degrees. 112 undergraduate majors. Total enrollment: 1,709. Undergraduates: 1,391. Freshmen: 382. Both federal and institutional methodology are used as a basis for awarding need-based institutional aid.

UNDERGRADUATE EXPENSES for 2006–07 ***Application fee:*** $60. ***Comprehensive fee:*** $48,240 includes full-time tuition ($35,280), mandatory fees ($808), and room and board ($12,152). ***College room only:*** $8056. Full-time tuition and fees vary according to course load. Room and board charges vary according to board plan. ***Part-time tuition:*** $1176 per credit. ***Part-time fees:*** $404 per term. Part-time tuition and fees vary according to course load. ***Payment plan:*** Installment.

FRESHMAN FINANCIAL AID (Fall 2006, est.) 232 applied for aid; of those 83% were deemed to have need. 100% of freshmen with need received aid; of those 90% had need fully met. ***Average percent of need met:*** 94% (excluding resources awarded to replace EFC). ***Average financial aid package:*** $26,119 (excluding resources awarded to replace EFC).

UNDERGRADUATE FINANCIAL AID (Fall 2006, est.) 802 applied for aid; of those 88% were deemed to have need. 100% of undergraduates with need received aid; of those 80% had need fully met. ***Average percent of need met:*** 91% (excluding resources awarded to replace EFC). ***Average financial aid package:*** $26,435 (excluding resources awarded to replace EFC). 1% of all full-time undergraduates had no need and received non-need-based gift aid.

GIFT AID (NEED-BASED) ***Total amount:*** $14,075,337 (5% federal, 2% state, 91% institutional, 2% external sources). ***Receiving aid:*** Freshmen: 47% (178); All full-time undergraduates: 51% (644). ***Average award:*** Freshmen: $22,008; Undergraduates: $21,856. ***Scholarships, grants, and awards:*** Federal Pell, FSEOG, state, private, college/university gift aid from institutional funds.

GIFT AID (NON-NEED-BASED) ***Total amount:*** $15,000 (50% state, 40% institutional, 10% external sources). ***Receiving aid:*** Undergraduates: 5. ***Average award:*** Undergraduates: $3000. ***Tuition waivers:*** Full or partial for employees or children of employees.

LOANS ***Student loans:*** $4,625,302 (90% need-based, 10% non-need-based). 49% of past graduating class borrowed through all loan programs. *Average indebtedness per student:* $45,300. ***Average need-based loan:*** Freshmen: $2329; Undergraduates: $3392. ***Parent loans:*** $4,463,946 (80% need-based, 20% non-need-based). ***Programs:*** FFEL (Subsidized and Unsubsidized Stafford, PLUS), Perkins, college/university, Achiever Loans, Signature Loans, CitiAssist Loans.

WORK-STUDY ***Federal work-study:*** Total amount: $934,702; 568 jobs averaging $1646. ***State or other work-study/employment:*** Total amount: $85,606 (82% need-based, 18% non-need-based). 44 part-time jobs averaging $1585.

APPLYING FOR FINANCIAL AID ***Required financial aid forms:*** FAFSA, CSS Financial Aid PROFILE, state aid form, noncustodial (divorced/separated) parent's statement. ***Financial aid deadline:*** 2/1. ***Notification date:*** 4/1. Students must reply by 5/1.

CONTACT Ms. Heather McDonnell, Director of Financial Aid, Sarah Lawrence College, One Mead Way, Bronxville, NY 10708, 914-395-2570 or toll-free 800-888-2858. *Fax:* 914-395-2676. *E-mail:* hmcdonn@sarahlawrence.edu.

SAVANNAH COLLEGE OF ART AND DESIGN

Savannah, GA

Tuition & fees: $24,890 **Average undergraduate aid package: $10,400**

ABOUT THE INSTITUTION Independent, coed. Awards: bachelor's and master's degrees and post-bachelor's certificates. 21 undergraduate majors. Total enrollment: 8,236. Undergraduates: 6,913. Freshmen: 1,481. Federal methodology is used as a basis for awarding need-based institutional aid.

UNDERGRADUATE EXPENSES for 2007–08 ***Application fee:*** $50. ***Comprehensive fee:*** $34,905 includes full-time tuition ($24,390), mandatory fees ($500), and room and board ($10,015). ***College room only:*** $6460. ***Part-time tuition:*** $2710 per course.

FRESHMAN FINANCIAL AID (Fall 2006, est.) 1002 applied for aid; of those 76% were deemed to have need. 98% of freshmen with need received aid; of those 42% had need fully met. ***Average percent of need met:*** 10% (excluding resources awarded to replace EFC). ***Average financial aid package:*** $9500 (excluding resources awarded to replace EFC). 36% of all full-time freshmen had no need and received non-need-based gift aid.

UNDERGRADUATE FINANCIAL AID (Fall 2006, est.) 3,939 applied for aid; of those 80% were deemed to have need. 99% of undergraduates with need received aid; of those 39% had need fully met. ***Average percent of need met:*** 12% (excluding resources awarded to replace EFC). ***Average financial aid package:*** $10,400 (excluding resources awarded to replace EFC). 29% of all full-time undergraduates had no need and received non-need-based gift aid.

GIFT AID (NEED-BASED) ***Total amount:*** $5,339,066 (66% federal, 1% state, 33% institutional). ***Receiving aid:*** Freshmen: 13% (184); All full-time undergraduates: 18% (1,055). ***Average award:*** Freshmen: $3700; Undergraduates: $4500. ***Scholarships, grants, and awards:*** Federal Pell, FSEOG, state, private, college/university gift aid from institutional funds.

GIFT AID (NON-NEED-BASED) ***Total amount:*** $29,396,909 (9% state, 90% institutional, 1% external sources). ***Receiving aid:*** Freshmen: 47% (674); Undergraduates: 44% (2,669). ***Average award:*** Freshmen: $5500; Undergraduates: $8250. ***Scholarships, grants, and awards by category:*** *Academic Interests/Achievement:* architecture, general academic interests/achievements, humanities. *Creative Arts/Performance:* art/fine arts, general creative arts/performance. *Special Achievements/Activities:* general special achievements/activities. *Special Characteristics:* general special characteristics.

LOANS ***Student loans:*** $39,208,261 (45% need-based, 55% non-need-based). 92% of past graduating class borrowed through all loan programs. *Average indebtedness per student:* $28,000. ***Average need-based loan:*** Freshmen: $2800; Undergraduates: $4750. ***Parent loans:*** $37,561,536 (100% non-need-based). ***Programs:*** Federal Direct (Subsidized and Unsubsidized Stafford, PLUS), Perkins.

WORK-STUDY ***Federal work-study:*** Total amount: $350,000. ***State or other work-study/employment:*** Total amount: $104,001 (100% non-need-based). 214 part-time jobs averaging $2095.

ATHLETIC AWARDS Total amount: $3,135,255 (100% non-need-based).

APPLYING FOR FINANCIAL AID ***Required financial aid forms:*** FAFSA, institution's own form, state aid form. ***Financial aid deadline (priority):*** 4/1. ***Notification date:*** Continuous. Students must reply within 4 weeks of notification.

CONTACT Ms. Cindy Bradley, Director of Financial Aid, Savannah College of Art and Design, PO Box 3146, 342 Bull Street, Savannah, GA 31402-3146, 912-525-6119 or toll-free 800-869-7223. *Fax:* 912-525-6263. *E-mail:* cbradley@scad.edu.

SAVANNAH STATE UNIVERSITY

Savannah, GA

CONTACT Mark Adkins, Director of Financial Aid, Savannah State University, PO Box 20523, Savannah, GA 31404, 912-356-2253 or toll-free 800-788-0478. *Fax:* 912-353-3150. *E-mail:* finaid@savstate.edu.

SCHOOL OF THE ART INSTITUTE OF CHICAGO

Chicago, IL

CONTACT Financial Aid Office, School of the Art Institute of Chicago, 37 South Wabash, Chicago, IL 60603-3103, 312-899-5106 or toll-free 800-232-SAIC.

SCHOOL OF THE MUSEUM OF FINE ARTS, BOSTON

Boston, MA

ABOUT THE INSTITUTION Independent, coed. Awards: bachelor's and master's degrees and post-bachelor's certificates. 20 undergraduate majors. Total enrollment: 733. Undergraduates: 634. Freshmen: 114.

GIFT AID (NEED-BASED) ***Scholarships, grants, and awards:*** Federal Pell, FSEOG, state, private, college/university gift aid from institutional funds.

GIFT AID (NON-NEED-BASED) ***Scholarships, grants, and awards by category:*** *Creative Arts/Performance:* art/fine arts. *Special Characteristics:* general special characteristics.

LOANS ***Programs:*** FFEL (Subsidized and Unsubsidized Stafford, PLUS), state.

WORK-STUDY ***Federal work-study:*** Total amount: $253,572; 139 jobs averaging $2173.

APPLYING FOR FINANCIAL AID ***Required financial aid forms:*** FAFSA, institution's own form.

CONTACT Ms. Elizabeth Goreham, Director of Financial Aid, School of the Museum of Fine Arts, Boston, 230 The Fenway, Boston, MA 02115, 617-369-3684 or toll-free 800-643-6078 (in-state). *Fax:* 617-369-3041.

SCHOOL OF VISUAL ARTS

New York, NY

Tuition & fees: $22,080 | **Average undergraduate aid package: $12,498**

ABOUT THE INSTITUTION Proprietary, coed. Awards: bachelor's and master's degrees. 9 undergraduate majors. Total enrollment: 3,715. Undergraduates: 3,308. Freshmen: 661. Federal methodology is used as a basis for awarding need-based institutional aid.

UNDERGRADUATE EXPENSES for 2006–07 ***Application fee:*** $50. ***Comprehensive fee:*** $34,380 includes full-time tuition ($22,080) and room and board ($12,300). ***College room only:*** $9800. Full-time tuition and fees vary according to program. Room and board charges vary according to board plan, gender, housing facility, and location. ***Part-time tuition:*** $740 per credit. ***Payment plan:*** Installment.

FRESHMAN FINANCIAL AID (Fall 2006, est.) 460 applied for aid; of those 85% were deemed to have need. 96% of freshmen with need received aid; of those 1% had need fully met. ***Average percent of need met:*** 41% (excluding resources awarded to replace EFC). ***Average financial aid package:*** $11,366 (excluding resources awarded to replace EFC). 3% of all full-time freshmen had no need and received non-need-based gift aid.

UNDERGRADUATE FINANCIAL AID (Fall 2006, est.) 1,881 applied for aid; of those 89% were deemed to have need. 99% of undergraduates with need received aid; of those 2% had need fully met. ***Average percent of need met:*** 42% (excluding resources awarded to replace EFC). ***Average financial aid package:*** $12,498 (excluding resources awarded to replace EFC). 5% of all full-time undergraduates had no need and received non-need-based gift aid.

GIFT AID (NEED-BASED) ***Total amount:*** $8,179,331 (37% federal, 20% state, 40% institutional, 3% external sources). ***Receiving aid:*** Freshmen: 35% (233); All full-time undergraduates: 37% (1,099). ***Average award:*** Freshmen: $6067. ***Scholarships, grants, and awards:*** Federal Pell, FSEOG, state, private, college/university gift aid from institutional funds.

GIFT AID (NON-NEED-BASED) ***Total amount:*** $990,119 (3% state, 84% institutional, 13% external sources). ***Receiving aid:*** Freshmen: 8% (56); Undergraduates: 10% (313). ***Average award:*** Freshmen: $7632; Undergraduates: $6238. ***Scholarships, grants, and awards by category:*** *Creative Arts/Performance:* 156 awards ($661,514 total): art/fine arts. ***Tuition waivers:*** Full or partial for employees or children of employees.

LOANS ***Student loans:*** $20,561,629 (95% need-based, 5% non-need-based). 71% of past graduating class borrowed through all loan programs. *Average indebtedness per student:* $30,600. ***Average need-based loan:*** Freshmen: $3063; Undergraduates: $4031. ***Parent loans:*** $7,961,754 (93% need-based, 7% non-need-based). ***Programs:*** FFEL (Subsidized and Unsubsidized Stafford, PLUS), Perkins, alternative loans.

WORK-STUDY ***Federal work-study:*** Total amount: $649,111; 186 jobs averaging $3490. ***State or other work-study/employment:*** Total amount: $364,395 (87% need-based, 13% non-need-based).

APPLYING FOR FINANCIAL AID ***Required financial aid forms:*** FAFSA, state aid form. ***Financial aid deadline:*** 3/1 (priority: 2/1). ***Notification date:*** Continuous beginning 2/15. Students must reply within 4 weeks of notification.

CONTACT William Berrios, Director of Financial Aid, School of Visual Arts, 209 East 23rd Street, New York, NY 10010, 212-592-2043 or toll-free 800-436-4204. *Fax:* 212-592-2029. *E-mail:* wberrios@sva.edu.

SCHREINER UNIVERSITY

Kerrville, TX

ABOUT THE INSTITUTION Independent Presbyterian, coed. Awards: associate, bachelor's, and master's degrees and post-bachelor's certificates. 33 undergraduate majors. Total enrollment: 842. Undergraduates: 793. Freshmen: 212.

GIFT AID (NEED-BASED) ***Scholarships, grants, and awards:*** Federal Pell, FSEOG, state, private, college/university gift aid from institutional funds.

GIFT AID (NON-NEED-BASED) ***Scholarships, grants, and awards by category:*** *Academic Interests/Achievement:* biological sciences, business, education, English, general academic interests/achievements, mathematics, physical sciences, religion/biblical studies, social sciences. *Creative Arts/Performance:* art/fine arts, journalism/publications, music, theater/drama. *Special Achievements/Activities:* community service, leadership, religious involvement. *Special Characteristics:* children of faculty/staff, ethnic background, general special characteristics, international students, local/state students, religious affiliation.

LOANS ***Programs:*** FFEL (Subsidized and Unsubsidized Stafford, PLUS), state, Sallie Mae Signature Loan, alternative loans.

APPLYING FOR FINANCIAL AID ***Required financial aid forms:*** FAFSA, institution's own form.

CONTACT Toni Bryant, Director of Financial Aid, Schreiner University, 2100 Memorial Boulevard, Kerrville, TX 78028, 830-792-7217 or toll-free 800-343-4919. *Fax:* 830-792-7226. *E-mail:* finaid@schreiner.edu.

SCRIPPS COLLEGE

Claremont, CA

Tuition & fees: $33,700 | **Average undergraduate aid package: $29,642**

ABOUT THE INSTITUTION Independent, women only. Awards: bachelor's degrees and post-bachelor's certificates. 57 undergraduate majors. Total enrollment: 890. Undergraduates: 869. Freshmen: 223. Both federal and institutional methodology are used as a basis for awarding need-based institutional aid.

UNDERGRADUATE EXPENSES for 2006–07 ***Application fee:*** $50. ***Comprehensive fee:*** $43,800 includes full-time tuition ($33,506), mandatory fees ($194), and room and board ($10,100). ***College room only:*** $5400. Full-time tuition and fees vary according to program. Room and board charges vary according to board plan. ***Part-time tuition:*** $4188 per course. Part-time tuition and fees vary according to program. ***Payment plan:*** Installment.

FRESHMAN FINANCIAL AID (Fall 2006, est.) 134 applied for aid; of those 70% were deemed to have need. 100% of freshmen with need received aid; of those

100% had need fully met. ***Average percent of need met:*** 100% (excluding resources awarded to replace EFC). ***Average financial aid package:*** $29,145 (excluding resources awarded to replace EFC). 6% of all full-time freshmen had no need and received non-need-based gift aid.

UNDERGRADUATE FINANCIAL AID (Fall 2006, est.) 443 applied for aid; of those 79% were deemed to have need. 100% of undergraduates with need received aid; of those 100% had need fully met. ***Average percent of need met:*** 100% (excluding resources awarded to replace EFC). ***Average financial aid package:*** $29,642 (excluding resources awarded to replace EFC). 9% of all full-time undergraduates had no need and received non-need-based gift aid.

GIFT AID (NEED-BASED) ***Total amount:*** $9,123,232 (4% federal, 7% state, 85% institutional, 4% external sources). ***Receiving aid:*** Freshmen: 42% (94); All full-time undergraduates: 41% (351). ***Average award:*** Freshmen: $25,927; Undergraduates: $25,057. ***Scholarships, grants, and awards:*** Federal Pell, FSEOG, state, private, college/university gift aid from institutional funds.

GIFT AID (NON-NEED-BASED) ***Total amount:*** $1,354,530 (1% state, 86% institutional, 13% external sources). ***Receiving aid:*** Freshmen: 7% (16); Undergraduates: 5% (42). ***Average award:*** Freshmen: $13,291; Undergraduates: $15,854. ***Scholarships, grants, and awards by category:*** *Academic Interests/Achievement:* 124 awards ($2,125,305 total): general academic interests/achievements. ***Tuition waivers:*** Full or partial for employees or children of employees. ***ROTC:*** Army cooperative, Air Force cooperative.

LOANS ***Student loans:*** $1,944,627 (53% need-based, 47% non-need-based). 42% of past graduating class borrowed through all loan programs. *Average indebtedness per student:* $12,071. ***Average need-based loan:*** Freshmen: $2910; Undergraduates: $3789. ***Parent loans:*** $1,815,032 (100% non-need-based). ***Programs:*** FFEL (Subsidized and Unsubsidized Stafford, PLUS), Perkins, college/university.

WORK-STUDY ***Federal work-study:*** Total amount: $485,913; 299 jobs averaging $1582.

APPLYING FOR FINANCIAL AID ***Required financial aid forms:*** FAFSA, CSS Financial Aid PROFILE, noncustodial (divorced/separated) parent's statement, business/farm supplement, verification worksheet, federal income tax form(s). ***Financial aid deadline (priority):*** 2/1. ***Notification date:*** 4/1. Students must reply by 5/1 or within 2 weeks of notification.

CONTACT Sean Smith, Director of Financial Aid, Scripps College, 1030 Columbia Avenue, PMB 1293, Claremont, CA 91711-3948, 909-621-8275 or toll-free 800-770-1333. *Fax:* 909-607-7742. *E-mail:* finaid@scrippscollege.edu.

SEATTLE PACIFIC UNIVERSITY

Seattle, WA

Tuition & fees: $23,391 **Average undergraduate aid package: $19,709**

ABOUT THE INSTITUTION Independent Free Methodist, coed. Awards: bachelor's, master's, and doctoral degrees and post-master's certificates. 54 undergraduate majors. Total enrollment: 3,830. Undergraduates: 2,979. Freshmen: 622. Federal methodology is used as a basis for awarding need-based institutional aid.

UNDERGRADUATE EXPENSES for 2006–07 ***Application fee:*** $45. ***Comprehensive fee:*** $31,209 includes full-time tuition ($23,055), mandatory fees ($336), and room and board ($7818). ***College room only:*** $4212. Room and board charges vary according to board plan and housing facility. ***Part-time tuition:*** $641 per credit. Part-time tuition and fees vary according to course load. ***Payment plan:*** Installment.

FRESHMAN FINANCIAL AID (Fall 2006, est.) 500 applied for aid; of those 77% were deemed to have need. 100% of freshmen with need received aid; of those 15% had need fully met. ***Average percent of need met:*** 79% (excluding resources awarded to replace EFC). ***Average financial aid package:*** $19,043 (excluding resources awarded to replace EFC). 31% of all full-time freshmen had no need and received non-need-based gift aid.

UNDERGRADUATE FINANCIAL AID (Fall 2006, est.) 2,101 applied for aid; of those 82% were deemed to have need. 100% of undergraduates with need received aid; of those 12% had need fully met. ***Average percent of need met:*** 82% (excluding resources awarded to replace EFC). ***Average financial aid package:*** $19,709 (excluding resources awarded to replace EFC). 29% of all full-time undergraduates had no need and received non-need-based gift aid.

GIFT AID (NEED-BASED) ***Total amount:*** $22,270,435 (9% federal, 7% state, 78% institutional, 6% external sources). ***Receiving aid:*** Freshmen: 61% (377); All full-time undergraduates: 60% (1,680). ***Average award:*** Freshmen: $17,299; Undergraduates: $15,522. ***Scholarships, grants, and awards:*** Federal Pell, FSEOG, state, private, college/university gift aid from institutional funds.

GIFT AID (NON-NEED-BASED) ***Total amount:*** $6,063,462 (1% state, 95% institutional, 4% external sources). ***Average award:*** Freshmen: $10,675; Undergraduates: $10,640. ***Scholarships, grants, and awards by category:*** *Academic Interests/Achievement:* 646 awards ($3,190,941 total): engineering/technologies, general academic interests/achievements. *Creative Arts/Performance:* 29 awards ($37,333 total): art/fine arts, performing arts. *Special Characteristics:* 221 awards ($755,733 total): children and siblings of alumni, children of faculty/staff, general special characteristics, international students, relatives of clergy, religious affiliation. ***Tuition waivers:*** Full or partial for employees or children of employees, senior citizens. ***ROTC:*** Army cooperative, Naval cooperative, Air Force cooperative.

LOANS ***Student loans:*** $13,147,727 (84% need-based, 16% non-need-based). 67% of past graduating class borrowed through all loan programs. *Average indebtedness per student:* $22,709. ***Average need-based loan:*** Freshmen: $4951; Undergraduates: $5160. ***Parent loans:*** $3,799,258 (76% need-based, 24% non-need-based). ***Programs:*** FFEL (Subsidized and Unsubsidized Stafford, PLUS), Perkins, Federal Nursing, college/university.

WORK-STUDY ***Federal work-study:*** Total amount: $755,386; 375 jobs averaging $1442. ***State or other work-study/employment:*** Total amount: $3,150,577 (100% need-based). 413 part-time jobs averaging $1923.

ATHLETIC AWARDS Total amount: $1,671,823 (63% need-based, 37% non-need-based).

APPLYING FOR FINANCIAL AID ***Required financial aid form:*** FAFSA. ***Financial aid deadline (priority):*** 4/1. ***Notification date:*** Continuous beginning 3/15. Students must reply by 5/1 or within 4 weeks of notification.

CONTACT Mr. Jordan Grant, Director of Student Financial Services, Seattle Pacific University, 3307 Third Avenue West, Seattle, WA 98119-1997, 206-281-2469 or toll-free 800-366-3344. *E-mail:* grantj@spu.edu.

SEATTLE UNIVERSITY

Seattle, WA

Tuition & fees: $24,615 **Average undergraduate aid package: $23,740**

ABOUT THE INSTITUTION Independent Roman Catholic, coed. Awards: bachelor's, master's, doctoral, and first professional degrees and post-bachelor's, post-master's, and first professional certificates. 56 undergraduate majors. Total enrollment: 7,226. Undergraduates: 4,160. Freshmen: 787. Federal methodology is used as a basis for awarding need-based institutional aid.

UNDERGRADUATE EXPENSES for 2006–07 ***Application fee:*** $45. ***Comprehensive fee:*** $32,118 includes full-time tuition ($24,615) and room and board ($7503). ***College room only:*** $4818. Full-time tuition and fees vary according to course load. Room and board charges vary according to board plan. ***Part-time tuition:*** $547 per credit. Part-time tuition and fees vary according to course load.

FRESHMAN FINANCIAL AID (Fall 2006, est.) 699 applied for aid; of those 72% were deemed to have need. 100% of freshmen with need received aid; of those 11% had need fully met. ***Average percent of need met:*** 82% (excluding resources awarded to replace EFC). ***Average financial aid package:*** $23,000 (excluding resources awarded to replace EFC). 2% of all full-time freshmen had no need and received non-need-based gift aid.

UNDERGRADUATE FINANCIAL AID (Fall 2006, est.) 3,227 applied for aid; of those 79% were deemed to have need. 99% of undergraduates with need received aid; of those 8% had need fully met. ***Average percent of need met:*** 74% (excluding resources awarded to replace EFC). ***Average financial aid package:*** $23,740 (excluding resources awarded to replace EFC). 4% of all full-time undergraduates had no need and received non-need-based gift aid.

GIFT AID (NEED-BASED) ***Total amount:*** $27,899,659 (14% federal, 81% institutional, 5% external sources). ***Receiving aid:*** Freshmen: 34% (270); All full-time undergraduates: 35% (1,364). ***Average award:*** Freshmen: $11,400; Undergraduates: $9346. ***Scholarships, grants, and awards:*** Federal Pell, FSEOG, state, private, college/university gift aid from institutional funds, Federal Nursing.

GIFT AID (NON-NEED-BASED) ***Total amount:*** $5,738,587 (30% federal, 1% state, 51% institutional, 18% external sources). ***Receiving aid:*** Freshmen: 31% (245); Undergraduates: 34% (1,312). ***Average award:*** Freshmen: $6089; Undergraduates: $8692. ***Scholarships, grants, and awards by category:*** *Academic Interests/Achievement:* 800 awards ($5,422,207 total): general academic interests/achievements. *Creative Arts/Performance:* 13 awards ($11,925 total): music. *Special Achievements/Activities:* 25 awards ($603,074 total): leadership. *Special Characteristics:* 402 awards ($2,594,224 total): children and siblings of alumni, children of educators, children of faculty/staff, members of minority groups. ***Tuition waivers:*** Full or partial for employees or children of employees. ***ROTC:*** Army, Air Force cooperative.

LOANS ***Student loans:*** $19,715,081 (62% need-based, 38% non-need-based). 76% of past graduating class borrowed through all loan programs. *Average indebtedness per student:* $18,329. ***Average need-based loan:*** Freshmen: $3716; Undergraduates: $4460. ***Parent loans:*** $3,930,258 (7% need-based, 93% non-need-based). ***Programs:*** Federal Direct (Subsidized and Unsubsidized Stafford, PLUS), Perkins, Federal Nursing.

WORK-STUDY ***Federal work-study:*** Total amount: $2,971,855; 704 jobs averaging $3899. ***State or other work-study/employment:*** Total amount: $3,862,138 (100% need-based). 830 part-time jobs averaging $5119.

ATHLETIC AWARDS Total amount: $1,277,585 (22% need-based, 78% non-need-based).

APPLYING FOR FINANCIAL AID ***Required financial aid form:*** FAFSA. ***Financial aid deadline (priority):*** 2/1. ***Notification date:*** Continuous beginning 3/21.

CONTACT Mr. James White, Director of Student Financial Services, Seattle University, Broadway & Madison, Seattle, WA 98122-4460, 206-296-2000 or toll-free 800-542-0833 (in-state), 800-426-7123 (out-of-state). *Fax:* 206-296-5755. *E-mail:* financial-aid@seattleu.edu.

SETON HALL UNIVERSITY

South Orange, NJ

CONTACT Office of Enrollment Services, Seton Hall University, 400 South Orange Avenue, South Orange, NJ 07079, 973-761-9350 or toll-free 800-THE HALL (out-of-state). *Fax:* 973-275-2040. *E-mail:* thehall@shu.edu.

SETON HILL UNIVERSITY

Greensburg, PA

Tuition & fees: $23,380 **Average undergraduate aid package: $18,760**

ABOUT THE INSTITUTION Independent Roman Catholic, coed. Awards: bachelor's and master's degrees and post-bachelor's and post-master's certificates. 91 undergraduate majors. Total enrollment: 1,895. Undergraduates: 1,549. Freshmen: 314. Federal methodology is used as a basis for awarding need-based institutional aid.

UNDERGRADUATE EXPENSES for 2006–07 ***Application fee:*** $35. ***Comprehensive fee:*** $30,610 includes full-time tuition ($23,180), mandatory fees ($200), and room and board ($7230). Room and board charges vary according to board plan and housing facility. ***Part-time tuition:*** $615 per credit. ***Part-time fees:*** $100 per term. Part-time tuition and fees vary according to course load. ***Payment plans:*** Installment, deferred payment.

FRESHMAN FINANCIAL AID (Fall 2006, est.) 297 applied for aid; of those 96% were deemed to have need. 100% of freshmen with need received aid; of those 20% had need fully met. ***Average percent of need met:*** 81% (excluding resources awarded to replace EFC). ***Average financial aid package:*** $18,632 (excluding resources awarded to replace EFC). 3% of all full-time freshmen had no need and received non-need-based gift aid.

UNDERGRADUATE FINANCIAL AID (Fall 2006, est.) 1,008 applied for aid; of those 95% were deemed to have need. 100% of undergraduates with need received aid; of those 20% had need fully met. ***Average percent of need met:*** 76% (excluding resources awarded to replace EFC). ***Average financial aid package:*** $18,760 (excluding resources awarded to replace EFC). 2% of all full-time undergraduates had no need and received non-need-based gift aid.

GIFT AID (NEED-BASED) ***Total amount:*** $12,701,628 (13% federal, 18% state, 66% institutional, 3% external sources). ***Receiving aid:*** Freshmen: 91% (286); All full-time undergraduates: 75% (957). ***Average award:*** Freshmen: $14,500; Undergraduates: $14,660. ***Scholarships, grants, and awards:*** Federal Pell, FSEOG, state, private, college/university gift aid from institutional funds.

GIFT AID (NON-NEED-BASED) ***Total amount:*** $416,219 (1% state, 99% institutional). ***Receiving aid:*** Freshmen: 13% (40); Undergraduates: 8% (105). ***Average award:*** Freshmen: $10,988; Undergraduates: $13,562. ***Scholarships, grants, and awards by category:*** *Academic Interests/Achievement:* 498 awards ($2,872,372 total): biological sciences, business, communication, computer science, education, English, foreign languages, general academic interests/achievements, home economics, humanities, mathematics, physical sciences, premedicine, religion/biblical studies, social sciences. *Creative Arts/Performance:* 37 awards ($20,075 total): applied art and design, art/fine arts, creative writing, journalism/publications, music, performing arts, theater/drama. *Special Achievements/Activities:* 356 awards ($500,113 total): community service, general special achievements/activities, leadership, religious involvement. *Special Characteristics:* 199 awards ($554,050 total): adult students, children and siblings of alumni, children of faculty/staff, children with a deceased or disabled parent, international students, parents of current students, siblings of current students. ***Tuition waivers:*** Full or partial for employees or children of employees. ***ROTC:*** Army cooperative, Air Force cooperative.

LOANS ***Student loans:*** $6,910,082 (52% need-based, 48% non-need-based). 82% of past graduating class borrowed through all loan programs. *Average indebtedness per student:* $24,657. ***Average need-based loan:*** Freshmen: $3250; Undergraduates: $4100. ***Parent loans:*** $1,576,945 (75% need-based, 25% non-need-based). ***Programs:*** FFEL (Subsidized and Unsubsidized Stafford, PLUS), Perkins, college/university, alternative loans.

WORK-STUDY ***Federal work-study:*** Total amount: $822,167; 346 jobs averaging $1236. ***State or other work-study/employment:*** Total amount: $235,004 (35% need-based, 65% non-need-based). 211 part-time jobs averaging $1500.

ATHLETIC AWARDS Total amount: $3,416,561 (65% need-based, 35% non-need-based).

APPLYING FOR FINANCIAL AID ***Required financial aid forms:*** FAFSA, institution's own form, state aid form. ***Financial aid deadline (priority):*** 6/1. ***Notification date:*** Continuous beginning 11/1. Students must reply by 5/1 or within 2 weeks of notification.

CONTACT Maryann Dudas, Director of Financial Aid, Seton Hill University, Seton Hill Drive, Greensburg, PA 15601, 724-838-4293 or toll-free 800-826-6234. *Fax:* 724-830-1194. *E-mail:* dudas@setonhill.edu.

SEWANEE: THE UNIVERSITY OF THE SOUTH

Sewanee, TN

Tuition & fees: $30,660 **Average undergraduate aid package: $21,439**

ABOUT THE INSTITUTION Independent Episcopal, coed. Awards: bachelor's, master's, doctoral, and first professional degrees and post-bachelor's, post-master's, and first professional certificates. 41 undergraduate majors. Total enrollment: 1,611. Undergraduates: 1,518. Freshmen: 412. Both federal and institutional methodology are used as a basis for awarding need-based institutional aid.

UNDERGRADUATE EXPENSES for 2007–08 ***Application fee:*** $45. ***Comprehensive fee:*** $39,440 includes full-time tuition ($30,438), mandatory fees ($222), and room and board ($8780). ***College room only:*** $4560.

FRESHMAN FINANCIAL AID (Fall 2006, est.) 234 applied for aid; of those 67% were deemed to have need. 100% of freshmen with need received aid; of those 77% had need fully met. ***Average percent of need met:*** 94% (excluding resources awarded to replace EFC). ***Average financial aid package:*** $24,809 (excluding resources awarded to replace EFC). 18% of all full-time freshmen had no need and received non-need-based gift aid.

UNDERGRADUATE FINANCIAL AID (Fall 2006, est.) 737 applied for aid; of those 93% were deemed to have need. 100% of undergraduates with need received aid; of those 85% had need fully met. ***Average percent of need met:*** 97% (excluding resources awarded to replace EFC). ***Average financial aid package:*** $21,439 (excluding resources awarded to replace EFC). 22% of all full-time undergraduates had no need and received non-need-based gift aid.

GIFT AID (NEED-BASED) ***Total amount:*** $11,611,449 (6% federal, 6% state, 84% institutional, 4% external sources). ***Receiving aid:*** Freshmen: 38% (157); All full-time undergraduates: 45% (666). ***Average award:*** Freshmen: $21,201; Undergraduates: $17,947. ***Scholarships, grants, and awards:*** Federal Pell, FSEOG, state, private, college/university gift aid from institutional funds.

GIFT AID (NON-NEED-BASED) ***Total amount:*** $4,717,751 (5% state, 90% institutional, 5% external sources). ***Average award:*** Freshmen: $12,517; Undergraduates: $11,871. ***Scholarships, grants, and awards by category:*** *Academic Interests/Achievement:* 377 awards ($4,114,028 total): general academic interests/achievements. *Special Characteristics:* 148 awards ($387,750 total): children of faculty/staff, ethnic background, members of minority groups, relatives of clergy.

LOANS ***Student loans:*** $2,004,045 (86% need-based, 14% non-need-based). 47% of past graduating class borrowed through all loan programs. *Average indebtedness per student:* $16,866. ***Average need-based loan:*** Freshmen: $3096;

Undergraduates: $3226. ***Parent loans:*** $3,385,525 (51% need-based, 49% non-need-based). ***Programs:*** FFEL (Subsidized and Unsubsidized Stafford, PLUS), Perkins, state, college/university, private alternative loans.

WORK-STUDY ***Federal work-study:*** Total amount: $376,398; 334 jobs averaging $1109. ***State or other work-study/employment:*** Total amount: $86,500 (57% need-based, 43% non-need-based). 79 part-time jobs averaging $1085.

APPLYING FOR FINANCIAL AID ***Required financial aid forms:*** FAFSA, institution's own form, Student and/or Parent U.S. Income Tax Returns if applicable. ***Financial aid deadline (priority):*** 3/1. ***Notification date:*** 4/1. Students must reply within 4 weeks of notification.

CONTACT Mr. David R. Gelinas, Director of Financial Aid, Sewanee: The University of the South, 735 University Avenue, Sewanee, TN 37383-1000, 931-598-1312 or toll-free 800-522-2234. *Fax:* 931-598-3273.

SHASTA BIBLE COLLEGE

Redding, CA

Tuition & fees: $7580 **Average undergraduate aid package: $5544**

ABOUT THE INSTITUTION Independent nondenominational, coed. Awards: associate, bachelor's, and master's degrees. 3 undergraduate majors. Total enrollment: 109. Undergraduates: 94. Freshmen: 10. Federal methodology is used as a basis for awarding need-based institutional aid.

UNDERGRADUATE EXPENSES for 2007–08 ***Application fee:*** $35. ***Tuition:*** full-time $7200; part-time $225 per unit. ***Required fees:*** full-time $380; $380 per year part-time.

FRESHMAN FINANCIAL AID (Fall 2005) 13 applied for aid; of those 85% were deemed to have need. 100% of freshmen with need received aid; of those 27% had need fully met. ***Average percent of need met:*** 25% (excluding resources awarded to replace EFC). ***Average financial aid package:*** $5544 (excluding resources awarded to replace EFC).

UNDERGRADUATE FINANCIAL AID (Fall 2005) 38 applied for aid; of those 89% were deemed to have need. 100% of undergraduates with need received aid; of those 9% had need fully met. ***Average percent of need met:*** 25% (excluding resources awarded to replace EFC). ***Average financial aid package:*** $5544 (excluding resources awarded to replace EFC). 11% of all full-time undergraduates had no need and received non-need-based gift aid.

GIFT AID (NEED-BASED) ***Total amount:*** $182,778 (71% federal, 29% state). ***Receiving aid:*** Freshmen: 85% (11); All full-time undergraduates: 89% (34). ***Average award:*** Freshmen: $4050; Undergraduates: $4050. ***Scholarships, grants, and awards:*** Federal Pell, FSEOG, state, private, college/university gift aid from institutional funds.

GIFT AID (NON-NEED-BASED) ***Total amount:*** $6000 (17% institutional, 83% external sources). ***Receiving aid:*** Undergraduates: 21% (8). ***Average award:*** Undergraduates: $1650. ***Scholarships, grants, and awards by category:*** *Academic Interests/Achievement:* 27 awards ($20,598 total): education. *Creative Arts/Performance:* 11 awards ($7225 total): general creative arts/performance. *Special Achievements/Activities:* general special achievements/activities. *Special Characteristics:* 18 awards ($34,065 total): relatives of clergy, veterans.

WORK-STUDY ***Federal work-study:*** Total amount: $10,344; 19 jobs averaging $1200. ***State or other work-study/employment:*** Total amount: $11,256 (100% non-need-based). 5 part-time jobs averaging $1000.

APPLYING FOR FINANCIAL AID ***Required financial aid forms:*** FAFSA, institution's own form, state aid form. ***Financial aid deadline:*** Continuous. ***Notification date:*** Continuous beginning 7/2. Students must reply within 3 weeks of notification.

CONTACT Connie Barton, Financial Aid Administrator, Shasta Bible College, 2951 Goodwater Avenue, Redding, CA 96002, 530-221-4275 or toll-free 800-800-45BC (in-state), 800-800-6929 (out-of-state). *Fax:* 530-221-6929. *E-mail:* finaid@shasta.edu.

SHAWNEE STATE UNIVERSITY

Portsmouth, OH

CONTACT Patricia Moore, Director of Financial Aid, Shawnee State University, 940 Second Street, Portsmouth, OH 45662-4344, 740-351-3245 or toll-free 800-959-2SSU. *E-mail:* pmoore@shawnee.edu.

SHAW UNIVERSITY

Raleigh, NC

Tuition & fees: $10,020 **Average undergraduate aid package: $8992**

ABOUT THE INSTITUTION Independent Baptist, coed. Awards: associate, bachelor's, master's, and first professional degrees. 36 undergraduate majors. Total enrollment: 2,882. Undergraduates: 2,669. Freshmen: 723. Federal methodology is used as a basis for awarding need-based institutional aid.

UNDERGRADUATE EXPENSES for 2006–07 ***Application fee:*** $25. ***Comprehensive fee:*** $16,430 includes full-time tuition ($8280), mandatory fees ($1740), and room and board ($6410). ***College room only:*** $3010. ***Part-time tuition:*** $345 per semester hour. ***Part-time fees:*** $41 per semester hour; $265 per term.

FRESHMAN FINANCIAL AID (Fall 2005) 593 applied for aid; of those 94% were deemed to have need. 100% of freshmen with need received aid; of those 9% had need fully met. ***Average percent of need met:*** 63% (excluding resources awarded to replace EFC). ***Average financial aid package:*** $8846 (excluding resources awarded to replace EFC). 7% of all full-time freshmen had no need and received non-need-based gift aid.

UNDERGRADUATE FINANCIAL AID (Fall 2005) 2,197 applied for aid; of those 94% were deemed to have need. 99% of undergraduates with need received aid; of those 10% had need fully met. ***Average percent of need met:*** 63% (excluding resources awarded to replace EFC). ***Average financial aid package:*** $8992 (excluding resources awarded to replace EFC). 5% of all full-time undergraduates had no need and received non-need-based gift aid.

GIFT AID (NEED-BASED) ***Total amount:*** $12,187,663 (52% federal, 33% state, 10% institutional, 5% external sources). ***Receiving aid:*** Freshmen: 88% (545); All full-time undergraduates: 89% (1,986). ***Average award:*** Freshmen: $6242; Undergraduates: $5898. ***Scholarships, grants, and awards:*** Federal Pell, FSEOG, state, private, college/university gift aid from institutional funds, United Negro College Fund.

GIFT AID (NON-NEED-BASED) ***Total amount:*** $485,926 (3% federal, 28% state, 45% institutional, 24% external sources). ***Receiving aid:*** Freshmen: 4% (27); Undergraduates: 4% (98). ***Average award:*** Freshmen: $8993; Undergraduates: $9333. ***Scholarships, grants, and awards by category:*** *Academic Interests/Achievement:* $37,042 total: biological sciences, computer science, education, engineering/technologies, general academic interests/achievements, mathematics, physical sciences. *Creative Arts/Performance:* $82,904 total: music, performing arts. *Special Characteristics:* children of faculty/staff, general special characteristics. ***ROTC:*** Army cooperative, Air Force cooperative.

LOANS ***Student loans:*** $14,754,615 (86% need-based, 14% non-need-based). 96% of past graduating class borrowed through all loan programs. *Average indebtedness per student:* $15,982. ***Average need-based loan:*** Freshmen: $2596; Undergraduates: $3394. ***Parent loans:*** $838,951 (44% need-based, 56% non-need-based). ***Programs:*** Federal Direct (Subsidized and Unsubsidized Stafford, PLUS), Perkins, college/university, state loans (for Education majors).

WORK-STUDY ***Federal work-study:*** Total amount: $417,747; 347 jobs averaging $1120.

ATHLETIC AWARDS Total amount: $2,011,503 (72% need-based, 28% non-need-based).

APPLYING FOR FINANCIAL AID ***Required financial aid forms:*** FAFSA, institution's own form, state aid form. ***Financial aid deadline:*** 6/1 (priority: 3/1). ***Notification date:*** Continuous.

CONTACT Rochelle King, Director of Financial Aid, Shaw University, 118 East South Street, Raleigh, NC 27601-2399, 919-546-8565 or toll-free 800-214-6683. *Fax:* 919-546-8356. *E-mail:* rking@shawu.edu.

SHELDON JACKSON COLLEGE

Sitka, AK

CONTACT Ms. Louise Driver, Financial Aid Director, Sheldon Jackson College, 801 Lincoln Street, Sitka, AK 99835-7699, 800-747-5206 or toll-free 800-478-4556. *Fax:* 907-747-6366. *E-mail:* ldriver@sj-alaska.edu.

SHENANDOAH UNIVERSITY

Winchester, VA

Tuition & fees: $21,240 **Average undergraduate aid package: $15,222**

ABOUT THE INSTITUTION Independent United Methodist, coed. Awards: associate, bachelor's, master's, doctoral, and first professional degrees and post-bachelor's and post-master's certificates. 36 undergraduate majors. Total enrollment: 3,105. Undergraduates: 1,522. Freshmen: 307. Federal methodology is used as a basis for awarding need-based institutional aid.

UNDERGRADUATE EXPENSES for 2006–07 ***Application fee:*** $30. ***Comprehensive fee:*** $28,890 includes full-time tuition ($21,090), mandatory fees ($150), and room and board ($7650). Full-time tuition and fees vary according to course load and program. Room and board charges vary according to board plan and housing facility. ***Part-time tuition:*** $610 per credit hour. Part-time tuition and fees vary according to course load and program. ***Payment plan:*** Installment.

FRESHMAN FINANCIAL AID (Fall 2006, est.) 325 applied for aid; of those 100% were deemed to have need. 100% of freshmen with need received aid; of those 19% had need fully met. ***Average percent of need met:*** 86% (excluding resources awarded to replace EFC). ***Average financial aid package:*** $15,063 (excluding resources awarded to replace EFC). 14% of all full-time freshmen had no need and received non-need-based gift aid.

UNDERGRADUATE FINANCIAL AID (Fall 2006, est.) 931 applied for aid; of those 100% were deemed to have need. 100% of undergraduates with need received aid; of those 20% had need fully met. ***Average percent of need met:*** 85% (excluding resources awarded to replace EFC). ***Average financial aid package:*** $15,222 (excluding resources awarded to replace EFC). 11% of all full-time undergraduates had no need and received non-need-based gift aid.

GIFT AID (NEED-BASED) ***Total amount:*** $3,229,879 (37% federal, 2% state, 50% institutional, 11% external sources). ***Receiving aid:*** Freshmen: 43% (168); All full-time undergraduates: 58% (884). ***Average award:*** Freshmen: $5022; Undergraduates: $7265. ***Scholarships, grants, and awards:*** Federal Pell, FSEOG, state, private, college/university gift aid from institutional funds, Federal Nursing.

GIFT AID (NON-NEED-BASED) ***Total amount:*** $8,617,943 (20% state, 80% institutional). ***Receiving aid:*** Freshmen: 31% (122); Undergraduates: 41% (623). ***Average award:*** Freshmen: $4500; Undergraduates: $4100. ***Scholarships, grants, and awards by category:*** *Academic Interests/Achievement:* 748 awards ($2,901,102 total): business, general academic interests/achievements. *Creative Arts/Performance:* 378 awards ($12,477,982 total): dance, music, performing arts, theater/drama. *Special Characteristics:* 216 awards ($879,024 total): children of faculty/staff, local/state students, relatives of clergy, religious affiliation. ***Tuition waivers:*** Full or partial for employees or children of employees.

LOANS ***Student loans:*** $7,703,823 (56% need-based, 44% non-need-based). 85% of past graduating class borrowed through all loan programs. *Average indebtedness per student:* $19,518. ***Average need-based loan:*** Freshmen: $4229; Undergraduates: $6109. ***Parent loans:*** $5,138,271 (76% need-based, 24% non-need-based). ***Programs:*** Federal Direct (Subsidized and Unsubsidized Stafford, PLUS), Perkins, Federal Nursing, college/university.

WORK-STUDY ***Federal work-study:*** Total amount: $627,690; 412 jobs averaging $1500. ***State or other work-study/employment:*** Total amount: $297,450 (100% non-need-based). 240 part-time jobs averaging $1500.

APPLYING FOR FINANCIAL AID ***Required financial aid forms:*** FAFSA, state aid form. ***Financial aid deadline (priority):*** 2/15. ***Notification date:*** Continuous beginning 3/15. Students must reply within 2 weeks of notification.

CONTACT Nancy Bragg, Director of Financial Aid, Shenandoah University, 1460 University Drive, Winchester, VA 22601-5195, 540-665-4538 or toll-free 800-432-2266. *Fax:* 540-665-4939. *E-mail:* nbragg@su.edu.

SHEPHERD UNIVERSITY

Shepherdstown, WV

Tuition & fees (WV res): $4348 Average undergraduate aid package: $8674

ABOUT THE INSTITUTION State-supported, coed. Awards: bachelor's and master's degrees. 22 undergraduate majors. Total enrollment: 4,091. Undergraduates: 3,970. Freshmen: 699. Federal methodology is used as a basis for awarding need-based institutional aid.

UNDERGRADUATE EXPENSES for 2006–07 ***Application fee:*** $35. ***Tuition, state resident:*** full-time $4348; part-time $177 per credit hour. ***Tuition, nonresident:*** full-time $11,464; part-time $473 per credit hour. Full-time tuition and fees vary according to degree level, program, and reciprocity agreements. Part-time tuition and fees vary according to degree level and program. ***College room and board:*** $6456. Room and board charges vary according to board plan and housing facility. ***Payment plan:*** Installment.

FRESHMAN FINANCIAL AID (Fall 2006, est.) 571 applied for aid; of those 58% were deemed to have need. 96% of freshmen with need received aid. ***Average percent of need met:*** 70% (excluding resources awarded to replace EFC). ***Average financial aid package:*** $7677 (excluding resources awarded to replace EFC). 21% of all full-time freshmen had no need and received non-need-based gift aid.

UNDERGRADUATE FINANCIAL AID (Fall 2006, est.) 2,347 applied for aid; of those 62% were deemed to have need. 96% of undergraduates with need received aid; of those 20% had need fully met. ***Average percent of need met:*** 74% (excluding resources awarded to replace EFC). ***Average financial aid package:*** $8674 (excluding resources awarded to replace EFC). 19% of all full-time undergraduates had no need and received non-need-based gift aid.

GIFT AID (NEED-BASED) ***Total amount:*** $3,278,428 (68% federal, 28% state, 4% institutional). ***Receiving aid:*** Freshmen: 22% (151); All full-time undergraduates: 24% (743). ***Average award:*** Freshmen: $3627; Undergraduates: $3529. ***Scholarships, grants, and awards:*** Federal Pell, FSEOG, state, private, college/university gift aid from institutional funds.

GIFT AID (NON-NEED-BASED) ***Total amount:*** $4,117,230 (39% state, 54% institutional, 7% external sources). ***Receiving aid:*** Freshmen: 16% (109); Undergraduates: 11% (327). ***Average award:*** Freshmen: $6842; Undergraduates: $7458. ***Scholarships, grants, and awards by category:*** *Academic Interests/Achievement:* 274 awards ($541,132 total): biological sciences, business, communication, computer science, education, engineering/technologies, English, foreign languages, general academic interests/achievements, health fields, home economics, humanities, mathematics, physical sciences, premedicine, social sciences. *Creative Arts/Performance:* 54 awards ($203,292 total): applied art and design, art/fine arts, music, performing arts. *Special Achievements/Activities:* 29 awards ($19,650 total): leadership. *Special Characteristics:* 26 awards ($141,206 total): ethnic background, members of minority groups, veterans' children. ***Tuition waivers:*** Full or partial for minority students, senior citizens. ***ROTC:*** Air Force cooperative.

LOANS ***Student loans:*** $12,013,156 (42% need-based, 58% non-need-based). 61% of past graduating class borrowed through all loan programs. *Average indebtedness per student:* $17,357. ***Average need-based loan:*** Freshmen: $2368; Undergraduates: $3584. ***Parent loans:*** $3,605,542 (100% non-need-based). ***Programs:*** Federal Direct (Subsidized and Unsubsidized Stafford, PLUS), Perkins.

WORK-STUDY ***Federal work-study:*** Total amount: $286,124; 183 jobs averaging $1500. ***State or other work-study/employment:*** Total amount: $661,354 (100% non-need-based). 325 part-time jobs averaging $3000.

ATHLETIC AWARDS Total amount: $805,763 (100% non-need-based).

APPLYING FOR FINANCIAL AID ***Required financial aid forms:*** FAFSA, state aid form. ***Financial aid deadline (priority):*** 3/1. ***Notification date:*** Continuous beginning 3/30. Students must reply within 2 weeks of notification.

CONTACT Financial Aid Office, Shepherd University, PO Box 3210, Shepherdstown, WV 25443-3210, 304-876-5470 or toll-free 800-344-5231. *Fax:* 304-876-5238. *E-mail:* faoweb@shepherd.edu.

SHIMER COLLEGE

Chicago, IL

Tuition & fees: $21,000 Average undergraduate aid package: $11,652

ABOUT THE INSTITUTION Independent, coed. Awards: bachelor's degrees and post-bachelor's certificates. 7 undergraduate majors. Total enrollment: 138. Undergraduates: 126. Freshmen: 26. Both federal and institutional methodology are used as a basis for awarding need-based institutional aid.

UNDERGRADUATE EXPENSES for 2006–07 ***Application fee:*** $25. ***Comprehensive fee:*** $29,049 includes full-time tuition ($21,000) and room and board ($8049).

FRESHMAN FINANCIAL AID (Fall 2005) 8 applied for aid; of those 100% were deemed to have need. 100% of freshmen with need received aid; of those 12% had need fully met. ***Average financial aid package:*** $10,736 (excluding resources awarded to replace EFC). 22% of all full-time freshmen had no need and received non-need-based gift aid.

UNDERGRADUATE FINANCIAL AID (Fall 2005) 85 applied for aid; of those 100% were deemed to have need. 100% of undergraduates with need received aid; of those 2% had need fully met. ***Average financial aid package:*** $11,652 (excluding resources awarded to replace EFC). 11% of all full-time undergraduates had no need and received non-need-based gift aid.

GIFT AID (NEED-BASED) ***Total amount:*** $645,501 (25% federal, 21% state, 54% institutional). ***Receiving aid:*** Freshmen: 78% (7); All full-time undergraduates: 80% (74). ***Average award:*** Freshmen: $5412; Undergraduates: $4010. ***Scholarships, grants, and awards:*** Federal Pell, FSEOG, state, private, college/university gift aid from institutional funds.

GIFT AID (NON-NEED-BASED) ***Total amount:*** $15,104 (100% institutional). ***Receiving aid:*** Freshmen: 22% (2); Undergraduates: 11% (10). ***Average award:*** Freshmen: $12,000; Undergraduates: $7066. ***Scholarships, grants, and awards by category:*** *Academic Interests/Achievement:* 1 award ($20,760 total): general academic interests/achievements. *Creative Arts/Performance:* art/fine arts, creative writing, theater/drama. *Special Achievements/Activities:* hobbies/interests. *Special Characteristics:* 2 awards ($1500 total): children and siblings of alumni, out-of-state students.

LOANS ***Student loans:*** $667,833 (97% need-based, 3% non-need-based). 3% of past graduating class borrowed through all loan programs. ***Average need-based loan:*** Freshmen: $4339; Undergraduates: $4267. ***Parent loans:*** $39,000 (82% need-based, 18% non-need-based). ***Programs:*** FFEL (Subsidized and Unsubsidized Stafford, PLUS), Perkins, Sallie Mae Signature Loans, TERI Loans.

WORK-STUDY ***Federal work-study:*** Total amount: $85,900; 49 jobs averaging $1900. ***State or other work-study/employment:*** Total amount: $13,750 (100% non-need-based). 12 part-time jobs averaging $625.

APPLYING FOR FINANCIAL AID ***Required financial aid forms:*** FAFSA, institution's own form. ***Financial aid deadline (priority):*** 3/1. ***Notification date:*** Continuous beginning 2/1. Students must reply by 5/1 or within 2 weeks of notification.

CONTACT Janet Henthorn, Director of Financial Aid, Shimer College, 3424 South State Street, Chicago, IL 60616, 312-235-3507 or toll-free 800-215-7173. *Fax:* 312-235-3502. *E-mail:* j.henthorn@shimer.edu.

SHIPPENSBURG UNIVERSITY OF PENNSYLVANIA

Shippensburg, PA

Tuition & fees (PA res): $6549 **Average undergraduate aid package: $6536**

ABOUT THE INSTITUTION State-supported, coed. Awards: bachelor's and master's degrees and post-master's certificates. 33 undergraduate majors. Total enrollment: 7,516. Undergraduates: 6,423. Freshmen: 1,503. Federal methodology is used as a basis for awarding need-based institutional aid.

UNDERGRADUATE EXPENSES for 2006–07 ***Application fee:*** $30. ***Tuition, state resident:*** full-time $5038; part-time $210 per credit hour. ***Tuition, nonresident:*** full-time $12,598; part-time $525 per credit hour. ***Required fees:*** full-time $1511; $20 per credit hour or $192 per term part-time. ***College room and board:*** $5962; ***Room only:*** $3420. Room and board charges vary according to board plan and housing facility. ***Payment plan:*** Installment.

FRESHMAN FINANCIAL AID (Fall 2006, est.) 1261 applied for aid; of those 65% were deemed to have need. 95% of freshmen with need received aid; of those 12% had need fully met. ***Average percent of need met:*** 61% (excluding resources awarded to replace EFC). ***Average financial aid package:*** $5775 (excluding resources awarded to replace EFC). 10% of all full-time freshmen had no need and received non-need-based gift aid.

UNDERGRADUATE FINANCIAL AID (Fall 2006, est.) 4,520 applied for aid; of those 67% were deemed to have need. 96% of undergraduates with need received aid; of those 21% had need fully met. ***Average percent of need met:*** 69% (excluding resources awarded to replace EFC). ***Average financial aid package:*** $6536 (excluding resources awarded to replace EFC). 35% of all full-time undergraduates had no need and received non-need-based gift aid.

GIFT AID (NEED-BASED) ***Total amount:*** $9,456,191 (35% federal, 56% state, 3% institutional, 6% external sources). ***Receiving aid:*** Freshmen: 38% (571); All full-time undergraduates: 36% (2,181). ***Average award:*** Freshmen: $4634; Undergraduates: $4485. ***Scholarships, grants, and awards:*** Federal Pell, FSEOG, state, private, college/university gift aid from institutional funds, ACG/SMART (Academic Competitiveness Grant).

GIFT AID (NON-NEED-BASED) ***Total amount:*** $874,869 (3% federal, 2% state, 34% institutional, 61% external sources). ***Receiving aid:*** Freshmen: 2% (34); Undergraduates: 2% (135). ***Average award:*** Freshmen: $2009; Undergraduates: $647. ***Scholarships, grants, and awards by category:*** *Academic Interests/Achievement:* 395 awards ($731,187 total): biological sciences, business, communication, computer science, education, English, general academic interests/achievements, social sciences. ***Tuition waivers:*** Full or partial for employees or children of employees, senior citizens. ***ROTC:*** Army.

LOANS ***Student loans:*** $21,352,884 (53% need-based, 47% non-need-based). 70% of past graduating class borrowed through all loan programs. *Average indebtedness per student:* $18,505. ***Average need-based loan:*** Freshmen: $2590; Undergraduates: $3394. ***Parent loans:*** $6,458,600 (16% need-based, 84% non-need-based). ***Programs:*** FFEL (Subsidized and Unsubsidized Stafford, PLUS), Perkins, college/university, alternative loans.

WORK-STUDY ***Federal work-study:*** Total amount: $324,198; 198 jobs averaging $1637. ***State or other work-study/employment:*** Total amount: $700,000 (21% need-based, 79% non-need-based). 333 part-time jobs averaging $2102.

ATHLETIC AWARDS Total amount: $513,806 (48% need-based, 52% non-need-based).

APPLYING FOR FINANCIAL AID ***Required financial aid form:*** FAFSA. ***Financial aid deadline (priority):*** 3/15. ***Notification date:*** Continuous beginning 2/15. Students must reply within 2 weeks of notification.

CONTACT Mr. Peter D'Annibale, Director of Financial Aid and Scholarships, Shippensburg University of Pennsylvania, 1871 Old Main Drive, Shippensburg, PA 17257-2299, 717-477-1131 or toll-free 800-822-8028 (in-state). *Fax:* 717-477-4028. *E-mail:* finaid@ship.edu.

SHORTER COLLEGE

Rome, GA

ABOUT THE INSTITUTION Independent Baptist, coed. Awards: bachelor's degrees. 38 undergraduate majors. Total enrollment: 1,044. Undergraduates: 1,044. Freshmen: 302.

GIFT AID (NEED-BASED) ***Scholarships, grants, and awards:*** Federal Pell, FSEOG, private, college/university gift aid from institutional funds.

GIFT AID (NON-NEED-BASED) ***Scholarships, grants, and awards by category:*** *Academic Interests/Achievement:* English, foreign languages, general academic interests/achievements, religion/biblical studies. *Creative Arts/Performance:* art/fine arts, music, theater/drama. *Special Achievements/Activities:* religious involvement. *Special Characteristics:* children of faculty/staff, children of union members/company employees, local/state students, out-of-state students, religious affiliation, siblings of current students.

LOANS ***Programs:*** FFEL (Subsidized and Unsubsidized Stafford, PLUS), Perkins.

WORK-STUDY ***Federal work-study:*** Total amount: $146,085; 109 jobs averaging $1340. ***State or other work-study/employment:*** Total amount: $93,865 (4% need-based, 96% non-need-based). 78 part-time jobs averaging $1203.

APPLYING FOR FINANCIAL AID ***Required financial aid forms:*** FAFSA, institution's own form, state aid form.

CONTACT Mr. Jared Smith, Director of Financial Aid, Shorter College, 315 Shorter Avenue, Rome, GA 30165, 706-233-7227 or toll-free 800-868-6980. *Fax:* 706-233-7314. *E-mail:* phawkins@shorter.edu.

SH'OR YOSHUV RABBINICAL COLLEGE

Lawrence, NY

CONTACT Office of Financial Aid, Sh'or Yoshuv Rabbinical College, 1526 Central Avenue, Far Rockaway, NY 11691-4002, 718-327-2048.

SIENA COLLEGE

Loudonville, NY

CONTACT Mary K. Lawyer, Assistant Vice President for Financial Aid, Siena College, 515 Loudon Road, Loudonville, NY 12211-1462, 518-783-2427 or toll-free 888-AT-SIENA. *Fax:* 518-783-2410. *E-mail:* aid@siena.edu.

SIENA HEIGHTS UNIVERSITY

Adrian, MI

CONTACT Office of Financial Aid, Siena Heights University, 1247 East Siena Heights Drive, Adrian, MI 49221, 517-264-7130 or toll-free 800-521-0009.

SIERRA NEVADA COLLEGE

Incline Village, NV

CONTACT Dorothy Caruso, Director of Financial Aid, Sierra Nevada College, 999 Tahoe Boulevard, Incline Village, NV 89451, 775-831-1314 Ext. 4066 or toll-free 775-831-1314 (in-state). *Fax:* 775-831-1347. *E-mail:* dcaruso@sierranevada.edu.

SILICON VALLEY UNIVERSITY

San Jose, CA

CONTACT Financial Aid Office, Silicon Valley University, 3590 North First Street, Suite 320, San Jose, CA 95134, 408-435-8989.

SILVER LAKE COLLEGE

Manitowoc, WI

Tuition & fees: $18,288 **Average undergraduate aid package: $12,054**

ABOUT THE INSTITUTION Independent Roman Catholic, coed. Awards: associate, bachelor's, and master's degrees and post-bachelor's certificates. 24 undergraduate majors. Total enrollment: 939. Undergraduates: 628. Freshmen: 31. Federal methodology is used as a basis for awarding need-based institutional aid.

UNDERGRADUATE EXPENSES for 2007–08 ***Application fee:*** $35. ***Tuition:*** full-time $17,980; part-time $565 per credit.

FRESHMAN FINANCIAL AID (Fall 2006, est.) 29 applied for aid; of those 90% were deemed to have need. 100% of freshmen with need received aid; of those 27% had need fully met. ***Average percent of need met:*** 82% (excluding resources awarded to replace EFC). ***Average financial aid package:*** $14,873 (excluding resources awarded to replace EFC). 7% of all full-time freshmen had no need and received non-need-based gift aid.

UNDERGRADUATE FINANCIAL AID (Fall 2006, est.) 149 applied for aid; of those 91% were deemed to have need. 100% of undergraduates with need received aid; of those 18% had need fully met. ***Average percent of need met:*** 68% (excluding resources awarded to replace EFC). ***Average financial aid package:*** $12,054 (excluding resources awarded to replace EFC). 10% of all full-time undergraduates had no need and received non-need-based gift aid.

GIFT AID (NEED-BASED) ***Total amount:*** $1,286,400 (33% federal, 13% state, 51% institutional, 3% external sources). ***Receiving aid:*** Freshmen: 87% (26); All full-time undergraduates: 77% (130). ***Average award:*** Freshmen: $11,027; Undergraduates: $9215. ***Scholarships, grants, and awards:*** Federal Pell, FSEOG, state, private, college/university gift aid from institutional funds.

GIFT AID (NON-NEED-BASED) ***Total amount:*** $137,623 (8% federal, 87% institutional, 5% external sources). ***Receiving aid:*** Freshmen: 3% (1); Undergraduates: 4% (7). ***Average award:*** Freshmen: $5500; Undergraduates: $5444. ***Scholarships, grants, and awards by category:*** *Academic Interests/Achievement:* 60 awards ($213,583 total): general academic interests/achievements. *Creative Arts/Performance:* 17 awards ($27,500 total): applied art and design, art/fine arts, music. *Special Achievements/Activities:* 39 awards ($36,250 total): religious involvement. *Special Characteristics:* 11 awards ($20,800 total): international students, local/state students.

LOANS ***Student loans:*** $1,747,021 (83% need-based, 17% non-need-based). 71% of past graduating class borrowed through all loan programs. *Average indebtedness per student:* $19,116. ***Average need-based loan:*** Freshmen: $2533; Undergraduates: $3944. ***Parent loans:*** $111,571 (22% need-based, 78% non-need-based). ***Programs:*** FFEL (Subsidized and Unsubsidized Stafford, PLUS).

WORK-STUDY ***Federal work-study:*** Total amount: $117,058; 60 jobs averaging $1951.

ATHLETIC AWARDS Total amount: $51,000 (67% need-based, 33% non-need-based).

APPLYING FOR FINANCIAL AID ***Required financial aid form:*** FAFSA. ***Financial aid deadline (priority):*** 3/15. ***Notification date:*** Continuous beginning 3/15. Students must reply within 2 weeks of notification.

CONTACT Ms. Mickey Shea, Financial Aid Specialist, Silver Lake College, 2406 South Alverno Road, Manitowoc, WI 54220-9319, 920-686-6122 or toll-free 800-236-4752 Ext. 175 (in-state). *Fax:* 920-684-7082. *E-mail:* financialaid@silver.sl.edu.

SIMMONS COLLEGE

Boston, MA

Tuition & fees: $26,705 **Average undergraduate aid package: $14,473**

ABOUT THE INSTITUTION Independent, undergraduate: women only; graduate: coed. Awards: bachelor's, master's, and doctoral degrees and post-bachelor's and post-master's certificates. 52 undergraduate majors. Total enrollment: 4,849. Undergraduates: 2,009. Freshmen: 436. Federal methodology is used as a basis for awarding need-based institutional aid.

UNDERGRADUATE EXPENSES for 2006–07 ***Application fee:*** $35. ***Comprehensive fee:*** $37,415 includes full-time tuition ($25,914), mandatory fees ($791), and room and board ($10,710). Full-time tuition and fees vary according to course load. Room and board charges vary according to board plan. ***Part-time tuition:*** $809 per hour. Part-time tuition and fees vary according to course load. ***Payment plan:*** Installment.

FRESHMAN FINANCIAL AID (Fall 2006, est.) 349 applied for aid; of those 89% were deemed to have need. 99% of freshmen with need received aid; of those 6% had need fully met. ***Average percent of need met:*** 52% (excluding resources awarded to replace EFC). ***Average financial aid package:*** $14,638 (excluding resources awarded to replace EFC). 4% of all full-time freshmen had no need and received non-need-based gift aid.

UNDERGRADUATE FINANCIAL AID (Fall 2006, est.) 1,410 applied for aid; of those 90% were deemed to have need. 97% of undergraduates with need received aid; of those 3% had need fully met. ***Average percent of need met:*** 48% (excluding resources awarded to replace EFC). ***Average financial aid package:*** $14,473 (excluding resources awarded to replace EFC). 2% of all full-time undergraduates had no need and received non-need-based gift aid.

GIFT AID (NEED-BASED) ***Total amount:*** $16,310,055 (10% federal, 4% state, 86% institutional). ***Receiving aid:*** Freshmen: 59% (250); All full-time undergraduates: 61% (1,101). ***Average award:*** Freshmen: $8985; Undergraduates: $10,063. ***Scholarships, grants, and awards:*** Federal Pell, FSEOG, state, private, college/university gift aid from institutional funds.

GIFT AID (NON-NEED-BASED) ***Total amount:*** $3,969,417 (83% institutional, 17% external sources). ***Receiving aid:*** Freshmen: 29% (125); Undergraduates: 21% (371). ***Average award:*** Freshmen: $10,893; Undergraduates: $11,235. ***Scholarships, grants, and awards by category:*** *Academic Interests/Achievement:* 90 awards ($1,155,500 total): general academic interests/achievements. *Special Achievements/Activities:* 730 awards ($4,957,400 total): community service, general special achievements/activities. *Special Characteristics:* 66 awards ($126,000 total): children and siblings of alumni, general special characteristics. ***Tuition waivers:*** Full or partial for employees or children of employees, adult students, senior citizens. ***ROTC:*** Army cooperative.

LOANS ***Student loans:*** $14,629,033 (39% need-based, 61% non-need-based). 90% of past graduating class borrowed through all loan programs. *Average indebtedness per student:* $26,300. ***Average need-based loan:*** Freshmen: $2883; Undergraduates: $2838. ***Parent loans:*** $5,345,531 (100% non-need-based). ***Programs:*** FFEL (Subsidized and Unsubsidized Stafford, PLUS), Perkins, state, college/university.

WORK-STUDY ***Federal work-study:*** Total amount: $1,447,000; 451 jobs averaging $2500.

APPLYING FOR FINANCIAL AID ***Required financial aid form:*** FAFSA. ***Financial aid deadline (priority):*** 2/15. ***Notification date:*** Continuous beginning 3/15. Students must reply by 5/1 or within 4 weeks of notification.

CONTACT Diane M. Hallisey, Director of Student Financial Services, Simmons College, 300 The Fenway, Boston, MA 02115, 617-521-2001 or toll-free 800-345-8468 (out-of-state). *Fax:* 617-521-3195. *E-mail:* hallisey@simmons.edu.

SIMON'S ROCK COLLEGE OF BARD

Great Barrington, MA

CONTACT Ms. Ann Gitto Murtagh, Director of Financial Aid, Simon's Rock College of Bard, 84 Alford Road, Great Barrington, MA 01230-9702, 413-528-0771 or toll-free 800-235-7186. *Fax:* 413-528-7339. *E-mail:* agitto@simons-rock.edu.

SIMPSON COLLEGE

Indianola, IA

Tuition & fees: $23,596 **Average undergraduate aid package: $19,902**

ABOUT THE INSTITUTION Independent United Methodist, coed. Awards: bachelor's degrees. 50 undergraduate majors. Total enrollment: 2,060. Undergraduates: 2,031. Freshmen: 412. Federal methodology is used as a basis for awarding need-based institutional aid.

UNDERGRADUATE EXPENSES for 2007–08 ***Comprehensive fee:*** $30,251 includes full-time tuition ($23,251), mandatory fees ($345), and room and board ($6655). ***College room only:*** $3194. ***Part-time tuition:*** $265 per credit hour.

FRESHMAN FINANCIAL AID (Fall 2006, est.) 412 applied for aid; of those 85% were deemed to have need. 100% of freshmen with need received aid; of those 22% had need fully met. ***Average percent of need met:*** 87% (excluding resources awarded to replace EFC). ***Average financial aid package:*** $20,105 (excluding resources awarded to replace EFC). 15% of all full-time freshmen had no need and received non-need-based gift aid.

UNDERGRADUATE FINANCIAL AID (Fall 2006, est.) 1,522 applied for aid; of those 86% were deemed to have need. 100% of undergraduates with need received aid; of those 24% had need fully met. ***Average percent of need met:*** 85% (excluding resources awarded to replace EFC). ***Average financial aid package:*** $19,902 (excluding resources awarded to replace EFC). 14% of all full-time undergraduates had no need and received non-need-based gift aid.

GIFT AID (NEED-BASED) ***Total amount:*** $18,672,364 (8% federal, 18% state, 71% institutional, 3% external sources). ***Receiving aid:*** Freshmen: 85% (351); All full-time undergraduates: 86% (1,311). ***Average award:*** Freshmen: $15,121; Undergraduates: $13,526. ***Scholarships, grants, and awards:*** Federal Pell, FSEOG, state, private, college/university gift aid from institutional funds.

GIFT AID (NON-NEED-BASED) ***Total amount:*** $2,682,033 (1% federal, 1% state, 93% institutional, 5% external sources). ***Receiving aid:*** Freshmen: 11% (46); Undergraduates: 11% (165). ***Average award:*** Freshmen: $10,160; Undergraduates: $9594. ***Scholarships, grants, and awards by category:*** *Academic Interests/Achievement:* $5,703,949 total: general academic interests/achievements. *Creative Arts/Performance:* $605,769 total: art/fine arts, music, theater/drama. *Special Achievements/Activities:* $283,432 total: community service, leadership, religious involvement. *Special Characteristics:* $1,608,727 total: adult students, children and siblings of alumni, children of educators, children of faculty/staff, ethnic background, international students, members of minority groups, relatives of clergy, religious affiliation, siblings of current students, twins.

LOANS ***Student loans:*** $12,218,316 (64% need-based, 36% non-need-based). 89% of past graduating class borrowed through all loan programs. *Average indebtedness per student:* $24,644. ***Average need-based loan:*** Freshmen: $3176; Undergraduates: $3962. ***Parent loans:*** $1,550,722 (23% need-based, 77% non-need-based). ***Programs:*** FFEL (Subsidized and Unsubsidized Stafford, PLUS), Perkins, state, college/university, alternative loans.

WORK-STUDY ***Federal work-study:*** Total amount: $287,718; 598 jobs averaging $529. ***State or other work-study/employment:*** Total amount: $589,127 (38% need-based, 62% non-need-based). 814 part-time jobs averaging $727.

APPLYING FOR FINANCIAL AID ***Required financial aid form:*** FAFSA. ***Financial aid deadline:*** Continuous. ***Notification date:*** Continuous beginning 3/15. Students must reply by 5/1 or within 3 weeks of notification.

CONTACT Tracie Pavon, Assistant Vice President of Financial Aid, Simpson College, 701 North C Street, Indianola, IA 50125-1297, 515-961-1630 Ext. 1596 or toll-free 800-362-2454 (in-state), 800-362-2454 Ext. 1624 (out-of-state). *Fax:* 515-961-1300. *E-mail:* pavon@simpson.edu.

SIMPSON UNIVERSITY

Redding, CA

Tuition & fees: $18,600 **Average undergraduate aid package: $7750**

ABOUT THE INSTITUTION Independent religious, coed. Awards: associate, bachelor's, and master's degrees. 20 undergraduate majors. Total enrollment: 1,015. Undergraduates: 862. Freshmen: 164. Federal methodology is used as a basis for awarding need-based institutional aid.

UNDERGRADUATE EXPENSES for 2007–08 ***Application fee:*** $20. ***Comprehensive fee:*** $25,000 includes full-time tuition ($18,600) and room and board ($6400).

FRESHMAN FINANCIAL AID (Fall 2005) 143 applied for aid; of those 99% were deemed to have need. 100% of freshmen with need received aid; of those 23% had need fully met. ***Average percent of need met:*** 55% (excluding resources awarded to replace EFC). ***Average financial aid package:*** $9912 (excluding resources awarded to replace EFC). 13% of all full-time freshmen had no need and received non-need-based gift aid.

UNDERGRADUATE FINANCIAL AID (Fall 2005) 814 applied for aid; of those 98% were deemed to have need. 100% of undergraduates with need received aid; of those 14% had need fully met. ***Average percent of need met:*** 45% (excluding resources awarded to replace EFC). ***Average financial aid package:*** $7750 (excluding resources awarded to replace EFC). 5% of all full-time undergraduates had no need and received non-need-based gift aid.

GIFT AID (NEED-BASED) ***Total amount:*** $4,056,275 (30% federal, 59% state, 10% institutional, 1% external sources). ***Receiving aid:*** Freshmen: 87% (141); All full-time undergraduates: 78% (651). ***Average award:*** Freshmen: $10,240; Undergraduates: $8514. ***Scholarships, grants, and awards:*** Federal Pell, FSEOG, state, private, college/university gift aid from institutional funds.

GIFT AID (NON-NEED-BASED) ***Total amount:*** $3,449,714 (97% institutional, 3% external sources). ***Receiving aid:*** Freshmen: 87% (141); Undergraduates: 79% (659). ***Average award:*** Freshmen: $4000; Undergraduates: $2000. ***Scholarships, grants, and awards by category:*** *Academic Interests/Achievement:* general academic interests/achievements. *Creative Arts/Performance:* music. *Special Achievements/Activities:* leadership, religious involvement. *Special Characteristics:* children of faculty/staff, general special characteristics, members of minority groups, out-of-state students, relatives of clergy, religious affiliation, siblings of current students, spouses of current students.

LOANS ***Student loans:*** $5,217,413 (59% need-based, 41% non-need-based). 89% of past graduating class borrowed through all loan programs. *Average indebtedness per student:* $17,940. ***Average need-based loan:*** Freshmen: $2625; Undergraduates: $4200. ***Parent loans:*** $1,700,536 (100% non-need-based). ***Programs:*** FFEL (Subsidized and Unsubsidized Stafford, PLUS), Perkins, alternative loans.

WORK-STUDY ***Federal work-study:*** Total amount: $109,800; jobs available.

ATHLETIC AWARDS Total amount: $149,908 (100% non-need-based).

APPLYING FOR FINANCIAL AID ***Required financial aid forms:*** FAFSA, institution's own form, if selected for verification, additional forms such as income tax forms may be required. ***Financial aid deadline (priority):*** 3/2. ***Notification date:*** Continuous beginning 3/16. Students must reply within 3 weeks of notification.

CONTACT Mr. James Herberger, Director of Enrollment Management, Simpson University, 2211 College View Drive, Redding, CA 96003-8606, 530-224-5600 or toll-free 800-598-2493. *Fax:* 530-226-4870. *E-mail:* financialaid@simpsonunivieristy.edu.

SINTE GLESKA UNIVERSITY

Rosebud, SD

CONTACT Office of Financial Aid, Sinte Gleska University, PO Box 490, Rosebud, SD 57570-0490, 605-747-4258. *Fax:* 605-747-2098.

SKIDMORE COLLEGE

Saratoga Springs, NY

ABOUT THE INSTITUTION Independent, coed. Awards: bachelor's and master's degrees. 42 undergraduate majors. Total enrollment: 2,816. Undergraduates: 2,759. Freshmen: 672.

GIFT AID (NEED-BASED) ***Scholarships, grants, and awards:*** Federal Pell, FSEOG, state, college/university gift aid from institutional funds.

GIFT AID (NON-NEED-BASED) ***Scholarships, grants, and awards by category:*** *Academic Interests/Achievement:* biological sciences, computer science, mathematics, physical sciences. *Creative Arts/Performance:* music. *Special Characteristics:* children of faculty/staff.

LOANS ***Programs:*** FFEL (Subsidized and Unsubsidized Stafford, PLUS), Perkins.

WORK-STUDY ***Federal work-study:*** Total amount: $540,000; 500 jobs averaging $1080. ***State or other work-study/employment:*** Total amount: $520,000 (100% non-need-based). 650 part-time jobs averaging $800.

APPLYING FOR FINANCIAL AID ***Required financial aid forms:*** FAFSA, CSS Financial Aid PROFILE.

CONTACT Mr. Robert D. Shorb, Director of Student Aid and Family Finance, Skidmore College, 815 North Broadway, Saratoga Springs, NY 12866-1632, 518-580-5750 or toll-free 800-867-6007. *Fax:* 518-580-5752. *E-mail:* rshorb@skidmore.edu.

SLIPPERY ROCK UNIVERSITY OF PENNSYLVANIA

Slippery Rock, PA

Tuition & fees (PA res): $6363 **Average undergraduate aid package: $7546**

ABOUT THE INSTITUTION State-supported, coed. Awards: bachelor's, master's, and doctoral degrees and post-bachelor's certificates. 43 undergraduate majors. Total enrollment: 8,230. Undergraduates: 7,545. Freshmen: 1,432. Federal methodology is used as a basis for awarding need-based institutional aid.

UNDERGRADUATE EXPENSES for 2006–07 ***Application fee:*** $25. ***Tuition, state resident:*** full-time $5038; part-time $210 per credit hour. ***Tuition, nonresident:*** full-time $7558; part-time $525 per credit. ***Required fees:*** full-time $1325; $85 per credit or $295 per term part-time. Full-time tuition and fees vary according to course load and degree level. Part-time tuition and fees vary according to course load and degree level. ***College room and board:*** $4998; ***Room only:*** $2822. Room and board charges vary according to board plan, housing facility, and location. ***Payment plan:*** Installment.

FRESHMAN FINANCIAL AID (Fall 2006, est.) 1326 applied for aid; of those 73% were deemed to have need. 99% of freshmen with need received aid; of those 44% had need fully met. ***Average percent of need met:*** 66% (excluding resources awarded to replace EFC). ***Average financial aid package:*** $7136 (excluding resources awarded to replace EFC). 22% of all full-time freshmen had no need and received non-need-based gift aid.

UNDERGRADUATE FINANCIAL AID (Fall 2006, est.) 6,239 applied for aid; of those 75% were deemed to have need. 98% of undergraduates with need received aid; of those 46% had need fully met. ***Average percent of need met:*** 72% (excluding resources awarded to replace EFC). ***Average financial aid package:*** $7546 (excluding resources awarded to replace EFC). 18% of all full-time undergraduates had no need and received non-need-based gift aid.

GIFT AID (NEED-BASED) ***Total amount:*** $13,725,976 (41% federal, 55% state, 4% external sources). ***Receiving aid:*** Freshmen: 47% (666); All full-time undergraduates: 46% (3,229). ***Average award:*** Freshmen: $3268; Undergraduates: $3164. ***Scholarships, grants, and awards:*** Federal Pell, FSEOG, state, private, college/university gift aid from institutional funds.

GIFT AID (NON-NEED-BASED) ***Total amount:*** $3,914,599 (25% institutional, 75% external sources). ***Receiving aid:*** Freshmen: 27% (381); Undergraduates: 16% (1,117). ***Average award:*** Freshmen: $4909; Undergraduates: $5629. ***Scholarships, grants, and awards by category:*** *Academic Interests/Achievement:* biological sciences, business, communication, computer science, education, English, general academic interests/achievements, health fields, physical sciences, social sciences. *Creative Arts/Performance:* applied art and design, art/fine arts, dance, music, performing arts, theater/drama. *Special Achievements/Activities:* community service, general special achievements/activities, leadership. *Special Characteristics:* children and siblings of alumni, children of faculty/staff, children of union members/company employees, ethnic background, general special characteristics, local/state students, members of minority groups, out-of-state students, previous college experience. ***Tuition waivers:*** Full or partial for minority students, employees or children of employees, senior citizens. ***ROTC:*** Army.

LOANS ***Student loans:*** $31,129,136 (52% need-based, 48% non-need-based). 81% of past graduating class borrowed through all loan programs. *Average indebtedness per student:* $21,025. ***Average need-based loan:*** Freshmen: $2754; Undergraduates: $3448. ***Parent loans:*** $5,056,385 (100% non-need-based). ***Programs:*** FFEL (Subsidized and Unsubsidized Stafford, PLUS), Perkins.

WORK-STUDY ***Federal work-study:*** Total amount: $589,549; jobs available. ***State or other work-study/employment:*** Total amount: $1,590,378 (100% non-need-based). Part-time jobs available.

ATHLETIC AWARDS Total amount: $665,577 (100% non-need-based).

APPLYING FOR FINANCIAL AID ***Required financial aid form:*** FAFSA. ***Financial aid deadline (priority):*** 2/15. ***Notification date:*** Continuous beginning 6/1.

CONTACT Ms. Patty A. Hladio, Director of Financial Aid, Slippery Rock University of Pennsylvania, 1 Morrow Way, Slippery Rock, PA 16057, 724-738-2044 or toll-free 800-SRU-9111. *Fax:* 724-738-2922. *E-mail:* financial.aid@sru.edu.

SMITH COLLEGE

Northampton, MA

Tuition & fees: $32,558 **Average undergraduate aid package: $32,659**

ABOUT THE INSTITUTION Independent, undergraduate: women only; graduate: coed. Awards: bachelor's, master's, and doctoral degrees and post-bachelor's and post-master's certificates. 51 undergraduate majors. Total enrollment: 3,092. Undergraduates: 2,634. Freshmen: 674. Both federal and institutional methodology are used as a basis for awarding need-based institutional aid.

UNDERGRADUATE EXPENSES for 2006–07 ***Application fee:*** $60. ***Comprehensive fee:*** $43,438 includes full-time tuition ($32,320), mandatory fees ($238), and room and board ($10,880). ***Part-time tuition:*** $1010 per credit hour.

FRESHMAN FINANCIAL AID (Fall 2006, est.) 495 applied for aid; of those 80% were deemed to have need. 100% of freshmen with need received aid; of those 100% had need fully met. ***Average percent of need met:*** 100% (excluding resources awarded to replace EFC). ***Average financial aid package:*** $32,307 (excluding resources awarded to replace EFC). 9% of all full-time freshmen had no need and received non-need-based gift aid.

UNDERGRADUATE FINANCIAL AID (Fall 2006, est.) 2,011 applied for aid; of those 80% were deemed to have need. 100% of undergraduates with need received aid; of those 100% had need fully met. ***Average percent of need met:*** 100% (excluding resources awarded to replace EFC). ***Average financial aid package:*** $32,659 (excluding resources awarded to replace EFC). 7% of all full-time undergraduates had no need and received non-need-based gift aid.

GIFT AID (NEED-BASED) ***Total amount:*** $43,945,475 (6% federal, 2% state, 90% institutional, 2% external sources). ***Receiving aid:*** Freshmen: 59% (397); All full-time undergraduates: 59% (1,609). ***Average award:*** Freshmen: $28,223; Undergraduates: $26,372. ***Scholarships, grants, and awards:*** Federal Pell, FSEOG, state, college/university gift aid from institutional funds.

GIFT AID (NON-NEED-BASED) ***Total amount:*** $1,266,104 (63% institutional, 37% external sources). ***Receiving aid:*** Undergraduates: 6. ***Average award:*** Freshmen: $4792; Undergraduates: $4304. ***Scholarships, grants, and awards by category:*** *Academic Interests/Achievement:* 86 awards ($469,250 total): engineering/technologies, general academic interests/achievements. *Special Characteristics:* 13 awards ($147,301 total): local/state students. ***ROTC:*** Army cooperative, Air Force cooperative.

LOANS ***Student loans:*** $9,752,925 (84% need-based, 16% non-need-based). 71% of past graduating class borrowed through all loan programs. *Average indebtedness per student:* $19,760. ***Average need-based loan:*** Freshmen: $2834; Undergraduates: $4977. ***Parent loans:*** $6,335,427 (100% non-need-based). ***Programs:*** Federal Direct (Subsidized and Unsubsidized Stafford), FFEL (PLUS), Perkins, state, college/university.

WORK-STUDY ***Federal work-study:*** Total amount: $2,749,752; jobs available. ***State or other work-study/employment:*** Total amount: $575,877 (79% need-based, 21% non-need-based). 219 part-time jobs averaging $1961.

APPLYING FOR FINANCIAL AID ***Required financial aid forms:*** FAFSA, CSS Financial Aid PROFILE, noncustodial (divorced/separated) parent's statement, business/farm supplement. ***Financial aid deadline:*** 2/1. ***Notification date:*** 4/1.

CONTACT Deborah Luekens, Director of Student Financial Services, Smith College, College Hall, Northampton, MA 01063, 413-585-2530 or toll-free 800-383-3232. *Fax:* 413-585-2566. *E-mail:* sfs@smith.edu.

SOJOURNER-DOUGLASS COLLEGE

Baltimore, MD

Tuition & fees: $6748 **Average undergraduate aid package: $4130**

ABOUT THE INSTITUTION Independent, coed, primarily women. Awards: bachelor's and master's degrees (offers only evening and weekend programs). 18 undergraduate majors. Total enrollment: 1,124. Undergraduates: 1,060. Freshmen: 169. Federal methodology is used as a basis for awarding need-based institutional aid.

UNDERGRADUATE EXPENSES for 2006–07 ***Tuition:*** full-time $6540; part-time $363 per credit. ***Required fees:*** full-time $208; $104 per term part-time. Part-time tuition and fees vary according to course load. ***Payment plan:*** Installment.

FRESHMAN FINANCIAL AID (Fall 2005) 589 applied for aid; of those 90% were deemed to have need. 100% of freshmen with need received aid. ***Average percent of need met:*** 50% (excluding resources awarded to replace EFC). ***Average financial aid package:*** $2831 (excluding resources awarded to replace EFC). 46% of all full-time freshmen had no need and received non-need-based gift aid.

UNDERGRADUATE FINANCIAL AID (Fall 2005) 1,045 applied for aid; of those 97% were deemed to have need. 100% of undergraduates with need received aid. ***Average percent of need met:*** 50% (excluding resources awarded to replace EFC). ***Average financial aid package:*** $4130 (excluding resources awarded to replace EFC). 46% of all full-time undergraduates had no need and received non-need-based gift aid.

GIFT AID (NEED-BASED) ***Total amount:*** $3,312,169 (69% federal, 31% state). ***Receiving aid:*** Freshmen: 83% (488); All full-time undergraduates: 90% (939).

Average award: Freshmen: $2394; Undergraduates: $2394. ***Scholarships, grants, and awards:*** Federal Pell, FSEOG, state, college/university gift aid from institutional funds.

GIFT AID (NON-NEED-BASED) ***Total amount:*** $443,170 (100% institutional). ***Receiving aid:*** Freshmen: 50% (292); Undergraduates: 47% (486). ***Average award:*** Freshmen: $515; Undergraduates: $919. ***Tuition waivers:*** Full or partial for employees or children of employees.

LOANS ***Student loans:*** $5,952,500 (100% need-based). 70% of past graduating class borrowed through all loan programs. ***Average need-based loan:*** Freshmen: $2487; Undergraduates: $4783. ***Parent loans:*** $9300 (100% need-based). ***Programs:*** FFEL (Subsidized and Unsubsidized Stafford, PLUS), college/university.

WORK-STUDY ***Federal work-study:*** Total amount: $152,680; 29 jobs averaging $5222.

APPLYING FOR FINANCIAL AID ***Required financial aid forms:*** FAFSA, institution's own form. ***Financial aid deadline:*** Continuous.

CONTACT Ms. Rebecca Chalk, Financial Aid Director, Sojourner-Douglass College, 200 North Central Avenue, Baltimore, MD 21202, 410-276-0306 Ext. 258. *Fax:* 410-276-0148. *E-mail:* rchalk@host.sdc.edu.

SOKA UNIVERSITY OF AMERICA

Aliso Viejo, CA

CONTACT Financial Aid Office, Soka University of America, 1 University Drive, Aliso Viejo, CA 92656, 949-480-4000 or toll-free 949-480-4150 (in-state), 888-600-SOKA (out-of-state).

SONOMA STATE UNIVERSITY

Rohnert Park, CA

Tuition & fees (CA res): $3648 **Average undergraduate aid package: $9971**

ABOUT THE INSTITUTION State-supported, coed. Awards: bachelor's and master's degrees. 64 undergraduate majors. Total enrollment: 7,749. Undergraduates: 6,599. Freshmen: 1,053. Federal methodology is used as a basis for awarding need-based institutional aid.

UNDERGRADUATE EXPENSES for 2006–07 ***Application fee:*** $55. ***Tuition, state resident:*** full-time $0. ***Tuition, nonresident:*** full-time $10,170.

FRESHMAN FINANCIAL AID (Fall 2005) 455 applied for aid; of those 64% were deemed to have need. 93% of freshmen with need received aid; of those 26% had need fully met. ***Average percent of need met:*** 80% (excluding resources awarded to replace EFC). ***Average financial aid package:*** $9960 (excluding resources awarded to replace EFC). 8% of all full-time freshmen had no need and received non-need-based gift aid.

UNDERGRADUATE FINANCIAL AID (Fall 2005) 2,884 applied for aid; of those 76% were deemed to have need. 95% of undergraduates with need received aid; of those 25% had need fully met. ***Average percent of need met:*** 79% (excluding resources awarded to replace EFC). ***Average financial aid package:*** $9971 (excluding resources awarded to replace EFC). 3% of all full-time undergraduates had no need and received non-need-based gift aid.

GIFT AID (NEED-BASED) ***Total amount:*** $8,324,647 (45% federal, 55% state). ***Receiving aid:*** Freshmen: 12% (180); All full-time undergraduates: 23% (1,437). ***Average award:*** Freshmen: $6231; Undergraduates: $5100. ***Scholarships, grants, and awards:*** Federal Pell, FSEOG, state, private, college/university gift aid from institutional funds.

GIFT AID (NON-NEED-BASED) ***Total amount:*** $832,359 (12% state, 23% institutional, 65% external sources). ***Receiving aid:*** Freshmen: 7% (112); Undergraduates: 7% (440). ***Average award:*** Freshmen: $1692; Undergraduates: $1457. ***Scholarships, grants, and awards by category:*** *Academic Interests/Achievement:* 100 awards ($98,700 total): area/ethnic studies, biological sciences, business, communication, computer science, education, English, foreign languages, general academic interests/achievements, health fields, humanities, mathematics, physical sciences, premedicine, social sciences. *Creative Arts/Performance:* 30 awards ($34,150 total): applied art and design, art/fine arts, cinema/film/broadcasting, creative writing, dance, journalism/publications, music, performing arts, theater/drama. *Special Achievements/Activities:* 2 awards ($1250 total): community service, leadership, memberships. *Special Characteristics:* 51 awards ($59,150 total): adult students, children and siblings of alumni, children of educators, children of faculty/staff, children of public servants, children of union members/company employees, children of workers in trades, ethnic background, first-generation college students, general special characteristics, handicapped students, international students, local/state students, married students, members of minority groups, out-of-state students, previous college experience, veterans. ***ROTC:*** Army cooperative, Air Force cooperative.

LOANS ***Student loans:*** $11,894,695 (59% need-based, 41% non-need-based). 12% of past graduating class borrowed through all loan programs. *Average indebtedness per student:* $8210. ***Average need-based loan:*** Freshmen: $2352; Undergraduates: $3935. ***Parent loans:*** $6,633,961 (100% non-need-based). ***Programs:*** Federal Direct (Subsidized and Unsubsidized Stafford, PLUS), Perkins.

WORK-STUDY ***Federal work-study:*** Total amount: $434,821; 176 jobs averaging $2470. ***State or other work-study/employment:*** Total amount: $1,600,000 (100% non-need-based). 694 part-time jobs averaging $2305.

ATHLETIC AWARDS Total amount: $124,837 (100% non-need-based).

APPLYING FOR FINANCIAL AID ***Required financial aid form:*** FAFSA. ***Financial aid deadline (priority):*** 1/31. ***Notification date:*** Continuous beginning 3/15. Students must reply within 4 weeks of notification.

CONTACT Susan Gutierrez, Director of Financial Aid, Sonoma State University, 1801 East Cotati Avenue, Rohnert Park, CA 94928-3609, 707-664-2287. *Fax:* 707-664-4242. *E-mail:* susan.gutierrez@sonoma.edu.

SOUTH CAROLINA STATE UNIVERSITY

Orangeburg, SC

ABOUT THE INSTITUTION State-supported, coed. Awards: bachelor's, master's, and doctoral degrees and post-bachelor's and post-master's certificates. 49 undergraduate majors. Total enrollment: 4,384. Undergraduates: 3,839. Freshmen: 881.

GIFT AID (NEED-BASED) ***Scholarships, grants, and awards:*** Federal Pell, FSEOG, state, private, college/university gift aid from institutional funds.

GIFT AID (NON-NEED-BASED) ***Scholarships, grants, and awards by category:*** *Academic Interests/Achievement:* general academic interests/achievements. *Creative Arts/Performance:* music.

LOANS ***Programs:*** FFEL (Subsidized and Unsubsidized Stafford, PLUS), Perkins, college/university.

APPLYING FOR FINANCIAL AID ***Required financial aid form:*** FAFSA.

CONTACT Sandra S. Davis, Director of Financial Aid, South Carolina State University, 300 College Street Northeast, Orangeburg, SC 29117, 803-536-7067 or toll-free 800-260-5956. *Fax:* 803-536-8420. *E-mail:* sdavis@scsu.edu.

SOUTH DAKOTA SCHOOL OF MINES AND TECHNOLOGY

Rapid City, SD

ABOUT THE INSTITUTION State-supported, coed. Awards: associate, bachelor's, master's, and doctoral degrees. 17 undergraduate majors. Total enrollment: 2,124. Undergraduates: 1,870. Freshmen: 285.

GIFT AID (NEED-BASED) ***Scholarships, grants, and awards:*** Federal Pell, college/university gift aid from institutional funds, LEAP.

GIFT AID (NON-NEED-BASED) ***Scholarships, grants, and awards by category:*** *Academic Interests/Achievement:* computer science, engineering/technologies, mathematics.

LOANS ***Programs:*** FFEL (Subsidized and Unsubsidized Stafford, PLUS), Perkins.

APPLYING FOR FINANCIAL AID ***Required financial aid forms:*** FAFSA, freshmen scholarship application form.

CONTACT David W. Martin, Financial Aid Director, South Dakota School of Mines and Technology, 501 East Saint Joseph Street, Rapid City, SD 57701-3995, 605-394-2274 or toll-free 800-544-8162 Ext. 2414. *Fax:* 605-394-1268. *E-mail:* david.martin@sdsmt.edu.

SOUTH DAKOTA STATE UNIVERSITY

Brookings, SD

Tuition & fees (SD res): $5052 **Average undergraduate aid package: $7714**

ABOUT THE INSTITUTION State-supported, coed. Awards: associate, bachelor's, master's, doctoral, and first professional degrees and post-bachelor's and post-master's certificates. 80 undergraduate majors. Total enrollment: 11,303. Undergraduates: 9,897. Freshmen: 1,917. Federal methodology is used as a basis for awarding need-based institutional aid.

UNDERGRADUATE EXPENSES for 2006–07 ***Application fee:*** $20. ***Tuition, state resident:*** full-time $2382; part-time $79.40 per credit. ***Tuition, nonresident:*** full-time $3573; part-time $119.10 per credit. ***Required fees:*** full-time $2670; $89 per credit. Full-time tuition and fees vary according to course load, location, program, and reciprocity agreements. Part-time tuition and fees vary according to course load, location, program, and reciprocity agreements. ***College room and board:*** $5029; ***Room only:*** $2240. Room and board charges vary according to board plan and housing facility. Note: as of fall 2006, new non-resident freshman and transfer students will be paying less; 30 credits for these students will be $3573, or $119.10 per credit. Fees are the same for all students. ***Payment plans:*** Installment, deferred payment.

FRESHMAN FINANCIAL AID (Fall 2006, est.) 1562 applied for aid; of those 90% were deemed to have need. 100% of freshmen with need received aid; of those 71% had need fully met. ***Average percent of need met:*** 87% (excluding resources awarded to replace EFC). ***Average financial aid package:*** $6364 (excluding resources awarded to replace EFC). 22% of all full-time freshmen had no need and received non-need-based gift aid.

UNDERGRADUATE FINANCIAL AID (Fall 2006, est.) 6,570 applied for aid; of those 92% were deemed to have need. 100% of undergraduates with need received aid; of those 79% had need fully met. ***Average percent of need met:*** 84% (excluding resources awarded to replace EFC). ***Average financial aid package:*** $7714 (excluding resources awarded to replace EFC). 12% of all full-time undergraduates had no need and received non-need-based gift aid.

GIFT AID (NEED-BASED) ***Total amount:*** $13,572,094 (61% federal, 5% state, 23% institutional, 11% external sources). ***Receiving aid:*** Freshmen: 40% (729); All full-time undergraduates: 39% (3,092). ***Average award:*** Freshmen: $3312; Undergraduates: $3365. ***Scholarships, grants, and awards:*** Federal Pell, FSEOG, state, private, college/university gift aid from institutional funds, United Negro College Fund, Federal Nursing, Federal SMART grants and Fed Academic Compositeness Grants.

GIFT AID (NON-NEED-BASED) ***Total amount:*** $3,575,817 (16% federal, 12% state, 48% institutional, 24% external sources). ***Receiving aid:*** Freshmen: 57% (1,046); Undergraduates: 48% (3,809). ***Average award:*** Freshmen: $1816; Undergraduates: $1728. ***Scholarships, grants, and awards by category:*** *Academic Interests/Achievement:* 2,127 awards ($2,256,747 total): agriculture, area/ethnic studies, biological sciences, business, communication, computer science, education, engineering/technologies, English, foreign languages, general academic interests/achievements, health fields, home economics, humanities, international studies, mathematics, military science, physical sciences, premedicine, social sciences. *Creative Arts/Performance:* 261 awards ($224,721 total): art/fine arts, debating, general creative arts/performance, journalism/publications, music, performing arts, theater/drama. *Special Achievements/Activities:* 74 awards ($58,090 total): community service, general special achievements/activities, hobbies/interests, junior miss, leadership, memberships, rodeo. *Special Characteristics:* 145 awards ($209,380 total): adult students, children of faculty/staff, children of workers in trades, ethnic background, first-generation college students, general special characteristics, handicapped students, international students, members of minority groups, veterans, veterans' children. ***Tuition waivers:*** Full or partial for children of alumni, senior citizens. ***ROTC:*** Army, Air Force.

LOANS ***Student loans:*** $44,200,662 (59% need-based, 41% non-need-based). 81% of past graduating class borrowed through all loan programs. *Average indebtedness per student:* $20,682. ***Average need-based loan:*** Freshmen: $2914; Undergraduates: $4027. ***Parent loans:*** $3,400,633 (100% non-need-based). ***Programs:*** FFEL (Subsidized and Unsubsidized Stafford, PLUS), Perkins, Federal Nursing, college/university, Health Professions Loans.

WORK-STUDY ***Federal work-study:*** Total amount: $770,598; 659 jobs averaging $1019. ***State or other work-study/employment:*** Total amount: $2,999,949 (100% non-need-based). 2,180 part-time jobs averaging $1320.

ATHLETIC AWARDS Total amount: $1,795,277 (55% need-based, 45% non-need-based).

APPLYING FOR FINANCIAL AID ***Required financial aid form:*** FAFSA. ***Financial aid deadline (priority):*** 3/15. ***Notification date:*** Continuous beginning 4/1. Students must reply within 3 weeks of notification.

CONTACT Mr. Jay Larsen, Director of Financial Aid, South Dakota State University, Box 2201 ADM 106, Brookings, SD 57007, 605-688-4703 or toll-free 800-952-3541. *Fax:* 605-688-5882. *E-mail:* jay.larsen@sdstate.edu.

SOUTHEASTERN BAPTIST COLLEGE

Laurel, MS

CONTACT Financial Aid Officer, Southeastern Baptist College, 4229 Highway 15 North, Laurel, MS 39440-1096, 601-426-6346.

SOUTHEASTERN BAPTIST THEOLOGICAL SEMINARY

Wake Forest, NC

CONTACT H. Allan Moseley, Vice President of Student Services/Dean of Students, Southeastern Baptist Theological Seminary, PO Box 1889, Wake Forest, NC 27588, 919-556-3101 Ext. 306 or toll-free 800-284-6317. *Fax:* 919-556-0998. *E-mail:* deanofstudents@sebts.edu.

SOUTHEASTERN BIBLE COLLEGE

Birmingham, AL

ABOUT THE INSTITUTION Independent nondenominational, coed. Awards: bachelor's degrees (associate). 8 undergraduate majors. Total enrollment: 208. Undergraduates: 208. Freshmen: 60.

GIFT AID (NEED-BASED) ***Scholarships, grants, and awards:*** Federal Pell, FSEOG.

GIFT AID (NON-NEED-BASED) ***Scholarships, grants, and awards by category:*** *Academic Interests/Achievement:* general academic interests/achievements. *Creative Arts/Performance:* music. *Special Characteristics:* children of faculty/staff, local/state students, veterans.

LOANS ***Programs:*** FFEL (Subsidized and Unsubsidized Stafford, PLUS).

WORK-STUDY ***Federal work-study:*** Total amount: $15,000; 10 jobs averaging $1200. ***State or other work-study/employment:*** Total amount: $20,000 (100% non-need-based). 10 part-time jobs averaging $2000.

APPLYING FOR FINANCIAL AID ***Required financial aid forms:*** FAFSA, institution's own form, state aid form.

CONTACT Ms. Joanne Belin, Financial Aid Administrator, Southeastern Bible College, 2545 Valleydale Road, Birmingham, AL 35244, 205-970-9215 or toll-free 800-749-8878 (in-state). *E-mail:* jbelin@sebc.edu.

SOUTHEASTERN COLLEGE OF THE ASSEMBLIES OF GOD

Lakeland, FL

See Southeastern University.

SOUTHEASTERN LOUISIANA UNIVERSITY

Hammond, LA

Tuition & fees (LA res): $3423 **Average undergraduate aid package: $4317**

ABOUT THE INSTITUTION State-supported, coed. Awards: associate, bachelor's, and master's degrees. 48 undergraduate majors. Total enrollment: 15,118. Undergraduates: 13,552. Freshmen: 2,888. Federal methodology is used as a basis for awarding need-based institutional aid.

UNDERGRADUATE EXPENSES for 2006–07 ***Application fee:*** $20. ***Tuition, state resident:*** full-time $2216; part-time $92 per credit hour. ***Tuition, nonresident:*** full-time $7544; part-time $314 per credit hour. ***Required fees:*** full-time $1207; $50 per credit hour. Full-time tuition and fees vary according to course load. Part-time tuition and fees vary according to course load. ***College room and board:*** $5750; ***Room only:*** $3600. Room and board charges vary according to board plan and housing facility. ***Payment plans:*** Installment, deferred payment.

FRESHMAN FINANCIAL AID (Fall 2005) 1898 applied for aid; of those 68% were deemed to have need. 72% of freshmen with need received aid. ***Average financial aid package:*** $3886 (excluding resources awarded to replace EFC). 5% of all full-time freshmen had no need and received non-need-based gift aid.

UNDERGRADUATE FINANCIAL AID (Fall 2005) 9,322 applied for aid; of those 77% were deemed to have need. 91% of undergraduates with need received aid. ***Average financial aid package:*** $4317 (excluding resources awarded to replace EFC). 2% of all full-time undergraduates had no need and received non-need-based gift aid.

GIFT AID (NEED-BASED) ***Total amount:*** $15,297,745 (100% federal). ***Receiving aid:*** Freshmen: 33% (721); All full-time undergraduates: 37% (4,444). ***Average award:*** Freshmen: $2855; Undergraduates: $2888. ***Scholarships, grants, and awards:*** Federal Pell, FSEOG, state, private, college/university gift aid from institutional funds, Federal Nursing.

GIFT AID (NON-NEED-BASED) ***Total amount:*** $9,290,924 (79% state, 18% institutional, 3% external sources). ***Receiving aid:*** Freshmen: 26% (571); Undergraduates: 18% (2,146). ***Average award:*** Freshmen: $1528; Undergraduates: $1564. ***Scholarships, grants, and awards by category:*** *Academic Interests/Achievement:* 1,772 awards ($1,414,894 total): biological sciences, business, communication, computer science, education, engineering/technologies, English, foreign languages, general academic interests/achievements, health fields, home economics, humanities, international studies, library science, mathematics, physical sciences, premedicine, social sciences. *Creative Arts/Performance:* 285 awards ($222,250 total): art/fine arts, cinema/film/broadcasting, dance, debating, music. *Special Achievements/Activities:* 236 awards ($74,270 total): cheerleading/drum major, leadership, memberships, rodeo. *Special Characteristics:* 840 awards ($1,402,024 total): children of faculty/staff, handicapped students, out-of-state students, veterans' children. ***Tuition waivers:*** Full or partial for employees or children of employees, senior citizens. ***ROTC:*** Army cooperative.

LOANS ***Student loans:*** $37,782,753 (56% need-based, 44% non-need-based). 63% of past graduating class borrowed through all loan programs. *Average indebtedness per student:* $19,006. ***Average need-based loan:*** Freshmen: $2305; Undergraduates: $3281. ***Parent loans:*** $721,357 (100% non-need-based). ***Programs:*** FFEL (Subsidized and Unsubsidized Stafford, PLUS), Perkins, college/university.

WORK-STUDY ***Federal work-study:*** Total amount: $643,347; 526 jobs averaging $1223. ***State or other work-study/employment:*** Total amount: $1,569,702 (100% non-need-based). 1,136 part-time jobs averaging $1382.

ATHLETIC AWARDS Total amount: $1,200,551 (100% non-need-based).

APPLYING FOR FINANCIAL AID ***Required financial aid form:*** FAFSA. ***Financial aid deadline (priority):*** 5/1. ***Notification date:*** Continuous. Students must reply within 2 weeks of notification.

CONTACT Rosie Toney, Director of Financial Aid, Southeastern Louisiana University, SLU 10768, Hammond, LA 70402, 985-549-5309 or toll-free 800-222-7358. *Fax:* 985-549-5077. *E-mail:* finaid@selu.edu.

SOUTHEASTERN OKLAHOMA STATE UNIVERSITY

Durant, OK

Tuition & fees (OK res): $3574 **Average undergraduate aid package: $1368**

ABOUT THE INSTITUTION State-supported, coed. Awards: bachelor's and master's degrees and post-master's certificates. 54 undergraduate majors. Total enrollment: 3,872. Undergraduates: 3,533. Freshmen: 616. Federal methodology is used as a basis for awarding need-based institutional aid.

UNDERGRADUATE EXPENSES for 2006–07 ***Application fee:*** $20. ***Tuition, state resident:*** full-time $2897. ***Tuition, nonresident:*** full-time $8169. Full-time tuition and fees vary according to course level. Part-time tuition and fees vary according to course level and course load. ***College room and board:*** $5348; ***Room only:*** $2566.

FRESHMAN FINANCIAL AID (Fall 2005) 463 applied for aid; of those 97% were deemed to have need. 97% of freshmen with need received aid; of those 38% had need fully met. ***Average percent of need met:*** 63% (excluding resources awarded to replace EFC). ***Average financial aid package:*** $1086 (excluding resources awarded to replace EFC). 3% of all full-time freshmen had no need and received non-need-based gift aid.

UNDERGRADUATE FINANCIAL AID (Fall 2005) 1,640 applied for aid; of those 98% were deemed to have need. 96% of undergraduates with need received aid; of those 66% had need fully met. ***Average percent of need met:*** 66% (excluding resources awarded to replace EFC). ***Average financial aid package:*** $1368 (excluding resources awarded to replace EFC). 2% of all full-time undergraduates had no need and received non-need-based gift aid.

GIFT AID (NEED-BASED) ***Total amount:*** $5,196,090 (90% federal, 10% state). ***Receiving aid:*** Freshmen: 50% (264); All full-time undergraduates: 46% (985). ***Average award:*** Freshmen: $1254; Undergraduates: $1302. ***Scholarships, grants, and awards:*** Federal Pell, FSEOG, state, private, college/university gift aid from institutional funds.

GIFT AID (NON-NEED-BASED) ***Total amount:*** $1,926,161 (5% state, 12% institutional, 83% external sources). ***Receiving aid:*** Freshmen: 32% (171); Undergraduates: 21% (463). ***Average award:*** Freshmen: $950; Undergraduates: $1002. ***Scholarships, grants, and awards by category:*** *Academic Interests/Achievement:* 300 awards ($256,676 total): biological sciences, business, computer science, education, engineering/technologies, general academic interests/achievements, mathematics, physical sciences, social sciences. *Creative Arts/Performance:* 103 awards ($98,335 total): music, theater/drama. *Special Achievements/Activities:* 4 awards ($2678 total): cheerleading/drum major. *Special Characteristics:* 887 awards ($2,427,821 total): children and siblings of alumni, out-of-state students.

LOANS ***Student loans:*** $7,710,313 (73% need-based, 27% non-need-based). 35% of past graduating class borrowed through all loan programs. *Average indebtedness per student:* $6430. ***Average need-based loan:*** Freshmen: $1149; Undergraduates: $1986. ***Parent loans:*** $280,866 (100% non-need-based). ***Programs:*** FFEL (Subsidized and Unsubsidized Stafford, PLUS), Perkins, college/university.

WORK-STUDY ***Federal work-study:*** Total amount: $154,724; 301 jobs averaging $514. ***State or other work-study/employment:*** Total amount: $758,403 (100% non-need-based). 676 part-time jobs averaging $1121.

ATHLETIC AWARDS Total amount: $601,960 (100% non-need-based).

APPLYING FOR FINANCIAL AID ***Required financial aid forms:*** FAFSA, institution's own form. ***Financial aid deadline (priority):*** 3/1. ***Notification date:*** Continuous beginning 4/15. Students must reply within 2 weeks of notification.

CONTACT Sherry Foster, Director of Student Financial Aid, Southeastern Oklahoma State University, 1405 North 4th Avenue, PMB 4113, Durant, OK 74701-0609, 580-745-2186 or toll-free 800-435-1327. *Fax:* 580-745-7469. *E-mail:* sfoster@sosu.edu.

SOUTHEASTERN UNIVERSITY

Washington, DC

CONTACT Hope Gibbs, Assistant Director of Financial Aid, Southeastern University, 501 I Street, SW, Washington, DC 20024-2788, 202-488-8162 Ext. 234. *E-mail:* hgibbs@admin.seu.edu.

SOUTHEASTERN UNIVERSITY

Lakeland, FL

Tuition & fees: $13,480 **Average undergraduate aid package: $7079**

ABOUT THE INSTITUTION Independent religious, coed. Awards: bachelor's degrees. 23 undergraduate majors. Total enrollment: 2,901. Undergraduates: 2,810. Freshmen: 575. Federal methodology is used as a basis for awarding need-based institutional aid.

UNDERGRADUATE EXPENSES for 2007–08 ***Application fee:*** $40. ***Comprehensive fee:*** $19,910 includes full-time tuition ($13,000), mandatory fees ($480), and room and board ($6430). ***College room only:*** $3400. ***Part-time tuition:*** $515 per credit.

FRESHMAN FINANCIAL AID (Fall 2005) 496 applied for aid; of those 79% were deemed to have need. 96% of freshmen with need received aid; of those 12% had need fully met. ***Average percent of need met:*** 52% (excluding resources awarded to replace EFC). ***Average financial aid package:*** $6953 (excluding resources awarded to replace EFC). 29% of all full-time freshmen had no need and received non-need-based gift aid.

UNDERGRADUATE FINANCIAL AID (Fall 2005) 1,841 applied for aid; of those 81% were deemed to have need. 98% of undergraduates with need received aid; of those 11% had need fully met. ***Average percent of need met:*** 52% (excluding resources awarded to replace EFC). ***Average financial aid package:*** $7079 (excluding resources awarded to replace EFC). 26% of all full-time undergraduates had no need and received non-need-based gift aid.

GIFT AID (NEED-BASED) ***Total amount:*** $7,327,308 (27% federal, 43% state, 19% institutional, 11% external sources). ***Receiving aid:*** Freshmen: 59% (371); All full-time undergraduates: 63% (1,337). ***Average award:*** Freshmen: $5217; Undergraduates: $4966. ***Scholarships, grants, and awards:*** Federal Pell, FSEOG, state, private, college/university gift aid from institutional funds.

GIFT AID (NON-NEED-BASED) ***Total amount:*** $2,638,696 (53% state, 23% institutional, 24% external sources). ***Receiving aid:*** Freshmen: 6% (38); Undergraduates: 6% (131). ***Average award:*** Freshmen: $8815; Undergraduates: $9333. ***Scholarships, grants, and awards by category:*** *Academic Interests/*

Achievement: 744 awards ($1,281,106 total): communication, general academic interests/achievements, religion/biblical studies. *Creative Arts/Performance:* 151 awards ($200,881 total): journalism/publications, music, theater/drama. *Special Achievements/Activities:* religious involvement. *Special Characteristics:* 85 awards ($172,485 total): children of faculty/staff, general special characteristics, siblings of current students. ***ROTC:*** Army cooperative, Air Force cooperative.

LOANS ***Student loans:*** $12,384,005 (66% need-based, 34% non-need-based). 92% of past graduating class borrowed through all loan programs. *Average indebtedness per student:* $21,569. ***Average need-based loan:*** Freshmen: $2239; Undergraduates: $2981. ***Parent loans:*** $4,476,727 (37% need-based, 63% non-need-based). ***Programs:*** FFEL (Subsidized and Unsubsidized Stafford, PLUS), Perkins.

WORK-STUDY ***Federal work-study:*** Total amount: $126,923; 85 jobs averaging $1545.

APPLYING FOR FINANCIAL AID ***Required financial aid forms:*** FAFSA, institution's own form, state aid form, state aid form (for FL residents only). ***Financial aid deadline (priority):*** 4/15. ***Notification date:*** Continuous beginning 2/1. Students must reply by 5/1 or within 4 weeks of notification.

CONTACT Ms. Carol B. Bradley, Financial Aid Director, Southeastern University, 1000 Longfellow Boulevard, Lakeland, FL 33801-6099, 863-667-5000 or toll-free 800-500-8760. *Fax:* 863-667-5200. *E-mail:* cbradley@seuniversity.edu.

SOUTHEAST MISSOURI STATE UNIVERSITY

Cape Girardeau, MO

Tuition & fees (MO res): $5505   Average undergraduate aid package: $6522

ABOUT THE INSTITUTION State-supported, coed. Awards: associate, bachelor's, and master's degrees and post-master's certificates. 69 undergraduate majors. Total enrollment: 10,477. Undergraduates: 8,977. Freshmen: 1,518. Federal methodology is used as a basis for awarding need-based institutional aid.

UNDERGRADUATE EXPENSES for 2006–07 ***Application fee:*** $20. ***Tuition, state resident:*** full-time $5034; part-time $167.80 per credit hour. ***Tuition, nonresident:*** full-time $9159; part-time $305.30 per credit hour. ***Required fees:*** full-time $471; $15.70 per credit hour. Full-time tuition and fees vary according to course load and location. Part-time tuition and fees vary according to course load and location. ***College room and board:*** $5647; ***Room only:*** $3363. Room and board charges vary according to board plan and housing facility. ***Payment plans:*** Installment, deferred payment.

FRESHMAN FINANCIAL AID (Fall 2005) 1203 applied for aid; of those 71% were deemed to have need. 99% of freshmen with need received aid; of those 21% had need fully met. ***Average percent of need met:*** 62% (excluding resources awarded to replace EFC). ***Average financial aid package:*** $6132 (excluding resources awarded to replace EFC). 20% of all full-time freshmen had no need and received non-need-based gift aid.

UNDERGRADUATE FINANCIAL AID (Fall 2005) 4,797 applied for aid; of those 76% were deemed to have need. 99% of undergraduates with need received aid; of those 21% had need fully met. ***Average percent of need met:*** 65% (excluding resources awarded to replace EFC). ***Average financial aid package:*** $6522 (excluding resources awarded to replace EFC). 13% of all full-time undergraduates had no need and received non-need-based gift aid.

GIFT AID (NEED-BASED) ***Total amount:*** $11,640,422 (58% federal, 9% state, 28% institutional, 5% external sources). ***Receiving aid:*** Freshmen: 46% (713); All full-time undergraduates: 40% (2,680). ***Average award:*** Freshmen: $4316; Undergraduates: $4258. ***Scholarships, grants, and awards:*** Federal Pell, FSEOG, state, private, college/university gift aid from institutional funds.

GIFT AID (NON-NEED-BASED) ***Total amount:*** $4,814,246 (3% federal, 10% state, 76% institutional, 11% external sources). ***Receiving aid:*** Freshmen: 6% (87); Undergraduates: 3% (223). ***Average award:*** Freshmen: $3415; Undergraduates: $3790. ***Scholarships, grants, and awards by category:*** *Academic Interests/Achievement:* 858 awards ($2,983,799 total): agriculture, biological sciences, business, communication, computer science, education, English, foreign languages, general academic interests/achievements, health fields, home economics, humanities, international studies, mathematics, military science, physical sciences, premedicine, religion/biblical studies, social sciences. *Creative Arts/Performance:* 124 awards ($69,900 total): music, theater/drama. *Special Achievements/Activities:* 201 awards ($331,744 total): cheerleading/drum major, general special achievements/activities, leadership. *Special Characteristics:* 238 awards ($657,637 total): adult students, children of faculty/staff, first-generation college students, general special characteristics, international students, members of minority groups, out-of-state students, previous college experience. ***Tuition waivers:*** Full or partial for employees or children of employees, senior citizens. ***ROTC:*** Air Force.

LOANS ***Student loans:*** $25,006,661 (67% need-based, 33% non-need-based). 63% of past graduating class borrowed through all loan programs. *Average indebtedness per student:* $17,198. ***Average need-based loan:*** Freshmen: $2582; Undergraduates: $3664. ***Parent loans:*** $7,906,631 (19% need-based, 81% non-need-based). ***Programs:*** FFEL (Subsidized and Unsubsidized Stafford, PLUS), Perkins, state.

WORK-STUDY ***Federal work-study:*** Total amount: $320,713; 147 jobs averaging $2181. ***State or other work-study/employment:*** Total amount: $2,068,439 (20% need-based, 80% non-need-based). 910 part-time jobs averaging $2273.

ATHLETIC AWARDS Total amount: $2,139,434 (34% need-based, 66% non-need-based).

APPLYING FOR FINANCIAL AID ***Required financial aid form:*** FAFSA. ***Financial aid deadline (priority):*** 3/1. ***Notification date:*** Continuous beginning 4/1. Students must reply within 3 weeks of notification.

CONTACT Barbara Garner, Customer Service Supervisor, Southeast Missouri State University, One University Plaza, Cape Girardeau, MO 63701, 573-651-2840. *Fax:* 573-651-5006.

SOUTHERN ADVENTIST UNIVERSITY

Collegedale, TN

Tuition & fees: $15,596   Average undergraduate aid package: $14,965

ABOUT THE INSTITUTION Independent Seventh-day Adventist, coed. Awards: associate, bachelor's, and master's degrees. 62 undergraduate majors. Total enrollment: 2,593. Undergraduates: 2,451. Freshmen: 567. Federal methodology is used as a basis for awarding need-based institutional aid.

UNDERGRADUATE EXPENSES for 2007–08 ***Application fee:*** $25. ***Comprehensive fee:*** $20,330 includes full-time tuition ($15,086), mandatory fees ($510), and room and board ($4734). ***College room only:*** $2734. ***Part-time tuition:*** $638 per semester hour. ***Part-time fees:*** $255 per term.

FRESHMAN FINANCIAL AID (Fall 2005) 317 applied for aid; of those 76% were deemed to have need. 100% of freshmen with need received aid; of those 50% had need fully met. ***Average percent of need met:*** 85% (excluding resources awarded to replace EFC). ***Average financial aid package:*** $16,414 (excluding resources awarded to replace EFC). 11% of all full-time freshmen had no need and received non-need-based gift aid.

UNDERGRADUATE FINANCIAL AID (Fall 2005) 856 applied for aid; of those 84% were deemed to have need. 100% of undergraduates with need received aid; of those 45% had need fully met. ***Average percent of need met:*** 83% (excluding resources awarded to replace EFC). ***Average financial aid package:*** $14,965 (excluding resources awarded to replace EFC). 8% of all full-time undergraduates had no need and received non-need-based gift aid.

GIFT AID (NEED-BASED) ***Total amount:*** $4,160,764 (47% federal, 4% state, 49% institutional). ***Receiving aid:*** Freshmen: 33% (142); All full-time undergraduates: 25% (358). ***Average award:*** Freshmen: $4294; Undergraduates: $2318. ***Scholarships, grants, and awards:*** Federal Pell, FSEOG, state, private, college/university gift aid from institutional funds.

GIFT AID (NON-NEED-BASED) ***Total amount:*** $10,596,746 (1% federal, 5% state, 44% institutional, 50% external sources). ***Average award:*** Freshmen: $8043; Undergraduates: $3665. ***Scholarships, grants, and awards by category:*** *Academic Interests/Achievement:* 1,006 awards ($1,426,168 total): business, communication, education, English, general academic interests/achievements, health fields, mathematics, religion/biblical studies. *Creative Arts/Performance:* 156 awards ($159,556 total): art/fine arts, journalism/publications, music, theater/drama. *Special Achievements/Activities:* 320 awards ($175,719 total): community service, general special achievements/activities, leadership, religious involvement. *Special Characteristics:* 521 awards ($424,212 total): children and siblings of alumni, general special characteristics, international students, local/state students, members of minority groups, out-of-state students, siblings of current students, spouses of current students.

LOANS ***Student loans:*** $9,647,653 (47% need-based, 53% non-need-based). 67% of past graduating class borrowed through all loan programs. *Average indebtedness per student:* $10,935. ***Average need-based loan:*** Freshmen: $4644; Undergraduates: $6026. ***Parent loans:*** $1,439,829 (100% non-need-based). ***Programs:*** FFEL (Subsidized and Unsubsidized Stafford, PLUS), Perkins, Federal Nursing, college/university.

WORK-STUDY ***Federal work-study:*** Total amount: $1,221,284; 566 jobs averaging $2158. ***State or other work-study/employment:*** Part-time jobs available.

APPLYING FOR FINANCIAL AID ***Required financial aid form:*** FAFSA. ***Financial aid deadline (priority):*** 3/1. ***Notification date:*** Continuous beginning 2/15. Students must reply within 2 weeks of notification.

CONTACT Mr. Marc Grundy, Director of Student Finance Office, Southern Adventist University, PO Box 370, Collegedale, TN 37315-0370, 423-236-2875 or toll-free 800-768-8437. *Fax:* 423-236-1835.

SOUTHERN ARKANSAS UNIVERSITY–MAGNOLIA

Magnolia, AR

Tuition & fees (AR res): $4650 **Average undergraduate aid package: $4127**

ABOUT THE INSTITUTION State-supported, coed. Awards: associate, bachelor's, and master's degrees. 45 undergraduate majors. Total enrollment: 3,057. Undergraduates: 2,803. Freshmen: 651. Federal methodology is used as a basis for awarding need-based institutional aid.

UNDERGRADUATE EXPENSES for 2006–07 ***Tuition, state resident:*** full-time $4260; part-time $142 per credit hour. ***Tuition, nonresident:*** full-time $6450; part-time $249 per credit hour. ***Required fees:*** full-time $390; $390 per year part-time. ***College room and board:*** $3970; ***Room only:*** $2024.

FRESHMAN FINANCIAL AID (Fall 2006, est.) 371 applied for aid; of those 86% were deemed to have need. 98% of freshmen with need received aid; of those 82% had need fully met. ***Average percent of need met:*** 100% (excluding resources awarded to replace EFC). ***Average financial aid package:*** $1532 (excluding resources awarded to replace EFC). 16% of all full-time freshmen had no need and received non-need-based gift aid.

UNDERGRADUATE FINANCIAL AID (Fall 2006, est.) 1,762 applied for aid; of those 90% were deemed to have need. 97% of undergraduates with need received aid; of those 82% had need fully met. ***Average percent of need met:*** 100% (excluding resources awarded to replace EFC). ***Average financial aid package:*** $4127 (excluding resources awarded to replace EFC). 11% of all full-time undergraduates had no need and received non-need-based gift aid.

GIFT AID (NEED-BASED) ***Total amount:*** $4,995,614 (88% federal, 12% state). ***Receiving aid:*** Freshmen: 36% (209); All full-time undergraduates: 63% (1,470). ***Average award:*** Freshmen: $3210; Undergraduates: $3284. ***Scholarships, grants, and awards:*** Federal Pell, FSEOG, state, private, college/university gift aid from institutional funds.

GIFT AID (NON-NEED-BASED) ***Total amount:*** $4,080,435 (89% institutional, 11% external sources). ***Receiving aid:*** Freshmen: 50% (295); Undergraduates: 39% (919). ***Average award:*** Freshmen: $3901; Undergraduates: $4365. ***Scholarships, grants, and awards by category:*** *Academic Interests/Achievement:* 592 awards ($2,364,267 total): agriculture, business, computer science, education, English, foreign languages, general academic interests/achievements, health fields, mathematics, physical sciences, social sciences. *Creative Arts/Performance:* 28 awards ($63,285 total): art/fine arts, dance, music, theater/drama. *Special Achievements/Activities:* 51 awards ($116,711 total): cheerleading/drum major, leadership, rodeo. *Special Characteristics:* 493 awards ($841,562 total): adult students, children and siblings of alumni, children of faculty/staff, members of minority groups, out-of-state students.

LOANS ***Student loans:*** $7,475,652 (57% need-based, 43% non-need-based). 61% of past graduating class borrowed through all loan programs. *Average indebtedness per student:* $14,423. ***Average need-based loan:*** Freshmen: $2003; Undergraduates: $3187. ***Parent loans:*** $181,944 (100% non-need-based). ***Programs:*** FFEL (Subsidized and Unsubsidized Stafford, PLUS), Perkins.

WORK-STUDY ***Federal work-study:*** Total amount: $2,732,719; 1,090 jobs averaging $2407. ***State or other work-study/employment:*** Total amount: $1,178,965 (100% non-need-based). 429 part-time jobs averaging $2464.

ATHLETIC AWARDS Total amount: $659,303 (100% non-need-based).

APPLYING FOR FINANCIAL AID ***Required financial aid form:*** FAFSA. ***Financial aid deadline (priority):*** 7/1. ***Notification date:*** Continuous beginning 4/1. Students must reply within 2 weeks of notification.

CONTACT Ms. Bronwyn C. Sneed, Director of Student Aid, Southern Arkansas University–Magnolia, PO Box 9344, Magnolia, AR 71754-9344, 870-235-4023 or toll-free 800-332-7286 (in-state). *Fax:* 870-235-4913. *E-mail:* bcsneed@saumag.edu.

SOUTHERN BAPTIST THEOLOGICAL SEMINARY

Louisville, KY

Tuition & fees: N/R **Average undergraduate aid package: $335**

ABOUT THE INSTITUTION Independent Southern Baptist, coed. Awards: associate and bachelor's degrees. Total enrollment: 475. Undergraduates: 475. Institutional methodology is used as a basis for awarding need-based institutional aid.

UNDERGRADUATE FINANCIAL AID (Fall 2005) 76 applied for aid; of those 93% were deemed to have need. 100% of undergraduates with need received aid. ***Average percent of need met:*** 7% (excluding resources awarded to replace EFC). ***Average financial aid package:*** $335 (excluding resources awarded to replace EFC).

GIFT AID (NEED-BASED) ***Total amount:*** $275,101 (9% institutional, 91% external sources). ***Receiving aid:*** All full-time undergraduates: 13% (71). ***Average award:*** Undergraduates: $335. ***Scholarships, grants, and awards:*** state, private, college/university gift aid from institutional funds, all other sources aid as long as the school does not need to participate in Title IV program.

LOANS ***Student loans:*** $1,135,788 (100% need-based). 29% of past graduating class borrowed through all loan programs. *Average indebtedness per student:* $7281. ***Programs:*** college/university, Non-Title IV loan programs such as Sallie Mae "Signature" Loan and Nellie Mae "Excel" loan.

APPLYING FOR FINANCIAL AID ***Required financial aid forms:*** institution's own form, scholarship application form(s). ***Financial aid deadline (priority):*** 7/15. ***Notification date:*** 8/1.

CONTACT Mr. David Schrock, Supervisor of Student Life, Southern Baptist Theological Seminary, Financial Aid Office, 2825 Lexington Road, Louisville, KY 40280, 502-897-4206. *Fax:* 502-897-4031. *E-mail:* financialaid@sbts.edu.

SOUTHERN CALIFORNIA INSTITUTE OF ARCHITECTURE

Los Angeles, CA

ABOUT THE INSTITUTION Independent, coed. Awards: bachelor's, master's, and first professional degrees. 1 undergraduate major. Total enrollment: 438. Undergraduates: 232. Freshmen: 11.

GIFT AID (NEED-BASED) ***Scholarships, grants, and awards:*** Federal Pell, FSEOG, state, private, college/university gift aid from institutional funds.

GIFT AID (NON-NEED-BASED) ***Scholarships, grants, and awards by category:*** *Academic Interests/Achievement:* architecture.

LOANS ***Programs:*** FFEL (Subsidized and Unsubsidized Stafford, PLUS), alternative loans.

WORK-STUDY ***Federal work-study:*** Total amount: $125,852; jobs available (averaging $3000). ***State or other work-study/employment:*** Total amount: $11,386 (100% non-need-based). Part-time jobs available (averaging $3000).

APPLYING FOR FINANCIAL AID ***Required financial aid forms:*** FAFSA, institution's own form.

CONTACT Lina Johnson, Financial Aid Director, Southern California Institute of Architecture, 960 East 3rd Street, Los Angeles, CA 90013, 213-613-2200 Ext. 345 or toll-free 800-774-7242. *Fax:* 213-613-2260. *E-mail:* financialaid@sciarc.edu.

SOUTHERN CALIFORNIA SEMINARY

El Cajon, CA

CONTACT Financial Aid Office, Southern California Seminary, 2075 East Madison Avenue, El Cajon, CA 92019, 619-442-9841.

SOUTHERN CHRISTIAN UNIVERSITY

Montgomery, AL

See Regions University.

SOUTHERN CONNECTICUT STATE UNIVERSITY

New Haven, CT

Tuition & fees (CT res): $6591 **Average undergraduate aid package: $6986**

ABOUT THE INSTITUTION State-supported, coed. Awards: bachelor's, master's, and doctoral degrees and post-master's certificates. 39 undergraduate majors. Total enrollment: 12,326. Undergraduates: 8,577. Freshmen: 1,531. Federal methodology is used as a basis for awarding need-based institutional aid.

UNDERGRADUATE EXPENSES for 2007–08 ***Application fee:*** $50. ***Tuition, state resident:*** full-time $3346. ***Tuition, nonresident:*** full-time $10,831. ***College room and board:*** $8432; ***Room only:*** $4668.

FRESHMAN FINANCIAL AID (Fall 2006, est.) 1255 applied for aid; of those 63% were deemed to have need. 95% of freshmen with need received aid; of those 37% had need fully met. ***Average percent of need met:*** 80% (excluding resources awarded to replace EFC). ***Average financial aid package:*** $6930 (excluding resources awarded to replace EFC). 6% of all full-time freshmen had no need and received non-need-based gift aid.

UNDERGRADUATE FINANCIAL AID (Fall 2006, est.) 5,745 applied for aid; of those 61% were deemed to have need. 96% of undergraduates with need received aid; of those 40% had need fully met. ***Average percent of need met:*** 82% (excluding resources awarded to replace EFC). ***Average financial aid package:*** $6986 (excluding resources awarded to replace EFC). 4% of all full-time undergraduates had no need and received non-need-based gift aid.

GIFT AID (NEED-BASED) ***Total amount:*** $12,373,793 (39% federal, 22% state, 36% institutional, 3% external sources). ***Receiving aid:*** Freshmen: 32% (492); All full-time undergraduates: 33% (2,293). ***Average award:*** Freshmen: $5606; Undergraduates: $5085. ***Scholarships, grants, and awards:*** Federal Pell, FSEOG, state, college/university gift aid from institutional funds.

GIFT AID (NON-NEED-BASED) ***Total amount:*** $1,912,511 (1% federal, 1% state, 77% institutional, 21% external sources). ***Receiving aid:*** Freshmen: 13% (193); Undergraduates: 7% (514). ***Average award:*** Freshmen: $2642; Undergraduates: $2903. ***Scholarships, grants, and awards by category:*** *Special Characteristics:* children of faculty/staff, veterans. ***ROTC:*** Army cooperative, Air Force cooperative.

LOANS ***Student loans:*** $25,048,601 (86% need-based, 14% non-need-based). 58% of past graduating class borrowed through all loan programs. *Average indebtedness per student:* $15,197. ***Average need-based loan:*** Freshmen: $2859; Undergraduates: $3429. ***Parent loans:*** $9,738,711 (19% need-based, 81% non-need-based). ***Programs:*** FFEL (Subsidized and Unsubsidized Stafford, PLUS), Perkins.

WORK-STUDY ***Federal work-study:*** Total amount: $189,501; 139 jobs averaging $3086. ***State or other work-study/employment:*** 3 part-time jobs averaging $2589.

ATHLETIC AWARDS Total amount: $1,035,651 (35% need-based, 65% non-need-based).

APPLYING FOR FINANCIAL AID ***Required financial aid form:*** FAFSA. ***Financial aid deadline:*** 3/9. ***Notification date:*** Continuous beginning 3/9. Students must reply within 2 weeks of notification.

CONTACT Avon Dennis, Director of Financial Aid, Southern Connecticut State University, Wintergreen Building, 501 Crescent Street, New Haven, CT 06515-1355, 203-392-5448. *Fax:* 203-392-5229. *E-mail:* dennisa1@southernet.edu.

SOUTHERN ILLINOIS UNIVERSITY CARBONDALE

Carbondale, IL

Tuition & fees (IL res): $8071 **Average undergraduate aid package: $10,570**

ABOUT THE INSTITUTION State-supported, coed. Awards: associate, bachelor's, master's, doctoral, and first professional degrees and post-bachelor's and first professional certificates. 89 undergraduate majors. Total enrollment: 21,003. Undergraduates: 16,294. Freshmen: 2,380. Federal methodology is used as a basis for awarding need-based institutional aid.

UNDERGRADUATE EXPENSES for 2007–08 ***Application fee:*** $30. ***Tuition, state resident:*** full-time $5808; part-time $211.60 per semester hour. ***Tuition, nonresident:*** full-time $14,520; part-time $529 per semester hour. ***College room and board:*** $6666; ***Room only:*** $3650.

FRESHMAN FINANCIAL AID (Fall 2006, est.) 1907 applied for aid; of those 74% were deemed to have need. 98% of freshmen with need received aid; of those 87% had need fully met. ***Average percent of need met:*** 95% (excluding resources awarded to replace EFC). ***Average financial aid package:*** $10,608 (excluding resources awarded to replace EFC). 8% of all full-time freshmen had no need and received non-need-based gift aid.

UNDERGRADUATE FINANCIAL AID (Fall 2006, est.) 10,181 applied for aid; of those 81% were deemed to have need. 99% of undergraduates with need received aid; of those 88% had need fully met. ***Average percent of need met:*** 96% (excluding resources awarded to replace EFC). ***Average financial aid package:*** $10,570 (excluding resources awarded to replace EFC). 15% of all full-time undergraduates had no need and received non-need-based gift aid.

GIFT AID (NEED-BASED) ***Total amount:*** $39,114,106 (40% federal, 54% state, 5% institutional, 1% external sources). ***Receiving aid:*** Freshmen: 45% (1,055); All full-time undergraduates: 45% (6,444). ***Average award:*** Freshmen: $6381; Undergraduates: $5999. ***Scholarships, grants, and awards:*** Federal Pell, FSEOG, state, private, college/university gift aid from institutional funds.

GIFT AID (NON-NEED-BASED) ***Total amount:*** $17,307,648 (35% federal, 33% state, 24% institutional, 8% external sources). ***Receiving aid:*** Freshmen: 24% (567); Undergraduates: 27% (3,950). ***Average award:*** Freshmen: $5036; Undergraduates: $3063. ***Scholarships, grants, and awards by category:*** *Academic Interests/Achievement:* 3,428 awards ($7,224,042 total): agriculture, architecture, area/ethnic studies, biological sciences, business, communication, computer science, education, engineering/technologies, English, foreign languages, general academic interests/achievements, health fields, home economics, humanities, international studies, mathematics, military science, physical sciences, premedicine, religion/biblical studies, social sciences. *Creative Arts/Performance:* 160 awards ($610,348 total): applied art and design, art/fine arts, cinema/film/broadcasting, creative writing, dance, debating, general creative arts/performance, journalism/publications, music, performing arts, theater/drama. *Special Achievements/Activities:* 72 awards ($26,402 total): cheerleading/drum major, community service, general special achievements/activities, leadership. *Special Characteristics:* 190 awards ($306,693 total): children and siblings of alumni, children of educators, children of faculty/staff, children of public servants, children with a deceased or disabled parent, general special characteristics, handicapped students, international students, public servants, spouses of deceased or disabled public servants, veterans. ***ROTC:*** Army, Air Force.

LOANS ***Student loans:*** $53,495,727 (60% need-based, 40% non-need-based). 42% of past graduating class borrowed through all loan programs. *Average indebtedness per student:* $15,748. ***Average need-based loan:*** Freshmen: $3735; Undergraduates: $3942. ***Parent loans:*** $9,874,039 (10% need-based, 90% non-need-based). ***Programs:*** Federal Direct (Subsidized and Unsubsidized Stafford, PLUS), Perkins, college/university.

WORK-STUDY ***Federal work-study:*** Total amount: $2,174,000; 1,957 jobs averaging $1297. ***State or other work-study/employment:*** Total amount: $5,688,178 (12% need-based, 88% non-need-based). 4,390 part-time jobs averaging $1848.

ATHLETIC AWARDS Total amount: $2,884,762 (30% need-based, 70% non-need-based).

APPLYING FOR FINANCIAL AID ***Required financial aid form:*** FAFSA. ***Financial aid deadline (priority):*** 4/1. ***Notification date:*** Continuous. Students must reply within 3 weeks of notification.

CONTACT Billie Jo Hamilton, Director of Financial Aid, Southern Illinois University Carbondale, Woody Hall, Third Floor, B-Wing, Carbondale, IL 62901-4702, 618-453-3102. *Fax:* 618-453-4606. *E-mail:* hamilton@siu.edu.

SOUTHERN ILLINOIS UNIVERSITY EDWARDSVILLE

Edwardsville, IL

Tuition & fees (IL res): $7118 **Average undergraduate aid package: $9077**

ABOUT THE INSTITUTION State-supported, coed. Awards: bachelor's, master's, and first professional degrees and post-bachelor's, post-master's, and first professional certificates. 43 undergraduate majors. Total enrollment: 13,449. Undergraduates: 10,960. Freshmen: 1,794. Federal methodology is used as a basis for awarding need-based institutional aid.

UNDERGRADUATE EXPENSES for 2007–08 ***Application fee:*** $30. ***Tuition, state resident:*** full-time $5938. ***Tuition, nonresident:*** full-time $13,075. ***College room and board:*** $6500; ***Room only:*** $3970.

FRESHMAN FINANCIAL AID (Fall 2005) 1285 applied for aid; of those 69% were deemed to have need. 94% of freshmen with need received aid; of those 35% had need fully met. ***Average percent of need met:*** 79% (excluding resources awarded to replace EFC). ***Average financial aid package:*** $8945 (excluding resources awarded to replace EFC). 13% of all full-time freshmen had no need and received non-need-based gift aid.

UNDERGRADUATE FINANCIAL AID (Fall 2005) 6,414 applied for aid; of those 75% were deemed to have need. 96% of undergraduates with need received aid; of those 26% had need fully met. ***Average percent of need met:*** 76% (excluding resources awarded to replace EFC). ***Average financial aid package:*** $9077 (excluding resources awarded to replace EFC). 10% of all full-time undergraduates had no need and received non-need-based gift aid.

GIFT AID (NEED-BASED) ***Total amount:*** $19,954,712 (41% federal, 51% state, 4% institutional, 4% external sources). ***Receiving aid:*** Freshmen: 36% (616); All full-time undergraduates: 36% (3,373). ***Average award:*** Freshmen: $5543; Undergraduates: $5557. ***Scholarships, grants, and awards:*** Federal Pell, FSEOG, state, private, college/university gift aid from institutional funds, Federal Nursing.

GIFT AID (NON-NEED-BASED) ***Total amount:*** $2,765,312 (5% federal, 53% state, 20% institutional, 22% external sources). ***Receiving aid:*** Freshmen: 3% (53); Undergraduates: 2% (163). ***Average award:*** Freshmen: $3882; Undergraduates: $3923. ***Scholarships, grants, and awards by category:*** *Academic Interests/Achievement:* business, education, general academic interests/achievements, health fields. *Creative Arts/Performance:* art/fine arts, dance, music, theater/drama. *Special Characteristics:* children of faculty/staff. ***ROTC:*** Army, Air Force.

LOANS ***Student loans:*** $29,518,806 (61% need-based, 39% non-need-based). 20% of past graduating class borrowed through all loan programs. *Average indebtedness per student:* $17,491. ***Average need-based loan:*** Freshmen: $2876; Undergraduates: $3702. ***Parent loans:*** $4,956,172 (21% need-based, 79% non-need-based). ***Programs:*** Federal Direct (Subsidized and Unsubsidized Stafford, PLUS), FFEL (PLUS), Perkins, Federal Nursing, college/university, alternative loans.

WORK-STUDY ***Federal work-study:*** Total amount: $868,891; 507 jobs averaging $1713. ***State or other work-study/employment:*** Total amount: $11,019,894 (12% need-based, 88% non-need-based). 1,544 part-time jobs averaging $880.

ATHLETIC AWARDS Total amount: $340,283 (35% need-based, 65% non-need-based).

APPLYING FOR FINANCIAL AID ***Required financial aid form:*** FAFSA. ***Financial aid deadline (priority):*** 3/1. ***Notification date:*** Continuous beginning 3/15. Students must reply within 2 weeks of notification.

CONTACT Sharon Berry, Director of Financial Aid, Southern Illinois University Edwardsville, Campus Box 1060, Rendleman Hall, Room 2308, Edwardsville, IL 62026-1060, 618-650-3834 or toll-free 800-447-SIUE. *Fax:* 618-650-3885. *E-mail:* shaberr@siue.edu.

SOUTHERN METHODIST COLLEGE

Orangeburg, SC

Tuition & fees: $5800 **Average undergraduate aid package: $2025**

ABOUT THE INSTITUTION Independent religious, coed. Awards: associate and bachelor's degrees. 2 undergraduate majors. Total enrollment: 77. Undergraduates: 77. Freshmen: 5. Both federal and institutional methodology are used as a basis for awarding need-based institutional aid.

UNDERGRADUATE EXPENSES for 2006–07 ***Application fee:*** $25. ***Comprehensive fee:*** $10,200 includes full-time tuition ($5200), mandatory fees ($600), and room and board ($4400). Full-time tuition and fees vary according to class time and course load. Room and board charges vary according to housing facility. ***Part-time tuition:*** $220 per semester hour. ***Part-time fees:*** $25 per semester hour. Part-time tuition and fees vary according to class time and course load. ***Payment plan:*** Installment.

FRESHMAN FINANCIAL AID (Fall 2005) 26 applied for aid; of those 92% were deemed to have need. 100% of freshmen with need received aid. ***Average percent of need met:*** 92% (excluding resources awarded to replace EFC). ***Average financial aid package:*** $2025 (excluding resources awarded to replace EFC).

UNDERGRADUATE FINANCIAL AID (Fall 2005) 56 applied for aid; of those 100% were deemed to have need. 100% of undergraduates with need received aid. ***Average percent of need met:*** 75% (excluding resources awarded to replace EFC). ***Average financial aid package:*** $2025 (excluding resources awarded to replace EFC).

GIFT AID (NEED-BASED) ***Total amount:*** $18,040 (42% institutional, 58% external sources). ***Receiving aid:*** Freshmen: 24; All full-time undergraduates: 56. ***Average award:*** Freshmen: $2625; Undergraduates: $5000. ***Scholarships, grants, and awards:*** Federal Pell, FSEOG, private, college/university gift aid from institutional funds.

GIFT AID (NON-NEED-BASED) ***Receiving aid:*** Freshmen: 24. ***Scholarships, grants, and awards by category:*** *Academic Interests/Achievement:* $4000 total: education, religion/biblical studies. *Special Achievements/Activities:* $4600 total: religious involvement. *Special Characteristics:* 5,000 awards ($18,000 total): relatives of clergy. ***Tuition waivers:*** Full or partial for employees or children of employees.

LOANS ***Student loans:*** $189,631 (100% need-based). 77% of past graduating class borrowed through all loan programs. *Average indebtedness per student:* $12,600. ***Average need-based loan:*** Freshmen: $4000; Undergraduates: $4000. ***Programs:*** Federal Direct (Subsidized and Unsubsidized Stafford, PLUS).

WORK-STUDY ***Federal work-study:*** Total amount: $7622; 13 jobs averaging $562.

APPLYING FOR FINANCIAL AID ***Required financial aid forms:*** FAFSA, institution's own form. ***Financial aid deadline:*** 3/15. ***Notification date:*** Continuous beginning 4/5. Students must reply within 2 weeks of notification.

CONTACT Terry H. Lynch, Financial Aid Officer, Southern Methodist College, PO Box 1027, 541 Broughton Street, Orangeburg, SC 29116, 803-534-7826 Ext. 1326 or toll-free 800-360-1503. *Fax:* 803-534-7827. *E-mail:* tlynch@smcollege.edu.

SOUTHERN METHODIST UNIVERSITY

Dallas, TX

Tuition & fees: $30,880 **Average undergraduate aid package: $24,824**

ABOUT THE INSTITUTION Independent religious, coed. Awards: bachelor's, master's, doctoral, and first professional degrees and post-bachelor's certificates. 77 undergraduate majors. Total enrollment: 10,941. Undergraduates: 6,296. Freshmen: 1,371. Both federal and institutional methodology are used as a basis for awarding need-based institutional aid.

UNDERGRADUATE EXPENSES for 2007–08 ***Application fee:*** $60. ***Comprehensive fee:*** $41,705 includes full-time tuition ($27,400), mandatory fees ($3480), and room and board ($10,825). ***College room only:*** $6730. ***Part-time tuition:*** $1145 per credit hour. ***Part-time fees:*** $146 per credit hour.

FRESHMAN FINANCIAL AID (Fall 2006, est.) 600 applied for aid; of those 69% were deemed to have need. 100% of freshmen with need received aid; of those 46% had need fully met. ***Average percent of need met:*** 91% (excluding resources awarded to replace EFC). ***Average financial aid package:*** $25,764 (excluding resources awarded to replace EFC). 45% of all full-time freshmen had no need and received non-need-based gift aid.

UNDERGRADUATE FINANCIAL AID (Fall 2006, est.) 2,543 applied for aid; of those 82% were deemed to have need. 100% of undergraduates with need received aid; of those 38% had need fully met. ***Average percent of need met:*** 90% (excluding resources awarded to replace EFC). ***Average financial aid package:*** $24,824 (excluding resources awarded to replace EFC). 34% of all full-time undergraduates had no need and received non-need-based gift aid.

GIFT AID (NEED-BASED) ***Total amount:*** $37,003,947 (9% federal, 12% state, 78% institutional, 1% external sources). ***Receiving aid:*** Freshmen: 24% (323); All full-time undergraduates: 29% (1,732). ***Average award:*** Freshmen: $15,256; Undergraduates: $14,892. ***Scholarships, grants, and awards:*** Federal Pell, FSEOG, state, private, college/university gift aid from institutional funds.

GIFT AID (NON-NEED-BASED) ***Total amount:*** $16,081,628 (96% institutional, 4% external sources). ***Receiving aid:*** Freshmen: 25% (349); Undergraduates: 21% (1,221). ***Average award:*** Freshmen: $10,048; Undergraduates: $11,453. ***Scholarships, grants, and awards by category:*** *Academic Interests/Achievement:* area/ethnic studies, biological sciences, business, communication, computer science, engineering/technologies, English, foreign languages, general academic interests/achievements, humanities, international studies, mathematics, physical sciences, religion/biblical studies, social sciences. *Creative Arts/Performance:* art/fine arts, cinema/film/broadcasting, creative writing, dance, journalism/publications, music, theater/drama. *Special Achievements/Activities:* general special achievements/activities. *Special Characteristics:* children of faculty/staff, relatives of clergy. ***ROTC:*** Army, Air Force cooperative.

LOANS ***Student loans:*** $13,124,864 (64% need-based, 36% non-need-based). 47% of past graduating class borrowed through all loan programs. *Average indebtedness per student:* $17,424. ***Average need-based loan:*** Freshmen: $1968;

Undergraduates: $3191. ***Parent loans:*** $14,059,553 (30% need-based, 70% non-need-based). ***Programs:*** FFEL (Subsidized and Unsubsidized Stafford, PLUS), Perkins, state, college/university.

WORK-STUDY ***Federal work-study:*** Total amount: $3,183,932; 1,304 jobs averaging $2442. ***State or other work-study/employment:*** Total amount: $242,156 (45% need-based, 55% non-need-based). 46 part-time jobs averaging $2365.

ATHLETIC AWARDS Total amount: $8,284,408 (38% need-based, 62% non-need-based).

APPLYING FOR FINANCIAL AID ***Required financial aid forms:*** FAFSA, CSS Financial Aid PROFILE, noncustodial (divorced/separated) parent's statement, business/farm supplement. ***Financial aid deadline (priority):*** 2/15. ***Notification date:*** Continuous beginning 3/15.

CONTACT Marc Peterson, Director of Financial Aid, Southern Methodist University, PO Box 750181, Dallas, TX 75275, 214-768-3016 or toll-free 800-323-0672. *Fax:* 214-768-0202. *E-mail:* mpeterso@smu.edu.

SOUTHERN NAZARENE UNIVERSITY

Bethany, OK

Tuition & fees: $15,024 **Average undergraduate aid package: N/A**

ABOUT THE INSTITUTION Independent Nazarene, coed. Awards: associate, bachelor's, and master's degrees. 64 undergraduate majors. Total enrollment: 2,218. Undergraduates: 1,793. Freshmen: 284. Federal methodology is used as a basis for awarding need-based institutional aid.

UNDERGRADUATE EXPENSES for 2006–07 ***Application fee:*** $25. ***One-time required fee:*** $350. ***Comprehensive fee:*** $20,402 includes full-time tuition ($14,400), mandatory fees ($624), and room and board ($5378). ***College room only:*** $2458. ***Part-time tuition:*** $507 per credit hour. ***Part-time fees:*** $23 per credit hour.

FRESHMAN FINANCIAL AID (Fall 2006, est.) 275 applied for aid; of those 93% were deemed to have need. 96% of freshmen with need received aid.

UNDERGRADUATE FINANCIAL AID (Fall 2006, est.) 1,548 applied for aid; of those 94% were deemed to have need. 96% of undergraduates with need received aid.

GIFT AID (NEED-BASED) ***Total amount:*** $6,469,284 (26% federal, 9% state, 57% institutional, 8% external sources). ***Scholarships, grants, and awards:*** Federal Pell, FSEOG, state, private, college/university gift aid from institutional funds.

GIFT AID (NON-NEED-BASED) ***Scholarships, grants, and awards by category:*** *Academic Interests/Achievement:* biological sciences, business, communication, education, English, general academic interests/achievements, mathematics, religion/biblical studies. *Creative Arts/Performance:* music, performing arts. *Special Characteristics:* children and siblings of alumni, children of faculty/staff, local/state students, religious affiliation. ***ROTC:*** Army cooperative, Air Force cooperative.

LOANS ***Student loans:*** $13,535,553 (100% need-based). 75% of past graduating class borrowed through all loan programs. ***Parent loans:*** $2,579,654 (100% need-based). ***Programs:*** FFEL (Subsidized and Unsubsidized Stafford, PLUS), Perkins, alternative.

WORK-STUDY ***Federal work-study:*** Total amount: $193,000; 96 jobs averaging $2000. ***State or other work-study/employment:*** Total amount: $378,000 (100% need-based). 126 part-time jobs averaging $3000.

ATHLETIC AWARDS Total amount: $1,607,000 (100% need-based).

APPLYING FOR FINANCIAL AID ***Required financial aid forms:*** FAFSA, institution's own form. ***Financial aid deadline (priority):*** 3/1. ***Notification date:*** Continuous beginning 3/15. Students must reply within 2 weeks of notification.

CONTACT Director of Financial Assistance, Southern Nazarene University, 6729 Northwest 39th Expressway, Bethany, OK 73008, 405-491-6310 or toll-free 800-648-9899. *Fax:* 405-717-6271. *E-mail:* finaid@snu.edu.

SOUTHERN NEW HAMPSHIRE UNIVERSITY

Manchester, NH

Tuition & fees: $23,346 **Average undergraduate aid package: $14,302**

ABOUT THE INSTITUTION Independent, coed. Awards: associate, bachelor's, master's, and doctoral degrees and post-bachelor's certificates. 37 undergraduate majors. Total enrollment: 3,490. Undergraduates: 1,686. Freshmen: 484. Federal methodology is used as a basis for awarding need-based institutional aid.

UNDERGRADUATE EXPENSES for 2007–08 ***Application fee:*** $35. ***Comprehensive fee:*** $32,316 includes full-time tuition ($23,016), mandatory fees ($330), and room and board ($8970). ***College room only:*** $6400. ***Part-time tuition:*** $959 per credit.

FRESHMAN FINANCIAL AID (Fall 2006, est.) 409 applied for aid; of those 84% were deemed to have need. 100% of freshmen with need received aid; of those 5% had need fully met. ***Average percent of need met:*** 71% (excluding resources awarded to replace EFC). ***Average financial aid package:*** $15,320 (excluding resources awarded to replace EFC). 15% of all full-time freshmen had no need and received non-need-based gift aid.

UNDERGRADUATE FINANCIAL AID (Fall 2006, est.) 1,267 applied for aid; of those 87% were deemed to have need. 100% of undergraduates with need received aid; of those 6% had need fully met. ***Average percent of need met:*** 68% (excluding resources awarded to replace EFC). ***Average financial aid package:*** $14,302 (excluding resources awarded to replace EFC). 18% of all full-time undergraduates had no need and received non-need-based gift aid.

GIFT AID (NEED-BASED) ***Total amount:*** $10,238,336 (10% federal, 2% state, 85% institutional, 3% external sources). ***Receiving aid:*** Freshmen: 69% (333); All full-time undergraduates: 64% (1,056). ***Average award:*** Freshmen: $11,188; Undergraduates: $9607. ***Scholarships, grants, and awards:*** Federal Pell, FSEOG, state, private, college/university gift aid from institutional funds.

GIFT AID (NON-NEED-BASED) ***Total amount:*** $1,279,374 (94% institutional, 6% external sources). ***Receiving aid:*** Freshmen: 5% (22); Undergraduates: 4% (70). ***Average award:*** Freshmen: $4143; Undergraduates: $3476. ***Scholarships, grants, and awards by category:*** *Academic Interests/Achievement:* 528 awards ($2,075,313 total): general academic interests/achievements. *Special Achievements/Activities:* 389 awards ($418,750 total): leadership, memberships. *Special Characteristics:* 90 awards ($85,600 total): children and siblings of alumni, children of faculty/staff, general special characteristics, international students, local/state students, previous college experience, siblings of current students, veterans, veterans' children. ***ROTC:*** Army cooperative, Air Force cooperative.

LOANS ***Student loans:*** $13,307,974 (53% need-based, 47% non-need-based). ***Average need-based loan:*** Freshmen: $2652; Undergraduates: $3877. ***Parent loans:*** $4,452,020 (29% need-based, 71% non-need-based). ***Programs:*** FFEL (Subsidized and Unsubsidized Stafford, PLUS), Perkins.

WORK-STUDY ***Federal work-study:*** Total amount: $1,083,229; 568 jobs averaging $695.

ATHLETIC AWARDS Total amount: $1,468,553 (34% need-based, 66% non-need-based).

APPLYING FOR FINANCIAL AID ***Required financial aid form:*** FAFSA. ***Financial aid deadline (priority):*** 3/15. ***Notification date:*** Continuous beginning 3/1. Students must reply within 3 weeks of notification.

CONTACT Financial Aid Office, Southern New Hampshire University, 2500 North River Road, Manchester, NH 03106, 603-645-9645 or toll-free 800-642-4968. *Fax:* 603-645-9639. *E-mail:* finaid@snhu.edu.

SOUTHERN OREGON UNIVERSITY

Ashland, OR

Tuition & fees (OR res): $4986 **Average undergraduate aid package: $8196**

ABOUT THE INSTITUTION State-supported, coed. Awards: bachelor's and master's degrees and post-bachelor's certificates. 40 undergraduate majors. Total enrollment: 4,675. Undergraduates: 4,130. Freshmen: 762. Federal methodology is used as a basis for awarding need-based institutional aid.

UNDERGRADUATE EXPENSES for 2006–07 ***Application fee:*** $50. ***Tuition, state resident:*** full-time $4986; part-time $108 per credit. ***Tuition, nonresident:*** full-time $14,691; part-time $108 per credit. ***Required fees:*** $25 per credit. ***College room and board:*** $6468.

FRESHMAN FINANCIAL AID (Fall 2006, est.) 510 applied for aid; of those 76% were deemed to have need. 100% of freshmen with need received aid; of those 17% had need fully met. ***Average percent of need met:*** 66% (excluding resources awarded to replace EFC). ***Average financial aid package:*** $7606 (excluding resources awarded to replace EFC). 18% of all full-time freshmen had no need and received non-need-based gift aid.

UNDERGRADUATE FINANCIAL AID (Fall 2006, est.) 2,313 applied for aid; of those 85% were deemed to have need. 100% of undergraduates with need received aid; of those 14% had need fully met. ***Average percent of need met:*** 65% (excluding resources awarded to replace EFC). ***Average financial aid package:*** $8196 (excluding resources awarded to replace EFC). 10% of all full-time undergraduates had no need and received non-need-based gift aid.

GIFT AID (NEED-BASED) ***Total amount:*** $8,429,390 (52% federal, 13% state, 23% institutional, 12% external sources). ***Receiving aid:*** Freshmen: 47% (337); All full-time undergraduates: 48% (1,615). ***Average award:*** Freshmen: $6440; Undergraduates: $5781. ***Scholarships, grants, and awards:*** Federal Pell, FSEOG, state, private, college/university gift aid from institutional funds.

GIFT AID (NON-NEED-BASED) ***Total amount:*** $1,230,528 (79% institutional, 21% external sources). ***Receiving aid:*** Freshmen: 6% (42); Undergraduates: 3% (109). ***Average award:*** Freshmen: $9313; Undergraduates: $9437. ***Scholarships, grants, and awards by category:*** *Academic Interests/Achievement:* 529 awards ($809,649 total): biological sciences, business, education, English, foreign languages, general academic interests/achievements, health fields, mathematics, physical sciences, social sciences. *Creative Arts/Performance:* 53 awards ($35,072 total): art/fine arts, creative writing, journalism/publications, music, theater/drama. *Special Achievements/Activities:* 9 awards ($13,424 total): community service, general special achievements/activities, hobbies/interests, leadership, memberships. *Special Characteristics:* 95 awards ($406,715 total): adult students, international students, members of minority groups.

LOANS ***Student loans:*** $13,030,512 (81% need-based, 19% non-need-based). 70% of past graduating class borrowed through all loan programs. *Average indebtedness per student:* $22,851. ***Average need-based loan:*** Freshmen: $2376; Undergraduates: $3673. ***Parent loans:*** $5,154,240 (32% need-based, 68% non-need-based). ***Programs:*** Federal Direct (Subsidized and Unsubsidized Stafford, PLUS), Perkins, state, college/university.

WORK-STUDY ***Federal work-study:*** Total amount: $650,874; 566 jobs averaging $1339.

ATHLETIC AWARDS Total amount: $241,221 (67% need-based, 33% non-need-based).

APPLYING FOR FINANCIAL AID ***Required financial aid form:*** FAFSA. ***Financial aid deadline (priority):*** 3/1. ***Notification date:*** Continuous beginning 4/1. Students must reply within 2 weeks of notification.

CONTACT Peg Blake, Associate Director of Financial Aid, Southern Oregon University, 1250 Siskiyou Boulevard, Ashland, OR 97520, 541-552-6754 or toll-free 800-482-7672 (in-state). *Fax:* 541-552-6035. *E-mail:* blakep@sou.edu.

SOUTHERN POLYTECHNIC STATE UNIVERSITY

Marietta, GA

Tuition & fees (GA res): $3348 **Average undergraduate aid package: $2710**

ABOUT THE INSTITUTION State-supported, coed. Awards: associate, bachelor's, and master's degrees and post-bachelor's certificates. 23 undergraduate majors. Total enrollment: 4,206. Undergraduates: 3,680. Freshmen: 450. Federal methodology is used as a basis for awarding need-based institutional aid.

UNDERGRADUATE EXPENSES for 2006–07 ***Application fee:*** $20. ***Tuition, state resident:*** full-time $2780; part-time $117 per credit hour. ***Tuition, nonresident:*** full-time $11,115; part-time $468 per credit hour. ***Required fees:*** full-time $568; $284 per term part-time. Full-time tuition and fees vary according to course load and student level. Part-time tuition and fees vary according to course load. ***College room and board:*** $5610; ***Room only:*** $3210. Room and board charges vary according to board plan, housing facility, and student level. ***Payment plan:*** Guaranteed tuition.

FRESHMAN FINANCIAL AID (Fall 2005) 328 applied for aid; of those 64% were deemed to have need. 98% of freshmen with need received aid; of those 35% had need fully met. ***Average percent of need met:*** 76% (excluding resources awarded to replace EFC). ***Average financial aid package:*** $2207 (excluding resources awarded to replace EFC). 1% of all full-time freshmen had no need and received non-need-based gift aid.

UNDERGRADUATE FINANCIAL AID (Fall 2005) 1,885 applied for aid; of those 76% were deemed to have need. 96% of undergraduates with need received aid; of those 55% had need fully met. ***Average percent of need met:*** 71% (excluding resources awarded to replace EFC). ***Average financial aid package:*** $2710 (excluding resources awarded to replace EFC). 1% of all full-time undergraduates had no need and received non-need-based gift aid.

GIFT AID (NEED-BASED) ***Total amount:*** $2,245,998 (94% federal, 6% external sources). ***Receiving aid:*** Freshmen: 22% (103); All full-time undergraduates: 25% (795). ***Average award:*** Freshmen: $2367; Undergraduates: $2437. ***Scholarships, grants, and awards:*** Federal Pell, FSEOG, state, private, college/university gift aid from institutional funds.

GIFT AID (NON-NEED-BASED) ***Total amount:*** $3,355,326 (94% state, 6% external sources). ***Receiving aid:*** Freshmen: 42% (194); Undergraduates: 31% (990). ***Average award:*** Freshmen: $1800; Undergraduates: $3445. ***Tuition waivers:*** Full or partial for senior citizens. ***ROTC:*** Army cooperative, Naval cooperative, Air Force cooperative.

LOANS ***Student loans:*** $6,970,950 (52% need-based, 48% non-need-based). 50% of past graduating class borrowed through all loan programs. *Average indebtedness per student:* $28,364. ***Average need-based loan:*** Freshmen: $2375; Undergraduates: $3306. ***Parent loans:*** $616,719 (100% non-need-based). ***Programs:*** FFEL (Subsidized and Unsubsidized Stafford, PLUS), state.

WORK-STUDY ***Federal work-study:*** Total amount: $149,467; 17 jobs averaging $3239.

ATHLETIC AWARDS Total amount: $190,131 (100% non-need-based).

APPLYING FOR FINANCIAL AID ***Required financial aid form:*** FAFSA. ***Financial aid deadline (priority):*** 3/15. ***Notification date:*** Continuous beginning 6/1. Students must reply by 8/15.

CONTACT Gary W. Bush, Director of Financial Aid, Southern Polytechnic State University, 1100 South Marietta Parkway, Marietta, GA 30060-2896, 678-915-7290 or toll-free 800-635-3204. *Fax:* 678-915-4227. *E-mail:* gbush@spsu.edu.

SOUTHERN UNIVERSITY AND AGRICULTURAL AND MECHANICAL COLLEGE

Baton Rouge, LA

ABOUT THE INSTITUTION State-supported, coed. Awards: associate, bachelor's, master's, and doctoral degrees and post-master's certificates. 65 undergraduate majors. Total enrollment: 8,619. Undergraduates: 7,331. Freshmen: 1,140.

GIFT AID (NEED-BASED) ***Scholarships, grants, and awards:*** Federal Pell, FSEOG, state, private, college/university gift aid from institutional funds, Federal work study, LEAP, TOPS, and T.H. Harris.

GIFT AID (NON-NEED-BASED) ***Scholarships, grants, and awards by category:*** *Academic Interests/Achievement:* general academic interests/achievements.

LOANS ***Programs:*** Federal Direct (Subsidized and Unsubsidized Stafford, PLUS), FFEL (Subsidized and Unsubsidized Stafford, PLUS), college/university.

WORK-STUDY ***Federal work-study:*** Total amount: $559,748; 900 jobs averaging $1800. ***State or other work-study/employment:*** Total amount: $268,286 (100% need-based). 300 part-time jobs averaging $2500.

APPLYING FOR FINANCIAL AID ***Required financial aid forms:*** FAFSA, institution's own form.

CONTACT Mr. Phillip Rodgers Sr., Director of Financial Aid, Southern University and Agricultural and Mechanical College, PO Box 9961, Baton Rouge, LA 70813, 225-771-2790 or toll-free 800-256-1531. *Fax:* 225-771-5898. *E-mail:* phillip_rodgers@cxs.subr.edu.

SOUTHERN UNIVERSITY AT NEW ORLEANS

New Orleans, LA

CONTACT Director of Financial Aid, Southern University at New Orleans, 6400 Press Drive, New Orleans, LA 70126, 504-286-5263. *Fax:* 504-286-5213.

SOUTHERN UTAH UNIVERSITY

Cedar City, UT

Tuition & fees (UT res): $4068 **Average undergraduate aid package: $5471**

ABOUT THE INSTITUTION State-supported, coed. Awards: associate, bachelor's, and master's degrees. 49 undergraduate majors. Total enrollment: 7,029. Undergraduates: 6,601. Freshmen: 1,269. Federal methodology is used as a basis for awarding need-based institutional aid.

UNDERGRADUATE EXPENSES for 2006–07 ***Application fee:*** $40. ***Tuition, state resident:*** full-time $3,564. ***Tuition, nonresident:*** full-time $10,602. Part-time tuition and fees vary according to course load. ***College room and board:*** $4154. Room and board charges vary according to board plan and housing facility. ***Payment plan:*** Installment.

FRESHMAN FINANCIAL AID (Fall 2005) 637 applied for aid; of those 78% were deemed to have need. 99% of freshmen with need received aid; of those 12% had need fully met. ***Average percent of need met:*** 67% (excluding resources awarded to replace EFC). ***Average financial aid package:*** $4710 (excluding resources awarded to replace EFC). 44% of all full-time freshmen had no need and received non-need-based gift aid.

UNDERGRADUATE FINANCIAL AID (Fall 2005) 3,122 applied for aid; of those 89% were deemed to have need. 99% of undergraduates with need received aid; of those 9% had need fully met. ***Average percent of need met:*** 69% (excluding resources awarded to replace EFC). ***Average financial aid package:*** $5471 (excluding resources awarded to replace EFC). 28% of all full-time undergraduates had no need and received non-need-based gift aid.

GIFT AID (NEED-BASED) ***Total amount:*** $8,620,757 (79% federal, 2% state, 10% institutional, 9% external sources). ***Receiving aid:*** Freshmen: 48% (492); All full-time undergraduates: 64% (2,733). ***Average award:*** Freshmen: $4075; Undergraduates: $3790. ***Scholarships, grants, and awards:*** Federal Pell, FSEOG, state, private, college/university gift aid from institutional funds.

GIFT AID (NON-NEED-BASED) ***Average award:*** Freshmen: $3813; Undergraduates: $3530. ***Scholarships, grants, and awards by category:*** *Academic Interests/Achievement:* business, communication, education, general academic interests/achievements. *Creative Arts/Performance:* dance, general creative arts/performance, journalism/publications, music, performing arts, theater/drama. *Special Achievements/Activities:* cheerleading/drum major, general special achievements/activities, leadership. *Special Characteristics:* ethnic background. ***Tuition waivers:*** Full or partial for employees or children of employees. ***ROTC:*** Army.

LOANS ***Student loans:*** $8,605,314 (80% need-based, 20% non-need-based). 35% of past graduating class borrowed through all loan programs. *Average indebtedness per student:* $9223. ***Average need-based loan:*** Freshmen: $2118; Undergraduates: $3571. ***Parent loans:*** $420,572 (100% non-need-based). ***Programs:*** FFEL (Subsidized and Unsubsidized Stafford, PLUS), Perkins, college/university.

WORK-STUDY ***Federal work-study:*** Total amount: $284,347; jobs available. ***State or other work-study/employment:*** Total amount: $147,723 (100% need-based). Part-time jobs available.

ATHLETIC AWARDS Total amount: $1,115,332 (100% non-need-based).

APPLYING FOR FINANCIAL AID ***Required financial aid forms:*** FAFSA, institution's own form. ***Financial aid deadline:*** Continuous. ***Notification date:*** 2/1.

CONTACT Paul Morris, Director of Financial Aid, Southern Utah University, 351 West Center Street, Cedar City, UT 84720-2498, 435-586-7734. *Fax:* 435-586-7736. *E-mail:* morris@suu.edu.

SOUTHERN VERMONT COLLEGE

Bennington, VT

Tuition & fees: $15,100 **Average undergraduate aid package: $12,689**

ABOUT THE INSTITUTION Independent, coed. Awards: associate and bachelor's degrees. 14 undergraduate majors. Total enrollment: 390. Undergraduates: 390. Freshmen: 74. Both federal and institutional methodology are used as a basis for awarding need-based institutional aid.

UNDERGRADUATE EXPENSES for 2006–07 ***Application fee:*** $30. ***Comprehensive fee:*** $22,450 includes full-time tuition ($15,100) and room and board ($7350). ***College room only:*** $3400. Room and board charges vary according to board plan. ***Part-time tuition:*** $420 per credit. ***Payment plan:*** Installment.

FRESHMAN FINANCIAL AID (Fall 2006, est.) 95 applied for aid; of those 85% were deemed to have need. 100% of freshmen with need received aid; of those 10% had need fully met. ***Average percent of need met:*** 71% (excluding resources awarded to replace EFC). ***Average financial aid package:*** $14,074 (excluding resources awarded to replace EFC). 6% of all full-time freshmen had no need and received non-need-based gift aid.

UNDERGRADUATE FINANCIAL AID (Fall 2006, est.) 287 applied for aid; of those 91% were deemed to have need. 100% of undergraduates with need received aid; of those 12% had need fully met. ***Average percent of need met:*** 65% (excluding resources awarded to replace EFC). ***Average financial aid package:*** $12,689 (excluding resources awarded to replace EFC). 5% of all full-time undergraduates had no need and received non-need-based gift aid.

GIFT AID (NEED-BASED) ***Total amount:*** $2,189,021 (21% federal, 15% state, 57% institutional, 7% external sources). ***Receiving aid:*** Freshmen: 76% (76); All full-time undergraduates: 73% (240). ***Average award:*** Freshmen: $11,630; Undergraduates: $9088. ***Scholarships, grants, and awards:*** Federal Pell, FSEOG, state, private, college/university gift aid from institutional funds.

GIFT AID (NON-NEED-BASED) ***Total amount:*** $202,519 (86% institutional, 14% external sources). ***Receiving aid:*** Freshmen: 1% (1); Undergraduates: 1% (3). ***Average award:*** Freshmen: $3833; Undergraduates: $3461. ***Scholarships, grants, and awards by category:*** *Academic Interests/Achievement:* 110 awards ($322,250 total): general academic interests/achievements. *Special Achievements/Activities:* 18 awards ($34,000 total): community service, leadership. *Special Characteristics:* children of faculty/staff, first-generation college students. ***Tuition waivers:*** Full or partial for employees or children of employees.

LOANS ***Student loans:*** $1,554,492 (84% need-based, 16% non-need-based). 85% of past graduating class borrowed through all loan programs. *Average indebtedness per student:* $20,244. ***Average need-based loan:*** Freshmen: $2819; Undergraduates: $4231. ***Parent loans:*** $489,523 (44% need-based, 56% non-need-based). ***Programs:*** FFEL (Subsidized and Unsubsidized Stafford, PLUS).

WORK-STUDY ***Federal work-study:*** Total amount: $85,469; 71 jobs averaging $1200. ***State or other work-study/employment:*** Total amount: $1050 (100% non-need-based).

APPLYING FOR FINANCIAL AID ***Required financial aid forms:*** FAFSA, institution's own form. ***Financial aid deadline (priority):*** 5/1. ***Notification date:*** Continuous. Students must reply within 2 weeks of notification.

CONTACT Office of Financial Aid, Southern Vermont College, 982 Mansion Drive, Bennington, VT 05201, 802-447-6306 or toll-free 800-378-2782. *Fax:* 802-447-4695. *E-mail:* financialaid@svc.edu.

SOUTHERN VIRGINIA UNIVERSITY

Buena Vista, VA

ABOUT THE INSTITUTION Independent Latter-day Saints, coed. Awards: bachelor's degrees. 13 undergraduate majors. Total enrollment: 749. Undergraduates: 749. Freshmen: 242.

GIFT AID (NEED-BASED) ***Scholarships, grants, and awards:*** Federal Pell, FSEOG, state, private, college/university gift aid from institutional funds.

GIFT AID (NON-NEED-BASED) ***Scholarships, grants, and awards by category:*** *Academic Interests/Achievement:* general academic interests/achievements. *Creative Arts/Performance:* art/fine arts. *Special Achievements/Activities:* religious involvement. *Special Characteristics:* children of faculty/staff, international students.

LOANS ***Programs:*** FFEL (Subsidized and Unsubsidized Stafford, PLUS), alternative loans.

WORK-STUDY ***Federal work-study:*** Total amount: $112,813; 154 jobs averaging $1000. ***State or other work-study/employment:*** Total amount: $42,880 (51% need-based, 49% non-need-based).

APPLYING FOR FINANCIAL AID ***Required financial aid forms:*** FAFSA, Virginia Tuition Assistance Grant (VA residents only).

CONTACT Jessica Massie, Financial Aid Specialist, Southern Virginia University, One University Hill Drive, Buena Vista, VA 24416, 540-261-4351 or toll-free 800-229-8420. *Fax:* 540-261-8559. *E-mail:* finaid@southernvirginia.edu.

SOUTHERN WESLEYAN UNIVERSITY

Central, SC

Tuition & fees: $16,150 **Average undergraduate aid package: $7859**

ABOUT THE INSTITUTION Independent religious, coed. Awards: associate, bachelor's, and master's degrees. 34 undergraduate majors. Total enrollment: 2,557. Undergraduates: 1,802. Freshmen: 135. Federal methodology is used as a basis for awarding need-based institutional aid.

UNDERGRADUATE EXPENSES for 2006–07 ***Application fee:*** $25. ***Comprehensive fee:*** $21,950 includes full-time tuition ($15,700), mandatory fees ($450), and room and board ($5800). ***College room only:*** $2150. Full-time tuition and fees vary according to course load, degree level, and location. Room and board charges vary according to board plan and housing facility. ***Part-time tuition:*** $480 per credit hour. ***Part-time fees:*** $225 per term. Part-time tuition and fees vary according to course load and degree level. ***Payment plan:*** Installment.

FRESHMAN FINANCIAL AID (Fall 2006, est.) 121 applied for aid; of those 87% were deemed to have need. 100% of freshmen with need received aid; of those

37% had need fully met. ***Average percent of need met:*** 79% (excluding resources awarded to replace EFC). ***Average financial aid package:*** $13,314 (excluding resources awarded to replace EFC). 18% of all full-time freshmen had no need and received non-need-based gift aid.

UNDERGRADUATE FINANCIAL AID (Fall 2006, est.) 1,901 applied for aid; of those 71% were deemed to have need. 99% of undergraduates with need received aid; of those 15% had need fully met. ***Average percent of need met:*** 57% (excluding resources awarded to replace EFC). ***Average financial aid package:*** $7859 (excluding resources awarded to replace EFC). 12% of all full-time undergraduates had no need and received non-need-based gift aid.

GIFT AID (NEED-BASED) ***Total amount:*** $5,314,295 (34% federal, 24% state, 26% institutional, 16% external sources). ***Receiving aid:*** Freshmen: 81% (105); All full-time undergraduates: 53% (1,110). ***Average award:*** Freshmen: $10,434; Undergraduates: $5471. ***Scholarships, grants, and awards:*** Federal Pell, FSEOG, state, private, college/university gift aid from institutional funds.

GIFT AID (NON-NEED-BASED) ***Total amount:*** $1,114,765 (30% state, 42% institutional, 28% external sources). ***Receiving aid:*** Freshmen: 20% (26); Undergraduates: 6% (130). ***Average award:*** Freshmen: $7903; Undergraduates: $7552. ***Scholarships, grants, and awards by category:*** *Academic Interests/Achievement:* biological sciences, business, computer science, education, English, general academic interests/achievements, humanities, mathematics, physical sciences, premedicine, religion/biblical studies, social sciences. *Creative Arts/Performance:* art/fine arts, creative writing, journalism/publications, music, theater/drama. *Special Achievements/Activities:* community service, leadership, religious involvement. *Special Characteristics:* children of faculty/staff, ethnic background, members of minority groups, relatives of clergy, religious affiliation, siblings of current students. ***Tuition waivers:*** Full or partial for employees or children of employees, senior citizens. ***ROTC:*** Army cooperative, Air Force cooperative.

LOANS ***Student loans:*** $9,664,155 (75% need-based, 25% non-need-based). 97% of past graduating class borrowed through all loan programs. *Average indebtedness per student:* $18,072. ***Average need-based loan:*** Freshmen: $3202; Undergraduates: $3623. ***Parent loans:*** $712,747 (46% need-based, 54% non-need-based). ***Programs:*** FFEL (Subsidized and Unsubsidized Stafford, PLUS), Perkins.

WORK-STUDY ***Federal work-study:*** Total amount: $238,567; 137 jobs averaging $1150. ***State or other work-study/employment:*** Total amount: $111,065 (2% need-based, 98% non-need-based). 60 part-time jobs averaging $1150.

ATHLETIC AWARDS Total amount: $833,110 (61% need-based, 39% non-need-based).

APPLYING FOR FINANCIAL AID ***Required financial aid forms:*** FAFSA, institution's own form. ***Financial aid deadline (priority):*** 3/31. ***Notification date:*** Continuous. Students must reply within 2 weeks of notification.

CONTACT Mrs. Sherri Peters, Financial Aid Associate, Southern Wesleyan University, 907 Wesleyan Drive, Central, SC 29630-1020, 800-289-1292 Ext. 5517 or toll-free 800-289-1292 Ext. 5550. *Fax:* 864-644-5970. *E-mail:* finaid@swu.edu.

SOUTH UNIVERSITY

Montgomery, AL

Tuition & fees: $15,800 **Average undergraduate aid package: $5146**

ABOUT THE INSTITUTION Proprietary, coed. Awards: associate, bachelor's, and master's degrees. 9 undergraduate majors. Total enrollment: 446. Undergraduates: 435. Freshmen: 76. Federal methodology is used as a basis for awarding need-based institutional aid.

UNDERGRADUATE EXPENSES for 2007–08 ***Application fee:*** $25. ***Tuition:*** full-time $15,800; part-time $3950 per term.

FRESHMAN FINANCIAL AID (Fall 2006, est.) 48 applied for aid; of those 100% were deemed to have need. 100% of freshmen with need received aid. ***Average percent of need met:*** 45% (excluding resources awarded to replace EFC). ***Average financial aid package:*** $5146 (excluding resources awarded to replace EFC).

UNDERGRADUATE FINANCIAL AID (Fall 2006, est.) 268 applied for aid; of those 100% were deemed to have need. 100% of undergraduates with need received aid. ***Average percent of need met:*** 45% (excluding resources awarded to replace EFC). ***Average financial aid package:*** $5146 (excluding resources awarded to replace EFC).

GIFT AID (NEED-BASED) ***Total amount:*** $1,910,060 (99% federal, 1% state). ***Receiving aid:*** Freshmen: 70% (37); All full-time undergraduates: 70% (206). ***Average award:*** Freshmen: $3819; Undergraduates: $3819. ***Scholarships, grants, and awards:*** Federal Pell, FSEOG, state.

LOANS ***Student loans:*** $7,053,796 (100% need-based). 89% of past graduating class borrowed through all loan programs. *Average indebtedness per student:* $9600. ***Average need-based loan:*** Freshmen: $2625; Undergraduates: $2625. ***Parent loans:*** $736,837 (100% need-based). ***Programs:*** Federal Direct (Subsidized and Unsubsidized Stafford), FFEL (Subsidized and Unsubsidized Stafford, PLUS), Perkins, college/university.

WORK-STUDY ***Federal work-study:*** Total amount: $54,000; 21 jobs averaging $2213.

APPLYING FOR FINANCIAL AID ***Required financial aid form:*** FAFSA. ***Financial aid deadline:*** Continuous. ***Notification date:*** Continuous beginning 9/1.

CONTACT James Berry, Director of Financial Aid, South University, 5355 Vaughn Road, Montgomery, AL 36116-1120, 334-395-8800. *Fax:* 334-395-8859. *E-mail:* jberry@southuniversity.edu.

SOUTH UNIVERSITY

Tampa, FL

CONTACT Financial Aid Office, South University, 4401 N. Himes Avenue, Tampa, FL 33614, 813-393-3800 or toll-free 800-846-1472 (in-state).

SOUTH UNIVERSITY

West Palm Beach, FL

CONTACT Lisa Hartman, Director of Financial Aid, South University, 1760 North Congress Avenue, West Palm Beach, FL 33409, 561-697-9200 Ext. 230 or toll-free 866-629-2902 (in-state), 866-629-9200 (out-of-state). *Fax:* 561-697-9944. *E-mail:* lhartman@southcollege.edu.

SOUTH UNIVERSITY

Savannah, GA

CONTACT Ms. Anne Gaglia, Director of Financial Services, South University, 709 Mall Boulevard, Savannah, GA 31406-4881, 912-201-8011 or toll-free 866-629-2901. *Fax:* 912-201-8072. *E-mail:* gaglia@southuniversity.edu.

SOUTH UNIVERSITY

Columbia, SC

CONTACT Sandra Gundlach, Financial Aid Coordinator, South University, 3810 Main Street, Columbia, SC 29203, 803-799-9082 or toll-free 866-629-3031. *Fax:* 803-799-9005.

SOUTHWEST BAPTIST UNIVERSITY

Bolivar, MO

Tuition & fees: $14,100 **Average undergraduate aid package: $10,617**

ABOUT THE INSTITUTION Independent Southern Baptist, coed. Awards: associate, bachelor's, master's, and doctoral degrees and post-master's certificates. 41 undergraduate majors. Total enrollment: 3,503. Undergraduates: 2,730. Freshmen: 508. Federal methodology is used as a basis for awarding need-based institutional aid.

UNDERGRADUATE EXPENSES for 2006–07 ***Application fee:*** $30. ***Comprehensive fee:*** $18,300 includes full-time tuition ($13,300), mandatory fees ($800), and room and board ($4200). ***College room only:*** $2200. Room and board charges vary according to board plan and housing facility. ***Part-time tuition:*** $500 per hour. Part-time tuition and fees vary according to course load. ***Payment plan:*** Installment.

FRESHMAN FINANCIAL AID (Fall 2006, est.) 414 applied for aid; of those 78% were deemed to have need. 99% of freshmen with need received aid; of those 29% had need fully met. ***Average percent of need met:*** 67% (excluding resources awarded to replace EFC). ***Average financial aid package:*** $10,869 (excluding resources awarded to replace EFC). 26% of all full-time freshmen had no need and received non-need-based gift aid.

UNDERGRADUATE FINANCIAL AID (Fall 2006, est.) 1,494 applied for aid; of those 82% were deemed to have need. 100% of undergraduates with need received aid; of those 22% had need fully met. ***Average percent of need met:*** 63% (excluding resources awarded to replace EFC). ***Average financial aid package:*** $10,617 (excluding resources awarded to replace EFC). 23% of all full-time undergraduates had no need and received non-need-based gift aid.

GIFT AID (NEED-BASED) ***Total amount:*** $2,812,869 (81% federal, 12% state, 7% institutional). ***Receiving aid:*** Freshmen: 26% (122); All full-time undergraduates: 35% (636). ***Average award:*** Freshmen: $3479; Undergraduates: $3502. ***Scholarships, grants, and awards:*** Federal Pell, FSEOG, state, private, college/university gift aid from institutional funds.

GIFT AID (NON-NEED-BASED) ***Total amount:*** $7,285,610 (2% state, 88% institutional, 10% external sources). ***Receiving aid:*** Freshmen: 62% (289); Undergraduates: 54% (993). ***Average award:*** Freshmen: $6241; Undergraduates: $5647. ***Scholarships, grants, and awards by category:*** *Academic Interests/Achievement:* 1,459 awards ($3,861,430 total): general academic interests/achievements. *Creative Arts/Performance:* 158 awards ($174,000 total): art/fine arts, debating, general creative arts/performance, music, theater/drama. *Special Achievements/Activities:* 227 awards ($411,500 total): religious involvement. *Special Characteristics:* 1,224 awards ($1,541,233 total): general special characteristics, local/state students, relatives of clergy. ***Tuition waivers:*** Full or partial for employees or children of employees. ***ROTC:*** Army cooperative.

LOANS ***Student loans:*** $8,154,025 (55% need-based, 45% non-need-based). 67% of past graduating class borrowed through all loan programs. *Average indebtedness per student:* $18,380. ***Average need-based loan:*** Freshmen: $3533; Undergraduates: $4210. ***Parent loans:*** $1,248,097 (100% non-need-based). ***Programs:*** FFEL (Subsidized and Unsubsidized Stafford, PLUS), Perkins, Federal Nursing, state, alternative loans.

WORK-STUDY ***Federal work-study:*** Total amount: $458,460; 530 jobs averaging $982.

ATHLETIC AWARDS Total amount: $1,435,374 (100% non-need-based).

APPLYING FOR FINANCIAL AID ***Required financial aid forms:*** FAFSA, institution's own form. ***Financial aid deadline (priority):*** 3/15. ***Notification date:*** Continuous beginning 3/1. Students must reply within 2 weeks of notification.

CONTACT Mr. Brad Gamble, Director of Financial Aid, Southwest Baptist University, 1600 University Avenue, Bolivar, MO 65613-2597, 417-328-1823 or toll-free 800-526-5859. *Fax:* 417-328-1514. *E-mail:* bgamble@sbuniv.edu.

SOUTHWESTERN ADVENTIST UNIVERSITY

Keene, TX

CONTACT Student Financial Services, Southwestern Adventist University, PO Box 567, Keene, TX 76059, 817-645-3921 Ext. 262 or toll-free 800-433-2240. *Fax:* 817-556-4744.

SOUTHWESTERN ASSEMBLIES OF GOD UNIVERSITY

Waxahachie, TX

CONTACT Financial Aid Office, Southwestern Assemblies of God University, 1200 Sycamore Street, Waxahachie, TX 75165-2397, 972-937-4010 Ext. 1140 or toll-free 888-937-7248. *Fax:* 972-937-4001. *E-mail:* finaid@sagu.edu.

SOUTHWESTERN CHRISTIAN COLLEGE

Terrell, TX

CONTACT Financial Aid Office, Southwestern Christian College, PO Box 10, Terrell, TX 75160, 972-524-3341. *Fax:* 972-563-7133.

SOUTHWESTERN CHRISTIAN UNIVERSITY

Bethany, OK

ABOUT THE INSTITUTION Independent religious, coed. Awards: associate, bachelor's, and master's degrees. 10 undergraduate majors. Total enrollment: 199. Undergraduates: 128. Freshmen: 32.

GIFT AID (NEED-BASED) ***Scholarships, grants, and awards:*** Federal Pell, FSEOG, state, private, college/university gift aid from institutional funds.

GIFT AID (NON-NEED-BASED) ***Scholarships, grants, and awards by category:*** *Academic Interests/Achievement:* business, education, general academic interests/achievements, religion/biblical studies. *Creative Arts/Performance:* music, theater/drama. *Special Achievements/Activities:* cheerleading/drum major, religious involvement. *Special Characteristics:* children and siblings of alumni, children of faculty/staff, relatives of clergy, religious affiliation.

LOANS ***Programs:*** FFEL (Subsidized and Unsubsidized Stafford, PLUS).

WORK-STUDY ***Federal work-study:*** Total amount: $70,000; 60 jobs averaging $1500. ***State or other work-study/employment:*** Total amount: $15,000 (100% non-need-based). 10 part-time jobs averaging $1000.

APPLYING FOR FINANCIAL AID ***Required financial aid form:*** FAFSA.

CONTACT Mr. Mark Arthur, Financial Aid Director, Southwestern Christian University, PO Box 340, Bethany, OK 73008, 405-789-7661 Ext. 3456. *Fax:* 405-495-0078. *E-mail:* mark@swcu.edu.

SOUTHWESTERN COLLEGE

Phoenix, AZ

CONTACT Mr. Pete Leonard, Director of Enrollment Management, Southwestern College, 2625 East Cactus Road, Phoenix, AZ 85032-7097, 602-992-6101 Ext. 114 or toll-free 800-247-2697. *Fax:* 602-404-2159.

SOUTHWESTERN COLLEGE

Winfield, KS

CONTACT Director of Financial Aid, Southwestern College, 100 College Street, Winfield, KS 67156-2499, 620-229-6215 or toll-free 800-846-1543. *Fax:* 620-229-6363. *E-mail:* finaid@sckans.edu.

SOUTHWESTERN OKLAHOMA STATE UNIVERSITY

Weatherford, OK

CONTACT Mr. Thomas M. Ratliff, Director of Student Financial Services, Southwestern Oklahoma State University, 100 Campus Drive, Weatherford, OK 73096-3098, 580-774-3786. *Fax:* 580-774-7066. *E-mail:* ratlift@swosu.edu.

SOUTHWESTERN UNIVERSITY

Georgetown, TX

Tuition & fees: $25,740 **Average undergraduate aid package: $20,432**

ABOUT THE INSTITUTION Independent Methodist, coed. Awards: bachelor's degrees. 45 undergraduate majors. Total enrollment: 1,277. Undergraduates: 1,277. Freshmen: 345. Both federal and institutional methodology are used as a basis for awarding need-based institutional aid.

UNDERGRADUATE EXPENSES for 2007–08 ***Application fee:*** $40. ***Comprehensive fee:*** $34,450 includes full-time tuition ($25,740) and room and board ($8710). ***College room only:*** $4410. ***Part-time tuition:*** $1075 per semester hour.

FRESHMAN FINANCIAL AID (Fall 2006, est.) 257 applied for aid; of those 72% were deemed to have need. 100% of freshmen with need received aid; of those 58% had need fully met. ***Average percent of need met:*** 95% (excluding resources awarded to replace EFC). ***Average financial aid package:*** $22,249 (excluding resources awarded to replace EFC). 30% of all full-time freshmen had no need and received non-need-based gift aid.

UNDERGRADUATE FINANCIAL AID (Fall 2006, est.) 783 applied for aid; of those 80% were deemed to have need. 100% of undergraduates with need received aid; of those 48% had need fully met. ***Average percent of need met:*** 90% (excluding resources awarded to replace EFC). ***Average financial aid package:*** $20,432 (excluding resources awarded to replace EFC). 30% of all full-time undergraduates had no need and received non-need-based gift aid.

GIFT AID (NEED-BASED) ***Total amount:*** $9,050,373 (7% federal, 14% state, 71% institutional, 8% external sources). ***Receiving aid:*** Freshmen: 54% (185); All full-time undergraduates: 50% (620). ***Average award:*** Freshmen: $17,048; Undergraduates: $14,399. ***Scholarships, grants, and awards:*** Federal Pell, FSEOG, state, private, college/university gift aid from institutional funds.

GIFT AID (NON-NEED-BASED) ***Total amount:*** $3,495,395 (1% federal, 91% institutional, 8% external sources). ***Receiving aid:*** Freshmen: 32% (112); Undergraduates: 29% (357). ***Average award:*** Freshmen: $9561; Undergraduates: $8387. ***Scholarships, grants, and awards by category:*** *Academic Interests/Achievement:* 703 awards ($5,342,120 total): general academic interests/

achievements. *Creative Arts/Performance:* 111 awards ($426,650 total): art/fine arts, music, performing arts, theater/drama. *Special Characteristics:* 43 awards ($599,115 total): children of faculty/staff, relatives of clergy.

LOANS ***Student loans:*** $4,542,518 (88% need-based, 12% non-need-based). 56% of past graduating class borrowed through all loan programs. *Average indebtedness per student:* $22,652. ***Average need-based loan:*** Freshmen: $3762; Undergraduates: $4732. ***Parent loans:*** $7,504,058 (55% need-based, 45% non-need-based). ***Programs:*** FFEL (Subsidized and Unsubsidized Stafford, PLUS), Perkins, state, college/university.

WORK-STUDY ***Federal work-study:*** Total amount: $498,374; 232 jobs averaging $2148. ***State or other work-study/employment:*** Total amount: $1,079,460 (50% need-based, 50% non-need-based). 220 part-time jobs averaging $2451.

APPLYING FOR FINANCIAL AID ***Required financial aid form:*** FAFSA. ***Financial aid deadline:*** 3/1 (priority: 3/1). ***Notification date:*** Continuous beginning 3/1. Students must reply by 5/1 or within 2 weeks of notification.

CONTACT Mr. James P. Gaeta, Director of Financial Aid, Southwestern University, PO Box 770, Georgetown, TX 78627-0770, 512-863-1259 or toll-free 800-252-3166. *E-mail:* gaetaj@southwestern.edu.

SOUTHWEST MINNESOTA STATE UNIVERSITY

Marshall, MN

Tuition & fees (MN res): $6240 **Average undergraduate aid package: $7381**

ABOUT THE INSTITUTION State-supported, coed. Awards: associate, bachelor's, and master's degrees. 50 undergraduate majors. Total enrollment: 6,126. Undergraduates: 5,605. Freshmen: 553. Federal methodology is used as a basis for awarding need-based institutional aid.

UNDERGRADUATE EXPENSES for 2006–07 ***Application fee:*** $20. ***Tuition, state resident:*** full-time $5400; part-time $174.25 per credit. ***Required fees:*** full-time $840; $32.71 per credit. Part-time tuition and fees vary according to class time and course load. ***College room and board:*** $5360; ***Room only:*** $3360. Room and board charges vary according to board plan and housing facility. ***Payment plan:*** Installment.

FRESHMAN FINANCIAL AID (Fall 2006, est.) 385 applied for aid; of those 78% were deemed to have need. 99% of freshmen with need received aid; of those 24% had need fully met. ***Average percent of need met:*** 58% (excluding resources awarded to replace EFC). ***Average financial aid package:*** $7647 (excluding resources awarded to replace EFC). 18% of all full-time freshmen had no need and received non-need-based gift aid.

UNDERGRADUATE FINANCIAL AID (Fall 2006, est.) 1,782 applied for aid; of those 79% were deemed to have need. 99% of undergraduates with need received aid; of those 33% had need fully met. ***Average percent of need met:*** 62% (excluding resources awarded to replace EFC). ***Average financial aid package:*** $7381 (excluding resources awarded to replace EFC). 2% of all full-time undergraduates had no need and received non-need-based gift aid.

GIFT AID (NEED-BASED) ***Total amount:*** $4,373,657 (55% federal, 44% state, 1% institutional). ***Receiving aid:*** Freshmen: 42% (208); All full-time undergraduates: 45% (1,022). ***Average award:*** Freshmen: $4581; Undergraduates: $4135. ***Scholarships, grants, and awards:*** Federal Pell, FSEOG, state, private, college/university gift aid from institutional funds.

GIFT AID (NON-NEED-BASED) ***Total amount:*** $2,251,663 (10% federal, 60% institutional, 30% external sources). ***Receiving aid:*** Freshmen: 42% (212); Undergraduates: 28% (645). ***Average award:*** Freshmen: $2430; Undergraduates: $1722. ***Scholarships, grants, and awards by category:*** *Academic Interests/Achievement:* 1,102 awards ($939,365 total): agriculture, biological sciences, business, communication, computer science, education, English, general academic interests/achievements, international studies, library science, mathematics, physical sciences, premedicine, social sciences. *Creative Arts/Performance:* 93 awards ($45,489 total): art/fine arts, creative writing, debating, journalism/publications, music, performing arts, theater/drama. *Special Achievements/Activities:* 455 awards ($674,749 total): general special achievements/activities, hobbies/interests, leadership. *Special Characteristics:* 142 awards ($172,175 total): children and siblings of alumni, children of union members/company employees, ethnic background, first-generation college students, general special characteristics, handicapped students, international students, local/state students, members of minority groups, previous college experience, veterans, veterans' children. ***Tuition waivers:*** Full or partial for employees or children of employees.

LOANS ***Student loans:*** $9,624,279 (45% need-based, 55% non-need-based). 76% of past graduating class borrowed through all loan programs. *Average indebtedness per student:* $16,438. ***Average need-based loan:*** Freshmen: $2518; Undergraduates: $3507. ***Parent loans:*** $548,335 (100% non-need-based). ***Programs:*** FFEL (Subsidized and Unsubsidized Stafford, PLUS), Perkins, state.

WORK-STUDY ***Federal work-study:*** Total amount: $250,092; 109 jobs averaging $2158. ***State or other work-study/employment:*** Total amount: $401,975 (100% need-based). 224 part-time jobs averaging $2048.

ATHLETIC AWARDS Total amount: $484,389 (100% non-need-based).

APPLYING FOR FINANCIAL AID ***Required financial aid forms:*** FAFSA, institution's own form. ***Financial aid deadline (priority):*** 3/1. ***Notification date:*** Continuous beginning 4/1.

CONTACT David Vikander, Director of Financial Aid, Southwest Minnesota State University, 1501 State Street, Marshall, MN 56258, 507-537-6281 or toll-free 800-642-0684. *Fax:* 507-537-6275. *E-mail:* vikander@southwestmsu.edu.

SPALDING UNIVERSITY

Louisville, KY

CONTACT Director of Student Financial Services, Spalding University, 851 South Fourth Street, Louisville, KY 40203, 502-588-7185 or toll-free 800-896-8941 Ext. 2111. *Fax:* 502-585-7128. *E-mail:* onestop@spalding.edu.

SPELMAN COLLEGE

Atlanta, GA

Tuition & fees: $17,005 **Average undergraduate aid package: $10,500**

ABOUT THE INSTITUTION Independent, women only. Awards: bachelor's degrees. 25 undergraduate majors. Total enrollment: 2,290. Undergraduates: 2,290. Freshmen: 569. Federal methodology is used as a basis for awarding need-based institutional aid.

UNDERGRADUATE EXPENSES for 2007–08 ***Application fee:*** $35. ***Comprehensive fee:*** $25,755 includes full-time tuition ($14,470), mandatory fees ($2535), and room and board ($8750). ***Part-time tuition:*** $603 per credit hour.

FRESHMAN FINANCIAL AID (Fall 2006, est.) 488 applied for aid; of those 89% were deemed to have need. 100% of freshmen with need received aid; of those 1% had need fully met. ***Average percent of need met:*** 67% (excluding resources awarded to replace EFC). ***Average financial aid package:*** $10,500 (excluding resources awarded to replace EFC). 1% of all full-time freshmen had no need and received non-need-based gift aid.

UNDERGRADUATE FINANCIAL AID (Fall 2006, est.) 1,929 applied for aid; of those 82% were deemed to have need. 100% of undergraduates with need received aid; of those 3% had need fully met. ***Average percent of need met:*** 67% (excluding resources awarded to replace EFC). ***Average financial aid package:*** $10,500 (excluding resources awarded to replace EFC). 1% of all full-time undergraduates had no need and received non-need-based gift aid.

GIFT AID (NEED-BASED) ***Total amount:*** $11,103,370 (23% federal, 12% state, 37% institutional, 28% external sources). ***Receiving aid:*** Freshmen: 61% (326); All full-time undergraduates: 57% (1,185). ***Average award:*** Freshmen: $2500; Undergraduates: $2500. ***Scholarships, grants, and awards:*** Federal Pell, FSEOG, state, private, college/university gift aid from institutional funds, United Negro College Fund.

GIFT AID (NON-NEED-BASED) ***Receiving aid:*** Freshmen: 12% (65); Undergraduates: 15% (325). ***Average award:*** Freshmen: $24,000; Undergraduates: $24,000. ***Scholarships, grants, and awards by category:*** *Academic Interests/Achievement:* 276 awards ($2,561,803 total): biological sciences, general academic interests/achievements, mathematics, physical sciences. *Creative Arts/Performance:* 11 awards ($14,365 total): dance, music, theater/drama. *Special Achievements/Activities:* 80 awards ($483,823 total): community service. *Special Characteristics:* 1 award ($5000 total). ***ROTC:*** Army, Naval, Air Force cooperative.

LOANS ***Student loans:*** $11,520,118 (100% need-based). 75% of past graduating class borrowed through all loan programs. *Average indebtedness per student:* $23,500. ***Average need-based loan:*** Freshmen: $2625; Undergraduates: $6226. ***Parent loans:*** $15,194,148 (100% need-based). ***Programs:*** FFEL (Subsidized and Unsubsidized Stafford, PLUS), Perkins.

WORK-STUDY ***Federal work-study:*** Total amount: $227,365; 172 jobs averaging $882. ***State or other work-study/employment:*** Total amount: $20,000 (100% need-based). 200 part-time jobs averaging $625.

APPLYING FOR FINANCIAL AID ***Required financial aid forms:*** FAFSA, institution's own form. ***Financial aid deadline (priority):*** 3/1. ***Notification date:*** 2/15.

CONTACT Lenora J. Jackson, Director, Student Financial Services, Spelman College, 350 Spelman Lane, SW, PO Box 771, Atlanta, GA 30314-4399, 404-270-5212 or toll-free 800-982-2411. *Fax:* 404-270-5220. *E-mail:* lenoraj@spelman.edu.

SPRING ARBOR UNIVERSITY

Spring Arbor, MI

Tuition & fees: $17,386 **Average undergraduate aid package: $15,163**

ABOUT THE INSTITUTION Independent Free Methodist, coed. Awards: associate, bachelor's, and master's degrees. 32 undergraduate majors. Total enrollment: 3,714. Undergraduates: 2,609. Freshmen: 335. Federal methodology is used as a basis for awarding need-based institutional aid.

UNDERGRADUATE EXPENSES for 2006–07 ***Application fee:*** $30. ***Comprehensive fee:*** $23,456 includes full-time tuition ($16,990), mandatory fees ($396), and room and board ($6070). ***College room only:*** $2850. Full-time tuition and fees vary according to course load and program. Room and board charges vary according to board plan, housing facility, and location. ***Part-time tuition:*** $400 per credit. ***Part-time fees:*** $153 per term. Part-time tuition and fees vary according to course load, program, and reciprocity agreements. ***Payment plan:*** Installment.

FRESHMAN FINANCIAL AID (Fall 2006, est.) 304 applied for aid; of those 87% were deemed to have need. 100% of freshmen with need received aid; of those 57% had need fully met. ***Average percent of need met:*** 93% (excluding resources awarded to replace EFC). ***Average financial aid package:*** $17,088 (excluding resources awarded to replace EFC). 15% of all full-time freshmen had no need and received non-need-based gift aid.

UNDERGRADUATE FINANCIAL AID (Fall 2006, est.) 1,594 applied for aid; of those 84% were deemed to have need. 98% of undergraduates with need received aid; of those 45% had need fully met. ***Average percent of need met:*** 84% (excluding resources awarded to replace EFC). ***Average financial aid package:*** $15,163 (excluding resources awarded to replace EFC). 5% of all full-time undergraduates had no need and received non-need-based gift aid.

GIFT AID (NEED-BASED) ***Total amount:*** $13,118,932 (18% federal, 18% state, 64% institutional). ***Receiving aid:*** Freshmen: 76% (256); All full-time undergraduates: 64% (1,237). ***Average award:*** Freshmen: $10,079; Undergraduates: $8679. ***Scholarships, grants, and awards:*** Federal Pell, FSEOG, state, private, college/university gift aid from institutional funds.

GIFT AID (NON-NEED-BASED) ***Total amount:*** $960,022 (55% state, 45% external sources). ***Receiving aid:*** Freshmen: 47% (158); Undergraduates: 19% (375). ***Average award:*** Freshmen: $1826; Undergraduates: $1815. ***Scholarships, grants, and awards by category:*** *Academic Interests/Achievement:* 890 awards ($2,973,447 total): general academic interests/achievements. *Creative Arts/Performance:* 205 awards ($109,818 total): art/fine arts. *Special Achievements/Activities:* junior miss. *Special Characteristics:* 305 awards ($1,067,901 total): adult students, children of faculty/staff, international students, members of minority groups, relatives of clergy, religious affiliation. ***Tuition waivers:*** Full or partial for employees or children of employees, senior citizens. ***ROTC:*** Army, Air Force cooperative.

LOANS ***Student loans:*** $15,986,841 (45% need-based, 55% non-need-based). 89% of past graduating class borrowed through all loan programs. *Average indebtedness per student:* $13,230. ***Average need-based loan:*** Freshmen: $3185; Undergraduates: $4161. ***Parent loans:*** $1,085,513 (100% need-based). ***Programs:*** FFEL (Subsidized and Unsubsidized Stafford, PLUS), Perkins, Michigan Loan Program and Alternative Loans.

WORK-STUDY ***Federal work-study:*** Total amount: $82,067; 386 jobs averaging $700. ***State or other work-study/employment:*** 44 part-time jobs averaging $465.

ATHLETIC AWARDS Total amount: $1,026,016 (100% need-based).

APPLYING FOR FINANCIAL AID ***Required financial aid form:*** FAFSA. ***Financial aid deadline (priority):*** 3/1. ***Notification date:*** Continuous beginning 4/1. Students must reply within 2 weeks of notification.

CONTACT Lois M. Hardy, Director of Financial Aid, Spring Arbor University, 106 East Main Street, Spring Arbor, MI 49283-9799, 517-750-6468 or toll-free 800-968-0011. *Fax:* 517-750-6620.

SPRINGFIELD COLLEGE

Springfield, MA

CONTACT Edward J. Ciosek, Director of Financial Aid, Springfield College, 263 Alden Street, Springfield, MA 01109-3797, 413-748-3108 or toll-free 800-343-1257 (out-of-state). *Fax:* 413-748-3462. *E-mail:* edward_j_ciosek@spfldcol.edu.

SPRING HILL COLLEGE

Mobile, AL

Tuition & fees: $22,000 **Average undergraduate aid package: $19,730**

ABOUT THE INSTITUTION Independent Roman Catholic (Jesuit), coed. Awards: associate, bachelor's, and master's degrees and post-bachelor's certificates. 40 undergraduate majors. Total enrollment: 1,446. Undergraduates: 1,218. Freshmen: 349. Federal methodology is used as a basis for awarding need-based institutional aid.

UNDERGRADUATE EXPENSES for 2006–07 ***Application fee:*** $25. ***Comprehensive fee:*** $30,120 includes full-time tuition ($20,650), mandatory fees ($1350), and room and board ($8120). ***College room only:*** $4200. Room and board charges vary according to board plan and housing facility. ***Part-time tuition:*** $773 per semester hour. ***Part-time fees:*** $44 per semester hour. ***Payment plan:*** Installment.

FRESHMAN FINANCIAL AID (Fall 2006, est.) 282 applied for aid; of those 81% were deemed to have need. 100% of freshmen with need received aid; of those 72% had need fully met. ***Average percent of need met:*** 86% (excluding resources awarded to replace EFC). ***Average financial aid package:*** $21,532 (excluding resources awarded to replace EFC). 30% of all full-time freshmen had no need and received non-need-based gift aid.

UNDERGRADUATE FINANCIAL AID (Fall 2006, est.) 844 applied for aid; of those 83% were deemed to have need. 100% of undergraduates with need received aid; of those 76% had need fully met. ***Average percent of need met:*** 80% (excluding resources awarded to replace EFC). ***Average financial aid package:*** $19,730 (excluding resources awarded to replace EFC). 31% of all full-time undergraduates had no need and received non-need-based gift aid.

GIFT AID (NEED-BASED) ***Total amount:*** $10,329,096 (10% federal, 2% state, 87% institutional, 1% external sources). ***Receiving aid:*** Freshmen: 66% (228); All full-time undergraduates: 61% (674). ***Average award:*** Freshmen: $16,415; Undergraduates: $14,269. ***Scholarships, grants, and awards:*** Federal Pell, FSEOG, state, private, college/university gift aid from institutional funds.

GIFT AID (NON-NEED-BASED) ***Total amount:*** $4,581,998 (1% state, 98% institutional, 1% external sources). ***Receiving aid:*** Freshmen: 48% (166); Undergraduates: 48% (529). ***Average award:*** Freshmen: $12,683; Undergraduates: $11,182. ***Scholarships, grants, and awards by category:*** *Academic Interests/Achievement:* 779 awards ($2,289,190 total): general academic interests/achievements. *Special Achievements/Activities:* community service. *Special Characteristics:* children of faculty/staff, siblings of current students. ***Tuition waivers:*** Full or partial for employees or children of employees. ***ROTC:*** Army cooperative, Air Force cooperative.

LOANS ***Student loans:*** $4,695,667 (74% need-based, 26% non-need-based). 77% of past graduating class borrowed through all loan programs. *Average indebtedness per student:* $12,864. ***Average need-based loan:*** Freshmen: $3239; Undergraduates: $4241. ***Parent loans:*** $1,649,870 (22% need-based, 78% non-need-based). ***Programs:*** FFEL (Subsidized and Unsubsidized Stafford, PLUS), alternative loans (i.e., Citiassist, Signature, etc.).

WORK-STUDY ***Federal work-study:*** Total amount: $254,520; jobs available. ***State or other work-study/employment:*** Total amount: $96,260 (39% need-based, 61% non-need-based). Part-time jobs available.

ATHLETIC AWARDS Total amount: $3,302,714 (82% need-based, 18% non-need-based).

APPLYING FOR FINANCIAL AID ***Required financial aid forms:*** FAFSA, institution's own form, state aid form. ***Financial aid deadline (priority):*** 3/1. ***Notification date:*** Continuous beginning 2/15. Students must reply by 5/1 or within 2 weeks of notification.

CONTACT Ellen Foster, Director, Financial Aid, Spring Hill College, 4000 Dauphin Street, Mobile, AL 36608, 251-380-3460 or toll-free 800-SHC-6704. *Fax:* 251-460-2176. *E-mail:* efoster@shc.edu.

STANFORD UNIVERSITY

Stanford, CA

Tuition & fees: $32,994 **Average undergraduate aid package: $29,234**

ABOUT THE INSTITUTION Independent, coed. Awards: bachelor's, master's, doctoral, and first professional degrees. 68 undergraduate majors. Total enrollment: 17,747. Undergraduates: 6,422. Freshmen: 1,646. Both federal and institutional methodology are used as a basis for awarding need-based institutional aid.

UNDERGRADUATE EXPENSES for 2006–07 ***Application fee:*** $75. ***Comprehensive fee:*** $43,361 includes full-time tuition ($32,994) and room and board ($10,367). ***College room only:*** $5571. Room and board charges vary according to board plan.

FRESHMAN FINANCIAL AID (Fall 2005) 963 applied for aid; of those 73% were deemed to have need. 99% of freshmen with need received aid; of those 77% had need fully met. ***Average percent of need met:*** 100% (excluding resources awarded to replace EFC). ***Average financial aid package:*** $30,088 (excluding resources awarded to replace EFC). 5% of all full-time freshmen had no need and received non-need-based gift aid.

UNDERGRADUATE FINANCIAL AID (Fall 2005) 3,530 applied for aid; of those 86% were deemed to have need. 99% of undergraduates with need received aid; of those 78% had need fully met. ***Average percent of need met:*** 100% (excluding resources awarded to replace EFC). ***Average financial aid package:*** $29,234 (excluding resources awarded to replace EFC). 11% of all full-time undergraduates had no need and received non-need-based gift aid.

GIFT AID (NEED-BASED) ***Total amount:*** $74,667,175 (5% federal, 6% state, 83% institutional, 6% external sources). ***Receiving aid:*** Freshmen: 42% (685); All full-time undergraduates: 43% (2,914). ***Average award:*** Freshmen: $26,639; Undergraduates: $25,315. ***Scholarships, grants, and awards:*** Federal Pell, FSEOG, state, private, college/university gift aid from institutional funds.

GIFT AID (NON-NEED-BASED) ***Total amount:*** $8,482,845 (9% federal, 39% institutional, 52% external sources). ***Receiving aid:*** Freshmen: 2% (28); Undergraduates: 2% (125). ***Average award:*** Freshmen: $3039; Undergraduates: $3639. ***Tuition waivers:*** Full or partial for employees or children of employees. ***ROTC:*** Army cooperative, Naval cooperative, Air Force cooperative.

LOANS ***Student loans:*** $11,801,616 (81% need-based, 19% non-need-based). 46% of past graduating class borrowed through all loan programs. *Average indebtedness per student:* $15,758. ***Average need-based loan:*** Freshmen: $1950; Undergraduates: $2193. ***Parent loans:*** $11,889,242 (100% non-need-based). ***Programs:*** FFEL (Subsidized and Unsubsidized Stafford, PLUS), Perkins, GATE Loans.

WORK-STUDY ***Federal work-study:*** Total amount: $2,665,893; 930 jobs averaging $2877. ***State or other work-study/employment:*** Total amount: $1,310,726 (100% need-based). 847 part-time jobs averaging $1617.

ATHLETIC AWARDS Total amount: $13,310,637 (5% need-based, 95% non-need-based).

APPLYING FOR FINANCIAL AID ***Required financial aid forms:*** FAFSA, CSS Financial Aid PROFILE, noncustodial (divorced/separated) parent's statement. ***Financial aid deadline (priority):*** 2/15. ***Notification date:*** Continuous beginning 4/3. Students must reply by 5/1.

CONTACT Financial Aid Office, Stanford University, 355 Galvez Street, Stanford, CA 94305-3021, 650-723-3058. *Fax:* 650-725-0540. *E-mail:* financialaid@lists.stanford.edu.

STATE UNIVERSITY OF NEW YORK AT BINGHAMTON

Binghamton, NY

Tuition & fees (NY res): $5910 **Average undergraduate aid package: $11,878**

ABOUT THE INSTITUTION State-supported, coed. Awards: bachelor's, master's, and doctoral degrees and post-master's certificates. 56 undergraduate majors. Total enrollment: 14,373. Undergraduates: 11,523. Freshmen: 2,415. Federal methodology is used as a basis for awarding need-based institutional aid.

UNDERGRADUATE EXPENSES for 2006–07 ***Application fee:*** $40. ***Tuition, state resident:*** full-time $4350; part-time $181 per credit hour. ***Tuition, nonresident:*** full-time $10,610; part-time $442 per credit hour. ***Required fees:*** full-time $1560; $136.50 per credit hour. ***College room and board:*** $8588; ***Room only:*** $5268. Room and board charges vary according to board plan and housing facility. ***Payment plan:*** Installment.

FRESHMAN FINANCIAL AID (Fall 2006, est.) 1823 applied for aid; of those 55% were deemed to have need. 99% of freshmen with need received aid; of those 89% had need fully met. ***Average percent of need met:*** 78% (excluding resources awarded to replace EFC). ***Average financial aid package:*** $11,224 (excluding resources awarded to replace EFC). 7% of all full-time freshmen had no need and received non-need-based gift aid.

UNDERGRADUATE FINANCIAL AID (Fall 2006, est.) 7,390 applied for aid; of those 69% were deemed to have need. 99% of undergraduates with need received aid; of those 77% had need fully met. ***Average percent of need met:*** 78% (excluding resources awarded to replace EFC). ***Average financial aid package:*** $11,878 (excluding resources awarded to replace EFC). 4% of all full-time undergraduates had no need and received non-need-based gift aid.

GIFT AID (NEED-BASED) ***Total amount:*** $23,941,650 (40% federal, 52% state, 2% institutional, 6% external sources). ***Receiving aid:*** Freshmen: 38% (878); All full-time undergraduates: 40% (4,454). ***Average award:*** Freshmen: $5302; Undergraduates: $5027. ***Scholarships, grants, and awards:*** Federal Pell, FSEOG, state, private, college/university gift aid from institutional funds.

GIFT AID (NON-NEED-BASED) ***Total amount:*** $3,269,036 (21% state, 79% institutional). ***Receiving aid:*** Freshmen: 14% (321); Undergraduates: 10% (1,066). ***Average award:*** Freshmen: $991; Undergraduates: $3203. ***Scholarships, grants, and awards by category:*** *Academic Interests/Achievement:* 501 awards ($2,203,687 total): biological sciences, business, computer science, engineering/technologies, English, foreign languages, general academic interests/achievements, health fields, international studies, mathematics, physical sciences, premedicine. *Creative Arts/Performance:* 10 awards ($12,800 total): creative writing, general creative arts/performance, music, performing arts, theater/drama. *Special Achievements/Activities:* 36 awards ($69,875 total): community service, general special achievements/activities, leadership, memberships. *Special Characteristics:* 185 awards ($190,900 total): children with a deceased or disabled parent, ethnic background, local/state students, members of minority groups, out-of-state students. ***Tuition waivers:*** Full or partial for employees or children of employees. ***ROTC:*** Air Force cooperative.

LOANS ***Student loans:*** $41,216,031 (100% need-based). 58% of past graduating class borrowed through all loan programs. *Average indebtedness per student:* $15,167. ***Average need-based loan:*** Freshmen: $2768; Undergraduates: $4261. ***Parent loans:*** $48,568,550 (100% need-based). ***Programs:*** Federal Direct (Subsidized and Unsubsidized Stafford, PLUS), Perkins, Federal Nursing, college/university.

WORK-STUDY ***Federal work-study:*** Total amount: $2,249,450; 1,467 jobs averaging $1401.

ATHLETIC AWARDS Total amount: $2,121,971 (100% non-need-based).

APPLYING FOR FINANCIAL AID ***Required financial aid forms:*** FAFSA, state aid form. ***Financial aid deadline (priority):*** 2/1. ***Notification date:*** Continuous. Students must reply within 2 weeks of notification.

CONTACT Mr. Dennis Chavez, Director of Student Financial Aid and Employment, State University of New York at Binghamton, PO Box 6011, Binghamton, NY 13902-6011, 607-777-2428.

STATE UNIVERSITY OF NEW YORK AT BUFFALO

Buffalo, NY

See University at Buffalo, the State University of New York.

STATE UNIVERSITY OF NEW YORK AT FREDONIA

Fredonia, NY

Tuition & fees (NY res): $5482 **Average undergraduate aid package: $8065**

ABOUT THE INSTITUTION State-supported, coed. Awards: bachelor's and master's degrees. 74 undergraduate majors. Total enrollment: 5,540. Undergraduates: 5,046. Freshmen: 1,077. Federal methodology is used as a basis for awarding need-based institutional aid.

UNDERGRADUATE EXPENSES for 2006–07 ***Application fee:*** $40. ***Tuition, state resident:*** full-time $4350; part-time $181 per credit hour. ***Tuition, nonresident:***

full-time $10,610; part-time $442 per credit hour. ***Required fees:*** full-time $1132; $47 per credit hour. ***College room and board:*** $8120; ***Room only:*** $4750. Room and board charges vary according to board plan and housing facility. ***Payment plan:*** Installment.

FRESHMAN FINANCIAL AID (Fall 2006, est.) 887 applied for aid; of those 70% were deemed to have need. 98% of freshmen with need received aid; of those 24% had need fully met. ***Average percent of need met:*** 69% (excluding resources awarded to replace EFC). ***Average financial aid package:*** $7750 (excluding resources awarded to replace EFC). 10% of all full-time freshmen had no need and received non-need-based gift aid.

UNDERGRADUATE FINANCIAL AID (Fall 2006, est.) 4,073 applied for aid; of those 73% were deemed to have need. 99% of undergraduates with need received aid; of those 30% had need fully met. ***Average percent of need met:*** 75% (excluding resources awarded to replace EFC). ***Average financial aid package:*** $8065 (excluding resources awarded to replace EFC). 6% of all full-time undergraduates had no need and received non-need-based gift aid.

GIFT AID (NEED-BASED) ***Total amount:*** $10,312,964 (36% federal, 48% state, 10% institutional, 6% external sources). ***Receiving aid:*** Freshmen: 55% (554); All full-time undergraduates: 56% (2,676). ***Average award:*** Freshmen: $3483; Undergraduates: $3150. ***Scholarships, grants, and awards:*** Federal Pell, FSEOG, state, private, college/university gift aid from institutional funds.

GIFT AID (NON-NEED-BASED) ***Receiving aid:*** Freshmen: 16% (161); Undergraduates: 10% (489). ***Average award:*** Freshmen: $1448; Undergraduates: $1714. ***Scholarships, grants, and awards by category:*** *Academic Interests/Achievement:* 381 awards ($407,177 total): biological sciences, business, communication, computer science, education, English, foreign languages, general academic interests/achievements, humanities, international studies, mathematics, physical sciences, social sciences. *Creative Arts/Performance:* 102 awards ($65,825 total): applied art and design, art/fine arts, dance, music, performing arts, theater/drama. *Special Achievements/Activities:* 31 awards ($108,050 total): general special achievements/activities, leadership. *Special Characteristics:* 132 awards ($166,100 total): children and siblings of alumni, ethnic background, general special characteristics, international students, local/state students, members of minority groups, out-of-state students, parents of current students, previous college experience, veterans, veterans' children.

LOANS ***Student loans:*** $24,654,614 (45% need-based, 55% non-need-based). 79% of past graduating class borrowed through all loan programs. *Average indebtedness per student:* $22,303. ***Average need-based loan:*** Freshmen: $3057; Undergraduates: $4201. ***Parent loans:*** $3,392,884 (100% non-need-based). ***Programs:*** FFEL (Subsidized and Unsubsidized Stafford, PLUS), Perkins, alternative (private) loans.

WORK-STUDY ***Federal work-study:*** Total amount: $272,731; 262 jobs averaging $1632. ***State or other work-study/employment:*** 850 part-time jobs averaging $1950.

APPLYING FOR FINANCIAL AID ***Required financial aid forms:*** FAFSA, state aid form. ***Financial aid deadline:*** 5/15 (priority: 1/31). ***Notification date:*** Continuous beginning 3/10. Students must reply within 4 weeks of notification.

CONTACT Amy Beers, Financial Aid Advisor, State University of New York at Fredonia, 2nd Floor Maytum Hall, Fredonia, NY 14063, 716-673-3253 or toll-free 800-252-1212. *Fax:* 716-673-3785. *E-mail:* beers@fredonia.edu.

STATE UNIVERSITY OF NEW YORK AT NEW PALTZ

New Paltz, NY

Tuition & fees (NY res): $5340 **Average undergraduate aid package: $2367**

ABOUT THE INSTITUTION State-supported, coed. Awards: bachelor's and master's degrees and post-master's certificates. 73 undergraduate majors. Total enrollment: 7,699. Undergraduates: 6,263. Freshmen: 999. Federal methodology is used as a basis for awarding need-based institutional aid.

UNDERGRADUATE EXPENSES for 2006–07 ***Application fee:*** $40. ***Tuition, state resident:*** full-time $4350; part-time $181 per credit. ***Tuition, nonresident:*** full-time $10,610; part-time $442 per credit. ***Required fees:*** full-time $990; $28.60 per credit or $160 per term part-time. ***College room and board:*** $7630; ***Room only:*** $4840.

FRESHMAN FINANCIAL AID (Fall 2005) 889 applied for aid; of those 62% were deemed to have need. 99% of freshmen with need received aid; of those 18% had need fully met. ***Average percent of need met:*** 65% (excluding resources awarded to replace EFC). ***Average financial aid package:*** $2040 (excluding resources awarded to replace EFC). 5% of all full-time freshmen had no need and received non-need-based gift aid.

UNDERGRADUATE FINANCIAL AID (Fall 2005) 4,375 applied for aid; of those 70% were deemed to have need. 99% of undergraduates with need received aid; of those 23% had need fully met. ***Average percent of need met:*** 67% (excluding resources awarded to replace EFC). ***Average financial aid package:*** $2367 (excluding resources awarded to replace EFC). 3% of all full-time undergraduates had no need and received non-need-based gift aid.

GIFT AID (NEED-BASED) ***Total amount:*** $12,038,358 (43% federal, 57% state). ***Receiving aid:*** Freshmen: 45% (473); All full-time undergraduates: 46% (2,630). ***Average award:*** Freshmen: $2289; Undergraduates: $2429. ***Scholarships, grants, and awards:*** Federal Pell, FSEOG, state, private, college/university gift aid from institutional funds.

GIFT AID (NON-NEED-BASED) ***Total amount:*** $1,014,570 (20% federal, 17% state, 16% institutional, 47% external sources). ***Receiving aid:*** Freshmen: 8% (86); Undergraduates: 5% (261). ***Average award:*** Freshmen: $1700; Undergraduates: $1744. ***Scholarships, grants, and awards by category:*** *Academic Interests/Achievement:* computer science, education, engineering/technologies, English, health fields, humanities, mathematics, physical sciences, premedicine. *Special Characteristics:* members of minority groups.

LOANS ***Student loans:*** $17,201,972 (58% need-based, 42% non-need-based). 75% of past graduating class borrowed through all loan programs. *Average indebtedness per student:* $1900. ***Average need-based loan:*** Freshmen: $2084; Undergraduates: $940. ***Parent loans:*** $6,646,216 (100% non-need-based). ***Programs:*** FFEL (Subsidized and Unsubsidized Stafford, PLUS), Perkins, private.

WORK-STUDY ***Federal work-study:*** Total amount: $1,056,594; 1,249 jobs averaging $846. ***State or other work-study/employment:*** Total amount: $578,665 (100% non-need-based). 480 part-time jobs averaging $1206.

APPLYING FOR FINANCIAL AID ***Required financial aid forms:*** FAFSA, state aid form. ***Financial aid deadline (priority):*** 3/15. ***Notification date:*** Continuous beginning 4/1. Students must reply within 4 weeks of notification.

CONTACT Mr. Daniel Sistarenik, Director of Financial Aid, State University of New York at New Paltz, 200 Hawk Drive, Suite 2, HAB 603B, New Paltz, NY 12561-2437, 845-257-3250 or toll-free 888-639-7589 (in-state). *Fax:* 845-257-3568. *E-mail:* sistared@newpaltz.edu.

STATE UNIVERSITY OF NEW YORK AT OSWEGO

Oswego, NY

Tuition & fees (NY res): $5322 **Average undergraduate aid package: $8486**

ABOUT THE INSTITUTION State-supported, coed. Awards: bachelor's and master's degrees and post-master's certificates. 63 undergraduate majors. Total enrollment: 8,183. Undergraduates: 7,096. Freshmen: 1,347. Federal methodology is used as a basis for awarding need-based institutional aid.

UNDERGRADUATE EXPENSES for 2006–07 ***Application fee:*** $40. ***Tuition, state resident:*** full-time $4350; part-time $181 per credit hour. ***Tuition, nonresident:*** full-time $10,610; part-time $442 per credit hour. ***Required fees:*** full-time $972; $31.28 per credit hour. Part-time tuition and fees vary according to class time, course load, and location. ***College room and board:*** $8940; ***Room only:*** $5490. Room and board charges vary according to board plan and housing facility. ***Payment plan:*** Installment.

FRESHMAN FINANCIAL AID (Fall 2005) 1207 applied for aid; of those 70% were deemed to have need. 98% of freshmen with need received aid; of those 38% had need fully met. ***Average percent of need met:*** 70% (excluding resources awarded to replace EFC). ***Average financial aid package:*** $7132 (excluding resources awarded to replace EFC). 23% of all full-time freshmen had no need and received non-need-based gift aid.

UNDERGRADUATE FINANCIAL AID (Fall 2005) 5,667 applied for aid; of those 75% were deemed to have need. 98% of undergraduates with need received aid; of those 43% had need fully met. ***Average percent of need met:*** 82% (excluding resources awarded to replace EFC). ***Average financial aid package:*** $8486 (excluding resources awarded to replace EFC). 19% of all full-time undergraduates had no need and received non-need-based gift aid.

GIFT AID (NEED-BASED) ***Total amount:*** $16,555,988 (39% federal, 48% state, 10% institutional, 3% external sources). ***Receiving aid:*** Freshmen: 58% (778);

All full-time undergraduates: 58% (3,853). ***Average award:*** Freshmen: $4701; Undergraduates: $3880. ***Scholarships, grants, and awards:*** Federal Pell, FSEOG, state.

GIFT AID (NON-NEED-BASED) ***Total amount:*** $1,949,006 (2% federal, 1% state, 84% institutional, 13% external sources). ***Receiving aid:*** Freshmen: 26% (349); Undergraduates: 14% (950). ***Average award:*** Freshmen: $4250; Undergraduates: $5744. ***Scholarships, grants, and awards by category:*** *Academic Interests/Achievement:* 1,272 awards ($3,250,036 total): area/ethnic studies, biological sciences, business, communication, computer science, education, English, foreign languages, general academic interests/achievements, humanities, international studies, mathematics, physical sciences, premedicine, social sciences. ***ROTC:*** Army cooperative.

LOANS ***Student loans:*** $30,794,813 (78% need-based, 22% non-need-based). 82% of past graduating class borrowed through all loan programs. *Average indebtedness per student:* $21,467. ***Average need-based loan:*** Freshmen: $2506; Undergraduates: $4555. ***Parent loans:*** $6,316,618 (60% need-based, 40% non-need-based). ***Programs:*** FFEL (Subsidized and Unsubsidized Stafford, PLUS), Perkins.

WORK-STUDY ***Federal work-study:*** Total amount: $392,958; 396 jobs averaging $992. ***State or other work-study/employment:*** Total amount: $1,755,236 (79% need-based, 21% non-need-based). 1,254 part-time jobs averaging $1107.

APPLYING FOR FINANCIAL AID ***Required financial aid forms:*** FAFSA, state aid form. ***Financial aid deadline (priority):*** 4/1. ***Notification date:*** Continuous beginning 3/1. Students must reply by 5/1 or within 3 weeks of notification.

CONTACT Mark C. Humbert, Director of Financial Aid, State University of New York at Oswego, 206 Culkin Hall, Oswego, NY 13126, 315-312-2248. *Fax:* 315-312-3696.

STATE UNIVERSITY OF NEW YORK AT PLATTSBURGH

Plattsburgh, NY

Tuition & fees (NY res): $5337 **Average undergraduate aid package: $9473**

ABOUT THE INSTITUTION State-supported, coed. Awards: bachelor's and master's degrees and post-master's certificates. 47 undergraduate majors. Total enrollment: 6,217. Undergraduates: 5,567. Freshmen: 1,105. Both federal and institutional methodology are used as a basis for awarding need-based institutional aid.

UNDERGRADUATE EXPENSES for 2006–07 ***Application fee:*** $40. ***Tuition, state resident:*** full-time $4350; part-time $181 per credit hour. ***Tuition, nonresident:*** full-time $10,610; part-time $442 per credit hour. ***Required fees:*** full-time $987; $41.20 per credit hour. Part-time tuition and fees vary according to course load. ***College room and board:*** $7728; ***Room only:*** $4800. Room and board charges vary according to board plan. ***Payment plans:*** Installment, deferred payment.

FRESHMAN FINANCIAL AID (Fall 2005) 854 applied for aid; of those 72% were deemed to have need. 99% of freshmen with need received aid; of those 28% had need fully met. ***Average percent of need met:*** 85% (excluding resources awarded to replace EFC). ***Average financial aid package:*** $8628 (excluding resources awarded to replace EFC). 30% of all full-time freshmen had no need and received non-need-based gift aid.

UNDERGRADUATE FINANCIAL AID (Fall 2005) 4,119 applied for aid; of those 76% were deemed to have need. 98% of undergraduates with need received aid; of those 31% had need fully met. ***Average percent of need met:*** 90% (excluding resources awarded to replace EFC). ***Average financial aid package:*** $9473 (excluding resources awarded to replace EFC). 26% of all full-time undergraduates had no need and received non-need-based gift aid.

GIFT AID (NEED-BASED) ***Total amount:*** $11,616,602 (40% federal, 46% state, 10% institutional, 4% external sources). ***Receiving aid:*** Freshmen: 57% (587); All full-time undergraduates: 52% (2,744). ***Average award:*** Freshmen: $5034; Undergraduates: $4226. ***Scholarships, grants, and awards:*** Federal Pell, FSEOG, state, private, college/university gift aid from institutional funds.

GIFT AID (NON-NEED-BASED) ***Total amount:*** $2,514,350 (1% federal, 17% state, 79% institutional, 3% external sources). ***Receiving aid:*** Freshmen: 25% (254); Undergraduates: 18% (973). ***Average award:*** Freshmen: $4199; Undergraduates: $5258. ***Scholarships, grants, and awards by category:*** *Academic Interests/Achievement:* 1,905 awards ($3,355,304 total): area/ethnic studies, biological sciences, business, communication, computer science, education, engineering/technologies, English, general academic interests/achievements, health fields, home economics, humanities, international studies, mathematics, physical sciences, premedicine, social sciences. *Creative Arts/Performance:* 35 awards ($62,898 total): art/fine arts, journalism/publications, music, theater/drama. *Special Achievements/Activities:* 24 awards ($45,000 total): community service, general special achievements/activities, leadership. *Special Characteristics:* 885 awards ($1,927,159 total): international students, out-of-state students. ***Tuition waivers:*** Full or partial for employees or children of employees.

LOANS ***Student loans:*** $21,870,875 (79% need-based, 21% non-need-based). 74% of past graduating class borrowed through all loan programs. *Average indebtedness per student:* $17,596. ***Average need-based loan:*** Freshmen: $3975; Undergraduates: $6184. ***Parent loans:*** $4,225,180 (63% need-based, 37% non-need-based). ***Programs:*** Federal Direct (Subsidized and Unsubsidized Stafford, PLUS), Perkins, Federal Nursing, college/university, alternative loans, short-term emergency loans from Student Association.

WORK-STUDY ***Federal work-study:*** Total amount: $365,000; 331 jobs averaging $1100.

APPLYING FOR FINANCIAL AID ***Required financial aid forms:*** FAFSA, state aid form. ***Financial aid deadline (priority):*** 2/15. ***Notification date:*** Continuous beginning 3/15. Students must reply within 6 weeks of notification.

CONTACT Mr. Todd Moravec, Financial Aid Director, State University of New York at Plattsburgh, 101 Broad Street, Kehoe Administration Building 406, Plattsburgh, NY 12901-2681, 518-564-2072 or toll-free 888-673-0012 (in-state). *Fax:* 518-564-4079. *E-mail:* todd.moravec@plattsburgh.edu.

STATE UNIVERSITY OF NEW YORK COLLEGE AT BROCKPORT

Brockport, NY

ABOUT THE INSTITUTION State-supported, coed. Awards: bachelor's and master's degrees and post-bachelor's and post-master's certificates. 112 undergraduate majors. Total enrollment: 8,312. Undergraduates: 6,916. Freshmen: 1,017.

GIFT AID (NEED-BASED) ***Scholarships, grants, and awards:*** Federal Pell, FSEOG, state, private, college/university gift aid from institutional funds.

GIFT AID (NON-NEED-BASED) ***Scholarships, grants, and awards by category:*** *Academic Interests/Achievement:* biological sciences, business, communication, computer science, education, English, foreign languages, general academic interests/achievements, health fields, international studies, mathematics, military science, physical sciences, social sciences. *Creative Arts/Performance:* art/fine arts, creative writing, dance, general creative arts/performance, journalism/publications, performing arts, theater/drama. *Special Achievements/Activities:* community service, general special achievements/activities, leadership, religious involvement. *Special Characteristics:* children and siblings of alumni, ethnic background, first-generation college students, general special characteristics, international students, local/state students, married students, members of minority groups, out-of-state students, religious affiliation, veterans.

LOANS ***Programs:*** Federal Direct (Subsidized and Unsubsidized Stafford, PLUS), Perkins, Federal Nursing, alternative loans.

APPLYING FOR FINANCIAL AID ***Required financial aid forms:*** FAFSA, state aid form.

CONTACT Mr. J. Scott Atkinson, Associate Vice President for Enrollment Management and Student Affairs, State University of New York College at Brockport, 350 New Campus Drive, Brockport, NY 14420-2937, 585-395-2501. *Fax:* 585-395-5445. *E-mail:* satkinso@brockport.edu.

STATE UNIVERSITY OF NEW YORK COLLEGE AT CORTLAND

Cortland, NY

ABOUT THE INSTITUTION State-supported, coed. Awards: bachelor's and master's degrees and post-bachelor's and post-master's certificates. 57 undergraduate majors. Total enrollment: 6,995. Undergraduates: 5,960. Freshmen: 1,091.

GIFT AID (NEED-BASED) ***Scholarships, grants, and awards:*** Federal Pell, FSEOG, state, private, college/university gift aid from institutional funds.

GIFT AID (NON-NEED-BASED) ***Scholarships, grants, and awards by category:*** *Academic Interests/Achievement:* general academic interests/achievements. *Creative Arts/Performance:* music, theater/drama. *Special Achievements/Activities:* general special achievements/activities, leadership. *Special Characteristics:* children and siblings of alumni, members of minority groups.

LOANS ***Programs:*** Federal Direct (Subsidized and Unsubsidized Stafford, PLUS), FFEL (Subsidized and Unsubsidized Stafford, PLUS), Perkins.

APPLYING FOR FINANCIAL AID ***Required financial aid form:*** FAFSA.

CONTACT David Canaski, Financial Aid Office, State University of New York College at Cortland, PO Box 2000, Cortland, NY 13045-0900, 607-753-4717. *Fax:* 607-753-5990. *E-mail:* finaid@em.cortland.edu.

STATE UNIVERSITY OF NEW YORK COLLEGE AT GENESEO

Geneseo, NY

Tuition & fees (NY res): $5560 **Average undergraduate aid package: $9526**

ABOUT THE INSTITUTION State-supported, coed. Awards: bachelor's and master's degrees. 45 undergraduate majors. Total enrollment: 5,530. Undergraduates: 5,358. Freshmen: 1,085. Federal methodology is used as a basis for awarding need-based institutional aid.

UNDERGRADUATE EXPENSES for 2006–07 ***Application fee:*** $40. ***Tuition, state resident:*** full-time $4350; part-time $181 per credit hour. ***Tuition, nonresident:*** full-time $10,610; part-time $442 per credit hour. ***Required fees:*** full-time $1210; $50.25 per credit hour. Part-time tuition and fees vary according to course load. ***College room and board:*** $7788. Room and board charges vary according to board plan and housing facility. ***Payment plans:*** Installment, deferred payment.

FRESHMAN FINANCIAL AID (Fall 2006, est.) 872 applied for aid; of those 49% were deemed to have need. 100% of freshmen with need received aid; of those 73% had need fully met. ***Average percent of need met:*** 73% (excluding resources awarded to replace EFC). ***Average financial aid package:*** $9055 (excluding resources awarded to replace EFC). 2% of all full-time freshmen had no need and received non-need-based gift aid.

UNDERGRADUATE FINANCIAL AID (Fall 2006, est.) 3,900 applied for aid; of those 60% were deemed to have need. 100% of undergraduates with need received aid; of those 86% had need fully met. ***Average percent of need met:*** 86% (excluding resources awarded to replace EFC). ***Average financial aid package:*** $9526 (excluding resources awarded to replace EFC). 5% of all full-time undergraduates had no need and received non-need-based gift aid.

GIFT AID (NEED-BASED) ***Total amount:*** $7,625,413 (37% federal, 63% state). ***Receiving aid:*** Freshmen: 31% (338); All full-time undergraduates: 37% (1,952). ***Average award:*** Freshmen: $2036; Undergraduates: $2646. ***Scholarships, grants, and awards:*** Federal Pell, FSEOG, state, private, college/university gift aid from institutional funds.

GIFT AID (NON-NEED-BASED) ***Total amount:*** $2,209,018 (1% federal, 27% state, 38% institutional, 34% external sources). ***Receiving aid:*** Freshmen: 18% (190); Undergraduates: 10% (545). ***Average award:*** Freshmen: $1930; Undergraduates: $1375. ***Scholarships, grants, and awards by category:*** *Academic Interests/Achievement:* 421 awards ($371,724 total): area/ethnic studies, biological sciences, business, communication, computer science, education, English, foreign languages, general academic interests/achievements, humanities, mathematics, physical sciences, premedicine, social sciences. *Creative Arts/Performance:* 44 awards ($22,050 total): applied art and design, art/fine arts, creative writing, dance, general creative arts/performance, journalism/publications, music, performing arts, theater/drama. *Special Achievements/Activities:* 18 awards ($9350 total): community service, general special achievements/activities, leadership. *Special Characteristics:* 38 awards ($26,177 total): adult students, local/state students, members of minority groups. ***ROTC:*** Army cooperative, Air Force cooperative.

LOANS ***Student loans:*** $19,443,003 (49% need-based, 51% non-need-based). 71% of past graduating class borrowed through all loan programs. *Average indebtedness per student:* $17,000. ***Average need-based loan:*** Freshmen: $4603; Undergraduates: $5307. ***Parent loans:*** $3,083,685 (100% non-need-based). ***Programs:*** FFEL (Subsidized and Unsubsidized Stafford, PLUS), Perkins, state, alternative loans.

WORK-STUDY ***Federal work-study:*** Total amount: $552,938; 420 jobs averaging $1400.

APPLYING FOR FINANCIAL AID ***Required financial aid forms:*** FAFSA, state aid form. ***Financial aid deadline:*** 2/15 (priority: 2/15). ***Notification date:*** Continuous beginning 3/15. Students must reply by 5/1 or within 3 weeks of notification.

CONTACT Archie Cureton, Director of Financial Aid, State University of New York College at Geneseo, 1 College Circle, Erwin Hall 104, Geneseo, NY 14454, 585-245-5731 or toll-free 866-245-5211. *Fax:* 585-245-5717. *E-mail:* cureton@geneseo.edu.

STATE UNIVERSITY OF NEW YORK COLLEGE AT OLD WESTBURY

Old Westbury, NY

Tuition & fees (NY res): $5076 **Average undergraduate aid package: $6438**

ABOUT THE INSTITUTION State-supported, coed. Awards: bachelor's and master's degrees. 42 undergraduate majors. Total enrollment: 3,450. Undergraduates: 3,411. Freshmen: 416. Both federal and institutional methodology are used as a basis for awarding need-based institutional aid.

UNDERGRADUATE EXPENSES for 2006–07 ***Application fee:*** $40. ***Tuition, state resident:*** full-time $4350; part-time $181 per credit. ***Tuition, nonresident:*** full-time $10,610; part-time $442 per credit. ***Required fees:*** full-time $726; $164.90 per course. Part-time tuition and fees vary according to course load. ***College room and board:*** $8083; ***Room only:*** $5793. Room and board charges vary according to board plan and housing facility. ***Payment plan:*** Installment.

FRESHMAN FINANCIAL AID (Fall 2006, est.) 349 applied for aid; of those 99% were deemed to have need. ***Average percent of need met:*** 46% (excluding resources awarded to replace EFC). ***Average financial aid package:*** $6880 (excluding resources awarded to replace EFC).

UNDERGRADUATE FINANCIAL AID (Fall 2006, est.) 2,105 applied for aid; of those 100% were deemed to have need. ***Average percent of need met:*** 45% (excluding resources awarded to replace EFC). ***Average financial aid package:*** $6438 (excluding resources awarded to replace EFC). 1% of all full-time undergraduates had no need and received non-need-based gift aid.

GIFT AID (NEED-BASED) ***Total amount:*** $9,093,483 (46% federal, 53% state, 1% institutional). ***Receiving aid:*** Freshmen: 75% (308); All full-time undergraduates: 63% (1,755). ***Average award:*** Freshmen: $5864; Undergraduates: $4791. ***Scholarships, grants, and awards:*** Federal Pell, FSEOG, state, private, college/university gift aid from institutional funds.

GIFT AID (NON-NEED-BASED) ***Total amount:*** $23,497 (100% external sources). ***Receiving aid:*** Freshmen: 5% (19); Undergraduates: 2% (56). ***Average award:*** Undergraduates: $2600. ***Scholarships, grants, and awards by category:*** *Academic Interests/Achievement:* biological sciences, health fields, physical sciences. ***Tuition waivers:*** Full or partial for senior citizens. ***ROTC:*** Army cooperative, Air Force cooperative.

LOANS ***Student loans:*** $5,927,860 (95% need-based, 5% non-need-based). 49% of past graduating class borrowed through all loan programs. *Average indebtedness per student:* $15,533. ***Average need-based loan:*** Freshmen: $1592; Undergraduates: $2294. ***Parent loans:*** $1,026,737 (92% need-based, 8% non-need-based). ***Programs:*** FFEL (Subsidized and Unsubsidized Stafford, PLUS), Perkins.

WORK-STUDY ***Federal work-study:*** Total amount: $184,003; 245 jobs averaging $751.

APPLYING FOR FINANCIAL AID ***Required financial aid forms:*** FAFSA, institution's own form, state aid form, income documentation. ***Financial aid deadline (priority):*** 4/12. ***Notification date:*** Continuous beginning 4/25. Students must reply within 2 weeks of notification.

CONTACT Ms. Dee Darrell, Financial Aid Assistant, State University of New York College at Old Westbury, PO Box 210, Old Westbury, NY 11568-0210, 516-876-3222. *Fax:* 516-876-3008. *E-mail:* finaid@oldwestbury.edu.

STATE UNIVERSITY OF NEW YORK COLLEGE AT ONEONTA

Oneonta, NY

Tuition & fees (NY res): $5412 **Average undergraduate aid package: $9838**

ABOUT THE INSTITUTION State-supported, coed. Awards: bachelor's and master's degrees and post-bachelor's and post-master's certificates. 71 undergraduate majors. Total enrollment: 5,786. Undergraduates: 5,596. Freshmen: 1,118. Federal methodology is used as a basis for awarding need-based institutional aid.

UNDERGRADUATE EXPENSES for 2006–07 ***Application fee:*** $40. ***Tuition, state resident:*** full-time $4350; part-time $181 per semester hour. ***Tuition, nonresident:***

full-time $10,610; part-time $442 per semester hour. ***Required fees:*** full-time $1062; $34.35 per semester hour. ***College room and board:*** $7696; ***Room only:*** $4378.

FRESHMAN FINANCIAL AID (Fall 2006, est.) 943 applied for aid; of those 63% were deemed to have need. 97% of freshmen with need received aid; of those 17% had need fully met. ***Average percent of need met:*** 60% (excluding resources awarded to replace EFC). ***Average financial aid package:*** $8828 (excluding resources awarded to replace EFC). 27% of all full-time freshmen had no need and received non-need-based gift aid.

UNDERGRADUATE FINANCIAL AID (Fall 2006, est.) 4,343 applied for aid; of those 72% were deemed to have need. 97% of undergraduates with need received aid; of those 19% had need fully met. ***Average percent of need met:*** 65% (excluding resources awarded to replace EFC). ***Average financial aid package:*** $9838 (excluding resources awarded to replace EFC). 22% of all full-time undergraduates had no need and received non-need-based gift aid.

GIFT AID (NEED-BASED) ***Total amount:*** $12,558,739 (38% federal, 49% state, 7% institutional, 6% external sources). ***Receiving aid:*** Freshmen: 45% (506); All full-time undergraduates: 49% (2,653). ***Average award:*** Freshmen: $3980; Undergraduates: $3791. ***Scholarships, grants, and awards:*** Federal Pell, FSEOG, state, private, college/university gift aid from institutional funds.

GIFT AID (NON-NEED-BASED) ***Total amount:*** $255,421 (55% institutional, 45% external sources). ***Average award:*** Freshmen: $3543; Undergraduates: $5223. ***Scholarships, grants, and awards by category:*** *Academic Interests/Achievement:* 45 awards ($40,000 total): biological sciences, education, general academic interests/achievements, home economics, international studies, physical sciences, premedicine. *Creative Arts/Performance:* 18 awards ($10,000 total): journalism/publications, music. *Special Achievements/Activities:* 37 awards ($31,500 total): community service, general special achievements/activities, leadership. *Special Characteristics:* 33 awards ($37,000 total): adult students, children and siblings of alumni, ethnic background, general special characteristics, handicapped students, international students, local/state students, members of minority groups.

LOANS ***Student loans:*** $23,964,737 (51% need-based, 49% non-need-based). 77% of past graduating class borrowed through all loan programs. *Average indebtedness per student:* $12,100. ***Average need-based loan:*** Freshmen: $3393; Undergraduates: $4499. ***Parent loans:*** $7,698,096 (100% need-based). ***Programs:*** FFEL (Subsidized and Unsubsidized Stafford, PLUS), Perkins.

WORK-STUDY ***Federal work-study:*** Total amount: $380,000; 317 jobs averaging $1200. ***State or other work-study/employment:*** Part-time jobs available.

ATHLETIC AWARDS Total amount: $3750 (100% non-need-based).

APPLYING FOR FINANCIAL AID ***Required financial aid forms:*** FAFSA, state aid form. ***Financial aid deadline (priority):*** 3/15. ***Notification date:*** Continuous beginning 3/1.

CONTACT Mr. Bill Goodhue, Director of Financial Aid, State University of New York College at Oneonta, Ravine Parkway, Oneonta, NY 13820, 607-436-2992 or toll-free 800-SUNY-123. *Fax:* 607-436-2659. *E-mail:* goodhucw@oneonta.edu.

STATE UNIVERSITY OF NEW YORK COLLEGE AT POTSDAM

Potsdam, NY

Tuition & fees (NY res): $5357 **Average undergraduate aid package: $12,256**

ABOUT THE INSTITUTION State-supported, coed. Awards: bachelor's and master's degrees. 37 undergraduate majors. Total enrollment: 4,332. Undergraduates: 3,670. Freshmen: 749. Federal methodology is used as a basis for awarding need-based institutional aid.

UNDERGRADUATE EXPENSES for 2006–07 ***Application fee:*** $40. ***Tuition, state resident:*** full-time $4350; part-time $181 per credit hour. ***Tuition, nonresident:*** full-time $10,610; part-time $442 per credit hour. ***Required fees:*** full-time $1007; $46.30 per credit hour. ***College room and board:*** $8220; ***Room only:*** $4720. Room and board charges vary according to board plan and housing facility. ***Payment plan:*** Installment.

FRESHMAN FINANCIAL AID (Fall 2006, est.) 654 applied for aid; of those 75% were deemed to have need. 100% of freshmen with need received aid; of those 85% had need fully met. ***Average percent of need met:*** 85% (excluding resources awarded to replace EFC). ***Average financial aid package:*** $12,479 (excluding resources awarded to replace EFC). 19% of all full-time freshmen had no need and received non-need-based gift aid.

UNDERGRADUATE FINANCIAL AID (Fall 2006, est.) 2,953 applied for aid; of those 77% were deemed to have need. 99% of undergraduates with need received aid; of those 82% had need fully met. ***Average percent of need met:*** 82% (excluding resources awarded to replace EFC). ***Average financial aid package:*** $12,256 (excluding resources awarded to replace EFC). 12% of all full-time undergraduates had no need and received non-need-based gift aid.

GIFT AID (NEED-BASED) ***Total amount:*** $10,466,101 (39% federal, 46% state, 11% institutional, 4% external sources). ***Receiving aid:*** Freshmen: 62% (464); All full-time undergraduates: 60% (2,073). ***Average award:*** Freshmen: $6239; Undergraduates: $4836. ***Scholarships, grants, and awards:*** Federal Pell, FSEOG, state, private, college/university gift aid from institutional funds, VESID Awards, Veterans Administration Rehabilitation Awards, Bureau of Indian Affairs Grant.

GIFT AID (NON-NEED-BASED) ***Total amount:*** $2,410,716 (17% federal, 6% state, 72% institutional, 5% external sources). ***Receiving aid:*** Freshmen: 40% (297); Undergraduates: 30% (1,042). ***Average award:*** Freshmen: $2756; Undergraduates: $3347. ***Scholarships, grants, and awards by category:*** *Academic Interests/Achievement:* 383 awards ($1,002,280 total): biological sciences, business, communication, computer science, education, engineering/technologies, English, foreign languages, general academic interests/achievements, humanities, mathematics, physical sciences, social sciences. *Creative Arts/Performance:* 108 awards ($151,400 total): art/fine arts, dance, music, performing arts, theater/drama. *Special Achievements/Activities:* 281 awards ($440,410 total): community service, general special achievements/activities, leadership. *Special Characteristics:* 152 awards ($138,550 total): adult students, children and siblings of alumni, children of faculty/staff, ethnic background, handicapped students, local/state students, members of minority groups, previous college experience. ***Tuition waivers:*** Full or partial for minority students, employees or children of employees. ***ROTC:*** Army cooperative, Air Force cooperative.

LOANS ***Student loans:*** $15,858,763 (52% need-based, 48% non-need-based). 77% of past graduating class borrowed through all loan programs. *Average indebtedness per student:* $17,495. ***Average need-based loan:*** Freshmen: $3641; Undergraduates: $4258. ***Parent loans:*** $6,035,608 (100% non-need-based). ***Programs:*** Federal Direct (Subsidized and Unsubsidized Stafford, PLUS), Perkins, college/university, alternative loans.

WORK-STUDY ***Federal work-study:*** Total amount: $453,652; 347 jobs averaging $1200.

APPLYING FOR FINANCIAL AID ***Required financial aid forms:*** FAFSA, state aid form. ***Financial aid deadline:*** 5/1 (priority: 3/1). ***Notification date:*** Continuous beginning 2/15. Students must reply within 4 weeks of notification.

CONTACT Susan C. Aldrich, Director of Financial Aid, State University of New York College at Potsdam, 44 Pierrepont Avenue, Potsdam, NY 13676, 315-267-2162 or toll-free 877-POTSDAM. *Fax:* 315-267-3067. *E-mail:* aldricsc@potsdam.edu.

STATE UNIVERSITY OF NEW YORK COLLEGE OF AGRICULTURE AND TECHNOLOGY AT COBLESKILL

Cobleskill, NY

Tuition & fees (NY res): $5650 **Average undergraduate aid package: $7045**

ABOUT THE INSTITUTION State-supported, coed. Awards: associate and bachelor's degrees. 46 undergraduate majors. Total enrollment: 2,506. Undergraduates: 2,506. Freshmen: 962. Federal methodology is used as a basis for awarding need-based institutional aid.

UNDERGRADUATE EXPENSES for 2006–07 ***Application fee:*** $40. ***Tuition, state resident:*** full-time $4350; part-time $181 per credit hour. ***Tuition, nonresident:*** full-time $10,610; part-time $442 per credit hour. ***Required fees:*** full-time $1300; $12.10 per credit. Full-time tuition and fees vary according to degree level. Part-time tuition and fees vary according to degree level. ***College room and board:*** $8630. Room and board charges vary according to board plan and housing facility. ***Payment plan:*** Installment.

FRESHMAN FINANCIAL AID (Fall 2005) 654 applied for aid; of those 61% were deemed to have need. 97% of freshmen with need received aid; of those 12% had need fully met. ***Average percent of need met:*** 59% (excluding resources awarded to replace EFC). ***Average financial aid package:*** $6923 (excluding resources awarded to replace EFC).

UNDERGRADUATE FINANCIAL AID (Fall 2005) 2,016 applied for aid; of those 81% were deemed to have need. 99% of undergraduates with need received

aid; of those 6% had need fully met. ***Average percent of need met:*** 61% (excluding resources awarded to replace EFC). ***Average financial aid package:*** $7045 (excluding resources awarded to replace EFC).

GIFT AID (NEED-BASED) ***Total amount:*** $17,558,581 (16% federal, 84% state). ***Receiving aid:*** Freshmen: 271; All full-time undergraduates: 66% (1,584). ***Average award:*** Freshmen: $4492; Undergraduates: $4532. ***Scholarships, grants, and awards:*** Federal Pell, FSEOG, state, private, college/university gift aid from institutional funds.

GIFT AID (NON-NEED-BASED) ***Total amount:*** $500,681 (23% institutional). ***Receiving aid:*** Freshmen: 86; Undergraduates: 6% (156). ***Tuition waivers:*** Full or partial for employees or children of employees.

LOANS ***Student loans:*** $6,644,683 (100% need-based). 88% of past graduating class borrowed through all loan programs. *Average indebtedness per student:* $22,463. ***Average need-based loan:*** Freshmen: $2832; Undergraduates: $3228. ***Parent loans:*** $2,827,567 (100% need-based). ***Programs:*** FFEL (Subsidized and Unsubsidized Stafford, PLUS), Perkins.

WORK-STUDY ***Federal work-study:*** Total amount: $97,193; 190 jobs averaging $1150. ***State or other work-study/employment:*** Part-time jobs available.

APPLYING FOR FINANCIAL AID ***Required financial aid forms:*** FAFSA, state aid form. ***Financial aid deadline:*** 3/1. ***Notification date:*** 4/1. Students must reply within 2 weeks of notification.

CONTACT Richard Young, Director of Financial Aid, State University of New York College of Agriculture and Technology at Cobleskill, Knapp Hall, Cobleskill, NY 12043, 518-255-5623 or toll-free 800-295-8988. *Fax:* 518-255-5844.

STATE UNIVERSITY OF NEW YORK COLLEGE OF ENVIRONMENTAL SCIENCE AND FORESTRY

Syracuse, NY

Tuition & fees (NY res): $5069 Average undergraduate aid package: $12,450

ABOUT THE INSTITUTION State-supported, coed. Awards: associate, bachelor's, master's, and doctoral degrees. 48 undergraduate majors. Total enrollment: 2,069. Undergraduates: 1,544. Freshmen: 242. Federal methodology is used as a basis for awarding need-based institutional aid.

UNDERGRADUATE EXPENSES for 2007–08 ***Application fee:*** $40. ***Tuition, state resident:*** full-time $4350; part-time $181 per credit hour. ***Tuition, nonresident:*** full-time $10,610; part-time $442 per credit hour. ***College room and board:*** $10,600; ***Room only:*** $5210.

FRESHMAN FINANCIAL AID (Fall 2006, est.) 228 applied for aid; of those 91% were deemed to have need. 100% of freshmen with need received aid; of those 100% had need fully met. ***Average percent of need met:*** 100% (excluding resources awarded to replace EFC). ***Average financial aid package:*** $11,150 (excluding resources awarded to replace EFC). 12% of all full-time freshmen had no need and received non-need-based gift aid.

UNDERGRADUATE FINANCIAL AID (Fall 2006, est.) 1,226 applied for aid; of those 89% were deemed to have need. 92% of undergraduates with need received aid; of those 100% had need fully met. ***Average percent of need met:*** 100% (excluding resources awarded to replace EFC). ***Average financial aid package:*** $12,450 (excluding resources awarded to replace EFC). 5% of all full-time undergraduates had no need and received non-need-based gift aid.

GIFT AID (NEED-BASED) ***Total amount:*** $4,256,000 (42% federal, 38% state, 15% institutional, 5% external sources). ***Receiving aid:*** Freshmen: 66% (160); All full-time undergraduates: 73% (982). ***Average award:*** Freshmen: $4800; Undergraduates: $6500. ***Scholarships, grants, and awards:*** Federal Pell, FSEOG, state, private, college/university gift aid from institutional funds.

GIFT AID (NON-NEED-BASED) ***Total amount:*** $508,000 (20% federal, 11% state, 49% institutional, 20% external sources). ***Receiving aid:*** Freshmen: 12% (28); Undergraduates: 5% (68). ***Average award:*** Freshmen: $2500; Undergraduates: $2000. ***Scholarships, grants, and awards by category:*** *Academic Interests/Achievement:* 108 awards ($150,000 total): agriculture, architecture, biological sciences, engineering/technologies, physical sciences, premedicine. *Special Achievements/Activities:* leadership. *Special Characteristics:* 42 awards ($90,000 total): members of minority groups. ***ROTC:*** Army cooperative, Air Force cooperative.

LOANS ***Student loans:*** $8,000,000 (54% need-based, 46% non-need-based). 92% of past graduating class borrowed through all loan programs. *Average indebtedness per student:* $19,000. ***Average need-based loan:*** Freshmen: $4625; Undergraduates: $6400. ***Parent loans:*** $2,450,000 (25% need-based, 75% non-need-based). ***Programs:*** FFEL (Subsidized and Unsubsidized Stafford, PLUS), Perkins, college/university.

WORK-STUDY ***Federal work-study:*** Total amount: $350,000; 310 jobs averaging $1129. ***State or other work-study/employment:*** Total amount: $200,000 (100% non-need-based). 120 part-time jobs averaging $1667.

APPLYING FOR FINANCIAL AID ***Required financial aid forms:*** FAFSA, state aid form. ***Financial aid deadline (priority):*** 3/1. ***Notification date:*** 4/1. Students must reply within 2 weeks of notification.

CONTACT Mr. John E. View, Director of Financial Aid, State University of New York College of Environmental Science and Forestry, One Forestry Drive, 115 Bray Hall, Syracuse, NY 13210-2779, 315-470-6671 or toll-free 800-777-7373. *Fax:* 315-470-4734. *E-mail:* jeview@esf.edu.

STATE UNIVERSITY OF NEW YORK DOWNSTATE MEDICAL CENTER

Brooklyn, NY

Tuition & fees (NY res): $4745 Average undergraduate aid package: $12,500

ABOUT THE INSTITUTION State-supported, coed. Awards: bachelor's, master's, doctoral, and first professional degrees and post-bachelor's and post-master's certificates. 6 undergraduate majors. Total enrollment: 1,609. Undergraduates: 350. Federal methodology is used as a basis for awarding need-based institutional aid.

UNDERGRADUATE EXPENSES for 2006–07 ***Application fee:*** $30. ***Tuition, state resident:*** full-time $4745; part-time $181 per credit. ***Tuition, nonresident:*** full-time $11,005; part-time $442 per credit. ***College room and board:*** $12,260.

UNDERGRADUATE FINANCIAL AID (Fall 2005) 302 applied for aid; of those 100% were deemed to have need. 100% of undergraduates with need received aid. ***Average percent of need met:*** 50% (excluding resources awarded to replace EFC). ***Average financial aid package:*** $12,500 (excluding resources awarded to replace EFC).

GIFT AID (NEED-BASED) ***Total amount:*** $841,750 (66% federal, 28% state, 6% external sources). ***Receiving aid:*** All full-time undergraduates: 97. ***Average award:*** Undergraduates: $2729. ***Scholarships, grants, and awards:*** Federal Pell, FSEOG.

LOANS ***Student loans:*** $1,469,803 (53% need-based, 47% non-need-based). ***Average need-based loan:*** Undergraduates: $4186. ***Parent loans:*** $40,518 (100% need-based). ***Programs:*** FFEL (Subsidized and Unsubsidized Stafford, PLUS), Perkins, Federal Nursing.

WORK-STUDY ***Federal work-study:*** Total amount: $156,095; 79 jobs averaging $8.

APPLYING FOR FINANCIAL AID ***Financial aid deadline (priority):*** 3/1.

CONTACT Financial Aid Office, State University of New York Downstate Medical Center, 450 Clarkson Avenue, Brooklyn, NY 11203-2098, 718-270-2488. *Fax:* 718-270-7592. *E-mail:* finaid1@downstate.edu.

STATE UNIVERSITY OF NEW YORK INSTITUTE OF TECHNOLOGY

Utica, NY

ABOUT THE INSTITUTION State-supported, coed. Awards: bachelor's and master's degrees and post-master's certificates. 19 undergraduate majors. Total enrollment: 2,587. Undergraduates: 2,069. Freshmen: 132.

GIFT AID (NEED-BASED) ***Scholarships, grants, and awards:*** Federal Pell, FSEOG, state.

GIFT AID (NON-NEED-BASED) ***Scholarships, grants, and awards by category:*** *Academic Interests/Achievement:* computer science, engineering/technologies, general academic interests/achievements. *Special Characteristics:* local/state students, members of minority groups, previous college experience.

LOANS ***Programs:*** Federal Direct (Subsidized and Unsubsidized Stafford, PLUS), Perkins, Federal Nursing.

WORK-STUDY ***Federal work-study:*** Total amount: $161,000; 100 jobs averaging $1400.

APPLYING FOR FINANCIAL AID ***Required financial aid forms:*** FAFSA, state aid form.

CONTACT Director of Financial Aid, State University of New York Institute of Technology, PO Box 3050, Utica, NY 13504-3050, 315-792-7210 or toll-free 800-SUNYTEC. *Fax:* 315-792-7220. *E-mail:* @sunyit.edu.

STATE UNIVERSITY OF NEW YORK MARITIME COLLEGE

Throggs Neck, NY

CONTACT Ms. Madeline Aponte, Director of Financial Aid, State University of New York Maritime College, 6 Pennyfield Avenue, Throgs Neck, NY 10465-4198, 718-409-7267 or toll-free 800-654-1874 (in-state), 800-642-1874 (out-of-state). *Fax:* 718-409-7275. *E-mail:* finaid@sunymaritime.edu.

STATE UNIVERSITY OF NEW YORK UPSTATE MEDICAL UNIVERSITY

Syracuse, NY

ABOUT THE INSTITUTION State-supported, coed. Awards: bachelor's, master's, doctoral, and first professional degrees and post-master's certificates. 8 undergraduate majors. Total enrollment: 1,236. Undergraduates: 255. Entering class: 159.

GIFT AID (NEED-BASED) ***Scholarships, grants, and awards:*** Federal Pell, FSEOG, college/university gift aid from institutional funds, State Grants.

GIFT AID (NON-NEED-BASED) ***Scholarships, grants, and awards by category:*** *Academic Interests/Achievement:* health fields.

LOANS ***Programs:*** FFEL (Subsidized and Unsubsidized Stafford, PLUS), Perkins.

APPLYING FOR FINANCIAL AID ***Required financial aid form:*** FAFSA.

CONTACT Office of Financial Aid, State University of New York Upstate Medical University, 155 Elizabeth Blackwell Street, Syracuse, NY 13210-2375, 315-464-4329 or toll-free 800-736-2171. *E-mail:* finaid@upstate.edu.

STEPHEN F. AUSTIN STATE UNIVERSITY

Nacogdoches, TX

Tuition & fees (TX res): $5232 **Average undergraduate aid package: $4732**

ABOUT THE INSTITUTION State-supported, coed. Awards: bachelor's, master's, and doctoral degrees. 73 undergraduate majors. Total enrollment: 11,756. Undergraduates: 10,158. Freshmen: 2,246. Federal methodology is used as a basis for awarding need-based institutional aid.

UNDERGRADUATE EXPENSES for 2006–07 ***Application fee:*** $35. ***Tuition, state resident:*** full-time $4050; part-time $135 per credit hour. ***Tuition, nonresident:*** full-time $12,300; part-time $410 per credit hour. ***Required fees:*** full-time $1182; $111 per credit hour or $11 per term part-time. Full-time tuition and fees vary according to course load. Part-time tuition and fees vary according to course load. ***College room and board:*** $6544. Room and board charges vary according to board plan and housing facility. ***Payment plan:*** Installment.

FRESHMAN FINANCIAL AID (Fall 2005) 1341 applied for aid; of those 68% were deemed to have need. 99% of freshmen with need received aid; of those 20% had need fully met. ***Average percent of need met:*** 95% (excluding resources awarded to replace EFC). ***Average financial aid package:*** $4361 (excluding resources awarded to replace EFC). 9% of all full-time freshmen had no need and received non-need-based gift aid.

UNDERGRADUATE FINANCIAL AID (Fall 2005) 5,504 applied for aid; of those 74% were deemed to have need. 99% of undergraduates with need received aid; of those 21% had need fully met. ***Average percent of need met:*** 95% (excluding resources awarded to replace EFC). ***Average financial aid package:*** $4732 (excluding resources awarded to replace EFC). 5% of all full-time undergraduates had no need and received non-need-based gift aid.

GIFT AID (NEED-BASED) ***Total amount:*** $18,212,158 (55% federal, 25% state, 20% institutional). ***Receiving aid:*** Freshmen: 44% (767); All full-time undergraduates: 47% (3,541). ***Average award:*** Freshmen: $2424; Undergraduates: $2241. ***Scholarships, grants, and awards:*** Federal Pell, FSEOG, state, private, college/university gift aid from institutional funds.

GIFT AID (NON-NEED-BASED) ***Total amount:*** $9,831,420 (1% federal, 2% state, 69% institutional, 28% external sources). ***Receiving aid:*** Freshmen: 52% (908); Undergraduates: 54% (4,049). ***Average award:*** Freshmen: $2791; Undergraduates: $2578. ***Scholarships, grants, and awards by category:*** *Academic Interests/Achievement:* agriculture, biological sciences, business, communication, computer science, education, general academic interests/achievements, health fields, home economics, mathematics, military science, physical sciences, premedicine. *Creative Arts/Performance:* applied art and design, art/fine arts, journalism/publications, music, theater/drama. *Special Achievements/Activities:* cheerleading/drum major, general special achievements/activities, hobbies/interests, leadership, rodeo. *Special Characteristics:* adult students, children of union members/company employees, first-generation college students, general special characteristics, local/state students, previous college experience, religious affiliation. ***Tuition waivers:*** Full or partial for employees or children of employees. ***ROTC:*** Army.

LOANS ***Student loans:*** $48,498,743 (42% need-based, 58% non-need-based). 67% of past graduating class borrowed through all loan programs. *Average indebtedness per student:* $19,177. ***Average need-based loan:*** Freshmen: $1219; Undergraduates: $2085. ***Parent loans:*** $6,729,942 (100% non-need-based). ***Programs:*** FFEL (Subsidized and Unsubsidized Stafford, PLUS), Perkins, state, college/university, alternative loans.

WORK-STUDY ***Federal work-study:*** Total amount: $704,397; 520 jobs averaging $1355. ***State or other work-study/employment:*** Total amount: $78,273 (100% need-based). 53 part-time jobs averaging $1477.

ATHLETIC AWARDS Total amount: $2,154,127 (100% non-need-based).

APPLYING FOR FINANCIAL AID ***Required financial aid forms:*** FAFSA, institution's own form. ***Financial aid deadline (priority):*** 4/1. ***Notification date:*** Continuous beginning 4/1. Students must reply within 6 weeks of notification.

CONTACT Office of Financial Aid, Stephen F. Austin State University, PO Box 13052, SFA Station, Nacogdoches, TX 75962, 936-468-2403 or toll-free 800-731-2902. *Fax:* 936-468-1048. *E-mail:* finaid@sfasu.edu.

STEPHENS COLLEGE

Columbia, MO

Tuition & fees: $20,500 **Average undergraduate aid package: $14,579**

ABOUT THE INSTITUTION Independent, undergraduate: women only; graduate: coed. Awards: bachelor's and master's degrees and post-bachelor's certificates. 35 undergraduate majors. Total enrollment: 964. Undergraduates: 845. Freshmen: 225. Federal methodology is used as a basis for awarding need-based institutional aid.

UNDERGRADUATE EXPENSES for 2006–07 ***Application fee:*** $25. ***Comprehensive fee:*** $28,475 includes full-time tuition ($20,500) and room and board ($7975). ***College room only:*** $4760. Room and board charges vary according to board plan, gender, and housing facility. ***Part-time tuition:*** $235 per hour. ***Payment plan:*** Installment.

FRESHMAN FINANCIAL AID (Fall 2006, est.) 195 applied for aid; of those 85% were deemed to have need. 100% of freshmen with need received aid; of those 14% had need fully met. ***Average percent of need met:*** 80% (excluding resources awarded to replace EFC). ***Average financial aid package:*** $16,787 (excluding resources awarded to replace EFC). 19% of all full-time freshmen had no need and received non-need-based gift aid.

UNDERGRADUATE FINANCIAL AID (Fall 2006, est.) 569 applied for aid; of those 88% were deemed to have need. 100% of undergraduates with need received aid; of those 12% had need fully met. ***Average percent of need met:*** 78% (excluding resources awarded to replace EFC). ***Average financial aid package:*** $14,579 (excluding resources awarded to replace EFC). 21% of all full-time undergraduates had no need and received non-need-based gift aid.

GIFT AID (NEED-BASED) ***Total amount:*** $6,045,138 (11% federal, 5% state, 82% institutional, 2% external sources). ***Receiving aid:*** Freshmen: 50% (109); All full-time undergraduates: 55% (361). ***Average award:*** Freshmen: $5644; Undergraduates: $6526. ***Scholarships, grants, and awards:*** Federal Pell, FSEOG, state, private, college/university gift aid from institutional funds, Federal Academic Competitiveness Grant, Federal SMART Grant.

GIFT AID (NON-NEED-BASED) ***Total amount:*** $1,643,090 (1% state, 97% institutional, 2% external sources). ***Receiving aid:*** Freshmen: 75% (164); Undergraduates: 68% (449). ***Average award:*** Freshmen: $9696; Undergraduates: $8629. ***Scholarships, grants, and awards by category:*** *Academic Interests/Achievement:* 521 awards ($3,385,807 total): general academic interests/achievements. *Creative Arts/Performance:* 73 awards ($358,500 total): creative writing, dance, performing arts, theater/drama. *Special Achievements/Activities:* 364 awards ($744,036 total): leadership. *Special Characteristics:* 176 awards ($295,576 total): children and siblings of alumni, children of faculty/staff, local/state students, out-of-state students, parents of current students, siblings of current students. ***Tuition waivers:*** Full or partial for employees or children of employees. ***ROTC:*** Army cooperative, Air Force cooperative.

LOANS ***Student loans:*** $2,727,065 (75% need-based, 25% non-need-based). 69% of past graduating class borrowed through all loan programs. *Average indebtedness per student:* $18,810. ***Average need-based loan:*** Freshmen: $2981; Undergraduates: $4183. ***Parent loans:*** $1,698,363 (64% need-based, 36% non-need-based). ***Programs:*** FFEL (Subsidized and Unsubsidized Stafford, PLUS), Perkins, alternative loans.

WORK-STUDY ***Federal work-study:*** Total amount: $60,085; 45 jobs averaging $1335. ***State or other work-study/employment:*** Total amount: $198,284 (100% non-need-based). 168 part-time jobs averaging $1180.

ATHLETIC AWARDS Total amount: $198,950 (76% need-based, 24% non-need-based).

APPLYING FOR FINANCIAL AID ***Required financial aid form:*** FAFSA. ***Financial aid deadline (priority):*** 3/15. ***Notification date:*** Continuous beginning 3/1.

CONTACT Mrs. Rachel Touchatt, Financial Aid Director, Stephens College, 1200 East Broadway, Campus Box 2124, Columbia, MO 65215-0002, 800-876-7207. *Fax:* 573-876-2320. *E-mail:* finaid@stephens.edu.

STERLING COLLEGE

Sterling, KS

CONTACT Ms. Jodi Lightner, Director of Financial Aid, Sterling College, PO Box 98, Sterling, KS 67579-0098, 620-278-4207 or toll-free 800-346-1017. *Fax:* 620-278-4416. *E-mail:* jlightner@sterling.edu.

STERLING COLLEGE

Craftsbury Common, VT

Tuition & fees: $17,780 **Average undergraduate aid package: $17,710**

ABOUT THE INSTITUTION Independent, coed. Awards: associate and bachelor's degrees. 85 undergraduate majors. Total enrollment: 105. Undergraduates: 105. Freshmen: 21. Both federal and institutional methodology are used as a basis for awarding need-based institutional aid.

UNDERGRADUATE EXPENSES for 2006–07 ***Application fee:*** $35. ***Comprehensive fee:*** $24,300 includes full-time tuition ($17,430), mandatory fees ($350), and room and board ($6520). ***College room only:*** $2970. Full-time tuition and fees vary according to course load. Room and board charges vary according to board plan. ***Part-time tuition:*** $545 per credit. Part-time tuition and fees vary according to course load. ***Payment plan:*** Installment.

FRESHMAN FINANCIAL AID (Fall 2006, est.) 21 applied for aid; of those 71% were deemed to have need. 100% of freshmen with need received aid; of those 20% had need fully met. ***Average percent of need met:*** 91% (excluding resources awarded to replace EFC). ***Average financial aid package:*** $17,547 (excluding resources awarded to replace EFC). 10% of all full-time freshmen had no need and received non-need-based gift aid.

UNDERGRADUATE FINANCIAL AID (Fall 2006, est.) 79 applied for aid; of those 90% were deemed to have need. 100% of undergraduates with need received aid; of those 10% had need fully met. ***Average percent of need met:*** 86% (excluding resources awarded to replace EFC). ***Average financial aid package:*** $17,710 (excluding resources awarded to replace EFC). 5% of all full-time undergraduates had no need and received non-need-based gift aid.

GIFT AID (NEED-BASED) ***Total amount:*** $526,065 ***Receiving aid:*** Freshmen: 71% (15); All full-time undergraduates: 72% (71). ***Average award:*** Freshmen: $11,596; Undergraduates: $10,189. ***Scholarships, grants, and awards:*** Federal Pell, FSEOG, state, private, college/university gift aid from institutional funds.

GIFT AID (NON-NEED-BASED) ***Total amount:*** $49,360 ***Receiving aid:*** Undergraduates: 1% (1). ***Average award:*** Freshmen: $1000; Undergraduates: $1200. ***Scholarships, grants, and awards by category:*** *Academic Interests/Achievement:* 7 awards ($16,500 total): general academic interests/achievements. *Special Achievements/Activities:* 16 awards ($71,290 total): general special achievements/activities. *Special Characteristics:* 53 awards ($103,000 total): general special characteristics, local/state students, previous college experience. ***Tuition waivers:*** Full or partial for employees or children of employees, senior citizens.

LOANS ***Student loans:*** $459,728 (91% need-based, 9% non-need-based). 40% of past graduating class borrowed through all loan programs. *Average indebtedness per student:* $15,880. ***Average need-based loan:*** Freshmen: $2709; Undergraduates: $4241. ***Parent loans:*** $120,924 (85% need-based, 15% non-need-based). ***Programs:*** FFEL (Subsidized and Unsubsidized Stafford, PLUS).

WORK-STUDY ***Federal work-study:*** Total amount: $15,072; 33 jobs averaging $457. ***State or other work-study/employment:*** Total amount: $146,935 (77% need-based, 23% non-need-based). 98 part-time jobs averaging $1751.

APPLYING FOR FINANCIAL AID ***Required financial aid forms:*** FAFSA, institution's own form, state aid form. ***Financial aid deadline:*** Continuous. ***Notification date:*** Continuous beginning 1/31. Students must reply by 5/1 or within 2 weeks of notification.

CONTACT Barbara Stuart, Associate Director of Financial Aid, Sterling College, PO Box 72, Craftsbury Common, VT 05827, 800-648-3591 Ext. 2 or toll-free 800-648-3591 Ext. 100. *Fax:* 802-586-2596. *E-mail:* bstuart@sterlingcollege.edu.

STETSON UNIVERSITY

DeLand, FL

Tuition & fees: $28,780 **Average undergraduate aid package: $22,727**

ABOUT THE INSTITUTION Independent, coed. Awards: bachelor's, master's, and first professional degrees and post-master's and first professional certificates. 60 undergraduate majors. Total enrollment: 3,762. Undergraduates: 2,273. Freshmen: 567. Federal methodology is used as a basis for awarding need-based institutional aid.

UNDERGRADUATE EXPENSES for 2007–08 ***Application fee:*** $40. ***Comprehensive fee:*** $36,748 includes full-time tuition ($27,100), mandatory fees ($1680), and room and board ($7968). ***College room only:*** $4548. ***Part-time tuition:*** $825 per credit hour.

FRESHMAN FINANCIAL AID (Fall 2006, est.) 421 applied for aid; of those 82% were deemed to have need. 100% of freshmen with need received aid; of those 39% had need fully met. ***Average percent of need met:*** 87% (excluding resources awarded to replace EFC). ***Average financial aid package:*** $23,644 (excluding resources awarded to replace EFC). 35% of all full-time freshmen had no need and received non-need-based gift aid.

UNDERGRADUATE FINANCIAL AID (Fall 2006, est.) 1,345 applied for aid; of those 86% were deemed to have need. 99% of undergraduates with need received aid; of those 31% had need fully met. ***Average percent of need met:*** 83% (excluding resources awarded to replace EFC). ***Average financial aid package:*** $22,727 (excluding resources awarded to replace EFC). 38% of all full-time undergraduates had no need and received non-need-based gift aid.

GIFT AID (NEED-BASED) ***Total amount:*** $17,538,205 (11% federal, 23% state, 65% institutional, 1% external sources). ***Receiving aid:*** Freshmen: 60% (342); All full-time undergraduates: 52% (1,125). ***Average award:*** Freshmen: $17,685; Undergraduates: $16,231. ***Scholarships, grants, and awards:*** Federal Pell, FSEOG, state, private, college/university gift aid from institutional funds.

GIFT AID (NON-NEED-BASED) ***Total amount:*** $13,748,545 (1% federal, 28% state, 70% institutional, 1% external sources). ***Receiving aid:*** Freshmen: 16% (91); Undergraduates: 11% (230). ***Average award:*** Freshmen: $11,912; Undergraduates: $10,809. ***Scholarships, grants, and awards by category:*** *Academic Interests/Achievement:* area/ethnic studies, biological sciences, business, communication, computer science, education, English, foreign languages, general academic interests/achievements, humanities, mathematics, military science, physical sciences, premedicine, religion/biblical studies, social sciences. *Creative Arts/Performance:* applied art and design, art/fine arts, music, theater/drama. *Special Achievements/Activities:* cheerleading/drum major, community service, general special achievements/activities, leadership, religious involvement. *Special Characteristics:* children and siblings of alumni, children of faculty/staff, ethnic background, general special characteristics, international students, local/state students, members of minority groups. ***ROTC:*** Army cooperative.

LOANS ***Student loans:*** $8,373,069 (64% need-based, 36% non-need-based). 55% of past graduating class borrowed through all loan programs. *Average indebtedness per student:* $22,000. ***Average need-based loan:*** Freshmen: $3499; Undergraduates: $4842. ***Parent loans:*** $2,101,777 (30% need-based, 70% non-need-based). ***Programs:*** FFEL (Subsidized and Unsubsidized Stafford, PLUS), Perkins, college/university.

WORK-STUDY ***Federal work-study:*** Total amount: $1,301,243; 534 jobs averaging $2437. ***State or other work-study/employment:*** Total amount: $704,896 (21% need-based, 79% non-need-based). 219 part-time jobs averaging $3219.

ATHLETIC AWARDS Total amount: $2,826,245 (31% need-based, 69% non-need-based).

APPLYING FOR FINANCIAL AID ***Required financial aid forms:*** FAFSA, institution's own form. ***Financial aid deadline (priority):*** 3/15. ***Notification date:*** Continuous beginning 2/15. Students must reply within 2 weeks of notification.

CONTACT Lois Hicks Williams, Associate Dean of Admissions and Financial Aid, Stetson University, 421 North Woodland Boulevard, DeLand, FL 32723, 386-822-7120 or toll-free 800-688-0101. *Fax:* 386-822-7126. *E-mail:* finaid@stetson.edu.

STEVENS-HENAGER COLLEGE

Boise, ID

CONTACT Financial Aid Office, Stevens-Henager College, 730 Americana Boulevard, Boise, ID 83702, 801-345-0700.

STEVENS INSTITUTE OF TECHNOLOGY

Hoboken, NJ

ABOUT THE INSTITUTION Independent, coed. Awards: bachelor's, master's, and doctoral degrees and post-bachelor's certificates. 26 undergraduate majors. Total enrollment: 4,829. Undergraduates: 1,853. Freshmen: 483.

GIFT AID (NEED-BASED) ***Scholarships, grants, and awards:*** Federal Pell, FSEOG, state, private, college/university gift aid from institutional funds.

GIFT AID (NON-NEED-BASED) ***Scholarships, grants, and awards by category:*** *Academic Interests/Achievement:* business, computer science, engineering/technologies, general academic interests/achievements, humanities, mathematics, physical sciences, premedicine. *Creative Arts/Performance:* art/fine arts, journalism/publications, music, performing arts, theater/drama. *Special Characteristics:* children and siblings of alumni, children of educators, children of faculty/staff, international students, local/state students, members of minority groups.

LOANS ***Programs:*** Federal Direct (Subsidized and Unsubsidized Stafford, PLUS), Perkins, state, Sallie Mae Signature Loans, TERI Loans, NJ Class Loans, CitiAssist Loans.

WORK-STUDY ***Federal work-study:*** Total amount: $500,000; 818 jobs averaging $1269.

APPLYING FOR FINANCIAL AID ***Required financial aid form:*** FAFSA.

CONTACT Ms. Adrienne Hynek, Associate Director of Financial Aid, Stevens Institute of Technology, Castle Point on Hudson, Hoboken, NJ 07030, 201-216-5555 or toll-free 800-458-5323. *Fax:* 201-216-8050. *E-mail:* ahynek@stevens.edu.

STILLMAN COLLEGE

Tuscaloosa, AL

CONTACT Jacqueline S. Morris, Director of Financial Aid, Stillman College, PO Box 1430, Tuscaloosa, AL 35403, 205-366-8950 or toll-free 800-841-5722. *Fax:* 205-247-8106.

STONEHILL COLLEGE

Easton, MA

Tuition & fees: $26,345 **Average undergraduate aid package: $19,235**

ABOUT THE INSTITUTION Independent Roman Catholic, coed. Awards: bachelor's and master's degrees. 32 undergraduate majors. Total enrollment: 2,386. Undergraduates: 2,371. Freshmen: 594. Both federal and institutional methodology are used as a basis for awarding need-based institutional aid.

UNDERGRADUATE EXPENSES for 2006–07 ***Application fee:*** $55. ***Comprehensive fee:*** $37,385 includes full-time tuition ($26,345) and room and board ($11,040). ***College room only:*** $8990. ***Part-time tuition:*** $890 per course. ***Part-time fees:*** $25 per term. Part-time tuition and fees vary according to course load. ***Payment plans:*** Tuition prepayment, installment.

FRESHMAN FINANCIAL AID (Fall 2006, est.) 504 applied for aid; of those 79% were deemed to have need. 100% of freshmen with need received aid; of those 38% had need fully met. ***Average percent of need met:*** 84% (excluding resources awarded to replace EFC). ***Average financial aid package:*** $19,839 (excluding resources awarded to replace EFC). 23% of all full-time freshmen had no need and received non-need-based gift aid.

UNDERGRADUATE FINANCIAL AID (Fall 2006, est.) 1,758 applied for aid; of those 83% were deemed to have need. 100% of undergraduates with need received aid; of those 28% had need fully met. ***Average percent of need met:*** 81% (excluding resources awarded to replace EFC). ***Average financial aid package:*** $19,235 (excluding resources awarded to replace EFC). 23% of all full-time undergraduates had no need and received non-need-based gift aid.

GIFT AID (NEED-BASED) ***Total amount:*** $18,550,029 (7% federal, 4% state, 85% institutional, 4% external sources). ***Receiving aid:*** Freshmen: 64% (382); All full-time undergraduates: 61% (1,382). ***Average award:*** Freshmen: $15,010; Undergraduates: $13,974. ***Scholarships, grants, and awards:*** Federal Pell, FSEOG, state, private, college/university gift aid from institutional funds.

GIFT AID (NON-NEED-BASED) ***Total amount:*** $3,529,110 (5% federal, 84% institutional, 11% external sources). ***Receiving aid:*** Freshmen: 9% (53); Undergraduates: 7% (151). ***Average award:*** Freshmen: $14,995; Undergraduates: $13,187. ***Scholarships, grants, and awards by category:*** *Academic Interests/Achievement:* 1,268 awards ($8,251,461 total): general academic interests/achievements. *Special Characteristics:* 166 awards ($1,772,443 total): children of faculty/staff, members of minority groups, relatives of clergy, siblings of current students. ***Tuition waivers:*** Full or partial for employees or children of employees. ***ROTC:*** Army.

LOANS ***Student loans:*** $12,880,063 (62% need-based, 38% non-need-based). 73% of past graduating class borrowed through all loan programs. *Average indebtedness per student:* $21,595. ***Average need-based loan:*** Freshmen: $5148; Undergraduates: $5374. ***Parent loans:*** $8,667,727 (25% need-based, 75% non-need-based). ***Programs:*** Federal Direct (Subsidized and Unsubsidized Stafford, PLUS), Perkins, state.

WORK-STUDY ***Federal work-study:*** Total amount: $1,639,707; 911 jobs averaging $1800. ***State or other work-study/employment:*** Total amount: $747,558 (22% need-based, 78% non-need-based). 163 part-time jobs averaging $2718.

ATHLETIC AWARDS Total amount: $1,520,517 (54% need-based, 46% non-need-based).

APPLYING FOR FINANCIAL AID ***Required financial aid forms:*** FAFSA, CSS Financial Aid PROFILE, noncustodial (divorced/separated) parent's statement, business/farm supplement. ***Financial aid deadline (priority):*** 2/1. ***Notification date:*** 4/1. Students must reply by 5/1.

CONTACT Rhonda Nickley, Office Manager, Stonehill College, 320 Washington Street, Easton, MA 02357, 508-565-1088. *Fax:* 508-565-1426. *E-mail:* finaid@stonehill.edu.

STONY BROOK UNIVERSITY, STATE UNIVERSITY OF NEW YORK

Stony Brook, NY

Tuition & fees (NY res): $5631 **Average undergraduate aid package: $8200**

ABOUT THE INSTITUTION State-supported, coed. Awards: bachelor's, master's, doctoral, and first professional degrees and post-bachelor's, post-master's, and first professional certificates. 58 undergraduate majors. Total enrollment: 22,522. Undergraduates: 14,847. Freshmen: 2,718. Federal methodology is used as a basis for awarding need-based institutional aid.

UNDERGRADUATE EXPENSES for 2006–07 ***Application fee:*** $40. ***Tuition, state resident:*** full-time $4350; part-time $181 per credit. ***Tuition, nonresident:*** full-time $10,610; part-time $442 per credit. ***Required fees:*** full-time $1281; $62.10 per credit. ***College room and board:*** $8394. Room and board charges vary according to board plan and housing facility. ***Payment plan:*** Installment.

FRESHMAN FINANCIAL AID (Fall 2005) 2021 applied for aid; of those 68% were deemed to have need. 98% of freshmen with need received aid; of those 8% had need fully met. ***Average percent of need met:*** 65% (excluding resources awarded to replace EFC). ***Average financial aid package:*** $8012 (excluding resources awarded to replace EFC). 20% of all full-time freshmen had no need and received non-need-based gift aid.

UNDERGRADUATE FINANCIAL AID (Fall 2005) 9,369 applied for aid; of those 79% were deemed to have need. 97% of undergraduates with need received aid; of those 9% had need fully met. ***Average percent of need met:*** 65% (excluding resources awarded to replace EFC). ***Average financial aid package:*** $8200 (excluding resources awarded to replace EFC). 12% of all full-time undergraduates had no need and received non-need-based gift aid.

GIFT AID (NEED-BASED) ***Total amount:*** $35,918,729 (44% federal, 51% state, 3% institutional, 2% external sources). ***Receiving aid:*** Freshmen: 52% (1,280); All full-time undergraduates: 51% (6,598). ***Average award:*** Freshmen: $5844; Undergraduates: $5357. ***Scholarships, grants, and awards:*** Federal Pell, FSEOG, state, private, college/university gift aid from institutional funds.

GIFT AID (NON-NEED-BASED) ***Total amount:*** $4,217,195 (6% federal, 13% state, 66% institutional, 15% external sources). ***Receiving aid:*** Freshmen: 2%

(51); Undergraduates: 1% (162). ***Average award:*** Freshmen: $2602; Undergraduates: $2468. ***Scholarships, grants, and awards by category:*** *Academic Interests/Achievement:* 1,343 awards ($3,987,794 total): area/ethnic studies, biological sciences, business, computer science, engineering/technologies, English, general academic interests/achievements, health fields, physical sciences, social sciences. *Creative Arts/Performance:* 12 awards ($23,200 total): music, theater/drama. *Special Achievements/Activities:* general special achievements/activities. *Special Characteristics:* 10 awards ($22,500 total): children and siblings of alumni. ***ROTC:*** Army cooperative, Air Force cooperative.

LOANS ***Student loans:*** $40,932,481 (70% need-based, 30% non-need-based). 59% of past graduating class borrowed through all loan programs. *Average indebtedness per student:* $14,816. ***Average need-based loan:*** Freshmen: $2952; Undergraduates: $4070. ***Parent loans:*** $6,288,040 (32% need-based, 68% non-need-based). ***Programs:*** FFEL (Subsidized and Unsubsidized Stafford, PLUS), Perkins.

WORK-STUDY ***Federal work-study:*** Total amount: $582,114; 393 jobs averaging $1485. ***State or other work-study/employment:*** Total amount: $4,236,382 (39% need-based, 61% non-need-based). 1,713 part-time jobs averaging $1817.

ATHLETIC AWARDS Total amount: $2,413,426 (33% need-based, 67% non-need-based).

APPLYING FOR FINANCIAL AID ***Required financial aid forms:*** FAFSA, supplemental admissions essay for honors and Wise. ***Financial aid deadline (priority):*** 3/1. ***Notification date:*** Continuous beginning 3/7. Students must reply within 2 weeks of notification.

CONTACT Jacqueline Pascariello, Director of Financial Aid and Student Employment, Stony Brook University, State University of New York, 180 Administration Building, Stony Brook, NY 11794-0851, 631-632-6840 or toll-free 800-872-7869 (out-of-state). *Fax:* 631-632-9525.

STRATFORD UNIVERSITY

Falls Church, VA

CONTACT Financial Aid Office, Stratford University, 7777 Leesburg Pike, Suite 100 South, Falls Church, VA 22043, 703-821-8570 or toll-free 800-444-0804.

STRAYER UNIVERSITY

Washington, DC

CONTACT Ms. Marjorie Arrington, Director of Financial Aid, Strayer University, 1133 15th Street, NW, Washington, DC 20005-2603, 703-558-7020 or toll-free 888-4-STRAYER. *Fax:* 703-741-3710. *E-mail:* ma@strayer.edu.

SUFFOLK UNIVERSITY

Boston, MA

Tuition & fees: $22,690 **Average undergraduate aid package: $13,452**

ABOUT THE INSTITUTION Independent, coed. Awards: associate, bachelor's, master's, doctoral, and first professional degrees and post-bachelor's, post-master's, and first professional certificates (doctoral degree in law). 61 undergraduate majors. Total enrollment: 8,863. Undergraduates: 5,214. Freshmen: 1,307. Both federal and institutional methodology are used as a basis for awarding need-based institutional aid.

UNDERGRADUATE EXPENSES for 2006–07 ***Application fee:*** $50. ***Comprehensive fee:*** $35,446 includes full-time tuition ($22,610), mandatory fees ($80), and room and board ($12,756). ***College room only:*** $10,596. Room and board charges vary according to board plan and housing facility. ***Part-time tuition:*** $596 per credit. ***Part-time fees:*** $10 per term. ***Payment plans:*** Installment, deferred payment.

FRESHMAN FINANCIAL AID (Fall 2006, est.) 968 applied for aid; of those 80% were deemed to have need. 100% of freshmen with need received aid; of those 13% had need fully met. ***Average percent of need met:*** 68% (excluding resources awarded to replace EFC). ***Average financial aid package:*** $13,387 (excluding resources awarded to replace EFC). 6% of all full-time freshmen had no need and received non-need-based gift aid.

UNDERGRADUATE FINANCIAL AID (Fall 2006, est.) 3,053 applied for aid; of those 82% were deemed to have need. 100% of undergraduates with need received aid; of those 12% had need fully met. ***Average percent of need met:*** 63% (excluding resources awarded to replace EFC). ***Average financial aid package:*** $13,452 (excluding resources awarded to replace EFC). 8% of all full-time undergraduates had no need and received non-need-based gift aid.

GIFT AID (NEED-BASED) ***Total amount:*** $17,081,189 (19% federal, 9% state, 68% institutional, 4% external sources). ***Receiving aid:*** Freshmen: 57% (682); All full-time undergraduates: 50% (2,248). ***Average award:*** Freshmen: $8123; Undergraduates: $7503. ***Scholarships, grants, and awards:*** Federal Pell, FSEOG, state, private, college/university gift aid from institutional funds.

GIFT AID (NON-NEED-BASED) ***Total amount:*** $5,875,185 (99% institutional, 1% external sources). ***Receiving aid:*** Freshmen: 27% (319); Undergraduates: 19% (836). ***Average award:*** Freshmen: $6425; Undergraduates: $5799. ***Scholarships, grants, and awards by category:*** *Academic Interests/Achievement:* 1,006 awards ($4,779,058 total): general academic interests/achievements. *Special Achievements/Activities:* 3 awards ($9000 total): community service. *Special Characteristics:* 137 awards ($214,050 total): children and siblings of alumni, children of faculty/staff, siblings of current students. ***Tuition waivers:*** Full or partial for employees or children of employees, senior citizens. ***ROTC:*** Army cooperative.

LOANS ***Student loans:*** $35,713,966 (33% need-based, 67% non-need-based). ***Average need-based loan:*** Freshmen: $3622; Undergraduates: $4349. ***Programs:*** Federal Direct (Subsidized and Unsubsidized Stafford, PLUS), Perkins, state, college/university.

WORK-STUDY ***Federal work-study:*** Total amount: $1,663,800; 779 jobs averaging $2158. ***State or other work-study/employment:*** Total amount: $907,501 (100% non-need-based). 448 part-time jobs averaging $2284.

APPLYING FOR FINANCIAL AID ***Required financial aid forms:*** FAFSA, institution's own form. ***Financial aid deadline:*** 3/1 (priority: 3/1). ***Notification date:*** Continuous beginning 3/1. Students must reply within 2 weeks of notification.

CONTACT Ms. Christine A. Perry, Director of Financial Aid, Suffolk University, 8 Ashburton Place, Boston, MA 02108, 617-573-8470 or toll-free 800-6-SUFFOLK. *Fax:* 617-720-3579. *E-mail:* finaid@suffolk.edu.

SULLIVAN UNIVERSITY

Louisville, KY

CONTACT Charlene Geiser, Financial Planning Office, Sullivan University, 3101 Bardstown Road, Louisville, KY 40205, 502-456-6504 Ext. 311 or toll-free 800-844-1354. *Fax:* 502-456-0040. *E-mail:* cgeiser@sullivan.edu.

SUL ROSS STATE UNIVERSITY

Alpine, TX

CONTACT Ms. Rena Gallego, Director of Financial Assistance and Recruiting, Sul Ross State University, PO Box C-113, Alpine, TX 79832, 915-837-8059 or toll-free 888-722-7778.

SUSQUEHANNA UNIVERSITY

Selinsgrove, PA

CONTACT Helen S. Nunn, Director of Financial Aid, Susquehanna University, 514 University Avenue, Selinsgrove, PA 17870, 570-372-4450 or toll-free 800-326-9672. *Fax:* 570-372-2722. *E-mail:* nunn@susqu.edu.

SWARTHMORE COLLEGE

Swarthmore, PA

Tuition & fees: $33,232 **Average undergraduate aid package: $30,369**

ABOUT THE INSTITUTION Independent, coed. Awards: bachelor's degrees. 44 undergraduate majors. Total enrollment: 1,484. Undergraduates: 1,484. Freshmen: 370. Institutional methodology is used as a basis for awarding need-based institutional aid.

UNDERGRADUATE EXPENSES for 2006–07 ***Application fee:*** $60. ***Comprehensive fee:*** $43,532 includes full-time tuition ($32,912), mandatory fees ($320), and room and board ($10,300). ***College room only:*** $5280. Room and board charges vary according to board plan. ***Payment plan:*** Installment.

FRESHMAN FINANCIAL AID (Fall 2006, est.) 250 applied for aid; of those 72% were deemed to have need. 100% of freshmen with need received aid; of those 100% had need fully met. ***Average percent of need met:*** 100% (excluding

resources awarded to replace EFC). ***Average financial aid package:*** $30,596 (excluding resources awarded to replace EFC). 1% of all full-time freshmen had no need and received non-need-based gift aid.

UNDERGRADUATE FINANCIAL AID (Fall 2006, est.) 793 applied for aid; of those 91% were deemed to have need. 100% of undergraduates with need received aid; of those 100% had need fully met. ***Average percent of need met:*** 100% (excluding resources awarded to replace EFC). ***Average financial aid package:*** $30,369 (excluding resources awarded to replace EFC). 1% of all full-time undergraduates had no need and received non-need-based gift aid.

GIFT AID (NEED-BASED) ***Total amount:*** $18,935,244 (4% federal, 1% state, 92% institutional, 3% external sources). ***Receiving aid:*** Freshmen: 49% (181); All full-time undergraduates: 49% (719). ***Average award:*** Freshmen: $27,403; Undergraduates: $26,411. ***Scholarships, grants, and awards:*** Federal Pell, FSEOG, state, private, college/university gift aid from institutional funds.

GIFT AID (NON-NEED-BASED) ***Total amount:*** $845,119 (43% institutional, 57% external sources). ***Average award:*** Freshmen: $33,232; Undergraduates: $32,912. ***Scholarships, grants, and awards by category:*** *Academic Interests/Achievement:* 12 awards ($374,352 total): general academic interests/achievements. ***Tuition waivers:*** Full or partial for employees or children of employees. ***ROTC:*** Army cooperative, Air Force cooperative.

LOANS ***Student loans:*** $1,891,589 (88% need-based, 12% non-need-based). 32% of past graduating class borrowed through all loan programs. *Average indebtedness per student:* $13,404. ***Average need-based loan:*** Freshmen: $2249; Undergraduates: $3121. ***Parent loans:*** $2,737,182 (100% non-need-based). ***Programs:*** FFEL (Subsidized and Unsubsidized Stafford, PLUS), Perkins, state, college/university.

WORK-STUDY ***Federal work-study:*** Total amount: $880,068; 632 jobs averaging $1574. ***State or other work-study/employment:*** Total amount: $416,656 (71% need-based, 29% non-need-based). Part-time jobs available.

APPLYING FOR FINANCIAL AID ***Required financial aid forms:*** FAFSA, institution's own form, CSS Financial Aid PROFILE, state aid form, noncustodial (divorced/separated) parent's statement, business/farm supplement, federal tax return, W2 statement, year-end paycheck stub. ***Financial aid deadline:*** 2/15 (priority: 2/15). ***Notification date:*** 4/1. Students must reply by 5/1.

CONTACT Laura Talbot, Director of Financial Aid, Swarthmore College, 500 College Avenue, Swarthmore, PA 19081-1397, 610-328-8358 or toll-free 800-667-3110. *Fax:* 610-328-8673. *E-mail:* finaid@swarthmore.edu.

SWEDISH INSTITUTE, COLLEGE OF HEALTH SCIENCES

New York, NY

CONTACT Financial Aid Office, Swedish Institute, College of Health Sciences, 226 West 26th Street, New York, NY 10001-6700, 212-924-5900.

SWEET BRIAR COLLEGE

Sweet Briar, VA

Tuition & fees: $25,015 **Average undergraduate aid package: $15,150**

ABOUT THE INSTITUTION Independent, women only. Awards: bachelor's and master's degrees. 34 undergraduate majors. Total enrollment: 751. Undergraduates: 739. Freshmen: 190. Federal methodology is used as a basis for awarding need-based institutional aid.

UNDERGRADUATE EXPENSES for 2007–08 ***Application fee:*** $40. ***Comprehensive fee:*** $35,055 includes full-time tuition ($24,740), mandatory fees ($275), and room and board ($10,040). ***College room only:*** $4030.

FRESHMAN FINANCIAL AID (Fall 2006, est.) 137 applied for aid; of those 77% were deemed to have need. ***Average percent of need met:*** 91% (excluding resources awarded to replace EFC). ***Average financial aid package:*** $16,143 (excluding resources awarded to replace EFC). 40% of all full-time freshmen had no need and received non-need-based gift aid.

UNDERGRADUATE FINANCIAL AID (Fall 2006, est.) 359 applied for aid; of those 100% were deemed to have need. ***Average percent of need met:*** 83% (excluding resources awarded to replace EFC). ***Average financial aid package:*** $15,150 (excluding resources awarded to replace EFC). 49% of all full-time undergraduates had no need and received non-need-based gift aid.

GIFT AID (NEED-BASED) ***Total amount:*** $3,889,124 (8% federal, 19% state, 69% institutional, 4% external sources). ***Receiving aid:*** Freshmen: 53% (102); All full-time undergraduates: 42% (238). ***Average award:*** Freshmen: $15,077; Undergraduates: $14,467. ***Scholarships, grants, and awards:*** Federal Pell, FSEOG, state, private, college/university gift aid from institutional funds.

GIFT AID (NON-NEED-BASED) ***Total amount:*** $3,335,034 (11% state, 88% institutional, 1% external sources). ***Receiving aid:*** Freshmen: 40% (76); Undergraduates: 49% (279). ***Average award:*** Freshmen: $11,387; Undergraduates: $11,150. ***Scholarships, grants, and awards by category:*** *Academic Interests/Achievement:* 306 awards ($3,506,707 total): general academic interests/achievements, premedicine. *Creative Arts/Performance:* 1 award ($1000 total): art/fine arts, general creative arts/performance, music. *Special Achievements/Activities:* 6 awards ($3000 total): community service. *Special Characteristics:* 238 awards ($1,722,180 total): adult students, general special characteristics, international students, local/state students.

LOANS ***Student loans:*** $1,524,614 (65% need-based, 35% non-need-based). 54% of past graduating class borrowed through all loan programs. *Average indebtedness per student:* $5496. ***Average need-based loan:*** Freshmen: $4252; Undergraduates: $4382. ***Parent loans:*** $2,686,199 (54% need-based, 46% non-need-based). ***Programs:*** Federal Direct (Subsidized and Unsubsidized Stafford, PLUS), Perkins, college/university.

WORK-STUDY ***Federal work-study:*** Total amount: $56,615; 59 jobs averaging $877. ***State or other work-study/employment:*** Total amount: $90,695 (100% need-based). 88 part-time jobs averaging $919.

APPLYING FOR FINANCIAL AID ***Required financial aid forms:*** FAFSA, state aid form. ***Financial aid deadline (priority):*** 3/1. ***Notification date:*** Continuous beginning 3/1. Students must reply by 5/1 or within 2 weeks of notification.

CONTACT Bobbi Carpenter, Director of Financial Aid, Sweet Briar College, Box AS, Sweet Briar, VA 24595, 800-381-6156 or toll-free 800-381-6142. *Fax:* 434-381-6450. *E-mail:* bcarpenter@sbc.edu.

SYRACUSE UNIVERSITY

Syracuse, NY

Tuition & fees: $29,965 **Average undergraduate aid package: $23,600**

ABOUT THE INSTITUTION Independent, coed. Awards: bachelor's, master's, doctoral, and first professional degrees and post-master's certificates. 147 undergraduate majors. Total enrollment: 17,492. Undergraduates: 11,546. Freshmen: 3,054. Both federal and institutional methodology are used as a basis for awarding need-based institutional aid.

UNDERGRADUATE EXPENSES for 2006–07 ***Application fee:*** $70. ***Comprehensive fee:*** $40,385 includes full-time tuition ($28,820), mandatory fees ($1145), and room and board ($10,420). ***College room only:*** $5390. Room and board charges vary according to board plan and housing facility. ***Part-time tuition:*** $1255 per credit hour. ***Payment plan:*** Installment.

FRESHMAN FINANCIAL AID (Fall 2006, est.) 2240 applied for aid; of those 81% were deemed to have need. 100% of freshmen with need received aid; of those 65% had need fully met. ***Average percent of need met:*** 85% (excluding resources awarded to replace EFC). ***Average financial aid package:*** $23,100 (excluding resources awarded to replace EFC). 13% of all full-time freshmen had no need and received non-need-based gift aid.

UNDERGRADUATE FINANCIAL AID (Fall 2006, est.) ***Average percent of need met:*** 82% (excluding resources awarded to replace EFC). ***Average financial aid package:*** $23,600 (excluding resources awarded to replace EFC). 15% of all full-time undergraduates had no need and received non-need-based gift aid.

GIFT AID (NEED-BASED) ***Total amount:*** $116,178,369 (9% federal, 7% state, 81% institutional, 3% external sources). ***Receiving aid:*** Freshmen: 54% (1,634). ***Average award:*** Freshmen: $17,845; Undergraduates: $16,391. ***Scholarships, grants, and awards:*** Federal Pell, FSEOG, state, college/university gift aid from institutional funds.

GIFT AID (NON-NEED-BASED) ***Total amount:*** $16,698,635 (94% institutional, 6% external sources). ***Receiving aid:*** Freshmen: 4% (123). ***Average award:*** Freshmen: $9500; Undergraduates: $9200. ***Scholarships, grants, and awards by category:*** *Academic Interests/Achievement:* general academic interests/achievements. *Creative Arts/Performance:* art/fine arts, music. ***Tuition waivers:*** Full or partial for employees or children of employees. ***ROTC:*** Army, Air Force.

LOANS ***Student loans:*** $51,119,946 (90% need-based, 10% non-need-based). 64% of past graduating class borrowed through all loan programs. *Average indebtedness per student:* $23,500. ***Average need-based loan:*** Freshmen: $3900; Undergraduates: $5400. ***Parent loans:*** $28,234,163 (75% need-based, 25% non-need-based). ***Programs:*** FFEL (Subsidized and Unsubsidized Stafford, PLUS), Perkins.

WORK-STUDY ***Federal work-study:*** Total amount: $3,300,000; jobs available (averaging $1300). ***State or other work-study/employment:*** Part-time jobs available.

ATHLETIC AWARDS Total amount: $10,816,810 (37% need-based, 63% non-need-based).

APPLYING FOR FINANCIAL AID ***Required financial aid forms:*** FAFSA, CSS Financial Aid PROFILE, noncustodial (divorced/separated) parent's statement, business/farm supplement. ***Financial aid deadline:*** 2/1. ***Notification date:*** 4/1. Students must reply by 5/1.

CONTACT Mr. Christopher Walsh, Executive Director of Financial Aid, Syracuse University, 200 Archbold Gymnasium, Syracuse, NY 13244-1140, 315-443-1513. *E-mail:* finmail@syr.edu.

TABOR COLLEGE

Hillsboro, KS

ABOUT THE INSTITUTION Independent Mennonite Brethren, coed. Awards: associate, bachelor's, and master's degrees. 53 undergraduate majors. Total enrollment: 603. Undergraduates: 599. Freshmen: 131.

GIFT AID (NEED-BASED) ***Scholarships, grants, and awards:*** Federal Pell, FSEOG, state, private, college/university gift aid from institutional funds.

GIFT AID (NON-NEED-BASED) ***Scholarships, grants, and awards by category:*** *Academic Interests/Achievement:* biological sciences, business, communication, computer science, education, English, general academic interests/achievements, humanities, mathematics, premedicine, religion/biblical studies, social sciences. *Creative Arts/Performance:* music, performing arts, theater/drama. *Special Achievements/Activities:* cheerleading/drum major, general special achievements/activities, religious involvement. *Special Characteristics:* children and siblings of alumni, children of faculty/staff, general special characteristics, international students, local/state students, out-of-state students, religious affiliation.

LOANS ***Programs:*** FFEL (Subsidized and Unsubsidized Stafford, PLUS), Perkins.

WORK-STUDY ***Federal work-study:*** Total amount: $98,109; 147 jobs averaging $667. ***State or other work-study/employment:*** Part-time jobs available.

APPLYING FOR FINANCIAL AID ***Required financial aid forms:*** FAFSA, state aid form, admissions application.

CONTACT Mr. Bruce Jost, Director of Student Financial Assistance, Tabor College, 400 South Jefferson, Hillsboro, KS 67063, 620-947-3121 Ext. 1726 or toll-free 800-822-6799. *Fax:* 620-947-6276. *E-mail:* brucej@tabor.edu.

TALLADEGA COLLEGE

Talladega, AL

CONTACT K. Michael Francois, Director of Financial Aid, Talladega College, 627 West Battle Street, Talladega, AL 35160, 256-761-6341 or toll-free 800-762-2468 (in-state), 800-633-2440 (out-of-state). *Fax:* 256-761-6462.

TALMUDICAL ACADEMY OF NEW JERSEY

Adelphia, NJ

CONTACT Office of Financial Aid, Talmudical Academy of New Jersey, Route 524, Adelphia, NJ 07710, 732-431-1600.

TALMUDICAL INSTITUTE OF UPSTATE NEW YORK

Rochester, NY

CONTACT Mrs. Ella Berenstein, Financial Aid Administrator, Talmudical Institute of Upstate New York, 769 Park Avenue, Rochester, NY 14607-3046, 716-473-2810.

TALMUDICAL SEMINARY OHOLEI TORAH

Brooklyn, NY

CONTACT Financial Aid Administrator, Talmudical Seminary Oholei Torah, 667 Eastern Parkway, Brooklyn, NY 11213-3310, 718-774-5050.

TALMUDICAL YESHIVA OF PHILADELPHIA

Philadelphia, PA

CONTACT Rabbi Uri Mandelbaum, Director of Student Financial Aid/Registrar, Talmudical Yeshiva of Philadelphia, 6063 Drexel Road, Philadelphia, PA 19131-1296, 215-473-1212. *E-mail:* typp@juno.com.

TALMUDIC COLLEGE OF FLORIDA

Miami Beach, FL

CONTACT Rabbi Ira Hill, Director of Financial Aid, Talmudic College of Florida, 1910 Alton Road, Miami Beach, FL 33139, 305-534-7050 or toll-free 888-825-6834. *Fax:* 305-534-8444.

TARLETON STATE UNIVERSITY

Stephenville, TX

Tuition & fees (TX res): $4626 **Average undergraduate aid package: $8162**

ABOUT THE INSTITUTION State-supported, coed. Awards: associate, bachelor's, master's, and doctoral degrees. 77 undergraduate majors. Total enrollment: 9,464. Undergraduates: 7,864. Freshmen: 1,278. Federal methodology is used as a basis for awarding need-based institutional aid.

UNDERGRADUATE EXPENSES for 2006–07 ***Application fee:*** $25. ***Tuition, state resident:*** full-time $3600; part-time $120 per credit hour. ***Tuition, nonresident:*** full-time $9100; part-time $395 per credit hour. ***Required fees:*** full-time $1026; $10 per credit hour or $24 per term part-time. Full-time tuition and fees vary according to course load. Part-time tuition and fees vary according to course load. ***College room and board:*** $5802; ***Room only:*** $3106. Room and board charges vary according to board plan and housing facility. ***Payment plan:*** Installment.

FRESHMAN FINANCIAL AID (Fall 2005) 1009 applied for aid; of those 90% were deemed to have need. 100% of freshmen with need received aid; of those 59% had need fully met. ***Average percent of need met:*** 50% (excluding resources awarded to replace EFC). ***Average financial aid package:*** $7874 (excluding resources awarded to replace EFC). 29% of all full-time freshmen had no need and received non-need-based gift aid.

UNDERGRADUATE FINANCIAL AID (Fall 2005) 4,916 applied for aid; of those 96% were deemed to have need. 100% of undergraduates with need received aid; of those 52% had need fully met. ***Average percent of need met:*** 60% (excluding resources awarded to replace EFC). ***Average financial aid package:*** $8162 (excluding resources awarded to replace EFC). 17% of all full-time undergraduates had no need and received non-need-based gift aid.

GIFT AID (NEED-BASED) ***Total amount:*** $9,842,061 (73% federal, 16% state, 11% institutional). ***Receiving aid:*** Freshmen: 33% (434); All full-time undergraduates: 40% (2,770). ***Average award:*** Freshmen: $3811; Undergraduates: $3272. ***Scholarships, grants, and awards:*** Federal Pell, FSEOG, state, private, college/university gift aid from institutional funds.

GIFT AID (NON-NEED-BASED) ***Total amount:*** $3,725,200 (50% institutional, 50% external sources). ***Receiving aid:*** Freshmen: 26% (351); Undergraduates: 23% (1,639). ***Average award:*** Freshmen: $4101; Undergraduates: $3959. ***Scholarships, grants, and awards by category:*** *Academic Interests/Achievement:* general academic interests/achievements. *Creative Arts/Performance:* music, theater/drama. *Special Achievements/Activities:* rodeo. *Special Characteristics:* children of faculty/staff. ***Tuition waivers:*** Full or partial for employees or children of employees, senior citizens. ***ROTC:*** Army.

LOANS ***Student loans:*** $24,091,919 (54% need-based, 46% non-need-based). 60% of past graduating class borrowed through all loan programs. *Average indebtedness per student:* $16,776. ***Average need-based loan:*** Freshmen: $2204; Undergraduates: $3347. ***Parent loans:*** $3,234,487 (100% non-need-based). ***Programs:*** FFEL (Subsidized and Unsubsidized Stafford, PLUS), college/university.

WORK-STUDY ***Federal work-study:*** Total amount: $185,812; 73 jobs available. ***State or other work-study/employment:*** Total amount: $1,751,745 (2% need-based, 98% non-need-based). 10 part-time jobs averaging $3300.

ATHLETIC AWARDS Total amount: $694,535 (100% non-need-based).

APPLYING FOR FINANCIAL AID ***Required financial aid forms:*** FAFSA, institution's own form. ***Financial aid deadline (priority):*** 6/1. ***Notification date:*** Continuous. Students must reply within 2 weeks of notification.

CONTACT Ms. Betty Murray, Director of Student Financial Aid, Tarleton State University, Box T-0310, Stephenville, TX 76402, 254-968-9070 or toll-free 800-687-8236 (in-state). *Fax:* 254-968-9600. *E-mail:* finaid@tarleton.edu.

TAYLOR UNIVERSITY

Upland, IN

Tuition & fees: $22,028 **Average undergraduate aid package: $14,752**

ABOUT THE INSTITUTION Independent interdenominational, coed. Awards: associate, bachelor's, and master's degrees. 74 undergraduate majors. Total enrollment: 1,854. Undergraduates: 1,854. Freshmen: 493. Both federal and institutional methodology are used as a basis for awarding need-based institutional aid.

UNDERGRADUATE EXPENSES for 2006–07 ***Application fee:*** $25. ***Comprehensive fee:*** $27,895 includes full-time tuition ($21,800), mandatory fees ($228), and room and board ($5867). ***College room only:*** $2868. Full-time tuition and fees vary according to course load. Room and board charges vary according to board plan and housing facility. ***Part-time tuition:*** $780 per credit. ***Part-time fees:*** $68 per year. Part-time tuition and fees vary according to course load. ***Payment plan:*** Installment.

FRESHMAN FINANCIAL AID (Fall 2006, est.) 377 applied for aid; of those 80% were deemed to have need. 100% of freshmen with need received aid; of those 23% had need fully met. ***Average percent of need met:*** 77% (excluding resources awarded to replace EFC). ***Average financial aid package:*** $15,135 (excluding resources awarded to replace EFC). 23% of all full-time freshmen had no need and received non-need-based gift aid.

UNDERGRADUATE FINANCIAL AID (Fall 2006, est.) 1,253 applied for aid; of those 83% were deemed to have need. 100% of undergraduates with need received aid; of those 19% had need fully met. ***Average percent of need met:*** 75% (excluding resources awarded to replace EFC). ***Average financial aid package:*** $14,752 (excluding resources awarded to replace EFC). 22% of all full-time undergraduates had no need and received non-need-based gift aid.

GIFT AID (NEED-BASED) ***Total amount:*** $10,102,526 (11% federal, 10% state, 69% institutional, 10% external sources). ***Receiving aid:*** Freshmen: 58% (284); All full-time undergraduates: 53% (962). ***Average award:*** Freshmen: $12,690; Undergraduates: $11,854. ***Scholarships, grants, and awards:*** Federal Pell, FSEOG, state, private, college/university gift aid from institutional funds.

GIFT AID (NON-NEED-BASED) ***Total amount:*** $2,679,591 (1% state, 81% institutional, 18% external sources). ***Receiving aid:*** Freshmen: 8% (37); Undergraduates: 6% (107). ***Average award:*** Freshmen: $5078; Undergraduates: $4607. ***Scholarships, grants, and awards by category:*** *Academic Interests/Achievement:* 760 awards ($2,984,561 total): general academic interests/achievements. *Creative Arts/Performance:* 88 awards ($187,400 total): music, theater/drama. *Special Achievements/Activities:* 84 awards ($410,628 total): leadership. *Special Characteristics:* 691 awards ($1,919,678 total): children and siblings of alumni, children of faculty/staff, ethnic background, international students, religious affiliation. ***Tuition waivers:*** Full or partial for employees or children of employees, senior citizens.

LOANS ***Student loans:*** $7,290,688 (67% need-based, 33% non-need-based). 60% of past graduating class borrowed through all loan programs. *Average indebtedness per student:* $17,712. ***Average need-based loan:*** Freshmen: $3548; Undergraduates: $4070. ***Parent loans:*** $14,467,503 (26% need-based, 74% non-need-based). ***Programs:*** FFEL (Subsidized and Unsubsidized Stafford, PLUS), Perkins, college/university.

WORK-STUDY ***Federal work-study:*** Total amount: $257,902; 773 jobs averaging $334.

ATHLETIC AWARDS Total amount: $1,281,174 (55% need-based, 45% non-need-based).

APPLYING FOR FINANCIAL AID ***Required financial aid forms:*** FAFSA, institution's own form. ***Financial aid deadline:*** 3/10. ***Notification date:*** Continuous beginning 3/1. Students must reply by 5/1.

CONTACT Mr. Timothy A. Nace, Director of Financial Aid, Taylor University, 236 West Reade Avenue, Upland, IN 46989-1001, 765-998-5358 or toll-free 800-882-3456. *Fax:* 765-998-4910. *E-mail:* tmnace@taylor.edu.

TAYLOR UNIVERSITY FORT WAYNE

Fort Wayne, IN

Tuition & fees: $19,056 **Average undergraduate aid package: $16,287**

ABOUT THE INSTITUTION Independent interdenominational, coed. Awards: associate, bachelor's, and master's degrees and post-bachelor's certificates. 16 undergraduate majors. Total enrollment: 975. Undergraduates: 975. Freshmen: 91. Both federal and institutional methodology are used as a basis for awarding need-based institutional aid.

UNDERGRADUATE EXPENSES for 2006–07 ***Application fee:*** $20. ***Comprehensive fee:*** $24,236 includes full-time tuition ($18,940), mandatory fees ($116), and room and board ($5180). ***College room only:*** $2300. Room and board charges vary according to board plan. ***Part-time tuition:*** $269 per credit hour. ***Part-time fees:*** $52 per year. Part-time tuition and fees vary according to course load. ***Payment plan:*** Installment.

FRESHMAN FINANCIAL AID (Fall 2006, est.) 76 applied for aid; of those 89% were deemed to have need. 100% of freshmen with need received aid; of those 19% had need fully met. ***Average percent of need met:*** 79% (excluding resources awarded to replace EFC). ***Average financial aid package:*** $16,174 (excluding resources awarded to replace EFC). 10% of all full-time freshmen had no need and received non-need-based gift aid.

UNDERGRADUATE FINANCIAL AID (Fall 2006, est.) 300 applied for aid; of those 91% were deemed to have need. 100% of undergraduates with need received aid; of those 17% had need fully met. ***Average percent of need met:*** 80% (excluding resources awarded to replace EFC). ***Average financial aid package:*** $16,287 (excluding resources awarded to replace EFC). 12% of all full-time undergraduates had no need and received non-need-based gift aid.

GIFT AID (NEED-BASED) ***Total amount:*** $3,360,234 (16% federal, 29% state, 54% institutional, 1% external sources). ***Receiving aid:*** Freshmen: 78% (67); All full-time undergraduates: 80% (271). ***Average award:*** Freshmen: $12,487; Undergraduates: $12,193. ***Scholarships, grants, and awards:*** Federal Pell, FSEOG, state, private, college/university gift aid from institutional funds, endowed-donor scholarships.

GIFT AID (NON-NEED-BASED) ***Total amount:*** $388,708 (1% federal, 4% state, 91% institutional, 4% external sources). ***Receiving aid:*** Freshmen: 8% (7); Undergraduates: 7% (23). ***Average award:*** Freshmen: $10,497; Undergraduates: $6774. ***Scholarships, grants, and awards by category:*** *Academic Interests/Achievement:* 157 awards ($654,536 total): business, general academic interests/achievements. *Creative Arts/Performance:* 11 awards ($22,000 total): music. *Special Achievements/Activities:* 36 awards ($69,570 total): leadership. *Special Characteristics:* 262 awards ($379,921 total): children and siblings of alumni, children of faculty/staff, general special characteristics, local/state students, relatives of clergy, spouses of current students. ***Tuition waivers:*** Full or partial for children of alumni, employees or children of employees, senior citizens.

LOANS ***Student loans:*** $2,146,499 (73% need-based, 27% non-need-based). 78% of past graduating class borrowed through all loan programs. *Average indebtedness per student:* $20,780. ***Average need-based loan:*** Freshmen: $3729; Undergraduates: $4069. ***Parent loans:*** $1,646,129 (35% need-based, 65% non-need-based). ***Programs:*** FFEL (Subsidized and Unsubsidized Stafford, PLUS), Perkins, college/university.

WORK-STUDY ***Federal work-study:*** Total amount: $124,554; 157 jobs averaging $1582.

ATHLETIC AWARDS Total amount: $11,049 (41% need-based, 59% non-need-based).

APPLYING FOR FINANCIAL AID ***Required financial aid forms:*** FAFSA, institution's own form. ***Financial aid deadline (priority):*** 3/1. ***Notification date:*** Continuous beginning 3/1. Students must reply by 5/1 or within 2 weeks of notification.

CONTACT Mr. Paul Johnston, Director of Financial Aid, Taylor University Fort Wayne, 1025 West Rudisill Boulevard, Fort Wayne, IN 46807-2197, 260-744-8691 or toll-free 800-233-3922. *Fax:* 260-744-8850. *E-mail:* pljohnston@fw.taylor.edu.

TEIKYO LORETTO HEIGHTS UNIVERSITY

Denver, CO

CONTACT Financial Aid Office, Teikyo Loretto Heights University, 3001 South Federal Boulevard, Denver, CO 80236, 303-936-4200.

TELSHE YESHIVA–CHICAGO

Chicago, IL

CONTACT Office of Financial Aid, Telshe Yeshiva–Chicago, 3535 West Foster Avenue, Chicago, IL 60625-5598, 773-463-7738.

TEMPLE BAPTIST COLLEGE

Cincinnati, OH

CONTACT Financial Aid Office, Temple Baptist College, 11965 Kenn Road, Cincinnati, OH 45240, 513-851-3800.

TEMPLE UNIVERSITY

Philadelphia, PA

Tuition & fees (PA res): $10,180 Average undergraduate aid package: $13,308

ABOUT THE INSTITUTION State-related, coed. Awards: associate, bachelor's, master's, doctoral, and first professional degrees and post-master's and first professional certificates. 118 undergraduate majors. Total enrollment: 33,865. Undergraduates: 24,674. Freshmen: 3,888. Federal methodology is used as a basis for awarding need-based institutional aid.

UNDERGRADUATE EXPENSES for 2006–07 ***Application fee:*** $50. ***Tuition, state resident:*** full-time $9680; part-time $375 per credit. ***Tuition, nonresident:*** full-time $17,724; part-time $631 per credit. ***Required fees:*** full-time $500; $122 per term part-time. Full-time tuition and fees vary according to course load, program, and reciprocity agreements. Part-time tuition and fees vary according to course load, program, and reciprocity agreements. ***College room and board:*** $8230; ***Room only:*** $5404. Room and board charges vary according to board plan and housing facility. ***Payment plan:*** Installment.

FRESHMAN FINANCIAL AID (Fall 2005) 3586 applied for aid; of those 74% were deemed to have need. 98% of freshmen with need received aid; of those 34% had need fully met. ***Average percent of need met:*** 88% (excluding resources awarded to replace EFC). ***Average financial aid package:*** $13,836 (excluding resources awarded to replace EFC). 24% of all full-time freshmen had no need and received non-need-based gift aid.

UNDERGRADUATE FINANCIAL AID (Fall 2005) 18,741 applied for aid; of those 76% were deemed to have need. 94% of undergraduates with need received aid; of those 37% had need fully met. ***Average percent of need met:*** 89% (excluding resources awarded to replace EFC). ***Average financial aid package:*** $13,308 (excluding resources awarded to replace EFC). 21% of all full-time undergraduates had no need and received non-need-based gift aid.

GIFT AID (NEED-BASED) ***Total amount:*** $67,251,560 (35% federal, 30% state, 35% institutional). ***Receiving aid:*** Freshmen: 67% (2,581); All full-time undergraduates: 64% (13,405). ***Average award:*** Freshmen: $5084; Undergraduates: $4746. ***Scholarships, grants, and awards:*** Federal Pell, FSEOG, state, private, college/university gift aid from institutional funds, Federal Nursing.

GIFT AID (NON-NEED-BASED) ***Total amount:*** $52,945,010 (12% institutional, 88% external sources). ***Receiving aid:*** Freshmen: 40% (1,554); Undergraduates: 32% (6,621). ***Average award:*** Freshmen: $4616; Undergraduates: $4603. ***Scholarships, grants, and awards by category:*** *Academic Interests/Achievement:* general academic interests/achievements. *Creative Arts/Performance:* art/fine arts, general creative arts/performance, music, performing arts. *Special Achievements/Activities:* cheerleading/drum major. *Special Characteristics:* general special characteristics. ***Tuition waivers:*** Full or partial for employees or children of employees. ***ROTC:*** Army, Naval cooperative, Air Force cooperative.

LOANS ***Student loans:*** $90,741,395 (65% need-based, 35% non-need-based). 70% of past graduating class borrowed through all loan programs. *Average indebtedness per student:* $27,355. ***Average need-based loan:*** Freshmen: $2552; Undergraduates: $3500. ***Parent loans:*** $568,979 (100% non-need-based). ***Programs:*** FFEL (Subsidized and Unsubsidized Stafford, PLUS), Perkins, Federal Nursing, college/university.

WORK-STUDY ***Federal work-study:*** Total amount: $1,674,882; jobs available.

ATHLETIC AWARDS Total amount: $5,991,728 (100% non-need-based).

APPLYING FOR FINANCIAL AID ***Required financial aid form:*** FAFSA. ***Financial aid deadline (priority):*** 3/1. ***Notification date:*** Continuous beginning 2/15. Students must reply by 5/1 or within 3 weeks of notification.

CONTACT Dr. John F. Morris, Director, Student Financial Services, Temple University, Conwell Hall, Ground Floor, 1801 North Broad Street, Philadelphia, PA 19122-6096, 215-204-8760 or toll-free 888-340-2222. *Fax:* 215-204-2016. *E-mail:* john.morris@temple.edu.

TENNESSEE STATE UNIVERSITY

Nashville, TN

Tuition & fees (TN res): $4564 Average undergraduate aid package: $2978

ABOUT THE INSTITUTION State-supported, coed. Awards: associate, bachelor's, master's, and doctoral degrees. 59 undergraduate majors. Total enrollment: 9,038. Undergraduates: 7,112. Freshmen: 988. Federal methodology is used as a basis for awarding need-based institutional aid.

UNDERGRADUATE EXPENSES for 2006–07 ***Application fee:*** $15. ***Tuition, state resident:*** full-time $4564. ***Tuition, nonresident:*** full-time $14,258. Full-time tuition and fees vary according to course load. Part-time tuition and fees vary according to course load and program. ***College room and board:*** $5000; ***Room only:*** $2840. Room and board charges vary according to board plan and housing facility.

FRESHMAN FINANCIAL AID (Fall 2005) 760 applied for aid; of those 92% were deemed to have need. 98% of freshmen with need received aid; of those 47% had need fully met. ***Average percent of need met:*** 86% (excluding resources awarded to replace EFC). ***Average financial aid package:*** $6485 (excluding resources awarded to replace EFC).

UNDERGRADUATE FINANCIAL AID (Fall 2005) 5,210 applied for aid; of those 87% were deemed to have need. 98% of undergraduates with need received aid; of those 60% had need fully met. ***Average percent of need met:*** 83% (excluding resources awarded to replace EFC). ***Average financial aid package:*** $2978 (excluding resources awarded to replace EFC). 7% of all full-time undergraduates had no need and received non-need-based gift aid.

GIFT AID (NEED-BASED) ***Total amount:*** $15,971,958 (90% federal, 10% state). ***Receiving aid:*** Freshmen: 452; All full-time undergraduates: 49% (2,907). ***Average award:*** Undergraduates: $1208. ***Scholarships, grants, and awards:*** Federal Pell, FSEOG, state, private, college/university gift aid from institutional funds.

GIFT AID (NON-NEED-BASED) ***Total amount:*** $11,468,761 (13% state, 87% institutional). ***Receiving aid:*** Freshmen: 262; Undergraduates: 27% (1,592). ***Average award:*** Freshmen: $6286; Undergraduates: $7208. ***Scholarships, grants, and awards by category:*** *Academic Interests/Achievement:* general academic interests/achievements. *Creative Arts/Performance:* music. *Special Achievements/Activities:* general special achievements/activities. *Special Characteristics:* local/state students, members of minority groups. ***Tuition waivers:*** Full or partial for minority students, employees or children of employees, senior citizens. ***ROTC:*** Army cooperative, Naval cooperative, Air Force.

LOANS ***Student loans:*** $44,894,731 (54% need-based, 46% non-need-based). 79% of past graduating class borrowed through all loan programs. *Average indebtedness per student:* $21,644. ***Parent loans:*** $6,743,814 (100% non-need-based). ***Programs:*** Federal Direct (Subsidized and Unsubsidized Stafford), FFEL (Subsidized and Unsubsidized Stafford, PLUS), Perkins, college/university.

WORK-STUDY ***Federal work-study:*** Total amount: $1,028,943; 566 jobs averaging $1755. ***State or other work-study/employment:*** Part-time jobs available.

ATHLETIC AWARDS Total amount: $1,975,315 (100% non-need-based).

APPLYING FOR FINANCIAL AID ***Required financial aid form:*** FAFSA. ***Financial aid deadline (priority):*** 4/1. ***Notification date:*** Continuous beginning 4/15. Students must reply within 3 weeks of notification.

CONTACT Mary Chambliss, Director of Financial Aid, Tennessee State University, 3500 John Merritt Boulevard, Nashville, TN 37209-1561, 615-963-5772. *Fax:* 615-963-5108.

TENNESSEE TECHNOLOGICAL UNIVERSITY

Cookeville, TN

Tuition & fees (TN res): $4590 Average undergraduate aid package: $3156

ABOUT THE INSTITUTION State-supported, coed. Awards: bachelor's, master's, and doctoral degrees and post-bachelor's certificates. 67 undergraduate majors. Total enrollment: 9,733. Undergraduates: 7,569. Freshmen: 1,527. Federal methodology is used as a basis for awarding need-based institutional aid.

UNDERGRADUATE EXPENSES for 2006–07 ***Application fee:*** $15. ***Tuition, state resident:*** full-time $4590; part-time $168 per hour. ***Tuition, nonresident:*** full-time $14,284; part-time $589 per hour. ***Required fees:*** $50 per hour. Full-time tuition and fees vary according to program. Part-time tuition and fees vary according to course load and program. ***College room and board:*** $5964; ***Room only:*** $3020. Room and board charges vary according to board plan and housing facility. ***Payment plan:*** Installment.

FRESHMAN FINANCIAL AID (Fall 2006, est.) 1202 applied for aid; of those 62% were deemed to have need. 99% of freshmen with need received aid; of those 30% had need fully met. ***Average percent of need met:*** 87% (excluding resources awarded to replace EFC). ***Average financial aid package:*** $8466 (excluding resources awarded to replace EFC). 26% of all full-time freshmen had no need and received non-need-based gift aid.

UNDERGRADUATE FINANCIAL AID (Fall 2006, est.) 5,691 applied for aid; of those 63% were deemed to have need. 99% of undergraduates with need received aid; of those 31% had need fully met. ***Average percent of need met:*** 82% (excluding resources awarded to replace EFC). ***Average financial aid package:*** $3156 (excluding resources awarded to replace EFC). 24% of all full-time undergraduates had no need and received non-need-based gift aid.

GIFT AID (NEED-BASED) ***Total amount:*** $7,511,380 (80% federal, 20% state). ***Receiving aid:*** Freshmen: 26% (399); All full-time undergraduates: 28% (1,874). ***Average award:*** Freshmen: $4125; Undergraduates: $2624. ***Scholarships, grants, and awards:*** Federal Pell, FSEOG, state, private, college/university gift aid from institutional funds, United Negro College Fund.

GIFT AID (NON-NEED-BASED) ***Total amount:*** $20,649,607 (59% state, 32% institutional, 9% external sources). ***Receiving aid:*** Freshmen: 43% (647); Undergraduates: 33% (2,193). ***Average award:*** Freshmen: $5485; Undergraduates: $3830. ***Scholarships, grants, and awards by category:*** *Academic Interests/Achievement:* 2,376 awards ($2,710,275 total): agriculture, biological sciences, business, communication, computer science, education, engineering/technologies, English, foreign languages, general academic interests/achievements, health fields, home economics, humanities, international studies, mathematics, military science, physical sciences, premedicine, social sciences. *Creative Arts/Performance:* 145 awards ($260,864 total): art/fine arts, debating, music. *Special Achievements/Activities:* 2,816 awards ($7,118,878 total): cheerleading/drum major, general special achievements/activities. *Special Characteristics:* 1,805 awards ($3,018,378 total): children and siblings of alumni, children of educators, children of faculty/staff, children of public servants, ethnic background, first-generation college students, local/state students, members of minority groups, out-of-state students, public servants. ***Tuition waivers:*** Full or partial for employees or children of employees. ***ROTC:*** Army, Air Force cooperative.

LOANS ***Student loans:*** $16,001,320 (57% need-based, 43% non-need-based). 30% of past graduating class borrowed through all loan programs. *Average indebtedness per student:* $15,195. ***Average need-based loan:*** Freshmen: $908; Undergraduates: $3137. ***Parent loans:*** $1,511,068 (100% non-need-based). ***Programs:*** Federal Direct (Subsidized and Unsubsidized Stafford), FFEL (PLUS), Perkins, college/university.

WORK-STUDY ***Federal work-study:*** Total amount: $430,464; 333 jobs averaging $1184. ***State or other work-study/employment:*** Total amount: $2,020,467 (100% non-need-based). 507 part-time jobs averaging $1786.

ATHLETIC AWARDS Total amount: $3,994,091 (100% non-need-based).

APPLYING FOR FINANCIAL AID ***Required financial aid form:*** FAFSA. ***Financial aid deadline (priority):*** 3/15. ***Notification date:*** Continuous beginning 4/1. Students must reply within 2 weeks of notification.

CONTACT Lester McKenzie, Director of Financial Aid, Tennessee Technological University, Box 5076, 1000 North Dixie Avenue, Cookeville, TN 38501, 931-372-3073 or toll-free 800-255-8881. *Fax:* 931-372-6309. *E-mail:* lmckenzie@tntech.edu.

TENNESSEE TEMPLE UNIVERSITY

Chattanooga, TN

CONTACT Mr. Michael Sapienza, Director of Financial Aid, Tennessee Temple University, 1815 Union Avenue, Chattanooga, TN 37404-3587, 423-493-4208 or toll-free 800-553-4050. *Fax:* 423-493-4497. *E-mail:* michaels@mail.tntemple.edu.

TENNESSEE WESLEYAN COLLEGE

Athens, TN

Tuition & fees: $15,550 **Average undergraduate aid package: $12,158**

ABOUT THE INSTITUTION Independent United Methodist, coed. Awards: bachelor's degrees (profile includes information for both the main and branch campuses). 40 undergraduate majors. Total enrollment: 874. Undergraduates: 874. Freshmen: 161. Federal methodology is used as a basis for awarding need-based institutional aid.

UNDERGRADUATE EXPENSES for 2007–08 ***Application fee:*** $25. ***Comprehensive fee:*** $21,250 includes full-time tuition ($15,000), mandatory fees ($550), and room and board ($5700). ***Part-time tuition:*** $405 per credit hour. ***Part-time fees:*** $10 per credit hour.

FRESHMAN FINANCIAL AID (Fall 2006, est.) 160 applied for aid; of those 82% were deemed to have need. 100% of freshmen with need received aid; of those 23% had need fully met. ***Average percent of need met:*** 69% (excluding resources awarded to replace EFC). ***Average financial aid package:*** $12,076 (excluding resources awarded to replace EFC). 18% of all full-time freshmen had no need and received non-need-based gift aid.

UNDERGRADUATE FINANCIAL AID (Fall 2006, est.) 695 applied for aid; of those 85% were deemed to have need. 99% of undergraduates with need received aid; of those 21% had need fully met. ***Average percent of need met:*** 67% (excluding resources awarded to replace EFC). ***Average financial aid package:*** $12,158 (excluding resources awarded to replace EFC). 17% of all full-time undergraduates had no need and received non-need-based gift aid.

GIFT AID (NEED-BASED) ***Total amount:*** $4,217,266 (23% federal, 33% state, 40% institutional, 4% external sources). ***Receiving aid:*** Freshmen: 82% (131); All full-time undergraduates: 78% (576). ***Average award:*** Freshmen: $10,601; Undergraduates: $9431. ***Scholarships, grants, and awards:*** Federal Pell, FSEOG, state, private, college/university gift aid from institutional funds.

GIFT AID (NON-NEED-BASED) ***Total amount:*** $900,575 (48% state, 47% institutional, 5% external sources). ***Receiving aid:*** Freshmen: 16% (25); Undergraduates: 13% (94). ***Average award:*** Freshmen: $8463; Undergraduates: $8679. ***Scholarships, grants, and awards by category:*** *Academic Interests/Achievement:* 459 awards ($1,644,413 total): biological sciences, business, communication, computer science, education, English, foreign languages, general academic interests/achievements, health fields, humanities, international studies, mathematics, physical sciences, premedicine, religion/biblical studies, social sciences. *Creative Arts/Performance:* 37 awards ($73,671 total): music. *Special Achievements/Activities:* 43 awards ($31,406 total): cheerleading/drum major, general special achievements/activities, junior miss, memberships, religious involvement. *Special Characteristics:* 127 awards ($226,366 total): children of faculty/staff, general special characteristics, international students, members of minority groups, relatives of clergy, religious affiliation.

LOANS ***Student loans:*** $3,489,095 (76% need-based, 24% non-need-based). 65% of past graduating class borrowed through all loan programs. *Average indebtedness per student:* $16,490. ***Average need-based loan:*** Freshmen: $2455; Undergraduates: $3932. ***Parent loans:*** $713,834 (35% need-based, 65% non-need-based). ***Programs:*** FFEL (Subsidized and Unsubsidized Stafford, PLUS), Perkins, state, United Methodist Student Loans.

WORK-STUDY ***Federal work-study:*** Total amount: $64,712; 88 jobs averaging $848. ***State or other work-study/employment:*** Total amount: $25,274 (6% need-based, 94% non-need-based). 33 part-time jobs averaging $766.

ATHLETIC AWARDS Total amount: $2,123,934 (62% need-based, 38% non-need-based).

APPLYING FOR FINANCIAL AID ***Required financial aid forms:*** FAFSA, institution's own form. ***Financial aid deadline:*** Continuous. ***Notification date:*** Continuous beginning 2/15. Students must reply within 2 weeks of notification.

CONTACT Mr. Bob Perry, Director of Financial Aid, Tennessee Wesleyan College, PO Box 40, Athens, TN 37371-0040, 423-746-5209 or toll-free 800-PICK-TWC. *Fax:* 423-744-9968. *E-mail:* rkperry@twcnet.edu.

TEXAS A&M INTERNATIONAL UNIVERSITY

Laredo, TX

CONTACT Laura Elizondo, Director of Financial Aid, Texas A&M International University, 5201 University Boulevard, Laredo, TX 78041, 956-326-2225 or toll-free 888-489-2648. *Fax:* 956-326-2224. *E-mail:* laura@tamiu.edu.

TEXAS A&M UNIVERSITY

College Station, TX

ABOUT THE INSTITUTION State-supported, coed. Awards: bachelor's, master's, doctoral, and first professional degrees and post-bachelor's certificates. 107 undergraduate majors. Total enrollment: 45,380. Undergraduates: 36,580. Freshmen: 7,804.

GIFT AID (NEED-BASED) ***Scholarships, grants, and awards:*** Federal Pell, FSEOG, state, private, college/university gift aid from institutional funds.

GIFT AID (NON-NEED-BASED) ***Scholarships, grants, and awards by category:*** *Academic Interests/Achievement:* agriculture, architecture, biological sciences, business, computer science, education, engineering/technologies, general academic interests/achievements, health fields, physical sciences. *Creative Arts/Performance:* journalism/publications, performing arts, theater/drama. *Special Achievements/Activities:* general special achievements/activities, leadership, memberships, rodeo. *Special Characteristics:* children of faculty/staff, veterans, veterans' children.

LOANS ***Programs:*** FFEL (Subsidized and Unsubsidized Stafford, PLUS), Perkins, state, college/university.

WORK-STUDY ***Federal work-study:*** Total amount: $2,409,192; 1,068 jobs averaging $2256. ***State or other work-study/employment:*** Total amount: $524,142 (100% need-based). 225 part-time jobs averaging $2330.

APPLYING FOR FINANCIAL AID ***Required financial aid form:*** FAFSA.

CONTACT Financial Aid Office, Texas A&M University, Department of Student Financial Aid, PO Box 30016, College Station, TX 77842-3016, 979-845-3236. *Fax:* 979-847-9061. *E-mail:* financialaid@tamu.edu.

TEXAS A&M UNIVERSITY AT GALVESTON

Galveston, TX

Tuition & fees (TX res): $4743 Average undergraduate aid package: $11,082

ABOUT THE INSTITUTION State-supported, coed. Awards: bachelor's and master's degrees. 12 undergraduate majors. Total enrollment: 1,553. Undergraduates: 1,520. Freshmen: 423. Federal methodology is used as a basis for awarding need-based institutional aid.

UNDERGRADUATE EXPENSES for 2006–07 ***Application fee:*** $45. ***Tuition, state resident:*** full-time $3735; part-time $124.50 per credit hour. ***Tuition, nonresident:*** full-time $12,015; part-time $400.50 per credit hour. ***Required fees:*** full-time $1008; $504 per term part-time. Full-time tuition and fees vary according to course load and program. Part-time tuition and fees vary according to course load and program. ***College room and board:*** $4870; ***Room only:*** $1958. Room and board charges vary according to board plan and housing facility. ***Payment plan:*** Installment.

FRESHMAN FINANCIAL AID (Fall 2006, est.) 245 applied for aid; of those 82% were deemed to have need. 95% of freshmen with need received aid; of those 24% had need fully met. ***Average percent of need met:*** 15% (excluding resources awarded to replace EFC). ***Average financial aid package:*** $11,057 (excluding resources awarded to replace EFC). 2% of all full-time freshmen had no need and received non-need-based gift aid.

UNDERGRADUATE FINANCIAL AID (Fall 2006, est.) 785 applied for aid; of those 91% were deemed to have need. 94% of undergraduates with need received aid; of those 26% had need fully met. ***Average percent of need met:*** 20% (excluding resources awarded to replace EFC). ***Average financial aid package:*** $11,082 (excluding resources awarded to replace EFC). 1% of all full-time undergraduates had no need and received non-need-based gift aid.

GIFT AID (NEED-BASED) ***Total amount:*** $1,357,404 (71% federal, 23% state, 6% institutional). ***Receiving aid:*** Freshmen: 25% (104); All full-time undergraduates: 29% (396). ***Average award:*** Freshmen: $4190; Undergraduates: $4653. ***Scholarships, grants, and awards:*** Federal Pell, FSEOG, state, private, college/university gift aid from institutional funds.

GIFT AID (NON-NEED-BASED) ***Total amount:*** $121,813 (16% state, 84% institutional). ***Receiving aid:*** Freshmen: 2% (9); Undergraduates: 4% (57). ***Average award:*** Freshmen: $7824; Undergraduates: $6147. ***Scholarships, grants, and awards by category:*** *Academic Interests/Achievement:* 100 awards ($100,000 total): general academic interests/achievements. *Special Achievements/Activities:* 35 awards ($42,000 total): leadership. ***ROTC:*** Naval.

LOANS ***Student loans:*** $5,677,182 (33% need-based, 67% non-need-based). 86% of past graduating class borrowed through all loan programs. *Average indebtedness per student:* $15,793. ***Average need-based loan:*** Freshmen: $2550; Undergraduates: $3307. ***Parent loans:*** $2,104,152 (3% need-based, 97% non-need-based). ***Programs:*** FFEL (Subsidized and Unsubsidized Stafford, PLUS), Perkins, college/university, alternative loans.

WORK-STUDY ***Federal work-study:*** Total amount: $27,117; 22 jobs averaging $1933.

APPLYING FOR FINANCIAL AID ***Required financial aid form:*** FAFSA. ***Financial aid deadline:*** Continuous. ***Notification date:*** 3/15. Students must reply within 3 weeks of notification.

CONTACT Dennis Carlton, Director for Financial Aid, Texas A&M University at Galveston, PO Box 1675, Galveston, TX 77553-1675, 409-740-4500 or toll-free 87—SEAAGGIE. *Fax:* 409-740-4959. *E-mail:* carltond@tamug.tamu.edu.

TEXAS A&M UNIVERSITY–COMMERCE

Commerce, TX

Tuition & fees (TX res): $5242 Average undergraduate aid package: $7348

ABOUT THE INSTITUTION State-supported, coed. Awards: bachelor's, master's, and doctoral degrees. 67 undergraduate majors. Total enrollment: 8,556. Undergraduates: 5,263. Federal methodology is used as a basis for awarding need-based institutional aid.

UNDERGRADUATE EXPENSES for 2006–07 ***Application fee:*** $25. ***Tuition, state resident:*** full-time $4136; part-time $117 per credit. ***Tuition, nonresident:*** full-time $12,416; part-time $392 per credit. Full-time tuition and fees vary according to course load. Part-time tuition and fees vary according to course load. ***College room and board:*** $5740; ***Room only:*** $2600. Room and board charges vary according to board plan and housing facility. ***Payment plan:*** Installment.

FRESHMAN FINANCIAL AID (Fall 2006, est.) 474 applied for aid; of those 75% were deemed to have need. 99% of freshmen with need received aid; of those 28% had need fully met. ***Average percent of need met:*** 65% (excluding resources awarded to replace EFC). ***Average financial aid package:*** $7292 (excluding resources awarded to replace EFC). 21% of all full-time freshmen had no need and received non-need-based gift aid.

UNDERGRADUATE FINANCIAL AID (Fall 2006, est.) 3,245 applied for aid; of those 84% were deemed to have need. 99% of undergraduates with need received aid; of those 25% had need fully met. ***Average percent of need met:*** 65% (excluding resources awarded to replace EFC). ***Average financial aid package:*** $7348 (excluding resources awarded to replace EFC). 11% of all full-time undergraduates had no need and received non-need-based gift aid.

GIFT AID (NEED-BASED) ***Total amount:*** $10,991,490 (63% federal, 22% state, 12% institutional, 3% external sources). ***Receiving aid:*** Freshmen: 62% (350); All full-time undergraduates: 62% (2,585). ***Average award:*** Freshmen: $6012; Undergraduates: $4522. ***Scholarships, grants, and awards:*** Federal Pell, FSEOG, state, private, college/university gift aid from institutional funds.

GIFT AID (NON-NEED-BASED) ***Total amount:*** $981,500 (3% state, 74% institutional, 23% external sources). ***Average award:*** Freshmen: $1978; Undergraduates: $2160. ***Scholarships, grants, and awards by category:*** *Academic Interests/Achievement:* agriculture, general academic interests/achievements. *Creative Arts/Performance:* art/fine arts, journalism/publications, music, theater/drama. *Special Achievements/Activities:* cheerleading/drum major, general special achievements/activities, leadership. ***Tuition waivers:*** Full or partial for senior citizens.

LOANS ***Student loans:*** $18,762,084 (87% need-based, 13% non-need-based). 69% of past graduating class borrowed through all loan programs. *Average indebtedness per student:* $19,032. ***Average need-based loan:*** Freshmen: $2122; Undergraduates: $3619. ***Parent loans:*** $1,106,775 (49% need-based, 51% non-need-based). ***Programs:*** Federal Direct (Subsidized and Unsubsidized Stafford), FFEL (Subsidized and Unsubsidized Stafford, PLUS), Perkins, state.

WORK-STUDY ***Federal work-study:*** Total amount: $214,970; 83 jobs averaging $2590. ***State or other work-study/employment:*** Total amount: $98,655 (100% need-based). 37 part-time jobs averaging $2666.

ATHLETIC AWARDS Total amount: $804,907 (66% need-based, 34% non-need-based).

APPLYING FOR FINANCIAL AID ***Required financial aid form:*** FAFSA. ***Financial aid deadline (priority):*** 4/1. ***Notification date:*** Continuous. Students must reply within 2 weeks of notification.

CONTACT Dalinda Laster, Director of Financial Aid, Texas A&M University–Commerce, PO Box 3011, Commerce, TX 75429, 903-886-5091 or toll-free 800-331-3878. *Fax:* 903-886-5098. *E-mail:* dolly_laster@tamu-commerce.edu.

TEXAS A&M UNIVERSITY–CORPUS CHRISTI

Corpus Christi, TX

Tuition & fees (TX res): $5148 **Average undergraduate aid package: $7017**

ABOUT THE INSTITUTION State-supported, coed. Awards: bachelor's, master's, and doctoral degrees. 62 undergraduate majors. Total enrollment: 8,585. Undergraduates: 6,903. Freshmen: 1,160. Federal methodology is used as a basis for awarding need-based institutional aid.

UNDERGRADUATE EXPENSES for 2006–07 ***Application fee:*** $30. ***Tuition, state resident:*** full-time $3720. ***Tuition, nonresident:*** full-time $10,392.

FRESHMAN FINANCIAL AID (Fall 2006, est.) 864 applied for aid; of those 75% were deemed to have need. 96% of freshmen with need received aid; of those 11% had need fully met. ***Average percent of need met:*** 62% (excluding resources awarded to replace EFC). ***Average financial aid package:*** $6974 (excluding resources awarded to replace EFC). 15% of all full-time freshmen had no need and received non-need-based gift aid.

UNDERGRADUATE FINANCIAL AID (Fall 2006, est.) 3,833 applied for aid; of those 82% were deemed to have need. 96% of undergraduates with need received aid; of those 10% had need fully met. ***Average percent of need met:*** 62% (excluding resources awarded to replace EFC). ***Average financial aid package:*** $7017 (excluding resources awarded to replace EFC). 10% of all full-time undergraduates had no need and received non-need-based gift aid.

GIFT AID (NEED-BASED) ***Total amount:*** $10,829,543 (69% federal, 25% state, 6% institutional). ***Receiving aid:*** Freshmen: 47% (533); All full-time undergraduates: 43% (2,353). ***Average award:*** Freshmen: $4495; Undergraduates: $4112. ***Scholarships, grants, and awards:*** Federal Pell, FSEOG, state, college/university gift aid from institutional funds.

GIFT AID (NON-NEED-BASED) ***Total amount:*** $2,396,379 (65% institutional, 35% external sources). ***Receiving aid:*** Freshmen: 20% (225); Undergraduates: 13% (715). ***Average award:*** Freshmen: $3410; Undergraduates: $4854. ***Scholarships, grants, and awards by category:*** *Academic Interests/Achievement:* general academic interests/achievements. *Creative Arts/Performance:* art/fine arts. ***ROTC:*** Army.

LOANS ***Student loans:*** $21,002,214 (54% need-based, 46% non-need-based). 62% of past graduating class borrowed through all loan programs. *Average indebtedness per student:* $18,625. ***Average need-based loan:*** Freshmen: $3282; Undergraduates: $4041. ***Parent loans:*** $4,993,215 (100% non-need-based). ***Programs:*** FFEL (Subsidized and Unsubsidized Stafford, PLUS), Perkins, state, college/university.

WORK-STUDY ***Federal work-study:*** Total amount: $417,184; jobs available. ***State or other work-study/employment:*** Total amount: $74,438 (100% need-based). 6 part-time jobs averaging $2400.

ATHLETIC AWARDS Total amount: $1,217,618 (100% non-need-based).

APPLYING FOR FINANCIAL AID ***Required financial aid form:*** FAFSA. ***Financial aid deadline (priority):*** 4/1. ***Notification date:*** 5/1. Students must reply within 2 weeks of notification.

CONTACT Financial Aid Adviser, Texas A&M University–Corpus Christi, 6300 Ocean Drive, Corpus Christi, TX 78412-5503, 361-825-2338 or toll-free 800-482-6822. *Fax:* 361-825-6095. *E-mail:* faoweb@tamucc.edu.

TEXAS A&M UNIVERSITY–KINGSVILLE

Kingsville, TX

Tuition & fees: N/R **Average undergraduate aid package: $6500**

ABOUT THE INSTITUTION State-supported, coed. Awards: bachelor's, master's, and doctoral degrees and post-bachelor's certificates. 72 undergraduate majors. Total enrollment: 7,126. Undergraduates: 5,645. Freshmen: 887. Federal methodology is used as a basis for awarding need-based institutional aid.

FRESHMAN FINANCIAL AID (Fall 2005) 1248 applied for aid; of those 89% were deemed to have need. 100% of freshmen with need received aid; of those 64% had need fully met. ***Average percent of need met:*** 99% (excluding resources awarded to replace EFC). ***Average financial aid package:*** $6625 (excluding resources awarded to replace EFC).

UNDERGRADUATE FINANCIAL AID (Fall 2005) 4,449 applied for aid; of those 95% were deemed to have need. 100% of undergraduates with need received aid; of those 69% had need fully met. ***Average financial aid package:*** $6500 (excluding resources awarded to replace EFC).

GIFT AID (NEED-BASED) ***Total amount:*** $12,441,317 (69% federal, 18% state, 8% institutional, 5% external sources). ***Receiving aid:*** Freshmen: 62% (999); All full-time undergraduates: 84% (3,937). ***Average award:*** Freshmen: $6625; Undergraduates: $6500. ***Scholarships, grants, and awards:*** Federal Pell, FSEOG, state, private, college/university gift aid from institutional funds.

GIFT AID (NON-NEED-BASED) ***Receiving aid:*** Freshmen: 20% (319); Undergraduates: 63% (2,941). ***Scholarships, grants, and awards by category:*** *Special Achievements/Activities:* rodeo. *Special Characteristics:* general special characteristics. ***ROTC:*** Army.

LOANS ***Student loans:*** $26,579,876 (100% need-based). 46% of past graduating class borrowed through all loan programs. *Average indebtedness per student:* $2867. ***Average need-based loan:*** Freshmen: $3875; Undergraduates: $3875. ***Parent loans:*** $594,722 (100% need-based). ***Programs:*** FFEL (Subsidized and Unsubsidized Stafford, PLUS), Perkins, state, alternative loans.

WORK-STUDY ***Federal work-study:*** Total amount: $519,510; jobs available. ***State or other work-study/employment:*** Total amount: $84,426 (100% need-based). Part-time jobs available.

ATHLETIC AWARDS Total amount: $3,012,939 (100% need-based).

APPLYING FOR FINANCIAL AID ***Required financial aid form:*** FAFSA. ***Financial aid deadline:*** Continuous. ***Notification date:*** Continuous beginning 4/1. Students must reply within 2 weeks of notification.

CONTACT Felipe Leal, Interim Director, Financial Aid, Texas A&M University–Kingsville, 700 University Boulevard, Kingsville, TX 78363, 361-593-2883 or toll-free 800-687-6000. *Fax:* 361-593-3036.

TEXAS A&M UNIVERSITY–TEXARKANA

Texarkana, TX

Tuition & fees (TX res): $2644 **Average undergraduate aid package: N/A**

ABOUT THE INSTITUTION State-supported, coed. Awards: bachelor's and master's degrees. 19 undergraduate majors. Total enrollment: 1,670. Undergraduates: 1,006. Federal methodology is used as a basis for awarding need-based institutional aid.

UNDERGRADUATE EXPENSES for 2006–07 ***Tuition, state resident:*** full-time $2208; part-time $92 per credit hour. ***Tuition, nonresident:*** full-time $8808; part-time $367 per credit hour. ***Required fees:*** full-time $436; $17.50 per credit hour or $8 per term part-time. Full-time tuition and fees vary according to course level, course load, and student level. Part-time tuition and fees vary according to course level, course load, and student level. ***Payment plan:*** Installment.

GIFT AID (NEED-BASED) ***Total amount:*** $1,199,620 (75% federal, 22% state, 3% external sources). ***Scholarships, grants, and awards:*** Federal Pell, FSEOG, state, private, college/university gift aid from institutional funds.

GIFT AID (NON-NEED-BASED) ***Total amount:*** $348,770 (100% institutional). ***Scholarships, grants, and awards by category:*** *Academic Interests/Achievement:* business, education, English, general academic interests/achievements, mathematics, social sciences. *Special Achievements/Activities:* community service, general special achievements/activities, leadership, memberships. *Special Characteristics:* first-generation college students.

LOANS ***Student loans:*** $1,213,025 (69% need-based, 31% non-need-based). ***Programs:*** FFEL (Subsidized and Unsubsidized Stafford, PLUS), college/university.

WORK-STUDY ***Federal work-study:*** Total amount: $24,186; jobs available.

APPLYING FOR FINANCIAL AID ***Required financial aid forms:*** FAFSA, institution's own form, state aid form. ***Financial aid deadline (priority):*** 5/1. ***Notification date:*** Continuous beginning 6/1. Students must reply within 6 weeks of notification.

CONTACT Marilyn Raney, Director of Financial Aid and Veterans' Services, Texas A&M University–Texarkana, 2600 North Robison Road, Texarkana, TX 75505, 903-223-3060. *Fax:* 903-223-3118. *E-mail:* marilyn.raney@tamut.edu.

TEXAS CHIROPRACTIC COLLEGE

Pasadena, TX

CONTACT Arthur Goudeau, Financial Aid Director, Texas Chiropractic College, 5912 Spencer Highway, Pasadena, TX 77505, 281-998-6022 or toll-free 800-468-6839. *Fax:* 281-991-5237. *E-mail:* agoudeau@txchiro.edu.

TEXAS CHRISTIAN UNIVERSITY

Fort Worth, TX

Tuition & fees: $23,020 **Average undergraduate aid package: $14,771**

ABOUT THE INSTITUTION Independent religious, coed. Awards: bachelor's, master's, doctoral, and first professional degrees and post-bachelor's and first professional certificates. 86 undergraduate majors. Total enrollment: 8,865. Undergraduates: 7,267. Freshmen: 1,652. Federal methodology is used as a basis for awarding need-based institutional aid.

UNDERGRADUATE EXPENSES for 2006–07 ***Application fee:*** $40. ***Comprehensive fee:*** $30,540 includes full-time tuition ($22,980), mandatory fees ($40), and room and board ($7520). ***College room only:*** $4320. Room and board charges vary according to board plan and housing facility. ***Payment plan:*** Installment.

FRESHMAN FINANCIAL AID (Fall 2005) 862 applied for aid; of those 70% were deemed to have need. 100% of freshmen with need received aid; of those 48% had need fully met. ***Average percent of need met:*** 76% (excluding resources awarded to replace EFC). ***Average financial aid package:*** $14,337 (excluding resources awarded to replace EFC). 24% of all full-time freshmen had no need and received non-need-based gift aid.

UNDERGRADUATE FINANCIAL AID (Fall 2005) 3,672 applied for aid; of those 80% were deemed to have need. 99% of undergraduates with need received aid; of those 43% had need fully met. ***Average percent of need met:*** 73% (excluding resources awarded to replace EFC). ***Average financial aid package:*** $14,771 (excluding resources awarded to replace EFC). 22% of all full-time undergraduates had no need and received non-need-based gift aid.

GIFT AID (NEED-BASED) ***Total amount:*** $23,951,840 (12% federal, 23% state, 58% institutional, 7% external sources). ***Receiving aid:*** Freshmen: 34% (545); All full-time undergraduates: 37% (2,528). ***Average award:*** Freshmen: $10,448; Undergraduates: $10,347. ***Scholarships, grants, and awards:*** Federal Pell, FSEOG, state, private, college/university gift aid from institutional funds, United Negro College Fund.

GIFT AID (NON-NEED-BASED) ***Total amount:*** $20,395,303 (79% institutional, 21% external sources). ***Receiving aid:*** Freshmen: 19% (307); Undergraduates: 17% (1,142). ***Average award:*** Freshmen: $8096; Undergraduates: $8747. ***Scholarships, grants, and awards by category:*** *Academic Interests/Achievement:* 2,237 awards ($13,332,112 total): education, engineering/technologies, general academic interests/achievements, international studies, military science, premedicine, religion/biblical studies. *Creative Arts/Performance:* 261 awards ($1,588,840 total): art/fine arts, cinema/film/broadcasting, dance, journalism/publications, music, performing arts, theater/drama. *Special Achievements/Activities:* 454 awards ($2,419,397 total): general special achievements/activities, leadership. *Special Characteristics:* 720 awards ($7,663,436 total): adult students, children of faculty/staff, children of union members/company employees, international students, local/state students, out-of-state students, relatives of clergy, religious affiliation. ***Tuition waivers:*** Full or partial for employees or children of employees. ***ROTC:*** Army, Air Force.

LOANS ***Student loans:*** $28,047,214 (75% need-based, 25% non-need-based). 47% of past graduating class borrowed through all loan programs. *Average indebtedness per student:* $23,220. ***Average need-based loan:*** Freshmen: $4790; Undergraduates: $5970. ***Parent loans:*** $26,819,745 (39% need-based, 61% non-need-based). ***Programs:*** FFEL (Subsidized and Unsubsidized Stafford, PLUS), Perkins, Federal Nursing, state.

WORK-STUDY ***Federal work-study:*** Total amount: $2,925,570; 1,250 jobs averaging $2340. ***State or other work-study/employment:*** Total amount: $47,186 (100% need-based). 25 part-time jobs averaging $2400.

ATHLETIC AWARDS Total amount: $7,839,143 (40% need-based, 60% non-need-based).

APPLYING FOR FINANCIAL AID ***Required financial aid forms:*** FAFSA, institution's own form. ***Financial aid deadline:*** 5/1 (priority: 5/1). ***Notification date:*** Continuous.

CONTACT Michael Scott, Director, Scholarships and Student Financial Aid, Texas Christian University, PO Box 297012, Fort Worth, TX 76129-0002, 817-257-7858 or toll-free 800-828-3764. *Fax:* 817-257-7462. *E-mail:* m.scott@tcu.edu.

TEXAS COLLEGE

Tyler, TX

CONTACT Mrs. Ruth Jordan, Financial Aid Office, Texas College, 2404 North Grand Avenue, Tyler, TX 75702, 903-593-8311 Ext. 2210 or toll-free 800-306-6299 (out-of-state). *Fax:* 903-596-0001. *E-mail:* rjordanW@texascollege.edu.

TEXAS LUTHERAN UNIVERSITY

Seguin, TX

Tuition & fees: $18,840 **Average undergraduate aid package: $13,740**

ABOUT THE INSTITUTION Independent religious, coed. Awards: bachelor's degrees and post-bachelor's certificates. 42 undergraduate majors. Total enrollment: 1,429. Undergraduates: 1,429. Freshmen: 387. Federal methodology is used as a basis for awarding need-based institutional aid.

UNDERGRADUATE EXPENSES for 2006–07 ***Application fee:*** $25. ***Comprehensive fee:*** $24,440 includes full-time tuition ($18,720), mandatory fees ($120), and room and board ($5600). ***College room only:*** $2600. Full-time tuition and fees vary according to course load. Room and board charges vary according to board plan, housing facility, and location. ***Part-time tuition:*** $630 per credit hour. ***Part-time fees:*** $60 per term. Part-time tuition and fees vary according to course load. ***Payment plan:*** Installment.

FRESHMAN FINANCIAL AID (Fall 2005) 343 applied for aid; of those 80% were deemed to have need. 100% of freshmen with need received aid; of those 26% had need fully met. ***Average percent of need met:*** 74% (excluding resources awarded to replace EFC). ***Average financial aid package:*** $14,256 (excluding resources awarded to replace EFC). 27% of all full-time freshmen had no need and received non-need-based gift aid.

UNDERGRADUATE FINANCIAL AID (Fall 2005) 1,102 applied for aid; of those 85% were deemed to have need. 100% of undergraduates with need received aid; of those 23% had need fully met. ***Average percent of need met:*** 72% (excluding resources awarded to replace EFC). ***Average financial aid package:*** $13,740 (excluding resources awarded to replace EFC). 24% of all full-time undergraduates had no need and received non-need-based gift aid.

GIFT AID (NEED-BASED) ***Total amount:*** $9,530,448 (13% federal, 25% state, 59% institutional, 3% external sources). ***Receiving aid:*** Freshmen: 67% (249); All full-time undergraduates: 63% (810). ***Average award:*** Freshmen: $6019; Undergraduates: $6040. ***Scholarships, grants, and awards:*** Federal Pell, FSEOG, state, private, college/university gift aid from institutional funds.

GIFT AID (NON-NEED-BASED) ***Total amount:*** $1,929,935 (95% institutional, 5% external sources). ***Receiving aid:*** Freshmen: 73% (273); Undergraduates: 72% (917). ***Average award:*** Freshmen: $6202; Undergraduates: $5881. ***Scholarships, grants, and awards by category:*** *Academic Interests/Achievement:* 730 awards ($3,913,780 total): general academic interests/achievements. *Creative Arts/Performance:* 219 awards ($402,030 total): journalism/publications, music, theater/drama. *Special Achievements/Activities:* 239 awards ($423,410 total): general special achievements/activities, leadership, religious involvement. *Special Characteristics:* 662 awards ($935,855 total): children and siblings of alumni, children of faculty/staff, first-generation college students, general special characteristics, international students, religious affiliation. ***Tuition waivers:*** Full or partial for children of alumni, employees or children of employees. ***ROTC:*** Army cooperative, Air Force cooperative.

LOANS ***Student loans:*** $7,702,505 (86% need-based, 14% non-need-based). 71% of past graduating class borrowed through all loan programs. *Average indebtedness per student:* $26,707. ***Average need-based loan:*** Freshmen: $2988; Undergraduates: $4191. ***Parent loans:*** $3,883,550 (72% need-based, 28% non-need-based). ***Programs:*** FFEL (Subsidized and Unsubsidized Stafford, PLUS), Perkins, state, alternative loans.

WORK-STUDY ***Federal work-study:*** Total amount: $426,513; 404 jobs averaging $1000. ***State or other work-study/employment:*** Total amount: $320,378 (6% need-based, 94% non-need-based). 17 part-time jobs averaging $1077.

APPLYING FOR FINANCIAL AID ***Required financial aid form:*** FAFSA. ***Financial aid deadline (priority):*** 4/1. ***Notification date:*** Continuous beginning 3/1. Students must reply within 2 weeks of notification.

CONTACT Debbie Mattke, Assistant Director Financial Aid, Texas Lutheran University, 1000 West Court Street, Seguin, TX 78155-5999, 830-372-8075 or toll-free 800-771-8521. *Fax:* 830-372-8096. *E-mail:* dmattke@tlu.edu.

TEXAS SOUTHERN UNIVERSITY

Houston, TX

ABOUT THE INSTITUTION State-supported, coed. Awards: bachelor's, master's, doctoral, and first professional degrees. 106 undergraduate majors. Total enrollment: 11,224. Undergraduates: 9,053. Freshmen: 1,756.

GIFT AID (NEED-BASED) ***Scholarships, grants, and awards:*** Federal Pell, FSEOG, state, private, college/university gift aid from institutional funds, United Negro College Fund, Federal Nursing.

GIFT AID (NON-NEED-BASED) ***Scholarships, grants, and awards by category:*** *Academic Interests/Achievement:* business, communication, engineering/technologies, general academic interests/achievements.

LOANS ***Programs:*** FFEL (Subsidized and Unsubsidized Stafford, PLUS), Perkins.

WORK-STUDY ***Federal work-study:*** Total amount: $729,525; 225 jobs averaging $4000. ***State or other work-study/employment:*** Total amount: $22,046 (100% need-based). 29 part-time jobs averaging $4000.

APPLYING FOR FINANCIAL AID ***Required financial aid forms:*** FAFSA, institution's own form.

CONTACT Financial Aid Office, Texas Southern University, 3100 Cleburne, Houston, TX 77004-4584, 713-313-7011. *Fax:* 713-313-1858.

TEXAS STATE UNIVERSITY-SAN MARCOS

San Marcos, TX

Tuition & fees (TX res): $5652   Average undergraduate aid package: $9695

ABOUT THE INSTITUTION State-supported, coed. Awards: bachelor's, master's, and doctoral degrees and post-bachelor's certificates. 94 undergraduate majors. Total enrollment: 27,485. Undergraduates: 23,568. Freshmen: 2,959. Federal methodology is used as a basis for awarding need-based institutional aid.

UNDERGRADUATE EXPENSES for 2006–07 ***Application fee:*** $40. ***Tuition, state resident:*** full-time $4140; part-time $138 per semester hour. ***Tuition, nonresident:*** full-time $12,390; part-time $413 per semester hour. ***Required fees:*** full-time $1512; $38 per semester hour or $221 per term part-time. Full-time tuition and fees vary according to course load. Part-time tuition and fees vary according to course load. ***College room and board:*** $5878; ***Room only:*** $3730. Room and board charges vary according to board plan and housing facility. ***Payment plan:*** Installment.

FRESHMAN FINANCIAL AID (Fall 2006, est.) 2005 applied for aid; of those 70% were deemed to have need. 98% of freshmen with need received aid; of those 14% had need fully met. ***Average percent of need met:*** 67% (excluding resources awarded to replace EFC). ***Average financial aid package:*** $10,209 (excluding resources awarded to replace EFC). 4% of all full-time freshmen had no need and received non-need-based gift aid.

UNDERGRADUATE FINANCIAL AID (Fall 2006, est.) 13,064 applied for aid; of those 77% were deemed to have need. 97% of undergraduates with need received aid; of those 15% had need fully met. ***Average percent of need met:*** 65% (excluding resources awarded to replace EFC). ***Average financial aid package:*** $9695 (excluding resources awarded to replace EFC). 2% of all full-time undergraduates had no need and received non-need-based gift aid.

GIFT AID (NEED-BASED) ***Total amount:*** $31,332,524 (55% federal, 45% state). ***Receiving aid:*** Freshmen: 33% (953); All full-time undergraduates: 35% (6,782). ***Average award:*** Freshmen: $4823; Undergraduates: $4203. ***Scholarships, grants, and awards:*** Federal Pell, FSEOG, state, college/university gift aid from institutional funds.

GIFT AID (NON-NEED-BASED) ***Total amount:*** $6,818,696 (35% institutional, 65% external sources). ***Receiving aid:*** Freshmen: 13% (389); Undergraduates: 6% (1,118). ***Average award:*** Freshmen: $1862; Undergraduates: $2386. ***Scholarships, grants, and awards by category:*** *Academic Interests/Achievement:* agriculture, business, education, English, general academic interests/achievements, home economics, international studies, military science. *Creative Arts/Performance:* applied art and design, journalism/publications, music, theater/drama. *Special Characteristics:* children and siblings of alumni, first-generation college students, handicapped students. ***Tuition waivers:*** Full or partial for employees or children of employees. ***ROTC:*** Army, Air Force.

LOANS ***Student loans:*** $60,939,224 (64% need-based, 36% non-need-based). 60% of past graduating class borrowed through all loan programs. *Average indebtedness per student:* $16,420. ***Average need-based loan:*** Freshmen: $2886; Undergraduates: $3895. ***Parent loans:*** $75,096,173 (100% non-need-based). ***Programs:*** Federal Direct (Subsidized and Unsubsidized Stafford, PLUS), FFEL (Subsidized and Unsubsidized Stafford, PLUS), Perkins, state, college/university.

WORK-STUDY ***Federal work-study:*** Total amount: $1,015,463; 883 jobs averaging $1150. ***State or other work-study/employment:*** Total amount: $168,388 (100% need-based). 157 part-time jobs averaging $1073.

ATHLETIC AWARDS Total amount: $2,449,489 (100% non-need-based).

APPLYING FOR FINANCIAL AID ***Required financial aid form:*** FAFSA. ***Financial aid deadline (priority):*** 4/1. ***Notification date:*** Continuous. Students must reply within 3 weeks of notification.

CONTACT Ms. Mariko Gomez, Director of Financial Aid, Texas State University-San Marcos, 601 University Drive, San Marcos, TX 78666-4602, 512-245-2315. *Fax:* 512-245-7920. *E-mail:* mg01@txstate.edu.

TEXAS TECH UNIVERSITY

Lubbock, TX

Tuition & fees (TX res): $6459   Average undergraduate aid package: $7424

ABOUT THE INSTITUTION State-supported, coed. Awards: bachelor's, master's, doctoral, and first professional degrees. 110 undergraduate majors. Total enrollment: 27,996. Undergraduates: 22,851. Freshmen: 3,918. Federal methodology is used as a basis for awarding need-based institutional aid.

UNDERGRADUATE EXPENSES for 2006–07 ***Application fee:*** $50. ***Tuition, state resident:*** full-time $4050; part-time $135 per credit hour. ***Tuition, nonresident:*** full-time $12,300; part-time $410 per credit hour. ***Required fees:*** full-time $2409; $59.50 per credit hour or $354 per term part-time. Full-time tuition and fees vary according to course load, program, and reciprocity agreements. Part-time tuition and fees vary according to course load, program, and reciprocity agreements. ***College room and board:*** $7288; ***Room only:*** $3883. Room and board charges vary according to board plan and housing facility. ***Payment plan:*** Installment.

FRESHMAN FINANCIAL AID (Fall 2005) 2721 applied for aid; of those 52% were deemed to have need. 98% of freshmen with need received aid; of those 6% had need fully met. ***Average percent of need met:*** 60% (excluding resources awarded to replace EFC). ***Average financial aid package:*** $5812 (excluding resources awarded to replace EFC). 6% of all full-time freshmen had no need and received non-need-based gift aid.

UNDERGRADUATE FINANCIAL AID (Fall 2005) 13,370 applied for aid; of those 63% were deemed to have need. 98% of undergraduates with need received aid; of those 5% had need fully met. ***Average percent of need met:*** 61% (excluding resources awarded to replace EFC). ***Average financial aid package:*** $7424 (excluding resources awarded to replace EFC). 3% of all full-time undergraduates had no need and received non-need-based gift aid.

GIFT AID (NEED-BASED) ***Total amount:*** $26,845,575 (50% federal, 47% state, 3% institutional). ***Receiving aid:*** Freshmen: 17% (649); All full-time undergraduates: 27% (5,664). ***Average award:*** Freshmen: $5249; Undergraduates: $4598. ***Scholarships, grants, and awards:*** Federal Pell, FSEOG, state, private, college/university gift aid from institutional funds.

GIFT AID (NON-NEED-BASED) ***Total amount:*** $10,860,597 (61% institutional, 39% external sources). ***Receiving aid:*** Freshmen: 18% (657); Undergraduates: 10% (2,089). ***Average award:*** Freshmen: $2123; Undergraduates: $1848. ***Scholarships, grants, and awards by category:*** *Academic Interests/Achievement:* agriculture, architecture, biological sciences, business, communication, computer science, education, engineering/technologies, English, foreign languages, general academic interests/achievements, home economics, humanities, international studies, mathematics, military science, physical sciences, premedicine, social sciences. *Creative Arts/Performance:* applied art and design, art/fine arts, dance, journalism/publications, music, performing arts, theater/drama. *Special Achievements/Activities:* community service, memberships, rodeo. *Special Characteristics:* children of faculty/staff, first-generation college students, handicapped students, out-of-state students, veterans, veterans' children. ***Tuition waivers:*** Full or partial for employees or children of employees, senior citizens. ***ROTC:*** Army, Air Force.

LOANS ***Student loans:*** $72,695,342 (44% need-based, 56% non-need-based). 55% of past graduating class borrowed through all loan programs. *Average indebtedness per student:* $21,355. ***Average need-based loan:*** Freshmen: $2831; Undergraduates: $3914. ***Parent loans:*** $19,992,692 (100% non-need-based). ***Programs:*** FFEL (Subsidized and Unsubsidized Stafford, PLUS), Perkins, state, college/university.

WORK-STUDY ***Federal work-study:*** Total amount: $710,192. ***State or other work-study/employment:*** Total amount: $1348 (100% need-based).

ATHLETIC AWARDS Total amount: $4,001,864 (100% non-need-based).

APPLYING FOR FINANCIAL AID ***Required financial aid form:*** FAFSA. ***Financial aid deadline (priority):*** 4/15. ***Notification date:*** Continuous beginning 4/1. Students must reply within 2 weeks of notification.

CONTACT Becky Wilson, Managing Director, Student Financial Aid, Texas Tech University, PO Box 45011, Lubbock, TX 79409-5011, 806-742-0454. *Fax:* 806-742-0880.

TEXAS WESLEYAN UNIVERSITY

Fort Worth, TX

CONTACT Mrs. Dean Carpenter, Director of Financial Aid, Texas Wesleyan University, 1201 Wesleyan Street, Fort Worth, TX 76105-1536, 817-531-4420 or toll-free 800-580-8980 (in-state). *Fax:* 817-531-4231. *E-mail:* finaid@txwes.edu.

TEXAS WOMAN'S UNIVERSITY

Denton, TX

Tuition & fees (TX res): $5832 **Average undergraduate aid package: $9778**

ABOUT THE INSTITUTION State-supported, coed, primarily women. Awards: bachelor's, master's, and doctoral degrees and post-master's certificates. 37 undergraduate majors. Total enrollment: 11,832. Undergraduates: 6,675. Freshmen: 812. Federal methodology is used as a basis for awarding need-based institutional aid.

UNDERGRADUATE EXPENSES for 2007–08 ***Application fee:*** $30. ***Tuition, state resident:*** full-time $4290; part-time $143 per hour. ***Tuition, nonresident:*** full-time $12,540; part-time $418 per hour. ***College room and board:*** $5846; ***Room only:*** $3825.

FRESHMAN FINANCIAL AID (Fall 2006, est.) 632 applied for aid; of those 76% were deemed to have need. 100% of freshmen with need received aid; of those 68% had need fully met. ***Average percent of need met:*** 96% (excluding resources awarded to replace EFC). ***Average financial aid package:*** $9712 (excluding resources awarded to replace EFC). 10% of all full-time freshmen had no need and received non-need-based gift aid.

UNDERGRADUATE FINANCIAL AID (Fall 2006, est.) 3,550 applied for aid; of those 82% were deemed to have need. 99% of undergraduates with need received aid; of those 42% had need fully met. ***Average percent of need met:*** 98% (excluding resources awarded to replace EFC). ***Average financial aid package:*** $9778 (excluding resources awarded to replace EFC). 20% of all full-time undergraduates had no need and received non-need-based gift aid.

GIFT AID (NEED-BASED) ***Total amount:*** $18,257,931 (42% federal, 21% state, 37% institutional). ***Receiving aid:*** Freshmen: 39% (317); All full-time undergraduates: 44% (2,113). ***Average award:*** Freshmen: $3604; Undergraduates: $4445. ***Scholarships, grants, and awards:*** Federal Pell, FSEOG, state, private, college/university gift aid from institutional funds.

GIFT AID (NON-NEED-BASED) ***Total amount:*** $1,239,876 (28% institutional, 72% external sources). ***Receiving aid:*** Freshmen: 40% (323); Undergraduates: 21% (994). ***Average award:*** Freshmen: $763; Undergraduates: $1852. ***Scholarships, grants, and awards by category:*** *Academic Interests/Achievement:* 1,679 awards ($1,881,415 total): biological sciences, business, communication, computer science, education, English, foreign languages, general academic interests/achievements, health fields, home economics, humanities, library science, mathematics, physical sciences, premedicine, social sciences. *Creative Arts/Performance:* 84 awards ($86,310 total): applied art and design, art/fine arts, cinema/film/broadcasting, dance, journalism/publications, music, theater/drama. *Special Characteristics:* 76 awards ($124,860 total): international students. ***ROTC:*** Army cooperative, Air Force cooperative.

LOANS ***Student loans:*** $24,824,673 (8% need-based, 92% non-need-based). 58% of past graduating class borrowed through all loan programs. *Average indebtedness per student:* $19,409. ***Average need-based loan:*** Freshmen: $2126; Undergraduates: $3673. ***Parent loans:*** $1,433,643 (27% need-based, 73% non-need-based). ***Programs:*** FFEL (Subsidized and Unsubsidized Stafford, PLUS), Perkins, Federal Nursing, state, college/university, alternative loans.

WORK-STUDY ***Federal work-study:*** Total amount: $350,000; 223 jobs averaging $1781. ***State or other work-study/employment:*** Total amount: $482,331 (15% need-based, 85% non-need-based). 517 part-time jobs averaging $3651.

ATHLETIC AWARDS Total amount: $452,080 (23% need-based, 77% non-need-based).

APPLYING FOR FINANCIAL AID ***Required financial aid form:*** FAFSA. ***Financial aid deadline (priority):*** 4/1. ***Notification date:*** 5/1. Students must reply within 3 weeks of notification.

CONTACT Mr. Governor Jackson, Director of Financial Aid, Texas Woman's University, PO Box 425408, Denton, TX 76204-5408, 940-898-3051 or toll-free 888-948-9984. *Fax:* 940-898-3068. *E-mail:* gjackson@twu.edu.

THIEL COLLEGE

Greenville, PA

Tuition & fees: $18,720 **Average undergraduate aid package: $11,403**

ABOUT THE INSTITUTION Independent religious, coed. Awards: associate and bachelor's degrees. 40 undergraduate majors. Total enrollment: 1,279. Undergraduates: 1,279. Freshmen: 365. Federal methodology is used as a basis for awarding need-based institutional aid.

UNDERGRADUATE EXPENSES for 2006–07 ***Application fee:*** $35. ***Comprehensive fee:*** $26,294 includes full-time tuition ($17,160), mandatory fees ($1560), and room and board ($7574). ***College room only:*** $3900. Full-time tuition and fees vary according to course load. Room and board charges vary according to board plan and housing facility. ***Part-time tuition:*** $550 per credit hour. ***Part-time fees:*** $45 per credit hour; $60 per term. Part-time tuition and fees vary according to course load. ***Payment plan:*** Installment.

FRESHMAN FINANCIAL AID (Fall 2006, est.) 326 applied for aid; of those 95% were deemed to have need. 100% of freshmen with need received aid; of those 35% had need fully met. ***Average percent of need met:*** 80% (excluding resources awarded to replace EFC). ***Average financial aid package:*** $12,924 (excluding resources awarded to replace EFC). 4% of all full-time freshmen had no need and received non-need-based gift aid.

UNDERGRADUATE FINANCIAL AID (Fall 2006, est.) 1,136 applied for aid; of those 94% were deemed to have need. 100% of undergraduates with need received aid; of those 34% had need fully met. ***Average percent of need met:*** 71% (excluding resources awarded to replace EFC). ***Average financial aid package:*** $11,403 (excluding resources awarded to replace EFC). 4% of all full-time undergraduates had no need and received non-need-based gift aid.

GIFT AID (NEED-BASED) ***Total amount:*** $11,441,344 (13% federal, 17% state, 68% institutional, 2% external sources). ***Receiving aid:*** Freshmen: 85% (310); All full-time undergraduates: 89% (1,068). ***Average award:*** Freshmen: $12,377; Undergraduates: $10,713. ***Scholarships, grants, and awards:*** Federal Pell, FSEOG, state, private, college/university gift aid from institutional funds.

GIFT AID (NON-NEED-BASED) ***Total amount:*** $563,120 (1% state, 97% institutional, 2% external sources). ***Receiving aid:*** Freshmen: 85% (310); Undergraduates: 89% (1,068). ***Average award:*** Freshmen: $7356; Undergraduates: $7292. ***Scholarships, grants, and awards by category:*** *Academic Interests/Achievement:* biological sciences, business, computer science, education, English, general academic interests/achievements, mathematics, physical sciences, religion/biblical studies. *Creative Arts/Performance:* 10 awards ($5750 total): music. *Special Achievements/Activities:* leadership. *Special Characteristics:* children and siblings of alumni, children of faculty/staff, relatives of clergy, religious affiliation, siblings of current students. ***Tuition waivers:*** Full or partial for employees or children of employees, senior citizens.

LOANS ***Student loans:*** $5,609,169 (87% need-based, 13% non-need-based). 81% of past graduating class borrowed through all loan programs. *Average indebtedness per student:* $21,427. ***Average need-based loan:*** Freshmen: $3474; Undergraduates: $3358. ***Parent loans:*** $1,859,913 (97% need-based, 3% non-need-based). ***Programs:*** FFEL (Subsidized and Unsubsidized Stafford, PLUS), Perkins, college/university.

WORK-STUDY ***Federal work-study:*** Total amount: $137,750; 154 jobs averaging $1013. ***State or other work-study/employment:*** Total amount: $206,480 (94% need-based, 6% non-need-based). 416 part-time jobs averaging $1014.

APPLYING FOR FINANCIAL AID ***Required financial aid forms:*** FAFSA, state aid form. ***Financial aid deadline (priority):*** 3/15. ***Notification date:*** Continuous beginning 2/15. Students must reply within 15 weeks of notification.

CONTACT Ms. Cynthia H. Farrell, Director of Financial Aid, Thiel College, 75 College Avenue, Greenville, PA 16125-2181, 724-589-2178 or toll-free 800-248-4435. *Fax:* 724-589-2850. *E-mail:* cfarrell@thiel.edu.

THOMAS AQUINAS COLLEGE

Santa Paula, CA

Tuition & fees: $20,400 **Average undergraduate aid package: $16,202**

ABOUT THE INSTITUTION Independent Roman Catholic, coed. Awards: bachelor's degrees. 4 undergraduate majors. Total enrollment: 351. Undergraduates: 351. Freshmen: 104. Institutional methodology is used as a basis for awarding need-based institutional aid.

UNDERGRADUATE EXPENSES for 2007–08 ***Comprehensive fee:*** $27,000 includes full-time tuition ($20,400) and room and board ($6600).

FRESHMAN FINANCIAL AID (Fall 2006, est.) 79 applied for aid; of those 91% were deemed to have need. 100% of freshmen with need received aid; of those 100% had need fully met. ***Average percent of need met:*** 100% (excluding resources awarded to replace EFC). ***Average financial aid package:*** $14,700 (excluding resources awarded to replace EFC).

UNDERGRADUATE FINANCIAL AID (Fall 2006, est.) 253 applied for aid; of those 94% were deemed to have need. 100% of undergraduates with need received aid; of those 100% had need fully met. ***Average percent of need met:*** 100% (excluding resources awarded to replace EFC). ***Average financial aid package:*** $16,202 (excluding resources awarded to replace EFC).

GIFT AID (NEED-BASED) ***Total amount:*** $2,497,319 (8% federal, 13% state, 76% institutional, 3% external sources). ***Receiving aid:*** Freshmen: 60% (62); All full-time undergraduates: 60% (211). ***Average award:*** Freshmen: $11,271; Undergraduates: $11,821. ***Scholarships, grants, and awards:*** Federal Pell, state, private, college/university gift aid from institutional funds.

GIFT AID (NON-NEED-BASED) ***Total amount:*** $51,441 (6% state, 94% external sources). ***Receiving aid:*** Freshmen: 1% (1); Undergraduates: 1% (2).

LOANS ***Student loans:*** $900,165 (76% need-based, 24% non-need-based). 65% of past graduating class borrowed through all loan programs. *Average indebtedness per student:* $14,000. ***Average need-based loan:*** Freshmen: $2611; Undergraduates: $3326. ***Parent loans:*** $252,604 (16% need-based, 84% non-need-based). ***Programs:*** FFEL (Subsidized and Unsubsidized Stafford, PLUS), college/university, Canada Student Loans.

WORK-STUDY ***State or other work-study/employment:*** Total amount: $671,688 (97% need-based, 3% non-need-based). 213 part-time jobs averaging $3152.

APPLYING FOR FINANCIAL AID ***Required financial aid forms:*** FAFSA, institution's own form, state aid form, noncustodial (divorced/separated) parent's statement, income tax returns. ***Financial aid deadline:*** 3/2. ***Notification date:*** Continuous beginning 1/1. Students must reply within 2 weeks of notification.

CONTACT Mr. Gregory Becher, Director of Financial Aid, Thomas Aquinas College, 10000 North Ojai Road, Santa Paula, CA 93060-9980, 805-525-4419 Ext. 235 or toll-free 800-634-9797. *Fax:* 805-525-9342. *E-mail:* gbecher@thomasaquinas.edu.

THOMAS COLLEGE

Waterville, ME

Tuition & fees: $17,730 **Average undergraduate aid package: $14,840**

ABOUT THE INSTITUTION Independent, coed. Awards: associate, bachelor's, and master's degrees (associate). 16 undergraduate majors. Total enrollment: 957. Undergraduates: 766. Freshmen: 221. Federal methodology is used as a basis for awarding need-based institutional aid.

UNDERGRADUATE EXPENSES for 2006–07 ***Application fee:*** $50. ***Comprehensive fee:*** $25,160 includes full-time tuition ($17,280), mandatory fees ($450), and room and board ($7430). Room and board charges vary according to board plan and housing facility. ***Part-time tuition:*** $720 per credit hour. ***Payment plan:*** Deferred payment.

FRESHMAN FINANCIAL AID (Fall 2006, est.) 189 applied for aid; of those 97% were deemed to have need. 100% of freshmen with need received aid; of those 15% had need fully met. ***Average percent of need met:*** 85% (excluding resources awarded to replace EFC). ***Average financial aid package:*** $16,850 (excluding resources awarded to replace EFC). 5% of all full-time freshmen had no need and received non-need-based gift aid.

UNDERGRADUATE FINANCIAL AID (Fall 2006, est.) 562 applied for aid; of those 96% were deemed to have need. 99% of undergraduates with need received aid; of those 21% had need fully met. ***Average percent of need met:*** 85% (excluding resources awarded to replace EFC). ***Average financial aid package:*** $14,840 (excluding resources awarded to replace EFC). 7% of all full-time undergraduates had no need and received non-need-based gift aid.

GIFT AID (NEED-BASED) ***Total amount:*** $5,404,266 (19% federal, 6% state, 75% institutional). ***Receiving aid:*** Freshmen: 96% (183); All full-time undergraduates: 90% (532). ***Average award:*** Freshmen: $13,579; Undergraduates: $7792. ***Scholarships, grants, and awards:*** Federal Pell, FSEOG, state, private, college/university gift aid from institutional funds.

GIFT AID (NON-NEED-BASED) ***Total amount:*** $415,496 (41% institutional, 59% external sources). ***Receiving aid:*** Freshmen: 36% (68); Undergraduates: 17% (101). ***Average award:*** Freshmen: $4500; Undergraduates: $6217. ***Scholarships, grants, and awards by category:*** *Academic Interests/Achievement:* 178 awards ($1,238,680 total): general academic interests/achievements. ***Tuition waivers:*** Full or partial for employees or children of employees.

LOANS ***Student loans:*** $4,399,732 (47% need-based, 53% non-need-based). 83% of past graduating class borrowed through all loan programs. *Average indebtedness per student:* $21,025. ***Average need-based loan:*** Freshmen: $3190; Undergraduates: $3779. ***Parent loans:*** $601,410 (100% non-need-based). ***Programs:*** Federal Direct (Subsidized and Unsubsidized Stafford, PLUS), Perkins.

WORK-STUDY ***Federal work-study:*** Total amount: $198,931; 118 jobs averaging $1685.

APPLYING FOR FINANCIAL AID ***Required financial aid form:*** FAFSA. ***Financial aid deadline (priority):*** 2/15. ***Notification date:*** Continuous beginning 3/15. Students must reply within 2 weeks of notification.

CONTACT Jeannine Bosse, Associate Director of Student Financial Aid, Thomas College, 180 West River Road, Waterville, ME 04901-5097, 800-339-7001. *Fax:* 207-859-1114. *E-mail:* sfsassistant@thomas.edu.

THOMAS EDISON STATE COLLEGE

Trenton, NJ

ABOUT THE INSTITUTION State-supported, coed. Awards: associate, bachelor's, and master's degrees (offers only distance learning degree programs). Total enrollment: 13,173. Undergraduates: 12,729.

GIFT AID (NEED-BASED) ***Scholarships, grants, and awards:*** Federal Pell, state, private.

LOANS ***Programs:*** FFEL (Subsidized and Unsubsidized Stafford, PLUS), private educational loans.

APPLYING FOR FINANCIAL AID ***Required financial aid forms:*** FAFSA, institution's own form.

CONTACT Financial Aid Office, Thomas Edison State College, 101 West State Street, Trenton, NJ 08608, 609-633-9658 or toll-free 888-442-8372. *Fax:* 609-633-6489.

THOMAS JEFFERSON UNIVERSITY

Philadelphia, PA

ABOUT THE INSTITUTION Independent, coed. Awards: bachelor's, master's, and doctoral degrees and post-bachelor's certificates. 8 undergraduate majors. Total enrollment: 2,867. Undergraduates: 1,057. Freshmen: 29.

GIFT AID (NEED-BASED) ***Scholarships, grants, and awards:*** Federal Pell, FSEOG, state, private, college/university gift aid from institutional funds, Scholarships for Disadvantaged Students (SDS).

GIFT AID (NON-NEED-BASED) ***Scholarships, grants, and awards by category:*** *Academic Interests/Achievement:* general academic interests/achievements, health fields. *Special Characteristics:* members of minority groups, veterans.

LOANS ***Programs:*** FFEL (Subsidized and Unsubsidized Stafford, PLUS), Perkins, Federal Nursing, college/university.

WORK-STUDY ***Federal work-study:*** Total amount: $107,286; 120 jobs averaging $2000.

APPLYING FOR FINANCIAL AID ***Required financial aid forms:*** FAFSA, institution's own form, parent and student income tax returns.

CONTACT Susan Batchelor, University Director of Financial Aid, Thomas Jefferson University, 1025 Walnut Street, Room G-1, College Building, Philadelphia, PA 19107, 215-955-2867 or toll-free 877-533-3247. *E-mail:* financial.aid@jefferson.edu.

THOMAS MORE COLLEGE

Crestview Hills, KY

Tuition & fees: $21,220 **Average undergraduate aid package: $17,720**

ABOUT THE INSTITUTION Independent Roman Catholic, coed. Awards: associate, bachelor's, and master's degrees. 42 undergraduate majors. Total enrollment: 1,400. Undergraduates: 1,325. Freshmen: 169. Federal methodology is used as a basis for awarding need-based institutional aid.

UNDERGRADUATE EXPENSES for 2007–08 ***Application fee:*** $25. ***Comprehensive fee:*** $27,470 includes full-time tuition ($20,500), mandatory fees ($720), and room and board ($6250). ***College room only:*** $2900. ***Part-time tuition:*** $490 per credit. ***Part-time fees:*** $30 per credit; $15 per term.

FRESHMAN FINANCIAL AID (Fall 2005) 190 applied for aid; of those 100% were deemed to have need. 100% of freshmen with need received aid; of those 100% had need fully met. ***Average percent of need met:*** 90% (excluding resources awarded to replace EFC). ***Average financial aid package:*** $17,950 (excluding resources awarded to replace EFC). 5% of all full-time freshmen had no need and received non-need-based gift aid.

UNDERGRADUATE FINANCIAL AID (Fall 2005) 828 applied for aid; of those 100% were deemed to have need. 100% of undergraduates with need received aid; of those 100% had need fully met. ***Average percent of need met:*** 82% (excluding resources awarded to replace EFC). ***Average financial aid package:*** $17,720 (excluding resources awarded to replace EFC). 13% of all full-time undergraduates had no need and received non-need-based gift aid.

GIFT AID (NEED-BASED) ***Total amount:*** $1,978,934 (39% federal, 56% state, 5% institutional). ***Receiving aid:*** Freshmen: 81% (179); All full-time undergraduates: 64% (727). ***Average award:*** Freshmen: $4709; Undergraduates: $4431. ***Scholarships, grants, and awards:*** Federal Pell, FSEOG, state, private, college/university gift aid from institutional funds.

GIFT AID (NON-NEED-BASED) ***Total amount:*** $6,146,636 (10% state, 75% institutional, 15% external sources). ***Receiving aid:*** Freshmen: 86% (190); Undergraduates: 73% (818). ***Average award:*** Freshmen: $7088; Undergraduates: $6770. ***Scholarships, grants, and awards by category:*** *Academic Interests/Achievement:* 716 awards ($2,419,995 total): general academic interests/achievements, social sciences. *Creative Arts/Performance:* 13 awards ($17,480 total): art/fine arts, theater/drama. *Special Achievements/Activities:* 38 awards ($58,350 total): leadership, religious involvement. *Special Characteristics:* 287 awards ($727,955 total): adult students, children and siblings of alumni, children of faculty/staff, members of minority groups, religious affiliation. ***ROTC:*** Army cooperative, Air Force cooperative.

LOANS ***Student loans:*** $5,381,932 (38% need-based, 62% non-need-based). 82% of past graduating class borrowed through all loan programs. *Average indebtedness per student:* $22,165. ***Average need-based loan:*** Freshmen: $1756; Undergraduates: $2301. ***Parent loans:*** $1,160,176 (100% non-need-based). ***Programs:*** FFEL (Subsidized and Unsubsidized Stafford, PLUS), Perkins, Federal Nursing, college/university.

WORK-STUDY ***Federal work-study:*** Total amount: $118,511; 96 jobs averaging $1235. ***State or other work-study/employment:*** Total amount: $215,497 (100% non-need-based). 47 part-time jobs averaging $4585.

APPLYING FOR FINANCIAL AID ***Required financial aid forms:*** FAFSA, institution's own form. ***Financial aid deadline (priority):*** 3/15. ***Notification date:*** Continuous beginning 3/1. Students must reply by 5/1.

CONTACT Ms. Mary Givhan, Director of Financial Aid, Thomas More College, 333 Thomas More Parkway, Crestview Hills, KY 41017-3495, 859-344-3531 or toll-free 800-825-4557. *Fax:* 859-344-3638. *E-mail:* mary.givhan@thomasmore.edu.

THOMAS MORE COLLEGE OF LIBERAL ARTS

Merrimack, NH

Tuition & fees: $11,150 **Average undergraduate aid package: $11,339**

ABOUT THE INSTITUTION Independent religious, coed. Awards: bachelor's degrees. 4 undergraduate majors. Total enrollment: 86. Undergraduates: 86. Freshmen: 21. Federal methodology is used as a basis for awarding need-based institutional aid.

UNDERGRADUATE EXPENSES for 2006–07 ***Comprehensive fee:*** $19,150 includes full-time tuition ($11,100), mandatory fees ($50), and room and board ($8000). ***Part-time tuition:*** $225 per credit hour. ***Payment plan:*** Installment.

FRESHMAN FINANCIAL AID (Fall 2006, est.) 22 applied for aid; of those 82% were deemed to have need. 100% of freshmen with need received aid; of those 83% had need fully met. ***Average percent of need met:*** 67% (excluding resources awarded to replace EFC). ***Average financial aid package:*** $9842 (excluding resources awarded to replace EFC). 22% of all full-time freshmen had no need and received non-need-based gift aid.

UNDERGRADUATE FINANCIAL AID (Fall 2006, est.) 94 applied for aid; of those 69% were deemed to have need. 100% of undergraduates with need received aid; of those 85% had need fully met. ***Average percent of need met:*** 81% (excluding resources awarded to replace EFC). ***Average financial aid package:*** $11,339 (excluding resources awarded to replace EFC). 28% of all full-time undergraduates had no need and received non-need-based gift aid.

GIFT AID (NEED-BASED) ***Total amount:*** $260,286 (29% federal, 3% state, 65% institutional, 3% external sources). ***Receiving aid:*** Freshmen: 78% (18); All full-time undergraduates: 68% (65). ***Average award:*** Freshmen: $6150; Undergraduates: $5676. ***Scholarships, grants, and awards:*** Federal Pell, FSEOG, state, private, college/university gift aid from institutional funds.

GIFT AID (NON-NEED-BASED) ***Total amount:*** $332,213 (100% institutional). ***Receiving aid:*** Freshmen: 57% (13); Undergraduates: 51% (49). ***Average award:*** Freshmen: $5508; Undergraduates: $4937. ***Scholarships, grants, and awards by category:*** *Academic Interests/Achievement:* 67 awards ($306,713 total): general academic interests/achievements. ***Tuition waivers:*** Full or partial for employees or children of employees.

LOANS ***Student loans:*** $451,581 (39% need-based, 61% non-need-based). 79% of past graduating class borrowed through all loan programs. *Average indebtedness per student:* $21,417. ***Average need-based loan:*** Freshmen: $2042; Undergraduates: $3295. ***Parent loans:*** $119,505 (65% need-based, 35% non-need-based). ***Programs:*** FFEL (Subsidized and Unsubsidized Stafford, PLUS).

WORK-STUDY ***State or other work-study/employment:*** Total amount: $65,550 (71% need-based, 29% non-need-based). 56 part-time jobs averaging $1170.

APPLYING FOR FINANCIAL AID ***Required financial aid form:*** FAFSA. ***Financial aid deadline:*** Continuous. ***Notification date:*** Continuous beginning 3/15. Students must reply within 2 weeks of notification.

CONTACT Clinton A. Hanson Jr., Director of Financial Aid, Thomas More College of Liberal Arts, 6 Manchester Street, Merrimack, NH 03054-4818, 603-880-8308 Ext. 23 or toll-free 800-880-8308. *Fax:* 603-546-0180. *E-mail:* chanson@thomasmorecollege.edu.

THOMAS UNIVERSITY

Thomasville, GA

CONTACT Ms. Angela Keys, Director of Financial Aid, Thomas University, 1501 Millpond Road, Thomasville, GA 31792-7499, 229-226-1621 Ext. 216 or toll-free 800-538-9784. *Fax:* 229-227-6919. *E-mail:* akeys@thomasu.edu.

TIFFIN UNIVERSITY

Tiffin, OH

Tuition & fees: $15,870 **Average undergraduate aid package: $13,044**

ABOUT THE INSTITUTION Independent, coed. Awards: associate, bachelor's, and master's degrees. 21 undergraduate majors. Total enrollment: 1,977. Undergraduates: 1,437. Freshmen: 332. Federal methodology is used as a basis for awarding need-based institutional aid.

UNDERGRADUATE EXPENSES for 2006–07 ***Application fee:*** $20. ***Comprehensive fee:*** $22,645 includes full-time tuition ($15,870) and room and board ($6775). ***College room only:*** $3525. ***Part-time tuition:*** $529 per credit hour.

FRESHMAN FINANCIAL AID (Fall 2006, est.) 299 applied for aid; of those 90% were deemed to have need. 100% of freshmen with need received aid; of those 17% had need fully met. ***Average percent of need met:*** 17% (excluding resources awarded to replace EFC). ***Average financial aid package:*** $16,949 (excluding resources awarded to replace EFC). 10% of all full-time freshmen had no need and received non-need-based gift aid.

UNDERGRADUATE FINANCIAL AID (Fall 2006, est.) 1,222 applied for aid; of those 90% were deemed to have need. 100% of undergraduates with need received aid; of those 14% had need fully met. ***Average percent of need met:*** 14% (excluding resources awarded to replace EFC). ***Average financial aid***

package: $13,044 (excluding resources awarded to replace EFC). 11% of all full-time undergraduates had no need and received non-need-based gift aid.

GIFT AID (NEED-BASED) ***Total amount:*** $8,261,194 (21% federal, 23% state, 54% institutional, 2% external sources). ***Receiving aid:*** Freshmen: 41% (136); All full-time undergraduates: 55% (719). ***Average award:*** Freshmen: $5359; Undergraduates: $5041. ***Scholarships, grants, and awards:*** Federal Pell, FSEOG, state, private, college/university gift aid from institutional funds.

GIFT AID (NON-NEED-BASED) ***Receiving aid:*** Freshmen: 68% (227); Undergraduates: 83% (1,084). ***Average award:*** Freshmen: $10,079; Undergraduates: $7123. ***Scholarships, grants, and awards by category:*** *Academic Interests/Achievement:* 669 awards ($2,291,946 total): general academic interests/achievements. *Creative Arts/Performance:* 85 awards ($173,250 total): music, performing arts, theater/drama. *Special Achievements/Activities:* 23 awards ($25,625 total): cheerleading/drum major. *Special Characteristics:* 16 awards ($122,508 total): children of faculty/staff. ***ROTC:*** Army cooperative, Air Force cooperative.

LOANS ***Student loans:*** $12,323,111 (100% need-based). 86% of past graduating class borrowed through all loan programs. *Average indebtedness per student:* $19,624. ***Average need-based loan:*** Freshmen: $2461; Undergraduates: $3833. ***Parent loans:*** $959,524 (100% need-based). ***Programs:*** FFEL (Subsidized and Unsubsidized Stafford, PLUS), Perkins, college/university.

WORK-STUDY ***Federal work-study:*** Total amount: $4,481,139; jobs available.

ATHLETIC AWARDS Total amount: $163,849 (100% need-based).

APPLYING FOR FINANCIAL AID ***Required financial aid form:*** FAFSA. ***Financial aid deadline (priority):*** 1/1. ***Notification date:*** Continuous beginning 2/15. Students must reply within 2 weeks of notification.

CONTACT Ashley Runion, Office Manager, Tiffin University, 155 Miami Street, Tiffin, OH 44883, 419-448-3279 or toll-free 800-968-6446. *Fax:* 419-443-5006. *E-mail:* runiona@tiffin.edu.

TOCCOA FALLS COLLEGE

Toccoa Falls, GA

ABOUT THE INSTITUTION Independent interdenominational, coed. Awards: associate and bachelor's degrees. 22 undergraduate majors. Total enrollment: 939. Undergraduates: 939. Freshmen: 191.

GIFT AID (NEED-BASED) ***Scholarships, grants, and awards:*** Federal Pell, FSEOG, state, private, college/university gift aid from institutional funds.

GIFT AID (NON-NEED-BASED) ***Scholarships, grants, and awards by category:*** *Academic Interests/Achievement:* business, communication, education, general academic interests/achievements, religion/biblical studies. *Creative Arts/Performance:* music. *Special Achievements/Activities:* leadership. *Special Characteristics:* children of faculty/staff, ethnic background, general special characteristics, international students, married students, relatives of clergy, religious affiliation, siblings of current students.

LOANS ***Programs:*** FFEL (Subsidized and Unsubsidized Stafford, PLUS), Perkins, college/university.

WORK-STUDY ***Federal work-study:*** Total amount: $492,805; 369 jobs averaging $1336. ***State or other work-study/employment:*** Total amount: $208,120 (100% non-need-based). 154 part-time jobs averaging $1351.

APPLYING FOR FINANCIAL AID ***Required financial aid forms:*** FAFSA, institution's own form.

CONTACT Vince Welch, Director of Financial Aid, Toccoa Falls College, PO Box 800900, Toccoa Falls, GA 30598, 706-886-7299 Ext. 5234. *Fax:* 706-282-6041. *E-mail:* vwelch@tfc.edu.

TORAH TEMIMAH TALMUDICAL SEMINARY

Brooklyn, NY

CONTACT Financial Aid Office, Torah Temimah Talmudical Seminary, 507 Ocean Parkway, Brooklyn, NY 11218-5913, 718-853-8500.

TOUGALOO COLLEGE

Tougaloo, MS

CONTACT Director of Financial Aid, Tougaloo College, 500 West County Line Road, Tougaloo, MS 39174, 601-977-6134 or toll-free 888-42GALOO. *Fax:* 601-977-6164.

TOURO COLLEGE

New York, NY

CONTACT Office of Financial Aid, Touro College, 27 West 23rd Street, New York, NY 10010, 212-463-0400.

TOURO UNIVERSITY INTERNATIONAL

Cypress, CA

CONTACT Financial Aid Office, Touro University International, 5665 Plaza Drive, 3rd Floor, Cypress, CA 90630, 714-816-0366.

TOWSON UNIVERSITY

Towson, MD

Tuition & fees (MD res): $7164 **Average undergraduate aid package: $7887**

ABOUT THE INSTITUTION State-supported, coed. Awards: bachelor's, master's, and doctoral degrees and post-bachelor's and post-master's certificates. 50 undergraduate majors. Total enrollment: 18,921. Undergraduates: 15,374. Freshmen: 2,696. Federal methodology is used as a basis for awarding need-based institutional aid.

UNDERGRADUATE EXPENSES for 2006–07 ***Application fee:*** $45. ***Tuition, state resident:*** full-time $5180; part-time $225 per credit. ***Tuition, nonresident:*** full-time $14,538; part-time $544 per credit. ***Required fees:*** full-time $1984; $71 per credit. ***College room and board:*** $7506; ***Room only:*** $4500.

FRESHMAN FINANCIAL AID (Fall 2006, est.) 1923 applied for aid; of those 65% were deemed to have need. 95% of freshmen with need received aid; of those 20% had need fully met. ***Average percent of need met:*** 64% (excluding resources awarded to replace EFC). ***Average financial aid package:*** $7320 (excluding resources awarded to replace EFC). 7% of all full-time freshmen had no need and received non-need-based gift aid.

UNDERGRADUATE FINANCIAL AID (Fall 2006, est.) 7,741 applied for aid; of those 72% were deemed to have need. 95% of undergraduates with need received aid; of those 19% had need fully met. ***Average percent of need met:*** 66% (excluding resources awarded to replace EFC). ***Average financial aid package:*** $7887 (excluding resources awarded to replace EFC). 3% of all full-time undergraduates had no need and received non-need-based gift aid.

GIFT AID (NEED-BASED) ***Total amount:*** $23,057,669 (30% federal, 36% state, 30% institutional, 4% external sources). ***Receiving aid:*** Freshmen: 29% (791); All full-time undergraduates: 27% (3,572). ***Average award:*** Freshmen: $6127; Undergraduates: $5710. ***Scholarships, grants, and awards:*** Federal Pell, FSEOG, state, private, college/university gift aid from institutional funds.

GIFT AID (NON-NEED-BASED) ***Total amount:*** $11,315,218 (9% state, 66% institutional, 25% external sources). ***Receiving aid:*** Freshmen: 20% (543); Undergraduates: 13% (1,721). ***Average award:*** Freshmen: $4532; Undergraduates: $4000. ***Scholarships, grants, and awards by category:*** *Academic Interests/Achievement:* general academic interests/achievements. *Creative Arts/Performance:* art/fine arts, dance, music, theater/drama. ***ROTC:*** Army cooperative, Air Force cooperative.

LOANS ***Student loans:*** $24,462,119 (67% need-based, 33% non-need-based). 49% of past graduating class borrowed through all loan programs. *Average indebtedness per student:* $12,472. ***Average need-based loan:*** Freshmen: $2875; Undergraduates: $3640. ***Parent loans:*** $32,535,632 (21% need-based, 79% non-need-based). ***Programs:*** Federal Direct (Subsidized and Unsubsidized Stafford, PLUS), Perkins.

WORK-STUDY ***Federal work-study:*** Total amount: $580,088; jobs available. ***State or other work-study/employment:*** Part-time jobs available.

ATHLETIC AWARDS Total amount: $4,077,311 (6% need-based, 94% non-need-based).

APPLYING FOR FINANCIAL AID ***Required financial aid form:*** FAFSA. ***Financial aid deadline:*** 3/1 (priority: 1/31). ***Notification date:*** Continuous beginning 3/21. Students must reply within 2 weeks of notification.

CONTACT Vince Pecora, Director of Financial Aid, Towson University, 8000 York Road, Towson, MD 21252-0001, 410-704-4236 or toll-free 888-4TOWSON. *E-mail:* finaid@towson.edu.

TRANSYLVANIA UNIVERSITY

Lexington, KY

Tuition & fees: $22,300 **Average undergraduate aid package: $17,629**

ABOUT THE INSTITUTION Independent religious, coed. Awards: bachelor's degrees. 31 undergraduate majors. Total enrollment: 1,117. Undergraduates: 1,117. Freshmen: 293. Federal methodology is used as a basis for awarding need-based institutional aid.

UNDERGRADUATE EXPENSES for 2007–08 ***Application fee:*** $30. ***Comprehensive fee:*** $29,430 includes full-time tuition ($22,300) and room and board ($7130). ***Part-time tuition:*** $2385 per course. ***Part-time fees:*** $80 per course.

FRESHMAN FINANCIAL AID (Fall 2006, est.) 239 applied for aid; of those 86% were deemed to have need. 100% of freshmen with need received aid; of those 33% had need fully met. ***Average percent of need met:*** 87% (excluding resources awarded to replace EFC). ***Average financial aid package:*** $18,044 (excluding resources awarded to replace EFC). 28% of all full-time freshmen had no need and received non-need-based gift aid.

UNDERGRADUATE FINANCIAL AID (Fall 2006, est.) 788 applied for aid; of those 87% were deemed to have need. 100% of undergraduates with need received aid; of those 28% had need fully met. ***Average percent of need met:*** 85% (excluding resources awarded to replace EFC). ***Average financial aid package:*** $17,629 (excluding resources awarded to replace EFC). 37% of all full-time undergraduates had no need and received non-need-based gift aid.

GIFT AID (NEED-BASED) ***Total amount:*** $9,209,289 (9% federal, 27% state, 62% institutional, 2% external sources). ***Receiving aid:*** Freshmen: 70% (202); All full-time undergraduates: 62% (678). ***Average award:*** Freshmen: $14,935; Undergraduates: $13,708. ***Scholarships, grants, and awards:*** Federal Pell, FSEOG, state, private, college/university gift aid from institutional funds.

GIFT AID (NON-NEED-BASED) ***Total amount:*** $4,627,019 (16% state, 81% institutional, 3% external sources). ***Receiving aid:*** Freshmen: 10% (30); Undergraduates: 8% (89). ***Average award:*** Freshmen: $11,257; Undergraduates: $12,157. ***Scholarships, grants, and awards by category:*** *Academic Interests/Achievement:* 1,053 awards ($7,484,220 total): computer science, general academic interests/achievements. *Creative Arts/Performance:* 51 awards ($126,850 total): art/fine arts, music. *Special Achievements/Activities:* 278 awards ($707,772 total): general special achievements/activities, religious involvement. *Special Characteristics:* 137 awards ($728,152 total): children of faculty/staff, members of minority groups, out-of-state students, relatives of clergy, religious affiliation. ***ROTC:*** Army cooperative, Air Force cooperative.

LOANS ***Student loans:*** $3,444,642 (69% need-based, 31% non-need-based). 58% of past graduating class borrowed through all loan programs. *Average indebtedness per student:* $17,616. ***Average need-based loan:*** Freshmen: $3338; Undergraduates: $3957. ***Parent loans:*** $1,677,386 (22% need-based, 78% non-need-based). ***Programs:*** FFEL (Subsidized and Unsubsidized Stafford, PLUS), Perkins, college/university.

WORK-STUDY ***Federal work-study:*** Total amount: $498,944; 413 jobs averaging $1208. ***State or other work-study/employment:*** Total amount: $317,540 (25% need-based, 75% non-need-based). 52 part-time jobs averaging $6107.

APPLYING FOR FINANCIAL AID ***Required financial aid form:*** FAFSA. ***Financial aid deadline (priority):*** 3/1. ***Notification date:*** Continuous beginning 3/15. Students must reply within 2 weeks of notification.

CONTACT Mr. Dave Cecil, Director of Financial Aid, Transylvania University, 300 North Broadway, Lexington, KY 40508-1797, 859-233-8239 or toll-free 800-872-6798. *Fax:* 859-281-3650. *E-mail:* dcecil@transy.edu.

TREVECCA NAZARENE UNIVERSITY

Nashville, TN

Tuition & fees: $14,774 **Average undergraduate aid package: $8846**

ABOUT THE INSTITUTION Independent Nazarene, coed. Awards: associate, bachelor's, master's, and doctoral degrees and post-master's certificates. 36 undergraduate majors. Total enrollment: 2,217. Undergraduates: 1,247. Freshmen: 244. Federal methodology is used as a basis for awarding need-based institutional aid.

UNDERGRADUATE EXPENSES for 2006–07 ***Application fee:*** $25. ***Comprehensive fee:*** $21,244 includes full-time tuition ($14,774) and room and board ($6470). ***College room only:*** $2920. Full-time tuition and fees vary according to course load. Room and board charges vary according to board plan. ***Part-time tuition:*** $569 per semester hour. Part-time tuition and fees vary according to course load. ***Payment plan:*** Installment.

FRESHMAN FINANCIAL AID (Fall 2005) 180 applied for aid; of those 86% were deemed to have need. 66% of freshmen with need received aid; of those 26% had need fully met. ***Average percent of need met:*** 47% (excluding resources awarded to replace EFC). ***Average financial aid package:*** $10,502 (excluding resources awarded to replace EFC). 52% of all full-time freshmen had no need and received non-need-based gift aid.

UNDERGRADUATE FINANCIAL AID (Fall 2005) 893 applied for aid; of those 86% were deemed to have need. 82% of undergraduates with need received aid; of those 17% had need fully met. ***Average percent of need met:*** 52% (excluding resources awarded to replace EFC). ***Average financial aid package:*** $8846 (excluding resources awarded to replace EFC). 28% of all full-time undergraduates had no need and received non-need-based gift aid.

GIFT AID (NEED-BASED) ***Total amount:*** $4,919,908 (22% federal, 9% state, 66% institutional, 3% external sources). ***Receiving aid:*** Freshmen: 41% (97); All full-time undergraduates: 53% (540). ***Average award:*** Freshmen: $8176; Undergraduates: $6388. ***Scholarships, grants, and awards:*** Federal Pell, FSEOG, state, private, college/university gift aid from institutional funds.

GIFT AID (NON-NEED-BASED) ***Total amount:*** $2,307,897 (9% state, 84% institutional, 7% external sources). ***Receiving aid:*** Freshmen: 9% (21); Undergraduates: 7% (73). ***Average award:*** Freshmen: $8486; Undergraduates: $8622. ***Scholarships, grants, and awards by category:*** *Academic Interests/Achievement:* business, communication, education, general academic interests/achievements, physical sciences, religion/biblical studies, social sciences. *Creative Arts/Performance:* music, theater/drama. *Special Achievements/Activities:* general special achievements/activities. *Special Characteristics:* children and siblings of alumni, general special characteristics, relatives of clergy, religious affiliation. ***Tuition waivers:*** Full or partial for employees or children of employees, senior citizens. ***ROTC:*** Army cooperative.

LOANS ***Student loans:*** $3,926,400 (73% need-based, 27% non-need-based). 77% of past graduating class borrowed through all loan programs. *Average indebtedness per student:* $16,072. ***Average need-based loan:*** Freshmen: $3820; Undergraduates: $4342. ***Parent loans:*** $1,667,759 (100% non-need-based). ***Programs:*** FFEL (Subsidized and Unsubsidized Stafford, PLUS), Perkins, college/university.

WORK-STUDY ***Federal work-study:*** Total amount: $82,360; jobs available.

ATHLETIC AWARDS Total amount: $723,468 (100% non-need-based).

APPLYING FOR FINANCIAL AID ***Required financial aid form:*** FAFSA. ***Financial aid deadline (priority):*** 3/1. ***Notification date:*** Continuous beginning 3/1. Students must reply by 8/29.

CONTACT Eddie White, Assistant Director of Financial Aid, Trevecca Nazarene University, 333 Murfreesboro Road, Nashville, TN 37210-2834, 615-248-1242 or toll-free 888-210-4TNU. *Fax:* 615-248-7728. *E-mail:* ewhite@trevecca.edu.

TRINITY BAPTIST COLLEGE

Jacksonville, FL

CONTACT Mr. Donald Schaffer, Financial Aid Administrator, Trinity Baptist College, 800 Hammond Boulevard, Jacksonville, FL 32221, 904-596-2445 or toll-free 800-786-2206 (out-of-state). *Fax:* 904-596-2531. *E-mail:* financialaid@tbc.edu.

TRINITY BIBLE COLLEGE

Ellendale, ND

CONTACT Rhonda Miller, Financial Aid Associate, Trinity Bible College, 50 South 6th Avenue, Ellendale, ND 58436-7150, 888-822-2329 Ext. 2781 or toll-free 888-TBC-2DAY. *Fax:* 701-349-5786. *E-mail:* financialaid@trinitybiblecollege.edu.

TRINITY CHRISTIAN COLLEGE

Palos Heights, IL

CONTACT L. Denise Coleman, Director of Financial Aid, Trinity Christian College, 6601 West College Drive, Palos Heights, IL 60463-0929, 708-239-4706 or toll-free 800-748-0085. *E-mail:* financial.aid@trnty.edu.

TRINITY COLLEGE
Hartford, CT

Tuition & fees: $35,130 **Average undergraduate aid package: $25,590**

ABOUT THE INSTITUTION Independent, coed. Awards: bachelor's and master's degrees. 44 undergraduate majors. Total enrollment: 2,528. Undergraduates: 2,353. Freshmen: 609. Both federal and institutional methodology are used as a basis for awarding need-based institutional aid.

UNDERGRADUATE EXPENSES for 2006–07 ***Application fee:*** $60. ***Comprehensive fee:*** $44,100 includes full-time tuition ($33,440), mandatory fees ($1690), and room and board ($8970). Full-time tuition and fees vary according to program. Room and board charges vary according to board plan. ***Part-time tuition:*** $1240 per credit hour. Part-time tuition and fees vary according to program. ***Payment plan:*** Installment.

FRESHMAN FINANCIAL AID (Fall 2005) 322 applied for aid; of those 86% were deemed to have need. 100% of freshmen with need received aid; of those 100% had need fully met. ***Average percent of need met:*** 100% (excluding resources awarded to replace EFC). ***Average financial aid package:*** $27,916 (excluding resources awarded to replace EFC). 1% of all full-time freshmen had no need and received non-need-based gift aid.

UNDERGRADUATE FINANCIAL AID (Fall 2005) 1,068 applied for aid; of those 85% were deemed to have need. 100% of undergraduates with need received aid; of those 100% had need fully met. ***Average percent of need met:*** 100% (excluding resources awarded to replace EFC). ***Average financial aid package:*** $25,590 (excluding resources awarded to replace EFC). 1% of all full-time undergraduates had no need and received non-need-based gift aid.

GIFT AID (NEED-BASED) ***Total amount:*** $22,864,488 (4% federal, 3% state, 91% institutional, 2% external sources). ***Receiving aid:*** Freshmen: 46% (264); All full-time undergraduates: 42% (833). ***Average award:*** Freshmen: $25,914; Undergraduates: $23,183. ***Scholarships, grants, and awards:*** Federal Pell, FSEOG, state, private, college/university gift aid from institutional funds, Federal ACG and Federal SMART Grants.

GIFT AID (NON-NEED-BASED) ***Total amount:*** $536,800 (100% institutional). ***Receiving aid:*** Freshmen: 1% (6); Undergraduates: 1% (14). ***Average award:*** Freshmen: $30,380; Undergraduates: $27,442. ***Scholarships, grants, and awards by category:*** *Academic Interests/Achievement:* 3 awards ($3000 total): general academic interests/achievements. *Special Achievements/Activities:* 10 awards ($320,000 total): leadership. ***Tuition waivers:*** Full or partial for employees or children of employees, adult students. ***ROTC:*** Army cooperative.

LOANS ***Student loans:*** $6,102,944 (55% need-based, 45% non-need-based). 42% of past graduating class borrowed through all loan programs. *Average indebtedness per student:* $18,122. ***Average need-based loan:*** Freshmen: $2669; Undergraduates: $4250. ***Parent loans:*** $4,901,893 (100% non-need-based). ***Programs:*** FFEL (Subsidized and Unsubsidized Stafford, PLUS), Perkins, college/university, alternative loans.

WORK-STUDY ***Federal work-study:*** Total amount: $1,054,538; 694 jobs averaging $1520.

APPLYING FOR FINANCIAL AID ***Required financial aid forms:*** FAFSA, CSS Financial Aid PROFILE, noncustodial (divorced/separated) parent's statement, business/farm supplement, federal income tax form(s). ***Financial aid deadline:*** 3/1 (priority: 2/1). ***Notification date:*** 4/1. Students must reply by 5/1 or within 2 weeks of notification.

CONTACT Ms. Kelly O'Brien, Director of Financial Aid, Trinity College, 300 Summit Street, Hartford, CT 06106-3100, 860-297-2046. *Fax:* 860-987-6296.

TRINITY COLLEGE OF FLORIDA
New Port Richey, FL

ABOUT THE INSTITUTION Independent nondenominational, coed. Awards: associate and bachelor's degrees. 8 undergraduate majors. Total enrollment: 182. Undergraduates: 182. Freshmen: 19.

GIFT AID (NEED-BASED) ***Scholarships, grants, and awards:*** Federal Pell, FSEOG, state, private, college/university gift aid from institutional funds.

GIFT AID (NON-NEED-BASED) ***Scholarships, grants, and awards by category:*** *Academic Interests/Achievement:* religion/biblical studies. *Special Achievements/Activities:* community service, leadership, religious involvement.

LOANS ***Programs:*** FFEL (Subsidized and Unsubsidized Stafford, PLUS).

APPLYING FOR FINANCIAL AID ***Required financial aid forms:*** FAFSA, institution's own form.

CONTACT Sue Wayne, Director of Financial Aid, Trinity College of Florida, 2430 Welbilt Boulevard, New Port Richey, FL 34655, 727-376-6911 Ext. 310 or toll-free 800-388-0869. *Fax:* 727-376-0781.

TRINITY COLLEGE OF NURSING AND HEALTH SCIENCES
Rock Island, IL

ABOUT THE INSTITUTION Independent, coed. Awards: associate and bachelor's degrees (general education requirements are taken off campus, usually at Black Hawk College, Eastern Iowa Community College District and Western Illinois University). 5 undergraduate majors. Total enrollment: 211. Undergraduates: 211. Freshmen: 3.

GIFT AID (NEED-BASED) ***Scholarships, grants, and awards:*** Federal Pell, FSEOG, state, college/university gift aid from institutional funds.

LOANS ***Programs:*** FFEL (Subsidized and Unsubsidized Stafford, PLUS), Federal Nursing.

WORK-STUDY ***Federal work-study:*** 5 jobs averaging $1500.

APPLYING FOR FINANCIAL AID ***Required financial aid forms:*** FAFSA, institution's own form.

CONTACT Angela Sumpler, Assistant Director of Learner Services, Trinity College of Nursing and Health Sciences, 2122 25th Avenue, Rock Island, IL 61201, 309-779-7733. *Fax:* 309-779-7796. *E-mail:* sumplera@trinityqc.com.

TRINITY INTERNATIONAL UNIVERSITY
Deerfield, IL

Tuition & fees: $20,106 **Average undergraduate aid package: $17,823**

ABOUT THE INSTITUTION Independent religious, coed. Awards: bachelor's, master's, doctoral, and first professional degrees and post-bachelor's certificates. 38 undergraduate majors. Total enrollment: 2,855. Undergraduates: 1,247. Freshmen: 166. Federal methodology is used as a basis for awarding need-based institutional aid.

UNDERGRADUATE EXPENSES for 2006–07 ***Application fee:*** $25. ***Comprehensive fee:*** $26,656 includes full-time tuition ($19,800), mandatory fees ($306), and room and board ($6550). ***College room only:*** $3620. Full-time tuition and fees vary according to location. Room and board charges vary according to board plan and housing facility. ***Part-time tuition:*** $820 per hour. ***Part-time fees:*** $153 per year. Part-time tuition and fees vary according to location. ***Payment plan:*** Installment.

FRESHMAN FINANCIAL AID (Fall 2006, est.) 144 applied for aid; of those 90% were deemed to have need. 100% of freshmen with need received aid; of those 19% had need fully met. ***Average percent of need met:*** 85% (excluding resources awarded to replace EFC). ***Average financial aid package:*** $19,509 (excluding resources awarded to replace EFC). 16% of all full-time freshmen had no need and received non-need-based gift aid.

UNDERGRADUATE FINANCIAL AID (Fall 2006, est.) 796 applied for aid; of those 89% were deemed to have need. 100% of undergraduates with need received aid; of those 19% had need fully met. ***Average percent of need met:*** 78% (excluding resources awarded to replace EFC). ***Average financial aid package:*** $17,823 (excluding resources awarded to replace EFC). 12% of all full-time undergraduates had no need and received non-need-based gift aid.

GIFT AID (NEED-BASED) ***Total amount:*** $4,703,449 (23% federal, 24% state, 51% institutional, 2% external sources). ***Receiving aid:*** Freshmen: 74% (122); All full-time undergraduates: 70% (653). ***Average award:*** Freshmen: $9778; Undergraduates: $9546. ***Scholarships, grants, and awards:*** Federal Pell, FSEOG, state, private, college/university gift aid from institutional funds.

GIFT AID (NON-NEED-BASED) ***Total amount:*** $2,242,020 (100% institutional). ***Receiving aid:*** Freshmen: 77% (126); Undergraduates: 63% (587). ***Average award:*** Freshmen: $5636; Undergraduates: $7082. ***Scholarships, grants, and awards by category:*** *Academic Interests/Achievement:* 255 awards ($992,500 total): general academic interests/achievements. *Creative Arts/Performance:* 90 awards ($696,121 total): music. *Special Characteristics:* 228 awards ($171,500 total): children and siblings of alumni, members of minority groups, religious affiliation. ***Tuition waivers:*** Full or partial for employees or children of employees.

LOANS ***Student loans:*** $4,877,253 (57% need-based, 43% non-need-based). 75% of past graduating class borrowed through all loan programs. *Average indebtedness per student:* $17,794. ***Average need-based loan:*** Freshmen: $1814;

Undergraduates: $2862. ***Parent loans:*** $901,279 (100% need-based). ***Programs:*** Federal Direct (Subsidized and Unsubsidized Stafford, PLUS), Perkins.

WORK-STUDY ***Federal work-study:*** Total amount: $662,856; 350 jobs averaging $1878.

ATHLETIC AWARDS Total amount: $2,516,075 (100% non-need-based).

APPLYING FOR FINANCIAL AID ***Required financial aid form:*** FAFSA. ***Financial aid deadline (priority):*** 4/1. ***Notification date:*** Continuous beginning 2/15. Students must reply within 4 weeks of notification.

CONTACT Dr. Ron Campbell, Director of Financial Aid, Trinity International University, 2065 Half Day Road, Deerfield, IL 60015-1284, 847-317-8060 or toll-free 800-822-3225 (out-of-state). *Fax:* 847-317-7081. *E-mail:* finaid@tiu.edu.

TRINITY LIFE BIBLE COLLEGE

Sacramento, CA

CONTACT Financial Aid Office, Trinity Life Bible College, 5225 Hillsdale Boulevard, Sacramento, CA 95842, 916-348-4689.

TRINITY LUTHERAN COLLEGE

Issaquah, WA

ABOUT THE INSTITUTION Independent Lutheran, coed. Awards: associate and bachelor's degrees and post-bachelor's certificates. 9 undergraduate majors. Total enrollment: 115. Undergraduates: 115.

GIFT AID (NEED-BASED) ***Scholarships, grants, and awards:*** Federal Pell, FSEOG, college/university gift aid from institutional funds.

GIFT AID (NON-NEED-BASED) ***Scholarships, grants, and awards by category:*** *Academic Interests/Achievement:* general academic interests/achievements, religion/biblical studies. *Creative Arts/Performance:* general creative arts/performance, music. *Special Achievements/Activities:* leadership, religious involvement. *Special Characteristics:* children of faculty/staff, international students, religious affiliation.

LOANS ***Programs:*** FFEL (Subsidized and Unsubsidized Stafford, PLUS), college/university.

APPLYING FOR FINANCIAL AID ***Required financial aid forms:*** FAFSA, institution's own form.

CONTACT Ms. Susan Dalgleish, Director of Financial Aid, Trinity Lutheran College, 4221 228th Avenue SE, Issaquah, WA 98029-9299, 425-961-5514 or toll-free 800-843-5659. *Fax:* 425-392-0404. *E-mail:* finaid@tlc.edu.

TRINITY UNIVERSITY

San Antonio, TX

CONTACT Director of Financial Aid, Trinity University, 715 Stadium Drive, San Antonio, TX 78212-7200, 210-999-8315 or toll-free 800-TRINITY. *Fax:* 210-999-8316. *E-mail:* financialaid@trinity.edu.

TRINITY (WASHINGTON) UNIVERSITY

Washington, DC

CONTACT Catherine H. Geier, Director of Student Financial Services, Trinity (Washington) University, 125 Michigan Avenue, NE, Washington, DC 20017-1094, 202-884-9530 or toll-free 800-IWANTTC. *Fax:* 202-884-9524. *E-mail:* financialaid@trinitydc.edu.

TRI-STATE BIBLE COLLEGE

South Point, OH

CONTACT Financial Aid Office, Tri-State Bible College, 506 Margaret Street, PO Box 445, South Point, OH 45680-8402, 740-377-2520.

TRI-STATE UNIVERSITY

Angola, IN

Tuition & fees: $21,210 **Average undergraduate aid package: $15,450**

ABOUT THE INSTITUTION Independent, coed. Awards: associate, bachelor's, and master's degrees. 42 undergraduate majors. Total enrollment: 1,210. Undergraduates: 1,203. Freshmen: 319. Federal methodology is used as a basis for awarding need-based institutional aid.

UNDERGRADUATE EXPENSES for 2006–07 ***Comprehensive fee:*** $27,450 includes full-time tuition ($21,210) and room and board ($6240). ***Part-time tuition:*** $663 per credit hour. ***Payment plan:*** Installment.

FRESHMAN FINANCIAL AID (Fall 2006, est.) 319 applied for aid; of those 67% were deemed to have need. 100% of freshmen with need received aid; of those 98% had need fully met. ***Average percent of need met:*** 87% (excluding resources awarded to replace EFC). ***Average financial aid package:*** $17,990 (excluding resources awarded to replace EFC). 1% of all full-time freshmen had no need and received non-need-based gift aid.

UNDERGRADUATE FINANCIAL AID (Fall 2006, est.) 1,068 applied for aid; of those 71% were deemed to have need. 100% of undergraduates with need received aid; of those 94% had need fully met. ***Average percent of need met:*** 78% (excluding resources awarded to replace EFC). ***Average financial aid package:*** $15,450 (excluding resources awarded to replace EFC). 2% of all full-time undergraduates had no need and received non-need-based gift aid.

GIFT AID (NEED-BASED) ***Total amount:*** $5,097,495 (22% federal, 37% state, 41% institutional). ***Receiving aid:*** Freshmen: 67% (215); All full-time undergraduates: 42% (453). ***Average award:*** Freshmen: $4807; Undergraduates: $4395. ***Scholarships, grants, and awards:*** Federal Pell, FSEOG, state, private, college/university gift aid from institutional funds.

GIFT AID (NON-NEED-BASED) ***Total amount:*** $7,112,517 (96% institutional, 4% external sources). ***Receiving aid:*** Freshmen: 67% (215); Undergraduates: 70% (756). ***Average award:*** Freshmen: $1833; Undergraduates: $2882. ***Scholarships, grants, and awards by category:*** *Academic Interests/Achievement:* general academic interests/achievements. *Special Characteristics:* children and siblings of alumni, children of faculty/staff, members of minority groups. ***Tuition waivers:*** Full or partial for employees or children of employees.

LOANS ***Student loans:*** $3,692,442 (69% need-based, 31% non-need-based). 76% of past graduating class borrowed through all loan programs. *Average indebtedness per student:* $15,780. ***Average need-based loan:*** Freshmen: $2613; Undergraduates: $3616. ***Parent loans:*** $1,131,381 (100% non-need-based). ***Programs:*** FFEL (Subsidized and Unsubsidized Stafford, PLUS), alternative loans.

WORK-STUDY ***Federal work-study:*** Total amount: $1,128,660; 629 jobs averaging $1794.

APPLYING FOR FINANCIAL AID ***Required financial aid form:*** FAFSA. ***Financial aid deadline (priority):*** 3/10. ***Notification date:*** Continuous beginning 2/20. Students must reply by 5/1 or within 2 weeks of notification.

CONTACT Kim Bennett, Director of Financial Aid, Tri-State University, 1 University Avenue, Angola, IN 46703-1764, 260-665-4175 or toll-free 800-347-4TSU. *Fax:* 260-665-4511. *E-mail:* admit@tristate.edu.

TROY UNIVERSITY

Troy, AL

Tuition & fees (AL res): $4104 **Average undergraduate aid package: $3766**

ABOUT THE INSTITUTION State-supported, coed. Awards: associate, bachelor's, and master's degrees and post-master's certificates. 50 undergraduate majors. Total enrollment: 27,938. Undergraduates: 20,069. Freshmen: 2,636. Federal methodology is used as a basis for awarding need-based institutional aid.

UNDERGRADUATE EXPENSES for 2006–07 ***Application fee:*** $30. ***Tuition, state resident:*** full-time $4004; part-time $170 per credit hour. ***Tuition, nonresident:*** full-time $8008; part-time $340 per credit hour. ***Required fees:*** full-time $100; $50 per term part-time. ***College room and board:*** $5491; ***Room only:*** $2863. Room and board charges vary according to board plan and housing facility. ***Payment plan:*** Installment.

FRESHMAN FINANCIAL AID (Fall 2005) 972 applied for aid; of those 100% were deemed to have need. 100% of freshmen with need received aid. ***Average financial aid package:*** $3002 (excluding resources awarded to replace EFC). 28% of all full-time freshmen had no need and received non-need-based gift aid.

UNDERGRADUATE FINANCIAL AID (Fall 2005) 9,139 applied for aid; of those 100% were deemed to have need. 100% of undergraduates with need received aid. ***Average financial aid package:*** $3766 (excluding resources awarded to replace EFC). 15% of all full-time undergraduates had no need and received non-need-based gift aid.

GIFT AID (NEED-BASED) ***Total amount:*** $24,365,877 (100% federal). ***Receiving aid:*** Freshmen: 37% (618); All full-time undergraduates: 31% (6,040). ***Average award:*** Freshmen: $3299; Undergraduates: $3260. ***Scholarships, grants, and awards:*** Federal Pell, FSEOG, state, private, college/university gift aid from institutional funds.

GIFT AID (NON-NEED-BASED) ***Total amount:*** $20,347,248 (33% institutional, 67% external sources). ***Receiving aid:*** Freshmen: 22% (362); Undergraduates: 8% (1,634). ***Average award:*** Freshmen: $2504; Undergraduates: $2280. ***Scholarships, grants, and awards by category:*** *Academic Interests/Achievement:* general academic interests/achievements. *Creative Arts/Performance:* music, theater/drama. *Special Achievements/Activities:* leadership. *Special Characteristics:* general special characteristics. ***Tuition waivers:*** Full or partial for employees or children of employees. ***ROTC:*** Army, Air Force.

LOANS ***Student loans:*** $157,977,364 (100% need-based). 78% of past graduating class borrowed through all loan programs. ***Average need-based loan:*** Freshmen: $2906; Undergraduates: $4007. ***Parent loans:*** $4,381,641 (100% need-based). ***Programs:*** FFEL (Subsidized and Unsubsidized Stafford, PLUS), Perkins.

WORK-STUDY ***Federal work-study:*** Total amount: $1,063,440; 550 jobs averaging $2000.

ATHLETIC AWARDS Total amount: $2,919,825 (100% non-need-based).

APPLYING FOR FINANCIAL AID ***Required financial aid forms:*** FAFSA, institution's own form. ***Financial aid deadline (priority):*** 3/1. ***Notification date:*** Continuous beginning 6/1. Students must reply within 2 weeks of notification.

CONTACT Ms. Carol Supri, Director of Financial Aid, Troy University, 131 Adams Administration Bldg., Troy, AL 36082, 334-670-3186 or toll-free 800-551-9716. *Fax:* 334-670-3702. *E-mail:* csupri@troy.edu.

TRUMAN STATE UNIVERSITY

Kirksville, MO

ABOUT THE INSTITUTION State-supported, coed. Awards: bachelor's and master's degrees. 56 undergraduate majors. Total enrollment: 5,762. Undergraduates: 5,524. Freshmen: 1,367.

GIFT AID (NEED-BASED) ***Scholarships, grants, and awards:*** Federal Pell, FSEOG, state, private, college/university gift aid from institutional funds.

GIFT AID (NON-NEED-BASED) ***Scholarships, grants, and awards by category:*** *Academic Interests/Achievement:* biological sciences, business, communication, education, English, foreign languages, general academic interests/achievements, mathematics, military science, physical sciences, premedicine, social sciences. *Creative Arts/Performance:* art/fine arts, debating, music, theater/drama. *Special Achievements/Activities:* leadership. *Special Characteristics:* children and siblings of alumni, children of faculty/staff, ethnic background, international students.

LOANS ***Programs:*** FFEL (Subsidized and Unsubsidized Stafford, PLUS), Perkins, Federal Nursing, state, college/university.

WORK-STUDY ***Federal work-study:*** Total amount: $414,424; 346 jobs averaging $886. ***State or other work-study/employment:*** Total amount: $1,614,051 (100% non-need-based). 1,733 part-time jobs averaging $904.

APPLYING FOR FINANCIAL AID ***Required financial aid forms:*** FAFSA, institution's own form.

CONTACT Ms. Melinda Wood, Director of Financial Aid, Truman State University, 103 McClain Hall, Kirksville, MO 63501-4221, 660-785-4130 or toll-free 800-892-7792 (in-state). *Fax:* 660-785-7389. *E-mail:* mwood@truman.edu.

TUFTS UNIVERSITY

Medford, MA

Tuition & fees: $34,730 **Average undergraduate aid package: $27,064**

ABOUT THE INSTITUTION Independent, coed. Awards: bachelor's, master's, doctoral, and first professional degrees and post-master's certificates. 64 undergraduate majors. Total enrollment: 9,638. Undergraduates: 4,995. Freshmen: 1,281. Both federal and institutional methodology are used as a basis for awarding need-based institutional aid.

UNDERGRADUATE EXPENSES for 2006–07 ***Application fee:*** $70. ***Comprehensive fee:*** $44,500 includes full-time tuition ($33,906), mandatory fees ($824), and room and board ($9770). ***College room only:*** $5020. Room and board charges vary according to board plan. ***Payment plans:*** Tuition prepayment, installment.

FRESHMAN FINANCIAL AID (Fall 2006, est.) 675 applied for aid; of those 72% were deemed to have need. 100% of freshmen with need received aid; of those 100% had need fully met. ***Average percent of need met:*** 100% (excluding resources awarded to replace EFC). ***Average financial aid package:*** $26,302 (excluding resources awarded to replace EFC). 2% of all full-time freshmen had no need and received non-need-based gift aid.

UNDERGRADUATE FINANCIAL AID (Fall 2006, est.) 2,235 applied for aid; of those 84% were deemed to have need. 100% of undergraduates with need received aid; of those 100% had need fully met. ***Average percent of need met:*** 100% (excluding resources awarded to replace EFC). ***Average financial aid package:*** $27,064 (excluding resources awarded to replace EFC). 2% of all full-time undergraduates had no need and received non-need-based gift aid.

GIFT AID (NEED-BASED) ***Total amount:*** $42,334,080 (6% federal, 2% state, 88% institutional, 4% external sources). ***Receiving aid:*** Freshmen: 34% (442); All full-time undergraduates: 35% (1,730). ***Average award:*** Freshmen: $23,907; Undergraduates: $23,680. ***Scholarships, grants, and awards:*** Federal Pell, FSEOG, state, private, college/university gift aid from institutional funds.

GIFT AID (NON-NEED-BASED) ***Total amount:*** $912,163 (13% federal, 3% state, 6% institutional, 78% external sources). ***Receiving aid:*** Freshmen: 2% (31); Undergraduates: 2% (95). ***Average award:*** Freshmen: $500; Undergraduates: $500. ***Scholarships, grants, and awards by category:*** *Academic Interests/Achievement:* 159 awards ($177,750 total): general academic interests/achievements. *Special Characteristics:* children of faculty/staff. ***Tuition waivers:*** Full or partial for employees or children of employees. ***ROTC:*** Army cooperative, Naval cooperative, Air Force cooperative.

LOANS ***Student loans:*** $8,555,810 (90% need-based, 10% non-need-based). 36% of past graduating class borrowed through all loan programs. *Average indebtedness per student:* $14,200. ***Average need-based loan:*** Freshmen: $2512; Undergraduates: $3756. ***Parent loans:*** $12,840,915 (100% non-need-based). ***Programs:*** FFEL (Subsidized and Unsubsidized Stafford, PLUS), Perkins, state, college/university.

WORK-STUDY ***Federal work-study:*** Total amount: $2,767,199; 1,777 jobs averaging $1555. ***State or other work-study/employment:*** Total amount: $140,550 (100% need-based). 75 part-time jobs averaging $1884.

APPLYING FOR FINANCIAL AID ***Required financial aid forms:*** FAFSA, CSS Financial Aid PROFILE, noncustodial (divorced/separated) parent's statement, business/farm supplement, federal income tax form(s). ***Financial aid deadline:*** 2/15. ***Notification date:*** 4/5. Students must reply by 5/1.

CONTACT Patricia C. Reilly, Director of Financial Aid, Tufts University, Dowling Hall, Medford, MA 02155, 617-627-2000. *Fax:* 617-627-3987. *E-mail:* patricia.reilly@tufts.edu.

TULANE UNIVERSITY

New Orleans, LA

Tuition & fees: $34,896 **Average undergraduate aid package: $25,945**

ABOUT THE INSTITUTION Independent, coed. Awards: associate, bachelor's, master's, doctoral, and first professional degrees and post-bachelor's certificates. 85 undergraduate majors. Total enrollment: 10,606. Undergraduates: 6,533. Freshmen: 1,115. Both federal and institutional methodology are used as a basis for awarding need-based institutional aid.

UNDERGRADUATE EXPENSES for 2006–07 ***Application fee:*** $55. ***Comprehensive fee:*** $43,293 includes full-time tuition ($34,896) and room and board ($8397). ***College room only:*** $4987. Room and board charges vary according to board plan and housing facility. ***Part-time tuition:*** $1421 per credit hour. ***Part-time fees:*** $40 per term. ***Payment plan:*** Installment.

FRESHMAN FINANCIAL AID (Fall 2005) 898 applied for aid; of those 69% were deemed to have need. 100% of freshmen with need received aid; of those 52% had need fully met. ***Average percent of need met:*** 89% (excluding resources awarded to replace EFC). ***Average financial aid package:*** $25,580 (excluding resources awarded to replace EFC).

UNDERGRADUATE FINANCIAL AID (Fall 2005) 2,988 applied for aid; of those 77% were deemed to have need. 99% of undergraduates with need received aid; of those 49% had need fully met. ***Average percent of need met:*** 88% (excluding resources awarded to replace EFC). ***Average financial aid package:*** $25,945 (excluding resources awarded to replace EFC). 36% of all full-time undergraduates had no need and received non-need-based gift aid.

GIFT AID (NEED-BASED) ***Total amount:*** $38,768,069 (7% federal, 1% state, 88% institutional, 4% external sources). ***Receiving aid:*** Freshmen: 600; All full-time undergraduates: 42% (2,195). ***Average award:*** Freshmen: $18,805;

Undergraduates: $19,182. ***Scholarships, grants, and awards:*** Federal Pell, FSEOG, state, private, college/university gift aid from institutional funds, Academic Competitiveness Grant (ACG), Science and Mathematics Access to Retain Talent (SMART) Grant.

GIFT AID (NON-NEED-BASED) ***Total amount:*** $35,588,483 (2% state, 84% institutional, 14% external sources). ***Receiving aid:*** Freshmen: 239; Undergraduates: 12% (607). ***Average award:*** Freshmen: $19,733; Undergraduates: $17,308. ***Scholarships, grants, and awards by category:*** *Academic Interests/Achievement:* 2,494 awards ($46,600,717 total): general academic interests/achievements. *Special Achievements/Activities:* 7 awards ($147,900 total): community service. *Special Characteristics:* 1,213 awards ($6,935,807 total): children of faculty/staff, local/state students. ***Tuition waivers:*** Full or partial for employees or children of employees. ***ROTC:*** Army, Naval, Air Force.

LOANS ***Student loans:*** $17,796,215 (61% need-based, 39% non-need-based). 43% of past graduating class borrowed through all loan programs. *Average indebtedness per student:* $21,202. ***Average need-based loan:*** Freshmen: $4321; Undergraduates: $5765. ***Parent loans:*** $9,291,351 (12% need-based, 88% non-need-based). ***Programs:*** FFEL (Subsidized and Unsubsidized Stafford, PLUS), Perkins.

WORK-STUDY ***Federal work-study:*** Total amount: $938,262; 956 jobs averaging $2065. ***State or other work-study/employment:*** Total amount: $444,513 (31% need-based, 69% non-need-based). 99 part-time jobs averaging $6764.

ATHLETIC AWARDS Total amount: $4,740,213 (100% non-need-based).

APPLYING FOR FINANCIAL AID ***Required financial aid forms:*** FAFSA, CSS Financial Aid PROFILE, noncustodial (divorced/separated) parent's statement, business/farm supplement. ***Financial aid deadline:*** 2/1 (priority: 1/15). ***Notification date:*** Continuous beginning 3/1. Students must reply by 5/1 or within 2 weeks of notification.

CONTACT Mr. Michael T. Goodman, Director of Financial Aid, Tulane University, 6823 St. Charles Avenue, New Orleans, LA 70118-5669, 504-865-5723 or toll-free 800-873-9283. *E-mail:* finaid@tulane.edu.

TUSCULUM COLLEGE

Greeneville, TN

ABOUT THE INSTITUTION Independent Presbyterian, coed. Awards: bachelor's and master's degrees. 27 undergraduate majors. Total enrollment: 2,923. Undergraduates: 2,600. Freshmen: 333.

GIFT AID (NEED-BASED) ***Scholarships, grants, and awards:*** Federal Pell, FSEOG, state, private, college/university gift aid from institutional funds.

GIFT AID (NON-NEED-BASED) ***Scholarships, grants, and awards by category:*** *Academic Interests/Achievement:* general academic interests/achievements. *Creative Arts/Performance:* music. *Special Achievements/Activities:* cheerleading/drum major, community service, leadership. *Special Characteristics:* adult students, children of faculty/staff, local/state students.

LOANS ***Programs:*** FFEL (Subsidized and Unsubsidized Stafford, PLUS), Perkins.

WORK-STUDY ***Federal work-study:*** Total amount: $270,136; 259 jobs averaging $1040. ***State or other work-study/employment:*** Total amount: $291,788 (100% non-need-based). 220 part-time jobs averaging $1332.

APPLYING FOR FINANCIAL AID ***Required financial aid form:*** FAFSA.

CONTACT Mr. J. Pat Shannon, Director of Financial Aid, Tusculum College, 5049 Tusculum Station, Greeneville, TN 37743-9997, 423-636-7377 or toll-free 800-729-0256. *Fax:* 615-250-4968. *E-mail:* pshannon@tusculum.edu.

TUSKEGEE UNIVERSITY

Tuskegee, AL

Tuition & fees: $14,615 **Average undergraduate aid package: $13,824**

ABOUT THE INSTITUTION Independent, coed. Awards: bachelor's, master's, doctoral, and first professional degrees. 43 undergraduate majors. Total enrollment: 2,842. Undergraduates: 2,420. Freshmen: 697. Federal methodology is used as a basis for awarding need-based institutional aid.

UNDERGRADUATE EXPENSES for 2007–08 ***Application fee:*** $25. ***Comprehensive fee:*** $21,398 includes full-time tuition ($14,150), mandatory fees ($465), and room and board ($6783). ***Part-time tuition:*** $510 per credit hour.

FRESHMAN FINANCIAL AID (Fall 2005) 635 applied for aid; of those 85% were deemed to have need. 92% of freshmen with need received aid; of those 70% had need fully met. ***Average percent of need met:*** 85% (excluding resources awarded to replace EFC). ***Average financial aid package:*** $13,824 (excluding resources awarded to replace EFC). 36% of all full-time freshmen had no need and received non-need-based gift aid.

UNDERGRADUATE FINANCIAL AID (Fall 2005) 2,519 applied for aid; of those 85% were deemed to have need. 92% of undergraduates with need received aid; of those 70% had need fully met. ***Average percent of need met:*** 85% (excluding resources awarded to replace EFC). ***Average financial aid package:*** $13,824 (excluding resources awarded to replace EFC). 32% of all full-time undergraduates had no need and received non-need-based gift aid.

GIFT AID (NEED-BASED) ***Total amount:*** $5,459,147 (98% federal, 2% institutional). ***Receiving aid:*** Freshmen: 56% (422); All full-time undergraduates: 61% (1,675). ***Average award:*** Freshmen: $8000; Undergraduates: $8000. ***Scholarships, grants, and awards:*** Federal Pell, FSEOG, state, private, college/university gift aid from institutional funds, United Negro College Fund, Federal Nursing.

GIFT AID (NON-NEED-BASED) ***Total amount:*** $3,408,097 (45% institutional, 55% external sources). ***Receiving aid:*** Freshmen: 36% (273); Undergraduates: 35% (951). ***Average award:*** Freshmen: $6000; Undergraduates: $6000. ***Scholarships, grants, and awards by category:*** *Academic Interests/Achievement:* 1,714 awards ($9,086,319 total): general academic interests/achievements. *Creative Arts/Performance:* 108 awards ($68,400 total): music. *Special Characteristics:* 36 awards ($157,002 total): children of faculty/staff, local/state students. ***ROTC:*** Army, Air Force.

LOANS ***Student loans:*** $16,456,358 (53% need-based, 47% non-need-based). 91% of past graduating class borrowed through all loan programs. *Average indebtedness per student:* $30,000. ***Average need-based loan:*** Freshmen: $5625; Undergraduates: $6006. ***Parent loans:*** $3,098,631 (100% non-need-based). ***Programs:*** FFEL (Subsidized and Unsubsidized Stafford, PLUS), Perkins.

WORK-STUDY ***Federal work-study:*** Total amount: $830,097; 525 jobs averaging $1879. ***State or other work-study/employment:*** Total amount: $1,318,823 (100% non-need-based). 425 part-time jobs averaging $4739.

ATHLETIC AWARDS Total amount: $1,145,218 (100% non-need-based).

APPLYING FOR FINANCIAL AID ***Required financial aid forms:*** FAFSA, institution's own form. ***Financial aid deadline (priority):*** 3/31. ***Notification date:*** Continuous beginning 4/15. Students must reply within 2 weeks of notification.

CONTACT Mr. A. D. James Jr., Director of Student Financial Services, Tuskegee University, Office of Student Financial Services, Tuskegee, AL 36088, 334-727-8201 or toll-free 800-622-6531. *Fax:* 334-724-4227. *E-mail:* jamesad@tuskegee.edu.

UNION COLLEGE

Barbourville, KY

Tuition & fees: $15,650 **Average undergraduate aid package: $14,262**

ABOUT THE INSTITUTION Independent United Methodist, coed. Awards: bachelor's and master's degrees. 21 undergraduate majors. Total enrollment: 1,389. Undergraduates: 653. Freshmen: 207. Federal methodology is used as a basis for awarding need-based institutional aid.

UNDERGRADUATE EXPENSES for 2006–07 ***Application fee:*** $20. ***Comprehensive fee:*** $20,650 includes full-time tuition ($15,290), mandatory fees ($360), and room and board ($5000). ***College room only:*** $2000. Room and board charges vary according to board plan and student level. ***Part-time tuition:*** $270 per hour. ***Part-time fees:*** $15 per semester hour. ***Payment plan:*** Installment.

FRESHMAN FINANCIAL AID (Fall 2006, est.) 197 applied for aid; of those 94% were deemed to have need. 99% of freshmen with need received aid; of those 26% had need fully met. ***Average percent of need met:*** 77% (excluding resources awarded to replace EFC). ***Average financial aid package:*** $13,326 (excluding resources awarded to replace EFC). 5% of all full-time freshmen had no need and received non-need-based gift aid.

UNDERGRADUATE FINANCIAL AID (Fall 2006, est.) 597 applied for aid; of those 95% were deemed to have need. 100% of undergraduates with need received aid; of those 26% had need fully met. ***Average percent of need met:*** 79% (excluding resources awarded to replace EFC). ***Average financial aid package:*** $14,262 (excluding resources awarded to replace EFC). 4% of all full-time undergraduates had no need and received non-need-based gift aid.

GIFT AID (NEED-BASED) ***Total amount:*** $3,915,791 (33% federal, 41% state, 22% institutional, 4% external sources). ***Receiving aid:*** Freshmen: 90% (185); All full-time undergraduates: 91% (565). ***Average award:*** Freshmen: $9839; Undergraduates: $9476. ***Scholarships, grants, and awards:*** Federal Pell, FSEOG, state, college/university gift aid from institutional funds.

GIFT AID (NON-NEED-BASED) ***Total amount:*** $314,036 (100% state). ***Receiving aid:*** Freshmen: 17% (35); Undergraduates: 12% (75). ***Average award:*** Freshmen: $14,058; Undergraduates: $12,998. ***Scholarships, grants, and awards by category:*** *Academic Interests/Achievement:* 294 awards ($606,248 total): general academic interests/achievements. *Creative Arts/Performance:* 16 awards ($31,750 total): music. *Special Achievements/Activities:* 17 awards ($68,783 total): cheerleading/drum major. *Special Characteristics:* 30 awards ($64,065 total): children and siblings of alumni, religious affiliation. ***Tuition waivers:*** Full or partial for employees or children of employees, senior citizens. ***ROTC:*** Army cooperative.

LOANS ***Student loans:*** $3,245,090 (62% need-based, 38% non-need-based). 100% of past graduating class borrowed through all loan programs. *Average indebtedness per student:* $22,434. ***Average need-based loan:*** Freshmen: $3577; Undergraduates: $4884. ***Parent loans:*** $325,261 (100% need-based). ***Programs:*** FFEL (Subsidized and Unsubsidized Stafford, PLUS), Perkins, college/university.

WORK-STUDY ***Federal work-study:*** Total amount: $169,237; 158 jobs averaging $1124. ***State or other work-study/employment:*** Part-time jobs available.

ATHLETIC AWARDS Total amount: $2,395,366 (100% need-based).

APPLYING FOR FINANCIAL AID ***Required financial aid form:*** FAFSA. ***Financial aid deadline (priority):*** 3/15. ***Notification date:*** Continuous beginning 4/1. Students must reply within 2 weeks of notification.

CONTACT Mrs. Sue Buttery, Associate Dean of Financial Aid and Admission, Union College, 310 College Street, Barbourville, KY 40906-1499, 606-546-1224 or toll-free 800-489-8646. *Fax:* 606-546-1556. *E-mail:* sbuttery@unionky.edu.

UNION COLLEGE

Lincoln, NE

Tuition & fees: $15,230 **Average undergraduate aid package: $12,234**

ABOUT THE INSTITUTION Independent Seventh-day Adventist, coed. Awards: associate, bachelor's, and master's degrees. 54 undergraduate majors. Total enrollment: 982. Undergraduates: 912. Freshmen: 192. Federal methodology is used as a basis for awarding need-based institutional aid.

UNDERGRADUATE EXPENSES for 2006–07 ***Comprehensive fee:*** $19,448 includes full-time tuition ($14,790), mandatory fees ($440), and room and board ($4218). ***College room only:*** $2898. ***Part-time tuition:*** $625 per semester hour. ***Payment plan:*** Installment.

FRESHMAN FINANCIAL AID (Fall 2005) ***Average percent of need met:*** 74% (excluding resources awarded to replace EFC). ***Average financial aid package:*** $11,989 (excluding resources awarded to replace EFC).

UNDERGRADUATE FINANCIAL AID (Fall 2005) ***Average percent of need met:*** 71% (excluding resources awarded to replace EFC). ***Average financial aid package:*** $12,234 (excluding resources awarded to replace EFC).

GIFT AID (NON-NEED-BASED) ***Total amount:*** $2,542,544 (2% state, 54% institutional, 44% external sources). ***Average award:*** Freshmen: $3714; Undergraduates: $3699. ***Scholarships, grants, and awards by category:*** *Academic Interests/Achievement:* general academic interests/achievements. *Creative Arts/Performance:* music. *Special Achievements/Activities:* community service, leadership, religious involvement. ***Tuition waivers:*** Full or partial for employees or children of employees.

LOANS ***Student loans:*** $4,468,348 (83% need-based, 17% non-need-based). 64% of past graduating class borrowed through all loan programs. *Average indebtedness per student:* $23,379. ***Average need-based loan:*** Freshmen: $3472; Undergraduates: $4442. ***Parent loans:*** $845,235 (27% need-based, 73% non-need-based).

WORK-STUDY ***Federal work-study:*** Total amount: $278,409; 172 jobs averaging $1663. ***State or other work-study/employment:*** Total amount: $993,084 (100% need-based).

APPLYING FOR FINANCIAL AID ***Notification date:*** Continuous. Students must reply within 3 weeks of notification.

CONTACT Mr. John C. Burdick, IV, Director of Financial Aid, Union College, 3800 South 48th Street, Lincoln, NE 68506-4300, 800-228-4600. *Fax:* 402-486-2895. *E-mail:* financialaid@ucollege.edu.

UNION COLLEGE

Schenectady, NY

Comprehensive fee: $44,043 **Average undergraduate aid package: $26,330**

ABOUT THE INSTITUTION Independent, coed. Awards: bachelor's degrees. 28 undergraduate majors. Total enrollment: 2,212. Undergraduates: 2,212. Freshmen: 560. Both federal and institutional methodology are used as a basis for awarding need-based institutional aid.

UNDERGRADUATE EXPENSES for 2006–07 ***Application fee:*** $50. ***Comprehensive fee:*** $44,043. ***Payment plan:*** Installment.

GIFT AID (NEED-BASED) ***Total amount:*** $21,758,642 (6% federal, 5% state, 87% institutional, 2% external sources). ***Receiving aid:*** Freshmen: 46% (254); All full-time undergraduates: 48% (1,017). ***Average award:*** Freshmen: $23,287; Undergraduates: $21,368. ***Scholarships, grants, and awards:*** Federal Pell, FSEOG, state, private, college/university gift aid from institutional funds.

GIFT AID (NON-NEED-BASED) ***Total amount:*** $2,932,518 (4% federal, 4% state, 92% institutional). ***Receiving aid:*** Freshmen: 3% (19); Undergraduates: 1% (28). ***Average award:*** Freshmen: $10,850; Undergraduates: $12,200. ***Scholarships, grants, and awards by category:*** *Academic Interests/Achievement:* 64 awards ($785,000 total): general academic interests/achievements. ***Tuition waivers:*** Full or partial for employees or children of employees, senior citizens. ***ROTC:*** Army cooperative, Naval cooperative, Air Force cooperative.

LOANS ***Student loans:*** $4,713,539 (86% need-based, 14% non-need-based). 53% of past graduating class borrowed through all loan programs. *Average indebtedness per student:* $22,602. ***Average need-based loan:*** Freshmen: $2967; Undergraduates: $4596. ***Parent loans:*** $3,351,399 (100% non-need-based). ***Programs:*** FFEL (Subsidized and Unsubsidized Stafford, PLUS), Perkins, college/university.

APPLYING FOR FINANCIAL AID ***Required financial aid forms:*** FAFSA, CSS Financial Aid PROFILE, state aid form, business/farm supplement, non custodial (divorced/separated) parent's statement. ***Financial aid deadline:*** 2/1. ***Notification date:*** 4/1. Students must reply by 5/1.

CONTACT Ms. Beth Post, Director of Financial Aid and Family Financing, Union College, Grant Hall, Schenectady, NY 12308-2311, 518-388-6123 or toll-free 888-843-6688 (in-state). *Fax:* 518-388-8052. *E-mail:* financialaid@union.edu.

UNION INSTITUTE & UNIVERSITY

Cincinnati, OH

CONTACT Ms. Rebecca Zackerman, Director of Financial Aid, Union Institute & University, 440 East McMillan Street, Cincinnati, OH 45206-1925, 513-861-6400 or toll-free 800-486-3116. *Fax:* 513-861-0779. *E-mail:* bzackerman@tui.edu.

UNION UNIVERSITY

Jackson, TN

Tuition & fees: $17,900 **Average undergraduate aid package: $14,089**

ABOUT THE INSTITUTION Independent Southern Baptist, coed. Awards: associate, bachelor's, master's, and doctoral degrees and post-master's certificates. 66 undergraduate majors. Total enrollment: 2,934. Undergraduates: 2,096. Freshmen: 424. Federal methodology is used as a basis for awarding need-based institutional aid.

UNDERGRADUATE EXPENSES for 2007–08 ***Application fee:*** $25. ***Tuition:*** full-time $17,900; part-time $630 per credit hour.

FRESHMAN FINANCIAL AID (Fall 2005) 368 applied for aid; of those 79% were deemed to have need. 100% of freshmen with need received aid. ***Average financial aid package:*** $16,748 (excluding resources awarded to replace EFC). 28% of all full-time freshmen had no need and received non-need-based gift aid.

UNDERGRADUATE FINANCIAL AID (Fall 2005) 1,400 applied for aid; of those 83% were deemed to have need. 100% of undergraduates with need received aid. ***Average financial aid package:*** $14,089 (excluding resources awarded to replace EFC). 27% of all full-time undergraduates had no need and received non-need-based gift aid.

GIFT AID (NEED-BASED) ***Total amount:*** $3,649,924 (38% federal, 19% state, 40% institutional, 3% external sources). ***Receiving aid:*** Freshmen: 52% (209); All full-time undergraduates: 51% (757). ***Average award:*** Freshmen: $4857; Undergraduates: $4385. ***Scholarships, grants, and awards:*** Federal Pell, FSEOG, state, private, college/university gift aid from institutional funds.

GIFT AID (NON-NEED-BASED) ***Total amount:*** $10,140,704 (22% state, 71% institutional, 7% external sources). ***Receiving aid:*** Freshmen: 72% (287); Undergraduates: 63% (936). ***Average award:*** Freshmen: $7807; Undergraduates: $7659. ***Scholarships, grants, and awards by category:*** *Academic Interests/Achievement:* 739 awards ($3,874,198 total): business, communication, education, engineering/technologies, general academic interests/achievements, mathematics, premedicine, religion/biblical studies. *Creative Arts/Performance:* 91 awards ($308,897 total): art/fine arts, cinema/film/broadcasting, journalism/publications, music, theater/drama. *Special Achievements/Activities:* 664 awards ($785,904 total): cheerleading/drum major, leadership. *Special Characteristics:* 472 awards ($1,405,010 total): children and siblings of alumni, children of faculty/staff, ethnic background, relatives of clergy, religious affiliation, siblings of current students.

LOANS ***Student loans:*** $7,382,135 (50% need-based, 50% non-need-based). 56% of past graduating class borrowed through all loan programs. *Average indebtedness per student:* $21,088. ***Average need-based loan:*** Freshmen: $2737; Undergraduates: $4434. ***Parent loans:*** $1,788,169 (100% non-need-based). ***Programs:*** FFEL (Subsidized and Unsubsidized Stafford, PLUS), Perkins, college/university, alternative loans.

WORK-STUDY ***Federal work-study:*** Total amount: $140,000; 128 jobs averaging $1100. ***State or other work-study/employment:*** Total amount: $350,000 (100% non-need-based). 339 part-time jobs averaging $1220.

ATHLETIC AWARDS Total amount: $1,673,009 (100% non-need-based).

APPLYING FOR FINANCIAL AID ***Required financial aid forms:*** FAFSA, institution's own form. ***Financial aid deadline:*** Continuous. ***Notification date:*** Continuous beginning 12/1. Students must reply by 5/1 or within 2 weeks of notification.

CONTACT John Thomas Brandt, Director of Financial Aid, Union University, 1050 Union University Drive, Jackson, TN 38305-3697, 731-661-5015 or toll-free 800-33-UNION. *Fax:* 731-661-5570. *E-mail:* jbrandt@uu.edu.

UNITED STATES SPORTS ACADEMY

Daphne, AL

CONTACT Financial Aid Office, United States Sports Academy, One Academy Drive, Daphne, AL 36526-7055, 251-626-3303.

UNITED TALMUDICAL SEMINARY

Brooklyn, NY

CONTACT Financial Aid Office, United Talmudical Seminary, 82 Lee Avenue, Brooklyn, NY 11211-7900, 718-963-9770 Ext. 309.

UNITY COLLEGE

Unity, ME

Tuition & fees: $19,630 **Average undergraduate aid package: $14,593**

ABOUT THE INSTITUTION Independent, coed. Awards: associate and bachelor's degrees. 14 undergraduate majors. Total enrollment: 562. Undergraduates: 562. Freshmen: 160. Federal methodology is used as a basis for awarding need-based institutional aid.

UNDERGRADUATE EXPENSES for 2007–08 ***Application fee:*** $25. ***Tuition:*** full-time $18,630.

FRESHMAN FINANCIAL AID (Fall 2006, est.) 144 applied for aid; of those 91% were deemed to have need. 100% of freshmen with need received aid; of those 35% had need fully met. ***Average percent of need met:*** 77% (excluding resources awarded to replace EFC). ***Average financial aid package:*** $14,904 (excluding resources awarded to replace EFC). 13% of all full-time freshmen had no need and received non-need-based gift aid.

UNDERGRADUATE FINANCIAL AID (Fall 2006, est.) 477 applied for aid; of those 91% were deemed to have need. 100% of undergraduates with need received aid; of those 36% had need fully met. ***Average percent of need met:*** 78% (excluding resources awarded to replace EFC). ***Average financial aid package:*** $14,593 (excluding resources awarded to replace EFC). 15% of all full-time undergraduates had no need and received non-need-based gift aid.

GIFT AID (NEED-BASED) ***Total amount:*** $3,603,214 (21% federal, 7% state, 66% institutional, 6% external sources). ***Receiving aid:*** Freshmen: 86% (131); All full-time undergraduates: 81% (435). ***Average award:*** Freshmen: $9558; Undergraduates: $8211. ***Scholarships, grants, and awards:*** Federal Pell, FSEOG, state, private, college/university gift aid from institutional funds.

GIFT AID (NON-NEED-BASED) ***Total amount:*** $345,484 (1% federal, 6% state, 80% institutional, 13% external sources). ***Receiving aid:*** Freshmen: 2% (3); Undergraduates: 4% (21). ***Average award:*** Freshmen: $9363; Undergraduates: $8706. ***Scholarships, grants, and awards by category:*** *Academic Interests/Achievement:* 258 awards ($934,300 total): general academic interests/achievements. *Special Achievements/Activities:* 115 awards ($113,125 total): community service, leadership. *Special Characteristics:* 55 awards ($117,895 total): children of educators, general special characteristics, local/state students, members of minority groups. ***ROTC:*** Army cooperative.

LOANS ***Student loans:*** $4,495,897 (67% need-based, 33% non-need-based). ***Average need-based loan:*** Freshmen: $5033; Undergraduates: $6149. ***Parent loans:*** $851,943 (43% need-based, 57% non-need-based). ***Programs:*** FFEL (Subsidized and Unsubsidized Stafford, PLUS), Perkins.

WORK-STUDY ***Federal work-study:*** Total amount: $473,016; 326 jobs averaging $1451. ***State or other work-study/employment:*** Total amount: $9500 (100% non-need-based). 8 part-time jobs averaging $1188.

APPLYING FOR FINANCIAL AID ***Required financial aid form:*** FAFSA. ***Financial aid deadline:*** Continuous. ***Notification date:*** Continuous beginning 3/10. Students must reply within 2 weeks of notification.

CONTACT Mr. Rand E. Newell, Director of Financial Aid, Unity College, 90 Quaker Hill Road, Unity, ME 04988, 207-948-3131 Ext. 201. *Fax:* 207-948-6277. *E-mail:* rnewell@unity.edu.

UNIVERSIDAD ADVENTISTA DE LAS ANTILLAS

Mayagüez, PR

CONTACT Mr. Heriberto Juarbe, Director of Financial Aid, Universidad Adventista de las Antillas, Box 118, Mayagüez, PR 00681-0118, 787-834-9595 Ext. 2200. *Fax:* 787-834-9597.

UNIVERSIDAD DEL ESTE

Carolina, PR

CONTACT Mr. Clotilde Santiago, Director of Financial Aid, Universidad del Este, Apartado 2010, Carolina, PR 00928, 787-257-7373 Ext. 3300.

UNIVERSIDAD DEL TURABO

Gurabo, PR

CONTACT Ms. Ivette Vázquez Ríos, Directora Oficina de Asistencia Económica, Universidad del Turabo, Apartado 3030, Gurabo, PR 00778-3030, 787-743-7979 Ext. 4352. *Fax:* 787-743-7979.

UNIVERSIDAD FLET

Miami, FL

CONTACT Financial Aid Office, Universidad FLET, 14540 SW 136th Street, Suite 200, Miami, FL 33186, 305-232-5880 or toll-free 888-376-3538.

UNIVERSIDAD METROPOLITANA

San Juan, PR

CONTACT Economic Assistant Director, Universidad Metropolitana, Call Box 21150, Rio Piedras, PR 00928-1150, 787-766-1717 Ext. 6586 or toll-free 800-747-8362 (out-of-state).

UNIVERSITY AT ALBANY, STATE UNIVERSITY OF NEW YORK

Albany, NY

Tuition & fees (NY res): $5939 **Average undergraduate aid package: $8399**

ABOUT THE INSTITUTION State-supported, coed. Awards: bachelor's, master's, and doctoral degrees and post-master's certificates. 69 undergraduate majors. Total enrollment: 17,434. Undergraduates: 12,457. Freshmen: 2,423. Federal methodology is used as a basis for awarding need-based institutional aid.

UNDERGRADUATE EXPENSES for 2006–07 ***Application fee:*** $40. ***Tuition, state resident:*** full-time $4350; part-time $181 per credit. ***Tuition, nonresident:*** full-time $10,610; part-time $442 per credit. Part-time tuition and fees vary according to course load. ***College room and board:*** $8605; ***Room only:*** $5269. Room and board charges vary according to board plan and housing facility. ***Payment plan:*** Installment.

FRESHMAN FINANCIAL AID (Fall 2006, est.) 2026 applied for aid; of those 66% were deemed to have need. 99% of freshmen with need received aid; of those 26% had need fully met. ***Average percent of need met:*** 78% (excluding resources awarded to replace EFC). ***Average financial aid package:*** $8763 (excluding resources awarded to replace EFC). 6% of all full-time freshmen had no need and received non-need-based gift aid.

UNDERGRADUATE FINANCIAL AID (Fall 2006, est.) 8,729 applied for aid; of those 73% were deemed to have need. 99% of undergraduates with need received aid; of those 30% had need fully met. ***Average percent of need met:*** 79% (excluding resources awarded to replace EFC). ***Average financial aid package:*** $8399 (excluding resources awarded to replace EFC). 6% of all full-time undergraduates had no need and received non-need-based gift aid.

GIFT AID (NEED-BASED) ***Total amount:*** $27,158,536 (43% federal, 49% state, 6% institutional, 2% external sources). ***Receiving aid:*** Freshmen: 52% (1,245); All full-time undergraduates: 50% (5,780). ***Average award:*** Freshmen: $5425; Undergraduates: $4767. ***Scholarships, grants, and awards:*** Federal Pell, FSEOG, state.

GIFT AID (NON-NEED-BASED) ***Total amount:*** $3,756,194 (3% federal, 29% state, 58% institutional, 10% external sources). ***Receiving aid:*** Freshmen: 2% (51); Undergraduates: 2% (177). ***Average award:*** Freshmen: $3202; Undergraduates: $3107. ***Scholarships, grants, and awards by category:*** *Academic Interests/Achievement:* 1,382 awards ($3,719,742 total): general academic interests/achievements. ***Tuition waivers:*** Full or partial for senior citizens. ***ROTC:*** Army, Air Force cooperative.

LOANS ***Student loans:*** $45,621,455 (49% need-based, 51% non-need-based). 64% of past graduating class borrowed through all loan programs. *Average indebtedness per student:* $11,856. ***Average need-based loan:*** Freshmen: $3371; Undergraduates: $4225. ***Parent loans:*** $9,686,235 (100% non-need-based). ***Programs:*** FFEL (Subsidized and Unsubsidized Stafford, PLUS), Perkins.

WORK-STUDY ***Federal work-study:*** Total amount: $1,802,126; 1,223 jobs averaging $1474. ***State or other work-study/employment:*** Total amount: $1,248,996 (61% need-based, 39% non-need-based). 255 part-time jobs averaging $4898.

ATHLETIC AWARDS Total amount: $2,837,249 (28% need-based, 72% non-need-based).

APPLYING FOR FINANCIAL AID ***Required financial aid forms:*** FAFSA, NY state residents should apply for TAP online at www.tapweb.org. ***Financial aid deadline:*** 4/15. ***Notification date:*** Continuous beginning 3/15. Students must reply by 5/1 or within 2 weeks of notification.

CONTACT Brenda Wright, Director of Financial Aid, University at Albany, State University of New York, 1400 Washington Avenue, Campus Center B52, Albany, NY 12222-0001, 518-442-5757 or toll-free 800-293-7869 (in-state). *Fax:* 518-442-5295. *E-mail:* faoweb@albany.edu.

UNIVERSITY AT BUFFALO, THE STATE UNIVERSITY OF NEW YORK

Buffalo, NY

Tuition & fees (NY res): $6128   Average undergraduate aid package: $6079

ABOUT THE INSTITUTION State-supported, coed. Awards: bachelor's, master's, doctoral, and first professional degrees and post-master's and first professional certificates. 81 undergraduate majors. Total enrollment: 27,220. Undergraduates: 18,165. Freshmen: 3,230. Federal methodology is used as a basis for awarding need-based institutional aid.

UNDERGRADUATE EXPENSES for 2006–07 ***Application fee:*** $40. ***Tuition, state resident:*** full-time $4350; part-time $181 per credit hour. ***Tuition, nonresident:*** full-time $10,610; part-time $442 per credit hour. ***Required fees:*** full-time $1778; $76 per credit hour. Part-time tuition and fees vary according to course load. ***College room and board:*** $8108; ***Room only:*** $5008. Room and board charges vary according to board plan and housing facility. ***Payment plan:*** Installment.

FRESHMAN FINANCIAL AID (Fall 2006, est.) 2673 applied for aid; of those 68% were deemed to have need. 100% of freshmen with need received aid; of those 19% had need fully met. ***Average percent of need met:*** 66% (excluding resources awarded to replace EFC). ***Average financial aid package:*** $5581 (excluding resources awarded to replace EFC). 7% of all full-time freshmen had no need and received non-need-based gift aid.

UNDERGRADUATE FINANCIAL AID (Fall 2006, est.) 13,023 applied for aid; of those 73% were deemed to have need. 100% of undergraduates with need received aid; of those 28% had need fully met. ***Average percent of need met:*** 69% (excluding resources awarded to replace EFC). ***Average financial aid package:*** $6079 (excluding resources awarded to replace EFC). 6% of all full-time undergraduates had no need and received non-need-based gift aid.

GIFT AID (NEED-BASED) ***Total amount:*** $38,632,224 (43% federal, 51% state, 2% institutional, 4% external sources). ***Receiving aid:*** Freshmen: 48% (1,669); All full-time undergraduates: 51% (8,742). ***Average award:*** Freshmen: $2654; Undergraduates: $2311. ***Scholarships, grants, and awards:*** Federal Pell, FSEOG, state, private, college/university gift aid from institutional funds, Federal Nursing.

GIFT AID (NON-NEED-BASED) ***Total amount:*** $8,106,680 (1% state, 99% institutional). ***Receiving aid:*** Freshmen: 11% (368); Undergraduates: 8% (1,461). ***Average award:*** Freshmen: $2825; Undergraduates: $2728. ***Scholarships, grants, and awards by category:*** *Academic Interests/Achievement:* general academic interests/achievements. *Creative Arts/Performance:* music. *Special Achievements/Activities:* general special achievements/activities. *Special Characteristics:* local/state students. ***Tuition waivers:*** Full or partial for minority students. ***ROTC:*** Army cooperative.

LOANS ***Student loans:*** $64,420,286 (47% need-based, 53% non-need-based). 92% of past graduating class borrowed through all loan programs. *Average indebtedness per student:* $19,062. ***Average need-based loan:*** Freshmen: $2742; Undergraduates: $3878. ***Parent loans:*** $8,169,795 (100% non-need-based). ***Programs:*** Federal Direct (Subsidized and Unsubsidized Stafford, PLUS), Perkins, Federal Nursing, college/university.

WORK-STUDY ***Federal work-study:*** Total amount: $1,366,220; 840 jobs averaging $1626. ***State or other work-study/employment:*** Total amount: $5,944,372 (100% non-need-based). 1,096 part-time jobs averaging $5424.

ATHLETIC AWARDS Total amount: $12,756,588 (100% non-need-based).

APPLYING FOR FINANCIAL AID ***Required financial aid forms:*** FAFSA, state aid form. ***Financial aid deadline (priority):*** 3/1. ***Notification date:*** Continuous beginning 5/1.

CONTACT Customer Service Department, University at Buffalo, the State University of New York, 232 Capen Hall, Buffalo, NY 14260, 716-645-2450 or toll-free 888-UB-ADMIT. *Fax:* 716-645-7760. *E-mail:* src@buffalo.edu.

UNIVERSITY OF ADVANCING TECHNOLOGY

Tempe, AZ

CONTACT Director of Financial Aid, University of Advancing Technology, 2625 West Baseline Road, Tempe, AZ 85283-1042, 602-383-8228 or toll-free 800-658-5744 (out-of-state).

THE UNIVERSITY OF AKRON

Akron, OH

Tuition & fees (OH res): $8382   Average undergraduate aid package: $6632

ABOUT THE INSTITUTION State-supported, coed. Awards: bachelor's, master's, doctoral, and first professional degrees and post-bachelor's and first professional certificates (associate). 235 undergraduate majors. Total enrollment: 21,882. Undergraduates: 18,016. Freshmen: 3,763. Federal methodology is used as a basis for awarding need-based institutional aid.

UNDERGRADUATE EXPENSES for 2006–07 ***Application fee:*** $30. ***Tuition, state resident:*** full-time $7218; part-time $301 per credit. ***Tuition, nonresident:*** full-time $16,467; part-time $609 per credit. ***Required fees:*** full-time $1164; $49 per credit. Full-time tuition and fees vary according to course load, degree level, and location. Part-time tuition and fees vary according to course load, degree level, and location. ***College room and board:*** $7640; ***Room only:*** $4764. Room and board charges vary according to board plan and housing facility. ***Payment plan:*** Installment.

FRESHMAN FINANCIAL AID (Fall 2005) 2420 applied for aid; of those 81% were deemed to have need. 100% of freshmen with need received aid; of those 6% had need fully met. ***Average percent of need met:*** 44% (excluding resources awarded to replace EFC). ***Average financial aid package:*** $5866 (excluding resources awarded to replace EFC). 8% of all full-time freshmen had no need and received non-need-based gift aid.

UNDERGRADUATE FINANCIAL AID (Fall 2005) 10,109 applied for aid; of those 81% were deemed to have need. 100% of undergraduates with need received aid; of those 5% had need fully met. ***Average percent of need met:*** 48%

(excluding resources awarded to replace EFC). ***Average financial aid package:*** $6632 (excluding resources awarded to replace EFC). 5% of all full-time undergraduates had no need and received non-need-based gift aid.

GIFT AID (NEED-BASED) ***Total amount:*** $22,712,970 (77% federal, 23% state). ***Receiving aid:*** Freshmen: 34% (988); All full-time undergraduates: 35% (4,373). ***Average award:*** Freshmen: $4096; Undergraduates: $4063. ***Scholarships, grants, and awards:*** Federal Pell, FSEOG, state, college/university gift aid from institutional funds.

GIFT AID (NON-NEED-BASED) ***Total amount:*** $14,619,807 (11% state, 62% institutional, 27% external sources). ***Receiving aid:*** Freshmen: 35% (1,028); Undergraduates: 29% (3,535). ***Average award:*** Freshmen: $3133; Undergraduates: $3264. ***Scholarships, grants, and awards by category:*** *Academic Interests/Achievement:* 2,377 awards ($5,786,032 total): biological sciences, business, communication, computer science, education, engineering/technologies, English, foreign languages, general academic interests/achievements, health fields, home economics, humanities, international studies, mathematics, military science, physical sciences, premedicine, social sciences. *Creative Arts/Performance:* 248 awards ($342,896 total): applied art and design, art/fine arts, creative writing, dance, debating, general creative arts/performance, journalism/publications, music, performing arts, theater/drama. *Special Achievements/Activities:* 115 awards ($276,327 total): community service, general special achievements/activities, leadership, memberships. *Special Characteristics:* 950 awards ($2,502,172 total): adult students, general special characteristics, handicapped students, international students, local/state students, members of minority groups, out-of-state students. ***Tuition waivers:*** Full or partial for employees or children of employees, senior citizens. ***ROTC:*** Army, Air Force cooperative.

LOANS ***Student loans:*** $63,053,590 (56% need-based, 44% non-need-based). 60% of past graduating class borrowed through all loan programs. *Average indebtedness per student:* $16,105. ***Average need-based loan:*** Freshmen: $2578; Undergraduates: $3482. ***Parent loans:*** $10,292,219 (100% non-need-based). ***Programs:*** FFEL (Subsidized and Unsubsidized Stafford, PLUS), Perkins, Federal Nursing, college/university.

WORK-STUDY ***Federal work-study:*** Total amount: $1,214,520; 763 jobs averaging $1592. ***State or other work-study/employment:*** Total amount: $4,371,510 (100% non-need-based). 2,750 part-time jobs averaging $1590.

ATHLETIC AWARDS Total amount: $4,634,598 (100% non-need-based).

APPLYING FOR FINANCIAL AID ***Required financial aid forms:*** FAFSA, institution's own form. ***Financial aid deadline (priority):*** 2/1. ***Notification date:*** Continuous beginning 4/1. Students must reply within 2 weeks of notification.

CONTACT Mr. Doug McNutt, Director of Financial Aid, The University of Akron, Office of Student Financial Aid, Akron, OH 44325-6211, 330-972-6334 or toll-free 800-655-4884. *Fax:* 330-972-7139. *E-mail:* mcnuttd@uakron.edu.

THE UNIVERSITY OF ALABAMA

Tuscaloosa, AL

Tuition & fees (AL res): $5278 **Average undergraduate aid package: $8542**

ABOUT THE INSTITUTION State-supported, coed. Awards: bachelor's, master's, doctoral, and first professional degrees and post-bachelor's and post-master's certificates. 77 undergraduate majors. Total enrollment: 23,838. Undergraduates: 19,471. Freshmen: 4,378. Federal methodology is used as a basis for awarding need-based institutional aid.

UNDERGRADUATE EXPENSES for 2006–07 ***Application fee:*** $35. ***Tuition, state resident:*** full-time $5278. ***Tuition, nonresident:*** full-time $15,294. Full-time tuition and fees vary according to course load. Part-time tuition and fees vary according to course load. ***College room and board:*** $5380; ***Room only:*** $3400. Room and board charges vary according to board plan and housing facility. ***Payment plans:*** Installment, deferred payment.

FRESHMAN FINANCIAL AID (Fall 2006, est.) 2824 applied for aid; of those 43% were deemed to have need. 98% of freshmen with need received aid; of those 19% had need fully met. ***Average percent of need met:*** 65% (excluding resources awarded to replace EFC). ***Average financial aid package:*** $7518 (excluding resources awarded to replace EFC). 37% of all full-time freshmen had no need and received non-need-based gift aid.

UNDERGRADUATE FINANCIAL AID (Fall 2006, est.) 11,769 applied for aid; of those 48% were deemed to have need. 97% of undergraduates with need received aid; of those 15% had need fully met. ***Average percent of need met:*** 67% (excluding resources awarded to replace EFC). ***Average financial aid package:*** $8542 (excluding resources awarded to replace EFC). 29% of all full-time undergraduates had no need and received non-need-based gift aid.

GIFT AID (NEED-BASED) ***Total amount:*** $11,440,755 (95% federal, 1% state, 4% institutional). ***Receiving aid:*** Freshmen: 16% (585); All full-time undergraduates: 19% (3,028). ***Average award:*** Freshmen: $3652; Undergraduates: $3480. ***Scholarships, grants, and awards:*** Federal Pell, FSEOG, state, private, college/university gift aid from institutional funds, Federal Nursing.

GIFT AID (NON-NEED-BASED) ***Total amount:*** $38,258,900 (47% institutional, 53% external sources). ***Receiving aid:*** Freshmen: 12% (447); Undergraduates: 10% (1,524). ***Average award:*** Freshmen: $3939; Undergraduates: $3450. ***Scholarships, grants, and awards by category:*** *Academic Interests/Achievement:* 8,504 awards ($16,020,718 total): area/ethnic studies, biological sciences, business, communication, computer science, education, engineering/technologies, English, foreign languages, general academic interests/achievements, home economics, library science, mathematics, military science, physical sciences, premedicine, social sciences. *Creative Arts/Performance:* 601 awards ($717,715 total): art/fine arts, cinema/film/broadcasting, creative writing, dance, debating, journalism/publications, music, theater/drama. *Special Achievements/Activities:* 233 awards ($942,896 total): cheerleading/drum major, community service, general special achievements/activities, hobbies/interests, junior miss. *Special Characteristics:* 169 awards ($307,024 total): children of union members/company employees, general special characteristics, international students, out-of-state students, spouses of deceased or disabled public servants. ***Tuition waivers:*** Full or partial for employees or children of employees. ***ROTC:*** Army, Air Force.

LOANS ***Student loans:*** $77,306,710 (45% need-based, 55% non-need-based). 41% of past graduating class borrowed through all loan programs. *Average indebtedness per student:* $18,653. ***Average need-based loan:*** Freshmen: $3220; Undergraduates: $4288. ***Parent loans:*** $11,615,617 (100% non-need-based). ***Programs:*** Federal Direct (Subsidized and Unsubsidized Stafford, PLUS), Perkins, college/university.

WORK-STUDY ***Federal work-study:*** Total amount: $1,551,015; 590 jobs averaging $2629.

ATHLETIC AWARDS Total amount: $6,823,428 (100% non-need-based).

APPLYING FOR FINANCIAL AID ***Required financial aid form:*** FAFSA. ***Financial aid deadline (priority):*** 3/1. ***Notification date:*** 4/1. Students must reply within 3 weeks of notification.

CONTACT Helen Leathers, Associate Director of Financial Aid, The University of Alabama, Box 870162, Tuscaloosa, AL 35487-0162, 205-348-6756 or toll-free 800-933-BAMA. *Fax:* 205-348-2989. *E-mail:* helen.leathers@ua.edu.

THE UNIVERSITY OF ALABAMA AT BIRMINGHAM

Birmingham, AL

Tuition & fees (AL res): $4792 **Average undergraduate aid package: $14,304**

ABOUT THE INSTITUTION State-supported, coed. Awards: bachelor's, master's, doctoral, and first professional degrees and post-bachelor's and post-master's certificates. 48 undergraduate majors. Total enrollment: 16,561. Undergraduates: 11,284. Freshmen: 1,531. Institutional methodology is used as a basis for awarding need-based institutional aid.

UNDERGRADUATE EXPENSES for 2006–07 ***Application fee:*** $30. ***Tuition, state resident:*** full-time $3960; part-time $132 per credit hour. ***Tuition, nonresident:*** full-time $9900; part-time $330 per credit hour. Full-time tuition and fees vary according to course load and program. Part-time tuition and fees vary according to course load and program. ***College room and board:*** $7111; ***Room only:*** $3427. Room and board charges vary according to board plan, housing facility, and student level.

FRESHMAN FINANCIAL AID (Fall 2005) 1001 applied for aid; of those 72% were deemed to have need. 98% of freshmen with need received aid; of those 15% had need fully met. ***Average percent of need met:*** 36% (excluding resources awarded to replace EFC). ***Average financial aid package:*** $14,145 (excluding resources awarded to replace EFC). 26% of all full-time freshmen had no need and received non-need-based gift aid.

UNDERGRADUATE FINANCIAL AID (Fall 2005) 5,081 applied for aid; of those 81% were deemed to have need. 99% of undergraduates with need received aid; of those 14% had need fully met. ***Average percent of need met:*** 40% (excluding resources awarded to replace EFC). ***Average financial aid package:*** $14,304 (excluding resources awarded to replace EFC). 19% of all full-time undergraduates had no need and received non-need-based gift aid.

GIFT AID (NEED-BASED) ***Total amount:*** $11,158,299 (96% federal, 1% state, 3% institutional). ***Receiving aid:*** Freshmen: 27% (414); All full-time undergraduates: 31% (2,477). ***Average award:*** Freshmen: $3265; Undergraduates: $3309. ***Scholarships, grants, and awards:*** Federal Pell, FSEOG, state, private, college/university gift aid from institutional funds, United Negro College Fund.

GIFT AID (NON-NEED-BASED) ***Total amount:*** $6,307,332 (2% state, 78% institutional, 20% external sources). ***Receiving aid:*** Freshmen: 20% (309); Undergraduates: 14% (1,113). ***Average award:*** Freshmen: $9983; Undergraduates: $9814. ***Scholarships, grants, and awards by category:*** *Academic Interests/Achievement:* business, communication, computer science, engineering/technologies, general academic interests/achievements, health fields, mathematics. *Creative Arts/Performance:* art/fine arts, music, performing arts, theater/drama. *Special Achievements/Activities:* cheerleading/drum major, junior miss, leadership, memberships, religious involvement. *Special Characteristics:* adult students, children and siblings of alumni, children of current students, children of educators, children of faculty/staff, children of public servants, children of union members/company employees, children of workers in trades, children with a deceased or disabled parent, ethnic background, first-generation college students, general special characteristics, handicapped students, local/state students, married students, members of minority groups, out-of-state students, parents of current students, previous college experience, public servants, relatives of clergy, religious affiliation, siblings of current students, spouses of current students, spouses of deceased or disabled public servants, twins, veterans, veterans' children. ***Tuition waivers:*** Full or partial for employees or children of employees. ***ROTC:*** Army, Air Force cooperative.

LOANS ***Student loans:*** $34,346,749 (60% need-based, 40% non-need-based). 53% of past graduating class borrowed through all loan programs. *Average indebtedness per student:* $17,650. ***Average need-based loan:*** Freshmen: $2637; Undergraduates: $3876. ***Parent loans:*** $4,870,949 (100% non-need-based). ***Programs:*** Federal Direct (Subsidized and Unsubsidized Stafford, PLUS), Perkins, state, college/university.

WORK-STUDY ***Federal work-study:*** Total amount: $1,882,322; jobs available.

ATHLETIC AWARDS Total amount: $3,714,237 (100% non-need-based).

APPLYING FOR FINANCIAL AID ***Required financial aid forms:*** FAFSA, institution's own form. ***Financial aid deadline (priority):*** 4/1. ***Notification date:*** Continuous beginning 4/1. Students must reply within 4 weeks of notification.

CONTACT Ms. Janet B. May, Financial Aid Director, The University of Alabama at Birmingham, Hill University Center 317, 1530 3rd Avenue South, Birmingham, AL 35294-1150, 205-934-8132 or toll-free 800-421-8743.

THE UNIVERSITY OF ALABAMA IN HUNTSVILLE

Huntsville, AL

Tuition & fees (AL res): $4848 **Average undergraduate aid package: $6191**

ABOUT THE INSTITUTION State-supported, coed. Awards: bachelor's, master's, and doctoral degrees and post-bachelor's and post-master's certificates. 29 undergraduate majors. Total enrollment: 7,091. Undergraduates: 5,719. Freshmen: 838. Both federal and institutional methodology are used as a basis for awarding need-based institutional aid.

UNDERGRADUATE EXPENSES for 2006–07 ***Application fee:*** $30. ***Tuition, state resident:*** full-time $4848; part-time $1086 per term. ***Tuition, nonresident:*** full-time $10,224; part-time $2286 per term. Full-time tuition and fees vary according to course load. Part-time tuition and fees vary according to course load. ***College room and board:*** $5110; ***Room only:*** $4560. Room and board charges vary according to board plan and housing facility. ***Payment plan:*** Deferred payment.

FRESHMAN FINANCIAL AID (Fall 2006, est.) 725 applied for aid; of those 46% were deemed to have need. 100% of freshmen with need received aid; of those 19% had need fully met. ***Average percent of need met:*** 64% (excluding resources awarded to replace EFC). ***Average financial aid package:*** $5941 (excluding resources awarded to replace EFC). 34% of all full-time freshmen had no need and received non-need-based gift aid.

UNDERGRADUATE FINANCIAL AID (Fall 2006, est.) 3,097 applied for aid; of those 53% were deemed to have need. 99% of undergraduates with need received aid; of those 19% had need fully met. ***Average percent of need met:*** 65% (excluding resources awarded to replace EFC). ***Average financial aid package:*** $6191 (excluding resources awarded to replace EFC). 21% of all full-time undergraduates had no need and received non-need-based gift aid.

GIFT AID (NEED-BASED) ***Total amount:*** $5,222,087 (77% federal, 1% state, 18% institutional, 4% external sources). ***Receiving aid:*** Freshmen: 36% (286); All full-time undergraduates: 31% (1,222). ***Average award:*** Freshmen: $4118; Undergraduates: $3692. ***Scholarships, grants, and awards:*** Federal Pell, FSEOG, state, private, college/university gift aid from institutional funds, Federal Nursing.

GIFT AID (NON-NEED-BASED) ***Total amount:*** $2,588,369 (90% institutional, 10% external sources). ***Receiving aid:*** Freshmen: 5% (39); Undergraduates: 2% (89). ***Average award:*** Freshmen: $2569; Undergraduates: $2636. ***Scholarships, grants, and awards by category:*** *Academic Interests/Achievement:* 1,682 awards ($3,387,353 total): business, computer science, education, engineering/technologies, English, general academic interests/achievements, health fields, humanities, physical sciences, social sciences. *Creative Arts/Performance:* 63 awards ($59,100 total): art/fine arts, music. *Special Achievements/Activities:* 475 awards ($1,295,495 total): cheerleading/drum major, community service, general special achievements/activities, junior miss, leadership. *Special Characteristics:* 35 awards ($75,000 total): general special characteristics, local/state students, members of minority groups. ***Tuition waivers:*** Full or partial for employees or children of employees. ***ROTC:*** Army cooperative.

LOANS ***Student loans:*** $14,001,599 (64% need-based, 36% non-need-based). 30% of past graduating class borrowed through all loan programs. *Average indebtedness per student:* $20,273. ***Average need-based loan:*** Freshmen: $3236; Undergraduates: $4462. ***Parent loans:*** $1,166,901 (35% need-based, 65% non-need-based). ***Programs:*** Federal Direct (Subsidized and Unsubsidized Stafford, PLUS).

WORK-STUDY ***Federal work-study:*** Total amount: $237,079; 69 jobs averaging $3435.

ATHLETIC AWARDS Total amount: $1,100,431 (17% need-based, 83% non-need-based).

APPLYING FOR FINANCIAL AID ***Required financial aid form:*** FAFSA. ***Financial aid deadline:*** 7/31 (priority: 4/1). ***Notification date:*** Continuous beginning 4/1. Students must reply within 2 weeks of notification.

CONTACT Mr. Andrew Weaver, Director of Student Financial Services, The University of Alabama in Huntsville, Office of Financial Aid, 301 Sparkman Drive, Huntsville, AL 35899, 256-824-6241 or toll-free 800-UAH-CALL. *Fax:* 256-824-6212. *E-mail:* finaid@uah.edu.

UNIVERSITY OF ALASKA ANCHORAGE

Anchorage, AK

CONTACT Theodore E. Malone, Director of Student Financial Aid, University of Alaska Anchorage, PO Box 141608, Anchorage, AK 99514-1608, 907-786-1520. *Fax:* 907-786-6122.

UNIVERSITY OF ALASKA FAIRBANKS

Fairbanks, AK

Tuition & fees (AK res): $4308 **Average undergraduate aid package: $8905**

ABOUT THE INSTITUTION State-supported, coed. Awards: associate, bachelor's, master's, and doctoral degrees. 68 undergraduate majors. Total enrollment: 8,341. Undergraduates: 7,274. Freshmen: 887. Federal methodology is used as a basis for awarding need-based institutional aid.

UNDERGRADUATE EXPENSES for 2007–08 ***Application fee:*** $40. ***Tuition, state resident:*** full-time $3600; part-time $128 per credit. ***Tuition, nonresident:*** full-time $11,970; part-time $407 per credit. ***Required fees:*** full-time $708; $7.56 per credit or $48 per term part-time. ***College room and board:*** $6030; ***Room only:*** $3440.

FRESHMAN FINANCIAL AID (Fall 2006, est.) 736 applied for aid; of those 39% were deemed to have need. 89% of freshmen with need received aid; of those 29% had need fully met. ***Average percent of need met:*** 64% (excluding resources awarded to replace EFC). ***Average financial aid package:*** $7973 (excluding resources awarded to replace EFC). 13% of all full-time freshmen had no need and received non-need-based gift aid.

UNDERGRADUATE FINANCIAL AID (Fall 2006, est.) 3,176 applied for aid; of those 44% were deemed to have need. 89% of undergraduates with need received aid; of those 28% had need fully met. ***Average percent of need met:*** 67% (excluding resources awarded to replace EFC). ***Average financial aid package:*** $8905 (excluding resources awarded to replace EFC). 12% of all full-time undergraduates had no need and received non-need-based gift aid.

GIFT AID (NEED-BASED) ***Total amount:*** $3,860,182 (87% federal, 8% institutional, 5% external sources). ***Receiving aid:*** Freshmen: 24% (183); All full-time undergraduates: 26% (859). ***Average award:*** Freshmen: $4112; Undergraduates: $4013. ***Scholarships, grants, and awards:*** Federal Pell, FSEOG, state, private, college/university gift aid from institutional funds, Native Non-Profit Corporations.

GIFT AID (NON-NEED-BASED) ***Total amount:*** $1,319,895 (1% federal, 79% institutional, 20% external sources). ***Receiving aid:*** Freshmen: 2% (16); Undergraduates: 3% (85). ***Average award:*** Freshmen: $2205; Undergraduates: $2775. ***Scholarships, grants, and awards by category:*** *Academic Interests/Achievement:* 1,691 awards ($2,735,612 total): general academic interests/achievements. *Creative Arts/Performance:* 91 awards ($161,457 total): art/fine arts, creative writing, music, theater/drama. *Special Achievements/Activities:* 7 awards ($10,232 total): community service, general special achievements/activities. *Special Characteristics:* 577 awards ($574,202 total): children and siblings of alumni, children of faculty/staff, members of minority groups. ***ROTC:*** Army.

LOANS ***Student loans:*** $15,182,511 (69% need-based, 31% non-need-based). 52% of past graduating class borrowed through all loan programs. *Average indebtedness per student:* $24,656. ***Average need-based loan:*** Freshmen: $5972; Undergraduates: $6397. ***Parent loans:*** $232,625 (37% need-based, 63% non-need-based). ***Programs:*** FFEL (Subsidized and Unsubsidized Stafford, PLUS), state.

WORK-STUDY ***Federal work-study:*** Total amount: $366,961; 200 jobs averaging $1835.

ATHLETIC AWARDS Total amount: $863,008 (18% need-based, 82% non-need-based).

APPLYING FOR FINANCIAL AID ***Required financial aid form:*** FAFSA. ***Financial aid deadline (priority):*** 2/15. ***Notification date:*** Continuous beginning 3/1. Students must reply within 2 weeks of notification.

CONTACT Tamara Hornbuckle, Financial Aid Officer, University of Alaska Fairbanks, 101 Eielson Building, PO Box 756360, Fairbanks, AK 99775-6360, 907-474-6628 or toll-free 800-478-1823. *Fax:* 907-474-7065. *E-mail:* fntmh@uaf.edu.

UNIVERSITY OF ALASKA SOUTHEAST

Juneau, AK

ABOUT THE INSTITUTION State-supported, coed. Awards: associate, bachelor's, and master's degrees. 17 undergraduate majors. Total enrollment: 2,965. Undergraduates: 2,753. Freshmen: 183.

GIFT AID (NEED-BASED) ***Scholarships, grants, and awards:*** Federal Pell, FSEOG, state, private, college/university gift aid from institutional funds.

GIFT AID (NON-NEED-BASED) ***Scholarships, grants, and awards by category:*** *Academic Interests/Achievement:* biological sciences, business, communication, computer science, education, general academic interests/achievements, humanities, mathematics, social sciences. *Creative Arts/Performance:* performing arts. *Special Achievements/Activities:* general special achievements/activities, leadership. *Special Characteristics:* ethnic background, first-generation college students.

LOANS ***Programs:*** FFEL (Subsidized and Unsubsidized Stafford, PLUS), state.

WORK-STUDY ***Federal work-study:*** Total amount: $76,829; 36 jobs averaging $2134.

APPLYING FOR FINANCIAL AID ***Required financial aid form:*** FAFSA.

CONTACT Ms. Barbara Carlson Burnett, Financial Aid Director, University of Alaska Southeast, 11120 Glacier Highway, Juneau, AK 99801-8680, 907-796-6296 or toll-free 877-796-4827. *Fax:* 907-796-6250. *E-mail:* barbara.burnett@uas.alaska.edu.

THE UNIVERSITY OF ARIZONA

Tucson, AZ

Tuition & fees (AZ res): $4766 Average undergraduate aid package: $8078

ABOUT THE INSTITUTION State-supported, coed. Awards: bachelor's, master's, doctoral, and first professional degrees and post-bachelor's certificates. 128 undergraduate majors. Total enrollment: 36,805. Undergraduates: 28,442. Freshmen: 6,009. Federal methodology is used as a basis for awarding need-based institutional aid.

UNDERGRADUATE EXPENSES for 2006–07 ***Application fee:*** $25. ***Tuition, state resident:*** full-time $4594; part-time $290 per credit hour. ***Tuition, nonresident:*** full-time $14,800; part-time $667 per credit hour. Full-time tuition and fees vary according to course load. Part-time tuition and fees vary according to course load. ***College room and board:*** $7850; ***Room only:*** $4350. Room and board charges vary according to board plan and housing facility.

FRESHMAN FINANCIAL AID (Fall 2005) 3513 applied for aid; of those 61% were deemed to have need. 95% of freshmen with need received aid; of those 18% had need fully met. ***Average percent of need met:*** 64% (excluding resources awarded to replace EFC). ***Average financial aid package:*** $7443 (excluding resources awarded to replace EFC). 34% of all full-time freshmen had no need and received non-need-based gift aid.

UNDERGRADUATE FINANCIAL AID (Fall 2005) 13,543 applied for aid; of those 74% were deemed to have need. 95% of undergraduates with need received aid; of those 16% had need fully met. ***Average percent of need met:*** 64% (excluding resources awarded to replace EFC). ***Average financial aid package:*** $8078 (excluding resources awarded to replace EFC). 19% of all full-time undergraduates had no need and received non-need-based gift aid.

GIFT AID (NEED-BASED) ***Total amount:*** $55,339,461 (33% federal, 1% state, 48% institutional, 18% external sources). ***Receiving aid:*** Freshmen: 33% (1,918); All full-time undergraduates: 34% (8,470). ***Average award:*** Freshmen: $6308; Undergraduates: $6031. ***Scholarships, grants, and awards:*** Federal Pell, FSEOG, state, private, college/university gift aid from institutional funds, Federal Nursing.

GIFT AID (NON-NEED-BASED) ***Total amount:*** $33,592,277 (73% institutional, 27% external sources). ***Receiving aid:*** Freshmen: 5% (314); Undergraduates: 3% (830). ***Average award:*** Freshmen: $4363; Undergraduates: $5105. ***Scholarships, grants, and awards by category:*** *Academic Interests/Achievement:* agriculture, architecture, biological sciences, business, education, engineering/technologies, general academic interests/achievements, humanities, military science, physical sciences, religion/biblical studies. *Creative Arts/Performance:* art/fine arts, dance, music, performing arts, theater/drama. *Special Achievements/Activities:* leadership. *Special Characteristics:* children of faculty/staff, ethnic background, international students. ***Tuition waivers:*** Full or partial for employees or children of employees. ***ROTC:*** Army, Naval, Air Force.

LOANS ***Student loans:*** $58,586,877 (81% need-based, 19% non-need-based). 44% of past graduating class borrowed through all loan programs. *Average indebtedness per student:* $17,392. ***Average need-based loan:*** Freshmen: $2870; Undergraduates: $4137. ***Parent loans:*** $23,202,175 (56% need-based, 44% non-need-based). ***Programs:*** FFEL (Subsidized and Unsubsidized Stafford, PLUS), Perkins, Federal Nursing, college/university.

WORK-STUDY ***Federal work-study:*** Total amount: $1,514,996; jobs available. ***State or other work-study/employment:*** Total amount: $11,315,672 (47% need-based, 53% non-need-based). Part-time jobs available.

CONTACT Student Financial Aid Office, The University of Arizona, PO Box 210066, Tucson, AZ 85721-0066, 520-621-1858. *Fax:* 520-621-9473. *E-mail:* askaid@arizona.edu.

UNIVERSITY OF ARKANSAS

Fayetteville, AR

Tuition & fees (AR res): $5808 Average undergraduate aid package: $8068

ABOUT THE INSTITUTION State-supported, coed. Awards: bachelor's, master's, doctoral, and first professional degrees and post-bachelor's and post-master's certificates. 75 undergraduate majors. Total enrollment: 17,926. Undergraduates: 14,350. Freshmen: 2,784. Federal methodology is used as a basis for awarding need-based institutional aid.

UNDERGRADUATE EXPENSES for 2006–07 ***Application fee:*** $40. ***Tuition, state resident:*** full-time $4590; part-time $153 per hour. ***Tuition, nonresident:*** full-time $12,724; part-time $424 per hour. Full-time tuition and fees vary according to program. Part-time tuition and fees vary according to program. ***College room and board:*** $6522; ***Room only:*** $3904. Room and board charges vary according to board plan and housing facility. ***Payment plan:*** Installment.

FRESHMAN FINANCIAL AID (Fall 2006, est.) 1558 applied for aid; of those 64% were deemed to have need. 97% of freshmen with need received aid; of those 21% had need fully met. ***Average percent of need met:*** 74% (excluding resources awarded to replace EFC). ***Average financial aid package:*** $7805 (excluding resources awarded to replace EFC). 20% of all full-time freshmen had no need and received non-need-based gift aid.

UNDERGRADUATE FINANCIAL AID (Fall 2006, est.) 6,077 applied for aid; of those 74% were deemed to have need. 96% of undergraduates with need received aid; of those 17% had need fully met. ***Average percent of need met:*** 73% (excluding resources awarded to replace EFC). ***Average financial aid***

package: $8068 (excluding resources awarded to replace EFC). 18% of all full-time undergraduates had no need and received non-need-based gift aid.

GIFT AID (NEED-BASED) ***Total amount:*** $12,122,656 (75% federal, 23% state, 2% institutional). ***Receiving aid:*** Freshmen: 22% (587); All full-time undergraduates: 23% (2,703). ***Average award:*** Freshmen: $4115; Undergraduates: $3953. ***Scholarships, grants, and awards:*** Federal Pell, FSEOG, state, private, college/university gift aid from institutional funds.

GIFT AID (NON-NEED-BASED) ***Total amount:*** $24,687,096 (20% state, 71% institutional, 9% external sources). ***Receiving aid:*** Freshmen: 19% (527); Undergraduates: 13% (1,574). ***Average award:*** Freshmen: $6073; Undergraduates: $5845. ***Scholarships, grants, and awards by category:*** *Academic Interests/Achievement:* general academic interests/achievements. *Creative Arts/Performance:* music, theater/drama. *Special Achievements/Activities:* community service, general special achievements/activities, leadership. *Special Characteristics:* children and siblings of alumni, children of faculty/staff, ethnic background, international students, out-of-state students, previous college experience. ***Tuition waivers:*** Full or partial for employees or children of employees, senior citizens. ***ROTC:*** Army, Air Force.

LOANS ***Student loans:*** $31,986,524 (51% need-based, 49% non-need-based). 46% of past graduating class borrowed through all loan programs. *Average indebtedness per student:* $18,170. ***Average need-based loan:*** Freshmen: $2973; Undergraduates: $4292. ***Parent loans:*** $6,732,103 (100% non-need-based). ***Programs:*** FFEL (Subsidized and Unsubsidized Stafford, PLUS), Perkins, state, college/university, alternative loans.

WORK-STUDY ***Federal work-study:*** Total amount: $2,550,939; 1,211 jobs averaging $1853.

ATHLETIC AWARDS Total amount: $3,759,177 (100% non-need-based).

APPLYING FOR FINANCIAL AID ***Required financial aid form:*** FAFSA. ***Financial aid deadline (priority):*** 3/15. ***Notification date:*** Continuous beginning 4/1. Students must reply within 4 weeks of notification.

CONTACT Kattie Wing, Director of Financial Aid, University of Arkansas, 114 Silas H. Hunt Hall, Fayetteville, AR 72701-1201, 479-575-3806 or toll-free 800-377-5346 (in-state), 800-377-8632 (out-of-state). *E-mail:* kattie@uark.edu.

UNIVERSITY OF ARKANSAS AT FORT SMITH

Fort Smith, AR

CONTACT Tammy Malone, Interim Financial Aid Director, University of Arkansas at Fort Smith, 5210 Grand Avenue, Fort Smith, AR 72913, 479-788-7099 or toll-free 888-512-5466. *Fax:* 479-788-7095. *E-mail:* tmalone@uafortsmith.edu.

UNIVERSITY OF ARKANSAS AT LITTLE ROCK

Little Rock, AR

CONTACT Financial Aid Office, University of Arkansas at Little Rock, 2801 South University Avenue, Little Rock, AR 72204-1099, 501-569-3127 or toll-free 800-482-8892 (in-state).

UNIVERSITY OF ARKANSAS AT MONTICELLO

Monticello, AR

Tuition & fees (AR res): $4150 **Average undergraduate aid package: N/A**

ABOUT THE INSTITUTION State-supported, coed. Awards: associate, bachelor's, and master's degrees and post-bachelor's certificates. 33 undergraduate majors. Total enrollment: 3,179. Undergraduates: 3,064. Freshmen: 694. Federal methodology is used as a basis for awarding need-based institutional aid.

UNDERGRADUATE EXPENSES for 2006–07 ***Tuition, state resident:*** full-time $3150; part-time $315 per hour. ***Tuition, nonresident:*** full-time $7080. ***Required fees:*** full-time $1000; $38 per hour. Full-time tuition and fees vary according to location and program. Part-time tuition and fees vary according to location and program. ***College room and board:*** $3440; ***Room only:*** $1400. Room and board charges vary according to board plan and housing facility. ***Payment plan:*** Guaranteed tuition.

GIFT AID (NEED-BASED) ***Total amount:*** $7,414,857 (71% federal, 11% state, 13% institutional, 5% external sources). ***Scholarships, grants, and awards:*** Federal Pell, FSEOG, state, private, college/university gift aid from institutional funds.

GIFT AID (NON-NEED-BASED) ***Total amount:*** $1,442,463 (9% state, 76% institutional, 15% external sources). ***Scholarships, grants, and awards by category:*** *Academic Interests/Achievement:* 314 awards ($965,455 total): general academic interests/achievements. *Creative Arts/Performance:* 182 awards ($388,053 total): debating, journalism/publications, music. *Special Achievements/Activities:* 122 awards ($113,860 total): cheerleading/drum major, general special achievements/activities, leadership, rodeo. *Special Characteristics:* 293 awards ($847,730 total): children of faculty/staff, out-of-state students. ***Tuition waivers:*** Full or partial for employees or children of employees, senior citizens. ***ROTC:*** Army.

LOANS ***Student loans:*** $7,383,429 (65% need-based, 35% non-need-based). ***Parent loans:*** $204,326 (100% non-need-based). ***Programs:*** FFEL (Subsidized and Unsubsidized Stafford, PLUS), Perkins.

WORK-STUDY ***Federal work-study:*** Total amount: $171,320; 188 jobs averaging $911. ***State or other work-study/employment:*** Total amount: $329,867 (100% non-need-based). 274 part-time jobs averaging $1204.

ATHLETIC AWARDS Total amount: $646,742 (68% need-based, 32% non-need-based).

APPLYING FOR FINANCIAL AID ***Required financial aid forms:*** FAFSA, institution's own form. ***Financial aid deadline:*** Continuous. ***Notification date:*** Continuous beginning 3/1. Students must reply within 2 weeks of notification.

CONTACT Susan Brewer, Director of Financial Aid, University of Arkansas at Monticello, PO Box 3470, Monticello, AR 71656, 870-460-1050 or toll-free 800-844-1826 (in-state). *Fax:* 870-460-1450. *E-mail:* brewers@uamont.edu.

UNIVERSITY OF ARKANSAS AT PINE BLUFF

Pine Bluff, AR

ABOUT THE INSTITUTION State-supported, coed. Awards: associate, bachelor's, and master's degrees. 52 undergraduate majors. Total enrollment: 3,128. Undergraduates: 3,051. Freshmen: 723.

GIFT AID (NEED-BASED) ***Scholarships, grants, and awards:*** Federal Pell, FSEOG, state.

GIFT AID (NON-NEED-BASED) ***Scholarships, grants, and awards by category:*** *Academic Interests/Achievement:* agriculture, biological sciences, business, education, English, general academic interests/achievements, mathematics. *Creative Arts/Performance:* art/fine arts, music. *Special Achievements/Activities:* leadership.

LOANS ***Programs:*** FFEL (Subsidized and Unsubsidized Stafford, PLUS), signature loans.

WORK-STUDY ***Federal work-study:*** Total amount: $328,969; 328 jobs averaging $1000. ***State or other work-study/employment:*** Total amount: $9720 (100% non-need-based).

APPLYING FOR FINANCIAL AID ***Required financial aid forms:*** FAFSA, institution's own form, verification worksheet.

CONTACT Mrs. Carolyn Iverson, Director of Financial Aid, University of Arkansas at Pine Bluff, 1200 North University Drive, PO Box 4985, Pine Bluff, AR 71601, 870-575-8303 or toll-free 800-264-6585. *Fax:* 870-575-4622. *E-mail:* iverson_c@uapb.edu.

UNIVERSITY OF ARKANSAS FOR MEDICAL SCIENCES

Little Rock, AR

Tuition & fees: N/R **Average undergraduate aid package: $3000**

ABOUT THE INSTITUTION State-supported, coed. Awards: associate, bachelor's, master's, doctoral, and first professional degrees (bachelor's degree is upper-level). 10 undergraduate majors. Total enrollment: 2,016. Undergraduates: 683. Federal methodology is used as a basis for awarding need-based institutional aid.

UNDERGRADUATE FINANCIAL AID (Fall 2005) 734 applied for aid; of those 93% were deemed to have need. 83% of undergraduates with need received aid. ***Average percent of need met:*** 62% (excluding resources awarded to replace EFC). ***Average financial aid package:*** $3000 (excluding resources awarded to replace EFC).

GIFT AID (NEED-BASED) ***Total amount:*** $1,311,551 (65% federal, 19% state, 12% institutional, 4% external sources). ***Average award:*** Undergraduates: $500. ***Scholarships, grants, and awards:*** Federal Pell, FSEOG, state, private, college/university gift aid from institutional funds.

GIFT AID (NON-NEED-BASED) ***ROTC:*** Army cooperative.

LOANS ***Student loans:*** $11,208,628 (49% need-based, 51% non-need-based). *Average indebtedness per student:* $7000. ***Average need-based loan:*** Undergraduates: $4000. ***Parent loans:*** $513,433 (100% need-based). ***Programs:*** FFEL (Subsidized and Unsubsidized Stafford, PLUS), Perkins, Federal Nursing.

WORK-STUDY ***Federal work-study:*** Total amount: $19,400; 9 jobs averaging $1201.

CONTACT Mr. Paul Carter, Director of Financial Aid, University of Arkansas for Medical Sciences, 4301 West Markham Street, MS 601, Little Rock, AR 72205, 501-686-5451. *Fax:* 501-686-5661. *E-mail:* pvcarter@uams.edu.

UNIVERSITY OF BALTIMORE

Baltimore, MD

ABOUT THE INSTITUTION State-supported, coed. Awards: bachelor's, master's, doctoral, and first professional degrees and post-bachelor's and post-master's certificates. 29 undergraduate majors. Total enrollment: 4,948. Undergraduates: 2,116.

GIFT AID (NEED-BASED) ***Scholarships, grants, and awards:*** Federal Pell, FSEOG, state, private, college/university gift aid from institutional funds.

GIFT AID (NON-NEED-BASED) ***Scholarships, grants, and awards by category:*** *Academic Interests/Achievement:* business, English, general academic interests/achievements. *Special Achievements/Activities:* community service, memberships. *Special Characteristics:* handicapped students.

LOANS ***Programs:*** FFEL (Subsidized and Unsubsidized Stafford, PLUS), Perkins, college/university.

WORK-STUDY ***Federal work-study:*** Total amount: $385,606; 105 jobs averaging $3672. ***State or other work-study/employment:*** Total amount: $72,319 (100% non-need-based).

APPLYING FOR FINANCIAL AID ***Required financial aid forms:*** FAFSA, institution's own form.

CONTACT Financial Aid Office, University of Baltimore, 1420 North Charles Street, CH 123, Baltimore, MD 21201-5779, 410-837-4763 or toll-free 877-APPLYUB. *Fax:* 410-837-5493.

UNIVERSITY OF BRIDGEPORT

Bridgeport, CT

Tuition & fees: $21,710 **Average undergraduate aid package: $19,830**

ABOUT THE INSTITUTION Independent, coed. Awards: associate, bachelor's, master's, doctoral, and first professional degrees and post-master's certificates. 32 undergraduate majors. Total enrollment: 4,018. Undergraduates: 1,694. Freshmen: 313. Federal methodology is used as a basis for awarding need-based institutional aid.

UNDERGRADUATE EXPENSES for 2006–07 ***Application fee:*** $25. ***Comprehensive fee:*** $31,310 includes full-time tuition ($20,250), mandatory fees ($1460), and room and board ($9600). ***College room only:*** $5000. Full-time tuition and fees vary according to program. Room and board charges vary according to board plan and student level. ***Part-time tuition:*** $675 per credit. ***Part-time fees:*** $70 per term. Part-time tuition and fees vary according to program. ***Payment plans:*** Installment, deferred payment.

FRESHMAN FINANCIAL AID (Fall 2006, est.) 254 applied for aid; of those 100% were deemed to have need. 100% of freshmen with need received aid; of those 8% had need fully met. ***Average percent of need met:*** 52% (excluding resources awarded to replace EFC). ***Average financial aid package:*** $20,453 (excluding resources awarded to replace EFC). 20% of all full-time freshmen had no need and received non-need-based gift aid.

UNDERGRADUATE FINANCIAL AID (Fall 2006, est.) 913 applied for aid; of those 99% were deemed to have need. 100% of undergraduates with need received aid; of those 9% had need fully met. ***Average percent of need met:*** 52% (excluding resources awarded to replace EFC). ***Average financial aid package:*** $19,830 (excluding resources awarded to replace EFC). 2% of all full-time undergraduates had no need and received non-need-based gift aid.

GIFT AID (NEED-BASED) ***Total amount:*** $5,743,012 (38% federal, 12% state, 50% institutional). ***Receiving aid:*** Freshmen: 74% (229); All full-time undergraduates: 65% (791). ***Average award:*** Freshmen: $6536; Undergraduates: $7574. ***Scholarships, grants, and awards:*** Federal Pell, FSEOG, state, college/university gift aid from institutional funds.

GIFT AID (NON-NEED-BASED) ***Total amount:*** $5,188,695 (96% institutional, 4% external sources). ***Receiving aid:*** Freshmen: 79% (245); Undergraduates: 60% (729). ***Average award:*** Freshmen: $13,448; Undergraduates: $13,748. ***Scholarships, grants, and awards by category:*** *Academic Interests/Achievement:* 672 awards ($4,253,801 total): general academic interests/achievements. *Creative Arts/Performance:* 2 awards ($39,450 total): applied art and design, music. *Special Achievements/Activities:* leadership. *Special Characteristics:* 198 awards ($1,631,572 total): children of faculty/staff, international students, local/state students, previous college experience. ***Tuition waivers:*** Full or partial for employees or children of employees, senior citizens. ***ROTC:*** Army.

LOANS ***Student loans:*** $11,340,598 (42% need-based, 58% non-need-based). ***Average need-based loan:*** Freshmen: $4078; Undergraduates: $5077. ***Parent loans:*** $3,580,616 (100% non-need-based). ***Programs:*** FFEL (Subsidized and Unsubsidized Stafford, PLUS), Perkins.

WORK-STUDY ***Federal work-study:*** Total amount: $364,919; 182 jobs averaging $2000. ***State or other work-study/employment:*** Total amount: $222,038 (100% non-need-based).

ATHLETIC AWARDS Total amount: $1,985,868 (100% non-need-based).

APPLYING FOR FINANCIAL AID ***Required financial aid forms:*** FAFSA, institution's own form. ***Financial aid deadline (priority):*** 4/15. ***Notification date:*** Continuous beginning 3/5. Students must reply within 4 weeks of notification.

CONTACT Kathleen E. Gailor, Director of Financial Aid, University of Bridgeport, 126 Park Avenue, Bridgeport, CT 06604, 203-576-4568 or toll-free 800-EXCEL-UB (in-state), 800-243-9496 (out-of-state). *Fax:* 203-576-4570. *E-mail:* finaid@bridgeport.edu.

UNIVERSITY OF CALIFORNIA, BERKELEY

Berkeley, CA

Tuition & fees (CA res): $6654 **Average undergraduate aid package: $15,710**

ABOUT THE INSTITUTION State-supported, coed. Awards: bachelor's, master's, doctoral, and first professional degrees. 93 undergraduate majors. Total enrollment: 33,933. Undergraduates: 23,863. Freshmen: 4,157. Both federal and institutional methodology are used as a basis for awarding need-based institutional aid.

UNDERGRADUATE EXPENSES for 2006–07 ***Application fee:*** $60. ***Tuition, state resident:*** full-time $0. ***Tuition, nonresident:*** full-time $18,684. Full-time tuition and fees vary according to program. ***College room and board:*** $13,074. Room and board charges vary according to board plan and housing facility. ***Payment plan:*** Installment.

FRESHMAN FINANCIAL AID (Fall 2006, est.) 3242 applied for aid; of those 64% were deemed to have need. 99% of freshmen with need received aid; of those 66% had need fully met. ***Average percent of need met:*** 92% (excluding resources awarded to replace EFC). ***Average financial aid package:*** $17,250 (excluding resources awarded to replace EFC). 7% of all full-time freshmen had no need and received non-need-based gift aid.

UNDERGRADUATE FINANCIAL AID (Fall 2006, est.) 14,420 applied for aid; of those 79% were deemed to have need. 99% of undergraduates with need received aid; of those 60% had need fully met. ***Average percent of need met:*** 89% (excluding resources awarded to replace EFC). ***Average financial aid package:*** $15,710 (excluding resources awarded to replace EFC). 6% of all full-time undergraduates had no need and received non-need-based gift aid.

GIFT AID (NEED-BASED) ***Total amount:*** $129,128,798 (20% federal, 28% state, 44% institutional, 8% external sources). ***Receiving aid:*** Freshmen: 48% (2,001); All full-time undergraduates: 48% (11,008). ***Average award:*** Freshmen: $12,651; Undergraduates: $11,541. ***Scholarships, grants, and awards:*** Federal Pell, FSEOG, state, private, college/university gift aid from institutional funds.

GIFT AID (NON-NEED-BASED) ***Total amount:*** $13,810,324 (6% federal, 1% state, 33% institutional, 60% external sources). ***Receiving aid:*** Freshmen: 2% (63); Undergraduates: 1% (229). ***Average award:*** Freshmen: $2136; Undergraduates: $2991. ***Scholarships, grants, and awards by category:*** *Academic Interests/Achievement:* engineering/technologies, general academic interests/achievements. ***ROTC:*** Army, Naval, Air Force.

LOANS ***Student loans:*** $42,114,198 (73% need-based, 27% non-need-based). 44% of past graduating class borrowed through all loan programs. *Average indebtedness per student:* $14,751. ***Average need-based loan:*** Freshmen: $3989; Undergraduates: $4761. ***Parent loans:*** $28,635,142 (12% need-based, 88% non-need-based). ***Programs:*** Federal Direct (Subsidized and Unsubsidized Stafford, PLUS), Perkins.

WORK-STUDY ***Federal work-study:*** Total amount: $10,755,994; jobs available. ***State or other work-study/employment:*** Total amount: $5,456,528 (100% need-based). Part-time jobs available.

ATHLETIC AWARDS Total amount: $7,068,524 (24% need-based, 76% non-need-based).

APPLYING FOR FINANCIAL AID ***Required financial aid forms:*** FAFSA, state aid form, State Cal Grants. ***Financial aid deadline:*** 3/2 (priority: 3/2).

CONTACT Sandy Jensen, Administrative Services Coordinator, University of California, Berkeley, 225 Sproul Hall, Berkeley, CA 94720-1960, 510-642-0649. *Fax:* 510-643-5526.

UNIVERSITY OF CALIFORNIA, DAVIS

Davis, CA

ABOUT THE INSTITUTION State-supported, coed. Awards: bachelor's, master's, doctoral, and first professional degrees and post-bachelor's and post-master's certificates. 83 undergraduate majors. Total enrollment: 29,628. Undergraduates: 23,458. Freshmen: 5,528.

GIFT AID (NEED-BASED) ***Scholarships, grants, and awards:*** Federal Pell, FSEOG, state, private, college/university gift aid from institutional funds, Federal Nursing.

GIFT AID (NON-NEED-BASED) ***Scholarships, grants, and awards by category:*** *Academic Interests/Achievement:* agriculture, general academic interests/achievements.

LOANS ***Programs:*** Federal Direct (Subsidized and Unsubsidized Stafford, PLUS), Perkins, college/university.

WORK-STUDY ***Federal work-study:*** Total amount: $1,833,566; jobs available. ***State or other work-study/employment:*** Total amount: $275,003 (100% need-based).

APPLYING FOR FINANCIAL AID ***Required financial aid forms:*** FAFSA, state aid form.

CONTACT Lora Jo Bossio, Director of Financial Aid, University of California, Davis, One Shields Avenue, 1100 Dutton Hall, Davis, CA 95616, 530-752-2396. *Fax:* 530-752-7339.

UNIVERSITY OF CALIFORNIA, IRVINE

Irvine, CA

Tuition & fees (CA res): $6141 **Average undergraduate aid package: $13,221**

ABOUT THE INSTITUTION State-supported, coed. Awards: bachelor's, master's, doctoral, and first professional degrees and post-bachelor's certificates. 66 undergraduate majors. Total enrollment: 25,229. Undergraduates: 20,719. Freshmen: 4,836. Federal methodology is used as a basis for awarding need-based institutional aid.

UNDERGRADUATE EXPENSES for 2006–07 ***Application fee:*** $60. ***Tuition, state resident:*** full-time $0. ***Tuition, nonresident:*** full-time $18,684. ***College room and board:*** $9815.

FRESHMAN FINANCIAL AID (Fall 2006, est.) 3603 applied for aid; of those 64% were deemed to have need. 92% of freshmen with need received aid; of those 47% had need fully met. ***Average percent of need met:*** 83% (excluding resources awarded to replace EFC). ***Average financial aid package:*** $13,006 (excluding resources awarded to replace EFC). 3% of all full-time freshmen had no need and received non-need-based gift aid.

UNDERGRADUATE FINANCIAL AID (Fall 2006, est.) 12,616 applied for aid; of those 78% were deemed to have need. 96% of undergraduates with need received aid; of those 44% had need fully met. ***Average percent of need met:*** 84% (excluding resources awarded to replace EFC). ***Average financial aid package:*** $13,221 (excluding resources awarded to replace EFC). 4% of all full-time undergraduates had no need and received non-need-based gift aid.

GIFT AID (NEED-BASED) ***Total amount:*** $88,299,817 (22% federal, 35% state, 41% institutional, 2% external sources). ***Receiving aid:*** Freshmen: 39% (1,885); All full-time undergraduates: 42% (8,445). ***Average award:*** Freshmen: $10,038; Undergraduates: $10,339. ***Scholarships, grants, and awards:*** Federal Pell, FSEOG, state, private, college/university gift aid from institutional funds.

GIFT AID (NON-NEED-BASED) ***Total amount:*** $9,225,083 (3% federal, 7% state, 78% institutional, 12% external sources). ***Receiving aid:*** Freshmen: 1% (32); Undergraduates: 97. ***Average award:*** Freshmen: $8614; Undergraduates: $8163. ***Scholarships, grants, and awards by category:*** *Academic Interests/Achievement:* 813 awards ($4,829,440 total): computer science, engineering/technologies, general academic interests/achievements, humanities. *Creative Arts/Performance:* 88 awards ($167,174 total): art/fine arts, dance, general creative arts/performance, music. ***ROTC:*** Army cooperative, Air Force cooperative.

LOANS ***Student loans:*** $35,813,039 (73% need-based, 27% non-need-based). 52% of past graduating class borrowed through all loan programs. *Average indebtedness per student:* $13,587. ***Average need-based loan:*** Freshmen: $5458; Undergraduates: $5495. ***Parent loans:*** $34,010,783 (21% need-based, 79% non-need-based). ***Programs:*** Federal Direct (Subsidized and Unsubsidized Stafford, PLUS), Perkins, college/university, private loans.

WORK-STUDY ***Federal work-study:*** Total amount: $3,480,301; 3,046 jobs averaging $1421. ***State or other work-study/employment:*** Part-time jobs available.

ATHLETIC AWARDS Total amount: $2,202,057 (21% need-based, 79% non-need-based).

APPLYING FOR FINANCIAL AID ***Required financial aid forms:*** FAFSA, state aid form. ***Financial aid deadline:*** 5/1 (priority: 3/2). ***Notification date:*** Continuous beginning 4/1.

CONTACT Penny Harrell, Associate Director of Student Services, University of California, Irvine, Office of Financial Aid and Scholarships, 102 Administration Building, Irvine, CA 92697-2825, 949-824-8262. *Fax:* 949-824-4876. *E-mail:* finaid@uci.edu.

UNIVERSITY OF CALIFORNIA, LOS ANGELES

Los Angeles, CA

Tuition & fees (CA res): $7143 **Average undergraduate aid package: $14,329**

ABOUT THE INSTITUTION State-supported, coed. Awards: bachelor's, master's, doctoral, and first professional degrees. 150 undergraduate majors. Total enrollment: 38,218. Undergraduates: 25,432. Freshmen: 4,811. Both federal and institutional methodology are used as a basis for awarding need-based institutional aid.

UNDERGRADUATE EXPENSES for 2006–07 ***Application fee:*** $60. ***Tuition, state resident:*** full-time $0. ***Tuition, nonresident:*** full-time $18,827. ***College room and board:*** $11,141. Room and board charges vary according to board plan and housing facility.

FRESHMAN FINANCIAL AID (Fall 2006, est.) 2722 applied for aid; of those 82% were deemed to have need. 100% of freshmen with need received aid; of those 32% had need fully met. ***Average percent of need met:*** 81% (excluding resources awarded to replace EFC). ***Average financial aid package:*** $15,446 (excluding resources awarded to replace EFC). 6% of all full-time freshmen had no need and received non-need-based gift aid.

UNDERGRADUATE FINANCIAL AID (Fall 2006, est.) 13,747 applied for aid; of those 90% were deemed to have need. 100% of undergraduates with need received aid; of those 35% had need fully met. ***Average percent of need met:*** 82% (excluding resources awarded to replace EFC). ***Average financial aid package:*** $14,329 (excluding resources awarded to replace EFC). 4% of all full-time undergraduates had no need and received non-need-based gift aid.

GIFT AID (NEED-BASED) ***Total amount:*** $127,649,396 (22% federal, 33% state, 41% institutional, 4% external sources). ***Receiving aid:*** Freshmen: 45% (2,111); All full-time undergraduates: 47% (11,557). ***Average award:*** Freshmen: $12,276; Undergraduates: $10,944. ***Scholarships, grants, and awards:*** Federal Pell, FSEOG, state, private, college/university gift aid from institutional funds, United Negro College Fund, Federal Nursing.

GIFT AID (NON-NEED-BASED) ***Total amount:*** $6,546,748 (6% federal, 7% state, 64% institutional, 23% external sources). ***Receiving aid:*** Freshmen: 1% (50); Undergraduates: 1% (126). ***Average award:*** Freshmen: $4054; Undergraduates: $3938. ***Scholarships, grants, and awards by category:*** *Academic Interests/Achievement:* general academic interests/achievements. *Special Achievements/Activities:* general special achievements/activities. ***ROTC:*** Army, Naval, Air Force.

LOANS ***Student loans:*** $54,957,273 (82% need-based, 18% non-need-based). 46% of past graduating class borrowed through all loan programs. *Average indebtedness per student:* $15,996. ***Average need-based loan:*** Freshmen: $5222;

Undergraduates: $5539. ***Parent loans:*** $20,171,595 (20% need-based, 80% non-need-based). ***Programs:*** FFEL (Subsidized and Unsubsidized Stafford, PLUS), Perkins, Federal Nursing, state, college/university.

WORK-STUDY ***Federal work-study:*** Total amount: $5,717,900; 2,735 jobs averaging $2127. ***State or other work-study/employment:*** Total amount: $673,836 (100% need-based). 600 part-time jobs averaging $1040.

ATHLETIC AWARDS Total amount: $7,194,718 (27% need-based, 73% non-need-based).

APPLYING FOR FINANCIAL AID ***Required financial aid form:*** FAFSA. ***Financial aid deadline:*** Continuous. ***Notification date:*** Continuous beginning 3/15.

CONTACT Ms. Yolanda Tan, Administrative Assistant, University of California, Los Angeles, Financial Aid Office, A-129 Murphy Hall, 405 Hilgard Avenue, Los Angeles, CA 90095-1435, 310-206-0404. *E-mail:* finaid@saonet.ucla.edu.

UNIVERSITY OF CALIFORNIA, RIVERSIDE

Riverside, CA

Tuition & fees (CA res): $6591 **Average undergraduate aid package: $13,933**

ABOUT THE INSTITUTION State-supported, coed. Awards: bachelor's, master's, and doctoral degrees. 59 undergraduate majors. Total enrollment: 16,875. Undergraduates: 14,792. Freshmen: 3,594. Federal methodology is used as a basis for awarding need-based institutional aid.

UNDERGRADUATE EXPENSES for 2006–07 ***Application fee:*** $60. ***Tuition, state resident:*** full-time $0. ***Tuition, nonresident:*** full-time $18,684. ***College room and board:*** $10,200. Room and board charges vary according to board plan and housing facility. ***Payment plan:*** Deferred payment.

FRESHMAN FINANCIAL AID (Fall 2006, est.) 2941 applied for aid; of those 78% were deemed to have need. 96% of freshmen with need received aid; of those 56% had need fully met. ***Average percent of need met:*** 90% (excluding resources awarded to replace EFC). ***Average financial aid package:*** $15,335 (excluding resources awarded to replace EFC). 2% of all full-time freshmen had no need and received non-need-based gift aid.

UNDERGRADUATE FINANCIAL AID (Fall 2006, est.) 10,511 applied for aid; of those 85% were deemed to have need. 97% of undergraduates with need received aid; of those 42% had need fully met. ***Average percent of need met:*** 83% (excluding resources awarded to replace EFC). ***Average financial aid package:*** $13,933 (excluding resources awarded to replace EFC). 1% of all full-time undergraduates had no need and received non-need-based gift aid.

GIFT AID (NEED-BASED) ***Total amount:*** $84,415,011 (25% federal, 36% state, 38% institutional, 1% external sources). ***Receiving aid:*** Freshmen: 55% (1,962); All full-time undergraduates: 55% (7,824). ***Average award:*** Freshmen: $12,306; Undergraduates: $10,678. ***Scholarships, grants, and awards:*** Federal Pell, FSEOG, state, private, college/university gift aid from institutional funds.

GIFT AID (NON-NEED-BASED) ***Total amount:*** $5,223,016 (4% federal, 2% state, 87% institutional, 7% external sources). ***Receiving aid:*** Freshmen: 1% (32); Undergraduates: 1% (97). ***Average award:*** Freshmen: $6466; Undergraduates: $6025. ***Scholarships, grants, and awards by category:*** *Academic Interests/Achievement:* agriculture, area/ethnic studies, biological sciences, business, education, engineering/technologies, English, general academic interests/achievements, humanities, mathematics, physical sciences, premedicine, social sciences. *Creative Arts/Performance:* art/fine arts, creative writing, dance, music, theater/drama. ***ROTC:*** Army cooperative, Air Force cooperative.

LOANS ***Student loans:*** $32,927,029 (82% need-based, 18% non-need-based). 62% of past graduating class borrowed through all loan programs. *Average indebtedness per student:* $14,965. ***Average need-based loan:*** Freshmen: $4007; Undergraduates: $5209. ***Parent loans:*** $18,303,606 (33% need-based, 67% non-need-based). ***Programs:*** Federal Direct (Subsidized and Unsubsidized Stafford, PLUS), Perkins, college/university.

WORK-STUDY ***Federal work-study:*** Total amount: $4,792,957; 2,040 jobs averaging $2321. ***State or other work-study/employment:*** Part-time jobs available.

ATHLETIC AWARDS Total amount: $1,918,832 (26% need-based, 74% non-need-based).

APPLYING FOR FINANCIAL AID ***Required financial aid forms:*** FAFSA, state aid form. ***Financial aid deadline:*** 3/2 (priority: 3/2). ***Notification date:*** Continuous beginning 3/1. Students must reply by 5/1 or within 3 weeks of notification.

CONTACT Ms. Sheryl Hayes, Director of Financial Aid, University of California, Riverside, 1156 Hinderaker Hall, Riverside, CA 92521-0209, 951-827-3879. *E-mail:* finaid@ucr.edu.

UNIVERSITY OF CALIFORNIA, SAN DIEGO

La Jolla, CA

Tuition & fees (CA res): $6685 **Average undergraduate aid package: $13,745**

ABOUT THE INSTITUTION State-supported, coed. Awards: bachelor's, master's, doctoral, and first professional degrees. 76 undergraduate majors. Total enrollment: 26,465. Undergraduates: 21,369. Freshmen: 4,589. Federal methodology is used as a basis for awarding need-based institutional aid.

UNDERGRADUATE EXPENSES for 2006–07 ***Application fee:*** $60. ***Tuition, state resident:*** full-time $0. ***Tuition, nonresident:*** full-time $18,684. Full-time tuition and fees vary according to location. ***College room and board:*** $9657. Room and board charges vary according to board plan and location. ***Payment plans:*** Installment, deferred payment.

FRESHMAN FINANCIAL AID (Fall 2006, est.) 3264 applied for aid; of those 69% were deemed to have need. 94% of freshmen with need received aid; of those 21% had need fully met. ***Average percent of need met:*** 82% (excluding resources awarded to replace EFC). ***Average financial aid package:*** $13,701 (excluding resources awarded to replace EFC). 2% of all full-time freshmen had no need and received non-need-based gift aid.

UNDERGRADUATE FINANCIAL AID (Fall 2006, est.) 13,009 applied for aid; of those 83% were deemed to have need. 95% of undergraduates with need received aid; of those 27% had need fully met. ***Average percent of need met:*** 83% (excluding resources awarded to replace EFC). ***Average financial aid package:*** $13,745 (excluding resources awarded to replace EFC). 3% of all full-time undergraduates had no need and received non-need-based gift aid.

GIFT AID (NEED-BASED) ***Total amount:*** $98,350,065 (27% federal, 38% state, 32% institutional, 3% external sources). ***Receiving aid:*** Freshmen: 45% (1,919); All full-time undergraduates: 46% (9,400). ***Average award:*** Freshmen: $10,233; Undergraduates: $10,034. ***Scholarships, grants, and awards:*** Federal Pell, FSEOG, state, private, college/university gift aid from institutional funds, Federal Academic Competitive Grant and Federal National Smart Grant.

GIFT AID (NON-NEED-BASED) ***Total amount:*** $6,961,829 (8% federal, 9% state, 66% institutional, 17% external sources). ***Receiving aid:*** Freshmen: 1% (31); Undergraduates: 81. ***Average award:*** Freshmen: $7275; Undergraduates: $6799. ***Scholarships, grants, and awards by category:*** *Academic Interests/Achievement:* 543 awards ($843,238 total): biological sciences, communication, computer science, education, engineering/technologies, general academic interests/achievements, mathematics, physical sciences, social sciences. *Creative Arts/Performance:* 9 awards ($10,700 total): cinema/film/broadcasting, dance, journalism/publications, performing arts, theater/drama. *Special Achievements/Activities:* 191 awards ($205,296 total): community service, general special achievements/activities, leadership. *Special Characteristics:* 163 awards ($228,631 total): ethnic background, first-generation college students, general special characteristics, handicapped students, members of minority groups, veterans' children. ***ROTC:*** Army cooperative.

LOANS ***Student loans:*** $45,406,298 (82% need-based, 18% non-need-based). 46% of past graduating class borrowed through all loan programs. *Average indebtedness per student:* $15,170. ***Average need-based loan:*** Freshmen: $4273; Undergraduates: $5072. ***Parent loans:*** $15,362,872 (23% need-based, 77% non-need-based). ***Programs:*** FFEL (Subsidized and Unsubsidized Stafford, PLUS), Perkins, college/university, alternative loans.

WORK-STUDY ***Federal work-study:*** Total amount: $7,942,942; 5,040 jobs averaging $1934.

APPLYING FOR FINANCIAL AID ***Required financial aid forms:*** FAFSA, state aid form. ***Financial aid deadline (priority):*** 3/2. ***Notification date:*** Continuous beginning 3/15.

CONTACT Mr. Vincent De Anda, Director of Financial Aid Office, University of California, San Diego, 9500 Gilman Drive-0013, La Jolla, CA 92093-0013, 858-534-3800. *Fax:* 858-534-5459. *E-mail:* vdeanda@ucsd.edu.

UNIVERSITY OF CALIFORNIA, SANTA BARBARA

Santa Barbara, CA

Tuition & fees (CA res): $7277 **Average undergraduate aid package: $13,437**

ABOUT THE INSTITUTION State-supported, coed. Awards: bachelor's, master's, and doctoral degrees and first professional certificates. 71 undergraduate majors.

Total enrollment: 21,062. Undergraduates: 18,212. Freshmen: 4,096. Both federal and institutional methodology are used as a basis for awarding need-based institutional aid.

UNDERGRADUATE EXPENSES for 2006–07 ***Application fee:*** $60. ***Tuition, state resident:*** full-time $0. ***Tuition, nonresident:*** full-time $18,684. ***College room and board:*** $11,178; ***Room only:*** $8798.

FRESHMAN FINANCIAL AID (Fall 2005) 2831 applied for aid; of those 68% were deemed to have need. 90% of freshmen with need received aid; of those 46% had need fully met. ***Average percent of need met:*** 82% (excluding resources awarded to replace EFC). ***Average financial aid package:*** $14,055 (excluding resources awarded to replace EFC). 1% of all full-time freshmen had no need and received non-need-based gift aid.

UNDERGRADUATE FINANCIAL AID (Fall 2005) 10,521 applied for aid; of those 78% were deemed to have need. 94% of undergraduates with need received aid; of those 39% had need fully met. ***Average percent of need met:*** 82% (excluding resources awarded to replace EFC). ***Average financial aid package:*** $13,437 (excluding resources awarded to replace EFC). 2% of all full-time undergraduates had no need and received non-need-based gift aid.

GIFT AID (NEED-BASED) ***Total amount:*** $68,221,587 (20% federal, 41% state, 37% institutional, 2% external sources). ***Receiving aid:*** Freshmen: 40% (1,537); All full-time undergraduates: 38% (6,560). ***Average award:*** Freshmen: $11,328; Undergraduates: $10,220. ***Scholarships, grants, and awards:*** Federal Pell, FSEOG, state, private, college/university gift aid from institutional funds, endowed scholarships.

GIFT AID (NON-NEED-BASED) ***Total amount:*** $3,705,721 (4% federal, 24% state, 55% institutional, 17% external sources). ***Receiving aid:*** Freshmen: 1% (36); Undergraduates: 77. ***Average award:*** Freshmen: $7109; Undergraduates: $5771. ***Scholarships, grants, and awards by category:*** *Academic Interests/Achievement:* general academic interests/achievements. ***ROTC:*** Army.

LOANS ***Student loans:*** $37,117,624 (79% need-based, 21% non-need-based). ***Average need-based loan:*** Freshmen: $5515; Undergraduates: $5807. ***Parent loans:*** $26,743,168 (22% need-based, 78% non-need-based). ***Programs:*** Federal Direct (Subsidized and Unsubsidized Stafford, PLUS), Perkins.

WORK-STUDY ***Federal work-study:*** Total amount: $2,295,869; jobs available.

ATHLETIC AWARDS Total amount: $2,287,023 (20% need-based, 80% non-need-based).

APPLYING FOR FINANCIAL AID ***Required financial aid form:*** FAFSA. ***Financial aid deadline (priority):*** 3/2. ***Notification date:*** Continuous beginning 3/15. Students must reply by 8/15.

CONTACT Office of Financial Aid, University of California, Santa Barbara, 2103 SAASB (Student Affairs/Administrative Services Building), Santa Barbara, CA 93106-3180, 805-893-2432. *Fax:* 805-893-8793.

UNIVERSITY OF CALIFORNIA, SANTA CRUZ

Santa Cruz, CA

Tuition & fees (CA res): $7962 **Average undergraduate aid package: $14,422**

ABOUT THE INSTITUTION State-supported, coed. Awards: bachelor's, master's, and doctoral degrees and post-bachelor's certificates. 76 undergraduate majors. Total enrollment: 15,364. Undergraduates: 13,961. Freshmen: 3,350. Both federal and institutional methodology are used as a basis for awarding need-based institutional aid.

UNDERGRADUATE EXPENSES for 2006–07 ***Application fee:*** $60. ***Tuition, state resident:*** full-time $0. ***Tuition, nonresident:*** full-time $18,168. ***College room and board:*** $11,805. Room and board charges vary according to board plan and housing facility. ***Payment plans:*** Installment, deferred payment.

FRESHMAN FINANCIAL AID (Fall 2006, est.) 2464 applied for aid; of those 67% were deemed to have need. 93% of freshmen with need received aid; of those 49% had need fully met. ***Average percent of need met:*** 86% (excluding resources awarded to replace EFC). ***Average financial aid package:*** $14,955 (excluding resources awarded to replace EFC). 2% of all full-time freshmen had no need and received non-need-based gift aid.

UNDERGRADUATE FINANCIAL AID (Fall 2006, est.) 8,470 applied for aid; of those 77% were deemed to have need. 95% of undergraduates with need received aid; of those 48% had need fully met. ***Average percent of need met:*** 87% (excluding resources awarded to replace EFC). ***Average financial aid package:*** $14,422 (excluding resources awarded to replace EFC). 2% of all full-time undergraduates had no need and received non-need-based gift aid.

GIFT AID (NEED-BASED) ***Total amount:*** $57,966,351 (21% federal, 33% state, 44% institutional, 2% external sources). ***Receiving aid:*** Freshmen: 40% (1,326); All full-time undergraduates: 40% (5,384). ***Average award:*** Freshmen: $11,525; Undergraduates: $10,582. ***Scholarships, grants, and awards:*** Federal Pell, FSEOG, state, private.

GIFT AID (NON-NEED-BASED) ***Total amount:*** $3,784,074 (2% federal, 9% state, 65% institutional, 24% external sources). ***Receiving aid:*** Freshmen: 14; Undergraduates: 1% (71). ***Average award:*** Freshmen: $8117; Undergraduates: $7603. ***Scholarships, grants, and awards by category:*** *Creative Arts/Performance:* music. ***Tuition waivers:*** Full or partial for employees or children of employees. ***ROTC:*** Army cooperative, Naval cooperative, Air Force cooperative.

LOANS ***Student loans:*** $30,477,218 (76% need-based, 24% non-need-based). 51% of past graduating class borrowed through all loan programs. *Average indebtedness per student:* $14,381. ***Average need-based loan:*** Freshmen: $4746; Undergraduates: $5168. ***Parent loans:*** $18,842,395 (14% need-based, 86% non-need-based). ***Programs:*** Federal Direct (Subsidized and Unsubsidized Stafford, PLUS), Perkins.

WORK-STUDY ***Federal work-study:*** Total amount: $7,226,591.

APPLYING FOR FINANCIAL AID ***Required financial aid forms:*** FAFSA, state aid form. ***Financial aid deadline:*** 6/1 (priority: 3/17). ***Notification date:*** Continuous beginning 4/1. Students must reply within 4 weeks of notification.

CONTACT Ms. Ann Draper, Director of Financial Aid, University of California, Santa Cruz, 201 Hahn Student Services Building, Santa Cruz, CA 95064, 831-459-4358. *Fax:* 831-459-4631. *E-mail:* ann@ucsc.edu.

UNIVERSITY OF CENTRAL ARKANSAS

Conway, AR

CONTACT Cheryl Lyons, Director of Student Aid, University of Central Arkansas, 201 Donaghey Avenue, Conway, AR 72035, 501-450-3140 or toll-free 800-243-8245 (in-state). *Fax:* 501-450-5168. *E-mail:* clyons@uca.edu.

UNIVERSITY OF CENTRAL FLORIDA

Orlando, FL

Tuition & fees (FL res): $3492 **Average undergraduate aid package: $6068**

ABOUT THE INSTITUTION State-supported, coed. Awards: associate, bachelor's, master's, and doctoral degrees and post-bachelor's certificates. 81 undergraduate majors. Total enrollment: 46,719. Undergraduates: 39,545. Freshmen: 6,666. Federal methodology is used as a basis for awarding need-based institutional aid.

UNDERGRADUATE EXPENSES for 2006–07 ***Application fee:*** $30. ***Tuition, state resident:*** full-time $3492; part-time $116.40 per credit. ***Tuition, nonresident:*** full-time $17,017; part-time $567.54 per credit. Full-time tuition and fees vary according to course load. Part-time tuition and fees vary according to course load. ***College room and board:*** $8000; ***Room only:*** $4600. Room and board charges vary according to board plan and housing facility. ***Payment plans:*** Tuition prepayment, deferred payment.

FRESHMAN FINANCIAL AID (Fall 2005) 4123 applied for aid; of those 78% were deemed to have need. 98% of freshmen with need received aid; of those 21% had need fully met. ***Average percent of need met:*** 53% (excluding resources awarded to replace EFC). ***Average financial aid package:*** $5374 (excluding resources awarded to replace EFC). 6% of all full-time freshmen had no need and received non-need-based gift aid.

UNDERGRADUATE FINANCIAL AID (Fall 2005) 17,169 applied for aid; of those 87% were deemed to have need. 95% of undergraduates with need received aid; of those 13% had need fully met. ***Average percent of need met:*** 54% (excluding resources awarded to replace EFC). ***Average financial aid package:*** $6068 (excluding resources awarded to replace EFC). 3% of all full-time undergraduates had no need and received non-need-based gift aid.

GIFT AID (NEED-BASED) ***Total amount:*** $31,847,118 (67% federal, 18% state, 15% institutional). ***Receiving aid:*** Freshmen: 21% (1,255); All full-time undergraduates: 26% (7,550). ***Average award:*** Freshmen: $3398; Undergraduates: $3425. ***Scholarships, grants, and awards:*** Federal Pell, FSEOG, state, private, college/university gift aid from institutional funds.

GIFT AID (NON-NEED-BASED) ***Total amount:*** $55,650,697 (80% state, 13% institutional, 7% external sources). ***Receiving aid:*** Freshmen: 48% (2,912); Undergraduates: 33% (9,323). ***Average award:*** Freshmen: $2101; Undergraduates: $2183. ***Scholarships, grants, and awards by category:*** *Academic Interests/*

Achievement: general academic interests/achievements. *Creative Arts/Performance:* cinema/film/broadcasting, music, theater/drama. *Special Achievements/Activities:* general special achievements/activities, leadership. *Special Characteristics:* first-generation college students. ***Tuition waivers:*** Full or partial for employees or children of employees, senior citizens. ***ROTC:*** Army, Air Force.

LOANS ***Student loans:*** $70,762,325 (57% need-based, 43% non-need-based). 42% of past graduating class borrowed through all loan programs. *Average indebtedness per student:* $12,876. ***Average need-based loan:*** Freshmen: $2496; Undergraduates: $4245. ***Parent loans:*** $6,280,665 (100% non-need-based). ***Programs:*** FFEL (Subsidized and Unsubsidized Stafford, PLUS), Perkins.

WORK-STUDY ***Federal work-study:*** Total amount: $1,212,594; jobs available. ***State or other work-study/employment:*** Part-time jobs available.

ATHLETIC AWARDS Total amount: $1,879,267 (100% non-need-based).

APPLYING FOR FINANCIAL AID ***Required financial aid form:*** FAFSA. ***Financial aid deadline:*** 6/30 (priority: 3/1). ***Notification date:*** Continuous beginning 3/15. Students must reply within 3 weeks of notification.

CONTACT Ms. Lisa Minnick, Associate Director, Student Financial Assistance, University of Central Florida, 4000 Central Florida Boulevard, Orlando, FL 32816-0113, 407-823-2827. *Fax:* 407-823-5241. *E-mail:* lminnick@mail.ucf.edu.

UNIVERSITY OF CENTRAL MISSOURI

Warrensburg, MO

Tuition & fees (MO res): $5835 Average undergraduate aid package: $7341

ABOUT THE INSTITUTION State-supported, coed. Awards: associate, bachelor's, and master's degrees and post-bachelor's and post-master's certificates. 72 undergraduate majors. Total enrollment: 10,711. Undergraduates: 8,970. Freshmen: 1,592. Federal methodology is used as a basis for awarding need-based institutional aid.

UNDERGRADUATE EXPENSES for 2006–07 ***Application fee:*** $30. ***Tuition, state resident:*** full-time $5835; part-time $195.50 per credit. ***Tuition, nonresident:*** full-time $11,250; part-time $375 per credit. ***Required fees:*** $14 per credit. Full-time tuition and fees vary according to course load and location. ***College room and board:*** $5109; ***Room only:*** $4606. Room and board charges vary according to board plan and housing facility. ***Payment plans:*** Installment, deferred payment.

FRESHMAN FINANCIAL AID (Fall 2005) 1241 applied for aid; of those 64% were deemed to have need. 97% of freshmen with need received aid; of those 27% had need fully met. ***Average percent of need met:*** 72% (excluding resources awarded to replace EFC). ***Average financial aid package:*** $6006 (excluding resources awarded to replace EFC). 34% of all full-time freshmen had no need and received non-need-based gift aid.

UNDERGRADUATE FINANCIAL AID (Fall 2005) 6,107 applied for aid; of those 73% were deemed to have need. 98% of undergraduates with need received aid; of those 38% had need fully met. ***Average percent of need met:*** 90% (excluding resources awarded to replace EFC). ***Average financial aid package:*** $7341 (excluding resources awarded to replace EFC). 30% of all full-time undergraduates had no need and received non-need-based gift aid.

GIFT AID (NEED-BASED) ***Total amount:*** $8,174,669 (95% federal, 5% state). ***Receiving aid:*** Freshmen: 27% (400); All full-time undergraduates: 36% (2,575). ***Average award:*** Freshmen: $3183; Undergraduates: $3200. ***Scholarships, grants, and awards:*** Federal Pell, FSEOG, state, private, college/university gift aid from institutional funds.

GIFT AID (NON-NEED-BASED) ***Total amount:*** $12,048,621 (5% federal, 8% state, 49% institutional, 38% external sources). ***Receiving aid:*** Freshmen: 36% (538); Undergraduates: 32% (2,298). ***Average award:*** Freshmen: $3269; Undergraduates: $3230. ***Scholarships, grants, and awards by category:*** *Academic Interests/Achievement:* 455 awards ($185,000 total): agriculture, area/ethnic studies, biological sciences, business, communication, computer science, education, engineering/technologies, English, foreign languages, general academic interests/achievements, health fields, home economics, humanities, library science, mathematics, military science, physical sciences, premedicine, religion/biblical studies, social sciences. *Creative Arts/Performance:* 705 awards ($230,000 total): applied art and design, art/fine arts, cinema/film/broadcasting, creative writing, debating, journalism/publications, music, performing arts, theater/drama. *Special Achievements/Activities:* 60 awards ($40,000 total): cheerleading/drum major, leadership. *Special Characteristics:* 546 awards ($536,450 total): adult students, children and siblings of alumni, children of faculty/staff, ethnic background, members of minority groups, out-of-state students, previous college experience. ***Tuition waivers:*** Full or partial for children of alumni, employees or children of employees, senior citizens. ***ROTC:*** Army, Air Force cooperative.

LOANS ***Student loans:*** $27,668,328 (52% need-based, 48% non-need-based). 65% of past graduating class borrowed through all loan programs. *Average indebtedness per student:* $9576. ***Average need-based loan:*** Freshmen: $2261; Undergraduates: $4084. ***Parent loans:*** $9,625,001 (100% non-need-based). ***Programs:*** Federal Direct (Subsidized and Unsubsidized Stafford, PLUS), Perkins, state.

WORK-STUDY ***Federal work-study:*** Total amount: $367,061; 353 jobs averaging $991. ***State or other work-study/employment:*** 1,042 part-time jobs averaging $1694.

ATHLETIC AWARDS Total amount: $1,849,940 (100% non-need-based).

APPLYING FOR FINANCIAL AID ***Required financial aid form:*** FAFSA. ***Financial aid deadline (priority):*** 4/1. ***Notification date:*** Continuous beginning 3/1. Students must reply within 3 weeks of notification.

CONTACT Mr. Phil Shreves, Director of Student Financial Assistance, University of Central Missouri, Office of Financial Aid, Administration Building 104, Warrensburg, MO 64093, 660-543-4040 or toll-free 800-729-2678 (in-state). *Fax:* 660-543-8080. *E-mail:* fedaid@ucmovmb.edu.

UNIVERSITY OF CENTRAL OKLAHOMA

Edmond, OK

Tuition & fees (OK res): $3539 Average undergraduate aid package: $6005

ABOUT THE INSTITUTION State-supported, coed. Awards: bachelor's and master's degrees. 86 undergraduate majors. Total enrollment: 15,723. Undergraduates: 14,429. Freshmen: 2,193. Federal methodology is used as a basis for awarding need-based institutional aid.

UNDERGRADUATE EXPENSES for 2006–07 ***Application fee:*** $25. ***Tuition, state resident:*** full-time $3027; part-time $100.90 per semester hour. ***Tuition, nonresident:*** full-time $8412; part-time $280.40 per semester hour. ***Required fees:*** full-time $512; $17.05 per semester hour. Full-time tuition and fees vary according to course load, degree level, program, and student level. Part-time tuition and fees vary according to course load, degree level, program, and student level. ***College room and board:*** $4763; ***Room only:*** $2383. Room and board charges vary according to board plan and housing facility. ***Payment plans:*** Installment, deferred payment.

FRESHMAN FINANCIAL AID (Fall 2005) 1246 applied for aid; of those 72% were deemed to have need. 89% of freshmen with need received aid; of those 10% had need fully met. ***Average percent of need met:*** 64% (excluding resources awarded to replace EFC). ***Average financial aid package:*** $5121 (excluding resources awarded to replace EFC). 10% of all full-time freshmen had no need and received non-need-based gift aid.

UNDERGRADUATE FINANCIAL AID (Fall 2005) 6,412 applied for aid; of those 80% were deemed to have need. 93% of undergraduates with need received aid; of those 10% had need fully met. ***Average percent of need met:*** 67% (excluding resources awarded to replace EFC). ***Average financial aid package:*** $6005 (excluding resources awarded to replace EFC). 7% of all full-time undergraduates had no need and received non-need-based gift aid.

GIFT AID (NEED-BASED) ***Total amount:*** $15,280,540 (65% federal, 24% state, 2% institutional, 9% external sources). ***Receiving aid:*** Freshmen: 41% (756); All full-time undergraduates: 43% (4,515). ***Average award:*** Freshmen: $5254; Undergraduates: $6150. ***Scholarships, grants, and awards:*** Federal Pell, FSEOG, state, private, college/university gift aid from institutional funds.

GIFT AID (NON-NEED-BASED) ***Total amount:*** $2,316,652 (35% state, 10% institutional, 55% external sources). ***Receiving aid:*** Freshmen: 2% (38); Undergraduates: 2% (225). ***Average award:*** Freshmen: $2319; Undergraduates: $2169. ***Scholarships, grants, and awards by category:*** *Academic Interests/Achievement:* biological sciences, business, computer science, education, foreign languages, general academic interests/achievements, health fields, home economics, mathematics, military science, physical sciences, social sciences. *Creative Arts/Performance:* applied art and design, art/fine arts, journalism/publications, music, theater/drama. *Special Achievements/Activities:* general special achievements/activities, leadership. *Special Characteristics:* ethnic background, members of minority groups. ***Tuition waivers:*** Full or partial for employees or children of employees. ***ROTC:*** Army.

LOANS ***Student loans:*** $31,076,969 (87% need-based, 13% non-need-based). 50% of past graduating class borrowed through all loan programs. *Average indebtedness per student:* $16,211. ***Average need-based loan:*** Freshmen: $2241;

Undergraduates: $3727. ***Parent loans:*** $1,382,538 (54% need-based, 46% non-need-based). ***Programs:*** FFEL (Subsidized and Unsubsidized Stafford, PLUS), Perkins.

WORK-STUDY ***Federal work-study:*** Total amount: $428,006; 199 jobs averaging $1947.

ATHLETIC AWARDS Total amount: $562,425 (58% need-based, 42% non-need-based).

APPLYING FOR FINANCIAL AID ***Required financial aid forms:*** FAFSA, institution's own form. ***Financial aid deadline (priority):*** 5/31. ***Notification date:*** Continuous beginning 5/1. Students must reply by 6/30 or within 4 weeks of notification.

CONTACT Ms. Becky Garrett, Assistant Director, Technical Services, University of Central Oklahoma, 100 North University Drive, Edmond, OK 73034-5209, 405-974-3334 or toll-free 800-254-4215. *Fax:* 405-340-7658. *E-mail:* bgarrett@ucok.edu.

UNIVERSITY OF CHARLESTON

Charleston, WV

Tuition & fees: $21,000 **Average undergraduate aid package: $18,300**

ABOUT THE INSTITUTION Independent, coed. Awards: associate, bachelor's, and master's degrees. 27 undergraduate majors. Total enrollment: 1,202. Undergraduates: 1,074. Freshmen: 315. Federal methodology is used as a basis for awarding need-based institutional aid.

UNDERGRADUATE EXPENSES for 2006–07 ***Application fee:*** $25. ***Comprehensive fee:*** $28,600 includes full-time tuition ($21,000) and room and board ($7600). ***College room only:*** $4175. Room and board charges vary according to board plan and housing facility. ***Part-time tuition:*** $380 per credit. ***Part-time fees:*** $75 per term. Part-time tuition and fees vary according to program. ***Payment plan:*** Installment.

FRESHMAN FINANCIAL AID (Fall 2006, est.) 284 applied for aid; of those 84% were deemed to have need. 100% of freshmen with need received aid; of those 39% had need fully met. ***Average percent of need met:*** 85% (excluding resources awarded to replace EFC). ***Average financial aid package:*** $17,500 (excluding resources awarded to replace EFC). 10% of all full-time freshmen had no need and received non-need-based gift aid.

UNDERGRADUATE FINANCIAL AID (Fall 2006, est.) 873 applied for aid; of those 90% were deemed to have need. 100% of undergraduates with need received aid; of those 42% had need fully met. ***Average percent of need met:*** 79% (excluding resources awarded to replace EFC). ***Average financial aid package:*** $18,300 (excluding resources awarded to replace EFC). 15% of all full-time undergraduates had no need and received non-need-based gift aid.

GIFT AID (NEED-BASED) ***Total amount:*** $3,410,088 (35% federal, 19% state, 44% institutional, 2% external sources). ***Receiving aid:*** Freshmen: 35% (107); All full-time undergraduates: 51% (511). ***Average award:*** Freshmen: $8550; Undergraduates: $6975. ***Scholarships, grants, and awards:*** Federal Pell, FSEOG, state, private, college/university gift aid from institutional funds, Council of Independent Colleges Tuition Exchange grants, Tuition Exchange Inc. grants.

GIFT AID (NON-NEED-BASED) ***Total amount:*** $8,931,724 (2% federal, 8% state, 87% institutional, 3% external sources). ***Receiving aid:*** Freshmen: 76% (230); Undergraduates: 61% (610). ***Average award:*** Freshmen: $11,797; Undergraduates: $14,338. ***Scholarships, grants, and awards by category:*** *Academic Interests/Achievement:* general academic interests/achievements, military science. *Creative Arts/Performance:* 30 awards ($30,000 total): music. *Special Achievements/Activities:* cheerleading/drum major, community service, general special achievements/activities, leadership. *Special Characteristics:* children and siblings of alumni, children of educators, children of faculty/staff, international students, local/state students. ***Tuition waivers:*** Full or partial for employees or children of employees, senior citizens. ***ROTC:*** Army.

LOANS ***Student loans:*** $5,765,769 (45% need-based, 55% non-need-based). 82% of past graduating class borrowed through all loan programs. *Average indebtedness per student:* $24,310. ***Average need-based loan:*** Freshmen: $3850; Undergraduates: $6195. ***Parent loans:*** $926,100 (100% non-need-based). ***Programs:*** FFEL (Subsidized and Unsubsidized Stafford, PLUS), Perkins, Federal Nursing, alternative loans.

WORK-STUDY ***Federal work-study:*** Total amount: $125,000; jobs available (averaging $975). ***State or other work-study/employment:*** Part-time jobs available (averaging $850).

ATHLETIC AWARDS Total amount: $2,268,889 (79% need-based, 21% non-need-based).

APPLYING FOR FINANCIAL AID ***Required financial aid forms:*** FAFSA, institution's own form, state aid form. ***Financial aid deadline (priority):*** 3/1. ***Notification date:*** Continuous beginning 3/15. Students must reply by 5/1 or within 4 weeks of notification.

CONTACT Ms. Janet M. Ruge, Director of Financial Aid, University of Charleston, 2300 MacCorkle Avenue SE, Charleston, WV 25304-1099, 304-357-4759 or toll-free 800-995-GOUC. *Fax:* 304-357-4769. *E-mail:* janetruge@ucwv.edu.

UNIVERSITY OF CHICAGO

Chicago, IL

CONTACT Office of College Aid, University of Chicago, 1116 East 59th Street, Room 203, Chicago, IL 60637, 773-702-8666. *Fax:* 773-702-5846.

UNIVERSITY OF CINCINNATI

Cincinnati, OH

ABOUT THE INSTITUTION State-supported, coed. Awards: associate, bachelor's, master's, doctoral, and first professional degrees and post-bachelor's certificates. 142 undergraduate majors. Total enrollment: 27,932. Undergraduates: 19,512. Freshmen: 3,914.

GIFT AID (NEED-BASED) ***Scholarships, grants, and awards:*** Federal Pell, FSEOG, state, private, college/university gift aid from institutional funds, Federal Nursing.

GIFT AID (NON-NEED-BASED) ***Scholarships, grants, and awards by category:*** *Academic Interests/Achievement:* architecture, area/ethnic studies, biological sciences, business, communication, computer science, education, engineering/technologies, English, foreign languages, general academic interests/achievements, health fields, humanities, mathematics, military science, physical sciences, premedicine, social sciences. *Creative Arts/Performance:* applied art and design, art/fine arts, music. *Special Achievements/Activities:* general special achievements/activities. *Special Characteristics:* children of faculty/staff, members of minority groups, out-of-state students.

LOANS ***Programs:*** Federal Direct (Subsidized and Unsubsidized Stafford, PLUS), FFEL (Subsidized and Unsubsidized Stafford, PLUS), Perkins, Federal Nursing, state, college/university.

WORK-STUDY ***Federal work-study:*** Total amount: $3,714,943; jobs available.

APPLYING FOR FINANCIAL AID ***Required financial aid form:*** FAFSA.

CONTACT Mrs. Martha Geiger, Student Financial Aid Associate Director, University of Cincinnati, 2624 Clifton Avenue, Cincinnati, OH 45221, 513-556-2441. *Fax:* 513-556-9171. *E-mail:* martha.geiger@uc.edu.

UNIVERSITY OF COLORADO AT BOULDER

Boulder, CO

Tuition & fees (CO res): $5643 **Average undergraduate aid package: $10,362**

ABOUT THE INSTITUTION State-supported, coed. Awards: bachelor's, master's, doctoral, and first professional degrees. 60 undergraduate majors. Total enrollment: 31,399. Undergraduates: 26,163. Freshmen: 5,645. Federal methodology is used as a basis for awarding need-based institutional aid.

UNDERGRADUATE EXPENSES for 2006–07 ***Application fee:*** $50. ***Tuition, state resident:*** full-time $4554. ***Tuition, nonresident:*** full-time $22,450. Full-time tuition and fees vary according to program. Part-time tuition and fees vary according to course load and program. ***College room and board:*** $8300. Room and board charges vary according to board plan, location, and student level. ***Payment plan:*** Deferred payment.

FRESHMAN FINANCIAL AID (Fall 2006, est.) 3736 applied for aid; of those 61% were deemed to have need. 97% of freshmen with need received aid; of those 80% had need fully met. ***Average percent of need met:*** 94% (excluding resources awarded to replace EFC). ***Average financial aid package:*** $8458 (excluding resources awarded to replace EFC). 22% of all full-time freshmen had no need and received non-need-based gift aid.

UNDERGRADUATE FINANCIAL AID (Fall 2006, est.) 14,134 applied for aid; of those 58% were deemed to have need. 97% of undergraduates with need received aid; of those 70% had need fully met. ***Average percent of need met:*** 92% (excluding resources awarded to replace EFC). ***Average financial aid package:*** $10,362 (excluding resources awarded to replace EFC). 17% of all full-time undergraduates had no need and received non-need-based gift aid.

GIFT AID (NEED-BASED) ***Total amount:*** $38,248,720 (33% federal, 14% state, 47% institutional, 6% external sources). ***Receiving aid:*** Freshmen: 22% (1,233); All full-time undergraduates: 21% (4,918). ***Average award:*** Freshmen: $7686; Undergraduates: $7177. ***Scholarships, grants, and awards:*** Federal Pell, FSEOG, state, private, college/university gift aid from institutional funds.

GIFT AID (NON-NEED-BASED) ***Total amount:*** $11,097,441 (18% federal, 1% state, 61% institutional, 20% external sources). ***Receiving aid:*** Freshmen: 2% (93); Undergraduates: 1% (189). ***Average award:*** Freshmen: $5338; Undergraduates: $5969. ***Scholarships, grants, and awards by category:*** *Academic Interests/Achievement:* architecture, area/ethnic studies, biological sciences, business, communication, computer science, education, engineering/technologies, English, foreign languages, general academic interests/achievements, health fields, humanities, international studies, mathematics, military science, physical sciences, premedicine, social sciences. *Creative Arts/Performance:* art/fine arts, cinema/film/broadcasting, creative writing, dance, journalism/publications, music, performing arts, theater/drama. *Special Achievements/Activities:* community service, general special achievements/activities, leadership. *Special Characteristics:* first-generation college students, general special characteristics, local/state students. ***Tuition waivers:*** Full or partial for senior citizens. ***ROTC:*** Army, Naval, Air Force.

LOANS ***Student loans:*** $58,459,549 (65% need-based, 35% non-need-based). 40% of past graduating class borrowed through all loan programs. *Average indebtedness per student:* $17,141. ***Average need-based loan:*** Freshmen: $3468; Undergraduates: $4947. ***Parent loans:*** $105,311,911 (43% need-based, 57% non-need-based). ***Programs:*** Federal Direct (Subsidized and Unsubsidized Stafford, PLUS), Perkins, college/university, private lenders.

WORK-STUDY ***Federal work-study:*** Total amount: $1,255,567; 1,184 jobs averaging $1757. ***State or other work-study/employment:*** Total amount: $1,796,289 (96% need-based, 4% non-need-based). 931 part-time jobs averaging $2045.

ATHLETIC AWARDS Total amount: $4,793,428 (33% need-based, 67% non-need-based).

APPLYING FOR FINANCIAL AID ***Required financial aid forms:*** FAFSA, income tax form(s). ***Financial aid deadline (priority):*** 4/1. ***Notification date:*** Continuous beginning 2/1. Students must reply within 3 weeks of notification.

CONTACT Gwen E. Pomper, Director of Financial Aid, University of Colorado at Boulder, University Campus Box 77, Boulder, CO 80309, 303-492-8223. *Fax:* 303-492-0838. *E-mail:* finaid@colorado.edu.

UNIVERSITY OF COLORADO AT COLORADO SPRINGS

Colorado Springs, CO

ABOUT THE INSTITUTION State-supported, coed. Awards: bachelor's, master's, and doctoral degrees and post-bachelor's certificates. 34 undergraduate majors. Total enrollment: 8,583. Undergraduates: 6,296. Freshmen: 755.

GIFT AID (NEED-BASED) ***Scholarships, grants, and awards:*** Federal Pell, FSEOG, state, private, college/university gift aid from institutional funds.

GIFT AID (NON-NEED-BASED) ***Scholarships, grants, and awards by category:*** *Academic Interests/Achievement:* biological sciences, business, computer science, education, engineering/technologies, English, general academic interests/achievements, health fields, mathematics, military science, physical sciences, premedicine. *Special Achievements/Activities:* community service, leadership. *Special Characteristics:* children and siblings of alumni, ethnic background, first-generation college students, general special characteristics, handicapped students, out-of-state students.

LOANS ***Programs:*** FFEL (Subsidized and Unsubsidized Stafford, PLUS), Perkins, college/university.

WORK-STUDY ***Federal work-study:*** Total amount: $257,554; 72 jobs averaging $3577. ***State or other work-study/employment:*** Total amount: $787,747 (84% need-based, 16% non-need-based). 220 part-time jobs averaging $3580.

APPLYING FOR FINANCIAL AID ***Required financial aid form:*** FAFSA.

CONTACT Ms. Lee Ingalls-Noble, Director of Financial Aid, University of Colorado at Colorado Springs, 1420 Austin Bluffs Parkway, Colorado Springs, CO 80933-7150, 719-262-3466 or toll-free 800-990-8227 Ext. 3383.

UNIVERSITY OF COLORADO AT DENVER AND HEALTH SCIENCES CENTER–DOWNTOWN DENVER CAMPUS

Denver, CO

ABOUT THE INSTITUTION State-supported, coed. Awards: bachelor's, master's, doctoral, and first professional degrees and post-master's certificates. 30 undergraduate majors. Total enrollment: 19,766. Undergraduates: 10,387. Freshmen: 808.

GIFT AID (NEED-BASED) ***Scholarships, grants, and awards:*** Federal Pell, FSEOG, state, private, college/university gift aid from institutional funds.

GIFT AID (NON-NEED-BASED) ***Scholarships, grants, and awards by category:*** *Academic Interests/Achievement:* business, engineering/technologies, general academic interests/achievements. *Creative Arts/Performance:* general creative arts/performance. *Special Achievements/Activities:* leadership. *Special Characteristics:* children of faculty/staff, first-generation college students, general special characteristics, handicapped students, members of minority groups.

LOANS ***Programs:*** FFEL (Subsidized and Unsubsidized Stafford, PLUS), Perkins, Federal Nursing, alternative loans.

APPLYING FOR FINANCIAL AID ***Required financial aid forms:*** FAFSA, institution's own form.

CONTACT Patrick McTee, Director of Financial Aid, University of Colorado at Denver and Health Sciences Center–Downtown Denver Campus, PO Box 173364, Denver, CO 80217-3364, 303-556-2886. *Fax:* 303-556-2325. *E-mail:* patrick.mctee@cudenver.edu.

UNIVERSITY OF CONNECTICUT

Storrs, CT

Tuition & fees (CT res): $8842 **Average undergraduate aid package: $10,507**

ABOUT THE INSTITUTION State-supported, coed. Awards: associate, bachelor's, master's, doctoral, and first professional degrees and post-bachelor's and post-master's certificates. 96 undergraduate majors. Total enrollment: 23,557. Undergraduates: 16,347. Freshmen: 3,241. Federal methodology is used as a basis for awarding need-based institutional aid.

UNDERGRADUATE EXPENSES for 2007–08 ***Application fee:*** $70. ***Tuition, state resident:*** full-time $6816; part-time $284 per credit. ***Tuition, nonresident:*** full-time $20,760; part-time $865 per credit. ***College room and board:*** $8850; ***Room only:*** $4698.

FRESHMAN FINANCIAL AID (Fall 2006, est.) 2577 applied for aid; of those 63% were deemed to have need. 98% of freshmen with need received aid; of those 19% had need fully met. ***Average percent of need met:*** 72% (excluding resources awarded to replace EFC). ***Average financial aid package:*** $10,740 (excluding resources awarded to replace EFC). 9% of all full-time freshmen had no need and received non-need-based gift aid.

UNDERGRADUATE FINANCIAL AID (Fall 2006, est.) 10,599 applied for aid; of those 72% were deemed to have need. 97% of undergraduates with need received aid; of those 22% had need fully met. ***Average percent of need met:*** 72% (excluding resources awarded to replace EFC). ***Average financial aid package:*** $10,507 (excluding resources awarded to replace EFC). 7% of all full-time undergraduates had no need and received non-need-based gift aid.

GIFT AID (NEED-BASED) ***Total amount:*** $44,974,891 (18% federal, 19% state, 59% institutional, 4% external sources). ***Receiving aid:*** Freshmen: 39% (1,275); All full-time undergraduates: 37% (5,693). ***Average award:*** Freshmen: $6805; Undergraduates: $6443. ***Scholarships, grants, and awards:*** Federal Pell, FSEOG, state, private, college/university gift aid from institutional funds.

GIFT AID (NON-NEED-BASED) ***Total amount:*** $8,721,392 (78% institutional, 22% external sources). ***Receiving aid:*** Freshmen: 35% (1,116); Undergraduates: 22% (3,440). ***Average award:*** Freshmen: $5530; Undergraduates: $5061. ***Scholarships, grants, and awards by category:*** *Academic Interests/Achievement:* 2,534 awards ($13,462,303 total): agriculture, biological sciences, business, computer science, education, engineering/technologies, English, foreign languages, general academic interests/achievements, health fields, humanities, international studies, mathematics, physical sciences, premedicine, religion/biblical studies, social sciences. *Creative Arts/Performance:* 101 awards ($194,702 total): art/fine arts, music, theater/drama. *Special Achievements/Activities:* 443

awards ($3,282,654 total): community service, leadership. *Special Characteristics:* 475 awards ($2,834,131 total): adult students, children of faculty/staff, veterans. ***ROTC:*** Army, Air Force.

LOANS ***Student loans:*** $56,193,391 (75% need-based, 25% non-need-based). 60% of past graduating class borrowed through all loan programs. *Average indebtedness per student:* $20,030. ***Average need-based loan:*** Freshmen: $3998; Undergraduates: $4732. ***Parent loans:*** $22,646,127 (30% need-based, 70% non-need-based). ***Programs:*** FFEL (Subsidized and Unsubsidized Stafford, PLUS), Perkins, state.

WORK-STUDY ***Federal work-study:*** Total amount: $2,452,963; 1,796 jobs averaging $1365. ***State or other work-study/employment:*** Total amount: $11,000,000 (28% need-based, 72% non-need-based). 5,489 part-time jobs averaging $2004.

ATHLETIC AWARDS Total amount: $7,383,763 (23% need-based, 77% non-need-based).

APPLYING FOR FINANCIAL AID ***Required financial aid form:*** FAFSA. ***Financial aid deadline (priority):*** 3/1. ***Notification date:*** Continuous. Students must reply within 4 weeks of notification.

CONTACT Client Service Staff, University of Connecticut, 233 Glenbrook Road, Unit 4116, Storrs, CT 06269-4116, 860-486-2819.

UNIVERSITY OF DALLAS

Irving, TX

Tuition & fees: $23,267 **Average undergraduate aid package: $17,668**

ABOUT THE INSTITUTION Independent Roman Catholic, coed. Awards: bachelor's, master's, and doctoral degrees and post-bachelor's and post-master's certificates. 32 undergraduate majors. Total enrollment: 2,941. Undergraduates: 1,188. Freshmen: 315. Federal methodology is used as a basis for awarding need-based institutional aid.

UNDERGRADUATE EXPENSES for 2007–08 ***Application fee:*** $40. ***Comprehensive fee:*** $30,882 includes full-time tuition ($21,819), mandatory fees ($1448), and room and board ($7615). ***College room only:*** $4240. ***Part-time tuition:*** $975 per credit hour. ***Part-time fees:*** $1448 per year.

FRESHMAN FINANCIAL AID (Fall 2005) 202 applied for aid; of those 79% were deemed to have need. 100% of freshmen with need received aid; of those 31% had need fully met. ***Average percent of need met:*** 85% (excluding resources awarded to replace EFC). ***Average financial aid package:*** $18,840 (excluding resources awarded to replace EFC). 35% of all full-time freshmen had no need and received non-need-based gift aid.

UNDERGRADUATE FINANCIAL AID (Fall 2005) 767 applied for aid; of those 83% were deemed to have need. 100% of undergraduates with need received aid; of those 29% had need fully met. ***Average percent of need met:*** 82% (excluding resources awarded to replace EFC). ***Average financial aid package:*** $17,668 (excluding resources awarded to replace EFC). 32% of all full-time undergraduates had no need and received non-need-based gift aid.

GIFT AID (NEED-BASED) ***Total amount:*** $7,482,305 (13% federal, 12% state, 74% institutional, 1% external sources). ***Receiving aid:*** Freshmen: 62% (159); All full-time undergraduates: 60% (629). ***Average award:*** Freshmen: $13,363; Undergraduates: $11,968. ***Scholarships, grants, and awards:*** Federal Pell, FSEOG, state, private, college/university gift aid from institutional funds.

GIFT AID (NON-NEED-BASED) ***Total amount:*** $3,684,203 (1% state, 96% institutional, 3% external sources). ***Receiving aid:*** Freshmen: 14% (37); Undergraduates: 12% (127). ***Average award:*** Freshmen: $9438; Undergraduates: $9087. ***Scholarships, grants, and awards by category:*** *Academic Interests/Achievement:* 1,170 awards ($6,467,100 total): business, education, foreign languages, general academic interests/achievements, mathematics, physical sciences, religion/biblical studies. *Creative Arts/Performance:* 56 awards ($98,500 total): art/fine arts, theater/drama. *Special Achievements/Activities:* 219 awards ($445,680 total): leadership, religious involvement. *Special Characteristics:* 17 awards ($276,266 total): children of faculty/staff, religious affiliation, siblings of current students. ***ROTC:*** Army cooperative, Air Force cooperative.

LOANS ***Student loans:*** $4,810,555 (66% need-based, 34% non-need-based). 65% of past graduating class borrowed through all loan programs. *Average indebtedness per student:* $24,737. ***Average need-based loan:*** Freshmen: $2823; Undergraduates: $3815. ***Parent loans:*** $1,461,876 (27% need-based, 73% non-need-based). ***Programs:*** FFEL (Subsidized and Unsubsidized Stafford, PLUS), Perkins, state.

WORK-STUDY ***Federal work-study:*** Total amount: $324,164; 279 jobs averaging $1161. ***State or other work-study/employment:*** Total amount: $96,834 (11% need-based, 89% non-need-based). 129 part-time jobs averaging $750.

APPLYING FOR FINANCIAL AID ***Required financial aid forms:*** FAFSA, institution's own form. ***Financial aid deadline (priority):*** 3/1. ***Notification date:*** Continuous. Students must reply by 5/1 or within 2 weeks of notification.

CONTACT Curt Eley, Dean of Enrollment Management, University of Dallas, 1845 East Northgate Drive, Irving, TX 75062, 972-721-5266 or toll-free 800-628-6999. *Fax:* 972-721-5017. *E-mail:* ugadmis@udallas.edu.

UNIVERSITY OF DAYTON

Dayton, OH

Tuition & fees: $23,970 **Average undergraduate aid package: $11,850**

ABOUT THE INSTITUTION Independent Roman Catholic, coed. Awards: bachelor's, master's, doctoral, and first professional degrees and post-master's certificates. 74 undergraduate majors. Total enrollment: 10,503. Undergraduates: 7,473. Freshmen: 1,738. Both federal and institutional methodology are used as a basis for awarding need-based institutional aid.

UNDERGRADUATE EXPENSES for 2006–07 ***Comprehensive fee:*** $31,160 includes full-time tuition ($23,000), mandatory fees ($970), and room and board ($7190). ***College room only:*** $4300. Full-time tuition and fees vary according to program. Room and board charges vary according to board plan, housing facility, and student level. ***Part-time tuition:*** $767 per credit hour. ***Part-time fees:*** $25 per term. Part-time tuition and fees vary according to course load and program. ***Payment plan:*** Deferred payment.

FRESHMAN FINANCIAL AID (Fall 2005) 1539 applied for aid; of those 72% were deemed to have need. 99% of freshmen with need received aid; of those 47% had need fully met. ***Average percent of need met:*** 98% (excluding resources awarded to replace EFC). ***Average financial aid package:*** $13,091 (excluding resources awarded to replace EFC). 20% of all full-time freshmen had no need and received non-need-based gift aid.

UNDERGRADUATE FINANCIAL AID (Fall 2005) 6,441 applied for aid; of those 75% were deemed to have need. 95% of undergraduates with need received aid; of those 52% had need fully met. ***Average percent of need met:*** 97% (excluding resources awarded to replace EFC). ***Average financial aid package:*** $11,850 (excluding resources awarded to replace EFC). 15% of all full-time undergraduates had no need and received non-need-based gift aid.

GIFT AID (NEED-BASED) ***Total amount:*** $37,264,789 (9% federal, 9% state, 78% institutional, 4% external sources). ***Receiving aid:*** Freshmen: 53% (1,058); All full-time undergraduates: 58% (3,981). ***Average award:*** Freshmen: $9927; Undergraduates: $8509. ***Scholarships, grants, and awards:*** Federal Pell, FSEOG, state, private, college/university gift aid from institutional funds.

GIFT AID (NON-NEED-BASED) ***Total amount:*** $19,203,621 (5% federal, 8% state, 81% institutional, 6% external sources). ***Receiving aid:*** Freshmen: 53% (1,057); Undergraduates: 58% (3,992). ***Average award:*** Freshmen: $8300; Undergraduates: $6150. ***Scholarships, grants, and awards by category:*** *Academic Interests/Achievement:* 5,488 awards ($29,188,581 total): business, education, engineering/technologies, general academic interests/achievements, humanities. *Creative Arts/Performance:* 103 awards ($340,610 total): art/fine arts, music. *Special Achievements/Activities:* 52 awards ($120,030 total): general special achievements/activities. *Special Characteristics:* 364 awards ($6,211,780 total): children of faculty/staff, religious affiliation. ***Tuition waivers:*** Full or partial for employees or children of employees, senior citizens. ***ROTC:*** Army, Air Force cooperative.

LOANS ***Student loans:*** $28,393,306 (86% need-based, 14% non-need-based). 76% of past graduating class borrowed through all loan programs. *Average indebtedness per student:* $20,731. ***Average need-based loan:*** Freshmen: $3004; Undergraduates: $3092. ***Parent loans:*** $9,306,831 (73% need-based, 27% non-need-based). ***Programs:*** FFEL (Subsidized and Unsubsidized Stafford, PLUS), Perkins, state, college/university.

WORK-STUDY ***Federal work-study:*** Total amount: $1,133,800; 827 jobs averaging $1371. ***State or other work-study/employment:*** Total amount: $4,209,792 (100% non-need-based). 2,783 part-time jobs averaging $1831.

ATHLETIC AWARDS Total amount: $2,524,511 (39% need-based, 61% non-need-based).

APPLYING FOR FINANCIAL AID ***Required financial aid form:*** FAFSA. ***Financial aid deadline (priority):*** 3/31. ***Notification date:*** Continuous beginning 3/1.

CONTACT Jeff Daniels, Director of Scholarships and Financial Aid, University of Dayton, 300 College Park Drive, Dayton, OH 45469-1305, 937-229-4311 or toll-free 800-837-7433. *Fax:* 937-229-4338. *E-mail:* jdaniels@udayton.edu.

UNIVERSITY OF DELAWARE

Newark, DE

Tuition & fees (DE res): $7740 **Average undergraduate aid package: $9891**

ABOUT THE INSTITUTION State-related, coed. Awards: associate, bachelor's, master's, and doctoral degrees. 133 undergraduate majors. Total enrollment: 19,742. Undergraduates: 16,296. Freshmen: 3,164. Federal methodology is used as a basis for awarding need-based institutional aid.

UNDERGRADUATE EXPENSES for 2006–07 ***Application fee:*** $60. ***Tuition, state resident:*** full-time $6980; part-time $291 per credit. ***Tuition, nonresident:*** full-time $17,690; part-time $737 per credit. ***College room and board:*** $7366; ***Room only:*** $4336. Room and board charges vary according to housing facility. ***Payment plan:*** Installment.

FRESHMAN FINANCIAL AID (Fall 2005) 2513 applied for aid; of those 51% were deemed to have need. 98% of freshmen with need received aid; of those 56% had need fully met. ***Average percent of need met:*** 79% (excluding resources awarded to replace EFC). ***Average financial aid package:*** $9706 (excluding resources awarded to replace EFC). 16% of all full-time freshmen had no need and received non-need-based gift aid.

UNDERGRADUATE FINANCIAL AID (Fall 2005) 8,257 applied for aid; of those 62% were deemed to have need. 98% of undergraduates with need received aid; of those 56% had need fully met. ***Average percent of need met:*** 79% (excluding resources awarded to replace EFC). ***Average financial aid package:*** $9891 (excluding resources awarded to replace EFC). 17% of all full-time undergraduates had no need and received non-need-based gift aid.

GIFT AID (NEED-BASED) ***Total amount:*** $19,695,244 (21% federal, 27% state, 37% institutional, 15% external sources). ***Receiving aid:*** Freshmen: 26% (929); All full-time undergraduates: 24% (3,650). ***Average award:*** Freshmen: $5197; Undergraduates: $5236. ***Scholarships, grants, and awards:*** Federal Pell, FSEOG, state, private, college/university gift aid from institutional funds.

GIFT AID (NON-NEED-BASED) ***Total amount:*** $14,212,162 (6% state, 76% institutional, 18% external sources). ***Receiving aid:*** Freshmen: 20% (705); Undergraduates: 11% (1,611). ***Average award:*** Freshmen: $4525; Undergraduates: $4204. ***Scholarships, grants, and awards by category:*** *Academic Interests/Achievement:* agriculture, biological sciences, business, communication, computer science, education, engineering/technologies, English, foreign languages, general academic interests/achievements, health fields, humanities, international studies, mathematics, military science, physical sciences, premedicine, religion/biblical studies, social sciences. *Creative Arts/Performance:* applied art and design, art/fine arts, music, theater/drama. *Special Achievements/Activities:* cheerleading/drum major, community service, general special achievements/activities, leadership. *Special Characteristics:* children and siblings of alumni, children of faculty/staff, children of public servants, ethnic background, first-generation college students, general special characteristics, local/state students, members of minority groups. ***Tuition waivers:*** Full or partial for employees or children of employees, senior citizens. ***ROTC:*** Army, Air Force.

LOANS ***Student loans:*** $48,510,348 (48% need-based, 52% non-need-based). 44% of past graduating class borrowed through all loan programs. *Average indebtedness per student:* $17,200. ***Average need-based loan:*** Freshmen: $4513; Undergraduates: $5367. ***Parent loans:*** $21,258,918 (24% need-based, 76% non-need-based). ***Programs:*** Federal Direct (Subsidized and Unsubsidized Stafford, PLUS), Perkins, Federal Nursing.

WORK-STUDY ***Federal work-study:*** Total amount: $1,786,558; jobs available. ***State or other work-study/employment:*** Total amount: $261,616 (74% need-based, 26% non-need-based). Part-time jobs available.

ATHLETIC AWARDS Total amount: $5,991,557 (19% need-based, 81% non-need-based).

APPLYING FOR FINANCIAL AID ***Required financial aid form:*** FAFSA. ***Financial aid deadline:*** 3/15 (priority: 2/1). ***Notification date:*** Continuous beginning 3/15. Students must reply by 5/1 or within 3 weeks of notification.

CONTACT Mr. Johnie A. Burton, Director of Scholarships and Financial Aid, University of Delaware, 224 Hullihen Hall, Newark, DE 19716, 302-831-8081. *E-mail:* jburton@udel.edu.

UNIVERSITY OF DENVER

Denver, CO

Tuition & fees: $30,372 **Average undergraduate aid package: $20,757**

ABOUT THE INSTITUTION Independent, coed. Awards: bachelor's, master's, doctoral, and first professional degrees. 68 undergraduate majors. Total enrollment: 10,374. Undergraduates: 4,877. Freshmen: 1,103. Federal methodology is used as a basis for awarding need-based institutional aid.

UNDERGRADUATE EXPENSES for 2006–07 ***Application fee:*** $50. ***Comprehensive fee:*** $39,600 includes full-time tuition ($29,628), mandatory fees ($744), and room and board ($9228). ***College room only:*** $5676. Full-time tuition and fees vary according to class time, course load, and program. Room and board charges vary according to board plan and housing facility. ***Part-time tuition:*** $823 per quarter hour. Part-time tuition and fees vary according to class time, course load, and program. ***Payment plan:*** Deferred payment.

FRESHMAN FINANCIAL AID (Fall 2005) 667 applied for aid; of those 73% were deemed to have need. 100% of freshmen with need received aid; of those 15% had need fully met. ***Average percent of need met:*** 75% (excluding resources awarded to replace EFC). ***Average financial aid package:*** $21,878 (excluding resources awarded to replace EFC). 37% of all full-time freshmen had no need and received non-need-based gift aid.

UNDERGRADUATE FINANCIAL AID (Fall 2005) 2,322 applied for aid; of those 81% were deemed to have need. 100% of undergraduates with need received aid; of those 12% had need fully met. ***Average percent of need met:*** 69% (excluding resources awarded to replace EFC). ***Average financial aid package:*** $20,757 (excluding resources awarded to replace EFC). 33% of all full-time undergraduates had no need and received non-need-based gift aid.

GIFT AID (NEED-BASED) ***Total amount:*** $33,251,943 (8% federal, 5% state, 86% institutional, 1% external sources). ***Receiving aid:*** Freshmen: 44% (481); All full-time undergraduates: 42% (1,836). ***Average award:*** Freshmen: $18,049; Undergraduates: $16,473. ***Scholarships, grants, and awards:*** Federal Pell, FSEOG, state, private, college/university gift aid from institutional funds.

GIFT AID (NON-NEED-BASED) ***Total amount:*** $15,551,068 (87% institutional, 13% external sources). ***Receiving aid:*** Freshmen: 6% (67); Undergraduates: 5% (199). ***Average award:*** Freshmen: $8650; Undergraduates: $8289. ***Scholarships, grants, and awards by category:*** *Academic Interests/Achievement:* business. *Creative Arts/Performance:* art/fine arts, debating, music, theater/drama. *Special Achievements/Activities:* community service, leadership. *Special Characteristics:* children of faculty/staff, local/state students. ***Tuition waivers:*** Full or partial for employees or children of employees. ***ROTC:*** Army cooperative, Air Force cooperative.

LOANS ***Student loans:*** $16,636,950 (63% need-based, 37% non-need-based). 47% of past graduating class borrowed through all loan programs. *Average indebtedness per student:* $27,008. ***Average need-based loan:*** Freshmen: $2868; Undergraduates: $3816. ***Parent loans:*** $4,515,159 (33% need-based, 67% non-need-based). ***Programs:*** Federal Direct (Subsidized and Unsubsidized Stafford, PLUS), FFEL (Subsidized and Unsubsidized Stafford, PLUS), Perkins, college/university.

WORK-STUDY ***Federal work-study:*** Total amount: $779,897; 461 jobs averaging $1806. ***State or other work-study/employment:*** Total amount: $413,575 (52% need-based, 48% non-need-based). 237 part-time jobs averaging $1732.

ATHLETIC AWARDS Total amount: $5,897,619 (15% need-based, 85% non-need-based).

APPLYING FOR FINANCIAL AID ***Required financial aid form:*** FAFSA. ***Financial aid deadline (priority):*** 3/1. ***Notification date:*** Continuous beginning 3/15. Students must reply within 4 weeks of notification.

CONTACT Ms. Barbara McFall, Director of Financial Aid, University of Denver, Office of Financial Aid, 2197 S. University Boulevard, Denver, CO 80208, 303-871-2342 or toll-free 800-525-9495 (out-of-state). *Fax:* 303-871-2341. *E-mail:* bmcfall@du.edu.

UNIVERSITY OF DETROIT MERCY

Detroit, MI

Tuition & fees: $23,970 **Average undergraduate aid package: $25,272**

ABOUT THE INSTITUTION Independent Roman Catholic (Jesuit), coed. Awards: associate, bachelor's, master's, doctoral, and first professional degrees and post-bachelor's, post-master's, and first professional certificates. 64 undergraduate majors. Total enrollment: 5,521. Undergraduates: 3,311. Freshmen: 461. Federal methodology is used as a basis for awarding need-based institutional aid.

UNDERGRADUATE EXPENSES for 2006–07 ***Application fee:*** $25. ***Comprehensive fee:*** $31,592 includes full-time tuition ($23,400), mandatory fees ($570), and

room and board ($7622). ***College room only:*** $4460. ***Part-time tuition:*** $575 per credit hour. ***Payment plans:*** Installment, deferred payment.

FRESHMAN FINANCIAL AID (Fall 2006, est.) 436 applied for aid; of those 91% were deemed to have need. 100% of freshmen with need received aid; of those 33% had need fully met. ***Average percent of need met:*** 91% (excluding resources awarded to replace EFC). ***Average financial aid package:*** $26,028 (excluding resources awarded to replace EFC). 10% of all full-time freshmen had no need and received non-need-based gift aid.

UNDERGRADUATE FINANCIAL AID (Fall 2006, est.) 1,672 applied for aid; of those 93% were deemed to have need. 100% of undergraduates with need received aid; of those 26% had need fully met. ***Average percent of need met:*** 82% (excluding resources awarded to replace EFC). ***Average financial aid package:*** $25,272 (excluding resources awarded to replace EFC). 7% of all full-time undergraduates had no need and received non-need-based gift aid.

GIFT AID (NEED-BASED) ***Total amount:*** $25,959,747 (14% federal, 13% state, 72% institutional, 1% external sources). ***Receiving aid:*** Freshmen: 75% (360); All full-time undergraduates: 72% (1,388). ***Average award:*** Freshmen: $21,788; Undergraduates: $21,402. ***Scholarships, grants, and awards:*** Federal Pell, FSEOG, state, private, college/university gift aid from institutional funds.

GIFT AID (NON-NEED-BASED) ***Total amount:*** $6,224,515 (99% institutional, 1% external sources). ***Receiving aid:*** Freshmen: 82% (395); Undergraduates: 71% (1,369). ***Average award:*** Freshmen: $15,695; Undergraduates: $14,704. ***Scholarships, grants, and awards by category:*** *Academic Interests/Achievement:* general academic interests/achievements. *Creative Arts/Performance:* theater/drama. *Special Achievements/Activities:* religious involvement. *Special Characteristics:* children and siblings of alumni, children of faculty/staff, members of minority groups. ***Tuition waivers:*** Full or partial for children of alumni, employees or children of employees.

LOANS ***Student loans:*** $52,877,754 (44% need-based, 56% non-need-based). ***Average need-based loan:*** Freshmen: $3399; Undergraduates: $3355. ***Parent loans:*** $1,459,350 (29% need-based, 71% non-need-based). ***Programs:*** FFEL (Subsidized and Unsubsidized Stafford, PLUS), Perkins, Federal Nursing.

WORK-STUDY ***Federal work-study:*** Total amount: $908,433; jobs available. ***State or other work-study/employment:*** Total amount: $939,512 (8% need-based, 92% non-need-based). Part-time jobs available.

ATHLETIC AWARDS Total amount: $2,691,548 (82% need-based, 18% non-need-based).

APPLYING FOR FINANCIAL AID ***Required financial aid form:*** FAFSA. ***Financial aid deadline (priority):*** 3/1. ***Notification date:*** Continuous. Students must reply within 4 weeks of notification.

CONTACT Sandy Ross, Director of Financial Aid and Scholarships, University of Detroit Mercy, 4001 West McNichols Road, Detroit, MI 48221-3038, 313-993-3350 or toll-free 800-635-5020 (out-of-state). *Fax:* 313-993-3347.

UNIVERSITY OF DUBUQUE

Dubuque, IA

CONTACT Mr. Timothy Kremer, Director of Financial Aid, University of Dubuque, 2000 University Avenue, Dubuque, IA 52001-5050, 563-589-3170 or toll-free 800-722-5583 (in-state). *Fax:* 563-589-3690.

UNIVERSITY OF EVANSVILLE

Evansville, IN

Tuition & fees: $22,980 **Average undergraduate aid package: $21,129**

ABOUT THE INSTITUTION Independent religious, coed. Awards: associate, bachelor's, and master's degrees. 86 undergraduate majors. Total enrollment: 2,879. Undergraduates: 2,813. Freshmen: 644. Federal methodology is used as a basis for awarding need-based institutional aid.

UNDERGRADUATE EXPENSES for 2006–07 ***Application fee:*** $35. ***Comprehensive fee:*** $30,100 includes full-time tuition ($22,370), mandatory fees ($610), and room and board ($7120). ***College room only:*** $3540. Room and board charges vary according to board plan and housing facility. ***Part-time tuition:*** $615 per hour. ***Part-time fees:*** $35 per term. Part-time tuition and fees vary according to course load. ***Payment plan:*** Installment.

FRESHMAN FINANCIAL AID (Fall 2006, est.) 555 applied for aid; of those 83% were deemed to have need. 100% of freshmen with need received aid; of those 32% had need fully met. ***Average percent of need met:*** 96% (excluding resources awarded to replace EFC). ***Average financial aid package:*** $22,031 (excluding resources awarded to replace EFC). 25% of all full-time freshmen had no need and received non-need-based gift aid.

UNDERGRADUATE FINANCIAL AID (Fall 2006, est.) 2,059 applied for aid; of those 85% were deemed to have need. 100% of undergraduates with need received aid; of those 31% had need fully met. ***Average percent of need met:*** 92% (excluding resources awarded to replace EFC). ***Average financial aid package:*** $21,129 (excluding resources awarded to replace EFC). 24% of all full-time undergraduates had no need and received non-need-based gift aid.

GIFT AID (NEED-BASED) ***Total amount:*** $26,095,120 (8% federal, 19% state, 66% institutional, 7% external sources). ***Receiving aid:*** Freshmen: 70% (451); All full-time undergraduates: 69% (1,696). ***Average award:*** Freshmen: $18,363; Undergraduates: $16,163. ***Scholarships, grants, and awards:*** Federal Pell, FSEOG, state, private, college/university gift aid from institutional funds.

GIFT AID (NON-NEED-BASED) ***Total amount:*** $6,968,340 (93% institutional, 7% external sources). ***Receiving aid:*** Freshmen: 57% (364); Undergraduates: 49% (1,222). ***Average award:*** Freshmen: $12,046; Undergraduates: $11,086. ***Scholarships, grants, and awards by category:*** *Academic Interests/Achievement:* 869 awards ($6,753,357 total): biological sciences, business, communication, computer science, education, engineering/technologies, English, foreign languages, general academic interests/achievements, health fields, humanities, international studies, mathematics, physical sciences, premedicine, religion/biblical studies, social sciences. *Creative Arts/Performance:* 229 awards ($1,906,536 total): art/fine arts, music, theater/drama. *Special Achievements/Activities:* 106 awards ($471,430 total): leadership. *Special Characteristics:* 314 awards ($3,131,690 total): children and siblings of alumni, children of faculty/staff, international students, members of minority groups, religious affiliation, siblings of current students. ***Tuition waivers:*** Full or partial for minority students, children of alumni, employees or children of employees, senior citizens.

LOANS ***Student loans:*** $8,638,729 (92% need-based, 8% non-need-based). 65% of past graduating class borrowed through all loan programs. *Average indebtedness per student:* $20,368. ***Average need-based loan:*** Freshmen: $4102; Undergraduates: $4990. ***Parent loans:*** $5,018,138 (82% need-based, 18% non-need-based). ***Programs:*** FFEL (Subsidized and Unsubsidized Stafford, PLUS), Perkins, Federal Nursing, college/university.

WORK-STUDY ***Federal work-study:*** Total amount: $486,298; 388 jobs averaging $1253. ***State or other work-study/employment:*** Total amount: $92,966 (1% need-based, 99% non-need-based). 74 part-time jobs averaging $1256.

ATHLETIC AWARDS Total amount: $3,231,243 (41% need-based, 59% non-need-based).

APPLYING FOR FINANCIAL AID ***Required financial aid form:*** FAFSA. ***Financial aid deadline (priority):*** 3/10. ***Notification date:*** Continuous beginning 3/21. Students must reply by 5/1.

CONTACT Ms. JoAnn E. Laugel, Director of Financial Aid, University of Evansville, 1800 Lincoln Avenue, Evansville, IN 47722, 812-488-2364 or toll-free 800-423-8633 Ext. 2468. *Fax:* 812-488-2028. *E-mail:* jl25@evansville.edu.

THE UNIVERSITY OF FINDLAY

Findlay, OH

Tuition & fees: $22,796 **Average undergraduate aid package: $14,900**

ABOUT THE INSTITUTION Independent religious, coed. Awards: associate, bachelor's, and master's degrees. 58 undergraduate majors. Total enrollment: 6,182. Undergraduates: 4,926. Freshmen: 673. Federal methodology is used as a basis for awarding need-based institutional aid.

UNDERGRADUATE EXPENSES for 2006–07 ***Comprehensive fee:*** $30,588 includes full-time tuition ($21,836), mandatory fees ($960), and room and board ($7792). ***College room only:*** $3906. Full-time tuition and fees vary according to location and program. ***Part-time tuition:*** $481 per semester hour. ***Part-time fees:*** $130 per term. Part-time tuition and fees vary according to location and program. ***Payment plan:*** Installment.

FRESHMAN FINANCIAL AID (Fall 2006, est.) 495 applied for aid; of those 88% were deemed to have need. 100% of freshmen with need received aid; of those 20% had need fully met. ***Average percent of need met:*** 87% (excluding resources awarded to replace EFC). ***Average financial aid package:*** $17,213 (excluding resources awarded to replace EFC). 18% of all full-time freshmen had no need and received non-need-based gift aid.

UNDERGRADUATE FINANCIAL AID (Fall 2006, est.) 2,102 applied for aid; of those 88% were deemed to have need. 100% of undergraduates with need received aid; of those 20% had need fully met. ***Average percent of need met:***

84% (excluding resources awarded to replace EFC). ***Average financial aid package:*** $14,900 (excluding resources awarded to replace EFC). 20% of all full-time undergraduates had no need and received non-need-based gift aid.

GIFT AID (NEED-BASED) ***Total amount:*** $16,852,056 (12% federal, 7% state, 81% institutional). ***Receiving aid:*** Freshmen: 65% (434); All full-time undergraduates: 71% (1,805). ***Average award:*** Freshmen: $9930; Undergraduates: $9300. ***Scholarships, grants, and awards:*** Federal Pell, FSEOG, state, college/university gift aid from institutional funds.

GIFT AID (NON-NEED-BASED) ***Total amount:*** $10,200,604 (17% state, 76% institutional, 7% external sources). ***Receiving aid:*** Freshmen: 65% (434); Undergraduates: 73% (1,843). ***Average award:*** Freshmen: $9359; Undergraduates: $7500. ***Scholarships, grants, and awards by category:*** *Academic Interests/Achievement:* 1,900 awards ($16,400,000 total): general academic interests/achievements. *Creative Arts/Performance:* 170 awards ($160,000 total): music, theater/drama. *Special Characteristics:* 145 awards ($1,455,000 total): children of faculty/staff. ***Tuition waivers:*** Full or partial for children of alumni, employees or children of employees, senior citizens. ***ROTC:*** Army cooperative, Air Force cooperative.

LOANS ***Student loans:*** $21,171,000 (36% need-based, 64% non-need-based). 85% of past graduating class borrowed through all loan programs. *Average indebtedness per student:* $19,000. ***Average need-based loan:*** Freshmen: $2500; Undergraduates: $4000. ***Parent loans:*** $2,391,746 (100% non-need-based). ***Programs:*** FFEL (Subsidized and Unsubsidized Stafford, PLUS), Perkins, college/university.

WORK-STUDY ***Federal work-study:*** Total amount: $350,000; 420 jobs averaging $830. ***State or other work-study/employment:*** Total amount: $340,000 (100% non-need-based). 300 part-time jobs averaging $850.

ATHLETIC AWARDS Total amount: $2,347,434 (100% non-need-based).

APPLYING FOR FINANCIAL AID ***Required financial aid form:*** FAFSA. ***Financial aid deadline:*** 3/1. ***Notification date:*** Continuous beginning 3/1. Students must reply within 2 weeks of notification.

CONTACT Mr. Arman Habegger, Director of Financial Aid, The University of Findlay, 1000 North Main Street, Findlay, OH 45840-3695, 419-434-4791 or toll-free 800-548-0932. *Fax:* 419-434-4344. *E-mail:* finaid@findlay.edu.

UNIVERSITY OF FLORIDA

Gainesville, FL

Tuition & fees (FL res): $3206 Average undergraduate aid package: $10,653

ABOUT THE INSTITUTION State-supported, coed. Awards: bachelor's, master's, doctoral, and first professional degrees. 98 undergraduate majors. Total enrollment: 50,822. Undergraduates: 35,110. Freshmen: 6,702. Federal methodology is used as a basis for awarding need-based institutional aid.

UNDERGRADUATE EXPENSES for 2006–07 ***Application fee:*** $30. ***Tuition, state resident:*** full-time $3206; part-time $111 per credit hour. ***Tuition, nonresident:*** full-time $17,790; part-time $593 per credit hour. ***College room and board:*** $6590; ***Room only:*** $4170. Room and board charges vary according to board plan and student level. ***Payment plan:*** Tuition prepayment.

FRESHMAN FINANCIAL AID (Fall 2005) 4350 applied for aid; of those 51% were deemed to have need. 98% of freshmen with need received aid; of those 30% had need fully met. ***Average percent of need met:*** 84% (excluding resources awarded to replace EFC). ***Average financial aid package:*** $10,511 (excluding resources awarded to replace EFC). 58% of all full-time freshmen had no need and received non-need-based gift aid.

UNDERGRADUATE FINANCIAL AID (Fall 2005) 16,014 applied for aid; of those 76% were deemed to have need. 100% of undergraduates with need received aid; of those 33% had need fully met. ***Average percent of need met:*** 81% (excluding resources awarded to replace EFC). ***Average financial aid package:*** $10,653 (excluding resources awarded to replace EFC). 53% of all full-time undergraduates had no need and received non-need-based gift aid.

GIFT AID (NEED-BASED) ***Total amount:*** $37,818,278 (60% federal, 15% state, 25% institutional). ***Receiving aid:*** Freshmen: 18% (1,312); All full-time undergraduates: 24% (7,641). ***Average award:*** Freshmen: $5451; Undergraduates: $4696. ***Scholarships, grants, and awards:*** Federal Pell, FSEOG, state, private, college/university gift aid from institutional funds.

GIFT AID (NON-NEED-BASED) ***Total amount:*** $121,745,210 (1% federal, 58% state, 15% institutional, 26% external sources). ***Receiving aid:*** Freshmen: 25% (1,810); Undergraduates: 29% (9,349). ***Average award:*** Freshmen: $5071; Undergraduates: $4565. ***Scholarships, grants, and awards by category:*** *Academic Interests/Achievement:* agriculture, architecture, business, communication, computer science, education, engineering/technologies, general academic interests/achievements, health fields, military science. *Creative Arts/Performance:* art/fine arts, dance, general creative arts/performance, journalism/publications, music, performing arts, theater/drama. *Special Achievements/Activities:* community service, general special achievements/activities, leadership. *Special Characteristics:* children of faculty/staff, members of minority groups, out-of-state students. ***Tuition waivers:*** Full or partial for employees or children of employees, senior citizens. ***ROTC:*** Army, Air Force.

LOANS ***Student loans:*** $49,425,372 (53% need-based, 47% non-need-based). 44% of past graduating class borrowed through all loan programs. *Average indebtedness per student:* $15,045. ***Average need-based loan:*** Freshmen: $3240; Undergraduates: $4198. ***Parent loans:*** $5,450,530 (100% non-need-based). ***Programs:*** Federal Direct (Subsidized and Unsubsidized Stafford, PLUS), Perkins, college/university.

WORK-STUDY ***Federal work-study:*** Total amount: $2,242,046; 1,274 jobs averaging $1760. ***State or other work-study/employment:*** Total amount: $6,387,123 (100% non-need-based). 4,044 part-time jobs averaging $1580.

ATHLETIC AWARDS Total amount: $3,611,412 (100% non-need-based).

APPLYING FOR FINANCIAL AID ***Required financial aid form:*** FAFSA. ***Financial aid deadline (priority):*** 3/15. ***Notification date:*** Continuous beginning 4/1.

CONTACT Ms. Karen L. Fooks, Director of Student Financial Affairs, University of Florida, S-107 Criser Hall, PO Box 114025, Gainesville, FL 32611-4025, 352-392-1271. *Fax:* 352-392-2861. *E-mail:* kfooks@ufl.edu.

UNIVERSITY OF GEORGIA

Athens, GA

Tuition & fees (GA res): $4964 Average undergraduate aid package: $7767

ABOUT THE INSTITUTION State-supported, coed. Awards: associate, bachelor's, master's, doctoral, and first professional degrees. 144 undergraduate majors. Total enrollment: 33,959. Undergraduates: 25,437. Freshmen: 5,064. Federal methodology is used as a basis for awarding need-based institutional aid.

UNDERGRADUATE EXPENSES for 2006–07 ***Application fee:*** $50. ***Tuition, state resident:*** full-time $3892; part-time $163 per credit. ***Tuition, nonresident:*** full-time $16,968; part-time $707 per credit. ***Required fees:*** full-time $1072; $536 per term part-time. Full-time tuition and fees vary according to course load, location, program, and reciprocity agreements. Part-time tuition and fees vary according to course load, location, program, and reciprocity agreements. ***College room and board:*** $6848; ***Room only:*** $3704. Room and board charges vary according to board plan and housing facility.

FRESHMAN FINANCIAL AID (Fall 2006, est.) 3046 applied for aid; of those 46% were deemed to have need. 99% of freshmen with need received aid; of those 38% had need fully met. ***Average percent of need met:*** 78% (excluding resources awarded to replace EFC). ***Average financial aid package:*** $7854 (excluding resources awarded to replace EFC). 7% of all full-time freshmen had no need and received non-need-based gift aid.

UNDERGRADUATE FINANCIAL AID (Fall 2006, est.) 10,604 applied for aid; of those 58% were deemed to have need. 98% of undergraduates with need received aid; of those 30% had need fully met. ***Average percent of need met:*** 72% (excluding resources awarded to replace EFC). ***Average financial aid package:*** $7767 (excluding resources awarded to replace EFC). 6% of all full-time undergraduates had no need and received non-need-based gift aid.

GIFT AID (NEED-BASED) ***Total amount:*** $30,793,741 (34% federal, 60% state, 2% institutional, 4% external sources). ***Receiving aid:*** Freshmen: 27% (1,340); All full-time undergraduates: 22% (5,176). ***Average award:*** Freshmen: $6723; Undergraduates: $6022. ***Scholarships, grants, and awards:*** Federal Pell, FSEOG, state, private, college/university gift aid from institutional funds.

GIFT AID (NON-NEED-BASED) ***Total amount:*** $67,670,984 (91% state, 5% institutional, 4% external sources). ***Receiving aid:*** Freshmen: 7% (375); Undergraduates: 4% (942). ***Average award:*** Freshmen: $1992; Undergraduates: $1905. ***Scholarships, grants, and awards by category:*** *Academic Interests/Achievement:* 21,510 awards ($87,395,917 total): agriculture, business, education, general academic interests/achievements. *Creative Arts/Performance:* 117 awards ($130,370 total): music. *Special Characteristics:* 101 awards ($167,500 total): local/state students. ***Tuition waivers:*** Full or partial for senior citizens. ***ROTC:*** Army, Air Force.

LOANS ***Student loans:*** $39,101,275 (52% need-based, 48% non-need-based). 41% of past graduating class borrowed through all loan programs. *Average indebtedness per student:* $13,478. ***Average need-based loan:*** Freshmen: $2481;

Undergraduates: $3728. ***Parent loans:*** $12,352,885 (19% need-based, 81% non-need-based). ***Programs:*** Federal Direct (Subsidized and Unsubsidized Stafford, PLUS), Perkins, state, college/university.

WORK-STUDY ***Federal work-study:*** Total amount: $1,051,511; 410 jobs averaging $2565.

ATHLETIC AWARDS Total amount: $5,229,460 (22% need-based, 78% non-need-based).

APPLYING FOR FINANCIAL AID ***Required financial aid form:*** FAFSA. ***Financial aid deadline (priority):*** 3/1. ***Notification date:*** Continuous beginning 3/15. Students must reply within 2 weeks of notification.

CONTACT Ms. Susan D. Little, Director of Student Affairs, University of Georgia, 220 Holmes/Hunter Academic Building, Athens, GA 30602-6114, 706-542-8208. *Fax:* 706-542-8217. *E-mail:* slittle@uga.edu.

UNIVERSITY OF GREAT FALLS

Great Falls, MT

Tuition & fees: $16,350 **Average undergraduate aid package: $11,886**

ABOUT THE INSTITUTION Independent Roman Catholic, coed. Awards: associate, bachelor's, and master's degrees. 76 undergraduate majors. Total enrollment: 716. Undergraduates: 632. Freshmen: 121. Federal methodology is used as a basis for awarding need-based institutional aid.

UNDERGRADUATE EXPENSES for 2007–08 ***Application fee:*** $35. ***Comprehensive fee:*** $22,150 includes full-time tuition ($15,450), mandatory fees ($900), and room and board ($5800). ***College room only:*** $2700. ***Part-time tuition:*** $490 per credit. ***Part-time fees:*** $30 per credit.

FRESHMAN FINANCIAL AID (Fall 2006, est.) 106 applied for aid; of those 78% were deemed to have need. 100% of freshmen with need received aid; of those 1% had need fully met. ***Average percent of need met:*** 46% (excluding resources awarded to replace EFC). ***Average financial aid package:*** $10,701 (excluding resources awarded to replace EFC). 3% of all full-time freshmen had no need and received non-need-based gift aid.

UNDERGRADUATE FINANCIAL AID (Fall 2006, est.) 409 applied for aid; of those 84% were deemed to have need. 100% of undergraduates with need received aid; of those 1% had need fully met. ***Average percent of need met:*** 50% (excluding resources awarded to replace EFC). ***Average financial aid package:*** $11,886 (excluding resources awarded to replace EFC). 3% of all full-time undergraduates had no need and received non-need-based gift aid.

GIFT AID (NEED-BASED) ***Total amount:*** $1,139,503 (90% federal, 10% state). ***Receiving aid:*** Freshmen: 47% (57); All full-time undergraduates: 54% (250). ***Average award:*** Freshmen: $3410; Undergraduates: $3719. ***Scholarships, grants, and awards:*** Federal Pell, FSEOG, state, private, college/university gift aid from institutional funds.

GIFT AID (NON-NEED-BASED) ***Total amount:*** $446,201 (59% institutional, 41% external sources). ***Receiving aid:*** Freshmen: 63% (76); Undergraduates: 68% (316). ***Average award:*** Freshmen: $3385; Undergraduates: $3459. ***Scholarships, grants, and awards by category:*** *Academic Interests/Achievement:* 382 awards ($1,071,203 total): biological sciences, business, computer science, education, general academic interests/achievements, humanities, mathematics, physical sciences, premedicine, religion/biblical studies, social sciences. *Creative Arts/Performance:* 23 awards ($42,750 total): art/fine arts, dance, music. *Special Achievements/Activities:* 36 awards ($50,805 total): cheerleading/drum major, religious involvement. *Special Characteristics:* 81 awards ($217,484 total): children of current students, children of faculty/staff, ethnic background, first-generation college students, international students, parents of current students, religious affiliation, siblings of current students, spouses of current students.

LOANS ***Student loans:*** $3,623,200 (50% need-based, 50% non-need-based). 83% of past graduating class borrowed through all loan programs. *Average indebtedness per student:* $26,450. ***Average need-based loan:*** Freshmen: $2598; Undergraduates: $4168. ***Parent loans:*** $419,284 (100% non-need-based). ***Programs:*** FFEL (Subsidized and Unsubsidized Stafford, PLUS), Perkins.

WORK-STUDY ***Federal work-study:*** Total amount: $104,126; jobs available. ***State or other work-study/employment:*** Total amount: $96,710 (100% non-need-based). Part-time jobs available.

ATHLETIC AWARDS Total amount: $847,479 (100% non-need-based).

APPLYING FOR FINANCIAL AID ***Required financial aid form:*** FAFSA. ***Financial aid deadline (priority):*** 4/1. ***Notification date:*** Continuous beginning 3/15. Students must reply within 3 weeks of notification.

CONTACT Kerri Koteskey, Director of Financial Aid, University of Great Falls, 1301 20th Street South, Great Falls, MT 59405, 406-791-5237 or toll-free 800-856-9544. *Fax:* 406-791-5242. *E-mail:* kkoteskey01@ugf.edu.

UNIVERSITY OF GUAM

Mangilao, GU

CONTACT Office of Financial Aid, University of Guam, UOG Station, Mangilao, GU 96923, 671-735-2280.

UNIVERSITY OF HARTFORD

West Hartford, CT

Tuition & fees: $26,996 **Average undergraduate aid package: $16,790**

ABOUT THE INSTITUTION Independent, coed. Awards: associate, bachelor's, master's, and doctoral degrees and post-bachelor's and post-master's certificates. 77 undergraduate majors. Total enrollment: 7,308. Undergraduates: 5,602. Freshmen: 1,478. Federal methodology is used as a basis for awarding need-based institutional aid.

UNDERGRADUATE EXPENSES for 2007–08 ***Application fee:*** $35. ***Comprehensive fee:*** $37,414 includes full-time tuition ($25,806), mandatory fees ($1190), and room and board ($10,418). ***College room only:*** $6424. ***Part-time tuition:*** $380 per credit.

FRESHMAN FINANCIAL AID (Fall 2005) 1111 applied for aid; of those 91% were deemed to have need. 100% of freshmen with need received aid; of those 27% had need fully met. ***Average percent of need met:*** 66% (excluding resources awarded to replace EFC). ***Average financial aid package:*** $16,153 (excluding resources awarded to replace EFC). 26% of all full-time freshmen had no need and received non-need-based gift aid.

UNDERGRADUATE FINANCIAL AID (Fall 2005) 3,095 applied for aid; of those 93% were deemed to have need. 100% of undergraduates with need received aid; of those 26% had need fully met. ***Average percent of need met:*** 72% (excluding resources awarded to replace EFC). ***Average financial aid package:*** $16,790 (excluding resources awarded to replace EFC). 30% of all full-time undergraduates had no need and received non-need-based gift aid.

GIFT AID (NEED-BASED) ***Total amount:*** $34,892,944 (8% federal, 6% state, 83% institutional, 3% external sources). ***Receiving aid:*** Freshmen: 50% (726); All full-time undergraduates: 46% (2,138). ***Average award:*** Freshmen: $12,864; Undergraduates: $12,322. ***Scholarships, grants, and awards:*** Federal Pell, FSEOG, state, private, college/university gift aid from institutional funds.

GIFT AID (NON-NEED-BASED) ***Total amount:*** $13,724,883 (98% institutional, 2% external sources). ***Receiving aid:*** Freshmen: 22% (322); Undergraduates: 28% (1,286). ***Average award:*** Freshmen: $6949; Undergraduates: $7169. ***Scholarships, grants, and awards by category:*** *Academic Interests/Achievement:* 3,176 awards ($21,955,957 total): general academic interests/achievements, health fields, premedicine. *Creative Arts/Performance:* 578 awards ($5,798,894 total): art/fine arts, dance, music, performing arts, theater/drama. *Special Achievements/Activities:* community service. *Special Characteristics:* adult students, children of current students, children of faculty/staff, children of union members/company employees, children with a deceased or disabled parent, ethnic background, first-generation college students, handicapped students, international students, local/state students, members of minority groups, parents of current students, previous college experience, religious affiliation, siblings of current students, twins. ***ROTC:*** Army cooperative, Air Force cooperative.

LOANS ***Student loans:*** $14,859,466 (93% need-based, 7% non-need-based). 66% of past graduating class borrowed through all loan programs. *Average indebtedness per student:* $25,553. ***Average need-based loan:*** Freshmen: $3987; Undergraduates: $4504. ***Parent loans:*** $11,293,384 (100% need-based). ***Programs:*** FFEL (Subsidized and Unsubsidized Stafford, PLUS), Perkins.

WORK-STUDY ***Federal work-study:*** Total amount: $350,564; 411 jobs averaging $1699. ***State or other work-study/employment:*** Total amount: $922,631 (80% need-based, 20% non-need-based). 87 part-time jobs averaging $10,487.

ATHLETIC AWARDS Total amount: $3,699,153 (23% need-based, 77% non-need-based).

APPLYING FOR FINANCIAL AID ***Required financial aid form:*** FAFSA. ***Financial aid deadline (priority):*** 2/1. ***Notification date:*** Continuous beginning 3/1. Students must reply by 5/1.

CONTACT Financial Aid Office, University of Hartford, 200 Bloomfield Avenue, West Hartford, CT 06117-1599, 860-768-4296 or toll-free 800-947-4303. *Fax:* 860-768-4961. *E-mail:* finaid@hartford.edu.

UNIVERSITY OF HAWAII AT HILO

Hilo, HI

Tuition & fees (HI res): $3148 **Average undergraduate aid package: $6555**

ABOUT THE INSTITUTION State-supported, coed. Awards: bachelor's and master's degrees and post-bachelor's certificates. 29 undergraduate majors. Total enrollment: 3,507. Undergraduates: 3,276. Freshmen: 470. Federal methodology is used as a basis for awarding need-based institutional aid.

UNDERGRADUATE EXPENSES for 2006–07 ***Application fee:*** $50. ***Tuition, state resident:*** full-time $3000; part-time $125 per credit hour. ***Tuition, nonresident:*** full-time $9552; part-time $398 per credit hour. ***Required fees:*** full-time $148; $40.50 per term part-time. Full-time tuition and fees vary according to reciprocity agreements. Part-time tuition and fees vary according to course load. ***College room and board:*** $6292; ***Room only:*** $3190. Room and board charges vary according to board plan and housing facility.

FRESHMAN FINANCIAL AID (Fall 2006, est.) 204 applied for aid; of those 99% were deemed to have need. 100% of freshmen with need received aid; of those 9% had need fully met. ***Average percent of need met:*** 51% (excluding resources awarded to replace EFC). ***Average financial aid package:*** $5283 (excluding resources awarded to replace EFC). 1% of all full-time freshmen had no need and received non-need-based gift aid.

UNDERGRADUATE FINANCIAL AID (Fall 2006, est.) 1,236 applied for aid; of those 98% were deemed to have need. 100% of undergraduates with need received aid; of those 13% had need fully met. ***Average percent of need met:*** 67% (excluding resources awarded to replace EFC). ***Average financial aid package:*** $6555 (excluding resources awarded to replace EFC). 1% of all full-time undergraduates had no need and received non-need-based gift aid.

GIFT AID (NEED-BASED) ***Total amount:*** $3,881,023 (95% federal, 3% state, 2% institutional). ***Receiving aid:*** Freshmen: 39% (133); All full-time undergraduates: 50% (895). ***Average award:*** Freshmen: $3863; Undergraduates: $3625. ***Scholarships, grants, and awards:*** Federal Pell, FSEOG, state, private, college/university gift aid from institutional funds.

GIFT AID (NON-NEED-BASED) ***Total amount:*** $2,141,331 (12% institutional, 88% external sources). ***Receiving aid:*** Freshmen: 13% (45); Undergraduates: 12% (214). ***Average award:*** Freshmen: $775; Undergraduates: $1215. ***Scholarships, grants, and awards by category:*** *Academic Interests/Achievement:* 48 awards ($60,530 total): agriculture, business, computer science, English, general academic interests/achievements, health fields, social sciences. *Creative Arts/Performance:* 3 awards ($900 total): art/fine arts, music, performing arts, theater/drama. *Special Achievements/Activities:* 10 awards ($37,306 total): community service, general special achievements/activities, leadership.

LOANS ***Student loans:*** $7,384,705 (54% need-based, 46% non-need-based). 34% of past graduating class borrowed through all loan programs. *Average indebtedness per student:* $11,206. ***Average need-based loan:*** Freshmen: $2933; Undergraduates: $4153. ***Parent loans:*** $347,982 (100% non-need-based). ***Programs:*** FFEL (Subsidized and Unsubsidized Stafford, PLUS), Perkins, state.

WORK-STUDY ***Federal work-study:*** Total amount: $323,793; 192 jobs averaging $1686. ***State or other work-study/employment:*** Total amount: $1,106,305 (100% non-need-based). 399 part-time jobs averaging $2773.

ATHLETIC AWARDS Total amount: $426,304 (100% non-need-based).

APPLYING FOR FINANCIAL AID ***Required financial aid form:*** FAFSA. ***Financial aid deadline (priority):*** 3/1. ***Notification date:*** Continuous beginning 4/1. Students must reply within 3 weeks of notification.

CONTACT Financial Aid Director, University of Hawaii at Hilo, 200 West Kawili Street, Hilo, HI 96720-4091, 808-974-7324 or toll-free 808-974-7414 (in-state), 800-897-4456 (out-of-state). *Fax:* 808-933-0861. *E-mail:* uhhfao@hawaii.edu.

UNIVERSITY OF HAWAII AT MANOA

Honolulu, HI

Tuition & fees (HI res): $5390 **Average undergraduate aid package: $7573**

ABOUT THE INSTITUTION State-supported, coed. Awards: bachelor's, master's, doctoral, and first professional degrees and post-bachelor's certificates. 87 undergraduate majors. Total enrollment: 20,357. Undergraduates: 14,037. Freshmen: 1,775. Federal methodology is used as a basis for awarding need-based institutional aid.

UNDERGRADUATE EXPENSES for 2007–08 ***Application fee:*** $50. ***Tuition, state resident:*** full-time $5136; part-time $214 per credit hour. ***Tuition, nonresident:*** full-time $14,400; part-time $600 per credit hour. ***College room and board:*** $7185; ***Room only:*** $4527.

FRESHMAN FINANCIAL AID (Fall 2006, est.) 1085 applied for aid; of those 50% were deemed to have need. 95% of freshmen with need received aid; of those 32% had need fully met. ***Average percent of need met:*** 69% (excluding resources awarded to replace EFC). ***Average financial aid package:*** $7177 (excluding resources awarded to replace EFC). 23% of all full-time freshmen had no need and received non-need-based gift aid.

UNDERGRADUATE FINANCIAL AID (Fall 2006, est.) 6,365 applied for aid; of those 62% were deemed to have need. 96% of undergraduates with need received aid; of those 28% had need fully met. ***Average percent of need met:*** 68% (excluding resources awarded to replace EFC). ***Average financial aid package:*** $7573 (excluding resources awarded to replace EFC). 21% of all full-time undergraduates had no need and received non-need-based gift aid.

GIFT AID (NEED-BASED) ***Total amount:*** $10,082,285 (84% federal, 3% state, 8% institutional, 5% external sources). ***Receiving aid:*** Freshmen: 27% (442); All full-time undergraduates: 27% (3,100). ***Average award:*** Freshmen: $4856; Undergraduates: $4744. ***Scholarships, grants, and awards:*** Federal Pell, FSEOG, state, private, college/university gift aid from institutional funds, Federal Nursing.

GIFT AID (NON-NEED-BASED) ***Total amount:*** $2,519,126 (15% institutional, 85% external sources). ***Receiving aid:*** Freshmen: 9% (141); Undergraduates: 6% (740). ***Average award:*** Freshmen: $4741; Undergraduates: $4464. ***Scholarships, grants, and awards by category:*** *Academic Interests/Achievement:* general academic interests/achievements. *Creative Arts/Performance:* art/fine arts, dance, journalism/publications, music, performing arts, theater/drama. ***ROTC:*** Army, Air Force.

LOANS ***Student loans:*** $19,949,000 (60% need-based, 40% non-need-based). 27% of past graduating class borrowed through all loan programs. *Average indebtedness per student:* $11,748. ***Average need-based loan:*** Freshmen: $2559; Undergraduates: $3760. ***Parent loans:*** $9,655,062 (100% non-need-based). ***Programs:*** FFEL (Subsidized and Unsubsidized Stafford, PLUS), Perkins, Federal Nursing, state, college/university.

WORK-STUDY ***Federal work-study:*** Total amount: $640,045; 292 jobs averaging $2192.

ATHLETIC AWARDS Total amount: $3,815,222 (1% need-based, 99% non-need-based).

APPLYING FOR FINANCIAL AID ***Required financial aid forms:*** FAFSA, institution's own form. ***Financial aid deadline (priority):*** 3/1. ***Notification date:*** Continuous beginning 3/28. Students must reply within 2 weeks of notification.

CONTACT Linda Clemons, Director of Financial Aid Services, University of Hawaii at Manoa, 2600 Campus Road, Suite 112, Honolulu, HI 96822, 808-956-3989 or toll-free 800-823-9771. *Fax:* 808-956-3985. *E-mail:* finaid@hawaii.edu.

UNIVERSITY OF HAWAII–WEST OAHU

Pearl City, HI

CONTACT Student Services Office, University of Hawaii–West Oahu, 96-129 Ala Ike, Pearl City, HI 96782-3366, 808-454-4700 or toll-free 808-454 Ext. 4700 (in-state). *Fax:* 808-453-6075.

UNIVERSITY OF HOUSTON

Houston, TX

CONTACT Financial Aid Office, University of Houston, 4800 Calhoun Road, Houston, TX 77204-2160, 713-743-1010. *Fax:* 713-743-9098.

UNIVERSITY OF HOUSTON–CLEAR LAKE

Houston, TX

CONTACT Lynda McKendree, Director of Financial Aid and Veterans' Affairs, University of Houston–Clear Lake, 2700 Bay Area Boulevard, Houston, TX 77058-1098, 281-283-2485. *Fax:* 281-283-2502. *E-mail:* mckendree@cl.uh.edu.

UNIVERSITY OF HOUSTON–DOWNTOWN

Houston, TX

CONTACT Office of Scholarships and Financial Aid, University of Houston–Downtown, One Main Street, Suite 330 South, Houston, TX 77002-1001, 713-221-8041. *Fax:* 713-221-8468. *E-mail:* uhd.finaid@dt.uh.edu.

UNIVERSITY OF HOUSTON–VICTORIA

Victoria, TX

Tuition & fees (TX res): $4680 Average undergraduate aid package: $6514

ABOUT THE INSTITUTION State-supported, coed. Awards: bachelor's and master's degrees and post-bachelor's and post-master's certificates. 10 undergraduate majors. Total enrollment: 2,652. Undergraduates: 1,315. Federal methodology is used as a basis for awarding need-based institutional aid.

UNDERGRADUATE EXPENSES for 2006–07 ***Tuition, state resident:*** full-time $3570; part-time $119 per semester hour. ***Tuition, nonresident:*** full-time $11,820; part-time $394 per semester hour. ***Required fees:*** full-time $1110; $42 per semester hour. Full-time tuition and fees vary according to course load. Part-time tuition and fees vary according to course load. ***Payment plan:*** Installment.

UNDERGRADUATE FINANCIAL AID (Fall 2005) 577 applied for aid; of those 47% were deemed to have need. 89% of undergraduates with need received aid; of those 7% had need fully met. ***Average percent of need met:*** 49% (excluding resources awarded to replace EFC). ***Average financial aid package:*** $6514 (excluding resources awarded to replace EFC). 4% of all full-time undergraduates had no need and received non-need-based gift aid.

GIFT AID (NEED-BASED) ***Total amount:*** $2,353,403 (57% federal, 4% state, 22% institutional, 17% external sources). ***Receiving aid:*** All full-time undergraduates: 31% (231). ***Average award:*** Undergraduates: $3630. ***Scholarships, grants, and awards:*** Federal Pell, FSEOG, state, private, college/university gift aid from institutional funds.

GIFT AID (NON-NEED-BASED) ***Total amount:*** $170,650 (1% federal, 50% institutional, 49% external sources). ***Receiving aid:*** Undergraduates: 2. ***Average award:*** Undergraduates: $5083. ***Scholarships, grants, and awards by category:*** *Academic Interests/Achievement:* 77 awards ($42,850 total): biological sciences, business, communication, computer science, education, general academic interests/achievements, humanities, mathematics, social sciences. *Special Achievements/Activities:* 10 awards ($11,900 total): community service, leadership, memberships. *Special Characteristics:* 2 awards ($4000 total): first-generation college students. ***Tuition waivers:*** Full or partial for senior citizens.

LOANS ***Student loans:*** $3,916,157 (76% need-based, 24% non-need-based). ***Average need-based loan:*** Undergraduates: $3944. ***Parent loans:*** $13,630 (100% non-need-based). ***Programs:*** FFEL (Subsidized and Unsubsidized Stafford, PLUS), state.

WORK-STUDY ***Federal work-study:*** Total amount: $35,093; 22 jobs averaging $1610. ***State or other work-study/employment:*** Total amount: $11,648 (100% need-based). 6 part-time jobs averaging $1941.

APPLYING FOR FINANCIAL AID ***Required financial aid form:*** FAFSA. ***Financial aid deadline (priority):*** 4/15. ***Notification date:*** Continuous beginning 5/20. Students must reply within 3 weeks of notification.

CONTACT Carolyn Mallory, Financial Aid Director, University of Houston–Victoria, 3007 North Ben Wilson, Victoria, TX 77901-5731, 361-570-4131 or toll-free 877-970-4848 Ext. 110. *Fax:* 361-570-4132. *E-mail:* malloryc@uhv.edu.

UNIVERSITY OF IDAHO

Moscow, ID

Tuition & fees (ID res): $4200 Average undergraduate aid package: $9471

ABOUT THE INSTITUTION State-supported, coed. Awards: bachelor's, master's, doctoral, and first professional degrees and post-master's certificates. 109 undergraduate majors. Total enrollment: 11,739. Undergraduates: 9,127. Freshmen: 1,621. Federal methodology is used as a basis for awarding need-based institutional aid.

UNDERGRADUATE EXPENSES for 2006–07 ***Application fee:*** $40. ***Tuition, state resident:*** full-time $0. ***Tuition, nonresident:*** full-time $9600; part-time $140 per credit. ***Required fees:*** full-time $4200; $200 per credit. Full-time tuition and fees vary according to degree level and program. Part-time tuition and fees vary according to course load, degree level, and program. ***College room and board:*** $5696. Room and board charges vary according to board plan and housing facility. ***Payment plans:*** Installment, deferred payment.

FRESHMAN FINANCIAL AID (Fall 2005) 1322 applied for aid; of those 73% were deemed to have need. 99% of freshmen with need received aid; of those 29% had need fully met. ***Average percent of need met:*** 76% (excluding resources awarded to replace EFC). ***Average financial aid package:*** $8572 (excluding resources awarded to replace EFC). 36% of all full-time freshmen had no need and received non-need-based gift aid.

UNDERGRADUATE FINANCIAL AID (Fall 2005) 6,253 applied for aid; of those 80% were deemed to have need. 98% of undergraduates with need received aid; of those 25% had need fully met. ***Average percent of need met:*** 75% (excluding resources awarded to replace EFC). ***Average financial aid package:*** $9471 (excluding resources awarded to replace EFC). 26% of all full-time undergraduates had no need and received non-need-based gift aid.

GIFT AID (NEED-BASED) ***Total amount:*** $10,850,362 (87% federal, 13% institutional). ***Receiving aid:*** Freshmen: 32% (549); All full-time undergraduates: 37% (3,146). ***Average award:*** Freshmen: $3035; Undergraduates: $3145. ***Scholarships, grants, and awards:*** Federal Pell, FSEOG, state, private, college/university gift aid from institutional funds.

GIFT AID (NON-NEED-BASED) ***Total amount:*** $8,112,323 (1% state, 77% institutional, 22% external sources). ***Receiving aid:*** Freshmen: 50% (850); Undergraduates: 42% (3,585). ***Average award:*** Freshmen: $3009; Undergraduates: $3577. ***Scholarships, grants, and awards by category:*** *Academic Interests/Achievement:* 7,500 awards ($17,000,000 total): agriculture, architecture, biological sciences, business, communication, computer science, education, engineering/technologies, English, foreign languages, general academic interests/achievements, home economics, humanities, mathematics, military science, physical sciences, premedicine, social sciences. *Creative Arts/Performance:* 300 awards ($600,000 total): applied art and design, art/fine arts, creative writing, dance, general creative arts/performance, journalism/publications, music, performing arts, theater/drama. *Special Achievements/Activities:* 70 awards ($100,000 total): cheerleading/drum major, general special achievements/activities, junior miss, leadership, rodeo. *Special Characteristics:* 400 awards ($300,000 total): children and siblings of alumni, children of faculty/staff, ethnic background, first-generation college students, general special characteristics, handicapped students, international students, local/state students, members of minority groups, out-of-state students. ***Tuition waivers:*** Full or partial for minority students, children of alumni, employees or children of employees, senior citizens. ***ROTC:*** Army, Naval, Air Force cooperative.

LOANS ***Student loans:*** $35,119,841 (57% need-based, 43% non-need-based). 69% of past graduating class borrowed through all loan programs. *Average indebtedness per student:* $20,002. ***Average need-based loan:*** Freshmen: $3341; Undergraduates: $5864. ***Parent loans:*** $3,483,767 (100% non-need-based). ***Programs:*** Federal Direct (Subsidized and Unsubsidized Stafford, PLUS), Perkins, college/university.

WORK-STUDY ***Federal work-study:*** Total amount: $616,392; 411 jobs averaging $1500. ***State or other work-study/employment:*** Total amount: $375,664 (100% need-based). 250 part-time jobs averaging $1500.

ATHLETIC AWARDS Total amount: $3,734,912 (100% non-need-based).

APPLYING FOR FINANCIAL AID ***Required financial aid form:*** FAFSA. ***Financial aid deadline (priority):*** 2/15. ***Notification date:*** Continuous beginning 3/30. Students must reply within 4 weeks of notification.

CONTACT Mr. Dan Davenport, Director of Admissions and Financial Aid, University of Idaho, Financial Aid Office, Moscow, ID 83844-4291, 208-885-6312 or toll-free 888-884-3246. *Fax:* 208-885-5592. *E-mail:* dand@uidaho.edu.

UNIVERSITY OF ILLINOIS AT CHICAGO

Chicago, IL

Tuition & fees (IL res): $9742 Average undergraduate aid package: $11,482

ABOUT THE INSTITUTION State-supported, coed. Awards: bachelor's, master's, doctoral, and first professional degrees and first professional certificates. 76 undergraduate majors. Total enrollment: 24,654. Undergraduates: 15,006. Freshmen: 2,852. Federal methodology is used as a basis for awarding need-based institutional aid.

UNDERGRADUATE EXPENSES for 2006–07 ***Application fee:*** $40. ***Tuition, state resident:*** full-time $6780. ***Tuition, nonresident:*** full-time $19,170. Full-time tuition and fees vary according to program. Part-time tuition and fees vary according to program. ***College room and board:*** $7446. Room and board charges vary according to board plan and housing facility. ***Payment plans:*** Guaranteed tuition, installment.

FRESHMAN FINANCIAL AID (Fall 2006, est.) 2234 applied for aid; of those 73% were deemed to have need. 99% of freshmen with need received aid; of those 67% had need fully met. ***Average percent of need met:*** 94% (excluding resources awarded to replace EFC). ***Average financial aid package:*** $10,892 (excluding resources awarded to replace EFC). 8% of all full-time freshmen had no need and received non-need-based gift aid.

UNDERGRADUATE FINANCIAL AID (Fall 2006, est.) 9,685 applied for aid; of those 79% were deemed to have need. 99% of undergraduates with need received aid; of those 62% had need fully met. ***Average percent of need met:*** 92% (excluding resources awarded to replace EFC). ***Average financial aid package:*** $11,482 (excluding resources awarded to replace EFC). 8% of all full-time undergraduates had no need and received non-need-based gift aid.

GIFT AID (NEED-BASED) ***Total amount:*** $59,721,156 (28% federal, 42% state, 29% institutional, 1% external sources). ***Receiving aid:*** Freshmen: 43% (1,206); All full-time undergraduates: 43% (5,914). ***Average award:*** Freshmen: $9749; Undergraduates: $9319. ***Scholarships, grants, and awards:*** Federal Pell, FSEOG, state, private, college/university gift aid from institutional funds.

GIFT AID (NON-NEED-BASED) ***Total amount:*** $3,081,145 (2% federal, 40% state, 46% institutional, 12% external sources). ***Receiving aid:*** Freshmen: 17% (485); Undergraduates: 11% (1,558). ***Average award:*** Freshmen: $2694; Undergraduates: $3787. ***Scholarships, grants, and awards by category:*** *Academic Interests/Achievement:* 1,411 awards ($1,925,371 total): architecture, business, general academic interests/achievements. *Creative Arts/Performance:* 135 awards ($405,418 total): applied art and design, art/fine arts, music, performing arts, theater/drama. *Special Achievements/Activities:* 197 awards ($752,499 total): general special achievements/activities. *Special Characteristics:* 1 award ($500 total): general special characteristics. ***Tuition waivers:*** Full or partial for employees or children of employees, senior citizens. ***ROTC:*** Army, Naval cooperative, Air Force cooperative.

LOANS ***Student loans:*** $30,457,380 (94% need-based, 6% non-need-based). 55% of past graduating class borrowed through all loan programs. *Average indebtedness per student:* $15,897. ***Average need-based loan:*** Freshmen: $3343; Undergraduates: $4258. ***Parent loans:*** $9,877,002 (58% need-based, 42% non-need-based). ***Programs:*** Federal Direct (Subsidized and Unsubsidized Stafford, PLUS), Perkins, Federal Nursing, college/university, private/alternative loans.

WORK-STUDY ***Federal work-study:*** Total amount: $1,339,512; 835 jobs averaging $1604. ***State or other work-study/employment:*** Total amount: $4,212,262 (100% non-need-based). 2,736 part-time jobs averaging $1540.

ATHLETIC AWARDS Total amount: $2,156,188 (25% need-based, 75% non-need-based).

APPLYING FOR FINANCIAL AID ***Required financial aid form:*** FAFSA. ***Financial aid deadline (priority):*** 3/1. ***Notification date:*** Continuous beginning 3/15. Students must reply within 2 weeks of notification.

CONTACT Deidre Rush, Associate Director of Financial Aid, University of Illinois at Chicago, 1200 West Harrison, M/C 334, Chicago, IL 60607-7128, 312-996-5563. *Fax:* 312-996-3385. *E-mail:* aroche@uic.edu.

UNIVERSITY OF ILLINOIS AT SPRINGFIELD

Springfield, IL

Tuition & fees (IL res): $7244 Average undergraduate aid package: $8233

ABOUT THE INSTITUTION State-supported, coed. Awards: bachelor's, master's, and doctoral degrees and post-bachelor's and post-master's certificates. 19 undergraduate majors. Total enrollment: 4,761. Undergraduates: 2,758. Freshmen: 243. Federal methodology is used as a basis for awarding need-based institutional aid.

UNDERGRADUATE EXPENSES for 2006–07 ***Application fee:*** $40. ***Tuition, state resident:*** full-time $5580; part-time $186 per credit hour. ***Tuition, nonresident:*** full-time $14,730; part-time $491 per credit hour. ***Required fees:*** full-time $1664; $597 per term part-time. ***College room and board:*** $7495; ***Room only:*** $3400. Room and board charges vary according to board plan and housing facility. Tuition for 2006-07 reflects the new Guaranteed tuition rate. ***Payment plans:*** Guaranteed tuition, installment.

FRESHMAN FINANCIAL AID (Fall 2005) 133 applied for aid; of those 56% were deemed to have need. 99% of freshmen with need received aid; of those 52% had need fully met. ***Average percent of need met:*** 84% (excluding resources awarded to replace EFC). ***Average financial aid package:*** $7923 (excluding resources awarded to replace EFC). 42% of all full-time freshmen had no need and received non-need-based gift aid.

UNDERGRADUATE FINANCIAL AID (Fall 2005) 1,180 applied for aid; of those 78% were deemed to have need. 98% of undergraduates with need received aid; of those 34% had need fully met. ***Average percent of need met:*** 82% (excluding resources awarded to replace EFC). ***Average financial aid package:*** $8233 (excluding resources awarded to replace EFC). 15% of all full-time undergraduates had no need and received non-need-based gift aid.

GIFT AID (NEED-BASED) ***Total amount:*** $5,025,269 (34% federal, 51% state, 13% institutional, 2% external sources). ***Receiving aid:*** Freshmen: 26% (36); All full-time undergraduates: 42% (644). ***Average award:*** Freshmen: $4667; Undergraduates: $5221. ***Scholarships, grants, and awards:*** Federal Pell, FSEOG, state, private, college/university gift aid from institutional funds.

GIFT AID (NON-NEED-BASED) ***Total amount:*** $816,941 (2% federal, 40% state, 52% institutional, 6% external sources). ***Receiving aid:*** Freshmen: 53% (72); Undergraduates: 27% (414). ***Average award:*** Freshmen: $2819; Undergraduates: $3444. ***Scholarships, grants, and awards by category:*** *Academic Interests/Achievement:* 594 awards ($1,056,990 total): agriculture, biological sciences, business, communication, computer science, education, engineering/technologies, English, foreign languages, general academic interests/achievements, health fields, humanities, international studies, mathematics, physical sciences, social sciences. *Creative Arts/Performance:* 5 awards ($3500 total): applied art and design, art/fine arts, general creative arts/performance, journalism/publications, music, performing arts. *Special Achievements/Activities:* 18 awards ($17,750 total): community service, general special achievements/activities, leadership, memberships. *Special Characteristics:* 86 awards ($206,683 total): adult students, children of educators, children of faculty/staff, children of union members/company employees, children of workers in trades, children with a deceased or disabled parent, ethnic background, first-generation college students, general special characteristics, international students, local/state students, members of minority groups, out-of-state students, public servants, veterans, veterans' children. ***Tuition waivers:*** Full or partial for employees or children of employees, senior citizens.

LOANS ***Student loans:*** $6,449,965 (85% need-based, 15% non-need-based). 55% of past graduating class borrowed through all loan programs. *Average indebtedness per student:* $12,696. ***Average need-based loan:*** Freshmen: $2324; Undergraduates: $4018. ***Parent loans:*** $803,671 (58% need-based, 42% non-need-based). ***Programs:*** FFEL (Subsidized and Unsubsidized Stafford, PLUS), Perkins, college/university.

WORK-STUDY ***Federal work-study:*** Total amount: $144,356; 74 jobs averaging $1951. ***State or other work-study/employment:*** Total amount: $754,583 (100% non-need-based). 320 part-time jobs averaging $2358.

ATHLETIC AWARDS Total amount: $332,862 (52% need-based, 48% non-need-based).

APPLYING FOR FINANCIAL AID ***Required financial aid form:*** FAFSA. ***Financial aid deadline:*** 11/15 (priority: 4/1). ***Notification date:*** Continuous beginning 1/1. Students must reply within 3 weeks of notification.

CONTACT Mr. Gerard Joseph, Director of Financial Aid, University of Illinois at Springfield, One University Plaza, MS UHB 1015, Financial Aid Office, Room 1015, Springfield, IL 627-5407, 217-206-6724 or toll-free 888-977-4847. *Fax:* 217-206-7376. *E-mail:* finaid@uis.edu.

UNIVERSITY OF ILLINOIS AT URBANA–CHAMPAIGN

Champaign, IL

Tuition & fees (IL res): $11,130 Average undergraduate aid package: $10,180

ABOUT THE INSTITUTION State-supported, coed. Awards: bachelor's, master's, doctoral, and first professional degrees and post-master's certificates. 155 undergraduate majors. Total enrollment: 42,728. Undergraduates: 31,472. Freshmen: 7,172. Federal methodology is used as a basis for awarding need-based institutional aid.

UNDERGRADUATE EXPENSES for 2007–08 ***Application fee:*** $40. ***Tuition, state resident:*** full-time $8440. ***Tuition, nonresident:*** full-time $22,526. ***College room and board:*** $8196. Entering degree-seeking students are guaranteed the same tuition rates for 4 years.

FRESHMAN FINANCIAL AID (Fall 2005) 5155 applied for aid; of those 61% were deemed to have need. 95% of freshmen with need received aid; of those

51% had need fully met. ***Average percent of need met:*** 90% (excluding resources awarded to replace EFC). ***Average financial aid package:*** $9733 (excluding resources awarded to replace EFC). 18% of all full-time freshmen had no need and received non-need-based gift aid.

UNDERGRADUATE FINANCIAL AID (Fall 2005) 16,969 applied for aid; of those 71% were deemed to have need. 97% of undergraduates with need received aid; of those 45% had need fully met. ***Average percent of need met:*** 87% (excluding resources awarded to replace EFC). ***Average financial aid package:*** $10,180 (excluding resources awarded to replace EFC). 15% of all full-time undergraduates had no need and received non-need-based gift aid.

GIFT AID (NEED-BASED) ***Total amount:*** $61,662,615 (21% federal, 41% state, 30% institutional, 8% external sources). ***Receiving aid:*** Freshmen: 25% (1,848); All full-time undergraduates: 26% (7,651). ***Average award:*** Freshmen: $6996; Undergraduates: $6531. ***Scholarships, grants, and awards:*** Federal Pell, FSEOG, state, private, college/university gift aid from institutional funds, United Negro College Fund.

GIFT AID (NON-NEED-BASED) ***Total amount:*** $10,841,297 (2% federal, 9% state, 57% institutional, 32% external sources). ***Receiving aid:*** Freshmen: 20% (1,521); Undergraduates: 16% (4,908). ***Average award:*** Freshmen: $3687; Undergraduates: $3773. ***Scholarships, grants, and awards by category:*** *Academic Interests/Achievement:* agriculture, architecture, area/ethnic studies, biological sciences, business, communication, computer science, education, engineering/technologies, English, foreign languages, general academic interests/achievements, health fields, humanities, international studies, library science, mathematics, military science, physical sciences, social sciences. *Creative Arts/Performance:* applied art and design, art/fine arts, cinema/film/broadcasting, creative writing, dance, general creative arts/performance, journalism/publications, music, performing arts, theater/drama. *Special Achievements/Activities:* community service, general special achievements/activities, leadership, memberships. *Special Characteristics:* children and siblings of alumni, children of faculty/staff, children with a deceased or disabled parent, ethnic background, first-generation college students, general special characteristics, handicapped students, local/state students, members of minority groups, out-of-state students, veterans, veterans' children. ***ROTC:*** Army, Naval, Air Force.

LOANS ***Student loans:*** $67,964,217 (92% need-based, 8% non-need-based). 51% of past graduating class borrowed through all loan programs. *Average indebtedness per student:* $15,413. ***Average need-based loan:*** Freshmen: $3554; Undergraduates: $4196. ***Parent loans:*** $39,734,084 (56% need-based, 44% non-need-based). ***Programs:*** Federal Direct (Subsidized and Unsubsidized Stafford, PLUS), Perkins, college/university, alternative loans.

WORK-STUDY ***Federal work-study:*** Total amount: $1,857,558; 1,456 jobs averaging $1276. ***State or other work-study/employment:*** Total amount: $14,662,049 (47% need-based, 53% non-need-based). 8,462 part-time jobs averaging $1732.

ATHLETIC AWARDS Total amount: $4,853,974 (31% need-based, 69% non-need-based).

APPLYING FOR FINANCIAL AID ***Required financial aid form:*** FAFSA. ***Financial aid deadline (priority):*** 3/15. ***Notification date:*** 3/15.

CONTACT Daniel Mann, Director of Student Financial Aid, University of Illinois at Urbana–Champaign, Student Services Arcade Building, 620 East John Street, Champaign, IL 61820-5711, 217-333-0100.

UNIVERSITY OF INDIANAPOLIS

Indianapolis, IN

CONTACT Ms. Linda B. Handy, Director of Financial Aid, University of Indianapolis, 1400 East Hanna Avenue, Indianapolis, IN 46227-3697, 317-788-3217 or toll-free 800-232-8634 Ext. 3216. *Fax:* 317-788-6136. *E-mail:* handy@uindy.edu.

THE UNIVERSITY OF IOWA

Iowa City, IA

Tuition & fees (IA res): $6293 **Average undergraduate aid package: $7480**

ABOUT THE INSTITUTION State-supported, coed. Awards: bachelor's, master's, doctoral, and first professional degrees and post-master's and first professional certificates. 144 undergraduate majors. Total enrollment: 28,816. Undergraduates: 20,738. Freshmen: 4,289. Federal methodology is used as a basis for awarding need-based institutional aid.

UNDERGRADUATE EXPENSES for 2007–08 ***Application fee:*** $40. ***Tuition, state resident:*** full-time $5376; part-time $224 per semester hour. ***Tuition, nonresident:*** full-time $18,548; part-time $773 per semester hour.

FRESHMAN FINANCIAL AID (Fall 2006, est.) 3008 applied for aid; of those 66% were deemed to have need. 95% of freshmen with need received aid; of those 99% had need fully met. ***Average percent of need met:*** 99% (excluding resources awarded to replace EFC). ***Average financial aid package:*** $7226 (excluding resources awarded to replace EFC). 23% of all full-time freshmen had no need and received non-need-based gift aid.

UNDERGRADUATE FINANCIAL AID (Fall 2006, est.) 13,330 applied for aid; of those 75% were deemed to have need. 94% of undergraduates with need received aid; of those 97% had need fully met. ***Average percent of need met:*** 97% (excluding resources awarded to replace EFC). ***Average financial aid package:*** $7480 (excluding resources awarded to replace EFC). 14% of all full-time undergraduates had no need and received non-need-based gift aid.

GIFT AID (NEED-BASED) ***Total amount:*** $26,379,738 (36% federal, 5% state, 52% institutional, 7% external sources). ***Receiving aid:*** Freshmen: 31% (1,212); All full-time undergraduates: 31% (5,606). ***Average award:*** Freshmen: $4488; Undergraduates: $4472. ***Scholarships, grants, and awards:*** Federal Pell, FSEOG, state, college/university gift aid from institutional funds.

GIFT AID (NON-NEED-BASED) ***Total amount:*** $12,162,692 (11% federal, 7% state, 57% institutional, 25% external sources). ***Receiving aid:*** Freshmen: 26% (1,001); Undergraduates: 16% (2,916). ***Average award:*** Freshmen: $1865; Undergraduates: $2209. ***Scholarships, grants, and awards by category:*** *Academic Interests/Achievement:* general academic interests/achievements. ***ROTC:*** Army, Air Force.

LOANS ***Student loans:*** $74,958,783 (38% need-based, 62% non-need-based). 61% of past graduating class borrowed through all loan programs. *Average indebtedness per student:* $20,234. ***Average need-based loan:*** Freshmen: $2892; Undergraduates: $3799. ***Parent loans:*** $29,910,543 (100% non-need-based). ***Programs:*** Federal Direct (Subsidized and Unsubsidized Stafford, PLUS), Perkins, Federal Nursing.

WORK-STUDY ***Federal work-study:*** Total amount: $2,201,594; jobs available. ***State or other work-study/employment:*** Total amount: $13,733 (100% need-based). Part-time jobs available.

ATHLETIC AWARDS Total amount: $6,238,442 (100% non-need-based).

APPLYING FOR FINANCIAL AID ***Required financial aid forms:*** FAFSA, institution's own form. ***Financial aid deadline:*** Continuous. ***Notification date:*** Continuous beginning 3/1.

CONTACT Mark Warner, Director of Student Financial Aid, The University of Iowa, 208 Calvin Hall, Iowa City, IA 52242, 319-335-3127 or toll-free 800-553-4692.

UNIVERSITY OF JUDAISM

Bel Air, CA

Tuition & fees: $20,300 **Average undergraduate aid package: $19,860**

ABOUT THE INSTITUTION Independent Jewish, coed. Awards: bachelor's and master's degrees. 8 undergraduate majors. Total enrollment: 291. Undergraduates: 115. Freshmen: 18. Both federal and institutional methodology are used as a basis for awarding need-based institutional aid.

UNDERGRADUATE EXPENSES for 2006–07 ***Application fee:*** $35. ***Comprehensive fee:*** $31,078 includes full-time tuition ($19,440), mandatory fees ($860), and room and board ($10,778). Room and board charges vary according to board plan. ***Part-time tuition:*** $810 per credit. ***Payment plan:*** Installment.

FRESHMAN FINANCIAL AID (Fall 2006, est.) 16 applied for aid; of those 100% were deemed to have need. 100% of freshmen with need received aid; of those 100% had need fully met. ***Average percent of need met:*** 99% (excluding resources awarded to replace EFC). ***Average financial aid package:*** $19,860 (excluding resources awarded to replace EFC). 12% of all full-time freshmen had no need and received non-need-based gift aid.

UNDERGRADUATE FINANCIAL AID (Fall 2006, est.) 95 applied for aid; of those 100% were deemed to have need. 100% of undergraduates with need received aid; of those 100% had need fully met. ***Average percent of need met:*** 100% (excluding resources awarded to replace EFC). ***Average financial aid package:*** $19,860 (excluding resources awarded to replace EFC). 6% of all full-time undergraduates had no need and received non-need-based gift aid.

GIFT AID (NEED-BASED) ***Total amount:*** $334,934 (40% federal, 32% state, 21% institutional, 7% external sources). ***Receiving aid:*** Freshmen: 47% (8); All full-time undergraduates: 32% (35). ***Average award:*** Freshmen: $6330; Undergraduates: $6499. ***Scholarships, grants, and awards:*** Federal Pell, FSEOG, state, private, college/university gift aid from institutional funds.

GIFT AID (NON-NEED-BASED) ***Total amount:*** $418,506 (100% institutional). ***Receiving aid:*** Freshmen: 24% (4); Undergraduates: 28% (30). ***Average award:*** Freshmen: $6370; Undergraduates: $4269. ***Scholarships, grants, and awards by category:*** *Academic Interests/Achievement:* 10 awards ($41,435 total): general academic interests/achievements, premedicine. *Special Achievements/Activities:* 2 awards ($2000 total): leadership.

LOANS ***Student loans:*** $398,654 (53% need-based, 47% non-need-based). 41% of past graduating class borrowed through all loan programs. *Average indebtedness per student:* $17,000. ***Average need-based loan:*** Freshmen: $2406; Undergraduates: $4386. ***Parent loans:*** $133,439 (100% need-based). ***Programs:*** FFEL (Subsidized and Unsubsidized Stafford, PLUS), alternative loans.

WORK-STUDY ***Federal work-study:*** Total amount: $59,529; 26 jobs averaging $2091. ***State or other work-study/employment:*** Total amount: $18,602,183 (1% need-based, 99% non-need-based). Part-time jobs available.

APPLYING FOR FINANCIAL AID ***Required financial aid forms:*** FAFSA, institution's own form, parent and student income tax returns. ***Financial aid deadline (priority):*** 3/2. ***Notification date:*** Continuous beginning 3/15. Students must reply within 3 weeks of notification.

CONTACT Larisa Zadoyen, Director of Financial Aid, University of Judaism, 15600 Mulholland Drive, Bel Air, CA 90077-1599, 310-476-9777 Ext. 252 or toll-free 888-853-6763. *Fax:* 310-476-4613. *E-mail:* finaid@uj.edu.

UNIVERSITY OF KANSAS

Lawrence, KS

Tuition & fees (KS res): $6153 Average undergraduate aid package: $7594

ABOUT THE INSTITUTION State-supported, coed. Awards: bachelor's, master's, doctoral, and first professional degrees and post-master's certificates (University of Kansas is a single institution with academic programs and facilities at two primary locations: Lawrence and Kansas City.). 103 undergraduate majors. Total enrollment: 28,924. Undergraduates: 21,353. Freshmen: 4,153. Federal methodology is used as a basis for awarding need-based institutional aid.

UNDERGRADUATE EXPENSES for 2006–07 ***Application fee:*** $30. ***Tuition, state resident:*** full-time $5513; part-time $183.75 per credit hour. ***Tuition, nonresident:*** full-time $14,483; part-time $482.75 per credit hour. ***Required fees:*** full-time $640; $53.33 per credit hour. Full-time tuition and fees vary according to program and reciprocity agreements. Part-time tuition and fees vary according to program and reciprocity agreements. ***College room and board:*** $5747; ***Room only:*** $2997. Room and board charges vary according to board plan and housing facility. ***Payment plan:*** Installment.

FRESHMAN FINANCIAL AID (Fall 2005) 3300 applied for aid; of those 47% were deemed to have need. 95% of freshmen with need received aid; of those 91% had need fully met. ***Average percent of need met:*** 62% (excluding resources awarded to replace EFC). ***Average financial aid package:*** $6281 (excluding resources awarded to replace EFC). 43% of all full-time freshmen had no need and received non-need-based gift aid.

UNDERGRADUATE FINANCIAL AID (Fall 2005) 14,331 applied for aid; of those 52% were deemed to have need. 96% of undergraduates with need received aid; of those 28% had need fully met. ***Average percent of need met:*** 70% (excluding resources awarded to replace EFC). ***Average financial aid package:*** $7594 (excluding resources awarded to replace EFC). 23% of all full-time undergraduates had no need and received non-need-based gift aid.

GIFT AID (NEED-BASED) ***Total amount:*** $17,635,653 (51% federal, 9% state, 39% institutional, 1% external sources). ***Receiving aid:*** Freshmen: 25% (1,014); All full-time undergraduates: 26% (4,760). ***Average award:*** Freshmen: $3393; Undergraduates: $3602. ***Scholarships, grants, and awards:*** Federal Pell, FSEOG, state, private, college/university gift aid from institutional funds.

GIFT AID (NON-NEED-BASED) ***Total amount:*** $12,424,866 (77% institutional, 23% external sources). ***Receiving aid:*** Freshmen: 16% (643); Undergraduates: 10% (1,889). ***Average award:*** Freshmen: $3003; Undergraduates: $3238. ***Scholarships, grants, and awards by category:*** *Academic Interests/Achievement:* architecture, area/ethnic studies, biological sciences, business, communication, computer science, education, engineering/technologies, English, foreign languages, general academic interests/achievements, health fields, humanities, international studies, library science, mathematics, military science, physical sciences, premedicine, religion/biblical studies, social sciences. *Creative Arts/Performance:* applied art and design, art/fine arts, cinema/film/broadcasting, creative writing, dance, debating, general creative arts/performance, journalism/publications, music, performing arts, theater/drama. *Special Achievements/Activities:* community service, general special achievements/activities, leadership. *Special Characteristics:* adult students, children of faculty/staff, ethnic background, first-generation college students, general special characteristics, international students, local/state students, married students, members of minority groups, out-of-state students, previous college experience. ***Tuition waivers:*** Full or partial for employees or children of employees. ***ROTC:*** Army, Naval, Air Force.

LOANS ***Student loans:*** $57,389,026 (50% need-based, 50% non-need-based). 39% of past graduating class borrowed through all loan programs. *Average indebtedness per student:* $18,869. ***Average need-based loan:*** Freshmen: $2198; Undergraduates: $2922. ***Parent loans:*** $24,980,747 (100% non-need-based). ***Programs:*** Federal Direct (Subsidized and Unsubsidized Stafford, PLUS), Perkins, college/university.

WORK-STUDY ***Federal work-study:*** Total amount: $1,340,682; 396 jobs averaging $3386. ***State or other work-study/employment:*** Total amount: $467,696 (100% non-need-based). 106 part-time jobs averaging $4412.

ATHLETIC AWARDS Total amount: $5,835,173 (100% non-need-based).

APPLYING FOR FINANCIAL AID ***Required financial aid form:*** FAFSA. ***Financial aid deadline (priority):*** 3/1. ***Notification date:*** Continuous beginning 4/1. Students must reply within 2 weeks of notification.

CONTACT Ms. Brenda Maigaard, Director of Student Financial Aid, University of Kansas, Office of Student Financial Aid, 50 Strong Hall, 1450 Jayhawk Boulevard, Lawrence, KS 66045-7535, 785-864-4700 or toll-free 888-686-7323 (in-state). *Fax:* 785-864-5469. *E-mail:* osfa@ku.edu.

UNIVERSITY OF KENTUCKY

Lexington, KY

ABOUT THE INSTITUTION State-supported, coed. Awards: bachelor's, master's, doctoral, and first professional degrees and post-master's certificates. 80 undergraduate majors. Total enrollment: 26,382. Undergraduates: 19,292. Freshmen: 4,190.

GIFT AID (NEED-BASED) ***Scholarships, grants, and awards:*** Federal Pell, FSEOG, state, private, college/university gift aid from institutional funds.

GIFT AID (NON-NEED-BASED) ***Scholarships, grants, and awards by category:*** *Academic Interests/Achievement:* agriculture, architecture, biological sciences, business, communication, education, engineering/technologies, foreign languages, general academic interests/achievements, health fields, home economics, mathematics, military science, physical sciences. *Creative Arts/Performance:* applied art and design, art/fine arts, debating, general creative arts/performance, journalism/publications, music, performing arts. *Special Achievements/Activities:* cheerleading/drum major, general special achievements/activities, leadership. *Special Characteristics:* adult students, children and siblings of alumni, children of educators, children of faculty/staff, children of public servants, children of union members/company employees, children of workers in trades, children with a deceased or disabled parent, ethnic background, first-generation college students, general special characteristics, handicapped students, international students, members of minority groups, spouses of deceased or disabled public servants, veterans, veterans' children.

LOANS ***Programs:*** Federal Direct (Subsidized and Unsubsidized Stafford, PLUS), FFEL (Subsidized and Unsubsidized Stafford, PLUS), Perkins, Federal Nursing, college/university.

WORK-STUDY ***Federal work-study:*** Total amount: $964,642; 489 jobs averaging $2038. ***State or other work-study/employment:*** Part-time jobs available.

APPLYING FOR FINANCIAL AID ***Required financial aid form:*** FAFSA.

CONTACT Ms. Lynda S. George, Director of Financial Aid, University of Kentucky, 128 Funkhouser Building, Lexington, KY 40506-0054, 859-257-3172 Ext. 241 or toll-free 800-432-0967 (in-state). *Fax:* 859-257-4398. *E-mail:* lgeorge@email.uky.edu.

UNIVERSITY OF LA VERNE

La Verne, CA

Tuition & fees: $25,590 Average undergraduate aid package: $20,615

ABOUT THE INSTITUTION Independent, coed. Awards: associate, bachelor's, master's, doctoral, and first professional degrees and post-bachelor's and post-master's certificates (also offers continuing education program with significant enrollment not reflected in profile). 48 undergraduate majors. Total enrollment: 3,876. Undergraduates: 1,685. Freshmen: 319. Federal methodology is used as a basis for awarding need-based institutional aid.

UNDERGRADUATE EXPENSES for 2007–08 ***Application fee:*** $50. ***Comprehensive fee:*** $35,340 includes full-time tuition ($25,590) and room and board ($9750). ***College room only:*** $5100. ***Part-time tuition:*** $720 per unit.

FRESHMAN FINANCIAL AID (Fall 2006, est.) 287 applied for aid; of those 92% were deemed to have need. 94% of freshmen with need received aid; of those 7% had need fully met. ***Average percent of need met:*** 64% (excluding resources awarded to replace EFC). ***Average financial aid package:*** $18,223 (excluding resources awarded to replace EFC). 21% of all full-time freshmen had no need and received non-need-based gift aid.

UNDERGRADUATE FINANCIAL AID (Fall 2006, est.) 1,306 applied for aid; of those 97% were deemed to have need. 100% of undergraduates with need received aid; of those 13% had need fully met. ***Average percent of need met:*** 68% (excluding resources awarded to replace EFC). ***Average financial aid package:*** $20,615 (excluding resources awarded to replace EFC). 37% of all full-time undergraduates had no need and received non-need-based gift aid.

GIFT AID (NEED-BASED) ***Total amount:*** $21,951,563 (11% federal, 25% state, 63% institutional, 1% external sources). ***Receiving aid:*** Freshmen: 81% (254); All full-time undergraduates: 75% (1,184). ***Average award:*** Freshmen: $10,033; Undergraduates: $10,763. ***Scholarships, grants, and awards:*** Federal Pell, FSEOG, state, private, college/university gift aid from institutional funds.

GIFT AID (NON-NEED-BASED) ***Total amount:*** $2,144,098 (99% institutional, 1% external sources). ***Receiving aid:*** Freshmen: 55% (174); Undergraduates: 69% (1,088). ***Average award:*** Freshmen: $8810; Undergraduates: $6972. ***Scholarships, grants, and awards by category:*** *Academic Interests/Achievement:* 1,682 awards ($12,349,260 total): general academic interests/achievements. *Creative Arts/Performance:* 53 awards ($195,200 total): art/fine arts, debating, journalism/publications, music, theater/drama. *Special Achievements/Activities:* 13 awards ($82,455 total): community service, leadership. *Special Characteristics:* 133 awards ($66,250 total): children and siblings of alumni, children of faculty/staff, ethnic background, first-generation college students, general special characteristics, international students, religious affiliation. ***ROTC:*** Army cooperative.

LOANS ***Student loans:*** $5,701,805 (95% need-based, 5% non-need-based). 66% of past graduating class borrowed through all loan programs. *Average indebtedness per student:* $28,856. ***Average need-based loan:*** Freshmen: $2445; Undergraduates: $3447. ***Parent loans:*** $3,112,998 (83% need-based, 17% non-need-based). ***Programs:*** FFEL (Subsidized and Unsubsidized Stafford, PLUS), Perkins, college/university, alternative loans.

WORK-STUDY ***Federal work-study:*** Total amount: $598,551; 249 jobs averaging $2189. ***State or other work-study/employment:*** 215 part-time jobs available.

APPLYING FOR FINANCIAL AID ***Required financial aid forms:*** FAFSA, state aid form. ***Financial aid deadline (priority):*** 3/2. ***Notification date:*** Continuous beginning 3/3. Students must reply within 1 week of notification.

CONTACT Leatha Webster, Director of Financial Aid, University of La Verne, 1950 3rd Street, La Verne, CA 91750-4443, 909-593-3511 Ext. 4180 or toll-free 800-876-4858. *Fax:* 909-392-2751. *E-mail:* websterl@ulv.edu.

UNIVERSITY OF LOUISIANA AT LAFAYETTE

Lafayette, LA

Tuition & fees (LA res): $3382 **Average undergraduate aid package: $5722**

ABOUT THE INSTITUTION State-supported, coed. Awards: bachelor's, master's, and doctoral degrees and post-master's certificates. 89 undergraduate majors. Total enrollment: 16,302. Undergraduates: 14,923. Freshmen: 2,914. Federal methodology is used as a basis for awarding need-based institutional aid.

UNDERGRADUATE EXPENSES for 2006–07 ***Application fee:*** $25. ***Tuition, state resident:*** full-time $3382; part-time $93.75 per credit hour. ***Tuition, nonresident:*** full-time $9592; part-time $350.25 per credit hour. Full-time tuition and fees vary according to course load. Part-time tuition and fees vary according to course load. ***College room and board:*** $3770. Room and board charges vary according to housing facility. ***Payment plan:*** Deferred payment.

FRESHMAN FINANCIAL AID (Fall 2005) 2488 applied for aid; of those 58% were deemed to have need. 97% of freshmen with need received aid; of those 13% had need fully met. ***Average percent of need met:*** 56% (excluding resources awarded to replace EFC). ***Average financial aid package:*** $4876 (excluding resources awarded to replace EFC). 10% of all full-time freshmen had no need and received non-need-based gift aid.

UNDERGRADUATE FINANCIAL AID (Fall 2005) 9,470 applied for aid; of those 67% were deemed to have need. 97% of undergraduates with need received aid; of those 9% had need fully met. ***Average percent of need met:*** 55% (excluding resources awarded to replace EFC). ***Average financial aid package:*** $5722 (excluding resources awarded to replace EFC). 5% of all full-time undergraduates had no need and received non-need-based gift aid.

GIFT AID (NEED-BASED) ***Total amount:*** $12,837,628 (99% federal, 1% state). ***Receiving aid:*** Freshmen: 47% (1,284); All full-time undergraduates: 42% (5,191). ***Average award:*** Freshmen: $3864; Undergraduates: $3770. ***Scholarships, grants, and awards:*** Federal Pell, FSEOG, state, college/university gift aid from institutional funds.

GIFT AID (NON-NEED-BASED) ***Total amount:*** $15,437,520 (74% state, 18% institutional, 8% external sources). ***Receiving aid:*** Freshmen: 7% (183); Undergraduates: 4% (447). ***Average award:*** Freshmen: $1499; Undergraduates: $1494. ***Scholarships, grants, and awards by category:*** *Academic Interests/Achievement:* 1,565 awards ($2,762,238 total): general academic interests/achievements. *Creative Arts/Performance:* general creative arts/performance. *Special Achievements/Activities:* general special achievements/activities. ***Tuition waivers:*** Full or partial for children of alumni, employees or children of employees, senior citizens. ***ROTC:*** Army.

LOANS ***Student loans:*** $27,343,837 (63% need-based, 37% non-need-based). ***Average need-based loan:*** Freshmen: $2220; Undergraduates: $3591. ***Parent loans:*** $1,310,135 (100% non-need-based). ***Programs:*** FFEL (Subsidized and Unsubsidized Stafford, PLUS), Perkins, Federal Nursing.

WORK-STUDY ***Federal work-study:*** Total amount: $829,182; 572 jobs averaging $1450. ***State or other work-study/employment:*** Total amount: $325,098 (100% non-need-based). 237 part-time jobs averaging $1372.

ATHLETIC AWARDS Total amount: $1,576,632 (100% non-need-based).

APPLYING FOR FINANCIAL AID ***Required financial aid form:*** FAFSA. ***Financial aid deadline (priority):*** 5/1. ***Notification date:*** Continuous beginning 4/1. Students must reply within 2 weeks of notification.

CONTACT Cindy S. Perez, Director of Financial Aid, University of Louisiana at Lafayette, PO Box 41206, Lafayette, LA 70504-1206, 337-482-6497 or toll-free 800-752-6553 (in-state). *Fax:* 337-482-6502. *E-mail:* cperez@louisiana.edu.

UNIVERSITY OF LOUISIANA AT MONROE

Monroe, LA

CONTACT Roslynn Pogue, Assistant Director, Financial Aid, University of Louisiana at Monroe, 700 University Avenue, Monroe, LA 71209, 318-342-5320 or toll-free 800-372-5272 (in-state), 800-372-5127 (out-of-state). *Fax:* 318-342-3539. *E-mail:* sspogue@ulm.edu.

UNIVERSITY OF LOUISVILLE

Louisville, KY

Tuition & fees (KY res): $6252 **Average undergraduate aid package: $8857**

ABOUT THE INSTITUTION State-supported, coed. Awards: associate, bachelor's, master's, doctoral, and first professional degrees and post-bachelor's and post-master's certificates. 50 undergraduate majors. Total enrollment: 20,804. Undergraduates: 14,995. Freshmen: 2,443. Federal methodology is used as a basis for awarding need-based institutional aid.

UNDERGRADUATE EXPENSES for 2006–07 ***Application fee:*** $30. ***Tuition, state resident:*** full-time $6252; part-time $261 per hour. ***Tuition, nonresident:*** full-time $16,072; part-time $670 per hour. Full-time tuition and fees vary according to reciprocity agreements. Part-time tuition and fees vary according to course load and reciprocity agreements. ***College room and board:*** $5096; ***Room only:*** $3396. Room and board charges vary according to board plan and housing facility. ***Payment plan:*** Installment.

FRESHMAN FINANCIAL AID (Fall 2006, est.) 1704 applied for aid; of those 80% were deemed to have need. 99% of freshmen with need received aid; of those 21% had need fully met. ***Average percent of need met:*** 57% (excluding resources awarded to replace EFC). ***Average financial aid package:*** $9110 (excluding resources awarded to replace EFC). 20% of all full-time freshmen had no need and received non-need-based gift aid.

UNDERGRADUATE FINANCIAL AID (Fall 2006, est.) 7,073 applied for aid; of those 87% were deemed to have need. 98% of undergraduates with need received aid; of those 14% had need fully met. ***Average percent of need met:*** 55% (excluding resources awarded to replace EFC). ***Average financial aid***

package: $8857 (excluding resources awarded to replace EFC). 15% of all full-time undergraduates had no need and received non-need-based gift aid.

GIFT AID (NEED-BASED) ***Total amount:*** $32,932,104 (29% federal, 25% state, 26% institutional, 20% external sources). ***Receiving aid:*** Freshmen: 54% (1,278); All full-time undergraduates: 44% (5,066). ***Average award:*** Freshmen: $6517; Undergraduates: $5828. ***Scholarships, grants, and awards:*** Federal Pell, FSEOG, state, private, college/university gift aid from institutional funds.

GIFT AID (NON-NEED-BASED) ***Total amount:*** $20,302,951 (30% state, 51% institutional, 19% external sources). ***Receiving aid:*** Freshmen: 8% (201); Undergraduates: 4% (427). ***Average award:*** Freshmen: $6153; Undergraduates: $5847. ***Scholarships, grants, and awards by category:*** *Academic Interests/Achievement:* general academic interests/achievements. *Creative Arts/Performance:* general creative arts/performance. *Special Achievements/Activities:* general special achievements/activities, memberships. *Special Characteristics:* general special characteristics. ***Tuition waivers:*** Full or partial for employees or children of employees, senior citizens. ***ROTC:*** Army, Air Force.

LOANS ***Student loans:*** $36,668,551 (82% need-based, 18% non-need-based). 40% of past graduating class borrowed through all loan programs. *Average indebtedness per student:* $10,906. ***Average need-based loan:*** Freshmen: $2549; Undergraduates: $3813. ***Parent loans:*** $2,656,084 (46% need-based, 54% non-need-based). ***Programs:*** FFEL (Subsidized and Unsubsidized Stafford, PLUS), Perkins, Federal Nursing, college/university.

WORK-STUDY ***Federal work-study:*** Total amount: $1,381,138; jobs available.

ATHLETIC AWARDS Total amount: $6,220,289 (35% need-based, 65% non-need-based).

APPLYING FOR FINANCIAL AID ***Required financial aid form:*** FAFSA. ***Financial aid deadline (priority):*** 3/15. ***Notification date:*** Continuous beginning 4/1. Students must reply by 5/1.

CONTACT Ms. Patricia O. Arauz, Director of Financial Aid, University of Louisville, 2301 South Third Street, Louisville, KY 40292-0001, 502-852-6145 or toll-free 502-852-6531 (in-state), 800-334-8635 (out-of-state). *Fax:* 502-852-0182. *E-mail:* finaid@louisville.edu.

UNIVERSITY OF MAINE

Orono, ME

Tuition & fees (ME res): $7464 Average undergraduate aid package: $10,946

ABOUT THE INSTITUTION State-supported, coed. Awards: bachelor's, master's, and doctoral degrees and post-master's certificates. 106 undergraduate majors. Total enrollment: 11,435. Undergraduates: 9,179. Freshmen: 1,753. Federal methodology is used as a basis for awarding need-based institutional aid.

UNDERGRADUATE EXPENSES for 2006–07 ***Application fee:*** $40. ***Tuition, state resident:*** full-time $5970; part-time $199 per credit hour. ***Tuition, nonresident:*** full-time $16,920; part-time $564 per credit hour. ***Required fees:*** full-time $1494; $139 per term part-time. Full-time tuition and fees vary according to reciprocity agreements. Part-time tuition and fees vary according to reciprocity agreements. ***College room and board:*** $7125; ***Room only:*** $3593. Room and board charges vary according to board plan and housing facility. ***Payment plan:*** Installment.

FRESHMAN FINANCIAL AID (Fall 2006, est.) 1890 applied for aid; of those 76% were deemed to have need. 99% of freshmen with need received aid; of those 34% had need fully met. ***Average percent of need met:*** 90% (excluding resources awarded to replace EFC). ***Average financial aid package:*** $11,269 (excluding resources awarded to replace EFC). 22% of all full-time freshmen had no need and received non-need-based gift aid.

UNDERGRADUATE FINANCIAL AID (Fall 2006, est.) 6,329 applied for aid; of those 79% were deemed to have need. 99% of undergraduates with need received aid; of those 33% had need fully met. ***Average percent of need met:*** 89% (excluding resources awarded to replace EFC). ***Average financial aid package:*** $10,946 (excluding resources awarded to replace EFC). 20% of all full-time undergraduates had no need and received non-need-based gift aid.

GIFT AID (NEED-BASED) ***Total amount:*** $21,251,101 (44% federal, 14% state, 33% institutional, 9% external sources). ***Receiving aid:*** Freshmen: 54% (1,184); All full-time undergraduates: 50% (3,820). ***Average award:*** Freshmen: $6358; Undergraduates: $5419. ***Scholarships, grants, and awards:*** Federal Pell, FSEOG, state, private, college/university gift aid from institutional funds.

GIFT AID (NON-NEED-BASED) ***Total amount:*** $4,399,358 (20% institutional, 80% external sources). ***Receiving aid:*** Freshmen: 5% (113); Undergraduates: 4% (286). ***Average award:*** Freshmen: $5769; Undergraduates: $6752. ***Scholarships, grants, and awards by category:*** *Academic Interests/Achievement:* 786 awards ($1,980,211 total): biological sciences, business, communication, computer science, education, engineering/technologies, English, general academic interests/achievements, humanities, mathematics, military science, physical sciences, social sciences. *Creative Arts/Performance:* applied art and design, art/fine arts, creative writing, journalism/publications, music, performing arts, theater/drama. *Special Achievements/Activities:* community service, general special achievements/activities, leadership, memberships. *Special Characteristics:* children and siblings of alumni, children of faculty/staff, children of union members/company employees, children with a deceased or disabled parent, ethnic background, international students, local/state students, members of minority groups, out-of-state students, previous college experience, public servants, veterans, veterans' children. ***Tuition waivers:*** Full or partial for employees or children of employees. ***ROTC:*** Army, Naval.

LOANS ***Student loans:*** $38,298,358 (52% need-based, 48% non-need-based). 75% of past graduating class borrowed through all loan programs. *Average indebtedness per student:* $21,795. ***Average need-based loan:*** Freshmen: $3240; Undergraduates: $4365. ***Parent loans:*** $5,937,061 (100% non-need-based). ***Programs:*** FFEL (Subsidized and Unsubsidized Stafford, PLUS), Perkins, state, college/university.

WORK-STUDY ***Federal work-study:*** Total amount: $3,635,939; 1,699 jobs averaging $2140.

ATHLETIC AWARDS Total amount: $1,434,046 (28% need-based, 72% non-need-based).

APPLYING FOR FINANCIAL AID ***Required financial aid form:*** FAFSA. ***Financial aid deadline (priority):*** 3/1. ***Notification date:*** Continuous beginning 3/15. Students must reply by 5/1 or within 2 weeks of notification.

CONTACT Ms. Peggy L. Crawford, Director of Student Aid, University of Maine, 5781 Wingate Hall, Orono, ME 04469, 207-581-1324 or toll-free 877-486-2364. *Fax:* 207-581-3261. *E-mail:* peggy.crawford@umit.maine.edu.

THE UNIVERSITY OF MAINE AT AUGUSTA

Augusta, ME

CONTACT Sherry McCollett, Financial Aid Counselor, The University of Maine at Augusta, 46 University Drive, Augusta, ME 04330-9410, 207-621-3455 or toll-free 877-862-1234 Ext. 3185 (in-state). *Fax:* 207-621-3116. *E-mail:* sherrym@maine.edu.

UNIVERSITY OF MAINE AT FARMINGTON

Farmington, ME

Tuition & fees (ME res): $6408 Average undergraduate aid package: $8281

ABOUT THE INSTITUTION State-supported, coed. Awards: bachelor's degrees. 40 undergraduate majors. Total enrollment: 2,424. Undergraduates: 2,424. Freshmen: 520. Federal methodology is used as a basis for awarding need-based institutional aid.

UNDERGRADUATE EXPENSES for 2006–07 ***Application fee:*** $40. ***Tuition, state resident:*** full-time $5824; part-time $182 per credit hour. ***Tuition, nonresident:*** full-time $13,536; part-time $423 per credit hour. ***Required fees:*** full-time $584; $75 per term part-time. Full-time tuition and fees vary according to course load, reciprocity agreements, and student level. Part-time tuition and fees vary according to course load, reciprocity agreements, and student level. ***College room and board:*** $6312; ***Room only:*** $3360. Room and board charges vary according to board plan and housing facility. ***Payment plan:*** Installment.

FRESHMAN FINANCIAL AID (Fall 2006, est.) 499 applied for aid; of those 80% were deemed to have need. 92% of freshmen with need received aid; of those 10% had need fully met. ***Average percent of need met:*** 75% (excluding resources awarded to replace EFC). ***Average financial aid package:*** $8880 (excluding resources awarded to replace EFC). 2% of all full-time freshmen had no need and received non-need-based gift aid.

UNDERGRADUATE FINANCIAL AID (Fall 2006, est.) 1,809 applied for aid; of those 81% were deemed to have need. 99% of undergraduates with need received aid; of those 18% had need fully met. ***Average percent of need met:*** 75% (excluding resources awarded to replace EFC). ***Average financial aid package:*** $8281 (excluding resources awarded to replace EFC). 3% of all full-time undergraduates had no need and received non-need-based gift aid.

GIFT AID (NEED-BASED) ***Total amount:*** $5,337,508 (50% federal, 18% state, 31% institutional, 1% external sources). ***Receiving aid:*** Freshmen: 63% (326); All full-time undergraduates: 54% (1,169). ***Average award:*** Freshmen: $4975;

Undergraduates: $4142. ***Scholarships, grants, and awards:*** Federal Pell, FSEOG, state, private, college/university gift aid from institutional funds.

GIFT AID (NON-NEED-BASED) ***Total amount:*** $1,956,136 (28% institutional, 72% external sources). ***Receiving aid:*** Freshmen: 49% (252); Undergraduates: 26% (558). ***Average award:*** Freshmen: $1864; Undergraduates: $1758. ***Scholarships, grants, and awards by category:*** *Academic Interests/Achievement:* general academic interests/achievements. *Special Characteristics:* children of faculty/staff, members of minority groups, out-of-state students, veterans' children. ***Tuition waivers:*** Full or partial for minority students, employees or children of employees, senior citizens.

LOANS ***Student loans:*** $10,541,647 (53% need-based, 47% non-need-based). 81% of past graduating class borrowed through all loan programs. *Average indebtedness per student:* $16,555. ***Average need-based loan:*** Freshmen: $2958; Undergraduates: $3812. ***Parent loans:*** $1,023,141 (100% non-need-based). ***Programs:*** FFEL (Subsidized and Unsubsidized Stafford, PLUS), Perkins, college/university, Educators For Maine Loans.

WORK-STUDY ***Federal work-study:*** Total amount: $750,513; 505 jobs averaging $1447. ***State or other work-study/employment:*** Total amount: $966,523 (100% non-need-based). 494 part-time jobs averaging $1957.

APPLYING FOR FINANCIAL AID ***Required financial aid form:*** FAFSA. ***Financial aid deadline (priority):*** 3/1. ***Notification date:*** Continuous beginning 3/15. Students must reply within 2 weeks of notification.

CONTACT Mr. Ronald P. Milliken, Director of Financial Aid, University of Maine at Farmington, 224 Main Street, Farmington, ME 04938-1990, 207-778-7105. *Fax:* 207-778-8178. *E-mail:* milliken@maine.edu.

UNIVERSITY OF MAINE AT FORT KENT

Fort Kent, ME

Tuition & fees: N/R **Average undergraduate aid package: $7307**

ABOUT THE INSTITUTION State-supported, coed. Awards: associate and bachelor's degrees. 25 undergraduate majors. Total enrollment: 1,076. Undergraduates: 1,076. Federal methodology is used as a basis for awarding need-based institutional aid.

FRESHMAN FINANCIAL AID (Fall 2006, est.) 131 applied for aid; of those 86% were deemed to have need. 98% of freshmen with need received aid; of those 25% had need fully met. ***Average percent of need met:*** 63% (excluding resources awarded to replace EFC). ***Average financial aid package:*** $6136 (excluding resources awarded to replace EFC).

UNDERGRADUATE FINANCIAL AID (Fall 2006, est.) 485 applied for aid; of those 88% were deemed to have need. 94% of undergraduates with need received aid; of those 30% had need fully met. ***Average percent of need met:*** 74% (excluding resources awarded to replace EFC). ***Average financial aid package:*** $7307 (excluding resources awarded to replace EFC). 5% of all full-time undergraduates had no need and received non-need-based gift aid.

GIFT AID (NEED-BASED) ***Total amount:*** $2,180,970 (63% federal, 10% state, 10% institutional, 17% external sources). ***Receiving aid:*** Freshmen: 110; All full-time undergraduates: 51% (389). ***Average award:*** Freshmen: $3911; Undergraduates: $4211. ***Scholarships, grants, and awards:*** Federal Pell, FSEOG, state, private, college/university gift aid from institutional funds.

GIFT AID (NON-NEED-BASED) ***Total amount:*** $192,213 (13% institutional, 87% external sources). ***Receiving aid:*** Undergraduates: 1% (5). ***Average award:*** Freshmen: $4114; Undergraduates: $4259. ***Scholarships, grants, and awards by category:*** *Academic Interests/Achievement:* business, computer science, education, English, foreign languages, general academic interests/achievements, health fields, humanities, mathematics, social sciences. *Creative Arts/Performance:* general creative arts/performance, performing arts. *Special Achievements/Activities:* general special achievements/activities. *Special Characteristics:* adult students, children of faculty/staff, general special characteristics, international students, members of minority groups. ***Tuition waivers:*** Full or partial for employees or children of employees.

LOANS ***Student loans:*** $2,010,233 (60% need-based, 40% non-need-based). 81% of past graduating class borrowed through all loan programs. *Average indebtedness per student:* $10,483. ***Average need-based loan:*** Freshmen: $2772; Undergraduates: $4502. ***Parent loans:*** $176,162 (100% non-need-based). ***Programs:*** FFEL (Subsidized and Unsubsidized Stafford, PLUS), Perkins, state.

WORK-STUDY ***Federal work-study:*** Total amount: $140,027; 119 jobs averaging $1500. ***State or other work-study/employment:*** Total amount: $1,450,675 (93% need-based, 7% non-need-based). 44 part-time jobs averaging $1500.

APPLYING FOR FINANCIAL AID ***Required financial aid form:*** FAFSA. ***Financial aid deadline (priority):*** 3/1. ***Notification date:*** Continuous beginning 3/1.

CONTACT Ellen Cost, Director of Financial Aid, University of Maine at Fort Kent, 23 University Drive, Fort Kent, ME 04743-1292, 207-834-7606 or toll-free 888-TRY-UMFK. *Fax:* 207-834-7841. *E-mail:* ecost@maine.edu.

UNIVERSITY OF MAINE AT MACHIAS

Machias, ME

CONTACT Ms. Stephanie Larrabee, Director of Financial Aid, University of Maine at Machias, 9 O'Brien Avenue, Machias, ME 04654, 207-255-1203 or toll-free 888-GOTOUMM (in-state), 888-468-6866 (out-of-state). *Fax:* 207-255-4864.

UNIVERSITY OF MAINE AT PRESQUE ISLE

Presque Isle, ME

ABOUT THE INSTITUTION State-supported, coed. Awards: associate and bachelor's degrees. 28 undergraduate majors. Total enrollment: 1,548. Undergraduates: 1,548. Freshmen: 211.

GIFT AID (NEED-BASED) ***Scholarships, grants, and awards:*** Federal Pell, FSEOG, state, private, college/university gift aid from institutional funds.

GIFT AID (NON-NEED-BASED) ***Scholarships, grants, and awards by category:*** *Academic Interests/Achievement:* general academic interests/achievements. *Creative Arts/Performance:* art/fine arts. *Special Achievements/Activities:* community service. *Special Characteristics:* children of faculty/staff, ethnic background, international students, veterans' children.

LOANS ***Programs:*** Federal Direct (Subsidized and Unsubsidized Stafford, PLUS), Perkins, state, college/university.

WORK-STUDY ***Federal work-study:*** Total amount: $450,200; 283 jobs averaging $1318.

APPLYING FOR FINANCIAL AID ***Required financial aid form:*** FAFSA.

CONTACT Christopher A. R. Bill, (Acting) Director of Financial Aid, University of Maine at Presque Isle, 181 Main Street, Presque Isle, ME 04769-2888, 207-768-9511. *Fax:* 207-768-9608. *E-mail:* chris@maine.edu.

UNIVERSITY OF MANAGEMENT AND TECHNOLOGY

Arlington, VA

CONTACT Financial Aid Office, University of Management and Technology, 1901 North Fort Myer Drive, Arlington, VA 22209, 703-516-0035 or toll-free 800-924-4885 (in-state). *E-mail:* info@umtweb.edu.

UNIVERSITY OF MARY

Bismarck, ND

ABOUT THE INSTITUTION Independent Roman Catholic, coed. Awards: associate, bachelor's, master's, and doctoral degrees. 37 undergraduate majors. Total enrollment: 2,765. Undergraduates: 2,106. Freshmen: 343.

GIFT AID (NEED-BASED) ***Scholarships, grants, and awards:*** Federal Pell, FSEOG, state, private, college/university gift aid from institutional funds.

GIFT AID (NON-NEED-BASED) ***Scholarships, grants, and awards by category:*** *Academic Interests/Achievement:* general academic interests/achievements. *Creative Arts/Performance:* debating, music, theater/drama. *Special Characteristics:* children of faculty/staff.

LOANS ***Programs:*** FFEL (Subsidized and Unsubsidized Stafford, PLUS), Perkins, Federal Nursing, college/university.

APPLYING FOR FINANCIAL AID ***Required financial aid form:*** FAFSA.

CONTACT Dave Hanson, Director of Financial Aid, University of Mary, 7500 University Drive, Bismarck, ND 58504-9652, 701-255-7500 Ext. 8079 or toll-free 800-288-6279. *Fax:* 701-255-7687.

UNIVERSITY OF MARY HARDIN-BAYLOR

Belton, TX

ABOUT THE INSTITUTION Independent Southern Baptist, coed. Awards: bachelor's and master's degrees. 52 undergraduate majors. Total enrollment: 2,738. Undergraduates: 2,600. Freshmen: 470.

GIFT AID (NEED-BASED) ***Scholarships, grants, and awards:*** Federal Pell, FSEOG, state, private, college/university gift aid from institutional funds.

GIFT AID (NON-NEED-BASED) ***Scholarships, grants, and awards by category:*** *Academic Interests/Achievement:* biological sciences, business, communication, computer science, education, English, foreign languages, general academic interests/achievements, health fields, humanities, international studies, mathematics, physical sciences, premedicine, religion/biblical studies, social sciences. *Creative Arts/Performance:* art/fine arts, music. *Special Achievements/Activities:* cheerleading/drum major, community service, leadership, religious involvement. *Special Characteristics:* children and siblings of alumni, children of faculty/staff, ethnic background, handicapped students, international students, local/state students, members of minority groups, out-of-state students, relatives of clergy, religious affiliation.

LOANS ***Programs:*** FFEL (Subsidized and Unsubsidized Stafford, PLUS), Perkins, state, college/university.

WORK-STUDY ***Federal work-study:*** Total amount: $412,981; 209 jobs averaging $2300. ***State or other work-study/employment:*** Total amount: $378,837 (27% need-based, 73% non-need-based). 201 part-time jobs averaging $2300.

APPLYING FOR FINANCIAL AID ***Required financial aid form:*** FAFSA.

CONTACT Ms. Kelly Graves, Assistant Director of Financial Aid, University of Mary Hardin-Baylor, Box 8080, UMHB Station, Belton, TX 76513, 254-295-4517 or toll-free 800-727-8642. *Fax:* 254-295-5049. *E-mail:* kgraves@umhb.edu.

UNIVERSITY OF MARYLAND, BALTIMORE COUNTY

Baltimore, MD

Tuition & fees (MD res): $8622 Average undergraduate aid package: $9876

ABOUT THE INSTITUTION State-supported, coed. Awards: bachelor's, master's, and doctoral degrees and post-bachelor's certificates. 57 undergraduate majors. Total enrollment: 11,798. Undergraduates: 9,416. Freshmen: 1,429. Federal methodology is used as a basis for awarding need-based institutional aid.

UNDERGRADUATE EXPENSES for 2006–07 ***Application fee:*** $50. ***Tuition, state resident:*** full-time $6484; part-time $270 per credit hour. ***Tuition, nonresident:*** full-time $15,216; part-time $633 per credit hour. ***Required fees:*** full-time $2138; $94 per credit hour. ***College room and board:*** $8381; ***Room only:*** $5127.

FRESHMAN FINANCIAL AID (Fall 2005) 951 applied for aid; of those 64% were deemed to have need. 100% of freshmen with need received aid; of those 34% had need fully met. ***Average percent of need met:*** 80% (excluding resources awarded to replace EFC). ***Average financial aid package:*** $10,204 (excluding resources awarded to replace EFC). 23% of all full-time freshmen had no need and received non-need-based gift aid.

UNDERGRADUATE FINANCIAL AID (Fall 2005) 4,592 applied for aid; of those 77% were deemed to have need. 100% of undergraduates with need received aid; of those 37% had need fully met. ***Average percent of need met:*** 73% (excluding resources awarded to replace EFC). ***Average financial aid package:*** $9876 (excluding resources awarded to replace EFC). 8% of all full-time undergraduates had no need and received non-need-based gift aid.

GIFT AID (NEED-BASED) ***Total amount:*** $17,679,048 (31% federal, 37% state, 28% institutional, 4% external sources). ***Receiving aid:*** Freshmen: 36% (516); All full-time undergraduates: 36% (2,890). ***Average award:*** Freshmen: $4860; Undergraduates: $6652. ***Scholarships, grants, and awards:*** Federal Pell, FSEOG, state, private, college/university gift aid from institutional funds.

GIFT AID (NON-NEED-BASED) ***Total amount:*** $12,550,703 (7% state, 89% institutional, 4% external sources). ***Receiving aid:*** Freshmen: 8% (118); Undergraduates: 4% (315). ***Average award:*** Freshmen: $4001; Undergraduates: $3484. ***Scholarships, grants, and awards by category:*** *Academic Interests/Achievement:* 1,304 awards ($10,978,019 total): biological sciences, computer science, engineering/technologies, English, foreign languages, general academic interests/achievements, humanities, mathematics, physical sciences. *Creative Arts/Performance:* 36 awards ($49,400 total): art/fine arts, cinema/film/broadcasting, creative writing, dance, music, performing arts, theater/drama. ***ROTC:*** Army cooperative.

LOANS ***Student loans:*** $22,144,240 (47% need-based, 53% non-need-based). 55% of past graduating class borrowed through all loan programs. *Average indebtedness per student:* $19,910. ***Average need-based loan:*** Freshmen: $3196; Undergraduates: $4338. ***Parent loans:*** $9,925,848 (100% non-need-based). ***Programs:*** FFEL (Subsidized and Unsubsidized Stafford, PLUS), Perkins.

WORK-STUDY ***Federal work-study:*** Total amount: $143,788; 69 jobs averaging $2083. ***State or other work-study/employment:*** Total amount: $863,999 (56% need-based, 44% non-need-based).

ATHLETIC AWARDS Total amount: $1,959,093 (22% need-based, 78% non-need-based).

APPLYING FOR FINANCIAL AID ***Required financial aid form:*** FAFSA. ***Financial aid deadline (priority):*** 2/14. ***Notification date:*** Continuous beginning 3/15.

CONTACT Stephanie Johnson, Director, University of Maryland, Baltimore County, 1000 Hilltop Circle, Baltimore, MD 21250, 410-455-2387 or toll-free 800-UMBC-4U2 (in-state), 800-862-2402 (out-of-state). *Fax:* 410-455-1094. *E-mail:* finaid@umbc.edu.

UNIVERSITY OF MARYLAND, COLLEGE PARK

College Park, MD

Tuition & fees (MD res): $7906 Average undergraduate aid package: $10,722

ABOUT THE INSTITUTION State-supported, coed. Awards: bachelor's, master's, doctoral, and first professional degrees and post-bachelor's and post-master's certificates. 92 undergraduate majors. Total enrollment: 35,300. Undergraduates: 25,373. Freshmen: 4,211. Federal methodology is used as a basis for awarding need-based institutional aid.

UNDERGRADUATE EXPENSES for 2006–07 ***Application fee:*** $55. ***Tuition, state resident:*** full-time $6566; part-time $273 per credit hour. ***Tuition, nonresident:*** full-time $20,005; part-time $834 per credit hour. ***Required fees:*** full-time $1340; $309 per term part-time. Part-time tuition and fees vary according to course load. ***College room and board:*** $8422; ***Room only:*** $4997. Room and board charges vary according to board plan. ***Payment plans:*** Installment, deferred payment.

FRESHMAN FINANCIAL AID (Fall 2006, est.) 2826 applied for aid; of those 56% were deemed to have need. 95% of freshmen with need received aid; of those 28% had need fully met. ***Average percent of need met:*** 69% (excluding resources awarded to replace EFC). ***Average financial aid package:*** $12,078 (excluding resources awarded to replace EFC). 18% of all full-time freshmen had no need and received non-need-based gift aid.

UNDERGRADUATE FINANCIAL AID (Fall 2006, est.) 12,467 applied for aid; of those 72% were deemed to have need. 95% of undergraduates with need received aid; of those 27% had need fully met. ***Average percent of need met:*** 67% (excluding resources awarded to replace EFC). ***Average financial aid package:*** $10,722 (excluding resources awarded to replace EFC). 10% of all full-time undergraduates had no need and received non-need-based gift aid.

GIFT AID (NEED-BASED) ***Total amount:*** $33,680,258 (34% federal, 36% state, 30% institutional). ***Receiving aid:*** Freshmen: 28% (1,115); All full-time undergraduates: 26% (6,084). ***Average award:*** Freshmen: $6321; Undergraduates: $5443. ***Scholarships, grants, and awards:*** Federal Pell, FSEOG, state, private, college/university gift aid from institutional funds.

GIFT AID (NON-NEED-BASED) ***Total amount:*** $31,585,711 (14% state, 63% institutional, 23% external sources). ***Receiving aid:*** Freshmen: 22% (879); Undergraduates: 13% (3,059). ***Average award:*** Freshmen: $5336; Undergraduates: $2845. ***Scholarships, grants, and awards by category:*** *Academic Interests/Achievement:* 4,079 awards ($15,639,305 total): agriculture, architecture, biological sciences, business, communication, computer science, education, engineering/technologies, English, foreign languages, general academic interests/achievements, health fields, humanities, international studies, library science, mathematics, military science, physical sciences, premedicine, social sciences. *Creative Arts/Performance:* 57 awards ($430,727 total): applied art and design, art/fine arts, dance, music, performing arts, theater/drama. *Special Achievements/Activities:* 71 awards ($310,469 total): cheerleading/drum major. *Special Characteristics:* 1,595 awards ($6,262,700 total): adult students, out-of-state students. ***Tuition waivers:*** Full or partial for employees or children of employees. ***ROTC:*** Army, Naval cooperative, Air Force.

LOANS ***Student loans:*** $61,530,015 (71% need-based, 29% non-need-based). 44% of past graduating class borrowed through all loan programs. *Average indebtedness per student:* $17,731. ***Average need-based loan:*** Freshmen: $3062; Undergraduates: $4075. ***Parent loans:*** $22,779,101 (39% need-based, 61% non-need-based). ***Programs:*** FFEL (Subsidized and Unsubsidized Stafford, PLUS), Perkins, college/university.

WORK-STUDY ***Federal work-study:*** Total amount: $1,069,500; 821 jobs averaging $1303.

APPLYING FOR FINANCIAL AID ***Required financial aid form:*** FAFSA. ***Financial aid deadline (priority):*** 2/15. ***Notification date:*** Continuous beginning 4/1.

CONTACT Sarah Bauder, Director of Financial Aid, University of Maryland, College Park, 0102 Lee Building, College Park, MD 20742, 301-314-8279 or toll-free 800-422-5867. *Fax:* 301-314-9587. *E-mail:* sbauder@umd.edu.

UNIVERSITY OF MARYLAND EASTERN SHORE

Princess Anne, MD

CONTACT Mr. James W. Kellam, Director of Financial Aid, University of Maryland Eastern Shore, Backbone Road, Princess Anne, MD 21853-1299, 410-651-6172. *Fax:* 410-651-7670. *E-mail:* jwkellam@umes.edu.

UNIVERSITY OF MARYLAND UNIVERSITY COLLEGE

Adelphi, MD

Tuition & fees (MD res): $5520 Average undergraduate aid package: $5925

ABOUT THE INSTITUTION State-supported, coed. Awards: associate, bachelor's, master's, and doctoral degrees and post-bachelor's certificates (offers primarily part-time evening and weekend degree programs at more than 30 off-campus locations in Maryland and the Washington, DC area, and more than 180 military communities in Europe and Asia with military enrollment not reflected in this profile; associate of arts program available to military students only). 19 undergraduate majors. Total enrollment: 33,096. Undergraduates: 22,898. Freshmen: 1,382. Federal methodology is used as a basis for awarding need-based institutional aid.

UNDERGRADUATE EXPENSES for 2006–07 ***Application fee:*** $30. ***Tuition, state resident:*** full-time $5520; part-time $230 per semester hour. ***Tuition, nonresident:*** full-time $10,656; part-time $444 per semester hour. ***Payment plan:*** Installment.

FRESHMAN FINANCIAL AID (Fall 2005) 59 applied for aid; of those 98% were deemed to have need. 64% of freshmen with need received aid. ***Average percent of need met:*** 13% (excluding resources awarded to replace EFC). ***Average financial aid package:*** $3909 (excluding resources awarded to replace EFC).

UNDERGRADUATE FINANCIAL AID (Fall 2005) 1,640 applied for aid; of those 96% were deemed to have need. 87% of undergraduates with need received aid; of those .4% had need fully met. ***Average percent of need met:*** 22% (excluding resources awarded to replace EFC). ***Average financial aid package:*** $5925 (excluding resources awarded to replace EFC).

GIFT AID (NEED-BASED) ***Total amount:*** $7,069,477 (77% federal, 12% state, 11% institutional). ***Receiving aid:*** Freshmen: 22% (24); All full-time undergraduates: 28% (756). ***Average award:*** Freshmen: $2589; Undergraduates: $3131. ***Scholarships, grants, and awards:*** Federal Pell, FSEOG, state, private, college/university gift aid from institutional funds.

GIFT AID (NON-NEED-BASED) ***Total amount:*** $1,158,321 (5% state, 61% institutional, 34% external sources). ***Receiving aid:*** Undergraduates: 9% (230). ***Scholarships, grants, and awards by category:*** *Academic Interests/Achievement:* general academic interests/achievements. *Special Achievements/Activities:* general special achievements/activities. ***Tuition waivers:*** Full or partial for employees or children of employees, senior citizens.

LOANS ***Student loans:*** $44,013,797 (46% need-based, 54% non-need-based). ***Average need-based loan:*** Freshmen: $2527; Undergraduates: $4157. ***Parent loans:*** $167,664 (100% non-need-based). ***Programs:*** Federal Direct (Subsidized and Unsubsidized Stafford, PLUS), Perkins.

WORK-STUDY ***Federal work-study:*** Total amount: $543,345; jobs available. ***State or other work-study/employment:*** Total amount: $388,037 (100% non-need-based). Part-time jobs available.

APPLYING FOR FINANCIAL AID ***Required financial aid form:*** FAFSA. ***Financial aid deadline (priority):*** 6/1. ***Notification date:*** Continuous beginning 5/1. Students must reply within 2 weeks of notification.

CONTACT Cheryl Storie, Financial Aid Counselor, University of Maryland University College, 3501 University Boulevard East, Adelphi, MD 20783, 301-985-7847 or toll-free 800-888-8682 (in-state). *Fax:* 301-985-7462. *E-mail:* finaid@umuc.edu.

UNIVERSITY OF MARY WASHINGTON

Fredericksburg, VA

ABOUT THE INSTITUTION State-supported, coed. Awards: bachelor's and master's degrees and post-bachelor's certificates. 40 undergraduate majors. Total enrollment: 4,862. Undergraduates: 4,183. Freshmen: 931.

GIFT AID (NEED-BASED) ***Scholarships, grants, and awards:*** Federal Pell, FSEOG, state, college/university gift aid from institutional funds.

GIFT AID (NON-NEED-BASED) ***Scholarships, grants, and awards by category:*** *Academic Interests/Achievement:* business, computer science, education, English, foreign languages, general academic interests/achievements, humanities, mathematics, physical sciences, religion/biblical studies, social sciences. *Creative Arts/Performance:* art/fine arts, dance, journalism/publications, music, theater/drama. *Special Achievements/Activities:* leadership. *Special Characteristics:* adult students, children and siblings of alumni, children of faculty/staff, local/state students.

LOANS ***Programs:*** FFEL (Subsidized and Unsubsidized Stafford, PLUS), Perkins.

APPLYING FOR FINANCIAL AID ***Required financial aid form:*** FAFSA.

CONTACT Ms. Debra J. Harber, Associate Dean for Financial Aid, University of Mary Washington, 1301 College Avenue, Fredericksburg, VA 22401-5358, 540-654-2468 or toll-free 800-468-5614. *Fax:* 540-654-1858. *E-mail:* dharber@umw.edu.

UNIVERSITY OF MASSACHUSETTS AMHERST

Amherst, MA

Tuition & fees (MA res): $9595 Average undergraduate aid package: $11,265

ABOUT THE INSTITUTION State-supported, coed. Awards: associate, bachelor's, master's, and doctoral degrees and post-master's certificates. 85 undergraduate majors. Total enrollment: 25,593. Undergraduates: 19,823. Freshmen: 4,249. Federal methodology is used as a basis for awarding need-based institutional aid.

UNDERGRADUATE EXPENSES for 2006–07 ***Application fee:*** $40. ***Tuition, state resident:*** full-time $1714; part-time $71.50 per credit. ***Tuition, nonresident:*** full-time $9937; part-time $414 per credit. ***Required fees:*** full-time $7881; $1,689 per term part-time. Full-time tuition and fees vary according to course load, reciprocity agreements, and student level. Part-time tuition and fees vary according to course load. ***College room and board:*** $6989; ***Room only:*** $3905. Room and board charges vary according to board plan and housing facility. ***Payment plan:*** Installment.

FRESHMAN FINANCIAL AID (Fall 2005) 2820 applied for aid; of those 65% were deemed to have need. 96% of freshmen with need received aid; of those 16% had need fully met. ***Average percent of need met:*** 82% (excluding resources awarded to replace EFC). ***Average financial aid package:*** $10,220 (excluding resources awarded to replace EFC). 1% of all full-time freshmen had no need and received non-need-based gift aid.

UNDERGRADUATE FINANCIAL AID (Fall 2005) 12,566 applied for aid; of those 74% were deemed to have need. 97% of undergraduates with need received aid; of those 27% had need fully met. ***Average percent of need met:*** 87% (excluding resources awarded to replace EFC). ***Average financial aid package:*** $11,265 (excluding resources awarded to replace EFC). 2% of all full-time undergraduates had no need and received non-need-based gift aid.

GIFT AID (NEED-BASED) ***Total amount:*** $45,293,362 (29% federal, 15% state, 49% institutional, 7% external sources). ***Receiving aid:*** Freshmen: 32% (1,425); All full-time undergraduates: 39% (6,963). ***Average award:*** Freshmen: $6646; Undergraduates: $7164. ***Scholarships, grants, and awards:*** Federal Pell, FSEOG, state, private, college/university gift aid from institutional funds.

GIFT AID (NON-NEED-BASED) ***Total amount:*** $5,084,871 (1% federal, 5% state, 42% institutional, 52% external sources). ***Receiving aid:*** Freshmen: 2% (74); Undergraduates: 2% (399). ***Average award:*** Freshmen: $3177; Undergraduates: $4714. ***Scholarships, grants, and awards by category:*** *Academic Interests/Achievement:* agriculture, architecture, biological sciences, business, communication, computer science, education, engineering/technologies, English, general academic interests/achievements, health fields, humanities, mathematics, military science, physical sciences, premedicine, social sciences. *Creative Arts/Performance:* art/fine arts, dance, journalism/publications, music, theater/drama. *Special Achievements/Activities:* cheerleading/drum major, general special achievements/activities, leadership. *Special Characteristics:* children and siblings of alumni, children of faculty/staff, handicapped students, veterans. ***Tuition waivers:*** Full or partial for employees or children of employees, senior citizens. ***ROTC:*** Army, Air Force.

LOANS ***Student loans:*** $72,151,131 (57% need-based, 43% non-need-based). 56% of past graduating class borrowed through all loan programs. *Average indebtedness per student:* $14,094. ***Average need-based loan:*** Freshmen: $2913; Undergraduates: $4026. ***Parent loans:*** $24,269,992 (20% need-based, 80% non-need-based). ***Programs:*** Federal Direct (Subsidized and Unsubsidized Stafford, PLUS), Perkins, state.

WORK-STUDY ***Federal work-study:*** Total amount: $8,681,420; 4,940 jobs averaging $1684.

ATHLETIC AWARDS Total amount: $4,388,736 (38% need-based, 62% non-need-based).

APPLYING FOR FINANCIAL AID ***Required financial aid form:*** FAFSA. ***Financial aid deadline (priority):*** 3/1. ***Notification date:*** Continuous beginning 4/1.

CONTACT Office of Financial Aid Services, University of Massachusetts Amherst, 255 Whitmore Administration Building, Amherst, MA 01003, 413-545-0801.

UNIVERSITY OF MASSACHUSETTS BOSTON

Boston, MA

Tuition & fees (MA res): $8546 **Average undergraduate aid package: $11,160**

ABOUT THE INSTITUTION State-supported, coed. Awards: bachelor's, master's, and doctoral degrees and post-bachelor's and post-master's certificates. 41 undergraduate majors. Total enrollment: 12,362. Undergraduates: 9,246. Freshmen: 974. Federal methodology is used as a basis for awarding need-based institutional aid.

UNDERGRADUATE EXPENSES for 2006–07 ***Application fee:*** $40. ***Tuition, state resident:*** full-time $1714; part-time $71.50 per credit. ***Tuition, nonresident:*** full-time $9758; part-time $406.50 per credit. ***Required fees:*** full-time $6832; $284 per credit hour. Full-time tuition and fees vary according to class time, course load, program, reciprocity agreements, and student level. Part-time tuition and fees vary according to class time, course load, program, reciprocity agreements, and student level. ***Payment plan:*** Installment.

FRESHMAN FINANCIAL AID (Fall 2005) 629 applied for aid; of those 84% were deemed to have need. 99% of freshmen with need received aid; of those 52% had need fully met. ***Average percent of need met:*** 85% (excluding resources awarded to replace EFC). ***Average financial aid package:*** $9777 (excluding resources awarded to replace EFC). 2% of all full-time freshmen had no need and received non-need-based gift aid.

UNDERGRADUATE FINANCIAL AID (Fall 2005) 3,901 applied for aid; of those 87% were deemed to have need. 100% of undergraduates with need received aid; of those 59% had need fully met. ***Average percent of need met:*** 89% (excluding resources awarded to replace EFC). ***Average financial aid package:*** $11,160 (excluding resources awarded to replace EFC). 1% of all full-time undergraduates had no need and received non-need-based gift aid.

GIFT AID (NEED-BASED) ***Total amount:*** $16,083,200 (48% federal, 23% state, 26% institutional, 3% external sources). ***Receiving aid:*** Freshmen: 66% (475); All full-time undergraduates: 53% (2,914). ***Average award:*** Freshmen: $5545; Undergraduates: $4929. ***Scholarships, grants, and awards:*** Federal Pell, FSEOG, state, private, college/university gift aid from institutional funds.

GIFT AID (NON-NEED-BASED) ***Total amount:*** $792,490 (4% federal, 11% state, 72% institutional, 13% external sources). ***Receiving aid:*** Freshmen: 2% (16); Undergraduates: 1% (44). ***Average award:*** Freshmen: $4089; Undergraduates: $4875. ***Scholarships, grants, and awards by category:*** *Academic Interests/Achievement:* general academic interests/achievements. *Special Achievements/Activities:* general special achievements/activities. ***Tuition waivers:*** Full or partial for employees or children of employees, senior citizens.

LOANS ***Student loans:*** $30,019,359 (73% need-based, 27% non-need-based). 92% of past graduating class borrowed through all loan programs. *Average indebtedness per student:* $18,755. ***Average need-based loan:*** Freshmen: $2878; Undergraduates: $5088. ***Parent loans:*** $1,511,928 (40% need-based, 60% non-need-based). ***Programs:*** Federal Direct (Subsidized and Unsubsidized Stafford, PLUS), Perkins, state.

WORK-STUDY ***Federal work-study:*** Total amount: $3,291,269; jobs available.

APPLYING FOR FINANCIAL AID ***Required financial aid form:*** FAFSA. ***Financial aid deadline (priority):*** 3/1. ***Notification date:*** Continuous beginning 4/1.

CONTACT Judy L. Keyes, Director of Financial Aid Services, University of Massachusetts Boston, 100 Morrissey Boulevard, Boston, MA 02125-3393, 617-287-6300. *Fax:* 617-287-6323. *E-mail:* judy.keyes@umb.edu.

UNIVERSITY OF MASSACHUSETTS DARTMOUTH

North Dartmouth, MA

Tuition & fees (MA res): $8309 **Average undergraduate aid package: $11,200**

ABOUT THE INSTITUTION State-supported, coed. Awards: bachelor's, master's, and doctoral degrees and post-bachelor's and post-master's certificates. 48 undergraduate majors. Total enrollment: 8,756. Undergraduates: 7,626. Freshmen: 1,789. Federal methodology is used as a basis for awarding need-based institutional aid.

UNDERGRADUATE EXPENSES for 2006–07 ***Application fee:*** $40; $55 for nonresidents. ***Tuition, state resident:*** full-time $1417; part-time $59.04 per credit. ***Tuition, nonresident:*** full-time $8099; part-time $337.46 per credit. ***Required fees:*** full-time $6892; $294.15 per credit. Full-time tuition and fees vary according to reciprocity agreements. Part-time tuition and fees vary according to course load and reciprocity agreements. ***College room and board:*** $8162; ***Room only:*** $5400. Room and board charges vary according to board plan and housing facility. ***Payment plan:*** Installment.

FRESHMAN FINANCIAL AID (Fall 2006, est.) 1400 applied for aid; of those 79% were deemed to have need. 98% of freshmen with need received aid; of those 56% had need fully met. ***Average percent of need met:*** 94% (excluding resources awarded to replace EFC). ***Average financial aid package:*** $11,010 (excluding resources awarded to replace EFC). 2% of all full-time freshmen had no need and received non-need-based gift aid.

UNDERGRADUATE FINANCIAL AID (Fall 2006, est.) 5,200 applied for aid; of those 83% were deemed to have need. 96% of undergraduates with need received aid; of those 63% had need fully met. ***Average percent of need met:*** 94% (excluding resources awarded to replace EFC). ***Average financial aid package:*** $11,200 (excluding resources awarded to replace EFC). 4% of all full-time undergraduates had no need and received non-need-based gift aid.

GIFT AID (NEED-BASED) ***Total amount:*** $21,980,000 (23% federal, 18% state, 55% institutional, 4% external sources). ***Receiving aid:*** Freshmen: 45% (800); All full-time undergraduates: 52% (3,450). ***Average award:*** Freshmen: $5900; Undergraduates: $5850. ***Scholarships, grants, and awards:*** Federal Pell, FSEOG, state, private, college/university gift aid from institutional funds.

GIFT AID (NON-NEED-BASED) ***Total amount:*** $3,170,000 (95% institutional, 5% external sources). ***Receiving aid:*** Freshmen: 3% (47); Undergraduates: 5% (310). ***Average award:*** Freshmen: $3000; Undergraduates: $2500. ***Scholarships, grants, and awards by category:*** *Academic Interests/Achievement:* 637 awards ($1,600,000 total): general academic interests/achievements. *Special Achievements/Activities:* 121 awards ($59,200 total): community service. *Special Characteristics:* 270 awards ($425,500 total): adult students, children of faculty/staff, children with a deceased or disabled parent, first-generation college students, members of minority groups, veterans. ***Tuition waivers:*** Full or partial for employees or children of employees, senior citizens. ***ROTC:*** Army cooperative.

LOANS ***Student loans:*** $34,500,000 (72% need-based, 28% non-need-based). 65% of past graduating class borrowed through all loan programs. *Average indebtedness per student:* $16,214. ***Average need-based loan:*** Freshmen: $6100; Undergraduates: $6400. ***Parent loans:*** $4,500,000 (67% need-based, 33% non-need-based). ***Programs:*** Federal Direct (Subsidized and Unsubsidized Stafford, PLUS), Perkins, Federal Nursing, state.

WORK-STUDY ***Federal work-study:*** Total amount: $850,000; 1,006 jobs averaging $1215. ***State or other work-study/employment:*** Total amount: $4,200,000 (76% need-based, 24% non-need-based). 1,300 part-time jobs averaging $3153.

APPLYING FOR FINANCIAL AID ***Required financial aid form:*** FAFSA. ***Financial aid deadline (priority):*** 3/1. ***Notification date:*** Continuous beginning 3/25.

CONTACT Bruce Palmer, Director of Financial Aid, University of Massachusetts Dartmouth, 285 Old Westport Road, North Dartmouth, MA 02747-2300, 508-999-8643. *Fax:* 508-999-8935. *E-mail:* financialaid@umassd.edu.

UNIVERSITY OF MASSACHUSETTS LOWELL
Lowell, MA

Tuition & fees (MA res): $8444 Average undergraduate aid package: $8783

ABOUT THE INSTITUTION State-supported, coed. Awards: associate, bachelor's, master's, and doctoral degrees and post-master's certificates. 38 undergraduate majors. Total enrollment: 11,208. Undergraduates: 8,649. Freshmen: 1,234. Federal methodology is used as a basis for awarding need-based institutional aid.

UNDERGRADUATE EXPENSES for 2006–07 ***Application fee:*** $40. ***Tuition, state resident:*** full-time $1454; part-time $60.58 per credit. ***Tuition, nonresident:*** full-time $8567; part-time $356.96 per credit. ***Required fees:*** full-time $6990; $302.92 per credit. ***College room and board:*** $6365; ***Room only:*** $3955. Room and board charges vary according to board plan and housing facility. ***Payment plan:*** Installment.

FRESHMAN FINANCIAL AID (Fall 2005) 764 applied for aid; of those 63% were deemed to have need. 99% of freshmen with need received aid; of those 67% had need fully met. ***Average percent of need met:*** 92% (excluding resources awarded to replace EFC). ***Average financial aid package:*** $8300 (excluding resources awarded to replace EFC). 2% of all full-time freshmen had no need and received non-need-based gift aid.

UNDERGRADUATE FINANCIAL AID (Fall 2005) 3,992 applied for aid; of those 70% were deemed to have need. 98% of undergraduates with need received aid; of those 70% had need fully met. ***Average percent of need met:*** 93% (excluding resources awarded to replace EFC). ***Average financial aid package:*** $8783 (excluding resources awarded to replace EFC). 3% of all full-time undergraduates had no need and received non-need-based gift aid.

GIFT AID (NEED-BASED) ***Total amount:*** $8,190,579 (50% federal, 26% state, 24% institutional). ***Receiving aid:*** Freshmen: 41% (441); All full-time undergraduates: 42% (2,379). ***Average award:*** Freshmen: $4572; Undergraduates: $4457. ***Scholarships, grants, and awards:*** Federal Pell, FSEOG, state, private, college/university gift aid from institutional funds.

GIFT AID (NON-NEED-BASED) ***Total amount:*** $2,517,021 (1% state, 75% institutional, 24% external sources). ***Receiving aid:*** Freshmen: 2% (16); Undergraduates: 1% (76). ***Average award:*** Freshmen: $2157; Undergraduates: $3792. ***Scholarships, grants, and awards by category:*** *Academic Interests/Achievement:* computer science, engineering/technologies, general academic interests/achievements, health fields, humanities. *Creative Arts/Performance:* music. *Special Achievements/Activities:* community service, general special achievements/activities. *Special Characteristics:* general special characteristics. ***Tuition waivers:*** Full or partial for employees or children of employees, senior citizens. ***ROTC:*** Air Force.

LOANS ***Student loans:*** $22,367,428 (39% need-based, 61% non-need-based). 57% of past graduating class borrowed through all loan programs. *Average indebtedness per student:* $14,833. ***Average need-based loan:*** Freshmen: $3358; Undergraduates: $4275. ***Parent loans:*** $4,384,105 (100% non-need-based). ***Programs:*** Federal Direct (Subsidized and Unsubsidized Stafford, PLUS), Perkins, state.

WORK-STUDY ***Federal work-study:*** Total amount: $415,304; 74 jobs averaging $3316. ***State or other work-study/employment:*** Total amount: $1,902,256 (100% need-based). 682 part-time jobs averaging $3154.

ATHLETIC AWARDS Total amount: $971,203 (100% non-need-based).

APPLYING FOR FINANCIAL AID ***Required financial aid form:*** FAFSA. ***Financial aid deadline (priority):*** 3/1. ***Notification date:*** Continuous beginning 3/24.

CONTACT Mr. Richard Barrett, Director of Financial Aid, University of Massachusetts Lowell, 883 Broadway Street, Room 102, Lowell, MA 01854, 978-934-4226 or toll-free 800-410-4607. *E-mail:* richard_barrett@uml.edu.

UNIVERSITY OF MEMPHIS
Memphis, TN

ABOUT THE INSTITUTION State-supported, coed. Awards: bachelor's, master's, doctoral, and first professional degrees and post-bachelor's, post-master's, and first professional certificates. 66 undergraduate majors. Total enrollment: 20,562. Undergraduates: 15,984. Freshmen: 2,093.

GIFT AID (NEED-BASED) ***Scholarships, grants, and awards:*** Federal Pell, FSEOG, state, college/university gift aid from institutional funds.

GIFT AID (NON-NEED-BASED) ***Scholarships, grants, and awards by category:*** *Academic Interests/Achievement:* biological sciences, business, communication, education, engineering/technologies, English, general academic interests/achievements, health fields, humanities, international studies, mathematics, military science, physical sciences, premedicine, social sciences. *Creative Arts/Performance:* art/fine arts, cinema/film/broadcasting, dance, journalism/publications, music. *Special Achievements/Activities:* cheerleading/drum major, general special achievements/activities, leadership. *Special Characteristics:* adult students, children of educators, children of faculty/staff, children of public servants, handicapped students, members of minority groups, public servants.

LOANS ***Programs:*** Federal Direct (Subsidized and Unsubsidized Stafford, PLUS), Perkins, college/university.

APPLYING FOR FINANCIAL AID ***Required financial aid form:*** FAFSA.

CONTACT Richard Ritzman, Director of Student Financial Aid, University of Memphis, Wilder Tower 103, Memphis, TN 38152, 901-678-2832 or toll-free 800-669-2678 (out-of-state). *Fax:* 901-678-3590. *E-mail:* rritzman@memphis.edu.

UNIVERSITY OF MIAMI
Coral Gables, FL

Tuition & fees: $33,070 Average undergraduate aid package: $25,088

ABOUT THE INSTITUTION Independent, coed. Awards: bachelor's, master's, doctoral, and first professional degrees and post-bachelor's and post-master's certificates. 125 undergraduate majors. Total enrollment: 15,670. Undergraduates: 10,509. Freshmen: 2,062. Both federal and institutional methodology are used as a basis for awarding need-based institutional aid.

UNDERGRADUATE EXPENSES for 2007–08 ***Application fee:*** $65. ***Comprehensive fee:*** $42,676 includes full-time tuition ($32,422), mandatory fees ($648), and room and board ($9606). ***College room only:*** $5762. ***Part-time tuition:*** $1350 per credit.

FRESHMAN FINANCIAL AID (Fall 2006, est.) 1297 applied for aid; of those 77% were deemed to have need. 100% of freshmen with need received aid; of those 36% had need fully met. ***Average percent of need met:*** 82% (excluding resources awarded to replace EFC). ***Average financial aid package:*** $24,674 (excluding resources awarded to replace EFC). 27% of all full-time freshmen had no need and received non-need-based gift aid.

UNDERGRADUATE FINANCIAL AID (Fall 2006, est.) 5,621 applied for aid; of those 86% were deemed to have need. 100% of undergraduates with need received aid; of those 30% had need fully met. ***Average percent of need met:*** 79% (excluding resources awarded to replace EFC). ***Average financial aid package:*** $25,088 (excluding resources awarded to replace EFC). 23% of all full-time undergraduates had no need and received non-need-based gift aid.

GIFT AID (NEED-BASED) ***Total amount:*** $79,756,683 (10% federal, 16% state, 72% institutional, 2% external sources). ***Receiving aid:*** Freshmen: 48% (977); All full-time undergraduates: 49% (4,697). ***Average award:*** Freshmen: $18,286; Undergraduates: $18,272. ***Scholarships, grants, and awards:*** Federal Pell, FSEOG, state, private, college/university gift aid from institutional funds, Federal Nursing.

GIFT AID (NON-NEED-BASED) ***Total amount:*** $53,347,361 (25% state, 72% institutional, 3% external sources). ***Receiving aid:*** Freshmen: 17% (347); Undergraduates: 14% (1,308). ***Average award:*** Freshmen: $15,760; Undergraduates: $15,683. ***Scholarships, grants, and awards by category:*** *Academic Interests/Achievement:* 4,331 awards ($65,610,142 total): architecture, biological sciences, business, communication, computer science, education, engineering/technologies, English, foreign languages, general academic interests/achievements, health fields, international studies, mathematics, physical sciences, social sciences. *Creative Arts/Performance:* 500 awards ($7,245,647 total): art/fine arts, cinema/film/broadcasting, debating, music, performing arts, theater/drama. *Special Characteristics:* 820 awards ($18,427,037 total): children of faculty/staff, international students. ***ROTC:*** Army, Air Force.

LOANS ***Student loans:*** $53,641,670 (65% need-based, 35% non-need-based). 58% of past graduating class borrowed through all loan programs. *Average indebtedness per student:* $24,673. ***Average need-based loan:*** Freshmen: $3823; Undergraduates: $5073. ***Parent loans:*** $12,482,936 (28% need-based, 72% non-need-based). ***Programs:*** FFEL (Subsidized and Unsubsidized Stafford, PLUS), Perkins, Federal Nursing, college/university, private alternative loans.

WORK-STUDY ***Federal work-study:*** Total amount: $5,864,560; 2,170 jobs averaging $2703. ***State or other work-study/employment:*** Total amount: $1,170,340 (24% need-based, 76% non-need-based). 251 part-time jobs averaging $4663.

ATHLETIC AWARDS Total amount: $8,504,379 (35% need-based, 65% non-need-based).

APPLYING FOR FINANCIAL AID ***Required financial aid form:*** FAFSA. ***Financial aid deadline (priority):*** 2/1. ***Notification date:*** Continuous beginning 3/1.

CONTACT Mr. James M. Bauer, Assistant Dean of Enrollment and Director of Financial Assistance, University of Miami, Rhodes House, Building 37R, Coral Gables, FL 33124-5240, 305-284-5212. *Fax:* 305-284-4491. *E-mail:* jbauer@miami.edu.

UNIVERSITY OF MICHIGAN

Ann Arbor, MI

Tuition & fees (MI res): $9798 **Average undergraduate aid package: $11,111**

ABOUT THE INSTITUTION State-supported, coed. Awards: bachelor's, master's, doctoral, and first professional degrees and post-bachelor's and post-master's certificates. 124 undergraduate majors. Total enrollment: 40,025. Undergraduates: 25,555. Freshmen: 5,060. Federal methodology is used as a basis for awarding need-based institutional aid.

UNDERGRADUATE EXPENSES for 2006–07 ***Application fee:*** $40. ***Tuition, state resident:*** full-time $9609. ***Tuition, nonresident:*** full-time $28,381. Full-time tuition and fees vary according to course load, degree level, location, program, and student level. Part-time tuition and fees vary according to course load, degree level, location, program, and student level. ***College room and board:*** $7838. Room and board charges vary according to board plan and housing facility. ***Payment plan:*** Installment.

FRESHMAN FINANCIAL AID (Fall 2005) 3438 applied for aid; of those 86% were deemed to have need. 100% of freshmen with need received aid; of those 90% had need fully met. ***Average percent of need met:*** 90% (excluding resources awarded to replace EFC). ***Average financial aid package:*** $9317 (excluding resources awarded to replace EFC). 36% of all full-time freshmen had no need and received non-need-based gift aid.

UNDERGRADUATE FINANCIAL AID (Fall 2005) 13,751 applied for aid; of those 84% were deemed to have need. 100% of undergraduates with need received aid; of those 90% had need fully met. ***Average percent of need met:*** 90% (excluding resources awarded to replace EFC). ***Average financial aid package:*** $11,111 (excluding resources awarded to replace EFC). 28% of all full-time undergraduates had no need and received non-need-based gift aid.

GIFT AID (NEED-BASED) ***Total amount:*** $50,931,411 (21% federal, 79% institutional). ***Receiving aid:*** Freshmen: 26% (1,607); All full-time undergraduates: 26% (6,410). ***Average award:*** Freshmen: $7883; Undergraduates: $7946. ***Scholarships, grants, and awards:*** Federal Pell, FSEOG, state, private, college/university gift aid from institutional funds.

GIFT AID (NON-NEED-BASED) ***Total amount:*** $73,207,342 (6% federal, 18% state, 54% institutional, 22% external sources). ***Receiving aid:*** Freshmen: 40% (2,458); Undergraduates: 30% (7,384). ***Average award:*** Freshmen: $4902; Undergraduates: $5716. ***Scholarships, grants, and awards by category:*** *Academic Interests/Achievement:* architecture, area/ethnic studies, biological sciences, business, communication, computer science, education, engineering/technologies, English, foreign languages, general academic interests/achievements, health fields, humanities, international studies, library science, mathematics, military science, physical sciences, premedicine, social sciences. *Creative Arts/Performance:* journalism/publications, music, theater/drama. *Special Achievements/Activities:* community service, general special achievements/activities, leadership. *Special Characteristics:* children of faculty/staff, children of workers in trades, handicapped students, international students, local/state students, members of minority groups, out-of-state students. ***Tuition waivers:*** Full or partial for senior citizens. ***ROTC:*** Army, Air Force.

LOANS ***Student loans:*** $85,437,973 (51% need-based, 49% non-need-based). 44% of past graduating class borrowed through all loan programs. *Average indebtedness per student:* $23,533. ***Average need-based loan:*** Freshmen: $4686; Undergraduates: $5885. ***Parent loans:*** $20,326,513 (100% non-need-based). ***Programs:*** Federal Direct (Subsidized and Unsubsidized Stafford, PLUS), Perkins, Federal Nursing, state, college/university, MI-Loan Program, Health Professions Student Loans (HPSL).

WORK-STUDY ***Federal work-study:*** Total amount: $12,724,180; 5,199 jobs averaging $2447. ***State or other work-study/employment:*** Total amount: $1,094,300 (100% need-based). 502 part-time jobs averaging $2180.

ATHLETIC AWARDS Total amount: $12,053,175 (100% non-need-based).

APPLYING FOR FINANCIAL AID ***Required financial aid forms:*** FAFSA, CSS Financial Aid PROFILE, federal income tax form(s). ***Financial aid deadline:*** 4/30. ***Notification date:*** Continuous beginning 3/15.

CONTACT Financial Aid Counseling and Advising Office, University of Michigan, 2011 Student Activities Building, Ann Arbor, MI 48109-1316, 734-763-6600. *Fax:* 734-647-3081. *E-mail:* financial.aid@umich.edu.

UNIVERSITY OF MICHIGAN–DEARBORN

Dearborn, MI

Tuition & fees (MI res): $7392 **Average undergraduate aid package: $4390**

ABOUT THE INSTITUTION State-supported, coed. Awards: bachelor's and master's degrees and post-bachelor's certificates. 53 undergraduate majors. Total enrollment: 8,566. Undergraduates: 6,612. Freshmen: 802. Federal methodology is used as a basis for awarding need-based institutional aid.

UNDERGRADUATE EXPENSES for 2006–07 ***Application fee:*** $30. ***Tuition, state resident:*** full-time $7259; part-time $267.70 per credit hour. ***Tuition, nonresident:*** full-time $16,054; part-time $628.30 per credit hour. ***Required fees:*** full-time $133; $133.15 per term part-time. Full-time tuition and fees vary according to course level, course load, program, and student level. Part-time tuition and fees vary according to course level, course load, program, and student level. ***Payment plan:*** Installment.

FRESHMAN FINANCIAL AID (Fall 2006, est.) 570 applied for aid; of those 59% were deemed to have need. 100% of freshmen with need received aid; of those 12% had need fully met. ***Average percent of need met:*** 47% (excluding resources awarded to replace EFC). ***Average financial aid package:*** $3825 (excluding resources awarded to replace EFC). 80% of all full-time freshmen had no need and received non-need-based gift aid.

UNDERGRADUATE FINANCIAL AID (Fall 2006, est.) 2,879 applied for aid; of those 76% were deemed to have need. 100% of undergraduates with need received aid; of those 14% had need fully met. ***Average percent of need met:*** 44% (excluding resources awarded to replace EFC). ***Average financial aid package:*** $4390 (excluding resources awarded to replace EFC). 37% of all full-time undergraduates had no need and received non-need-based gift aid.

GIFT AID (NEED-BASED) ***Total amount:*** $6,595,467 (74% federal, 7% state, 19% institutional). ***Receiving aid:*** Freshmen: 28% (220); All full-time undergraduates: 32% (1,491). ***Average award:*** Freshmen: $3817; Undergraduates: $4054. ***Scholarships, grants, and awards:*** Federal Pell, FSEOG, state, private, college/university gift aid from institutional funds.

GIFT AID (NON-NEED-BASED) ***Total amount:*** $5,626,637 (27% state, 62% institutional, 11% external sources). ***Receiving aid:*** Freshmen: 35% (276); Undergraduates: 17% (799). ***Average award:*** Freshmen: $3068; Undergraduates: $3133. ***Scholarships, grants, and awards by category:*** *Academic Interests/Achievement:* 533 awards ($1,396,359 total): biological sciences, business, communication, computer science, education, engineering/technologies, foreign languages, general academic interests/achievements, international studies, mathematics, physical sciences, social sciences. *Creative Arts/Performance:* 34 awards ($24,434 total): art/fine arts, cinema/film/broadcasting, creative writing, debating, general creative arts/performance, journalism/publications. *Special Achievements/Activities:* 153 awards ($791,270 total): community service, general special achievements/activities, leadership, memberships. *Special Characteristics:* 232 awards ($983,367 total): children and siblings of alumni, children of current students, children of faculty/staff, children of workers in trades, ethnic background, general special characteristics, handicapped students, members of minority groups, out-of-state students, previous college experience. ***Tuition waivers:*** Full or partial for employees or children of employees, senior citizens. ***ROTC:*** Army cooperative, Naval cooperative, Air Force cooperative.

LOANS ***Student loans:*** $18,971,927 (53% need-based, 47% non-need-based). 56% of past graduating class borrowed through all loan programs. *Average indebtedness per student:* $22,908. ***Average need-based loan:*** Freshmen: $2732; Undergraduates: $4185. ***Parent loans:*** $768,490 (100% non-need-based). ***Programs:*** Federal Direct (Subsidized and Unsubsidized Stafford, PLUS), Perkins, state, college/university, alternative loans.

WORK-STUDY ***Federal work-study:*** Total amount: $130,000; 79 jobs averaging $1646. ***State or other work-study/employment:*** Total amount: $61,261 (100% need-based). 47 part-time jobs averaging $1303.

ATHLETIC AWARDS Total amount: $80,625 (100% non-need-based).

APPLYING FOR FINANCIAL AID ***Required financial aid form:*** FAFSA. ***Financial aid deadline (priority):*** 2/14. ***Notification date:*** Continuous beginning 3/15. Students must reply within 3 weeks of notification.

CONTACT Cheryl Powell, Associate Director, University of Michigan–Dearborn, 4901 Evergreen Road, 1183 UC, Dearborn, MI 48128-1491, 313-593-5300. *Fax:* 313-593-5313. *E-mail:* jamason@umd.umich.edu.

UNIVERSITY OF MICHIGAN–FLINT

Flint, MI

Tuition & fees (MI res): $6902   Average undergraduate aid package: $7228

ABOUT THE INSTITUTION State-supported, coed. Awards: bachelor's, master's, and first professional degrees. 77 undergraduate majors. Total enrollment: 6,527. Undergraduates: 5,600. Freshmen: 524. Federal methodology is used as a basis for awarding need-based institutional aid.

UNDERGRADUATE EXPENSES for 2006–07 ***Application fee:*** $30. ***Tuition, state resident:*** full-time $6568; part-time $259 per credit. ***Tuition, nonresident:*** full-time $12,818; part-time $518 per credit. ***Required fees:*** full-time $334; $129 per term part-time. Full-time tuition and fees vary according to course level, course load, degree level, and program. Part-time tuition and fees vary according to course level, degree level, and program.

FRESHMAN FINANCIAL AID (Fall 2005) 390 applied for aid; of those 66% were deemed to have need. 96% of freshmen with need received aid; of those 23% had need fully met. ***Average percent of need met:*** 65% (excluding resources awarded to replace EFC). ***Average financial aid package:*** $6369 (excluding resources awarded to replace EFC). 7% of all full-time freshmen had no need and received non-need-based gift aid.

UNDERGRADUATE FINANCIAL AID (Fall 2005) 2,529 applied for aid; of those 80% were deemed to have need. 97% of undergraduates with need received aid; of those 17% had need fully met. ***Average percent of need met:*** 60% (excluding resources awarded to replace EFC). ***Average financial aid package:*** $7228 (excluding resources awarded to replace EFC). 2% of all full-time undergraduates had no need and received non-need-based gift aid.

GIFT AID (NEED-BASED) ***Total amount:*** $6,919,682 (72% federal, 4% state, 20% institutional, 4% external sources). ***Receiving aid:*** Freshmen: 30% (149); All full-time undergraduates: 36% (1,212). ***Average award:*** Freshmen: $3867; Undergraduates: $4278. ***Scholarships, grants, and awards:*** Federal Pell, FSEOG, state, private, college/university gift aid from institutional funds.

GIFT AID (NON-NEED-BASED) ***Total amount:*** $1,144,249 (100% state). ***Receiving aid:*** Freshmen: 33% (168); Undergraduates: 32% (1,105). ***Average award:*** Freshmen: $2338; Undergraduates: $2353. ***Scholarships, grants, and awards by category:*** *Academic Interests/Achievement:* biological sciences, business, communication, computer science, education, engineering/technologies, English, foreign languages, general academic interests/achievements, health fields, humanities, international studies, mathematics, physical sciences, premedicine, social sciences. *Creative Arts/Performance:* art/fine arts, music, theater/drama. *Special Achievements/Activities:* community service, general special achievements/activities, hobbies/interests, leadership. *Special Characteristics:* adult students, children and siblings of alumni, children of union members/company employees, ethnic background, first-generation college students, general special characteristics, handicapped students, international students, local/state students, members of minority groups. ***Tuition waivers:*** Full or partial for minority students, employees or children of employees, senior citizens.

LOANS ***Student loans:*** $19,450,009 (100% need-based). 24% of past graduating class borrowed through all loan programs. *Average indebtedness per student:* $19,315. ***Average need-based loan:*** Freshmen: $2960; Undergraduates: $4105. ***Parent loans:*** $400,221 (100% non-need-based). ***Programs:*** Federal Direct (Subsidized and Unsubsidized Stafford, PLUS), Perkins, state, alternative loans.

WORK-STUDY ***Federal work-study:*** Total amount: $552,006; 343 jobs averaging $1755. ***State or other work-study/employment:*** Total amount: $155,714 (100% need-based). 85 part-time jobs averaging $1847.

APPLYING FOR FINANCIAL AID ***Required financial aid form:*** FAFSA. ***Financial aid deadline (priority):*** 3/1. ***Notification date:*** Continuous beginning 3/15.

CONTACT Financial Aid Office, University of Michigan–Flint, Room 277 UPAV, Flint, MI 48502-1950, 810-762-3444 or toll-free 800-942-5636 (in-state). *Fax:* 810-766-6757. *E-mail:* financial_aid@list.flint.umich.edu.

UNIVERSITY OF MINNESOTA, CROOKSTON

Crookston, MN

Tuition & fees (MN res): $9065   Average undergraduate aid package: $10,998

ABOUT THE INSTITUTION State-supported, coed. Awards: associate and bachelor's degrees. 32 undergraduate majors. Total enrollment: 2,414. Undergraduates: 2,414. Freshmen: 216. Federal methodology is used as a basis for awarding need-based institutional aid.

UNDERGRADUATE EXPENSES for 2007–08 ***Application fee:*** $30. ***Tuition, state resident:*** full-time $6525; part-time $215 per credit. ***Tuition, nonresident:*** full-time $6525; part-time $215 per credit. ***College room and board:*** $5750; ***Room only:*** $2725.

FRESHMAN FINANCIAL AID (Fall 2006, est.) 181 applied for aid; of those 79% were deemed to have need. 100% of freshmen with need received aid; of those 47% had need fully met. ***Average percent of need met:*** 87% (excluding resources awarded to replace EFC). ***Average financial aid package:*** $11,764 (excluding resources awarded to replace EFC). 17% of all full-time freshmen had no need and received non-need-based gift aid.

UNDERGRADUATE FINANCIAL AID (Fall 2006, est.) 726 applied for aid; of those 82% were deemed to have need. 98% of undergraduates with need received aid; of those 42% had need fully met. ***Average percent of need met:*** 83% (excluding resources awarded to replace EFC). ***Average financial aid package:*** $10,998 (excluding resources awarded to replace EFC). 9% of all full-time undergraduates had no need and received non-need-based gift aid.

GIFT AID (NEED-BASED) ***Total amount:*** $3,493,996 (32% federal, 34% state, 30% institutional, 4% external sources). ***Receiving aid:*** Freshmen: 62% (133); All full-time undergraduates: 58% (515). ***Average award:*** Freshmen: $7967; Undergraduates: $6551. ***Scholarships, grants, and awards:*** Federal Pell, FSEOG, state, college/university gift aid from institutional funds, AGG/SMART Grants.

GIFT AID (NON-NEED-BASED) ***Total amount:*** $206,854 (84% institutional, 16% external sources). ***Receiving aid:*** Freshmen: 21% (45); Undergraduates: 16% (142). ***Average award:*** Freshmen: $2759; Undergraduates: $2875. ***Scholarships, grants, and awards by category:*** *Academic Interests/Achievement:* agriculture, biological sciences, business, communication, computer science, education, engineering/technologies, general academic interests/achievements, health fields, premedicine. *Special Achievements/Activities:* general special achievements/activities, leadership. *Special Characteristics:* children and siblings of alumni, children of faculty/staff, ethnic background, general special characteristics, members of minority groups, out-of-state students, previous college experience. ***ROTC:*** Air Force cooperative.

LOANS ***Student loans:*** $4,442,763 (80% need-based, 20% non-need-based). ***Average need-based loan:*** Freshmen: $5306; Undergraduates: $6583. ***Parent loans:*** $167,736 (100% non-need-based). ***Programs:*** Federal Direct (Subsidized and Unsubsidized Stafford, PLUS), Perkins, state, college/university.

WORK-STUDY ***Federal work-study:*** Total amount: $156,215; 91 jobs averaging $1669. ***State or other work-study/employment:*** Total amount: $76,170 (100% need-based). 76 part-time jobs averaging $1017.

ATHLETIC AWARDS Total amount: $323,300 (100% non-need-based).

APPLYING FOR FINANCIAL AID ***Required financial aid form:*** FAFSA. ***Financial aid deadline (priority):*** 2/15. ***Notification date:*** 3/15.

CONTACT Melissa Dingmann, Director of Financial Aid, University of Minnesota, Crookston, 170 Owen Hall, Crookston, MN 56716-5001, 218-281-8563 or toll-free 800-862-6466. *Fax:* 218-281-8575. *E-mail:* dingmann@umcrookston.edu.

UNIVERSITY OF MINNESOTA, DULUTH

Duluth, MN

ABOUT THE INSTITUTION State-supported, coed. Awards: bachelor's, master's, and first professional degrees. 69 undergraduate majors. Total enrollment: 11,090. Undergraduates: 10,372. Freshmen: 2,315.

GIFT AID (NEED-BASED) ***Scholarships, grants, and awards:*** Federal Pell, FSEOG, state, private, college/university gift aid from institutional funds.

LOANS ***Programs:*** Federal Direct (Subsidized and Unsubsidized Stafford, PLUS), Perkins, state, college/university, Primary Care Loans.

WORK-STUDY ***Federal work-study:*** Total amount: $386,521; 159 jobs averaging $2431. ***State or other work-study/employment:*** Total amount: $522,572 (100% need-based). 249 part-time jobs averaging $2099.

APPLYING FOR FINANCIAL AID ***Required financial aid form:*** FAFSA.

CONTACT Ms. Brenda Herzig, Director of Financial Aid, University of Minnesota, Duluth, 10 University Drive, 184 Darland Administration Building, Duluth, MN 55812-2496, 218-726-8000 or toll-free 800-232-1339. *Fax:* 218-726-8219.

UNIVERSITY OF MINNESOTA, MORRIS

Morris, MN

ABOUT THE INSTITUTION State-supported, coed. Awards: bachelor's degrees. 42 undergraduate majors. Total enrollment: 1,740. Undergraduates: 1,740. Freshmen: 377.

GIFT AID (NEED-BASED) ***Scholarships, grants, and awards:*** Federal Pell, FSEOG, state, private, college/university gift aid from institutional funds.

GIFT AID (NON-NEED-BASED) ***Scholarships, grants, and awards by category:*** *Academic Interests/Achievement:* general academic interests/achievements. *Creative Arts/Performance:* music. *Special Achievements/Activities:* general special achievements/activities. *Special Characteristics:* ethnic background, international students, members of minority groups, veterans, veterans' children.

LOANS ***Programs:*** Federal Direct (Subsidized and Unsubsidized Stafford, PLUS), Perkins, state, college/university.

WORK-STUDY ***Federal work-study:*** Total amount: $395,617; 432 jobs averaging $916. ***State or other work-study/employment:*** Total amount: $445,766 (44% need-based, 56% non-need-based). 516 part-time jobs averaging $863.

APPLYING FOR FINANCIAL AID ***Required financial aid form:*** FAFSA.

CONTACT Ms. Pam Engebretson, Director of Financial Aid, University of Minnesota, Morris, 600 East 4th Street, Morris, MN 56267, 320-589-6035 or toll-free 800-992-8863. *Fax:* 320-589-1673. *E-mail:* finaid@morris.umn.edu.

UNIVERSITY OF MINNESOTA, TWIN CITIES CAMPUS

Minneapolis, MN

Tuition & fees (MN res): $9173 **Average undergraduate aid package: $11,969**

ABOUT THE INSTITUTION State-supported, coed. Awards: bachelor's, master's, doctoral, and first professional degrees and post-bachelor's, post-master's, and first professional certificates. 132 undergraduate majors. Total enrollment: 50,402. Undergraduates: 32,113. Freshmen: 5,439. Federal methodology is used as a basis for awarding need-based institutional aid.

UNDERGRADUATE EXPENSES for 2006–07 ***Application fee:*** $45. ***Tuition, state resident:*** full-time $7588; part-time $291.85 per credit. ***Tuition, nonresident:*** full-time $19,218; part-time $739.15 per credit. Full-time tuition and fees vary according to program and reciprocity agreements. Part-time tuition and fees vary according to course load, program, and reciprocity agreements. ***College room and board:*** $6996; ***Room only:*** $4042. Room and board charges vary according to board plan, housing facility, and location. ***Payment plan:*** Installment.

FRESHMAN FINANCIAL AID (Fall 2006, est.) 4143 applied for aid; of those 65% were deemed to have need. 98% of freshmen with need received aid; of those 57% had need fully met. ***Average percent of need met:*** 88% (excluding resources awarded to replace EFC). ***Average financial aid package:*** $12,148 (excluding resources awarded to replace EFC). 16% of all full-time freshmen had no need and received non-need-based gift aid.

UNDERGRADUATE FINANCIAL AID (Fall 2006, est.) 17,575 applied for aid; of those 73% were deemed to have need. 97% of undergraduates with need received aid; of those 52% had need fully met. ***Average percent of need met:*** 85% (excluding resources awarded to replace EFC). ***Average financial aid package:*** $11,969 (excluding resources awarded to replace EFC). 12% of all full-time undergraduates had no need and received non-need-based gift aid.

GIFT AID (NEED-BASED) ***Total amount:*** $70,281,245 (28% federal, 32% state, 35% institutional, 5% external sources). ***Receiving aid:*** Freshmen: 37% (2,030); All full-time undergraduates: 34% (8,977). ***Average award:*** Freshmen: $8394; Undergraduates: $7596. ***Scholarships, grants, and awards:*** Federal Pell, FSEOG, state, private, college/university gift aid from institutional funds, Federal Nursing.

GIFT AID (NON-NEED-BASED) ***Total amount:*** $13,762,863 (85% institutional, 15% external sources). ***Receiving aid:*** Freshmen: 14% (755); Undergraduates: 10% (2,562). ***Average award:*** Freshmen: $4209; Undergraduates: $4566. ***Scholarships, grants, and awards by category:*** *Academic Interests/Achievement:* agriculture, architecture, area/ethnic studies, biological sciences, business, communication, computer science, education, engineering/technologies, English, foreign languages, general academic interests/achievements, health fields, home economics, humanities, international studies, library science, mathematics, military science, physical sciences, premedicine, religion/biblical studies, social sciences. *Creative Arts/Performance:* general creative arts/performance. *Special Achievements/Activities:* hobbies/interests, leadership. *Special Characteristics:* general special characteristics. ***Tuition waivers:*** Full or partial for senior citizens. ***ROTC:*** Army, Naval, Air Force.

LOANS ***Student loans:*** $103,521,456 (75% need-based, 25% non-need-based). ***Average need-based loan:*** Freshmen: $6370; Undergraduates: $7742. ***Parent loans:*** $20,152,677 (100% non-need-based). ***Programs:*** Federal Direct (Subsidized and Unsubsidized Stafford, PLUS), Perkins, Federal Nursing, state, college/university.

WORK-STUDY ***Federal work-study:*** Total amount: $3,964,835; jobs available. ***State or other work-study/employment:*** Total amount: $10,334,281 (100% need-based). Part-time jobs available.

ATHLETIC AWARDS Total amount: $6,738,932 (100% non-need-based).

APPLYING FOR FINANCIAL AID ***Required financial aid forms:*** FAFSA, institution's own form. ***Financial aid deadline:*** Continuous. ***Notification date:*** Continuous.

CONTACT Mr. John Kellogg, Institutional Research and Reporting, University of Minnesota, Twin Cities Campus, 318 Morrill Hall, 100 Church Street SE, Minneapolis, MN 55455, 612-625-3387 or toll-free 800-752-1000. *E-mail:* j-kell@umn.edu.

UNIVERSITY OF MISSISSIPPI

Oxford, MS

CONTACT Ms. Laura Diven-Brown, Director of Financial Aid, University of Mississippi, 257 Martindale Center, University, MS 38677, 662-915-5788 or toll-free 800-653-6477 (in-state). *Fax:* 662-915-1164. *E-mail:* ldivenbr@olemiss.edu.

UNIVERSITY OF MISSISSIPPI MEDICAL CENTER

Jackson, MS

CONTACT Minetta Veazey, Administrative Secretary, University of Mississippi Medical Center, 2500 North State Street, Jackson, MS 39216, 601-984-1117. *Fax:* 601-984-6984. *E-mail:* mveazey@registrar.umsmed.edu.

UNIVERSITY OF MISSOURI–COLUMBIA

Columbia, MO

Tuition & fees (MO res): $7308 **Average undergraduate aid package: $11,452**

ABOUT THE INSTITUTION State-supported, coed. Awards: bachelor's, master's, doctoral, and first professional degrees and post-master's and first professional certificates. 124 undergraduate majors. Total enrollment: 28,253. Undergraduates: 21,551. Freshmen: 4,838. Federal methodology is used as a basis for awarding need-based institutional aid.

UNDERGRADUATE EXPENSES for 2006–07 ***Application fee:*** $45. ***Tuition, state resident:*** full-time $6364; part-time $227.30 per credit hour. ***Tuition, nonresident:*** full-time $15,946; part-time $569.50 per credit hour. ***Required fees:*** full-time $944; $33.60 per credit hour. Full-time tuition and fees vary according to course load, program, and reciprocity agreements. Part-time tuition and fees vary according to course load, program, and reciprocity agreements. ***College room and board:*** $6977; ***Room only:*** $3837. Room and board charges vary according to board plan and housing facility. ***Payment plan:*** Installment.

FRESHMAN FINANCIAL AID (Fall 2006, est.) 3389 applied for aid; of those 62% were deemed to have need. 99% of freshmen with need received aid; of those 21% had need fully met. ***Average percent of need met:*** 89% (excluding resources awarded to replace EFC). ***Average financial aid package:*** $12,611 (excluding resources awarded to replace EFC). 29% of all full-time freshmen had no need and received non-need-based gift aid.

UNDERGRADUATE FINANCIAL AID (Fall 2006, est.) 12,547 applied for aid; of those 69% were deemed to have need. 99% of undergraduates with need received aid; of those 22% had need fully met. ***Average percent of need met:*** 86% (excluding resources awarded to replace EFC). ***Average financial aid package:*** $11,452 (excluding resources awarded to replace EFC). 23% of all full-time undergraduates had no need and received non-need-based gift aid.

GIFT AID (NEED-BASED) ***Total amount:*** $41,868,708 (29% federal, 10% state, 46% institutional, 15% external sources). ***Receiving aid:*** Freshmen: 39% (1,880); All full-time undergraduates: 35% (7,089). ***Average award:*** Freshmen: $6759;

Undergraduates: $6154. ***Scholarships, grants, and awards:*** Federal Pell, FSEOG, state, private, college/university gift aid from institutional funds, Outside.

GIFT AID (NON-NEED-BASED) ***Total amount:*** $23,389,847 (5% federal, 13% state, 53% institutional, 29% external sources). ***Receiving aid:*** Freshmen: 5% (233); Undergraduates: 3% (581). ***Average award:*** Freshmen: $4310; Undergraduates: $4310. ***Scholarships, grants, and awards by category:*** *Academic Interests/Achievement:* agriculture, biological sciences, business, communication, computer science, education, engineering/technologies, English, foreign languages, general academic interests/achievements, health fields, home economics, mathematics, premedicine, religion/biblical studies, social sciences. *Creative Arts/Performance:* journalism/publications, music, theater/drama. *Special Achievements/Activities:* general special achievements/activities. *Special Characteristics:* children and siblings of alumni, international students, members of minority groups, out-of-state students. ***Tuition waivers:*** Full or partial for employees or children of employees, senior citizens. ***ROTC:*** Army, Naval, Air Force.

LOANS ***Student loans:*** $73,003,734 (59% need-based, 41% non-need-based). 59% of past graduating class borrowed through all loan programs. *Average indebtedness per student:* $18,983. ***Average need-based loan:*** Freshmen: $3018; Undergraduates: $4001. ***Parent loans:*** $29,577,150 (42% need-based, 58% non-need-based). ***Programs:*** Federal Direct (Subsidized and Unsubsidized Stafford, PLUS), FFEL (PLUS), Perkins, Federal Nursing, state, college/university, Outside.

WORK-STUDY ***Federal work-study:*** Total amount: $1,815,769; 1,188 jobs averaging $1528.

ATHLETIC AWARDS Total amount: $5,142,611 (34% need-based, 66% non-need-based).

APPLYING FOR FINANCIAL AID ***Required financial aid form:*** FAFSA. ***Financial aid deadline (priority):*** 3/1. ***Notification date:*** Continuous beginning 4/1. Students must reply within 4 weeks of notification.

CONTACT Lori A. Hartman, Associate Director, Student Financial Aid, University of Missouri–Columbia, 11 Jesse Hall, Columbia, MO 65211, 573-882-7506 or toll-free 800-225-6075 (in-state). *Fax:* 573-884-5335. *E-mail:* finaldinfo@missouri.edu.

UNIVERSITY OF MISSOURI–KANSAS CITY

Kansas City, MO

Tuition & fees (MO res): $7592 Average undergraduate aid package: $9867

ABOUT THE INSTITUTION State-supported, coed. Awards: bachelor's, master's, doctoral, and first professional degrees and post-master's and first professional certificates. 50 undergraduate majors. Total enrollment: 14,213. Undergraduates: 9,383. Freshmen: 956. Federal methodology is used as a basis for awarding need-based institutional aid.

UNDERGRADUATE EXPENSES for 2006–07 ***Application fee:*** $35. ***Tuition, state resident:*** full-time $6819; part-time $227.30 per credit hour. ***Tuition, nonresident:*** full-time $17,085; part-time $569.50 per credit hour. ***Required fees:*** full-time $773; $29.72 per credit hour. Full-time tuition and fees vary according to course load, program, and student level. Part-time tuition and fees vary according to course load, program, and student level. ***College room and board:*** $6823. Room and board charges vary according to board plan and housing facility. ***Payment plan:*** Installment.

FRESHMAN FINANCIAL AID (Fall 2006, est.) 863 applied for aid; of those 68% were deemed to have need. 99% of freshmen with need received aid; of those 59% had need fully met. ***Average percent of need met:*** 58% (excluding resources awarded to replace EFC). ***Average financial aid package:*** $11,419 (excluding resources awarded to replace EFC). 22% of all full-time freshmen had no need and received non-need-based gift aid.

UNDERGRADUATE FINANCIAL AID (Fall 2006, est.) 4,935 applied for aid; of those 73% were deemed to have need. 100% of undergraduates with need received aid; of those 43% had need fully met. ***Average percent of need met:*** 51% (excluding resources awarded to replace EFC). ***Average financial aid package:*** $9867 (excluding resources awarded to replace EFC). 13% of all full-time undergraduates had no need and received non-need-based gift aid.

GIFT AID (NEED-BASED) ***Total amount:*** $14,216,175 (50% federal, 7% state, 34% institutional, 9% external sources). ***Receiving aid:*** Freshmen: 46% (426); All full-time undergraduates: 41% (2,336). ***Average award:*** Freshmen: $7070; Undergraduates: $5630. ***Scholarships, grants, and awards:*** Federal Pell, FSEOG, state, private, college/university gift aid from institutional funds, United Negro College Fund, Federal Nursing.

GIFT AID (NON-NEED-BASED) ***Total amount:*** $5,903,004 (4% federal, 8% state, 81% institutional, 7% external sources). ***Receiving aid:*** Freshmen: 37% (345); Undergraduates: 21% (1,203). ***Average award:*** Freshmen: $4070; Undergraduates: $4124. ***Scholarships, grants, and awards by category:*** *Academic Interests/Achievement:* general academic interests/achievements. *Creative Arts/Performance:* debating, general creative arts/performance, music, performing arts. *Special Achievements/Activities:* general special achievements/activities. *Special Characteristics:* ethnic background, members of minority groups, out-of-state students. ***Tuition waivers:*** Full or partial for employees or children of employees. ***ROTC:*** Army, Air Force cooperative.

LOANS ***Student loans:*** $37,085,428 (68% need-based, 32% non-need-based). 97% of past graduating class borrowed through all loan programs. *Average indebtedness per student:* $18,227. ***Average need-based loan:*** Freshmen: $3251; Undergraduates: $6018. ***Parent loans:*** $2,095,909 (19% need-based, 81% non-need-based). ***Programs:*** FFEL (Subsidized and Unsubsidized Stafford, PLUS), Perkins, Federal Nursing, state, college/university.

WORK-STUDY ***Federal work-study:*** Total amount: $1,999,009; jobs available.

ATHLETIC AWARDS Total amount: $1,638,519 (15% need-based, 85% non-need-based).

APPLYING FOR FINANCIAL AID ***Required financial aid form:*** FAFSA. ***Financial aid deadline (priority):*** 3/1. ***Notification date:*** Continuous beginning 4/1. Students must reply within 2 weeks of notification.

CONTACT Jan Brandow, Financial Aid and Scholarships Office, University of Missouri–Kansas City, 5100 Rockhill Road, Kansas City, MO 64110-2499, 816-235-1154 or toll-free 800-775-8652 (out-of-state). *Fax:* 816-235-5511.

UNIVERSITY OF MISSOURI–ROLLA

Rolla, MO

CONTACT Mr. Robert W. Whites, Director of Student Financial Assistance, University of Missouri–Rolla, G1 Parker Hall, Rolla, MO 65409, 573-341-4282 or toll-free 800-522-0938. *Fax:* 573-341-4274. *E-mail:* bobw@umr.edu.

UNIVERSITY OF MISSOURI–ST. LOUIS

St. Louis, MO

Tuition & fees (MO res): $7968 Average undergraduate aid package: $10,458

ABOUT THE INSTITUTION State-supported, coed. Awards: bachelor's, master's, doctoral, and first professional degrees and post-bachelor's certificates. 71 undergraduate majors. Total enrollment: 15,540. Undergraduates: 12,470. Freshmen: 526. Federal methodology is used as a basis for awarding need-based institutional aid.

UNDERGRADUATE EXPENSES for 2006–07 ***Application fee:*** $35. ***Tuition, state resident:*** full-time $6819; part-time $227.30 per credit hour. ***Tuition, nonresident:*** full-time $17,085; part-time $569.50 per credit hour. ***Required fees:*** full-time $1149; $44.04 per credit hour. Full-time tuition and fees vary according to course load, program, and reciprocity agreements. Part-time tuition and fees vary according to course load, program, and reciprocity agreements. ***College room and board:*** $7178; ***Room only:*** $5298. Room and board charges vary according to board plan and housing facility. ***Payment plan:*** Installment.

FRESHMAN FINANCIAL AID (Fall 2006, est.) 337 applied for aid; of those 84% were deemed to have need. 100% of freshmen with need received aid; of those 24% had need fully met. ***Average percent of need met:*** 72% (excluding resources awarded to replace EFC). ***Average financial aid package:*** $11,022 (excluding resources awarded to replace EFC). 16% of all full-time freshmen had no need and received non-need-based gift aid.

UNDERGRADUATE FINANCIAL AID (Fall 2006, est.) 3,645 applied for aid; of those 86% were deemed to have need. 99% of undergraduates with need received aid; of those 12% had need fully met. ***Average percent of need met:*** 66% (excluding resources awarded to replace EFC). ***Average financial aid package:*** $10,458 (excluding resources awarded to replace EFC). 11% of all full-time undergraduates had no need and received non-need-based gift aid.

GIFT AID (NEED-BASED) ***Total amount:*** $12,338,817 (58% federal, 9% state, 29% institutional, 4% external sources). ***Receiving aid:*** Freshmen: 46% (221); All full-time undergraduates: 36% (2,036). ***Average award:*** Freshmen: $6757; Undergraduates: $4593. ***Scholarships, grants, and awards:*** Federal Pell, FSEOG, state, private, college/university gift aid from institutional funds, Federal Nursing.

GIFT AID (NON-NEED-BASED) ***Total amount:*** $3,598,355 (1% federal, 6% state, 88% institutional, 5% external sources). ***Receiving aid:*** Freshmen: 10%

(48); Undergraduates: 4% (200). ***Average award:*** Freshmen: $5797; Undergraduates: $4670. ***Scholarships, grants, and awards by category:*** *Academic Interests/Achievement:* biological sciences, business, communication, computer science, education, engineering/technologies, English, foreign languages, general academic interests/achievements, health fields, humanities, international studies, mathematics. *Creative Arts/Performance:* art/fine arts, music. *Special Achievements/Activities:* memberships. *Special Characteristics:* ethnic background, general special characteristics, local/state students, members of minority groups. ***Tuition waivers:*** Full or partial for employees or children of employees, senior citizens. ***ROTC:*** Army cooperative, Air Force cooperative.

LOANS ***Student loans:*** $37,844,111 (86% need-based, 14% non-need-based). 65% of past graduating class borrowed through all loan programs. *Average indebtedness per student:* $18,143. ***Average need-based loan:*** Freshmen: $2666; Undergraduates: $4279. ***Parent loans:*** $6,182,935 (57% need-based, 43% non-need-based). ***Programs:*** FFEL (Subsidized and Unsubsidized Stafford, PLUS), Perkins, Federal Nursing.

WORK-STUDY ***Federal work-study:*** Total amount: $341,015; 97 jobs averaging $3242.

ATHLETIC AWARDS Total amount: $704,265 (31% need-based, 69% non-need-based).

APPLYING FOR FINANCIAL AID ***Required financial aid form:*** FAFSA. ***Financial aid deadline (priority):*** 4/1. ***Notification date:*** Continuous beginning 4/1. Students must reply within 2 weeks of notification.

CONTACT Samantha Ruffini, Senior Associate Director, Student Financial Aid, University of Missouri–St. Louis, One University Boulevard, 327 MSC, St. Louis, MO 63121-4400, 314-516-6893 or toll-free 888-GO2-UMSL (in-state). *Fax:* 314-516-5408. *E-mail:* ruffinis@umsl.edu.

UNIVERSITY OF MOBILE

Mobile, AL

CONTACT Marie Thomas, Director of Financial Aid, University of Mobile, PO Box 13220, Mobile, AL 36663-0220, 251-442-2370 or toll-free 800-946-7267. *Fax:* 251-442-2498.

THE UNIVERSITY OF MONTANA

Missoula, MT

Tuition & fees (MT res): $4977 Average undergraduate aid package: $7866

ABOUT THE INSTITUTION State-supported, coed. Awards: associate, bachelor's, master's, doctoral, and first professional degrees and post-master's certificates. 119 undergraduate majors. Total enrollment: 13,558. Undergraduates: 11,431. Federal methodology is used as a basis for awarding need-based institutional aid.

UNDERGRADUATE EXPENSES for 2006–07 ***Application fee:*** $30. ***Tuition, state resident:*** full-time $3686; part-time $164 per credit. ***Tuition, nonresident:*** full-time $13,193; part-time $573 per credit. ***Required fees:*** full-time $1291; $40 per credit. Full-time tuition and fees vary according to degree level, location, program, reciprocity agreements, and student level. Part-time tuition and fees vary according to course load, degree level, location, and student level. ***College room and board:*** $5860; ***Room only:*** $2660. Room and board charges vary according to board plan and housing facility. ***Payment plans:*** Installment, deferred payment.

FRESHMAN FINANCIAL AID (Fall 2005) 1782 applied for aid; of those 71% were deemed to have need. 99% of freshmen with need received aid; of those 15% had need fully met. ***Average percent of need met:*** 70% (excluding resources awarded to replace EFC). ***Average financial aid package:*** $6740 (excluding resources awarded to replace EFC). 23% of all full-time freshmen had no need and received non-need-based gift aid.

UNDERGRADUATE FINANCIAL AID (Fall 2005) 7,752 applied for aid; of those 76% were deemed to have need. 99% of undergraduates with need received aid; of those 17% had need fully met. ***Average percent of need met:*** 75% (excluding resources awarded to replace EFC). ***Average financial aid package:*** $7866 (excluding resources awarded to replace EFC). 17% of all full-time undergraduates had no need and received non-need-based gift aid.

GIFT AID (NEED-BASED) ***Total amount:*** $15,022,468 (88% federal, 6% state, 6% institutional). ***Receiving aid:*** Freshmen: 38% (838); All full-time undergraduates: 42% (4,277). ***Average award:*** Freshmen: $3327; Undergraduates: $3504. ***Scholarships, grants, and awards:*** Federal Pell, FSEOG, state, private, college/university gift aid from institutional funds.

GIFT AID (NON-NEED-BASED) ***Total amount:*** $5,676,340 (49% institutional, 51% external sources). ***Receiving aid:*** Freshmen: 6% (142); Undergraduates: 3% (279). ***Average award:*** Freshmen: $2991; Undergraduates: $4195. ***Scholarships, grants, and awards by category:*** *Academic Interests/Achievement:* 1,011 awards ($1,458,715 total): biological sciences, business, computer science, education, English, foreign languages, general academic interests/achievements, health fields, humanities, international studies, mathematics, military science, physical sciences, premedicine, social sciences. *Creative Arts/Performance:* 126 awards ($191,483 total): art/fine arts, creative writing, dance, journalism/publications, music, performing arts, theater/drama. *Special Achievements/Activities:* 82 awards ($525,895 total): cheerleading/drum major, leadership, rodeo. *Special Characteristics:* 842 awards ($4,965,764 total): children and siblings of alumni, children with a deceased or disabled parent, general special characteristics, international students, members of minority groups, out-of-state students, veterans. ***Tuition waivers:*** Full or partial for minority students, employees or children of employees, senior citizens. ***ROTC:*** Army.

LOANS ***Student loans:*** $34,726,718 (100% need-based). 70% of past graduating class borrowed through all loan programs. *Average indebtedness per student:* $15,185. ***Average need-based loan:*** Freshmen: $3426; Undergraduates: $5012. ***Parent loans:*** $6,240,721 (100% non-need-based). ***Programs:*** FFEL (Subsidized and Unsubsidized Stafford, PLUS), Perkins.

WORK-STUDY ***Federal work-study:*** Total amount: $2,232,099; 1,098 jobs averaging $1977. ***State or other work-study/employment:*** Total amount: $419,535 (100% need-based). Part-time jobs available.

ATHLETIC AWARDS Total amount: $2,314,746 (100% non-need-based).

APPLYING FOR FINANCIAL AID ***Required financial aid forms:*** FAFSA, UM Supplemental Information Sheet. ***Financial aid deadline (priority):*** 2/15. ***Notification date:*** Continuous beginning 4/1. Students must reply within 4 weeks of notification.

CONTACT Mick Hanson, Director of Financial Aid, The University of Montana, Enrollment Services, Missoula, MT 59812-0002, 406-243-5373 or toll-free 800-462-8636. *Fax:* 406-243-4930. *E-mail:* faid@mso.umt.edu.

THE UNIVERSITY OF MONTANA–WESTERN

Dillon, MT

CONTACT Arlene Williams, Financial Aid Director, The University of Montana–Western, 710 South Atlantic Street, Dillon, MT 59725, 406-683-7511 or toll-free 866-869-6668 (in-state), 877-683-7493 (out-of-state). *Fax:* 406-683-7493. *E-mail:* a_williams@umwestern.edu.

UNIVERSITY OF MONTEVALLO

Montevallo, AL

CONTACT Ms. Maria Parker, Director of Student Financial Aid, University of Montevallo, Station 6050, Montevallo, AL 35115, 205-665-6050 or toll-free 800-292-4349. *Fax:* 205-665-6047. *E-mail:* finaid@montevallo.edu.

UNIVERSITY OF NEBRASKA AT KEARNEY

Kearney, NE

Tuition & fees (NE res): $4765 Average undergraduate aid package: $7227

ABOUT THE INSTITUTION State-supported, coed. Awards: bachelor's and master's degrees and post-master's certificates. 41 undergraduate majors. Total enrollment: 6,468. Undergraduates: 5,276. Freshmen: 1,014. Federal methodology is used as a basis for awarding need-based institutional aid.

UNDERGRADUATE EXPENSES for 2006–07 ***Application fee:*** $45. ***Tuition, state resident:*** full-time $3885; part-time $129.50 per hour. ***Tuition, nonresident:*** full-time $7958; part-time $265.25 per hour. ***Required fees:*** full-time $880; $17.50 per hour or $64 per term part-time. Full-time tuition and fees vary according to course level, course load, degree level, and location. Part-time tuition and fees vary according to course level, course load, degree level, and location. ***College room and board:*** $5686. Room and board charges vary according to board plan and housing facility. ***Payment plan:*** Installment.

FRESHMAN FINANCIAL AID (Fall 2005) 839 applied for aid; of those 74% were deemed to have need. 98% of freshmen with need received aid; of those 31%

had need fully met. ***Average percent of need met:*** 74% (excluding resources awarded to replace EFC). ***Average financial aid package:*** $7162 (excluding resources awarded to replace EFC). 8% of all full-time freshmen had no need and received non-need-based gift aid.

UNDERGRADUATE FINANCIAL AID (Fall 2005) 3,598 applied for aid; of those 80% were deemed to have need. 97% of undergraduates with need received aid; of those 32% had need fully met. ***Average percent of need met:*** 79% (excluding resources awarded to replace EFC). ***Average financial aid package:*** $7227 (excluding resources awarded to replace EFC). 30% of all full-time undergraduates had no need and received non-need-based gift aid.

GIFT AID (NEED-BASED) ***Total amount:*** $6,426,544 (67% federal, 11% state, 22% institutional). ***Receiving aid:*** Freshmen: 42% (436); All full-time undergraduates: 39% (1,935). ***Average award:*** Freshmen: $3219; Undergraduates: $3176. ***Scholarships, grants, and awards:*** Federal Pell, FSEOG, state, private, college/university gift aid from institutional funds.

GIFT AID (NON-NEED-BASED) ***Total amount:*** $3,113,105 (55% institutional, 45% external sources). ***Receiving aid:*** Freshmen: 36% (378); Undergraduates: 30% (1,478). ***Average award:*** Freshmen: $1753; Undergraduates: $1994. ***Scholarships, grants, and awards by category:*** *Academic Interests/Achievement:* 3 awards ($2200 total): communication. *Creative Arts/Performance:* 89 awards ($63,874 total): applied art and design, art/fine arts, debating, journalism/publications, music. *Special Achievements/Activities:* 15 awards ($3120 total): cheerleading/drum major. *Special Characteristics:* 469 awards ($812,191 total): children of faculty/staff, ethnic background, first-generation college students, international students, out-of-state students, veterans, veterans' children. ***Tuition waivers:*** Full or partial for employees or children of employees.

LOANS ***Student loans:*** $14,465,329 (59% need-based, 41% non-need-based). 74% of past graduating class borrowed through all loan programs. *Average indebtedness per student:* $16,175. ***Average need-based loan:*** Freshmen: $2573; Undergraduates: $3590. ***Parent loans:*** $2,808,073 (100% non-need-based). ***Programs:*** FFEL (Subsidized and Unsubsidized Stafford, PLUS), Perkins.

WORK-STUDY ***Federal work-study:*** Total amount: $569,382; 325 jobs averaging $1088.

ATHLETIC AWARDS Total amount: $684,532 (100% non-need-based).

APPLYING FOR FINANCIAL AID ***Required financial aid forms:*** FAFSA, institution's own form. ***Financial aid deadline (priority):*** 4/1. ***Notification date:*** Continuous beginning 3/15.

CONTACT Financial Aid Office, University of Nebraska at Kearney, Memorial Student Affairs Building, 905 West 25th Street, Kearney, NE 68849-0001, 308-865-8520 or toll-free 800-532-7639. *Fax:* 308-865-8096.

UNIVERSITY OF NEBRASKA AT OMAHA

Omaha, NE

Tuition & fees (NE res): $5118 **Average undergraduate aid package: N/A**

ABOUT THE INSTITUTION State-supported, coed. Awards: bachelor's, master's, and doctoral degrees and post-bachelor's and post-master's certificates. 73 undergraduate majors. Total enrollment: 13,906. Undergraduates: 11,156. Freshmen: 1,708. Federal methodology is used as a basis for awarding need-based institutional aid.

UNDERGRADUATE EXPENSES for 2006–07 ***Application fee:*** $45. ***Tuition, state resident:*** full-time $4380; part-time $146 per semester hour. ***Tuition, nonresident:*** full-time $12,908; part-time $430.25 per semester hour. ***Required fees:*** full-time $738; $24.50 per semester hour or $89.20 per term part-time. Full-time tuition and fees vary according to course load. Part-time tuition and fees vary according to course load. ***College room and board:*** $6630; ***Room only:*** $4110. Room and board charges vary according to board plan. ***Payment plans:*** Installment, deferred payment.

FRESHMAN FINANCIAL AID (Fall 2006, est.) 1272 applied for aid; of those 64% were deemed to have need. 99% of freshmen with need received aid.

UNDERGRADUATE FINANCIAL AID (Fall 2006, est.) 5,748 applied for aid; of those 71% were deemed to have need. 100% of undergraduates with need received aid.

GIFT AID (NEED-BASED) ***Total amount:*** $15,410,000 (47% federal, 9% state, 32% institutional, 12% external sources). ***Receiving aid:*** Freshmen: 27% (497); All full-time undergraduates: 34% (3,195). ***Scholarships, grants, and awards:*** Federal Pell, FSEOG, state, private, college/university gift aid from institutional funds.

GIFT AID (NON-NEED-BASED) ***Receiving aid:*** Freshmen: 37% (668); Undergraduates: 31% (2,833). ***Scholarships, grants, and awards by category:*** *Academic Interests/Achievement:* biological sciences, business, communication, computer science, education, engineering/technologies, English, foreign languages, general academic interests/achievements, home economics, mathematics, physical sciences, premedicine, social sciences. *Creative Arts/Performance:* art/fine arts, creative writing, debating, journalism/publications, music, performing arts, theater/drama. *Special Achievements/Activities:* general special achievements/activities, leadership, memberships. *Special Characteristics:* adult students, children and siblings of alumni, children of faculty/staff, ethnic background, first-generation college students, handicapped students, international students, members of minority groups, out-of-state students, veterans' children. ***Tuition waivers:*** Full or partial for employees or children of employees. ***ROTC:*** Army cooperative, Air Force.

LOANS ***Student loans:*** $43,312,000 (45% need-based, 55% non-need-based). 48% of past graduating class borrowed through all loan programs. *Average indebtedness per student:* $18,800. ***Parent loans:*** $2,000,000 (100% non-need-based). ***Programs:*** FFEL (Subsidized and Unsubsidized Stafford, PLUS), Perkins, college/university.

WORK-STUDY ***Federal work-study:*** Total amount: $680,000; 400 jobs averaging $1700.

ATHLETIC AWARDS Total amount: $772,622 (100% need-based).

APPLYING FOR FINANCIAL AID ***Required financial aid form:*** FAFSA. ***Financial aid deadline (priority):*** 3/1. ***Notification date:*** Continuous beginning 4/1. Students must reply within 2 weeks of notification.

CONTACT Office of Financial Aid, University of Nebraska at Omaha, 103 Eppley Administration Building, 6001 Dodge Street, Omaha, NE 68182-0187, 402-554-2327 or toll-free 800-858-8648 (in-state). *Fax:* 402-554-3472. *E-mail:* finaid@unomaha.edu.

UNIVERSITY OF NEBRASKA–LINCOLN

Lincoln, NE

ABOUT THE INSTITUTION State-supported, coed. Awards: associate, bachelor's, master's, doctoral, and first professional degrees and post-bachelor's and post-master's certificates. 128 undergraduate majors. Total enrollment: 22,106. Undergraduates: 17,371. Freshmen: 3,849.

GIFT AID (NEED-BASED) ***Scholarships, grants, and awards:*** Federal Pell, FSEOG, state, private, college/university gift aid from institutional funds.

GIFT AID (NON-NEED-BASED) ***Scholarships, grants, and awards by category:*** *Academic Interests/Achievement:* agriculture, architecture, biological sciences, business, computer science, education, engineering/technologies, English, foreign languages, general academic interests/achievements, health fields, home economics, humanities, international studies, mathematics, physical sciences, premedicine, social sciences. *Creative Arts/Performance:* art/fine arts, cinema/film/broadcasting, dance, journalism/publications, music, performing arts, theater/drama. *Special Achievements/Activities:* cheerleading/drum major, community service, leadership. *Special Characteristics:* children and siblings of alumni, ethnic background, handicapped students, international students, members of minority groups, out-of-state students, veterans' children.

LOANS ***Programs:*** Federal Direct (Subsidized and Unsubsidized Stafford, PLUS), Perkins, college/university.

APPLYING FOR FINANCIAL AID ***Required financial aid form:*** FAFSA.

CONTACT Ms. Jo Tederman, Assistant Director of Scholarships and Financial Aid, University of Nebraska–Lincoln, 16 Canfield Administration Building, PO Box 880411, Lincoln, NE 68588-0411, 402-472-2030 or toll-free 800-742-8800. *Fax:* 402-472-9826.

UNIVERSITY OF NEBRASKA MEDICAL CENTER

Omaha, NE

Tuition & fees (NE res): $4830 **Average undergraduate aid package: $7999**

ABOUT THE INSTITUTION State-supported, coed. Awards: bachelor's, master's, doctoral, and first professional degrees and post-bachelor's, post-master's, and first professional certificates. 7 undergraduate majors. Total enrollment: 2,995. Undergraduates: 851. Federal methodology is used as a basis for awarding need-based institutional aid.

UNDERGRADUATE EXPENSES for 2006–07 ***Application fee:*** $45. ***Tuition, state resident:*** full-time $4530; part-time $151 per semester hour. ***Tuition, nonresident:*** full-time $13,440; part-time $448 per semester hour. ***Required fees:*** full-time $300; $105 per semester hour.

UNDERGRADUATE FINANCIAL AID (Fall 2005) 833 applied for aid; of those 85% were deemed to have need. 99% of undergraduates with need received aid; of those 16% had need fully met. ***Average percent of need met:*** 63% (excluding resources awarded to replace EFC). ***Average financial aid package:*** $7999 (excluding resources awarded to replace EFC). 19% of all full-time undergraduates had no need and received non-need-based gift aid.

GIFT AID (NEED-BASED) ***Total amount:*** $3,512,364 (22% federal, 53% state, 25% external sources). ***Receiving aid:*** All full-time undergraduates: 59% (588). ***Average award:*** Undergraduates: $4425. ***Scholarships, grants, and awards:*** Federal Pell, FSEOG, state, private, college/university gift aid from institutional funds.

GIFT AID (NON-NEED-BASED) ***Receiving aid:*** Undergraduates: 4% (39). ***Average award:*** Undergraduates: $7839. ***ROTC:*** Army cooperative, Air Force cooperative.

LOANS ***Student loans:*** $6,553,403 (100% need-based). 73% of past graduating class borrowed through all loan programs. *Average indebtedness per student:* $26,226. ***Average need-based loan:*** Undergraduates: $4799. ***Parent loans:*** $993,577 (100% need-based). ***Programs:*** FFEL (Subsidized and Unsubsidized Stafford, PLUS), Perkins, Federal Nursing, state, college/university.

WORK-STUDY ***Federal work-study:*** Total amount: $28,006; 59 jobs averaging $474.

APPLYING FOR FINANCIAL AID ***Required financial aid forms:*** FAFSA, institution's own form. ***Financial aid deadline (priority):*** 3/15. ***Notification date:*** Continuous beginning 4/1. Students must reply within 2 weeks of notification.

CONTACT Judi Walker, Director of Financial Aid, University of Nebraska Medical Center, 984265 Nebraska Medical Center, Omaha, NE 68198-4265, 402-559-6409 or toll-free 800-626-8431 Ext. 6468. *Fax:* 402-559-6796. *E-mail:* jdwalker@unmc.edu.

UNIVERSITY OF NEVADA, LAS VEGAS

Las Vegas, NV

ABOUT THE INSTITUTION State-supported, coed. Awards: bachelor's, master's, doctoral, and first professional degrees and post-bachelor's and post-master's certificates. 86 undergraduate majors. Total enrollment: 27,933. Undergraduates: 21,853. Freshmen: 2,768.

GIFT AID (NEED-BASED) ***Scholarships, grants, and awards:*** Federal Pell, FSEOG, state, private, college/university gift aid from institutional funds.

GIFT AID (NON-NEED-BASED) ***Scholarships, grants, and awards by category:*** *Academic Interests/Achievement:* architecture, biological sciences, business, communication, computer science, education, engineering/technologies, English, general academic interests/achievements, health fields, humanities, international studies, mathematics, physical sciences, premedicine, social sciences. *Creative Arts/Performance:* applied art and design, art/fine arts, cinema/film/broadcasting, dance, journalism/publications, music, performing arts, theater/drama. *Special Achievements/Activities:* cheerleading/drum major, community service, general special achievements/activities, hobbies/interests, leadership, memberships, rodeo. *Special Characteristics:* children and siblings of alumni, children of faculty/staff, children of public servants, children of workers in trades, ethnic background, first-generation college students, general special characteristics, handicapped students, international students, local/state students, members of minority groups, out-of-state students.

LOANS ***Programs:*** Federal Direct (Subsidized and Unsubsidized Stafford, PLUS), Perkins, state, college/university.

WORK-STUDY ***Federal work-study:*** Total amount: $1,100,000; 300 jobs averaging $3100. ***State or other work-study/employment:*** Total amount: $5,800,000 (28% need-based, 72% non-need-based). 300 part-time jobs averaging $3000.

APPLYING FOR FINANCIAL AID ***Required financial aid forms:*** FAFSA, institution's own form.

CONTACT Director of Student Financial Services, University of Nevada, Las Vegas, 4505 Maryland Parkway, Box 452016, Las Vegas, NV 89154-2016, 702-895-3424. *Fax:* 702-895-1353.

UNIVERSITY OF NEVADA, RENO

Reno, NV

ABOUT THE INSTITUTION State-supported, coed. Awards: bachelor's, master's, doctoral, and first professional degrees and post-bachelor's, post-master's, and first professional certificates. 97 undergraduate majors. Total enrollment: 16,663. Undergraduates: 13,134. Freshmen: 2,357.

GIFT AID (NEED-BASED) ***Scholarships, grants, and awards:*** Federal Pell, FSEOG, private, college/university gift aid from institutional funds.

GIFT AID (NON-NEED-BASED) ***Scholarships, grants, and awards by category:*** *Academic Interests/Achievement:* agriculture, biological sciences, business, computer science, education, engineering/technologies, English, foreign languages, general academic interests/achievements, health fields, humanities, international studies, mathematics, military science, physical sciences, premedicine, social sciences. *Creative Arts/Performance:* applied art and design, art/fine arts, creative writing, dance, debating, general creative arts/performance, journalism/publications, music, performing arts, theater/drama. *Special Achievements/Activities:* cheerleading/drum major. *Special Characteristics:* adult students, children and siblings of alumni, ethnic background, first-generation college students, local/state students, married students, members of minority groups.

LOANS ***Programs:*** FFEL (Subsidized and Unsubsidized Stafford, PLUS), Perkins, Federal Nursing, college/university.

APPLYING FOR FINANCIAL AID ***Required financial aid form:*** FAFSA.

CONTACT Dr. Nancee Langley, Director of Student Financial Aid, University of Nevada, Reno, Student Services Building, Room 316, Mail Stop 076, Reno, NV 89557, 775-784-4666 Ext. 3009 or toll-free 866-263-8232. *Fax:* 775-784-1025. *E-mail:* langley@unr.edu.

UNIVERSITY OF NEW ENGLAND

Biddeford, ME

Tuition & fees: $23,790 **Average undergraduate aid package: $22,472**

ABOUT THE INSTITUTION Independent, coed. Awards: associate, bachelor's, master's, and first professional degrees and post-bachelor's and post-master's certificates. 38 undergraduate majors. Total enrollment: 3,379. Undergraduates: 1,856. Freshmen: 481. Federal methodology is used as a basis for awarding need-based institutional aid.

UNDERGRADUATE EXPENSES for 2006–07 ***Application fee:*** $40. ***Comprehensive fee:*** $33,045 includes full-time tuition ($22,940), mandatory fees ($850), and room and board ($9255). Room and board charges vary according to housing facility and location. ***Part-time tuition:*** $825 per credit. ***Payment plan:*** Installment.

FRESHMAN FINANCIAL AID (Fall 2006, est.) 453 applied for aid; of those 90% were deemed to have need. 100% of freshmen with need received aid; of those 50% had need fully met. ***Average percent of need met:*** 86% (excluding resources awarded to replace EFC). ***Average financial aid package:*** $22,497 (excluding resources awarded to replace EFC). 15% of all full-time freshmen had no need and received non-need-based gift aid.

UNDERGRADUATE FINANCIAL AID (Fall 2006, est.) 1,456 applied for aid; of those 92% were deemed to have need. 100% of undergraduates with need received aid; of those 51% had need fully met. ***Average percent of need met:*** 85% (excluding resources awarded to replace EFC). ***Average financial aid package:*** $22,472 (excluding resources awarded to replace EFC). 16% of all full-time undergraduates had no need and received non-need-based gift aid.

GIFT AID (NEED-BASED) ***Total amount:*** $15,160,925 (10% federal, 3% state, 80% institutional, 7% external sources). ***Receiving aid:*** Freshmen: 85% (406); All full-time undergraduates: 82% (1,329). ***Average award:*** Freshmen: $12,817; Undergraduates: $11,311. ***Scholarships, grants, and awards:*** Federal Pell, FSEOG, state, private, college/university gift aid from institutional funds.

GIFT AID (NON-NEED-BASED) ***Total amount:*** $2,318,083 (96% institutional, 4% external sources). ***Receiving aid:*** Freshmen: 6% (29); Undergraduates: 5% (82). ***Average award:*** Freshmen: $8271; Undergraduates: $7274. ***Scholarships, grants, and awards by category:*** *Academic Interests/Achievement:* 1,682 awards ($7,782,848 total): biological sciences, business, education, English, general academic interests/achievements, health fields, humanities, international studies, mathematics, physical sciences, premedicine, social sciences. *Special Achievements/Activities:* 16 awards ($13,500 total): community service, general special achievements/activities, leadership. *Special Characteristics:* 11 awards ($12,750 total): children and siblings of alumni, ethnic background, members of minority groups, siblings of current students. ***Tuition waivers:*** Full or partial for children of alumni, employees or children of employees. ***ROTC:*** Army cooperative.

LOANS ***Student loans:*** $17,618,295 (72% need-based, 28% non-need-based). 87% of past graduating class borrowed through all loan programs. *Average indebtedness per student:* $39,014. ***Average need-based loan:*** Freshmen: $9154; Undergraduates: $11,112. ***Parent loans:*** $3,807,747 (47% need-based, 53% non-need-based). ***Programs:*** FFEL (Subsidized and Unsubsidized Stafford, PLUS), Perkins, Federal Nursing, state, college/university.

WORK-STUDY ***Federal work-study:*** Total amount: $1,462,831; 792 jobs averaging $1847. ***State or other work-study/employment:*** Total amount: $53,250 (33% need-based, 67% non-need-based). 30 part-time jobs averaging $10,167.

APPLYING FOR FINANCIAL AID ***Required financial aid form:*** FAFSA. ***Financial aid deadline (priority):*** 5/1. ***Notification date:*** Continuous beginning 2/1.

CONTACT John R. Bowie, Director of Financial Aid, University of New England, 11 Hills Beach Road, Biddeford, ME 04005, 207-602-2342 or toll-free 800-477-4UNE. *Fax:* 207-602-5946. *E-mail:* finaid@une.edu.

UNIVERSITY OF NEW HAMPSHIRE

Durham, NH

Tuition & fees (NH res): $10,401 Average undergraduate aid package: $15,688

ABOUT THE INSTITUTION State-supported, coed. Awards: associate, bachelor's, master's, and doctoral degrees and post-master's certificates. 142 undergraduate majors. Total enrollment: 14,848. Undergraduates: 11,971. Freshmen: 3,079. Federal methodology is used as a basis for awarding need-based institutional aid.

UNDERGRADUATE EXPENSES for 2006–07 ***Application fee:*** $45. ***Tuition, state resident:*** full-time $8240; part-time $343 per credit. ***Tuition, nonresident:*** full-time $20,690; part-time $862 per credit. ***Required fees:*** full-time $2161; $20 per term part-time. ***College room and board:*** $7584; ***Room only:*** $4606.

FRESHMAN FINANCIAL AID (Fall 2005) 2125 applied for aid; of those 72% were deemed to have need. 99% of freshmen with need received aid; of those 28% had need fully met. ***Average percent of need met:*** 84% (excluding resources awarded to replace EFC). ***Average financial aid package:*** $15,617 (excluding resources awarded to replace EFC). 25% of all full-time freshmen had no need and received non-need-based gift aid.

UNDERGRADUATE FINANCIAL AID (Fall 2005) 7,506 applied for aid; of those 79% were deemed to have need. 99% of undergraduates with need received aid; of those 24% had need fully met. ***Average percent of need met:*** 80% (excluding resources awarded to replace EFC). ***Average financial aid package:*** $15,688 (excluding resources awarded to replace EFC). 23% of all full-time undergraduates had no need and received non-need-based gift aid.

GIFT AID (NEED-BASED) ***Total amount:*** $27,430,832 (24% federal, 4% state, 51% institutional, 21% external sources). ***Receiving aid:*** Freshmen: 38% (1,000); All full-time undergraduates: 35% (3,647). ***Average award:*** Freshmen: $2935; Undergraduates: $2448. ***Scholarships, grants, and awards:*** Federal Pell, FSEOG, state, private, college/university gift aid from institutional funds.

GIFT AID (NON-NEED-BASED) ***Total amount:*** $13,087,249 (100% institutional). ***Receiving aid:*** Freshmen: 8% (221); Undergraduates: 4% (452). ***Average award:*** Freshmen: $5695; Undergraduates: $6479. ***Scholarships, grants, and awards by category:*** *Academic Interests/Achievement:* agriculture, business, education, engineering/technologies, English, general academic interests/achievements, health fields, humanities, mathematics, military science. *Creative Arts/Performance:* art/fine arts, dance, music, theater/drama. *Special Achievements/Activities:* community service. *Special Characteristics:* children and siblings of alumni, children of faculty/staff, handicapped students, international students, local/state students. ***ROTC:*** Army, Air Force.

LOANS ***Student loans:*** $66,354,146 (44% need-based, 56% non-need-based). 72% of past graduating class borrowed through all loan programs. *Average indebtedness per student:* $23,928. ***Average need-based loan:*** Freshmen: $2209; Undergraduates: $3321. ***Parent loans:*** $17,341,674 (100% non-need-based). ***Programs:*** FFEL (Subsidized and Unsubsidized Stafford, PLUS), Perkins, state, college/university.

WORK-STUDY ***Federal work-study:*** Total amount: $7,949,915; 3,134 jobs averaging $2190. ***State or other work-study/employment:*** Total amount: $5,312,876 (100% non-need-based). 2,875 part-time jobs averaging $1867.

ATHLETIC AWARDS Total amount: $5,544,212 (100% non-need-based).

APPLYING FOR FINANCIAL AID ***Required financial aid form:*** FAFSA. ***Financial aid deadline (priority):*** 3/1. ***Notification date:*** Continuous beginning 3/1.

CONTACT Susan K. Allen, Director of Financial Aid, University of New Hampshire, 11 Garrison Avenue, Stoke Hall, Durham, NH 03824, 603-862-3600. *Fax:* 603-862-1947. *E-mail:* financial.aid@unh.edu.

UNIVERSITY OF NEW HAMPSHIRE AT MANCHESTER

Manchester, NH

Tuition & fees (NH res): $7788 Average undergraduate aid package: $7739

ABOUT THE INSTITUTION State-supported, coed. Awards: associate, bachelor's, and master's degrees. 13 undergraduate majors. Total enrollment: 1,013. Undergraduates: 1,013. Freshmen: 107. Federal methodology is used as a basis for awarding need-based institutional aid.

UNDERGRADUATE EXPENSES for 2006–07 ***Application fee:*** $45. ***Tuition, state resident:*** full-time $7580; part-time $316 per credit. ***Tuition, nonresident:*** full-time $19,170; part-time $799 per credit. Full-time tuition and fees vary according to course load and program. Part-time tuition and fees vary according to course load and program.

FRESHMAN FINANCIAL AID (Fall 2005) 91 applied for aid; of those 65% were deemed to have need. 95% of freshmen with need received aid; of those 7% had need fully met. ***Average percent of need met:*** 54% (excluding resources awarded to replace EFC). ***Average financial aid package:*** $5864 (excluding resources awarded to replace EFC).

UNDERGRADUATE FINANCIAL AID (Fall 2005) 466 applied for aid; of those 74% were deemed to have need. 97% of undergraduates with need received aid; of those 11% had need fully met. ***Average percent of need met:*** 55% (excluding resources awarded to replace EFC). ***Average financial aid package:*** $7739 (excluding resources awarded to replace EFC). 1% of all full-time undergraduates had no need and received non-need-based gift aid.

GIFT AID (NEED-BASED) ***Total amount:*** $513,270 (57% federal, 13% state, 10% institutional, 20% external sources). ***Receiving aid:*** Freshmen: 13% (16); All full-time undergraduates: 13% (103). ***Average award:*** Freshmen: $776; Undergraduates: $715. ***Scholarships, grants, and awards:*** Federal Pell, FSEOG, state, private, college/university gift aid from institutional funds.

GIFT AID (NON-NEED-BASED) ***Total amount:*** $47,468 (100% institutional). ***Receiving aid:*** Undergraduates: 1. ***Average award:*** Undergraduates: $500. ***Scholarships, grants, and awards by category:*** *Academic Interests/Achievement:* general academic interests/achievements. *Special Characteristics:* children of faculty/staff. ***Tuition waivers:*** Full or partial for employees or children of employees, senior citizens. ***ROTC:*** Army cooperative, Air Force cooperative.

LOANS ***Student loans:*** $2,598,262 (48% need-based, 52% non-need-based). 66% of past graduating class borrowed through all loan programs. *Average indebtedness per student:* $17,562. ***Average need-based loan:*** Freshmen: $1827; Undergraduates: $3430. ***Parent loans:*** $111,325 (100% non-need-based). ***Programs:*** FFEL (Subsidized and Unsubsidized Stafford, PLUS), Perkins, state, college/university.

WORK-STUDY ***Federal work-study:*** Total amount: $171,491; 80 jobs averaging $2117.

APPLYING FOR FINANCIAL AID ***Required financial aid form:*** FAFSA. ***Financial aid deadline (priority):*** 3/1. ***Notification date:*** Continuous beginning 4/1.

CONTACT Jodi Abad, Assistant Director of Financial Aid, University of New Hampshire at Manchester, French Hall, 400 Commercial Street, Manchester, NH 03101-1113, 603-641-4146. *Fax:* 603-641-4125.

UNIVERSITY OF NEW HAVEN

West Haven, CT

Tuition & fees: $24,645 Average undergraduate aid package: $15,576

ABOUT THE INSTITUTION Independent, coed. Awards: associate, bachelor's, and master's degrees and post-bachelor's and post-master's certificates. 48 undergraduate majors. Total enrollment: 4,649. Undergraduates: 2,877. Freshmen: 706. Federal methodology is used as a basis for awarding need-based institutional aid.

UNDERGRADUATE EXPENSES for 2006–07 ***Application fee:*** $50. ***Comprehensive fee:*** $34,775 includes full-time tuition ($24,000), mandatory fees ($645), and room and board ($10,130). ***College room only:*** $6170. Full-time tuition and fees vary according to class time, course load, and program. Room and board charges vary according to board plan and housing facility. ***Part-time tuition:*** $800 per credit hour. Part-time tuition and fees vary according to class time, course load, and program. ***Payment plan:*** Installment.

FRESHMAN FINANCIAL AID (Fall 2006, est.) 624 applied for aid; of those 88% were deemed to have need. 100% of freshmen with need received aid; of those 13% had need fully met. ***Average percent of need met:*** 70% (excluding resources awarded to replace EFC). ***Average financial aid package:*** $16,402 (excluding resources awarded to replace EFC). 15% of all full-time freshmen had no need and received non-need-based gift aid.

UNDERGRADUATE FINANCIAL AID (Fall 2006, est.) 2,082 applied for aid; of those 90% were deemed to have need. 100% of undergraduates with need received aid; of those 12% had need fully met. ***Average percent of need met:*** 66% (excluding resources awarded to replace EFC). ***Average financial aid package:*** $15,576 (excluding resources awarded to replace EFC). 12% of all full-time undergraduates had no need and received non-need-based gift aid.

GIFT AID (NEED-BASED) ***Total amount:*** $20,584,221 (9% federal, 9% state, 78% institutional, 4% external sources). ***Receiving aid:*** Freshmen: 77% (534); All full-time undergraduates: 75% (1,817). ***Average award:*** Freshmen: $13,551; Undergraduates: $11,986. ***Scholarships, grants, and awards:*** Federal Pell, FSEOG, state, college/university gift aid from institutional funds.

GIFT AID (NON-NEED-BASED) ***Total amount:*** $1,864,434 (100% institutional). ***Receiving aid:*** Freshmen: 8% (56); Undergraduates: 7% (166). ***Average award:*** Freshmen: $13,909; Undergraduates: $14,830. ***Scholarships, grants, and awards by category:*** *Special Achievements/Activities:* general special achievements/ activities. ***Tuition waivers:*** Full or partial for employees or children of employees.

LOANS ***Student loans:*** $24,576,878 (28% need-based, 72% non-need-based). 75% of past graduating class borrowed through all loan programs. *Average indebtedness per student:* $35,118. ***Average need-based loan:*** Freshmen: $3437; Undergraduates: $4295. ***Parent loans:*** $4,591,835 (100% non-need-based). ***Programs:*** FFEL (Subsidized and Unsubsidized Stafford, PLUS), Perkins.

WORK-STUDY ***Federal work-study:*** Total amount: $200,000.

ATHLETIC AWARDS Total amount: $1,506,794 (49% need-based, 51% non-need-based).

APPLYING FOR FINANCIAL AID ***Required financial aid forms:*** FAFSA, institution's own form. ***Financial aid deadline:*** 3/1 (priority: 3/1). ***Notification date:*** Continuous beginning 3/15. Students must reply by 5/1 or within 2 weeks of notification.

CONTACT Mr. Christopher Hourigan, Director of Institutional Research, University of New Haven, 300 Boston Post Road, West Haven, CT 06516-1916, 203-932-7139 or toll-free 800-DIAL-UNH. *Fax:* 203-931-6050. *E-mail:* finaid@newhaven.edu.

UNIVERSITY OF NEW MEXICO

Albuquerque, NM

CONTACT Office of Student Financial Aid, University of New Mexico, Mesa Vista Hall North, Albuquerque, NM 87131, 505-277-2041 or toll-free 800-CALLUNM (in-state). *Fax:* 505-277-6326. *E-mail:* finaid@unm.edu.

UNIVERSITY OF NEW ORLEANS

New Orleans, LA

Tuition & fees (LA res): $3810 **Average undergraduate aid package: $7119**

ABOUT THE INSTITUTION State-supported, coed. Awards: bachelor's, master's, and doctoral degrees and post-bachelor's certificates. 50 undergraduate majors. Total enrollment: 11,747. Undergraduates: 9,156. Freshmen: 1,021. Federal methodology is used as a basis for awarding need-based institutional aid.

UNDERGRADUATE EXPENSES for 2007–08 ***Application fee:*** $40. ***Tuition, state resident:*** full-time $3292; part-time $521 per course. ***Tuition, nonresident:*** full-time $10,336; part-time $1859 per course. ***Required fees:*** full-time $518; $53 per hour. ***College room and board:*** $4734.

FRESHMAN FINANCIAL AID (Fall 2006, est.) 951 applied for aid; of those 78% were deemed to have need. 62% of freshmen with need received aid; of those 17% had need fully met. ***Average percent of need met:*** 64% (excluding resources awarded to replace EFC). ***Average financial aid package:*** $5031 (excluding resources awarded to replace EFC). 46% of all full-time freshmen had no need and received non-need-based gift aid.

UNDERGRADUATE FINANCIAL AID (Fall 2006, est.) 5,745 applied for aid; of those 85% were deemed to have need. 71% of undergraduates with need received aid; of those 14% had need fully met. ***Average percent of need met:*** 72% (excluding resources awarded to replace EFC). ***Average financial aid package:*** $7119 (excluding resources awarded to replace EFC). 18% of all full-time undergraduates had no need and received non-need-based gift aid.

GIFT AID (NEED-BASED) ***Total amount:*** $12,330,587 (93% federal, 7% state). ***Receiving aid:*** Freshmen: 35% (337); All full-time undergraduates: 36% (2,522). ***Average award:*** Freshmen: $3739; Undergraduates: $3801. ***Scholarships, grants, and awards:*** Federal Pell, FSEOG, state, private, college/university gift aid from institutional funds.

GIFT AID (NON-NEED-BASED) ***Total amount:*** $5,928,598 (100% state). ***Receiving aid:*** Freshmen: 15% (139); Undergraduates: 10% (709). ***Average award:*** Freshmen: $2480; Undergraduates: $2530. ***Scholarships, grants, and awards by category:*** *Academic Interests/Achievement:* 2,419 awards ($9,327,304 total): communication, computer science, education, foreign languages, general academic interests/achievements, international studies, mathematics, military science, physical sciences. *Creative Arts/Performance:* 38 awards ($123,534 total): general creative arts/performance, music, theater/drama. *Special Achievements/Activities:* 91 awards ($589,365 total): general special achievements/ activities, leadership. *Special Characteristics:* 2,263 awards ($6,762,788 total): adult students, children and siblings of alumni, children of public servants, children with a deceased or disabled parent, international students, local/state students, members of minority groups, out-of-state students, previous college experience, public servants, veterans' children. ***ROTC:*** Army cooperative, Naval cooperative, Air Force cooperative.

LOANS ***Student loans:*** $18,511,889 (56% need-based, 44% non-need-based). 36% of past graduating class borrowed through all loan programs. *Average indebtedness per student:* $22,350. ***Average need-based loan:*** Freshmen: $2477; Undergraduates: $3570. ***Parent loans:*** $191,956 (100% non-need-based). ***Programs:*** FFEL (Subsidized and Unsubsidized Stafford, PLUS), Perkins, college/ university.

WORK-STUDY ***Federal work-study:*** Total amount: $419,851; 167 jobs averaging $2514. ***State or other work-study/employment:*** Part-time jobs available.

ATHLETIC AWARDS Total amount: $608,355 (100% non-need-based).

APPLYING FOR FINANCIAL AID ***Required financial aid forms:*** FAFSA, institution's own form. ***Financial aid deadline (priority):*** 5/15. ***Notification date:*** Continuous beginning 4/20. Students must reply within 4 weeks of notification.

CONTACT Ms. Emily London-Jones, Director of Student Financial Aid, University of New Orleans, Administration Building, Room 1005, New Orleans, LA 70148, 504-280-6687 or toll-free 800-256-5866 (out-of-state). *Fax:* 504-280-3973. *E-mail:* elondon@uno.edu.

UNIVERSITY OF NORTH ALABAMA

Florence, AL

Tuition & fees (AL res): $4651 **Average undergraduate aid package: $4354**

ABOUT THE INSTITUTION State-supported, coed. Awards: bachelor's and master's degrees and post-master's certificates. 38 undergraduate majors. Total enrollment: 6,810. Undergraduates: 5,600. Freshmen: 1,019. Federal methodology is used as a basis for awarding need-based institutional aid.

UNDERGRADUATE EXPENSES for 2006–07 ***Application fee:*** $25. ***Tuition, state resident:*** full-time $3768; part-time $147 per credit hour. ***Tuition, nonresident:*** full-time $7536; part-time $294 per credit hour. Full-time tuition and fees vary according to course load. Part-time tuition and fees vary according to course load. ***College room and board:*** $4372; ***Room only:*** $2060. Room and board charges vary according to board plan and housing facility. ***Payment plan:*** Installment.

FRESHMAN FINANCIAL AID (Fall 2006, est.) 582 applied for aid; of those 79% were deemed to have need. 96% of freshmen with need received aid; of those 26% had need fully met. ***Average percent of need met:*** 40% (excluding resources awarded to replace EFC). ***Average financial aid package:*** $3565 (excluding resources awarded to replace EFC).

UNDERGRADUATE FINANCIAL AID (Fall 2006, est.) 3,125 applied for aid; of those 81% were deemed to have need. 94% of undergraduates with need received aid; of those 41% had need fully met. ***Average percent of need met:*** 66% (excluding resources awarded to replace EFC). ***Average financial aid package:*** $4354 (excluding resources awarded to replace EFC).

GIFT AID (NEED-BASED) ***Total amount:*** $4,337,331 (99% federal, 1% state). ***Receiving aid:*** Freshmen: 29% (285); All full-time undergraduates: 31% (1,481).

Average award: Freshmen: $3975; Undergraduates: $2894. ***Scholarships, grants, and awards:*** Federal Pell, FSEOG, state, private, college/university gift aid from institutional funds.

GIFT AID (NON-NEED-BASED) ***Total amount:*** $2,652,546 (80% institutional, 20% external sources). ***Scholarships, grants, and awards by category:*** *Academic Interests/Achievement:* general academic interests/achievements. *Creative Arts/Performance:* art/fine arts, journalism/publications, music. *Special Achievements/Activities:* cheerleading/drum major, general special achievements/activities, leadership. *Special Characteristics:* children of faculty/staff, first-generation college students, general special characteristics, out-of-state students. ***Tuition waivers:*** Full or partial for employees or children of employees, senior citizens. ***ROTC:*** Army.

LOANS ***Student loans:*** $14,883,734 (53% need-based, 47% non-need-based). ***Average need-based loan:*** Freshmen: $2254; Undergraduates: $3416. ***Parent loans:*** $670,680 (100% non-need-based). ***Programs:*** FFEL (Subsidized and Unsubsidized Stafford, PLUS), Perkins.

WORK-STUDY ***Federal work-study:*** Total amount: $315,234; 214 jobs averaging $1240.

ATHLETIC AWARDS Total amount: $1,160,571 (100% non-need-based).

APPLYING FOR FINANCIAL AID ***Required financial aid form:*** FAFSA. ***Financial aid deadline (priority):*** 4/1. ***Notification date:*** 5/31. Students must reply within 2 weeks of notification.

CONTACT Mr. Ben Baker, Director of Student Financial Services, University of North Alabama, UNA Box 5014, Florence, AL 35632-0001, 256-765-4278 or toll-free 800-TALKUNA. *Fax:* 256-765-4920. *E-mail:* bjbaker@una.edu.

THE UNIVERSITY OF NORTH CAROLINA AT ASHEVILLE

Asheville, NC

Tuition & fees (NC res): $3882 Average undergraduate aid package: $8231

ABOUT THE INSTITUTION State-supported, coed. Awards: bachelor's and master's degrees and post-bachelor's certificates. 29 undergraduate majors. Total enrollment: 3,635. Undergraduates: 3,609. Freshmen: 572. Federal methodology is used as a basis for awarding need-based institutional aid.

UNDERGRADUATE EXPENSES for 2006–07 ***Application fee:*** $50. ***Tuition, state resident:*** full-time $2172. ***Tuition, nonresident:*** full-time $12,297. Full-time tuition and fees vary according to course load. Part-time tuition and fees vary according to course load. ***College room and board:*** $5880; ***Room only:*** $3200. Room and board charges vary according to housing facility.

FRESHMAN FINANCIAL AID (Fall 2006, est.) 392 applied for aid; of those 51% were deemed to have need. 99% of freshmen with need received aid; of those 32% had need fully met. ***Average percent of need met:*** 76% (excluding resources awarded to replace EFC). ***Average financial aid package:*** $6464 (excluding resources awarded to replace EFC). 7% of all full-time freshmen had no need and received non-need-based gift aid.

UNDERGRADUATE FINANCIAL AID (Fall 2006, est.) 1,787 applied for aid; of those 65% were deemed to have need. 99% of undergraduates with need received aid; of those 41% had need fully met. ***Average percent of need met:*** 80% (excluding resources awarded to replace EFC). ***Average financial aid package:*** $8231 (excluding resources awarded to replace EFC). 6% of all full-time undergraduates had no need and received non-need-based gift aid.

GIFT AID (NEED-BASED) ***Total amount:*** $4,433,257 (49% federal, 32% state, 19% institutional). ***Receiving aid:*** Freshmen: 34% (191); All full-time undergraduates: 36% (1,031). ***Average award:*** Freshmen: $4052; Undergraduates: $4106. ***Scholarships, grants, and awards:*** Federal Pell, FSEOG, state, private, college/university gift aid from institutional funds.

GIFT AID (NON-NEED-BASED) ***Total amount:*** $1,139,292 (19% federal, 49% state, 32% institutional). ***Receiving aid:*** Freshmen: 5% (29); Undergraduates: 5% (145). ***Average award:*** Freshmen: $3214; Undergraduates: $3639. ***Scholarships, grants, and awards by category:*** *Academic Interests/Achievement:* 209 awards ($569,408 total): biological sciences, business, communication, computer science, education, engineering/technologies, English, general academic interests/achievements, health fields, mathematics, physical sciences, premedicine, social sciences. *Creative Arts/Performance:* 26 awards ($14,641 total): art/fine arts, general creative arts/performance, music, theater/drama. *Special Achievements/Activities:* 62 awards ($123,642 total): community service, general special achievements/activities, junior miss, leadership. *Special Characteristics:* 30 awards ($108,187 total): adult students, children and siblings of alumni, children of faculty/staff, ethnic background, first-generation college students, general special characteristics, handicapped students, international students, local/state students, members of minority groups, veterans, veterans' children. ***Tuition waivers:*** Full or partial for employees or children of employees, senior citizens.

LOANS ***Student loans:*** $6,485,962 (71% need-based, 29% non-need-based). 46% of past graduating class borrowed through all loan programs. *Average indebtedness per student:* $14,211. ***Average need-based loan:*** Freshmen: $2488; Undergraduates: $3848. ***Parent loans:*** $1,423,995 (21% need-based, 79% non-need-based). ***Programs:*** Federal Direct (Subsidized and Unsubsidized Stafford, PLUS), Perkins, state, college/university.

WORK-STUDY ***Federal work-study:*** Total amount: $96,132; 61 jobs averaging $1576.

ATHLETIC AWARDS Total amount: $878,442 (24% need-based, 76% non-need-based).

APPLYING FOR FINANCIAL AID ***Required financial aid form:*** FAFSA. ***Financial aid deadline (priority):*** 3/1. ***Notification date:*** Continuous beginning 3/15. Students must reply within 2 weeks of notification.

CONTACT Ms. Elizabeth D. Bartlett, Associate Director of Financial Aid, The University of North Carolina at Asheville, 1 University Heights, Asheville, NC 28804-8510, 828-232-6535 or toll-free 800-531-9842. *Fax:* 828-251-2294. *E-mail:* bbartlett@unca.edu.

THE UNIVERSITY OF NORTH CAROLINA AT CHAPEL HILL

Chapel Hill, NC

Tuition & fees (NC res): $5033 Average undergraduate aid package: $10,575

ABOUT THE INSTITUTION State-supported, coed. Awards: bachelor's, master's, doctoral, and first professional degrees and post-master's certificates. 61 undergraduate majors. Total enrollment: 27,717. Undergraduates: 17,124. Freshmen: 3,807. Both federal and institutional methodology are used as a basis for awarding need-based institutional aid.

UNDERGRADUATE EXPENSES for 2006–07 ***Application fee:*** $70. ***Tuition, state resident:*** full-time $3455. ***Tuition, nonresident:*** full-time $18,103. Full-time tuition and fees vary according to program. Part-time tuition and fees vary according to course load and program. ***College room and board:*** $6846; ***Room only:*** $3960. Room and board charges vary according to board plan, housing facility, and location. ***Payment plans:*** Installment, deferred payment.

FRESHMAN FINANCIAL AID (Fall 2005) 2840 applied for aid; of those 43% were deemed to have need. 98% of freshmen with need received aid; of those 95% had need fully met. ***Average percent of need met:*** 100% (excluding resources awarded to replace EFC). ***Average financial aid package:*** $10,103 (excluding resources awarded to replace EFC). 20% of all full-time freshmen had no need and received non-need-based gift aid.

UNDERGRADUATE FINANCIAL AID (Fall 2005) 10,209 applied for aid; of those 51% were deemed to have need. 99% of undergraduates with need received aid; of those 95% had need fully met. ***Average percent of need met:*** 100% (excluding resources awarded to replace EFC). ***Average financial aid package:*** $10,575 (excluding resources awarded to replace EFC). 17% of all full-time undergraduates had no need and received non-need-based gift aid.

GIFT AID (NEED-BASED) ***Total amount:*** $39,621,533 (19% federal, 18% state, 53% institutional, 10% external sources). ***Receiving aid:*** Freshmen: 32% (1,193); All full-time undergraduates: 32% (5,053). ***Average award:*** Freshmen: $8366; Undergraduates: $7528. ***Scholarships, grants, and awards:*** Federal Pell, FSEOG, state, private, college/university gift aid from institutional funds.

GIFT AID (NON-NEED-BASED) ***Total amount:*** $14,886,884 (5% federal, 13% state, 36% institutional, 46% external sources). ***Receiving aid:*** Freshmen: 17% (622); Undergraduates: 10% (1,579). ***Average award:*** Freshmen: $4510; Undergraduates: $6361. ***Scholarships, grants, and awards by category:*** *Academic Interests/Achievement:* business, communication, education, English, general academic interests/achievements, health fields, mathematics. *Creative Arts/Performance:* applied art and design, art/fine arts, journalism/publications, music, theater/drama. *Special Achievements/Activities:* community service, general special achievements/activities, leadership. *Special Characteristics:* children of faculty/staff, international students, out-of-state students, relatives of clergy, religious affiliation. ***Tuition waivers:*** Full or partial for employees or children of employees, senior citizens. ***ROTC:*** Army, Naval, Air Force.

LOANS ***Student loans:*** $27,254,182 (68% need-based, 32% non-need-based). ***Average need-based loan:*** Freshmen: $2471; Undergraduates: $4111. ***Parent***

loans: $9,584,211 (34% need-based, 66% non-need-based). ***Programs:*** FFEL (Subsidized and Unsubsidized Stafford, PLUS), Perkins, state, college/university, alternative loans.

WORK-STUDY ***Federal work-study:*** Total amount: $1,563,343; 867 jobs averaging $1803.

ATHLETIC AWARDS Total amount: $6,378,418 (26% need-based, 74% non-need-based).

APPLYING FOR FINANCIAL AID ***Required financial aid forms:*** FAFSA, CSS Financial Aid PROFILE. ***Financial aid deadline (priority):*** 3/1. ***Notification date:*** Continuous beginning 3/15. Students must reply by 5/1.

CONTACT Ms. Shirley A. Ort, Associate Provost and Director, Office of Scholarships and Student Aid, The University of North Carolina at Chapel Hill, PO Box 1080, Chapel Hill, NC 27514, 919-962-9246. *E-mail:* sao@unc.edu.

THE UNIVERSITY OF NORTH CAROLINA AT CHARLOTTE

Charlotte, NC

Tuition & fees (NC res): $3895 Average undergraduate aid package: $8527

ABOUT THE INSTITUTION State-supported, coed. Awards: bachelor's, master's, and doctoral degrees and post-master's certificates. 71 undergraduate majors. Total enrollment: 21,519. Undergraduates: 17,032. Freshmen: 2,798. Federal methodology is used as a basis for awarding need-based institutional aid.

UNDERGRADUATE EXPENSES for 2006–07 ***Application fee:*** $50. ***Tuition, state resident:*** full-time $2344; part-time $97.66 per credit hour. ***Tuition, nonresident:*** full-time $12,756; part-time $531.50 per credit hour. ***Required fees:*** full-time $1551; $65 per credit hour. Full-time tuition and fees vary according to course load. Part-time tuition and fees vary according to course load. ***College room and board:*** $5790; ***Room only:*** $2940. Room and board charges vary according to board plan and housing facility.

FRESHMAN FINANCIAL AID (Fall 2005) 1770 applied for aid; of those 69% were deemed to have need. 94% of freshmen with need received aid; of those 25% had need fully met. ***Average percent of need met:*** 66% (excluding resources awarded to replace EFC). ***Average financial aid package:*** $7190 (excluding resources awarded to replace EFC). 18% of all full-time freshmen had no need and received non-need-based gift aid.

UNDERGRADUATE FINANCIAL AID (Fall 2005) 7,689 applied for aid; of those 78% were deemed to have need. 96% of undergraduates with need received aid; of those 33% had need fully met. ***Average percent of need met:*** 64% (excluding resources awarded to replace EFC). ***Average financial aid package:*** $8527 (excluding resources awarded to replace EFC). 15% of all full-time undergraduates had no need and received non-need-based gift aid.

GIFT AID (NEED-BASED) ***Total amount:*** $19,703,469 (57% federal, 37% state, 2% institutional, 4% external sources). ***Receiving aid:*** Freshmen: 37% (995); All full-time undergraduates: 36% (4,626). ***Average award:*** Freshmen: $4323; Undergraduates: $4083. ***Scholarships, grants, and awards:*** Federal Pell, FSEOG, state, private, college/university gift aid from institutional funds.

GIFT AID (NON-NEED-BASED) ***Total amount:*** $1,644,722 (28% state, 25% institutional, 47% external sources). ***Receiving aid:*** Freshmen: 9% (240); Undergraduates: 5% (651). ***Average award:*** Freshmen: $5854; Undergraduates: $5772. ***Scholarships, grants, and awards by category:*** *Academic Interests/Achievement:* 170 awards ($528,000 total): architecture, business, computer science, education, engineering/technologies, general academic interests/achievements, health fields, humanities, mathematics, military science. *Creative Arts/Performance:* 30 awards ($42,500 total): music, performing arts. *Special Characteristics:* 54 awards ($56,000 total): adult students. ***Tuition waivers:*** Full or partial for senior citizens. ***ROTC:*** Army, Air Force.

LOANS ***Student loans:*** $41,759,710 (52% need-based, 48% non-need-based). 56% of past graduating class borrowed through all loan programs. *Average indebtedness per student:* $17,730. ***Average need-based loan:*** Freshmen: $2768; Undergraduates: $3862. ***Parent loans:*** $6,026,987 (100% non-need-based). ***Programs:*** FFEL (Subsidized and Unsubsidized Stafford, PLUS), Perkins, state, college/university.

WORK-STUDY ***Federal work-study:*** Total amount: $679,643; 530 jobs averaging $1282. ***State or other work-study/employment:*** Total amount: $2,298,246 (100% non-need-based). 1,825 part-time jobs averaging $1611.

ATHLETIC AWARDS Total amount: $1,894,032 (34% need-based, 66% non-need-based).

APPLYING FOR FINANCIAL AID ***Required financial aid form:*** FAFSA. ***Financial aid deadline (priority):*** 4/1. ***Notification date:*** 4/2. Students must reply within 3 weeks of notification.

CONTACT Anthony D. Carter, Director of Financial Aid, The University of North Carolina at Charlotte, 9201 University City Boulevard, Charlotte, NC 28223-0001, 704-687-2461. *Fax:* 704-687-3132. *E-mail:* finaid@email.uncc.edu.

THE UNIVERSITY OF NORTH CAROLINA AT GREENSBORO

Greensboro, NC

Tuition & fees (NC res): $4029 Average undergraduate aid package: $7837

ABOUT THE INSTITUTION State-supported, coed. Awards: bachelor's, master's, and doctoral degrees. 76 undergraduate majors. Total enrollment: 16,728. Undergraduates: 12,921. Freshmen: 2,426. Federal methodology is used as a basis for awarding need-based institutional aid.

UNDERGRADUATE EXPENSES for 2007–08 ***Application fee:*** $45. ***Tuition, state resident:*** full-time $2458; part-time $307.25 per credit hour. ***Tuition, nonresident:*** full-time $13,726; part-time $1,715.75 per credit hour. ***College room and board:*** $6051; ***Room only:*** $3427.

FRESHMAN FINANCIAL AID (Fall 2006, est.) 1853 applied for aid; of those 89% were deemed to have need. 96% of freshmen with need received aid; of those 24% had need fully met. ***Average percent of need met:*** 54% (excluding resources awarded to replace EFC). ***Average financial aid package:*** $7480 (excluding resources awarded to replace EFC). 5% of all full-time freshmen had no need and received non-need-based gift aid.

UNDERGRADUATE FINANCIAL AID (Fall 2006, est.) 7,641 applied for aid; of those 97% were deemed to have need. 97% of undergraduates with need received aid; of those 23% had need fully met. ***Average percent of need met:*** 58% (excluding resources awarded to replace EFC). ***Average financial aid package:*** $7837 (excluding resources awarded to replace EFC). 5% of all full-time undergraduates had no need and received non-need-based gift aid.

GIFT AID (NEED-BASED) ***Total amount:*** $13,689,248 (86% federal, 7% state, 7% institutional). ***Receiving aid:*** Freshmen: 31% (743); All full-time undergraduates: 31% (3,435). ***Average award:*** Freshmen: $4716; Undergraduates: $4399. ***Scholarships, grants, and awards:*** Federal Pell, FSEOG, state, private, college/university gift aid from institutional funds.

GIFT AID (NON-NEED-BASED) ***Total amount:*** $12,897,736 (69% state, 31% institutional). ***Receiving aid:*** Freshmen: 44% (1,059); Undergraduates: 38% (4,166). ***Average award:*** Freshmen: $4120; Undergraduates: $3763. ***Scholarships, grants, and awards by category:*** *Academic Interests/Achievement:* 320 awards ($600,000 total): biological sciences, business, communication, education, English, foreign languages, general academic interests/achievements, health fields, home economics, humanities, library science, mathematics, physical sciences, premedicine, religion/biblical studies, social sciences. *Creative Arts/Performance:* 100 awards ($350,000 total): art/fine arts, cinema/film/broadcasting, dance, music, performing arts, theater/drama. *Special Achievements/Activities:* 25 awards ($30,000 total): community service, general special achievements/activities, junior miss, leadership, religious involvement. *Special Characteristics:* 500 awards ($500,000 total): adult students, ethnic background, general special characteristics, handicapped students, members of minority groups, out-of-state students, religious affiliation, veterans, veterans' children. ***ROTC:*** Army cooperative, Air Force cooperative.

LOANS ***Student loans:*** $39,697,880 (50% need-based, 50% non-need-based). 61% of past graduating class borrowed through all loan programs. *Average indebtedness per student:* $19,146. ***Average need-based loan:*** Freshmen: $2514; Undergraduates: $3786. ***Parent loans:*** $13,502,329 (100% non-need-based). ***Programs:*** FFEL (Subsidized and Unsubsidized Stafford, PLUS), Perkins, college/university.

WORK-STUDY ***Federal work-study:*** Total amount: $616,587; 837 jobs averaging $737.

ATHLETIC AWARDS Total amount: $1,729,592 (100% non-need-based).

APPLYING FOR FINANCIAL AID ***Required financial aid form:*** FAFSA. ***Financial aid deadline (priority):*** 3/1. ***Notification date:*** Continuous beginning 3/15. Students must reply within 3 weeks of notification.

CONTACT Mr. Bruce Cabiness, Associate Director of Financial Aid, The University of North Carolina at Greensboro, PO Box 26170, Greensboro, NC 27402-6170, 336-334-5702. *Fax:* 336-334-3010. *E-mail:* bruce_cabiness@uncg.edu.

THE UNIVERSITY OF NORTH CAROLINA AT PEMBROKE

Pembroke, NC

Tuition & fees (NC res): $5262 **Average undergraduate aid package: $7044**

ABOUT THE INSTITUTION State-supported, coed. Awards: bachelor's and master's degrees. 42 undergraduate majors. Total enrollment: 5,827. Undergraduates: 5,158. Freshmen: 955. Federal methodology is used as a basis for awarding need-based institutional aid.

UNDERGRADUATE EXPENSES for 2006–07 ***Application fee:*** $40. ***Tuition, state resident:*** full-time $3809. ***Tuition, nonresident:*** full-time $13,187. Full-time tuition and fees vary according to course load and location. Part-time tuition and fees vary according to course load and location. ***College room and board:*** $5517. Room and board charges vary according to board plan and housing facility. ***Payment plan:*** Installment.

FRESHMAN FINANCIAL AID (Fall 2006, est.) 833 applied for aid; of those 80% were deemed to have need. 98% of freshmen with need received aid; of those 12% had need fully met. ***Average percent of need met:*** 62% (excluding resources awarded to replace EFC). ***Average financial aid package:*** $6557 (excluding resources awarded to replace EFC). 6% of all full-time freshmen had no need and received non-need-based gift aid.

UNDERGRADUATE FINANCIAL AID (Fall 2006, est.) 3,215 applied for aid; of those 84% were deemed to have need. 97% of undergraduates with need received aid; of those 13% had need fully met. ***Average percent of need met:*** 65% (excluding resources awarded to replace EFC). ***Average financial aid package:*** $7044 (excluding resources awarded to replace EFC). 4% of all full-time undergraduates had no need and received non-need-based gift aid.

GIFT AID (NEED-BASED) ***Total amount:*** $11,831,918 (52% federal, 34% state, 8% institutional, 6% external sources). ***Receiving aid:*** Freshmen: 63% (589); All full-time undergraduates: 60% (2,293). ***Average award:*** Freshmen: $4921; Undergraduates: $4678. ***Scholarships, grants, and awards:*** Federal Pell, FSEOG, state, private, college/university gift aid from institutional funds.

GIFT AID (NON-NEED-BASED) ***Total amount:*** $217,219 (100% institutional). ***Receiving aid:*** Freshmen: 5% (48); Undergraduates: 3% (125). ***Average award:*** Freshmen: $1182; Undergraduates: $1367. ***Scholarships, grants, and awards by category:*** *Academic Interests/Achievement:* 114 awards ($178,729 total): business, communication, education, English, general academic interests/achievements, health fields, physical sciences. *Creative Arts/Performance:* 48 awards ($20,500 total): journalism/publications, music. *Special Characteristics:* 7 awards ($17,500 total): children and siblings of alumni, general special characteristics. ***Tuition waivers:*** Full or partial for senior citizens. ***ROTC:*** Army, Air Force.

LOANS ***Student loans:*** $16,129,412 (55% need-based, 45% non-need-based). 72% of past graduating class borrowed through all loan programs. *Average indebtedness per student:* $16,296. ***Average need-based loan:*** Freshmen: $2426; Undergraduates: $3422. ***Parent loans:*** $1,277,851 (100% non-need-based). ***Programs:*** FFEL (Subsidized and Unsubsidized Stafford, PLUS), Perkins, college/university.

WORK-STUDY ***Federal work-study:*** Total amount: $330,506; 393 jobs averaging $1500. ***State or other work-study/employment:*** Total amount: $18,528 (100% need-based). 29 part-time jobs averaging $1500.

ATHLETIC AWARDS Total amount: $1,022,190 (100% need-based).

APPLYING FOR FINANCIAL AID ***Required financial aid form:*** FAFSA. ***Financial aid deadline:*** Continuous. ***Notification date:*** 4/15.

CONTACT Mildred Weber, Associate Director of Financial Aid, The University of North Carolina at Pembroke, PO Box 1510, Pembroke, NC 28372, 910-521-6612 or toll-free 800-949-UNCP. *Fax:* 910-775-4159. *E-mail:* mildred.weber@uncp.edu.

THE UNIVERSITY OF NORTH CAROLINA WILMINGTON

Wilmington, NC

Tuition & fees (NC res): $4160 **Average undergraduate aid package: $6283**

ABOUT THE INSTITUTION State-supported, coed. Awards: bachelor's, master's, and doctoral degrees. 62 undergraduate majors. Total enrollment: 11,793. Undergraduates: 10,759. Freshmen: 1,987. Federal methodology is used as a basis for awarding need-based institutional aid.

UNDERGRADUATE EXPENSES for 2006–07 ***Application fee:*** $45. ***Tuition, state resident:*** full-time $2221. ***Tuition, nonresident:*** full-time $12,156. Full-time tuition and fees vary according to course load. Part-time tuition and fees vary according to course load. ***College room and board:*** $6722. Room and board charges vary according to board plan and housing facility. ***Payment plan:*** Installment.

FRESHMAN FINANCIAL AID (Fall 2005) 1012 applied for aid; of those 54% were deemed to have need. 100% of freshmen with need received aid; of those 67% had need fully met. ***Average percent of need met:*** 88% (excluding resources awarded to replace EFC). ***Average financial aid package:*** $5411 (excluding resources awarded to replace EFC). 1% of all full-time freshmen had no need and received non-need-based gift aid.

UNDERGRADUATE FINANCIAL AID (Fall 2005) 4,975 applied for aid; of those 60% were deemed to have need. 100% of undergraduates with need received aid; of those 61% had need fully met. ***Average percent of need met:*** 86% (excluding resources awarded to replace EFC). ***Average financial aid package:*** $6283 (excluding resources awarded to replace EFC). 2% of all full-time undergraduates had no need and received non-need-based gift aid.

GIFT AID (NEED-BASED) ***Total amount:*** $9,957,769 (7% federal, 49% state, 19% institutional, 25% external sources). ***Receiving aid:*** Freshmen: 23% (438); All full-time undergraduates: 26% (2,457). ***Average award:*** Freshmen: $3763; Undergraduates: $3663. ***Scholarships, grants, and awards:*** Federal Pell, FSEOG, state, private, college/university gift aid from institutional funds, F. Academic Competitiveness Grant (ACG), F. National Science and Mathematics Access to Retain Talent.

GIFT AID (NON-NEED-BASED) ***Total amount:*** $1,713,235 (53% state, 47% institutional). ***Receiving aid:*** Freshmen: 2; Undergraduates: 16. ***Average award:*** Freshmen: $1619; Undergraduates: $1549. ***Scholarships, grants, and awards by category:*** *Academic Interests/Achievement:* 133 awards ($275,315 total): biological sciences, business, communication, computer science, education, English, foreign languages, general academic interests/achievements, health fields, humanities, international studies, mathematics, physical sciences, social sciences. *Creative Arts/Performance:* 21 awards ($14,500 total): art/fine arts, cinema/film/broadcasting, creative writing, music, theater/drama. *Special Achievements/Activities:* 63 awards ($14,430 total): cheerleading/drum major, general special achievements/activities, leadership. *Special Characteristics:* local/state students. ***Tuition waivers:*** Full or partial for employees or children of employees, senior citizens.

LOANS ***Student loans:*** $24,242,992 (52% need-based, 48% non-need-based). 52% of past graduating class borrowed through all loan programs. *Average indebtedness per student:* $15,620. ***Average need-based loan:*** Freshmen: $2793; Undergraduates: $3788. ***Parent loans:*** $15,113,230 (100% non-need-based). ***Programs:*** Federal Direct (Subsidized and Unsubsidized Stafford, PLUS), Perkins, state, college/university.

WORK-STUDY ***Federal work-study:*** Total amount: $404,269; 279 jobs averaging $3000.

ATHLETIC AWARDS Total amount: $1,530,044 (29% need-based, 71% non-need-based).

APPLYING FOR FINANCIAL AID ***Required financial aid form:*** FAFSA. ***Financial aid deadline:*** Continuous. ***Notification date:*** Continuous beginning 4/1. Students must reply within 3 weeks of notification.

CONTACT Emily Bliss, Director of Financial Aid and Veterans' Services Office, The University of North Carolina Wilmington, 601 South College Road, Wilmington, NC 28403-5951, 910-962-3177 or toll-free 800-228-5571 (out-of-state). *Fax:* 910-962-3851. *E-mail:* finaid@uncw.edu.

UNIVERSITY OF NORTH DAKOTA

Grand Forks, ND

Tuition & fees (ND res): $5792 **Average undergraduate aid package: $7032**

ABOUT THE INSTITUTION State-supported, coed. Awards: bachelor's, master's, doctoral, and first professional degrees and post-master's certificates. 86 undergraduate majors. Total enrollment: 12,834. Undergraduates: 10,376. Freshmen: 1,900. Federal methodology is used as a basis for awarding need-based institutional aid.

UNDERGRADUATE EXPENSES for 2006–07 ***Application fee:*** $35. ***Tuition, state resident:*** full-time $4786. ***Tuition, nonresident:*** full-time $12,780. Full-time tuition and fees vary according to degree level, program, and reciprocity agreements. Part-time tuition and fees vary according to course load, degree level, program, and reciprocity agreements. ***College room and board:*** $5085; ***Room only:*** $2137. Room and board charges vary according to board plan and housing facility. ***Payment plan:*** Deferred payment.

FRESHMAN FINANCIAL AID (Fall 2006, est.) 1628 applied for aid; of those 69% were deemed to have need. 99% of freshmen with need received aid; of those 27% had need fully met. ***Average percent of need met:*** 37% (excluding resources awarded to replace EFC). ***Average financial aid package:*** $6316 (excluding resources awarded to replace EFC). 24% of all full-time freshmen had no need and received non-need-based gift aid.

UNDERGRADUATE FINANCIAL AID (Fall 2006, est.) 7,285 applied for aid; of those 74% were deemed to have need. 98% of undergraduates with need received aid; of those 23% had need fully met. ***Average percent of need met:*** 32% (excluding resources awarded to replace EFC). ***Average financial aid package:*** $7032 (excluding resources awarded to replace EFC). 21% of all full-time undergraduates had no need and received non-need-based gift aid.

GIFT AID (NEED-BASED) ***Total amount:*** $8,940,102 (67% federal, 5% state, 13% institutional, 15% external sources). ***Receiving aid:*** Freshmen: 34% (629); All full-time undergraduates: 31% (2,636). ***Average award:*** Freshmen: $2977; Undergraduates: $2938. ***Scholarships, grants, and awards:*** Federal Pell, FSEOG, state, private, college/university gift aid from institutional funds, Federal Nursing.

GIFT AID (NON-NEED-BASED) ***Total amount:*** $1,395,551 (1% federal, 6% state, 63% institutional, 30% external sources). ***Receiving aid:*** Freshmen: 8% (148); Undergraduates: 7% (591). ***Average award:*** Freshmen: $989; Undergraduates: $1103. ***Scholarships, grants, and awards by category:*** *Academic Interests/Achievement:* biological sciences, business, communication, computer science, education, engineering/technologies, English, foreign languages, general academic interests/achievements, health fields, humanities, international studies, mathematics, military science, physical sciences, premedicine, social sciences. *Creative Arts/Performance:* art/fine arts, debating, music, theater/drama. *Special Achievements/Activities:* general special achievements/activities, leadership, memberships. *Special Characteristics:* children of faculty/staff, ethnic background, general special characteristics, handicapped students, international students, members of minority groups, veterans' children. ***Tuition waivers:*** Full or partial for minority students, employees or children of employees, senior citizens. ***ROTC:*** Army, Air Force.

LOANS ***Student loans:*** $40,835,532 (77% need-based, 23% non-need-based). ***Average need-based loan:*** Freshmen: $3851; Undergraduates: $4955. ***Parent loans:*** $2,553,576 (39% need-based, 61% non-need-based). ***Programs:*** FFEL (Subsidized and Unsubsidized Stafford, PLUS), Perkins, Federal Nursing, alternative commercial loans.

WORK-STUDY ***Federal work-study:*** Total amount: $2,509,003; jobs available.

ATHLETIC AWARDS Total amount: $1,310,930 (16% need-based, 84% non-need-based).

APPLYING FOR FINANCIAL AID ***Required financial aid form:*** FAFSA. ***Financial aid deadline (priority):*** 3/15. ***Notification date:*** Continuous beginning 5/15. Students must reply within 4 weeks of notification.

CONTACT Ms. Robin Holden, Director of Student Financial Aid Office, University of North Dakota, 264 Centennial Drive Stop 8371, Grand Forks, ND 58202, 701-777-3121 or toll-free 800-CALL UND. *Fax:* 701-777-2040. *E-mail:* robin.holden@mail.und.nodak.edu.

UNIVERSITY OF NORTHERN COLORADO

Greeley, CO

Tuition & fees (CO res): $3950 **Average undergraduate aid package: $10,075**

ABOUT THE INSTITUTION State-supported, coed. Awards: bachelor's, master's, and doctoral degrees (specialist). 42 undergraduate majors. Total enrollment: 12,981. Undergraduates: 10,799. Freshmen: 2,521. Federal methodology is used as a basis for awarding need-based institutional aid.

UNDERGRADUATE EXPENSES for 2006–07 ***Application fee:*** $40. ***Tuition, state resident:*** full-time $3276; part-time $136.50 per credit hour. ***Tuition, nonresident:*** full-time $11,858; part-time $494 per credit hour. ***Required fees:*** full-time $674; $33.70 per credit hour. Full-time tuition and fees vary according to program. Part-time tuition and fees vary according to program. ***College room and board:*** $6832; ***Room only:*** $3260. Room and board charges vary according to board plan and housing facility. ***Payment plan:*** Deferred payment.

FRESHMAN FINANCIAL AID (Fall 2005) 2134 applied for aid; of those 50% were deemed to have need. 99% of freshmen with need received aid; of those 44% had need fully met. ***Average percent of need met:*** 90% (excluding resources awarded to replace EFC). ***Average financial aid package:*** $8383 (excluding resources awarded to replace EFC). 12% of all full-time freshmen had no need and received non-need-based gift aid.

UNDERGRADUATE FINANCIAL AID (Fall 2005) 7,245 applied for aid; of those 56% were deemed to have need. 99% of undergraduates with need received aid; of those 56% had need fully met. ***Average percent of need met:*** 100% (excluding resources awarded to replace EFC). ***Average financial aid package:*** $10,075 (excluding resources awarded to replace EFC). 10% of all full-time undergraduates had no need and received non-need-based gift aid.

GIFT AID (NEED-BASED) ***Total amount:*** $8,715,560 (60% federal, 25% state, 15% institutional). ***Receiving aid:*** Freshmen: 20% (504); All full-time undergraduates: 23% (2,125). ***Average award:*** Freshmen: $3603; Undergraduates: $3920. ***Scholarships, grants, and awards:*** Federal Pell, FSEOG, state, private, college/university gift aid from institutional funds.

GIFT AID (NON-NEED-BASED) ***Total amount:*** $9,451,204 (11% state, 33% institutional, 56% external sources). ***Receiving aid:*** Freshmen: 24% (587); Undergraduates: 17% (1,548). ***Average award:*** Freshmen: $3237; Undergraduates: $2786. ***Scholarships, grants, and awards by category:*** *Academic Interests/Achievement:* 899 awards ($939,840 total): biological sciences, business, communication, education, English, general academic interests/achievements, health fields, home economics, mathematics, military science, physical sciences, social sciences. *Creative Arts/Performance:* 105 awards ($56,654 total): dance, music, performing arts, theater/drama. *Special Characteristics:* 3,999 awards ($8,389,854 total): adult students, children and siblings of alumni, children of faculty/staff, children of union members/company employees, ethnic background, general special characteristics, handicapped students, international students, local/state students, members of minority groups, out-of-state students, veterans. ***ROTC:*** Army, Air Force.

LOANS ***Student loans:*** $31,310,247 (44% need-based, 56% non-need-based). ***Average need-based loan:*** Freshmen: $2732; Undergraduates: $3673. ***Parent loans:*** $38,518,997 (100% non-need-based). ***Programs:*** FFEL (Subsidized and Unsubsidized Stafford, PLUS), Perkins, college/university.

WORK-STUDY ***Federal work-study:*** Total amount: $725,619; 249 jobs averaging $1538. ***State or other work-study/employment:*** Total amount: $9,096,609 (19% need-based, 81% non-need-based). 677 part-time jobs averaging $1568.

ATHLETIC AWARDS Total amount: $703,170 (100% non-need-based).

APPLYING FOR FINANCIAL AID ***Required financial aid form:*** FAFSA. ***Financial aid deadline (priority):*** 3/1. ***Notification date:*** Continuous beginning 4/15. Students must reply within 4 weeks of notification.

CONTACT Donni Clark, Director of Student Financial Resources, University of Northern Colorado, Carter Hall 1005, Campus Box 33, Greeley, CO 80639, 970-351-2502 or toll-free 888-700-4UNC (in-state). *Fax:* 970-351-3737. *E-mail:* sfr@unco.edu.

UNIVERSITY OF NORTHERN IOWA

Cedar Falls, IA

Tuition & fees (IA res): $6112 **Average undergraduate aid package: $6992**

ABOUT THE INSTITUTION State-supported, coed. Awards: bachelor's, master's, and doctoral degrees. 112 undergraduate majors. Total enrollment: 12,327. Undergraduates: 10,727. Freshmen: 1,768. Federal methodology is used as a basis for awarding need-based institutional aid.

UNDERGRADUATE EXPENSES for 2006–07 ***Application fee:*** $30. ***Tuition, state resident:*** full-time $5086; part-time $212 per hour. ***Tuition, nonresident:*** full-time $13,002; part-time $542 per hour. ***Required fees:*** full-time $1026; $461 per term part-time. Full-time tuition and fees vary according to course load. Part-time tuition and fees vary according to course load. ***College room and board:*** $5740; ***Room only:*** $2695. Room and board charges vary according to board plan and housing facility. ***Payment plan:*** Installment.

FRESHMAN FINANCIAL AID (Fall 2006, est.) 1442 applied for aid; of those 69% were deemed to have need. 96% of freshmen with need received aid; of those 19% had need fully met. ***Average percent of need met:*** 64% (excluding resources awarded to replace EFC). ***Average financial aid package:*** $6283 (excluding resources awarded to replace EFC). 16% of all full-time freshmen had no need and received non-need-based gift aid.

UNDERGRADUATE FINANCIAL AID (Fall 2006, est.) 7,516 applied for aid; of those 74% were deemed to have need. 96% of undergraduates with need received aid; of those 21% had need fully met. ***Average percent of need met:*** 65% (excluding resources awarded to replace EFC). ***Average financial aid***

package: $6992 (excluding resources awarded to replace EFC). 9% of all full-time undergraduates had no need and received non-need-based gift aid.

GIFT AID (NEED-BASED) ***Total amount:*** $10,734,694 (69% federal, 7% state, 24% institutional). ***Receiving aid:*** Freshmen: 39% (654); All full-time undergraduates: 34% (3,243). ***Average award:*** Freshmen: $2836; Undergraduates: $2888. ***Scholarships, grants, and awards:*** Federal Pell, FSEOG, state, private, college/university gift aid from institutional funds.

GIFT AID (NON-NEED-BASED) ***Total amount:*** $6,920,878 (5% state, 70% institutional, 25% external sources). ***Receiving aid:*** Freshmen: 28% (474); Undergraduates: 15% (1,451). ***Average award:*** Freshmen: $2164; Undergraduates: $3083. ***Scholarships, grants, and awards by category:*** *Academic Interests/Achievement:* biological sciences, business, education, general academic interests/achievements, mathematics, physical sciences, social sciences. *Creative Arts/Performance:* applied art and design, art/fine arts, music, theater/drama. *Special Achievements/Activities:* leadership. *Special Characteristics:* general special characteristics, members of minority groups. ***ROTC:*** Army.

LOANS ***Student loans:*** $50,947,855 (46% need-based, 54% non-need-based). 79% of past graduating class borrowed through all loan programs. *Average indebtedness per student:* $21,561. ***Average need-based loan:*** Freshmen: $2780; Undergraduates: $4056. ***Parent loans:*** $18,681,024 (100% non-need-based). ***Programs:*** Federal Direct (Subsidized and Unsubsidized Stafford, PLUS), Perkins, state, alternative loans.

WORK-STUDY ***Federal work-study:*** Total amount: $1,010,226; 476 jobs averaging $1829. ***State or other work-study/employment:*** Total amount: $247,429 (57% need-based, 43% non-need-based). 122 part-time jobs averaging $2053.

ATHLETIC AWARDS Total amount: $2,840,520 (100% non-need-based).

APPLYING FOR FINANCIAL AID ***Required financial aid form:*** FAFSA. ***Financial aid deadline:*** Continuous. ***Notification date:*** Continuous beginning 3/1.

CONTACT Joyce Morrow, Associate Director Enrollment Services, University of Northern Iowa, 255 Gilchrist Hall, Cedar Falls, IA 50614-0024, 319-273-2700 or toll-free 800-772-2037. *Fax:* 319-273-6950. *E-mail:* joyce.morrow@uni.edu.

UNIVERSITY OF NORTHERN VIRGINIA

Manassas, VA

CONTACT Financial Aid Office, University of Northern Virginia, 10021 Balls Ford Road, Manassas, VA 20109, 703-392-0771.

UNIVERSITY OF NORTH FLORIDA

Jacksonville, FL

Tuition & fees (FL res): $3353 **Average undergraduate aid package: $1310**

ABOUT THE INSTITUTION State-supported, coed. Awards: associate, bachelor's, master's, and doctoral degrees and post-bachelor's and post-master's certificates (doctoral degree in education only). 50 undergraduate majors. Total enrollment: 15,954. Undergraduates: 14,124. Freshmen: 1,824. Federal methodology is used as a basis for awarding need-based institutional aid.

UNDERGRADUATE EXPENSES for 2006–07 ***Application fee:*** $30. ***Tuition, state resident:*** full-time $3353; part-time $111.75 per semester hour. ***Tuition, nonresident:*** full-time $14,995; part-time $499.82 per semester hour. ***College room and board:*** $6268; ***Room only:*** $3866. Room and board charges vary according to board plan and housing facility. ***Payment plan:*** Deferred payment.

FRESHMAN FINANCIAL AID (Fall 2006, est.) 1232 applied for aid; of those 55% were deemed to have need. 99% of freshmen with need received aid; of those 39% had need fully met. ***Average percent of need met:*** 92% (excluding resources awarded to replace EFC). ***Average financial aid package:*** $1271 (excluding resources awarded to replace EFC). 12% of all full-time freshmen had no need and received non-need-based gift aid.

UNDERGRADUATE FINANCIAL AID (Fall 2006, est.) 4,925 applied for aid; of those 58% were deemed to have need. 98% of undergraduates with need received aid; of those 22% had need fully met. ***Average percent of need met:*** 91% (excluding resources awarded to replace EFC). ***Average financial aid package:*** $1310 (excluding resources awarded to replace EFC). 11% of all full-time undergraduates had no need and received non-need-based gift aid.

GIFT AID (NEED-BASED) ***Total amount:*** $14,104,254 (58% federal, 39% state, 2% institutional, 1% external sources). ***Receiving aid:*** Freshmen: 21% (469); All full-time undergraduates: 19% (1,893). ***Average award:*** Freshmen: $861; Undergraduates: $955. ***Scholarships, grants, and awards:*** Federal Pell, FSEOG, college/university gift aid from institutional funds, 2+2 Scholarships (jointly sponsored with Florida Community College at Jacksonville).

GIFT AID (NON-NEED-BASED) ***Total amount:*** $11,593,555 (1% federal, 91% state, 3% institutional, 5% external sources). ***Receiving aid:*** Freshmen: 26% (579); Undergraduates: 15% (1,454). ***Average award:*** Freshmen: $1141; Undergraduates: $1099. ***Scholarships, grants, and awards by category:*** *Academic Interests/Achievement:* 841 awards ($2,326,298 total): business, computer science, education, engineering/technologies, general academic interests/achievements, health fields, international studies. *Creative Arts/Performance:* 60 awards ($66,570 total): art/fine arts, music. *Special Achievements/Activities:* 14 awards ($21,428 total): community service, general special achievements/activities, leadership. *Special Characteristics:* 17 awards ($40,607 total): first-generation college students, general special characteristics, international students, members of minority groups, out-of-state students. ***Tuition waivers:*** Full or partial for employees or children of employees, senior citizens. ***ROTC:*** Naval cooperative.

LOANS ***Student loans:*** $22,061,451 (72% need-based, 28% non-need-based). 43% of past graduating class borrowed through all loan programs. *Average indebtedness per student:* $16,707. ***Average need-based loan:*** Freshmen: $1343; Undergraduates: $1408. ***Parent loans:*** $1,504,550 (44% need-based, 56% non-need-based). ***Programs:*** FFEL (Subsidized and Unsubsidized Stafford, PLUS).

WORK-STUDY ***Federal work-study:*** Total amount: $149,217; 50 jobs averaging $2984.

ATHLETIC AWARDS Total amount: $858,626 (16% need-based, 84% non-need-based).

APPLYING FOR FINANCIAL AID ***Required financial aid forms:*** FAFSA, financial aid transcript (for transfers). ***Financial aid deadline (priority):*** 4/1. ***Notification date:*** Continuous beginning 3/15. Students must reply within 2 weeks of notification.

CONTACT Mrs. Janice Nowak, Director of Financial Aid, University of North Florida, 4567 St. Johns Bluff Road, South, Jacksonville, FL 32224-2645, 904-620-2604. *E-mail:* jnowak@unf.edu.

UNIVERSITY OF NORTH TEXAS

Denton, TX

CONTACT Mrs. Carolyn Cunningham, Director of Financial Aid, University of North Texas, PO Box 311370, Denton, TX 76203-1370, 940-565-2302 or toll-free 800-868-8211 (in-state). *Fax:* 940-565-2738.

UNIVERSITY OF NOTRE DAME

Notre Dame, IN

Tuition & fees: $35,187 **Average undergraduate aid package: $28,373**

ABOUT THE INSTITUTION Independent Roman Catholic, coed. Awards: bachelor's, master's, doctoral, and first professional degrees. 55 undergraduate majors. Total enrollment: 11,603. Undergraduates: 8,352. Freshmen: 2,039. Both federal and institutional methodology are used as a basis for awarding need-based institutional aid.

UNDERGRADUATE EXPENSES for 2007–08 ***Application fee:*** $50. ***Comprehensive fee:*** $44,477 includes full-time tuition ($34,680), mandatory fees ($507), and room and board ($9290). ***Part-time tuition:*** $1445 per credit.

FRESHMAN FINANCIAL AID (Fall 2006, est.) 1395 applied for aid; of those 71% were deemed to have need. 100% of freshmen with need received aid; of those 99% had need fully met. ***Average percent of need met:*** 100% (excluding resources awarded to replace EFC). ***Average financial aid package:*** $28,331 (excluding resources awarded to replace EFC). 1% of all full-time freshmen had no need and received non-need-based gift aid.

UNDERGRADUATE FINANCIAL AID (Fall 2006, est.) 4,901 applied for aid; of those 80% were deemed to have need. 100% of undergraduates with need received aid; of those 95% had need fully met. ***Average percent of need met:*** 99% (excluding resources awarded to replace EFC). ***Average financial aid package:*** $28,373 (excluding resources awarded to replace EFC). 3% of all full-time undergraduates had no need and received non-need-based gift aid.

GIFT AID (NEED-BASED) ***Total amount:*** $74,510,611 (7% federal, 88% institutional, 5% external sources). ***Receiving aid:*** Freshmen: 46% (947); All full-time undergraduates: 45% (3,746). ***Average award:*** Freshmen: $22,361;

Undergraduates: $20,791. ***Scholarships, grants, and awards:*** Federal Pell, FSEOG, state, private, college/university gift aid from institutional funds, Federal ACG and SMART Grants.

GIFT AID (NON-NEED-BASED) ***Total amount:*** $14,471,928 (33% federal, 1% state, 29% institutional, 37% external sources). ***Receiving aid:*** Freshmen: 32% (644); Undergraduates: 29% (2,375). ***Average award:*** Freshmen: $3688; Undergraduates: $5491. ***Scholarships, grants, and awards by category:*** *Special Characteristics:* 257 awards ($7,613,037 total): children of faculty/staff. ***ROTC:*** Army, Naval, Air Force.

LOANS ***Student loans:*** $38,873,334 (49% need-based, 51% non-need-based). 57% of past graduating class borrowed through all loan programs. *Average indebtedness per student:* $26,285. ***Average need-based loan:*** Freshmen: $3020; Undergraduates: $4696. ***Parent loans:*** $11,545,181 (2% need-based, 98% non-need-based). ***Programs:*** FFEL (Subsidized and Unsubsidized Stafford, PLUS), Perkins, Notre Dame Undergraduate Loan.

WORK-STUDY ***Federal work-study:*** Total amount: $3,465,147; 1,757 jobs averaging $2112. ***State or other work-study/employment:*** Total amount: $10,189,355 (6% need-based, 94% non-need-based). 4,083 part-time jobs averaging $2496.

ATHLETIC AWARDS Total amount: $12,379,179 (14% need-based, 86% non-need-based).

APPLYING FOR FINANCIAL AID ***Required financial aid forms:*** FAFSA, CSS Financial Aid PROFILE, business/farm supplement, income tax form(s), W-2 forms. ***Financial aid deadline:*** 2/15. ***Notification date:*** 4/1. Students must reply by 5/1.

CONTACT Mr. Joseph A. Russo, Director, Student Financial Strategies, University of Notre Dame, 115 Main Building, Notre Dame, IN 46556, 574-631-6436. *Fax:* 574-631-6899. *E-mail:* finaid.1@nd.edu.

UNIVERSITY OF OKLAHOMA

Norman, OK

Tuition & fees (OK res): $5110 **Average undergraduate aid package: $9316**

ABOUT THE INSTITUTION State-supported, coed. Awards: bachelor's, master's, doctoral, and first professional degrees and post-master's certificates. 104 undergraduate majors. Total enrollment: 26,002. Undergraduates: 19,600. Freshmen: 3,342. Federal methodology is used as a basis for awarding need-based institutional aid.

UNDERGRADUATE EXPENSES for 2006–07 ***Application fee:*** $40. ***Tuition, state resident:*** full-time $3006; part-time $100.20 per credit hour. ***Tuition, nonresident:*** full-time $11,295; part-time $376.50 per credit hour. ***Required fees:*** full-time $2104; $62.40 per credit hour or $116.50 per term part-time. Full-time tuition and fees vary according to course load, location, program, and reciprocity agreements. Part-time tuition and fees vary according to course load, location, program, and reciprocity agreements. ***College room and board:*** $6863; ***Room only:*** $3753. Room and board charges vary according to board plan and housing facility. ***Payment plan:*** Installment.

FRESHMAN FINANCIAL AID (Fall 2005) 1889 applied for aid; of those 80% were deemed to have need. 100% of freshmen with need received aid; of those 50% had need fully met. ***Average percent of need met:*** 87% (excluding resources awarded to replace EFC). ***Average financial aid package:*** $9234 (excluding resources awarded to replace EFC). 14% of all full-time freshmen had no need and received non-need-based gift aid.

UNDERGRADUATE FINANCIAL AID (Fall 2005) 9,257 applied for aid; of those 91% were deemed to have need. 100% of undergraduates with need received aid; of those 51% had need fully met. ***Average percent of need met:*** 87% (excluding resources awarded to replace EFC). ***Average financial aid package:*** $9316 (excluding resources awarded to replace EFC). 11% of all full-time undergraduates had no need and received non-need-based gift aid.

GIFT AID (NEED-BASED) ***Total amount:*** $24,432,800 (53% federal, 24% state, 14% institutional, 9% external sources). ***Receiving aid:*** Freshmen: 11% (368); All full-time undergraduates: 17% (2,949). ***Average award:*** Freshmen: $3770; Undergraduates: $3830. ***Scholarships, grants, and awards:*** Federal Pell, FSEOG, state, private, college/university gift aid from institutional funds, United Negro College Fund.

GIFT AID (NON-NEED-BASED) ***Total amount:*** $8,974,516 (11% federal, 51% state, 22% institutional, 16% external sources). ***Receiving aid:*** Freshmen: 30% (949); Undergraduates: 20% (3,533). ***Average award:*** Freshmen: $951; Undergraduates: $1008. ***Scholarships, grants, and awards by category:*** *Academic Interests/Achievement:* 8,197 awards ($17,357,952 total): architecture, area/ethnic studies, biological sciences, business, communication, computer science, education, engineering/technologies, foreign languages, general academic interests/achievements, humanities, international studies, mathematics, physical sciences, social sciences. *Creative Arts/Performance:* 131 awards ($1,245,606 total): art/fine arts, dance, journalism/publications, music, performing arts, theater/drama. *Special Achievements/Activities:* 66 awards ($116,445 total): leadership. *Special Characteristics:* 599 awards ($1,162,500 total): children and siblings of alumni, members of minority groups, previous college experience. ***Tuition waivers:*** Full or partial for employees or children of employees, senior citizens. ***ROTC:*** Army, Naval, Air Force.

LOANS ***Student loans:*** $50,283,840 (98% need-based, 2% non-need-based). 52% of past graduating class borrowed through all loan programs. *Average indebtedness per student:* $19,206. ***Average need-based loan:*** Freshmen: $3408; Undergraduates: $4639. ***Parent loans:*** $11,480,063 (97% need-based, 3% non-need-based). ***Programs:*** FFEL (Subsidized and Unsubsidized Stafford, PLUS), Perkins, college/university, alternative loans.

WORK-STUDY ***Federal work-study:*** Total amount: $1,598,716; 682 jobs averaging $2344.

ATHLETIC AWARDS Total amount: $4,476,390 (41% need-based, 59% non-need-based).

APPLYING FOR FINANCIAL AID ***Required financial aid form:*** FAFSA. ***Financial aid deadline:*** Continuous. ***Notification date:*** Continuous beginning 3/15. Students must reply within 6 weeks of notification.

CONTACT Financial Aid Assistant, University of Oklahoma, 1000 Asp Avenue, Room 216, Norman, OK 73019-4078, 405-325-4521 or toll-free 800-234-6868. *Fax:* 405-325-0819. *E-mail:* financialaid@ou.edu.

UNIVERSITY OF OREGON

Eugene, OR

Tuition & fees (OR res): $5838 **Average undergraduate aid package: $7671**

ABOUT THE INSTITUTION State-supported, coed. Awards: bachelor's, master's, doctoral, and first professional degrees and post-bachelor's and post-master's certificates. 95 undergraduate majors. Total enrollment: 20,348. Undergraduates: 16,529. Freshmen: 3,423. Federal methodology is used as a basis for awarding need-based institutional aid.

UNDERGRADUATE EXPENSES for 2006–07 ***Application fee:*** $50. ***Tuition, state resident:*** full-time $4341; part-time $107 per credit hour. ***Tuition, nonresident:*** full-time $16,755; part-time $433 per credit hour. Full-time tuition and fees vary according to class time, course load, program, and reciprocity agreements. Part-time tuition and fees vary according to class time, course load, program, and reciprocity agreements. ***College room and board:*** $7827. Room and board charges vary according to board plan and housing facility. ***Payment plan:*** Installment.

FRESHMAN FINANCIAL AID (Fall 2005) 2139 applied for aid; of those 59% were deemed to have need. 93% of freshmen with need received aid; of those 20% had need fully met. ***Average percent of need met:*** 55% (excluding resources awarded to replace EFC). ***Average financial aid package:*** $6938 (excluding resources awarded to replace EFC). 11% of all full-time freshmen had no need and received non-need-based gift aid.

UNDERGRADUATE FINANCIAL AID (Fall 2005) 8,718 applied for aid; of those 70% were deemed to have need. 94% of undergraduates with need received aid; of those 19% had need fully met. ***Average percent of need met:*** 64% (excluding resources awarded to replace EFC). ***Average financial aid package:*** $7671 (excluding resources awarded to replace EFC). 6% of all full-time undergraduates had no need and received non-need-based gift aid.

GIFT AID (NEED-BASED) ***Total amount:*** $14,458,615 (78% federal, 20% state, 2% institutional). ***Receiving aid:*** Freshmen: 16% (537); All full-time undergraduates: 21% (3,129). ***Average award:*** Freshmen: $4297; Undergraduates: $4231. ***Scholarships, grants, and awards:*** Federal Pell, FSEOG, state, private, college/university gift aid from institutional funds.

GIFT AID (NON-NEED-BASED) ***Total amount:*** $8,697,375 (94% institutional, 6% external sources). ***Receiving aid:*** Freshmen: 17% (575); Undergraduates: 10% (1,564). ***Average award:*** Freshmen: $1893; Undergraduates: $1859. ***Scholarships, grants, and awards by category:*** *Academic Interests/Achievement:* architecture, biological sciences, business, education, foreign languages, general academic interests/achievements, physical sciences, social sciences. *Creative Arts/Performance:* art/fine arts, dance, journalism/publications, music, performing arts, theater/drama. *Special Achievements/Activities:* general special achievements/activities. *Special Characteristics:* general special characteristics, international students, local/state students. ***Tuition waivers:*** Full or partial for employees or children of employees. ***ROTC:*** Army, Air Force cooperative.

LOANS ***Student loans:*** $41,018,524 (56% need-based, 44% non-need-based). 59% of past graduating class borrowed through all loan programs. *Average indebtedness per student:* $18,813. ***Average need-based loan:*** Freshmen: $3649; Undergraduates: $4465. ***Parent loans:*** $30,486,867 (20% need-based, 80% non-need-based). ***Programs:*** Federal Direct (Subsidized and Unsubsidized Stafford, PLUS), Perkins, college/university.

WORK-STUDY ***Federal work-study:*** Total amount: $3,023,213; 2,077 jobs averaging $1456. ***State or other work-study/employment:*** Total amount: $201,351 (100% need-based). 107 part-time jobs averaging $1882.

ATHLETIC AWARDS Total amount: $5,197,954 (100% non-need-based).

APPLYING FOR FINANCIAL AID ***Required financial aid form:*** FAFSA. ***Financial aid deadline (priority):*** 3/1. ***Notification date:*** Continuous beginning 4/1. Students must reply within 4 weeks of notification.

CONTACT Elizabeth Bickford, Director of Financial Aid, University of Oregon, 1278 University of Oregon, 260 Oregon Hall, Eugene, OR 97403-1278, 541-346-3221 or toll-free 800-232-3825 (in-state). *Fax:* 541-346-1175. *E-mail:* ebick@uoregon.edu.

UNIVERSITY OF PENNSYLVANIA

Philadelphia, PA

Tuition & fees: $34,156 **Average undergraduate aid package: $28,633**

ABOUT THE INSTITUTION Independent, coed. Awards: associate, bachelor's, master's, doctoral, and first professional degrees and post-bachelor's, post-master's, and first professional certificates (also offers evening program with significant enrollment not reflected in profile). 95 undergraduate majors. Total enrollment: 18,809. Undergraduates: 9,730. Freshmen: 2,373. Institutional methodology is used as a basis for awarding need-based institutional aid.

UNDERGRADUATE EXPENSES for 2006–07 ***Application fee:*** $70. ***Comprehensive fee:*** $43,960 includes full-time tuition ($30,598), mandatory fees ($3558), and room and board ($9804). ***College room only:*** $6022. Room and board charges vary according to board plan and housing facility. Part-time tuition and fees vary according to course load. ***Payment plan:*** Installment.

FRESHMAN FINANCIAL AID (Fall 2005) 1296 applied for aid; of those 80% were deemed to have need. 100% of freshmen with need received aid; of those 100% had need fully met. ***Average percent of need met:*** 100% (excluding resources awarded to replace EFC). ***Average financial aid package:*** $27,948 (excluding resources awarded to replace EFC).

UNDERGRADUATE FINANCIAL AID (Fall 2005) 4,632 applied for aid; of those 90% were deemed to have need. 100% of undergraduates with need received aid; of those 100% had need fully met. ***Average percent of need met:*** 100% (excluding resources awarded to replace EFC). ***Average financial aid package:*** $28,633 (excluding resources awarded to replace EFC).

GIFT AID (NEED-BASED) ***Total amount:*** $91,316,000 (6% federal, 2% state, 88% institutional, 4% external sources). ***Receiving aid:*** Freshmen: 40% (957); All full-time undergraduates: 41% (3,897). ***Average award:*** Freshmen: $24,291; Undergraduates: $23,580. ***Scholarships, grants, and awards:*** Federal Pell, FSEOG, state, private, college/university gift aid from institutional funds.

GIFT AID (NON-NEED-BASED) ***Total amount:*** $6,145,000 (1% federal, 1% state, 98% external sources). ***Tuition waivers:*** Full or partial for employees or children of employees. ***ROTC:*** Army cooperative, Naval, Air Force cooperative.

LOANS ***Student loans:*** $31,402,000 (46% need-based, 54% non-need-based). 41% of past graduating class borrowed through all loan programs. *Average indebtedness per student:* $20,927. ***Average need-based loan:*** Freshmen: $2785; Undergraduates: $3713. ***Parent loans:*** $15,077,000 (60% need-based, 40% non-need-based). ***Programs:*** FFEL (Subsidized and Unsubsidized Stafford, PLUS), Perkins, Federal Nursing, college/university, supplemental third-party loans (guaranteed by institution).

WORK-STUDY ***Federal work-study:*** Total amount: $9,654,000.

APPLYING FOR FINANCIAL AID ***Required financial aid forms:*** FAFSA, institution's own form, CSS Financial Aid PROFILE, noncustodial (divorced/separated) parent's statement, business/farm supplement, parent and student most recently completed income tax. ***Financial aid deadline (priority):*** 2/1. ***Notification date:*** 4/1. Students must reply by 5/1.

CONTACT Mr. William Schilling, Director of Financial Aid, University of Pennsylvania, 212 Franklin Building, 3451 Walnut Street, Philadelphia, PA 19104-6270, 215-898-6784. *Fax:* 215-573-2208. *E-mail:* schilling@sfs.upenn.edu.

UNIVERSITY OF PHOENIX–ATLANTA CAMPUS

Sandy Springs, GA

Tuition & fees: $11,558 **Average undergraduate aid package: $4348**

ABOUT THE INSTITUTION Proprietary, coed. Awards: bachelor's and master's degrees. 23 undergraduate majors. Total enrollment: 2,518. Undergraduates: 1,827. Freshmen: 67. Both federal and institutional methodology are used as a basis for awarding need-based institutional aid.

UNDERGRADUATE EXPENSES for 2006–07 ***Application fee:*** $45. ***Tuition:*** full-time $11,558; part-time $385 per credit. ***Payment plan:*** Deferred payment.

FRESHMAN FINANCIAL AID (Fall 2005) ***Average financial aid package:*** $2712 (excluding resources awarded to replace EFC).

UNDERGRADUATE FINANCIAL AID (Fall 2005) ***Average financial aid package:*** $4348 (excluding resources awarded to replace EFC).

GIFT AID (NEED-BASED) ***Total amount:*** $1,998,998 (100% federal). ***Receiving aid:*** Freshmen: 167; All full-time undergraduates: 885. ***Average award:*** Freshmen: $1952; Undergraduates: $2249. ***Scholarships, grants, and awards:*** Federal Pell, FSEOG, state, private, college/university gift aid from institutional funds, Academic Competitiveness Grant and National Science and Mathematics Access to Retain Talent (SMART).

GIFT AID (NON-NEED-BASED) ***Receiving aid:*** Freshmen: 1; Undergraduates: 52. ***Scholarships, grants, and awards by category:*** *Academic Interests/Achievement:* business, communication, computer science, health fields, social sciences. ***Tuition waivers:*** Full or partial for employees or children of employees.

LOANS ***Student loans:*** $20,137,332 (44% need-based, 56% non-need-based). ***Average need-based loan:*** Undergraduates: $6122. ***Programs:*** FFEL (Subsidized and Unsubsidized Stafford, PLUS), Perkins.

APPLYING FOR FINANCIAL AID ***Required financial aid forms:*** FAFSA, institution's own form. ***Financial aid deadline:*** Continuous. ***Notification date:*** Continuous beginning 7/1.

CONTACT ACS/AFS, University of Phoenix–Atlanta Campus, 875 West Elliot Road, Suite 116, Tempe, AZ 85284, 480-735-3000 or toll-free 800-776-4867 (in-state), 800-228-7240 (out-of-state). *Fax:* 480-940-2060.

UNIVERSITY OF PHOENIX–BAY AREA CAMPUS

Pleasanton, CA

Tuition & fees: $13,390 **Average undergraduate aid package: $3866**

ABOUT THE INSTITUTION Proprietary, coed. Awards: associate, bachelor's, and master's degrees. 24 undergraduate majors. Total enrollment: 3,139. Undergraduates: 2,249. Freshmen: 68. Both federal and institutional methodology are used as a basis for awarding need-based institutional aid.

UNDERGRADUATE EXPENSES for 2006–07 ***Application fee:*** $45. ***Tuition:*** full-time $13,390; part-time $446 per credit. ***Payment plan:*** Deferred payment.

FRESHMAN FINANCIAL AID (Fall 2005) ***Average financial aid package:*** $2109 (excluding resources awarded to replace EFC).

UNDERGRADUATE FINANCIAL AID (Fall 2005) ***Average financial aid package:*** $3866 (excluding resources awarded to replace EFC).

GIFT AID (NEED-BASED) ***Total amount:*** $1,539,725 (76% federal, 24% state). ***Receiving aid:*** Freshmen: 51; All full-time undergraduates: 584. ***Average award:*** Freshmen: $1542; Undergraduates: $2673. ***Scholarships, grants, and awards:*** Federal Pell, FSEOG, state, private, college/university gift aid from institutional funds, Academic Competitiveness Grant and National Science and Mathematics Access to Retain Talent (SMART).

GIFT AID (NON-NEED-BASED) ***Receiving aid:*** Freshmen: 1; Undergraduates: 42. ***Scholarships, grants, and awards by category:*** *Academic Interests/Achievement:* business, computer science, health fields, social sciences. ***Tuition waivers:*** Full or partial for employees or children of employees.

LOANS ***Student loans:*** $22,470,063 (43% need-based, 57% non-need-based). ***Programs:*** FFEL (Subsidized and Unsubsidized Stafford, PLUS), Perkins.

APPLYING FOR FINANCIAL AID ***Required financial aid forms:*** FAFSA, institution's own form. ***Financial aid deadline:*** Continuous. ***Notification date:*** Continuous beginning 7/1.

CONTACT ACS/AFS, University of Phoenix–Bay Area Campus, 875 West Elliot Road, Suite 116, Tempe, AZ 85284, 480-735-3000 or toll-free 877-4-STUDENT. *Fax:* 480-940-2060.

UNIVERSITY OF PHOENIX–BOSTON CAMPUS

Braintree, MA

Tuition & fees: $13,050 **Average undergraduate aid package: $3659**

ABOUT THE INSTITUTION Proprietary, coed. Awards: bachelor's and master's degrees. 3 undergraduate majors. Total enrollment: 634. Undergraduates: 468. Freshmen: 29. Both federal and institutional methodology are used as a basis for awarding need-based institutional aid.

UNDERGRADUATE EXPENSES for 2006–07 ***Application fee:*** $45. ***Tuition:*** full-time $13,050; part-time $435 per credit. ***Payment plan:*** Deferred payment.

FRESHMAN FINANCIAL AID (Fall 2005) ***Average financial aid package:*** $1857 (excluding resources awarded to replace EFC).

UNDERGRADUATE FINANCIAL AID (Fall 2005) ***Average financial aid package:*** $3659 (excluding resources awarded to replace EFC).

GIFT AID (NEED-BASED) ***Total amount:*** $242,523 (99% federal, 1% state). ***Receiving aid:*** Freshmen: 33; All full-time undergraduates: 140. ***Average award:*** Freshmen: $1101; Undergraduates: $1732. ***Scholarships, grants, and awards:*** Federal Pell, FSEOG, state, private, college/university gift aid from institutional funds, Academic Competitiveness Grant and National Science and Mathematics Access to Retain Talent (SMART).

GIFT AID (NON-NEED-BASED) ***Receiving aid:*** Freshmen: 2; Undergraduates: 14. ***Scholarships, grants, and awards by category:*** *Academic Interests/Achievement:* business, computer science, health fields. ***Tuition waivers:*** Full or partial for employees or children of employees.

LOANS ***Student loans:*** $3,650,668 (47% need-based, 53% non-need-based). ***Programs:*** FFEL (Subsidized and Unsubsidized Stafford, PLUS), Perkins.

APPLYING FOR FINANCIAL AID ***Required financial aid forms:*** FAFSA, institution's own form. ***Financial aid deadline:*** Continuous. ***Notification date:*** Continuous beginning 7/1.

CONTACT ACS/AFS, University of Phoenix–Boston Campus, 875 West Elliot Road, Suite 116, Tempe, AZ 85284, 480-735-3000 or toll-free 800-228-7240. *Fax:* 480-940-2060.

UNIVERSITY OF PHOENIX–CENTRAL FLORIDA CAMPUS

Maitland, FL

Tuition & fees: $10,058 **Average undergraduate aid package: $4244**

ABOUT THE INSTITUTION Proprietary, coed. Awards: bachelor's and master's degrees. 15 undergraduate majors. Total enrollment: 2,072. Undergraduates: 1,562. Freshmen: 62. Both federal and institutional methodology are used as a basis for awarding need-based institutional aid.

UNDERGRADUATE EXPENSES for 2006–07 ***Application fee:*** $45. ***Tuition:*** full-time $10,058. ***Payment plan:*** Deferred payment.

FRESHMAN FINANCIAL AID (Fall 2005) ***Average financial aid package:*** $2776 (excluding resources awarded to replace EFC).

UNDERGRADUATE FINANCIAL AID (Fall 2005) ***Average financial aid package:*** $4244 (excluding resources awarded to replace EFC).

GIFT AID (NEED-BASED) ***Total amount:*** $1,283,616 (97% federal, 3% state). ***Receiving aid:*** Freshmen: 50; All full-time undergraduates: 574. ***Average award:*** Freshmen: $1983; Undergraduates: $2236. ***Scholarships, grants, and awards:*** Federal Pell, FSEOG, state, private, college/university gift aid from institutional funds, Academic Competitiveness Grant and National Science and Mathematics Access to Retain Talent (SMART).

GIFT AID (NON-NEED-BASED) ***Receiving aid:*** Freshmen: 1; Undergraduates: 20. ***Scholarships, grants, and awards by category:*** *Academic Interests/Achievement:* business, computer science, health fields, social sciences. ***Tuition waivers:*** Full or partial for employees or children of employees.

LOANS ***Student loans:*** $14,824,149 (44% need-based, 56% non-need-based). ***Programs:*** FFEL (Subsidized and Unsubsidized Stafford, PLUS), Perkins.

APPLYING FOR FINANCIAL AID ***Required financial aid forms:*** FAFSA, institution's own form. ***Financial aid deadline:*** Continuous. ***Notification date:*** Continuous beginning 7/1.

CONTACT ACS/AFS, University of Phoenix–Central Florida Campus, 875 West Elliot Road, Suite 116, Tempe, AZ 85284, 480-735-3000 or toll-free 800-776-4867 (in-state), 800-228-7240 (out-of-state). *Fax:* 480-940-2060.

UNIVERSITY OF PHOENIX–CENTRAL MASSACHUSETTS CAMPUS

Westborough, MA

Tuition & fees: $13,050 **Average undergraduate aid package: $3557**

ABOUT THE INSTITUTION Proprietary, coed. Awards: bachelor's and master's degrees. 4 undergraduate majors. Total enrollment: 267. Undergraduates: 189. Freshmen: 7. Both federal and institutional methodology are used as a basis for awarding need-based institutional aid.

UNDERGRADUATE EXPENSES for 2006–07 ***Application fee:*** $45. ***Tuition:*** full-time $13,050; part-time $435 per credit. ***Payment plan:*** Deferred payment.

FRESHMAN FINANCIAL AID (Fall 2005) ***Average financial aid package:*** $1798 (excluding resources awarded to replace EFC).

UNDERGRADUATE FINANCIAL AID (Fall 2005) ***Average financial aid package:*** $3557 (excluding resources awarded to replace EFC).

GIFT AID (NEED-BASED) ***Total amount:*** $78,939 (100% federal). ***Receiving aid:*** Freshmen: 6; All full-time undergraduates: 34. ***Average award:*** Freshmen: $1385; Undergraduates: $2322. ***Scholarships, grants, and awards:*** Federal Pell, FSEOG, state, private, college/university gift aid from institutional funds, Academic Competitiveness Grant and National Science and Mathematics Access to retain talent (Smart).

GIFT AID (NON-NEED-BASED) ***Receiving aid:*** Undergraduates: 5. ***Scholarships, grants, and awards by category:*** *Academic Interests/Achievement:* business. ***Tuition waivers:*** Full or partial for employees or children of employees.

LOANS ***Student loans:*** $1,254,104 (41% need-based, 59% non-need-based). ***Programs:*** FFEL (Subsidized and Unsubsidized Stafford, PLUS), Perkins.

APPLYING FOR FINANCIAL AID ***Required financial aid forms:*** FAFSA, institution's own form. ***Financial aid deadline:*** Continuous. ***Notification date:*** Continuous beginning 7/1.

CONTACT ACS/AFS, University of Phoenix–Central Massachusetts Campus, 875 West Elliot Road, Suite 116, Tempe, AZ 85284, 480-735-3000 or toll-free 800-776-4867 (in-state), 800-228-7240 (out-of-state). *Fax:* 480-940-2060.

UNIVERSITY OF PHOENIX–CENTRAL VALLEY CAMPUS

Fresno, CA

ABOUT THE INSTITUTION Proprietary, coed. Awards: bachelor's and master's degrees and post-bachelor's certificates. 8 undergraduate majors. Total enrollment: 2,145. Undergraduates: 1,780. Freshmen: 53.

GIFT AID (NEED-BASED) ***Scholarships, grants, and awards:*** Federal Pell, FSEOG, state, private, college/university gift aid from institutional funds, Academic Competitiveness Grant and National Science and Mathematics Access to Retain Talent (SMART).

GIFT AID (NON-NEED-BASED) ***Scholarships, grants, and awards by category:*** *Academic Interests/Achievement:* business, computer science.

LOANS ***Programs:*** FFEL (Subsidized and Unsubsidized Stafford, PLUS), Perkins.

APPLYING FOR FINANCIAL AID ***Required financial aid form:*** institution's own form.

CONTACT ACS/AFS, University of Phoenix–Central Valley Campus, 875 West Elliot Road, Suite 116, Tempe, AZ 85284, 480-735-3000 or toll-free 888-776-4867 (in-state), 888-228-7240 (out-of-state). *Fax:* 480-940-2060.

UNIVERSITY OF PHOENIX–CHARLOTTE CAMPUS

Charlotte, NC

Tuition & fees: $10,770 **Average undergraduate aid package: $4289**

ABOUT THE INSTITUTION Proprietary, coed. Awards: bachelor's and master's degrees. 1 undergraduate major. Total enrollment: 1,604. Undergraduates: 1,074. Freshmen: 43. Both federal and institutional methodology are used as a basis for awarding need-based institutional aid.

UNDERGRADUATE EXPENSES for 2006–07 ***Application fee:*** $45. ***Tuition:*** full-time $10,770; part-time $359 per credit. ***Payment plan:*** Deferred payment.

FRESHMAN FINANCIAL AID (Fall 2005) ***Average financial aid package:*** $2744 (excluding resources awarded to replace EFC).

UNDERGRADUATE FINANCIAL AID (Fall 2005) ***Average financial aid package:*** $4289 (excluding resources awarded to replace EFC).

GIFT AID (NEED-BASED) ***Total amount:*** $1,166,116 (100% federal). ***Receiving aid:*** Freshmen: 89; All full-time undergraduates: 521. ***Average award:*** Freshmen: $2014; Undergraduates: $2238. ***Scholarships, grants, and awards:*** Federal Pell, FSEOG, state, private, college/university gift aid from institutional funds, Academic Competitiveness Grant and National Science and Mathematics Access to Retain Talent (SMART).

GIFT AID (NON-NEED-BASED) ***Receiving aid:*** Undergraduates: 17. ***Scholarships, grants, and awards by category:*** *Academic Interests/Achievement:* business, computer science. ***Tuition waivers:*** Full or partial for employees or children of employees.

LOANS ***Student loans:*** $11,832,642 (44% need-based, 56% non-need-based). ***Programs:*** FFEL (Subsidized and Unsubsidized Stafford, PLUS), Perkins.

APPLYING FOR FINANCIAL AID ***Required financial aid form:*** institution's own form. ***Financial aid deadline:*** Continuous. ***Notification date:*** Continuous beginning 7/1.

CONTACT ACS/AFS, University of Phoenix–Charlotte Campus, 875 West Elliot Road, Suite 116, Tempe, AZ 85284, 480-735-3000 or toll-free 800-776-4867 (in-state), 800-228-7240 (out-of-state). *Fax:* 480-940-2060.

UNIVERSITY OF PHOENIX–CHICAGO CAMPUS

Schaumburg, IL

Tuition & fees: $11,190 **Average undergraduate aid package: $3787**

ABOUT THE INSTITUTION Proprietary, coed. Awards: bachelor's and master's degrees. 9 undergraduate majors. Total enrollment: 1,590. Undergraduates: 1,320. Freshmen: 69. Both federal and institutional methodology are used as a basis for awarding need-based institutional aid.

UNDERGRADUATE EXPENSES for 2006–07 ***Application fee:*** $45. ***Tuition:*** full-time $11,190; part-time $373 per credit. ***Payment plan:*** Deferred payment.

FRESHMAN FINANCIAL AID (Fall 2005) ***Average financial aid package:*** $2404 (excluding resources awarded to replace EFC).

UNDERGRADUATE FINANCIAL AID (Fall 2005) ***Average financial aid package:*** $3787 (excluding resources awarded to replace EFC).

GIFT AID (NEED-BASED) ***Total amount:*** $992,614 (100% federal). ***Receiving aid:*** Freshmen: 88; All full-time undergraduates: 470. ***Average award:*** Freshmen: $1564; Undergraduates: $2112. ***Scholarships, grants, and awards:*** Federal Pell, FSEOG, state, private, college/university gift aid from institutional funds, Academic Competitiveness Grant and National Science and Mathematics Access to Retain Talent (SMART).

GIFT AID (NON-NEED-BASED) ***Receiving aid:*** Undergraduates: 25. ***Scholarships, grants, and awards by category:*** *Academic Interests/Achievement:* business, computer science. ***Tuition waivers:*** Full or partial for employees or children of employees.

LOANS ***Student loans:*** $11,249,674 (42% need-based, 58% non-need-based). ***Programs:*** FFEL (Subsidized and Unsubsidized Stafford, PLUS), Perkins.

APPLYING FOR FINANCIAL AID ***Required financial aid form:*** institution's own form. ***Financial aid deadline:*** Continuous. ***Notification date:*** Continuous beginning 7/1.

CONTACT ACS/AFS, University of Phoenix–Chicago Campus, 875 West Elliot Road, Suite 116, Tempe, AZ 85284, 480-735-3000 or toll-free 800-776-4867 (in-state), 800-228-7240 (out-of-state). *Fax:* 480-940-2060.

UNIVERSITY OF PHOENIX–CINCINNATI CAMPUS

West Chester, OH

Tuition & fees: $11,910 **Average undergraduate aid package: $3974**

ABOUT THE INSTITUTION Proprietary, coed. Awards: bachelor's and master's degrees. 26 undergraduate majors. Total enrollment: 646. Undergraduates: 462. Freshmen: 32. Both federal and institutional methodology are used as a basis for awarding need-based institutional aid.

UNDERGRADUATE EXPENSES for 2006–07 ***Application fee:*** $45. ***Tuition:*** full-time $11,910; part-time $397 per credit. ***Payment plan:*** Deferred payment.

FRESHMAN FINANCIAL AID (Fall 2005) ***Average financial aid package:*** $1987 (excluding resources awarded to replace EFC).

UNDERGRADUATE FINANCIAL AID (Fall 2005) ***Average financial aid package:*** $3974 (excluding resources awarded to replace EFC).

GIFT AID (NEED-BASED) ***Total amount:*** $325,929 (100% federal). ***Receiving aid:*** Freshmen: 37; All full-time undergraduates: 175. ***Average award:*** Freshmen: $1265; Undergraduates: $1862. ***Scholarships, grants, and awards:*** Federal Pell, FSEOG, state, private, college/university gift aid from institutional funds, Academic Competitiveness Grant and National Science and Mathematics Access to Retain Talent (SMART).

GIFT AID (NON-NEED-BASED) ***Receiving aid:*** Freshmen: 1; Undergraduates: 8. ***Scholarships, grants, and awards by category:*** *Academic Interests/Achievement:* business, computer science. ***Tuition waivers:*** Full or partial for employees or children of employees.

LOANS ***Student loans:*** $4,167,722 (46% need-based, 54% non-need-based). ***Programs:*** FFEL (Subsidized and Unsubsidized Stafford, PLUS), Perkins.

APPLYING FOR FINANCIAL AID ***Required financial aid forms:*** FAFSA, institution's own form. ***Financial aid deadline:*** Continuous. ***Notification date:*** Continuous beginning 7/1.

CONTACT ACS/AFS, University of Phoenix–Cincinnati Campus, 875 West Elliot Road, Suite 116, Tempe, AZ 85284, 480-735-3000 or toll-free 800-776-4867 (in-state), 800-228-7240 (out-of-state). *Fax:* 480-940-2060.

UNIVERSITY OF PHOENIX–CLEVELAND CAMPUS

Independence, OH

Tuition & fees: $11,910 **Average undergraduate aid package: $4211**

ABOUT THE INSTITUTION Proprietary, coed. Awards: bachelor's and master's degrees. 26 undergraduate majors. Total enrollment: 865. Undergraduates: 663. Freshmen: 41. Both federal and institutional methodology are used as a basis for awarding need-based institutional aid.

UNDERGRADUATE EXPENSES for 2006–07 ***Application fee:*** $45. ***Tuition:*** full-time $11,910. ***Payment plan:*** Deferred payment.

FRESHMAN FINANCIAL AID (Fall 2005) ***Average financial aid package:*** $2732 (excluding resources awarded to replace EFC).

UNDERGRADUATE FINANCIAL AID (Fall 2005) ***Average financial aid package:*** $4211 (excluding resources awarded to replace EFC).

GIFT AID (NEED-BASED) ***Total amount:*** $710,479 (100% federal). ***Receiving aid:*** Freshmen: 47; All full-time undergraduates: 313. ***Average award:*** Freshmen: $2020; Undergraduates: $2270. ***Scholarships, grants, and awards:*** Federal Pell, FSEOG, state, private, college/university gift aid from institutional funds, Academic Competitiveness Grant and National Science and Mathematics Access to Retain Talent (SMART).

GIFT AID (NON-NEED-BASED) ***Receiving aid:*** Undergraduates: 7. ***Scholarships, grants, and awards by category:*** *Academic Interests/Achievement:* business, computer science, health fields, social sciences. ***Tuition waivers:*** Full or partial for employees or children of employees.

LOANS ***Student loans:*** $6,558,624 (46% need-based, 54% non-need-based). ***Programs:*** FFEL (Subsidized and Unsubsidized Stafford, PLUS), Perkins.

APPLYING FOR FINANCIAL AID ***Required financial aid forms:*** FAFSA, institution's own form. ***Financial aid deadline:*** Continuous. ***Notification date:*** Continuous beginning 7/1.

CONTACT ACS/AFS, University of Phoenix–Cleveland Campus, 875 West Elliot Road, Suite 116, Tempe, AZ 85284, 480-735-3000 or toll-free 800-776-4867 (in-state), 800-228-7240 (out-of-state). *Fax:* 480-940-2060.

UNIVERSITY OF PHOENIX–COLUMBUS GEORGIA CAMPUS

Columbus, GA

Tuition & fees: $10,500 **Average undergraduate aid package: $4527**

ABOUT THE INSTITUTION Proprietary, coed. Awards: bachelor's and master's degrees. 8 undergraduate majors. Total enrollment: 819. Undergraduates: 752. Freshmen: 36. Both federal and institutional methodology are used as a basis for awarding need-based institutional aid.

UNDERGRADUATE EXPENSES for 2006–07 ***Application fee:*** $45. ***Tuition:*** full-time $10,500; part-time $350 per credit. ***Payment plan:*** Deferred payment.

FRESHMAN FINANCIAL AID (Fall 2005) ***Average financial aid package:*** $2720 (excluding resources awarded to replace EFC).

UNDERGRADUATE FINANCIAL AID (Fall 2005) ***Average financial aid package:*** $4527 (excluding resources awarded to replace EFC).

GIFT AID (NEED-BASED) ***Total amount:*** $1,298,120 (100% federal). ***Receiving aid:*** Freshmen: 108; All full-time undergraduates: 519. ***Average award:*** Freshmen: $1948; Undergraduates: $2501. ***Scholarships, grants, and awards:*** Federal Pell, FSEOG, state, private, college/university gift aid from institutional funds, Academic Competitiveness Grant and National Science and Mathematics Access to Retain Talent (SMART).

GIFT AID (NON-NEED-BASED) ***Receiving aid:*** Undergraduates: 13. ***Scholarships, grants, and awards by category:*** *Academic Interests/Achievement:* business, computer science, health fields. ***Tuition waivers:*** Full or partial for employees or children of employees.

LOANS ***Student loans:*** $5,504,999 (46% need-based, 54% non-need-based). ***Programs:*** FFEL (Subsidized and Unsubsidized Stafford, PLUS), Perkins.

APPLYING FOR FINANCIAL AID ***Required financial aid forms:*** FAFSA, institution's own form. ***Financial aid deadline:*** Continuous. ***Notification date:*** Continuous beginning 7/1.

CONTACT ACS/AFS, University of Phoenix–Columbus Georgia Campus, 875 West Elliot Road, Suite 116, Tempe, AZ 85284, 480-735-3000 or toll-free 800-776-4867 (in-state), 800-228-7240 (out-of-state). *Fax:* 480-940-2060.

UNIVERSITY OF PHOENIX–COLUMBUS OHIO CAMPUS

Columbus, OH

Tuition & fees: $10,080 **Average undergraduate aid package: $3460**

ABOUT THE INSTITUTION Proprietary, coed. Awards: bachelor's and master's degrees. 27 undergraduate majors. Total enrollment: 471. Undergraduates: 326. Freshmen: 13. Both federal and institutional methodology are used as a basis for awarding need-based institutional aid.

UNDERGRADUATE EXPENSES for 2006–07 ***Application fee:*** $45. ***Tuition:*** full-time $10,080. ***Payment plan:*** Deferred payment.

FRESHMAN FINANCIAL AID (Fall 2005) ***Average financial aid package:*** $1934 (excluding resources awarded to replace EFC).

UNDERGRADUATE FINANCIAL AID (Fall 2005) ***Average financial aid package:*** $3460 (excluding resources awarded to replace EFC).

GIFT AID (NEED-BASED) ***Total amount:*** $231,885 (100% federal). ***Receiving aid:*** Freshmen: 34; All full-time undergraduates: 132. ***Average award:*** Freshmen: $1388; Undergraduates: $1757. ***Scholarships, grants, and awards:*** Federal Pell, FSEOG, state, private, college/university gift aid from institutional funds, Academic Competitiveness Grant and National Science and Mathematics Access to Retain Talent (SMART).

GIFT AID (NON-NEED-BASED) ***Receiving aid:*** Undergraduates: 10. ***Scholarships, grants, and awards by category:*** *Academic Interests/Achievement:* business, computer science. ***Tuition waivers:*** Full or partial for employees or children of employees.

LOANS ***Student loans:*** $3,283,397 (45% need-based, 55% non-need-based). ***Programs:*** FFEL (Subsidized and Unsubsidized Stafford, PLUS), Perkins.

APPLYING FOR FINANCIAL AID ***Required financial aid forms:*** FAFSA, institution's own form. ***Financial aid deadline:*** Continuous. ***Notification date:*** Continuous beginning 7/1.

CONTACT ACS/AFS, University of Phoenix–Columbus Ohio Campus, 875 West Elliot Road, Suite 116, Tempe, AZ 85284, 480-735-3000 or toll-free 800-776-4867 (in-state), 800-228-7240 (out-of-state). *Fax:* 480-940-2060.

UNIVERSITY OF PHOENIX–DALLAS CAMPUS

Dallas, TX

Tuition & fees: $11,190 **Average undergraduate aid package: $4159**

ABOUT THE INSTITUTION Proprietary, coed. Awards: bachelor's and master's degrees. 22 undergraduate majors. Total enrollment: 2,539. Undergraduates: 1,975. Freshmen: 82. Both federal and institutional methodology are used as a basis for awarding need-based institutional aid.

UNDERGRADUATE EXPENSES for 2006–07 ***Application fee:*** $45. ***Tuition:*** full-time $11,190; part-time $373 per credit. Full-time tuition and fees vary according to program. ***Payment plan:*** Deferred payment.

FRESHMAN FINANCIAL AID (Fall 2005) ***Average financial aid package:*** $2509 (excluding resources awarded to replace EFC).

UNDERGRADUATE FINANCIAL AID (Fall 2005) ***Average financial aid package:*** $4159 (excluding resources awarded to replace EFC).

GIFT AID (NEED-BASED) ***Total amount:*** $2,095,599 (100% federal). ***Receiving aid:*** Freshmen: 156; All full-time undergraduates: 966. ***Average award:*** Freshmen: $1807; Undergraduates: $2169. ***Scholarships, grants, and awards:*** Federal Pell, FSEOG, state, private, college/university gift aid from institutional funds, Academic Competitiveness Grant and National Science and Mathematics Access to Retain Talent (SMART).

GIFT AID (NON-NEED-BASED) ***Receiving aid:*** Undergraduates: 47. ***Scholarships, grants, and awards by category:*** *Academic Interests/Achievement:* business, computer science, health fields, social sciences. ***Tuition waivers:*** Full or partial for employees or children of employees.

LOANS ***Student loans:*** $19,765,855 (46% need-based, 54% non-need-based). ***Programs:*** FFEL (Subsidized and Unsubsidized Stafford, PLUS), Perkins.

APPLYING FOR FINANCIAL AID ***Required financial aid forms:*** FAFSA, institution's own form. ***Financial aid deadline:*** Continuous. ***Notification date:*** Continuous beginning 7/1.

CONTACT ACS/AFS, University of Phoenix–Dallas Campus, 875 West Elliot Road, Suite 116, Tempe, AZ 85284, 480-735-3000 or toll-free 800-776-4867 (in-state), 800-228-7240 (out-of-state). *Fax:* 480-940-2060.

UNIVERSITY OF PHOENIX–DENVER CAMPUS

Lone Tree, CO

Tuition & fees: $9750 **Average undergraduate aid package: $4347**

ABOUT THE INSTITUTION Proprietary, coed. Awards: bachelor's and master's degrees and post-master's certificates. 23 undergraduate majors. Total enrollment: 2,948. Undergraduates: 1,645. Freshmen: 39. Both federal and institutional methodology are used as a basis for awarding need-based institutional aid.

UNDERGRADUATE EXPENSES for 2006–07 ***Application fee:*** $45. ***Tuition:*** full-time $9750. ***Payment plan:*** Deferred payment.

FRESHMAN FINANCIAL AID (Fall 2005) ***Average financial aid package:*** $2757 (excluding resources awarded to replace EFC).

UNDERGRADUATE FINANCIAL AID (Fall 2005) ***Average financial aid package:*** $4347 (excluding resources awarded to replace EFC).

GIFT AID (NEED-BASED) ***Total amount:*** $1,024,162 (100% federal). ***Receiving aid:*** Freshmen: 34; All full-time undergraduates: 458. ***Average award:*** Freshmen: $2372; Undergraduates: $2226. ***Scholarships, grants, and awards:*** Federal Pell, FSEOG, state, private, college/university gift aid from institutional funds, Academic Competitiveness Grant and National Science and Mathematics Access to Retain Talent (SMART).

GIFT AID (NON-NEED-BASED) ***Receiving aid:*** Freshmen: 1; Undergraduates: 31. ***Scholarships, grants, and awards by category:*** *Academic Interests/Achievement:* business, computer science, health fields, social sciences. ***Tuition waivers:*** Full or partial for employees or children of employees.

LOANS ***Student loans:*** $25,476,170 (42% need-based, 58% non-need-based). ***Programs:*** FFEL (Subsidized and Unsubsidized Stafford, PLUS), Perkins.

APPLYING FOR FINANCIAL AID ***Required financial aid forms:*** FAFSA, institution's own form. ***Financial aid deadline:*** Continuous. ***Notification date:*** Continuous beginning 7/1.

CONTACT ACS/AFS, University of Phoenix–Denver Campus, 875 West Elliot Road, Suite 116, Tempe, AZ 85284, 480-735-3000 or toll-free 800-776-4867 (in-state), 800-228-7240 (out-of-state). *Fax:* 480-940-2060.

UNIVERSITY OF PHOENIX–FORT LAUDERDALE CAMPUS

Fort Lauderdale, FL

Tuition & fees: $10,058 **Average undergraduate aid package: $4226**

ABOUT THE INSTITUTION Proprietary, coed. Awards: bachelor's and master's degrees. 14 undergraduate majors. Total enrollment: 3,121. Undergraduates: 2,343. Freshmen: 148. Both federal and institutional methodology are used as a basis for awarding need-based institutional aid.

UNDERGRADUATE EXPENSES for 2006–07 ***Application fee:*** $45. ***Tuition:*** full-time $10,058. ***Payment plan:*** Deferred payment.

FRESHMAN FINANCIAL AID (Fall 2005) ***Average financial aid package:*** $2761 (excluding resources awarded to replace EFC).

UNDERGRADUATE FINANCIAL AID (Fall 2005) ***Average financial aid package:*** $4226 (excluding resources awarded to replace EFC).

GIFT AID (NEED-BASED) ***Total amount:*** $1,873,029 (99% federal, 1% state). ***Receiving aid:*** Freshmen: 109; All full-time undergraduates: 818. ***Average award:*** Freshmen: $2038; Undergraduates: $2290. ***Scholarships, grants, and awards:*** Federal Pell, FSEOG, state, private, college/university gift aid from institutional funds, Academic Competitiveness Grant and National Science and Mathematics Access to Retain Talent (SMART).

GIFT AID (NON-NEED-BASED) ***Receiving aid:*** Freshmen: 2; Undergraduates: 20. ***Scholarships, grants, and awards by category:*** *Academic Interests/Achievement:* business, computer science, education, health fields, social sciences. ***Tuition waivers:*** Full or partial for employees or children of employees.

LOANS ***Student loans:*** $19,817,245 (44% need-based, 56% non-need-based). ***Programs:*** FFEL (Subsidized and Unsubsidized Stafford, PLUS), Perkins.

APPLYING FOR FINANCIAL AID ***Required financial aid forms:*** FAFSA, institution's own form. ***Financial aid deadline:*** Continuous. ***Notification date:*** Continuous beginning 7/1.

CONTACT ACS/AFS, University of Phoenix–Fort Lauderdale Campus, 875 West Elliot Road, Suite 116, Tempe, AZ 85284, 480-735-3000 or toll-free 800-228-7240. *Fax:* 480-940-2060.

UNIVERSITY OF PHOENIX–HAWAII CAMPUS

Honolulu, HI

Tuition & fees: $11,700 **Average undergraduate aid package: $4557**

ABOUT THE INSTITUTION Proprietary, coed. Awards: bachelor's and master's degrees (courses conducted at 121 campuses and learning centers in 25 states). 29 undergraduate majors. Total enrollment: 1,730. Undergraduates: 796. Freshmen: 14. Both federal and institutional methodology are used as a basis for awarding need-based institutional aid.

UNDERGRADUATE EXPENSES for 2006–07 ***Application fee:*** $45. ***Tuition:*** full-time $11,700. ***Payment plan:*** Deferred payment.

FRESHMAN FINANCIAL AID (Fall 2005) ***Average financial aid package:*** $2796 (excluding resources awarded to replace EFC).

UNDERGRADUATE FINANCIAL AID (Fall 2005) ***Average financial aid package:*** $4557 (excluding resources awarded to replace EFC).

GIFT AID (NEED-BASED) ***Total amount:*** $780,161 (100% federal). ***Receiving aid:*** Freshmen: 50; All full-time undergraduates: 348. ***Average award:*** Freshmen: $1895; Undergraduates: $2242. ***Scholarships, grants, and awards:*** Federal Pell, FSEOG, state, private, college/university gift aid from institutional funds, Academic Competitiveness Grant and National Science and Mathematics Access to Retain Talent (SMART).

GIFT AID (NON-NEED-BASED) ***Total amount:*** $6,245,010 (99% federal, 1% state). ***Receiving aid:*** Freshmen: 1; Undergraduates: 14. ***Scholarships, grants, and awards by category:*** *Academic Interests/Achievement:* business, computer science, health fields, social sciences. ***Tuition waivers:*** Full or partial for employees or children of employees.

LOANS ***Student loans:*** $10,498,366 (48% need-based, 52% non-need-based). ***Programs:*** FFEL (Subsidized and Unsubsidized Stafford, PLUS), Perkins.

APPLYING FOR FINANCIAL AID ***Required financial aid forms:*** FAFSA, institution's own form. ***Financial aid deadline:*** Continuous. ***Notification date:*** Continuous beginning 7/1.

CONTACT ACS/AFS, University of Phoenix–Hawaii Campus, 875 West Elliot Road, Suite 116, Tempe, AZ 85284, 480-735-3000 or toll-free 800-776-4867 (in-state), 800-228-7240 (out-of-state). *Fax:* 480-940-2060.

UNIVERSITY OF PHOENIX–HOUSTON CAMPUS

Houston, TX

Tuition & fees: $11,190 **Average undergraduate aid package: $4713**

ABOUT THE INSTITUTION Proprietary, coed. Awards: bachelor's and master's degrees. 27 undergraduate majors. Total enrollment: 4,532. Undergraduates: 3,702. Freshmen: 134. Both federal and institutional methodology are used as a basis for awarding need-based institutional aid.

UNDERGRADUATE EXPENSES for 2006–07 ***Application fee:*** $45. ***Tuition:*** full-time $11,190; part-time $373 per credit. ***Payment plan:*** Deferred payment.

FRESHMAN FINANCIAL AID (Fall 2005) ***Average financial aid package:*** $2872 (excluding resources awarded to replace EFC).

UNDERGRADUATE FINANCIAL AID (Fall 2005) ***Average financial aid package:*** $4713 (excluding resources awarded to replace EFC).

GIFT AID (NEED-BASED) ***Total amount:*** $4,103,007 (100% federal). ***Receiving aid:*** Freshmen: 226; All full-time undergraduates: 1,707. ***Average award:*** Freshmen: $2009; Undergraduates: $2404. ***Scholarships, grants, and awards:*** Federal Pell, FSEOG, state, private, college/university gift aid from institutional funds, Academic Competitiveness Grant and National Science and Mathematics Access to Retain Talent (SMART).

GIFT AID (NON-NEED-BASED) ***Receiving aid:*** Freshmen: 6; Undergraduates: 83. ***Scholarships, grants, and awards by category:*** *Academic Interests/Achievement:* business, computer science, health fields, social sciences. ***Tuition waivers:*** Full or partial for employees or children of employees.

LOANS ***Student loans:*** $33,926,013 (46% need-based, 54% non-need-based). ***Programs:*** FFEL (Subsidized and Unsubsidized Stafford, PLUS), Perkins.

APPLYING FOR FINANCIAL AID ***Required financial aid forms:*** FAFSA, institution's own form. ***Financial aid deadline:*** Continuous. ***Notification date:*** Continuous beginning 7/1.

CONTACT ACS/AFS, University of Phoenix–Houston Campus, 875 West Elliot Road, Suite 116, Tempe, AZ 85284, 480-735-3000 or toll-free 800-776-4867 (in-state), 800-228-7240 (out-of-state). *Fax:* 480-940-2060.

UNIVERSITY OF PHOENIX–IDAHO CAMPUS

Meridian, ID

Tuition & fees: $10,200 **Average undergraduate aid package: $4067**

ABOUT THE INSTITUTION Proprietary, coed. Awards: bachelor's and master's degrees. 23 undergraduate majors. Total enrollment: 659. Undergraduates: 532. Freshmen: 4. Both federal and institutional methodology are used as a basis for awarding need-based institutional aid.

UNDERGRADUATE EXPENSES for 2006–07 ***Application fee:*** $45. ***Tuition:*** full-time $10,200; part-time $340 per credit. ***Payment plan:*** Deferred payment.

FRESHMAN FINANCIAL AID (Fall 2005) ***Average financial aid package:*** $2118 (excluding resources awarded to replace EFC).

UNDERGRADUATE FINANCIAL AID (Fall 2005) ***Average financial aid package:*** $4067 (excluding resources awarded to replace EFC).

GIFT AID (NEED-BASED) ***Total amount:*** $641,732 (100% federal). ***Receiving aid:*** Freshmen: 35; All full-time undergraduates: 299. ***Average award:*** Freshmen: $1543; Undergraduates: $2146. ***Scholarships, grants, and awards:*** Federal Pell, FSEOG, state, private, college/university gift aid from institutional funds, Academic Competitiveness Grant and National Science and Mathematics Access to Retain Talent (SMART).

GIFT AID (NON-NEED-BASED) ***Receiving aid:*** Undergraduates: 6. ***Scholarships, grants, and awards by category:*** *Academic Interests/Achievement:* business, computer science, health fields. ***Tuition waivers:*** Full or partial for employees or children of employees.

LOANS ***Student loans:*** $2,634,574 (90% need-based, 10% non-need-based). ***Programs:*** FFEL (Subsidized and Unsubsidized Stafford, PLUS), Perkins.

APPLYING FOR FINANCIAL AID ***Required financial aid forms:*** FAFSA, institution's own form. ***Financial aid deadline:*** Continuous. ***Notification date:*** Continuous beginning 7/1.

CONTACT ACS/AFS, University of Phoenix–Idaho Campus, 875 West Elliot Road, Suite 116, Tempe, AZ 85284, 480-735-3000 or toll-free 800-776-4867 (in-state), 800-228-7240 (out-of-state). *Fax:* 480-940-2060.

UNIVERSITY OF PHOENIX–INDIANAPOLIS CAMPUS

Indianapolis, IN

Tuition & fees: $10,320 **Average undergraduate aid package: $4196**

ABOUT THE INSTITUTION Proprietary, coed. Awards: bachelor's and master's degrees. 30 undergraduate majors. Total enrollment: 602. Undergraduates: 497. Freshmen: 41. Both federal and institutional methodology are used as a basis for awarding need-based institutional aid.

UNDERGRADUATE EXPENSES for 2006–07 ***Application fee:*** $45. ***Tuition:*** full-time $10,320; part-time $336 per credit. ***Payment plan:*** Deferred payment.

FRESHMAN FINANCIAL AID (Fall 2005) ***Average financial aid package:*** $2925 (excluding resources awarded to replace EFC).

UNDERGRADUATE FINANCIAL AID (Fall 2005) ***Average financial aid package:*** $4196 (excluding resources awarded to replace EFC).

GIFT AID (NEED-BASED) ***Total amount:*** $569,989 (100% federal). ***Receiving aid:*** Freshmen: 65; All full-time undergraduates: 255. ***Average award:*** Freshmen: $1963; Undergraduates: $2235. ***Scholarships, grants, and awards:*** Federal Pell, FSEOG, state, private, college/university gift aid from institutional funds, Academic Competitiveness Grant and National Science and Mathematics Access to Retain Talent (SMART).

GIFT AID (NON-NEED-BASED) ***Receiving aid:*** Freshmen: 1; Undergraduates: 15. ***Scholarships, grants, and awards by category:*** *Academic Interests/Achievement:* business, computer science, health fields, social sciences. ***Tuition waivers:*** Full or partial for employees or children of employees.

LOANS ***Student loans:*** $4,177,298 (43% need-based, 57% non-need-based). ***Programs:*** FFEL (Subsidized and Unsubsidized Stafford, PLUS), Perkins.

APPLYING FOR FINANCIAL AID ***Required financial aid forms:*** FAFSA, institution's own form. ***Financial aid deadline:*** Continuous. ***Notification date:*** Continuous beginning 7/1.

CONTACT ACS/AFS, University of Phoenix–Indianapolis Campus, 875 West Elliot Road, Suite 116, Tempe, AZ 85284, 480-735-3000 or toll-free 800-776-4867 (in-state), 800-228-7240 (out-of-state). *Fax:* 480-940-2060.

UNIVERSITY OF PHOENIX–KANSAS CITY CAMPUS

Kansas City, MO

Tuition & fees: $11,064 **Average undergraduate aid package: $4111**

ABOUT THE INSTITUTION Proprietary, coed. Awards: bachelor's and master's degrees. 21 undergraduate majors. Total enrollment: 1,201. Undergraduates: 928. Freshmen: 33. Both federal and institutional methodology are used as a basis for awarding need-based institutional aid.

UNDERGRADUATE EXPENSES for 2006–07 ***Application fee:*** $45. ***Tuition:*** full-time $11,064; part-time $373 per credit. ***Payment plan:*** Deferred payment.

FRESHMAN FINANCIAL AID (Fall 2005) ***Average financial aid package:*** $2473 (excluding resources awarded to replace EFC).

UNDERGRADUATE FINANCIAL AID (Fall 2005) ***Average financial aid package:*** $4111 (excluding resources awarded to replace EFC).

GIFT AID (NEED-BASED) ***Total amount:*** $1,040,238 (100% federal). ***Receiving aid:*** Freshmen: 69; All full-time undergraduates: 471. ***Average award:*** Freshmen: $1978; Undergraduates: $2209. ***Scholarships, grants, and awards:*** Federal Pell, FSEOG, state, private, college/university gift aid from institutional funds, Academic Competitiveness Grant and National Science and Mathematics Access to Retain Talent (SMART).

GIFT AID (NON-NEED-BASED) ***Receiving aid:*** Undergraduates: 8. ***Scholarships, grants, and awards by category:*** *Academic Interests/Achievement:* business, computer science, health fields, social sciences. ***Tuition waivers:*** Full or partial for employees or children of employees.

LOANS ***Student loans:*** $8,981,200 (46% need-based, 54% non-need-based). ***Programs:*** FFEL (Subsidized and Unsubsidized Stafford, PLUS), Perkins.

APPLYING FOR FINANCIAL AID ***Required financial aid forms:*** FAFSA, institution's own form. ***Financial aid deadline:*** Continuous. ***Notification date:*** Continuous beginning 7/1.

CONTACT ACS/AFS, University of Phoenix–Kansas City Campus, 875 West Elliot Road, Suite 116, Tempe, AZ 85284, 480-735-3000 or toll-free 800-776-4867 (in-state), 800-228-7240 (out-of-state). *Fax:* 480-940-2060.

UNIVERSITY OF PHOENIX–LITTLE ROCK CAMPUS

Little Rock, AR

Tuition & fees: $9750 **Average undergraduate aid package: $4311**

ABOUT THE INSTITUTION Proprietary, coed. Awards: bachelor's and master's degrees. 5 undergraduate majors. Total enrollment: 498. Undergraduates: 328. Freshmen: 21. Both federal and institutional methodology are used as a basis for awarding need-based institutional aid.

UNDERGRADUATE EXPENSES for 2006–07 ***Application fee:*** $45. ***Tuition:*** full-time $9750; part-time $325 per credit. ***Payment plan:*** Deferred payment.

FRESHMAN FINANCIAL AID (Fall 2005) ***Average financial aid package:*** $2649 (excluding resources awarded to replace EFC).

UNDERGRADUATE FINANCIAL AID (Fall 2005) ***Average financial aid package:*** $4311 (excluding resources awarded to replace EFC).

GIFT AID (NEED-BASED) ***Total amount:*** $446,668 (100% federal). ***Receiving aid:*** Freshmen: 39; All full-time undergraduates: 211. ***Average award:*** Freshmen: $1939; Undergraduates: $2117. ***Scholarships, grants, and awards:*** Federal Pell, FSEOG, state, private, college/university gift aid from institutional funds, Academic Competitiveness Grant and National Science and Mathematics Access to Retain Talent (SMART).

GIFT AID (NON-NEED-BASED) ***Receiving aid:*** Freshmen: 1; Undergraduates: 7. ***Scholarships, grants, and awards by category:*** *Academic Interests/Achievement:* business, communication, computer science, social sciences. ***Tuition waivers:*** Full or partial for employees or children of employees.

LOANS ***Student loans:*** $3,944,137 (48% need-based, 52% non-need-based). ***Programs:*** FFEL (Subsidized and Unsubsidized Stafford, PLUS), Perkins.

APPLYING FOR FINANCIAL AID ***Required financial aid forms:*** FAFSA, institution's own form. ***Financial aid deadline:*** Continuous. ***Notification date:*** Continuous beginning 7/1.

CONTACT ACS/AFS, University of Phoenix–Little Rock Campus, 875 West Elliot Road, Suite 116, Tempe, AZ 85284, 480-735-3000 or toll-free 800-776-4867 (in-state), 800-228-7240 (out-of-state). *Fax:* 480-940-2060.

UNIVERSITY OF PHOENIX–LOUISIANA CAMPUS

Metairie, LA

Tuition & fees: $9090 **Average undergraduate aid package: $4656**

ABOUT THE INSTITUTION Proprietary, coed. Awards: bachelor's and master's degrees. 31 undergraduate majors. Total enrollment: 2,747. Undergraduates: 2,085. Freshmen: 114. Both federal and institutional methodology are used as a basis for awarding need-based institutional aid.

UNDERGRADUATE EXPENSES for 2006–07 ***Application fee:*** $110. ***Tuition:*** full-time $9090; part-time $303 per credit. ***Payment plan:*** Deferred payment.

FRESHMAN FINANCIAL AID (Fall 2005) ***Average financial aid package:*** $3011 (excluding resources awarded to replace EFC).

UNDERGRADUATE FINANCIAL AID (Fall 2005) ***Average financial aid package:*** $4656 (excluding resources awarded to replace EFC).

GIFT AID (NEED-BASED) ***Total amount:*** $2,689,604 (100% federal). ***Receiving aid:*** Freshmen: 179; All full-time undergraduates: 1,099. ***Average award:*** Freshmen: $1938; Undergraduates: $2447. ***Scholarships, grants, and awards:*** Federal Pell, FSEOG, state, private, college/university gift aid from institutional funds, Academic Competitiveness Grant and National Science and Mathematics Access to Retain Talent (SMART).

GIFT AID (NON-NEED-BASED) ***Receiving aid:*** Freshmen: 2; Undergraduates: 35. ***Scholarships, grants, and awards by category:*** *Academic Interests/Achievement:* business, computer science, health fields, social sciences. ***Tuition waivers:*** Full or partial for employees or children of employees.

LOANS ***Student loans:*** $14,831,035 (47% need-based, 53% non-need-based). ***Programs:*** FFEL (Subsidized and Unsubsidized Stafford, PLUS), Perkins.

APPLYING FOR FINANCIAL AID ***Required financial aid forms:*** FAFSA, institution's own form. ***Financial aid deadline:*** Continuous. ***Notification date:*** Continuous beginning 7/1.

CONTACT ACS/AFS, University of Phoenix–Louisiana Campus, 875 West Elliot Road, Suite 116, Tempe, AZ 85284, 480-735-3000 or toll-free 800-776-4867 (in-state), 800-228-7240 (out-of-state). *Fax:* 480-940-2060.

UNIVERSITY OF PHOENIX–MARYLAND CAMPUS

Columbia, MD

Tuition & fees: $11,820 **Average undergraduate aid package: $3797**

ABOUT THE INSTITUTION Proprietary, coed. Awards: bachelor's and master's degrees. 22 undergraduate majors. Total enrollment: 1,823. Undergraduates: 1,434. Freshmen: 70. Both federal and institutional methodology are used as a basis for awarding need-based institutional aid.

UNDERGRADUATE EXPENSES for 2006–07 ***Application fee:*** $45. ***Tuition:*** full-time $11,820. ***Payment plan:*** Deferred payment.

FRESHMAN FINANCIAL AID (Fall 2005) ***Average financial aid package:*** $2362 (excluding resources awarded to replace EFC).

UNDERGRADUATE FINANCIAL AID (Fall 2005) ***Average financial aid package:*** $3797 (excluding resources awarded to replace EFC).

GIFT AID (NEED-BASED) ***Total amount:*** $828,848 (100% federal). ***Receiving aid:*** Freshmen: 86; All full-time undergraduates: 400. ***Average award:*** Freshmen: $1682; Undergraduates: $2072. ***Scholarships, grants, and awards:*** Federal Pell, FSEOG, state, private, college/university gift aid from institutional funds, Academic Competitiveness Grant and National Science and Mathematics Access to Retain Talent (SMART).

GIFT AID (NON-NEED-BASED) ***Receiving aid:*** Freshmen: 3; Undergraduates: 27. ***Scholarships, grants, and awards by category:*** *Academic Interests/Achievement:* business, computer science. ***Tuition waivers:*** Full or partial for employees or children of employees.

LOANS ***Student loans:*** $10,574,074 (45% need-based, 55% non-need-based). ***Programs:*** FFEL (Subsidized and Unsubsidized Stafford, PLUS), Perkins.

APPLYING FOR FINANCIAL AID ***Required financial aid forms:*** FAFSA, institution's own form. ***Financial aid deadline:*** Continuous. ***Notification date:*** Continuous beginning 7/1.

CONTACT ACS/AFS, University of Phoenix–Maryland Campus, 875 West Elliot Road, Suite 116, Tempe, AZ 85284, 480-735-3000 or toll-free 800-776-4867 (in-state), 800-228-7240 (out-of-state). *Fax:* 480-940-2060.

UNIVERSITY OF PHOENIX–METRO DETROIT CAMPUS

Troy, MI

Tuition & fees: $11,700 **Average undergraduate aid package: $4337**

ABOUT THE INSTITUTION Proprietary, coed. Awards: bachelor's and master's degrees. 22 undergraduate majors. Total enrollment: 3,918. Undergraduates: 2,948. Freshmen: 275. Both federal and institutional methodology are used as a basis for awarding need-based institutional aid.

UNDERGRADUATE EXPENSES for 2006–07 ***Application fee:*** $45. ***Tuition:*** full-time $11,700. ***Payment plan:*** Deferred payment.

FRESHMAN FINANCIAL AID (Fall 2005) ***Average financial aid package:*** $2632 (excluding resources awarded to replace EFC).

UNDERGRADUATE FINANCIAL AID (Fall 2005) ***Average financial aid package:*** $4337 (excluding resources awarded to replace EFC).

GIFT AID (NEED-BASED) ***Total amount:*** $3,584,212 (100% federal). ***Receiving aid:*** Freshmen: 350; All full-time undergraduates: 1,501. ***Average award:*** Freshmen: $1962; Undergraduates: $2388. ***Scholarships, grants, and awards:*** Federal Pell, FSEOG, state, private, college/university gift aid from institutional funds, Academic Competitiveness Grant and National Science and Mathematics Access to Retain Talent (SMART).

GIFT AID (NON-NEED-BASED) ***Receiving aid:*** Freshmen: 3; Undergraduates: 52. ***Scholarships, grants, and awards by category:*** *Academic Interests/Achievement:* business, computer science, health fields, social sciences. ***Tuition waivers:*** Full or partial for employees or children of employees.

LOANS ***Student loans:*** $28,938,774 (46% need-based, 54% non-need-based). ***Programs:*** FFEL (Subsidized and Unsubsidized Stafford, PLUS), Perkins.

APPLYING FOR FINANCIAL AID ***Required financial aid forms:*** FAFSA, institution's own form. ***Financial aid deadline:*** Continuous. ***Notification date:*** Continuous beginning 7/1.

CONTACT ACS/AFS, University of Phoenix–Metro Detroit Campus, 875 West Elliot Road, Suite 116, Tempe, AZ 85284, 480-735-3000 or toll-free 800-776-4867 (in-state), 800-228-7240 (out-of-state). *Fax:* 480-940-2060.

UNIVERSITY OF PHOENIX–NASHVILLE CAMPUS

Nashville, TN

Tuition & fees: $10,470 **Average undergraduate aid package: $3865**

ABOUT THE INSTITUTION Proprietary, coed. Awards: bachelor's and master's degrees. 11 undergraduate majors. Total enrollment: 1,290. Undergraduates: 957. Freshmen: 46. Both federal and institutional methodology are used as a basis for awarding need-based institutional aid.

UNDERGRADUATE EXPENSES for 2006–07 ***Application fee:*** $45. ***Tuition:*** full-time $10,470; part-time $349 per credit. ***Payment plan:*** Deferred payment.

FRESHMAN FINANCIAL AID (Fall 2005) ***Average financial aid package:*** $2406 (excluding resources awarded to replace EFC).

UNDERGRADUATE FINANCIAL AID (Fall 2005) ***Average financial aid package:*** $3865 (excluding resources awarded to replace EFC).

GIFT AID (NEED-BASED) ***Total amount:*** $855,514 (100% federal). ***Receiving aid:*** Freshmen: 88; All full-time undergraduates: 418. ***Average award:*** Freshmen: $1611; Undergraduates: $2047. ***Scholarships, grants, and awards:*** Federal Pell, FSEOG, state, private, college/university gift aid from institutional funds, Academic Competitiveness Grant and National Science and Mathematics Access to Retain Talent (SMART).

GIFT AID (NON-NEED-BASED) ***Receiving aid:*** Freshmen: 1; Undergraduates: 7. ***Scholarships, grants, and awards by category:*** *Academic Interests/Achievement:* business, communication, computer science, education, health fields, social sciences. ***Tuition waivers:*** Full or partial for employees or children of employees.

LOANS ***Student loans:*** $9,071,863 (44% need-based, 56% non-need-based). ***Programs:*** FFEL (Subsidized and Unsubsidized Stafford, PLUS), Perkins.

APPLYING FOR FINANCIAL AID ***Required financial aid forms:*** FAFSA, institution's own form. ***Financial aid deadline:*** Continuous. ***Notification date:*** Continuous beginning 7/1.

CONTACT ACS/AFS, University of Phoenix–Nashville Campus, 875 West Elliot Road, Suite 116, Tempe, AZ 85284, 480-735-3000 or toll-free 800-776-4867 (in-state), 800-228-7240 (out-of-state). *Fax:* 480-940-2060.

UNIVERSITY OF PHOENIX–NEVADA CAMPUS

Las Vegas, NV

Tuition & fees: $10,200 **Average undergraduate aid package: $4273**

ABOUT THE INSTITUTION Proprietary, coed. Awards: bachelor's and master's degrees and post-master's certificates. 27 undergraduate majors. Total enrollment: 3,484. Undergraduates: 2,379. Freshmen: 76. Both federal and institutional methodology are used as a basis for awarding need-based institutional aid.

UNDERGRADUATE EXPENSES for 2006–07 ***Application fee:*** $45. ***Tuition:*** full-time $10,200. ***Payment plan:*** Deferred payment.

FRESHMAN FINANCIAL AID (Fall 2005) ***Average financial aid package:*** $2530 (excluding resources awarded to replace EFC).

UNDERGRADUATE FINANCIAL AID (Fall 2005) ***Average financial aid package:*** $4273 (excluding resources awarded to replace EFC).

GIFT AID (NEED-BASED) ***Total amount:*** $20,732,223 (10% federal). ***Receiving aid:*** Freshmen: 124; All full-time undergraduates: 935. ***Average award:*** Freshmen: $1852; Undergraduates: $2217. ***Scholarships, grants, and awards:*** Federal Pell, FSEOG, state.

GIFT AID (NON-NEED-BASED) ***Receiving aid:*** Freshmen: 2; Undergraduates: 30. ***Scholarships, grants, and awards by category:*** *Academic Interests/Achievement:* business, computer science, education, health fields, social sciences. ***Tuition waivers:*** Full or partial for employees or children of employees.

LOANS ***Student loans:*** $27,274,266 (44% need-based, 56% non-need-based). ***Programs:*** Federal Direct (Unsubsidized Stafford, PLUS), Perkins.

APPLYING FOR FINANCIAL AID ***Required financial aid forms:*** FAFSA, institution's own form. ***Financial aid deadline:*** Continuous. ***Notification date:*** Continuous.

CONTACT ACS/AFS, University of Phoenix–Nevada Campus, 875 West Elliot Road, Suite 116, Tempe, AZ 85284, 480-735-3000 or toll-free 800-776-4867 (in-state), 800-228-7240 (out-of-state). *Fax:* 480-940-2060.

UNIVERSITY OF PHOENIX–NEW MEXICO CAMPUS

Albuquerque, NM

Tuition & fees: $9750 **Average undergraduate aid package: $5497**

ABOUT THE INSTITUTION Proprietary, coed. Awards: bachelor's and master's degrees. 12 undergraduate majors. Total enrollment: 4,586. Undergraduates: 3,537. Freshmen: 150. Both federal and institutional methodology are used as a basis for awarding need-based institutional aid.

UNDERGRADUATE EXPENSES for 2006–07 ***Application fee:*** $45. ***Tuition:*** full-time $9750. ***Payment plan:*** Deferred payment.

FRESHMAN FINANCIAL AID (Fall 2005) ***Average financial aid package:*** $3440 (excluding resources awarded to replace EFC).

UNDERGRADUATE FINANCIAL AID (Fall 2005) ***Average financial aid package:*** $5497 (excluding resources awarded to replace EFC).

GIFT AID (NEED-BASED) ***Total amount:*** $6,393,535 (100% federal). ***Receiving aid:*** Freshmen: 268; All full-time undergraduates: 2,327. ***Average award:*** Freshmen: $2166; Undergraduates: $2748. ***Scholarships, grants, and awards:*** Federal Pell, FSEOG, state, private, college/university gift aid from institutional funds, Academic Competitiveness Grant and National Science and Mathematics Access to Retain Talent (SMART).

GIFT AID (NON-NEED-BASED) ***Receiving aid:*** Undergraduates: 66. ***Scholarships, grants, and awards by category:*** *Academic Interests/Achievement:* business, computer science, health fields, social sciences. ***Tuition waivers:*** Full or partial for employees or children of employees.

LOANS ***Student loans:*** $38,957,858 (47% need-based, 53% non-need-based). ***Programs:*** FFEL (Subsidized and Unsubsidized Stafford, PLUS), Perkins.

APPLYING FOR FINANCIAL AID ***Required financial aid forms:*** FAFSA, institution's own form. ***Financial aid deadline:*** Continuous. ***Notification date:*** Continuous beginning 7/1.

CONTACT ACS/AFS, University of Phoenix–New Mexico Campus, 875 West Elliot Road, Suite 116, Tempe, AZ 85284, 480-735-3000 or toll-free 800-776-4867 (in-state), 800-228-7240 (out-of-state). *Fax:* 480-940-2060.

UNIVERSITY OF PHOENIX–NORTHERN VIRGINIA CAMPUS

Reston, VA

ABOUT THE INSTITUTION Proprietary, coed. Awards: bachelor's and master's degrees. 15 undergraduate majors. Total enrollment: 938. Undergraduates: 717. Freshmen: 7.

GIFT AID (NEED-BASED) ***Scholarships, grants, and awards:*** Federal Pell, FSEOG, state, private, college/university gift aid from institutional funds, Academic Competitiveness Grant and National Science and Mathematics Access to Retain Talent (SMART).

GIFT AID (NON-NEED-BASED) ***Scholarships, grants, and awards by category:*** *Academic Interests/Achievement:* business, computer science, health fields, social sciences.

LOANS ***Programs:*** FFEL (Subsidized and Unsubsidized Stafford, PLUS).

APPLYING FOR FINANCIAL AID ***Required financial aid form:*** institution's own form.

CONTACT ACS/AFS, University of Phoenix–Northern Virginia Campus, 875 W. Elliott Road, Suite 116, Tempe, AZ 85284, 480-735-3000 or toll-free 800-776-4867 (in-state), 800-228-7240 (out-of-state). *Fax:* 480-940-2060.

UNIVERSITY OF PHOENIX–NORTH FLORIDA CAMPUS

Jacksonville, FL

ABOUT THE INSTITUTION Proprietary, coed. Awards: bachelor's and master's degrees. 16 undergraduate majors. Total enrollment: 2,211. Undergraduates: 1,632. Freshmen: 35.

GIFT AID (NEED-BASED) ***Scholarships, grants, and awards:*** Federal Pell, FSEOG, state, private, college/university gift aid from institutional funds, Academic Competitiveness Grant and National Science and Mathematics Access to Retain Talent (SMART).

GIFT AID (NON-NEED-BASED) ***Scholarships, grants, and awards by category:*** *Academic Interests/Achievement:* business, computer science, health fields, social sciences.

LOANS ***Programs:*** FFEL (Subsidized and Unsubsidized Stafford, PLUS), Perkins.

APPLYING FOR FINANCIAL AID ***Required financial aid form:*** institution's own form.

CONTACT ACS/AFS, University of Phoenix–North Florida Campus, 875 West Elliot Road, Suite 116, Tempe, AZ 85284, 480-735-3000 or toll-free 800-776-4867 (in-state), 800-894-1758 (out-of-state). *Fax:* 480-940-2060.

UNIVERSITY OF PHOENIX–OKLAHOMA CITY CAMPUS

Oklahoma City, OK

Tuition & fees: $9750 **Average undergraduate aid package: $4443**

ABOUT THE INSTITUTION Proprietary, coed. Awards: bachelor's and master's degrees. 16 undergraduate majors. Total enrollment: 1,080. Undergraduates: 915. Freshmen: 76. Both federal and institutional methodology are used as a basis for awarding need-based institutional aid.

UNDERGRADUATE EXPENSES for 2006–07 ***Application fee:*** $45. ***Tuition:*** full-time $9750. ***Payment plan:*** Deferred payment.

FRESHMAN FINANCIAL AID (Fall 2005) ***Average financial aid package:*** $2731 (excluding resources awarded to replace EFC).

UNDERGRADUATE FINANCIAL AID (Fall 2005) ***Average financial aid package:*** $4443 (excluding resources awarded to replace EFC).

GIFT AID (NEED-BASED) ***Total amount:*** $1,441,737 (100% federal). ***Receiving aid:*** Freshmen: 145; All full-time undergraduates: 617. ***Average award:*** Freshmen: $1986; Undergraduates: $2337. ***Scholarships, grants, and awards:*** Federal Pell, FSEOG, state, private, college/university gift aid from institutional funds, Academic Competitiveness Grant and National Science and Mathematics Access to Retain Talent (SMART).

GIFT AID (NON-NEED-BASED) ***Receiving aid:*** Undergraduates: 13. ***Scholarships, grants, and awards by category:*** *Academic Interests/Achievement:* business, computer science, health fields, social sciences. ***Tuition waivers:*** Full or partial for employees or children of employees.

LOANS ***Student loans:*** $7,397,715 (47% need-based, 53% non-need-based). ***Programs:*** FFEL (Subsidized and Unsubsidized Stafford, PLUS), Perkins.

APPLYING FOR FINANCIAL AID ***Required financial aid forms:*** FAFSA, institution's own form. ***Financial aid deadline:*** Continuous. ***Notification date:*** Continuous beginning 7/1.

CONTACT ACS/AFS, University of Phoenix–Oklahoma City Campus, 875 West Elliot Road, Suite 116, Tempe, AZ 85284, 480-735-3000 or toll-free 800-776-4867 (in-state), 800-228-7240 (out-of-state). *Fax:* 480-940-2060.

UNIVERSITY OF PHOENIX ONLINE CAMPUS

Phoenix, AZ

Tuition & fees: $14,180 **Average undergraduate aid package: $3846**

ABOUT THE INSTITUTION Proprietary, coed. Awards: associate, bachelor's, master's, and doctoral degrees and post-bachelor's and post-master's certificates. 8 undergraduate majors. Total enrollment: 160,150. Undergraduates: 113,387. Freshmen: 11,518. Both federal and institutional methodology are used as a basis for awarding need-based institutional aid.

UNDERGRADUATE EXPENSES for 2006–07 ***Application fee:*** $45. ***Tuition:*** full-time $14,180; part-time $473 per credit. Full-time tuition and fees vary according to program. ***Payment plan:*** Deferred payment.

FRESHMAN FINANCIAL AID (Fall 2005) ***Average financial aid package:*** $2200 (excluding resources awarded to replace EFC).

UNDERGRADUATE FINANCIAL AID (Fall 2005) ***Average financial aid package:*** $3846 (excluding resources awarded to replace EFC).

GIFT AID (NEED-BASED) ***Total amount:*** $59,662,765 (98% federal, 2% state). ***Receiving aid:*** Freshmen: 8,423; All full-time undergraduates: 31,089. ***Average award:*** Freshmen: $1655; Undergraduates: $1919. ***Scholarships, grants, and awards:*** Federal Pell, FSEOG, state, private, college/university gift aid from institutional funds, Academic Competitiveness Grant and National Science and Mathematics Access to Retain Talent (SMART).

GIFT AID (NON-NEED-BASED) ***Receiving aid:*** Freshmen: 73; Undergraduates: 1,874. ***Scholarships, grants, and awards by category:*** *Academic Interests/Achievement:* business, communication, computer science, education, health fields, social sciences. ***Tuition waivers:*** Full or partial for employees or children of employees.

LOANS ***Student loans:*** $801,454,170 (46% need-based, 54% non-need-based). ***Programs:*** FFEL (Subsidized and Unsubsidized Stafford, PLUS), Perkins.

APPLYING FOR FINANCIAL AID ***Required financial aid forms:*** FAFSA, institution's own form. ***Financial aid deadline:*** Continuous. ***Notification date:*** Continuous beginning 7/1.

CONTACT ACS/AFS, University of Phoenix Online Campus, 875 West Elliot Road, Suite 116, Tempe, AZ 85284, 480-735-3000 or toll-free 800-776-4867 (in-state), 800-228-7240 (out-of-state). *Fax:* 480-940-2060.

UNIVERSITY OF PHOENIX–OREGON CAMPUS

Tigard, OR

Tuition & fees: $10,770 **Average undergraduate aid package: $4213**

ABOUT THE INSTITUTION Proprietary, coed. Awards: bachelor's and master's degrees. 18 undergraduate majors. Total enrollment: 1,836. Undergraduates: 1,481. Freshmen: 26. Both federal and institutional methodology are used as a basis for awarding need-based institutional aid.

UNDERGRADUATE EXPENSES for 2006–07 ***Application fee:*** $45. ***Tuition:*** full-time $10,770. ***Payment plan:*** Deferred payment.

FRESHMAN FINANCIAL AID (Fall 2005) ***Average financial aid package:*** $2512 (excluding resources awarded to replace EFC).

UNDERGRADUATE FINANCIAL AID (Fall 2005) ***Average financial aid package:*** $4213 (excluding resources awarded to replace EFC).

GIFT AID (NEED-BASED) ***Total amount:*** $1,330,535 (100% federal). ***Receiving aid:*** Freshmen: 57; All full-time undergraduates: 574. ***Average award:*** Freshmen: $1762; Undergraduates: $23,181. ***Scholarships, grants, and awards:*** Federal Pell, FSEOG, state, private, college/university gift aid from institutional funds, Academic Competitiveness Grant and National Science and Mathematics Access to Retain Talent (SMART).

GIFT AID (NON-NEED-BASED) ***Receiving aid:*** Freshmen: 1; Undergraduates: 21. ***Scholarships, grants, and awards by category:*** *Academic Interests/Achievement:* business, computer science, health fields, social sciences. ***Tuition waivers:*** Full or partial for employees or children of employees.

LOANS ***Student loans:*** $14,298,341 (45% need-based, 55% non-need-based). ***Programs:*** FFEL (Subsidized and Unsubsidized Stafford, PLUS), Perkins.

APPLYING FOR FINANCIAL AID ***Required financial aid forms:*** FAFSA, institution's own form. ***Financial aid deadline:*** Continuous. ***Notification date:*** Continuous.

CONTACT ACS/AFS, University of Phoenix–Oregon Campus, 875 West Elliot Road, Suite 116, Tempe, AZ 85284, 480-735-3000 or toll-free 800-776-4867 (in-state), 800-228-7240 (out-of-state). *Fax:* 480-940-2060.

UNIVERSITY OF PHOENIX–PHILADELPHIA CAMPUS

Wayne, PA

Tuition & fees: $13,050 **Average undergraduate aid package: $3973**

ABOUT THE INSTITUTION Proprietary, coed. Awards: bachelor's and master's degrees. 25 undergraduate majors. Total enrollment: 1,611. Undergraduates: 1,270. Freshmen: 138. Both federal and institutional methodology are used as a basis for awarding need-based institutional aid.

UNDERGRADUATE EXPENSES for 2006–07 ***Application fee:*** $45. ***Tuition:*** full-time $13,050. ***Payment plan:*** Deferred payment.

FRESHMAN FINANCIAL AID (Fall 2005) ***Average financial aid package:*** $2307 (excluding resources awarded to replace EFC).

UNDERGRADUATE FINANCIAL AID (Fall 2005) ***Average financial aid package:*** $3973 (excluding resources awarded to replace EFC).

GIFT AID (NEED-BASED) ***Total amount:*** $1,075,473 (97% federal, 3% state). ***Receiving aid:*** Freshmen: 133; All full-time undergraduates: 534. ***Average award:*** Freshmen: $1743; Undergraduates: $2014. ***Scholarships, grants, and awards:*** Federal Pell, FSEOG, state, private, college/university gift aid from institutional funds, Academic Competitiveness Grant and National Science and Mathematics Access to Retain Talent (SMART).

GIFT AID (NON-NEED-BASED) ***Receiving aid:*** Freshmen: 1; Undergraduates: 11. ***Scholarships, grants, and awards by category:*** *Academic Interests/Achievement:* business, computer science. ***Tuition waivers:*** Full or partial for employees or children of employees.

LOANS ***Student loans:*** $10,278,745 (48% need-based, 52% non-need-based). ***Programs:*** FFEL (Subsidized and Unsubsidized Stafford, PLUS), Perkins.

APPLYING FOR FINANCIAL AID ***Required financial aid forms:*** FAFSA, institution's own form. ***Financial aid deadline:*** Continuous. ***Notification date:*** Continuous beginning 7/1.

CONTACT ACS/AFS, University of Phoenix–Philadelphia Campus, 875 West Elliot Road, Suite 116, Tempe, AZ 85284, 480-735-3000 or toll-free 800-776-4867 (in-state), 800-228-7240 (out-of-state). *Fax:* 480-940-2060.

UNIVERSITY OF PHOENIX–PHOENIX CAMPUS

Phoenix, AZ

Tuition & fees: $9630 **Average undergraduate aid package: $4921**

ABOUT THE INSTITUTION Proprietary, coed. Awards: bachelor's and master's degrees and post-bachelor's and post-master's certificates. 25 undergraduate majors. Total enrollment: 8,497. Undergraduates: 4,910. Freshmen: 144. Both federal and institutional methodology are used as a basis for awarding need-based institutional aid.

UNDERGRADUATE EXPENSES for 2006–07 ***Application fee:*** $45. ***Tuition:*** full-time $9630. ***Payment plan:*** Deferred payment.

FRESHMAN FINANCIAL AID (Fall 2005) ***Average financial aid package:*** $2763 (excluding resources awarded to replace EFC).

UNDERGRADUATE FINANCIAL AID (Fall 2005) ***Average financial aid package:*** $4921 (excluding resources awarded to replace EFC).

GIFT AID (NEED-BASED) ***Total amount:*** $3,661,938 (94% federal, 6% state). ***Receiving aid:*** Freshmen: 134; All full-time undergraduates: 1,609. ***Average award:*** Freshmen: $1854; Undergraduates: $2276. ***Scholarships, grants, and awards:*** Federal Pell, FSEOG, state, private, college/university gift aid from institutional funds, Academic Competitiveness Grant and National Science and Mathematics Access to Retain Talent (SMART).

GIFT AID (NON-NEED-BASED) ***Receiving aid:*** Freshmen: 12; Undergraduates: 632. ***Scholarships, grants, and awards by category:*** *Academic Interests/Achievement:* business, communication, computer science, education, health fields, social sciences. ***Tuition waivers:*** Full or partial for employees or children of employees.

LOANS ***Student loans:*** $52,761,300 (45% need-based, 55% non-need-based). ***Programs:*** FFEL (Subsidized and Unsubsidized Stafford, PLUS), Perkins.

APPLYING FOR FINANCIAL AID ***Required financial aid forms:*** FAFSA, institution's own form. ***Financial aid deadline:*** Continuous. ***Notification date:*** Continuous beginning 7/1.

CONTACT ACS/AFS, University of Phoenix–Phoenix Campus, 875 West Elliot Road, Suite 116, Tempe, AZ 85284, 480-735-3000 or toll-free 800-776-4867 (in-state), 800-228-7240 (out-of-state). *Fax:* 480-940-2060.

UNIVERSITY OF PHOENIX–PITTSBURGH CAMPUS

Pittsburgh, PA

Tuition & fees: $13,050 **Average undergraduate aid package: $3829**

ABOUT THE INSTITUTION Proprietary, coed. Awards: bachelor's and master's degrees. 24 undergraduate majors. Total enrollment: 408. Undergraduates: 301. Freshmen: 7. Both federal and institutional methodology are used as a basis for awarding need-based institutional aid.

UNDERGRADUATE EXPENSES for 2006–07 ***Application fee:*** $45. ***Tuition:*** full-time $13,050. ***Payment plan:*** Deferred payment.

FRESHMAN FINANCIAL AID (Fall 2005) ***Average financial aid package:*** $2171 (excluding resources awarded to replace EFC).

UNDERGRADUATE FINANCIAL AID (Fall 2005) ***Average financial aid package:*** $3829 (excluding resources awarded to replace EFC).

GIFT AID (NEED-BASED) ***Total amount:*** $318,666 (96% federal, 4% state). ***Receiving aid:*** Freshmen: 33; All full-time undergraduates: 166. ***Average award:*** Freshmen: $1714; Undergraduates: $1920. ***Scholarships, grants, and awards:*** Federal Pell, FSEOG, state, private, college/university gift aid from institutional funds, Academic Competitiveness Grant and National Science and Mathematics Access to Retain Talent (SMART).

GIFT AID (NON-NEED-BASED) ***Receiving aid:*** Undergraduates: 8. ***Scholarships, grants, and awards by category:*** *Academic Interests/Achievement:* business, computer science, health fields, social sciences. ***Tuition waivers:*** Full or partial for employees or children of employees.

LOANS ***Student loans:*** $3,313,740 (50% need-based, 50% non-need-based). ***Programs:*** FFEL (Subsidized and Unsubsidized Stafford, PLUS), Perkins.

APPLYING FOR FINANCIAL AID ***Required financial aid forms:*** FAFSA, institution's own form. ***Financial aid deadline:*** Continuous. ***Notification date:*** Continuous beginning 7/1.

CONTACT ACS/AFS, University of Phoenix–Pittsburgh Campus, 875 West Elliot Road, Suite 116, Tempe, AZ 85284, 480-735-3000 or toll-free 800-776-4867 (in-state), 800-228-7240 (out-of-state). *Fax:* 480-940-2060.

UNIVERSITY OF PHOENIX–PUERTO RICO CAMPUS

Guaynabo, PR

Tuition & fees: $5880 **Average undergraduate aid package: $5862**

ABOUT THE INSTITUTION Proprietary, coed. Awards: bachelor's and master's degrees (courses conducted at 121 campuses and learning centers in 25 states). 2 undergraduate majors. Total enrollment: 2,853. Undergraduates: 1,113. Freshmen: 53. Both federal and institutional methodology are used as a basis for awarding need-based institutional aid.

UNDERGRADUATE EXPENSES for 2006–07 ***Application fee:*** $45. ***Tuition:*** full-time $5880. ***Payment plan:*** Deferred payment.

FRESHMAN FINANCIAL AID (Fall 2005) ***Average financial aid package:*** $3272 (excluding resources awarded to replace EFC).

UNDERGRADUATE FINANCIAL AID (Fall 2005) ***Average financial aid package:*** $5862 (excluding resources awarded to replace EFC).

GIFT AID (NEED-BASED) ***Total amount:*** $1,626,925 (100% federal). ***Receiving aid:*** Freshmen: 111; All full-time undergraduates: 620. ***Average award:*** Freshmen: $2186; Undergraduates: $2624. ***Scholarships, grants, and awards:*** Federal Pell, FSEOG, state, private, college/university gift aid from institutional funds, Academic Competitiveness Grant and National Science and Mathematics Access to Retain Talent (SMART).

GIFT AID (NON-NEED-BASED) ***Receiving aid:*** Undergraduates: 26. ***Scholarships, grants, and awards by category:*** *Academic Interests/Achievement:* business. ***Tuition waivers:*** Full or partial for employees or children of employees.

LOANS ***Student loans:*** $21,146,658 (50% need-based, 50% non-need-based). ***Programs:*** FFEL (Subsidized and Unsubsidized Stafford, PLUS), Perkins.

APPLYING FOR FINANCIAL AID ***Required financial aid forms:*** FAFSA, institution's own form. ***Financial aid deadline:*** Continuous. ***Notification date:*** Continuous beginning 7/1.

CONTACT ACS/AFS, University of Phoenix–Puerto Rico Campus, 875 West Elliot Road, Suite 116, Tempe, AZ 85284, 480-735-3000 or toll-free 800-776-4867 (in-state), 800-228-7240 (out-of-state). *Fax:* 480-940-2060.

UNIVERSITY OF PHOENIX–RALEIGH CAMPUS

Raleigh, NC

Tuition & fees: $10,770 **Average undergraduate aid package: $4157**

ABOUT THE INSTITUTION Proprietary, coed. Awards: bachelor's and master's degrees. 8 undergraduate majors. Total enrollment: 526. Undergraduates: 326. Freshmen: 32. Both federal and institutional methodology are used as a basis for awarding need-based institutional aid.

UNDERGRADUATE EXPENSES for 2006–07 ***Application fee:*** $45. ***Tuition:*** full-time $10,770; part-time $359 per credit. ***Payment plan:*** Deferred payment.

FRESHMAN FINANCIAL AID (Fall 2005) ***Average financial aid package:*** $2801 (excluding resources awarded to replace EFC).

UNDERGRADUATE FINANCIAL AID (Fall 2005) ***Average financial aid package:*** $4157 (excluding resources awarded to replace EFC).

GIFT AID (NEED-BASED) ***Total amount:*** $233,349 (100% federal). ***Receiving aid:*** Freshmen: 18; All full-time undergraduates: 103. ***Average award:*** Freshmen: $1775; Undergraduates: $2266. ***Scholarships, grants, and awards:*** Federal Pell, FSEOG, state, private, college/university gift aid from institutional funds, Academic Competitiveness Grant and National Science and Mathematics Access to Retain Talent (SMART).

GIFT AID (NON-NEED-BASED) ***Receiving aid:*** Freshmen: 1; Undergraduates: 7. ***Scholarships, grants, and awards by category:*** *Academic Interests/Achievement:* business, computer science. ***Tuition waivers:*** Full or partial for employees or children of employees.

LOANS ***Student loans:*** $2,805,632 (43% need-based, 57% non-need-based). ***Programs:*** FFEL (Subsidized and Unsubsidized Stafford, PLUS), Perkins.

APPLYING FOR FINANCIAL AID ***Required financial aid forms:*** FAFSA, institution's own form. ***Financial aid deadline:*** Continuous. ***Notification date:*** Continuous beginning 7/1.

CONTACT ACS/AFS, University of Phoenix–Raleigh Campus, 875 West Elliot Road, Suite 116, Tempe, AZ 85284, 480-735-3000 or toll-free 800-776-4867 (in-state), 800-228-7240 (out-of-state). *Fax:* 480-940-2060.

UNIVERSITY OF PHOENIX–RICHMOND CAMPUS

Richmond, VA

Tuition & fees: $11,820 **Average undergraduate aid package: $3228**

ABOUT THE INSTITUTION Proprietary, coed. Awards: bachelor's and master's degrees. 20 undergraduate majors. Total enrollment: 351. Undergraduates: 227. Freshmen: 16. Both federal and institutional methodology are used as a basis for awarding need-based institutional aid.

UNDERGRADUATE EXPENSES for 2006–07 ***Application fee:*** $45. ***Tuition:*** full-time $11,820; part-time $394 per credit. ***Payment plan:*** Deferred payment.

FRESHMAN FINANCIAL AID (Fall 2005) ***Average financial aid package:*** $1890 (excluding resources awarded to replace EFC).

UNDERGRADUATE FINANCIAL AID (Fall 2005) ***Average financial aid package:*** $3228 (excluding resources awarded to replace EFC).

GIFT AID (NEED-BASED) ***Total amount:*** $230,057 (100% federal). ***Receiving aid:*** Freshmen: 25; All full-time undergraduates: 131. ***Average award:*** Freshmen: $1465; Undergraduates: $1756. ***Scholarships, grants, and awards:*** Federal Pell, FSEOG, state, private, college/university gift aid from institutional funds, Academic Competitiveness Grant and National Science and Mathematics Access to Retain Talent (SMART).

GIFT AID (NON-NEED-BASED) ***Receiving aid:*** Undergraduates: 8. ***Scholarships, grants, and awards by category:*** *Academic Interests/Achievement:* business, computer science. ***Tuition waivers:*** Full or partial for employees or children of employees.

LOANS ***Student loans:*** $2,162,979 (46% need-based, 54% non-need-based). ***Programs:*** FFEL (Subsidized and Unsubsidized Stafford, PLUS), Perkins, Academic Competitiveness Grant and National Science and Mathematics Access to Retain Talent (SMART).

APPLYING FOR FINANCIAL AID ***Required financial aid forms:*** FAFSA, institution's own form. ***Financial aid deadline:*** Continuous. ***Notification date:*** Continuous beginning 7/1.

CONTACT ACS/AFS, University of Phoenix–Richmond Campus, 875 West Elliot Road, Suite 116, Tempe, AZ 85284, 480-735-3000 or toll-free 800-776-4867 (in-state), 800-228-7240 (out-of-state). *Fax:* 480-940-2060.

UNIVERSITY OF PHOENIX–SACRAMENTO VALLEY CAMPUS

Sacramento, CA

Tuition & fees: $12,900 **Average undergraduate aid package: $4481**

ABOUT THE INSTITUTION Proprietary, coed. Awards: bachelor's and master's degrees. 27 undergraduate majors. Total enrollment: 4,585. Undergraduates: 3,480. Freshmen: 117. Both federal and institutional methodology are used as a basis for awarding need-based institutional aid.

UNDERGRADUATE EXPENSES for 2006–07 ***Application fee:*** $45. ***Tuition:*** full-time $12,900. ***Payment plan:*** Deferred payment.

FRESHMAN FINANCIAL AID (Fall 2005) ***Average financial aid package:*** $2138 (excluding resources awarded to replace EFC).

UNDERGRADUATE FINANCIAL AID (Fall 2005) ***Average financial aid package:*** $4481 (excluding resources awarded to replace EFC).

GIFT AID (NEED-BASED) ***Total amount:*** $3,860,570 (76% federal, 24% state). ***Receiving aid:*** Freshmen: 111; All full-time undergraduates: 1,392. ***Average award:*** Freshmen: $1674; Undergraduates: $2773. ***Scholarships, grants, and awards:*** Federal Pell, FSEOG, state, private, college/university gift aid from institutional funds, Academic Competitiveness Grant and National Science and Mathematics Access to Retain Talent (SMART).

GIFT AID (NON-NEED-BASED) ***Receiving aid:*** Freshmen: 1; Undergraduates: 84. ***Scholarships, grants, and awards by category:*** *Academic Interests/Achievement:* business, communication, computer science, health fields, social sciences. ***Tuition waivers:*** Full or partial for employees or children of employees.

LOANS ***Student loans:*** $34,982,494 (46% need-based, 54% non-need-based). ***Programs:*** FFEL (Subsidized and Unsubsidized Stafford, PLUS), Perkins.

APPLYING FOR FINANCIAL AID ***Required financial aid forms:*** FAFSA, institution's own form. ***Financial aid deadline:*** Continuous. ***Notification date:*** Continuous beginning 7/1.

CONTACT ACS/AFS, University of Phoenix–Sacramento Valley Campus, 875 West Elliot Road, Suite 116, Tempe, AZ 85284, 480-735-3000 or toll-free 800-776-4867 (in-state), 800-228-7240 (out-of-state). *Fax:* 480-940-2060.

UNIVERSITY OF PHOENIX–ST. LOUIS CAMPUS

St. Louis, MO

Tuition & fees: $11,910 **Average undergraduate aid package: $3888**

ABOUT THE INSTITUTION Proprietary, coed. Awards: bachelor's and master's degrees. 28 undergraduate majors. Total enrollment: 964. Undergraduates: 834. Freshmen: 26. Both federal and institutional methodology are used as a basis for awarding need-based institutional aid.

UNDERGRADUATE EXPENSES for 2006–07 ***Application fee:*** $45. ***Tuition:*** full-time $11,910. ***Payment plan:*** Deferred payment.

FRESHMAN FINANCIAL AID (Fall 2005) ***Average financial aid package:*** $2451 (excluding resources awarded to replace EFC).

UNDERGRADUATE FINANCIAL AID (Fall 2005) ***Average financial aid package:*** $3888 (excluding resources awarded to replace EFC).

GIFT AID (NEED-BASED) ***Total amount:*** $1,048,955 (100% federal). ***Receiving aid:*** Freshmen: 103; All full-time undergraduates: 494. ***Average award:*** Freshmen: $1757; Undergraduates: $2123. ***Scholarships, grants, and awards:*** Federal Pell, FSEOG, state, private, college/university gift aid from institutional funds, Academic Competitiveness Grant and National Science and Mathematics Access to Retain Talent (SMART).

GIFT AID (NON-NEED-BASED) ***Receiving aid:*** Undergraduates: 16. ***Scholarships, grants, and awards by category:*** *Academic Interests/Achievement:* business, computer science. ***Tuition waivers:*** Full or partial for employees or children of employees.

LOANS ***Student loans:*** $6,383,050 (48% need-based, 52% non-need-based). ***Programs:*** FFEL (Subsidized and Unsubsidized Stafford, PLUS), Perkins.

APPLYING FOR FINANCIAL AID ***Required financial aid forms:*** FAFSA, institution's own form. ***Financial aid deadline:*** Continuous. ***Notification date:*** Continuous beginning 7/1.

CONTACT ACS/AFS, University of Phoenix–St. Louis Campus, 875 West Elliot Road, Suite 116, Tempe, AZ 85284, 480-735-3000 or toll-free 800-776-4867 (in-state), 800-228-7240 (out-of-state). *Fax:* 480-940-2060.

UNIVERSITY OF PHOENIX–SAN DIEGO CAMPUS

San Diego, CA

Tuition & fees: $12,450 **Average undergraduate aid package: $4180**

ABOUT THE INSTITUTION Proprietary, coed. Awards: bachelor's and master's degrees. 12 undergraduate majors. Total enrollment: 3,781. Undergraduates: 2,780. Freshmen: 37. Both federal and institutional methodology are used as a basis for awarding need-based institutional aid.

UNDERGRADUATE EXPENSES for 2006–07 ***Application fee:*** $45. ***Tuition:*** full-time $12,450. ***Payment plan:*** Deferred payment.

FRESHMAN FINANCIAL AID (Fall 2005) ***Average financial aid package:*** $2830 (excluding resources awarded to replace EFC).

UNDERGRADUATE FINANCIAL AID (Fall 2005) ***Average financial aid package:*** $4180 (excluding resources awarded to replace EFC).

GIFT AID (NEED-BASED) ***Total amount:*** $2,378,001 (85% federal, 15% state). ***Receiving aid:*** Freshmen: 72; All full-time undergraduates: 941. ***Average award:*** Freshmen: $2073; Undergraduates: $2527. ***Scholarships, grants, and awards:*** Federal Pell, FSEOG, state, private, college/university gift aid from institutional funds, Academic Competitiveness Grant and National Science and Mathematics Access to Retain Talent (SMART).

GIFT AID (NON-NEED-BASED) ***Receiving aid:*** Freshmen: 3; Undergraduates: 62. ***Scholarships, grants, and awards by category:*** *Academic Interests/Achievement:* business, communication, computer science, health fields, social sciences. ***Tuition waivers:*** Full or partial for employees or children of employees.

LOANS ***Student loans:*** $28,953,484 (45% need-based, 55% non-need-based). ***Programs:*** FFEL (Subsidized and Unsubsidized Stafford, PLUS), Perkins.

APPLYING FOR FINANCIAL AID ***Required financial aid forms:*** FAFSA, institution's own form. ***Financial aid deadline:*** Continuous. ***Notification date:*** Continuous beginning 7/1.

CONTACT ACS/AFS, University of Phoenix–San Diego Campus, 875 West Elliot Road, Suite 116, Tempe, AZ 85284, 480-735-3000 or toll-free 888-776-4867 (in-state), 888-228-7240 (out-of-state). *Fax:* 480-940-2060.

UNIVERSITY OF PHOENIX–SOUTHERN ARIZONA CAMPUS

Tucson, AZ

Tuition & fees: $9990 **Average undergraduate aid package: $4838**

ABOUT THE INSTITUTION Proprietary, coed. Awards: bachelor's and master's degrees and post-master's certificates. 12 undergraduate majors. Total enrollment: 2,839. Undergraduates: 2,096. Freshmen: 52. Both federal and institutional methodology are used as a basis for awarding need-based institutional aid.

UNDERGRADUATE EXPENSES for 2006–07 ***Application fee:*** $45. ***Tuition:*** full-time $9990; part-time $333 per credit. ***Payment plan:*** Deferred payment.

FRESHMAN FINANCIAL AID (Fall 2005) ***Average financial aid package:*** $3335 (excluding resources awarded to replace EFC).

UNDERGRADUATE FINANCIAL AID (Fall 2005) ***Average financial aid package:*** $4838 (excluding resources awarded to replace EFC).

GIFT AID (NEED-BASED) ***Total amount:*** $2,150,848 (95% federal, 5% state). ***Receiving aid:*** Freshmen: 59; All full-time undergraduates: 866. ***Average award:*** Freshmen: $2459; Undergraduates: $2484. ***Scholarships, grants, and awards:***

Federal Pell, FSEOG, state, private, college/university gift aid from institutional funds, Academic Competitiveness Grant and National Science and Mathematics Access to Retain Talent (SMART).

GIFT AID (NON-NEED-BASED) ***Receiving aid:*** Undergraduates: 33. ***Scholarships, grants, and awards by category:*** *Academic Interests/Achievement:* business, computer science, education, health fields, social sciences. ***Tuition waivers:*** Full or partial for employees or children of employees.

LOANS ***Student loans:*** $19,369,633 (46% need-based, 54% non-need-based). ***Programs:*** FFEL (Subsidized and Unsubsidized Stafford, PLUS), Perkins.

APPLYING FOR FINANCIAL AID ***Required financial aid forms:*** FAFSA, institution's own form. ***Financial aid deadline:*** Continuous. ***Notification date:*** Continuous beginning 7/1.

CONTACT ACS/AFS, University of Phoenix–Southern Arizona Campus, 875 West Elliot Road, Suite 116, Tempe, AZ 85284, 480-735-3000 or toll-free 800-776-4867 (in-state), 800-228-7240 (out-of-state). *Fax:* 480-940-2060.

UNIVERSITY OF PHOENIX–SOUTHERN CALIFORNIA CAMPUS

Costa Mesa, CA

Tuition & fees: $13,710 **Average undergraduate aid package: $4394**

ABOUT THE INSTITUTION Proprietary, coed. Awards: bachelor's and master's degrees. 11 undergraduate majors. Total enrollment: 14,760. Undergraduates: 11,166. Freshmen: 244. Both federal and institutional methodology are used as a basis for awarding need-based institutional aid.

UNDERGRADUATE EXPENSES for 2006–07 ***Application fee:*** $45. ***Tuition:*** full-time $13,710. ***Payment plan:*** Deferred payment.

FRESHMAN FINANCIAL AID (Fall 2005) ***Average financial aid package:*** $2486 (excluding resources awarded to replace EFC).

UNDERGRADUATE FINANCIAL AID (Fall 2005) ***Average financial aid package:*** $4394 (excluding resources awarded to replace EFC).

GIFT AID (NEED-BASED) ***Total amount:*** $13,210,134 (82% federal, 18% state). ***Receiving aid:*** Freshmen: 457; All full-time undergraduates: 4,911. ***Average award:*** Freshmen: $1925; Undergraduates: $2690. ***Scholarships, grants, and awards:*** Federal Pell, FSEOG, state, private, college/university gift aid from institutional funds, Academic Competitiveness Grant and National Science and Mathematics Access to Retain Talent (SMART).

GIFT AID (NON-NEED-BASED) ***Receiving aid:*** Freshmen: 4; Undergraduates: 165. ***Scholarships, grants, and awards by category:*** *Academic Interests/Achievement:* business, computer science, health fields, social sciences. ***Tuition waivers:*** Full or partial for employees or children of employees.

LOANS ***Student loans:*** $118,269,032 (47% need-based, 53% non-need-based). ***Programs:*** FFEL (Subsidized and Unsubsidized Stafford, PLUS), Perkins.

APPLYING FOR FINANCIAL AID ***Required financial aid forms:*** FAFSA, institution's own form. ***Financial aid deadline:*** Continuous. ***Notification date:*** Continuous beginning 7/1.

CONTACT ACS/AFS, University of Phoenix–Southern California Campus, 875 West Elliot Road, Suite 116, Tempe, AZ 85284, 480-735-3000 or toll-free 800-776-4867 (in-state), 800-228-7240 (out-of-state). *Fax:* 480-940-2060.

UNIVERSITY OF PHOENIX–SOUTHERN COLORADO CAMPUS

Colorado Springs, CO

Tuition & fees: $9750 **Average undergraduate aid package: $4814**

ABOUT THE INSTITUTION Proprietary, coed. Awards: bachelor's and master's degrees. 18 undergraduate majors. Total enrollment: 1,090. Undergraduates: 618. Freshmen: 17. Both federal and institutional methodology are used as a basis for awarding need-based institutional aid.

UNDERGRADUATE EXPENSES for 2006–07 ***Application fee:*** $45. ***Tuition:*** full-time $9750. ***Payment plan:*** Deferred payment.

FRESHMAN FINANCIAL AID (Fall 2005) ***Average financial aid package:*** $3121 (excluding resources awarded to replace EFC).

UNDERGRADUATE FINANCIAL AID (Fall 2005) ***Average financial aid package:*** $4814 (excluding resources awarded to replace EFC).

GIFT AID (NEED-BASED) ***Total amount:*** $497,190 (100% federal). ***Receiving aid:*** Freshmen: 15; All full-time undergraduates: 233. ***Average award:*** Freshmen: $2135; Undergraduates: $2134. ***Scholarships, grants, and awards:*** Federal Pell, FSEOG, state, private, college/university gift aid from institutional funds, Academic Competitiveness Grant and National Science and Mathematics Access to Retain Talent (SMART).

GIFT AID (NON-NEED-BASED) ***Receiving aid:*** Freshmen: 1; Undergraduates: 14. ***Scholarships, grants, and awards by category:*** *Academic Interests/Achievement:* business, communication, computer science, social sciences. ***Tuition waivers:*** Full or partial for employees or children of employees.

LOANS ***Student loans:*** $9,218,970 (45% need-based, 55% non-need-based). ***Programs:*** FFEL (Subsidized and Unsubsidized Stafford, PLUS), Perkins.

APPLYING FOR FINANCIAL AID ***Required financial aid forms:*** FAFSA, institution's own form. ***Financial aid deadline:*** Continuous. ***Notification date:*** Continuous beginning 7/1.

CONTACT ACS/AFS, University of Phoenix–Southern Colorado Campus, 875 West Elliot Road, Suite 116, Tempe, AZ 85284, 480-735-3000 or toll-free 800-776-4867 (in-state), 800-228-7240 (out-of-state). *Fax:* 480-940-2060.

UNIVERSITY OF PHOENIX–SPOKANE CAMPUS

Spokane Valley, WA

Tuition & fees: $10,260 **Average undergraduate aid package: $4005**

ABOUT THE INSTITUTION Proprietary, coed. Awards: bachelor's and master's degrees. 4 undergraduate majors. Total enrollment: 294. Undergraduates: 254. Freshmen: 14. Both federal and institutional methodology are used as a basis for awarding need-based institutional aid.

UNDERGRADUATE EXPENSES for 2006–07 ***Application fee:*** $45. ***Tuition:*** full-time $10,260; part-time $342 per credit. ***Payment plan:*** Deferred payment.

FRESHMAN FINANCIAL AID (Fall 2005) ***Average financial aid package:*** $2144 (excluding resources awarded to replace EFC).

UNDERGRADUATE FINANCIAL AID (Fall 2005) ***Average financial aid package:*** $4005 (excluding resources awarded to replace EFC).

GIFT AID (NEED-BASED) ***Total amount:*** $312,367 (100% federal). ***Receiving aid:*** Freshmen: 21; All full-time undergraduates: 143. ***Average award:*** Freshmen: $1765; Undergraduates: $2184. ***Scholarships, grants, and awards:*** Federal Pell, FSEOG, state, private, college/university gift aid from institutional funds, Academic Competitiveness Grant and National Science and Mathematics Access to Retain Talent (SMART).

GIFT AID (NON-NEED-BASED) ***Receiving aid:*** Undergraduates: 7. ***Scholarships, grants, and awards by category:*** *Academic Interests/Achievement:* business, computer science. ***Tuition waivers:*** Full or partial for employees or children of employees.

LOANS ***Student loans:*** $2,110,086 (49% need-based, 51% non-need-based). ***Programs:*** FFEL (Subsidized and Unsubsidized Stafford, PLUS), Perkins.

APPLYING FOR FINANCIAL AID ***Required financial aid forms:*** FAFSA, institution's own form. ***Financial aid deadline:*** Continuous. ***Notification date:*** Continuous beginning 7/1.

CONTACT ACS/AFS, University of Phoenix–Spokane Campus, 875 West Elliot Road, Suite 116, Tempe, AZ 85284, 480-735-3000 or toll-free 800-697-8223 (in-state), 800-228-7240 (out-of-state). *Fax:* 480-940-2060.

UNIVERSITY OF PHOENIX–SPRINGFIELD CAMPUS

Springfield, MO

Tuition & fees: $9750 **Average undergraduate aid package: $4044**

ABOUT THE INSTITUTION Proprietary, coed. Awards: bachelor's and master's degrees. 27 undergraduate majors. Total enrollment: 305. Undergraduates: 265. Freshmen: 12. Both federal and institutional methodology are used as a basis for awarding need-based institutional aid.

UNDERGRADUATE EXPENSES for 2006–07 ***Application fee:*** $45. ***Tuition:*** full-time $9750; part-time $325 per credit. ***Payment plan:*** Deferred payment.

FRESHMAN FINANCIAL AID (Fall 2005) ***Average financial aid package:*** $2881 (excluding resources awarded to replace EFC).

UNDERGRADUATE FINANCIAL AID (Fall 2005) ***Average financial aid package:*** $4044 (excluding resources awarded to replace EFC).

GIFT AID (NEED-BASED) ***Total amount:*** $414,268 (100% federal). ***Receiving aid:*** Freshmen: 46; All full-time undergraduates: 184. ***Average award:*** Freshmen: $1990; Undergraduates: $2251. ***Scholarships, grants, and awards:*** Federal Pell, FSEOG, state, private, college/university gift aid from institutional funds, Academic Competitiveness Grant and National Science and Mathematics Access to Retain Talent (SMART).

GIFT AID (NON-NEED-BASED) ***Receiving aid:*** Freshmen: 1; Undergraduates: 5. ***Scholarships, grants, and awards by category:*** *Academic Interests/Achievement:* business, communication, computer science, health fields, social sciences. ***Tuition waivers:*** Full or partial for employees or children of employees.

LOANS ***Student loans:*** $2,147,155 (46% need-based, 54% non-need-based). ***Programs:*** FFEL (Subsidized and Unsubsidized Stafford, PLUS), Perkins.

APPLYING FOR FINANCIAL AID ***Required financial aid forms:*** FAFSA, institution's own form. ***Financial aid deadline:*** Continuous. ***Notification date:*** Continuous beginning 7/1.

CONTACT ACS/AFS, University of Phoenix–Springfield Campus, 875 West Elliot Road, Suite 116, Tempe, AZ 85284, 480-735-3000 or toll-free 800-776-4867 (in-state), 800-228-7240 (out-of-state). *Fax:* 480-940-2060.

UNIVERSITY OF PHOENIX–TULSA CAMPUS

Tulsa, OK

Tuition & fees: $9750 | **Average undergraduate aid package: $4528**

ABOUT THE INSTITUTION Proprietary, coed. Awards: bachelor's and master's degrees. 16 undergraduate majors. Total enrollment: 1,169. Undergraduates: 1,018. Freshmen: 60. Both federal and institutional methodology are used as a basis for awarding need-based institutional aid.

UNDERGRADUATE EXPENSES for 2006–07 ***Application fee:*** $45. ***Tuition:*** full-time $9750. ***Payment plan:*** Deferred payment.

FRESHMAN FINANCIAL AID (Fall 2005) ***Average financial aid package:*** $2778 (excluding resources awarded to replace EFC).

UNDERGRADUATE FINANCIAL AID (Fall 2005) ***Average financial aid package:*** $4528 (excluding resources awarded to replace EFC).

GIFT AID (NEED-BASED) ***Total amount:*** $1,834,664 (100% federal). ***Receiving aid:*** Freshmen: 160; All full-time undergraduates: 799. ***Average award:*** Freshmen: $1904; Undergraduates: $2296. ***Scholarships, grants, and awards:*** Federal Pell, FSEOG, state, private, college/university gift aid from institutional funds, Academic Competitiveness Grant and National Science and Mathematics Access to Retain Talent (SMART).

GIFT AID (NON-NEED-BASED) ***Receiving aid:*** Undergraduates: 15. ***Scholarships, grants, and awards by category:*** *Academic Interests/Achievement:* business, computer science, health fields, social sciences. ***Tuition waivers:*** Full or partial for employees or children of employees.

LOANS ***Student loans:*** $9,612,252 (47% need-based, 53% non-need-based). ***Programs:*** FFEL (Subsidized and Unsubsidized Stafford, PLUS), Perkins.

APPLYING FOR FINANCIAL AID ***Required financial aid forms:*** FAFSA, institution's own form. ***Financial aid deadline:*** Continuous. ***Notification date:*** Continuous beginning 7/1.

CONTACT ACS/AFS, University of Phoenix–Tulsa Campus, 875 West Elliot Road, Suite 116, Tempe, AZ 85284, 480-735-3000 or toll-free 800-776-4867 (in-state), 800-228-7240 (out-of-state). *Fax:* 480-940-2060.

UNIVERSITY OF PHOENIX–UTAH CAMPUS

Salt Lake City, UT

Tuition & fees: $10,200 | **Average undergraduate aid package: $4810**

ABOUT THE INSTITUTION Proprietary, coed. Awards: bachelor's and master's degrees. 17 undergraduate majors. Total enrollment: 3,986. Undergraduates: 2,559. Freshmen: 50. Both federal and institutional methodology are used as a basis for awarding need-based institutional aid.

UNDERGRADUATE EXPENSES for 2006–07 ***Application fee:*** $45. ***Tuition:*** full-time $10,200. ***Payment plan:*** Deferred payment.

FRESHMAN FINANCIAL AID (Fall 2005) ***Average financial aid package:*** $2597 (excluding resources awarded to replace EFC).

UNDERGRADUATE FINANCIAL AID (Fall 2005) ***Average financial aid package:*** $4810 (excluding resources awarded to replace EFC).

GIFT AID (NEED-BASED) ***Total amount:*** $2,338,566 (100% federal). ***Receiving aid:*** Freshmen: 73; All full-time undergraduates: 1,040. ***Average award:*** Freshmen: $2049; Undergraduates: $2249. ***Scholarships, grants, and awards:*** Federal Pell, FSEOG, state, private, college/university gift aid from institutional funds, Academic Competitiveness Grant and National Science and Mathematics Access to Retain Talent (SMART).

GIFT AID (NON-NEED-BASED) ***Receiving aid:*** Undergraduates: 25. ***Scholarships, grants, and awards by category:*** *Academic Interests/Achievement:* business, communication, computer science, education, health fields, social sciences. ***Tuition waivers:*** Full or partial for employees or children of employees.

LOANS ***Student loans:*** $27,945,167 (48% need-based, 52% non-need-based). ***Programs:*** FFEL (Subsidized and Unsubsidized Stafford, PLUS), Perkins.

APPLYING FOR FINANCIAL AID ***Required financial aid forms:*** FAFSA, institution's own form. ***Financial aid deadline:*** Continuous. ***Notification date:*** Continuous beginning 7/1.

CONTACT ACS/AFS, University of Phoenix–Utah Campus, 875 West Elliot Road, Suite 116, Tempe, AZ 85284, 480-735-3000 or toll-free 800-776-4867 (in-state), 800-228-7240 (out-of-state). *Fax:* 480-940-2060.

UNIVERSITY OF PHOENIX–WASHINGTON CAMPUS

Seattle, WA

Tuition & fees: $11,190 | **Average undergraduate aid package: $3681**

ABOUT THE INSTITUTION Proprietary, coed. Awards: bachelor's and master's degrees. 24 undergraduate majors. Total enrollment: 1,758. Undergraduates: 1,430. Freshmen: 19. Both federal and institutional methodology are used as a basis for awarding need-based institutional aid.

UNDERGRADUATE EXPENSES for 2006–07 ***Application fee:*** $45. ***Tuition:*** full-time $11,190. ***Payment plan:*** Deferred payment.

FRESHMAN FINANCIAL AID (Fall 2005) ***Average financial aid package:*** $2506 (excluding resources awarded to replace EFC).

UNDERGRADUATE FINANCIAL AID (Fall 2005) ***Average financial aid package:*** $3681 (excluding resources awarded to replace EFC).

GIFT AID (NEED-BASED) ***Total amount:*** $926,083 (100% federal). ***Receiving aid:*** Freshmen: 52; All full-time undergraduates: 455. ***Average award:*** Freshmen: $2004; Undergraduates: $2035. ***Scholarships, grants, and awards:*** Federal Pell, FSEOG, state, private, college/university gift aid from institutional funds, Academic Competitiveness Grant and National Science and Mathematics Access to Retain Talent (SMART).

GIFT AID (NON-NEED-BASED) ***Receiving aid:*** Undergraduates: 17. ***Scholarships, grants, and awards by category:*** *Academic Interests/Achievement:* business, computer science, social sciences. ***Tuition waivers:*** Full or partial for employees or children of employees.

LOANS ***Student loans:*** $12,620,326 (44% need-based, 56% non-need-based). ***Programs:*** FFEL (Subsidized and Unsubsidized Stafford, PLUS), Perkins.

APPLYING FOR FINANCIAL AID ***Required financial aid forms:*** FAFSA, institution's own form. ***Financial aid deadline:*** Continuous. ***Notification date:*** Continuous beginning 7/1.

CONTACT ACS/AFS, University of Phoenix–Washington Campus, 875 West Elliot Road, Suite 116, Tempe, AZ 85284, 480-735-3000 or toll-free 800-776-4867 (in-state), 800-228-7240 (out-of-state). *Fax:* 480-940-2060.

UNIVERSITY OF PHOENIX–WEST FLORIDA CAMPUS

Temple Terrace, FL

Tuition & fees: $10,058 | **Average undergraduate aid package: $4157**

ABOUT THE INSTITUTION Proprietary, coed. Awards: bachelor's and master's degrees. 10 undergraduate majors. Total enrollment: 2,659. Undergraduates: 1,983. Freshmen: 99. Both federal and institutional methodology are used as a basis for awarding need-based institutional aid.

UNDERGRADUATE EXPENSES for 2006–07 ***Application fee:*** $45. ***Tuition:*** full-time $10,058. ***Payment plan:*** Deferred payment.

FRESHMAN FINANCIAL AID (Fall 2005) ***Average financial aid package:*** $2736 (excluding resources awarded to replace EFC).

UNDERGRADUATE FINANCIAL AID (Fall 2005) ***Average financial aid package:*** $4157 (excluding resources awarded to replace EFC).

GIFT AID (NEED-BASED) ***Total amount:*** $1,579,322 (98% federal, 2% state). ***Receiving aid:*** Freshmen: 106; All full-time undergraduates: 694. ***Average award:*** Freshmen: $1885; Undergraduates: $2276. ***Scholarships, grants, and awards:*** Federal Pell, FSEOG, state, private, college/university gift aid from institutional funds, Academic Competitiveness Grant and National Science and Mathematics Access to Retain Talent (SMART).

GIFT AID (NON-NEED-BASED) ***Receiving aid:*** Freshmen: 2; Undergraduates: 30. ***Scholarships, grants, and awards by category:*** *Academic Interests/Achievement:* business, computer science, education, health fields, social sciences. ***Tuition waivers:*** Full or partial for employees or children of employees.

LOANS ***Student loans:*** $18,466,531 (43% need-based, 57% non-need-based). ***Programs:*** FFEL (Subsidized and Unsubsidized Stafford, PLUS), Perkins.

APPLYING FOR FINANCIAL AID ***Required financial aid forms:*** FAFSA, institution's own form. ***Financial aid deadline:*** Continuous. ***Notification date:*** Continuous beginning 7/1.

CONTACT ACS/AFS, University of Phoenix–West Florida Campus, 875 West Elliot Road, Suite 116, Tempe, AZ 85284, 480-735-3000 or toll-free 800-776-4867 (in-state), 800-228-7240 (out-of-state). *Fax:* 480-940-2060.

UNIVERSITY OF PHOENIX–WEST MICHIGAN CAMPUS

Walker, MI

Tuition & fees: $11,400 **Average undergraduate aid package: $4167**

ABOUT THE INSTITUTION Proprietary, coed. Awards: bachelor's and master's degrees. 14 undergraduate majors. Total enrollment: 1,004. Undergraduates: 812. Freshmen: 26. Both federal and institutional methodology are used as a basis for awarding need-based institutional aid.

UNDERGRADUATE EXPENSES for 2006–07 ***Application fee:*** $45. ***Tuition:*** full-time $11,400. ***Payment plan:*** Deferred payment.

FRESHMAN FINANCIAL AID (Fall 2005) ***Average financial aid package:*** $2558 (excluding resources awarded to replace EFC).

UNDERGRADUATE FINANCIAL AID (Fall 2005) ***Average financial aid package:*** $4167 (excluding resources awarded to replace EFC).

GIFT AID (NEED-BASED) ***Total amount:*** $998,466 (100% federal). ***Receiving aid:*** Freshmen: 65; All full-time undergraduates: 254. ***Average award:*** Freshmen: $1831; Undergraduates: $2327. ***Scholarships, grants, and awards:*** Federal Pell, FSEOG, state, private, college/university gift aid from institutional funds, Academic Competitiveness Grant and National Science and Mathematics Access to Retain Talent (SMART).

GIFT AID (NON-NEED-BASED) ***Receiving aid:*** Freshmen: 1; Undergraduates: 17. ***Scholarships, grants, and awards by category:*** *Academic Interests/Achievement:* business, computer science, health fields, social sciences. ***Tuition waivers:*** Full or partial for employees or children of employees.

LOANS ***Student loans:*** $4,753,953 (71% need-based, 29% non-need-based). ***Programs:*** FFEL (Subsidized and Unsubsidized Stafford, PLUS), Perkins.

APPLYING FOR FINANCIAL AID ***Required financial aid forms:*** FAFSA, institution's own form. ***Financial aid deadline:*** Continuous. ***Notification date:*** Continuous beginning 7/1.

CONTACT ACS/AFS, University of Phoenix–West Michigan Campus, 875 West Elliot Road, Suite 116, Tempe, AZ 85284, 480-735-3000 or toll-free 800-776-4867 (in-state), 800-228-7240 (out-of-state). *Fax:* 480-940-2060.

UNIVERSITY OF PHOENIX–WICHITA CAMPUS

Wichita, KS

Tuition & fees: $10,770 **Average undergraduate aid package: $3923**

ABOUT THE INSTITUTION Proprietary, coed. Awards: bachelor's and master's degrees. 4 undergraduate majors. Total enrollment: 406. Undergraduates: 339. Freshmen: 34. Both federal and institutional methodology are used as a basis for awarding need-based institutional aid.

UNDERGRADUATE EXPENSES for 2006–07 ***Application fee:*** $45. ***Tuition:*** full-time $10,770; part-time $359 per credit. ***Payment plan:*** Deferred payment.

FRESHMAN FINANCIAL AID (Fall 2005) ***Average financial aid package:*** $2476 (excluding resources awarded to replace EFC).

UNDERGRADUATE FINANCIAL AID (Fall 2005) ***Average financial aid package:*** $3923 (excluding resources awarded to replace EFC).

GIFT AID (NEED-BASED) ***Total amount:*** $521,690 (100% federal). ***Receiving aid:*** Freshmen: 65; All full-time undergraduates: 254. ***Average award:*** Freshmen: $1699; Undergraduates: $2054. ***Scholarships, grants, and awards:*** Federal Pell, FSEOG, state, private, college/university gift aid from institutional funds, Academic Competitiveness Grant and National Science and Mathematics Access to Retain Talent (SMART).

GIFT AID (NON-NEED-BASED) ***Receiving aid:*** Undergraduates: 3. ***Scholarships, grants, and awards by category:*** *Academic Interests/Achievement:* business, computer science, health fields, social sciences. ***Tuition waivers:*** Full or partial for employees or children of employees.

LOANS ***Student loans:*** $2,626,712 (48% need-based, 52% non-need-based). ***Programs:*** FFEL (Subsidized and Unsubsidized Stafford, PLUS), Perkins.

APPLYING FOR FINANCIAL AID ***Required financial aid forms:*** FAFSA, institution's own form. ***Financial aid deadline:*** Continuous. ***Notification date:*** Continuous beginning 7/1.

CONTACT ACS/AFS, University of Phoenix–Wichita Campus, 875 West Elliot Road, Suite 116, Tempe, AZ 85284, 480-735-3000 or toll-free 800-776-4867 (in-state), 800-228-7240 (out-of-state). *Fax:* 480-940-2060.

UNIVERSITY OF PHOENIX–WISCONSIN CAMPUS

Brookfield, WI

Tuition & fees: $11,010 **Average undergraduate aid package: $3918**

ABOUT THE INSTITUTION Proprietary, coed. Awards: bachelor's and master's degrees. 11 undergraduate majors. Total enrollment: 1,132. Undergraduates: 883. Freshmen: 15. Both federal and institutional methodology are used as a basis for awarding need-based institutional aid.

UNDERGRADUATE EXPENSES for 2006–07 ***Application fee:*** $45. ***Tuition:*** full-time $11,010; part-time $367 per credit. ***Payment plan:*** Deferred payment.

FRESHMAN FINANCIAL AID (Fall 2005) ***Average financial aid package:*** $2650 (excluding resources awarded to replace EFC).

UNDERGRADUATE FINANCIAL AID (Fall 2005) ***Average financial aid package:*** $3918 (excluding resources awarded to replace EFC).

GIFT AID (NEED-BASED) ***Total amount:*** $1,052,614 (100% federal). ***Receiving aid:*** Freshmen: 103; All full-time undergraduates: 472. ***Average award:*** Freshmen: $1957; Undergraduates: $2230. ***Scholarships, grants, and awards:*** Federal Pell, FSEOG, state, private, college/university gift aid from institutional funds, Academic Competitiveness Grant and National Science and Mathematics Access to Retain Talent (SMART).

GIFT AID (NON-NEED-BASED) ***Receiving aid:*** Undergraduates: 15. ***Scholarships, grants, and awards by category:*** *Academic Interests/Achievement:* business, computer science. ***Tuition waivers:*** Full or partial for employees or children of employees.

LOANS ***Student loans:*** $8,371,062 (45% need-based, 55% non-need-based). ***Programs:*** FFEL (Subsidized and Unsubsidized Stafford, PLUS), Perkins.

APPLYING FOR FINANCIAL AID ***Required financial aid forms:*** FAFSA, institution's own form. ***Financial aid deadline:*** Continuous. ***Notification date:*** Continuous beginning 7/1.

CONTACT ACS/AFS, University of Phoenix–Wisconsin Campus, 875 West Elliot Road, Suite 116, Tempe, AZ 85284, 480-735-3000 or toll-free 800-776-4867 (in-state), 800-228-7240 (out-of-state). *Fax:* 480-940-2060.

UNIVERSITY OF PITTSBURGH

Pittsburgh, PA

Tuition & fees (PA res): $12,138 **Average undergraduate aid package: $9087**

ABOUT THE INSTITUTION State-related, coed. Awards: bachelor's, master's, doctoral, and first professional degrees and post-bachelor's and post-master's certificates. 86 undergraduate majors. Total enrollment: 26,860. Undergraduates: 17,246. Freshmen: 3,396. Federal methodology is used as a basis for awarding need-based institutional aid.

UNDERGRADUATE EXPENSES for 2006–07 ***Application fee:*** $35. ***Tuition, state resident:*** full-time $11,368; part-time $473 per credit. ***Tuition, nonresident:*** full-time $20,686; part-time $861 per credit. ***Required fees:*** full-time $770;

$189 per term part-time. Full-time tuition and fees vary according to degree level and program. Part-time tuition and fees vary according to degree level and program. ***College room and board:*** $7800; ***Room only:*** $4790. Room and board charges vary according to board plan and housing facility. ***Payment plans:*** Installment, deferred payment.

FRESHMAN FINANCIAL AID (Fall 2006, est.) 2738 applied for aid; of those 69% were deemed to have need. 98% of freshmen with need received aid; of those 42% had need fully met. ***Average percent of need met:*** 80% (excluding resources awarded to replace EFC). ***Average financial aid package:*** $9309 (excluding resources awarded to replace EFC). 7% of all full-time freshmen had no need and received non-need-based gift aid.

UNDERGRADUATE FINANCIAL AID (Fall 2006, est.) 11,048 applied for aid; of those 79% were deemed to have need. 98% of undergraduates with need received aid; of those 37% had need fully met. ***Average percent of need met:*** 79% (excluding resources awarded to replace EFC). ***Average financial aid package:*** $9087 (excluding resources awarded to replace EFC). 7% of all full-time undergraduates had no need and received non-need-based gift aid.

GIFT AID (NEED-BASED) ***Total amount:*** $43,331,353 (23% federal, 33% state, 30% institutional, 14% external sources). ***Receiving aid:*** Freshmen: 44% (1,492); All full-time undergraduates: 43% (6,616). ***Average award:*** Freshmen: $8533; Undergraduates: $7273. ***Scholarships, grants, and awards:*** Federal Pell, FSEOG, state, private, college/university gift aid from institutional funds.

GIFT AID (NON-NEED-BASED) ***Total amount:*** $15,165,971 (5% state, 69% institutional, 26% external sources). ***Receiving aid:*** Freshmen: 25% (859); Undergraduates: 18% (2,848). ***Average award:*** Freshmen: $13,110; Undergraduates: $11,038. ***Scholarships, grants, and awards by category:*** *Academic Interests/Achievement:* 1,020 awards ($11,258,000 total): general academic interests/achievements. *Special Characteristics:* children of faculty/staff. ***Tuition waivers:*** Full or partial for employees or children of employees. ***ROTC:*** Army, Naval cooperative, Air Force.

LOANS ***Student loans:*** $75,860,095 (46% need-based, 54% non-need-based). ***Average need-based loan:*** Freshmen: $3789; Undergraduates: $4673. ***Parent loans:*** $19,336,484 (68% need-based, 32% non-need-based). ***Programs:*** FFEL (Subsidized and Unsubsidized Stafford, PLUS), Perkins, Federal Nursing, college/university.

WORK-STUDY ***Federal work-study:*** Total amount: $2,500,000; jobs available.

ATHLETIC AWARDS Total amount: $5,890,566 (42% need-based, 58% non-need-based).

APPLYING FOR FINANCIAL AID ***Required financial aid forms:*** FAFSA, institution's own form. ***Financial aid deadline:*** 6/1 (priority: 3/1). ***Notification date:*** Continuous beginning 3/15.

CONTACT Dr. Betsy A. Porter, Director, Office of Admissions and Financial Aid, University of Pittsburgh, 4227 Fifth Avenue, First Floor, Alumni Hall, Pittsburgh, PA 15260, 412-624-7488. *Fax:* 412-648-8815. *E-mail:* oafa@pitt.edu.

UNIVERSITY OF PITTSBURGH AT BRADFORD

Bradford, PA

Tuition & fees (PA res): $10,894   Average undergraduate aid package: $12,000

ABOUT THE INSTITUTION State-related, coed. Awards: associate and bachelor's degrees. 25 undergraduate majors. Total enrollment: 1,319. Undergraduates: 1,319. Freshmen: 339. Federal methodology is used as a basis for awarding need-based institutional aid.

UNDERGRADUATE EXPENSES for 2006–07 ***Application fee:*** $35. ***Tuition, state resident:*** full-time $10,184; part-time $424 per credit. ***Tuition, nonresident:*** full-time $19,776; part-time $824 per credit. ***Required fees:*** full-time $710; $105 per term part-time. Full-time tuition and fees vary according to course load and program. Part-time tuition and fees vary according to course load and program. ***College room and board:*** $6650. Room and board charges vary according to board plan and housing facility. ***Payment plan:*** Installment.

FRESHMAN FINANCIAL AID (Fall 2006, est.) 306 applied for aid; of those 87% were deemed to have need. 100% of freshmen with need received aid; of those 18% had need fully met. ***Average percent of need met:*** 76% (excluding resources awarded to replace EFC). ***Average financial aid package:*** $11,400 (excluding resources awarded to replace EFC). 17% of all full-time freshmen had no need and received non-need-based gift aid.

UNDERGRADUATE FINANCIAL AID (Fall 2006, est.) 1,058 applied for aid; of those 87% were deemed to have need. 100% of undergraduates with need received aid; of those 22% had need fully met. ***Average percent of need met:*** 78% (excluding resources awarded to replace EFC). ***Average financial aid package:*** $12,000 (excluding resources awarded to replace EFC). 11% of all full-time undergraduates had no need and received non-need-based gift aid.

GIFT AID (NEED-BASED) ***Total amount:*** $3,419,581 (41% federal, 57% state, 2% institutional). ***Receiving aid:*** Freshmen: 58% (194); All full-time undergraduates: 59% (653). ***Average award:*** Freshmen: $4000; Undergraduates: $4000. ***Scholarships, grants, and awards:*** Federal Pell, FSEOG, state, private, college/university gift aid from institutional funds, Academic Competitiveness Grant and National SMART Grants.

GIFT AID (NON-NEED-BASED) ***Total amount:*** $4,394,739 (7% state, 79% institutional, 14% external sources). ***Receiving aid:*** Freshmen: 61% (205); Undergraduates: 58% (644). ***Average award:*** Freshmen: $4000; Undergraduates: $4000. ***Scholarships, grants, and awards by category:*** *Academic Interests/Achievement:* biological sciences, business, communication, computer science, education, engineering/technologies, English, general academic interests/achievements, health fields, humanities, mathematics, physical sciences, premedicine, social sciences. ***Tuition waivers:*** Full or partial for employees or children of employees. ***ROTC:*** Army cooperative.

LOANS ***Student loans:*** $7,347,002 (46% need-based, 54% non-need-based). 89% of past graduating class borrowed through all loan programs. *Average indebtedness per student:* $27,684. ***Average need-based loan:*** Freshmen: $2625; Undergraduates: $4281. ***Parent loans:*** $1,475,175 (100% non-need-based). ***Programs:*** FFEL (Subsidized and Unsubsidized Stafford, PLUS), Perkins.

WORK-STUDY ***Federal work-study:*** Total amount: $187,668; 200 jobs averaging $1400. ***State or other work-study/employment:*** Total amount: $100,000 (100% non-need-based). 10 part-time jobs averaging $1400.

APPLYING FOR FINANCIAL AID ***Required financial aid form:*** FAFSA. ***Financial aid deadline (priority):*** 3/1. ***Notification date:*** Continuous beginning 4/1. Students must reply within 2 weeks of notification.

CONTACT Melissa Ibañez, Director of Financial Aid, University of Pittsburgh at Bradford, 300 Campus Drive, Bradford, PA 16701-2812, 814-362-7550 or toll-free 800-872-1787. *Fax:* 814-362-7578. *E-mail:* ibanez@exchange.upb.pitt.edu.

UNIVERSITY OF PITTSBURGH AT GREENSBURG

Greensburg, PA

Tuition & fees (PA res): $11,612   Average undergraduate aid package: $8243

ABOUT THE INSTITUTION State-related, coed. Awards: bachelor's degrees. 22 undergraduate majors. Total enrollment: 1,796. Undergraduates: 1,796. Freshmen: 424. Federal methodology is used as a basis for awarding need-based institutional aid.

UNDERGRADUATE EXPENSES for 2006–07 ***Application fee:*** $45. ***Tuition, state resident:*** full-time $10,898; part-time $424 per credit. ***Tuition, nonresident:*** full-time $20,490; part-time $824 per credit. ***Required fees:*** full-time $714; $123 per term part-time. ***College room and board:*** $6680; ***Room only:*** $4350. Room and board charges vary according to board plan and housing facility. ***Payment plan:*** Installment.

FRESHMAN FINANCIAL AID (Fall 2006, est.) 349 applied for aid; of those 79% were deemed to have need. 100% of freshmen with need received aid; of those 57% had need fully met. ***Average percent of need met:*** 61% (excluding resources awarded to replace EFC). ***Average financial aid package:*** $8176 (excluding resources awarded to replace EFC). 9% of all full-time freshmen had no need and received non-need-based gift aid.

UNDERGRADUATE FINANCIAL AID (Fall 2006, est.) 1,187 applied for aid; of those 81% were deemed to have need. 100% of undergraduates with need received aid; of those 39% had need fully met. ***Average percent of need met:*** 60% (excluding resources awarded to replace EFC). ***Average financial aid package:*** $8243 (excluding resources awarded to replace EFC). 4% of all full-time undergraduates had no need and received non-need-based gift aid.

GIFT AID (NEED-BASED) ***Total amount:*** $4,069,230 (28% federal, 51% state, 18% institutional, 3% external sources). ***Receiving aid:*** Freshmen: 56% (227); All full-time undergraduates: 48% (744). ***Average award:*** Freshmen: $5658; Undergraduates: $5232. ***Scholarships, grants, and awards:*** Federal Pell, FSEOG, state, private, college/university gift aid from institutional funds, United Negro College Fund.

GIFT AID (NON-NEED-BASED) ***Total amount:*** $177,576 (2% state, 94% institutional, 4% external sources). ***Receiving aid:*** Freshmen: 53% (216); Undergraduates: 43% (677). ***Average award:*** Freshmen: $2855; Undergraduates: $3025. ***Scholarships, grants, and awards by category:*** *Academic Interests/Achievement:* 186 awards ($514,750 total): general academic interests/achievements. *Special Achievements/Activities:* 24 awards ($32,700 total): general special achievements/activities, leadership. *Special Characteristics:* 103 awards ($164,000 total). ***Tuition waivers:*** Full or partial for employees or children of employees, senior citizens. ***ROTC:*** Army cooperative, Air Force cooperative.

LOANS ***Student loans:*** $6,704,529 (85% need-based, 15% non-need-based). 79% of past graduating class borrowed through all loan programs. *Average indebtedness per student:* $15,260. ***Average need-based loan:*** Freshmen: $3400; Undergraduates: $3992. ***Parent loans:*** $1,909,440 (64% need-based, 36% non-need-based). ***Programs:*** FFEL (Subsidized and Unsubsidized Stafford, PLUS), Perkins.

WORK-STUDY ***Federal work-study:*** Total amount: $228,460; 78 jobs averaging $2100.

APPLYING FOR FINANCIAL AID ***Required financial aid forms:*** FAFSA, institution's own form, state aid form. ***Financial aid deadline (priority):*** 2/15. ***Notification date:*** Continuous beginning 3/15. Students must reply within 3 weeks of notification.

CONTACT Ms. Brandi S. Darr, Director of Admissions and Financial Aid, University of Pittsburgh at Greensburg, 150 Finoli Drive, Greensburg, PA 15601-5860, 724-836-7167. *E-mail:* upgadmit@pitt.edu.

UNIVERSITY OF PITTSBURGH AT JOHNSTOWN

Johnstown, PA

Tuition & fees (PA res): $10,876 Average undergraduate aid package: $9398

ABOUT THE INSTITUTION State-related, coed. Awards: associate and bachelor's degrees. 50 undergraduate majors. Total enrollment: 3,142. Undergraduates: 3,142. Freshmen: 790. Federal methodology is used as a basis for awarding need-based institutional aid.

UNDERGRADUATE EXPENSES for 2006–07 ***Application fee:*** $45. ***Tuition, state resident:*** full-time $10,184; part-time $424 per credit. ***Tuition, nonresident:*** full-time $19,776; part-time $824 per credit. ***Required fees:*** full-time $692; $87 per term part-time. Full-time tuition and fees vary according to program and student level. Part-time tuition and fees vary according to program and student level. ***College room and board:*** $6200; ***Room only:*** $3800. Room and board charges vary according to board plan and housing facility. ***Payment plan:*** Installment.

FRESHMAN FINANCIAL AID (Fall 2006, est.) 703 applied for aid; of those 87% were deemed to have need. 92% of freshmen with need received aid; of those 10% had need fully met. ***Average percent of need met:*** 49% (excluding resources awarded to replace EFC). ***Average financial aid package:*** $8638 (excluding resources awarded to replace EFC). 4% of all full-time freshmen had no need and received non-need-based gift aid.

UNDERGRADUATE FINANCIAL AID (Fall 2006, est.) 2,747 applied for aid; of those 86% were deemed to have need. 94% of undergraduates with need received aid; of those 7% had need fully met. ***Average percent of need met:*** 52% (excluding resources awarded to replace EFC). ***Average financial aid package:*** $9398 (excluding resources awarded to replace EFC). 3% of all full-time undergraduates had no need and received non-need-based gift aid.

GIFT AID (NEED-BASED) ***Total amount:*** $7,751,475 (33% federal, 61% state, 4% institutional, 2% external sources). ***Receiving aid:*** Freshmen: 59% (473); All full-time undergraduates: 65% (1,887). ***Average award:*** Freshmen: $4549; Undergraduates: $4502. ***Scholarships, grants, and awards:*** Federal Pell, FSEOG, state, private, college/university gift aid from institutional funds.

GIFT AID (NON-NEED-BASED) ***Total amount:*** $2,286,326 (9% state, 77% institutional, 14% external sources). ***Receiving aid:*** Freshmen: 40% (320); Undergraduates: 25% (710). ***Average award:*** Freshmen: $2973; Undergraduates: $2890. ***Scholarships, grants, and awards by category:*** *Academic Interests/Achievement:* 177 awards ($561,315 total): general academic interests/achievements. *Special Achievements/Activities:* 108 awards ($149,500 total): leadership. *Special Characteristics:* 149 awards ($1,295,223 total): children of faculty/staff. ***Tuition waivers:*** Full or partial for employees or children of employees.

LOANS ***Student loans:*** $14,489,607 (49% need-based, 51% non-need-based). 90% of past graduating class borrowed through all loan programs. *Average indebtedness per student:* $23,609. ***Average need-based loan:*** Freshmen: $2570; Undergraduates: $3155. ***Parent loans:*** $4,078,712 (100% non-need-based). ***Programs:*** FFEL (Subsidized and Unsubsidized Stafford, PLUS), Perkins.

WORK-STUDY ***Federal work-study:*** Total amount: $624,348; 372 jobs averaging $1678. ***State or other work-study/employment:*** Total amount: $312,117 (5% need-based, 95% non-need-based). 332 part-time jobs averaging $941.

ATHLETIC AWARDS Total amount: $460,076 (100% non-need-based).

APPLYING FOR FINANCIAL AID ***Required financial aid form:*** FAFSA. ***Financial aid deadline (priority):*** 4/1. ***Notification date:*** Continuous beginning 3/15. Students must reply within 2 weeks of notification.

CONTACT Ms. Julie A. Salem, Director of Student Financial Aid, University of Pittsburgh at Johnstown, 125 Biddle Hall, Johnstown, PA 15904-2990, 814-269-7045 or toll-free 800-765-4875. *Fax:* 814-269-7061. *E-mail:* jasalem@pitt.edu.

UNIVERSITY OF PORTLAND

Portland, OR

ABOUT THE INSTITUTION Independent Roman Catholic, coed. Awards: bachelor's and master's degrees and post-master's certificates. 42 undergraduate majors. Total enrollment: 3,478. Undergraduates: 2,907. Freshmen: 725.

GIFT AID (NEED-BASED) ***Scholarships, grants, and awards:*** Federal Pell, FSEOG, state, private, college/university gift aid from institutional funds.

GIFT AID (NON-NEED-BASED) ***Scholarships, grants, and awards by category:*** *Academic Interests/Achievement:* biological sciences, business, communication, computer science, education, engineering/technologies, English, foreign languages, general academic interests/achievements, health fields, humanities, mathematics, military science, physical sciences, premedicine, religion/biblical studies, social sciences. *Creative Arts/Performance:* music, performing arts, theater/drama. *Special Achievements/Activities:* community service. *Special Characteristics:* children of faculty/staff, relatives of clergy.

LOANS ***Programs:*** FFEL (Subsidized and Unsubsidized Stafford, PLUS), Perkins, Federal Nursing, college/university.

WORK-STUDY ***Federal work-study:*** Total amount: $1,408,167; 848 jobs averaging $1819. ***State or other work-study/employment:*** Total amount: $14,940 (78% need-based, 22% non-need-based). 9 part-time jobs averaging $1660.

APPLYING FOR FINANCIAL AID ***Required financial aid forms:*** FAFSA, institution's own form.

CONTACT Ms. Tracy Reisinger, Director of Financial Aid, University of Portland, 5000 North Willamette Boulevard, Portland, OR 97203-5798, 503-943-7311 or toll-free 888-627-5601 (out-of-state). *Fax:* 503-943-7508. *E-mail:* reisinge@up.edu.

UNIVERSITY OF PUERTO RICO, AGUADILLA UNIVERSITY COLLEGE

Aguadilla, PR

CONTACT Director of Financial Aid, University of Puerto Rico, Aguadilla University College, PO Box 250-160, Aguadilla, PR 00604-0160, 787-890-2681 Ext. 273.

UNIVERSITY OF PUERTO RICO AT ARECIBO

Arecibo, PR

CONTACT Mr. Luis Rodriguez, Director of Financial Aid, University of Puerto Rico at Arecibo, PO Box 4010, Arecibo, PR 00613, 787-878-2830 Ext. 2008.

UNIVERSITY OF PUERTO RICO AT BAYAMÓN

Bayamón, PR

CONTACT Financial Aid Director, University of Puerto Rico at Bayamón, 170 Carr 174 Parque Indust Minillas, Bayamon, PR 00959-1919, 787-786-2885 Ext. 2434.

UNIVERSITY OF PUERTO RICO AT HUMACAO

Humacao, PR

CONTACT Larry Cruz, Director of Financial Aid, University of Puerto Rico at Humacao, HUC Station, Humacao, PR 00791-4300, 787-850-9342.

UNIVERSITY OF PUERTO RICO AT PONCE

Ponce, PR

CONTACT Carmelo Vega Montes, Director of Financial Aid, University of Puerto Rico at Ponce, Box 7186, Ponce, PR 00732-7186, 787-844-8181. *Fax:* 787-840-8108.

UNIVERSITY OF PUERTO RICO AT UTUADO

Utuado, PR

CONTACT Edgar Salva, Director of Student Financial Assistance, University of Puerto Rico at Utuado, Call Box 2500, Utuado, PR 00641, 787-894-2828. *Fax:* 787-894-2891.

UNIVERSITY OF PUERTO RICO, CAYEY UNIVERSITY COLLEGE

Cayey, PR

CONTACT Mr. Hector Maldonado Otero, Director of Financial Aid, University of Puerto Rico, Cayey University College, Antonio Barcelo, Cayey, PR 00736, 787-738-2161. *Fax:* 787-263-0676.

UNIVERSITY OF PUERTO RICO, MAYAGÜEZ CAMPUS

Mayagüez, PR

ABOUT THE INSTITUTION Commonwealth-supported, coed. Awards: bachelor's, master's, and doctoral degrees. 62 undergraduate majors. Total enrollment: 12,380. Undergraduates: 11,305. Freshmen: 2,239.

GIFT AID (NEED-BASED) ***Scholarships, grants, and awards:*** Federal Pell, FSEOG, state, private, college/university gift aid from institutional funds.

GIFT AID (NON-NEED-BASED) ***Scholarships, grants, and awards by category:*** *Academic Interests/Achievement:* military science. *Creative Arts/Performance:* dance, music. *Special Achievements/Activities:* cheerleading/drum major.

LOANS ***Programs:*** FFEL (Subsidized and Unsubsidized Stafford), college/university.

APPLYING FOR FINANCIAL AID ***Required financial aid forms:*** FAFSA, institution's own form, noncustodial (divorced/separated) parent's statement, business/farm supplement.

CONTACT Ms. Ana I. Rodríguez, Director of Financial Aid, University of Puerto Rico, Mayagüez Campus, PO Box 9000, Mayagüez, PR 00681-9000, 787-265-3863. *Fax:* 787-265-1920. *E-mail:* a_rodriguez@rumad.uprm.edu.

UNIVERSITY OF PUERTO RICO, MEDICAL SCIENCES CAMPUS

San Juan, PR

Tuition & fees: N/R **Average undergraduate aid package: $4851**

ABOUT THE INSTITUTION Commonwealth-supported, coed, primarily women. Awards: associate, bachelor's, master's, doctoral, and first professional degrees and post-bachelor's and first professional certificates (bachelor's degree is upper-level). 14 undergraduate majors. Total enrollment: 2,289. Undergraduates: 442. Both federal and institutional methodology are used as a basis for awarding need-based institutional aid.

UNDERGRADUATE FINANCIAL AID (Fall 2005) 308 applied for aid; of those 88% were deemed to have need. 100% of undergraduates with need received aid; of those 7% had need fully met. ***Average percent of need met:*** 52% (excluding resources awarded to replace EFC). ***Average financial aid package:*** $4851 (excluding resources awarded to replace EFC).

GIFT AID (NEED-BASED) ***Total amount:*** $1,011,742 (82% federal, 8% state, 10% external sources). ***Receiving aid:*** Entering class: 47% (102); All full-time undergraduates: 57% (254). ***Average award:*** Freshmen: $4375; Undergraduates: $4450. ***Scholarships, grants, and awards:*** Federal Pell, FSEOG, state, college/university gift aid from institutional funds, Department of Health and Human Services Scholarships.

GIFT AID (NON-NEED-BASED) ***Scholarships, grants, and awards by category:*** *Academic Interests/Achievement:* general academic interests/achievements.

LOANS ***Student loans:*** $274,453 (100% need-based). 23% of past graduating class borrowed through all loan programs. *Average indebtedness per student:* $3491. ***Average need-based loan:*** Freshmen: $2225; Undergraduates: $3351. ***Programs:*** FFEL (Subsidized and Unsubsidized Stafford), Perkins, alternative loans.

WORK-STUDY ***Federal work-study:*** Total amount: $26,462; 26 jobs averaging $980.

APPLYING FOR FINANCIAL AID ***Required financial aid forms:*** FAFSA, institution's own form. ***Financial aid deadline:*** 5/15. ***Notification date:*** Continuous beginning 8/1. Students must reply within 2 weeks of notification.

CONTACT Zoraida Figueroa, Financial Aid Director, University of Puerto Rico, Medical Sciences Campus, Terreno Centro Médico-Edificio Decanato Farmacia y Estudiantes, PO Box 365067, Rio Piedras, PR 00936-5067, 787-763-2525. *Fax:* 787-282-7117. *E-mail:* zfigueroa@rcm.upr.edu.

UNIVERSITY OF PUERTO RICO, RÍO PIEDRAS

San Juan, PR

CONTACT Mr. Efraim Williams, EDP Manager, University of Puerto Rico, Río Piedras, PO Box 23353, San Juan, PR 00931, 787-764-0000 Ext. 5573.

UNIVERSITY OF PUGET SOUND

Tacoma, WA

Tuition & fees: $30,060 **Average undergraduate aid package: $22,740**

ABOUT THE INSTITUTION Independent, coed. Awards: bachelor's, master's, and first professional degrees and post-master's certificates. 40 undergraduate majors. Total enrollment: 2,819. Undergraduates: 2,539. Freshmen: 678. Federal methodology is used as a basis for awarding need-based institutional aid.

UNDERGRADUATE EXPENSES for 2006–07 ***Application fee:*** $40. ***Comprehensive fee:*** $37,730 includes full-time tuition ($29,870), mandatory fees ($190), and room and board ($7670). ***College room only:*** $4190. Full-time tuition and fees vary according to course load. Room and board charges vary according to board plan and housing facility. ***Part-time tuition:*** $3770 per unit. Part-time tuition and fees vary according to course load. ***Payment plans:*** Installment, deferred payment.

FRESHMAN FINANCIAL AID (Fall 2006, est.) 488 applied for aid; of those 80% were deemed to have need. 100% of freshmen with need received aid; of those 31% had need fully met. ***Average percent of need met:*** 84% (excluding resources awarded to replace EFC). ***Average financial aid package:*** $23,409 (excluding resources awarded to replace EFC). 27% of all full-time freshmen had no need and received non-need-based gift aid.

UNDERGRADUATE FINANCIAL AID (Fall 2006, est.) 1,723 applied for aid; of those 86% were deemed to have need. 100% of undergraduates with need received aid; of those 28% had need fully met. ***Average percent of need met:*** 82% (excluding resources awarded to replace EFC). ***Average financial aid package:*** $22,740 (excluding resources awarded to replace EFC). 28% of all full-time undergraduates had no need and received non-need-based gift aid.

GIFT AID (NEED-BASED) ***Total amount:*** $24,414,072 (8% federal, 3% state, 85% institutional, 4% external sources). ***Receiving aid:*** Freshmen: 56% (381); All full-time undergraduates: 58% (1,447). ***Average award:*** Freshmen: $19,282; Undergraduates: $17,238. ***Scholarships, grants, and awards:*** Federal Pell, FSEOG, state, private, college/university gift aid from institutional funds.

GIFT AID (NON-NEED-BASED) ***Total amount:*** $4,612,001 (95% institutional, 5% external sources). ***Receiving aid:*** Freshmen: 29% (199); Undergraduates: 29% (723). ***Average award:*** Freshmen: $6353; Undergraduates: $6380. ***Scholarships, grants, and awards by category:*** *Academic Interests/Achievement:* 736 awards ($3,880,932 total): biological sciences, business, communication, computer science, English, foreign languages, general academic interests/achievements, humanities, international studies, mathematics, physical sciences, premedicine, social sciences. *Creative Arts/Performance:* 54 awards ($174,750 total): art/fine arts, debating, music, theater/drama. *Special Achievements/Activities:* 6 awards ($16,500 total): leadership, religious involvement. *Special Characteristics:* 24 awards ($548,345 total): children of faculty/staff, international students. ***Tuition waivers:*** Full or partial for employees or children of employees. ***ROTC:*** Army cooperative.

LOANS ***Student loans:*** $10,584,246 (90% need-based, 10% non-need-based). 59% of past graduating class borrowed through all loan programs. *Average indebtedness per student:* $26,762. ***Average need-based loan:*** Freshmen: $3966; Undergraduates: $5756. ***Parent loans:*** $4,924,986 (73% need-based, 27% non-need-based). ***Programs:*** FFEL (Subsidized and Unsubsidized Stafford, PLUS), Perkins, Alaska Loans.

WORK-STUDY ***Federal work-study:*** Total amount: $1,334,000; 519 jobs averaging $2570. ***State or other work-study/employment:*** Total amount: $2,069,017 (100% need-based). 875 part-time jobs averaging $2365.

APPLYING FOR FINANCIAL AID ***Required financial aid form:*** FAFSA. ***Financial aid deadline (priority):*** 2/1. ***Notification date:*** Continuous beginning 3/15. Students must reply by 5/1.

CONTACT Maggie A. Mittuch, Associate Vice President for Student Financial Services, University of Puget Sound, 1500 North Warner Street #1039, Tacoma, WA 98416-1039, 253-879-3214 or toll-free 800-396-7191. *Fax:* 253-879-8508. *E-mail:* mmittuch@ups.edu.

UNIVERSITY OF REDLANDS

Redlands, CA

Tuition & fees: $28,776 **Average undergraduate aid package: $25,693**

ABOUT THE INSTITUTION Independent, coed. Awards: bachelor's and master's degrees and post-bachelor's and post-master's certificates. 42 undergraduate majors. Total enrollment: 2,407. Undergraduates: 2,313. Freshmen: 613. Federal methodology is used as a basis for awarding need-based institutional aid.

UNDERGRADUATE EXPENSES for 2006–07 ***Application fee:*** $45. ***Comprehensive fee:*** $38,136 includes full-time tuition ($28,476), mandatory fees ($300), and room and board ($9360). ***College room only:*** $5221. Room and board charges vary according to board plan and housing facility. ***Part-time tuition:*** $890 per credit. ***Part-time fees:*** $150 per term. Part-time tuition and fees vary according to course load. ***Payment plan:*** Installment.

FRESHMAN FINANCIAL AID (Fall 2006, est.) 493 applied for aid; of those 82% were deemed to have need. 100% of freshmen with need received aid; of those 49% had need fully met. ***Average percent of need met:*** 95% (excluding resources awarded to replace EFC). ***Average financial aid package:*** $27,366 (excluding resources awarded to replace EFC). 25% of all full-time freshmen had no need and received non-need-based gift aid.

UNDERGRADUATE FINANCIAL AID (Fall 2006, est.) 1,838 applied for aid; of those 85% were deemed to have need. 100% of undergraduates with need received aid; of those 42% had need fully met. ***Average percent of need met:*** 91% (excluding resources awarded to replace EFC). ***Average financial aid package:*** $25,693 (excluding resources awarded to replace EFC). 22% of all full-time undergraduates had no need and received non-need-based gift aid.

GIFT AID (NEED-BASED) ***Total amount:*** $29,221,338 (7% federal, 15% state, 78% institutional). ***Receiving aid:*** Freshmen: 65% (398); All full-time undergraduates: 67% (1,539). ***Average award:*** Freshmen: $20,405; Undergraduates: $18,296. ***Scholarships, grants, and awards:*** Federal Pell, FSEOG, state, private, college/university gift aid from institutional funds.

GIFT AID (NON-NEED-BASED) ***Total amount:*** $4,307,963 (100% institutional). ***Receiving aid:*** Freshmen: 31% (187); Undergraduates: 27% (621). ***Average award:*** Freshmen: $11,055; Undergraduates: $10,219. ***Scholarships, grants, and awards by category:*** *Academic Interests/Achievement:* general academic interests/achievements. *Creative Arts/Performance:* art/fine arts, creative writing, debating, music. *Special Achievements/Activities:* general special achievements/activities. *Special Characteristics:* international students. ***Tuition waivers:*** Full or partial for employees or children of employees. ***ROTC:*** Army cooperative, Air Force cooperative.

LOANS ***Student loans:*** $19,523,778 (53% need-based, 47% non-need-based). 75% of past graduating class borrowed through all loan programs. *Average indebtedness per student:* $15,125. ***Average need-based loan:*** Freshmen: $4625; Undergraduates: $5640. ***Parent loans:*** $3,709,953 (74% need-based, 26% non-need-based). ***Programs:*** FFEL (Subsidized and Unsubsidized Stafford, PLUS), Perkins, college/university, alternative loans.

WORK-STUDY ***Federal work-study:*** Total amount: $2,381,515; jobs available. ***State or other work-study/employment:*** Total amount: $252,402 (100% non-need-based). Part-time jobs available.

APPLYING FOR FINANCIAL AID ***Required financial aid forms:*** FAFSA, state aid form. ***Financial aid deadline (priority):*** 2/15. ***Notification date:*** Continuous beginning 2/28. Students must reply by 5/1.

CONTACT Mr. Craig Slaughter, Director of Financial Aid, University of Redlands, PO Box 3080, Redlands, CA 92373-0999, 909-748-8261 or toll-free 800-455-5064. *Fax:* 909-335-4089. *E-mail:* financialaid@redlands.edu.

UNIVERSITY OF RHODE ISLAND

Kingston, RI

Tuition & fees (RI res): $7724 **Average undergraduate aid package: $12,707**

ABOUT THE INSTITUTION State-supported, coed. Awards: bachelor's, master's, doctoral, and first professional degrees and post-bachelor's certificates. 76 undergraduate majors. Total enrollment: 15,062. Undergraduates: 11,875. Freshmen: 2,780. Federal methodology is used as a basis for awarding need-based institutional aid.

UNDERGRADUATE EXPENSES for 2006–07 ***Application fee:*** $50. ***Tuition, state resident:*** full-time $5656; part-time $236 per credit. ***Tuition, nonresident:*** full-time $19,356; part-time $807 per credit. ***Required fees:*** full-time $2068; $66 per credit or $48 per term part-time. Full-time tuition and fees vary according to reciprocity agreements. Part-time tuition and fees vary according to reciprocity agreements. ***College room and board:*** $8466; ***Room only:*** $4814. Room and board charges vary according to board plan and housing facility. ***Payment plan:*** Installment.

FRESHMAN FINANCIAL AID (Fall 2006, est.) 2244 applied for aid; of those 77% were deemed to have need. 78% of freshmen with need received aid; of those 86% had need fully met. ***Average percent of need met:*** 71% (excluding resources awarded to replace EFC). ***Average financial aid package:*** $13,735 (excluding resources awarded to replace EFC). 7% of all full-time freshmen had no need and received non-need-based gift aid.

UNDERGRADUATE FINANCIAL AID (Fall 2006, est.) 8,355 applied for aid; of those 83% were deemed to have need. 74% of undergraduates with need received aid; of those 70% had need fully met. ***Average percent of need met:*** 63% (excluding resources awarded to replace EFC). ***Average financial aid package:*** $12,707 (excluding resources awarded to replace EFC). 5% of all full-time undergraduates had no need and received non-need-based gift aid.

GIFT AID (NEED-BASED) ***Total amount:*** $35,324,405 (20% federal, 9% state, 67% institutional, 4% external sources). ***Receiving aid:*** Freshmen: 49% (1,349); All full-time undergraduates: 50% (5,088). ***Average award:*** Freshmen: $6460; Undergraduates: $6156. ***Scholarships, grants, and awards:*** Federal Pell, FSEOG, state, private, college/university gift aid from institutional funds.

GIFT AID (NON-NEED-BASED) ***Total amount:*** $2,459,325 (93% institutional, 7% external sources). ***Receiving aid:*** Freshmen: 8% (218); Undergraduates: 5% (540). ***Average award:*** Freshmen: $4645; Undergraduates: $4937. ***Scholarships, grants, and awards by category:*** *Academic Interests/Achievement:* general academic interests/achievements. *Creative Arts/Performance:* music. *Special Achievements/Activities:* general special achievements/activities. *Special Characteristics:* general special characteristics. ***Tuition waivers:*** Full or partial for minority students, employees or children of employees, senior citizens. ***ROTC:*** Army.

LOANS ***Student loans:*** $52,605,280 (79% need-based, 21% non-need-based). 56% of past graduating class borrowed through all loan programs. *Average indebtedness per student:* $16,200. ***Average need-based loan:*** Freshmen: $7114; Undergraduates: $7299. ***Parent loans:*** $15,326,821 (67% need-based, 33% non-need-based). ***Programs:*** Federal Direct (Subsidized and Unsubsidized Stafford, PLUS), Perkins, Federal Nursing, state, college/university.

WORK-STUDY ***Federal work-study:*** Total amount: $960,000; jobs available. ***State or other work-study/employment:*** Part-time jobs available.

ATHLETIC AWARDS Total amount: $4,173,590 (97% need-based, 3% non-need-based).

APPLYING FOR FINANCIAL AID ***Required financial aid form:*** FAFSA. ***Financial aid deadline (priority):*** 3/1. ***Notification date:*** Continuous beginning 3/31. Students must reply by 5/1 or within 2 weeks of notification.

CONTACT Mr. Horace J. Amaral Jr., Director of Enrollment Services, University of Rhode Island, Green Hall, Kingston, RI 02881, 401-874-9500.

UNIVERSITY OF RICHMOND

Richmond, VA

Tuition & fees: $37,610 **Average undergraduate aid package: $27,205**

ABOUT THE INSTITUTION Independent, coed. Awards: associate, bachelor's, master's, and first professional degrees and post-bachelor's certificates. 53 undergraduate majors. Total enrollment: 3,554. Undergraduates: 2,857. Freshmen: 757. Federal methodology is used as a basis for awarding need-based institutional aid.

UNDERGRADUATE EXPENSES for 2007–08 ***Application fee:*** $50. ***Comprehensive fee:*** $44,810 includes full-time tuition ($37,610) and room and board ($7200). ***College room only:*** $3230. ***Part-time tuition:*** $1500 per semester hour.

FRESHMAN FINANCIAL AID (Fall 2006, est.) 420 applied for aid; of those 74% were deemed to have need. 100% of freshmen with need received aid; of those 95% had need fully met. ***Average percent of need met:*** 100% (excluding resources awarded to replace EFC). ***Average financial aid package:*** $31,115 (excluding resources awarded to replace EFC). 5% of all full-time freshmen had no need and received non-need-based gift aid.

UNDERGRADUATE FINANCIAL AID (Fall 2006, est.) 1,353 applied for aid; of those 76% were deemed to have need. 100% of undergraduates with need received aid; of those 94% had need fully met. ***Average percent of need met:*** 100% (excluding resources awarded to replace EFC). ***Average financial aid package:*** $27,205 (excluding resources awarded to replace EFC). 14% of all full-time undergraduates had no need and received non-need-based gift aid.

GIFT AID (NEED-BASED) ***Total amount:*** $23,921,715 (3% federal, 3% state, 92% institutional, 2% external sources). ***Receiving aid:*** Freshmen: 41% (309); All full-time undergraduates: 34% (1,015). ***Average award:*** Freshmen: $27,929; Undergraduates: $24,286. ***Scholarships, grants, and awards:*** Federal Pell, FSEOG, state, private, college/university gift aid from institutional funds.

GIFT AID (NON-NEED-BASED) ***Total amount:*** $8,979,715 (6% federal, 6% state, 83% institutional, 5% external sources). ***Receiving aid:*** Freshmen: 4% (29); Undergraduates: 3% (79). ***Average award:*** Freshmen: $29,185; Undergraduates: $15,959. ***Scholarships, grants, and awards by category:*** *Academic Interests/Achievement:* 216 awards ($4,285,922 total): biological sciences, computer science, general academic interests/achievements, mathematics, physical sciences. *Creative Arts/Performance:* 14 awards ($85,800 total): art/fine arts, dance, music, performing arts, theater/drama. *Special Achievements/Activities:* 25 awards ($52,500 total): community service. *Special Characteristics:* 56 awards ($1,403,025 total): members of minority groups. ***ROTC:*** Army.

LOANS ***Student loans:*** $7,668,782 (30% need-based, 70% non-need-based). 39% of past graduating class borrowed through all loan programs. *Average indebtedness per student:* $17,165. ***Average need-based loan:*** Freshmen: $2587; Undergraduates: $2830. ***Parent loans:*** $3,869,947 (1% need-based, 99% non-need-based). ***Programs:*** Federal Direct (Subsidized and Unsubsidized Stafford, PLUS), Perkins.

WORK-STUDY ***Federal work-study:*** Total amount: $333,751; 213 jobs averaging $1570.

ATHLETIC AWARDS Total amount: $6,325,423 (14% need-based, 86% non-need-based).

APPLYING FOR FINANCIAL AID ***Required financial aid forms:*** FAFSA, institution's own form. ***Financial aid deadline:*** 2/25. ***Notification date:*** 4/1. Students must reply within 4 weeks of notification.

CONTACT Financial Aid Office, University of Richmond, Sarah Brunet Hall, 28 Westhampton Way, University of Richmond, VA 23173, 804-289-8438 or toll-free 800-700-1662. *Fax:* 804-287-6003. *E-mail:* finaid@richmond.edu.

UNIVERSITY OF RIO GRANDE

Rio Grande, OH

CONTACT Dr. John Hill, Director of Financial Aid, University of Rio Grande, 218 North College Avenue, Rio Grande, OH 45674, 740-245-7218 or toll-free 800-282-7201 (in-state). *Fax:* 740-245-7102.

UNIVERSITY OF ROCHESTER

Rochester, NY

Tuition & fees: $35,190 **Average undergraduate aid package: $26,667**

ABOUT THE INSTITUTION Independent, coed. Awards: bachelor's, master's, doctoral, and first professional degrees and post-bachelor's, post-master's, and first professional certificates. 50 undergraduate majors. Total enrollment: 8,846. Undergraduates: 4,904. Freshmen: 1,219. Institutional methodology is used as a basis for awarding need-based institutional aid.

UNDERGRADUATE EXPENSES for 2007–08 ***Application fee:*** $50. ***Comprehensive fee:*** $45,830 includes full-time tuition ($34,380), mandatory fees ($810), and room and board ($10,640). ***College room only:*** $6200. ***Part-time tuition:*** $1075 per credit hour.

FRESHMAN FINANCIAL AID (Fall 2006, est.) 793 applied for aid; of those 77% were deemed to have need. 100% of freshmen with need received aid; of those 100% had need fully met. ***Average percent of need met:*** 100% (excluding resources awarded to replace EFC). ***Average financial aid package:*** $27,987 (excluding resources awarded to replace EFC). 33% of all full-time freshmen had no need and received non-need-based gift aid.

UNDERGRADUATE FINANCIAL AID (Fall 2006, est.) 2,716 applied for aid; of those 81% were deemed to have need. 100% of undergraduates with need received aid; of those 43% had need fully met. ***Average percent of need met:*** 86% (excluding resources awarded to replace EFC). ***Average financial aid package:*** $26,667 (excluding resources awarded to replace EFC). 32% of all full-time undergraduates had no need and received non-need-based gift aid.

GIFT AID (NEED-BASED) ***Total amount:*** $53,509,301 (5% federal, 6% state, 85% institutional, 4% external sources). ***Receiving aid:*** Freshmen: 55% (603); All full-time undergraduates: 54% (2,185). ***Average award:*** Freshmen: $23,608; Undergraduates: $21,489. ***Scholarships, grants, and awards:*** Federal Pell, FSEOG, state, college/university gift aid from institutional funds.

GIFT AID (NON-NEED-BASED) ***Total amount:*** $4,647,541 (3% state, 91% institutional, 6% external sources). ***Receiving aid:*** Freshmen: 8% (84); Undergraduates: 5% (210). ***Average award:*** Freshmen: $9014; Undergraduates: $8877. ***Scholarships, grants, and awards by category:*** *Academic Interests/Achievement:* biological sciences, engineering/technologies, general academic interests/achievements, humanities, mathematics, military science, physical sciences, social sciences. *Creative Arts/Performance:* general creative arts/performance, music. *Special Achievements/Activities:* general special achievements/activities, leadership. *Special Characteristics:* children and siblings of alumni, children of faculty/staff, general special characteristics, international students. ***ROTC:*** Army cooperative, Naval, Air Force cooperative.

LOANS ***Student loans:*** $21,708,578 (78% need-based, 22% non-need-based). 56% of past graduating class borrowed through all loan programs. *Average indebtedness per student:* $27,497. ***Average need-based loan:*** Freshmen: $4220; Undergraduates: $5059. ***Parent loans:*** $7,110,646 (70% need-based, 30% non-need-based). ***Programs:*** Federal Direct (Subsidized and Unsubsidized Stafford, PLUS), Perkins, Federal Nursing, college/university, alternative loans.

WORK-STUDY ***Federal work-study:*** Total amount: $3,835,195; 1,692 jobs averaging $2225. ***State or other work-study/employment:*** Total amount: $542,850 (92% need-based, 8% non-need-based).

APPLYING FOR FINANCIAL AID ***Required financial aid forms:*** FAFSA, CSS Financial Aid PROFILE, state aid form, noncustodial (divorced/separated) parent's statement, business/farm supplement. ***Financial aid deadline (priority):*** 2/1. ***Notification date:*** 4/1. Students must reply by 5/1.

CONTACT Charles W. Puls, Director of Financial Aid, University of Rochester, Office of Financial Aid, 314 Meliora Hall, Box 270261, Rochester, NY 14627, 585-275-3226 or toll-free 888-822-2256. *Fax:* 585-756-7664. *E-mail:* cpuls@finaid.rochester.edu.

UNIVERSITY OF ST. FRANCIS

Joliet, IL

Tuition & fees: $19,540 **Average undergraduate aid package: $16,063**

ABOUT THE INSTITUTION Independent Roman Catholic, coed. Awards: bachelor's and master's degrees. 43 undergraduate majors. Total enrollment: 2,060. Undergraduates: 1,289. Freshmen: 182. Federal methodology is used as a basis for awarding need-based institutional aid.

UNDERGRADUATE EXPENSES for 2006–07 ***Application fee:*** $30. ***Comprehensive fee:*** $26,820 includes full-time tuition ($19,150), mandatory fees ($390), and room and board ($7280). ***Part-time tuition:*** $625 per credit hour.

FRESHMAN FINANCIAL AID (Fall 2006, est.) 170 applied for aid; of those 84% were deemed to have need. 100% of freshmen with need received aid; of those 85% had need fully met. ***Average percent of need met:*** 78% (excluding

resources awarded to replace EFC). ***Average financial aid package:*** $17,703 (excluding resources awarded to replace EFC). 21% of all full-time freshmen had no need and received non-need-based gift aid.

UNDERGRADUATE FINANCIAL AID (Fall 2006, est.) 1,048 applied for aid; of those 85% were deemed to have need. 100% of undergraduates with need received aid; of those 76% had need fully met. ***Average percent of need met:*** 80% (excluding resources awarded to replace EFC). ***Average financial aid package:*** $16,063 (excluding resources awarded to replace EFC). 12% of all full-time undergraduates had no need and received non-need-based gift aid.

GIFT AID (NEED-BASED) ***Total amount:*** $7,774,017 (13% federal, 30% state, 56% institutional, 1% external sources). ***Receiving aid:*** Freshmen: 62% (112); All full-time undergraduates: 59% (709). ***Average award:*** Freshmen: $7960; Undergraduates: $7575. ***Scholarships, grants, and awards:*** Federal Pell, FSEOG, state, private, college/university gift aid from institutional funds.

GIFT AID (NON-NEED-BASED) ***Total amount:*** $2,878,662 (3% federal, 3% state, 91% institutional, 3% external sources). ***Receiving aid:*** Freshmen: 77% (141); Undergraduates: 68% (814). ***Average award:*** Freshmen: $5721; Undergraduates: $5806. ***Scholarships, grants, and awards by category:*** *Academic Interests/Achievement:* 1,146 awards ($4,745,960 total): biological sciences, communication, education, general academic interests/achievements, health fields, social sciences. *Creative Arts/Performance:* 32 awards ($15,182 total): applied art and design, art/fine arts, music. *Special Achievements/Activities:* 598 awards ($304,885 total): community service, general special achievements/activities, leadership, religious involvement. *Special Characteristics:* 253 awards ($202,103 total): children and siblings of alumni, children of educators, ethnic background, first-generation college students, religious affiliation, siblings of current students.

LOANS ***Student loans:*** $5,300,717 (56% need-based, 44% non-need-based). 86% of past graduating class borrowed through all loan programs. *Average indebtedness per student:* $18,547. ***Average need-based loan:*** Freshmen: $3108; Undergraduates: $4366. ***Parent loans:*** $2,009,010 (57% need-based, 43% non-need-based). ***Programs:*** Federal Direct (Subsidized and Unsubsidized Stafford, PLUS), Perkins, alternative loans.

WORK-STUDY ***Federal work-study:*** Total amount: $515,373; 282 jobs averaging $1828. ***State or other work-study/employment:*** Total amount: $424,563 (100% non-need-based). 237 part-time jobs averaging $1791.

ATHLETIC AWARDS Total amount: $2,684,566 (43% need-based, 57% non-need-based).

APPLYING FOR FINANCIAL AID ***Required financial aid forms:*** FAFSA, institution's own form. ***Financial aid deadline (priority):*** 4/1. ***Notification date:*** Continuous beginning 3/5. Students must reply within 3 weeks of notification.

CONTACT Mrs. Mary V. Shaw, Director of Financial Aid Services, University of St. Francis, 500 North Wilcox Street, Joliet, IL 60435-6188, 815-740-3403 or toll-free 800-735-3500. *Fax:* 815-740-3822. *E-mail:* mshaw@stfrancis.edu.

UNIVERSITY OF SAINT FRANCIS

Fort Wayne, IN

Tuition & fees: $18,478 **Average undergraduate aid package: $13,008**

ABOUT THE INSTITUTION Independent Roman Catholic, coed. Awards: associate, bachelor's, and master's degrees and post-bachelor's certificates. 52 undergraduate majors. Total enrollment: 2,039. Undergraduates: 1,784. Freshmen: 362. Federal methodology is used as a basis for awarding need-based institutional aid.

UNDERGRADUATE EXPENSES for 2006–07 ***Application fee:*** $20. ***Comprehensive fee:*** $24,312 includes full-time tuition ($17,760), mandatory fees ($718), and room and board ($5834). Full-time tuition and fees vary according to course load. Room and board charges vary according to housing facility. ***Part-time tuition:*** $560 per hour. ***Part-time fees:*** $17 per hour. Part-time tuition and fees vary according to course load. ***Payment plans:*** Installment, deferred payment.

FRESHMAN FINANCIAL AID (Fall 2005) 292 applied for aid; of those 85% were deemed to have need. 100% of freshmen with need received aid; of those 29% had need fully met. ***Average percent of need met:*** 78% (excluding resources awarded to replace EFC). ***Average financial aid package:*** $13,139 (excluding resources awarded to replace EFC). 15% of all full-time freshmen had no need and received non-need-based gift aid.

UNDERGRADUATE FINANCIAL AID (Fall 2005) 1,181 applied for aid; of those 87% were deemed to have need. 100% of undergraduates with need received aid; of those 27% had need fully met. ***Average percent of need met:*** 77% (excluding resources awarded to replace EFC). ***Average financial aid package:*** $13,008 (excluding resources awarded to replace EFC). 13% of all full-time undergraduates had no need and received non-need-based gift aid.

GIFT AID (NEED-BASED) ***Total amount:*** $9,907,221 (15% federal, 40% state, 30% institutional, 15% external sources). ***Receiving aid:*** Freshmen: 84% (248); All full-time undergraduates: 85% (1,022). ***Average award:*** Freshmen: $10,487; Undergraduates: $9487. ***Scholarships, grants, and awards:*** Federal Pell, FSEOG, state, private, college/university gift aid from institutional funds.

GIFT AID (NON-NEED-BASED) ***Total amount:*** $1,315,738 (1% state, 53% institutional, 46% external sources). ***Receiving aid:*** Freshmen: 15% (45); Undergraduates: 12% (142). ***Average award:*** Freshmen: $12,304; Undergraduates: $11,062. ***Scholarships, grants, and awards by category:*** *Academic Interests/Achievement:* 584 awards ($2,052,795 total): biological sciences, business, communication, education, English, general academic interests/achievements, health fields, mathematics, physical sciences, premedicine, religion/biblical studies, social sciences. *Creative Arts/Performance:* 199 awards ($559,492 total): art/fine arts, dance, debating, music. *Special Achievements/Activities:* 69 awards ($66,991 total): cheerleading/drum major, religious involvement. *Special Characteristics:* 143 awards ($435,208 total): children and siblings of alumni, children of faculty/staff, siblings of current students, spouses of current students. ***Tuition waivers:*** Full or partial for children of alumni, employees or children of employees, senior citizens.

LOANS ***Student loans:*** $10,037,517 (69% need-based, 31% non-need-based). 97% of past graduating class borrowed through all loan programs. *Average indebtedness per student:* $21,352. ***Average need-based loan:*** Freshmen: $2380; Undergraduates: $3209. ***Parent loans:*** $1,821,464 (33% need-based, 67% non-need-based). ***Programs:*** FFEL (Subsidized and Unsubsidized Stafford, PLUS), Perkins.

WORK-STUDY ***Federal work-study:*** Total amount: $1,171,399; 891 jobs averaging $1521. ***State or other work-study/employment:*** Part-time jobs available.

ATHLETIC AWARDS Total amount: $2,431,699 (74% need-based, 26% non-need-based).

APPLYING FOR FINANCIAL AID ***Required financial aid form:*** FAFSA. ***Financial aid deadline:*** 6/30 (priority: 3/10). ***Notification date:*** Continuous beginning 3/1. Students must reply within 2 weeks of notification.

CONTACT Jamie McGrath, Director of Financial Aid, University of Saint Francis, 2701 Spring Street, Fort Wayne, IN 46808, 260-434-3283 or toll-free 800-729-4732. *Fax:* 260-434-7526.

UNIVERSITY OF SAINT MARY

Leavenworth, KS

CONTACT Mrs. Judy Wiedower, Financial Aid Director, University of Saint Mary, 4100 South Fourth Street, Leavenworth, KS 66048, 913-758-6314 or toll-free 800-752-7043 (out-of-state). *Fax:* 913-758-6146. *E-mail:* wiedower@hub.smcks.edu.

UNIVERSITY OF ST. THOMAS

St. Paul, MN

Tuition & fees: $24,808 **Average undergraduate aid package: $17,223**

ABOUT THE INSTITUTION Independent Roman Catholic, coed. Awards: bachelor's, master's, doctoral, and first professional degrees and post-bachelor's and post-master's certificates. 83 undergraduate majors. Total enrollment: 10,712. Undergraduates: 5,807. Freshmen: 1,299. Both federal and institutional methodology are used as a basis for awarding need-based institutional aid.

UNDERGRADUATE EXPENSES for 2006–07 ***Comprehensive fee:*** $31,690 includes full-time tuition ($24,368), mandatory fees ($440), and room and board ($6882). ***College room only:*** $4042. Full-time tuition and fees vary according to class time, course load, and program. Room and board charges vary according to board plan, housing facility, and student level. ***Part-time tuition:*** $761 per credit hour. Part-time tuition and fees vary according to class time, course load, and program. ***Payment plans:*** Installment, deferred payment.

FRESHMAN FINANCIAL AID (Fall 2006, est.) 991 applied for aid; of those 74% were deemed to have need. 100% of freshmen with need received aid; of those 32% had need fully met. ***Average percent of need met:*** 79% (excluding resources awarded to replace EFC). ***Average financial aid package:*** $17,014 (excluding resources awarded to replace EFC). 18% of all full-time freshmen had no need and received non-need-based gift aid.

UNDERGRADUATE FINANCIAL AID (Fall 2006, est.) 3,764 applied for aid; of those 79% were deemed to have need. 99% of undergraduates with need received aid; of those 24% had need fully met. ***Average percent of need met:*** 78% (excluding resources awarded to replace EFC). ***Average financial aid package:*** $17,223 (excluding resources awarded to replace EFC). 10% of all full-time undergraduates had no need and received non-need-based gift aid.

GIFT AID (NEED-BASED) ***Total amount:*** $31,152,321 (8% federal, 11% state, 78% institutional, 3% external sources). ***Receiving aid:*** Freshmen: 56% (732); All full-time undergraduates: 49% (2,865). ***Average award:*** Freshmen: $11,441; Undergraduates: $10,430. ***Scholarships, grants, and awards:*** Federal Pell, FSEOG, state, private, college/university gift aid from institutional funds.

GIFT AID (NON-NEED-BASED) ***Total amount:*** $7,166,356 (1% federal, 3% state, 91% institutional, 5% external sources). ***Receiving aid:*** Freshmen: 12% (158); Undergraduates: 8% (446). ***Average award:*** Freshmen: $9525; Undergraduates: $8326. ***Scholarships, grants, and awards by category:*** *Academic Interests/Achievement:* 2,402 awards ($13,984,159 total): biological sciences, business, education, English, general academic interests/achievements, humanities, international studies, mathematics, physical sciences, religion/biblical studies, social sciences. *Creative Arts/Performance:* 66 awards ($600,742 total): journalism/publications, music. *Special Characteristics:* general special characteristics. ***Tuition waivers:*** Full or partial for employees or children of employees, senior citizens. ***ROTC:*** Army cooperative, Naval cooperative, Air Force.

LOANS ***Student loans:*** $28,756,595 (55% need-based, 45% non-need-based). 66% of past graduating class borrowed through all loan programs. *Average indebtedness per student:* $31,065. ***Average need-based loan:*** Freshmen: $2591; Undergraduates: $4343. ***Parent loans:*** $8,190,521 (25% need-based, 75% non-need-based). ***Programs:*** FFEL (Subsidized and Unsubsidized Stafford, PLUS), Perkins, state, alternative loans.

WORK-STUDY ***Federal work-study:*** Total amount: $2,293,927; 829 jobs averaging $2767. ***State or other work-study/employment:*** Total amount: $1,923,997 (100% need-based). 730 part-time jobs averaging $2636.

APPLYING FOR FINANCIAL AID ***Required financial aid form:*** FAFSA. ***Financial aid deadline:*** Continuous. ***Notification date:*** Continuous beginning 3/1. Students must reply within 3 weeks of notification.

CONTACT Ms. Ginny Reese, Associate Director, Student Financial Services, University of St. Thomas, 2115 Summit Avenue, FOL100, St. Paul, MN 55105-1096, 651-962-6557 or toll-free 800-328-6819 Ext. 26150. *Fax:* 651-962-6599. *E-mail:* vmreese@stthomas.edu.

UNIVERSITY OF ST. THOMAS

Houston, TX

Tuition & fees: $17,868 **Average undergraduate aid package: $13,302**

ABOUT THE INSTITUTION Independent Roman Catholic, coed. Awards: bachelor's, master's, doctoral, and first professional degrees. 36 undergraduate majors. Total enrollment: 3,607. Undergraduates: 1,805. Freshmen: 302. Federal methodology is used as a basis for awarding need-based institutional aid.

UNDERGRADUATE EXPENSES for 2006–07 ***Application fee:*** $35. ***Comprehensive fee:*** $24,568 includes full-time tuition ($17,700), mandatory fees ($168), and room and board ($6700). ***College room only:*** $4000. Full-time tuition and fees vary according to course load. Room and board charges vary according to board plan and housing facility. ***Part-time tuition:*** $590 per credit hour. ***Part-time fees:*** $84 per term. Part-time tuition and fees vary according to course load. ***Payment plans:*** Installment, deferred payment.

FRESHMAN FINANCIAL AID (Fall 2006, est.) 189 applied for aid; of those 86% were deemed to have need. 99% of freshmen with need received aid; of those 16% had need fully met. ***Average percent of need met:*** 68% (excluding resources awarded to replace EFC). ***Average financial aid package:*** $13,452 (excluding resources awarded to replace EFC). 25% of all full-time freshmen had no need and received non-need-based gift aid.

UNDERGRADUATE FINANCIAL AID (Fall 2006, est.) 831 applied for aid; of those 88% were deemed to have need. 100% of undergraduates with need received aid; of those 13% had need fully met. ***Average percent of need met:*** 64% (excluding resources awarded to replace EFC). ***Average financial aid package:*** $13,302 (excluding resources awarded to replace EFC). 20% of all full-time undergraduates had no need and received non-need-based gift aid.

GIFT AID (NEED-BASED) ***Total amount:*** $7,166,134 (21% federal, 32% state, 47% institutional). ***Receiving aid:*** Freshmen: 55% (160); All full-time undergraduates: 54% (711). ***Average award:*** Freshmen: $10,463; Undergraduates: $9624. ***Scholarships, grants, and awards:*** Federal Pell, FSEOG, state, college/university gift aid from institutional funds.

GIFT AID (NON-NEED-BASED) ***Total amount:*** $2,316,081 (89% institutional, 11% external sources). ***Receiving aid:*** Freshmen: 15% (43); Undergraduates: 10% (132). ***Average award:*** Freshmen: $8508; Undergraduates: $7064. ***Scholarships, grants, and awards by category:*** *Academic Interests/Achievement:* 314 awards ($2,052,884 total): biological sciences, English, foreign languages, general academic interests/achievements, mathematics, physical sciences, social sciences. *Creative Arts/Performance:* debating, music, theater/drama. *Special Achievements/Activities:* community service. *Special Characteristics:* children of educators, children of faculty/staff, general special characteristics, international students, members of minority groups, relatives of clergy, religious affiliation. ***Tuition waivers:*** Full or partial for employees or children of employees, senior citizens. ***ROTC:*** Army cooperative.

LOANS ***Student loans:*** $5,060,767 (48% need-based, 52% non-need-based). 65% of past graduating class borrowed through all loan programs. *Average indebtedness per student:* $19,668. ***Average need-based loan:*** Freshmen: $2535; Undergraduates: $4001. ***Parent loans:*** $1,493,227 (100% non-need-based). ***Programs:*** FFEL (Subsidized and Unsubsidized Stafford, PLUS), Perkins.

WORK-STUDY ***Federal work-study:*** Total amount: $101,886; 37 jobs averaging $2754. ***State or other work-study/employment:*** Total amount: $9705 (100% need-based). 4 part-time jobs averaging $2426.

ATHLETIC AWARDS Total amount: $18,100 (25% need-based, 75% non-need-based).

APPLYING FOR FINANCIAL AID ***Required financial aid form:*** FAFSA. ***Financial aid deadline (priority):*** 3/1. ***Notification date:*** Continuous. Students must reply within 4 weeks of notification.

CONTACT Scott Moore, Dean of Scholarships and Financial Aid, University of St. Thomas, 3800 Montrose Boulevard, Houston, TX 77006-4696, 713-942-3465 or toll-free 800-856-8565. *Fax:* 713-525-2142. *E-mail:* finaid@stthom.edu.

UNIVERSITY OF SAN DIEGO

San Diego, CA

Tuition & fees: $32,564 **Average undergraduate aid package: $20,558**

ABOUT THE INSTITUTION Independent Roman Catholic, coed. Awards: bachelor's, master's, doctoral, and first professional degrees and post-bachelor's, post-master's, and first professional certificates. 35 undergraduate majors. Total enrollment: 7,483. Undergraduates: 4,962. Freshmen: 1,106. Federal methodology is used as a basis for awarding need-based institutional aid.

UNDERGRADUATE EXPENSES for 2007–08 ***Application fee:*** $55. ***Comprehensive fee:*** $43,524 includes full-time tuition ($32,300), mandatory fees ($264), and room and board ($10,960). ***Part-time tuition:*** $1115 per unit. ***Part-time fees:*** $56 per term.

FRESHMAN FINANCIAL AID (Fall 2005) 815 applied for aid; of those 85% were deemed to have need. 100% of freshmen with need received aid; of those 9% had need fully met. ***Average percent of need met:*** 68% (excluding resources awarded to replace EFC). ***Average financial aid package:*** $19,667 (excluding resources awarded to replace EFC). 8% of all full-time freshmen had no need and received non-need-based gift aid.

UNDERGRADUATE FINANCIAL AID (Fall 2005) 2,725 applied for aid; of those 82% were deemed to have need. 100% of undergraduates with need received aid; of those 24% had need fully met. ***Average percent of need met:*** 71% (excluding resources awarded to replace EFC). ***Average financial aid package:*** $20,558 (excluding resources awarded to replace EFC). 13% of all full-time undergraduates had no need and received non-need-based gift aid.

GIFT AID (NEED-BASED) ***Total amount:*** $34,201,967 (10% federal, 15% state, 72% institutional, 3% external sources). ***Receiving aid:*** Freshmen: 50% (565); All full-time undergraduates: 45% (2,166). ***Average award:*** Freshmen: $16,079; Undergraduates: $16,150. ***Scholarships, grants, and awards:*** Federal Pell, FSEOG, state, private, college/university gift aid from institutional funds, Federal Nursing.

GIFT AID (NON-NEED-BASED) ***Total amount:*** $7,535,349 (32% federal, 63% institutional, 5% external sources). ***Receiving aid:*** Freshmen: 26% (299); Undergraduates: 19% (889). ***Average award:*** Freshmen: $8663; Undergraduates: $7462. ***Scholarships, grants, and awards by category:*** *Academic Interests/Achievement:* 1,096 awards ($9,302,093 total): general academic interests/achievements. *Creative Arts/Performance:* 14 awards ($92,950 total): music.

Special Achievements/Activities: 114 awards ($158,950 total). *Special Characteristics:* 57 awards ($1,331,401 total): children of faculty/staff. ***ROTC:*** Army cooperative, Naval, Air Force cooperative.

LOANS ***Student loans:*** $16,829,041 (88% need-based, 12% non-need-based). 45% of past graduating class borrowed through all loan programs. *Average indebtedness per student:* $28,842. ***Average need-based loan:*** Freshmen: $4295; Undergraduates: $5073. ***Parent loans:*** $17,437,879 (100% need-based). ***Programs:*** FFEL (Subsidized and Unsubsidized Stafford, PLUS), Perkins, college/university.

WORK-STUDY ***Federal work-study:*** Total amount: $1,535,353; 619 jobs averaging $2480. ***State or other work-study/employment:*** Total amount: $2,991,993 (16% need-based, 84% non-need-based). 958 part-time jobs averaging $3123.

ATHLETIC AWARDS Total amount: $3,871,492 (24% need-based, 76% non-need-based).

APPLYING FOR FINANCIAL AID ***Required financial aid form:*** FAFSA. ***Financial aid deadline (priority):*** 2/20. ***Notification date:*** Continuous beginning 3/1. Students must reply within 3 weeks of notification.

CONTACT Judith Lewis Logue, Director of Financial Aid Services, University of San Diego, 5998 Alcala Park, San Diego, CA 92110-2492, 619-260-4514 or toll-free 800-248-4873.

UNIVERSITY OF SAN FRANCISCO

San Francisco, CA

Tuition & fees: $31,180 **Average undergraduate aid package: $22,062**

ABOUT THE INSTITUTION Independent Roman Catholic (Jesuit), coed. Awards: bachelor's, master's, doctoral, and first professional degrees and post-master's certificates. 64 undergraduate majors. Total enrollment: 8,549. Undergraduates: 5,384. Freshmen: 1,078. Federal methodology is used as a basis for awarding need-based institutional aid.

UNDERGRADUATE EXPENSES for 2007–08 ***Application fee:*** $55. ***Comprehensive fee:*** $41,910 includes full-time tuition ($30,840), mandatory fees ($340), and room and board ($10,730). ***College room only:*** $7230. ***Part-time tuition:*** $1060 per unit. ***Part-time fees:*** $340 per year.

FRESHMAN FINANCIAL AID (Fall 2006, est.) 747 applied for aid; of those 85% were deemed to have need. 97% of freshmen with need received aid; of those 12% had need fully met. ***Average percent of need met:*** 64% (excluding resources awarded to replace EFC). ***Average financial aid package:*** $23,143 (excluding resources awarded to replace EFC). 3% of all full-time freshmen had no need and received non-need-based gift aid.

UNDERGRADUATE FINANCIAL AID (Fall 2006, est.) 2,932 applied for aid; of those 90% were deemed to have need. 98% of undergraduates with need received aid; of those 15% had need fully met. ***Average percent of need met:*** 62% (excluding resources awarded to replace EFC). ***Average financial aid package:*** $22,062 (excluding resources awarded to replace EFC). 3% of all full-time undergraduates had no need and received non-need-based gift aid.

GIFT AID (NEED-BASED) ***Total amount:*** $36,084,079 (11% federal, 17% state, 72% institutional). ***Receiving aid:*** Freshmen: 48% (516); All full-time undergraduates: 47% (2,206). ***Average award:*** Freshmen: $19,482; Undergraduates: $16,200. ***Scholarships, grants, and awards:*** Federal Pell, FSEOG, state, private, college/university gift aid from institutional funds, Federal Nursing.

GIFT AID (NON-NEED-BASED) ***Total amount:*** $7,113,480 (25% federal, 57% institutional, 18% external sources). ***Receiving aid:*** Freshmen: 12% (128); Undergraduates: 9% (402). ***Average award:*** Freshmen: $14,206; Undergraduates: $14,408. ***Scholarships, grants, and awards by category:*** *Academic Interests/Achievement:* general academic interests/achievements, military science. *Creative Arts/Performance:* general creative arts/performance. *Special Achievements/Activities:* general special achievements/activities. ***ROTC:*** Army, Air Force cooperative.

LOANS ***Student loans:*** $22,106,545 (56% need-based, 44% non-need-based). 64% of past graduating class borrowed through all loan programs. *Average indebtedness per student:* $28,000. ***Average need-based loan:*** Freshmen: $4181; Undergraduates: $5510. ***Parent loans:*** $15,293,500 (100% non-need-based). ***Programs:*** Federal Direct (Subsidized and Unsubsidized Stafford, PLUS), Perkins, Federal Nursing, college/university.

WORK-STUDY ***Federal work-study:*** Total amount: $1,746,895; 856 jobs averaging $3737. ***State or other work-study/employment:*** Total amount: $3,105,179 (100% need-based). 535 part-time jobs averaging $3512.

ATHLETIC AWARDS Total amount: $4,191,581 (100% non-need-based).

APPLYING FOR FINANCIAL AID ***Required financial aid form:*** FAFSA. ***Financial aid deadline (priority):*** 2/15. ***Notification date:*** Continuous beginning 4/1. Students must reply within 4 weeks of notification.

CONTACT Ms. Susan Murphy, Director of Financial Aid, University of San Francisco, 2130 Fulton Street, San Francisco, CA 94117-1080, 415-422-2620 or toll-free 415-422-6563 (in-state), 800-CALL USF (out-of-state). *Fax:* 415-422-6084. *E-mail:* murphy@usfca.edu.

UNIVERSITY OF SCIENCE AND ARTS OF OKLAHOMA

Chickasha, OK

Tuition & fees (OK res): $3720 **Average undergraduate aid package: $7300**

ABOUT THE INSTITUTION State-supported, coed. Awards: bachelor's degrees. 25 undergraduate majors. Total enrollment: 1,492. Undergraduates: 1,492. Freshmen: 246. Federal methodology is used as a basis for awarding need-based institutional aid.

UNDERGRADUATE EXPENSES for 2006–07 ***Application fee:*** $15. ***Tuition, state resident:*** full-time $2640; part-time $88 per hour. ***Tuition, nonresident:*** full-time $7740; part-time $258 per hour. ***Required fees:*** full-time $1080; $36 per hour. ***College room and board:*** $4360; ***Room only:*** $2290. Room and board charges vary according to board plan and housing facility. ***Payment plan:*** Installment.

FRESHMAN FINANCIAL AID (Fall 2006, est.) 187 applied for aid; of those 83% were deemed to have need. 99% of freshmen with need received aid; of those 14% had need fully met. ***Average percent of need met:*** 64% (excluding resources awarded to replace EFC). ***Average financial aid package:*** $6694 (excluding resources awarded to replace EFC). 19% of all full-time freshmen had no need and received non-need-based gift aid.

UNDERGRADUATE FINANCIAL AID (Fall 2006, est.) 787 applied for aid; of those 84% were deemed to have need. 97% of undergraduates with need received aid; of those 16% had need fully met. ***Average percent of need met:*** 65% (excluding resources awarded to replace EFC). ***Average financial aid package:*** $7300 (excluding resources awarded to replace EFC). 20% of all full-time undergraduates had no need and received non-need-based gift aid.

GIFT AID (NEED-BASED) ***Total amount:*** $2,827,433 (59% federal, 21% state, 5% institutional, 15% external sources). ***Receiving aid:*** Freshmen: 62% (147); All full-time undergraduates: 59% (602). ***Average award:*** Freshmen: $5579; Undergraduates: $5382. ***Scholarships, grants, and awards:*** Federal Pell, FSEOG, state, private, college/university gift aid from institutional funds, USAO Foundation Grants.

GIFT AID (NON-NEED-BASED) ***Total amount:*** $553,879 (42% state, 35% institutional, 23% external sources). ***Receiving aid:*** Freshmen: 5% (13); Undergraduates: 4% (45). ***Average award:*** Freshmen: $3918; Undergraduates: $4227. ***Scholarships, grants, and awards by category:*** *Academic Interests/Achievement:* 125 awards ($152,890 total): general academic interests/achievements. *Creative Arts/Performance:* 18 awards ($26,700 total): art/fine arts, music, theater/drama. *Special Achievements/Activities:* 14 awards ($8832 total): cheerleading/drum major, leadership. *Special Characteristics:* 84 awards ($244,788 total): children of faculty/staff, international students, out-of-state students, previous college experience. ***Tuition waivers:*** Full or partial for employees or children of employees, senior citizens.

LOANS ***Student loans:*** $2,221,593 (74% need-based, 26% non-need-based). 69% of past graduating class borrowed through all loan programs. *Average indebtedness per student:* $13,129. ***Average need-based loan:*** Freshmen: $1954; Undergraduates: $2860. ***Parent loans:*** $135,035 (18% need-based, 82% non-need-based). ***Programs:*** FFEL (Subsidized and Unsubsidized Stafford, PLUS), Perkins, college/university.

WORK-STUDY ***Federal work-study:*** Total amount: $232,343; 184 jobs averaging $1374.

ATHLETIC AWARDS Total amount: $583,294 (48% need-based, 52% non-need-based).

APPLYING FOR FINANCIAL AID ***Required financial aid forms:*** FAFSA, institution's own form. ***Financial aid deadline (priority):*** 3/15. ***Notification date:*** Continuous beginning 3/15. Students must reply within 4 weeks of notification.

CONTACT Nancy Moats, Director of Financial Aid, University of Science and Arts of Oklahoma, 1727 West Alabama, Chickasha, OK 73018-5322, 405-574-1251 or toll-free 800-933-8726 Ext. 1212. *Fax:* 405-574-1220.

THE UNIVERSITY OF SCRANTON

Scranton, PA

CONTACT Mr. William R. Burke, Director of Financial Aid, The University of Scranton, St. Thomas Hall 401, Scranton, PA 18510, 570-941-7887 or toll-free 888-SCRANTON. *Fax:* 570-941-4370. *E-mail:* finaid@scranton.edu.

UNIVERSITY OF SIOUX FALLS

Sioux Falls, SD

CONTACT Rachel Gunn, Financial Aid Counselor, University of Sioux Falls, 1101 West 22nd Street, Sioux Falls, SD 57105-1699, 605-331-6623 or toll-free 800-888-1047. *Fax:* 605-331-6615. *E-mail:* rachel.gunn@usiouxfalls.edu.

UNIVERSITY OF SOUTH ALABAMA

Mobile, AL

CONTACT Financial Aid Office, University of South Alabama, 307 University Boulevard, Mobile, AL 36688-0002, 251-460-6231 or toll-free 800-872-5247. *Fax:* 251-460-6517.

UNIVERSITY OF SOUTH CAROLINA

Columbia, SC

Tuition & fees (SC res): $7808   Average undergraduate aid package: $9840

ABOUT THE INSTITUTION State-supported, coed. Awards: bachelor's, master's, doctoral, and first professional degrees and post-bachelor's and post-master's certificates. 65 undergraduate majors. Total enrollment: 27,390. Undergraduates: 18,648. Freshmen: 3,697. Federal methodology is used as a basis for awarding need-based institutional aid.

UNDERGRADUATE EXPENSES for 2006–07 ***Application fee:*** $50. ***Tuition, state resident:*** full-time $7408; part-time $347 per credit hour. ***Tuition, nonresident:*** full-time $19,836; part-time $904 per credit hour. Full-time tuition and fees vary according to program. ***College room and board:*** $6520; ***Room only:*** $4003. Room and board charges vary according to board plan, housing facility, and location. ***Payment plans:*** Installment, deferred payment.

FRESHMAN FINANCIAL AID (Fall 2006, est.) 2644 applied for aid; of those 61% were deemed to have need. 100% of freshmen with need received aid; of those 32% had need fully met. ***Average percent of need met:*** 74% (excluding resources awarded to replace EFC). ***Average financial aid package:*** $9448 (excluding resources awarded to replace EFC). 46% of all full-time freshmen had no need and received non-need-based gift aid.

UNDERGRADUATE FINANCIAL AID (Fall 2006, est.) 10,240 applied for aid; of those 75% were deemed to have need. 99% of undergraduates with need received aid; of those 28% had need fully met. ***Average percent of need met:*** 73% (excluding resources awarded to replace EFC). ***Average financial aid package:*** $9840 (excluding resources awarded to replace EFC). 34% of all full-time undergraduates had no need and received non-need-based gift aid.

GIFT AID (NEED-BASED) ***Total amount:*** $35,260,633 (31% federal, 51% state, 10% institutional, 8% external sources). ***Receiving aid:*** Freshmen: 19% (683); All full-time undergraduates: 24% (3,927). ***Average award:*** Freshmen: $3469; Undergraduates: $3445. ***Scholarships, grants, and awards:*** Federal Pell, FSEOG, state, private, college/university gift aid from institutional funds, United Negro College Fund, Federal Nursing.

GIFT AID (NON-NEED-BASED) ***Total amount:*** $36,091,926 (61% state, 24% institutional, 15% external sources). ***Receiving aid:*** Freshmen: 40% (1,436); Undergraduates: 27% (4,357). ***Average award:*** Freshmen: $5665; Undergraduates: $5940. ***Scholarships, grants, and awards by category:*** *Academic Interests/Achievement:* 5,161 awards ($10,718,001 total): area/ethnic studies, biological sciences, business, communication, computer science, education, engineering/technologies, English, foreign languages, general academic interests/achievements, health fields, humanities, international studies, library science, mathematics, military science, physical sciences, premedicine, religion/biblical studies, social sciences. *Creative Arts/Performance:* 127 awards ($537,450 total): art/fine arts, debating, journalism/publications, music, theater/drama. *Special Achievements/Activities:* 218 awards ($118,237 total): cheerleading/drum major, community service, general special achievements/activities, leadership, religious involvement. *Special Characteristics:* 3,999 awards ($9,019,423 total): adult students, children and siblings of alumni, children of faculty/staff, children of union members/company employees, children of workers in trades, children with a deceased or disabled parent, ethnic background, first-generation college students, general special characteristics, handicapped students, international students, local/state students, members of minority groups, out-of-state students, relatives of clergy, religious affiliation, spouses of deceased or disabled public servants. ***Tuition waivers:*** Full or partial for employees or children of employees, senior citizens. ***ROTC:*** Army, Naval, Air Force.

LOANS ***Student loans:*** $56,672,882 (56% need-based, 44% non-need-based). 44% of past graduating class borrowed through all loan programs. *Average indebtedness per student:* $19,360. ***Average need-based loan:*** Freshmen: $1927; Undergraduates: $3552. ***Parent loans:*** $11,454,781 (13% need-based, 87% non-need-based). ***Programs:*** FFEL (Subsidized and Unsubsidized Stafford, PLUS), Perkins, Federal Nursing.

WORK-STUDY ***Federal work-study:*** Total amount: $1,465,133; 643 jobs averaging $2535. ***State or other work-study/employment:*** Total amount: $4,627,326 (100% non-need-based). Part-time jobs available.

ATHLETIC AWARDS Total amount: $5,858,283 (28% need-based, 72% non-need-based).

APPLYING FOR FINANCIAL AID ***Required financial aid form:*** FAFSA. ***Financial aid deadline (priority):*** 4/1. ***Notification date:*** Continuous beginning 4/1.

CONTACT Dr. Ed Miller, Financial Aid Director, University of South Carolina, 1714 College Street, Columbia, SC 29208, 803-777-8134 or toll-free 800-868-5872 (in-state). *Fax:* 803-777-0941.

UNIVERSITY OF SOUTH CAROLINA AIKEN

Aiken, SC

CONTACT Financial Aid Office, University of South Carolina Aiken, 471 University Parkway, Aiken, SC 29801, 803-641-3476 or toll-free 888-WOW-USCA.

UNIVERSITY OF SOUTH CAROLINA BEAUFORT

Beaufort, SC

CONTACT Sally Maybin, Financial Aid Director, University of South Carolina Beaufort, 801 Carteret Street, Beaufort, SC 29902, 843-521-3104. *Fax:* 843-521-4194. *E-mail:* smaybin@gwm.sc.edu.

UNIVERSITY OF SOUTH CAROLINA UPSTATE

Spartanburg, SC

Tuition & fees (SC res): $7314   Average undergraduate aid package: $7756

ABOUT THE INSTITUTION State-supported, coed. Awards: associate, bachelor's, and master's degrees. 20 undergraduate majors. Total enrollment: 4,610. Undergraduates: 4,574. Freshmen: 882. Federal methodology is used as a basis for awarding need-based institutional aid.

UNDERGRADUATE EXPENSES for 2006–07 ***Application fee:*** $40. ***Tuition, state resident:*** full-time $6958; part-time $299 per hour. ***Tuition, nonresident:*** full-time $14,396; part-time $618 per hour. Full-time tuition and fees vary according to course load. Part-time tuition and fees vary according to course load. ***College room and board:*** $5240; ***Room only:*** $3200. Room and board charges vary according to board plan and housing facility. ***Payment plan:*** Deferred payment.

FRESHMAN FINANCIAL AID (Fall 2006, est.) 632 applied for aid; of those 76% were deemed to have need. 100% of freshmen with need received aid; of those 19% had need fully met. ***Average percent of need met:*** 38% (excluding resources awarded to replace EFC). ***Average financial aid package:*** $8424 (excluding resources awarded to replace EFC). 2% of all full-time freshmen had no need and received non-need-based gift aid.

UNDERGRADUATE FINANCIAL AID (Fall 2006, est.) 2,976 applied for aid; of those 83% were deemed to have need. 99% of undergraduates with need received aid; of those 14% had need fully met. ***Average percent of need met:*** 42% (excluding resources awarded to replace EFC). ***Average financial aid package:*** $7756 (excluding resources awarded to replace EFC). 3% of all full-time undergraduates had no need and received non-need-based gift aid.

GIFT AID (NEED-BASED) ***Total amount:*** $5,873,570 (87% federal, 13% state). ***Receiving aid:*** Freshmen: 36% (281); All full-time undergraduates: 39% (1,477).

Average award: Freshmen: $4203; Undergraduates: $3709. ***Scholarships, grants, and awards:*** Federal Pell, FSEOG, state, private, college/university gift aid from institutional funds.

GIFT AID (NON-NEED-BASED) ***Total amount:*** $7,248,465 (88% state, 6% institutional, 6% external sources). ***Receiving aid:*** Freshmen: 52% (402); Undergraduates: 25% (950). ***Average award:*** Freshmen: $1934; Undergraduates: $2412. ***Scholarships, grants, and awards by category:*** *Academic Interests/Achievement:* 189 awards ($427,707 total): general academic interests/achievements. *Special Achievements/Activities:* 6 awards ($900 total). *Special Characteristics:* 68 awards ($30,800 total): first-generation college students. ***Tuition waivers:*** Full or partial for senior citizens. ***ROTC:*** Army cooperative.

LOANS ***Student loans:*** $17,675,424 (48% need-based, 52% non-need-based). 69% of past graduating class borrowed through all loan programs. *Average indebtedness per student:* $19,359. ***Average need-based loan:*** Freshmen: $2491; Undergraduates: $3745. ***Parent loans:*** $1,047,001 (100% need-based). ***Programs:*** FFEL (Subsidized and Unsubsidized Stafford, PLUS), Perkins, state.

WORK-STUDY ***Federal work-study:*** Total amount: $155,008; 97 jobs averaging $1598. ***State or other work-study/employment:*** Total amount: $357,719 (100% non-need-based). 344 part-time jobs averaging $1039.

ATHLETIC AWARDS Total amount: $812,894 (100% need-based).

APPLYING FOR FINANCIAL AID ***Required financial aid form:*** FAFSA. ***Financial aid deadline (priority):*** 3/1. ***Notification date:*** Continuous beginning 4/1. Students must reply within 2 weeks of notification.

CONTACT Kim Jenerette, Director of Financial Aid, University of South Carolina Upstate, 800 University Way, Spartanburg, SC 29303, 864-503-5340 or toll-free 800-277-8727. *Fax:* 864-503-5974. *E-mail:* kjenerette@uscupstate.edu.

THE UNIVERSITY OF SOUTH DAKOTA

Vermillion, SD

Tuition & fees (SD res): $5380 **Average undergraduate aid package: $5500**

ABOUT THE INSTITUTION State-supported, coed. Awards: associate, bachelor's, master's, doctoral, and first professional degrees and post-bachelor's and post-master's certificates. 61 undergraduate majors. Total enrollment: 8,746. Undergraduates: 6,468. Freshmen: 1,128. Federal methodology is used as a basis for awarding need-based institutional aid.

UNDERGRADUATE EXPENSES for 2006–07 ***Application fee:*** $20. ***Tuition, state resident:*** full-time $2,690; part-time $79.40 per credit hour. ***Tuition, nonresident:*** full-time $7569; part-time $252.30 per credit hour. ***Required fees:*** full-time $2,690; $89.65 per credit hour. Full-time tuition and fees vary according to course load and reciprocity agreements. Part-time tuition and fees vary according to course load and reciprocity agreements. ***College room and board:*** $4,964; ***Room only:*** $2,389. Room and board charges vary according to board plan and housing facility. ***Payment plan:*** Deferred payment.

FRESHMAN FINANCIAL AID (Fall 2005) 870 applied for aid; of those 69% were deemed to have need. 91% of freshmen with need received aid; of those 82% had need fully met. ***Average percent of need met:*** 73% (excluding resources awarded to replace EFC). ***Average financial aid package:*** $4200 (excluding resources awarded to replace EFC). 27% of all full-time freshmen had no need and received non-need-based gift aid.

UNDERGRADUATE FINANCIAL AID (Fall 2005) 3,693 applied for aid; of those 76% were deemed to have need. 95% of undergraduates with need received aid; of those 71% had need fully met. ***Average percent of need met:*** 73% (excluding resources awarded to replace EFC). ***Average financial aid package:*** $5500 (excluding resources awarded to replace EFC). 18% of all full-time undergraduates had no need and received non-need-based gift aid.

GIFT AID (NEED-BASED) ***Total amount:*** $4,867,240 (100% federal). ***Receiving aid:*** Freshmen: 23% (237); All full-time undergraduates: 28% (1,285). ***Average award:*** Freshmen: $3035; Undergraduates: $3086. ***Scholarships, grants, and awards:*** Federal Pell, FSEOG, private, college/university gift aid from institutional funds, Federal Nursing.

GIFT AID (NON-NEED-BASED) ***Total amount:*** $5,869,698 (14% federal, 5% state, 59% institutional, 22% external sources). ***Receiving aid:*** Freshmen: 27% (278); Undergraduates: 18% (797). ***Average award:*** Freshmen: $2950; Undergraduates: $3062. ***Scholarships, grants, and awards by category:*** *Academic Interests/Achievement:* biological sciences, business, communication, computer science, education, English, foreign languages, general academic interests/achievements, humanities, mathematics, military science, premedicine, social sciences. *Creative Arts/Performance:* art/fine arts, creative writing, debating, music, theater/drama. ***Tuition waivers:*** Full or partial for children of alumni, employees or children of employees, senior citizens. ***ROTC:*** Army.

LOANS ***Student loans:*** $21,251,036 (56% need-based, 44% non-need-based). 88% of past graduating class borrowed through all loan programs. *Average indebtedness per student:* $20,163. ***Average need-based loan:*** Freshmen: $2768; Undergraduates: $3772. ***Parent loans:*** $2,319,521 (100% non-need-based). ***Programs:*** FFEL (Subsidized and Unsubsidized Stafford, PLUS), Perkins, Federal Nursing, alternative loans.

WORK-STUDY ***Federal work-study:*** Total amount: $764,341; 603 jobs averaging $1267. ***State or other work-study/employment:*** Total amount: $1,217,718 (100% non-need-based). 750 part-time jobs averaging $1624.

ATHLETIC AWARDS Total amount: $961,330 (100% non-need-based).

APPLYING FOR FINANCIAL AID ***Required financial aid form:*** FAFSA. ***Financial aid deadline (priority):*** 3/15. ***Notification date:*** Continuous beginning 4/1. Students must reply within 3 weeks of notification.

CONTACT Julie Pier, Director of Student Financial Aid, The University of South Dakota, Belbas Center, 414 East Clark Street, Vermillion, SD 57069-2390, 605-677-5446 or toll-free 877-269-6837. *Fax:* 605-677-5238.

UNIVERSITY OF SOUTHERN CALIFORNIA

Los Angeles, CA

Tuition & fees: $33,892 **Average undergraduate aid package: $29,641**

ABOUT THE INSTITUTION Independent, coed. Awards: bachelor's, master's, doctoral, and first professional degrees and post-bachelor's, post-master's, and first professional certificates. 111 undergraduate majors. Total enrollment: 33,389. Undergraduates: 16,729. Freshmen: 2,763. Both federal and institutional methodology are used as a basis for awarding need-based institutional aid.

UNDERGRADUATE EXPENSES for 2006–07 ***Application fee:*** $65. ***Comprehensive fee:*** $44,036 includes full-time tuition ($33,314), mandatory fees ($578), and room and board ($10,144). ***College room only:*** $5580. Full-time tuition and fees vary according to program. Room and board charges vary according to board plan and housing facility. ***Part-time tuition:*** $1121 per term. ***Part-time fees:*** $289 per term. Part-time tuition and fees vary according to course load and program. ***Payment plans:*** Tuition prepayment, installment, deferred payment.

FRESHMAN FINANCIAL AID (Fall 2005) 1681 applied for aid; of those 65% were deemed to have need. 100% of freshmen with need received aid; of those 96% had need fully met. ***Average percent of need met:*** 100% (excluding resources awarded to replace EFC). ***Average financial aid package:*** $29,256 (excluding resources awarded to replace EFC). 25% of all full-time freshmen had no need and received non-need-based gift aid.

UNDERGRADUATE FINANCIAL AID (Fall 2005) 8,775 applied for aid; of those 78% were deemed to have need. 100% of undergraduates with need received aid; of those 95% had need fully met. ***Average percent of need met:*** 100% (excluding resources awarded to replace EFC). ***Average financial aid package:*** $29,641 (excluding resources awarded to replace EFC). 19% of all full-time undergraduates had no need and received non-need-based gift aid.

GIFT AID (NEED-BASED) ***Total amount:*** $149,470,564 (8% federal, 11% state, 78% institutional, 3% external sources). ***Receiving aid:*** Freshmen: 34% (938); All full-time undergraduates: 39% (6,241). ***Average award:*** Freshmen: $20,685; Undergraduates: $19,781. ***Scholarships, grants, and awards:*** Federal Pell, FSEOG, state, private, college/university gift aid from institutional funds.

GIFT AID (NON-NEED-BASED) ***Total amount:*** $39,250,250 (78% institutional, 22% external sources). ***Receiving aid:*** Freshmen: 23% (638); Undergraduates: 18% (2,844). ***Average award:*** Freshmen: $12,011; Undergraduates: $12,659. ***Scholarships, grants, and awards by category:*** *Academic Interests/Achievement:* 4,720 awards ($48,768,682 total): general academic interests/achievements. *Creative Arts/Performance:* 14 awards ($360,590 total): debating. *Special Achievements/Activities:* 50 awards ($595,000 total): leadership. *Special Characteristics:* 866 awards ($13,873,781 total): children and siblings of alumni, children of faculty/staff, international students, members of minority groups. ***Tuition waivers:*** Full or partial for employees or children of employees. ***ROTC:*** Army, Naval, Air Force.

LOANS ***Student loans:*** $50,412,947 (72% need-based, 28% non-need-based). 54% of past graduating class borrowed through all loan programs. *Average indebtedness per student:* $27,420. ***Average need-based loan:*** Freshmen: $3781; Undergraduates: $6099. ***Parent loans:*** $69,021,053 (100% non-need-based). ***Programs:*** FFEL (Subsidized and Unsubsidized Stafford, PLUS), Perkins, 'Credit Ready' and Credit Based loans.

WORK-STUDY ***Federal work-study:*** Total amount: $13,706,330; 4,994 jobs averaging $2745.

ATHLETIC AWARDS Total amount: $12,492,573 (22% need-based, 78% non-need-based).

APPLYING FOR FINANCIAL AID ***Required financial aid forms:*** FAFSA, CSS Financial Aid PROFILE, for 2007-2008: 2006 parent and student federal income tax forms and all schedules and W-2s, USC non-filing forms. ***Financial aid deadline (priority):*** 1/20. ***Notification date:*** Continuous beginning 3/15. Students must reply by 5/1.

CONTACT L. Katharine Harrington, Dean of Admission and Financial Aid, University of Southern California, University of Southern California, University Park Campus, Los Angeles, CA 90089-0914, 213-740-1111. *Fax:* 213-740-0680. *E-mail:* fao@usc.edu.

UNIVERSITY OF SOUTHERN INDIANA

Evansville, IN

Tuition & fees (IN res): $4520 **Average undergraduate aid package: $8561**

ABOUT THE INSTITUTION State-supported, coed. Awards: associate, bachelor's, and master's degrees and post-bachelor's certificates. 55 undergraduate majors. Total enrollment: 10,021. Undergraduates: 9,298. Freshmen: 2,105. Federal methodology is used as a basis for awarding need-based institutional aid.

UNDERGRADUATE EXPENSES for 2006–07 ***Application fee:*** $25. ***Tuition, state resident:*** full-time $4460; part-time $148.65 per credit hour. ***Tuition, nonresident:*** full-time $10,631; part-time $354.35 per credit hour. ***Required fees:*** full-time $60; $22.75 per term part-time. ***College room and board:*** $6492; ***Room only:*** $3234.

FRESHMAN FINANCIAL AID (Fall 2006, est.) 1731 applied for aid; of those 64% were deemed to have need. 100% of freshmen with need received aid; of those 13% had need fully met. ***Average percent of need met:*** 45% (excluding resources awarded to replace EFC). ***Average financial aid package:*** $7728 (excluding resources awarded to replace EFC). 12% of all full-time freshmen had no need and received non-need-based gift aid.

UNDERGRADUATE FINANCIAL AID (Fall 2006, est.) 5,802 applied for aid; of those 67% were deemed to have need. 100% of undergraduates with need received aid; of those 12% had need fully met. ***Average percent of need met:*** 46% (excluding resources awarded to replace EFC). ***Average financial aid package:*** $8561 (excluding resources awarded to replace EFC). 7% of all full-time undergraduates had no need and received non-need-based gift aid.

GIFT AID (NEED-BASED) ***Total amount:*** $14,194,940 (47% federal, 38% state, 3% institutional, 12% external sources). ***Receiving aid:*** Freshmen: 39% (789); All full-time undergraduates: 34% (2,569). ***Average award:*** Freshmen: $5366; Undergraduates: $5028. ***Scholarships, grants, and awards:*** Federal Pell, FSEOG, state, private, college/university gift aid from institutional funds.

GIFT AID (NON-NEED-BASED) ***Total amount:*** $2,889,877 (23% institutional, 77% external sources). ***Receiving aid:*** Freshmen: 3% (52); Undergraduates: 2% (114). ***Average award:*** Freshmen: $2038; Undergraduates: $2082. ***Scholarships, grants, and awards by category:*** *Academic Interests/Achievement:* 1,612 awards ($1,844,116 total): biological sciences, business, education, engineering/technologies, general academic interests/achievements, health fields, humanities, mathematics, premedicine, social sciences. *Creative Arts/Performance:* 46 awards ($47,696 total): art/fine arts, creative writing, theater/drama. *Special Achievements/Activities:* leadership. *Special Characteristics:* 377 awards ($851,965 total): children of faculty/staff, members of minority groups, out-of-state students, spouses of current students, veterans' children. ***ROTC:*** Army.

LOANS ***Student loans:*** $27,469,875 (71% need-based, 29% non-need-based). 40% of past graduating class borrowed through all loan programs. *Average indebtedness per student:* $15,623. ***Average need-based loan:*** Freshmen: $3319; Undergraduates: $4863. ***Parent loans:*** $4,163,713 (43% need-based, 57% non-need-based). ***Programs:*** FFEL (Subsidized and Unsubsidized Stafford, PLUS), Perkins.

WORK-STUDY ***Federal work-study:*** Total amount: $276,327; 114 jobs averaging $2424.

ATHLETIC AWARDS Total amount: $763,294 (40% need-based, 60% non-need-based).

APPLYING FOR FINANCIAL AID ***Required financial aid forms:*** FAFSA, institution's own form. ***Financial aid deadline:*** 3/1. ***Notification date:*** Continuous beginning 4/15.

CONTACT Financial Aid Counselor, University of Southern Indiana, 8600 University Boulevard, Evansville, IN 47712-3590, 812-464-1767 or toll-free 800-467-1965. *Fax:* 812-465-7154. *E-mail:* finaid@usi.edu.

UNIVERSITY OF SOUTHERN MAINE

Portland, ME

Tuition & fees (ME res): $6326 **Average undergraduate aid package: $9264**

ABOUT THE INSTITUTION State-supported, coed. Awards: associate, bachelor's, master's, doctoral, and first professional degrees and post-master's certificates. 46 undergraduate majors. Total enrollment: 10,478. Undergraduates: 8,287. Freshmen: 936. Federal methodology is used as a basis for awarding need-based institutional aid.

UNDERGRADUATE EXPENSES for 2006–07 ***Application fee:*** $40. ***Tuition, state resident:*** full-time $5400; part-time $180 per credit hour. ***Tuition, nonresident:*** full-time $14,640; part-time $488 per credit hour. Full-time tuition and fees vary according to course load, degree level, and reciprocity agreements. Part-time tuition and fees vary according to course load, degree level, and reciprocity agreements. ***College room and board:*** $7444; ***Room only:*** $3834. Room and board charges vary according to board plan, housing facility, and location. ***Payment plan:*** Installment.

FRESHMAN FINANCIAL AID (Fall 2006, est.) 753 applied for aid; of those 82% were deemed to have need. 96% of freshmen with need received aid; of those 14% had need fully met. ***Average percent of need met:*** 68% (excluding resources awarded to replace EFC). ***Average financial aid package:*** $8224 (excluding resources awarded to replace EFC). 11% of all full-time freshmen had no need and received non-need-based gift aid.

UNDERGRADUATE FINANCIAL AID (Fall 2006, est.) 3,840 applied for aid; of those 84% were deemed to have need. 97% of undergraduates with need received aid; of those 20% had need fully met. ***Average percent of need met:*** 72% (excluding resources awarded to replace EFC). ***Average financial aid package:*** $9264 (excluding resources awarded to replace EFC). 10% of all full-time undergraduates had no need and received non-need-based gift aid.

GIFT AID (NEED-BASED) ***Total amount:*** $11,850,348 (61% federal, 15% state, 12% institutional, 12% external sources). ***Receiving aid:*** Freshmen: 57% (503); All full-time undergraduates: 52% (2,470). ***Average award:*** Freshmen: $4564; Undergraduates: $4186. ***Scholarships, grants, and awards:*** Federal Pell, FSEOG, state, college/university gift aid from institutional funds.

GIFT AID (NON-NEED-BASED) ***Total amount:*** $1,495,206 (38% institutional, 62% external sources). ***Receiving aid:*** Freshmen: 3% (26); Undergraduates: 2% (85). ***Average award:*** Freshmen: $3010; Undergraduates: $4210. ***Scholarships, grants, and awards by category:*** *Academic Interests/Achievement:* general academic interests/achievements. *Creative Arts/Performance:* music, theater/drama. *Special Achievements/Activities:* community service. *Special Characteristics:* children of faculty/staff, general special characteristics, local/state students, out-of-state students. ***Tuition waivers:*** Full or partial for minority students, employees or children of employees. ***ROTC:*** Army cooperative, Air Force cooperative.

LOANS ***Student loans:*** $21,435,353 (68% need-based, 32% non-need-based). 59% of past graduating class borrowed through all loan programs. *Average indebtedness per student:* $22,000. ***Average need-based loan:*** Freshmen: $3261; Undergraduates: $4386. ***Parent loans:*** $3,374,373 (100% non-need-based). ***Programs:*** FFEL (Subsidized and Unsubsidized Stafford, PLUS), Perkins, Federal Nursing, college/university.

WORK-STUDY ***Federal work-study:*** Total amount: $4,119,213; jobs available.

APPLYING FOR FINANCIAL AID ***Required financial aid form:*** FAFSA. ***Financial aid deadline (priority):*** 2/15. ***Notification date:*** Continuous beginning 3/15. Students must reply within 2 weeks of notification.

CONTACT Mr. Keith P. Dubois, Director of Student Financial Aid, University of Southern Maine, 96 Falmouth Street, PO Box 9300, Portland, ME 04104-9300, 207-780-5122 or toll-free 800-800-4USM Ext. 5670. *Fax:* 207-780-5143. *E-mail:* dubois@maine.edu.

UNIVERSITY OF SOUTHERN MISSISSIPPI

Hattiesburg, MS

Tuition & fees (MS res): $4714 **Average undergraduate aid package: $9965**

ABOUT THE INSTITUTION State-supported, coed. Awards: bachelor's, master's, and doctoral degrees. 66 undergraduate majors. Total enrollment: 14,777. Undergraduates: 12,122. Freshmen: 1,587. Federal methodology is used as a basis for awarding need-based institutional aid.

UNDERGRADUATE EXPENSES for 2006–07 ***Tuition, state resident:*** full-time $4594; part-time $192 per credit hour. ***Tuition, nonresident:*** full-time $10,622; part-time $443 per credit hour. Part-time tuition and fees vary according to course load and degree level. ***College room and board:*** $5070; ***Room only:*** $3010. Room and board charges vary according to board plan and housing facility. ***Payment plan:*** Installment.

FRESHMAN FINANCIAL AID (Fall 2005) 1191 applied for aid; of those 79% were deemed to have need. 99% of freshmen with need received aid; of those 38% had need fully met. ***Average percent of need met:*** 90% (excluding resources awarded to replace EFC). ***Average financial aid package:*** $9192 (excluding resources awarded to replace EFC). 10% of all full-time freshmen had no need and received non-need-based gift aid.

UNDERGRADUATE FINANCIAL AID (Fall 2005) 7,887 applied for aid; of those 85% were deemed to have need. 100% of undergraduates with need received aid; of those 45% had need fully met. ***Average percent of need met:*** 93% (excluding resources awarded to replace EFC). ***Average financial aid package:*** $9965 (excluding resources awarded to replace EFC). 6% of all full-time undergraduates had no need and received non-need-based gift aid.

GIFT AID (NEED-BASED) ***Total amount:*** $30,332,762 (88% federal, 5% state, 3% institutional, 4% external sources). ***Receiving aid:*** Freshmen: 57% (885); All full-time undergraduates: 60% (6,207). ***Average award:*** Freshmen: $2631; Undergraduates: $2765. ***Scholarships, grants, and awards:*** Federal Pell, FSEOG, state, private, college/university gift aid from institutional funds.

GIFT AID (NON-NEED-BASED) ***Total amount:*** $9,005,969 (1% federal, 32% state, 42% institutional, 25% external sources). ***Receiving aid:*** Freshmen: 31% (488); Undergraduates: 25% (2,619). ***Average award:*** Freshmen: $2471; Undergraduates: $2039. ***Scholarships, grants, and awards by category:*** *Academic Interests/Achievement:* 2,482 awards ($1,915,663 total): general academic interests/achievements. *Creative Arts/Performance:* 553 awards ($467,707 total): art/fine arts, dance, music, theater/drama. *Special Achievements/Activities:* 145 awards ($96,450 total): cheerleading/drum major, leadership. *Special Characteristics:* 6,822 awards ($4,936,625 total): children and siblings of alumni, children of faculty/staff, ethnic background, local/state students, out-of-state students, veterans. ***Tuition waivers:*** Full or partial for children of alumni, employees or children of employees, senior citizens. ***ROTC:*** Army, Air Force.

LOANS ***Student loans:*** $43,044,088 (67% need-based, 33% non-need-based). 77% of past graduating class borrowed through all loan programs. *Average indebtedness per student:* $17,429. ***Average need-based loan:*** Freshmen: $2519; Undergraduates: $3006. ***Parent loans:*** $4,356,565 (20% need-based, 80% non-need-based). ***Programs:*** FFEL (Subsidized and Unsubsidized Stafford, PLUS), Perkins, Federal Nursing, college/university.

WORK-STUDY ***Federal work-study:*** Total amount: $178,497; 140 jobs averaging $1275.

ATHLETIC AWARDS Total amount: $2,099,554 (29% need-based, 71% non-need-based).

APPLYING FOR FINANCIAL AID ***Required financial aid forms:*** FAFSA, institution's own form, state aid form. ***Financial aid deadline (priority):*** 3/15. ***Notification date:*** Continuous. Students must reply within 2 weeks of notification.

CONTACT Mr. David Williamson, Assistant Director of Financial Aid, University of Southern Mississippi, 118 College Drive #5101, Hattiesburg, MS 39406-0001, 601-266-4774. *E-mail:* david.williamson@usm.edu.

UNIVERSITY OF SOUTH FLORIDA

Tampa, FL

Tuition & fees (FL res): $3490 **Average undergraduate aid package: $9025**

ABOUT THE INSTITUTION State-supported, coed. Awards: associate, bachelor's, master's, doctoral, and first professional degrees and post-bachelor's certificates. 84 undergraduate majors. Total enrollment: 43,636. Undergraduates: 34,438. Freshmen: 4,357. Federal methodology is used as a basis for awarding need-based institutional aid.

UNDERGRADUATE EXPENSES for 2006–07 ***Application fee:*** $30. ***Tuition, state resident:*** full-time $3416; part-time $114 per credit hour. ***Tuition, nonresident:*** full-time $16,115; part-time $537 per credit hour. ***Required fees:*** full-time $74; $37 per term part-time. Full-time tuition and fees vary according to course level, course load, and location. Part-time tuition and fees vary according to course level, course load, and location. ***College room and board:*** $7180; ***Room only:*** $3648. Room and board charges vary according to board plan, housing facility, and location. ***Payment plan:*** Installment.

FRESHMAN FINANCIAL AID (Fall 2005) 2396 applied for aid; of those 69% were deemed to have need. 100% of freshmen with need received aid; of those 16% had need fully met. ***Average percent of need met:*** 19% (excluding resources awarded to replace EFC). ***Average financial aid package:*** $8603 (excluding resources awarded to replace EFC). 16% of all full-time freshmen had no need and received non-need-based gift aid.

UNDERGRADUATE FINANCIAL AID (Fall 2005) 14,082 applied for aid; of those 80% were deemed to have need. 98% of undergraduates with need received aid; of those 17% had need fully met. ***Average percent of need met:*** 26% (excluding resources awarded to replace EFC). ***Average financial aid package:*** $9025 (excluding resources awarded to replace EFC). 8% of all full-time undergraduates had no need and received non-need-based gift aid.

GIFT AID (NEED-BASED) ***Total amount:*** $32,187,215 (70% federal, 21% state, 9% institutional). ***Receiving aid:*** Freshmen: 20% (847); All full-time undergraduates: 29% (6,894). ***Average award:*** Freshmen: $4541; Undergraduates: $4347. ***Scholarships, grants, and awards:*** Federal Pell, FSEOG, state, private, college/university gift aid from institutional funds.

GIFT AID (NON-NEED-BASED) ***Total amount:*** $61,347,603 (76% state, 19% institutional, 5% external sources). ***Receiving aid:*** Freshmen: 18% (788); Undergraduates: 15% (3,504). ***Average award:*** Freshmen: $4605; Undergraduates: $2530. ***Scholarships, grants, and awards by category:*** *Academic Interests/Achievement:* 3,682 awards ($5,881,838 total): architecture, biological sciences, business, communication, computer science, education, engineering/technologies, English, foreign languages, general academic interests/achievements, health fields, humanities, international studies, library science, mathematics, military science, physical sciences, premedicine, religion/biblical studies, social sciences. *Creative Arts/Performance:* applied art and design, art/fine arts, cinema/film/broadcasting, creative writing, dance, debating, journalism/publications, music, performing arts, theater/drama. *Special Achievements/Activities:* general special achievements/activities. *Special Characteristics:* general special characteristics. ***Tuition waivers:*** Full or partial for senior citizens. ***ROTC:*** Army, Naval, Air Force.

LOANS ***Student loans:*** $81,513,164 (53% need-based, 47% non-need-based). 53% of past graduating class borrowed through all loan programs. *Average indebtedness per student:* $17,995. ***Average need-based loan:*** Freshmen: $1849; Undergraduates: $4068. ***Parent loans:*** $5,306,188 (100% non-need-based). ***Programs:*** FFEL (Subsidized and Unsubsidized Stafford, PLUS), Perkins, college/university.

WORK-STUDY ***Federal work-study:*** Total amount: $2,825,189; 858 jobs averaging $3600.

ATHLETIC AWARDS Total amount: $3,140,933 (100% non-need-based).

APPLYING FOR FINANCIAL AID ***Required financial aid form:*** FAFSA. ***Financial aid deadline (priority):*** 3/1. ***Notification date:*** Continuous beginning 3/28. Students must reply within 4 weeks of notification.

CONTACT Mr. Leonard Gude, Director of Student Financial Aid, University of South Florida, 4202 East Fowler Avenue, SVC 1102, Tampa, FL 33620-6960, 813-974-4700 or toll-free 877-USF-BULLS. *Fax:* 813-974-5144. *E-mail:* lgude@admin.usf.edu.

THE UNIVERSITY OF TAMPA

Tampa, FL

Tuition & fees: $19,628 **Average undergraduate aid package: $14,968**

ABOUT THE INSTITUTION Independent, coed. Awards: associate, bachelor's, and master's degrees. 45 undergraduate majors. Total enrollment: 5,381. Undergraduates: 4,745. Freshmen: 1,194. Federal methodology is used as a basis for awarding need-based institutional aid.

UNDERGRADUATE EXPENSES for 2006–07 ***Application fee:*** $35. ***Comprehensive fee:*** $26,882 includes full-time tuition ($18,666), mandatory fees ($962), and room and board ($7254). ***College room only:*** $3354. Full-time tuition and fees vary according to class time. Room and board charges vary according to board plan and housing facility. ***Part-time tuition:*** $398 per hour. ***Part-time fees:*** $35 per term. Part-time tuition and fees vary according to class time. ***Payment plan:*** Installment.

FRESHMAN FINANCIAL AID (Fall 2006, est.) 814 applied for aid. of those 26% had need fully met. ***Average percent of need met:*** 80% (excluding resources awarded to replace EFC). ***Average financial aid package:*** $15,050 (excluding resources awarded to replace EFC). 15% of all full-time freshmen had no need and received non-need-based gift aid.

UNDERGRADUATE FINANCIAL AID (Fall 2006, est.) 2,846 applied for aid; of those 80% were deemed to have need. 100% of undergraduates with need received aid; of those 22% had need fully met. ***Average percent of need met:*** 79% (excluding resources awarded to replace EFC). ***Average financial aid package:*** $14,968 (excluding resources awarded to replace EFC). 11% of all full-time undergraduates had no need and received non-need-based gift aid.

GIFT AID (NEED-BASED) ***Total amount:*** $24,120,798 (14% federal, 16% state, 65% institutional, 5% external sources). ***Receiving aid:*** Freshmen: 48% (577); All full-time undergraduates: 50% (2,152). ***Average award:*** Freshmen: $7193; Undergraduates: $7008. ***Scholarships, grants, and awards:*** Federal Pell, FSEOG, state, private, college/university gift aid from institutional funds.

GIFT AID (NON-NEED-BASED) ***Total amount:*** $11,384,760 (21% state, 71% institutional, 8% external sources). ***Receiving aid:*** Freshmen: 47% (556); Undergraduates: 38% (1,639). ***Average award:*** Freshmen: $6255; Undergraduates: $6093. ***Scholarships, grants, and awards by category:*** *Academic Interests/Achievement:* biological sciences, business, communication, education, general academic interests/achievements, health fields, military science, social sciences. *Creative Arts/Performance:* art/fine arts, creative writing, journalism/publications, music, performing arts. *Special Achievements/Activities:* general special achievements/activities, leadership. *Special Characteristics:* children and siblings of alumni, children of faculty/staff, international students. ***Tuition waivers:*** Full or partial for employees or children of employees. ***ROTC:*** Army, Air Force cooperative.

LOANS ***Student loans:*** $20,030,206 (63% need-based, 37% non-need-based). 71% of past graduating class borrowed through all loan programs. *Average indebtedness per student:* $23,099. ***Average need-based loan:*** Freshmen: $3712; Undergraduates: $4946. ***Parent loans:*** $9,238,475 (63% need-based, 37% non-need-based). ***Programs:*** FFEL (Subsidized and Unsubsidized Stafford, PLUS), Perkins, state, college/university.

WORK-STUDY ***Federal work-study:*** Total amount: $462,637; jobs available (averaging $2000).

ATHLETIC AWARDS Total amount: $1,196,568 (53% need-based, 47% non-need-based).

APPLYING FOR FINANCIAL AID ***Required financial aid forms:*** FAFSA, state aid form. ***Financial aid deadline:*** Continuous. ***Notification date:*** Continuous beginning 2/1. Students must reply within 3 weeks of notification.

CONTACT Financial Aid Office, The University of Tampa, 401 West Kennedy Boulevard, Tampa, FL 33606-1490, 813-253-6219 or toll-free 888-646-2438 (in-state), 888-MINARET (out-of-state). *Fax:* 813-258-7439. *E-mail:* finaid@ut.edu.

THE UNIVERSITY OF TENNESSEE

Knoxville, TN

CONTACT Office of Financial Aid and Scholarships, The University of Tennessee, 115 Student Services Building, Knoxville, TN 37996-0210, 865-974-3131 or toll-free 800-221-8657 (in-state). *Fax:* 865-974-2175. *E-mail:* finaid@utk.edu.

THE UNIVERSITY OF TENNESSEE AT CHATTANOOGA

Chattanooga, TN

CONTACT Jonathan Looney, Financial Aid Director, The University of Tennessee at Chattanooga, 615 McCallie Avenue, Chattanooga, TN 37403-2598, 423-425-4677 or toll-free 800-UTC-MOCS (in-state). *Fax:* 423-425-2292. *E-mail:* jonathan-looney@utc.edu.

THE UNIVERSITY OF TENNESSEE AT MARTIN

Martin, TN

Tuition & fees (TN res): $4665 **Average undergraduate aid package: $9080**

ABOUT THE INSTITUTION State-supported, coed. Awards: bachelor's and master's degrees. 103 undergraduate majors. Total enrollment: 6,893. Undergraduates: 6,320. Freshmen: 1,231. Federal methodology is used as a basis for awarding need-based institutional aid.

UNDERGRADUATE EXPENSES for 2006–07 ***Application fee:*** $30. ***Tuition, state resident:*** full-time $3916; part-time $164 per credit hour. ***Tuition, nonresident:*** full-time $13,388; part-time $558 per credit hour. ***Required fees:*** full-time $749; $33 per credit hour. Part-time tuition and fees vary according to course load. ***College room and board:*** $4410; ***Room only:*** $2100. Room and board charges vary according to board plan and housing facility. ***Payment plan:*** Deferred payment.

FRESHMAN FINANCIAL AID (Fall 2006, est.) 1148 applied for aid; of those 69% were deemed to have need. 98% of freshmen with need received aid; of those 44% had need fully met. ***Average percent of need met:*** 79% (excluding resources awarded to replace EFC). ***Average financial aid package:*** $9368 (excluding resources awarded to replace EFC). 27% of all full-time freshmen had no need and received non-need-based gift aid.

UNDERGRADUATE FINANCIAL AID (Fall 2006, est.) 4,645 applied for aid; of those 69% were deemed to have need. 96% of undergraduates with need received aid; of those 40% had need fully met. ***Average percent of need met:*** 75% (excluding resources awarded to replace EFC). ***Average financial aid package:*** $9080 (excluding resources awarded to replace EFC). 21% of all full-time undergraduates had no need and received non-need-based gift aid.

GIFT AID (NEED-BASED) ***Total amount:*** $9,178,644 (70% federal, 26% state, 4% institutional). ***Receiving aid:*** Freshmen: 41% (494); All full-time undergraduates: 38% (1,936). ***Average award:*** Freshmen: $5119; Undergraduates: $4634. ***Scholarships, grants, and awards:*** Federal Pell, FSEOG, state, private, TN minority: Teaching fellowships; TN teachers; Sc.

GIFT AID (NON-NEED-BASED) ***Total amount:*** $11,242,722 (71% state, 24% institutional, 5% external sources). ***Receiving aid:*** Freshmen: 51% (612); Undergraduates: 31% (1,591). ***Average award:*** Freshmen: $5074; Undergraduates: $5147. ***Scholarships, grants, and awards by category:*** *Academic Interests/Achievement:* 597 awards ($984,626 total): agriculture, biological sciences, business, communication, computer science, education, engineering/technologies, English, general academic interests/achievements, health fields, home economics, humanities, mathematics, military science, physical sciences, premedicine, social sciences. *Creative Arts/Performance:* 147 awards ($126,466 total): art/fine arts, journalism/publications, music, theater/drama. *Special Achievements/Activities:* 624 awards ($498,897 total): cheerleading/drum major, general special achievements/activities, leadership, rodeo. *Special Characteristics:* 1,269 awards ($2,098,703 total): adult students, children of educators, children of faculty/staff, ethnic background, handicapped students, members of minority groups, out-of-state students. ***Tuition waivers:*** Full or partial for employees or children of employees, senior citizens. ***ROTC:*** Army.

LOANS ***Student loans:*** $14,406,246 (57% need-based, 43% non-need-based). 47% of past graduating class borrowed through all loan programs. *Average indebtedness per student:* $22,854. ***Average need-based loan:*** Freshmen: $2535; Undergraduates: $3895. ***Parent loans:*** $1,344,146 (100% non-need-based). ***Programs:*** FFEL (Subsidized and Unsubsidized Stafford, PLUS), Perkins.

WORK-STUDY ***Federal work-study:*** Total amount: $533,175; 265 jobs averaging $2011.

ATHLETIC AWARDS Total amount: $2,340,925 (100% non-need-based).

APPLYING FOR FINANCIAL AID ***Required financial aid form:*** FAFSA. ***Financial aid deadline:*** Continuous. ***Notification date:*** Continuous beginning 4/1. Students must reply within 2 weeks of notification.

CONTACT Sandra J. Neel, Director of Student Financial Assistance, The University of Tennessee at Martin, 205 Administration Building, Martin, TN 38238-1000, 731-881-7040 or toll-free 800-829-8861. *Fax:* 731-881-7036. *E-mail:* sneel@utm.edu.

THE UNIVERSITY OF TEXAS AT ARLINGTON

Arlington, TX

ABOUT THE INSTITUTION State-supported, coed. Awards: bachelor's, master's, and doctoral degrees and post-bachelor's and post-master's certificates. 60 undergraduate majors. Total enrollment: 24,825. Undergraduates: 19,205. Freshmen: 2,110.

GIFT AID (NEED-BASED) ***Scholarships, grants, and awards:*** Federal Pell, FSEOG, state, private, college/university gift aid from institutional funds, United Negro College Fund.

GIFT AID (NON-NEED-BASED) ***Scholarships, grants, and awards by category:*** *Academic Interests/Achievement:* architecture, biological sciences, business, communication, computer science, education, engineering/technologies, English, foreign languages, general academic interests/achievements, health fields, humanities, international studies, mathematics, military science, physical sciences, social sciences. *Creative Arts/Performance:* journalism/publications, music, theater/drama. *Special Achievements/Activities:* cheerleading/drum major, community service, general special achievements/activities, leadership. *Special Characteristics:* children with a deceased or disabled parent, first-generation college students, general special characteristics, handicapped students, public servants.

LOANS ***Programs:*** FFEL (Subsidized and Unsubsidized Stafford, PLUS), Perkins, state.

WORK-STUDY ***Federal work-study:*** Total amount: $4,153,507; 718 jobs averaging $1827.

APPLYING FOR FINANCIAL AID ***Required financial aid form:*** FAFSA.

CONTACT Karen Krause, Director of Financial Aid, The University of Texas at Arlington, PO Box 19199, Arlington, TX 76019, 817-272-3568. *Fax:* 817-272-3555. *E-mail:* kkrause@uta.edu.

THE UNIVERSITY OF TEXAS AT AUSTIN

Austin, TX

Tuition & fees (TX res): $7630 **Average undergraduate aid package: $10,900**

ABOUT THE INSTITUTION State-supported, coed. Awards: bachelor's, master's, doctoral, and first professional degrees. 104 undergraduate majors. Total enrollment: 49,697. Undergraduates: 37,037. Freshmen: 7,417. Federal methodology is used as a basis for awarding need-based institutional aid.

UNDERGRADUATE EXPENSES for 2006–07 ***Application fee:*** $60. ***Tuition, state resident:*** full-time $7630. ***Tuition, nonresident:*** full-time $20,364. Full-time tuition and fees vary according to course load and program. Part-time tuition and fees vary according to course load and program. ***College room and board:*** $8176. Room and board charges vary according to board plan, housing facility, and location. ***Payment plan:*** Installment.

FRESHMAN FINANCIAL AID (Fall 2006, est.) 4800 applied for aid; of those 86% were deemed to have need. 98% of freshmen with need received aid; of those 89% had need fully met. ***Average percent of need met:*** 89% (excluding resources awarded to replace EFC). ***Average financial aid package:*** $9800 (excluding resources awarded to replace EFC). 17% of all full-time freshmen had no need and received non-need-based gift aid.

UNDERGRADUATE FINANCIAL AID (Fall 2006, est.) 22,700 applied for aid; of those 80% were deemed to have need. 97% of undergraduates with need received aid; of those 86% had need fully met. ***Average percent of need met:*** 90% (excluding resources awarded to replace EFC). ***Average financial aid package:*** $10,900 (excluding resources awarded to replace EFC). 31% of all full-time undergraduates had no need and received non-need-based gift aid.

GIFT AID (NEED-BASED) ***Total amount:*** $95,950,000 (26% federal, 20% state, 47% institutional, 7% external sources). ***Receiving aid:*** Freshmen: 54% (3,950); All full-time undergraduates: 37% (12,320). ***Average award:*** Freshmen: $6800; Undergraduates: $6300. ***Scholarships, grants, and awards:*** Federal Pell, FSEOG, state, private, college/university gift aid from institutional funds, Federal Nursing.

GIFT AID (NON-NEED-BASED) ***Total amount:*** $43,855,500 (1% federal, 1% state, 78% institutional, 20% external sources). ***Average award:*** Freshmen: $3600; Undergraduates: $3300. ***Scholarships, grants, and awards by category:*** *Academic Interests/Achievement:* architecture, biological sciences, business, communication, computer science, education, general academic interests/achievements, humanities, mathematics, social sciences. *Creative Arts/Performance:* art/fine arts, dance, general creative arts/performance, journalism/publications, music, performing arts, theater/drama. *Special Achievements/Activities:* general special achievements/activities. *Special Characteristics:* first-generation college students, general special characteristics, handicapped students, out-of-state students, relatives of clergy. ***Tuition waivers:*** Full or partial for employees or children of employees, senior citizens. ***ROTC:*** Army, Naval, Air Force.

LOANS ***Student loans:*** $105,350,000 (76% need-based, 24% non-need-based). 39% of past graduating class borrowed through all loan programs. *Average indebtedness per student:* $16,800. ***Average need-based loan:*** Freshmen: $3800; Undergraduates: $4700. ***Parent loans:*** $48,000,000 (40% need-based, 60% non-need-based). ***Programs:*** FFEL (Subsidized and Unsubsidized Stafford, PLUS), Perkins, state.

WORK-STUDY ***Federal work-study:*** Total amount: $2,350,000; 1,425 jobs averaging $1650. ***State or other work-study/employment:*** Total amount: $14,950,000 (2% need-based, 98% non-need-based). 245 part-time jobs averaging $1270.

APPLYING FOR FINANCIAL AID ***Required financial aid form:*** FAFSA. ***Financial aid deadline (priority):*** 4/1. ***Notification date:*** Continuous beginning 4/1. Students must reply within 4 weeks of notification.

CONTACT Don C. Davis, Associate Director of Student Financial Services, The University of Texas at Austin, PO Box 7758, UT Station, Austin, TX 78713-7758, 512-475-6282. *Fax:* 512-475-6296. *E-mail:* dondavis@mail.utexas.edu.

THE UNIVERSITY OF TEXAS AT BROWNSVILLE

Brownsville, TX

Tuition & fees (TX res): $3657 **Average undergraduate aid package: $3467**

ABOUT THE INSTITUTION State-supported, coed. Awards: associate, bachelor's, and master's degrees. 35 undergraduate majors. Total enrollment: 15,688. Undergraduates: 14,867. Entering class: 1,749. Federal methodology is used as a basis for awarding need-based institutional aid.

UNDERGRADUATE EXPENSES for 2006–07 ***Tuition, state resident:*** full-time $2592; part-time $108 per credit hour. ***Tuition, nonresident:*** full-time $9192; part-time $383 per credit hour. ***College room and board: Room only:*** $2300.

UNDERGRADUATE FINANCIAL AID (Fall 2006, est.) 3,627 applied for aid; of those 94% were deemed to have need. 98% of undergraduates with need received aid. ***Average percent of need met:*** 29% (excluding resources awarded to replace EFC). ***Average financial aid package:*** $3467 (excluding resources awarded to replace EFC). 1% of all full-time undergraduates had no need and received non-need-based gift aid.

GIFT AID (NEED-BASED) ***Total amount:*** $12,442,354 (85% federal, 15% state). ***Receiving aid:*** Entering class: 73% (665); All full-time undergraduates: 70% (3,067). ***Average award:*** Freshmen: $2527; Undergraduates: $2564. ***Scholarships, grants, and awards:*** Federal Pell, FSEOG, state, private, college/university gift aid from institutional funds.

GIFT AID (NON-NEED-BASED) ***Total amount:*** $1,089,972 (15% state, 53% institutional, 32% external sources). ***Receiving aid:*** Freshmen: 28% (251); Undergraduates: 24% (1,060). ***Average award:*** Freshmen: $717; Undergraduates: $1855. ***Scholarships, grants, and awards by category:*** *Academic Interests/Achievement:* biological sciences, education, engineering/technologies, general academic interests/achievements, health fields, mathematics. *Creative Arts/Performance:* art/fine arts, music. *Special Characteristics:* general special characteristics.

LOANS ***Student loans:*** $10,445,219 (76% need-based, 24% non-need-based). ***Average need-based loan:*** Freshmen: $1233; Undergraduates: $1900. ***Parent loans:*** $40,728 (100% non-need-based). ***Programs:*** FFEL (Subsidized and Unsubsidized Stafford, PLUS), state, college/university.

WORK-STUDY ***Federal work-study:*** Total amount: $236,553; jobs available. ***State or other work-study/employment:*** Total amount: $45,303 (100% need-based). Part-time jobs available.

ATHLETIC AWARDS Total amount: $71,130 (100% non-need-based).

APPLYING FOR FINANCIAL AID ***Required financial aid form:*** FAFSA. ***Financial aid deadline (priority):*** 4/1. ***Notification date:*** 5/1. Students must reply by 7/1 or within 12 weeks of notification.

CONTACT Ms. Georgiana M. Velarde, Assistant Director of Financial Aid, The University of Texas at Brownsville, 80 Fort Brown, Tandy Building, Suite 206, Brownsville, TX 78520-4991, 956-882-8830 or toll-free 800-850-0160 (in-state). *Fax:* 956-882-8229. *E-mail:* georgiana.velarde@utb.edu.

THE UNIVERSITY OF TEXAS AT DALLAS

Richardson, TX

Tuition & fees (TX res): $7570 **Average undergraduate aid package: $9819**

ABOUT THE INSTITUTION State-supported, coed. Awards: bachelor's, master's, and doctoral degrees. 35 undergraduate majors. Total enrollment: 14,523. Undergraduates: 9,375. Freshmen: 1,085. Both federal and institutional methodology are used as a basis for awarding need-based institutional aid.

UNDERGRADUATE EXPENSES for 2006–07 ***Application fee:*** $50. ***Tuition, state resident:*** full-time $7570; part-time $252 per credit. ***Tuition, nonresident:***

full-time $15,820; part-time $527 per credit. Full-time tuition and fees vary according to course load, degree level, and program. Part-time tuition and fees vary according to course load, degree level, and program. ***College room and board:*** $6540. Room and board charges vary according to board plan and housing facility. ***Payment plan:*** Installment.

FRESHMAN FINANCIAL AID (Fall 2006, est.) 653 applied for aid; of those 62% were deemed to have need. 100% of freshmen with need received aid; of those 68% had need fully met. ***Average percent of need met:*** 91% (excluding resources awarded to replace EFC). ***Average financial aid package:*** $12,179 (excluding resources awarded to replace EFC). 41% of all full-time freshmen had no need and received non-need-based gift aid.

UNDERGRADUATE FINANCIAL AID (Fall 2006, est.) 3,690 applied for aid; of those 81% were deemed to have need. 100% of undergraduates with need received aid; of those 35% had need fully met. ***Average percent of need met:*** 75% (excluding resources awarded to replace EFC). ***Average financial aid package:*** $9819 (excluding resources awarded to replace EFC). 18% of all full-time undergraduates had no need and received non-need-based gift aid.

GIFT AID (NEED-BASED) ***Total amount:*** $16,571,906 (38% federal, 24% state, 35% institutional, 3% external sources). ***Receiving aid:*** Freshmen: 26% (279); All full-time undergraduates: 34% (2,224). ***Average award:*** Freshmen: $4946; Undergraduates: $4398. ***Scholarships, grants, and awards:*** Federal Pell, FSEOG, state, private, college/university gift aid from institutional funds.

GIFT AID (NON-NEED-BASED) ***Total amount:*** $12,283,840 (98% institutional, 2% external sources). ***Receiving aid:*** Freshmen: 20% (214); Undergraduates: 13% (842). ***Average award:*** Freshmen: $9091; Undergraduates: $8418. ***Scholarships, grants, and awards by category:*** *Academic Interests/Achievement:* biological sciences, business, computer science, engineering/technologies, general academic interests/achievements, mathematics, physical sciences. *Special Achievements/Activities:* general special achievements/activities, leadership. *Special Characteristics:* adult students, children of public servants, general special characteristics, handicapped students, international students, local/state students, members of minority groups, out-of-state students, public servants, veterans, veterans' children. ***Tuition waivers:*** Full or partial for senior citizens. ***ROTC:*** Army cooperative, Air Force cooperative.

LOANS ***Student loans:*** $33,499,259 (87% need-based, 13% non-need-based). 49% of past graduating class borrowed through all loan programs. *Average indebtedness per student:* $16,895. ***Average need-based loan:*** Freshmen: $4535; Undergraduates: $4845. ***Parent loans:*** $23,706,568 (66% need-based, 34% non-need-based). ***Programs:*** FFEL (Subsidized and Unsubsidized Stafford, PLUS), Perkins, state, college/university.

WORK-STUDY ***Federal work-study:*** Total amount: $2,393,146; 496 jobs averaging $4825. ***State or other work-study/employment:*** Total amount: $44,791 (100% need-based). 10 part-time jobs averaging $4479.

APPLYING FOR FINANCIAL AID ***Required financial aid form:*** FAFSA. ***Financial aid deadline (priority):*** 4/12. ***Notification date:*** Continuous beginning 3/1. Students must reply within 3 weeks of notification.

CONTACT Maria Ramos, Director of Financial Aid, The University of Texas at Dallas, 800 West Campbell Road, PO Box 830688, MC12, Richardson, TX 75083-0688, 972-883-2941 or toll-free 800-889-2443. *Fax:* 972-883-2947. *E-mail:* ramos@utdallas.edu.

THE UNIVERSITY OF TEXAS AT EL PASO

El Paso, TX

Tuition & fees (TX res): $5262 Average undergraduate aid package: $9606

ABOUT THE INSTITUTION State-supported, coed. Awards: bachelor's, master's, and doctoral degrees. 61 undergraduate majors. Total enrollment: 19,842. Undergraduates: 16,793. Freshmen: 2,517. Federal methodology is used as a basis for awarding need-based institutional aid.

UNDERGRADUATE EXPENSES for 2006–07 ***Tuition, state resident:*** full-time $4065. ***Tuition, nonresident:*** full-time $12,315. ***College room and board:*** ***Room only:*** $4185.

FRESHMAN FINANCIAL AID (Fall 2005) 1918 applied for aid; of those 78% were deemed to have need. 98% of freshmen with need received aid; of those 19% had need fully met. ***Average percent of need met:*** 74% (excluding resources awarded to replace EFC). ***Average financial aid package:*** $8691 (excluding resources awarded to replace EFC). 9% of all full-time freshmen had no need and received non-need-based gift aid.

UNDERGRADUATE FINANCIAL AID (Fall 2005) 7,571 applied for aid; of those 80% were deemed to have need. 98% of undergraduates with need received aid; of those 27% had need fully met. ***Average percent of need met:*** 76% (excluding resources awarded to replace EFC). ***Average financial aid package:*** $9606 (excluding resources awarded to replace EFC). 6% of all full-time undergraduates had no need and received non-need-based gift aid.

GIFT AID (NEED-BASED) ***Total amount:*** $41,125,842 (64% federal, 25% state, 11% institutional). ***Receiving aid:*** Freshmen: 61% (1,322); All full-time undergraduates: 47% (5,203). ***Average award:*** Freshmen: $5894; Undergraduates: $5201. ***Scholarships, grants, and awards:*** Federal Pell, FSEOG, state, private, college/university gift aid from institutional funds, United Negro College Fund, Federal Nursing.

GIFT AID (NON-NEED-BASED) ***Total amount:*** $4,776,887 (9% state, 70% institutional, 21% external sources). ***Receiving aid:*** Freshmen: 9% (186); Undergraduates: 5% (583). ***Average award:*** Freshmen: $996; Undergraduates: $1549. ***Scholarships, grants, and awards by category:*** *Academic Interests/Achievement:* biological sciences, business, communication, computer science, education, engineering/technologies, English, general academic interests/achievements, health fields, humanities, international studies, mathematics, military science, physical sciences. *Creative Arts/Performance:* applied art and design, art/fine arts, journalism/publications, music, performing arts, theater/drama. *Special Achievements/Activities:* cheerleading/drum major, leadership. *Special Characteristics:* ethnic background, international students, local/state students, members of minority groups, out-of-state students. ***ROTC:*** Army, Air Force.

LOANS ***Student loans:*** $50,095,072 (100% need-based). 47% of past graduating class borrowed through all loan programs. *Average indebtedness per student:* $6538. ***Average need-based loan:*** Freshmen: $2770; Undergraduates: $5093. ***Parent loans:*** $519,588 (100% non-need-based). ***Programs:*** FFEL (Subsidized and Unsubsidized Stafford, PLUS), Perkins, Federal Nursing, state, college/university.

WORK-STUDY ***Federal work-study:*** Total amount: $1,924,425; jobs available. ***State or other work-study/employment:*** Total amount: $178,274 (100% need-based). Part-time jobs available.

ATHLETIC AWARDS Total amount: $397,920 (100% non-need-based).

APPLYING FOR FINANCIAL AID ***Required financial aid forms:*** FAFSA, institution's own form. ***Financial aid deadline (priority):*** 3/15. ***Notification date:*** 6/30. Students must reply within 2 weeks of notification.

CONTACT Mr. Raul Lerma, Director of Financial Aid, The University of Texas at El Paso, 500 West University Avenue, El Paso, TX 79968-0001, 915-747-7378 or toll-free 877-746-4636.

THE UNIVERSITY OF TEXAS AT SAN ANTONIO

San Antonio, TX

Tuition & fees (TX res): $6699 Average undergraduate aid package: $6827

ABOUT THE INSTITUTION State-supported, coed. Awards: bachelor's, master's, and doctoral degrees. 56 undergraduate majors. Total enrollment: 28,380. Undergraduates: 24,399. Freshmen: 4,782. Federal methodology is used as a basis for awarding need-based institutional aid.

UNDERGRADUATE EXPENSES for 2007–08 ***Application fee:*** $40. ***Tuition, state resident:*** full-time $4530; part-time $151 per hour. ***Tuition, nonresident:*** full-time $12,780; part-time $426 per hour. ***Required fees:*** full-time $2169; $69.70 per hour or $721.45 per term part-time. ***College room and board:*** $8169; ***Room only:*** $5616.

FRESHMAN FINANCIAL AID (Fall 2005) 3455 applied for aid; of those 67% were deemed to have need. 95% of freshmen with need received aid; of those 22% had need fully met. ***Average percent of need met:*** 53% (excluding resources awarded to replace EFC). ***Average financial aid package:*** $6644 (excluding resources awarded to replace EFC). 6% of all full-time freshmen had no need and received non-need-based gift aid.

UNDERGRADUATE FINANCIAL AID (Fall 2005) 13,760 applied for aid; of those 77% were deemed to have need. 97% of undergraduates with need received aid; of those 20% had need fully met. ***Average percent of need met:*** 52% (excluding resources awarded to replace EFC). ***Average financial aid package:*** $6827 (excluding resources awarded to replace EFC). 4% of all full-time undergraduates had no need and received non-need-based gift aid.

GIFT AID (NEED-BASED) ***Total amount:*** $37,487,775 (64% federal, 22% state, 14% institutional). ***Receiving aid:*** Freshmen: 40% (1,756); All full-time undergraduates: 47% (8,262). ***Average award:*** Freshmen: $4812; Undergraduates: $3868. ***Scholarships, grants, and awards:*** Federal Pell, FSEOG, state, private, college/university gift aid from institutional funds.

GIFT AID (NON-NEED-BASED) ***Total amount:*** $5,862,475 (39% institutional, 61% external sources). ***Receiving aid:*** Freshmen: 14% (626); Undergraduates: 10% (1,810). ***Average award:*** Freshmen: $1512; Undergraduates: $1747. ***Scholarships, grants, and awards by category:*** *Academic Interests/Achievement:* agriculture, architecture, area/ethnic studies, biological sciences, business, communication, computer science, education, engineering/technologies, English, foreign languages, general academic interests/achievements, humanities, mathematics, physical sciences, social sciences. *Creative Arts/Performance:* art/fine arts, debating, music. *Special Achievements/Activities:* general special achievements/activities. *Special Characteristics:* ethnic background, general special characteristics, handicapped students, local/state students, out-of-state students. ***ROTC:*** Army, Air Force.

LOANS ***Student loans:*** $78,990,102 (53% need-based, 47% non-need-based). 63% of past graduating class borrowed through all loan programs. *Average indebtedness per student:* $16,888. ***Average need-based loan:*** Freshmen: $2367; Undergraduates: $3616. ***Parent loans:*** $10,196,047 (100% non-need-based). ***Programs:*** FFEL (Subsidized and Unsubsidized Stafford, PLUS), Perkins, state, college/university.

WORK-STUDY ***Federal work-study:*** Total amount: $1,140,281; 523 jobs averaging $2212. ***State or other work-study/employment:*** Total amount: $596,378 (100% need-based). 121 part-time jobs averaging $1256.

ATHLETIC AWARDS Total amount: $1,645,984 (100% non-need-based).

APPLYING FOR FINANCIAL AID ***Required financial aid forms:*** FAFSA, institution's own form. ***Financial aid deadline (priority):*** 3/31. ***Notification date:*** Continuous beginning 4/1. Students must reply within 4 weeks of notification.

CONTACT Kim Canady, Assistant Director of Student Financial Aid, The University of Texas at San Antonio, One UTSA Cirlce, San Antonio, TX 78249, 210-458-8000 or toll-free 800-669-0919. *Fax:* 210-458-4638. *E-mail:* financialaid@utsa.edu.

THE UNIVERSITY OF TEXAS AT TYLER

Tyler, TX

Tuition & fees (TX res): $4476 **Average undergraduate aid package: $7314**

ABOUT THE INSTITUTION State-supported, coed. Awards: bachelor's and master's degrees. 38 undergraduate majors. Total enrollment: 5,926. Undergraduates: 4,764. Freshmen: 594. Federal methodology is used as a basis for awarding need-based institutional aid.

UNDERGRADUATE EXPENSES for 2007–08 ***Application fee:*** $25. ***Tuition, state resident:*** full-time $3240; part-time $186.50 per semester hour. ***Tuition, nonresident:*** full-time $9912; part-time $464.50 per semester hour.

FRESHMAN FINANCIAL AID (Fall 2006, est.) 389 applied for aid; of those 63% were deemed to have need. 100% of freshmen with need received aid; of those 16% had need fully met. ***Average percent of need met:*** 51% (excluding resources awarded to replace EFC). ***Average financial aid package:*** $6442 (excluding resources awarded to replace EFC). 10% of all full-time freshmen had no need and received non-need-based gift aid.

UNDERGRADUATE FINANCIAL AID (Fall 2006, est.) 2,441 applied for aid; of those 78% were deemed to have need. 100% of undergraduates with need received aid; of those 21% had need fully met. ***Average percent of need met:*** 67% (excluding resources awarded to replace EFC). ***Average financial aid package:*** $7314 (excluding resources awarded to replace EFC). 7% of all full-time undergraduates had no need and received non-need-based gift aid.

GIFT AID (NEED-BASED) ***Total amount:*** $8,057,340 (63% federal, 16% state, 15% institutional, 6% external sources). ***Receiving aid:*** Freshmen: 35% (205); All full-time undergraduates: 42% (1,554). ***Average award:*** Freshmen: $4980; Undergraduates: $4395. ***Scholarships, grants, and awards:*** Federal Pell, FSEOG, state, private, college/university gift aid from institutional funds, Texas Grant, Institutional Grants (Education Affordability Prog).

GIFT AID (NON-NEED-BASED) ***Total amount:*** $2,468,136 (2% state, 62% institutional, 36% external sources). ***Receiving aid:*** Freshmen: 6% (34); Undergraduates: 3% (117). ***Average award:*** Freshmen: $2885; Undergraduates: $2198. ***Scholarships, grants, and awards by category:*** *Academic Interests/Achievement:* 937 awards ($2,125,306 total): communication, engineering/technologies, general academic interests/achievements, health fields. *Creative Arts/Performance:* 52 awards ($59,993 total): art/fine arts, music.

LOANS ***Student loans:*** $17,809,533 (69% need-based, 31% non-need-based). 44% of past graduating class borrowed through all loan programs. *Average indebtedness per student:* $11,286. ***Average need-based loan:*** Freshmen: $2146; Undergraduates: $3582. ***Parent loans:*** $6,565,583 (16% need-based, 84% non-need-based). ***Programs:*** FFEL (Subsidized and Unsubsidized Stafford, PLUS), state.

WORK-STUDY ***Federal work-study:*** Total amount: $246,778; 85 jobs averaging $2903. ***State or other work-study/employment:*** Total amount: $123,360 (45% need-based, 55% non-need-based). 23 part-time jobs averaging $2407.

APPLYING FOR FINANCIAL AID ***Required financial aid forms:*** FAFSA, institution's own form. ***Financial aid deadline (priority):*** 4/1. ***Notification date:*** Continuous beginning 4/15. Students must reply within 2 weeks of notification.

CONTACT Candice A. Lindsey, Associate Dean for Enrollment Management, Financial Aid, and Registrar's Office, The University of Texas at Tyler, 3900 University Boulevard Adm 213, Tyler, TX 75799-0001, 903-566-7221 or toll-free 800-UTTYLER (in-state). *Fax:* 903-566-7183. *E-mail:* clindsey@uttyler.edu.

THE UNIVERSITY OF TEXAS HEALTH SCIENCE CENTER AT HOUSTON

Houston, TX

Tuition & fees: N/R **Average undergraduate aid package: $8534**

ABOUT THE INSTITUTION State-supported, coed. Awards: bachelor's, master's, doctoral, and first professional degrees and post-master's certificates. 2 undergraduate majors. Total enrollment: 3,399. Undergraduates: 381. Federal methodology is used as a basis for awarding need-based institutional aid.

UNDERGRADUATE FINANCIAL AID (Fall 2005) 322 applied for aid; of those 78% were deemed to have need. 100% of undergraduates with need received aid; of those 18% had need fully met. ***Average percent of need met:*** 82% (excluding resources awarded to replace EFC). ***Average financial aid package:*** $8534 (excluding resources awarded to replace EFC).

GIFT AID (NEED-BASED) ***Total amount:*** $815,663 (40% federal, 6% state, 39% institutional, 15% external sources). ***Receiving aid:*** All full-time undergraduates: 34% (137). ***Average award:*** Undergraduates: $4016. ***Scholarships, grants, and awards:*** Federal Pell, FSEOG, state, private, college/university gift aid from institutional funds.

GIFT AID (NON-NEED-BASED) ***ROTC:*** Army cooperative.

LOANS ***Student loans:*** $2,949,429 (100% need-based). 51% of past graduating class borrowed through all loan programs. *Average indebtedness per student:* $22,812. ***Average need-based loan:*** Undergraduates: $11,941. ***Parent loans:*** $403,682 (100% need-based). ***Programs:*** FFEL (Subsidized and Unsubsidized Stafford, PLUS), Perkins, Federal Nursing, state, college/university, alternative loans.

APPLYING FOR FINANCIAL AID ***Required financial aid forms:*** FAFSA, supplemental form. ***Financial aid deadline:*** Continuous. ***Notification date:*** Continuous.

CONTACT Ms. Wanda Williams, Director, The University of Texas Health Science Center at Houston, PO Box 20036, Houston, TX 77225, 713-500-3860. *Fax:* 713-500-3863. *E-mail:* wanta.k.williams@uth.tmc.edu.

THE UNIVERSITY OF TEXAS HEALTH SCIENCE CENTER AT SAN ANTONIO

San Antonio, TX

CONTACT Robert T. Lawson, Financial Aid Administrator, The University of Texas Health Science Center at San Antonio, 7703 Floyd Curl Drive, MSC 7708, San Antonio, TX 78284, 210-567-0025. *Fax:* 210-567-6643.

THE UNIVERSITY OF TEXAS MEDICAL BRANCH

Galveston, TX

Tuition & fees (TX res): $4302 **Average undergraduate aid package: $7026**

ABOUT THE INSTITUTION State-supported, coed. Awards: bachelor's, master's, doctoral, and first professional degrees. 3 undergraduate majors. Total enrollment: 2,255. Undergraduates: 494. Federal methodology is used as a basis for awarding need-based institutional aid.

UNDERGRADUATE EXPENSES for 2006–07 ***Application fee:*** $30. ***Tuition, state resident:*** full-time $3600; part-time $120 per credit hour. ***Tuition, nonresident:*** full-time $11,850; part-time $395 per credit hour. Full-time tuition and fees vary according to program. ***College room and board: Room only:*** $3060. ***Payment plan:*** Installment.

UNDERGRADUATE FINANCIAL AID (Fall 2005) 362 applied for aid; of those 95% were deemed to have need. 100% of undergraduates with need received aid; of those 1% had need fully met. ***Average percent of need met:*** 81% (excluding resources awarded to replace EFC). ***Average financial aid package:*** $7026 (excluding resources awarded to replace EFC). 3% of all full-time undergraduates had no need and received non-need-based gift aid.

GIFT AID (NEED-BASED) ***Total amount:*** $911,694 (41% federal, 32% state, 21% institutional, 6% external sources). ***Receiving aid:*** All full-time undergraduates: 51% (255). ***Average award:*** Undergraduates: $3575. ***Scholarships, grants, and awards:*** Federal Pell, FSEOG, state, private, college/university gift aid from institutional funds.

GIFT AID (NON-NEED-BASED) ***Total amount:*** $6300 (48% institutional, 52% external sources). ***Receiving aid:*** Undergraduates: 34% (171). ***Average award:*** Undergraduates: $1000. ***Scholarships, grants, and awards by category:*** *Academic Interests/Achievement:* 16 awards ($177,762 total): health fields.

LOANS ***Student loans:*** $4,672,809 (96% need-based, 4% non-need-based). 73% of past graduating class borrowed through all loan programs. *Average indebtedness per student:* $25,083. ***Average need-based loan:*** Undergraduates: $6077. ***Parent loans:*** $27,000 (100% need-based). ***Programs:*** Federal Direct (Subsidized and Unsubsidized Stafford, PLUS), Perkins, Federal Nursing, state, college/university.

WORK-STUDY ***Federal work-study:*** Total amount: $44,654; 27 jobs averaging $1654.

APPLYING FOR FINANCIAL AID ***Required financial aid form:*** FAFSA. ***Financial aid deadline:*** Continuous. ***Notification date:*** Continuous. Students must reply within 4 weeks of notification.

CONTACT Mr. Carl Gordon, University Financial Aid Officer, The University of Texas Medical Branch, 301 University Boulevard, Galveston, TX 77555-1305, 409-772-1215. *Fax:* 409-772-4466. *E-mail:* enrollment.services@utmb.edu.

THE UNIVERSITY OF TEXAS OF THE PERMIAN BASIN

Odessa, TX

Tuition & fees: N/R **Average undergraduate aid package: $5815**

ABOUT THE INSTITUTION State-supported, coed. Awards: bachelor's and master's degrees. 24 undergraduate majors. Total enrollment: 2,695. Undergraduates: 2,012. Freshmen: 226. Federal methodology is used as a basis for awarding need-based institutional aid.

FRESHMAN FINANCIAL AID (Fall 2006, est.) 308 applied for aid; of those 66% were deemed to have need. 100% of freshmen with need received aid; of those 8% had need fully met. ***Average percent of need met:*** 6% (excluding resources awarded to replace EFC). ***Average financial aid package:*** $5468 (excluding resources awarded to replace EFC). 34% of all full-time freshmen had no need and received non-need-based gift aid.

UNDERGRADUATE FINANCIAL AID (Fall 2006, est.) 2,306 applied for aid; of those 72% were deemed to have need. 100% of undergraduates with need received aid; of those 21% had need fully met. ***Average percent of need met:*** 46% (excluding resources awarded to replace EFC). ***Average financial aid package:*** $5815 (excluding resources awarded to replace EFC). 12% of all full-time undergraduates had no need and received non-need-based gift aid.

GIFT AID (NEED-BASED) ***Total amount:*** $4,123,968 (75% federal, 16% state, 5% institutional, 4% external sources). ***Receiving aid:*** Freshmen: 45% (149); All full-time undergraduates: 44% (1,324). ***Average award:*** Freshmen: $3184; Undergraduates: $3129. ***Scholarships, grants, and awards:*** Federal Pell, FSEOG, state, private, college/university gift aid from institutional funds.

GIFT AID (NON-NEED-BASED) ***Total amount:*** $2,729,197 (3% federal, 7% state, 63% institutional, 27% external sources). ***Receiving aid:*** Freshmen: 57% (188); Undergraduates: 24% (738). ***Average award:*** Freshmen: $2271; Undergraduates: $895. ***Scholarships, grants, and awards by category:*** *Academic Interests/Achievement:* 1,389 awards ($1,334,000 total): general academic interests/achievements. *Creative Arts/Performance:* 16 awards ($2000 total): art/fine arts, dance, general creative arts/performance, music.

LOANS ***Student loans:*** $6,645,690 (83% need-based, 17% non-need-based). 23% of past graduating class borrowed through all loan programs. *Average indebtedness per student:* $12,611. ***Average need-based loan:*** Freshmen: $1625; Undergraduates: $4965. ***Parent loans:*** $116,887 (100% non-need-based). ***Programs:*** FFEL (Subsidized and Unsubsidized Stafford, PLUS), state.

WORK-STUDY ***Federal work-study:*** Total amount: $100,000; 75 jobs averaging $2350. ***State or other work-study/employment:*** Total amount: $20,000 (100% need-based). 12 part-time jobs averaging $650.

ATHLETIC AWARDS Total amount: $364,674 (100% non-need-based).

APPLYING FOR FINANCIAL AID ***Required financial aid form:*** FAFSA. ***Financial aid deadline (priority):*** 5/1. ***Notification date:*** Continuous beginning 5/1. Students must reply within 2 weeks of notification.

CONTACT Mr. Robert L. Vasquez, Director, Office of Student Financial Aid, The University of Texas of the Permian Basin, 4901 East University Blvd., Odessa, TX 79762, 432-552-2620 or toll-free 866-552-UTPB. *Fax:* 432-552-2621. *E-mail:* finaid@utpb.edu.

THE UNIVERSITY OF TEXAS–PAN AMERICAN

Edinburg, TX

Tuition & fees (TX res): $4165 **Average undergraduate aid package: $8072**

ABOUT THE INSTITUTION State-supported, coed. Awards: bachelor's, master's, and doctoral degrees and post-bachelor's and post-master's certificates. 58 undergraduate majors. Total enrollment: 17,337. Undergraduates: 15,076. Freshmen: 2,807. Federal methodology is used as a basis for awarding need-based institutional aid.

UNDERGRADUATE EXPENSES for 2006–07 ***Tuition, state resident:*** full-time $3268; part-time $113 per semester hour. ***Tuition, nonresident:*** full-time $11,250; part-time $388 per semester hour. ***Required fees:*** full-time $897; $449 per term part-time. ***College room and board:*** $5095; ***Room only:*** $3140. Room and board charges vary according to board plan and housing facility. ***Payment plan:*** Installment.

FRESHMAN FINANCIAL AID (Fall 2005) 1629 applied for aid; of those 95% were deemed to have need. 97% of freshmen with need received aid; of those 6% had need fully met. ***Average percent of need met:*** 70% (excluding resources awarded to replace EFC). ***Average financial aid package:*** $7324 (excluding resources awarded to replace EFC). 6% of all full-time freshmen had no need and received non-need-based gift aid.

UNDERGRADUATE FINANCIAL AID (Fall 2005) 8,509 applied for aid; of those 96% were deemed to have need. 97% of undergraduates with need received aid; of those 8% had need fully met. ***Average percent of need met:*** 85% (excluding resources awarded to replace EFC). ***Average financial aid package:*** $8072 (excluding resources awarded to replace EFC). 5% of all full-time undergraduates had no need and received non-need-based gift aid.

GIFT AID (NEED-BASED) ***Total amount:*** $47,907,551 (52% federal, 41% state, 5% institutional, 2% external sources). ***Receiving aid:*** Freshmen: 63% (1,437); All full-time undergraduates: 70% (7,448). ***Average award:*** Freshmen: $7426; Undergraduates: $8190. ***Scholarships, grants, and awards:*** Federal Pell, FSEOG, state, private, college/university gift aid from institutional funds.

GIFT AID (NON-NEED-BASED) ***Total amount:*** $2,252,524 (9% federal, 63% institutional, 28% external sources). ***Receiving aid:*** Freshmen: 2% (44); Undergraduates: 2% (196). ***Average award:*** Freshmen: $5024; Undergraduates: $4944. ***Scholarships, grants, and awards by category:*** *Academic Interests/Achievement:* 1,461 awards ($3,374,901 total): biological sciences, business, communication, computer science, education, engineering/technologies, English, general academic interests/achievements, health fields, mathematics, military science, premedicine, social sciences. *Creative Arts/Performance:* 101 awards ($51,260 total): art/fine arts, dance, journalism/publications, music, theater/drama. *Special Achievements/Activities:* 111 awards ($150,647 total): cheerleading/drum major, community service, general special achievements/activities, leadership, memberships. *Special Characteristics:* 82 awards ($72,550 total): ethnic background, general special characteristics, international students, local/state students, out-of-state students, veterans. ***Tuition waivers:*** Full or partial for senior citizens. ***ROTC:*** Army.

LOANS ***Student loans:*** $22,727,686 (100% need-based). 76% of past graduating class borrowed through all loan programs. *Average indebtedness per student:* $12,630. ***Average need-based loan:*** Freshmen: $2072; Undergraduates: $3946.

Parent loans: $220,642 (40% need-based, 60% non-need-based). ***Programs:*** FFEL (Subsidized and Unsubsidized Stafford, PLUS), Perkins, college/university.

WORK-STUDY ***Federal work-study:*** Total amount: $2,035,406; 899 jobs averaging $2264. ***State or other work-study/employment:*** Total amount: $182,673 (100% need-based). 141 part-time jobs averaging $1296.

ATHLETIC AWARDS Total amount: $811,054 (34% need-based, 66% non-need-based).

APPLYING FOR FINANCIAL AID ***Required financial aid form:*** FAFSA. ***Financial aid deadline (priority):*** 3/1. ***Notification date:*** Continuous beginning 3/15. Students must reply within 2 weeks of notification.

CONTACT Mrs. Elaine Rivera, Executive Director of Student Financial Services, The University of Texas–Pan American, 1201 West University Drive, Edinburg, TX 78541, 956-381-2190. *Fax:* 956-381-2396. *E-mail:* eriverall@panam.edu.

THE UNIVERSITY OF TEXAS SOUTHWESTERN MEDICAL CENTER AT DALLAS

Dallas, TX

Tuition & fees (TX res): $4105 **Average undergraduate aid package: N/A**

ABOUT THE INSTITUTION State-supported, coed. Awards: bachelor's, master's, doctoral, and first professional degrees and post-bachelor's certificates. 4 undergraduate majors. Total enrollment: 2,434. Undergraduates: 113. Federal methodology is used as a basis for awarding need-based institutional aid.

UNDERGRADUATE EXPENSES for 2007–08 ***Application fee:*** $10. ***Tuition, state resident:*** full-time $3300; part-time $158 per credit hour. ***Tuition, nonresident:*** full-time $11,640; part-time $436 per credit hour.

UNDERGRADUATE FINANCIAL AID (Fall 2006, est.) 89 applied for aid; of those 100% were deemed to have need. 100% of undergraduates with need received aid.

GIFT AID (NEED-BASED) ***Total amount:*** $214,298 (42% federal, 58% institutional). ***Scholarships, grants, and awards:*** Federal Pell, FSEOG, state, private, college/university gift aid from institutional funds.

GIFT AID (NON-NEED-BASED) ***Total amount:*** $22,016 (6% federal, 10% state, 24% institutional, 60% external sources). ***Scholarships, grants, and awards by category:*** *Special Achievements/Activities:* community service.

LOANS ***Student loans:*** $1,001,236 (100% need-based). 89% of past graduating class borrowed through all loan programs. *Average indebtedness per student:* $36,000. ***Parent loans:*** $16,062 (100% non-need-based). ***Programs:*** FFEL (Subsidized and Unsubsidized Stafford, PLUS), Perkins, state, college/university, alternative loans.

WORK-STUDY ***Federal work-study:*** Total amount: $19,326; 10 jobs averaging $1933.

APPLYING FOR FINANCIAL AID ***Required financial aid forms:*** FAFSA, we do not enroll freshmen, they must have 60-90 hours prior to attending U T Southwestern. ***Financial aid deadline (priority):*** 3/15. ***Notification date:*** 4/15. Students must reply within 2 weeks of notification.

CONTACT Ms. June M. Perry, Associate Director of Student Financial Aid, The University of Texas Southwestern Medical Center at Dallas, 5323 Harry Hines Boulevard, Dallas, TX 75390-9064, 214-648-3611. *Fax:* 214-648-3289. *E-mail:* june.perry@utsouthwestern.edu.

THE UNIVERSITY OF THE ARTS

Philadelphia, PA

CONTACT Office of Financial Aid, The University of the Arts, 320 South Broad Street, Philadelphia, PA 19102-4944, 800-616-ARTS Ext. 6170 or toll-free 800-616-ARTS. *E-mail:* finaid@uarts.edu.

UNIVERSITY OF THE CUMBERLANDS

Williamsburg, KY

Tuition & fees: $13,658 **Average undergraduate aid package: $16,447**

ABOUT THE INSTITUTION Independent Kentucky Baptist, coed. Awards: associate, bachelor's, and master's degrees. 34 undergraduate majors. Total enrollment: 1,884. Undergraduates: 1,525. Freshmen: 349. Federal methodology is used as a basis for awarding need-based institutional aid.

UNDERGRADUATE EXPENSES for 2007–08 ***Application fee:*** $30. ***Comprehensive fee:*** $20,284 includes full-time tuition ($13,298), mandatory fees ($360), and room and board ($6626). ***Part-time tuition:*** $430 per hour. ***Part-time fees:*** $65 per term.

FRESHMAN FINANCIAL AID (Fall 2006, est.) 326 applied for aid; of those 93% were deemed to have need. 100% of freshmen with need received aid; of those 70% had need fully met. ***Average percent of need met:*** 93% (excluding resources awarded to replace EFC). ***Average financial aid package:*** $16,137 (excluding resources awarded to replace EFC). 3% of all full-time freshmen had no need and received non-need-based gift aid.

UNDERGRADUATE FINANCIAL AID (Fall 2006, est.) 1,227 applied for aid; of those 93% were deemed to have need. 100% of undergraduates with need received aid; of those 70% had need fully met. ***Average percent of need met:*** 95% (excluding resources awarded to replace EFC). ***Average financial aid package:*** $16,447 (excluding resources awarded to replace EFC). 3% of all full-time undergraduates had no need and received non-need-based gift aid.

GIFT AID (NEED-BASED) ***Total amount:*** $8,548,970 (27% federal, 28% state, 44% institutional, 1% external sources). ***Receiving aid:*** Freshmen: 87% (304); All full-time undergraduates: 85% (1,145). ***Average award:*** Freshmen: $9334; Undergraduates: $8451. ***Scholarships, grants, and awards:*** Federal Pell, FSEOG, state, private, college/university gift aid from institutional funds.

GIFT AID (NON-NEED-BASED) ***Total amount:*** $3,799,742 (24% state, 66% institutional, 10% external sources). ***Receiving aid:*** Freshmen: 87% (304); Undergraduates: 85% (1,145). ***Average award:*** Freshmen: $6574; Undergraduates: $7155. ***Scholarships, grants, and awards by category:*** *Academic Interests/Achievement:* 860 awards ($3,116,065 total): general academic interests/achievements. *Creative Arts/Performance:* 105 awards ($231,290 total): art/fine arts, debating, music, theater/drama. *Special Achievements/Activities:* 151 awards ($198,150 total): cheerleading/drum major, community service, leadership, religious involvement. *Special Characteristics:* 225 awards ($413,595 total): children and siblings of alumni, children of faculty/staff, relatives of clergy, siblings of current students. ***ROTC:*** Army.

LOANS ***Student loans:*** $4,810,124 (68% need-based, 32% non-need-based). 72% of past graduating class borrowed through all loan programs. *Average indebtedness per student:* $19,497. ***Average need-based loan:*** Freshmen: $2572; Undergraduates: $3998. ***Parent loans:*** $805,530 (25% need-based, 75% non-need-based). ***Programs:*** FFEL (Subsidized and Unsubsidized Stafford, PLUS), Perkins, college/university.

WORK-STUDY ***Federal work-study:*** Total amount: $793,959; 431 jobs averaging $1842. ***State or other work-study/employment:*** Total amount: $309,231 (75% need-based, 25% non-need-based). 172 part-time jobs averaging $1798.

ATHLETIC AWARDS Total amount: $2,340,627 (60% need-based, 40% non-need-based).

APPLYING FOR FINANCIAL AID ***Required financial aid form:*** FAFSA. ***Financial aid deadline (priority):*** 3/1. ***Notification date:*** Continuous beginning 4/1. Students must reply within 2 weeks of notification.

CONTACT Mr. Steve Allen, Vice President of Student Financial Planning, University of the Cumberlands, 6190 College Station Drive, Williamsburg, KY 40769-1372, 606-549-2200 Ext. 4220 or toll-free 800-343-1609. *Fax:* 606-539-4220. *E-mail:* finplan@ucumberlands.edu.

UNIVERSITY OF THE DISTRICT OF COLUMBIA

Washington, DC

ABOUT THE INSTITUTION District-supported, coed. Awards: associate, bachelor's, and master's degrees. 102 undergraduate majors. Total university enrollment: 992. Total unit enrollment: 5,534. Undergraduates: 5,300. Freshmen: 1,425.

GIFT AID (NEED-BASED) ***Scholarships, grants, and awards:*** Federal Pell, FSEOG, state, college/university gift aid from institutional funds.

GIFT AID (NON-NEED-BASED) ***Scholarships, grants, and awards by category:*** *Academic Interests/Achievement:* general academic interests/achievements. *Creative Arts/Performance:* music. *Special Characteristics:* children of faculty/staff.

LOANS ***Programs:*** FFEL (Subsidized and Unsubsidized Stafford, PLUS), Perkins, college/university.

APPLYING FOR FINANCIAL AID ***Required financial aid forms:*** FAFSA, district aid form, loan request form.

CONTACT Henry Anderson, Director, Officer of Financial Aid, University of the District of Columbia, 4200 Connecticut Avenue NW, Washington, DC 20008-1175, 202-274-6053. *E-mail:* henderson@udc.edu.

UNIVERSITY OF THE INCARNATE WORD

San Antonio, TX

Tuition & fees: $19,060 **Average undergraduate aid package: $12,349**

ABOUT THE INSTITUTION Independent Roman Catholic, coed. Awards: associate, bachelor's, master's, doctoral, and first professional degrees. 69 undergraduate majors. Total enrollment: 5,619. Undergraduates: 4,666. Freshmen: 621. Federal methodology is used as a basis for awarding need-based institutional aid.

UNDERGRADUATE EXPENSES for 2007–08 ***Application fee:*** $20. ***Comprehensive fee:*** $26,054 includes full-time tuition ($18,400), mandatory fees ($660), and room and board ($6994). ***College room only:*** $4080. ***Part-time tuition:*** $605 per semester hour. ***Part-time fees:*** $200 per term.

FRESHMAN FINANCIAL AID (Fall 2006, est.) 612 applied for aid; of those 81% were deemed to have need. 100% of freshmen with need received aid; of those 62% had need fully met. ***Average percent of need met:*** 69% (excluding resources awarded to replace EFC). ***Average financial aid package:*** $14,050 (excluding resources awarded to replace EFC). 19% of all full-time freshmen had no need and received non-need-based gift aid.

UNDERGRADUATE FINANCIAL AID (Fall 2006, est.) 2,764 applied for aid; of those 81% were deemed to have need. 100% of undergraduates with need received aid; of those 63% had need fully met. ***Average percent of need met:*** 64% (excluding resources awarded to replace EFC). ***Average financial aid package:*** $12,349 (excluding resources awarded to replace EFC). 15% of all full-time undergraduates had no need and received non-need-based gift aid.

GIFT AID (NEED-BASED) ***Total amount:*** $19,820,099 (23% federal, 22% state, 53% institutional, 2% external sources). ***Receiving aid:*** Freshmen: 80% (493); All full-time undergraduates: 72% (2,042). ***Average award:*** Freshmen: $10,321; Undergraduates: $8525. ***Scholarships, grants, and awards:*** Federal Pell, FSEOG, state, private, college/university gift aid from institutional funds, United Negro College Fund, Federal Nursing.

GIFT AID (NON-NEED-BASED) ***Total amount:*** $748,938 (96% institutional, 4% external sources). ***Receiving aid:*** Freshmen: 49% (303); Undergraduates: 44% (1,250). ***Average award:*** Freshmen: $4997; Undergraduates: $5160. ***Scholarships, grants, and awards by category:*** *Academic Interests/Achievement:* 1,756 awards ($6,294,863 total): general academic interests/achievements. *Creative Arts/Performance:* 83 awards ($168,204 total): art/fine arts, dance, music, theater/drama. *Special Achievements/Activities:* 24 awards ($39,500 total): religious involvement. *Special Characteristics:* 201 awards ($1,368,948 total): children of union members/company employees. ***ROTC:*** Army cooperative, Air Force cooperative.

LOANS ***Student loans:*** $16,013,233 (51% need-based, 49% non-need-based). 75% of past graduating class borrowed through all loan programs. *Average indebtedness per student:* $31,681. ***Average need-based loan:*** Freshmen: $2989; Undergraduates: $4238. ***Parent loans:*** $508,648 (95% need-based, 5% non-need-based). ***Programs:*** FFEL (Subsidized and Unsubsidized Stafford, PLUS), Perkins, Federal Nursing, state, alternative loans.

WORK-STUDY ***Federal work-study:*** Total amount: $445,135; 416 jobs averaging $1982. ***State or other work-study/employment:*** 19 part-time jobs averaging $3425.

ATHLETIC AWARDS Total amount: $2,101,075 (26% need-based, 74% non-need-based).

APPLYING FOR FINANCIAL AID ***Required financial aid form:*** FAFSA. ***Financial aid deadline (priority):*** 4/1. ***Notification date:*** Continuous beginning 2/15. Students must reply within 2 weeks of notification.

CONTACT Ms. Amy Carcanagues, Director of Financial Assistance, University of the Incarnate Word, 4301 Broadway, Box 308, San Antonio, TX 78209, 210-829-6008 or toll-free 800-749-WORD. *Fax:* 210-283-5053. *E-mail:* amyc@uiwtx.edu.

UNIVERSITY OF THE OZARKS

Clarksville, AR

Tuition & fees: $14,950 **Average undergraduate aid package: $16,560**

ABOUT THE INSTITUTION Independent Presbyterian, coed. Awards: bachelor's degrees. 35 undergraduate majors. Total enrollment: 622. Undergraduates: 622. Freshmen: 165. Both federal and institutional methodology are used as a basis for awarding need-based institutional aid.

UNDERGRADUATE EXPENSES for 2006–07 ***Comprehensive fee:*** $20,210 includes full-time tuition ($14,470), mandatory fees ($480), and room and board ($5260). ***Part-time tuition:*** $605 per credit hour.

FRESHMAN FINANCIAL AID (Fall 2006, est.) 115 applied for aid; of those 93% were deemed to have need. 100% of freshmen with need received aid; of those 19% had need fully met. ***Average percent of need met:*** 70% (excluding resources awarded to replace EFC). ***Average financial aid package:*** $12,963 (excluding resources awarded to replace EFC). 35% of all full-time freshmen had no need and received non-need-based gift aid.

UNDERGRADUATE FINANCIAL AID (Fall 2006, est.) 329 applied for aid; of those 94% were deemed to have need. 100% of undergraduates with need received aid; of those 14% had need fully met. ***Average percent of need met:*** 61% (excluding resources awarded to replace EFC). ***Average financial aid package:*** $16,560 (excluding resources awarded to replace EFC). 47% of all full-time undergraduates had no need and received non-need-based gift aid.

GIFT AID (NEED-BASED) ***Total amount:*** $3,473,310 (17% federal, 6% state, 73% institutional, 4% external sources). ***Receiving aid:*** Freshmen: 65% (107); All full-time undergraduates: 53% (308). ***Average award:*** Freshmen: $12,977; Undergraduates: $11,942. ***Scholarships, grants, and awards:*** Federal Pell, FSEOG, state, private, college/university gift aid from institutional funds.

GIFT AID (NON-NEED-BASED) ***Total amount:*** $2,815,888 (2% state, 97% institutional, 1% external sources). ***Receiving aid:*** Freshmen: 62% (101); Undergraduates: 48% (278). ***Average award:*** Freshmen: $15,964; Undergraduates: $17,911. ***Scholarships, grants, and awards by category:*** *Academic Interests/Achievement:* 324 awards ($1,490,955 total): biological sciences, business, communication, education, English, general academic interests/achievements, humanities, mathematics, premedicine, religion/biblical studies, social sciences. *Creative Arts/Performance:* 41 awards ($122,562 total): art/fine arts, music, theater/drama. *Special Achievements/Activities:* 170 awards ($440,569 total): leadership. *Special Characteristics:* 220 awards ($721,211 total): children and siblings of alumni, children of faculty/staff, general special characteristics, international students, members of minority groups, relatives of clergy, religious affiliation, siblings of current students.

LOANS ***Student loans:*** $1,551,776 (93% need-based, 7% non-need-based). 53% of past graduating class borrowed through all loan programs. *Average indebtedness per student:* $18,292. ***Average need-based loan:*** Freshmen: $2288; Undergraduates: $3957. ***Parent loans:*** $588,918 (57% need-based, 43% non-need-based). ***Programs:*** FFEL (Subsidized and Unsubsidized Stafford, PLUS), Perkins, college/university.

WORK-STUDY ***Federal work-study:*** Total amount: $139,790; 122 jobs averaging $806. ***State or other work-study/employment:*** Total amount: $270,458 (24% need-based, 76% non-need-based). 209 part-time jobs averaging $1494.

APPLYING FOR FINANCIAL AID ***Required financial aid form:*** FAFSA. ***Financial aid deadline (priority):*** 2/15. ***Notification date:*** Continuous beginning 3/15. Students must reply within 2 weeks of notification.

CONTACT Ms. Jana D. Hart, Director of Financial Aid, University of the Ozarks, 415 North College Avenue, Clarksville, AR 72830-2880, 479-979-1221 or toll-free 800-264-8636. *Fax:* 479-979-1417. *E-mail:* jhart@ozarks.edu.

UNIVERSITY OF THE PACIFIC

Stockton, CA

Tuition & fees: $27,350 **Average undergraduate aid package: $24,110**

ABOUT THE INSTITUTION Independent, coed. Awards: bachelor's, master's, doctoral, and first professional degrees. 54 undergraduate majors. Total enrollment: 6,251. Undergraduates: 3,535. Freshmen: 878. Federal methodology is used as a basis for awarding need-based institutional aid.

UNDERGRADUATE EXPENSES for 2006–07 ***Application fee:*** $60. ***Comprehensive fee:*** $36,050 includes full-time tuition ($26,920), mandatory fees ($430), and room and board ($8700). ***College room only:*** $4350. Room and board charges vary according to board plan and housing facility. ***Part-time tuition:*** $930 per unit. Part-time tuition and fees vary according to course load. ***Payment plan:*** Deferred payment.

FRESHMAN FINANCIAL AID (Fall 2006, est.) 699 applied for aid; of those 80% were deemed to have need. 100% of freshmen with need received aid; of those

30% had need fully met. ***Average financial aid package:*** $23,192 (excluding resources awarded to replace EFC). 20% of all full-time freshmen had no need and received non-need-based gift aid.

UNDERGRADUATE FINANCIAL AID (Fall 2006, est.) 2,605 applied for aid; of those 87% were deemed to have need. 100% of undergraduates with need received aid; of those 26% had need fully met. ***Average financial aid package:*** $24,110 (excluding resources awarded to replace EFC). 14% of all full-time undergraduates had no need and received non-need-based gift aid.

GIFT AID (NEED-BASED) ***Total amount:*** $37,977,920 (11% federal, 23% state, 66% institutional). ***Receiving aid:*** Freshmen: 63% (552); All full-time undergraduates: 62% (2,152). ***Average award:*** Freshmen: $17,907; Undergraduates: $17,482. ***Scholarships, grants, and awards:*** Federal Pell, FSEOG, state, private, college/university gift aid from institutional funds.

GIFT AID (NON-NEED-BASED) ***Total amount:*** $4,138,958 (100% institutional). ***Average award:*** Freshmen: $8615; Undergraduates: $8588. ***Scholarships, grants, and awards by category:*** *Academic Interests/Achievement:* 1,361 awards ($11,500,000 total): general academic interests/achievements. *Creative Arts/Performance:* 132 awards ($788,000 total): music. *Special Achievements/Activities:* 32 awards ($80,000 total): religious involvement. ***Tuition waivers:*** Full or partial for employees or children of employees. ***ROTC:*** Air Force cooperative.

LOANS ***Student loans:*** $11,944,677 (88% need-based, 12% non-need-based). ***Average need-based loan:*** Freshmen: $3113; Undergraduates: $4941. ***Parent loans:*** $6,779,115 (80% need-based, 20% non-need-based). ***Programs:*** Federal Direct (Subsidized and Unsubsidized Stafford, PLUS), FFEL (Subsidized and Unsubsidized Stafford, PLUS), Perkins, state.

WORK-STUDY ***Federal work-study:*** Total amount: $3,149,220; 2,315 jobs averaging $1921. ***State or other work-study/employment:*** Part-time jobs available.

ATHLETIC AWARDS Total amount: $4,112,945 (33% need-based, 67% non-need-based).

APPLYING FOR FINANCIAL AID ***Required financial aid form:*** FAFSA. ***Financial aid deadline (priority):*** 2/15. ***Notification date:*** Continuous beginning 3/15.

CONTACT Lynn Fox, Director of Financial Aid, University of the Pacific, 3601 Pacific Avenue, Stockton, CA 95211-0197, 209-946-2421 or toll-free 800-959-2867.

UNIVERSITY OF THE SACRED HEART

San Juan, PR

CONTACT Ms. Maria Torres, Director of Financial Aid, University of the Sacred Heart, PO Box 12383, San Juan, PR 00914-0383, 787-728-1515 Ext. 3605.

UNIVERSITY OF THE SCIENCES IN PHILADELPHIA

Philadelphia, PA

Tuition & fees: $25,392 **Average undergraduate aid package: $11,801**

ABOUT THE INSTITUTION Independent, coed. Awards: bachelor's, master's, doctoral, and first professional degrees. 16 undergraduate majors. Total enrollment: 2,857. Undergraduates: 2,020. Freshmen: 501. Federal methodology is used as a basis for awarding need-based institutional aid.

UNDERGRADUATE EXPENSES for 2006–07 ***Application fee:*** $45. ***Comprehensive fee:*** $35,328 includes full-time tuition ($24,144), mandatory fees ($1248), and room and board ($9936). ***College room only:*** $6070. Full-time tuition and fees vary according to degree level and program. Room and board charges vary according to board plan. ***Part-time tuition:*** $1006 per credit. ***Part-time fees:*** $39 per credit. Part-time tuition and fees vary according to course load and degree level. ***Payment plans:*** Tuition prepayment, installment.

FRESHMAN FINANCIAL AID (Fall 2005) 501 applied for aid; of those 79% were deemed to have need. 100% of freshmen with need received aid; of those 59% had need fully met. ***Average percent of need met:*** 95% (excluding resources awarded to replace EFC). ***Average financial aid package:*** $16,087 (excluding resources awarded to replace EFC). 21% of all full-time freshmen had no need and received non-need-based gift aid.

UNDERGRADUATE FINANCIAL AID (Fall 2005) 1,523 applied for aid; of those 90% were deemed to have need. 100% of undergraduates with need received aid; of those 47% had need fully met. ***Average percent of need met:*** 52% (excluding resources awarded to replace EFC). ***Average financial aid package:*** $11,801 (excluding resources awarded to replace EFC). 41% of all full-time undergraduates had no need and received non-need-based gift aid.

GIFT AID (NEED-BASED) ***Total amount:*** $5,112,969 (7% federal, 9% state, 82% institutional, 2% external sources). ***Receiving aid:*** Freshmen: 76% (379); All full-time undergraduates: 36% (625). ***Average award:*** Freshmen: $6611; Undergraduates: $8744. ***Scholarships, grants, and awards:*** Federal Pell, FSEOG, state, college/university gift aid from institutional funds.

GIFT AID (NON-NEED-BASED) ***Receiving aid:*** Freshmen: 79% (394); Undergraduates: 75% (1,316). ***Average award:*** Freshmen: $7189; Undergraduates: $6432. ***Scholarships, grants, and awards by category:*** *Academic Interests/Achievement:* 1,748 awards ($55,016,798 total): general academic interests/achievements. ***Tuition waivers:*** Full or partial for employees or children of employees. ***ROTC:*** Army cooperative, Air Force cooperative.

LOANS ***Student loans:*** $5,576,820 (18% need-based, 82% non-need-based). 24% of past graduating class borrowed through all loan programs. *Average indebtedness per student:* $36,145. ***Average need-based loan:*** Freshmen: $2856; Undergraduates: $4561. ***Parent loans:*** $1,138,162 (100% need-based). ***Programs:*** FFEL (Subsidized and Unsubsidized Stafford, PLUS), Perkins.

WORK-STUDY ***Federal work-study:*** Total amount: $612,856; 975 jobs averaging $682. ***State or other work-study/employment:*** Total amount: $22,743 (100% need-based). Part-time jobs available.

ATHLETIC AWARDS Total amount: $146,643 (100% non-need-based).

APPLYING FOR FINANCIAL AID ***Required financial aid form:*** FAFSA. ***Financial aid deadline:*** 3/15 (priority: 3/15). ***Notification date:*** Continuous. Students must reply within 2 weeks of notification.

CONTACT Ms. Paula Lehrberger, Director of Financial Aid, University of the Sciences in Philadelphia, 600 South 43rd Street, Philadelphia, PA 19104-4495, 215-596-8894 or toll-free 888-996-8747 (in-state). *Fax:* 215-596-8554.

UNIVERSITY OF THE SOUTH

Sewanee, TN

See Sewanee: The University of the South.

UNIVERSITY OF THE VIRGIN ISLANDS

Saint Thomas, VI

Tuition & fees (VI res): $3726 **Average undergraduate aid package: $4800**

ABOUT THE INSTITUTION Territory-supported, coed. Awards: associate, bachelor's, and master's degrees. 23 undergraduate majors. Total enrollment: 2,487. Undergraduates: 2,272. Freshmen: 380. Federal methodology is used as a basis for awarding need-based institutional aid.

UNDERGRADUATE EXPENSES for 2006–07 ***Application fee:*** $25. ***Tuition, state resident:*** full-time $3300; part-time $110 per credit. ***Tuition, nonresident:*** full-time $9900; part-time $330 per credit. ***Required fees:*** full-time $426; $316 per year part-time. Full-time tuition and fees vary according to course load, degree level, and program. Part-time tuition and fees vary according to course load, degree level, and program. ***College room and board:*** $7550; ***Room only:*** $1100. Room and board charges vary according to board plan and housing facility.

FRESHMAN FINANCIAL AID (Fall 2005) 261 applied for aid; of those 81% were deemed to have need. 96% of freshmen with need received aid; of those 3% had need fully met. ***Average financial aid package:*** $4145 (excluding resources awarded to replace EFC). 2% of all full-time freshmen had no need and received non-need-based gift aid.

UNDERGRADUATE FINANCIAL AID (Fall 2005) 1,150 applied for aid; of those 99% were deemed to have need. 84% of undergraduates with need received aid; of those 2% had need fully met. ***Average financial aid package:*** $4800 (excluding resources awarded to replace EFC). 1% of all full-time undergraduates had no need and received non-need-based gift aid.

GIFT AID (NEED-BASED) ***Total amount:*** $2,780,082 (92% federal, 8% institutional). ***Receiving aid:*** Freshmen: 60% (189); All full-time undergraduates: 76% (912). ***Average award:*** Freshmen: $2400; Undergraduates: $2657. ***Scholarships, grants, and awards:*** Federal Pell, FSEOG, state, college/university gift aid from institutional funds, Federal Nursing.

GIFT AID (NON-NEED-BASED) ***Total amount:*** $552,215 (100% institutional). ***Receiving aid:*** Freshmen: 9% (29); Undergraduates: 8% (101). ***Average award:*** Freshmen: $5090; Undergraduates: $4590. ***Scholarships, grants, and awards by category:*** *Academic Interests/Achievement:* 122 awards ($552,215 total).

Special Characteristics: $145,000 total: children of faculty/staff, veterans. ***Tuition waivers:*** Full or partial for employees or children of employees, senior citizens. ***ROTC:*** Army.

LOANS ***Student loans:*** $1,483,783 (81% need-based, 19% non-need-based). 36% of past graduating class borrowed through all loan programs. *Average indebtedness per student:* $8782. ***Average need-based loan:*** Freshmen: $2050; Undergraduates: $2800. ***Parent loans:*** $224,625 (100% need-based). ***Programs:*** Federal Direct (Subsidized and Unsubsidized Stafford, PLUS), Perkins, college/university.

WORK-STUDY ***Federal work-study:*** Total amount: $92,767; 51 jobs averaging $1819. ***State or other work-study/employment:*** Total amount: $77,593 (100% need-based). 31 part-time jobs averaging $2217.

ATHLETIC AWARDS Total amount: $27,438 (100% non-need-based).

APPLYING FOR FINANCIAL AID ***Required financial aid form:*** FAFSA. ***Financial aid deadline (priority):*** 3/1. ***Notification date:*** Continuous beginning 4/1. Students must reply within 2 weeks of notification.

CONTACT Mavis M. Gilchrist, Director of Financial Aid, University of the Virgin Islands, RR #2, Box 10,000, Kingshill, St. Croix, VI 00850, 340-692-4186. *Fax:* 340-692-4145. *E-mail:* mgilchr@uvi.edu.

UNIVERSITY OF THE WEST

Rosemead, CA

CONTACT Dr. Teresa Ku, Director of Student Services, University of the West, 1409 Walnut Grove Avenue, Rosemead, CA 91770, 626-571-8811 Ext. 355. *Fax:* 626-571-1413. *E-mail:* naikuangk@hlu.edu.

THE UNIVERSITY OF TOLEDO

Toledo, OH

ABOUT THE INSTITUTION State-supported, coed. Awards: associate, bachelor's, master's, doctoral, and first professional degrees and post-bachelor's and post-master's certificates. 173 undergraduate majors. Total enrollment: 19,374. Undergraduates: 16,067. Freshmen: 3,432.

GIFT AID (NEED-BASED) ***Scholarships, grants, and awards:*** Federal Pell, FSEOG, state, private, college/university gift aid from institutional funds.

GIFT AID (NON-NEED-BASED) ***Scholarships, grants, and awards by category:*** *Academic Interests/Achievement:* biological sciences, business, communication, education, engineering/technologies, English, foreign languages, general academic interests/achievements, health fields, humanities, international studies, library science, mathematics, physical sciences, premedicine, social sciences. *Creative Arts/Performance:* art/fine arts, general creative arts/performance, music, performing arts, theater/drama. *Special Achievements/Activities:* cheerleading/drum major, general special achievements/activities, hobbies/interests, leadership, memberships, religious involvement. *Special Characteristics:* adult students, children and siblings of alumni, children of faculty/staff, children of public servants, children of union members/company employees, ethnic background, general special characteristics, handicapped students, international students, members of minority groups, previous college experience, public servants, religious affiliation, veterans, veterans' children.

LOANS ***Programs:*** Federal Direct (Subsidized and Unsubsidized Stafford, PLUS), Perkins, alternative loans.

WORK-STUDY ***Federal work-study:*** Total amount: $1,468,920; 470 jobs averaging $1705.

APPLYING FOR FINANCIAL AID ***Required financial aid form:*** FAFSA.

CONTACT Lisa Hasselschwert, Interim Director, The University of Toledo, 2801 West Bancroft Street, 1200 Rocket Hall, MS-314, Toledo, OH 43606, 419-530-8700 or toll-free 800-5TOLEDO (in-state). *Fax:* 419-530-5835. *E-mail:* lhassel@utnet.utoledo.edu.

UNIVERSITY OF TULSA

Tulsa, OK

Tuition & fees: $21,770 **Average undergraduate aid package: $22,586**

ABOUT THE INSTITUTION Independent religious, coed. Awards: bachelor's, master's, doctoral, and first professional degrees and post-bachelor's and first professional certificates. 54 undergraduate majors. Total enrollment: 4,125. Undergraduates: 2,882. Freshmen: 660. Federal methodology is used as a basis for awarding need-based institutional aid.

UNDERGRADUATE EXPENSES for 2007–08 ***Application fee:*** $35. ***Comprehensive fee:*** $29,174 includes full-time tuition ($21,690), mandatory fees ($80), and room and board ($7404). ***College room only:*** $4090. ***Part-time tuition:*** $778 per credit hour. ***Part-time fees:*** $3 per credit hour.

FRESHMAN FINANCIAL AID (Fall 2005) 594 applied for aid; of those 55% were deemed to have need. 100% of freshmen with need received aid; of those 48% had need fully met. ***Average percent of need met:*** 87% (excluding resources awarded to replace EFC). ***Average financial aid package:*** $22,431 (excluding resources awarded to replace EFC). 33% of all full-time freshmen had no need and received non-need-based gift aid.

UNDERGRADUATE FINANCIAL AID (Fall 2005) 2,410 applied for aid; of those 49% were deemed to have need. 100% of undergraduates with need received aid; of those 49% had need fully met. ***Average percent of need met:*** 87% (excluding resources awarded to replace EFC). ***Average financial aid package:*** $22,586 (excluding resources awarded to replace EFC). 36% of all full-time undergraduates had no need and received non-need-based gift aid.

GIFT AID (NEED-BASED) ***Total amount:*** $2,988,679 (58% federal, 21% state, 21% institutional). ***Receiving aid:*** Freshmen: 20% (132); All full-time undergraduates: 22% (584). ***Average award:*** Freshmen: $5056; Undergraduates: $4716. ***Scholarships, grants, and awards:*** Federal Pell, FSEOG, state, private, college/university gift aid from institutional funds.

GIFT AID (NON-NEED-BASED) ***Total amount:*** $19,579,853 (1% federal, 10% state, 83% institutional, 6% external sources). ***Receiving aid:*** Freshmen: 48% (314); Undergraduates: 39% (1,064). ***Average award:*** Freshmen: $10,464; Undergraduates: $11,342. ***Scholarships, grants, and awards by category:*** *Academic Interests/Achievement:* 1,759 awards ($8,871,742 total): biological sciences, business, communication, computer science, education, engineering/technologies, English, foreign languages, general academic interests/achievements, health fields, international studies, mathematics, physical sciences, premedicine, religion/biblical studies, social sciences. *Creative Arts/Performance:* 213 awards ($1,146,700 total): art/fine arts, music, performing arts, theater/drama. *Special Achievements/Activities:* 83 awards ($148,200 total): cheerleading/drum major, community service, leadership. *Special Characteristics:* 799 awards ($3,861,500 total): children and siblings of alumni, children of faculty/staff, relatives of clergy, religious affiliation, siblings of current students. ***ROTC:*** Air Force cooperative.

LOANS ***Student loans:*** $9,451,302 (51% need-based, 49% non-need-based). 54% of past graduating class borrowed through all loan programs. *Average indebtedness per student:* $12,411. ***Average need-based loan:*** Freshmen: $5136; Undergraduates: $5918. ***Parent loans:*** $3,195,079 (100% non-need-based). ***Programs:*** FFEL (Subsidized and Unsubsidized Stafford, PLUS), Perkins.

WORK-STUDY ***Federal work-study:*** Total amount: $1,638,357; 643 jobs averaging $2700. ***State or other work-study/employment:*** Total amount: $17,500 (100% non-need-based). 8 part-time jobs averaging $2200.

ATHLETIC AWARDS Total amount: $5,495,923 (100% non-need-based).

APPLYING FOR FINANCIAL AID ***Required financial aid forms:*** FAFSA, institution's own form. ***Financial aid deadline (priority):*** 4/1. ***Notification date:*** Continuous beginning 3/1. Students must reply by 5/1 or within 2 weeks of notification.

CONTACT Ms. Vicki Hendrickson, Director of Student Financial Services, University of Tulsa, 600 South College, Tulsa, OK 74104, 918-631-2526 or toll-free 800-331-3050. *Fax:* 918-631-5105. *E-mail:* vicki-hendrickson@utulsa.edu.

UNIVERSITY OF UTAH

Salt Lake City, UT

ABOUT THE INSTITUTION State-supported, coed. Awards: bachelor's, master's, doctoral, and first professional degrees and post-bachelor's and post-master's certificates. 128 undergraduate majors. Total enrollment: 28,619. Undergraduates: 22,155. Freshmen: 2,838.

GIFT AID (NEED-BASED) ***Scholarships, grants, and awards:*** Federal Pell, FSEOG, state, private, college/university gift aid from institutional funds.

GIFT AID (NON-NEED-BASED) ***Scholarships, grants, and awards by category:*** *Academic Interests/Achievement:* architecture, area/ethnic studies, biological sciences, business, communication, computer science, education, engineering/technologies, English, foreign languages, general academic interests/achievements, health fields, humanities, international studies, mathematics, military science, physical sciences, social sciences. *Creative Arts/Performance:* art/fine arts, cinema/film/broadcasting, creative writing, dance, journalism/publications, music, performing arts, theater/drama. *Special Achievements/Activities:* cheerleading/drum major, general special achievements/activities, leadership. *Special Characteristics:* children of faculty/staff, children of public servants, children with a deceased or disabled parent, ethnic background, first-generation college students, handicapped students, out-of-state students, spouses of deceased or disabled public servants.

LOANS ***Programs:*** FFEL (Subsidized and Unsubsidized Stafford, PLUS), Perkins, Federal Nursing, college/university, alternative loans.

WORK-STUDY ***Federal work-study:*** Total amount: $1,500,000; 427 jobs averaging $3500.

APPLYING FOR FINANCIAL AID ***Required financial aid forms:*** FAFSA, institution's own form.

CONTACT Amy Capps, Assistant Director, University of Utah, 201 South 1460 East, Room 105, Salt Lake City, UT 84112-9055, 801-581-6211 or toll-free 800-444-8638. *Fax:* 801-585-6350. *E-mail:* fawin1@saff.utah.edu.

UNIVERSITY OF VERMONT

Burlington, VT

Tuition & fees (VT res): $11,324 Average undergraduate aid package: $15,408

ABOUT THE INSTITUTION State-supported, coed. Awards: bachelor's, master's, doctoral, and first professional degrees and post-bachelor's and post-master's certificates. 99 undergraduate majors. Total enrollment: 11,870. Undergraduates: 10,082. Freshmen: 2,190. Federal methodology is used as a basis for awarding need-based institutional aid.

UNDERGRADUATE EXPENSES for 2006–07 ***Application fee:*** $45. ***Tuition, state resident:*** full-time $9832; part-time $410 per credit hour. ***Tuition, nonresident:*** full-time $24,816; part-time $1034 per credit hour. Part-time tuition and fees vary according to course load. ***College room and board:*** $7642; ***Room only:*** $5150. Room and board charges vary according to board plan. ***Payment plans:*** Installment, deferred payment.

FRESHMAN FINANCIAL AID (Fall 2005) 1711 applied for aid; of those 75% were deemed to have need. 100% of freshmen with need received aid; of those 24% had need fully met. ***Average percent of need met:*** 82% (excluding resources awarded to replace EFC). ***Average financial aid package:*** $16,068 (excluding resources awarded to replace EFC). 30% of all full-time freshmen had no need and received non-need-based gift aid.

UNDERGRADUATE FINANCIAL AID (Fall 2005) 5,681 applied for aid; of those 83% were deemed to have need. 99% of undergraduates with need received aid; of those 20% had need fully met. ***Average percent of need met:*** 78% (excluding resources awarded to replace EFC). ***Average financial aid package:*** $15,408 (excluding resources awarded to replace EFC). 16% of all full-time undergraduates had no need and received non-need-based gift aid.

GIFT AID (NEED-BASED) ***Total amount:*** $45,014,696 (14% federal, 7% state, 74% institutional, 5% external sources). ***Receiving aid:*** Freshmen: 48% (1,151); All full-time undergraduates: 48% (4,099). ***Average award:*** Freshmen: $11,369; Undergraduates: $10,770. ***Scholarships, grants, and awards:*** Federal Pell, FSEOG, state, private, college/university gift aid from institutional funds, Federal Nursing.

GIFT AID (NON-NEED-BASED) ***Total amount:*** $4,087,996 (80% institutional, 20% external sources). ***Receiving aid:*** Freshmen: 2% (59); Undergraduates: 2% (178). ***Average award:*** Freshmen: $1939; Undergraduates: $2157. ***Scholarships, grants, and awards by category:*** *Academic Interests/Achievement:* 3,882 awards ($8,427,445 total): agriculture, area/ethnic studies, business, computer science, education, engineering/technologies, English, foreign languages, general academic interests/achievements, health fields, home economics, humanities, international studies, mathematics, military science, physical sciences, social sciences. *Creative Arts/Performance:* 18 awards ($14,083 total): debating, music, theater/drama. *Special Achievements/Activities:* 73 awards ($183,569 total): community service, memberships. *Special Characteristics:* 84 awards ($284,255 total): ethnic background, first-generation college students. ***Tuition waivers:*** Full or partial for employees or children of employees, senior citizens. ***ROTC:*** Army.

LOANS ***Student loans:*** $36,984,180 (60% need-based, 40% non-need-based). 59% of past graduating class borrowed through all loan programs. *Average indebtedness per student:* $23,328. ***Average need-based loan:*** Freshmen: $5737; Undergraduates: $5978. ***Parent loans:*** $28,683,412 (100% non-need-based). ***Programs:*** FFEL (Subsidized and Unsubsidized Stafford, PLUS), Perkins, Federal Nursing, state, college/university.

WORK-STUDY ***Federal work-study:*** Total amount: $1,576,167; 2,019 jobs averaging $1426. ***State or other work-study/employment:*** Total amount: $23,768,650 (100% need-based).

ATHLETIC AWARDS Total amount: $3,241,523 (27% need-based, 73% non-need-based).

APPLYING FOR FINANCIAL AID ***Required financial aid form:*** FAFSA. ***Financial aid deadline (priority):*** 2/10. ***Notification date:*** Continuous beginning 3/15. Students must reply within 4 weeks of notification.

CONTACT Student Financial Services, University of Vermont, 221 Waterman Building, South Prospect Street, Burlington, VT 05405-0160, 802-656-5700. *Fax:* 802-656-4076. *E-mail:* financialaid@uvm.edu.

UNIVERSITY OF VIRGINIA

Charlottesville, VA

Tuition & fees (VA res): $7845 Average undergraduate aid package: $15,687

ABOUT THE INSTITUTION State-supported, coed. Awards: bachelor's, master's, doctoral, and first professional degrees and post-master's certificates. 52 undergraduate majors. Total enrollment: 24,068. Undergraduates: 14,676. Freshmen: 3,095. Federal methodology is used as a basis for awarding need-based institutional aid.

UNDERGRADUATE EXPENSES for 2006–07 ***Application fee:*** $60. ***Tuition, state resident:*** full-time $6129. ***Tuition, nonresident:*** full-time $24,229. Part-time tuition and fees vary according to course load. ***College room and board:*** $6909; ***Room only:*** $3639. Room and board charges vary according to board plan and housing facility. ***Payment plan:*** Installment.

FRESHMAN FINANCIAL AID (Fall 2006, est.) 1642 applied for aid; of those 43% were deemed to have need. 100% of freshmen with need received aid; of those 100% had need fully met. ***Average percent of need met:*** 100% (excluding resources awarded to replace EFC). ***Average financial aid package:*** $15,553 (excluding resources awarded to replace EFC). 11% of all full-time freshmen had no need and received non-need-based gift aid.

UNDERGRADUATE FINANCIAL AID (Fall 2006, est.) 5,279 applied for aid; of those 60% were deemed to have need. 100% of undergraduates with need received aid; of those 100% had need fully met. ***Average percent of need met:*** 100% (excluding resources awarded to replace EFC). ***Average financial aid package:*** $15,687 (excluding resources awarded to replace EFC). 12% of all full-time undergraduates had no need and received non-need-based gift aid.

GIFT AID (NEED-BASED) ***Total amount:*** $31,576,378 (10% federal, 13% state, 71% institutional, 6% external sources). ***Receiving aid:*** Freshmen: 20% (614); All full-time undergraduates: 19% (2,550). ***Average award:*** Freshmen: $12,589; Undergraduates: $12,523. ***Scholarships, grants, and awards:*** Federal Pell, FSEOG, state, private, college/university gift aid from institutional funds.

GIFT AID (NON-NEED-BASED) ***Total amount:*** $6,205,548 (6% state, 32% institutional, 62% external sources). ***Receiving aid:*** Freshmen: 3% (103); Undergraduates: 2% (304). ***Average award:*** Freshmen: $7660; Undergraduates: $8228. ***Scholarships, grants, and awards by category:*** *Academic Interests/Achievement:* general academic interests/achievements. ***Tuition waivers:*** Full or partial for employees or children of employees, senior citizens. ***ROTC:*** Army, Naval, Air Force.

LOANS ***Student loans:*** $19,667,945 (51% need-based, 49% non-need-based). 31% of past graduating class borrowed through all loan programs. *Average indebtedness per student:* $12,726. ***Average need-based loan:*** Freshmen: $3626; Undergraduates: $4376. ***Parent loans:*** $8,542,935 (2% need-based, 98% non-need-based). ***Programs:*** Federal Direct (Subsidized and Unsubsidized Stafford, PLUS), Perkins, Federal Nursing, college/university.

WORK-STUDY ***Federal work-study:*** Total amount: $1,257,005; 567 jobs averaging $2161.

ATHLETIC AWARDS Total amount: $8,445,701 (29% need-based, 71% non-need-based).

APPLYING FOR FINANCIAL AID ***Required financial aid forms:*** FAFSA, institution's own form. ***Financial aid deadline (priority):*** 3/1. ***Notification date:*** 4/5. Students must reply by 5/1.

CONTACT Ms. Yvonne B. Hubbard, Director, Student Financial Services, University of Virginia, PO Box 400207, Charlottesville, VA 22904-4207, 434-982-6000. *E-mail:* faid@virginia.edu.

THE UNIVERSITY OF VIRGINIA'S COLLEGE AT WISE

Wise, VA

CONTACT Bill Wendle, Director of Financial Aid, The University of Virginia's College at Wise, 1 College Avenue, Wise, VA 24293, 276-328-0103 or toll-free 888-282-9324. *Fax:* 276-328-0251. *E-mail:* wdw8m@uvawise.edu.

UNIVERSITY OF WASHINGTON

Seattle, WA

Tuition & fees (WA res): $5988 Average undergraduate aid package: $12,000

ABOUT THE INSTITUTION State-supported, coed. Awards: bachelor's, master's, doctoral, and first professional degrees and first professional certificates. 155 undergraduate majors. Total enrollment: 39,524. Undergraduates: 27,836. Freshmen: 5,475. Federal methodology is used as a basis for awarding need-based institutional aid.

UNDERGRADUATE EXPENSES for 2006–07 ***Application fee:*** $50. ***Tuition, state resident:*** full-time $5988. ***Tuition, nonresident:*** full-time $21,286. Full-time tuition and fees vary according to course load. Part-time tuition and fees vary according to course load. ***College room and board:*** $6561. Room and board charges vary according to board plan and housing facility.

FRESHMAN FINANCIAL AID (Fall 2006, est.) 3650 applied for aid; of those 55% were deemed to have need. 88% of freshmen with need received aid; of those 66% had need fully met. ***Average percent of need met:*** 88% (excluding resources awarded to replace EFC). ***Average financial aid package:*** $11,000 (excluding resources awarded to replace EFC). 4% of all full-time freshmen had no need and received non-need-based gift aid.

UNDERGRADUATE FINANCIAL AID (Fall 2006, est.) 15,700 applied for aid; of those 73% were deemed to have need. 75% of undergraduates with need received aid; of those 59% had need fully met. ***Average percent of need met:*** 86% (excluding resources awarded to replace EFC). ***Average financial aid package:*** $12,000 (excluding resources awarded to replace EFC). 2% of all full-time undergraduates had no need and received non-need-based gift aid.

GIFT AID (NEED-BASED) ***Total amount:*** $61,643,000 (34% federal, 42% state, 19% institutional, 5% external sources). ***Receiving aid:*** Freshmen: 20% (1,100); All full-time undergraduates: 26% (6,200). ***Average award:*** Freshmen: $5100; Undergraduates: $8500. ***Scholarships, grants, and awards:*** Federal Pell, FSEOG, state, private, college/university gift aid from institutional funds.

GIFT AID (NON-NEED-BASED) ***Total amount:*** $9,040,000 (1% federal, 6% state, 56% institutional, 37% external sources). ***Receiving aid:*** Freshmen: 3% (150); Undergraduates: 3% (770). ***Average award:*** Freshmen: $3200; Undergraduates: $4500. ***Scholarships, grants, and awards by category:*** *Academic Interests/Achievement:* architecture, biological sciences, business, communication, engineering/technologies, English, foreign languages, general academic interests/achievements, health fields, humanities, mathematics, physical sciences, social sciences. *Creative Arts/Performance:* art/fine arts, creative writing, dance, general creative arts/performance, journalism/publications, music, performing arts, theater/drama. *Special Achievements/Activities:* community service, general special achievements/activities, leadership. *Special Characteristics:* international students. ***Tuition waivers:*** Full or partial for senior citizens. ***ROTC:*** Army, Naval, Air Force.

LOANS ***Student loans:*** $50,500,000 (75% need-based, 25% non-need-based). 50% of past graduating class borrowed through all loan programs. *Average indebtedness per student:* $15,900. ***Average need-based loan:*** Freshmen: $2800; Undergraduates: $4200. ***Parent loans:*** $27,500,000 (27% need-based, 73% non-need-based). ***Programs:*** Federal Direct (Subsidized and Unsubsidized Stafford, PLUS), Perkins, Federal Nursing, college/university.

WORK-STUDY ***Federal work-study:*** Total amount: $2,700,000; 855 jobs averaging $2690. ***State or other work-study/employment:*** Total amount: $550,000 (100% need-based). 156 part-time jobs averaging $3000.

ATHLETIC AWARDS Total amount: $3,200,000 (53% need-based, 47% non-need-based).

APPLYING FOR FINANCIAL AID ***Required financial aid form:*** FAFSA. ***Financial aid deadline (priority):*** 2/28. ***Notification date:*** 3/31.

CONTACT Office of Student Financial Aid, University of Washington, Box 355880, Seattle, WA 98195-5880, 206-543-6101. *E-mail:* osfa@u.washington.edu.

UNIVERSITY OF WASHINGTON, BOTHELL

Bothell, WA

CONTACT Financial Aid Office, University of Washington, Bothell, 18115 Campus Way NE, Bothell, WA 98011-8246, 425-352-5000.

UNIVERSITY OF WASHINGTON, TACOMA

Tacoma, WA

CONTACT Financial Aid Office, University of Washington, Tacoma, 1900 Commerce Street, Tacoma, WA 98402-3100, 253-692-4000 or toll-free 800-736-7750 (out-of-state).

THE UNIVERSITY OF WEST ALABAMA

Livingston, AL

Tuition & fees (AL res): $4326 Average undergraduate aid package: $10,222

ABOUT THE INSTITUTION State-supported, coed. Awards: associate, bachelor's, and master's degrees. 19 undergraduate majors. Total enrollment: 3,633. Undergraduates: 1,821. Freshmen: 354. Federal methodology is used as a basis for awarding need-based institutional aid.

UNDERGRADUATE EXPENSES for 2007–08 ***Application fee:*** $20. ***Tuition, state resident:*** full-time $3838. ***Tuition, nonresident:*** full-time $7676. ***College room and board:*** $3438; ***Room only:*** $1746.

FRESHMAN FINANCIAL AID (Fall 2005) of those 74% had need fully met. ***Average percent of need met:*** 74% (excluding resources awarded to replace EFC). ***Average financial aid package:*** $6145 (excluding resources awarded to replace EFC). 10% of all full-time freshmen had no need and received non-need-based gift aid.

UNDERGRADUATE FINANCIAL AID (Fall 2005) 1,516 applied for aid; of those 84% were deemed to have need. 84% of undergraduates with need received aid; of those 49% had need fully met. ***Average percent of need met:*** 85% (excluding resources awarded to replace EFC). ***Average financial aid package:*** $10,222 (excluding resources awarded to replace EFC). 14% of all full-time undergraduates had no need and received non-need-based gift aid.

GIFT AID (NEED-BASED) ***Total amount:*** $2,765,822 (99% federal, 1% state). ***Receiving aid:*** All full-time undergraduates: 47% (866). ***Average award:*** Freshmen: $6431; Undergraduates: $3761. ***Scholarships, grants, and awards:*** Federal Pell, FSEOG, state, private, college/university gift aid from institutional funds.

GIFT AID (NON-NEED-BASED) ***Total amount:*** $2,504,115 (67% institutional, 33% external sources). ***Receiving aid:*** Freshmen: 64% (230); Undergraduates: 20% (374). ***Average award:*** Freshmen: $1500; Undergraduates: $3144. ***Scholarships, grants, and awards by category:*** *Academic Interests/Achievement:* business, computer science, education, English, general academic interests/achievements. *Creative Arts/Performance:* creative writing, dance, journalism/publications, music. *Special Achievements/Activities:* cheerleading/drum major, rodeo. *Special Characteristics:* children of faculty/staff, first-generation college students. ***ROTC:*** Army cooperative, Air Force cooperative.

LOANS ***Student loans:*** $5,118,008 (42% need-based, 58% non-need-based). 62% of past graduating class borrowed through all loan programs. *Average indebtedness per student:* $16,043. ***Average need-based loan:*** Freshmen: $2625; Undergraduates: $4239. ***Parent loans:*** $162,333 (100% non-need-based). ***Programs:*** FFEL (Subsidized and Unsubsidized Stafford, PLUS), Perkins.

WORK-STUDY ***Federal work-study:*** Total amount: $199,970; 176 jobs averaging $1221.

ATHLETIC AWARDS Total amount: $684,185 (100% non-need-based).

APPLYING FOR FINANCIAL AID ***Required financial aid form:*** FAFSA. ***Financial aid deadline (priority):*** 4/1. ***Notification date:*** Continuous beginning 5/1. Students must reply within 4 weeks of notification.

CONTACT Mr. Don Rainer, Director of Financial Aid, The University of West Alabama, Station 3, Livingston, AL 35470, 205-652-3576 or toll-free 800-621-7742 (in-state), 800-621-8044 (out-of-state). *Fax:* 205-652-3847. *E-mail:* drainer@uwa.edu.

UNIVERSITY OF WEST FLORIDA

Pensacola, FL

Tuition & fees (FL res): $3311 **Average undergraduate aid package: N/A**

ABOUT THE INSTITUTION State-supported, coed. Awards: associate, bachelor's, master's, and doctoral degrees (specialists). 55 undergraduate majors. Total enrollment: 9,819. Undergraduates: 8,254. Freshmen: 1,186. Federal methodology is used as a basis for awarding need-based institutional aid.

UNDERGRADUATE EXPENSES for 2006–07 ***Application fee:*** $30. ***Tuition, state resident:*** full-time $2211; part-time $110.39 per semester hour. ***Tuition, nonresident:*** full-time $14,778; part-time $527.27 per semester hour. Full-time tuition and fees vary according to location and reciprocity agreements. Part-time tuition and fees vary according to location and reciprocity agreements. ***College room and board:*** $6600. Room and board charges vary according to housing facility. ***Payment plans:*** Tuition prepayment, deferred payment.

GIFT AID (NEED-BASED) ***Total amount:*** $8,127,684 (70% federal, 19% state, 11% institutional). ***Scholarships, grants, and awards:*** Federal Pell, FSEOG, state, college/university gift aid from institutional funds.

GIFT AID (NON-NEED-BASED) ***Total amount:*** $7,856,150 (78% state, 15% institutional, 7% external sources). ***Scholarships, grants, and awards by category:*** *Academic Interests/Achievement:* 1,050 awards ($1,056,806 total): biological sciences, business, general academic interests/achievements, military science. *Creative Arts/Performance:* 100 awards ($74,750 total): applied art and design, art/fine arts, music, theater/drama. *Special Characteristics:* 70 awards ($73,900 total): children and siblings of alumni, first-generation college students, handicapped students, members of minority groups. ***Tuition waivers:*** Full or partial for employees or children of employees, senior citizens. ***ROTC:*** Army, Air Force.

LOANS ***Student loans:*** $16,847,344 (63% need-based, 37% non-need-based). ***Parent loans:*** $1,170,398 (100% non-need-based). ***Programs:*** Federal Direct (Subsidized and Unsubsidized Stafford, PLUS), Perkins, college/university.

WORK-STUDY ***Federal work-study:*** Total amount: $299,824; 224 jobs averaging $1434. ***State or other work-study/employment:*** 1,545 part-time jobs available.

ATHLETIC AWARDS Total amount: $862,948 (100% non-need-based).

APPLYING FOR FINANCIAL AID ***Required financial aid forms:*** FAFSA, institution's own form. ***Financial aid deadline:*** Continuous. ***Notification date:*** Continuous beginning 3/1.

CONTACT Ms. Georganne E. Major, Coordinator, University of West Florida, 11000 University Parkway, Pensacola, FL 32514-5750, 850-474-2397 or toll-free 800-263-1074. *E-mail:* gmajor@uwf.edu.

UNIVERSITY OF WEST GEORGIA

Carrollton, GA

Tuition & fees (GA res): $3460 **Average undergraduate aid package: $6590**

ABOUT THE INSTITUTION State-supported, coed. Awards: bachelor's, master's, and doctoral degrees and post-master's certificates. 51 undergraduate majors. Total enrollment: 10,163. Undergraduates: 8,475. Freshmen: 2,024. Federal methodology is used as a basis for awarding need-based institutional aid.

UNDERGRADUATE EXPENSES for 2006–07 ***Application fee:*** $20. ***Tuition, state resident:*** full-time $2560; part-time $107 per semester hour. ***Tuition, nonresident:*** full-time $10,242; part-time $427 per semester hour. ***Required fees:*** full-time $900; $27.42 per semester hour or $121 per term part-time. Full-time tuition and fees vary according to course load. Part-time tuition and fees vary according to course load. ***College room and board:*** $5162; ***Room only:*** $2458. Room and board charges vary according to board plan and housing facility. ***Payment plan:*** Guaranteed tuition.

FRESHMAN FINANCIAL AID (Fall 2006, est.) 1394 applied for aid; of those 65% were deemed to have need. 99% of freshmen with need received aid; of those 18% had need fully met. ***Average percent of need met:*** 65% (excluding resources awarded to replace EFC). ***Average financial aid package:*** $6612 (excluding resources awarded to replace EFC). 2% of all full-time freshmen had no need and received non-need-based gift aid.

UNDERGRADUATE FINANCIAL AID (Fall 2006, est.) 5,092 applied for aid; of those 68% were deemed to have need. 99% of undergraduates with need received aid; of those 19% had need fully met. ***Average percent of need met:*** 61% (excluding resources awarded to replace EFC). ***Average financial aid package:*** $6590 (excluding resources awarded to replace EFC). 2% of all full-time undergraduates had no need and received non-need-based gift aid.

GIFT AID (NEED-BASED) ***Total amount:*** $13,191,225 (59% federal, 38% state, 1% institutional, 2% external sources). ***Receiving aid:*** Freshmen: 47% (804); All full-time undergraduates: 39% (2,716). ***Average award:*** Freshmen: $5018; Undergraduates: $3341. ***Scholarships, grants, and awards:*** Federal Pell, FSEOG, state, private, college/university gift aid from institutional funds.

GIFT AID (NON-NEED-BASED) ***Total amount:*** $6,351,142 (91% state, 6% institutional, 3% external sources). ***Receiving aid:*** Freshmen: 18% (304); Undergraduates: 18% (1,280). ***Average award:*** Freshmen: $2979; Undergraduates: $2019. ***Scholarships, grants, and awards by category:*** *Academic Interests/Achievement:* biological sciences, business, communication, computer science, education, English, foreign languages, general academic interests/achievements, health fields, humanities, mathematics, physical sciences, social sciences. *Creative Arts/Performance:* art/fine arts, debating, journalism/publications, music, theater/drama. *Special Achievements/Activities:* community service, memberships, religious involvement. *Special Characteristics:* adult students, children and siblings of alumni, children of union members/company employees, ethnic background, handicapped students, international students, local/state students, members of minority groups, previous college experience. ***Tuition waivers:*** Full or partial for senior citizens. ***ROTC:*** Army.

LOANS ***Student loans:*** $16,371,677 (52% need-based, 48% non-need-based). 60% of past graduating class borrowed through all loan programs. *Average indebtedness per student:* $14,781. ***Average need-based loan:*** Freshmen: $2589; Undergraduates: $3401. ***Parent loans:*** $1,876,333 (100% non-need-based). ***Programs:*** Federal Direct (Subsidized and Unsubsidized Stafford, PLUS), Perkins, state.

WORK-STUDY ***Federal work-study:*** Total amount: $930,997; 704 jobs averaging $1605. ***State or other work-study/employment:*** Part-time jobs available.

ATHLETIC AWARDS Total amount: $751,167 (45% need-based, 55% non-need-based).

APPLYING FOR FINANCIAL AID ***Required financial aid form:*** FAFSA. ***Financial aid deadline (priority):*** 4/1. ***Notification date:*** Continuous beginning 3/1. Students must reply by 5/1.

CONTACT Kimberly Jordan, Director of Financial Aid, University of West Georgia, Aycock Hall, Carrollton, GA 30118, 678-839-6421. *Fax:* 678-839-6422. *E-mail:* kjordan@westga.edu.

UNIVERSITY OF WISCONSIN–EAU CLAIRE

Eau Claire, WI

ABOUT THE INSTITUTION State-supported, coed. Awards: associate, bachelor's, and master's degrees and post-bachelor's and post-master's certificates. 48 undergraduate majors. Total enrollment: 10,505. Undergraduates: 10,031. Freshmen: 2,024.

GIFT AID (NEED-BASED) ***Scholarships, grants, and awards:*** Federal Pell, FSEOG, state, private, college/university gift aid from institutional funds, Federal Nursing.

GIFT AID (NON-NEED-BASED) ***Scholarships, grants, and awards by category:*** *Academic Interests/Achievement:* biological sciences, business, communication, computer science, education, English, foreign languages, general academic interests/achievements, health fields, international studies, mathematics, physical sciences, premedicine, social sciences. *Creative Arts/Performance:* debating, music, theater/drama. *Special Achievements/Activities:* community service, general special achievements/activities, hobbies/interests, leadership, memberships. *Special Characteristics:* adult students, ethnic background, first-generation college students, general special characteristics, international students, local/state students, members of minority groups, previous college experience.

LOANS ***Programs:*** Federal Direct (Subsidized and Unsubsidized Stafford, PLUS), Perkins, college/university, alternative loans.

APPLYING FOR FINANCIAL AID ***Required financial aid form:*** FAFSA.

CONTACT Ms. Kathleen Sahlhoff, Director of Financial Aid, University of Wisconsin–Eau Claire, 115 Schofield Hall, Eau Claire, WI 54701, 715-836-3373. *Fax:* 715-836-3846.

UNIVERSITY OF WISCONSIN–GREEN BAY

Green Bay, WI

Tuition & fees (WI res): $5716 **Average undergraduate aid package: $8095**

ABOUT THE INSTITUTION State-supported, coed. Awards: associate, bachelor's, and master's degrees and post-bachelor's certificates. 35 undergraduate majors. Total enrollment: 5,803. Undergraduates: 5,661. Freshmen: 1,025. Federal methodology is used as a basis for awarding need-based institutional aid.

UNDERGRADUATE EXPENSES for 2006–07 ***Application fee:*** $35. ***Tuition, state resident:*** full-time $4568; part-time $190 per credit. ***Tuition, nonresident:*** full-time $12,042; part-time $502 per credit. ***Required fees:*** full-time $1148; $75 per credit. ***College room and board:*** $4700; ***Room only:*** $3000.

FRESHMAN FINANCIAL AID (Fall 2006, est.) 875 applied for aid; of those 67% were deemed to have need. 95% of freshmen with need received aid; of those 37% had need fully met. ***Average percent of need met:*** 76% (excluding resources awarded to replace EFC). ***Average financial aid package:*** $7559 (excluding resources awarded to replace EFC). 4% of all full-time freshmen had no need and received non-need-based gift aid.

UNDERGRADUATE FINANCIAL AID (Fall 2006, est.) 3,670 applied for aid; of those 74% were deemed to have need. 96% of undergraduates with need received aid; of those 45% had need fully met. ***Average percent of need met:*** 80% (excluding resources awarded to replace EFC). ***Average financial aid package:*** $8095 (excluding resources awarded to replace EFC). 2% of all full-time undergraduates had no need and received non-need-based gift aid.

GIFT AID (NEED-BASED) ***Total amount:*** $7,553,321 (49% federal, 35% state, 2% institutional, 14% external sources). ***Receiving aid:*** Freshmen: 35% (357); All full-time undergraduates: 33% (1,501). ***Average award:*** Freshmen: $4492; Undergraduates: $4837. ***Scholarships, grants, and awards:*** Federal Pell, FSEOG, state, private, college/university gift aid from institutional funds.

GIFT AID (NON-NEED-BASED) ***Total amount:*** $741,284 (9% state, 24% institutional, 67% external sources). ***Receiving aid:*** Freshmen: 19% (188); Undergraduates: 20% (912). ***Average award:*** Freshmen: $1466; Undergraduates: $2715. ***Scholarships, grants, and awards by category:*** *Academic Interests/Achievement:* 200 awards ($250,000 total): area/ethnic studies, biological sciences, business, communication, engineering/technologies, general academic interests/achievements, physical sciences, social sciences. *Creative Arts/Performance:* 30 awards ($20,400 total): art/fine arts, dance, music, theater/drama. *Special Achievements/Activities:* community service, leadership. *Special Characteristics:* adult students, children of public servants, ethnic background, veterans. ***ROTC:*** Army cooperative.

LOANS ***Student loans:*** $15,723,510 (52% need-based, 48% non-need-based). 68% of past graduating class borrowed through all loan programs. *Average indebtedness per student:* $17,000. ***Average need-based loan:*** Freshmen: $3154; Undergraduates: $3957. ***Parent loans:*** $1,512,164 (100% non-need-based). ***Programs:*** FFEL (Subsidized and Unsubsidized Stafford, PLUS), Perkins.

WORK-STUDY ***Federal work-study:*** Total amount: $444,942; jobs available. ***State or other work-study/employment:*** Part-time jobs available.

ATHLETIC AWARDS Total amount: $1,837,003 (77% need-based, 23% non-need-based).

APPLYING FOR FINANCIAL AID ***Required financial aid form:*** FAFSA. ***Financial aid deadline (priority):*** 4/15. ***Notification date:*** Continuous. Students must reply within 3 weeks of notification.

CONTACT Mr. Ron Ronnenberg, Director of Financial Aid, University of Wisconsin–Green Bay, 2420 Nicolet Drive, Green Bay, WI 54311-7001, 920-465-2073 or toll-free 888-367-8942 (out-of-state). *E-mail:* ronnenbr@uwgb.edu.

UNIVERSITY OF WISCONSIN–LA CROSSE

La Crosse, WI

Tuition & fees (WI res): $5555 Average undergraduate aid package: $5461

ABOUT THE INSTITUTION State-supported, coed. Awards: associate, bachelor's, and master's degrees. 42 undergraduate majors. Total enrollment: 9,818. Undergraduates: 8,306. Freshmen: 1,743. Federal methodology is used as a basis for awarding need-based institutional aid.

UNDERGRADUATE EXPENSES for 2006–07 ***Application fee:*** $35. ***Tuition, state resident:*** full-time $5555; part-time $244.17 per credit hour. ***Tuition, nonresident:*** full-time $12,873; part-time $555.61 per credit hour. Full-time tuition and fees vary according to program and reciprocity agreements. Part-time tuition and fees vary according to course load, program, and reciprocity agreements. ***College room and board:*** $4970; ***Room only:*** $2840. Room and board charges vary according to board plan. ***Payment plan:*** Installment.

FRESHMAN FINANCIAL AID (Fall 2005) 1760 applied for aid; of those 42% were deemed to have need. 92% of freshmen with need received aid; of those 17% had need fully met. ***Average percent of need met:*** 68% (excluding resources awarded to replace EFC). ***Average financial aid package:*** $4692 (excluding resources awarded to replace EFC). 3% of all full-time freshmen had no need and received non-need-based gift aid.

UNDERGRADUATE FINANCIAL AID (Fall 2005) 5,996 applied for aid; of those 53% were deemed to have need. 94% of undergraduates with need received aid; of those 25% had need fully met. ***Average percent of need met:*** 74% (excluding resources awarded to replace EFC). ***Average financial aid package:*** $5461 (excluding resources awarded to replace EFC). 2% of all full-time undergraduates had no need and received non-need-based gift aid.

GIFT AID (NEED-BASED) ***Total amount:*** $7,217,605 (50% federal, 38% state, 6% institutional, 6% external sources). ***Receiving aid:*** Freshmen: 16% (297); All full-time undergraduates: 17% (1,294). ***Average award:*** Freshmen: $4117; Undergraduates: $4176. ***Scholarships, grants, and awards:*** Federal Pell, FSEOG, state, private, college/university gift aid from institutional funds.

GIFT AID (NON-NEED-BASED) ***Total amount:*** $2,726,627 (17% federal, 21% state, 4% institutional, 58% external sources). ***Receiving aid:*** Freshmen: 4% (71); Undergraduates: 4% (298). ***Average award:*** Freshmen: $1238; Undergraduates: $1096. ***Scholarships, grants, and awards by category:*** *Academic Interests/Achievement:* area/ethnic studies, biological sciences, business, communication, computer science, education, English, foreign languages, general academic interests/achievements, health fields, mathematics, military science, physical sciences, social sciences. *Creative Arts/Performance:* art/fine arts, music, theater/drama. *Special Achievements/Activities:* community service, leadership, memberships. *Special Characteristics:* adult students, children and siblings of alumni, children of union members/company employees, ethnic background, first-generation college students, general special characteristics, international students, local/state students, members of minority groups, out-of-state students, veterans' children. ***Tuition waivers:*** Full or partial for minority students. ***ROTC:*** Army.

LOANS ***Student loans:*** $30,187,862 (49% need-based, 51% non-need-based). 63% of past graduating class borrowed through all loan programs. *Average indebtedness per student:* $16,793. ***Average need-based loan:*** Freshmen: $2814; Undergraduates: $3608. ***Parent loans:*** $2,807,340 (100% non-need-based). ***Programs:*** FFEL (Subsidized and Unsubsidized Stafford, PLUS), Perkins, state, college/university.

WORK-STUDY ***Federal work-study:*** Total amount: $488,397; 479 jobs averaging $1242. ***State or other work-study/employment:*** Total amount: $2,474,775 (100% non-need-based). 1,072 part-time jobs averaging $2415.

APPLYING FOR FINANCIAL AID ***Required financial aid forms:*** FAFSA, institution's own form. ***Financial aid deadline (priority):*** 3/15. ***Notification date:*** Continuous beginning 3/10. Students must reply by 5/10 or within 3 weeks of notification.

CONTACT Louise Janke, Associate Director of Financial Aid, University of Wisconsin–La Crosse, 1725 State Street, La Crosse, WI 54601-3742, 608-785-8604. *Fax:* 608-785-8843. *E-mail:* janke.loui@uwlax.edu.

UNIVERSITY OF WISCONSIN–MADISON

Madison, WI

Tuition & fees (WI res): $6726 Average undergraduate aid package: $11,818

ABOUT THE INSTITUTION State-supported, coed. Awards: bachelor's, master's, doctoral, and first professional degrees and post-master's and first professional certificates. 136 undergraduate majors. Total enrollment: 41,466. Undergraduates: 30,055. Freshmen: 5,643. Both federal and institutional methodology are used as a basis for awarding need-based institutional aid.

UNDERGRADUATE EXPENSES for 2006–07 ***Application fee:*** $35. ***Tuition, state resident:*** full-time $6000; part-time $282 per credit. ***Tuition, nonresident:*** full-time $20,000; part-time $866 per credit. ***Required fees:*** full-time $726; $32.25 per credit. Full-time tuition and fees vary according to degree level and reciprocity agreements. Part-time tuition and fees vary according to course load, degree level, and reciprocity agreements. ***College room and board:*** $6920. Room and board charges vary according to board plan, housing facility, and location.

FRESHMAN FINANCIAL AID (Fall 2006, est.) 4016 applied for aid; of those 44% were deemed to have need. 95% of freshmen with need received aid; of those 33% had need fully met. ***Average financial aid package:*** $11,469 (excluding resources awarded to replace EFC). 22% of all full-time freshmen had no need and received non-need-based gift aid.

UNDERGRADUATE FINANCIAL AID (Fall 2006, est.) 14,438 applied for aid; of those 60% were deemed to have need. 96% of undergraduates with need received aid; of those 27% had need fully met. ***Average financial aid package:***

$11,818 (excluding resources awarded to replace EFC). 14% of all full-time undergraduates had no need and received non-need-based gift aid.

GIFT AID (NEED-BASED) ***Total amount:*** $24,812,190 (51% federal, 26% state, 23% institutional). ***Receiving aid:*** Freshmen: 23% (1,232); All full-time undergraduates: 23% (6,479). ***Average award:*** Freshmen: $3725; Undergraduates: $3829. ***Scholarships, grants, and awards:*** Federal Pell, FSEOG, state, private, college/university gift aid from institutional funds.

GIFT AID (NON-NEED-BASED) ***Total amount:*** $25,010,747 (10% federal, 18% state, 42% institutional, 30% external sources). ***Receiving aid:*** Freshmen: 17% (919); Undergraduates: 10% (2,790). ***Average award:*** Freshmen: $2989; Undergraduates: $3135. ***Scholarships, grants, and awards by category:*** *Academic Interests/Achievement:* general academic interests/achievements. *Creative Arts/Performance:* general creative arts/performance. *Special Achievements/Activities:* general special achievements/activities. *Special Characteristics:* general special characteristics. ***ROTC:*** Army, Naval, Air Force.

LOANS ***Student loans:*** $76,110,744 (55% need-based, 45% non-need-based). 47% of past graduating class borrowed through all loan programs. *Average indebtedness per student:* $20,282. ***Average need-based loan:*** Freshmen: $4345; Undergraduates: $4801. ***Parent loans:*** $14,239,691 (100% non-need-based). ***Programs:*** FFEL (Subsidized and Unsubsidized Stafford, PLUS), Perkins, Federal Nursing, state, college/university.

WORK-STUDY ***Federal work-study:*** Total amount: $8,807,296; 3,894 jobs averaging $2640.

ATHLETIC AWARDS Total amount: $7,100,000 (100% non-need-based).

APPLYING FOR FINANCIAL AID ***Required financial aid forms:*** FAFSA, institution's own form. ***Financial aid deadline:*** Continuous. ***Notification date:*** Continuous beginning 4/1. Students must reply within 3 weeks of notification.

CONTACT Office of Student Financial Services, University of Wisconsin–Madison, 432 North Murray Street, Madison, WI 53706-1380, 608-262-3060. *Fax:* 608-262-9068. *E-mail:* finaid@das.wisc.edu.

UNIVERSITY OF WISCONSIN–MILWAUKEE

Milwaukee, WI

Tuition & fees (WI res): $7392 **Average undergraduate aid package: $6266**

ABOUT THE INSTITUTION State-supported, coed. Awards: bachelor's, master's, and doctoral degrees and post-bachelor's and post-master's certificates. 105 undergraduate majors. Total enrollment: 28,309. Undergraduates: 23,595. Freshmen: 4,090. Federal methodology is used as a basis for awarding need-based institutional aid.

UNDERGRADUATE EXPENSES for 2006–07 ***Application fee:*** $35. ***Tuition, state resident:*** full-time $6630; part-time $244.50 per credit. ***Tuition, nonresident:*** full-time $16,232; part-time $644.58 per credit. Full-time tuition and fees vary according to location, program, and reciprocity agreements. Part-time tuition and fees vary according to course load, location, program, and reciprocity agreements. ***College room and board:*** $5314; ***Room only:*** $3304. Room and board charges vary according to board plan and housing facility. ***Payment plan:*** Installment.

FRESHMAN FINANCIAL AID (Fall 2006, est.) 2900 applied for aid; of those 73% were deemed to have need. 96% of freshmen with need received aid; of those 25% had need fully met. ***Average percent of need met:*** 48% (excluding resources awarded to replace EFC). ***Average financial aid package:*** $5275 (excluding resources awarded to replace EFC). 1% of all full-time freshmen had no need and received non-need-based gift aid.

UNDERGRADUATE FINANCIAL AID (Fall 2006, est.) 16,319 applied for aid; of those 81% were deemed to have need. 84% of undergraduates with need received aid; of those 27% had need fully met. ***Average percent of need met:*** 58% (excluding resources awarded to replace EFC). ***Average financial aid package:*** $6266 (excluding resources awarded to replace EFC). 1% of all full-time undergraduates had no need and received non-need-based gift aid.

GIFT AID (NEED-BASED) ***Total amount:*** $26,188,629 (59% federal, 40% state, 1% institutional). ***Receiving aid:*** Freshmen: 20% (749); All full-time undergraduates: 23% (4,710). ***Average award:*** Freshmen: $5471; Undergraduates: $5107. ***Scholarships, grants, and awards:*** Federal Pell, FSEOG, state, private, Federal Nursing.

GIFT AID (NON-NEED-BASED) ***Total amount:*** $7,809,312 (53% federal, 1% state, 23% institutional, 23% external sources). ***Receiving aid:*** Freshmen: 11% (403); Undergraduates: 7% (1,544). ***Average award:*** Freshmen: $2532; Undergraduates: $2628. ***Scholarships, grants, and awards by category:*** *Academic Interests/Achievement:* general academic interests/achievements. *Creative Arts/Performance:* general creative arts/performance. *Special Achievements/Activities:* general special achievements/activities. *Special Characteristics:* general special characteristics. ***Tuition waivers:*** Full or partial for senior citizens. ***ROTC:*** Army cooperative, Air Force cooperative.

LOANS ***Student loans:*** $84,529,139 (48% need-based, 52% non-need-based). 74% of past graduating class borrowed through all loan programs. *Average indebtedness per student:* $16,683. ***Average need-based loan:*** Freshmen: $2990; Undergraduates: $3926. ***Parent loans:*** $8,249,065 (100% non-need-based). ***Programs:*** FFEL (Subsidized and Unsubsidized Stafford, PLUS), Perkins, Federal Nursing, alternative loans.

WORK-STUDY ***Federal work-study:*** Total amount: $351,785; jobs available.

ATHLETIC AWARDS Total amount: $364,381 (100% non-need-based).

APPLYING FOR FINANCIAL AID ***Required financial aid form:*** FAFSA. ***Financial aid deadline (priority):*** 3/1. ***Notification date:*** Continuous beginning 3/20.

CONTACT Ms. Jane Hojan-Clark, Director of Financial Aid and Student Employment Services, University of Wisconsin–Milwaukee, Mellencamp Hall 162, Milwaukee, WI 53201, 414-229-6300. *E-mail:* jhojan@uwm.edu.

UNIVERSITY OF WISCONSIN–OSHKOSH

Oshkosh, WI

CONTACT Ms. Sheila Denney, Financial Aid Counselor, University of Wisconsin–Oshkosh, 800 Algoma Boulevard, Oshkosh, WI 54901, 920-424-3377. *E-mail:* denney@uwosh.edu.

UNIVERSITY OF WISCONSIN–PARKSIDE

Kenosha, WI

ABOUT THE INSTITUTION State-supported, coed. Awards: bachelor's and master's degrees. 37 undergraduate majors. Total enrollment: 4,914. Undergraduates: 4,802. Freshmen: 906.

GIFT AID (NEED-BASED) ***Scholarships, grants, and awards:*** Federal Pell, FSEOG, state, private, college/university gift aid from institutional funds.

GIFT AID (NON-NEED-BASED) ***Scholarships, grants, and awards by category:*** *Academic Interests/Achievement:* biological sciences, business, communication, education, engineering/technologies, English, foreign languages, general academic interests/achievements, health fields, mathematics, physical sciences, premedicine. *Creative Arts/Performance:* applied art and design, art/fine arts, music, theater/drama. *Special Achievements/Activities:* community service, leadership. *Special Characteristics:* adult students, children of union members/company employees, children of workers in trades, ethnic background, general special characteristics, international students, local/state students, members of minority groups.

LOANS ***Programs:*** FFEL (Subsidized and Unsubsidized Stafford, PLUS), Perkins, state.

WORK-STUDY ***State or other work-study/employment:*** Total amount: $391,305 (100% need-based).

APPLYING FOR FINANCIAL AID ***Required financial aid form:*** FAFSA.

CONTACT Dr. Randall McCready, Director of Financial Aid and Scholarships, University of Wisconsin–Parkside, 900 Wood Road, Kenosha, WI 53141-2000, 262-595-2574. *Fax:* 262-595-2216. *E-mail:* randall.mccready@uwp.edu.

UNIVERSITY OF WISCONSIN–PLATTEVILLE

Platteville, WI

CONTACT Elizabeth Tucker, Director of Financial Aid, University of Wisconsin–Platteville, 1 University Plaza, Platteville, WI 53818-3099, 608-342-1836 or toll-free 800-362-5515. *Fax:* 608-342-1281. *E-mail:* tucker@uwplatt.edu.

UNIVERSITY OF WISCONSIN–RIVER FALLS

River Falls, WI

CONTACT Mr. David Woodward, Director of Financial Aid, University of Wisconsin–River Falls, 410 South Third Street, River Falls, WI 54022-5001, 715-425-3272. *Fax:* 715-425-0708.

UNIVERSITY OF WISCONSIN–STEVENS POINT

Stevens Point, WI

Tuition & fees (WI res): $5459 **Average undergraduate aid package: $6887**

ABOUT THE INSTITUTION State-supported, coed. Awards: associate, bachelor's, and master's degrees. 55 undergraduate majors. Total enrollment: 8,842. Undergraduates: 8,612. Freshmen: 1,638. Federal methodology is used as a basis for awarding need-based institutional aid.

UNDERGRADUATE EXPENSES for 2006–07 ***Application fee:*** $35. ***Tuition, state resident:*** full-time $4568; part-time $190 per credit. ***Tuition, nonresident:*** full-time $12,042; part-time $502 per credit. ***Required fees:*** full-time $891; $79 per credit. Full-time tuition and fees vary according to course load and reciprocity agreements. Part-time tuition and fees vary according to course load and reciprocity agreements. ***College room and board:*** $4542; ***Room only:*** $2726. ***Payment plan:*** Installment.

FRESHMAN FINANCIAL AID (Fall 2005) 1298 applied for aid; of those 52% were deemed to have need. 95% of freshmen with need received aid; of those 68% had need fully met. ***Average percent of need met:*** 98% (excluding resources awarded to replace EFC). ***Average financial aid package:*** $5462 (excluding resources awarded to replace EFC). 7% of all full-time freshmen had no need and received non-need-based gift aid.

UNDERGRADUATE FINANCIAL AID (Fall 2005) 7,131 applied for aid; of those 56% were deemed to have need. 97% of undergraduates with need received aid; of those 74% had need fully met. ***Average percent of need met:*** 96% (excluding resources awarded to replace EFC). ***Average financial aid package:*** $6887 (excluding resources awarded to replace EFC). 6% of all full-time undergraduates had no need and received non-need-based gift aid.

GIFT AID (NEED-BASED) ***Total amount:*** $9,945,735 (59% federal, 35% state, 4% institutional, 2% external sources). ***Receiving aid:*** Freshmen: 20% (313); All full-time undergraduates: 25% (2,069). ***Average award:*** Freshmen: $4036; Undergraduates: $4489. ***Scholarships, grants, and awards:*** Federal Pell, FSEOG, state, college/university gift aid from institutional funds.

GIFT AID (NON-NEED-BASED) ***Total amount:*** $1,475,022 (3% state, 48% institutional, 49% external sources). ***Receiving aid:*** Freshmen: 4% (67); Undergraduates: 5% (386). ***Average award:*** Freshmen: $1905; Undergraduates: $1987. ***Scholarships, grants, and awards by category:*** *Academic Interests/Achievement:* 939 awards ($587,777 total): agriculture, architecture, biological sciences, business, communication, computer science, education, engineering/technologies, English, foreign languages, general academic interests/achievements, health fields, home economics, humanities, international studies, mathematics, military science, physical sciences, premedicine, social sciences. *Creative Arts/Performance:* 59 awards ($33,650 total): applied art and design, creative writing, dance, music, performing arts, theater/drama. *Special Achievements/Activities:* 25 awards ($19,950 total): general special achievements/activities, leadership. *Special Characteristics:* 7 awards ($31,240 total): adult students, ethnic background, general special characteristics, international students, members of minority groups, out-of-state students, veterans. ***Tuition waivers:*** Full or partial for children of alumni, senior citizens. ***ROTC:*** Army.

LOANS ***Student loans:*** $25,640,416 (61% need-based, 39% non-need-based). 69% of past graduating class borrowed through all loan programs. *Average indebtedness per student:* $17,025. ***Average need-based loan:*** Freshmen: $3232; Undergraduates: $4235. ***Parent loans:*** $1,760,639 (6% need-based, 94% non-need-based). ***Programs:*** Perkins, college/university.

WORK-STUDY ***Federal work-study:*** Total amount: $2,484,644; 945 jobs averaging $1310.

APPLYING FOR FINANCIAL AID ***Required financial aid form:*** FAFSA. ***Financial aid deadline (priority):*** 6/15. ***Notification date:*** Continuous. Students must reply within 4 weeks of notification.

CONTACT Mr. Paul Watson, Interim Director of Financial Aid, University of Wisconsin–Stevens Point, 105 Student Services Center, Stevens Point, WI 54481-3897, 715-346-4771. *Fax:* 715-346-3526. *E-mail:* pwatson@uwsp.edu.

UNIVERSITY OF WISCONSIN–STOUT

Menomonie, WI

Tuition & fees (WI res): $6963 **Average undergraduate aid package: $8113**

ABOUT THE INSTITUTION State-supported, coed. Awards: bachelor's and master's degrees and post-master's certificates. 30 undergraduate majors. Total enrollment: 8,327. Undergraduates: 7,492. Freshmen: 1,506. Federal methodology is used as a basis for awarding need-based institutional aid.

UNDERGRADUATE EXPENSES for 2007–08 ***Application fee:*** $35. ***Tuition, state resident:*** full-time $5087; part-time $170 per credit. ***Tuition, nonresident:*** full-time $12,737; part-time $425 per credit. ***College room and board:*** $4884; ***Room only:*** $2990.

FRESHMAN FINANCIAL AID (Fall 2006, est.) 1176 applied for aid; of those 64% were deemed to have need. 100% of freshmen with need received aid; of those 49% had need fully met. ***Average percent of need met:*** 83% (excluding resources awarded to replace EFC). ***Average financial aid package:*** $7402 (excluding resources awarded to replace EFC). 2% of all full-time freshmen had no need and received non-need-based gift aid.

UNDERGRADUATE FINANCIAL AID (Fall 2006, est.) 5,082 applied for aid; of those 69% were deemed to have need. 100% of undergraduates with need received aid; of those 52% had need fully met. ***Average percent of need met:*** 85% (excluding resources awarded to replace EFC). ***Average financial aid package:*** $8113 (excluding resources awarded to replace EFC). 2% of all full-time undergraduates had no need and received non-need-based gift aid.

GIFT AID (NEED-BASED) ***Total amount:*** $7,222,391 (62% federal, 36% state, 1% institutional, 1% external sources). ***Receiving aid:*** Freshmen: 22% (318); All full-time undergraduates: 22% (1,521). ***Average award:*** Freshmen: $4388; Undergraduates: $4456. ***Scholarships, grants, and awards:*** Federal Pell, FSEOG, state, private, college/university gift aid from institutional funds, Bureau of Indian Affairs Grants, GEAR UP grants.

GIFT AID (NON-NEED-BASED) ***Total amount:*** $2,258,101 (10% federal, 2% state, 18% institutional, 70% external sources). ***Receiving aid:*** Freshmen: 23% (339); Undergraduates: 11% (758). ***Average award:*** Freshmen: $1433; Undergraduates: $1330. ***Scholarships, grants, and awards by category:*** *Academic Interests/Achievement:* 242 awards ($208,035 total): business, education, engineering/technologies, general academic interests/achievements, home economics, international studies, mathematics, physical sciences. *Creative Arts/Performance:* 14 awards ($3600 total): applied art and design, art/fine arts, music. *Special Achievements/Activities:* 20 awards ($10,475 total): community service, general special achievements/activities, memberships. *Special Characteristics:* 36 awards ($26,450 total): adult students, first-generation college students, handicapped students, international students, local/state students, members of minority groups, out-of-state students, previous college experience, veterans, veterans' children.

LOANS ***Student loans:*** $27,986,004 (48% need-based, 52% non-need-based). 72% of past graduating class borrowed through all loan programs. *Average indebtedness per student:* $21,665. ***Average need-based loan:*** Freshmen: $3371; Undergraduates: $4339. ***Parent loans:*** $3,392,722 (100% non-need-based). ***Programs:*** FFEL (Subsidized and Unsubsidized Stafford, PLUS), Perkins, alternative educational loans.

WORK-STUDY ***Federal work-study:*** Total amount: $2,689,185; 1,249 jobs averaging $1493.

APPLYING FOR FINANCIAL AID ***Required financial aid form:*** FAFSA. ***Financial aid deadline (priority):*** 3/15. ***Notification date:*** Continuous beginning 4/1. Students must reply within 4 weeks of notification.

CONTACT Beth A. Resech, Director of Financial Aid, University of Wisconsin–Stout, 210 Bowman Hall, Menomonie, WI 54751, 715-232-1363 or toll-free 800-HI-STOUT (in-state). *Fax:* 715-232-5246. *E-mail:* resechb@uwstout.edu.

UNIVERSITY OF WISCONSIN–SUPERIOR

Superior, WI

Tuition & fees (WI res): $5567 **Average undergraduate aid package: $6809**

ABOUT THE INSTITUTION State-supported, coed. Awards: bachelor's and master's degrees (associate, educational specialist). 63 undergraduate majors. Total enrollment: 2,924. Undergraduates: 2,626. Freshmen: 312. Federal methodology is used as a basis for awarding need-based institutional aid.

UNDERGRADUATE EXPENSES for 2006–07 ***Application fee:*** $35. ***Tuition, state resident:*** full-time $4558; part-time $340 per credit. ***Tuition, nonresident:*** full-time $12,043; part-time $652 per credit. ***Required fees:*** full-time $1009; $287.66 per unit. Full-time tuition and fees vary according to reciprocity agreements. Part-time tuition and fees vary according to reciprocity agreements. ***College room and board:*** $4576; ***Room only:*** $2668. Room and board charges vary according to board plan and housing facility. ***Payment plan:*** Installment.

FRESHMAN FINANCIAL AID (Fall 2006, est.) 224 applied for aid; of those 74% were deemed to have need. 96% of freshmen with need received aid; of those 30% had need fully met. ***Average financial aid package:*** $5303 (excluding resources awarded to replace EFC). 4% of all full-time freshmen had no need and received non-need-based gift aid.

UNDERGRADUATE FINANCIAL AID (Fall 2006, est.) 1,486 applied for aid; of those 81% were deemed to have need. 98% of undergraduates with need received aid; of those 29% had need fully met. ***Average financial aid package:*** $6809 (excluding resources awarded to replace EFC). 3% of all full-time undergraduates had no need and received non-need-based gift aid.

GIFT AID (NEED-BASED) ***Total amount:*** $3,353,536 (70% federal, 30% state). ***Receiving aid:*** Freshmen: 26% (71); All full-time undergraduates: 34% (710). ***Average award:*** Freshmen: $5495; Undergraduates: $3949. ***Scholarships, grants, and awards:*** Federal Pell, FSEOG, state, private, college/university gift aid from institutional funds.

GIFT AID (NON-NEED-BASED) ***Total amount:*** $1,030,879 (2% state, 66% institutional, 32% external sources). ***Receiving aid:*** Freshmen: 25% (68); Undergraduates: 14% (291). ***Average award:*** Freshmen: $2329; Undergraduates: $2180. ***Scholarships, grants, and awards by category:*** *Academic Interests/Achievement:* biological sciences, business, communication, computer science, education, English, general academic interests/achievements, health fields, humanities, mathematics, physical sciences, social sciences. *Special Characteristics:* general special characteristics. ***ROTC:*** Air Force cooperative.

LOANS ***Student loans:*** $8,626,431 (53% need-based, 47% non-need-based). 72% of past graduating class borrowed through all loan programs. *Average indebtedness per student:* $20,114. ***Average need-based loan:*** Freshmen: $2743; Undergraduates: $4117. ***Parent loans:*** $628,601 (100% non-need-based). ***Programs:*** Federal Direct (Subsidized and Unsubsidized Stafford, PLUS), Perkins, state, college/university.

WORK-STUDY ***Federal work-study:*** Total amount: $344,000; 298 jobs averaging $840. ***State or other work-study/employment:*** Part-time jobs available.

APPLYING FOR FINANCIAL AID ***Required financial aid form:*** FAFSA. ***Financial aid deadline (priority):*** 4/15. ***Notification date:*** Continuous beginning 3/15.

CONTACT Financial Aid Office, University of Wisconsin–Superior, Belknap and Catlin, PO Box 2000, Superior, WI 54880-4500, 715-394-8200 or toll-free 715-394-8230 (in-state).

UNIVERSITY OF WISCONSIN–WHITEWATER

Whitewater, WI

Tuition & fees (WI res): $6407 Average undergraduate aid package: $6773

ABOUT THE INSTITUTION State-supported, coed. Awards: associate, bachelor's, and master's degrees. 56 undergraduate majors. Total enrollment: 10,502. Undergraduates: 9,210. Freshmen: 1,805. Federal methodology is used as a basis for awarding need-based institutional aid.

UNDERGRADUATE EXPENSES for 2006–07 ***Application fee:*** $35. ***One-time required fee:*** $100. ***Tuition, state resident:*** full-time $5568; part-time $232 per credit. ***Tuition, nonresident:*** full-time $13,042; part-time $543 per credit. ***Required fees:*** full-time $839; $35 per credit. Full-time tuition and fees vary according to degree level and reciprocity agreements. ***College room and board:*** $4190; ***Room only:*** $2440. Room and board charges vary according to board plan. ***Payment plan:*** Installment.

FRESHMAN FINANCIAL AID (Fall 2006, est.) 1458 applied for aid; of those 64% were deemed to have need. 95% of freshmen with need received aid; of those 44% had need fully met. ***Average percent of need met:*** 69% (excluding resources awarded to replace EFC). ***Average financial aid package:*** $5691 (excluding resources awarded to replace EFC). 8% of all full-time freshmen had no need and received non-need-based gift aid.

UNDERGRADUATE FINANCIAL AID (Fall 2006, est.) 5,779 applied for aid; of those 67% were deemed to have need. 94% of undergraduates with need received aid; of those 53% had need fully met. ***Average percent of need met:*** 76% (excluding resources awarded to replace EFC). ***Average financial aid package:*** $6773 (excluding resources awarded to replace EFC). 5% of all full-time undergraduates had no need and received non-need-based gift aid.

GIFT AID (NEED-BASED) ***Total amount:*** $9,380,000 (59% federal, 41% state). ***Receiving aid:*** Freshmen: 20% (350); All full-time undergraduates: 21% (1,713). ***Average award:*** Freshmen: $5253; Undergraduates: $5108. ***Scholarships, grants, and awards:*** Federal Pell, FSEOG, state, private, college/university gift aid from institutional funds.

GIFT AID (NON-NEED-BASED) ***Total amount:*** $2,671,000 (3% federal, 4% state, 26% institutional, 67% external sources). ***Receiving aid:*** Freshmen: 14% (249); Undergraduates: 6% (515). ***Average award:*** Freshmen: $2212; Undergraduates: $2353. ***Scholarships, grants, and awards by category:*** *Academic Interests/Achievement:* biological sciences, business, communication, computer science, education, English, foreign languages, general academic interests/achievements, humanities, mathematics, physical sciences, premedicine, social sciences. *Creative Arts/Performance:* art/fine arts, cinema/film/broadcasting, creative writing, journalism/publications, music, theater/drama. *Special Achievements/Activities:* leadership. *Special Characteristics:* adult students, ethnic background, handicapped students, international students, local/state students, members of minority groups, out-of-state students. ***Tuition waivers:*** Full or partial for children of alumni, senior citizens. ***ROTC:*** Army, Air Force.

LOANS ***Student loans:*** $31,500,000 (49% need-based, 51% non-need-based). 65% of past graduating class borrowed through all loan programs. *Average indebtedness per student:* $17,712. ***Average need-based loan:*** Freshmen: $3020; Undergraduates: $3884. ***Parent loans:*** $375,000 (100% non-need-based). ***Programs:*** Federal Direct (Subsidized and Unsubsidized Stafford, PLUS), Perkins.

WORK-STUDY ***Federal work-study:*** Total amount: $656,000; 606 jobs averaging $1083. ***State or other work-study/employment:*** Total amount: $3,000,000 (100% non-need-based). 1,675 part-time jobs averaging $1490.

APPLYING FOR FINANCIAL AID ***Required financial aid form:*** FAFSA. ***Financial aid deadline (priority):*** 3/15. ***Notification date:*** Continuous beginning 4/1. Students must reply within 3 weeks of notification.

CONTACT Ms. Carol Miller, Director of Financial Aid, University of Wisconsin–Whitewater, 800 West Main Street, Whitewater, WI 53190-1790, 262-472-1130. *Fax:* 262-472-5655.

UNIVERSITY OF WYOMING

Laramie, WY

Tuition & fees (WY res): $3554 Average undergraduate aid package: $7012

ABOUT THE INSTITUTION State-supported, coed. Awards: bachelor's, master's, doctoral, and first professional degrees and post-master's certificates. 78 undergraduate majors. Total enrollment: 13,203. Undergraduates: 9,468. Freshmen: 1,574. Federal methodology is used as a basis for awarding need-based institutional aid.

UNDERGRADUATE EXPENSES for 2007–08 ***Application fee:*** $40. ***Tuition, state resident:*** full-time $2820; part-time $94 per credit hour. ***Tuition, nonresident:*** full-time $9660; part-time $322 per credit hour. ***Required fees:*** full-time $734; $176 per term part-time. ***College room and board:*** $7274; ***Room only:*** $3158.

FRESHMAN FINANCIAL AID (Fall 2005) 1335 applied for aid; of those 89% were deemed to have need. 92% of freshmen with need received aid; of those 15% had need fully met. ***Average percent of need met:*** 76% (excluding resources awarded to replace EFC). ***Average financial aid package:*** $6702 (excluding resources awarded to replace EFC). 27% of all full-time freshmen had no need and received non-need-based gift aid.

UNDERGRADUATE FINANCIAL AID (Fall 2005) 5,695 applied for aid; of those 74% were deemed to have need. 97% of undergraduates with need received aid; of those 11% had need fully met. ***Average percent of need met:*** 76% (excluding resources awarded to replace EFC). ***Average financial aid package:*** $7012 (excluding resources awarded to replace EFC). 16% of all full-time undergraduates had no need and received non-need-based gift aid.

GIFT AID (NEED-BASED) ***Total amount:*** $7,554,844 (87% federal, 1% state, 4% institutional, 8% external sources). ***Receiving aid:*** Freshmen: 35% (499); All full-time undergraduates: 27% (2,576). ***Average award:*** Freshmen: $2565; Undergraduates: $3296. ***Scholarships, grants, and awards:*** Federal Pell, FSEOG, state, private, college/university gift aid from institutional funds.

GIFT AID (NON-NEED-BASED) ***Total amount:*** $16,294,078 (10% federal, 49% state, 18% institutional, 23% external sources). ***Receiving aid:*** Freshmen: 63% (902); Undergraduates: 29% (2,755). ***Average award:*** Freshmen: $2382; Undergraduates: $3487. ***Scholarships, grants, and awards by category:*** *Academic Interests/Achievement:* 4,037 awards ($5,522,444 total): agriculture, business, communication, computer science, education, engineering/technologies, English, foreign languages, general academic interests/achievements, health fields, home economics, international studies, mathematics, military science, physical sciences, social sciences. *Creative Arts/Performance:* 457 awards ($503,851 total): dance, debating, music, theater/drama. *Special Achievements/Activities:* 191 awards ($242,698 total): cheerleading/drum major, junior miss, leadership, rodeo. *Special Characteristics:* 1,774 awards ($6,522,128 total):

adult students, children and siblings of alumni, ethnic background, first-generation college students, handicapped students, international students, local/state students, out-of-state students, veterans. ***ROTC:*** Army, Air Force.

LOANS ***Student loans:*** $23,292,569 (58% need-based, 42% non-need-based). 44% of past graduating class borrowed through all loan programs. *Average indebtedness per student:* $16,855. ***Average need-based loan:*** Freshmen: $2826; Undergraduates: $3731. ***Parent loans:*** $2,850,098 (100% non-need-based). ***Programs:*** FFEL (Subsidized and Unsubsidized Stafford, PLUS), Perkins, alternative loans.

WORK-STUDY ***Federal work-study:*** Total amount: $457,701; 371 jobs averaging $1233.

ATHLETIC AWARDS Total amount: $2,781,490 (100% non-need-based).

APPLYING FOR FINANCIAL AID ***Required financial aid form:*** FAFSA. ***Financial aid deadline (priority):*** 2/1. ***Notification date:*** Continuous beginning 3/15. Students must reply within 3 weeks of notification.

CONTACT Mr. David Gruen, Director of Student Financial Aid, University of Wyoming, Department 3335, 1000 East University Avenue, Laramie, WY 82071-3335, 307-766-2116 or toll-free 800-342-5996. *Fax:* 307-766-3800. *E-mail:* finaid@uwyo.edu.

UPPER IOWA UNIVERSITY

Fayette, IA

CONTACT Jobyna Johnston, Director of Financial Aid, Upper Iowa University, Parker Fox Hall, Box 1859, Fayette, IA 52142-1859, 563-425-5393 or toll-free 800-553-4150 Ext. 2. *Fax:* 563-425-5277. *E-mail:* jobyna@uiu.edu.

URBANA UNIVERSITY

Urbana, OH

Tuition & fees: $16,254 **Average undergraduate aid package: $13,285**

ABOUT THE INSTITUTION Independent, coed. Awards: associate, bachelor's, and master's degrees. 28 undergraduate majors. Total enrollment: 1,551. Undergraduates: 1,461. Freshmen: 279. Federal methodology is used as a basis for awarding need-based institutional aid.

UNDERGRADUATE EXPENSES for 2006–07 ***Application fee:*** $25. ***Comprehensive fee:*** $22,866 includes full-time tuition ($16,254) and room and board ($6612). ***College room only:*** $2234. ***Part-time tuition:*** $337 per semester hour.

FRESHMAN FINANCIAL AID (Fall 2006, est.) 316 applied for aid; of those 83% were deemed to have need. 81% of freshmen with need received aid; of those 30% had need fully met. ***Average percent of need met:*** 60% (excluding resources awarded to replace EFC). ***Average financial aid package:*** $13,224 (excluding resources awarded to replace EFC). 18% of all full-time freshmen had no need and received non-need-based gift aid.

UNDERGRADUATE FINANCIAL AID (Fall 2006, est.) 941 applied for aid; of those 81% were deemed to have need. 92% of undergraduates with need received aid; of those 89% had need fully met. ***Average percent of need met:*** 63% (excluding resources awarded to replace EFC). ***Average financial aid package:*** $13,285 (excluding resources awarded to replace EFC). 65% of all full-time undergraduates had no need and received non-need-based gift aid.

GIFT AID (NEED-BASED) ***Total amount:*** $2,123,662 (58% federal, 42% state). ***Receiving aid:*** Freshmen: 56% (196); All full-time undergraduates: 65% (615). ***Average award:*** Freshmen: $1804; Undergraduates: $2676. ***Scholarships, grants, and awards:*** Federal Pell, FSEOG, state, private, college/university gift aid from institutional funds.

GIFT AID (NON-NEED-BASED) ***Total amount:*** $2,558,106 (18% state, 69% institutional, 13% external sources). ***Receiving aid:*** Freshmen: 4% (15); Undergraduates: 6% (56). ***Scholarships, grants, and awards by category:*** *Academic Interests/Achievement:* 129 awards ($346,781 total): general academic interests/achievements. *Creative Arts/Performance:* 47 awards ($200,350 total): music. *Special Achievements/Activities:* community service, leadership, religious involvement. *Special Characteristics:* 68 awards ($301,491 total): children and siblings of alumni, children of faculty/staff, religious affiliation, spouses of current students.

LOANS ***Student loans:*** $6,690,385 (100% need-based). 89% of past graduating class borrowed through all loan programs. *Average indebtedness per student:* $21,125. ***Average need-based loan:*** Freshmen: $3702; Undergraduates: $4680. ***Parent loans:*** $1,735,561 (100% need-based). ***Programs:*** FFEL (Subsidized and Unsubsidized Stafford, PLUS), Perkins.

WORK-STUDY ***Federal work-study:*** Total amount: $121,977; 181 jobs averaging $1200.

ATHLETIC AWARDS Total amount: $2,569,163 (100% non-need-based).

APPLYING FOR FINANCIAL AID ***Required financial aid forms:*** FAFSA, institution's own form. ***Financial aid deadline (priority):*** 4/1. ***Notification date:*** Continuous beginning 3/1. Students must reply within 4 weeks of notification.

CONTACT Mrs. Amy M. Barnhart, Director of Financial Aid, Urbana University, 579 College Way, Urbana, OH 43078-2091, 937-484-1359 or toll-free 800-7-URBANA. *Fax:* 937-652-6870. *E-mail:* abarnhart@urbana.edu.

URSINUS COLLEGE

Collegeville, PA

Tuition & fees: $33,350 **Average undergraduate aid package: $24,109**

ABOUT THE INSTITUTION Independent, coed. Awards: bachelor's degrees. 36 undergraduate majors. Total enrollment: 1,589. Undergraduates: 1,589. Freshmen: 405. Both federal and institutional methodology are used as a basis for awarding need-based institutional aid.

UNDERGRADUATE EXPENSES for 2006–07 ***Application fee:*** $50. ***Comprehensive fee:*** $40,950 includes full-time tuition ($33,200), mandatory fees ($150), and room and board ($7600). ***Part-time tuition:*** $1038 per credit hour. ***Payment plan:*** Installment.

FRESHMAN FINANCIAL AID (Fall 2005) 337 applied for aid; of those 97% were deemed to have need. 100% of freshmen with need received aid; of those 75% had need fully met. ***Average percent of need met:*** 80% (excluding resources awarded to replace EFC). ***Average financial aid package:*** $22,364 (excluding resources awarded to replace EFC). 13% of all full-time freshmen had no need and received non-need-based gift aid.

UNDERGRADUATE FINANCIAL AID (Fall 2005) 1,292 applied for aid; of those 96% were deemed to have need. 100% of undergraduates with need received aid; of those 68% had need fully met. ***Average percent of need met:*** 80% (excluding resources awarded to replace EFC). ***Average financial aid package:*** $24,109 (excluding resources awarded to replace EFC). 13% of all full-time undergraduates had no need and received non-need-based gift aid.

GIFT AID (NEED-BASED) ***Total amount:*** $22,505,893 (5% federal, 7% state, 86% institutional, 2% external sources). ***Receiving aid:*** Freshmen: 78% (326); All full-time undergraduates: 80% (1,245). ***Average award:*** Freshmen: $18,719; Undergraduates: $18,211. ***Scholarships, grants, and awards:*** Federal Pell, FSEOG, state, private, college/university gift aid from institutional funds, Office of Vocational Rehabilitation Awards.

GIFT AID (NON-NEED-BASED) ***Total amount:*** $3,993,359 (86% institutional, 14% external sources). ***Receiving aid:*** Freshmen: 12% (49); Undergraduates: 12% (187). ***Average award:*** Freshmen: $10,500; Undergraduates: $9500. ***Scholarships, grants, and awards by category:*** *Academic Interests/Achievement:* 118 awards ($3,993,359 total): general academic interests/achievements. *Creative Arts/Performance:* 12 awards ($100,000 total): art/fine arts, creative writing, music, theater/drama. *Special Achievements/Activities:* 60 awards ($350,000 total): leadership. *Special Characteristics:* 60 awards ($527,000 total): children of faculty/staff, international students, siblings of current students. ***Tuition waivers:*** Full or partial for employees or children of employees, senior citizens.

LOANS ***Student loans:*** $11,086,386 (100% need-based). 77% of past graduating class borrowed through all loan programs. *Average indebtedness per student:* $26,997. ***Average need-based loan:*** Freshmen: $2745; Undergraduates: $4998. ***Parent loans:*** $3,669,751 (100% need-based). ***Programs:*** FFEL (Subsidized and Unsubsidized Stafford, PLUS), Perkins, college/university.

WORK-STUDY ***Federal work-study:*** Total amount: $1,430,125; 637 jobs averaging $1540. ***State or other work-study/employment:*** Total amount: $684,405 (100% need-based).

APPLYING FOR FINANCIAL AID ***Required financial aid forms:*** FAFSA, CSS Financial Aid PROFILE. ***Financial aid deadline:*** 2/15. ***Notification date:*** 3/15. Students must reply by 5/1.

CONTACT Ms. Suzanne B. Sparrow, Director of Student Financial Services, Ursinus College, PO Box 1000, Collegeville, PA 19426-1000, 610-409-3600 Ext. 2242. *Fax:* 610-409-3662. *E-mail:* ssparrow@ursinus.edu.

URSULINE COLLEGE

Pepper Pike, OH

CONTACT Ms. Mary Lynn Perri, Director of Financial Aid and Enrollment Services, Ursuline College, 2550 Lander Road, Mullen Building, Room 202b, Pepper Pike, OH 44124-4398, 440-646-8330 or toll-free 888-URSULINE.

UTAH STATE UNIVERSITY

Logan, UT

Tuition & fees (UT res): $3949 **Average undergraduate aid package: $6455**

ABOUT THE INSTITUTION State-supported, coed. Awards: associate, bachelor's, master's, and doctoral degrees and post-bachelor's and post-master's certificates. 121 undergraduate majors. Total enrollment: 14,444. Undergraduates: 12,779. Freshmen: 2,562. Federal methodology is used as a basis for awarding need-based institutional aid.

UNDERGRADUATE EXPENSES for 2006–07 ***Application fee:*** $40. ***Tuition, state resident:*** full-time $3378. ***Tuition, nonresident:*** full-time $10,878. Full-time tuition and fees vary according to course load and student level. Part-time tuition and fees vary according to course load and student level. ***College room and board:*** $4400; ***Room only:*** $1550. Room and board charges vary according to board plan and housing facility. ***Payment plan:*** Deferred payment.

FRESHMAN FINANCIAL AID (Fall 2006, est.) 1002 applied for aid; of those 75% were deemed to have need. 99% of freshmen with need received aid; of those 25% had need fully met. ***Average percent of need met:*** 61% (excluding resources awarded to replace EFC). ***Average financial aid package:*** $5680 (excluding resources awarded to replace EFC). 6% of all full-time freshmen had no need and received non-need-based gift aid.

UNDERGRADUATE FINANCIAL AID (Fall 2006, est.) 5,912 applied for aid; of those 88% were deemed to have need. 97% of undergraduates with need received aid; of those 8% had need fully met. ***Average percent of need met:*** 65% (excluding resources awarded to replace EFC). ***Average financial aid package:*** $6455 (excluding resources awarded to replace EFC). 2% of all full-time undergraduates had no need and received non-need-based gift aid.

GIFT AID (NEED-BASED) ***Receiving aid:*** Freshmen: 16% (387); All full-time undergraduates: 35% (3,651). ***Average award:*** Freshmen: $3153; Undergraduates: $3683. ***Scholarships, grants, and awards:*** Federal Pell, FSEOG, state, private, college/university gift aid from institutional funds.

GIFT AID (NON-NEED-BASED) ***Receiving aid:*** Freshmen: 18% (424); Undergraduates: 14% (1,509). ***Average award:*** Freshmen: $1932; Undergraduates: $1755. ***Scholarships, grants, and awards by category:*** *Academic Interests/Achievement:* 5,264 awards ($15,956,023 total): agriculture, architecture, biological sciences, business, communication, computer science, education, engineering/technologies, English, foreign languages, general academic interests/achievements, health fields, home economics, humanities, international studies, library science, mathematics, physical sciences, premedicine, social sciences. *Creative Arts/Performance:* 110 awards ($338,958 total): applied art and design, art/fine arts, general creative arts/performance, journalism/publications, music, performing arts, theater/drama. *Special Characteristics:* 475 awards ($1,728,616 total): children and siblings of alumni, children of faculty/staff, international students. ***Tuition waivers:*** Full or partial for minority students, children of alumni, employees or children of employees, adult students, senior citizens. ***ROTC:*** Army, Air Force.

LOANS ***Student loans:*** $18,014,067 (75% need-based, 25% non-need-based). 25% of past graduating class borrowed through all loan programs. *Average indebtedness per student:* $11,040. ***Average need-based loan:*** Freshmen: $2749; Undergraduates: $4103. ***Parent loans:*** $582,632 (100% non-need-based). ***Programs:*** FFEL (Subsidized and Unsubsidized Stafford, PLUS), Perkins, college/university.

WORK-STUDY ***Federal work-study:*** Total amount: $615,510; 324 jobs averaging $1900. ***State or other work-study/employment:*** Part-time jobs available.

ATHLETIC AWARDS Total amount: $2,524,905 (100% non-need-based).

APPLYING FOR FINANCIAL AID ***Required financial aid forms:*** FAFSA, institution's own form, Federal Tax Forms. ***Financial aid deadline:*** Continuous. ***Notification date:*** Continuous beginning 4/1. Students must reply within 4 weeks of notification.

CONTACT Tamara Allen, Associate Director of Financial Aid, Utah State University, Old Main Hill, Logan, UT 84322, 435-797-3369 or toll-free 800-488-8108. *Fax:* 435-797-0654. *E-mail:* tamara.allen@usu.edu.

UTAH VALLEY STATE COLLEGE

Orem, UT

CONTACT Mr. Michael H. Johnson, Director of Financial Aid, Utah Valley State College, Mail Code—164, 800 West 1200 South Street, Orem, UT 84058-0001, 801-222-8442. *Fax:* 801-222-8448.

U.T.A. MESIVTA OF KIRYAS JOEL

Monroe, NY

CONTACT Financial Aid Office, U.T.A. Mesivta of Kiryas Joel, 33 Forest Road, Suite 101, Monroe, NY 10950, 845-873-9901.

UTICA COLLEGE

Utica, NY

ABOUT THE INSTITUTION Independent, coed. Awards: bachelor's, master's, and first professional degrees. 44 undergraduate majors. Total enrollment: 2,952. Undergraduates: 2,429. Freshmen: 496.

GIFT AID (NEED-BASED) ***Scholarships, grants, and awards:*** Federal Pell, FSEOG, state, private, college/university gift aid from institutional funds, Federal Nursing.

GIFT AID (NON-NEED-BASED) ***Scholarships, grants, and awards by category:*** *Academic Interests/Achievement:* general academic interests/achievements.

LOANS ***Programs:*** Federal Direct (Subsidized and Unsubsidized Stafford, PLUS), Perkins, GATE Loans.

WORK-STUDY ***Federal work-study:*** Total amount: $1,400,403; 872 jobs averaging $1512. ***State or other work-study/employment:*** Total amount: $546,126 (80% need-based, 20% non-need-based). 367 part-time jobs averaging $1540.

APPLYING FOR FINANCIAL AID ***Required financial aid forms:*** FAFSA, state aid form.

CONTACT Mrs. Elizabeth C. Wilson, Director of Financial Aid, Utica College, 1600 Burrstone Road, Utica, NY 13502-4892, 800-782-8884. *Fax:* 315-792-3368.

VALDOSTA STATE UNIVERSITY

Valdosta, GA

Tuition & fees (GA res): $3490 **Average undergraduate aid package: $13,183**

ABOUT THE INSTITUTION State-supported, coed. Awards: associate, bachelor's, master's, and doctoral degrees and post-master's certificates. 49 undergraduate majors. Total enrollment: 10,888. Undergraduates: 9,489. Freshmen: 2,059. Federal methodology is used as a basis for awarding need-based institutional aid.

UNDERGRADUATE EXPENSES for 2007–08 ***Application fee:*** $40. ***Tuition, state resident:*** full-time $2560; part-time $107 per hour. ***Tuition, nonresident:*** full-time $10,242; part-time $427 per hour. ***College room and board:*** $5680; ***Room only:*** $2880.

FRESHMAN FINANCIAL AID (Fall 2006, est.) 1618 applied for aid; of those 70% were deemed to have need. 100% of freshmen with need received aid; of those 19% had need fully met. ***Average percent of need met:*** 67% (excluding resources awarded to replace EFC). ***Average financial aid package:*** $7332 (excluding resources awarded to replace EFC). 1% of all full-time freshmen had no need and received non-need-based gift aid.

UNDERGRADUATE FINANCIAL AID (Fall 2006, est.) 6,563 applied for aid; of those 77% were deemed to have need. 99% of undergraduates with need received aid; of those 55% had need fully met. ***Average percent of need met:*** 76% (excluding resources awarded to replace EFC). ***Average financial aid package:*** $13,183 (excluding resources awarded to replace EFC). 1% of all full-time undergraduates had no need and received non-need-based gift aid.

GIFT AID (NEED-BASED) ***Total amount:*** $17,499,856 (51% federal, 45% state, 1% institutional, 3% external sources). ***Receiving aid:*** Freshmen: 61% (1,059); All full-time undergraduates: 52% (3,936). ***Average award:*** Freshmen: $5387; Undergraduates: $4665. ***Scholarships, grants, and awards:*** Federal Pell, FSEOG, state, private, college/university gift aid from institutional funds.

GIFT AID (NON-NEED-BASED) ***Total amount:*** $8,789,327 (97% state, 1% institutional, 2% external sources). ***Receiving aid:*** Freshmen: 31% (528); Undergraduates: 17% (1,282). ***Average award:*** Freshmen: $1182; Undergraduates: $1445. ***Scholarships, grants, and awards by category:*** *Academic Interests/Achievement:* 354 awards ($165,500 total): biological sciences, business, communication, computer science, education, engineering/technologies, English, foreign languages, general academic interests/achievements, health fields, humanities, library science, mathematics, military science, physical sciences, premedicine, social sciences. *Creative Arts/Performance:* 65 awards ($50,000 total): art/fine arts, music, theater/drama. *Special Achievements/Activities:* 80 awards ($65,000 total): community service, general special achievements/activities, hobbies/interests. *Special Characteristics:* 36 awards ($32,200 total): children of public servants, general special characteristics, international students, members of minority groups. ***ROTC:*** Air Force.

LOANS ***Student loans:*** $34,149,454 (79% need-based, 21% non-need-based). 65% of past graduating class borrowed through all loan programs. *Average indebtedness per student:* $16,220. ***Average need-based loan:*** Freshmen: $2419; Undergraduates: $3241. ***Parent loans:*** $34,201,473 (62% need-based, 38% non-need-based). ***Programs:*** Federal Direct (Subsidized and Unsubsidized Stafford, PLUS), FFEL (Subsidized and Unsubsidized Stafford, PLUS), college/university.

WORK-STUDY ***Federal work-study:*** Total amount: $544,920; 265 jobs averaging $2225.

ATHLETIC AWARDS Total amount: $732,867 (42% need-based, 58% non-need-based).

APPLYING FOR FINANCIAL AID ***Required financial aid form:*** FAFSA. ***Financial aid deadline (priority):*** 5/1. ***Notification date:*** Continuous beginning 5/15.

CONTACT Mr. Douglas R. Tanner, Director of Financial Aid, Valdosta State University, 1500 North Patterson Street, Valdosta, GA 31698, 229-333-5935 or toll-free 800-618-1878 Ext. 1. *Fax:* 229-333-5430.

VALLEY CITY STATE UNIVERSITY

Valley City, ND

Tuition & fees (ND res): $5307 **Average undergraduate aid package: $5672**

ABOUT THE INSTITUTION State-supported, coed. Awards: bachelor's degrees. 40 undergraduate majors. Total enrollment: 1,037. Undergraduates: 959. Freshmen: 178. Federal methodology is used as a basis for awarding need-based institutional aid.

UNDERGRADUATE EXPENSES for 2006–07 ***Application fee:*** $35. ***Tuition, state resident:*** full-time $3753; part-time $126 per semester hour. ***Tuition, nonresident:*** full-time $10,021; part-time $335 per semester hour. Full-time tuition and fees vary according to course load, location, program, and reciprocity agreements. Part-time tuition and fees vary according to course load, location, program, and reciprocity agreements. ***College room and board:*** $3716; ***Room only:*** $1436. Room and board charges vary according to board plan and housing facility.

FRESHMAN FINANCIAL AID (Fall 2006, est.) 164 applied for aid; of those 100% were deemed to have need. 100% of freshmen with need received aid; of those 43% had need fully met. ***Average percent of need met:*** 48% (excluding resources awarded to replace EFC). ***Average financial aid package:*** $5525 (excluding resources awarded to replace EFC). 54% of all full-time freshmen had no need and received non-need-based gift aid.

UNDERGRADUATE FINANCIAL AID (Fall 2006, est.) 572 applied for aid; of those 100% were deemed to have need. 83% of undergraduates with need received aid; of those 36% had need fully met. ***Average percent of need met:*** 42% (excluding resources awarded to replace EFC). ***Average financial aid package:*** $5672 (excluding resources awarded to replace EFC). 35% of all full-time undergraduates had no need and received non-need-based gift aid.

GIFT AID (NEED-BASED) ***Total amount:*** $1,043,924 (61% federal, 5% state, 22% institutional, 12% external sources). ***Receiving aid:*** Freshmen: 78% (139); All full-time undergraduates: 54% (357). ***Average award:*** Freshmen: $2857; Undergraduates: $2726. ***Scholarships, grants, and awards:*** Federal Pell, FSEOG, state, private, college/university gift aid from institutional funds.

GIFT AID (NON-NEED-BASED) ***Total amount:*** $192,093 (2% state, 66% institutional, 32% external sources). ***Receiving aid:*** Freshmen: 9% (16); Undergraduates: 8% (56). ***Average award:*** Freshmen: $1614; Undergraduates: $1236. ***Scholarships, grants, and awards by category:*** *Academic Interests/Achievement:* 330 awards ($349,829 total): biological sciences, business, communication, computer science, education, English, general academic interests/achievements, library science, mathematics, physical sciences, social sciences. *Creative Arts/Performance:* 53 awards ($20,908 total): applied art and design, art/fine arts, journalism/publications, music, theater/drama. *Special Achievements/Activities:* 152 awards ($142,975 total): general special achievements/activities. *Special Characteristics:* 23 awards ($34,135 total): children of faculty/staff. ***Tuition waivers:*** Full or partial for children of alumni, employees or children of employees.

LOANS ***Student loans:*** $3,093,575 (62% need-based, 38% non-need-based). 63% of past graduating class borrowed through all loan programs. *Average indebtedness per student:* $15,544. ***Average need-based loan:*** Freshmen: $2491; Undergraduates: $3471. ***Parent loans:*** $88,288 (26% need-based, 74% non-need-based). ***Programs:*** FFEL (Subsidized and Unsubsidized Stafford, PLUS), Perkins, college/university.

WORK-STUDY ***Federal work-study:*** Total amount: $68,202; 64 jobs averaging $1229. ***State or other work-study/employment:*** Total amount: $391,050 (100% non-need-based). 237 part-time jobs averaging $1650.

ATHLETIC AWARDS Total amount: $142,085 (31% need-based, 69% non-need-based).

APPLYING FOR FINANCIAL AID ***Required financial aid form:*** FAFSA. ***Financial aid deadline (priority):*** 3/15. ***Notification date:*** Continuous beginning 2/1. Students must reply within 4 weeks of notification.

CONTACT Betty Kuss Schumacher, Director of Financial Aid, Valley City State University, 101 College Street SW, Valley City, ND 58072, 701-845-7412 or toll-free 800-532-8641 Ext. 37101. *Fax:* 701-845-7410. *E-mail:* betty.schumacher@vcsu.edu.

VALLEY FORGE CHRISTIAN COLLEGE

Phoenixville, PA

Tuition & fees: $12,600 **Average undergraduate aid package: $8067**

ABOUT THE INSTITUTION Independent Assemblies of God, coed. Awards: associate and bachelor's degrees. 6 undergraduate majors. Total enrollment: 925. Undergraduates: 925. Freshmen: 180. Federal methodology is used as a basis for awarding need-based institutional aid.

UNDERGRADUATE EXPENSES for 2007–08 ***Application fee:*** $25. ***Comprehensive fee:*** $19,342 includes full-time tuition ($11,650), mandatory fees ($950), and room and board ($6742). ***College room only:*** $3282. ***Part-time tuition:*** $449 per credit.

FRESHMAN FINANCIAL AID (Fall 2006, est.) 194 applied for aid; of those 91% were deemed to have need. 98% of freshmen with need received aid; of those 8% had need fully met. ***Average percent of need met:*** 48% (excluding resources awarded to replace EFC). ***Average financial aid package:*** $7373 (excluding resources awarded to replace EFC). 39% of all full-time freshmen had no need and received non-need-based gift aid.

UNDERGRADUATE FINANCIAL AID (Fall 2006, est.) 789 applied for aid; of those 89% were deemed to have need. 99% of undergraduates with need received aid; of those 11% had need fully met. ***Average percent of need met:*** 54% (excluding resources awarded to replace EFC). ***Average financial aid package:*** $8067 (excluding resources awarded to replace EFC). 21% of all full-time undergraduates had no need and received non-need-based gift aid.

GIFT AID (NEED-BASED) ***Total amount:*** $3,911,371 (26% federal, 22% state, 39% institutional, 13% external sources). ***Receiving aid:*** Freshmen: 55% (165); All full-time undergraduates: 70% (631). ***Average award:*** Freshmen: $5194; Undergraduates: $5225. ***Scholarships, grants, and awards:*** Federal Pell, FSEOG, state, private, college/university gift aid from institutional funds.

GIFT AID (NON-NEED-BASED) ***Receiving aid:*** Freshmen: 3% (8); Undergraduates: 4% (36). ***Average award:*** Freshmen: $4581; Undergraduates: $6873. ***Scholarships, grants, and awards by category:*** *Academic Interests/Achievement:* 161 awards ($298,836 total): general academic interests/achievements. *Creative Arts/Performance:* 372 awards ($470,075 total): art/fine arts, music. *Special Achievements/Activities:* 404 awards ($356,185 total): general special achievements/activities, leadership. *Special Characteristics:* 238 awards ($324,083 total): children of current students, children of faculty/staff, general special characteristics, married students, relatives of clergy, siblings of current students, spouses of current students.

LOANS ***Student loans:*** $6,695,561 (37% need-based, 63% non-need-based). 91% of past graduating class borrowed through all loan programs. *Average indebtedness per student:* $24,253. ***Average need-based loan:*** Freshmen: $2461; Undergraduates: $3497. ***Parent loans:*** $1,363,900 (100% non-need-based). ***Programs:*** FFEL (Subsidized and Unsubsidized Stafford, PLUS), Perkins.

WORK-STUDY ***Federal work-study:*** Total amount: $70,973; 58 jobs averaging $1224.

APPLYING FOR FINANCIAL AID ***Required financial aid form:*** FAFSA. ***Financial aid deadline (priority):*** 5/1. ***Notification date:*** Continuous beginning 3/1. Students must reply within 3 weeks of notification.

CONTACT Mrs. Evie Meyer, Director of Financial Aid, Valley Forge Christian College, 1401 Charlestown Road, Phoenixville, PA 19460-2399, 610-917-1417 or toll-free 800-432-8322. *Fax:* 610-917-2069. *E-mail:* eemeyer@vfcc.edu.

VALPARAISO UNIVERSITY

Valparaiso, IN

Tuition & fees: $24,000 **Average undergraduate aid package: $18,608**

ABOUT THE INSTITUTION Independent religious, coed. Awards: associate, bachelor's, master's, and first professional degrees and post-bachelor's and post-master's certificates. 86 undergraduate majors. Total enrollment: 3,868. Undergraduates: 2,960. Freshmen: 762. Both federal and institutional methodology are used as a basis for awarding need-based institutional aid.

UNDERGRADUATE EXPENSES for 2006–07 ***Application fee:*** $30. ***Comprehensive fee:*** $30,640 includes full-time tuition ($23,200), mandatory fees ($800), and room and board ($6640). ***College room only:*** $4140. Room and board charges vary according to housing facility and student level. ***Part-time tuition:*** $1100 per credit hour. ***Part-time fees:*** $20 per credit hour. Part-time tuition and fees vary according to course load. ***Payment plans:*** Installment, deferred payment.

FRESHMAN FINANCIAL AID (Fall 2006, est.) 681 applied for aid; of those 80% were deemed to have need. 100% of freshmen with need received aid; of those 29% had need fully met. ***Average percent of need met:*** 89% (excluding resources awarded to replace EFC). ***Average financial aid package:*** $19,817 (excluding resources awarded to replace EFC). 24% of all full-time freshmen had no need and received non-need-based gift aid.

UNDERGRADUATE FINANCIAL AID (Fall 2006, est.) 1,643 applied for aid; of those 85% were deemed to have need. 100% of undergraduates with need received aid; of those 32% had need fully met. ***Average percent of need met:*** 85% (excluding resources awarded to replace EFC). ***Average financial aid package:*** $18,608 (excluding resources awarded to replace EFC). 35% of all full-time undergraduates had no need and received non-need-based gift aid.

GIFT AID (NEED-BASED) ***Total amount:*** $26,200,000 (10% federal, 10% state, 74% institutional, 6% external sources). ***Receiving aid:*** Freshmen: 71% (539); All full-time undergraduates: 66% (1,339). ***Average award:*** Freshmen: $15,728; Undergraduates: $13,418. ***Scholarships, grants, and awards:*** Federal Pell, FSEOG, state, private, college/university gift aid from institutional funds.

GIFT AID (NON-NEED-BASED) ***Total amount:*** $6,340,000 (91% institutional, 9% external sources). ***Receiving aid:*** Freshmen: 25% (189); Undergraduates: 27% (545). ***Average award:*** Freshmen: $9473; Undergraduates: $8138. ***Scholarships, grants, and awards by category:*** *Academic Interests/Achievement:* 1,900 awards ($14,000,000 total): business, engineering/technologies, foreign languages, general academic interests/achievements, health fields, physical sciences, religion/biblical studies. *Creative Arts/Performance:* 200 awards ($210,000 total): art/fine arts, music, performing arts, theater/drama. *Special Achievements/Activities:* 400 awards ($1,155,000 total): general special achievements/activities, religious involvement. *Special Characteristics:* 1,910 awards ($4,935,000 total): children and siblings of alumni, children of faculty/staff, international students, relatives of clergy, religious affiliation. ***Tuition waivers:*** Full or partial for employees or children of employees. ***ROTC:*** Air Force cooperative.

LOANS ***Student loans:*** $14,580,000 (82% need-based, 18% non-need-based). 69% of past graduating class borrowed through all loan programs. *Average indebtedness per student:* $25,524. ***Average need-based loan:*** Freshmen: $4676; Undergraduates: $5377. ***Parent loans:*** $3,300,000 (100% non-need-based). ***Programs:*** Federal Direct (Subsidized and Unsubsidized Stafford, PLUS), Perkins, college/university.

WORK-STUDY ***Federal work-study:*** Total amount: $530,000; 500 jobs averaging $1060. ***State or other work-study/employment:*** Total amount: $1,000,000 (20% need-based, 80% non-need-based). 775 part-time jobs averaging $1032.

ATHLETIC AWARDS Total amount: $1,150,000 (87% need-based, 13% non-need-based).

APPLYING FOR FINANCIAL AID ***Required financial aid form:*** FAFSA. ***Financial aid deadline (priority):*** 3/1. ***Notification date:*** Continuous beginning 3/1.

CONTACT Ms. Phyllis Schroeder, Interim Director of Financial Aid, Valparaiso University, 1700 Chapel Drive, Valparaiso, IN 46383-6493, 219-464-5015 or toll-free 888-GO-VALPO. *Fax:* 219-464-5012. *E-mail:* phyllis.schroeder@valpo.edu.

VANDERBILT UNIVERSITY

Nashville, TN

Tuition & fees: $33,440 **Average undergraduate aid package: $33,896**

ABOUT THE INSTITUTION Independent, coed. Awards: bachelor's, master's, doctoral, and first professional degrees. 56 undergraduate majors. Total enrollment: 11,607. Undergraduates: 6,378. Freshmen: 1,590. Both federal and institutional methodology are used as a basis for awarding need-based institutional aid.

UNDERGRADUATE EXPENSES for 2006–07 ***Application fee:*** $50. ***Comprehensive fee:*** $44,330 includes full-time tuition ($32,620), mandatory fees ($820), and room and board ($10,890). ***College room only:*** $7100. Room and board charges vary according to board plan. ***Payment plans:*** Tuition prepayment, installment.

FRESHMAN FINANCIAL AID (Fall 2006, est.) 840 applied for aid; of those 87% were deemed to have need. 100% of freshmen with need received aid; of those 96% had need fully met. ***Average percent of need met:*** 100% (excluding resources awarded to replace EFC). ***Average financial aid package:*** $34,594 (excluding resources awarded to replace EFC). 13% of all full-time freshmen had no need and received non-need-based gift aid.

UNDERGRADUATE FINANCIAL AID (Fall 2006, est.) 2,839 applied for aid; of those 92% were deemed to have need. 100% of undergraduates with need received aid; of those 95% had need fully met. ***Average percent of need met:*** 99% (excluding resources awarded to replace EFC). ***Average financial aid package:*** $33,896 (excluding resources awarded to replace EFC). 13% of all full-time undergraduates had no need and received non-need-based gift aid.

GIFT AID (NEED-BASED) ***Total amount:*** $80,231,040 (3% federal, 4% state, 90% institutional, 3% external sources). ***Receiving aid:*** Freshmen: 42% (663); All full-time undergraduates: 38% (2,450). ***Average award:*** Freshmen: $27,956; Undergraduates: $27,012. ***Scholarships, grants, and awards:*** Federal Pell, FSEOG, state, private, college/university gift aid from institutional funds.

GIFT AID (NON-NEED-BASED) ***Total amount:*** $16,012,275 (6% state, 90% institutional, 4% external sources). ***Receiving aid:*** Freshmen: 27% (434); Undergraduates: 20% (1,251). ***Average award:*** Freshmen: $13,621; Undergraduates: $17,485. ***Scholarships, grants, and awards by category:*** *Academic Interests/Achievement:* education, engineering/technologies, general academic interests/achievements, humanities. *Creative Arts/Performance:* 52 awards ($344,234 total): journalism/publications, music. *Special Characteristics:* 144 awards ($3,191,412 total): local/state students, members of minority groups. ***Tuition waivers:*** Full or partial for employees or children of employees. ***ROTC:*** Army, Naval, Air Force cooperative.

LOANS ***Student loans:*** $11,852,903 (89% need-based, 11% non-need-based). 38% of past graduating class borrowed through all loan programs. *Average indebtedness per student:* $19,429. ***Average need-based loan:*** Freshmen: $3341; Undergraduates: $4145. ***Parent loans:*** $8,545,978 (50% need-based, 50% non-need-based). ***Programs:*** FFEL (Subsidized and Unsubsidized Stafford, PLUS), Perkins, Federal Nursing, college/university, Undergrad Education Loan.

WORK-STUDY ***Federal work-study:*** Total amount: $1,846,479; jobs available.

ATHLETIC AWARDS Total amount: $7,730,111 (35% need-based, 65% non-need-based).

APPLYING FOR FINANCIAL AID ***Required financial aid forms:*** FAFSA, CSS Financial Aid PROFILE, noncustodial (divorced/separated) parent's statement. ***Financial aid deadline (priority):*** 2/1. ***Notification date:*** 4/1. Students must reply by 5/1.

CONTACT David Mohning, Director of Financial Aid, Vanderbilt University, 2309 West End Avenue, Nashville, TN 37235, 615-322-3591 or toll-free 800-288-0432. *Fax:* 615-343-8512. *E-mail:* finaid@vanderbilt.edu.

VANDERCOOK COLLEGE OF MUSIC

Chicago, IL

Tuition & fees: $17,890 **Average undergraduate aid package: N/A**

ABOUT THE INSTITUTION Independent, coed. Awards: bachelor's and master's degrees. 1 undergraduate major. Total enrollment: 227. Undergraduates: 150. Freshmen: 22. Federal methodology is used as a basis for awarding need-based institutional aid.

UNDERGRADUATE EXPENSES for 2006–07 ***Application fee:*** $35. ***Comprehensive fee:*** $25,940 includes full-time tuition ($17,120), mandatory fees ($770), and room and board ($8050). ***Part-time tuition:*** $590 per credit hour.

GIFT AID (NEED-BASED) ***Total amount:*** $329,813 (38% federal, 51% state, 11% institutional). ***Scholarships, grants, and awards:*** Federal Pell, FSEOG, state, private, college/university gift aid from institutional funds.

GIFT AID (NON-NEED-BASED) ***Total amount:*** $488,759 (1% federal, 29% state, 60% institutional, 10% external sources). ***Scholarships, grants, and awards by category:*** *Academic Interests/Achievement:* education, general academic interests/achievements. *Creative Arts/Performance:* 130 awards ($206,125 total): music. *Special Characteristics:* 1 award ($14,620 total): ethnic background.

LOANS ***Student loans:*** $807,601 (40% need-based, 60% non-need-based). ***Parent loans:*** $361,227 (100% non-need-based). ***Programs:*** FFEL (Subsidized and Unsubsidized Stafford, PLUS).

WORK-STUDY ***Federal work-study:*** Total amount: $3000; 7 jobs averaging $500. ***State or other work-study/employment:*** Total amount: $35,500 (100% non-need-based). 37 part-time jobs averaging $959.

APPLYING FOR FINANCIAL AID ***Required financial aid form:*** FAFSA. ***Financial aid deadline (priority):*** 4/1. ***Notification date:*** 4/1. Students must reply within 2 weeks of notification.

CONTACT Ms. D. Denny, Director of Financial Aid, VanderCook College of Music, 3140 South Federal Street, Chicago, IL 60616-3731, 312-225-6288 Ext. 233 or toll-free 800-448-2655. *Fax:* 312-225-5211. *E-mail:* ddenny@vandercook.edu.

VANGUARD UNIVERSITY OF SOUTHERN CALIFORNIA

Costa Mesa, CA

Tuition & fees: $21,564 **Average undergraduate aid package: $19,883**

ABOUT THE INSTITUTION Independent religious, coed. Awards: bachelor's and master's degrees. 37 undergraduate majors. Total enrollment: 2,146. Undergraduates: 1,854. Freshmen: 396. Federal methodology is used as a basis for awarding need-based institutional aid.

UNDERGRADUATE EXPENSES for 2006–07 ***Application fee:*** $45. ***One-time required fee:*** $70. ***Tuition:*** full-time $21,094; part-time $879 per credit hour. ***Required fees:*** full-time $470; $35 per term part-time. Full-time tuition and fees vary according to course load. Part-time tuition and fees vary according to course load. Room and board charges vary according to board plan and housing facility. ***Payment plan:*** Installment.

FRESHMAN FINANCIAL AID (Fall 2006, est.) 354 applied for aid; of those 76% were deemed to have need. 100% of freshmen with need received aid; of those 11% had need fully met. ***Average percent of need met:*** 73% (excluding resources awarded to replace EFC). ***Average financial aid package:*** $20,573 (excluding resources awarded to replace EFC). 16% of all full-time freshmen had no need and received non-need-based gift aid.

UNDERGRADUATE FINANCIAL AID (Fall 2006, est.) 1,364 applied for aid; of those 75% were deemed to have need. 100% of undergraduates with need received aid; of those 12% had need fully met. ***Average percent of need met:*** 68% (excluding resources awarded to replace EFC). ***Average financial aid package:*** $19,883 (excluding resources awarded to replace EFC). 19% of all full-time undergraduates had no need and received non-need-based gift aid.

GIFT AID (NEED-BASED) ***Total amount:*** $11,466,931 (11% federal, 23% state, 63% institutional, 3% external sources). ***Receiving aid:*** Freshmen: 53% (218); All full-time undergraduates: 54% (792). ***Average award:*** Freshmen: $15,944; Undergraduates: $14,050. ***Scholarships, grants, and awards:*** Federal Pell, FSEOG, state, private, college/university gift aid from institutional funds.

GIFT AID (NON-NEED-BASED) ***Total amount:*** $2,216,383 (95% institutional, 5% external sources). ***Receiving aid:*** Freshmen: 48% (198); Undergraduates: 55% (797). ***Average award:*** Freshmen: $8552; Undergraduates: $7522. ***Scholarships, grants, and awards by category:*** *Academic Interests/Achievement:* 907 awards ($5,231,946 total): general academic interests/achievements. *Creative Arts/Performance:* 259 awards ($660,290 total): debating, music, theater/drama. *Special Characteristics:* 31 awards ($539,357 total): children of faculty/staff. ***Tuition waivers:*** Full or partial for employees or children of employees. ***ROTC:*** Air Force cooperative.

LOANS ***Student loans:*** $7,115,872 (69% need-based, 31% non-need-based). 74% of past graduating class borrowed through all loan programs. *Average indebtedness per student:* $16,979. ***Average need-based loan:*** Freshmen: $3292; Undergraduates: $4099. ***Parent loans:*** $952,193 (84% need-based, 16% non-need-based). ***Programs:*** FFEL (Subsidized and Unsubsidized Stafford, PLUS), Perkins, college/university.

WORK-STUDY ***Federal work-study:*** Total amount: $156,535; 63 jobs averaging $2402. ***State or other work-study/employment:*** Total amount: $100,788 (78% need-based, 22% non-need-based). 32 part-time jobs averaging $3388.

ATHLETIC AWARDS Total amount: $1,624,900 (36% need-based, 64% non-need-based).

APPLYING FOR FINANCIAL AID ***Required financial aid forms:*** FAFSA, state aid form. ***Financial aid deadline:*** 3/2. ***Notification date:*** 3/15. Students must reply within 3 weeks of notification.

CONTACT Amberley Wolf, Director of Undergraduate Admissions, Vanguard University of Southern California, 55 Fair Drive, Costa Mesa, CA 92626-6597, 800-722-6279. *Fax:* 714-966-5471. *E-mail:* admissions@vanguard.edu.

VASSAR COLLEGE

Poughkeepsie, NY

Tuition & fees: $36,030 **Average undergraduate aid package: $27,982**

ABOUT THE INSTITUTION Independent, coed. Awards: bachelor's and master's degrees. 51 undergraduate majors. Total enrollment: 2,424. Undergraduates: 2,423. Freshmen: 668. Both federal and institutional methodology are used as a basis for awarding need-based institutional aid.

UNDERGRADUATE EXPENSES for 2006–07 ***Application fee:*** $60. ***Comprehensive fee:*** $44,160 includes full-time tuition ($35,520), mandatory fees ($510), and room and board ($8130). ***College room only:*** $4310. Room and board charges vary according to board plan and housing facility. ***Part-time tuition:*** $4180 per course. ***Part-time fees:*** $250 per year. Part-time tuition and fees vary according to course load. ***Payment plan:*** Installment.

FRESHMAN FINANCIAL AID (Fall 2006, est.) 422 applied for aid; of those 72% were deemed to have need. 100% of freshmen with need received aid; of those 100% had need fully met. ***Average percent of need met:*** 100% (excluding resources awarded to replace EFC). ***Average financial aid package:*** $27,803 (excluding resources awarded to replace EFC).

UNDERGRADUATE FINANCIAL AID (Fall 2006, est.) 1,489 applied for aid; of those 84% were deemed to have need. 100% of undergraduates with need received aid; of those 100% had need fully met. ***Average percent of need met:*** 100% (excluding resources awarded to replace EFC). ***Average financial aid package:*** $27,982 (excluding resources awarded to replace EFC).

GIFT AID (NEED-BASED) ***Total amount:*** $28,449,345 (4% federal, 2% state, 92% institutional, 2% external sources). ***Receiving aid:*** Freshmen: 46% (302); All full-time undergraduates: 53% (1,228). ***Average award:*** Freshmen: $23,920; Undergraduates: $22,754. ***Scholarships, grants, and awards:*** Federal Pell, FSEOG, state, private, college/university gift aid from institutional funds.

GIFT AID (NON-NEED-BASED) ***Total amount:*** $145,656 (8% federal, 14% state, 78% external sources). ***Tuition waivers:*** Full or partial for employees or children of employees.

LOANS ***Student loans:*** $6,195,608 (62% need-based, 38% non-need-based). 59% of past graduating class borrowed through all loan programs. *Average indebtedness per student:* $19,313. ***Average need-based loan:*** Freshmen: $2283; Undergraduates: $3378. ***Parent loans:*** $4,627,789 (100% non-need-based). ***Programs:*** FFEL (Subsidized and Unsubsidized Stafford, PLUS), Perkins, college/university.

WORK-STUDY ***Federal work-study:*** Total amount: $1,469,557; 798 jobs averaging $1951. ***State or other work-study/employment:*** Total amount: $668,297 (98% need-based, 2% non-need-based). 362 part-time jobs averaging $1920.

APPLYING FOR FINANCIAL AID ***Required financial aid forms:*** FAFSA, institution's own form, CSS Financial Aid PROFILE, state aid form, noncustodial (divorced/separated) parent's statement, business/farm supplement. ***Financial aid deadline:*** 2/1. ***Notification date:*** 3/29. Students must reply by 5/1.

CONTACT Mr. Michael Fraher, Director of Financial Aid, Vassar College, 124 Raymond Avenue, Poughkeepsie, NY 12604, 845-437-5322 or toll-free 800-827-7270. *Fax:* 845-437-5325. *E-mail:* mafraher@vassar.edu.

VAUGHN COLLEGE OF AERONAUTICS AND TECHNOLOGY

Flushing, NY

ABOUT THE INSTITUTION Independent, coed, primarily men. Awards: associate and bachelor's degrees. 9 undergraduate majors. Total enrollment: 1,097. Undergraduates: 1,097. Freshmen: 199.

GIFT AID (NEED-BASED) ***Scholarships, grants, and awards:*** Federal Pell, FSEOG, state, private, college/university gift aid from institutional funds.

WORK-STUDY ***Federal work-study:*** Total amount: $55,000; jobs available. ***State or other work-study/employment:*** Part-time jobs available.

APPLYING FOR FINANCIAL AID ***Required financial aid forms:*** FAFSA, state aid form.

CONTACT Sinu Jacob, Acting Director of Financial Aid, Vaughn College of Aeronautics and Technology, 8601 23rd Avenue, Flushing, NY 11369-1037, 718-429-6600 Ext. 187 or toll-free 800-776-2376 Ext. 145 (in-state).

VENNARD COLLEGE

University Park, IA

CONTACT Office of Financial Aid, Vennard College, PO Box 29, University Park, IA 52595, 641-673-8391 or toll-free 800-686-8391.

VERMONT TECHNICAL COLLEGE

Randolph Center, VT

Tuition & fees (area res): $8704 **Average undergraduate aid package: $9628**

ABOUT THE INSTITUTION State-supported, coed. Awards: associate and bachelor's degrees. 20 undergraduate majors. Total enrollment: 1,454. Undergraduates: 1,454. Freshmen: 253. Federal methodology is used as a basis for awarding need-based institutional aid.

UNDERGRADUATE EXPENSES for 2006–07 ***Application fee:*** $35. ***Tuition, area resident:*** full-time $8184. ***Tuition, state resident:*** full-time $12,264; part-time $341 per credit. ***Tuition, nonresident:*** full-time $15,600; part-time $650 per credit. Full-time tuition and fees vary according to course load and program. Part-time tuition and fees vary according to program. ***College room and board:*** $6942; ***Room only:*** $4134. Room and board charges vary according to board plan. ***Payment plan:*** Installment.

FRESHMAN FINANCIAL AID (Fall 2006, est.) 218 applied for aid; of those 77% were deemed to have need. 100% of freshmen with need received aid; of those 21% had need fully met. ***Average percent of need met:*** 66% (excluding resources awarded to replace EFC). ***Average financial aid package:*** $9238 (excluding resources awarded to replace EFC). 2% of all full-time freshmen had no need and received non-need-based gift aid.

UNDERGRADUATE FINANCIAL AID (Fall 2006, est.) 845 applied for aid; of those 86% were deemed to have need. 99% of undergraduates with need received aid; of those 15% had need fully met. ***Average percent of need met:*** 67% (excluding resources awarded to replace EFC). ***Average financial aid package:*** $9628 (excluding resources awarded to replace EFC). 3% of all full-time undergraduates had no need and received non-need-based gift aid.

GIFT AID (NEED-BASED) ***Total amount:*** $3,059,316 (39% federal, 31% state, 15% institutional, 15% external sources). ***Receiving aid:*** Freshmen: 53% (132); All full-time undergraduates: 53% (549). ***Average award:*** Freshmen: $5006; Undergraduates: $4847. ***Scholarships, grants, and awards:*** Federal Pell, FSEOG, state, private, college/university gift aid from institutional funds.

GIFT AID (NON-NEED-BASED) ***Total amount:*** $297,722 (61% institutional, 39% external sources). ***Receiving aid:*** Freshmen: 2% (6); Undergraduates: 2% (19). ***Average award:*** Freshmen: $6408; Undergraduates: $5257. ***Scholarships, grants, and awards by category:*** *Academic Interests/Achievement:* 24 awards ($132,490 total): general academic interests/achievements. ***Tuition waivers:*** Full or partial for employees or children of employees. ***ROTC:*** Army cooperative.

LOANS ***Student loans:*** $5,954,440 (83% need-based, 17% non-need-based). 90% of past graduating class borrowed through all loan programs. *Average indebtedness per student:* $25,456. ***Average need-based loan:*** Freshmen: $2648; Undergraduates: $3036. ***Parent loans:*** $2,337,287 (60% need-based, 40% non-need-based). ***Programs:*** Federal Direct (Subsidized and Unsubsidized Stafford, PLUS), FFEL (Subsidized and Unsubsidized Stafford, PLUS), Perkins.

WORK-STUDY ***Federal work-study:*** Total amount: $155,711; 154 jobs averaging $1010. ***State or other work-study/employment:*** Part-time jobs available.

APPLYING FOR FINANCIAL AID ***Required financial aid forms:*** FAFSA, state aid form. ***Financial aid deadline (priority):*** 3/1. ***Notification date:*** 4/1. Students must reply within 2 weeks of notification.

CONTACT Catherine R. McCullough, Director of Financial Aid, Vermont Technical College, PO Box 500, Randolph Center, VT 05061-0500, 802-728-1248 or toll-free 800-442-VTC1. *Fax:* 802-728-1390.

VILLA JULIE COLLEGE

Stevenson, MD

Tuition & fees: $16,770 **Average undergraduate aid package: $12,883**

ABOUT THE INSTITUTION Independent, coed. Awards: associate, bachelor's, and master's degrees. 50 undergraduate majors. Total enrollment: 3,123. Undergraduates: 2,927. Freshmen: 648. Institutional methodology is used as a basis for awarding need-based institutional aid.

UNDERGRADUATE EXPENSES for 2006–07 ***Application fee:*** $25. ***Comprehensive fee:*** $25,958 includes full-time tuition ($15,700), mandatory fees ($1070), and room and board ($9188). ***College room only:*** $6188. Room and board charges vary according to board plan and housing facility. ***Part-time tuition:*** $425 per credit. ***Part-time fees:*** $75 per term. ***Payment plans:*** Installment, deferred payment.

FRESHMAN FINANCIAL AID (Fall 2006, est.) 523 applied for aid; of those 79% were deemed to have need. 100% of freshmen with need received aid; of those 31% had need fully met. ***Average percent of need met:*** 75% (excluding resources awarded to replace EFC). ***Average financial aid package:*** $14,046 (excluding resources awarded to replace EFC). 27% of all full-time freshmen had no need and received non-need-based gift aid.

UNDERGRADUATE FINANCIAL AID (Fall 2006, est.) 1,768 applied for aid; of those 80% were deemed to have need. 100% of undergraduates with need received aid; of those 29% had need fully met. ***Average percent of need met:*** 74% (excluding resources awarded to replace EFC). ***Average financial aid package:*** $12,883 (excluding resources awarded to replace EFC). 26% of all full-time undergraduates had no need and received non-need-based gift aid.

GIFT AID (NEED-BASED) ***Total amount:*** $13,165,125 (12% federal, 26% state, 59% institutional, 3% external sources). ***Receiving aid:*** Freshmen: 63% (405); All full-time undergraduates: 56% (1,344). ***Average award:*** Freshmen: $12,227; Undergraduates: $10,319. ***Scholarships, grants, and awards:*** Federal Pell, FSEOG, state, private, college/university gift aid from institutional funds.

GIFT AID (NON-NEED-BASED) ***Total amount:*** $5,320,957 (5% state, 88% institutional, 7% external sources). ***Receiving aid:*** Freshmen: 14% (91); Undergraduates: 10% (243). ***Average award:*** Freshmen: $7802; Undergraduates: $6476. ***Scholarships, grants, and awards by category:*** *Academic Interests/Achievement:* business, computer science, general academic interests/achievements. ***Tuition waivers:*** Full or partial for employees or children of employees. ***ROTC:*** Army cooperative.

LOANS ***Student loans:*** $9,732,250 (48% need-based, 52% non-need-based). 68% of past graduating class borrowed through all loan programs. *Average indebtedness per student:* $15,580. ***Average need-based loan:*** Freshmen: $2513; Undergraduates: $3713. ***Parent loans:*** $18,665,323 (100% need-based). ***Programs:*** FFEL (Subsidized and Unsubsidized Stafford, PLUS), Perkins.

WORK-STUDY ***Federal work-study:*** Total amount: $288,529.

APPLYING FOR FINANCIAL AID ***Required financial aid form:*** FAFSA. ***Financial aid deadline (priority):*** 2/15. ***Notification date:*** Continuous beginning 3/15. Students must reply by 5/1 or within 2 weeks of notification.

CONTACT Ms. Debra Bottomms, Director of Financial Aid, Villa Julie College, 1525 Greenspring Valley Road, Stevenson, MD 21153, 443-334-2559 or toll-free 877-468-6852 (in-state), 877-468-3852 (out-of-state). *Fax:* 443-334-2600. *E-mail:* fa-deb1@mail.vjc.edu.

VILLANOVA UNIVERSITY

Villanova, PA

ABOUT THE INSTITUTION Independent Roman Catholic, coed. Awards: associate, bachelor's, master's, doctoral, and first professional degrees. 44 undergraduate majors. Total enrollment: 10,456. Undergraduates: 7,254. Freshmen: 1,638.

GIFT AID (NEED-BASED) ***Scholarships, grants, and awards:*** Federal Pell, FSEOG, state, private, college/university gift aid from institutional funds, endowed and restricted grants.

GIFT AID (NON-NEED-BASED) ***Scholarships, grants, and awards by category:*** *Academic Interests/Achievement:* general academic interests/achievements, international studies, military science. *Special Achievements/Activities:* general special achievements/activities. *Special Characteristics:* children of educators, children of faculty/staff, general special characteristics, members of minority groups, religious affiliation.

LOANS ***Programs:*** FFEL (Subsidized and Unsubsidized Stafford, PLUS), Perkins, Federal Nursing, Villanova Loan.

WORK-STUDY ***Federal work-study:*** Total amount: $3,342,674; 1,586 jobs averaging $2108. ***State or other work-study/employment:*** Total amount: $16,000 (100% need-based). 8 part-time jobs averaging $2000.

APPLYING FOR FINANCIAL AID ***Required financial aid forms:*** FAFSA, institution's own form, W-2 forms, federal income tax forms.

CONTACT Bonnie Lee Behm, Director of Financial Assistance, Villanova University, 800 Lancaster Avenue, Villanova, PA 19085-1699, 610-519-4010. *Fax:* 610-519-7599.

VIRGINIA COLLEGE AT BIRMINGHAM

Birmingham, AL

CONTACT Vice President, Campus Administration, Virginia College at Birmingham, 65 Bagby Drive, Birmingham, AL 35209, 205-802-1200. *Fax:* 205-271-8273.

VIRGINIA COMMONWEALTH UNIVERSITY

Richmond, VA

Tuition & fees (VA res): $4227 **Average undergraduate aid package: $7246**

ABOUT THE INSTITUTION State-supported, coed. Awards: bachelor's, master's, doctoral, and first professional degrees and post-bachelor's, post-master's, and first professional certificates. 55 undergraduate majors. Total enrollment: 30,381. Undergraduates: 21,260. Freshmen: 3,540. Federal methodology is used as a basis for awarding need-based institutional aid.

UNDERGRADUATE EXPENSES for 2006–07 ***Application fee:*** $30. ***Tuition, state resident:*** full-time $4227; part-time $176.15 per credit. ***Tuition, nonresident:*** full-time $15,904; part-time $663 per credit. ***Required fees:*** $70.65 per credit. ***College room and board:*** $7473; ***Room only:*** $4273. Room and board charges vary according to board plan. ***Payment plan:*** Installment.

FRESHMAN FINANCIAL AID (Fall 2005) 2197 applied for aid; of those 64% were deemed to have need. 100% of freshmen with need received aid; of those 4% had need fully met. ***Average percent of need met:*** 49% (excluding resources awarded to replace EFC). ***Average financial aid package:*** $7285 (excluding resources awarded to replace EFC). 13% of all full-time freshmen had no need and received non-need-based gift aid.

UNDERGRADUATE FINANCIAL AID (Fall 2005) 10,966 applied for aid; of those 67% were deemed to have need. 100% of undergraduates with need received aid; of those 8% had need fully met. ***Average percent of need met:*** 53% (excluding resources awarded to replace EFC). ***Average financial aid package:*** $7246 (excluding resources awarded to replace EFC). 9% of all full-time undergraduates had no need and received non-need-based gift aid.

GIFT AID (NEED-BASED) ***Total amount:*** $24,047,168 (50% federal, 46% state, 4% institutional). ***Receiving aid:*** Freshmen: 32% (1,131); All full-time undergraduates: 32% (5,325). ***Average award:*** Freshmen: $4431; Undergraduates: $4165. ***Scholarships, grants, and awards:*** Federal Pell, FSEOG, state, private, college/university gift aid from institutional funds, Federal Nursing.

GIFT AID (NON-NEED-BASED) ***Total amount:*** $13,136,745 (13% federal, 1% state, 26% institutional, 60% external sources). ***Receiving aid:*** Freshmen: 11% (379); Undergraduates: 7% (1,260). ***Average award:*** Freshmen: $3927; Undergraduates: $4874. ***Scholarships, grants, and awards by category:*** *Academic Interests/Achievement:* business, communication, computer science, education, engineering/technologies, foreign languages, general academic interests/achievements, health fields, mathematics, military science. *Creative Arts/Performance:* applied art and design, art/fine arts, dance, music, performing arts, theater/drama. *Special Characteristics:* children of union members/company employees, general special characteristics, veterans' children. ***Tuition waivers:*** Full or partial for employees or children of employees, senior citizens. ***ROTC:*** Army cooperative.

LOANS ***Student loans:*** $56,608,789 (47% need-based, 53% non-need-based). 68% of past graduating class borrowed through all loan programs. *Average indebtedness per student:* $20,737. ***Average need-based loan:*** Freshmen: $2949; Undergraduates: $3737. ***Parent loans:*** $10,062,556 (100% non-need-based). ***Programs:*** Federal Direct (Subsidized and Unsubsidized Stafford, PLUS), Perkins, Federal Nursing, college/university.

WORK-STUDY ***Federal work-study:*** Total amount: $1,055,503; 666 jobs averaging $2658.

ATHLETIC AWARDS Total amount: $1,197,718 (100% non-need-based).

APPLYING FOR FINANCIAL AID ***Required financial aid form:*** FAFSA. ***Notification date:*** 3/15. Students must reply by 5/1 or within 2 weeks of notification.

CONTACT Financial Aid Office, Virginia Commonwealth University, 901 West Franklin Street, Richmond, VA 23284-9005, 804-828-6669 or toll-free 800-841-3638. *Fax:* 804-828-6186. *E-mail:* faidmail@vcu.edu.

VIRGINIA INTERMONT COLLEGE

Bristol, VA

Tuition & fees: $17,845 **Average undergraduate aid package: $10,251**

ABOUT THE INSTITUTION Independent religious, coed. Awards: associate and bachelor's degrees. 41 undergraduate majors. Total enrollment: 916. Undergraduates: 916. Freshmen: 85. Federal methodology is used as a basis for awarding need-based institutional aid.

UNDERGRADUATE EXPENSES for 2006–07 ***Application fee:*** $25. ***Comprehensive fee:*** $23,940 includes full-time tuition ($16,895), mandatory fees ($950), and room and board ($6095). ***College room only:*** $2900. Full-time tuition and fees vary according to class time and program. Room and board charges vary according to housing facility. ***Part-time tuition:*** $220 per credit. ***Part-time fees:*** $50 per credit. Part-time tuition and fees vary according to class time, course level, course load, and program. ***Payment plan:*** Installment.

FRESHMAN FINANCIAL AID (Fall 2005) 144 applied for aid; of those 83% were deemed to have need. 100% of freshmen with need received aid; of those 10% had need fully met. ***Average percent of need met:*** 55% (excluding resources awarded to replace EFC). ***Average financial aid package:*** $11,514 (excluding resources awarded to replace EFC). 24% of all full-time freshmen had no need and received non-need-based gift aid.

UNDERGRADUATE FINANCIAL AID (Fall 2005) 803 applied for aid; of those 92% were deemed to have need. 100% of undergraduates with need received aid; of those 9% had need fully met. ***Average percent of need met:*** 54% (excluding resources awarded to replace EFC). ***Average financial aid package:*** $10,251 (excluding resources awarded to replace EFC). 16% of all full-time undergraduates had no need and received non-need-based gift aid.

GIFT AID (NEED-BASED) ***Total amount:*** $4,113,893 (28% federal, 22% state, 43% institutional, 7% external sources). ***Receiving aid:*** Freshmen: 9% (17); All full-time undergraduates: 73% (689). ***Average award:*** Freshmen: $9637; Undergraduates: $7543. ***Scholarships, grants, and awards:*** Federal Pell, FSEOG, state, private, college/university gift aid from institutional funds.

GIFT AID (NON-NEED-BASED) ***Total amount:*** $859,945 (15% state, 82% institutional, 3% external sources). ***Receiving aid:*** Freshmen: 5% (9); Undergraduates: 4% (39). ***Average award:*** Freshmen: $7703; Undergraduates: $7875. ***Scholarships, grants, and awards by category:*** *Academic Interests/Achievement:* general academic interests/achievements. *Creative Arts/Performance:* applied art and design, art/fine arts, dance, general creative arts/performance, music, performing arts, theater/drama. *Special Achievements/Activities:* cheerleading/drum major. *Special Characteristics:* children and siblings of alumni, children of current students, children of faculty/staff, first-generation college students, members of minority groups, religious affiliation, siblings of current students. ***Tuition waivers:*** Full or partial for employees or children of employees, senior citizens.

LOANS ***Student loans:*** $4,696,600 (86% need-based, 14% non-need-based). 79% of past graduating class borrowed through all loan programs. *Average indebtedness per student:* $20,051. ***Average need-based loan:*** Freshmen: $2396; Undergraduates: $3556. ***Parent loans:*** $1,351,907 (54% need-based, 46% non-need-based). ***Programs:*** FFEL (Subsidized and Unsubsidized Stafford, PLUS), Perkins, alternative loans.

WORK-STUDY ***Federal work-study:*** Total amount: $121,878; 220 jobs averaging $750.

ATHLETIC AWARDS Total amount: $2,140,379 (48% need-based, 52% non-need-based).

APPLYING FOR FINANCIAL AID ***Required financial aid forms:*** FAFSA, state aid form. ***Financial aid deadline (priority):*** 3/1. ***Notification date:*** Continuous beginning 2/15. Students must reply within 3 weeks of notification.

CONTACT Ms. Denise Posey, Director of Financial Aid, Virginia Intermont College, 1013 Moore Street, Bristol, VA 24201-4298, 276-466-7872 or toll-free 800-451-1842. *Fax:* 276-669-5763.

VIRGINIA MILITARY INSTITUTE

Lexington, VA

Tuition & fees (VA res): $7609 Average undergraduate aid package: $13,960

ABOUT THE INSTITUTION State-supported, coed, primarily men. Awards: bachelor's degrees. 14 undergraduate majors. Total enrollment: 1,362. Undergraduates: 1,362. Freshmen: 363. Federal methodology is used as a basis for awarding need-based institutional aid.

UNDERGRADUATE EXPENSES for 2006–07 ***Application fee:*** $35. ***One-time required fee:*** $1864. ***Tuition, state resident:*** full-time $4776. ***Tuition, nonresident:*** full-time $19,585. ***College room and board:*** $5930. ***Payment plan:*** Installment.

FRESHMAN FINANCIAL AID (Fall 2005) 240 applied for aid; of those 70% were deemed to have need. 99% of freshmen with need received aid; of those 35% had need fully met. ***Average percent of need met:*** 90% (excluding resources awarded to replace EFC). ***Average financial aid package:*** $12,749 (excluding resources awarded to replace EFC). 17% of all full-time freshmen had no need and received non-need-based gift aid.

UNDERGRADUATE FINANCIAL AID (Fall 2005) 769 applied for aid; of those 76% were deemed to have need. 99% of undergraduates with need received aid; of those 55% had need fully met. ***Average percent of need met:*** 90% (excluding resources awarded to replace EFC). ***Average financial aid package:*** $13,960 (excluding resources awarded to replace EFC). 20% of all full-time undergraduates had no need and received non-need-based gift aid.

GIFT AID (NEED-BASED) ***Total amount:*** $4,467,228 (12% federal, 15% state, 68% institutional, 5% external sources). ***Receiving aid:*** Freshmen: 36% (142); All full-time undergraduates: 32% (454). ***Average award:*** Freshmen: $10,235; Undergraduates: $16,821. ***Scholarships, grants, and awards:*** Federal Pell, FSEOG, state, private, college/university gift aid from institutional funds.

GIFT AID (NON-NEED-BASED) ***Total amount:*** $5,637,675 (71% federal, 19% institutional, 10% external sources). ***Receiving aid:*** Freshmen: 5% (20); Undergraduates: 9% (124). ***Average award:*** Freshmen: $2789; Undergraduates: $4667. ***Scholarships, grants, and awards by category:*** *Academic Interests/Achievement:* 125 awards ($900,000 total): biological sciences, business, computer science, engineering/technologies, English, general academic interests/achievements, international studies, mathematics, military science, premedicine. *Creative Arts/Performance:* 12 awards ($6000 total): music. *Special Achievements/Activities:* 15 awards ($75,000 total): general special achievements/activities, leadership. *Special Characteristics:* 300 awards ($1,250,000 total): children and siblings of alumni, children of faculty/staff, general special characteristics, local/state students, out-of-state students. ***ROTC:*** Army, Naval, Air Force.

LOANS ***Student loans:*** $3,050,131 (39% need-based, 61% non-need-based). 45% of past graduating class borrowed through all loan programs. *Average indebtedness per student:* $11,754. ***Average need-based loan:*** Freshmen: $3392; Undergraduates: $3676. ***Parent loans:*** $1,809,175 (100% non-need-based). ***Programs:*** Federal Direct (Subsidized and Unsubsidized Stafford, PLUS), Perkins.

WORK-STUDY ***Federal work-study:*** Total amount: $36,650; 42 jobs averaging $873.

ATHLETIC AWARDS Total amount: $1,352,060 (6% need-based, 94% non-need-based).

APPLYING FOR FINANCIAL AID ***Required financial aid forms:*** FAFSA, institution's own form. ***Financial aid deadline (priority):*** 3/1. ***Notification date:*** Continuous beginning 3/15. Students must reply by 5/1.

CONTACT Col. Timothy P. Golden, Director of Financial Aid, Virginia Military Institute, 306 Carroll Hall, Lexington, VA 24450, 540-464-7208 or toll-free 800-767-4207. *Fax:* 540-464-7629. *E-mail:* goldentp@vmi.edu.

VIRGINIA POLYTECHNIC INSTITUTE AND STATE UNIVERSITY

Blacksburg, VA

Tuition & fees (VA res): $6973 Average undergraduate aid package: $8171

ABOUT THE INSTITUTION State-supported, coed. Awards: associate, bachelor's, master's, doctoral, and first professional degrees. 66 undergraduate majors. Total enrollment: 28,470. Undergraduates: 21,997. Freshmen: 5,085. Institutional methodology is used as a basis for awarding need-based institutional aid.

UNDERGRADUATE EXPENSES for 2006–07 ***Application fee:*** $50. ***Tuition, state resident:*** full-time $5450; part-time $227 per credit hour. ***Tuition, nonresident:*** full-time $17,406; part-time $725.25 per credit hour. ***Required fees:*** full-time $1523; $255.50 per term part-time. ***College room and board:*** $4700; ***Room only:*** $2578. Room and board charges vary according to board plan and location. ***Payment plan:*** Installment.

FRESHMAN FINANCIAL AID (Fall 2005) 3678 applied for aid; of those 63% were deemed to have need. 80% of freshmen with need received aid; of those 14% had need fully met. ***Average percent of need met:*** 60% (excluding resources awarded to replace EFC). ***Average financial aid package:*** $8786 (excluding resources awarded to replace EFC). 9% of all full-time freshmen had no need and received non-need-based gift aid.

UNDERGRADUATE FINANCIAL AID (Fall 2005) 13,146 applied for aid; of those 63% were deemed to have need. 90% of undergraduates with need received aid; of those 21% had need fully met. ***Average percent of need met:*** 68% (excluding resources awarded to replace EFC). ***Average financial aid package:*** $8171 (excluding resources awarded to replace EFC). 4% of all full-time undergraduates had no need and received non-need-based gift aid.

GIFT AID (NON-NEED-BASED) ***Total amount:*** $17,815,363 (100% external sources). ***Receiving aid:*** Freshmen: 9% (457); Undergraduates: 6% (1,271). ***Average award:*** Freshmen: $2253; Undergraduates: $2133. ***Scholarships, grants, and awards by category:*** *Academic Interests/Achievement:* agriculture, architecture, area/ethnic studies, biological sciences, business, communication, computer science, education, engineering/technologies, English, foreign languages, general academic interests/achievements, health fields, home economics, humanities, international studies, mathematics, military science, physical sciences, premedicine, religion/biblical studies, social sciences. *Creative Arts/Performance:* applied art and design, art/fine arts, cinema/film/broadcasting, creative writing, journalism/publications, music, performing arts, theater/drama. *Special Achievements/Activities:* cheerleading/drum major, community service, general special achievements/activities, leadership, memberships, religious involvement. *Special Characteristics:* children of faculty/staff, first-generation college students, local/state students, members of minority groups, out-of-state students, twins, veterans' children. ***Tuition waivers:*** Full or partial for senior citizens. ***ROTC:*** Army, Naval, Air Force.

LOANS ***Student loans:*** $54,796,031 (45% need-based, 55% non-need-based). 52% of past graduating class borrowed through all loan programs. *Average indebtedness per student:* $19,807. ***Average need-based loan:*** Freshmen: $3363; Undergraduates: $3899. ***Parent loans:*** $21,048,117 (100% non-need-based).

WORK-STUDY ***Federal work-study:*** Total amount: $923,578; 829 jobs averaging $1114. ***State or other work-study/employment:*** Total amount: $6,600,899 (100% non-need-based). 4,268 part-time jobs averaging $1547.

ATHLETIC AWARDS Total amount: $4,916,012 (100% non-need-based).

APPLYING FOR FINANCIAL AID ***Financial aid deadline (priority):*** 3/11. ***Notification date:*** Continuous beginning 3/30. Students must reply by 5/1 or within 4 weeks of notification.

CONTACT Dr. Barry Simmons, Director, Virginia Polytechnic Institute and State University, 300 Student Service Building, Virginia Tech, Blacksburg, VA 24061, 540-231-5179. *Fax:* 540-231-9139. *E-mail:* simmonsb@vt.edu.

VIRGINIA STATE UNIVERSITY

Petersburg, VA

Tuition & fees (VA res): $5440 Average undergraduate aid package: $9678

ABOUT THE INSTITUTION State-supported, coed. Awards: associate, bachelor's, master's, and doctoral degrees and post-master's certificates. 33 undergraduate majors. Total enrollment: 4,872. Undergraduates: 4,306. Freshmen: 827. Federal methodology is used as a basis for awarding need-based institutional aid.

UNDERGRADUATE EXPENSES for 2006–07 ***Application fee:*** $25. ***Tuition, state resident:*** full-time $3007; part-time $181 per semester hour. ***Tuition, nonresident:*** full-time $10,079; part-time $417 per semester hour. Full-time tuition and fees vary according to course load. Part-time tuition and fees vary according to course load. ***College room and board:*** $6884; ***Room only:*** $4047. Room and board charges vary according to housing facility. ***Payment plan:*** Installment.

FRESHMAN FINANCIAL AID (Fall 2005) 935 applied for aid; of those 90% were deemed to have need. 100% of freshmen with need received aid; of those 30% had need fully met. ***Average percent of need met:*** 70% (excluding resources awarded to replace EFC). ***Average financial aid package:*** $8452 (excluding resources awarded to replace EFC). 15% of all full-time freshmen had no need and received non-need-based gift aid.

UNDERGRADUATE FINANCIAL AID (Fall 2005) 4,048 applied for aid; of those 90% were deemed to have need. 100% of undergraduates with need received aid; of those 15% had need fully met. ***Average percent of need met:*** 68% (excluding resources awarded to replace EFC). ***Average financial aid package:*** $9678 (excluding resources awarded to replace EFC). 10% of all full-time undergraduates had no need and received non-need-based gift aid.

GIFT AID (NEED-BASED) ***Total amount:*** $12,091,273 (63% federal, 29% state, 8% institutional). ***Receiving aid:*** Freshmen: 63% (631); All full-time undergraduates: 63% (2,732). ***Average award:*** Freshmen: $4626; Undergraduates: $4500. ***Scholarships, grants, and awards:*** Federal Pell, FSEOG, state, private, college/university gift aid from institutional funds.

GIFT AID (NON-NEED-BASED) ***Total amount:*** $3,694,380 (5% federal, 28% state, 44% institutional, 23% external sources). ***Receiving aid:*** Freshmen: 21% (208); Undergraduates: 19% (819). ***Scholarships, grants, and awards by category:*** *Academic Interests/Achievement:* 500 awards ($1500 total): agriculture, architecture, area/ethnic studies, biological sciences, business, communication, computer science, education, engineering/technologies, English, general academic interests/achievements, health fields, home economics, humanities, mathematics, military science, physical sciences, premedicine, social sciences. *Creative Arts/Performance:* 100 awards ($1500 total): applied art and design, art/fine arts, dance, music, performing arts. *Special Achievements/Activities:* cheerleading/drum major, community service, hobbies/interests, leadership, religious involvement. ***Tuition waivers:*** Full or partial for senior citizens. ***ROTC:*** Army.

LOANS ***Student loans:*** $24,551,132 (48% need-based, 52% non-need-based). 90% of past graduating class borrowed through all loan programs. *Average indebtedness per student:* $28,250. ***Average need-based loan:*** Freshmen: $2500; Undergraduates: $5925. ***Parent loans:*** $5,201,136 (100% non-need-based). ***Programs:*** FFEL (Subsidized and Unsubsidized Stafford, PLUS), Perkins, college/university.

WORK-STUDY ***Federal work-study:*** Total amount: $537,863; 400 jobs averaging $2000.

ATHLETIC AWARDS Total amount: $521,948 (100% non-need-based).

APPLYING FOR FINANCIAL AID ***Required financial aid forms:*** FAFSA, institution's own form. ***Financial aid deadline (priority):*** 3/31. ***Notification date:*** Continuous beginning 4/1. Students must reply within 2 weeks of notification.

CONTACT Henry DeBose, Director, Virginia State University, PO Box 9031, Petersburg, VA 23806-2096, 804-524-5992 or toll-free 800-871-7611. *Fax:* 804-524-6818. *E-mail:* hedebose@vsu.edu.

VIRGINIA UNION UNIVERSITY

Richmond, VA

Tuition & fees: N/R **Average undergraduate aid package: $14,661**

ABOUT THE INSTITUTION Independent Baptist, coed. Awards: bachelor's, master's, doctoral, and first professional degrees. 22 undergraduate majors. Total enrollment: 1,700. Undergraduates: 1,344. Freshmen: 341. Federal methodology is used as a basis for awarding need-based institutional aid.

FRESHMAN FINANCIAL AID (Fall 2006, est.) 318 applied for aid; of those 88% were deemed to have need. 100% of freshmen with need received aid; of those 34% had need fully met. ***Average percent of need met:*** 81% (excluding resources awarded to replace EFC). ***Average financial aid package:*** $15,174 (excluding resources awarded to replace EFC). 1% of all full-time freshmen had no need and received non-need-based gift aid.

UNDERGRADUATE FINANCIAL AID (Fall 2006, est.) 1,048 applied for aid. of those 27% had need fully met. ***Average percent of need met:*** 67% (excluding resources awarded to replace EFC). ***Average financial aid package:*** $14,661 (excluding resources awarded to replace EFC). 1% of all full-time undergraduates had no need and received non-need-based gift aid.

GIFT AID (NEED-BASED) ***Receiving aid:*** Freshmen: 54% (176); All full-time undergraduates: 52% (618). ***Average award:*** Freshmen: $3766; Undergraduates: $3857. ***Scholarships, grants, and awards:*** Federal Pell, FSEOG, state, private, college/university gift aid from institutional funds.

GIFT AID (NON-NEED-BASED) ***Receiving aid:*** Freshmen: 58% (187); Undergraduates: 51% (611). ***Average award:*** Freshmen: $5483; Undergraduates: $5179. ***Scholarships, grants, and awards by category:*** *Academic Interests/Achievement:* 114 awards ($818,306 total): general academic interests/achievements. ***Tuition waivers:*** Full or partial for employees or children of employees. ***ROTC:*** Army cooperative.

LOANS ***Student loans:*** 98% of past graduating class borrowed through all loan programs. *Average indebtedness per student:* $17,568. ***Average need-based loan:*** Freshmen: $2669; Undergraduates: $3770. ***Programs:*** Federal Direct (Subsidized and Unsubsidized Stafford), FFEL (PLUS), Perkins.

WORK-STUDY ***Federal work-study:*** 260 jobs averaging $1678.

APPLYING FOR FINANCIAL AID ***Required financial aid forms:*** FAFSA, state aid form. ***Financial aid deadline (priority):*** 5/1. ***Notification date:*** Continuous. Students must reply within 2 weeks of notification.

CONTACT Mrs. Phenie Golatt, Director of Financial Aid, Virginia Union University, 1500 North Lombardy Street, Richmond, VA 23220-1170, 804-257-5882 or toll-free 800-368-3227 (out-of-state). *E-mail:* pgolatt@vuu.edu.

VIRGINIA UNIVERSITY OF LYNCHBURG

Lynchburg, VA

CONTACT Financial Aid Office, Virginia University of Lynchburg, 2058 Garfield Avenue, Lynchburg, VA 24501-6417, 804-528-5276.

VIRGINIA WESLEYAN COLLEGE

Norfolk, VA

Tuition & fees: $23,136 **Average undergraduate aid package: $16,496**

ABOUT THE INSTITUTION Independent United Methodist, coed. Awards: bachelor's degrees. 44 undergraduate majors. Total enrollment: 1,414. Undergraduates: 1,414. Freshmen: 371. Federal methodology is used as a basis for awarding need-based institutional aid.

UNDERGRADUATE EXPENSES for 2006–07 ***Application fee:*** $40. ***Comprehensive fee:*** $29,986 includes full-time tuition ($22,976), mandatory fees ($160), and room and board ($6850). Full-time tuition and fees vary according to class time. Room and board charges vary according to board plan and housing facility. ***Part-time tuition:*** $957 per semester hour. Part-time tuition and fees vary according to class time. ***Payment plans:*** Installment, deferred payment.

FRESHMAN FINANCIAL AID (Fall 2006, est.) 254 applied for aid; of those 100% were deemed to have need. 100% of freshmen with need received aid; of those 3% had need fully met. ***Average percent of need met:*** 69% (excluding resources awarded to replace EFC). ***Average financial aid package:*** $17,594 (excluding resources awarded to replace EFC). 25% of all full-time freshmen had no need and received non-need-based gift aid.

UNDERGRADUATE FINANCIAL AID (Fall 2006, est.) 732 applied for aid; of those 100% were deemed to have need. 100% of undergraduates with need received aid; of those 5% had need fully met. ***Average percent of need met:*** 68% (excluding resources awarded to replace EFC). ***Average financial aid package:*** $16,496 (excluding resources awarded to replace EFC). 26% of all full-time undergraduates had no need and received non-need-based gift aid.

GIFT AID (NEED-BASED) ***Total amount:*** $1,185,208 (87% federal, 7% state, 6% institutional). ***Receiving aid:*** Freshmen: 27% (102); All full-time undergraduates: 26% (308). ***Average award:*** Freshmen: $1825; Undergraduates: $1856. ***Scholarships, grants, and awards:*** Federal Pell, FSEOG, state, private, college/university gift aid from institutional funds, United Negro College Fund.

GIFT AID (NON-NEED-BASED) ***Total amount:*** $11,065,911 (19% state, 78% institutional, 3% external sources). ***Receiving aid:*** Freshmen: 68% (254); Undergraduates: 62% (728). ***Average award:*** Freshmen: $8566; Undergraduates: $7151. ***Scholarships, grants, and awards by category:*** *Academic Interests/Achievement:* general academic interests/achievements. *Creative Arts/Performance:* music. *Special Achievements/Activities:* leadership, religious involvement. *Special Characteristics:* children of faculty/staff, relatives of clergy, religious affiliation. ***Tuition waivers:*** Full or partial for employees or children of employees, senior citizens. ***ROTC:*** Army cooperative.

LOANS ***Student loans:*** $6,866,665 (42% need-based, 58% non-need-based). 72% of past graduating class borrowed through all loan programs. *Average indebtedness per student:* $18,604. ***Average need-based loan:*** Freshmen: $2765; Undergraduates: $3912. ***Parent loans:*** $3,603,239 (100% non-need-based). ***Programs:*** FFEL (Subsidized and Unsubsidized Stafford, PLUS), Perkins, alternative loans.

WORK-STUDY ***Federal work-study:*** Total amount: $187,559; 142 jobs averaging $1500.

APPLYING FOR FINANCIAL AID ***Required financial aid forms:*** FAFSA, state aid form. ***Financial aid deadline (priority):*** 3/1. ***Notification date:*** Continuous beginning 2/1. Students must reply by 5/1 or within 2 weeks of notification.

CONTACT Mrs. Angie T. Hawkins, Director of Financial Aid, Virginia Wesleyan College, 1584 Wesleyan Drive, Norfolk, VA 23502-5599, 757-455-3345 or toll-free 800-737-8684. *Fax:* 757-455-6779. *E-mail:* finaid@vwc.edu.

VITERBO UNIVERSITY

La Crosse, WI

CONTACT Ms. Terry Norman, Director of Financial Aid, Viterbo University, 900 Viterbo Drive, La Crosse, WI 54601-4797, 608-796-3900 or toll-free 800-VITERBO Ext. 3010. *Fax:* 608-796-3050. *E-mail:* twnorman@viterbo.edu.

VOORHEES COLLEGE

Denmark, SC

CONTACT Augusta L. Kitchen, Director of Financial Aid, Voorhees College, PO Box 678, Denmark, SC 29042, 803-703-7109 Ext. 7106 or toll-free 800-446-6250. *Fax:* 803-793-0831. *E-mail:* akitchen@voorhees.edu.

WABASH COLLEGE

Crawfordsville, IN

Tuition & fees: $24,792 **Average undergraduate aid package: $20,607**

ABOUT THE INSTITUTION Independent, men only. Awards: bachelor's degrees. 24 undergraduate majors. Total enrollment: 874. Undergraduates: 874. Freshmen: 268. Both federal and institutional methodology are used as a basis for awarding need-based institutional aid.

UNDERGRADUATE EXPENSES for 2006–07 ***Application fee:*** $30. ***Comprehensive fee:*** $31,856 includes full-time tuition ($24,342), mandatory fees ($450), and room and board ($7064). ***College room only:*** $2877. Room and board charges vary according to board plan and housing facility. ***Part-time tuition:*** $4057 per course. Part-time tuition and fees vary according to course load. ***Payment plans:*** Tuition prepayment, installment.

FRESHMAN FINANCIAL AID (Fall 2006, est.) 253 applied for aid; of those 87% were deemed to have need. 100% of freshmen with need received aid; of those 100% had need fully met. ***Average percent of need met:*** 100% (excluding resources awarded to replace EFC). ***Average financial aid package:*** $22,581 (excluding resources awarded to replace EFC). 15% of all full-time freshmen had no need and received non-need-based gift aid.

UNDERGRADUATE FINANCIAL AID (Fall 2006, est.) 713 applied for aid; of those 88% were deemed to have need. 100% of undergraduates with need received aid; of those 100% had need fully met. ***Average percent of need met:*** 100% (excluding resources awarded to replace EFC). ***Average financial aid package:*** $20,607 (excluding resources awarded to replace EFC). 25% of all full-time undergraduates had no need and received non-need-based gift aid.

GIFT AID (NEED-BASED) ***Total amount:*** $10,128,520 (5% federal, 13% state, 79% institutional, 3% external sources). ***Receiving aid:*** Freshmen: 81% (216); All full-time undergraduates: 70% (611). ***Average award:*** Freshmen: $17,550; Undergraduates: $16,577. ***Scholarships, grants, and awards:*** Federal Pell, state, private, college/university gift aid from institutional funds.

GIFT AID (NON-NEED-BASED) ***Total amount:*** $3,828,022 (1% state, 82% institutional, 17% external sources). ***Receiving aid:*** Freshmen: 29% (77); Undergraduates: 36% (310). ***Average award:*** Freshmen: $13,228; Undergraduates: $12,030. ***Scholarships, grants, and awards by category:*** *Academic Interests/Achievement:* 638 awards ($6,309,657 total): education, general academic interests/achievements. *Creative Arts/Performance:* 64 awards ($156,754 total): art/fine arts, creative writing, journalism/publications, music, theater/drama. *Special Achievements/Activities:* 32 awards ($669,442 total): community service, leadership. *Special Characteristics:* 47 awards ($655,024 total): children of faculty/staff, international students. ***Tuition waivers:*** Full or partial for employees or children of employees.

LOANS ***Student loans:*** $3,179,565 (62% need-based, 38% non-need-based). 89% of past graduating class borrowed through all loan programs. *Average indebtedness per student:* $18,137. ***Average need-based loan:*** Freshmen: $3660; Undergraduates: $4206. ***Programs:*** FFEL (Subsidized and Unsubsidized Stafford, PLUS), college/university.

WORK-STUDY ***State or other work-study/employment:*** Total amount: $1,832,845 (69% need-based, 31% non-need-based). 823 part-time jobs averaging $2227.

APPLYING FOR FINANCIAL AID ***Required financial aid forms:*** FAFSA, CSS Financial Aid PROFILE, noncustodial (divorced/separated) parent's statement, federal income tax form(s), W-2 forms. ***Financial aid deadline:*** 3/1 (priority: 2/15). ***Notification date:*** 3/31. Students must reply by 5/1 or within 2 weeks of notification.

CONTACT Mr. Clint Gasaway, Financial Aid Director, Wabash College, PO Box 352, Crawfordsville, IN 47933-0352, 800-718-9746 or toll-free 800-345-5385. *Fax:* 765-361-6166. *E-mail:* financialaid@wabash.edu.

WAGNER COLLEGE

Staten Island, NY

Tuition & fees: $27,400 **Average undergraduate aid package: $14,734**

ABOUT THE INSTITUTION Independent, coed. Awards: bachelor's and master's degrees and post-master's certificates. 35 undergraduate majors. Total enrollment: 2,280. Undergraduates: 1,941. Freshmen: 529. Federal methodology is used as a basis for awarding need-based institutional aid.

UNDERGRADUATE EXPENSES for 2006–07 ***Application fee:*** $50. ***Comprehensive fee:*** $35,800 includes full-time tuition ($27,300), mandatory fees ($100), and room and board ($8400). ***Part-time tuition:*** $3410 per unit.

FRESHMAN FINANCIAL AID (Fall 2006, est.) 408 applied for aid; of those 92% were deemed to have need. 100% of freshmen with need received aid; of those 22% had need fully met. ***Average percent of need met:*** 73% (excluding resources awarded to replace EFC). ***Average financial aid package:*** $14,960 (excluding resources awarded to replace EFC). 30% of all full-time freshmen had no need and received non-need-based gift aid.

UNDERGRADUATE FINANCIAL AID (Fall 2006, est.) 1,274 applied for aid; of those 78% were deemed to have need. 100% of undergraduates with need received aid; of those 54% had need fully met. ***Average percent of need met:*** 78% (excluding resources awarded to replace EFC). ***Average financial aid package:*** $14,734 (excluding resources awarded to replace EFC). 34% of all full-time undergraduates had no need and received non-need-based gift aid.

GIFT AID (NEED-BASED) ***Total amount:*** $9,306,741 (6% federal, 9% state, 83% institutional, 2% external sources). ***Receiving aid:*** Freshmen: 69% (365); All full-time undergraduates: 52% (967). ***Average award:*** Freshmen: $10,430; Undergraduates: $10,759. ***Scholarships, grants, and awards:*** Federal Pell, FSEOG, state, private, college/university gift aid from institutional funds.

GIFT AID (NON-NEED-BASED) ***Total amount:*** $5,806,569 (2% state, 98% institutional). ***Receiving aid:*** Freshmen: 6% (31); Undergraduates: 14% (271). ***Average award:*** Freshmen: $8857; Undergraduates: $8670. ***Scholarships, grants, and awards by category:*** *Academic Interests/Achievement:* 1,196 awards ($8,328,013 total): general academic interests/achievements. *Creative Arts/Performance:* 232 awards ($1,901,531 total): music, theater/drama. *Special Achievements/Activities:* 304 awards ($3,693,782 total): general special achievements/activities, leadership. *Special Characteristics:* 93 awards ($679,270 total): children of faculty/staff, international students, siblings of current students. ***Tuition waivers:*** Full or partial for employees or children of employees. ***ROTC:*** Army cooperative.

LOANS ***Student loans:*** $9,792,998 (78% need-based, 22% non-need-based). ***Average need-based loan:*** Freshmen: $2451; Undergraduates: $4464. ***Parent loans:*** $5,358,451 (68% need-based, 32% non-need-based). ***Programs:*** FFEL (Subsidized and Unsubsidized Stafford, PLUS), Perkins, Federal Nursing.

WORK-STUDY ***Federal work-study:*** Total amount: $577,782; 670 jobs averaging $1176. ***State or other work-study/employment:*** Part-time jobs available.

ATHLETIC AWARDS Total amount: $4,979,956 (45% need-based, 55% non-need-based).

APPLYING FOR FINANCIAL AID ***Required financial aid forms:*** FAFSA, institution's own form. ***Financial aid deadline (priority):*** 2/15. ***Notification date:*** Continuous beginning 3/1. Students must reply within 3 weeks of notification.

CONTACT Mr. Angelo Araimo, Vice President for Enrollment and Planning, Wagner College, One Campus Road, Staten Island, NY 10301, 718-390-3411 or toll-free 800-221-1010 (out-of-state). *Fax:* 718-390-3105.

WAKE FOREST UNIVERSITY

Winston-Salem, NC

Tuition & fees: $34,330 **Average undergraduate aid package: $24,745**

ABOUT THE INSTITUTION Independent, coed. Awards: bachelor's, master's, doctoral, and first professional degrees. 37 undergraduate majors. Total enrollment: 6,739. Undergraduates: 4,332. Freshmen: 1,122. Institutional methodology is used as a basis for awarding need-based institutional aid.

UNDERGRADUATE EXPENSES for 2007–08 ***Application fee:*** $50. ***Comprehensive fee:*** $43,830 includes full-time tuition ($34,230), mandatory fees ($100), and room and board ($9500). ***College room only:*** $6000. ***Part-time tuition:*** $1420 per credit hour.

FRESHMAN FINANCIAL AID (Fall 2005) 573 applied for aid; of those 80% were deemed to have need. 100% of freshmen with need received aid; of those 44% had need fully met. ***Average percent of need met:*** 87% (excluding resources awarded to replace EFC). ***Average financial aid package:*** $24,308 (excluding resources awarded to replace EFC). 2% of all full-time freshmen had no need and received non-need-based gift aid.

UNDERGRADUATE FINANCIAL AID (Fall 2005) 1,774 applied for aid; of those 90% were deemed to have need. 100% of undergraduates with need received aid; of those 38% had need fully met. ***Average percent of need met:*** 86% (excluding resources awarded to replace EFC). ***Average financial aid package:*** $24,745 (excluding resources awarded to replace EFC). 8% of all full-time undergraduates had no need and received non-need-based gift aid.

GIFT AID (NEED-BASED) ***Total amount:*** $23,020,205 (7% federal, 10% state, 76% institutional, 7% external sources). ***Receiving aid:*** Freshmen: 36% (407); All full-time undergraduates: 34% (1,433). ***Average award:*** Freshmen: $19,484; Undergraduates: $18,632. ***Scholarships, grants, and awards:*** Federal Pell, FSEOG, state, private, college/university gift aid from institutional funds.

GIFT AID (NON-NEED-BASED) ***Total amount:*** $6,386,893 (1% federal, 13% state, 57% institutional, 29% external sources). ***Receiving aid:*** Freshmen: 26% (287); Undergraduates: 15% (648). ***Average award:*** Freshmen: $11,765; Undergraduates: $10,837. ***Scholarships, grants, and awards by category:*** *Academic Interests/Achievement:* biological sciences, business, education, English, foreign languages, general academic interests/achievements, international studies, mathematics, military science, physical sciences, premedicine, religion/biblical studies. *Creative Arts/Performance:* art/fine arts, creative writing, dance, debating, general creative arts/performance, journalism/publications, music, performing arts, theater/drama. *Special Achievements/Activities:* cheerleading/drum major, community service, leadership, memberships, religious involvement. *Special Characteristics:* children and siblings of alumni, children of faculty/staff, general special characteristics, handicapped students, international students, local/state students, members of minority groups, relatives of clergy, religious affiliation. ***ROTC:*** Army.

LOANS ***Student loans:*** $15,805,337 (78% need-based, 22% non-need-based). 37% of past graduating class borrowed through all loan programs. *Average indebtedness per student:* $20,655. ***Average need-based loan:*** Freshmen: $6402; Undergraduates: $7648. ***Parent loans:*** $8,762,990 (74% need-based, 26% non-need-based). ***Programs:*** FFEL (Subsidized and Unsubsidized Stafford, PLUS), Perkins, state, college/university, private alternative loans.

WORK-STUDY ***Federal work-study:*** Total amount: $1,861,973; 983 jobs averaging $1818. ***State or other work-study/employment:*** Part-time jobs available.

ATHLETIC AWARDS Total amount: $8,599,178 (35% need-based, 65% non-need-based).

APPLYING FOR FINANCIAL AID ***Required financial aid forms:*** FAFSA, CSS Financial Aid PROFILE, state aid form, noncustodial (divorced/separated) parent's statement. ***Financial aid deadline:*** 3/1 (priority: 2/1). ***Notification date:*** Continuous beginning 4/1. Students must reply by 5/1 or within 4 weeks of notification.

CONTACT Adam Holyfield, Assistant Director, Wake Forest University, PO Box 7246, Reynolda Station, Winston-Salem, NC 27109-7246, 336-758-5154. *Fax:* 336-758-4924. *E-mail:* financial-aid@wfu.edu.

WALDEN UNIVERSITY

Minneapolis, MN

CONTACT Financial Aid Office, Walden University, 155 Fifth Avenue South, Minneapolis, MN 55401, 800-444-6795 or toll-free 866-492-5336 (out-of-state). *Fax:* 410-843-6211. *E-mail:* finaid@waldenu.edu.

WALDORF COLLEGE

Forest City, IA

ABOUT THE INSTITUTION Independent Lutheran, coed. Awards: bachelor's degrees. 31 undergraduate majors. Total enrollment: 670. Undergraduates: 670. Freshmen: 172.

GIFT AID (NEED-BASED) ***Scholarships, grants, and awards:*** Federal Pell, FSEOG, state, private, college/university gift aid from institutional funds.

GIFT AID (NON-NEED-BASED) ***Scholarships, grants, and awards by category:*** *Academic Interests/Achievement:* communication, general academic interests/achievements. *Creative Arts/Performance:* music, theater/drama. *Special Achievements/Activities:* cheerleading/drum major, junior miss, leadership. *Special Characteristics:* children of faculty/staff, religious affiliation.

LOANS ***Programs:*** Federal Direct (Subsidized and Unsubsidized Stafford, PLUS), Perkins, state, alternative loans.

APPLYING FOR FINANCIAL AID ***Required financial aid form:*** FAFSA.

CONTACT Duane Polsdofer, Director of Financial Aid, Waldorf College, 106 South 6th Street, Forest City, IA 50436, 641-585-8120 or toll-free 800-292-1903. *Fax:* 641-585-8125.

WALLA WALLA COLLEGE

College Place, WA

Tuition & fees: $21,014 **Average undergraduate aid package: $17,608**

ABOUT THE INSTITUTION Independent Seventh-day Adventist, coed. Awards: associate, bachelor's, and master's degrees. 64 undergraduate majors. Total enrollment: 1,876. Undergraduates: 1,635. Freshmen: 323. Both federal and institutional methodology are used as a basis for awarding need-based institutional aid.

UNDERGRADUATE EXPENSES for 2006–07 ***Application fee:*** $40. ***Comprehensive fee:*** $25,724 includes full-time tuition ($20,810), mandatory fees ($204), and room and board ($4710). ***College room only:*** $2547. ***Part-time tuition:*** $516 per credit.

FRESHMAN FINANCIAL AID (Fall 2005) 265 applied for aid; of those 68% were deemed to have need. 100% of freshmen with need received aid; of those 23% had need fully met. ***Average percent of need met:*** 87% (excluding resources awarded to replace EFC). ***Average financial aid package:*** $16,300 (excluding resources awarded to replace EFC). 29% of all full-time freshmen had no need and received non-need-based gift aid.

UNDERGRADUATE FINANCIAL AID (Fall 2005) 1,301 applied for aid; of those 74% were deemed to have need. 100% of undergraduates with need received aid; of those 18% had need fully met. ***Average percent of need met:*** 87% (excluding resources awarded to replace EFC). ***Average financial aid package:*** $17,608 (excluding resources awarded to replace EFC). 18% of all full-time undergraduates had no need and received non-need-based gift aid.

GIFT AID (NEED-BASED) ***Total amount:*** $9,675,128 (18% federal, 8% state, 50% institutional, 24% external sources). ***Receiving aid:*** Freshmen: 55% (149); All full-time undergraduates: 54% (783). ***Average award:*** Freshmen: $6007; Undergraduates: $6775. ***Scholarships, grants, and awards:*** Federal Pell, FSEOG, state, private, college/university gift aid from institutional funds.

GIFT AID (NON-NEED-BASED) ***Total amount:*** $2,097,589 (40% institutional, 60% external sources). ***Receiving aid:*** Freshmen: 60% (162); Undergraduates: 49% (721). ***Average award:*** Freshmen: $3714; Undergraduates: $2939. ***Scholarships, grants, and awards by category:*** *Academic Interests/Achievement:* 582 awards ($1,046,715 total): biological sciences, education, general academic interests/achievements, social sciences. *Creative Arts/Performance:* 70 awards ($53,708 total): general creative arts/performance, music. *Special Achievements/Activities:* 161 awards ($204,393 total): community service, leadership. *Special Characteristics:* 78 awards ($577,371 total): children of faculty/staff, ethnic background.

LOANS ***Student loans:*** $8,399,120 (88% need-based, 12% non-need-based). 69% of past graduating class borrowed through all loan programs. *Average*

indebtedness per student: $32,283. ***Average need-based loan:*** Freshmen: $5753; Undergraduates: $6094. ***Parent loans:*** $1,560,732 (45% need-based, 55% non-need-based). ***Programs:*** FFEL (Subsidized and Unsubsidized Stafford, PLUS), Perkins, Federal Nursing, college/university.

WORK-STUDY ***Federal work-study:*** Total amount: $1,618,755; 690 jobs averaging $2463. ***State or other work-study/employment:*** Total amount: $112,965 (100% need-based). 72 part-time jobs averaging $2582.

APPLYING FOR FINANCIAL AID ***Required financial aid forms:*** FAFSA, institution's own form. ***Financial aid deadline:*** Continuous. ***Notification date:*** Continuous beginning 3/15.

CONTACT Ms. Nancy Caldera, Associate Director of Financial Aid, Walla Walla College, 204 South College Avenue, College Place, WA 99324-1198, 509-527-2315 or toll-free 800-541-8900. *Fax:* 509-527-2556. *E-mail:* caldna@wwc.edu.

WALSH COLLEGE OF ACCOUNTANCY AND BUSINESS ADMINISTRATION

Troy, MI

Tuition & fees: $9526 **Average undergraduate aid package: $11,123**

ABOUT THE INSTITUTION Independent, coed. Awards: bachelor's and master's degrees. 5 undergraduate majors. Total enrollment: 3,105. Undergraduates: 909. Federal methodology is used as a basis for awarding need-based institutional aid.

UNDERGRADUATE EXPENSES for 2006–07 ***Application fee:*** $25. ***Tuition:*** full-time $9288; part-time $258 per credit. ***Required fees:*** full-time $238; $119 per contact hour. ***Payment plan:*** Deferred payment.

UNDERGRADUATE FINANCIAL AID (Fall 2005) 152 applied for aid; of those 91% were deemed to have need. 98% of undergraduates with need received aid. ***Average percent of need met:*** 48% (excluding resources awarded to replace EFC). ***Average financial aid package:*** $11,123 (excluding resources awarded to replace EFC). 8% of all full-time undergraduates had no need and received non-need-based gift aid.

GIFT AID (NEED-BASED) ***Total amount:*** $674,574 (46% federal, 26% state, 27% institutional, 1% external sources). ***Receiving aid:*** All full-time undergraduates: 35% (86). ***Average award:*** Undergraduates: $5712. ***Scholarships, grants, and awards:*** Federal Pell, FSEOG, state, private, college/university gift aid from institutional funds.

GIFT AID (NON-NEED-BASED) ***Total amount:*** $185,762 (2% state, 93% institutional, 5% external sources). ***Receiving aid:*** Undergraduates: 11% (27). ***Average award:*** Undergraduates: $1745. ***Scholarships, grants, and awards by category:*** *Academic Interests/Achievement:* business. *Special Characteristics:* $128,454 total: previous college experience. ***Tuition waivers:*** Full or partial for employees or children of employees.

LOANS ***Student loans:*** $2,349,675 (96% need-based, 4% non-need-based). 45% of past graduating class borrowed through all loan programs. *Average indebtedness per student:* $10,472. ***Average need-based loan:*** Undergraduates: $7094. ***Programs:*** FFEL (Subsidized and Unsubsidized Stafford, PLUS), alternative loans.

WORK-STUDY ***State or other work-study/employment:*** Part-time jobs available.

APPLYING FOR FINANCIAL AID ***Required financial aid forms:*** FAFSA, institution's own form. ***Financial aid deadline:*** Continuous. ***Notification date:*** Continuous beginning 6/1.

CONTACT Howard Thomas, Director of Student Financial Resources, Walsh College of Accountancy and Business Administration, 3838 Livernois Road, PO Box 7006, Troy, MI 48007-7006, 248-823-1285 or toll-free 800-925-7401 (in-state). *Fax:* 248-524-2520. *E-mail:* hthomas@walshcollege.edu.

WALSH UNIVERSITY

North Canton, OH

Tuition & fees: $18,900 **Average undergraduate aid package: $11,262**

ABOUT THE INSTITUTION Independent Roman Catholic, coed. Awards: associate, bachelor's, and master's degrees. 37 undergraduate majors. Total enrollment: 2,396. Undergraduates: 2,078. Freshmen: 479. Federal methodology is used as a basis for awarding need-based institutional aid.

UNDERGRADUATE EXPENSES for 2007–08 ***Application fee:*** $25. ***Comprehensive fee:*** $26,330 includes full-time tuition ($18,300), mandatory fees ($600), and room and board ($7430). ***College room only:*** $5100. ***Part-time tuition:*** $600 per credit hour. ***Part-time fees:*** $20 per credit hour.

FRESHMAN FINANCIAL AID (Fall 2006, est.) 396 applied for aid; of those 86% were deemed to have need. 100% of freshmen with need received aid; of those 60% had need fully met. ***Average percent of need met:*** 81% (excluding resources awarded to replace EFC). ***Average financial aid package:*** $13,625 (excluding resources awarded to replace EFC). 18% of all full-time freshmen had no need and received non-need-based gift aid.

UNDERGRADUATE FINANCIAL AID (Fall 2006, est.) 1,202 applied for aid; of those 87% were deemed to have need. 100% of undergraduates with need received aid; of those 52% had need fully met. ***Average percent of need met:*** 83% (excluding resources awarded to replace EFC). ***Average financial aid package:*** $11,262 (excluding resources awarded to replace EFC). 13% of all full-time undergraduates had no need and received non-need-based gift aid.

GIFT AID (NEED-BASED) ***Total amount:*** $5,455,857 (27% federal, 19% state, 54% institutional). ***Receiving aid:*** Freshmen: 70% (318); All full-time undergraduates: 72% (1,019). ***Average award:*** Freshmen: $6722; Undergraduates: $5827. ***Scholarships, grants, and awards:*** Federal Pell, FSEOG, state, private, college/university gift aid from institutional funds.

GIFT AID (NON-NEED-BASED) ***Total amount:*** $7,101,021 (13% state, 81% institutional, 6% external sources). ***Receiving aid:*** Freshmen: 72% (326); Undergraduates: 65% (921). ***Average award:*** Freshmen: $5233; Undergraduates: $4834. ***Scholarships, grants, and awards by category:*** *Academic Interests/Achievement:* 494 awards ($1,110,550 total): biological sciences, business, communication, computer science, education, English, foreign languages, general academic interests/achievements, health fields, humanities, international studies, mathematics, physical sciences, premedicine, religion/biblical studies, social sciences. *Creative Arts/Performance:* 3 awards ($1500 total): music. *Special Achievements/Activities:* 35 awards ($28,963 total): leadership, religious involvement. *Special Characteristics:* 102 awards ($206,940 total): children and siblings of alumni, children of faculty/staff, international students, local/state students, members of minority groups, out-of-state students, siblings of current students.

LOANS ***Student loans:*** $9,535,402 (55% need-based, 45% non-need-based). 79% of past graduating class borrowed through all loan programs. *Average indebtedness per student:* $18,775. ***Average need-based loan:*** Freshmen: $2117; Undergraduates: $4220. ***Parent loans:*** $915,004 (11% need-based, 89% non-need-based). ***Programs:*** FFEL (Subsidized and Unsubsidized Stafford), Perkins, state, college/university.

WORK-STUDY ***Federal work-study:*** Total amount: $196,000; 182 jobs averaging $1480. ***State or other work-study/employment:*** Total amount: $77,755 (100% non-need-based). 30 part-time jobs averaging $1418.

ATHLETIC AWARDS Total amount: $1,186,959 (100% non-need-based).

APPLYING FOR FINANCIAL AID ***Required financial aid forms:*** FAFSA, institution's own form. ***Financial aid deadline:*** Continuous. ***Notification date:*** Continuous beginning 3/15. Students must reply within 4 weeks of notification.

CONTACT Holly Van Gilder, Director of Financial Aid, Walsh University, 2020 East Maple NW, North Canton, OH 44720-3396, 330-490-7147 or toll-free 800-362-9846 (in-state), 800-362-8846 (out-of-state). *Fax:* 330-490-7372. *E-mail:* hvangilder@walsh.edu.

WARNER PACIFIC COLLEGE

Portland, OR

Tuition & fees: $22,408 **Average undergraduate aid package: $19,963**

ABOUT THE INSTITUTION Independent religious, coed. Awards: associate, bachelor's, and master's degrees and post-bachelor's certificates. 34 undergraduate majors. Total enrollment: 740. Undergraduates: 720. Freshmen: 76. Federal methodology is used as a basis for awarding need-based institutional aid.

UNDERGRADUATE EXPENSES for 2006–07 ***Application fee:*** $50. ***Comprehensive fee:*** $28,148 includes full-time tuition ($20,480), mandatory fees ($1928), and room and board ($5740). Full-time tuition and fees vary according to course load, location, and reciprocity agreements. Room and board charges vary according to board plan and housing facility. Part-time tuition and fees vary according to course load, location, and reciprocity agreements.

FRESHMAN FINANCIAL AID (Fall 2006, est.) 66 applied for aid; of those 92% were deemed to have need. 100% of freshmen with need received aid; of those 16% had need fully met. ***Average percent of need met:*** 74% (excluding

resources awarded to replace EFC). ***Average financial aid package:*** $13,887 (excluding resources awarded to replace EFC). 4% of all full-time freshmen had no need and received non-need-based gift aid.

UNDERGRADUATE FINANCIAL AID (Fall 2006, est.) 312 applied for aid; of those 95% were deemed to have need. 100% of undergraduates with need received aid; of those 18% had need fully met. ***Average percent of need met:*** 76% (excluding resources awarded to replace EFC). ***Average financial aid package:*** $19,963 (excluding resources awarded to replace EFC). 3% of all full-time undergraduates had no need and received non-need-based gift aid.

GIFT AID (NEED-BASED) ***Total amount:*** $2,616,996 (18% federal, 6% state, 68% institutional, 8% external sources). ***Receiving aid:*** Freshmen: 78% (53); All full-time undergraduates: 74% (246). ***Average award:*** Freshmen: $4840; Undergraduates: $5209. ***Scholarships, grants, and awards:*** Federal Pell, FSEOG, state, private, college/university gift aid from institutional funds.

GIFT AID (NON-NEED-BASED) ***Total amount:*** $200,909 (2% state, 92% institutional, 6% external sources). ***Receiving aid:*** Freshmen: 84% (57); Undergraduates: 75% (249). ***Average award:*** Freshmen: $8590; Undergraduates: $6579. ***Scholarships, grants, and awards by category:*** *Academic Interests/Achievement:* 194 awards ($938,826 total): biological sciences, general academic interests/achievements, humanities, mathematics, physical sciences, religion/biblical studies, social sciences. *Creative Arts/Performance:* 45 awards ($69,620 total): music, theater/drama. *Special Achievements/Activities:* 37 awards ($68,090 total): leadership. *Special Characteristics:* 185 awards ($264,210 total): children and siblings of alumni, members of minority groups, religious affiliation. ***ROTC:*** Army cooperative, Air Force cooperative.

LOANS ***Student loans:*** $2,239,470 (80% need-based, 20% non-need-based). 79% of past graduating class borrowed through all loan programs. *Average indebtedness per student:* $24,717. ***Average need-based loan:*** Freshmen: $3431; Undergraduates: $4705. ***Parent loans:*** $634,307 (37% need-based, 63% non-need-based). ***Programs:*** FFEL (Subsidized and Unsubsidized Stafford, PLUS), Perkins.

WORK-STUDY ***Federal work-study:*** Total amount: $251,378; 194 jobs averaging $1296.

ATHLETIC AWARDS Total amount: $506,563 (88% need-based, 12% non-need-based).

APPLYING FOR FINANCIAL AID ***Required financial aid form:*** FAFSA. ***Financial aid deadline:*** Continuous. ***Notification date:*** Continuous beginning 3/1. Students must reply within 2 weeks of notification.

CONTACT Cynthia Pollard, Director of Financial Aid, Warner Pacific College, 2219 Southeast 68th Avenue, Portland, OR 97215-4099, 503-517-1018 or toll-free 800-582-7885 (in-state), 800-804-1510 (out-of-state). *E-mail:* cpollard@warnerpacific.edu.

WARNER SOUTHERN COLLEGE

Lake Wales, FL

CONTACT Student Financial Services, Warner Southern College, 13895 Highway 27, Lake Wales, FL 33859, 863-638-7202 or toll-free 800-949-7248 (in-state). *Fax:* 863-638-7603. *E-mail:* financialaid@warner.edu.

WARREN WILSON COLLEGE

Swannanoa, NC

Tuition & fees: $21,084 **Average undergraduate aid package: $14,705**

ABOUT THE INSTITUTION Independent religious, coed. Awards: bachelor's and master's degrees. 27 undergraduate majors. Total enrollment: 908. Undergraduates: 841. Freshmen: 221. Both federal and institutional methodology are used as a basis for awarding need-based institutional aid.

UNDERGRADUATE EXPENSES for 2007–08 ***Comprehensive fee:*** $27,784 includes full-time tuition ($21,084) and room and board ($6700).

FRESHMAN FINANCIAL AID (Fall 2006, est.) 168 applied for aid; of those 77% were deemed to have need. 100% of freshmen with need received aid; of those 17% had need fully met. ***Average percent of need met:*** 75% (excluding resources awarded to replace EFC). ***Average financial aid package:*** $14,683 (excluding resources awarded to replace EFC). 18% of all full-time freshmen had no need and received non-need-based gift aid.

UNDERGRADUATE FINANCIAL AID (Fall 2006, est.) 595 applied for aid; of those 82% were deemed to have need. 100% of undergraduates with need received aid; of those 14% had need fully met. ***Average percent of need met:*** 73% (excluding resources awarded to replace EFC). ***Average financial aid package:*** $14,705 (excluding resources awarded to replace EFC). 14% of all full-time undergraduates had no need and received non-need-based gift aid.

GIFT AID (NEED-BASED) ***Total amount:*** $4,616,272 (15% federal, 6% state, 73% institutional, 6% external sources). ***Receiving aid:*** Freshmen: 48% (113); All full-time undergraduates: 48% (443). ***Average award:*** Freshmen: $10,606; Undergraduates: $9519. ***Scholarships, grants, and awards:*** Federal Pell, FSEOG, state, college/university gift aid from institutional funds.

GIFT AID (NON-NEED-BASED) ***Total amount:*** $731,140 (14% state, 64% institutional, 22% external sources). ***Receiving aid:*** Freshmen: 35% (81); Undergraduates: 25% (228). ***Average award:*** Freshmen: $3792; Undergraduates: $3727. ***Scholarships, grants, and awards by category:*** *Academic Interests/Achievement:* 144 awards ($310,682 total): general academic interests/achievements. *Creative Arts/Performance:* 22 awards ($14,250 total): art/fine arts, creative writing. *Special Achievements/Activities:* 44 awards ($71,673 total): community service, general special achievements/activities, leadership. *Special Characteristics:* 88 awards ($213,392 total): children of faculty/staff, general special characteristics, local/state students, previous college experience, religious affiliation.

LOANS ***Student loans:*** $2,392,897 (86% need-based, 14% non-need-based). 35% of past graduating class borrowed through all loan programs. *Average indebtedness per student:* $15,713. ***Average need-based loan:*** Freshmen: $2007; Undergraduates: $3538. ***Parent loans:*** $1,408,436 (76% need-based, 24% non-need-based). ***Programs:*** FFEL (Subsidized and Unsubsidized Stafford, PLUS), Perkins, college/university.

WORK-STUDY ***Federal work-study:*** Total amount: $850,000; 370 jobs averaging $2297. ***State or other work-study/employment:*** Total amount: $850,000 (29% need-based, 71% non-need-based). 400 part-time jobs averaging $2125.

APPLYING FOR FINANCIAL AID ***Required financial aid forms:*** FAFSA, institution's own form, state aid form. ***Financial aid deadline (priority):*** 4/1. ***Notification date:*** Continuous beginning 3/1. Students must reply by 5/1 or within 3 weeks of notification.

CONTACT Admissions Office, Warren Wilson College, PO Box 9000, Asheville, NC 28815-9000, 800-934-3536. *Fax:* 828-298-1440.

WARTBURG COLLEGE

Waverly, IA

Tuition & fees: $22,410 **Average undergraduate aid package: $17,098**

ABOUT THE INSTITUTION Independent Lutheran, coed. Awards: bachelor's degrees. 52 undergraduate majors. Total enrollment: 1,769. Undergraduates: 1,769. Freshmen: 505. Federal methodology is used as a basis for awarding need-based institutional aid.

UNDERGRADUATE EXPENSES for 2006–07 ***Application fee:*** $20. ***Comprehensive fee:*** $29,125 includes full-time tuition ($21,980), mandatory fees ($430), and room and board ($6715). ***College room only:*** $3205. Room and board charges vary according to board plan and housing facility. ***Part-time tuition:*** $810 per credit. ***Part-time fees:*** $50 per term. Part-time tuition and fees vary according to course load. ***Payment plan:*** Installment.

FRESHMAN FINANCIAL AID (Fall 2005) 464 applied for aid; of those 86% were deemed to have need. 100% of freshmen with need received aid; of those 36% had need fully met. ***Average percent of need met:*** 90% (excluding resources awarded to replace EFC). ***Average financial aid package:*** $17,853 (excluding resources awarded to replace EFC). 22% of all full-time freshmen had no need and received non-need-based gift aid.

UNDERGRADUATE FINANCIAL AID (Fall 2005) 1,568 applied for aid; of those 87% were deemed to have need. 100% of undergraduates with need received aid; of those 29% had need fully met. ***Average percent of need met:*** 85% (excluding resources awarded to replace EFC). ***Average financial aid package:*** $17,098 (excluding resources awarded to replace EFC). 23% of all full-time undergraduates had no need and received non-need-based gift aid.

GIFT AID (NEED-BASED) ***Total amount:*** $16,921,407 (6% federal, 15% state, 69% institutional, 10% external sources). ***Receiving aid:*** Freshmen: 77% (398); All full-time undergraduates: 78% (1,354). ***Average award:*** Freshmen: $13,851; Undergraduates: $12,455. ***Scholarships, grants, and awards:*** Federal Pell, FSEOG, state, private, college/university gift aid from institutional funds.

GIFT AID (NON-NEED-BASED) ***Total amount:*** $4,903,335 (83% institutional, 17% external sources). ***Receiving aid:*** Freshmen: 12% (61); Undergraduates: 9% (163). ***Average award:*** Freshmen: $14,105; Undergraduates: $12,721. ***Scholarships, grants, and awards by category:*** *Academic Interests/Achievement:*

biological sciences, business, communication, computer science, education, English, general academic interests/achievements, international studies, mathematics, physical sciences, religion/biblical studies. *Creative Arts/Performance:* art/fine arts, journalism/publications, music. *Special Achievements/Activities:* junior miss. *Special Characteristics:* children and siblings of alumni, children of faculty/staff, ethnic background, international students, members of minority groups, out-of-state students, religious affiliation, siblings of current students. ***Tuition waivers:*** Full or partial for employees or children of employees, senior citizens.

LOANS ***Student loans:*** $10,351,141 (58% need-based, 42% non-need-based). 84% of past graduating class borrowed through all loan programs. *Average indebtedness per student:* $22,122. ***Average need-based loan:*** Freshmen: $3966; Undergraduates: $4786. ***Parent loans:*** $1,212,455 (50% need-based, 50% non-need-based). ***Programs:*** FFEL (Subsidized and Unsubsidized Stafford, PLUS), Perkins, alternative loans.

WORK-STUDY ***Federal work-study:*** Total amount: $687,975; 382 jobs averaging $1801. ***State or other work-study/employment:*** Total amount: $1,200,733 (100% non-need-based). 628 part-time jobs averaging $1911.

APPLYING FOR FINANCIAL AID ***Required financial aid form:*** FAFSA. ***Financial aid deadline (priority):*** 3/1. ***Notification date:*** Continuous beginning 3/21. Students must reply within 2 weeks of notification.

CONTACT Ms. Jennifer Sassman, Director of Financial Aid, Wartburg College, 100 Wartburg Boulevard, PO Box 1003, Waverly, IA 50677-0903, 319-352-8262 or toll-free 800-772-2085. *Fax:* 319-352-8514. *E-mail:* jennifer.sassman@wartburg.edu.

WASHBURN UNIVERSITY

Topeka, KS

CONTACT Annita Huff, Director of Financial Aid, Washburn University, 1700 SW College Avenue, Topeka, KS 66621, 785-231-1151 or toll-free 800-332-0291 (in-state). *E-mail:* zzahuff@washburn.edu.

WASHINGTON & JEFFERSON COLLEGE

Washington, PA

Tuition & fees: $28,080 **Average undergraduate aid package: $19,096**

ABOUT THE INSTITUTION Independent, coed. Awards: associate and bachelor's degrees. 27 undergraduate majors. Total enrollment: 1,515. Undergraduates: 1,515. Freshmen: 455. Both federal and institutional methodology are used as a basis for awarding need-based institutional aid.

UNDERGRADUATE EXPENSES for 2006–07 ***Application fee:*** $25. ***Comprehensive fee:*** $35,682 includes full-time tuition ($27,680), mandatory fees ($400), and room and board ($7602). ***College room only:*** $4442. Room and board charges vary according to board plan and housing facility. ***Part-time tuition:*** $865 per credit hour. ***Payment plans:*** Installment, deferred payment.

FRESHMAN FINANCIAL AID (Fall 2006, est.) 419 applied for aid; of those 84% were deemed to have need. 100% of freshmen with need received aid; of those 19% had need fully met. ***Average percent of need met:*** 80% (excluding resources awarded to replace EFC). ***Average financial aid package:*** $19,380 (excluding resources awarded to replace EFC). 16% of all full-time freshmen had no need and received non-need-based gift aid.

UNDERGRADUATE FINANCIAL AID (Fall 2006, est.) 1,263 applied for aid; of those 87% were deemed to have need. 92% of undergraduates with need received aid; of those 29% had need fully met. ***Average percent of need met:*** 74% (excluding resources awarded to replace EFC). ***Average financial aid package:*** $19,096 (excluding resources awarded to replace EFC). 19% of all full-time undergraduates had no need and received non-need-based gift aid.

GIFT AID (NEED-BASED) ***Total amount:*** $13,904,862 (6% federal, 11% state, 80% institutional, 3% external sources). ***Receiving aid:*** Freshmen: 67% (304); All full-time undergraduates: 63% (935). ***Average award:*** Freshmen: $14,800; Undergraduates: $14,301. ***Scholarships, grants, and awards:*** Federal Pell, FSEOG, state, private, college/university gift aid from institutional funds, ACG and SMART Grants.

GIFT AID (NON-NEED-BASED) ***Total amount:*** $3,104,950 (98% institutional, 2% external sources). ***Receiving aid:*** Freshmen: 7% (34); Undergraduates: 6% (87). ***Average award:*** Freshmen: $9519; Undergraduates: $9297. ***Scholarships, grants, and awards by category:*** *Academic Interests/Achievement:* 1,152 awards ($10,999,350 total): business, general academic interests/achievements. *Special Characteristics:* 38 awards ($1,380,690 total): children and siblings of alumni, children of faculty/staff. ***Tuition waivers:*** Full or partial for employees or children of employees. ***ROTC:*** Army cooperative, Air Force cooperative.

LOANS ***Student loans:*** $9,359,550 (63% need-based, 37% non-need-based). 75% of past graduating class borrowed through all loan programs. *Average indebtedness per student:* $20,000. ***Average need-based loan:*** Freshmen: $2696; Undergraduates: $3725. ***Parent loans:*** $1,547,346 (48% need-based, 52% non-need-based). ***Programs:*** FFEL (Subsidized and Unsubsidized Stafford, PLUS), Perkins, college/university.

WORK-STUDY ***Federal work-study:*** Total amount: $863,981; 615 jobs averaging $1590. ***State or other work-study/employment:*** Total amount: $200,000 (100% non-need-based). 180 part-time jobs averaging $1020.

APPLYING FOR FINANCIAL AID ***Required financial aid form:*** FAFSA. ***Financial aid deadline (priority):*** 3/1. ***Notification date:*** Continuous beginning 3/1. Students must reply by 5/1.

CONTACT Michelle Vettorel, Director of Financial Aid, Washington & Jefferson College, 60 South Lincoln Street, Washington, PA 15301-4801, 724-503-1001 Ext. 6019 or toll-free 888-WANDJAY. *Fax:* 724-250-3340. *E-mail:* mvettorel@washjeff.edu.

WASHINGTON AND LEE UNIVERSITY

Lexington, VA

Tuition & fees: $31,875 **Average undergraduate aid package: $27,934**

ABOUT THE INSTITUTION Independent, coed. Awards: bachelor's, master's, and first professional degrees. 39 undergraduate majors. Total enrollment: 2,148. Undergraduates: 1,752. Freshmen: 450. Both federal and institutional methodology are used as a basis for awarding need-based institutional aid.

UNDERGRADUATE EXPENSES for 2006–07 ***Application fee:*** $50. ***Comprehensive fee:*** $40,795 includes full-time tuition ($31,175), mandatory fees ($700), and room and board ($8920). ***College room only:*** $4690. Room and board charges vary according to housing facility and student level.

FRESHMAN FINANCIAL AID (Fall 2006, est.) 234 applied for aid; of those 70% were deemed to have need. 100% of freshmen with need received aid; of those 93% had need fully met. ***Average percent of need met:*** 99% (excluding resources awarded to replace EFC). ***Average financial aid package:*** $28,588 (excluding resources awarded to replace EFC). 7% of all full-time freshmen had no need and received non-need-based gift aid.

UNDERGRADUATE FINANCIAL AID (Fall 2006, est.) 708 applied for aid; of those 84% were deemed to have need. 99% of undergraduates with need received aid; of those 97% had need fully met. ***Average percent of need met:*** 99% (excluding resources awarded to replace EFC). ***Average financial aid package:*** $27,934 (excluding resources awarded to replace EFC). 11% of all full-time undergraduates had no need and received non-need-based gift aid.

GIFT AID (NEED-BASED) ***Total amount:*** $12,313,869 (3% federal, 2% state, 91% institutional, 4% external sources). ***Receiving aid:*** Freshmen: 32% (146); All full-time undergraduates: 30% (528). ***Average award:*** Freshmen: $24,390; Undergraduates: $23,075. ***Scholarships, grants, and awards:*** Federal Pell, FSEOG, state, private, college/university gift aid from institutional funds.

GIFT AID (NON-NEED-BASED) ***Total amount:*** $6,595,672 (1% federal, 7% state, 87% institutional, 5% external sources). ***Receiving aid:*** Freshmen: 10% (46); Undergraduates: 10% (180). ***Average award:*** Freshmen: $18,097; Undergraduates: $16,109. ***Scholarships, grants, and awards by category:*** *Academic Interests/Achievement:* general academic interests/achievements. *Special Characteristics:* local/state students. ***Tuition waivers:*** Full or partial for employees or children of employees. ***ROTC:*** Army cooperative.

LOANS ***Student loans:*** $3,036,628 (73% need-based, 27% non-need-based). 31% of past graduating class borrowed through all loan programs. *Average indebtedness per student:* $21,846. ***Average need-based loan:*** Freshmen: $2479; Undergraduates: $4148. ***Parent loans:*** $4,425,068 (59% need-based, 41% non-need-based). ***Programs:*** FFEL (Subsidized and Unsubsidized Stafford, PLUS), Perkins, college/university.

WORK-STUDY ***Federal work-study:*** Total amount: $193,685; 139 jobs averaging $1394. ***State or other work-study/employment:*** Total amount: $489,715 (72% need-based, 28% non-need-based). 363 part-time jobs averaging $1349.

APPLYING FOR FINANCIAL AID ***Required financial aid forms:*** FAFSA, CSS Financial Aid PROFILE, noncustodial (divorced/separated) parent's statement, business/farm supplement. ***Financial aid deadline (priority):*** 2/1. ***Notification date:*** 4/3. Students must reply by 5/1.

CONTACT John DeCourcy, Director, Financial Aid, Washington and Lee University, Gilliam House, 204 West Washington Street, Lexington, VA 24450, 540-458-8729. *Fax:* 540-458-8614.

WASHINGTON BIBLE COLLEGE

Lanham, MD

Tuition & fees: N/R **Average undergraduate aid package: $5000**

ABOUT THE INSTITUTION Independent nondenominational, coed. Awards: associate and bachelor's degrees. 8 undergraduate majors. Total enrollment: 331. Undergraduates: 331. Both federal and institutional methodology are used as a basis for awarding need-based institutional aid.

UNDERGRADUATE EXPENSES for 2007–08 ***Application fee:*** $25. ***Tuition:*** part-time $380 per credit.

FRESHMAN FINANCIAL AID (Fall 2005) 16 applied for aid; of those 75% were deemed to have need. 100% of freshmen with need received aid. ***Average percent of need met:*** 65% (excluding resources awarded to replace EFC). ***Average financial aid package:*** $8050 (excluding resources awarded to replace EFC). 22% of all full-time freshmen had no need and received non-need-based gift aid.

UNDERGRADUATE FINANCIAL AID (Fall 2005) 120 applied for aid; of those 83% were deemed to have need. 100% of undergraduates with need received aid. ***Average percent of need met:*** 85% (excluding resources awarded to replace EFC). ***Average financial aid package:*** $5000 (excluding resources awarded to replace EFC). 18% of all full-time undergraduates had no need and received non-need-based gift aid.

GIFT AID (NEED-BASED) ***Total amount:*** $370,640 (46% federal, 13% state, 38% institutional, 3% external sources). ***Receiving aid:*** Freshmen: 61% (11); All full-time undergraduates: 44% (63). ***Average award:*** Freshmen: $2245; Undergraduates: $500. ***Scholarships, grants, and awards:*** Federal Pell, FSEOG, state, private, college/university gift aid from institutional funds.

GIFT AID (NON-NEED-BASED) ***Total amount:*** $93,294 (100% institutional). ***Receiving aid:*** Freshmen: 67% (12); Undergraduates: 63% (90). ***Average award:*** Freshmen: $3048; Undergraduates: $2000. ***Scholarships, grants, and awards by category:*** *Academic Interests/Achievement:* 64 awards ($13,700 total): general academic interests/achievements, religion/biblical studies. *Creative Arts/Performance:* 18 awards ($25,880 total): music. *Special Achievements/Activities:* 23 awards ($13,365 total): general special achievements/activities, leadership, religious involvement. *Special Characteristics:* 54 awards ($105,945 total): children of faculty/staff, international students, relatives of clergy, siblings of current students, spouses of current students, veterans, veterans' children.

LOANS ***Student loans:*** $732,210 (47% need-based, 53% non-need-based). 50% of past graduating class borrowed through all loan programs. *Average indebtedness per student:* $9095. ***Average need-based loan:*** Freshmen: $2625; Undergraduates: $4625. ***Parent loans:*** $108,307 (100% non-need-based). ***Programs:*** FFEL (Subsidized and Unsubsidized Stafford, PLUS).

WORK-STUDY ***Federal work-study:*** Total amount: $46,863; 34 jobs averaging $1378.

APPLYING FOR FINANCIAL AID ***Required financial aid forms:*** FAFSA, institution's own form, CSS Financial Aid PROFILE. ***Financial aid deadline (priority):*** 6/1. ***Notification date:*** Continuous beginning 7/1. Students must reply within 2 weeks of notification.

CONTACT Diane Marineau, Director of Financial Aid, Washington Bible College, 6511 Princess Garden Parkway, Lanham, MD 20706-3599, 301-552-1400 Ext. 1222 or toll-free 877-793-7227 Ext. 1212. *Fax:* 301-552-2775. *E-mail:* dmarineau@bible.edu.

WASHINGTON COLLEGE

Chestertown, MD

Tuition & fees: $30,200 **Average undergraduate aid package: $16,314**

ABOUT THE INSTITUTION Independent, coed. Awards: bachelor's and master's degrees. 34 undergraduate majors. Total enrollment: 1,381. Undergraduates: 1,307. Freshmen: 314. Both federal and institutional methodology are used as a basis for awarding need-based institutional aid.

UNDERGRADUATE EXPENSES for 2006–07 ***Application fee:*** $45. ***Comprehensive fee:*** $36,650 includes full-time tuition ($29,640), mandatory fees ($560), and room and board ($6450). ***College room only:*** $3250. Full-time tuition and fees vary according to program and reciprocity agreements. Room and board charges vary according to board plan and housing facility. ***Part-time tuition:*** $1235 per credit. Part-time tuition and fees vary according to course load and program. ***Payment plans:*** Tuition prepayment, installment.

FRESHMAN FINANCIAL AID (Fall 2005) 202 applied for aid; of those 63% were deemed to have need. 100% of freshmen with need received aid; of those 70% had need fully met. ***Average percent of need met:*** 85% (excluding resources awarded to replace EFC). ***Average financial aid package:*** $15,528 (excluding resources awarded to replace EFC). 35% of all full-time freshmen had no need and received non-need-based gift aid.

UNDERGRADUATE FINANCIAL AID (Fall 2005) 753 applied for aid; of those 74% were deemed to have need. 100% of undergraduates with need received aid; of those 73% had need fully met. ***Average percent of need met:*** 90% (excluding resources awarded to replace EFC). ***Average financial aid package:*** $16,314 (excluding resources awarded to replace EFC). 40% of all full-time undergraduates had no need and received non-need-based gift aid.

GIFT AID (NEED-BASED) ***Total amount:*** $7,146,777 (6% federal, 11% state, 83% institutional). ***Receiving aid:*** Freshmen: 36% (123); All full-time undergraduates: 43% (545). ***Average award:*** Freshmen: $13,881; Undergraduates: $14,939. ***Scholarships, grants, and awards:*** Federal Pell, FSEOG, state, private, college/university gift aid from institutional funds.

GIFT AID (NON-NEED-BASED) ***Total amount:*** $6,180,803 (5% state, 86% institutional, 9% external sources). ***Receiving aid:*** Freshmen: 26% (90); Undergraduates: 32% (400). ***Average award:*** Freshmen: $9266; Undergraduates: $10,743. ***Scholarships, grants, and awards by category:*** *Academic Interests/Achievement:* general academic interests/achievements. *Creative Arts/Performance:* 12 awards ($18,000 total): creative writing. *Special Achievements/Activities:* 580 awards ($5,800,000 total): memberships. *Special Characteristics:* 54 awards ($1,394,736 total): children of faculty/staff, children of union members/company employees, international students. ***Tuition waivers:*** Full or partial for minority students, employees or children of employees.

LOANS ***Student loans:*** $4,917,689 (37% need-based, 63% non-need-based). 58% of past graduating class borrowed through all loan programs. *Average indebtedness per student:* $19,800. ***Average need-based loan:*** Freshmen: $3219; Undergraduates: $4583. ***Parent loans:*** $5,151,756 (100% non-need-based). ***Programs:*** FFEL (Subsidized and Unsubsidized Stafford, PLUS), Perkins, college/university.

WORK-STUDY ***Federal work-study:*** Total amount: $298,401; 238 jobs averaging $1455.

APPLYING FOR FINANCIAL AID ***Required financial aid forms:*** FAFSA, institution's own form, federal income tax form(s). ***Financial aid deadline (priority):*** 2/15. ***Notification date:*** Continuous beginning 3/1. Students must reply by 5/1.

CONTACT Ms. Jean M. Narcum, Director of Financial Aid, Washington College, 300 Washington Avenue, Chestertown, MD 21620-1197, 410-778-7214 or toll-free 800-422-1782. *Fax:* 410-778-7287. *E-mail:* jnarcum2@washcoll.edu.

WASHINGTON STATE UNIVERSITY

Pullman, WA

Tuition & fees (WA res): $6447 **Average undergraduate aid package: $9929**

ABOUT THE INSTITUTION State-supported, coed. Awards: bachelor's, master's, doctoral, and first professional degrees and post-bachelor's and post-master's certificates. 130 undergraduate majors. Total enrollment: 23,655. Undergraduates: 19,554. Freshmen: 2,856. Federal methodology is used as a basis for awarding need-based institutional aid.

UNDERGRADUATE EXPENSES for 2006–07 ***Application fee:*** $50. ***Tuition, state resident:*** full-time $5432; part-time $294 per credit. ***Tuition, nonresident:*** full-time $15,072; part-time $776 per credit. Part-time tuition and fees vary according to course load. ***College room and board:*** $6890; ***Room only:*** $3390. Room and board charges vary according to board plan, housing facility, and location. ***Payment plan:*** Installment.

FRESHMAN FINANCIAL AID (Fall 2005) 2013 applied for aid; of those 61% were deemed to have need. 98% of freshmen with need received aid; of those 27% had need fully met. ***Average percent of need met:*** 72% (excluding resources awarded to replace EFC). ***Average financial aid package:*** $8297 (excluding resources awarded to replace EFC). 7% of all full-time freshmen had no need and received non-need-based gift aid.

UNDERGRADUATE FINANCIAL AID (Fall 2005) 11,218 applied for aid; of those 74% were deemed to have need. 98% of undergraduates with need received aid; of those 32% had need fully met. ***Average percent of need met:*** 78%

(excluding resources awarded to replace EFC). ***Average financial aid package:*** $9929 (excluding resources awarded to replace EFC). 6% of all full-time undergraduates had no need and received non-need-based gift aid.

GIFT AID (NEED-BASED) ***Total amount:*** $34,567,480 (40% federal, 50% state, 10% institutional). ***Receiving aid:*** Freshmen: 22% (633); All full-time undergraduates: 32% (5,336). ***Average award:*** Freshmen: $5236; Undergraduates: $5866. ***Scholarships, grants, and awards:*** Federal Pell, FSEOG, state, private, college/university gift aid from institutional funds.

GIFT AID (NON-NEED-BASED) ***Total amount:*** $12,100,739 (8% state, 32% institutional, 60% external sources). ***Receiving aid:*** Freshmen: 23% (669); Undergraduates: 17% (2,773). ***Average award:*** Freshmen: $1839; Undergraduates: $2089. ***Scholarships, grants, and awards by category:*** *Academic Interests/Achievement:* agriculture, architecture, area/ethnic studies, biological sciences, business, communication, computer science, education, engineering/technologies, English, foreign languages, general academic interests/achievements, health fields, home economics, humanities, international studies, mathematics, military science, physical sciences, premedicine, social sciences. *Creative Arts/Performance:* applied art and design, art/fine arts, cinema/film/broadcasting, creative writing, general creative arts/performance, journalism/publications, music, performing arts, theater/drama. *Special Achievements/Activities:* community service, general special achievements/activities, junior miss, leadership, memberships, religious involvement, rodeo. *Special Characteristics:* children and siblings of alumni, children of faculty/staff, children of public servants, children with a deceased or disabled parent, first-generation college students, handicapped students, international students, out-of-state students, public servants, religious affiliation, veterans. ***Tuition waivers:*** Full or partial for children of alumni, employees or children of employees. ***ROTC:*** Army, Naval cooperative, Air Force.

LOANS ***Student loans:*** $60,337,710 (53% need-based, 47% non-need-based). ***Average need-based loan:*** Freshmen: $3073; Undergraduates: $4448. ***Parent loans:*** $25,960,153 (100% non-need-based). ***Programs:*** FFEL (Subsidized and Unsubsidized Stafford, PLUS), Perkins, Federal Nursing, college/university, alternative loans.

WORK-STUDY ***Federal work-study:*** Total amount: $512,726; 368 jobs averaging $1396. ***State or other work-study/employment:*** Total amount: $1,711,538 (100% need-based). 1,124 part-time jobs averaging $1523.

ATHLETIC AWARDS Total amount: $5,003,563 (100% non-need-based).

APPLYING FOR FINANCIAL AID ***Required financial aid form:*** FAFSA. ***Financial aid deadline (priority):*** 3/1. ***Notification date:*** 4/15.

CONTACT Financial Aid Office, Washington State University, Office of Student Financial Aid, PO Box 641068, Pullman, WA 99164-1068, 509-335-9711 or toll-free 888-468-6978. *E-mail:* finaid@wsu.edu.

WASHINGTON UNIVERSITY IN ST. LOUIS

St. Louis, MO

Tuition & fees: $35,524 **Average undergraduate aid package: $27,310**

ABOUT THE INSTITUTION Independent, coed. Awards: bachelor's, master's, doctoral, and first professional degrees and post-bachelor's certificates. 167 undergraduate majors. Total enrollment: 13,355. Undergraduates: 7,386. Freshmen: 1,470. Both federal and institutional methodology are used as a basis for awarding need-based institutional aid.

UNDERGRADUATE EXPENSES for 2007–08 ***Application fee:*** $55. ***Comprehensive fee:*** $46,776 includes full-time tuition ($34,500), mandatory fees ($1024), and room and board ($11,252). ***College room only:*** $7102.

FRESHMAN FINANCIAL AID (Fall 2006, est.) 994 applied for aid; of those 60% were deemed to have need. 98% of freshmen with need received aid; of those 100% had need fully met. ***Average percent of need met:*** 100% (excluding resources awarded to replace EFC). ***Average financial aid package:*** $27,621 (excluding resources awarded to replace EFC). 20% of all full-time freshmen had no need and received non-need-based gift aid.

UNDERGRADUATE FINANCIAL AID (Fall 2006, est.) 4,392 applied for aid; of those 61% were deemed to have need. 99% of undergraduates with need received aid; of those 100% had need fully met. ***Average percent of need met:*** 100% (excluding resources awarded to replace EFC). ***Average financial aid package:*** $27,310 (excluding resources awarded to replace EFC). 14% of all full-time undergraduates had no need and received non-need-based gift aid.

GIFT AID (NEED-BASED) ***Total amount:*** $59,103,776 (4% federal, 1% state, 90% institutional, 5% external sources). ***Receiving aid:*** Freshmen: 39% (574); All full-time undergraduates: 42% (2,592). ***Average award:*** Freshmen: $23,691; Undergraduates: $22,802. ***Scholarships, grants, and awards:*** Federal Pell, FSEOG, state, private, college/university gift aid from institutional funds, United Negro College Fund.

GIFT AID (NON-NEED-BASED) ***Total amount:*** $5,506,229 (3% federal, 7% state, 73% institutional, 17% external sources). ***Receiving aid:*** Freshmen: 4% (63); Undergraduates: 3% (206). ***Average award:*** Freshmen: $9178; Undergraduates: $5975. ***Scholarships, grants, and awards by category:*** *Academic Interests/Achievement:* architecture, biological sciences, business, communication, computer science, education, engineering/technologies, English, foreign languages, general academic interests/achievements, health fields, humanities, international studies, mathematics, military science, physical sciences, premedicine, religion/biblical studies, social sciences. *Creative Arts/Performance:* applied art and design, art/fine arts, cinema/film/broadcasting, creative writing, dance, music, performing arts, theater/drama. ***ROTC:*** Army, Air Force cooperative.

LOANS ***Student loans:*** $14,458,905 (94% need-based, 6% non-need-based). 41% of past graduating class borrowed through all loan programs. ***Average need-based loan:*** Freshmen: $4375; Undergraduates: $5954. ***Parent loans:*** $2,540,294 (71% need-based, 29% non-need-based). ***Programs:*** FFEL (Subsidized and Unsubsidized Stafford, PLUS), Perkins, state, college/university.

WORK-STUDY ***Federal work-study:*** Total amount: $2,136,676; 1,123 jobs averaging $1903.

APPLYING FOR FINANCIAL AID ***Required financial aid forms:*** FAFSA, CSS Financial Aid PROFILE, noncustodial (divorced/separated) parent's statement, student and parent 1040 tax return or signed waiver if there is no tax return. ***Financial aid deadline:*** 2/15. ***Notification date:*** 4/1. Students must reply by 5/1 or within 2 weeks of notification.

CONTACT Mr. William Witbrodt, Director of Financial Aid, Washington University in St. Louis, Campus Box 1041, One Brookings Drive, St. Louis, MO 63130-4899, 314-935-5900 or toll-free 800-638-0700. *Fax:* 314-935-4037. *E-mail:* financial@wustl.edu.

WATKINS COLLEGE OF ART AND DESIGN

Nashville, TN

Tuition & fees: $12,720 **Average undergraduate aid package: $9000**

ABOUT THE INSTITUTION Independent, coed. Awards: bachelor's degrees. 5 undergraduate majors. Total enrollment: 393. Undergraduates: 375. Freshmen: 40. Federal methodology is used as a basis for awarding need-based institutional aid.

UNDERGRADUATE EXPENSES for 2006–07 ***Application fee:*** $50. ***Tuition:*** full-time $12,000; part-time $500 per hour. ***Required fees:*** full-time $720; $30 per hour.

FRESHMAN FINANCIAL AID (Fall 2006, est.) 45 applied for aid; of those 100% were deemed to have need. 89% of freshmen with need received aid; of those 5% had need fully met. ***Average percent of need met:*** 60% (excluding resources awarded to replace EFC). ***Average financial aid package:*** $4778 (excluding resources awarded to replace EFC).

UNDERGRADUATE FINANCIAL AID (Fall 2006, est.) 156 applied for aid; of those 100% were deemed to have need. 100% of undergraduates with need received aid; of those 2% had need fully met. ***Average percent of need met:*** 60% (excluding resources awarded to replace EFC). ***Average financial aid package:*** $9000 (excluding resources awarded to replace EFC).

GIFT AID (NEED-BASED) ***Total amount:*** $424,038 (51% federal, 26% state, 23% institutional). ***Receiving aid:*** Freshmen: 51% (23); All full-time undergraduates: 40% (85). ***Average award:*** Freshmen: $1500; Undergraduates: $1500. ***Scholarships, grants, and awards:*** Federal Pell, FSEOG, state, college/university gift aid from institutional funds.

GIFT AID (NON-NEED-BASED) ***Total amount:*** $213,526 (67% state, 29% institutional, 4% external sources). ***Receiving aid:*** Freshmen: 58% (26); Undergraduates: 21% (45). ***Scholarships, grants, and awards by category:*** *Academic Interests/Achievement:* 3 awards ($30,000 total): general academic interests/achievements. *Creative Arts/Performance:* 4 awards ($8500 total): applied art and design, art/fine arts, cinema/film/broadcasting. *Special Achievements/Activities:* 10 awards ($25,000 total): general special achievements/activities.

LOANS ***Student loans:*** $1,636,865 (46% need-based, 54% non-need-based). 50% of past graduating class borrowed through all loan programs. *Average indebtedness per student:* $18,000. ***Average need-based loan:*** Freshmen: $2625;

Undergraduates: $4000. ***Parent loans:*** $629,700 (100% non-need-based). ***Programs:*** FFEL (Subsidized and Unsubsidized Stafford, PLUS), private alternative loans.

WORK-STUDY ***Federal work-study:*** Total amount: $20,000; 15 jobs averaging $1500. ***State or other work-study/employment:*** Total amount: $20,000 (100% non-need-based). 15 part-time jobs averaging $1500.

APPLYING FOR FINANCIAL AID ***Required financial aid forms:*** FAFSA, institution's own form. ***Financial aid deadline (priority):*** 4/1. ***Notification date:*** Continuous beginning 5/1. Students must reply within 1 week of notification.

CONTACT Lyle Jones, Financial Aid Coordinator, Watkins College of Art and Design, 2298 Metrocenter Boulevard, Nashville, TN 37228, 615-383-4848 Ext. 7421. *Fax:* 615-383-4849. *E-mail:* financialaid@watkins.edu.

WAYLAND BAPTIST UNIVERSITY

Plainview, TX

Tuition & fees: $10,800 **Average undergraduate aid package: $9569**

ABOUT THE INSTITUTION Independent Baptist, coed. Awards: associate, bachelor's, and master's degrees (branch locations in Anchorage, AK; Amarillo, TX; Luke Airforce Base, AZ; Glorieta, NM; Aiea, HI; Lubbock, TX; San Antonio, TX; Wichita Falls, TX). 27 undergraduate majors. Total enrollment: 1,072. Undergraduates: 962. Freshmen: 215. Federal methodology is used as a basis for awarding need-based institutional aid.

UNDERGRADUATE EXPENSES for 2006–07 ***Application fee:*** $35. ***Comprehensive fee:*** $14,384 includes full-time tuition ($10,200), mandatory fees ($600), and room and board ($3584). ***College room only:*** $1276. Full-time tuition and fees vary according to course load and location. Room and board charges vary according to board plan and housing facility. ***Part-time tuition:*** $340 per credit hour. ***Part-time fees:*** $50 per term. Part-time tuition and fees vary according to course load and location. ***Payment plan:*** Installment.

FRESHMAN FINANCIAL AID (Fall 2006, est.) 195 applied for aid; of those 84% were deemed to have need. 95% of freshmen with need received aid; of those 16% had need fully met. ***Average percent of need met:*** 65% (excluding resources awarded to replace EFC). ***Average financial aid package:*** $9195 (excluding resources awarded to replace EFC). 19% of all full-time freshmen had no need and received non-need-based gift aid.

UNDERGRADUATE FINANCIAL AID (Fall 2006, est.) 717 applied for aid; of those 85% were deemed to have need. 97% of undergraduates with need received aid; of those 18% had need fully met. ***Average percent of need met:*** 67% (excluding resources awarded to replace EFC). ***Average financial aid package:*** $9569 (excluding resources awarded to replace EFC). 22% of all full-time undergraduates had no need and received non-need-based gift aid.

GIFT AID (NEED-BASED) ***Total amount:*** $4,161,646 (33% federal, 25% state, 39% institutional, 3% external sources). ***Receiving aid:*** Freshmen: 73% (153); All full-time undergraduates: 73% (575). ***Average award:*** Freshmen: $7525; Undergraduates: $6981. ***Scholarships, grants, and awards:*** Federal Pell, FSEOG, state, private, college/university gift aid from institutional funds.

GIFT AID (NON-NEED-BASED) ***Total amount:*** $1,769,821 (1% state, 95% institutional, 4% external sources). ***Receiving aid:*** Freshmen: 10% (21); Undergraduates: 8% (65). ***Average award:*** Freshmen: $8885; Undergraduates: $9290. ***Scholarships, grants, and awards by category:*** *Academic Interests/Achievement:* 330 awards ($1,088,783 total): biological sciences, business, communication, education, English, general academic interests/achievements, mathematics, physical sciences, religion/biblical studies, social sciences. *Creative Arts/Performance:* 132 awards ($190,633 total): art/fine arts, journalism/publications, music, theater/drama. *Special Achievements/Activities:* 119 awards ($52,812 total): cheerleading/drum major, leadership, memberships, religious involvement. *Special Characteristics:* 456 awards ($663,414 total): children and siblings of alumni, children of faculty/staff, ethnic background, general special characteristics, international students, local/state students, members of minority groups, relatives of clergy, religious affiliation. ***Tuition waivers:*** Full or partial for employees or children of employees. ***ROTC:*** Army cooperative, Air Force cooperative.

LOANS ***Student loans:*** $3,266,650 (79% need-based, 21% non-need-based). 35% of past graduating class borrowed through all loan programs. *Average indebtedness per student:* $23,896. ***Average need-based loan:*** Freshmen: $2321; Undergraduates: $3231. ***Parent loans:*** $368,819 (29% need-based, 71% non-need-based). ***Programs:*** FFEL (Subsidized and Unsubsidized Stafford, PLUS), Perkins, state.

WORK-STUDY ***Federal work-study:*** Total amount: $156,203; 185 jobs averaging $1450. ***State or other work-study/employment:*** Total amount: $37,599 (100% non-need-based). 331 part-time jobs averaging $499.

ATHLETIC AWARDS Total amount: $342,410 (100% non-need-based).

APPLYING FOR FINANCIAL AID ***Required financial aid forms:*** FAFSA, institution's own form. ***Financial aid deadline (priority):*** 5/1. ***Notification date:*** Continuous beginning 2/15. Students must reply within 3 weeks of notification.

CONTACT Karen LaQuey, Director of Financial Aid, Wayland Baptist University, 1900 West 7th Street, Plainview, TX 79072-6998, 806-291-3520 or toll-free 800-588-1928. *Fax:* 806-291-1956. *E-mail:* laquey@wbu.edu.

WAYNESBURG COLLEGE

Waynesburg, PA

Tuition & fees: $15,780 **Average undergraduate aid package: $12,405**

ABOUT THE INSTITUTION Independent religious, coed. Awards: associate, bachelor's, and master's degrees. 50 undergraduate majors. Total enrollment: 2,159. Undergraduates: 1,616. Freshmen: 380. Federal methodology is used as a basis for awarding need-based institutional aid.

UNDERGRADUATE EXPENSES for 2006–07 ***Application fee:*** $20. ***Comprehensive fee:*** $22,150 includes full-time tuition ($15,440), mandatory fees ($340), and room and board ($6370). ***College room only:*** $3250. Full-time tuition and fees vary according to class time. Room and board charges vary according to board plan. ***Part-time tuition:*** $650 per credit. ***Part-time fees:*** $15 per credit. Part-time tuition and fees vary according to class time, course load, and location. ***Payment plans:*** Installment, deferred payment.

FRESHMAN FINANCIAL AID (Fall 2006, est.) 323 applied for aid; of those 89% were deemed to have need. 99% of freshmen with need received aid; of those 22% had need fully met. ***Average percent of need met:*** 81% (excluding resources awarded to replace EFC). ***Average financial aid package:*** $12,743 (excluding resources awarded to replace EFC). 13% of all full-time freshmen had no need and received non-need-based gift aid.

UNDERGRADUATE FINANCIAL AID (Fall 2006, est.) 1,327 applied for aid; of those 87% were deemed to have need. 98% of undergraduates with need received aid; of those 29% had need fully met. ***Average percent of need met:*** 80% (excluding resources awarded to replace EFC). ***Average financial aid package:*** $12,405 (excluding resources awarded to replace EFC). 13% of all full-time undergraduates had no need and received non-need-based gift aid.

GIFT AID (NEED-BASED) ***Total amount:*** $10,751,183 (16% federal, 26% state, 54% institutional, 4% external sources). ***Receiving aid:*** Freshmen: 76% (285); All full-time undergraduates: 78% (1,099). ***Average award:*** Freshmen: $10,156; Undergraduates: $9588. ***Scholarships, grants, and awards:*** Federal Pell, FSEOG, state, private, college/university gift aid from institutional funds.

GIFT AID (NON-NEED-BASED) ***Total amount:*** $1,235,981 (1% federal, 94% institutional, 5% external sources). ***Receiving aid:*** Freshmen: 7% (26); Undergraduates: 6% (82). ***Average award:*** Freshmen: $11,197; Undergraduates: $10,495. ***Scholarships, grants, and awards by category:*** *Academic Interests/Achievement:* 60 awards ($2000 total): biological sciences, business, communication, computer science, education, English, general academic interests/achievements, international studies, mathematics, religion/biblical studies. *Creative Arts/Performance:* 4 awards ($2000 total): music. *Special Achievements/Activities:* 65 awards ($2100 total): community service. *Special Characteristics:* 50 awards ($500,000 total): children of faculty/staff. ***Tuition waivers:*** Full or partial for employees or children of employees. ***ROTC:*** Army cooperative.

LOANS ***Student loans:*** $8,878,127 (61% need-based, 39% non-need-based). 88% of past graduating class borrowed through all loan programs. *Average indebtedness per student:* $20,000. ***Average need-based loan:*** Freshmen: $2706; Undergraduates: $3576. ***Parent loans:*** $1,886,456 (25% need-based, 75% non-need-based). ***Programs:*** FFEL (Subsidized and Unsubsidized Stafford, PLUS), Perkins, Federal Nursing.

WORK-STUDY ***Federal work-study:*** Total amount: $185,246; 275 jobs averaging $1300.

APPLYING FOR FINANCIAL AID ***Required financial aid form:*** FAFSA. ***Financial aid deadline:*** Continuous. ***Notification date:*** Continuous beginning 2/15. Students must reply within 2 weeks of notification.

CONTACT Matthew C. Stokan, Director of Financial Aid, Waynesburg College, 51 West College Street, Waynesburg, PA 15370-1222, 724-852-3208 or toll-free 800-225-7393. *Fax:* 724-627-6416. *E-mail:* mstokan@waynesburg.edu.

WAYNE STATE COLLEGE

Wayne, NE

Tuition & fees (NE res): $4013 Average undergraduate aid package: $4027

ABOUT THE INSTITUTION State-supported, coed. Awards: bachelor's and master's degrees and post-master's certificates. 75 undergraduate majors. Total enrollment: 3,407. Undergraduates: 2,748. Freshmen: 611. Federal methodology is used as a basis for awarding need-based institutional aid.

UNDERGRADUATE EXPENSES for 2006–07 ***Application fee:*** $30. ***Tuition, state resident:*** full-time $3075; part-time $102.50 per credit hour. ***Tuition, nonresident:*** full-time $6150; part-time $205 per credit hour. ***Required fees:*** full-time $938; $37.25 per credit hour. Full-time tuition and fees vary according to course level and course load. Part-time tuition and fees vary according to course level and course load. ***College room and board:*** $4470; ***Room only:*** $2170. Room and board charges vary according to board plan and housing facility. ***Payment plan:*** Installment.

FRESHMAN FINANCIAL AID (Fall 2006, est.) 520 applied for aid; of those 74% were deemed to have need. 98% of freshmen with need received aid; of those 25% had need fully met. ***Average percent of need met:*** 31% (excluding resources awarded to replace EFC). ***Average financial aid package:*** $3882 (excluding resources awarded to replace EFC). 5% of all full-time freshmen had no need and received non-need-based gift aid.

UNDERGRADUATE FINANCIAL AID (Fall 2006, est.) 2,053 applied for aid; of those 77% were deemed to have need. 99% of undergraduates with need received aid; of those 30% had need fully met. ***Average percent of need met:*** 36% (excluding resources awarded to replace EFC). ***Average financial aid package:*** $4027 (excluding resources awarded to replace EFC). 5% of all full-time undergraduates had no need and received non-need-based gift aid.

GIFT AID (NEED-BASED) ***Total amount:*** $3,428,344 (83% federal, 16% state, 1% institutional). ***Receiving aid:*** Freshmen: 41% (249); All full-time undergraduates: 42% (1,063). ***Average award:*** Freshmen: $1476; Undergraduates: $1597. ***Scholarships, grants, and awards:*** Federal Pell, FSEOG, state, college/university gift aid from institutional funds.

GIFT AID (NON-NEED-BASED) ***Total amount:*** $1,382,183 (52% institutional, 48% external sources). ***Receiving aid:*** Freshmen: 29% (174); Undergraduates: 23% (579). ***Average award:*** Freshmen: $695; Undergraduates: $1150. ***Scholarships, grants, and awards by category:*** *Academic Interests/Achievement:* biological sciences, business, communication, computer science, education, English, foreign languages, general academic interests/achievements, health fields, home economics, humanities, mathematics, physical sciences, premedicine, social sciences. *Creative Arts/Performance:* applied art and design, art/fine arts, creative writing, debating, general creative arts/performance, journalism/publications, music, performing arts, theater/drama. *Special Achievements/Activities:* general special achievements/activities, leadership. *Special Characteristics:* children of faculty/staff, children with a deceased or disabled parent, ethnic background, general special characteristics, local/state students, members of minority groups, out-of-state students, veterans, veterans' children. ***Tuition waivers:*** Full or partial for minority students, employees or children of employees. ***ROTC:*** Army.

LOANS ***Student loans:*** $9,430,179 (57% need-based, 43% non-need-based). ***Average need-based loan:*** Freshmen: $1415; Undergraduates: $1855. ***Parent loans:*** $1,003,087 (100% non-need-based). ***Programs:*** FFEL (Subsidized and Unsubsidized Stafford, PLUS), Perkins.

WORK-STUDY ***Federal work-study:*** Total amount: $129,475; 112 jobs averaging $1200.

ATHLETIC AWARDS Total amount: $319,981 (100% non-need-based).

APPLYING FOR FINANCIAL AID ***Required financial aid forms:*** FAFSA, institution's own form. ***Financial aid deadline (priority):*** 4/1. ***Notification date:*** Continuous beginning 3/15. Students must reply within 4 weeks of notification.

CONTACT Mrs. Kyle M. Rose, Director of Financial Aid, Wayne State College, 1111 Main Street, Wayne, NE 68787, 402-375-7230 or toll-free 800-228-9972 (in-state). *Fax:* 402-375-7067. *E-mail:* kyrose1@wsc.edu.

WAYNE STATE UNIVERSITY

Detroit, MI

Tuition & fees (MI res): $6812 Average undergraduate aid package: $6958

ABOUT THE INSTITUTION State-supported, coed. Awards: bachelor's, master's, doctoral, and first professional degrees and post-bachelor's and post-master's certificates. 83 undergraduate majors. Total enrollment: 33,137. Undergraduates: 20,737. Freshmen: 2,878. Federal methodology is used as a basis for awarding need-based institutional aid.

UNDERGRADUATE EXPENSES for 2006–07 ***Application fee:*** $30. ***Tuition, state resident:*** full-time $6012; part-time $200.40 per credit hour. ***Tuition, nonresident:*** full-time $13,770; part-time $459.50 per credit hour. ***Required fees:*** full-time $800; $16.75 per semester hour or $148.50 per term part-time. ***College room and board:*** $6575. Room and board charges vary according to housing facility. ***Payment plan:*** Installment.

FRESHMAN FINANCIAL AID (Fall 2005) 1851 applied for aid; of those 79% were deemed to have need. 99% of freshmen with need received aid; of those 7% had need fully met. ***Average percent of need met:*** 50% (excluding resources awarded to replace EFC). ***Average financial aid package:*** $6233 (excluding resources awarded to replace EFC). 11% of all full-time freshmen had no need and received non-need-based gift aid.

UNDERGRADUATE FINANCIAL AID (Fall 2005) 7,660 applied for aid; of those 85% were deemed to have need. 98% of undergraduates with need received aid; of those 7% had need fully met. ***Average percent of need met:*** 64% (excluding resources awarded to replace EFC). ***Average financial aid package:*** $6958 (excluding resources awarded to replace EFC). 9% of all full-time undergraduates had no need and received non-need-based gift aid.

GIFT AID (NEED-BASED) ***Total amount:*** $19,883,216 (90% federal, 5% state, 5% institutional). ***Receiving aid:*** Freshmen: 43% (1,051); All full-time undergraduates: 38% (4,469). ***Average award:*** Freshmen: $3623; Undergraduates: $3330. ***Scholarships, grants, and awards:*** Federal Pell, FSEOG, state, private, college/university gift aid from institutional funds.

GIFT AID (NON-NEED-BASED) ***Total amount:*** $15,450,305 (1% federal, 20% state, 75% institutional, 4% external sources). ***Receiving aid:*** Freshmen: 31% (755); Undergraduates: 26% (3,056). ***Average award:*** Freshmen: $3333; Undergraduates: $4769. ***Scholarships, grants, and awards by category:*** *Academic Interests/Achievement:* 14 awards ($20,547 total): communication. *Creative Arts/Performance:* 529 awards ($771,221 total): art/fine arts, dance, debating, music, theater/drama. *Special Achievements/Activities:* general special achievements/activities. ***Tuition waivers:*** Full or partial for employees or children of employees, senior citizens. ***ROTC:*** Air Force cooperative.

LOANS ***Student loans:*** $56,236,951 (92% need-based, 8% non-need-based). 50% of past graduating class borrowed through all loan programs. *Average indebtedness per student:* $19,329. ***Average need-based loan:*** Freshmen: $2338; Undergraduates: $3629. ***Parent loans:*** $1,694,829 (100% need-based). ***Programs:*** FFEL (Subsidized and Unsubsidized Stafford, PLUS), Perkins, Federal Nursing, state, college/university.

WORK-STUDY ***Federal work-study:*** Total amount: $362,773; 417 jobs averaging $1423. ***State or other work-study/employment:*** Total amount: $106,864 (100% need-based). 189 part-time jobs averaging $1146.

ATHLETIC AWARDS Total amount: $2,354,518 (100% non-need-based).

APPLYING FOR FINANCIAL AID ***Required financial aid forms:*** FAFSA, income tax forms, W-2 forms. ***Financial aid deadline (priority):*** 3/1. ***Notification date:*** Continuous beginning 4/15. Students must reply within 2 weeks of notification.

CONTACT Catherine Kay, Interim Director of Scholarships and Financial Aid, Wayne State University, 3W HNJ Student Services Building, Detroit, MI 48202, 313-577-3378 or toll-free 877-978 Ext. 4636 (in-state), 800-WSU-INFO (out-of-state). *Fax:* 313-577-6648.

WEBBER INTERNATIONAL UNIVERSITY

Babson Park, FL

Tuition & fees: $15,900 Average undergraduate aid package: $15,080

ABOUT THE INSTITUTION Independent, coed. Awards: associate, bachelor's, and master's degrees. 11 undergraduate majors. Total enrollment: 617. Undergraduates: 560. Freshmen: 148. Federal methodology is used as a basis for awarding need-based institutional aid.

UNDERGRADUATE EXPENSES for 2006–07 ***Application fee:*** $35. ***Comprehensive fee:*** $20,890 includes full-time tuition ($15,900) and room and board ($4990). ***College room only:*** $2900. Full-time tuition and fees vary according to class time and course load. Room and board charges vary according to board plan. ***Part-time tuition:*** $200 per credit hour. Part-time tuition and fees vary according to course load. ***Payment plan:*** Installment.

FRESHMAN FINANCIAL AID (Fall 2006, est.) 111 applied for aid; of those 72% were deemed to have need. 100% of freshmen with need received aid; of those 35% had need fully met. ***Average percent of need met:*** 74% (excluding

resources awarded to replace EFC). ***Average financial aid package:*** $16,104 (excluding resources awarded to replace EFC). 44% of all full-time freshmen had no need and received non-need-based gift aid.

UNDERGRADUATE FINANCIAL AID (Fall 2006, est.) 381 applied for aid; of those 72% were deemed to have need. 100% of undergraduates with need received aid; of those 28% had need fully met. ***Average percent of need met:*** 85% (excluding resources awarded to replace EFC). ***Average financial aid package:*** $15,080 (excluding resources awarded to replace EFC). 31% of all full-time undergraduates had no need and received non-need-based gift aid.

GIFT AID (NEED-BASED) ***Total amount:*** $1,996,666 (33% federal, 50% state, 15% institutional, 2% external sources). ***Receiving aid:*** Freshmen: 55% (80); All full-time undergraduates: 55% (275). ***Average award:*** Freshmen: $13,789; Undergraduates: $11,208. ***Scholarships, grants, and awards:*** Federal Pell, FSEOG, state, private, college/university gift aid from institutional funds.

GIFT AID (NON-NEED-BASED) ***Total amount:*** $1,028,583 (48% state, 50% institutional, 2% external sources). ***Receiving aid:*** Freshmen: 55% (80); Undergraduates: 55% (272). ***Average award:*** Freshmen: $7391; Undergraduates: $4421. ***Scholarships, grants, and awards by category:*** *Academic Interests/Achievement:* 241 awards ($466,548 total): business, general academic interests/achievements. *Creative Arts/Performance:* 40 awards ($37,375 total): general creative arts/performance, journalism/publications. *Special Achievements/Activities:* 401 awards ($2,097,855 total): cheerleading/drum major, community service, general special achievements/activities, leadership, memberships. *Special Characteristics:* 146 awards ($290,593 total): children and siblings of alumni, children of faculty/staff, first-generation college students, general special characteristics, international students, local/state students, siblings of current students. ***Tuition waivers:*** Full or partial for children of alumni, employees or children of employees, adult students, senior citizens.

LOANS ***Student loans:*** $2,159,131 (86% need-based, 14% non-need-based). 75% of past graduating class borrowed through all loan programs. *Average indebtedness per student:* $23,642. ***Average need-based loan:*** Freshmen: $2535; Undergraduates: $3578. ***Parent loans:*** $534,042 (58% need-based, 42% non-need-based). ***Programs:*** FFEL (Subsidized and Unsubsidized Stafford, PLUS), Perkins, alternative loans.

WORK-STUDY ***Federal work-study:*** Total amount: $37,248; 44 jobs averaging $813. ***State or other work-study/employment:*** Total amount: $63,896 (22% need-based, 78% non-need-based). 36 part-time jobs averaging $1051.

ATHLETIC AWARDS Total amount: $2,133,380 (54% need-based, 46% non-need-based).

APPLYING FOR FINANCIAL AID ***Required financial aid forms:*** FAFSA, state aid form. ***Financial aid deadline:*** 8/1 (priority: 5/1). ***Notification date:*** Continuous beginning 4/1. Students must reply within 4 weeks of notification.

CONTACT Ms. Kathleen Wilson, Director of Financial Aid, Webber International University, PO Box 96, Babson Park, FL 33827-0096, 863-638-2930 or toll-free 800-741-1844. *Fax:* 863-638-1317. *E-mail:* wilson@webber.edu.

WEBB INSTITUTE

Glen Cove, NY

ABOUT THE INSTITUTION Independent, coed. Awards: bachelor's degrees. 1 undergraduate major. Total enrollment: 87. Undergraduates: 87. Freshmen: 24.

GIFT AID (NEED-BASED) ***Scholarships, grants, and awards:*** Federal Pell, private, college/university gift aid from institutional funds.

LOANS ***Programs:*** FFEL (Subsidized and Unsubsidized Stafford, PLUS).

APPLYING FOR FINANCIAL AID ***Required financial aid form:*** FAFSA.

CONTACT Stephen P Ostendorff, Director of Financial Aid, Webb Institute, Crescent Beach Road, Glen Cove, NY 11542-1398, 516-671-2213 Ext. 104. *Fax:* 516-674-9838. *E-mail:* sostendo@webb-institute.edu.

WEBER STATE UNIVERSITY

Ogden, UT

CONTACT Mr. Richard O. Effiong, Financial Aid Director, Weber State University, 120 Student Service Center, 1136 University Circle, Ogden, UT 84408-1136, 801-626-7569 or toll-free 800-634-6568 (in-state), 800-848-7770 (out-of-state). *E-mail:* finaid@weber.edu.

WEBSTER UNIVERSITY

St. Louis, MO

Tuition & fees: $18,240 **Average undergraduate aid package: $17,988**

ABOUT THE INSTITUTION Independent, coed. Awards: bachelor's, master's, and doctoral degrees and post-bachelor's and post-master's certificates. 56 undergraduate majors. Total enrollment: 7,840. Undergraduates: 3,567. Freshmen: 444. Federal methodology is used as a basis for awarding need-based institutional aid.

UNDERGRADUATE EXPENSES for 2006–07 ***Application fee:*** $25. ***Comprehensive fee:*** $25,643 includes full-time tuition ($18,240) and room and board ($7403). ***College room only:*** $3944. Full-time tuition and fees vary according to program. Room and board charges vary according to board plan and housing facility. ***Part-time tuition:*** $465 per credit hour. Part-time tuition and fees vary according to location. ***Payment plan:*** Installment.

FRESHMAN FINANCIAL AID (Fall 2006, est.) 401 applied for aid; of those 85% were deemed to have need. 100% of freshmen with need received aid. ***Average financial aid package:*** $18,807 (excluding resources awarded to replace EFC). 24% of all full-time freshmen had no need and received non-need-based gift aid.

UNDERGRADUATE FINANCIAL AID (Fall 2006, est.) 2,027 applied for aid; of those 86% were deemed to have need. 100% of undergraduates with need received aid. ***Average financial aid package:*** $17,988 (excluding resources awarded to replace EFC). 19% of all full-time undergraduates had no need and received non-need-based gift aid.

GIFT AID (NEED-BASED) ***Total amount:*** $19,198,776 (12% federal, 7% state, 54% institutional, 27% external sources). ***Receiving aid:*** Freshmen: 68% (290); All full-time undergraduates: 58% (1,465). ***Average award:*** Freshmen: $5585; Undergraduates: $5077. ***Scholarships, grants, and awards:*** Federal Pell, FSEOG, state, private, college/university gift aid from institutional funds.

GIFT AID (NON-NEED-BASED) ***Total amount:*** $4,499,895 (2% state, 66% institutional, 32% external sources). ***Receiving aid:*** Freshmen: 58% (248); Undergraduates: 42% (1,065). ***Average award:*** Freshmen: $8301; Undergraduates: $6846. ***Scholarships, grants, and awards by category:*** *Academic Interests/Achievement:* 1,447 awards ($7,750,316 total): education, general academic interests/achievements, humanities, international studies. *Creative Arts/Performance:* 130 awards ($142,000 total): art/fine arts, creative writing, debating, music, theater/drama. *Special Achievements/Activities:* 129 awards ($288,240 total): leadership. *Special Characteristics:* 57 awards ($293,180 total): international students. ***Tuition waivers:*** Full or partial for employees or children of employees. ***ROTC:*** Army cooperative, Air Force cooperative.

LOANS ***Student loans:*** $14,086,545 (89% need-based, 11% non-need-based). 58% of past graduating class borrowed through all loan programs. *Average indebtedness per student:* $22,690. ***Average need-based loan:*** Freshmen: $2632; Undergraduates: $4078. ***Parent loans:*** $3,239,028 (77% need-based, 23% non-need-based). ***Programs:*** FFEL (Subsidized and Unsubsidized Stafford, PLUS), Perkins.

WORK-STUDY ***Federal work-study:*** Total amount: $1,040,744; 514 jobs averaging $2086. ***State or other work-study/employment:*** Total amount: $666,232 (57% need-based, 43% non-need-based). 544 part-time jobs averaging $1272.

APPLYING FOR FINANCIAL AID ***Required financial aid forms:*** FAFSA, institution's own form. ***Financial aid deadline (priority):*** 4/1. ***Notification date:*** Continuous beginning 2/10. Students must reply within 2 weeks of notification.

CONTACT Marilynn Shelton, Financial Aid Counselor, Webster University, Financial Aid Office, 470 East Lockwood Avenue, St. Louis, MO 63119, 314-968-6992 Ext. 7671 or toll-free 800-75-ENROL. *Fax:* 314-968-7125. *E-mail:* sheltoma@webster.edu.

WELLESLEY COLLEGE

Wellesley, MA

Tuition & fees: $33,072 **Average undergraduate aid package: $29,797**

ABOUT THE INSTITUTION Independent, women only. Awards: bachelor's degrees (double bachelor's degree with Massachusetts Institute of Technology). 54 undergraduate majors. Total enrollment: 2,318. Undergraduates: 2,318. Freshmen: 586. Both federal and institutional methodology are used as a basis for awarding need-based institutional aid.

UNDERGRADUATE EXPENSES for 2006–07 ***Application fee:*** $50. ***Comprehensive fee:*** $43,288 includes full-time tuition ($32,384), mandatory fees ($688), and room and board ($10,216). ***College room only:*** $5176. Room and board charges vary according to board plan. ***Payment plans:*** Tuition prepayment, installment.

FRESHMAN FINANCIAL AID (Fall 2006, est.) 420 applied for aid; of those 78% were deemed to have need. 100% of freshmen with need received aid; of those 100% had need fully met. ***Average percent of need met:*** 100% (excluding resources awarded to replace EFC). ***Average financial aid package:*** $29,793 (excluding resources awarded to replace EFC).

UNDERGRADUATE FINANCIAL AID (Fall 2006, est.) 1,522 applied for aid; of those 87% were deemed to have need. 100% of undergraduates with need received aid; of those 100% had need fully met. ***Average percent of need met:*** 100% (excluding resources awarded to replace EFC). ***Average financial aid package:*** $29,797 (excluding resources awarded to replace EFC).

GIFT AID (NEED-BASED) ***Total amount:*** $35,003,467 (3% federal, 1% state, 92% institutional, 4% external sources). ***Receiving aid:*** Freshmen: 53% (313); All full-time undergraduates: 58% (1,262). ***Average award:*** Freshmen: $28,524; Undergraduates: $27,508. ***Scholarships, grants, and awards:*** Federal Pell, FSEOG, state, private, college/university gift aid from institutional funds.

GIFT AID (NON-NEED-BASED) ***Total amount:*** $584,152 (100% external sources). ***Tuition waivers:*** Full or partial for employees or children of employees. ***ROTC:*** Army cooperative, Air Force cooperative.

LOANS ***Student loans:*** $4,244,341 (80% need-based, 20% non-need-based). 55% of past graduating class borrowed through all loan programs. *Average indebtedness per student:* $10,206. ***Average need-based loan:*** Freshmen: $2397; Undergraduates: $3245. ***Parent loans:*** $5,675,237 (100% non-need-based). ***Programs:*** FFEL (Subsidized and Unsubsidized Stafford, PLUS), Perkins, state, college/university.

WORK-STUDY ***Federal work-study:*** Total amount: $898,604; 764 jobs averaging $1167. ***State or other work-study/employment:*** Total amount: $400,618 (100% need-based). 263 part-time jobs averaging $1216.

APPLYING FOR FINANCIAL AID ***Required financial aid forms:*** FAFSA, institution's own form, CSS Financial Aid PROFILE, noncustodial (divorced/separated) parent's statement, business/farm supplement, federal income tax form(s), W-2 forms. ***Financial aid deadline (priority):*** 1/15. ***Notification date:*** 4/1. Students must reply by 5/1.

CONTACT Ms. Kathryn Osmond, Director of Financial Aid, Wellesley College, 106 Central Street, Wellesley, MA 02481-8203, 781-283-2360. *Fax:* 781-283-3946. *E-mail:* finaid@wellesley.edu.

WELLS COLLEGE

Aurora, NY

Tuition & fees: $16,680 **Average undergraduate aid package: $17,562**

ABOUT THE INSTITUTION Independent, coed, primarily women. Awards: bachelor's degrees. 40 undergraduate majors. Total enrollment: 481. Undergraduates: 481. Freshmen: 167. Federal methodology is used as a basis for awarding need-based institutional aid.

UNDERGRADUATE EXPENSES for 2006–07 ***Application fee:*** $40. ***Comprehensive fee:*** $24,180 includes full-time tuition ($15,580), mandatory fees ($1100), and room and board ($7500). ***College room only:*** $3750. ***Part-time tuition:*** $650 per credit hour.

FRESHMAN FINANCIAL AID (Fall 2006, est.) 155 applied for aid; of those 89% were deemed to have need. 100% of freshmen with need received aid; of those 25% had need fully met. ***Average percent of need met:*** 90% (excluding resources awarded to replace EFC). ***Average financial aid package:*** $17,747 (excluding resources awarded to replace EFC). 7% of all full-time freshmen had no need and received non-need-based gift aid.

UNDERGRADUATE FINANCIAL AID (Fall 2006, est.) 403 applied for aid; of those 88% were deemed to have need. 100% of undergraduates with need received aid; of those 23% had need fully met. ***Average percent of need met:*** 89% (excluding resources awarded to replace EFC). ***Average financial aid package:*** $17,562 (excluding resources awarded to replace EFC). 12% of all full-time undergraduates had no need and received non-need-based gift aid.

GIFT AID (NEED-BASED) ***Total amount:*** $4,428,433 (16% federal, 13% state, 67% institutional, 4% external sources). ***Receiving aid:*** Freshmen: 83% (138); All full-time undergraduates: 76% (356). ***Average award:*** Freshmen: $13,557; Undergraduates: $12,439. ***Scholarships, grants, and awards:*** Federal Pell, FSEOG, state, private, college/university gift aid from institutional funds.

GIFT AID (NON-NEED-BASED) ***Total amount:*** $305,063 (5% state, 87% institutional, 8% external sources). ***Average award:*** Freshmen: $5458; Undergraduates: $4940. ***Scholarships, grants, and awards by category:*** *Academic Interests/Achievement:* 20 awards ($90,000 total): general academic interests/achievements. *Special Achievements/Activities:* 16 awards ($80,000 total): leadership. *Special Characteristics:* 6 awards ($13,750 total): children and siblings of alumni. ***ROTC:*** Army cooperative, Air Force cooperative.

LOANS ***Student loans:*** $1,794,006 (75% need-based, 25% non-need-based). 79% of past graduating class borrowed through all loan programs. *Average indebtedness per student:* $20,923. ***Average need-based loan:*** Freshmen: $3355; Undergraduates: $4383. ***Parent loans:*** $728,944 (100% non-need-based). ***Programs:*** FFEL (Subsidized and Unsubsidized Stafford, PLUS), Perkins.

WORK-STUDY ***Federal work-study:*** Total amount: $110,000; 78 jobs averaging $1400. ***State or other work-study/employment:*** Total amount: $450,467 (81% need-based, 19% non-need-based). 300 part-time jobs averaging $1500.

APPLYING FOR FINANCIAL AID ***Required financial aid form:*** FAFSA. ***Financial aid deadline (priority):*** 2/15. ***Notification date:*** 3/1. Students must reply by 5/1.

CONTACT Ms. Cathleen A. Patella, Director of Financial Aid, Wells College, Route 90, Aurora, NY 13026, 315-364-3289 or toll-free 800-952-9355. *Fax:* 315-364-3227. *E-mail:* cpatella@wells.edu.

WENTWORTH INSTITUTE OF TECHNOLOGY

Boston, MA

Tuition & fees: $19,300 **Average undergraduate aid package: $7625**

ABOUT THE INSTITUTION Independent, coed. Awards: associate and bachelor's degrees. 21 undergraduate majors. Total enrollment: 3,613. Undergraduates: 3,613. Freshmen: 792. Federal methodology is used as a basis for awarding need-based institutional aid.

UNDERGRADUATE EXPENSES for 2006–07 ***Application fee:*** $30. ***Comprehensive fee:*** $28,600 includes full-time tuition ($19,300) and room and board ($9300). Full-time tuition and fees vary according to student level. Room and board charges vary according to board plan. Part-time tuition and fees vary according to class time, course load, and degree level. ***Payment plan:*** Installment.

FRESHMAN FINANCIAL AID (Fall 2006, est.) 976 applied for aid; of those 60% were deemed to have need. 100% of freshmen with need received aid; of those 4% had need fully met. ***Average percent of need met:*** 40% (excluding resources awarded to replace EFC). ***Average financial aid package:*** $8443 (excluding resources awarded to replace EFC). 7% of all full-time freshmen had no need and received non-need-based gift aid.

UNDERGRADUATE FINANCIAL AID (Fall 2006, est.) 3,278 applied for aid; of those 56% were deemed to have need. 100% of undergraduates with need received aid; of those 4% had need fully met. ***Average percent of need met:*** 46% (excluding resources awarded to replace EFC). ***Average financial aid package:*** $7625 (excluding resources awarded to replace EFC). 4% of all full-time undergraduates had no need and received non-need-based gift aid.

GIFT AID (NEED-BASED) ***Total amount:*** $10,890,039 (19% federal, 4% state, 72% institutional, 5% external sources). ***Receiving aid:*** Freshmen: 17% (170); All full-time undergraduates: 11% (369). ***Average award:*** Freshmen: $1484; Undergraduates: $1396. ***Scholarships, grants, and awards:*** Federal Pell, FSEOG, state, private, college/university gift aid from institutional funds.

GIFT AID (NON-NEED-BASED) ***Total amount:*** $3,254,564 (98% institutional, 2% external sources). ***Receiving aid:*** Freshmen: 60% (584); Undergraduates: 45% (1,490). ***Average award:*** Freshmen: $5500; Undergraduates: $5217. ***Tuition waivers:*** Full or partial for employees or children of employees. ***ROTC:*** Army cooperative, Air Force cooperative.

LOANS ***Student loans:*** $13,977,827 (82% need-based, 18% non-need-based). 80% of past graduating class borrowed through all loan programs. *Average indebtedness per student:* $20,928. ***Average need-based loan:*** Freshmen: $2533; Undergraduates: $3559. ***Parent loans:*** $4,397,238 (91% need-based, 9% non-need-based). ***Programs:*** FFEL (Subsidized and Unsubsidized Stafford, PLUS), Perkins, state.

WORK-STUDY ***Federal work-study:*** Total amount: $2,422,590; 800 jobs averaging $1600.

APPLYING FOR FINANCIAL AID ***Required financial aid forms:*** FAFSA, state aid form. ***Financial aid deadline (priority):*** 3/1. ***Notification date:*** Continuous beginning 3/15. Students must reply within 2 weeks of notification.

CONTACT Shelle Riehl, Director of Financial Aid, Wentworth Institute of Technology, 550 Huntington Avenue, Boston, MA 02115-5998, 617-989-4033 or toll-free 800-556-0610. *Fax:* 617-989-4201. *E-mail:* shahanriehlr@wir.edu.

WESLEYAN COLLEGE

Macon, GA

ABOUT THE INSTITUTION Independent United Methodist, undergraduate: women only; graduate: coed. Awards: bachelor's and master's degrees. 31 undergraduate majors. Total enrollment: 636. Undergraduates: 540. Freshmen: 96.

GIFT AID (NEED-BASED) ***Scholarships, grants, and awards:*** Federal Pell, FSEOG, state, private, college/university gift aid from institutional funds.

GIFT AID (NON-NEED-BASED) ***Scholarships, grants, and awards by category:*** *Academic Interests/Achievement:* biological sciences, business, communication, education, English, foreign languages, general academic interests/achievements, humanities, mathematics, premedicine, religion/biblical studies, social sciences. *Creative Arts/Performance:* art/fine arts, music, theater/drama. *Special Achievements/Activities:* community service, general special achievements/activities, leadership, religious involvement. *Special Characteristics:* adult students, children and siblings of alumni, children of current students, children of faculty/staff, ethnic background, first-generation college students, general special characteristics, handicapped students, international students, out-of-state students, parents of current students, relatives of clergy, religious affiliation, siblings of current students, spouses of current students.

LOANS ***Programs:*** FFEL (Subsidized and Unsubsidized Stafford, PLUS), Perkins, college/university, various Alternative or Private Education Loans.

WORK-STUDY ***Federal work-study:*** Total amount: $51,804; 97 jobs averaging $1200. ***State or other work-study/employment:*** Total amount: $90,689 (8% need-based, 92% non-need-based). 147 part-time jobs averaging $1200.

APPLYING FOR FINANCIAL AID ***Required financial aid forms:*** FAFSA, institution's own form, state aid form.

CONTACT Quintress L. Hollis, Director of Financial Aid, Wesleyan College, 4760 Forsyth Road, Macon, GA 31210-4462, 478-757-5205 or toll-free 800-447-6610. *Fax:* 478-757-4030. *E-mail:* sjones@wesleyancollege.edu.

WESLEYAN UNIVERSITY

Middletown, CT

Tuition & fees: $35,144 **Average undergraduate aid package: $29,465**

ABOUT THE INSTITUTION Independent, coed. Awards: bachelor's, master's, and doctoral degrees and post-master's certificates. 48 undergraduate majors. Total enrollment: 3,220. Undergraduates: 2,813. Freshmen: 720. Both federal and institutional methodology are used as a basis for awarding need-based institutional aid.

UNDERGRADUATE EXPENSES for 2006–07 ***Application fee:*** $55. ***Comprehensive fee:*** $44,684 includes full-time tuition ($34,844), mandatory fees ($300), and room and board ($9540). ***College room only:*** $5808.

FRESHMAN FINANCIAL AID (Fall 2005) 352 applied for aid; of those 88% were deemed to have need. 100% of freshmen with need received aid; of those 100% had need fully met. ***Average percent of need met:*** 100% (excluding resources awarded to replace EFC). ***Average financial aid package:*** $29,476 (excluding resources awarded to replace EFC).

UNDERGRADUATE FINANCIAL AID (Fall 2005) 1,390 applied for aid; of those 95% were deemed to have need. 100% of undergraduates with need received aid; of those 100% had need fully met. ***Average percent of need met:*** 100% (excluding resources awarded to replace EFC). ***Average financial aid package:*** $29,465 (excluding resources awarded to replace EFC).

GIFT AID (NEED-BASED) ***Total amount:*** $30,155,774 (6% federal, 1% state, 90% institutional, 3% external sources). ***Receiving aid:*** Freshmen: 41% (291); All full-time undergraduates: 45% (1,232). ***Average award:*** Freshmen: $25,765; Undergraduates: $24,927. ***Scholarships, grants, and awards:*** Federal Pell, FSEOG, state, private, college/university gift aid from institutional funds.

GIFT AID (NON-NEED-BASED) ***ROTC:*** Air Force cooperative.

LOANS ***Student loans:*** $6,206,591 (100% need-based). 39% of past graduating class borrowed through all loan programs. *Average indebtedness per student:* $23,375. ***Average need-based loan:*** Freshmen: $2881; Undergraduates: $4812. ***Programs:*** FFEL (Subsidized and Unsubsidized Stafford, PLUS), Perkins, college/university.

WORK-STUDY ***Federal work-study:*** Total amount: $2,068,814; 1,028 jobs averaging $2012. ***State or other work-study/employment:*** Total amount: $329,156 (100% need-based). 130 part-time jobs averaging $1838.

APPLYING FOR FINANCIAL AID ***Required financial aid forms:*** FAFSA, CSS Financial Aid PROFILE, noncustodial (divorced/separated) parent's statement, business/farm supplement. ***Financial aid deadline:*** 2/15. ***Notification date:*** 4/1. Students must reply by 5/1 or within 2 weeks of notification.

CONTACT Jennifer Garratt Lawton, Director of Financial Aid, Wesleyan University, 237 High Street, Middletown, CT 06459-0260, 860-685-2800. *Fax:* 860-685-2801. *E-mail:* finaid@wesleyan.edu.

WESLEY COLLEGE

Dover, DE

Tuition & fees: $17,579 **Average undergraduate aid package: $15,250**

ABOUT THE INSTITUTION Independent United Methodist, coed. Awards: associate, bachelor's, and master's degrees and post-bachelor's and post-master's certificates. 18 undergraduate majors. Total enrollment: 2,306. Undergraduates: 2,128. Freshmen: 499. Federal methodology is used as a basis for awarding need-based institutional aid.

UNDERGRADUATE EXPENSES for 2007–08 ***Application fee:*** $25. ***Comprehensive fee:*** $25,379 includes full-time tuition ($16,750), mandatory fees ($829), and room and board ($7800). ***Part-time tuition:*** $610 per credit. ***Part-time fees:*** $20 per term.

FRESHMAN FINANCIAL AID (Fall 2005) 461 applied for aid; of those 95% were deemed to have need. 100% of freshmen with need received aid. ***Average percent of need met:*** 85% (excluding resources awarded to replace EFC). ***Average financial aid package:*** $15,250 (excluding resources awarded to replace EFC). 9% of all full-time freshmen had no need and received non-need-based gift aid.

UNDERGRADUATE FINANCIAL AID (Fall 2005) 1,751 applied for aid; of those 91% were deemed to have need. 100% of undergraduates with need received aid. ***Average percent of need met:*** 80% (excluding resources awarded to replace EFC). ***Average financial aid package:*** $15,250 (excluding resources awarded to replace EFC). 5% of all full-time undergraduates had no need and received non-need-based gift aid.

GIFT AID (NEED-BASED) ***Total amount:*** $3,361,227 (34% federal, 4% state, 62% institutional). ***Receiving aid:*** Freshmen: 83% (412); All full-time undergraduates: 73% (1,345). ***Average award:*** Freshmen: $6500; Undergraduates: $6500. ***Scholarships, grants, and awards:*** Federal Pell, FSEOG, state, private, college/university gift aid from institutional funds.

GIFT AID (NON-NEED-BASED) ***Receiving aid:*** Freshmen: 35% (175); Undergraduates: 63% (1,150). ***Average award:*** Freshmen: $2500; Undergraduates: $2500. ***Scholarships, grants, and awards by category:*** *Academic Interests/Achievement:* 25 awards ($5000 total): general academic interests/achievements. *Special Achievements/Activities:* 20 awards ($2500 total): community service, general special achievements/activities, leadership, religious involvement. ***ROTC:*** Army cooperative.

LOANS ***Student loans:*** $2,812,402 (100% need-based). 90% of past graduating class borrowed through all loan programs. *Average indebtedness per student:* $19,500. ***Average need-based loan:*** Freshmen: $2200; Undergraduates: $4250. ***Parent loans:*** $4,522,203 (100% need-based). ***Programs:*** Federal Direct (Subsidized and Unsubsidized Stafford, PLUS), FFEL (Subsidized and Unsubsidized Stafford, PLUS), Perkins, state, college/university.

WORK-STUDY ***Federal work-study:*** Total amount: $346,977; 189 jobs averaging $2250. ***State or other work-study/employment:*** Part-time jobs available.

APPLYING FOR FINANCIAL AID ***Required financial aid forms:*** FAFSA, institution's own form. ***Financial aid deadline (priority):*** 4/15. ***Notification date:*** Continuous. Students must reply within 2 weeks of notification.

CONTACT James Marks, Director of Student Financial Planning, Wesley College, 120 North State Street, Dover, DE 19901-3875, 302-736-2334 or toll-free 800-937-5398 Ext. 2400 (out-of-state). *Fax:* 302-736-2594. *E-mail:* marksja@wesley.edu.

WESLEY COLLEGE

Florence, MS

Tuition & fees: $8040 **Average undergraduate aid package: $5950**

ABOUT THE INSTITUTION Independent Congregational Methodist, coed. Awards: bachelor's degrees. 2 undergraduate majors. Total enrollment: 80. Undergraduates: 80. Freshmen: 19. Federal methodology is used as a basis for awarding need-based institutional aid.

UNDERGRADUATE EXPENSES for 2006–07 ***Application fee:*** $20. ***Comprehensive fee:*** $11,680 includes full-time tuition ($7360), mandatory fees ($680), and room and board ($3640). Full-time tuition and fees vary according to course load and program. ***Part-time tuition:*** $230 per credit hour. ***Part-time fees:*** $204 per term. Part-time tuition and fees vary according to course load and program. ***Payment plan:*** Installment.

FRESHMAN FINANCIAL AID (Fall 2006, est.) 15 applied for aid; of those 100% were deemed to have need. 100% of freshmen with need received aid. ***Average percent of need met:*** 55% (excluding resources awarded to replace EFC). ***Average financial aid package:*** $3090 (excluding resources awarded to replace EFC).

UNDERGRADUATE FINANCIAL AID (Fall 2006, est.) 60 applied for aid; of those 97% were deemed to have need. 100% of undergraduates with need received aid. ***Average percent of need met:*** 70% (excluding resources awarded to replace EFC). ***Average financial aid package:*** $5950 (excluding resources awarded to replace EFC). 6% of all full-time undergraduates had no need and received non-need-based gift aid.

GIFT AID (NEED-BASED) ***Total amount:*** $180,892 (96% federal, 4% state). ***Receiving aid:*** Freshmen: 59% (10); All full-time undergraduates: 64% (49). ***Average award:*** Freshmen: $2530; Undergraduates: $3025. ***Scholarships, grants, and awards:*** Federal Pell, FSEOG, state, college/university gift aid from institutional funds.

GIFT AID (NON-NEED-BASED) ***Total amount:*** $83,973 (62% institutional, 38% external sources). ***Average award:*** Undergraduates: $2040. ***Scholarships, grants, and awards by category:*** *Academic Interests/Achievement:* 8 awards ($4176 total): general academic interests/achievements. *Creative Arts/Performance:* 6 awards ($500 total): music. *Special Achievements/Activities:* 25 awards ($652 total): leadership, religious involvement. ***Tuition waivers:*** Full or partial for employees or children of employees.

LOANS ***Student loans:*** $463,400 (56% need-based, 44% non-need-based). 67% of past graduating class borrowed through all loan programs. *Average indebtedness per student:* $6750. ***Average need-based loan:*** Freshmen: $2100; Undergraduates: $3940. ***Parent loans:*** $45,300 (100% need-based). ***Programs:*** Federal Direct (Subsidized and Unsubsidized Stafford, PLUS), FFEL (Subsidized and Unsubsidized Stafford, PLUS), Perkins, alternative loans.

WORK-STUDY ***Federal work-study:*** Total amount: $25,296; 19 jobs averaging $1331.

APPLYING FOR FINANCIAL AID ***Required financial aid form:*** FAFSA. ***Financial aid deadline (priority):*** 8/20. ***Notification date:*** Continuous beginning 5/1. Students must reply within 2 weeks of notification.

CONTACT William Devore Jr., Director of Financial Aid, Wesley College, PO Box 1070, Florence, MS 39073-1070, 601-845-4086 or toll-free 800-748-9972. *Fax:* 601-845-2266. *E-mail:* wdevore@wesleycollege.edu.

WEST CHESTER UNIVERSITY OF PENNSYLVANIA

West Chester, PA

CONTACT Financial Aid Office, West Chester University of Pennsylvania, 138 E.O. Bull Center, West Chester, PA 19383, 610-436-2627 or toll-free 877-315-2165 (in-state). *Fax:* 610-436-2574.

WESTERN CAROLINA UNIVERSITY

Cullowhee, NC

Tuition & fees (NC res): $4609   **Average undergraduate aid package: $6857**

ABOUT THE INSTITUTION State-supported, coed. Awards: bachelor's, master's, and doctoral degrees and post-master's certificates. 66 undergraduate majors. Total enrollment: 8,861. Undergraduates: 7,146. Freshmen: 1,568. Federal methodology is used as a basis for awarding need-based institutional aid.

UNDERGRADUATE EXPENSES for 2006–07 ***Application fee:*** $40. ***Tuition, state resident:*** full-time $1,972; part-time $278.03 per hour. ***Tuition, nonresident:*** full-time $11,487; part-time $1,457.53 per hour. Part-time tuition and fees vary according to course load. ***College room and board:*** $5210; ***Room only:*** $2660. Room and board charges vary according to board plan and housing facility. ***Payment plan:*** Installment.

FRESHMAN FINANCIAL AID (Fall 2006, est.) 1144 applied for aid; of those 69% were deemed to have need. 99% of freshmen with need received aid; of those 34% had need fully met. ***Average percent of need met:*** 73% (excluding resources awarded to replace EFC). ***Average financial aid package:*** $6623 (excluding resources awarded to replace EFC). 9% of all full-time freshmen had no need and received non-need-based gift aid.

UNDERGRADUATE FINANCIAL AID (Fall 2006, est.) 4,297 applied for aid; of those 70% were deemed to have need. 98% of undergraduates with need received aid; of those 43% had need fully met. ***Average percent of need met:*** 79% (excluding resources awarded to replace EFC). ***Average financial aid package:*** $6857 (excluding resources awarded to replace EFC). 8% of all full-time undergraduates had no need and received non-need-based gift aid.

GIFT AID (NEED-BASED) ***Total amount:*** $12,620,577 (40% federal, 39% state, 14% institutional, 7% external sources). ***Receiving aid:*** Freshmen: 49% (774); All full-time undergraduates: 47% (2,895). ***Average award:*** Freshmen: $4702; Undergraduates: $4383. ***Scholarships, grants, and awards:*** Federal Pell, FSEOG, state, private, college/university gift aid from institutional funds.

GIFT AID (NON-NEED-BASED) ***Total amount:*** $2,649,044 (43% state, 28% institutional, 29% external sources). ***Receiving aid:*** Freshmen: 5% (71); Undergraduates: 4% (239). ***Average award:*** Freshmen: $1178; Undergraduates: $1333. ***Scholarships, grants, and awards by category:*** *Academic Interests/Achievement:* 726 awards ($843,391 total): biological sciences, business, communication, education, English, general academic interests/achievements, health fields, mathematics, social sciences. *Creative Arts/Performance:* 228 awards ($59,974 total): art/fine arts, music, theater/drama. *Special Characteristics:* 100 awards ($70,808 total): ethnic background, handicapped students, local/state students, members of minority groups. ***Tuition waivers:*** Full or partial for employees or children of employees, senior citizens.

LOANS ***Student loans:*** $16,728,570 (64% need-based, 36% non-need-based). 59% of past graduating class borrowed through all loan programs. *Average indebtedness per student:* $17,964. ***Average need-based loan:*** Freshmen: $2296; Undergraduates: $3183. ***Parent loans:*** $6,311,258 (34% need-based, 66% non-need-based). ***Programs:*** Federal Direct (Subsidized and Unsubsidized Stafford, PLUS), Perkins.

WORK-STUDY ***Federal work-study:*** Total amount: $593,313; 505 jobs averaging $1175.

ATHLETIC AWARDS Total amount: $2,027,959 (41% need-based, 59% non-need-based).

APPLYING FOR FINANCIAL AID ***Required financial aid forms:*** FAFSA, institution's own form. ***Financial aid deadline (priority):*** 3/31. ***Notification date:*** Continuous beginning 4/1.

CONTACT Ms. Nancy B. Dillard, Director of Financial Aid, Western Carolina University, 224 Killian Annex, Cullowhee, NC 28723, 828-227-7292 or toll-free 877-WCU4YOU. *Fax:* 828-227-7042. *E-mail:* dillard@email.wcu.edu.

WESTERN CONNECTICUT STATE UNIVERSITY

Danbury, CT

Tuition & fees (CT res): $6731   **Average undergraduate aid package: $6813**

ABOUT THE INSTITUTION State-supported, coed. Awards: associate, bachelor's, master's, and doctoral degrees. 39 undergraduate majors. Total enrollment: 6,086. Undergraduates: 5,384. Freshmen: 870. Federal methodology is used as a basis for awarding need-based institutional aid.

UNDERGRADUATE EXPENSES for 2006–07 ***Application fee:*** $50. ***Tuition, state resident:*** full-time $3187; part-time $304 per semester hour. ***Tuition, nonresident:*** full-time $10,315; part-time $304 per semester hour. ***Required fees:*** full-time $3544; $60 per term part-time. Full-time tuition and fees vary according to reciprocity agreements. ***College room and board:*** $7784; ***Room only:*** $4516. Room and board charges vary according to housing facility. ***Payment plan:*** Installment.

FRESHMAN FINANCIAL AID (Fall 2005) 610 applied for aid; of those 66% were deemed to have need. 94% of freshmen with need received aid; of those 33% had need fully met. ***Average percent of need met:*** 69% (excluding resources awarded to replace EFC). ***Average financial aid package:*** $6917 (excluding resources awarded to replace EFC). 6% of all full-time freshmen had no need and received non-need-based gift aid.

UNDERGRADUATE FINANCIAL AID (Fall 2005) 2,631 applied for aid; of those 69% were deemed to have need. 93% of undergraduates with need received aid; of those 24% had need fully met. ***Average percent of need met:*** 60% (excluding resources awarded to replace EFC). ***Average financial aid package:*** $6813 (excluding resources awarded to replace EFC). 37% of all full-time undergraduates had no need and received non-need-based gift aid.

GIFT AID (NEED-BASED) ***Total amount:*** $5,607,165 (35% federal, 60% state, 1% institutional, 4% external sources). ***Receiving aid:*** Freshmen: 45% (345); All full-time undergraduates: 37% (1,488). ***Average award:*** Freshmen: $4613; Undergraduates: $3603. ***Scholarships, grants, and awards:*** Federal Pell, FSEOG, state, private, college/university gift aid from institutional funds.

GIFT AID (NON-NEED-BASED) ***Total amount:*** $652,466 (49% institutional, 51% external sources). ***Receiving aid:*** Freshmen: 5% (36); Undergraduates: 2% (92). ***Average award:*** Freshmen: $3856; Undergraduates: $4077. ***Scholarships, grants, and awards by category:*** *Academic Interests/Achievement:* 45 awards ($170,015 total): general academic interests/achievements. ***Tuition waivers:*** Full or partial for employees or children of employees, senior citizens. ***ROTC:*** Army cooperative, Air Force cooperative.

LOANS ***Student loans:*** $12,120,358 (100% need-based). 47% of past graduating class borrowed through all loan programs. *Average indebtedness per student:* $6005. ***Average need-based loan:*** Freshmen: $2422; Undergraduates: $3313. ***Parent loans:*** $2,309,809 (100% need-based). ***Programs:*** FFEL (Subsidized and Unsubsidized Stafford, PLUS), Perkins.

WORK-STUDY ***Federal work-study:*** Total amount: $215,334; 78 jobs averaging $1180. ***State or other work-study/employment:*** Total amount: $973,470 (6% need-based, 94% non-need-based). 417 part-time jobs averaging $2273.

APPLYING FOR FINANCIAL AID ***Required financial aid forms:*** FAFSA, institution's own form. ***Financial aid deadline:*** 4/15 (priority: 3/15). ***Notification date:*** Continuous. Students must reply by 5/1 or within 2 weeks of notification.

CONTACT Nancy Barton, Director of Financial Aid, Western Connecticut State University, 181 White Street, Danbury, CT 06810-6860, 203-837-8580 or toll-free 877-837-9278. *Fax:* 203-837-8528. *E-mail:* bartonn@wcsu.edu.

WESTERN GOVERNORS UNIVERSITY

Salt Lake City, UT

CONTACT Stacey Ludwig-Hardman, Director of Academic Services, Western Governors University, 2040 East Murray Holladay Road, Suite #106, Salt Lake City, UT 84117, 801-274-3280 or toll-free 877-435-7948. *Fax:* 801-274-3305. *E-mail:* shardman@wgu.edu.

WESTERN ILLINOIS UNIVERSITY

Macomb, IL

Tuition & fees (IL res): $7411 **Average undergraduate aid package: $8525**

ABOUT THE INSTITUTION State-supported, coed. Awards: bachelor's, master's, and doctoral degrees and post-bachelor's and post-master's certificates. 53 undergraduate majors. Total enrollment: 13,602. Undergraduates: 11,334. Freshmen: 1,922. Federal methodology is used as a basis for awarding need-based institutional aid.

UNDERGRADUATE EXPENSES for 2006–07 ***Application fee:*** $30. ***Tuition, state resident:*** full-time $5439; part-time $181.30 per semester hour. ***Tuition, nonresident:*** full-time $8158; part-time $271.95 per semester hour. ***Required fees:*** full-time $1972; $49.47 per semester hour. Full-time tuition and fees vary according to course load, location, and student level. Part-time tuition and fees vary according to course load, location, and student level. ***College room and board:*** $6446; ***Room only:*** $3876. Room and board charges vary according to board plan, housing facility, and student level. ***Payment plan:*** Guaranteed tuition.

FRESHMAN FINANCIAL AID (Fall 2006, est.) 1449 applied for aid; of those 69% were deemed to have need. 97% of freshmen with need received aid; of those 39% had need fully met. ***Average percent of need met:*** 61% (excluding resources awarded to replace EFC). ***Average financial aid package:*** $6972 (excluding resources awarded to replace EFC). 5% of all full-time freshmen had no need and received non-need-based gift aid.

UNDERGRADUATE FINANCIAL AID (Fall 2006, est.) 7,217 applied for aid; of those 76% were deemed to have need. 98% of undergraduates with need received aid; of those 41% had need fully met. ***Average percent of need met:*** 65% (excluding resources awarded to replace EFC). ***Average financial aid package:*** $8525 (excluding resources awarded to replace EFC). 5% of all full-time undergraduates had no need and received non-need-based gift aid.

GIFT AID (NEED-BASED) ***Total amount:*** $26,403,707 (40% federal, 52% state, 6% institutional, 2% external sources). ***Receiving aid:*** Freshmen: 36% (684); All full-time undergraduates: 38% (3,903). ***Average award:*** Freshmen: $6596; Undergraduates: $6780. ***Scholarships, grants, and awards:*** Federal Pell, FSEOG, state, private, college/university gift aid from institutional funds.

GIFT AID (NON-NEED-BASED) ***Total amount:*** $4,701,536 (33% federal, 35% state, 26% institutional, 6% external sources). ***Average award:*** Freshmen: $3403; Undergraduates: $2394. ***Scholarships, grants, and awards by category:*** *Academic Interests/Achievement:* 3,032 awards ($2,072,459 total): agriculture, biological sciences, business, education, foreign languages, general academic interests/achievements, home economics, mathematics, physical sciences, social sciences. *Creative Arts/Performance:* 476 awards ($479,510 total): applied art and design, cinema/film/broadcasting, dance, debating, journalism/publications, music, performing arts, theater/drama. *Special Achievements/Activities:* 356 awards ($176,680 total): community service, leadership. *Special Characteristics:* 1,269 awards ($1,916,300 total): children of faculty/staff, general special characteristics, international students, members of minority groups, veterans' children. ***Tuition waivers:*** Full or partial for employees or children of employees, senior citizens. ***ROTC:*** Army.

LOANS ***Student loans:*** $37,062,831 (61% need-based, 39% non-need-based). 62% of past graduating class borrowed through all loan programs. *Average indebtedness per student:* $16,400. ***Average need-based loan:*** Freshmen: $2408; Undergraduates: $3674. ***Parent loans:*** $9,424,157 (59% need-based, 41% non-need-based). ***Programs:*** FFEL (Subsidized and Unsubsidized Stafford, PLUS), Perkins, college/university.

WORK-STUDY ***Federal work-study:*** Total amount: $399,242; 230 jobs averaging $1736. ***State or other work-study/employment:*** Total amount: $1,341,437 (63% need-based, 37% non-need-based). 1,567 part-time jobs averaging $856.

ATHLETIC AWARDS Total amount: $2,033,381 (51% need-based, 49% non-need-based).

APPLYING FOR FINANCIAL AID ***Required financial aid form:*** FAFSA. ***Financial aid deadline (priority):*** 2/15. ***Notification date:*** Continuous beginning 1/15.

CONTACT Financial Aid Office, Western Illinois University, 1 University Circle, 127 Sherman Hall, Macomb, IL 61455-1390, 309-298-2446 or toll-free 877-742-5948. *Fax:* 309-298-2353. *E-mail:* financial_aid@doss.wiu.edu.

WESTERN KENTUCKY UNIVERSITY

Bowling Green, KY

ABOUT THE INSTITUTION State-supported, coed. Awards: associate, bachelor's, and master's degrees and post-bachelor's, post-master's, and first professional certificates. 85 undergraduate majors. Total enrollment: 18,660. Undergraduates: 16,063. Freshmen: 3,235.

GIFT AID (NEED-BASED) ***Scholarships, grants, and awards:*** Federal Pell, FSEOG, state, private, college/university gift aid from institutional funds, United Negro College Fund.

GIFT AID (NON-NEED-BASED) ***Scholarships, grants, and awards by category:*** *Academic Interests/Achievement:* agriculture, biological sciences, business, communication, education, engineering/technologies, English, foreign languages, general academic interests/achievements, health fields, home economics, library science, mathematics, military science, physical sciences, premedicine, social sciences. *Creative Arts/Performance:* art/fine arts, cinema/film/broadcasting, dance, debating, general creative arts/performance, journalism/publications, music, theater/drama. *Special Achievements/Activities:* general special achievements/activities, leadership, memberships. *Special Characteristics:* adult students, children of union members/company employees, ethnic background, general special characteristics, handicapped students, international students, local/state students, members of minority groups, out-of-state students, religious affiliation, veterans, veterans' children.

LOANS ***Programs:*** FFEL (Subsidized and Unsubsidized Stafford, PLUS), Perkins, alternative loans.

APPLYING FOR FINANCIAL AID ***Required financial aid form:*** FAFSA.

CONTACT Cindy Burnette, Student Financial Assistance Director, Western Kentucky University, Potter Hall, Room 317, 1906 College Heights Blvd., Bowling Green, KY 42101-1018, 270-745-2758 or toll-free 800-495-8463 (in-state). *Fax:* 270-745-6586. *E-mail:* cindy.burnette@wku.edu.

WESTERN MICHIGAN UNIVERSITY

Kalamazoo, MI

CONTACT Mr. David Ladd, Associate Director of Student Financial Aid, Western Michigan University, 1903 West Michigan Avenue, Faunce Student Services Building, Room 3306, Kalamazoo, MI 49008-5337, 269-387-6000. *E-mail:* david.ladd@wmich.edu.

WESTERN NEW ENGLAND COLLEGE

Springfield, MA

Tuition & fees: $37,658 **Average undergraduate aid package: $15,179**

ABOUT THE INSTITUTION Independent, coed. Awards: associate, bachelor's, master's, and first professional degrees. 35 undergraduate majors. Total enrollment: 3,653. Undergraduates: 2,813. Freshmen: 738. Federal methodology is used as a basis for awarding need-based institutional aid.

UNDERGRADUATE EXPENSES for 2007–08 ***Application fee:*** $50. ***Comprehensive fee:*** $47,656 includes full-time tuition ($35,940), mandatory fees ($1718), and room and board ($9998). ***Part-time tuition:*** $481 per credit hour.

FRESHMAN FINANCIAL AID (Fall 2006, est.) 665 applied for aid; of those 82% were deemed to have need. 99% of freshmen with need received aid; of those 14% had need fully met. ***Average percent of need met:*** 73% (excluding resources awarded to replace EFC). ***Average financial aid package:*** $16,485 (excluding resources awarded to replace EFC). 10% of all full-time freshmen had no need and received non-need-based gift aid.

UNDERGRADUATE FINANCIAL AID (Fall 2006, est.) 2,156 applied for aid; of those 81% were deemed to have need. 98% of undergraduates with need received aid; of those 13% had need fully met. ***Average percent of need met:*** 68% (excluding resources awarded to replace EFC). ***Average financial aid package:*** $15,179 (excluding resources awarded to replace EFC). 10% of all full-time undergraduates had no need and received non-need-based gift aid.

GIFT AID (NEED-BASED) ***Total amount:*** $16,910,833 (8% federal, 3% state, 86% institutional, 3% external sources). ***Receiving aid:*** Freshmen: 75% (542); All full-time undergraduates: 70% (1,693). ***Average award:*** Freshmen: $11,683; Undergraduates: $10,317. ***Scholarships, grants, and awards:*** Federal Pell, FSEOG, state, private, college/university gift aid from institutional funds.

GIFT AID (NON-NEED-BASED) ***Total amount:*** $1,759,837 (100% institutional). ***Receiving aid:*** Freshmen: 5% (36); Undergraduates: 3% (77). ***Average award:*** Freshmen: $9072; Undergraduates: $7772. ***Scholarships, grants, and awards by category:*** *Academic Interests/Achievement:* business, engineering/technologies, general academic interests/achievements. *Creative Arts/Performance:* 1 award ($500 total): music. *Special Achievements/Activities:* community service, leadership. *Special Characteristics:* children of faculty/staff, children of union members/company employees, international students, local/state students, members of minority groups, out-of-state students, siblings of current students. ***ROTC:*** Army, Air Force cooperative.

LOANS ***Student loans:*** $25,541,044 (29% need-based, 71% non-need-based). ***Average need-based loan:*** Freshmen: $3816; Undergraduates: $4540. ***Parent loans:*** $4,778,743 (100% non-need-based). ***Programs:*** Federal Direct (Subsidized and Unsubsidized Stafford, PLUS), FFEL (PLUS), Perkins, state.

WORK-STUDY ***Federal work-study:*** Total amount: $1,613,917; 831 jobs averaging $1942. ***State or other work-study/employment:*** Total amount: $600,000 (100% non-need-based). Part-time jobs available.

APPLYING FOR FINANCIAL AID ***Required financial aid forms:*** FAFSA, federal income tax form(s) and W2's. ***Financial aid deadline (priority):*** 4/15. ***Notification date:*** Continuous beginning 3/15. Students must reply by 5/1 or within 2 weeks of notification.

CONTACT Mrs. Kathy M. Chambers, Associate Director of Student Administrative Services, Western New England College, 1215 Wilbraham Road, Springfield, MA 01119-2684, 413-796-2080 or toll-free 800-325-1122 Ext. 1321. *Fax:* 413-796-2081. *E-mail:* finaid@wnec.edu.

WESTERN NEW MEXICO UNIVERSITY

Silver City, NM

CONTACT Debra Reyes, Grant Counselor, Western New Mexico University, PO Box 680, Silver City, NM 88062, 505-538-6173 or toll-free 800-872-WNMU (in-state).

WESTERN OREGON UNIVERSITY

Monmouth, OR

Tuition & fees (OR res): $4683 **Average undergraduate aid package: $6902**

ABOUT THE INSTITUTION State-supported, coed. Awards: associate, bachelor's, and master's degrees and post-bachelor's certificates. 35 undergraduate majors. Total enrollment: 4,885. Undergraduates: 4,183. Freshmen: 805. Federal methodology is used as a basis for awarding need-based institutional aid.

UNDERGRADUATE EXPENSES for 2006–07 ***Application fee:*** $50. ***Tuition, state resident:*** full-time $3510; part-time $192 per credit. ***Tuition, nonresident:*** full-time $13,650; part-time $237 per credit. ***College room and board:*** $7030. Room and board charges vary according to board plan and housing facility. ***Payment plan:*** Deferred payment.

FRESHMAN FINANCIAL AID (Fall 2006, est.) 563 applied for aid; of those 76% were deemed to have need. 100% of freshmen with need received aid; of those 21% had need fully met. ***Average percent of need met:*** 66% (excluding resources awarded to replace EFC). ***Average financial aid package:*** $6317 (excluding resources awarded to replace EFC). 25% of all full-time freshmen had no need and received non-need-based gift aid.

UNDERGRADUATE FINANCIAL AID (Fall 2006, est.) 2,737 applied for aid; of those 80% were deemed to have need. 100% of undergraduates with need received aid; of those 18% had need fully met. ***Average percent of need met:*** 66% (excluding resources awarded to replace EFC). ***Average financial aid package:*** $6902 (excluding resources awarded to replace EFC). 21% of all full-time undergraduates had no need and received non-need-based gift aid.

GIFT AID (NEED-BASED) ***Total amount:*** $7,075,960 (54% federal, 16% state, 7% institutional, 23% external sources). ***Receiving aid:*** Freshmen: 57% (343); All full-time undergraduates: 53% (1,586). ***Average award:*** Freshmen: $5101; Undergraduates: $4740. ***Scholarships, grants, and awards:*** Federal Pell, FSEOG, state, private, college/university gift aid from institutional funds.

GIFT AID (NON-NEED-BASED) ***Total amount:*** $907,337 (1% state, 22% institutional, 77% external sources). ***Receiving aid:*** Freshmen: 6% (34); Undergraduates: 3% (100). ***Average award:*** Freshmen: $8319; Undergraduates: $8156. ***Scholarships, grants, and awards by category:*** *Academic Interests/Achievement:* 472 awards ($726,421 total): biological sciences, business, education, general academic interests/achievements, mathematics, physical sciences, social sciences. *Creative Arts/Performance:* 28 awards ($24,317 total): art/fine arts, dance, music, performing arts, theater/drama. *Special Achievements/Activities:* 168 awards ($289,614 total): general special achievements/activities. *Special Characteristics:* 9 awards ($55,458 total): international students, veterans. ***Tuition waivers:*** Full or partial for employees or children of employees. ***ROTC:*** Army, Air Force cooperative.

LOANS ***Student loans:*** $15,049,077 (71% need-based, 29% non-need-based). 60% of past graduating class borrowed through all loan programs. *Average indebtedness per student:* $19,337. ***Average need-based loan:*** Freshmen: $2314; Undergraduates: $3670. ***Parent loans:*** $6,408,159 (27% need-based, 73% non-need-based). ***Programs:*** Federal Direct (Subsidized and Unsubsidized Stafford, PLUS), Perkins, college/university.

WORK-STUDY ***Federal work-study:*** Total amount: $199,599; 234 jobs averaging $853.

ATHLETIC AWARDS Total amount: $263,677 (57% need-based, 43% non-need-based).

APPLYING FOR FINANCIAL AID ***Required financial aid form:*** FAFSA. ***Financial aid deadline (priority):*** 3/1. ***Notification date:*** Continuous beginning 3/20. Students must reply within 2 weeks of notification.

CONTACT Ms. Donna Fossum, Director of Financial Aid, Western Oregon University, 345 North Monmouth Avenue, Monmouth, OR 97361, 503-838-8475 or toll-free 877-877-1593. *Fax:* 503-838-8200. *E-mail:* finaid@wou.edu.

WESTERN STATE COLLEGE OF COLORADO

Gunnison, CO

ABOUT THE INSTITUTION State-supported, coed. Awards: bachelor's degrees. 75 undergraduate majors. Total enrollment: 2,094. Undergraduates: 2,094. Freshmen: 515.

GIFT AID (NEED-BASED) ***Scholarships, grants, and awards:*** Federal Pell, FSEOG, state, private, college/university gift aid from institutional funds.

GIFT AID (NON-NEED-BASED) ***Scholarships, grants, and awards by category:*** *Academic Interests/Achievement:* general academic interests/achievements. *Creative Arts/Performance:* art/fine arts, music. *Special Achievements/Activities:* leadership. *Special Characteristics:* children and siblings of alumni.

LOANS ***Programs:*** FFEL (Subsidized and Unsubsidized Stafford, PLUS), Perkins.

WORK-STUDY ***Federal work-study:*** Total amount: $210,000; 200 jobs averaging $1050. ***State or other work-study/employment:*** Total amount: $605,000 (34% need-based, 66% non-need-based). 161 part-time jobs averaging $1273.

APPLYING FOR FINANCIAL AID ***Required financial aid form:*** FAFSA.

CONTACT Marty Somero, Director, Financial Aid, Western State College of Colorado, Room 207, Taylor Hall, Gunnison, CO 81231, 970-943-3026 or toll-free 800-876-5309. *Fax:* 970-943-3086. *E-mail:* msomero@western.edu.

WESTERN WASHINGTON UNIVERSITY

Bellingham, WA

Tuition & fees (WA res): $5002 Average undergraduate aid package: $9310

ABOUT THE INSTITUTION State-supported, coed. Awards: bachelor's and master's degrees and post-bachelor's certificates. 98 undergraduate majors. Total enrollment: 14,035. Undergraduates: 12,838. Freshmen: 2,425. Federal methodology is used as a basis for awarding need-based institutional aid.

UNDERGRADUATE EXPENSES for 2006–07 ***Application fee:*** $50. ***Tuition, state resident:*** full-time $3894; part-time $145 per credit. ***Tuition, nonresident:*** full-time $14,441; part-time $497 per credit. Full-time tuition and fees vary according to location. Part-time tuition and fees vary according to location. ***College room and board:*** $6785; ***Room only:*** $4409. Room and board charges vary according to board plan and housing facility. ***Payment plan:*** Installment.

FRESHMAN FINANCIAL AID (Fall 2006, est.) 1646 applied for aid; of those 54% were deemed to have need. 96% of freshmen with need received aid; of those 31% had need fully met. ***Average percent of need met:*** 88% (excluding resources awarded to replace EFC). ***Average financial aid package:*** $8879 (excluding resources awarded to replace EFC). 2% of all full-time freshmen had no need and received non-need-based gift aid.

UNDERGRADUATE FINANCIAL AID (Fall 2006, est.) 6,855 applied for aid; of those 66% were deemed to have need. 97% of undergraduates with need received aid; of those 34% had need fully met. ***Average percent of need met:*** 87% (excluding resources awarded to replace EFC). ***Average financial aid package:*** $9310 (excluding resources awarded to replace EFC). 2% of all full-time undergraduates had no need and received non-need-based gift aid.

GIFT AID (NEED-BASED) ***Total amount:*** $19,600,332 (37% federal, 44% state, 12% institutional, 7% external sources). ***Receiving aid:*** Freshmen: 29% (699); All full-time undergraduates: 29% (3,435). ***Average award:*** Freshmen: $6161; Undergraduates: $6172. ***Scholarships, grants, and awards:*** Federal Pell, FSEOG, state, private, college/university gift aid from institutional funds.

GIFT AID (NON-NEED-BASED) ***Total amount:*** $1,917,804 (8% federal, 5% state, 29% institutional, 58% external sources). ***Receiving aid:*** Freshmen: 2% (52); Undergraduates: 1% (131). ***Average award:*** Freshmen: $964; Undergraduates: $1651. ***Scholarships, grants, and awards by category:*** *Academic Interests/Achievement:* biological sciences, business, communication, computer science, education, engineering/technologies, English, foreign languages, general academic interests/achievements, health fields, humanities, library science, mathematics, physical sciences, premedicine, social sciences. *Creative Arts/Performance:* applied art and design, art/fine arts, cinema/film/broadcasting, creative writing, dance, general creative arts/performance, journalism/publications, music, performing arts, theater/drama. *Special Achievements/Activities:* community service, leadership, memberships. *Special Characteristics:* children of public servants, children of union members/company employees, ethnic background, general special characteristics, international students, local/state students, members of minority groups, previous college experience, veterans. ***Tuition waivers:*** Full or partial for employees or children of employees.

LOANS ***Student loans:*** $27,523,080 (60% need-based, 40% non-need-based). 54% of past graduating class borrowed through all loan programs. *Average indebtedness per student:* $14,887. ***Average need-based loan:*** Freshmen: $2897; Undergraduates: $4198. ***Parent loans:*** $19,573,477 (13% need-based, 87% non-need-based). ***Programs:*** Federal Direct (Subsidized and Unsubsidized Stafford, PLUS), FFEL (PLUS), Perkins, college/university, alternative loans.

WORK-STUDY ***Federal work-study:*** Total amount: $564,849; 274 jobs averaging $2843. ***State or other work-study/employment:*** Total amount: $1,216,889 (100% need-based). 364 part-time jobs averaging $3124.

ATHLETIC AWARDS Total amount: $979,040 (36% need-based, 64% non-need-based).

APPLYING FOR FINANCIAL AID ***Required financial aid form:*** FAFSA. ***Financial aid deadline (priority):*** 2/15. ***Notification date:*** 5/1. Students must reply within 3 weeks of notification.

CONTACT Ms. Fidele Dent, Office Support Supervisor II, Student Financial Resources, Western Washington University, OM 255 MS 9006, Bellingham, WA 98225-9006, 360-650-3470. *E-mail:* financialaid@wwu.edu.

WESTFIELD STATE COLLEGE

Westfield, MA

Tuition & fees (MA res): $5657 Average undergraduate aid package: $6395

ABOUT THE INSTITUTION State-supported, coed. Awards: bachelor's and master's degrees and post-bachelor's and post-master's certificates. 49 undergraduate majors. Total enrollment: 5,345. Undergraduates: 4,667. Freshmen: 1,185. Federal methodology is used as a basis for awarding need-based institutional aid.

UNDERGRADUATE EXPENSES for 2006–07 ***Application fee:*** $25. ***Tuition, state resident:*** full-time $970. ***Tuition, nonresident:*** full-time $7050. ***College room and board:*** $6470.

FRESHMAN FINANCIAL AID (Fall 2005) 1005 applied for aid; of those 60% were deemed to have need. 98% of freshmen with need received aid; of those 16% had need fully met. ***Average percent of need met:*** 76% (excluding resources awarded to replace EFC). ***Average financial aid package:*** $6097 (excluding resources awarded to replace EFC). 1% of all full-time freshmen had no need and received non-need-based gift aid.

UNDERGRADUATE FINANCIAL AID (Fall 2005) 2,959 applied for aid; of those 65% were deemed to have need. 99% of undergraduates with need received aid; of those 24% had need fully met. ***Average percent of need met:*** 78% (excluding resources awarded to replace EFC). ***Average financial aid package:*** $6395 (excluding resources awarded to replace EFC). 1% of all full-time undergraduates had no need and received non-need-based gift aid.

GIFT AID (NEED-BASED) ***Total amount:*** $6,136,153 (37% federal, 36% state, 24% institutional, 3% external sources). ***Receiving aid:*** Freshmen: 36% (418); All full-time undergraduates: 32% (1,325). ***Average award:*** Freshmen: $4153; Undergraduates: $4053. ***Scholarships, grants, and awards:*** Federal Pell, FSEOG, state, private.

GIFT AID (NON-NEED-BASED) ***Total amount:*** $704,539 (20% state, 41% institutional, 39% external sources). ***Receiving aid:*** Freshmen: 13% (149); Undergraduates: 7% (292). ***Average award:*** Freshmen: $5657; Undergraduates: $4341. ***Scholarships, grants, and awards by category:*** *Academic Interests/Achievement:* 137 awards ($507,141 total): general academic interests/achievements. ***ROTC:*** Army cooperative, Air Force cooperative.

LOANS ***Student loans:*** $12,171,730 (56% need-based, 44% non-need-based). ***Average need-based loan:*** Freshmen: $2535; Undergraduates: $3318. ***Parent loans:*** $3,098,674 (26% need-based, 74% non-need-based). ***Programs:*** FFEL (Subsidized and Unsubsidized Stafford, PLUS), Perkins, state.

WORK-STUDY ***Federal work-study:*** Total amount: $366,753; 357 jobs averaging $1027.

APPLYING FOR FINANCIAL AID ***Required financial aid form:*** FAFSA. ***Financial aid deadline (priority):*** 3/1. ***Notification date:*** 4/15.

CONTACT Catherine Ryan, Financial Aid Director, Westfield State College, 333 Western Avenue, Westfield, MA 01086, 413-572-5218 or toll-free 800-322-8401 (in-state).

WEST LIBERTY STATE COLLEGE

West Liberty, WV

Tuition & fees (WV res): $3996 Average undergraduate aid package: N/A

ABOUT THE INSTITUTION State-supported, coed. Awards: associate and bachelor's degrees. 35 undergraduate majors. Total enrollment: 2,246. Undergraduates: 2,241. Freshmen: 421. Federal methodology is used as a basis for awarding need-based institutional aid.

UNDERGRADUATE EXPENSES for 2006–07 ***Tuition, state resident:*** full-time $3946; part-time $159.08 per hour. ***Tuition, nonresident:*** full-time $9630; part-time $395.92 per hour. ***College room and board:*** $5734; ***Room only:*** $3292. Room and board charges vary according to board plan and housing facility. ***Payment plans:*** Installment, deferred payment.

GIFT AID (NEED-BASED) ***Total amount:*** $3,504,951 (69% federal, 30% state, 1% institutional). ***Scholarships, grants, and awards:*** Federal Pell, FSEOG, state, private, college/university gift aid from institutional funds.

GIFT AID (NON-NEED-BASED) ***Total amount:*** $1,839,117 (55% state, 32% institutional, 13% external sources). ***Scholarships, grants, and awards by category:*** *Academic Interests/Achievement:* 273 awards ($604,597 total): business, communication, education, English, general academic interests/achievements, health fields, mathematics, physical sciences. *Creative Arts/Performance:* 69 awards ($155,061 total): art/fine arts, music, theater/drama. *Special Achievements/Activities:* cheerleading/drum major. *Special Characteristics:* 7 awards ($5954 total): children and siblings of alumni, children of faculty/staff. ***Tuition waivers:*** Full or partial for employees or children of employees, senior citizens.

LOANS ***Student loans:*** $8,959,279 (43% need-based, 57% non-need-based). *Average indebtedness per student:* $13,800. ***Parent loans:*** $946,046 (100% non-need-based). ***Programs:*** Federal Direct (Subsidized and Unsubsidized Stafford, PLUS), Perkins, Federal Nursing, alternative loans.

WORK-STUDY ***Federal work-study:*** Total amount: $130,000; 139 jobs averaging $952. ***State or other work-study/employment:*** Total amount: $219,633 (100% non-need-based). 55 part-time jobs averaging $3993.

ATHLETIC AWARDS Total amount: $428,625 (100% non-need-based).

APPLYING FOR FINANCIAL AID ***Required financial aid form:*** FAFSA. ***Financial aid deadline (priority):*** 3/1. ***Notification date:*** Continuous. Students must reply within 2 weeks of notification.

CONTACT Mr. Scott A. Cook, Director of Financial Aid, West Liberty State College, PO Box 295, West Liberty, WV 26074-0295, 304-336-8016 or toll-free 800-732-6204 Ext. 8076. *Fax:* 304-336-8088. *E-mail:* cookscot@westliberty.edu.

WESTMINSTER CHOIR COLLEGE OF RIDER UNIVERSITY

Princeton, NJ

CONTACT Student Financial Services, Westminster Choir College of Rider University, 2083 Lawrenceville Road, Lawrenceville, NJ 08648, 609-896-5360 or toll-free 800-96-CHOIR. *Fax:* 609-219-4487. *E-mail:* finaid@rider.edu.

WESTMINSTER COLLEGE

Fulton, MO

Tuition & fees: $15,030 **Average undergraduate aid package: $14,264**

ABOUT THE INSTITUTION Independent religious, coed. Awards: bachelor's degrees. 28 undergraduate majors. Total enrollment: 953. Undergraduates: 953. Freshmen: 278. Federal methodology is used as a basis for awarding need-based institutional aid.

UNDERGRADUATE EXPENSES for 2006–07 ***Comprehensive fee:*** $21,170 includes full-time tuition ($14,600), mandatory fees ($430), and room and board ($6140). ***College room only:*** $3170. Room and board charges vary according to board plan and housing facility. ***Part-time tuition:*** $750 per credit hour. ***Payment plan:*** Installment.

FRESHMAN FINANCIAL AID (Fall 2006, est.) 194 applied for aid; of those 77% were deemed to have need. 100% of freshmen with need received aid; of those 63% had need fully met. ***Average percent of need met:*** 87% (excluding resources awarded to replace EFC). ***Average financial aid package:*** $14,117 (excluding resources awarded to replace EFC). 44% of all full-time freshmen had no need and received non-need-based gift aid.

UNDERGRADUATE FINANCIAL AID (Fall 2006, est.) 612 applied for aid; of those 83% were deemed to have need. 100% of undergraduates with need received aid; of those 58% had need fully met. ***Average percent of need met:*** 85% (excluding resources awarded to replace EFC). ***Average financial aid package:*** $14,264 (excluding resources awarded to replace EFC). 43% of all full-time undergraduates had no need and received non-need-based gift aid.

GIFT AID (NEED-BASED) ***Total amount:*** $9,808,088 (7% federal, 5% state, 79% institutional, 9% external sources). ***Receiving aid:*** Freshmen: 53% (148); All full-time undergraduates: 55% (508). ***Average award:*** Freshmen: $11,535; Undergraduates: $10,643. ***Scholarships, grants, and awards:*** Federal Pell, FSEOG, state, private, college/university gift aid from institutional funds.

GIFT AID (NON-NEED-BASED) ***Average award:*** Freshmen: $9729; Undergraduates: $8771. ***Scholarships, grants, and awards by category:*** *Academic Interests/Achievement:* 601 awards ($4,069,755 total): general academic interests/achievements. *Creative Arts/Performance:* 7 awards ($7000 total): music. *Special Achievements/Activities:* 233 awards ($379,348 total): general special achievements/activities, leadership. *Special Characteristics:* 270 awards ($1,714,693 total): children and siblings of alumni, children of faculty/staff, ethnic background, international students, local/state students, relatives of clergy, religious affiliation, siblings of current students, twins. ***Tuition waivers:*** Full or partial for children of alumni, employees or children of employees. ***ROTC:*** Army cooperative, Air Force cooperative.

LOANS ***Student loans:*** $2,650,544 (49% need-based, 51% non-need-based). 64% of past graduating class borrowed through all loan programs. *Average indebtedness per student:* $16,477. ***Average need-based loan:*** Freshmen: $2645; Undergraduates: $3614. ***Parent loans:*** $1,143,842 (100% non-need-based). ***Programs:*** FFEL (Subsidized and Unsubsidized Stafford, PLUS), Perkins.

WORK-STUDY ***Federal work-study:*** Total amount: $90,000; 136 jobs averaging $662. ***State or other work-study/employment:*** Total amount: $205,000 (100% non-need-based). 149 part-time jobs averaging $1376.

APPLYING FOR FINANCIAL AID ***Required financial aid form:*** FAFSA. ***Financial aid deadline (priority):*** 2/15. ***Notification date:*** Continuous beginning 2/28. Students must reply within 3 weeks of notification.

CONTACT Ms. Aimee Bristow, Director of Financial Aid, Westminster College, 501 Westminster Avenue, Fulton, MO 65251-1299, 800-475-3361. *Fax:* 573-592-5255. *E-mail:* bristoa@westminster-mo.edu.

WESTMINSTER COLLEGE

New Wilmington, PA

Tuition & fees: $24,325 **Average undergraduate aid package: $20,157**

ABOUT THE INSTITUTION Independent religious, coed. Awards: bachelor's and master's degrees. 52 undergraduate majors. Total enrollment: 1,593. Undergraduates: 1,464. Freshmen: 359. Federal methodology is used as a basis for awarding need-based institutional aid.

UNDERGRADUATE EXPENSES for 2006–07 ***Application fee:*** $35. ***Comprehensive fee:*** $31,395 includes full-time tuition ($23,220), mandatory fees ($1105), and room and board ($7070). ***Part-time tuition:*** $730 per semester hour.

FRESHMAN FINANCIAL AID (Fall 2006, est.) 288 applied for aid; of those 88% were deemed to have need. 100% of freshmen with need received aid; of those 26% had need fully met. ***Average percent of need met:*** 91% (excluding resources awarded to replace EFC). ***Average financial aid package:*** $21,108 (excluding resources awarded to replace EFC). 18% of all full-time freshmen had no need and received non-need-based gift aid.

UNDERGRADUATE FINANCIAL AID (Fall 2006, est.) 1,136 applied for aid; of those 91% were deemed to have need. 100% of undergraduates with need received aid; of those 29% had need fully met. ***Average percent of need met:*** 88% (excluding resources awarded to replace EFC). ***Average financial aid package:*** $20,157 (excluding resources awarded to replace EFC). 20% of all full-time undergraduates had no need and received non-need-based gift aid.

GIFT AID (NEED-BASED) ***Total amount:*** $16,310,113 (7% federal, 13% state, 75% institutional, 5% external sources). ***Receiving aid:*** Freshmen: 80% (249); All full-time undergraduates: 78% (1,025). ***Average award:*** Freshmen: $17,435; Undergraduates: $15,900. ***Scholarships, grants, and awards:*** Federal Pell, FSEOG, state, private, college/university gift aid from institutional funds.

GIFT AID (NON-NEED-BASED) ***Total amount:*** $2,695,380 (98% institutional, 2% external sources). ***Receiving aid:*** Freshmen: 78% (243); Undergraduates: 74% (983). ***Average award:*** Freshmen: $10,715; Undergraduates: $9780. ***Scholarships, grants, and awards by category:*** *Academic Interests/Achievement:* 1,105 awards ($8,605,983 total): general academic interests/achievements. *Creative Arts/Performance:* 178 awards ($177,275 total): cinema/film/broadcasting, general creative arts/performance, music, theater/drama. *Special*

Characteristics: 393 awards ($1,090,483 total): children and siblings of alumni, general special characteristics, international students, religious affiliation. ***ROTC:*** Army cooperative.

LOANS ***Student loans:*** $6,852,217 (95% need-based, 5% non-need-based). 80% of past graduating class borrowed through all loan programs. *Average indebtedness per student:* $23,592. ***Average need-based loan:*** Freshmen: $3576; Undergraduates: $4183. ***Parent loans:*** $2,221,974 (87% need-based, 13% non-need-based). ***Programs:*** FFEL (Subsidized and Unsubsidized Stafford, PLUS), Perkins, Resource Loans.

WORK-STUDY ***Federal work-study:*** Total amount: $544,860; 343 jobs averaging $1591. ***State or other work-study/employment:*** Total amount: $301,527 (67% need-based, 33% non-need-based). 173 part-time jobs averaging $1743.

APPLYING FOR FINANCIAL AID ***Required financial aid forms:*** FAFSA, institution's own form. ***Financial aid deadline (priority):*** 5/1. ***Notification date:*** Continuous beginning 11/1. Students must reply by 5/1 or within 3 weeks of notification.

CONTACT Mrs. Cheryl A. Gerber, Director of Financial Aid, Westminster College, South Market Street, New Wilmington, PA 16172-0001, 724-946-7102 or toll-free 800-942-8033 (in-state). *Fax:* 724-946-6171. *E-mail:* gerberca@westminster.edu.

WESTMINSTER COLLEGE

Salt Lake City, UT

Tuition & fees: $21,030 **Average undergraduate aid package: $15,651**

ABOUT THE INSTITUTION Independent, coed. Awards: bachelor's and master's degrees and post-bachelor's certificates. 33 undergraduate majors. Total enrollment: 2,479. Undergraduates: 1,959. Freshmen: 375. Federal methodology is used as a basis for awarding need-based institutional aid.

UNDERGRADUATE EXPENSES for 2006–07 ***Application fee:*** $40. ***Comprehensive fee:*** $27,170 includes full-time tuition ($20,640), mandatory fees ($390), and room and board ($6140). Full-time tuition and fees vary according to course load. Room and board charges vary according to board plan. ***Part-time tuition:*** $860 per credit hour. ***Part-time fees:*** $220 per term. ***Payment plans:*** Installment, deferred payment.

FRESHMAN FINANCIAL AID (Fall 2005) 244 applied for aid; of those 82% were deemed to have need. 100% of freshmen with need received aid; of those 85% had need fully met. ***Average percent of need met:*** 92% (excluding resources awarded to replace EFC). ***Average financial aid package:*** $15,920 (excluding resources awarded to replace EFC). 35% of all full-time freshmen had no need and received non-need-based gift aid.

UNDERGRADUATE FINANCIAL AID (Fall 2005) 1,323 applied for aid; of those 89% were deemed to have need. 100% of undergraduates with need received aid; of those 46% had need fully met. ***Average percent of need met:*** 88% (excluding resources awarded to replace EFC). ***Average financial aid package:*** $15,651 (excluding resources awarded to replace EFC). 29% of all full-time undergraduates had no need and received non-need-based gift aid.

GIFT AID (NEED-BASED) ***Total amount:*** $11,117,345 (16% federal, 1% state, 76% institutional, 7% external sources). ***Receiving aid:*** Freshmen: 63% (199); All full-time undergraduates: 70% (1,169). ***Average award:*** Freshmen: $10,499; Undergraduates: $9154. ***Scholarships, grants, and awards:*** Federal Pell, FSEOG, state, private, college/university gift aid from institutional funds, United Negro College Fund.

GIFT AID (NON-NEED-BASED) ***Total amount:*** $4,859,640 (75% institutional, 25% external sources). ***Receiving aid:*** Freshmen: 8% (26); Undergraduates: 7% (112). ***Average award:*** Freshmen: $8031; Undergraduates: $6998. ***Scholarships, grants, and awards by category:*** *Academic Interests/Achievement:* 1,713 awards ($11,521,710 total): biological sciences, business, communication, computer science, education, English, general academic interests/achievements, health fields, humanities, international studies, mathematics, military science, physical sciences, premedicine, social sciences. *Creative Arts/Performance:* 43 awards ($107,000 total): art/fine arts, journalism/publications, music, theater/drama. *Special Characteristics:* 106 awards ($285,000 total): adult students, children and siblings of alumni, children of faculty/staff, children of public servants, ethnic background, first-generation college students, handicapped students, international students, local/state students, members of minority groups, public servants, relatives of clergy, religious affiliation, siblings of current students, spouses of current students, veterans, veterans' children. ***Tuition waivers:*** Full or partial for employees or children of employees. ***ROTC:*** Army cooperative, Naval cooperative, Air Force cooperative.

LOANS ***Student loans:*** $10,083,587 (78% need-based, 21% non-need-based). 64% of past graduating class borrowed through all loan programs. *Average indebtedness per student:* $16,450. ***Average need-based loan:*** Freshmen: $3218; Undergraduates: $4122. ***Parent loans:*** $770,943 (44% need-based, 56% non-need-based). ***Programs:*** FFEL (Subsidized and Unsubsidized Stafford, PLUS), Perkins.

WORK-STUDY ***Federal work-study:*** Total amount: $405,925; 248 jobs averaging $2050. ***State or other work-study/employment:*** Total amount: $450,000 (100% non-need-based).

ATHLETIC AWARDS Total amount: $78,500 (35% need-based, 65% non-need-based).

APPLYING FOR FINANCIAL AID ***Required financial aid form:*** FAFSA. ***Financial aid deadline (priority):*** 4/15. ***Notification date:*** Continuous beginning 3/15. Students must reply within 3 weeks of notification.

CONTACT Craig Green, Director of Financial Aid, Westminster College, 1840 South 1300 East, Salt Lake City, UT 84105, 801-832-2500 or toll-free 800-748-4753 (out-of-state). *Fax:* 801-832-2502. *E-mail:* cgreen@westminstercollege.edu.

WESTMONT COLLEGE

Santa Barbara, CA

Tuition & fees: $29,470 **Average undergraduate aid package: $20,266**

ABOUT THE INSTITUTION Independent nondenominational, coed. Awards: bachelor's degrees and post-bachelor's certificates. 43 undergraduate majors. Total enrollment: 1,337. Undergraduates: 1,332. Freshmen: 329. Federal methodology is used as a basis for awarding need-based institutional aid.

UNDERGRADUATE EXPENSES for 2006–07 ***Application fee:*** $50. ***Comprehensive fee:*** $38,702 includes full-time tuition ($28,700), mandatory fees ($770), and room and board ($9232). ***College room only:*** $5672. Room and board charges vary according to board plan. ***Payment plan:*** Installment.

FRESHMAN FINANCIAL AID (Fall 2006, est.) 248 applied for aid; of those 77% were deemed to have need. 99% of freshmen with need received aid; of those 11% had need fully met. ***Average percent of need met:*** 69% (excluding resources awarded to replace EFC). ***Average financial aid package:*** $20,388 (excluding resources awarded to replace EFC). 29% of all full-time freshmen had no need and received non-need-based gift aid.

UNDERGRADUATE FINANCIAL AID (Fall 2006, est.) 853 applied for aid; of those 83% were deemed to have need. 100% of undergraduates with need received aid; of those 9% had need fully met. ***Average percent of need met:*** 69% (excluding resources awarded to replace EFC). ***Average financial aid package:*** $20,266 (excluding resources awarded to replace EFC). 31% of all full-time undergraduates had no need and received non-need-based gift aid.

GIFT AID (NEED-BASED) ***Total amount:*** $9,683,585 (7% federal, 17% state, 71% institutional, 5% external sources). ***Receiving aid:*** Freshmen: 57% (186); All full-time undergraduates: 53% (699). ***Average award:*** Freshmen: $16,475; Undergraduates: $14,968. ***Scholarships, grants, and awards:*** Federal Pell, FSEOG, state, private, college/university gift aid from institutional funds.

GIFT AID (NON-NEED-BASED) ***Total amount:*** $3,436,758 (93% institutional, 7% external sources). ***Receiving aid:*** Freshmen: 5% (18); Undergraduates: 4% (55). ***Average award:*** Freshmen: $10,939; Undergraduates: $10,869. ***Scholarships, grants, and awards by category:*** *Academic Interests/Achievement:* 801 awards ($5,050,779 total): general academic interests/achievements. *Creative Arts/Performance:* 77 awards ($76,586 total): art/fine arts, music, theater/drama. *Special Achievements/Activities:* 57 awards ($87,250 total): general special achievements/activities, leadership. *Special Characteristics:* 255 awards ($1,525,916 total): children of faculty/staff, ethnic background, international students. ***Tuition waivers:*** Full or partial for employees or children of employees. ***ROTC:*** Army cooperative, Air Force cooperative.

LOANS ***Student loans:*** $5,440,144 (75% need-based, 25% non-need-based). 67% of past graduating class borrowed through all loan programs. *Average indebtedness per student:* $16,801. ***Average need-based loan:*** Freshmen: $3715; Undergraduates: $5690. ***Parent loans:*** $2,638,915 (22% need-based, 78% non-need-based). ***Programs:*** FFEL (Subsidized and Unsubsidized Stafford, PLUS), Perkins, college/university, alternative loans.

WORK-STUDY ***Federal work-study:*** Total amount: $248,769; 169 jobs averaging $910.

ATHLETIC AWARDS Total amount: $717,074 (53% need-based, 47% non-need-based).

APPLYING FOR FINANCIAL AID ***Required financial aid form:*** FAFSA. ***Financial aid deadline (priority):*** 3/1. ***Notification date:*** 3/1. Students must reply by 5/1 or within 2 weeks of notification.

CONTACT Mrs. Diane L. Horvath, Director of Financial Aid, Westmont College, 955 La Paz Road, Santa Barbara, CA 93108, 805-565-6061 or toll-free 800-777-9011. *Fax:* 805-565-7157. *E-mail:* dhorvath@westmont.edu.

WEST SUBURBAN COLLEGE OF NURSING

Oak Park, IL

CONTACT Ms. Ruth Rehwadt, Director of Financial Aid, West Suburban College of Nursing, 3 Erie Court, Oak Park, IL 60302, 708-287-8100.

WEST TEXAS A&M UNIVERSITY

Canyon, TX

ABOUT THE INSTITUTION State-supported, coed. Awards: bachelor's, master's, and doctoral degrees. 59 undergraduate majors. Total enrollment: 7,412. Undergraduates: 5,895. Freshmen: 919.

GIFT AID (NEED-BASED) ***Scholarships, grants, and awards:*** Federal Pell, FSEOG, state, college/university gift aid from institutional funds.

GIFT AID (NON-NEED-BASED) ***Scholarships, grants, and awards by category:*** *Academic Interests/Achievement:* agriculture, biological sciences, business, communication, computer science, education, English, foreign languages, general academic interests/achievements, health fields, humanities, mathematics, physical sciences, social sciences. *Creative Arts/Performance:* art/fine arts, dance, debating, journalism/publications, music, theater/drama. *Special Achievements/Activities:* cheerleading/drum major, leadership, memberships, rodeo. *Special Characteristics:* children of faculty/staff, first-generation college students, handicapped students.

LOANS ***Programs:*** FFEL (Subsidized and Unsubsidized Stafford, PLUS), Perkins, state, college/university.

APPLYING FOR FINANCIAL AID ***Required financial aid forms:*** FAFSA, scholarship application form(s).

CONTACT Mr. Jim Reed, Director of Financial Aid, West Texas A&M University, WTAMU Box 60939, Canyon, TX 79016-0001, 806-651-2055 or toll-free 800-99-WTAMU. *Fax:* 806-651-2924. *E-mail:* jreed@mail.wtamu.edu.

WEST VIRGINIA STATE UNIVERSITY

Institute, WV

CONTACT Mrs. Mary Blizzard, Director, Office of Student Financial Assistance, West Virginia State University, PO Box 1000, Ferrell Hall 324, Institute, WV 25112-1000, 304-766-3131 or toll-free 800-987-2112.

WEST VIRGINIA UNIVERSITY

Morgantown, WV

Tuition & fees (WV res): $4476 Average undergraduate aid package: $5977

ABOUT THE INSTITUTION State-supported, coed. Awards: bachelor's, master's, doctoral, and first professional degrees. 75 undergraduate majors. Total enrollment: 27,115. Undergraduates: 20,590. Freshmen: 4,828. Federal methodology is used as a basis for awarding need-based institutional aid.

UNDERGRADUATE EXPENSES for 2006–07 ***Application fee:*** $25. ***Tuition, state resident:*** full-time $4476; part-time $186 per credit hour. ***Tuition, nonresident:*** full-time $13,840; part-time $576 per credit hour. Full-time tuition and fees vary according to location, program, and reciprocity agreements. Part-time tuition and fees vary according to course load, location, program, and reciprocity agreements. ***College room and board:*** $6630; ***Room only:*** $3500. Room and board charges vary according to board plan, housing facility, and location. ***Payment plan:*** Installment.

FRESHMAN FINANCIAL AID (Fall 2005) 3503 applied for aid; of those 79% were deemed to have need. 96% of freshmen with need received aid; of those 45% had need fully met. ***Average percent of need met:*** 85% (excluding resources awarded to replace EFC). ***Average financial aid package:*** $4911 (excluding resources awarded to replace EFC). 27% of all full-time freshmen had no need and received non-need-based gift aid.

UNDERGRADUATE FINANCIAL AID (Fall 2005) 14,547 applied for aid; of those 92% were deemed to have need. 93% of undergraduates with need received aid; of those 26% had need fully met. ***Average percent of need met:*** 87% (excluding resources awarded to replace EFC). ***Average financial aid package:*** $5977 (excluding resources awarded to replace EFC). 36% of all full-time undergraduates had no need and received non-need-based gift aid.

GIFT AID (NEED-BASED) ***Total amount:*** $21,289,186 (64% federal, 24% state, 12% institutional). ***Receiving aid:*** Freshmen: 34% (1,523); All full-time undergraduates: 37% (6,754). ***Average award:*** Freshmen: $3064; Undergraduates: $3152. ***Scholarships, grants, and awards:*** Federal Pell, FSEOG, state, private, college/university gift aid from institutional funds.

GIFT AID (NON-NEED-BASED) ***Total amount:*** $24,352,422 (1% federal, 72% state, 19% institutional, 8% external sources). ***Receiving aid:*** Freshmen: 37% (1,683); Undergraduates: 30% (5,592). ***Average award:*** Freshmen: $5400; Undergraduates: $3100. ***Scholarships, grants, and awards by category:*** *Academic Interests/Achievement:* 3,000 awards ($5,000,000 total): agriculture, architecture, area/ethnic studies, biological sciences, business, communication, computer science, education, engineering/technologies, English, foreign languages, general academic interests/achievements, health fields, home economics, humanities, international studies, library science, mathematics, military science, physical sciences, premedicine, religion/biblical studies, social sciences. *Creative Arts/Performance:* 100 awards ($660,000 total): art/fine arts, debating, music, theater/drama. *Special Achievements/Activities:* 12 awards ($35,000 total): general special achievements/activities, leadership. *Special Characteristics:* 500 awards ($1,100,000 total): children of faculty/staff, children of union members/company employees, children of workers in trades, ethnic background, general special characteristics, international students, local/state students, members of minority groups. ***Tuition waivers:*** Full or partial for employees or children of employees, senior citizens. ***ROTC:*** Army, Air Force.

LOANS ***Student loans:*** $66,922,976 (47% need-based, 53% non-need-based). 50% of past graduating class borrowed through all loan programs. *Average indebtedness per student:* $20,100. ***Average need-based loan:*** Freshmen: $3624; Undergraduates: $4123. ***Parent loans:*** $33,906,614 (100% non-need-based). ***Programs:*** Federal Direct (Subsidized and Unsubsidized Stafford, PLUS), Perkins, college/university.

WORK-STUDY ***Federal work-study:*** Total amount: $1,733,494; 1,665 jobs averaging $1003. ***State or other work-study/employment:*** Total amount: $519,510 (100% non-need-based). 1,230 part-time jobs averaging $1070.

ATHLETIC AWARDS Total amount: $4,945,432 (100% non-need-based).

APPLYING FOR FINANCIAL AID ***Required financial aid form:*** FAFSA. ***Financial aid deadline:*** 3/1. ***Notification date:*** Continuous beginning 3/15. Students must reply within 4 weeks of notification.

CONTACT Kaye Widney, Director of Financial Aid, West Virginia University, PO Box 6004, Morgantown, WV 26506-6004, 304-293-5242 or toll-free 800-344-9881. *Fax:* 304-293-4890. *E-mail:* kaye.widney@mail.wvu.edu.

WEST VIRGINIA UNIVERSITY INSTITUTE OF TECHNOLOGY

Montgomery, WV

CONTACT Nina M. Morton, Director of Financial Aid, West Virginia University Institute of Technology, 405 Fayette Pike, Montgomery, WV 25136, 304-442-3032 or toll-free 888-554-8324.

WEST VIRGINIA WESLEYAN COLLEGE

Buckhannon, WV

Tuition & fees: $20,980 Average undergraduate aid package: $21,248

ABOUT THE INSTITUTION Independent religious, coed. Awards: bachelor's and master's degrees. 64 undergraduate majors. Total enrollment: 1,222. Undergraduates: 1,176. Freshmen: 291. Federal methodology is used as a basis for awarding need-based institutional aid.

UNDERGRADUATE EXPENSES for 2007–08 ***Application fee:*** $35. ***Comprehensive fee:*** $27,140 includes full-time tuition ($20,980) and room and board ($6160).

FRESHMAN FINANCIAL AID (Fall 2006, est.) 258 applied for aid; of those 85% were deemed to have need. 100% of freshmen with need received aid; of those 32% had need fully met. ***Average percent of need met:*** 86% (excluding resources awarded to replace EFC). ***Average financial aid package:*** $20,750 (excluding resources awarded to replace EFC). 24% of all full-time freshmen had no need and received non-need-based gift aid.

UNDERGRADUATE FINANCIAL AID (Fall 2006, est.) 942 applied for aid; of those 91% were deemed to have need. 100% of undergraduates with need received aid; of those 33% had need fully met. ***Average percent of need met:*** 86% (excluding resources awarded to replace EFC). ***Average financial aid package:*** $21,248 (excluding resources awarded to replace EFC). 25% of all full-time undergraduates had no need and received non-need-based gift aid.

GIFT AID (NEED-BASED) ***Total amount:*** $11,333,306 (10% federal, 4% state, 82% institutional, 4% external sources). ***Receiving aid:*** Freshmen: 76% (219); All full-time undergraduates: 75% (857). ***Average award:*** Freshmen: $15,886; Undergraduates: $14,881. ***Scholarships, grants, and awards:*** Federal Pell, FSEOG, state, private, college/university gift aid from institutional funds, Federal Nursing.

GIFT AID (NON-NEED-BASED) ***Total amount:*** $3,903,861 (30% state, 57% institutional, 13% external sources). ***Receiving aid:*** Freshmen: 22% (63); Undergraduates: 20% (227). ***Average award:*** Freshmen: $8007; Undergraduates: $7815. ***Scholarships, grants, and awards by category:*** *Academic Interests/Achievement:* English, general academic interests/achievements, physical sciences. *Creative Arts/Performance:* art/fine arts, music, performing arts, theater/drama. *Special Achievements/Activities:* community service, leadership, religious involvement. *Special Characteristics:* children and siblings of alumni, children of faculty/staff, general special characteristics, international students, members of minority groups, relatives of clergy, religious affiliation.

LOANS ***Student loans:*** $4,464,988 (77% need-based, 23% non-need-based). 69% of past graduating class borrowed through all loan programs. *Average indebtedness per student:* $19,090. ***Average need-based loan:*** Freshmen: $2121; Undergraduates: $4009. ***Parent loans:*** $1,456,714 (34% need-based, 66% non-need-based). ***Programs:*** FFEL (Subsidized and Unsubsidized Stafford, PLUS), Perkins, Federal Nursing, college/university.

WORK-STUDY ***Federal work-study:*** Total amount: $718,400; jobs available. ***State or other work-study/employment:*** Total amount: $619,900 (100% non-need-based). Part-time jobs available.

ATHLETIC AWARDS Total amount: $2,155,299 (66% need-based, 34% non-need-based).

APPLYING FOR FINANCIAL AID ***Required financial aid form:*** FAFSA. ***Financial aid deadline (priority):*** 2/15. ***Notification date:*** Continuous beginning 3/1. Students must reply within 4 weeks of notification.

CONTACT Ms. Tammy Crites, Director of Institutional Research, West Virginia Wesleyan College, 59 College Avenue, Buckhannon, WV 26201, 304-473-8186 or toll-free 800-722-9933 (out-of-state). *Fax:* 304-473-8187. *E-mail:* crites_t@wvwc.edu.

WESTWOOD COLLEGE–ANNANDALE CAMPUS

Annandale, VA

CONTACT Financial Aid Office, Westwood College–Annandale Campus, 7611 Little River Turnpike, 3rd Floor, Annandale, VA 22003, 706-642-3770 or toll-free 800-281-2978.

WESTWOOD COLLEGE–ARLINGTON BALLSTON CAMPUS

Arlington, VA

CONTACT Financial Aid Office, Westwood College–Arlington Ballston Campus, 1901 North Ft. Myer Drive, Arlington, VA 22209, 800-281-2978.

WESTWOOD COLLEGE–ATLANTA NORTHLAKE

Atlanta, GA

CONTACT Financial Aid Office, Westwood College–Atlanta Northlake, 2220 Parklake Drive, Suite 175, Atlanta, GA 30345, 404-962-2999.

WHEATON COLLEGE

Wheaton, IL

Tuition & fees: $22,450 **Average undergraduate aid package: $19,307**

ABOUT THE INSTITUTION Independent nondenominational, coed. Awards: bachelor's, master's, and doctoral degrees and post-bachelor's certificates. 38 undergraduate majors. Total enrollment: 2,924. Undergraduates: 2,365. Freshmen: 572. Both federal and institutional methodology are used as a basis for awarding need-based institutional aid.

UNDERGRADUATE EXPENSES for 2006–07 ***Application fee:*** $50. ***Comprehensive fee:*** $29,490 includes full-time tuition ($22,450) and room and board ($7040). ***College room only:*** $4160. Room and board charges vary according to board plan and housing facility. ***Part-time tuition:*** $623 per credit hour. Part-time tuition and fees vary according to course load. ***Payment plans:*** Installment, deferred payment.

FRESHMAN FINANCIAL AID (Fall 2006, est.) 449 applied for aid; of those 58% were deemed to have need. 99% of freshmen with need received aid; of those 38% had need fully met. ***Average percent of need met:*** 86% (excluding resources awarded to replace EFC). ***Average financial aid package:*** $19,359 (excluding resources awarded to replace EFC). 25% of all full-time freshmen had no need and received non-need-based gift aid.

UNDERGRADUATE FINANCIAL AID (Fall 2006, est.) 1,699 applied for aid; of those 65% were deemed to have need. 98% of undergraduates with need received aid; of those 34% had need fully met. ***Average percent of need met:*** 85% (excluding resources awarded to replace EFC). ***Average financial aid package:*** $19,307 (excluding resources awarded to replace EFC). 20% of all full-time undergraduates had no need and received non-need-based gift aid.

GIFT AID (NEED-BASED) ***Total amount:*** $14,574,198 (9% federal, 3% state, 82% institutional, 6% external sources). ***Receiving aid:*** Freshmen: 39% (219); All full-time undergraduates: 40% (919). ***Average award:*** Freshmen: $14,687; Undergraduates: $13,562. ***Scholarships, grants, and awards:*** Federal Pell, FSEOG, state, college/university gift aid from institutional funds.

GIFT AID (NON-NEED-BASED) ***Total amount:*** $1,495,725 (2% federal, 1% state, 74% institutional, 23% external sources). ***Receiving aid:*** Freshmen: 20% (111); Undergraduates: 17% (398). ***Average award:*** Freshmen: $5102; Undergraduates: $5021. ***Scholarships, grants, and awards by category:*** *Academic Interests/Achievement:* 20 awards ($56,372 total): English, general academic interests/achievements, physical sciences, premedicine. *Creative Arts/Performance:* 32 awards ($189,595 total): music. *Special Characteristics:* handicapped students. ***Tuition waivers:*** Full or partial for employees or children of employees. ***ROTC:*** Army.

LOANS ***Student loans:*** $7,618,314 (83% need-based, 17% non-need-based). 57% of past graduating class borrowed through all loan programs. *Average indebtedness per student:* $19,343. ***Average need-based loan:*** Freshmen: $4464; Undergraduates: $5585. ***Programs:*** FFEL (Subsidized and Unsubsidized Stafford, PLUS), Perkins, college/university, alternative loans.

WORK-STUDY ***Federal work-study:*** Total amount: $448,887; 427 jobs averaging $719.

APPLYING FOR FINANCIAL AID ***Required financial aid forms:*** FAFSA, institution's own form. ***Financial aid deadline (priority):*** 2/15. ***Notification date:*** Continuous beginning 3/1.

CONTACT Mrs. Donna Peltz, Director of Financial Aid, Wheaton College, 501 College Avenue, Wheaton, IL 60187-5593, 630-752-5021 or toll-free 800-222-2419 (out-of-state). *E-mail:* finaid@wheaton.edu.

WHEATON COLLEGE

Norton, MA

Tuition & fees: $34,610 **Average undergraduate aid package: $25,229**

ABOUT THE INSTITUTION Independent, coed. Awards: bachelor's degrees. 37 undergraduate majors. Total enrollment: 1,561. Undergraduates: 1,561. Freshmen: 410. Institutional methodology is used as a basis for awarding need-based institutional aid.

UNDERGRADUATE EXPENSES for 2006–07 ***Application fee:*** $55. ***Comprehensive fee:*** $42,760 includes full-time tuition ($34,365), mandatory fees ($245), and room and board ($8150). ***College room only:*** $4300. ***Payment plans:*** Tuition prepayment, installment.

FRESHMAN FINANCIAL AID (Fall 2006, est.) 267 applied for aid; of those 85% were deemed to have need. 100% of freshmen with need received aid; of those 50% had need fully met. ***Average percent of need met:*** 96% (excluding resources awarded to replace EFC). ***Average financial aid package:*** $25,556 (excluding resources awarded to replace EFC). 11% of all full-time freshmen had no need and received non-need-based gift aid.

UNDERGRADUATE FINANCIAL AID (Fall 2006, est.) 1,081 applied for aid; of those 77% were deemed to have need. 100% of undergraduates with need received aid; of those 67% had need fully met. ***Average percent of need met:*** 98% (excluding resources awarded to replace EFC). ***Average financial aid package:*** $25,229 (excluding resources awarded to replace EFC). 13% of all full-time undergraduates had no need and received non-need-based gift aid.

GIFT AID (NEED-BASED) ***Total amount:*** $16,165,817 (5% federal, 3% state, 89% institutional, 3% external sources). ***Receiving aid:*** Freshmen: 52% (215); All full-time undergraduates: 48% (779). ***Average award:*** Freshmen: $20,360; Undergraduates: $19,121. ***Scholarships, grants, and awards:*** Federal Pell, FSEOG, state, private, college/university gift aid from institutional funds.

GIFT AID (NON-NEED-BASED) ***Total amount:*** $2,821,786 (90% institutional, 10% external sources). ***Receiving aid:*** Freshmen: 1; Undergraduates: 1. ***Average award:*** Freshmen: $14,226; Undergraduates: $12,146. ***Scholarships, grants, and awards by category:*** *Academic Interests/Achievement:* 432 awards ($3,910,370 total): general academic interests/achievements. ***Tuition waivers:*** Full or partial for employees or children of employees. ***ROTC:*** Army cooperative.

LOANS ***Student loans:*** $5,951,927 (60% need-based, 40% non-need-based). 55% of past graduating class borrowed through all loan programs. *Average indebtedness per student:* $23,880. ***Average need-based loan:*** Freshmen: $3546; Undergraduates: $4451. ***Parent loans:*** $4,928,160 (100% non-need-based). ***Programs:*** FFEL (Subsidized and Unsubsidized Stafford, PLUS), Perkins, state, college/university, MEFA, TERI, CitiAssist, Signature, alternative loans.

WORK-STUDY ***Federal work-study:*** Total amount: $1,288,951; 698 jobs averaging $1846. ***State or other work-study/employment:*** Total amount: $598,395 (32% need-based, 68% non-need-based). 299 part-time jobs averaging $2000.

APPLYING FOR FINANCIAL AID ***Required financial aid forms:*** FAFSA, CSS Financial Aid PROFILE, noncustodial (divorced/separated) parent's statement, business/farm supplement, federal income tax form(s). ***Financial aid deadline:*** 2/1. ***Notification date:*** 4/1. Students must reply by 5/1.

CONTACT Ms. Susan Beard, Director of Financial Aid Programs, Wheaton College, East Main Street, Norton, MA 02766, 508-286-8232 or toll-free 800-394-6003. *Fax:* 508-286-3787. *E-mail:* sfs@wheatonma.edu.

WHEELING JESUIT UNIVERSITY

Wheeling, WV

Tuition & fees: $23,490 **Average undergraduate aid package: $19,168**

ABOUT THE INSTITUTION Independent Roman Catholic (Jesuit), coed. Awards: bachelor's, master's, and doctoral degrees. 54 undergraduate majors. Total enrollment: 1,402. Undergraduates: 1,203. Freshmen: 284. Both federal and institutional methodology are used as a basis for awarding need-based institutional aid.

UNDERGRADUATE EXPENSES for 2007–08 ***Application fee:*** $25. ***Comprehensive fee:*** $30,720 includes full-time tuition ($22,690), mandatory fees ($800), and room and board ($7230). ***College room only:*** $3350. ***Part-time tuition:*** $556 per credit hour.

FRESHMAN FINANCIAL AID (Fall 2006, est.) 263 applied for aid; of those 87% were deemed to have need. 100% of freshmen with need received aid; of those 40% had need fully met. ***Average percent of need met:*** 94% (excluding resources awarded to replace EFC). ***Average financial aid package:*** $21,339 (excluding resources awarded to replace EFC). 19% of all full-time freshmen had no need and received non-need-based gift aid.

UNDERGRADUATE FINANCIAL AID (Fall 2006, est.) 903 applied for aid; of those 88% were deemed to have need. 100% of undergraduates with need received aid; of those 34% had need fully met. ***Average percent of need met:*** 85% (excluding resources awarded to replace EFC). ***Average financial aid package:*** $19,168 (excluding resources awarded to replace EFC). 12% of all full-time undergraduates had no need and received non-need-based gift aid.

GIFT AID (NEED-BASED) ***Total amount:*** $3,594,906 (29% federal, 8% state, 63% institutional). ***Receiving aid:*** Freshmen: 65% (186); All full-time undergraduates: 63% (623). ***Average award:*** Freshmen: $6451; Undergraduates: $5709. ***Scholarships, grants, and awards:*** Federal Pell, FSEOG, state, private, college/university gift aid from institutional funds, Federal Nursing.

GIFT AID (NON-NEED-BASED) ***Total amount:*** $8,944,369 (6% state, 89% institutional, 5% external sources). ***Receiving aid:*** Freshmen: 77% (220); Undergraduates: 72% (713). ***Average award:*** Freshmen: $11,081; Undergraduates: $9608. ***Scholarships, grants, and awards by category:*** *Academic Interests/Achievement:* 831 awards ($7,234,882 total): education, English, general academic interests/achievements, health fields, premedicine. *Creative Arts/Performance:* 35 awards ($56,200 total): music. *Special Achievements/Activities:* 101 awards ($311,843 total): community service, general special achievements/activities. *Special Characteristics:* 396 awards ($1,273,731 total): children and siblings of alumni, children of faculty/staff, children of union members/company employees, general special characteristics, international students, religious affiliation.

LOANS ***Student loans:*** $3,780,598 (59% need-based, 41% non-need-based). 93% of past graduating class borrowed through all loan programs. *Average indebtedness per student:* $23,218. ***Average need-based loan:*** Freshmen: $3087; Undergraduates: $3980. ***Parent loans:*** $767,112 (100% non-need-based). ***Programs:*** FFEL (Subsidized and Unsubsidized Stafford, PLUS), Perkins, Federal Nursing, alternative loans.

WORK-STUDY ***Federal work-study:*** Total amount: $239,560; 154 jobs averaging $1556. ***State or other work-study/employment:*** Total amount: $267,449 (100% non-need-based). 177 part-time jobs averaging $1511.

ATHLETIC AWARDS Total amount: $709,673 (100% non-need-based).

APPLYING FOR FINANCIAL AID ***Required financial aid forms:*** FAFSA, institution's own form. ***Financial aid deadline (priority):*** 3/1. ***Notification date:*** Continuous beginning 3/15. Students must reply within 2 weeks of notification.

CONTACT Christie Tomczyk, Director of Financial Aid, Wheeling Jesuit University, 316 Washington Avenue, Wheeling, WV 26003-6295, 304-243-2304 or toll-free 800-624-6992 Ext. 2359. *Fax:* 304-243-4397. *E-mail:* finaid@wju.edu.

WHEELOCK COLLEGE

Boston, MA

Tuition & fees: $24,890 **Average undergraduate aid package: $16,823**

ABOUT THE INSTITUTION Independent, coed, primarily women. Awards: associate, bachelor's, and master's degrees and post-bachelor's and post-master's certificates. 8 undergraduate majors. Total enrollment: 1,023. Undergraduates: 728. Freshmen: 234. Both federal and institutional methodology are used as a basis for awarding need-based institutional aid.

UNDERGRADUATE EXPENSES for 2006–07 ***Application fee:*** $35. ***Comprehensive fee:*** $34,800 includes full-time tuition ($24,235), mandatory fees ($655), and room and board ($9910). ***Part-time tuition:*** $757 per credit. ***Payment plans:*** Tuition prepayment, installment.

FRESHMAN FINANCIAL AID (Fall 2006, est.) 174 applied for aid; of those 100% were deemed to have need. 100% of freshmen with need received aid; of those 3% had need fully met. ***Average percent of need met:*** 64% (excluding resources awarded to replace EFC). ***Average financial aid package:*** $15,101 (excluding resources awarded to replace EFC). 9% of all full-time freshmen had no need and received non-need-based gift aid.

UNDERGRADUATE FINANCIAL AID (Fall 2006, est.) 629 applied for aid; of those 99% were deemed to have need. 100% of undergraduates with need received aid; of those 2% had need fully met. ***Average percent of need met:*** 58% (excluding resources awarded to replace EFC). ***Average financial aid package:*** $16,823 (excluding resources awarded to replace EFC). 6% of all full-time undergraduates had no need and received non-need-based gift aid.

GIFT AID (NEED-BASED) ***Total amount:*** $5,514,523 (12% federal, 6% state, 82% institutional). ***Receiving aid:*** Freshmen: 82% (147); All full-time undergraduates: 87% (591). ***Average award:*** Freshmen: $10,227; Undergraduates: $9482. ***Scholarships, grants, and awards:*** Federal Pell, FSEOG, state, private, college/university gift aid from institutional funds.

GIFT AID (NON-NEED-BASED) ***Total amount:*** $1,820,285 (1% federal, 8% state, 83% institutional, 8% external sources). ***Receiving aid:*** Freshmen: 19% (34); Undergraduates: 9% (61). ***Average award:*** Freshmen: $6695; Undergraduates: $11,231. ***Scholarships, grants, and awards by category:*** *Academic Interests/Achievement:* 185 awards ($924,800 total). ***Tuition waivers:*** Full or partial for employees or children of employees.

LOANS ***Student loans:*** $2,921,611 (77% need-based, 23% non-need-based). 94% of past graduating class borrowed through all loan programs. *Average indebtedness per student:* $18,231. ***Average need-based loan:*** Freshmen: $2825; Undergraduates: $4482. ***Parent loans:*** $1,638,967 (100% non-need-based). ***Programs:*** FFEL (Subsidized and Unsubsidized Stafford, PLUS), Perkins, state, college/university.

WORK-STUDY ***Federal work-study:*** Total amount: $146,333.

APPLYING FOR FINANCIAL AID ***Required financial aid form:*** FAFSA. ***Financial aid deadline (priority):*** 2/15. ***Notification date:*** Continuous beginning 3/15. Students must reply by 5/1 or within 2 weeks of notification.

CONTACT Melissa Holster, Director of Financial Aid, Wheelock College, 200 The Riverway, Boston, MA 02215-4176, 617-879-2205 or toll-free 800-734-5212 (out-of-state). *E-mail:* mholster@wheelock.edu.

WHITMAN COLLEGE

Walla Walla, WA

Tuition & fees: $30,806 **Average undergraduate aid package: $22,300**

ABOUT THE INSTITUTION Independent, coed. Awards: bachelor's degrees. 27 undergraduate majors. Total enrollment: 1,455. Undergraduates: 1,455. Freshmen: 366. Both federal and institutional methodology are used as a basis for awarding need-based institutional aid.

UNDERGRADUATE EXPENSES for 2006–07 ***Application fee:*** $45. ***Comprehensive fee:*** $38,646 includes full-time tuition ($30,530), mandatory fees ($276), and room and board ($7840). ***College room only:*** $3600. Room and board charges vary according to board plan and housing facility. ***Part-time tuition:*** $1280 per credit. ***Payment plan:*** Deferred payment.

FRESHMAN FINANCIAL AID (Fall 2006, est.) 240 applied for aid; of those 78% were deemed to have need. 100% of freshmen with need received aid; of those 84% had need fully met. ***Average percent of need met:*** 99% (excluding resources awarded to replace EFC). ***Average financial aid package:*** $22,000 (excluding resources awarded to replace EFC). 23% of all full-time freshmen had no need and received non-need-based gift aid.

UNDERGRADUATE FINANCIAL AID (Fall 2006, est.) 702 applied for aid; of those 91% were deemed to have need. 100% of undergraduates with need received aid; of those 56% had need fully met. ***Average percent of need met:*** 91% (excluding resources awarded to replace EFC). ***Average financial aid package:*** $22,300 (excluding resources awarded to replace EFC). 27% of all full-time undergraduates had no need and received non-need-based gift aid.

GIFT AID (NEED-BASED) ***Total amount:*** $11,857,800 (7% federal, 2% state, 91% institutional). ***Receiving aid:*** Freshmen: 51% (186); All full-time undergraduates: 45% (641). ***Average award:*** Freshmen: $16,500; Undergraduates: $17,300. ***Scholarships, grants, and awards:*** Federal Pell, FSEOG, state, private, college/university gift aid from institutional funds.

GIFT AID (NON-NEED-BASED) ***Total amount:*** $5,410,650 (4% state, 83% institutional, 13% external sources). ***Receiving aid:*** Freshmen: 14% (52); Undergraduates: 17% (238). ***Average award:*** Freshmen: $5550; Undergraduates: $9200. ***Scholarships, grants, and awards by category:*** *Academic Interests/Achievement:* 524 awards ($4,499,000 total): general academic interests/achievements. *Creative Arts/Performance:* 47 awards ($122,600 total): art/fine arts, debating, music, theater/drama. *Special Characteristics:* 175 awards ($4,247,026 total): ethnic background, international students. ***Tuition waivers:*** Full or partial for employees or children of employees.

LOANS ***Student loans:*** $3,500,650 (66% need-based, 34% non-need-based). 61% of past graduating class borrowed through all loan programs. *Average indebtedness per student:* $16,300. ***Average need-based loan:*** Freshmen: $3750; Undergraduates: $4450. ***Parent loans:*** $2,500,000 (100% non-need-based). ***Programs:*** FFEL (Subsidized and Unsubsidized Stafford, PLUS), Perkins, alternative loans.

WORK-STUDY ***Federal work-study:*** Total amount: $975,150; 523 jobs averaging $2073. ***State or other work-study/employment:*** Total amount: $315,500 (27% need-based, 73% non-need-based). 198 part-time jobs averaging $1495.

APPLYING FOR FINANCIAL AID ***Required financial aid forms:*** FAFSA, CSS Financial Aid PROFILE. ***Financial aid deadline:*** 2/1 (priority: 11/15). ***Notification date:*** Continuous beginning 12/20. Students must reply within 3 weeks of notification.

CONTACT Tyson Harlow, Financial Aid Assistant, Whitman College, 345 Boyer Avenue, Walla Walla, WA 99362-2046, 509-527-5178 or toll-free 877-462-9448. *Fax:* 509-527-4967.

WHITTIER COLLEGE

Whittier, CA

ABOUT THE INSTITUTION Independent, coed. Awards: bachelor's, master's, and first professional degrees. 25 undergraduate majors. Total enrollment: 1,307. Undergraduates: 1,307. Freshmen: 394.

GIFT AID (NEED-BASED) ***Scholarships, grants, and awards:*** Federal Pell, FSEOG, state, private, college/university gift aid from institutional funds.

GIFT AID (NON-NEED-BASED) ***Scholarships, grants, and awards by category:*** *Academic Interests/Achievement:* general academic interests/achievements. *Creative Arts/Performance:* art/fine arts, music, theater/drama. *Special Characteristics:* children and siblings of alumni, children of faculty/staff, international students.

LOANS ***Programs:*** Federal Direct (PLUS), FFEL (Subsidized and Unsubsidized Stafford, PLUS), Perkins, alternative financing loans.

WORK-STUDY ***Federal work-study:*** Total amount: $1,414,331; jobs available. ***State or other work-study/employment:*** Total amount: $732,684 (72% need-based, 28% non-need-based). Part-time jobs available.

APPLYING FOR FINANCIAL AID ***Required financial aid forms:*** FAFSA, CSS Financial Aid PROFILE.

CONTACT Mr. Vernon Bridges, Director of Student Financing, Whittier College, 13406 East Philadelphia Street, PO Box 634, Whittier, CA 90608-0634, 562-907-4285. *Fax:* 562-464-4560. *E-mail:* vbridges@whittier.edu.

WHITWORTH UNIVERSITY

Spokane, WA

Tuition & fees: $25,692 **Average undergraduate aid package: $17,200**

ABOUT THE INSTITUTION Independent Presbyterian, coed. Awards: bachelor's and master's degrees. 43 undergraduate majors. Total enrollment: 2,504. Undergraduates: 2,256. Freshmen: 470. Federal methodology is used as a basis for awarding need-based institutional aid.

UNDERGRADUATE EXPENSES for 2007–08 ***Comprehensive fee:*** $32,986 includes full-time tuition ($25,382), mandatory fees ($310), and room and board ($7294).

FRESHMAN FINANCIAL AID (Fall 2006, est.) 406 applied for aid; of those 80% were deemed to have need. 99% of freshmen with need received aid; of those 22% had need fully met. ***Average percent of need met:*** 81% (excluding resources awarded to replace EFC). ***Average financial aid package:*** $16,975 (excluding resources awarded to replace EFC). 29% of all full-time freshmen had no need and received non-need-based gift aid.

UNDERGRADUATE FINANCIAL AID (Fall 2006, est.) 1,510 applied for aid; of those 85% were deemed to have need. 100% of undergraduates with need received aid; of those 24% had need fully met. ***Average percent of need met:*** 82% (excluding resources awarded to replace EFC). ***Average financial aid package:*** $17,200 (excluding resources awarded to replace EFC). 28% of all full-time undergraduates had no need and received non-need-based gift aid.

GIFT AID (NEED-BASED) ***Total amount:*** $16,823,615 (10% federal, 11% state, 73% institutional, 6% external sources). ***Receiving aid:*** Freshmen: 67% (313); All full-time undergraduates: 67% (1,237). ***Average award:*** Freshmen: $13,090; Undergraduates: $12,833. ***Scholarships, grants, and awards:*** Federal Pell, FSEOG, state, private, college/university gift aid from institutional funds.

GIFT AID (NON-NEED-BASED) ***Total amount:*** $5,424,305 (5% federal, 1% state, 87% institutional, 7% external sources). ***Receiving aid:*** Freshmen: 11% (51); Undergraduates: 8% (152). ***Average award:*** Freshmen: $10,105; Undergraduates: $8864. ***Scholarships, grants, and awards by category:*** *Academic Interests/Achievement:* 1,290 awards ($9,206,073 total): biological sciences, computer science, general academic interests/achievements, military science, physical sciences, premedicine. *Creative Arts/Performance:* 165 awards ($320,215 total): art/fine arts, journalism/publications, music, theater/drama. *Special Achievements/Activities:* 42 awards ($43,400 total): religious involvement. *Special Characteristics:* 405 awards ($1,294,106 total): children and siblings of alumni, ethnic background, international students, members of minority groups, relatives of clergy, siblings of current students. ***ROTC:*** Army cooperative.

LOANS ***Student loans:*** $8,889,911 (76% need-based, 24% non-need-based). 73% of past graduating class borrowed through all loan programs. *Average indebtedness per student:* $18,478. ***Average need-based loan:*** Freshmen: $4066; Undergraduates: $4763. ***Parent loans:*** $2,832,730 (29% need-based, 71% non-need-based). ***Programs:*** Federal Direct (Subsidized and Unsubsidized Stafford, PLUS), FFEL (PLUS), Perkins, college/university.

WORK-STUDY ***Federal work-study:*** Total amount: $1,153,942; 510 jobs averaging $2140. ***State or other work-study/employment:*** Total amount: $614,569 (98% need-based, 2% non-need-based). 199 part-time jobs averaging $2894.

APPLYING FOR FINANCIAL AID ***Required financial aid form:*** FAFSA. ***Financial aid deadline (priority):*** 3/1. ***Notification date:*** Continuous beginning 3/1.

CONTACT Ms. Wendy Z. Olson, Director of Financial Aid, Whitworth University, 300 West Hawthorne Road, Spokane, WA 99251-0001, 509-777-4306 or toll-free 800-533-4668 (out-of-state). *Fax:* 509-777-3725. *E-mail:* wolson@whitworth.edu.

WICHITA STATE UNIVERSITY

Wichita, KS

Tuition & fees (KS res): $4481 **Average undergraduate aid package: $5160**

ABOUT THE INSTITUTION State-supported, coed. Awards: associate, bachelor's, master's, and doctoral degrees and post-bachelor's and post-master's certificates. 56 undergraduate majors. Total enrollment: 14,298. Undergraduates: 11,203. Freshmen: 1,259. Federal methodology is used as a basis for awarding need-based institutional aid.

UNDERGRADUATE EXPENSES for 2006–07 ***Application fee:*** $30. ***Tuition, state resident:*** full-time $3673; part-time $122.45 per credit hour. ***Tuition, nonresident:*** full-time $11,020; part-time $367.35 per credit hour. ***Required fees:*** full-time $808; $26.95 per credit hour or $17 per term part-time. Full-time tuition and fees vary according to course load. Part-time tuition and fees vary according to course load. ***College room and board:*** $5276. Room and board charges vary according to board plan and housing facility. ***Payment plan:*** Installment.

FRESHMAN FINANCIAL AID (Fall 2005) 828 applied for aid; of those 98% were deemed to have need. 94% of freshmen with need received aid; of those 17% had need fully met. ***Average percent of need met:*** 39% (excluding resources awarded to replace EFC). ***Average financial aid package:*** $4775 (excluding resources awarded to replace EFC). 21% of all full-time freshmen had no need and received non-need-based gift aid.

UNDERGRADUATE FINANCIAL AID (Fall 2005) 5,198 applied for aid; of those 99% were deemed to have need. 95% of undergraduates with need received aid; of those 13% had need fully met. ***Average percent of need met:*** 54% (excluding resources awarded to replace EFC). ***Average financial aid package:*** $5160 (excluding resources awarded to replace EFC). 10% of all full-time undergraduates had no need and received non-need-based gift aid.

GIFT AID (NEED-BASED) ***Total amount:*** $9,874,812 (86% federal, 13% state, 1% external sources). ***Receiving aid:*** Freshmen: 30% (352); All full-time undergraduates: 33% (2,464). ***Average award:*** Freshmen: $3110; Undergraduates: $3308. ***Scholarships, grants, and awards:*** Federal Pell, FSEOG, state, private, college/university gift aid from institutional funds, Bureau of Indian Affairs Grants.

GIFT AID (NON-NEED-BASED) ***Total amount:*** $5,594,301 (86% institutional, 14% external sources). ***Receiving aid:*** Freshmen: 40% (460); Undergraduates: 20% (1,501). ***Average award:*** Freshmen: $1688; Undergraduates: $1514. ***Scholarships, grants, and awards by category:*** *Academic Interests/Achievement:* area/ethnic studies, biological sciences, business, communication, computer science, education, engineering/technologies, English, foreign languages, general academic interests/achievements, health fields, humanities, international studies, mathematics, physical sciences, premedicine, social sciences. *Creative Arts/Performance:* applied art and design, art/fine arts, creative writing, dance, debating, journalism/publications, music, performing arts, theater/drama. *Special Achievements/Activities:* cheerleading/drum major, general special achievements/activities, leadership, memberships. *Special Characteristics:* adult students, first-generation college students, international students, members of minority groups. ***Tuition waivers:*** Full or partial for employees or children of employees, senior citizens.

LOANS ***Student loans:*** $43,786,135 (54% need-based, 46% non-need-based). 58% of past graduating class borrowed through all loan programs. *Average indebtedness per student:* $21,368. ***Average need-based loan:*** Freshmen: $2360; Undergraduates: $3873. ***Parent loans:*** $815,385 (100% non-need-based). ***Programs:*** FFEL (Subsidized and Unsubsidized Stafford, PLUS), Perkins, college/university.

WORK-STUDY ***Federal work-study:*** Total amount: $432,839; 195 jobs averaging $2576. ***State or other work-study/employment:*** Total amount: $92,293 (100% need-based). Part-time jobs available.

ATHLETIC AWARDS Total amount: $1,343,663 (100% non-need-based).

APPLYING FOR FINANCIAL AID ***Required financial aid forms:*** FAFSA, state aid form, scholarship application form(s). ***Financial aid deadline (priority):*** 3/1. ***Notification date:*** Continuous beginning 3/15. Students must reply within 2 weeks of notification.

CONTACT Deborah D. Byers, Director of Financial Aid, Wichita State University, 1845 Fairmount, Wichita, KS 67260-0024, 316-978-3430 or toll-free 800-362-2594. *Fax:* 316-978-3396.

WIDENER UNIVERSITY

Chester, PA

Tuition & fees: $26,750 **Average undergraduate aid package: $20,437**

ABOUT THE INSTITUTION Independent, coed. Awards: associate, bachelor's, master's, doctoral, and first professional degrees. 70 undergraduate majors. Total enrollment: 6,460. Undergraduates: 3,220. Freshmen: 752. Both federal and institutional methodology are used as a basis for awarding need-based institutional aid.

UNDERGRADUATE EXPENSES for 2006–07 ***Application fee:*** $35. ***Comprehensive fee:*** $36,390 includes full-time tuition ($26,350), mandatory fees ($400), and room and board ($9640). ***College room only:*** $4800. Full-time tuition and fees vary according to class time, course load, and program. Room and board charges vary according to board plan and housing facility. ***Part-time tuition:*** $878 per credit. ***Payment plan:*** Installment.

FRESHMAN FINANCIAL AID (Fall 2006, est.) 637 applied for aid; of those 90% were deemed to have need. 100% of freshmen with need received aid; of those 21% had need fully met. ***Average percent of need met:*** 81% (excluding resources awarded to replace EFC). ***Average financial aid package:*** $21,998 (excluding resources awarded to replace EFC). 14% of all full-time freshmen had no need and received non-need-based gift aid.

UNDERGRADUATE FINANCIAL AID (Fall 2006, est.) 2,070 applied for aid; of those 91% were deemed to have need. 100% of undergraduates with need received aid; of those 54% had need fully met. ***Average percent of need met:*** 77% (excluding resources awarded to replace EFC). ***Average financial aid package:*** $20,437 (excluding resources awarded to replace EFC). 14% of all full-time undergraduates had no need and received non-need-based gift aid.

GIFT AID (NEED-BASED) ***Total amount:*** $28,319,459 (12% federal, 11% state, 71% institutional, 6% external sources). ***Receiving aid:*** Freshmen: 68% (506); All full-time undergraduates: 65% (1,588). ***Average award:*** Freshmen: $8983; Undergraduates: $8392. ***Scholarships, grants, and awards:*** Federal Pell, FSEOG, state, private, college/university gift aid from institutional funds, Federal Nursing.

GIFT AID (NON-NEED-BASED) ***Total amount:*** $3,436,567 (5% federal, 84% institutional, 11% external sources). ***Receiving aid:*** Freshmen: 68% (503); Undergraduates: 61% (1,486). ***Average award:*** Freshmen: $9329; Undergraduates: $8107. ***Scholarships, grants, and awards by category:*** *Academic Interests/Achievement:* 2,157 awards ($13,807,096 total): biological sciences, business, communication, computer science, education, engineering/technologies, English, foreign languages, general academic interests/achievements, health fields, humanities, international studies, mathematics, military science, physical sciences, premedicine, social sciences. *Creative Arts/Performance:* 41 awards ($80,000 total): music. *Special Achievements/Activities:* 108 awards ($431,920 total): community service, general special achievements/activities, leadership. *Special Characteristics:* 118 awards ($2,814,910 total): adult students, children and siblings of alumni, children of faculty/staff, ethnic background, international students, siblings of current students, veterans. ***Tuition waivers:*** Full or partial for employees or children of employees, senior citizens. ***ROTC:*** Army, Naval cooperative, Air Force cooperative.

LOANS ***Student loans:*** $21,700,382 (92% need-based, 8% non-need-based). 88% of past graduating class borrowed through all loan programs. *Average indebtedness per student:* $29,514. ***Average need-based loan:*** Freshmen: $3640; Undergraduates: $4656. ***Parent loans:*** $6,268,976 (88% need-based, 12% non-need-based). ***Programs:*** FFEL (Subsidized and Unsubsidized Stafford, PLUS), Perkins.

WORK-STUDY ***Federal work-study:*** Total amount: $2,678,789; 1,437 jobs averaging $1864. ***State or other work-study/employment:*** 337 part-time jobs averaging $1092.

APPLYING FOR FINANCIAL AID ***Required financial aid form:*** FAFSA. ***Financial aid deadline (priority):*** 2/15. ***Notification date:*** Continuous beginning 3/15. Students must reply within 4 weeks of notification.

CONTACT Thomas K Malloy, Director of Financial Aid, Widener University, One University Place, Chester, PA 19013-5792, 610-499-4174 or toll-free 888-WIDENER. *Fax:* 610-499-4687. *E-mail:* finaidmc@widener.edu.

WILBERFORCE UNIVERSITY

Wilberforce, OH

CONTACT Director of Financial Aid, Wilberforce University, 1055 North Bickett Road, Wilberforce, OH 45384, 937-708-5727 or toll-free 800-367-8568. *Fax:* 937-376-4752.

WILEY COLLEGE

Marshall, TX

CONTACT Cecelia Jones, Interim Director of Financial Aid, Wiley College, 711 Wiley Avenue, Marshall, TX 75670-5199, 903-927-3210 or toll-free 800-658-6889. *Fax:* 903-927-3366.

WILKES UNIVERSITY

Wilkes-Barre, PA

Tuition & fees: $22,990 **Average undergraduate aid package: $17,368**

ABOUT THE INSTITUTION Independent, coed. Awards: bachelor's, master's, and first professional degrees. 37 undergraduate majors. Total enrollment: 4,777. Undergraduates: 2,245. Freshmen: 580. Federal methodology is used as a basis for awarding need-based institutional aid.

UNDERGRADUATE EXPENSES for 2006–07 ***Application fee:*** $40. ***Comprehensive fee:*** $32,850 includes full-time tuition ($21,830), mandatory fees ($1160), and room and board ($9860). ***College room only:*** $5940. Room and board charges vary according to board plan and housing facility. ***Part-time tuition:*** $605 per credit. ***Part-time fees:*** $50 per credit. ***Payment plans:*** Installment, deferred payment.

FRESHMAN FINANCIAL AID (Fall 2006, est.) 540 applied for aid; of those 89% were deemed to have need. 99% of freshmen with need received aid; of those 12% had need fully met. ***Average percent of need met:*** 78% (excluding resources awarded to replace EFC). ***Average financial aid package:*** $17,746 (excluding resources awarded to replace EFC). 13% of all full-time freshmen had no need and received non-need-based gift aid.

UNDERGRADUATE FINANCIAL AID (Fall 2006, est.) 2,001 applied for aid; of those 89% were deemed to have need. 99% of undergraduates with need received aid; of those 19% had need fully met. ***Average percent of need met:*** 79% (excluding resources awarded to replace EFC). ***Average financial aid package:*** $17,368 (excluding resources awarded to replace EFC). 13% of all full-time undergraduates had no need and received non-need-based gift aid.

GIFT AID (NEED-BASED) ***Total amount:*** $22,770,752 (8% federal, 16% state, 75% institutional, 1% external sources). ***Receiving aid:*** Freshmen: 84% (479); All full-time undergraduates: 82% (1,757). ***Average award:*** Freshmen: $14,372; Undergraduates: $13,383. ***Scholarships, grants, and awards:*** Federal Pell, FSEOG, state, private, college/university gift aid from institutional funds.

GIFT AID (NON-NEED-BASED) ***Total amount:*** $2,676,285 (1% federal, 1% state, 97% institutional, 1% external sources). ***Receiving aid:*** Freshmen: 68% (386); Undergraduates: 62% (1,331). ***Average award:*** Freshmen: $9492; Undergraduates: $9240. ***Scholarships, grants, and awards by category:*** *Academic Interests/Achievement:* biological sciences, business, communication, education, engineering/technologies, English, general academic interests/achievements, health fields, humanities, international studies, mathematics, premedicine, social sciences. *Creative Arts/Performance:* music, performing arts, theater/drama. *Special Achievements/Activities:* general special achievements/activities, leadership. *Special Characteristics:* adult students, children of faculty/staff. ***Tuition waivers:*** Full or partial for employees or children of employees. ***ROTC:*** Army cooperative, Air Force.

LOANS ***Student loans:*** $17,797,158 (92% need-based, 8% non-need-based). 86% of past graduating class borrowed through all loan programs. *Average indebtedness per student:* $27,729. ***Average need-based loan:*** Freshmen: $2081; Undergraduates: $2859. ***Parent loans:*** $3,029,119 (87% need-based, 13% non-need-based). ***Programs:*** FFEL (Subsidized and Unsubsidized Stafford, PLUS), Perkins, Federal Nursing, state, college/university, Gulf Oil Loan Fund, Rulison Evans Loan Fund.

WORK-STUDY ***Federal work-study:*** Total amount: $1,788,113; 1,096 jobs averaging $1631. ***State or other work-study/employment:*** Total amount: $259,581 (65% need-based, 35% non-need-based). 170 part-time jobs averaging $1527.

APPLYING FOR FINANCIAL AID ***Required financial aid form:*** FAFSA. ***Financial aid deadline (priority):*** 3/1. ***Notification date:*** Continuous.

CONTACT Michael Frantz, Vice President Enrollment Services, Wilkes University, 84 W South Street, Wilkes-Barre, PA 18766, 570-408-4000 or toll-free 800-945-5378 Ext. 4400. *Fax:* 570-408-3000. *E-mail:* michael.frantz@wilkes.edu.

WILLAMETTE UNIVERSITY

Salem, OR

Tuition & fees: $30,018 **Average undergraduate aid package: $26,640**

ABOUT THE INSTITUTION Independent United Methodist, coed. Awards: bachelor's, master's, and first professional degrees and post-bachelor's and first professional certificates. 40 undergraduate majors. Total enrollment: 2,747. Undergraduates: 2,055. Freshmen: 482. Institutional methodology is used as a basis for awarding need-based institutional aid.

UNDERGRADUATE EXPENSES for 2006–07 ***Application fee:*** $50. ***Comprehensive fee:*** $37,268 includes full-time tuition ($30,018) and room and board ($7250). Full-time tuition and fees vary according to course load. Room and board charges vary according to board plan and housing facility. ***Part-time tuition:*** $3753 per course. Part-time tuition and fees vary according to course load. ***Payment plan:*** Installment.

FRESHMAN FINANCIAL AID (Fall 2006, est.) 393 applied for aid; of those 81% were deemed to have need. 100% of freshmen with need received aid; of those 25% had need fully met. ***Average percent of need met:*** 92% (excluding resources awarded to replace EFC). ***Average financial aid package:*** $26,019 (excluding resources awarded to replace EFC). 28% of all full-time freshmen had no need and received non-need-based gift aid.

UNDERGRADUATE FINANCIAL AID (Fall 2006, est.) 1,363 applied for aid; of those 88% were deemed to have need. 100% of undergraduates with need received aid; of those 29% had need fully met. ***Average percent of need met:*** 93% (excluding resources awarded to replace EFC). ***Average financial aid package:*** $26,640 (excluding resources awarded to replace EFC). 31% of all full-time undergraduates had no need and received non-need-based gift aid.

GIFT AID (NEED-BASED) ***Total amount:*** $25,155,449 (6% federal, 2% state, 87% institutional, 5% external sources). ***Receiving aid:*** Freshmen: 66% (314); All full-time undergraduates: 62% (1,178). ***Average award:*** Freshmen: $20,120; Undergraduates: $20,273. ***Scholarships, grants, and awards:*** Federal Pell, FSEOG, state, private, college/university gift aid from institutional funds, United Negro College Fund.

GIFT AID (NON-NEED-BASED) ***Total amount:*** $6,207,892 (97% institutional, 3% external sources). ***Receiving aid:*** Freshmen: 27% (128); Undergraduates: 15% (293). ***Average award:*** Freshmen: $9693; Undergraduates: $10,115. ***Scholarships, grants, and awards by category:*** *Academic Interests/Achievement:* general academic interests/achievements. *Creative Arts/Performance:* debating, music, theater/drama. *Special Achievements/Activities:* community service, leadership. *Special Characteristics:* international students, members of minority groups. ***Tuition waivers:*** Full or partial for employees or children of employees. ***ROTC:*** Air Force cooperative.

LOANS ***Student loans:*** $6,768,831 (92% need-based, 8% non-need-based). 56% of past graduating class borrowed through all loan programs. *Average indebtedness per student:* $25,240. ***Average need-based loan:*** Freshmen: $4010; Undergraduates: $4491. ***Parent loans:*** $5,874,124 (100% need-based). ***Programs:*** FFEL (Subsidized and Unsubsidized Stafford, PLUS), Perkins, state.

WORK-STUDY ***Federal work-study:*** Total amount: $1,479,200; 787 jobs averaging $1761. ***State or other work-study/employment:*** 437 part-time jobs averaging $1323.

APPLYING FOR FINANCIAL AID ***Required financial aid forms:*** FAFSA, state aid form. ***Financial aid deadline (priority):*** 2/1. ***Notification date:*** 3/30. Students must reply by 5/1 or within 2 weeks of notification.

CONTACT Patty Hoban, Director of Financial Aid, Willamette University, 900 State Street, Salem, OR 97301-3931, 503-370-6273 or toll-free 877-542-2787. *Fax:* 503-370-6588. *E-mail:* phoban@willamette.edu.

WILLIAM CAREY COLLEGE

Hattiesburg, MS

Tuition & fees: $8715 **Average undergraduate aid package: $12,700**

ABOUT THE INSTITUTION Independent Southern Baptist, coed. Awards: bachelor's and master's degrees. 32 undergraduate majors. Total enrollment: 2,493. Undergraduates: 1,653. Freshmen: 127. Federal methodology is used as a basis for awarding need-based institutional aid.

UNDERGRADUATE EXPENSES for 2006–07 ***Application fee:*** $20. ***Comprehensive fee:*** $12,330 includes full-time tuition ($8400), mandatory fees ($315), and room and board ($3615). ***College room only:*** $1305. Full-time tuition and fees vary according to degree level and location. Room and board charges vary according to board plan, housing facility, and location. ***Part-time tuition:*** $280 per hour. Part-time tuition and fees vary according to degree level and location. ***Payment plan:*** Deferred payment.

UNDERGRADUATE FINANCIAL AID (Fall 2006, est.) 1,573 applied for aid; of those 100% were deemed to have need. 100% of undergraduates with need received aid; of those 97% had need fully met. ***Average percent of need met:*** 85% (excluding resources awarded to replace EFC). ***Average financial aid package:*** $12,700 (excluding resources awarded to replace EFC). 9% of all full-time undergraduates had no need and received non-need-based gift aid.

GIFT AID (NEED-BASED) ***Total amount:*** $4,720,000 (68% federal, 23% state, 9% external sources). ***Receiving aid:*** All full-time undergraduates: 85% (1,569). ***Average award:*** Undergraduates: $6000. ***Scholarships, grants, and awards:*** Federal Pell, FSEOG, state, private, college/university gift aid from institutional funds.

GIFT AID (NON-NEED-BASED) ***Total amount:*** $4,000,000 (100% institutional). ***Receiving aid:*** Undergraduates: 37% (687). ***Average award:*** Undergraduates: $6000. ***Scholarships, grants, and awards by category:*** *Academic Interests/Achievement:* 850 awards ($3,500,000 total): general academic interests/achievements. *Creative Arts/Performance:* 80 awards ($370,000 total): art/fine arts, debating, journalism/publications, music, theater/drama. *Special Achievements/Activities:* 200 awards ($150,000 total): cheerleading/drum major, junior miss, leadership, religious involvement. *Special Characteristics:* 180 awards ($250,000 total): children and siblings of alumni, children of educators, children of faculty/staff, first-generation college students, international students, relatives of clergy, religious affiliation, veterans. ***Tuition waivers:*** Full or partial for employees or children of employees. ***ROTC:*** Army cooperative, Air Force cooperative.

LOANS ***Student loans:*** $19,500,000 (100% need-based). 85% of past graduating class borrowed through all loan programs. *Average indebtedness per student:* $17,000. ***Average need-based loan:*** Undergraduates: $5000. ***Parent loans:*** $150,000 (100% need-based). ***Programs:*** FFEL (Subsidized and Unsubsidized Stafford, PLUS), Perkins, Federal Nursing, college/university.

WORK-STUDY ***Federal work-study:*** Total amount: $370,000; 230 jobs averaging $1700. ***State or other work-study/employment:*** Total amount: $112,000 (100% non-need-based). 65 part-time jobs averaging $1700.

ATHLETIC AWARDS Total amount: $750,000 (100% non-need-based).

APPLYING FOR FINANCIAL AID ***Required financial aid form:*** FAFSA. ***Financial aid deadline (priority):*** 4/1. ***Notification date:*** Continuous beginning 5/1. Students must reply within 2 weeks of notification.

CONTACT Ms. Brenda Pittman, Associate Director of Financial Aid, William Carey College, 498 Tuscan Avenue, Hattiesburg, MS 39401-5499, 601-318-6153 or toll-free 800-962-5991 (in-state).

WILLIAM JESSUP UNIVERSITY

Rocklin, CA

CONTACT Kristi Kindberg, Financial Aid Administrator, William Jessup University, 790 South 12th Street, San Jose, CA 95112-2381, 408-278-4328 or toll-free 800-355-7522. *Fax:* 408-293-9299. *E-mail:* finaid@sjchristian.edu.

WILLIAM JEWELL COLLEGE

Liberty, MO

Tuition & fees: $21,400 **Average undergraduate aid package: $15,639**

ABOUT THE INSTITUTION Independent Baptist, coed. Awards: bachelor's degrees (also offers evening program with significant enrollment not reflected in profile). 42 undergraduate majors. Total enrollment: 1,404. Undergraduates: 1,404. Freshmen: 248. Federal methodology is used as a basis for awarding need-based institutional aid.

UNDERGRADUATE EXPENSES for 2007–08 ***Application fee:*** $25. ***Comprehensive fee:*** $27,240 includes full-time tuition ($21,400) and room and board ($5840). ***College room only:*** $2459. ***Part-time tuition:*** $700 per credit hour.

FRESHMAN FINANCIAL AID (Fall 2006, est.) 216 applied for aid; of those 81% were deemed to have need. 100% of freshmen with need received aid. ***Average financial aid package:*** $16,761 (excluding resources awarded to replace EFC).

UNDERGRADUATE FINANCIAL AID (Fall 2006, est.) 890 applied for aid; of those 83% were deemed to have need. 100% of undergraduates with need received aid. ***Average financial aid package:*** $15,639 (excluding resources awarded to replace EFC).

GIFT AID (NEED-BASED) ***Total amount:*** $6,964,945 (12% federal, 7% state, 73% institutional, 8% external sources). ***Receiving aid:*** Freshmen: 71% (175); All full-time undergraduates: 64% (736). ***Average award:*** Freshmen: $13,139; Undergraduates: $11,444. ***Scholarships, grants, and awards:*** Federal Pell, FSEOG, state, college/university gift aid from institutional funds.

GIFT AID (NON-NEED-BASED) ***Total amount:*** $2,576,220 (3% state, 89% institutional, 8% external sources). ***Receiving aid:*** Freshmen: 48% (118); Undergraduates: 45% (519). ***Scholarships, grants, and awards by category:*** *Academic Interests/Achievement:* 665 awards ($3,813,030 total): general academic interests/achievements. *Creative Arts/Performance:* 225 awards ($646,569 total): art/fine arts, debating, journalism/publications, music, theater/drama. *Special Achievements/Activities:* 90 awards ($207,522 total): cheerleading/drum major, religious involvement. *Special Characteristics:* 176 awards ($636,028 total): children and siblings of alumni, children of faculty/staff, siblings of current students.

LOANS ***Student loans:*** $5,474,475 (87% need-based, 13% non-need-based). 79% of past graduating class borrowed through all loan programs. *Average indebtedness per student:* $18,093. ***Average need-based loan:*** Freshmen: $4118; Undergraduates: $5047. ***Parent loans:*** $2,822,966 (76% need-based, 24% non-need-based). ***Programs:*** FFEL (Subsidized and Unsubsidized Stafford, PLUS), Perkins, Federal Nursing, non-Federal alternative loans (non-college).

WORK-STUDY ***Federal work-study:*** Total amount: $611,375; 386 jobs averaging $1584. ***State or other work-study/employment:*** Total amount: $125,811 (100% non-need-based). 170 part-time jobs averaging $740.

ATHLETIC AWARDS Total amount: $2,148,039 (63% need-based, 37% non-need-based).

APPLYING FOR FINANCIAL AID ***Required financial aid form:*** FAFSA. ***Financial aid deadline (priority):*** 3/1. ***Notification date:*** Continuous beginning 2/15. Students must reply within 2 weeks of notification.

CONTACT Sue Armstrong, Director of Financial Aid, William Jewell College, 500 College Hill, Box 1014, T37, Brown Hall, Liberty, MO 64068, 816-415-5973 or toll-free 888-2JEWELL. *Fax:* 816-415-5006. *E-mail:* armstrongs@william.jewell.edu.

WILLIAM PATERSON UNIVERSITY OF NEW JERSEY

Wayne, NJ

Tuition & fees (NJ res): $9422 **Average undergraduate aid package: $11,611**

ABOUT THE INSTITUTION State-supported, coed. Awards: bachelor's and master's degrees and post-bachelor's and post-master's certificates. 53 undergraduate majors. Total enrollment: 10,600. Undergraduates: 8,863. Freshmen: 1,390. Federal methodology is used as a basis for awarding need-based institutional aid.

UNDERGRADUATE EXPENSES for 2006–07 ***Application fee:*** $50. ***Tuition, state resident:*** full-time $5782; part-time $185.83 per credit. ***Tuition, nonresident:*** full-time $11,730; part-time $379.83 per credit. ***Required fees:*** full-time $3640; $117.17 per credit. ***College room and board:*** $9380; ***Room only:*** $6240. Room and board charges vary according to board plan and housing facility. ***Payment plan:*** Installment.

FRESHMAN FINANCIAL AID (Fall 2006, est.) 953 applied for aid; of those 75% were deemed to have need. 94% of freshmen with need received aid; of those 52% had need fully met. ***Average financial aid package:*** $12,477 (excluding resources awarded to replace EFC). 7% of all full-time freshmen had no need and received non-need-based gift aid.

UNDERGRADUATE FINANCIAL AID (Fall 2006, est.) 4,798 applied for aid; of those 75% were deemed to have need. 97% of undergraduates with need received aid; of those 52% had need fully met. ***Average financial aid package:*** $11,611 (excluding resources awarded to replace EFC). 8% of all full-time undergraduates had no need and received non-need-based gift aid.

GIFT AID (NEED-BASED) ***Total amount:*** $13,500,000 (42% federal, 53% state, 5% institutional). ***Receiving aid:*** Freshmen: 33% (397); All full-time undergraduates: 28% (1,960). ***Average award:*** Freshmen: $6991; Undergraduates: $6344. ***Scholarships, grants, and awards:*** Federal Pell, FSEOG, state, college/university gift aid from institutional funds.

GIFT AID (NON-NEED-BASED) ***Total amount:*** $6,587,000 (4% state, 91% institutional, 5% external sources). ***Receiving aid:*** Freshmen: 40% (488); Undergraduates: 32% (2,263). ***Average award:*** Freshmen: $6999; Undergraduates: $6915. ***Scholarships, grants, and awards by category:*** *Academic Interests/Achievement:* 844 awards ($4,959,434 total): general academic interests/achievements. *Creative Arts/Performance:* 12 awards ($3300 total): music. *Special Characteristics:* general special characteristics. ***Tuition waivers:*** Full or partial for employees or children of employees, senior citizens. ***ROTC:*** Air Force cooperative.

LOANS ***Student loans:*** $38,700,000 (36% need-based, 64% non-need-based). 64% of past graduating class borrowed through all loan programs. *Average indebtedness per student:* $18,386. ***Average need-based loan:*** Freshmen: $2503; Undergraduates: $3674. ***Parent loans:*** $5,200,000 (100% non-need-based). ***Programs:*** FFEL (Subsidized and Unsubsidized Stafford, PLUS), Perkins.

WORK-STUDY ***Federal work-study:*** Total amount: $300,000; 220 jobs averaging $1136. ***State or other work-study/employment:*** Total amount: $278,000 (100% non-need-based). 192 part-time jobs averaging $1300.

APPLYING FOR FINANCIAL AID ***Required financial aid form:*** FAFSA. ***Financial aid deadline:*** 4/1 (priority: 4/1). ***Notification date:*** Continuous beginning 3/1. Students must reply within 2 weeks of notification.

CONTACT Robert Baumel, Director of Financial Aid, William Paterson University of New Jersey, 300 Pompton Road, Raubinger Hall, Wayne, NJ 07470, 973-720-2928 or toll-free 877-WPU-EXCEL (in-state). *E-mail:* baumelr@wpunj.edu.

WILLIAM PENN UNIVERSITY

Oskaloosa, IA

ABOUT THE INSTITUTION Independent religious, coed. Awards: associate and bachelor's degrees. 39 undergraduate majors. Total enrollment: 1,861. Undergraduates: 1,861. Freshmen: 433.

GIFT AID (NEED-BASED) ***Scholarships, grants, and awards:*** Federal Pell, FSEOG, state, private, college/university gift aid from institutional funds.

GIFT AID (NON-NEED-BASED) ***Scholarships, grants, and awards by category:*** *Academic Interests/Achievement:* general academic interests/achievements. *Creative Arts/Performance:* dance, journalism/publications, music, theater/drama. *Special Achievements/Activities:* cheerleading/drum major, general special achievements/activities, junior miss, leadership, religious involvement. *Special Characteristics:* children and siblings of alumni, children of faculty/staff, general special characteristics, international students.

LOANS ***Programs:*** FFEL (Subsidized and Unsubsidized Stafford, PLUS), Perkins, state, college/university.

WORK-STUDY ***Federal work-study:*** Total amount: $657,564; 511 jobs averaging $1287. ***State or other work-study/employment:*** Total amount: $1103 (100% need-based). 1 part-time job averaging $1103.

APPLYING FOR FINANCIAL AID ***Required financial aid form:*** FAFSA.

CONTACT Cyndi Peiffer, Director of Financial Aid, William Penn University, 201 Trueblood Avenue, Oskaloosa, IA 52577-1799, 641-673-1060 or toll-free 800-779-7366. *Fax:* 641-673-1115. *E-mail:* peifferc@wmpenn.edu.

WILLIAMS BAPTIST COLLEGE

Walnut Ridge, AR

Tuition & fees: $10,370 **Average undergraduate aid package: $9633**

ABOUT THE INSTITUTION Independent Southern Baptist, coed. Awards: associate and bachelor's degrees. 26 undergraduate majors. Total enrollment: 629. Undergraduates: 629. Freshmen: 128. Federal methodology is used as a basis for awarding need-based institutional aid.

UNDERGRADUATE EXPENSES for 2007–08 ***Application fee:*** $20. ***Comprehensive fee:*** $15,070 includes full-time tuition ($9700), mandatory fees ($670), and room and board ($4700).

FRESHMAN FINANCIAL AID (Fall 2005) 116 applied for aid; of those 76% were deemed to have need. 100% of freshmen with need received aid. ***Average financial aid package:*** $9321 (excluding resources awarded to replace EFC). 28% of all full-time freshmen had no need and received non-need-based gift aid.

UNDERGRADUATE FINANCIAL AID (Fall 2005) 433 applied for aid; of those 78% were deemed to have need. 100% of undergraduates with need received aid. ***Average financial aid package:*** $9633 (excluding resources awarded to replace EFC). 24% of all full-time undergraduates had no need and received non-need-based gift aid.

GIFT AID (NEED-BASED) ***Total amount:*** $994,707 (71% federal, 29% state). ***Receiving aid:*** Freshmen: 46% (59); All full-time undergraduates: 51% (242). ***Average award:*** Freshmen: $2635; Undergraduates: $2856. ***Scholarships, grants, and awards:*** Federal Pell, FSEOG, state, private, college/university gift aid from institutional funds.

GIFT AID (NON-NEED-BASED) ***Total amount:*** $1,547,388 (9% state, 73% institutional, 18% external sources). ***Receiving aid:*** Freshmen: 69% (88); Undergraduates: 65% (310). ***Average award:*** Freshmen: $3931; Undergraduates: $3703. ***Scholarships, grants, and awards by category:*** *Academic Interests/Achievement:* 389 awards ($1,014,430 total): biological sciences, business, education, general academic interests/achievements, humanities, religion/biblical studies. *Creative Arts/Performance:* 36 awards ($40,542 total): art/fine arts, music. *Special Achievements/Activities:* 14 awards ($3800 total): cheerleading/drum major. *Special Characteristics:* 161 awards ($115,248 total): children of faculty/staff, international students, members of minority groups, relatives of clergy, religious affiliation. ***ROTC:*** Army cooperative.

LOANS ***Student loans:*** $1,664,834 (58% need-based, 42% non-need-based). 83% of past graduating class borrowed through all loan programs. *Average indebtedness per student:* $14,739. ***Average need-based loan:*** Freshmen: $1986; Undergraduates: $3344. ***Parent loans:*** $180,617 (100% non-need-based). ***Programs:*** Federal Direct (Subsidized and Unsubsidized Stafford, PLUS).

WORK-STUDY ***Federal work-study:*** Total amount: $216,295; 199 jobs averaging $1058. ***State or other work-study/employment:*** Total amount: $33,838 (100% non-need-based). 37 part-time jobs averaging $915.

ATHLETIC AWARDS Total amount: $385,496 (100% non-need-based).

APPLYING FOR FINANCIAL AID ***Required financial aid form:*** FAFSA. ***Financial aid deadline:*** Continuous. ***Notification date:*** Continuous beginning 4/1. Students must reply within 2 weeks of notification.

CONTACT Barbara Turner, Director of Financial Aid, Williams Baptist College, 60 West Fulbright Avenue, PO Box 3734, Walnut Ridge, AR 72476, 870-759-4112 or toll-free 800-722-4434. *Fax:* 870-759-4209. *E-mail:* bturner@wbcoll.edu.

WILLIAMS COLLEGE

Williamstown, MA

Tuition & fees: $33,700 **Average undergraduate aid package: $32,979**

ABOUT THE INSTITUTION Independent, coed. Awards: bachelor's and master's degrees. 33 undergraduate majors. Total enrollment: 2,049. Undergraduates: 2,003. Freshmen: 534. Institutional methodology is used as a basis for awarding need-based institutional aid.

UNDERGRADUATE EXPENSES for 2006–07 ***Application fee:*** $60. ***Comprehensive fee:*** $42,650 includes full-time tuition ($33,478), mandatory fees ($222), and room and board ($8950). ***College room only:*** $4540. Room and board charges vary according to board plan. ***Payment plan:*** Installment.

FRESHMAN FINANCIAL AID (Fall 2006, est.) 317 applied for aid; of those 78% were deemed to have need. 100% of freshmen with need received aid; of those 100% had need fully met. ***Average percent of need met:*** 100% (excluding resources awarded to replace EFC). ***Average financial aid package:*** $33,948 (excluding resources awarded to replace EFC).

UNDERGRADUATE FINANCIAL AID (Fall 2006, est.) 1,015 applied for aid; of those 84% were deemed to have need. 100% of undergraduates with need received aid; of those 100% had need fully met. ***Average percent of need met:*** 100% (excluding resources awarded to replace EFC). ***Average financial aid package:*** $32,979 (excluding resources awarded to replace EFC).

GIFT AID (NEED-BASED) ***Total amount:*** $25,137,573 (5% federal, 1% state, 91% institutional, 3% external sources). ***Receiving aid:*** Freshmen: 46% (245); All full-time undergraduates: 43% (842). ***Average award:*** Freshmen: $31,819; Undergraduates: $29,713. ***Scholarships, grants, and awards:*** Federal Pell, FSEOG, state, private, college/university gift aid from institutional funds.

GIFT AID (NON-NEED-BASED) ***Total amount:*** $1,171,912 (100% external sources).

LOANS ***Student loans:*** $2,018,569 (83% need-based, 17% non-need-based). 41% of past graduating class borrowed through all loan programs. *Average indebtedness per student:* $9943. ***Average need-based loan:*** Freshmen: $2093;

Undergraduates: $3136. ***Parent loans:*** $4,616,797 (100% non-need-based). ***Programs:*** Federal Direct (Subsidized and Unsubsidized Stafford, PLUS), Perkins, college/university.

WORK-STUDY ***Federal work-study:*** Total amount: $758,451; 444 jobs averaging $1572. ***State or other work-study/employment:*** Total amount: $1,552,160 (31% need-based, 69% non-need-based). 338 part-time jobs averaging $1589.

APPLYING FOR FINANCIAL AID ***Required financial aid forms:*** FAFSA, CSS Financial Aid PROFILE, noncustodial (divorced/separated) parent's statement, business/farm supplement, parent and student federal tax returns and W2 statements. ***Financial aid deadline:*** 2/1. ***Notification date:*** 4/1. Students must reply by 5/1.

CONTACT Paul J. Boyer, Director of Financial Aid, Williams College, PO Box 37, Williamstown, MA 01267, 413-597-4181. *Fax:* 413-597-2999. *E-mail:* paul.j.boyer@williams.edu.

WILLIAMSON CHRISTIAN COLLEGE

Franklin, TN

CONTACT Jeanie Maguire, Director of Financial Aid, Williamson Christian College, 200 Seaboard Lane, Franklin, TN 37067, 615-771-7821. *Fax:* 615-771-7810. *E-mail:* info@williamsoncc.edu.

WILLIAM WOODS UNIVERSITY

Fulton, MO

ABOUT THE INSTITUTION Independent religious, coed. Awards: associate, bachelor's, and master's degrees and post-master's certificates. 46 undergraduate majors. Total enrollment: 2,893. Undergraduates: 1,162. Freshmen: 196.

GIFT AID (NEED-BASED) ***Scholarships, grants, and awards:*** Federal Pell, FSEOG, state, college/university gift aid from institutional funds.

GIFT AID (NON-NEED-BASED) ***Scholarships, grants, and awards by category:*** *Academic Interests/Achievement:* general academic interests/achievements, health fields. *Creative Arts/Performance:* art/fine arts, journalism/publications, performing arts, theater/drama. *Special Achievements/Activities:* general special achievements/activities, leadership. *Special Characteristics:* children and siblings of alumni, children of faculty/staff, relatives of clergy, religious affiliation, siblings of current students.

LOANS ***Programs:*** FFEL (Subsidized and Unsubsidized Stafford, PLUS), Perkins, college/university.

WORK-STUDY ***Federal work-study:*** Total amount: $274,233; 302 jobs averaging $1278. ***State or other work-study/employment:*** Total amount: $192,474 (16% need-based, 84% non-need-based). 169 part-time jobs averaging $847.

APPLYING FOR FINANCIAL AID ***Required financial aid forms:*** FAFSA, institution's own form.

CONTACT Deana Ready, Director of Student Financial Services, William Woods University, One University Avenue, Fulton, MO 65251, 573-592-4232 or toll-free 800-995-3159 Ext. 4221. *Fax:* 573-592-1180.

WILMINGTON COLLEGE

New Castle, DE

CONTACT J. Lynn Iocono, Director of Financial Aid, Wilmington College, 320 DuPont Highway, New Castle, DE 19720, 302-328-9437 or toll-free 877-967-5464. *Fax:* 302-328-5902.

WILMINGTON COLLEGE

Wilmington, OH

CONTACT Donna Barton, Coordinator of Financial Aid, Wilmington College, Pyle Center Box 1184, Wilmington, OH 45177, 937-382-6661 Ext. 466 or toll-free 800-341-9318. *Fax:* 937-383-8564.

WILSON COLLEGE

Chambersburg, PA

Tuition & fees: $21,830	Average undergraduate aid package: $16,860

ABOUT THE INSTITUTION Independent religious, women only. Awards: associate and bachelor's degrees. 23 undergraduate majors. Total enrollment: 770. Undergraduates: 765. Freshmen: 79. Both federal and institutional methodology are used as a basis for awarding need-based institutional aid.

UNDERGRADUATE EXPENSES for 2006–07 ***Application fee:*** $35. ***Comprehensive fee:*** $29,746 includes full-time tuition ($21,330), mandatory fees ($500), and room and board ($7916). ***College room only:*** $4078. Room and board charges vary according to board plan. ***Part-time tuition:*** $2136 per course. ***Part-time fees:*** $35 per course; $40 per term. Part-time tuition and fees vary according to course load. ***Payment plan:*** Installment.

FRESHMAN FINANCIAL AID (Fall 2006, est.) 63 applied for aid; of those 92% were deemed to have need. 100% of freshmen with need received aid; of those 24% had need fully met. ***Average percent of need met:*** 77% (excluding resources awarded to replace EFC). ***Average financial aid package:*** $15,863 (excluding resources awarded to replace EFC). 21% of all full-time freshmen had no need and received non-need-based gift aid.

UNDERGRADUATE FINANCIAL AID (Fall 2006, est.) 289 applied for aid; of those 92% were deemed to have need. 100% of undergraduates with need received aid; of those 18% had need fully met. ***Average percent of need met:*** 77% (excluding resources awarded to replace EFC). ***Average financial aid package:*** $16,860 (excluding resources awarded to replace EFC). 22% of all full-time undergraduates had no need and received non-need-based gift aid.

GIFT AID (NEED-BASED) ***Total amount:*** $3,833,632 (16% federal, 19% state, 62% institutional, 3% external sources). ***Receiving aid:*** Freshmen: 76% (58); All full-time undergraduates: 72% (254). ***Average award:*** Freshmen: $12,686; Undergraduates: $13,100. ***Scholarships, grants, and awards:*** Federal Pell, FSEOG, state, private, college/university gift aid from institutional funds.

GIFT AID (NON-NEED-BASED) ***Total amount:*** $1,078,893 (5% state, 82% institutional, 13% external sources). ***Receiving aid:*** Freshmen: 12% (9); Undergraduates: 7% (24). ***Average award:*** Freshmen: $15,324; Undergraduates: $14,808. ***Scholarships, grants, and awards by category:*** *Academic Interests/Achievement:* 348 awards ($2,846,096 total): biological sciences, business, communication, computer science, education, English, foreign languages, general academic interests/achievements, humanities, international studies, mathematics, physical sciences, premedicine, religion/biblical studies, social sciences. *Creative Arts/Performance:* 1 award ($1800 total): music. *Special Achievements/Activities:* 21 awards ($96,790 total): community service, leadership. *Special Characteristics:* 115 awards ($486,338 total): adult students, children and siblings of alumni, children of current students, children of faculty/staff, international students, local/state students, relatives of clergy, religious affiliation, veterans. ***Tuition waivers:*** Full or partial for employees or children of employees. ***ROTC:*** Army cooperative.

LOANS ***Student loans:*** $3,422,947 (66% need-based, 34% non-need-based). 92% of past graduating class borrowed through all loan programs. *Average indebtedness per student:* $26,224. ***Average need-based loan:*** Freshmen: $3321; Undergraduates: $4520. ***Parent loans:*** $1,150,086 (36% need-based, 64% non-need-based). ***Programs:*** FFEL (Subsidized and Unsubsidized Stafford, PLUS), Perkins, college/university.

WORK-STUDY ***Federal work-study:*** Total amount: $45,844; 60 jobs averaging $1500. ***State or other work-study/employment:*** Total amount: $138,742 (28% need-based, 72% non-need-based). 101 part-time jobs averaging $1500.

APPLYING FOR FINANCIAL AID ***Required financial aid forms:*** FAFSA, institution's own form. ***Financial aid deadline (priority):*** 4/30. ***Notification date:*** Continuous beginning 3/1. Students must reply within 2 weeks of notification.

CONTACT Linda Brittain, Associate Dean of Enrollment, Wilson College, 1015 Philadelphia Avenue, Chambersburg, PA 17201-1285, 717-262-2016 or toll-free 800-421-8402. *Fax:* 717-262-2546. *E-mail:* finaid@wilson.edu.

WINGATE UNIVERSITY

Wingate, NC

Tuition & fees: $17,650	Average undergraduate aid package: $15,049

ABOUT THE INSTITUTION Independent Baptist, coed. Awards: bachelor's, master's, and first professional degrees. 39 undergraduate majors. Total enrollment: 1,809. Undergraduates: 1,390. Freshmen: 385. Both federal and institutional methodology are used as a basis for awarding need-based institutional aid.

UNDERGRADUATE EXPENSES for 2006–07 ***Application fee:*** $30. ***Comprehensive fee:*** $24,400 includes full-time tuition ($16,600), mandatory fees ($1050), and room and board ($6750). ***College room only:*** $3375. Room and board charges vary according to board plan. ***Part-time tuition:*** $550 per credit hour. ***Part-time fees:*** $175 per term. Part-time tuition and fees vary according to course load. ***Payment plan:*** Installment.

FRESHMAN FINANCIAL AID (Fall 2006, est.) 336 applied for aid; of those 70% were deemed to have need. 100% of freshmen with need received aid; of those 27% had need fully met. ***Average percent of need met:*** 81% (excluding resources awarded to replace EFC). ***Average financial aid package:*** $15,348 (excluding resources awarded to replace EFC). 31% of all full-time freshmen had no need and received non-need-based gift aid.

UNDERGRADUATE FINANCIAL AID (Fall 2006, est.) 1,131 applied for aid; of those 73% were deemed to have need. 100% of undergraduates with need received aid; of those 28% had need fully met. ***Average percent of need met:*** 80% (excluding resources awarded to replace EFC). ***Average financial aid package:*** $15,049 (excluding resources awarded to replace EFC). 30% of all full-time undergraduates had no need and received non-need-based gift aid.

GIFT AID (NEED-BASED) ***Total amount:*** $3,949,131 (30% federal, 25% state, 45% institutional). ***Receiving aid:*** Freshmen: 57% (221); All full-time undergraduates: 51% (692). ***Average award:*** Freshmen: $6442; Undergraduates: $5240. ***Scholarships, grants, and awards:*** Federal Pell, FSEOG, state, private, college/university gift aid from institutional funds.

GIFT AID (NON-NEED-BASED) ***Total amount:*** $7,013,195 (21% state, 72% institutional, 7% external sources). ***Receiving aid:*** Freshmen: 58% (225); Undergraduates: 59% (793). ***Average award:*** Freshmen: $3951; Undergraduates: $4623. ***Scholarships, grants, and awards by category:*** *Academic Interests/Achievement:* 1,205 awards ($4,915,230 total): general academic interests/achievements. *Creative Arts/Performance:* 29 awards ($89,250 total): music. *Special Achievements/Activities:* 56 awards ($26,041 total): religious involvement. *Special Characteristics:* 17 awards ($7500 total): children and siblings of alumni, relatives of clergy, religious affiliation. ***Tuition waivers:*** Full or partial for employees or children of employees. ***ROTC:*** Army cooperative, Air Force cooperative.

LOANS ***Student loans:*** $10,268,625 (45% need-based, 55% non-need-based). 45% of past graduating class borrowed through all loan programs. *Average indebtedness per student:* $2424. ***Average need-based loan:*** Freshmen: $2252; Undergraduates: $3619. ***Parent loans:*** $2,473,020 (100% non-need-based). ***Programs:*** FFEL (Subsidized and Unsubsidized Stafford, PLUS).

WORK-STUDY ***Federal work-study:*** Total amount: $128,883; 164 jobs averaging $786. ***State or other work-study/employment:*** Total amount: $279,000 (100% non-need-based). 373 part-time jobs averaging $560.

ATHLETIC AWARDS Total amount: $1,924,713 (100% non-need-based).

APPLYING FOR FINANCIAL AID ***Required financial aid form:*** FAFSA. ***Financial aid deadline (priority):*** 5/1. ***Notification date:*** Continuous. Students must reply within 4 weeks of notification.

CONTACT Teresa G. Williams, Director of Financial Planning, Wingate University, Campus Box 3001, Wingate, NC 28174, 704-233-8209 or toll-free 800-755-5550. *Fax:* 704-233-9396. *E-mail:* tgwilliam@wingate.edu.

WINONA STATE UNIVERSITY

Winona, MN

Tuition & fees (MN res): $7100 **Average undergraduate aid package: $6066**

ABOUT THE INSTITUTION State-supported, coed. Awards: associate, bachelor's, and master's degrees and post-master's certificates. 104 undergraduate majors. Total enrollment: 8,220. Undergraduates: 7,608. Freshmen: 1,727. Federal methodology is used as a basis for awarding need-based institutional aid.

UNDERGRADUATE EXPENSES for 2006–07 ***Application fee:*** $20. ***Tuition, state resident:*** full-time $5386. ***Tuition, nonresident:*** full-time $9686. ***College room and board:*** $6300. ***Payment plan:*** Installment.

FRESHMAN FINANCIAL AID (Fall 2005) 1329 applied for aid; of those 68% were deemed to have need. 97% of freshmen with need received aid; of those 10% had need fully met. ***Average percent of need met:*** 35% (excluding resources awarded to replace EFC). ***Average financial aid package:*** $4893 (excluding resources awarded to replace EFC). 30% of all full-time freshmen had no need and received non-need-based gift aid.

UNDERGRADUATE FINANCIAL AID (Fall 2005) 4,857 applied for aid; of those 74% were deemed to have need. 98% of undergraduates with need received aid; of those 9% had need fully met. ***Average percent of need met:*** 40% (excluding resources awarded to replace EFC). ***Average financial aid package:*** $6066 (excluding resources awarded to replace EFC). 16% of all full-time undergraduates had no need and received non-need-based gift aid.

GIFT AID (NEED-BASED) ***Total amount:*** $6,411,684 (55% federal, 42% state, 3% institutional). ***Receiving aid:*** Freshmen: 23% (390); All full-time undergraduates: 26% (1,781). ***Average award:*** Freshmen: $3341; Undergraduates: $3244. ***Scholarships, grants, and awards:*** Federal Pell, FSEOG, state, private, college/university gift aid from institutional funds.

GIFT AID (NON-NEED-BASED) ***Total amount:*** $5,623,956 (60% institutional, 40% external sources). ***Receiving aid:*** Freshmen: 30% (508); Undergraduates: 17% (1,161). ***Average award:*** Freshmen: $1642; Undergraduates: $2370. ***Scholarships, grants, and awards by category:*** *Academic Interests/Achievement:* 1,631 awards ($2,457,617 total): general academic interests/achievements. *Creative Arts/Performance:* 12 awards ($6450 total): art/fine arts, debating, music, theater/drama. *Special Characteristics:* 1,437 awards ($2,574,069 total): children and siblings of alumni, children of faculty/staff, local/state students, members of minority groups, out-of-state students. ***Tuition waivers:*** Full or partial for employees or children of employees. ***ROTC:*** Army cooperative.

LOANS ***Student loans:*** $33,249,752 (39% need-based, 61% non-need-based). 71% of past graduating class borrowed through all loan programs. *Average indebtedness per student:* $20,889. ***Average need-based loan:*** Freshmen: $2304; Undergraduates: $3499. ***Parent loans:*** $3,197,234 (100% non-need-based). ***Programs:*** FFEL (Subsidized and Unsubsidized Stafford, PLUS), Perkins, state, college/university.

WORK-STUDY ***Federal work-study:*** Total amount: $338,065; 174 jobs averaging $1943. ***State or other work-study/employment:*** Total amount: $3,660,029 (21% need-based, 79% non-need-based). 385 part-time jobs averaging $2007.

ATHLETIC AWARDS Total amount: $464,929 (100% non-need-based).

APPLYING FOR FINANCIAL AID ***Required financial aid form:*** FAFSA. ***Financial aid deadline:*** Continuous. ***Notification date:*** 5/1. Students must reply within 3 weeks of notification.

CONTACT Cindy Groth, Counselor, Winona State University, PO Box 5838, Winona, MN 55987-5838, 507-457-5090 Ext. 5561 or toll-free 800-DIAL WSU.

WINSTON-SALEM BIBLE COLLEGE

Winston-Salem, NC

CONTACT Financial Aid Office, Winston-Salem Bible College, 4117 Northampton Drive, PO Box 777, Winston-Salem, NC 27102-0777, 336-744-0900.

WINSTON-SALEM STATE UNIVERSITY

Winston-Salem, NC

Tuition & fees (NC res): $3109 **Average undergraduate aid package: $3447**

ABOUT THE INSTITUTION State-supported, coed. Awards: bachelor's and master's degrees. 41 undergraduate majors. Total enrollment: 5,650. Undergraduates: 5,329. Freshmen: 992. Federal methodology is used as a basis for awarding need-based institutional aid.

UNDERGRADUATE EXPENSES for 2006–07 ***Application fee:*** $40. ***Tuition, state resident:*** full-time $1651. ***Tuition, nonresident:*** full-time $10,291. Full-time tuition and fees vary according to degree level. Part-time tuition and fees vary according to course load and location. ***College room and board:*** $5476; ***Room only:*** $3270. Room and board charges vary according to board plan and housing facility. ***Payment plan:*** Installment.

FRESHMAN FINANCIAL AID (Fall 2005) 890 applied for aid; of those 98% were deemed to have need. 86% of freshmen with need received aid; of those 1% had need fully met. ***Average percent of need met:*** 69% (excluding resources awarded to replace EFC). ***Average financial aid package:*** $3782 (excluding resources awarded to replace EFC). 4% of all full-time freshmen had no need and received non-need-based gift aid.

UNDERGRADUATE FINANCIAL AID (Fall 2005) 4,220 applied for aid; of those 97% were deemed to have need. 97% of undergraduates with need received aid; of those 4% had need fully met. ***Average percent of need met:*** 82% (excluding resources awarded to replace EFC). ***Average financial aid package:*** $3447 (excluding resources awarded to replace EFC). 2% of all full-time undergraduates had no need and received non-need-based gift aid.

GIFT AID (NEED-BASED) ***Total amount:*** $13,707,259 (74% federal, 26% state). ***Receiving aid:*** Freshmen: 69% (722); All full-time undergraduates: 82% (3,789). ***Average award:*** Freshmen: $2768; Undergraduates: $2666. ***Scholarships, grants, and awards:*** Federal Pell, FSEOG, state, private, college/university gift aid from institutional funds, United Negro College Fund.

GIFT AID (NON-NEED-BASED) ***Total amount:*** $2,768,643 (19% state, 42% institutional, 39% external sources). ***Receiving aid:*** Freshmen: 9% (99); Undergraduates: 6% (282). ***Average award:*** Freshmen: $4514; Undergraduates: $4099. ***Scholarships, grants, and awards by category:*** *Academic Interests/Achievement:* 658 awards ($1,818,795 total): business, computer science, education, general academic interests/achievements, health fields, mathematics. *Creative Arts/Performance:* 58 awards ($147,891 total): music. *Special Achievements/Activities:* 20 awards ($4400 total): cheerleading/drum major. *Special Characteristics:* 39 awards ($19,700 total): adult students, first-generation college students. ***Tuition waivers:*** Full or partial for employees or children of employees, senior citizens. ***ROTC:*** Army, Air Force.

LOANS ***Student loans:*** $22,275,221 (57% need-based, 43% non-need-based). 80% of past graduating class borrowed through all loan programs. *Average indebtedness per student:* $10,200. ***Average need-based loan:*** Freshmen: $2523; Undergraduates: $3501. ***Parent loans:*** $2,705,925 (100% non-need-based). ***Programs:*** FFEL (Subsidized and Unsubsidized Stafford, PLUS), Perkins, state, college/university.

WORK-STUDY ***Federal work-study:*** Total amount: $584,269; 333 jobs averaging $1755. ***State or other work-study/employment:*** Total amount: $417,832 (100% non-need-based). 220 part-time jobs averaging $2780.

ATHLETIC AWARDS Total amount: $539,039 (100% non-need-based).

APPLYING FOR FINANCIAL AID ***Required financial aid form:*** FAFSA. ***Financial aid deadline:*** 4/1 (priority: 3/1). ***Notification date:*** 3/15. Students must reply within 2 weeks of notification.

CONTACT Raymond Solomon, Director of Financial Aid Office, Winston-Salem State University, 601 Martin Luther King Jr. Drive, PO Box 19524, Winston-Salem, NC 27110-0003, 336-750-3299 or toll-free 800-257-4052. *Fax:* 336-750-3297.

WINTHROP UNIVERSITY

Rock Hill, SC

Tuition & fees (SC res): $9500 **Average undergraduate aid package: $8815**

ABOUT THE INSTITUTION State-supported, coed. Awards: bachelor's and master's degrees. 32 undergraduate majors. Total enrollment: 6,292. Undergraduates: 5,111. Freshmen: 1,183. Federal methodology is used as a basis for awarding need-based institutional aid.

UNDERGRADUATE EXPENSES for 2006–07 ***Application fee:*** $40. ***Tuition, state resident:*** full-time $9500; part-time $396 per semester hour. ***Tuition, nonresident:*** full-time $17,564; part-time $732 per semester hour. Full-time tuition and fees vary according to degree level. Part-time tuition and fees vary according to degree level. ***College room and board:*** $5570; ***Room only:*** $3560. Room and board charges vary according to board plan and housing facility. ***Payment plan:*** Installment.

FRESHMAN FINANCIAL AID (Fall 2006, est.) 981 applied for aid; of those 73% were deemed to have need. 99% of freshmen with need received aid; of those 22% had need fully met. ***Average percent of need met:*** 70% (excluding resources awarded to replace EFC). ***Average financial aid package:*** $9737 (excluding resources awarded to replace EFC). 5% of all full-time freshmen had no need and received non-need-based gift aid.

UNDERGRADUATE FINANCIAL AID (Fall 2006, est.) 3,394 applied for aid; of those 80% were deemed to have need. 98% of undergraduates with need received aid; of those 21% had need fully met. ***Average percent of need met:*** 63% (excluding resources awarded to replace EFC). ***Average financial aid package:*** $8815 (excluding resources awarded to replace EFC). 10% of all full-time undergraduates had no need and received non-need-based gift aid.

GIFT AID (NEED-BASED) ***Total amount:*** $14,697,140 (31% federal, 49% state, 18% institutional, 2% external sources). ***Receiving aid:*** Freshmen: 58% (688); All full-time undergraduates: 49% (2,254). ***Average award:*** Freshmen: $7828; Undergraduates: $6624. ***Scholarships, grants, and awards:*** Federal Pell, FSEOG, state, private, college/university gift aid from institutional funds.

GIFT AID (NON-NEED-BASED) ***Total amount:*** $8,076,123 (50% state, 40% institutional, 10% external sources). ***Receiving aid:*** Freshmen: 8% (92); Undergraduates: 5% (231). ***Average award:*** Freshmen: $5288; Undergraduates: $3480. ***Scholarships, grants, and awards by category:*** *Academic Interests/Achievement:* 454 awards ($1,713,784 total): general academic interests/achievements. *Creative Arts/Performance:* 142 awards ($136,024 total): art/fine arts, dance, music, performing arts, theater/drama. *Special Characteristics:* 4 awards ($4250 total): children of faculty/staff. ***Tuition waivers:*** Full or partial for employees or children of employees, senior citizens. ***ROTC:*** Army cooperative.

LOANS ***Student loans:*** $21,564,835 (42% need-based, 58% non-need-based). ***Average need-based loan:*** Freshmen: $2763; Undergraduates: $3860. ***Parent loans:*** $3,238,510 (100% non-need-based). ***Programs:*** Federal Direct (Subsidized and Unsubsidized Stafford), FFEL (PLUS), Perkins.

WORK-STUDY ***Federal work-study:*** Total amount: $225,000; 285 jobs averaging $789. ***State or other work-study/employment:*** Total amount: $1,725,800 (100% non-need-based). Part-time jobs available (averaging $1000).

ATHLETIC AWARDS Total amount: $1,444,885 (30% need-based, 70% non-need-based).

APPLYING FOR FINANCIAL AID ***Required financial aid form:*** FAFSA. ***Financial aid deadline (priority):*** 3/1. ***Notification date:*** Continuous beginning 3/15. Students must reply within 4 weeks of notification.

CONTACT Ms. Leah Sturgis, Assistant Director, Office of Financial Aid, Winthrop University, 119 Tillman Hall, Rock Hill, SC 29733, 803-323-2189 or toll-free 800-763-0230. *Fax:* 803-323-2557. *E-mail:* finaid@winthrop.edu.

WISCONSIN LUTHERAN COLLEGE

Milwaukee, WI

Tuition & fees: $19,564 **Average undergraduate aid package: $14,709**

ABOUT THE INSTITUTION Independent religious, coed. Awards: bachelor's degrees. 20 undergraduate majors. Total enrollment: 741. Undergraduates: 741. Freshmen: 198. Federal methodology is used as a basis for awarding need-based institutional aid.

UNDERGRADUATE EXPENSES for 2007–08 ***Application fee:*** $20. ***Comprehensive fee:*** $26,474 includes full-time tuition ($19,430), mandatory fees ($134), and room and board ($6910). ***College room only:*** $3680.

FRESHMAN FINANCIAL AID (Fall 2006, est.) 166 applied for aid; of those 87% were deemed to have need. 100% of freshmen with need received aid; of those 21% had need fully met. ***Average percent of need met:*** 81% (excluding resources awarded to replace EFC). ***Average financial aid package:*** $14,213 (excluding resources awarded to replace EFC). 24% of all full-time freshmen had no need and received non-need-based gift aid.

UNDERGRADUATE FINANCIAL AID (Fall 2006, est.) 578 applied for aid; of those 91% were deemed to have need. 100% of undergraduates with need received aid; of those 30% had need fully met. ***Average percent of need met:*** 84% (excluding resources awarded to replace EFC). ***Average financial aid package:*** $14,709 (excluding resources awarded to replace EFC). 22% of all full-time undergraduates had no need and received non-need-based gift aid.

GIFT AID (NEED-BASED) ***Total amount:*** $5,549,959 (8% federal, 10% state, 79% institutional, 3% external sources). ***Receiving aid:*** Freshmen: 73% (145); All full-time undergraduates: 75% (523). ***Average award:*** Freshmen: $11,094; Undergraduates: $10,604. ***Scholarships, grants, and awards:*** Federal Pell, FSEOG, state, private, college/university gift aid from institutional funds.

GIFT AID (NON-NEED-BASED) ***Total amount:*** $1,378,667 (94% institutional, 6% external sources). ***Receiving aid:*** Freshmen: 10% (19); Undergraduates: 9% (64). ***Average award:*** Freshmen: $14,251; Undergraduates: $11,600. ***Scholarships, grants, and awards by category:*** *Academic Interests/Achievement:* 661 awards ($4,166,626 total): biological sciences, business, communication, education, general academic interests/achievements, international studies, mathematics, social sciences. *Creative Arts/Performance:* 71 awards ($80,000 total): art/fine arts, music, theater/drama. *Special Achievements/Activities:* 14 awards ($18,499 total): general special achievements/activities, leadership. *Special Characteristics:* 42 awards ($421,104 total): children of faculty/staff, ethnic background, international students, members of minority groups. ***ROTC:*** Army cooperative, Naval cooperative, Air Force cooperative.

LOANS ***Student loans:*** $3,051,081 (70% need-based, 30% non-need-based). 71% of past graduating class borrowed through all loan programs. *Average indebtedness per student:* $14,028. ***Average need-based loan:*** Freshmen: $2485; Undergraduates: $3618. ***Parent loans:*** $1,472,685 (20% need-based, 80% non-need-based). ***Programs:*** FFEL (Subsidized and Unsubsidized Stafford, PLUS), alternative loans.

WORK-STUDY ***Federal work-study:*** Total amount: $440,287; 255 jobs averaging $1699. ***State or other work-study/employment:*** Total amount: $128,445 (35% need-based, 65% non-need-based). 25 part-time jobs averaging $5200.

APPLYING FOR FINANCIAL AID ***Required financial aid forms:*** FAFSA, institution's own form. ***Financial aid deadline (priority):*** 3/1. ***Notification date:*** Continuous beginning 3/15. Students must reply within 2 weeks of notification.

CONTACT Mrs. Linda Loeffel, Director of Financial Aid, Wisconsin Lutheran College, 8800 West Bluemound Road, Milwaukee, WI 53226-4699, 414-443-8842 or toll-free 888-WIS LUTH. *Fax:* 414-443-8514. *E-mail:* linda_loeffel@wlc.edu.

WITTENBERG UNIVERSITY

Springfield, OH

Tuition & fees: $31,400 **Average undergraduate aid package: $20,155**

ABOUT THE INSTITUTION Independent religious, coed. Awards: bachelor's and master's degrees. 38 undergraduate majors. Total enrollment: 2,089. Undergraduates: 2,059. Freshmen: 574. Federal methodology is used as a basis for awarding need-based institutional aid.

UNDERGRADUATE EXPENSES for 2007–08 ***Application fee:*** $40. ***Comprehensive fee:*** $39,270 includes full-time tuition ($31,100), mandatory fees ($300), and room and board ($7870). ***College room only:*** $4110.

FRESHMAN FINANCIAL AID (Fall 2005) 426 applied for aid; of those 84% were deemed to have need. 99% of freshmen with need received aid; of those 38% had need fully met. ***Average percent of need met:*** 88% (excluding resources awarded to replace EFC). ***Average financial aid package:*** $22,839 (excluding resources awarded to replace EFC). 28% of all full-time freshmen had no need and received non-need-based gift aid.

UNDERGRADUATE FINANCIAL AID (Fall 2005) 1,657 applied for aid; of those 87% were deemed to have need. 100% of undergraduates with need received aid; of those 28% had need fully met. ***Average percent of need met:*** 83% (excluding resources awarded to replace EFC). ***Average financial aid package:*** $20,155 (excluding resources awarded to replace EFC). 24% of all full-time undergraduates had no need and received non-need-based gift aid.

GIFT AID (NEED-BASED) ***Total amount:*** $23,667,614 (6% federal, 7% state, 84% institutional, 3% external sources). ***Receiving aid:*** Freshmen: 71% (354); All full-time undergraduates: 73% (1,432). ***Average award:*** Freshmen: $17,875; Undergraduates: $16,528. ***Scholarships, grants, and awards:*** Federal Pell, FSEOG, state, private, college/university gift aid from institutional funds.

GIFT AID (NON-NEED-BASED) ***Total amount:*** $5,348,632 (6% state, 92% institutional, 2% external sources). ***Average award:*** Freshmen: $11,221; Undergraduates: $10,371. ***Scholarships, grants, and awards by category:*** *Academic Interests/Achievement:* general academic interests/achievements. *Creative Arts/Performance:* art/fine arts, dance, music, theater/drama. *Special Achievements/Activities:* community service, general special achievements/activities, leadership. *Special Characteristics:* adult students, children and siblings of alumni, children of faculty/staff, ethnic background, international students, local/state students, members of minority groups, relatives of clergy, religious affiliation. ***ROTC:*** Army cooperative, Air Force cooperative.

LOANS ***Student loans:*** $9,459,122 (94% need-based, 6% non-need-based). 69% of past graduating class borrowed through all loan programs. *Average indebtedness per student:* $24,298. ***Average need-based loan:*** Freshmen: $4168; Undergraduates: $4614. ***Parent loans:*** $5,113,888 (87% need-based, 13% non-need-based). ***Programs:*** FFEL (Subsidized and Unsubsidized Stafford, PLUS), Perkins, college/university, alternative loans.

WORK-STUDY ***Federal work-study:*** Total amount: $966,900; 515 jobs averaging $1757. ***State or other work-study/employment:*** Total amount: $1,380,104 (69% need-based, 31% non-need-based). 835 part-time jobs averaging $2785.

APPLYING FOR FINANCIAL AID ***Required financial aid form:*** FAFSA. ***Financial aid deadline (priority):*** 3/15. ***Notification date:*** Continuous beginning 3/1. Students must reply by 5/1 or within 2 weeks of notification.

CONTACT Mr. J. Randy Green, Director of Financial Aid, Wittenberg University, PO Box 720, Springfield, OH 45501-0720, 937-327-7321 or toll-free 800-677-7558 Ext. 6314. *Fax:* 937-327-6379. *E-mail:* jgreen@wittenberg.edu.

WOFFORD COLLEGE

Spartanburg, SC

ABOUT THE INSTITUTION Independent religious, coed. Awards: bachelor's degrees. 30 undergraduate majors. Total enrollment: 1,240. Undergraduates: 1,240. Freshmen: 378.

GIFT AID (NEED-BASED) ***Scholarships, grants, and awards:*** Federal Pell, FSEOG, state, private, college/university gift aid from institutional funds.

GIFT AID (NON-NEED-BASED) ***Scholarships, grants, and awards by category:*** *Academic Interests/Achievement:* general academic interests/achievements. *Creative Arts/Performance:* music. *Special Achievements/Activities:* cheerleading/drum major, community service, general special achievements/activities, leadership, religious involvement. *Special Characteristics:* children of faculty/staff, general special characteristics, relatives of clergy.

LOANS ***Programs:*** FFEL (Subsidized and Unsubsidized Stafford, PLUS), Perkins, state.

WORK-STUDY ***Federal work-study:*** Total amount: $283,559; jobs available. ***State or other work-study/employment:*** Part-time jobs available.

APPLYING FOR FINANCIAL AID ***Required financial aid form:*** FAFSA.

CONTACT Donna D. Hawkins, Director of Financial Aid, Wofford College, Campus PO Box 171, 429 North Church Street, Spartanburg, SC 29303-3663, 864-597-4160. *Fax:* 864-597-4149. *E-mail:* hawkinsdd@wofford.edu.

WOODBURY COLLEGE

Montpelier, VT

ABOUT THE INSTITUTION Independent, coed. Awards: associate and bachelor's degrees. 4 undergraduate majors. Total enrollment: 132. Undergraduates: 105. Freshmen: 5.

GIFT AID (NEED-BASED) ***Scholarships, grants, and awards:*** Federal Pell, FSEOG, state, private, college/university gift aid from institutional funds.

LOANS ***Programs:*** Federal Direct (Subsidized and Unsubsidized Stafford, PLUS).

WORK-STUDY ***Federal work-study:*** Total amount: $2248; jobs available.

APPLYING FOR FINANCIAL AID ***Required financial aid forms:*** FAFSA, institution's own form, state aid form.

CONTACT Marcy Spaulding, Financial Aid Director, Woodbury College, 660 Elm Street, Montpelier, VT 05602, 800-639-6039 Ext. 245 or toll-free 800-639-6039 (in-state). *E-mail:* admissions@woodbury-college.edu.

WOODBURY UNIVERSITY

Burbank, CA

Tuition & fees: $23,572 **Average undergraduate aid package: $16,591**

ABOUT THE INSTITUTION Independent, coed. Awards: bachelor's and master's degrees. 17 undergraduate majors. Total enrollment: 1,485. Undergraduates: 1,310. Freshmen: 135. Federal methodology is used as a basis for awarding need-based institutional aid.

UNDERGRADUATE EXPENSES for 2006–07 ***Application fee:*** $35. ***Comprehensive fee:*** $31,676 includes full-time tuition ($23,232), mandatory fees ($340), and room and board ($8104). ***College room only:*** $4952. Full-time tuition and fees vary according to program. Room and board charges vary according to board plan and housing facility. ***Part-time tuition:*** $758 per unit. ***Part-time fees:*** $340 per term. Part-time tuition and fees vary according to class time, course load, and program. ***Payment plans:*** Installment, deferred payment.

FRESHMAN FINANCIAL AID (Fall 2005) 100 applied for aid; of those 94% were deemed to have need. 100% of freshmen with need received aid; of those 5% had need fully met. ***Average percent of need met:*** 62% (excluding resources awarded to replace EFC). ***Average financial aid package:*** $17,485 (excluding resources awarded to replace EFC). 30% of all full-time freshmen had no need and received non-need-based gift aid.

UNDERGRADUATE FINANCIAL AID (Fall 2005) 757 applied for aid; of those 93% were deemed to have need. 100% of undergraduates with need received aid; of those 5% had need fully met. ***Average percent of need met:*** 58% (excluding resources awarded to replace EFC). ***Average financial aid package:*** $16,591 (excluding resources awarded to replace EFC). 17% of all full-time undergraduates had no need and received non-need-based gift aid.

GIFT AID (NEED-BASED) ***Total amount:*** $10,928,565 (19% federal, 32% state, 47% institutional, 2% external sources). ***Receiving aid:*** Freshmen: 70% (94); All full-time undergraduates: 79% (675). ***Average award:*** Freshmen: $15,185; Undergraduates: $12,929. ***Scholarships, grants, and awards:*** Federal Pell, FSEOG, state, private, college/university gift aid from institutional funds.

GIFT AID (NON-NEED-BASED) ***Total amount:*** $866,990 (1% state, 86% institutional, 13% external sources). ***Receiving aid:*** Freshmen: 3% (4); Undergraduates: 2% (15). ***Average award:*** Freshmen: $8186; Undergraduates: $11,714. ***Scholarships, grants, and awards by category:*** *Academic Interests/Achievement:* 751 awards ($3,846,203 total): general academic interests/achievements. *Creative Arts/Performance:* 1 award ($11,788 total): applied art and design. ***Tuition waivers:*** Full or partial for employees or children of employees.

LOANS ***Student loans:*** $10,910,335 (88% need-based, 12% non-need-based). 87% of past graduating class borrowed through all loan programs. *Average indebtedness per student:* $27,115. ***Average need-based loan:*** Freshmen: $2686; Undergraduates: $4494. ***Parent loans:*** $3,708,811 (55% need-based, 45% non-need-based). ***Programs:*** FFEL (Subsidized and Unsubsidized Stafford, PLUS), Perkins, alternative loans.

WORK-STUDY ***Federal work-study:*** Total amount: $118,108; 117 jobs averaging $1204.

APPLYING FOR FINANCIAL AID ***Required financial aid forms:*** FAFSA, institution's own form. ***Financial aid deadline:*** Continuous. ***Notification date:*** Continuous beginning 3/15. Students must reply within 2 weeks of notification.

CONTACT Celeastia Williams, Director of Enrollment Services, Woodbury University, 7500 Glenoaks Boulevard, Burbank, CA 91510, 818-767-0888 Ext. 273 or toll-free 800-784-WOOD. *Fax:* 818-767-4816.

WORCESTER POLYTECHNIC INSTITUTE

Worcester, MA

Tuition & fees: $33,318 **Average undergraduate aid package: $24,103**

ABOUT THE INSTITUTION Independent, coed. Awards: bachelor's, master's, and doctoral degrees and post-bachelor's and post-master's certificates. 48 undergraduate majors. Total enrollment: 3,918. Undergraduates: 2,866. Freshmen: 777. Both federal and institutional methodology are used as a basis for awarding need-based institutional aid.

UNDERGRADUATE EXPENSES for 2006–07 ***Application fee:*** $60. ***Comprehensive fee:*** $43,268 includes full-time tuition ($32,818), mandatory fees ($500), and room and board ($9950). ***College room only:*** $5840. Full-time tuition and fees vary according to degree level. Room and board charges vary according to board plan and housing facility. ***Part-time tuition:*** $2736 per unit. Part-time tuition and fees vary according to course load and degree level. ***Payment plans:*** Installment, deferred payment.

FRESHMAN FINANCIAL AID (Fall 2006, est.) 690 applied for aid; of those 87% were deemed to have need. 99% of freshmen with need received aid; of those 38% had need fully met. ***Average percent of need met:*** 65% (excluding resources awarded to replace EFC). ***Average financial aid package:*** $21,654 (excluding resources awarded to replace EFC). 20% of all full-time freshmen had no need and received non-need-based gift aid.

UNDERGRADUATE FINANCIAL AID (Fall 2006, est.) 2,152 applied for aid; of those 91% were deemed to have need. 98% of undergraduates with need received aid; of those 33% had need fully met. ***Average percent of need met:*** 69% (excluding resources awarded to replace EFC). ***Average financial aid package:*** $24,103 (excluding resources awarded to replace EFC). 18% of all full-time undergraduates had no need and received non-need-based gift aid.

GIFT AID (NEED-BASED) ***Total amount:*** $32,555,784 (5% federal, 3% state, 86% institutional, 6% external sources). ***Receiving aid:*** Freshmen: 76% (590); All full-time undergraduates: 67% (1,879). ***Average award:*** Freshmen: $16,607; Undergraduates: $16,372. ***Scholarships, grants, and awards:*** Federal Pell, FSEOG, state, private, college/university gift aid from institutional funds.

GIFT AID (NON-NEED-BASED) ***Total amount:*** $8,794,801 (84% institutional, 16% external sources). ***Receiving aid:*** Freshmen: 23% (178); Undergraduates: 16% (439). ***Average award:*** Freshmen: $12,273; Undergraduates: $16,324. ***Scholarships, grants, and awards by category:*** *Academic Interests/Achievement:* 1,404 awards ($15,645,429 total): general academic interests/achievements, premedicine. *Special Characteristics:* 37 awards ($127,640 total): children of workers in trades. ***Tuition waivers:*** Full or partial for employees or children of employees. ***ROTC:*** Army, Naval cooperative, Air Force.

LOANS ***Student loans:*** $21,053,859 (48% need-based, 52% non-need-based). 82% of past graduating class borrowed through all loan programs. *Average indebtedness per student:* $34,409. ***Average need-based loan:*** Freshmen: $4923; Undergraduates: $6446. ***Parent loans:*** $7,097,384 (100% non-need-based). ***Programs:*** FFEL (Subsidized and Unsubsidized Stafford, PLUS), Perkins, state, college/university.

WORK-STUDY ***Federal work-study:*** Total amount: $502,759; 553 jobs averaging $909. ***State or other work-study/employment:*** Part-time jobs available.

APPLYING FOR FINANCIAL AID ***Required financial aid forms:*** FAFSA, CSS Financial Aid PROFILE, noncustodial (divorced/separated) parent's statement, federal income tax form(s) and W-2 statements. ***Financial aid deadline:*** 2/1 (priority: 2/1). ***Notification date:*** 4/1. Students must reply by 5/1.

CONTACT Office of Financial Aid, Worcester Polytechnic Institute, 100 Institute Road, Worcester, MA 01609-2280, 508-831-5469. *Fax:* 508-831-5039. *E-mail:* finaid@wpi.edu.

WORCESTER STATE COLLEGE

Worcester, MA

ABOUT THE INSTITUTION State-supported, coed. Awards: bachelor's and master's degrees and post-bachelor's certificates. 23 undergraduate majors. Total enrollment: 5,440. Undergraduates: 4,626. Freshmen: 684.

GIFT AID (NEED-BASED) ***Scholarships, grants, and awards:*** Federal Pell, FSEOG, state, private, college/university gift aid from institutional funds.

GIFT AID (NON-NEED-BASED) ***Scholarships, grants, and awards by category:*** *Academic Interests/Achievement:* biological sciences, business, education, English, foreign languages, health fields. *Creative Arts/Performance:* art/fine arts. *Special Achievements/Activities:* community service, general special achievements/activities. *Special Characteristics:* children and siblings of alumni, children of faculty/staff, children with a deceased or disabled parent, general special characteristics, handicapped students, local/state students, veterans.

LOANS ***Programs:*** FFEL (Subsidized and Unsubsidized Stafford, PLUS), Perkins, Massachusetts No-Interest Loans (NIL).

APPLYING FOR FINANCIAL AID ***Required financial aid forms:*** FAFSA, institution's own form.

CONTACT Jayne McGinn, Director of Financial Aid, Worcester State College, 486 Chandler Street, Worcester, MA 01602, 508-929-8058 or toll-free 866-WSC-CALL. *Fax:* 508-929-8194. *E-mail:* jmcginn@worcester.edu.

WRIGHT STATE UNIVERSITY

Dayton, OH

CONTACT Mr. David R. Darr, Director of Financial Aid, Wright State University, Colonel Glenn Highway, Dayton, OH 45435, 937-873-5721 or toll-free 800-247-1770.

XAVIER UNIVERSITY

Cincinnati, OH

Tuition & fees: $23,880 **Average undergraduate aid package: $15,224**

ABOUT THE INSTITUTION Independent Roman Catholic, coed. Awards: associate, bachelor's, master's, and doctoral degrees and post-bachelor's and post-master's certificates. 56 undergraduate majors. Total enrollment: 6,666. Undergraduates: 3,910. Freshmen: 813. Federal methodology is used as a basis for awarding need-based institutional aid.

UNDERGRADUATE EXPENSES for 2006–07 ***Application fee:*** $35. ***Comprehensive fee:*** $32,520 includes full-time tuition ($23,270), mandatory fees ($610), and room and board ($8640). ***College room only:*** $4710. Full-time tuition and fees vary according to course load, program, and student level. Room and board charges vary according to board plan and housing facility. ***Part-time tuition:*** $446 per credit hour. Part-time tuition and fees vary according to course load. ***Payment plans:*** Installment, deferred payment.

FRESHMAN FINANCIAL AID (Fall 2006, est.) 623 applied for aid; of those 74% were deemed to have need. 100% of freshmen with need received aid; of those 27% had need fully met. ***Average percent of need met:*** 80% (excluding resources awarded to replace EFC). ***Average financial aid package:*** $15,823 (excluding resources awarded to replace EFC). 30% of all full-time freshmen had no need and received non-need-based gift aid.

UNDERGRADUATE FINANCIAL AID (Fall 2006, est.) 2,280 applied for aid; of those 80% were deemed to have need. 100% of undergraduates with need received aid; of those 25% had need fully met. ***Average percent of need met:*** 75% (excluding resources awarded to replace EFC). ***Average financial aid package:*** $15,224 (excluding resources awarded to replace EFC). 30% of all full-time undergraduates had no need and received non-need-based gift aid.

GIFT AID (NEED-BASED) ***Total amount:*** $18,981,087 (9% federal, 8% state, 77% institutional, 6% external sources). ***Receiving aid:*** Freshmen: 56% (454); All full-time undergraduates: 52% (1,754). ***Average award:*** Freshmen: $11,203; Undergraduates: $10,536. ***Scholarships, grants, and awards:*** Federal Pell, FSEOG, state, private, college/university gift aid from institutional funds.

GIFT AID (NON-NEED-BASED) ***Total amount:*** $12,704,636 (6% state, 83% institutional, 11% external sources). ***Receiving aid:*** Freshmen: 12% (94);

Undergraduates: 9% (312). ***Average award:*** Freshmen: $10,323; Undergraduates: $9056. ***Scholarships, grants, and awards by category:*** *Academic Interests/Achievement:* 2,077 awards ($15,486,335 total): foreign languages, general academic interests/achievements, mathematics, military science, physical sciences, social sciences. *Creative Arts/Performance:* 144 awards ($451,605 total): art/fine arts, music, performing arts, theater/drama. *Special Characteristics:* 294 awards ($1,200,140 total): children and siblings of alumni, international students, members of minority groups, siblings of current students. ***Tuition waivers:*** Full or partial for employees or children of employees, senior citizens. ***ROTC:*** Army, Air Force cooperative.

LOANS ***Student loans:*** $14,649,663 (67% need-based, 33% non-need-based). 59% of past graduating class borrowed through all loan programs. *Average indebtedness per student:* $21,753. ***Average need-based loan:*** Freshmen: $3785; Undergraduates: $4543. ***Parent loans:*** $4,571,528 (31% need-based, 69% non-need-based). ***Programs:*** FFEL (Subsidized and Unsubsidized Stafford, PLUS), Perkins.

WORK-STUDY ***Federal work-study:*** Total amount: $1,227,232; 609 jobs averaging $2015. ***State or other work-study/employment:*** Total amount: $127,000 (6% need-based, 94% non-need-based). 126 part-time jobs averaging $1008.

ATHLETIC AWARDS Total amount: $3,016,517 (34% need-based, 66% non-need-based).

APPLYING FOR FINANCIAL AID ***Required financial aid form:*** FAFSA. ***Financial aid deadline (priority):*** 2/15. ***Notification date:*** Continuous beginning 2/15. Students must reply by 5/1.

CONTACT Office of Financial Aid, Xavier University, 3800 Victory Parkway, Cincinnati, OH 45207-5411, 513-745-3142 or toll-free 800-344-4698. *Fax:* 513-745-2806.

XAVIER UNIVERSITY OF LOUISIANA

New Orleans, LA

ABOUT THE INSTITUTION Independent Roman Catholic, coed. Awards: bachelor's, master's, and first professional degrees. 54 undergraduate majors. Total enrollment: 3,012. Undergraduates: 2,272. Freshmen: 444.

GIFT AID (NEED-BASED) ***Scholarships, grants, and awards:*** Federal Pell, FSEOG, state, private, college/university gift aid from institutional funds, United Negro College Fund.

GIFT AID (NON-NEED-BASED) ***Scholarships, grants, and awards by category:*** *Academic Interests/Achievement:* biological sciences, business, computer science, education, engineering/technologies, foreign languages, general academic interests/achievements, humanities, mathematics, physical sciences, premedicine, social sciences. *Creative Arts/Performance:* art/fine arts, music, performing arts. *Special Achievements/Activities:* religious involvement. *Special Characteristics:* children of faculty/staff.

LOANS ***Programs:*** Federal Direct (Subsidized and Unsubsidized Stafford, PLUS), FFEL (Subsidized and Unsubsidized Stafford, PLUS), Perkins.

APPLYING FOR FINANCIAL AID ***Required financial aid form:*** FAFSA.

CONTACT Mrs. Mildred Higgins, Financial Aid Director, Xavier University of Louisiana, One Drexel Drive, New Orleans, LA 70125-1098, 504-520-7517 or toll-free 877-XAVIERU.

YALE UNIVERSITY

New Haven, CT

Tuition & fees: $33,030	Average undergraduate aid package: $32,533

ABOUT THE INSTITUTION Independent, coed. Awards: bachelor's, master's, doctoral, and first professional degrees and post-master's certificates. 67 undergraduate majors. Total enrollment: 11,416. Undergraduates: 5,333. Freshmen: 1,315. Both federal and institutional methodology are used as a basis for awarding need-based institutional aid.

UNDERGRADUATE EXPENSES for 2006–07 ***Application fee:*** $75. ***Comprehensive fee:*** $43,050 includes full-time tuition ($33,030) and room and board ($10,020). ***Payment plan:*** Installment.

FRESHMAN FINANCIAL AID (Fall 2006, est.) 780 applied for aid; of those 72% were deemed to have need. 100% of freshmen with need received aid; of those 100% had need fully met. ***Average percent of need met:*** 100% (excluding resources awarded to replace EFC). ***Average financial aid package:*** $32,260 (excluding resources awarded to replace EFC).

UNDERGRADUATE FINANCIAL AID (Fall 2006, est.) 2,521 applied for aid; of those 91% were deemed to have need. 100% of undergraduates with need received aid; of those 100% had need fully met. ***Average percent of need met:*** 100% (excluding resources awarded to replace EFC). ***Average financial aid package:*** $32,533 (excluding resources awarded to replace EFC).

GIFT AID (NEED-BASED) ***Total amount:*** $68,359,114 (5% federal, 88% institutional, 7% external sources). ***Receiving aid:*** Freshmen: 42% (555); All full-time undergraduates: 42% (2,260). ***Average award:*** Freshmen: $31,468; Undergraduates: $30,055. ***Scholarships, grants, and awards:*** Federal Pell, FSEOG, state, private, college/university gift aid from institutional funds, United Negro College Fund.

GIFT AID (NON-NEED-BASED) ***ROTC:*** Army cooperative, Air Force cooperative.

LOANS ***Student loans:*** $4,743,662 (100% need-based). 32% of past graduating class borrowed through all loan programs. *Average indebtedness per student:* $13,344. ***Average need-based loan:*** Freshmen: $1168; Undergraduates: $1996. ***Parent loans:*** $7,905,423 (100% need-based). ***Programs:*** FFEL (Subsidized and Unsubsidized Stafford, PLUS), Perkins, state, college/university.

WORK-STUDY ***Federal work-study:*** Total amount: $1,907,214; 883 jobs averaging $2179. ***State or other work-study/employment:*** Total amount: $2,163,823 (100% need-based). 655 part-time jobs averaging $3028.

APPLYING FOR FINANCIAL AID ***Required financial aid forms:*** FAFSA, CSS Financial Aid PROFILE, noncustodial (divorced/separated) parent's statement, business/farm supplement, parent tax returns. ***Financial aid deadline:*** 3/1 (priority: 3/1). ***Notification date:*** 4/1. Students must reply by 5/1 or within 1 week of notification.

CONTACT Student Financial Services, Yale University, PO Box 208288, New Haven, CT 06520-8288, 203-432-0371. *Fax:* 203-432-0359. *E-mail:* sfs@yale.edu.

YESHIVA AND KOLEL BAIS MEDRASH ELYON

Monsey, NY

CONTACT Financial Aid Office, Yeshiva and Kolel Bais Medrash Elyon, 73 Main Street, Monsey, NY 10952, 845-356-7064.

YESHIVA AND KOLLEL HARBOTZAS TORAH

Brooklyn, NY

CONTACT Financial Aid Office, Yeshiva And Kollel Harbotzas Torah, 1049 East 15th Street, Brooklyn, NY 11230, 718-692-0208.

YESHIVA BETH MOSHE

Scranton, PA

CONTACT Financial Aid Office, Yeshiva Beth Moshe, 930 Hickory Street, Scranton, PA 18505-2124, 717-346-1747.

YESHIVA COLLEGE OF THE NATION'S CAPITAL

Silver Spring, MD

CONTACT Financial Aid Office, Yeshiva College of the Nation's Capital, 1216 Arcola Avenue, Silver Spring, MD 20902, 301-593-2534.

YESHIVA DERECH CHAIM

Brooklyn, NY

CONTACT Financial Aid Office, Yeshiva Derech Chaim, 1573 39th Street, Brooklyn, NY 11218, 718-438-5426.

YESHIVA D'MONSEY RABBINICAL COLLEGE

Monsey, NY

CONTACT Financial Aid Office, Yeshiva D'Monsey Rabbinical College, 2 Roman Boulevard, Monsey, NY 10952, 914-352-5852.

YESHIVA GEDDOLAH OF GREATER DETROIT RABBINICAL COLLEGE

Oak Park, MI

CONTACT Rabbi P. Rushnawitz, Executive Administrator, Yeshiva Geddolah of Greater Detroit Rabbinical College, 24600 Greenfield Road, Oak Park, MI 48237-1544, 810-968-3360. *Fax:* 810-968-8613.

YESHIVA GEDOLAH IMREI YOSEF D'SPINKA

Brooklyn, NY

CONTACT Financial Aid Office, Yeshiva Gedolah Imrei Yosef D'Spinka, 1466 56th Street, Brooklyn, NY 11219, 718-851-8721.

YESHIVA GEDOLAH RABBINICAL COLLEGE

Miami Beach, FL

CONTACT Financial Aid Office, Yeshiva Gedolah Rabbinical College, 1140 Alton Road, Miami Beach, FL 33139, 305-673-5664.

YESHIVA KARLIN STOLIN RABBINICAL INSTITUTE

Brooklyn, NY

CONTACT Mr. Daniel Ross, Financial Aid Administrator, Yeshiva Karlin Stolin Rabbinical Institute, 1818 Fifty-fourth Street, Brooklyn, NY 11204, 718-232-7800 Ext. 116. *Fax:* 718-331-4833.

YESHIVA OF NITRA RABBINICAL COLLEGE

Mount Kisco, NY

CONTACT Mr. Yosef Rosen, Financial Aid Administrator, Yeshiva of Nitra Rabbinical College, 194 Division Avenue, Mount Kisco, NY 10549, 718-384-5460. *Fax:* 718-387-9400.

YESHIVA OF THE TELSHE ALUMNI

Riverdale, NY

CONTACT Financial Aid Office, Yeshiva of the Telshe Alumni, 4904 Independence Avenue, Riverdale, NY 10471, 718-601-3523.

YESHIVA OHR ELCHONON CHABAD/WEST COAST TALMUDICAL SEMINARY

Los Angeles, CA

CONTACT Ms. Hendy Tauber, Director of Financial Aid, Yeshiva Ohr Elchonon Chabad/West Coast Talmudical Seminary, 7215 Waring Avenue, Los Angeles, CA 90046-7660, 213-937-3763. *Fax:* 213-937-9456.

YESHIVA SHAAREI TORAH OF ROCKLAND

Suffern, NY

CONTACT Financial Aid Office, Yeshiva Shaarei Torah of Rockland, 91 West Carlton Road, Suffern, NY 10901, 845-352-3431.

YESHIVA SHAAR HATORAH TALMUDIC RESEARCH INSTITUTE

Kew Gardens, NY

CONTACT Mr. Yoel Yankelewitz, Executive Director, Financial Aid, Yeshiva Shaar Hatorah Talmudic Research Institute, 117-06 84th Avenue, Kew Gardens, NY 11418-1469, 718-846-1940.

YESHIVAS NOVOMINSK

Brooklyn, NY

CONTACT Financial Aid Office, Yeshivas Novominsk, 1569 47th Street, Brooklyn, NY 11219, 718-438-2727.

YESHIVATH VIZNITZ

Monsey, NY

CONTACT Financial Aid Office, Yeshivath Viznitz, Phyllis Terrace, PO Box 446, Monsey, NY 10952, 914-356-1010.

YESHIVATH ZICHRON MOSHE

South Fallsburg, NY

CONTACT Ms. Miryom R. Miller, Director of Financial Aid, Yeshivath Zichron Moshe, Laurel Park Road, South Fallsburg, NY 12779, 914-434-5240. *Fax:* 914-434-1009. *E-mail:* lehus@aol.com.

YESHIVAT MIKDASH MELECH

Brooklyn, NY

CONTACT Financial Aid Office, Yeshivat Mikdash Melech, 1326 Ocean Parkway, Brooklyn, NY 11230-5601, 718-339-1090.

YESHIVA TORAS CHAIM TALMUDICAL SEMINARY

Denver, CO

CONTACT Office of Financial Aid, Yeshiva Toras Chaim Talmudical Seminary, 1400 Quitman Street, Denver, CO 80204-1415, 303-629-8200.

YESHIVA UNIVERSITY

New York, NY

CONTACT Jean Belmont, Director of Student Finances, Yeshiva University, 500 West 185th Street, Room 121, New York, NY 10033-3201, 212-960-5269. *Fax:* 212-960-0037. *E-mail:* jbelmont@ymail.yu.edu.

YORK COLLEGE

York, NE

CONTACT Deb Lowry, Director of Financial Aid, York College, 1125 East 8th Street, York, NE 68467, 402-363-5624 or toll-free 800-950-9675. *Fax:* 402-363-5623.

YORK COLLEGE OF PENNSYLVANIA

York, PA

Tuition & fees: $11,160 **Average undergraduate aid package: $8670**

ABOUT THE INSTITUTION Independent, coed. Awards: associate, bachelor's, and master's degrees. 59 undergraduate majors. Total enrollment: 5,664. Undergraduates: 5,367. Freshmen: 1,116. Federal methodology is used as a basis for awarding need-based institutional aid.

UNDERGRADUATE EXPENSES for 2006–07 ***Application fee:*** $30. ***Comprehensive fee:*** $18,110 includes full-time tuition ($10,160), mandatory fees ($1000), and room and board ($6950). ***College room only:*** $3900. Full-time tuition and fees vary according to course load and program. Room and board charges vary according to housing facility. ***Part-time tuition:*** $318 per credit hour. ***Part-time fees:*** $195 per term. Part-time tuition and fees vary according to course load and program. ***Payment plans:*** Tuition prepayment, installment.

FRESHMAN FINANCIAL AID (Fall 2006, est.) 931 applied for aid; of those 62% were deemed to have need. 99% of freshmen with need received aid; of those 29% had need fully met. ***Average percent of need met:*** 74% (excluding resources awarded to replace EFC). ***Average financial aid package:*** $8611 (excluding resources awarded to replace EFC). 18% of all full-time freshmen had no need and received non-need-based gift aid.

UNDERGRADUATE FINANCIAL AID (Fall 2006, est.) 3,517 applied for aid; of those 67% were deemed to have need. 98% of undergraduates with need received aid; of those 31% had need fully met. ***Average percent of need met:*** 73% (excluding resources awarded to replace EFC). ***Average financial aid package:*** $8670 (excluding resources awarded to replace EFC). 10% of all full-time undergraduates had no need and received non-need-based gift aid.

GIFT AID (NEED-BASED) ***Total amount:*** $9,338,962 (25% federal, 32% state, 38% institutional, 5% external sources). ***Receiving aid:*** Freshmen: 38% (415); All full-time undergraduates: 35% (1,598). ***Average award:*** Freshmen: $4325; Undergraduates: $4342. ***Scholarships, grants, and awards:*** Federal Pell, FSEOG, state, private, college/university gift aid from institutional funds.

GIFT AID (NON-NEED-BASED) ***Total amount:*** $1,449,483 (1% state, 87% institutional, 12% external sources). ***Receiving aid:*** Freshmen: 26% (283); Undergraduates: 13% (597). ***Average award:*** Freshmen: $2682; Undergraduates: $3055. ***Scholarships, grants, and awards by category:*** *Academic Interests/Achievement:* 595 awards ($2,113,682 total): general academic interests/achievements. *Creative Arts/Performance:* 20 awards ($15,080 total): music. *Special Achievements/Activities:* 10 awards ($33,870 total): community service, memberships. *Special Characteristics:* 35 awards ($58,091 total): children and siblings of alumni, children of union members/company employees, international students, members of minority groups. ***Tuition waivers:*** Full or partial for employees or children of employees. ***ROTC:*** Army cooperative.

LOANS ***Student loans:*** $16,340,080 (49% need-based, 51% non-need-based). 70% of past graduating class borrowed through all loan programs. *Average indebtedness per student:* $20,639. ***Average need-based loan:*** Freshmen: $4151; Undergraduates: $5147. ***Parent loans:*** $4,281,047 (55% need-based, 45% non-need-based). ***Programs:*** Federal Direct (Subsidized and Unsubsidized Stafford, PLUS), FFEL (Subsidized and Unsubsidized Stafford, PLUS), Perkins, Federal Nursing, college/university.

WORK-STUDY ***Federal work-study:*** Total amount: $352,878; 267 jobs averaging $1458. ***State or other work-study/employment:*** Total amount: $46,000 (23% need-based, 77% non-need-based). 37 part-time jobs averaging $1277.

APPLYING FOR FINANCIAL AID ***Required financial aid form:*** FAFSA. ***Financial aid deadline (priority):*** 3/1. ***Notification date:*** Continuous beginning 3/1. Students must reply within 4 weeks of notification.

CONTACT Calvin Williams, Director of Financial Aid, York College of Pennsylvania, Country Club Road, York, PA 17405-7199, 717-849-1682 or toll-free 800-455-8018. *Fax:* 717-849-1607. *E-mail:* financialaid@ycp.edu.

YORK COLLEGE OF THE CITY UNIVERSITY OF NEW YORK

Jamaica, NY

ABOUT THE INSTITUTION State and locally supported, coed. Awards: bachelor's degrees. 36 undergraduate majors. Total enrollment: 6,185. Undergraduates: 6,185. Freshmen: 693.

GIFT AID (NEED-BASED) ***Scholarships, grants, and awards:*** Federal Pell, FSEOG, state, private.

LOANS ***Programs:*** Federal Direct (Subsidized and Unsubsidized Stafford, PLUS), Perkins, college/university.

WORK-STUDY ***Federal work-study:*** Total amount: $627,550; jobs available.

APPLYING FOR FINANCIAL AID ***Required financial aid forms:*** FAFSA, state aid form.

CONTACT Ms. Cathy Tsiapanos, Director of Student Financial Services, York College of the City University of New York, 94-20 Guy R. Brewer Boulevard, Jamaica, NY 11451-0001, 718-262-2238. *E-mail:* ctsia@york.cuny.edu.

YOUNGSTOWN STATE UNIVERSITY

Youngstown, OH

Tuition & fees (OH res): $6697 **Average undergraduate aid package: N/A**

ABOUT THE INSTITUTION State-supported, coed. Awards: associate, bachelor's, master's, and doctoral degrees and post-bachelor's certificates. 120 undergraduate majors. Total enrollment: 13,178. Undergraduates: 11,987. Freshmen: 2,352. Federal methodology is used as a basis for awarding need-based institutional aid.

UNDERGRADUATE EXPENSES for 2006–07 ***Application fee:*** $30. ***Tuition, area resident:*** part-time $269 per credit. ***Tuition, state resident:*** full-time $6468. ***Tuition, nonresident:*** full-time $11,976; part-time $498.98 per credit. ***Required fees:*** full-time $229; $9.54 per credit. Full-time tuition and fees vary according to course load. Part-time tuition and fees vary according to course load. ***College room and board:*** $6490. Room and board charges vary according to board plan and housing facility. ***Payment plan:*** Installment.

GIFT AID (NEED-BASED) ***Total amount:*** $18,941,934 (70% federal, 21% state, 9% institutional). ***Scholarships, grants, and awards:*** Federal Pell, FSEOG, state, private, college/university gift aid from institutional funds.

GIFT AID (NON-NEED-BASED) ***Total amount:*** $10,505,261 (2% federal, 22% state, 46% institutional, 30% external sources). ***Scholarships, grants, and awards by category:*** *Academic Interests/Achievement:* business, computer science, education, engineering/technologies, English, general academic interests/achievements, health fields, humanities, military science. *Creative Arts/Performance:* music, theater/drama. *Special Achievements/Activities:* cheerleading/drum major, leadership. *Special Characteristics:* adult students, children and siblings of alumni, children of faculty/staff, children of union members/company employees, children of workers in trades, children with a deceased or disabled parent, handicapped students, members of minority groups, spouses of deceased or disabled public servants, veterans, veterans' children. ***Tuition waivers:*** Full or partial for employees or children of employees, senior citizens. ***ROTC:*** Army, Air Force cooperative.

LOANS ***Student loans:*** $51,875,000 (88% need-based, 12% non-need-based). ***Parent loans:*** $5,231,389 (100% non-need-based). ***Programs:*** FFEL (Subsidized and Unsubsidized Stafford, PLUS), Perkins, state, Charles E. Schell Foundation loans.

WORK-STUDY ***Federal work-study:*** Total amount: $662,019; 286 jobs averaging $2314. ***State or other work-study/employment:*** Part-time jobs available.

ATHLETIC AWARDS Total amount: $2,936,551 (100% non-need-based).

APPLYING FOR FINANCIAL AID ***Required financial aid forms:*** FAFSA, institution's own form. ***Financial aid deadline (priority):*** 2/15. ***Notification date:*** 5/1. Students must reply within 4 weeks of notification.

CONTACT Ms. Beth Bartlett, Administrative Assistant, Youngstown State University, One University Plaza, Youngstown, OH 44555, 330-941-3504 or toll-free 877-468-6978. *Fax:* 330-941-1659. *E-mail:* babartlett@ysu.edu.

ZION BIBLE INSTITUTE

Barrington, RI

CONTACT Financial Aid Office, Zion Bible Institute, 27 Middle Highway, Barrington, RI 02806, 401-246-0900 or toll-free 800-356-4014.

Appendix

State Scholarship and Grant Programs

Each state government has established one or more state-administered financial aid programs for qualified students. In many instances, these state programs are restricted to legal residents of the state. However, they often are available to out-of-state students who will be or are attending colleges or universities within the state. In addition to residential status, other qualifications frequently exist.

Gift aid and forgivable loan programs open to undergraduate students for all states and the District of Columbia are described on the following pages. They are arranged in alphabetical order, first by state name, then by program name. The annotation for each program provides information about the program, eligibility, and the contact addresses for applications or further information. Unless otherwise stated, this information refers to awards for 2006–07. Information is provided by the state-sponsoring agency in response to *Peterson's Annual Survey of Non-institutional Aid*, which was conducted between November 2006 and March 2007. Information is accurate when Peterson's receives it. However, it is always advisable to check with the sponsor to ascertain that the information remains correct.

You should write to the address given for each program to request that award details for 2007–08 be sent to you as soon as they are available. Descriptive information, brochures, and application forms for state scholarship programs are usually available from the financial aid offices of public colleges or universities within the specific state. High school guidance offices often have information and relevant forms for awards for which high school seniors may be eligible. Increasingly, state government agencies are putting state scholarship information on state government agency Web sites. In searching state government Web sites, however, you should be aware that the higher education agency in many states is separate from the state's general education office, which is often responsible only for elementary and secondary education. Also, the page at public university Web sites that provides information about student financial aid frequently has a list of state-sponsored scholarships and financial aid programs. College and university Web sites can be easily accessed through www.petersons.com.

Names of scholarship programs are frequently used inconsistently or become abbreviated in popular usage. Many programs have variant names by which they are known. The program's sponsor has approved the title of the program that Peterson's uses in this guide, yet this name may differ from the program's official name or from its most commonly used name.

In addition to the grant aid and forgivable loan programs listed on the following pages, states may also offer internship or work-study programs, graduate fellowships and grants, or low-interest loans. If you are interested in learning more about these other kinds of programs, the state education office that supplies information or applications for the undergraduate scholarship programs listed here should be able to provide information about other kinds of higher education financial aid programs that are sponsored by the state.

ALABAMA

Air Force ROTC College Scholarship. Scholarship program provides three- and four-year scholarships in three different types to high school seniors. All scholarship cadets receive a nontaxable monthly allowance (stipend) during the academic year. The monthly stipend is $250 for freshmen, $300 for sophomores, $350 for juniors and $400 for seniors. For more details refer to Web Site: http://www.afrotc.com/scholarships/hsschol/types.php. *Award:* Scholarship for use in freshman, sophomore, junior, or senior year; renewable. *Award amount:* $9000–$15,000. *Number of awards:* 2000–4000. *Eligibility Requirements:* Applicant must be age 17-30 and enrolled or expecting to enroll full-time at a four-year institution or university. Applicant must have 3.0 GPA or higher. Available to U.S. citizens. Applicant must have served in the Air Force. *Application Requirements:* Application, interview, test scores, transcript. *Deadline:* January 13.

Contact Ty Christian, Chief Air Force ROTC Advertising Manager, Air Force Reserve Officer Training Corps, 551 East Maxwell Boulevard, Maxwell Air Force Base, AL 36112-6106. *E-mail:* ty.christian@maxwell.af.mil. *Phone:* 334-953-2278. *Fax:* 334-953-4384. *Web site:* www.afrotc.com.

Alabama G.I. Dependents Scholarship Program. Full scholarship for dependents of Alabama disabled, prisoner of war, or missing-in-action veterans. Child or stepchild must initiate training before 26th birthday; age 30 deadline may apply in certain situations. No age deadline for spouses or widows. *Award:* Scholarship for use in freshman, sophomore, junior, or senior year; renewable. *Award amount:* varies. *Number of awards:* varies. *Eligibility Requirements:* Applicant must be age 30 or under; enrolled or expecting to enroll full- or part-time at a four-year institution or university; resident of Alabama and studying in Alabama. Available to U.S. and non-U.S. citizens. Applicant or parent must meet one or more of the following requirements: general military experience; retired from active duty; disabled or killed as a result of military service; prisoner of war; or missing in action. *Application Requirements:* Application, transcript. *Deadline:* varies.

Contact Willie E. Moore, Scholarship Administrator, Alabama Department of Veterans Affairs, PO Box 1509, Montgomery, AL 36102-1509. *E-mail:* wmoore@va.state.al.us. *Phone:* 334-242-5077. *Fax:* 334-242-5102. *Web site:* www.va.state.al.us.

Alabama National Guard Educational Assistance Program. Renewable award aids Alabama residents who are members of the Alabama National Guard and are enrolled in an accredited college in Alabama. Forms must be signed by a representative of the Alabama Military Department and financial aid officer. Recipient must be in a degree-seeking program. *Award:* Scholarship for use in freshman, sophomore, junior, senior, graduate, or postgraduate years; renewable. *Award amount:* up to $1000. *Number of awards:* varies. *Eligibility Requirements:* Applicant must be enrolled or expecting to enroll full- or part-time at a two-year, four-year, or technical institution or university; resident of Alabama and studying in Alabama. Available to U.S. citizens. Applicant must have served in the Air Force National Guard or Army National Guard. *Application Requirements:* Application, references, transcript. *Deadline:* continuous.

Contact William Wall, Associate Executive Director for Student Assistance, Alabama Commission on Higher Education, PO Box 302000, Montgomery, AL 36130-2000. *E-mail:* wwall@ache.state.al.us. *Phone:* 334-242-2271. *Fax:* 334-242-0268. *Web site:* www.ache.state.al.us.

Alabama Student Grant Program. Nonrenewable awards available to Alabama residents for undergraduate study at certain independent colleges within the state. Both full and half-time students are eligible. Deadlines: September 15, January 15, and February 15. *Award:* Grant for use in freshman, sophomore, junior, or senior year; not renewable. *Award amount:* up to $1200. *Number of awards:* varies. *Eligibility Requirements:* Applicant must be enrolled or expecting to enroll full- or part-time at a four-year institution or university; resident of Alabama and studying in Alabama. Available to U.S. citizens. *Application Requirements:* Application, references, test scores, transcript. *Deadline:* varies.

Contact William Wall, Associate Executive Director for Student Assistance, ACHE, Alabama Commission on Higher Education, PO Box 302000, Montgomery, AL 36130-2000. *E-mail:* wwall@ache.state.al.us. *Phone:* 334-242-2271. *Fax:* 334-242-0268. *Web site:* www.ache.state.al.us.

Police Officers and Firefighters Survivors Education Assistance Program-Alabama. Provides tuition, fees, books, and supplies to dependents of full-time police officers and firefighters killed in the line of duty. Must attend any Alabama public college as an undergraduate. Must be Alabama resident. Renewable. *Award:* Scholarship for use in freshman, sophomore, junior, or senior year; renewable. *Award amount:* $2000–$5000. *Number of awards:* 15–30. *Eligibility Requirements:* Applicant must be enrolled or expecting to enroll full- or part-time at a two-year, four-year, or technical institution or university; single; resident of Alabama and studying in Alabama. Applicant or parent of applicant must have employment or volunteer experience in police/firefighting. Available to U.S. citizens. *Application Requirements:* Application, references, transcript. *Deadline:* continuous.

Contact William Wall, Associate Executive Director for Student Assistance, ACHE, Alabama Commission on Higher Education, PO Box 302000, Montgomery, AL 36130-2000. *E-mail:* wwall@ache.state.al.us. *Phone:* 334-242-2273. *Fax:* 334-242-0268. *Web site:* www.ache.state.al.us.

ALASKA

GEAR UP Alaska Scholarship. Scholarship provides up to $7000 each year for up to four years of undergraduate study (up to $3500 each year for half-time study). Applicant must be an Alaska high school senior or have an diploma or GED. Must be under the age of 22 years. For more details visit: http://www.eed.state.ak.us/gearup/scholarship.html. *Award:* Scholarship for use in freshman, sophomore, junior, or senior year; not renewable. *Award amount:* $3500–$7000. *Number of awards:* varies. *Eligibility Requirements:* Applicant must be high school student; age 22 or under; planning to enroll or expecting to enroll full- or part-time at a two-year or four-year institution or university and resident of Alaska. Available to U.S. citizens. *Application Requirements:* Application, financial need analysis, references, transcript. *Deadline:* May 31.

Contact Scholarship Committee, Alaska State Department of Education, 801 West 10th Street, Suite 200, PO Box 110500, Juneau, AK 99811-0500. *E-mail:* customer_service@acpe.state.ak.us. *Phone:* 907-465-2800. *Fax:* 907-465-4156. *Web site:* www.eed.state.ak.us.

ARIZONA

Arizona Private Postsecondary Education Student Financial Assistance Program. Provides grants to financially needy Arizona Community College graduates, to attend a private postsecondary baccalaureate degree-granting institution. *Award:* Forgivable loan for use in freshman, sophomore, junior, or senior year; renewable. *Award amount:* $1000–$1500. *Number of awards:* varies. *Eligibility Requirements:* Applicant must be enrolled or expecting to enroll full-time at a four-year institution or university; resident of Arizona and studying in Arizona. Available to U.S. citizens. *Application Requirements:* Application, financial need analysis, transcript, promissory note. *Deadline:* June 30.

Contact Danny Lee, PFAP Program Manager, Arizona Commission for Postsecondary Education, 2020 North Central Avenue, Suite 550, Phoenix, AZ 85004-4503. *E-mail:* dan_lee@azhighered.org. *Phone:* 602-258-2435 Ext. 103. *Fax:* 602-258-2483. *Web site:* www.azhighered.gov.

Leveraging Educational Assistance Partnership. Grants to financially needy students, who enroll in and attend postsecondary education or training in Arizona schools. Program was formerly known as the State Student Incentive Grant or SSIG Program. *Award:* Grant for use in freshman, sophomore, junior, senior, or graduate year; not renewable. *Award amount:* $700–$2500. *Number of awards:* varies. *Eligibility Requirements:* Applicant must be enrolled or expecting to enroll full- or part-time at a two-year, four-year, or technical institution or university; resident of Arizona and studying in Arizona. Available to U.S. citizens. *Application Requirements:* Application, financial need analysis. *Deadline:* April 30.

Contact Mila A. Zaporteza, Business Manager and LEAP Financial Aid Manager, Arizona Commission for Postsecondary Education, 2020 North Central Avenue, Suite 550, Phoenix, AZ 85004-4503. *E-mail:* mila@azhighered.org. *Phone:* 602-258-2435 Ext. 102. *Fax:* 602-258-2483. *Web site:* www.azhighered.gov.

ARKANSAS

Arkansas Academic Challenge Scholarship Program. Awards for Arkansas residents who are graduating high school seniors to study at an Arkansas institution. Must have at least a 2.75 GPA, meet minimum ACT composite score standards, and have financial need. Renewable up to three additional years. *Award:* Scholarship for use in freshman, sophomore, junior, or senior year; renewable. *Award amount:* $2500–$3500. *Number of awards:* 7000–10,000. *Eligibility Requirements:* Applicant must be enrolled or expecting to enroll full-time at a two-year or four-year institution or university; resident of Arkansas and studying in Arkansas. Available to U.S. citizens. *Application Requirements:* Application, financial need analysis, test scores, transcript. *Deadline:* June 1.

Contact Tara Smith, Director of Financial Aid, Arkansas Department of Higher Education, 114 East Capitol, Little Rock, AR 72201. *E-mail:* finaid@adhe.arknet.edu. *Phone:* 800-547-8839. *Fax:* 501-371-2001. *Web site:* www.adhe.edu.

Arkansas Health Education Grant Program (ARHEG). Award provides assistance to Arkansas residents pursuing professional degrees in dentistry, optometry, veterinary medicine, podiatry, chiropractic medicine, or osteopathic medicine at out-of-state, accredited institutions (programs that are unavailable in Arkansas). *Academic Fields/Career Goals:* Animal/Veterinary Sciences; Dental Health/Services; Health and Medical Sciences. *Award:* Grant for use in freshman, sophomore, junior, senior, or graduate year; renewable. *Award amount:* $5000–$14,600. *Number of awards:* 258–288. *Eligibility Requirements:* Applicant must be enrolled or expecting to enroll full-time at a four-year institution or university and resident of Arkansas. Available to U.S. citizens. *Application Requirements:* Application, affidavit of Arkansas residency. *Deadline:* continuous.

Contact Tara Smith, Director of Financial Aid, Arkansas Department of Higher Education, 114 East Capitol Avenue, Little Rock, AR 72201-3818. *E-mail:* taras@adhe.edu. *Phone:* 501-371-2013. *Fax:* 501-371-2002. *Web site:* www.adhe.edu.

Governor's Scholars-Arkansas. Awards for outstanding Arkansas high school seniors. Must be an Arkansas resident and have a high school GPA of at least 3.5 or have scored at least 27 on the ACT. Award is $4000 per year for four years of full-time undergraduate study. Applicants who attain 32 or above on ACT, 1410 or above on SAT and have an academic 3.50 GPA, or are selected as National Merit or National Achievement finalists may receive an award equal to tuition, mandatory fees, room, and board up to $10,000 per year at any Arkansas institution. *Award:* Scholarship for use in freshman, sophomore, junior, or senior year; renewable. *Award amount:* $4000–$10,000. *Number of awards:* up to 325. *Eligibility Requirements:* Applicant must be enrolled or expecting to enroll full-time at a two-year or four-year institution or university; resident of Arkansas and studying in Arkansas. Applicant must have 3.5 GPA or higher. Available to U.S. citizens. *Application Requirements:* Application, test scores, transcript. *Deadline:* February 1.

Contact Tara Smith, Director of Financial Aid, Arkansas Department of Higher Education, 114 East Capitol, Little Rock, AR 72201. *E-mail:* taras@adhe.edu. *Phone:* 501-371-2050. *Fax:* 501-371-2001. *Web site:* www.adhe.edu.

Law Enforcement Officers' Dependents Scholarship-Arkansas. Scholarship for dependents, under 23 years old, of Arkansas law-enforcement officers killed or permanently disabled in the line of duty. Renewable award is a waiver of tuition, fees, and room at two- or four-year Arkansas institution. Submit birth certificate, death certificate, and claims commission report of findings of fact. Proof of disability from State Claims Commission may also be submitted. *Award:* Scholarship for use in freshman, sophomore, junior, or senior year; renewable. *Award amount:* $2000–$2500. *Number of awards:* 27–32. *Eligibility Requirements:* Applicant must be age 23 or under; enrolled or expecting to enroll full- or part-time at a two-year, four-year, or technical institution or university; resident of Arkansas and studying in Arkansas. Applicant or parent of applicant must have employment or volunteer experience in police/firefighting. Available to U.S. citizens. *Application Requirements:* Application. *Deadline:* continuous.

Contact Tara Smith, Director of Financial Aid, Arkansas Department of Higher Education, 114 East Capitol Avenue, Little Rock, AR 72201. *E-mail:* taras@adhe.edu. *Phone:* 501-371-2050. *Fax:* 501-371-2001. *Web site:* www.adhe.edu.

Military Dependent's Scholarship Program-Arkansas. Available to Arkansas residents whose parent or spouse was classified either as missing in action, killed in action, or a prisoner-of-war. Must attend state-supported institution in Arkansas. Renewable waiver of tuition, fees, room and board. Submit proof of casualty. *Award:* Scholarship for use in freshman, sophomore, junior, or senior year; renewable. *Award amount:* up to $2500. *Number of awards:* 1. *Eligibility Requirements:* Applicant must be enrolled or expecting to enroll full-time at a two-year, four-year, or technical institution or university; resident of Arkansas and studying in Arkansas. Available to U.S. citizens. Applicant or parent must meet one or more of the following requirements: general military experience; retired from active duty; disabled or killed as a result of military service; prisoner of war; or missing in action. *Application Requirements:* Application, references, report of casualty. *Deadline:* continuous.

Contact Tara Smith, Director of Financial Aid, Arkansas Department of Higher Education, 114 East Capitol Avenue, Little Rock, AR 72201. *E-mail:* taras@adhe.edu. *Phone:* 501-371-2050. *Fax:* 501-371-2001. *Web site:* www.adhe.edu.

Robert C. Byrd Honors Scholarship-Arkansas. Applicant must be a graduate of a public or private school or receive a recognized equivalent of a high school diploma. Must be a resident of Arkansas. Must be admitted to an institution of higher education, demonstrate outstanding academic achievement and show promise of continued academic achievement. Award is $1500 for each academic year for a maximum of four years. *Award:* Scholarship for use in freshman, sophomore, junior, or senior year; renewable. *Award amount:* $1500. *Number of awards:* 62. *Eligibility Requirements:* Applicant must be high school student; planning to enroll or expecting to enroll full-time at a two-year, four-year, or technical institution or university and resident of Arkansas. Available to U.S. citizens. *Application Requirements:* Application, transcript. *Deadline:* February 16.

Contact Program Coordinator, Arkansas State Department of Education, Four Capitol Mall, Little Rock, AR 72201. *E-mail:* ade.communications@arkansas.gov. *Phone:* 501-682-4475. *Web site:* arkansased.org.

Second Effort Scholarship. Awarded to those scholars who achieved one of the 10 highest scores on the Arkansas High School Diploma Test (GED). Must be at least age 18 and not have graduated from high school. Students do not apply for this award, they are contacted by the Arkansas Department of Higher Education. *Award:* Scholarship for use in freshman year; renewable. *Award amount:* up to $1000. *Number of awards:* 10. *Eligibility Requirements:* Applicant must be age 18 and over; enrolled or expecting to enroll full- or part-time at a four-year institution or university; resident of Arkansas and studying in Arkansas. Applicant must have 2.5 GPA or higher. Available to U.S. citizens. *Application Requirements:* Application. *Deadline:* varies.

Contact Tara Smith, Director of Financial Aid, Arkansas Department of Higher Education, 114 East Capitol Avenue, Little Rock, AR 72120. *E-mail:* taras@adhe.edu. *Phone:* 501-371-2050. *Fax:* 501-371-2001. *Web site:* www.adhe.edu.

CALIFORNIA

Cal Grant C. Award for California residents who are enrolled in a short-term vocational training program. Program must lead to a recognized degree or certificate. Course length must be a minimum of 4 months and no longer than 24 months. Students must be attending an approved California institution and show financial need. *Award:* Grant for use in freshman or sophomore year; renewable. *Award amount:* $576–$3168. *Number of awards:* up to 7761. *Eligibility Requirements:* Applicant must be enrolled or expecting to enroll full- or part-time at a two-year or technical institution; resident of California and studying in California. Available to U.S. citizens. *Application Requirements:* Application, financial need analysis, GPA verification. *Deadline:* March 2.

Contact Student Support Services Branch, California Student Aid Commission, PO Box 419027, Rancho Cordova, CA 95741-9027. *E-mail:* custsvcs@csac.ca.gov. *Phone:* 916-526-7590. *Fax:* 916-526-8002. *Web site:* www.csac.ca.gov.

Child Development Teacher and Supervisor Grant Program. Award is for those students pursuing an approved course of study leading to a Child Development Permit issued by the California Commission on Teacher Credentialing. In exchange for each year funding is received, recipients agree to provide one year of service in a licensed childcare center. *Academic Fields/Career Goals:* Education. *Award:* Grant for use in freshman, sophomore, junior, senior, or graduate year; renewable. *Award amount:* $1000–$2000. *Number of awards:* up to 300. *Eligibility Requirements:* Applicant must be enrolled or expecting to enroll full- or part-time at a two-year or four-year institution or university; resident of California and studying in California. Applicant or parent of applicant must have employment or volunteer experience in teaching. Available to U.S. citizens. *Application Requirements:* Application, financial need analysis, references, GPA verification. *Deadline:* June 30.

Contact Diana Fuentes-Michel, Executive Director, California Student Aid Commission, PO Box 419027, Rancho Cordova, CA 95741-9027. *E-mail:* studentsupport@csac.ca.gov. *Phone:* 916-526-7268. *Fax:* 916-526-8002. *Web site:* www.csac.ca.gov.

Competitive Cal Grant A. Award for California residents who are not recent high school graduates attending an approved college or university within the state. Must show financial need and meet minimum 3.0 GPA requirement. *Award:* Grant for use in freshman, sophomore, junior, or senior year; renewable. *Award amount:* $2772–$6636. *Number of awards:* 22,500. *Eligibility Requirements:* Applicant must be enrolled or expecting to enroll full- or part-time at a two-year or four-year institution or university; resident of California and studying in California. Applicant must have 3.0 GPA or higher. Available to U.S. citizens. *Application Requirements:* Application, financial need analysis, GPA verification. *Deadline:* March 2.

Contact Student Support Services Branch, California Student Aid Commission, PO Box 419027, Rancho Cordova, CA 95741-9027. *E-mail:* custsvcs@csac.ca.gov. *Phone:* 916-526-7590. *Fax:* 916-526-8002. *Web site:* www.csac.ca.gov.

Cooperative Agencies Resources for Education Program. Renewable award available to California resident attending a two-year California community college. Must have no more than 70 degree-applicable units, currently receive CALWORKS/TANF, and have at least one child under fourteen years of age. Must be in EOPS, single head of household, and 18 or older. Contact local college EOPS-CARE office. *Award:* Grant for use in freshman or sophomore year; renewable. *Award amount:* varies. *Number of awards:* 10,000–11,000. *Eligibility Requirements:* Applicant must be age 18 and over; enrolled or expecting to enroll full-time at a two-year institution; single; resident of California and studying in California. Available to U.S. citizens. *Application Requirements:* Application, financial need analysis, test scores, transcript. *Deadline:* varies.

Contact Cheryl Fong, CARE Coordinator, California Community Colleges, 1102 Q Street, Sacramento, CA 95814-6511. *E-mail:* cfong@cccco.edu. *Phone:* 916-323-5954. *Fax:* 916-327-8232. *Web site:* www.cccco.edu.

Entitlement Cal Grant B. Provide grant funds for access costs for low-income students in an amount not to exceed $1551. Must be California residents and enroll in an undergraduate academic program of not less than one academic year at a qualifying postsecondary institution. Must show financial need and meet the minimum 2.0 GPA requirement. *Award:* Grant for use in freshman, sophomore, junior, or senior year; renewable. *Award amount:* $700–$1551. *Number of awards:* varies. *Eligibility Requirements:* Applicant must be age 23 or under; enrolled or expecting to enroll full- or part-time at a two-year, four-year, or technical institution or university; resident of California and studying in California. Available to U.S. citizens. *Application Requirements:* Application, financial need analysis. *Deadline:* March 2.

Contact Student Support Services Branch, California Student Aid Commission, PO Box 419027, Rancho Cordova, CA 95741-9027. *E-mail:* custsvcs@csac.ca.gov. *Phone:* 916-526-7590. *Fax:* 916-526-8002. *Web site:* www.csac.ca.gov.

Law Enforcement Personnel Dependents Scholarship. Provides college grants to needy dependents of California law enforcement officers, officers and employees of the Department of Corrections and Department of Youth Authority, and firefighters killed or disabled in the line of duty. *Award:* Grant for use in freshman, sophomore, junior, or senior year; renewable. *Award amount:* $100–$11,259. *Number of awards:* varies. *Eligibility Requirements:* Applicant must be enrolled or expecting to enroll full- or part-time at a two-year or four-year institution or university; resident of California and studying in California. Applicant or parent of applicant must have employment or volunteer experience in police/firefighting. Available to U.S. citizens. *Application Requirements:* Application, financial need analysis, transcript, birth certificate, death certificate of parents or spouse, police report. *Deadline:* continuous.

Contact Specialized Programs Operations Branch, California Student Aid Commission, PO Box 419029, Rancho Cordova, CA 95741-9027. *E-mail:* custsvcs@csac.ca.gov. *Phone:* 916-526-7590. *Fax:* 916-526-8002. *Web site:* www.csac.ca.gov.

COLORADO

American Legion Auxiliary Department of Colorado Department President's Scholarship for Junior Member. Open to children, spouses, grandchildren, great-grandchildren of veterans, and veterans who served in the armed forces during eligibility dates for membership in the American Legion. Applicants must be Colorado residents who have been accepted by an accredited school in Colorado. *Award:* Scholarship for use in freshman year; not renewable. *Award amount:* up to $500. *Number of awards:* 1–2. *Eligibility Requirements:* Applicant must be high school student; planning to enroll or expecting to enroll full- or part-time at a four-year institution or university and resident of Colorado. Available to U.S. citizens. Applicant must have general military experience. *Application Requirements:* Application, essay, references, transcript. *Deadline:* April 15.

Contact Jean Lennie, Department Secretary and Treasurer, American Legion Auxiliary, Department of Colorado, 7465 East First Avenue, Suite D, Denver, CO 80230. *E-mail:* ala@coloradolegion.org. *Phone:* 303-367-5388. *Fax:* 303-367-0688. *Web site:* www.coloradolegion.org.

American Legion Auxiliary Department of Colorado Past President Parley Nurses Scholarship. Open to children, spouses, grandchildren, great-grandchildren of veterans, and veterans who served in the armed forces during eligibility dates for membership in the American Legion. Applicants must be Colorado residents who have been accepted by an accredited school of nursing in Colorado. *Academic Fields/Career Goals:* Nursing. *Award:* Scholarship for use in freshman, sophomore, junior, senior, or graduate year; not renewable. *Award amount:* up to $500. *Number of awards:* 3–5. *Eligibility Requirements:* Applicant must be enrolled or expecting to enroll full- or part-time at a four-year institution or university; resident of Colorado and studying in Colorado. Applicant or parent of applicant must be member of American Legion or Auxiliary. Available to U.S. citizens. Applicant or parent must meet one or more of the following requirements: general military experience; retired from active duty; disabled or killed as a result of military service; prisoner of war; or missing in action. *Application Requirements:* Application, essay, financial need analysis, references. *Deadline:* April 1.

Contact Department of Colorado, American Legion Auxiliary, Department of Colorado, 7465 East First Avenue, Suite D, Denver, CO 80230. *E-mail:* ala@coloradolegion.org. *Phone:* 303-367-5388. *Web site:* www.coloradolegion.org.

Colorado Student Grant. Assists Colorado residents attending eligible public, private, or vocational institutions within the state. Application deadlines vary by institution. Renewable award for undergraduates. Contact the financial aid office at the college/institution for more information and an application. *Award:* Grant for use in freshman, sophomore, junior, or senior year; renewable. *Award amount:* $1500–$5000. *Number of awards:* varies. *Eligibility Requirements:* Applicant must be enrolled or expecting to enroll full- or part-time at a two-year, four-year, or technical institution or university; resident of Colorado and studying in Colorado. Available to U.S. citizens. *Application Requirements:* Application, financial need analysis. *Deadline:* varies.

Contact Tobin Bliss, Financial Aid Director, Colorado Commission on Higher Education, 1380 Lawrence Street, Suite 1200, Denver, CO 80204-2059. *E-mail:* tobin.bliss@cche.state.co.us. *Phone:* 303-866-2723. *Web site:* www.state.co.us/cche.

Colorado Undergraduate Merit Scholarships. Renewable awards for students attending Colorado state-supported institutions at the undergraduate level. Must demonstrate superior scholarship or talent. Contact college financial aid office for complete information and deadlines. *Award:* Scholarship for use in freshman, sophomore, junior, or senior year; renewable. *Award amount:* $1230. *Number of awards:* 10,823. *Eligibility Requirements:* Applicant must be enrolled or expecting to enroll full- or part-time at a two-year, four-year, or technical institution or university; resident of Colorado and studying in Colorado. Applicant must have 3.0 GPA or higher. Available to U.S. citizens. *Application Requirements:* Application, test scores, transcript. *Deadline:* varies.

Contact Tobin Bliss, Financial Aid Director, Colorado Commission on Higher Education, 1380 Lawrence Street, Suite 1200, Denver, CO 80204-2059. *E-mail:* tobin.bliss@cche.state.co.us. *Phone:* 303-866-2723. *Web site:* www.state.co.us/cche.

Governor's Opportunity Scholarship. Scholarship available for the most needy first-time freshman whose parents' adjusted gross income is less than $26,000. Must be U.S. citizen or permanent legal resident. Work-study is part of the program. *Award:* Scholarship for use in freshman year; renewable. *Award amount:* up to $10,700. *Number of awards:* 250. *Eligibility Requirements:* Applicant must be high school student; planning to enroll or expecting to enroll full-time at a two-year, four-year, or technical institution or university; resident of Colorado and studying in Colorado. Available to U.S. citizens. *Application Requirements:* Application, financial need analysis, test scores, transcript. *Deadline:* continuous.

Contact Tobin Bliss, Financial Aid Director, Colorado Commission on Higher Education, 1380 Lawrence Street, Suite 1200, Denver, CO 80204-2059. *E-mail:* tobin.bliss@cche.state.co.us. *Phone:* 303-866-2723. *Web site:* www.state.co.us/cche.

Western Undergraduate Exchange (WUE) Program. Students can enroll in designated two- and four-year undergraduate programs at public institutions in participating states at reduced tuition level. Students can apply directly to the admissions office at participating institution, and should indicate he/she want to be considered as a WUE student. *Award:* Scholarship for use in freshman, sophomore, junior, or senior year; renewable. *Award amount:* varies. *Number of awards:* varies. *Eligibility Requirements:* Applicant must be enrolled or expecting to enroll full- or part-time at a two-year or four-year institution; resident of Alaska, Arizona, California, Colorado, Hawaii, Idaho, Montana, Nevada, New Mexico, North Dakota, Oregon, South Dakota, Utah, Washington, or Wyoming and studying in Alaska, Arizona, California, Colorado, Hawaii, Idaho, Montana, Nevada, New Mexico, North Dakota, Oregon, or South Dakota. Available to U.S. citizens. *Application Requirements:* Application. *Deadline:* varies.

Contact Margo Schultz, Program Coordinator, Western Interstate Commission for Higher Education, PO Box 9752, Boulder, CO 80301-9752. *E-mail:* info-sep@wiche.edu. *Phone:* 303-541-0270. *Web site:* www.wiche.edu.

CONNECTICUT

Capitol Scholarship Program. Award for Connecticut residents attending eligible institutions in Connecticut or in a state with reciprocity with Connecticut (Massachusetts, New Hampshire, Pennsylvania, Rhode Island, Vermont, or Washington, D.C). Must be U.S. citizen or permanent resident alien who is a high school senior or graduate. Must rank in top 20% of class or score at least 1800 on SAT. Must show financial need. *Award:* Scholarship for use in freshman, sophomore, junior, or senior year; renewable. *Award amount:* \$500–\$3000. *Number of awards:* varies. *Eligibility Requirements:* Applicant must be enrolled or expecting to enroll full- or part-time at a two-year, four-year, or technical institution or university; resident of Connecticut and studying in Connecticut, District of Columbia, Maine, Massachusetts, New Hampshire, Pennsylvania, Rhode Island, or Vermont. Applicant must have 3.5 GPA or higher. Available to U.S. citizens. *Application Requirements:* Application, financial need analysis, test scores. *Deadline:* February 15.

Contact Suzanne Schilling, Connecticut Department of Higher Education, 61 Woodland Street, Hartford, CT 06105-2326. *E-mail:* csp@ctdhe.org. *Phone:* 860-947-1855. *Fax:* 860-947-1311. *Web site:* www.ctdhe.org.

Connecticut Aid to Public College Students Grant. Award for Connecticut residents attending public colleges or universities within the state. Renewable awards based on financial need. Application deadline varies by institution. Apply at college financial aid office. *Award:* Grant for use in freshman, sophomore, junior, or senior year; renewable. *Award amount:* varies. *Number of awards:* 1. *Eligibility Requirements:* Applicant must be enrolled or expecting to enroll full- or part-time at a two-year or four-year institution or university; resident of Connecticut and studying in Connecticut. Available to U.S. citizens. *Application Requirements:* Application, financial need analysis. *Deadline:* varies.

Contact Suzanne Schilling, Connecticut Department of Higher Education, 61 Woodland Street, Hartford, CT 06105. *Phone:* 860-947-1855. *Fax:* 860-947-1311. *Web site:* www.ctdhe.org.

Connecticut Army National Guard 100% Tuition Waiver. Program is for any active member of the Connecticut Army National Guard in good standing. Must be a resident of Connecticut attending any Connecticut state (public) university, community-technical college or regional vocational-technical school. *Award:* Scholarship for use in freshman, sophomore, junior, or senior year; not renewable. *Award amount:* varies. *Number of awards:* varies. *Eligibility Requirements:* Applicant must be age 17-65; enrolled or expecting to enroll full- or part-time at a two-year, four-year, or technical institution or university; resident of Connecticut and studying in Connecticut. Available to U.S. and non-U.S. citizens. Applicant must have served in the Army National Guard. *Application Requirements:* Application. *Deadline:* July 1.

Contact Capt. Jeremy Lingenfelser, Education Services Officer, Connecticut Army National Guard, 360 Broad Street, Hartford, CT 06105-3795. *E-mail:* education@ct.ngb.army.mil. *Phone:* 860-524-4816. *Fax:* 860-524-4904. *Web site:* www.ct.ngb.army.mil.

Connecticut Independent College Student Grants. Award for Connecticut residents attending an independent college or university within the state on at least a half-time basis. Renewable awards based on financial need. Application deadline varies by institution. Apply at college financial aid office. *Award:* Grant for use in freshman, sophomore, junior, or senior year; renewable. *Award amount:* up to \$8500. *Number of awards:* varies. *Eligibility Requirements:* Applicant must be enrolled or expecting to enroll full- or part-time at a two-year or four-year institution or university; resident of Connecticut and studying in Connecticut. Available to U.S. citizens. *Application Requirements:* Application, financial need analysis. *Deadline:* varies.

Contact Suzanne Schilling, Connecticut Department of Higher Education, 61 Woodland Street, Hartford, CT 06105-2326. *Phone:* 860-947-1855. *Fax:* 860-947-1311. *Web site:* www.ctdhe.org.

Minority Teacher Incentive Grant Program. Program provides up to \$5,000 a year for two years of full-time study in a teacher preparation program, for the junior or senior year at a Connecticut college or university. Applicant must be African American, Hispanic/Latino, Asian American or Native American heritage, and be nominated by the Education Dean. Program graduates who teach in Connecticut public schools may be eligible for loan reimbursement stipends up to \$2,500 per year for up to four years. *Academic Fields/Career Goals:* Education. *Award:* Grant for use in junior or senior year; renewable. *Award amount:* up to \$5000. *Number of awards:* 1. *Eligibility Requirements:* Applicant must be American Indian/Alaska Native, Asian/Pacific Islander, Black (non-Hispanic), or Hispanic; enrolled or expecting to enroll full-time at a four-year institution or university and studying in Connecticut. Available to U.S. citizens. *Application Requirements:* Application. *Deadline:* October 1.

Contact Suzanne Schilling, Connecticut Department of Higher Education, 61 Woodland Street, Hartford, CT 06105. *E-mail:* mtip@ctdhe.org. *Phone:* 860-947-1855. *Fax:* 860-947-1311. *Web site:* www.ctdhe.org.

DELAWARE

Charles L. Hebner Memorial Scholarship. Award for legal residents of Delaware who plan to enroll full-time at the University of Delaware or Delaware State University. Must pursue their career in humanities or social sciences. Must have combined score of 1350 on the SAT. Full tuition, fees, room, board, and books at the University of Delaware or Delaware State University. Renewable for up to three additional years. One award every year per school. Deadline: March 13. *Academic Fields/Career Goals:* Humanities; Social Sciences. *Award:* Scholarship for use in freshman, sophomore, junior, or senior year; renewable. *Award amount:* varies. *Number of awards:* 1. *Eligibility Requirements:* Applicant must be high school student; planning to enroll or expecting to enroll full-time at a two-year, four-year, or technical institution or university; resident of Delaware and studying in Delaware. Applicant must have 2.5 GPA or higher. Available to U.S. and non-U.S. citizens. *Application Requirements:* Application, transcript. *Deadline:* April 2.

Contact Maureen Laffey, Director, Delaware Department of Education, Carvel State Office Building, 820 North French Street, Wilmington, DE 19801. *E-mail:* DHEC@doe.k12.de.us. *Phone:* 302-577-5240. *Fax:* 302-577-6765. *Web site:* www.doe.k12.de.us.

Christa McAuliffe Teacher Scholarship Loan-Delaware. Award for legal residents of Delaware who are U.S. citizens or eligible non-citizens. Must be full-time students enrolled at a Delaware college in an undergraduate program leading to teacher certification. High school seniors must rank in upper half of class and have a combined score of 1570 on the SAT. Undergraduates must have at least a 2.75 cumulative GPA. For details visit: http://www.doe.k12.de.us. *Academic Fields/Career Goals:* Education. *Award:* Forgivable loan for use in freshman, sophomore, junior, or senior year; renewable. *Award amount:* \$1000–

$5000. *Number of awards:* 1–60. *Eligibility Requirements:* Applicant must be enrolled or expecting to enroll full-time at a four-year institution or university; resident of Delaware and studying in Delaware. Applicant must have 2.5 GPA or higher. Available to U.S. citizens. *Application Requirements:* Application, essay, test scores, transcript. *Deadline:* March 30.

Contact Carylin Brinkley, Program Administrator, Delaware Higher Education Commission, Carvel State Office Building, 820 North French Street, Fifth Floor, Wilmington, DE 19801. *E-mail:* cbrinkley@doe.k12.de.us. *Phone:* 302-577-5240. *Fax:* 302-577-6765. *Web site:* www.doe.k12.de.us.

Delaware Nursing Incentive Scholarship Loan. Award for legal residents of Delaware who are U.S. citizens or eligible non-citizens. Must be full-time student enrolled in an accredited program leading to certification as an RN or LPN. High school seniors must rank in upper half of class with at least a 2.5 cumulative GPA. *Academic Fields/Career Goals:* Nursing. *Award:* Forgivable loan for use in freshman, sophomore, junior, or senior year; renewable. *Award amount:* $1000–$5000. *Number of awards:* 1–40. *Eligibility Requirements:* Applicant must be enrolled or expecting to enroll full- or part-time at a two-year or four-year institution and resident of Delaware. Applicant must have 2.5 GPA or higher. Available to U.S. citizens. *Application Requirements:* Application, essay, test scores, transcript. *Deadline:* March 30.

Contact Carylin Brinkley, Program Administrator, Delaware Higher Education Commission, Carvel State Office Building, 820 North French Street, Fifth Floor, Wilmington, DE 19801. *E-mail:* cbrinkley@doe.k12.de.us. *Phone:* 302-577-5240. *Fax:* 302-577-6765. *Web site:* www.doe.k12.de.us.

Delaware Solid Waste Authority John P. "Pat" Healy Scholarship. Award for legal residents of Delaware who are U.S. citizens or eligible non-citizens. Must be high school seniors or full-time college students in their freshman or sophomore years. Must major in either environmental engineering or environmental sciences at a Delaware college. Selection based on financial need, academic performance, community and school involvement, and leadership ability. *Academic Fields/Career Goals:* Engineering-Related Technologies; Environmental Science. *Award:* Scholarship for use in freshman or sophomore year; renewable. *Award amount:* $2000. *Number of awards:* 1. *Eligibility Requirements:* Applicant must be enrolled or expecting to enroll full-time at a two-year or four-year institution or university; resident of Delaware and studying in Delaware. Applicant must have 3.0 GPA or higher. Available to U.S. citizens. *Application Requirements:* Application, financial need analysis, FAFSA, SAR. *Deadline:* March 15.

Contact Carylin Brinkley, Program Administrator, Delaware Higher Education Commission, Carvel State Office Building, 820 North French Street, Fifth Floor, Wilmington, DE 19801. *E-mail:* cbrinkley@doe.k12.de.us. *Phone:* 302-577-5240. *Fax:* 302-577-6765. *Web site:* www.doe.k12.de.us.

Diamond State Scholarship. Award of $1250 per year and renewable for up to three additional years. Must be a legal residents of Delaware. Must be a high school senior ranking in upper quarter of class. Deadline: March 31. Degree program enrollment must be on a full-time basis. *Award:* Scholarship for use in freshman, sophomore, junior, or senior year; renewable. *Award amount:* $1250–$5000. *Number of awards:* 50. *Eligibility Requirements:* Applicant must be high school student; planning to enroll or expecting to enroll full-time at a two-year, four-year, or technical institution or university and resident of Delaware. Available to U.S. and non-U.S. citizens. *Application Requirements:* Application, transcript. *Deadline:* June 15.

Contact Maureen Laffey, Director, Delaware Department of Education, 820 North French Street, Carvel State Office Building, Wilmington, DE 19801. *E-mail:* DHEC@doe.k12.de.us. *Phone:* 302-577-5240. *Fax:* 302-577-6765. *Web site:* www.doe.k12.de.us.

Diamond State Scholarship. Award for legal residents of Delaware who are U.S. citizens or eligible non-citizens. Must be enrolled as a full-time student in a degree program at a nonprofit, regionally accredited institution. High school seniors who rank in upper quarter of class, combined score of at least 1800 on the SAT. Visit: www.doe.k12.de.us for details. *Award:* Scholarship for use in freshman year; renewable. *Award amount:* $1250. *Number of awards:* 50–200. *Eligibility Requirements:* Applicant must be high school student; planning to enroll or expecting to enroll full-time at a four-year institution or university and resident of Delaware. Applicant must have 3.5 GPA or higher. Available to U.S. citizens. *Application Requirements:* Application, essay, test scores, transcript. *Deadline:* March 30.

Contact Carylin Brinkley, Program Administrator, Delaware Higher Education Commission, Carvel State Office Building, 820 North French Street, Fifth Floor, Wilmington, DE 19801. *E-mail:* cbrinkley@doe.k12.de.us. *Phone:* 302-577-5240. *Fax:* 302-577-6765. *Web site:* www.doe.k12.de.us.

Educational Benefits for Children of Deceased Veterans and Others. Award for legal residents of Delaware. Must be a child of deceased U.S. military veterans or state police officers whose cause of death was service related or of military veterans held prisoner of war or declared missing in action. Must be 16 to 24 years old. Applicant must be a U.S. citizen or eligible non-citizen. Must attain full- or part-time undergraduate student admission at a public institution in Delaware. Award must not exceed tuition and fees at a Delaware public institution. *Award:* Grant for use in freshman, sophomore, junior, or senior year; renewable. *Award amount:* varies. *Number of awards:* varies. *Eligibility Requirements:* Applicant must be age 16-24; enrolled or expecting to enroll full- or part-time at a two-year or four-year institution or university; resident of Delaware and studying in Delaware. Available to U.S. and non-U.S. citizens. Applicant or parent must meet one or more of the following requirements: general military experience; retired from active duty; disabled or killed as a result of military service; prisoner of war; or missing in action. *Application Requirements:* Application, transcript. *Deadline:* varies.

Contact Maureen Laffey, Director, Delaware Department of Education, Carvel State Office Building, 820 North French Street, Wilmington, DE 19801. *E-mail:* DHEC@doe.k12.de.us. *Phone:* 302-577-5240. *Fax:* 302-577-6765. *Web site:* www.doe.k12.de.us.

Educational Benefits for Children of Deceased Veterans and Others. Award for children of deceased veterans and others, must have been a resident of the state of Delaware for three or more years prior to the date of application, must be between the ages of 16 and 24. If the applicants parent is a member of the armed forces, the parent must have been a resident of Delaware at the time of death or declaration of missing in action or prisoner of war status. *Award:* Grant for use in freshman, sophomore, junior, or senior year; renewable. *Award amount:* varies. *Number of awards:* varies. *Eligibility Requirements:* Applicant must be age 16-24; enrolled or expecting to enroll full-time at a two-year or four-year institution or university and resident of Delaware. Applicant or parent of applicant must have employment or volunteer experience in police/firefighting. Available to U.S. citizens. Applicant or parent must meet one or more of the following requirements: general military experience; retired from active duty; disabled or killed as a result of military service; prisoner of war; or missing in action. *Application Requirements:*

Application, verification of service-related death. *Deadline:* continuous.

Contact Carylin Brinkley, Program Administrator, Delaware Higher Education Commission, Carvel State Office Building, 820 North French Street, Fifth Floor, Wilmington, DE 19801. *E-mail:* cbrinkley@doe.k12.de.us. *Phone:* 302-577-5240. *Fax:* 302-577-6765. *Web site:* www.doe.k12.de.us.

Governor's Workforce Development Grant. Award for residents of Delaware and a U.S. citizen or an eligible non-citizen. Must be employed by a company in Delaware that contributes to the Blue Collar Training Fund Program. Must attend a participating college in Delaware on a part-time basis. Individual income must not exceed $32,417 annually. Full-time students are not eligible. The maximum Governor's Workforce Development Grant for one academic year is $2000 for part-time undergraduate study. Applications are due by the end of the free drop/add period each term. *Award:* Grant for use in freshman, sophomore, junior, or senior year; not renewable. *Award amount:* $2000. *Number of awards:* 1. *Eligibility Requirements:* Applicant must be age 18 and over; enrolled or expecting to enroll part-time at a two-year or four-year institution or university; resident of Delaware and studying in Delaware. Available to U.S. and non-U.S. citizens. *Application Requirements:* Application, transcript. *Deadline:* varies.

Contact Maureen Laffey, Director, Delaware Department of Education, Carvel State Office Building, 820 North French Street, Wilmington, DE 19801. *E-mail:* DHEC@doe.k12.de.us. *Phone:* 302-577-5240. *Fax:* 302-577-6765. *Web site:* www.doe.k12.de.us.

Legislative Essay Scholarship. Award for legal residents of Delaware who are U.S. citizens or eligible non-citizens. Must be high school seniors in public or private schools or in home school programs who plans to enroll full-time at a nonprofit, regionally accredited college. Must submit an essay on topic: "The Declaration of Independence states that all men are created equal." How true was this concept then and is it true today?". *Award:* Prize for use in freshman year; not renewable. *Award amount:* $1000–$10,000. *Number of awards:* up to 62. *Eligibility Requirements:* Applicant must be high school student; planning to enroll or expecting to enroll full- or part-time at a two-year, four-year, or technical institution or university and resident of Delaware. Available to U.S. citizens. *Application Requirements:* Application, applicant must enter a contest, essay. *Deadline:* November 30.

Contact Carylin Brinkley, Program Administrator, Delaware Higher Education Commission, Carvel State Office Building, 820 North French Street, Fifth Floor, Wilmington, DE 19801. *E-mail:* cbrinkley@doe.k12.de.us. *Phone:* 302-577-5240. *Fax:* 302-577-6765. *Web site:* www.doe.k12.de.us.

Legislative Essay Scholarship. Applicant must be a legal resident of Delaware. High school seniors in public or private schools or in home school programs can apply. Must be planning to enroll full-time at a nonprofit, regionally accredited college. Up to 62 nonrenewable awards of $1000 for each state senatorial and representative legislative district are awarded annually. *Award:* Scholarship for use in freshman year; not renewable. *Award amount:* $1000. *Number of awards:* 62. *Eligibility Requirements:* Applicant must be high school student; planning to enroll or expecting to enroll full-time at a four-year institution or university and resident of Delaware. Available to U.S. and non-U.S. citizens. *Application Requirements:* Application, essay. *Deadline:* November 30.

Contact Maureen Laffey, Director, Delaware Department of Education, Carvel State Office Building, 820 North French Street, Wilmington, DE 19801. *E-mail:* DHEC@doe.k12.de.us. *Phone:* 302-577-5240. *Fax:* 302-577-6765. *Web site:* www.doe.k12.de.us.

Robert C. Byrd Honors Scholarship-Delaware. Award for legal residents of Delaware who are U.S. citizens or eligible non-citizens. For high school seniors who rank in upper quarter of class or GED recipients with a minimum score of 300, combined score of at least 1800 on the SAT. Must be enrolled at least half-time at a nonprofit, regionally accredited institution. *Award:* Scholarship for use in freshman year; renewable. *Award amount:* $1500. *Number of awards:* 20. *Eligibility Requirements:* Applicant must be high school student; planning to enroll or expecting to enroll full-time at a two-year or four-year institution or university and resident of Delaware. Applicant must have 3.5 GPA or higher. Available to U.S. citizens. *Application Requirements:* Application, essay, test scores, transcript. *Deadline:* March 30.

Contact Carylin Brinkley, Program Administrator, Delaware Higher Education Commission, Carvel State Office Building, 820 North French Street, Fifth Floor, Wilmington, DE 19801. *E-mail:* cbrinkley@doe.k12.de.us. *Phone:* 302-577-5240. *Fax:* 302-577-6765. *Web site:* www.doe.k12.de.us.

Scholarship Incentive Program (ScIP). Award for legal residents of Delaware who plan to enroll full-time in an undergraduate degree program at a nonprofit regionally accredited institution college in Delaware or Pennsylvania. Must have a minimum cumulative, unweighted GPA of 2.5. Graduate students attending the University of Delaware or Delaware State University are not eligible. Awards for undergraduate is $700 to $2200, depending on GPA and for graduate is $1000. Deadline varies. *Award:* Grant for use in freshman, sophomore, junior, senior, or graduate year; not renewable. *Award amount:* $700–$2200. *Number of awards:* up to 2. *Eligibility Requirements:* Applicant must be enrolled or expecting to enroll full-time at a two-year or four-year institution or university; resident of Delaware and studying in Delaware or Pennsylvania. Applicant must have 2.5 GPA or higher. Available to U.S. and non-U.S. citizens. *Application Requirements:* Application, transcript. *Deadline:* varies.

Contact Maureen Laffey, Director, Delaware Department of Education, Carvel State Office Building, 820 North French Street, Wilmington, DE 19801. *E-mail:* DHEC@doe.k12.de.us. *Phone:* 302-577-5240. *Fax:* 302-577-6765. *Web site:* www.doe.k12.de.us.

Scholarship Incentive Program-Delaware. Award for legal residents of Delaware who are U.S. citizens or eligible non-citizens. Must demonstrate substantial financial need and enroll full-time in an undergraduate degree program at a nonprofit, regionally accredited institution or college in Delaware or Pennsylvania. Minimum GPA 2.5. For details visit: www.doe.k12.de.us. *Award:* Grant for use in freshman, sophomore, junior, senior, or graduate year; not renewable. *Award amount:* $700–$2200. *Number of awards:* 1000–1300. *Eligibility Requirements:* Applicant must be enrolled or expecting to enroll full-time at a two-year or four-year institution or university; resident of Delaware and studying in Delaware or Pennsylvania. Applicant must have 2.5 GPA or higher. Available to U.S. citizens. *Application Requirements:* Application, financial need analysis, transcript, FAFSA. *Deadline:* April 15.

Contact Carylin Brinkley, Program Administrator, Delaware Higher Education Commission, Carvel State Office Building, 820 North French Street, Fifth Floor, Wilmington, DE 19801. *E-mail:* cbrinkley@doe.k12.de.us. *Phone:* 302-577-5240. *Fax:* 302-577-6765. *Web site:* www.doe.k12.de.us.

State Tuition Assistance. Award providing tuition assistance for any member of the Air or Army National Guard attending a Delaware two-year or four-year college. Awards are renewable. Applicant's minimum GPA must be 2.0. *Award:* Scholarship for use in freshman, sophomore, junior, or senior year; renewable. *Award amount:* up to $10,000. *Number of awards:* 1–300. *Eligibility Requirements:* Applicant must be enrolled or expecting to enroll full- or part-time at a two-year or four-year institution or university and studying in Delaware. Applicant must have 2.5 GPA or higher. Available to U.S. citizens. Applicant must have served in the Air Force National Guard or Army National Guard. *Application Requirements:* Application, transcript. *Deadline:* July 1.

Contact Robert Csizmadia, State Tuition Assistance Manager, Delaware National Guard, 1st Regiment Road, Wilmington, DE 19808-2191. *E-mail:* robert.csizmadi@de.ngb.army.mil. *Phone:* 302-326-7012. *Fax:* 302-326-7029. *Web site:* www.delawarenationalguard.com.

DISTRICT OF COLUMBIA

American Council of the Blind Scholarships. Merit-based award available to undergraduate students who are legally blind in both eyes. Submit certificate of legal blindness and proof of acceptance at an accredited postsecondary institution. *Award:* Scholarship for use in freshman, sophomore, junior, or senior year; renewable. *Award amount:* $500–$3000. *Number of awards:* 26. *Eligibility Requirements:* Applicant must be enrolled or expecting to enroll full- or part-time at a four-year institution or university. Applicant must be visually impaired. Applicant must have 3.5 GPA or higher. Available to U.S. citizens. *Application Requirements:* Application, autobiography, essay, references, transcript, evidence of legal blindness. *Deadline:* March 1.

Contact Terry Pacheco, Scholarship Coordinator, American Council of the Blind, 1155 15th Street, NW, Suite 1004, Washington, DC 20005. *E-mail:* info@acb.org. *Phone:* 202-467-5081. *Fax:* 202-467-5085. *Web site:* www.acb.org.

Bureau of Indian Affairs Higher Education Grant Program. Grants are provided to supplement financial assistance to eligible American Indian/Alaska Native students entering college seeking a baccalaureate degree. A student must be a member of, or at least one-quarter degree Indian blood descendent of a member of an American Indian tribe who are eligible for the special programs and services provided by the United States through the Bureau of Indian Affairs to Indians because of their status as Indians. *Award:* Grant for use in freshman year; not renewable. *Award amount:* varies. *Number of awards:* varies. *Eligibility Requirements:* Applicant must be American Indian/Alaska Native; high school student and planning to enroll or expecting to enroll full-time at a two-year or four-year institution or university. Available to U.S. citizens. *Application Requirements:* Application, references, test scores, transcript. *Deadline:* varies.

Contact Office of Indian Education Programs, Bureau of Indian Affairs Office of Indian Education Programs, 1849 C Street, NW, MS 3512 MB, Washington, DC 20240-0001. *Phone:* 202-208-3478. *Web site:* www.oiep.bia.edu.

Costas G. Lemonopoulos Scholarship. Scholarships to children of NALC members attending public, four-year colleges or universities supported by the state of Florida or St. Petersburg Junior College. Scholarships are renewable one time. Deadline: June 1. *Award:* Scholarship for use in freshman, sophomore, junior, or senior year; renewable. *Award amount:* varies. *Number of awards:* 1–20. *Eligibility Requirements:* Applicant must be enrolled or expecting to enroll full-time at a two-year or four-year institution or university and studying in Florida. Available to U.S. citizens. *Application Requirements:* Application, references, transcript. *Deadline:* June 1.

Contact Ann Porch, Membership Committee, National Association of Letter Carriers, 100 Indiana Avenue, NW, Washington, DC 20001-2144. *E-mail:* nalcinf@nalc.org. *Phone:* 202-393-4695. *Fax:* 202-737-1540. *Web site:* www.nalc.org.

DC Leveraging Educational Assistance Partnership Program (LEAP). Grant available to District of Columbia residents enrolled in undergraduate program. Must attend an eligible college at least half-time. Grant value is $1500. Deadline: last Friday in June. *Award:* Grant for use in freshman, sophomore, junior, or senior year; renewable. *Award amount:* $250–$1500. *Number of awards:* 2274–2300. *Eligibility Requirements:* Applicant must be enrolled or expecting to enroll full- or part-time at a two-year, four-year, or technical institution or university and resident of District of Columbia. Available to U.S. citizens. *Application Requirements:* Application, financial need analysis, transcript, SAR, FAFSA. *Deadline:* varies.

Contact Ms. Carol Talley, Scholarship Committee, District of Columbia State Education Office, 441 Fourth Street, NW, Suite 350 North, Washington, DC 20001. *Phone:* 202-724-7784. *Web site:* www.seo.dc.gov.

Robert C. Byrd Honors Scholarship-District of Columbia. Federally funded, state administered program to recognize exceptionally able high school seniors who show promise of continued excellence in postsecondary education. Must be a U.S. citizen and permanent resident of District of Columbia. Minimum 3.2 GPA required. Must show promise of continued success, and acceptance at an accredited institution of higher education in the United States. Must be school's nominee. Renewable of the scholarship is based on satisfactory academic staying. *Award:* Scholarship for use in freshman, sophomore, junior, or senior year; renewable. *Award amount:* $1500. *Number of awards:* 10. *Eligibility Requirements:* Applicant must be high school student; planning to enroll or expecting to enroll full-time at a four-year institution or university and resident of District of Columbia. Available to U.S. citizens. *Application Requirements:* Application, interview, test scores, transcript, 250-word essay on "Life Goals," nominee from. *Deadline:* March 30.

Contact Michon Peck, Director of Student Affairs, District of Columbia Public Schools, 825 North Capitol Street, NE, Ninth Floor, PO Box 92240, Washington, DC 20002. *E-mail:* michon.peck@k12.dc.us. *Phone:* 202-442-5110. *Fax:* 202-442-5094. *Web site:* www.k12.dc.us.

Scholarship For Service (SFS) Program. A unique program designed to increase and strengthen the cadre of federal information assurance professionals. This program provides scholarships that fully fund the typical costs that students pay for books, tuition, and room and board while attending an approved institution of higher learning. Participants receive stipends of up to $8000 for undergraduate and $12,000 for graduate students. *Award:* Scholarship for use in freshman, sophomore, junior, senior, or graduate year; renewable. *Award amount:* up to $12,000. *Number of awards:* 1. *Eligibility Requirements:* Applicant must be enrolled or expecting to enroll full-time at a four-year institution or university. Available to U.S. citizens. *Application Requirements:* Application. *Deadline:* varies.

Contact Kathy Roberson, Scholarship For Service Program Office, Office of Personnel Management, 8610 Broadway, Suite 305, San Antonio, TX 78217-6352. *E-mail:* karobers@opm.gov. *Phone:* 210-805-2423 Ext. 506. *Web site:* www.sfs.opm.gov.

FLORIDA

Access to Better Learning and Education Grant. Grant program provides tuition assistance to Florida undergraduate students enrolled in degree programs at eligible private Florida colleges or universities. Must be U.S. citizen or eligible non-citizen and must meet Florida residency requirements. Participating institution determines application procedures, deadlines, and student eligibility. *Award:* Grant for use in freshman, sophomore, junior, or senior year; renewable. *Award amount:* varies. *Number of awards:* varies. *Eligibility Requirements:* Applicant must be enrolled or expecting to enroll full-time at a four-year institution or university; resident of Florida and studying in Florida. Available to U.S. citizens. *Application Requirements:* Application. *Deadline:* varies.

Contact Theresa Antworth, State Programs Director, Florida Department of Education, Office of Student Financial Assistance, 1940 North Monroe Street, Suite 70, Tallahassee, FL 32303-4759. *E-mail:* osfa@fldoe.org. *Phone:* 850-410-5180. *Fax:* 850-487-6244. *Web site:* www.floridastudentfinancialaid.org.

Critical Teacher Shortage Student Loan Forgiveness Program-Florida. Award program provides financial assistance to eligible Florida teachers who hold a valid Florida teachers certificate or Florida department of health license, by assisting them in the repayment of undergraduate and graduate educational loans that led to certification in a critical teacher shortage subject area. Must teach full-time at a publicly-funded school. *Academic Fields/Career Goals:* Education. *Award:* Forgivable loan for use in freshman, sophomore, junior, senior, or graduate year; renewable. *Award amount:* up to $5000. *Number of awards:* varies. *Eligibility Requirements:* Applicant must be enrolled or expecting to enroll full- or part-time at a two-year or four-year institution or university and resident of Florida. Applicant or parent of applicant must have employment or volunteer experience in teaching. Available to U.S. citizens. *Application Requirements:* Application, transcript. *Deadline:* July 15.

Contact Theresa Antworth, State Programs Director, Florida Department of Education, Office of Student Financial Assistance, 1940 North Monroe Street, Suite 70, Tallahassee, FL 32303-4759. *E-mail:* osfa@fldoe.org. *Phone:* 850-410-5180. *Fax:* 850-487-6244. *Web site:* www.floridastudentfinancialaid.org.

Ethics in Business Scholarship. Scholarship program provides assistance to undergraduate college students, who enroll at community colleges and eligible independent postsecondary educational institutions. Scholarships are funded by private and state contributions. Awards are dependent on private, matching funds. *Award:* Scholarship for use in freshman, sophomore, junior, or senior year; not renewable. *Award amount:* varies. *Number of awards:* varies. *Eligibility Requirements:* Applicant must be enrolled or expecting to enroll full-time at a two-year or four-year institution or university and studying in Florida. Available to U.S. citizens. *Application Requirements:* Application. *Deadline:* varies.

Contact Theresa Antworth, State Programs Director, Florida Department of Education, Office of Student Financial Assistance, 1940 North Monroe Street, Suite 70, Tallahassee, FL 32303-4759. *E-mail:* osfa@fldoe.org. *Phone:* 850-410-5180. *Fax:* 850-487-6244. *Web site:* www.floridastudentfinancialaid.org.

First Generation Matching Grant Program. Need-based grants to undergraduate students who are enrolled in state universities and whose parents have not earned baccalaureate degrees. Available state funds are contingent upon matching contributions from private sources on a dollar-for-dollar basis. *Award:* Grant for use in freshman, sophomore, junior, or senior year; renewable. *Award amount:* varies. *Number of awards:* varies. *Eligibility Requirements:* Applicant must be enrolled or expecting to enroll full- or part-time at an institution or university; resident of Florida and studying in Florida. Available to U.S. citizens. *Application Requirements:* Application, financial need analysis. *Deadline:* varies.

Contact Theresa Antworth, State Programs Director, Florida Department of Education, Office of Student Financial Assistance, 1940 North Monroe Street, Suite 70, Tallahassee, FL 32303-4759. *E-mail:* osfa@fldoe.org. *Phone:* 850-410-5180. *Fax:* 850-487-6244. *Web site:* www.floridastudentfinancialaid.org.

Florida Postsecondary Student Assistance Grant. Scholarships to degree-seeking, resident, undergraduate students who demonstrate substantial financial need and are enrolled in eligible degree-granting private colleges and universities not eligible under the Florida Private Student Assistance Grant. FSAG is a decentralized program, and each participating institution determines application procedures, deadlines, student eligibility. Number of awards varies. *Award:* Grant for use in freshman, sophomore, junior, or senior year; renewable. *Award amount:* $200–$1722. *Number of awards:* varies. *Eligibility Requirements:* Applicant must be enrolled or expecting to enroll full-time at a two-year or four-year institution or university; resident of Florida and studying in Florida. Available to U.S. citizens. *Application Requirements:* Application, financial need analysis. *Deadline:* varies.

Contact Theresa Antworth, State Programs Director, Florida Department of Education, Office of Student Financial Assistance, 1940 North Monroe Street, Suite 70, Tallahassee, FL 32303-4759. *E-mail:* osfa@fldoe.org. *Phone:* 850-410-5180. *Fax:* 850-487-6244. *Web site:* www.floridastudentfinancialaid.org.

Florida Private Student Assistance Grant. Grants for Florida residents who are U.S. citizens or eligible non-citizens attending eligible private, nonprofit, four-year colleges and universities. Must be a full-time student and demonstrate substantial financial need. For renewal, must have earned a minimum cumulative GPA of 2.0 at the last institution attended. *Award:* Grant for use in freshman, sophomore, junior, or senior year; renewable. *Award amount:* $200–$1722. *Number of awards:* varies. *Eligibility Requirements:* Applicant must be enrolled or expecting to enroll full-time at a four-year institution or university; resident of Florida and studying in Florida. Available to U.S. citizens. *Application Requirements:* Application, financial need analysis. *Deadline:* varies.

Contact Theresa Antworth, State Programs Director, Florida Department of Education, Office of Student Financial Assistance, 1940 North Monroe Street, Suite 70, Tallahassee, FL 32303-4759. *E-mail:* osfa@fldoe.org. *Phone:* 850-410-5180. *Fax:* 850-487-6244. *Web site:* www.floridastudentfinancialaid.org.

Florida Public Student Assistance Grant. Grants for Florida residents, U.S. citizens or eligible non-citizens who attend state universities and public community colleges. For renewal, must have earned a minimum cumulative GPA of 2.0 at the last institution attended. Students with documented disabilities are able to qualify for part-time status. *Award:* Grant for use in freshman, sophomore, junior, or senior year; renewable. *Award amount:* $200–$1722. *Number of awards:* varies. *Eligibility Requirements:* Applicant must be enrolled or expecting to enroll full- or part-time at a two-year or four-year institution or university; resident of Florida and studying in Florida. Available to U.S. citizens. *Application Requirements:* Application, financial need analysis. *Deadline:* varies.

Contact Theresa Antworth, State Programs Director, Florida Department of Education, Office of Student Financial Assistance, 1940 North Monroe Street, Suite 70, Tallahassee, FL 32303-4759. *E-mail:* osfa@fldoe.org. *Phone:* 850-410-5180. *Fax:* 850-487-6244. *Web site:* www.floridastudentfinancialaid.org.

Florida Work Experience Program. Need-based program providing eligible Florida students work experiences that will complement and reinforce their educational and career goals. Must maintain GPA of 2.0. Postsecondary institution will determine applicant's eligibility, number of hours to be worked per week, and the award amount. *Award:* Grant for use in freshman, sophomore, junior, or senior year; renewable. *Award amount:* varies. *Number of awards:* varies. *Eligibility Requirements:* Applicant must be enrolled or expecting to enroll full- or part-time at a two-year or four-year institution or university; resident of Florida and studying in Florida. Available to U.S. citizens. *Application Requirements:* Application, financial need analysis. *Deadline:* varies.

Contact Theresa Antworth, State Programs Director, Florida Department of Education, Office of Student Financial Assistance, 1940 North Monroe Street, Suite 70, Tallahassee, FL 32303-4759. *E-mail:* osfa@fldoe.org. *Phone:* 850-410-5180. *Fax:* 850-487-6244. *Web site:* www.floridastudentfinancialaid.org.

Jose Marti Scholarship Challenge Grant Fund. Award available to Hispanic-American students who were born in, or whose parent were born in a Hispanic country. Must have lived in Florida for one year, be enrolled full-time in Florida at an eligible school, and have a GPA of 3.0 or above. Must be U.S. citizen or eligible non-citizen. Deadline: April 1. Free Application for Federal Student Aid must be processed by May 15. *Award:* Scholarship for use in freshman, sophomore, junior, senior, or graduate year; renewable. *Award amount:* $2000. *Number of awards:* varies. *Eligibility Requirements:* Applicant must be of Hispanic heritage; enrolled or expecting to enroll full-time at a two-year, four-year, or technical institution or university; resident of Florida and studying in Florida. Applicant must have 3.0 GPA or higher. Available to U.S. citizens. *Application Requirements:* Application, financial need analysis. *Deadline:* April 1.

Contact Theresa Antworth, State Programs Director, Florida Department of Education, Office of Student Financial Assistance, 1940 North Monroe Street, Suite 70, Tallahassee, FL 32303-4759. *E-mail:* osfa@fldoe.org. *Phone:* 850-410-5180. *Fax:* 850-487-6244. *Web site:* www.floridastudentfinancialaid.org.

Mary McLeod Bethune Scholarship. Renewable award to Florida students with a GPA of 3.0 or above, who will attend Bethune-Cookman College, Edward Waters College, Florida A&M University, or Florida Memorial University. Must not have previously received a baccalaureate degree. Must demonstrate financial need as specified by the institution. *Award:* Scholarship for use in freshman, sophomore, junior, or senior year; renewable. *Award amount:* $3000. *Number of awards:* varies. *Eligibility Requirements:* Applicant must be enrolled or expecting to enroll full-time at a two-year or four-year institution or university; resident of Florida and studying in Florida. Applicant must have 3.0 GPA or higher. Available to U.S. citizens. *Application Requirements:* Application, financial need analysis. *Deadline:* varies.

Contact Theresa Antworth, State Programs Director, Florida Department of Education, Office of Student Financial Assistance, 1940 North Monroe Street, Suite 70, Tallahassee, FL 32303-4759. *E-mail:* osfa@fldoe.org. *Phone:* 850-410-5180. *Fax:* 850-487-6244. *Web site:* www.floridastudentfinancialaid.org.

Robert C. Byrd Honors Scholarship-Florida. One applicant per high school may be nominated by the Florida high school principal or designee by May 15. Must be U.S. citizen or eligible non-citizen and Florida resident. Application must be submitted in the same year as graduation. Must meet selective service system registration requirements. May attend any postsecondary accredited institution. Deadline: April 15. *Award:* Scholarship for use in freshman, sophomore, junior, or senior year; renewable. *Award amount:* $1500. *Number of awards:* varies. *Eligibility Requirements:* Applicant must be high school student; planning to enroll or expecting to enroll full-time at a technical institution and resident of Florida. Available to U.S. citizens. *Application Requirements:* Application, references, test scores, transcript. *Deadline:* April 15.

Contact Theresa Antworth, State Programs Director, Florida Department of Education, Office of Student Financial Assistance, 1940 North Monroe Street, Suite 70, Tallahassee, FL 32303-4759. *E-mail:* osfa@fldoe.org. *Phone:* 850-410-5180. *Fax:* 850-487-6244. *Web site:* www.floridastudentfinancialaid.org.

Rosewood Family Scholarship Fund. Renewable award for eligible minority students to enable them to attend a Florida public postsecondary institution on a full-time basis. Preference given to direct descendants of African-American Rosewood families affected by the incidents of January 1923. Must be Black, Hispanic, Asian, Pacific Islander, American Indian, or Alaska Native. Must not have previously received a baccalaureate degree. *Award:* Scholarship for use in freshman, sophomore, junior, or senior year; renewable. *Award amount:* up to $4000. *Number of awards:* up to 25. *Eligibility Requirements:* Applicant must be American Indian/Alaska Native, Asian/Pacific Islander, Black (non-Hispanic), or Hispanic; enrolled or expecting to enroll full-time at a two-year, four-year, or technical institution or university and studying in Florida. Available to U.S. citizens. *Application Requirements:* Application, financial need analysis. *Deadline:* April 1.

Contact Theresa Antworth, State Programs Director, Florida Department of Education, Office of Student Financial Assistance, 1940 North Monroe Street, Suite 70, Tallahassee, FL 32303-4759. *E-mail:* osfa@fldoe.org. *Phone:* 850-410-5180. *Fax:* 850-487-6244. *Web site:* www.floridastudentfinancialaid.org.

Scholarships for Children & Spouses of Deceased or Disabled Veterans or Servicemembers. Renewable scholarships for children and spouses of deceased or disabled veterans and service members. Children must be between the ages of 16 and 22, and attend an eligible Florida public, nonpublic postsecondary institution or enrolled part-time. Must ensure that the Florida Department of Veteran's Affairs certifies the applicant's eligibility. Must maintain GPA of 2.0. *Award:* Scholarship for use in freshman, sophomore, junior, or senior year; renewable. *Award amount:* varies. *Number of awards:* varies. *Eligibility Requirements:* Applicant must be age 16-22; enrolled or expecting to enroll full- or part-time at a two-year, four-year, or technical institution or university; resident of Florida and studying in Florida. Available to U.S. citizens. Applicant or parent must meet one or more of the following requirements: general military experience; retired from active duty; disabled or killed as a result of military service; prisoner of war; or missing in action. *Application Requirements:* Application. *Deadline:* April 1.

Contact Theresa Antworth, State Programs Director, Florida Department of Education, Office of Student Financial Assistance, 1940 North Monroe Street, Suite 70, Tallahassee, FL 32303-4759. *E-mail:* osfa@fldoe.org. *Phone:* 850-410-5180. *Fax:* 850-487-6244. *Web site:* www.floridastudentfinancialaid.org.

William L. Boyd IV Florida Resident Access Grant. Renewable awards to Florida undergraduate students attending an eligible private, nonprofit Florida college or university. Postsecondary institution will determine applicant's eligibility. Renewal applicant must have earned a minimum institutional GPA of 2.0. *Award:* Grant for use in freshman, sophomore, junior, or senior year; renewable. *Award amount:* $3000. *Number of awards:* varies. *Eligibility Requirements:* Applicant must be enrolled or expecting to enroll full-time at a four-year institution or university; resident of Florida and studying in Florida. Available to U.S. citizens. *Application Requirements:* Application. *Deadline:* varies.

Contact Theresa Antworth, State Programs Director, Florida Department of Education, Office of Student Financial Assistance, 1940 North Monroe Street, Suite 70, Tallahassee, FL 32303-4759. *E-mail:* osfa@fldoe.org.

Phone: 850-410-5180. *Fax:* 850-487-6244. *Web site:* www.floridastudentfinancialaid.org.

GEORGIA

American Indian Nurse Scholarship Awards. Renewable award of $1000 per semester. Currently able to fund between 10 and 15 students per semester. Intended originally to benefit females only, the program has expanded to include males and the career goals now include not only nursing careers, but jobs in health care and health education, as well. *Academic Fields/Career Goals:* Health Administration; Nursing. *Award:* Scholarship for use in freshman, sophomore, junior, senior, graduate, or postgraduate years; renewable. *Award amount:* $500–$1000. *Number of awards:* 10–15. *Eligibility Requirements:* Applicant must be American Indian/Alaska Native and enrolled or expecting to enroll full-time at a two-year, four-year, or technical institution or university. Applicant must have 2.5 GPA or higher. Available to U.S. citizens. *Application Requirements:* Application, autobiography, financial need analysis, photo, references, transcript. *Deadline:* continuous.

Contact Mrs. Joe Calvin, American Indian Nurse Scholarship Awards Consultant, National Society of The Colonial Dames of America, Nine Cross Creek Drive, Birmingham, AL 35213. *E-mail:* info@nscda.org. *Phone:* 205-871-4072. *Web site:* www.nscda.org.

Department of Human Resources Federal Stafford Loan with the Service Cancelable Loan Option. Forgivable loan of $4000 is awarded to current Department of Human Resources employee who will be enrolled in a baccalaureate or advanced nursing degree program at an eligible participating school in Georgia. Loans are cancelled upon two calendar years of service as a registered nurse for the Georgia DHR or any Georgia county board of health. *Academic Fields/Career Goals:* Nursing. *Award:* Forgivable loan for use in freshman, sophomore, junior, senior, or graduate year; not renewable. *Award amount:* $4000. *Number of awards:* 1. *Eligibility Requirements:* Applicant must be enrolled or expecting to enroll full- or part-time at a four-year institution or university; resident of Georgia and studying in Georgia. Available to U.S. citizens. *Application Requirements:* Application, financial need analysis. *Deadline:* June 4.

Contact Peggy Matthews, Manager, GSFA Originations, State of Georgia, 2082 East Exchange Place, Suite 230, Tucker, GA 30084-5305. *E-mail:* peggy@gsfc.org. *Phone:* 770-724-9230. *Fax:* 770-724-9225. *Web site:* www.gsfc.org.

GAE GFIE Scholarship for Aspiring Teachers. Scholarships will be awarded to graduating seniors who currently attend a fully accredited public Georgia high school and will attend a fully accredited Georgia college or university within the next twelve months. Must have a 3.0 GPA. Must submit three letters of recommendation. Must have plans to enter the teaching profession. *Academic Fields/Career Goals:* Education. *Award:* Scholarship for use in freshman year; not renewable. *Award amount:* $1000. *Number of awards:* 10–20. *Eligibility Requirements:* Applicant must be high school student; planning to enroll or expecting to enroll full-time at a two-year or four-year institution or university; resident of Georgia and studying in Georgia. Applicant must have 3.0 GPA or higher. Available to U.S. and non-U.S. citizens. *Application Requirements:* Application, transcript. *Deadline:* varies.

Contact Sally Bennett, Professional Development Specialist, Georgia Association of Educators, 100 Crescent Centre Parkway, Suite 500, Tucker, GA 30084-7049. *E-mail:* sally.bennett@gae.org. *Phone:* 678-837-1103. *Web site:* www.gae.org.

Georgia Leveraging Educational Assistance Partnership Grant Program. Awards based on financial need. Recipients must be eligible for the Federal Pell Grant. Renewable award for Georgia residents enrolled in a state postsecondary institution. Must be U.S. citizen. *Award:* Grant for use in freshman, sophomore, junior, or senior year; renewable. *Award amount:* up to $2000. *Number of awards:* 3000–3500. *Eligibility Requirements:* Applicant must be enrolled or expecting to enroll full- or part-time at a two-year, four-year, or technical institution or university; resident of Georgia and studying in Georgia. Available to U.S. citizens. *Application Requirements:* Application, financial need analysis. *Deadline:* continuous.

Contact Mr. Tracy Ireland, Vice President, Georgia Student Finance Commission, 2082 East Exchange Place, Suite 100, Tucker, GA 30084. *E-mail:* billf@gsfc.org. *Phone:* 770-724-9000. *Web site:* www.gsfc.org.

Georgia National Guard Service Cancelable Loan Program. Forgivable loans will be awarded to residents of Georgia maintaining good military standing as an eligible member of the Georgia National Guard who are enrolled at least half-time in an undergraduate degree program at an eligible college, university or technical school within the state of Georgia. *Award:* Forgivable loan for use in freshman, sophomore, junior, or senior year; not renewable. *Award amount:* $150–$1821. *Number of awards:* 200–250. *Eligibility Requirements:* Applicant must be enrolled or expecting to enroll full- or part-time at a two-year, four-year, or technical institution or university; resident of Georgia and studying in Georgia. Available to U.S. citizens. Applicant must have served in the Air Force National Guard or Army National Guard. *Application Requirements:* Application, financial need analysis. *Deadline:* June 4.

Contact Peggy Matthews, Manager, GSFA Originations, State of Georgia, 2082 East Exchange Place, Suite 230, Tucker, GA 30084-5305. *E-mail:* peggy@gsfc.org. *Phone:* 770-724-9230. *Fax:* 770-724-9225. *Web site:* www.gsfc.org.

Georgia PROMISE Teacher Scholarship Program. Renewable, forgivable loans for junior undergraduates at Georgia colleges who have been accepted for enrollment into a teacher education program leading to initial certification. Minimum cumulative 3.0 GPA required. Recipient must teach at a Georgia public school for one year for each $1500 awarded. Available to seniors for renewal only. Write for deadlines. *Academic Fields/Career Goals:* Education. *Award:* Forgivable loan for use in junior or senior year; renewable. *Award amount:* $3000–$6000. *Number of awards:* 700–1500. *Eligibility Requirements:* Applicant must be enrolled or expecting to enroll full- or part-time at a four-year institution or university; resident of Georgia and studying in Georgia. Applicant must have 3.0 GPA or higher. Available to U.S. citizens. *Application Requirements:* Application, transcript, Selective Service registration, official certification of admittance into an approved teacher education program in Georgia. *Deadline:* continuous.

Contact Stan DeWitt, Manager of Teacher Scholarships, Georgia Student Finance Commission, 2082 East Exchange Place, Suite 100, Tucker, GA 30084. *E-mail:* stand@gsfc.org. *Phone:* 770-724-9060. *Fax:* 770-724-9031. *Web site:* www.gsfc.org.

Georgia Public Safety Memorial Grant/Law Enforcement Personnel Department Grant. Award for children of Georgia law enforcement officers, prison guards, or fire fighters killed or permanently disabled in the line of duty. Must attend an accredited postsecondary Georgia school. Complete the Law Enforcement Personnel Dependents application. *Award:* Grant for use in freshman, sophomore, junior, or senior year; renewable. *Award amount:* $1000–$8000. *Number of awards:* 20–40. *Eligibility*

Requirements: Applicant must be enrolled or expecting to enroll full-time at a two-year, four-year, or technical institution or university; resident of Georgia and studying in Georgia. Applicant or parent of applicant must have employment or volunteer experience in police/firefighting. Available to U.S. citizens. *Application Requirements:* Application, financial need analysis, selective service registration. *Deadline:* continuous.

Contact Mr. Tracy Irleand, Vice President, Georgia Student Finance Commission, 2082 East Exchange Place, Suite 100, Tucker, GA 30084. *E-mail:* tracyi@gsfc.org. *Phone:* 770-724-9000. *Web site:* www.gsfc.org.

Georgia Tuition Equalization Grant (GTEG). Award for Georgia residents pursuing undergraduate study at an accredited two- or four-year Georgia private institution. Available to residents of Georgia who live near the State borders to attend certain four-year public colleges out-of-state, so that a four-year public college. Award is $1000 per academic year. *Award:* Grant for use in freshman, sophomore, junior, or senior year; renewable. *Award amount:* $1000. *Number of awards:* 1. *Eligibility Requirements:* Applicant must be enrolled or expecting to enroll full-time at a two-year or four-year institution or university; resident of Georgia and studying in Alabama, Florida, Georgia, or Tennessee. Available to U.S. citizens. *Application Requirements:* Application, social security number. *Deadline:* continuous.

Contact Mr. Tracy Ireland, Vice President, Georgia Student Finance Commission, 2082 East Exchange Place, Suite 100, Tucker, GA 30084. *E-mail:* tracyi@gsfc.org. *Phone:* 770-724-9000. *Web site:* www.gsfc.org.

Governor's Scholarship-Georgia. Award to assist students selected as Georgia scholars, STAR students, valedictorians, and salutatorians. For use at two- and four-year colleges and universities in Georgia. Recipients are selected as entering freshmen. Renewable award of up to $1000. Minimum 3.0 GPA required. *Award:* Scholarship for use in freshman, sophomore, junior, or senior year; renewable. *Award amount:* up to $1000. *Number of awards:* 900–3000. *Eligibility Requirements:* Applicant must be high school student; planning to enroll or expecting to enroll full-time at a two-year or four-year institution or university; resident of Georgia and studying in Georgia. Applicant must have 3.0 GPA or higher. Available to U.S. citizens. *Application Requirements:* Application, transcript. *Deadline:* continuous.

Contact Mr. Tracy Ireland, Vice President, Georgia Student Finance Commission, 2082 East Exchange Place, Suite 100, Tucker, GA 30084. *E-mail:* tracyi@gsfc.org. *Phone:* 770-724-9000. *Web site:* www.gsfc.org.

HOPE—Helping Outstanding Pupils Educationally. Grant program for Georgia residents who are college undergraduates to attend an accredited two or four-year Georgia institution. Tuition and fees may be covered by the grant. Minimum 3.0 GPA required. Renewable if student maintains grades and reapplies. Write for deadlines. *Award:* Scholarship for use in freshman, sophomore, junior, or senior year; renewable. *Award amount:* $300–$3900. *Number of awards:* 140,000–170,000. *Eligibility Requirements:* Applicant must be enrolled or expecting to enroll full- or part-time at a two-year or four-year institution or university; resident of Georgia and studying in Georgia. Applicant must have 3.0 GPA or higher. Available to U.S. citizens. *Application Requirements:* Application. *Deadline:* continuous.

Contact Mr. Tracy Ireland, Vice President, Georgia Student Finance Commission, 2082 East Exchange Place, Suite 100, Tucker, GA 30084. *E-mail:* tracyi@gsfc.org. *Phone:* 770-724-9000. *Web site:* www.gsfc.org.

Intellectual Capital Partnership Program, ICAPP. Forgivable loans will be awarded to undergraduate students who are residents of Georgia studying high-tech related fields at a Georgia institution. Repayment for every $2500 that is awarded is one-year service in a high-tech field in Georgia. Can be enrolled in a certificate or degree program. *Academic Fields/Career Goals:* Trade/Technical Specialties. *Award:* Forgivable loan for use in freshman, sophomore, junior, or senior year; not renewable. *Award amount:* $7000–$10,000. *Number of awards:* up to 328. *Eligibility Requirements:* Applicant must be enrolled or expecting to enroll full- or part-time at a two-year or four-year institution or university; resident of Georgia and studying in Georgia. Available to U.S. citizens. *Application Requirements:* Application, financial need analysis. *Deadline:* June 3.

Contact Peggy Matthews, Manager, GSFA Originations, State of Georgia, 2082 East Exchange Place, Suite 230, Tucker, GA 30084-5305. *E-mail:* peggy@gsfc.org. *Phone:* 770-724-9230. *Fax:* 770-724-9225. *Web site:* www.gsfc.org.

Ladders in Nursing Career Service Cancelable Loan Program. Forgivable loans of $3000 are awarded to students who agree to serve for one calendar year at an approved site within the state of Georgia. Eligible applicants will be residents of Georgia who are studying nursing at a Georgia institution. *Academic Fields/Career Goals:* Nursing. *Award:* Forgivable loan for use in freshman, sophomore, junior, senior, or graduate year; not renewable. *Award amount:* $3000. *Number of awards:* 5. *Eligibility Requirements:* Applicant must be enrolled or expecting to enroll full- or part-time at a two-year, four-year, or technical institution or university; resident of Georgia and studying in Georgia. Available to U.S. citizens. *Application Requirements:* Application, financial need analysis. *Deadline:* June 3.

Contact Peggy Matthews, Manager, GSFA Originations, State of Georgia, 2082 East Exchange Place, Suite 230, Tucker, GA 30084-5305. *E-mail:* peggy@gsfc.org. *Phone:* 770-724-9230. *Fax:* 770-724-9225. *Web site:* www.gsfc.org.

Northeast Georgia Pilot Nurse Service Cancelable Loan. Awards up to 100 forgivable loans between $2500 and $4500 to undergraduate students who are residents of Georgia studying nursing in Georgia. Loans can be repaid by working as a nurse in northeast Georgia. *Academic Fields/Career Goals:* Nursing. *Award:* Forgivable loan for use in freshman, sophomore, junior, or senior year; not renewable. *Award amount:* $2500–$4500. *Number of awards:* up to 100. *Eligibility Requirements:* Applicant must be enrolled or expecting to enroll full-time at a four-year institution or university; resident of Georgia and studying in Georgia. Available to U.S. citizens. *Application Requirements:* Application, financial need analysis. *Deadline:* June 3.

Contact Peggy Matthews, Manager, GSFA Originations, State of Georgia, 2082 East Exchange Place, Suite 230, Tucker, GA 30084-5305. *E-mail:* peggy@gsfc.org. *Phone:* 770-724-9230. *Fax:* 770-724-9225. *Web site:* www.gsfc.org.

Registered Nurse Service Cancelable Loan Program. Forgivable loans will be awarded to undergraduate students who are residents of Georgia studying nursing in a two-year or four-year school in Georgia. Loans can be repaid by working as a registered nurse in the state of Georgia. *Academic Fields/Career Goals:* Nursing. *Award:* Forgivable loan for use in freshman, sophomore, junior, or senior year; not renewable. *Award amount:* $200–$4500. *Number of awards:* 15. *Eligibility Requirements:* Applicant must be enrolled or expecting to enroll full- or part-time at a two-year or four-year institution or university; resident of Georgia and studying in Georgia. Available to U.S. citizens. *Application Requirements:* Application, financial need analysis. *Deadline:* June 3.

Contact Peggy Matthews, Manager, GSFA Originations, State of Georgia, 2082 East Exchange Place, Suite 230, Tucker, GA 30084-5305. *E-mail:* peggy@gsfc.org. *Phone:* 770-724-9230. *Fax:* 770-724-9225. *Web site:* www.gsfc.org.

Robert C. Byrd Honors Scholarship-Georgia. Complete the application provided by the Georgia Department of Education. Renewable awards for outstanding graduating Georgia high school seniors to be used for full-time undergraduate study at eligible U.S. institution. Must a legal resident of Georgia and a U.S. citizen. *Award:* Scholarship for use in freshman, sophomore, junior, or senior year; renewable. *Award amount:* up to $1500. *Number of awards:* 600–720. *Eligibility Requirements:* Applicant must be high school student; planning to enroll or expecting to enroll full-time at a two-year or four-year institution or university; resident of Georgia and studying in Georgia. Available to U.S. citizens. *Application Requirements:* Application, transcript. *Deadline:* February 1.

Contact Mr. Tracy Ireland, Vice President, Georgia Student Finance Commission, 2082 East Exchange Place, Suite 100, Tucker, GA 30084. *E-mail:* tracyi@gsfc.org. *Phone:* 770-724-9000. *Web site:* www.gsfc.org.

Service-Cancelable Stafford Loan-Georgia. Scholarship assists Georgia students enrolled in critical fields of study in allied health. For use at GSFA-approved schools. Awards $3500 forgivable loan for dentistry students only. Contact school financial aid officer for more details. *Academic Fields/Career Goals:* Dental Health/Services; Health and Medical Sciences; Nursing; Therapy/Rehabilitation. *Award:* Forgivable loan for use in freshman, sophomore, junior, senior, or graduate year; not renewable. *Award amount:* $2000–$4500. *Number of awards:* 500–1200. *Eligibility Requirements:* Applicant must be enrolled or expecting to enroll full- or part-time at a two-year, four-year, or technical institution or university; resident of Georgia and studying in Georgia. Available to U.S. citizens. *Application Requirements:* Application, financial need analysis. *Deadline:* continuous.

Contact Peggy Matthews, Manager, GSFA Originations, State of Georgia, 2082 East Exchange Place, Suite 230, Tucker, GA 30084-5305. *E-mail:* peggy@gsfc.org. *Phone:* 770-724-9230. *Fax:* 770-724-9225. *Web site:* www.gsfc.org.

HAWAII

Hawaii State Student Incentive Grant. Grants are given to residents of Hawaii who are enrolled in a participating Hawaiian state school. Funds are for undergraduate tuition only. Applicants must submit a financial need analysis. *Award:* Grant for use in freshman, sophomore, junior, or senior year; renewable. *Award amount:* $200–$2000. *Number of awards:* 470. *Eligibility Requirements:* Applicant must be enrolled or expecting to enroll full- or part-time at a two-year, four-year, or technical institution or university; resident of Hawaii and studying in Hawaii. Available to U.S. citizens. *Application Requirements:* Application, financial need analysis. *Deadline:* continuous.

Contact Janine Oyama, Financial Aid Specialist, Hawaii State Postsecondary Education Commission, University of Hawaii, Honolulu, HI 96822. *Phone:* 808-956-6066.

Robert C. Byrd Honors Scholarship-Hawaii. Scholarship is available to students planning to attend college. The scholarship is federally funded, state-administered and recognizes exceptional high school seniors who show promise of continued excellence in the postsecondary educational system. Must have a minimum GPA of 3.2 and 1270 SAT. Applicant must be a legal resident of the State of Hawaii. Hawaii residents who are attending high school in another state are eligible to apply. Deadline: March 17. *Award:* Scholarship for use in freshman, sophomore, junior, or senior year; renewable. *Award amount:* $1500. *Number of awards:* 28. *Eligibility Requirements:* Applicant must be high school student; planning to enroll or expecting to enroll full-time at a two-year, four-year, or technical institution or university and resident of Hawaii. Available to U.S. citizens. *Application Requirements:* Application, transcript, community service. *Deadline:* March 17.

Contact Deanna Helber, Education Specialist, Hawaii Department of Education, 641 18th Avenue, Building V, Room 201, Honolulu, HI 96816-4444. *E-mail:* dee_helber@notes.k12.hi.us. *Phone:* 808-735-6222. *Fax:* 808-733-9890. *Web site:* doe.k12.hi.us.

IDAHO

Education Incentive Loan Forgiveness Contract-Idaho. Renewable award assists Idaho residents enrolling in teacher education or nursing programs within the state. Must rank in top 15 percent of high school graduating class, have a 3.0 GPA or above, and agree to work in Idaho for two years. Deadlines vary. Contact financial aid office at institution of choice. *Academic Fields/Career Goals:* Education; Nursing. *Award:* Forgivable loan for use in freshman year; renewable. *Award amount:* varies. *Number of awards:* 13–45. *Eligibility Requirements:* Applicant must be high school student; planning to enroll or expecting to enroll full-time at a two-year or four-year institution or university; resident of Idaho and studying in Idaho. Applicant must have 3.0 GPA or higher. Available to U.S. citizens. *Application Requirements:* Application, test scores, transcript. *Deadline:* varies.

Contact Dana Kelly, Program Manager, Idaho State Board of Education, PO Box 83720, Boise, ID 83720-0037. *E-mail:* dana.kelly@osbe.idaho.gov. *Phone:* 208-332-1574. *Web site:* www.boardofed.idaho.gov.

Freedom Scholarship. Scholarship for children of Idaho citizens determined by the federal government to have been prisoners of war, missing in action, or killed in action or died of injuries or wounds sustained in action in southeast Asia, including Korea, or who shall become so hereafter, in any area of armed conflicts. Applicant must attend an Idaho public college or university and meet all requirements for regular admission. The award value and the number of awards granted varies. Deadline: January 15. *Award:* Scholarship for use in freshman, sophomore, junior, senior, graduate, or postgraduate years; not renewable. *Award amount:* varies. *Number of awards:* varies. *Eligibility Requirements:* Applicant must be enrolled or expecting to enroll full- or part-time at a two-year, four-year, or technical institution or university; resident of Idaho and studying in Idaho. Available to U.S. citizens. Applicant or parent must meet one or more of the following requirements: general military experience; retired from active duty; disabled or killed as a result of military service; prisoner of war; or missing in action. *Application Requirements:* Application. *Deadline:* January 15.

Contact Dana Kelly, Program Manager, Idaho State Board of Education, PO Box 83720, Boise, ID 83720-0037. *E-mail:* dana.kelly@osbe.idaho.gov. *Phone:* 208-332-1574. *Web site:* www.boardofed.idaho.gov.

Idaho Minority and "At Risk" Student Scholarship. Renewable award for Idaho residents who are disabled or members of a minority group and have financial need. Must attend one of eight postsecondary institutions in the state for undergraduate study. Deadlines vary by institution. Must be a U.S. citizen and be a graduate of an Idaho high school. Contact college financial aid office. *Award:* Scholarship for use in freshman, sophomore, junior, or senior year; renewable. *Award amount:* $3000. *Number of awards:* 35–40. *Eligibility Requirements:* Applicant must be American Indian/Alaska Native, Asian/Pacific Islander, Black (non-Hispanic), or Hispanic; enrolled or expecting to enroll full-time at a two-year, four-year, or technical institution or university; resident of Idaho and studying in Idaho. Applicant must be hearing impaired, physically disabled, or visually impaired. Available to U.S. citizens. *Application Requirements:* Application, financial need analysis, transcript. *Deadline:* varies.

Contact Dana Kelly, Program Manager, Idaho State Board of Education, PO Box 83720, Boise, ID 83720-0037. *E-mail:* dana.kelly@osbe.idaho.gov. *Phone:* 208-332-1574. *Web site:* www.boardofed.idaho.gov.

Idaho Promise Category A Scholarship Program. Renewable award available to Idaho residents who are graduating high school seniors. Must attend an approved Idaho institute of higher education on full-time basis. Must have a cumulative GPA of 3.5 or above and an ACT score of 28 or above. Scholarship value is $3000. Deadline: January 15. *Award:* Scholarship for use in freshman year; renewable. *Award amount:* $3000. *Number of awards:* 25. *Eligibility Requirements:* Applicant must be high school student; planning to enroll or expecting to enroll full-time at a two-year, four-year, or technical institution or university; resident of Idaho and studying in Idaho. Applicant must have 3.5 GPA or higher. Available to U.S. citizens. *Application Requirements:* Application, applicant must enter a contest, test scores. *Deadline:* January 15.

Contact Lynn Humphrey, Manager, Student Aid Programs, Idaho State Board of Education, PO Box 83720, Boise, ID 83720-0037. *E-mail:* lhumphre@osbe.state.id.us. *Phone:* 208-334-2270. *Fax:* 208-334-2632. *Web site:* www.boardofed.idaho.gov.

Idaho Promise Category B Scholarship Program. Available to Idaho residents entering college for the first time prior to the age of 22. Must have completed high school or its equivalent in Idaho and have a minimum GPA of 3.0 or an ACT score of 20 or higher. Scholarship limited to two years or four semesters. *Award:* Scholarship for use in freshman or sophomore year; renewable. *Award amount:* $500. *Number of awards:* varies. *Eligibility Requirements:* Applicant must be age 21 or under; enrolled or expecting to enroll full-time at a two-year, four-year, or technical institution or university; resident of Idaho and studying in Idaho. Applicant must have 3.0 GPA or higher. Available to U.S. citizens. *Application Requirements:* Application, transcript. *Deadline:* continuous.

Contact Lynn Humphrey, Manager, Student Aid Programs, Idaho State Board of Education, PO Box 83720, Boise, ID 83720-0037. *Phone:* 208-334-2270. *Fax:* 208-334-2632. *Web site:* www.boardofed.idaho.gov.

Leveraging Educational Assistance State Partnership Program (LEAP). One-time award assists students attending participating Idaho trade schools, colleges, and universities majoring in any field except theology or divinity. Must be U.S. citizen or permanent resident, and show financial need. Deadlines vary by institution. *Award:* Grant for use in freshman, sophomore, junior, senior, or graduate year; not renewable. *Award amount:* $400–$5000. *Number of awards:* varies. *Eligibility Requirements:* Applicant must be enrolled or expecting to enroll full- or part-time at a two-year, four-year, or technical institution or university; resident of Idaho and studying in Idaho. Available to U.S. citizens. *Application Requirements:* Application, financial need analysis, self-addressed stamped envelope. *Deadline:* varies.

Contact Lynn Humphrey, Manager, Student Aid Programs, Idaho State Board of Education, PO Box 83720, Boise, ID 83720-0037. *Phone:* 208-334-2270. *Fax:* 208-334-2632. *Web site:* www.boardofed.idaho.gov.

Public Safety Officer Dependent Scholarship. Scholarship for dependents of full-time Idaho public safety officers who were killed or disabled in the line of duty. Recipients will attend an Idaho postsecondary institution with a full waiver of fees. Scholarship value is $500. Deadline: January 15. *Award:* Scholarship for use in freshman year; renewable. *Award amount:* up to $500. *Number of awards:* varies. *Eligibility Requirements:* Applicant must be enrolled or expecting to enroll full- or part-time at a two-year or four-year institution or university; resident of Idaho and studying in Idaho. Applicant or parent of applicant must have employment or volunteer experience in police/firefighting. Available to U.S. citizens. Applicant must have general military experience. *Application Requirements:* Application. *Deadline:* January 15.

Contact Dana Kelly, Program Manager, Idaho State Board of Education, PO Box 83720, Boise, ID 83720-0037. *E-mail:* dana.kelly@osbe.idaho.gov. *Phone:* 208-332-1574. *Web site:* www.boardofed.idaho.gov.

ILLINOIS

Golden Apple Scholars of Illinois. 100 scholars are selected annually. Scholars receive $7000 a year for four years. Applicants must be between 17 and 21 and maintain a GPA of 2.5. Eligible applicants must be residents of Illinois studying in Illinois. Deadline: December 1. Recipients must agree to teach in high-need Illinois schools. *Academic Fields/Career Goals:* Education. *Award:* Scholarship for use in freshman, sophomore, junior, or senior year; not renewable. *Award amount:* $4500. *Number of awards:* 100. *Eligibility Requirements:* Applicant must be age 17-21; enrolled or expecting to enroll full-time at a four-year institution or university; resident of Illinois and studying in Illinois. Applicant must have 2.5 GPA or higher. Available to U.S. citizens. *Application Requirements:* Application, autobiography, essay, interview, photo, references, test scores, transcript. *Deadline:* December 1.

Contact Pat Kilduff, Director of Recruitment and Placement, Golden Apple Foundation, 8 South Michigan Avenue, Suite 700, Chicago, IL 60603-3318. *E-mail:* kilduff@goldenapple.org. *Phone:* 312-407-0006. *Fax:* 312-407-0344. *Web site:* www.goldenapple.org.

Grant Program for Dependents of Police, Fire, or Correctional Officers. Awards dependents of police, fire, and correctional officers killed or disabled in line of duty. Provides for tuition and fees at approved Illinois institutions. Must be resident of Illinois. The number of grants made through this program and the individual dollar amount awarded are subject to sufficient annual appropriations by the Illinois General Assembly and the governor. Deadline varies. *Award:* Grant for use in freshman, sophomore, junior, senior, graduate, or postgraduate years; renewable. *Award amount:* varies. *Number of awards:* varies. *Eligibility Requirements:* Applicant must be enrolled or expecting to enroll full- or part-time at a two-year, four-year, or technical institution or university; resident of Illinois and studying in Illinois. Available to U.S. citizens. *Application Requirements:* Application, proof of status. *Deadline:* varies.

Contact College Zone Counselor, Illinois Student Assistance Commission (ISAC), 1755 Lake Cook Road, Deerfield, IL 60015-5209. *E-mail:* collegezone@isac.org. *Phone:* 800-899-4722. *Web site:* www.collegezone.org.

Higher Education License Plate Program-HELP. Need-based grants for students who attend Illinois institutions. Funds for the program are raised by the sale of special license plates commemorating the institutions. Must be Illinois resident. May be eligible to receive the grant for the equivalent of 10 semesters of full-time enrollment. The number of grants made through this program and the individual dollar amount awarded varies. *Award:* Grant for use in freshman, sophomore, junior, or senior year; not renewable. *Award amount:* varies. *Number* *of awards:* varies. *Eligibility Requirements:* Applicant must be enrolled or expecting to enroll full- or part-time at a two-year or four-year institution or university; resident of Illinois and studying in Illinois. Available to U.S. citizens. *Application Requirements:* Application, financial need analysis, FAFSA. *Deadline:* varies.

Contact College Zone Counselor, Illinois Student Assistance Commission (ISAC), 1755 Lake Cook Road, Deerfield, IL 60015-5209. *E-mail:* collegezone@isac.org. *Phone:* 800-899-4722. *Web site:* www.collegezone.org.

Illinois College Savings Bond Bonus Incentive Grant Program. Program offers Illinois college savings bond holders a grant for each year of bond maturity payable upon bond redemption if at least 70 percent of proceeds are used to attend college in Illinois. The amount of grant will depend on the amount of the bond, ranging from a $40 to $440 grant per $5000 of the bond. Applications are accepted between August 1 and May 30 of the academic year in which the bonds matured, or in the academic year immediately following maturity. *Award:* Grant for use in freshman, sophomore, junior, senior, graduate, or postgraduate years; not renewable. *Award amount:* $40–$440. *Number of awards:* varies. *Eligibility Requirements:* Applicant must be enrolled or expecting to enroll full- or part-time at a two-year, four-year, or technical institution or university and studying in Illinois. Available to U.S. citizens. *Application Requirements:* Application. *Deadline:* May 30.

Contact College Zone Counselor, Illinois Student Assistance Commission (ISAC), 1755 Lake Cook Road, Deerfield, IL 60015-5209. *E-mail:* collegezone@isac.org. *Phone:* 800-899-4722. *Web site:* www.collegezone.org.

Illinois Department of Public Health Center for Rural Health Allied Health Care Professional Scholarship Program. Scholarship for Illinois student who wants to be a nurse practitioner, physician assistant, or certified nurse midwife. Funding available for up to two years. Must fulfill an obligation to practice full-time in a designated shortage area as an allied healthcare professional in Illinois for one year for each year of scholarship funding. *Academic Fields/Career Goals:* Health and Medical Sciences; Nursing. *Award:* Scholarship for use in freshman, sophomore, junior, or senior year; renewable. *Award amount:* up to $7500. *Number of awards:* varies. *Eligibility Requirements:* Applicant must be enrolled or expecting to enroll full- or part-time at a two-year or four-year institution or university; resident of Illinois and studying in Illinois. Available to U.S. citizens. *Application Requirements:* Application, financial need analysis. *Deadline:* May 15.

Contact Marcia Franklin, Department of Public Health, Illinois Student Assistance Commission (ISAC), 535 West Jefferson Street, Springfield, IL 62761. *Phone:* 217-782-1624. *Web site:* www.collegezone.org.

Illinois Department of Public Health Center for Rural Health Nursing Education Scholarship Program. Scholarship for Illinois students pursuing a certificate, diploma, or degree in nursing. Must demonstrate financial need. Provides up to four years of financial aid in return for full- or part-time employment as a licensed practical or registered nurse in Illinois upon graduation. Must remain employed in Illinois for a period equivalent to the educational time that was supported by the scholarship. Deadline: May 31. *Academic Fields/Career Goals:* Health and Medical Sciences; Nursing. *Award:* Scholarship for use in freshman, sophomore, junior, or senior year; renewable. *Award amount:* $1500–$6000. *Number of awards:* varies. *Eligibility Requirements:* Applicant must be enrolled or expecting to enroll full- or part-time at a two-year or four-year institution or university; resident of Illinois and studying in Illinois. Available to U.S. citizens. *Application Requirements:* Application, financial need analysis, transcript. *Deadline:* May 31.

Contact Illinois Department of Public Health, Illinois Student Assistance Commission (ISAC), 535 West Jefferson Street, Springfield, IL 62761-0001. *Phone:* 212-782-1624. *Web site:* www.collegezone.org.

Illinois Future Teachers Corps Program. Scholarships are available for students planning to become teachers in Illinois. Students must be Illinois residents, enrolled or accepted as a junior or above in a Teacher Education Program at an Illinois college or university. By receiving the award, students agree to teach for five years at either a public, private, or parochial Illinois preschool, or at a public elementary or secondary school. *Academic Fields/Career Goals:* Education. *Award:* Forgivable loan for use in junior, senior, or graduate year; renewable. *Award amount:* up to $15,000. *Number of awards:* 1150. *Eligibility Requirements:* Applicant must be enrolled or expecting to enroll full- or part-time at a four-year institution or university; resident of Illinois and studying in Illinois. Applicant must have 2.5 GPA or higher. Available to U.S. citizens. *Application Requirements:* Application, financial need analysis, FAFSA. *Deadline:* March 1.

Contact College Zone Counselor, Illinois Student Assistance Commission (ISAC), 1755 Lake Cook Road, Deerfield, IL 60015-5209. *E-mail:* collegezone@isac.org. *Phone:* 800-899-4722. *Web site:* www.collegezone.org.

Illinois General Assembly Scholarship. Scholarships available for Illinois students enrolled at an Illinois four-year state-supported college. Must contact the general assembly member for eligibility criteria. Deadline varies. *Award:* Scholarship for use in freshman, sophomore, junior, or senior year; not renewable. *Award amount:* varies. *Number of awards:* varies. *Eligibility Requirements:* Applicant must be enrolled or expecting to enroll full- or part-time at a four-year institution or university; resident of Illinois and studying in Illinois. Available to U.S. citizens. *Application Requirements:* Application. *Deadline:* varies.

Contact College Zone Counselor, Illinois Student Assistance Commission (ISAC), 1755 Lake Cook Road, Deerfield, IL 60015-5209. *E-mail:* collegezone@isac.org. *Phone:* 800-899-4722. *Web site:* www.collegezone.org.

Illinois Monetary Award Program. The program provides grants, which do not need to be repaid. Awards to Illinois residents who demonstrate financial need, based on the information provided on the Free Application for Federal Student Aid. The number of grants made through this program, and the individual dollar amount awarded, are subject to sufficient annual appropriations by the Illinois General Assembly. Deadlines: August 15 and September 30. *Award:* Grant for use in freshman, sophomore, junior, or senior year; renewable. *Award amount:* $2365. *Number of awards:* 146,853. *Eligibility Requirements:* Applicant must be enrolled or expecting to enroll full- or part-time at a two-year, four-year, or technical institution or university; resident of Illinois and studying in Illinois. Available to U.S. citizens. *Application Requirements:* Financial need analysis, FAFSA online. *Deadline:* varies.

Contact College Zone Counselor, Illinois Student Assistance Commission (ISAC), 1755 Lake Cook Road, Deerfield, IL 60015-5209. *E-mail:* collegezone@isac.org. *Phone:* 800-899-4722. *Web site:* www.collegezone.org.

Illinois National Guard Grant Program. Members of the Illinois National Guard are eligible to receive the grant. The grant can pay for eligible tuition and certain fees for undergraduate or graduate study at Illinois two- or four-year public colleges. It can be used for a maximum of the equivalent of four academic years of full-time enrollment. Deadlines: October 1 of the academic year for full year, March 1 for second/third term, or June 15 for the summer term. *Award:* Grant for use in freshman, sophomore, junior, senior, or graduate year; renewable. *Award amount:* varies. *Number of awards:* varies. *Eligibility Requirements:* Applicant must be enrolled or expecting to enroll full- or part-time at a two-year or four-year institution or university; resident of Illinois and studying in Illinois. Available to U.S. citizens. Applicant must have served in the Air Force National Guard or Army National Guard. *Application Requirements:* Application, documentation of service. *Deadline:* varies.

Contact College Zone Counselor, Illinois Student Assistance Commission (ISAC), 1755 Lake Cook Road, Deerfield, IL 60015-5209. *E-mail:* collegezone@isac.org. *Phone:* 800-899-4722. *Web site:* www.collegezone.org.

Illinois Special Education Teacher Tuition Waiver. Teachers or students who are pursuing a career in special education as public, private or parochial preschool, elementary or secondary school teachers in Illinois may be eligible for this program. This program will exempt such individuals from paying tuition and mandatory fees at an eligible institution, for up to four years. The number of scholarships and the individual dollar amount awarded are subject to sufficient annual appropriations by the Illinois General Assembly. Deadline: March 1. *Academic Fields/Career Goals:* Special Education. *Award:* Forgivable loan for use in freshman, sophomore, junior, senior, or graduate year; renewable. *Award amount:* varies. *Number of awards:* up to 250. *Eligibility Requirements:* Applicant must be enrolled or expecting to enroll full- or part-time at a four-year institution or university; resident of Illinois and studying in Illinois. Available to U.S. citizens. *Application Requirements:* Application. *Deadline:* March 1.

Contact College Zone Counselor, Illinois Student Assistance Commission (ISAC), 1755 Lake Cook Road, Deerfield, IL 60015-5209. *E-mail:* collegezone@isac.org. *Phone:* 800-899-4722. *Web site:* www.collegezone.org.

Illinois Student-to-Student Program of Matching Grants. Grant is available to undergraduates at participating state-supported colleges through voluntary contributions from students and matching grants from the state. The number of grants made through this program, and the individual dollar amount awarded, are subject to sufficient annual appropriations by the Illinois General Assembly. Contact financial aid office at the institution. *Award:* Grant for use in freshman, sophomore, junior, or senior year; not renewable. *Award amount:* varies. *Number of awards:* varies. *Eligibility Requirements:* Applicant must be enrolled or expecting to enroll full- or part-time at a two-year or four-year institution or university; resident of Illinois and studying in Illinois. Available to U.S. citizens. *Application Requirements:* Application, financial need analysis. *Deadline:* varies.

Contact College Zone Counselor, Illinois Student Assistance Commission (ISAC), 1755 Lake Cook Road, Deerfield, IL 60015-5209. *E-mail:* collegezone@isac.org. *Phone:* 800-899-4722. *Web site:* www.collegezone.org.

Illinois Veteran Grant Program-IVG. Awards qualified veterans and pays eligible tuition and fees for study in Illinois public universities or community colleges. Program eligibility units are based on the enrolled hours for a particular term, not the dollar amount of the benefits paid. Applications are available at college financial aid office and can be submitted any time during the academic year for which assistance is being requested. *Award:* Grant for use in freshman, sophomore, junior, senior, or graduate year; renewable. *Award amount:* $1400–$1600. *Number of awards:* 11,000–13,000. *Eligibility Requirements:* Applicant must be enrolled or expecting to enroll full- or part-time at a two-year or four-year institution or university; resident of Illinois and studying in Illinois. Available to U.S. citizens. Applicant must have general military experience. *Application Requirements:* Application. *Deadline:* continuous.

Contact College Zone Counselor, Illinois Student Assistance Commission (ISAC), 1755 Lake Cook Road, Deerfield, IL 60015-5209. *E-mail:* collegezone@isac.org. *Phone:* 800-899-4722. *Web site:* www.collegezone.org.

Merit Recognition Scholarship (MRS) Program. Awards students who were ranked in the top 5 percent of their high school class or scored among the top 5 percent of scores in the ACT, SAT or Prairie state achievement exam. May be eligible to receive an one-time, nonrenewable scholarship of $1000. The number of scholarships granted varies. *Award:* Scholarship for use in freshman year; not renewable. *Award amount:* up to $1000. *Number of awards:* varies. *Eligibility Requirements:* Applicant must be high school student; planning to enroll or expecting to enroll full- or part-time at a two-year or four-year institution or university; resident of Illinois and studying in Illinois. Applicant must have 3.5 GPA or higher. Available to U.S. citizens. *Application Requirements:* Application. *Deadline:* varies.

Contact College Zone Counselor, Illinois Student Assistance Commission (ISAC), 1755 Lake Cook Road, Deerfield, IL 60015-5209. *E-mail:* collegezone@isac.org. *Phone:* 800-899-4722. *Web site:* www.collegezone.org.

MIA/POW Scholarships. One-time award for spouse, child, or step-child of veterans who are missing in action or were a prisoner of war. Must be enrolled at a state-supported school in Illinois. Candidate must be U.S. citizen. Must apply and be accepted before beginning of school. Also for children and spouses of veterans who are determined to be 100 percent disabled as established by the Veterans Administration. Scholarship value and the number of awards granted varies. Deadline: continuous. *Award:* Scholarship for use in freshman, sophomore, junior, senior, or graduate year; renewable. *Award amount:* varies. *Number of awards:* varies. *Eligibility Requirements:* Applicant must be enrolled or expecting to enroll full- or part-time at a two-year or four-year institution or university; resident of Illinois and studying in Illinois. Available to U.S. citizens. Applicant or parent must meet one or more of the following requirements: general military experience; retired from active duty; disabled or killed as a result of military service; prisoner of war; or missing in action. *Application Requirements:* Application. *Deadline:* continuous.

Contact Ms. Tracy Mahan, Grants Section, Illinois Department of Veterans Affairs, 833 South Spring Street, Springfield, IL 62794-9432. *Phone:* 217-782-3564. *Fax:* 217-782-4161. *Web site:* www.state.il.us/agency/dva.

Minority Teachers of Illinois Scholarship Program. The program awards students who are planning to become school teachers and are of African American/Black, Hispanic American, Asian American or Native American origin. May qualify for up to $5000 per year. The number of scholarships and the individual dollar amount awarded are subject to sufficient annual appropriations by the Illinois General Assembly and the governor. Deadline: March 1. *Academic Fields/Career Goals:* Education; Special Education. *Award:* Forgivable loan for use in freshman, sophomore, junior, senior, graduate, or postgraduate years; renewable. *Award amount:* up to $5000. *Number of awards:* 450–550. *Eligibility Requirements:* Applicant must be American Indian/Alaska Native, Asian/Pacific Islander, Black (non-Hispanic), or Hispanic; enrolled or expecting to enroll full- or part-time at a two-year or four-year institution or university; resident of Illinois and studying in Illinois. Applicant must have 2.5 GPA or higher. Available to U.S. citizens. *Application Requirements:* Application. *Deadline:* March 1.

Contact College Zone Counselor, Illinois Student Assistance Commission (ISAC), 1755 Lake Cook Road, Deerfield, IL 60015-5209.

E-mail: collegezone@isac.org. *Phone:* 800-899-4722. *Web site:* www.collegezone.org.

Paul Douglas Teacher Scholarship (PDTS) Program. Program enables and encourages outstanding high school graduates to pursue teaching careers at the preschool, elementary or secondary school level by providing financial assistance. Deadline: August 1. *Academic Fields/Career Goals:* Education. *Award:* Scholarship for use in freshman year; not renewable. *Award amount:* varies. *Number of awards:* varies. *Eligibility Requirements:* Applicant must be enrolled or expecting to enroll full-time at a four-year institution or university; resident of Illinois and studying in Illinois. Available to U.S. citizens. *Application Requirements:* Application, financial need analysis. *Deadline:* August 1.

Contact College Zone Counselor, Illinois Student Assistance Commission (ISAC), 1755 Lake Cook Road, Deerfield, IL 60015-5209. *E-mail:* collegezone@isac.org. *Phone:* 800-899-4722. *Web site:* www.collegezone.org.

Silas Purnell Illinois Incentive for Access Program. Students whose information provided on the FAFSA results in a calculated zero expected family contribution when they are college freshmen may be eligible to receive the grant of up to $500. To apply, the student must complete the FAFSA as soon as possible after January 1, prior to the academic year that starts on or after July 1. *Award:* Grant for use in freshman year; not renewable. *Award amount:* up to $500. *Number of awards:* varies. *Eligibility Requirements:* Applicant must be enrolled or expecting to enroll full- or part-time at a two-year, four-year, or technical institution or university; resident of Illinois and studying in Illinois. Available to U.S. citizens. *Application Requirements:* Financial need analysis, FAFSA. *Deadline:* July 1.

Contact College Zone Counselor, Illinois Student Assistance Commission (ISAC), 1755 Lake Cook Road, Deerfield, IL 60015-5209. *E-mail:* collegezone@isac.org. *Phone:* 800-899-4722. *Web site:* www.collegezone.org.

Veterans' Children Educational Opportunities. Award for each child of age 18 or younger of a veteran who died or became totally disabled as a result of service during World War I, World War II, Korean, or Vietnam War. Must be studying in Illinois. Death must be service-connected. Disability must be rated 100 percent for two or more years. Grant value is $250. Deadline: June 30. *Award:* Grant for use in freshman year; not renewable. *Award amount:* $250. *Number of awards:* varies. *Eligibility Requirements:* Applicant must be age 10-18; enrolled or expecting to enroll full- or part-time at a two-year or four-year institution or university; resident of Illinois and studying in Illinois. Available to U.S. citizens. Applicant or parent must meet one or more of the following requirements: general military experience; retired from active duty; disabled or killed as a result of military service; prisoner of war; or missing in action. *Application Requirements:* Application. *Deadline:* June 30.

Contact Tracy Mahan, Grants Section, Illinois Department of Veterans Affairs, 833 South Spring Street, Springfield, IL 62794-9432. *Phone:* 217-782-3564. *Fax:* 217-782-4161. *Web site:* www.state.il.us/agency/dva.

INDIANA

Child of Disabled Veteran Grant or Purple Heart Recipient Grant. Free tuition at Indiana state-supported colleges or universities for children of disabled veterans or Purple Heart recipients. Must submit Form DD214 or service record. Dollar amount and number of awards varies. *Award:* Grant for use in freshman, sophomore, junior, senior, graduate, or postgraduate years; renewable. *Award amount:* varies. *Number of awards:* varies. *Eligibility Requirements:* Applicant must be enrolled or expecting to enroll full- or part-time at a two-year or four-year institution or university; resident of Indiana and studying in Indiana. Available to U.S. citizens. Applicant or parent must meet one or more of the following requirements: general military experience; retired from active duty; disabled or killed as a result of military service; prisoner of war; or missing in action. *Application Requirements:* Application. *Deadline:* continuous.

Contact Jon Brinkley, State Service Officer, Indiana Department of Veterans Affairs, 302 West Washington Street, Room E-120, Indianapolis, IN 46204-2738. *E-mail:* jbrinkley@dva.state.in.us. *Phone:* 317-232-3910. *Fax:* 317-232-7721. *Web site:* www.ai.org/veteran.

Department of Veterans Affairs Free Tuition for Children of POW/MIA's in Vietnam. Renewable award for residents of Indiana who are the children of veterans declared missing in action or prisoner-of-war after January 1, 1960. Provides tuition at Indiana state-supported institutions for undergraduate study. *Award:* Grant for use in freshman, sophomore, junior, senior, graduate, or postgraduate years; renewable. *Award amount:* varies. *Number of awards:* varies. *Eligibility Requirements:* Applicant must be age 24 or under; enrolled or expecting to enroll full- or part-time at a two-year or four-year institution or university; resident of Indiana and studying in Indiana. Available to U.S. citizens. Applicant or parent must meet one or more of the following requirements: general military experience; retired from active duty; disabled or killed as a result of military service; prisoner of war; or missing in action. *Application Requirements:* Application. *Deadline:* March 10.

Contact Jon Brinkley, State Service Officer, Indiana Department of Veterans Affairs, 302 West Washington Street, Room E-120, Indianapolis, IN 46204-2738. *E-mail:* jbrinkley@dva.state.in.us. *Phone:* 317-232-3910. *Fax:* 317-232-7721. *Web site:* www.ai.org/veteran.

Frank O'Bannon Grant Program. The Higher Education Award (Frank O'Bannon) is a need-based, tuition-restricted program for students attending Indiana public, private, or proprietary institutions seeking a first undergraduate degree. Students (and parents of dependent students) who are U.S. citizens and Indiana residents must file the FAFSA yearly by the March 10 deadline. *Award:* Grant for use in freshman, sophomore, junior, or senior year; not renewable. *Award amount:* $200–$5172. *Number of awards:* 38,000–70,239. *Eligibility Requirements:* Applicant must be enrolled or expecting to enroll full-time at a two-year, four-year, or technical institution or university; resident of Indiana and studying in Indiana. Available to U.S. citizens. *Application Requirements:* Application, financial need analysis, FAFSA. *Deadline:* March 10.

Contact Grants Counselor, State Student Assistance Commission of Indiana (SSACI), 150 West Market Street, Suite 500, Indianapolis, IN 46204-2805. *E-mail:* grants@ssaci.state.in.us. *Phone:* 317-232-2350. *Fax:* 317-232-3260. *Web site:* www.in.gov/ssaci.

Hoosier Scholar Award. The Hoosier Scholar Award is a $500 nonrenewable award. Based on the size of the senior class, one to three scholars are selected by the guidance counselor(s) of each accredited high school in Indiana. The award is based on academic merit and may be used for any educational expense at an eligible Indiana institution of higher education. *Award:* Scholarship for use in freshman year; not renewable. *Award amount:* $500. *Number of awards:* 689–840. *Eligibility Requirements:* Applicant must be high school student; planning to enroll or expecting to enroll full-time at a two-year or four-year institution or university; resident of Indiana and studying in Indiana. Applicant must have 3.5 GPA or higher. Available to U.S. citizens. *Application Requirements:* Application, references. *Deadline:* March 10.

Contact Ada Sparkman, Program Coordinator, State Student Assistance Commission of Indiana (SSACI), 150 West Market Street, Suite 500, Indianapolis, IN 46204-2805. *Phone:* 317-232-2350. *Fax:* 317-232-3260. *Web site:* www.in.gov/ssaci.

Indiana National Guard Supplemental Grant. The award is a supplement to the Indiana Higher Education Grant program. Applicants must be members of the Indiana National Guard. All Guard paperwork must be completed prior to the start of each semester. The FAFSA must be received by March 10. Award covers certain tuition and fees at select public colleges. *Award:* Grant for use in freshman, sophomore, junior, or senior year; not renewable. *Award amount:* $200–$7110. *Number of awards:* 503–925. *Eligibility Requirements:* Applicant must be enrolled or expecting to enroll full- or part-time at a two-year or four-year institution or university; resident of Indiana and studying in Indiana. Available to U.S. citizens. Applicant must have served in the Air Force National Guard or Army National Guard. *Application Requirements:* Application. *Deadline:* March 10.

Contact Kathryn Moore, Grants Counselor, State Student Assistance Commission of Indiana (SSACI), 150 West Market Street, Suite 500, Indianapolis, IN 46204-2805. *E-mail:* grants@ssaci.state.in.us. *Phone:* 317-232-2350. *Fax:* 317-232-2360. *Web site:* www.in.gov/ssaci.

Indiana Nursing Scholarship Fund. Need-based tuition funding for nursing students enrolled full- or part-time at an eligible Indiana institution. Must be a U.S. citizen and an Indiana resident and have a minimum 2.0 GPA or meet the minimum requirements for the nursing program. Upon graduation, recipients must practice as a nurse in an Indiana health care setting for two years. *Academic Fields/Career Goals:* Nursing. *Award:* Scholarship for use in freshman, sophomore, junior, or senior year; not renewable. *Award amount:* $200–$5000. *Number of awards:* 490–690. *Eligibility Requirements:* Applicant must be enrolled or expecting to enroll full- or part-time at a two-year or four-year institution or university; resident of Indiana and studying in Indiana. Available to U.S. citizens. *Application Requirements:* Application, financial need analysis, FAFSA. *Deadline:* continuous.

Contact Yvonne Heflin, Director, Special Programs, State Student Assistance Commission of Indiana (SSACI), 150 West Market Street, Suite 500, Indianapolis, IN 46204-2805. *Phone:* 317-232-2350. *Fax:* 317-232-3260. *Web site:* www.in.gov/ssaci.

Part-time Grant Program. Program is designed to encourage part-time undergraduates to start and complete their associate or baccalaureate degrees or certificates by subsidizing part-time tuition costs. It is a term-based award that is based on need. State residency requirements must be met and a FAFSA must be filed. Eligibility is determined at the institutional level subject to approval by SSACI. *Award:* Grant for use in freshman, sophomore, junior, or senior year; not renewable. *Award amount:* $50–$4000. *Number of awards:* 4680–6700. *Eligibility Requirements:* Applicant must be enrolled or expecting to enroll part-time at a two-year, four-year, or technical institution or university; resident of Indiana and studying in Indiana. Available to U.S. citizens. *Application Requirements:* Application, financial need analysis. *Deadline:* continuous.

Contact Grants Counselor, State Student Assistance Commission of Indiana (SSACI), 150 West Market Street, Suite 500, Indianapolis, IN 46204-2805. *E-mail:* grants@ssaci.state.in.us. *Phone:* 317-232-2350. *Fax:* 317-232-3260. *Web site:* www.in.gov/ssaci.

Twenty-first Century Scholars Gear Up Summer Scholarship. Grant of up to $3000 that pays for summer school tuition and regularly assessed course fees (does not cover other costs such as textbooks or room and board). *Award:* Scholarship for use in freshman, sophomore, junior, or senior year; not renewable. *Award amount:* up to $3000. *Number of awards:* 1. *Eligibility Requirements:* Applicant must be enrolled or expecting to enroll full-time at a two-year or four-year institution or university; resident of Indiana and studying in Indiana. Available to U.S. citizens. *Application Requirements:* Application, must be in twenty-first century scholars program, have high school diploma. *Deadline:* varies.

Contact GEAR UP Coordinator, Office of Twenty-first Century Scholars, State Student Assistance Commission of Indiana (SSACI), 150 West Market Street, Suite 500, Indianapolis, IN 46204. *E-mail:* 21stscholars@ssaci.in.gov. *Phone:* 317-234-1394. *Web site:* www.in.gov/ssaci.

IOWA

Governor Terry E. Branstad Iowa State Fair Scholarship. Awards up to four scholarships ranging from $500 to $1000 to students graduating from an Iowa high school. Must actively participate at the Iowa State fair. For more details see Web site: http://www.iowacollegeaid.org. *Award:* Scholarship for use in freshman year; not renewable. *Award amount:* $500–$1000. *Number of awards:* up to 4. *Eligibility Requirements:* Applicant must be high school student; planning to enroll or expecting to enroll full- or part-time at a four-year institution or university; resident of Iowa and studying in Iowa. Available to U.S. citizens. *Application Requirements:* Application, essay, financial need analysis, references, transcript. *Deadline:* May 1.

Contact Misty Thompson, Program Planner, Iowa College Student Aid Commission, 200 Tenth Street, Fourth Floor, Des Moines, IA 50309-3609. *E-mail:* misty.thompson@iowa.gov. *Phone:* 515-725-3424. *Web site:* www.iowacollegeaid.gov.

Iowa Grants. Statewide need-based program to assist high-need Iowa residents. Recipients must demonstrate a high level of financial need to receive awards ranging from $100 to $1000. Awards are prorated for students enrolled for less than full-time. Awards must be used at Iowa postsecondary institutions. *Award:* Grant for use in freshman, sophomore, junior, or senior year; not renewable. *Award amount:* $100–$1000. *Number of awards:* varies. *Eligibility Requirements:* Applicant must be enrolled or expecting to enroll full- or part-time at a two-year, four-year, or technical institution or university; resident of Iowa and studying in Iowa. Available to U.S. citizens. *Application Requirements:* Application, financial need analysis. *Deadline:* continuous.

Contact Julie Leeper, Director, Program Administration, Iowa College Student Aid Commission, 200 Tenth Street, Fourth Floor, Des Moines, IA 50309-3609. *E-mail:* icsac@max.state.ia.us. *Phone:* 515-725-3420. *Web site:* www.iowacollegeaid.gov.

Iowa National Guard Education Assistance Program. Program provides postsecondary tuition assistance to members of Iowa National Guard Units. Must study at a postsecondary institution in Iowa. Contact the office for additional information. *Award:* Grant for use in freshman, sophomore, junior, or senior year; not renewable. *Award amount:* up to $1200. *Number of awards:* varies. *Eligibility Requirements:* Applicant must be enrolled or expecting to enroll full- or part-time at a two-year, four-year, or technical institution or university; resident of Iowa and studying in Iowa. Available to U.S. citizens. Applicant must have served in the Air Force National Guard or Army National Guard. *Application Requirements:* Application. *Deadline:* continuous.

Contact Julie Leeper, Director, Program Administration, Iowa College Student Aid Commission, 200 Tenth Street, Fourth Floor, Des Moines, IA 50309-3609. *E-mail:* icsac@max.state.ia.us. *Phone:* 515-242-3370. *Web site:* www.iowacollegeaid.gov.

Iowa Teacher Shortage Forgivable Loan Program. Forgivable loan assists students who will teach in Iowa secondary schools. Must be an Iowa resident attending an Iowa postsecondary institution. Contact the office for additional information. *Academic Fields/ Career Goals:* Education. *Award:* Forgivable loan for use in freshman, sophomore, junior, or senior year; not renewable. *Award amount:* $2686. *Number of awards:* varies. *Eligibility Requirements:* Applicant must be enrolled or expecting to enroll full- or part-time at a four-year institution or university; resident of Iowa and studying in Iowa. Applicant or parent of applicant must have employment or volunteer experience in teaching. Available to U.S. citizens. *Application Requirements:* Application, financial need analysis. *Deadline:* continuous.

Contact Julie Leeper, Director, Program Administration, Iowa College Student Aid Commission, 200 Tenth Street, Fourth Floor, Des Moines, IA 50309-3609. *E-mail:* icsac@max.state.ia.us. *Phone:* 515-725-3420. *Web site:* www.iowacollegeaid.gov.

Iowa Tuition Grant Program. Program assists students who attend independent postsecondary institutions in Iowa. Iowa residents currently enrolled, or planning to enroll, for at least 3 semester hours at one of the eligible Iowa postsecondary institutions may apply. Awards currently range from $100 to $4000. Grants may not exceed the difference between independent college and university tuition and fees and the average tuition and fees at the three public Regent universities. *Award:* Grant for use in freshman, sophomore, junior, or senior year; not renewable. *Award amount:* $100–$4000. *Number of awards:* varies. *Eligibility Requirements:* Applicant must be enrolled or expecting to enroll full- or part-time at a two-year or four-year institution or university; resident of Iowa and studying in Iowa. Available to U.S. citizens. *Application Requirements:* Application, financial need analysis. *Deadline:* July 1.

Contact Julie Leeper, Director, Program Administration, Iowa College Student Aid Commission, 200 Tenth Street, Fourth Floor, Des Moines, IA 50309-3609. *E-mail:* icsac@max.state.ia.us. *Phone:* 515-725-3420. *Web site:* www.iowacollegeaid.gov.

Iowa Vocational Rehabilitation. Provides vocational rehabilitation services to individuals with disabilities who need these services in order to maintain, retain, or obtain employment compatible with their disabilities. Must be Iowa resident. *Award:* Grant for use in freshman, sophomore, junior, senior, graduate, or postgraduate years; renewable. *Award amount:* $4000. *Number of awards:* 4000. *Eligibility Requirements:* Applicant must be enrolled or expecting to enroll full- or part-time at a two-year, four-year, or technical institution or university and resident of Iowa. Applicant must be hearing impaired, learning disabled, physically disabled, or visually impaired. Available to U.S. and non-U.S. citizens. *Application Requirements:* Application, interview. *Deadline:* varies.

Contact Ralph Childers, Policy and Workforce Initiatives Coordinator, Iowa Division of Vocational Rehabilitation Services, Division of Vocational Rehabilitation Services, 510 East 12th Street, Des Moines, IA 50319. *E-mail:* ralph.childers@iowa.gov. *Phone:* 515-281-4151. *Fax:* 515-281-4703. *Web site:* www.ivrs.iowa.gov.

Iowa Vocational-Technical Tuition Grant Program. Program provides need-based financial assistance to Iowa residents enrolled in career education (vocational-technical), and career option programs at Iowa area community colleges. Grants range from $150 to $1250, depending on the length of the program, financial need, and available funds. *Award:* Grant for use in freshman or sophomore year; not renewable. *Award amount:* $150–$1200. *Number of awards:* varies. *Eligibility Requirements:* Applicant must be enrolled or expecting to enroll full- or part-time at a technical institution; resident of Iowa and studying in Iowa. Available to U.S. citizens. *Application Requirements:* Application, financial need analysis. *Deadline:* July 1.

Contact Julie Leeper, Director, Program Administration, Iowa College Student Aid Commission, 200 Tenth Street, Fourth Floor, Des Moines, IA 50309-3609. *E-mail:* julie.leeper@iowa.gov. *Phone:* 515-725-3420. *Web site:* www.iowacollegeaid.gov.

State of Iowa Scholarship Program. Program provides recognition and financial honorarium to Iowa's academically talented high school seniors. Honorary scholarships are presented to all qualified candidates. Approximately 1700 top-ranking candidates are designated as State of Iowa scholars every March, from an applicant pool of nearly 5000 high school seniors. Must be used at an Iowa postsecondary institution. Minimum 3.5 GPA required. *Award:* Scholarship for use in freshman year; not renewable. *Award amount:* varies. *Number of awards:* up to 1700. *Eligibility Requirements:* Applicant must be high school student; planning to enroll or expecting to enroll full-time at a two-year, four-year, or technical institution or university; resident of Iowa and studying in Iowa. Applicant must have 3.5 GPA or higher. Available to U.S. citizens. *Application Requirements:* Application, test scores. *Deadline:* November 1.

Contact Misty Thompson, Program Planner, Iowa College Student Aid Commission, 200 Tenth Street, Fourth Floor, Des Moines, IA 50309-3609. *E-mail:* misty.thompson@iowa.gov. *Phone:* 515-725-3424. *Web site:* www.iowacollegeaid.gov.

KANSAS

Kansas Educational Benefits for Children of MIA, POW, and Deceased Veterans of the Vietnam War. Scholarship awarded to students who are children of veterans. Must show proof of parent's status as missing in action, prisoner of war, or killed in action in the Vietnam War. Kansas residence required of veteran at time of entry to service. Must attend a state-supported postsecondary school. *Award:* Scholarship for use in freshman, sophomore, junior, or senior year; not renewable. *Award amount:* varies. *Number of awards:* 1. *Eligibility Requirements:* Applicant must be enrolled or expecting to enroll full- or part-time at a two-year, four-year, or technical institution or university and studying in Kansas. Available to U.S. citizens. Applicant or parent must meet one or more of the following requirements: general military experience; retired from active duty; disabled or killed as a result of military service; prisoner of war; or missing in action. *Application Requirements:* Application, report of casualty, birth certificate, school acceptance letter, military discharge of veteran. *Deadline:* varies.

Contact Wayne Bollig, Program Director, Kansas Commission on Veterans Affairs, 700 Jackson, SW, Suite 701, Topeka, KS 66603-3743. *E-mail:* bhayes@kcva.org. *Phone:* 785-296-3976. *Fax:* 785-296-1462. *Web site:* www.kcva.org.

Ted and Nora Anderson Scholarships. Scholarship of $250 for each semester (one year only) given to the children of American Legion members or Auxiliary members who are holding membership for the past three consecutive years. Children of a deceased member can also apply. Parent of the applicant must be a veteran. Must be high school seniors or college freshmen or sophomores in a Kansas institution. Scholarship for use at an approved college, university, or trade school in Kansas. Must maintain a C average in college. *Award:* Scholarship for use in freshman or sophomore year; not renewable. *Award amount:* $250–$500. *Number of awards:* 4. *Eligibility Requirements:* Applicant must be enrolled or expecting to enroll full-time at a two-year, four-year, or technical institution or university; resident of Kansas and studying in Kansas. Applicant or parent of applicant must be member of American Legion or Auxiliary. Available to U.S.

citizens. Applicant or parent must meet one or more of the following requirements: general military experience; retired from active duty; disabled or killed as a result of military service; prisoner of war; or missing in action. *Application Requirements:* Application, essay, financial need analysis, photo, references, transcript. *Deadline:* February 15.

Contact Jim Gravenstein, Chairman of the Scholarship Committee, American Legion, Department of Kansas, 1314 Topeka Boulevard, SW, Topeka, KS 66612. *Phone:* 785-232-9315. *Fax:* 785-232-1399. *Web site:* www.ksamlegion.org.

KENTUCKY

College Access Program (CAP) Grant. Award for U.S. citizen and Kentucky resident with no previous college degree. Applicants seeking degrees in religion are not eligible. Must demonstrate financial need and submit Free Application for Federal Student Aid. Expected family contribution (EFC) towards the students educational expenses cannot exceed $3850. Deadline: March 15. *Award:* Grant for use in freshman, sophomore, junior, or senior year; not renewable. *Award amount:* $79–$1900. *Number of awards:* 35,000–40,000. *Eligibility Requirements:* Applicant must be enrolled or expecting to enroll full- or part-time at a two-year, four-year, or technical institution or university; resident of Kentucky and studying in Kentucky. Available to U.S. citizens. *Application Requirements:* Application, financial need analysis, FAFSA. *Deadline:* March 15.

Contact Michael D. Morgan, Program Coordinator, Kentucky Higher Education Assistance Authority (KHEAA), PO Box 798, Frankfort, KY 40602-0798. *E-mail:* mmorgan@kheaa.com. *Phone:* 502-696-7394. *Fax:* 502-696-7373. *Web site:* www.kheaa.com.

Department of Veterans Affairs Tuition Waiver-KY KRS 164-507. The scholarship is given to college students. The applicant must be under the age of 23. Must be residents of Kentucky. *Award:* Scholarship for use in freshman, sophomore, junior, or senior year; not renewable. *Award amount:* varies. *Number of awards:* 350. *Eligibility Requirements:* Applicant must be age 23 or under; enrolled or expecting to enroll full-time at a two-year or four-year institution or university and resident of Kentucky. Available to U.S. citizens. *Application Requirements:* Application, resume. *Deadline:* varies.

Contact Barbara A. Hale, Administrative Specialist, Kentucky Department of Veterans Affairs, 321 West Main Street, Suite 390, Louisville, KY 40213-9095. *E-mail:* barbaraa.hale@ky.gov. *Phone:* 502-595-4447. *Fax:* 502-595-4448. *Web site:* www.kdva.net.

Early Childhood Development Scholarship. Awards scholarship with conditional service commitment for part-time students currently employed by participating ECD facility or providing training in ECD for an approved organization. *Academic Fields/Career Goals:* Child and Family Studies; Education. *Award:* Scholarship for use in freshman, sophomore, junior, or senior year; not renewable. *Award amount:* up to $1800. *Number of awards:* 900–1000. *Eligibility Requirements:* Applicant must be enrolled or expecting to enroll part-time at a four-year institution or university; resident of Kentucky and studying in Kentucky. Available to U.S. citizens. *Application Requirements:* Application, resume. *Deadline:* continuous.

Contact Early Childhood Development Authority, Kentucky Higher Education Assistance Authority (KHEAA), 275 East Main Street, 2W-E, Frankfort, KY 40621. *Phone:* 502-564-8099. *Web site:* www.kheaa.com.

Education At Work Scholarship. Scholarships available for Kentucky residents enrolled in a Kentucky postsecondary institution. Should have received services from the state Office for the Blind, Office of Employment and Training, Office of Career and Technical Education, Office of Vocational Rehabilitation or Kentucky Adult Education in the past three years. Must submit an application, two character references, and an essay of under 600 words. *Award:* Scholarship for use in freshman, sophomore, junior, senior, or graduate year; not renewable. *Award amount:* $1000. *Number of awards:* 20–36. *Eligibility Requirements:* Applicant must be enrolled or expecting to enroll full- or part-time at a two-year, four-year, or technical institution or university; resident of Kentucky and studying in Kentucky. Available to U.S. citizens. *Application Requirements:* Application, essay, references. *Deadline:* continuous.

Contact Wynee Hecker, Program Coordinator, Kentucky Higher Education Assistance Authority (KHEAA), 500 Mero Street, Second Floor, Frankfort, KY 40601. *E-mail:* wyneej.hecker@ky.gov. *Phone:* 502-564-6606 Ext. 128. *Web site:* www.kheaa.com.

Environmental Protection Scholarships. Renewable awards for college juniors, seniors, and graduate students for tuition, fees, and room and board at a Kentucky state university. Minimum 2.5 GPA required. Must agree to work full-time for the Kentucky Natural Resources and Environmental Protection Cabinet upon graduation. Interview is required. *Academic Fields/Career Goals:* Biology; Earth Science; Environmental Science. *Award:* Scholarship for use in junior, senior, or graduate year; renewable. *Award amount:* $15,500–$22,700. *Number of awards:* 1–4. *Eligibility Requirements:* Applicant must be enrolled or expecting to enroll full-time at a four-year institution or university and studying in Kentucky. Applicant must have 3.0 GPA or higher. Available to U.S. and non-U.S. citizens. *Application Requirements:* Application, essay, interview, references, transcript, proof of valid work permit for non-U.S. citizens. *Deadline:* February 15.

Contact James Kipp, Scholarship Program Coordinator, Kentucky Natural Resources and Environmental Protection Cabinet, 233 Mining/Mineral Resources Building, Lexington, KY 40506-0107. *E-mail:* kipp@uky.edu. *Phone:* 859-257-1299. *Fax:* 859-323-1049. *Web site:* www.uky.edu/waterresources.

GED Incentive Program Tuition Discount. Tuition waivers available to Kentucky students who earned their GED in one year after having been out of high school three years and signing a learning contract with their employer. Award is $250 tuition discount each semester for a maximum of four semesters at a Kentucky public college or university. *Award:* Scholarship for use in freshman, sophomore, junior, or senior year; renewable. *Award amount:* $250–$1000. *Number of awards:* varies. *Eligibility Requirements:* Applicant must be enrolled or expecting to enroll part-time at a two-year or four-year institution or university; resident of Kentucky and studying in Kentucky. Available to U.S. citizens. *Application Requirements:* Application, learning contract with employer, GED certificate. *Deadline:* continuous.

Contact B.J. Helton, Senior Associate, Kentucky Higher Education Assistance Authority (KHEAA), 1024 Capital Center Drive, Suite 250, Frankfort, KY 40601. *E-mail:* bj.helton@ky.gov. *Phone:* 502-564-5114 Ext. 103. *Web site:* www.kheaa.com.

Kentucky Department of Agriculture Agribusiness/Governor's Scholars Program Scholarship. Scholarships available for alumni of the governor's scholars program. Must agree to pursue an education and career in agriculture or agribusiness. Must be a resident of Kentucky. *Academic Fields/Career Goals:* Agribusiness; Agriculture. *Award:* Scholarship for use in freshman, sophomore, junior, or senior year; not renewable. *Award amount:* $300–$3000. *Number of awards:* 10–30. *Eligibility Requirements:* Applicant must be enrolled or expecting to enroll full-time at a two-year or four-year institution or university; resident of Kentucky and studying in Kentucky. Available to U.S. citizens. *Application Requirements:* Application, essay, financial need analysis, references, transcript. *Deadline:* March 29.

Contact Kim Sisk, Governor's Scholars Program, Kentucky Higher Education Assistance Authority (KHEAA), 1024 Capital Center Drive, Suite 210, Frankfort, KY 40601-8204. *E-mail:* kim.goins@ky.gov. *Phone:* 502-573-1618. *Web site:* www.kheaa.com.

Kentucky Department of Agriculture Scholarship. Scholarship available for youth exhibitor who has participated in a state-sponsored district livestock show. Four exhibitors in each species (dairy, beef, sheep, hogs, goats, horses) will be chosen in a random drawing from a list of Future Farmers of America and 4-H show participants. Must be a Kentucky resident. *Award:* Scholarship for use in freshman, sophomore, junior, or senior year; not renewable. *Award amount:* $500. *Number of awards:* 24. *Eligibility Requirements:* Applicant must be enrolled or expecting to enroll full- or part-time at a two-year, four-year, or technical institution or university; resident of Kentucky and must have an interest in animal/agricultural competition. Available to U.S. citizens. *Application Requirements:* Applicant must enter a contest. *Deadline:* varies.

Contact Linda Renschler, Director, Kentucky Higher Education Assistance Authority (KHEAA), PO Box 798, Frankfort, KY 40602-0798. *E-mail:* lrenschler@kheaa.com. *Phone:* 502-696-7400. *Fax:* 502-696-7373. *Web site:* www.kheaa.com.

Kentucky Department of Vocational Rehabilitation. Grant provides services necessary to secure employment. Eligible individual must possess physical or mental impairment that results in a substantial impediment to employment; benefit from vocational rehabilitation services in terms of an employment outcome; and require vocational rehabilitation services to prepare for, enter, or retain employment. *Award:* Grant for use in freshman, sophomore, junior, senior, graduate, or postgraduate years; renewable. *Award amount:* varies. *Number of awards:* varies. *Eligibility Requirements:* Applicant must be enrolled or expecting to enroll full- or part-time at a two-year, four-year, or technical institution or university. Applicant must be learning disabled or physically disabled. Available to U.S. and non-U.S. citizens. *Application Requirements:* Application, financial need analysis, interview, transcript. *Deadline:* continuous.

Contact Charles Tuckett, Program Administrator, Kentucky Department of Vocational Rehabilitation, 209 Saint Clair Street, Frankfort, KY 40601. *E-mail:* marianu.spencer@mail.state.ky.us. *Phone:* 502-595-3423. *Fax:* 502-564-6745. *Web site:* ovr.ky.gov.

Kentucky Educational Excellence Scholarship (KEES). Annual award based on GPA and highest ACT or SAT score received at the time of high school graduation. Awards are renewable, if required cumulative GPA is maintained at a Kentucky postsecondary school. Must be a Kentucky resident, and a graduate of a Kentucky high school. *Award:* Scholarship for use in freshman, sophomore, junior, or senior year; renewable. *Award amount:* varies. *Number of awards:* 60,000–65,000. *Eligibility Requirements:* Applicant must be high school student; planning to enroll or expecting to enroll full- or part-time at a two-year, four-year, or technical institution or university; resident of Kentucky and studying in Kentucky. Applicant must have 2.5 GPA or higher. Available to U.S. citizens. *Application Requirements:* Application, test scores, transcript. *Deadline:* continuous.

Contact Linda Renschler, Director, Kentucky Higher Education Assistance Authority (KHEAA), PO Box 798, Frankfort, KY 40602-0798. *E-mail:* lrenschler@kheaa.com. *Phone:* 502-696-7400. *Fax:* 502-696-7373. *Web site:* www.kheaa.com.

Kentucky Minority Educator Recruitment and Retention (KMERR) Scholarship. Scholarship for minority teacher candidates who rank in the upper half of their class or have a minimum 2.5 GPA. Must be a U.S. citizen and Kentucky resident enrolled in one of Kentucky's eight public institutions. Must teach one semester in Kentucky for each semester the scholarship is received. *Academic Fields/Career Goals:* Education. *Award:* Forgivable loan for use in freshman, sophomore, junior, senior, or graduate year; renewable. *Award amount:* $2500–$5000. *Number of awards:* 300. *Eligibility Requirements:* Applicant must be American Indian/Alaska Native, Asian/Pacific Islander, Black (non-Hispanic), or Hispanic; enrolled or expecting to enroll full-time at a two-year or four-year institution or university; resident of Kentucky and studying in Kentucky. Applicant must have 2.5 GPA or higher. Available to U.S. citizens. *Application Requirements:* Application, essay, references, test scores, transcript. *Deadline:* continuous.

Contact Michael Dailey, Division Director, Kentucky Department of Education, 500 Mero Street, 17th Floor, Frankfort, KY 40601. *E-mail:* michael.dailey@education.ky.gov. *Phone:* 502-564-1479. *Fax:* 502-564-6952. *Web site:* www.kde.state.ky.us.

Kentucky Teacher Scholarship Program. Awards Kentucky residents attending Kentucky institutions and pursuing initial teacher certification programs. Must teach one semester for each semester of award received. In critical shortage areas, must teach one semester for every two semesters of award received. Must submit Free Application for Federal Student Aid. Deadline: May 1. *Academic Fields/Career Goals:* Education. *Award:* Scholarship for use in freshman, sophomore, junior, senior, or graduate year; renewable. *Award amount:* $325–$5000. *Number of awards:* 600–700. *Eligibility Requirements:* Applicant must be enrolled or expecting to enroll full-time at a two-year or four-year institution or university; resident of Kentucky and studying in Kentucky. Available to U.S. citizens. *Application Requirements:* Application, financial need analysis. *Deadline:* May 1.

Contact Tim Phelps, Student Aid Branch Manager, Kentucky Higher Education Assistance Authority (KHEAA), PO Box 798, Frankfort, KY 40602. *E-mail:* tphelps@kheaa.com. *Phone:* 502-696-7393. *Fax:* 502-696-7496. *Web site:* www.kheaa.com.

Kentucky Transportation Cabinet Civil Engineering Scholarship Program. Cabinet awards scholarships to qualified Kentucky residents who wish to study civil engineering at Kentucky State University, Western Kentucky University, University of Louisville or University of Louisville. Applicant should be a graduate of an accredited Kentucky high school / high school graduates who are Kentucky residents. *Academic Fields/Career Goals:* Civil Engineering. *Award:* Scholarship for use in freshman, sophomore, junior, senior, or graduate year; renewable. *Award amount:* $4000–$4500. *Number of awards:* 10–20. *Eligibility Requirements:* Applicant must be enrolled or expecting to enroll full-time at a four-year institution or university; resident of Kentucky and studying in Kentucky. Applicant must have 2.5 GPA or higher. Available to U.S. and non-U.S. citizens. *Application Requirements:* Application, essay, interview, references, test scores, transcript. *Deadline:* March 1.

Contact Jo Anne Tingle, Scholarship Program Manager, Kentucky Transportation Cabinet, 200 Metro Street, Suite E6-S1-00, Frankfort, KY 40622. *E-mail:* jo.tingle@ky.gov. *Phone:* 502-564-3020. *Fax:* 502-564-2277. *Web site:* www.transportation.ky.gov.

Kentucky Tuition Grant (KTG). Grants available to Kentucky residents who are full-time undergraduates at an independent college within the state. Must not be enrolled in a religion program. Based on financial need. Must submit Free Application for Federal Student Aid. Deadline: March 15. *Award:* Grant for use in freshman, sophomore, junior, or senior year; not renewable. *Award amount:* $200–$2900. *Number of awards:* 10,000–12,000. *Eligibility Requirements:* Applicant must be enrolled or expecting to enroll full-time at a two-year or four-year institution or university; resident of Kentucky and studying in Kentucky. Available to U.S. citizens. *Application Requirements:* Application, financial need analysis, FAFSA. *Deadline:* March 15.

Contact Tim Phelps, Student Aid Branch Manager, Kentucky Higher Education Assistance Authority (KHEAA), PO Box 798, Frankfort, KY 40602-0798. *E-mail:* tphelps@kheaa.com. *Phone:* 502-696-7393. *Fax:* 502-696-7496. *Web site:* www.kheaa.com.

Laura Blackburn Memorial Scholarship. Scholarship to the child, grandchild, or great grandchild of a veteran who served in the Armed Forces. Applicant must be a Kentucky resident. Deadline: March 31. *Award:* Scholarship for use in freshman year; not renewable. *Award amount:* $1000. *Number of awards:* varies. *Eligibility Requirements:* Applicant must be enrolled or expecting to enroll full-time at a four-year institution or university and resident of Kentucky. Available to U.S. citizens. Applicant or parent must meet one or more of the following requirements: Army experience; retired from active duty; disabled or killed as a result of military service; prisoner of war; or missing in action. *Application Requirements:* Application, financial need analysis, transcript. *Deadline:* March 31.

Contact Betty Cook, Secretary and Treasurer, American Legion Auxiliary, Department of Kentucky, PO BOX 2123, Louisville, KY 40201. *Phone:* 270-932-7533. *Fax:* 270-932-7672. *Web site:* www.kylegion.org.

Minority Educator Recruitment and Retention Scholarship. Conversion loan or scholarship providing up to $5000 per academic year to minority students majoring in teacher education and pursuing initial teacher certification. Must be repaid with interest if scholarship requirements are not met. *Academic Fields/Career Goals:* Education; Special Education. *Award:* Forgivable loan for use in freshman, sophomore, junior, senior, or graduate year; not renewable. *Award amount:* up to $5000. *Number of awards:* 200–300. *Eligibility Requirements:* Applicant must be American Indian/Alaska Native, Asian/Pacific Islander, Black (non-Hispanic), or Hispanic; enrolled or expecting to enroll full-time at a two-year or four-year institution or university; resident of Kentucky and studying in Kentucky. Applicant must have 2.5 GPA or higher. Available to U.S. citizens. *Application Requirements:* Application. *Deadline:* continuous.

Contact Natasha Murray, Program Director, Kentucky Higher Education Assistance Authority (KHEAA), 500 Metro Street, Frankfort, KY 40601. *E-mail:* natasha.murray@education.ky.gov. *Phone:* 502-564-1479. *Web site:* www.kheaa.com.

Robert C. Byrd Honors Scholarship-Kentucky. Scholarship available to high school seniors who show past high achievement and potential for continued academic success. Must have applied for admission or have been accepted for enrollment at a public or private nonprofit postsecondary school. Must be a Kentucky resident. Deadline: second Friday in March. *Award:* Scholarship for use in freshman, sophomore, junior, or senior year; renewable. *Award amount:* up to $1500. *Number of awards:* varies. *Eligibility Requirements:* Applicant must be high school student; planning to enroll or expecting to enroll full-time at a two-year or four-year institution or university and resident of Kentucky. Applicant must have 3.5 GPA or higher. Available to U.S. citizens. *Application Requirements:* Application, test scores. *Deadline:* varies.

Contact Donna Melton, Scholarship committee, Kentucky Department of Education, 500 Mero Street, 19th Floor, Frankfort, KY 40601. *E-mail:* dmelton@kde.state.ky.us. *Phone:* 502-564-1479. *Web site:* www.kde.state.ky.us.

Touchstone Energy All "A" Classic Scholarship. Award of $1000 for senior student in good standing at a Kentucky high school which is a member of the All Classic. Applicant must be a U.S. citizen and must plan to attend a postsecondary institution in Kentucky in the upcoming year as a full-time student and be drug free. Deadline: December 2. *Award:* Scholarship for use in freshman year; not renewable. *Award amount:* $1000. *Number of awards:* 12. *Eligibility Requirements:* Applicant must be high school student; planning to enroll or expecting to enroll full-time at a two-year, four-year, or technical institution or university; resident of Kentucky and studying in Kentucky. Available to U.S. citizens. *Application Requirements:* Application, essay, photo, references, transcript. *Deadline:* December 2.

Contact David Cowden, Chairperson of Scholarship Committee, Kentucky Touchstone Energy Cooperatives, 1320 Lincoln Road, Lewisport, KY 42351. *E-mail:* allaclassic@alltel.net. *Phone:* 859-744-4812. *Web site:* www.ekpc.com.

Women in Rural Electrification (WIRE) Scholarships. Scholarship available to Kentucky students who are juniors or seniors in a Kentucky college or university and have 60 credit hours by fall semester. Immediate family of student must be served by one of the state's 24 rural electric distribution cooperatives. Awards based on academic achievement, extracurricular activities, career goals, recommendations. *Award:* Scholarship for use in junior or senior year; not renewable. *Award amount:* $1000. *Number of awards:* 3. *Eligibility Requirements:* Applicant must be enrolled or expecting to enroll full- or part-time at a four-year institution or university; resident of Kentucky and studying in Kentucky. Available to U.S. citizens. *Application Requirements:* Application. *Deadline:* June 15.

Contact Ellie Hobgood, W.I.R.E. Scholarships, South Kentucky Rural Electric Cooperative Corporation, PO Box 32170, Louisville, KY 40232. *Phone:* 800-264-5112. *Web site:* www.skrecc.com.

LOUISIANA

Leveraging Educational Assistance Program (LEAP). Apply by completing the FAFSA each year. Eligibility is determined by the institution the student attends. Must be a resident of Louisiana and must be attending an institution in Louisiana. *Award:* Grant for use in freshman, sophomore, junior, or senior year; renewable. *Award amount:* $200–$2000. *Number of awards:* 3000–4000. *Eligibility Requirements:* Applicant must be enrolled or expecting to enroll full- or part-time at a two-year, four-year, or technical institution or university; resident of Louisiana and studying in Louisiana. Available to U.S. citizens. *Application Requirements:* Application, financial need analysis. *Deadline:* varies.

Contact Public Information, Louisiana Office of Student Financial Assistance, PO Box 91202, Baton Rouge, LA 70821-9202. *E-mail:* custserv@osfa.state.la.us. *Phone:* 800-259-5626 Ext. 1012. *Fax:* 225-922-0790. *Web site:* www.osfa.state.la.us.

Louisiana Department of Veterans Affairs State Aid Program. Tuition exemption at any state supported college, university, or technical institute for children (dependents between the ages of 18-25) of veterans that are rated 90% or above service connected disabled by the U.S. Department of Veterans Affairs. Tuition exemption also available for the surviving spouse and children (dependents between the ages of 18-25) of veterans who died on active duty, in line of duty, or where death was the result of a disability incurred in or aggravated by military service. For residents of Louisiana who are attending a Louisiana institution. *Award:* Grant for use in freshman, sophomore, junior, senior, graduate, or postgraduate years; renewable. *Award amount:* varies. *Number of awards:* varies. *Eligibility Requirements:* Applicant must be age 18-25; enrolled or expecting to enroll full-time at a two-year, four-year, or technical institution or university; resident of Louisiana and studying in Louisiana. Available to U.S. citizens. Applicant or parent must meet one or more of the following requirements: general military experience; retired from active duty; disabled or killed as a result of military service; prisoner of war; or missing in action. *Application Requirements:* Application. *Deadline:* continuous.

Contact Richard Blackwell, Veterans Affairs Regional Manager, Louisiana Department of Veterans Affairs. *E-mail:* rblackwell@vetaffairs.com. *Phone:* 225-922-0500. *Web site:* www.vetaffairs.com.

Louisiana National Guard State Tuition Exemption Program. Renewable award for college undergraduates to receive tuition exemption upon satisfactory performance in the Louisiana National Guard. Applicant must attend a state-funded institution in Louisiana, be a resident and registered voter in Louisiana, meet the academic and residency requirements of the university attended, and provide documentation of Louisiana National Guard enlistment. The exemption can be used for up to 15 semesters. Minimum 2.5 GPA required. *Award:* Scholarship for use in freshman, sophomore, junior, or senior year; renewable. *Award amount:* varies. *Number of awards:* varies. *Eligibility Requirements:* Applicant must be enrolled or expecting to enroll full- or part-time at a two-year, four-year, or technical institution or university; resident of Louisiana and studying in Louisiana. Applicant must have 2.5 GPA or higher. Available to U.S. citizens. Applicant must have served in the Air Force National Guard or Army National Guard. *Application Requirements:* Application, test scores, transcript. *Deadline:* continuous.

Contact Jona M. Hughes, Education Services Officer, Louisiana National Guard-State of Louisiana, Joint Task Force LA, Building 35, Jackson Barracks, JI-PD, New Orleans, LA 70146-0330. *E-mail:* hughesj@la-arng.ngb.army.mil. *Phone:* 504-278-8531 Ext. 8304. *Fax:* 504-278-8025. *Web site:* www.la.ngb.army.mil.

Rockefeller State Wildlife Scholarship. Awarded to high school graduates, college undergraduates and graduate students majoring in forestry, wildlife or marine science. Renewable up to five years as an undergraduate and two years as a graduate. Must have at least a 2.5 GPA and have taken the ACT or SAT. *Academic Fields/Career Goals:* Animal/Veterinary Sciences; Marine Biology; Natural Resources; Natural Sciences. *Award:* Scholarship for use in freshman, sophomore, junior, senior, or graduate year; renewable. *Award amount:* $1000. *Number of awards:* 64. *Eligibility Requirements:* Applicant must be enrolled or expecting to enroll full-time at a four-year institution or university; resident of Louisiana and studying in Louisiana. Applicant must have 2.5 GPA or higher. Available to U.S. citizens. *Application Requirements:* Application, test scores, transcript, FAFSA. *Deadline:* July 1.

Contact Public Information, Louisiana Office of Student Financial Assistance, PO Box 91202, Baton Rouge, LA 70821-9202. *E-mail:* custserv@osfa.state.la.us. *Phone:* 800-259-5626 Ext. 1012. *Fax:* 225-922-0790. *Web site:* www.osfa.state.la.us.

TOPS Honors Award. Program awards an amount equal to tuition plus an $800 per year stipend to students attending a Louisiana public institution, or an amount equal to the weighted average public tuition plus an $800 per year stipend to students attending a LAICU private institution. Must have a minimum high school GPA of 3.5 based on TOPS core curriculum, ACT score of 27, and complete a 16.5 unit core curriculum. Must be resident of Louisiana. *Award:* Scholarship for use in freshman, sophomore, junior, or senior year; renewable. *Award amount:* varies. *Number of awards:* varies. *Eligibility Requirements:* Applicant must be enrolled or expecting to enroll full-time at a two-year, four-year, or technical institution or university; resident of Louisiana and studying in Louisiana. Applicant must have 3.5 GPA or higher. Available to U.S. citizens. *Application Requirements:* Application, test scores. *Deadline:* July 1.

Contact Public Information, Louisiana Office of Student Financial Assistance, PO Box 91202, Baton Rouge, LA 70821-9202. *E-mail:* custserv@osfa.state.la.us. *Phone:* 800-259-5626 Ext. 1012. *Fax:* 225-922-0790. *Web site:* www.osfa.state.la.us.

TOPS Performance Award. Program awards an amount equal to tuition including a $400 annual stipend to students attending a Louisiana public institution, or an amount equal to the weighted average public tuition and a $400 annual stipend to students attending a LAICU private institution. Must have a minimum high school GPA of 3.5 based on the TOPS core curriculum, an ACT score of 23 and completion of a 16.5 unit core curriculum. Must be a Louisiana resident. *Award:* Scholarship for use in freshman, sophomore, junior, or senior year; renewable. *Award amount:* varies. *Number of awards:* varies. *Eligibility Requirements:* Applicant must be high school student; planning to enroll or expecting to enroll full-time at a two-year, four-year, or technical institution or university; resident of Louisiana and studying in Louisiana. Applicant must have 3.5 GPA or higher. Available to U.S. citizens. *Application Requirements:* Application, test scores. *Deadline:* July 1.

Contact Public Information, Louisiana Office of Student Financial Assistance, PO Box 91202, Baton Rouge, LA 70821-9202. *E-mail:* custserv@osfa.state.la.us. *Phone:* 800-259-5626 Ext. 1012. *Fax:* 225-922-0790. *Web site:* www.osfa.state.la.us.

TOPS Tech Award. Program awards an amount equal to tuition for up to two years of technical training at a Louisiana postsecondary institution that offers a vocational or technical education certificate or diploma program, or a non-academic degree program. Must have a 2.5 high school GPA based on TOPS Tech core curriculum, an ACT score of 17, and complete the TOPS-Tech core curriculum. Must be a Louisiana resident. *Award:* Scholarship for use in freshman or sophomore year; renewable. *Award amount:* varies. *Number of awards:* varies. *Eligibility Requirements:* Applicant must be enrolled or expecting to enroll full-time at a technical institution; resident of Louisiana and studying in Louisiana. Applicant must have 2.5 GPA or higher. Available to U.S. citizens. *Application Requirements:* Application, test scores, FAFSA. *Deadline:* July 1.

Contact Public Information, Louisiana Office of Student Financial Assistance, PO Box 91202, Baton Rouge, LA 70821-9202. *E-mail:* custserv@osfa.state.la.us. *Phone:* 800-259-5626 Ext. 1012. *Fax:* 225-922-0790. *Web site:* www.osfa.state.la.us.

Tuition Opportunity Program for Students. Program awards an amount equal to tuition fee to students attending a Louisiana public institution, or an amount equal to the weighted average public tuition fee to students attending a LAICU private institution. Must have a minimum high school GPA of 2.5 based on the TOPS core curriculum, the prior year's state average

ACT score, and complete a 16.5 unit core curriculum. Must be a Louisiana resident. Number of awards given varies each year. *Award:* Scholarship for use in freshman, sophomore, junior, or senior year; renewable. *Award amount:* $879–$4434. *Number of awards:* varies. *Eligibility Requirements:* Applicant must be enrolled or expecting to enroll full-time at a two-year, four-year, or technical institution or university; resident of Louisiana and studying in Louisiana. Applicant must have 2.5 GPA or higher. Available to U.S. citizens. *Application Requirements:* Application, test scores. *Deadline:* July 1.

Contact Public Information, Louisiana Office of Student Financial Assistance, PO Box 91202, Baton Rouge, LA 70821-9202. *E-mail:* custserv@osfa.state.la.us. *Phone:* 800-259-5626 Ext. 1012. *Fax:* 225-922-0790. *Web site:* www.osfa.state.la.us.

MAINE

American Legion Auxiliary Department of Maine Daniel E. Lambert Memorial Scholarship. Scholarships to assist young men and women in continuing their education beyond high school. Must demonstrate financial need, must be a resident of the State of Maine, U.S. citizen, and parent must be a veteran. *Award:* Scholarship for use in freshman year; not renewable. *Award amount:* $1000. *Number of awards:* up to 2. *Eligibility Requirements:* Applicant must be enrolled or expecting to enroll full-time at a four-year institution or university and resident of Maine. Available to U.S. citizens. Applicant or parent must meet one or more of the following requirements: general military experience; retired from active duty; disabled or killed as a result of military service; prisoner of war; or missing in action. *Application Requirements:* Application, financial need analysis. *Deadline:* May 1.

Contact Madeline Sweet, Secretary, American Legion Auxiliary, Department of Maine, 21 College Avenue, PO Box 887, Waterville, ME 04901. *E-mail:* legionme@me.acadia.net. *Phone:* 207-873-3229. *Fax:* 207-469-0598. *Web site:* www.mainelegion.org.

American Legion Auxiliary Department of Maine Past Presidents' Parley Nurses Scholarship. One-time award for child, grandchild, sister, or brother of veteran. Must be resident of Maine and wishing to continue education at accredited school in medical field. Must submit photo, doctor's statement, and evidence of civic activity. Minimum 3.5 GPA required. *Academic Fields/Career Goals:* Health and Medical Sciences; Nursing. *Award:* Scholarship for use in freshman, sophomore, junior, or senior year; not renewable. *Award amount:* $300. *Number of awards:* 1. *Eligibility Requirements:* Applicant must be age 18 and over; enrolled or expecting to enroll full-time at a two-year, four-year, or technical institution or university and resident of Maine. Applicant or parent of applicant must have employment or volunteer experience in community service. Applicant must have 3.5 GPA or higher. Available to U.S. citizens. Applicant or parent must meet one or more of the following requirements: general military experience; retired from active duty; disabled or killed as a result of military service; prisoner of war; or missing in action. *Application Requirements:* Application, photo, references, transcript, doctor's statement. *Deadline:* March 31.

Contact Madeline Sweet, Secretary, American Legion Auxiliary, Department of Maine, 21 College Avenue, PO Box 887, Waterville, ME 04901. *E-mail:* legionme@me.acadia.net. *Phone:* 207-873-3229. *Fax:* 207-469-0598. *Web site:* www.mainelegion.org.

American Legion Auxiliary, Department of Maine National President's Scholarship. Scholarships to children of veterans who served in the Armed Forces during the eligibility dates for The American Legion. One $2500, one $2000, and one $1000 in scholarships will be awarded. Applicant must complete 50 hours of community service during his/her high school years. For more details and application visit: http://www.legion-aux.org/uploads/docs/National%20Presidents06_07.doc. *Award:* Scholarship for use in freshman year; not renewable. *Award amount:* $1000–$2500. *Number of awards:* 3. *Eligibility Requirements:* Applicant must be high school student; planning to enroll or expecting to enroll full-time at a four-year institution or university and resident of Maine. Applicant or parent of applicant must have employment or volunteer experience in community service. Available to U.S. citizens. Applicant or parent must meet one or more of the following requirements: general military experience; retired from active duty; disabled or killed as a result of military service; prisoner of war; or missing in action. *Application Requirements:* Application, essay, references, test scores, transcript. *Deadline:* March 1.

Contact Madeline Sweet, Secretary, American Legion Auxiliary, Department of Maine, 21 College Avenue, PO Box 887, Waterville, ME 04901. *E-mail:* legionme@me.acadia.net. *Phone:* 207-873-3229. *Fax:* 207-469-0598. *Web site:* www.mainelegion.org.

Early College For ME. Scholarship for high school students who have not made plans for college but are academically capable of success in college. Recipients are selected by their school principal or director. Students must be entering a Maine Community College. Refer to Web site: http://www.mccs.me.edu/scholarships.html. *Award:* Scholarship for use in freshman year; not renewable. *Award amount:* $2000. *Number of awards:* 200. *Eligibility Requirements:* Applicant must be high school student; planning to enroll or expecting to enroll full-time at a two-year or four-year institution or university; resident of Maine and studying in Maine. Available to U.S. citizens. *Application Requirements:* Application, financial need analysis, references, transcript. *Deadline:* varies.

Contact Charles P. Collins, State Director, Center for Career Development, Maine Community College System, 323 State Street, Augusta, ME 04330. *E-mail:* ccollins@mccs.me.edu. *Phone:* 207-767-5210 Ext. 4115. *Fax:* 207-629-4048. *Web site:* www.mccs.me.edu.

Educators for Maine Forgivable Loan Program. Forgivable loan for residents of Maine who are high school seniors, college students, or college graduates with a minimum 3.0 GPA, studying or preparing to study teacher education. Must teach in Maine upon graduation. Award based on merit. For application information see Web site: http://www.famemaine.com. *Academic Fields/Career Goals:* Education. *Award:* Forgivable loan for use in freshman, sophomore, junior, senior, or graduate year; renewable. *Award amount:* $2000–$3000. *Number of awards:* varies. *Eligibility Requirements:* Applicant must be enrolled or expecting to enroll full-time at a two-year or four-year institution and resident of Maine. Applicant must have 3.0 GPA or higher. Available to U.S. citizens. *Application Requirements:* Application, essay, test scores, transcript. *Deadline:* May 15.

Contact Tammy Holman, Manager, Education Finance Programs, Finance Authority of Maine, 5 Community Drive, PO Box 949, Augusta, ME 04332-0949. *E-mail:* education@famemaine.com. *Phone:* 207-623-3263. *Fax:* 207-623-0095. *Web site:* www.famemaine.com.

Maine Antique Power Scholarship. Scholarship of $400 is available each year to second-year students enrolled in an automotive technology program. *Award:* Scholarship for use in sophomore year; not renewable. *Award amount:* $400. *Number* *of awards:* varies. *Eligibility Requirements:* Applicant must be enrolled or expecting to enroll full-time at a two-year or technical institution; resident of Maine and studying in Maine. Available to U.S. citizens. *Application Requirements:* Application. *Deadline:* varies.

Contact Scholarship Committee, Maine Community College System, 323 State Street, Augusta, ME 04330. *E-mail:* info@mccs.me.edu. *Phone:* 207-629-4000. *Fax:* 207-629-4048. *Web site:* www.mccs.me.edu.

State of Maine Grant Program. Scholarship for residents of Maine, attending an eligible school in Connecticut, Maine, Massachusetts, New Hampshire, Pennsylvania, Rhode Island, Washington, D.C., or Vermont. Award based on need. Must apply annually. Complete Free Application for Federal Student Aid to apply. One-time award of $600 to $1450 for undergraduate study. See Web site: http://www.famemaine.com. *Award:* Grant for use in freshman, sophomore, junior, or senior year; not renewable. *Award amount:* $600–$1450. *Number of awards:* varies. *Eligibility Requirements:* Applicant must be enrolled or expecting to enroll full- or part-time at a two-year, four-year, or technical institution or university; resident of Maine and studying in Connecticut, District of Columbia, Maine, Massachusetts, New Hampshire, Pennsylvania, Rhode Island, or Vermont. Applicant must have 2.5 GPA or higher. Available to U.S. citizens. *Application Requirements:* Application, financial need analysis, FAFSA. *Deadline:* May 1.

Contact Customer Service, Finance Authority of Maine, 5 Community Drive, Augusta, ME 04332. *E-mail:* education@famemaine.com. *Web site:* www.famemaine.com.

Tuition Waiver Programs. Provides tuition waivers for children and spouses of EMS personnel, firefighters, and law enforcement officers who have been killed in the line of duty and for students who were foster children under the custody of the Department of Human Services when they graduated from high school. Waivers valid at the University of Maine System, the Maine Technical College System, and Maine Maritime Academy. Applicant must reside and study in Maine. *Award:* Grant for use in freshman, sophomore, junior, or senior year; renewable. *Award amount:* varies. *Number of awards:* varies. *Eligibility Requirements:* Applicant must be enrolled or expecting to enroll full- or part-time at a four-year institution or university; resident of Maine and studying in Maine. Applicant or parent of applicant must have employment or volunteer experience in designated career field or police/firefighting. Available to U.S. citizens. *Application Requirements:* Application, letter from the Department of Human Services documenting that applicant is in their custody and residing in foster care at the time of graduation from high school or its equivalent. *Deadline:* continuous.

Contact Tammy Holman, Customer Associate, Finance Authority of Maine, 5 Community Drive, Augusta, ME 04332. *E-mail:* trisha@famemaine.com. *Phone:* 207-623-3263. *Fax:* 207-623-0095. *Web site:* www.famemaine.com.

Veterans Dependents Educational Benefits-Maine. Tuition waiver award for dependents or spouses of veterans who were prisoners of war, missing in action, or permanently disabled as a result of service. Veteran must have been Maine resident at service entry for five years preceding application. For use at Maine University system, technical colleges and Maine Maritime. Must be high school graduate. Must submit birth certificate and proof of VA disability of veteran. Award renewable for eight semesters for those under 22 years of age. number and value of awards varies. *Award:* Scholarship for use in freshman, sophomore, junior, or senior year; not renewable. *Award amount:* varies. *Number of awards:* varies. *Eligibility Requirements:* Applicant must be age 21-22; enrolled or expecting to enroll full- or part-time at a two-year or technical institution or university; resident of Maine and studying in Maine. Available to U.S. and non-U.S. citizens. Applicant or parent must meet one or more of the following requirements: general military experience; retired from active duty; disabled or killed as a result of military service; prisoner of war; or missing in action. *Application Requirements:* Application, birth certificate. *Deadline:* continuous.

Contact Peter Ogden, Director, Maine Bureau of Veterans Services, State House, Station 117, Augusta, ME 04333-0117. *E-mail:* mainebzs@maine.gov. *Phone:* 207-626-4464. *Fax:* 207-626-4471. *Web site:* www.state.me.us.

MARYLAND

Charles W. Riley Fire and Emergency Medical Services Tuition Reimbursement Program. Award intended to reimburse members of rescue organizations serving Maryland communities for tuition costs of course work towards a degree or certificate in fire service or medical technology. Must attend a two- or four-year school in Maryland. Minimum 2.0 GPA. The scholarship values up to $6500. *Academic Fields/Career Goals:* Fire Sciences; Health and Medical Sciences; Trade/Technical Specialties. *Award:* Scholarship for use in freshman, sophomore, junior, or senior year; not renewable. *Award amount:* up to $6500. *Number of awards:* up to 150. *Eligibility Requirements:* Applicant must be enrolled or expecting to enroll full- or part-time at a two-year or four-year institution or university; resident of Maryland and studying in Maryland. Applicant or parent of applicant must have employment or volunteer experience in police/firefighting. Available to U.S. citizens. *Application Requirements:* Application, transcript, tuition receipt/proof of enrollment in specified degree program. *Deadline:* July 1.

Contact Gerrie Rogers, Office of Student Financial Assistance, Maryland Higher Education Commission, 839 Bestgate Road, Suite 400, Annapolis, MD 21401-3013. *E-mail:* grogers@mhec.state.md.us. *Phone:* 410-260-4574. *Fax:* 410-260-3203. *Web site:* www.mhec.state.md.us.

Delegate Scholarship Program-Maryland. Delegate scholarships help Maryland residents attending Maryland degree-granting institutions, certain career schools, or nursing diploma schools. May attend out-of-state institution if Maryland Higher Education Commission deems major to be unique and not offered at a Maryland institution. Free Application for Federal Student Aid may be required. Students interested in this program should apply by contacting their legislative district delegate. *Award:* Scholarship for use in freshman, sophomore, junior, senior, or graduate year; not renewable. *Award amount:* $200–$8650. *Number of awards:* up to 3500. *Eligibility Requirements:* Applicant must be enrolled or expecting to enroll full- or part-time at a two-year, four-year, or technical institution or university; resident of Maryland and studying in Maryland. Available to U.S. citizens. *Application Requirements:* Application, FAFSA. *Deadline:* continuous.

Contact Office of Student Financial Assistance, Maryland Higher Education Commission, 839 Bestgate Road, Suite 400, Annapolis, MD 21401-3013. *E-mail:* osfamail@mhec.state.md.us. *Phone:* 800-974-1024. *Fax:* 410-260-3200. *Web site:* www.mhec.state.md.us.

Distinguished Scholar Award-Maryland. Renewable award for Maryland students enrolled full-time at Maryland institutions. National Merit Scholar Finalists automatically offered award. Others may qualify for the award in satisfying criteria of a minimum 3.7 GPA or in combination with high test scores, or for Talent in Arts competition in categories of music, drama, dance, or visual arts. Must maintain annual 3.0 GPA in college for award to be renewed. Contact for further details. *Award:* Scholarship for use in freshman, sophomore, junior, or senior year; renewable. *Award amount:* up to $3000. *Number of awards:* up to 1400. *Eligibility Requirements:* Applicant must be high school student; planning to enroll or expecting to enroll full-time at a two-year or four-year institution or university; resident of Maryland and studying in Maryland. Applicant must have 3.5 GPA or higher. Available to U.S. citizens. *Application Requirements:* Application, test scores, transcript. *Deadline:* varies.

Contact Maura Sappington, Program Administrator, Maryland Higher Education Commission, 839 Bestgate Road, Suite 400, Annapolis, MD 21401-3013. *E-mail:* msappington@mhec.state.md.us. *Phone:* 410-260-4545. *Fax:* 410-260-3200. *Web site:* www.mhec.state.md.us.

Distinguished Scholar Community College Transfer Program. Scholarship available for Maryland residents who have completed 60 credit hours or an AA degree at a Maryland community college and are transferring to a Maryland four-year institution. Deadline varies. *Award:* Scholarship for use in freshman or sophomore year; renewable. *Award amount:* $3000. *Number of awards:* 50. *Eligibility Requirements:* Applicant must be enrolled or expecting to enroll full-time at a two-year institution; resident of Maryland and studying in Maryland. Available to U.S. citizens. *Application Requirements:* Application, transcript. *Deadline:* varies.

Contact Andrea E. Mansfield, Director, Maryland Higher Education Commission, 839 Bestgate Road, Suite 400, Annapolis, MD 21401-3013. *E-mail:* amansfie@mhec.state.md.us. *Phone:* 410-260-4558. *Fax:* 410-260-3202. *Web site:* www.mhec.state.md.us.

Educational Assistance Grants-Maryland. Award for Maryland residents accepted or enrolled in a full-time undergraduate degree or certificate program at a Maryland institution or hospital nursing school. Must submit financial aid form by March 1. Must earn 2.0 GPA in college to maintain award. *Award:* Grant for use in freshman, sophomore, junior, or senior year; renewable. *Award amount:* $400–$2700. *Number of awards:* 15,000–30,000. *Eligibility Requirements:* Applicant must be enrolled or expecting to enroll full-time at a two-year or four-year institution or university; resident of Maryland and studying in Maryland. Available to U.S. citizens. *Application Requirements:* Application, financial need analysis. *Deadline:* March 1.

Contact Office of Student Financial Assistance, Maryland Higher Education Commission, 839 Bestgate Road, Suite 400, Annapolis, MD 21401-3013. *E-mail:* osfamail@mhec.state.md.us. *Phone:* 800-974-1024. *Fax:* 410-260-3200. *Web site:* www.mhec.state.md.us.

Edward T. Conroy Memorial Scholarship Program. Scholarship for dependents of deceased or 100 percent disabled U.S. Armed Forces personnel; the son, daughter, or surviving spouse of a victim of the September 11, 2001 terrorist attacks who died as a result of the attacks on the World Trade Center in New York City, the attack on the Pentagon in Virginia, or the crash of United Airlines Flight 93 in Pennsylvania; a POW/MIA of the Vietnam Conflict or his/her son or daughter; the son, daughter or surviving spouse (who has not remarried) of a state or local public safety employee or volunteer who died in the line of duty; or a state or local public safety employee or volunteer who was 100 percent disabled in the line of duty. Must be Maryland resident at time of disability. Submit applicable VA certification. Must be at least 16 years of age and attend Maryland institution. Deadline: July 30. *Award:* Scholarship for use in freshman, sophomore, junior, senior, or graduate year; renewable. *Award amount:* $7200–$8550. *Number of awards:* up to 70. *Eligibility Requirements:* Applicant must be age 16-24; enrolled or expecting to enroll full- or part-time at a two-year or four-year institution or university; resident of Maryland and studying in Maryland. Applicant or parent of applicant must have employment or volunteer experience in police/firefighting. Available to U.S. citizens. Applicant or parent must meet one or more of the following requirements: general military experience; retired from active duty; disabled or killed as a result of military service; prisoner of war; or missing in action. *Application Requirements:* Application, birth and death certificate, and disability papers. *Deadline:* July 30.

Contact Margaret Crutchley, Office of Student Financial Assistance, Maryland Higher Education Commission, 839 Bestgate Road, Suite 400, Annapolis, MD 21401-3013. *E-mail:* osfamail@mhec.state.md.us. *Phone:* 410-260-4545. *Fax:* 410-260-3203. *Web site:* www.mhec.state.md.us.

Graduate and Professional Scholarship Program-Maryland. Graduate and professional scholarships provide need-based financial assistance to students attending a Maryland school of medicine, dentistry, law, pharmacy, social work, or nursing. Funds are provided to specific Maryland colleges and universities. Students must demonstrate financial need and be Maryland residents. Contact institution financial aid office for more information. *Academic Fields/Career Goals:* Dental Health/Services; Health and Medical Sciences; Law/Legal Services; Nursing; Social Services. *Award:* Scholarship for use in freshman, sophomore, junior, senior, graduate, or postgraduate years; renewable. *Award amount:* $1000–$5000. *Number of awards:* 40–200. *Eligibility Requirements:* Applicant must be enrolled or expecting to enroll full- or part-time at a four-year institution or university; resident of Maryland and studying in Maryland. Available to U.S. citizens. *Application Requirements:* Application, financial need analysis, contact institution financial aid office. *Deadline:* March 1.

Contact Andrea E. Mansfield, Director, Maryland Higher Education Commission, 839 Bestgate Road, Suite 400, Annapolis, MD 21401-3013. *E-mail:* amansfie@mhec.state.md.us. *Phone:* 410-260-4558. *Fax:* 410-260-3202. *Web site:* www.mhec.state.md.us.

Guaranteed Access Grant-Maryland. Award for Maryland resident enrolling full-time in an undergraduate program at a Maryland institution. Must be under 21 at time of first award and begin college within one year of completing high school in Maryland with a minimum 2.5 GPA. Must have an annual family income less than 130 percent of the federal poverty level guideline. *Award:* Grant for use in freshman, sophomore, junior, or senior year; renewable. *Award amount:* $400–$14,300. *Number of awards:* up to 1000. *Eligibility Requirements:* Applicant must be age 21 or under; enrolled or expecting to enroll full-time at a two-year or four-year institution or university; resident of Maryland and studying in Maryland. Applicant must have 2.5 GPA or higher. Available to U.S. citizens. *Application Requirements:* Application, financial need analysis, transcript. *Deadline:* continuous.

Contact Theresa Lowe, Office of Student Financial Assistance, Maryland Higher Education Commission, 839 Bestgate Road, Suite 400, Annapolis, MD 21401-3013. *E-mail:* osfamail@mhec.state.md.us. *Phone:* 410-260-4555. *Fax:* 410-260-3200. *Web site:* www.mhec.state.md.us.

Janet L. Hoffmann Loan Assistance Repayment Program. Provides assistance for repayment of loan debt to Maryland residents working full-time in nonprofit organizations and state or local governments. Must submit Employment Verification Form and Lender Verification Form. *Academic Fields/Career Goals:* Education; Law/Legal Services; Nursing; Social Services; Therapy/

Rehabilitation. *Award:* Grant for use in freshman, sophomore, junior, senior, or graduate year; not renewable. *Award amount:* up to $10,000. *Number of awards:* up to 700. *Eligibility Requirements:* Applicant must be enrolled or expecting to enroll full-time at a four-year institution or university; resident of Maryland and studying in Maryland. Available to U.S. citizens. *Application Requirements:* Application, transcript, IRS 1040 form. *Deadline:* September 30.

Contact Tamika McKelvin, Office of Student Financial Assistance, Maryland Higher Education Commission, 839 Bestgate Road, Suite 400, Annapolis, MD 21401. *E-mail:* tmckelvil@mhec.state.md.us. *Phone:* 410-260-4546. *Fax:* 410-260-3203. *Web site:* www.mhec.state.md.us.

J.F. Tolbert Memorial Student Grant Program. Awards of up to $500 granted to Maryland residents attending a private career school in Maryland. The scholarship deadline continues. *Award:* Grant for use in freshman or sophomore year; not renewable. *Award amount:* up to $500. *Number of awards:* 400. *Eligibility Requirements:* Applicant must be enrolled or expecting to enroll full-time at a technical institution; resident of Maryland and studying in Maryland. Available to U.S. citizens. *Application Requirements:* Application, financial need analysis. *Deadline:* continuous.

Contact Glenda Hamlet, Office of Student Financial Assistance, Maryland Higher Education Commission, 839 Bestgate Road, Suite 400, Annapolis, MD 21401-3013. *E-mail:* osfamail@mhec.state.md.us. *Phone:* 800-974-1024. *Fax:* 410-260-3200. *Web site:* www.mhec.state.md.us.

Part-time Grant Program-Maryland. Funds provided to Maryland colleges and universities. Eligible students must be enrolled on a part-time basis (6 to 11 credits) in an undergraduate degree program. Must demonstrate financial need and also be Maryland resident. Contact financial aid office at institution for more information. *Award:* Grant for use in freshman, sophomore, junior, or senior year; renewable. *Award amount:* $200–$1500. *Number of awards:* 1800–9000. *Eligibility Requirements:* Applicant must be enrolled or expecting to enroll part-time at a two-year or four-year institution or university; resident of Maryland and studying in Maryland. Available to U.S. citizens. *Application Requirements:* Application, financial need analysis. *Deadline:* March 1.

Contact Andrea E. Mansfield, Director, Maryland Higher Education Commission, 839 Bestgate Road, Suite 400, Annapolis, MD 21401-3013. *E-mail:* amansfie@mhec.state.md.us. *Phone:* 410-260-4558. *Fax:* 410-260-3202. *Web site:* www.mhec.state.md.us.

Robert C. Byrd Honors Scholarship-Maryland. Scholarship amount changes each year, however, it has ranged from $1000 to $1500. Amount received by the students is based on the total cost of attendance at each institution of higher education. Awarded on merit basis. Students in the top 1 percent of the graduating class may be nominated by the principal or headmaster. Must be admitted to an institution of higher education as full-time students and be Maryland residents. *Award:* Scholarship for use in freshman year; not renewable. *Award amount:* $1000–$1500. *Number of awards:* varies. *Eligibility Requirements:* Applicant must be high school student; planning to enroll or expecting to enroll full-time at a four-year institution or university and resident of Maryland. Available to U.S. citizens. *Application Requirements:* Application. *Deadline:* varies.

Contact William Cappe, Scholarship Coordinator, Maryland State Department of Education, 200 West Baltimore Street, Baltimore, MD 21201. *E-mail:* wcappe@msde.state.md.us. *Phone:* 888-246-0016. *Web site:* www.msde.state.md.us.

Senatorial Scholarships-Maryland. Renewable award for Maryland residents attending a Maryland degree-granting institution, nursing diploma school, or certain private career schools. May be used out-of-state only if Maryland Higher Education Commission deems major to be unique and not offered at Maryland institution. The scholarship value is $200 to $2000. *Award:* Scholarship for use in freshman, sophomore, junior, senior, or graduate year; renewable. *Award amount:* $200–$2000. *Number of awards:* up to 7000. *Eligibility Requirements:* Applicant must be enrolled or expecting to enroll full- or part-time at a two-year, four-year, or technical institution or university; resident of Maryland and studying in Maryland. Available to U.S. citizens. *Application Requirements:* Financial need analysis, test scores, application to legislative district senator. *Deadline:* March 1.

Contact Office of Student Financial Assistance, Maryland Higher Education Commission, 839 Bestgate Road, Suite 400, Annapolis, MD 21401-3013. *E-mail:* osfamail@mhec.state.md.us. *Phone:* 800-974-1024. *Fax:* 410-260-3202. *Web site:* www.mhec.state.md.us.

Tuition Reduction for Non-Resident Nursing Students. Available to nonresidents of Maryland who attend a two-year or four-year public institution in Maryland. It is renewable provided student maintains academic requirements designated by institution attended. Recipient must agree to serve as a full-time nurse in a hospital or related institution for two to four years. *Academic Fields/Career Goals:* Nursing. *Award:* Scholarship for use in freshman, sophomore, junior, or senior year; renewable. *Award amount:* varies. *Number of awards:* varies. *Eligibility Requirements:* Applicant must be enrolled or expecting to enroll full- or part-time at a two-year or four-year institution and studying in Maryland. Available to U.S. citizens. *Application Requirements:* Application. *Deadline:* varies.

Contact Andrea E. Mansfield, Director, Maryland Higher Education Commission, 839 Bestgate Road, Suite 400, Annapolis, MD 21401-3013. *E-mail:* amansfie@mhec.state.md.us. *Phone:* 410-260-4558. *Fax:* 410-260-3202. *Web site:* www.mhec.state.md.us.

Tuition Waiver for Foster Care Recipients. Applicant must be a high school graduate or recipient of a GED under the age of 20. Applicant must either have resided in a foster care home in Maryland at time of high school graduation or GED reception, or until 14th birthday and had been adopted after 14th birthday. Applicant, if status approved, will be exempt from paying tuition and mandatory fees at a public college in Maryland. *Award:* Grant for use in freshman, sophomore, junior, senior, or graduate year; renewable. *Award amount:* varies. *Number of awards:* varies. *Eligibility Requirements:* Applicant must be age 20 or under; enrolled or expecting to enroll full- or part-time at a two-year or four-year institution or university; resident of Maryland and studying in Maryland. Available to U.S. citizens. *Application Requirements:* Application, financial need analysis, must inquire at financial aid office of schools. *Deadline:* March 1.

Contact Andrea E. Mansfield, Director, Maryland Higher Education Commission, 839 Bestgate Road, Suite 400, Annapolis, MD 21401-3013. *E-mail:* amansfie@mhec.state.md.us. *Phone:* 410-260-4558. *Fax:* 410-260-3202. *Web site:* www.mhec.state.md.us.

Veterans of the Afghanistan and Iraq Conflicts Scholarship Program. Provides financial assistance to Maryland resident U.S. Armed Forces personnel who served in Afghanistan or Iraq Conflicts and their children or spouses who are attending Maryland institutions. *Award:* Scholarship for use in freshman, sophomore, junior, or senior year; renewable. *Award amount:* $8850. *Number of awards:* 75. *Eligibility Requirements:* Applicant must be enrolled or expecting to enroll full- or part-time at a two-year or four-year institution; resident of Maryland and studying in Maryland.

Available to U.S. citizens. Applicant or parent must meet one or more of the following requirements: general military experience; retired from active duty; disabled or killed as a result of military service; prisoner of war; or missing in action. *Application Requirements:* Application, financial need analysis, birth certificate/marriage certificate, documentation of military order. *Deadline:* March 1.

Contact Andrea E. Mansfield, Director, Maryland Higher Education Commission, 839 Bestgate Road, Suite 400, Annapolis, MD 21401-3013. *E-mail:* amansfie@mhec.state.md.us. *Phone:* 410-260-4558. *Fax:* 410-260-3202. *Web site:* www.mhec.state.md.us.

Workforce Shortage Student Assistance Grant Program. Scholarship of $4000 available to students who will be required to major in specific areas and will be obligated to serve in the state of Maryland after completion of degree. June 1 is the deadline. *Award:* Scholarship for use in freshman, sophomore, junior, senior, or graduate year; renewable. *Award amount:* $4000. *Number of awards:* 1300. *Eligibility Requirements:* Applicant must be enrolled or expecting to enroll full- or part-time at a two-year or four-year institution or university; resident of Maryland and studying in Maryland. Available to U.S. citizens. *Application Requirements:* Application, financial need analysis, transcript, certain majors require additional documentation. *Deadline:* June 1.

Contact Andrea E. Mansfield, Director, Maryland Higher Education Commission, 839 Bestgate Road, Suite 400, Annapolis, MD 21401-3013. *E-mail:* amansfie@mhec.state.md.us. *Phone:* 410-260-4558. *Fax:* 410-260-3202. *Web site:* www.mhec.state.md.us.

MASSACHUSETTS

Agnes M. Lindsay Scholarship. Scholarships for students with demonstrated financial need who are from rural areas of Massachusetts and attend public institutions of higher education in Massachusetts. *Award:* Scholarship for use in freshman, sophomore, junior, or senior year; not renewable. *Award amount:* varies. *Number of awards:* varies. *Eligibility Requirements:* Applicant must be enrolled or expecting to enroll full-time at a two-year or four-year institution or university; resident of Massachusetts and studying in Massachusetts. Available to U.S. citizens. *Application Requirements:* Application, financial need analysis. *Deadline:* varies.

Contact Robert Brun, Director of Scholarships and Grants, Massachusetts Office of Student Financial Assistance, 454 Broadway, Suite 200, Revere, MA 02151. *E-mail:* osfa@osfa.mass.edu. *Phone:* 617-727-9420. *Fax:* 617-727-0667. *Web site:* www.osfa.mass.edu.

Christian A. Herter Memorial Scholarship. Renewable award for Massachusetts residents, who are in the tenth and eleventh grades, and whose socio-economic backgrounds and environment may inhibit their ability to attain educational goals. Must exhibit severe personal or family-related difficulties, medical problems, or have overcome a personal obstacle. Provides up to 50 percent of the student's calculated need, as determined by Federal methodology, at the college of their choice within the continental United States. *Award:* Scholarship for use in freshman, sophomore, junior, or senior year; renewable. *Award amount:* up to $15,000. *Number of awards:* 25. *Eligibility Requirements:* Applicant must be high school student; planning to enroll or expecting to enroll full-time at a two-year, four-year, or technical institution or university and resident of Massachusetts. Applicant must be physically disabled. Applicant must have 2.5 GPA or higher. Available to U.S. citizens. *Application Requirements:* Application, autobiography, financial need analysis, interview, references. *Deadline:* varies.

Contact Robert Brun, Director of Scholarships and Grants, Massachusetts Office of Student Financial Assistance, 454 Broadway, Suite 200, Revere, MA 02151. *E-mail:* osfa@osfa.mass.edu. *Phone:* 617-727-9420. *Fax:* 617-727-0667. *Web site:* www.osfa.mass.edu.

Department of Education Scholarship for Programs in China. Scholarships offered to students who are pursuing Chinese language programs in China. Must be a U.S. citizen enrolled in a CIEE program. Students must have the equivalent of two years study in Chinese language documented. Deadlines: April 1 and November 1. For more details see Web site: http://www.ciee.org/study/scholarships.aspx#china. *Academic Fields/Career Goals:* Education. *Award:* Scholarship for use in junior, senior, or graduate year; not renewable. *Award amount:* varies. *Number of awards:* varies. *Eligibility Requirements:* Applicant must be enrolled or expecting to enroll full-time at a four-year institution or university and must have an interest in foreign language. Applicant must have 3.0 GPA or higher. Available to U.S. citizens. *Application Requirements:* Application, essay, financial need analysis, references, transcript. *Deadline:* varies.

Contact Scholarship Committee, Council for International Educational Exchange, Three Copley Place, Second Floor, Boston, MA 02116. *E-mail:* scholarships@ciee.org. *Phone:* 800-407-8839. *Fax:* 617-247-2911. *Web site:* www.ciee.org/study.

Early Childhood Educators Scholarship Program. Scholarship to provide financial assistance for currently employed early childhood educators and providers who enroll in an associate or bachelor degree program in Early Childhood Education or related programs. Awards are not based on financial need. Individuals taking their first college-level ECE course are eligible for 100 percent tuition, while subsequent ECE courses are awarded at 50 percent tuition. Can be used for one class each semester. *Academic Fields/Career Goals:* Education. *Award:* Scholarship for use in freshman, sophomore, junior, or senior year; not renewable. *Award amount:* $200–$4050. *Number of awards:* varies. *Eligibility Requirements:* Applicant must be enrolled or expecting to enroll full- or part-time at a four-year institution or university. Available to U.S. citizens. *Application Requirements:* Application. *Deadline:* varies.

Contact Robert Brun, Director of Scholarships and Grants, Massachusetts Office of Student Financial Assistance, 454 Broadway, Suite 200, Revere, MA 02151. *E-mail:* osfa@osfa.mass.edu. *Phone:* 617-727-9420. *Fax:* 617-727-0667. *Web site:* www.osfa.mass.edu.

Hemophilia Federation of America. One-time scholarship for persons with hemophilia, attending either full-time or part-time in any accredited two- or four-year college, university, or vocation/technical school in the United States. Scholarship value is $1500. Deadline: April 1. *Award:* Scholarship for use in freshman, sophomore, junior, or senior year; not renewable. *Award amount:* $1500. *Number of awards:* 1–3. *Eligibility Requirements:* Applicant must be enrolled or expecting to enroll full- or part-time at a two-year, four-year, or technical institution or university. Applicant must be physically disabled. Available to U.S. citizens. *Application Requirements:* Application. *Deadline:* April 1.

Contact Sandy Aultman, Hemophilia Federation of America, LA Kelley Communications, 1045 West Pinhook Road, Suite 101, Lafayette, LA 70503. *Phone:* 337-261-9787. *Fax:* 337-261-1787. *Web site:* www.kelleycom.com.

John and Abigail Adams Scholarship. Scholarship to reward and inspire student achievement, attract more high-performing students to Massachusetts public higher education, and provide families of college-bound students with financial assistance. Must be a U.S. citizen or an eligible non-citizen. There is no application process for the scholarship. Students who are eligible will be notified in the fall of their senior year in high school. *Award:* Scholarship for use in freshman year; not renewable. *Award amount:* varies. *Number of awards:* varies. *Eligibility Requirements:* Applicant must be high school student; planning to enroll or expecting to enroll full-time at a two-year or four-year institution or university; resident of Massachusetts and studying in Massachusetts. Applicant must have 3.0 GPA or higher. Available to U.S. citizens. *Application Requirements: Deadline:* varies.

Contact Robert Brun, Director of Scholarships and Grants, Massachusetts Office of Student Financial Assistance, 454 Broadway, Suite 200, Revere, MA 02151. *E-mail:* osfa@osfa.mass.edu. *Phone:* 617-727-9420. *Fax:* 617-727-0667. *Web site:* www.osfa.mass.edu.

Massachusetts Assistance for Student Success Program. The program provides need-based financial assistance to Massachusetts residents to attend undergraduate postsecondary institutions in Connecticut, Maine, Massachusetts, New Hampshire, Pennsylvania, Rhode Island, Vermont, and District of Columbia. High school seniors may apply. Expected Family Contribution (EFC) should be between 0 to $3850. Timely filing of FAFSA required. *Award:* Grant for use in freshman, sophomore, junior, or senior year; not renewable. *Award amount:* $300–$2400. *Number of awards:* 25,000–30,000. *Eligibility Requirements:* Applicant must be enrolled or expecting to enroll full-time at a two-year, four-year, or technical institution or university; resident of Massachusetts and studying in Connecticut, District of Columbia, Maine, Massachusetts, New Hampshire, Pennsylvania, Rhode Island, or Vermont. Available to U.S. citizens. *Application Requirements:* Financial need analysis, FAFSA. *Deadline:* May 1.

Contact Robert Brun, Director of Scholarships and Grants, Massachusetts Office of Student Financial Assistance, 454 Broadway, Suite 200, Revere, MA 02151. *E-mail:* osfa@osfa.mass.edu. *Phone:* 617-727-9420. *Fax:* 617-727-0667. *Web site:* www.osfa.mass.edu.

Massachusetts Cash Grant Program. A need-based grant to assist with mandatory fees and non-state supported tuition. This supplemental award is available to Massachusetts residents, who are undergraduates at public two-year, four-year colleges and universities in Massachusetts. Must file FAFSA before May 1. Contact college financial aid office for information. *Award:* Grant for use in freshman, sophomore, junior, or senior year; not renewable. *Award amount:* varies. *Number of awards:* varies. *Eligibility Requirements:* Applicant must be enrolled or expecting to enroll full-time at a two-year or four-year institution or university and resident of Massachusetts. Available to U.S. citizens. *Application Requirements:* Application, financial need analysis, FAFSA. *Deadline:* continuous.

Contact Robert Brun, Director of Scholarships and Grants, Massachusetts Office of Student Financial Assistance, 454 Broadway, Suite 200, Revere, MA 02151. *E-mail:* osfa@osfa.mass.edu. *Phone:* 617-727-9420. *Fax:* 617-727-0667. *Web site:* www.osfa.mass.edu.

Massachusetts Gilbert Matching Student Grant Program. Must be permanent Massachusetts resident for at least one year and attending an independent, regionally accredited Massachusetts school or school of nursing full time. File the Free Application for Federal Student Aid after January 1. Contact college financial aid office for complete details and deadlines. *Award:* Grant for use in freshman, sophomore, junior, or senior year; not renewable. *Award amount:* $200–$2500. *Number of awards:* varies. *Eligibility Requirements:* Applicant must be enrolled or expecting to enroll full-time at a four-year institution or university; resident of Massachusetts and studying in Massachusetts. Available to U.S. citizens. *Application Requirements:* Financial need analysis, FAFSA. *Deadline:* varies.

Contact Robert Brun, Director of Scholarships and Grants, Massachusetts Office of Student Financial Assistance, Director of Scholarships and Grants, Revere, MA 02151. *E-mail:* rbrun@osfa.mass.edu. *Phone:* 617-727-9420. *Fax:* 617-727-0667. *Web site:* www.osfa.mass.edu.

Massachusetts Part-time Grant Program. Award for permanent Massachusetts residents who have enrolled part-time for at least one year in a state-approved postsecondary school. First the recipient must not have a bachelor's degree. FAFSA must be filed before May 1. Contact college financial aid office for further information. *Award:* Grant for use in freshman, sophomore, junior, or senior year; not renewable. *Award amount:* $200–$1150. *Number of awards:* 200. *Eligibility Requirements:* Applicant must be enrolled or expecting to enroll part-time at a two-year, four-year, or technical institution or university and resident of Massachusetts. Available to U.S. citizens. *Application Requirements:* Application, financial need analysis, FAFSA. *Deadline:* varies.

Contact Robert Brun, Director of Scholarships and Grants, Massachusetts Office of Student Financial Assistance, 454 Broadway, Suite 200, Revere, MA 02151. *E-mail:* osfa@osfa.mass.edu. *Phone:* 617-727-9420. *Fax:* 617-727-0667. *Web site:* www.osfa.mass.edu.

Massachusetts Public Service Grant Program. Scholarships for children and/or spouses of deceased members of fire, police, and corrections departments, who were killed in the line of duty. Awards Massachusetts residents attending Massachusetts institutions. Applicant should have not received a prior bachelor's degree or its equivalent. *Award:* Grant for use in freshman, sophomore, junior, or senior year; not renewable. *Award amount:* varies. *Number of awards:* varies. *Eligibility Requirements:* Applicant must be enrolled or expecting to enroll full-time at a four-year institution or university and resident of Massachusetts. Applicant or parent of applicant must have employment or volunteer experience in police/firefighting. Available to U.S. and non-U.S. citizens. Applicant must have general military experience. *Application Requirements:* Application, financial need analysis, copy of birth certificate, copy of veteran's death certificate, proof that death was service-related. *Deadline:* May 1.

Contact Alison Leary, Director of Scholarships and Grants, Massachusetts Office of Student Financial Assistance, 454 Broadway, Suite 200, Revere, MA 02151. *E-mail:* osfa@osfa.mass.edu. *Phone:* 617-727-9420. *Fax:* 617-727-0667. *Web site:* www.osfa.mass.edu.

New England Regional Student Program. Scholarship for residents of New England. Students pay reduced out-of-state tuition at public colleges or universities in other New England states when enrolling in certain majors not offered at public institutions in home state. Deadline: college application deadline. *Award:* Scholarship for use in freshman, sophomore, junior, senior, or graduate year; renewable. *Award amount:* varies. *Number of awards:* varies. *Eligibility Requirements:* Applicant must be enrolled or expecting to enroll full- or part-time at a two-year or four-year institution or university and resident of Connecticut, Maine, Massachusetts, New Hampshire, Rhode Island, or Vermont. Available to U.S. citizens. *Application Requirements:* College application. *Deadline:* continuous.

Contact Wendy Lindsay, Senior Director of Regional Student Program, New England Board of Higher Education, 45 Temple Place, Boston, MA 02111-1305. *E-mail:* tuitionbreak@nebhe.org. *Phone:* 617-357-9620 Ext. 111. *Fax:* 617-338-1577. *Web site:* www.nebhe.org.

Paraprofessional Teacher Preparation Grant. Grant providing financial aid assistance to Massachusetts residents, who are currently employed as paraprofessionals in Massachusetts public schools and wish to obtain higher education and become certified as full-time teachers. *Academic Fields/Career Goals:* Education. *Award:* Grant for use in freshman, sophomore, junior, or senior year; not renewable. *Award amount:* $250–$7500. *Number of awards:* varies. *Eligibility Requirements:* Applicant must be enrolled or expecting to enroll full- or part-time at a two-year or four-year institution or university and resident of Massachusetts. Available to U.S. citizens. *Application Requirements:* Application, written proof of employment as a paraprofessional, FAFSA. *Deadline:* September 15.

Contact Robert Brun, Director of Scholarships and Grants, Massachusetts Office of Student Financial Assistance, 454 Broadway, Suite 200, Revere, MA 02151. *E-mail:* osfa@osfa.mass.edu. *Phone:* 617-727-9420. *Fax:* 617-727-0667. *Web site:* www.osfa.mass.edu.

Tuition Waiver (General)-Massachusetts. Need-based tuition waiver for full-time students. Must attend a Massachusetts public institution of higher education and be a permanent Massachusetts resident. File the FAFSA after January 1. Award is for undergraduate study. Contact school financial aid office for more information. *Award:* Scholarship for use in freshman, sophomore, junior, or senior year; renewable. *Award amount:* varies. *Number of awards:* varies. *Eligibility Requirements:* Applicant must be age 24 or under; enrolled or expecting to enroll full-time at a two-year or four-year institution and resident of Massachusetts. Available to U.S. and non-Canadian citizens. *Application Requirements:* Application, financial need analysis, FAFSA. *Deadline:* varies.

Contact Robert Brun, Director of Scholarships and Grants, Massachusetts Office of Student Financial Assistance, 454 Broadway, Suite 200, Revere, MA 02151. *E-mail:* osfa@osfa.mass.edu. *Phone:* 617-727-9420. *Fax:* 617-727-0667. *Web site:* www.osfa.mass.edu.

MICHIGAN

Children of Veterans Tuition Grant. Awards available for students who are children of a disabled or deceased Michigan veteran. Must be enrolled at least half-time in a degree-granting Michigan public or private nonprofit institution. Must be a U.S. citizen or permanent resident and must be residing in Michigan. *Award:* Grant for use in freshman, sophomore, junior, or senior year; renewable. *Award amount:* up to $2800. *Number of awards:* varies. *Eligibility Requirements:* Applicant must be age 17-25; enrolled or expecting to enroll part-time at a two-year or four-year institution or university; resident of Michigan and studying in Michigan. Available to U.S. citizens. Applicant or parent must meet one or more of the following requirements: general military experience; retired from active duty; disabled or killed as a result of military service; prisoner of war; or missing in action. *Application Requirements:* Application. *Deadline:* varies.

Contact Program Director, Michigan Bureau of Student Financial Assistance, PO Box 30462, Lansing, MI 48909-7962. *E-mail:* osg@michigan.gov. *Phone:* 888-447-2687. *Web site:* www.michigan.gov/studentaid.

Michigan Adult Part-Time Grant. Grant is intended for financially needy, independent undergraduates who have been out of high school for at least two years. Must be Michigan resident. Deadlines determined by college. *Award:* Grant for use in freshman, sophomore, junior, or senior year; renewable. *Award amount:* up to $600. *Number of awards:* varies. *Eligibility Requirements:* Applicant must be enrolled or expecting to enroll part-time at a two-year or four-year institution or university; resident of Michigan and studying in Michigan. Available to U.S. citizens. *Application Requirements:* Financial need analysis. *Deadline:* varies.

Contact Program Director, Michigan Bureau of Student Financial Assistance, PO Box 30462, Lansing, MI 48909-7962. *E-mail:* osg@michigan.gov. *Phone:* 888-447-2687. *Web site:* www.michigan.gov/studentaid.

Michigan Competitive Scholarship. Renewable award of $1300 for undergraduate study at a Michigan institution. Awards limited to tuition. Must maintain a C average and meet the college's academic progress requirements. Must file Free Application for Federal Student Aid. Deadline: March 1. Must be Michigan resident. *Award:* Scholarship for use in freshman, sophomore, junior, or senior year; renewable. *Award amount:* $100–$1300. *Number of awards:* varies. *Eligibility Requirements:* Applicant must be enrolled or expecting to enroll full- or part-time at a two-year or four-year institution or university; resident of Michigan and studying in Michigan. Available to U.S. citizens. *Application Requirements:* Application, financial need analysis, test scores, FAFSA. *Deadline:* March 1.

Contact Scholarship and Grant Director, Michigan Bureau of Student Financial Assistance, PO Box 30466, Lansing, MI 48909-7962. *E-mail:* osg@michigan.gov. *Phone:* 888-447-2687. *Web site:* www.michigan.gov/studentaid.

Michigan Educational Opportunity Grant. Need-based program for Michigan residents who are at least half-time undergraduates attending public Michigan colleges. Must maintain good academic standing. Deadline determined by college. Award of up to $1000. *Award:* Grant for use in freshman, sophomore, junior, or senior year; renewable. *Award amount:* up to $1000. *Number of awards:* varies. *Eligibility Requirements:* Applicant must be enrolled or expecting to enroll full- or part-time at an institution or university; resident of Michigan and studying in Michigan. Available to U.S. citizens. *Application Requirements:* Financial need analysis. *Deadline:* varies.

Contact Program Director, Michigan Bureau of Student Financial Assistance, PO Box 30462, Lansing, MI 48909-7962. *E-mail:* osg@michigan.gov. *Phone:* 888-447-2687. *Web site:* www.michigan.gov/studentaid.

Michigan Indian Tuition Waiver. Renewable award provides free tuition for Native-American of 1/4 or more blood degree who attend a Michigan public college or university. Must be a Michigan resident for at least one year. The tuition waiver program covers full-time, part-time or summer school student attending a public, state, community, junior college, public college, or public university. Deadline: continuous. *Award:* Scholarship for use in freshman, sophomore, junior, senior, graduate, or postgraduate years; renewable. *Award amount:* varies. *Number of awards:* varies. *Eligibility Requirements:* Applicant must be American Indian/Alaska Native; enrolled or expecting to enroll full- or part-time at a two-year, four-year, or technical institution or university; resident of Michigan and studying in Michigan. Available to U.S. citizens. *Application Requirements:* Application, driver's license, transcript, tribal certification, proof of residency. *Deadline:* continuous.

Contact Christin McKerchie, Executive Assistant to Programs, Inter-Tribal Council of Michigan Inc., 2956 Ashmun Street, Suite A, Sault Ste. Marie, MI 49783. *Phone:* 906-632-6896 Ext. 136. *Fax:* 906-632-6878. *Web site:* www.itcmi.org.

Michigan Merit Award. Scholarship for students scoring well on state's standardized assessment tests. Students will have four years from high school graduation to use the award. *Award:* Scholarship for use in freshman, sophomore, junior, or senior year; not renewable. *Award amount:* $1000–$2500. *Number of awards:* varies. *Eligibility Requirements:* Applicant must be enrolled or expecting to enroll full- or part-time at a two-year, four-year, or technical institution or university and resident of Michigan. Available to U.S. citizens. *Application Requirements:* Test scores. *Deadline:* varies.

Contact Program Director, Michigan Bureau of Student Financial Assistance, PO Box 30466, Lansing, MI 48909-7962. *E-mail:* osg@michigan.gov. *Phone:* 888-447-2687. *Web site:* www.michigan.gov/studentaid.

Michigan Nursing Scholarship. Scholarship for students enrolled in an LPN, associate degree in nursing, bachelor of science in nursing, or master of science in nursing programs. Colleges determine application procedure and select recipients. Recipients must fulfill in-state work commitment or repay scholarship. *Academic Fields/Career Goals:* Nursing. *Award:* Scholarship for use in freshman, sophomore, junior, senior, or graduate year; renewable. *Award amount:* up to $4000. *Number of awards:* varies. *Eligibility Requirements:* Applicant must be enrolled or expecting to enroll full- or part-time at a two-year or four-year institution or university; resident of Michigan and studying in Michigan. Available to U.S. citizens. *Application Requirements: Deadline:* varies.

Contact Program Director, Michigan Bureau of Student Financial Assistance, PO Box 30462, Lansing, MI 48909-7962. *E-mail:* osg@michigan.gov. *Phone:* 888-447-2687. *Web site:* www.michigan.gov/studentaid.

Michigan Promise Scholarship. Scholarship available for students who have taken the state's assessment test. Students who meet or exceed state assessment test may receive $1000 during each of their first two years of college and another $2000 after completing two years with at least a 2.5 GPA. Students who do not meet or exceed state assessment test may receive $4000 after completing two years of postsecondary study with at least a 2.5 GPA. Must be a Michigan resident enrolled at an approved Michigan postsecondary institution. *Award:* Scholarship for use in freshman, sophomore, or junior year; not renewable. *Award amount:* up to $4000. *Number of awards:* varies. *Eligibility Requirements:* Applicant must be enrolled or expecting to enroll full- or part-time at a two-year, four-year, or technical institution or university; resident of Michigan and studying in Michigan. Available to U.S. citizens. *Application Requirements:* Test scores. *Deadline:* varies.

Contact Program Director, Michigan Bureau of Student Financial Assistance, PO Box 30462, Lansing, MI 48909-7962. *E-mail:* osg@michigan.gov. *Phone:* 888-447-2687. *Web site:* www.michigan.gov/studentaid.

Michigan Tuition Grant. Need-based program. Students must attend a Michigan private, nonprofit, degree-granting college. Must file the Free Application for Federal Student Aid and meet the college's academic progress requirements. Deadline: March 1. Must be Michigan resident. Renewable award of $2100. *Award:* Grant for use in freshman, sophomore, junior, senior, or graduate year; renewable. *Award amount:* $100–$2100. *Number of awards:* varies. *Eligibility Requirements:* Applicant must be enrolled or expecting to enroll full- or part-time at a two-year or four-year institution or university; resident of Michigan and studying in Michigan. Available to U.S. citizens. *Application Requirements:* Financial need analysis, FAFSA. *Deadline:* March 1.

Contact Scholarship and Grant Director, Michigan Bureau of Student Financial Assistance, PO Box 30462, Lansing, MI 48909-7962. *E-mail:* osg@michigan.gov. *Phone:* 888-447-2687. *Web site:* www.michigan.gov/studentaid.

Michigan Veterans Trust Fund Tuition Grant Program. Provides grants for the emergency needs of veterans, tuition grants to dependents of disabled and deceased veterans, and emergency education loans to veterans and their children. Tuition grants are available to sons and daughters of totally disabled or deceased service-connected veterans attending Michigan institutions of higher education. Refer to Web Site: http://www.michigan.gov/textonly/0,2964,7-153-10366_10871-44121—,00.html for details. *Award:* Grant for use in freshman, sophomore, junior, or senior year; renewable. *Award amount:* up to $2800. *Number of awards:* varies. *Eligibility Requirements:* Applicant must be age 17-25; enrolled or expecting to enroll full-time at a two-year, four-year, or technical institution or university; resident of Michigan and studying in Michigan. Available to U.S. citizens. Applicant or parent must meet one or more of the following requirements: general military experience; retired from active duty; disabled or killed as a result of military service; prisoner of war; or missing in action. *Application Requirements:* Application. *Deadline:* continuous.

Contact Mary Kay Bitten, Scholarship Committee, Michigan Veterans Trust Fund, 3423 North, Martin Luther King Jr. Boulevard, Lansing, MI 48909-7962. *Phone:* 517-335-1636. *Fax:* 517-335-1631. *Web site:* www.michigan.gov/dmva.

Tuition Incentive Program (TIP). Award for Michigan residents who receive or have received Medicaid for required period of time through the Department of Human Services. Scholarship provides two years tuition towards an associate degree at a Michigan college or university and $2000 total assistance for third and fourth years. Must apply before graduating from high school or earning a general education development diploma. *Award:* Grant for use in freshman, sophomore, junior, or senior year; renewable. *Award amount:* varies. *Number of awards:* varies. *Eligibility Requirements:* Applicant must be enrolled or expecting to enroll full- or part-time at a two-year or four-year institution or university; resident of Michigan and studying in Michigan. Available to U.S. citizens. *Application Requirements:* Application, Medicaid eligibility for specified period of time. *Deadline:* continuous.

Contact Program Director, Michigan Bureau of Student Financial Assistance, PO Box 30462, Lansing, MI 48909-7962. *E-mail:* osg@michigan.gov. *Phone:* 888-447-2687. *Web site:* www.michigan.gov/studentaid.

MINNESOTA

Leadership, Excellence and Dedicated Service Scholarship. Scholarship will award a maximum of thirty $1000 to selected high school seniors who become a member of the Minnesota National Guard and complete the application process. The award recognizes demonstrated leadership, community services and potential for success in the Minnesota National Guard. Deadline: March 15. *Award:* Scholarship for use in freshman year; not renewable. *Award amount:* $1000. *Number of awards:* 30. *Eligibility Requirements:* Applicant must be high school student; planning to enroll or expecting to enroll full- or part-time at a two-year, four-year, or technical institution or university and must have an interest in leadership. Applicant or parent of applicant must have employment or volunteer experience in community service. Available to U.S. citizens. Applicant must have served in the Air Force National Guard or Army National Guard. *Application Requirements:* Essay, resume, references, transcript. *Deadline:* March 15.

Contact Barbara O'Reilly, Education Services Officer, Minnesota Department of Military Affairs, 20 West 12th Street, Veterans Services Building, St. Paul, MN 55155-2098. *E-mail:* barbara.oreilly@mn.ngb.army.mil. *Phone:* 651-282-4508. *Web site:* www.minnesotanationalguard.org.

Minnesota Indian Scholarship Program. Applicant must be one quarter Native-American and a resident of Minnesota. Must re-apply for scholarship annually. *Award:* Scholarship for use in freshman, sophomore, junior, senior, or graduate year; renewable. *Award amount:* $3300–$4000. *Number of awards:* 6–700. *Eligibility Requirements:* Applicant must be American Indian/Alaska Native; enrolled or expecting to enroll full-time at a two-year, four-year, or technical institution or university; resident of Minnesota and studying in Minnesota. Available to U.S. citizens. *Application Requirements:* Application, financial need analysis. *Deadline:* July 1.

Contact Yvonne Novack, Director, Minnesota Indian Scholarship Office, 1500 Highway 36W, Roseville, MN 55113-4266. *E-mail:* cfl.indianeducation@state.mn.us. *Phone:* 800-657-3927. *Web site:* www.mheso.state.mn.us.

Minnesota Reciprocal Agreement. Renewable tuition waiver for Minnesota residents. Waives all or part of non-resident tuition surcharge at public institutions in Iowa, Kansas, Michigan, Missouri, Nebraska, North Dakota, South Dakota, and Wisconsin. Deadline: last day of academic term. *Award:* Scholarship for use in freshman, sophomore, junior, senior, graduate, or postgraduate years; renewable. *Award amount:* varies. *Number of awards:* varies. *Eligibility Requirements:* Applicant must be enrolled or expecting to enroll full- or part-time at a two-year, four-year, or technical institution or university; resident of Minnesota and studying in Iowa, Kansas, Michigan, Missouri, Nebraska, North Dakota, South Dakota, or Wisconsin. Available to U.S. citizens. *Application Requirements:* Application. *Deadline:* varies.

Contact Ginny Dodds, Manager, Minnesota Higher Education Services Office, 1450 Energy Park Drive, Suite 350, St. Paul, MN 55108-5227. *Phone:* 651-642-0567 Ext. 1. *Web site:* www.getreadyforcollege.org.

Minnesota State Grant Program. Need-based grant program available for Minnesota residents attending Minnesota colleges. Student covers 46% of cost with remainder covered by Pell Grant, parent contribution and state grant. Students apply with FAFSA and college administers the program on campus. *Award:* Grant for use in freshman, sophomore, junior, or senior year; not renewable. *Award amount:* $100–$8372. *Number of awards:* 71,000–75,000. *Eligibility Requirements:* Applicant must be age 17 and over; enrolled or expecting to enroll full- or part-time at a two-year, four-year, or technical institution or university; resident of Minnesota and studying in Minnesota. Available to U.S. citizens. *Application Requirements:* Application, financial need analysis. *Deadline:* varies.

Contact Scholarship Committee, Minnesota Higher Education Services Office, 1450 Energy Park Drive, Suite 350, St. Paul, MN 55108. *Phone:* 651-642-0567. *Web site:* www.getreadyforcollege.org.

Minnesota State Veterans' Dependents Assistance Program. Tuition assistance to dependents of persons considered to be prisoner-of-war or missing in action after August 1, 1958. Must be Minnesota resident attending Minnesota two- or four-year school. *Award:* Scholarship for use in freshman, sophomore, junior, or senior year; renewable. *Award amount:* varies. *Number of awards:* varies. *Eligibility Requirements:* Applicant must be enrolled or expecting to enroll full- or part-time at a two-year or four-year institution; resident of Minnesota and studying in Minnesota. Available to U.S. citizens. Applicant or parent must meet one or more of the following requirements: general military experience; retired from active duty; disabled or killed as a result of military service; prisoner of war; or missing in action. *Application Requirements:* Application. *Deadline:* continuous.

Contact Ginny Dodds, Manager, Minnesota Higher Education Services Office, 1450 Energy Park Drive, Suite 350, Saint Paul, MN 55108-5227. *E-mail:* ginny.dodds@state.mn.us. *Phone:* 651-642-0567 Ext. 3410. *Fax:* 651-642-0675. *Web site:* www.getreadyforcollege.org.

Postsecondary Child Care Grant Program-Minnesota. Grant available for students not receiving MFIP. Based on financial need. Cannot exceed actual child care costs or maximum award chart (based on income). Must be Minnesota resident. For use at Minnesota two- or four-year school, including public technical colleges. *Award:* Grant for use in freshman, sophomore, junior, or senior year; renewable. *Award amount:* $100–$2300. *Number of awards:* varies. *Eligibility Requirements:* Applicant must be enrolled or expecting to enroll full- or part-time at a two-year, four-year, or technical institution or university; resident of Minnesota and studying in Minnesota. Available to U.S. citizens. *Application Requirements:* Application, financial need analysis. *Deadline:* continuous.

Contact Ginny Dodds, Manager, Minnesota Higher Education Services Office, 1450 Energy Park Drive, Suite 350, St. Paul, MN 55108-5227. *Phone:* 651-642-0567 Ext. 3410. *Fax:* 651-642-0675. *Web site:* www.getreadyforcollege.org.

Safety Officers' Survivor Grant Program. Grant for eligible survivors of Minnesota public safety officers killed in the line of duty. Safety officers who have been permanently or totally disabled in the line of duty are also eligible. Must be used at a Minnesota institution participating in State Grant Program. Write for details. Must submit proof of death or disability and Public Safety Officers Benefit Fund Certificate. Must apply each year. Can be renewed for four years. *Award:* Grant for use in freshman, sophomore, junior, or senior year; renewable. *Award amount:* up to $9438. *Number of awards:* 1. *Eligibility Requirements:* Applicant must be age 23 or under; enrolled or expecting to enroll full- or part-time at a two-year, four-year, or technical institution or university; resident of Minnesota and studying in Minnesota. Applicant or parent of applicant must have employment or volunteer experience in police/firefighting. Available to U.S. citizens. *Application Requirements:* Application, proof of death/disability. *Deadline:* continuous.

Contact Ginny Dodds, Manager, Minnesota Higher Education Services Office, 1450 Energy Park Drive, Suite 350, St. Paul, MN 55108-5227. *Phone:* 651-642-0567 Ext. 1. *Web site:* www.getreadyforcollege.org.

MISSISSIPPI

Critical Needs Teacher Loan/Scholarship. Eligible applicants will agree to employment immediately upon degree completion as a full-time classroom teacher in a public school located in a critical teacher shortage area in the state of Mississippi. Must verify the intention to pursue a first bachelor's degree in teacher education. Award covers tuition and required fees, average cost of room and meals plus allowance for books. Must be enrolled at a Mississippi college or university. *Academic Fields/Career Goals:* Education; Psychology; Therapy/Rehabilitation. *Award:* Forgivable loan for use in junior or senior year; not renewable. *Award amount:* varies. *Number of awards:* varies. *Eligibility Requirements:* Applicant must be enrolled or expecting to enroll full- or part-time at a four-year institution or university and studying in Mississippi. Applicant must have 2.5 GPA or higher. Available to U.S. and non-U.S. citizens. *Application Requirements:* Application, test scores, transcript. *Deadline:* March 31.

Contact Mary J. Covington, Mississippi Student Financial Aid, Mississippi State Student Financial Aid, 3825 Ridgewood Road, Jackson, MS 39211-6453. *E-mail:* sfa@ihl.state.ms.us. *Phone:* 800-327-2980. *Web site:* www.ihl.state.ms.us.

Gulf Coast Research Laboratory Minority Summer Grant. Grants to minority freshmen, sophomore, junior, or senior student at a Mississippi college or university majoring in marine and environmental sciences. Provide tuition and stipend. Deadline: March 31. *Academic Fields/Career Goals:* Environmental Science; Marine Biology. *Award:* Grant for use in freshman, sophomore, junior, or senior year; renewable. *Award amount:* varies. *Number* *of awards:* varies. *Eligibility Requirements:* Applicant must be enrolled or expecting to enroll full-time at a four-year institution or university; resident of Mississippi and studying in Mississippi. Available to U.S. citizens. *Application Requirements:* Application, transcript. *Deadline:* March 31.

Contact Mary J. Covington, Mississippi Student Financial Aid, Mississippi State Student Financial Aid, 3825 Ridgewood Road, Jackson, MS 39211-6453. *E-mail:* sfa@ihl.state.ms.us. *Phone:* 800-327-2980. *Web site:* www.ihl.state.ms.us.

Higher Education Legislative Plan (HELP). Eligible applicant must be resident of Mississippi and be freshman and/or sophomore student who graduated from high school within the immediate past two years. Must demonstrate need as determined by the results of the Free Application for Federal Student Aid, documenting an average family adjusted gross income of $36,500 or less over the prior two years. Must be enrolled full-time at a Mississippi college or university, have a GPA of 2.5 and have scored 20 on the ACT. *Award:* Scholarship for use in freshman or sophomore year; renewable. *Award amount:* varies. *Number of awards:* varies. *Eligibility Requirements:* Applicant must be enrolled or expecting to enroll full-time at a four-year institution or university; resident of Mississippi and studying in Mississippi. Applicant must have 2.5 GPA or higher. Available to U.S. citizens. *Application Requirements:* Application, financial need analysis, test scores, transcript, FAFSA. *Deadline:* March 31.

Contact Mary J. Covington, Mississippi Student Financial Aid, Mississippi State Student Financial Aid, 3825 Ridgewood Road, Jackson, MS 39211-6453. *E-mail:* sfa@ihl.state.ms.us. *Phone:* 800-327-2980. *Web site:* www.ihl.state.ms.us.

Mississippi Eminent Scholars Grant. Award for high-school seniors who are residents of Mississippi. Applicants must achieve a GPA of 3.5 and must have scored 29 on the ACT. Must enroll full-time at an eligible Mississippi college or university. *Award:* Grant for use in freshman, sophomore, junior, or senior year; renewable. *Award amount:* up to $2500. *Number of awards:* varies. *Eligibility Requirements:* Applicant must be enrolled or expecting to enroll full-time at a two-year or four-year institution or university; resident of Mississippi and studying in Mississippi. Applicant must have 3.5 GPA or higher. Available to U.S. citizens. *Application Requirements:* Application, test scores, transcript. *Deadline:* September 15.

Contact Mary J. Covington, Mississippi Student Financial Aid, Mississippi State Student Financial Aid, 3825 Ridgewood Road, Jackson, MS 39211-6453. *E-mail:* sfa@ihl.state.ms.us. *Phone:* 800-327-2980. *Web site:* www.ihl.state.ms.us.

Mississippi Health Care Professions Loan/Scholarship Program. Renewable award for junior and senior undergraduates studying psychology, speech pathology or occupational therapy. Must be Mississippi residents attending four-year universities in Mississippi. Must fulfill work obligation in Mississippi or pay back as loan. Renewable award for graduate student enrolled in physical therapy. *Academic Fields/Career Goals:* Health and Medical Sciences; Psychology; Therapy/Rehabilitation. *Award:* Forgivable loan for use in junior, senior, or graduate year; renewable. *Award amount:* $1500–$6000. *Number of awards:* varies. *Eligibility Requirements:* Applicant must be enrolled or expecting to enroll full-time at a four-year institution or university; resident of Mississippi and studying in Mississippi. Available to U.S. citizens. *Application Requirements:* Application, driver's license, references, transcript. *Deadline:* March 31.

Contact Susan Eckels, Program Administrator, Mississippi State Student Financial Aid, 3825 Ridgewood Road, Jackson, MS 39211-6453. *E-mail:* sme@ihl.state.ms.us. *Phone:* 601-432-6997. *Web site:* www.ihl.state.ms.us.

Mississippi Leveraging Educational Assistance Partnership (LEAP). Award for Mississippi residents enrolled for full-time study at a Mississippi college or university. Based on financial need. Contact college financial aid office. The award value and deadline varies. *Award:* Grant for use in freshman, sophomore, junior, or senior year; renewable. *Award amount:* varies. *Number of awards:* varies. *Eligibility Requirements:* Applicant must be enrolled or expecting to enroll full-time at a two-year or four-year institution or university; resident of Mississippi and studying in Mississippi. Available to U.S. citizens. *Application Requirements:* Application, financial need analysis, FAFSA. *Deadline:* varies.

Contact Mary J. Covington, Mississippi Student Financial Aid, Mississippi State Student Financial Aid, 3825 Ridgewood Road, Jackson, MS 39211-6453. *E-mail:* sfa@ihl.state.ms.us. *Phone:* 800-327-2980. *Web site:* www.ihl.state.ms.us.

Mississippi Resident Tuition Assistance Grant. Must be a resident of Mississippi enrolled full-time at an eligible Mississippi college or university. Must maintain a minimum 2.5 GPA each semester. MTAG awards may be up to $500 per academic year for freshman and sophomores and $1000 per academic year for juniors and seniors. *Award:* Grant for use in freshman, sophomore, junior, or senior year; renewable. *Award amount:* $500–$1000. *Number of awards:* varies. *Eligibility Requirements:* Applicant must be enrolled or expecting to enroll full-time at a two-year or four-year institution or university; resident of Mississippi and studying in Mississippi. Applicant must have 2.5 GPA or higher. Available to U.S. citizens. *Application Requirements:* Application, test scores, transcript. *Deadline:* September 15.

Contact Mary J. Covington, Mississippi Student Financial Aid, Mississippi State Student Financial Aid, 3825 Ridgewood Road, Jackson, MS 39211-6453. *E-mail:* sfa@ihl.state.ms.us. *Phone:* 800-327-2980. *Web site:* www.ihl.state.ms.us.

Nursing Education Loan/Scholarship-BSN. Award available to junior and senior students pursuing a baccalaureate degree in nursing as well as to the licensed registered nurse who wishes to continue his/her education to the baccalaureate degree. Includes transcript and references with application. Must agree to employment in professional nursing (patient care) in Mississippi. Deadline: March 31. *Academic Fields/Career Goals:* Nursing. *Award:* Forgivable loan for use in junior or senior year; renewable. *Award amount:* $4000–$8000. *Number of awards:* varies. *Eligibility Requirements:* Applicant must be enrolled or expecting to enroll full- or part-time at a four-year institution or university; resident of Mississippi and studying in Mississippi. Applicant must have 2.5 GPA or higher. Available to U.S. citizens. *Application Requirements:* Application, driver's license, financial need analysis, references, transcript. *Deadline:* March 31.

Contact Mary J. Covington, Mississippi Student Financial Aid, Mississippi State Student Financial Aid, 3825 Ridgewood Road, Jackson, MS 39211-6453. *E-mail:* sfa@ihl.state.ms.us. *Phone:* 800-327-2980. *Web site:* www.ihl.state.ms.us.

William Winter Teacher Scholar Loan. Scholarship available to a junior or senior student at a four-year Mississippi college or university. Applicants must enroll in a program of study leading to a Class "A" teacher educator license. *Academic Fields/Career Goals:* Education. *Award:* Scholarship for use in junior or senior year; renewable. *Award amount:* up to $4000. *Number of awards:* varies. *Eligibility Requirements:* Applicant must be enrolled or expecting to enroll full-time at a four-year institution or university; resident of Mississippi and studying in Mississippi. Applicant must have 2.5 GPA or higher. Available to U.S. citizens. *Application Requirements:* Application. *Deadline:* March 31.

Contact Mary J. Covington, Mississippi Student Financial Aid, Mississippi State Student Financial Aid, 3825 Ridgewood Road, Jackson, MS 39211-6453. *E-mail:* sfa@ihl.state.ms.us. *Phone:* 800-327-2980. *Web site:* www.ihl.state.ms.us.

MISSOURI

ACES/PRIMO Program. Program of the Missouri Area Health Education Centers (MAHEC) And the Primary Care Resource Initiative for Missouri students interested in Primary Care. Applicant should have a minimum GPA of 3.0. *Academic Fields/Career Goals:* Health and Medical Sciences. *Award:* Forgivable loan for use in freshman, sophomore, junior, senior, graduate, or postgraduate years; not renewable. *Award amount:* $3000–$5000. *Number of awards:* 100. *Eligibility Requirements:* Applicant must be enrolled or expecting to enroll full- or part-time at a four-year institution or university. Applicant must have 3.0 GPA or higher. Available to U.S. and non-U.S. citizens. *Application Requirements:* Application, driver's license, proof of Missouri residency. *Deadline:* June 30.

Contact Jan Shipley, Programs Director, Missouri Department of Health and Senior Services, 1101 Yuane Avenue, Rolla, MO 65401. *Phone:* 573-364-4797. *Fax:* 573-364-8972. *Web site:* www.dhss.mo.gov.

Charles Gallagher Student Assistance Program. Program was the first state grant program to provide need-based grants for Missouri citizens to access Missouri postsecondary education. Must be a full-time undergraduate student at a participating Missouri postsecondary school, working toward a first baccalaureate degree. Must be a Missouri resident and a U.S. citizen. Must maintain satisfactory academic progress as defined by the school. *Award:* Grant for use in freshman, sophomore, junior, or senior year; not renewable. *Award amount:* $1500. *Number of awards:* varies. *Eligibility Requirements:* Applicant must be enrolled or expecting to enroll full-time at a two-year, four-year, or technical institution or university; resident of Missouri and studying in Missouri. Available to U.S. citizens. *Application Requirements:* Financial need analysis, FAFSA. *Deadline:* April 1.

Contact MDHE Information Center, Missouri Department of Higher Education, 3515 Amazonas Drive, Jefferson City, MO 65109-5717. *E-mail:* info@dhe.mo.gov. *Phone:* 800-473-6757 Ext. 1. *Fax:* 573-751-6635. *Web site:* www.dhe.mo.gov.

Environmental Education Scholarship Program (EESP). Scholarship to minority and other underrepresented students pursuing a bachelor's or master's degree in an environmental course of study. Must be a Missouri resident having a cumulative high school GPA of 3.0 or if enrolled in college, must have cumulative GPA of 2.5. Deadline: June 1. *Academic Fields/Career Goals:* Environmental Science. *Award:* Scholarship for use in freshman, sophomore, junior, senior, or graduate year; not renewable. *Award amount:* varies. *Number of awards:* varies. *Eligibility Requirements:* Applicant must be American Indian/Alaska Native, Asian/Pacific Islander, Black (non-Hispanic), or Hispanic; enrolled or expecting to enroll full-time at a four-year institution or university and resident of Missouri. Applicant must have 3.0 GPA or higher. Available to U.S. citizens. *Application Requirements:* Application, essay, references, transcript. *Deadline:* June 1.

Contact Toni Clark, Office Support, Missouri Department of Natural Resources, Environmental Educational Scholarship Program, PO Box 176, Jefferson City, MO 65102. *Phone:* 800-361-4827. *Web site:* www.dnr.mo.gov.

Lillie Lois Ford Scholarship Fund. Two awards of $1000 each are given each year to one boy and one girl. Applicant must have attended a full session of Missouri Boys/Girls State or Missouri Cadet Patrol Academy. Must be a Missouri resident of age below 21, attending an accredited college/university as a full-time student. Must be an unmarried descendant of a veteran having served at least 90 days on active duty in the Army, Air Force, Navy, Marine Corps or Coast Guard of the United States. Deadline: April 20. *Award:* Scholarship for use in freshman year; not renewable. *Award amount:* $1000. *Number of awards:* 2. *Eligibility Requirements:* Applicant must be high school student; age 21 or under; planning to enroll or expecting to enroll full-time at a four-year institution or university; single and resident of Missouri. Available to U.S. citizens. Applicant or parent must meet one or more of the following requirements: general military experience; retired from active duty; disabled or killed as a result of military service; prisoner of war; or missing in action. *Application Requirements:* Application, financial need analysis, test scores, copy of the veteran's discharge certificate. *Deadline:* April 20.

Contact John Doane, Chairman, Education and Scholarship Committee, American Legion, Department of Missouri, PO Box 179, Jefferson City, MO 65102-0179. *Phone:* 417-924-8186. *Web site:* www.missourilegion.org.

Marguerite Ross Barnett Memorial Scholarship. Scholarship was established for students who are employed while attending school part-time. Must be enrolled at least half-time but less than full-time at a participating Missouri postsecondary school, be employed and compensated for at least 20 hours per week, be 18 years of age, be a Missouri resident and a U.S. citizen or an eligible non-citizen. *Award:* Scholarship for use in freshman, sophomore, junior, or senior year; renewable. *Award amount:* varies. *Number of awards:* varies. *Eligibility Requirements:* Applicant must be age 18 and over; enrolled or expecting to enroll part-time at a two-year, four-year, or technical institution or university; resident of Missouri and studying in Missouri. Available to U.S. and non-U.S. citizens. *Application Requirements:* Application, financial need analysis. *Deadline:* varies.

Contact MDHE Information Center, Missouri Department of Higher Education, 3515 Amazonas Drive, Jefferson City, MO 65109-5717. *E-mail:* info@dhe.mo.gov. *Phone:* 800-473-6757 Ext. 1. *Fax:* 573-751-6635. *Web site:* www.dhe.mo.gov.

Missouri College Guarantee Program. Grant is based on demonstrated financial need, as well as high school and college academic achievement. Must have a high school GPA of 2.5 or higher, be enrolled full-time at a participating Missouri postsecondary school, be a Missouri resident and a U.S. citizen. Must have participated in high school extracurricular activities. *Award:* Scholarship for use in freshman, sophomore, junior, or senior year; not renewable. *Award amount:* varies. *Number of awards:* varies. *Eligibility Requirements:* Applicant must be enrolled or expecting to enroll full-time at a two-year or four-year institution or university; resident of Missouri and studying in Missouri. Applicant must have 2.5 GPA or higher. Available to U.S. citizens. *Application Requirements:* Financial need analysis, test scores, FAFSA. *Deadline:* varies.

Contact MDHE Information Center, Missouri Department of Higher Education, 3515 Amazonas Drive, Jefferson City, MO 65109-5717. *E-mail:* info@dhe.mo.gov. *Phone:* 800-473-6757 Ext. 1. *Fax:* 573-751-6635. *Web site:* www.dhe.mo.gov.

Missouri Higher Education Academic Scholarship (Bright Flight). Program encourages top-ranked high school seniors to attend approved Missouri postsecondary schools. Must be a Missouri resident and a

U.S. citizen. Must have a composite score on the ACT or the SAT in the top three percent of all Missouri students taking those tests. Annual scholarship of $2000 is awarded in two payments of $1000 each semester. *Award:* Scholarship for use in freshman, sophomore, junior, or senior year; renewable. *Award amount:* $2000. *Number of awards:* varies. *Eligibility Requirements:* Applicant must be high school student; planning to enroll or expecting to enroll full-time at a two-year, four-year, or technical institution or university; resident of Missouri and studying in Missouri. Available to U.S. citizens. *Application Requirements:* Test scores. *Deadline:* varies.

Contact MDHE Information Center, Missouri Department of Higher Education, 3515 Amazonas Drive, Jefferson City, MO 65109-5717. *E-mail:* info@dhe.mo.gov. *Phone:* 800-473-6757 Ext. 1. *Fax:* 573-751-6635. *Web site:* www.dhe.mo.gov.

Missouri Minority Teaching Scholarship. Scholarship is competitive and is a renewable award of $3000 for up to four years. Must be a Missouri resident, be African American, Asian American, Hispanic American, or Native American, be a high school senior, college student or returning adult. For details refer to Web Site: http://www.dese.mo.gov/divteachqual/scholarships/mmts_cover.pdf. *Academic Fields/Career Goals:* Education. *Award:* Scholarship for use in freshman, sophomore, junior, or senior year; renewable. *Award amount:* $3000. *Number of awards:* varies. *Eligibility Requirements:* Applicant must be American Indian/Alaska Native, Asian/Pacific Islander, Black (non-Hispanic), or Hispanic; enrolled or expecting to enroll full-time at a four-year institution or university; resident of Missouri and studying in Missouri. Applicant must have 3.0 GPA or higher. Available to U.S. citizens. *Application Requirements:* Application, essay, financial need analysis, resume, references, test scores, transcript. *Deadline:* February 15.

Contact Laura Harrison, Administrative Assistant, Missouri Department of Elementary and Secondary Education, PO Box 480, Jefferson City, MO 65102-0480. *E-mail:* laura.harrison@dese.mo.gov. *Phone:* 573-751-1668. *Fax:* 573-526-3580. *Web site:* www.dese.mo.gov.

Missouri Teacher Education Scholarship (General). Nonrenewable award for Missouri high school seniors or Missouri resident college students. Must attend approved teacher training program at a participating Missouri institution. Must rank in top 15 percent of high school class on ACT/SAT. Merit-based award. Recipients must commit to teach in Missouri for five years at a public elementary or secondary school or award must be repaid. *Academic Fields/Career Goals:* Education. *Award:* Scholarship for use in freshman, sophomore, junior, or senior year; not renewable. *Award amount:* up to $2000. *Number of awards:* 200–240. *Eligibility Requirements:* Applicant must be enrolled or expecting to enroll full-time at a two-year or four-year institution or university; resident of Missouri and studying in Missouri. Applicant must have 3.5 GPA or higher. Available to U.S. citizens. *Application Requirements:* Application, essay, resume, references, test scores, transcript. *Deadline:* February 15.

Contact Laura Harrison, Administrative Assistant II, Missouri Department of Elementary and Secondary Education, PO Box 480, Jefferson City, MO 65102-0480. *E-mail:* laura.harrison@dese.mo.gov. *Phone:* 573-751-1668. *Fax:* 573-526-3580. *Web site:* www.dese.mo.gov.

Primary Care Resource Initiative for Missouri Loan Program. Forgivable loans for Missouri residents attending Missouri institutions pursuing a degree as a primary care physician or dentist, studying for a bachelors degree as a dental hygienist, or a master of science degree in nursing leading to certification as an Advanced Practice Nurse. To be forgiven participant must work in a Missouri health professional shortage area. *Academic Fields/Career Goals:* Dental Health/Services; Health and Medical Sciences; Nursing. *Award:* Forgivable loan for use in freshman, sophomore, junior, senior, graduate, or postgraduate years; not renewable. *Award amount:* $3000–$25,000. *Number of awards:* 100. *Eligibility Requirements:* Applicant must be enrolled or expecting to enroll full- or part-time at a four-year institution or university; resident of Missouri and studying in Missouri. Applicant must have 3.0 GPA or higher. Available to U.S. and non-U.S. citizens. *Application Requirements:* Application, driver's license, proof of Missouri residency. *Deadline:* June 30.

Contact Kristie Frank, Health Program Representative, Missouri Department of Health and Senior Services, PO Box 570, Jefferson City, MO 65102-0570. *E-mail:* frank@dhss.mo.gov. *Phone:* 800-891-7415. *Fax:* 573-522-8146. *Web site:* www.dhss.mo.gov.

Robert C. Byrd Honors Scholarship-Missouri. Award for Missouri high school seniors who are residents of Missouri. The amount of the award per student each year depends on the amount the state is allotted by the U.S. Department of Education. The highest amount of award per student is $1500. Students must rank in top 10 percent of high school class and score in top 10 percent of ACT test. *Award:* Scholarship for use in freshman year; renewable. *Award amount:* $1100–$1500. *Number of awards:* 100–150. *Eligibility Requirements:* Applicant must be high school student; planning to enroll or expecting to enroll full-time at a two-year, four-year, or technical institution or university and resident of Missouri. Applicant must have 3.5 GPA or higher. Available to U.S. citizens. *Application Requirements:* Application, test scores, transcript. *Deadline:* April 15.

Contact Laura Harrison, Administrative Assistant II, Missouri Department of Elementary and Secondary Education, PO Box 480, Jefferson City, MO 65102-0480. *E-mail:* laura.harrison@dese.mo.gov. *Phone:* 573-751-1668. *Fax:* 573-526-3580. *Web site:* www.dese.mo.gov.

Teacher Education Scholarship. The scholarship is a competitive, one-time, nonrenewable award of $2000 to be used in one academic year. Applicants must be a Missouri resident and a high school senior or student enrolled fulltime at a community or four-year college or university in Missouri. Deadline: February 15. *Award:* Scholarship for use in freshman, sophomore, junior, or senior year; not renewable. *Award amount:* $2000. *Number of awards:* varies. *Eligibility Requirements:* Applicant must be enrolled or expecting to enroll full- or part-time at a four-year institution or university; resident of Missouri and studying in Missouri. Available to U.S. citizens. *Application Requirements:* Application, essay, references, test scores, transcript. *Deadline:* February 15.

Contact Laura Harrison, Administrative Assistant, Missouri State Department of Elementary/Secondary Education, 205 Jefferson Street, Seventh Floor, PO Box 480, Jefferson City, MO 65102. *E-mail:* Laura.Harrison@dese.mo.gov. *Phone:* 573-751-1668. *Fax:* 573-526-3580. *Web site:* www.dese.mo.gov.

MONTANA

Montana Higher Education Opportunity Grant. This grant is awarded based on need to undergraduate students attending either part-time or full-time who are residents of Montana and attending participating Montana schools. Awards are limited to the most needy students. A specific major or program of study is not required. This grant does not need to be repaid, and students may apply each year. Apply by filing FAFSA by March 1 and contacting the financial aid office at the admitting college. *Award:* Grant for use in freshman, sophomore, junior, or senior year; not renewable. *Award amount:* $400–$600. *Number of awards:* up to 800. *Eligibility Requirements:* Applicant must be enrolled or expecting to enroll full- or part-time at a two-year or four-year institution or university; resident of Montana and studying in Montana. Available to U.S. citizens. *Application Requirements:* Application, financial need analysis, resume, FAFSA. *Deadline:* March 1.

Contact Janice Kirkpatrick, Grants and Scholarship Coordinator, Montana Guaranteed Student Loan Program, Office of Commissioner of Higher Education, PO Box 203101, Helena, MT 59620-3101. *E-mail:* jkirkpatrick@mgslp.state.mt.us. *Phone:* 406-444-0638. *Fax:* 406-444-1869. *Web site:* www.mgslp.state.mt.us.

Montana Tuition Assistance Program-Baker Grant. Need-based grant for Montana residents attending participating Montana schools who have earned at least $2575 during the previous calendar year. Must be enrolled full time. Grant does not need to be repaid. Award covers the first undergraduate degree or certificate. Apply by filing FAFSA by March 1 and contacting the financial aid office at the admitting college. *Award:* Grant for use in freshman, sophomore, junior, or senior year; not renewable. *Award amount:* $100–$1000. *Number of awards:* 1000–3000. *Eligibility Requirements:* Applicant must be enrolled or expecting to enroll full-time at a two-year or four-year institution or university; resident of Montana and studying in Montana. Available to U.S. citizens. *Application Requirements:* Application, financial need analysis, resume, FAFSA. *Deadline:* March 1.

Contact Janice Kirkpatrick, Grants and Scholarship Coordinator, Montana Guaranteed Student Loan Program, Office of Commissioner of Higher Education, PO Box 203101, Helena, MT 59620-3101. *E-mail:* jkirkpatrick@mgslp.state.mt.us. *Phone:* 406-444-0638. *Fax:* 406-444-1869. *Web site:* www.mgslp.state.mt.us.

Montana University System Honor Scholarship. Scholarship will be awarded annually to high school seniors graduating from accredited Montana high schools. The MUS Honor Scholarship is a four year renewable scholarship that waives the tuition and registration fee at one of the Montana University System campuses or one of the three community colleges (Flathead Valley in Kalispell, Miles in Miles City or Dawson in Glendive). The scholarship must be used within 9 months after high school graduation. Deadline: January 31. *Award:* Scholarship for use in freshman, sophomore, junior, or senior year; renewable. *Award amount:* varies. *Number of awards:* varies. *Eligibility Requirements:* Applicant must be high school student; planning to enroll or expecting to enroll full- or part-time at a two-year or four-year institution or university; resident of Montana and studying in Montana. Applicant must have 3.5 GPA or higher. Available to U.S. citizens. *Application Requirements:* Application, test scores, transcript. *Deadline:* January 31.

Contact Janice Kirkpatrick, Grant and Scholarship Coordinator, Montana Guaranteed Student Loan Program, Office of Commissioner of Higher Education, PO Box 203101, Helena, MT 59620-3101. *E-mail:* jkirkpatrick@mgslp.state.mt.us. *Phone:* 406-444-0638. *Fax:* 406-444-1869. *Web site:* www.mgslp.state.mt.us.

NEBRASKA

Nebraska State Grant. Available to undergraduates attending a participating postsecondary institution in Nebraska. Available to Pell Grant recipients only. Nebraska residency required. Awards determined by each participating institution. Contact financial aid office at institution for application and additional information. *Award:* Grant for use in freshman, sophomore, junior, or senior year; not renewable. *Award amount:* $100–$1032. *Number of awards:* varies. *Eligibility Requirements:* Applicant must be enrolled or expecting to enroll full- or part-time at a two-year, four-year, or technical institution or university; resident of Nebraska and studying in Nebraska. Available to U.S. citizens. *Application Requirements:* Application, financial need analysis. *Deadline:* continuous.

Contact J. Ritchie Morrow, Financial Aid Coordinator, State of Nebraska Coordinating Commission for Postsecondary Education, 140 North Eighth Street, Suite 300, PO Box 95005, Lincoln, NE 68509-5005. *E-mail:* rmorrow@ccpe.st.ne.us. *Phone:* 402-471-0032. *Fax:* 402-471-2886. *Web site:* www.ccpe.state.ne.us.

NEVADA

Governor Guinn Millennium Scholarship. Scholarship for high school graduates with a diploma from a Nevada public or private high school in the graduating class of the year 2000 or later. Must complete high school with at least 3.25 GPA. *Award:* Scholarship for use in freshman, sophomore, junior, or senior year; not renewable. *Award amount:* $10,000. *Number of awards:* 1. *Eligibility Requirements:* Applicant must be enrolled or expecting to enroll full-time at a two-year or four-year institution and resident of Nevada. Available to U.S. citizens. *Application Requirements:* Application. *Deadline:* varies.

Contact Christy Thurston, Office Assistant, Nevada Office of the State Treasurer, 555 East Washington Avenue, Suite 4600, Las Vegas, NV 89101. *E-mail:* info@nevadatreasurer.gov. *Phone:* 702-486-3383. *Fax:* 702-486-3246. *Web site:* www.nevadatreasurer.gov.

Nevada Student Incentive Grant. Grants awarded to undergraduate and graduate students who are Nevada residents pursuing their first degree. Recipients must be enrolled at least halftime and have financial need. Awards may range from $200 to $4000. Any field of study eligible. High school students may not apply. *Award:* Grant for use in freshman, sophomore, junior, senior, or graduate year; not renewable. *Award amount:* $200–$4000. *Number of awards:* 400–800. *Eligibility Requirements:* Applicant must be enrolled or expecting to enroll full- or part-time at a two-year, four-year, or technical institution or university; resident of Nevada and studying in Nevada. Available to U.S. citizens. *Application Requirements:* Application, financial need analysis. *Deadline:* continuous.

Contact Bill Arensdorf, Director, Nevada Department of Education, 700 East Fifth Street, Carson City, NV 89701. *E-mail:* warensdorf@doe.nv.gov. *Phone:* 775-687-9200. *Fax:* 775-687-9101. *Web site:* www.doe.nv.gov.

University and Community College System of Nevada NASA Space Grant and Fellowship Program. The grant provides graduate fellowships and undergraduate scholarship to qualified student majoring in aerospace science, technology and related fields. Must be Nevada resident studying at a Nevada college/university. Minimum 2.5 GPA required. *Academic Fields/Career Goals:* Aviation/Aerospace; Chemical Engineering; Computer Science/Data Processing; Engineering/Technology; Physical Sciences and Math. *Award:* Scholarship for use in freshman, sophomore, junior, senior, or graduate year; not renewable. *Award amount:* $2500–$30,000. *Number of awards:* 1–20. *Eligibility Requirements:* Applicant must be enrolled or expecting to enroll full-time at a two-year or four-year institution or university; resident of Nevada and studying in Nevada. Applicant must have 3.0 GPA or higher. Available to U.S. citizens. *Application Requirements:* Application, autobiography, essay, resume, references, transcript, project proposal, budget. *Deadline:* April 13.

Contact Cindy Routh, Program Coordinator, NASA Nevada Space Grant Consortium,

2215 Raggio Parkway, Reno, NV 89512. *E-mail:* nvsg@dri.edu. *Phone:* 775-673-7674. *Fax:* 775-673-7485. *Web site:* www.unr.edu/spacegrant.

NEW HAMPSHIRE

Leveraged Incentive Grant Program. Grants to provide assistance on the basis of merit and need to full-time undergraduate New Hampshire students at New Hampshire accredited institutions. Must be a New Hampshire resident, and demonstrate financial need as determined by the federal formula and by merit as determined by the institution. Must be a sophomore, junior or senior undergraduate student. *Award:* Grant for use in sophomore, junior, or senior year; not renewable. *Award amount:* $250–$7500. *Number of awards:* varies. *Eligibility Requirements:* Applicant must be enrolled or expecting to enroll full-time at a two-year, four-year, or technical institution or university; resident of New Hampshire and studying in New Hampshire. Available to U.S. citizens. *Application Requirements:* Application, financial need analysis. *Deadline:* varies.

Contact Judith A. Knapp, Scholarship Coordinator, New Hampshire Postsecondary Education Commission, Three Barrell Court, Suite 300, Concord, NH 03301-8543. *E-mail:* jknapp@pec.state.nh.us. *Phone:* 603-271-2555. *Fax:* 603-271-2696. *Web site:* www.nh.gov/postsecondary.

New Hampshire Incentive Program (NHIP). Grants to provide financial assistance to New Hampshire students attending eligible institutions in New England. Must demonstrate financial need. May be a part- or full-time undergraduate student with no previous bachelor's degree. For more details see Web site: http://www.nh.gov/postsecondary/financial/NHIP.html. *Award:* Grant for use in freshman, sophomore, junior, or senior year; renewable. *Award amount:* $125–$1000. *Number of awards:* 3000–4300. *Eligibility Requirements:* Applicant must be enrolled or expecting to enroll full- or part-time at a four-year institution or university; resident of New Hampshire and studying in Connecticut, Maine, Massachusetts, New Hampshire, Rhode Island, or Vermont. Available to U.S. citizens. *Application Requirements:* Application, financial need analysis, FAFSA. *Deadline:* May 1.

Contact Sherrie Tucker, Program Assistant, New Hampshire Postsecondary Education Commission, Three Barrell Court, Suite 300, Concord, NH 03301-8512. *E-mail:* stucker@pec.state.nh.us. *Phone:* 603-271-2555 Ext. 355. *Fax:* 603-271-2696. *Web site:* www.nh.gov/postsecondary.

Scholarships for Orphans of Veterans-New Hampshire. Scholarship to provide financial assistance (room, board, books and supplies) to children of parent(s) who served in World War II, Korean Conflict, Vietnam (Southeast Asian Conflict) or the Gulf Wars, or any other operation for which the armed forces expeditionary medal or theater of operations service medal was awarded to the veteran. For more details refer to Web site: http://www.nh.gov/postsecondary/financial/War_Orphans.html. *Award:* Scholarship for use in freshman, sophomore, junior, or senior year; renewable. *Award amount:* up to $2500. *Number of awards:* 1–10. *Eligibility Requirements:* Applicant must be age 16-25; enrolled or expecting to enroll full-time at a two-year or four-year institution or university; resident of New Hampshire and studying in New Hampshire. Available to U.S. citizens. Applicant or parent must meet one or more of the following requirements: general military experience; retired from active duty; disabled or killed as a result of military service; prisoner of war; or missing in action. *Application Requirements:* Application. *Deadline:* varies.

Contact Melanie K. Deshaies, Program Assistant, New Hampshire Postsecondary Education Commission, Three Barrell Court, Suite 300, Concord, NH 03301-8543. *E-mail:* mdeshaies@pec.state.nh.us. *Phone:* 603-271-2555 Ext. 356. *Fax:* 603-271-2696. *Web site:* www.nh.gov/postsecondary.

Workforce Incentive Program. The program provides incentive for students to pursue careers in critical workforce shortage areas at appropriate New Hampshire institutions and to encourage students to then seek employment in New Hampshire after completion of their career program. May be a part- or full-time student in an approved program, and should demonstrate financial need as determined by the institution. For more details, visit: http://www.nh.gov/postsecondary/financial/WIP.html. *Academic Fields/Career Goals:* Education; Foreign Language; Nursing; Special Education. *Award:* Forgivable loan for use in freshman, sophomore, junior, senior, graduate, or postgraduate years; not renewable. *Award amount:* varies. *Number of awards:* varies. *Eligibility Requirements:* Applicant must be enrolled or expecting to enroll full- or part-time at a four-year institution or university; resident of New Hampshire and studying in New Hampshire. Available to U.S. citizens. *Application Requirements:* Application. *Deadline:* varies.

Contact Judith A. Knapp, Scholarship Coordinator, New Hampshire Postsecondary Education Commission, Three Barrell Court, Suite 300, Concord, NH 03301-8543. *E-mail:* jknapp@pec.state.nh.us. *Phone:* 603-271-2555. *Fax:* 603-271-2696. *Web site:* www.nh.gov/postsecondary.

NEW JERSEY

Dana Christmas Scholarship for Heroism. Honors young New Jersey residents for acts of heroism. Scholarship is a nonrenewable award of up to $10,000 for 5 students. This scholarship may be used for undergraduate or graduate study. Deadline varies. *Award:* Scholarship for use in freshman, sophomore, junior, senior, or graduate year; not renewable. *Award amount:* up to $10,000. *Number of awards:* up to 5. *Eligibility Requirements:* Applicant must be age 21 or under; enrolled or expecting to enroll full- or part-time at a two-year, four-year, or technical institution or university and resident of New Jersey. Available to U.S. citizens. *Application Requirements:* Application. *Deadline:* varies.

Contact Gisele Joachim, Director, Financial Aid Services, New Jersey Higher Education Student Assistance Authority, Four Quakerbridge Plaza, PO Box 540, Trenton, NJ 08625. *E-mail:* gjoachim@hesaa.org. *Phone:* 800-792-8670 Ext. 2349. *Fax:* 609-588-7389. *Web site:* www.hesaa.org.

Edward J. Bloustein Distinguished Scholars. Renewable scholarship for students who are placed in top 10 percent of their classes and have a minimum combined SAT score of 1260, or ranked first, second or third in their classes as of end of junior year. Must be New Jersey resident and must attend a New Jersey two-year college, four-year college or university, or approved programs at proprietary institutions. Secondary schools must forward to HESAA, the names and class standings for all nominees. Award value is $1000 and deadline varies. *Award:* Scholarship for use in freshman, sophomore, junior, senior, or graduate year; renewable. *Award amount:* up to $1000. *Number of awards:* varies. *Eligibility Requirements:* Applicant must be high school student; planning to enroll or expecting to enroll full-time at a two-year or four-year institution or university; resident of New Jersey and studying in New Jersey. Available to U.S. citizens. *Application Requirements:* Test scores, nomination by high school. *Deadline:* varies.

Contact Carol Muka, Assistant Director of Grants and Scholarships, New Jersey Higher Education Student Assistance Authority, PO Box 540, Trenton, NJ 08625. *E-mail:* cmuka@hesaa.org. *Phone:* 800-792-8670 Ext. 3266. *Fax:* 609-588-2228. *Web site:* www.hesaa.org.

Law Enforcement Officer Memorial Scholarship. Scholarships for full-time undergraduate study at approved New Jersey institutions for the dependent children of New Jersey law enforcement officers killed in the line of duty. Value of scholarship will be established annually. Deadline varies. *Award:* Scholarship for use in freshman, sophomore, junior, or senior year; renewable. *Award amount:* varies. *Number of awards:* varies. *Eligibility Requirements:* Applicant must be enrolled or expecting to enroll full-time at a four-year institution or university; resident of New Jersey and studying in New Jersey. Applicant or parent of applicant must have employment or volunteer experience in police/firefighting. Available to U.S. citizens. *Application Requirements:* Application. *Deadline:* varies.

Contact Carol Muka, Assistant Director of Grants and Scholarships, New Jersey Higher Education Student Assistance Authority, PO Box 540, Trenton, NJ 08625. *E-mail:* cmuka@hesaa.org. *Phone:* 800-792-8670 Ext. 3266. *Fax:* 609-588-2228. *Web site:* www.hesaa.org.

New Jersey Educational Opportunity Fund Grants. Grants up to $4350 per year. Must be a New Jersey resident for at least twelve consecutive months and attend a New Jersey institution. Must be from a disadvantaged background as defined by EOF guidelines. EOF grant applicants must also apply for financial aid. EOF recipients may qualify for the Martin Luther King Physician/Dentistry Scholarships for graduate study at a professional institution. *Academic Fields/Career Goals:* Dental Health/Services; Health and Medical Sciences. *Award:* Grant for use in freshman, sophomore, junior, senior, or graduate year; renewable. *Award amount:* $200–$4350. *Number of awards:* varies. *Eligibility Requirements:* Applicant must be enrolled or expecting to enroll full-time at a four-year institution or university; resident of New Jersey and studying in New Jersey. Available to U.S. citizens. *Application Requirements:* Application, financial need analysis. *Deadline:* continuous.

Contact Glenn Lang, EOF Executive Director, University of Medicine and Dentistry of NJ School of Osteopathic Medicine, 40 East Laurel Road, Primary Care Center 119, Trenton, NJ 08625-0542. *E-mail:* glang@che.state.nj.us. *Phone:* 609-984-2709. *Fax:* 609-292-7225. *Web site:* www.umdnj.edu.

New Jersey Student Tuition Assistance Reward Scholarship II. Scholarship for high school graduates who plan to pursue a baccalaureate degree at a New Jersey four-year public institution. Scholarship will cover the cost of tuition and approved fees for up to 18 credits per semester when combined with other state, federal and institutional aid. Deadline varies. *Award:* Scholarship for use in junior or senior year; renewable. *Award amount:* varies. *Number of awards:* varies. *Eligibility Requirements:* Applicant must be enrolled or expecting to enroll full-time at a four-year institution; resident of New Jersey and studying in New Jersey. Applicant must have 3.0 GPA or higher. Available to U.S. citizens. *Application Requirements:* FAFSA. *Deadline:* varies.

Contact Cathleen Lewis, Assistant Director, Client Services, New Jersey Higher Education Student Assistance Authority, Fourth Quaker Bridge Plaza, PO Box 540, Trenton, NJ 08625-0540. *E-mail:* clewis@hesaa.org. *Phone:* 609-588-3280. *Fax:* 609-588-2228. *Web site:* www.hesaa.org.

New Jersey War Orphans Tuition Assistance. Scholarship to children of those service personnel who died while in the military or due to service-connected disabilities, or who are officially listed as missing in action by the U.S. Department of Defense may claim $500 per year for four years of college or equivalent training. To qualify, the child must be a resident of New Jersey for at least one year immediately preceding the filing of the application and be between the ages of 16 and 21 at the time of application. *Award:* Scholarship for use in freshman, sophomore, junior, or senior year; renewable. *Award amount:* $500. *Number of awards:* varies. *Eligibility Requirements:* Applicant must be high school student; age 16-21; planning to enroll or expecting to enroll full-time at a four-year institution or university and resident of New Jersey. Available to U.S. citizens. Applicant or parent must meet one or more of the following requirements: general military experience; retired from active duty; disabled or killed as a result of military service; prisoner of war; or missing in action. *Application Requirements:* Application, transcript. *Deadline:* varies.

Contact Patricia Richter, Grants Manager, New Jersey Department of Military and Veterans Affairs, PO Box 340, Trenton, NJ 08625-0340. *E-mail:* patricia.richter@njdmava.state.nj.us. *Phone:* 609-530-6854. *Fax:* 609-530-6970. *Web site:* www.state.nj.us/military.

New Jersey World Trade Center Scholarship. Scholarship was established by the legislature to aid the dependent children and surviving spouses of New Jersey residents who were killed in the terrorist attacks, or who are missing and officially presumed dead as a direct result of the attacks; applies to instate and out-of-state institutions for students seeking undergraduate degrees. Deadline: March 1 for fall, October 1 for spring. *Award:* Scholarship for use in freshman, sophomore, junior, or senior year; renewable. *Award amount:* up to $6500. *Number of awards:* varies. *Eligibility Requirements:* Applicant must be enrolled or expecting to enroll full-time at a four-year institution or university and resident of New Jersey. Available to U.S. citizens. *Application Requirements:* Application. *Deadline:* varies.

Contact Giselle Joachim, Director of Financial Aid Services, New Jersey Higher Education Student Assistance Authority, PO Box 540, Trenton, NJ 08625. *E-mail:* gjoachim@hesaa.org. *Phone:* 800-792-8670 Ext. 2349. *Fax:* 609-588-7389. *Web site:* www.hesaa.org.

NJ Student Tuition Assistance Reward Scholarship. Scholarship for students who graduate in the top 20 percent of their high school class. Recipients may be awarded up to five semesters of tuition (up to 15 credits per term) and approved fees at one of New Jersey's nineteen county colleges. *Award:* Scholarship for use in freshman, sophomore, junior, or senior year; renewable. *Award amount:* varies. *Number of awards:* varies. *Eligibility Requirements:* Applicant must be enrolled or expecting to enroll full-time at a two-year or four-year institution or university; resident of New Jersey and studying in New Jersey. Applicant must have 3.0 GPA or higher. Available to U.S. citizens. *Application Requirements:* Application, transcript. *Deadline:* varies.

Contact Carol Muka, Assistant Director of Grants and Scholarships, New Jersey Higher Education Student Assistance Authority, PO Box 540, Trenton, NJ 08625. *E-mail:* cmuka@hessa.org. *Phone:* 800-792-8670 Ext. 3266. *Fax:* 609-588-2228. *Web site:* www.hesaa.org.

Outstanding Scholar Recruitment Program. Awards students who meet the eligibility criteria and who are enrolled as first-time freshmen at participating New Jersey institutions receive annual scholarship awards of up to $7500. Deadline varies. *Award:* Scholarship for use in freshman, sophomore, junior, or senior year; renewable. *Award amount:* $2500–$7500. *Number of awards:* varies. *Eligibility Requirements:* Applicant must be enrolled or expecting to enroll full-time at a four-year institution or university; resident of New Jersey and studying in New Jersey. Available to U.S. citizens. *Application Requirements:* Application. *Deadline:* varies.

Contact Carol Muka, Assistant Director of Grants and Scholarships, New Jersey Higher Education Student Assistance Authority, PO Box 540, Trenton, NJ 08625. *E-mail:*

cmuka@hesaa.org. *Phone:* 800-792-8670 Ext. 3266. *Fax:* 609-588-2228. *Web site:* www.hesaa.org.

Part-time Tuition Aid Grant (TAG) for County Colleges. Provides financial aid to eligible part-time undergraduate students enrolled for 6 to 11 credits at participating New Jersey community colleges. Deadlines: March 1 for spring and October 1 for fall. *Award:* Grant for use in freshman, sophomore, junior, or senior year; not renewable. *Award amount:* $381–$571. *Number of awards:* varies. *Eligibility Requirements:* Applicant must be enrolled or expecting to enroll part-time at a two-year or four-year institution or university; resident of New Jersey and studying in New Jersey. Available to U.S. citizens. *Application Requirements:* Application, financial need analysis. *Deadline:* varies.

Contact Sherri Fox, Acting Director of Grants and Scholarships, New Jersey Higher Education Student Assistance Authority, PO Box 540, Trenton, NJ 08625. *Phone:* 800-792-8670. *Fax:* 609-588-2228. *Web site:* www.hesaa.org.

POW-MIA Tuition Benefit Program. Free undergraduate college tuition provided to any child born or adopted before or during the period of time his or her parent was officially declared a prisoner of war (POW) or person missing in action (MIA) after January 1, 1960. The POW-MIA must have been a New Jersey resident at the time he or she entered the service or whose official residence is in N.J. The child must attend either a public or private institution in New Jersey. A copy of DD 1300 must be furnished with the application. *Award:* Scholarship for use in freshman, sophomore, junior, or senior year; renewable. *Award amount:* varies. *Number of awards:* varies. *Eligibility Requirements:* Applicant must be enrolled or expecting to enroll full-time at a two-year, four-year, or technical institution or university; resident of New Jersey and studying in New Jersey. Applicant must have 2.5 GPA or higher. Available to U.S. citizens. Applicant or parent must meet one or more of the following requirements: general military experience; retired from active duty; disabled or killed as a result of military service; prisoner of war; or missing in action. *Application Requirements:* Application, transcript, copy of DD 1300. *Deadline:* varies.

Contact Patricia Richter, Grants Manager, New Jersey Department of Military and Veterans Affairs, PO Box 340, Trenton, NJ 08625-0340. *E-mail:* patricia.richter@njdmava.state.nj.us. *Phone:* 609-530-6854. *Fax:* 609-530-6970. *Web site:* www.state.nj.us/military.

Survivor Tuition Benefits Program. The scholarship provides tuition fees for spouses and dependents of law enforcement officers, fire, or emergency services personnel killed in the line of duty. Eligible recipients may attend any independent institution in the state; however, the annual value of the grant cannot exceed the highest tuition charged at a New Jersey public institution. Deadline varies. *Award:* Scholarship for use in freshman, sophomore, junior, or senior year; renewable. *Award amount:* varies. *Number of awards:* varies. *Eligibility Requirements:* Applicant must be enrolled or expecting to enroll full- or part-time at a two-year or four-year institution or university; resident of New Jersey and studying in New Jersey. Applicant or parent of applicant must have employment or volunteer experience in police/firefighting. Available to U.S. citizens. *Application Requirements:* Application. *Deadline:* varies.

Contact Carol Muka, Scholarship Coordinator, New Jersey Higher Education Student Assistance Authority, PO Box 540, Trenton, NJ 08625. *E-mail:* cmuka@hesaa.org. *Phone:* 800-792-8670 Ext. 3266. *Fax:* 609-588-2228. *Web site:* www.hesaa.org.

Tuition Aid Grant. The program provides tuition fees to eligible undergraduate students attending participating instate institutions. Deadlines: March 1 for fall, October 1 for spring. *Award:* Grant for use in freshman, sophomore, junior, or senior year; not renewable. *Award amount:* $868–$7272. *Number of awards:* varies. *Eligibility Requirements:* Applicant must be enrolled or expecting to enroll full-time at a two-year or four-year institution or university; resident of New Jersey and studying in New Jersey. Available to U.S. citizens. *Application Requirements:* Application, financial need analysis. *Deadline:* varies.

Contact Sherri Fox, Acting Director of Grants and Scholarships, New Jersey Higher Education Student Assistance Authority, PO Box 540, Trenton, NJ 08625. *Phone:* 800-792-8670. *Fax:* 609-588-2228. *Web site:* www.hesaa.org.

Urban Scholars. Renewable scholarship to high achieving students attending public secondary schools in the urban and economically distressed areas of New Jersey. Students must rank in the top 10 percent of their class and have a GPA of at least 3.0 at the end of their junior year. Must be New Jersey resident and attend a New Jersey two-year college, four-year college or university, or approved programs at proprietary institutions. Students do not apply directly for scholarship consideration. Deadline varies. *Award:* Scholarship for use in freshman, sophomore, junior, or senior year; renewable. *Award amount:* up to $1000. *Number of awards:* varies. *Eligibility Requirements:* Applicant must be enrolled or expecting to enroll full-time at a two-year or four-year institution or university; resident of New Jersey and studying in New Jersey. Applicant must have 3.0 GPA or higher. Available to U.S. citizens. *Application Requirements:* Test scores, nomination by school. *Deadline:* varies.

Contact Carol Muka, Assistant Director of Grants and Scholarships, New Jersey Higher Education Student Assistance Authority, PO Box 540, Trenton, NJ 08625. *E-mail:* cmuka@hesaa.org. *Phone:* 800-792-8670 Ext. 3266. *Fax:* 609-588-2228. *Web site:* www.hesaa.org.

Veterans Tuition Credit Program-New Jersey. Award for veterans who served in the armed forces between December 31, 1960, and May 7, 1975. Must have been a New Jersey resident at time of induction or discharge or for two years immediately prior to application. *Award:* Scholarship for use in freshman, sophomore, junior, or senior year; renewable. *Award amount:* $200–$400. *Number of awards:* varies. *Eligibility Requirements:* Applicant must be enrolled or expecting to enroll full- or part-time at a two-year, four-year, or technical institution or university and resident of New Jersey. Available to U.S. citizens. Applicant must have general military experience. *Application Requirements:* Application. *Deadline:* varies.

Contact Patricia Richter, Grants Manager, New Jersey Department of Military and Veterans Affairs, PO Box 340, Trenton, NJ 08625-0340. *E-mail:* patricia.richter@njdmava.state.nj.us. *Phone:* 609-530-6854. *Fax:* 609-530-6970. *Web site:* www.state.nj.us/military.

NEW MEXICO

Allied Health Student Loan Program-New Mexico. Award to increase the number if physician assistants in areas of the state which have experienced shortages of health practitioners, by making educational loans to students seeking certification/licensers in an eligible health field. As a condition of each loan, the student shall declare his/her intent to practice as a health professional in a designated shortage area. For every year of service, a portion of the loan will be forgiven. *Academic Fields/Career Goals:* Dental Health/Services; Health and Medical Sciences; Nursing; Social Sciences; Therapy/Rehabilitation. *Award:* Forgivable loan for use in freshman, sophomore, junior, or senior year; renewable. *Award amount:* up to $12,000. *Number of awards:* 1–40. *Eligibility Requirements:*

Applicant must be enrolled or expecting to enroll full- or part-time at a four-year institution or university; resident of New Mexico and studying in New Mexico. Available to U.S. citizens. *Application Requirements:* Application, financial need analysis, transcript, FAFSA. *Deadline:* July 1.

Contact Ofelia Morales, Director of Financial Aid, New Mexico Commission on Higher Education, 1068 Cerrillos Road, Santa Fe, NM 87505. *E-mail:* ofelia.morales@state.nm.us. *Phone:* 505-476-6506. *Fax:* 505-476-6511. *Web site:* www.hed.state.nm.us.

Amigo Scholars Program for Non-residents. Scholarship for non-resident high school graduates. Applicant must have high school GPA of 3.5 or higher, ACT composite score of 23 or SAT of 1060. Must be a U.S. citizen. Deadline: May 1. *Award:* Scholarship for use in freshman year; renewable. *Award amount:* varies. *Number of awards:* varies. *Eligibility Requirements:* Applicant must be high school student and planning to enroll or expecting to enroll full- or part-time at a four-year institution or university. Available to U.S. citizens. *Application Requirements:* Application, resume. *Deadline:* May 1.

Contact Robert Romero, Financial Aid Advisor, University of New Mexico, Mesa Vista Hall, Room 3019, Albuquerque, NM 87131. *E-mail:* schol@unm.edu. *Phone:* 505-277-6090. *Fax:* 505-277-5325. *Web site:* www.unm.edu.

Children of Deceased Veterans Scholarship-New Mexico. Award for New Mexico residents who are children of veterans killed or disabled as a result of service, prisoner of war, or veterans missing in action. Must be between ages of 16 to 26. For use at New Mexico schools for undergraduate study. Should submit parent's death certificate and DD form 214. *Award:* Scholarship for use in freshman, sophomore, junior, or senior year; renewable. *Award amount:* $300. *Number of awards:* varies. *Eligibility Requirements:* Applicant must be age 16-26; enrolled or expecting to enroll full- or part-time at a two-year or four-year institution or university; resident of New Mexico and studying in New Mexico. Available to U.S. citizens. Applicant or parent must meet one or more of the following requirements: general military experience; retired from active duty; disabled or killed as a result of military service; prisoner of war; or missing in action. *Application Requirements:* Application, transcript, death certificate or notice of casualty, DD form 214. *Deadline:* continuous.

Contact Alan Martinez, Director, State Benefits Division, New Mexico Veterans Service Commission, Bataan Memorial Building, 300 Galisteo, Room 142, Santa Fe, NM 87504. *E-mail:* alan.martinez@state.nm.us. *Phone:* 505-827-6300. *Fax:* 505-827-6372. *Web site:* www.dvs.state.nm.us.

College Affordability Grant. The purpose of the grant is to encourage New Mexico students with financial need, who do not qualify for other state grants and scholarships, to attend and complete educational programs at a New Mexico public college or university. Student must have unmet need after all other financial aid has been awarded. Student may not be receiving any other state grants or scholarships. Renewable upon satisfactory academic progress. Grant value is $1000. Deadline: continuous. *Award:* Grant for use in freshman, sophomore, junior, or senior year; renewable. *Award amount:* up to $1000. *Number of awards:* varies. *Eligibility Requirements:* Applicant must be enrolled or expecting to enroll full- or part-time at a two-year or four-year institution or university; resident of New Mexico and studying in New Mexico. Available to U.S. citizens. *Application Requirements:* Financial need analysis. *Deadline:* continuous.

Contact Ofelia Morales, Director of Financial Aid, New Mexico Commission on Higher Education, 1068 Cerrillos Road, Santa Fe, NM 87505. *Phone:* 505-476-6506. *Web site:* www.hed.state.nm.us.

Legislative Endowment Scholarships. Renewable scholarships to provide aid for undergraduate students with substantial financial need who are attending public postsecondary institutions in New Mexico. Four-year schools may award up to $2500 per academic year, two-year schools may award up to $1000 per academic year. Deadlines: set by each institution. *Award:* Scholarship for use in freshman, sophomore, junior, or senior year; renewable. *Award amount:* $1000–$2500. *Number of awards:* varies. *Eligibility Requirements:* Applicant must be enrolled or expecting to enroll full- or part-time at a two-year or four-year institution or university; resident of New Mexico and studying in New Mexico. Available to U.S. citizens. *Application Requirements:* Application, financial need analysis, FAFSA. *Deadline:* varies.

Contact Ofelia Morales, Director of Financial Aid, New Mexico Commission on Higher Education, 1068 Cerrillos Road, Santa Fe, NM 87505. *E-mail:* ofelia.morales@state.nm.us. *Phone:* 505-476-6506. *Fax:* 505-476-6511. *Web site:* www.hed.state.nm.us.

Lottery Success Scholarships. Renewable Scholarship for New Mexico high school graduates or GED recipients who plan to attend an eligible New Mexico public college or university. Must be enrolled full-time and maintain 2.5 GPA. *Award:* Scholarship for use in freshman, sophomore, junior, or senior year; renewable. *Award amount:* varies. *Number of awards:* 1. *Eligibility Requirements:* Applicant must be high school student; planning to enroll or expecting to enroll full-time at a four-year institution or university; resident of New Mexico and studying in New Mexico. Applicant must have 2.5 GPA or higher. Available to U.S. citizens. *Application Requirements:* Application, FAFSA. *Deadline:* varies.

Contact Ofelia Morales, Director of Financial Aid, New Mexico Commission on Higher Education, 1068 Cerrillos Road, Santa Fe, NM 87505. *E-mail:* ofelia.morales@state.nm.us. *Phone:* 505-476-6506. *Fax:* 505-476-6511. *Web site:* www.hed.state.nm.us.

New Mexico Competitive Scholarship. Scholarships for non-resident or non-citizen of the United States to encourage out-of-state students, who have demonstrated high academic achievement in high school, to enroll in public four-year universities in New Mexico. Renewable for up to four years. High School GPA and ACT varies. For details visit: http://fin.hed.state.nm.us. *Award:* Scholarship for use in freshman, sophomore, junior, or senior year; renewable. *Award amount:* varies. *Number of awards:* varies. *Eligibility Requirements:* Applicant must be high school student; planning to enroll or expecting to enroll full-time at a four-year institution or university and studying in New Mexico. Available to Canadian and non-U.S. citizens. *Application Requirements:* Application, essay, references, test scores. *Deadline:* varies.

Contact Ofelia Morales, Director of Financial Aid, New Mexico Commission on Higher Education, 1068 Cerrillos Road, Santa Fe, NM 87505. *E-mail:* ofelia.morales@state.nm.us. *Phone:* 505-476-6506. *Fax:* 505-476-6511. *Web site:* www.hed.state.nm.us.

New Mexico Scholars' Program. Renewable award program created to encourage New Mexico high school students to attend public postsecondary institutions or the following private colleges in New Mexico: College of Santa Fe, St. John's College, College of the Southwest. For details visit: http://fin.hed.state.nm.us. Deadlines: set by each institution. *Award:* Scholarship for use in freshman, sophomore, junior, or senior year; renewable. *Award amount:* varies. *Number of awards:* 1. *Eligibility Requirements:* Applicant must be age 21 or under; enrolled or expecting to enroll full-time at a two-year or four-year institution; resident of New Mexico and studying in New

Mexico. Available to U.S. citizens. *Application Requirements:* Application, financial need analysis, test scores, FAFSA. *Deadline:* varies.

Contact Ofelia Morales, Director of Financial Aid, New Mexico Commission on Higher Education, 1068 Cerrillos Road, Santa Fe, NM 87505. *E-mail:* ofelia.morales@state.nm.us. *Phone:* 505-476-6506. *Fax:* 505-476-6511. *Web site:* www.hed.state.nm.us.

New Mexico Student Incentive Grant. Grant created to provide aid for undergraduate students with substantial financial need who are attending public colleges or universities or the following eligible colleges in New Mexico: College of Santa Fe, St. John's College, College of the Southwest, Institute of American Indian Art, Crownpoint Institute of Technology, Dine College and Southwestern Indian Polytechnic Institute. Part-time students are eligible for prorated awards. *Award:* Grant for use in freshman, sophomore, junior, or senior year; not renewable. *Award amount:* $200–$2500. *Number of awards:* varies. *Eligibility Requirements:* Applicant must be enrolled or expecting to enroll full- or part-time at a two-year, four-year, or technical institution or university; resident of New Mexico and studying in New Mexico. Available to U.S. citizens. *Application Requirements:* Application, financial need analysis. *Deadline:* varies.

Contact Ofelia Morales, Director of Financial Aid, New Mexico Commission on Higher Education, 1068 Cerrillos Road, Santa Fe, NM 87505. *E-mail:* ofelia.morales@state.nm.us. *Phone:* 505-476-6506. *Fax:* 505-476-6511. *Web site:* www.hed.state.nm.us.

New Mexico Vietnam Veteran Scholarship. Award for Vietnam veterans who are New Mexico residents for minimum of ten years and attending state funded postsecondary schools. Must have been awarded the Vietnam Campaign medal. Must submit DD 214 and discharge papers. *Award:* Scholarship for use in freshman, sophomore, junior, or senior year; renewable. *Award amount:* varies. *Number of awards:* varies. *Eligibility Requirements:* Applicant must be enrolled or expecting to enroll full- or part-time at a two-year, four-year, or technical institution or university; resident of New Mexico and studying in New Mexico. Available to U.S. citizens. Applicant must have general military experience. *Application Requirements:* Application, copy of DD214. *Deadline:* continuous.

Contact Alan Martinez, Director, State Benefits Division, New Mexico Veterans Service Commission, Bataan Memorial Building, 300 Galisteo, Room 142, Santa Fe, NM 87504. *E-mail:* alan.martinez@state.nm.us. *Phone:* 505-827-6300. *Fax:* 505-827-6372. *Web site:* www.dvs.state.nm.us.

Nursing Student Loan-For-Service Program. Award to increase the number of nurses in areas of the state which have experienced shortages by making educational loans to students entering nursing programs. As a condition of each loan, the student shall declare his/her intent to practice as a health professional in a designated shortage area. For every year of service, a portion of the loan will be forgiven. Deadline: July 1. *Academic Fields/Career Goals:* Nursing. *Award:* Forgivable loan for use in freshman, sophomore, junior, or senior year; renewable. *Award amount:* up to $12,000. *Number of awards:* varies. *Eligibility Requirements:* Applicant must be enrolled or expecting to enroll full- or part-time at a four-year institution or university; resident of New Mexico and studying in New Mexico. Available to U.S. citizens. *Application Requirements:* Application, financial need analysis, transcript, FAFSA. *Deadline:* July 1.

Contact Ofelia Morales, Director of Financial Aid, New Mexico Commission on Higher Education, 1068 Cerrillos Road, Santa Fe, NM 87505. *E-mail:* ofelia.morales@state.nm.us. *Phone:* 505-476-6506. *Fax:* 505-476-6511. *Web site:* www.hed.state.nm.us.

Vietnam Veterans' Scholarship Program. Renewable scholarship program created to provide aid for Vietnam veterans who are undergraduate and graduate students attending public postsecondary institutions or select private colleges in New Mexico. College includes: College of Santa Fe, St. John's College and College of the Southwest. *Award:* Scholarship for use in freshman, sophomore, junior, senior, or graduate year; renewable. *Award amount:* varies. *Number of awards:* 1. *Eligibility Requirements:* Applicant must be enrolled or expecting to enroll full-time at a two-year or four-year institution; resident of New Mexico and studying in New Mexico. Available to U.S. citizens. Applicant must have general military experience. *Application Requirements:* Application, certification by the NM Veteran's commission. *Deadline:* varies.

Contact Ofelia Morales, Director of Financial Aid, New Mexico Commission on Higher Education, 1068 Cerrillos Road, Santa Fe, NM 87505. *E-mail:* ofelia.morales@state.nm.us. *Phone:* 505-476-6506. *Fax:* 505-476-6511. *Web site:* www.hed.state.nm.us.

NEW YORK

American-Scandinavian Foundation Translation Prize. Two prizes are awarded for outstanding English translations of poetry, fiction, drama or literary prose originally written in Danish, Finnish, Icelandic, Norwegian or Swedish. One-time award of $2000. *Award:* Prize for use in freshman, sophomore, junior, senior, graduate, or postgraduate years; not renewable. *Award amount:* $2000. *Number of awards:* 2. *Eligibility Requirements:* Applicant must be enrolled or expecting to enroll full- or part-time at a two-year, four-year, or technical institution or university and must have an interest in Scandinavian language. Available to U.S. citizens. *Application Requirements:* Application, applicant must enter a contest, resume. *Deadline:* June 1.

Contact Ellen McKey, Director of Fellowships and Grants, American-Scandinavian Foundation, 58 Park Avenue, New York, NY 10016. *E-mail:* info@amscan.org. *Phone:* 212-879-9779. *Fax:* 212-686-2115. *Web site:* www.amscan.org.

Broome and Allen Boys Camp and Scholarship Fund. The Broome and Allen Scholarship is awarded to students of Sephardic origin or those working in Sephardic studies. Both graduate and undergraduate degree candidates as well as those doing research projects will be considered. It is awarded for one year and must be renewed for successive years. Enclose copy of tax returns with application. Deadline: May 15. *Award:* Scholarship for use in freshman, sophomore, junior, senior, graduate, or postgraduate years; not renewable. *Award amount:* $500–$2000. *Number of awards:* 20–60. *Eligibility Requirements:* Applicant must be Jewish and enrolled or expecting to enroll full- or part-time at a two-year, four-year, or technical institution or university. Available to U.S. and non-U.S. citizens. *Application Requirements:* Application, essay, financial need analysis, references, transcript, copy of tax returns. *Deadline:* May 15.

Contact Ms. Ellen Cohen, Membership & Outreach Coordinator, American Sephardi Foundation, 15 West 16th Street, New York, NY 10011. *E-mail:* ecohen@asf.cjh.org. *Phone:* 212-294-8350 Ext. 4. *Fax:* 212-294-8348. *Web site:* www.americansephardifederation.org.

New York Aid for Part-time Study (APTS). Renewable scholarship provides tuition assistance to part-time undergraduate students who are New York residents, meet income eligibility requirements and are attending New York accredited institutions. Deadline varies. Must be U.S. citizen. *Award:* Grant for use in freshman, sophomore, junior, or senior year; renewable. *Award amount:* up to $2000. *Number of awards:* varies. *Eligibility Requirements:*

Applicant must be enrolled or expecting to enroll part-time at a two-year or four-year institution or university; resident of New York and studying in New York. Available to U.S. citizens. *Application Requirements:* Application, financial need analysis. *Deadline:* varies.

Contact Student Information, New York State Higher Education Services Corporation, 99 Washington Avenue, Room 1320, Albany, NY 12255. *Phone:* 518-473-3887. *Fax:* 518-474-2839. *Web site:* www.hesc.com.

New York Lottery Leaders of Tomorrow (Lot) Scholarship. Scholarship to one eligible graduating senior from every participating public and private high school in New York State is awarded a $4000, four-year college scholarship. Scholarships can only be used toward the cost of attendance. For more details visit: http://www.nylottery.org/storelayoutimages/lot_overview.pdf. *Award:* Scholarship for use in freshman, sophomore, junior, or senior year; renewable. *Award amount:* $1000. *Number of awards:* varies. *Eligibility Requirements:* Applicant must be high school student; planning to enroll or expecting to enroll full-time at a two-year, four-year, or technical institution or university; resident of New York and studying in New York. Applicant must have 3.0 GPA or higher. Available to U.S. citizens. *Application Requirements:* Application, essay, transcript. *Deadline:* March 9.

Contact New York Lottery LOT Scholarships, New York Lottery, One Broadway Center, PO Box 7540, Schenectady, NY 12301-7540. *E-mail:* lotscholar@lottery.state.ny.us. *Phone:* 518-388-3415. *Fax:* 518-388-3423. *Web site:* www.nylottery.org/lot.

New York Memorial Scholarships for Families of Deceased Police Officers, Fire Fighters and Peace Officers. Renewable scholarship for families of New York police officers, peace officers, emergency medical service workers or firefighters who died in the line of duty. Provides up to the cost of SUNY educational expenses. *Award:* Scholarship for use in freshman, sophomore, junior, or senior year; renewable. *Award amount:* varies. *Number of awards:* varies. *Eligibility Requirements:* Applicant must be enrolled or expecting to enroll full-time at a four-year institution or university; resident of New York and studying in New York. Applicant or parent of applicant must have employment or volunteer experience in police/firefighting. Available to U.S. citizens. *Application Requirements:* Application, financial need analysis, transcript. *Deadline:* May 1.

Contact Adrienne Day, Associate HESC Information Representative, New York State Higher Education Services Corporation, 99 Washington Avenue, Room 1320, Albany, NY 12255. *E-mail:* aday@hesc.com. *Phone:* 518-474-2991. *Web site:* www.hesc.com.

New York State Aid to Native Americans. Award for enrolled members of a New York State tribe and their children who are attending or planning to attend a New York State college and who are New York State residents. Deadlines: July 15 for the fall semester, December 31 for the spring semester, and May 20 for summer session. *Award:* Scholarship for use in freshman, sophomore, junior, or senior year; renewable. *Award amount:* varies. *Number of awards:* varies. *Eligibility Requirements:* Applicant must be American Indian/Alaska Native; enrolled or expecting to enroll full- or part-time at a four-year institution or university; resident of New York and studying in New York. Available to U.S. citizens. *Application Requirements:* Application, financial need analysis, references, transcript. *Deadline:* varies.

Contact Native American Education Unit, New York State Education Department, New York State Higher Education Services Corporation, EBA Room 374, Albany, NY 12234. *Phone:* 518-474-0537. *Web site:* www.hesc.com.

New York State Tuition Assistance Program. Award for New York state residents attending a New York postsecondary institution. Must be full-time student in approved program with tuition over $200 per year. Must show financial need and not be in default in any other state program. Renewable award of $500 to $5000 dependent on family income and tuition charged. *Award:* Grant for use in freshman, sophomore, junior, or senior year; renewable. *Award amount:* $500–$5000. *Number of awards:* 350,000–360,000. *Eligibility Requirements:* Applicant must be enrolled or expecting to enroll full-time at a two-year or four-year institution or university; resident of New York and studying in New York. Available to U.S. citizens. *Application Requirements:* Application, financial need analysis. *Deadline:* May 1.

Contact Student Information, New York State Higher Education Services Corporation, 99 Washington Avenue, Room 1320, Albany, NY 12255. *Web site:* www.hesc.com.

New York Vietnam/Persian Gulf/Afghanistan Veterans Tuition Awards. Scholarship for veterans who served in Vietnam, the Persian Gulf, or Afghanistan. Must be a New York resident attending a New York institution. Deadline: May 1. Must establish eligibility by September 1. *Award:* Scholarship for use in freshman, sophomore, junior, or senior year; renewable. *Award amount:* varies. *Number of awards:* varies. *Eligibility Requirements:* Applicant must be enrolled or expecting to enroll full- or part-time at a four-year institution or university; resident of New York and studying in New York. Available to U.S. citizens. Applicant must have general military experience. *Application Requirements:* Application, financial need analysis, transcript. *Deadline:* May 1.

Contact Adrienne Day, Associate HESC Information Representative, New York State Higher Education Services Corporation, 99 Washington Avenue, Room 1320, Albany, NY 12255. *E-mail:* aday@hesc.com. *Phone:* 518-474-2991. *Web site:* www.hesc.com.

Regents Award for Child of Veteran. Award for students whose parent, as a result of service in U.S. Armed Forces during war or national emergency, died; suffered a 40 percent or more disability; or is classified as missing in action or a prisoner of war. Veteran must be current New York State resident or have been so at time of death. Student must be a New York resident, attending, or planning to attend, college in New York State. Must establish eligibility before applying for payment. *Award:* Scholarship for use in freshman, sophomore, junior, or senior year; not renewable. *Award amount:* $450. *Number of awards:* varies. *Eligibility Requirements:* Applicant must be enrolled or expecting to enroll full-time at a two-year or four-year institution or university; resident of New York and studying in New York. Available to U.S. citizens. Applicant or parent must meet one or more of the following requirements: general military experience; retired from active duty; disabled or killed as a result of military service; prisoner of war; or missing in action. *Application Requirements:* Application, proof of eligibility. *Deadline:* May 1.

Contact Rita McGivern, Student Information, New York State Higher Education Services Corporation, 99 Washington Avenue, Room 1320, Albany, NY 12255. *E-mail:* rmcgivern@hesc.com. *Web site:* www.hesc.com.

Regents Professional Opportunity Scholarship. Scholarship for New York residents beginning or already enrolled in an approved degree-bearing program of study in New York that leads to licensure in a particular profession. See the Web site for the list of eligible professions. Must be U.S. citizen or permanent resident. Award recipients must agree to practice upon licensure in their profession in New York for 12 months for each annual payment received. Priority given to economically disadvantaged members of minority groups underrepresented in the professions. *Academic Fields/Career Goals:* Accounting; Architecture; Dental Health/Services; Engineering/Technology; Health and Medical Sciences; Interior Design; Landscape Architecture; Law/Legal Services; Nursing; Pharmacy; Psychology; Social Services. *Award:* Scholarship for use in freshman, sophomore, junior, senior, or graduate year; renewable. *Award amount:* up to $5000. *Number of awards:* 220. *Eligibility Requirements:* Applicant must be enrolled or expecting to enroll full-time at a two-year or four-year institution or university; resident of New York and studying in New York. Available to U.S. citizens. *Application Requirements:* Application. *Deadline:* May 31.

Contact Lewis J. Hall, Coordinator, New York State Education Department, Room 1078 EBA, Albany, NY 12234. *E-mail:* scholar@mail.nysed.gov. *Phone:* 518-486-1319. *Fax:* 518-486-5346. *Web site:* www.highered.nysed.gov/.

Regents Professional Opportunity Scholarships. Award for New York State residents pursuing career in certain licensed professions. Must attend New York State college. Priority given to economically disadvantaged members of minority group underrepresented in chosen profession and graduates of SEEK, College Discovery, EOP, and HEOP. Must work in New York State in chosen profession one year for each annual payment. Scholarships are awarded to undergraduate or graduate students, depending on the program. *Award:* Scholarship for use in freshman, sophomore, junior, senior, or graduate year; not renewable. *Award amount:* $1000–$5000. *Number of awards:* 220. *Eligibility Requirements:* Applicant must be enrolled or expecting to enroll full-time at a two-year or four-year institution or university; resident of New York and studying in New York. Available to U.S. citizens. *Application Requirements:* Application. *Deadline:* May 3.

Contact New York State Education Department, Bureau of HEOP/VATEA/Scholarships, New York State Higher Education Services Corporation, Education Building Addition Room 1071, Albany, NY 12234. *Phone:* 518-486-1319. *Web site:* www.hesc.com.

Scholarship for Academic Excellence. Renewable award for New York residents. Scholarship winners must attend a college or university in New York. 2000 scholarships are for $1500 and 6000 are for $500. The selection criteria used are based on Regents test scores or rank in class or local exam. Must be U.S. citizen or permanent resident. *Award:* Scholarship for use in freshman, sophomore, junior, or senior year; renewable. *Award amount:* $500–$1500. *Number of awards:* up to 8000. *Eligibility Requirements:* Applicant must be high school student; planning to enroll or expecting to enroll full-time at a two-year or four-year institution or university; resident of New York and studying in New York. Available to U.S. citizens. *Application Requirements:* Application. *Deadline:* December 19.

Contact Lewis J. Hall, Supervisor, New York State Education Department, Room 1078 EBA, Albany, NY 12234. *E-mail:* scholar@mail.nysed.gov. *Phone:* 518-486-1319. *Fax:* 518-486-5346. *Web site:* www.highered.nysed.gov/.

Scholarships for Academic Excellence. Renewable awards of up to $1500 for academically outstanding New York State high school graduates planning to attend an approved postsecondary institution in New York State. For full-time study only. Contact high school guidance counselor to apply. *Award:* Scholarship for use in freshman, sophomore, junior, or senior year; renewable. *Award amount:* $500–$1500. *Number of awards:* 8000. *Eligibility Requirements:* Applicant must be high school student; planning to enroll or expecting to enroll full-time at a four-year institution or university; resident of New York and studying in New York. Available to U.S. citizens. *Application Requirements:* Application. *Deadline:* varies.

Contact Rita McGivern, Student Information, New York State Higher Education Services Corporation, 99 Washington Avenue, Room 1320, Albany, NY 12255. *E-mail:* rmcgivern@hesc.com. *Web site:* www.hesc.com.

World Trade Center Memorial Scholarship. Renewable awards of up to the cost of educational expenses at a State University of New York four-year college. Available to the children, spouses and financial dependents of victims who died or were severely disabled as a result of the September 11, 2001 terrorist attacks on the U.S. and the rescue and recovery efforts. *Award:* Scholarship for use in freshman, sophomore, junior, or senior year; renewable. *Award amount:* varies. *Number of awards:* varies. *Eligibility Requirements:* Applicant must be enrolled or expecting to enroll full-time at a four-year institution or university; resident of New York and studying in New York. Available to U.S. citizens. *Application Requirements:* Application, financial need analysis, references, transcript. *Deadline:* May 1.

Contact HESC Scholarship Unit, New York State Higher Education Services Corporation, 99 Washington Avenue, Room 1320, Albany, NY 12255. *Phone:* 518-402-6494. *Web site:* www.hesc.com.

NORTH CAROLINA

Federal Supplemental Educational Opportunity Grant Program. Applicant must have exceptional financial need to qualify for this award. Amount of financial need is determined by the educational institution the student attends. Available only to undergraduate students. Recipient must be a U.S. citizen or permanent resident. Priority is given to a students who receive Federal Pell Grants. *Award:* Grant for use in freshman, sophomore, junior, or senior year; not renewable. *Award amount:* $100–$4400. *Number of awards:* varies. *Eligibility Requirements:* Applicant must be enrolled or expecting to enroll full-time at a four-year institution or university. Available to U.S. citizens. *Application Requirements:* Application, financial need analysis, transcript, student's total financial aid package developed through the school the student attends. *Deadline:* continuous.

Contact Federal Student Aid Information Center, College Foundation of North Carolina Inc., PO Box 84, Washington, DC 20044. *Phone:* 800-433-3243. *Web site:* www.cfnc.org.

North Carolina Community College Grant Program. Annual award for North Carolina residents enrolled at least part-time in a North Carolina community college curriculum program. Priority given to those enrolled in college transferable curriculum programs, persons seeking new job skills, women in non-traditional curricula, and those participating in an ABE, GED, or high school diploma program. Contact financial aid office of institution the student attends for information and deadline. Must complete Free Application for Federal Student Aid. *Award:* Grant for use in freshman or sophomore year; renewable. *Award amount:* $683. *Number of awards:* varies. *Eligibility Requirements:* Applicant must be enrolled or expecting to enroll full- or part-time at a two-year or technical institution; resident of North Carolina and studying in North Carolina. Available to U.S. citizens. *Application Requirements:* Application, financial need analysis, FAFSA. *Deadline:* varies.

Contact Bill Carswell, Manager, Scholarship and Grants Division, North Carolina State Education Assistance Authority, PO Box 14103, Research Triangle Park, NC 27709.

E-mail: carswellb@ncseaa.edu. *Phone:* 919-549-8614. *Fax:* 919-248-4687. *Web site:* www.ncseaa.edu.

North Carolina Division of Services for the Blind Rehabilitation Services. Financial assistance is available for North Carolina residents who are blind or visually impaired and who require vocational rehabilitation to help find employment. Tuition and other assistance provided based on need. Open to U.S. citizens and legal residents of United States. Applicants goal must be to work after receiving vocational services. To apply, contact the local DSB office and apply for vocational rehabilitation services. *Award:* Scholarship for use in freshman, sophomore, junior, or senior year; renewable. *Award amount:* varies. *Number of awards:* varies. *Eligibility Requirements:* Applicant must be enrolled or expecting to enroll full- or part-time at a two-year, four-year, or technical institution or university and resident of North Carolina. Applicant must be visually impaired. Available to U.S. and non-U.S. citizens. *Application Requirements:* Application, financial need analysis, interview, proof of eligibility. *Deadline:* continuous.

Contact JoAnn Strader, Chief of Rehabilitation Field Services, North Carolina Division of Services for the Blind, 2601 Mail Service Center, Raleigh, NC 27699-2601. *E-mail:* joann.strader@ncmail.net. *Phone:* 919-733-9700. *Fax:* 919-715-8771. *Web site:* www.dhhs.state.nc.us/dsb.

North Carolina Legislative Tuition Grant Program (NCLTG). Renewable aid for North Carolina residents attending approved private colleges or universities within the state. Must be enrolled full-time in an undergraduate program not leading to a religious vocation. Contact college financial aid office for deadlines. *Award:* Grant for use in freshman, sophomore, junior, or senior year; renewable. *Award amount:* $1950. *Number of awards:* varies. *Eligibility Requirements:* Applicant must be enrolled or expecting to enroll full-time at a two-year or four-year institution or university; resident of North Carolina and studying in North Carolina. Available to U.S. citizens. *Application Requirements:* Application. *Deadline:* varies.

Contact Bill Carswell, Manager of Scholarship and Grant Division, North Carolina State Education Assistance Authority, PO Box 13663, Research Triangle Park, NC 27709. *E-mail:* carswellb@ncseaa.edu. *Phone:* 919-549-8614. *Fax:* 919-248-4687. *Web site:* www.ncseaa.edu.

North Carolina National Guard Tuition Assistance Program. Scholarship for members of the North Carolina Air and Army National Guard who will remain in the service for two years following the period for which assistance is provided. Applicants must reapply for each academic period. For use at approved North Carolina institutions. Deadline: last day of late registration period set by the school. *Award:* Grant for use in freshman, sophomore, junior, senior, or graduate year; not renewable. *Award amount:* up to $2000. *Number of awards:* varies. *Eligibility Requirements:* Applicant must be enrolled or expecting to enroll full- or part-time at a two-year, four-year, or technical institution or university and studying in North Carolina. Available to U.S. citizens. Applicant must have served in the Air Force National Guard or Army National Guard. *Application Requirements:* Application. *Deadline:* varies.

Contact Capt. Miriam Gray, Education Services Officer, North Carolina National Guard, 4105 Reedy Creek Road, Raleigh, NC 27607-6410. *E-mail:* miriam.gray@nc.ngb.army.mil. *Phone:* 800-621-4136 Ext. 6272. *Fax:* 919-664-6520. *Web site:* www.nc.ngb.army.mil.

North Carolina Sheriffs' Association Undergraduate Criminal Justice Scholarships. One-time award for full-time North Carolina resident undergraduate students majoring in criminal justice at a University of North Carolina school. Priority given to child of any North Carolina law enforcement officer. Letter of recommendation from county sheriff required. *Academic Fields/Career Goals:* Criminal Justice/Criminology; Law Enforcement/Police Administration. *Award:* Scholarship for use in freshman, sophomore, junior, or senior year; not renewable. *Award amount:* $1000–$2000. *Number of awards:* up to 10. *Eligibility Requirements:* Applicant must be enrolled or expecting to enroll full-time at a four-year institution or university; resident of North Carolina and studying in North Carolina. Applicant or parent of applicant must have employment or volunteer experience in police/firefighting. Available to U.S. citizens. *Application Requirements:* Application, financial need analysis, references, transcript, statement of career goals. *Deadline:* continuous.

Contact Nolita Goldston, Assistant, Scholarship and Grant Division, North Carolina State Education Assistance Authority, PO Box 13663, Research Triangle Park, NC 27709. *E-mail:* ngoldston@ncseaa.edu. *Phone:* 919-549-8614. *Fax:* 919-248-4687. *Web site:* www.ncseaa.edu.

North Carolina Student Loan Program for Health, Science, and Mathematics. Renewable award for North Carolina residents studying health-related fields, or science or math education. Based on merit, need, and promise of service as a health professional or educator in an underserved area of North Carolina. Need two co-signers. Submit surety statement. *Academic Fields/Career Goals:* Dental Health/Services; Health Administration; Health and Medical Sciences; Nursing; Physical Sciences and Math; Therapy/Rehabilitation. *Award:* Forgivable loan for use in freshman, junior, senior, or graduate year; renewable. *Award amount:* $3000–$8500. *Number of awards:* 1. *Eligibility Requirements:* Applicant must be enrolled or expecting to enroll full-time at a two-year or four-year institution or university and resident of North Carolina. Available to U.S. citizens. *Application Requirements:* Application, financial need analysis, transcript. *Deadline:* June 1.

Contact Edna Williams, Manager, Selection and Origination, HSM Loan Program, North Carolina State Education Assistance Authority, PO Box 14223, Research Triangle Park, NC 27709. *E-mail:* eew@ncseaa.edu. *Phone:* 800-700-1775 Ext. 4658. *Web site:* www.ncseaa.edu.

North Carolina Teaching Fellows Scholarship Program. Award for North Carolina high school seniors planning to pursue teacher training studies. Must agree to teach in a North Carolina public or government school for four years or repay award. For more details visit Web site: http://www.teachingfellows.org. *Academic Fields/Career Goals:* Education. *Award:* Forgivable loan for use in freshman, sophomore, junior, or senior year; renewable. *Award amount:* $6500. *Number of awards:* 500. *Eligibility Requirements:* Applicant must be high school student; planning to enroll or expecting to enroll full-time at a four-year institution or university; resident of North Carolina and studying in North Carolina. Applicant must have 3.5 GPA or higher. Available to U.S. citizens. *Application Requirements:* Application, essay, interview, references, test scores, transcript. *Deadline:* varies.

Contact Sherry Woodruff, Program Officer, North Carolina Teaching Fellows Commission, 3739 National Drive, Suite 100, Raleigh, NC 27612. *E-mail:* tfellows@ncforum.org. *Phone:* 919-781-6833 Ext. 103. *Fax:* 919-781-6527. *Web site:* www.teachingfellows.org.

North Carolina Veterans Scholarships Class I-B. Awards for children of veterans rated by USDVA as 100 percent disabled due to wartime service as defined in the law, and currently or at time of death drawing compensation for such disability. Parent must have been a North Carolina resident at time of entry into service. Duration of the scholarship is four academic years (8 semesters) if used within 8 years. No limit on number awarded each year. *Award:* Scholarship for use in freshman, sophomore, junior, or senior year; renewable. *Award amount:* $1500. *Number of awards:* varies. *Eligibility Requirements:* Applicant must be enrolled or expecting to enroll full- or part-time at a two-year, four-year, or technical institution or university and studying in North Carolina. Available to U.S. citizens. Applicant or parent must meet one or more of the following requirements: general military experience; retired from active duty; disabled or killed as a result of military service; prisoner of war; or missing in action. *Application Requirements:* Application, financial need analysis, interview, transcript. *Deadline:* continuous.

Contact Charles Smith, Assistant Secretary, North Carolina Division of Veterans Affairs, 325 North Salisbury Street, Raleigh, NC 27603. *E-mail:* charlie.smith@ncmail.net. *Phone:* 919-733-3851. *Fax:* 919-733-2834. *Web site:* www.doa.state.nc.us/vets/va.htm.

North Carolina Veterans Scholarships Class II. Awards for children of veterans rated by USDVA as much as 20 percent but less than 100 percent disabled due to wartime service as defined in the law, or awarded Purple Heart Medal for wounds received. Parent must have been a North Carolina resident at time of entry into service. Duration of the scholarship is four academic years (8 semesters) if used within 8 years. Free tuition and exemption from certain mandatory fees as set forth in the law in Public, Community and Technical Colleges. *Award:* Scholarship for use in freshman, sophomore, junior, or senior year; renewable. *Award amount:* $4500. *Number of awards:* up to 100. *Eligibility Requirements:* Applicant must be enrolled or expecting to enroll full- or part-time at a two-year, four-year, or technical institution or university and studying in North Carolina. Available to U.S. citizens. Applicant or parent must meet one or more of the following requirements: general military experience; retired from active duty; disabled or killed as a result of military service; prisoner of war; or missing in action. *Application Requirements:* Application, financial need analysis, interview, transcript. *Deadline:* continuous.

Contact Charles Smith, Assistant Secretary, North Carolina Division of Veterans Affairs, 325 North Salisbury Street, Raleigh, NC 27603. *E-mail:* charlie.smith@ncmail.net. *Phone:* 919-733-3851. *Fax:* 919-733-2834. *Web site:* www.doa.state.nc.us/vets/va.htm.

North Carolina Veterans Scholarships Class III. Awards for children of a deceased war veteran, who was honorably discharged and who does not qualify under any other provision within this synopsis or veteran who served in a combat zone or waters adjacent to a combat zone and received a campaign badge or medal and who does not qualify under any other provision within this synopsis. Duration of the scholarship is four academic years (8 semesters) if used within 8 years. For more details, visit: http://www.doa.state.nc.us/vets/scholarship.htm. *Award:* Scholarship for use in freshman, sophomore, junior, or senior year; renewable. *Award amount:* $4500. *Number of awards:* up to 100. *Eligibility Requirements:* Applicant must be enrolled or expecting to enroll full- or part-time at a two-year, four-year, or technical institution or university and studying in North Carolina. Available to U.S. citizens. Applicant or parent must meet one or more of the following requirements: general military experience; retired from active duty; disabled or killed as a result of military service; prisoner of war; or missing in action. *Application Requirements:* Application, financial need analysis, interview, transcript. *Deadline:* March 31.

Contact Charles Smith, Assistant Secretary, North Carolina Division of Veterans Affairs, 325 North Salisbury Street, Raleigh, NC 27603. *E-mail:* charlie.smith@ncmail.net. *Phone:* 919-733-3851. *Fax:* 919-733-2834. *Web site:* www.doa.state.nc.us/vets/va.htm.

North Carolina Veterans Scholarships Class IV. Awards for children of veterans, who were prisoner of war or missing in action. Duration of the scholarship is four academic years (8 semesters) if used within 8 years. No limit on number awarded each year. Award value is $4500 per nine-month academic year in private colleges and junior colleges. For more details, visit: http://www.doa.state.nc.us/vets/scholarship.htm. *Award:* Scholarship for use in freshman, sophomore, junior, or senior year; renewable. *Award amount:* $4500. *Number of awards:* varies. *Eligibility Requirements:* Applicant must be enrolled or expecting to enroll full- or part-time at a two-year, four-year, or technical institution or university and studying in North Carolina. Available to U.S. citizens. Applicant or parent must meet one or more of the following requirements: general military experience; retired from active duty; disabled or killed as a result of military service; prisoner of war; or missing in action. *Application Requirements:* Application, financial need analysis, interview, transcript. *Deadline:* March 31.

Contact Charles Smith, Assistant Secretary, North Carolina Division of Veterans Affairs, 325 North Salisbury Street, Raleigh, NC 27603. *E-mail:* charlie.smith@ncmail.net. *Phone:* 919-733-3851. *Fax:* 919-733-2834. *Web site:* www.doa.state.nc.us/vets/va.htm.

Nurse Education Scholarship Loan Program (NESLP). Must be U.S. citizen and North Carolina resident. Award available through financial aid offices of North Carolina colleges and universities that offer programs to prepare students for licensure in the state as LPN or RN. Recipients enter contract with the State of North Carolina to work full time as a licensed nurse. Loans not repaid through service must be repaid in cash. Award based upon financial need. Maximum award for students enrolled in Associate Degree Nursing and Practical Nurse Education programs is $3000. Maximum award for students enrolled in a baccalaureate program is $5000. *Academic Fields/Career Goals:* Nursing. *Award:* Forgivable loan for use in freshman, sophomore, junior, or senior year; renewable. *Award amount:* $400–$5000. *Number of awards:* varies. *Eligibility Requirements:* Applicant must be enrolled or expecting to enroll full- or part-time at a four-year institution or university; resident of North Carolina and studying in North Carolina. Available to U.S. citizens. *Application Requirements:* Application, financial need analysis. *Deadline:* continuous.

Contact Bill Carswell, Manager of Scholarship and Grant Division, North Carolina State Education Assistance Authority, PO Box 14103, Research Triangle Park, NC 27709. *E-mail:* carswellb@ncseaa.edu. *Phone:* 919-549-8614. *Fax:* 919-248-4687. *Web site:* www.ncseaa.edu.

State Contractual Scholarship Fund Program-North Carolina. Renewable award for North Carolina residents already attending an approved private college or university in the state in pursuit of an undergraduate degree. Must have financial need. Contact college financial aid office for deadline and information. May not be enrolled in a program leading to a religious vocation. *Award:* Scholarship for use in freshman, sophomore, junior, or senior year; renewable. *Award amount:* up to $1250. *Number of awards:* varies. *Eligibility Requirements:* Applicant must be enrolled or expecting to enroll full- or part-time at a four-year institution or university; resident of North Carolina and studying in North Carolina. Available to U.S. citizens. *Application Requirements:* Application, financial need analysis. *Deadline:* varies.

Contact Bill Carswell, Manager of Scholarship and Grant Division, North Carolina State

Education Assistance Authority, PO Box 13663, Research Triangle Park, NC 27709. *E-mail:* carswellb@ncseaa.edu. *Phone:* 919-549-8614. *Fax:* 919-248-4687. *Web site:* www.ncseaa.edu.

Teacher Assistant Scholarship Fund. Funding to attend a public or private four-year college or university in North Carolina with an approved teacher education program. Applicant must be employed full-time as a teacher assistant in an instructional area while pursuing licensure and maintain employment to remain eligible. Refer to Web site for further details: http://www.ncseaa.edu/tas.htm. *Academic Fields/Career Goals:* Education. *Award:* Scholarship for use in freshman, sophomore, junior, or senior year; renewable. *Award amount:* $600–$3600. *Number of awards:* varies. *Eligibility Requirements:* Applicant must be enrolled or expecting to enroll full- or part-time at a four-year institution or university; resident of North Carolina and studying in North Carolina. Applicant must have 2.5 GPA or higher. Available to U.S. citizens. *Application Requirements:* Application, financial need analysis, transcript, FAFSA. *Deadline:* March 31.

Contact Rashonn Albritton, Processing Assistant, North Carolina State Education Assistance Authority, PO Box 13663, Research Triangle Park, NC 27709. *E-mail:* ralbritton@ncseaa.edu. *Phone:* 919-549-8614. *Fax:* 919-248-4687. *Web site:* www.ncseaa.edu.

University of North Carolina Need Based Grant. Grants available for eligible students attending one of the 16 campuses of the University of North Carolina. Students must be enrolled in at least 6 credit hours at one of the 16 constituent institutions of The University of North Carolina. Award amounts vary, based on legislative appropriations. No formal deadline has been established. *Award:* Grant for use in freshman, sophomore, junior, or senior year; not renewable. *Award amount:* varies. *Number of awards:* varies. *Eligibility Requirements:* Applicant must be enrolled or expecting to enroll full- or part-time at a four-year institution or university; resident of North Carolina and studying in North Carolina. Available to U.S. citizens. *Application Requirements:* Financial need analysis. *Deadline:* continuous.

Contact Scholarship Coordinator, College Foundation of North Carolina Inc., 2917 Highwoods Boulevard, PO Box 41966, Raleigh, NC 27604. *E-mail:* programinformation@cfnc.org. *Phone:* 866-866-2362. *Fax:* 919-248-4687. *Web site:* www.cfnc.org.

University of North Carolina Need-Based Grant. Applicants must be enrolled in at least 6 credit hours at one of sixteen UNC system universities. Eligibility based on need; award varies, consideration for grant automatic when FAFSA is filed. Late applications may be denied due to insufficient funds. *Award:* Grant for use in freshman, sophomore, junior, or senior year; renewable. *Award amount:* varies. *Number of awards:* 1. *Eligibility Requirements:* Applicant must be enrolled or expecting to enroll full- or part-time at an institution or university; resident of North Carolina and studying in North Carolina. Available to U.S. citizens. *Application Requirements:* Application, financial need analysis, FAFSA. *Deadline:* varies.

Contact Bill Carswell, Manager of Scholarship and Grant Division, North Carolina State Education Assistance Authority, PO Box 13663, Research Triangle Park, NC 27709. *E-mail:* carswellb@ncseaa.edu. *Phone:* 919-549-8614. *Fax:* 919-248-4687. *Web site:* www.ncseaa.edu.

NORTH DAKOTA

North Dakota Indian Scholarship Program. The scholarship assists American Indian students in obtaining a college education by providing scholarships ranging in amount from $500 to $2000 per year. The scholarship is based upon scholastic ability and unmet financial need. Must be a resident of North Dakota, must be enrolled full-time, and may not have a GPA below 2.0. *Award:* Scholarship for use in freshman, sophomore, junior, senior, or graduate year; renewable. *Award amount:* $500–$2000. *Number of awards:* 150–175. *Eligibility Requirements:* Applicant must be American Indian/Alaska Native; enrolled or expecting to enroll full-time at a two-year or four-year institution or university; resident of North Dakota and studying in North Dakota. Applicant must have 3.5 GPA or higher. Available to U.S. citizens. *Application Requirements:* Application, financial need analysis, transcript, proof of tribal enrollment, budget completed by a financial aid officer at the institution being attended. *Deadline:* July 15.

Contact Rhonda Schauer, Coordinator of American Indian Higher Education, State of North Dakota, 919 South Seventh Street, Suite 300, Bismarck, ND 58504-5881. *E-mail:* rhonda.schauer@ndus.nodak.edu. *Phone:* 701-328-9661. *Web site:* www.ndus.nodak.edu.

North Dakota Scholars Program. Provides scholarships equal to cost of tuition at the public colleges in North Dakota for North Dakota residents. Must score at or above the 95th percentile on ACT and rank in top twenty percent of high school graduation class. Must take ACT in fall. For high school seniors with a minimum 3.5 GPA. Deadline: October or June ACT test date. *Award:* Scholarship for use in freshman year; renewable. *Award amount:* varies. *Number of awards:* 15–20. *Eligibility Requirements:* Applicant must be high school student; planning to enroll or expecting to enroll full-time at a two-year or four-year institution or university; resident of North Dakota and studying in North Dakota. Applicant must have 3.5 GPA or higher. Available to U.S. citizens. *Application Requirements:* Application, references, test scores, transcript. *Deadline:* varies.

Contact Peggy Wipf, Director of Financial Aid, State of North Dakota, 600 East Boulevard Avenue, Department 215, Bismarck, ND 58505-0230. *E-mail:* peggy.wipf@ndus.nodak.edu. *Phone:* 701-328-4114. *Web site:* www.ndus.nodak.edu.

North Dakota State Student Incentive Grant Program. Aids North Dakota residents attending an approved college or university in North Dakota. Must be enrolled in a program of at least nine months in length. Must be a U.S. citizen. Deadline: March 15. *Award:* Grant for use in freshman, sophomore, junior, or senior year; renewable. *Award amount:* up to $600. *Number of awards:* 2500–2600. *Eligibility Requirements:* Applicant must be enrolled or expecting to enroll full-time at a two-year or four-year institution or university; resident of North Dakota and studying in North Dakota. Available to U.S. citizens. *Application Requirements:* Application, financial need analysis. *Deadline:* March 15.

Contact Peggy Wipf, Director of Financial Aid, State of North Dakota, 600 East Boulevard Avenue, Department 215, Bismarck, ND 58505-0230. *Phone:* 701-328-4114. *Web site:* www.ndus.nodak.edu.

OHIO

Accountancy Board of Ohio Educational Assistance Program. Program intended for minority students or students with financial need. Applicant must be enrolled as accounting major at an accredited Ohio college or university in a five-year degree program. Applicant must be an Ohio resident. Please refer to Web site for further details: http://acc.ohio.gov/educasst.html. *Academic Fields/Career Goals:* Accounting. *Award:* Scholarship for use in sophomore, junior, or senior year; not renewable. *Award amount:* $7700. *Number of awards:* varies. *Eligibility Requirements:* Applicant must be enrolled or expecting to enroll full- or part-time at a four-year institution or university; resident of Ohio and studying in Ohio. Available to U.S. citizens. *Application Requirements:* Application, financial need analysis, transcript, FAFSA. *Deadline:* November 15.

Contact Kay Sedgmer, Scholarship Secretary, Accountancy Board of Ohio, Accountancy Board of Ohio, 77 South High Street, 18th Floor, Columbus, OH 43215-6128. *E-mail:* kay.sedgmer@acc.state.oh.us. *Phone:* 614-466-4135. *Fax:* 614-466-2628. *Web site:* acc.ohio.gov.

Ohio Academic Scholarship Program. Award for academically outstanding Ohio residents planning to attend an approved Ohio college. Must be a high school senior intending to enroll full-time. Award is renewable for up to four years. Must rank in upper quarter of class or have a minimum GPA of 3.5. *Award:* Scholarship for use in freshman, sophomore, junior, or senior year; renewable. *Award amount:* $2205. *Number of awards:* 1000. *Eligibility Requirements:* Applicant must be high school student; planning to enroll or expecting to enroll full-time at a two-year or four-year institution; resident of Ohio and studying in Ohio. Applicant must have 3.5 GPA or higher. Available to U.S. citizens. *Application Requirements:* Application, test scores, transcript. *Deadline:* February 23.

Contact Jathiya Abdullah, Program Administrator, Ohio Board of Regents, 30 East Broad Street, 36th Floor, Columbus, OH 43215-3414. *E-mail:* jabdullah@regents.state.oh.us. *Phone:* 614-752-9528. *Fax:* 614-752-5903. *Web site:* www.regents.ohio.gov.

Ohio Environmental Science & Engineering Scholarships. Merit-based, non-renewable, tuition-only scholarships given to undergraduate students admitted to Ohio state or private colleges and universities who can demonstrate their knowledge and commitment to careers in environmental sciences or environmental engineering. Deadline: June 1. *Academic Fields/Career Goals:* Environmental Science. *Award:* Scholarship for use in senior year; not renewable. *Award amount:* $1250–$2500. *Number of awards:* 18. *Eligibility Requirements:* Applicant must be enrolled or expecting to enroll full- or part-time at a two-year or four-year institution or university; resident of Ohio and studying in Ohio. Applicant must have 3.0 GPA or higher. Available to U.S. citizens. *Application Requirements:* Application, essay, resume, references, self-addressed stamped envelope, transcript. *Deadline:* June 1.

Contact Mr. Lynn E. Elfner, Chief Executive Officer, Ohio Academy of Science/Ohio Environmental Education Fund, 1500 West Third Avenue, Suite 228, Columbus, OH 43212-2817. *E-mail:* oas@iwaynet.net. *Phone:* 614-488-2228. *Fax:* 614-488-7629. *Web site:* www.ohiosci.org.

Ohio Instructional Grant. Award for low- and middle-income Ohio residents attending an approved college or school in Ohio or Pennsylvania. Must be enrolled full-time and have financial need. May be used for any course of study except theology. *Award:* Grant for use in freshman, sophomore, junior, or senior year; renewable. *Award amount:* $78–$5466. *Number of awards:* varies. *Eligibility Requirements:* Applicant must be enrolled or expecting to enroll full-time at a two-year or four-year institution or university; resident of Ohio and studying in Ohio or Pennsylvania. Available to U.S. citizens. *Application Requirements:* Application, financial need analysis. *Deadline:* October 1.

Contact Lamar Burch, Program Administrator, Ohio Board of Regents, 30 East Broad Street, 36th Floor, Columbus, OH 43215-3414. *E-mail:* lburch@regents.state.oh.us. *Phone:* 614-752-9489. *Fax:* 614-752-5903. *Web site:* www.regents.ohio.gov.

Ohio Missing in Action and Prisoners of War Orphans Scholarship. Renewable award aids children of Vietnam conflict servicemen who have been classified as missing in action or prisoner of war. Applicants must be under the age of 25 and be enrolled full-time at an Ohio college. Full tuition awards. Dollar value of each award varies. *Award:* Scholarship for use in freshman, sophomore, junior, or senior year; renewable. *Award amount:* varies. *Number of awards:* 1–5. *Eligibility Requirements:* Applicant must be age 25 or under; enrolled or expecting to enroll full-time at a four-year institution or university; resident of Ohio and studying in Ohio. Available to U.S. citizens. Applicant or parent must meet one or more of the following requirements: general military experience; retired from active duty; disabled or killed as a result of military service; prisoner of war; or missing in action. *Application Requirements:* Application. *Deadline:* July 1.

Contact Jathiya Abdullah, Program Administrator, Ohio Board of Regents, 30 East Broad Street, 36th Floor, Columbus, OH 43215-3414. *E-mail:* jabdullah@regents.state.oh.us. *Phone:* 614-752-9528. *Fax:* 614-752-5903. *Web site:* www.regents.ohio.gov.

Ohio National Guard Scholarship Program. Scholarships are for undergraduate studies at an approved Ohio postsecondary institution. Applicants must enlist for six years of Selective Service Reserve Duty in the Ohio National Guard. Scholarship pays 100% instructional and general fees for public institutions and an average of cost of public schools is available for private schools. Must be 18 years of age or older. Award is renewable. Deadlines: July 1, November 1, February 1, April 1. *Award:* Scholarship for use in freshman, sophomore, junior, or senior year; renewable. *Award amount:* up to $3000. *Number of awards:* 3500–8000. *Eligibility Requirements:* Applicant must be age 18 and over; enrolled or expecting to enroll full- or part-time at a two-year, four-year, or technical institution or university and studying in Ohio. Available to U.S. citizens. Applicant must have served in the Air Force National Guard or Army National Guard. *Application Requirements:* Application. *Deadline:* varies.

Contact Toni Davis, Grants Administrator, Ohio National Guard, 2825 West Dublin Granville Road, Columbus, OH 43235-2789. *E-mail:* toni.davis@tagoh.gov. *Phone:* 614-336-7032. *Fax:* 614-336-7318. *Web site:* www.ongsp.org.

Ohio Safety Officers College Memorial Fund. Renewable award covering up to full tuition is available to children and surviving spouses of peace officers and fire fighters killed in the line of duty in any state. Children must be under 26 years of age. Dollar value of each award varies. Must be an Ohio resident and enroll full-time or part-time at an Ohio college or university. *Award:* Scholarship for use in freshman, sophomore, junior, or senior year; renewable. *Award amount:* varies. *Number of awards:* 50–65. *Eligibility Requirements:* Applicant must be age 25 or under; enrolled or expecting to enroll full- or part-time at a two-year or four-year institution or university; resident of Ohio and studying in Ohio. Applicant or parent of applicant must have employment or volunteer experience in police/firefighting. Available to U.S. citizens. *Application Requirements: Deadline:* continuous.

Contact Barbara Thoma, Program Administrator, Ohio Board of Regents, 30 East Broad Street, 36th Floor, Columbus, OH 43215-3414. *E-mail:* bthoma@regents.state.oh.us. *Phone:* 614-752-9535. *Fax:* 614-752-5903. *Web site:* www.regents.ohio.gov.

Ohio Student Choice Grant Program. Renewable award available to Ohio residents attending private colleges within the state. Must be enrolled full-time in a bachelor's degree program. Do not apply to state. Dollar value of each award varies. Check with financial aid office of college. *Award:* Grant for use in freshman, sophomore, junior, or senior year; renewable. *Award amount:* up to $900. *Number of awards:* varies. *Eligibility Requirements:* Applicant must be enrolled or expecting to enroll full-time at a four-year institution or university; resident of Ohio and studying in Ohio. Available to U.S. citizens. *Application Requirements: Deadline:* continuous.

Contact Barbara Thoma, Program Administrator, Ohio Board of Regents, 30 East Broad Street, 36th Floor, Columbus, OH 43215-3414. *E-mail:* bthoma@regents.state.oh.us. *Phone:* 614-752-9535. *Fax:* 614-752-5903. *Web site:* www.regents.ohio.gov.

Ohio War Orphans Scholarship. Aids Ohio residents attending an eligible college in Ohio. Must be between the ages of 16-25, the child of a disabled or deceased veteran, and enrolled full-time. Renewable up to five years. Amount of award varies. Must include Form DD214. *Award:* Scholarship for use in freshman, sophomore, junior, or senior year; renewable. *Award amount:* varies. *Number of awards:* 300–450. *Eligibility Requirements:* Applicant must be age 16-25; enrolled or expecting to enroll full-time at a two-year or four-year institution or university; resident of Ohio and studying in Ohio. Available to U.S. citizens. Applicant or parent must meet one or more of the following requirements: general military experience; retired from active duty; disabled or killed as a result of military service; prisoner of war; or missing in action. *Application Requirements:* Application. *Deadline:* July 1.

Contact Jathiya Abdullah, Program Administrator, Ohio Board of Regents, 30 East Broad Street, 36th Floor, Columbus, OH 43215-3414. *E-mail:* jabdullah@regents.state.oh.us. *Phone:* 614-752-9528. *Fax:* 614-752-5903. *Web site:* www.regents.ohio.gov.

Part-time Student Instructional Grant. Renewable grants for part-time undergraduates who are Ohio residents. Award amounts vary. Must attend an Ohio institution. *Award:* Grant for use in freshman, sophomore, junior, or senior year; renewable. *Award amount:* varies. *Number of awards:* varies. *Eligibility Requirements:* Applicant must be enrolled or expecting to enroll part-time at a two-year or four-year institution or university; resident of Ohio and studying in Ohio. Available to U.S. citizens. *Application Requirements:* Application, financial need analysis. *Deadline:* continuous.

Contact Barbara Thoma, Program Administrator, Ohio Board of Regents, 30 East Broad Street, 36th Floor, Columbus, OH 43215-3414. *E-mail:* bmethene@regents.state.oh.us. *Phone:* 614-752-9535. *Fax:* 614-752-5903. *Web site:* www.regents.ohio.gov.

Robert C. Byrd Honors Scholarship-Ohio. Renewable award for graduating high school seniors who demonstrate outstanding academic achievement. Each Ohio high school receives applications by January of each year. School can submit one application for every 200 students in the senior class. Deadline: second Friday in March. *Award:* Scholarship for use in freshman, sophomore, junior, or senior year; renewable. *Award amount:* up to $1500. *Number of awards:* varies. *Eligibility Requirements:* Applicant must be high school student; planning to enroll or expecting to enroll full-time at a two-year or four-year institution or university; resident of Ohio and studying in Ohio. Applicant must have 3.5 GPA or higher. Available to U.S. citizens. *Application Requirements:* Application, test scores. *Deadline:* varies.

Contact Mr. Mark Lynskey, Program Administrator, Ohio Department of Education, 25 South Front Street, 2nd Floor, Columbus, OH 43215. *Phone:* 614-466-2650. *Web site:* www.ode.state.oh.us.

Student Workforce Development Grant Program. Provides tuition assistance to Ohio students. Students must be pursuing an associate or bachelor's degree and must not have been enrolled full-time in a private career school prior to July 1, 2000. *Award:* Grant for use in freshman, sophomore, junior, or senior year; renewable. *Award amount:* $300. *Number of awards:* 1. *Eligibility Requirements:* Applicant must be enrolled or expecting to enroll full-time at a four-year institution or university; resident of Ohio and studying in Ohio. Available to U.S. citizens. *Application Requirements: Deadline:* varies.

Contact Barbara Thoma, Program Administrator, Ohio Board of Regents, 30 East Broad Street, 36th Floor, Columbus, OH 43215-3414. *E-mail:* bthoma@regents.state.oh.us. *Phone:* 614-752-9535. *Fax:* 614-752-5903. *Web site:* www.regents.ohio.gov.

OKLAHOMA

Academic Scholars Program. The program encourages students of high academic ability to attend institutions in Oklahoma. Renewable up to four years. ACT or SAT scores must fall between 99.5 and 100th percentiles, or applicant must be designated as a National Merit scholar or finalist. Oklahoma public institutions can also select institutional nominees. *Award:* Scholarship for use in freshman, sophomore, junior, or senior year; renewable. *Award amount:* $1800–$5500. *Number of awards:* varies. *Eligibility Requirements:* Applicant must be high school student; planning to enroll or expecting to enroll full-time at a two-year or four-year institution or university and studying in Oklahoma. Available to U.S. citizens. *Application Requirements:* Application, test scores, transcript. *Deadline:* continuous.

Contact Scholarship Programs Coordinator, Oklahoma State Regents for Higher Education, PO Box 108850, Oklahoma City, OK 73101-8850. *E-mail:* studentinfo@osrhe.edu. *Phone:* 800-858-1840. *Fax:* 405-225-9230. *Web site:* www.okhighered.org.

Future Teacher Scholarship-Oklahoma. Open to outstanding Oklahoma high school graduates who agree to teach in shortage areas. Must rank in top 15 percent of graduating class or score above 85th percentile on ACT or similar test, or be accepted in an educational program. Students nominated by institution. Reapply to renew. Must attend college/university in Oklahoma. Deadline varies. *Academic Fields/Career Goals:* Education. *Award:* Scholarship for use in freshman, sophomore, junior, senior, or graduate year; renewable. *Award amount:* $500–$1500. *Number of awards:* varies. *Eligibility Requirements:* Applicant must be enrolled or expecting to enroll full- or part-time at a two-year or four-year institution or university; resident of Oklahoma and studying in Oklahoma. Available to U.S. and non-U.S. citizens. *Application Requirements:* Application, essay, test scores, transcript. *Deadline:* varies.

Contact Scholarship Programs Coordinator, Oklahoma State Regents for Higher Education, PO Box 108850, Oklahoma City, OK 73101-8850. *E-mail:* studentinfo@osrhe.edu. *Phone:* 800-858-1840. *Fax:* 405-225-9230. *Web site:* www.okhighered.org.

Oklahoma Tuition Aid Grant. Award for Oklahoma residents enrolled at an Oklahoma institution at least part time each semester in a degree program. May be enrolled in two- or four-year or approved vocational-technical institution. Award of up to $1000 per year. Application is made through FAFSA. *Award:* Grant for use in freshman, sophomore, junior, or senior year; renewable. *Award amount:* $200–$1000. *Number of awards:* 23,000. *Eligibility Requirements:* Applicant must be enrolled or expecting to enroll full- or part-time at a two-year, four-year, or technical institution or university; resident of Oklahoma and studying in Oklahoma. Available to U.S. citizens. *Application Requirements:* Application, financial need analysis, FAFSA. *Deadline:* varies.

Contact Alicia Harris, Scholarship Programs Coordinator, Oklahoma State Regents for Higher Education, PO Box 3020, Oklahoma City, OK 73101-3020. *E-mail:* aharris@osrhe.edu. *Phone:* 405-225-9131. *Fax:* 405-225-9230. *Web site:* www.okhighered.org.

Regional University Baccalaureate Scholarship. Renewable award for Oklahoma residents attending one of 11 participating Oklahoma public universities.

Must have an ACT composite score of at least 30 or be a National Merit semifinalist or commended student. In addition to the award amount, each recipient will receive a resident tuition waiver from the institution. Must maintain a 3.25 GPA. Deadlines vary depending upon the institution attended. *Award:* Scholarship for use in freshman, sophomore, junior, or senior year; renewable. *Award amount:* $3000. *Number of awards:* varies. *Eligibility Requirements:* Applicant must be enrolled or expecting to enroll full-time at an institution or university; resident of Oklahoma and studying in Oklahoma. Available to U.S. citizens. *Application Requirements:* Application. *Deadline:* varies.

Contact Alicia Harris, Scholarship Programs Coordinator, Oklahoma State Regents for Higher Education, PO Box 108850, Oklahoma City, OK 73101-8850. *E-mail:* aharris@osrhe.edu. *Phone:* 405-225-9131. *Fax:* 405-225-9230. *Web site:* www.okhighered.org.

Robert C. Byrd Honors Scholarship-Oklahoma. Scholarships available to high school seniors. Applicants must be U.S. citizens or national, or be permanent residents of the United States. Must be legal residents of Oklahoma. Must have a minimum ACT composite score of 32 and/or a minimum SAT combined score of 1420 and/or 2130 or a minimum GED score of 700. Deadline: March 16. Application URL: http://www.sde.state.ok.us/pro/Byrd/application.pdf. *Award:* Scholarship for use in freshman year; not renewable. *Award amount:* $1500. *Number of awards:* 10. *Eligibility Requirements:* Applicant must be high school student; planning to enroll or expecting to enroll full-time at a four-year institution or university and resident of Oklahoma. Available to U.S. citizens. *Application Requirements:* Application, essay, references, transcript. *Deadline:* March 9.

Contact Certification Specialist, Oklahoma State Department of Education, 2500 North Lincoln Boulevard, Suite 212, Oklahoma City, OK 73105-4599. *Phone:* 405-521-2808. *Web site:* www.sde.state.ok.us.

OREGON

American Ex-Prisoner of War Scholarships: Peter Connacher Memorial Scholarship. Renewable award for American prisoners-of-war and their descendants. Written proof of prisoner-of-war status and discharge papers from the U.S. Armed Forces must accompany application. Statement of relationship between applicant and former prisoner-of-war is required. See Web site at http://www.osac.state.or.us for details. *Award:* Scholarship for use in freshman, sophomore, junior, or senior year; renewable. *Award amount:* varies. *Number of awards:* varies. *Eligibility Requirements:* Applicant must be enrolled or expecting to enroll full-time at a two-year or four-year institution and resident of Oregon. Available to U.S. citizens. Applicant or parent must meet one or more of the following requirements: general military experience; retired from active duty; disabled or killed as a result of military service; prisoner of war; or missing in action. *Application Requirements:* Application, essay, financial need analysis, transcript, activities chart. *Deadline:* March 1.

Contact Director of Grant Programs, Oregon Student Assistance Commission, 1500 Valley River Drive, Suite 100, Eugene, OR 97401-7020. *Phone:* 800-452-8807 Ext. 7395. *Web site:* www.osac.state.or.us.

Children, Adult, and Family Services Scholarship. Award for graduating high school seniors currently in foster care or participating in Independent Living Program (ILP) or GED recipients or continuing college students formerly in foster care. Only for Oregon public colleges. Visit Web site: http://www.osac.state.or.us for more details. *Award:* Scholarship for use in freshman, sophomore, junior, senior, or graduate year; renewable. *Award amount:* varies. *Number of awards:* varies. *Eligibility Requirements:* Applicant must be enrolled or expecting to enroll full-time at a two-year or four-year institution or university; resident of Oregon and studying in Oregon. Available to U.S. citizens. *Application Requirements:* Application, essay, financial need analysis, references, transcript, activity chart. *Deadline:* March 1.

Contact Director of Grant Programs, Oregon Student Assistance Commission, 1500 Valley River Drive, Suite 100, Eugene, OR 97401-7020. *Phone:* 800-452-8807 Ext. 7395. *Web site:* www.osac.state.or.us.

Dorothy Campbell Memorial Scholarship. Renewable award for female Oregon high school graduates with a minimum 2.75 GPA. Must submit essay describing strong, continuing interest in golf and the contribution that sport has made to applicant's development. *Award:* Scholarship for use in freshman, sophomore, junior, or senior year; renewable. *Award amount:* varies. *Number of awards:* varies. *Eligibility Requirements:* Applicant must be enrolled or expecting to enroll full-time at a four-year institution; female; resident of Oregon; studying in Oregon and must have an interest in golf. Available to U.S. citizens. *Application Requirements:* Application, essay, financial need analysis, transcript, activity chart. *Deadline:* March 1.

Contact Director of Grant Programs, Oregon Student Assistance Commission, 1500 Valley River Drive, Suite 100, Eugene, OR 97401-7020. *Phone:* 800-452-8807 Ext. 7395. *Web site:* www.osac.state.or.us.

Glenn Jackson Scholars Scholarships (OCF). Award for graduating high school seniors who are dependents of employees or retirees of Oregon Department of Transportation or Parks and Recreation Department. Employees must have worked in their department at least three years as of the March 1 scholarship deadline. Award for maximum twelve undergraduate quarters or six quarters at a two-year institution. Visit Web site http://www.osac.state.or.us for more details. *Award:* Scholarship for use in freshman, sophomore, junior, or senior year; renewable. *Award amount:* varies. *Number of awards:* varies. *Eligibility Requirements:* Applicant must be high school student; planning to enroll or expecting to enroll full- or part-time at a four-year institution and resident of Oregon. Applicant or parent of applicant must be affiliated with Oregon Department of Transportation Parks and Recreation. Applicant or parent of applicant must have employment or volunteer experience in designated career field. Available to U.S. citizens. *Application Requirements:* Application, essay, financial need analysis, references, transcript, activity chart. *Deadline:* March 1.

Contact Director of Grant Programs, Oregon Student Assistance Commission, 1500 Valley River Drive, Suite 100, Eugene, OR 97401-7020. *Phone:* 800-452-8807 Ext. 7395. *Web site:* www.osac.state.or.us.

Lawrence R. Foster Memorial Scholarship. One-time award to students enrolled or planning to enroll in a public health degree program. First preference given to those working in the public health field and those pursuing a graduate degree in public health. Undergraduates entering junior or senior year health programs may apply if seeking a public health career, and not private practice. Prefer applicants from diverse cultures. Must provide three references. Additional essay required. Must be resident of Oregon. *Academic Fields/Career Goals:* Health and Medical Sciences. *Award:* Scholarship for use in junior, senior, graduate, or postgraduate years; renewable. *Award amount:* varies. *Number of awards:* varies. *Eligibility Requirements:* Applicant must be enrolled or expecting to enroll full- or part-time at a four-year institution and resident of Oregon. Available to U.S. citizens. *Application Requirements:* Application, essay, financial need analysis, references, transcript, activity chart. *Deadline:* March 1.

Contact Director of Grant Programs, Oregon Student Assistance Commission, 1500 Valley River Drive, Suite 100, Eugene, OR 97401-7020. *Phone:* 800-452-8807 Ext. 7395. *Web site:* www.osac.state.or.us.

Oregon Occupational Safety and Health Division Workers Memorial Scholarship. Available to Oregon residents who are high school graduates or GED recipients, and either who are the dependents or spouses of an Oregon worker who was killed or permanently disabled on the job. Submit essay of 500 words or less titled, "How has the injury or death of your parent or spouse affected or influenced your decision to further your education?ö. *Award:* Scholarship for use in freshman, sophomore, junior, senior, or graduate year; renewable. *Award amount:* varies. *Number of awards:* varies. *Eligibility Requirements:* Applicant must be enrolled or expecting to enroll full-time at a four-year institution or university and resident of Oregon. Applicant or parent of applicant must have employment or volunteer experience in designated career field. Available to U.S. citizens. *Application Requirements:* Application, essay, financial need analysis, test scores, transcript, social security number or workers compensation claim. *Deadline:* March 1.

Contact Director of Grant Programs, Oregon Student Assistance Commission, 1500 Valley River Drive, Suite 100, Eugene, OR 97401-7020. *Phone:* 800-452-8807 Ext. 7395. *Web site:* www.osac.state.or.us.

Oregon Scholarship Fund Community College Student Award. Scholarship open to Oregon residents enrolled or planning to enroll in Oregon community college programs. May apply for one additional year. *Award:* Scholarship for use in freshman or sophomore year; renewable. *Award amount:* varies. *Number of awards:* varies. *Eligibility Requirements:* Applicant must be enrolled or expecting to enroll full-time at a two-year institution; resident of Oregon and studying in Oregon. Available to U.S. citizens. *Application Requirements:* Application, essay, financial need analysis, transcript, activity chart. *Deadline:* March 1.

Contact Director of Grant Programs, Oregon Student Assistance Commission, 1500 Valley River Drive, Suite 100, Eugene, OR 97401-7020. *Phone:* 800-452-8807 Ext. 7395. *Web site:* www.osac.state.or.us.

Oregon Scholarship Fund Transfer Student Award. Award open to Oregon residents who are currently enrolled in their second year at a community college and are planning to transfer to a four-year college in Oregon. Prior recipients may apply for one additional year. *Award:* Scholarship for use in sophomore or junior year; renewable. *Award amount:* varies. *Number of awards:* varies. *Eligibility Requirements:* Applicant must be enrolled or expecting to enroll full-time at a two-year or four-year institution; resident of Oregon and studying in Oregon. Available to U.S. citizens. *Application Requirements:* Application, essay, financial need analysis, transcript, activity chart. *Deadline:* March 1.

Contact Director of Grant Programs, Oregon Student Assistance Commission, 1500 Valley River Drive, Suite 100, Eugene, OR 97401-7020. *Phone:* 800-452-8807 Ext. 7395. *Web site:* www.osac.state.or.us.

Oregon Student Assistance Commission Employee and Dependent Scholarship. Award for current permanent employees of the OSAC, who are past initial trial service or legally dependent children of current permanent employees at the time of the March 1 scholarship deadline or legally dependent children of an employee who retires, is permanently disabled, or deceased directly from employment at OSAC. Dependents must enroll full-time and employees must enroll at least half-time. Must reapply each year for up to four years. *Award:* Scholarship for use in freshman, sophomore, junior, or senior year; not renewable. *Award amount:* varies. *Number of awards:* 1. *Eligibility Requirements:* Applicant must be enrolled or expecting to enroll full- or part-time at a four-year institution and resident of Oregon. Available to U.S. citizens. *Application Requirements:* Application, essay, transcript, activities chart. *Deadline:* March 1.

Contact Director of Grant Programs, Oregon Student Assistance Commission, 1500 Valley River Drive, Suite 100, Eugene, OR 97401-7020. *Phone:* 800-452-8807 Ext. 7395. *Web site:* www.osac.state.or.us.

Oregon Trucking Association Safety Council Scholarship. One-time award available to a child of an Oregon Trucking Association member, or child of employee of member. Applicants must be Oregon residents who are graduating high school seniors from an Oregon high school. *Award:* Scholarship for use in freshman year; not renewable. *Award amount:* varies. *Number of awards:* 4. *Eligibility Requirements:* Applicant must be high school student; planning to enroll or expecting to enroll full-time at a four-year institution and resident of Oregon. Applicant or parent of applicant must be affiliated with Oregon Trucking Association. Applicant or parent of applicant must have employment or volunteer experience in designated career field. Available to U.S. citizens. *Application Requirements:* Application, essay, financial need analysis, references, transcript, activity chart. *Deadline:* March 1.

Contact Director of Grant Programs, Oregon Student Assistance Commission, 1500 Valley River Drive, Suite 100, Eugene, OR 97401-7020. *Phone:* 800-452-8807 Ext. 7395. *Web site:* www.osac.state.or.us.

Oregon Veterans' Education Aid. To be eligible, veteran must have served in U.S. armed forces 90 days and been discharged under honorable conditions. Must be U.S. citizen and Oregon resident. Korean War veteran or received campaign or expeditionary medal or ribbon awarded by U.S. armed forces for services after June 30, 1958. Full-time students receive $50 per month, and part-time students receive $35 per month. *Award:* Grant for use in freshman, sophomore, junior, senior, graduate, or postgraduate years; not renewable. *Award amount:* $150. *Number of awards:* up to 100. *Eligibility Requirements:* Applicant must be enrolled or expecting to enroll full-time at a two-year, four-year, or technical institution or university; resident of Oregon and studying in Oregon. Available to U.S. citizens. Applicant or parent must meet one or more of the following requirements: general military experience; retired from active duty; disabled or killed as a result of military service; prisoner of war; or missing in action. *Application Requirements:* Application, certified copy of DD Form 214. *Deadline:* continuous.

Contact Loriann Sheridan, Educational Aid Coordinator, Oregon Department of Veterans Affairs, 700 Summer Street, NE, Salem, OR 97301-1289. *E-mail:* sheridl@odva.state.or.us. *Phone:* 503-373-2085. *Fax:* 503-373-2393. *Web site:* www.odva.state.or.us.

Robert C. Byrd Honors Scholarship-Oregon. Renewable award available to Oregon high school seniors with a GPA of at least 3.85 or a GED score of 3300 and ACT scores of at least 29 or SAT combined math and critical reading scores of 1300. See Web site: http://www.osac.state.or.us for more information. Deadline: March 1. *Award:* Scholarship for use in freshman, sophomore, junior, or senior year; renewable. *Award amount:* varies. *Number of awards:* 15–75. *Eligibility Requirements:* Applicant must be high school student; planning to enroll or expecting to enroll full-time at a two-year or four-year institution and resident of Oregon. Available to U.S. citizens. *Application Requirements:* Application, essay, financial need analysis, test scores, transcript, activity chart. *Deadline:* March 1.

Contact Scholarship and Access Programs, Oregon Student Assistance Commission, 1500 Valley River Drive, Suite 100, Eugene, OR 97401-7020. *Phone:* 541-687-7395. *Web site:* www.osac.state.or.us.

PENNSYLVANIA

Armed Forces Loan Forgiveness Program. Loan forgiveness for non-residents of Pennsylvania who served in Armed Forces in an active duty status between September 11, 2001 and June 30, 2007. Must be a student who either left a PA approved institution of postsecondary education due to call to active duty, or was living in PA at time of enlistment, or enlisted in military immediately after attending a PA approved institution of postsecondary education. Number of loans forgiven varies. Deadline: December 31. *Award:* Forgivable loan for use in freshman, sophomore, junior, or senior year; not renewable. *Award amount:* up to $2500. *Number of awards:* varies. *Eligibility Requirements:* Applicant must be enrolled or expecting to enroll full- or part-time at a two-year, four-year, or technical institution or university. Available to U.S. citizens. Applicant or parent must meet one or more of the following requirements: general military experience; retired from active duty; disabled or killed as a result of military service; prisoner of war; or missing in action. *Application Requirements:* Application. *Deadline:* December 31.

Contact Keith R. New, Director, Communications and Press Office, Pennsylvania Higher Education Assistance Agency, 1200 North Seventh Street, Harrisburg, PA 17102-1444. *E-mail:* knew@pheaa.org. *Phone:* 717-720-2509. *Fax:* 717-720-3903. *Web site:* www.pheaa.org.

New Economy Technology and SciTech Scholarships. Renewable award for Pennsylvania residents pursuing a degree in science or technology at a PHEAA-approved two- or four-year Pennsylvania college or university. Must maintain minimum GPA of 3.0. Must commence employment in Pennsylvania in a field related to degree within one year after graduation, and work one year for each year the scholarship was awarded. *Academic Fields/Career Goals:* Science, Technology, and Society. *Award:* Scholarship for use in freshman, sophomore, junior, or senior year; renewable. *Award amount:* varies. *Number of awards:* varies. *Eligibility Requirements:* Applicant must be enrolled or expecting to enroll full-time at a two-year, four-year, or technical institution or university; resident of Pennsylvania and studying in Pennsylvania. Applicant must have 3.0 GPA or higher. Available to U.S. citizens. *Application Requirements:* Application, FAFSA. *Deadline:* December 31.

Contact PHEAA State Grant and Special Programs Division, Pennsylvania Higher Education Assistance Agency, 1200 North Seventh Street, Harrisburg, PA 17102-1444. *Phone:* 800-692-7392. *Web site:* www.pheaa.org.

Pennsylvania State Grants. Award for Pennsylvania residents attending an approved postsecondary institution as undergraduates in a program of at least two years duration. Renewable for up to eight semesters if applicants show continued need and academic progress. Must submit Free Application for Federal Student Aid. Number of awards granted varies annually. Scholarship value is $3500 to $4500. Deadlines: May 1 and August 1. *Award:* Grant for use in freshman, sophomore, junior, or senior year; renewable. *Award amount:* $3500–$4500. *Number of awards:* varies. *Eligibility Requirements:* Applicant must be enrolled or expecting to enroll full- or part-time at a two-year, four-year, or technical institution or university and resident of Pennsylvania. Available to U.S. citizens. *Application Requirements:* Financial need analysis, FAFSA. *Deadline:* varies.

Contact Keith New, Director of Communications and Press Office, Pennsylvania Higher Education Assistance Agency, 1200 North Seventh Street, Harrisburg, PA 17102-1444. *Phone:* 717-720-2509. *Fax:* 717-720-3903. *Web site:* www.pheaa.org.

Postsecondary Education Gratuity Program. The program offers waiver of tuition and fees for children of Pennsylvania police officers, firefighters, rescue or ambulance squad members, corrections facility employees, or National Guard members who died in line of duty after January 1, 1976. *Award:* Grant for use in freshman, sophomore, junior, or senior year; renewable. *Award amount:* varies. *Number of awards:* varies. *Eligibility Requirements:* Applicant must be age 25 or under; enrolled or expecting to enroll full-time at a two-year or four-year institution or university; resident of Pennsylvania and studying in Pennsylvania. Applicant or parent of applicant must have employment or volunteer experience in police/firefighting. Available to U.S. citizens. Applicant or parent must meet one or more of the following requirements: Air Force National Guard or Army National Guard experience; retired from active duty; disabled or killed as a result of military service; prisoner of war; or missing in action. *Application Requirements:* Application. *Deadline:* March 31.

Contact Keith R. New, Director, Communications and Press Office, Pennsylvania Higher Education Assistance Agency, 1200 North Seventh Street, Harrisburg, PA 17102-1444. *E-mail:* knew@pheaa.org. *Phone:* 717-720-2509. *Fax:* 717-720-3903. *Web site:* www.pheaa.org.

Robert C. Byrd Honors Scholarship-Pennsylvania. Awards Pennsylvania residents who are graduating high school seniors. Must rank in the top 5 percent of graduating class, have at least a 3.5 GPA and score 1150 or above on the SAT, 25 or above on the ACT, or 355 or above on the GED. Renewable award and the amount granted varies. Applicants are expected to be a full-time freshman student enrolled at an eligible institution of higher education, following high school graduation. Deadline: May 1. *Award:* Scholarship for use in freshman, sophomore, junior, or senior year; renewable. *Award amount:* $1500. *Number of awards:* varies. *Eligibility Requirements:* Applicant must be high school student; planning to enroll or expecting to enroll full-time at a four-year institution or university and resident of Pennsylvania. Applicant must have 3.5 GPA or higher. Available to U.S. citizens. *Application Requirements:* Application, references, test scores, transcript. *Deadline:* May 1.

Contact Keith R. New, Director of Communications and Press Office, Pennsylvania Higher Education Assistance Agency, 1200 North Seventh Street, Harrisburg, PA 17102. *Phone:* 717-720-2509. *Fax:* 717-720-3903. *Web site:* www.pheaa.org.

Veterans Grant-Pennsylvania. Renewable awards for Pennsylvania residents who are qualified veterans attending an approved undergraduate program full-time. Number of awards granted varies annually. Award ranges from $800 to $3500. Deadlines: May 1 and August 1. *Award:* Grant for use in freshman, sophomore, junior, or senior year; renewable. *Award amount:* $800–$3500. *Number of awards:* varies. *Eligibility Requirements:* Applicant must be enrolled or expecting to enroll full-time at a two-year, four-year, or technical institution or university and resident of Pennsylvania. Available to U.S. citizens. Applicant must have general military experience. *Application Requirements:* FAFSA. *Deadline:* varies.

Contact Keith R. New, Director, Communications and Press Office, Pennsylvania Higher Education Assistance Agency, 1200 North Seventh Street, Harrisburg, PA 17102-1444. *E-mail:* knew@pheaa.org. *Phone:* 717-720-2509. *Fax:* 717-720-3903. *Web site:* www.pheaa.org.

PUERTO RICO

Robert C. Byrd Honors Scholarship-Puerto Rico. Grant is sponsored by the Puerto Rico Department of Education and is granted to gifted students. These are students chosen from public and private schools who graduate from high school and are admitted to an accredited university in Puerto Rico or in the United States and who show promise to complete a college career. It is granted for a period of four years if the student maintains a satisfactory academic progress. Must be a U.S. citizen and rank in the upper quarter of class or have a minimum 3.5 GPA. *Award:* Scholarship for use in freshman year; renewable. *Award amount:* up to $1500. *Number of awards:* 74–85. *Eligibility Requirements:* Applicant must be high school student; planning to enroll or expecting to enroll full-time at a four-year institution or university and resident of Puerto Rico. Applicant must have 3.5 GPA or higher. Available to U.S. citizens. *Application Requirements:* Application, financial need analysis, interview, portfolio, references, test scores, transcript. *Deadline:* May 30.

Contact Marta Colon-Rivera, Coordinator, Puerto Rico Department of Education, PO Box 19900, San Juan, PR 00910-1900. *E-mail:* colon_mm@de.gobierno.pr. *Phone:* 787-759-8313. *Fax:* 787-758-2281.

RHODE ISLAND

Rhode Island State Grant Program. Grants for residents of Rhode Island attending an approved school in United States. Based on need. Renewable for up to four years if in good academic standing. *Award:* Grant for use in freshman, sophomore, junior, or senior year; renewable. *Award amount:* $300–$1400. *Number of awards:* 10,000–12,900. *Eligibility Requirements:* Applicant must be enrolled or expecting to enroll full- or part-time at a two-year, four-year, or technical institution or university and resident of Rhode Island. Available to U.S. citizens. *Application Requirements:* Application, financial need analysis. *Deadline:* March 1.

Contact Ms. Mary Ann Welch, Director of Program Administration, Rhode Island Higher Education Assistance Authority, 560 Jefferson Boulevard, Warwick, RI 02886. *E-mail:* mawelch@riheaa.org. *Phone:* 401-736-1171. *Fax:* 401-736-1178. *Web site:* www.riheaa.org.

SOUTH CAROLINA

Educational Assistance for Certain War Veteran's Dependents-South Carolina. The State of South Carolina does not appropriated any funds for this program. All children who qualify may receive these benefits, regardless of financial need, up to and including their twenty-sixth birthday. Dollar Value and Total number of awards varies. *Award:* Scholarship for use in freshman, sophomore, junior, senior, graduate, or postgraduate years; not renewable. *Award amount:* varies. *Number of awards:* varies. *Eligibility Requirements:* Applicant must be age 26 or under; enrolled or expecting to enroll full- or part-time at a two-year, four-year, or technical institution or university and studying in South Carolina. Available to U.S. citizens. *Application Requirements:* Application, transcript. *Deadline:* continuous.

Contact Dianne Coley, Free Tuition Assistant, South Carolina Division of Veterans Affairs, South Carolina Governor's Office, 1205 Pendleton Street, Suite 369, Columbia, SC 29201. *E-mail:* va@oepp.sc.gov. *Phone:* 803-255-4317. *Fax:* 803-255-4257. *Web site:* www.govoepp.state.sc.us/vetaff.htm.

Palmetto Fellows Scholarship Program. Renewable award for qualified high school seniors in South Carolina to attend a four-year South Carolina institution. The scholarship must be applied directly towards the cost of attendance, less any other gift aid received. For more details, refer to Web site: http://www.che.sc.gov/New_Web/GoingToCollege/PF_Hm.htm. *Award:* Scholarship for use in freshman, sophomore, junior, or senior year; renewable. *Award amount:* up to $6700. *Number of awards:* varies. *Eligibility Requirements:* Applicant must be high school student; planning to enroll or expecting to enroll full-time at a four-year institution or university; resident of South Carolina and studying in South Carolina. Applicant must have 3.5 GPA or higher. Available to U.S. citizens. *Application Requirements:* Application, test scores, transcript. *Deadline:* December 15.

Contact Ms. Melissa Santilly, Coordinator, South Carolina Commission on Higher Education, 1333 Main Street, Suite 200, Columbia, SC 29201. *E-mail:* msantilli@che.sc.gov. *Phone:* 803-737-2128. *Fax:* 803-737-3610. *Web site:* www.che.sc.gov.

Robert C. Byrd Honors Scholarship-South Carolina. Renewable award of $1500 for a graduating high school senior from South Carolina, who will be attending a two- or four-year institution. Applicants should be superior students who demonstrate academic achievement and show promise of continued success at a post-secondary institution. Interested applicants should contact their high school counselors after the first week of December for an application. *Award:* Scholarship for use in freshman, sophomore, junior, or senior year; renewable. *Award amount:* varies. *Number of awards:* varies. *Eligibility Requirements:* Applicant must be high school student; planning to enroll or expecting to enroll full-time at a two-year or four-year institution and resident of South Carolina. Applicant must have 3.5 GPA or higher. Available to U.S. citizens. *Application Requirements:* Application, test scores, ACT or SAT scores. *Deadline:* February 1.

Contact Beth Cope, Program Coordinator, South Carolina Department of Education, 1424 Senate Street, Columbia, SC 29201. *E-mail:* bcope@sde.state.sc.us. *Phone:* 803-734-8116. *Fax:* 803-734-4387. *Web site:* www.ed.sc.gov.

South Carolina HOPE Scholarship. A merit-based scholarship for eligible first-time entering freshman attending a four-year South Carolina institution. Minimum GPA of 3.0 required. Must be a resident of South Carolina. For more information visit Web site: http://www.che.sc.gov/New_Web/GoingToCollege/HOPE_Hm.htm. *Award:* Scholarship for use in freshman year; not renewable. *Award amount:* $2650. *Number of awards:* varies. *Eligibility Requirements:* Applicant must be enrolled or expecting to enroll full-time at a four-year institution or university; resident of South Carolina and studying in South Carolina. Applicant must have 3.0 GPA or higher. Available to U.S. citizens. *Application Requirements:* Transcript. *Deadline:* continuous.

Contact Karen Wham, Life and Hope Scholarship Coordinator, South Carolina Commission on Higher Education, 1333 Main Street, Suite 200, Columbia, SC 29201. *E-mail:* kwham@che.sc.gov. *Phone:* 803-737-4544. *Fax:* 803-737-3610. *Web site:* www.che.sc.gov.

South Carolina Need-Based Grants Program. Award based on results of FAFSA. A student may receive up to $2500 annually for full-time and up to $1250 annually for part-time study. The grant must be applied directly towards the cost-of-attendance at the college for a maximum of eight full-time equivalent terms. *Award:* Grant for use in freshman, sophomore, junior, senior, or graduate year; renewable. *Award amount:* $1250–$2500. *Number of awards:* 1–23,485. *Eligibility Requirements:* Applicant must be enrolled or expecting to enroll full- or part-time at a two-year, four-year, or technical institution or university; resident of South Carolina and studying in South Carolina. Available to U.S. citizens. *Application Requirements:* Application, financial need analysis. *Deadline:* continuous.

Contact Dr. Karen Woodfaulk, Director of Student Service, South Carolina Commission on Higher Education, 1333 Main Street, Suite 200, Columbia, SC 29201. *E-mail:* kwoodfaulk@che.sc.gov. *Phone:* 803-737-2244. *Fax:* 803-737-2297. *Web site:* www.che.sc.gov.

South Carolina Teacher Loan Program. One-time awards for South Carolina residents attending four-year postsecondary institutions in South Carolina. Recipients must teach in the South Carolina public school system in a critical-need area after graduation. 20 percent of loan forgiven for each year of service. Write for additional requirements. *Academic Fields/Career Goals:* Education; Special Education. *Award:* Forgivable loan for use in freshman, sophomore, junior, senior, or graduate year; not renewable. *Award amount:* $2500–$5000. *Number of awards:* up to 1121. *Eligibility Requirements:* Applicant must be enrolled or expecting to enroll full- or part-time at a four-year institution or university; resident of South Carolina and studying in South Carolina. Applicant must have 3.0 GPA or higher. Available to U.S. citizens. *Application Requirements:* Application, references, test scores, promissory note. *Deadline:* June 1.

Contact Jennifer Jones-Gaddy, Vice President, South Carolina Student Loan Corporation, PO Box 21487, Columbia, SC 29221. *E-mail:* jgaddy@slc.sc.edu. *Phone:* 803-798-0916. *Fax:* 803-772-9410. *Web site:* www.scstudentloan.org.

South Carolina Tuition Grants Program. Award assists South Carolina residents attending one of twenty approved South Carolina independent colleges. Freshmen must be in upper 3/4 of high school class or have SAT score of at least 900 or ACT of 19 or 2.0 final GAP on SC uniform grading scale. Upper-class students must complete 24 semester hours per year to be eligible. *Award:* Grant for use in freshman, sophomore, junior, or senior year; renewable. *Award amount:* $100–$3100. *Number of awards:* up to 12,000. *Eligibility Requirements:* Applicant must be enrolled or expecting to enroll full-time at a two-year or four-year institution or university; resident of South Carolina and studying in South Carolina. Available to U.S. citizens. *Application Requirements:* Application, financial need analysis, test scores, transcript, FAFSA. *Deadline:* June 30.

Contact Toni Cave, Financial Aid Counselor, South Carolina Tuition Grants Commission, 101 Business Park Boulevard, Suite 2100, Columbia, SC 29203-9498. *E-mail:* toni@sctuitiongrants.org. *Phone:* 803-896-1120. *Fax:* 803-896-1126. *Web site:* www.sctuitiongrants.com.

SOUTH DAKOTA

Haines Memorial Scholarship. One-time scholarship for South Dakota public university students who are sophomores, juniors, or seniors having at least a 2.5 GPA and majoring in a teacher education program. Must include resume with application. Must be South Dakota resident. *Academic Fields/Career Goals:* Education. *Award:* Scholarship for use in sophomore, junior, or senior year; not renewable. *Award amount:* $2150. *Number of awards:* 1. *Eligibility Requirements:* Applicant must be enrolled or expecting to enroll full-time at an institution or university; resident of South Dakota and studying in South Dakota. Applicant must have 2.5 GPA or higher. Available to U.S. citizens. *Application Requirements:* Application, autobiography, essay, resume. *Deadline:* February 9.

Contact Janelle Toman, Director of Institutional Research, South Dakota Board of Regents, 306 East Capitol Avenue, Suite 200, Pierre, SD 57501-2545. *E-mail:* info@sdbor.edu. *Phone:* 605-773-3455. *Fax:* 605-773-2422. *Web site:* www.sdbor.edu.

South Dakota Opportunity Scholarship. The scholarship is worth up to $5000 over four years to students who take a rigorous college-prep curriculum while in high school and stay in the state for their postsecondary education. *Award:* Scholarship for use in freshman, sophomore, junior, or senior year; renewable. *Award amount:* up to $1000. *Number of awards:* 1000. *Eligibility Requirements:* Applicant must be enrolled or expecting to enroll full-time at a two-year, four-year, or technical institution or university; resident of South Dakota and studying in South Dakota. Applicant must have 3.0 GPA or higher. Available to U.S. citizens. *Application Requirements:* Application, test scores, transcript. *Deadline:* September 1.

Contact Janelle Toman, Director of Institutional Research, South Dakota Board of Regents, 306 East Capitol Avenue, Suite 200, Pierre, SD 57501-2545. *E-mail:* info@sdbor.edu. *Phone:* 605-773-3455. *Fax:* 605-773-2422. *Web site:* www.sdbor.edu.

TENNESSEE

ASPIRE Award. $1500 supplement to the Tennessee HOPE scholarship. Must meet Tennessee HOPE Scholarship requirements and student's parents must have an Adjusted Gross Income on their federal tax return of $36000 or less. *Award:* Scholarship for use in freshman, sophomore, junior, or senior year; renewable. *Award amount:* up to $1500. *Number of awards:* varies. *Eligibility Requirements:* Applicant must be enrolled or expecting to enroll full- or part-time at a two-year or four-year institution or university; resident of Tennessee and studying in Tennessee. Applicant must have 3.0 GPA or higher. Available to U.S. citizens. *Application Requirements:* Application, financial need analysis. *Deadline:* September 1.

Contact Robert Biggers, Lottery Scholarship Program Administrator, Tennessee Student Assistance Corporation, 404 James Robertson Parkway, Suite 1510, Nashville, TN 37243-0820. *E-mail:* tsac.aidinfo@state.tn.us. *Phone:* 800-342-1663. *Fax:* 615-741-6101. *Web site:* www.collegepaystn.com.

Christa McAuliffe Scholarship Program. Scholarship to assist and support Tennessee students who have demonstrated a commitment to a career in educating the youth of Tennessee. Offered to college seniors for a period of one academic year. Must have a high school GPA of minimum 3.5. Must have attained scores on either the ACT or SAT which meet or exceed the national norms. *Academic Fields/Career Goals:* Education. *Award:* Scholarship for use in senior year; renewable. *Award amount:* up to $500. *Number of awards:* up to 1. *Eligibility Requirements:* Applicant must be enrolled or expecting to enroll full-time at a four-year institution or university and studying in Tennessee. Available to U.S. citizens. *Application Requirements:* Application. *Deadline:* April 1.

Contact Scholarship Committee, Tennessee Student Assistance Corporation, 404 James Robertson Parkway, Suite 1510, Parkway Towers, Nashville, TN 37243-0820. *Phone:* 615-741-1346. *Fax:* 615-741-6101. *Web site:* www.collegepaystn.com.

Dependent Children Scholarship Program. Scholarship aid for Tennessee residents who are dependent children of a Tennessee law enforcement officer, fireman, or an emergency medical service technician who has been killed or totally and permanently disabled while performing duties within the scope of such employment. The scholarship awarded to full-time undergraduate students for a maximum of four academic years or the period required for the completion of the program of study. *Award:* Scholarship for use in freshman, sophomore, junior, or senior year; renewable. *Award amount:* varies. *Number of awards:* up to 30. *Eligibility Requirements:* Applicant must be enrolled or expecting to enroll full-time at a two-year or four-year institution or university and resident of Tennessee. Applicant or parent of applicant must have employment or volunteer experience in police/firefighting. Available to U.S. citizens.

Application Requirements: Application, FAFSA. *Deadline:* July 15.

Contact Scholarship Committee, Tennessee Student Assistance Corporation, 404 James Robertson Parkway, Suite 1510, Parkway Towers, Nashville, TN 37243-0820. *Phone:* 615-741-1346. *Fax:* 615-741-6101. *Web site:* www.collegepaystn.com.

Minority Teaching Fellows Program/Tennessee. Forgivable loan for minority Tennessee residents pursuing teaching careers. High school applicant minimum 2.75 GPA. Must be in the top quarter of the class or score an 18 on ACT. College applicant minimum 2.5 GPA required. Submit statement of intent, application, test scores, transcripts, and two letters of recommendation. Must teach one year for each year the award is received, or repay loan. *Academic Fields/Career Goals:* Education; Special Education. *Award:* Forgivable loan for use in freshman, sophomore, junior, or senior year; renewable. *Award amount:* up to $5000. *Number of awards:* 19–29. *Eligibility Requirements:* Applicant must be American Indian/Alaska Native, Asian/Pacific Islander, Black (non-Hispanic), or Hispanic; enrolled or expecting to enroll full-time at a two-year or four-year institution or university; resident of Tennessee and studying in Tennessee. Available to U.S. citizens. *Application Requirements:* Application, essay, references, test scores, transcript, statement of intent, separate sheet identifying extracurricular activities, leadership positions, and length of time involved. *Deadline:* April 15.

Contact Mike McCormack, Scholarship Coordinator, Tennessee Student Assistance Corporation, Parkway Towers, 404 James Robertson Parkway, Suite 1950, Nashville, TN 37243-0820. *E-mail:* mike.mccormack@state.tn.us. *Phone:* 615-741-1346. *Fax:* 615-741-6101. *Web site:* www.collegepaystn.com.

Ned McWherter Scholars Program. Award for Tennessee high school seniors with high academic ability. Must have minimum high school GPA of 3.5 and a score of 29 on the ACT or SAT equivalent. Must attend a College or university in Tennessee. Must be a permanent U.S. citizen and resident of Tennessee. *Award:* Scholarship for use in freshman, sophomore, junior, or senior year; renewable. *Award amount:* up to $6000. *Number of awards:* up to 180. *Eligibility Requirements:* Applicant must be enrolled or expecting to enroll full-time at a two-year, four-year, or technical institution or university; resident of Tennessee and studying in Tennessee. Applicant must have 3.5 GPA or higher. Available to U.S. citizens. *Application Requirements:* Application, test scores, transcript. *Deadline:* February 15.

Contact Kathy Stripling, Scholarship Coordinator, Tennessee Student Assistance Corporation, 404 James Robertson Parkway, Suite 1510, Parkway Towers, Nashville, TN 37243-0820. *E-mail:* kathy.stripling@state.tn.us. *Phone:* 615-741-1346. *Fax:* 615-741-6101. *Web site:* www.collegepaystn.com.

Tennessee Education Lottery Scholarship Program General Assembly Merit Scholarship. $1000 supplement to base award per semester, maximum one thousand dollars ($1000). Entering freshmen must have 3.75 GPA and 29 ACT (1280 SAT). Must be a U.S. citizen and must reside in Tennessee. *Award:* Scholarship for use in freshman, sophomore, junior, or senior year; renewable. *Award amount:* up to $1000. *Number of awards:* varies. *Eligibility Requirements:* Applicant must be enrolled or expecting to enroll full- or part-time at a two-year or four-year institution or university; resident of Tennessee and studying in Tennessee. Available to U.S. citizens. *Application Requirements:* Application. *Deadline:* September 1.

Contact Robert Biggers, Lottery Scholarship Program Administrator, Tennessee Student Assistance Corporation, 404 James Robertson Parkway, Suite 1510, Nashville, TN 37243-0820. *E-mail:* tsac.aidinfo@state.tn.us. *Phone:* 800-342-1663. *Fax:* 615-741-6101. *Web site:* www.collegepaystn.com.

Tennessee Education Lottery Scholarship Program Tennessee HOPE Access Grant. Non-renewable award of $2650 for students at four-year colleges or $1700 for students at two-year colleges. Entering freshmen must have a minimum GPA of 2.75 and parents income must be $36,000 or less. Recipients will be eligible for Tennessee HOPE Scholarship by meeting HOPE Scholarship renewal criteria. *Award:* Scholarship for use in freshman, sophomore, junior, or senior year; not renewable. *Award amount:* $1700–$2650. *Number of awards:* varies. *Eligibility Requirements:* Applicant must be enrolled or expecting to enroll full- or part-time at a two-year or four-year institution or university; resident of Tennessee and studying in Tennessee. Available to U.S. citizens. *Application Requirements:* Application, financial need analysis. *Deadline:* September 1.

Contact Robert Biggers, Lottery Scholarship Program Administrator, Tennessee Student Assistance Corporation, 404 James Robertson Parkway, Suite 1510, Nashville, TN 37243-0820. *E-mail:* tsac.aidinfo@state.tn.us. *Phone:* 800-342-1663. *Fax:* 615-741-6101. *Web site:* www.collegepaystn.com.

Tennessee Education Lottery Scholarship Program Tennessee HOPE Scholarship. Award of $3800 per year for students at four-year colleges or $1900 per year for students at two-year colleges. *Award:* Scholarship for use in freshman, sophomore, junior, or senior year; renewable. *Award amount:* $1900–$3800. *Number of awards:* varies. *Eligibility Requirements:* Applicant must be enrolled or expecting to enroll full- or part-time at a two-year or four-year institution or university; resident of Tennessee and studying in Tennessee. Applicant must have 3.0 GPA or higher. Available to U.S. citizens. *Application Requirements:* Application. *Deadline:* September 1.

Contact Robert Biggers, Lottery Scholarship Program Administrator, Tennessee Student Assistance Corporation, 404 James Robertson Parkway, Suite 1510, Nashville, TN 37243-0820. *E-mail:* tsac.aidinfo@state.tn.us. *Phone:* 800-342-1663. *Fax:* 615-741-6101. *Web site:* www.collegepaystn.com.

Tennessee Education Lottery Scholarship Program Wilder-Naifeh Technical Skills Grant. Award of $1500 for students enrolled in Tennessee Technology Centers. Cannot be prior recipient of Tennessee HOPE Scholarship. *Award:* Scholarship for use in freshman or sophomore year; renewable. *Award amount:* up to $1500. *Number of awards:* varies. *Eligibility Requirements:* Applicant must be enrolled or expecting to enroll full- or part-time at a technical institution; resident of Tennessee and studying in Tennessee. Available to U.S. citizens. *Application Requirements:* Application. *Deadline:* varies.

Contact Robert Biggers, Lottery Scholarship Program Administrator, Tennessee Student Assistance Corporation, 404 James Robertson Parkway, Suite 1510, Nashville, TN 37243-0820. *E-mail:* tsac.aidinfo@state.tn.us. *Phone:* 800-342-1663. *Fax:* 615-741-6101. *Web site:* www.collegepaystn.com.

Tennessee Student Assistance Award Program. Assists Tennessee residents attending an approved college or university within the state. Complete a Free Application for Federal Student Aid form. Apply by January 1. FAFSA must be processed by May 1 for priority consideration. *Award:* Grant for use in freshman, sophomore, junior, or senior year; renewable. *Award amount:* $100–$2130. *Number of awards:* 26,000. *Eligibility Requirements:* Applicant must be enrolled or expecting to enroll full- or part-time at a two-year, four-year, or technical institution or university; resident of Tennessee and studying in Tennessee. Available to U.S. citizens. *Application*

Requirements: Application, financial need analysis. *Deadline:* May 1.

Contact Naomi Derryberry, Grant and Scholarship Administrator, Tennessee Student Assistance Corporation, 404 James Robertson Parkway, Suite 1950, Parkway Towers, Nashville, TN 37243-0820. *E-mail:* naomi.derryberry@state.tn.us. *Phone:* 615-741-1346. *Fax:* 615-741-6101. *Web site:* www.collegepaystn.com.

Tennessee Teaching Scholars Program. Forgivable loan for college juniors, seniors, and college graduates admitted to an education program in Tennessee with a minimum GPA of 2.75. Students must commit to teach in a Tennessee public school one year for each year of the award. Must be a U.S. citizen and resident of Tennessee. *Academic Fields/Career Goals:* Education. *Award:* Forgivable loan for use in junior, senior, or graduate year; renewable. *Award amount:* up to $4500. *Number of awards:* varies. *Eligibility Requirements:* Applicant must be enrolled or expecting to enroll full- or part-time at a four-year institution or university; resident of Tennessee and studying in Tennessee. Available to U.S. citizens. *Application Requirements:* Application, references, test scores, transcript. *Deadline:* April 15.

Contact Mike McCormack, Scholarship Administrator, Tennessee Student Assistance Corporation, 404 James Robertson Parkway, Suite 1510, Parkway Towers, Nashville, TN 37243-0820. *E-mail:* mike.mccormack@state.tn.us. *Phone:* 615-741-1346. *Fax:* 615-741-6101. *Web site:* www.collegepaystn.com.

TEXAS

Conditional Grant Program. Renewable award to students who are considered economically disadvantaged based on federal guidelines. The maximum amount awarded per semester is $3000 not to exceed $6000 per academic year. *Academic Fields/Career Goals:* Civil Engineering; Computer Science/Data Processing. *Award:* Grant for use in freshman, sophomore, junior, or senior year; renewable. *Award amount:* $3000–$6000. *Number of awards:* varies. *Eligibility Requirements:* Applicant must be enrolled or expecting to enroll full-time at a four-year institution or university; resident of Texas and studying in Texas. Applicant must have 2.5 GPA or higher. Available to U.S. citizens. *Application Requirements:* Application, essay, interview, references, test scores, transcript. *Deadline:* March 1.

Contact Minnie Brown, Program Coordinator, Texas Department of Transportation, 125 East 11th Street, Austin, TX 78701-2483. *E-mail:* mbrown2@dot.state.tx.us. *Phone:* 512-416-4979. *Fax:* 512-416-4980. *Web site:* www.txdot.gov.

Outstanding Rural Scholar Program. Award enables rural communities to sponsor a student going into health professions. The students must agree to work in that community once they receive their degree. Must be Texas resident entering a Texas institution on a full-time basis. Must demonstrate financial need. Deadline varies. *Academic Fields/Career Goals:* Health and Medical Sciences. *Award:* Scholarship for use in freshman, sophomore, junior, or senior year; renewable. *Award amount:* varies. *Number of awards:* varies. *Eligibility Requirements:* Applicant must be enrolled or expecting to enroll full-time at a four-year institution or university; resident of Texas and studying in Texas. Applicant must have 3.0 GPA or higher. Available to U.S. citizens. *Application Requirements:* Application, financial need analysis, transcript, nomination. *Deadline:* varies.

Contact Office of Rural Community Affairs, Texas Higher Education Coordinating Board, PO Box 1708, Austin, TX 78767. *E-mail:* grantinfo@thecb.state.tx.us. *Phone:* 512-479-8891. *Web site:* www.collegefortexans.com.

Texas National Guard Tuition Assistance Program. Provides exemption from the payment of tuition to certain members of the Texas National Guard, Texas Air Guard or the State Guard. Must be Texas resident and attend school in Texas. Deadline varies. *Award:* Scholarship for use in freshman, sophomore, junior, or senior year; renewable. *Award amount:* varies. *Number of awards:* varies. *Eligibility Requirements:* Applicant must be enrolled or expecting to enroll full- or part-time at a four-year institution or university; resident of Texas and studying in Texas. Available to U.S. citizens. Applicant must have served in the Air Force National Guard or Army National Guard. *Application Requirements:* Application. *Deadline:* varies.

Contact State Adjutant General's Office, Texas Higher Education Coordinating Board, PO Box 5218, Austin, TX 78763-5218. *E-mail:* education.office@tx.ngb.army.mil. *Phone:* 512-465-5515. *Web site:* www.collegefortexans.com.

Toward Excellence Access and Success (TEXAS Grant). Renewable aid for students enrolled in a public or private nonprofit, trade school, college or university in Texas. Must be a resident of Texas and have minimum 2.5 GPA. Based on need. Amount of award is determined by the financial aid office of each school. Deadlines vary. Contact the college/university financial aid office for application information. *Award:* Grant for use in freshman, sophomore, junior, or senior year; renewable. *Award amount:* $1670–$4750. *Number of awards:* varies. *Eligibility Requirements:* Applicant must be enrolled or expecting to enroll full- or part-time at a two-year, four-year, or technical institution or university; resident of Texas and studying in Texas. Applicant must have 2.5 GPA or higher. Available to U.S. citizens. *Application Requirements:* Financial need analysis, transcript. *Deadline:* varies.

Contact Financial Aid Office, Texas Higher Education Coordinating Board, PO Box 12788, Austin, TX 78711-2788. *E-mail:* grantinfo@thecb.state.tx.us. *Phone:* 512-427-6101. *Fax:* 512-427-6127. *Web site:* www.collegefortexans.com.

Tuition Equalization Grant (TEG) Program. Renewable award for Texas residents enrolled full-time at an independent college or university within the state. Based on financial need. Maintain an overall college GPA of at least 2.5. Deadlines vary by institution. Must not be receiving athletic scholarship. Contact college/university financial aid office for application information. Nonresidents who are National Merit Finalists may also receive awards. *Award:* Grant for use in freshman, sophomore, junior, senior, or graduate year; renewable. *Award amount:* $2900. *Number of awards:* 30,000. *Eligibility Requirements:* Applicant must be enrolled or expecting to enroll full-time at a two-year or four-year institution or university; resident of Texas and studying in Texas. Applicant must have 2.5 GPA or higher. Available to U.S. citizens. *Application Requirements:* Financial need analysis, FAFSA. *Deadline:* varies.

Contact Financial Aid Office, Texas Higher Education Coordinating Board, PO Box 12788, Austin, TX 78711-2788. *E-mail:* grantinfo@thecb.state.tx.us. *Phone:* 512-427-6101. *Fax:* 512-427-6127. *Web site:* www.collegefortexans.com.

Vanessa Rudloff Scholarship Program. Scholarships of $1000 awarded to qualified members of TWLE or a family member (spouse, child, brother, sister, niece, nephew or grandchild) of a TWLE member. For details refer to Web Site: http://www.twle.net/ *Academic Fields/Career Goals:* Criminal Justice/Criminology. *Award:* Scholarship for use in freshman, sophomore, junior, senior, graduate, or postgraduate years; not renewable. *Award amount:* $1000. *Number of awards:* 4. *Eligibility Requirements:* Applicant must be enrolled or expecting to enroll full- or part-time at a two-year, four-year, or technical institution or university.

Applicant must have 3.0 GPA or higher. Available to U.S. and non-U.S. citizens. *Application Requirements:* Application, essay, references. *Deadline:* April 15.

Contact Glenda Baker, Scholarship Awards Chairperson, Texas Women in Law Enforcement, 12605 Rhea Court, Austin, TX 78727. *E-mail:* gbakerab@aol.com. *Web site:* www.twle.com.

UTAH

New Century Scholarship. Scholarship for qualified high school graduates of Utah. Must attend Utah state-operated college. Award depends on number of hours student enrolled. Please contact for further eligibility requirements. Eligible recipients receive an award equal to 75 percent of tuition for 60 credit hours toward the completion of a bachelor's degree. For more details see Web site: http://www.utahsbr.edu. *Award:* Scholarship for use in freshman, sophomore, junior, or senior year; renewable. *Award amount:* \$1300–\$3400. *Number of awards:* 1. *Eligibility Requirements:* Applicant must be enrolled or expecting to enroll full- or part-time at a four-year institution or university; resident of Utah and studying in Utah. Available to U.S. citizens. *Application Requirements:* Application, transcript, GPA/copy of enrollment verification from an eligible Utah 4-year institution, verification from registrar of completion of requirements for associates degree. *Deadline:* continuous.

Contact Charles Downer, Compliance Officer, Utah State Board of Regents, Board of Regents Building, The Gateway, 60 South 400 West, Salt Lake City, UT 84101-1284. *E-mail:* cdowner@utahsbr.edu. *Phone:* 801-321-7221. *Fax:* 801-366-8470. *Web site:* www.utahsbr.edu.

Terrill H. Bell Teaching Incentive Loan. Designed to provide financial assistance to outstanding Utah students pursuing a degree in education. The incentive loan funds full-time tuition and general fees for eight semesters. After graduation/certification the loan may be forgiven if the recipient teaches in a Utah public school or accredited private school (K-12). Dollar value varies. Loan forgiveness is done on a year-for-year basis. For more details see Web site: http://www.utahsbr.edu. *Academic Fields/Career Goals:* Education. *Award:* Forgivable loan for use in freshman, sophomore, junior, senior, or graduate year; renewable. *Award amount:* varies. *Number of awards:* 365. *Eligibility Requirements:* Applicant must be enrolled or expecting to enroll full-time at a two-year or four-year institution or university; resident of Utah and studying in Utah. Available to U.S. citizens. *Application Requirements:* Application, essay, references, test scores, transcript. *Deadline:* varies.

Contact Charles Downer, Compliance Officer, Utah State Board of Regents, Board of Regents Building, The Gateway, 60 South 400 West, Salt Lake City, UT 84101-1284. *E-mail:* cdowner@utahsbr.edu. *Phone:* 801-321-7221. *Fax:* 801-366-8470. *Web site:* www.utahsbr.edu.

T.H. Bell Teaching Incentive Loan-Utah. Renewable awards for Utah residents who are high school seniors wishing to pursue teaching careers. The award value varies depending upon tuition and fees at a Utah institution. Must agree to teach in a Utah public school or pay back loan through monthly installments. Must be a U.S. citizen. Deadline: April 27. *Academic Fields/Career Goals:* Education; Special Education. *Award:* Forgivable loan for use in freshman year; renewable. *Award amount:* varies. *Number of awards:* 25–50. *Eligibility Requirements:* Applicant must be high school student; planning to enroll or expecting to enroll full-time at a four-year institution or university; resident of Utah and studying in Utah. Available to U.S. citizens. *Application Requirements:* Application, essay, test scores, transcript. *Deadline:* April 27.

Contact Diane DeMan, Executive Secretary, Utah State Office of Education, 250 East 500 South, PO Box 144200, Salt Lake City, UT 84111. *Phone:* 801-538-7741. *Fax:* 801-538-7973. *Web site:* www.schools.utah.gov.

Utah Centennial Opportunity Program for Education. The award is available to students with substantial financial need for use at any of the participating Utah institutions. The student must be a Utah resident. Contact the financial aid office of the participating institution for requirements and deadlines. *Award:* Grant for use in freshman, sophomore, junior, or senior year; not renewable. *Award amount:* \$300–\$5000. *Number of awards:* up to 2102. *Eligibility Requirements:* Applicant must be enrolled or expecting to enroll full- or part-time at a two-year, four-year, or technical institution or university; resident of Utah and studying in Utah. Available to U.S. citizens. *Application Requirements:* Financial need analysis. *Deadline:* continuous.

Contact Ms. Lynda L. Reid, Student Aid Specialist III, Utah Higher Education Assistance Authority, 60 South 400 West, The Board of Regents Building, The Gateway, Salt Lake City, UT 84101-1284. *E-mail:* lreid@utahsbr.edu. *Phone:* 801-321-7207. *Fax:* 801-366-8470. *Web site:* www.uheaa.org.

Utah Leveraging Educational Assistance Partnership. The award is available to students with substantial financial need for use at any of the participating Utah institutions. The student must be a Utah resident. Contact the financial aid office of the participating institution for requirements and deadlines. *Award:* Grant for use in freshman, sophomore, junior, or senior year; not renewable. *Award amount:* \$300–\$2500. *Number of awards:* 1–3886. *Eligibility Requirements:* Applicant must be enrolled or expecting to enroll full- or part-time at a two-year, four-year, or technical institution or university; resident of Utah and studying in Utah. Available to U.S. citizens. *Application Requirements:* Financial need analysis. *Deadline:* continuous.

Contact Ms. Lynda L. Reid, Student Aid Specialist III, Utah Higher Education Assistance Authority, 60 South 400 West, The Board of Regents Building, The Gateway, Salt Lake City, UT 84101-1284. *E-mail:* lreid@utahsbr.edu. *Phone:* 801-321-7207. *Fax:* 801-366-8470. *Web site:* www.uheaa.org.

VERMONT

Vermont Incentive Grants. Renewable grants for Vermont residents based on financial need. Must meet needs test. Must be college undergraduate or graduate student enrolled full-time at an approved post secondary institution. Only available to U.S. citizens or permanent residents. *Award:* Grant for use in freshman, sophomore, junior, senior, or graduate year; renewable. *Award amount:* \$500–\$9900. *Number of awards:* varies. *Eligibility Requirements:* Applicant must be enrolled or expecting to enroll full-time at a two-year, four-year, or technical institution or university and resident of Vermont. Available to U.S. citizens. *Application Requirements:* Application, financial need analysis, FAFSA. *Deadline:* continuous.

Contact Grant Program, Vermont Student Assistance Corporation, PO Box 2000, Winooski, VT 05404-2000. *Phone:* 802-655-9602. *Fax:* 802-654-3765. *Web site:* services.vsac.org.

Vermont Non-Degree Student Grant Program. Need-based, renewable grants for Vermont residents enrolled in non-degree programs in a college, vocational school, or high school adult program, that will improve employability or encourage further study. Award available for two semesters per year, up to \$885 per semester. *Award:* Grant for use in freshman, sophomore, junior, or senior year; renewable. *Award amount:* \$885. *Number of awards:* varies. *Eligibility Requirements:* Applicant must be enrolled or expecting to enroll full- or part-time at a two-year, four-year, or technical institution or university and resident of Vermont. Available to U.S. citizens. *Application Requirements:* Application, financial need analysis. *Deadline:* continuous.

Contact Grant Program, Vermont Student Assistance Corporation, PO Box 2000, Winooski, VT 05404-2000. *E-mail:* info@vsac.org. *Web site:* services.vsac.org.

Vermont Part-time Student Grants. For undergraduates carrying less than twelve credits per semester who have not received a bachelors degree. Must be Vermont resident. Based on financial need. Complete Vermont Financial Aid Packet to apply. May be used at any approved post secondary institution. *Award:* Grant for use in freshman, sophomore, junior, or senior year; renewable. *Award amount:* $250–$7420. *Number of awards:* varies. *Eligibility Requirements:* Applicant must be enrolled or expecting to enroll part-time at a four-year institution or university and resident of Vermont. Available to U.S. citizens. *Application Requirements:* Application, financial need analysis. *Deadline:* continuous.

Contact Grant Program, Vermont Student Assistance Corporation, PO Box 2000, Winooski, VT 05404-2000. *Phone:* 802-655-9602. *Fax:* 802-654-3765. *Web site:* services.vsac.org.

Vermont Teacher Diversity Scholarship Program. Loan forgiveness program for students from diverse racial and ethnic backgrounds who attend college in Vermont with a goal of becoming public school teachers. Preference will be given to residents of Vermont. Deadline: April 5. *Academic Fields/Career Goals:* Education. *Award:* Forgivable loan for use in freshman, sophomore, junior, senior, or graduate year; not renewable. *Award amount:* $4000. *Number of awards:* 4. *Eligibility Requirements:* Applicant must be American Indian/Alaska Native, Asian/Pacific Islander, Black (non-Hispanic), or Hispanic; enrolled or expecting to enroll full- or part-time at a four-year institution or university and studying in Vermont. Available to U.S. citizens. *Application Requirements:* Application, resume, references, transcript. *Deadline:* April 5.

Contact Ms. Phyl Newbeck, Director, Vermont Teacher Diversity Scholarship Program, PO Box 359, Waterbury, VT 05676-0359. *Phone:* 802-241-3379. *Fax:* 802-241-3369. *Web site:* willow.vsc.edu/teacherdiversity/.

VIRGINIA

College Scholarship Assistance Program. Need-based scholarship for undergraduate study by a Virginia resident at a participating Virginia two- or four-year college, or university. Contact financial aid office at the participating Virginia public or nonprofit private institution. *Award:* Grant for use in freshman, sophomore, junior, or senior year; renewable. *Award amount:* $400–$5000. *Number of awards:* varies. *Eligibility Requirements:* Applicant must be enrolled or expecting to enroll full- or part-time at a two-year or four-year institution or university; resident of Virginia and studying in Virginia. Available to U.S. citizens. *Application Requirements:* Application, financial need analysis, Virginia domicile; enroll at Virginia public or participating non-profit private institution; FAFSA. *Deadline:* varies.

Contact Lee Andes, Assistant Director for Financial Aid, State Council of Higher Education for Virginia, James Monroe Building, 101 North 14th Street, 10th Floor, Richmond, VA 23219. *E-mail:* leeandes@schev.edu. *Phone:* 804-225-2614. *Fax:* 804-225-2604. *Web site:* www.schev.edu.

Gheens Foundation Scholarship. The scholarship supports students from Louisville, Kentucky, who are enrolled in a HBCU participating school. Please visit Web site for more information: http://www.uncf.org. *Award:* Scholarship for use in freshman, sophomore, junior, senior, or graduate year; not renewable. *Award amount:* up to $2000. *Number of awards:* varies. *Eligibility Requirements:* Applicant must be Black (non-Hispanic); enrolled or expecting to enroll full- or part-time at a four-year institution or university and resident of Kentucky. Applicant must have 2.5 GPA or higher. Available to U.S. citizens. *Application Requirements:* Application, financial need analysis, transcript. *Deadline:* varies.

Contact Rebecca Bennett, Director, Program Services, United Negro College Fund, 8260 Willow Oaks Corporate Drive, Fairfax, VA 22031-8044. *E-mail:* rebecca.bennett@uncf.org. *Phone:* 800-331-2244. *Web site:* www.uncf.org.

Mary Marshall Practical Nursing Scholarships. Award for practical nursing students who are Virginia residents. Must attend a nursing program in Virginia. Recipient must agree to work in Virginia after graduation. Minimum 3.0 GPA required. Scholarship value and the number of scholarships granted varies annually. Deadline: June 30. *Academic Fields/Career Goals:* Nursing. *Award:* Scholarship for use in freshman, sophomore, junior, or senior year; not renewable. *Award amount:* varies. *Number of awards:* varies. *Eligibility Requirements:* Applicant must be enrolled or expecting to enroll full- or part-time at a four-year institution or university; resident of Virginia and studying in Virginia. Applicant must have 3.0 GPA or higher. Available to U.S. citizens. *Application Requirements:* Application, financial need analysis, references, transcript. *Deadline:* June 30.

Contact Office of Health Policy and Planning, Virginia Department of Health, Office of Health Policy and Planning, 109 Governor Street, Suite 1016 East, Richmond, VA 23219. *Web site:* www.vdh.virginia.gov.

Mary Marshall Registered Nursing Program Scholarships. Award for registered nursing students who are Virginia residents. Must attend a nursing program in Virginia. Recipient must agree to work in Virginia after graduation. Minimum 3.0 GPA required. The amount of each scholarship award is dependent upon the amount of money appropriated by the Virginia General Assembly and the number of qualified applicants. Deadline: June 30. *Academic Fields/Career Goals:* Nursing. *Award:* Scholarship for use in freshman, sophomore, junior, or senior year; not renewable. *Award amount:* varies. *Number of awards:* 60–100. *Eligibility Requirements:* Applicant must be enrolled or expecting to enroll full- or part-time at a four-year institution or university; resident of Virginia and studying in Virginia. Applicant must have 3.0 GPA or higher. Available to U.S. citizens. *Application Requirements:* Application, financial need analysis, references, transcript. *Deadline:* June 30.

Contact Scholarship Coordinator, Virginia Department of Health, Office of Health Policy and Planning, 109 Governor Street, Suite 1016 East, Richmond, VA 23219. *Web site:* www.vdh.virginia.gov.

NRA Youth Educational Summit (YES) Scholarships. Awards for Youth Educational Summit participants based on the initial application, on-site debate, and degree of participation during the week-long event. Must be graduating high school seniors enrolled in undergraduate program. Must have a minimum GPA of 3.0. Scholarship values from $1000 to $10,000. Deadline: March 1. *Award:* Scholarship for use in freshman year; not renewable. *Award amount:* $1000–$10,000. *Number of awards:* 1–6. *Eligibility Requirements:* Applicant must be high school student and planning to enroll or expecting to enroll full- or part-time at a two-year, four-year, or technical institution or university. Applicant must have 3.0 GPA or higher. Available to U.S. citizens. *Application Requirements:* Application, applicant must enter a contest, essay, references, transcript. *Deadline:* March 1.

Contact Event Services Manager, National Rifle Association, 11250 Waples Mill Road, Fairfax, VA 22030. *E-mail:* fnra@nrahq.org.

Phone: 703-267-1354. *Fax:* 703-267-3743. *Web site:* www.nrafoundation.org.

Nurse Practitioners/Nurse Midwife Program Scholarships. One-time award for nurse practitioner/nurse midwife students who have been residents of Virginia for at least one year. Must attend a nursing program in Virginia. Recipient must agree to work in an underserved community in Virginia following graduation. The amount of each scholarship award is dependent upon the amount of funds appropriated by the Virginia General Assembly. Minimum 3.0 GPA required. Deadline: June 30. *Academic Fields/Career Goals:* Nursing. *Award:* Scholarship for use in freshman, sophomore, junior, senior, graduate, or postgraduate years; not renewable. *Award amount:* varies. *Number of awards:* varies. *Eligibility Requirements:* Applicant must be enrolled or expecting to enroll full- or part-time at a four-year institution or university and resident of Virginia. Applicant must have 3.0 GPA or higher. Available to U.S. citizens. *Application Requirements:* Application, financial need analysis, references, transcript. *Deadline:* June 30.

Contact Scholarship Coordinator, Virginia Department of Health, Office of Health Policy and Planning, 109 Governor Street, Suite 1016 East, Richmond, VA 23219. *Web site:* www.vdh.virginia.gov.

Pennsylvania State Employees Scholarship Fund. Scholarships for UNCF students from Pennsylvania. Funds may be used for tuition, room and board, books, or to repay federal student loans. Minimum 2.5 GPA required. Prospective applicants should complete the Student Profile found at Web site: http://www.uncf.org. *Award:* Scholarship for use in freshman, sophomore, junior, or senior year; not renewable. *Award amount:* up to $4000. *Number of awards:* 20. *Eligibility Requirements:* Applicant must be Black (non-Hispanic); enrolled or expecting to enroll full-time at a four-year institution or university and resident of Pennsylvania. Applicant must have 2.5 GPA or higher. Available to U.S. citizens. *Application Requirements:* Application, financial need analysis. *Deadline:* July 14.

Contact Rebecca Bennett, Director, Program Services, United Negro College Fund, 8260 Willow Oaks Corporate Drive, Fairfax, VA 22031-8044. *E-mail:* rebecca.bennett@uncf.org. *Phone:* 800-331-2244. *Web site:* www.uncf.org.

Southside Virginia Tobacco Teacher Scholarship/Loan. Need-based scholarship for Southside Virginia natives to pursue a degree in K-12 teacher education in any four-year U.S. institution and then return to the Southside region to live and work. Must teach in Southside Virginia public school for scholarship/loan forgiveness. *Academic Fields/Career Goals:* Education. *Award:* Forgivable loan for use in freshman, sophomore, junior, or senior year; renewable. *Award amount:* up to $4000. *Number of awards:* varies. *Eligibility Requirements:* Applicant must be enrolled or expecting to enroll full- or part-time at a two-year or four-year institution or university; resident of Virginia and studying in Virginia. Available to U.S. citizens. *Application Requirements:* Application, financial need analysis, FAFSA.

Contact Christine Fields, Scholarship committee, State Council of Higher Education for Virginia, PO Box 1987, Abingdon, VA 24212. *Phone:* 276-619-4376 Ext. 4002. *Web site:* www.schev.edu.

State Department Federal Credit Union Annual Scholarship Program. Scholarships available to members who are currently enrolled in a degree program and have completed 12 credit hours of coursework at an accredited college or university. Must have an account in good standing in their name with SDFCU, have a minimum 2.5 GPA, submit official cumulative transcripts, and describe need for financial assistance to continue their education. *Award:* Scholarship for use in freshman, sophomore, junior, or senior year; renewable. *Award amount:* varies. *Number of awards:* varies. *Eligibility Requirements:* Applicant must be enrolled or expecting to enroll full-time at a four-year institution or university. Applicant must have 2.5 GPA or higher. Available to U.S. citizens. *Application Requirements:* Application, applicant must enter a contest, financial need analysis, transcript, personal statement. *Deadline:* April 13.

Contact Scholarship Coordinator, State Department Federal Credit Union Annual Scholarship Program, SDFCU, 1630 King Street, Alexandria, VA 22314. *E-mail:* sdfcu@sdfcu.org. *Phone:* 703-706-5019. *Web site:* www.sdfcu.org.

Virginia Commonwealth Award. Need-based award for undergraduate or graduate study at a Virginia public two- or four-year college, or university. Undergraduates must be Virginia residents. The application and awards process are administered by the financial aid office at the Virginia public institution where student is enrolled. Dollar value of each award varies. Contact financial aid office for application and deadlines. *Award:* Grant for use in freshman, sophomore, junior, senior, or graduate year; renewable. *Award amount:* varies. *Number of awards:* varies. *Eligibility Requirements:* Applicant must be enrolled or expecting to enroll full- or part-time at a two-year or four-year institution or university; resident of Virginia and studying in Virginia. Available to U.S. citizens. *Application Requirements:* Application, financial need analysis, FAFSA. *Deadline:* varies.

Contact Lee Andes, Assistant Director for Financial Aid, State Council of Higher Education for Virginia, James Monroe Building, 101 North 14th Street, 10th Floor, Richmond, VA 23219. *E-mail:* leeandes@schev.edu. *Phone:* 804-225-2614. *Fax:* 804-225-2604. *Web site:* www.schev.edu.

Virginia Guaranteed Assistance Program. Awards to undergraduate students proportional to their need, up to full tuition, fees and book allowance. Must be a graduate of a Virginia high school, not home-schooled. High school GPA of 2.5 required. Must be enrolled full-time in a Virginia 2- or 4-year institution and demonstrate financial need. Contact financial aid office of your institution for application process and deadlines. Must maintain minimum college GPA of 2.0 for renewal awards. *Award:* Scholarship for use in freshman, sophomore, junior, or senior year; renewable. *Award amount:* varies. *Number of awards:* varies. *Eligibility Requirements:* Applicant must be enrolled or expecting to enroll full-time at a two-year or four-year institution or university; resident of Virginia and studying in Virginia. Applicant must have 2.5 GPA or higher. Available to U.S. citizens. *Application Requirements:* Application, financial need analysis, transcript, FAFSA. *Deadline:* varies.

Contact Lee Andes, Assistant Director for Financial Aid, State Council of Higher Education for Virginia, James Monroe Building, 101 North 14th Street, 10th Floor, Richmond, VA 23219. *E-mail:* leeandes@schev.edu. *Phone:* 804-225-2614. *Fax:* 804-225-2604. *Web site:* www.schev.edu.

Virginia Teaching Scholarship Loan Program. Forgivable loan for Virginia resident students enrolled full- or part-time in a Virginia institution pursuing a teaching degree. The loan is forgiven if the student teaches for four semesters in any Virginia public school in the critical shortage fields identified by the State Council of Higher Education. Must maintain a minimum GPA of 2.7. Must be nominated by the Education Department of the eligible institution. *Academic Fields/Career Goals:* Education. *Award:* Forgivable loan for use in sophomore, junior, senior, or graduate year; not renewable. *Award amount:* up to $3720. *Number of awards:* varies. *Eligibility Requirements:* Applicant must be enrolled or expecting to enroll full- or part-time at a four-year institution or university; resident of Virginia and studying in Virginia. Available to U.S. citizens. *Application Requirements:* Application, references. *Deadline:* varies.

Contact Lee Andes, Assistant Director for Financial Aid, State Council of Higher Education for Virginia, James Monroe Building, 101 North 14th Street, 10th Floor, Richmond, VA 23219. *E-mail:* leeandes@schev.edu. *Phone:* 804-225-2614. *Fax:* 804-225-2604. *Web site:* www.schev.edu.

Virginia Tuition Assistance Grant Program (Private Institutions). Renewable awards of approximately $1900 to $2750 each for undergraduate, graduate, and first professional degree students attending an approved private, nonprofit college within Virginia. Must be a Virginia resident and be enrolled full-time. Not to be used for religious study. Deadline: July 31. Others are wait-listed. Information and application available from participating Virginia colleges financial aid office. *Award:* Grant for use in freshman, sophomore, junior, senior, or graduate year; renewable. *Award amount:* $1900–$2750. *Number of awards:* 18,600. *Eligibility Requirements:* Applicant must be enrolled or expecting to enroll full-time at a four-year institution or university; resident of Virginia and studying in Virginia. Available to U.S. citizens. *Application Requirements:* Application, demonstrate one-year of Virginia domicile and full-time enrollment at a participating Virginia non-profit private institution. *Deadline:* July 31.

Contact Lee Andes, Assistant Director for Financial Aid, State Council of Higher Education for Virginia, James Monroe Building, 101 North 14th Street, 10th Floor, Richmond, VA 23219. *E-mail:* leeandes@schev.edu. *Phone:* 804-225-2614. *Fax:* 804-225-2604. *Web site:* www.schev.edu.

Virginia War Orphans Education Program. Scholarships for postsecondary students between ages 16 and 25 to attend Virginia state-supported institutions. Must be child or surviving child of veteran who has either been permanently or totally disabled due to war or other armed conflict; died as a result of war or other armed conflict; or been listed as a POW or MIA. Parent must also meet Virginia residency requirements. *Award:* Scholarship for use in freshman, sophomore, junior, senior, or graduate year; renewable. *Award amount:* varies. *Number of awards:* varies. *Eligibility Requirements:* Applicant must be age 16-25; enrolled or expecting to enroll full-time at a two-year, four-year, or technical institution or university; resident of Virginia and studying in Virginia. Available to U.S. citizens. Applicant or parent must meet one or more of the following requirements: general military experience; retired from active duty; disabled or killed as a result of military service; prisoner of war; or missing in action. *Application Requirements:* Application, references. *Deadline:* varies.

Contact Doris Sullivan, Coordinator, Virginia Department of Veterans Services, Poff Federal Building, 270 Franklin Road, SW, Room 503, Roanoke, VA 24011-2215. *Phone:* 540-857-7101 Ext. 213. *Fax:* 540-857-7573. *Web site:* www.dvs.virginia.gov.

Walter Reed Smith Scholarship. Award for full-time female undergraduate students who are descendant of a Confederate soldier, studying nutrition, home economics, nursing, business administration, or computer science in accredited college or university. Minimum 3.0 GPA required. Submit letter of endorsement from sponsoring chapter of the United Daughters of the Confederacy. Deadline: March 15. *Academic Fields/Career Goals:* Business/Consumer Services; Computer Science/Data Processing; Food Science/Nutrition; Home Economics; Nursing. *Award:* Scholarship for use in freshman, sophomore, junior, or senior year; renewable. *Award amount:* $800–$1000. *Number of awards:* 1–2. *Eligibility Requirements:* Applicant must be enrolled or expecting to enroll full-time at a four-year institution or university and female. Applicant or parent of applicant must be member of United Daughters of the Confederacy. Applicant must have 3.0 GPA or higher. Available to U.S. citizens. Applicant or parent must meet one or more of the following requirements: Air Force, Army, or Navy experience; retired from active duty; disabled or killed as a result of military service; prisoner of war; or missing in action. *Application Requirements:* Application, essay, financial need analysis, photo, references, self-addressed stamped envelope, transcript, copy of applicant's birth certificate, copy of confederate ancestor's proof of service. *Deadline:* March 15.

Contact Deanna Bryant, Second Vice President General, United Daughters of the Confederacy, 328 North Boulevard, Richmond, VA 23220-4009. *E-mail:* hqudc@rcn.com. *Phone:* 804-355-1636. *Fax:* 804-353-1396. *Web site:* www.hqudc.org.

WASHINGTON

American Indian Endowed Scholarship. Awarded to financially needy undergraduate and graduate students with close social and cultural ties with a Native-American community. Must be Washington resident, enrolled full-time at Washington school. Deadline: May 15. *Award:* Scholarship for use in freshman, sophomore, junior, senior, or graduate year; renewable. *Award amount:* $500–$2000. *Number of awards:* 15. *Eligibility Requirements:* Applicant must be American Indian/Alaska Native; enrolled or expecting to enroll full-time at a two-year, four-year, or technical institution or university; resident of Washington and studying in Washington. Available to U.S. citizens. *Application Requirements:* Application, financial need analysis. *Deadline:* May 15.

Contact Ann Lee, Program Manager, Washington Higher Education Coordinating Board, 917 Lakeridge Way, PO Box 43430, Olympia, WA 98504-3430. *E-mail:* annl@hecb.wa.gov. *Phone:* 360-755-7843. *Fax:* 360-753-7808. *Web site:* www.hecb.wa.gov.

Educational Opportunity Grant. Annual grants of $2500 to encourage financially needy, placebound students to complete bachelor's degree. Must be unable to continue education due to family or work commitments, health concerns, financial needs or other similar factors. Must be Washington residents, and have completed two years of college. Grants can only be used at eligible four-year colleges in Washington. Applications are accepted from the beginning of April through the following months until funds are depleted. *Award:* Grant for use in junior or senior year; renewable. *Award amount:* $2500. *Number of awards:* 1300. *Eligibility Requirements:* Applicant must be enrolled or expecting to enroll full-time at a four-year institution; resident of Washington and studying in Washington. Available to U.S. citizens. *Application Requirements:* Application, financial need analysis. *Deadline:* continuous.

Contact Dawn Cypriano-McAferty, Program Manager, Washington Higher Education Coordinating Board, 917 Lakeridge Way, PO Box 43430, Olympia, WA 98504-3430. *E-mail:* eog@hecb.wa.gov. *Phone:* 360-753-7800. *Fax:* 360-753-7808. *Web site:* www.hecb.wa.gov.

Future Teachers Conditional Scholarship and Loan Repayment Program. The program is designed to encourage outstanding students and paraprofessionals to become teachers. Participants must agree to teach in Washington K-12 schools, in return for conditional scholarships or loan repayments. Additional consideration is given to individuals seeking certification or additional endorsements in teacher subject shortage areas, as well as to individuals with demonstrated bilingual ability. Must be residents of Washington and attend an institution in Washington. *Academic Fields/Career Goals:* Education. *Award:* Forgivable loan for use in freshman, sophomore, junior, or senior year; renewable. *Award amount:* $2600–$5800. *Number of awards:* 50. *Eligibility Requirements:* Applicant must be enrolled or expecting to enroll full- or part-time at a two-year or four-year institution or university; resident of Washington and studying in Washington. Available to U.S. citizens. *Application Requirements:* Application, essay, references, transcript, bilingual verification (if applicable). *Deadline:* October 15.

Contact Mary Knutson, Program Coordinator, Washington Higher Education Coordinating Board, 917 Lakeridge Way, PO Box 43430, Olympia, WA 98504-3430. *E-mail:* futureteachers@hecb.wa.gov. *Phone:* 360-753-7845. *Fax:* 360-753-7808. *Web site:* www.hecb.wa.gov.

Health Professional Scholarship Program. The program was created to attract and retain health professionals, to serve in critical shortage areas in Washington state. Must sign a promissory note agreeing to serve for a minimum of three years in a designated shortage area in Washington state or pay back funds at double penalty with the interest. *Academic Fields/Career Goals:* Health and Medical Sciences. *Award:* Forgivable loan for use in junior, senior, or graduate year; renewable. *Award amount:* varies. *Number of awards:* varies. *Eligibility Requirements:* Applicant must be enrolled or expecting to enroll full- or part-time at a four-year institution or university. Available to U.S. citizens. *Application Requirements:* Application, references, transcript. *Deadline:* April 30.

Contact Kathy McVay, Program Administrator, Washington Higher Education Coordinating Board, PO Box 47834, Olympia, WA 98504-7834. *E-mail:* kathy.mcvay@doh.wa.gov. *Phone:* 360-236-2816. *Web site:* www.hecb.wa.gov.

Robert C. Byrd Honors Scholarship-Washington. Scholarship for high school seniors who demonstrate outstanding academic achievement and show promise of continued academic excellence. Must be Washington residents. *Award:* Scholarship for use in freshman, sophomore, junior, or senior year; not renewable. *Award amount:* $1500–$6000. *Number of awards:* varies. *Eligibility Requirements:* Applicant must be high school student; planning to enroll or expecting to enroll full-time at a four-year institution or university and resident of Washington. Available to U.S. citizens. *Application Requirements:* Application, transcript. *Deadline:* varies.

Contact Kara Larson, Superintendent of Public Instruction, Washington Higher Education Coordinating Board, PO Box 47200, Olympia, WA 98504-7200. *E-mail:* kara.larson@k12.wa.us. *Phone:* 360-725-6225. *Web site:* www.hecb.wa.gov.

State Need Grant. The program helps Washington's lowest-income undergraduate students to pursue degrees, hone skills, or retrain for new careers. Students with family incomes equal to or less than 50 percent of the state median are eligible for up to 100 percent of the maximum grant. Students with family incomes between 51 percent and 65 percent of the state median are eligible for up to 75 percent of the maximum grant. *Award:* Grant for use in freshman, sophomore, junior, or senior year; renewable. *Award amount:* $553–$5156. *Number of awards:* 55,000. *Eligibility Requirements:* Applicant must be enrolled or expecting to enroll full- or part-time at a two-year or four-year institution or university; resident of Washington and studying in Washington. Available to U.S. citizens. *Application Requirements:* Application, financial need analysis, FAFSA. *Deadline:* continuous.

Contact Karola Longoria, Administrative Assistant, Student Financial Assist, Washington Higher Education Coordinating Board, 917 Lakeridge Way, PO Box 43430, Olympia, WA 98504-3430. *E-mail:* karolal@hecb.wa.gov. *Phone:* 360-753-7850. *Fax:* 360-753-7808. *Web site:* www.hecb.wa.gov.

Washington Award for Vocational Excellence. Award for students who are currently a state resident enrolled in a Washington State high school, skills center, or public community or technical college. Recipients of this annual award receive monetary grants, based on availability of funds. *Award:* Grant for use in freshman or sophomore year; renewable. *Award amount:* varies. *Number of awards:* 147. *Eligibility Requirements:* Applicant must be enrolled or expecting to enroll full- or part-time at a two-year, four-year, or technical institution or university; resident of Washington and studying in Washington. Available to U.S. and non-U.S. citizens. *Application Requirements:* Application, essay, references. *Deadline:* March 2.

Contact Lee Williams, Program Administrator, Washington State Workforce Training and Education Coordinating Board, 128 Tenth Avenue, SW, PO Box 43105, Olympia, WA 98504-3105. *E-mail:* lwilliams@wtb.wa.gov. *Phone:* 360-586-3321. *Fax:* 360-586-5862. *Web site:* www.wtb.wa.gov.

Washington Award for Vocational Excellence (WAVE). Award to honor vocational students from the districts of Washington. Grants for up to two years of undergraduate resident tuition. Must be enrolled in Washington high school, skills center, or technical college at time of application. Must complete 360 hours in single vocational program in high school or one year at technical college. Contact principal or guidance counselor for more information. *Award:* Grant for use in freshman, sophomore, junior, or senior year; renewable. *Award amount:* $2586–$5887. *Number of awards:* 147. *Eligibility Requirements:* Applicant must be enrolled or expecting to enroll full-time at a two-year, four-year, or technical institution or university; resident of Washington and studying in Washington. Available to U.S. citizens. *Application Requirements:* Application. *Deadline:* February 16.

Contact Ann Lee, Program Manager, Washington Higher Education Coordinating Board, 917 Lakeridge Way, PO Box 43430, Olympia, WA 98504-3430. *E-mail:* annl@hecb.wa.gov. *Phone:* 360-753-7843. *Fax:* 360-753-7808. *Web site:* www.hecb.wa.gov.

Washington Scholars Program. Awards high school students from the legislative districts of Washington. Must be enrolled in college or university in Washington. Scholarships equal up to four years of full-time resident undergraduate tuition and fees. Contact principal or guidance counselor for more information. *Award:* Grant for use in freshman, sophomore, junior, or senior year; renewable. *Award amount:* $2586–$5887. *Number of awards:* 147. *Eligibility Requirements:* Applicant must be high school student; planning to enroll or expecting to enroll full-time at a four-year institution or university; resident of Washington and studying in Washington. Available to U.S. citizens. *Application Requirements:* Application. *Deadline:* continuous.

Contact Ann Lee, Program Manager, Washington Higher Education Coordinating Board, 917 Lakeridge Way, PO Box 43430, Olympia, WA 98504-3430. *E-mail:* annl@hecb.wa.gov. *Phone:* 360-753-7843. *Fax:* 360-753-7808. *Web site:* www.hecb.wa.gov.

WICHE Professional Student Exchange. Scholarship for students at senior year of undergraduate degree or above. Must be residents of Washington. Must return to Washington and serve for a minimum of four years. Deadline: October 15. *Award:* Scholarship for use in senior, graduate, or postgraduate years; renewable. *Award amount:* $13,600–$17,000. *Number of awards:* 14. *Eligibility Requirements:* Applicant must be enrolled or expecting to enroll full-time at an institution or university; resident of Washington and studying in Washington. Available to U.S. citizens.

Application Requirements: Application, financial need analysis, transcript. *Deadline:* October 15.

Contact Dawn McAferty, Program Manager, Washington Higher Education Coordinating Board, 917 Lakeridge Way, PO Box 43430, Olympia, WA 98504. *E-mail:* dawnc@hecb.wa.gov. *Phone:* 360-753-7846. *Fax:* 360-704-6246. *Web site:* www.hecb.wa.gov.

WEST VIRGINIA

Robert C. Byrd Honors Scholarship-West Virginia. Award for West Virginia residents who have demonstrated outstanding academic achievement. Must be a graduating high school senior. May apply for renewal consideration for a total of four years of assistance. For full-time study only. *Award:* Scholarship for use in freshman, sophomore, junior, or senior year; renewable. *Award amount:* $1500. *Number of awards:* 36. *Eligibility Requirements:* Applicant must be high school student; planning to enroll or expecting to enroll full-time at a two-year, four-year, or technical institution or university and resident of West Virginia. Applicant must have 3.5 GPA or higher. Available to U.S. citizens. *Application Requirements:* Application, test scores, transcript, letter of acceptance from a college/university. *Deadline:* March 1.

Contact Darlene Elmore, Scholarship Coordinator, West Virginia Higher Education Policy Commission-Office of Financial Aid and Outreach Services, 1018 Kanawha Boulevard, East, Suite 700, Charleston, WV 25301. *E-mail:* elmore@hepc.wvnet.edu. *Web site:* www.hepc.wvnet.edu.

Underwood-Smith Teacher Scholarship Program. Award for West Virginia residents at West Virginia institutions pursuing teaching careers. Must have a 3.5 GPA after completion of two years of course work. Must teach two years in West Virginia public schools for each year the award is received. Recipients will be required to sign an agreement acknowledging an understanding of the program's requirements and their willingness to repay the award if appropriate teaching service is not rendered. *Academic Fields/Career Goals:* Education. *Award:* Scholarship for use in junior, senior, or graduate year; renewable. *Award amount:* $1620–$5000. *Number of awards:* 53. *Eligibility Requirements:* Applicant must be enrolled or expecting to enroll full-time at a four-year institution or university; resident of West Virginia and studying in West Virginia. Applicant must have 3.5 GPA or higher. Available to U.S. citizens. *Application Requirements:* Application, essay, references. *Deadline:* March 1.

Contact Darlene Elmore, Scholarship Coordinator, West Virginia Higher Education Policy Commission-Office of Financial Aid and Outreach Services, 1018 Kanawha Boulevard, East, Suite 700, Charleston, WV 25301. *E-mail:* elmore@hepc.wvnet.edu. *Web site:* www.hepc.wvnet.edu.

West Virginia Engineering, Science and Technology Scholarship Program. Award for full-time students attending West Virginia institutions, pursuing a degree in engineering, science, or technology. Must be a resident of West Virginia. Must have a 3.0 GPA, and after graduation, must work in the fields of engineering, science, or technology in West Virginia one year for each year the award was received. *Academic Fields/Career Goals:* Electrical Engineering/Electronics; Engineering/Technology; Engineering-Related Technologies; Science, Technology, and Society. *Award:* Scholarship for use in freshman, sophomore, junior, or senior year; renewable. *Award amount:* up to $3000. *Number of awards:* varies. *Eligibility Requirements:* Applicant must be enrolled or expecting to enroll full-time at a two-year, four-year, or technical institution or university; resident of West Virginia and studying in West Virginia. Applicant must have 3.0 GPA or higher. Available to U.S. citizens. *Application Requirements:* Application, essay, test scores, transcript. *Deadline:* March 1.

Contact Darlene Elmore, Scholarship Coordinator, West Virginia Higher Education Policy Commission-Office of Financial Aid and Outreach Services, 1018 Kanawha Boulevard East, Suite 700, Charleston, WV 25301. *E-mail:* elmore@hepc.wvnet.edu. *Phone:* 304-558-4618. *Fax:* 304-558-4622. *Web site:* www.hepc.wvnet.edu.

West Virginia Higher Education Grant Program. Award available for West Virginia resident for one year immediately preceding the date of application, high school graduate or the equivalent, demonstrate financial need, and enroll as a full-time undergraduate at an approved university or college located in West Virginia or Pennsylvania. *Award:* Grant for use in freshman year; not renewable. *Award amount:* $375–$3358. *Number of awards:* 10,755–11,000. *Eligibility Requirements:* Applicant must be high school student; planning to enroll or expecting to enroll full-time at a four-year institution or university; resident of West Virginia and studying in Pennsylvania or West Virginia. Available to U.S. citizens. *Application Requirements:* Application, financial need analysis, references, test scores, transcript. *Deadline:* March 1.

Contact Daniel Crockett, Director of Student and Educational Services, West Virginia Higher Education Policy Commission-Office of Financial Aid and Outreach Services, 1018 Kanawha Boulevard East, Suite 700, Charleston, WV 25301-2827. *E-mail:* crockett@hepc.wvnet.edu. *Phone:* 888-825-5707. *Fax:* 304-558-4622. *Web site:* www.hepc.wvnet.edu.

WISCONSIN

Handicapped Student Grant-Wisconsin. One-time award available to residents of Wisconsin who have severe or profound hearing or visual impairment. Must be enrolled at least half-time at a nonprofit institution. If the handicap prevents the student from attending a Wisconsin school, the award may be used out-of-state in a specialized college. Refer to Web site for further details: http://www.heab.state.wi.us. *Award:* Grant for use in freshman, sophomore, junior, or senior year; not renewable. *Award amount:* $250–$1800. *Number of awards:* varies. *Eligibility Requirements:* Applicant must be enrolled or expecting to enroll full- or part-time at a four-year institution or university and resident of Wisconsin. Applicant must be hearing impaired or visually impaired. Available to U.S. citizens. *Application Requirements:* Application, financial need analysis. *Deadline:* continuous.

Contact Sandy Thomas, Program Coordinator, Wisconsin Higher Educational Aids Board, PO Box 7885, Madison, WI 53707-7885. *E-mail:* sandy.thomas@heab.state.wi.us. *Phone:* 608-266-0888. *Fax:* 608-267-2808. *Web site:* www.heab.state.wi.us.

Minority Undergraduate Retention Grant-Wisconsin. The grant provides financial assistance to African-American, Native-American, Hispanic, and former citizens of Laos, Vietnam, and Cambodia, for study in Wisconsin. Must be Wisconsin resident, enrolled at least half-time in Wisconsin Technical College System schools, non-profit independent colleges and universities, and tribal colleges. Refer to Web site for further details: http://www.heab.state.wi.us. *Award:* Grant for use in sophomore, junior, senior, or graduate year; not renewable. *Award amount:* $250–$2500. *Number of awards:* varies. *Eligibility Requirements:* Applicant must be American Indian/Alaska Native, Asian/Pacific Islander, Black (non-Hispanic), or Hispanic; enrolled or expecting to enroll full- or part-time at a two-year, four-year, or technical institution or university; resident of Wisconsin and studying in Wisconsin. Available to U.S.

and non-U.S. citizens. *Application Requirements:* Application, financial need analysis. *Deadline:* continuous.

Contact Mary Lou Kuzdas, Program Coordinator, Wisconsin Higher Educational Aids Board, PO Box 7885, Madison, WI 53707-7885. *E-mail:* mary.kuzdas@heab.state.wi.us. *Phone:* 608-267-2212. *Fax:* 608-267-2808. *Web site:* www.heab.state.wi.us.

Nursing Student Loan Program. The program provides forgivable loans to students enrolled in a nursing program. Must be Wisconsin residents studying in Wisconsin. Deadline is last day on which the student is enrolled. Refer to Web site for further details: http://www.heab.state.wi.us. *Academic Fields/Career Goals:* Nursing. *Award:* Forgivable loan for use in freshman, sophomore, junior, or senior year; renewable. *Award amount:* $250–$3000. *Number of awards:* 150–1800. *Eligibility Requirements:* Applicant must be enrolled or expecting to enroll full- or part-time at a two-year, four-year, or technical institution or university; resident of Wisconsin and studying in Wisconsin. Available to U.S. citizens. *Application Requirements:* Application, financial need analysis. *Deadline:* varies.

Contact Cindy Lehrman, Program Coordinator, Wisconsin Higher Educational Aids Board, PO Box 7885, Madison, WI 53707-7885. *E-mail:* cindy.lehrman@heab.state.wi.us. *Phone:* 608-267-2209. *Fax:* 608-267-2808. *Web site:* www.heab.state.wi.us.

Talent Incentive Program Grant. Grant assists residents of Wisconsin who are attending a nonprofit institution in Wisconsin, and who have substantial financial need. Must meet income criteria, be considered economically and educationally disadvantaged, and be enrolled at least half-time. Refer to Web site for further details: http://www.heab.state.wi.us. *Award:* Grant for use in freshman, sophomore, junior, or senior year; renewable. *Award amount:* $250–$1800. *Number of awards:* varies. *Eligibility Requirements:* Applicant must be enrolled or expecting to enroll full- or part-time at a two-year or four-year institution or university; resident of Wisconsin and studying in Wisconsin. Available to U.S. citizens. *Application Requirements:* Application, financial need analysis, nomination. *Deadline:* continuous.

Contact John Whitt, Program Coordinator, Wisconsin Higher Educational Aids Board, PO Box 7885, Madison, WI 53707-7885. *E-mail:* john.whitt@heab.state.wi.us. *Phone:* 608-266-1665. *Fax:* 608-267-2808. *Web site:* www.heab.state.wi.us.

Teacher of the Visually Impaired Loan Program. Forgivable loans to students who enroll in programs that lead to certification as a teacher of the visually impaired or an orientation and mobility instructor. Must be a Wisconsin resident. For study in Wisconsin, Illinois, Iowa, Michigan, and Minnesota. Refer to Web site for further details: http://www.heab.state.wi.us. *Academic Fields/Career Goals:* Special Education. *Award:* Forgivable loan for use in freshman, sophomore, junior, senior, or graduate year; not renewable. *Award amount:* $250–$10,000. *Number of awards:* varies. *Eligibility Requirements:* Applicant must be enrolled or expecting to enroll full- or part-time at a two-year, four-year, or technical institution or university; resident of Wisconsin and studying in Illinois, Iowa, Michigan, Minnesota, or Wisconsin. Available to U.S. citizens. *Application Requirements:* Application, financial need analysis. *Deadline:* continuous.

Contact John Whitt, Program Coordinator, Wisconsin Higher Educational Aids Board, PO Box 7885, Madison, WI 53707-7885. *E-mail:* john.whitt@heab.state.wi.us. *Phone:* 608-266-1665. *Fax:* 608-267-2808. *Web site:* www.heab.state.wi.us.

Veterans Education (VetEd) Reimbursement Grant. Open only to Wisconsin veterans enrolled at approved schools for undergraduate study. Benefit is based on length of time serving on active duty in the armed forces (active duty for training does not apply). Pre-application due no later than 30 days after the start of semester. Application deadline no later than 60 days after the course completion. Veterans may be reimbursed up to 100 percent of tuition and fees. *Award:* Grant for use in freshman, sophomore, junior, or senior year; renewable. *Award amount:* up to $3365. *Number of awards:* varies. *Eligibility Requirements:* Applicant must be enrolled or expecting to enroll full- or part-time at a two-year, four-year, or technical institution or university and resident of Wisconsin. Available to U.S. citizens. Applicant must have served in the Air Force, Army, Coast Guard, Marine Corps, or Navy. *Application Requirements:* Application. *Deadline:* varies.

Contact Mr. Joe Bertalan, Supervisor, Wisconsin Department of Veterans Affairs, PO Box 7843, Madison, WI 53707-7843. *Phone:* 800-947-8387. *Web site:* www.dva.state.wi.us.

Wisconsin Academic Excellence Scholarship. Renewable award for high school seniors with the highest GPA in graduating class. Must be a Wisconsin resident. Award covers tuition for up to four years. Must maintain 3.0 GPA for renewal. Scholarships value is $2250 each. Must attend a nonprofit Wisconsin institution full-time. Refer to Web site for further details: http://www.heab.state.wi.us. *Award:* Scholarship for use in freshman, sophomore, junior, or senior year; renewable. *Award amount:* up to $2250. *Number of awards:* varies. *Eligibility Requirements:* Applicant must be enrolled or expecting to enroll full-time at a two-year, four-year, or technical institution or university; resident of Wisconsin and studying in Wisconsin. Applicant must have 3.5 GPA or higher. Available to U.S. citizens. *Application Requirements:* Transcript. *Deadline:* continuous.

Contact Alice Winters, Program Coordinator, Wisconsin Higher Educational Aids Board, PO Box 7885, Madison, WI 53707-7885. *E-mail:* alice.winters@heab.state.wi.us. *Phone:* 608-267-2213. *Fax:* 608-267-2808. *Web site:* www.heab.state.wi.us.

Wisconsin Higher Education Grants (WHEG). Grants for residents of Wisconsin enrolled at least half-time in degree or certificate programs at University of Wisconsin or Wisconsin Technical College. Must show financial need. Refer to Web site for further details: http://www.heab.state.wi.us. *Award:* Grant for use in freshman, sophomore, junior, or senior year; not renewable. *Award amount:* $250–$3000. *Number of awards:* varies. *Eligibility Requirements:* Applicant must be enrolled or expecting to enroll full- or part-time at a two-year, four-year, or technical institution or university; resident of Wisconsin and studying in Wisconsin. Available to U.S. citizens. *Application Requirements:* Application, financial need analysis. *Deadline:* continuous.

Contact Sandra Thomas, Program Coordinator, Wisconsin Higher Educational Aids Board, PO Box 7885, Madison, WI 53707-7885. *E-mail:* sandy.thomas@heab.state.wi.us. *Phone:* 608-266-0888. *Fax:* 608-267-2808. *Web site:* www.heab.state.wi.us.

Wisconsin Native American/Indian Student Assistance Grant. Grants for Wisconsin residents who are at least one-quarter American Indian. Must be attending a college or university within the state. Refer to Web site for further details: http://www.heab.state.wi.us. *Award:* Grant for use in freshman, sophomore, junior, senior, graduate, or postgraduate years; not renewable. *Award amount:* $250–$1100. *Number of awards:* varies. *Eligibility Requirements:* Applicant must be American Indian/Alaska Native; enrolled or expecting to enroll full- or part-time at a two-year, four-year, or technical institution or university; resident of Wisconsin and studying in Wisconsin. Available to U.S. citizens.

Application Requirements: Application, financial need analysis. *Deadline:* continuous.

Contact Sandra Thomas, Program Coordinator, Wisconsin Higher Educational Aids Board, PO Box 7885, Madison, WI 53707-7885. *E-mail:* sandy.thomas@heab.state.wi.us. *Phone:* 608-266-0888. *Fax:* 608-267-2808. *Web site:* www.heab.state.wi.us.

WYOMING

Douvas Memorial Scholarship. Available to Wyoming residents who are first-generation Americans. Must be between 18 and 22 years old. Must be used at any Wyoming public institution of higher education for study in freshman year. *Award:* Scholarship for use in freshman year; not renewable. *Award amount:* $500. *Number of awards:* 1. *Eligibility Requirements:* Applicant must be age 18-22; enrolled or expecting to enroll full- or part-time at a two-year or four-year institution or university; resident of Wyoming and studying in Wyoming. Available to U.S. citizens. *Application Requirements:* Application. *Deadline:* March 24.

Contact Gerry Maas, Director, Health and Safety, Wyoming Department of Education, 2300 Capitol Avenue, Hathaway Building, Second Floor, Cheyenne, WY 82002-0050. *E-mail:* gmaas@educ.state.wy.us. *Phone:* 307-777-6282. *Fax:* 307-777-6234.

Hathaway Scholarship. Scholarship for Wyoming students to pursue postsecondary education within the state. *Award:* Scholarship for use in freshman, sophomore, junior, or senior year; not renewable. *Award amount:* $1000. *Number of awards:* 1. *Eligibility Requirements:* Applicant must be enrolled or expecting to enroll full-time at a two-year or four-year institution or university and resident of Wyoming. Available to U.S. citizens. *Application Requirements:* Application. *Deadline:* varies.

Contact Gerry Maas, Director, Health and Safety, Wyoming Department of Education, 2300 Capitol Avenue, Hathaway Building, Second Floor, Cheyenne, WY 82002-0050. *E-mail:* gmaas@educ.state.wy.us. *Phone:* 307-777-6282. *Fax:* 307-777-6234.

Superior Student in Education Scholarship-Wyoming. Scholarship available each year to sixteen new Wyoming high school graduates who plan to teach in Wyoming. The award covers costs of undergraduate tuition at the University of Wyoming or any Wyoming community college. *Academic Fields/Career Goals:* Education. *Award:* Scholarship for use in freshman, sophomore, junior, or senior year; renewable. *Award amount:* varies. *Number of awards:* 16. *Eligibility Requirements:* Applicant must be high school student; planning to enroll or expecting to enroll full-time at a four-year institution or university; resident of Wyoming and studying in Wyoming. Applicant must have 3.0 GPA or higher. Available to U.S. citizens. *Application Requirements:* Application, references, test scores, transcript. *Deadline:* October 31.

Contact Joel Anne Berrigan, Assistant Director, Scholarships, State of Wyoming, administered by University of Wyoming, Student Financial Aid, Department 3335, 1000 East University Avenue, Laramie, WY 82071-3335. *E-mail:* finaid@uwyo.edu. *Phone:* 307-766-2117. *Fax:* 307-766-3800. *Web site:* www.uwyo.edu/scholarships.

Vietnam Veterans Award-Wyoming. Scholarship available to Wyoming residents who served in the armed forces between August 5, 1964, and May 7, 1975, and received a Vietnam service medal. *Award:* Scholarship for use in freshman, sophomore, junior, or senior year; renewable. *Award amount:* varies. *Number of awards:* varies. *Eligibility Requirements:* Applicant must be enrolled or expecting to enroll full- or part-time at a two-year or four-year institution or university and resident of Wyoming. Available to U.S. citizens. Applicant must have general military experience. *Application Requirements:* Application. *Deadline:* continuous.

Contact Joel Anne Berrigan, Assistant Director, Scholarships, State of Wyoming, administered by University of Wyoming, Student Financial Aid, Department 3335, 1000 East University Avenue, Laramie, WY 82071-3335. *E-mail:* finaid@uwyo.edu. *Phone:* 307-766-2117. *Fax:* 307-766-3800. *Web site:* www.uwyo.edu/scholarships.

Indexes

Non-Need Scholarships for Undergraduates

Academic Interests/ Achievements

Agriculture

Abilene Christian University, TX
Arkansas State University, AR
Arkansas Tech University, AR
Auburn University, AL
Berry College, GA
Brigham Young University, UT
California Polytechnic State University, San Luis Obispo, CA
California State University, Chico, CA
California State University, Fresno, CA
California State University, Stanislaus, CA
Clemson University, SC
Dickinson State University, ND
Dordt College, IA
Eastern Michigan University, MI
Fort Lewis College, CO
Illinois State University, IL
Louisiana State University and Agricultural and Mechanical College, LA
Louisiana Tech University, LA
Lubbock Christian University, TX
Michigan State University, MI
Middle Tennessee State University, TN
Mississippi State University, MS
Missouri State University, MO
Montana State University, MT
Morehead State University, KY
Murray State University, KY
New Mexico State University, NM
North Carolina State University, NC
North Dakota State University, ND
Northwestern Oklahoma State University, OK
The Ohio State University, OH
Oklahoma Panhandle State University, OK
Oklahoma State University, OK
Purdue University, IN
Sam Houston State University, TX
South Dakota State University, SD
Southeast Missouri State University, MO
Southern Arkansas University–Magnolia, AR
Southern Illinois University Carbondale, IL
Southwest Minnesota State University, MN
State University of New York College of Environmental Science and Forestry, NY
Stephen F. Austin State University, TX
Tennessee Technological University, TN
Texas A&M University–Commerce, TX
Texas State University-San Marcos, TX
Texas Tech University, TX
The University of Arizona, AZ
University of California, Riverside, CA
University of Central Missouri, MO
University of Connecticut, CT
University of Delaware, DE
University of Florida, FL
University of Georgia, GA
University of Hawaii at Hilo, HI
University of Idaho, ID
University of Illinois at Springfield, IL
University of Illinois at Urbana–Champaign, IL
University of Maryland, College Park, MD
University of Massachusetts Amherst, MA
University of Minnesota, Crookston, MN
University of Minnesota, Twin Cities Campus, MN
University of Missouri–Columbia, MO
University of New Hampshire, NH
The University of Tennessee at Martin, TN
The University of Texas at San Antonio, TX
University of Vermont, VT
University of Wisconsin–Stevens Point, WI
University of Wyoming, WY
Utah State University, UT
Virginia Polytechnic Institute and State University, VA
Virginia State University, VA
Washington State University, WA
Western Illinois University, IL
West Virginia University, WV

Architecture

Arizona State University, AZ
Auburn University, AL
California College of the Arts, CA
California Polytechnic State University, San Luis Obispo, CA
City College of the City University of New York, NY
Clemson University, SC
Cooper Union for the Advancement of Science and Art, NY
Drury University, MO
Eastern Michigan University, MI
Georgia Institute of Technology, GA
Illinois Institute of Technology, IL
James Madison University, VA
Kent State University, OH
Lawrence Technological University, MI
Louisiana State University and Agricultural and Mechanical College, LA
Louisiana Tech University, LA
Miami University, OH
Michigan State University, MI
Mississippi State University, MS
Montana State University, MT
North Dakota State University, ND
The Ohio State University, OH
Oklahoma State University, OK
Portland State University, OR
Rice University, TX
Savannah College of Art and Design, GA
Southern Illinois University Carbondale, IL
State University of New York College of Environmental Science and Forestry, NY
Texas Tech University, TX
The University of Arizona, AZ
University of Colorado at Boulder, CO
University of Florida, FL
University of Idaho, ID
University of Illinois at Chicago, IL
University of Illinois at Urbana–Champaign, IL
University of Kansas, KS
University of Maryland, College Park, MD
University of Massachusetts Amherst, MA
University of Miami, FL
University of Michigan, MI
University of Minnesota, Twin Cities Campus, MN
The University of North Carolina at Charlotte, NC
University of Oklahoma, OK
University of Oregon, OR
University of South Florida, FL
The University of Texas at Austin, TX
The University of Texas at San Antonio, TX
University of Washington, WA
University of Wisconsin–Stevens Point, WI
Utah State University, UT
Virginia Polytechnic Institute and State University, VA
Virginia State University, VA
Washington State University, WA
Washington University in St. Louis, MO
West Virginia University, WV

Area/Ethnic Studies

Arizona State University, AZ
Brigham Young University, UT
Brigham Young University–Hawaii, HI
California State University, Chico, CA
California State University, Fresno, CA
California State University, Stanislaus, CA
City College of the City University of New York, NY

The College of New Rochelle, NY
Felician College, NJ
Fort Lewis College, CO
Furman University, SC
Indiana University of Pennsylvania, PA
Kent State University, OH
Mississippi State University, MS
Montana State University, MT
Northern Arizona University, AZ
The Ohio State University, OH
Ohio University, OH
Ohio University–Chillicothe, OH
Ohio University–Eastern, OH
Ohio University–Lancaster, OH
Ohio University–Southern Campus, OH
Ohio University–Zanesville, OH
Ohio Wesleyan University, OH
Oklahoma State University, OK
Ouachita Baptist University, AR
Portland State University, OR
Purchase College, State University of New York, NY
Radford University, VA
Rice University, TX
The Richard Stockton College of New Jersey, NJ
Saint Louis University, MO
Sonoma State University, CA
South Dakota State University, SD
Southern Illinois University Carbondale, IL
Southern Methodist University, TX
State University of New York at Oswego, NY
State University of New York at Plattsburgh, NY
State University of New York College at Geneseo, NY
Stetson University, FL
Stony Brook University, State University of New York, NY
The University of Alabama, AL
University of California, Riverside, CA
University of Central Missouri, MO
University of Colorado at Boulder, CO
University of Illinois at Urbana–Champaign, IL
University of Kansas, KS
University of Michigan, MI
University of Minnesota, Twin Cities Campus, MN
University of Oklahoma, OK
University of South Carolina, SC
The University of Texas at San Antonio, TX
University of Vermont, VT
University of Wisconsin–Green Bay, WI
University of Wisconsin–La Crosse, WI
Virginia Polytechnic Institute and State University, VA
Virginia State University, VA
Washington State University, WA
West Virginia University, WV
Wichita State University, KS

Biological Sciences

Abilene Christian University, TX
Alabama State University, AL
Alderson-Broaddus College, WV
Alfred University, NY
Antioch College, OH
Arizona State University, AZ
Arkansas State University, AR
Armstrong Atlantic State University, GA
Auburn University, AL
Augsburg College, MN
Augustana College, IL
Augustana College, SD
Augusta State University, GA
Austin College, TX
Austin Peay State University, TN
Averett University, VA
Azusa Pacific University, CA
Bard College, NY
Barton College, NC
Bellarmine University, KY
Bethel College, IN
Birmingham-Southern College, AL
Black Hills State University, SD
Bloomfield College, NJ
Bloomsburg University of Pennsylvania, PA
Blue Mountain College, MS
Boise State University, ID
Bowie State University, MD
Bowling Green State University, OH
Brenau University, GA
Brevard College, NC
Brigham Young University, UT
Brigham Young University–Hawaii, HI
Bryan College, TN
Buena Vista University, IA
Butler University, IN
California Polytechnic State University, San Luis Obispo, CA
California State University, Chico, CA
California State University, Fresno, CA
California State University, Los Angeles, CA
California State University, San Bernardino, CA
California State University, Stanislaus, CA
Calvin College, MI
Campbellsville University, KY
Carroll College, WI
Carson-Newman College, TN
Carthage College, WI
Case Western Reserve University, OH
Centenary College of Louisiana, LA
Central College, IA
Central Methodist University, MO
Central Michigan University, MI
Chapman University, CA
Chatham University, PA
City College of the City University of New York, NY
Clarion University of Pennsylvania, PA
Clarkson University, NY
Clemson University, SC
Coastal Carolina University, SC
Coe College, IA
College of Charleston, SC
The College of New Rochelle, NY
College of Staten Island of the City University of New York, NY
College of the Southwest, NM
The College of Wooster, OH
The Colorado College, CO
Colorado State University-Pueblo, CO
Columbia College, MO
Columbus State University, GA
Concordia University, IL
Concordia University, NE
Concordia University at Austin, TX
Concordia University, St. Paul, MN
Dana College, NE
Davidson College, NC
Davis & Elkins College, WV
Denison University, OH
DeSales University, PA
Dickinson State University, ND
Dordt College, IA
Drury University, MO
D'Youville College, NY
Eastern Michigan University, MI
East Tennessee State University, TN
East Texas Baptist University, TX
Elizabethtown College, PA
Elmhurst College, IL
Elon University, NC
Emmanuel College, MA
Emporia State University, KS
Erskine College, SC
Fairfield University, CT
Felician College, NJ
Fitchburg State College, MA
Florida Gulf Coast University, FL
Fort Lewis College, CO
Framingham State College, MA
Francis Marion University, SC
Freed-Hardeman University, TN
Friends University, KS
Frostburg State University, MD
Furman University, SC
Gannon University, PA
Gardner-Webb University, NC
George Fox University, OR
Georgia Institute of Technology, GA
Georgia Southern University, GA
Glenville State College, WV
Green Mountain College, VT
Grove City College, PA
Guilford College, NC
Hampden-Sydney College, VA
Hardin-Simmons University, TX
Hawai'i Pacific University, HI
Hillsdale College, MI
Idaho State University, ID
Illinois Institute of Technology, IL
Illinois State University, IL
Indiana University of Pennsylvania, PA
Jacksonville State University, AL
James Madison University, VA
Kalamazoo College, MI
Kent State University, OH
King's College, PA
Lake Forest College, IL
Lambuth University, TN
Lebanon Valley College, PA
Lee University, TN
Lewis-Clark State College, ID
Limestone College, SC
Lincoln University, PA
Lindenwood University, MO
Lindsey Wilson College, KY
Lipscomb University, TN
Lock Haven University of Pennsylvania, PA
Longwood University, VA
Louisiana State University and Agricultural and Mechanical College, LA

Louisiana Tech University, LA
Lycoming College, PA
MacMurray College, IL
Macon State College, GA
Maine Maritime Academy, ME
Malone College, OH
Manhattan College, NY
Mansfield University of Pennsylvania, PA
Marquette University, WI
Maryville University of Saint Louis, MO
Massachusetts College of Liberal Arts, MA
Mayville State University, ND
McKendree College, IL
McMurry University, TX
Mercer University, GA
Meredith College, NC
Mesa State College, CO
Metropolitan State College of Denver, CO
Michigan State University, MI
Michigan Technological University, MI
Middle Tennessee State University, TN
Millersville University of Pennsylvania, PA
Mills College, CA
Mississippi State University, MS
Missouri State University, MO
Missouri Valley College, MO
Molloy College, NY
Montana State University, MT
Montana State University–Billings, MT
Montclair State University, NJ
Moravian College, PA
Morehead State University, KY
Mount St. Mary's College, CA
Murray State University, KY
New England College, NH
New Jersey City University, NJ
New Mexico State University, NM
North Carolina State University, NC
North Central College, IL
North Dakota State University, ND
Northeastern Illinois University, IL
Northeastern State University, OK
Northern Arizona University, AZ
Northern Illinois University, IL
Northern Michigan University, MI
Northern State University, SD
North Georgia College & State University, GA
North Greenville University, SC
Northwestern College, IA
Northwestern College, MN
Northwestern Oklahoma State University, OK
Northwestern State University of Louisiana, LA
Northwest Nazarene University, ID
The Ohio State University, OH
Ohio University, OH
Ohio University–Chillicothe, OH
Ohio University–Eastern, OH
Ohio University–Lancaster, OH
Ohio University–Southern Campus, OH
Ohio University–Zanesville, OH
Ohio Wesleyan University, OH
Oklahoma State University, OK
Oral Roberts University, OK
Ouachita Baptist University, AR
Palmer College of Chiropractic, IA
Piedmont College, GA
Pittsburg State University, KS
Point Loma Nazarene University, CA
Purchase College, State University of New York, NY
Radford University, VA
Randolph College, VA
Regis University, CO
Rice University, TX
The Richard Stockton College of New Jersey, NJ
Ripon College, WI
Rivier College, NH
Rochester Institute of Technology, NY
Rockhurst University, MO
Sacred Heart University, CT
St. Cloud State University, MN
St. Edward's University, TX
St. John Fisher College, NY
Saint Louis University, MO
Saint Vincent College, PA
Salisbury University, MD
Sam Houston State University, TX
Seton Hill University, PA
Shaw University, NC
Shepherd University, WV
Shippensburg University of Pennsylvania, PA
Slippery Rock University of Pennsylvania, PA
Sonoma State University, CA
South Dakota State University, SD
Southeastern Louisiana University, LA
Southeastern Oklahoma State University, OK
Southeast Missouri State University, MO
Southern Illinois University Carbondale, IL
Southern Methodist University, TX
Southern Nazarene University, OK
Southern Oregon University, OR
Southern Wesleyan University, SC
Southwest Minnesota State University, MN
Spelman College, GA
State University of New York at Binghamton, NY
State University of New York at Fredonia, NY
State University of New York at Oswego, NY
State University of New York at Plattsburgh, NY
State University of New York College at Geneseo, NY
State University of New York College at Old Westbury, NY
State University of New York College at Oneonta, NY
State University of New York College at Potsdam, NY
State University of New York College of Environmental Science and Forestry, NY
Stephen F. Austin State University, TX
Stetson University, FL
Stony Brook University, State University of New York, NY
Tennessee Technological University, TN
Tennessee Wesleyan College, TN
Texas Tech University, TX
Texas Woman's University, TX
Thiel College, PA
The University of Akron, OH
The University of Alabama, AL
The University of Arizona, AZ
University of California, Riverside, CA
University of California, San Diego, CA
University of Central Missouri, MO
University of Central Oklahoma, OK
University of Colorado at Boulder, CO
University of Connecticut, CT
University of Delaware, DE
University of Evansville, IN
University of Great Falls, MT
University of Houston–Victoria, TX
University of Idaho, ID
University of Illinois at Springfield, IL
University of Illinois at Urbana–Champaign, IL
University of Kansas, KS
University of Maine, ME
University of Maryland, Baltimore County, MD
University of Maryland, College Park, MD
University of Massachusetts Amherst, MA
University of Miami, FL
University of Michigan, MI
University of Michigan–Dearborn, MI
University of Michigan–Flint, MI
University of Minnesota, Crookston, MN
University of Minnesota, Twin Cities Campus, MN
University of Missouri–Columbia, MO
University of Missouri–St. Louis, MO
The University of Montana, MT
University of Nebraska at Omaha, NE
University of New England, ME
The University of North Carolina at Asheville, NC
The University of North Carolina at Greensboro, NC
The University of North Carolina Wilmington, NC
University of North Dakota, ND
University of Northern Colorado, CO
University of Northern Iowa, IA
University of Oklahoma, OK
University of Oregon, OR
University of Pittsburgh at Bradford, PA
University of Puget Sound, WA
University of Richmond, VA
University of Rochester, NY
University of St. Francis, IL
University of Saint Francis, IN
University of St. Thomas, MN
University of St. Thomas, TX
University of South Carolina, SC
The University of South Dakota, SD
University of Southern Indiana, IN
University of South Florida, FL
The University of Tampa, FL
The University of Tennessee at Martin, TN
The University of Texas at Austin, TX
The University of Texas at Brownsville, TX
The University of Texas at Dallas, TX
The University of Texas at El Paso, TX
The University of Texas at San Antonio, TX
The University of Texas–Pan American, TX
University of the Ozarks, AR
University of Tulsa, OK

University of Washington, WA
University of West Florida, FL
University of West Georgia, GA
University of Wisconsin–Green Bay, WI
University of Wisconsin–La Crosse, WI
University of Wisconsin–Stevens Point, WI
University of Wisconsin–Superior, WI
University of Wisconsin–Whitewater, WI
Utah State University, UT
Valdosta State University, GA
Valley City State University, ND
Virginia Military Institute, VA
Virginia Polytechnic Institute and State University, VA
Virginia State University, VA
Wake Forest University, NC
Walla Walla College, WA
Walsh University, OH
Warner Pacific College, OR
Wartburg College, IA
Washington State University, WA
Washington University in St. Louis, MO
Wayland Baptist University, TX
Waynesburg College, PA
Wayne State College, NE
Western Carolina University, NC
Western Illinois University, IL
Western Oregon University, OR
Western Washington University, WA
Westminster College, UT
West Virginia University, WV
Whitworth University, WA
Wichita State University, KS
Widener University, PA
Wilkes University, PA
Williams Baptist College, AR
Wilson College, PA
Wisconsin Lutheran College, WI

Business

Abilene Christian University, TX
Adams State College, CO
Alabama State University, AL
Albion College, MI
Alderson-Broaddus College, WV
Alfred University, NY
Alliant International University, CA
Arizona State University, AZ
Arkansas State University, AR
Auburn University, AL
Augsburg College, MN
Augustana College, IL
Augustana College, SD
Augusta State University, GA
Austin College, TX
Austin Peay State University, TN
Averett University, VA
Barton College, NC
Baylor University, TX
Bellarmine University, KY
Bethel College, IN
Birmingham-Southern College, AL
Black Hills State University, SD
Bloomfield College, NJ
Bloomsburg University of Pennsylvania, PA
Blue Mountain College, MS
Boise State University, ID
Bowie State University, MD
Bowling Green State University, OH
Brenau University, GA
Brevard College, NC
Brigham Young University, UT
Brigham Young University–Hawaii, HI
Bryan College, TN
Bucknell University, PA
Buena Vista University, IA
Butler University, IN
California Polytechnic State University, San Luis Obispo, CA
California State University, Chico, CA
California State University, Fresno, CA
California State University, Fullerton, CA
California State University, Los Angeles, CA
California State University, Northridge, CA
California State University, San Bernardino, CA
California State University, Stanislaus, CA
Calvin College, MI
Campbellsville University, KY
Carroll College, WI
Carson-Newman College, TN
Case Western Reserve University, OH
Centenary College of Louisiana, LA
Central College, IA
Central Methodist University, MO
Central Michigan University, MI
Central State University, OH
Central Washington University, WA
Chatham University, PA
Christopher Newport University, VA
Clarion University of Pennsylvania, PA
Clarkson University, NY
Clearwater Christian College, FL
Cleary University, MI
Clemson University, SC
Coastal Carolina University, SC
Coe College, IA
College Misericordia, PA
College of Charleston, SC
The College of New Rochelle, NY
College of St. Catherine, MN
The College of Saint Rose, NY
College of Staten Island of the City University of New York, NY
College of the Southwest, NM
Colorado School of Mines, CO
Colorado State University-Pueblo, CO
Columbia College, MO
Columbia College Chicago, IL
Columbia International University, SC
Columbus State University, GA
Concordia University, IL
Concordia University, NE
Concordia University at Austin, TX
Concordia University, St. Paul, MN
Concord University, WV
Creighton University, NE
Dakota State University, SD
Dallas Baptist University, TX
Dana College, NE
Daniel Webster College, NH
Davis & Elkins College, WV
DeSales University, PA
Dickinson State University, ND
Dordt College, IA
Dowling College, NY
Drury University, MO
D'Youville College, NY
Eastern Michigan University, MI
East Tennessee State University, TN
East Texas Baptist University, TX
Elizabethtown College, PA
Elmhurst College, IL
Elon University, NC
Emporia State University, KS
Endicott College, MA
Erskine College, SC
Evangel University, MO
Fairfield University, CT
Felician College, NJ
Fitchburg State College, MA
Five Towns College, NY
Flagler College, FL
Florida Atlantic University, FL
Florida Gulf Coast University, FL
Florida Metropolitan University–Pinellas Campus, FL
Fort Lewis College, CO
Francis Marion University, SC
Freed-Hardeman University, TN
Friends University, KS
Frostburg State University, MD
Furman University, SC
Gannon University, PA
Gardner-Webb University, NC
Georgia College & State University, GA
Georgia Southern University, GA
Glenville State College, WV
Gonzaga University, WA
Grace College, IN
Grace University, NE
Green Mountain College, VT
Grove City College, PA
Hardin-Simmons University, TX
Hawai'i Pacific University, HI
Hillsdale College, MI
Husson College, ME
Idaho State University, ID
Illinois Institute of Technology, IL
Illinois State University, IL
Indiana University of Pennsylvania, PA
Jacksonville State University, AL
James Madison University, VA
Juniata College, PA
Kean University, NJ
Kent State University, OH
Kentucky Christian University, KY
Kettering University, MI
King's College, PA
Kutztown University of Pennsylvania, PA
Lakeland College, WI
Lambuth University, TN
Lawrence Technological University, MI
Lee University, TN
Lewis-Clark State College, ID
Limestone College, SC
Lincoln University, PA
Lindenwood University, MO
Lindsey Wilson College, KY
Lipscomb University, TN
Longwood University, VA
Louisiana State University and Agricultural and Mechanical College, LA
Louisiana Tech University, LA
Lubbock Christian University, TX
Lycoming College, PA
Macon State College, GA

Maine Maritime Academy, ME
Malone College, OH
Manchester College, IN
Manhattan College, NY
Maranatha Baptist Bible College, WI
Marquette University, WI
Maryville University of Saint Louis, MO
Marywood University, PA
Massachusetts College of Liberal Arts, MA
Mayville State University, ND
McKendree College, IL
McMurry University, TX
Mercer University, GA
Meredith College, NC
Mesa State College, CO
Metropolitan State College of Denver, CO
Michigan State University, MI
Michigan Technological University, MI
Middle Tennessee State University, TN
Midwestern State University, TX
Millersville University of Pennsylvania, PA
Millsaps College, MS
Milwaukee School of Engineering, WI
Minnesota State University Mankato, MN
Minot State University, ND
Mississippi State University, MS
Missouri State University, MO
Missouri Valley College, MO
Molloy College, NY
Monmouth University, NJ
Montana State University, MT
Montana State University–Billings, MT
Montana Tech of The University of Montana, MT
Montclair State University, NJ
Moravian College, PA
Morehead State University, KY
Mount Mary College, WI
Mount Vernon Nazarene University, OH
Murray State University, KY
Myers University, OH
The National Hispanic University, CA
New England College, NH
New Jersey City University, NJ
New Mexico State University, NM
North Carolina State University, NC
North Central College, IL
North Dakota State University, ND
Northeastern Illinois University, IL
Northeastern State University, OK
Northern Arizona University, AZ
Northern Illinois University, IL
Northern Michigan University, MI
Northern State University, SD
North Georgia College & State University, GA
Northwestern College, IA
Northwestern Oklahoma State University, OK
Northwest Nazarene University, ID
Northwood University, MI
Northwood University, Florida Campus, FL
Northwood University, Texas Campus, TX
Ohio Christian University, OH
The Ohio State University, OH
Ohio University, OH
Ohio University–Chillicothe, OH
Ohio University–Eastern, OH
Ohio University–Lancaster, OH
Ohio University–Southern Campus, OH
Ohio University–Zanesville, OH
Ohio Wesleyan University, OH
Oklahoma State University, OK
Olivet College, MI
Oral Roberts University, OK
Ouachita Baptist University, AR
Pittsburg State University, KS
Point Loma Nazarene University, CA
Portland State University, OR
Providence College, RI
Radford University, VA
Rhodes College, TN
The Richard Stockton College of New Jersey, NJ
Ripon College, WI
Rivier College, NH
Rochester Institute of Technology, NY
Rockhurst University, MO
Sacred Heart University, CT
St. Cloud State University, MN
St. Edward's University, TX
St. John Fisher College, NY
Saint Louis University, MO
Saint Vincent College, PA
Salisbury University, MD
Sam Houston State University, TX
Santa Clara University, CA
Seton Hill University, PA
Shenandoah University, VA
Shepherd University, WV
Shippensburg University of Pennsylvania, PA
Slippery Rock University of Pennsylvania, PA
Sonoma State University, CA
South Dakota State University, SD
Southeastern Louisiana University, LA
Southeastern Oklahoma State University, OK
Southeast Missouri State University, MO
Southern Adventist University, TN
Southern Arkansas University–Magnolia, AR
Southern Illinois University Carbondale, IL
Southern Illinois University Edwardsville, IL
Southern Methodist University, TX
Southern Nazarene University, OK
Southern Oregon University, OR
Southern Utah University, UT
Southern Wesleyan University, SC
Southwest Minnesota State University, MN
State University of New York at Binghamton, NY
State University of New York at Fredonia, NY
State University of New York at Oswego, NY
State University of New York at Plattsburgh, NY
State University of New York College at Geneseo, NY
State University of New York College at Potsdam, NY
Stephen F. Austin State University, TX
Stetson University, FL
Stony Brook University, State University of New York, NY
Taylor University Fort Wayne, IN
Tennessee Technological University, TN
Tennessee Wesleyan College, TN
Texas A&M University–Texarkana, TX
Texas State University-San Marcos, TX
Texas Tech University, TX
Texas Woman's University, TX
Thiel College, PA
Trevecca Nazarene University, TN
Union University, TN
The University of Akron, OH
The University of Alabama, AL
The University of Alabama at Birmingham, AL
The University of Alabama in Huntsville, AL
The University of Arizona, AZ
University of California, Riverside, CA
University of Central Missouri, MO
University of Central Oklahoma, OK
University of Colorado at Boulder, CO
University of Connecticut, CT
University of Dallas, TX
University of Dayton, OH
University of Delaware, DE
University of Denver, CO
University of Evansville, IN
University of Florida, FL
University of Georgia, GA
University of Great Falls, MT
University of Hawaii at Hilo, HI
University of Houston–Victoria, TX
University of Idaho, ID
University of Illinois at Chicago, IL
University of Illinois at Springfield, IL
University of Illinois at Urbana–Champaign, IL
University of Kansas, KS
University of Maine, ME
University of Maine at Fort Kent, ME
University of Maryland, College Park, MD
University of Massachusetts Amherst, MA
University of Miami, FL
University of Michigan, MI
University of Michigan–Dearborn, MI
University of Michigan–Flint, MI
University of Minnesota, Crookston, MN
University of Minnesota, Twin Cities Campus, MN
University of Missouri–Columbia, MO
University of Missouri–St. Louis, MO
The University of Montana, MT
University of Nebraska at Omaha, NE
University of New England, ME
University of New Hampshire, NH
The University of North Carolina at Asheville, NC
The University of North Carolina at Chapel Hill, NC
The University of North Carolina at Charlotte, NC
The University of North Carolina at Greensboro, NC
The University of North Carolina at Pembroke, NC
The University of North Carolina Wilmington, NC
University of North Dakota, ND
University of Northern Colorado, CO

University of Northern Iowa, IA
University of North Florida, FL
University of Oklahoma, OK
University of Oregon, OR
University of Phoenix–Atlanta Campus, GA
University of Phoenix–Bay Area Campus, CA
University of Phoenix–Boston Campus, MA
University of Phoenix–Central Florida Campus, FL
University of Phoenix–Central Massachusetts Campus, MA
University of Phoenix–Charlotte Campus, NC
University of Phoenix–Chicago Campus, IL
University of Phoenix–Cincinnati Campus, OH
University of Phoenix–Cleveland Campus, OH
University of Phoenix–Columbus Georgia Campus, GA
University of Phoenix–Columbus Ohio Campus, OH
University of Phoenix–Dallas Campus, TX
University of Phoenix–Denver Campus, CO
University of Phoenix–Fort Lauderdale Campus, FL
University of Phoenix–Hawaii Campus, HI
University of Phoenix–Houston Campus, TX
University of Phoenix–Idaho Campus, ID
University of Phoenix–Indianapolis Campus, IN
University of Phoenix–Kansas City Campus, MO
University of Phoenix–Little Rock Campus, AR
University of Phoenix–Louisiana Campus, LA
University of Phoenix–Maryland Campus, MD
University of Phoenix–Metro Detroit Campus, MI
University of Phoenix–Nashville Campus, TN
University of Phoenix–Nevada Campus, NV
University of Phoenix–New Mexico Campus, NM
University of Phoenix–Oklahoma City Campus, OK
University of Phoenix Online Campus, AZ
University of Phoenix–Oregon Campus, OR
University of Phoenix–Philadelphia Campus, PA
University of Phoenix–Phoenix Campus, AZ
University of Phoenix–Pittsburgh Campus, PA
University of Phoenix–Puerto Rico Campus, PR
University of Phoenix–Raleigh Campus, NC
University of Phoenix–Richmond Campus, VA
University of Phoenix–Sacramento Valley Campus, CA
University of Phoenix–St. Louis Campus, MO
University of Phoenix–San Diego Campus, CA
University of Phoenix–Southern Arizona Campus, AZ
University of Phoenix–Southern California Campus, CA
University of Phoenix–Southern Colorado Campus, CO
University of Phoenix–Spokane Campus, WA
University of Phoenix–Springfield Campus, MO
University of Phoenix–Tulsa Campus, OK
University of Phoenix–Utah Campus, UT
University of Phoenix–Washington Campus, WA
University of Phoenix–West Florida Campus, FL
University of Phoenix–West Michigan Campus, MI
University of Phoenix–Wichita Campus, KS
University of Phoenix–Wisconsin Campus, WI
University of Pittsburgh at Bradford, PA
University of Puget Sound, WA
University of Saint Francis, IN
University of St. Thomas, MN
University of South Carolina, SC
The University of South Dakota, SD
University of Southern Indiana, IN
University of South Florida, FL
The University of Tampa, FL
The University of Tennessee at Martin, TN
The University of Texas at Austin, TX
The University of Texas at Dallas, TX
The University of Texas at El Paso, TX
The University of Texas at San Antonio, TX
The University of Texas–Pan American, TX
University of the Ozarks, AR
University of Tulsa, OK
University of Vermont, VT
University of Washington, WA
The University of West Alabama, AL
University of West Florida, FL
University of West Georgia, GA
University of Wisconsin–Green Bay, WI
University of Wisconsin–La Crosse, WI
University of Wisconsin–Stevens Point, WI
University of Wisconsin–Stout, WI
University of Wisconsin–Superior, WI
University of Wisconsin–Whitewater, WI
University of Wyoming, WY
Utah State University, UT
Valdosta State University, GA
Valley City State University, ND
Valparaiso University, IN
Villa Julie College, MD
Virginia Commonwealth University, VA
Virginia Military Institute, VA
Virginia Polytechnic Institute and State University, VA
Virginia State University, VA
Wake Forest University, NC
Walsh College of Accountancy and Business Administration, MI
Walsh University, OH
Wartburg College, IA
Washington & Jefferson College, PA
Washington State University, WA
Washington University in St. Louis, MO
Wayland Baptist University, TX
Waynesburg College, PA
Wayne State College, NE
Webber International University, FL
Western Carolina University, NC
Western Illinois University, IL
Western New England College, MA
Western Oregon University, OR
Western Washington University, WA
West Liberty State College, WV
Westminster College, UT
West Virginia University, WV
Wichita State University, KS
Widener University, PA
Wilkes University, PA
Williams Baptist College, AR
Wilson College, PA
Winston-Salem State University, NC
Wisconsin Lutheran College, WI
Youngstown State University, OH

Communication

Abilene Christian University, TX
Adelphi University, NY
Albion College, MI
Alderson-Broaddus College, WV
Alfred University, NY
Alliant International University, CA
Arizona State University, AZ
Arkansas State University, AR
Auburn University, AL
Augsburg College, MN
Augustana College, IL
Augustana College, SD
Augusta State University, GA
Austin College, TX
Barton College, NC
Baylor University, TX
Bethel College, IN
Black Hills State University, SD
Bloomsburg University of Pennsylvania, PA
Boise State University, ID
Bowie State University, MD
Bowling Green State University, OH
Brenau University, GA
Brigham Young University, UT
Brigham Young University–Hawaii, HI
Bryan College, TN
Butler University, IN
California Polytechnic State University, San Luis Obispo, CA
California State University, Chico, CA
California State University, Fresno, CA
California State University, Fullerton, CA
California State University, Los Angeles, CA
California State University, Northridge, CA
California State University, Stanislaus, CA
Calvin College, MI
Campbellsville University, KY
Case Western Reserve University, OH
Centenary College of Louisiana, LA
Central College, IA
Central Methodist University, MO
Central Michigan University, MI
Central Washington University, WA
Chatham University, PA
Christopher Newport University, VA
City College of the City University of New York, NY

Clarion University of Pennsylvania, PA
Clemson University, SC
College of Charleston, SC
The College of New Rochelle, NY
Columbia College Chicago, IL
Columbia International University, SC
Columbus State University, GA
Concordia University, IL
Concordia University, NE
Concordia University, St. Paul, MN
Concord University, WV
Dakota State University, SD
Dallas Baptist University, TX
Dana College, NE
Denison University, OH
DeSales University, PA
Dickinson State University, ND
Dordt College, IA
Drury University, MO
East Central University, OK
Eastern Michigan University, MI
East Texas Baptist University, TX
Elizabethtown College, PA
Elmhurst College, IL
Elon University, NC
Emporia State University, KS
Evangel University, MO
Fitchburg State College, MA
Flagler College, FL
Fort Lewis College, CO
Franklin Pierce University, NH
Friends University, KS
Frostburg State University, MD
Furman University, SC
Gardner-Webb University, NC
Georgia Southern University, GA
Grove City College, PA
Harding University, AR
Hardin-Simmons University, TX
Hastings College, NE
Hawai'i Pacific University, HI
Hofstra University, NY
Idaho State University, ID
Illinois Institute of Technology, IL
Illinois State University, IL
Indiana University of Pennsylvania, PA
Ithaca College, NY
Jacksonville State University, AL
Johnson Bible College, TN
Kent State University, OH
King's College, PA
Kutztown University of Pennsylvania, PA
Lambuth University, TN
Lee University, TN
Lehigh University, PA
Limestone College, SC
Lincoln University, PA
Lindenwood University, MO
Lipscomb University, TN
Lock Haven University of Pennsylvania, PA
Louisiana State University and Agricultural and Mechanical College, LA
Lubbock Christian University, TX
Lycoming College, PA
Macon State College, GA
Malone College, OH
Mansfield University of Pennsylvania, PA
Marquette University, WI
Marywood University, PA
Massachusetts College of Liberal Arts, MA
McMurry University, TX
Mesa State College, CO
Metropolitan State College of Denver, CO
Michigan State University, MI
Michigan Technological University, MI
Middle Tennessee State University, TN
Midwestern State University, TX
Millersville University of Pennsylvania, PA
Milligan College, TN
Milwaukee School of Engineering, WI
Minot State University, ND
Mississippi State University, MS
Missouri State University, MO
Missouri Valley College, MO
Molloy College, NY
Monmouth University, NJ
Montana State University, MT
Montana State University–Billings, MT
Montclair State University, NJ
Morehead State University, KY
Mount Mary College, WI
Murray State University, KY
New England College, NH
New England School of Communications, ME
New Jersey City University, NJ
New Mexico State University, NM
North Central College, IL
North Dakota State University, ND
Northeastern Illinois University, IL
Northeastern State University, OK
Northern Arizona University, AZ
Northern Illinois University, IL
Northern Michigan University, MI
North Greenville University, SC
Northwestern College, IA
Northwestern Oklahoma State University, OK
The Ohio State University, OH
Ohio University, OH
Ohio University–Chillicothe, OH
Ohio University–Eastern, OH
Ohio University–Lancaster, OH
Ohio University–Southern Campus, OH
Ohio University–Zanesville, OH
Ohio Wesleyan University, OH
Oklahoma State University, OK
Olivet College, MI
Oral Roberts University, OK
Ouachita Baptist University, AR
Pittsburg State University, KS
Point Loma Nazarene University, CA
Radford University, VA
Rivier College, NH
Rochester Institute of Technology, NY
Rockhurst University, MO
St. Cloud State University, MN
St. Edward's University, TX
Saint Louis University, MO
Salisbury University, MD
Sam Houston State University, TX
Seton Hill University, PA
Shepherd University, WV
Shippensburg University of Pennsylvania, PA
Slippery Rock University of Pennsylvania, PA
Sonoma State University, CA
South Dakota State University, SD
Southeastern Louisiana University, LA
Southeastern University, FL
Southeast Missouri State University, MO
Southern Adventist University, TN
Southern Illinois University Carbondale, IL
Southern Methodist University, TX
Southern Nazarene University, OK
Southern Utah University, UT
Southwest Minnesota State University, MN
State University of New York at Fredonia, NY
State University of New York at Oswego, NY
State University of New York at Plattsburgh, NY
State University of New York College at Geneseo, NY
State University of New York College at Potsdam, NY
Stephen F. Austin State University, TX
Stetson University, FL
Tennessee Technological University, TN
Tennessee Wesleyan College, TN
Texas Tech University, TX
Texas Woman's University, TX
Trevecca Nazarene University, TN
Union University, TN
The University of Akron, OH
The University of Alabama, AL
The University of Alabama at Birmingham, AL
University of California, San Diego, CA
University of Central Missouri, MO
University of Colorado at Boulder, CO
University of Delaware, DE
University of Evansville, IN
University of Florida, FL
University of Houston–Victoria, TX
University of Idaho, ID
University of Illinois at Springfield, IL
University of Illinois at Urbana–Champaign, IL
University of Kansas, KS
University of Maine, ME
University of Maryland, College Park, MD
University of Massachusetts Amherst, MA
University of Miami, FL
University of Michigan, MI
University of Michigan–Dearborn, MI
University of Michigan–Flint, MI
University of Minnesota, Crookston, MN
University of Minnesota, Twin Cities Campus, MN
University of Missouri–Columbia, MO
University of Missouri–St. Louis, MO
University of Nebraska at Kearney, NE
University of Nebraska at Omaha, NE
University of New Orleans, LA
The University of North Carolina at Asheville, NC
The University of North Carolina at Chapel Hill, NC
The University of North Carolina at Greensboro, NC
The University of North Carolina at Pembroke, NC
The University of North Carolina Wilmington, NC

University of North Dakota, ND
University of Northern Colorado, CO
University of Oklahoma, OK
University of Phoenix–Atlanta Campus, GA
University of Phoenix–Little Rock Campus, AR
University of Phoenix–Nashville Campus, TN
University of Phoenix Online Campus, AZ
University of Phoenix–Phoenix Campus, AZ
University of Phoenix–Sacramento Valley Campus, CA
University of Phoenix–San Diego Campus, CA
University of Phoenix–Southern Colorado Campus, CO
University of Phoenix–Springfield Campus, MO
University of Phoenix–Utah Campus, UT
University of Pittsburgh at Bradford, PA
University of Puget Sound, WA
University of St. Francis, IL
University of Saint Francis, IN
University of South Carolina, SC
The University of South Dakota, SD
University of South Florida, FL
The University of Tampa, FL
The University of Tennessee at Martin, TN
The University of Texas at Austin, TX
The University of Texas at El Paso, TX
The University of Texas at San Antonio, TX
The University of Texas at Tyler, TX
The University of Texas–Pan American, TX
University of the Ozarks, AR
University of Tulsa, OK
University of Washington, WA
University of West Georgia, GA
University of Wisconsin–Green Bay, WI
University of Wisconsin–La Crosse, WI
University of Wisconsin–Stevens Point, WI
University of Wisconsin–Superior, WI
University of Wisconsin–Whitewater, WI
University of Wyoming, WY
Utah State University, UT
Valdosta State University, GA
Valley City State University, ND
Virginia Commonwealth University, VA
Virginia Polytechnic Institute and State University, VA
Virginia State University, VA
Walsh University, OH
Wartburg College, IA
Washington State University, WA
Washington University in St. Louis, MO
Wayland Baptist University, TX
Waynesburg College, PA
Wayne State College, NE
Wayne State University, MI
Western Carolina University, NC
Western Washington University, WA
West Liberty State College, WV
Westminster College, UT
West Virginia University, WV
Wichita State University, KS
Widener University, PA
Wilkes University, PA
Wilson College, PA
Wisconsin Lutheran College, WI

Computer Science

Alderson-Broaddus College, WV
Alliant International University, CA
Arizona State University, AZ
Arkansas State University, AR
Armstrong Atlantic State University, GA
Auburn University, AL
Augsburg College, MN
Augustana College, SD
Augusta State University, GA
Azusa Pacific University, CA
Barton College, NC
Baylor University, TX
Bethel College, IN
Birmingham-Southern College, AL
Black Hills State University, SD
Bloomfield College, NJ
Bloomsburg University of Pennsylvania, PA
Boise State University, ID
Bowie State University, MD
Bowling Green State University, OH
Brigham Young University, UT
Brigham Young University–Hawaii, HI
Bryan College, TN
Buena Vista University, IA
Butler University, IN
California Polytechnic State University, San Luis Obispo, CA
California State University, Chico, CA
California State University, Los Angeles, CA
California State University, Northridge, CA
California State University, San Bernardino, CA
California State University, Stanislaus, CA
Calvin College, MI
Campbellsville University, KY
Carroll College, WI
Carthage College, WI
Case Western Reserve University, OH
Central College, IA
Central Methodist University, MO
Central Michigan University, MI
Central State University, OH
Central Washington University, WA
Christopher Newport University, VA
City College of the City University of New York, NY
Clarion University of Pennsylvania, PA
Clarke College, IA
Clarkson University, NY
Clemson University, SC
Cogswell Polytechnical College, CA
College Misericordia, PA
College of Charleston, SC
College of Staten Island of the City University of New York, NY
Colorado School of Mines, CO
Colorado State University-Pueblo, CO
Columbus State University, GA
Concordia University, IL
Concordia University, NE
Dakota State University, SD
Dallas Baptist University, TX
Daniel Webster College, NH
Davis & Elkins College, WV
DeSales University, PA
Dickinson State University, ND
Dordt College, IA
Eastern Michigan University, MI
East Tennessee State University, TN
East Texas Baptist University, TX
Elizabethtown College, PA
Elmhurst College, IL
Elon University, NC
Emporia State University, KS
Evangel University, MO
Felician College, NJ
Fitchburg State College, MA
Florida Metropolitan University–Pinellas Campus, FL
Fort Lewis College, CO
Freed-Hardeman University, TN
Friends University, KS
Frostburg State University, MD
Furman University, SC
Gardner-Webb University, NC
Georgia College & State University, GA
Georgia Institute of Technology, GA
Graceland University, IA
Harding University, AR
Husson College, ME
Idaho State University, ID
Illinois Institute of Technology, IL
Illinois State University, IL
Indiana University of Pennsylvania, PA
Jacksonville State University, AL
James Madison University, VA
Johnson C. Smith University, NC
Kent State University, OH
Kettering University, MI
King's College, PA
Kutztown University of Pennsylvania, PA
Lambuth University, TN
Lawrence Technological University, MI
Limestone College, SC
Lincoln University, PA
Lindenwood University, MO
Longwood University, VA
Louisiana State University and Agricultural and Mechanical College, LA
Louisiana Tech University, LA
Lubbock Christian University, TX
Lycoming College, PA
Malone College, OH
Manhattan College, NY
Massachusetts College of Liberal Arts, MA
McMurry University, TX
Meredith College, NC
Mesa State College, CO
Metropolitan State College of Denver, CO
Michigan State University, MI
Michigan Technological University, MI
Middle Tennessee State University, TN
Midwestern State University, TX
Millersville University of Pennsylvania, PA
Milligan College, TN
Mills College, CA
Milwaukee School of Engineering, WI
Minnesota State University Mankato, MN
Minot State University, ND
Mississippi State University, MS
Missouri State University, MO
Missouri Valley College, MO
Monmouth University, NJ
Montana State University, MT
Montana State University–Billings, MT

Montana Tech of The University of Montana, MT
Moravian College, PA
Mount Vernon Nazarene University, OH
Murray State University, KY
The National Hispanic University, CA
New England College, NH
New Mexico State University, NM
North Central College, IL
North Dakota State University, ND
Northeastern Illinois University, IL
Northeastern State University, OK
Northern Arizona University, AZ
Northern Illinois University, IL
Northern Michigan University, MI
Northwestern College, IA
Northwestern Oklahoma State University, OK
Northwest Nazarene University, ID
The Ohio State University, OH
Ohio University, OH
Ohio University–Chillicothe, OH
Ohio University–Eastern, OH
Ohio University–Lancaster, OH
Ohio University–Southern Campus, OH
Ohio University–Zanesville, OH
Ohio Wesleyan University, OH
Oklahoma State University, OK
Ouachita Baptist University, AR
Pittsburg State University, KS
Polytechnic University, Brooklyn Campus, NY
Portland State University, OR
Purchase College, State University of New York, NY
Purdue University, IN
Radford University, VA
Rice University, TX
The Richard Stockton College of New Jersey, NJ
Ripon College, WI
Rivier College, NH
Rochester Institute of Technology, NY
Rockhurst University, MO
Rollins College, FL
Sacred Heart University, CT
St. Cloud State University, MN
St. Edward's University, TX
Saint Louis University, MO
Saint Vincent College, PA
Salisbury University, MD
Sam Houston State University, TX
Seton Hill University, PA
Shaw University, NC
Shepherd University, WV
Shippensburg University of Pennsylvania, PA
Slippery Rock University of Pennsylvania, PA
Sonoma State University, CA
South Dakota State University, SD
Southeastern Louisiana University, LA
Southeastern Oklahoma State University, OK
Southeast Missouri State University, MO
Southern Arkansas University–Magnolia, AR
Southern Illinois University Carbondale, IL
Southern Methodist University, TX
Southern Wesleyan University, SC
Southwest Minnesota State University, MN
State University of New York at Binghamton, NY
State University of New York at Fredonia, NY
State University of New York at New Paltz, NY
State University of New York at Oswego, NY
State University of New York at Plattsburgh, NY
State University of New York College at Geneseo, NY
State University of New York College at Potsdam, NY
Stephen F. Austin State University, TX
Stetson University, FL
Stony Brook University, State University of New York, NY
Tennessee Technological University, TN
Tennessee Wesleyan College, TN
Texas Tech University, TX
Texas Woman's University, TX
Thiel College, PA
Transylvania University, KY
The University of Akron, OH
The University of Alabama, AL
The University of Alabama at Birmingham, AL
The University of Alabama in Huntsville, AL
University of California, Irvine, CA
University of California, San Diego, CA
University of Central Missouri, MO
University of Central Oklahoma, OK
University of Colorado at Boulder, CO
University of Connecticut, CT
University of Delaware, DE
University of Evansville, IN
University of Florida, FL
University of Great Falls, MT
University of Hawaii at Hilo, HI
University of Houston–Victoria, TX
University of Idaho, ID
University of Illinois at Springfield, IL
University of Illinois at Urbana–Champaign, IL
University of Kansas, KS
University of Maine, ME
University of Maine at Fort Kent, ME
University of Maryland, Baltimore County, MD
University of Maryland, College Park, MD
University of Massachusetts Amherst, MA
University of Massachusetts Lowell, MA
University of Miami, FL
University of Michigan, MI
University of Michigan–Dearborn, MI
University of Michigan–Flint, MI
University of Minnesota, Crookston, MN
University of Minnesota, Twin Cities Campus, MN
University of Missouri–Columbia, MO
University of Missouri–St. Louis, MO
The University of Montana, MT
University of Nebraska at Omaha, NE
University of New Orleans, LA
The University of North Carolina at Asheville, NC
The University of North Carolina at Charlotte, NC
The University of North Carolina Wilmington, NC
University of North Dakota, ND
University of North Florida, FL
University of Oklahoma, OK
University of Phoenix–Atlanta Campus, GA
University of Phoenix–Bay Area Campus, CA
University of Phoenix–Boston Campus, MA
University of Phoenix–Central Florida Campus, FL
University of Phoenix–Charlotte Campus, NC
University of Phoenix–Chicago Campus, IL
University of Phoenix–Cincinnati Campus, OH
University of Phoenix–Cleveland Campus, OH
University of Phoenix–Columbus Georgia Campus, GA
University of Phoenix–Columbus Ohio Campus, OH
University of Phoenix–Dallas Campus, TX
University of Phoenix–Denver Campus, CO
University of Phoenix–Fort Lauderdale Campus, FL
University of Phoenix–Hawaii Campus, HI
University of Phoenix–Houston Campus, TX
University of Phoenix–Idaho Campus, ID
University of Phoenix–Indianapolis Campus, IN
University of Phoenix–Kansas City Campus, MO
University of Phoenix–Little Rock Campus, AR
University of Phoenix–Louisiana Campus, LA
University of Phoenix–Maryland Campus, MD
University of Phoenix–Metro Detroit Campus, MI
University of Phoenix–Nashville Campus, TN
University of Phoenix–Nevada Campus, NV
University of Phoenix–New Mexico Campus, NM
University of Phoenix–Oklahoma City Campus, OK
University of Phoenix Online Campus, AZ
University of Phoenix–Oregon Campus, OR
University of Phoenix–Philadelphia Campus, PA
University of Phoenix–Phoenix Campus, AZ
University of Phoenix–Pittsburgh Campus, PA
University of Phoenix–Raleigh Campus, NC
University of Phoenix–Richmond Campus, VA
University of Phoenix–Sacramento Valley Campus, CA
University of Phoenix–St. Louis Campus, MO

University of Phoenix–San Diego Campus, CA
University of Phoenix–Southern Arizona Campus, AZ
University of Phoenix–Southern California Campus, CA
University of Phoenix–Southern Colorado Campus, CO
University of Phoenix–Spokane Campus, WA
University of Phoenix–Springfield Campus, MO
University of Phoenix–Tulsa Campus, OK
University of Phoenix–Utah Campus, UT
University of Phoenix–Washington Campus, WA
University of Phoenix–West Florida Campus, FL
University of Phoenix–West Michigan Campus, MI
University of Phoenix–Wichita Campus, KS
University of Phoenix–Wisconsin Campus, WI
University of Pittsburgh at Bradford, PA
University of Puget Sound, WA
University of Richmond, VA
University of South Carolina, SC
The University of South Dakota, SD
University of South Florida, FL
The University of Tennessee at Martin, TN
The University of Texas at Austin, TX
The University of Texas at Dallas, TX
The University of Texas at El Paso, TX
The University of Texas at San Antonio, TX
The University of Texas–Pan American, TX
University of Tulsa, OK
University of Vermont, VT
The University of West Alabama, AL
University of West Georgia, GA
University of Wisconsin–La Crosse, WI
University of Wisconsin–Stevens Point, WI
University of Wisconsin–Superior, WI
University of Wisconsin–Whitewater, WI
University of Wyoming, WY
Utah State University, UT
Valdosta State University, GA
Valley City State University, ND
Villa Julie College, MD
Virginia Commonwealth University, VA
Virginia Military Institute, VA
Virginia Polytechnic Institute and State University, VA
Virginia State University, VA
Walsh University, OH
Wartburg College, IA
Washington State University, WA
Washington University in St. Louis, MO
Waynesburg College, PA
Wayne State College, NE
Western Washington University, WA
Westminster College, UT
West Virginia University, WV
Whitworth University, WA
Wichita State University, KS
Widener University, PA
Wilson College, PA
Winston-Salem State University, NC
Youngstown State University, OH

Education

Abilene Christian University, TX
Adams State College, CO
Alabama State University, AL
Albion College, MI
Alderson-Broaddus College, WV
Alfred University, NY
Alliant International University, CA
Antioch College, OH
Arizona State University, AZ
Arkansas State University, AR
Armstrong Atlantic State University, GA
Auburn University, AL
Augsburg College, MN
Augustana College, IL
Augustana College, SD
Augusta State University, GA
Aurora University, IL
Austin College, TX
Austin Peay State University, TN
Averett University, VA
The Baptist College of Florida, FL
Barton College, NC
Baylor University, TX
Bellarmine University, KY
Berry College, GA
Bethel College, IN
Birmingham-Southern College, AL
Black Hills State University, SD
Bloomfield College, NJ
Bloomsburg University of Pennsylvania, PA
Blue Mountain College, MS
Boise State University, ID
Boston University, MA
Bowling Green State University, OH
Brenau University, GA
Brevard College, NC
Brigham Young University, UT
Brigham Young University–Hawaii, HI
Bryan College, TN
Buena Vista University, IA
Butler University, IN
California Polytechnic State University, San Luis Obispo, CA
California State University, Chico, CA
California State University, Fresno, CA
California State University, Los Angeles, CA
California State University, Northridge, CA
California State University, San Bernardino, CA
California State University, Stanislaus, CA
Calvin College, MI
Campbellsville University, KY
Carroll College, WI
Carson-Newman College, TN
Catawba College, NC
Centenary College of Louisiana, LA
Central College, IA
Central Methodist University, MO
Central Michigan University, MI
Central State University, OH
Central Washington University, WA
Chatham University, PA
Christopher Newport University, VA
City College of the City University of New York, NY
Clarion University of Pennsylvania, PA
Clearwater Christian College, FL
Clemson University, SC
Coastal Carolina University, SC
College Misericordia, PA
College of Charleston, SC
The College of New Rochelle, NY
College of St. Catherine, MN
The College of Saint Rose, NY
College of Staten Island of the City University of New York, NY
College of the Southwest, NM
Columbia College, MO
Columbia College Chicago, IL
Columbia International University, SC
Columbus State University, GA
Concordia University, IL
Concordia University, NE
Concordia University at Austin, TX
Concord University, WV
Creighton University, NE
Dakota State University, SD
Dallas Baptist University, TX
Dana College, NE
Davidson College, NC
Davis & Elkins College, WV
DeSales University, PA
Dickinson State University, ND
Dominican College, NY
Dordt College, IA
Dowling College, NY
Drury University, MO
D'Youville College, NY
Eastern Michigan University, MI
East Tennessee State University, TN
East Texas Baptist University, TX
Elizabethtown College, PA
Elmhurst College, IL
Elon University, NC
Emmanuel College, MA
Emporia State University, KS
Endicott College, MA
Erskine College, SC
Evangel University, MO
Fairfield University, CT
Felician College, NJ
Fitchburg State College, MA
Five Towns College, NY
Flagler College, FL
Florida Gulf Coast University, FL
Fort Lewis College, CO
Framingham State College, MA
Francis Marion University, SC
Freed-Hardeman University, TN
Friends University, KS
Frostburg State University, MD
Furman University, SC
Gannon University, PA
Gardner-Webb University, NC
George Fox University, OR
Georgia College & State University, GA
Georgia Southern University, GA
Glenville State College, WV
Grace University, NE
Green Mountain College, VT
Grove City College, PA
Hampden-Sydney College, VA
Hardin-Simmons University, TX
Hillsdale College, MI
Husson College, ME
Idaho State University, ID

Illinois State University, IL
Indiana University of Pennsylvania, PA
Jacksonville State University, AL
James Madison University, VA
Jarvis Christian College, TX
Johnson Bible College, TN
Kean University, NJ
Kent State University, OH
Kentucky Christian University, KY
King's College, PA
Kutztown University of Pennsylvania, PA
Lambuth University, TN
Lawrence Technological University, MI
Lee University, TN
Lewis-Clark State College, ID
Limestone College, SC
Lincoln University, PA
Lindenwood University, MO
Lindsey Wilson College, KY
Lipscomb University, TN
Lock Haven University of Pennsylvania, PA
Longwood University, VA
Louisiana State University and Agricultural and Mechanical College, LA
Louisiana Tech University, LA
Lubbock Christian University, TX
Lycoming College, PA
MacMurray College, IL
Macon State College, GA
Malone College, OH
Mansfield University of Pennsylvania, PA
Maryville University of Saint Louis, MO
Marywood University, PA
Massachusetts College of Liberal Arts, MA
Mayville State University, ND
McMurry University, TX
Mercer University, GA
Meredith College, NC
Mesa State College, CO
Messenger College, MO
Metropolitan State College of Denver, CO
Miami University, OH
Michigan State University, MI
Michigan Technological University, MI
Middle Tennessee State University, TN
Midwestern State University, TX
Millersville University of Pennsylvania, PA
Minot State University, ND
Mississippi State University, MS
Missouri State University, MO
Missouri Valley College, MO
Molloy College, NY
Monmouth University, NJ
Montana State University, MT
Montana State University–Billings, MT
Montclair State University, NJ
Morehead State University, KY
Mount Mary College, WI
Mount St. Mary's College, CA
Mount Vernon Nazarene University, OH
Murray State University, KY
The National Hispanic University, CA
New England College, NH
New Jersey City University, NJ
New Mexico State University, NM
North Carolina State University, NC
North Central College, IL
North Dakota State University, ND
Northeastern Illinois University, IL
Northeastern State University, OK
Northern Arizona University, AZ
Northern Illinois University, IL
Northern Michigan University, MI
Northern State University, SD
North Georgia College & State University, GA
North Greenville University, SC
Northwestern College, IA
Northwestern Oklahoma State University, OK
Northwestern State University of Louisiana, LA
Northwest Nazarene University, ID
Ohio Christian University, OH
The Ohio State University, OH
Ohio University, OH
Ohio University–Chillicothe, OH
Ohio University–Eastern, OH
Ohio University–Lancaster, OH
Ohio University–Southern Campus, OH
Ohio University–Zanesville, OH
Ohio Valley University, WV
Ohio Wesleyan University, OH
Oklahoma Panhandle State University, OK
Oklahoma State University, OK
Olivet College, MI
Oral Roberts University, OK
Ouachita Baptist University, AR
Pacific Union College, CA
Piedmont College, GA
Pittsburg State University, KS
Point Loma Nazarene University, CA
Portland State University, OR
Purdue University, IN
Radford University, VA
Randolph College, VA
The Richard Stockton College of New Jersey, NJ
Ripon College, WI
Rivier College, NH
Sacred Heart University, CT
St. Cloud State University, MN
St. Edward's University, TX
Saint Louis University, MO
Salisbury University, MD
Sam Houston State University, TX
Seton Hill University, PA
Shasta Bible College, CA
Shaw University, NC
Shepherd University, WV
Shippensburg University of Pennsylvania, PA
Slippery Rock University of Pennsylvania, PA
Sonoma State University, CA
South Dakota State University, SD
Southeastern Louisiana University, LA
Southeastern Oklahoma State University, OK
Southeast Missouri State University, MO
Southern Adventist University, TN
Southern Arkansas University–Magnolia, AR
Southern Illinois University Carbondale, IL
Southern Illinois University Edwardsville, IL
Southern Methodist College, SC
Southern Nazarene University, OK
Southern Oregon University, OR
Southern Utah University, UT
Southern Wesleyan University, SC
Southwest Minnesota State University, MN
State University of New York at Fredonia, NY
State University of New York at New Paltz, NY
State University of New York at Oswego, NY
State University of New York at Plattsburgh, NY
State University of New York College at Geneseo, NY
State University of New York College at Oneonta, NY
State University of New York College at Potsdam, NY
Stephen F. Austin State University, TX
Stetson University, FL
Tennessee Technological University, TN
Tennessee Wesleyan College, TN
Texas A&M University–Texarkana, TX
Texas Christian University, TX
Texas State University-San Marcos, TX
Texas Tech University, TX
Texas Woman's University, TX
Thiel College, PA
Trevecca Nazarene University, TN
Union University, TN
The University of Akron, OH
The University of Alabama, AL
The University of Alabama in Huntsville, AL
The University of Arizona, AZ
University of California, Riverside, CA
University of California, San Diego, CA
University of Central Missouri, MO
University of Central Oklahoma, OK
University of Colorado at Boulder, CO
University of Connecticut, CT
University of Dallas, TX
University of Dayton, OH
University of Delaware, DE
University of Evansville, IN
University of Florida, FL
University of Georgia, GA
University of Great Falls, MT
University of Houston–Victoria, TX
University of Idaho, ID
University of Illinois at Springfield, IL
University of Illinois at Urbana–Champaign, IL
University of Kansas, KS
University of Maine, ME
University of Maine at Fort Kent, ME
University of Maryland, College Park, MD
University of Massachusetts Amherst, MA
University of Miami, FL
University of Michigan, MI
University of Michigan–Dearborn, MI
University of Michigan–Flint, MI
University of Minnesota, Crookston, MN
University of Minnesota, Twin Cities Campus, MN
University of Missouri–Columbia, MO
University of Missouri–St. Louis, MO
The University of Montana, MT
University of Nebraska at Omaha, NE

University of New England, ME
University of New Hampshire, NH
University of New Orleans, LA
The University of North Carolina at Asheville, NC
The University of North Carolina at Chapel Hill, NC
The University of North Carolina at Charlotte, NC
The University of North Carolina at Greensboro, NC
The University of North Carolina at Pembroke, NC
The University of North Carolina Wilmington, NC
University of North Dakota, ND
University of Northern Colorado, CO
University of Northern Iowa, IA
University of North Florida, FL
University of Oklahoma, OK
University of Oregon, OR
University of Phoenix–Fort Lauderdale Campus, FL
University of Phoenix–Nashville Campus, TN
University of Phoenix–Nevada Campus, NV
University of Phoenix Online Campus, AZ
University of Phoenix–Phoenix Campus, AZ
University of Phoenix–Southern Arizona Campus, AZ
University of Phoenix–Utah Campus, UT
University of Phoenix–West Florida Campus, FL
University of Pittsburgh at Bradford, PA
University of St. Francis, IL
University of Saint Francis, IN
University of St. Thomas, MN
University of South Carolina, SC
The University of South Dakota, SD
University of Southern Indiana, IN
University of South Florida, FL
The University of Tampa, FL
The University of Tennessee at Martin, TN
The University of Texas at Austin, TX
The University of Texas at Brownsville, TX
The University of Texas at El Paso, TX
The University of Texas at San Antonio, TX
The University of Texas–Pan American, TX
University of the Ozarks, AR
University of Tulsa, OK
University of Vermont, VT
The University of West Alabama, AL
University of West Georgia, GA
University of Wisconsin–La Crosse, WI
University of Wisconsin–Stevens Point, WI
University of Wisconsin–Stout, WI
University of Wisconsin–Superior, WI
University of Wisconsin–Whitewater, WI
University of Wyoming, WY
Utah State University, UT
Valdosta State University, GA
Valley City State University, ND
Vanderbilt University, TN
VanderCook College of Music, IL
Virginia Commonwealth University, VA
Virginia Polytechnic Institute and State University, VA
Virginia State University, VA
Wabash College, IN
Wake Forest University, NC
Walla Walla College, WA
Walsh University, OH
Wartburg College, IA
Washington State University, WA
Washington University in St. Louis, MO
Wayland Baptist University, TX
Waynesburg College, PA
Wayne State College, NE
Webster University, MO
Western Carolina University, NC
Western Illinois University, IL
Western Oregon University, OR
Western Washington University, WA
West Liberty State College, WV
Westminster College, UT
West Virginia University, WV
Wheeling Jesuit University, WV
Wichita State University, KS
Widener University, PA
Wilkes University, PA
Williams Baptist College, AR
Wilson College, PA
Winston-Salem State University, NC
Wisconsin Lutheran College, WI
Youngstown State University, OH

Engineering/Technologies

Alfred University, NY
Arizona State University, AZ
Arkansas State University, AR
Arkansas Tech University, AR
Armstrong Atlantic State University, GA
Auburn University, AL
Austin College, TX
Averett University, VA
Baylor University, TX
Bluefield State College, WV
Boise State University, ID
Boston University, MA
Bowie State University, MD
Bowling Green State University, OH
Brigham Young University, UT
Bryant University, RI
Bucknell University, PA
Butler University, IN
California Polytechnic State University, San Luis Obispo, CA
California State University, Chico, CA
California State University, Fresno, CA
California State University, Fullerton, CA
California State University, Los Angeles, CA
California State University, Northridge, CA
Calvin College, MI
Carthage College, WI
Case Western Reserve University, OH
Centenary College of Louisiana, LA
Central Michigan University, MI
Central State University, OH
Central Washington University, WA
Christian Brothers University, TN
City College of the City University of New York, NY
Clarkson University, NY
Clemson University, SC
Cleveland State University, OH
Cogswell Polytechnical College, CA
College of Charleston, SC
The College of New Jersey, NJ
The College of Saint Rose, NY
College of Staten Island of the City University of New York, NY
Colorado School of Mines, CO
Colorado State University-Pueblo, CO
Cooper Union for the Advancement of Science and Art, NY
Daniel Webster College, NH
Davis & Elkins College, WV
Dordt College, IA
Eastern Michigan University, MI
East Tennessee State University, TN
Elizabethtown College, PA
Elon University, NC
Emmanuel College, MA
Emporia State University, KS
Evangel University, MO
Fairfield University, CT
Florida Atlantic University, FL
Florida Gulf Coast University, FL
Freed-Hardeman University, TN
Frostburg State University, MD
Furman University, SC
Gannon University, PA
Geneva College, PA
The George Washington University, DC
Georgia Institute of Technology, GA
Georgia Southern University, GA
Gonzaga University, WA
Graceland University, IA
Grove City College, PA
Harding University, AR
Idaho State University, ID
Illinois Institute of Technology, IL
Illinois State University, IL
Indiana University of Pennsylvania, PA
James Madison University, VA
The Johns Hopkins University, MD
Kettering University, MI
Lakeland College, WI
Lawrence Technological University, MI
Lindenwood University, MO
Lipscomb University, TN
Loras College, IA
Louisiana State University and Agricultural and Mechanical College, LA
Louisiana Tech University, LA
Macon State College, GA
Maine Maritime Academy, ME
Marquette University, WI
Mercer University, GA
Mesa State College, CO
Metropolitan State College of Denver, CO
Miami University, OH
Michigan State University, MI
Michigan Technological University, MI
Middle Tennessee State University, TN
Midwestern State University, TX
Milwaukee School of Engineering, WI
Minnesota State University Mankato, MN
Mississippi State University, MS
Montana State University, MT
Montana State University–Billings, MT
Montana Tech of The University of Montana, MT
Murray State University, KY
New England College, NH

New Mexico State University, NM
North Carolina State University, NC
North Dakota State University, ND
Northeastern University, MA
Northern Arizona University, AZ
Northern Illinois University, IL
Northern Michigan University, MI
Northwestern College, IA
Northwestern State University of Louisiana, LA
The Ohio State University, OH
Ohio University, OH
Ohio University–Chillicothe, OH
Ohio University–Eastern, OH
Ohio University–Lancaster, OH
Ohio University–Southern Campus, OH
Ohio University–Zanesville, OH
Ohio Wesleyan University, OH
Oklahoma State University, OK
Oral Roberts University, OK
Ouachita Baptist University, AR
Pittsburg State University, KS
Point Loma Nazarene University, CA
Polytechnic University, Brooklyn Campus, NY
Portland State University, OR
Purdue University, IN
Rice University, TX
Rochester Institute of Technology, NY
Rollins College, FL
St. Cloud State University, MN
Saint Louis University, MO
Sam Houston State University, TX
Santa Clara University, CA
Seattle Pacific University, WA
Shaw University, NC
Shepherd University, WV
Smith College, MA
South Dakota State University, SD
Southeastern Louisiana University, LA
Southeastern Oklahoma State University, OK
Southern Illinois University Carbondale, IL
Southern Methodist University, TX
State University of New York at Binghamton, NY
State University of New York at New Paltz, NY
State University of New York at Plattsburgh, NY
State University of New York College at Potsdam, NY
State University of New York College of Environmental Science and Forestry, NY
Stony Brook University, State University of New York, NY
Tennessee Technological University, TN
Texas Christian University, TX
Texas Tech University, TX
Union University, TN
The University of Akron, OH
The University of Alabama, AL
The University of Alabama at Birmingham, AL
The University of Alabama in Huntsville, AL
The University of Arizona, AZ
University of California, Berkeley, CA
University of California, Irvine, CA
University of California, Riverside, CA
University of California, San Diego, CA
University of Central Missouri, MO
University of Colorado at Boulder, CO
University of Connecticut, CT
University of Dayton, OH
University of Delaware, DE
University of Evansville, IN
University of Florida, FL
University of Idaho, ID
University of Illinois at Springfield, IL
University of Illinois at Urbana–Champaign, IL
University of Kansas, KS
University of Maine, ME
University of Maryland, Baltimore County, MD
University of Maryland, College Park, MD
University of Massachusetts Amherst, MA
University of Massachusetts Lowell, MA
University of Miami, FL
University of Michigan, MI
University of Michigan–Dearborn, MI
University of Michigan–Flint, MI
University of Minnesota, Crookston, MN
University of Minnesota, Twin Cities Campus, MN
University of Missouri–Columbia, MO
University of Missouri–St. Louis, MO
University of Nebraska at Omaha, NE
University of New Hampshire, NH
The University of North Carolina at Asheville, NC
The University of North Carolina at Charlotte, NC
University of North Dakota, ND
University of North Florida, FL
University of Oklahoma, OK
University of Pittsburgh at Bradford, PA
University of Rochester, NY
University of South Carolina, SC
University of Southern Indiana, IN
University of South Florida, FL
The University of Tennessee at Martin, TN
The University of Texas at Brownsville, TX
The University of Texas at Dallas, TX
The University of Texas at El Paso, TX
The University of Texas at San Antonio, TX
The University of Texas at Tyler, TX
The University of Texas–Pan American, TX
University of Tulsa, OK
University of Vermont, VT
University of Washington, WA
University of Wisconsin–Green Bay, WI
University of Wisconsin–Stevens Point, WI
University of Wisconsin–Stout, WI
University of Wyoming, WY
Utah State University, UT
Valdosta State University, GA
Valparaiso University, IN
Vanderbilt University, TN
Virginia Commonwealth University, VA
Virginia Military Institute, VA
Virginia Polytechnic Institute and State University, VA
Virginia State University, VA
Washington State University, WA
Washington University in St. Louis, MO
Western New England College, MA
Western Washington University, WA
West Virginia University, WV
Wichita State University, KS
Widener University, PA
Wilkes University, PA
Youngstown State University, OH

English

Abilene Christian University, TX
Adams State College, CO
Alfred University, NY
Alliant International University, CA
Arizona State University, AZ
Arkansas State University, AR
Armstrong Atlantic State University, GA
Auburn University, AL
Augsburg College, MN
Augustana College, SD
Augusta State University, GA
Austin College, TX
Averett University, VA
Barton College, NC
Baylor University, TX
Berry College, GA
Bethel College, IN
Black Hills State University, SD
Bloomfield College, NJ
Bloomsburg University of Pennsylvania, PA
Blue Mountain College, MS
Boise State University, ID
Bowling Green State University, OH
Brevard College, NC
Brigham Young University, UT
Brigham Young University–Hawaii, HI
Bryan College, TN
Butler University, IN
California Polytechnic State University, San Luis Obispo, CA
California State University, Chico, CA
California State University, Fresno, CA
California State University, Los Angeles, CA
California State University, Northridge, CA
California State University, Stanislaus, CA
Calvin College, MI
Campbellsville University, KY
Case Western Reserve University, OH
Centenary College of Louisiana, LA
Central Methodist University, MO
Central Michigan University, MI
Central Washington University, WA
Chatham University, PA
Christopher Newport University, VA
City College of the City University of New York, NY
Clarion University of Pennsylvania, PA
Clemson University, SC
College of Charleston, SC
The College of New Rochelle, NY
College of St. Catherine, MN
The College of Saint Rose, NY
College of the Southwest, NM
Columbia College, MO
Columbia International University, SC
Columbus State University, GA
Concordia University, IL
Concordia University, NE
Concordia University, St. Paul, MN
Concord University, WV

Dakota State University, SD
Dana College, NE
Denison University, OH
DeSales University, PA
Dickinson State University, ND
Dordt College, IA
Drury University, MO
D'Youville College, NY
Eastern Michigan University, MI
East Tennessee State University, TN
East Texas Baptist University, TX
Elizabethtown College, PA
Elmhurst College, IL
Emporia State University, KS
Erskine College, SC
Evangel University, MO
Felician College, NJ
Fitchburg State College, MA
Flagler College, FL
Fort Lewis College, CO
Francis Marion University, SC
Freed-Hardeman University, TN
Friends University, KS
Frostburg State University, MD
Furman University, SC
Gannon University, PA
Gardner-Webb University, NC
Georgia College & State University, GA
Georgia Southern University, GA
Glenville State College, WV
Graceland University, IA
Green Mountain College, VT
Grove City College, PA
Harding University, AR
Hardin-Simmons University, TX
Hillsdale College, MI
Idaho State University, ID
Illinois State University, IL
Indiana University of Pennsylvania, PA
Jacksonville State University, AL
James Madison University, VA
Kalamazoo College, MI
Kent State University, OH
King's College, PA
Kutztown University of Pennsylvania, PA
Lakeland College, WI
Lambuth University, TN
Lewis-Clark State College, ID
Limestone College, SC
Lincoln University, PA
Lindenwood University, MO
Lindsey Wilson College, KY
Lipscomb University, TN
Lock Haven University of Pennsylvania, PA
Longwood University, VA
Louisiana State University and Agricultural and Mechanical College, LA
Louisiana Tech University, LA
Lubbock Christian University, TX
Lycoming College, PA
MacMurray College, IL
Malone College, OH
Manchester College, IN
Massachusetts College of Liberal Arts, MA
Mayville State University, ND
McMurry University, TX
Mercer University, GA
Meredith College, NC
Mesa State College, CO
Methodist University, NC
Metropolitan State College of Denver, CO
Michigan State University, MI
Middle Tennessee State University, TN
Midwestern State University, TX
Millersville University of Pennsylvania, PA
Minot State University, ND
Mississippi State University, MS
Missouri Valley College, MO
Molloy College, NY
Montana State University, MT
Montana State University–Billings, MT
Montclair State University, NJ
Morehead State University, KY
Mount Mary College, WI
Murray State University, KY
New England College, NH
New Mexico State University, NM
North Central College, IL
North Dakota State University, ND
Northeastern Illinois University, IL
Northeastern State University, OK
Northern Arizona University, AZ
Northern Illinois University, IL
Northern Michigan University, MI
Northern State University, SD
North Georgia College & State University, GA
Northwestern College, IA
Northwestern Oklahoma State University, OK
Northwest Nazarene University, ID
The Ohio State University, OH
Ohio University, OH
Ohio University–Chillicothe, OH
Ohio University–Eastern, OH
Ohio University–Lancaster, OH
Ohio University–Southern Campus, OH
Ohio University–Zanesville, OH
Ohio Valley University, WV
Ohio Wesleyan University, OH
Oklahoma Panhandle State University, OK
Oklahoma State University, OK
Olivet College, MI
Ouachita Baptist University, AR
Piedmont College, GA
Pittsburg State University, KS
Purchase College, State University of New York, NY
Radford University, VA
Randolph College, VA
Rice University, TX
Ripon College, WI
Rivier College, NH
Rockhurst University, MO
Sacred Heart University, CT
St. Cloud State University, MN
St. Edward's University, TX
St. John Fisher College, NY
Saint Louis University, MO
Salisbury University, MD
Sam Houston State University, TX
Seton Hill University, PA
Shepherd University, WV
Shippensburg University of Pennsylvania, PA
Slippery Rock University of Pennsylvania, PA
Sonoma State University, CA
South Dakota State University, SD
Southeastern Louisiana University, LA
Southeast Missouri State University, MO
Southern Adventist University, TN
Southern Arkansas University–Magnolia, AR
Southern Illinois University Carbondale, IL
Southern Methodist University, TX
Southern Nazarene University, OK
Southern Oregon University, OR
Southern Wesleyan University, SC
Southwest Minnesota State University, MN
State University of New York at Binghamton, NY
State University of New York at Fredonia, NY
State University of New York at New Paltz, NY
State University of New York at Oswego, NY
State University of New York at Plattsburgh, NY
State University of New York College at Geneseo, NY
State University of New York College at Potsdam, NY
Stetson University, FL
Stony Brook University, State University of New York, NY
Tennessee Technological University, TN
Tennessee Wesleyan College, TN
Texas A&M University–Texarkana, TX
Texas State University-San Marcos, TX
Texas Tech University, TX
Texas Woman's University, TX
Thiel College, PA
The University of Akron, OH
The University of Alabama, AL
The University of Alabama in Huntsville, AL
University of California, Riverside, CA
University of Central Missouri, MO
University of Colorado at Boulder, CO
University of Connecticut, CT
University of Delaware, DE
University of Evansville, IN
University of Hawaii at Hilo, HI
University of Idaho, ID
University of Illinois at Springfield, IL
University of Illinois at Urbana–Champaign, IL
University of Kansas, KS
University of Maine, ME
University of Maine at Fort Kent, ME
University of Maryland, Baltimore County, MD
University of Maryland, College Park, MD
University of Massachusetts Amherst, MA
University of Miami, FL
University of Michigan, MI
University of Michigan–Flint, MI
University of Minnesota, Twin Cities Campus, MN
University of Missouri–Columbia, MO
University of Missouri–St. Louis, MO
The University of Montana, MT
University of Nebraska at Omaha, NE
University of New England, ME
University of New Hampshire, NH

The University of North Carolina at Asheville, NC
The University of North Carolina at Chapel Hill, NC
The University of North Carolina at Greensboro, NC
The University of North Carolina at Pembroke, NC
The University of North Carolina Wilmington, NC
University of North Dakota, ND
University of Northern Colorado, CO
University of Pittsburgh at Bradford, PA
University of Puget Sound, WA
University of Saint Francis, IN
University of St. Thomas, MN
University of St. Thomas, TX
University of South Carolina, SC
The University of South Dakota, SD
University of South Florida, FL
The University of Tennessee at Martin, TN
The University of Texas at El Paso, TX
The University of Texas at San Antonio, TX
The University of Texas–Pan American, TX
University of the Ozarks, AR
University of Tulsa, OK
University of Vermont, VT
University of Washington, WA
The University of West Alabama, AL
University of West Georgia, GA
University of Wisconsin–La Crosse, WI
University of Wisconsin–Stevens Point, WI
University of Wisconsin–Superior, WI
University of Wisconsin–Whitewater, WI
University of Wyoming, WY
Utah State University, UT
Valdosta State University, GA
Valley City State University, ND
Virginia Military Institute, VA
Virginia Polytechnic Institute and State University, VA
Virginia State University, VA
Wake Forest University, NC
Walsh University, OH
Wartburg College, IA
Washington State University, WA
Washington University in St. Louis, MO
Wayland Baptist University, TX
Waynesburg College, PA
Wayne State College, NE
Western Carolina University, NC
Western Washington University, WA
West Liberty State College, WV
Westminster College, UT
West Virginia University, WV
West Virginia Wesleyan College, WV
Wheaton College, IL
Wheeling Jesuit University, WV
Wichita State University, KS
Widener University, PA
Wilkes University, PA
Wilson College, PA
Youngstown State University, OH

Foreign Languages

Abilene Christian University, TX
Adams State College, CO
Adelphi University, NY
Alfred University, NY
Alliant International University, CA
Arizona State University, AZ
Armstrong Atlantic State University, GA
Auburn University, AL
Augsburg College, MN
Augustana College, SD
Austin College, TX
Averett University, VA
Baylor University, TX
Black Hills State University, SD
Bloomsburg University of Pennsylvania, PA
Boise State University, ID
Boston University, MA
Bowling Green State University, OH
Brigham Young University, UT
Brigham Young University–Hawaii, HI
Bryan College, TN
Butler University, IN
California Polytechnic State University, San Luis Obispo, CA
California State University, Chico, CA
California State University, Fresno, CA
California State University, Los Angeles, CA
California State University, San Bernardino, CA
California State University, Stanislaus, CA
Calvin College, MI
Carthage College, WI
Centenary College of Louisiana, LA
Central College, IA
Central Methodist University, MO
Central Michigan University, MI
Central Washington University, WA
Christopher Newport University, VA
City College of the City University of New York, NY
Clarion University of Pennsylvania, PA
Clarke College, IA
Clemson University, SC
Coe College, IA
College of Charleston, SC
The College of New Rochelle, NY
College of St. Catherine, MN
The College of Saint Rose, NY
Concordia University, IL
Dana College, NE
Davidson College, NC
Denison University, OH
DeSales University, PA
Dickinson State University, ND
Dordt College, IA
Eastern Michigan University, MI
East Texas Baptist University, TX
Edgewood College, WI
Elizabethtown College, PA
Elmhurst College, IL
Emmanuel College, MA
Emporia State University, KS
Erskine College, SC
Evangel University, MO
Fairfield University, CT
Flagler College, FL
Friends University, KS
Frostburg State University, MD
Furman University, SC
Gannon University, PA
Gardner-Webb University, NC
Georgia College & State University, GA
Georgia Southern University, GA
Grove City College, PA
Hardin-Simmons University, TX
Hillsdale College, MI
Idaho State University, ID
Illinois State University, IL
Indiana University of Pennsylvania, PA
Kalamazoo College, MI
King's College, PA
Kutztown University of Pennsylvania, PA
Lake Forest College, IL
Lambuth University, TN
Lindenwood University, MO
Lock Haven University of Pennsylvania, PA
Louisiana State University and Agricultural and Mechanical College, LA
Louisiana Tech University, LA
Lubbock Christian University, TX
Lycoming College, PA
MacMurray College, IL
Malone College, OH
Manchester College, IN
Manhattan College, NY
Marquette University, WI
Marywood University, PA
Mercer University, GA
Meredith College, NC
Metropolitan State College of Denver, CO
Michigan State University, MI
Middle Tennessee State University, TN
Millersville University of Pennsylvania, PA
Mississippi State University, MS
Missouri State University, MO
Montana State University, MT
Montclair State University, NJ
Moravian College, PA
Murray State University, KY
New Mexico State University, NM
North Central College, IL
Northeastern Illinois University, IL
Northeastern State University, OK
Northern Arizona University, AZ
Northern Illinois University, IL
Northern Michigan University, MI
Northern State University, SD
Northwestern College, IA
Northwestern Oklahoma State University, OK
The Ohio State University, OH
Ohio University, OH
Ohio University–Chillicothe, OH
Ohio University–Eastern, OH
Ohio University–Lancaster, OH
Ohio University–Southern Campus, OH
Ohio University–Zanesville, OH
Ohio Wesleyan University, OH
Oklahoma State University, OK
Olivet College, MI
Ouachita Baptist University, AR
Piedmont College, GA
Pittsburg State University, KS
Portland State University, OR
Rice University, TX
Ripon College, WI
Rivier College, NH
Rockhurst University, MO
St. Edward's University, TX
St. John Fisher College, NY
Saint Louis University, MO

Salisbury University, MD
Sam Houston State University, TX
Seton Hill University, PA
Shepherd University, WV
Sonoma State University, CA
South Dakota State University, SD
Southeastern Louisiana University, LA
Southeast Missouri State University, MO
Southern Arkansas University–Magnolia, AR
Southern Illinois University Carbondale, IL
Southern Methodist University, TX
Southern Oregon University, OR
State University of New York at Binghamton, NY
State University of New York at Fredonia, NY
State University of New York at Oswego, NY
State University of New York College at Geneseo, NY
State University of New York College at Potsdam, NY
Stetson University, FL
Tennessee Technological University, TN
Tennessee Wesleyan College, TN
Texas Tech University, TX
Texas Woman's University, TX
The University of Akron, OH
The University of Alabama, AL
University of Central Missouri, MO
University of Central Oklahoma, OK
University of Colorado at Boulder, CO
University of Connecticut, CT
University of Dallas, TX
University of Delaware, DE
University of Evansville, IN
University of Idaho, ID
University of Illinois at Springfield, IL
University of Illinois at Urbana–Champaign, IL
University of Kansas, KS
University of Maine at Fort Kent, ME
University of Maryland, Baltimore County, MD
University of Maryland, College Park, MD
University of Miami, FL
University of Michigan, MI
University of Michigan–Dearborn, MI
University of Michigan–Flint, MI
University of Minnesota, Twin Cities Campus, MN
University of Missouri–Columbia, MO
University of Missouri–St. Louis, MO
The University of Montana, MT
University of Nebraska at Omaha, NE
University of New Orleans, LA
The University of North Carolina at Greensboro, NC
The University of North Carolina Wilmington, NC
University of North Dakota, ND
University of Oklahoma, OK
University of Oregon, OR
University of Puget Sound, WA
University of St. Thomas, TX
University of South Carolina, SC
The University of South Dakota, SD
University of South Florida, FL
The University of Texas at San Antonio, TX
University of Tulsa, OK
University of Vermont, VT
University of Washington, WA
University of West Georgia, GA
University of Wisconsin–La Crosse, WI
University of Wisconsin–Stevens Point, WI
University of Wisconsin–Whitewater, WI
University of Wyoming, WY
Utah State University, UT
Valdosta State University, GA
Valparaiso University, IN
Virginia Commonwealth University, VA
Virginia Polytechnic Institute and State University, VA
Wake Forest University, NC
Walsh University, OH
Washington State University, WA
Washington University in St. Louis, MO
Wayne State College, NE
Western Illinois University, IL
Western Washington University, WA
West Virginia University, WV
Wichita State University, KS
Widener University, PA
Wilson College, PA
Xavier University, OH

Health Fields

Alabama State University, AL
Alderson-Broaddus College, WV
Allen College, IA
Arizona State University, AZ
Arkansas State University, AR
Armstrong Atlantic State University, GA
Auburn University, AL
Augsburg College, MN
Augustana College, SD
Augusta State University, GA
Austin College, TX
Averett University, VA
Azusa Pacific University, CA
Barton College, NC
Bastyr University, WA
Baylor University, TX
Bellarmine University, KY
Bethel College, IN
Birmingham-Southern College, AL
Black Hills State University, SD
Bloomfield College, NJ
Bloomsburg University of Pennsylvania, PA
Boise State University, ID
Bowling Green State University, OH
Brenau University, GA
Brevard College, NC
Brigham Young University, UT
California Polytechnic State University, San Luis Obispo, CA
California State University, Chico, CA
California State University, Fresno, CA
California State University, Los Angeles, CA
California State University, San Bernardino, CA
California State University, Stanislaus, CA
Calvin College, MI
Carroll College, WI
Carthage College, WI
Case Western Reserve University, OH
Centenary College of Louisiana, LA
Central College, IA
Central Methodist University, MO
Central Michigan University, MI
Central Washington University, WA
Clemson University, SC
College Misericordia, PA
College of Charleston, SC
The College of New Rochelle, NY
College of St. Catherine, MN
College of Staten Island of the City University of New York, NY
Colorado State University-Pueblo, CO
Columbus State University, GA
Concordia University, NE
Dana College, NE
Davis & Elkins College, WV
DeSales University, PA
Dickinson State University, ND
Dominican College, NY
Drury University, MO
D'Youville College, NY
Eastern Michigan University, MI
East Tennessee State University, TN
East Texas Baptist University, TX
Elizabethtown College, PA
Elmhurst College, IL
Emmanuel College, MA
Emporia State University, KS
Endicott College, MA
Felician College, NJ
Fitchburg State College, MA
Florida Gulf Coast University, FL
Florida Metropolitan University–Pinellas Campus, FL
Francis Marion University, SC
Friends University, KS
Frostburg State University, MD
Furman University, SC
Gardner-Webb University, NC
Georgia College & State University, GA
Georgia Southern University, GA
Grace University, NE
Hampden-Sydney College, VA
Harding University, AR
Hardin-Simmons University, TX
Hawai'i Pacific University, HI
Hillsdale College, MI
Houston Baptist University, TX
Husson College, ME
Idaho State University, ID
Illinois State University, IL
Indiana University of Pennsylvania, PA
Jacksonville State University, AL
James Madison University, VA
Kean University, NJ
Kent State University, OH
King's College, PA
Lewis-Clark State College, ID
Lindenwood University, MO
Louisiana Tech University, LA
Lycoming College, PA
MacMurray College, IL
Macon State College, GA
Malone College, OH
Mansfield University of Pennsylvania, PA
Marquette University, WI
Maryville University of Saint Louis, MO
Marywood University, PA

Massachusetts College of Liberal Arts, MA
Medcenter One College of Nursing, ND
Medical College of Georgia, GA
Mesa State College, CO
Metropolitan State College of Denver, CO
Michigan State University, MI
Middle Tennessee State University, TN
Midwestern State University, TX
Midwestern University, Glendale Campus, AZ
Millersville University of Pennsylvania, PA
Milligan College, TN
Milwaukee School of Engineering, WI
Minot State University, ND
Mississippi State University, MS
Missouri State University, MO
Molloy College, NY
Monmouth University, NJ
Montana State University, MT
Montana State University–Billings, MT
Montana Tech of The University of Montana, MT
Moravian College, PA
Morehead State University, KY
Mount Mary College, WI
Mount Vernon Nazarene University, OH
Murray State University, KY
New Mexico State University, NM
North Dakota State University, ND
Northeastern State University, OK
Northern Arizona University, AZ
Northern Illinois University, IL
Northern Michigan University, MI
North Georgia College & State University, GA
Northwestern College, IA
Northwestern Oklahoma State University, OK
Northwest Nazarene University, ID
Ohio Christian University, OH
The Ohio State University, OH
Ohio University, OH
Ohio University–Chillicothe, OH
Ohio University–Eastern, OH
Ohio University–Lancaster, OH
Ohio University–Southern Campus, OH
Ohio University–Zanesville, OH
Ohio Wesleyan University, OH
Oklahoma Panhandle State University, OK
Oral Roberts University, OK
Oregon Health & Science University, OR
Ouachita Baptist University, AR
Palmer College of Chiropractic, IA
Piedmont College, GA
Pittsburg State University, KS
Point Loma Nazarene University, CA
Purdue University, IN
Radford University, VA
The Richard Stockton College of New Jersey, NJ
Rochester Institute of Technology, NY
Rockhurst University, MO
Sacred Heart University, CT
St. Cloud State University, MN
Saint Francis Medical Center College of Nursing, IL
Saint Louis University, MO
Salisbury University, MD
Shepherd University, WV
Slippery Rock University of Pennsylvania, PA
Sonoma State University, CA
South Dakota State University, SD
Southeastern Louisiana University, LA
Southeast Missouri State University, MO
Southern Adventist University, TN
Southern Arkansas University–Magnolia, AR
Southern Illinois University Carbondale, IL
Southern Illinois University Edwardsville, IL
Southern Oregon University, OR
State University of New York at Binghamton, NY
State University of New York at New Paltz, NY
State University of New York at Plattsburgh, NY
State University of New York College at Old Westbury, NY
Stephen F. Austin State University, TX
Stony Brook University, State University of New York, NY
Tennessee Technological University, TN
Tennessee Wesleyan College, TN
Texas Woman's University, TX
The University of Akron, OH
The University of Alabama at Birmingham, AL
The University of Alabama in Huntsville, AL
University of Central Missouri, MO
University of Central Oklahoma, OK
University of Colorado at Boulder, CO
University of Connecticut, CT
University of Delaware, DE
University of Evansville, IN
University of Florida, FL
University of Hartford, CT
University of Hawaii at Hilo, HI
University of Illinois at Springfield, IL
University of Illinois at Urbana–Champaign, IL
University of Kansas, KS
University of Maine at Fort Kent, ME
University of Maryland, College Park, MD
University of Massachusetts Amherst, MA
University of Massachusetts Lowell, MA
University of Miami, FL
University of Michigan, MI
University of Michigan–Flint, MI
University of Minnesota, Crookston, MN
University of Minnesota, Twin Cities Campus, MN
University of Missouri–Columbia, MO
University of Missouri–St. Louis, MO
The University of Montana, MT
University of New England, ME
University of New Hampshire, NH
The University of North Carolina at Asheville, NC
The University of North Carolina at Chapel Hill, NC
The University of North Carolina at Charlotte, NC
The University of North Carolina at Greensboro, NC
The University of North Carolina at Pembroke, NC
The University of North Carolina Wilmington, NC
University of North Dakota, ND
University of Northern Colorado, CO
University of North Florida, FL
University of Phoenix–Atlanta Campus, GA
University of Phoenix–Bay Area Campus, CA
University of Phoenix–Boston Campus, MA
University of Phoenix–Central Florida Campus, FL
University of Phoenix–Cleveland Campus, OH
University of Phoenix–Columbus Georgia Campus, GA
University of Phoenix–Dallas Campus, TX
University of Phoenix–Denver Campus, CO
University of Phoenix–Fort Lauderdale Campus, FL
University of Phoenix–Hawaii Campus, HI
University of Phoenix–Houston Campus, TX
University of Phoenix–Idaho Campus, ID
University of Phoenix–Indianapolis Campus, IN
University of Phoenix–Kansas City Campus, MO
University of Phoenix–Louisiana Campus, LA
University of Phoenix–Metro Detroit Campus, MI
University of Phoenix–Nashville Campus, TN
University of Phoenix–Nevada Campus, NV
University of Phoenix–New Mexico Campus, NM
University of Phoenix–Oklahoma City Campus, OK
University of Phoenix Online Campus, AZ
University of Phoenix–Oregon Campus, OR
University of Phoenix–Phoenix Campus, AZ
University of Phoenix–Pittsburgh Campus, PA
University of Phoenix–Sacramento Valley Campus, CA
University of Phoenix–San Diego Campus, CA
University of Phoenix–Southern Arizona Campus, AZ
University of Phoenix–Southern California Campus, CA
University of Phoenix–Springfield Campus, MO
University of Phoenix–Tulsa Campus, OK
University of Phoenix–Utah Campus, UT
University of Phoenix–West Florida Campus, FL
University of Phoenix–West Michigan Campus, MI
University of Phoenix–Wichita Campus, KS
University of Pittsburgh at Bradford, PA
University of St. Francis, IL
University of Saint Francis, IN
University of South Carolina, SC
University of Southern Indiana, IN
University of South Florida, FL

The University of Tampa, FL
The University of Tennessee at Martin, TN
The University of Texas at Brownsville, TX
The University of Texas at El Paso, TX
The University of Texas at Tyler, TX
The University of Texas Medical Branch, TX
The University of Texas–Pan American, TX
University of Tulsa, OK
University of Vermont, VT
University of Washington, WA
University of West Georgia, GA
University of Wisconsin–La Crosse, WI
University of Wisconsin–Stevens Point, WI
University of Wisconsin–Superior, WI
University of Wyoming, WY
Utah State University, UT
Valdosta State University, GA
Valparaiso University, IN
Virginia Commonwealth University, VA
Virginia Polytechnic Institute and State University, VA
Virginia State University, VA
Walsh University, OH
Washington State University, WA
Washington University in St. Louis, MO
Wayne State College, NE
Western Carolina University, NC
Western Washington University, WA
West Liberty State College, WV
Westminster College, UT
West Virginia University, WV
Wheeling Jesuit University, WV
Wichita State University, KS
Widener University, PA
Wilkes University, PA
Winston-Salem State University, NC
Youngstown State University, OH

Home Economics

Arizona State University, AZ
Auburn University, AL
Averett University, VA
Baylor University, TX
Bowling Green State University, OH
Brigham Young University, UT
California Polytechnic State University, San Luis Obispo, CA
Carson-Newman College, TN
College of St. Catherine, MN
Eastern Michigan University, MI
Framingham State College, MA
Idaho State University, ID
Illinois State University, IL
Indiana University of Pennsylvania, PA
Jacksonville State University, AL
Lambuth University, TN
Lipscomb University, TN
Louisiana State University and Agricultural and Mechanical College, LA
Louisiana Tech University, LA
Middle Tennessee State University, TN
Mississippi State University, MS
Missouri State University, MO
Montana State University, MT
Montclair State University, NJ
Mount Mary College, WI
Mount Vernon Nazarene University, OH
New Mexico State University, NM
North Dakota State University, ND
Northeastern State University, OK
Northern Arizona University, AZ
The Ohio State University, OH
Ohio University, OH
Ohio University–Chillicothe, OH
Ohio University–Eastern, OH
Ohio University–Lancaster, OH
Ohio University–Southern Campus, OH
Ohio University–Zanesville, OH
Oklahoma State University, OK
Ouachita Baptist University, AR
Pittsburg State University, KS
Point Loma Nazarene University, CA
Sam Houston State University, TX
Seton Hill University, PA
Shepherd University, WV
South Dakota State University, SD
Southeastern Louisiana University, LA
Southeast Missouri State University, MO
Southern Illinois University Carbondale, IL
State University of New York at Plattsburgh, NY
State University of New York College at Oneonta, NY
Stephen F. Austin State University, TX
Tennessee Technological University, TN
Texas State University-San Marcos, TX
Texas Tech University, TX
Texas Woman's University, TX
The University of Akron, OH
The University of Alabama, AL
University of Central Missouri, MO
University of Central Oklahoma, OK
University of Idaho, ID
University of Minnesota, Twin Cities Campus, MN
University of Missouri–Columbia, MO
University of Nebraska at Omaha, NE
The University of North Carolina at Greensboro, NC
University of Northern Colorado, CO
The University of Tennessee at Martin, TN
University of Vermont, VT
University of Wisconsin–Stevens Point, WI
University of Wisconsin–Stout, WI
University of Wyoming, WY
Utah State University, UT
Virginia Polytechnic Institute and State University, VA
Virginia State University, VA
Washington State University, WA
Wayne State College, NE
Western Illinois University, IL
West Virginia University, WV

Humanities

Alderson-Broaddus College, WV
Alfred University, NY
Alliant International University, CA
Antioch College, OH
Arizona State University, AZ
Arkansas State University, AR
Armstrong Atlantic State University, GA
Auburn University, AL
Augustana College, SD
Austin College, TX
Austin Peay State University, TN
Averett University, VA
Barton College, NC
Baylor University, TX
Berry College, GA
Black Hills State University, SD
Bloomfield College, NJ
Bloomsburg University of Pennsylvania, PA
Boise State University, ID
Bowling Green State University, OH
Brenau University, GA
Brigham Young University, UT
Brigham Young University–Hawaii, HI
Bryan College, TN
Buena Vista University, IA
Butler University, IN
California Polytechnic State University, San Luis Obispo, CA
California State University, Chico, CA
California State University, Fresno, CA
California State University, Fullerton, CA
California State University, Stanislaus, CA
Calvin College, MI
Campbellsville University, KY
Carroll College, WI
Case Western Reserve University, OH
Centenary College of Louisiana, LA
Central College, IA
Central Methodist University, MO
Central Michigan University, MI
Christopher Newport University, VA
City College of the City University of New York, NY
Clarion University of Pennsylvania, PA
Clarkson University, NY
Clemson University, SC
Coastal Carolina University, SC
College of Charleston, SC
The College of New Rochelle, NY
College of St. Catherine, MN
College of the Holy Cross, MA
College of the Southwest, NM
Columbia College, MO
Columbus State University, GA
Concordia University, NE
Dallas Baptist University, TX
Denison University, OH
DeSales University, PA
Dickinson State University, ND
Dordt College, IA
Drury University, MO
D'Youville College, NY
Eastern Michigan University, MI
Elizabethtown College, PA
Elmhurst College, IL
Emmanuel College, MA
Emporia State University, KS
Evangel University, MO
Flagler College, FL
Florida Gulf Coast University, FL
Fort Lewis College, CO
Francis Marion University, SC
Freed-Hardeman University, TN
Fresno Pacific University, CA
Friends University, KS
Frostburg State University, MD
Furman University, SC
Gannon University, PA
Gardner-Webb University, NC
Georgia College & State University, GA
Georgia Southern University, GA
Hardin-Simmons University, TX
Hillsdale College, MI

Idaho State University, ID
Illinois Institute of Technology, IL
Illinois State University, IL
Indiana University of Pennsylvania, PA
Jacksonville State University, AL
James Madison University, VA
Kean University, NJ
King's College, PA
Kutztown University of Pennsylvania, PA
Lambuth University, TN
Lawrence Technological University, MI
Lewis-Clark State College, ID
Limestone College, SC
Lincoln University, PA
Lindenwood University, MO
Longwood University, VA
Louisiana State University and Agricultural and Mechanical College, LA
Louisiana Tech University, LA
Lubbock Christian University, TX
Lycoming College, PA
Malone College, OH
Manchester College, IN
Massachusetts College of Liberal Arts, MA
Mesa State College, CO
Metropolitan State College of Denver, CO
Michigan Technological University, MI
Middle Tennessee State University, TN
Millersville University of Pennsylvania, PA
Minot State University, ND
Mississippi State University, MS
Missouri Valley College, MO
Monmouth University, NJ
Montana State University, MT
Montana State University–Billings, MT
Montclair State University, NJ
Morehead State University, KY
Mount Mary College, WI
Murray State University, KY
New England College, NH
New Mexico State University, NM
North Carolina State University, NC
North Central College, IL
North Dakota State University, ND
Northeastern State University, OK
Northern Arizona University, AZ
Northern Illinois University, IL
Northern State University, SD
North Georgia College & State University, GA
Northwestern College, IA
Northwestern Oklahoma State University, OK
Northwestern State University of Louisiana, LA
The Ohio State University, OH
Ohio University, OH
Ohio University–Chillicothe, OH
Ohio University–Eastern, OH
Ohio University–Lancaster, OH
Ohio University–Southern Campus, OH
Ohio University–Zanesville, OH
Ohio Wesleyan University, OH
Oklahoma State University, OK
Ouachita Baptist University, AR
Piedmont College, GA
Point Loma Nazarene University, CA
Portland State University, OR
Purchase College, State University of New York, NY
Purdue University, IN
Radford University, VA
Rensselaer Polytechnic Institute, NY
Rhodes College, TN
Rice University, TX
The Richard Stockton College of New Jersey, NJ
Ripon College, WI
Rivier College, NH
Rockhurst University, MO
Sacred Heart University, CT
St. Edward's University, TX
St. John Fisher College, NY
Saint Louis University, MO
Salisbury University, MD
Sam Houston State University, TX
Savannah College of Art and Design, GA
Seton Hill University, PA
Shepherd University, WV
Sonoma State University, CA
South Dakota State University, SD
Southeastern Louisiana University, LA
Southeast Missouri State University, MO
Southern Illinois University Carbondale, IL
Southern Methodist University, TX
Southern Wesleyan University, SC
State University of New York at Fredonia, NY
State University of New York at New Paltz, NY
State University of New York at Oswego, NY
State University of New York at Plattsburgh, NY
State University of New York College at Geneseo, NY
State University of New York College at Potsdam, NY
Stetson University, FL
Tennessee Technological University, TN
Tennessee Wesleyan College, TN
Texas Tech University, TX
Texas Woman's University, TX
The University of Akron, OH
The University of Alabama in Huntsville, AL
The University of Arizona, AZ
University of California, Irvine, CA
University of California, Riverside, CA
University of Central Missouri, MO
University of Colorado at Boulder, CO
University of Connecticut, CT
University of Dayton, OH
University of Delaware, DE
University of Evansville, IN
University of Great Falls, MT
University of Houston–Victoria, TX
University of Idaho, ID
University of Illinois at Springfield, IL
University of Illinois at Urbana–Champaign, IL
University of Kansas, KS
University of Maine, ME
University of Maine at Fort Kent, ME
University of Maryland, Baltimore County, MD
University of Maryland, College Park, MD
University of Massachusetts Amherst, MA
University of Massachusetts Lowell, MA
University of Michigan, MI
University of Michigan–Flint, MI
University of Minnesota, Twin Cities Campus, MN
University of Missouri–St. Louis, MO
The University of Montana, MT
University of New England, ME
University of New Hampshire, NH
The University of North Carolina at Charlotte, NC
The University of North Carolina at Greensboro, NC
The University of North Carolina Wilmington, NC
University of North Dakota, ND
University of Oklahoma, OK
University of Pittsburgh at Bradford, PA
University of Puget Sound, WA
University of Rochester, NY
University of St. Thomas, MN
University of South Carolina, SC
The University of South Dakota, SD
University of Southern Indiana, IN
University of South Florida, FL
The University of Tennessee at Martin, TN
The University of Texas at Austin, TX
The University of Texas at El Paso, TX
The University of Texas at San Antonio, TX
University of the Ozarks, AR
University of Vermont, VT
University of Washington, WA
University of West Georgia, GA
University of Wisconsin–Stevens Point, WI
University of Wisconsin–Superior, WI
University of Wisconsin–Whitewater, WI
Utah State University, UT
Valdosta State University, GA
Vanderbilt University, TN
Virginia Polytechnic Institute and State University, VA
Virginia State University, VA
Walsh University, OH
Warner Pacific College, OR
Washington State University, WA
Washington University in St. Louis, MO
Wayne State College, NE
Webster University, MO
Western Washington University, WA
Westminster College, UT
West Virginia University, WV
Wichita State University, KS
Widener University, PA
Wilkes University, PA
Williams Baptist College, AR
Wilson College, PA
Youngstown State University, OH

International Studies

Alfred University, NY
Alliant International University, CA
Antioch College, OH
Arkansas Tech University, AR
Armstrong Atlantic State University, GA
Auburn University, AL
Augsburg College, MN
Augustana College, SD
Austin College, TX

Barton College, NC
Baylor University, TX
Bloomsburg University of Pennsylvania, PA
Boise State University, ID
Bowling Green State University, OH
Brigham Young University, UT
Brigham Young University–Hawaii, HI
Buena Vista University, IA
Butler University, IN
California Polytechnic State University, San Luis Obispo, CA
California State University, Chico, CA
California State University, Stanislaus, CA
Calvin College, MI
Carroll College, WI
Case Western Reserve University, OH
Central College, IA
Central Washington University, WA
Chatham University, PA
City College of the City University of New York, NY
Clarion University of Pennsylvania, PA
Clemson University, SC
College of Staten Island of the City University of New York, NY
Colorado State University-Pueblo, CO
Columbia International University, SC
Columbus State University, GA
Concordia University at Austin, TX
Culver-Stockton College, MO
Dana College, NE
D'Youville College, NY
Elizabethtown College, PA
Frostburg State University, MD
Furman University, SC
Gannon University, PA
Georgia College & State University, GA
Georgia Southern University, GA
Grace University, NE
Hampshire College, MA
Hillsdale College, MI
Idaho State University, ID
Illinois State University, IL
Indiana University of Pennsylvania, PA
James Madison University, VA
Kean University, NJ
Kent State University, OH
Keuka College, NY
Lambuth University, TN
Lawrence Technological University, MI
Lindenwood University, MO
Lock Haven University of Pennsylvania, PA
Lycoming College, PA
Malone College, OH
Mercer University, GA
Michigan State University, MI
Middle Tennessee State University, TN
Mississippi State University, MS
Monmouth University, NJ
Montclair State University, NJ
Murray State University, KY
New England College, NH
North Central College, IL
Northern Arizona University, AZ
Northern Illinois University, IL
Northern Michigan University, MI
Northern State University, SD
Northwestern Oklahoma State University, OK
The Ohio State University, OH
Ohio University, OH
Ohio University–Chillicothe, OH
Ohio University–Eastern, OH
Ohio University–Lancaster, OH
Ohio University–Southern Campus, OH
Ohio University–Zanesville, OH
Ohio Wesleyan University, OH
Oklahoma State University, OK
Ouachita Baptist University, AR
Portland State University, OR
Rice University, TX
Rochester Institute of Technology, NY
St. Ambrose University, IA
St. Cloud State University, MN
St. Edward's University, TX
Saint Louis University, MO
South Dakota State University, SD
Southeastern Louisiana University, LA
Southeast Missouri State University, MO
Southern Illinois University Carbondale, IL
Southern Methodist University, TX
Southwest Minnesota State University, MN
State University of New York at Binghamton, NY
State University of New York at Fredonia, NY
State University of New York at Oswego, NY
State University of New York at Plattsburgh, NY
State University of New York College at Oneonta, NY
Tennessee Technological University, TN
Tennessee Wesleyan College, TN
Texas Christian University, TX
Texas State University-San Marcos, TX
Texas Tech University, TX
The University of Akron, OH
University of Colorado at Boulder, CO
University of Connecticut, CT
University of Delaware, DE
University of Evansville, IN
University of Illinois at Springfield, IL
University of Illinois at Urbana–Champaign, IL
University of Kansas, KS
University of Maryland, College Park, MD
University of Miami, FL
University of Michigan, MI
University of Michigan–Dearborn, MI
University of Michigan–Flint, MI
University of Minnesota, Twin Cities Campus, MN
University of Missouri–St. Louis, MO
The University of Montana, MT
University of New England, ME
University of New Orleans, LA
The University of North Carolina Wilmington, NC
University of North Dakota, ND
University of North Florida, FL
University of Oklahoma, OK
University of Puget Sound, WA
University of St. Thomas, MN
University of South Carolina, SC
University of South Florida, FL
The University of Texas at El Paso, TX
University of Tulsa, OK
University of Vermont, VT
University of Wisconsin–Stevens Point, WI
University of Wisconsin–Stout, WI
University of Wyoming, WY
Utah State University, UT
Virginia Military Institute, VA
Virginia Polytechnic Institute and State University, VA
Wake Forest University, NC
Walsh University, OH
Wartburg College, IA
Washington State University, WA
Washington University in St. Louis, MO
Waynesburg College, PA
Webster University, MO
Westminster College, UT
West Virginia University, WV
Wichita State University, KS
Widener University, PA
Wilkes University, PA
Wilson College, PA
Wisconsin Lutheran College, WI

Library Science

Arkansas State University, AR
California Polytechnic State University, San Luis Obispo, CA
Clarion University of Pennsylvania, PA
Emporia State University, KS
Illinois State University, IL
Kent State University, OH
Kutztown University of Pennsylvania, PA
Lindenwood University, MO
Lock Haven University of Pennsylvania, PA
Louisiana Tech University, LA
Mayville State University, ND
Mississippi State University, MS
Murray State University, KY
Northeastern State University, OK
Northern Arizona University, AZ
Northwestern Oklahoma State University, OK
Radford University, VA
Sam Houston State University, TX
Southeastern Louisiana University, LA
Southwest Minnesota State University, MN
Texas Woman's University, TX
The University of Alabama, AL
University of Central Missouri, MO
University of Illinois at Urbana–Champaign, IL
University of Kansas, KS
University of Maryland, College Park, MD
University of Michigan, MI
University of Minnesota, Twin Cities Campus, MN
The University of North Carolina at Greensboro, NC
University of South Carolina, SC
University of South Florida, FL
Utah State University, UT
Valdosta State University, GA
Valley City State University, ND
Western Washington University, WA
West Virginia University, WV

Mathematics

Abilene Christian University, TX
Alabama State University, AL
Albion College, MI

Alderson-Broaddus College, WV
Alfred University, NY
Antioch College, OH
Arizona State University, AZ
Arkansas State University, AR
Armstrong Atlantic State University, GA
Auburn University, AL
Augsburg College, MN
Augustana College, IL
Augustana College, SD
Augusta State University, GA
Aurora University, IL
Austin Peay State University, TN
Averett University, VA
Bard College, NY
Barton College, NC
Baylor University, TX
Bethel College, IN
Birmingham-Southern College, AL
Black Hills State University, SD
Bloomfield College, NJ
Bloomsburg University of Pennsylvania, PA
Blue Mountain College, MS
Boise State University, ID
Bowie State University, MD
Bowling Green State University, OH
Brevard College, NC
Brigham Young University, UT
Brigham Young University–Hawaii, HI
Bryan College, TN
Buena Vista University, IA
Butler University, IN
California Polytechnic State University, San Luis Obispo, CA
California State University, Chico, CA
California State University, Fresno, CA
California State University, Fullerton, CA
California State University, Los Angeles, CA
California State University, Northridge, CA
California State University, Stanislaus, CA
Calvin College, MI
Campbellsville University, KY
Carroll College, WI
Carson-Newman College, TN
Carthage College, WI
Case Western Reserve University, OH
Centenary College of Louisiana, LA
Central College, IA
Central Methodist University, MO
Central Michigan University, MI
Central Washington University, WA
Chatham University, PA
Christopher Newport University, VA
City College of the City University of New York, NY
Clarion University of Pennsylvania, PA
Clarkson University, NY
Clemson University, SC
Coastal Carolina University, SC
College of Charleston, SC
The College of New Rochelle, NY
College of St. Catherine, MN
The College of Saint Rose, NY
College of Staten Island of the City University of New York, NY
College of the Southwest, NM
The College of Wooster, OH
The Colorado College, CO
Colorado School of Mines, CO
Colorado State University-Pueblo, CO
Concordia University, IL
Concordia University, NE
Concordia University, St. Paul, MN
Dakota State University, SD
Dallas Baptist University, TX
Dana College, NE
Davidson College, NC
DeSales University, PA
Dickinson State University, ND
Dordt College, IA
Drury University, MO
Duke University, NC
Eastern Michigan University, MI
East Tennessee State University, TN
East Texas Baptist University, TX
Elizabethtown College, PA
Elmhurst College, IL
Elon University, NC
Emmanuel College, MA
Emporia State University, KS
Erskine College, SC
Evangel University, MO
Felician College, NJ
Fitchburg State College, MA
Florida Gulf Coast University, FL
Fort Lewis College, CO
Francis Marion University, SC
Freed-Hardeman University, TN
Friends University, KS
Frostburg State University, MD
Furman University, SC
Gannon University, PA
Gardner-Webb University, NC
George Fox University, OR
The George Washington University, DC
Georgia College & State University, GA
Georgia Southern University, GA
Glenville State College, WV
Hardin-Simmons University, TX
Heidelberg College, OH
Hillsdale College, MI
Idaho State University, ID
Illinois Institute of Technology, IL
Illinois State University, IL
Indiana University of Pennsylvania, PA
Jacksonville State University, AL
James Madison University, VA
Johnson C. Smith University, NC
Kalamazoo College, MI
Kent State University, OH
Kettering University, MI
King's College, PA
Knox College, IL
Kutztown University of Pennsylvania, PA
Lambuth University, TN
Lawrence Technological University, MI
Lewis-Clark State College, ID
Limestone College, SC
Lincoln University, PA
Lindenwood University, MO
Lindsey Wilson College, KY
Lipscomb University, TN
Lock Haven University of Pennsylvania, PA
Longwood University, VA
Louisiana State University and Agricultural and Mechanical College, LA
Louisiana Tech University, LA
Lycoming College, PA
Malone College, OH
Manhattan College, NY
Manhattanville College, NY
Mansfield University of Pennsylvania, PA
Marquette University, WI
Marywood University, PA
Massachusetts College of Liberal Arts, MA
Mayville State University, ND
McMurry University, TX
Meredith College, NC
Mesa State College, CO
Metropolitan State College of Denver, CO
Michigan State University, MI
Michigan Technological University, MI
Middle Tennessee State University, TN
Midwestern State University, TX
Millersville University of Pennsylvania, PA
Milligan College, TN
Mills College, CA
Minnesota State University Mankato, MN
Minot State University, ND
Mississippi State University, MS
Missouri State University, MO
Missouri Valley College, MO
Molloy College, NY
Monmouth University, NJ
Montana State University, MT
Montana State University–Billings, MT
Montana Tech of The University of Montana, MT
Montclair State University, NJ
Moravian College, PA
Mount Mary College, WI
Mount Olive College, NC
Murray State University, KY
New England College, NH
New Jersey City University, NJ
New Mexico State University, NM
North Carolina State University, NC
North Central College, IL
North Dakota State University, ND
Northeastern Illinois University, IL
Northeastern State University, OK
Northern Arizona University, AZ
Northern Illinois University, IL
Northern Michigan University, MI
Northern State University, SD
North Georgia College & State University, GA
Northwestern College, IA
Northwestern Oklahoma State University, OK
Northwestern State University of Louisiana, LA
Northwest Nazarene University, ID
The Ohio State University, OH
Ohio University, OH
Ohio University–Chillicothe, OH
Ohio University–Eastern, OH
Ohio University–Lancaster, OH
Ohio University–Southern Campus, OH
Ohio University–Zanesville, OH
Ohio Wesleyan University, OH
Oklahoma Panhandle State University, OK
Oklahoma State University, OK
Ouachita Baptist University, AR
Piedmont College, GA
Pittsburg State University, KS

Point Loma Nazarene University, CA
Purchase College, State University of New York, NY
Purdue University, IN
Radford University, VA
Randolph College, VA
Rensselaer Polytechnic Institute, NY
Rice University, TX
The Richard Stockton College of New Jersey, NJ
Ripon College, WI
Rivier College, NH
Rochester Institute of Technology, NY
Rockhurst University, MO
Rollins College, FL
Sacred Heart University, CT
St. Cloud State University, MN
St. Edward's University, TX
St. John Fisher College, NY
Saint Louis University, MO
Saint Vincent College, PA
Salisbury University, MD
Sam Houston State University, TX
Seton Hill University, PA
Shaw University, NC
Shepherd University, WV
Sonoma State University, CA
South Dakota State University, SD
Southeastern Louisiana University, LA
Southeastern Oklahoma State University, OK
Southeast Missouri State University, MO
Southern Adventist University, TN
Southern Arkansas University–Magnolia, AR
Southern Illinois University Carbondale, IL
Southern Methodist University, TX
Southern Nazarene University, OK
Southern Oregon University, OR
Southern Wesleyan University, SC
Southwest Minnesota State University, MN
Spelman College, GA
State University of New York at Binghamton, NY
State University of New York at Fredonia, NY
State University of New York at New Paltz, NY
State University of New York at Oswego, NY
State University of New York at Plattsburgh, NY
State University of New York College at Geneseo, NY
State University of New York College at Potsdam, NY
Stephen F. Austin State University, TX
Stetson University, FL
Tennessee Technological University, TN
Tennessee Wesleyan College, TN
Texas A&M University–Texarkana, TX
Texas Tech University, TX
Texas Woman's University, TX
Thiel College, PA
Union University, TN
The University of Akron, OH
The University of Alabama, AL
The University of Alabama at Birmingham, AL
University of California, Riverside, CA
University of California, San Diego, CA
University of Central Missouri, MO
University of Central Oklahoma, OK
University of Colorado at Boulder, CO
University of Connecticut, CT
University of Dallas, TX
University of Delaware, DE
University of Evansville, IN
University of Great Falls, MT
University of Houston–Victoria, TX
University of Idaho, ID
University of Illinois at Springfield, IL
University of Illinois at Urbana–Champaign, IL
University of Kansas, KS
University of Maine, ME
University of Maine at Fort Kent, ME
University of Maryland, Baltimore County, MD
University of Maryland, College Park, MD
University of Massachusetts Amherst, MA
University of Miami, FL
University of Michigan, MI
University of Michigan–Dearborn, MI
University of Michigan–Flint, MI
University of Minnesota, Twin Cities Campus, MN
University of Missouri–Columbia, MO
University of Missouri–St. Louis, MO
The University of Montana, MT
University of Nebraska at Omaha, NE
University of New England, ME
University of New Hampshire, NH
University of New Orleans, LA
The University of North Carolina at Asheville, NC
The University of North Carolina at Chapel Hill, NC
The University of North Carolina at Charlotte, NC
The University of North Carolina at Greensboro, NC
The University of North Carolina Wilmington, NC
University of North Dakota, ND
University of Northern Colorado, CO
University of Northern Iowa, IA
University of Oklahoma, OK
University of Pittsburgh at Bradford, PA
University of Puget Sound, WA
University of Richmond, VA
University of Rochester, NY
University of Saint Francis, IN
University of St. Thomas, MN
University of St. Thomas, TX
University of South Carolina, SC
The University of South Dakota, SD
University of Southern Indiana, IN
University of South Florida, FL
The University of Tennessee at Martin, TN
The University of Texas at Austin, TX
The University of Texas at Brownsville, TX
The University of Texas at Dallas, TX
The University of Texas at El Paso, TX
The University of Texas at San Antonio, TX
The University of Texas–Pan American, TX
University of the Ozarks, AR
University of Tulsa, OK
University of Vermont, VT
University of Washington, WA
University of West Georgia, GA
University of Wisconsin–La Crosse, WI
University of Wisconsin–Stevens Point, WI
University of Wisconsin–Stout, WI
University of Wisconsin–Superior, WI
University of Wisconsin–Whitewater, WI
University of Wyoming, WY
Utah State University, UT
Valdosta State University, GA
Valley City State University, ND
Virginia Commonwealth University, VA
Virginia Military Institute, VA
Virginia Polytechnic Institute and State University, VA
Virginia State University, VA
Wake Forest University, NC
Walsh University, OH
Warner Pacific College, OR
Wartburg College, IA
Washington State University, WA
Washington University in St. Louis, MO
Wayland Baptist University, TX
Waynesburg College, PA
Wayne State College, NE
Western Carolina University, NC
Western Illinois University, IL
Western Oregon University, OR
Western Washington University, WA
West Liberty State College, WV
Westminster College, UT
West Virginia University, WV
Wichita State University, KS
Widener University, PA
Wilkes University, PA
Wilson College, PA
Winston-Salem State University, NC
Wisconsin Lutheran College, WI
Xavier University, OH

Military Science

Alfred University, NY
Arizona State University, AZ
Arkansas State University, AR
Armstrong Atlantic State University, GA
Augusta State University, GA
Austin Peay State University, TN
Baylor University, TX
Black Hills State University, SD
Boise State University, ID
Boston College, MA
Bowie State University, MD
Bowling Green State University, OH
Brigham Young University, UT
California Polytechnic State University, San Luis Obispo, CA
California State University, Fullerton, CA
Carson-Newman College, TN
Central Michigan University, MI
Central Washington University, WA
Christopher Newport University, VA
Clarkson University, NY
Clemson University, SC
College of the Holy Cross, MA
Colorado School of Mines, CO
Columbus State University, GA
Creighton University, NE
Dana College, NE

DeSales University, PA
Dickinson College, PA
East Tennessee State University, TN
Elon University, NC
Florida Institute of Technology, FL
Furman University, SC
Georgia Southern University, GA
Gonzaga University, WA
Idaho State University, ID
Illinois Institute of Technology, IL
Illinois State University, IL
Jacksonville State University, AL
James Madison University, VA
Kent State University, OH
Lawrence Technological University, MI
Lehigh University, PA
Lindenwood University, MO
Louisiana State University and Agricultural and Mechanical College, LA
Louisiana Tech University, LA
Manhattan College, NY
Mercer University, GA
Michigan State University, MI
Middle Tennessee State University, TN
Mississippi State University, MS
Missouri State University, MO
Missouri Valley College, MO
Montana State University, MT
New Mexico State University, NM
North Carolina Agricultural and Technical State University, NC
North Dakota State University, ND
Northern Arizona University, AZ
Northern Michigan University, MI
North Georgia College & State University, GA
North Greenville University, SC
Northwest Nazarene University, ID
The Ohio State University, OH
Ohio University, OH
Ohio University–Chillicothe, OH
Ohio University–Eastern, OH
Ohio University–Lancaster, OH
Ohio University–Southern Campus, OH
Ohio University–Zanesville, OH
Oklahoma State University, OK
Pittsburg State University, KS
Providence College, RI
Purdue University, IN
Radford University, VA
Rensselaer Polytechnic Institute, NY
Ripon College, WI
Rochester Institute of Technology, NY
St. Edward's University, TX
Saint Louis University, MO
Sam Houston State University, TX
Santa Clara University, CA
South Dakota State University, SD
Southeast Missouri State University, MO
Southern Illinois University Carbondale, IL
Stephen F. Austin State University, TX
Stetson University, FL
Tennessee Technological University, TN
Texas Christian University, TX
Texas State University-San Marcos, TX
Texas Tech University, TX
The University of Akron, OH
The University of Alabama, AL
The University of Arizona, AZ
University of Central Missouri, MO
University of Central Oklahoma, OK
University of Charleston, WV
University of Colorado at Boulder, CO
University of Delaware, DE
University of Florida, FL
University of Idaho, ID
University of Illinois at Urbana–Champaign, IL
University of Kansas, KS
University of Maine, ME
University of Maryland, College Park, MD
University of Massachusetts Amherst, MA
University of Michigan, MI
University of Minnesota, Twin Cities Campus, MN
The University of Montana, MT
University of New Hampshire, NH
University of New Orleans, LA
The University of North Carolina at Charlotte, NC
University of North Dakota, ND
University of Northern Colorado, CO
University of Rochester, NY
University of San Francisco, CA
University of South Carolina, SC
The University of South Dakota, SD
University of South Florida, FL
The University of Tampa, FL
The University of Tennessee at Martin, TN
The University of Texas at El Paso, TX
The University of Texas–Pan American, TX
University of Vermont, VT
University of West Florida, FL
University of Wisconsin–La Crosse, WI
University of Wisconsin–Stevens Point, WI
University of Wyoming, WY
Valdosta State University, GA
Virginia Commonwealth University, VA
Virginia Military Institute, VA
Virginia Polytechnic Institute and State University, VA
Virginia State University, VA
Wake Forest University, NC
Washington State University, WA
Washington University in St. Louis, MO
Westminster College, UT
West Virginia University, WV
Whitworth University, WA
Widener University, PA
Xavier University, OH
Youngstown State University, OH

Physical Sciences

Abilene Christian University, TX
Adams State College, CO
Alderson-Broaddus College, WV
Alfred University, NY
Antioch College, OH
Arizona State University, AZ
Arkansas State University, AR
Armstrong Atlantic State University, GA
Auburn University, AL
Augsburg College, MN
Augustana College, IL
Augustana College, SD
Augusta State University, GA
Austin College, TX
Averett University, VA
Bard College, NY
Barton College, NC
Baylor University, TX
Bethel College, IN
Birmingham-Southern College, AL
Black Hills State University, SD
Bloomfield College, NJ
Bloomsburg University of Pennsylvania, PA
Boise State University, ID
Bowling Green State University, OH
Brevard College, NC
Brigham Young University, UT
Brigham Young University–Hawaii, HI
Bryan College, TN
Bucknell University, PA
Butler University, IN
California Polytechnic State University, San Luis Obispo, CA
California State University, Chico, CA
California State University, Los Angeles, CA
California State University, Stanislaus, CA
Calvin College, MI
Campbellsville University, KY
Carroll College, WI
Carthage College, WI
Case Western Reserve University, OH
Centenary College of Louisiana, LA
Central College, IA
Central Methodist University, MO
Central Michigan University, MI
Central State University, OH
Central Washington University, WA
Chapman University, CA
Chatham University, PA
Clarion University of Pennsylvania, PA
Clarkson University, NY
Clemson University, SC
Coe College, IA
College Misericordia, PA
College of Charleston, SC
The College of New Jersey, NJ
The College of New Rochelle, NY
College of St. Catherine, MN
College of Staten Island of the City University of New York, NY
The College of Wooster, OH
The Colorado College, CO
Colorado School of Mines, CO
Columbia College, MO
Columbus State University, GA
Concordia University, NE
Concordia University, St. Paul, MN
Davidson College, NC
Davis & Elkins College, WV
Denison University, OH
DeSales University, PA
Dickinson State University, ND
Dominican University, IL
Dordt College, IA
Drury University, MO
Eastern Michigan University, MI
East Texas Baptist University, TX
Elizabethtown College, PA
Elmhurst College, IL
Elon University, NC
Emmanuel College, MA
Emporia State University, KS
Evangel University, MO
Fairfield University, CT

Florida Atlantic University, FL
Florida Gulf Coast University, FL
Fort Lewis College, CO
Framingham State College, MA
Freed-Hardeman University, TN
Friends University, KS
Frostburg State University, MD
Furman University, SC
Gardner-Webb University, NC
George Fox University, OR
Georgia College & State University, GA
Georgia Institute of Technology, GA
Graceland University, IA
Grove City College, PA
Hampshire College, MA
Hardin-Simmons University, TX
Heidelberg College, OH
Hillsdale College, MI
Idaho State University, ID
Illinois Institute of Technology, IL
Illinois State University, IL
Indiana University of Pennsylvania, PA
Jacksonville State University, AL
James Madison University, VA
Jamestown College, ND
Kalamazoo College, MI
Kent State University, OH
Kettering University, MI
King's College, PA
Kutztown University of Pennsylvania, PA
Lake Forest College, IL
Lambuth University, TN
Lawrence Technological University, MI
Lewis-Clark State College, ID
Limestone College, SC
Lincoln University, PA
Lindenwood University, MO
Lock Haven University of Pennsylvania, PA
Loras College, IA
Louisiana State University and Agricultural and Mechanical College, LA
Louisiana Tech University, LA
Lubbock Christian University, TX
Lycoming College, PA
MacMurray College, IL
Malone College, OH
Mansfield University of Pennsylvania, PA
Massachusetts College of Liberal Arts, MA
Mayville State University, ND
McMurry University, TX
Meredith College, NC
Mesa State College, CO
Metropolitan State College of Denver, CO
Michigan State University, MI
Michigan Technological University, MI
Middle Tennessee State University, TN
Millersville University of Pennsylvania, PA
Mills College, CA
Minnesota State University Mankato, MN
Mississippi State University, MS
Missouri State University, MO
Missouri Valley College, MO
Montana State University, MT
Montana State University–Billings, MT
Montana Tech of The University of Montana, MT
Montclair State University, NJ
Moravian College, PA
Morehead State University, KY
Mount Mary College, WI
Mount Vernon Nazarene University, OH
New Mexico State University, NM
North Carolina State University, NC
North Central College, IL
North Dakota State University, ND
Northeastern Illinois University, IL
Northeastern State University, OK
Northern Arizona University, AZ
Northern Illinois University, IL
Northern Michigan University, MI
Northern State University, SD
North Georgia College & State University, GA
Northwestern College, IA
Northwestern Oklahoma State University, OK
Northwestern State University of Louisiana, LA
Northwest Nazarene University, ID
Oberlin College, OH
The Ohio State University, OH
Ohio University, OH
Ohio University–Chillicothe, OH
Ohio University–Eastern, OH
Ohio University–Lancaster, OH
Ohio University–Southern Campus, OH
Ohio University–Zanesville, OH
Ohio Wesleyan University, OH
Oklahoma Panhandle State University, OK
Oklahoma State University, OK
Ouachita Baptist University, AR
Pittsburg State University, KS
Portland State University, OR
Purdue University, IN
Radford University, VA
Randolph College, VA
Regis University, CO
Rice University, TX
The Richard Stockton College of New Jersey, NJ
Ripon College, WI
Rochester Institute of Technology, NY
Rockhurst University, MO
Rollins College, FL
Sacred Heart University, CT
St. Cloud State University, MN
St. Edward's University, TX
St. John Fisher College, NY
Saint Louis University, MO
Saint Vincent College, PA
Salisbury University, MD
Sam Houston State University, TX
Seton Hill University, PA
Shaw University, NC
Shepherd University, WV
Slippery Rock University of Pennsylvania, PA
Sonoma State University, CA
South Dakota State University, SD
Southeastern Louisiana University, LA
Southeastern Oklahoma State University, OK
Southeast Missouri State University, MO
Southern Arkansas University–Magnolia, AR
Southern Illinois University Carbondale, IL
Southern Methodist University, TX
Southern Oregon University, OR
Southern Wesleyan University, SC
Southwest Minnesota State University, MN
Spelman College, GA
State University of New York at Binghamton, NY
State University of New York at Fredonia, NY
State University of New York at New Paltz, NY
State University of New York at Oswego, NY
State University of New York at Plattsburgh, NY
State University of New York College at Geneseo, NY
State University of New York College at Old Westbury, NY
State University of New York College at Oneonta, NY
State University of New York College at Potsdam, NY
State University of New York College of Environmental Science and Forestry, NY
Stephen F. Austin State University, TX
Stetson University, FL
Stony Brook University, State University of New York, NY
Tennessee Technological University, TN
Tennessee Wesleyan College, TN
Texas Tech University, TX
Texas Woman's University, TX
Thiel College, PA
Trevecca Nazarene University, TN
The University of Akron, OH
The University of Alabama, AL
The University of Alabama in Huntsville, AL
The University of Arizona, AZ
University of California, Riverside, CA
University of California, San Diego, CA
University of Central Missouri, MO
University of Central Oklahoma, OK
University of Colorado at Boulder, CO
University of Connecticut, CT
University of Dallas, TX
University of Delaware, DE
University of Evansville, IN
University of Great Falls, MT
University of Idaho, ID
University of Illinois at Springfield, IL
University of Illinois at Urbana–Champaign, IL
University of Kansas, KS
University of Maine, ME
University of Maryland, Baltimore County, MD
University of Maryland, College Park, MD
University of Massachusetts Amherst, MA
University of Miami, FL
University of Michigan, MI
University of Michigan–Dearborn, MI
University of Michigan–Flint, MI
University of Minnesota, Twin Cities Campus, MN
The University of Montana, MT
University of Nebraska at Omaha, NE
University of New England, ME
University of New Orleans, LA

The University of North Carolina at Asheville, NC
The University of North Carolina at Greensboro, NC
The University of North Carolina at Pembroke, NC
The University of North Carolina Wilmington, NC
University of North Dakota, ND
University of Northern Colorado, CO
University of Northern Iowa, IA
University of Oklahoma, OK
University of Oregon, OR
University of Pittsburgh at Bradford, PA
University of Puget Sound, WA
University of Richmond, VA
University of Rochester, NY
University of Saint Francis, IN
University of St. Thomas, MN
University of St. Thomas, TX
University of South Carolina, SC
University of South Florida, FL
The University of Tennessee at Martin, TN
The University of Texas at Dallas, TX
The University of Texas at El Paso, TX
The University of Texas at San Antonio, TX
University of Tulsa, OK
University of Vermont, VT
University of Washington, WA
University of West Georgia, GA
University of Wisconsin–Green Bay, WI
University of Wisconsin–La Crosse, WI
University of Wisconsin–Stevens Point, WI
University of Wisconsin–Stout, WI
University of Wisconsin–Superior, WI
University of Wisconsin–Whitewater, WI
University of Wyoming, WY
Utah State University, UT
Valdosta State University, GA
Valley City State University, ND
Valparaiso University, IN
Virginia Polytechnic Institute and State University, VA
Virginia State University, VA
Wake Forest University, NC
Walsh University, OH
Warner Pacific College, OR
Wartburg College, IA
Washington State University, WA
Washington University in St. Louis, MO
Wayland Baptist University, TX
Wayne State College, NE
Western Illinois University, IL
Western Oregon University, OR
Western Washington University, WA
West Liberty State College, WV
Westminster College, UT
West Virginia University, WV
West Virginia Wesleyan College, WV
Wheaton College, IL
Whitworth University, WA
Wichita State University, KS
Widener University, PA
Wilson College, PA
Xavier University, OH

Premedicine

Albion College, MI
Alderson-Broaddus College, WV
Alfred University, NY
Arizona State University, AZ
Arkansas State University, AR
Auburn University, AL
Augustana College, SD
Austin College, TX
Averett University, VA
Baylor University, TX
Birmingham-Southern College, AL
Blue Mountain College, MS
Boise State University, ID
Brevard College, NC
Brigham Young University, UT
Bryan College, TN
California State University, Stanislaus, CA
Calvin College, MI
Campbellsville University, KY
Carroll College, WI
Carthage College, WI
Case Western Reserve University, OH
Centenary College of Louisiana, LA
Central Methodist University, MO
Central Washington University, WA
Chatham University, PA
City College of the City University of New York, NY
Clarion University of Pennsylvania, PA
Clearwater Christian College, FL
Clemson University, SC
Coe College, IA
College of Charleston, SC
The College of New Rochelle, NY
College of St. Catherine, MN
The College of Saint Rose, NY
College of Staten Island of the City University of New York, NY
Colorado State University-Pueblo, CO
Concordia University, NE
Dallas Baptist University, TX
Dana College, NE
Davidson College, NC
DeSales University, PA
Dickinson State University, ND
Dordt College, IA
Drury University, MO
D'Youville College, NY
Elizabethtown College, PA
Elmhurst College, IL
Elon University, NC
Emporia State University, KS
Erskine College, SC
Evangel University, MO
Felician College, NJ
Francis Marion University, SC
Freed-Hardeman University, TN
Friends University, KS
Frostburg State University, MD
Furman University, SC
Gannon University, PA
Gardner-Webb University, NC
Hampden-Sydney College, VA
Hardin-Simmons University, TX
Hillsdale College, MI
Idaho State University, ID
Illinois Institute of Technology, IL
Illinois State University, IL
Indiana University of Pennsylvania, PA
James Madison University, VA
Juniata College, PA
King's College, PA
Lambuth University, TN
Lindenwood University, MO
Lindsey Wilson College, KY
Lipscomb University, TN
Louisiana State University and Agricultural and Mechanical College, LA
Lycoming College, PA
Malone College, OH
McMurry University, TX
Michigan Technological University, MI
Middle Tennessee State University, TN
Mills College, CA
Mississippi State University, MS
Missouri State University, MO
Missouri Valley College, MO
Montana State University–Billings, MT
North Central College, IL
North Dakota State University, ND
Northeastern State University, OK
Northern Arizona University, AZ
Northern Michigan University, MI
North Georgia College & State University, GA
Northwestern College, IA
Northwestern Oklahoma State University, OK
Northwest Nazarene University, ID
The Ohio State University, OH
Ohio University, OH
Ohio University–Chillicothe, OH
Ohio University–Eastern, OH
Ohio University–Lancaster, OH
Ohio University–Southern Campus, OH
Ohio University–Zanesville, OH
Ohio Wesleyan University, OH
Oklahoma State University, OK
Ouachita Baptist University, AR
Piedmont College, GA
Providence College, RI
Radford University, VA
Randolph College, VA
Ripon College, WI
Rivier College, NH
Rochester Institute of Technology, NY
Rockhurst University, MO
Sacred Heart University, CT
Saint Louis University, MO
Salisbury University, MD
Seton Hill University, PA
Shepherd University, WV
Sonoma State University, CA
South Dakota State University, SD
Southeastern Louisiana University, LA
Southeast Missouri State University, MO
Southern Illinois University Carbondale, IL
Southern Wesleyan University, SC
Southwest Minnesota State University, MN
State University of New York at Binghamton, NY
State University of New York at New Paltz, NY
State University of New York at Oswego, NY
State University of New York at Plattsburgh, NY
State University of New York College at Geneseo, NY

State University of New York College at Oneonta, NY
State University of New York College of Environmental Science and Forestry, NY
Stephen F. Austin State University, TX
Stetson University, FL
Sweet Briar College, VA
Tennessee Technological University, TN
Tennessee Wesleyan College, TN
Texas Christian University, TX
Texas Tech University, TX
Texas Woman's University, TX
Union University, TN
The University of Akron, OH
The University of Alabama, AL
University of California, Riverside, CA
University of Central Missouri, MO
University of Colorado at Boulder, CO
University of Connecticut, CT
University of Delaware, DE
University of Evansville, IN
University of Great Falls, MT
University of Hartford, CT
University of Idaho, ID
University of Judaism, CA
University of Kansas, KS
University of Maryland, College Park, MD
University of Massachusetts Amherst, MA
University of Michigan, MI
University of Michigan–Flint, MI
University of Minnesota, Crookston, MN
University of Minnesota, Twin Cities Campus, MN
University of Missouri–Columbia, MO
The University of Montana, MT
University of Nebraska at Omaha, NE
University of New England, ME
The University of North Carolina at Asheville, NC
The University of North Carolina at Greensboro, NC
University of North Dakota, ND
University of Pittsburgh at Bradford, PA
University of Puget Sound, WA
University of Saint Francis, IN
University of South Carolina, SC
The University of South Dakota, SD
University of Southern Indiana, IN
University of South Florida, FL
The University of Tennessee at Martin, TN
The University of Texas–Pan American, TX
University of the Ozarks, AR
University of Tulsa, OK
University of Wisconsin–Stevens Point, WI
University of Wisconsin–Whitewater, WI
Utah State University, UT
Valdosta State University, GA
Virginia Military Institute, VA
Virginia Polytechnic Institute and State University, VA
Virginia State University, VA
Wake Forest University, NC
Walsh University, OH
Washington State University, WA
Washington University in St. Louis, MO
Wayne State College, NE
Western Washington University, WA
Westminster College, UT
West Virginia University, WV
Wheaton College, IL
Wheeling Jesuit University, WV
Whitworth University, WA
Wichita State University, KS
Widener University, PA
Wilkes University, PA
Wilson College, PA
Worcester Polytechnic Institute, MA

Religion/Biblical Studies

Abilene Christian University, TX
Alderson-Broaddus College, WV
Augsburg College, MN
Augustana College, IL
Augustana College, SD
Austin College, TX
Austin Graduate School of Theology, TX
Averett University, VA
Azusa Pacific University, CA
Baptist Bible College, MO
The Baptist College of Florida, FL
Barton College, NC
Baylor University, TX
Belmont University, TN
Berry College, GA
Bethel College, IN
Bloomfield College, NJ
Bloomsburg University of Pennsylvania, PA
Blue Mountain College, MS
Brevard College, NC
Brigham Young University, UT
Brigham Young University–Hawaii, HI
Bryan College, TN
Calvin College, MI
Campbellsville University, KY
Carson-Newman College, TN
Case Western Reserve University, OH
Centenary College of Louisiana, LA
Central College, IA
Central Methodist University, MO
Christopher Newport University, VA
Clearwater Christian College, FL
The College of New Rochelle, NY
Columbia College, MO
Columbia International University, SC
Concordia University, CA
Concordia University, IL
Concordia University, NE
Concordia University, St. Paul, MN
Dallas Baptist University, TX
Dana College, NE
Davis & Elkins College, WV
DeSales University, PA
Dordt College, IA
Eastern Michigan University, MI
East Texas Baptist University, TX
Elizabethtown College, PA
Elmhurst College, IL
Elon University, NC
Emmanuel College, MA
Erskine College, SC
Eugene Bible College, OR
Evangel University, MO
Faulkner University, AL
Felician College, NJ
Flagler College, FL
Florida Gulf Coast University, FL
Freed-Hardeman University, TN
Fresno Pacific University, CA
Friends University, KS
Furman University, SC
Gannon University, PA
Gardner-Webb University, NC
Geneva College, PA
George Fox University, OR
Grace University, NE
Grove City College, PA
Hampden-Sydney College, VA
Hardin-Simmons University, TX
Hastings College, NE
Hellenic College, MA
Hillsdale College, MI
Houston Baptist University, TX
Idaho State University, ID
James Madison University, VA
Johnson Bible College, TN
Kentucky Christian University, KY
King's College, PA
LaGrange College, GA
Lakeland College, WI
Lambuth University, TN
Lee University, TN
Limestone College, SC
Lindsey Wilson College, KY
Lipscomb University, TN
Lubbock Christian University, TX
Lycoming College, PA
MacMurray College, IL
Malone College, OH
Manhattan Christian College, KS
Maranatha Baptist Bible College, WI
Marywood University, PA
McKendree College, IL
McMurry University, TX
Mercer University, GA
Meredith College, NC
Messenger College, MO
Milligan College, TN
Mississippi State University, MS
Missouri Baptist University, MO
Missouri State University, MO
Montclair State University, NJ
Mount Vernon Nazarene University, OH
Nazarene Bible College, CO
North Central College, IL
Northern Arizona University, AZ
North Greenville University, SC
Northwestern College, IA
Northwest Nazarene University, ID
Ohio Christian University, OH
Ohio Valley University, WV
Ohio Wesleyan University, OH
Oklahoma Baptist University, OK
Oral Roberts University, OK
Ouachita Baptist University, AR
Piedmont College, GA
Point Loma Nazarene University, CA
Ripon College, WI
Roanoke Bible College, NC
Rockhurst University, MO
St. Edward's University, TX
Saint Francis University, PA
Saint Louis University, MO
Seton Hill University, PA
Southeastern University, FL
Southeast Missouri State University, MO
Southern Adventist University, TN
Southern Illinois University Carbondale, IL
Southern Methodist College, SC

Southern Methodist University, TX
Southern Nazarene University, OK
Southern Wesleyan University, SC
Stetson University, FL
Tennessee Wesleyan College, TN
Texas Christian University, TX
Thiel College, PA
Trevecca Nazarene University, TN
Union University, TN
The University of Arizona, AZ
University of Central Missouri, MO
University of Connecticut, CT
University of Dallas, TX
University of Delaware, DE
University of Evansville, IN
University of Great Falls, MT
University of Kansas, KS
University of Minnesota, Twin Cities Campus, MN
University of Missouri–Columbia, MO
The University of North Carolina at Greensboro, NC
University of Saint Francis, IN
University of St. Thomas, MN
University of South Carolina, SC
University of South Florida, FL
University of the Ozarks, AR
University of Tulsa, OK
Valparaiso University, IN
Virginia Polytechnic Institute and State University, VA
Wake Forest University, NC
Walsh University, OH
Warner Pacific College, OR
Wartburg College, IA
Washington Bible College, MD
Washington University in St. Louis, MO
Wayland Baptist University, TX
Waynesburg College, PA
West Virginia University, WV
Williams Baptist College, AR
Wilson College, PA

Social Sciences

Abilene Christian University, TX
Alderson-Broaddus College, WV
Alfred University, NY
Alliant International University, CA
Antioch College, OH
Arizona State University, AZ
Arkansas State University, AR
Auburn University, AL
Augsburg College, MN
Augustana College, IL
Augustana College, SD
Augusta State University, GA
Austin College, TX
Austin Peay State University, TN
Barton College, NC
Baylor University, TX
Bethel College, IN
Black Hills State University, SD
Bloomfield College, NJ
Bloomsburg University of Pennsylvania, PA
Blue Mountain College, MS
Boise State University, ID
Bowling Green State University, OH
Brevard College, NC
Brigham Young University, UT
Brigham Young University–Hawaii, HI
Bryan College, TN
Butler University, IN
California Polytechnic State University, San Luis Obispo, CA
California State University, Chico, CA
California State University, Fresno, CA
California State University, Fullerton, CA
California State University, Los Angeles, CA
California State University, Northridge, CA
California State University, Stanislaus, CA
Calvin College, MI
Campbellsville University, KY
Carroll College, WI
Case Western Reserve University, OH
Centenary College of Louisiana, LA
Central Methodist University, MO
Central Michigan University, MI
Chatham University, PA
City College of the City University of New York, NY
Clarion University of Pennsylvania, PA
Clemson University, SC
College Misericordia, PA
College of Charleston, SC
The College of New Rochelle, NY
College of St. Catherine, MN
The College of Saint Rose, NY
College of the Southwest, NM
The College of Wooster, OH
Colorado State University-Pueblo, CO
Columbia College, MO
Concordia University, CA
Concordia University, NE
Concordia University, St. Paul, MN
Concord University, WV
Dana College, NE
Daniel Webster College, NH
DeSales University, PA
Dickinson State University, ND
Dordt College, IA
Drury University, MO
D'Youville College, NY
Eastern Michigan University, MI
East Tennessee State University, TN
Elizabethtown College, PA
Elon University, NC
Emmanuel College, MA
Emporia State University, KS
Erskine College, SC
Evangel University, MO
Felician College, NJ
Fitchburg State College, MA
Flagler College, FL
Florida Atlantic University, FL
Florida Gulf Coast University, FL
Fort Lewis College, CO
Francis Marion University, SC
Fresno Pacific University, CA
Friends University, KS
Frostburg State University, MD
Furman University, SC
Gannon University, PA
Gardner-Webb University, NC
Georgia College & State University, GA
Georgia Southern University, GA
Glenville State College, WV
Green Mountain College, VT
Grove City College, PA
Hampshire College, MA
Hardin-Simmons University, TX
Hawai'i Pacific University, HI
Hillsdale College, MI
Idaho State University, ID
Illinois Institute of Technology, IL
Illinois State University, IL
Indiana University of Pennsylvania, PA
Jacksonville State University, AL
James Madison University, VA
Kalamazoo College, MI
Kent State University, OH
King's College, PA
Lambuth University, TN
Lewis-Clark State College, ID
Limestone College, SC
Lincoln University, PA
Lindenwood University, MO
Lock Haven University of Pennsylvania, PA
Longwood University, VA
Louisiana Tech University, LA
Lubbock Christian University, TX
Lycoming College, PA
MacMurray College, IL
Macon State College, GA
Malone College, OH
Massachusetts College of Liberal Arts, MA
McMurry University, TX
Mesa State College, CO
Metropolitan State College of Denver, CO
Michigan State University, MI
Michigan Technological University, MI
Middle Tennessee State University, TN
Midwestern State University, TX
Millersville University of Pennsylvania, PA
Minot State University, ND
Mississippi State University, MS
Missouri State University, MO
Missouri Valley College, MO
Monmouth University, NJ
Montana State University, MT
Montana State University–Billings, MT
Montclair State University, NJ
Morehead State University, KY
Mount Mary College, WI
New England College, NH
New Mexico State University, NM
North Carolina State University, NC
North Central College, IL
North Dakota State University, ND
Northeastern Illinois University, IL
Northeastern State University, OK
Northern Arizona University, AZ
Northern Illinois University, IL
Northern Michigan University, MI
Northern State University, SD
Northwestern College, IA
Northwestern Oklahoma State University, OK
Northwest Nazarene University, ID
The Ohio State University, OH
Ohio University, OH
Ohio University–Chillicothe, OH
Ohio University–Eastern, OH
Ohio University–Lancaster, OH
Ohio University–Southern Campus, OH
Ohio University–Zanesville, OH
Ohio Wesleyan University, OH
Oklahoma State University, OK

Ouachita Baptist University, AR
Pittsburg State University, KS
Point Loma Nazarene University, CA
Portland State University, OR
Purchase College, State University of New York, NY
Radford University, VA
Randolph College, VA
Rice University, TX
The Richard Stockton College of New Jersey, NJ
Ripon College, WI
Rivier College, NH
Rochester Institute of Technology, NY
Rockhurst University, MO
St. Cloud State University, MN
St. Edward's University, TX
Saint Francis University, PA
Saint Louis University, MO
Saint Vincent College, PA
Salisbury University, MD
Sam Houston State University, TX
Seton Hill University, PA
Shepherd University, WV
Shippensburg University of Pennsylvania, PA
Slippery Rock University of Pennsylvania, PA
Sonoma State University, CA
South Dakota State University, SD
Southeastern Louisiana University, LA
Southeastern Oklahoma State University, OK
Southeast Missouri State University, MO
Southern Arkansas University–Magnolia, AR
Southern Illinois University Carbondale, IL
Southern Methodist University, TX
Southern Oregon University, OR
Southern Wesleyan University, SC
Southwest Minnesota State University, MN
State University of New York at Fredonia, NY
State University of New York at Oswego, NY
State University of New York at Plattsburgh, NY
State University of New York College at Geneseo, NY
State University of New York College at Potsdam, NY
Stetson University, FL
Stony Brook University, State University of New York, NY
Tennessee Technological University, TN
Tennessee Wesleyan College, TN
Texas A&M University–Texarkana, TX
Texas Tech University, TX
Texas Woman's University, TX
Thomas More College, KY
Trevecca Nazarene University, TN
The University of Akron, OH
The University of Alabama, AL
The University of Alabama in Huntsville, AL
University of California, Riverside, CA
University of California, San Diego, CA
University of Central Missouri, MO
University of Central Oklahoma, OK
University of Colorado at Boulder, CO
University of Connecticut, CT
University of Delaware, DE
University of Evansville, IN
University of Great Falls, MT
University of Hawaii at Hilo, HI
University of Houston–Victoria, TX
University of Idaho, ID
University of Illinois at Springfield, IL
University of Illinois at Urbana–Champaign, IL
University of Kansas, KS
University of Maine, ME
University of Maine at Fort Kent, ME
University of Maryland, College Park, MD
University of Massachusetts Amherst, MA
University of Miami, FL
University of Michigan, MI
University of Michigan–Dearborn, MI
University of Michigan–Flint, MI
University of Minnesota, Twin Cities Campus, MN
University of Missouri–Columbia, MO
The University of Montana, MT
University of Nebraska at Omaha, NE
University of New England, ME
The University of North Carolina at Asheville, NC
The University of North Carolina at Greensboro, NC
The University of North Carolina Wilmington, NC
University of North Dakota, ND
University of Northern Colorado, CO
University of Northern Iowa, IA
University of Oklahoma, OK
University of Oregon, OR
University of Phoenix–Atlanta Campus, GA
University of Phoenix–Bay Area Campus, CA
University of Phoenix–Central Florida Campus, FL
University of Phoenix–Cleveland Campus, OH
University of Phoenix–Dallas Campus, TX
University of Phoenix–Denver Campus, CO
University of Phoenix–Fort Lauderdale Campus, FL
University of Phoenix–Hawaii Campus, HI
University of Phoenix–Houston Campus, TX
University of Phoenix–Indianapolis Campus, IN
University of Phoenix–Kansas City Campus, MO
University of Phoenix–Little Rock Campus, AR
University of Phoenix–Louisiana Campus, LA
University of Phoenix–Metro Detroit Campus, MI
University of Phoenix–Nashville Campus, TN
University of Phoenix–Nevada Campus, NV
University of Phoenix–New Mexico Campus, NM
University of Phoenix–Oklahoma City Campus, OK
University of Phoenix Online Campus, AZ
University of Phoenix–Oregon Campus, OR
University of Phoenix–Phoenix Campus, AZ
University of Phoenix–Pittsburgh Campus, PA
University of Phoenix–Sacramento Valley Campus, CA
University of Phoenix–San Diego Campus, CA
University of Phoenix–Southern Arizona Campus, AZ
University of Phoenix–Southern California Campus, CA
University of Phoenix–Southern Colorado Campus, CO
University of Phoenix–Springfield Campus, MO
University of Phoenix–Tulsa Campus, OK
University of Phoenix–Utah Campus, UT
University of Phoenix–Washington Campus, WA
University of Phoenix–West Florida Campus, FL
University of Phoenix–West Michigan Campus, MI
University of Phoenix–Wichita Campus, KS
University of Pittsburgh at Bradford, PA
University of Puget Sound, WA
University of Rochester, NY
University of St. Francis, IL
University of Saint Francis, IN
University of St. Thomas, MN
University of St. Thomas, TX
University of South Carolina, SC
The University of South Dakota, SD
University of Southern Indiana, IN
University of South Florida, FL
The University of Tampa, FL
The University of Tennessee at Martin, TN
The University of Texas at Austin, TX
The University of Texas at San Antonio, TX
The University of Texas–Pan American, TX
University of the Ozarks, AR
University of Tulsa, OK
University of Vermont, VT
University of Washington, WA
University of West Georgia, GA
University of Wisconsin–Green Bay, WI
University of Wisconsin–La Crosse, WI
University of Wisconsin–Stevens Point, WI
University of Wisconsin–Superior, WI
University of Wisconsin–Whitewater, WI
University of Wyoming, WY
Utah State University, UT
Valdosta State University, GA
Valley City State University, ND
Virginia Polytechnic Institute and State University, VA
Virginia State University, VA
Walla Walla College, WA
Walsh University, OH
Warner Pacific College, OR
Washington State University, WA
Washington University in St. Louis, MO
Wayland Baptist University, TX
Wayne State College, NE
Western Carolina University, NC
Western Illinois University, IL

Western Oregon University, OR
Western Washington University, WA
Westminster College, UT
West Virginia University, WV
Wichita State University, KS
Widener University, PA
Wilkes University, PA
Wilson College, PA
Wisconsin Lutheran College, WI
Xavier University, OH

Creative Arts/Performance

Applied Art and Design

Arcadia University, PA
Arizona State University, AZ
The Art Institute of Portland, OR
Auburn University, AL
Bloomfield College, NJ
Bowie State University, MD
Brenau University, GA
Brigham Young University, UT
California College of the Arts, CA
California Institute of the Arts, CA
California Polytechnic State University, San Luis Obispo, CA
California State University, Chico, CA
Carthage College, WI
Central Michigan University, MI
Central Washington University, WA
Chester College of New England, NH
City College of the City University of New York, NY
Claflin University, SC
Clemson University, SC
College for Creative Studies, MI
The College of New Rochelle, NY
Colorado State University-Pueblo, CO
Columbia College, MO
Columbia College Chicago, IL
Concordia University, CA
Converse College, SC
Corcoran College of Art and Design, DC
Dana College, NE
Eastern Michigan University, MI
Fashion Institute of Technology, NY
Flagler College, FL
Friends University, KS
Georgia College & State University, GA
Grace College, IN
Graceland University, IA
Illinois State University, IL
Indiana University of Pennsylvania, PA
Kean University, NJ
Keene State College, NH
Kutztown University of Pennsylvania, PA
La Roche College, PA
Lindenwood University, MO
Lindsey Wilson College, KY
Louisiana State University and Agricultural and Mechanical College, LA
Massachusetts College of Liberal Arts, MA
Memphis College of Art, TN
Meredith College, NC
Minnesota State University Mankato, MN
Mississippi State University, MS
Missouri State University, MO
Mount Ida College, MA
Mount Mary College, WI
Murray State University, KY
New England College, NH
New Mexico State University, NM
North Carolina School of the Arts, NC
Northeastern State University, OK
Northern Illinois University, IL
Northern Michigan University, MI
North Georgia College & State University, GA
Ohio University, OH
Ohio University–Chillicothe, OH
Ohio University–Eastern, OH
Ohio University–Lancaster, OH
Ohio University–Southern Campus, OH
Ohio University–Zanesville, OH
Oral Roberts University, OK
Otis College of Art and Design, CA
Radford University, VA
Rice University, TX
The Richard Stockton College of New Jersey, NJ
Ringling College of Art and Design, FL
Rivier College, NH
Rochester Institute of Technology, NY
Sacred Heart University, CT
St. Cloud State University, MN
Saint Mary-of-the-Woods College, IN
Salisbury University, MD
Seton Hill University, PA
Shepherd University, WV
Silver Lake College, WI
Slippery Rock University of Pennsylvania, PA
Sonoma State University, CA
Southern Illinois University Carbondale, IL
State University of New York at Fredonia, NY
State University of New York College at Geneseo, NY
Stephen F. Austin State University, TX
Stetson University, FL
Texas State University-San Marcos, TX
Texas Tech University, TX
Texas Woman's University, TX
The University of Akron, OH
University of Bridgeport, CT
University of Central Missouri, MO
University of Central Oklahoma, OK
University of Delaware, DE
University of Idaho, ID
University of Illinois at Chicago, IL
University of Illinois at Springfield, IL
University of Illinois at Urbana–Champaign, IL
University of Kansas, KS
University of Maine, ME
University of Maryland, College Park, MD
University of Nebraska at Kearney, NE
The University of North Carolina at Chapel Hill, NC
University of Northern Iowa, IA
University of St. Francis, IL
University of South Florida, FL
The University of Texas at El Paso, TX
University of West Florida, FL
University of Wisconsin–Stevens Point, WI
University of Wisconsin–Stout, WI
Utah State University, UT
Valley City State University, ND
Virginia Commonwealth University, VA
Virginia Intermont College, VA
Virginia Polytechnic Institute and State University, VA
Virginia State University, VA
Washington State University, WA
Washington University in St. Louis, MO
Watkins College of Art and Design, TN
Wayne State College, NE
Western Illinois University, IL
Western Washington University, WA
Wichita State University, KS
Woodbury University, CA

Art/Fine Arts

Abilene Christian University, TX
Adams State College, CO
Adelphi University, NY
Alabama State University, AL
Albion College, MI
Alderson-Broaddus College, WV
Alfred University, NY
Alma College, MI
Alverno College, WI
Anderson University, IN
Arcadia University, PA
Arizona State University, AZ
Arkansas State University, AR
Armstrong Atlantic State University, GA
Auburn University, AL
Augustana College, IL
Augustana College, SD
Augusta State University, GA
Austin College, TX
Austin Peay State University, TN
Averett University, VA
Baker University, KS
Barton College, NC
Baylor University, TX
Bellarmine University, KY
Berry College, GA
Bethany College, KS
Bethany Lutheran College, MN
Bethel College, IN
Bethel College, KS
Bethel University, MN
Birmingham-Southern College, AL
Black Hills State University, SD
Bloomfield College, NJ
Bluffton University, OH
Boise State University, ID
Boston University, MA
Bowie State University, MD
Bowling Green State University, OH
Bradley University, IL
Brenau University, GA
Brevard College, NC
Brigham Young University, UT
Brigham Young University–Hawaii, HI
Bryan College, TN
Bucknell University, PA
Buena Vista University, IA
Butler University, IN
California College of the Arts, CA
California Institute of the Arts, CA
California Polytechnic State University, San Luis Obispo, CA
California State University, Chico, CA
California State University, Fresno, CA
California State University, Fullerton, CA

California State University, Los Angeles, CA
California State University, San Bernardino, CA
California State University, Stanislaus, CA
Calvin College, MI
Campbellsville University, KY
Campbell University, NC
Canisius College, NY
Carroll College, WI
Carson-Newman College, TN
Carthage College, WI
Case Western Reserve University, OH
Cedar Crest College, PA
Centenary College of Louisiana, LA
Central College, IA
Central Michigan University, MI
Central Washington University, WA
Chapman University, CA
Chester College of New England, NH
Christopher Newport University, VA
City College of the City University of New York, NY
Claflin University, SC
Clarion University of Pennsylvania, PA
Clarke College, IA
Clemson University, SC
The Cleveland Institute of Art, OH
Cleveland State University, OH
Coastal Carolina University, SC
Coe College, IA
College for Creative Studies, MI
College of Charleston, SC
The College of New Jersey, NJ
The College of New Rochelle, NY
College of Notre Dame of Maryland, MD
College of St. Catherine, MN
The College of Saint Rose, NY
College of Staten Island of the City University of New York, NY
College of Visual Arts, MN
Colorado State University, CO
Colorado State University-Pueblo, CO
Columbia College, MO
Columbia College Chicago, IL
Columbus College of Art & Design, OH
Columbus State University, GA
Concordia University, IL
Concordia University, NE
Concordia University, St. Paul, MN
Concord University, WV
Cooper Union for the Advancement of Science and Art, NY
Cornell College, IA
Creighton University, NE
Culver-Stockton College, MO
Cumberland University, TN
Dana College, NE
Davidson College, NC
Davis & Elkins College, WV
Denison University, OH
Dickinson State University, ND
Doane College, NE
Drake University, IA
Drury University, MO
Eastern Michigan University, MI
East Tennessee State University, TN
Edgewood College, WI
Elizabethtown College, PA
Elmhurst College, IL
Elon University, NC
Emporia State University, KS
Endicott College, MA
Eureka College, IL
Evangel University, MO
Fairfield University, CT
Flagler College, FL
Florida Gulf Coast University, FL
Fort Lewis College, CO
Francis Marion University, SC
Franklin College, IN
Freed-Hardeman University, TN
Fresno Pacific University, CA
Friends University, KS
Frostburg State University, MD
Furman University, SC
George Fox University, OR
Georgetown College, KY
Georgia College & State University, GA
Georgia Southern University, GA
Goucher College, MD
Grace College, IN
Grand Valley State University, MI
Grand View College, IA
Green Mountain College, VT
Gustavus Adolphus College, MN
Harding University, AR
Hardin-Simmons University, TX
Hastings College, NE
Hendrix College, AR
Hillsdale College, MI
Hobart and William Smith Colleges, NY
Hofstra University, NY
Hope College, MI
Houghton College, NY
Houston Baptist University, TX
Huntington University, IN
Idaho State University, ID
Illinois College, IL
Illinois State University, IL
Illinois Wesleyan University, IL
Indiana State University, IN
Indiana University of Pennsylvania, PA
Iowa Wesleyan College, IA
Jacksonville State University, AL
James Madison University, VA
Jamestown College, ND
Johnson Bible College, TN
Judson College, AL
Judson College, IL
Kalamazoo College, MI
Kean University, NJ
Keene State College, NH
Kent State University, OH
Kentucky Wesleyan College, KY
Knox College, IL
Kutztown University of Pennsylvania, PA
Lake Forest College, IL
Lakeland College, WI
Lesley University, MA
Lewis-Clark State College, ID
Limestone College, SC
Lindenwood University, MO
Lipscomb University, TN
Lock Haven University of Pennsylvania, PA
Longwood University, VA
Louisiana State University and Agricultural and Mechanical College, LA
Lourdes College, OH
Loyola University Chicago, IL
Lubbock Christian University, TX
Lycoming College, PA
Lyme Academy College of Fine Arts, CT
Lyon College, AR
MacMurray College, IL
Maine College of Art, ME
Mansfield University of Pennsylvania, PA
Maryville University of Saint Louis, MO
Marywood University, PA
Massachusetts College of Liberal Arts, MA
McMurry University, TX
Memphis College of Art, TN
Mercer University, GA
Meredith College, NC
Mesa State College, CO
Messiah College, PA
Metropolitan State College of Denver, CO
Miami University, OH
Midwestern State University, TX
Millersville University of Pennsylvania, PA
Milligan College, TN
Millsaps College, MS
Mills College, CA
Minnesota State University Mankato, MN
Mississippi State University, MS
Missouri State University, MO
Molloy College, NY
Montana State University, MT
Montana State University–Billings, MT
Montclair State University, NJ
Montreat College, NC
Morehead State University, KY
Morningside College, IA
Mount Ida College, MA
Mount Mary College, WI
Mount Mercy College, IA
Mount Olive College, NC
Mount St. Mary's University, MD
Mount Union College, OH
Murray State University, KY
Nazareth College of Rochester, NY
Nebraska Wesleyan University, NE
New England College, NH
New Jersey City University, NJ
Newman University, KS
New Mexico State University, NM
North Central College, IL
North Dakota State University, ND
Northeastern Illinois University, IL
Northeastern State University, OK
Northern Arizona University, AZ
Northern Illinois University, IL
Northern State University, SD
Northland College, WI
Northwestern College, IA
Northwestern Oklahoma State University, OK
Northwestern State University of Louisiana, LA
Northwest Nazarene University, ID
Ohio University, OH
Ohio University–Chillicothe, OH
Ohio University–Eastern, OH
Ohio University–Lancaster, OH
Ohio University–Southern Campus, OH
Ohio University–Zanesville, OH
Ohio Wesleyan University, OH

Oklahoma Baptist University, OK
Oklahoma Panhandle State University, OK
Oklahoma State University, OK
Olivet College, MI
Oral Roberts University, OK
Oregon College of Art & Craft, OR
Otis College of Art and Design, CA
Ouachita Baptist University, AR
Pacific Lutheran University, WA
Pacific Northwest College of Art, OR
Piedmont College, GA
Point Loma Nazarene University, CA
Portland State University, OR
Purchase College, State University of New York, NY
Radford University, VA
Randolph College, VA
Reinhardt College, GA
Rhodes College, TN
Rice University, TX
The Richard Stockton College of New Jersey, NJ
Ringling College of Art and Design, FL
Ripon College, WI
Rivier College, NH
Roanoke College, VA
Roberts Wesleyan College, NY
Rochester Institute of Technology, NY
Rollins College, FL
Rosemont College, PA
Sacred Heart University, CT
Sage College of Albany, NY
St. Ambrose University, IA
St. Cloud State University, MN
Saint Francis University, PA
St. Gregory's University, OK
Saint John's University, MN
Saint Louis University, MO
Saint Mary-of-the-Woods College, IN
Saint Mary's College, IN
Saint Michael's College, VT
St. Norbert College, WI
San Diego State University, CA
San Francisco Art Institute, CA
Savannah College of Art and Design, GA
School of Visual Arts, NY
Seattle Pacific University, WA
Seton Hill University, PA
Shepherd University, WV
Shimer College, IL
Silver Lake College, WI
Simpson College, IA
Slippery Rock University of Pennsylvania, PA
Sonoma State University, CA
South Dakota State University, SD
Southeastern Louisiana University, LA
Southern Adventist University, TN
Southern Arkansas University–Magnolia, AR
Southern Illinois University Carbondale, IL
Southern Illinois University Edwardsville, IL
Southern Methodist University, TX
Southern Oregon University, OR
Southern Wesleyan University, SC
Southwest Baptist University, MO
Southwestern University, TX
Southwest Minnesota State University, MN
Spring Arbor University, MI
State University of New York at Fredonia, NY
State University of New York at Plattsburgh, NY
State University of New York College at Geneseo, NY
State University of New York College at Potsdam, NY
Stephen F. Austin State University, TX
Stetson University, FL
Sweet Briar College, VA
Syracuse University, NY
Temple University, PA
Tennessee Technological University, TN
Texas A&M University–Commerce, TX
Texas A&M University–Corpus Christi, TX
Texas Christian University, TX
Texas Tech University, TX
Texas Woman's University, TX
Thomas More College, KY
Towson University, MD
Transylvania University, KY
Union University, TN
The University of Akron, OH
The University of Alabama, AL
The University of Alabama at Birmingham, AL
The University of Alabama in Huntsville, AL
University of Alaska Fairbanks, AK
The University of Arizona, AZ
University of California, Irvine, CA
University of California, Riverside, CA
University of Central Missouri, MO
University of Central Oklahoma, OK
University of Colorado at Boulder, CO
University of Connecticut, CT
University of Dallas, TX
University of Dayton, OH
University of Delaware, DE
University of Denver, CO
University of Evansville, IN
University of Florida, FL
University of Great Falls, MT
University of Hartford, CT
University of Hawaii at Hilo, HI
University of Hawaii at Manoa, HI
University of Idaho, ID
University of Illinois at Chicago, IL
University of Illinois at Springfield, IL
University of Illinois at Urbana–Champaign, IL
University of Kansas, KS
University of La Verne, CA
University of Maine, ME
University of Maryland, Baltimore County, MD
University of Maryland, College Park, MD
University of Massachusetts Amherst, MA
University of Miami, FL
University of Michigan–Dearborn, MI
University of Michigan–Flint, MI
University of Missouri–St. Louis, MO
The University of Montana, MT
University of Nebraska at Kearney, NE
University of Nebraska at Omaha, NE
University of New Hampshire, NH
University of North Alabama, AL
The University of North Carolina at Asheville, NC
The University of North Carolina at Chapel Hill, NC
The University of North Carolina at Greensboro, NC
The University of North Carolina Wilmington, NC
University of North Dakota, ND
University of Northern Iowa, IA
University of North Florida, FL
University of Oklahoma, OK
University of Oregon, OR
University of Puget Sound, WA
University of Redlands, CA
University of Richmond, VA
University of St. Francis, IL
University of Saint Francis, IN
University of Science and Arts of Oklahoma, OK
University of South Carolina, SC
The University of South Dakota, SD
University of Southern Indiana, IN
University of Southern Mississippi, MS
University of South Florida, FL
The University of Tampa, FL
The University of Tennessee at Martin, TN
The University of Texas at Austin, TX
The University of Texas at Brownsville, TX
The University of Texas at El Paso, TX
The University of Texas at San Antonio, TX
The University of Texas at Tyler, TX
The University of Texas of the Permian Basin, TX
The University of Texas–Pan American, TX
University of the Cumberlands, KY
University of the Incarnate Word, TX
University of the Ozarks, AR
University of Tulsa, OK
University of Washington, WA
University of West Florida, FL
University of West Georgia, GA
University of Wisconsin–Green Bay, WI
University of Wisconsin–La Crosse, WI
University of Wisconsin–Stout, WI
University of Wisconsin–Whitewater, WI
Ursinus College, PA
Utah State University, UT
Valdosta State University, GA
Valley City State University, ND
Valley Forge Christian College, PA
Valparaiso University, IN
Virginia Commonwealth University, VA
Virginia Intermont College, VA
Virginia Polytechnic Institute and State University, VA
Virginia State University, VA
Wabash College, IN
Wake Forest University, NC
Warren Wilson College, NC
Wartburg College, IA
Washington State University, WA
Washington University in St. Louis, MO
Watkins College of Art and Design, TN
Wayland Baptist University, TX
Wayne State College, NE
Wayne State University, MI
Webster University, MO

Western Carolina University, NC
Western Oregon University, OR
Western Washington University, WA
West Liberty State College, WV
Westminster College, UT
Westmont College, CA
West Virginia University, WV
West Virginia Wesleyan College, WV
Whitman College, WA
Whitworth University, WA
Wichita State University, KS
William Carey College, MS
William Jewell College, MO
Williams Baptist College, AR
Winona State University, MN
Winthrop University, SC
Wisconsin Lutheran College, WI
Wittenberg University, OH
Xavier University, OH

Cinema/Film/Broadcasting

Arizona State University, AZ
Arkansas State University, AR
Auburn University, AL
Azusa Pacific University, CA
Baker University, KS
Baylor University, TX
Bloomfield College, NJ
Bowling Green State University, OH
Brenau University, GA
Brigham Young University, UT
Butler University, IN
California Institute of the Arts, CA
California Polytechnic State University, San Luis Obispo, CA
California State University, Chico, CA
Central Michigan University, MI
Chapman University, CA
City College of the City University of New York, NY
The College of New Rochelle, NY
Colorado State University-Pueblo, CO
Columbia College Chicago, IL
DeSales University, PA
Eastern Michigan University, MI
Five Towns College, NY
Flagler College, FL
Florida State University, FL
Freed-Hardeman University, TN
Georgia Southern University, GA
Grace University, NE
Harding University, AR
Illinois State University, IL
James Madison University, VA
Kalamazoo College, MI
Keene State College, NH
Lindenwood University, MO
Marywood University, PA
Massachusetts College of Liberal Arts, MA
Mississippi State University, MS
Montana State University, MT
Montclair State University, NJ
Morehead State University, KY
Morningside College, IA
Mount Union College, OH
North Carolina School of the Arts, NC
North Central College, IL
Northern Arizona University, AZ
Northwestern Oklahoma State University, OK
Northwestern State University of Louisiana, LA
Ohio University, OH
Ohio University–Chillicothe, OH
Ohio University–Eastern, OH
Ohio University–Lancaster, OH
Ohio University–Southern Campus, OH
Ohio University–Zanesville, OH
Oral Roberts University, OK
Purchase College, State University of New York, NY
Radford University, VA
Rochester Institute of Technology, NY
St. Cloud State University, MN
Saint Joseph's College, IN
Sonoma State University, CA
Southeastern Louisiana University, LA
Southern Illinois University Carbondale, IL
Southern Methodist University, TX
Texas Christian University, TX
Texas Woman's University, TX
Union University, TN
The University of Alabama, AL
University of California, San Diego, CA
University of Central Florida, FL
University of Central Missouri, MO
University of Colorado at Boulder, CO
University of Illinois at Urbana–Champaign, IL
University of Kansas, KS
University of Maryland, Baltimore County, MD
University of Miami, FL
University of Michigan–Dearborn, MI
The University of North Carolina at Greensboro, NC
The University of North Carolina Wilmington, NC
University of South Florida, FL
University of Wisconsin–Whitewater, WI
Virginia Polytechnic Institute and State University, VA
Washington State University, WA
Washington University in St. Louis, MO
Watkins College of Art and Design, TN
Western Illinois University, IL
Western Washington University, WA
Westminster College, PA

Creative Writing

Alderson-Broaddus College, WV
Arizona State University, AZ
Arkansas Tech University, AR
Auburn University, AL
Augustana College, IL
Augusta State University, GA
Austin Peay State University, TN
Bowling Green State University, OH
Brenau University, GA
Brigham Young University, UT
Brigham Young University–Hawaii, HI
Bucknell University, PA
California College of the Arts, CA
California Institute of the Arts, CA
California Polytechnic State University, San Luis Obispo, CA
California State University, Chico, CA
Campbell University, NC
Case Western Reserve University, OH
Central Michigan University, MI
Chapman University, CA
Chester College of New England, NH
City College of the City University of New York, NY
Cleveland State University, OH
Coe College, IA
The College of New Rochelle, NY
Colorado State University, CO
Columbia College Chicago, IL
Creighton University, NE
Davidson College, NC
DeSales University, PA
Dickinson State University, ND
Drury University, MO
Duke University, NC
Eastern Michigan University, MI
Edgewood College, WI
Emporia State University, KS
Frostburg State University, MD
Furman University, SC
Georgia College & State University, GA
Graceland University, IA
Grove City College, PA
Hampshire College, MA
Hardin-Simmons University, TX
Hobart and William Smith Colleges, NY
Hood College, MD
Hope College, MI
Illinois State University, IL
Knox College, IL
Lake Forest College, IL
Lakeland College, WI
Lewis-Clark State College, ID
Lycoming College, PA
Maharishi University of Management, IA
Meredith College, NC
Mesa State College, CO
Michigan State University, MI
Minnesota State University Mankato, MN
Mississippi State University, MS
Mount Marty College, SD
Murray State University, KY
New England College, NH
Northeastern Illinois University, IL
Northern Arizona University, AZ
Northern Illinois University, IL
Northwestern State University of Louisiana, LA
The Ohio State University, OH
Oklahoma State University, OK
Purchase College, State University of New York, NY
Randolph College, VA
Rice University, TX
The Richard Stockton College of New Jersey, NJ
Rockhurst University, MO
Sacred Heart University, CT
St. Cloud State University, MN
Saint Mary-of-the-Woods College, IN
San Diego State University, CA
Seton Hill University, PA
Shimer College, IL
Sonoma State University, CA
Southern Illinois University Carbondale, IL
Southern Methodist University, TX
Southern Oregon University, OR
Southern Wesleyan University, SC
Southwest Minnesota State University, MN

State University of New York at Binghamton, NY
State University of New York College at Geneseo, NY
Stephens College, MO
The University of Akron, OH
The University of Alabama, AL
University of Alaska Fairbanks, AK
University of California, Riverside, CA
University of Central Missouri, MO
University of Colorado at Boulder, CO
University of Idaho, ID
University of Illinois at Urbana–Champaign, IL
University of Kansas, KS
University of Maine, ME
University of Maryland, Baltimore County, MD
University of Michigan–Dearborn, MI
The University of Montana, MT
University of Nebraska at Omaha, NE
The University of North Carolina Wilmington, NC
University of Redlands, CA
The University of South Dakota, SD
University of Southern Indiana, IN
University of South Florida, FL
The University of Tampa, FL
University of Washington, WA
The University of West Alabama, AL
University of Wisconsin–Stevens Point, WI
University of Wisconsin–Whitewater, WI
Ursinus College, PA
Virginia Polytechnic Institute and State University, VA
Wabash College, IN
Wake Forest University, NC
Warren Wilson College, NC
Washington College, MD
Washington State University, WA
Washington University in St. Louis, MO
Wayne State College, NE
Webster University, MO
Western Washington University, WA
Wichita State University, KS

Dance

Adelphi University, NY
Alma College, MI
Arizona State University, AZ
Baker University, KS
Birmingham-Southern College, AL
Boise State University, ID
Bowling Green State University, OH
Brenau University, GA
Brigham Young University, UT
Bucknell University, PA
Butler University, IN
California Institute of the Arts, CA
California Polytechnic State University, San Luis Obispo, CA
California State University, Chico, CA
Case Western Reserve University, OH
Cedar Crest College, PA
Centenary College of Louisiana, LA
Central Michigan University, MI
Chapman University, CA
Cleveland State University, OH
The College of New Rochelle, NY
The College of Wooster, OH
Colorado State University, CO
Columbia College Chicago, IL
Columbus State University, GA
Denison University, OH
DeSales University, PA
Duquesne University, PA
Eastern Michigan University, MI
Florida State University, FL
Friends University, KS
Frostburg State University, MD
Goucher College, MD
Hawai'i Pacific University, HI
Hendrix College, AR
Hobart and William Smith Colleges, NY
Hofstra University, NY
Hope College, MI
Indiana University of Pennsylvania, PA
Ithaca College, NY
James Madison University, VA
Keene State College, NH
Knox College, IL
Kutztown University of Pennsylvania, PA
Lambuth University, TN
Lindenwood University, MO
Manhattanville College, NY
Marymount Manhattan College, NY
Middle Tennessee State University, TN
Mississippi State University, MS
Missouri State University, MO
Missouri Valley College, MO
Montana State University, MT
Montclair State University, NJ
Murray State University, KY
New Jersey City University, NJ
North Carolina School of the Arts, NC
Northeastern Illinois University, IL
Northeastern State University, OK
Northern Illinois University, IL
Northwestern Oklahoma State University, OK
Northwestern State University of Louisiana, LA
The Ohio State University, OH
Ohio University, OH
Ohio University–Chillicothe, OH
Ohio University–Eastern, OH
Ohio University–Lancaster, OH
Ohio University–Southern Campus, OH
Ohio University–Zanesville, OH
Ohio Wesleyan University, OH
Pacific Lutheran University, WA
Palm Beach Atlantic University, FL
Purchase College, State University of New York, NY
Radford University, VA
The Richard Stockton College of New Jersey, NJ
St. Ambrose University, IA
St. Gregory's University, OK
Saint Mary-of-the-Woods College, IN
San Diego State University, CA
Santa Clara University, CA
Shenandoah University, VA
Slippery Rock University of Pennsylvania, PA
Sonoma State University, CA
Southeastern Louisiana University, LA
Southern Arkansas University–Magnolia, AR
Southern Illinois University Carbondale, IL
Southern Illinois University Edwardsville, IL
Southern Methodist University, TX
Southern Utah University, UT
Spelman College, GA
State University of New York at Fredonia, NY
State University of New York College at Geneseo, NY
State University of New York College at Potsdam, NY
Stephens College, MO
Texas Christian University, TX
Texas Tech University, TX
Texas Woman's University, TX
Towson University, MD
The University of Akron, OH
The University of Alabama, AL
The University of Arizona, AZ
University of California, Irvine, CA
University of California, Riverside, CA
University of California, San Diego, CA
University of Colorado at Boulder, CO
University of Florida, FL
University of Great Falls, MT
University of Hartford, CT
University of Hawaii at Manoa, HI
University of Idaho, ID
University of Illinois at Urbana–Champaign, IL
University of Kansas, KS
University of Maryland, Baltimore County, MD
University of Maryland, College Park, MD
University of Massachusetts Amherst, MA
The University of Montana, MT
University of New Hampshire, NH
The University of North Carolina at Greensboro, NC
University of Northern Colorado, CO
University of Oklahoma, OK
University of Oregon, OR
University of Richmond, VA
University of Saint Francis, IN
University of Southern Mississippi, MS
University of South Florida, FL
The University of Texas at Austin, TX
The University of Texas of the Permian Basin, TX
The University of Texas–Pan American, TX
University of the Incarnate Word, TX
University of Washington, WA
The University of West Alabama, AL
University of Wisconsin–Green Bay, WI
University of Wisconsin–Stevens Point, WI
University of Wyoming, WY
Virginia Commonwealth University, VA
Virginia Intermont College, VA
Virginia State University, VA
Wake Forest University, NC
Washington University in St. Louis, MO
Wayne State University, MI
Western Illinois University, IL
Western Oregon University, OR
Western Washington University, WA
Wichita State University, KS
Winthrop University, SC
Wittenberg University, OH

Debating

Abilene Christian University, TX
Alderson-Broaddus College, WV
Arizona State University, AZ
Arkansas State University, AR
Augustana College, IL
Austin Peay State University, TN
Azusa Pacific University, CA
Baker University, KS
Baylor University, TX
Berry College, GA
Bethany Lutheran College, MN
Bethel College, KS
Bethel University, MN
Boise State University, ID
Bowling Green State University, OH
California Polytechnic State University, San Luis Obispo, CA
California State University, Chico, CA
Carson-Newman College, TN
Cedarville University, OH
The College of New Rochelle, NY
College of the Southwest, NM
Concordia College, MN
Creighton University, NE
Culver-Stockton College, MO
Doane College, NE
Eastern Michigan University, MI
Emory University, GA
Emporia State University, KS
Evangel University, MO
Ferris State University, MI
Florida College, FL
George Fox University, OR
The George Washington University, DC
Georgia College & State University, GA
Gonzaga University, WA
Gustavus Adolphus College, MN
Harding University, AR
Hastings College, NE
Hillsdale College, MI
Idaho State University, ID
Illinois State University, IL
Kentucky Christian University, KY
Lewis & Clark College, OR
Lewis-Clark State College, ID
Linfield College, OR
Louisiana Tech University, LA
Loyola University Chicago, IL
Malone College, OH
Marist College, NY
Mercer University, GA
Methodist University, NC
Michigan State University, MI
Middle Tennessee State University, TN
Minnesota State University Mankato, MN
Mississippi State University, MS
Missouri State University, MO
Morehead State University, KY
Mount Union College, OH
Murray State University, KY
North Central College, IL
North Dakota State University, ND
Northeastern State University, OK
Northern Arizona University, AZ
Northern Illinois University, IL
Northwestern Oklahoma State University, OK
Northwest Nazarene University, ID
Northwest University, WA
Ohio University, OH
Ohio University–Chillicothe, OH
Ohio University–Eastern, OH
Ohio University–Lancaster, OH
Ohio University–Southern Campus, OH
Ohio University–Zanesville, OH
Oklahoma Panhandle State University, OK
Pacific Lutheran University, WA
Point Loma Nazarene University, CA
Regis University, CO
Rice University, TX
Ripon College, WI
Santa Clara University, CA
South Dakota State University, SD
Southeastern Louisiana University, LA
Southern Illinois University Carbondale, IL
Southwest Baptist University, MO
Southwest Minnesota State University, MN
Tennessee Technological University, TN
The University of Akron, OH
The University of Alabama, AL
University of Arkansas at Monticello, AR
University of Central Missouri, MO
University of Denver, CO
University of Kansas, KS
University of La Verne, CA
University of Miami, FL
University of Michigan–Dearborn, MI
University of Missouri–Kansas City, MO
University of Nebraska at Kearney, NE
University of Nebraska at Omaha, NE
University of North Dakota, ND
University of Puget Sound, WA
University of Redlands, CA
University of Saint Francis, IN
University of St. Thomas, TX
University of South Carolina, SC
The University of South Dakota, SD
University of Southern California, CA
University of South Florida, FL
The University of Texas at San Antonio, TX
University of the Cumberlands, KY
University of Vermont, VT
University of West Georgia, GA
University of Wyoming, WY
Vanguard University of Southern California, CA
Wake Forest University, NC
Wayne State College, NE
Wayne State University, MI
Webster University, MO
Western Illinois University, IL
West Virginia University, WV
Whitman College, WA
Wichita State University, KS
Willamette University, OR
William Carey College, MS
William Jewell College, MO
Winona State University, MN

Journalism/Publications

Abilene Christian University, TX
Albright College, PA
Alderson-Broaddus College, WV
Arizona State University, AZ
Arkansas State University, AR
Auburn University, AL
Austin Peay State University, TN
Averett University, VA
Baker University, KS
Baylor University, TX
Berry College, GA
Bethany Lutheran College, MN
Bethel College, IN
Boise State University, ID
Bowling Green State University, OH
Brenau University, GA
Brevard College, NC
Brigham Young University, UT
Brigham Young University–Hawaii, HI
Bryan College, TN
California Polytechnic State University, San Luis Obispo, CA
California State University, Chico, CA
California State University, Fresno, CA
California State University, Los Angeles, CA
California State University, Northridge, CA
Campbellsville University, KY
Campbell University, NC
Carroll College, WI
Carson-Newman College, TN
Central Michigan University, MI
Central Washington University, WA
The College of New Rochelle, NY
Colorado State University-Pueblo, CO
Columbia College Chicago, IL
Concordia University, St. Paul, MN
Concord University, WV
Dickinson State University, ND
Dordt College, IA
East Tennessee State University, TN
Elon University, NC
Faulkner University, AL
Ferris State University, MI
Florida College, FL
Franklin College, IN
Freed-Hardeman University, TN
Fresno Pacific University, CA
Frostburg State University, MD
Georgia College & State University, GA
Glenville State College, WV
Harding University, AR
Hardin-Simmons University, TX
Hawai'i Pacific University, HI
Hillsdale College, MI
Huntington University, IN
Indiana University of Pennsylvania, PA
Ithaca College, NY
Jacksonville State University, AL
James Madison University, VA
Kent State University, OH
Lakeland College, WI
LeMoyne-Owen College, TN
Lipscomb University, TN
Lock Haven University of Pennsylvania, PA
Louisiana State University and Agricultural and Mechanical College, LA
Louisiana Tech University, LA
Loyola University Chicago, IL
Lubbock Christian University, TX
Macon State College, GA
Malone College, OH
Mansfield University of Pennsylvania, PA
Marywood University, PA
Massachusetts College of Liberal Arts, MA
Mesa State College, CO

Michigan State University, MI
Middle Tennessee State University, TN
Mississippi State University, MS
Missouri State University, MO
Missouri Valley College, MO
Morehead State University, KY
Morningside College, IA
Mount Union College, OH
Murray State University, KY
Newman University, KS
New Mexico State University, NM
North Central College, IL
North Dakota State University, ND
Northeastern Illinois University, IL
Northeastern State University, OK
Northern Arizona University, AZ
Northern Illinois University, IL
North Greenville University, SC
Northwestern College, IA
Northwestern Oklahoma State University, OK
Northwestern State University of Louisiana, LA
Northwest Nazarene University, ID
Nyack College, NY
Oglethorpe University, GA
The Ohio State University, OH
Ohio University, OH
Ohio University–Chillicothe, OH
Ohio University–Eastern, OH
Ohio University–Lancaster, OH
Ohio University–Southern Campus, OH
Ohio University–Zanesville, OH
Ohio Valley University, WV
Oklahoma State University, OK
Olivet College, MI
Oral Roberts University, OK
Ouachita Baptist University, AR
Rice University, TX
The Richard Stockton College of New Jersey, NJ
Rivier College, NH
St. Cloud State University, MN
St. Gregory's University, OK
Saint Mary-of-the-Woods College, IN
San Diego State University, CA
Seton Hill University, PA
Sonoma State University, CA
South Dakota State University, SD
Southeastern University, FL
Southern Adventist University, TN
Southern Illinois University Carbondale, IL
Southern Methodist University, TX
Southern Oregon University, OR
Southern Utah University, UT
Southern Wesleyan University, SC
Southwest Minnesota State University, MN
State University of New York at Plattsburgh, NY
State University of New York College at Geneseo, NY
State University of New York College at Oneonta, NY
Stephen F. Austin State University, TX
Texas A&M University–Commerce, TX
Texas Christian University, TX
Texas Lutheran University, TX
Texas State University-San Marcos, TX
Texas Tech University, TX
Texas Woman's University, TX
Union University, TN
The University of Akron, OH
The University of Alabama, AL
University of Arkansas at Monticello, AR
University of California, San Diego, CA
University of Central Missouri, MO
University of Central Oklahoma, OK
University of Colorado at Boulder, CO
University of Florida, FL
University of Hawaii at Manoa, HI
University of Idaho, ID
University of Illinois at Springfield, IL
University of Illinois at Urbana–Champaign, IL
University of Kansas, KS
University of La Verne, CA
University of Maine, ME
University of Massachusetts Amherst, MA
University of Michigan, MI
University of Michigan–Dearborn, MI
University of Missouri–Columbia, MO
The University of Montana, MT
University of Nebraska at Kearney, NE
University of Nebraska at Omaha, NE
University of North Alabama, AL
The University of North Carolina at Chapel Hill, NC
The University of North Carolina at Pembroke, NC
University of Oklahoma, OK
University of Oregon, OR
University of St. Thomas, MN
University of South Carolina, SC
University of South Florida, FL
The University of Tampa, FL
The University of Tennessee at Martin, TN
The University of Texas at Austin, TX
The University of Texas at El Paso, TX
The University of Texas–Pan American, TX
University of Washington, WA
The University of West Alabama, AL
University of West Georgia, GA
University of Wisconsin–Whitewater, WI
Utah State University, UT
Valley City State University, ND
Vanderbilt University, TN
Virginia Polytechnic Institute and State University, VA
Wabash College, IN
Wake Forest University, NC
Wartburg College, IA
Washington State University, WA
Wayland Baptist University, TX
Wayne State College, NE
Webber International University, FL
Western Illinois University, IL
Western Washington University, WA
Westminster College, UT
Whitworth University, WA
Wichita State University, KS
William Carey College, MS
William Jewell College, MO

Music

Abilene Christian University, TX
Adams State College, CO
Adelphi University, NY
Agnes Scott College, GA
Alabama State University, AL
Albion College, MI
Alcorn State University, MS
Alderson-Broaddus College, WV
Alma College, MI
Alverno College, WI
Anderson University, IN
Andrews University, MI
Arizona State University, AZ
Arkansas State University, AR
Arkansas Tech University, AR
Armstrong Atlantic State University, GA
Asbury College, KY
Auburn University, AL
Augsburg College, MN
Augustana College, IL
Augustana College, SD
Augusta State University, GA
Aurora University, IL
Austin College, TX
Austin Peay State University, TN
Averett University, VA
Azusa Pacific University, CA
Baker University, KS
Baldwin-Wallace College, OH
Baptist Bible College, MO
The Baptist College of Florida, FL
Barton College, NC
Baylor University, TX
Bellarmine University, KY
Belmont University, TN
Beloit College, WI
Benedictine University, IL
Berklee College of Music, MA
Berry College, GA
Bethany College, KS
Bethany College, WV
Bethany Lutheran College, MN
Bethel College, IN
Bethel College, KS
Bethel University, MN
Bethesda Christian University, CA
Birmingham-Southern College, AL
Black Hills State University, SD
Bloomfield College, NJ
Blue Mountain College, MS
Bluffton University, OH
Boise State University, ID
Boston University, MA
Bowie State University, MD
Bowling Green State University, OH
Bradley University, IL
Brenau University, GA
Brevard College, NC
Bridgewater College, VA
Brigham Young University, UT
Brigham Young University–Hawaii, HI
Bryan College, TN
Bucknell University, PA
Buena Vista University, IA
Butler University, IN
California Institute of the Arts, CA
California Polytechnic State University, San Luis Obispo, CA
California State University, Chico, CA
California State University, East Bay, CA
California State University, Fresno, CA
California State University, Fullerton, CA
California State University, Los Angeles, CA

California State University, Northridge, CA
California State University, San Bernardino, CA
California State University, Stanislaus, CA
Calvin College, MI
Campbellsville University, KY
Campbell University, NC
Canisius College, NY
Capital University, OH
Carleton College, MN
Carroll College, WI
Carson-Newman College, TN
Carthage College, WI
Case Western Reserve University, OH
Catawba College, NC
The Catholic University of America, DC
Cedarville University, OH
Centenary College of Louisiana, LA
Central College, IA
Central Methodist University, MO
Central Michigan University, MI
Central State University, OH
Central Washington University, WA
Centre College, KY
Chapman University, CA
Christopher Newport University, VA
City College of the City University of New York, NY
Claflin University, SC
Clarke College, IA
Clear Creek Baptist Bible College, KY
Clearwater Christian College, FL
Cleveland Institute of Music, OH
Cleveland State University, OH
Coastal Carolina University, SC
Coe College, IA
College of Charleston, SC
The College of New Jersey, NJ
The College of New Rochelle, NY
College of St. Catherine, MN
College of Saint Mary, NE
The College of Saint Rose, NY
The College of St. Scholastica, MN
College of Staten Island of the City University of New York, NY
College of the Holy Cross, MA
College of the Southwest, NM
The College of William and Mary, VA
The College of Wooster, OH
Colorado School of Mines, CO
Colorado State University, CO
Colorado State University-Pueblo, CO
Columbia College, MO
Columbia College Chicago, IL
Columbia International University, SC
Columbus State University, GA
Concordia College, MN
Concordia University, CA
Concordia University, IL
Concordia University, NE
Concordia University at Austin, TX
Concordia University, St. Paul, MN
Concordia University Wisconsin, WI
Concord University, WV
Converse College, SC
Corban College, OR
Cornell College, IA
Crown College, MN
Culver-Stockton College, MO
Cumberland University, TN
Dakota State University, SD
Dallas Baptist University, TX
Dana College, NE
Davidson College, NC
Davis & Elkins College, WV
Delaware Valley College, PA
Denison University, OH
DeSales University, PA
Dickinson State University, ND
Doane College, NE
Dordt College, IA
Drake University, IA
Drury University, MO
Duquesne University, PA
East Central University, OK
Eastern Kentucky University, KY
Eastern Michigan University, MI
East Tennessee State University, TN
East Texas Baptist University, TX
Edgewood College, WI
Elizabethtown College, PA
Elmhurst College, IL
Elon University, NC
Emory University, GA
Emporia State University, KS
Erskine College, SC
Eugene Bible College, OR
Eureka College, IL
Evangel University, MO
Fairfield University, CT
Faulkner University, AL
Ferris State University, MI
Five Towns College, NY
Florida Atlantic University, FL
Florida College, FL
Florida Gulf Coast University, FL
Florida State University, FL
Fort Lewis College, CO
Francis Marion University, SC
Franklin & Marshall College, PA
Franklin College, IN
Freed-Hardeman University, TN
Fresno Pacific University, CA
Friends University, KS
Frostburg State University, MD
Furman University, SC
Gannon University, PA
Gardner-Webb University, NC
Geneva College, PA
George Fox University, OR
Georgetown College, KY
The George Washington University, DC
Georgia College & State University, GA
Georgia Southern University, GA
Glenville State College, WV
Gonzaga University, WA
Goucher College, MD
Grace Bible College, MI
Grace College, IN
Graceland University, IA
Grace University, NE
Grand Valley State University, MI
Grand View College, IA
Green Mountain College, VT
Grove City College, PA
Guilford College, NC
Gustavus Adolphus College, MN
Hampden-Sydney College, VA
Hanover College, IN
Harding University, AR
Hardin-Simmons University, TX
Hastings College, NE
Hawai'i Pacific University, HI
Heidelberg College, OH
Hendrix College, AR
Hillsdale College, MI
Hobart and William Smith Colleges, NY
Hofstra University, NY
Holy Names University, CA
Hope College, MI
Houghton College, NY
Houston Baptist University, TX
Huntington University, IN
Idaho State University, ID
Illinois College, IL
Illinois State University, IL
Illinois Wesleyan University, IL
Indiana University of Pennsylvania, PA
Iona College, NY
Iowa Wesleyan College, IA
Ithaca College, NY
Jackson State University, MS
Jacksonville State University, AL
James Madison University, VA
Jamestown College, ND
Johnson Bible College, TN
Johnson C. Smith University, NC
Judson College, AL
Judson College, IL
Kalamazoo College, MI
Kean University, NJ
Keene State College, NH
Kent State University, OH
Kentucky Christian University, KY
Kentucky Wesleyan College, KY
King College, TN
Knox College, IL
Kutztown University of Pennsylvania, PA
LaGrange College, GA
Lake Forest College, IL
Lakeland College, WI
Lambuth University, TN
Lancaster Bible College, PA
La Sierra University, CA
Lawrence University, WI
Lebanon Valley College, PA
Lee University, TN
Lehigh University, PA
LeMoyne-Owen College, TN
Lewis & Clark College, OR
Lewis-Clark State College, ID
Limestone College, SC
Lincoln University, PA
Lindenwood University, MO
Lindsey Wilson College, KY
Linfield College, OR
Lipscomb University, TN
Lock Haven University of Pennsylvania, PA
Longwood University, VA
Loras College, IA
Louisiana State University and Agricultural and Mechanical College, LA
Louisiana Tech University, LA
Lourdes College, OH
Loyola University Chicago, IL
Lubbock Christian University, TX
Luther College, IA

Lycoming College, PA
Lyon College, AR
MacMurray College, IL
Maharishi University of Management, IA
Malone College, OH
Manhattan Christian College, KS
Manhattan College, NY
Mannes College The New School for Music, NY
Mansfield University of Pennsylvania, PA
Marian College of Fond du Lac, WI
Marist College, NY
Martin Luther College, MN
Marywood University, PA
Massachusetts College of Liberal Arts, MA
Mayville State University, ND
McKendree College, IL
McMurry University, TX
Mercer University, GA
Meredith College, NC
Mesa State College, CO
Messiah College, PA
Methodist University, NC
Metropolitan State College of Denver, CO
Miami University, OH
Michigan State University, MI
Middle Tennessee State University, TN
Midwestern State University, TX
Millersville University of Pennsylvania, PA
Milligan College, TN
Millsaps College, MS
Mills College, CA
Minnesota State University Mankato, MN
Minot State University, ND
Mississippi State University, MS
Missouri Baptist University, MO
Missouri State University, MO
Missouri Valley College, MO
Molloy College, NY
Montana State University, MT
Montana State University–Billings, MT
Montclair State University, NJ
Montreat College, NC
Moravian College, PA
Morehead State University, KY
Morningside College, IA
Mount Aloysius College, PA
Mount Marty College, SD
Mount Mary College, WI
Mount Mercy College, IA
Mount Olive College, NC
Mount St. Mary's College, CA
Mount Union College, OH
Mount Vernon Nazarene University, OH
Murray State University, KY
Nazareth College of Rochester, NY
Nebraska Wesleyan University, NE
Neumann College, PA
New Jersey City University, NJ
Newman University, KS
New Mexico State University, NM
Nicholls State University, LA
North Carolina Agricultural and Technical State University, NC
North Carolina School of the Arts, NC
North Central College, IL
North Dakota State University, ND
Northeastern Illinois University, IL
Northeastern State University, OK
Northeastern University, MA
Northern Arizona University, AZ
Northern Illinois University, IL
Northern Michigan University, MI
Northern State University, SD
North Georgia College & State University, GA
North Greenville University, SC
Northland College, WI
Northwest Christian College, OR
Northwestern College, IA
Northwestern College, MN
Northwestern Oklahoma State University, OK
Northwestern State University of Louisiana, LA
Northwest Nazarene University, ID
Northwest University, WA
Nyack College, NY
Oberlin College, OH
Oglethorpe University, GA
Ohio Christian University, OH
The Ohio State University, OH
Ohio University, OH
Ohio University–Chillicothe, OH
Ohio University–Eastern, OH
Ohio University–Lancaster, OH
Ohio University–Southern Campus, OH
Ohio University–Zanesville, OH
Ohio Valley University, WV
Ohio Wesleyan University, OH
Oklahoma Baptist University, OK
Oklahoma Panhandle State University, OK
Oklahoma State University, OK
Olivet College, MI
Oral Roberts University, OK
Oregon State University, OR
Ouachita Baptist University, AR
Pacific Lutheran University, WA
Palm Beach Atlantic University, FL
Peabody Conservatory of Music of The Johns Hopkins University, MD
Pfeiffer University, NC
Philadelphia Biblical University, PA
Piedmont College, GA
Pittsburg State University, KS
Point Loma Nazarene University, CA
Portland State University, OR
Purchase College, State University of New York, NY
Purdue University, IN
Radford University, VA
Randolph College, VA
Reinhardt College, GA
Rhodes College, TN
Rice University, TX
The Richard Stockton College of New Jersey, NJ
Ripon College, WI
Roanoke College, VA
Roberts Wesleyan College, NY
Rockhurst University, MO
Rollins College, FL
Rowan University, NJ
Sacred Heart University, CT
St. Cloud State University, MN
Saint Francis University, PA
St. Gregory's University, OK
Saint John's University, MN
Saint Joseph's College, IN
Saint Louis University, MO
Saint Mary-of-the-Woods College, IN
Saint Mary's College, IN
Saint Mary's University of Minnesota, MN
St. Norbert College, WI
St. Olaf College, MN
Saint Vincent College, PA
Saint Xavier University, IL
Salisbury University, MD
Samford University, AL
San Diego State University, CA
Santa Clara University, CA
Seattle University, WA
Seton Hill University, PA
Shaw University, NC
Shenandoah University, VA
Shepherd University, WV
Silver Lake College, WI
Simpson College, IA
Simpson University, CA
Slippery Rock University of Pennsylvania, PA
Sonoma State University, CA
South Dakota State University, SD
Southeastern Louisiana University, LA
Southeastern Oklahoma State University, OK
Southeastern University, FL
Southeast Missouri State University, MO
Southern Adventist University, TN
Southern Arkansas University–Magnolia, AR
Southern Illinois University Carbondale, IL
Southern Illinois University Edwardsville, IL
Southern Methodist University, TX
Southern Nazarene University, OK
Southern Oregon University, OR
Southern Utah University, UT
Southern Wesleyan University, SC
Southwest Baptist University, MO
Southwestern University, TX
Southwest Minnesota State University, MN
Spelman College, GA
State University of New York at Binghamton, NY
State University of New York at Fredonia, NY
State University of New York at Plattsburgh, NY
State University of New York College at Geneseo, NY
State University of New York College at Oneonta, NY
State University of New York College at Potsdam, NY
Stephen F. Austin State University, TX
Stetson University, FL
Stony Brook University, State University of New York, NY
Sweet Briar College, VA
Syracuse University, NY
Tarleton State University, TX
Taylor University, IN
Taylor University Fort Wayne, IN
Temple University, PA
Tennessee State University, TN
Tennessee Technological University, TN

Tennessee Wesleyan College, TN
Texas A&M University–Commerce, TX
Texas Christian University, TX
Texas Lutheran University, TX
Texas State University-San Marcos, TX
Texas Tech University, TX
Texas Woman's University, TX
Thiel College, PA
Tiffin University, OH
Towson University, MD
Transylvania University, KY
Trevecca Nazarene University, TN
Trinity International University, IL
Troy University, AL
Tuskegee University, AL
Union College, KY
Union College, NE
Union University, TN
University at Buffalo, the State University of New York, NY
The University of Akron, OH
The University of Alabama, AL
The University of Alabama at Birmingham, AL
The University of Alabama in Huntsville, AL
University of Alaska Fairbanks, AK
The University of Arizona, AZ
University of Arkansas, AR
University of Arkansas at Monticello, AR
University of Bridgeport, CT
University of California, Irvine, CA
University of California, Riverside, CA
University of California, Santa Cruz, CA
University of Central Florida, FL
University of Central Missouri, MO
University of Central Oklahoma, OK
University of Charleston, WV
University of Colorado at Boulder, CO
University of Connecticut, CT
University of Dayton, OH
University of Delaware, DE
University of Denver, CO
University of Evansville, IN
The University of Findlay, OH
University of Florida, FL
University of Georgia, GA
University of Great Falls, MT
University of Hartford, CT
University of Hawaii at Hilo, HI
University of Hawaii at Manoa, HI
University of Idaho, ID
University of Illinois at Chicago, IL
University of Illinois at Springfield, IL
University of Illinois at Urbana–Champaign, IL
University of Kansas, KS
University of La Verne, CA
University of Maine, ME
University of Maryland, Baltimore County, MD
University of Maryland, College Park, MD
University of Massachusetts Amherst, MA
University of Massachusetts Lowell, MA
University of Miami, FL
University of Michigan, MI
University of Michigan–Flint, MI
University of Missouri–Columbia, MO
University of Missouri–Kansas City, MO
University of Missouri–St. Louis, MO
The University of Montana, MT
University of Nebraska at Kearney, NE
University of Nebraska at Omaha, NE
University of New Hampshire, NH
University of New Orleans, LA
University of North Alabama, AL
The University of North Carolina at Asheville, NC
The University of North Carolina at Chapel Hill, NC
The University of North Carolina at Charlotte, NC
The University of North Carolina at Greensboro, NC
The University of North Carolina at Pembroke, NC
The University of North Carolina Wilmington, NC
University of North Dakota, ND
University of Northern Colorado, CO
University of Northern Iowa, IA
University of North Florida, FL
University of Oklahoma, OK
University of Oregon, OR
University of Puget Sound, WA
University of Redlands, CA
University of Rhode Island, RI
University of Richmond, VA
University of Rochester, NY
University of St. Francis, IL
University of Saint Francis, IN
University of St. Thomas, MN
University of St. Thomas, TX
University of San Diego, CA
University of Science and Arts of Oklahoma, OK
University of South Carolina, SC
The University of South Dakota, SD
University of Southern Maine, ME
University of Southern Mississippi, MS
University of South Florida, FL
The University of Tampa, FL
The University of Tennessee at Martin, TN
The University of Texas at Austin, TX
The University of Texas at Brownsville, TX
The University of Texas at El Paso, TX
The University of Texas at San Antonio, TX
The University of Texas at Tyler, TX
The University of Texas of the Permian Basin, TX
The University of Texas–Pan American, TX
University of the Cumberlands, KY
University of the Incarnate Word, TX
University of the Ozarks, AR
University of the Pacific, CA
University of Tulsa, OK
University of Vermont, VT
University of Washington, WA
The University of West Alabama, AL
University of West Florida, FL
University of West Georgia, GA
University of Wisconsin–Green Bay, WI
University of Wisconsin–La Crosse, WI
University of Wisconsin–Stevens Point, WI
University of Wisconsin–Stout, WI
University of Wisconsin–Whitewater, WI
University of Wyoming, WY
Urbana University, OH
Ursinus College, PA
Utah State University, UT
Valdosta State University, GA
Valley City State University, ND
Valley Forge Christian College, PA
Valparaiso University, IN
Vanderbilt University, TN
VanderCook College of Music, IL
Vanguard University of Southern California, CA
Virginia Commonwealth University, VA
Virginia Intermont College, VA
Virginia Military Institute, VA
Virginia Polytechnic Institute and State University, VA
Virginia State University, VA
Virginia Wesleyan College, VA
Wabash College, IN
Wagner College, NY
Wake Forest University, NC
Walla Walla College, WA
Walsh University, OH
Warner Pacific College, OR
Wartburg College, IA
Washington Bible College, MD
Washington State University, WA
Washington University in St. Louis, MO
Wayland Baptist University, TX
Waynesburg College, PA
Wayne State College, NE
Wayne State University, MI
Webster University, MO
Wesley College, MS
Western Carolina University, NC
Western Illinois University, IL
Western New England College, MA
Western Oregon University, OR
Western Washington University, WA
West Liberty State College, WV
Westminster College, MO
Westminster College, PA
Westminster College, UT
Westmont College, CA
West Virginia University, WV
West Virginia Wesleyan College, WV
Wheaton College, IL
Wheeling Jesuit University, WV
Whitman College, WA
Whitworth University, WA
Wichita State University, KS
Widener University, PA
Wilkes University, PA
Willamette University, OR
William Carey College, MS
William Jewell College, MO
William Paterson University of New Jersey, NJ
Williams Baptist College, AR
Wilson College, PA
Wingate University, NC
Winona State University, MN
Winston-Salem State University, NC
Winthrop University, SC
Wisconsin Lutheran College, WI
Wittenberg University, OH
Xavier University, OH
York College of Pennsylvania, PA
Youngstown State University, OH

Performing Arts

Adelphi University, NY
Alabama State University, AL
Albion College, MI
Alderson-Broaddus College, WV
Alfred University, NY
Arizona State University, AZ
Arkansas State University, AR
Auburn University, AL
Augsburg College, MN
Augustana College, SD
Augusta State University, GA
Birmingham-Southern College, AL
Bloomfield College, NJ
Boise State University, ID
Bowling Green State University, OH
Brenau University, GA
Brigham Young University, UT
Bryan College, TN
Bucknell University, PA
California Institute of the Arts, CA
California Polytechnic State University, San Luis Obispo, CA
California State University, Chico, CA
Calvin College, MI
Carroll College, WI
Cedar Crest College, PA
Centenary College of Louisiana, LA
Central Michigan University, MI
Central Washington University, WA
Chapman University, CA
City College of the City University of New York, NY
Clarion University of Pennsylvania, PA
Clemson University, SC
Coe College, IA
College of Charleston, SC
The College of New Rochelle, NY
Columbia College Chicago, IL
Columbia International University, SC
Columbus State University, GA
Concordia University Wisconsin, WI
Corban College, OR
Cornell College, IA
Cumberland University, TN
Davis & Elkins College, WV
DeSales University, PA
Eastern Michigan University, MI
Edgewood College, WI
Elizabethtown College, PA
Elon University, NC
Emerson College, MA
Emory University, GA
Eureka College, IL
Fairfield University, CT
Flagler College, FL
Florida Atlantic University, FL
Fort Lewis College, CO
Franklin College, IN
Franklin Pierce University, NH
Freed-Hardeman University, TN
Friends University, KS
Frostburg State University, MD
Gannon University, PA
Georgetown College, KY
The George Washington University, DC
Georgia College & State University, GA
Goucher College, MD
Green Mountain College, VT
Hastings College, NE
Hobart and William Smith Colleges, NY
Idaho State University, ID
Illinois State University, IL
Indiana State University, IN
Indiana University of Pennsylvania, PA
Ithaca College, NY
Kentucky Christian University, KY
King College, TN
Lakeland College, WI
Lehigh University, PA
Limestone College, SC
Lindenwood University, MO
Louisiana State University and Agricultural and Mechanical College, LA
Louisiana Tech University, LA
Lubbock Christian University, TX
Manhattanville College, NY
Marymount Manhattan College, NY
Marywood University, PA
Massachusetts College of Liberal Arts, MA
Michigan State University, MI
Mississippi State University, MS
Missouri State University, MO
Missouri Valley College, MO
Molloy College, NY
Montclair State University, NJ
Mount Aloysius College, PA
New Mexico State University, NM
North Carolina School of the Arts, NC
Northeastern Illinois University, IL
Northeastern State University, OK
Northern Arizona University, AZ
Northern Illinois University, IL
Northwestern State University of Louisiana, LA
Northwest Nazarene University, ID
Northwest University, WA
Nyack College, NY
Oglethorpe University, GA
The Ohio State University, OH
Ohio University, OH
Ohio University–Chillicothe, OH
Ohio University–Eastern, OH
Ohio University–Lancaster, OH
Ohio University–Southern Campus, OH
Ohio University–Zanesville, OH
Ohio Valley University, WV
Oklahoma Baptist University, OK
Oklahoma Panhandle State University, OK
Ouachita Baptist University, AR
Purchase College, State University of New York, NY
Rice University, TX
The Richard Stockton College of New Jersey, NJ
Rockhurst University, MO
St. Andrews Presbyterian College, NC
St. Cloud State University, MN
Saint Louis University, MO
Saint Mary-of-the-Woods College, IN
San Diego State University, CA
Seattle Pacific University, WA
Seton Hill University, PA
Shaw University, NC
Shenandoah University, VA
Shepherd University, WV
Slippery Rock University of Pennsylvania, PA
Sonoma State University, CA
South Dakota State University, SD
Southern Illinois University Carbondale, IL
Southern Nazarene University, OK
Southern Utah University, UT
Southwestern University, TX
Southwest Minnesota State University, MN
State University of New York at Binghamton, NY
State University of New York at Fredonia, NY
State University of New York College at Geneseo, NY
State University of New York College at Potsdam, NY
Stephens College, MO
Temple University, PA
Texas Christian University, TX
Texas Tech University, TX
Tiffin University, OH
The University of Akron, OH
The University of Alabama at Birmingham, AL
The University of Arizona, AZ
University of California, San Diego, CA
University of Central Missouri, MO
University of Colorado at Boulder, CO
University of Florida, FL
University of Hartford, CT
University of Hawaii at Hilo, HI
University of Hawaii at Manoa, HI
University of Idaho, ID
University of Illinois at Chicago, IL
University of Illinois at Springfield, IL
University of Illinois at Urbana–Champaign, IL
University of Kansas, KS
University of Maine, ME
University of Maine at Fort Kent, ME
University of Maryland, Baltimore County, MD
University of Maryland, College Park, MD
University of Miami, FL
University of Missouri–Kansas City, MO
The University of Montana, MT
University of Nebraska at Omaha, NE
The University of North Carolina at Charlotte, NC
The University of North Carolina at Greensboro, NC
University of Northern Colorado, CO
University of Oklahoma, OK
University of Oregon, OR
University of Richmond, VA
University of South Florida, FL
The University of Tampa, FL
The University of Texas at Austin, TX
The University of Texas at El Paso, TX
University of Tulsa, OK
University of Washington, WA
University of Wisconsin–Stevens Point, WI
Utah State University, UT
Valparaiso University, IN
Virginia Commonwealth University, VA
Virginia Intermont College, VA
Virginia Polytechnic Institute and State University, VA
Virginia State University, VA
Wake Forest University, NC

Washington State University, WA
Washington University in St. Louis, MO
Wayne State College, NE
Western Illinois University, IL
Western Oregon University, OR
Western Washington University, WA
West Virginia Wesleyan College, WV
Wichita State University, KS
Wilkes University, PA
Winthrop University, SC
Xavier University, OH

Theater/Drama

Abilene Christian University, TX
Adams State College, CO
Adelphi University, NY
Alabama State University, AL
Albion College, MI
Alderson-Broaddus College, WV
Alma College, MI
Arcadia University, PA
Arizona State University, AZ
Arkansas State University, AR
Arkansas Tech University, AR
Auburn University, AL
Augsburg College, MN
Augustana College, IL
Augustana College, SD
Augusta State University, GA
Austin College, TX
Austin Peay State University, TN
Averett University, VA
Azusa Pacific University, CA
Baker University, KS
Barton College, NC
Baylor University, TX
Belmont Abbey College, NC
Berry College, GA
Bethany College, KS
Bethany Lutheran College, MN
Bethel College, IN
Bethel College, KS
Bethel University, MN
Birmingham-Southern College, AL
Black Hills State University, SD
Bloomfield College, NJ
Blue Mountain College, MS
Boise State University, ID
Boston University, MA
Bowling Green State University, OH
Bradley University, IL
Brenau University, GA
Brevard College, NC
Brigham Young University, UT
Brigham Young University–Hawaii, HI
Bryan College, TN
Bucknell University, PA
Buena Vista University, IA
Butler University, IN
California Institute of the Arts, CA
California Polytechnic State University, San Luis Obispo, CA
California State University, Chico, CA
California State University, Fresno, CA
California State University, Los Angeles, CA
California State University, San Bernardino, CA
Calvin College, MI
Campbellsville University, KY
Campbell University, NC
Carroll College, WI
Carthage College, WI
Case Western Reserve University, OH
Catawba College, NC
The Catholic University of America, DC
Cedar Crest College, PA
Centenary College of Louisiana, LA
Central College, IA
Central Methodist University, MO
Central Michigan University, MI
Central Washington University, WA
Centre College, KY
Chapman University, CA
Chatham University, PA
Christopher Newport University, VA
Clarion University of Pennsylvania, PA
Clarke College, IA
Clemson University, SC
Cleveland State University, OH
Coastal Carolina University, SC
Coe College, IA
College of Charleston, SC
The College of New Rochelle, NY
College of Staten Island of the City University of New York, NY
College of the Southwest, NM
The College of William and Mary, VA
The College of Wooster, OH
Colorado State University, CO
Columbia College Chicago, IL
Columbus State University, GA
Concordia College, MN
Concordia University, CA
Concordia University, NE
Concordia University, St. Paul, MN
Concord University, WV
Converse College, SC
Cornell College, IA
Culver-Stockton College, MO
Cumberland University, TN
Dana College, NE
Davidson College, NC
Davis & Elkins College, WV
Denison University, OH
DeSales University, PA
Dickinson State University, ND
Doane College, NE
Dordt College, IA
Drake University, IA
Drury University, MO
East Central University, OK
Eastern Michigan University, MI
East Tennessee State University, TN
East Texas Baptist University, TX
Edgewood College, WI
Elizabethtown College, PA
Elmhurst College, IL
Elon University, NC
Emporia State University, KS
Erskine College, SC
Eureka College, IL
Faulkner University, AL
Ferris State University, MI
Five Towns College, NY
Flagler College, FL
Florida College, FL
Florida State University, FL
Fort Lewis College, CO
Francis Marion University, SC
Franklin College, IN
Franklin Pierce University, NH
Freed-Hardeman University, TN
Fresno Pacific University, CA
Friends University, KS
Frostburg State University, MD
Furman University, SC
Gannon University, PA
Gardner-Webb University, NC
George Fox University, OR
Georgetown College, KY
The George Washington University, DC
Georgia College & State University, GA
Georgia Southern University, GA
Goucher College, MD
Grace College, IN
Graceland University, IA
Grand Valley State University, MI
Grand View College, IA
Green Mountain College, VT
Guilford College, NC
Gustavus Adolphus College, MN
Hanover College, IN
Hardin-Simmons University, TX
Hastings College, NE
Hendrix College, AR
Hillsdale College, MI
Hofstra University, NY
Hope College, MI
Huntington University, IN
Idaho State University, ID
Illinois College, IL
Illinois State University, IL
Illinois Wesleyan University, IL
Indiana University of Pennsylvania, PA
Ithaca College, NY
Jacksonville State University, AL
James Madison University, VA
Jamestown College, ND
Kalamazoo College, MI
Kean University, NJ
Keene State College, NH
Kent State University, OH
Kentucky Christian University, KY
Kentucky Wesleyan College, KY
King College, TN
Knox College, IL
Kutztown University of Pennsylvania, PA
LaGrange College, GA
Lake Forest College, IL
Lambuth University, TN
La Sierra University, CA
Lee University, TN
Lehigh University, PA
Lewis-Clark State College, ID
Limestone College, SC
Lindenwood University, MO
Lipscomb University, TN
Longwood University, VA
Louisiana State University and Agricultural and Mechanical College, LA
Louisiana Tech University, LA
Loyola University Chicago, IL
Lubbock Christian University, TX
Lycoming College, PA
Lyon College, AR
MacMurray College, IL
Malone College, OH

Marymount Manhattan College, NY
Marywood University, PA
Massachusetts College of Liberal Arts, MA
Mayville State University, ND
McMurry University, TX
Mercer University, GA
Mesa State College, CO
Messiah College, PA
Methodist University, NC
Metropolitan State College of Denver, CO
Miami University, OH
Michigan State University, MI
Middle Tennessee State University, TN
Midwestern State University, TX
Millsaps College, MS
Minnesota State University Mankato, MN
Minot State University, ND
Mississippi State University, MS
Missouri Baptist University, MO
Missouri State University, MO
Missouri Valley College, MO
Montana State University, MT
Montana State University–Billings, MT
Montclair State University, NJ
Montreat College, NC
Morehead State University, KY
Morningside College, IA
Mount Marty College, SD
Mount Mercy College, IA
Mount Union College, OH
Murray State University, KY
Nazareth College of Rochester, NY
Nebraska Wesleyan University, NE
New England College, NH
Newman University, KS
New Mexico State University, NM
Niagara University, NY
North Carolina Agricultural and Technical State University, NC
North Carolina School of the Arts, NC
North Central College, IL
North Dakota State University, ND
Northeastern Illinois University, IL
Northeastern State University, OK
Northern Arizona University, AZ
Northern Illinois University, IL
Northern Michigan University, MI
Northern State University, SD
North Greenville University, SC
Northwestern College, IA
Northwestern College, MN
Northwestern Oklahoma State University, OK
Northwestern State University of Louisiana, LA
Northwest Nazarene University, ID
Northwest University, WA
Nyack College, NY
Oglethorpe University, GA
The Ohio State University, OH
Ohio University, OH
Ohio University–Chillicothe, OH
Ohio University–Eastern, OH
Ohio University–Lancaster, OH
Ohio University–Southern Campus, OH
Ohio University–Zanesville, OH
Ohio Valley University, WV
Ohio Wesleyan University, OH
Oklahoma Panhandle State University, OK
Oklahoma State University, OK
Ouachita Baptist University, AR
Pacific Lutheran University, WA
Palm Beach Atlantic University, FL
Piedmont College, GA
Point Loma Nazarene University, CA
Portland State University, OR
Providence College, RI
Purchase College, State University of New York, NY
Radford University, VA
Randolph College, VA
Rhodes College, TN
The Richard Stockton College of New Jersey, NJ
Ripon College, WI
Rockhurst University, MO
Rollins College, FL
Russell Sage College, NY
St. Ambrose University, IA
St. Cloud State University, MN
St. Edward's University, TX
St. Gregory's University, OK
Saint John's University, MN
Saint Joseph's College, IN
Saint Louis University, MO
Saint Mary-of-the-Woods College, IN
Saint Mary's College, IN
Saint Mary's University of Minnesota, MN
St. Norbert College, WI
San Diego State University, CA
Santa Clara University, CA
Seton Hill University, PA
Shenandoah University, VA
Shimer College, IL
Simpson College, IA
Slippery Rock University of Pennsylvania, PA
Sonoma State University, CA
South Dakota State University, SD
Southeastern Oklahoma State University, OK
Southeastern University, FL
Southeast Missouri State University, MO
Southern Adventist University, TN
Southern Arkansas University–Magnolia, AR
Southern Illinois University Carbondale, IL
Southern Illinois University Edwardsville, IL
Southern Methodist University, TX
Southern Oregon University, OR
Southern Utah University, UT
Southern Wesleyan University, SC
Southwest Baptist University, MO
Southwestern University, TX
Southwest Minnesota State University, MN
Spelman College, GA
State University of New York at Binghamton, NY
State University of New York at Fredonia, NY
State University of New York at Plattsburgh, NY
State University of New York College at Geneseo, NY
State University of New York College at Potsdam, NY
Stephen F. Austin State University, TX
Stephens College, MO
Stetson University, FL
Stony Brook University, State University of New York, NY
Tarleton State University, TX
Taylor University, IN
Texas A&M University–Commerce, TX
Texas Christian University, TX
Texas Lutheran University, TX
Texas State University-San Marcos, TX
Texas Tech University, TX
Texas Woman's University, TX
Thomas More College, KY
Tiffin University, OH
Towson University, MD
Trevecca Nazarene University, TN
Troy University, AL
Union University, TN
The University of Akron, OH
The University of Alabama, AL
The University of Alabama at Birmingham, AL
University of Alaska Fairbanks, AK
The University of Arizona, AZ
University of Arkansas, AR
University of California, Riverside, CA
University of California, San Diego, CA
University of Central Florida, FL
University of Central Missouri, MO
University of Central Oklahoma, OK
University of Colorado at Boulder, CO
University of Connecticut, CT
University of Dallas, TX
University of Delaware, DE
University of Denver, CO
University of Detroit Mercy, MI
University of Evansville, IN
The University of Findlay, OH
University of Florida, FL
University of Hartford, CT
University of Hawaii at Hilo, HI
University of Hawaii at Manoa, HI
University of Idaho, ID
University of Illinois at Chicago, IL
University of Illinois at Urbana–Champaign, IL
University of Kansas, KS
University of La Verne, CA
University of Maine, ME
University of Maryland, Baltimore County, MD
University of Maryland, College Park, MD
University of Massachusetts Amherst, MA
University of Miami, FL
University of Michigan, MI
University of Michigan–Flint, MI
University of Missouri–Columbia, MO
The University of Montana, MT
University of Nebraska at Omaha, NE
University of New Hampshire, NH
University of New Orleans, LA
The University of North Carolina at Asheville, NC
The University of North Carolina at Chapel Hill, NC
The University of North Carolina at Greensboro, NC
The University of North Carolina Wilmington, NC

University of North Dakota, ND
University of Northern Colorado, CO
University of Northern Iowa, IA
University of Oklahoma, OK
University of Oregon, OR
University of Puget Sound, WA
University of Richmond, VA
University of St. Thomas, TX
University of Science and Arts of Oklahoma, OK
University of South Carolina, SC
The University of South Dakota, SD
University of Southern Indiana, IN
University of Southern Maine, ME
University of Southern Mississippi, MS
University of South Florida, FL
The University of Tennessee at Martin, TN
The University of Texas at Austin, TX
The University of Texas at El Paso, TX
The University of Texas–Pan American, TX
University of the Cumberlands, KY
University of the Incarnate Word, TX
University of the Ozarks, AR
University of Tulsa, OK
University of Vermont, VT
University of Washington, WA
University of West Florida, FL
University of West Georgia, GA
University of Wisconsin–Green Bay, WI
University of Wisconsin–La Crosse, WI
University of Wisconsin–Stevens Point, WI
University of Wisconsin–Whitewater, WI
University of Wyoming, WY
Ursinus College, PA
Utah State University, UT
Valdosta State University, GA
Valley City State University, ND
Valparaiso University, IN
Vanguard University of Southern California, CA
Virginia Commonwealth University, VA
Virginia Intermont College, VA
Virginia Polytechnic Institute and State University, VA
Wabash College, IN
Wagner College, NY
Wake Forest University, NC
Warner Pacific College, OR
Washington State University, WA
Washington University in St. Louis, MO
Wayland Baptist University, TX
Wayne State College, NE
Wayne State University, MI
Webster University, MO
Western Carolina University, NC
Western Illinois University, IL
Western Oregon University, OR
Western Washington University, WA
West Liberty State College, WV
Westminster College, PA
Westminster College, UT
Westmont College, CA
West Virginia University, WV
West Virginia Wesleyan College, WV
Whitman College, WA
Whitworth University, WA
Wichita State University, KS
Wilkes University, PA
Willamette University, OR
William Carey College, MS
William Jewell College, MO
Winona State University, MN
Winthrop University, SC
Wisconsin Lutheran College, WI
Wittenberg University, OH
Xavier University, OH
Youngstown State University, OH

Special Achievements/ Activities

Cheerleading/Drum Major

Abilene Christian University, TX
Alabama State University, AL
Arkansas State University, AR
Auburn University, AL
Azusa Pacific University, CA
Baker University, KS
Bellarmine University, KY
Bethany College, KS
Bethel College, IN
Bluefield State College, WV
Boise State University, ID
Brevard College, NC
Brigham Young University, UT
Brigham Young University–Hawaii, HI
Bryan College, TN
Campbellsville University, KY
Campbell University, NC
Central Methodist University, MO
Claflin University, SC
Cleveland State University, OH
Columbus State University, GA
Culver-Stockton College, MO
Dickinson State University, ND
Drury University, MO
East Central University, OK
East Texas Baptist University, TX
Evangel University, MO
Faulkner University, AL
Francis Marion University, SC
Friends University, KS
Gardner-Webb University, NC
Graceland University, IA
Harding University, AR
Hawai'i Pacific University, HI
Houston Baptist University, TX
Huntington University, IN
Iowa Wesleyan College, IA
James Madison University, VA
Lambuth University, TN
Lee University, TN
Limestone College, SC
Lindenwood University, MO
Lindsey Wilson College, KY
Lipscomb University, TN
Louisiana Tech University, LA
Lubbock Christian University, TX
McKendree College, IL
Methodist University, NC
Middle Tennessee State University, TN
Midwestern State University, TX
Milligan College, TN
Mississippi State University, MS
Missouri Baptist University, MO
Missouri State University, MO
Missouri Valley College, MO
Montana State University–Billings, MT
Morehead State University, KY
Morningside College, IA
Mountain State University, WV
Murray State University, KY
Northeastern State University, OK
North Georgia College & State University, GA
Northwestern Oklahoma State University, OK
Northwestern State University of Louisiana, LA
Northwest Nazarene University, ID
Northwood University, MI
The Ohio State University, OH
Oklahoma Panhandle State University, OK
Oklahoma State University, OK
Oral Roberts University, OK
St. Edward's University, TX
Saint Francis University, PA
Saint Joseph's College, IN
Saint Louis University, MO
Sam Houston State University, TX
Southeastern Louisiana University, LA
Southeastern Oklahoma State University, OK
Southeast Missouri State University, MO
Southern Arkansas University–Magnolia, AR
Southern Illinois University Carbondale, IL
Southern Utah University, UT
Stephen F. Austin State University, TX
Stetson University, FL
Temple University, PA
Tennessee Technological University, TN
Tennessee Wesleyan College, TN
Texas A&M University–Commerce, TX
Tiffin University, OH
Union College, KY
Union University, TN
The University of Alabama, AL
The University of Alabama at Birmingham, AL
The University of Alabama in Huntsville, AL
University of Arkansas at Monticello, AR
University of Central Missouri, MO
University of Charleston, WV
University of Delaware, DE
University of Great Falls, MT
University of Idaho, ID
University of Maryland, College Park, MD
University of Massachusetts Amherst, MA
The University of Montana, MT
University of Nebraska at Kearney, NE
University of North Alabama, AL
The University of North Carolina Wilmington, NC
University of Saint Francis, IN
University of Science and Arts of Oklahoma, OK
University of South Carolina, SC
University of Southern Mississippi, MS
The University of Tennessee at Martin, TN
The University of Texas at El Paso, TX
The University of Texas–Pan American, TX
University of the Cumberlands, KY
University of Tulsa, OK
The University of West Alabama, AL

University of Wyoming, WY
Virginia Intermont College, VA
Virginia Polytechnic Institute and State University, VA
Virginia State University, VA
Wake Forest University, NC
Wayland Baptist University, TX
Webber International University, FL
West Liberty State College, WV
Wichita State University, KS
William Carey College, MS
William Jewell College, MO
Williams Baptist College, AR
Winston-Salem State University, NC
Youngstown State University, OH

Community Service

Adelphi University, NY
Agnes Scott College, GA
Allen College, IA
Alliant International University, CA
Alverno College, WI
Arcadia University, PA
Arkansas State University, AR
Armstrong Atlantic State University, GA
Augsburg College, MN
Augusta State University, GA
Austin College, TX
Baylor University, TX
Bellarmine University, KY
Beloit College, WI
Bentley College, MA
Berry College, GA
Bethel University, MN
Bloomfield College, NJ
Boise State University, ID
Bradley University, IL
Brevard College, NC
Brigham Young University, UT
Brigham Young University–Hawaii, HI
Bryan College, TN
California Polytechnic State University, San Luis Obispo, CA
California State University, Chico, CA
California State University, Fresno, CA
California State University, Los Angeles, CA
California State University, San Bernardino, CA
California State University, Stanislaus, CA
Calvin College, MI
Canisius College, NY
Cedar Crest College, PA
Centenary College of Louisiana, LA
Central Washington University, WA
City College of the City University of New York, NY
Clark University, MA
Cleary University, MI
Clemson University, SC
College Misericordia, PA
The College of New Rochelle, NY
College of Notre Dame of Maryland, MD
College of St. Catherine, MN
College of St. Joseph, VT
College of Saint Mary, NE
The College of Saint Rose, NY
College of Staten Island of the City University of New York, NY
The College of Wooster, OH
Colorado State University-Pueblo, CO
Columbus State University, GA
Concord University, WV
Cornell College, IA
Dallas Baptist University, TX
Davidson College, NC
Edgewood College, WI
Elmhurst College, IL
Elon University, NC
Emmanuel College, MA
Endicott College, MA
Eugene Bible College, OR
Florida Gulf Coast University, FL
Frostburg State University, MD
Furman University, SC
Gannon University, PA
Georgia College & State University, GA
Georgia Southern University, GA
Green Mountain College, VT
Gustavus Adolphus College, MN
Hampshire College, MA
Hendrix College, AR
Hillsdale College, MI
Holy Names University, CA
Hood College, MD
Illinois State University, IL
Indiana University of Pennsylvania, PA
Iowa Wesleyan College, IA
Johnson Bible College, TN
Johnson C. Smith University, NC
Juniata College, PA
Kean University, NJ
Kent State University, OH
Kentucky Christian University, KY
Keuka College, NY
King's College, PA
Knox College, IL
Lakeland College, WI
Lewis & Clark College, OR
Lewis-Clark State College, ID
Lincoln Christian College, IL
Lindenwood University, MO
Lipscomb University, TN
Loyola University Chicago, IL
Malone College, OH
Manhattan College, NY
Manhattanville College, NY
Marymount University, VA
Maryville University of Saint Louis, MO
Marywood University, PA
McKendree College, IL
Menlo College, CA
Mercer University, GA
Meredith College, NC
Michigan State University, MI
Millersville University of Pennsylvania, PA
Milligan College, TN
Millsaps College, MS
Minnesota State University Mankato, MN
Missouri Valley College, MO
Molloy College, NY
Montclair State University, NJ
Morningside College, IA
Mount Ida College, MA
Mount St. Mary's College, CA
New England College, NH
Newman University, KS
Niagara University, NY
Nichols College, MA
North Central College, IL
Northeastern State University, OK
North Georgia College & State University, GA
Oglethorpe University, GA
Ohio Valley University, WV
Ohio Wesleyan University, OH
Oklahoma State University, OK
Olivet College, MI
Oral Roberts University, OK
Pacific Union College, CA
Peirce College, PA
Pitzer College, CA
Portland State University, OR
Providence College, RI
Randolph College, VA
Regis College, MA
Rhodes College, TN
Rice University, TX
The Richard Stockton College of New Jersey, NJ
Rochester Institute of Technology, NY
Rockhurst University, MO
Rosemont College, PA
Russell Sage College, NY
Sacred Heart University, CT
Sage College of Albany, NY
St. Cloud State University, MN
St. Edward's University, TX
St. John Fisher College, NY
Saint Joseph's College of Maine, ME
St. Lawrence University, NY
Saint Louis University, MO
Saint Mary-of-the-Woods College, IN
Saint Mary's College, IN
St. Olaf College, MN
San Diego State University, CA
Seton Hill University, PA
Simmons College, MA
Simpson College, IA
Slippery Rock University of Pennsylvania, PA
Sonoma State University, CA
South Dakota State University, SD
Southern Adventist University, TN
Southern Illinois University Carbondale, IL
Southern Oregon University, OR
Southern Vermont College, VT
Southern Wesleyan University, SC
Spelman College, GA
Spring Hill College, AL
State University of New York at Binghamton, NY
State University of New York at Plattsburgh, NY
State University of New York College at Geneseo, NY
State University of New York College at Oneonta, NY
State University of New York College at Potsdam, NY
Stetson University, FL
Suffolk University, MA
Sweet Briar College, VA
Texas A&M University–Texarkana, TX
Texas Tech University, TX
Tulane University, LA
Union College, NE
Unity College, ME

The University of Akron, OH
The University of Alabama, AL
The University of Alabama in Huntsville, AL
University of Alaska Fairbanks, AK
University of Arkansas, AR
University of California, San Diego, CA
University of Charleston, WV
University of Colorado at Boulder, CO
University of Connecticut, CT
University of Delaware, DE
University of Denver, CO
University of Florida, FL
University of Hartford, CT
University of Hawaii at Hilo, HI
University of Houston–Victoria, TX
University of Illinois at Springfield, IL
University of Illinois at Urbana–Champaign, IL
University of Kansas, KS
University of La Verne, CA
University of Maine, ME
University of Massachusetts Dartmouth, MA
University of Massachusetts Lowell, MA
University of Michigan, MI
University of Michigan–Dearborn, MI
University of Michigan–Flint, MI
University of New England, ME
University of New Hampshire, NH
The University of North Carolina at Asheville, NC
The University of North Carolina at Chapel Hill, NC
The University of North Carolina at Greensboro, NC
University of North Florida, FL
University of Richmond, VA
University of St. Francis, IL
University of St. Thomas, TX
University of South Carolina, SC
University of Southern Maine, ME
The University of Texas–Pan American, TX
The University of Texas Southwestern Medical Center at Dallas, TX
University of the Cumberlands, KY
University of Tulsa, OK
University of Vermont, VT
University of Washington, WA
University of West Georgia, GA
University of Wisconsin–Green Bay, WI
University of Wisconsin–La Crosse, WI
University of Wisconsin–Stout, WI
Urbana University, OH
Valdosta State University, GA
Virginia Polytechnic Institute and State University, VA
Virginia State University, VA
Wabash College, IN
Wake Forest University, NC
Walla Walla College, WA
Warren Wilson College, NC
Washington State University, WA
Waynesburg College, PA
Webber International University, FL
Wesley College, DE
Western Illinois University, IL
Western New England College, MA
Western Washington University, WA
West Virginia Wesleyan College, WV
Wheeling Jesuit University, WV
Widener University, PA
Willamette University, OR
Wilson College, PA
Wittenberg University, OH
York College of Pennsylvania, PA

Hobbies/Interests

Albright College, PA
Augusta State University, GA
Brevard College, NC
California State University, Chico, CA
California State University, San Bernardino, CA
Capital University, OH
Central Washington University, WA
The College of New Rochelle, NY
Corban College, OR
Edgewood College, WI
Eugene Bible College, OR
Hawai'i Pacific University, HI
Indiana University of Pennsylvania, PA
Mesa State College, CO
Michigan State University, MI
Millsaps College, MS
Missouri State University, MO
Missouri Valley College, MO
The Ohio State University, OH
Shimer College, IL
South Dakota State University, SD
Southern Oregon University, OR
Southwest Minnesota State University, MN
Stephen F. Austin State University, TX
The University of Alabama, AL
University of Michigan–Flint, MI
University of Minnesota, Twin Cities Campus, MN
Valdosta State University, GA
Virginia State University, VA

Junior Miss

Augsburg College, MN
Bethel University, MN
Birmingham-Southern College, AL
Bluefield State College, WV
Brigham Young University–Hawaii, HI
Campbellsville University, KY
Carroll College, WI
Cedar Crest College, PA
The College of New Rochelle, NY
Friends University, KS
Georgetown College, KY
Georgia Southern University, GA
Grace College, IN
Grand View College, IA
Gustavus Adolphus College, MN
Hardin-Simmons University, TX
Idaho State University, ID
Judson College, AL
Kentucky Wesleyan College, KY
Lebanon Valley College, PA
Lewis-Clark State College, ID
Lindenwood University, MO
Lindsey Wilson College, KY
Malone College, OH
McDaniel College, MD
McMurry University, TX
Mercer University, GA
Michigan State University, MI
Missouri Valley College, MO
Mount Vernon Nazarene University, OH
Murray State University, KY
Northeastern State University, OK
South Dakota State University, SD
Spring Arbor University, MI
Tennessee Wesleyan College, TN
The University of Alabama, AL
The University of Alabama at Birmingham, AL
The University of Alabama in Huntsville, AL
University of Idaho, ID
The University of North Carolina at Asheville, NC
The University of North Carolina at Greensboro, NC
University of Wyoming, WY
Wartburg College, IA
Washington State University, WA
William Carey College, MS

Leadership

Abilene Christian University, TX
Agnes Scott College, GA
Alabama State University, AL
Alderson-Broaddus College, WV
Alfred University, NY
Allen College, IA
Alliant International University, CA
Anderson University, IN
Andrews University, MI
Arcadia University, PA
Arkansas Tech University, AR
Asbury College, KY
Auburn University, AL
Augsburg College, MN
Augustana College, SD
Augusta State University, GA
Austin College, TX
Austin Peay State University, TN
Averett University, VA
Azusa Pacific University, CA
Babson College, MA
Baker University, KS
Baldwin-Wallace College, OH
Bard College, NY
Barton College, NC
Baylor University, TX
Becker College, MA
Bellarmine University, KY
Bethany College, WV
Bethel College, IN
Bethel University, MN
Bluefield State College, WV
Blue Mountain College, MS
Bluffton University, OH
Boise State University, ID
Boston University, MA
Bowdoin College, ME
Bowling Green State University, OH
Bradley University, IL
Brenau University, GA
Brevard College, NC
Brigham Young University, UT
Brigham Young University–Hawaii, HI
Bryan College, TN
Bucknell University, PA
Buena Vista University, IA

California Polytechnic State University, San Luis Obispo, CA
California State University, Chico, CA
California State University, Fullerton, CA
California State University, Northridge, CA
California State University, Stanislaus, CA
Campbellsville University, KY
Canisius College, NY
Capital University, OH
Carroll College, WI
Carson-Newman College, TN
Carthage College, WI
Case Western Reserve University, OH
Cedar Crest College, PA
Cedarville University, OH
Centenary College, NJ
Centenary College of Louisiana, LA
Central Methodist University, MO
Central Michigan University, MI
Central Pennsylvania College, PA
Central Washington University, WA
Chestnut Hill College, PA
Christian Brothers University, TN
Christopher Newport University, VA
City College of the City University of New York, NY
Claremont McKenna College, CA
Clarion University of Pennsylvania, PA
Clarke College, IA
Clarkson University, NY
Clearwater Christian College, FL
Clemson University, SC
College Misericordia, PA
The College of New Rochelle, NY
College of Notre Dame of Maryland, MD
College of St. Catherine, MN
College of St. Joseph, VT
College of Saint Mary, NE
The College of Wooster, OH
Colorado State University-Pueblo, CO
Columbia College, MO
Columbia College Chicago, IL
Columbia International University, SC
Columbus State University, GA
Concordia University at Austin, TX
Concordia University Wisconsin, WI
Concord University, WV
Converse College, SC
Corban College, OR
Cornell College, IA
Crown College, MN
Culver-Stockton College, MO
Cumberland University, TN
Curry College, MA
Dallas Baptist University, TX
Dana College, NE
Daniel Webster College, NH
Davidson College, NC
Davis & Elkins College, WV
Denison University, OH
DeSales University, PA
Dickinson College, PA
Dickinson State University, ND
Dominican University, IL
Dordt College, IA
Drury University, MO
Duke University, NC
Eastern Michigan University, MI
East Tennessee State University, TN
East Texas Baptist University, TX
Edgewood College, WI
Elmira College, NY
Elon University, NC
Embry-Riddle Aeronautical University, AZ
Embry-Riddle Aeronautical University, FL
Embry-Riddle Aeronautical University Worldwide, FL
Emmaus Bible College, IA
Endicott College, MA
Erskine College, SC
Eugene Bible College, OR
Eureka College, IL
Evangel University, MO
Faulkner University, AL
Fitchburg State College, MA
Flagler College, FL
Florida Gulf Coast University, FL
Fort Lewis College, CO
Franklin Pierce University, NH
Freed-Hardeman University, TN
Fresno Pacific University, CA
Friends University, KS
Frostburg State University, MD
Furman University, SC
Gannon University, PA
George Fox University, OR
Georgetown College, KY
Georgia College & State University, GA
Georgia Institute of Technology, GA
Georgia Southern University, GA
Gonzaga University, WA
Graceland University, IA
Grace University, NE
Green Mountain College, VT
Grove City College, PA
Gustavus Adolphus College, MN
Hampden-Sydney College, VA
Hampshire College, MA
Harding University, AR
Hardin-Simmons University, TX
Hawai'i Pacific University, HI
Hendrix College, AR
Hilbert College, NY
Hillsdale College, MI
Hobart and William Smith Colleges, NY
Hofstra University, NY
Hood College, MD
Husson College, ME
Idaho State University, ID
Illinois Institute of Technology, IL
Illinois State University, IL
Indiana University of Pennsylvania, PA
Iowa Wesleyan College, IA
Ithaca College, NY
Jackson State University, MS
James Madison University, VA
Jamestown College, ND
Johnson Bible College, TN
Johnson C. Smith University, NC
Judson College, IL
Juniata College, PA
Kean University, NJ
Kent State University, OH
Kentucky Christian University, KY
Kentucky Wesleyan College, KY
Keuka College, NY
King's College, PA
Kutztown University of Pennsylvania, PA
Kuyper College, MI
LaGrange College, GA
Lake Forest College, IL
Lakeland College, WI
Lancaster Bible College, PA
La Sierra University, CA
Lee University, TN
Le Moyne College, NY
Lewis-Clark State College, ID
Limestone College, SC
Lincoln Christian College, IL
Lindenwood University, MO
Lindsey Wilson College, KY
Linfield College, OR
Lipscomb University, TN
Lock Haven University of Pennsylvania, PA
Louisiana State University and Agricultural and Mechanical College, LA
Loyola University Chicago, IL
Lubbock Christian University, TX
Lycoming College, PA
Lyon College, AR
MacMurray College, IL
Malone College, OH
Manhattan Christian College, KS
Manhattan College, NY
Manhattanville College, NY
Mary Baldwin College, VA
Marymount University, VA
Maryville University of Saint Louis, MO
Marywood University, PA
Massachusetts College of Liberal Arts, MA
McDaniel College, MD
McKendree College, IL
Meredith College, NC
Messiah College, PA
Methodist University, NC
Miami University, OH
Michigan State University, MI
Michigan Technological University, MI
Middle Tennessee State University, TN
Midwestern State University, TX
Millsaps College, MS
Minnesota State University Mankato, MN
Mississippi State University, MS
Missouri Valley College, MO
Monmouth University, NJ
Montclair State University, NJ
Montreat College, NC
Moore College of Art & Design, PA
Moravian College, PA
Morehead State University, KY
Morningside College, IA
Mount Aloysius College, PA
Mount Ida College, MA
Mount Marty College, SD
Mount Mary College, WI
Mount Mercy College, IA
Mount Olive College, NC
Mount St. Mary's College, CA
Murray State University, KY
Myers University, OH
National University, CA
New England College, NH
Newman University, KS
New Mexico State University, NM
Nichols College, MA
Northeastern Illinois University, IL
Northeastern State University, OK

Northern Illinois University, IL
Northern Michigan University, MI
Northern State University, SD
North Georgia College & State University, GA
Northland College, WI
Northwest Christian College, OR
Northwestern College, MN
Northwestern Oklahoma State University, OK
Northwestern State University of Louisiana, LA
Northwest Nazarene University, ID
Northwood University, MI
Nova Southeastern University, FL
Nyack College, NY
Ohio Christian University, OH
The Ohio State University, OH
Ohio Valley University, WV
Ohio Wesleyan University, OH
Oklahoma Baptist University, OK
Oklahoma State University, OK
Olivet College, MI
Oral Roberts University, OK
Pacific Lutheran University, WA
Pacific Union College, CA
Peirce College, PA
Pfeiffer University, NC
Philadelphia Biblical University, PA
Piedmont College, GA
Pitzer College, CA
Portland State University, OR
Purdue University, IN
Quinnipiac University, CT
Radford University, VA
Randolph College, VA
Regis College, MA
Regis University, CO
Rice University, TX
The Richard Stockton College of New Jersey, NJ
Ripon College, WI
Roberts Wesleyan College, NY
Rochester Institute of Technology, NY
Rockhurst University, MO
Russell Sage College, NY
Sacred Heart University, CT
St. Andrews Presbyterian College, NC
St. Edward's University, TX
Saint Louis University, MO
Saint Mary-of-the-Woods College, IN
Saint Mary's University of Minnesota, MN
Saint Vincent College, PA
Saint Xavier University, IL
Sam Houston State University, TX
San Diego State University, CA
Seattle University, WA
Seton Hill University, PA
Shepherd University, WV
Simpson College, IA
Simpson University, CA
Slippery Rock University of Pennsylvania, PA
Sonoma State University, CA
South Dakota State University, SD
Southeastern Louisiana University, LA
Southeast Missouri State University, MO
Southern Adventist University, TN
Southern Arkansas University–Magnolia, AR
Southern Illinois University Carbondale, IL
Southern New Hampshire University, NH
Southern Oregon University, OR
Southern Utah University, UT
Southern Vermont College, VT
Southern Wesleyan University, SC
Southwest Minnesota State University, MN
State University of New York at Binghamton, NY
State University of New York at Fredonia, NY
State University of New York at Plattsburgh, NY
State University of New York College at Geneseo, NY
State University of New York College at Oneonta, NY
State University of New York College at Potsdam, NY
State University of New York College of Environmental Science and Forestry, NY
Stephen F. Austin State University, TX
Stephens College, MO
Stetson University, FL
Taylor University, IN
Taylor University Fort Wayne, IN
Texas A&M University at Galveston, TX
Texas A&M University–Commerce, TX
Texas A&M University–Texarkana, TX
Texas Christian University, TX
Texas Lutheran University, TX
Thiel College, PA
Thomas More College, KY
Trinity College, CT
Troy University, AL
Union College, NE
Union University, TN
Unity College, ME
The University of Akron, OH
The University of Alabama at Birmingham, AL
The University of Alabama in Huntsville, AL
The University of Arizona, AZ
University of Arkansas, AR
University of Arkansas at Monticello, AR
University of Bridgeport, CT
University of California, San Diego, CA
University of Central Florida, FL
University of Central Missouri, MO
University of Central Oklahoma, OK
University of Charleston, WV
University of Colorado at Boulder, CO
University of Connecticut, CT
University of Dallas, TX
University of Delaware, DE
University of Denver, CO
University of Evansville, IN
University of Florida, FL
University of Hawaii at Hilo, HI
University of Houston–Victoria, TX
University of Idaho, ID
University of Illinois at Springfield, IL
University of Illinois at Urbana–Champaign, IL
University of Judaism, CA
University of Kansas, KS
University of La Verne, CA
University of Maine, ME
University of Massachusetts Amherst, MA
University of Michigan, MI
University of Michigan–Dearborn, MI
University of Michigan–Flint, MI
University of Minnesota, Crookston, MN
University of Minnesota, Twin Cities Campus, MN
The University of Montana, MT
University of Nebraska at Omaha, NE
University of New England, ME
University of New Orleans, LA
University of North Alabama, AL
The University of North Carolina at Asheville, NC
The University of North Carolina at Chapel Hill, NC
The University of North Carolina at Greensboro, NC
The University of North Carolina Wilmington, NC
University of North Dakota, ND
University of Northern Iowa, IA
University of North Florida, FL
University of Oklahoma, OK
University of Pittsburgh at Greensburg, PA
University of Pittsburgh at Johnstown, PA
University of Puget Sound, WA
University of Rochester, NY
University of St. Francis, IL
University of Science and Arts of Oklahoma, OK
University of South Carolina, SC
University of Southern California, CA
University of Southern Indiana, IN
University of Southern Mississippi, MS
The University of Tampa, FL
The University of Tennessee at Martin, TN
The University of Texas at Dallas, TX
The University of Texas at El Paso, TX
The University of Texas–Pan American, TX
University of the Cumberlands, KY
University of the Ozarks, AR
University of Tulsa, OK
University of Washington, WA
University of Wisconsin–Green Bay, WI
University of Wisconsin–La Crosse, WI
University of Wisconsin–Stevens Point, WI
University of Wisconsin–Whitewater, WI
University of Wyoming, WY
Urbana University, OH
Ursinus College, PA
Valley Forge Christian College, PA
Virginia Military Institute, VA
Virginia Polytechnic Institute and State University, VA
Virginia State University, VA
Virginia Wesleyan College, VA
Wabash College, IN
Wagner College, NY
Wake Forest University, NC
Walla Walla College, WA
Walsh University, OH
Warner Pacific College, OR
Warren Wilson College, NC
Washington Bible College, MD
Washington State University, WA
Wayland Baptist University, TX

Wayne State College, NE
Webber International University, FL
Webster University, MO
Wells College, NY
Wesley College, DE
Wesley College, MS
Western Illinois University, IL
Western New England College, MA
Western Washington University, WA
Westminster College, MO
Westmont College, CA
West Virginia University, WV
West Virginia Wesleyan College, WV
Wichita State University, KS
Widener University, PA
Wilkes University, PA
Willamette University, OR
William Carey College, MS
Wilson College, PA
Wisconsin Lutheran College, WI
Wittenberg University, OH
Youngstown State University, OH

Memberships

Adelphi University, NY
Arcadia University, PA
Auburn University, AL
Averett University, VA
Birmingham-Southern College, AL
Blue Mountain College, MS
Boston University, MA
Brigham Young University, UT
California State University, Chico, CA
California State University, Stanislaus, CA
Carroll College, WI
Carson-Newman College, TN
Cedar Crest College, PA
Central Pennsylvania College, PA
Central Washington University, WA
The College of New Rochelle, NY
College of Notre Dame of Maryland, MD
College of St. Catherine, MN
Columbia College, MO
Concordia University, NE
Corban College, OR
Dallas Baptist University, TX
Delaware Valley College, PA
Eastern Michigan University, MI
East Tennessee State University, TN
Emory University, GA
Emporia State University, KS
Erskine College, SC
Flagler College, FL
Fresno Pacific University, CA
Georgia Southern University, GA
Gonzaga University, WA
Grove City College, PA
Hawai'i Pacific University, HI
Hood College, MD
Idaho State University, ID
Kettering University, MI
Laboratory Institute of Merchandising, NY
Lock Haven University of Pennsylvania, PA
Longwood University, VA
Loras College, IA
Loyola University Chicago, IL
Marymount University, VA
Massachusetts College of Liberal Arts, MA
Medcenter One College of Nursing, ND
Mercer University, GA
Michigan State University, MI
Midwestern State University, TX
Mississippi State University, MS
Missouri State University, MO
Molloy College, NY
Mount Marty College, SD
Newman University, KS
North Dakota State University, ND
Northern Michigan University, MI
Northwestern Oklahoma State University, OK
Northwestern State University of Louisiana, LA
Northwood University, MI
Northwood University, Florida Campus, FL
Northwood University, Texas Campus, TX
The Ohio State University, OH
Oklahoma State University, OK
Olivet College, MI
Oral Roberts University, OK
Peirce College, PA
Portland State University, OR
Ripon College, WI
Saint Louis University, MO
Saint Mary-of-the-Woods College, IN
Saint Mary's College of California, CA
Sonoma State University, CA
South Dakota State University, SD
Southeastern Louisiana University, LA
Southern New Hampshire University, NH
Southern Oregon University, OR
State University of New York at Binghamton, NY
Tennessee Wesleyan College, TN
Texas A&M University–Texarkana, TX
Texas Tech University, TX
The University of Akron, OH
The University of Alabama at Birmingham, AL
University of Houston–Victoria, TX
University of Illinois at Springfield, IL
University of Illinois at Urbana–Champaign, IL
University of Louisville, KY
University of Maine, ME
University of Michigan–Dearborn, MI
University of Missouri–St. Louis, MO
University of Nebraska at Omaha, NE
University of North Dakota, ND
The University of Texas–Pan American, TX
University of Vermont, VT
University of West Georgia, GA
University of Wisconsin–La Crosse, WI
University of Wisconsin–Stout, WI
Virginia Polytechnic Institute and State University, VA
Wake Forest University, NC
Washington College, MD
Washington State University, WA
Wayland Baptist University, TX
Webber International University, FL
Western Washington University, WA
Wichita State University, KS
York College of Pennsylvania, PA

Religious Involvement

Albright College, PA
Andrews University, MI
Augsburg College, MN
Austin College, TX
Averett University, VA
Azusa Pacific University, CA
Baker University, KS
Barton College, NC
Baylor University, TX
Bellarmine University, KY
Belmont Abbey College, NC
Berry College, GA
Bethany College, WV
Bethel College, IN
Bethel University, MN
Birmingham-Southern College, AL
Blue Mountain College, MS
Brigham Young University–Hawaii, HI
Bryan College, TN
Calvin College, MI
Campbellsville University, KY
Campbell University, NC
Canisius College, NY
Capital University, OH
Carroll College, WI
Carthage College, WI
Cedar Crest College, PA
Centenary College of Louisiana, LA
Central College, IA
Central Methodist University, MO
The College of New Rochelle, NY
College of Notre Dame of Maryland, MD
The College of Wooster, OH
Columbia College, MO
Concordia University, NE
Concordia University at Austin, TX
Corban College, OR
Cornell College, IA
Dallas Baptist University, TX
Dana College, NE
Davidson College, NC
Davis & Elkins College, WV
Drury University, MO
Eastern Michigan University, MI
East Texas Baptist University, TX
Elizabethtown College, PA
Elon University, NC
Emmaus Bible College, IA
Endicott College, MA
Eugene Bible College, OR
Evangel University, MO
Fairfield University, CT
Faulkner University, AL
Flagler College, FL
Fresno Pacific University, CA
Friends University, KS
Furman University, SC
Gardner-Webb University, NC
George Fox University, OR
Georgetown College, KY
Graceland University, IA
Grace University, NE
Green Mountain College, VT
Grove City College, PA
Guilford College, NC
Harding University, AR
Hawai'i Pacific University, HI
Heidelberg College, OH
Hellenic College, MA
Hendrix College, AR
Houghton College, NY
Iowa Wesleyan College, IA
Johnson Bible College, TN

Kentucky Christian University, KY
Kutztown University of Pennsylvania, PA
Kuyper College, MI
Lakeland College, WI
Lancaster Bible College, PA
Lee University, TN
Limestone College, SC
Lindsey Wilson College, KY
Lipscomb University, TN
Loras College, IA
MacMurray College, IL
Malone College, OH
Messenger College, MO
Millsaps College, MS
Missouri Baptist University, MO
Molloy College, NY
Moravian College, PA
Mount Marty College, SD
Mount Vernon Nazarene University, OH
Newman University, KS
North Central College, IL
North Dakota State University, ND
Northwest Christian College, OR
Northwest Nazarene University, ID
Nyack College, NY
Oglethorpe University, GA
Ohio Valley University, WV
Ohio Wesleyan University, OH
Oklahoma Baptist University, OK
Oral Roberts University, OK
Pacific Union College, CA
Palm Beach Atlantic University, FL
Pfeiffer University, NC
Philadelphia Biblical University, PA
Randolph College, VA
Reinhardt College, GA
Roanoke Bible College, NC
Rosemont College, PA
Sacred Heart University, CT
Saint Francis University, PA
St. Gregory's University, OK
Saint Joseph's College of Maine, ME
Saint Mary-of-the-Woods College, IN
St. Olaf College, MN
Seton Hill University, PA
Silver Lake College, WI
Simpson College, IA
Simpson University, CA
Southeastern University, FL
Southern Adventist University, TN
Southern Methodist College, SC
Southern Wesleyan University, SC
Southwest Baptist University, MO
Stetson University, FL
Tennessee Wesleyan College, TN
Texas Lutheran University, TX
Thomas More College, KY
Transylvania University, KY
Union College, NE
The University of Alabama at Birmingham, AL
University of Dallas, TX
University of Detroit Mercy, MI
University of Great Falls, MT
The University of North Carolina at Greensboro, NC
University of Puget Sound, WA
University of St. Francis, IL
University of Saint Francis, IN
University of South Carolina, SC
University of the Cumberlands, KY
University of the Incarnate Word, TX
University of the Pacific, CA
University of West Georgia, GA
Urbana University, OH
Valparaiso University, IN
Virginia Polytechnic Institute and State University, VA
Virginia State University, VA
Virginia Wesleyan College, VA
Wake Forest University, NC
Walsh University, OH
Washington Bible College, MD
Washington State University, WA
Wayland Baptist University, TX
Wesley College, DE
Wesley College, MS
West Virginia Wesleyan College, WV
Whitworth University, WA
William Carey College, MS
William Jewell College, MO
Wingate University, NC

Rodeo

Boise State University, ID
California Polytechnic State University, San Luis Obispo, CA
Dickinson State University, ND
Idaho State University, ID
Lewis-Clark State College, ID
Michigan State University, MI
Missouri State University, MO
Missouri Valley College, MO
Murray State University, KY
New Mexico State University, NM
Northwestern Oklahoma State University, OK
Oklahoma Panhandle State University, OK
Oklahoma State University, OK
Sam Houston State University, TX
South Dakota State University, SD
Southeastern Louisiana University, LA
Southern Arkansas University–Magnolia, AR
Stephen F. Austin State University, TX
Tarleton State University, TX
Texas A&M University–Kingsville, TX
Texas Tech University, TX
University of Arkansas at Monticello, AR
University of Idaho, ID
The University of Montana, MT
The University of Tennessee at Martin, TN
The University of West Alabama, AL
University of Wyoming, WY
Washington State University, WA

Special Characteristics

Adult Students

Agnes Scott College, GA
Allegheny College, PA
Anderson University, IN
Arkansas State University, AR
Arkansas Tech University, AR
Averett University, VA
Barton College, NC
Bellarmine University, KY
Berry College, GA
Bethel College, IN
Bloomfield College, NJ
Brigham Young University, UT
California State University, Chico, CA
Campbellsville University, KY
Carroll College, WI
The Catholic University of America, DC
Cedar Crest College, PA
Central Washington University, WA
Cleary University, MI
Coe College, IA
College of St. Catherine, MN
The College of Saint Rose, NY
Concordia University at Austin, TX
The Culinary Institute of America, NY
Faulkner University, AL
Fitchburg State College, MA
Florida Gulf Coast University, FL
Francis Marion University, SC
Franklin Pierce University, NH
Freed-Hardeman University, TN
Frostburg State University, MD
Gannon University, PA
Grace University, NE
Hastings College, NE
Indiana University of Pennsylvania, PA
Juniata College, PA
Kent State University, OH
Lancaster Bible College, PA
La Sierra University, CA
Lipscomb University, TN
Loyola University Chicago, IL
Marywood University, PA
Medaille College, NY
Mercer University, GA
Meredith College, NC
Messiah College, PA
Middle Tennessee State University, TN
Millsaps College, MS
Mississippi State University, MS
Missouri State University, MO
Monmouth University, NJ
Montana State University–Billings, MT
Moravian College, PA
Morehead State University, KY
Murray State University, KY
New Mexico State University, NM
North Central College, IL
Northeastern Illinois University, IL
Northern Illinois University, IL
Northwestern College, IA
Northwestern State University of Louisiana, LA
Ohio Christian University, OH
The Ohio State University, OH
Ohio Valley University, WV
Oklahoma State University, OK
Piedmont College, GA
Pitzer College, CA
Portland State University, OR
Randolph College, VA
Regis College, MA
The Richard Stockton College of New Jersey, NJ
St. Edward's University, TX
Saint Francis University, PA
Saint Mary-of-the-Woods College, IN
Seton Hill University, PA
Simpson College, IA

Sonoma State University, CA
South Dakota State University, SD
Southeast Missouri State University, MO
Southern Arkansas University–Magnolia, AR
Southern Oregon University, OR
Spring Arbor University, MI
State University of New York College at Geneseo, NY
State University of New York College at Oneonta, NY
State University of New York College at Potsdam, NY
Stephen F. Austin State University, TX
Sweet Briar College, VA
Texas Christian University, TX
Thomas More College, KY
The University of Akron, OH
The University of Alabama at Birmingham, AL
University of Central Missouri, MO
University of Connecticut, CT
University of Hartford, CT
University of Illinois at Springfield, IL
University of Kansas, KS
University of Maine at Fort Kent, ME
University of Maryland, College Park, MD
University of Massachusetts Dartmouth, MA
University of Michigan–Flint, MI
University of Nebraska at Omaha, NE
University of New Orleans, LA
The University of North Carolina at Asheville, NC
The University of North Carolina at Charlotte, NC
The University of North Carolina at Greensboro, NC
University of Northern Colorado, CO
University of South Carolina, SC
The University of Tennessee at Martin, TN
The University of Texas at Dallas, TX
University of West Georgia, GA
University of Wisconsin–Green Bay, WI
University of Wisconsin–La Crosse, WI
University of Wisconsin–Stevens Point, WI
University of Wisconsin–Stout, WI
University of Wisconsin–Whitewater, WI
University of Wyoming, WY
Westminster College, UT
Wichita State University, KS
Widener University, PA
Wilkes University, PA
Wilson College, PA
Winston-Salem State University, NC
Wittenberg University, OH
Youngstown State University, OH

Children and Siblings of Alumni

Adelphi University, NY
Albion College, MI
Alliant International University, CA
Alma College, MI
Arcadia University, PA
Arkansas State University, AR
Asbury College, KY
Auburn University, AL
Augsburg College, MN
Augustana College, IL
Augustana College, SD
Aurora University, IL
Averett University, VA
Baker University, KS
Baldwin-Wallace College, OH
Barton College, NC
Bemidji State University, MN
Benedictine University, IL
Bethany College, KS
Bethany College, WV
Bethel College, KS
Bethel University, MN
Bloomfield College, NJ
Boston University, MA
Bowling Green State University, OH
Bradley University, IL
Brigham Young University–Hawaii, HI
Bryan College, TN
Bryant University, RI
Calvin College, MI
Canisius College, NY
Capital University, OH
Carroll College, WI
Carson-Newman College, TN
Carthage College, WI
Cedar Crest College, PA
Cedarville University, OH
Centenary College, NJ
Central College, IA
Central Methodist University, MO
Central Michigan University, MI
Central Washington University, WA
Centre College, KY
Chapman University, CA
Chatham University, PA
Chestnut Hill College, PA
Christian Brothers University, TN
Clarke College, IA
Clearwater Christian College, FL
Cleveland State University, OH
Coe College, IA
College Misericordia, PA
College of St. Catherine, MN
The College of Saint Rose, NY
The College of St. Scholastica, MN
Colorado School of Mines, CO
Columbia College, MO
Columbia International University, SC
Concordia University, CA
Concordia University, IL
Concordia University, NE
Concordia University at Austin, TX
Converse College, SC
Corban College, OR
Crown College, MN
The Culinary Institute of America, NY
Culver-Stockton College, MO
Dakota State University, SD
Dickinson College, PA
Dominican University, IL
Dordt College, IA
Dowling College, NY
Drake University, IA
Drury University, MO
Duke University, NC
Duquesne University, PA
D'Youville College, NY
Eastern Kentucky University, KY
Eastern Michigan University, MI
East Texas Baptist University, TX
Elmhurst College, IL
Embry-Riddle Aeronautical University, AZ
Embry-Riddle Aeronautical University, FL
Emmanuel College, MA
Emporia State University, KS
Endicott College, MA
Erskine College, SC
Fairfield University, CT
Faulkner University, AL
Fitchburg State College, MA
Florida Institute of Technology, FL
Fort Lewis College, CO
Francis Marion University, SC
Franklin College, IN
Franklin Pierce University, NH
Friends University, KS
George Fox University, OR
Georgia Southern University, GA
Gonzaga University, WA
Graceland University, IA
Grace University, NE
Grand View College, IA
Green Mountain College, VT
Gustavus Adolphus College, MN
Gwynedd-Mercy College, PA
Hanover College, IN
Hilbert College, NY
Hofstra University, NY
Holy Names University, CA
Hood College, MD
Houghton College, NY
Houston Baptist University, TX
Huntington University, IN
Idaho State University, ID
Illinois Institute of Technology, IL
Indiana State University, IN
Iona College, NY
Iowa Wesleyan College, IA
Ithaca College, NY
James Madison University, VA
Juniata College, PA
Kent State University, OH
Kentucky Christian University, KY
Kentucky Wesleyan College, KY
Kettering University, MI
Keuka College, NY
Lake Forest College, IL
Lakeland College, WI
Lambuth University, TN
Lancaster Bible College, PA
Lawrence University, WI
Lebanon Valley College, PA
Le Moyne College, NY
Limestone College, SC
Lincoln University, PA
Lindsey Wilson College, KY
Lipscomb University, TN
Longwood University, VA
Loras College, IA
Louisiana State University and Agricultural and Mechanical College, LA
Luther College, IA
MacMurray College, IL
Malone College, OH
Manchester College, IN
Maranatha Baptist Bible College, WI
Marymount University, VA
Maryville University of Saint Louis, MO
Marywood University, PA

Medcenter One College of Nursing, ND
Messiah College, PA
Methodist University, NC
Michigan State University, MI
Michigan Technological University, MI
Mississippi State University, MS
Missouri Baptist University, MO
Missouri State University, MO
Missouri Valley College, MO
Molloy College, NY
Monmouth University, NJ
Montana State University–Billings, MT
Montclair State University, NJ
Moravian College, PA
Morehead State University, KY
Mount St. Mary's College, CA
Mount Union College, OH
Murray State University, KY
Nazareth College of Rochester, NY
New England College, NH
Newman University, KS
New Mexico State University, NM
New York Institute of Technology, NY
Nichols College, MA
Northeastern State University, OK
Northern Arizona University, AZ
Northwestern College, IA
Northwestern Oklahoma State University, OK
Northwest Nazarene University, ID
Northwood University, MI
Northwood University, Florida Campus, FL
Northwood University, Texas Campus, TX
Nyack College, NY
The Ohio State University, OH
Ohio Wesleyan University, OH
Oklahoma Baptist University, OK
Oklahoma State University, OK
Olivet College, MI
Oral Roberts University, OK
Ouachita Baptist University, AR
Pacific Lutheran University, WA
Palm Beach Atlantic University, FL
Peirce College, PA
Pfeiffer University, NC
Philadelphia Biblical University, PA
Pittsburg State University, KS
Rensselaer Polytechnic Institute, NY
Rice University, TX
Ripon College, WI
Rivier College, NH
Roanoke Bible College, NC
Roberts Wesleyan College, NY
Rockhurst University, MO
Rosemont College, PA
Russell Sage College, NY
St. John Fisher College, NY
Saint Joseph's College, IN
St. Joseph's College, New York, NY
St. Lawrence University, NY
Saint Mary-of-the-Woods College, IN
Saint Mary's College of California, CA
St. Mary's College of Maryland, MD
Saint Mary's University of Minnesota, MN
Salisbury University, MD
San Diego State University, CA
Santa Clara University, CA
Seattle Pacific University, WA
Seattle University, WA
Seton Hill University, PA
Shimer College, IL
Simmons College, MA
Simpson College, IA
Slippery Rock University of Pennsylvania, PA
Sonoma State University, CA
Southeastern Oklahoma State University, OK
Southern Adventist University, TN
Southern Arkansas University–Magnolia, AR
Southern Illinois University Carbondale, IL
Southern Nazarene University, OK
Southern New Hampshire University, NH
Southwest Minnesota State University, MN
State University of New York at Fredonia, NY
State University of New York College at Oneonta, NY
State University of New York College at Potsdam, NY
Stephens College, MO
Stetson University, FL
Stony Brook University, State University of New York, NY
Suffolk University, MA
Taylor University, IN
Taylor University Fort Wayne, IN
Tennessee Technological University, TN
Texas Lutheran University, TX
Texas State University-San Marcos, TX
Thiel College, PA
Thomas More College, KY
Trevecca Nazarene University, TN
Trinity International University, IL
Tri-State University, IN
Union College, KY
Union University, TN
The University of Alabama at Birmingham, AL
University of Alaska Fairbanks, AK
University of Arkansas, AR
University of Central Missouri, MO
University of Charleston, WV
University of Delaware, DE
University of Detroit Mercy, MI
University of Evansville, IN
University of Idaho, ID
University of Illinois at Urbana–Champaign, IL
University of La Verne, CA
University of Maine, ME
University of Massachusetts Amherst, MA
University of Michigan–Dearborn, MI
University of Michigan–Flint, MI
University of Minnesota, Crookston, MN
University of Missouri–Columbia, MO
The University of Montana, MT
University of Nebraska at Omaha, NE
University of New England, ME
University of New Hampshire, NH
University of New Orleans, LA
The University of North Carolina at Asheville, NC
The University of North Carolina at Pembroke, NC
University of Northern Colorado, CO
University of Oklahoma, OK
University of Rochester, NY
University of St. Francis, IL
University of Saint Francis, IN
University of South Carolina, SC
University of Southern California, CA
University of Southern Mississippi, MS
The University of Tampa, FL
University of the Cumberlands, KY
University of the Ozarks, AR
University of Tulsa, OK
University of West Florida, FL
University of West Georgia, GA
University of Wisconsin–La Crosse, WI
University of Wyoming, WY
Urbana University, OH
Utah State University, UT
Valparaiso University, IN
Virginia Intermont College, VA
Virginia Military Institute, VA
Wake Forest University, NC
Walsh University, OH
Warner Pacific College, OR
Wartburg College, IA
Washington & Jefferson College, PA
Washington State University, WA
Wayland Baptist University, TX
Webber International University, FL
Wells College, NY
West Liberty State College, WV
Westminster College, MO
Westminster College, PA
Westminster College, UT
West Virginia Wesleyan College, WV
Wheeling Jesuit University, WV
Whitworth University, WA
Widener University, PA
William Carey College, MS
William Jewell College, MO
Wilson College, PA
Wingate University, NC
Winona State University, MN
Wittenberg University, OH
Xavier University, OH
York College of Pennsylvania, PA
Youngstown State University, OH

Children of Current Students

Alliant International University, CA
Augustana College, SD
Bryan College, TN
Carroll College, WI
Central College, IA
College Misericordia, PA
The College of New Rochelle, NY
Columbia College, MO
Elmhurst College, IL
Franklin Pierce University, NH
Grace University, NE
Green Mountain College, VT
Huntington University, IN
Johnson Bible College, TN
Lancaster Bible College, PA
Marymount University, VA
Maryville University of Saint Louis, MO
Marywood University, PA
Missouri Baptist University, MO
Mount Aloysius College, PA
Mount Marty College, SD
Northwest University, WA
Palm Beach Atlantic University, FL

Rivier College, NH
Saint Mary-of-the-Woods College, IN
The University of Alabama at Birmingham, AL
University of Great Falls, MT
University of Hartford, CT
University of Michigan–Dearborn, MI
Valley Forge Christian College, PA
Virginia Intermont College, VA
Wilson College, PA

Children of Educators

Agnes Scott College, GA
Alfred University, NY
Allegheny College, PA
Aurora University, IL
Austin Peay State University, TN
Bard College, NY
Bennington College, VT
Brigham Young University–Hawaii, HI
Bryan College, TN
Campbellsville University, KY
Canisius College, NY
Carthage College, WI
Centenary College of Louisiana, LA
College of St. Catherine, MN
Columbia College, MO
Columbus College of Art & Design, OH
Concordia University, NE
Cornell College, IA
DeSales University, PA
Dowling College, NY
East Texas Baptist University, TX
Emmanuel College, MA
Endicott College, MA
Florida College, FL
Franklin Pierce University, NH
Gallaudet University, DC
Grand View College, IA
Hampden-Sydney College, VA
Hastings College, NE
Hendrix College, AR
Johnson Bible College, TN
Judson College, AL
King's College, PA
Lipscomb University, TN
Lycoming College, PA
Maranatha Baptist Bible College, WI
Mary Baldwin College, VA
Mississippi State University, MS
Moravian College, PA
Mount St. Mary's University, MD
New England College, NH
New York Institute of Technology, NY
Northern Arizona University, AZ
Northwest Nazarene University, ID
Pacific Lutheran University, WA
Palm Beach Atlantic University, FL
Pfeiffer University, NC
Rosemont College, PA
Saint Anselm College, NH
Saint Francis University, PA
Saint Mary's College of California, CA
Seattle University, WA
Simpson College, IA
Sonoma State University, CA
Southern Illinois University Carbondale, IL
Tennessee Technological University, TN
Unity College, ME
The University of Alabama at Birmingham, AL
University of Charleston, WV
University of Illinois at Springfield, IL
University of St. Francis, IL
University of St. Thomas, TX
The University of Tennessee at Martin, TN
William Carey College, MS

Children of Faculty/Staff

Abilene Christian University, TX
Adelphi University, NY
Agnes Scott College, GA
Alcorn State University, MS
Alderson-Broaddus College, WV
Alfred University, NY
Allegheny College, PA
Alliant International University, CA
Alma College, MI
Anderson University, IN
Andrews University, MI
Arkansas State University, AR
Arkansas Tech University, AR
Arlington Baptist College, TX
The Art Institute of Portland, OR
Asbury College, KY
Ashford University, IA
Auburn University, AL
Augustana College, IL
Augustana College, SD
Aurora University, IL
Austin College, TX
Austin Peay State University, TN
Azusa Pacific University, CA
Baker University, KS
Baptist Bible College, MO
Bard College, NY
Barton College, NC
Baylor University, TX
Becker College, MA
Bellarmine University, KY
Belmont Abbey College, NC
Belmont University, TN
Bemidji State University, MN
Bennington College, VT
Berklee College of Music, MA
Berry College, GA
Bethany College, WV
Bethany Lutheran College, MN
Bethel College, IN
Bethel College, KS
Bethel University, MN
Birmingham-Southern College, AL
Bloomsburg University of Pennsylvania, PA
Blue Mountain College, MS
Bluffton University, OH
Bowdoin College, ME
Bowling Green State University, OH
Bradley University, IL
Brenau University, GA
Brevard College, NC
Brigham Young University–Hawaii, HI
Bryan College, TN
Buena Vista University, IA
Cabrini College, PA
California State University, Chico, CA
California State University, Stanislaus, CA
Calvin College, MI
Campbell University, NC
Canisius College, NY
Capital University, OH
Carroll College, WI
Carthage College, WI
Case Western Reserve University, OH
Catawba College, NC
The Catholic University of America, DC
Cedarville University, OH
Centenary College, NJ
Centenary College of Louisiana, LA
Central College, IA
Central Methodist University, MO
Central Michigan University, MI
Central State University, OH
Centre College, KY
Chatham University, PA
Claflin University, SC
Clarion University of Pennsylvania, PA
Clarke College, IA
Clarkson University, NY
Cleary University, MI
Clemson University, SC
Coe College, IA
College Misericordia, PA
The College of New Rochelle, NY
College of St. Catherine, MN
The College of St. Scholastica, MN
College of the Holy Cross, MA
College of the Southwest, NM
College of Visual Arts, MN
The College of Wooster, OH
Colorado State University, CO
Columbia College, MO
Columbia College Chicago, IL
Columbus College of Art & Design, OH
Concordia University, CA
Concordia University, IL
Concordia University, NE
Concordia University at Austin, TX
Concordia University, St. Paul, MN
Concordia University Wisconsin, WI
Converse College, SC
Corban College, OR
Cornell College, IA
Creighton University, NE
Crown College, MN
The Culinary Institute of America, NY
Culver-Stockton College, MO
Cumberland University, TN
Dallas Baptist University, TX
Davidson College, NC
Davis & Elkins College, WV
DeSales University, PA
Dickinson College, PA
Dickinson State University, ND
Dominican College, NY
Dominican University, IL
Dordt College, IA
Dowling College, NY
Drury University, MO
Duquesne University, PA
D'Youville College, NY
East Central University, OK
Eastern Kentucky University, KY
East Texas Baptist University, TX
Elizabethtown College, PA
Elmira College, NY
Elon University, NC
Embry-Riddle Aeronautical University, AZ
Embry-Riddle Aeronautical University, FL

Embry-Riddle Aeronautical University Worldwide, FL
Emmanuel College, MA
Emmaus Bible College, IA
Emory University, GA
Emporia State University, KS
Erskine College, SC
Eureka College, IL
Evangel University, MO
Faulkner University, AL
Ferris State University, MI
Flagler College, FL
Florida College, FL
Florida Institute of Technology, FL
Fort Lewis College, CO
Framingham State College, MA
Francis Marion University, SC
Franklin & Marshall College, PA
Franklin College, IN
Franklin Pierce University, NH
Freed-Hardeman University, TN
Free Will Baptist Bible College, TN
Fresno Pacific University, CA
Furman University, SC
Gallaudet University, DC
Gardner-Webb University, NC
Geneva College, PA
George Fox University, OR
Georgetown College, KY
Georgetown University, DC
Georgia College & State University, GA
Georgia Institute of Technology, GA
Gonzaga University, WA
Grace Bible College, MI
Grace College, IN
Graceland University, IA
Grace University, NE
Grand Valley State University, MI
Grand View College, IA
Guilford College, NC
Hampden-Sydney College, VA
Hampshire College, MA
Hanover College, IN
Hardin-Simmons University, TX
Hastings College, NE
Heidelberg College, OH
Hendrix College, AR
Hillsdale College, MI
Hood College, MD
Houghton College, NY
Houston Baptist University, TX
Huntington University, IN
Idaho State University, ID
Illinois College, IL
Illinois Institute of Technology, IL
Illinois State University, IL
Illinois Wesleyan University, IL
Indiana State University, IN
Indiana University of Pennsylvania, PA
Iona College, NY
Iowa Wesleyan College, IA
Jackson State University, MS
James Madison University, VA
Jamestown College, ND
The Johns Hopkins University, MD
Johnson Bible College, TN
Johnson C. Smith University, NC
Judson College, AL
Juniata College, PA
Kent State University, OH
Kentucky Christian University, KY
Kentucky Wesleyan College, KY
Kettering University, MI
Keuka College, NY
King College, TN
King's College, PA
Kutztown University of Pennsylvania, PA
Kuyper College, MI
LaGrange College, GA
Lakeland College, WI
Lambuth University, TN
Lancaster Bible College, PA
La Sierra University, CA
Lawrence Technological University, MI
Lebanon Valley College, PA
Lee University, TN
LeMoyne-Owen College, TN
LeTourneau University, TX
Limestone College, SC
Lincoln Christian College, IL
Lincoln University, PA
Lindsey Wilson College, KY
Linfield College, OR
Lipscomb University, TN
Louisiana Tech University, LA
Lourdes College, OH
Loyola University New Orleans, LA
Lubbock Christian University, TX
Lycoming College, PA
Lyon College, AR
MacMurray College, IL
Maharishi University of Management, IA
Maine College of Art, ME
Maine Maritime Academy, ME
Malone College, OH
Manhattan Christian College, KS
Manhattan College, NY
Maranatha Baptist Bible College, WI
Marian College of Fond du Lac, WI
Marquette University, WI
Mary Baldwin College, VA
Marymount University, VA
Maryville University of Saint Louis, MO
Marywood University, PA
Massachusetts College of Art, MA
Massachusetts College of Pharmacy and Health Sciences, MA
Mayville State University, ND
McKendree College, IL
McMurry University, TX
Mercer University, GA
Meredith College, NC
Messiah College, PA
Methodist University, NC
Miami University, OH
Michigan State University, MI
Michigan Technological University, MI
Midwestern State University, TX
Milligan College, TN
Millsaps College, MS
Mills College, CA
Milwaukee School of Engineering, WI
Mississippi State University, MS
Missouri Baptist University, MO
Missouri State University, MO
Missouri Valley College, MO
Molloy College, NY
Monmouth University, NJ
Montana State University–Billings, MT
Montreat College, NC
Moravian College, PA
Morningside College, IA
Mount Holyoke College, MA
Mount Marty College, SD
Mount Mary College, WI
Mount Olive College, NC
Mount Saint Mary College, NY
Mount St. Mary's University, MD
Mount Union College, OH
Mount Vernon Nazarene University, OH
Murray State University, KY
Nazareth College of Rochester, NY
Nebraska Wesleyan University, NE
Neumann College, PA
New England College, NH
Newman University, KS
New Mexico State University, NM
New York Institute of Technology, NY
Niagara University, NY
Nicholls State University, LA
Nichols College, MA
North Central College, IL
North Dakota State University, ND
Northeastern Illinois University, IL
Northeastern State University, OK
Northern Arizona University, AZ
Northern Illinois University, IL
Northern Michigan University, MI
North Greenville University, SC
Northwest Christian College, OR
Northwestern College, IA
Northwestern College, MN
Northwestern Oklahoma State University, OK
Northwestern State University of Louisiana, LA
Northwest Nazarene University, ID
Northwest University, WA
Northwood University, MI
Northwood University, Florida Campus, FL
Northwood University, Texas Campus, TX
Nova Southeastern University, FL
Nyack College, NY
Oglethorpe University, GA
Ohio Christian University, OH
The Ohio State University, OH
Ohio University, OH
Ohio University–Chillicothe, OH
Ohio University–Eastern, OH
Ohio University–Lancaster, OH
Ohio University–Southern Campus, OH
Ohio University–Zanesville, OH
Ohio Valley University, WV
Ohio Wesleyan University, OH
Oklahoma Baptist University, OK
Oklahoma Panhandle State University, OK
Olivet College, MI
Oral Roberts University, OK
Ouachita Baptist University, AR
Pacific Lutheran University, WA
Palm Beach Atlantic University, FL
Pfeiffer University, NC
Philadelphia Biblical University, PA
Piedmont College, GA
Purdue University, IN
Quinnipiac University, CT
Radford University, VA

Randolph College, VA
Regis College, MA
Regis University, CO
Reinhardt College, GA
Rensselaer Polytechnic Institute, NY
Rhodes College, TN
Rice University, TX
The Richard Stockton College of New Jersey, NJ
Ripon College, WI
Roanoke Bible College, NC
Robert Morris University, PA
Roberts Wesleyan College, NY
Rochester Institute of Technology, NY
Rockhurst University, MO
Rosemont College, PA
Russell Sage College, NY
Rutgers, The State University of New Jersey, Camden, NJ
Rutgers, The State University of New Jersey, Newark, NJ
Rutgers, The State University of New Jersey, New Brunswick, NJ
Sacred Heart University, CT
Sage College of Albany, NY
St. Ambrose University, IA
Saint Anselm College, NH
St. Cloud State University, MN
St. Edward's University, TX
Saint Francis University, PA
St. John's College, NM
Saint Joseph's College, IN
St. Joseph's College, New York, NY
Saint Joseph's College of Maine, ME
St. Louis Christian College, MO
Saint Louis University, MO
Saint Mary-of-the-Woods College, IN
Saint Mary's College, IN
Saint Mary's College of California, CA
St. Mary's College of Maryland, MD
Saint Mary's University of Minnesota, MN
St. Norbert College, WI
Saint Vincent College, PA
Saint Xavier University, IL
Samford University, AL
San Diego State University, CA
Santa Clara University, CA
Seattle Pacific University, WA
Seattle University, WA
Seton Hill University, PA
Sewanee: The University of the South, TN
Shaw University, NC
Shenandoah University, VA
Simpson College, IA
Simpson University, CA
Slippery Rock University of Pennsylvania, PA
Sonoma State University, CA
South Dakota State University, SD
Southeastern Louisiana University, LA
Southeastern University, FL
Southeast Missouri State University, MO
Southern Arkansas University–Magnolia, AR
Southern Connecticut State University, CT
Southern Illinois University Carbondale, IL
Southern Illinois University Edwardsville, IL
Southern Methodist University, TX
Southern Nazarene University, OK
Southern New Hampshire University, NH
Southern Vermont College, VT
Southern Wesleyan University, SC
Southwestern University, TX
Spring Arbor University, MI
Spring Hill College, AL
State University of New York College at Potsdam, NY
Stephens College, MO
Stetson University, FL
Stonehill College, MA
Suffolk University, MA
Tarleton State University, TX
Taylor University, IN
Taylor University Fort Wayne, IN
Tennessee Technological University, TN
Tennessee Wesleyan College, TN
Texas Christian University, TX
Texas Lutheran University, TX
Texas Tech University, TX
Thiel College, PA
Thomas More College, KY
Tiffin University, OH
Transylvania University, KY
Tri-State University, IN
Tufts University, MA
Tulane University, LA
Tuskegee University, AL
Union University, TN
The University of Alabama at Birmingham, AL
University of Alaska Fairbanks, AK
The University of Arizona, AZ
University of Arkansas, AR
University of Arkansas at Monticello, AR
University of Bridgeport, CT
University of Central Missouri, MO
University of Charleston, WV
University of Connecticut, CT
University of Dallas, TX
University of Dayton, OH
University of Delaware, DE
University of Denver, CO
University of Detroit Mercy, MI
University of Evansville, IN
The University of Findlay, OH
University of Florida, FL
University of Great Falls, MT
University of Hartford, CT
University of Idaho, ID
University of Illinois at Springfield, IL
University of Illinois at Urbana–Champaign, IL
University of Kansas, KS
University of La Verne, CA
University of Maine, ME
University of Maine at Farmington, ME
University of Maine at Fort Kent, ME
University of Massachusetts Amherst, MA
University of Massachusetts Dartmouth, MA
University of Miami, FL
University of Michigan, MI
University of Michigan–Dearborn, MI
University of Minnesota, Crookston, MN
University of Nebraska at Kearney, NE
University of Nebraska at Omaha, NE
University of New Hampshire, NH
University of New Hampshire at Manchester, NH
University of North Alabama, AL
The University of North Carolina at Asheville, NC
The University of North Carolina at Chapel Hill, NC
University of North Dakota, ND
University of Northern Colorado, CO
University of Notre Dame, IN
University of Pittsburgh, PA
University of Pittsburgh at Johnstown, PA
University of Puget Sound, WA
University of Rochester, NY
University of Saint Francis, IN
University of St. Thomas, TX
University of San Diego, CA
University of Science and Arts of Oklahoma, OK
University of South Carolina, SC
University of Southern California, CA
University of Southern Indiana, IN
University of Southern Maine, ME
University of Southern Mississippi, MS
The University of Tampa, FL
The University of Tennessee at Martin, TN
University of the Cumberlands, KY
University of the Ozarks, AR
University of the Virgin Islands, VI
University of Tulsa, OK
The University of West Alabama, AL
Urbana University, OH
Ursinus College, PA
Utah State University, UT
Valley City State University, ND
Valley Forge Christian College, PA
Valparaiso University, IN
Vanguard University of Southern California, CA
Virginia Intermont College, VA
Virginia Military Institute, VA
Virginia Polytechnic Institute and State University, VA
Virginia Wesleyan College, VA
Wabash College, IN
Wagner College, NY
Wake Forest University, NC
Walla Walla College, WA
Walsh University, OH
Warren Wilson College, NC
Wartburg College, IA
Washington & Jefferson College, PA
Washington Bible College, MD
Washington College, MD
Washington State University, WA
Wayland Baptist University, TX
Waynesburg College, PA
Wayne State College, NE
Webber International University, FL
Western Illinois University, IL
Western New England College, MA
West Liberty State College, WV
Westminster College, MO
Westminster College, UT
Westmont College, CA
West Virginia University, WV
West Virginia Wesleyan College, WV
Wheeling Jesuit University, WV
Widener University, PA

Wilkes University, PA
William Carey College, MS
William Jewell College, MO
Williams Baptist College, AR
Wilson College, PA
Winona State University, MN
Winthrop University, SC
Wisconsin Lutheran College, WI
Wittenberg University, OH
Youngstown State University, OH

Children of Public Servants

California State University, San Bernardino, CA
Carthage College, WI
College of Staten Island of the City University of New York, NY
Dowling College, NY
Framingham State College, MA
Georgia Southern University, GA
Graceland University, IA
Mercer University, GA
Mississippi State University, MS
Monmouth University, NJ
New Mexico State University, NM
New York Institute of Technology, NY
Northern Arizona University, AZ
Northwestern State University of Louisiana, LA
The Ohio State University, OH
Peirce College, PA
St. Francis College, NY
San Diego State University, CA
Sonoma State University, CA
Southern Illinois University Carbondale, IL
Tennessee Technological University, TN
The University of Alabama at Birmingham, AL
University of Delaware, DE
University of New Orleans, LA
The University of Texas at Dallas, TX
University of Wisconsin–Green Bay, WI
Valdosta State University, GA
Washington State University, WA
Western Washington University, WA
Westminster College, UT

Children of Union Members/Company Employees

Alabama State University, AL
Auburn University, AL
Averett University, VA
Calvin College, MI
Central Michigan University, MI
The College of Saint Rose, NY
Columbia College, MO
Dowling College, NY
East Tennessee State University, TN
Emmanuel College, MA
Emporia State University, KS
Framingham State College, MA
Frostburg State University, MD
Georgia Institute of Technology, GA
Grand Valley State University, MI
Hofstra University, NY
Husson College, ME
Illinois State University, IL
Kent State University, OH
Kentucky Wesleyan College, KY
Kutztown University of Pennsylvania, PA
Massachusetts College of Art, MA
Mercer University, GA
Michigan State University, MI
Millersville University of Pennsylvania, PA
Minnesota State University Mankato, MN
Montana State University–Billings, MT
New Mexico State University, NM
Northern Michigan University, MI
The Ohio State University, OH
The Richard Stockton College of New Jersey, NJ
St. Cloud State University, MN
Slippery Rock University of Pennsylvania, PA
Sonoma State University, CA
Southwest Minnesota State University, MN
Stephen F. Austin State University, TX
Texas Christian University, TX
The University of Alabama, AL
The University of Alabama at Birmingham, AL
University of Hartford, CT
University of Illinois at Springfield, IL
University of Maine, ME
University of Michigan–Flint, MI
University of Northern Colorado, CO
University of South Carolina, SC
University of the Incarnate Word, TX
University of West Georgia, GA
University of Wisconsin–La Crosse, WI
Virginia Commonwealth University, VA
Washington College, MD
Western New England College, MA
Western Washington University, WA
West Virginia University, WV
Wheeling Jesuit University, WV
York College of Pennsylvania, PA
Youngstown State University, OH

Children of Workers in Trades

Baptist Bible College, MO
Dowling College, NY
Marywood University, PA
New Mexico State University, NM
The Ohio State University, OH
Sonoma State University, CA
South Dakota State University, SD
The University of Alabama at Birmingham, AL
University of Illinois at Springfield, IL
University of Michigan, MI
University of Michigan–Dearborn, MI
University of South Carolina, SC
West Virginia University, WV
Worcester Polytechnic Institute, MA
Youngstown State University, OH

Children with a Deceased or Disabled Parent

The Baptist College of Florida, FL
California State University, San Bernardino, CA
Clarke College, IA
The College of New Jersey, NJ
College of Staten Island of the City University of New York, NY
Columbia College, MO
Dickinson State University, ND
Erskine College, SC
Georgia College & State University, GA
Harding University, AR
Illinois State University, IL
Indiana State University, IN
Kent State University, OH
Lipscomb University, TN
Louisiana State University and Agricultural and Mechanical College, LA
Louisiana Tech University, LA
Marian College of Fond du Lac, WI
New Mexico State University, NM
Northeastern State University, OK
The Ohio State University, OH
St. Norbert College, WI
Santa Clara University, CA
Seton Hill University, PA
Southern Illinois University Carbondale, IL
State University of New York at Binghamton, NY
The University of Alabama at Birmingham, AL
University of Hartford, CT
University of Illinois at Springfield, IL
University of Illinois at Urbana–Champaign, IL
University of Maine, ME
University of Massachusetts Dartmouth, MA
The University of Montana, MT
University of New Orleans, LA
University of South Carolina, SC
Washington State University, WA
Wayne State College, NE
Youngstown State University, OH

Ethnic Background

Abilene Christian University, TX
Alabama State University, AL
Alderson-Broaddus College, WV
Alliant International University, CA
Arkansas State University, AR
Arkansas Tech University, AR
Armstrong Atlantic State University, GA
Asbury College, KY
Auburn University, AL
Augustana College, SD
Austin College, TX
Azusa Pacific University, CA
Baker University, KS
Bellarmine University, KY
Berry College, GA
Bethany College, WV
Bethel University, MN
Boise State University, ID
Bridgewater College, VA
Brigham Young University, UT
Brigham Young University–Hawaii, HI
Buena Vista University, IA
Cabarrus College of Health Sciences, NC
Cabrini College, PA
California State University, Chico, CA
California State University, Dominguez Hills, CA
California State University, San Bernardino, CA
California State University, Stanislaus, CA
California University of Pennsylvania, PA
Calvin College, MI
Capital University, OH
The Catholic University of America, DC
Cedarville University, OH

Centenary College, NJ
Centenary College of Louisiana, LA
Centre College, KY
Clarion University of Pennsylvania, PA
Clearwater Christian College, FL
Clemson University, SC
College of St. Catherine, MN
The College of Saint Rose, NY
Columbia International University, SC
Cornell College, IA
Dakota State University, SD
Dana College, NE
Dickinson State University, ND
Drake University, IA
Duke University, NC
Eastern Michigan University, MI
Elmhurst College, IL
Emmanuel College, MA
Erskine College, SC
Fairfield University, CT
Flagler College, FL
Florida Gulf Coast University, FL
Fort Lewis College, CO
Franklin College, IN
Fresno Pacific University, CA
Furman University, SC
Gannon University, PA
George Fox University, OR
Georgia Institute of Technology, GA
Grace College, IN
Grace University, NE
Grove City College, PA
Gustavus Adolphus College, MN
Hardin-Simmons University, TX
Hawai'i Pacific University, HI
Holy Names University, CA
Hood College, MD
Illinois College, IL
Illinois Institute of Technology, IL
Indiana University of Pennsylvania, PA
Johnson Bible College, TN
Johnson C. Smith University, NC
Juniata College, PA
Kent State University, OH
Kenyon College, OH
LaGrange College, GA
Lebanon Valley College, PA
Lesley University, MA
Lewis-Clark State College, ID
Lyon College, AR
Maharishi University of Management, IA
Manchester College, IN
Maryville University of Saint Louis, MO
Marywood University, PA
McMurry University, TX
Meredith College, NC
Michigan State University, MI
Michigan Technological University, MI
Millsaps College, MS
Minot State University, ND
Missouri State University, MO
Molloy College, NY
Montana State University–Billings, MT
Moravian College, PA
Mount Union College, OH
New England College, NH
New Mexico State University, NM
North Carolina Agricultural and Technical State University, NC
North Dakota State University, ND
Northern Illinois University, IL
Northland College, WI
Northwestern College, IA
Northwestern College, MN
Northwest Nazarene University, ID
The Ohio State University, OH
Ohio Valley University, WV
Ohio Wesleyan University, OH
Oklahoma State University, OK
Ouachita Baptist University, AR
Portland State University, OR
Regis University, CO
Rensselaer Polytechnic Institute, NY
Rhodes College, TN
Rice University, TX
The Richard Stockton College of New Jersey, NJ
Robert Morris University, PA
Sacred Heart University, CT
St. Gregory's University, OK
St. John Fisher College, NY
Saint Mary-of-the-Woods College, IN
St. Norbert College, WI
Sewanee: The University of the South, TN
Shepherd University, WV
Simpson College, IA
Slippery Rock University of Pennsylvania, PA
Sonoma State University, CA
South Dakota State University, SD
Southern Utah University, UT
Southern Wesleyan University, SC
Southwest Minnesota State University, MN
State University of New York at Binghamton, NY
State University of New York at Fredonia, NY
State University of New York College at Oneonta, NY
State University of New York College at Potsdam, NY
Stetson University, FL
Taylor University, IN
Tennessee Technological University, TN
Union University, TN
The University of Alabama at Birmingham, AL
The University of Arizona, AZ
University of Arkansas, AR
University of California, San Diego, CA
University of Central Missouri, MO
University of Central Oklahoma, OK
University of Delaware, DE
University of Great Falls, MT
University of Hartford, CT
University of Idaho, ID
University of Illinois at Springfield, IL
University of Illinois at Urbana–Champaign, IL
University of Kansas, KS
University of La Verne, CA
University of Maine, ME
University of Michigan–Dearborn, MI
University of Michigan–Flint, MI
University of Minnesota, Crookston, MN
University of Missouri–Kansas City, MO
University of Missouri–St. Louis, MO
University of Nebraska at Kearney, NE
University of Nebraska at Omaha, NE
University of New England, ME
The University of North Carolina at Asheville, NC
The University of North Carolina at Greensboro, NC
University of North Dakota, ND
University of Northern Colorado, CO
University of St. Francis, IL
University of South Carolina, SC
University of Southern Mississippi, MS
The University of Tennessee at Martin, TN
The University of Texas at El Paso, TX
The University of Texas at San Antonio, TX
The University of Texas–Pan American, TX
University of Vermont, VT
University of West Georgia, GA
University of Wisconsin–Green Bay, WI
University of Wisconsin–La Crosse, WI
University of Wisconsin–Stevens Point, WI
University of Wisconsin–Whitewater, WI
University of Wyoming, WY
VanderCook College of Music, IL
Walla Walla College, WA
Wartburg College, IA
Wayland Baptist University, TX
Wayne State College, NE
Western Carolina University, NC
Western Washington University, WA
Westminster College, MO
Westminster College, UT
Westmont College, CA
West Virginia University, WV
Whitman College, WA
Whitworth University, WA
Widener University, PA
Wisconsin Lutheran College, WI
Wittenberg University, OH

First-Generation College Students

Abilene Christian University, TX
Appalachian State University, NC
Arkansas State University, AR
Austin College, TX
Averett University, VA
Boise State University, ID
Bowie State University, MD
Brenau University, GA
Cabarrus College of Health Sciences, NC
California State University, Chico, CA
California State University, San Bernardino, CA
California State University, Stanislaus, CA
The Catholic University of America, DC
Central Michigan University, MI
Centre College, KY
College of the Southwest, NM
Colorado State University, CO
Colorado State University-Pueblo, CO
Creighton University, NE
Davis & Elkins College, WV
Dowling College, NY
Edgewood College, WI
Elon University, NC
Erskine College, SC
Fairfield University, CT
Flagler College, FL
Fort Lewis College, CO
Georgia Southern University, GA

Glenville State College, WV
Graceland University, IA
Guilford College, NC
Gustavus Adolphus College, MN
Idaho State University, ID
Illinois State University, IL
Kenyon College, OH
LaGrange College, GA
Lewis-Clark State College, ID
Limestone College, SC
Massachusetts College of Liberal Arts, MA
Meredith College, NC
Mesa State College, CO
Michigan State University, MI
Millsaps College, MS
Mississippi State University, MS
Missouri State University, MO
Monmouth University, NJ
Montana State University–Billings, MT
Montreat College, NC
Newman University, KS
Northern Arizona University, AZ
Northwestern College, IA
Oklahoma State University, OK
Ouachita Baptist University, AR
The Richard Stockton College of New Jersey, NJ
St. John Fisher College, NY
Saint Louis University, MO
Saint Mary-of-the-Woods College, IN
Salisbury University, MD
Sonoma State University, CA
South Dakota State University, SD
Southeast Missouri State University, MO
Southern Vermont College, VT
Southwest Minnesota State University, MN
Stephen F. Austin State University, TX
Tennessee Technological University, TN
Texas A&M University–Texarkana, TX
Texas Lutheran University, TX
Texas State University-San Marcos, TX
Texas Tech University, TX
The University of Alabama at Birmingham, AL
University of California, San Diego, CA
University of Central Florida, FL
University of Colorado at Boulder, CO
University of Delaware, DE
University of Great Falls, MT
University of Hartford, CT
University of Houston–Victoria, TX
University of Idaho, ID
University of Illinois at Springfield, IL
University of Illinois at Urbana–Champaign, IL
University of Kansas, KS
University of La Verne, CA
University of Massachusetts Dartmouth, MA
University of Michigan–Flint, MI
University of Nebraska at Kearney, NE
University of Nebraska at Omaha, NE
University of North Alabama, AL
The University of North Carolina at Asheville, NC
University of North Florida, FL
University of St. Francis, IL
University of South Carolina, SC
University of South Carolina Upstate, SC
The University of Texas at Austin, TX
University of Vermont, VT
The University of West Alabama, AL
University of West Florida, FL
University of Wisconsin–La Crosse, WI
University of Wisconsin–Stout, WI
University of Wyoming, WY
Virginia Intermont College, VA
Virginia Polytechnic Institute and State University, VA
Washington State University, WA
Webber International University, FL
Westminster College, UT
Wichita State University, KS
William Carey College, MS
Winston-Salem State University, NC

Handicapped Students

Alabama State University, AL
Appalachian State University, NC
Arkansas State University, AR
Augusta State University, GA
Austin College, TX
Boise State University, ID
Brigham Young University, UT
Bryan College, TN
California State University, Chico, CA
California State University, Fresno, CA
California State University, San Bernardino, CA
Calvin College, MI
The Catholic University of America, DC
Central College, IA
Central Washington University, WA
Clear Creek Baptist Bible College, KY
The College of St. Scholastica, MN
College of Staten Island of the City University of New York, NY
Columbia College Chicago, IL
Creighton University, NE
The Culinary Institute of America, NY
Delaware Valley College, PA
Dordt College, IA
Edgewood College, WI
Emmanuel College, MA
Emporia State University, KS
Florida Gulf Coast University, FL
Fort Lewis College, CO
Francis Marion University, SC
Gallaudet University, DC
Gardner-Webb University, NC
Georgia College & State University, GA
Georgia Institute of Technology, GA
Georgia Southern University, GA
Grand Valley State University, MI
Hofstra University, NY
Idaho State University, ID
James Madison University, VA
Kent State University, OH
Kutztown University of Pennsylvania, PA
Lock Haven University of Pennsylvania, PA
Massachusetts College of Liberal Arts, MA
Michigan State University, MI
Midwestern State University, TX
Mississippi State University, MS
Missouri State University, MO
Murray State University, KY
New Mexico State University, NM
North Carolina Agricultural and Technical State University, NC
Northern Arizona University, AZ
Northwestern College, IA
The Ohio State University, OH
Oklahoma State University, OK
Ouachita Baptist University, AR
Portland State University, OR
Roanoke Bible College, NC
Rowan University, NJ
Sacred Heart University, CT
St. Francis College, NY
St. Gregory's University, OK
Sam Houston State University, TX
San Diego State University, CA
Santa Clara University, CA
Sonoma State University, CA
South Dakota State University, SD
Southeastern Louisiana University, LA
Southern Illinois University Carbondale, IL
Southwest Minnesota State University, MN
State University of New York College at Oneonta, NY
State University of New York College at Potsdam, NY
Texas State University-San Marcos, TX
Texas Tech University, TX
The University of Akron, OH
The University of Alabama at Birmingham, AL
University of California, San Diego, CA
University of Hartford, CT
University of Idaho, ID
University of Illinois at Urbana–Champaign, IL
University of Massachusetts Amherst, MA
University of Michigan, MI
University of Michigan–Dearborn, MI
University of Michigan–Flint, MI
University of Nebraska at Omaha, NE
University of New Hampshire, NH
The University of North Carolina at Asheville, NC
The University of North Carolina at Greensboro, NC
University of North Dakota, ND
University of Northern Colorado, CO
University of South Carolina, SC
The University of Tennessee at Martin, TN
The University of Texas at Austin, TX
The University of Texas at Dallas, TX
The University of Texas at San Antonio, TX
University of West Florida, FL
University of West Georgia, GA
University of Wisconsin–Stout, WI
University of Wisconsin–Whitewater, WI
University of Wyoming, WY
Wake Forest University, NC
Washington State University, WA
Western Carolina University, NC
Westminster College, UT
Wheaton College, IL
Youngstown State University, OH

International Students

Agnes Scott College, GA
Alderson-Broaddus College, WV
Alfred University, NY
Allegheny College, PA
Alliant International University, CA
Anderson University, IN

Andrews University, MI
Arkansas Tech University, AR
Armstrong Atlantic State University, GA
Asbury College, KY
Ashford University, IA
Augsburg College, MN
Augustana College, IL
Augustana College, SD
Austin College, TX
Averett University, VA
Azusa Pacific University, CA
Baker University, KS
Barton College, NC
Bellarmine University, KY
Bemidji State University, MN
Bentley College, MA
Bethany College, KS
Bethany College, WV
Bethel College, IN
Bethel College, KS
Bethel University, MN
Bloomsburg University of Pennsylvania, PA
Bluffton University, OH
Boise State University, ID
Bowling Green State University, OH
Brenau University, GA
Bridgewater College, VA
Brigham Young University, UT
Brigham Young University–Hawaii, HI
Bryan College, TN
Buena Vista University, IA
California State University, Chico, CA
California University of Pennsylvania, PA
Calvin College, MI
Campbellsville University, KY
Canisius College, NY
Capital University, OH
Carroll College, WI
Centenary College of Louisiana, LA
Central College, IA
Central Methodist University, MO
Central Michigan University, MI
Chestnut Hill College, PA
Clarke College, IA
Clarkson University, NY
Clear Creek Baptist Bible College, KY
Coastal Carolina University, SC
Coe College, IA
College of Notre Dame of Maryland, MD
College of St. Catherine, MN
The College of St. Scholastica, MN
College of Staten Island of the City University of New York, NY
The College of Wooster, OH
Columbia College, MO
Columbia International University, SC
Concordia College, MN
Concordia University, IL
Concordia University, NE
Corban College, OR
Cornell College, IA
Crown College, MN
The Culinary Institute of America, NY
Culver-Stockton College, MO
Dana College, NE
Dickinson College, PA
Dickinson State University, ND
Dominican University, IL
Dordt College, IA
Duquesne University, PA
Eastern Michigan University, MI
East Texas Baptist University, TX
Elizabethtown College, PA
Elmira College, NY
Emmanuel College, MA
Emporia State University, KS
Endicott College, MA
Eugene Bible College, OR
Florida Gulf Coast University, FL
Fort Lewis College, CO
Francis Marion University, SC
Franklin Pierce University, NH
Free Will Baptist Bible College, TN
Fresno Pacific University, CA
Friends University, KS
Frostburg State University, MD
Furman University, SC
Gallaudet University, DC
Gannon University, PA
George Fox University, OR
Georgia College & State University, GA
Gonzaga University, WA
Graceland University, IA
Grace University, NE
Green Mountain College, VT
Gustavus Adolphus College, MN
Hanover College, IN
Harding University, AR
Hawai'i Pacific University, HI
Hendrix College, AR
Hillsdale College, MI
Holy Names University, CA
Hood College, MD
Houghton College, NY
Huntington University, IN
Illinois College, IL
Illinois Institute of Technology, IL
Illinois Wesleyan University, IL
Indiana University of Pennsylvania, PA
Iowa Wesleyan College, IA
James Madison University, VA
Jamestown College, ND
Johnson Bible College, TN
Juniata College, PA
Kent State University, OH
Kentucky Christian University, KY
Keuka College, NY
King's College, PA
Kuyper College, MI
Lancaster Bible College, PA
Lebanon Valley College, PA
LeTourneau University, TX
Lincoln University, PA
Lipscomb University, TN
MacMurray College, IL
Malone College, OH
Manchester College, IN
Marywood University, PA
Mayville State University, ND
McMurry University, TX
Mercer University, GA
Meredith College, NC
Mesa State College, CO
Michigan State University, MI
Michigan Technological University, MI
Midwestern State University, TX
Millersville University of Pennsylvania, PA
Minot State University, ND
Missouri State University, MO
Monmouth University, NJ
Montclair State University, NJ
Montreat College, NC
Moravian College, PA
Morningside College, IA
Mount Marty College, SD
Mount Mary College, WI
Mount Union College, OH
Mount Vernon Nazarene University, OH
Murray State University, KY
New England College, NH
Newman University, KS
New Mexico State University, NM
North Central College, IL
Northeastern University, MA
Northern Arizona University, AZ
Northern Illinois University, IL
Northwestern College, IA
Northwestern College, MN
Northwestern State University of Louisiana, LA
Northwest Nazarene University, ID
Northwest University, WA
Nyack College, NY
Ohio Christian University, OH
Ohio Valley University, WV
Ohio Wesleyan University, OH
Olivet College, MI
Oral Roberts University, OK
Ouachita Baptist University, AR
Pacific Lutheran University, WA
Philadelphia Biblical University, PA
Piedmont College, GA
Portland State University, OR
Quinnipiac University, CT
Ramapo College of New Jersey, NJ
Randolph College, VA
Regis College, MA
Rice University, TX
The Richard Stockton College of New Jersey, NJ
Ripon College, WI
Rivier College, NH
Roanoke Bible College, NC
Roberts Wesleyan College, NY
Rochester Institute of Technology, NY
Rowan University, NJ
St. Ambrose University, IA
Saint Francis University, PA
St. Gregory's University, OK
Saint John's University, MN
Saint Louis University, MO
Saint Mary-of-the-Woods College, IN
St. Norbert College, WI
St. Olaf College, MN
Saint Vincent College, PA
Seattle Pacific University, WA
Seton Hill University, PA
Silver Lake College, WI
Simpson College, IA
Sonoma State University, CA
South Dakota State University, SD
Southeast Missouri State University, MO
Southern Adventist University, TN
Southern Illinois University Carbondale, IL
Southern New Hampshire University, NH
Southern Oregon University, OR
Southwest Minnesota State University, MN

Spring Arbor University, MI
State University of New York at Fredonia, NY
State University of New York at Plattsburgh, NY
State University of New York College at Oneonta, NY
Stetson University, FL
Sweet Briar College, VA
Taylor University, IN
Tennessee Wesleyan College, TN
Texas Christian University, TX
Texas Lutheran University, TX
Texas Woman's University, TX
The University of Akron, OH
The University of Alabama, AL
The University of Arizona, AZ
University of Arkansas, AR
University of Bridgeport, CT
University of Charleston, WV
University of Evansville, IN
University of Great Falls, MT
University of Hartford, CT
University of Idaho, ID
University of Illinois at Springfield, IL
University of Kansas, KS
University of La Verne, CA
University of Maine, ME
University of Maine at Fort Kent, ME
University of Miami, FL
University of Michigan, MI
University of Michigan–Flint, MI
University of Missouri–Columbia, MO
The University of Montana, MT
University of Nebraska at Kearney, NE
University of Nebraska at Omaha, NE
University of New Hampshire, NH
University of New Orleans, LA
The University of North Carolina at Asheville, NC
The University of North Carolina at Chapel Hill, NC
University of North Dakota, ND
University of Northern Colorado, CO
University of North Florida, FL
University of Oregon, OR
University of Puget Sound, WA
University of Redlands, CA
University of Rochester, NY
University of St. Thomas, TX
University of Science and Arts of Oklahoma, OK
University of South Carolina, SC
University of Southern California, CA
The University of Tampa, FL
The University of Texas at Dallas, TX
The University of Texas at El Paso, TX
The University of Texas–Pan American, TX
University of the Ozarks, AR
University of Washington, WA
University of West Georgia, GA
University of Wisconsin–La Crosse, WI
University of Wisconsin–Stevens Point, WI
University of Wisconsin–Stout, WI
University of Wisconsin–Whitewater, WI
University of Wyoming, WY
Ursinus College, PA
Utah State University, UT
Valdosta State University, GA
Valparaiso University, IN
Wabash College, IN
Wagner College, NY
Wake Forest University, NC
Walsh University, OH
Wartburg College, IA
Washington Bible College, MD
Washington College, MD
Washington State University, WA
Wayland Baptist University, TX
Webber International University, FL
Webster University, MO
Western Illinois University, IL
Western New England College, MA
Western Oregon University, OR
Western Washington University, WA
Westminster College, MO
Westminster College, PA
Westminster College, UT
Westmont College, CA
West Virginia University, WV
West Virginia Wesleyan College, WV
Wheeling Jesuit University, WV
Whitman College, WA
Whitworth University, WA
Wichita State University, KS
Widener University, PA
Willamette University, OR
William Carey College, MS
Williams Baptist College, AR
Wilson College, PA
Wisconsin Lutheran College, WI
Wittenberg University, OH
Xavier University, OH
York College of Pennsylvania, PA

Local/State Students

Abilene Christian University, TX
Agnes Scott College, GA
Alabama State University, AL
Alcorn State University, MS
Allen College, IA
Alliant International University, CA
Antioch College, OH
Arkansas State University, AR
Auburn University, AL
Augustana College, SD
Augusta State University, GA
Austin College, TX
Averett University, VA
Barton College, NC
Bellarmine University, KY
Berry College, GA
Bethel College, KS
Boise State University, ID
Boston University, MA
Brevard College, NC
Brigham Young University, UT
Brigham Young University–Hawaii, HI
Bryan College, TN
Bryant University, RI
California State University, Chico, CA
California State University, Fresno, CA
California State University, Stanislaus, CA
Carthage College, WI
The Catholic University of America, DC
Centenary College, NJ
Centenary College of Louisiana, LA
Central Michigan University, MI
Central Washington University, WA
Clarion University of Pennsylvania, PA
Clarke College, IA
Clarkson University, NY
Clemson University, SC
Coastal Carolina University, SC
College of St. Catherine, MN
College of St. Joseph, VT
The College of Wooster, OH
Columbia College, MO
Columbus College of Art & Design, OH
Concordia University, NE
Cornell College, IA
Creighton University, NE
Culver-Stockton College, MO
Dakota State University, SD
Dana College, NE
Davis & Elkins College, WV
Dordt College, IA
Dowling College, NY
Duke University, NC
East Texas Baptist University, TX
Edgewood College, WI
Elizabethtown College, PA
Elmira College, NY
Emmanuel College, MA
Emory University, GA
Endicott College, MA
Flagler College, FL
Florida Gulf Coast University, FL
Florida State University, FL
Fort Lewis College, CO
Framingham State College, MA
Franklin Pierce University, NH
Frostburg State University, MD
Furman University, SC
Gardner-Webb University, NC
Georgetown College, KY
Georgia College & State University, GA
Georgia Institute of Technology, GA
Graceland University, IA
Grace University, NE
Grand Valley State University, MI
Green Mountain College, VT
Guilford College, NC
Hardin-Simmons University, TX
Hawai'i Pacific University, HI
Houghton College, NY
Idaho State University, ID
Laboratory Institute of Merchandising, NY
Lee University, TN
Lesley University, MA
LeTourneau University, TX
Lewis-Clark State College, ID
Limestone College, SC
Lock Haven University of Pennsylvania, PA
Longwood University, VA
Lourdes College, OH
Lyon College, AR
Macon State College, GA
Mansfield University of Pennsylvania, PA
Marywood University, PA
Massachusetts College of Liberal Arts, MA
Mayville State University, ND
McDaniel College, MD
McMurry University, TX
Medcenter One College of Nursing, ND
Mercer University, GA
Mesa State College, CO
Miami University, OH

Michigan State University, MI
Michigan Technological University, MI
Middle Tennessee State University, TN
Minnesota State University Mankato, MN
Minot State University, ND
Mississippi State University, MS
Monmouth University, NJ
Montana State University–Billings, MT
Morehead State University, KY
Mount Vernon Nazarene University, OH
Murray State University, KY
New England College, NH
New Mexico State University, NM
New York Institute of Technology, NY
Northern Arizona University, AZ
Nyack College, NY
Ohio Valley University, WV
Ohio Wesleyan University, OH
Oklahoma Baptist University, OK
Oklahoma Panhandle State University, OK
Ouachita Baptist University, AR
Randolph College, VA
Regis University, CO
The Richard Stockton College of New Jersey, NJ
Ripon College, WI
Roanoke College, VA
St. Cloud State University, MN
St. John Fisher College, NY
Saint Mary-of-the-Woods College, IN
Saint Michael's College, VT
San Diego State University, CA
Shenandoah University, VA
Silver Lake College, WI
Slippery Rock University of Pennsylvania, PA
Smith College, MA
Sonoma State University, CA
Southern Adventist University, TN
Southern Nazarene University, OK
Southern New Hampshire University, NH
Southwest Baptist University, MO
Southwest Minnesota State University, MN
State University of New York at Binghamton, NY
State University of New York at Fredonia, NY
State University of New York College at Geneseo, NY
State University of New York College at Oneonta, NY
State University of New York College at Potsdam, NY
Stephen F. Austin State University, TX
Stephens College, MO
Sterling College, VT
Stetson University, FL
Sweet Briar College, VA
Taylor University Fort Wayne, IN
Tennessee State University, TN
Tennessee Technological University, TN
Texas Christian University, TX
Tulane University, LA
Tuskegee University, AL
Unity College, ME
University at Buffalo, the State University of New York, NY
The University of Akron, OH
The University of Alabama at Birmingham, AL
The University of Alabama in Huntsville, AL
University of Bridgeport, CT
University of Charleston, WV
University of Colorado at Boulder, CO
University of Delaware, DE
University of Denver, CO
University of Georgia, GA
University of Hartford, CT
University of Idaho, ID
University of Illinois at Springfield, IL
University of Illinois at Urbana–Champaign, IL
University of Kansas, KS
University of Maine, ME
University of Michigan, MI
University of Michigan–Flint, MI
University of Missouri–St. Louis, MO
University of New Hampshire, NH
University of New Orleans, LA
The University of North Carolina at Asheville, NC
The University of North Carolina Wilmington, NC
University of Northern Colorado, CO
University of Oregon, OR
University of South Carolina, SC
University of Southern Maine, ME
University of Southern Mississippi, MS
The University of Texas at Dallas, TX
The University of Texas at El Paso, TX
The University of Texas at San Antonio, TX
The University of Texas–Pan American, TX
University of West Georgia, GA
University of Wisconsin–La Crosse, WI
University of Wisconsin–Stout, WI
University of Wisconsin–Whitewater, WI
University of Wyoming, WY
Vanderbilt University, TN
Virginia Military Institute, VA
Virginia Polytechnic Institute and State University, VA
Wake Forest University, NC
Walsh University, OH
Warren Wilson College, NC
Washington and Lee University, VA
Wayland Baptist University, TX
Wayne State College, NE
Webber International University, FL
Western Carolina University, NC
Western New England College, MA
Western Washington University, WA
Westminster College, MO
Westminster College, UT
West Virginia University, WV
Wilson College, PA
Winona State University, MN
Wittenberg University, OH

Married Students

Auburn University, AL
Brigham Young University–Hawaii, HI
California State University, Chico, CA
Columbia International University, SC
Eugene Bible College, OR
Franklin Pierce University, NH
Free Will Baptist Bible College, TN
Georgia Southern University, GA
Grace University, NE
Johnson Bible College, TN
Lancaster Bible College, PA
New Mexico State University, NM
Northwest University, WA
Ouachita Baptist University, AR
Roanoke Bible College, NC
Sonoma State University, CA
The University of Alabama at Birmingham, AL
University of Kansas, KS
Valley Forge Christian College, PA

Members of Minority Groups

Abilene Christian University, TX
Alabama State University, AL
Alcorn State University, MS
Allen College, IA
Alliant International University, CA
Appalachian State University, NC
Arkansas State University, AR
Augsburg College, MN
Augustana College, IL
Augustana College, SD
Austin Peay State University, TN
Baker University, KS
Baldwin-Wallace College, OH
Beloit College, WI
Bentley College, MA
Berry College, GA
Bethel College, IN
Bethel University, MN
Bluffton University, OH
Boise State University, ID
Bowling Green State University, OH
Bradley University, IL
Brigham Young University, UT
Brigham Young University–Hawaii, HI
Bryant University, RI
California State University, Chico, CA
California State University, Dominguez Hills, CA
California State University, Stanislaus, CA
California University of Pennsylvania, PA
Calvin College, MI
Capital University, OH
Carson-Newman College, TN
Carthage College, WI
Centenary College of Louisiana, LA
Central College, IA
Central Michigan University, MI
Clarion University of Pennsylvania, PA
Clarke College, IA
Clarkson University, NY
Clemson University, SC
College Misericordia, PA
The College of New Jersey, NJ
The College of Saint Rose, NY
The College of St. Scholastica, MN
College of Staten Island of the City University of New York, NY
The College of Wooster, OH
Concordia College, MN
Concordia University, NE
Cornell College, IA
Creighton University, NE
Crown College, MN
The Culinary Institute of America, NY
Dakota State University, SD

Dana College, NE
Denison University, OH
Dickinson State University, ND
Dordt College, IA
Drake University, IA
Duquesne University, PA
East Central University, OK
Eastern Kentucky University, KY
Eastern Michigan University, MI
East Tennessee State University, TN
Edgewood College, WI
Elizabethtown College, PA
Elmhurst College, IL
Emporia State University, KS
Erskine College, SC
Fairfield University, CT
Flagler College, FL
Florida Gulf Coast University, FL
Franklin & Marshall College, PA
Franklin College, IN
Fresno Pacific University, CA
Gannon University, PA
Gardner-Webb University, NC
George Fox University, OR
Georgia College & State University, GA
Georgia Institute of Technology, GA
Georgia Southern University, GA
Gonzaga University, WA
Graceland University, IA
Grace University, NE
Grand Valley State University, MI
Grove City College, PA
Gustavus Adolphus College, MN
Hanover College, IN
Hilbert College, NY
Idaho State University, ID
Illinois College, IL
Illinois State University, IL
Indiana State University, IN
Johnson Bible College, TN
Kent State University, OH
Kentucky Christian University, KY
Kettering University, MI
King College, TN
King's College, PA
Kuyper College, MI
Lawrence Technological University, MI
Lawrence University, WI
Le Moyne College, NY
Lesley University, MA
Lewis-Clark State College, ID
Lipscomb University, TN
Lock Haven University of Pennsylvania, PA
Lourdes College, OH
Loyola College in Maryland, MD
Luther College, IA
Lyon College, AR
Manchester College, IN
Mansfield University of Pennsylvania, PA
Maryville University of Saint Louis, MO
Mayville State University, ND
Mercer University, GA
Meredith College, NC
Mesa State College, CO
Miami University, OH
Michigan State University, MI
Michigan Technological University, MI
Middle Tennessee State University, TN
Millsaps College, MS
Minot State University, ND
Missouri State University, MO
Monmouth University, NJ
Montana State University–Billings, MT
Morehead State University, KY
Mount St. Mary's University, MD
Mount Vernon Nazarene University, OH
Murray State University, KY
Nebraska Wesleyan University, NE
New Mexico State University, NM
Nicholls State University, LA
North Carolina Agricultural and Technical State University, NC
Northern Illinois University, IL
Northern Michigan University, MI
Northwest Nazarene University, ID
The Ohio State University, OH
Ohio University, OH
Ohio University–Chillicothe, OH
Ohio University–Eastern, OH
Ohio University–Lancaster, OH
Ohio University–Southern Campus, OH
Ohio University–Zanesville, OH
Ohio Wesleyan University, OH
Ouachita Baptist University, AR
Pitzer College, CA
Polytechnic University, Brooklyn Campus, NY
Portland State University, OR
Quinnipiac University, CT
Regis University, CO
Rensselaer Polytechnic Institute, NY
The Richard Stockton College of New Jersey, NJ
Ripon College, WI
Roanoke College, VA
Robert Morris University, PA
Rochester Institute of Technology, NY
Rowan University, NJ
Sacred Heart University, CT
St. Ambrose University, IA
St. Cloud State University, MN
St. John Fisher College, NY
Saint Louis University, MO
Saint Mary-of-the-Woods College, IN
Saint Mary's University of Minnesota, MN
Saint Michael's College, VT
Saint Vincent College, PA
Seattle University, WA
Sewanee: The University of the South, TN
Shepherd University, WV
Simpson College, IA
Simpson University, CA
Slippery Rock University of Pennsylvania, PA
Sonoma State University, CA
South Dakota State University, SD
Southeast Missouri State University, MO
Southern Adventist University, TN
Southern Arkansas University–Magnolia, AR
Southern Oregon University, OR
Southern Wesleyan University, SC
Southwest Minnesota State University, MN
Spring Arbor University, MI
State University of New York at Binghamton, NY
State University of New York at Fredonia, NY
State University of New York at New Paltz, NY
State University of New York College at Geneseo, NY
State University of New York College at Oneonta, NY
State University of New York College at Potsdam, NY
State University of New York College of Environmental Science and Forestry, NY
Stetson University, FL
Stonehill College, MA
Tennessee State University, TN
Tennessee Technological University, TN
Tennessee Wesleyan College, TN
Thomas More College, KY
Transylvania University, KY
Trinity International University, IL
Tri-State University, IN
Unity College, ME
The University of Akron, OH
The University of Alabama at Birmingham, AL
The University of Alabama in Huntsville, AL
University of Alaska Fairbanks, AK
University of California, San Diego, CA
University of Central Missouri, MO
University of Central Oklahoma, OK
University of Delaware, DE
University of Detroit Mercy, MI
University of Evansville, IN
University of Florida, FL
University of Hartford, CT
University of Idaho, ID
University of Illinois at Springfield, IL
University of Illinois at Urbana–Champaign, IL
University of Kansas, KS
University of Maine, ME
University of Maine at Farmington, ME
University of Maine at Fort Kent, ME
University of Massachusetts Dartmouth, MA
University of Michigan, MI
University of Michigan–Dearborn, MI
University of Michigan–Flint, MI
University of Minnesota, Crookston, MN
University of Missouri–Columbia, MO
University of Missouri–Kansas City, MO
University of Missouri–St. Louis, MO
The University of Montana, MT
University of Nebraska at Omaha, NE
University of New England, ME
University of New Orleans, LA
The University of North Carolina at Asheville, NC
The University of North Carolina at Greensboro, NC
University of North Dakota, ND
University of Northern Colorado, CO
University of Northern Iowa, IA
University of North Florida, FL
University of Oklahoma, OK
University of Richmond, VA
University of St. Thomas, TX
University of South Carolina, SC
University of Southern California, CA
University of Southern Indiana, IN

The University of Tennessee at Martin, TN
The University of Texas at Dallas, TX
The University of Texas at El Paso, TX
University of the Ozarks, AR
University of West Florida, FL
University of West Georgia, GA
University of Wisconsin–La Crosse, WI
University of Wisconsin–Stevens Point, WI
University of Wisconsin–Stout, WI
University of Wisconsin–Whitewater, WI
Valdosta State University, GA
Vanderbilt University, TN
Virginia Intermont College, VA
Virginia Polytechnic Institute and State University, VA
Wake Forest University, NC
Walsh University, OH
Warner Pacific College, OR
Wartburg College, IA
Wayland Baptist University, TX
Wayne State College, NE
Western Carolina University, NC
Western Illinois University, IL
Western New England College, MA
Western Washington University, WA
Westminster College, UT
West Virginia University, WV
West Virginia Wesleyan College, WV
Whitworth University, WA
Wichita State University, KS
Willamette University, OR
Williams Baptist College, AR
Winona State University, MN
Wisconsin Lutheran College, WI
Wittenberg University, OH
Xavier University, OH
York College of Pennsylvania, PA
Youngstown State University, OH

Out-of-State Students

Abilene Christian University, TX
Alabama State University, AL
Allen College, IA
Appalachian State University, NC
Arkansas State University, AR
Arkansas Tech University, AR
Auburn University, AL
Aurora University, IL
Averett University, VA
Baker University, KS
Bellarmine University, KY
Bemidji State University, MN
Benedictine University, IL
Bethel University, MN
Bluffton University, OH
Boise State University, ID
Bridgewater College, VA
Brigham Young University, UT
Buena Vista University, IA
California State University, Chico, CA
Centenary College, NJ
Centenary College of Louisiana, LA
Central College, IA
Central Michigan University, MI
Central Pennsylvania College, PA
Coastal Carolina University, SC
College Misericordia, PA
The College of New Rochelle, NY
College of St. Catherine, MN
Concordia University Wisconsin, WI
Dana College, NE
Dordt College, IA
East Central University, OK
Eastern Michigan University, MI
Erskine College, SC
Eugene Bible College, OR
Flagler College, FL
Florida Gulf Coast University, FL
Fort Lewis College, CO
Francis Marion University, SC
Franklin College, IN
Friends University, KS
Frostburg State University, MD
Gardner-Webb University, NC
George Fox University, OR
Georgia College & State University, GA
Georgia Institute of Technology, GA
Grace University, NE
Grand Valley State University, MI
Gustavus Adolphus College, MN
Hampden-Sydney College, VA
Hanover College, IN
Hardin-Simmons University, TX
Hawai'i Pacific University, HI
Heidelberg College, OH
Idaho State University, ID
Illinois College, IL
Iowa Wesleyan College, IA
James Madison University, VA
Kent State University, OH
Kentucky Wesleyan College, KY
Lewis-Clark State College, ID
Limestone College, SC
Louisiana Tech University, LA
Lourdes College, OH
MacMurray College, IL
Massachusetts College of Liberal Arts, MA
Mayville State University, ND
McKendree College, IL
McMurry University, TX
Meredith College, NC
Mesa State College, CO
Miami University, OH
Michigan State University, MI
Michigan Technological University, MI
Midwestern State University, TX
Minnesota State University Mankato, MN
Minot State University, ND
Mississippi State University, MS
Missouri State University, MO
Monmouth University, NJ
Montana State University–Billings, MT
Morehead State University, KY
Morningside College, IA
Murray State University, KY
New College of Florida, FL
New Mexico State University, NM
Northern Arizona University, AZ
Northern Michigan University, MI
Northwestern State University of Louisiana, LA
Northwest Nazarene University, ID
Nyack College, NY
Ohio Christian University, OH
The Ohio State University, OH
Ohio Wesleyan University, OH
Oklahoma Baptist University, OK
Oklahoma Panhandle State University, OK
Oklahoma State University, OK
Ouachita Baptist University, AR
Piedmont College, GA
Portland State University, OR
Ramapo College of New Jersey, NJ
Ripon College, WI
Robert Morris University, PA
Roberts Wesleyan College, NY
St. Cloud State University, MN
Saint Mary-of-the-Woods College, IN
Saint Michael's College, VT
Saint Vincent College, PA
Shimer College, IL
Simpson University, CA
Slippery Rock University of Pennsylvania, PA
Sonoma State University, CA
Southeastern Louisiana University, LA
Southeastern Oklahoma State University, OK
Southeast Missouri State University, MO
Southern Adventist University, TN
Southern Arkansas University–Magnolia, AR
State University of New York at Binghamton, NY
State University of New York at Fredonia, NY
State University of New York at Plattsburgh, NY
Stephens College, MO
Tennessee Technological University, TN
Texas Christian University, TX
Texas Tech University, TX
Transylvania University, KY
The University of Akron, OH
The University of Alabama, AL
The University of Alabama at Birmingham, AL
University of Arkansas, AR
University of Arkansas at Monticello, AR
University of Central Missouri, MO
University of Florida, FL
University of Idaho, ID
University of Illinois at Springfield, IL
University of Illinois at Urbana–Champaign, IL
University of Kansas, KS
University of Maine, ME
University of Maine at Farmington, ME
University of Maryland, College Park, MD
University of Michigan, MI
University of Michigan–Dearborn, MI
University of Minnesota, Crookston, MN
University of Missouri–Columbia, MO
University of Missouri–Kansas City, MO
The University of Montana, MT
University of Nebraska at Kearney, NE
University of Nebraska at Omaha, NE
University of New Orleans, LA
University of North Alabama, AL
The University of North Carolina at Chapel Hill, NC
The University of North Carolina at Greensboro, NC
University of Northern Colorado, CO
University of North Florida, FL
University of Science and Arts of Oklahoma, OK
University of South Carolina, SC

University of Southern Indiana, IN
University of Southern Maine, ME
University of Southern Mississippi, MS
The University of Tennessee at Martin, TN
The University of Texas at Austin, TX
The University of Texas at Dallas, TX
The University of Texas at El Paso, TX
The University of Texas at San Antonio, TX
The University of Texas–Pan American, TX
University of Wisconsin–La Crosse, WI
University of Wisconsin–Stevens Point, WI
University of Wisconsin–Stout, WI
University of Wisconsin–Whitewater, WI
University of Wyoming, WY
Virginia Military Institute, VA
Virginia Polytechnic Institute and State University, VA
Walsh University, OH
Wartburg College, IA
Washington State University, WA
Wayne State College, NE
Western New England College, MA
Winona State University, MN

Parents of Current Students

Aurora University, IL
The College of New Rochelle, NY
Columbia College, MO
Franklin Pierce University, NH
Green Mountain College, VT
Gustavus Adolphus College, MN
Huntington University, IN
Johnson Bible College, TN
Malone College, OH
Marymount University, VA
Maryville University of Saint Louis, MO
Missouri Baptist University, MO
Mount Aloysius College, PA
Mount Marty College, SD
Mount Mary College, WI
New England College, NH
Northwest University, WA
Peirce College, PA
Saint Mary-of-the-Woods College, IN
Seton Hill University, PA
State University of New York at Fredonia, NY
Stephens College, MO
The University of Alabama at Birmingham, AL
University of Great Falls, MT
University of Hartford, CT

Previous College Experience

Abilene Christian University, TX
Alma College, MI
Alverno College, WI
Arkansas Tech University, AR
Bellarmine University, KY
Benedictine University, IL
Bethel College, KS
Bloomfield College, NJ
Boise State University, ID
Brevard College, NC
Carthage College, WI
Cedar Crest College, PA
Centenary College, NJ
Central College, IA
Central Washington University, WA
College Misericordia, PA
The College of New Rochelle, NY
College of St. Joseph, VT
The College of St. Scholastica, MN
Columbia College, MO
East Central University, OK
Eastern Michigan University, MI
East Texas Baptist University, TX
Elmira College, NY
Florida Institute of Technology, FL
Gardner-Webb University, NC
Grace University, NE
Hawai'i Pacific University, HI
Hendrix College, AR
Hood College, MD
Illinois College, IL
Illinois State University, IL
Lake Forest College, IL
Lancaster Bible College, PA
Lewis-Clark State College, ID
Lock Haven University of Pennsylvania, PA
Lourdes College, OH
MacMurray College, IL
Manchester College, IN
Manhattanville College, NY
McDaniel College, MD
McMurry University, TX
Memphis College of Art, TN
Meredith College, NC
Michigan Technological University, MI
Mississippi State University, MS
Monmouth University, NJ
Mount Mercy College, IA
New Mexico State University, NM
New York Institute of Technology, NY
The Ohio State University, OH
Oklahoma State University, OK
Ouachita Baptist University, AR
Pacific Lutheran University, WA
Palm Beach Atlantic University, FL
Peirce College, PA
The Richard Stockton College of New Jersey, NJ
Ripon College, WI
Saint Francis University, PA
Saint Louis University, MO
Slippery Rock University of Pennsylvania, PA
Sonoma State University, CA
Southeast Missouri State University, MO
Southern New Hampshire University, NH
Southwest Minnesota State University, MN
State University of New York at Fredonia, NY
State University of New York College at Potsdam, NY
Stephen F. Austin State University, TX
Sterling College, VT
The University of Alabama at Birmingham, AL
University of Arkansas, AR
University of Bridgeport, CT
University of Central Missouri, MO
University of Hartford, CT
University of Kansas, KS
University of Maine, ME
University of Michigan–Dearborn, MI
University of Minnesota, Crookston, MN
University of New Orleans, LA
University of Oklahoma, OK
University of Science and Arts of Oklahoma, OK
University of West Georgia, GA
University of Wisconsin–Stout, WI
Walsh College of Accountancy and Business Administration, MI
Warren Wilson College, NC
Western Washington University, WA

Public Servants

Arkansas Tech University, AR
College of Staten Island of the City University of New York, NY
Dowling College, NY
Hardin-Simmons University, TX
Hofstra University, NY
Louisiana Tech University, LA
Michigan State University, MI
Missouri Baptist University, MO
New York Institute of Technology, NY
Nicholls State University, LA
Northwestern State University of Louisiana, LA
Peirce College, PA
St. Francis College, NY
Southern Illinois University Carbondale, IL
Tennessee Technological University, TN
The University of Alabama at Birmingham, AL
University of Illinois at Springfield, IL
University of Maine, ME
University of New Orleans, LA
The University of Texas at Dallas, TX
Washington State University, WA
Westminster College, UT

Relatives of Clergy

Abilene Christian University, TX
Albion College, MI
Anderson University, IN
Arcadia University, PA
Augsburg College, MN
Austin College, TX
Averett University, VA
Azusa Pacific University, CA
Baker University, KS
Baptist Bible College, MO
Barton College, NC
Bethany College, KS
Bethany College, WV
Bethel College, IN
Bethel College, KS
Bethel University, MN
Birmingham-Southern College, AL
Bluffton University, OH
Boston University, MA
Brevard College, NC
Bryan College, TN
Campbellsville University, KY
Capital University, OH
Carson-Newman College, TN
Carthage College, WI
Cedar Crest College, PA
Centenary College of Louisiana, LA
Central Methodist University, MO
Claflin University, SC
Clarke College, IA
College Misericordia, PA
College of the Southwest, NM

Columbia International University, SC
Corban College, OR
Cornell College, IA
Crown College, MN
Dallas Baptist University, TX
Davidson College, NC
DeSales University, PA
Dominican College, NY
Drury University, MO
Duquesne University, PA
Elon University, NC
Emory University, GA
Erskine College, SC
Eugene Bible College, OR
Faulkner University, AL
Free Will Baptist Bible College, TN
Friends University, KS
Furman University, SC
Gardner-Webb University, NC
George Fox University, OR
Georgetown College, KY
Grace Bible College, MI
Grace College, IN
Grace University, NE
Green Mountain College, VT
Hardin-Simmons University, TX
Hastings College, NE
Hawai'i Pacific University, HI
Heidelberg College, OH
Hendrix College, AR
Houghton College, NY
Houston Baptist University, TX
Huntington University, IN
Iowa Wesleyan College, IA
Jamestown College, ND
Johnson Bible College, TN
Judson College, AL
Kentucky Wesleyan College, KY
King College, TN
King's College, PA
LaGrange College, GA
Lambuth University, TN
Lancaster Bible College, PA
La Sierra University, CA
LeTourneau University, TX
Lindsey Wilson College, KY
Lipscomb University, TN
Lycoming College, PA
Malone College, OH
Maranatha Baptist Bible College, WI
McMurry University, TX
Mercer University, GA
Messiah College, PA
Methodist University, NC
Millsaps College, MS
Missouri Baptist University, MO
Moravian College, PA
Mount Union College, OH
Mount Vernon Nazarene University, OH
Nebraska Wesleyan University, NE
Niagara University, NY
North Central College, IL
Northwest Christian College, OR
Northwestern College, MN
Northwest Nazarene University, ID
Northwest University, WA
Nyack College, NY
Ohio Christian University, OH
Ohio Valley University, WV
Ohio Wesleyan University, OH
Oklahoma Baptist University, OK
Oral Roberts University, OK
Ouachita Baptist University, AR
Pacific Lutheran University, WA
Palm Beach Atlantic University, FL
Philadelphia Biblical University, PA
Randolph College, VA
Regis College, MA
Rhodes College, TN
Roberts Wesleyan College, NY
Rosemont College, PA
Saint Mary's College of California, CA
Samford University, AL
Seattle Pacific University, WA
Sewanee: The University of the South, TN
Shasta Bible College, CA
Shenandoah University, VA
Simpson College, IA
Simpson University, CA
Southern Methodist College, SC
Southern Methodist University, TX
Southern Wesleyan University, SC
Southwest Baptist University, MO
Southwestern University, TX
Spring Arbor University, MI
Stonehill College, MA
Taylor University Fort Wayne, IN
Tennessee Wesleyan College, TN
Texas Christian University, TX
Thiel College, PA
Transylvania University, KY
Trevecca Nazarene University, TN
Union University, TN
The University of Alabama at Birmingham, AL
The University of North Carolina at Chapel Hill, NC
University of St. Thomas, TX
University of South Carolina, SC
The University of Texas at Austin, TX
University of the Cumberlands, KY
University of the Ozarks, AR
University of Tulsa, OK
Valley Forge Christian College, PA
Valparaiso University, IN
Virginia Wesleyan College, VA
Wake Forest University, NC
Washington Bible College, MD
Wayland Baptist University, TX
Westminster College, MO
Westminster College, UT
West Virginia Wesleyan College, WV
Whitworth University, WA
William Carey College, MS
Williams Baptist College, AR
Wilson College, PA
Wingate University, NC
Wittenberg University, OH

Religious Affiliation

Abilene Christian University, TX
Agnes Scott College, GA
Alabama State University, AL
Alderson-Broaddus College, WV
Arcadia University, PA
Armstrong Atlantic State University, GA
Augustana College, IL
Augustana College, SD
Averett University, VA
Azusa Pacific University, CA
Baldwin-Wallace College, OH
The Baptist College of Florida, FL
Barton College, NC
Bethany College, KS
Bethany College, WV
Bethel College, IN
Bethel College, KS
Bethel University, MN
Birmingham-Southern College, AL
Bluffton University, OH
Boston University, MA
Brevard College, NC
Bridgewater College, VA
Brigham Young University, UT
Brigham Young University–Hawaii, HI
Bryan College, TN
Buena Vista University, IA
Calvin College, MI
Campbellsville University, KY
Canisius College, NY
Capital University, OH
Carthage College, WI
The Catholic University of America, DC
Cedar Crest College, PA
Cedarville University, OH
Centenary College, NJ
Centenary College of Louisiana, LA
Central College, IA
Central Methodist University, MO
Chestnut Hill College, PA
Christian Brothers University, TN
Claflin University, SC
Clarke College, IA
Clearwater Christian College, FL
College Misericordia, PA
College of St. Catherine, MN
College of St. Joseph, VT
The College of St. Scholastica, MN
Columbia College, MO
Columbia International University, SC
Conception Seminary College, MO
Concordia University, CA
Concordia University, IL
Concordia University at Austin, TX
Concordia University, St. Paul, MN
Concordia University Wisconsin, WI
Cornell College, IA
Creighton University, NE
Culver-Stockton College, MO
Dallas Baptist University, TX
Dana College, NE
Davis & Elkins College, WV
DeSales University, PA
Doane College, NE
Dordt College, IA
Drury University, MO
Duquesne University, PA
Eastern Michigan University, MI
East Texas Baptist University, TX
Edgewood College, WI
Elizabethtown College, PA
Elmhurst College, IL
Emmanuel College, MA
Emory University, GA
Emporia State University, KS
Endicott College, MA
Erskine College, SC
Eureka College, IL

Evangel University, MO
Fairfield University, CT
Faulkner University, AL
Franklin College, IN
Fresno Pacific University, CA
Friends University, KS
Furman University, SC
Gannon University, PA
Geneva College, PA
George Fox University, OR
Georgetown College, KY
Georgia College & State University, GA
Grace College, IN
Graceland University, IA
Grace University, NE
Green Mountain College, VT
Hampden-Sydney College, VA
Hanover College, IN
Hardin-Simmons University, TX
Hastings College, NE
Hawai'i Pacific University, HI
Heidelberg College, OH
Holy Names University, CA
Houghton College, NY
Huntington University, IN
Illinois College, IL
Iona College, NY
Iowa Wesleyan College, IA
Jamestown College, ND
Jarvis Christian College, TX
Johnson Bible College, TN
Judson College, AL
Juniata College, PA
Kentucky Christian University, KY
Kentucky Wesleyan College, KY
LaGrange College, GA
Lakeland College, WI
Lambuth University, TN
Lancaster Bible College, PA
La Sierra University, CA
Lindsey Wilson College, KY
Loyola University Chicago, IL
Luther College, IA
Lyon College, AR
MacMurray College, IL
Malone College, OH
Manchester College, IN
Marywood University, PA
McKendree College, IL
McMurry University, TX
Medical College of Georgia, GA
Mercer University, GA
Meredith College, NC
Messenger College, MO
Messiah College, PA
Methodist University, NC
Michigan State University, MI
Millsaps College, MS
Missouri Baptist University, MO
Moravian College, PA
Mount Aloysius College, PA
Mount Marty College, SD
Mount Olive College, NC
Mount Vernon Nazarene University, OH
Northwest Christian College, OR
Northwestern College, IA
Northwest Nazarene University, ID
Northwest University, WA
Nyack College, NY
Ohio Christian University, OH
Ohio Valley University, WV
Ohio Wesleyan University, OH
Oklahoma Baptist University, OK
Olivet College, MI
Ouachita Baptist University, AR
Randolph College, VA
Regis College, MA
Rhodes College, TN
Ripon College, WI
Roanoke College, VA
Roberts Wesleyan College, NY
Rosemont College, PA
Sacred Heart University, CT
St. Edward's University, TX
St. Gregory's University, OK
Saint Mary-of-the-Woods College, IN
Saint Michael's College, VT
Seattle Pacific University, WA
Shenandoah University, VA
Simpson College, IA
Simpson University, CA
Southern Nazarene University, OK
Southern Wesleyan University, SC
Spring Arbor University, MI
Stephen F. Austin State University, TX
Taylor University, IN
Tennessee Wesleyan College, TN
Texas Christian University, TX
Texas Lutheran University, TX
Thiel College, PA
Thomas More College, KY
Transylvania University, KY
Trevecca Nazarene University, TN
Trinity International University, IL
Union College, KY
Union University, TN
The University of Alabama at Birmingham, AL
University of Dallas, TX
University of Dayton, OH
University of Evansville, IN
University of Great Falls, MT
University of Hartford, CT
University of La Verne, CA
The University of North Carolina at Chapel Hill, NC
The University of North Carolina at Greensboro, NC
University of St. Francis, IL
University of St. Thomas, TX
University of South Carolina, SC
University of the Ozarks, AR
University of Tulsa, OK
Urbana University, OH
Valparaiso University, IN
Virginia Intermont College, VA
Virginia Wesleyan College, VA
Wake Forest University, NC
Warner Pacific College, OR
Warren Wilson College, NC
Wartburg College, IA
Washington State University, WA
Wayland Baptist University, TX
Westminster College, MO
Westminster College, PA
Westminster College, UT
West Virginia Wesleyan College, WV
Wheeling Jesuit University, WV
William Carey College, MS
Williams Baptist College, AR
Wilson College, PA
Wingate University, NC
Wittenberg University, OH

Siblings of Current Students

Asbury College, KY
Augsburg College, MN
Augustana College, IL
Augustana College, SD
Aurora University, IL
Azusa Pacific University, CA
Baldwin-Wallace College, OH
Barton College, NC
Becker College, MA
Beloit College, WI
Benedictine University, IL
Bethel College, IN
Brevard College, NC
Bridgewater College, VA
Bryant University, RI
Buena Vista University, IA
Canisius College, NY
Capital University, OH
Carroll College, WI
Carson-Newman College, TN
Carthage College, WI
The Catholic University of America, DC
Cedar Crest College, PA
Centenary College, NJ
Central College, IA
Central Methodist University, MO
Chatham University, PA
Clarke College, IA
Clearwater Christian College, FL
Coe College, IA
College Misericordia, PA
The College of New Rochelle, NY
College of St. Catherine, MN
The College of Saint Rose, NY
The College of St. Scholastica, MN
Columbia College, MO
Concordia University, CA
Corban College, OR
Creighton University, NE
Crown College, MN
DeSales University, PA
Doane College, NE
Dominican University, IL
East Texas Baptist University, TX
Elizabethtown College, PA
Elmhurst College, IL
Elmira College, NY
Embry-Riddle Aeronautical University, FL
Emmanuel College, MA
Erskine College, SC
Eureka College, IL
Faulkner University, AL
Franklin College, IN
Franklin Pierce University, NH
Gonzaga University, WA
Grace University, NE
Green Mountain College, VT
Gustavus Adolphus College, MN
Gwynedd-Mercy College, PA
Hanover College, IN
Harding University, AR
Hardin-Simmons University, TX
Hastings College, NE

Hilbert College, NY
Hood College, MD
Houghton College, NY
Houston Baptist University, TX
Huntington University, IN
Iona College, NY
Ithaca College, NY
James Madison University, VA
Johnson Bible College, TN
Johnson C. Smith University, NC
Kentucky Wesleyan College, KY
Kettering University, MI
Keuka College, NY
King's College, PA
Lakeland College, WI
Lancaster Bible College, PA
La Sierra University, CA
Lee University, TN
Limestone College, SC
Loras College, IA
MacMurray College, IL
Malone College, OH
Marian College of Fond du Lac, WI
Marymount University, VA
Maryville University of Saint Louis, MO
Marywood University, PA
McDaniel College, MD
Mercer University, GA
Messiah College, PA
Missouri Baptist University, MO
Molloy College, NY
Mount Aloysius College, PA
Mount Marty College, SD
Mount Mary College, WI
Mount St. Mary's University, MD
Mount Vernon Nazarene University, OH
Nazareth College of Rochester, NY
Nebraska Wesleyan University, NE
New England College, NH
Newman University, KS
Nichols College, MA
Northwestern College, IA
Northwestern College, MN
Northwest Nazarene University, ID
Northwest University, WA
Northwood University, MI
Northwood University, Florida Campus, FL
Northwood University, Texas Campus, TX
Oglethorpe University, GA
Ohio Christian University, OH
Olivet College, MI
Oral Roberts University, OK
Pacific Union College, CA
Palm Beach Atlantic University, FL
Peirce College, PA
Philadelphia Biblical University, PA
Quinnipiac University, CT
Regis College, MA
Ripon College, WI
Rivier College, NH
Roberts Wesleyan College, NY
Rockhurst University, MO
Rosemont College, PA
Russell Sage College, NY
Sacred Heart University, CT
Saint Anselm College, NH
Saint Francis University, PA
Saint Joseph's College, IN
Saint Joseph's College of Maine, ME
St. Lawrence University, NY
Saint Louis University, MO
Saint Mary-of-the-Woods College, IN
Saint Mary's College, IN
Saint Michael's College, VT
Seton Hill University, PA
Simpson College, IA
Simpson University, CA
Southeastern University, FL
Southern Adventist University, TN
Southern New Hampshire University, NH
Southern Wesleyan University, SC
Spring Hill College, AL
Stephens College, MO
Stonehill College, MA
Suffolk University, MA
Thiel College, PA
Union University, TN
The University of Alabama at Birmingham, AL
University of Dallas, TX
University of Evansville, IN
University of Great Falls, MT
University of Hartford, CT
University of New England, ME
University of St. Francis, IL
University of Saint Francis, IN
University of the Cumberlands, KY
University of the Ozarks, AR
University of Tulsa, OK
Ursinus College, PA
Valley Forge Christian College, PA
Virginia Intermont College, VA
Wagner College, NY
Walsh University, OH
Wartburg College, IA
Washington Bible College, MD
Webber International University, FL
Western New England College, MA
Westminster College, MO
Westminster College, UT
Whitworth University, WA
Widener University, PA
William Jewell College, MO
Xavier University, OH

Spouses of Current Students

Arlington Baptist College, TX
Augustana College, SD
Aurora University, IL
Baptist Bible College, MO
The Baptist College of Florida, FL
Bethel College, IN
Boise State University, ID
Bryan College, TN
Canisius College, NY
Carroll College, WI
Central Methodist University, MO
The College of New Rochelle, NY
Columbia College, MO
Columbia International University, SC
Elmhurst College, IL
Eugene Bible College, OR
Franklin Pierce University, NH
Grace University, NE
Huntington University, IN
Jamestown College, ND
Johnson Bible College, TN
Lancaster Bible College, PA
Lee University, TN
LeTourneau University, TX
Malone College, OH
Maranatha Baptist Bible College, WI
Maryville University of Saint Louis, MO
Marywood University, PA
Messiah College, PA
Mount Aloysius College, PA
Mount Marty College, SD
Mount Vernon Nazarene University, OH
New Mexico State University, NM
Northwest University, WA
Nyack College, NY
Palm Beach Atlantic University, FL
Peirce College, PA
Roanoke Bible College, NC
Russell Sage College, NY
Saint Joseph's College of Maine, ME
Saint Mary-of-the-Woods College, IN
Simpson University, CA
Southern Adventist University, TN
Taylor University Fort Wayne, IN
The University of Alabama at Birmingham, AL
University of Great Falls, MT
University of Saint Francis, IN
University of Southern Indiana, IN
Urbana University, OH
Valley Forge Christian College, PA
Washington Bible College, MD
Westminster College, UT

Spouses of Deceased or Disabled Public Servants

College of Staten Island of the City University of New York, NY
Francis Marion University, SC
Louisiana Tech University, LA
Michigan State University, MI
Mississippi State University, MS
Missouri State University, MO
New York Institute of Technology, NY
Northeastern State University, OK
Northern Arizona University, AZ
Southern Illinois University Carbondale, IL
The University of Alabama, AL
The University of Alabama at Birmingham, AL
University of South Carolina, SC
Youngstown State University, OH

Twins

Becker College, MA
The Catholic University of America, DC
The College of Saint Rose, NY
Dominican University, IL
East Texas Baptist University, TX
Maryville University of Saint Louis, MO
Mount Aloysius College, PA
Ouachita Baptist University, AR
Randolph College, VA
Sacred Heart University, CT
Simpson College, IA
The University of Alabama at Birmingham, AL
University of Hartford, CT
Virginia Polytechnic Institute and State University, VA
Westminster College, MO

Veterans

Alabama State University, AL
Alliant International University, CA
Appalachian State University, NC
Arkansas State University, AR
Augustana College, SD
Austin Peay State University, TN
Barton College, NC
Boise State University, ID
Brigham Young University–Hawaii, HI
California University of Pennsylvania, PA
Cedarville University, OH
Central Michigan University, MI
Central State University, OH
Clarion University of Pennsylvania, PA
Columbia College, MO
Columbia International University, SC
The Culinary Institute of America, NY
Dickinson State University, ND
East Central University, OK
Emory University, GA
Emporia State University, KS
Eugene Bible College, OR
Excelsior College, NY
Framingham State College, MA
Francis Marion University, SC
Free Will Baptist Bible College, TN
Frostburg State University, MD
Furman University, SC
Maharishi University of Management, IA
Massachusetts College of Art, MA
McMurry University, TX
Michigan State University, MI
Midwestern State University, TX
Minot State University, ND
Missouri State University, MO
Monmouth University, NJ
Montana State University–Billings, MT
Mount Vernon Nazarene University, OH
The National Hispanic University, CA
New Mexico State University, NM
New York Institute of Technology, NY
Northern Illinois University, IL
Northwestern State University of Louisiana, LA
Northwest Nazarene University, ID
Ohio Christian University, OH
Oklahoma Panhandle State University, OK
Rochester Institute of Technology, NY
Saint Vincent College, PA
Shasta Bible College, CA
Sonoma State University, CA
South Dakota State University, SD
Southern Connecticut State University, CT
Southern Illinois University Carbondale, IL
Southern New Hampshire University, NH
Southwest Minnesota State University, MN
State University of New York at Fredonia, NY
Texas Tech University, TX
The University of Alabama at Birmingham, AL
University of Connecticut, CT
University of Illinois at Springfield, IL
University of Illinois at Urbana–Champaign, IL
University of Maine, ME
University of Massachusetts Amherst, MA
University of Massachusetts Dartmouth, MA
The University of Montana, MT
University of Nebraska at Kearney, NE
The University of North Carolina at Asheville, NC
The University of North Carolina at Greensboro, NC
University of Northern Colorado, CO
University of Southern Mississippi, MS
The University of Texas at Dallas, TX
The University of Texas–Pan American, TX
University of the Virgin Islands, VI
University of Wisconsin–Green Bay, WI
University of Wisconsin–Stevens Point, WI
University of Wisconsin–Stout, WI
University of Wyoming, WY
Washington Bible College, MD
Washington State University, WA
Wayne State College, NE
Western Oregon University, OR
Western Washington University, WA
Westminster College, UT
Widener University, PA
William Carey College, MS
Wilson College, PA
Youngstown State University, OH

Veterans' Children

Alabama State University, AL
Appalachian State University, NC
Arkansas State University, AR
Boise State University, ID
Brevard College, NC
Central Michigan University, MI
Central State University, OH
Coastal Carolina University, SC
College of Staten Island of the City University of New York, NY
Columbia International University, SC
Dickinson State University, ND
East Central University, OK
Emporia State University, KS
Eugene Bible College, OR
Excelsior College, NY
Fort Lewis College, CO
Francis Marion University, SC
Free Will Baptist Bible College, TN
Frostburg State University, MD
Glenville State College, WV
Indiana State University, IN
Maharishi University of Management, IA
Michigan State University, MI
Minot State University, ND
Mount Vernon Nazarene University, OH
The National Hispanic University, CA
New Mexico State University, NM
Northwestern State University of Louisiana, LA
Ohio Christian University, OH
Oklahoma Panhandle State University, OK
Saint Vincent College, PA
Shepherd University, WV
South Dakota State University, SD
Southeastern Louisiana University, LA
Southern New Hampshire University, NH
Southwest Minnesota State University, MN
State University of New York at Fredonia, NY
Texas Tech University, TX
The University of Alabama at Birmingham, AL
University of California, San Diego, CA
University of Illinois at Springfield, IL
University of Illinois at Urbana–Champaign, IL
University of Maine, ME
University of Maine at Farmington, ME
University of Nebraska at Kearney, NE
University of Nebraska at Omaha, NE
University of New Orleans, LA
The University of North Carolina at Asheville, NC
The University of North Carolina at Greensboro, NC
University of North Dakota, ND
University of Southern Indiana, IN
The University of Texas at Dallas, TX
University of Wisconsin–La Crosse, WI
University of Wisconsin–Stout, WI
Virginia Commonwealth University, VA
Virginia Polytechnic Institute and State University, VA
Washington Bible College, MD
Wayne State College, NE
Western Illinois University, IL
Westminster College, UT
Youngstown State University, OH

Athletic Grants for Undergraduates

Baseball

Abilene Christian University, TX M
Adelphi University, NY M
Alabama State University, AL M
Albertson College of Idaho, ID M
Alcorn State University, MS M
Alderson-Broaddus College, WV M
American International College, MA M
Anderson University, SC M
Appalachian State University, NC M
Arizona State University, AZ M
Arkansas State University, AR M
Arkansas Tech University, AR M
Armstrong Atlantic State University, GA M
Ashford University, IA M
Auburn University, AL M
Auburn University Montgomery, AL M
Augustana College, SD M
Austin Peay State University, TN M
Azusa Pacific University, CA M
Baker University, KS M
Barton College, NC M
Baylor University, TX M
Bellarmine University, KY M
Belmont Abbey College, NC M
Belmont University, TN M
Bemidji State University, MN M
Bentley College, MA M
Berry College, GA M
Bethany College, KS M
Bethel College, IN M
Bethune-Cookman College, FL M
Birmingham-Southern College, AL M
Blessing-Rieman College of Nursing, IL M,W
Bloomfield College, NJ M
Bloomsburg University of Pennsylvania, PA M
Bluefield State College, WV M
Bowling Green State University, OH M
Bradley University, IL M
Brevard College, NC M
Brigham Young University, UT M
Bryan College, TN M
Butler University, IN M
California Polytechnic State University, San Luis Obispo, CA M
California State University, Chico, CA M
California State University, Fresno, CA M
California State University, Fullerton, CA M
California State University, Los Angeles, CA M
California State University, Northridge, CA M
California State University, Sacramento, CA M
California State University, San Bernardino, CA M
California University of Pennsylvania, PA M
Campbellsville University, KY M
Campbell University, NC M
Canisius College, NY M
Carson-Newman College, TN M
Catawba College, NC M
Cedarville University, OH M
Centenary College of Louisiana, LA M
Central Methodist University, MO M
Central Michigan University, MI M
Central Washington University, WA M
Christian Brothers University, TN M
Clarion University of Pennsylvania, PA M
Cleveland State University, OH M
Coastal Carolina University, SC M
College of Charleston, SC M
The College of Saint Rose, NY M
College of the Ozarks, MO M
College of the Southwest, NM M
The College of William and Mary, VA M
Colorado School of Mines, CO M
Columbus State University, GA M
Concordia University, CA M
Concordia University, NE M
Concordia University, St. Paul, MN M
Concord University, WV M
Coppin State University, MD M
Corban College, OR M
Creighton University, NE M
Culver-Stockton College, MO M
Cumberland University, TN M
Dakota Wesleyan University, SD M
Dallas Baptist University, TX M
Dana College, NE M
Davidson College, NC M
Davis & Elkins College, WV M
Dickinson State University, ND M
Doane College, NE M
Dominican College, NY M
Dordt College, IA M
Dowling College, NY M
Drury University, MO M
Duke University, NC M
Duquesne University, PA M
East Central University, OK M
Eastern Illinois University, IL M
Eastern Kentucky University, KY M
Eastern Michigan University, MI M
East Tennessee State University, TN M
Elon University, NC M
Embry-Riddle Aeronautical University, FL M
Emporia State University, KS M
Erskine College, SC M
Evangel University, MO M
Fairfield University, CT M
Faulkner University, AL M
Felician College, NJ M
Flagler College, FL M
Florida Atlantic University, FL M
Florida College, FL M
Florida Gulf Coast University, FL M
Florida Institute of Technology, FL M
Florida State University, FL M
Francis Marion University, SC M
Franklin Pierce University, NH M
Freed-Hardeman University, TN M
Friends University, KS M
Furman University, SC M
Gannon University, PA M
Gardner-Webb University, NC M
Geneva College, PA M
George Mason University, VA M
Georgetown College, KY M
Georgetown University, DC M
The George Washington University, DC M
Georgia College & State University, GA M
Georgia Institute of Technology, GA M
Georgia Southern University, GA M
Gonzaga University, WA M
Grace College, IN M
Graceland University, IA M
Grand Valley State University, MI M
Grand View College, IA M
Harding University, AR M
Hastings College, NE M
Hawai'i Pacific University, HI M
Hofstra University, NY M
Houston Baptist University, TX M
Huntington University, IN M
Illinois Institute of Technology, IL M
Illinois State University, IL M
Indiana State University, IN M
Indiana University Bloomington, IN M
Indiana University of Pennsylvania, PA M

Iona College, NY M
Iowa Wesleyan College, IA M
Jackson State University, MS M
Jacksonville State University, AL M
James Madison University, VA M
Jamestown College, ND M
Judson College, IL M
Kent State University, OH M
Kentucky Wesleyan College, KY M
King College, TN M
Kutztown University of Pennsylvania, PA M
Lamar University, TX M
Lambuth University, TN M
Lehigh University, PA M
Le Moyne College, NY M
LeMoyne-Owen College, TN M
Lewis-Clark State College, ID M
Limestone College, SC M
Lindenwood University, MO M
Lindsey Wilson College, KY M
Lipscomb University, TN M
Lock Haven University of Pennsylvania, PA M
Longwood University, VA M
Louisiana State University and Agricultural and Mechanical College, LA M
Louisiana Tech University, LA M
Lubbock Christian University, TX M
Lyon College, AR M
Malone College, OH M
Manhattan College, NY M
Mansfield University of Pennsylvania, PA M
Marist College, NY M
Mayville State University, ND M
McKendree College, IL M
Mercer University, GA M
Mesa State College, CO M
Metropolitan State College of Denver, CO M
Miami University, OH M
Middle Tennessee State University, TN M
Millersville University of Pennsylvania, PA M
Milligan College, TN M
Minnesota State University Mankato, MN M
Minot State University, ND M
Mississippi State University, MS M
Missouri Baptist University, MO M
Missouri State University, MO M
Missouri Valley College, MO M
Molloy College, NY M
Monmouth University, NJ M
Montreat College, NC M
Morehead State University, KY M
Morningside College, IA M
Mount Marty College, SD M
Mount Olive College, NC M
Mount St. Mary's University, MD M
Mount Vernon Nazarene University, OH M
Murray State University, KY M
Newman University, KS M
New Mexico State University, NM M
New York Institute of Technology, NY M
Niagara University, NY M
Nicholls State University, LA M
North Carolina Agricultural and Technical State University, NC M
North Carolina State University, NC M
North Dakota State University, ND M
Northeastern State University, OK M
Northeastern University, MA M
Northern Illinois University, IL M
North Greenville University, SC M
Northwestern College, IA M
Northwestern Oklahoma State University, OK M
Northwestern State University of Louisiana, LA M
Northwest Nazarene University, ID M
Northwood University, MI M
Northwood University, Florida Campus, FL M
Northwood University, Texas Campus, TX M
Nova Southeastern University, FL M
Nyack College, NY M
The Ohio State University, OH M
Ohio University, OH M
Ohio Valley University, WV M
Oklahoma Baptist University, OK M
Oklahoma Panhandle State University, OK M
Oklahoma State University, OK M
Oral Roberts University, OK M
Oregon State University, OR M
Ouachita Baptist University, AR M
Penn State University Park, PA M
Pfeiffer University, NC M
Philadelphia University, PA M
Pikeville College, KY M
Pittsburg State University, KS M
Point Loma Nazarene University, CA M
Portland State University, OR M
Purdue University, IN M
Quinnipiac University, CT M
Radford University, VA M
Regis University, CO M
Rice University, TX M
Rockhurst University, MO M
Rollins College, FL M
Sacred Heart University, CT M
St. Ambrose University, IA M
St. Andrews Presbyterian College, NC M
St. Cloud State University, MN M
St. Edward's University, TX M
St. Francis College, NY M
St. Gregory's University, OK M
Saint Joseph's College, IN M
Saint Leo University, FL M
Saint Louis University, MO M
Saint Mary's College of California, CA M
Saint Vincent College, PA M
Saint Xavier University, IL M
Samford University, AL M
Sam Houston State University, TX M
San Diego State University, CA M
San Francisco State University, CA M,W
San Jose State University, CA M
Santa Clara University, CA M
Seton Hill University, PA M
Shaw University, NC M
Shepherd University, WV M
Shippensburg University of Pennsylvania, PA M
Slippery Rock University of Pennsylvania, PA M
Sonoma State University, CA M
South Dakota State University, SD M
Southeastern Louisiana University, LA M
Southeastern Oklahoma State University, OK M
Southeast Missouri State University, MO M
Southern Arkansas University–Magnolia, AR M
Southern Illinois University Carbondale, IL M
Southern Illinois University Edwardsville, IL M
Southern Nazarene University, OK M
Southern New Hampshire University, NH M
Southern Polytechnic State University, GA M
Southern Utah University, UT M
Southern Wesleyan University, SC M
Southwest Baptist University, MO M
Southwest Minnesota State University, MN M
Spring Arbor University, MI M
Spring Hill College, AL M
Stanford University, CA M
State University of New York at Binghamton, NY M
Stetson University, FL M
Stonehill College, MA M
Stony Brook University, State University of New York, NY M
Tarleton State University, TX M
Taylor University, IN M
Temple University, PA M
Tennessee Technological University, TN M
Tennessee Wesleyan College, TN M
Texas A&M University–Corpus Christi, TX M
Texas A&M University–Kingsville, TX M
Texas Christian University, TX M
Texas State University-San Marcos, TX M
Texas Tech University, TX M
Tiffin University, OH M
Towson University, MD M
Trevecca Nazarene University, TN M
Trinity International University, IL M
Troy University, AL M
Tulane University, LA M
Tuskegee University, AL M
Union College, KY M
Union University, TN M
University at Albany, State University of New York, NY M
University at Buffalo, the State University of New York, NY M
The University of Akron, OH M
The University of Alabama, AL M
The University of Alabama at Birmingham, AL M

School	Grants
The University of Alabama in Huntsville, AL	M
The University of Arizona, AZ	M
University of Arkansas, AR	M
University of Arkansas at Monticello, AR	M
University of Bridgeport, CT	M
University of California, Berkeley, CA	M
University of California, Irvine, CA	M
University of California, Los Angeles, CA	M
University of California, Riverside, CA	M
University of California, Santa Barbara, CA	M
University of Central Florida, FL	M
University of Central Missouri, MO	M
University of Central Oklahoma, OK	M
University of Charleston, WV	M
University of Connecticut, CT	M
University of Dayton, OH	M
University of Delaware, DE	M
University of Evansville, IN	M
The University of Findlay, OH	M
University of Florida, FL	M
University of Georgia, GA	M
University of Hartford, CT	M
University of Hawaii at Hilo, HI	M
University of Hawaii at Manoa, HI	M
University of Illinois at Chicago, IL	M
University of Illinois at Urbana–Champaign, IL	M
The University of Iowa, IA	M
University of Kansas, KS	M
University of Louisiana at Lafayette, LA	M
University of Louisville, KY	M
University of Maine, ME	M
University of Maryland, Baltimore County, MD	M
University of Maryland, College Park, MD	M
University of Massachusetts Amherst, MA	M
University of Miami, FL	M
University of Michigan, MI	M
University of Minnesota, Crookston, MN	M
University of Minnesota, Twin Cities Campus, MN	M
University of Missouri–Columbia, MO	M
University of Missouri–St. Louis, MO	M
University of Nebraska at Kearney, NE	M
University of Nebraska at Omaha, NE	M
University of New Haven, CT	M
University of New Orleans, LA	M
University of North Alabama, AL	M
The University of North Carolina at Asheville, NC	M
The University of North Carolina at Chapel Hill, NC	M
The University of North Carolina at Charlotte, NC	M
The University of North Carolina at Greensboro, NC	M
The University of North Carolina at Pembroke, NC	M
The University of North Carolina Wilmington, NC	M
University of North Dakota, ND	M
University of Northern Colorado, CO	M
University of Northern Iowa, IA	M
University of North Florida, FL	M
University of Notre Dame, IN	M
University of Oklahoma, OK	M
University of Pittsburgh, PA	M
University of Rhode Island, RI	M
University of Richmond, VA	M
University of St. Francis, IL	M
University of Saint Francis, IN	M
University of San Diego, CA	M
University of San Francisco, CA	M
University of Science and Arts of Oklahoma, OK	M
University of South Carolina, SC	M
University of South Carolina Upstate, SC	M
The University of South Dakota, SD	M
University of Southern California, CA	M
University of Southern Indiana, IN	M
University of Southern Mississippi, MS	M
University of South Florida, FL	M
The University of Tampa, FL	M
The University of Tennessee at Martin, TN	M
The University of Texas at Austin, TX	M
The University of Texas at Brownsville, TX	M
The University of Texas at San Antonio, TX	M
The University of Texas–Pan American, TX	M
University of the Cumberlands, KY	M
University of the Incarnate Word, TX	M
University of the Pacific, CA	M
University of the Sciences in Philadelphia, PA	M
University of Vermont, VT	M
University of Virginia, VA	M
University of Washington, WA	M
The University of West Alabama, AL	M
University of West Florida, FL	M
University of West Georgia, GA	M
Urbana University, OH	M
Valdosta State University, GA	M
Valley City State University, ND	M
Valparaiso University, IN	M
Vanderbilt University, TN	M
Vanguard University of Southern California, CA	M
Virginia Commonwealth University, VA	M
Virginia Intermont College, VA	M
Virginia Military Institute, VA	M
Virginia Polytechnic Institute and State University, VA	M
Virginia State University, VA	M
Wagner College, NY	M
Wake Forest University, NC	M
Walsh University, OH	M
Washington State University, WA	M
Wayland Baptist University, TX	M
Wayne State College, NE	M
Wayne State University, MI	M
Webber International University, FL	M
Western Carolina University, NC	M
Western Illinois University, IL	M
West Liberty State College, WV	M
Westmont College, CA	M
West Virginia University, WV	M
West Virginia Wesleyan College, WV	M
Wheeling Jesuit University, WV	M
Wichita State University, KS	M
William Carey College, MS	M
William Jewell College, MO	M
Williams Baptist College, AR	M
Wingate University, NC	M
Winona State University, MN	M
Winthrop University, SC	M
Xavier University, OH	M
Youngstown State University, OH	M

Basketball

School	Grants
Abilene Christian University, TX	M,W
Adams State College, CO	M,W
Adelphi University, NY	M,W
Alabama State University, AL	M,W
Albertson College of Idaho, ID	M,W
Alcorn State University, MS	M,W
Alderson-Broaddus College, WV	M,W
American International College, MA	M,W
Anderson University, SC	M,W
Appalachian State University, NC	M,W
Arizona State University, AZ	M,W
Arkansas State University, AR	M,W
Arkansas Tech University, AR	M,W
Armstrong Atlantic State University, GA	M,W
Asbury College, KY	M,W
Ashford University, IA	M,W
Assumption College, MA	M,W
Auburn University, AL	M,W
Auburn University Montgomery, AL	M,W
Augustana College, SD	M,W
Augusta State University, GA	M,W
Austin Peay State University, TN	M,W
Azusa Pacific University, CA	M,W
Baker University, KS	M,W
Barton College, NC	M,W
Baylor University, TX	M,W
Bellarmine University, KY	M,W
Belmont Abbey College, NC	M,W
Belmont University, TN	M,W
Bemidji State University, MN	M,W
Bentley College, MA	M,W
Berry College, GA	M,W
Bethany College, KS	M,W
Bethel College, IN	M,W
Bethel College, KS	M,W
Bethune-Cookman College, FL	M,W
Birmingham-Southern College, AL	M,W
Black Hills State University, SD	M,W
Blessing-Rieman College of Nursing, IL	M,W
Bloomfield College, NJ	M,W
Bloomsburg University of Pennsylvania, PA	M,W
Bluefield State College, WV	M,W
Blue Mountain College, MS	W
Boise State University, ID	M,W
Boston College, MA	M,W
Boston University, MA	M,W
Bowie State University, MD	M,W
Bowling Green State University, OH	M,W
Bradley University, IL	M,W

Brevard College, NC M,W
Brigham Young University, UT M,W
Brigham Young University–Hawaii, HI M
Bryan College, TN M,W
Bryant University, RI M,W
Bucknell University, PA M,W
Butler University, IN M,W
California Polytechnic State University, San Luis Obispo, CA M,W
California State University, Chico, CA M,W
California State University, Dominguez Hills, CA M,W
California State University, Fresno, CA M,W
California State University, Fullerton, CA M,W
California State University, Los Angeles, CA M,W
California State University, Northridge, CA M,W
California State University, Sacramento, CA M,W
California State University, San Bernardino, CA M,W
California University of Pennsylvania, PA M,W
Campbellsville University, KY M,W
Campbell University, NC M,W
Canisius College, NY M,W
Carson-Newman College, TN M,W
Catawba College, NC M,W
Cedarville University, OH M,W
Centenary College of Louisiana, LA M,W
Central Methodist University, MO M,W
Central Michigan University, MI M,W
Central State University, OH M,W
Central Washington University, WA M,W
Christian Brothers University, TN M,W
Claflin University, SC M,W
Clarion University of Pennsylvania, PA M,W
Clemson University, SC M,W
Cleveland State University, OH M,W
Coastal Carolina University, SC M,W
Colgate University, NY M,W
College of Charleston, SC M,W
College of Saint Mary, NE W
The College of Saint Rose, NY M,W
College of the Holy Cross, MA M,W
College of the Ozarks, MO M,W
The College of William and Mary, VA M,W
Colorado School of Mines, CO M,W
Colorado State University, CO M,W
Colorado State University-Pueblo, CO M,W
Columbia College, MO M,W
Columbus State University, GA M,W
Concordia University, CA M,W
Concordia University, NE M,W
Concordia University, St. Paul, MN M,W
Concord University, WV M,W
Converse College, SC W
Coppin State University, MD M,W
Corban College, OR M,W
Creighton University, NE M,W
Culver-Stockton College, MO M,W
Cumberland University, TN M,W
Dakota State University, SD M,W
Dakota Wesleyan University, SD M,W
Dana College, NE M,W
Davidson College, NC M,W
Davis & Elkins College, WV M,W
Dickinson State University, ND M,W
Doane College, NE M,W
Dominican College, NY M,W
Dordt College, IA M,W
Dowling College, NY M,W
Drake University, IA M,W
Drury University, MO M,W
Duke University, NC M,W
Duquesne University, PA M,W
East Central University, OK M,W
Eastern Illinois University, IL M,W
Eastern Kentucky University, KY M,W
Eastern Michigan University, MI M,W
East Tennessee State University, TN M,W
Elon University, NC M,W
Embry-Riddle Aeronautical University, FL M
Emporia State University, KS M,W
Erskine College, SC M,W
Evangel University, MO M,W
Fairfield University, CT M,W
Faulkner University, AL M
Felician College, NJ M,W
Ferris State University, MI M,W
Flagler College, FL M,W
Florida Atlantic University, FL M,W
Florida College, FL M
Florida Gulf Coast University, FL M,W
Florida Institute of Technology, FL M,W
Florida State University, FL M,W
Fort Lewis College, CO M,W
Francis Marion University, SC M,W
Franklin Pierce University, NH M,W
Freed-Hardeman University, TN M,W
Fresno Pacific University, CA M,W
Friends University, KS M,W
Furman University, SC M,W
Gannon University, PA M,W
Gardner-Webb University, NC M,W
Geneva College, PA M,W
George Mason University, VA M,W
Georgetown College, KY M,W
Georgetown University, DC M,W
The George Washington University, DC M,W
Georgia College & State University, GA M,W
Georgia Institute of Technology, GA M,W
Georgia Southern University, GA M,W
Glenville State College, WV M,W
Gonzaga University, WA M,W
Grace College, IN M,W
Graceland University, IA M,W
Grand Valley State University, MI M,W
Grand View College, IA M,W
Harding University, AR M,W
Hastings College, NE M,W
Hawai'i Pacific University, HI M
Hofstra University, NY M,W
Holy Names University, CA M,W
Houghton College, NY M,W
Houston Baptist University, TX M,W
Huntington University, IN M,W
Idaho State University, ID M,W
Illinois Institute of Technology, IL M,W
Illinois State University, IL M,W
Indiana State University, IN M,W
Indiana University Bloomington, IN M,W
Indiana University of Pennsylvania, PA M,W
Indiana University–Purdue University Indianapolis, IN M,W
Indiana University South Bend, IN M,W
Indiana University Southeast, IN M,W
Iona College, NY M,W
Iowa Wesleyan College, IA M,W
Jackson State University, MS M,W
Jacksonville State University, AL M,W
James Madison University, VA M,W
Jamestown College, ND M,W
Johnson C. Smith University, NC M,W
Judson College, AL W
Judson College, IL M,W
Kent State University, OH M,W
Kentucky Wesleyan College, KY M,W
King College, TN M,W
Kutztown University of Pennsylvania, PA M,W
Lake Superior State University, MI M,W
Lamar University, TX M,W
Lambuth University, TN M,W
Lee University, TN M,W
Lehigh University, PA M,W
Le Moyne College, NY M,W
LeMoyne-Owen College, TN M,W
Lesley University, MA M,W
Lewis-Clark State College, ID M,W
Limestone College, SC M,W
Lindenwood University, MO M,W
Lindsey Wilson College, KY M,W
Lipscomb University, TN M,W
Lock Haven University of Pennsylvania, PA M,W
Longwood University, VA M,W
Louisiana State University and Agricultural and Mechanical College, LA M,W
Louisiana Tech University, LA M,W
Loyola University Chicago, IL M,W
Loyola University New Orleans, LA M,W
Lubbock Christian University, TX M,W
Lyon College, AR M,W
Malone College, OH M,W
Manhattan College, NY M,W
Mansfield University of Pennsylvania, PA M,W
Marist College, NY M,W
Marquette University, WI M,W
Mayville State University, ND M,W
McKendree College, IL M,W
Mercer University, GA M,W
Mesa State College, CO M,W
Metropolitan State College of Denver, CO M,W
Miami University, OH M,W
Michigan State University, MI M,W
Michigan Technological University, MI M,W
Middle Tennessee State University, TN M,W
Midwestern State University, TX M,W
Millersville University of Pennsylvania, PA M,W
Milligan College, TN M,W
Minnesota State University Mankato, MN M,W

Minot State University, ND M,W
Mississippi State University, MS M,W
Missouri Baptist University, MO M,W
Missouri State University, MO M,W
Missouri Valley College, MO M,W
Molloy College, NY M,W
Monmouth University, NJ M,W
Montana State University, MT M,W
Montana State University–Billings, MT M,W
Montana Tech of The University of Montana, MT M,W
Montreat College, NC M,W
Morehead State University, KY M,W
Morningside College, IA M,W
Mountain State University, WV M
Mount Marty College, SD M,W
Mount Olive College, NC M,W
Mount St. Mary's University, MD M,W
Mount Vernon Nazarene University, OH M,W
Murray State University, KY M,W
Newman University, KS M,W
New Mexico State University, NM M,W
New York Institute of Technology, NY M,W
Niagara University, NY M,W
Nicholls State University, LA M,W
North Carolina Agricultural and Technical State University, NC M,W
North Carolina State University, NC M,W
North Dakota State University, ND M,W
Northeastern State University, OK M,W
Northeastern University, MA M,W
Northern Arizona University, AZ M,W
Northern Illinois University, IL M,W
Northern State University, SD M,W
North Georgia College & State University, GA M,W
North Greenville University, SC M,W
Northwest Christian College, OR M,W
Northwestern College, IA M,W
Northwestern Oklahoma State University, OK M,W
Northwestern State University of Louisiana, LA M,W
Northwest Nazarene University, ID M,W
Northwest University, WA M,W
Northwood University, MI M,W
Nova Southeastern University, FL M,W
Nyack College, NY M,W
The Ohio State University, OH M,W
Ohio University, OH M,W
Ohio Valley University, WV M,W
Oklahoma Baptist University, OK M,W
Oklahoma Panhandle State University, OK M,W
Oklahoma State University, OK M,W
Oral Roberts University, OK M,W
Oregon State University, OR M,W
Ouachita Baptist University, AR M,W
Paul Smith's College of Arts and Sciences, NY M,W
Penn State University Park, PA M,W
Pfeiffer University, NC M,W
Philadelphia University, PA M,W
Pikeville College, KY M,W
Pittsburg State University, KS M,W
Point Loma Nazarene University, CA M,W
Portland State University, OR M,W
Providence College, RI M,W
Purdue University, IN M,W
Purdue University Calumet, IN M,W
Quinnipiac University, CT M,W
Radford University, VA M,W
Regis University, CO M,W
Reinhardt College, GA M,W
Rice University, TX M,W
Robert Morris University, PA M,W
Roberts Wesleyan College, NY M,W
Rockhurst University, MO M,W
Rollins College, FL M,W
Sacred Heart University, CT M,W
St. Ambrose University, IA M,W
St. Andrews Presbyterian College, NC M,W
Saint Anselm College, NH M,W
St. Cloud State University, MN M,W
St. Edward's University, TX M,W
St. Francis College, NY M,W
Saint Francis University, PA M,W
St. Gregory's University, OK M,W
Saint Joseph's College, IN M,W
Saint Leo University, FL M,W
Saint Louis University, MO M,W
Saint Mary-of-the-Woods College, IN W
Saint Mary's College of California, CA M,W
Saint Michael's College, VT M,W
Saint Vincent College, PA M,W
Saint Xavier University, IL M
Samford University, AL M,W
Sam Houston State University, TX M,W
San Diego State University, CA M,W
San Francisco State University, CA M,W
San Jose State University, CA M,W
Santa Clara University, CA M,W
Seattle Pacific University, WA M,W
Seattle University, WA M,W
Seton Hill University, PA M,W
Shaw University, NC M,W
Shepherd University, WV M,W
Shippensburg University of Pennsylvania, PA M,W
Slippery Rock University of Pennsylvania, PA M,W
Sonoma State University, CA M,W
South Dakota State University, SD M,W
Southeastern Louisiana University, LA M,W
Southeastern Oklahoma State University, OK M,W
Southeast Missouri State University, MO M,W
Southern Arkansas University–Magnolia, AR M,W
Southern Illinois University Carbondale, IL M,W
Southern Illinois University Edwardsville, IL M,W
Southern Methodist University, TX M,W
Southern Nazarene University, OK M,W
Southern New Hampshire University, NH M,W
Southern Oregon University, OR M,W
Southern Polytechnic State University, GA M,W
Southern Utah University, UT M,W
Southern Wesleyan University, SC M,W
Southwest Baptist University, MO M,W
Southwest Minnesota State University, MN M,W
Spring Arbor University, MI M,W
Spring Hill College, AL M,W
Stanford University, CA M,W
State University of New York at Binghamton, NY M,W
Stephen F. Austin State University, TX M,W
Stetson University, FL M,W
Stonehill College, MA M,W
Stony Brook University, State University of New York, NY M,W
Syracuse University, NY M,W
Tarleton State University, TX M,W
Taylor University, IN M,W
Temple University, PA M,W
Tennessee State University, TN M,W
Tennessee Technological University, TN M,W
Tennessee Wesleyan College, TN M,W
Texas A&M University–Commerce, TX M,W
Texas A&M University–Corpus Christi, TX M,W
Texas A&M University–Kingsville, TX M,W
Texas Christian University, TX M,W
Texas State University-San Marcos, TX M,W
Texas Tech University, TX M,W
Texas Woman's University, TX W
Tiffin University, OH M,W
Towson University, MD M,W
Trevecca Nazarene University, TN M,W
Trinity International University, IL M,W
Troy University, AL M,W
Tulane University, LA M,W
Tuskegee University, AL M,W
Union College, KY M,W
Union University, TN M,W
Unity College, ME M
University at Albany, State University of New York, NY M,W
University at Buffalo, the State University of New York, NY M,W
The University of Akron, OH M,W
The University of Alabama, AL M,W
The University of Alabama at Birmingham, AL M,W
The University of Alabama in Huntsville, AL M,W
University of Alaska Fairbanks, AK M,W
The University of Arizona, AZ M,W
University of Arkansas, AR M,W
University of Arkansas at Monticello, AR M,W
University of Bridgeport, CT M,W
University of California, Berkeley, CA M,W
University of California, Irvine, CA M,W
University of California, Los Angeles, CA M,W
University of California, Riverside, CA M,W
University of California, Santa Barbara, CA M,W
University of Central Florida, FL M,W
University of Central Missouri, MO M,W
University of Central Oklahoma, OK M,W
University of Charleston, WV M,W

University of Colorado at Boulder, CO M,W
University of Connecticut, CT M,W
University of Dayton, OH M,W
University of Delaware, DE M,W
University of Denver, CO M,W
University of Detroit Mercy, MI M,W
University of Evansville, IN M,W
The University of Findlay, OH M,W
University of Florida, FL M,W
University of Georgia, GA M,W
University of Great Falls, MT M,W
University of Hartford, CT M,W
University of Hawaii at Hilo, HI M
University of Hawaii at Manoa, HI M,W
University of Idaho, ID M,W
University of Illinois at Chicago, IL M,W
University of Illinois at Springfield, IL M,W
University of Illinois at Urbana–Champaign, IL M,W
The University of Iowa, IA M,W
University of Kansas, KS M,W
University of Louisiana at Lafayette, LA M,W
University of Louisville, KY M,W
University of Maine, ME M,W
University of Maryland, Baltimore County, MD M,W
University of Maryland, College Park, MD M,W
University of Massachusetts Amherst, MA M,W
University of Massachusetts Lowell, MA M,W
University of Miami, FL M,W
University of Michigan, MI M,W
University of Michigan–Dearborn, MI M,W
University of Minnesota, Crookston, MN M,W
University of Minnesota, Twin Cities Campus, MN M,W
University of Missouri–Columbia, MO M,W
University of Missouri–Kansas City, MO M,W
University of Missouri–St. Louis, MO M,W
The University of Montana, MT M,W
University of Nebraska at Kearney, NE M,W
University of Nebraska at Omaha, NE M,W
University of New Hampshire, NH M,W
University of New Haven, CT M,W
University of New Orleans, LA M,W
University of North Alabama, AL M,W
The University of North Carolina at Asheville, NC M,W
The University of North Carolina at Chapel Hill, NC M,W
The University of North Carolina at Charlotte, NC M,W
The University of North Carolina at Greensboro, NC M,W
The University of North Carolina at Pembroke, NC M,W
The University of North Carolina Wilmington, NC M,W
University of North Dakota, ND M,W
University of Northern Colorado, CO M,W
University of Northern Iowa, IA M,W
University of North Florida, FL M,W
University of Notre Dame, IN M,W
University of Oklahoma, OK M,W
University of Oregon, OR M,W
University of Pittsburgh, PA M,W
University of Pittsburgh at Johnstown, PA M,W
University of Rhode Island, RI M,W
University of Richmond, VA M,W
University of St. Francis, IL M,W
University of Saint Francis, IN M,W
University of San Diego, CA M,W
University of San Francisco, CA M,W
University of Science and Arts of Oklahoma, OK M,W
University of South Carolina, SC M,W
University of South Carolina Upstate, SC M,W
The University of South Dakota, SD M,W
University of Southern California, CA M,W
University of Southern Indiana, IN M,W
University of Southern Mississippi, MS M,W
University of South Florida, FL M,W
The University of Tampa, FL M,W
The University of Tennessee at Martin, TN M,W
The University of Texas at Austin, TX M,W
The University of Texas at El Paso, TX M,W
The University of Texas at San Antonio, TX M,W
The University of Texas–Pan American, TX M,W
University of the Cumberlands, KY M,W
University of the Incarnate Word, TX M,W
University of the Pacific, CA M,W
University of the Sciences in Philadelphia, PA M,W
University of Tulsa, OK M,W
University of Vermont, VT M,W
University of Virginia, VA M,W
University of Washington, WA M,W
The University of West Alabama, AL M,W
University of West Florida, FL M,W
University of West Georgia, GA M,W
University of Wisconsin–Green Bay, WI M,W
University of Wisconsin–Madison, WI M,W
University of Wisconsin–Milwaukee, WI M,W
University of Wyoming, WY M,W
Urbana University, OH M,W
Utah State University, UT M,W
Valdosta State University, GA M,W
Valley City State University, ND M,W
Valparaiso University, IN M,W
Vanderbilt University, TN M,W
Vanguard University of Southern California, CA M,W
Virginia Commonwealth University, VA M,W
Virginia Intermont College, VA M,W
Virginia Military Institute, VA M
Virginia Polytechnic Institute and State University, VA M,W
Virginia State University, VA M,W
Virginia Union University, VA M,W
Wagner College, NY M,W
Wake Forest University, NC M,W
Walsh University, OH M,W
Warner Pacific College, OR M,W
Washington State University, WA M,W
Wayland Baptist University, TX M,W
Wayne State College, NE M,W
Wayne State University, MI M,W
Webber International University, FL M,W
Western Carolina University, NC M,W
Western Illinois University, IL M,W
Western Washington University, WA M,W
West Liberty State College, WV M,W
Westmont College, CA M,W
West Virginia University, WV M,W
West Virginia Wesleyan College, WV M,W
Wheeling Jesuit University, WV M,W
Wichita State University, KS M,W
William Carey College, MS M,W
William Jewell College, MO M,W
Williams Baptist College, AR M,W
Wingate University, NC M,W
Winona State University, MN M,W
Winston-Salem State University, NC M,W
Winthrop University, SC M,W
Xavier University, OH M,W
Youngstown State University, OH M,W

Bowling

Arkansas State University, AR W
Bethune-Cookman College, FL W
Jackson State University, MS W
Johnson C. Smith University, NC W
Lindenwood University, MO M,W
Lindsey Wilson College, KY M,W
McKendree College, IL M,W
Newman University, KS M,W
Pikeville College, KY M,W
Sacred Heart University, CT W
Shaw University, NC W
Virginia State University, VA W
Winston-Salem State University, NC M,W

Cheerleading

Anderson University, SC W
Austin Peay State University, TN M,W
Baker University, KS M,W
Bethany College, KS M,W
Bethel College, IN M,W
Brevard College, NC M,W
Brigham Young University, UT M,W
California State University, Fresno, CA M,W
Campbellsville University, KY M,W
Campbell University, NC W
Central State University, OH M,W
Culver-Stockton College, MO M,W
Cumberland University, TN M,W
Dakota Wesleyan University, SD M,W
Drake University, IA M,W
East Texas Baptist University, TX M,W
Emporia State University, KS M,W
Freed-Hardeman University, TN W
Gardner-Webb University, NC M,W
Georgetown College, KY W
Grace College, IN M,W
Hastings College, NE W
Hawai'i Pacific University, HI M,W
Hofstra University, NY M,W
Houston Baptist University, TX M,W
Kent State University, OH M,W
King College, TN M,W

School	Grant
Kutztown University of Pennsylvania, PA	W
Lambuth University, TN	M,W
Limestone College, SC	M,W
Lindenwood University, MO	M,W
Lindsey Wilson College, KY	M,W
Manhattan College, NY	M,W
McKendree College, IL	M,W
Mercer University, GA	M,W
Methodist University, NC	M,W
Metropolitan State College of Denver, CO	M,W
Middle Tennessee State University, TN	M,W
Midwestern State University, TX	M,W
Missouri Valley College, MO	M,W
Montana State University, MT	M,W
Newman University, KS	M,W
North Greenville University, SC	M,W
Northwestern Oklahoma State University, OK	M,W
Northwood University, MI	M,W
Nyack College, NY	M,W
Ohio Valley University, WV	W
Pfeiffer University, NC	M,W
Pittsburg State University, KS	M,W
St. Ambrose University, IA	W
Southeastern Louisiana University, LA	M,W
Southeast Missouri State University, MO	M,W
Southern Illinois University Carbondale, IL	M,W
Southern Nazarene University, OK	M,W
Tarleton State University, TX	M,W
Tennessee Technological University, TN	M,W
Tennessee Wesleyan College, TN	M,W
Texas A&M University–Commerce, TX	M,W
Tiffin University, OH	M,W
Union College, KY	M,W
Union University, TN	W
The University of Alabama, AL	M,W
The University of Alabama in Huntsville, AL	M,W
University of Central Florida, FL	M,W
University of Charleston, WV	W
University of Delaware, DE	M,W
University of Hawaii at Manoa, HI	W
University of Louisville, KY	M,W
University of Maryland, College Park, MD	W
University of Oregon, OR	M,W
University of Saint Francis, IN	M,W
University of Science and Arts of Oklahoma, OK	M,W
University of the Cumberlands, KY	M,W
University of West Georgia, GA	M,W
University of Wyoming, WY	M,W
Virginia Intermont College, VA	W
Wayland Baptist University, TX	M,W
Webber International University, FL	M,W
West Virginia University, WV	M,W
William Jewell College, MO	M,W

Crew

School	Grant
Boston University, MA	M,W
California State University, Sacramento, CA	M,W
Clemson University, SC	W
Creighton University, NE	W
Duke University, NC	W
Duquesne University, PA	W
Eastern Michigan University, MI	W
Florida Institute of Technology, FL	M,W
The George Washington University, DC	M,W
Indiana University Bloomington, IN	W
Lehigh University, PA	W
Lesley University, MA	M,W
Michigan State University, MI	W
Murray State University, KY	M,W
Northeastern University, MA	M,W
Nova Southeastern University, FL	W
Robert Morris University, PA	W
Sacred Heart University, CT	W
Saint Leo University, FL	M,W
Southern Methodist University, TX	W
Stanford University, CA	W
Syracuse University, NY	M,W
Temple University, PA	M,W
University at Buffalo, the State University of New York, NY	W
University of California, Berkeley, CA	M,W
University of California, Irvine, CA	M,W
University of Charleston, WV	M,W
University of Delaware, DE	W
The University of Iowa, IA	W
University of Kansas, KS	W
University of Louisville, KY	W
University of Massachusetts Amherst, MA	W
University of Miami, FL	W
The University of North Carolina at Chapel Hill, NC	W
University of Notre Dame, IN	W
University of Southern California, CA	W
The University of Tampa, FL	W
The University of Texas at Austin, TX	W
University of Tulsa, OK	W
University of Virginia, VA	W
University of Washington, WA	M,W
Washington State University, WA	W
Western Washington University, WA	M,W
West Virginia University, WV	W

Cross-Country Running

School	Grant
Abilene Christian University, TX	M,W
Adams State College, CO	M,W
Adelphi University, NY	M,W
Alabama State University, AL	M,W
Alcorn State University, MS	M,W
Alderson-Broaddus College, WV	M,W
Alliant International University, CA	M,W
Anderson University, SC	M,W
Appalachian State University, NC	M,W
Arizona State University, AZ	M,W
Arkansas State University, AR	M,W
Arkansas Tech University, AR	W
Asbury College, KY	M,W
Ashford University, IA	M,W
Auburn University, AL	M,W
Augustana College, SD	M,W
Augusta State University, GA	M,W
Austin Peay State University, TN	M,W
Azusa Pacific University, CA	M,W
Baker University, KS	M,W
Barton College, NC	M,W
Baylor University, TX	M,W
Bellarmine University, KY	M,W
Belmont Abbey College, NC	M,W
Belmont University, TN	M,W
Bentley College, MA	M,W
Berry College, GA	M,W
Bethany College, KS	M,W
Bethel College, IN	M,W
Bethel College, KS	M,W
Bethune-Cookman College, FL	M,W
Birmingham-Southern College, AL	M,W
Black Hills State University, SD	M,W
Bloomfield College, NJ	M
Bloomsburg University of Pennsylvania, PA	M,W
Bluefield State College, WV	M,W
Boise State University, ID	M,W
Boston College, MA	W
Boston University, MA	M,W
Bowie State University, MD	M,W
Bowling Green State University, OH	M,W
Bradley University, IL	M,W
Brenau University, GA	W
Brevard College, NC	M,W
Brigham Young University, UT	M,W
Brigham Young University–Hawaii, HI	M,W
Bryan College, TN	M,W
Butler University, IN	M,W
California Polytechnic State University, San Luis Obispo, CA	M,W
California State University, Chico, CA	M,W
California State University, Fresno, CA	M,W
California State University, Fullerton, CA	M,W
California State University, Los Angeles, CA	W
California State University, Northridge, CA	M,W
California State University, Sacramento, CA	M,W
California University of Pennsylvania, PA	M,W
Campbellsville University, KY	M,W
Campbell University, NC	M,W
Canisius College, NY	M,W
Carson-Newman College, TN	M,W
Catawba College, NC	M,W
Cedarville University, OH	M,W
Centenary College of Louisiana, LA	M,W
Central Methodist University, MO	M,W
Central Michigan University, MI	M,W
Central State University, OH	M,W
Central Washington University, WA	M,W
Clarion University of Pennsylvania, PA	M,W
Clemson University, SC	M,W
Cleveland State University, OH	W
Coastal Carolina University, SC	M,W
College of Charleston, SC	M,W
College of Saint Mary, NE	W
The College of Saint Rose, NY	M,W
College of the Southwest, NM	M,W
The College of William and Mary, VA	M,W
Colorado School of Mines, CO	M,W
Colorado State University, CO	M,W
Colorado State University-Pueblo, CO	W
Columbus State University, GA	M,W
Concordia University, CA	M,W
Concordia University, NE	M,W
Concordia University, St. Paul, MN	M,W

Concord University, WV	M,W
Converse College, SC	W
Coppin State University, MD	M,W
Corban College, OR	M,W
Creighton University, NE	M,W
Cumberland University, TN	M,W
Dakota State University, SD	M,W
Dakota Wesleyan University, SD	M,W
Dallas Baptist University, TX	W
Dana College, NE	M,W
Davidson College, NC	M,W
Davis & Elkins College, WV	M,W
Dickinson State University, ND	M,W
Doane College, NE	M,W
Dominican College, NY	M,W
Dordt College, IA	M,W
Drake University, IA	M,W
Drury University, MO	M,W
Duquesne University, PA	M,W
East Central University, OK	M,W
Eastern Illinois University, IL	M,W
Eastern Kentucky University, KY	M,W
Eastern Michigan University, MI	M,W
East Tennessee State University, TN	M,W
Elon University, NC	M,W
Emporia State University, KS	M,W
Erskine College, SC	M,W
Evangel University, MO	M,W
Felician College, NJ	M,W
Ferris State University, MI	M,W
Flagler College, FL	M,W
Florida Atlantic University, FL	M,W
Florida Institute of Technology, FL	M,W
Florida State University, FL	M,W
Fort Lewis College, CO	M,W
Francis Marion University, SC	M,W
Fresno Pacific University, CA	M,W
Friends University, KS	M,W
Furman University, SC	M,W
Gannon University, PA	M,W
Gardner-Webb University, NC	M,W
Geneva College, PA	M,W
George Mason University, VA	M,W
Georgetown College, KY	M,W
Georgetown University, DC	M,W
The George Washington University, DC	M,W
Georgia College & State University, GA	M,W
Georgia Institute of Technology, GA	M,W
Georgia Southern University, GA	W
Glenville State College, WV	M,W
Grace College, IN	M,W
Graceland University, IA	M,W
Grand Valley State University, MI	M,W
Grand View College, IA	M,W
Harding University, AR	M,W
Hastings College, NE	M,W
Hawai'i Pacific University, HI	M,W
Hofstra University, NY	M,W
Holy Names University, CA	M,W
Houghton College, NY	M,W
Huntington University, IN	M,W
Idaho State University, ID	M,W
Illinois Institute of Technology, IL	M,W
Illinois State University, IL	M,W
Indiana State University, IN	M,W
Indiana University Bloomington, IN	M,W
Indiana University of Pennsylvania, PA	M,W
Indiana University–Purdue University Indianapolis, IN	M,W
Iona College, NY	M,W
Jacksonville State University, AL	M,W
James Madison University, VA	M,W
Jamestown College, ND	M,W
Johnson C. Smith University, NC	M,W
Judson College, IL	M,W
Kent State University, OH	M,W
King College, TN	M,W
Kutztown University of Pennsylvania, PA	M,W
Lake Superior State University, MI	M,W
Lamar University, TX	M,W
Lambuth University, TN	M,W
Lee University, TN	M,W
Lehigh University, PA	M,W
Le Moyne College, NY	M,W
LeMoyne-Owen College, TN	M
Lewis-Clark State College, ID	M,W
Limestone College, SC	M,W
Lindenwood University, MO	M,W
Lindsey Wilson College, KY	M,W
Lipscomb University, TN	M,W
Lock Haven University of Pennsylvania, PA	M,W
Longwood University, VA	M,W
Louisiana State University and Agricultural and Mechanical College, LA	M,W
Louisiana Tech University, LA	M,W
Loyola University Chicago, IL	M,W
Lyon College, AR	M,W
Malone College, OH	M,W
Manhattan College, NY	M,W
Mansfield University of Pennsylvania, PA	M,W
Marist College, NY	M,W
Marquette University, WI	M,W
McKendree College, IL	M,W
Mercer University, GA	M,W
Mesa State College, CO	W
Miami University, OH	M,W
Michigan State University, MI	M,W
Middle Tennessee State University, TN	M,W
Millersville University of Pennsylvania, PA	M,W
Milligan College, TN	M,W
Minnesota State University Mankato, MN	M,W
Minot State University, ND	M,W
Mississippi State University, MS	M,W
Missouri Baptist University, MO	M,W
Missouri State University, MO	M,W
Missouri Valley College, MO	M,W
Molloy College, NY	M,W
Monmouth University, NJ	M,W
Montana State University, MT	M,W
Montana State University–Billings, MT	M,W
Montreat College, NC	M,W
Morehead State University, KY	M,W
Morningside College, IA	M,W
Mount Marty College, SD	M,W
Mount Olive College, NC	M,W
Mount St. Mary's University, MD	M,W
Murray State University, KY	M,W
Newman University, KS	M,W
New Mexico State University, NM	M,W
New York Institute of Technology, NY	M,W
Niagara University, NY	M,W
Nicholls State University, LA	M,W
North Carolina Agricultural and Technical State University, NC	M,W
North Carolina State University, NC	M,W
North Dakota State University, ND	M,W
Northeastern University, MA	M,W
Northern Arizona University, AZ	M,W
Northern State University, SD	M,W
North Greenville University, SC	M,W
Northwestern College, IA	M,W
Northwestern Oklahoma State University, OK	M,W
Northwestern State University of Louisiana, LA	M,W
Northwest Nazarene University, ID	M,W
Northwest University, WA	M,W
Northwood University, MI	M,W
Northwood University, Texas Campus, TX	M,W
Nova Southeastern University, FL	M,W
Nyack College, NY	M,W
The Ohio State University, OH	M,W
Ohio University, OH	M,W
Ohio Valley University, WV	M,W
Oklahoma Baptist University, OK	M,W
Oklahoma Panhandle State University, OK	M,W
Oklahoma State University, OK	M,W
Oral Roberts University, OK	M,W
Ouachita Baptist University, AR	W
Penn State University Park, PA	M,W
Pfeiffer University, NC	M,W
Pikeville College, KY	M,W
Pittsburg State University, KS	M,W
Point Loma Nazarene University, CA	M,W
Portland State University, OR	M,W
Providence College, RI	M,W
Purdue University, IN	M,W
Quinnipiac University, CT	M,W
Radford University, VA	M,W
Rice University, TX	M,W
Robert Morris University, PA	M,W
Roberts Wesleyan College, NY	M,W
Sacred Heart University, CT	M,W
St. Ambrose University, IA	M,W
St. Andrews Presbyterian College, NC	M,W
St. Cloud State University, MN	M
St. Francis College, NY	M,W
Saint Francis University, PA	M,W
St. Gregory's University, OK	M,W
Saint Joseph's College, IN	M,W
Saint Leo University, FL	M,W
Saint Louis University, MO	M,W
Saint Mary's College of California, CA	M,W
Saint Vincent College, PA	M,W
Saint Xavier University, IL	W
Samford University, AL	M,W
Sam Houston State University, TX	M,W
San Diego State University, CA	W
San Francisco State University, CA	M,W
San Jose State University, CA	M,W
Santa Clara University, CA	M,W
Seattle Pacific University, WA	M,W

Seattle University, WA	M,W
Seton Hill University, PA	M,W
Shaw University, NC	M,W
Shippensburg University of Pennsylvania, PA	M,W
Slippery Rock University of Pennsylvania, PA	M,W
Sonoma State University, CA	W
South Dakota State University, SD	M,W
Southeastern Louisiana University, LA	M,W
Southeastern Oklahoma State University, OK	W
Southeast Missouri State University, MO	M,W
Southern Arkansas University–Magnolia, AR	W
Southern Illinois University Carbondale, IL	M,W
Southern Illinois University Edwardsville, IL	M,W
Southern Methodist University, TX	M,W
Southern Nazarene University, OK	M,W
Southern New Hampshire University, NH	M,W
Southern Oregon University, OR	M,W
Southern Wesleyan University, SC	M,W
Southwest Baptist University, MO	M,W
Spring Arbor University, MI	M,W
Spring Hill College, AL	M,W
Stanford University, CA	M,W
State University of New York at Binghamton, NY	M,W
Stephen F. Austin State University, TX	M,W
Stetson University, FL	M,W
Stonehill College, MA	M,W
Stony Brook University, State University of New York, NY	M,W
Syracuse University, NY	M,W
Tarleton State University, TX	M,W
Taylor University, IN	M,W
Tennessee State University, TN	M,W
Tennessee Technological University, TN	M,W
Tennessee Wesleyan College, TN	M,W
Texas A&M University–Commerce, TX	M,W
Texas A&M University–Kingsville, TX	M,W
Texas Christian University, TX	M,W
Texas State University-San Marcos, TX	M,W
Texas Tech University, TX	M,W
Tiffin University, OH	M,W
Towson University, MD	M,W
Troy University, AL	M,W
Tulane University, LA	M,W
Union University, TN	W
Unity College, ME	M,W
University at Albany, State University of New York, NY	M,W
University at Buffalo, the State University of New York, NY	M,W
The University of Akron, OH	M,W
The University of Alabama, AL	M,W
The University of Alabama at Birmingham, AL	W
The University of Alabama in Huntsville, AL	M,W
University of Alaska Fairbanks, AK	M,W
The University of Arizona, AZ	M,W
University of Arkansas, AR	M,W
University of California, Berkeley, CA	M,W
University of California, Irvine, CA	M,W
University of California, Los Angeles, CA	M,W
University of California, Riverside, CA	M,W
University of California, Santa Barbara, CA	M,W
University of Central Florida, FL	M,W
University of Central Missouri, MO	M,W
University of Central Oklahoma, OK	M,W
University of Charleston, WV	M,W
University of Colorado at Boulder, CO	M,W
University of Connecticut, CT	M,W
University of Dayton, OH	M,W
University of Detroit Mercy, MI	M,W
University of Evansville, IN	M,W
The University of Findlay, OH	M,W
University of Florida, FL	M,W
University of Georgia, GA	M,W
University of Hartford, CT	M,W
University of Hawaii at Hilo, HI	M,W
University of Hawaii at Manoa, HI	W
University of Idaho, ID	M,W
University of Illinois at Chicago, IL	M,W
University of Illinois at Urbana–Champaign, IL	M,W
The University of Iowa, IA	M,W
University of Kansas, KS	M,W
University of Louisiana at Lafayette, LA	M,W
University of Louisville, KY	M,W
University of Maine, ME	M,W
University of Maryland, Baltimore County, MD	M,W
University of Maryland, College Park, MD	M,W
University of Massachusetts Amherst, MA	M,W
University of Massachusetts Lowell, MA	M,W
University of Miami, FL	M,W
University of Michigan, MI	M,W
University of Minnesota, Twin Cities Campus, MN	M,W
University of Missouri–Columbia, MO	M,W
University of Missouri–Kansas City, MO	M,W
The University of Montana, MT	M,W
University of Nebraska at Kearney, NE	M,W
University of Nebraska at Omaha, NE	W
University of New Hampshire, NH	M,W
University of New Haven, CT	M,W
University of New Orleans, LA	M,W
University of North Alabama, AL	M,W
The University of North Carolina at Asheville, NC	M,W
The University of North Carolina at Chapel Hill, NC	M,W
The University of North Carolina at Charlotte, NC	M,W
The University of North Carolina at Greensboro, NC	M,W
The University of North Carolina at Pembroke, NC	M,W
The University of North Carolina Wilmington, NC	M,W
University of Northern Colorado, CO	W
University of Northern Iowa, IA	M,W
University of North Florida, FL	M,W
University of Notre Dame, IN	M,W
University of Oklahoma, OK	M,W
University of Oregon, OR	M,W
University of Pittsburgh, PA	M,W
University of Rhode Island, RI	M,W
University of Richmond, VA	W
University of St. Francis, IL	W
University of Saint Francis, IN	M,W
University of San Diego, CA	M,W
University of San Francisco, CA	M,W
University of South Carolina, SC	W
University of South Carolina Upstate, SC	M,W
The University of South Dakota, SD	M,W
University of Southern California, CA	M,W
University of Southern Indiana, IN	M,W
University of Southern Mississippi, MS	M,W
University of South Florida, FL	M,W
The University of Tampa, FL	M,W
The University of Tennessee at Martin, TN	M,W
The University of Texas at Austin, TX	M,W
The University of Texas at El Paso, TX	M,W
The University of Texas at San Antonio, TX	M,W
The University of Texas–Pan American, TX	M,W
University of the Cumberlands, KY	M,W
University of the Incarnate Word, TX	M,W
University of the Pacific, CA	W
University of Tulsa, OK	M,W
University of Vermont, VT	M,W
University of Virginia, VA	M,W
University of Washington, WA	M,W
The University of West Alabama, AL	M,W
University of West Florida, FL	M,W
University of West Georgia, GA	M,W
University of Wisconsin–Green Bay, WI	M,W
University of Wisconsin–Madison, WI	M,W
University of Wisconsin–Milwaukee, WI	M,W
University of Wyoming, WY	M,W
Utah State University, UT	M,W
Valdosta State University, GA	M,W
Valparaiso University, IN	M,W
Vanderbilt University, TN	M,W
Vanguard University of Southern California, CA	M,W
Virginia Commonwealth University, VA	M,W
Virginia Intermont College, VA	M,W
Virginia Military Institute, VA	M,W
Virginia Polytechnic Institute and State University, VA	M,W
Virginia State University, VA	M,W
Virginia Union University, VA	M,W
Wagner College, NY	M,W
Wake Forest University, NC	M,W
Walsh University, OH	M,W
Warner Pacific College, OR	M,W
Washington State University, WA	M,W

Wayland Baptist University, TX M,W
Wayne State College, NE M,W
Wayne State University, MI M,W
Webber International University, FL M,W
Western Carolina University, NC M,W
Western Illinois University, IL M,W
Western Washington University, WA M,W
West Liberty State College, WV M,W
Westmont College, CA M,W
West Virginia University, WV W
West Virginia Wesleyan College, WV M,W
Wheeling Jesuit University, WV M,W
Wichita State University, KS M,W
William Jewell College, MO M,W
Wingate University, NC M
Winona State University, MN W
Winston-Salem State University, NC M,W
Winthrop University, SC M,W
Xavier University, OH M,W
Youngstown State University, OH M,W

Equestrian Sports

Auburn University, AL W
Baylor University, TX W
California State University, Fresno, CA W
Molloy College, NY M,W
Murray State University, KY M,W
Oklahoma State University, OK W
Sacred Heart University, CT W
St. Andrews Presbyterian College, NC M,W
Saint Mary-of-the-Woods College, IN W
Seton Hill University, PA M,W
Southern Methodist University, TX W
University of Georgia, GA M,W
University of South Carolina, SC W
Virginia Intermont College, VA M,W

Fencing

California State University, Fullerton, CA M,W
Cleveland State University, OH M,W
The Ohio State University, OH M,W
Penn State University Park, PA M,W
Sacred Heart University, CT W
Stanford University, CA M,W
Temple University, PA W
University of Detroit Mercy, MI M,W
University of Notre Dame, IN M,W
Wayne State University, MI M,W

Field Hockey

American International College, MA W
Appalachian State University, NC W
Bellarmine University, KY W
Bentley College, MA W
Bloomsburg University of Pennsylvania, PA W
Boston College, MA W
Boston University, MA W
Catawba College, NC W
Central Michigan University, MI W
Colgate University, NY W
The College of William and Mary, VA W
Davidson College, NC W
Duke University, NC W
Fairfield University, CT W
Franklin Pierce University, NH W
Hofstra University, NY W
Houghton College, NY W
Indiana University of Pennsylvania, PA W
James Madison University, VA W
Kent State University, OH W
Kutztown University of Pennsylvania, PA W
Lehigh University, PA W
Lindenwood University, MO W
Lock Haven University of Pennsylvania, PA W
Longwood University, VA W
Mansfield University of Pennsylvania, PA W
Miami University, OH W
Michigan State University, MI W
Millersville University of Pennsylvania, PA W
Missouri State University, MO W
Monmouth University, NJ W
Northeastern University, MA W
The Ohio State University, OH W
Ohio University, OH W
Penn State University Park, PA W
Philadelphia University, PA W
Providence College, RI W
Quinnipiac University, CT W
Radford University, VA W
Robert Morris University, PA W
Sacred Heart University, CT W
Saint Francis University, PA W
Saint Leo University, FL W
Saint Louis University, MO W
Saint Vincent College, PA W
Seton Hill University, PA W
Shippensburg University of Pennsylvania, PA W
Slippery Rock University of Pennsylvania, PA W
Stanford University, CA W
Stonehill College, MA W
Syracuse University, NY W
Temple University, PA W
Towson University, MD W
University at Albany, State University of New York, NY W
University of California, Berkeley, CA W
University of Connecticut, CT W
University of Delaware, DE W
The University of Iowa, IA W
University of Louisville, KY W
University of Maine, ME W
University of Maryland, Baltimore County, MD W
University of Maryland, College Park, MD W
University of Massachusetts Amherst, MA W
University of Massachusetts Lowell, MA W
University of Michigan, MI W
University of New Hampshire, NH W
The University of North Carolina at Chapel Hill, NC W
University of Rhode Island, RI W
University of Richmond, VA W
University of the Pacific, CA W
University of Vermont, VT W
University of Virginia, VA W
Virginia Commonwealth University, VA W
Wake Forest University, NC W

Football

Abilene Christian University, TX M
Adams State College, CO M
Alabama State University, AL M
Alcorn State University, MS M
American International College, MA M
Appalachian State University, NC M
Arizona State University, AZ M
Arkansas State University, AR M
Arkansas Tech University, AR M
Auburn University, AL M
Augustana College, SD M
Azusa Pacific University, CA M
Baker University, KS M
Baylor University, TX M
Bemidji State University, MN M
Bethany College, KS M
Bethel College, KS M
Bethune-Cookman College, FL M
Black Hills State University, SD M
Blessing-Rieman College of Nursing, IL M
Bloomsburg University of Pennsylvania, PA M
Boise State University, ID M
Boston College, MA M
Bowie State University, MD M
Bowling Green State University, OH M
Brigham Young University, UT M
California Polytechnic State University, San Luis Obispo, CA M
California State University, Fresno, CA M
California State University, Northridge, CA M
California State University, Sacramento, CA M
California University of Pennsylvania, PA M
Campbellsville University, KY M
Carson-Newman College, TN M
Catawba College, NC M
Central Methodist University, MO M
Central Michigan University, MI M
Central Washington University, WA M
Clarion University of Pennsylvania, PA M
Clemson University, SC M
Coastal Carolina University, SC M
The College of William and Mary, VA M
Colorado School of Mines, CO M
Colorado State University, CO M
Concordia University, NE M
Concordia University, St. Paul, MN M
Concord University, WV M
Culver-Stockton College, MO M
Cumberland University, TN M
Dakota State University, SD M
Dakota Wesleyan University, SD M
Dana College, NE M
Davidson College, NC M
Dickinson State University, ND M
Doane College, NE M
Duke University, NC M
East Central University, OK M
Eastern Illinois University, IL M

Eastern Kentucky University, KY M
Eastern Michigan University, MI M
Elon University, NC M
Emporia State University, KS M
Evangel University, MO M
Ferris State University, MI M
Florida Atlantic University, FL M
Florida State University, FL M
Fort Lewis College, CO M
Friends University, KS M
Furman University, SC M
Gardner-Webb University, NC M
Geneva College, PA M
Georgetown College, KY M
Georgetown University, DC M
Georgia Institute of Technology, GA M
Georgia Southern University, GA M
Glenville State College, WV M
Graceland University, IA M
Grand Valley State University, MI M
Harding University, AR M
Hastings College, NE M
Hillsdale College, MI M
Hofstra University, NY M
Idaho State University, ID M
Illinois State University, IL M
Indiana State University, IN M
Indiana University Bloomington, IN M
Indiana University of Pennsylvania, PA M
Iowa Wesleyan College, IA M
Jackson State University, MS M
Jacksonville State University, AL M
James Madison University, VA M
Jamestown College, ND M
Johnson C. Smith University, NC M
Kent State University, OH M
Kentucky Wesleyan College, KY M
Kutztown University of Pennsylvania, PA M
Lamar University, TX M
Lambuth University, TN M
Lehigh University, PA M
Lindenwood University, MO M
Lock Haven University of Pennsylvania, PA M
Louisiana State University and Agricultural and Mechanical College, LA M
Louisiana Tech University, LA M
Malone College, OH M
Mansfield University of Pennsylvania, PA M
Mayville State University, ND M
McKendree College, IL M
Mesa State College, CO M
Miami University, OH M
Michigan State University, MI M
Michigan Technological University, MI M
Middle Tennessee State University, TN M
Midwestern State University, TX M
Millersville University of Pennsylvania, PA M
Minnesota State University Mankato, MN M
Minot State University, ND M
Mississippi State University, MS M
Missouri State University, MO M
Missouri Valley College, MO M
Montana State University, MT M
Montana Tech of The University of Montana, MT M
Morningside College, IA M
Murray State University, KY M
New Mexico State University, NM M
Nicholls State University, LA M
North Carolina Agricultural and Technical State University, NC M
North Carolina State University, NC M
North Dakota State University, ND M
Northeastern State University, OK M
Northeastern University, MA M
Northern Arizona University, AZ M
Northern Illinois University, IL M
Northern State University, SD M
North Greenville University, SC M
Northwestern College, IA M
Northwestern Oklahoma State University, OK M
Northwestern State University of Louisiana, LA M
Northwood University, MI M
The Ohio State University, OH M
Ohio University, OH M
Oklahoma Panhandle State University, OK M
Oklahoma State University, OK M
Oregon State University, OR M
Ouachita Baptist University, AR M
Penn State University Park, PA M
Pikeville College, KY M
Pittsburg State University, KS M
Portland State University, OR M
Purdue University, IN M
Rice University, TX M
Sacred Heart University, CT M
St. Ambrose University, IA M
St. Cloud State University, MN M
Saint Joseph's College, IN M
Saint Xavier University, IL M
Samford University, AL M
Sam Houston State University, TX M
San Diego State University, CA M
San Jose State University, CA M
Seton Hill University, PA M
Shepherd University, WV M
Shippensburg University of Pennsylvania, PA M
Slippery Rock University of Pennsylvania, PA M
South Dakota State University, SD M
Southeastern Louisiana University, LA M
Southeastern Oklahoma State University, OK M
Southeast Missouri State University, MO M
Southern Arkansas University–Magnolia, AR M
Southern Illinois University Carbondale, IL M
Southern Methodist University, TX M
Southern Nazarene University, OK M
Southern Oregon University, OR M
Southern Utah University, UT M
Southwest Baptist University, MO M
Southwest Minnesota State University, MN M
Stanford University, CA M
Stephen F. Austin State University, TX M
Stonehill College, MA M
Stony Brook University, State University of New York, NY M
Syracuse University, NY M
Tarleton State University, TX M
Taylor University, IN M
Temple University, PA M
Tennessee State University, TN M
Tennessee Technological University, TN M
Texas A&M University–Commerce, TX M
Texas A&M University–Kingsville, TX M
Texas Christian University, TX M
Texas State University-San Marcos, TX M
Texas Tech University, TX M
Tiffin University, OH M
Towson University, MD M
Trinity International University, IL M
Troy University, AL M
Tulane University, LA M
Tuskegee University, AL M
Union College, KY M
University at Albany, State University of New York, NY M
University at Buffalo, the State University of New York, NY M
The University of Akron, OH M
The University of Alabama, AL M
The University of Alabama at Birmingham, AL M
The University of Arizona, AZ M
University of Arkansas, AR M
University of Arkansas at Monticello, AR M
University of California, Berkeley, CA M
University of California, Los Angeles, CA M
University of Central Florida, FL M
University of Central Missouri, MO M
University of Central Oklahoma, OK M
University of Charleston, WV M
University of Colorado at Boulder, CO M
University of Connecticut, CT M
University of Delaware, DE M
The University of Findlay, OH M
University of Florida, FL M
University of Georgia, GA M
University of Hawaii at Manoa, HI M
University of Idaho, ID M
University of Illinois at Urbana–Champaign, IL M
The University of Iowa, IA M
University of Kansas, KS M
University of Louisiana at Lafayette, LA M
University of Louisville, KY M
University of Maine, ME M
University of Maryland, College Park, MD M
University of Massachusetts Amherst, MA M
University of Miami, FL M

University of Michigan, MI M
University of Minnesota, Crookston, MN M
University of Minnesota, Twin Cities Campus, MN M
University of Missouri–Columbia, MO M
The University of Montana, MT M
University of Nebraska at Kearney, NE M
University of Nebraska at Omaha, NE M
University of New Hampshire, NH M
University of New Haven, CT M
University of North Alabama, AL M
The University of North Carolina at Chapel Hill, NC M
University of North Dakota, ND M
University of Northern Colorado, CO M
University of Northern Iowa, IA M
University of Notre Dame, IN M
University of Oklahoma, OK M
University of Oregon, OR M
University of Pittsburgh, PA M
University of Rhode Island, RI M
University of Richmond, VA M
University of St. Francis, IL M
University of Saint Francis, IN M
University of South Carolina, SC M
The University of South Dakota, SD M
University of Southern California, CA M
University of Southern Mississippi, MS M
University of South Florida, FL M
The University of Tennessee at Martin, TN M
The University of Texas at Austin, TX M
The University of Texas at El Paso, TX M
University of the Cumberlands, KY M
University of Tulsa, OK M
University of Virginia, VA M
University of Washington, WA M
The University of West Alabama, AL M
University of West Georgia, GA M
University of Wisconsin–Madison, WI M
University of Wyoming, WY M
Urbana University, OH M
Utah State University, UT M
Valdosta State University, GA M
Valley City State University, ND M
Vanderbilt University, TN M
Virginia Military Institute, VA M
Virginia Polytechnic Institute and State University, VA M
Virginia State University, VA M
Virginia Union University, VA M
Wagner College, NY M
Wake Forest University, NC M
Walsh University, OH M
Washington State University, WA M
Wayne State College, NE M
Wayne State University, MI M
Webber International University, FL M
Western Carolina University, NC M
Western Illinois University, IL M
Western Washington University, WA M
West Liberty State College, WV M
Westminster College, PA M
West Virginia University, WV M
West Virginia Wesleyan College, WV M
William Jewell College, MO M
Wingate University, NC M
Winona State University, MN M
Winston-Salem State University, NC M
Youngstown State University, OH M

Golf

Abilene Christian University, TX M
Adams State College, CO M
Adelphi University, NY M
Alabama State University, AL M
Albertson College of Idaho, ID M,W
Alcorn State University, MS M,W
Alderson-Broaddus College, WV M,W
Anderson University, SC M,W
Appalachian State University, NC M,W
Arizona State University, AZ M,W
Arkansas State University, AR M,W
Arkansas Tech University, AR M
Armstrong Atlantic State University, GA M
Ashford University, IA M,W
Auburn University, AL M,W
Austin Peay State University, TN M,W
Azusa Pacific University, CA M
Baker University, KS M,W
Barton College, NC M
Baylor University, TX M,W
Bellarmine University, KY M,W
Belmont Abbey College, NC M,W
Belmont University, TN M,W
Berry College, GA M,W
Bethany College, KS M
Bethel College, IN M,W
Bethel College, KS M,W
Bethune-Cookman College, FL M,W
Birmingham-Southern College, AL M,W
Bluefield State College, WV M
Boise State University, ID M,W
Bowling Green State University, OH M,W
Bradley University, IL M,W
Brevard College, NC M
Brigham Young University, UT M,W
Butler University, IN M,W
California Polytechnic State University, San Luis Obispo, CA M
California State University, Chico, CA M,W
California State University, Fresno, CA M
California State University, Northridge, CA M
California State University, Sacramento, CA M
California State University, San Bernardino, CA M
California University of Pennsylvania, PA M,W
Campbellsville University, KY M,W
Campbell University, NC M,W
Canisius College, NY M
Carson-Newman College, TN M
Catawba College, NC M
Cedarville University, OH M
Centenary College of Louisiana, LA M,W
Central State University, OH M,W
Clarion University of Pennsylvania, PA M
Clemson University, SC M
Cleveland State University, OH M
Coastal Carolina University, SC M,W
College of Charleston, SC M,W
College of the Southwest, NM M,W
Colorado School of Mines, CO M
Colorado State University, CO M,W
Colorado State University-Pueblo, CO M,W
Columbus State University, GA M
Concordia University, NE M,W
Concordia University, St. Paul, MN W
Concord University, WV M
Creighton University, NE M,W
Culver-Stockton College, MO M,W
Cumberland University, TN M,W
Dakota Wesleyan University, SD M,W
Dana College, NE W
Davidson College, NC M
Davis & Elkins College, WV M
Dickinson State University, ND M,W
Doane College, NE M,W
Dominican College, NY M
Dordt College, IA M
Drake University, IA M
Drury University, MO M,W
Duke University, NC M,W
Duquesne University, PA M
East Central University, OK M
Eastern Illinois University, IL M,W
Eastern Kentucky University, KY M,W
Eastern Michigan University, MI M,W
East Tennessee State University, TN M,W
Elon University, NC M,W
Embry-Riddle Aeronautical University, FL M
Evangel University, MO M,W
Ferris State University, MI M,W
Flagler College, FL M
Florida Atlantic University, FL M,W
Florida Gulf Coast University, FL M,W
Florida Institute of Technology, FL M,W
Florida State University, FL M,W
Fort Lewis College, CO M
Francis Marion University, SC M
Friends University, KS M
Furman University, SC M,W
Gannon University, PA M,W
Gardner-Webb University, NC M,W
George Mason University, VA M
Georgetown College, KY M,W
Georgetown University, DC M
The George Washington University, DC M
Georgia College & State University, GA M
Georgia Institute of Technology, GA M
Georgia Southern University, GA M
Glenville State College, WV M,W
Grace College, IN M
Graceland University, IA M,W
Grand Valley State University, MI M,W
Grand View College, IA M,W
Hastings College, NE M,W
Hawai'i Pacific University, HI M,W
Hofstra University, NY M,W
Holy Names University, CA M
Huntington University, IN M
Idaho State University, ID M,W
Illinois State University, IL M,W
Indiana University Bloomington, IN M,W
Indiana University of Pennsylvania, PA M

Indiana University–Purdue University Indianapolis, IN M
Iona College, NY M
Iowa Wesleyan College, IA M,W
Jackson State University, MS M,W
Jacksonville State University, AL M,W
Jamestown College, ND M,W
Johnson C. Smith University, NC M
Kent State University, OH M,W
Kentucky Wesleyan College, KY M,W
King College, TN M,W
Kutztown University of Pennsylvania, PA W
Lamar University, TX M,W
Lambuth University, TN M
Lee University, TN M
Lehigh University, PA M
Le Moyne College, NY M
LeMoyne-Owen College, TN M,W
Lewis-Clark State College, ID M,W
Limestone College, SC M,W
Lindenwood University, MO M,W
Lindsey Wilson College, KY M,W
Lipscomb University, TN M,W
Longwood University, VA M,W
Louisiana State University and Agricultural and Mechanical College, LA M,W
Louisiana Tech University, LA M
Loyola University Chicago, IL M,W
Lyon College, AR M,W
Malone College, OH M,W
Manhattan College, NY M
Marquette University, WI M
McKendree College, IL M,W
Mercer University, GA M,W
Mesa State College, CO W
Miami University, OH M
Michigan State University, MI M,W
Middle Tennessee State University, TN M,W
Millersville University of Pennsylvania, PA M
Milligan College, TN M
Minnesota State University Mankato, MN M,W
Mississippi State University, MS M,W
Missouri Baptist University, MO M
Missouri State University, MO M,W
Missouri Valley College, MO M,W
Monmouth University, NJ M,W
Montana State University, MT W
Montana Tech of The University of Montana, MT M,W
Montreat College, NC M
Morehead State University, KY M
Morningside College, IA M,W
Mount Olive College, NC M,W
Mount St. Mary's University, MD M,W
Mount Vernon Nazarene University, OH M
Murray State University, KY M,W
Newman University, KS M,W
New Mexico State University, NM M,W
Niagara University, NY M
Nicholls State University, LA M,W
North Carolina State University, NC M
North Dakota State University, ND W
Northeastern State University, OK M,W
Northern Arizona University, AZ W
Northern Illinois University, IL M,W
Northern State University, SD W
North Greenville University, SC M
Northwestern College, IA M,W
Northwestern Oklahoma State University, OK M,W
Northwest Nazarene University, ID M
Northwood University, MI M,W
Northwood University, Florida Campus, FL M,W
Northwood University, Texas Campus, TX M,W
Nova Southeastern University, FL M,W
Nyack College, NY M
The Ohio State University, OH M,W
Ohio University, OH M,W
Ohio Valley University, WV M
Oklahoma Baptist University, OK M,W
Oklahoma Panhandle State University, OK M,W
Oklahoma State University, OK M,W
Oral Roberts University, OK M,W
Oregon State University, OR M,W
Ouachita Baptist University, AR M
Penn State University Park, PA M,W
Pfeiffer University, NC M,W
Philadelphia University, PA M
Pikeville College, KY M,W
Pittsburg State University, KS M
Point Loma Nazarene University, CA M
Portland State University, OR M,W
Purdue University, IN M,W
Quinnipiac University, CT M
Radford University, VA M,W
Regis University, CO M,W
Reinhardt College, GA M
Rice University, TX M
Robert Morris University, PA M,W
Roberts Wesleyan College, NY M,W
Rockhurst University, MO M,W
Rollins College, FL M,W
Sacred Heart University, CT M,W
St. Ambrose University, IA M,W
St. Andrews Presbyterian College, NC M,W
St. Cloud State University, MN W
St. Edward's University, TX M,W
Saint Francis University, PA M,W
St. Gregory's University, OK M,W
Saint Joseph's College, IN M,W
Saint Leo University, FL M,W
Saint Louis University, MO M
Saint Mary's College of California, CA M
Saint Vincent College, PA M,W
Saint Xavier University, IL M
Samford University, AL M,W
Sam Houston State University, TX M,W
San Diego State University, CA M,W
San Jose State University, CA M,W
Santa Clara University, CA M,W
Seton Hill University, PA M,W
Slippery Rock University of Pennsylvania, PA M,W
South Dakota State University, SD M,W
Southeastern Louisiana University, LA M
Southeast Missouri State University, MO M
Southern Illinois University Carbondale, IL M,W
Southern Illinois University Edwardsville, IL M,W
Southern Methodist University, TX M,W
Southern Nazarene University, OK M,W
Southern Utah University, UT M
Southern Wesleyan University, SC M
Southwest Baptist University, MO M
Southwest Minnesota State University, MN W
Spring Arbor University, MI M
Spring Hill College, AL M,W
Stanford University, CA M,W
State University of New York at Binghamton, NY M
Stephen F. Austin State University, TX M
Stetson University, FL M,W
Tarleton State University, TX W
Taylor University, IN M
Temple University, PA M
Tennessee State University, TN M
Tennessee Technological University, TN M,W
Tennessee Wesleyan College, TN M
Texas A&M University–Commerce, TX M,W
Texas Christian University, TX M,W
Texas State University-San Marcos, TX M,W
Texas Tech University, TX M,W
Tiffin University, OH M,W
Towson University, MD M
Trevecca Nazarene University, TN M,W
Tulane University, LA M,W
Tuskegee University, AL M
Union College, KY M,W
Union University, TN M
University at Albany, State University of New York, NY W
The University of Akron, OH M
The University of Alabama, AL M,W
The University of Alabama at Birmingham, AL M,W
The University of Arizona, AZ M,W
University of Arkansas, AR M,W
University of Arkansas at Monticello, AR M
University of California, Berkeley, CA M,W
University of California, Irvine, CA M,W
University of California, Los Angeles, CA M,W
University of California, Santa Barbara, CA M
University of Central Florida, FL M,W
University of Central Missouri, MO M
University of Central Oklahoma, OK M,W
University of Charleston, WV M
University of Colorado at Boulder, CO M,W
University of Connecticut, CT M
University of Dayton, OH M,W
University of Denver, CO M,W
University of Detroit Mercy, MI M,W
University of Evansville, IN M
The University of Findlay, OH M,W
University of Florida, FL M,W
University of Georgia, GA M,W
University of Hartford, CT M,W
University of Hawaii at Hilo, HI M

University of Hawaii at Manoa, HI M,W
University of Idaho, ID M,W
University of Illinois at Urbana–Champaign, IL M,W
The University of Iowa, IA M,W
University of Kansas, KS M,W
University of Louisiana at Lafayette, LA M
University of Louisville, KY M,W
University of Maryland, College Park, MD M,W
University of Miami, FL W
University of Michigan, MI M,W
University of Minnesota, Twin Cities Campus, MN M,W
University of Missouri–Columbia, MO M,W
University of Missouri–Kansas City, MO M,W
University of Missouri–St. Louis, MO M,W
University of Nebraska at Kearney, NE M,W
University of New Haven, CT M
University of New Orleans, LA M,W
University of North Alabama, AL M
The University of North Carolina at Chapel Hill, NC M,W
The University of North Carolina at Charlotte, NC M
The University of North Carolina at Greensboro, NC M,W
The University of North Carolina at Pembroke, NC M
The University of North Carolina Wilmington, NC M,W
University of Northern Colorado, CO M,W
University of Northern Iowa, IA M,W
University of North Florida, FL M
University of Notre Dame, IN M,W
University of Oklahoma, OK M,W
University of Oregon, OR M,W
University of Rhode Island, RI M
University of Richmond, VA M,W
University of St. Francis, IL M,W
University of Saint Francis, IN M
University of San Diego, CA M
University of San Francisco, CA M,W
University of South Carolina, SC M,W
University of Southern California, CA M,W
University of Southern Indiana, IN M,W
University of Southern Mississippi, MS M,W
University of South Florida, FL M,W
The University of Tampa, FL M
The University of Tennessee at Martin, TN M
The University of Texas at Austin, TX M,W
The University of Texas at Brownsville, TX M,W
The University of Texas at El Paso, TX M
The University of Texas at San Antonio, TX M
The University of Texas–Pan American, TX M,W
University of the Cumberlands, KY M,W
University of the Incarnate Word, TX M,W
University of the Pacific, CA M
University of Tulsa, OK M,W
University of Virginia, VA M,W
University of Washington, WA M,W
University of West Florida, FL M
University of Wisconsin–Madison, WI M,W
University of Wyoming, WY M,W
Urbana University, OH M,W
Utah State University, UT M
Valdosta State University, GA M
Vanderbilt University, TN M,W
Virginia Commonwealth University, VA M
Virginia Intermont College, VA M
Virginia Military Institute, VA M
Virginia Polytechnic Institute and State University, VA M
Virginia State University, VA M,W
Virginia Union University, VA M
Wagner College, NY M,W
Wake Forest University, NC M,W
Walsh University, OH M,W
Washington State University, WA M,W
Wayland Baptist University, TX M
Wayne State College, NE M,W
Wayne State University, MI M
Webber International University, FL M,W
Western Carolina University, NC M,W
Western Illinois University, IL M
Western Washington University, WA M,W
West Liberty State College, WV M,W
West Virginia Wesleyan College, WV M
Wheeling Jesuit University, WV M,W
Wichita State University, KS M,W
William Jewell College, MO M,W
Williams Baptist College, AR M
Wingate University, NC M,W
Winona State University, MN M,W
Winthrop University, SC M,W
Xavier University, OH M,W
Youngstown State University, OH M

Gymnastics

Arizona State University, AZ W
Auburn University, AL W
Boise State University, ID W
Bowling Green State University, OH W
Brigham Young University, UT W
California Polytechnic State University, San Luis Obispo, CA W
California State University, Fullerton, CA W
California State University, Sacramento, CA W
Centenary College of Louisiana, LA W
Central Michigan University, MI W
The College of William and Mary, VA M,W
Eastern Michigan University, MI W
The George Washington University, DC W
Illinois State University, IL W
Kent State University, OH W
Louisiana State University and Agricultural and Mechanical College, LA W
Michigan State University, MI W
North Carolina State University, NC W
Northern Illinois University, IL W
The Ohio State University, OH M,W
Oregon State University, OR W
Penn State University Park, PA M,W
San Jose State University, CA W
Seattle Pacific University, WA W
Southeast Missouri State University, MO W
Southern Utah University, UT W
Stanford University, CA M,W
Temple University, PA M,W
Texas Woman's University, TX W
Towson University, MD W
The University of Alabama, AL W
The University of Arizona, AZ W
University of Arkansas, AR W
University of Bridgeport, CT W
University of California, Berkeley, CA M,W
University of California, Los Angeles, CA W
University of California, Santa Barbara, CA W
University of Denver, CO W
University of Florida, FL W
University of Georgia, GA W
University of Illinois at Chicago, IL M,W
University of Illinois at Urbana–Champaign, IL M,W
The University of Iowa, IA M,W
University of Maryland, College Park, MD W
University of Michigan, MI M,W
University of Minnesota, Twin Cities Campus, MN M,W
University of Missouri–Columbia, MO W
University of New Hampshire, NH W
The University of North Carolina at Chapel Hill, NC W
University of Oklahoma, OK M,W
University of Pittsburgh, PA W
University of Rhode Island, RI W
University of Washington, WA W
Utah State University, UT W
West Virginia University, WV W
Winona State University, MN W

Ice Hockey

American International College, MA M
Bemidji State University, MN M,W
Bentley College, MA M
Boston College, MA M
Boston University, MA M,W
Bowling Green State University, OH M
Canisius College, NY M
Clarkson University, NY M,W
Colgate University, NY M,W
The Colorado College, CO M
Dordt College, IA M
Ferris State University, MI M
Lake Superior State University, MI M
Lindenwood University, MO M,W
Miami University, OH M
Michigan State University, MI M
Michigan Technological University, MI M
Minnesota State University Mankato, MN M,W
Niagara University, NY M,W
Northeastern University, MA M,W
The Ohio State University, OH M,W
Providence College, RI M,W
Quinnipiac University, CT M,W
Rensselaer Polytechnic Institute, NY M,W
Robert Morris University, PA M
Sacred Heart University, CT M
St. Cloud State University, MN M,W

St. Lawrence University, NY M,W
The University of Alabama in Huntsville, AL M
University of Alaska Fairbanks, AK M
University of Connecticut, CT M,W
University of Denver, CO M
University of Maine, ME M,W
University of Massachusetts Amherst, MA M
University of Massachusetts Lowell, MA M
University of Michigan, MI M
University of Minnesota, Twin Cities Campus, MN M,W
University of Nebraska at Omaha, NE M
University of New Hampshire, NH M,W
University of North Dakota, ND M,W
University of Notre Dame, IN M
University of Vermont, VT M,W
University of Wisconsin–Madison, WI M,W
Wayne State University, MI M,W

Lacrosse

Adelphi University, NY M,W
American International College, MA W
Bellarmine University, KY M
Belmont Abbey College, NC M,W
Bentley College, MA M,W
Boston College, MA W
Boston University, MA W
Butler University, IN M
Canisius College, NY M,W
Colgate University, NY M,W
The College of William and Mary, VA W
Davidson College, NC W
Dominican College, NY M
Duke University, NC M,W
Duquesne University, PA W
Fairfield University, CT M,W
Gannon University, PA W
George Mason University, VA W
Georgetown University, DC M,W
Hofstra University, NY M,W
Indiana University of Pennsylvania, PA W
Iona College, NY W
James Madison University, VA W
The Johns Hopkins University, MD M,W
Lehigh University, PA M,W
Le Moyne College, NY M,W
Limestone College, SC M,W
Lindenwood University, MO M,W
Lock Haven University of Pennsylvania, PA W
Longwood University, VA W
Manhattan College, NY M,W
Marist College, NY M,W
Millersville University of Pennsylvania, PA W
Molloy College, NY M,W
Monmouth University, NJ W
Mount St. Mary's University, MD M,W
New York Institute of Technology, NY M
Niagara University, NY W
The Ohio State University, OH M,W
Penn State University Park, PA M,W
Pfeiffer University, NC M,W
Philadelphia University, PA W
Quinnipiac University, CT M,W
Regis University, CO W
Robert Morris University, PA M,W
Sacred Heart University, CT M,W
St. Andrews Presbyterian College, NC M,W
Saint Francis University, PA W
Saint Leo University, FL M
Saint Vincent College, PA M,W
Seton Hill University, PA M,W
Shippensburg University of Pennsylvania, PA W
Southern New Hampshire University, NH M,W
State University of New York at Binghamton, NY M,W
Stonehill College, MA W
Stony Brook University, State University of New York, NY M,W
Syracuse University, NY M,W
Temple University, PA W
Towson University, MD M,W
University at Albany, State University of New York, NY M,W
University of California, Berkeley, CA W
University of Delaware, DE M,W
University of Denver, CO M,W
University of Hartford, CT M
University of Maryland, Baltimore County, MD M,W
University of Maryland, College Park, MD M,W
University of Massachusetts Amherst, MA M,W
University of New Hampshire, NH W
University of New Haven, CT W
The University of North Carolina at Chapel Hill, NC M,W
University of Notre Dame, IN M,W
University of Oregon, OR W
University of Richmond, VA W
University of Vermont, VT M,W
University of Virginia, VA M,W
Vanderbilt University, TN W
Virginia Military Institute, VA M
Virginia Polytechnic Institute and State University, VA W
Wagner College, NY M,W
Wheeling Jesuit University, WV M
Wingate University, NC M

Riflery

Austin Peay State University, TN W
Birmingham-Southern College, AL W
Jacksonville State University, AL M,W
Lindenwood University, MO M,W
Mercer University, GA M,W
Morehead State University, KY M,W
Murray State University, KY M,W
North Georgia College & State University, GA M,W
Tennessee Technological University, TN M,W
Texas Christian University, TX W
University of Alaska Fairbanks, AK M,W
University of Missouri–Kansas City, MO M,W
University of San Francisco, CA M,W
The University of Tennessee at Martin, TN M,W
Virginia Military Institute, VA M,W
West Virginia University, WV M,W
Xavier University, OH M,W

Rugby

Eastern Illinois University, IL W
University of California, Berkeley, CA M

Skiing (Cross-Country)

Montana State University, MT M,W
St. Cloud State University, MN W
University of Alaska Fairbanks, AK M,W
University of Colorado at Boulder, CO M,W
University of Denver, CO M,W
University of New Hampshire, NH M,W
University of Vermont, VT M,W
University of Wisconsin–Green Bay, WI M,W

Skiing (Downhill)

Albertson College of Idaho, ID M,W
Davis & Elkins College, WV M,W
Montana State University, MT M,W
Paul Smith's College of Arts and Sciences, NY M,W
University of Colorado at Boulder, CO M,W
University of Denver, CO M,W
University of Massachusetts Amherst, MA M,W
University of New Hampshire, NH M,W
University of Vermont, VT M,W

Soccer

Adelphi University, NY M,W
Albertson College of Idaho, ID M,W
Alcorn State University, MS W
Alderson-Broaddus College, WV M
Alliant International University, CA M,W
American International College, MA M,W
Anderson University, SC M,W
Appalachian State University, NC M,W
Arizona State University, AZ W
Arkansas State University, AR W
Asbury College, KY M,W
Ashford University, IA M,W
Auburn University, AL W
Auburn University Montgomery, AL M,W
Augustana College, SD W
Austin Peay State University, TN W
Azusa Pacific University, CA M,W
Baker University, KS M,W
Barton College, NC M,W
Baylor University, TX W
Bellarmine University, KY M,W
Belmont Abbey College, NC M,W
Belmont University, TN M,W
Bemidji State University, MN W
Bentley College, MA M,W
Berry College, GA M,W
Bethany College, KS M,W
Bethel College, IN M,W
Bethel College, KS M,W
Birmingham-Southern College, AL M,W
Blessing-Rieman College of Nursing, IL M,W
Bloomfield College, NJ M,W
Bloomsburg University of Pennsylvania, PA M,W
Boston College, MA M,W
Boston University, MA M,W
Bowling Green State University, OH M,W
Bradley University, IL M
Brenau University, GA W
Brevard College, NC M,W

Brigham Young University, UT W
Bryan College, TN M,W
Butler University, IN M,W
California State University, Chico, CA M,W
California State University, Dominguez Hills, CA M,W
California State University, Fresno, CA M,W
California State University, Fullerton, CA M,W
California State University, Los Angeles, CA M,W
California State University, Northridge, CA M
California State University, Sacramento, CA M,W
California State University, San Bernardino, CA M,W
California University of Pennsylvania, PA M,W
Campbellsville University, KY M,W
Campbell University, NC M,W
Canisius College, NY M,W
Carson-Newman College, TN M,W
Catawba College, NC M,W
Cedarville University, OH M,W
Centenary College of Louisiana, LA M,W
Central Methodist University, MO M,W
Central Michigan University, MI W
Central Washington University, WA W
Christian Brothers University, TN M,W
Clemson University, SC M,W
Cleveland State University, OH M
Coastal Carolina University, SC M,W
Colgate University, NY M,W
College of Charleston, SC M,W
College of Saint Mary, NE W
The College of Saint Rose, NY M,W
College of the Southwest, NM M,W
The College of William and Mary, VA M,W
The Colorado College, CO W
Columbia College, MO M
Columbus State University, GA W
Concordia University, CA M,W
Concordia University, NE M,W
Concordia University, St. Paul, MN W
Concord University, WV W
Converse College, SC W
Corban College, OR M,W
Creighton University, NE M,W
Culver-Stockton College, MO M,W
Cumberland University, TN M,W
Dallas Baptist University, TX W
Dana College, NE M,W
Davidson College, NC M,W
Davis & Elkins College, WV M,W
Doane College, NE M,W
Dominican College, NY M,W
Dordt College, IA M,W
Dowling College, NY M
Drake University, IA M,W
Drury University, MO M,W
Duke University, NC M,W
Duquesne University, PA M,W
East Central University, OK W
Eastern Illinois University, IL M,W
Eastern Michigan University, MI W
East Tennessee State University, TN W
Elon University, NC M,W
Embry-Riddle Aeronautical University, FL M,W
Emporia State University, KS W
Erskine College, SC M,W
Fairfield University, CT M,W
Faulkner University, AL M,W
Felician College, NJ M,W
Flagler College, FL M,W
Florida Atlantic University, FL M,W
Florida Institute of Technology, FL M,W
Florida State University, FL W
Fort Lewis College, CO M,W
Francis Marion University, SC M,W
Franklin Pierce University, NH M,W
Freed-Hardeman University, TN M,W
Fresno Pacific University, CA M,W
Friends University, KS M,W
Furman University, SC M,W
Gannon University, PA M,W
Gardner-Webb University, NC M,W
Geneva College, PA M,W
George Mason University, VA M,W
Georgetown College, KY M,W
Georgetown University, DC M,W
The George Washington University, DC M,W
Georgia College & State University, GA W
Georgia Southern University, GA M,W
Gonzaga University, WA M,W
Grace College, IN M,W
Graceland University, IA M,W
Grand Valley State University, MI W
Grand View College, IA M,W
Harding University, AR M,W
Hastings College, NE M,W
Hawai'i Pacific University, HI M,W
Hofstra University, NY M,W
Holy Names University, CA M,W
Houghton College, NY M,W
Huntington University, IN M,W
Illinois Institute of Technology, IL M,W
Illinois State University, IL W
Indiana State University, IN W
Indiana University Bloomington, IN M,W
Indiana University of Pennsylvania, PA W
Indiana University–Purdue University Indianapolis, IN M,W
Iona College, NY M,W
Iowa Wesleyan College, IA M,W
Jackson State University, MS W
Jacksonville State University, AL W
James Madison University, VA M,W
Jamestown College, ND W
Judson College, IL M,W
Kent State University, OH W
Kentucky Wesleyan College, KY M,W
King College, TN M,W
Kutztown University of Pennsylvania, PA M,W
Lambuth University, TN M,W
Lee University, TN M,W
Lehigh University, PA M,W
Le Moyne College, NY M,W
Limestone College, SC M,W
Lindenwood University, MO M,W
Lindsey Wilson College, KY M,W
Lipscomb University, TN M,W
Lock Haven University of Pennsylvania, PA M,W
Longwood University, VA M,W
Louisiana State University and Agricultural and Mechanical College, LA W
Loyola University Chicago, IL M,W
Lyon College, AR M,W
Malone College, OH M,W
Manhattan College, NY M,W
Mansfield University of Pennsylvania, PA W
Marist College, NY M,W
Marquette University, WI M,W
Mayville State University, ND M,W
McKendree College, IL M,W
Mercer University, GA M,W
Mesa State College, CO W
Metropolitan State College of Denver, CO M,W
Miami University, OH W
Michigan State University, MI M
Middle Tennessee State University, TN W
Midwestern State University, TX M,W
Millersville University of Pennsylvania, PA M,W
Milligan College, TN M,W
Minnesota State University Mankato, MN W
Mississippi State University, MS W
Missouri Baptist University, MO M,W
Missouri State University, MO M,W
Missouri Valley College, MO M,W
Molloy College, NY M,W
Monmouth University, NJ M,W
Montana State University–Billings, MT M,W
Montreat College, NC M,W
Morehead State University, KY W
Morningside College, IA M,W
Mount Marty College, SD M,W
Mount Olive College, NC M,W
Mount St. Mary's University, MD M,W
Mount Vernon Nazarene University, OH M,W
Murray State University, KY W
Newman University, KS M,W
New York Institute of Technology, NY M,W
Niagara University, NY M,W
Nicholls State University, LA W
North Carolina State University, NC M,W
North Dakota State University, ND W
Northeastern State University, OK M,W
Northeastern University, MA M,W
Northern Arizona University, AZ W
Northern Illinois University, IL M,W
Northern State University, SD W
North Georgia College & State University, GA M,W
North Greenville University, SC M,W
Northwestern College, IA M,W
Northwestern Oklahoma State University, OK W
Northwestern State University of Louisiana, LA W
Northwest Nazarene University, ID W
Northwest University, WA M
Northwood University, MI M,W

Northwood University, Florida Campus, FL M,W
Northwood University, Texas Campus, TX M,W
Nova Southeastern University, FL M,W
Nyack College, NY M,W
The Ohio State University, OH M,W
Ohio University, OH W
Ohio Valley University, WV M,W
Oklahoma State University, OK W
Oral Roberts University, OK M,W
Oregon State University, OR M,W
Paul Smith's College of Arts and Sciences, NY M,W
Penn State University Park, PA M,W
Pfeiffer University, NC M,W
Philadelphia University, PA M,W
Point Loma Nazarene University, CA M,W
Portland State University, OR W
Providence College, RI M,W
Purdue University, IN W
Quinnipiac University, CT M,W
Radford University, VA M,W
Regis University, CO M,W
Reinhardt College, GA M,W
Rice University, TX W
Robert Morris University, PA M,W
Roberts Wesleyan College, NY M,W
Rockhurst University, MO M,W
Rollins College, FL M,W
Sacred Heart University, CT M,W
St. Ambrose University, IA M,W
St. Andrews Presbyterian College, NC M,W
St. Cloud State University, MN W
St. Edward's University, TX M,W
St. Francis College, NY M
Saint Francis University, PA M,W
St. Gregory's University, OK M,W
Saint Joseph's College, IN M,W
Saint Leo University, FL M,W
Saint Louis University, MO M,W
Saint Mary-of-the-Woods College, IN W
Saint Mary's College of California, CA M,W
Saint Vincent College, PA M,W
Saint Xavier University, IL M,W
Samford University, AL W
Sam Houston State University, TX W
San Diego State University, CA M,W
San Francisco State University, CA M,W
San Jose State University, CA M,W
Santa Clara University, CA M,W
Seattle Pacific University, WA M
Seattle University, WA M,W
Seton Hill University, PA M,W
Shepherd University, WV M,W
Shippensburg University of Pennsylvania, PA M,W
Slippery Rock University of Pennsylvania, PA M,W
Sonoma State University, CA M,W
South Dakota State University, SD W
Southeastern Louisiana University, LA W
Southeast Missouri State University, MO W
Southern Illinois University Edwardsville, IL M,W
Southern Methodist University, TX M,W
Southern Nazarene University, OK M,W
Southern New Hampshire University, NH M,W
Southern Oregon University, OR W
Southern Wesleyan University, SC M,W
Southwest Baptist University, MO W
Southwest Minnesota State University, MN W
Spring Arbor University, MI M,W
Spring Hill College, AL M,W
Stanford University, CA M,W
State University of New York at Binghamton, NY M,W
State University of New York College at Oneonta, NY M
Stephen F. Austin State University, TX W
Stetson University, FL M,W
Stonehill College, MA M,W
Stony Brook University, State University of New York, NY M,W
Syracuse University, NY M,W
Taylor University, IN M,W
Temple University, PA M,W
Tennessee Technological University, TN W
Tennessee Wesleyan College, TN M,W
Texas A&M University–Commerce, TX W
Texas Christian University, TX W
Texas State University-San Marcos, TX W
Texas Tech University, TX W
Texas Woman's University, TX W
Tiffin University, OH M,W
Towson University, MD M,W
Trevecca Nazarene University, TN M,W
Trinity International University, IL M,W
Troy University, AL W
Tulane University, LA W
Union College, KY M,W
Union University, TN M,W
Unity College, ME M
University at Albany, State University of New York, NY M,W
University at Buffalo, the State University of New York, NY M,W
The University of Akron, OH M
The University of Alabama, AL W
The University of Alabama at Birmingham, AL M,W
The University of Alabama in Huntsville, AL M,W
The University of Arizona, AZ W
University of Arkansas, AR W
University of Bridgeport, CT M,W
University of California, Berkeley, CA M,W
University of California, Irvine, CA M,W
University of California, Los Angeles, CA M,W
University of California, Santa Barbara, CA M,W
University of Central Florida, FL M,W
University of Central Missouri, MO W
University of Central Oklahoma, OK W
University of Charleston, WV M,W
University of Colorado at Boulder, CO W
University of Connecticut, CT M,W
University of Dayton, OH M,W
University of Delaware, DE M,W
University of Denver, CO M,W
University of Detroit Mercy, MI M,W
University of Evansville, IN M,W
The University of Findlay, OH M,W
University of Florida, FL W
University of Georgia, GA W
University of Great Falls, MT W
University of Hartford, CT M,W
University of Hawaii at Manoa, HI W
University of Idaho, ID W
University of Illinois at Chicago, IL M
University of Illinois at Springfield, IL M
University of Illinois at Urbana–Champaign, IL W
The University of Iowa, IA W
University of Kansas, KS W
University of Louisville, KY M,W
University of Maine, ME M,W
University of Maryland, Baltimore County, MD M,W
University of Maryland, College Park, MD M,W
University of Massachusetts Amherst, MA M,W
University of Miami, FL W
University of Michigan, MI W
University of Minnesota, Crookston, MN W
University of Minnesota, Twin Cities Campus, MN W
University of Missouri–Columbia, MO W
University of Missouri–Kansas City, MO M
University of Missouri–St. Louis, MO M,W
University of New Hampshire, NH M,W
University of New Haven, CT M,W
University of North Alabama, AL W
The University of North Carolina at Asheville, NC M,W
The University of North Carolina at Chapel Hill, NC M,W
The University of North Carolina at Charlotte, NC M,W
The University of North Carolina at Greensboro, NC M,W
The University of North Carolina at Pembroke, NC M,W
The University of North Carolina Wilmington, NC M,W
University of Northern Colorado, CO W
University of Northern Iowa, IA W
University of North Florida, FL M,W
University of Notre Dame, IN M,W
University of Oklahoma, OK W
University of Oregon, OR W
University of Pittsburgh, PA M,W
University of Rhode Island, RI M,W
University of Richmond, VA M,W
University of St. Francis, IL M,W
University of Saint Francis, IN M,W
University of San Diego, CA M,W
University of San Francisco, CA M,W
University of Science and Arts of Oklahoma, OK M,W
University of South Carolina, SC M,W
University of South Carolina Upstate, SC M,W
University of Southern California, CA W
University of Southern Indiana, IN M,W
University of South Florida, FL M,W

The University of Tampa, FL M,W
The University of Tennessee at Martin, TN W
The University of Texas at Austin, TX W
University of the Cumberlands, KY M,W
University of the Incarnate Word, TX M,W
University of the Pacific, CA W
University of Tulsa, OK M,W
University of Vermont, VT M,W
University of Virginia, VA M,W
University of Washington, WA M
University of West Florida, FL M,W
University of Wisconsin–Green Bay, WI M,W
University of Wisconsin–Madison, WI M,W
University of Wisconsin–Milwaukee, WI M,W
University of Wyoming, WY W
Urbana University, OH M,W
Utah State University, UT W
Valparaiso University, IN M,W
Vanderbilt University, TN M,W
Vanguard University of Southern California, CA M,W
Virginia Commonwealth University, VA M,W
Virginia Intermont College, VA M,W
Virginia Military Institute, VA M
Virginia Polytechnic Institute and State University, VA M,W
Wagner College, NY W
Wake Forest University, NC M,W
Walsh University, OH M,W
Washington State University, WA W
Wayne State College, NE W
Webber International University, FL M,W
Western Carolina University, NC W
Western Illinois University, IL M,W
Western Washington University, WA M,W
Westmont College, CA M,W
West Virginia University, WV M,W
West Virginia Wesleyan College, WV M,W
Wheeling Jesuit University, WV M,W
Whitman College, WA M,W
William Carey College, MS M,W
William Jewell College, MO M,W
Williams Baptist College, AR M,W
Wingate University, NC M
Winona State University, MN W
Winthrop University, SC M
Xavier University, OH M,W

Softball

Abilene Christian University, TX W
Adams State College, CO W
Adelphi University, NY W
Alabama State University, AL W
Albertson College of Idaho, ID W
Alcorn State University, MS W
Alderson-Broaddus College, WV W
American International College, MA W
Anderson University, SC W
Arizona State University, AZ W
Armstrong Atlantic State University, GA W
Ashford University, IA W
Auburn University, AL W
Augustana College, SD W
Austin Peay State University, TN W
Azusa Pacific University, CA W
Baker University, KS W
Barton College, NC W
Baylor University, TX W
Bellarmine University, KY W
Belmont Abbey College, NC W
Belmont University, TN W
Bemidji State University, MN W
Bentley College, MA W
Bethany College, KS W
Bethel College, IN W
Bethune-Cookman College, FL W
Birmingham-Southern College, AL W
Bloomfield College, NJ W
Bloomsburg University of Pennsylvania, PA W
Bluefield State College, WV W
Boston College, MA W
Boston University, MA W
Bowie State University, MD W
Bowling Green State University, OH W
Bradley University, IL W
Brenau University, GA W
Brevard College, NC W
Brigham Young University, UT W
Brigham Young University–Hawaii, HI W
Butler University, IN W
California Polytechnic State University, San Luis Obispo, CA W
California State University, Chico, CA W
California State University, Fresno, CA W
California State University, Fullerton, CA W
California State University, Northridge, CA W
California State University, Sacramento, CA W
California State University, San Bernardino, CA W
California University of Pennsylvania, PA W
Campbellsville University, KY W
Campbell University, NC W
Canisius College, NY W
Carson-Newman College, TN W
Catawba College, NC W
Cedarville University, OH W
Centenary College of Louisiana, LA W
Central Methodist University, MO W
Central Michigan University, MI W
Central Washington University, WA W
Christian Brothers University, TN W
Clarion University of Pennsylvania, PA W
Cleveland State University, OH W
Coastal Carolina University, SC W
Colgate University, NY W
College of Charleston, SC W
College of Saint Mary, NE W
The College of Saint Rose, NY W
College of the Southwest, NM W
Colorado School of Mines, CO W
Colorado State University, CO W
Colorado State University-Pueblo, CO W
Columbia College, MO W
Columbus State University, GA W
Concordia University, CA W
Concordia University, NE W
Concordia University, St. Paul, MN W
Corban College, OR W
Creighton University, NE W
Culver-Stockton College, MO W
Cumberland University, TN W
Dakota Wesleyan University, SD W
Dana College, NE W
Davis & Elkins College, WV W
Dickinson State University, ND W
Doane College, NE W
Dominican College, NY W
Dordt College, IA W
Dowling College, NY W
Drake University, IA W
East Central University, OK W
Eastern Illinois University, IL W
Eastern Kentucky University, KY W
Eastern Michigan University, MI W
East Tennessee State University, TN W
Elon University, NC W
Emporia State University, KS W
Erskine College, SC W
Evangel University, MO W
Fairfield University, CT W
Faulkner University, AL W
Felician College, NJ W
Ferris State University, MI W
Florida Atlantic University, FL W
Florida Gulf Coast University, FL W
Florida Institute of Technology, FL W
Florida State University, FL W
Fort Lewis College, CO W
Francis Marion University, SC W
Franklin Pierce University, NH W
Freed-Hardeman University, TN W
Friends University, KS W
Furman University, SC W
Gannon University, PA W
Gardner-Webb University, NC W
Geneva College, PA W
George Mason University, VA W
Georgetown College, KY W
Georgia College & State University, GA W
Georgia Institute of Technology, GA W
Georgia Southern University, GA W
Glenville State College, WV W
Grace College, IN W
Graceland University, IA W
Grand Valley State University, MI W
Grand View College, IA W
Hastings College, NE W
Hawai'i Pacific University, HI W
Hillsdale College, MI W
Hofstra University, NY W
Houston Baptist University, TX W
Huntington University, IN W
Illinois State University, IL W
Indiana State University, IN W
Indiana University Bloomington, IN W
Indiana University of Pennsylvania, PA W
Indiana University–Purdue University Indianapolis, IN W
Iona College, NY W
Iowa Wesleyan College, IA W
Jackson State University, MS W
Jacksonville State University, AL W
James Madison University, VA W
Jamestown College, ND W

Johnson C. Smith University, NC	W
Judson College, AL	W
Judson College, IL	W
Kent State University, OH	W
Kentucky Wesleyan College, KY	W
King College, TN	M,W
Kutztown University of Pennsylvania, PA	W
Lambuth University, TN	W
Lee University, TN	W
Lehigh University, PA	W
Le Moyne College, NY	W
LeMoyne-Owen College, TN	W
Limestone College, SC	W
Lindenwood University, MO	W
Lindsey Wilson College, KY	W
Lipscomb University, TN	W
Lock Haven University of Pennsylvania, PA	W
Longwood University, VA	W
Louisiana State University and Agricultural and Mechanical College, LA	W
Louisiana Tech University, LA	W
Loyola University Chicago, IL	W
Malone College, OH	W
Manhattan College, NY	W
Mansfield University of Pennsylvania, PA	W
Marist College, NY	W
Mayville State University, ND	W
McKendree College, IL	W
Mercer University, GA	W
Mesa State College, CO	W
Miami University, OH	W
Middle Tennessee State University, TN	W
Midwestern State University, TX	W
Millersville University of Pennsylvania, PA	W
Milligan College, TN	W
Minnesota State University Mankato, MN	W
Minot State University, ND	W
Mississippi State University, MS	W
Missouri Baptist University, MO	W
Missouri State University, MO	W
Missouri Valley College, MO	W
Molloy College, NY	W
Monmouth University, NJ	W
Montreat College, NC	W
Morehead State University, KY	W
Morningside College, IA	W
Mountain State University, WV	W
Mount Marty College, SD	W
Mount Olive College, NC	W
Mount St. Mary's University, MD	W
Mount Vernon Nazarene University, OH	W
Newman University, KS	W
New Mexico State University, NM	W
New York Institute of Technology, NY	W
Niagara University, NY	W
Nicholls State University, LA	W
North Carolina State University, NC	W
North Dakota State University, ND	W
Northeastern State University, OK	W
Northern Illinois University, IL	W
Northern State University, SD	W
North Greenville University, SC	W
Northwest Christian College, OR	W
Northwestern College, IA	W
Northwestern Oklahoma State University, OK	W
Northwestern State University of Louisiana, LA	W
Northwest Nazarene University, ID	W
Northwood University, MI	W
Northwood University, Florida Campus, FL	W
Northwood University, Texas Campus, TX	W
Nova Southeastern University, FL	W
Nyack College, NY	W
The Ohio State University, OH	W
Ohio University, OH	W
Ohio Valley University, WV	W
Oklahoma Baptist University, OK	W
Oklahoma Panhandle State University, OK	W
Oklahoma State University, OK	W
Oregon State University, OR	W
Ouachita Baptist University, AR	W
Pfeiffer University, NC	W
Philadelphia University, PA	W
Pikeville College, KY	W
Pittsburg State University, KS	W
Point Loma Nazarene University, CA	W
Portland State University, OR	W
Providence College, RI	W
Purdue University, IN	W
Quinnipiac University, CT	W
Radford University, VA	W
Regis University, CO	W
Reinhardt College, GA	W
Robert Morris University, PA	W
Rockhurst University, MO	W
Rollins College, FL	W
Sacred Heart University, CT	W
St. Ambrose University, IA	W
St. Andrews Presbyterian College, NC	W
St. Cloud State University, MN	W
St. Edward's University, TX	W
St. Francis College, NY	W
Saint Francis University, PA	W
St. Gregory's University, OK	W
Saint Joseph's College, IN	W
Saint Leo University, FL	W
Saint Louis University, MO	W
Saint Mary-of-the-Woods College, IN	W
Saint Mary's College of California, CA	W
Saint Vincent College, PA	W
Saint Xavier University, IL	W
Samford University, AL	W
Sam Houston State University, TX	M,W
San Diego State University, CA	W
San Francisco State University, CA	W
Santa Clara University, CA	W
Seattle University, WA	W
Seton Hill University, PA	W
Shaw University, NC	W
Shepherd University, WV	W
Shippensburg University of Pennsylvania, PA	W
Slippery Rock University of Pennsylvania, PA	W
Sonoma State University, CA	W
South Dakota State University, SD	W
Southeastern Louisiana University, LA	W
Southeastern Oklahoma State University, OK	W
Southeast Missouri State University, MO	W
Southern Arkansas University–Magnolia, AR	W
Southern Illinois University Carbondale, IL	W
Southern Illinois University Edwardsville, IL	W
Southern Nazarene University, OK	W
Southern New Hampshire University, NH	W
Southern Oregon University, OR	W
Southern Utah University, UT	W
Southern Wesleyan University, SC	W
Southwest Baptist University, MO	W
Southwest Minnesota State University, MN	W
Spring Arbor University, MI	W
Spring Hill College, AL	W
Stanford University, CA	W
State University of New York at Binghamton, NY	W
Stephen F. Austin State University, TX	W
Stetson University, FL	W
Stonehill College, MA	W
Stony Brook University, State University of New York, NY	W
Syracuse University, NY	W
Tarleton State University, TX	W
Taylor University, IN	W
Temple University, PA	M,W
Tennessee Technological University, TN	W
Tennessee Wesleyan College, TN	W
Texas A&M University–Kingsville, TX	W
Texas State University-San Marcos, TX	W
Texas Tech University, TX	W
Texas Woman's University, TX	W
Tiffin University, OH	W
Towson University, MD	W
Trevecca Nazarene University, TN	W
Trinity International University, IL	W
Troy University, AL	W
Union College, KY	W
Union University, TN	W
University at Albany, State University of New York, NY	W
University at Buffalo, the State University of New York, NY	W
The University of Akron, OH	W
The University of Alabama, AL	W
The University of Alabama at Birmingham, AL	W
The University of Alabama in Huntsville, AL	W
The University of Arizona, AZ	W
University of Arkansas, AR	W
University of Arkansas at Monticello, AR	W
University of Bridgeport, CT	W
University of California, Berkeley, CA	W
University of California, Los Angeles, CA	W

University of California, Riverside, CA W
University of California, Santa Barbara, CA W
University of Central Missouri, MO W
University of Central Oklahoma, OK W
University of Charleston, WV W
University of Connecticut, CT W
University of Dayton, OH W
University of Delaware, DE W
University of Detroit Mercy, MI W
University of Evansville, IN W
The University of Findlay, OH W
University of Florida, FL W
University of Hartford, CT W
University of Hawaii at Hilo, HI W
University of Hawaii at Manoa, HI W
University of Illinois at Chicago, IL W
University of Illinois at Springfield, IL W
University of Illinois at Urbana–Champaign, IL W
The University of Iowa, IA W
University of Kansas, KS W
University of Louisiana at Lafayette, LA W
University of Louisville, KY W
University of Maine, ME W
University of Maryland, Baltimore County, MD W
University of Maryland, College Park, MD W
University of Massachusetts Amherst, MA W
University of Michigan, MI W
University of Minnesota, Crookston, MN W
University of Minnesota, Twin Cities Campus, MN W
University of Missouri–Columbia, MO W
University of Missouri–Kansas City, MO W
University of Missouri–St. Louis, MO W
University of Nebraska at Kearney, NE W
University of Nebraska at Omaha, NE W
University of New Haven, CT W
University of North Alabama, AL W
The University of North Carolina at Chapel Hill, NC W
The University of North Carolina at Charlotte, NC W
The University of North Carolina at Greensboro, NC W
The University of North Carolina at Pembroke, NC W
The University of North Carolina Wilmington, NC W
University of North Dakota, ND W
University of Northern Colorado, CO W
University of Northern Iowa, IA W
University of North Florida, FL W
University of Notre Dame, IN W
University of Oklahoma, OK W
University of Oregon, OR W
University of Pittsburgh, PA W
University of Rhode Island, RI W
University of St. Francis, IL W
University of Saint Francis, IN W
University of Science and Arts of Oklahoma, OK W
University of South Carolina, SC W
University of South Carolina Upstate, SC W
The University of South Dakota, SD W
University of Southern Indiana, IN W
University of South Florida, FL W
The University of Tampa, FL W
The University of Tennessee at Martin, TN W
The University of Texas at Austin, TX W
The University of Texas at San Antonio, TX W
University of the Cumberlands, KY W
University of the Incarnate Word, TX W
University of the Pacific, CA W
University of the Sciences in Philadelphia, PA W
University of Tulsa, OK W
University of Vermont, VT W
University of Virginia, VA W
University of Washington, WA W
The University of West Alabama, AL W
University of West Florida, FL W
University of West Georgia, GA W
University of Wisconsin–Green Bay, WI W
University of Wisconsin–Madison, WI W
Urbana University, OH W
Utah State University, UT W
Valdosta State University, GA W
Valley City State University, ND W
Valparaiso University, IN W
Vanguard University of Southern California, CA W
Virginia Intermont College, VA W
Virginia State University, VA W
Virginia Union University, VA W
Wagner College, NY W
Walsh University, OH W
Wayne State College, NE W
Wayne State University, MI W
Webber International University, FL W
Western Illinois University, IL W
Western Washington University, WA W
West Liberty State College, WV W
West Virginia Wesleyan College, WV W
Wheeling Jesuit University, WV W
Wichita State University, KS W
William Carey College, MS W
William Jewell College, MO W
Williams Baptist College, AR W
Wingate University, NC W
Winona State University, MN W
Winston-Salem State University, NC W
Winthrop University, SC W
Youngstown State University, OH W

Swimming and Diving

Adelphi University, NY M,W
Arizona State University, AZ M,W
Asbury College, KY M,W
Auburn University, AL M,W
Bentley College, MA M,W
Bloomsburg University of Pennsylvania, PA M,W
Boston College, MA W
Boston University, MA M,W
Bowling Green State University, OH M,W
Brigham Young University, UT M,W
California State University, Fresno, CA W
California State University, Northridge, CA M,W
California State University, San Bernardino, CA M,W
California University of Pennsylvania, PA W
Canisius College, NY M,W
Catawba College, NC W
Centenary College of Louisiana, LA M,W
Clarion University of Pennsylvania, PA M,W
Clemson University, SC M,W
Cleveland State University, OH M,W
College of Charleston, SC M,W
The College of Saint Rose, NY M,W
The College of William and Mary, VA M
Colorado School of Mines, CO M,W
Colorado State University, CO W
Davidson College, NC M,W
Drury University, MO M,W
Duquesne University, PA M,W
Eastern Illinois University, IL M,W
Eastern Michigan University, MI M,W
Fairfield University, CT M,W
Florida Atlantic University, FL M,W
Florida State University, FL M,W
Gannon University, PA M,W
Gardner-Webb University, NC W
George Mason University, VA M,W
The George Washington University, DC M,W
Georgia Institute of Technology, GA M,W
Georgia Southern University, GA W
Grand Valley State University, MI M,W
Hillsdale College, MI W
Illinois Institute of Technology, IL M,W
Illinois State University, IL W
Indiana University Bloomington, IN M,W
Indiana University of Pennsylvania, PA W
Indiana University–Purdue University Indianapolis, IN M,W
Iona College, NY M,W
Kutztown University of Pennsylvania, PA M,W
Lambuth University, TN M,W
Lehigh University, PA M,W
Limestone College, SC W
Lindenwood University, MO M,W
Lock Haven University of Pennsylvania, PA W
Louisiana State University and Agricultural and Mechanical College, LA M,W
Manhattan College, NY W
Marist College, NY M,W
Metropolitan State College of Denver, CO M,W
Miami University, OH M,W
Michigan State University, MI M,W
Millersville University of Pennsylvania, PA W
Minnesota State University Mankato, MN M,W
Missouri State University, MO M,W
Morningside College, IA M,W

New Mexico State University, NM W
Niagara University, NY M,W
North Carolina Agricultural and Technical State University, NC W
North Carolina State University, NC M,W
Northeastern University, MA W
Northern Arizona University, AZ W
Northern Illinois University, IL M,W
The Ohio State University, OH M,W
Ohio University, OH M,W
Oregon State University, OR W
Ouachita Baptist University, AR M,W
Penn State University Park, PA M,W
Pfeiffer University, NC W
Purdue University, IN M,W
Radford University, VA W
Rice University, TX W
Sacred Heart University, CT W
St. Cloud State University, MN M,W
St. Francis College, NY M,W
Saint Francis University, PA M,W
Saint Leo University, FL M,W
Saint Louis University, MO M,W
San Diego State University, CA W
San Francisco State University, CA M,W
San Jose State University, CA W
Seattle University, WA M,W
Shippensburg University of Pennsylvania, PA M,W
Slippery Rock University of Pennsylvania, PA M,W
South Dakota State University, SD M,W
Southern Illinois University Carbondale, IL M,W
Southern Methodist University, TX M,W
Spring Hill College, AL M,W
Stanford University, CA M,W
State University of New York at Binghamton, NY M,W
Stony Brook University, State University of New York, NY M,W
Syracuse University, NY M,W
Texas Christian University, TX M,W
Towson University, MD M,W
Tulane University, LA W
University at Buffalo, the State University of New York, NY M,W
The University of Alabama, AL M,W
The University of Alabama at Birmingham, AL W
University of Alaska Fairbanks, AK W
The University of Arizona, AZ M,W
University of Arkansas, AR W
University of Bridgeport, CT W
University of California, Berkeley, CA M,W
University of California, Irvine, CA M,W
University of California, Los Angeles, CA W
University of California, Santa Barbara, CA M,W
University of Charleston, WV M,W
University of Connecticut, CT M,W
University of Delaware, DE W
University of Denver, CO M,W
University of Evansville, IN M,W
The University of Findlay, OH M,W
University of Florida, FL M,W
University of Georgia, GA M,W
University of Hawaii at Manoa, HI M,W
University of Illinois at Chicago, IL M,W
University of Illinois at Urbana–Champaign, IL W
The University of Iowa, IA M,W
University of Kansas, KS W
University of Louisville, KY M,W
University of Maine, ME W
University of Maryland, Baltimore County, MD M,W
University of Maryland, College Park, MD M,W
University of Massachusetts Amherst, MA M,W
University of Massachusetts Lowell, MA M
University of Miami, FL W
University of Michigan, MI M,W
University of Minnesota, Twin Cities Campus, MN M,W
University of Missouri–Columbia, MO M,W
University of Nebraska at Kearney, NE W
University of New Hampshire, NH W
The University of North Carolina at Chapel Hill, NC M,W
The University of North Carolina Wilmington, NC M,W
University of North Dakota, ND W
University of Northern Colorado, CO W
University of Northern Iowa, IA W
University of North Florida, FL W
University of Notre Dame, IN M,W
University of Pittsburgh, PA M,W
University of Rhode Island, RI M,W
University of Richmond, VA W
University of San Diego, CA W
University of South Carolina, SC M,W
The University of South Dakota, SD M
University of Southern California, CA M,W
The University of Texas at Austin, TX M,W
University of the Cumberlands, KY M,W
University of the Incarnate Word, TX W
University of the Pacific, CA M,W
University of Vermont, VT W
University of Virginia, VA M,W
University of Washington, WA M,W
University of Wisconsin–Green Bay, WI M,W
University of Wisconsin–Madison, WI M,W
University of Wisconsin–Milwaukee, WI M,W
University of Wyoming, WY M,W
Valparaiso University, IN M,W
Virginia Military Institute, VA M
Virginia Polytechnic Institute and State University, VA M,W
Wagner College, NY W
Washington State University, WA W
Wayne State University, MI M,W
Western Illinois University, IL M,W
West Virginia University, WV M,W
West Virginia Wesleyan College, WV M,W
Wheeling Jesuit University, WV M,W
Wingate University, NC M,W
Xavier University, OH M,W

Tennis

Abilene Christian University, TX M,W
Adelphi University, NY M,W
Alabama State University, AL M,W
Albertson College of Idaho, ID M,W
Alcorn State University, MS M,W
Alliant International University, CA M,W
Anderson University, SC M,W
Appalachian State University, NC M,W
Arizona State University, AZ M,W
Arkansas State University, AR W
Arkansas Tech University, AR W
Armstrong Atlantic State University, GA M,W
Asbury College, KY M,W
Auburn University, AL M,W
Auburn University Montgomery, AL M,W
Augusta State University, GA M,W
Austin Peay State University, TN M,W
Azusa Pacific University, CA M
Baker University, KS M,W
Barton College, NC M,W
Baylor University, TX M,W
Bellarmine University, KY M,W
Belmont Abbey College, NC M,W
Belmont University, TN M,W
Bemidji State University, MN W
Berry College, GA M,W
Bethany College, KS M,W
Bethel College, IN M,W
Bethel College, KS M,W
Bethune-Cookman College, FL M,W
Birmingham-Southern College, AL M,W
Bloomsburg University of Pennsylvania, PA M,W
Bluefield State College, WV M,W
Blue Mountain College, MS W
Boise State University, ID M,W
Boston College, MA W
Boston University, MA W
Bowie State University, MD W
Bowling Green State University, OH M,W
Bradley University, IL M,W
Brenau University, GA W
Brevard College, NC M,W
Brigham Young University, UT M,W
Brigham Young University–Hawaii, HI M,W
Bryan College, TN M,W
Butler University, IN M,W
California State University, Fresno, CA M,W
California State University, Fullerton, CA W
California State University, Los Angeles, CA W
California State University, Northridge, CA W
California State University, Sacramento, CA M,W
California University of Pennsylvania, PA W
Campbellsville University, KY M,W
Campbell University, NC M,W
Carson-Newman College, TN M,W
Catawba College, NC M,W
Cedarville University, OH M,W
Centenary College of Louisiana, LA M,W
Central State University, OH M,W
Clarion University of Pennsylvania, PA W
Clemson University, SC M,W
Cleveland State University, OH W
Coastal Carolina University, SC M,W

College of Charleston, SC	M,W
The College of William and Mary, VA	M,W
Colorado School of Mines, CO	M,W
Colorado State University, CO	W
Colorado State University-Pueblo, CO	M,W
Columbus State University, GA	M,W
Concordia University, NE	M,W
Concord University, WV	M,W
Converse College, SC	W
Coppin State University, MD	M,W
Creighton University, NE	M,W
Cumberland University, TN	M,W
Dallas Baptist University, TX	W
Davidson College, NC	M,W
Dordt College, IA	M,W
Dowling College, NY	M,W
Drake University, IA	M,W
Drury University, MO	M,W
Duke University, NC	M,W
Duquesne University, PA	M,W
East Central University, OK	M,W
Eastern Illinois University, IL	M,W
Eastern Kentucky University, KY	M,W
Eastern Michigan University, MI	W
East Tennessee State University, TN	M,W
Elon University, NC	M,W
Embry-Riddle Aeronautical University, FL	M
Emporia State University, KS	M,W
Erskine College, SC	M,W
Evangel University, MO	M,W
Fairfield University, CT	M,W
Ferris State University, MI	M,W
Flagler College, FL	M,W
Florida Atlantic University, FL	M,W
Florida Gulf Coast University, FL	M,W
Florida Institute of Technology, FL	M,W
Florida State University, FL	M,W
Francis Marion University, SC	M,W
Franklin Pierce University, NH	M,W
Freed-Hardeman University, TN	M,W
Friends University, KS	M,W
Furman University, SC	M,W
Gardner-Webb University, NC	M,W
Geneva College, PA	W
George Mason University, VA	M,W
Georgetown College, KY	M,W
Georgetown University, DC	W
The George Washington University, DC	M,W
Georgia College & State University, GA	M,W
Georgia Institute of Technology, GA	M,W
Georgia Southern University, GA	M,W
Gonzaga University, WA	M,W
Grace College, IN	M,W
Graceland University, IA	M,W
Grand Valley State University, MI	M,W
Harding University, AR	M,W
Hastings College, NE	M,W
Hawai'i Pacific University, HI	M,W
Hofstra University, NY	M,W
Huntington University, IN	M,W
Idaho State University, ID	M,W
Illinois State University, IL	M,W
Indiana State University, IN	M,W
Indiana University Bloomington, IN	M,W
Indiana University of Pennsylvania, PA	W
Indiana University–Purdue University Indianapolis, IN	M,W
Jackson State University, MS	M,W
Jacksonville State University, AL	M,W
Johnson C. Smith University, NC	M,W
Judson College, AL	W
Judson College, IL	M,W
King College, TN	M,W
Kutztown University of Pennsylvania, PA	M,W
Lake Superior State University, MI	M,W
Lamar University, TX	M,W
Lambuth University, TN	M,W
Lee University, TN	M,W
Lehigh University, PA	M,W
Le Moyne College, NY	M,W
LeMoyne-Owen College, TN	M,W
Lewis-Clark State College, ID	M,W
Limestone College, SC	M,W
Lindenwood University, MO	M,W
Lindsey Wilson College, KY	M,W
Lipscomb University, TN	M,W
Longwood University, VA	M,W
Louisiana State University and Agricultural and Mechanical College, LA	M,W
Louisiana Tech University, LA	W
Lyon College, AR	M,W
Malone College, OH	M,W
Manhattan College, NY	M,W
Marist College, NY	M,W
Marquette University, WI	M,W
McKendree College, IL	M,W
Mercer University, GA	M,W
Mesa State College, CO	M,W
Metropolitan State College of Denver, CO	M,W
Miami University, OH	W
Michigan State University, MI	M,W
Michigan Technological University, MI	W
Middle Tennessee State University, TN	M,W
Midwestern State University, TX	M,W
Millersville University of Pennsylvania, PA	M,W
Milligan College, TN	M,W
Minnesota State University Mankato, MN	M,W
Mississippi State University, MS	M,W
Missouri State University, MO	M,W
Missouri Valley College, MO	M,W
Molloy College, NY	W
Monmouth University, NJ	M,W
Montana State University, MT	M,W
Montana State University–Billings, MT	M,W
Montreat College, NC	M,W
Morehead State University, KY	M,W
Morningside College, IA	M,W
Mount Olive College, NC	M,W
Mount St. Mary's University, MD	M,W
Murray State University, KY	M,W
Newman University, KS	M,W
New Mexico State University, NM	M,W
Niagara University, NY	M,W
Nicholls State University, LA	W
North Carolina Agricultural and Technical State University, NC	M,W
North Carolina State University, NC	M,W
Northeastern State University, OK	W
Northeastern University, MA	M
Northern Arizona University, AZ	M,W
Northern Illinois University, IL	M,W
Northern State University, SD	W
North Georgia College & State University, GA	M,W
North Greenville University, SC	M,W
Northwestern State University of Louisiana, LA	W
Northwood University, MI	M,W
Northwood University, Florida Campus, FL	M,W
Nova Southeastern University, FL	W
The Ohio State University, OH	M,W
Oklahoma Baptist University, OK	M,W
Oklahoma State University, OK	M,W
Oral Roberts University, OK	M,W
Ouachita Baptist University, AR	M,W
Penn State University Park, PA	M,W
Pfeiffer University, NC	M,W
Philadelphia University, PA	M,W
Pikeville College, KY	M,W
Point Loma Nazarene University, CA	M,W
Portland State University, OR	M,W
Providence College, RI	W
Purdue University, IN	M,W
Quinnipiac University, CT	M,W
Radford University, VA	M,W
Reinhardt College, GA	M,W
Rice University, TX	M,W
Robert Morris University, PA	M,W
Roberts Wesleyan College, NY	M,W
Rockhurst University, MO	M,W
Rollins College, FL	M,W
Sacred Heart University, CT	M,W
St. Ambrose University, IA	M,W
St. Andrews Presbyterian College, NC	M,W
St. Cloud State University, MN	M,W
St. Edward's University, TX	M,W
St. Francis College, NY	M,W
Saint Francis University, PA	M,W
Saint Joseph's College, IN	M,W
Saint Leo University, FL	M,W
Saint Louis University, MO	M,W
Saint Mary's College of California, CA	M,W
Saint Vincent College, PA	M,W
Samford University, AL	M,W
Sam Houston State University, TX	M,W
San Diego State University, CA	M,W
San Jose State University, CA	W
Santa Clara University, CA	M,W
Seton Hill University, PA	M,W
Shaw University, NC	M,W
Shepherd University, WV	M,W
Shippensburg University of Pennsylvania, PA	W
Slippery Rock University of Pennsylvania, PA	W
Sonoma State University, CA	M,W
South Dakota State University, SD	M,W
Southeastern Louisiana University, LA	M,W
Southeastern Oklahoma State University, OK	M,W
Southeast Missouri State University, MO	W

Southern Arkansas University–Magnolia, AR W
Southern Illinois University Carbondale, IL M,W
Southern Illinois University Edwardsville, IL M,W
Southern Methodist University, TX M,W
Southern Nazarene University, OK M,W
Southern New Hampshire University, NH M,W
Southern Oregon University, OR W
Southern Utah University, UT W
Southwest Baptist University, MO M,W
Southwest Minnesota State University, MN W
Spring Arbor University, MI M,W
Spring Hill College, AL M,W
Stanford University, CA M,W
State University of New York at Binghamton, NY M,W
Stephen F. Austin State University, TX W
Stetson University, FL M,W
Stonehill College, MA M,W
Stony Brook University, State University of New York, NY M,W
Syracuse University, NY W
Tarleton State University, TX W
Taylor University, IN M,W
Temple University, PA M
Tennessee State University, TN M,W
Tennessee Technological University, TN M,W
Tennessee Wesleyan College, TN M,W
Texas A&M University–Kingsville, TX M,W
Texas Christian University, TX M,W
Texas State University-San Marcos, TX W
Texas Tech University, TX M,W
Tiffin University, OH M,W
Towson University, MD M,W
Troy University, AL M,W
Tulane University, LA M,W
Tuskegee University, AL M,W
Union College, KY M,W
University at Albany, State University of New York, NY W
University at Buffalo, the State University of New York, NY M,W
The University of Akron, OH M,W
The University of Alabama, AL M,W
The University of Alabama at Birmingham, AL M,W
The University of Alabama in Huntsville, AL M,W
The University of Arizona, AZ M,W
University of Arkansas, AR M,W
University of California, Berkeley, CA M,W
University of California, Irvine, CA M,W
University of California, Los Angeles, CA M,W
University of California, Riverside, CA M,W
University of California, Santa Barbara, CA M,W
University of Central Florida, FL M,W
University of Central Oklahoma, OK M,W
University of Charleston, WV M,W
University of Colorado at Boulder, CO M,W
University of Connecticut, CT M,W
University of Dayton, OH M,W
University of Denver, CO M,W
University of Detroit Mercy, MI W
University of Evansville, IN W
The University of Findlay, OH M,W
University of Florida, FL M,W
University of Georgia, GA M,W
University of Hartford, CT M,W
University of Hawaii at Hilo, HI M,W
University of Hawaii at Manoa, HI M,W
University of Idaho, ID M,W
University of Illinois at Chicago, IL M,W
University of Illinois at Springfield, IL M,W
University of Illinois at Urbana–Champaign, IL M,W
The University of Iowa, IA M,W
University of Kansas, KS W
University of Louisiana at Lafayette, LA M,W
University of Louisville, KY M,W
University of Maryland, Baltimore County, MD M,W
University of Maryland, College Park, MD M,W
University of Massachusetts Amherst, MA M,W
University of Massachusetts Lowell, MA M,W
University of Miami, FL M,W
University of Michigan, MI M,W
University of Minnesota, Twin Cities Campus, MN M,W
University of Missouri–Columbia, MO W
University of Missouri–Kansas City, MO M,W
University of Missouri–St. Louis, MO M,W
The University of Montana, MT M,W
University of Nebraska at Kearney, NE M,W
University of New Hampshire, NH W
University of New Haven, CT W
University of New Orleans, LA M,W
University of North Alabama, AL M,W
The University of North Carolina at Asheville, NC M,W
The University of North Carolina at Chapel Hill, NC M,W
The University of North Carolina at Charlotte, NC M,W
The University of North Carolina at Greensboro, NC M,W
The University of North Carolina at Pembroke, NC W
The University of North Carolina Wilmington, NC M,W
University of Northern Colorado, CO M,W
University of Northern Iowa, IA W
University of North Florida, FL M,W
University of Notre Dame, IN M,W
University of Oklahoma, OK M,W
University of Oregon, OR M,W
University of Pittsburgh, PA W
University of Rhode Island, RI W
University of Richmond, VA M,W
University of St. Francis, IL M,W
University of Saint Francis, IN M,W
University of San Diego, CA M,W
University of San Francisco, CA M,W
University of South Carolina, SC M,W
University of South Carolina Upstate, SC M,W
The University of South Dakota, SD M,W
University of Southern California, CA M,W
University of Southern Indiana, IN M,W
University of Southern Mississippi, MS M,W
University of South Florida, FL M,W
The University of Tampa, FL W
The University of Tennessee at Martin, TN M,W
The University of Texas at Austin, TX M,W
The University of Texas at El Paso, TX W
The University of Texas at San Antonio, TX M,W
The University of Texas–Pan American, TX M,W
University of the Cumberlands, KY M,W
University of the Incarnate Word, TX M,W
University of the Pacific, CA M,W
University of Tulsa, OK M,W
University of Virginia, VA M,W
University of Washington, WA M,W
University of West Florida, FL M,W
University of Wisconsin–Green Bay, WI M,W
University of Wisconsin–Madison, WI M,W
University of Wisconsin–Milwaukee, WI M,W
University of Wyoming, WY W
Utah State University, UT M,W
Valdosta State University, GA M,W
Valparaiso University, IN M,W
Vanderbilt University, TN M,W
Vanguard University of Southern California, CA M,W
Virginia Commonwealth University, VA M,W
Virginia Intermont College, VA M,W
Virginia Military Institute, VA M
Virginia Polytechnic Institute and State University, VA M,W
Virginia State University, VA M,W
Virginia Union University, VA M
Wagner College, NY M,W
Wake Forest University, NC M,W
Walsh University, OH M,W
Washington State University, WA W
Wayne State University, MI M,W
Webber International University, FL M,W
Western Carolina University, NC W
Western Illinois University, IL M,W
West Liberty State College, WV M,W
Westmont College, CA M,W
West Virginia University, WV W
West Virginia Wesleyan College, WV M,W
Wichita State University, KS M,W
William Jewell College, MO M,W
Wingate University, NC M,W
Winona State University, MN M,W
Winston-Salem State University, NC M,W
Winthrop University, SC M,W
Xavier University, OH M,W
Youngstown State University, OH M,W

Track and Field

Abilene Christian University, TX M,W
Adams State College, CO M,W

Adelphi University, NY	M,W
Alabama State University, AL	M,W
Alcorn State University, MS	M,W
Alliant International University, CA	M,W
Anderson University, SC	M,W
Appalachian State University, NC	M,W
Arizona State University, AZ	M,W
Arkansas State University, AR	M,W
Ashford University, IA	M,W
Auburn University, AL	M,W
Augustana College, SD	M,W
Austin Peay State University, TN	W
Azusa Pacific University, CA	M,W
Baker University, KS	M,W
Baylor University, TX	M,W
Bellarmine University, KY	M,W
Belmont University, TN	M,W
Bemidji State University, MN	M,W
Bentley College, MA	M,W
Berry College, GA	M,W
Bethany College, KS	M,W
Bethel College, IN	M,W
Bethel College, KS	M,W
Bethune-Cookman College, FL	M,W
Black Hills State University, SD	M,W
Bloomsburg University of Pennsylvania, PA	M,W
Boise State University, ID	M,W
Boston College, MA	M,W
Boston University, MA	M,W
Bowie State University, MD	M,W
Bowling Green State University, OH	M,W
Bradley University, IL	W
Brevard College, NC	M,W
Brigham Young University, UT	M,W
California Polytechnic State University, San Luis Obispo, CA	M,W
California State University, Chico, CA	M,W
California State University, Fresno, CA	M,W
California State University, Fullerton, CA	M,W
California State University, Los Angeles, CA	M,W
California State University, Northridge, CA	M,W
California State University, Sacramento, CA	M,W
California University of Pennsylvania, PA	M,W
Campbellsville University, KY	M,W
Campbell University, NC	M,W
Carson-Newman College, TN	M,W
Cedarville University, OH	M,W
Central Methodist University, MO	M,W
Central Michigan University, MI	M,W
Central State University, OH	M,W
Central Washington University, WA	M,W
Clarion University of Pennsylvania, PA	M,W
Clemson University, SC	M,W
Cleveland State University, OH	W
Coastal Carolina University, SC	M,W
College of the Southwest, NM	M,W
The College of William and Mary, VA	M,W
Colorado School of Mines, CO	M,W
Colorado State University, CO	M,W
Concordia University, NE	M,W
Concordia University, St. Paul, MN	M,W
Concord University, WV	M,W
Coppin State University, MD	M,W
Dakota State University, SD	M,W
Dakota Wesleyan University, SD	M,W
Dallas Baptist University, TX	W
Dana College, NE	M,W
Davidson College, NC	M,W
Dickinson State University, ND	M,W
Doane College, NE	M,W
Dordt College, IA	M,W
Drake University, IA	M,W
Duquesne University, PA	W
Eastern Illinois University, IL	M,W
Eastern Kentucky University, KY	M,W
Eastern Michigan University, MI	M,W
East Tennessee State University, TN	M,W
Elon University, NC	W
Emporia State University, KS	M,W
Evangel University, MO	M,W
Felician College, NJ	M,W
Ferris State University, MI	M,W
Florida Atlantic University, FL	W
Florida State University, FL	M,W
Fresno Pacific University, CA	M,W
Friends University, KS	M,W
Furman University, SC	M,W
Gardner-Webb University, NC	M,W
Geneva College, PA	M,W
George Mason University, VA	M,W
Georgetown College, KY	M,W
Georgetown University, DC	M,W
Georgia Institute of Technology, GA	M,W
Georgia Southern University, GA	W
Glenville State College, WV	M,W
Grace College, IN	M,W
Graceland University, IA	M,W
Grand Valley State University, MI	M,W
Grand View College, IA	M,W
Harding University, AR	M,W
Hastings College, NE	M,W
Hillsdale College, MI	M,W
Houghton College, NY	M,W
Huntington University, IN	M,W
Idaho State University, ID	M,W
Illinois State University, IL	M,W
Indiana State University, IN	M,W
Indiana University Bloomington, IN	M,W
Indiana University of Pennsylvania, PA	M,W
Iona College, NY	M,W
Iowa Wesleyan College, IA	M,W
Jackson State University, MS	M,W
James Madison University, VA	M,W
Jamestown College, ND	M,W
Johnson C. Smith University, NC	M,W
Kent State University, OH	M,W
King College, TN	M,W
Kutztown University of Pennsylvania, PA	M,W
Lake Superior State University, MI	M,W
Lamar University, TX	M,W
Lehigh University, PA	M,W
Lindenwood University, MO	M,W
Lindsey Wilson College, KY	M,W
Lock Haven University of Pennsylvania, PA	M,W
Louisiana State University and Agricultural and Mechanical College, LA	M,W
Louisiana Tech University, LA	M,W
Loyola University Chicago, IL	M,W
Malone College, OH	M,W
Manhattan College, NY	M,W
Mansfield University of Pennsylvania, PA	M,W
Marist College, NY	M,W
Marquette University, WI	M,W
McKendree College, IL	M,W
Miami University, OH	M,W
Michigan State University, MI	M,W
Middle Tennessee State University, TN	M,W
Millersville University of Pennsylvania, PA	M,W
Minnesota State University Mankato, MN	M,W
Minot State University, ND	M,W
Mississippi State University, MS	M,W
Missouri State University, MO	M,W
Missouri Valley College, MO	M,W
Monmouth University, NJ	M,W
Montana State University, MT	M,W
Morehead State University, KY	M,W
Morningside College, IA	M,W
Mount Marty College, SD	M,W
Mount St. Mary's University, MD	M,W
Murray State University, KY	M,W
New Mexico State University, NM	W
New York Institute of Technology, NY	M,W
Nicholls State University, LA	M,W
North Carolina Agricultural and Technical State University, NC	M,W
North Carolina State University, NC	M,W
North Dakota State University, ND	M,W
Northeastern University, MA	M,W
Northern Arizona University, AZ	M,W
Northern State University, SD	M,W
Northwestern College, IA	M,W
Northwestern State University of Louisiana, LA	M,W
Northwest Nazarene University, ID	M,W
Northwest University, WA	M,W
Northwood University, MI	M,W
Northwood University, Texas Campus, TX	M,W
The Ohio State University, OH	M,W
Ohio University, OH	M,W
Oklahoma Baptist University, OK	M,W
Oklahoma State University, OK	M,W
Oral Roberts University, OK	M,W
Penn State University Park, PA	M,W
Pittsburg State University, KS	M,W
Point Loma Nazarene University, CA	M,W
Portland State University, OR	M,W
Providence College, RI	M,W
Purdue University, IN	M,W
Quinnipiac University, CT	M,W
Radford University, VA	M,W
Rice University, TX	M,W
Robert Morris University, PA	M,W
Roberts Wesleyan College, NY	M,W
Sacred Heart University, CT	M,W
St. Ambrose University, IA	M,W
St. Cloud State University, MN	M,W
St. Francis College, NY	M,W
Saint Francis University, PA	M,W
St. Gregory's University, OK	M,W
Saint Joseph's College, IN	M,W

Samford University, AL M,W
Sam Houston State University, TX M,W
San Diego State University, CA W
San Francisco State University, CA M,W
Seattle Pacific University, WA M,W
Seattle University, WA M,W
Seton Hill University, PA M,W
Shaw University, NC M,W
Shippensburg University of Pennsylvania, PA M,W
Slippery Rock University of Pennsylvania, PA M,W
Sonoma State University, CA W
South Dakota State University, SD M,W
Southeastern Louisiana University, LA M,W
Southeast Missouri State University, MO M,W
Southern Illinois University Carbondale, IL M,W
Southern Illinois University Edwardsville, IL M,W
Southern Methodist University, TX M,W
Southern Nazarene University, OK M,W
Southern Oregon University, OR M,W
Southern Utah University, UT M,W
Spring Arbor University, MI M,W
Stanford University, CA M,W
State University of New York at Binghamton, NY M,W
Stephen F. Austin State University, TX M,W
Stonehill College, MA M,W
Stony Brook University, State University of New York, NY M,W
Syracuse University, NY M,W
Tarleton State University, TX M,W
Taylor University, IN M,W
Temple University, PA M,W
Tennessee State University, TN M,W
Tennessee Technological University, TN W
Texas A&M University–Commerce, TX M,W
Texas A&M University–Kingsville, TX M,W
Texas Christian University, TX M,W
Texas State University-San Marcos, TX M,W
Texas Tech University, TX M,W
Tiffin University, OH M,W
Towson University, MD M,W
Troy University, AL M
Tulane University, LA W
Tuskegee University, AL M,W
University at Albany, State University of New York, NY M,W
University at Buffalo, the State University of New York, NY M,W
The University of Akron, OH M,W
The University of Alabama, AL M,W
The University of Alabama at Birmingham, AL W
The University of Alabama in Huntsville, AL M,W
The University of Arizona, AZ M,W
University of Arkansas, AR M,W
University of California, Berkeley, CA M
University of California, Irvine, CA M,W
University of California, Los Angeles, CA M,W
University of California, Riverside, CA M,W
University of California, Santa Barbara, CA M,W
University of Central Florida, FL W
University of Central Missouri, MO M,W
University of Charleston, WV M,W
University of Colorado at Boulder, CO M,W
University of Connecticut, CT M,W
University of Dayton, OH W
University of Delaware, DE W
University of Detroit Mercy, MI M,W
The University of Findlay, OH M,W
University of Florida, FL M,W
University of Georgia, GA M,W
University of Hawaii at Manoa, HI W
University of Idaho, ID M,W
University of Illinois at Chicago, IL M,W
University of Illinois at Urbana–Champaign, IL M,W
The University of Iowa, IA M,W
University of Kansas, KS M,W
University of Louisiana at Lafayette, LA M,W
University of Louisville, KY M,W
University of Maine, ME M,W
University of Maryland, Baltimore County, MD M,W
University of Maryland, College Park, MD M,W
University of Massachusetts Amherst, MA M,W
University of Massachusetts Lowell, MA M,W
University of Miami, FL M,W
University of Michigan, MI M,W
University of Minnesota, Twin Cities Campus, MN M,W
University of Missouri–Columbia, MO M,W
University of Missouri–Kansas City, MO M,W
The University of Montana, MT M,W
University of Nebraska at Kearney, NE M,W
University of New Hampshire, NH M,W
University of New Haven, CT M,W
University of New Orleans, LA M,W
The University of North Carolina at Asheville, NC M,W
The University of North Carolina at Chapel Hill, NC M,W
The University of North Carolina at Charlotte, NC M,W
The University of North Carolina at Pembroke, NC M
The University of North Carolina Wilmington, NC M,W
University of North Dakota, ND M,W
University of Northern Colorado, CO M,W
University of Northern Iowa, IA M,W
University of North Florida, FL M,W
University of Notre Dame, IN M,W
University of Oklahoma, OK M,W
University of Oregon, OR M,W
University of Pittsburgh, PA M,W
University of Rhode Island, RI M,W
University of Richmond, VA W
University of St. Francis, IL W
University of Saint Francis, IN M,W
University of San Francisco, CA W
University of South Carolina, SC M,W
The University of South Dakota, SD M,W
University of Southern California, CA M,W
University of Southern Mississippi, MS M,W
University of South Florida, FL M,W
The University of Texas at Austin, TX M,W
The University of Texas at El Paso, TX M,W
The University of Texas at San Antonio, TX M,W
The University of Texas–Pan American, TX M,W
University of the Cumberlands, KY M,W
University of Tulsa, OK M,W
University of Vermont, VT M,W
University of Virginia, VA M,W
University of Washington, WA M,W
University of Wisconsin–Madison, WI M,W
University of Wisconsin–Milwaukee, WI M,W
University of Wyoming, WY M,W
Utah State University, UT M,W
Vanderbilt University, TN W
Vanguard University of Southern California, CA M,W
Virginia Commonwealth University, VA M,W
Virginia Intermont College, VA M,W
Virginia Military Institute, VA M,W
Virginia Polytechnic Institute and State University, VA M,W
Virginia State University, VA M,W
Virginia Union University, VA M,W
Wagner College, NY M,W
Wake Forest University, NC M,W
Walsh University, OH M,W
Washington State University, WA M,W
Wayland Baptist University, TX M,W
Wayne State College, NE M,W
Webber International University, FL M,W
Western Carolina University, NC M,W
Western Illinois University, IL M,W
Western Washington University, WA M,W
West Liberty State College, WV M,W
Westmont College, CA M,W
West Virginia University, WV W
West Virginia Wesleyan College, WV M,W
Wheeling Jesuit University, WV M,W
Wichita State University, KS M,W
William Jewell College, MO M,W
Winona State University, MN W
Winthrop University, SC M,W
Youngstown State University, OH M,W

Volleyball

Abilene Christian University, TX W
Adams State College, CO W
Adelphi University, NY W
Alabama State University, AL W
Albertson College of Idaho, ID W
Alcorn State University, MS W
Alderson-Broaddus College, WV W
Alliant International University, CA W
American International College, MA W
Anderson University, SC W
Appalachian State University, NC W
Arizona State University, AZ W
Arkansas State University, AR W

Arkansas Tech University, AR W
Armstrong Atlantic State University, GA W
Asbury College, KY W
Ashford University, IA W
Auburn University, AL W
Augustana College, SD W
Austin Peay State University, TN W
Azusa Pacific University, CA W
Baker University, KS W
Barton College, NC W
Baylor University, TX W
Bellarmine University, KY W
Belmont University, TN W
Bemidji State University, MN W
Bentley College, MA W
Bethany College, KS W
Bethel College, IN W
Bethel College, KS W
Bethune-Cookman College, FL W
Birmingham-Southern College, AL W
Black Hills State University, SD W
Blessing-Rieman College of Nursing, IL M,W
Bloomfield College, NJ W
Bluefield State College, WV W
Boise State University, ID W
Boston College, MA W
Bowie State University, MD W
Bowling Green State University, OH W
Bradley University, IL W
Brenau University, GA W
Brevard College, NC W
Brigham Young University, UT M,W
Brigham Young University–Hawaii, HI W
Bryan College, TN W
Butler University, IN W
California Polytechnic State University, San Luis Obispo, CA W
California State University, Dominguez Hills, CA W
California State University, Fresno, CA W
California State University, Fullerton, CA W
California State University, Los Angeles, CA W
California State University, Northridge, CA M,W
California State University, Sacramento, CA W
California State University, San Bernardino, CA W
California University of Pennsylvania, PA W
Campbellsville University, KY W
Campbell University, NC W
Canisius College, NY W
Carson-Newman College, TN W
Catawba College, NC W
Cedarville University, OH W
Centenary College of Louisiana, LA W
Central Methodist University, MO W
Central Michigan University, MI W
Central State University, OH W
Central Washington University, WA W
Christian Brothers University, TN W
Clarion University of Pennsylvania, PA W
Clemson University, SC W
Cleveland State University, OH W
Coastal Carolina University, SC W
Colgate University, NY W
College of Charleston, SC W
College of Saint Mary, NE W
The College of Saint Rose, NY W
College of the Ozarks, MO W
College of the Southwest, NM W
The College of William and Mary, VA W
Colorado School of Mines, CO W
Colorado State University, CO W
Colorado State University-Pueblo, CO W
Columbia College, MO W
Concordia University, CA W
Concordia University, NE W
Concordia University, St. Paul, MN W
Concord University, WV W
Converse College, SC W
Coppin State University, MD W
Corban College, OR W
Creighton University, NE W
Culver-Stockton College, MO W
Cumberland University, TN W
Dakota State University, SD W
Dakota Wesleyan University, SD W
Dallas Baptist University, TX W
Dana College, NE W
Davidson College, NC W
Davis & Elkins College, WV W
Dickinson State University, ND W
Doane College, NE W
Dominican College, NY W
Dordt College, IA W
Dowling College, NY W
Drake University, IA W
Drury University, MO W
Duke University, NC W
Duquesne University, PA W
Eastern Illinois University, IL W
Eastern Kentucky University, KY W
Eastern Michigan University, MI W
East Tennessee State University, TN W
Elon University, NC W
Embry-Riddle Aeronautical University, AZ W
Embry-Riddle Aeronautical University, FL W
Emporia State University, KS W
Evangel University, MO W
Fairfield University, CT W
Faulkner University, AL W
Ferris State University, MI W
Flagler College, FL W
Florida Atlantic University, FL W
Florida College, FL W
Florida Gulf Coast University, FL W
Florida Institute of Technology, FL W
Florida State University, FL W
Fort Lewis College, CO W
Francis Marion University, SC W
Franklin Pierce University, NH W
Freed-Hardeman University, TN W
Fresno Pacific University, CA W
Friends University, KS W
Furman University, SC W
Gannon University, PA W
Gardner-Webb University, NC W
Geneva College, PA W
George Mason University, VA M,W
Georgetown College, KY W
Georgetown University, DC W
The George Washington University, DC W
Georgia Institute of Technology, GA W
Georgia Southern University, GA W
Glenville State College, WV W
Gonzaga University, WA W
Grace College, IN W
Graceland University, IA M,W
Grand Valley State University, MI W
Grand View College, IA W
Harding University, AR W
Hastings College, NE W
Hawai'i Pacific University, HI W
Hillsdale College, MI W
Hofstra University, NY W
Holy Names University, CA M,W
Houghton College, NY W
Houston Baptist University, TX W
Huntington University, IN W
Idaho State University, ID W
Illinois Institute of Technology, IL W
Illinois State University, IL W
Indiana State University, IN W
Indiana University Bloomington, IN W
Indiana University of Pennsylvania, PA W
Indiana University–Purdue University Indianapolis, IN W
Indiana University Southeast, IN W
Iona College, NY W
Iowa Wesleyan College, IA W
Jackson State University, MS W
Jacksonville State University, AL W
James Madison University, VA W
Jamestown College, ND W
Johnson C. Smith University, NC W
Judson College, AL W
Judson College, IL W
Kent State University, OH W
Kentucky Wesleyan College, KY W
King College, TN W
Kutztown University of Pennsylvania, PA W
Lake Superior State University, MI W
Lamar University, TX W
Lambuth University, TN W
Lee University, TN W
Lehigh University, PA W
Le Moyne College, NY W
LeMoyne-Owen College, TN W
Lesley University, MA M,W
Lewis-Clark State College, ID W
Limestone College, SC W
Lindenwood University, MO M,W
Lindsey Wilson College, KY W
Lipscomb University, TN W
Lock Haven University of Pennsylvania, PA W
Louisiana State University and Agricultural and Mechanical College, LA W
Louisiana Tech University, LA W
Loyola University Chicago, IL M,W
Lubbock Christian University, TX W
Lyon College, AR W
Malone College, OH W

Manhattan College, NY	W
Marist College, NY	W
Marquette University, WI	W
Mayville State University, ND	W
McKendree College, IL	W
Mercer University, GA	W
Mesa State College, CO	W
Metropolitan State College of Denver, CO	W
Miami University, OH	W
Michigan State University, MI	W
Michigan Technological University, MI	W
Middle Tennessee State University, TN	W
Midwestern State University, TX	W
Millersville University of Pennsylvania, PA	W
Milligan College, TN	W
Minnesota State University Mankato, MN	W
Minot State University, ND	W
Mississippi State University, MS	W
Missouri Baptist University, MO	M,W
Missouri State University, MO	W
Missouri Valley College, MO	M,W
Molloy College, NY	W
Montana State University, MT	W
Montana State University–Billings, MT	W
Montana Tech of The University of Montana, MT	W
Montreat College, NC	W
Morehead State University, KY	W
Morningside College, IA	W
Mount Marty College, SD	W
Mount Olive College, NC	M,W
Mount Vernon Nazarene University, OH	W
Murray State University, KY	W
Newman University, KS	M,W
New Mexico State University, NM	W
New York Institute of Technology, NY	W
Niagara University, NY	W
Nicholls State University, LA	W
North Carolina Agricultural and Technical State University, NC	W
North Carolina State University, NC	W
North Dakota State University, ND	W
Northeastern University, MA	W
Northern Arizona University, AZ	W
Northern Illinois University, IL	W
Northern State University, SD	W
North Greenville University, SC	W
Northwestern College, IA	W
Northwestern State University of Louisiana, LA	W
Northwest Nazarene University, ID	W
Northwest University, WA	W
Northwood University, MI	W
Northwood University, Florida Campus, FL	W
Nova Southeastern University, FL	W
Nyack College, NY	W
The Ohio State University, OH	M,W
Ohio University, OH	W
Ohio Valley University, WV	W
Oklahoma Panhandle State University, OK	W
Oral Roberts University, OK	W
Oregon State University, OR	W
Ouachita Baptist University, AR	W
Penn State University Park, PA	M,W
Pfeiffer University, NC	W
Philadelphia University, PA	W
Pikeville College, KY	W
Pittsburg State University, KS	W
Point Loma Nazarene University, CA	W
Portland State University, OR	W
Providence College, RI	W
Purdue University, IN	W
Quinnipiac University, CT	W
Radford University, VA	W
Regis University, CO	W
Rice University, TX	W
Robert Morris University, PA	W
Roberts Wesleyan College, NY	W
Rockhurst University, MO	W
Rollins College, FL	W
Sacred Heart University, CT	M,W
St. Ambrose University, IA	M,W
St. Andrews Presbyterian College, NC	W
St. Cloud State University, MN	W
St. Edward's University, TX	W
St. Francis College, NY	W
Saint Francis University, PA	M,W
Saint Joseph's College, IN	W
Saint Leo University, FL	W
Saint Louis University, MO	W
Saint Mary's College of California, CA	W
Saint Vincent College, PA	W
Saint Xavier University, IL	W
Samford University, AL	W
Sam Houston State University, TX	W
San Diego State University, CA	W
San Francisco State University, CA	W
San Jose State University, CA	W
Santa Clara University, CA	W
Seattle Pacific University, WA	W
Seton Hill University, PA	W
Shaw University, NC	W
Shepherd University, WV	W
Shippensburg University of Pennsylvania, PA	W
Slippery Rock University of Pennsylvania, PA	W
Sonoma State University, CA	W
South Dakota State University, SD	W
Southeastern Louisiana University, LA	W
Southeastern Oklahoma State University, OK	W
Southeast Missouri State University, MO	W
Southern Arkansas University–Magnolia, AR	W
Southern Illinois University Carbondale, IL	W
Southern Illinois University Edwardsville, IL	W
Southern Methodist University, TX	W
Southern Nazarene University, OK	W
Southern New Hampshire University, NH	W
Southern Oregon University, OR	W
Southern Wesleyan University, SC	W
Southwest Baptist University, MO	W
Southwest Minnesota State University, MN	W
Spring Arbor University, MI	W
Spring Hill College, AL	W
Stanford University, CA	M,W
State University of New York at Binghamton, NY	W
Stephen F. Austin State University, TX	W
Stetson University, FL	W
Stonehill College, MA	W
Stony Brook University, State University of New York, NY	W
Syracuse University, NY	W
Tarleton State University, TX	W
Taylor University, IN	W
Temple University, PA	W
Tennessee Technological University, TN	W
Tennessee Wesleyan College, TN	W
Texas A&M University–Commerce, TX	W
Texas A&M University–Kingsville, TX	W
Texas Christian University, TX	W
Texas State University-San Marcos, TX	W
Texas Tech University, TX	W
Texas Woman's University, TX	W
Tiffin University, OH	W
Towson University, MD	W
Trevecca Nazarene University, TN	W
Trinity International University, IL	W
Troy University, AL	W
Tulane University, LA	W
Tuskegee University, AL	W
Union College, KY	W
Union University, TN	W
Unity College, ME	W
University at Albany, State University of New York, NY	W
University at Buffalo, the State University of New York, NY	W
The University of Akron, OH	W
The University of Alabama, AL	W
The University of Alabama at Birmingham, AL	W
The University of Alabama in Huntsville, AL	W
University of Alaska Fairbanks, AK	W
The University of Arizona, AZ	W
University of Arkansas, AR	W
University of Bridgeport, CT	W
University of California, Berkeley, CA	W
University of California, Irvine, CA	M,W
University of California, Los Angeles, CA	M,W
University of California, Riverside, CA	W
University of California, Santa Barbara, CA	M,W
University of Central Florida, FL	W
University of Central Missouri, MO	W
University of Central Oklahoma, OK	W
University of Charleston, WV	W
University of Colorado at Boulder, CO	W
University of Connecticut, CT	W
University of Dayton, OH	W
University of Delaware, DE	W
University of Denver, CO	W

University of Evansville, IN W
The University of Findlay, OH W
University of Florida, FL W
University of Georgia, GA W
University of Great Falls, MT W
University of Hartford, CT W
University of Hawaii at Hilo, HI W
University of Hawaii at Manoa, HI M,W
University of Idaho, ID W
University of Illinois at Chicago, IL W
University of Illinois at Springfield, IL W
University of Illinois at Urbana–Champaign, IL W
The University of Iowa, IA W
University of Kansas, KS W
University of Louisiana at Lafayette, LA W
University of Louisville, KY W
University of Maine, ME W
University of Maryland, Baltimore County, MD W
University of Maryland, College Park, MD W
University of Massachusetts Amherst, MA W
University of Massachusetts Lowell, MA W
University of Miami, FL W
University of Michigan, MI W
University of Michigan–Dearborn, MI W
University of Minnesota, Crookston, MN W
University of Minnesota, Twin Cities Campus, MN W
University of Missouri–Columbia, MO W
University of Missouri–Kansas City, MO W
University of Missouri–St. Louis, MO W
The University of Montana, MT W
University of Nebraska at Kearney, NE W
University of Nebraska at Omaha, NE W
University of New Hampshire, NH W
University of New Haven, CT M,W
University of New Orleans, LA W
University of North Alabama, AL W
The University of North Carolina at Asheville, NC W
The University of North Carolina at Chapel Hill, NC W
The University of North Carolina at Charlotte, NC W
The University of North Carolina at Greensboro, NC W
The University of North Carolina at Pembroke, NC W
The University of North Carolina Wilmington, NC W
University of North Dakota, ND W
University of Northern Colorado, CO W
University of Northern Iowa, IA W
University of North Florida, FL W
University of Notre Dame, IN W
University of Oklahoma, OK W
University of Oregon, OR W
University of Pittsburgh, PA W
University of Rhode Island, RI W
University of St. Francis, IL W
University of Saint Francis, IN W
University of San Diego, CA W
University of San Francisco, CA W
University of South Carolina, SC W
University of South Carolina Upstate, SC W
The University of South Dakota, SD W
University of Southern California, CA M,W
University of Southern Indiana, IN W
University of Southern Mississippi, MS W
University of South Florida, FL W
The University of Tampa, FL W
The University of Tennessee at Martin, TN W
The University of Texas at Austin, TX W
The University of Texas at Brownsville, TX W
The University of Texas at El Paso, TX W
The University of Texas at San Antonio, TX W
The University of Texas–Pan American, TX W
University of the Cumberlands, KY W
University of the Incarnate Word, TX W
University of the Pacific, CA M,W
University of the Sciences in Philadelphia, PA W
University of Tulsa, OK W
University of Virginia, VA W
University of Washington, WA W
The University of West Alabama, AL W
University of West Georgia, GA W
University of Wisconsin–Green Bay, WI W
University of Wisconsin–Madison, WI W
University of Wisconsin–Milwaukee, WI W
University of Wyoming, WY W
Urbana University, OH W
Utah State University, UT W
Valdosta State University, GA W
Valley City State University, ND W
Valparaiso University, IN W
Vanguard University of Southern California, CA W
Virginia Intermont College, VA W
Virginia Polytechnic Institute and State University, VA W
Virginia State University, VA W
Virginia Union University, VA W
Wagner College, NY W
Wake Forest University, NC W
Walsh University, OH W
Warner Pacific College, OR W
Washington State University, WA W
Wayland Baptist University, TX W
Wayne State College, NE W
Wayne State University, MI W
Western Carolina University, NC W
Western Illinois University, IL W
Western Washington University, WA W
West Liberty State College, WV W
Westmont College, CA W
West Virginia University, WV W
West Virginia Wesleyan College, WV W
Wheeling Jesuit University, WV W
Whitman College, WA M,W
Wichita State University, KS W
William Jewell College, MO W
Williams Baptist College, AR W
Wingate University, NC W
Winona State University, MN W
Winston-Salem State University, NC W
Winthrop University, SC W
Xavier University, OH W
Youngstown State University, OH W

Water Polo

Brigham Young University–Hawaii, HI M
Colorado State University, CO W
The George Washington University, DC M
Indiana University Bloomington, IN W
Iona College, NY W
Lindenwood University, MO M,W
Marist College, NY W
St. Francis College, NY M,W
San Diego State University, CA W
San Jose State University, CA W
Santa Clara University, CA M
Slippery Rock University of Pennsylvania, PA M,W
Stanford University, CA M,W
University of California, Berkeley, CA M,W
University of California, Irvine, CA M
University of California, Los Angeles, CA M,W
University of California, Santa Barbara, CA M,W
University of Hawaii at Manoa, HI W
University of Maryland, College Park, MD W
University of Southern California, CA M,W
University of the Pacific, CA M,W
Wagner College, NY W

Weight Lifting

Coppin State University, MD M,W

Wrestling

Adams State College, CO M
Anderson University, SC M
Appalachian State University, NC M
Arizona State University, AZ M
Augustana College, SD M
Bethel College, IN M
Bloomsburg University of Pennsylvania, PA M
Boise State University, ID M
Boston University, MA M
California Polytechnic State University, San Luis Obispo, CA M
California State University, Fresno, CA M
California State University, Fullerton, CA M
Campbellsville University, KY M
Campbell University, NC M
Carson-Newman College, TN M
Central Michigan University, MI M
Clarion University of Pennsylvania, PA M
Cleveland State University, OH M
Colorado School of Mines, CO M
Coppin State University, MD M
Cumberland University, TN M
Dakota Wesleyan University, SD M
Dana College, NE M

Davidson College, NC	M
Dickinson State University, ND	M
Duquesne University, PA	M
Eastern Illinois University, IL	M
Eastern Michigan University, MI	M
Embry-Riddle Aeronautical University, AZ	M
Gannon University, PA	M
Gardner-Webb University, NC	M
George Mason University, VA	M
Hofstra University, NY	M
Indiana University Bloomington, IN	M
Jamestown College, ND	M
Kent State University, OH	M
King College, TN	M
Kutztown University of Pennsylvania, PA	M
Lehigh University, PA	M
Limestone College, SC	M
Lindenwood University, MO	M
Lock Haven University of Pennsylvania, PA	M
McKendree College, IL	M
Michigan State University, MI	M
Millersville University of Pennsylvania, PA	M
Minnesota State University Mankato, MN	M
Missouri Baptist University, MO	M
Missouri Valley College, MO	M,W
Morningside College, IA	M
Newman University, KS	M
North Carolina State University, NC	M
North Dakota State University, ND	M
Northern Illinois University, IL	M
Northern State University, SD	M
Northwestern College, IA	M
The Ohio State University, OH	M
Ohio University, OH	M
Oklahoma State University, OK	M
Oregon State University, OR	M
Penn State University Park, PA	M
Portland State University, OR	M
Purdue University, IN	M
Sacred Heart University, CT	M
St. Cloud State University, MN	M
San Francisco State University, CA	M
Shippensburg University of Pennsylvania, PA	M
Slippery Rock University of Pennsylvania, PA	M
South Dakota State University, SD	M
Southern Connecticut State University, CT	M
Southern Illinois University Edwardsville, IL	M
Southern Oregon University, OR	M
Southwest Minnesota State University, MN	M
Stanford University, CA	M
State University of New York at Binghamton, NY	M
University at Buffalo, the State University of New York, NY	M
University of Central Missouri, MO	M
University of Central Oklahoma, OK	M
The University of Findlay, OH	M
University of Great Falls, MT	M
University of Illinois at Urbana–Champaign, IL	M
The University of Iowa, IA	M
University of Maryland, College Park, MD	M
University of Massachusetts Lowell, MA	M
University of Michigan, MI	M
University of Minnesota, Twin Cities Campus, MN	M
University of Missouri–Columbia, MO	M
University of Nebraska at Kearney, NE	M
University of Nebraska at Omaha, NE	M
The University of North Carolina at Chapel Hill, NC	M
The University of North Carolina at Greensboro, NC	M
The University of North Carolina at Pembroke, NC	M
University of Northern Colorado, CO	M
University of Northern Iowa, IA	M
University of Oklahoma, OK	M
University of Oregon, OR	M
University of Pittsburgh, PA	M
University of Pittsburgh at Johnstown, PA	M
University of the Cumberlands, KY	M,W
University of Virginia, VA	M
University of Wisconsin–Madison, WI	M
University of Wyoming, WY	M
Virginia Military Institute, VA	M
Virginia Polytechnic Institute and State University, VA	M
Wagner College, NY	M
West Liberty State College, WV	M
West Virginia University, WV	M

Co-op Programs

Alabama State University, AL
Albertson College of Idaho, ID
Alcorn State University, MS
Alfred University, NY
Anderson University, SC
Andrews University, MI
Antioch College, OH
Antioch University McGregor, OH
Arcadia University, PA
Arizona State University, AZ
Armstrong Atlantic State University, GA
Auburn University, AL
Auburn University Montgomery, AL
Augsburg College, MN
Augustana College, SD
Augusta State University, GA
Austin Peay State University, TN
Averett University, VA
Azusa Pacific University, CA
Barton College, NC
Bastyr University, WA
Becker College, MA
Belmont Abbey College, NC
Belmont University, TN
Bemidji State University, MN
Berry College, GA
Bethune-Cookman College, FL
Black Hills State University, SD
Bloomfield College, NJ
Bloomsburg University of Pennsylvania, PA
Boise State University, ID
Boston University, MA
Bowie State University, MD
Bowling Green State University, OH
Bradley University, IL
Brigham Young University, UT
Brigham Young University–Hawaii, HI
Burlington College, VT
Butler University, IN
Cabrini College, PA
California College of the Arts, CA
California Institute of Technology, CA
California Institute of the Arts, CA
California Polytechnic State University, San Luis Obispo, CA
California State University, Chico, CA
California State University, Dominguez Hills, CA
California State University, East Bay, CA
California State University, Fresno, CA
California State University, Fullerton, CA
California State University, Los Angeles, CA
California State University, Sacramento, CA
California State University, San Bernardino, CA
California State University, Stanislaus, CA
California University of Pennsylvania, PA
Calumet College of Saint Joseph, IN
Campbell University, NC
Capital University, OH
Carthage College, WI
Case Western Reserve University, OH
The Catholic University of America, DC
Central State University, OH
Central Washington University, WA
Champlain College, VT
Chatham University, PA
Chester College of New England, NH
Chestnut Hill College, PA
Christendom College, VA
Christopher Newport University, VA
City College of the City University of New York, NY
Claflin University, SC
Clarion University of Pennsylvania, PA
Clarke College, IA
Clarkson University, NY
Cleary University, MI
Clemson University, SC
Cleveland State University, OH
Coastal Carolina University, SC
College for Creative Studies, MI
College Misericordia, PA
College of Charleston, SC
The College of New Rochelle, NY
The College of Saint Thomas More, TX
College of Staten Island of the City University of New York, NY
College of the Ozarks, MO
The College of Wooster, OH
Colorado School of Mines, CO
Colorado State University, CO
Colorado State University-Pueblo, CO
Columbia College, MO
Columbia College Chicago, IL
Columbia International University, SC
Columbus State University, GA
Concordia College, MN
Concordia University, CA
Converse College, SC
Coppin State University, MD
Cornell University, NY
The Culinary Institute of America, NY
Cumberland University, TN
Dakota State University, SD
Daniel Webster College, NH
Davis & Elkins College, WV
Delaware Valley College, PA
Denison University, OH
Dickinson State University, ND
Doane College, NE
Dominican College, NY
Dowling College, NY
Drake University, IA
Drury University, MO
Eastern Kentucky University, KY
Eastern Michigan University, MI
East Tennessee State University, TN
Elmhurst College, IL
Embry-Riddle Aeronautical University, AZ
Embry-Riddle Aeronautical University, FL
Embry-Riddle Aeronautical University Worldwide, FL
Emory & Henry College, VA
Emory University, GA
Eugene Bible College, OR
Eureka College, IL
Fashion Institute of Technology, NY
Felician College, NJ
Ferris State University, MI
Five Towns College, NY
Florida Atlantic University, FL
Florida Gulf Coast University, FL
Florida Institute of Technology, FL
Florida Metropolitan University–Pinellas Campus, FL
Florida Metropolitan University–Tampa Campus, FL
Florida State University, FL
Fort Lewis College, CO
Franklin College, IN
Freed-Hardeman University, TN
Fresno Pacific University, CA
Friends University, KS
Gallaudet University, DC
Gannon University, PA
Gardner-Webb University, NC
Geneva College, PA
George Mason University, VA
Georgetown College, KY
The George Washington University, DC
Georgia Institute of Technology, GA
Georgia Southern University, GA
Glenville State College, WV
Grace College, IN
Graceland University, IA
Grace University, NE
Grand Valley State University, MI
Grand View College, IA
Green Mountain College, VT
Guilford College, NC
Gustavus Adolphus College, MN
Gwynedd-Mercy College, PA
Harding University, AR
Hawai'i Pacific University, HI
Hendrix College, AR
Hilbert College, NY
Husson College, ME
Illinois Institute of Technology, IL
Illinois State University, IL
Indiana State University, IN
Indiana University Bloomington, IN
Indiana University East, IN
Indiana University Northwest, IN
Indiana University of Pennsylvania, PA

Indiana University–Purdue University Indianapolis, IN
Jackson State University, MS
Jacksonville State University, AL
Jamestown College, ND
Jarvis Christian College, TX
John Jay College of Criminal Justice of the City University of New York, NY
Johnson Bible College, TN
Johnson C. Smith University, NC
Kean University, NJ
Keene State College, NH
Kent State University, OH
Kentucky Christian University, KY
Kettering University, MI
Keuka College, NY
King College, TN
Kuyper College, MI
Laboratory Institute of Merchandising, NY
Lake Superior State University, MI
Lamar University, TX
Lawrence Technological University, MI
Lehigh University, PA
Lehman College of the City University of New York, NY
LeMoyne-Owen College, TN
LeTourneau University, TX
Lewis-Clark State College, ID
Lexington College, IL
Life University, GA
Lincoln University, PA
Lindenwood University, MO
Lindsey Wilson College, KY
Lock Haven University of Pennsylvania, PA
Loras College, IA
Louisiana State University and Agricultural and Mechanical College, LA
Louisiana Tech University, LA
Lourdes College, OH
Lyndon State College, VT
Macon State College, GA
Magdalen College, NH
Maharishi University of Management, IA
Manhattan College, NY
Marian College of Fond du Lac, WI
Marist College, NY
Marquette University, WI
Maryville University of Saint Louis, MO
Massachusetts Institute of Technology, MA
Mayville State University, ND
Medgar Evers College of the City University of New York, NY
Menlo College, CA
Mercer University, GA
Meredith College, NC
Mesa State College, CO
Messenger College, MO
Methodist University, NC
Metropolitan State College of Denver, CO
Miami University, OH
Michigan State University, MI
Michigan Technological University, MI
Middle Tennessee State University, TN
Millersville University of Pennsylvania, PA
Milligan College, TN
Minot State University, ND
Mississippi State University, MS
Missouri State University, MO
Missouri Valley College, MO
Molloy College, NY
Monmouth University, NJ
Monroe College, NY
Monroe College, NY
Montana State University–Billings, MT
Montana Tech of The University of Montana, MT
Montclair State University, NJ
Montreat College, NC
Morehead State University, KY
Mountain State University, WV
Mount Holyoke College, MA
Mount Ida College, MA
Mount Marty College, SD
Mount Olive College, NC
Mount Saint Mary College, NY
Mount Union College, OH
Murray State University, KY
Myers University, OH
Naropa University, CO
The National Hispanic University, CA
Nazareth College of Rochester, NY
Neumann College, PA
New Jersey City University, NJ
Newman University, KS
New Mexico State University, NM
New York Institute of Technology, NY
New York University, NY
Niagara University, NY
Nicholls State University, LA
Nichols College, MA
North Carolina Agricultural and Technical State University, NC
North Carolina State University, NC
North Dakota State University, ND
Northeastern Illinois University, IL
Northeastern State University, OK
Northeastern University, MA
Northern Arizona University, AZ
Northern Illinois University, IL
Northern State University, SD
North Georgia College & State University, GA
Northland College, WI
Northwest Christian College, OR
Northwestern College, IA
Northwestern State University of Louisiana, LA
Northwest Nazarene University, ID
Northwest University, WA
Northwood University, MI
Oglethorpe University, GA
The Ohio State University, OH
Ohio University, OH
Oklahoma Baptist University, OK
Olivet College, MI
Oregon State University, OR
Otis College of Art and Design, CA
Ouachita Baptist University, AR
Pacific Lutheran University, WA
Pacific Union College, CA
Parsons The New School for Design, NY
Paul Smith's College of Arts and Sciences, NY
Peirce College, PA
Penn State Abington, PA
Penn State Altoona, PA
Penn State Berks, PA
Penn State Erie, The Behrend College, PA
Penn State Harrisburg, PA
Penn State University Park, PA
Pennsylvania College of Technology, PA
Pfeiffer University, NC
Philadelphia University, PA
Piedmont College, GA
Pittsburg State University, KS
Pitzer College, CA
Polytechnic University, Brooklyn Campus, NY
Portland State University, OR
Providence College, RI
Purdue University, IN
Purdue University Calumet, IN
Ramapo College of New Jersey, NJ
Reed College, OR
Regis University, CO
Reinhardt College, GA
Rensselaer Polytechnic Institute, NY
Robert Morris University, PA
Roberts Wesleyan College, NY
Rochester Institute of Technology, NY
Rockhurst University, MO
Rose-Hulman Institute of Technology, IN
Russell Sage College, NY
Rutgers, The State University of New Jersey, Camden, NJ
Rutgers, The State University of New Jersey, Newark, NJ
Rutgers, The State University of New Jersey, New Brunswick, NJ
Sacred Heart University, CT
Sage College of Albany, NY
St. Ambrose University, IA
St. Francis College, NY
Saint Joseph's College of Maine, ME
St. Joseph's College, Suffolk Campus, NY
Saint Louis University, MO
Saint Mary's College, IN
St. Mary's College of Maryland, MD
Saint Mary's University of Minnesota, MN
Saint Vincent College, PA
Saint Xavier University, IL
Samford University, AL
San Francisco Art Institute, CA
San Francisco State University, CA
San Jose State University, CA
Santa Clara University, CA
Seattle Pacific University, WA
Shasta Bible College, CA
Shenandoah University, VA
Shepherd University, WV
Shimer College, IL
Shippensburg University of Pennsylvania, PA
Silver Lake College, WI
Simmons College, MA
Simpson College, IA
Sonoma State University, CA
South Dakota State University, SD
Southern Connecticut State University, CT
Southern Illinois University Carbondale, IL
Southern Illinois University Edwardsville, IL
Southern Methodist College, SC
Southern Methodist University, TX
Southern New Hampshire University, NH
Southern Oregon University, OR
Southern Polytechnic State University, GA

Southern Utah University, UT
Southern Vermont College, VT
Southwest Baptist University, MO
State University of New York at New Paltz, NY
State University of New York at Oswego, NY
State University of New York at Plattsburgh, NY
State University of New York College of Agriculture and Technology at Cobleskill, NY
State University of New York College of Environmental Science and Forestry, NY
Stephens College, MO
Suffolk University, MA
Syracuse University, NY
Tarleton State University, TX
Taylor University, IN
Taylor University Fort Wayne, IN
Temple University, PA
Tennessee State University, TN
Tennessee Technological University, TN
Tennessee Wesleyan College, TN
Texas A&M University at Galveston, TX
Texas A&M University–Commerce, TX
Texas A&M University–Corpus Christi, TX
Texas A&M University–Kingsville, TX
Texas Tech University, TX
Texas Woman's University, TX
Thiel College, PA
Thomas Aquinas College, CA
Thomas College, ME
Thomas More College, KY
Towson University, MD
Tri-State University, IN
Tulane University, LA
Tuskegee University, AL
Union College, KY
Union College, NE
Union University, TN
Unity College, ME
University at Buffalo, the State University of New York, NY
The University of Akron, OH
The University of Alabama, AL
The University of Alabama at Birmingham, AL
The University of Alabama in Huntsville, AL
University of Alaska Fairbanks, AK
University of Arkansas, AR
University of Bridgeport, CT
University of California, Riverside, CA
University of California, San Diego, CA
University of California, Santa Barbara, CA
University of California, Santa Cruz, CA
University of Central Florida, FL
University of Central Missouri, MO
University of Colorado at Boulder, CO
University of Connecticut, CT
University of Dayton, OH
University of Delaware, DE
University of Denver, CO
University of Detroit Mercy, MI
University of Evansville, IN
The University of Findlay, OH
University of Florida, FL
University of Georgia, GA
University of Great Falls, MT
University of Hartford, CT
University of Hawaii at Manoa, HI
University of Idaho, ID
University of Illinois at Chicago, IL
University of Illinois at Springfield, IL
University of Illinois at Urbana–Champaign, IL
The University of Iowa, IA
University of Judaism, CA
University of Kansas, KS
University of Louisiana at Lafayette, LA
University of Louisville, KY
University of Maine, ME
University of Maryland, Baltimore County, MD
University of Maryland, College Park, MD
University of Maryland University College, MD
University of Massachusetts Amherst, MA
University of Massachusetts Boston, MA
University of Massachusetts Dartmouth, MA
University of Massachusetts Lowell, MA
University of Michigan, MI
University of Michigan–Dearborn, MI
University of Michigan–Flint, MI
University of Minnesota, Twin Cities Campus, MN
University of Missouri–Columbia, MO
University of Missouri–Kansas City, MO
University of Missouri–St. Louis, MO
The University of Montana, MT
University of Nebraska at Kearney, NE
University of Nebraska at Omaha, NE
University of New England, ME
University of New Hampshire, NH
University of New Haven, CT
University of New Orleans, LA
University of North Alabama, AL
The University of North Carolina at Charlotte, NC
The University of North Carolina at Pembroke, NC
The University of North Carolina Wilmington, NC
University of North Dakota, ND
University of Northern Colorado, CO
University of Northern Iowa, IA
University of North Florida, FL
University of Oklahoma, OK
University of Pittsburgh, PA
University of Pittsburgh at Johnstown, PA
University of Puget Sound, WA
University of Rhode Island, RI
University of Richmond, VA
University of Saint Francis, IN
University of San Francisco, CA
University of South Carolina, SC
University of South Carolina Upstate, SC
University of Southern California, CA
University of Southern Indiana, IN
University of Southern Maine, ME
University of Southern Mississippi, MS
University of South Florida, FL
The University of Tampa, FL
The University of Tennessee at Martin, TN
The University of Texas at Austin, TX
The University of Texas at Brownsville, TX
The University of Texas at Dallas, TX
The University of Texas at El Paso, TX
The University of Texas at San Antonio, TX
The University of Texas at Tyler, TX
The University of Texas–Pan American, TX
University of the Cumberlands, KY
University of the Ozarks, AR
University of the Pacific, CA
University of the Sciences in Philadelphia, PA
University of Vermont, VT
University of Virginia, VA
University of Washington, WA
University of West Florida, FL
University of West Georgia, GA
University of Wisconsin–La Crosse, WI
University of Wisconsin–Madison, WI
University of Wisconsin–Milwaukee, WI
University of Wisconsin–Stout, WI
University of Wisconsin–Superior, WI
University of Wisconsin–Whitewater, WI
Urbana University, OH
Utah State University, UT
Valdosta State University, GA
Valley City State University, ND
Valparaiso University, IN
Vanderbilt University, TN
Vassar College, NY
Vermont Technical College, VT
Villa Julie College, MD
Virginia Commonwealth University, VA
Virginia Polytechnic Institute and State University, VA
Virginia State University, VA
Virginia Union University, VA
Walla Walla College, WA
Warner Pacific College, OR
Warren Wilson College, NC
Washington Bible College, MD
Washington University in St. Louis, MO
Watkins College of Art and Design, TN
Wayne State College, NE
Wayne State University, MI
Webber International University, FL
Webster University, MO
Wentworth Institute of Technology, MA
Wesley College, DE
Western Carolina University, NC
Western Connecticut State University, CT
Western Washington University, WA
Westfield State College, MA
Westminster College, MO
Westminster College, UT
Whitman College, WA
Whitworth University, WA
Wichita State University, KS
Widener University, PA
Wilkes University, PA
Willamette University, OR
William Jewell College, MO
Wilson College, PA
Winston-Salem State University, NC
Winthrop University, SC
Wittenberg University, OH
Worcester Polytechnic Institute, MA
Xavier University, OH
York College of Pennsylvania, PA
Youngstown State University, OH

ROTC Programs

Air Force

Adelphi University, NY*
Agnes Scott College, GA*
Alabama State University, AL
Alverno College, WI*
American International College, MA*
Anderson University, SC*
Arizona State University, AZ
Arizona State University at the Polytechnic Campus, AZ*
Asbury College, KY*
Assumption College, MA*
Auburn University, AL
Auburn University Montgomery, AL*
Augsburg College, MN*
Austin Peay State University, TN*
Babson College, MA*
Baker University, KS*
Baldwin-Wallace College, OH*
Baylor University, TX
Becker College, MA*
Bellarmine University, KY*
Belmont Abbey College, NC*
Bentley College, MA*
Bethel College, IN*
Bethel University, MN*
Bethune-Cookman College, FL*
Birmingham-Southern College, AL*
Bloomsburg University of Pennsylvania, PA*
Boston College, MA*
Boston University, MA
Bowling Green State University, OH
Brandeis University, MA*
Bridgewater State College, MA*
Brigham Young University, UT
Brigham Young University–Hawaii, HI*
Bryn Mawr College, PA*
Butler University, IN*
Cabrini College, PA*
California Institute of Technology, CA*
California State University, Dominguez Hills, CA*
California State University, Fresno, CA
California State University, Los Angeles, CA*
California State University, Northridge, CA*
California State University, Sacramento, CA
California State University, San Bernardino, CA
Capital University, OH*
Carroll College, WI*
Carson-Newman College, TN*
Carthage College, WI*
Case Western Reserve University, OH*
The Catholic University of America, DC*
Cazenovia College, NY*
Cedarville University, OH*
Central Methodist University, MO*
Central Washington University, WA
Centre College, KY*
Chapman University, CA*
Chatham University, PA*
Christian Brothers University, TN*
City College of the City University of New York, NY*
Claremont McKenna College, CA*
Clarkson University, NY
Clark University, MA*
Clearwater Christian College, FL*
Clemson University, SC
Cleveland Institute of Music, OH*
Cleveland State University, OH*
Coe College, IA*
College Misericordia, PA*
College of Charleston, SC*
The College of New Jersey, NJ*
College of St. Catherine, MN*
College of Saint Mary, NE*
The College of St. Scholastica, MN*
College of the Holy Cross, MA*
Colorado State University, CO
Columbia College, MO*
Columbia University, School of General Studies, NY*
Concordia College, MN*
Concordia University, NE*
Concordia University at Austin, TX*
Concordia University, St. Paul, MN*
Corban College, OR*
Cornell University, NY
Creighton University, NE*
Dakota State University, SD*
Dallas Baptist University, TX*
Dana College, NE*
Daniel Webster College, NH*
Davidson College, NC*
Doane College, NE*
Dowling College, NY*
Drake University, IA*
Duke University, NC
Duquesne University, PA*
Eastern Kentucky University, KY*
Eastern Michigan University, MI*
Elmhurst College, IL*
Elmira College, NY*
Elon University, NC*
Embry-Riddle Aeronautical University, AZ
Embry-Riddle Aeronautical University, FL
Emory University, GA*
Endicott College, MA*
Fairfield University, CT*
Faulkner University, AL*
Fitchburg State College, MA*
Florida Atlantic University, FL*
Florida College, FL*
Florida State University, FL
Franklin Pierce University, NH*
Free Will Baptist Bible College, TN*
George Fox University, OR*
George Mason University, VA*
Georgetown College, KY*
Georgetown University, DC*
The George Washington University, DC*
Georgia Institute of Technology, GA
Grace University, NE*
Grand View College, IA*
Guilford College, NC*
Hamilton College, NY*
Harvard University, MA*
Harvey Mudd College, CA
Hawai'i Pacific University, HI*
Heidelberg College, OH*
Holy Names University, CA*
Illinois Institute of Technology, IL
Indiana State University, IN
Indiana University Bloomington, IN
Indiana University–Purdue University Indianapolis, IN*
Indiana University South Bend, IN*
Iona College, NY*
Ithaca College, NY*
James Madison University, VA*
John Jay College of Criminal Justice of the City University of New York, NY*
The Johns Hopkins University, MD*
Johnson C. Smith University, NC*
Kean University, NJ*
Keene State College, NH*
Kent State University, OH
La Roche College, PA*
Lawrence Technological University, MI*
Le Moyne College, NY*
LeMoyne-Owen College, TN*
Lewis-Clark State College, ID*
Lincoln University, PA*
Lindenwood University, MO*
Linfield College, OR*
Lipscomb University, TN*
Louisiana State University and Agricultural and Mechanical College, LA
Lourdes College, OH*
Loyola College in Maryland, MD*
Loyola University Chicago, IL*
Loyola University New Orleans, LA*
Lubbock Christian University, TX*
Lyndon State College, VT*
Malone College, OH*
Manhattan Christian College, KS*
Manhattan College, NY
Marquette University, WI
Mary Baldwin College, VA*
Marywood University, PA*
Massachusetts Institute of Technology, MA
Mayville State University, ND*
McKendree College, IL*

**program is offered at another college's campus*

McMurry University, TX*
Meredith College, NC*
Methodist University, NC*
Metropolitan State College of Denver, CO*
Miami University, OH
Michigan State University, MI
Michigan Technological University, MI
Middle Tennessee State University, TN*
Midwestern State University, TX*
Milwaukee School of Engineering, WI*
Mississippi State University, MS
Molloy College, NY*
Monmouth University, NJ*
Montana State University, MT
Montclair State University, NJ*
Mount Holyoke College, MA*
Mount Union College, OH*
National University, CA*
Nazareth College of Rochester, NY*
Nebraska Methodist College, NE*
Nebraska Wesleyan University, NE*
New England College, NH*
New Mexico State University, NM
New York Institute of Technology, NY
North Carolina Agricultural and Technical State University, NC
North Carolina State University, NC
North Central College, IL*
North Dakota State University, ND
Northeastern Illinois University, IL*
Northeastern University, MA*
Northern Arizona University, AZ
Northern Illinois University, IL*
Northwestern College, MN*
The Ohio State University, OH
Ohio University, OH
Ohio University–Chillicothe, OH*
Ohio University–Lancaster, OH*
Ohio Valley University, WV*
Ohio Wesleyan University, OH*
Oklahoma Baptist University, OK*
Oklahoma State University, OK
Oral Roberts University, OK*
Oregon State University, OR
Penn State Abington, PA*
Penn State Altoona, PA
Penn State University Park, PA
Philadelphia Biblical University, PA*
Pitzer College, CA*
Point Loma Nazarene University, CA*
Polytechnic University, Brooklyn Campus, NY*
Pomona College, CA*
Portland State University, OR*
Princeton University, NJ*
Purdue University, IN
Quinnipiac University, CT*
Ramapo College of New Jersey, NJ*
Regis University, CO*
Rensselaer Polytechnic Institute, NY
Rhodes College, TN*
Rice University, TX*
Rivier College, NH*
Robert Morris University, PA*
Roberts Wesleyan College, NY*
Rochester Institute of Technology, NY
Rose-Hulman Institute of Technology, IN
Russell Sage College, NY*
Rutgers, The State University of New Jersey, Camden, NJ*
Rutgers, The State University of New Jersey, Newark, NJ
Rutgers, The State University of New Jersey, New Brunswick, NJ
Saint Anselm College, NH*
St. Edward's University, TX*
St. Francis College, NY*
St. Gregory's University, OK*
St. John Fisher College, NY*
St. Joseph's College, Suffolk Campus, NY*
St. Lawrence University, NY*
Saint Leo University, FL*
Saint Louis University, MO
Saint Mary-of-the-Woods College, IN*
Saint Mary's College, IN*
Saint Mary's College of California, CA*
Saint Michael's College, VT*
Saint Vincent College, PA*
Saint Xavier University, IL*
Samford University, AL
San Diego State University, CA
San Francisco State University, CA*
San Jose State University, CA
Santa Clara University, CA*
Scripps College, CA*
Seattle Pacific University, WA*
Seattle University, WA*
Seton Hill University, PA*
Shaw University, NC*
Shepherd University, WV*
Smith College, MA*
Sonoma State University, CA*
South Dakota State University, SD
Southeastern University, FL*
Southeast Missouri State University, MO
Southern Connecticut State University, CT*
Southern Illinois University Carbondale, IL
Southern Illinois University Edwardsville, IL
Southern Methodist University, TX*
Southern Nazarene University, OK*
Southern New Hampshire University, NH*
Southern Polytechnic State University, GA*
Southern Wesleyan University, SC*
Spelman College, GA*
Spring Arbor University, MI*
Spring Hill College, AL*
Stanford University, CA*
State University of New York at Binghamton, NY*
State University of New York College at Geneseo, NY*
State University of New York College at Old Westbury, NY*
State University of New York College at Potsdam, NY*
State University of New York College of Environmental Science and Forestry, NY*
Stephens College, MO*
Stony Brook University, State University of New York, NY*
Swarthmore College, PA*
Syracuse University, NY
Temple University, PA*
Tennessee State University, TN
Tennessee Technological University, TN*
Texas Christian University, TX
Texas Lutheran University, TX*
Texas State University-San Marcos, TX
Texas Tech University, TX
Texas Woman's University, TX*
Thomas More College, KY*
Tiffin University, OH*
Towson University, MD*
Transylvania University, KY*
Troy University, AL
Tufts University, MA*
Tulane University, LA
Tuskegee University, AL
Union College, NY*
University at Albany, State University of New York, NY*
The University of Akron, OH*
The University of Alabama, AL
The University of Alabama at Birmingham, AL*
The University of Arizona, AZ
University of Arkansas, AR
University of California, Berkeley, CA
University of California, Irvine, CA*
University of California, Los Angeles, CA
University of California, Riverside, CA*
University of California, Santa Cruz, CA*
University of Central Florida, FL
University of Central Missouri, MO*
University of Colorado at Boulder, CO
University of Connecticut, CT
University of Dallas, TX*
University of Dayton, OH*
University of Delaware, DE
University of Denver, CO*
The University of Findlay, OH*
University of Florida, FL
University of Georgia, GA
University of Hartford, CT*
University of Hawaii at Manoa, HI
University of Idaho, ID*
University of Illinois at Chicago, IL*
University of Illinois at Urbana–Champaign, IL
The University of Iowa, IA
University of Kansas, KS
University of Louisville, KY
University of Maryland, College Park, MD
University of Massachusetts Amherst, MA
University of Massachusetts Lowell, MA
University of Miami, FL
University of Michigan, MI
University of Michigan–Dearborn, MI*
University of Minnesota, Crookston, MN*
University of Minnesota, Twin Cities Campus, MN
University of Missouri–Columbia, MO
University of Missouri–Kansas City, MO*
University of Missouri–St. Louis, MO*
University of Nebraska at Omaha, NE
University of Nebraska Medical Center, NE*
University of New Hampshire, NH
University of New Hampshire at Manchester, NH*
University of New Orleans, LA*
The University of North Carolina at Chapel Hill, NC
The University of North Carolina at Charlotte, NC

The University of North Carolina at Greensboro, NC*
The University of North Carolina at Pembroke, NC
University of North Dakota, ND
University of Northern Colorado, CO
University of Notre Dame, IN
University of Oklahoma, OK
University of Oregon, OR*
University of Pennsylvania, PA*
University of Pittsburgh, PA
University of Pittsburgh at Greensburg, PA*
University of Redlands, CA*
University of Rochester, NY*
University of St. Thomas, MN
University of San Diego, CA*
University of San Francisco, CA*
University of South Carolina, SC
University of Southern California, CA
University of Southern Maine, ME*
University of Southern Mississippi, MS
University of South Florida, FL
The University of Tampa, FL*
The University of Texas at Austin, TX
The University of Texas at Dallas, TX*
The University of Texas at El Paso, TX
The University of Texas at San Antonio, TX
University of the Incarnate Word, TX*
University of the Pacific, CA*
University of the Sciences in Philadelphia, PA*
University of Tulsa, OK*
University of Virginia, VA
University of Washington, WA
The University of West Alabama, AL*
University of West Florida, FL
University of Wisconsin–Madison, WI
University of Wisconsin–Milwaukee, WI*
University of Wisconsin–Superior, WI*
University of Wisconsin–Whitewater, WI
University of Wyoming, WY
Utah State University, UT
Valdosta State University, GA
Valparaiso University, IN*
Vanderbilt University, TN*
Vanguard University of Southern California, CA*
Virginia Military Institute, VA
Virginia Polytechnic Institute and State University, VA
Warner Pacific College, OR*
Washington & Jefferson College, PA*
Washington State University, WA
Washington University in St. Louis, MO*
Wayland Baptist University, TX*
Wayne State University, MI*
Webster University, MO*
Wellesley College, MA*
Wells College, NY*
Wentworth Institute of Technology, MA*
Wesleyan University, CT*
Western Connecticut State University, CT*
Western New England College, MA*
Western Oregon University, OR*
Westfield State College, MA*
Westminster College, MO*
Westminster College, UT*
Westmont College, CA*
West Virginia University, WV
Widener University, PA*
Wilkes University, PA
Willamette University, OR*
William Carey College, MS*
William Paterson University of New Jersey, NJ*
Wingate University, NC*
Winston-Salem State University, NC
Wisconsin Lutheran College, WI*
Wittenberg University, OH*
Worcester Polytechnic Institute, MA
Xavier University, OH*
Yale University, CT*
Youngstown State University, OH*

Army

Adelphi University, NY*
Agnes Scott College, GA*
Alabama State University, AL*
Albertson College of Idaho, ID*
Alcorn State University, MS
Alfred University, NY*
Allen College, IA*
Alliant International University, CA*
Alma College, MI*
Alverno College, WI*
American International College, MA*
Anderson University, SC*
Appalachian State University, NC
Arizona State University, AZ
Arizona State University at the Polytechnic Campus, AZ*
Arkansas State University, AR
Arkansas Tech University, AR*
Armstrong Atlantic State University, GA
Asbury College, KY*
Assumption College, MA*
Auburn University, AL
Auburn University Montgomery, AL
Augsburg College, MN*
Augusta State University, GA
Aurora University, IL*
Austin Peay State University, TN
Azusa Pacific University, CA*
Babson College, MA*
Baker University, KS*
Baptist Bible College, MO*
Becker College, MA*
Bellarmine University, KY*
Bellin College of Nursing, WI*
Belmont Abbey College, NC*
Belmont University, TN*
Benedictine University, IL*
Bentley College, MA*
Bethany Lutheran College, MN*
Bethel College, IN*
Bethel University, MN*
Bethune-Cookman College, FL*
Birmingham-Southern College, AL*
Black Hills State University, SD
Bloomfield College, NJ*
Bloomsburg University of Pennsylvania, PA
Boise State University, ID
Boston College, MA*
Boston University, MA
Bowling Green State University, OH
Bradley University, IL*
Brandeis University, MA*
Bridgewater State College, MA*
Brigham Young University, UT
Brigham Young University–Hawaii, HI*
Bryant University, RI
Bucknell University, PA
Butler University, IN
Cabrini College, PA*
California Institute of Technology, CA*
California Polytechnic State University, San Luis Obispo, CA
California State University, Dominguez Hills, CA*
California State University, Fresno, CA
California State University, Fullerton, CA
California State University, Los Angeles, CA*
California State University, Northridge, CA*
California State University, Sacramento, CA*
California State University, San Bernardino, CA
California University of Pennsylvania, PA
Calvin College, MI*
Campbellsville University, KY*
Campbell University, NC
Canisius College, NY
Capital University, OH
Carroll College, WI*
Carson-Newman College, TN
Carthage College, WI*
Case Western Reserve University, OH*
Catawba College, NC*
The Catholic University of America, DC*
Cazenovia College, NY*
Cedar Crest College, PA*
Cedarville University, OH*
Central Methodist University, MO*
Central Michigan University, MI
Central State University, OH
Central Washington University, WA
Centre College, KY*
Champlain College, VT*
Chapman University, CA*
Chatham University, PA*
Christian Brothers University, TN*
Christopher Newport University, VA
City College of the City University of New York, NY*
Claflin University, SC*
Claremont McKenna College, CA
Clarion University of Pennsylvania, PA*
Clarke College, IA*
Clarkson University, NY
Clark University, MA*
Clearwater Christian College, FL*
Clemson University, SC
Cleveland Institute of Music, OH*
Cleveland State University, OH*
Coe College, IA*
Colby College, ME*
Colgate University, NY*
College Misericordia, PA*
The College of New Jersey, NJ*
College of Notre Dame of Maryland, MD*
College of St. Catherine, MN*
College of Saint Mary, NE*
The College of Saint Thomas More, TX*
College of the Holy Cross, MA*
College of the Ozarks, MO

**program is offered at another college's campus*

The College of William and Mary, VA
The Colorado College, CO*
Colorado School of Mines, CO
Colorado State University, CO
Colorado State University-Pueblo, CO
Columbia College, MO*
Columbia University, School of General Studies, NY*
Columbus State University, GA
Concordia College, MN*
Concordia University, NE*
Concordia University at Austin, TX*
Concordia University, St. Paul, MN*
Converse College, SC*
Coppin State University, MD
Corban College, OR*
Cornell University, NY
Creighton University, NE
Cumberland University, TN
Curry College, MA*
Dakota State University, SD
Dallas Baptist University, TX*
Dana College, NE*
Daniel Webster College, NH*
Dartmouth College, NH*
Davidson College, NC
Denison University, OH*
DeSales University, PA*
Dickinson College, PA
Doane College, NE*
Drake University, IA
Drury University, MO*
Duke University, NC
Duquesne University, PA
D'Youville College, NY*
Eastern Illinois University, IL
Eastern Kentucky University, KY
Eastern Michigan University, MI
East Tennessee State University, TN
Elmhurst College, IL*
Elmira College, NY
Elon University, NC
Embry-Riddle Aeronautical University, AZ
Embry-Riddle Aeronautical University, FL
Emmanuel College, MA*
Emory University, GA*
Endicott College, MA*
Evangel University, MO
Fairfield University, CT*
Faulkner University, AL*
Ferris State University, MI*
Florida Atlantic University, FL*
Florida College, FL*
Florida Institute of Technology, FL
Florida State University, FL
Framingham State College, MA*
Franklin College, IN*
Franklin Pierce University, NH*
Free Will Baptist Bible College, TN*
Furman University, SC
Gannon University, PA
Gardner-Webb University, NC
Geneva College, PA*
George Mason University, VA
Georgetown College, KY*
Georgetown University, DC
The George Washington University, DC*
Georgia College & State University, GA*
Georgia Institute of Technology, GA
Georgia Southern University, GA
Gonzaga University, WA
Goucher College, MD*
Grace Bible College, MI*
Grace University, NE*
Grand View College, IA*
Grove City College, PA*
Guilford College, NC*
Gustavus Adolphus College, MN*
Hamilton College, NY*
Hampden-Sydney College, VA*
Hampshire College, MA*
Harding University, AR*
Harvard University, MA*
Harvey Mudd College, CA*
Hawai'i Pacific University, HI*
Heidelberg College, OH*
Hendrix College, AR*
Hilbert College, NY*
Hofstra University, NY
Holy Names University, CA*
Hood College, MD*
Hope College, MI*
Houghton College, NY*
Houston Baptist University, TX*
Husson College, ME*
Idaho State University, ID*
Illinois Institute of Technology, IL
Illinois State University, IL
Illinois Wesleyan University, IL*
Indiana State University, IN
Indiana University Bloomington, IN
Indiana University Kokomo, IN*
Indiana University Northwest, IN
Indiana University of Pennsylvania, PA
Indiana University–Purdue University Indianapolis, IN
Indiana University South Bend, IN*
Indiana University Southeast, IN
Iona College, NY*
Ithaca College, NY*
Jackson State University, MS
Jacksonville State University, AL
James Madison University, VA
The Johns Hopkins University, MD
Johnson C. Smith University, NC
Judson College, AL*
Judson College, IL*
Kalamazoo College, MI*
Kean University, NJ*
Kent State University, OH
Kentucky Wesleyan College, KY*
King's College, PA
Kutztown University of Pennsylvania, PA*
La Roche College, PA*
Lawrence Technological University, MI*
Lehigh University, PA
Lehman College of the City University of New York, NY*
Le Moyne College, NY*
LeMoyne-Owen College, TN*
Lewis-Clark State College, ID
Limestone College, SC*
Lincoln University, PA*
Lindenwood University, MO
Lipscomb University, TN*
Lock Haven University of Pennsylvania, PA
Longwood University, VA
Loras College, IA*
Louisiana State University and Agricultural and Mechanical College, LA
Louisiana Tech University, LA*
Lourdes College, OH*
Loyola College in Maryland, MD
Loyola University Chicago, IL*
Loyola University New Orleans, LA*
Lubbock Christian University, TX*
Lycoming College, PA*
Maine Maritime Academy, ME
Malone College, OH*
Manhattan Christian College, KS*
Manhattan College, NY*
Maranatha Baptist Bible College, WI
Marian College of Fond du Lac, WI
Marist College, NY
Marquette University, WI
Mary Baldwin College, VA
Marymount University, VA*
Maryville University of Saint Louis, MO*
Marywood University, PA*
Massachusetts Institute of Technology, MA
Mayville State University, ND*
McDaniel College, MD
McKendree College, IL*
Medaille College, NY*
Menlo College, CA*
Mercer University, GA
Meredith College, NC*
Methodist University, NC
Metropolitan State College of Denver, CO*
Miami University, OH*
Michigan State University, MI
Michigan Technological University, MI
Middlebury College, VT*
Middle Tennessee State University, TN
Millersville University of Pennsylvania, PA
Milligan College, TN*
Millsaps College, MS*
Milwaukee School of Engineering, WI*
Minnesota State University Mankato, MN
Mississippi State University, MS
Missouri Baptist University, MO*
Missouri State University, MO
Missouri Valley College, MO
Molloy College, NY*
Montana State University, MT
Montana Tech of The University of Montana, MT
Moravian College, PA*
Morehead State University, KY
Morningside College, IA*
Mount Holyoke College, MA*
Mount Marty College, SD*
Mount Mary College, WI*
Mount St. Mary's University, MD*
Mount Union College, OH*
Murray State University, KY*
National University, CA*
Nazareth College of Rochester, NY*
Nebraska Methodist College, NE*
Nebraska Wesleyan University, NE*
Neumann College, PA*
New England College, NH*
New England School of Communications, ME*
New Mexico State University, NM
New York Institute of Technology, NY
New York University, NY*

Niagara University, NY
Nichols College, MA*
North Carolina Agricultural and Technical State University, NC
North Carolina State University, NC
North Central College, IL*
North Dakota State University, ND
Northeastern Illinois University, IL*
Northeastern State University, OK
Northeastern University, MA
Northern Arizona University, AZ
Northern Illinois University, IL
Northern Michigan University, MI
North Georgia College & State University, GA
North Greenville University, SC*
Northwest Christian College, OR*
Northwestern College, MN*
Northwestern State University of Louisiana, LA
Northwest Nazarene University, ID
Northwest University, WA*
The Ohio State University, OH
Ohio University, OH
Ohio University–Chillicothe, OH*
Ohio University–Lancaster, OH*
Ohio Wesleyan University, OH*
Oklahoma State University, OK
Oregon Health & Science University, OR*
Oregon State University, OR
Ouachita Baptist University, AR
Pacific Lutheran University, WA
Penn State Abington, PA*
Penn State Altoona, PA
Penn State Berks, PA*
Penn State Erie, The Behrend College, PA*
Penn State Harrisburg, PA*
Penn State University Park, PA
Pennsylvania College of Technology, PA*
Pfeiffer University, NC*
Pittsburg State University, KS
Pitzer College, CA*
Point Loma Nazarene University, CA*
Polytechnic University, Brooklyn Campus, NY*
Pomona College, CA*
Portland State University, OR
Princeton University, NJ
Providence College, RI
Purdue University, IN
Quinnipiac University, CT*
Radford University, VA
Regis University, CO*
Rensselaer Polytechnic Institute, NY*
Rhodes College, TN*
Rice University, TX*
Ripon College, WI
Robert Morris University, PA
Roberts Wesleyan College, NY*
Rochester Institute of Technology, NY
Rockhurst University, MO*
Rose-Hulman Institute of Technology, IN
Rosemont College, PA*
Rowan University, NJ*
Russell Sage College, NY*
Rutgers, The State University of New Jersey, Camden, NJ*
Rutgers, The State University of New Jersey, Newark, NJ
Rutgers, The State University of New Jersey, New Brunswick, NJ
Sacred Heart University, CT
Saint Anselm College, NH*
St. Cloud State University, MN
St. Edward's University, TX*
St. Francis College, NY*
Saint Francis University, PA*
St. John Fisher College, NY*
Saint John's University, MN
Saint Joseph's College of Maine, ME*
St. Joseph's College, Suffolk Campus, NY*
St. Lawrence University, NY*
Saint Leo University, FL*
Saint Louis University, MO*
Saint Mary-of-the-Woods College, IN*
Saint Mary's College, IN*
Saint Mary's College of California, CA*
Saint Mary's University of Minnesota, MN*
Saint Michael's College, VT*
St. Norbert College, WI
Salisbury University, MD*
Salve Regina University, RI*
Samford University, AL*
Sam Houston State University, TX
San Diego State University, CA
San Francisco State University, CA*
San Jose State University, CA
Santa Clara University, CA
Scripps College, CA*
Seattle Pacific University, WA*
Seattle University, WA
Seton Hill University, PA*
Shaw University, NC*
Shippensburg University of Pennsylvania, PA
Simmons College, MA*
Slippery Rock University of Pennsylvania, PA
Smith College, MA*
Sonoma State University, CA*
South Dakota State University, SD
Southeastern Louisiana University, LA*
Southeastern University, FL*
Southern Connecticut State University, CT*
Southern Illinois University Carbondale, IL
Southern Illinois University Edwardsville, IL
Southern Methodist University, TX
Southern Nazarene University, OK*
Southern New Hampshire University, NH*
Southern Polytechnic State University, GA*
Southern Utah University, UT
Southern Wesleyan University, SC*
Southwest Baptist University, MO*
Spelman College, GA
Spring Arbor University, MI
Spring Hill College, AL*
Stanford University, CA*
State University of New York at Oswego, NY*
State University of New York College at Geneseo, NY*
State University of New York College at Old Westbury, NY*
State University of New York College at Potsdam, NY*
State University of New York College of Environmental Science and Forestry, NY*
Stephen F. Austin State University, TX
Stephens College, MO*
Stetson University, FL*
Stonehill College, MA
Stony Brook University, State University of New York, NY*
Suffolk University, MA*
Swarthmore College, PA*
Syracuse University, NY
Tarleton State University, TX
Temple University, PA
Tennessee State University, TN*
Tennessee Technological University, TN
Texas A&M University–Corpus Christi, TX
Texas A&M University–Kingsville, TX
Texas Christian University, TX
Texas Lutheran University, TX*
Texas State University-San Marcos, TX
Texas Tech University, TX
Texas Woman's University, TX*
Thomas More College, KY*
Tiffin University, OH*
Towson University, MD*
Transylvania University, KY*
Trevecca Nazarene University, TN*
Trinity College, CT*
Troy University, AL
Tufts University, MA*
Tulane University, LA
Tuskegee University, AL
Union College, KY*
Union College, NY*
Unity College, ME*
University at Albany, State University of New York, NY
University at Buffalo, the State University of New York, NY*
The University of Akron, OH
The University of Alabama, AL
The University of Alabama at Birmingham, AL
The University of Alabama in Huntsville, AL*
University of Alaska Fairbanks, AK
The University of Arizona, AZ
University of Arkansas, AR
University of Arkansas at Monticello, AR
University of Arkansas for Medical Sciences, AR*
University of Bridgeport, CT
University of California, Berkeley, CA
University of California, Irvine, CA*
University of California, Los Angeles, CA
University of California, Riverside, CA*
University of California, San Diego, CA*
University of California, Santa Barbara, CA
University of California, Santa Cruz, CA*
University of Central Florida, FL
University of Central Missouri, MO
University of Central Oklahoma, OK
University of Charleston, WV
University of Colorado at Boulder, CO
University of Connecticut, CT
University of Dallas, TX*
University of Dayton, OH
University of Delaware, DE
University of Denver, CO*

**program is offered at another college's campus*

The University of Findlay, OH*
University of Florida, FL
University of Georgia, GA
University of Hartford, CT*
University of Hawaii at Manoa, HI
University of Idaho, ID
University of Illinois at Chicago, IL
University of Illinois at Urbana–Champaign, IL
The University of Iowa, IA
University of Kansas, KS
University of La Verne, CA*
University of Louisiana at Lafayette, LA
University of Louisville, KY
University of Maine, ME
University of Maryland, Baltimore County, MD*
University of Maryland, College Park, MD
University of Massachusetts Amherst, MA
University of Massachusetts Dartmouth, MA*
University of Miami, FL
University of Michigan, MI
University of Michigan–Dearborn, MI*
University of Minnesota, Twin Cities Campus, MN
University of Missouri–Columbia, MO
University of Missouri–Kansas City, MO
University of Missouri–St. Louis, MO*
The University of Montana, MT
University of Nebraska at Omaha, NE*
University of Nebraska Medical Center, NE*
University of New England, ME*
University of New Hampshire, NH
University of New Hampshire at Manchester, NH*
University of New Orleans, LA*
University of North Alabama, AL
The University of North Carolina at Chapel Hill, NC
The University of North Carolina at Charlotte, NC
The University of North Carolina at Greensboro, NC*
The University of North Carolina at Pembroke, NC
University of North Dakota, ND
University of Northern Colorado, CO
University of Northern Iowa, IA
University of Notre Dame, IN
University of Oklahoma, OK
University of Oregon, OR
University of Pennsylvania, PA*
University of Pittsburgh, PA
University of Pittsburgh at Bradford, PA*
University of Pittsburgh at Greensburg, PA*
University of Puget Sound, WA*
University of Redlands, CA*
University of Rhode Island, RI
University of Richmond, VA
University of Rochester, NY*
University of St. Thomas, MN*
University of St. Thomas, TX*
University of San Diego, CA*
University of San Francisco, CA
University of South Carolina, SC
University of South Carolina Upstate, SC*
The University of South Dakota, SD
University of Southern California, CA
University of Southern Indiana, IN
University of Southern Maine, ME*
University of Southern Mississippi, MS
University of South Florida, FL
The University of Tampa, FL
The University of Tennessee at Martin, TN
The University of Texas at Austin, TX
The University of Texas at Dallas, TX*
The University of Texas at El Paso, TX
The University of Texas at San Antonio, TX
The University of Texas Health Science Center at Houston, TX*
The University of Texas–Pan American, TX
University of the Cumberlands, KY
University of the Incarnate Word, TX*
University of the Sciences in Philadelphia, PA*
University of the Virgin Islands, VI
University of Vermont, VT
University of Virginia, VA
University of Washington, WA
The University of West Alabama, AL*
University of West Florida, FL
University of West Georgia, GA
University of Wisconsin–Green Bay, WI*
University of Wisconsin–La Crosse, WI
University of Wisconsin–Madison, WI
University of Wisconsin–Milwaukee, WI*
University of Wisconsin–Stevens Point, WI
University of Wisconsin–Whitewater, WI
University of Wyoming, WY
Utah State University, UT
Vanderbilt University, TN
Vermont Technical College, VT*
Villa Julie College, MD*
Virginia Commonwealth University, VA*
Virginia Military Institute, VA
Virginia Polytechnic Institute and State University, VA
Virginia State University, VA
Virginia Union University, VA*
Virginia Wesleyan College, VA*
Wagner College, NY*
Wake Forest University, NC
Warner Pacific College, OR*
Washington & Jefferson College, PA*
Washington and Lee University, VA*
Washington State University, WA
Washington University in St. Louis, MO
Wayland Baptist University, TX*
Waynesburg College, PA*
Wayne State College, NE
Webster University, MO*
Wellesley College, MA*
Wells College, NY*
Wentworth Institute of Technology, MA*
Wesley College, DE*
Western Connecticut State University, CT*
Western Illinois University, IL
Western New England College, MA
Western Oregon University, OR
Westfield State College, MA*
Westminster College, MO*
Westminster College, PA*
Westminster College, UT*
Westmont College, CA*
West Virginia University, WV
Wheaton College, IL
Wheaton College, MA*
Whitworth University, WA*
Widener University, PA
Wilkes University, PA*
William Carey College, MS*
Williams Baptist College, AR*
Wilson College, PA*
Wingate University, NC*
Winona State University, MN*
Winston-Salem State University, NC
Winthrop University, SC*
Wisconsin Lutheran College, WI*
Wittenberg University, OH*
Worcester Polytechnic Institute, MA
Xavier University, OH
Yale University, CT*
York College of Pennsylvania, PA*
Youngstown State University, OH

Naval

Armstrong Atlantic State University, GA*
Auburn University, AL
Augsburg College, MN*
Babson College, MA*
Becker College, MA*
Belmont University, TN*
Boston College, MA*
Boston University, MA
Brigham Young University–Hawaii, HI*
The Catholic University of America, DC*
Chatham University, PA*
Christian Brothers University, TN*
Clark University, MA*
Cleveland State University, OH*
College of the Holy Cross, MA
Columbia College, MO*
Concordia University, St. Paul, MN*
Duke University, NC
Duquesne University, PA*
Eastern Michigan University, MI*
Embry-Riddle Aeronautical University, FL
Emory University, GA*
Florida State University, FL*
George Mason University, VA*
Georgetown University, DC*
The George Washington University, DC
Georgia Institute of Technology, GA
Guilford College, NC*
Harvard University, MA*
Husson College, ME*
Illinois Institute of Technology, IL
Indiana University–Purdue University Indianapolis, IN*
Indiana University South Bend, IN*
Indiana University Southeast, IN
Lawrence Technological University, MI*
Louisiana State University and Agricultural and Mechanical College, LA*
Louisiana Tech University, LA
Loyola University Chicago, IL*
Loyola University New Orleans, LA*
Maine Maritime Academy, ME
Marquette University, WI
Mary Baldwin College, VA*
Massachusetts Institute of Technology, MA
Miami University, OH
Milwaukee School of Engineering, WI*
Molloy College, NY*
New York University, NY*

ROTC Programs

Naval

North Carolina State University, NC
Northeastern University, MA*
The Ohio State University, OH
Oregon State University, OR
Penn State University Park, PA
Point Loma Nazarene University, CA*
Purdue University, IN
Rensselaer Polytechnic Institute, NY
Rice University, TX
Rochester Institute of Technology, NY*
Saint Mary's College, IN*
San Diego State University, CA
San Francisco State University, CA*
Seattle Pacific University, WA*
Southern Polytechnic State University, GA*
Spelman College, GA
Stanford University, CA*
Temple University, PA*
Tennessee State University, TN*
Texas A&M University at Galveston, TX
Tufts University, MA*
Tulane University, LA
Union College, NY*
The University of Arizona, AZ
University of California, Berkeley, CA
University of California, Los Angeles, CA
University of California, Santa Cruz, CA*
University of Colorado at Boulder, CO
University of Idaho, ID
University of Illinois at Chicago, IL*
University of Illinois at Urbana–Champaign, IL
University of Kansas, KS
University of Maine, ME
University of Maryland, College Park, MD*
University of Michigan–Dearborn, MI*
University of Minnesota, Twin Cities Campus, MN
University of Missouri–Columbia, MO
University of New Orleans, LA*
The University of North Carolina at Chapel Hill, NC
University of North Florida, FL*
University of Notre Dame, IN
University of Oklahoma, OK
University of Pennsylvania, PA
University of Pittsburgh, PA*
University of Rochester, NY
University of St. Thomas, MN*
University of San Diego, CA
University of South Carolina, SC
University of Southern California, CA
University of South Florida, FL
The University of Texas at Austin, TX
University of Virginia, VA
University of Washington, WA
University of Wisconsin–Madison, WI
Vanderbilt University, TN
Virginia Military Institute, VA
Virginia Polytechnic Institute and State University, VA
Washington State University, WA*
Westminster College, UT*
Widener University, PA*
Wisconsin Lutheran College, WI*
Worcester Polytechnic Institute, MA*

**program is offered at another college's campus*

Tuition Waivers

Adult Students

Albertson College of Idaho, ID
Augustana College, SD
Barton College, NC
California State University, Stanislaus, CA
Clarke College, IA
Concord University, WV
Converse College, SC
Coppin State University, MD
Cornell College, IA
Creighton University, NE
Dowling College, NY
Eureka College, IL
Goucher College, MD
Hastings College, NE
Hood College, MD
Juniata College, PA
Marquette University, WI
Medaille College, NY
Messiah College, PA
Mount Union College, OH
Nebraska Wesleyan University, NE
New England College, NH
Randolph College, VA
St. Ambrose University, IA
St. Andrews Presbyterian College, NC
St. Olaf College, MN
Simmons College, MA
Southern Adventist University, TN
Sweet Briar College, VA
Trinity College, CT
Utah State University, UT
Webber International University, FL
Wittenberg University, OH

Children of Alumni

Albertson College of Idaho, ID
Albion College, MI
Albright College, PA
Alliant International University, CA
Arkansas State University, AR
Augsburg College, MN
Baldwin-Wallace College, OH
Barton College, NC
Bethel College, KS
Cabrini College, PA
Canisius College, NY
Carthage College, WI
Central Michigan University, MI
Centre College, KY
Christian Brothers University, TN
Clarke College, IA
College of Saint Elizabeth, NJ
The College of St. Scholastica, MN
Columbia College, MO
Concordia University, IL
Coppin State University, MD
Dana College, NE
Dickinson State University, ND
Dominican University, IL
Dowling College, NY
Drake University, IA
Drury University, MO
D'Youville College, NY
Erskine College, SC
Eureka College, IL
Georgetown College, KY
Grace University, NE
Hilbert College, NY
Hillsdale College, MI
Hood College, MD
Jackson State University, MS
Kentucky Wesleyan College, KY
Lake Superior State University, MI
Lancaster Bible College, PA
Louisiana State University and Agricultural and Mechanical College, LA
Louisiana Tech University, LA
MacMurray College, IL
Marymount University, VA
Messiah College, PA
Michigan Technological University, MI
Minot State University, ND
Mississippi State University, MS
Missouri Baptist University, MO
Missouri State University, MO
Missouri Valley College, MO
Moravian College, PA
Morehead State University, KY
Morningside College, IA
Mount Union College, OH
Murray State University, KY
Nazareth College of Rochester, NY
New England College, NH
North Dakota State University, ND
Northwestern College, MN
Northwood University, MI
Northwood University, Florida Campus, FL
Northwood University, Texas Campus, TX
Ohio Wesleyan University, OH
Oklahoma State University, OK
Oral Roberts University, OK
Peirce College, PA
Philadelphia Biblical University, PA
Ripon College, WI
Roanoke Bible College, NC
Rockhurst University, MO
St. Ambrose University, IA
Saint Joseph's College, IN
South Dakota State University, SD
Taylor University Fort Wayne, IN
Texas Lutheran University, TX
Thomas More College, KY
University of Central Missouri, MO
University of Detroit Mercy, MI
University of Evansville, IN
The University of Findlay, OH
University of Idaho, ID
University of Louisiana at Lafayette, LA
University of New England, ME
University of Saint Francis, IN
The University of South Dakota, SD
University of Southern Mississippi, MS
University of Wisconsin–Stevens Point, WI
University of Wisconsin–Whitewater, WI
University of Wyoming, WY
Utah State University, UT
Valley City State University, ND
Washington State University, WA
Webber International University, FL
Westminster College, MO
Wittenberg University, OH

Minority Students

Assumption College, MA
Bloomsburg University of Pennsylvania, PA
Bridgewater College, VA
Concordia University, IL
Coppin State University, MD
Dickinson State University, ND
Dowling College, NY
Fort Lewis College, CO
Illinois State University, IL
Indiana University of Pennsylvania, PA
Lake Superior State University, MI
Lipscomb University, TN
Lock Haven University of Pennsylvania, PA
MacMurray College, IL
Mayville State University, ND
Messiah College, PA
Minot State University, ND
Montana State University, MT
Montana State University–Billings, MT
Nazareth College of Rochester, NY
North Dakota State University, ND
Northern Illinois University, IL
Portland State University, OR
St. Ambrose University, IA
Saint Joseph's College, IN
Shepherd University, WV
Slippery Rock University of Pennsylvania, PA
State University of New York College at Potsdam, NY
Tennessee State University, TN
University at Buffalo, the State University of New York, NY
University of Evansville, IN
University of Hawaii at Manoa, HI
University of Idaho, ID
University of Maine at Farmington, ME
University of Michigan–Flint, MI
The University of Montana, MT
University of North Dakota, ND
University of Rhode Island, RI
University of Southern Maine, ME
University of Wisconsin–La Crosse, WI

Utah State University, UT
Washington College, MD
Wayne State College, NE
Wittenberg University, OH

Senior Citizens

Adams State College, CO
Albertson College of Idaho, ID
Albright College, PA
Andrews University, MI
Arkansas State University, AR
Arkansas Tech University, AR
Armstrong Atlantic State University, GA
Asbury College, KY
Augsburg College, MN
Augustana College, SD
Augusta State University, GA
Aurora University, IL
Austin Peay State University, TN
Averett University, VA
Baker University, KS
Barton College, NC
Becker College, MA
Belmont Abbey College, NC
Belmont University, TN
Bemidji State University, MN
Berry College, GA
Bethel College, KS
Black Hills State University, SD
Bloomfield College, NJ
Bloomsburg University of Pennsylvania, PA
Boise State University, ID
Boston University, MA
Bowie State University, MD
Bowling Green State University, OH
Bradley University, IL
Brevard College, NC
Bridgewater College, VA
Cabrini College, PA
California State University, Chico, CA
California State University, Fullerton, CA
California State University, Los Angeles, CA
California State University, Northridge, CA
California State University, Sacramento, CA
California State University, Stanislaus, CA
Campbellsville University, KY
Capital University, OH
Cedarville University, OH
Central Michigan University, MI
Central State University, OH
Central Washington University, WA
Christopher Newport University, VA
City College of the City University of New York, NY
Clarke College, IA
Cleary University, MI
Clemson University, SC
Cleveland State University, OH
Coastal Carolina University, SC
College of Charleston, SC
The College of New Jersey, NJ
The College of New Rochelle, NY
College of St. Catherine, MN
College of Saint Elizabeth, NJ
College of St. Joseph, VT
College of Saint Mary, NE
The College of St. Scholastica, MN
College of Staten Island of the City University of New York, NY
The College of William and Mary, VA
Columbus State University, GA
Concordia University, IL
Concord University, WV
Connecticut College, CT
Converse College, SC
Coppin State University, MD
Cornell College, IA
Culver-Stockton College, MO
Dakota State University, SD
Dakota Wesleyan University, SD
DeSales University, PA
Dickinson State University, ND
Doane College, NE
Dominican College, NY
Dordt College, IA
Dowling College, NY
Drake University, IA
Drew University, NJ
Drury University, MO
Duquesne University, PA
D'Youville College, NY
East Central University, OK
Eastern Kentucky University, KY
East Tennessee State University, TN
Elmhurst College, IL
Emporia State University, KS
Eureka College, IL
Fitchburg State College, MA
Florida Atlantic University, FL
Florida Gulf Coast University, FL
Florida Institute of Technology, FL
Florida State University, FL
Framingham State College, MA
Francis Marion University, SC
Franklin College, IN
Freed-Hardeman University, TN
Fresno Pacific University, CA
Gannon University, PA
Gardner-Webb University, NC
George Fox University, OR
George Mason University, VA
Georgia College & State University, GA
Georgia Southern University, GA
Glenville State College, WV
Goucher College, MD
Grace University, NE
Grand View College, IA
Hanover College, IN
Harding University, AR
Hilbert College, NY
Hofstra University, NY
Houghton College, NY
Husson College, ME
Idaho State University, ID
Illinois State University, IL
Indiana State University, IN
Indiana University Northwest, IN
Iona College, NY
James Madison University, VA
Judson College, IL
Kean University, NJ
Keene State College, NH
Kent State University, OH
Kentucky Wesleyan College, KY
King College, TN
King's College, PA
Kutztown University of Pennsylvania, PA
Lake Superior State University, MI
Lancaster Bible College, PA
La Roche College, PA
Lebanon Valley College, PA
Lehigh University, PA
Lewis-Clark State College, ID
Lindenwood University, MO
Linfield College, OR
Lock Haven University of Pennsylvania, PA
Longwood University, VA
Loras College, IA
Louisiana Tech University, LA
Lourdes College, OH
Loyola University New Orleans, LA
MacMurray College, IL
Macon State College, GA
Malone College, OH
Mansfield University of Pennsylvania, PA
Marian College of Fond du Lac, WI
Marquette University, WI
Martin University, IN
Marymount University, VA
Maryville University of Saint Louis, MO
Marywood University, PA
Mayville State University, ND
Medaille College, NY
Messiah College, PA
Metropolitan State College of Denver, CO
Michigan Technological University, MI
Middle Tennessee State University, TN
Midwestern State University, TX
Minnesota State University Mankato, MN
Mississippi State University, MS
Missouri Baptist University, MO
Missouri State University, MO
Missouri Valley College, MO
Monmouth University, NJ
Montana State University, MT
Montana State University–Billings, MT
Montclair State University, NJ
Morehead State University, KY
Morningside College, IA
Mountain State University, WV
Mount Mary College, WI
Mount Vernon Nazarene University, OH
Murray State University, KY
Nebraska Wesleyan University, NE
New England College, NH
New Jersey City University, NJ
New Mexico State University, NM
New York Institute of Technology, NY
Niagara University, NY
Nichols College, MA
North Carolina Agricultural and Technical State University, NC
North Carolina State University, NC
North Central College, IL
North Dakota State University, ND
Northeastern State University, OK
Northeastern University, MA
Northern Michigan University, MI
North Georgia College & State University, GA
Northwestern College, MN
Northwestern Oklahoma State University, OK
Northwestern State University of Louisiana, LA
The Ohio State University, OH
Ohio University–Zanesville, OH

Ohio Valley University, WV
Oklahoma Baptist University, OK
Pacific Union College, CA
Penn State Abington, PA
Penn State Altoona, PA
Penn State Berks, PA
Penn State Erie, The Behrend College, PA
Penn State Harrisburg, PA
Pikeville College, KY
Point Loma Nazarene University, CA
Portland State University, OR
Providence College, RI
Purdue University Calumet, IN
Radford University, VA
Ramapo College of New Jersey, NJ
Reinhardt College, GA
The Richard Stockton College of New Jersey, NJ
Roanoke College, VA
Rockhurst University, MO
Rosemont College, PA
St. Ambrose University, IA
St. Andrews Presbyterian College, NC
St. Cloud State University, MN
St. Gregory's University, OK
St. Joseph's College, Suffolk Campus, NY
St. Olaf College, MN
Saint Vincent College, PA
Saint Xavier University, IL
Salisbury University, MD
San Francisco State University, CA
Seattle Pacific University, WA
Shasta Bible College, CA
Shepherd University, WV
Shippensburg University of Pennsylvania, PA
Simmons College, MA
Slippery Rock University of Pennsylvania, PA
South Dakota State University, SD
Southeastern Louisiana University, LA
Southeast Missouri State University, MO
Southern Adventist University, TN
Southern Illinois University Carbondale, IL
Southern Illinois University Edwardsville, IL
Southern Polytechnic State University, GA
Southern Wesleyan University, SC
Spring Arbor University, MI
State University of New York College at Old Westbury, NY
Sterling College, VT
Suffolk University, MA
Sweet Briar College, VA
Tarleton State University, TX
Taylor University, IN
Taylor University Fort Wayne, IN
Tennessee State University, TN
Texas A&M University–Commerce, TX
Texas Tech University, TX
Thiel College, PA
Trevecca Nazarene University, TN
Union College, KY
Union College, NY
University at Albany, State University of New York, NY
The University of Akron, OH
University of Arkansas, AR
University of Arkansas at Monticello, AR
University of Bridgeport, CT
University of Central Florida, FL
University of Central Missouri, MO
University of Charleston, WV
University of Colorado at Boulder, CO
University of Connecticut, CT
University of Dayton, OH
University of Delaware, DE
University of Evansville, IN
The University of Findlay, OH
University of Florida, FL
University of Georgia, GA
University of Great Falls, MT
University of Hartford, CT
University of Houston–Victoria, TX
University of Idaho, ID
University of Illinois at Chicago, IL
University of Illinois at Springfield, IL
University of Illinois at Urbana–Champaign, IL
University of Louisiana at Lafayette, LA
University of Louisville, KY
University of Maine at Farmington, ME
University of Maryland University College, MD
University of Massachusetts Amherst, MA
University of Massachusetts Boston, MA
University of Massachusetts Dartmouth, MA
University of Massachusetts Lowell, MA
University of Michigan, MI
University of Michigan–Dearborn, MI
University of Michigan–Flint, MI
University of Minnesota, Crookston, MN
University of Minnesota, Twin Cities Campus, MN
University of Missouri–Columbia, MO
University of Missouri–St. Louis, MO
The University of Montana, MT
University of New Hampshire at Manchester, NH
University of New Orleans, LA
University of North Alabama, AL
The University of North Carolina at Asheville, NC
The University of North Carolina at Chapel Hill, NC
The University of North Carolina at Charlotte, NC
The University of North Carolina at Pembroke, NC
The University of North Carolina Wilmington, NC
University of North Dakota, ND
University of North Florida, FL
University of Oklahoma, OK
University of Pittsburgh at Greensburg, PA
University of Rhode Island, RI
University of Saint Francis, IN
University of St. Thomas, MN
University of St. Thomas, TX
University of Science and Arts of Oklahoma, OK
University of South Carolina, SC
University of South Carolina Upstate, SC
The University of South Dakota, SD
University of Southern Mississippi, MS
University of South Florida, FL
The University of Tennessee at Martin, TN
The University of Texas at Austin, TX
The University of Texas at Dallas, TX
The University of Texas at Tyler, TX
The University of Texas–Pan American, TX
University of the Incarnate Word, TX
University of the Virgin Islands, VI
University of Vermont, VT
University of Virginia, VA
University of Washington, WA
University of West Florida, FL
University of West Georgia, GA
University of Wisconsin–Milwaukee, WI
University of Wisconsin–Stevens Point, WI
University of Wisconsin–Whitewater, WI
University of Wyoming, WY
Ursinus College, PA
Utah State University, UT
Valdosta State University, GA
Virginia Commonwealth University, VA
Virginia Intermont College, VA
Virginia Polytechnic Institute and State University, VA
Virginia State University, VA
Virginia Wesleyan College, VA
Wartburg College, IA
Wayne State University, MI
Webber International University, FL
Wesley College, DE
Western Carolina University, NC
Western Connecticut State University, CT
Western Illinois University, IL
Western New England College, MA
West Liberty State College, WV
West Virginia University, WV
Wichita State University, KS
Widener University, PA
William Paterson University of New Jersey, NJ
Williams Baptist College, AR
Winston-Salem State University, NC
Winthrop University, SC
Wittenberg University, OH
Xavier University, OH
Youngstown State University, OH

Tuition Payment Alternatives

Institution	Option
Abilene Christian University, TX	I,P
Adams State College, CO	D,I
Adelphi University, NY	D,I
Agnes Scott College, GA	I
Alabama State University, AL	D
Albion College, MI	D,I,P
Albright College, PA	I
Alderson-Broaddus College, WV	I
Alfred University, NY	D,I,P
Allegheny College, PA	I,P
Alliant International University, CA	I
Alma College, MI	D,I
Alverno College, WI	D,I
Amherst College, MA	D,I
Anderson University, SC	I
Andrews University, MI	I
Antioch College, OH	I
Antioch University Seattle, WA	I
Appalachian State University, NC	D,I
Arcadia University, PA	D,I
Arizona State University, AZ	I
Arizona State University at the Polytechnic Campus, AZ	I
Arkansas State University, AR	I
Arkansas Tech University, AR	D,I
Arlington Baptist College, TX	I
Armstrong Atlantic State University, GA	G
Asbury College, KY	D,I
Assumption College, MA	I
Auburn University Montgomery, AL	D
Augsburg College, MN	I
Augustana College, IL	I,P
Augustana College, SD	I
Augusta State University, GA	G
Aurora University, IL	D,I
Austin College, TX	I
Austin Graduate School of Theology, TX	I
Austin Peay State University, TN	I
Averett University, VA	I
Azusa Pacific University, CA	I
Babson College, MA	I
Baker University, KS	I
Baldwin-Wallace College, OH	D,I
Baptist Bible College, MO	I
The Baptist College of Florida, FL	I
Barnard College, NY	D,I
Barton College, NC	I
Baylor University, TX	I
Becker College, MA	I
Bellin College of Nursing, WI	I
Belmont Abbey College, NC	D,I
Belmont University, TN	D,I
Beloit College, WI	I
Bemidji State University, MN	I
Benedictine University, IL	D,I
Bennington College, VT	I
Bentley College, MA	I
Berklee College of Music, MA	I,P
Berry College, GA	I
Bethany Lutheran College, MN	I
Bethel College, KS	D,I
Birmingham-Southern College, AL	I
Black Hills State University, SD	D,I
Blessing-Rieman College of Nursing, IL	I
Bloomfield College, NJ	D,I
Bloomsburg University of Pennsylvania, PA	I
Blue Mountain College, MS	I
Bluffton University, OH	I
Boise State University, ID	D
Boston College, MA	I,P
Boston University, MA	I,P
Bowdoin College, ME	D,I
Bowie State University, MD	D,I
Bowling Green State University, OH	I
Bradley University, IL	I
Brandeis University, MA	I
Brenau University, GA	I
Brevard College, NC	I
Bridgewater College, VA	I
Bridgewater State College, MA	I
Brigham Young University, UT	D
Brigham Young University–Hawaii, HI	I
Bryan College, TN	I
Bryant University, RI	I
Bucknell University, PA	I
Butler University, IN	I
Cabrini College, PA	I
California College of the Arts, CA	D,I
California Institute of Technology, CA	D,I
California Institute of the Arts, CA	D
California Polytechnic State University, San Luis Obispo, CA	I
California State University, Chico, CA	D,I
California State University, Fullerton, CA	D,I
California State University, Los Angeles, CA	I
California State University, Sacramento, CA	I
California State University, Stanislaus, CA	D,I
California University of Pennsylvania, PA	I
Calvin College, MI	I,P
Campbellsville University, KY	I
Canisius College, NY	D,I,P
Capital University, OH	I
Carroll College, WI	I
Carthage College, WI	I
Case Western Reserve University, OH	I
Catawba College, NC	I
The Catholic University of America, DC	I,P
Cazenovia College, NY	I
Cedarville University, OH	I
Central College, IA	I
Central Methodist University, MO	I
Central Michigan University, MI	I
Central Pennsylvania College, PA	D
Central State University, OH	D,I
Central Washington University, WA	I
Centre College, KY	I
Champlain College, VT	I
Chapman University, CA	D,I,P
Chatham University, PA	I
Chester College of New England, NH	I
Christendom College, VA	I,P
Christian Brothers University, TN	D,I
Christopher Newport University, VA	I
City College of the City University of New York, NY	D
Claflin University, SC	I
Claremont McKenna College, CA	I,P
Clarke College, IA	D,I
Clarkson University, NY	I,P
Clark University, MA	I,P
Cleary University, MI	D,G,I
Clemson University, SC	I
Cleveland Institute of Music, OH	I
Cleveland State University, OH	I
Coastal Carolina University, SC	D,I
Cogswell Polytechnical College, CA	D
Colgate University, NY	D,I,P
College Misericordia, PA	D,I
College of Charleston, SC	I
The College of New Jersey, NJ	I
The College of New Rochelle, NY	I
College of Saint Elizabeth, NJ	I
College of St. Joseph, VT	I
College of Saint Mary, NE	D,I
The College of Saint Rose, NY	D
The College of St. Scholastica, MN	I
College of Staten Island of the City University of New York, NY	I
College of the Holy Cross, MA	I,P
College of the Ozarks, MO	I
College of the Southwest, NM	D
College of Visual Arts, MN	I
The College of William and Mary, VA	I
The College of Wooster, OH	I
The Colorado College, CO	I
Colorado School of Mines, CO	I
Colorado State University, CO	I
Columbia College, MO	D
Columbia International University, SC	I
Columbia University, School of General Studies, NY	I,P
Columbus College of Art & Design, OH	D,I
Columbus State University, GA	G
Conception Seminary College, MO	I
Concordia College, MN	I
Concordia University, CA	D,I

D = deferred payment system; G = guaranteed tuition rate; I = installment payments; P = prepayment locks in tuition rate

Institution	Plans
Concordia University, IL	I
Concordia University, NE	I
Concordia University at Austin, TX	I
Concordia University, St. Paul, MN	I
Concordia University Wisconsin, WI	D,G,I
Concord University, WV	I
Connecticut College, CT	I
Converse College, SC	I
Coppin State University, MD	D
Corban College, OR	I
Corcoran College of Art and Design, DC	I
Cornell College, IA	I
Cornell University, NY	I
Creighton University, NE	I
The Culinary Institute of America, NY	I
Culver-Stockton College, MO	I
Cumberland University, TN	D,I
Dakota State University, SD	D,I
Dakota Wesleyan University, SD	I
Dallas Baptist University, TX	I
Dana College, NE	D,I
Daniel Webster College, NH	I
Dartmouth College, NH	P
Davis & Elkins College, WV	I
Denison University, OH	I
DeSales University, PA	D,I
Dickinson College, PA	I
Doane College, NE	I
Dominican College, NY	D,I
Dominican University, IL	I
Dordt College, IA	I
Dowling College, NY	D,I
Drake University, IA	I
Drew University, NJ	D,I,P
Drury University, MO	D,I,P
Duquesne University, PA	I
D'Youville College, NY	D,G,I,P
Eastern Illinois University, IL	I
Eastern Kentucky University, KY	D
Eastern Michigan University, MI	I
East Tennessee State University, TN	D,I
East Texas Baptist University, TX	G,I
Elizabethtown College, PA	I
Elmhurst College, IL	I
Elmira College, NY	I,P
Elon University, NC	I
Embry-Riddle Aeronautical University, AZ	D,I
Embry-Riddle Aeronautical University, FL	D,I
Embry-Riddle Aeronautical University Worldwide, FL	D
Emerson College, MA	I
Emmanuel College, MA	I
Emory & Henry College, VA	I
Emory University, GA	I
Emporia State University, KS	D,I
Endicott College, MA	I
Erskine College, SC	I
Eugene Lang College The New School for Liberal Arts, NY	I
Eureka College, IL	I
Evangel University, MO	I
Excelsior College, NY	I
Fairfield University, CT	I
Ferris State University, MI	D,I
Fitchburg State College, MA	I
Florida Atlantic University, FL	D,I,P
Florida College, FL	I
Florida Institute of Technology, FL	I
Florida Metropolitan University–Pinellas Campus, FL	D,I
Florida State University, FL	I,P
Framingham State College, MA	I
Francis Marion University, SC	I
Franklin & Marshall College, PA	D,I
Franklin College, IN	I
Freed-Hardeman University, TN	I,P
Fresno Pacific University, CA	I
Furman University, SC	I
Gannon University, PA	D,I
Gardner-Webb University, NC	I
George Fox University, OR	I
George Mason University, VA	D,I
Georgetown College, KY	D
Georgetown University, DC	D,I
Georgia College & State University, GA	G
Georgia Institute of Technology, GA	G
Glenville State College, WV	I
Goddard College, VT	I
Gonzaga University, WA	D,I
Goucher College, MD	I,P
Grace Bible College, MI	I
Grace College, IN	I
Grace University, NE	I
Grand Valley State University, MI	D,I
Grand View College, IA	I
Green Mountain College, VT	I
Grinnell College, IA	I,P
Grove City College, PA	I
Guilford College, NC	I
Gustavus Adolphus College, MN	G,I,P
Hamilton College, NY	I
Hampden-Sydney College, VA	I
Hampshire College, MA	I
Hanover College, IN	I
Harding University, AR	I,P
Hardin-Simmons University, TX	D,G,I,P
Harvey Mudd College, CA	I
Hastings College, NE	D,I
Haverford College, PA	I
Hawai'i Pacific University, HI	I
Heidelberg College, OH	D,I
Hendrix College, AR	I
Heritage Bible College, NC	D,I
Hilbert College, NY	D,I
Hillsdale College, MI	D,I,P
Hobart and William Smith Colleges, NY	I,P
Hofstra University, NY	D,I
Holy Names University, CA	I
Hood College, MD	D,I,P
Hope College, MI	I
Houghton College, NY	I
Husson College, ME	I,P
Idaho State University, ID	D
Illinois College, IL	D,I
Illinois Institute of Technology, IL	I
Illinois State University, IL	G,I
Illinois Wesleyan University, IL	I
Indiana State University, IN	D,I
Indiana University Bloomington, IN	D
Indiana University East, IN	D
Indiana University Kokomo, IN	D
Indiana University Northwest, IN	D,I
Indiana University of Pennsylvania, PA	D,I
Indiana University–Purdue University Indianapolis, IN	D,I
Indiana University South Bend, IN	D
Indiana University Southeast, IN	D
Iona College, NY	I
Ithaca College, NY	I
Jackson State University, MS	I
James Madison University, VA	I
Jamestown College, ND	I
Jarvis Christian College, TX	D,I
Johnson Bible College, TN	I
Johnson C. Smith University, NC	I
Judson College, AL	I
Judson College, IL	I
Juniata College, PA	I
Kalamazoo College, MI	I
Kean University, NJ	D,I
Keene State College, NH	I
Kent State University, OH	D,I,P
Kentucky Christian University, KY	I
Kentucky Wesleyan College, KY	D,I
Kenyon College, OH	I
Kettering University, MI	I
Keuka College, NY	I
King College, TN	I
King's College, PA	D,I
Knox College, IL	I
Kutztown University of Pennsylvania, PA	D,I
Kuyper College, MI	I
LaGrange College, GA	I
Lake Forest College, IL	I
Lake Superior State University, MI	D,I
Lamar University, TX	I
Lancaster Bible College, PA	I
La Roche College, PA	I
Lebanon Valley College, PA	I,P
Lee University, TN	D
Lehigh University, PA	I,P
Le Moyne College, NY	D,I
LeMoyne-Owen College, TN	I
Lesley University, MA	I
LeTourneau University, TX	I
Lewis-Clark State College, ID	D
Lexington College, IL	G,I
Limestone College, SC	I
Lincoln Christian College, IL	D,I
Lincoln University, PA	D,I
Lindenwood University, MO	D,I
Linfield College, OR	I
Lipscomb University, TN	D,I
Lock Haven University of Pennsylvania, PA	D,I
Longwood University, VA	I
Loras College, IA	I
Louisiana State University and Agricultural and Mechanical College, LA	D
Louisiana Tech University, LA	D,I
Lourdes College, OH	D,I
Loyola University New Orleans, LA	I
Lubbock Christian University, TX	I
Luther College, IA	I
Lycoming College, PA	I
Lyndon State College, VT	I
MacMurray College, IL	I
Macon State College, GA	G

Institution	Payment
Maine Maritime Academy, ME	I
Malone College, OH	I
Manchester College, IN	I
Mansfield University of Pennsylvania, PA	D,I
Marian College of Fond du Lac, WI	I
Marist College, NY	I
Marquette University, WI	I
Martin Luther College, MN	I
Martin University, IN	I
Mary Baldwin College, VA	I
Marymount University, VA	I
Maryville University of Saint Louis, MO	D
Marywood University, PA	D,I
Massachusetts College of Art, MA	I
Massachusetts College of Pharmacy and Health Sciences, MA	I
Massachusetts Institute of Technology, MA	I
Mayville State University, ND	I
McDaniel College, MD	I
McMurry University, TX	I
Medaille College, NY	I
Medgar Evers College of the City University of New York, NY	D,I
Memphis College of Art, TN	I
Menlo College, CA	I
Mercer University, GA	I
Meredith College, NC	I
Mesa State College, CO	I
Messenger College, MO	I
Messiah College, PA	I
Metropolitan State College of Denver, CO	D,I
Miami University, OH	I
Michigan State University, MI	D
Michigan Technological University, MI	D,I
Middlebury College, VT	P
Middle Tennessee State University, TN	D
Midwestern State University, TX	I
Millersville University of Pennsylvania, PA	I
Milligan College, TN	I
Millsaps College, MS	D,I
Mills College, CA	I
Milwaukee School of Engineering, WI	I
Minnesota State University Mankato, MN	I
Minot State University, ND	I
Missouri Baptist University, MO	I
Missouri State University, MO	D,P
Missouri Valley College, MO	I
Molloy College, NY	I
Monmouth University, NJ	I
Monroe College, NY	I
Montana State University, MT	D,I
Montana State University–Billings, MT	I
Montana Tech of The University of Montana, MT	D,I
Montclair State University, NJ	I
Montreat College, NC	I
Moore College of Art & Design, PA	I
Moravian College, PA	I
Morehead State University, KY	D,I
Morningside College, IA	I
Mountain State University, WV	I
Mount Aloysius College, PA	I
Mount Holyoke College, MA	D,I,P
Mount Ida College, MA	I
Mount Marty College, SD	I
Mount Mary College, WI	I
Mount Mercy College, IA	I
Mount Saint Mary College, NY	I
Mount St. Mary's University, MD	I
Mount Union College, OH	I,P
Mount Vernon Nazarene University, OH	I
Murray State University, KY	I
Naropa University, CO	I
Nazareth College of Rochester, NY	I
Nebraska Wesleyan University, NE	D,I
New College of Florida, FL	D,I,P
New England College, NH	I
New Jersey City University, NJ	D
Newman University, KS	I
New Mexico State University, NM	D,I
The New School for Jazz and Contemporary Music, NY	I
New York Institute of Technology, NY	I
New York School of Interior Design, NY	I
New York University, NY	D,I
Niagara University, NY	D,I
Nicholls State University, LA	D,I
Nichols College, MA	I
North Carolina Agricultural and Technical State University, NC	I
North Carolina School of the Arts, NC	I
North Carolina State University, NC	I
North Central College, IL	I
North Dakota State University, ND	I
Northeastern University, MA	I
Northern Arizona University, AZ	I
Northern Illinois University, IL	I
Northern Michigan University, MI	D,I
Northern State University, SD	I
North Georgia College & State University, GA	G
Northwest Christian College, OR	D,I
Northwestern College, IA	I,P
Northwestern College, MN	I
Northwestern Oklahoma State University, OK	I
Northwestern State University of Louisiana, LA	I
Northwest University, WA	I
Northwood University, MI	I
Northwood University, Florida Campus, FL	I
Northwood University, Texas Campus, TX	I
Nova Southeastern University, FL	D,I
Oberlin College, OH	I
Oglethorpe University, GA	I,P
The Ohio State University, OH	I
Ohio University, OH	I
Ohio University–Zanesville, OH	I
Ohio Valley University, WV	I
Ohio Wesleyan University, OH	I
Oklahoma Baptist University, OK	I
Oklahoma Panhandle State University, OK	I
Oklahoma State University, OK	I
Olivet College, MI	I
Oral Roberts University, OK	I
Oregon State University, OR	D
Ouachita Baptist University, AR	D,G,I,P
Pacific Lutheran University, WA	I
Pacific Oaks College, CA	I
Pacific Union College, CA	G,I
Palm Beach Atlantic University, FL	I
Peabody Conservatory of Music of The Johns Hopkins University, MD	I
Peirce College, PA	I
Penn State Abington, PA	D
Penn State Altoona, PA	D
Penn State Berks, PA	D
Penn State Erie, The Behrend College, PA	D
Penn State Harrisburg, PA	D
Pennsylvania College of Technology, PA	D
Pfeiffer University, NC	I
Philadelphia Biblical University, PA	I
Philadelphia University, PA	D,I
Piedmont College, GA	I
Pikeville College, KY	I
Pittsburg State University, KS	I
Pitzer College, CA	D,I
Point Loma Nazarene University, CA	I
Polytechnic University, Brooklyn Campus, NY	D,G,I
Pomona College, CA	I
Portland State University, OR	I
Princeton University, NJ	D,I
Providence College, RI	I
Purdue University Calumet, IN	D
Quinnipiac University, CT	D,I
Radford University, VA	I
Ramapo College of New Jersey, NJ	I
Randolph College, VA	I
Reed College, OR	I
Regis College, MA	I
Regis University, CO	I
Reinhardt College, GA	I
Rensselaer Polytechnic Institute, NY	I
Rice University, TX	I
The Richard Stockton College of New Jersey, NJ	D,I
Ringling College of Art and Design, FL	I
Ripon College, WI	G,I
Roanoke Bible College, NC	D
Roanoke College, VA	I
Robert Morris University, PA	D,I
Roberts Wesleyan College, NY	I
Rochester Institute of Technology, NY	D,I,P
Rockhurst University, MO	D,I
Rollins College, FL	I
Rose-Hulman Institute of Technology, IN	I,P
Rosemont College, PA	I
Rowan University, NJ	D
Russell Sage College, NY	D,I
Rutgers, The State University of New Jersey, Newark, NJ	I
Rutgers, The State University of New Jersey, New Brunswick, NJ	I
Sacred Heart University, CT	I
Sage College of Albany, NY	D,I
St. Ambrose University, IA	I
St. Andrews Presbyterian College, NC	I
St. Cloud State University, MN	I

D = deferred payment system; G = guaranteed tuition rate; I = installment payments; P = prepayment locks in tuition rate

St. Edward's University, TX D,I
St. Francis College, NY D,I
Saint Francis Medical Center College of Nursing, IL I
Saint Francis University, PA I
St. Gregory's University, OK D,I
St. John Fisher College, NY D,I
St. John's College, MD I
St. John's College, NM I
Saint John's University, MN I,P
Saint Joseph's College, IN I
St. Joseph's College, New York, NY I
Saint Joseph's College of Maine, ME I
St. Joseph's College, Suffolk Campus, NY I
St. Lawrence University, NY D,I
Saint Leo University, FL I
Saint Louis University, MO I
Saint Mary-of-the-Woods College, IN I
Saint Mary's College of California, CA I
Saint Mary's University of Minnesota, MN I
Saint Michael's College, VT I
St. Norbert College, WI D,I
St. Olaf College, MN I
Saint Vincent College, PA I
Saint Xavier University, IL I
Salisbury University, MD I
Salve Regina University, RI I
Sam Houston State University, TX I
San Diego State University, CA I
San Francisco Art Institute, CA D
San Francisco State University, CA I
San Jose State University, CA I
Santa Clara University, CA D,I,P
Sarah Lawrence College, NY I
School of Visual Arts, NY I
Scripps College, CA I
Seattle Pacific University, WA I
Seton Hill University, PA D,I
Sewanee: The University of the South, TN D,I
Shasta Bible College, CA I
Shenandoah University, VA I
Shepherd University, WV I
Shippensburg University of Pennsylvania, PA I
Simmons College, MA I
Simpson College, IA I
Slippery Rock University of Pennsylvania, PA I
Sojourner-Douglass College, MD I
South Dakota State University, SD D,I
Southeastern Louisiana University, LA D,I
Southeastern University, FL I
Southeast Missouri State University, MO D,I
Southern Adventist University, TN D,I,P
Southern Illinois University Carbondale, IL G,I
Southern Illinois University Edwardsville, IL I
Southern Methodist College, SC I
Southern Methodist University, TX I,P
Southern New Hampshire University, NH I
Southern Polytechnic State University, GA G
Southern Utah University, UT I
Southern Vermont College, VT I
Southern Wesleyan University, SC I
Southwest Baptist University, MO I
Southwestern University, TX D,I
Southwest Minnesota State University, MN I
Spelman College, GA D
Spring Arbor University, MI I
Spring Hill College, AL I
State University of New York at Binghamton, NY I
State University of New York at Fredonia, NY I
State University of New York at Oswego, NY I
State University of New York at Plattsburgh, NY D,I
State University of New York College at Geneseo, NY D,I
State University of New York College at Old Westbury, NY I
State University of New York College at Potsdam, NY I
State University of New York College of Agriculture and Technology at Cobleskill, NY I
State University of New York College of Environmental Science and Forestry, NY D,I
Stephen F. Austin State University, TX I
Stephens College, MO I
Sterling College, VT I
Stetson University, FL I
Stonehill College, MA I,P
Stony Brook University, State University of New York, NY I
Suffolk University, MA D,I
Swarthmore College, PA I
Sweet Briar College, VA I
Syracuse University, NY I
Tarleton State University, TX I
Taylor University, IN I
Taylor University Fort Wayne, IN I
Temple University, PA I
Tennessee Technological University, TN I
Tennessee Wesleyan College, TN D,I
Texas A&M University at Galveston, TX I
Texas A&M University–Commerce, TX I
Texas A&M University–Texarkana, TX I
Texas Christian University, TX I
Texas Lutheran University, TX I
Texas State University-San Marcos, TX I
Texas Tech University, TX I
Texas Woman's University, TX I
Thiel College, PA I
Thomas College, ME D
Thomas More College, KY D,I
Thomas More College of Liberal Arts, NH I
Transylvania University, KY I
Trevecca Nazarene University, TN I
Trinity College, CT I
Trinity International University, IL I
Tri-State University, IN I
Troy University, AL I
Tufts University, MA I,P
Tulane University, LA I
Tuskegee University, AL I
Union College, KY I
Union College, NE I
Union College, NY I
Union University, TN D,I
Unity College, ME I
University at Albany, State University of New York, NY I
University at Buffalo, the State University of New York, NY I
The University of Akron, OH I
The University of Alabama, AL D,I
The University of Alabama in Huntsville, AL D
University of Arkansas, AR I
University of Arkansas at Monticello, AR G
University of Bridgeport, CT D,I
University of California, Berkeley, CA I
University of California, Riverside, CA D
University of California, San Diego, CA D,I
University of California, Santa Cruz, CA D,I
University of Central Florida, FL D,P
University of Central Missouri, MO D,I
University of Central Oklahoma, OK D,I
University of Charleston, WV I
University of Colorado at Boulder, CO D
University of Connecticut, CT D,I
University of Dallas, TX I
University of Dayton, OH D
University of Delaware, DE I
University of Denver, CO D
University of Detroit Mercy, MI D,I
University of Evansville, IN I
The University of Findlay, OH I
University of Florida, FL P
University of Great Falls, MT D,I
University of Hartford, CT I,P
University of Houston–Victoria, TX I
University of Idaho, ID D,I
University of Illinois at Chicago, IL G,I
University of Illinois at Springfield, IL G,I
University of Illinois at Urbana–Champaign, IL G
The University of Iowa, IA I
University of Judaism, CA I
University of Kansas, KS I
University of La Verne, CA D,I
University of Louisiana at Lafayette, LA D
University of Louisville, KY I
University of Maine, ME I
University of Maine at Farmington, ME I
University of Maryland, College Park, MD D,I
University of Maryland University College, MD I
University of Massachusetts Amherst, MA I
University of Massachusetts Boston, MA I

Institution	Code
University of Massachusetts Dartmouth, MA	I
University of Massachusetts Lowell, MA	I
University of Miami, FL	D,I,P
University of Michigan, MI	I
University of Michigan–Dearborn, MI	I
University of Minnesota, Crookston, MN	G,I
University of Minnesota, Twin Cities Campus, MN	I
University of Missouri–Columbia, MO	I
University of Missouri–Kansas City, MO	I
University of Missouri–St. Louis, MO	I
The University of Montana, MT	D,I
University of Nebraska at Kearney, NE	I
University of Nebraska at Omaha, NE	D,I
University of New England, ME	I
University of New Haven, CT	I
University of New Orleans, LA	D
University of North Alabama, AL	I
The University of North Carolina at Chapel Hill, NC	D,I
The University of North Carolina at Pembroke, NC	I
The University of North Carolina Wilmington, NC	I
University of North Dakota, ND	D
University of Northern Colorado, CO	D
University of Northern Iowa, IA	I
University of North Florida, FL	D
University of Oklahoma, OK	I
University of Oregon, OR	I
University of Pennsylvania, PA	I
University of Phoenix–Atlanta Campus, GA	D
University of Phoenix–Bay Area Campus, CA	D
University of Phoenix–Boston Campus, MA	D
University of Phoenix–Central Florida Campus, FL	D
University of Phoenix–Central Massachusetts Campus, MA	D
University of Phoenix–Charlotte Campus, NC	D
University of Phoenix–Chicago Campus, IL	D
University of Phoenix–Cincinnati Campus, OH	D
University of Phoenix–Cleveland Campus, OH	D
University of Phoenix–Columbus Georgia Campus, GA	D
University of Phoenix–Columbus Ohio Campus, OH	D
University of Phoenix–Dallas Campus, TX	D
University of Phoenix–Denver Campus, CO	D
University of Phoenix–Fort Lauderdale Campus, FL	D
University of Phoenix–Hawaii Campus, HI	D
University of Phoenix–Houston Campus, TX	D
University of Phoenix–Idaho Campus, ID	D
University of Phoenix–Indianapolis Campus, IN	D
University of Phoenix–Kansas City Campus, MO	D
University of Phoenix–Little Rock Campus, AR	D
University of Phoenix–Louisiana Campus, LA	D
University of Phoenix–Maryland Campus, MD	D
University of Phoenix–Metro Detroit Campus, MI	D
University of Phoenix–Nashville Campus, TN	D
University of Phoenix–Nevada Campus, NV	D
University of Phoenix–New Mexico Campus, NM	D
University of Phoenix–Oklahoma City Campus, OK	D
University of Phoenix Online Campus, AZ	D
University of Phoenix–Oregon Campus, OR	D
University of Phoenix–Philadelphia Campus, PA	D
University of Phoenix–Phoenix Campus, AZ	D
University of Phoenix–Pittsburgh Campus, PA	D
University of Phoenix–Puerto Rico Campus, PR	D
University of Phoenix–Raleigh Campus, NC	D
University of Phoenix–Richmond Campus, VA	D
University of Phoenix–Sacramento Valley Campus, CA	D
University of Phoenix–St. Louis Campus, MO	D
University of Phoenix–San Diego Campus, CA	D
University of Phoenix–Southern Arizona Campus, AZ	D
University of Phoenix–Southern California Campus, CA	D
University of Phoenix–Southern Colorado Campus, CO	D
University of Phoenix–Spokane Campus, WA	D
University of Phoenix–Springfield Campus, MO	D
University of Phoenix–Tulsa Campus, OK	D
University of Phoenix–Utah Campus, UT	D
University of Phoenix–Washington Campus, WA	D
University of Phoenix–West Florida Campus, FL	D
University of Phoenix–West Michigan Campus, MI	D
University of Phoenix–Wichita Campus, KS	D
University of Phoenix–Wisconsin Campus, WI	D
University of Pittsburgh, PA	D,I
University of Pittsburgh at Bradford, PA	I
University of Pittsburgh at Greensburg, PA	I
University of Pittsburgh at Johnstown, PA	I
University of Puget Sound, WA	D,I
University of Redlands, CA	I
University of Rhode Island, RI	I
University of Richmond, VA	D,I
University of Rochester, NY	I,P
University of Saint Francis, IN	D,I
University of St. Thomas, MN	D,I
University of St. Thomas, TX	D,I
University of San Diego, CA	I
University of Science and Arts of Oklahoma, OK	I
University of South Carolina, SC	D,I
University of South Carolina Upstate, SC	D
The University of South Dakota, SD	D
University of Southern California, CA	D,I,P
University of Southern Maine, ME	I
University of Southern Mississippi, MS	I
University of South Florida, FL	I
The University of Tampa, FL	I
The University of Tennessee at Martin, TN	D
The University of Texas at Austin, TX	I
The University of Texas at Dallas, TX	I
The University of Texas at San Antonio, TX	D,I
The University of Texas at Tyler, TX	I
The University of Texas Medical Branch, TX	I
The University of Texas–Pan American, TX	I
The University of Texas Southwestern Medical Center at Dallas, TX	I
University of the Cumberlands, KY	I
University of the Incarnate Word, TX	I
University of the Pacific, CA	D
University of the Sciences in Philadelphia, PA	I,P
University of Vermont, VT	D,I
University of Virginia, VA	I
The University of West Alabama, AL	D
University of West Florida, FL	D,P
University of West Georgia, GA	G
University of Wisconsin–La Crosse, WI	I
University of Wisconsin–Milwaukee, WI	I
University of Wisconsin–Stevens Point, WI	I
University of Wisconsin–Stout, WI	I
University of Wisconsin–Superior, WI	I
University of Wisconsin–Whitewater, WI	I
University of Wyoming, WY	D,I
Ursinus College, PA	I
Utah State University, UT	D
Valdosta State University, GA	G
Valparaiso University, IN	D,I
Vanderbilt University, TN	I,P
Vanguard University of Southern California, CA	I
Vassar College, NY	I

D = deferred payment system; G = guaranteed tuition rate; I = installment payments; P = prepayment locks in tuition rate

Vermont Technical College, VT	I
Villa Julie College, MD	D,I
Virginia Commonwealth University, VA	I
Virginia Intermont College, VA	I
Virginia Military Institute, VA	I
Virginia Polytechnic Institute and State University, VA	I
Virginia State University, VA	I
Virginia Wesleyan College, VA	D,I
Wabash College, IN	I,P
Walsh College of Accountancy and Business Administration, MI	D
Warren Wilson College, NC	I
Wartburg College, IA	I
Washington & Jefferson College, PA	D,I
Washington Bible College, MD	I
Washington College, MD	I,P
Washington State University, WA	I
Wayland Baptist University, TX	I
Waynesburg College, PA	D,I
Wayne State College, NE	I
Wayne State University, MI	I
Webber International University, FL	I
Webster University, MO	I
Wellesley College, MA	I,P
Wentworth Institute of Technology, MA	I
Wesley College, DE	I
Wesley College, MS	I
Western Carolina University, NC	I
Western Connecticut State University, CT	I
Western Illinois University, IL	G
Western New England College, MA	I,P
Western Oregon University, OR	D
Western Washington University, WA	I
West Liberty State College, WV	D,I
Westminster College, MO	I
Westminster College, UT	D,I
Westmont College, CA	I
West Virginia University, WV	I
Wheaton College, IL	D,I
Wheaton College, MA	I,P
Wheelock College, MA	I,P
Whitman College, WA	D
Whitworth University, WA	I
Wichita State University, KS	I
Widener University, PA	I
Wilkes University, PA	D,I
Willamette University, OR	I
William Carey College, MS	D
William Paterson University of New Jersey, NJ	I
Williams Baptist College, AR	I
Williams College, MA	I
Wilson College, PA	I
Wingate University, NC	I
Winona State University, MN	I
Winston-Salem State University, NC	I
Winthrop University, SC	I
Wisconsin Lutheran College, WI	I
Wittenberg University, OH	I
Woodbury University, CA	D,I
Worcester Polytechnic Institute, MA	D,I
Xavier University, OH	D,I
Yale University, CT	I
York College of Pennsylvania, PA	I,P
Youngstown State University, OH	I

Notes

Peterson's
Book Satisfaction Survey

Give Us Your Feedback

Thank you for choosing Peterson's as your source for personalized solutions for your education and career achievement. Please take a few minutes to answer the following questions. Your answers will go a long way in helping us to produce the most user-friendly and comprehensive resources to meet your individual needs.

When completed, please tear out this page and mail it to us at:

Publishing Department
Peterson's, a Nelnet company
2000 Lenox Drive
Lawrenceville, NJ 08648

You can also complete this survey online at **www.petersons.com/booksurvey.**

---

1. What is the ISBN of the book you have purchased? (The ISBN can be found on the book's back cover in the lower right-hand corner.) ____________________

2. Where did you purchase this book?

- ❑ Retailer, such as Barnes & Noble
- ❑ Online reseller, such as Amazon.com
- ❑ Petersons.com
- ❑ Other (please specify) ____________________

3. If you purchased this book on Petersons.com, please rate the following aspects of your online purchasing experience on a scale of 4 to 1 (4 = Excellent and 1 = Poor).

	4	**3**	**2**	**1**
Comprehensiveness of Peterson's Online Bookstore page	❑	❑	❑	❑
Overall online customer experience	❑	❑	❑	❑

4. Which category best describes you?

- ❑ High school student
- ❑ Parent of high school student
- ❑ College student
- ❑ Graduate/professional student
- ❑ Returning adult student
- ❑ Teacher
- ❑ Counselor
- ❑ Working professional/military
- ❑ Other (please specify) ____________________

5. Rate your overall satisfaction with this book.

Extremely Satisfied	Satisfied	Not Satisfied
❑	❑	❑

6. Rate each of the following aspects of this book on a scale of 4 to 1 (4 = Excellent and 1 = Poor).

	4	3	2	1
Comprehensiveness of the information	❑	❑	❑	❑
Accuracy of the information	❑	❑	❑	❑
Usability	❑	❑	❑	❑
Cover design	❑	❑	❑	❑
Book layout	❑	❑	❑	❑
Special features *(e.g., CD, flashcards, charts, etc.)*	❑	❑	❑	❑
Value for the money	❑	❑	❑	❑

7. This book was recommended by:

❑ Guidance counselor
❑ Parent/guardian
❑ Family member/relative
❑ Friend
❑ Teacher
❑ Not recommended by anyone—I found the book on my own
❑ Other (please specify) ______________________

8. Would you recommend this book to others?

Yes	Not Sure	No
❑	❑	❑

9. Please provide any additional comments.

____

____

____

____

____

Remember, you can tear out this page and mail it to us at:

Publishing Department
Peterson's, a Nelnet company
2000 Lenox Drive
Lawrenceville, NJ 08648

or you can complete the survey online at **www.petersons.com/booksurvey.**

Your feedback is important to us at Peterson's, and we thank you for your time!

If you would like us to keep in touch with you about new products and services, please include your e-mail address here: ______________________